DATE DUE

DEMCO 38-296

AMERICAN NATIONAL BIOGRAPHY

AMERICAN
NATIONAL BIOGRAPHY

Published under the auspices of the
AMERICAN COUNCIL OF LEARNED SOCIETIES

General Editors

John A. Garraty

Mark C. Carnes

VOLUME 19

OXFORD UNIVERSITY PRESS

New York   1999   Oxford

OXFORD UNIVERSITY PRESS

Oxford   New York
Athens   Auckland   Bangkok   Bogotá
Buenos Aires   Calcutta   Cape Town   Chennai
Dar es Salaam   Delhi   Florence   Hong Kong   Istanbul
Karachi   Kuala Lumpur   Madrid   Melbourne   Mexico City
Mumbai   Nairobi   Paris   São Paulo   Singapore
Taipei   Tokyo   Toronto   Warsaw
and associated companies in
Berlin   Ibadan

Published by Oxford University Press, Inc.,
198 Madison Avenue, New York, New York 10016
http://www.oup-usa.org

Funding for this publication was provided in part by
the Andrew W. Mellon Foundation, the Rockefeller Foundation,
and the National Endowment for the Humanities,
a federal agency.

Library of Congress Cataloging-in-Publication Data

American national biography / general editors, John A. Garraty, Mark C. Carnes
p.   cm.
"Published under the auspices of the American Council of Learned Societies."
Includes bibliographical references and index.
1. United States—Biography—Dictionaries.   I. Garraty, John Arthur,
1920–   .   II. Carnes, Mark C. (Mark Christopher), 1950–   .
III. American Council of Learned Societies.
CT213.A68   1998   98-20826   920.073—dc21   CIP
ISBN 0-19-520635-5 (set)
ISBN 0-19-512798-6 (vol. 19)

Printing (last digit): 9 8 7 6 5 4 3 2 1

Printed in the United States of America
on acid-free paper

R

ROUSSEAU, Lovell Harrison (4 Aug. 1818–7 Jan. 1869), military officer and congressman, was born near Stanford, Lincoln County, Kentucky; his parents' names are unknown. He briefly attended local schools and worked on neighboring farms before joining a construction crew to build a road from Lexington to Lancaster. Rousseau then studied law in Louisville. He moved to Bloomfield, Indiana, in 1840 and was admitted to the bar in February 1841. He took an immediate interest in politics and became affiliated with the Whig party. Rousseau was a member of the Indiana State House of Representatives in 1844 and 1845. Attached to the Second Indiana Infantry during the Mexican War, he held the rank of captain and in 1847 served with General Zachary Taylor at the battle of Buena Vista, where he lost nearly one-third of his men. Four days after his return from Mexico, in June 1847, Rousseau was elected to the Indiana State Senate.

In 1849 Rousseau moved to Louisville, Kentucky, where he began a successful career as a criminal lawyer. He was particularly adept in addressing juries. Continuing his interest in Republican politics, he was elected to the Kentucky State Senate in 1860. Firmly opposed to secession, he worked diligently to restrain Kentucky from joining the Confederacy; he succeeded, and his memorable speeches denouncing secessionists attracted national attention.

When the Civil War began in 1861, Rousseau resigned his legislative seat to join the military. He recruited troops for the Union cause and provided for their drill and equipment. He established headquarters at Camp Jo Holt in Indiana across the Ohio River from Louisville, and on 9 September he became a colonel in the Third Kentucky Infantry. On 1 October 1861 Rousseau was promoted to brigadier general of volunteers and attached to General Don Carlos Buell's army. He led a brigade of General Alexander M. McCook's division at the battle of Shiloh in 1862. Rousseau also participated in the battle of Perryville on 8 October 1862. For his bravery he won a promotion in 1862 to major general of volunteers and subsequently succeeded General Ormsby M. Mitchel in command of the fifth division of the Army of the Cumberland, serving in the battles of Stones River in late 1862 and early 1863 and at Chickamauga in 1863. From November 1863 until 30 November 1865, when he resigned his commission, Rousseau had command of the districts of Nashville and Middle Tennessee, during which time he raided Alabama and destroyed the Montgomery and Atlanta railway lines. He ably defended Fort Rosecrans at Nashville with 8,000 men against Confederate general John B. Hood.

Upon the conclusion of the Civil War, Rousseau returned to Kentucky and resumed his political career. He lost a campaign for the U.S. Senate to Democrat James Guthrie, a railroad president and former member of President Franklin Pierce's cabinet. Shortly thereafter, Rousseau was elected to the U.S. House of Representatives as a Republican; he served from 4 March 1865 to 21 July 1866, when he resigned after having been censured by the House for publicly assaulting Representative Josiah B. Grinnell, an Iowa Republican, with a cane in the Capitol corridors after a heated debate. In a poignant address to his constituents in the Fifth Congressional District, Rousseau explained his actions before and after the assault on Grinnell. The local Kentucky electorate, refusing to hold Rousseau accountable for his attack on Grinnell, sent the congressman back to the House, where he held a seat from 3 December 1866 to 3 March 1867.

Rousseau compiled a solid record as a national legislator. Because of his knowledge of military matters, he was a valuable member of the Committee on Military Affairs. He participated in the debates over Reconstruction policies for the South; in a noted speech of 11 June 1866, he abandoned any ties he had to Radical Republicanism. Rousseau denounced the vindictive measures that Radical Republicans such as Thaddeus Stevens of Pennsylvania wished to impose on the vanquished South. The independent-minded Kentuckian also opposed the Freedmen's Bureau, a temporary agency to provide aid to freedmen and deal with abandoned southern lands; it was the original federal civil rights department for African Americans, which became a branch of the Department of War. The debate hinged on conceptions of property rights and public purpose and the principle of using government action to promote the welfare of a class of people. For many, including Rousseau—who outlined his thoughts on the bill in a House speech on 3 February 1866—the matter was more of a state responsibility. The controversial Bureau Act passed in the House by two votes.

Shortly after his retirement from the House, Rousseau reentered military life. President Andrew Johnson appointed him brigadier general in the regular army on 27 March 1867; at the same time he received the brevet of major general in the U.S. Army for his wartime services. After the United States purchased Alaska from Russia in 1867 under provisions negotiated by Secretary of State William H. Seward, Rousseau was dispatched there to receive Alaska officially and assume control of the territory. In 1868 he was summoned to Washington to testify in the impeachment trial of President Johnson, but he did not arrive in time. On 28 July 1868, Rousseau became commander of the Department of the Gulf and the District of Louisiana during Reconstruction, earning a reputation for moderation and conciliation. His relaxed supervision and mild actions reflected the will of the white citizens of the state, giving Democrats wide latitude in several parishes. He died in New Orleans while serving in this capacity. He was survived by his wife and four children. His death brought to a close the life of a capable military officer and independent politician who gained national recognition during the Civil War and Reconstruction.

• Most of Rousseau's extant papers are in the Charles Lanman Collection at the Filson Club in Louisville, Ky. Others are scattered in the manuscript collections of various contemporaries, including several letters in the Andrew Johnson Papers in the Manuscripts Division of the Library of Congress. The main article on Rousseau is Joseph G. Dawson III, "General Lovell H. Rousseau and Louisiana Reconstruction," *Louisiana History* 20 (1979): 373–91. See also William E. Highsmith, "Louisiana during Reconstruction" (Ph.D. diss., Louisiana State Univ., 1953); James E. Sefton, *The United States Army and Reconstruction, 1865–1877* (1967); Joe Gray Taylor, *Louisiana Reconstructed, 1863–1877* (1974); and Dawson, *Army Generals and Reconstruction: Louisiana, 1862–1877* (1982; repr. 1994). Obituaries are in the *New York Times*, 9 Jan. 1869, the New Orleans *Times*, *Crescent*, *Daily Picayune*, and *Republican*, all 10 Jan. 1869, and the *Kentucky Statesman* (Lexington), 14 Jan. 1869.

LEONARD SCHLUP

ROVERE, Richard Halworth (5 May 1915–23 Nov. 1979), political columnist and author, was born in Jersey City, New Jersey, the son of Louis Halworth Rovere, an electrical engineer, and Ethel Roberts. Rovere attended public schools in New York City and Stony Brook School on Long Island before attending Bard College in Annandale-on-Hudson, New York, where he earned his B.A. in 1937. His writing career dated to his days at Bard, where he edited the campus newspaper, the *Bardian*. He became "an ardent Socialist," probably during his first year at Bard, before deciding in his junior year "to become a Communist, because the Communists seemed to me to be working harder than the Socialists" (*Final Reports*, p. 42). The Soviet pact with Nazi Germany in 1939 disillusioned Rovere, who abandoned the Communist party—although he apparently had never formally joined—and found a political home in the Democratic party. He retained his Socialist values, writing late in his life, "I would be some sort of Social Democrat if I lived in a country that had such a movement" (*Final Reports*, p. 43).

Combining his love of language and politics, Rovere embarked on a career in journalism and publishing. In 1937 he became an associate editor at *New Masses*, a Communist weekly in New York City, where he worked until 1939 when he abandoned Communism. He moved to the *Nation*, where he worked as an assistant editor. Rovere married Eleanor Alice Burgess in 1941; they had three children.

In 1943 Rovere became editor of *Common Sense*, the monthly bulletin of the League for Independent Political Action, but he left after less than a year, citing personality conflicts with the staff. The following year he began writing for *Harper's* and the *New Yorker*. Although his early *New Yorker* assignments were mostly nonpolitical, his successful dispatches on the 1948 presidential campaign convinced editors to hire Rovere as a regular political columnist. He began writing the "Letter from Washington" (later the "Affairs of State") column for the *New Yorker* in 1948 and continued the column on a roughly monthly basis for more than thirty years, his last column appearing in the 6 August 1979 issue. Rovere preferred to cover Washington, D.C., from his homes in New York City or the nearby Hudson River valley, where he lived most of his life. In place of on-site reporting, he used the printed record as his source for the sake of accuracy and detached objectivity.

Rovere expressed his wry sense of humor in his writing and found one of his jokes enshrined in American culture. In a 1962 essay for *Esquire* he announced the existence of an American Establishment, applying a British term to a group of Americans of a certain background who wore three-piece suits and joined famous clubs. He bolstered his argument with footnotes citing bogus books. To his surprise, the public received the piece as sociological gospel. The Library of Congress asked for his sources and sent a copy of the essay to Cuban leader Fidel Castro to give him insight into America's ruling class.

In addition to his magazine columns, Rovere wrote nine books, one published posthumously. His earliest works included *Howe & Hummel: Their True and Scandalous History* (1947) and *The General and the President, & the Future of American Foreign Policy* (1951, reprinted in 1965 as *The MacArthur Controversy and American Policy*), a collaboration with historian Arthur M. Schlesinger, Jr., that analyzed President Harry S. Truman's recall of General Douglas MacArthur from his command in Korea. His *Affairs of State: The Eisenhower Years* (1956) contributed to the historical record, offering forty-one essays on people and events surrounding the presidency during the years 1950 to 1956. In it he described then–vice president Richard M. Nixon as "a politician with an advertising man's approach to his work." In Nixon's approach, Rovere wrote, "Policies are products to be sold to the public—this one today, that one tomorrow, depending on the discounts and the state of the market." Rovere's most popular and widely acclaimed book was *Senator Joe McCarthy* (1959). Rovere argued that McCarthy had no agenda other than to champion whatever causes would win him the strongest support. He called McCarthy a "liar," a "barbarian," "in many ways the most gifted demagogue ever bred on these shores." His other books included *The American Establishment and Other Reports, Opinions, and Speculations* (1962), *The Goldwater Caper* (1965), *Waist Deep in the Big Muddy: Reflections on United States Policy* (1968), *Arrivals and Departures: A Journalist's Memoirs* (1976), and *Final Reports: Personal Reflections on Politics and History in Our Time* (1984).

Established as one of the country's top political journalists by the end of the 1950s, Rovere expanded his reputation and influence by working as American correspondent for *Spectator*, a London-based weekly review of politics, literature, theology, and art, from 1954 to 1962 and as a member of the board of editors of the *American Scholar* from 1958 to 1967. He joined the faculty of Columbia University as an associate professor of American civilization from 1957 to 1959 and lectured at Yale University in 1972 and 1973. He died in Poughkeepsie, New York.

Richard H. Rovere made his mark writing political commentary as a Washington outsider with a gift for elegant prose, evenhanded coverage, and wry humor, whose work contributed to the historical record. Schlesinger wrote, "For all his rather definite private feelings, he had an impressive ability to distance himself from the passions and personalities of his time." Or, as Schlesinger paraphrased Rovere, he preferred "a ringside seat when he could get one, but he did not want to be in the ring or in anyone's corner" (*Final Reports*, p. ix). Upon Rovere's death, William Shawn, editor at the *New Yorker*, described him as "among the fairest, most nearly objective, most brilliant writers on American politics. He wrote with tremendous skill, with care, with humor, with style. . . . He brought an extraordinary clarity of mind to bear on complex and confused political situations and made them comprehensible." Although not meant as history, Rovere's political profiles and books provide the valuable perspective of an intelligent, informed contemporary observer who not only recorded history but whose work may aid those who write it.

• Rovere's papers are in the Archive Division of the State Historical Society of Wisconsin in Madison. In addition to the works cited, Rovere served as advisory editor for *Loyalty and Security in a Democratic State* (1977). More information on Rovere's life can be found in Daniel Patrick Moynihan's lengthy review of *Final Reports* in the *New Yorker*, 17 Sept. 1984, pp. 134–40. The best and most widely available of Rovere's obituaries include the *New York Times* and the *Washington Post*, both 24 Nov. 1979. The *New York Times*, 3 Dec. 1979, editorialized on Rovere's death, focusing on his *Esquire* article depicting the American Establishment.

TODD KERSTETTER

ROWAN, Dan (2 July 1922–22 Sept. 1987), comedian, was born Dan Hale Rowan in Beggs, Oklahoma, the son of Sean John Rowan and Clella Hale, carnival workers. He was orphaned as a child and grew up at the McClelland Home in Pueblo, Colorado. He attended Central High School, where he played football, ran track, worked on the yearbook, and served as class president.

In 1940 Rowan traveled to Hollywood, hoping to break into show business. His first job was in the mailroom at Paramount, but he quickly advanced to become a junior writer. World War II interrupted his career plans, however; Rowan served as a fighter pilot with the Fifth Air Force Squadron in New Guinea. After the war Rowan took classes at the University of California and the University of Southern California. At this time, he was also a partner in a foreign-car dealership.

In 1952 Rowan was introduced to a struggling radio comedy writer and bartender named Dick Martin. Rowan and Martin hit it off, and after doing some writing for the comedy team of Noonan and Marshall they began planning a nightclub comedy act of their own that consisted of television takeoffs and character skits, with Rowan as straight man and Martin as clown. They performed in clubs in the Los Angeles area for three years, struggling to achieve notice. Finally, in 1956, Walter Winchell favorably reviewed their act in his syndicated newspaper column. They began to get better bookings and a measure of fame.

Strangely enough, the real-life Rowan and Martin were similar to their comic personas. Martin was a happy-go-lucky sort who belonged to all the clubs in town; Rowan was always the straight man, seriousminded, thoughtful, and concerned about the world around him. Yet the two men remained friends throughout their careers and rarely disagreed. Martin later noted that the two never had any kind of contract: they "just went and did [their act]."

In 1958 Rowan and Martin appeared in the Universal International film *Once upon a Horse*. The studio hoped they would be the next Abbott and Costello or Martin and Lewis, but lack of promotion resulted in the film's failing. The duo then signed their first television contract with NBC, but it was later canceled by mutual agreement.

Although Rowan and Martin appeared on "The Ed Sullivan Show" in 1960 and recorded the album *Rowan and Martin at Work* the same year, they still relied on nightclub appearances as their main source of income. In the early 1960s they performed only in the Reno, Lake Tahoe, and Las Vegas areas.

In 1966 Rowan and Martin substituted for the vacationing Dean Martin on his NBC show and earned the highest ratings of the summer. NBC offered them a chance to do a regular comedy variety show, but they insisted on a program that would not be restricted to the traditional variety-show format. They wanted an hour-long show made up completely of comedy. NBC executive Ed Friendly and independent television producer George Schlatter joined with Rowan and Martin in forming a production company to create a zany, fast-paced, hip comedy program. After recruiting George Wiles as director and Timex as a sponsor, the company produced the pilot for "Rowan and Martin's Laugh-In."

A reluctant NBC aired the pilot on 9 September 1967 and then gave Rowan and Martin the green light on their series. "Laugh-In" soon became a great success. The show featured running gags, comic cameos, short skits, bottom screen scrawls (subtitles that ran left to right across the bottom of the screen), political satire, and parodies. The excellent cast of improvisational comics included Ruth Buzzi, Henry Gibson, Arte Johnson, Judy Carne, Jo Anne Worley, Goldie Hawn, Alan Sues, Lily Tomlin, and Gary Owens; everyone from movie stars (John Wayne) to politicians (Richard Nixon) made guest appearances. The show was a huge hit with the younger generation, who identified with its hip humor and adopted its many catch phrases (including "You bet your bippy," "Look that up in your Funk and Wagnall's," "Here come de judge," and "Sock it to me").

Within three months "Laugh-In" had risen to fifth place in the Nielsen ratings; it was in first place by the end of the season. It won four Emmy awards and topped the ratings into the 1968–1969 season. The show lasted until 1973. In 1980 Schlatter tried to bring "Laugh-In" back without Rowan and Martin or their permission, and the team sued their former partner, winning $4.6 million.

In 1969 Rowan and Martin appeared in their second film, a horror spoof titled *The Maltese Bippy*. This attempt to translate their television formula to film was not a success.

After "Laugh-In" ended, Rowan and Martin began to drift apart. They parted amicably, making their last major appearance as a team on the "First Annual Ultra Quiz" (1981).

Rowan retired soon after in order to devote his time to travel and correspondence with writers. One was John D. MacDonald who, with Rowan, published *A Friendship* (1986), a collection of their letters from 1967 to 1974, focusing on their developing friendship.

Rowan was married three times: in 1946 to Phyllis Mathis, with whom he had three children, and, after their 1960 divorce, to Adriana van Ballegooyan in 1963. His third wife was Joanna (maiden name unknown). Rowan died in Englewood, Florida.

A *New York Times* editorial, printed a few days after Rowan's death, called "Laugh-In" "a cross between updated vaudeville and a psychedelic happening" (24 Sept. 1987). The article went on to say that Rowan's innovative career well displayed television's capacity "to renew and regenerate itself." As co-creator of one of the most original television programs of his time, Rowan went beyond being a straight man in a comedy team to a truly original entertainer.

• Biographies of Rowan appear in the *New York Times Biographical Service* and Ronald L. Smith, *Who's Who in Comedy* (1992). An excellent biography with detailed information about "Laugh-In" is in *Current Biography Yearbook* (1969). An obituary in the *New York Times*, 23 Sept. 1987, is also a good source.

JEFFREY S. MILLER

ROWAN, John (12 July 1773–14 July 1843), U.S. senator, was born in York, Pennsylvania, the son of Captain William Rowan, a sheriff, and Sarah Elizabeth Cooper. The Rowan family lost most of their resources during the revolutionary war by supporting the American cause. In 1783, feeling that the West offered a brighter future for them than did Pennsylvania, they set out for frontier Kentucky. John Rowan suffered from rheumatic pains as a youngster, and his family finally determined that he would have a difficult life

without the benefit of the best education available. Therefore, the Rowan family moved to Bardstown, Kentucky, in 1790 to allow John to attend Salem Academy, a school run by Dr. James Priestly. At the time, the Priestly school had the reputation as the best educational establishment west of the Allegheny Mountains.

After completing his studies at Salem Academy, Rowan was advised to study law. He went to Lexington, Kentucky, in about 1792 to study with George Nicholas, one of the leading lawyers in Kentucky and a personal friend of Thomas Jefferson. Rowan would later become friends with Jefferson when he went to Congress. In 1794 Rowan married Ann Lytle; they had nine children. By 1801 Rowan had established a reputation as a rising Kentucky lawyer and politician. However, in that year he participated in a duel with Dr. James Chambers over which of the two was the better scholar of dead languages. Chambers was killed, and Rowan suffered a temporary setback in his career.

While he was living in Frankfort from 1801 to 1806, Rowan established a lucrative legal practice that included numerous cases argued before the Kentucky Court of Appeals. In 1804 he was appointed secretary of state, a post he held for two years. In 1806 the voters from Bardstown elected him, a Federalist, as their representative to Congress. He served one term, returning to Kentucky in 1808.

During the years between his term in the House of Representatives and his selection to the Senate, Rowan practiced law and participated in politics. In 1818 he delivered the funeral oration for his old friend George Rogers Clark, and in 1819 he was the official host at a public dinner held in Louisville to honor James Monroe, Andrew Jackson, and their party. Rowan and Jackson had become close personal friends and remained friends until Rowan's death. When General Lafayette visited Kentucky in 1825, Rowan served on a committee to plan the visit. He was selected to welcome Lafayette to the state, and the Rowan family entertained him at their Bardstown home, "Federal Hill."

Rowan was a significant figure in the early years of Kentucky history and a national figure of some importance. The main Kentucky issue for which he is remembered is the Old Court–New Court or the Anti–Debtor Relief struggle. The issue was rooted in the relationship between Kentucky and Virginia and concerned the problem of land titles. Kentucky's separation agreement from Virginia guaranteed that all private rights and interests in the new state derived from Virginia law before the separation would be governed by Virginia's constitution. The problem was complicated by the fact that Virginia had been careless with most surveys before granting land to settlers and companies. This led to difficulties for settlers, sometimes forcing them to buy two or three times more land than they needed in order to save their homes. Rowan was the main leader of the Relief party, supporting state laws to relieve Kentuckians of the consequences of heavy debt burdens in the 1820s.

In 1819 Rowan was appointed a judge of the Kentucky Court of Appeals. Although his tenure on the Court of Appeals lasted only two years, it was significant in that he delivered several opinions for the court, earning him the title "Judge," which would remain with him throughout his life. His service on the court ended when he was elected to serve a term in the state legislature from 1822 to 1824.

In 1824 the state legislature elected Rowan to a six-year term in the U.S. Senate. With one term in Congress, a short stint on the Kentucky Court of Appeals, and experience in the Kentucky legislature behind him, he was now ready to take a more active part in the business of Congress. In 1826 he sponsored amendments to a bill on judiciary reform. The effect of the bill would have been to reduce the size of the judicial district in which Kentucky was located. He felt strongly that the U.S. government was founded on the principle of looking to the good of the whole by taking care of the best interests of the parts. He sponsored several bills relating to Kentucky, including one authorizing a subscription of stock by the United States for the Louisville and Portland Canal Company. Another, signed in 1827, authorized establishment of a deaf and dumb asylum in Kentucky and provided for a grant of land in the territories of Arkansas and Florida to be disposed of for the benefit of the asylum.

During his term in the Senate, Rowan received attention for his speech related to resolutions, supported by Senator Samuel A. Foote of Connecticut, regarding limiting the sale of public lands. In his speech Rowan advocated protection of two subjects very dear to him, slavery and states' rights, a topic he managed to work into most of his Senate speeches.

When Rowan first went to the Senate he was close to President John Quincy Adams, but a rift developed between them. By 1828 Rowan was openly speaking against the reelection of Adams and in favor of Jackson. When Rowan's term in the Senate ended, he was not returned, partly because of Henry Clay's opposition to him. Although Rowan and Clay were friends for many years, they had a falling out during the critical court struggle. Clay had become the Whig leader in Kentucky and used his influence to prevent Rowan's return to the Senate.

Following his return to Kentucky, Rowan split his time between Louisville and Bardstown, practicing law and overseeing his considerable real estate interests. In 1840 he was appointed as commissioner to adjust the claims of the citizens of the United States against Mexico. He went to Washington in 1840 and was still serving as commissioner in 1842, when he returned to Kentucky for a visit. During the visit, he became ill and was unable to return to Washington, D.C. He died at his Louisville home.

In March 1920 Federal Hill was purchased from the Rowan family by the state of Kentucky to become the first Kentucky state park, known as My Old Kentucky Home State Park. Myth suggests that Federal Hill inspired Stephen C. Foster, a cousin of the Rowans, to write "My Old Kentucky Home" while visiting there. While Foster did visit the Rowans in Louisville, there is no documentation that he visited Bardstown.

• Much of the material on Rowan is located in the Rowan collection of the Manuscript Division in the Kentucky Library at Western Kentucky University in Bowling Green. The published work with the most beneficial information regarding Rowan is Lucius Little, *Ben Hardin: His Times and Contemporaries* (1887). Numerous biographies of Rowan's contemporaries are helpful in explaining the man and his times. See, for example, Joseph Howard Parks, *Felix Grundy, Champion of Democracy* (1940); John Hopkins, ed., *The Papers of Henry Clay* (1969); *Biographical Sketch of the Honorable Lazarus W. Powell* (1868); Albert K. Kirwan, *John J. Crittenden: The Struggle for the Union* (1962); Charles Francis Adams, ed., *Memoirs of John Quincy Adams*, vols. 5 and 6 (repr. 1969); Cassius Marcellus Clay, *The Life of Cassius Marcellus Clay* (1886); and Thomas Clark, *The Kentucky* (1942). Several works contain information about Rowan's career as an attorney. Some of the better ones include H. Levin, *Lawyers and Lawmakers of Kentucky* (1897); Samuel Haycraft, *A History of Elizabethtown, Kentucky, and Its Surroundings* (1869); William B. Allen, *History of Kentucky* (1872); and L. F. Johnson, *Famous Kentucky Tragedies and Trials* (1916). Much information on the Kentucky court conflict is available in Arndt M. Stickles, *The Critical Court Struggle in Kentucky* (1929).

RANDALL CAPPS

ROWAN, Stephen Clegg (25 Dec. 1808–31 Mar. 1890), naval officer, was born near Dublin, Ireland, the son of John Rowan. His mother's maiden name was Clegg. While Rowan was still a boy, his family immigrated to the United States, but Rowan was compelled to remain in Ireland with his grandparents while recovering from severe burns resulting from an accident. After his recovery, Rowan, aged ten, joined his family at Piqua, Ohio, where they had settled. At age eighteen, having finished his schooling in Oxford, Ohio, Rowan was appointed a midshipman in the U.S. Navy. His first cruise, aboard the *Vincennes*, coincided with that vessel's four-year (1826–1830) circumnavigation of the globe, a first for an American man-of-war. Routine duties for Rowan followed this historic cruise, and in 1832 he was promoted to passed midshipman. During the Seminole War, he was actively involved in naval operations on Florida rivers and in Charlotte Harbor. Promotion to lieutenant came in 1837.

Following a year of coast survey duty, Rowan served aboard the *Delaware* off the coast of Brazil, then aboard the *Ontario*, cruising the Mediterranean. In 1845 he became executive officer of the *Cyane*, which was assigned to the Pacific Squadron. When war with Mexico began, Rowan was with the landing party that seized Monterey, California. Then the *Cyane* blockaded the harbor at San Diego, and Rowan landed with a detachment of sailors and marines and occupied the city. Rowan and his force joined Admiral Robert F. Stockton and participated in the engagements of Rio San Gabriel and the Mesa. He was wounded at the Mesa but recovered sufficiently to lead a night attack on the enemy positions at Mazatlán and to relieve a detachment of American soldiers under seige at San José. While operating in the Gulf of California, the *Cyane* captured twenty blockade-runners and destroyed several enemy gunboats.

Rowan was ordnance inspector at the New York Navy Yard from 1850 to 1853 and returned to that post in 1858–1861. During the interim he commanded the supply ship *Relief* and the receiving ship *North Carolina*. He was promoted to commander in 1855.

With the coming of the Civil War, Rowan was an experienced senior officer with an impressive record of accomplishment. As commander of the *Pawnee*, he participated in the unsuccessful expedition sent in 1861 to relieve Fort Sumter, then in the evacuation of Federal forces at the Navy Yard in Norfolk, Virginia. Following these setbacks, the Federals achieved a significant victory in the occupation of Alexandria, Virginia, on 23–24 May 1861 with the help of a naval force commanded by Rowan. According to Admiral Daniel Ammen, this first amphibious operation of the war exceeded in "dash" and "brilliance" any other that "occurred during the entire Civil War." In August and September 1861 Rowan, still commanding the *Pawnee*, participated in the Goldsborough expedition that captured the Confederate forts guarding Hatteras and Ocracoke inlets in North Carolina. Commanding the *Delaware*, he provided naval support for General Ambrose E. Burnside's capture of Roanoke Island in February 1862. Rowan followed with the destruction of Confederate works on the Pasquotank River, the defeat of an enemy naval fleet, and the capture of Elizabeth City and Edenton, North Carolina. He provided General Burnside with further support in the capture of Winston, New Bern, and Beaufort, North Carolina. In recognition of his "distinguished gallantry," Rowan was simultaneously promoted to captain and commodore on 16 July 1862. At the recommendation of President Abraham Lincoln, he also received the Thanks of Congress.

From July to September 1863 Rowan commanded the ironclad steamer *New Ironsides* of the South Atlantic Blockading Squadron, engaging enemy batteries at Forts Wagner and Moultrie from off Charleston. During March 1864 he was temporarily in command of the South Atlantic Squadron during the absence of Admiral John Adolphus Bernard Dahlgren.

When the war ended, Rowan was head of the Norfolk Navy Yard. He was promoted to rear admiral in 1866 and to vice admiral in 1870. From 1867 to 1870 he commanded the Asiatic Squadron, followed by command of the New York Navy Yard in 1872–1879. During the final ten years of his naval career he served as president of the Board of Naval Examiners (1879–1881); governor of the Naval Asylum in Philadelphia (1881); superintendent of the Naval Observatory (1882); and chairman of the Lighthouse Board (1883). Rowan retired in 1889 and died in Washington, D.C. He married Mary Stark, who died in 1875. They had one child who survived infancy.

• Information on Rowan is in RG 45 (Naval Records Collection), National Archives. Rowan's official Civil War correspondence is in *The Official Records of the Union and Confederate Navies in the War of the Rebellion* (30 vols., 1894–1922). A biography of Rowan is S. C. Ayers, *Sketch of the Life and Services of Vice Admiral S. C. Rowan* (1910). See also Lewis R. Hamersly, *The Records of Living Officers of the U.S. Navy and Marine Corps*, 4th ed. (1890). An obituary is in the *Washington, D.C., Evening Star*, 31 Mar. 1890.

NORMAN C. DELANEY

ROWE, James (1865–1933), gospel music song lyricist, was born in Devonshire, England, the son of John Rowe and Jane Gallard. His father died at age forty-eight, and Rowe left school at an early age to support his family. He held positions in the English government for several years but seems not to have had any special training or experience in music. He immigrated to the United States in 1890, settling first in New York City, where he worked for the New York Central Railroad Company. Later relocating to Albany, New York, he served as superintendent for the animal control department of the Mohawk and Hudson River Humane Society from 1900 to 1910. During this time he married Blanche Clapper.

Starting in about 1900 Rowe began to write poems and song lyrics. In 1912 he composed one of his first and most enduring songs, "Love Lifted Me," with music by Howard E. Smith. Still found in many modern hymnals, the song was written in Saugatuck, Connecticut, and encouraged Rowe to consider using gospel songs as an outlet for his lyrics. At the turn of the century there was a revolution of sorts in Protestant church music, with the advent of the new "gospel hymns" of the type popularized by evangelists Dwight Moody and Ira Sankey; the new hymns stressed personal salvation and were more lively and singable than older ones. Rowe was able to plug into this new scene and soon found his poems being set to music by some of the leading gospel composers of the day, including E. O. Excell and Charles H. Gabriel.

Rowe soon found that the center for the new gospel song movement was the South, where by the first decade of the twentieth century a number of independent publishers were producing hundreds of new songbooks, written in seven-shape note style. He soon mastered the idiom of southern gospel songs and began to write seriously for a number of companies. For a time he lived in Waco, Texas, where he wrote for the Trio Music Company; in Chattanooga, Tennessee, where he wrote for the A. J. Showalter Company; and in Lawrenceburg, Tennessee, where he wrote for the James D. Vaughan Company. His Lawrenceburg residence, from 1920 to 1927, was his longest in the South. During this time he also edited several periodicals published by the Vaughan company—then the largest gospel publisher in the South—and published secular poems in the *Lawrence News*, a local paper. He also sold poems to greeting card companies.

An idea of the scope of his activities may be gained from an ad he placed in a 1917 periodical offering to furnish poems to music at the rate of one dollar each; revising a poem cost a mere fifty cents. At this time Rowe claimed to have written some 6,000 published song poems; his later work probably doubled that total. Modern hymn and gospel books are still full of his collaborations from this period. They include "If I Could Only Hear My Mother Pray Again" (1922), "Is It Well with Your Soul?" (1922), "Somebody Needs Just You" (1920), "God Holds the Future" (1922), "Just One Way to the Gate" (1920), and "Give Me the Roses Now" (1925). In 1927 the Vaughan company published *Ready for Mornin' and Other Poems*, a substantial collection of Rowe's secular verse; in 1913 they published a small instruction book, *How to Write Song-Poems, Sacred and Secular*, in which Rowe gave practical advice on meter and prosody.

After the death of his wife in 1927, Rowe returned north, where he lived for a time in West Albany, New York, and then moved to Wells, Vermont. In later years he turned more to greeting card verse and edited collections of recitations and lectures. In 1931 he brought out *Twenty-Five Peppy Grange Songs*. He died probably in Wells.

• Information for this entry was drawn primarily from interviews conducted by the author with James Walbert, Stella Vaughan, Otis Knippers, and Harlan Daniel. References to Rowe are in George Pullen Jackson, *White Spirituals in the Southern Uplands* (1933), pp. 375–77.

CHARLES K. WOLFE

ROWE, John (1715–17 Feb. 1787), merchant, smuggler, and political trimmer during the American Revolution, was born in Exeter, England, the son of Joseph Rowe and Mary Hawker (occupations unknown). He took up residence in Boston, Massachusetts, by 1736 and remained there throughout his life. In 1743 he married Hannah Speakman, the twin sister of the first wife of the wealthy Cambridge merchant and future Loyalist Ralph Inman; they had no children. His wife's family had helped to found Trinity Church, Boston's second Anglican parish, and Rowe served on its vestry from 1761 until his death. These family associations may have helped to moderate Rowe's initial vigorous support of the patriot cause.

Newspaper advertisements suggest that Rowe was a general merchant whose store was fully stocked with English dry goods but who earned credits to pay for those manufactures by energetically plying a trade with the foreign West Indies. Since Rowe sometimes took the precaution of insuring his vessels against seizures by the Royal Navy and His Majesty's customs officers, we can assume that the persistent rumors that Rowe was an inveterate smuggler (that is, did not pay duty on foreign West Indies goods, mainly sugar and molasses) were true, despite the fact that he, along with many other Boston merchants in similar circumstances, signed an agreement in 1756 to inform on Dutch smugglers.

Rowe's smuggling interests also help to explain his active involvement in many of the protests of the Bos-

ton Society for the Encouraging of Trade and Commerce against increasingly strict enforcement of British mercantilist legislation during the early 1760s. Rowe was among the first to take up the cause of Benjamin Barons, a Boston customs collector who had connived with the local merchants to evade the Acts of Trade to enrich himself. James Otis's famous argument against the use of the Writs of Assistance was but one phase of the movement to reinstate Barons.

Rowe's intimacy with Barons caused his name to be mentioned as a smuggler in secret depositions, taken in part by Chief Justice Thomas Hutchinson, which were subsequently dispatched to England. Briggs Hallowell, a Boston merchant in London, saw these depositions at the Plantation Office; his account of their contents had just arrived in Boston in 1765, shortly before the second Stamp Act riot of 26 August that destroyed both the records of the vice-admiralty court and Hutchinson's North End mansion. Rowe later acknowledged helping to incite the riot (Peter O. Hutchinson, ed., *The Diary and Letters of Thomas Hutchinson*, vol. 1 [1971], p. 67).

While serving as a Boston selectman, Rowe was an early advocate of nonimportation as a response to the Townshend duties, but his ardor cooled after he successfully solicited the supply contract for the British troops after their arrival in Boston in 1768. Although he was a member of the merchants committee in charge of enforcing the nonimportation agreement, he was later embarrassed when customs documents published by Loyalist printer John Mein revealed that he himself had broken the compact. When staunch patriots sought to extend the nonimportation campaign in the winter of 1770, Rowe pronounced their proceedings "too severe."

Sensing an opportunity to disengage Rowe from the patriots, Hutchinson, now the acting governor, began to court him with flattering social invitations. Hutchinson's success with Rowe and other prominent people may help to account for the seeming calm that spread over Boston politics from 1770 until the Boston Tea Party in 1773. But Hutchinson never forgave Rowe for his role in orchestrating Boston's response to the Stamp Act. Hutchinson sent one of his London correspondents a coded message in 1771 suggesting customs officials might find a way to intercept a vessel owned by Rowe that was bound from London to Holland to pick up a cargo of illegal Dutch tea. However, nothing came of the effort.

Rowe reappeared at the center of Boston merchant politics in 1773 as the owner of one of the tea ships that were eligible to be confiscated together with their valuable cargoes if the duof tea aboard were not unloaded within the statutory twenty-day limit. Some of the accounts of the great mass meeting at Old South Meetinghouse on the night of the Tea Party, 16 December, quote Rowe as broadly hinting that "perhaps salt water and tea will mix tonight," but Rowe's own diary says he was "a little Unwell" and "staid home all Day & all the Evening."

Rowe remained in Boston after the outbreak of hostilities in April 1775, thereby earning the suspicion of his patriot neighbors. But when British troops evacuated the city at the end of the siege, Rowe alleged that they took away with them £2,260 of his property, probably blankets and other furnishings that were a disputed part of his supply contract.

Early in the war, Rowe imported coal from Great Britain contrary to the resolves of Congress, but he denied selling any to Boston's inhabitants. By 1779 his status in the merchant community was sufficiently restored that he was appointed at a Boston town meeting to a committee to fix prices.

An amiable and gregarious man, Rowe was a member of many Boston fraternal and charitable associations. He became a Freemason in 1740, master of his lodge in 1749, and grand master for North America in 1768. He was in constant demand as a guest at all the best tables in Boston; his diary makes clear that next to good food and good company, he enjoyed freshwater fishing most. He died in Boston.

Although perhaps not a leader of revolutionary events in Boston, Rowe was integrally involved in nearly everything that happened. The careful way in which Rowe weighed business interests against the ideological commitments of his friends and relations is perhaps more typical of North American merchants of the time than is generally realized. If Rowe was a trimmer, there were many like him.

• The only Rowe manuscripts to survive are the John Rowe Letterbook, 1759–1762, at the Baker Library, Harvard University Graduate School of Business Administration, and his diary at the Massachusetts Historical Society. Large parts of both have been published as *The Letters and Diary of John Rowe, Boston Merchant, 1759–1762, 1764–1779*, ed. Anne Rowe Cunningham (1903), and "The Diary of John Rowe," *Massachusetts Historical Society Proceedings*, 2d ser., 10 (1895): 20–108.

JOHN W. TYLER

ROWE, Peter Trimble (20 Nov. 1856–1 June 1942), Episcopal bishop, was born in Meadowvale, Canada West (now Mississauga, Ontario), the son of Peter Rowe, a taverner and farmer, and Mary Trimble. Rowe was reared in a poor household and spent most of his youth on his family's farm in Clarksburg (County Grey), Ontario. He also attended the local Anglican church and received religious instruction from a clergyman. By the time of his confirmation he was committed to entering the priesthood.

In 1875 Rowe enrolled in Trinity College (Toronto), but poor finances forced him to leave after one year of study. He subsequently worked as a lay missionary to the Ojibway on Manitoulin Island in Lake Huron. In 1878 he was ordained deacon. While a lay missionary, he also completed his college education. He graduated with a B.A. from Trinity in 1880 and two years later earned an M.A. from the same institution. Rowe advanced to the priesthood in 1880. He served for two years in the Diocese of Algoma (Ontario) as a missionary to the Garden River Indian Reserve on Lake Huron. In this frontier post he traveled great distances and acquired amazing powers of endurance, learning to survive winters in the wilderness. Much of his missionary work was medical. When visiting settlements, he often pulled teeth and delivered babies.

In 1882 Rowe married Dora Henriette Cary, a native of Quebec; they had two children. In that year he also came to the United States to oversee a mission in Sault Ste. Marie, Michigan. During his thirteen years in northern Michigan he founded seven missions. Also during that time, in 1894, he became an American citizen. In 1895, responding to aggressive missionary gains by the Roman Catholic church, the General Convention of the Episcopal Church created a missionary district in Alaska and elected Rowe as its first bishop. Bishop William Croswell Doane presided at his consecration, held on 30 November 1895 in St. George's Church, New York City.

Rowe was admirably qualified for the challenge to evangelize a territory of 600,000 square miles. Physically he was "a rugged, robust man, a real athlete" (W. J. Thompson quoted in Jenkins, p. 30). He had worked among Native Americans and learned to speak their languages. He had established new missions and traveled through wilderness areas. He knew how to drive dog teams and to attend to the medical needs of settlers in remote outposts. At the outset of his episcopate Rowe believed that his primary field of work would be among the native peoples of Alaska. The Klondike gold rush, followed by the "stampedes" in Nome and Fairbanks, quickly enlarged the scope of his episcopal duties. Beginning in 1897 he visited mining camps and boom towns, where he preached in saloons, in gambling halls, and in tents to gold prospectors "from almost every civilized nation on the earth." He opened the first makeshift hospitals and cared for migrants stricken with scurvy or typhoid. In Nome and in Fairbanks he built, with his hands, wood-frame churches.

Rowe's travels across Alaska were legendary. In his lifetime he was the most experienced traveler in the territory and was unsurpassed in his knowledge of the Alaskan terrain. Called to "the Lord's business," he typically covered more than 2,000 miles each year on dog-sled runs, traversing, in his words, "limitless reaches of unbroken ice and snow . . . through howling winds and Arctic cold." "As a musher," he once boasted in an interview, "I took a back seat to no one." In 1896 he led a party on the first recorded climb through the Chilkoot Pass and on a run down the treacherous Yukon rapids. Only at age seventy-four, in 1931, did he abandon snowshoes and sleds to travel his diocese by air.

In his first encounters with the natives of Alaska, Rowe was repelled by certain customs, such as polygamy and shamanism. He swiftly became, however, an uncompromising friend to the natives, whom he called "my people." He learned to speak Chinook and often preached to assemblies of Indians without interpreters. He founded hospitals and schools, including the first hospital for the Eskimos. He lobbied the U.S.

Congress on behalf of hunting and fishing rights for the natives and against canneries on the Yukon River that depleted supplies of salmon. Ultimately Rowe founded twenty-four missions in Alaska. Largely because of his efforts, in 1941 roughly one-half of the native population of Alaska were baptized members of the Episcopal church, and copies of the Bible, the Book of Common Prayer, and the Episcopal hymnal were to be found in every village above the Arctic Circle.

Although he declined four offers to serve other bishoprics, Rowe moved his diocesan office in 1926 from Sitka to Seattle. At the time of his death, in Victoria, British Columbia, he was the oldest active bishop within the Anglican Communion. Widely known as the "Bishop of the Snows," he had served as a missionary bishop in Alaska for forty-six years. He was survived by his second wife, Rose Fullerton (whom he had married in 1915 after the death of his first wife), their three children, and one child from his first marriage.

In his lifetime, Rowe was an honored figure in Alaska and in all quarters of the Episcopal church. His exceptional courage during perilous journeys across Alaska and his devotion to the spiritual and material welfare of his diocese earned him widespread adulation. Among his followers in Alaska he was "the great missionary bishop of the Church in our time" (*Alaskan Churchman*, p. 6). Rowe dedicated sixty-six years of his life to missionary work, an accomplishment remarkable for its length and for its association with the native peoples of Ontario, Michigan, the Yukon, and Alaska. His energetic and humanitarian achievements rank with those of Father Ivan Veniaminov of the Russian Orthodox church in the forefront of a 150-year history of missionary endeavors in Alaska.

• The Archives of the Episcopal Church, USA, in Austin, Tex., has a sizable collection of correspondence, annual reports, and other manuscripts relating to Rowe. He began, but never completed, an autobiography. Portions of it are included in the leading source of information on him, a biography by Thomas Jenkins, *The Man of Alaska* (1943). Late in life Rowe was the subject of numerous articles in newspapers and magazines, including the *New York Times*, 30 Nov. and 1 and 2 Dec. 1935; *Time*, 1 Dec. 1941, p. 44; and the Washington, D.C., *Sunday Star*, 31 May 1942. A descriptive account of Rowe's popularity and influence is in Ella Higginson, *Alaska: The Great Country*, 3d ed. (1926), pp. 211–12. An insightful assessment of his importance in the history of Alaska is in Melody Webb, *The Last Frontier* (1985), and, among Episcopal missionaries, in David L. Holmes, "The Domestic Missionary Movement in the Episcopal Church in the 19th Century," in *Beyond the Horizon*, ed. Charles R. Henery (1985). The most informative obituaries are in the *Alaskan Churchman*, Nov. 1942, and the *New York Times*, 2 June 1942.

JEFFREY CRONIN

ROWLAND, Henry Augustus (27 Nov. 1848–16 Apr. 1901), experimental physicist, was born in Honesdale, Pennsylvania, the son of Henry Augustus Rowland, Sr., a Presbyterian clergyman, and Harriet Heyer, the daughter of a New York merchant. In the spring of 1865 Rowland enrolled in the Phillips Academy at Andover, Massachusetts, to study Latin and Greek, with the intention of then entering Yale University, as had his father and grandfather, to become a clergyman. But by the fall of 1865 he had switched to the study of science and engineering at the Rensselaer Polytechnic Institute at Troy, New York, from which he graduated as a civil engineer in 1870.

After being employed as a railroad surveyor for one year and as a teacher at the College of Wooster in Ohio in 1871, he returned to Rensselaer as an instructor in physics in 1872 and became assistant professor of physics in 1874. His research at that time concerned the magnetic permeability of iron, steel, and nickel. Although his data were seriously distorted by hysteresis, he nevertheless was able to show that magnetic permeability varied with the magnetizing force, a result which won him recognition as a promising experimentalist.

In 1875 the founding president of the newly established Johns Hopkins University, Daniel Coit Gilman, appointed Rowland the university's first professor of physics. Rowland held this chair until his premature death in 1901. In planning his laboratory, he undertook a one-year journey in Europe with the aim of studying experimental and teaching methods at leading universities and examining their instrumentation. Rowland visited in particular James Clark Maxwell in Cambridge, England, and Hermann von Helmholtz in Berlin, Germany, working in the latter's laboratories for four months in the winter of 1875–1876. There he succeeded in demonstrating for the first time that moving charges on a rotating disc do in fact create magnetic effects like an electric current.

With the instruments and equipment he had purchased in Europe for more than $6,000, Rowland's physics laboratory became the best-equipped in the United States and attracted many students. Closely connected with his laboratory was a well-equipped workshop in which new apparatus could be produced. Between 1879 and 1901 Rowland had 165 graduate students, including forty-five doctoral students, thirty of whom later appeared in *American Men of Science*; in this sense he was instrumental in the establishment of the physics discipline in America. Rowland's research in the late 1870s was mostly concerned with precision measurement, such as the absolute value of the unit of electrical resistance. His 1873 value of the ohm was within .5 percent of the value adopted in 1905. Around 1880 he undertook the determination of the mechanical equivalent of heat, improving on James Prescott Joule's authoritative work of the 1840s. With these measurements, Rowland demonstrated his mastery of the art of designing physical apparatus and his experimental insight in avoiding potential systematic errors. For this work, he was awarded the Rumford Medal in 1884.

Rowland became most famous for his work on spectroscopy and diffraction gratings. In the early 1880s he improved the design of "ruling engines," which guide a sharp diamond point over a speculum metal surface and produce parallel ruled lines at a fixed spacing of roughly one-thousandth of a millimeter. The straightness of the lines was achieved by guiding the point along two parallel hardened metal rails; more difficult was its repositioning by exactly the same minute distance after each ruling for up to 110,000 lines in one grating. Rowland's success lay in using a very regular ruling screw up to twenty-five centimeters in length, made out of special flawless steel, in a painstaking grinding process that could take up to fourteen days without interruption to complete. Rowland claimed that "there was not an error of half a wave-length, although the screw was nine inches long." His ruled gratings were much more regular than those constructed by his American predecessors, Lewis Rutherfurd and William August Rogers, and were also free from periodic errors, which caused the appearance of pseudo-lines (called ghosts) in the diffraction spectra.

Over the course of his career Rowland produced three of these ruling engines. The first, built in the autumn of 1881, could rule up to 14,438 lines per inch. In 1889 and 1894 he constructed two others, which ruled 20,000 and 15,020 lines per inch respectively onto surfaces of up to twenty-five square inches. Each machine was driven mechanically by water power, which had greater regularity and higher reliability than electric power, and worked nonstop for up to fourteen days under permanent monitoring, until a complete grating was ruled. Commenting on Rowland's practical ingenuity, Rowland's successor at Johns Hopkins, Joseph Sweetman Ames, reported:

I have seen Rowland stand by the machine with a screw driver in his hand looking at the specimen of ruling and then say "I think I'll try this." Then he would poke his screw driver in, doing something which would be impossible for anyone else to understand clearly; and the chances were that after one or two such attacks on the machine it would work all right. When I would ask him what he had done, and why he had done it, he was never able to explain fully. The truth was that his knowledge of machines of all kinds was in part a process of instinct. (*Johns Hopkins University Alumni Magazine*, Jan. 1916, pp. 92–99)

In 1882 Rowland invented concave diffraction gratings. With the very slight radius of curvature of three to six meters, the regular pattern on the ruled speculum metal surface acted not only as a reflecting diffraction grating, but in addition had a focusing effect, thus obviating the use of convex glass lenses with their unwanted light absorption in the ultraviolet. Throughout the late nineteenth and early twentieth centuries, all major spectroscopists tried to get at least one of these gratings, which allowed work on a broader range of frequencies much more efficiently and at an increase of precision of roughly a factor of ten compared to other contemporary gratings. They were manufactured in Baltimore by Rowland's chief mechanician, Theodore Schneider, and passed a rigorous quality control by his assistant Lewis E. Jewell before being handed over to

the distributor, the instrument maker John A. Brashear in Pittsburgh, Pennsylvania, who also supplied the polished curved surfaces. By January 1901 between 250 and 300 gratings had been sold at cost to physical and chemical laboratories and astronomical observatories all over the world, in addition to those gratings that had been given away for free (probably a handful, at most).

Rowland was a founding member and from 1899 to 1901 the first president of the American Physical Society and became a member of the Legion of Honor in 1896. His diffraction gratings and photographic map of the solar spectrum won him the gold medal and a grand prize at the Paris world exhibition of 1890 and the National Academy of Sciences' Draper Medal. He served as a U.S. delegate at various international congresses concerned with the determination of electrical units and became a member of the National Academy of Sciences, a foreign member of the Royal Society of London and the Paris Académie des Sciences, as well as of about a dozen other learned societies and academies.

In 1890 Rowland married Henrietta Troup Harrison; they had three children. Also in 1890 Rowland learned that he had diabetes, which was then untreatable. His more commercially oriented activities at the end of his life, such as his work on the development and marketing of a multiplex telegraph, his occupation as chief design consultant for the installation of big electric generators at Niagara Falls, and his filing of at least nineteen patent claims, can be seen as an effort to assure the future livelihood of his family. He died in Baltimore. At his own request, his cremated ashes were masoned into the wall of his laboratory close to the ruling engine.

• Rowland's papers, including notebooks, drafts, correspondence, lectures, calculations, bills, patents, and other materials, are in the Milton S. Eisenhower Library of Johns Hopkins University. His papers have been collected in *Physical Papers of Henry Augustus Rowland*, ed. T. C. Mendenhall (1902), but this volume excludes his long tables of spectral wavelengths that were published in the *Astrophysical Journal*. The most detailed biographical study is Mendenhall's sketch in National Academy of Sciences, *Biographical Memoirs* 5 (1905): 115–40, which also includes a full bibliography. Retrospective general evaluations of his work can be found in *American Journal of Physics*, by H. F. Reid, 9 (1941): 117–19, and by Henry Crew, 17 (1949): 576f.; John D. Miller, "Rowland's Physics," *Physics Today* (July 1976): 39–46; and A. D. Moore, "Henry A. Rowland," *Scientific American* 246 (1982): 118–26.

On Rowland's trip to Europe see Samuel Reznick, *American Journal of Physics* 30 (1962): 877–86, and on his formative years see Reznick, "The Education of an American Scientist," *American Journal of Physics* 28 (1960): 155–62. For Rowland's important work in electromagnetism during his Berlin stay and its later impact, see John David Miller, "Rowland and the Nature of Electric Currents," *ISIS* 63 (1972): 4–27. For his role in precision spectroscopy, see Richard C. Henry and Peter Beer, eds., "Henry Rowland and Astronomical Spectroscopy," *Vistas in Astronomy* 29 (1986): 125–42; and Klaus Hentschel, "The Discovery of Solar Redshift by Rowland and Jewell in Baltimore around

1890," *Historical Studies in the Physical Sciences* 23, no. 2 (1993): 219–77. On Rowland's role in the establishment of the physics discipline in America, see Daniel J. Kevles, *The Physicists* (1987). An obituary is in the *Baltimore Sun*, 17 Apr. 1901.

KLAUS HENTSCHEL

ROWLANDSON, Mary White (c. 1637/38–5 Jan. 1710), author of the earliest full-length Indian captivity narrative, was born probably in England shortly before her parents, John White and Joan (maiden name unknown), landowners, immigrated to New England in 1639. Mary White was brought up in a comfortable household. When her father died in 1653, he was the wealthiest landowner in Lancaster, Massachusetts, with an estate valued at £389. Around 1656 she married Joseph Rowlandson, who was ordained in 1660 and became a prominent member of the Puritan clergy. They had three children (a fourth died in infancy).

When the frontier community of Lancaster was attacked in February 1676 during King Philip's War (1675–1676), Rowlandson, her three children, and other settlers were captured by Native Americans and held for ransom. Because of Rowlandson's position in New England society, her capture attracted considerable attention and led to special efforts to release her. She was ransomed in May 1676 for the sum of £20, and two of her children, Joseph and Mary, were released some weeks later. Her third child, six-year-old Sarah, died in captivity from wounds received during the initial attack. Rowlandson's three-month captivity forms the basis of her famous and popular captivity narrative, titled *The Sovereignty and Goodness of God* for its first three editions (all published in New England in 1682) and *A True History* for its fourth edition (London, 1682).

After the family was reunited, they moved to Boston for a short time because their home in Lancaster had been destroyed. In 1677 they moved to Wethersfield, Connecticut, where Rev. Joseph Rowlandson became the new minister. But on 24 November 1678, he died suddenly, just three days after delivering a powerful sermon whose text was bound with the early editions of his wife's narrative. He left his widow and children a substantial estate, including a large library.

Because Rowlandson's name was not mentioned after about March 1679, literary scholars assumed that she must have died shortly after her husband. However, recently recovered genealogical information proves that she disappeared as Mary Rowlandson only because she remarried and took her second husband's name. On 6 August 1679 she married Captain Samuel Talcott, a Harvard graduate and community leader. Little is known about her life after this except that in 1707 she testified in a notorious court case involving her son, Joseph, who was accused of selling his brother-in-law Nathaniel Wilson into servitude, presumably because Joseph stood to benefit from Wilson's estate if Wilson were declared legally dead. Rowlandson outlived both her spouses and died in Wethersfield.

Rowlandson's only literary work is her autobiographical narrative, which reveals her physical, spiritual, and psychological states as she reluctantly journeyed across what she called "the vast and desolate Wilderness." It is estimated that she traveled about 150 miles while a prisoner and journeyed as far north as New Hampshire. Although it has not been possible to confirm exactly when she composed this text, internal and external evidence suggests that she wrote it shortly after her release but did not publish it for several years. Like many later captives, she seems to have been persuaded to publish her private story for public reasons. In this case, the reasons were spiritual and political: her work exemplified the Puritan belief in providential affliction, and it lent support to the settlers' distrust and dislike of the Native Americans. And yet the work is actually much more complex, as it challenged these basic assumptions even as it reiterated them. As a woman, she could not initiate publication herself and was almost certainly aided in this endeavor by the prominent Puritan minister Increase Mather, who probably also wrote the anonymous preface to her text.

Critics have praised Rowlandson's narrative for its sophisticated form, pointing out both the underlying mythic structure of capture-initiation-return and the distinctive arrangement of its twenty separate episodes (or "removes," as Rowlandson termed them). Rowlandson also skillfully blends plot with psychological and spiritual analysis to produce an integrated textual structure. Her work became an immediate bestseller in New England and has remained the best-known and most anthologized Indian captivity narrative. It is considered a colonial classic, a rare example of a work by a seventeenth-century American woman writer, and a text that seems to accommodate almost endless reinterpretation.

• No manuscript of Rowlandson's text exists, and the first edition is no longer extant. The most authoritative edition is considered the fourth, *A True History* (1682), because it seems to have been typeset from the first edition (or possibly even from the manuscript). Rowlandson's captivity narrative is widely anthologized, though readers should be aware that anthologized versions do not necessarily follow the fourth, authoritative, edition.

Many studies of this narrative have been written; a selection of the more important ones includes Mitchell Robert Breitwieser, *American Puritanism and the Defense of Mourning: Religion, Grief, and Ethnology in Mary White Rowlandson's Captivity Narrative* (1990); Kathryn Zabelle Derounian, "Puritan Orthodoxy and the 'Survivor Syndrome' in Mary Rowlandson's Indian Captivity Narrative," *Early American Literature* 22 (1987): 82–93, and "The Publication, Promotion, and Distribution of Mary Rowlandson's Indian Captivity Narrative in the Seventeenth Century," *Early American Literature* 23 (1988): 239–61; David L. Greene, "New Light on Mary Rowlandson," *Early American Literature* 20 (1985): 24–38; Douglas Edward Leach, "The 'When's' of Mary Rowlandson's Captivity," *New England Quarterly* 34 (1961): 353–63; David L. Minter, "By Dens of Lions: Notes on Stylization in Early Puritan Captivity Narratives," *American*

Literature 45 (1973): 335–47; and Roy Harvey Pearce, "The Significances of the Captivity Narrative," *American Literature* 19 (1947): 1–20.

KATHRYN ZABELLE DEROUNIAN-STODOLA

ROWLEY, Thomas (1721–1796), politician and poet of the Green Mountain Boys, was born in Hebron, Connecticut, the son of poor farmers whose names are not known. Little is known of Rowley's early years. Rowley was himself an unremarkable small farmer until the age of forty-seven, when he moved with his family to the northern frontier of New England and helped to found the town of Danby. Elected the first town clerk in 1769, an office he held until 1782, Rowley taught himself surveying and traveled through much of the Green Mountains. The struggle between New Hampshire and New York for control of this region propelled Rowley into an active political career on the side of those settlers who favored independence from both provinces.

In 1771 Rowley's friend Ethan Allen, leader of the Green Mountain separatist movement, encouraged Rowley to turn his skill at improvised versifying to political topics. By 1774 Rowley was well known in New England as the bard of the Green Mountain Boys, the popular name for Allen's followers. Rowley was with Allen at the capture of Fort Ticonderoga in May 1775 and played an active role in organizing American forces in the north during the Revolution. In addition to serving as chair of the region's Committee of Safety for most of the Revolution, Rowley played a key role at the conventions that formed the independent state of Vermont and produced its constitution. He served on numerous committees and helped to draft petitions and public statements. An eloquent speaker, he apparently helped to persuade many who wavered in the separatist cause. A member of the first Vermont Assembly, Rowley emerged as one of the leaders of the more radical faction within the legislature, serving as chair of dozens of committees and pushing for the expropriation of the property of all Loyalists. Rowley served as a judge on the special court for the confiscation of Loyalist lands in 1778–1779. In addition he saw duty as a militia officer, county surveyor, and member of the assembly from 1778 to 1782. With the war's end, Rowley moved to Shoreham, Vermont, where he became the first town clerk and justice of the peace, positions he held from 1783 until his death.

While most of Rowley's poetry would strike modern ears as dreadful, and while he often slipped into Hudibrastic when he could not make a rhyme, contemporaries credited Rowley with "setting the mountains on fire" with his poetry. Newspapers from Pennsylvania to New Hampshire reprinted Rowley's poems, influencing other American nationalist poets such as Joel Barlow. Rowley's poems appealed to class antagonisms, calling on "you laboring hands" to rise up against political and economic elites and seize what was rightfully theirs. As Rowley wrote, "We value not New York with all their powers, / For here we'll stay and work, the land is ours." In addition to his political poems, which often doubled as promotional literature for Vermont land, Rowley wrote pastoral and religious poetry. The latter, which formed the bulk of his published work, was particularly popular among his fellow Methodists for its attacks on Calvinist predestination. "If I withhold my hand from what I am forbid, / Why then should I be dam'd for what I never did?" Rowley's poems glorified the independent yeoman farmer and fostered the image of America as an agrarian republic of smallholders. Rowley himself remained among that smallholding class until his death at his son's house in Benson, Vermont. His wife's name is unknown, though there are many poems in her memory. Together they had four children.

• Sources of original documents concerning Rowley are in Special Collections, Bailey/Howe Library, University of Vermont; the Vermont State Archives, Montpelier; the Vermont Historical Society, Montpelier; and the Danby town clerk's office. Political records can be found in E. P. Walton, ed., *Records of the Council of Safety, and Governor, and Council of the State of Vermont* (8 vols., 1873–1880), and Walter H. Crockett, ed., *Journals and Proceedings of the General Assembly of the State of Vermont, 1778–1781* (3 vols., 1924–1925). For collections of Rowley's poems, see *Selections and Miscellaneous Works of Thomas Rowley* (1802); J. C. Williams, *The History and Map of Danby, Vermont* (1869); and Abby M. Hemenway, ed., *Vermont Historical Gazetteer* (1868). See also Michael Bellesiles, *Revolutionary Outlaws: Ethan Allen and the Struggle for Independence on the Early American Frontier* (1993); Matt B. Jones, *Vermont in the Making, 1750–1777* (1968); and Chilton Williamson, *Vermont in Quandary, 1763–1825* (1949).

MICHAEL BELLESILES

ROWSON, Susanna Haswell (Feb. 1762–2 Mar. 1824), writer and educator, was born in Portsmouth, England, the daughter of William Haswell, naval officer, and Susanna Musgrave. Her mother died shortly after childbirth, and her father entrusted her to relatives when he was sent for naval duty in colonial Massachusetts. There he married Rachel Woodward and in 1766 brought the five-year-old Susanna to settle with the family in Hull, Massachusetts. Though she received no formal schooling, the child Susanna benefited from her father's good library. In 1775 the American patriots imprisoned Lieutenant Haswell and his family before returning them to England in 1778 in a prisoner exchange.

As a young refugee in London, Susanna Haswell was drawn to the theater. To help support the family she wrote songs for Vauxhall Gardens and in 1786 published her first novel, a conventional story of seduction and filial piety entitled *Victoria*. In the same year she married William Rowson, about whom little is known except that he played trumpet, sang, and acted on stage. Susanna Rowson's intense interest in and acquaintance with theater is reflected in *A Trip to Parnassus*, a lighthearted but critical poetic evaluation of actors at Covent Garden, published two years later. Also in 1788 she published *The Inquisitor*, a loosely structured, picaresque series of short stories or scenes in the sentimental tradition of Laurence Sterne.

Although Rowson remained married to William, family support fell on her shoulders, as he seemed unable to hold a job and later drank excessively. Failing to earn a living from the stage, Rowson pursued the writing of novels. In 1789 she anonymously published the unsuccessful *Mary, or The Test of Honour* and in 1791 published the novel with which her name today is identified, *Charlotte, a Tale of Truth*. This short but fast-moving sentimental story caused little stir until it was published in the United States in 1794 and became America's first bestseller. The simple plot of this novel concerns fifteen-year-old Charlotte, whose French teacher encourages her to run away to America with a handsome young army officer, Montraville, who has promised marriage. Once in New York, however, Montraville delays in honoring his commitment and soon falls in love with a beautiful heiress. Montraville's false friend, the scheming Belcour, tricks Montraville into believing that Charlotte is unfaithful and convinces Charlotte that Montraville has deserted her. In a pattern followed by literary heroines for another fifty years, the pregnant and forsaken Charlotte wanders through a snowstorm seeking assistance. After poor servants finally befriend her, Charlotte gives birth to a daughter and descends into insanity. Her father, who has learned of her whereabouts, arrives from England to take her home, but comes too late. Charlotte dies after receiving his forgiveness. American readers responded to the novel's American setting, its democratic disapproval of class snobbery, and its emphasis on the virtuous middle class. As readers came to believe in the truth of the novel, they made pilgrimages to Charlotte's supposed gravesite in New York. The novel went through more than 150 editions and various translations; it was copied, imitated, and dramatized.

In 1791 Rowson also published a collection of tales called *Mentoria*. The following year she published yet another novel, *Rebecca; or the Fille de Chambre*, also more popular in its later American version. This somewhat autobiographical work features a young woman who, forced to earn a living, suffers a cruel employer, then various adventures including a sea voyage to America and war experiences there. These early Rowson novels written in England contain themes that continued to run through Rowson's life's work: filial piety, contentment with one's station in life, sympathy for the fallen woman, the virtues of the middle classes, and the importance of women's education. They established literary patterns that women's literature followed through much of the nineteenth century.

In 1793 the Rowsons and other actors and actresses were recruited by Thomas Wignell into the New Theater Company of Chestnut Street in Philadelphia, formed to meet the growing demands of the postrevolutionary American theater audience. Thus Rowson returned permanently to the United States to enter the world of actors and musicians developing the arts in the new nation. In Philadelphia she continued writing while performing in over thirty-five roles. *Slaves in Algiers* (1793), Rowson's only surviving play, contained strong feminist statements that provoked a pamphlet attack by William Cobbett. *Trials of the Human Heart* (1794), an epistolary novel, contains a number of autobiographical scenes, but none rescued the work from its episodic structure and weak characterization. When the Wignell company faced financial failure in 1796, the Rowsons and their colleagues moved to the Boston Federal Street Theater. A year later that company too went bankrupt, and Rowson changed careers. Pursuing her abiding interest in women's education, she opened Boston's first academy for young women.

Mrs. Rowson's Young Ladies' Academy on Federal Street attracted the daughters of the socially prominent. Moving from Boston to Medford to Newton and back to Boston, her academy introduced a rigorous curriculum including geography, history, navigation, and music. With the unflagging energy that characterized her life, Rowson continued writing novels (*Reuben and Rachel; or, Tales of Old Times* in 1798 and *Sincerity* in 1803–1804), as well as poems, textbooks, and a collection of recitations from her academy's annual exhibition. Her sequel to *Charlotte Temple, Charlotte's Daughter; or, The Three Orphans*, was published posthumously in 1828 but never achieved the popularity of the original.

When she died in Boston, Rowson was mourned by the many Boston women she had educated and by readers of her popular novels. Distinguished among writers of her time for her interest in women, Rowson contributed substantially to the development of the literary, musical, poetic, and dramatic arts of the new Republic, expressing in various ways the American concern for freedom.

• Rowson papers can be found in the Barrett Collection, University of Virginia. Biography and criticism are found in Patricia Parker's *Susanna Rowson* (1986), Dorothy Weil's *In Defense of Women* (1976), and Cathy Davidson's edition of *Charlotte Temple* (1986). Bibliographies are by Robert W. G. Vail, *Susanna Haswell Rowson, the Author of Charlotte Temple: A Bibliographical Study* (1933), and Patricia Parker, *Early American Fiction: A Reference Guide* (1984). Obituaries are in the *Boston Evening Gazette*, 6 Mar. 1824, and in the *Columbian Centinel*, 10 Mar. 1824.

PATRICIA L. PARKER

ROYALL, Anne Newport (11 June 1769–1 Oct. 1854), travel writer and journalist, was born near Baltimore, Maryland, the daughter of William Newport and Mary (maiden name unknown). The Newports moved to the Pennsylvania frontier in 1772 and by 1775 were living near Hanna's Town, the Westmoreland County seat, after which time William Newport disappears from the records. Anne learned to read at an early age from her father and briefly attended school in a log cabin. After the death of her mother's second husband (c. 1782), she moved with her mother and her half brother to Middle River, Virginia. In 1787 she and her mother became domestics for William Royall of Sweet Springs Mountain, now in West Virginia.

Appreciating her intellect and wit, William Royall undertook Anne's education by introducing her to the works of Thomas Paine and Voltaire and by instructing her in the principles of Freemasonry. She married William Royall in 1797 and managed his estate until his death in December 1812. Selling the plantation the year after his death, she indulged a long-held desire to travel, spending most of the next decade in Alabama. No children had issued from the marriage.

Anne Royall turned to literature for a livelihood after relatives of William Royall succeeded in overturning his will in 1819, claiming that she had forged the will, treated her husband badly during their marriage, and cohabitated with him before marriage. She denied all but the last charge. While dodging creditors, Royall supported herself by writing about the rapidly expanding and developing nation. In preparation for what was to become *Letters from Alabama on Various Subjects* (1830), Royall gathered the letters she had written between 1817 and 1822 to her young lawyer friend Matthew Dunbar as she traveled through Kentucky, Tennessee, and Alabama. While still in Alabama, she began work on *The Tennessean* (1827), a historical romance describing a secret expedition of frontiersmen to Spanish-ruled New Mexico, which unsuccessfully combines the conventions of the domestic romance, dime novel, and shipwreck narrative. To support herself, Royall also petitioned the federal government for a pension as a revolutionary war widow.

Using Washington, D.C. as her home base, Royall traveled extensively from 1824 to 1830. Recording her journeys in nine published volumes, Royall described every substantial city and town in the United States. Her dauntless personality and her husband's Masonic connections enabled her to gather an impressive list of subscribers for *Sketches of History, Life, and Manners in the United States* (1826), signed "a Traveller," which traced her trip from Alabama to New England from 1823 through 1825. In this work she discussed politics, education, religion, and social vices, depicting in detail colleges, schools, churches, hospitals, almshouses, prisons, museums, theaters, and libraries. She also interviewed prominent citizens and included population, crop, and trade statistics. A signature mark of both her travel writing and her later journalism was the "pen portrait," a brief, vivid sketch of a celebrity's appearance and character. Royall's travel works demonstrate her talents as a roving correspondent: boundless curiosity, attention to detail, and investigative skills.

Except for *Sketches of History*, which is good-humored, her travel writing also reveals a liberal political philosophy and acerbic wit that some readers found offensive. In *The Black Book* (3 vols., 1828–1829), *Mrs. Royall's Pennsylvania* (2 vols., 1829), and *Mrs. Royall's Southern Tour* (3 vols., 1830–1831), she attacked, often fervently, political corruption, the enemies of Freemasonry, and Protestant evangelicals such as Ezra Stiles Ely and Lyman Beecher. In her *Southern Tour*, Royall dismissed tract literature and

missionary societies as "vile speculations to amass money" with the explanation that their promoters collect "money . . . from the poor and ignorant, and no man of sense would pay for the gospel which is to be had without a price" (vol. 3, p. 244). Despite her diatribes against opponents and flattery of subscribers, Royall's travel works are still of historical and social value.

Royall's revelations and her animosity toward evangelicals, whom she contemptuously labeled "Holy Rollers," "Holy Willies," and "Blackcoats," resulted in her widely publicized trial in 1829 on the obsolete charge of common scold or public nuisance. Royall was convicted for twice berating members of a neighboring evangelical congregation who tormented her with heckling and stones, "usually at night," noted Royall, "'when the out-pouring of divine goodness' is most powerful" (*Pennsylvania*, vol. 2, app., p. 2). Deeming the traditional punishment of a public dunking too ludicrous, Judge William Cranch fined Royall $10 and ordered her to post a $100 bond as a guarantee of her future conduct. Many journalists viewed the event as an attack on freedom of speech and the press, and two reporters for the *Washington National Intelligencer* paid her fine and bond. James Gordon Bennett (1795–1872), a Washington reporter who later founded the *New York Herald*, sat with Royall throughout the trial.

The infirmities of age and the hostile reception she sometimes met with on her 1830 tour of southern states encouraged Royall to settle in Washington and to abandon travel writing for the more sedentary occupation of journalist. With the help of Sarah Stack, a younger friend who acted as her assistant and companion, Royall began publishing on 3 December 1831 a four-page weekly newspaper called *Paul Pry*. Named after an 1825 English comedy by John Poole and printed in Royall's kitchen, *Paul Pry* contained ads, humorous and poetic fillers, local news, political news, and editorials. An independent newspaper, *Paul Pry* is notable for its exposés of government graft and the Bank of the United States, its editorials pleading for civil service and public health reforms, and its attacks on evangelicals and Anti-Masons. The last issue of *Paul Pry* appeared on 19 November 1836. It was succeeded on 2 December 1836 by the *Huntress*, in which Royall continued to expose ills and espouse causes. She denounced the beef monopoly, defended Catholic foreigners, berated legislators from blocking improvements in the western states, and argued against abolition. The *Huntress* also included a joke column and a literary page with poems and sketches reprinted from popular writers, including Dickens and Seba Smith, creator of the comic Yankee character, Major Jack Dowling. As Royall aged, she relied increasingly on others to assist with the paper, particularly John Henry Simmes, an orphan she took into her household. By 1854 Simmes was both printing and writing almost every issue. When he married in March 1854, Royall attempted to carry on without him, but publication of the paper ceased in May. In June 1854 Royall revived the paper in a pamphlet-size format, but the second series lasted for only three issues. In the final issue, which appeared on 24 July, Royall offered a prayer for the eternal "Union of these States" and noted that she had "thirty-one cents in the world" (quoted in James, p. 386). She died in Washington, D.C.

Royall's contemporaries viewed her as an eccentric—sometimes even as a figure of fun—because of her indifference to her appearance, her tart tongue, her strongly held and often unfashionable views, and her reformer's zeal. Frederick A. Packard of the *Hampden Journal* represented the views of many when he dismissed Royall as "a silly old hag" who belonged in "some asylum or work house" (18 July 1827). Yet Royall contributed significantly to social history and journalism. Her work not only contains valuable descriptions of institutions, customs, and personalities but also demonstrates the potency of the press as a watchdog of freedom against government corruption and abuse.

• The largest collection of Royall's papers, including the files of *Paul Pry* and the *Huntress*, is in the Library of Congress. The official records of her 1829 trial are in the National Archives, *U.S. v. Royall*, Records of the Circuit Court, District of Columbia. The best and most complete biography of Anne Royall is Bessie Rowland James, *Anne Royall's U.S.A.* (1972), but Alice S. Maxwell and Marion Dunlevy, *Virago!: The Story of Anne Newport Royall* (1985), should be consulted for an account of her trial. Although occasionally inaccurate, Sarah Harvey Porter, *The Life and Times of Anne Royall* (1909), and George S. Jackson, *Uncommon Scold* (1937), are still useful biographies. For an evaluation of Royall's contributions to journalism, see Madelon Golden Schilpp and Sharon M. Murphy, *Great Women of the Press* (1983), pp. 21–36.

JEANNE M. MALLOY

ROYALL, Kenneth Claiborne (24 July 1894–25 May 1971), lawyer and last U.S. secretary of war, was born in Goldsboro, North Carolina, the son of George Claiborne Royall, a wealthy manufacturer, and Clara Howard Jones. Royall attended local public schools in Goldsboro and completed his secondary education at the Episcopal High School in Alexandria, Virginia. He entered the University of North Carolina at Chapel Hill in 1911 and received a bachelor of arts degree in 1914. At the university, Royall majored in mathematics, captained the debating team, and graduated with Phi Beta Kappa honors. He continued his studies at Harvard Law School, where he served as an associate editor of the *Harvard Law Review* and earned an LL.B. in 1917.

In May 1917, less than a month after the United States entered World War I, Royall joined the army. Trained at Fort Oglethorpe, Georgia, he became a second lieutenant on 15 August. Just three days after receiving his commission, Royall married Margaret Best in Warsaw, North Carolina. The couple had three children, two of whom survived to adulthood. In January 1918 Royall was promoted to first lieutenant. He sailed for France with the 317th Field Artillery Reserve seven months later. Though he saw combat he was not wounded in the war.

Returning home to Goldsboro in February 1919, Royall opened a small law practice there by the end of the year. He soon established himself as one of the foremost trial lawyers in the area, and in 1937 he formed a partnership with several of North Carolina's finest attorneys (including former governor J. C. B. Ehringhaus and future U.S. senator Willis Smith). Instead of limiting himself to his successful law practice, Royall increasingly involved himself in Democratic politics. In 1926 he was elected to the North Carolina State Senate, where he chaired the Banking Committee and drafted the long-standing North Carolina Bank Liquidation Statute. He also served as president of the North Carolina Bar Association from 1929 to 1930 and as a Democratic presidential elector in 1940.

In June 1942 Royall retired from his law practice, received a colonel's commission in the U.S. Army, and assumed control of the Army Service Forces legal section. He rose to public prominence within a month of his appointment, when President Franklin D. Roosevelt appointed him defense counsel for eight German saboteurs who had been captured just after they landed from a submarine on Long Island. Royall appealed the saboteur case all the way to the U.S. Supreme Court, which ruled against him.

Royall quickly advanced up the army's hierarchy, in part because of the prominence he gained during the saboteur case. In 1943 he was made deputy fiscal director of Army Services and was promoted to the rank of brigadier general. In April 1945 he became special assistant to Secretary of War Henry Stimson, whom he had met during the saboteur case. As special assistant he coordinated legislative proposals and executive orders on procurement of army supplies, and he maintained contact with the Department of Justice in fraud cases involving War Department contractors. In November 1945 Royall received the Distinguished Service Medal for "perform[ing] exceptionally meritorious services . . . in positions of great responsibility."

When Under Secretary of War Robert Porter Patterson moved up to the secretary of war position in October 1945, he chose Royall as his under secretary. Royall's record shows that he was an exceptionally diligent under secretary. He settled nearly 480,000 delinquent contracts during his two years in office, earning a reputation as "the War Department's number one bulldog." Believing that the U.S. Army had been punitive in issuing courts-martial sentences during World War II, he reviewed 30,000 courts-martial cases as under secretary, reducing 80 percent of those sentences. Royall remained deeply committed to reforming the army's courts-martial policy and instituted a much more humane system in April 1947.

In July 1947 President Harry Truman appointed Royall secretary of war. However, the National Security Act of 1947 soon undermined Royall's autonomy by unifying all branches of the armed forces under the National Military Establishment (later the U.S. Department of Defense). In September James Forrestal became secretary of defense and joined Truman's cabinet, while Royall lost his cabinet position as his title was changed to secretary of the army. In this post, Royall assumed responsibility for operating all army bases and seacoast fortifications. He also enlarged the military mission of the U.S. Army in Europe by securing $500 million in additional funds for the support of American troops.

After resigning as secretary of the army in April 1949, Royall moved to New York City and became a partner in one of the nation's most prominent law firms, Dwight, Royall, Harris, Koegel, and Caskey. He became head of the firm in 1958, serving in that capacity until his retirement in January 1968.

In his later years, Royall was among the early southern proponents of desegregation in public schools. During a 1955 speech at the dedication of an armory in Goldsboro, he said North Carolina could solve its school desegregation problems peacefully "no matter how hopeless the situation looks to many in this state." He warned North Carolinians against abolishing the public school system, as some politicians had proposed after the Supreme Court's 1954 *Brown v. Board of Education* decision.

Royall rekindled his interest in politics during John F. Kennedy's administration, serving as a mediator between civil rights groups and local authorities during the 1963 racial flareups in Alabama and as a delegate to the 1964 Democratic National Convention. Royall died in Durham, North Carolina.

Although Royall did not participate in the complex task of postwar policy formulation, he was a master technician who fought corruption and ensured that various aspects of the military operated with the greatest efficiency possible. Perhaps best remembered for his booming voice and his six-foot-five frame, Royall earned the respect of his peers in the legal and military communities. In the 1950s and 1960s the Pentagon periodically called on Royall for advice about military matters. He also won the trust of politicians for his moderate conservatism and appreciation of political problems. Late in life, Truman wrote a personal letter that praised Royall's lifelong commitment to service: "In war and peace, you have served your government faithfully and well. As an officer with overseas combat service in both wars . . . you gained rich experience before you were called on to serve in various civilian capacities. . . . For your part in . . . activities of paramount importance to the national security, I tender you this assurance of heartfelt gratitude and appreciation."

• Files relating to Royall's tenure as secretary of war and secretary of the army have been declassified and are located in Washington, D.C., at the National Archives and Records Administration, Military Reference Branch. Correspondence, writings, speeches, financial records, and personal papers relating to all other aspects of his life are in the Southern Historical Collection at the University of North Carolina at Chapel Hill. A book-length study of Royall has yet to be published, but details of his military career appear in numerous studies of Truman and the Truman administration, including

Alfred Steinberg, *The Man from Missouri: The Life and Times of Harry S. Truman* (1962), Michael J. Lacey, ed., *The Truman Presidency* (1989), and Harry Truman, *Memoirs* (1955–1956). Perhaps the best short biography of Royall is his obituary in the *New York Times*, 27 May 1971. Other obituaries are in the *Durham Morning Herald*, 27 May 1971, and the *Goldsboro News-Argus*, 26 May 1971.

GREGORY M. SMITH

ROYCE, Josiah (20 Nov. 1855–14 Sept. 1916), philosopher and man of letters, was born in Grass Valley, California, the son of Josiah Royce, Sr., a farmer and salesman, and Sarah Eleanor Bayliss, a schoolteacher. His English-born parents came to the United States in early childhood. They were married in Rochester, New York, in 1845 and joined the Gold Rush to California in 1849. After much wandering and repeated financial misadventures, the family moved to San Francisco in 1866, where the father became a fruit vendor. Noted for his evangelical piety and considered "a little cracked in the head," the elder Royce often delivered impromptu sermons on street corners. Royce's mother, although also "intensely *spiritual . . . a mystic*," was more conventionally responsible, better-educated, and served as a strong model to her son.

The religious environment of the household had a profound impact on Royce. Although as a youth he underwent a skeptical crisis and afterward did not subscribe to traditional creeds or hold church membership, religion permeated his philosophy. He wrote in a homiletic style, alluded frequently to the Bible, and often stated philosophical problems in theological terminology. While the religious atmosphere he evoked sometimes endeared him to his contemporaries, his rhetoric may sound antiquated to readers today. He remains, however, a major figure in the "Golden Age" of American philosophy.

In 1870 Royce enrolled in the recently established University of California as a member of the "preparatory class," and the following year as a freshman he majored in civil engineering. Two years later he changed his major to the "classical course," which emphasized Greek, Latin, Hebrew, and modern languages, as well as mathematics and science. Courses in geology, taught by Joseph Le Conte, introduced Royce to naturalism and had an important influence on his thinking. During his final two years at Berkeley (B.A., 1875), Royce was repeatedly cited for exceptional scholarship. He won first prize in two rhetorical contests, served as an editor and frequent contributor to *The Berkeleyan*, was chosen class essayist, wrote a baccalaureate thesis on Aeschylus' *Prometheus Bound*, and delivered the classical commencement address, "On a Passage in Sophocles."

With the financial support of Bay Area businessmen, Royce spent the academic year of 1875–1876 in Germany, where he began his lifelong study of philosophy, principally under Wilhelm Wundt in Leipzig and Rudolf Hermann Lotze in Göttingen. When the Johns Hopkins University opened in 1876, Royce obtained one of its first graduate fellowships. The two years spent in Baltimore constitute one of his happiest and most productive periods. In 1878 he earned his Ph.D. with a thesis entitled "Of the Interdependence of the Principles of Knowledge: An Investigation of the Problems of Elementary Epistemology," a work, as he would later remember it, of "pure pragmatism." Here, Royce explored the logical conditions that facilitate all rational discourse, especially scientific discourse, and concluded that the goal of reasoning is not the discovery of "the truth," but the satisfaction, by means of ideal postulates, of the purposes of thought.

At this time Royce's interests were divided between literature and philosophy, although he definitely preferred philosophy. There being no academic posts available in the discipline, however, he accepted an instructorship in English at the University of California, a fate he likened to intellectual tuberculosis. Despite this exaggerated fear, these years in Berkeley (1878–1882) served as an effective apprenticeship; he established his competence as a teacher and, through many publications, his originality as a philosopher and literary critic. In 1880 he married Katharine Head, who remained his wife for thirty-six years and was the mother of his three sons.

With William James's help, Royce became a temporary instructor of philosophy at Harvard in 1882. In 1885, appointed an assistant professor, he published *The Religious Aspect of Philosophy*, a work that established the fundamental character of his philosophy. In it he abandoned his earlier pragmatism in favor of objective idealism and set off his famous "battle" with James for the "Absolute." Hailed as a radically new defense of theism, Royce's argument shares a kinship with romantic transcendentalism (subjective idealism), but his method of presentation differs from earlier efforts by being strictly logical. The conditions that make error possible, Royce argued, entail an infinity of rectifying truth: "all judgments, true or false, are but fragments, the whole being at once Absolute Truth and Absolute Knowledge."

His next two books were a history, *California from the Conquest in 1846 to the Second Vigilance Committee in San Francisco* (1886), and a novel, *The Feud of Oakfield Creek* (1887). The first is important for its indictment of John Charles Frémont as perpetrator of the Bear Flag War and the seizure of California. The novel, although flawed, remains a readable effort in regional fiction and Howellsian realism.

At the height of his youthful success, Royce suffered a nervous breakdown, manifested by an incapacitating depression, and was forced to take a leave of absence in 1888. To restore his health he embarked on a seven-month voyage around the world by way of Australia. In 1890–1891 he became entangled in controversies arising from his studies of California history and from a philosophical dispute with Francis Ellingwood Abbot. Throughout most of the 1890s, however, Royce was engaged in sustained philosophical growth—in his writing, in his teaching, and in important curricular innovations at Harvard. He became professor of the history of philosophy in 1892 and

chair of the department for four years in 1894. His books during this decade include a series of popular lectures, *The Spirit of Modern Philosophy* (1892), most important for its "double-aspect" theory of experience (the Worlds of Description and Appreciation); an address delivered to the Philosophical Union of the University of California, *The Conception of God* (1895, revised and reissued with a "Supplementary Essay" containing "The Principle of Individuation," 1897); and *Studies of Good and Evil: A Series of Essays upon Problems of Philosophy and of Life* (1898). Before the end of the century, he was reputed the most distinguished philosopher in the United States.

International recognition culminated with Royce's appointment, as the first American philosopher, to deliver the Gifford Lectures at the University of Aberdeen in 1899 and 1900, which were published as *The World and the Individual*, two massive volumes that appeared in 1899 and 1901. In the book, absolute idealism is formulated with arguments unsurpassed in the history of American philosophy. Here, Royce advanced an ontology whereby the real world is defined in terms of the purpose of thought. An idea is an intention or internal meaning that seeks realization in its object, its other, or external meaning. "*What is, or what is real, is as such the complete embodiment, in individual form and in final fulfillment, of the internal meaning of finite ideas.*" Royce argued that only an Absolute Experience or God could satisfy the completeness and finality demanded by this conception of reality. He eventually characterized his system as "absolute pragmatism" and extended it into all branches of philosophy, including nature, man, and the moral order.

For several years following *The World and the Individual*, Royce seems to have lost some of his momentum, and his works tended to stray. In 1903 he published *Outlines of Psychology*, an elementary treatise written for teachers. *Herbert Spencer: An Estimate and Review* (1904) is actually two historical essays, which, like *Outlines*, were composed for nontechnical readers. In 1906 he delivered a series of lectures at Johns Hopkins on "Some Aspects of Post-Kantian Idealism," posthumously published as *Lectures on Modern Idealism* (1919). Much of his teaching and research during and after these years centered on logic, but most of this work remains unpublished. At the same time, Royce's absolutism came increasingly under attack from pragmatists (principally James and John Dewey) and from realists (Ralph Barton Perry, A. O. Lovejoy, William Pepperell Montague, and others). In his personal life Royce also had to deal with a family crisis. His eldest son, who had suffered from psychotic episodes in childhood, became hopelessly schizophrenic, was hospitalized, and died two years after being permanently committed.

A "new growth" in Royce's thought can be traced to 1908 when he published *The Philosophy of Loyalty*, often thought to be his most enduring contribution to ethical theory. Developing further the voluntaristic features of his philosophical system, Royce now argued that loyalty—"*the willing and practical and thor-*

oughgoing devotion of a person to a cause"—is the summum bonum. Loyalty, not to be confused with obedience or conformity, makes the moral life possible; its opposite, disloyalty, is "moral suicide." The steady and uncompromising struggle to fulfill social commitments makes one truly an individual and unites that person with the human community. The effort to further the cause of loyalty—"*loyalty to loyalty*"—constitutes one's ultimate moral obligation. In *The Philosophy of Loyalty*, Royce answered James's pragmatism, which denies all ethical universals: seeking to quantify values, the pragmatist cries "*cash, cash*" in a world that is morally bankrupt. Loyalty is not only the will to believe, but the will to manifest "*the Eternal*" on the plane of human action.

Two collections of essays, *Race Questions, Provincialism, and Other American Problems* (1908) and *William James and Other Essays on the Philosophy of Life* (1911), extended Royce's philosophy of loyalty to other social and religious issues and continued his debate with pragmatism. *The Sources of Religious Insight* (Bross Lectures, 1912) iterated these positions, but in the penultimate lecture in this series, "The Religious Mission of Sorrow," Royce emphasized a leitmotif that runs throughout his work: the centrality of the problem of evil. This emphasis seems to have been the result of personal tragedies, professional disappointments, and failing health.

Early in 1911 Royce suffered a stroke and was incapacitated for several months. He recovered and wrote *The Problem of Christianity* (1913), the Hibbert Lectures he delivered that year at Manchester College, Oxford. Often regarded as Royce's most important work, this two-volume treatise subordinates the argument for absolutism; in its place, Royce reinterpreted traditional religious ideas and advanced a new epistemology. Always an idealist, he maintained that the true church is "invisible"; it is the spiritual Body of Christ. Thus, the "Universal Community" replaced the "Absolute" in Royce's metaphysical vocabulary. This community is literally a person; it may be loved as a person and is in fact the "Beloved Community." As such, it atones for the "moral burden," or fallen state, of humanity. Royce's theory of knowledge, derived partly from Charles S. Peirce, explained how communities can function as redemptive agencies. Dyadic relationships, such as perception and conception, tend to isolate, alienate, and mechanize human activity. Interpretation, on the other hand, a triadic relationship, is the *sine qua non* of human communities. Hence, the Beloved Community is also a Community of Interpretation.

Following *The Problem of Christianity*, the outbreak of World War I prompted Royce to apply his theory of interpretative communities to the problem of international strife. In *War and Insurance* (1914) he traced the cause of the war to nationalism in which an intense love for one's country is expressed in a murderous hatred of one's neighbors. Nationalism, Royce argued, illustrates the danger of dyadic social relationships. As a solution to this problem, he envisioned the creation of a worldwide community of interpretation that would promote interdependence, cooperation, and loyalty. He also advocated the formation of an international insurance corporation to protect independent nations from external aggression and help preserve world peace.

Before 1915, Royce shunned political activism. After the sinking of the *Lusitania*, however, he abandoned neutrality and became an outspoken advocate for the Allied cause against the Central Powers. Although, as always, a lover of German culture, he now denounced Germanic imperialism as the "enemy of the human race." These views are collected in his last book, in press at the time of his death, in Cambridge, Massachusetts, *The Hope of the Great Community* (1916).

A superficial acquaintance with Royce's ideas has induced some critics to characterize him as an ivory-tower optimist. Although it is true that he was indifferent to the radical social philosophies of his generation, Royce was not indifferent to politics. His was a thoroughly pragmatic, avowedly conservative philosophy that attacked social evils—such as racism, militarism, colonialism—and supported efforts to preserve the creative, interpretive energies of communal life. By criticizing, repairing, and fortifying the social order, Royce insisted, we actually and concretely sustain our own always endangered individuality. The idealism that Royce advanced was not the fatuous optimism of Voltaire's Dr. Pangloss. On the contrary, a profound loneliness and a sense of tragedy pervaded his writings; his constructive solutions to life's problems were not formulaic abstractions but carefully reasoned and heartfelt answers to questions arising from human need and sorrow.

• The papers of Josiah Royce are in the Harvard University Archives located in the Nathan Marsh Pusey Library. An important augmentation to this collection is described in John Clendenning and Frank M. Oppenheim, "New Documents on Josiah Royce," *Transactions of the Charles S. Peirce Society* (1990): 131–45. There is no standard edition of Royce's works; the best selection is *The Basic Writings of Josiah Royce*, ed. John J. McDermott (2 vols., 1969); volume 2 contains Ignas K. Skrupskelis, "Annotated Bibliography of the Published Works of Josiah Royce." Clendenning edited *The Letters of Josiah Royce* (1970) and wrote the only complete biography, *The Life and Thought of Josiah Royce* (1985). For critical studies of Royce's philosophy, see John E. Smith, *Royce's Social Infinite* (1950), James Harry Cotton, *Royce on the Human Self* (1954), Peter Fuss, *The Moral Philosophy of Josiah Royce* (1965), Bruce Kuklick, *The Rise of American Philosophy* (1977), and Oppenheim, *Royce's Mature Philosophy of Religion* (1987).

JOHN CLENDENNING

ROYCE, Sarah Eleanor Bayliss (2 Mar. 1819–23 Nov. 1891), pioneer, teacher, and writer, was born in Stratford-on-Avon, England, the daughter of Benjamin Bayliss, a tailor, and Mary Trimble (or Timbell). Her parents brought her as a baby with five older children to the United States in 1819. They lived for a time in Philadelphia before settling in Rochester, New York.

Sarah was educated as extensively as a woman then could be, with what her daughter would call an "old-style academy education" at the Albion Female Seminary. She then taught school, as she would at many other times in her life. She joined the Disciples of Christ and probably at church meetings met Josiah Royce, Sr., an Englishman whose family had lived for a time in Canada before coming to New York State. The two were married on 31 May 1845.

They resided for three years in Rochester, and there Royce bore their first daughter, Mary Eleanor. Her young husband's restlessness led them down the Ohio and out to a farming village in eastern Iowa, a move probably planned as a first step on the trail further west. In 1849 they took off in a wagon train for California. Royce was always spunky and never a whiner: "If we were going, let us go, and meet what we were to meet, bravely." Before long they were traveling alone, because Royce had refused to journey on the Sabbath. They endured real hardships. In the most difficult of situations, Royce imagined herself as Abraham's rejected wife, "in the wilderness walking wearily away from her fainting child among the dried up bushes." When she confronted another shrub, bursting aflame from a distant sagebrush fire, she felt again the days of Hagar and Ishmael and, now, of Moses before the burning bush.

The Royces entered California in October 1849. Their first stop, of only two months, was a settlement two or three miles above Placerville, where luck did not smile. If Josiah Royce came to California to pan for gold, we have no record of his ever finding any. If he came to make a merchant fortune, it eluded him. If he came to find good land to settle and claim for himself and his children, he was frustrated. Sarah Royce, however, either courted success or was of a disposition to make a success of whatever she found as they moved from camp to camp and town to town. In Sacramento, then a town of 10,000, Josiah Royce managed to build a wood floor under a tent to be their house and store, but the floods of January washed them out. Sarah Royce, only barely recovered from cholera, camped with her child in an abandoned house until the family could board a steamer and plow through miles of muddy waters among hordes of shivering, huddled refugees to arrive in gold rush San Francisco.

Sometime in the winter of 1850–1851 they were off again, this time to the Contra Costa shores of the Suisun Bay near Martinez. A series of other camps followed. During the first five years after they descended the mountains, Sarah Royce set up housekeeping in eight new places. In the spring of 1854 the Royces moved to Grass Valley where they organized their ninth California abode. They bought a piece of land, erected a small one-story house, planted an orchard, and sold fruit. Within a year Royce added the first surviving boy to their family of three girls; Josiah Royce, Jr., would become one of the greatest American philosophers.

Sarah Royce, who by then was running a school in her house, was the boy's teacher through his first eleven years. Far more than her husband, she was the boy's model, shepherding him through the roughness of a community that included near neighbors like the freethinking performer Lola Montez and her protégée, Lotta Crabtree. In contrast, the Royce household was a religious island, with family members active in the organization and support of the Disciples of Christ church. Sarah Royce moved the family to San Francisco so that Josiah, Jr., could go to high school and then to Oakland in 1870 when he entered the fledgling University of California, thus beginning an academic journey that would continue the rest of his life.

In 1884, when Josiah Royce, Jr., taught at Harvard during American philosophy's golden age, he was asked to write a history of California; for documentary assistance he encouraged his mother to compile from her "Pilgrim's Diary" a record of her journey across the plains, including accounts of her first years in California. He used the resulting manuscript in his history, and it was later published as *A Frontier Lady*. Her story, a vivid account of the westward transit, illuminates the life of a pioneer woman married to a restless man, expresses the determination of a strong, devout mother to encourage an intellectually gifted child under difficult conditions, stresses the importance of religion to people on the frontier, and describes the painful wresting of community out of a chaotic society.

Sarah Royce's later life was spent in Oakland, Berkeley, Los Gatos, and San Jose, where, after the death of her husband in 1889, she lived with her daughter Ruth, librarian for the San Jose State Normal School. Sarah died from complications of an accidental blow to the head in the San Jose post office.

• Letters by and to Royce in her later years are in the Josiah Royce Papers, Pusey Library, Harvard University. The basic source is Sarah Royce's own account, *A Frontier Lady: Recollections of the Gold Rush and Early California*, ed. Ralph Henry Gabriel (1932; repr. 1977). The most recent identification of places and events in Royce's life is in Robert V. Hine, *Josiah Royce: From Grass Valley to Harvard* (1992). An obituary and related articles are in the San Francisco *Call*, 24 and 25 Nov. 1891.

ROBERT V. HINE

ROYE, Edward James (3 Feb. 1815–28? Oct. 1871), fifth president of the Republic of Liberia, was born in Newark, Ohio, the son of John Roye, a wealthy merchant. His mother's name is unknown. His father died in 1829, leaving some personal property and land to Roye. He went to public schools in Ohio, attended Oberlin College, and taught for a few years in Chillicothe. He also tried his hand as a sheep trader and shopkeeper in various parts of the Middle West. After his mother died in 1840, he was influenced by the emigration movement to escape American prejudice. He rejected Haiti and instead went to Liberia in 1846 when an independent republic was proclaimed, taking with him a stock of goods.

At the time of Roye's arrival, the new republic faced a variety of ills. The dominant Americo-Liberians remained a small minority threatened by the local tribes;

Liberia was in financial straits; the colony's international position was in doubt; the colonists were involved in disputes with the Colonization Society; and various social divisions had developed. The more conservative element consisted mainly of light-skinned mulattoes, many of them adherents of the Colonization Society and some of them prominent traders and ship owners. The mulattoes were better educated than their darker-skinned neighbors, and some mulattoes had inherited property from their white fathers. They regarded themselves as a social elite entitled to the better jobs in commerce and government and defended their political interests by founding the True Liberian party, later known as the Republican party.

The darker-skinned settlers, who, in the main, made up the less affluent and lower class of immigrant population, were assigned land outside Monrovia, the main settlement, and they accused the Colonization Society's white agents of discriminating on the mulattoes' behalf. In the 1850s the dark-skinned elements formed the National True Whig party (NTWP), led by Roye, James S. Smith, and Edward Wilmot Blyden, in the upriver settlement of Clay Ashland. They called for the unification of all tribes and classes in the country and professed a more democratic outlook than the rival party.

The colonists faced all manner of difficulties: lack of capital, markets, and military resources; a difficult climate and soil; and tropical diseases for which no remedy was known. From the beginning they fought numerous wars with tribes of the coast and the hinterland. European colonial powers also threatened the new republic.

Roye became a leading merchant and ship owner and challenged the mulatto mercantile monopoly. Becoming one of the wealthiest men in the republic, he started the first shipping line to fly the Liberian flag and had a distinguished public career. He was a journalist, a member of the house of representatives in Liberia, and a government official in many capacities, including chief justice from 1865 to 1868, before being elected president in 1870 on his third attempt. A leader of the True Whigs, Roye was the first pure-blooded Negro elected to the presidency. According to Blyden, Roye had married "a pure Negro woman" from the United States, and she was the first woman who was not a mulatto to live in the presidential mansion.

With Roye's election, lower-class and darker-skinned Americo-Liberians and Congoes, freed slaves from ships captured by the American African Squadron, gained power at the expense of the light-skinned, upper-class Monrovian traders, and Roye was the major architect of the political change that propelled the government into economic development. He had become acquainted with Blyden, "the brilliant and controversial West Indian born Liberian" who spent "his entire life championing his race" (Lynch), in 1850, and they both resented the dominance of light-skinned Americo-Liberians in the country's government and mercantile life. With Blyden's help, Roye set forth a program of development for Liberia that called for a national banking system, education of the indigenous people, building of railroads to open the interior, incorporation of the native peoples contiguous to Liberia, and the formation of an alliance with distant interior tribes.

Roye's predecessor, James S. Payne, had seized the British ship *Elizabeth*, had been involved in border disputes with Sierra Leone, and was forced to pay an indemnity to Britain. After his election, Roye faced the problems of acquiring a loan to pay off the indemnity and settling the border disputes. He went to England in 1870 to request a loan of $500,000 from a London banking firm, offering future customs receipts as security. Consul General David Chinery, Speaker of the House of Representatives William S. Anderson, and Secretary of the Interior Hiliary Johnson carried out the negotiations. The terms were onerous—$150,000 discount, 7 percent interest, and repayment in fifteen years—and Liberia only received about $90,000 from the loan. Roye sanctioned the terms of the loan but failed to win the border dispute with Sierra Leone, a British colony. His mulatto Republican party opponents claimed he profited from the loan and gave away land.

Roye's troubles increased dangerously when he tried to extend his presidential term from two to four years. In 1869 the Republicans had maneuvered to keep Payne in office by amending the constitution to allow an additional two-year term. In 1870 Roye won a vote in the Liberian House to amend the constitution to allow for a four-year term, but the Republicans in the Liberian Senate refused to accept the amendment. In May 1871 a referendum was held, but the legislature ignored the electoral vote and, without a two-thirds majority, declared the constitution not amended. Angered, Roye in October 1871 issued a proclamation declaring the constitution amended on the basis of the 1869 vote and the presidential term extended to four years. A crisis developed when the Republicans claimed the proclamation was unconstitutional and nominated former president J. J. Roberts to take over when Roye's term ended. Believing he had a four-year term, Roye forbade the holding of the election.

Fighting broke out in Monrovia on 21 October 1871. A mulatto-led mob attacked Roye's house and imprisoned him and the other True Whig party leaders. Roye was deposed on 26 October 1871, then he escaped from prison, only to be recaptured. Some accounts were that Roye, carrying a portion of the loan money, tried to escape in a boat and was drowned when the boat capsized. Blyden later claimed a mulatto shot Roye while he was waiting for the boat. Roye's wife stated that, after his attempted escape, Roye was captured, beaten, then dragged through the streets and left to die in prison in Monrovia, the date unknown. It is unlikely that Roye had any of the loan money on him when he escaped. He was reportedly the richest man in Liberia, and most of his money was in British banks. He could have lived comfortably, had he escaped. Any money he carried on his person during the escape attempt, therefore, would probably have been his own cash.

Vice President J. S. Smith did not complete Roye's term. Instead, a junta that had helped stage the coup took over. The legislature proclaimed Roberts president in December 1871, and he served until 1875. He was succeeded by Payne, who served until 1877, when once again the True Whig party won the presidency. When Britain took over the customs offices (until 1912) to collect the loan, Liberia lost some of its legitimacy, and Roye was unjustly blamed for the loan and the political trouble. In fact, the crisis was the work of the light-skinned elite who did not want to share power with black-skinned Americo-Liberians.

Despite Roye's failings, his short administration marked a watershed. Although he was deposed, he had encouraged dark-skinned people to gain a share of government and to challenge the light-skinned politicians. He introduced the politics of patronage to the dark-skinned Americo-Liberians and the Congoes, and when the True Whig party returned to power in 1877, it remained in control until 1980. Patronage was thereafter extended to all Americo-Liberians, but the indigenous people continued to be excluded except for educating selected youths from the interior. Finally in 1980 the sons and daughters of the original settlers were overthrown.

• Archival materials on Roye are in the U.S. Consulate, Monrovia: Dispatches from U.S. Consuls in Monrovia, 1852–1906; the National Archives, Washington, D.C.; Historical Collections, Episcopal Church, Austin, Tex.; and the New-York Historical Society. Roye's economic development plans are in "Inaugural Address of President Edward James Roye," *Fifty-fourth Annual Report of the American Colonization Society* (1871). See also African Repository (the organ of the American Colonization Society), 1870–1872; *Fifty-fifth Annual Report of the American Colonization Society . . .* (1870–1872); C. Abayomi Cassell, *Liberia: History of the First African Republic* (1970); Sir Harry Hamilton Johnston, *Liberia*, vol. 1 (1906); Hollis R. Lynch, *Edward Wilmot Blyden: Pan-Negro Patriot 1832–1912* (1967); and James Bertin Webster and A. A. Boahen, *The Revolutionary Years: West Africa since 1800* (1967).

PETER J. DUIGNAN

RUBEY, William Walden (18 Dec. 1898–12 Apr. 1974), geologist, was born in Moberly, Missouri, the son of Ambrose Burnside Rubey, a store owner, and Alva Beatrice Walden. Rubey attended public schools in Moberly and enjoyed the woods and nature in his rural surroundings. He entered the University of Missouri in Columbia, intending to study forestry, but he soon changed his interest to geology and received an A.B. in 1920 in that field. In 1919 he married Susan Elsie Manovill; they had three children.

Rubey worked as an assistant valuation engineer for a consulting company in Pittsburgh, Pennsylvania, in 1920, but after a few months he left to work as a geologic aide with the U.S. Geological Survey. He undertook graduate work at Johns Hopkins University in 1921–1922 and at Yale University from 1922 to 1924, but, interrupted by work for the survey, he did not receive an advanced degree.

At the USGS from 1920 to 1960, Rubey advanced to its highest position of research geologist and from 1944 to 1945 was in charge of its division of areal geology and basic science. In his first years he carried out field work in the Eldorado oil field in Arkansas, in the rim area of the Black Hills in South Dakota and Wyoming, and on a cooperative program in Kansas with that state's geological survey. In the early 1930s he was assigned to a cooperative program with the Illinois State Geological Survey, for which he analyzed the dynamics of the streams. His report was lost in the state's files and, finally relocated, was published in 1952. In 1933, on special assignment with others, he studied the mineral resources of the area where Boulder (now Hoover) Dam was to be built. After the Illinois work, Rubey was transferred to the USGS section of general geology, where he concentrated on the region of southwestern Wyoming for many years of field work. He completed geologic maps of approximately 3,300 square miles, which represented four quadrangles, the topographic mapping unit of the USGS. The publication of these was delayed by a decision to enlarge the scale of the base maps, which required additional field work.

Rubey was especially concerned with geologic structure, stratigraphy, and the mechanism of sedimentation. He dealt with questions of stream capture and the evolution of badlands topography in relatively flat areas of the midwestern United States. He analyzed the settling of sediment grains in rivers and the relationship of particulate matter to stream flow and topography. He also dealt with the nature of compaction in sedimentary rocks. During his studies in Wyoming he identified commercial concentrations of vanadium and uranium, which became significant as strategic minerals during World War II. With Marion King Hubbert he presented a theory of the origin of overthrust faults in that region, with the explanation that fluid pressures at depth may reduce frictional resistance enough to allow low-angle faulting. He presented a theory that seawater and the atmosphere may have originated from the release of gases from the deep interior of the earth. This idea, first given as his presidential address to the Geological Society of America in 1950 and published in 1955, resulted in considerable discussion among geologists on a question not yet resolved. While living in Washington, D.C., Rubey held informal seminar-type evening meetings at his home, usually monthly, where local and visiting scientists discussed geologic topics.

Over many years Rubey served effectively on advisory committees and was recognized as one who came to the meetings well prepared. From his early geologic work in Arkansas he estimated the extent of the helium field in the midwestern United States, which caused the federal government to regulate its production. He was a diligent and patient member of a national committee that established the first American Stratigraphic Code for geologists in 1933. During World War II he was a liaison between the USGS and military forces, for which he provided information on water resources and other geological information. He served from 1957 to 1963 on the American Miscellaneous Committee, sponsored by the National Academy of Sciences and the National Research Council, which was involved with drilling to the earth's mantle at the Mohorovicic discontinuity. From 1960 to 1966 he was a member of the National Science Board of the National Science Foundation. In 1966 he was appointed to advise the U.S. Corps of Engineers, in which post he helped to determine the association of small earthquakes near Denver, Colorado, to the Rocky Mountain Arsenal Disposal well. He followed this with a study of the relationship of fluid injection with earthquake activity in Colorado for the Advanced Research Projects Agency. As a consultant to the National Aeronautics and Space Administration for some years, he was the director of its Lunar Science Institute from 1968 to 1971, when the first rock samples from the moon were obtained.

After having served as a visiting professor at several universities during the 1950s, Rubey accepted a position in 1960 as professor of geology and geophysics at the University of California, Los Angeles. There he conducted a much-appreciated seminar on broad questions in the earth sciences. He retired in 1966.

As noted by his biographers W. G. Ernst and Philip H. Abelson, Rubey was considered a competent generalist in geology, with an ability to relate physics to it. Of special significance to them was his kindness and helpfulness to others, as well as his modesty. He was, according to Ernst, "a perceptive, scholarly, and dedicated naturalist, as aware of the beauty to be found in the living environment as he was of geologic features" (p. 208). Among his scientific papers was one on barred owls and another on ravens. Elected to the National Academy of Sciences in 1945, Rubey was also a member of many scientific societies and often a hardworking officer of them, serving as president of the Geological Society of Washington (1948), the Geological Society of America (1949–1950), and the Washington Academy of Sciences (1957). He received the Award of Excellence (1943) and the Distinguished Service Medal (1958) of the Department of the Interior, the Penrose Medal of the Geological Society of America (1963), and the National Medal of Science (1965). Rubey died in Santa Monica, California.

• Rubey's personal papers are in the Manuscripts Division of the Library of Congress. Some archival records and field notebooks of Rubey are in the National Archives in papers of the U.S. Geological Survey. His delayed paper on the work in Illinois was "Geology and Mineral Resources of the Hardin and Brussels Quadrangles (Illinois)," *U.S. Geological Survey Professional Paper* 218 (1952). His published theory on seawater and atmosphere was "Development of the Hydrosphere and Atmosphere with Special Reference to Probable Composition of the Early Atmosphere," *Geological Society of America Special Paper* 62 (1955): 631–50. He also published, with M. King Hubbert, "Role of Fluid Pressure in Mechanics of Overthrust Faulting," *Geological Society of America Bulletin* 70 (1959): 115–206, in two parts. Biographical accounts are by Philip H. Abelson, in *American Philosophical Society Yearbook for 1975* (1976): 157–63; James Gilluly, in *Geological Society of America Memorials* 6 (1977): 1–6; and W. G. Ernst, in National Academy of Sciences, *Biographical Memoirs* 49 (1978): 205–23, with bibliography. An obituary is in the *New York Times*, 14 Apr. 1974.

ELIZABETH NOBLE SHOR

RUBICAM, Raymond (16 June 1892–8 May 1978), advertising agency executive, was born in Brooklyn, New York, the son of Joseph Rubicam, an import-exporter, and Sarah Maria Bodine. He was raised by older siblings following his mother's collapse after his father died when he was five. He left school in the eighth grade and lived in several states before settling in Philadelphia. Rubicam settled on a career in advertising at age twenty-three after a wide variety of jobs. F. Wallis Armstrong, his first employer, reflected advertising industry opinion: "A copywriter is a necessary evil, but an art director is just a damned luxury." For three years Rubicam wrote ad copy that gradually gained Armstrong's grudging respect. He married Regina McCloskey in 1916; they had three children.

In 1919 Rubicam accepted a job with N. W. Ayer and Son, then considered the nation's largest agency. Two of his print campaigns became industry classics: "The Instrument of Immortals" for Steinway pianos and "The Priceless Ingredient" for aspirin-maker E. R. Squibb. Both slogans were used for decades. When agency founder F. Wayland Ayer died, Rubicam and John Orr Young, a marketing man whom he had known at both Armstrong and Ayer, started their own agency.

Young & Rubicam began in Philadelphia in 1923. Because most agency directors came from account management departments, Rubicam's creative background made Y&R unique. So did Rubicam's belief that clients deserved excellence and his determination to encourage and reward excellence in advertising copy and graphics. "The way to sell is to get read first," he later wrote. "Mirror the reader to himself; and then show him afterwards how your product fits his needs."

The agency's campaign for its first major client, Postum, a noncaffeinated beverage, increased sales, won Harvard University's Bok Award for Advertising Excellence in 1925, and helped establish the firm's reputation. Y&R moved to New York in 1926. To strengthen the agency, Rubicam sought the best talent and often paid employees salaries higher than either he or Young earned. He expanded client service by establishing a merchandising department to teach clients how to sell their products more effectively.

The agency reflected Rubicam's working habits. Members of the creative staff kept their own hours but worked hard and long when needed. Each campaign began with a "gang-up," where writers, artists, and account staff sweated out the basic details, usually well into the night. Unlike other agencies, Y&R hired talented people without college degrees, sometimes without high school diplomas. It was the only agency where artists and writers, not administrators or account executives, had creative control of ads. To sustain creative quality, he set up a system in which seasoned copy supervisors trained junior writers.

During the depression, Rubicam resisted the grim, fear-ridden hard sell and created stylish, sometimes humorous ads with excellent art and advertising copy that sold by indirect persuasion. While other agencies folded or cut staff, Y&R grew. In 1932 he hired George Gallup, a Northwestern University professor, to develop the first audience-research department. Gallup chose to work for Y&R because the pollster said, Rubicam "was far more interested intellectually in how advertising works than the other [advertising] people I talked to."

In the late 1930s Rubicam declared, "It is more important to develop present business than to get new business." But he also rejected business. When George Washington Hill, the autocratic head of American Tobacco, tried to bully Rubicam about advertising practices, Rubicam resigned the $3 million tobacco account. He gave up a deodorant manufacturer's $2 million account when it pressured Gallup to alter his research findings.

Rubicam began publishing *Tide*, an advertising trade magazine, in 1931. He was chair of the American Association of Advertising Agencies in 1935, and in 1938 he became the youngest man to receive *Advertising and Selling* magazine's Gold Medal for distinguished services to advertising. An enthusiastic profile in 1935 concluded, "His foes respect him; the disinterested admire him; his friends adore him. He has the capability of setting a mark for everyone else to shoot at."

Rubicam became president and chief executive officer of Y&R in 1927; in 1934 Young retired. Company stock was entirely owned by its employees; Rubicam sold his shares back to the company when he retired in 1944. Y&R was then the country's second-largest advertising agency.

Rubicam later said that he retired at age fifty-two because the agency's growth took him too far from "planning and making ads" and meant he spent too much time with "chief executives, many of whom cared little about advertising and knew less" (*Advertising Age*, 1 July 1974, p. 39).

Rubicam, who had divorced his first wife in 1939, retired to Scottsdale, Arizona, with Bettina Hall, whom he had married in 1940, and their two children. He became actively involved in real-estate development and banking. He served as consultant to the Campbell Soup Company until 1962. In 1942 he was special assistant to the chair of the War Manpower Commission. He was a trustee of Colgate University (1947–1952) and the Committee for Economic Development (1946–1952) and was honorary trustee of both until his death.

In 1971 Rubicam reminded a packed audience at Y&R's New York headquarters that a great agency must excel in "integrity, thoroughness, and restlessness," that good ideas must be prized, and that "for-mula is another word for 'rut.'" In 1974 he became the second living person elected to the Advertising Hall of Fame, and in 1975 he was inducted into the Copywriters Hall of Fame. At a testimonial dinner celebrating Rubicam's eighty-fifth birthday, David Ogilvy, founder of Ogilvy & Mather, declared, "You taught me that advertising can sell without being dishonest." William Bernbach, of Doyle Dane Bernbach, said, "You taught me the importance of saying the right things in an ad—with freshness, with humor, with drama, with humanity." Rubicam died in Scottsdale.

Raymond Rubicam influenced advertising by his insistence on creating honest and persuasive copy and well-executed art, on finding better ways to reach and understand readers, and on expanding client services to help improve product sales.

• Unlike many other important people in advertising, Rubicam wrote neither an autobiography nor a book on advertising. The most complete study of his career in advertising is Stephen Fox, *The Mirror Makers* (1984). Rubicam's remembrances of life at Armstrong and Ayer appeared in a series of articles in *Advertising Age*, 9 Feb. 1970, pp. 47–49; 16 Feb. 1970, pp. 39–42; 2 Mar. 1970, pp. 48–50; 7 July 1975, pp. 21, 25; and 28 July 1975, pp. 43, 46–47. After his death, *Advertising Age* published an interview about his career at Y&R and his retirement ("Long-delayed Reminiscences of Ray Rubicam," 29 May 1978, pp. 29, 35) that had been conducted in 1958 but never approved for publication by Rubicam. For contemporary estimates, see George H. Allen, "In Sharper Focus: Raymond Rubicam," *Outlook*, Jan. 1935, pp. 63–64; *Advertising & Selling* award issue 1938, pp. 37–39; and Nathaniel Benson, "Raymond Rubicam, a close-up," *Forbes*, 1 Feb. 1944, pp. 14–15, 27. In his career reminiscences, *Giants, Pigmies and Other Advertising People* (1974), Draper Daniels wrote that "in the early 1940s, Young & Rubicam was heaven, or next door to it, and God's name was Raymond Rubicam." David Ogilvy included an appreciation of Rubicam in *Ogilvy on Advertising* (1983). A summary of his eighty-fifth birthday celebration appears in "Tributes and Memories for Raymond Rubicam," *Advertising Age*, 23 July 1977, pp. 46, 49.

Rubicam wrote in the foreword to Julian Lewis Watkins, *The 100 Greatest Advertisements, Who Wrote Them and What They Did* (1949), that "the best identification of a great ad is that its public is not only strongly sold by it, but that both the public and the advertising world remember it for a long time as an admirable piece of work." An obituary is in the *New York Times*, 9 May 1978; an appreciation of his life and contributions to advertising is in *Advertising Age*, 15 May 1978.

EILEEN MARGERUM

RUBIN, Jerry (14 July 1938–28 Nov. 1994), radical activist, was born in Cincinnati, Ohio, the son of Robert Rubin, a bread truck driver and Teamster business agent, and Esther Katz. Raised in an urban, liberal, Jewish household, Rubin worked at minor tasks for his high school newspaper before becoming a reporter for the *Cincinnati Post and Time Star*. He attended Oberlin College for a year as well as the University of Cincinnati, from which he graduated in 1960. In 1962–1963 Rubin studied sociology at Hebrew University in Israel.

He returned to the United States in early 1964 to begin graduate school in sociology at the University of California in Berkeley, but, inspired by the emerging radicalism centered in Berkeley, Rubin quit school to become a full-time civil rights picketer. On a student delegation to Cuba in 1964, Rubin heard revolutionary president Fidel Castro speak to a crowd of 200,000 and met with leftist guerrilla Che Guevara. A month after his return to Berkeley, Rubin took part in the campus Free Speech Movement against bureaucratic strictures on student political activity. In 1965 he headed the Berkeley Vietnam Day Committee, which organized a marathon teach-in by prominent international intellectuals against the Vietnam War. He also led an effort to block troop trains at the Oakland Army Terminal.

After an unsuccessful run for mayor of Berkeley, Rubin moved to New York in 1967. Already a public marijuana smoker, he first took LSD that same year. He concluded that psychedelic drugs had revolutionary potential. By then Rubin had already won a reputation for combining zaniness, theatricality, and humor with leftist politics, making him one of the "anticapitalist comics of the 1960s," as he later put it. In 1966, when subpoenaed by the House Committee on Un-American Activities, Rubin appeared in a full Continental army costume. While in New York Rubin teamed up with Abbie Hoffman, another whimsical New Leftist, for further antics. The two sought to fuse the new alternative culture—psychedelic drugs, long hair, sexual freedom, and rock music—with revolutionary politics. In their first act they threw wads of dollar bills from the visitors' deck at the New York Stock Exchange, causing trade to stop on the floor below as brokers scrambled to get the money. On 21 October 1967 they joined throngs of demonstrators in Washington, D.C., where they facetiously tried to "Levitate the Pentagon."

On New Year's Eve 1967, together with satirist Paul Krassner and singer Ed Sanders, Hoffman and Rubin devised the term "Yippie." While they sometimes spoke of a Youth International Party (YIP), there was no real organization behind the phrase. Rubin evoked an image of the Yippie as a "Marxist acidhead, the psychedelic Bolshevik," one who combined the hippie culture and political activism of 1960s youth. But Rubin and Hoffman were creations of the mass media, celebrities of the youth revolt, and not the type of movement leaders directly accountable to radical organizations and constituents. The Yippies therefore came in for severe criticism on the left. Many viewed Rubin and Hoffman as self-indulgent and fatuous, more interested in outlandish self-promotion than genuine revolutionary action. "It was mutual manipulation," Rubin later said in defense of his relationship to the media. "To interest the media I needed to express my politics frivolously. . . . If I had given a sober lecture on the history of Vietnam, the media would have turned off."

Rubin and Hoffman reached their apex of notoriety during the Chicago Seven trial of 1969–1970. In 1968 the Yippies had focused their attention on Chicago, where the Democratic party was to hold its convention to nominate its presidential candidate. Proclaiming a "politics of ecstasy" and a "Festival of Life," the Yippies tried to attract young people from around the country to Chicago to protest the Vietnam War. They put forward absurd slogans such as "Abandon the creeping meatball!" They nominated a pig for president. Only about 5,000 antiwar demonstrators actually went to Chicago, where the police, as many radicals had predicted, beat the demonstrators mercilessly.

In 1969 President Richard Nixon's administration indicted eight radicals, including Rubin and Hoffman, for conspiracy—holding them responsible, essentially, for the violence in Chicago. One defendant, Black Panther Bobby Seale, was later removed from the case. The long and contentious trial resulted in a guilty verdict against Rubin and four of the others on the charge of crossing state borders with intent to cause a riot. But that judgment was overturned in 1972 by the Seventh Circuit Court of Appeals, which found numerous errors in the judge's imperious handling of the case.

While his book *Do It!: Scenarios of the Revolution* (1970) was a bestseller, Rubin was no longer young, and the movements he thrived on were fading. Overwhelmed by a mood of personal crisis, he moved back to California, where he experimented with a mélange of therapeutic techniques, including Rolfing, Erhard Seminars Training (EST), acupuncture, hypnotism, gestalt therapy, and Reichian therapy. When he turned thirty-five, Rubin shaved his bushy beard and cut his hair. He began to undercut his earlier radicalism. In a 1976 editorial that he later called "a mistake," Rubin denied the entire premise of the Chicago Seven defense: "We WANTED disruption. We PLANNED it. We WERE NOT innocent victims. . . . Guilty as hell. Guilty as charged."

Rubin never renounced his opposition to the Vietnam War, but he did embrace capitalism with zeal. In 1978 he married Mimi Leonard, a former debutante who worked for ABC television in New York. The couple lived in a chic New York apartment, and Rubin worked briefly on Wall Street before heading the 500 Club, a "networking" facilitator for business executives. He was again a media symbol, this time of a purported generational transformation "from Yippie to yuppie." In a series of "Jerry versus Abbie" debates, Rubin even took to the stage against his old comrade Hoffman. Rubin was struck by a car on 15 November 1994 while jaywalking in Los Angeles, where he was residing, and he died two weeks later. Rubin, who was divorced in 1992, was survived by a son and daughter. At the time of his death, Rubin was a marketer and distributor of a nutritional beverage called Wow!

• Additional writings by Rubin include *We Are Everywhere* (1971), *Growing (Up) at 37* (1976), and, with Mimi Leonard, *The War between the Sheets* (1980). For criticism of the media politics of the Yippies, see especially Todd Gitlin, *The Whole*

World Is Watching (1980). On the countercultural left, see Abe Peck, *Uncovering the Sixties* (1985). An obituary is in the *New York Times*, 30 Nov. 1994.

CHRISTOPHER PHELPS

RUBINOW, Isaac Max (19 Apr. 1875–1 Sept. 1936), social insurance expert and Jewish social service administrator, was born in Grodno, Russia, the son of Max Simon Rubinow, a textile merchant, and Esther Shereshewsky. Little is known about Rubinow's childhood other than the fact that he migrated to the United States at the age of eighteen. Having a relatively privileged background, he was connected to a cosmopolitan network of kin, who facilitated his entry into American life. Rubinow enrolled in Columbia University, earning a B.A. in 1895 and an M.D. three years later. In 1899 he married Sophia Himowich; they had three children. As a doctor to New York City's poor between 1898 and 1903, Rubinow discovered that the illnesses and disabilities he treated were as much socioeconomic as physiological or pathological in origin. Eager to corroborate this hypothesis, he abandoned his medical practice and began to conduct the sort of investigative studies of the urban working class being done at the time by Charles Booth in England. He took graduate courses in mathematics while working for a Ph.D. in political science at Columbia. Under the direction of Edwin R. A. Seligman, Rubinow investigated trends in workers' wages and purchasing power and completed his doctorate in 1914.

From 1903 to 1904, Rubinow was an examiner for the U.S. Civil Service Commission. He then served as a researcher and statistician for the U.S. Department of Agriculture (1904–1907) and the U.S. Department of Commerce and Labor (1907–1908). For the next three years, he worked on a report of the commissioner of Labor Statistics, *Workmen's Insurance and Compensation Systems in Europe*. As a government employee, Rubinow published his first series of articles. Several focused on labor conditions and reforms in his homeland, including "The New Russian Workingmen's Compensation Act," which appeared in the *U.S. Labor Bulletin* 58 (1905): 955–59. Private groups began to seek his expertise, and from 1911 to 1916 Rubinow was chief statistician for the Ocean Accident & Guarantee Corporation. He also served as president of the Casualty Actuarial Society and lectured on social insurance at the New York School of Philanthropy, where he offered the first course devoted exclusively to this topic at any American university.

In 1913 Rubinow published *Social Insurance*, arguably the most impressive statistical and theoretical rationale for adopting new forms of protection for the poor and aged issued in the United States to that date. Rubinow hoped that the book would stimulate scholarly and public interest in workmen's compensation, widows' pensions, retirement annuities, and state-financed life insurance. In Rubinow's opinion, "The ideal purpose of social insurance, the purpose to which the best insurance systems tend (and the others slowly follow), is to prevent and finally eradicate poverty, and the subsequent need of relief, by meeting the problem at the origin, rather than waiting until the effects of destitution have begun to be felt" (p. 481). Rubinow's ideal, however, rested on assumptions that few of his contemporaries were prepared to accept. In "highly capitalized" societies, Rubinow argued, few working-class people could protect themselves from the risk of accidents, illness, and old-age dependency through commercial insurance. Citing the income and spending evidence given by radical academics such as Scott Nearing, he declared that only families with more than one wage-earner and fewer than two children could sustain a life above "the standard of physiological necessity and economic efficiency" (p. 45). Only a sweeping reorganization of social values and a dramatic redistribution of income, Rubinow contended, would remedy the situation. Such a scenario was unlikely. Without advocating class warfare, he encouraged Americans to acknowledge that "the class which needs social insurance cannot afford it, and the class that can afford it does not need it" (p. 491) and to be more supportive of social legislation.

Social Insurance became an immediate classic. For the rest of his life, Rubinow worked for better workmen's compensation laws, unemployment insurance, old-age pensions, and national health insurance programs. Along with a growing number of experts, he felt that these programs should be financed through public funds, taxes on employees' wages, and employers' contributions. Not all reformers shared Rubinow's position. Leaders of the American Association for Labor Legislation for instance, were greatly influenced between 1916 and 1920 by Rubinow's views on health insurance and mothers' pensions. Thereafter, however, AALL emphasized the "preventive" more than the "redistributionist" features of social insurance and laid less stress than Rubinow on class differences and the inevitable need for federal action. In 1916 Rubinow became executive secretary of the American Medical Association's Social Insurance Commission. A year later he was appointed director of the Bureau of Social Statistics of New York City's Department of Public Charities. In the meantime, he continued to lecture on social insurance at the New York School of Philanthropy and became a contributing editor of *Survey*. After World War I, Rubinow became increasingly involved in the second major cause of his career, the organization and promotion of social services in the Jewish community. From 1918 to 1922 Rubinow headed the Hadassah medical unit in Palestine, supervising the modernization of hospitals and clinics. He was director of the Jewish Welfare Society in Philadelphia for the next five years. Between 1925 and 1929 he edited the *Jewish Social Service Quarterly*, and he served as secretary of the B'nai B'rith in Cincinnati from 1929 until his death. In the latter capacity he was instrumental in launching an antidefamation movement and took steps to aid Jews who wished to flee Nazi Germany.

In 1934 Rubinow published *The Quest for Security*. Omitting tables, figures, and citations in setting forth his argument, Rubinow aimed the book at "the average intelligent and educated but not specialized adult mind," people who might be persuaded to make an "effort toward a more desirable social order" (p. vi). Rubinow viewed the book's format as an "experiment." Though a departure in style, much of the argument of *The Quest for Security* paralleled his earlier work. The definition and scope of "social insurance," for instance, remained unchanged, but there were subtle modifications in his argument. Rubinow was doubtful that trade unions were yet powerful enough to take a leadership role and, though he recognized the importance of their efforts, was loathe to entrust private insurance companies with social-insurance programs. Instead of invoking arguments that emphasized the plight of the wage worker, Rubinow analyzed the debate over means being waged by health-care organizations, old-age groups, and unions. Eschewing images of a utopian society, he appealed to New Dealers to do what was possible: "Surely it cannot be part of the philosophy of the New Deal that those who are left by the wayside of modern industrial civilization always remain objects of charity, whether private or public. Social insurance must therefore become—if it is not already—an essential aspect of the New Deal" (p. viii).

Taking note of Rubinow's message, Franklin D. Roosevelt wrote him to express "great interest" in his suggestions about the president's role in enacting social security legislation. But, though he exerted influence through his contacts with Paul Douglas and lectures he delivered at the University of Chicago in 1930, Rubinow did not play a central role in drafting the 1935 Social Security Act. As a member of the Ohio Commission on Unemployment Insurance (1932) and as chairman of the Cincinnati Board on Old Age Pensions (1934–1935), he was active at the grassroots level. He did not, however, serve on any of the technical or advisory boards set up to assist the Committee on Economic Security that drafted the omnibus legislation. Some have suggested that he was too pugnacious and "ethnic" to gain the confidence of those who had to accommodate diverse interests to get Social Security enacted. Rubinow died in New York City.

• Most biographical details of Rubinow's life appear in *Who Was Who in America* 1 (1942): 1064, and in his obituary in the *New York Times*, 3 Sept. 1936. Additional details can be gleaned from Rubinow's own writings. The significance of Rubinow's ideas and efforts to promote social insurance are discussed in Roy Lubove, *The Struggle for Social Security* (1968); Daniel J. Boorstin, *The Americans: The Democratic Experience* (1973); and W. Andrew Achenbaum, *Old Age in the New Land* (1978) and *Social Security* (1986).

W. ANDREW ACHENBAUM

RUBINSTEIN, Arthur (28 Jan. 1887–20 Dec. 1982), pianist, was born Artur Rubinstein in Lodz, Poland, the son of Izaak Rubinstein, a textile manufacturer, and Felicja Heiman. When he was two, his parents bought a piano so that his sisters, Jadzia and Hela, could learn to play. He observed their lessons, and by the age of

three he was playing piano four hand with them. His talent appeared so great that his mother took him to Berlin when he was four to play for the great violinist Joseph Joachim. Joachim was impressed with the boy and offered to help when Arthur was ready for serious musical study.

In the fall of 1896, after five years of study with a local piano teacher, Adolf Prechner, in Lodz, Rubinstein's parents sent him to Warsaw to study with Aleksander Rózycki, but the lessons were a disaster and he quickly returned to Lodz. The next year Arthur went to Berlin, where he again played for Joachim, who was director of the Hochschule für Musik. The ten-year-old Arthur was too young for admission to the Hochschule, but Joachim arranged for him to study privately with the pianist Heinrich Barth and other teachers from the school, including Max Bruch. Three years later Joachim invited Rubinstein to perform Mozart's Concerto in A Major, K. 488 in the Hochschule's main auditorium with Joachim conducting, although Rubinstein was still not enrolled in the school. His official debut came on 1 December 1900, when he played the same Mozart concerto and the Saint-Saëns Concerto No. 2 in G Minor with the Berlin Philharmonic under the direction of Josef Rebicek. The concert was a huge success. He made his Warsaw debut with the newly formed Warsaw Philharmonic in April 1902 and played for the composers Edvard Grieg and Pietro Mascagni at a private party a few days later.

By now, however, Arthur had discovered the opposite sex. That, combined with souring relations with his teacher Barth, led to a decline in his piano playing and exacerbated a lifelong aversion to practicing. An important recital at the Beethoven-Saal in Berlin in February 1903 was a failure. He spent that summer living at the Swiss home of the great Polish pianist Ignacy Paderewski, though Rubinstein did not formally study with him. Rubinstein completed his studies with Barth late that year, and in early 1904 the young pianist set out to experience life.

He soon became close friends with the violinist Paul Kochanski and the composer Karol Szymanowski. He made his Paris debut on 19 December 1904, with mixed success. There he met and played for Saint-Saëns. He made his U.S. debut with the Philadelphia Orchestra at New York's Carnegie Hall on 8 January 1906. He made his Russian debut in St. Petersburg (at the invitation of Alexander Glazunov) in 1909, his Vienna debut later that year, his official Italian debut in Rome in 1911, and his London debut in 1912. He toured Spain and South America in 1916, and he spent all of the 1916–1917 and 1917–1918 season in Spain, where he was very successful. He returned to the United States in 1919, and while there he made his first piano rolls for Aeolian Duo-Art. In his 1995 biography, Harvey Sachs quotes Rubinstein as saying that his U.S. tour was "a personal triumph and an artistic disaster. I knew everybody, I dined out, I was sidetracked by pretty girls, . . . [but] I neglected the piano." Rubinstein returned to the United States in 1920 and 1921 and then gave his first concerts in seventeen years in

Paris in 1923. He toured extensively throughout the 1920s, and made his first recordings for His Master's Voice in 1928. In 1932 he married Aniela (Nela) Mlynarska, the daughter of the great Polish conductor Emil Mlynarski. Rubinstein was forty-five, and she was twenty-three. They had five children, four of whom survived infancy.

Married life gave Rubinstein the discipline he needed to concentrate on his piano playing and hone his career. He had felt guilty for years about his failure to practice. In his book, *My Young Years* (1973), Rubinstein recalled that Barth, his old professor, had chastized his laziness, saying that if only he would work, he could play all the other pianists into the mud. "This phrase struck me," Rubinstein wrote; "it kept ringing in my ears for the rest of my life." Now, despite his success, he was increasingly unhappy with his own playing, and he vowed to settle down and work. Harold Schonberg quoted Rubinstein in *The Great Pianists* (1963) as asking himself, "Was it to be said of me that I *could* have been a great pianist? Was this the kind of legacy to leave to my wife and family?" Now Rubinstein worked on the piano as he had never worked before, and he made a triumphant reentry to the American concert scene in 1937.

Rubinstein had added discipline to his famous joie de vivre, and the combination made him a sensation on the concert stage. He loved the experience of performing before an audience, and audiences loved him. Although he made many outstanding recordings (his Chopin recordings are especially renowned), he felt lost playing in front of a bare microphone. Unlike his colleague Glenn Gould (who interviewed him in a famous 1971 *Look* magazine article), he needed the interaction and stimulus of a live audience to bring out the best in his playing.

With the outbreak of war in 1939 the Rubinstein family moved to the United States. Rubinstein had refused to play in Germany for years, and, shocked by the rise of Nazi Germany, he vowed never to play there again. The closest he came was a recital in 1968 in the Dutch town of Nijmegen, on the German border. In 1938 he also canceled all concerts in Italy and returned all of his Italian medals of honor to Mussolini to protest Italy's new anti-Semitic laws. Devastated by Germany's invasion of Poland, he became an active supporter of Polish Relief and gave benefit concerts to raise money for the Allied cause.

He settled in California. The violinist Jascha Heifetz and the cellist Emanuel Feuermann also lived there, and the three got together for informal evenings of chamber music and then for a series of extraordinary trio recordings for RCA Victor. "Not bad for local talent," Rubinstein quipped. After Feuermann's death Rubinstein and Heifetz joined cellist Gregor Piatigorsky for more recordings, concerts, and a film. *Life* magazine dubbed them the "Million Dollar Trio."

After the war Rubinstein's fame grew to legendary status. In his later years some critics referred to him as one of the last of the great Romantic pianists. Though certainly not of the German school of playing (represented by such pianists as Artur Schnabel, Wilhelm Kempf, and Wilhelm Backhaus), Rubinstein was not a throwback to highly Romantic players like Vladimir de Pachmann or Paderewski either, with their broken chords, highly individualistic rubato, and willingness to embellish the musical text. Rubinstein was a modern Romantic, cooler and more sparing in his use of Romantic devices than his forebears but still bigger than life onstage and a player in the grand tradition.

Rubinstein gave a series of ten Carnegie Hall recitals in 1961 to celebrate the upcoming twenty-fifth anniversary of his return to the United States in 1937. He continued to record and give concerts until he was eighty-nine years old. In 1975 he recorded the complete Beethoven piano concertos. He gave his last New York concert at Carnegie Hall on 15 March 1976, made his last recording the next month, and gave his last public concert at London's Wigmore Hall on 31 May 1976. By then he was almost completely blind. He left his wife, Nela, to live with Annabelle Whitestone in 1977, although he and Nela never divorced.

Rubinstein was long considered a champion of modern music, hissed for his playing of Debussy in 1904. He developed close ties with many composers, including Szymanowski, Igor Stravinsky, Manuel de Falla, Darius Milhaud, and Sergei Prokofiev. In addition to his many recordings, he made several films and wrote two volumes of memoirs (the first, comprising 478 pages, covered only his first thirty years). Among his many awards were election to the Academie des Beaux-Arts of the Institut de France in 1971, English knighthood, and the U.S. Medal of Freedom in 1976. He was also named a commander of the French Legion of Honor in 1970. He died at his home in Geneva, Switzerland.

• Rubinstein's personal papers are housed at the Library of Congress in Washington, D.C., and the Historical Museum of the City of Lodz in Poland. The best single source on Rubinstein is the Harvey Sachs biography, *Rubinstein: A Life* (1995), which contains a thorough bibliography, a discography compiled by Donald Manildi, and a list of Rubinstein's films and piano rolls. Rubinstein himself wrote two volumes of memoirs: *My Young Years* (1973) and *My Many Years* (1980). Both are fascinating reading but not always entirely accurate. See also Aylesa Forsee, *Artur Rubinstein: King of the Keyboard* (1969); Harold C. Schonberg, *The Great Pianists* (1963); Glenn Gould, "Rubinstein," *Look*, 9 Mar. 1971; Donald Henahan, "This Ageless Hero, Rubinstein," *New York Times Magazine*, 14 Mar. 1976; and Max Wilcox and John Rubinstein, "Arthur Rubinstein at 100" and Allan Kozinn, "The Rubinstein Legacy," *Keynote*, July 1987. Rubinstein's recordings are available on compact disc from BMG Classics, EMI, and Pearl, and his films are available on video cassette and laserdisc from London, Video Artists International, and Kultur. Obituaries and memorial editorials are in the *New York Times* and the *Washington Post*, both 21 Dec. 1982; the *Los Angeles Times*, 26 Dec. 1982; and the *Christian Science Monitor*, 27 Dec. 1982.

JOHN ANTHONY MALTESE

RUBINSTEIN, Helena (25 Dec. 1870–1 Apr. 1965), cosmetics entrepreneur, was born in Cracow, Poland, the daughter of Horace Rubinstein, a food broker, and

Augusta Silberfield. Helena and her sisters were taught the value and import of beauty by their mother. The daughters used jars of cream concocted by a chemist for their mother's friend, the actress Helena Modjeska. Rubinstein attended the University of Cracow. Her father wanted her to study medical science, but a brief stint of lab work in medical school in Zurich, Switzerland, made her physically ill. Her father relented; she could end her studies, but she should marry instead. Rubinstein balked at his choice of a 35-year-old widower. When her parents forbade her to marry the young man she chose, Rubinstein asked if she could live with her maternal uncle and his family in Australia. She packed pots of what would become a famous beauty cream for her personal use. In Australia, where sun damage ruined many a complexion, Rubinstein's skin looked especially beautiful. She found herself giving away the jars of cream. She decided that there was enough demand for the creams to start selling them as a business. With financial backing from Helen MacDonald, a satisfied customer, Rubinstein opened a shop in Melbourne, Australia.

Rubinstein used the loan from MacDonald to cover the cost of a large quantity of the cream, rent, and furnishings for the shop. She did the painting and decorating herself. Furthermore, she realized that different creams would help different kinds of skin. Without any formal training in chemistry, she experimented with different creams for different skin types. She gave a personal skin analysis with each jar of cream purchased. Newspaper coverage of her growing business netted her a surge of orders—so many that she was able to afford to bring over Jacob Lykusky, the chemist who had created the original formula. Accounts vary from two years to eight years as to how long it took her to repay the debt to MacDonald. She hired family members to run various parts of her business.

Ever receptive to refining her products, she traveled to Europe intermittently to study with skin care and nutrition experts. Throughout her meteoric rise, she focused on her work instead of relationships. Despite falling in love with American newspaperman Edward William Titus, she refused his initial marriage proposal, saying she wanted to open a salon in England before she married. When he asked again after she had opened a salon on London's Grafton Street, she agreed to the marriage. Their private civil ceremony took place in 1908. Edward continued his writing and even wrote advertising pieces for her products. After their children were born in 1909 and 1912, Rubinstein devoted more time to family matters, but by the time the youngest was two years old, she decided to expand her business by moving to Paris to open a salon. The next year her husband, worried about living in Europe during the escalating war years, convinced her to move to the United States. Rubinstein opened her New York salon, Maison de Beauté Valaze. By 1916 she began expanding her American market to other cities, opening salons in Philadelphia and San Francisco, and then in Boston, Washington, D.C., Chicago, and Los Angeles. She also opened a salon in Toronto, Canada.

She gained more publicity for her products when movie stars such as Theda Bara and Pola Negri began using them, with Rubinstein's direction. These stars popularized the "vamp" look, using mascara to highlight their eyes. Meanwhile Rubinstein also selected stores in which to sell her products and trained the women who would sell them.

In her autobiography, *My Life for Beauty* (1966), Rubinstein writes poignantly about giving up her life for her beauty business. At one point she hoped to solve problems in her marriage by selling the business. She did sell it to the Lehman Brothers for $7.3 million, but it was too late for the marriage, which ended in divorce about 1938. However, her decision proved fortuitous, for after the stock market crashed, Rubinstein was able to buy back the business for only $1.5 million.

She was less fortunate in her personal life, as she continued to suffer losses. The death of both of her parents before she had a chance for one last visit was emotionally difficult for her. A physician friend suggested that she recover in Europe. She returned revived and ready to try a new idea—"A Day of Beauty" in her salons. She also found some personal comfort, meeting a Georgian named Prince Artchil Gourielli-Tchkonia in 1935. She married him three years later, and they remained married for twenty years. They had homes in New York City and in Paris. They were fortunate to have left their Paris apartment in 1939, a year before the fall of France during World War II. Some people criticized Rubinstein for producing luxury goods during the war, but President Franklin D. Roosevelt agreed with Rubinstein that her products were keeping up the morale of the American women. In terms of innovations, Rubinstein tried a line of men's colognes named after her husband, but the House of Gourielli was an idea ahead of its time.

Despite her pain at the loss of her second husband in 1956 and her second son two years later, Rubinstein continued her active business life. Surviving a frightening robbery attempt at her New York apartment at the age of ninety-three, Rubinstein, whom associates addressed as "Madame," died in New York City. She will be remembered for the cosmetics business she started with a few pots of cream and turned into a business worth millions; estimates of its worth at the time of her death range from $17.5 to $60 million. She had laboratories and salons in fourteen countries. She had given some of her immense wealth to charities through the Helena Rubinstein Foundation. She also gave a large donation to create the Helena Rubinstein Pavilion at the Tel Aviv Art Museum in Israel, where a magnificent collection of miniature rooms is on display.

• Books about Helena Rubinstein include Margaret Allen, *Selling Dreams: Inside the Beauty Business* (1981), Maxene Fabe, *Beauty Millionaire: The Life of Helena Rubinstein* (1972), and Patrick O'Higgins, *Madame: An Intimate Biography of Helena Rubinstein* (1971). See also Elinor Slater and

Robert Slater's piece, "Helena Rubinstein," in *Great Jewish Women* (1994). A lengthy obituary is in the *New York Times*, 2 Apr. 1965.

SARA ALPERN

RUBLE, Olan G. (17 Feb. 1906–11 Nov. 1982), professor of physical education and women's basketball coach, was born Olan Guy Ruble near Chariton in Lucas County, Iowa, the son of Lon S. Ruble and Gertrude Curtis, farmers. Ruble attended a rural elementary school. Following graduation from Norwood High School in 1923, he earned a B.A. from Simpson College in 1928 and a master's degree from the University of Iowa in 1937. In 1930 he married Marguerite O'Neall, with whom he would have one child.

From 1928 to 1938 Ruble taught physical education and coached at several Iowa high schools. He was director of physical education at the Sioux City, Iowa, YMCA from 1938 to 1942, when he left to become a physical education instructor for the Eighty-second Detachment of the U.S. Army Air Force.

After his discharge in 1943, Ruble became director of physical education and health at Iowa Wesleyan College in Mount Pleasant. He held the post until 1950, when he was promoted to professor and appointed chair of the Division of Physical Education and Health; he later chaired the Division of Applied Sciences (1961–1965). Ruble taught physical education theory and kinesiology. Regarded as a fine teacher, he was named in 1971 the J. Raymond Chadwick Outstanding Teacher at Iowa Wesleyan. After retiring from teaching in 1974, he was honored as professor emeritus. At his retirement, several hundred of his former students returned to campus to honor him. He died eight years later in Wheaton, Illinois.

Although Ruble was appreciated and recognized for his teaching and administrative work at Iowa Wesleyan, his singular accomplishment there was as coach of women's basketball. Iowa Wesleyan was the first liberal arts college in the nation to consistently carry on a program of intercollegiate basketball for women. During his first years there Ruble coached football and men's basketball. Because of his skills as a men's coach, former players, area school superintendents, and parents pleaded with him to start a women's team. So in 1943 Ruble added to his other coaching duties responsibility for women's basketball. The players were former Iowa high school players. Their play was outstanding even in the first year, during which they played independent teams, a business school team, and some high school teams. By 1948 they were competing against teams across the Southeast and Midwest.

In the 1940s there were few women's basketball coaches, and Ruble was greatly appreciated for sharing his expertise at high school girls' basketball clinics and workshops for players, coaches, and officials around the state and beyond. Believing that the term *scholar-athlete* should embody a single ideal, he used team traveling opportunities to enhance the education of his players by often arranging side trips to historical areas. He had high expectations for his players, treated them with respect and care, and engendered great loyalty and devotion. Countering a spectator at a practice who remarked, "She runs like a boy," Ruble once said, "I'd rather say she runs like a girl should run" (Beran, p. 155).

Ruble and his Iowa Wesleyan Tigerettes participated in national and international competitions. They played college and business teams all over the United States and at Amateur Athletic Union (AAU) tourneys competed against fine teams from many other states and Mexico. Ruble led his Tigerettes to a 626–127 record. His team won more than twenty consecutive trips to the national AAU tournament, once finishing as runner-up and several times placing in the top four. Seventeen of his players were named All-Americans.

As a member of the U.S. Women's Olympic Committee from 1941 to 1976, Ruble worked assiduously to have women's basketball included in the Olympics. According to Tug Wilson, another long-time member of that committee, Ruble was a dominant figure in the crusade to win inclusion of women's basketball in the Olympics, which was finally achieved in 1976. He was two-time coach of the U.S. women's team, in 1965 and 1971, and assisted in coaching the women's team for the 1963 Pan-American Games in Winnipeg. In 1962 the third-ranked Tigerettes were selected to play the Russian National Team. When the Russian players arrived in Mount Pleasant, Ruble and his colleagues treated them to an Iowa small-town welcome, giving them a campus tour, holding a banquet in their honor, and, unfortunately for the Tigerettes, handing them two lopsided victories.

In recognition of his contributions to the field of women's basketball, Ruble was the first women's basketball coach inducted into the Helms National Hall of Fame, in 1967. He is the only coach to be in both the Helms Basketball Hall of Fame and the Iowa Football Coaches Hall of Fame. The Olan G. Ruble Memorial Scholarship Fund, initiated by a challenge pledge of $100,000 made by two former male student athletes who were greatly influenced by Ruble, was established in 1983 at Iowa Wesleyan to honor his lifelong work and achievements. As the president of Iowa Wesleyan, Louis Haselmeyer, said at the announcement of the Ruble scholarship, "He guided student athletes to great athletic achievements, but most of all he provided opportunities for them to grow and mature as worthwhile and contributing human beings." A highly enthusiastic and devoted man, Olan Guy Ruble dedicated himself to the development of young people through his teaching and coaching.

• For more information, see Janice A. Beran, *From Six on Six to Full Court Press, A Century of Iowa Girls' Basketball* (1993), and R. H. Chisholm, ed., *Iowa Girls Basketball Yearbook* (1948).

JANICE A. BERAN

RUBLEE, George (7 July 1868–26 Apr. 1957), corporate and international lawyer and presidential adviser, was born in Madison, Wisconsin, the son of Horace

Rublee, the editor and publisher of the *Milwaukee Sentinel*, and Kate Hopkins. George Rublee's first seven years were spent in Geneva, where his father served as U.S. minister to Switzerland. He graduated from Harvard with an A.B. in 1890, spent two years in Europe, and graduated from the Harvard Law School in 1895. Between 1895 and 1897 he worked at law firms in New York and Chicago and taught contract law at the Harvard Law School for one semester in 1896. His career significantly improved when he became the assistant of Victor Morawetz, an astute Wall Street financial lawyer, in January 1898. While working with Morawetz on the formation of the U.S. Steel Company, Rublee gained an in-depth knowledge of corporate and antitrust law that benefited his later work establishing the Federal Trade Commission.

In 1899 Rublee married Juliet Barrett; they had no children. By 1901 he had made a substantial fortune in the stock market. The Rublees spent the majority of 1903–1906 in Europe, with intermittent work in New York. While living near Stockholm during much of 1903, Rublee became a regular tennis partner of the crown prince of Sweden, later Gustav V. In 1906 Rublee studied diplomatic history in Paris at the École Libre des Sciences Politiques.

The Rublees returned to the United States in 1906 and purchased a home in Cornish, New Hampshire, an artist and literary community whose residents included the sculptor Augustus Saint-Gaudens; the etcher Stephen Parrish and his more famous son Maxfield Parrish; Norman Hapgood, publisher of *Collier's Weekly*; and Herbert Croly, editor of the *New Republic*. In late 1909 Hapgood invited Rublee to attend a strategy meeting with Louis Brandeis concerning the growing controversy over conservation policy that came to be known as the Ballinger-Pinchot affair. Rublee soon began assisting Brandeis at the congressional hearings in Washington, and he eventually wrote much of Brandeis's brief of the case. Rublee's private work on this highly publicized case marked the beginning of his behind-the-scenes influence in public affairs.

During the height of the progressive insurgency, Rublee served as an adviser to Robert Perkins Bass's successful campaign for governor of New Hampshire, and he advised Theodore Roosevelt throughout his Bull Moose campaign in 1912. Rublee moved to Washington in 1913, when Brandeis asked him to help draft President Woodrow Wilson's antitrust legislation. Rublee's version of the Federal Trade Commission, the centerpiece of which was the provision to outlaw "unfair methods of competition" rather than specific enumerated practices, was adopted by Wilson in 1914, and Rublee was appointed an original member of the commission in 1915. Rublee's confirmation, however, never passed the Senate, because Senator Jacob H. Gallinger of New Hampshire denounced Rublee, who had supported the senator's rival in 1914, as "personally obnoxious" and thus blocked the nomination by what was termed senatorial courtesy. Rublee

nevertheless served on the commission through January 1917 by recess appointment.

Rublee made a series of important contributions to Wilson's administration during World War I. He helped organize the Commercial Economy Board of the Advisory Council of National Defense, served as counselor to the Emergency Fleet Corporation, and was the U.S. Shipping Board representative on the Priorities Committee of the War Industries Board. In January 1918 Rublee and former congressman Raymond B. Stevens traveled to London, where they served as the U.S. delegates on the Allied Maritime Transport Council throughout the remainder of the war. This council allocated all available tonnage between the Allied powers in such a way as to make the most economical use of ships and their cargo. Rublee remained in Europe during the armistice period and was a member of the staff of the American Commission to Negotiate Peace.

In 1921 Rublee became a partner in Edward Burling and Harry Covington's recently established law firm in Washington, D.C. Rublee's public work resumed in 1928, when he went to Mexico to serve as adviser to Ambassador Dwight Morrow. Rublee was instrumental in helping Morrow reconcile the bloody rift between the Mexican government and the Catholic church. In 1930 Rublee assisted Morrow at the London Naval Conference on Disarmament, where the two succeeded in obtaining agreements from France and Italy on much of the disarmament proposals that were completely accepted by the United States, Britain, and Japan. Finally, Rublee served as Morrow's political adviser during his successful campaign for U.S. senator in 1930.

From 1930 to 1933, through the recommendation of the U.S. Department of State, Rublee served as special adviser to Colombian president Enrique Olaya Herrera. Rublee successfully arranged an agreement between the Colombian government and American oil companies over the Barco oil concession, and he gained U.S. support for Colombia's retention of the Letician Province of Colombia after Peru seized it in 1932. In 1933 Rublee served as arbitrator opposite Frank Morrison in a labor dispute in the anthracite coal industry, and from 1935 to 1938 he represented the International Committee of Bankers in the restructuring of Mexico's foreign debt.

Rublee's final and most important international appointment came in August 1938, when President Franklin Roosevelt appointed him to serve as the director of the Intergovernmental Committee on Political Refugees Coming from Germany, which was created out of the international Evian Conference in July 1938. Rublee, then seventy, had the very difficult task of trying to formulate an agreement with Germany for the orderly emigration of German Jews, an agreement that could not be formally recognized by either Germany or the Western powers. Rublee was particularly suited for the task because of his extensive work with European governments from 1918 to 1930 and because of his popularity among Latin American countries, the latter being the most likely area of resettlement for Germany's Jews. After four months of diplomatic maneuvering and a month of negotiation, Rublee reached an agreement with the Nazi government for the emigration of 400,000 German Jews over a five-year period. Some efforts to comply with this agreement were carried out until the war began in Europe in September 1939.

Rublee returned to his law practice in Washington in 1939 but continued to take an active interest in public affairs. In January 1940 Secretary of State Cordell Hull appointed Rublee chairman of a subcommittee of the Advisory Committee on Problems of Foreign Relations, on which he served throughout the war. From 1938 to 1944 he was a member of the Board of Overseers of Harvard and was president of the Harvard Alumni Association in 1947–1948. He was chevalier of the Legion of Honor of France and a commander of the Order of the Crown of Italy. Rublee died in New York City.

The distinguishing characteristic of Rublee's career is that he carried out his public service without thought of personal gain. Morrow described him as "a hard working fellow, without any thought of 'blue ribbons'," and the *New Republic* noted that Rublee was "not a politician nor an office-seeker" but rather "an ideal public servant." Rublee's low-profile approach to public affairs coupled with the breadth and depth of his involvement have resulted in his contributions being generally overlooked by historians.

• Rublee's private papers are at the Groton School archives in Groton, Mass., along with the letters he wrote to Endicott Peabody over the course of his life. Other significant sources for Rublee's correspondence include the Louis Brandeis Papers from the Brandeis Law Library at the University of Louisville (microfilmed) and the Dwight W. Morrow Papers at the Amherst College Library (microfilmed). Rublee's oral memoir, "The Reminiscences of George Rublee," at the Columbia University Oral History Office is also available on microfilm. Marc McClure, "George Rublee: A Voice of Reason" (master's thesis, Univ. of North Texas, 1996), treats Rublee's public work through 1919. Published sources that relate isolated events of Rublee's public work include Arthur Link, *Wilson: The New Freedom* (1956); Nelson Gaskill, *The Regulation of Competition* (1936); Charles Forcey, *The Crossroads of Liberalism: Croly, Weyl, Lippman, and the Progressive Era, 1900–1925* (1961); Gerald Gunther, *Learned Hand: The Man and the Judge* (1994); and Henry Feingold, *The Politics of Rescue* (1970).

MARC MCCLURE

RUBY, George T. (1841–31 Oct. 1882), African-American politician and newspaperman, was born in New York City, the son of Ebenezer Ruby, a clergyman and farmer, and Jemima (maiden name unknown). The family moved to the vicinity of Portland, Maine, in 1851. Little is known about Ruby's early life, although he claimed, and his later career supported his contention, to have received a liberal education.

In 1860 Ruby moved to Boston and was employed as a reporter on James Redpath's *Pine and Palm*. That newspaper supported Redpath's project promoting the emigration of black Americans to Haiti, and Ruby visited that island to report on the enterprise's results. His experiences in Haiti apparently convinced him that true freedom for blacks required economic self-sufficiency, an idea that he held to throughout his life.

Ruby returned to the United States in 1862, after the Haitian scheme collapsed, and moved to New Orleans, where he taught in the freedmen's schools in that city, including the American Missionary Association's Fort Douglas school and in St. Bernard Parish. At the Civil War's end, he joined the Freedmen's Bureau schools as a teacher and school agent. His efforts met serious local white resistance, including an attack by a white mob in East Feliciana Parish. In September 1866, after the failure of the Louisiana schools, Ruby moved to Texas, where the bureau schools employed him as a school organizer.

Ruby's school work gave him extensive contacts among the freedmen in the Galveston area, which served as a base of political support when he decided to enter politics after passage of the First Reconstruction Act on 2 March 1867. Ruby emerged immediately as one of his district's black leaders, joining the local Republican party and heading the Galveston chapter of the Union League. His ambitions brought him into conflict with white party leaders when he decided to run for a seat in the constitutional convention over their opposition. He easily defeated his conservative opponent, paving the way for his development as the most important black politician in Texas during Reconstruction.

In the constitutional convention of 1868 Ruby supported a public school system, the opening of public lands for black homesteaders, and prohibitions against any legal barriers to black freedom. The latter included a section forbidding the exclusion of blacks from public conveyances, places of public business, or businesses licensed by the state. Bipartisan white opposition purged this measure from the final document, but it showed Ruby's broad definition of black rights. Ruby also endorsed restricting the voting rights of former Confederates, believing that without such qualifications blacks would never secure fair treatment in the state. When the majority in the convention failed to place conditions on white voting, Ruby opposed the new constitution. Despite his position, however, he became a candidate for the state senate.

During the convention, Ruby became attached to the Radical or Davis wing of the Republican party. When white leaders divided into supporters of Governor Andrew J. Hamilton and General Edmund J. Davis, Ruby threw his support to Davis, believing that the former Union general would do more for black aspirations than Hamilton. Ruby's power expanded greatly in June 1868, when he seized control of the state Union League—by securing election as its president despite white opposition—and gave its support to the Davis faction. In the state elections of 1869 Ruby backed Davis's candidacy for governor and delivered a heavy black vote that put Davis in the governor's seat and himself in the state senate position from Galveston.

The removal of suffrage restrictions on white voters by the new constitution required Ruby to look for white support to supplement his firm position among black voters. As state senator, he sought that backing from Galveston's businesspeople by delivering state aid to their economic projects. He never forgot his original constituency, however, and worked equally hard to secure schools and protection for them. At the same time, Ruby exhibited national promise, traveling frequently to the North, where he participated in activities such as the Colored National Labor Convention in 1868 and the Colored Men's National Convention of 1872. On one of these trips he married Lucy (maiden name unknown), with whom he had three children.

The demographics of Ruby's district ultimately limited his promise. In 1873, never securing the white support he sought, Ruby gave in to party pressure to nominate a white Republican for his seat and refused to run for reelection. Ruby despaired of his prospects in Texas. He remained in Galveston through 1874 and, though nominated for a seat in the lower house, did not campaign and opposed his own nomination. He was ready for new opportunities.

In 1875 Ruby moved to New Orleans, where he was employed first by P. B. S. Pinchback's *State Register* then after 1878 by the *New Orleans Observer*, a paper supporting Senator John Sherman's presidential aspirations. Ruby actively campaigned for Sherman in Louisiana and Texas, but when Sherman failed to secure the presidential nomination in 1880, the *Observer* closed. Ruby was forced to start again, and he found local patrons who backed his publication of the *Republic* in support of local Republican congressional candidates.

In the late 1870s Ruby developed a new cause when he became a major proponent of black emigration from the South to Kansas. As a leader of the Exoduster movement, he repeatedly stated his belief that the only way to obtain the economic independence required for full freedom was to leave the South, seeking land in Kansas. On the verge once again of realizing his potential as a leader, Ruby's career was cut short when he died from an attack of malarial fever in New Orleans.

• Some of Ruby's letters are in the James P. Newcomb Papers at the American History Center, University of Texas at Austin. A useful study of Ruby's role as state senator is Randall B. Woods, "George T. Ruby: A Black Militant in the White Business Community," *Red River Valley Historical Review* 2 (1974): 269–80. The only overview of his entire career is Carl H. Moneyhon, "George T. Ruby and the Politics of Expediency in Texas," in *Southern Black Leaders of the Reconstruction Era*, ed. Howard N. Rabinowitz (1982).

CARL H. MONEYHON

RUBY, Jack L. (1911–3 Jan. 1967), assassin, was born Jack Rubenstein in Chicago, Illinois, the son of Joseph Rubenstein, a carpenter, and Fannie Turek Rutkowski, Yiddish-speaking Polish-Jewish immigrants.

Ruby gave a half-dozen different dates for his birth, but all in 1911. The fifth of eight living children, he grew to manhood in the midst of poverty in a violent slum, his father an irregularly employed alcoholic and his mother suffering from intermittent mental disease. Amid constant family tumult he finally completed the eighth grade. He was an emotional, quick-tempered, impulsive street brawler.

A nobody who aspired to be somebody, Ruby possessed neither the means nor the natural resources to achieve his goal. In this respect he was not much different from others born into unhappy families whose parents could not make a living. So Ruby began making a living any way that he could; a creature of society and his tainted environment, he sought to rid himself of their hobbling restraints. He did not have the ability to become a real gangster but was a hanger-on at pool halls, gymnasiums, and local establishments. The overriding desire of his life was to have others like him. He failed at every project or business enterprise he undertook throughout his life.

In the 1930s Ruby engaged in street peddling, selling racing sheets, and running sales promotions in the Chicago area. From 1937 until 1940 he worked as a union organizer for Local 20467 of the Scrap Iron and Junk Handlers Union. He then sold novelties and punch boards for gambling until drafted into the air force in 1943. Upon discharge in 1946 he returned to Chicago and sold novelties until 1947, when he moved to Dallas, Texas. That same year he changed his name to Jack Ruby.

Ruby was an undisciplined businessman, and his finances were often in a state of chaos. He ultimately became owner of the Carousel Club, a sleazy Dallas nightclub featuring striptease acts. He was noted for a volatile temper and sudden violent acts. He was a police buff, making friends of officers and in other ways ingratiating himself to those in positions of visible power.

Ruby was arrested several times for minor crimes, traffic tickets, and license violations and had a variety of charges made against him, some serious and a few bizarre. The files of Dallas district attorney Henry Wade contained a letter from the Society for the Prevention of Cruelty to Animals. Ruby had a dog named Sheba whom he sometimes referred to as his wife. The SPCA was concerned that Ruby was treating her that way. It had reason to believe it. Another complaint charged that at a fair Ruby publicly fondled the breasts of adolescent girls, remarking to friends, "I'm just breaking them in to come to work for me."

Ruby's notoriety, however, stems from his assassination of Lee Harvey Oswald and subsequent questions as to whether Oswald acted alone in the assassination of President John F. Kennedy. Questions also arose regarding Ruby's connection with the Federal Bureau of Investigation. FBI officials grudgingly admitted having contact with Ruby to enlist him as a criminal informant, but claimed he did not make the grade. The bureau, however, refused to release its records about Ruby's status as an informant. The processes of contact, enlistment, pay, and results would have generated Criminal Informant classification files 137 at the Dallas field office and FBI headquarters.

The assassination of Kennedy on 22 November 1963 in Dallas gave Ruby a serendipitous opportunity to be somebody. Oswald was arrested as a suspect in the assassination, and on 24 November the police announced they would move him from the city jail to the county jail at 10:00 A.M. A postal inspector arrived to complete his interrogation of Oswald, however, and delayed the transfer. At 11:15 the police escorted Oswald to the garage in the basement, where a van was waiting. Meanwhile Ruby stopped at the Western Union building opposite the police station at 11:17 to send money to one of his strippers. He then walked into the station basement with seventy police officers in the area as Oswald emerged, handcuffed to Detective James R. Leavelle. At 11:21 A.M. Ruby killed Oswald with a single fatal shot.

The killing unleashed a torrent of conspiracy speculation. In the aftermath federal officials launched a massive investigation of Ruby, at the same time focusing on Oswald as the lone assassin of the president. The official investigation conducted by the Warren Commission "found no evidence that . . . Jack Ruby was part of any conspiracy, domestic or foreign."

No evidence has been found to suggest that Oswald and Ruby had ever seen each other, let alone conspired together. Rumors of such a relationship lack any confirmation. In killing Oswald, however, Ruby eliminated any assassination trial in which evidence about Oswald's responsibility could be presented and tested. Ruby's action, then, accounts for subsequent controversies and for the ensuing legacy of disenchantment with government that is reflected in many polls.

The presumptions that the Mafia or the Central Intelligence Agency or Cuba was behind the assassination of Oswald through Ruby are contradicted by known and indisputable facts. Ruby's oft-cited remark to Chief Justice Earl Warren of the commission investigating the crime that if taken to Washington he would talk was prattle from a mind increasingly irrational. A psychiatrist who evaluated him for his defense counsel reported that Ruby had serious psychiatric problems and was "not now capable of cooperating intelligently in his own defense."

Ruby was tried for Oswald's murder, found guilty, and sentenced to death, unusual in a city where the typical sentence for gunshot murder was eight years in prison. The sentence was overturned on appeal in October 1966. While he awaited a second trial, Ruby became ill and was transferred to Parkland Memorial Hospital, where both Kennedy and Oswald had also been taken. There doctors discovered advanced stages of cancer of the brain. Ruby soon died in Dallas. Questions about Ruby remain; indeed, some have asked whether the illness so long undetected could have affected his behavior in 1963.

Ruby never married.

• Ruby left few papers. A vast federal collection of documents related to Ruby compiled by the assassination investigations is in the National Archives. The Texas Court of Inquiry deposited files in the state archives in Austin. The papers of most major figures involved in the investigation contain material on Ruby, including Gerald Ford in the Ford Library in Ann Arbor, Mich.; Richard Russell in Athens, Ga.; John Sherman Cooper in Lexington, Ky.; Earl Warren in the Library of Congress; Lyndon B. Johnson in the Johnson Library in Austin; Allen Dulles at Princeton University; and Texas attorney general Waggoner Carr at Baylor University. The psychiatric reports of Dr. L. J. West and Dr. R. L. Stubblefield are in the Cooper papers. The papers of critic and scholar Harold Weisberg, Frederick, Md., to be deposited in Hood College, contain essential files, along with his correspondence with District Attorney Henry Wade and his notes and aide memoirs on the Wade files and Ruby. The Warren Commission *Report* (1964) discusses Ruby throughout and includes a biography, pp. 779–806, while its twenty-six-volume *Hearings and Exhibits* (1964) contains essential exhibits and witness testimony. The House Select Committee on Assassinations *Report* of 1979 and its twelve volumes of reports and testimony are a recent addition to the National Archives. Almost every book on the assassination of President Kennedy discusses Ruby, most superficially and often distorted by theories. Four volumes on the trial itself that also discuss his life are Melvin M. Belli and Maurice C. Carroll, *Dallas Justice* (1964); John Kaplan and Jon R. Waltz, *The Trial of Jack Ruby* (1965); Garry Wills and Ovid Demaris, *Jack Ruby* (1968); and Elmer Gertz, *Moment of Madness: The People vs. Jack Ruby* (1968). Most volumes discussing Ruby are flawed by speculation, such as Renatus Hartogs and Lucy Freeman, *The Two Assassins* (1965); Seth Kantor, *The Ruby Cover-Up* (1978); and Mark Lane, *Rush to Judgment* (1966). A representative refutation of the speculators is in the objective refutation of Lane by Gertz, pp. 507–43, and Wills and Demaris, pp. 160–67, 208–46. The best approach to President Kennedy's assassination is through Harold Weisberg, *Whitewash* (1965) and *Never Again* (1995), and Sylvia Meagher, *Accessories after the Fact* (1967).

DAVID R. WRONE

RUDD, Daniel (7 Aug. 1854–4 Dec. 1933), newspaper editor and Catholic lay leader, was born in Bardstown, Kentucky, the son of Robert Rudd, a slave on the Rudd estate, and Elizabeth "Eliza" Hayden, a slave of the Hayden family in Bardstown. He was baptized a Catholic when an infant. Although little information exists about his early life, it may be conjectured that his Catholic upbringing was due chiefly to his mother who acted as sexton in the local church for more than sixty years. After the Civil War, he went to Springfield, Ohio, where an older brother had already established himself, to get a secondary school education. There is little information about Rudd until 1884 when he began a black newspaper, the *Ohio State Tribune*. In 1886 Rudd changed the name of the weekly newspaper to the *American Catholic Tribune*, proudly displaying on the editorial page the words "The only Catholic Journal owned and published by Colored men." The newspaper's focus was the Catholic church and the African American. Rudd's purpose was to demonstrate to African Americans that the Catholic church was truly the best hope of black Americans. He was convinced that Catholicism would elevate the cultural level of the black race and thus attract an enormous influx of black converts to the Catholic church. Believing that the authority structure of the church could change racist behavior and influence racist thought, he asserted, "The Catholic Church alone can break the color line. Our people should help her to do it." Although black Catholics could point to the Catholic church's teaching on the dignity of the person as inherently antiracist, Rudd made the case more directly for the usefulness of Roman Catholicism in changing the moral and religious status of African Americans. He published the following on the front page of his paper: "The Holy Roman Catholic Church offers to the oppressed Negro a material as well as spiritual refuge, superior to all the inducements of other organizations combined. . . . The distinctions and differences among men are unrecognized within the pale of the Church. . . . The Negro and the Caucasian are equally the children of one Father and as such, are equally welcomed, with equal rights, equal privileges."

On the other hand, Rudd used the newspaper to speak out forcefully against racial discrimination. He editorialized in favor of an integrated school system in Cincinnati, Ohio, and against segregated schools and institutions. Race pride was important to him, so he used his newspaper to highlight the achievements of leading African Americans of his day.

By 1887 Rudd had moved his weekly newspaper to Cincinnati, where he had a small staff of assistant editors and traveling correspondents who doubled as sales representatives. The paper in most editions ran to four pages. Front-page articles carried religious news from various black Catholic communities along with other items related to African Americans. A column or two was often dedicated to an exposition of Catholic belief or practice. Many articles were reprints from other newspapers, including items from the Catholic press and the African-American press. According to some estimates, the newspaper had as many as ten thousand subscribers in the period prior to the move to Detroit, Michigan. Rudd received the approbation of some members of the church hierarchy and some small contributions, but there is no indication of any long-term subsidy from Catholic leaders or laypeople.

Rudd also traveled across the country as a tireless lecturer. The message was usually the same: "the Catholic Church is not only a warm and true friend to the Colored people but is absolutely impartial in recognizing them as the equals of all." He spoke to varied audiences in places like Lexington, Kentucky, and Fort Wayne, Indiana (1887); Natchez, Mississippi, and Nashville, Tennessee (1891); Syracuse, New York (1895); and Lewiston, Maine (1896). Fluent in German, he spoke to German organizations such as the *Central Verein* in Toledo, Ohio, in 1886 and to students at a German orphanage in Linwood, Ohio, in 1890.

In the summer of 1889 Rudd was sent to Europe to participate in the Anti-Slavery Conference organized by Cardinal Charles-Martial Lavigerie, the primate of Africa. The trip was made possible, it seems, by a subvention from William Henry Elder, the archbishop of Cincinnati. Rudd was already in Germany when the conference which was to be held in Lucerne, Switzerland, was postponed; he nevertheless continued his trip to Lucerne, where he met with Cardinal Lavigerie, and to London, where he visited Cardinal Henry Edward Manning before returning to America.

Rudd was responsible for the five black Catholic lay congresses that were held between the years 1889 and 1894. He first called for a congress of black Catholics in the columns of his newspaper as early as 1888, writing, "Colored Catholics ought to unite. . . . Let leading Colored Catholics gather together from every city in the Union [where] they may get to know one another and take up the cause of the race." The first nationwide assembly of black Catholics, meeting in Washington, D.C., in early January 1889, was well attended and widely acclaimed. The second congress was held in Cincinnati in 1890 and the third in Philadelphia, Pennsylvania, in 1892. Rudd published the proceedings of these congresses on his own press. His influence in the last two congresses, held in Chicago, Illinois, in 1893 and in Baltimore, Maryland, in 1894, is less evident.

Rudd played other significant roles in American Catholicism and black journalism. He was on the steering committee for the first national Lay Catholic Congress held in Baltimore in November 1889 and was a founding member of the Catholic Press Association (1890) and the Afro-American Press Association and was actively involved in both. By 1894 he had moved the publication of the *American Catholic Tribune* to Detroit for unknown reasons. There are no extant copies of the newspaper dating after 1894, but only after 1897 did Rudd's name cease to appear as a publisher in the Detroit City Directory.

Under circumstances that are not clear Rudd had, according to census records, moved to Bolivar County in Mississippi by 1910. He later moved to eastern Arkansas where he acted as accountant and business manager for two well-to-do black farmers. He seemingly had little contact with the small black Catholic community in Arkansas centered around Pine Bluff. The black Catholic congresses had ceased to meet after 1894 for reasons that remain unclear, and Rudd thereafter was no longer an influential leader in the black Catholic movement. In his correspondence with John B. Morris, the bishop of Little Rock, he alluded to his former role and indicated his continued interest in the cause of black Catholics, even expressing a desire to represent the diocese at a meeting of the National Association for the Advancement of Colored People. In 1917 Rudd was the coauthor of a biography of Scott Bond, one of the successful black farmers of the region for whom he worked as an accountant. Rudd's attention in his later years seemingly centered on the furtherance of black business. After suffering a stroke, he returned to Bardstown in 1932, where he died.

A member of the first generation of postslavery African Americans, Rudd was one of the more significant figures in the history of black Catholics in the United States. Here was a former slave welcomed by two cardinals, a black man lecturing to white audiences both in the North and in the South. He began the longest running African-American Catholic newspaper in the country and single-handedly launched a black Catholic lay movement when he began the black lay congresses. From this effort emerged other black Catholic lay leaders from whom came the first articulation of a black Catholic theological position. As the first African-American Catholic layman to call publicly for the Catholic church to live up to its teachings on social justice and social equality, Rudd opened the way for later black Catholic activists in the civil rights movement.

Rudd never married. He could be difficult; many ecclesiastics and white lay leaders saw him as "pushy" because he would not accept circumstances that he deemed disrespectful to the black race. Among Catholic laymen of his time, he was unique; among black leaders of his generation, he was extraordinary; in the light of recent American Catholic history, he was prophetic.

• The only extant copies of Rudd's newspaper are in the Archdiocese of Philadelphia Archives in Overbrook, Pa. They are available on microfilm from the American Theological Library Association, Board of Microtext. Correspondence from Rudd is in the Archdiocese of Cincinnati Archives, the Little Rock Diocesan Archives, and the Josephite Archives in Baltimore. For the book Rudd wrote in collaboration with Theophilus Bond, see *From Slavery to Wealth, the Life of Scott Bond: The Rewards of Honesty, Industry, Economy, and Perseverance* (1917; repr. 1971). Information about Rudd is in Thomas Spalding, "The Negro Catholic Congresses, 1889–1894," *Catholic Historical Review* 55 (1969): 337–57. See also Joseph H. Lackner, "Daniel Rudd, Editor of the *American Catholic Tribune*, from Bardstown to Cincinnati," *Catholic Historical Review* 80 (1994): 258–81, and Cyprian Davis, *The History of Black Catholics in the United States* (1990).

CYPRIAN DAVIS

RUDERMAN, Yaakov Yitzchak (14 Feb. 1900–11 July 1987), yeshiva dean, was born in Dolhinov, Russia, the son of Yehuda Leib Ruderman and Shana (maiden name unknown). Ruderman received his initial education from his father, a rabbi and instructor of Bible and Talmud for young men. Enrolling in the famed Knesset Israel yeshiva in Slobodka, Lithuania, Ruderman was greatly influenced by the yeshiva's legendary spiritual counselor, Rabbi Nathan Zevi Finkel, known as the Alter of Slobodka.

As a yeshiva student Ruderman was highly regarded for his scholarship and piety and became acquainted with many of the great Talmud scholars of Eastern Europe, some of whom, like Rabbis Moshe Mordechai Epstein, Isser Zalman Meltzer, and Meir Atlas granted him rabbinical ordination in 1926. Ruderman's brilliant mind came to be widely acknowledged when, at the age of twenty-nine, he published *Avodat*

Levi, a highly regarded commentary on the laws of sacrifices. In August 1925 his piety and scholarship earned him the privilege of marrying Faige Kramer, the daughter of Rabbi Sheftel Kramer, an outstanding Lithuanian Talmud scholar. They had one child.

In 1930 Ruderman immigrated to the United States, where he joined his father-in-law as lecturer in Talmud at the Yeshiva of New Haven, headed by Rabbi Yehuda Levenberg. Shortly after his arrival, the yeshiva moved to Cleveland, though retaining its name, the Yeshiva of New Haven.

Two years later, in 1933, following a controversy regarding the administration of the yeshiva, Ruderman left his teaching position in Cleveland to become rabbi at Congregation Tiferet Israel in Baltimore. Shortly thereafter he established his own yeshiva called Ner Israel. With great steadfastness, Ruderman persevered in establishing a vibrant European-style yeshiva in the United States, the Ner Israel Rabbinical College. Unlike the Rabbi Isaac Elchanan Theological Seminary in New York City, which had begun to incorporate secular studies into the yeshiva program, the Ner Israel yeshiva devoted itself exclusively to the study of Talmud and other religious texts.

Employing many of the pedagogical techniques and the earnest devotion of his mentor, Rabbi Nathan Zevi Finkel, Ruderman inspired a generation of American rabbis, teachers, and learned laymen to provide noteworthy leadership in the Orthodox community. Ruderman's influence was felt not only in Baltimore but in Toronto, where his son-in-law, Rabbi Yaakov Weinberg, opened a branch school of the Ner Israel Rabbinical College. For the rest of his life, Ruderman successfully guided the affairs of Ner Israel as yeshiva dean. Within a few decades the yeshiva, which had started with only five students, grew in numbers and emerged as one of the preeminent American yeshiva academies.

A member of the rabbinic union Agudath ha-Rabbonim and a supporter of the philanthropic agency Ezrat Torah, Ruderman was closely aligned also with the Agudath Israel of America, an Orthodox political advocacy group, for which he served as a senior member of the Council of Torah Sages. In addition, he supported the activities of Torah U'mesorah National Society of Hebrew Day Schools and served on its rabbinic advisory board.

After a long illness, Ruderman died at his home on the campus of his beloved yeshiva in Baltimore. The funeral was attended by approximately 10,000 students and admirers. Ruderman's son-in-law succeeded him as yeshiva dean of the Ner Israel Rabbinical College.

• There are no personal papers or complete biographies of Ruderman. Brief accounts of his life and achievements can be found in *Who's Who in American Jewry* (1938); Asher Rand, *Toldoth Anshe Shem* (1950), p. 129; *Ha-Pardes* 3 (Feb. 1930): 26; and *Encyclopedia Judaica*. Obituaries and tributes are in the *Baltimore Jewish Times*, 17 July 1987; *Ha-Pardes* 62 (Oct. 1987): 25–26; and the *Jewish Observer*, Nov. 1987.

MOSHE SHERMAN

RUDGE, William Edwin (23 Nov. 1876–12 June 1931), printer and publisher, was born in Brooklyn, New York, the son of William Edwin Rudge, a printer, and Lavinia Knapp. William had a quiet childhood that was brought to a quick end at the age of thirteen when his father's declining health forced him to assume increasing responsibility in the family business. The elder Rudge was a competent printer whose mainstay was printing the weekly *Coal Trade Journal* (*CTJ*). William had begun working part-time in the business two years earlier, addressing wrappers for the *CTJ*. His father also gave him a couple of small presses, and William began to do his own small jobs.

At fifteen Rudge assumed total responsibility for the production of the *CTJ*. During this time he also began to attend night school to improve his education. His formal courses were in engineering, but he also took an interest in the humanities. He developed strong opinions on good and bad literature, scholarship, and the arts that he later put to good use in his publishing ventures. He made a success of running the printing shop, moving the company to larger premises with more modern presses in 1895. His father's tuberculosis flared in 1900, effectively ending his role in the business. Rudge assumed formal control at age twenty-three.

After the new works burned in 1905 Rudge moved to Manhattan. In 1906 he married Lillie May Gould of Mount Vernon, New York. They had two sons. The move to Manhattan proved providential, for Rudge was able to upgrade his printing equipment again and keep pace with developments. Rudge was interested in the history of the graphic arts and read widely, collecting many examples of printing craftsmanship. It was, therefore, natural that he became active in the Graphic Group, an organization of like-minded printers who were interested in the advancement of the printing art. Around 1913 most members of the Graphic Group joined the fledgling American Institute of Graphic Arts (AIGA) and slowly began to take over its direction. As a result, the AIGA adopted most of the goals and objectives of the Graphic Group, although the latter continued as a separate organization.

Rudge spent the decade of the 1910s and the war years building a strong organization. He began to gain a good reputation as a fine printer and businessman. In 1911 he tried his hand at publishing, producing John Cox Underwood's *The Lineage of the Rogers Family, England: Embracing John Rogers the Martyr*. Most of the early works bearing the Rudge imprints, however, were limited special editions that we would now describe as "vanity press" publications.

Rudge's efforts were increasingly directed toward producing a book that was of high quality and technical achievement. The first book that bears his distinct attention to quality bookmaking was Frederic W. Goudy's *The Alphabet*, printed for the Mitchell Kennerley publishing house in 1918. In 1920 Rudge moved the company to Mount Vernon, buying the building and two acres of the Triplex Glass Company. Extensive renovations of the building gave the company increased space to work on Rudge's commissions and pet printing projects.

Rudge was concerned with solving the problem of printing illustrations on uncoated paper. He felt the coated plates detracted from the overall look and feel of a work. He initially worked under license with Robert John's Aquatone process for printing lithography from a gelatine surface on metal plates. Since Aquatone was John's patented property, however, Rudge could never share his developments with his peers. The Smithsonian Institution approached him with a challenge to develop a more exacting process that could be used on their works, one that would be free for all to use and develop. Rudge was also interested in the design of books, writing in 1922: "There is no question but that it is harder to prepare and execute an advertising page that is clear and simple and *easy to read* than one that is crowded with too many display lines and unnecessary ornaments" (*Monotype: A Journal of Composing Room Efficiency*, Oct.–Nov. 1992).

In 1925 Rudge printed the five volumes of Mary Vaux Walcott's *North American Wildflowers* for the Smithsonian, using what was later called the Smithsonian Process for printing illustrations. This same year, Secretary of Commerce Herbert Hoover recognized Rudge as a printer of some repute, choosing him to represent the American printing industry at the Paris Exposition of Industrial and Decorative Arts. The subsidiary William Edwin Rudge, Publisher was also established in 1925, reflecting Rudge's increasing interest in making available significant works of literature, scholarship, and art. Works that appeared under this new imprint include George Moore's *Perronick the Fool* (1926), Wilmarth S. Lewis's facsimile edition of *The Commonplace Book of Horace Walpole* (1927), and Frederick A. Pottle's edition of *Private Papers of James Boswell from Malahide Castle* (1928).

Rudge's contribution to printing excellence can best be seen in the number of books his printing house produced over the years. He was an uncompromising critic of his work and a perfectionist. He assembled some of the top talent of his day, infusing them with his energy, vision, and desire to experiment with their art. He died in Mount Vernon after suffering complications from surgery to treat an internal disorder.

• The most extensive collection of Rudge's printings and publications can be found in the Printers Collection of the Library at the University of California at Santa Barbara. William J. Glick's examination of Rudge and his legacy, *William Edwin Rudge* (1984), used this collection heavily. Rudge also received a warm obituary in *Publishers Weekly*, 30 June 1931, p. 2869, and his career was examined in the *Saturday Evening Review of Literature*, 25 July 1931, p. 15.

JOHN J. DOHERTY

RUDITSKY, Barney (3 Jan. 1898–18 Oct. 1962), policeman and private detective, was born Barnett Ruditsky in London, England, the son of Phillip Ruditsky, a boot finisher, and Blooma Marin. He was taken as a child to South Africa by his parents, but the family then returned to England. About 1908, they moved to New York and settled in the East Side of Manhattan. In 1916 Ruditsky served with the U.S. Army along the Mexican border, and during World War I he was stationed in France.

Returning home at the end of the war, Ruditsky launched a highly publicized career with the New York Police Department. Joining the force in 1921, he demonstrated a singular flair for the dramatic. In 1923 the slender Ruditsky subdued a much larger, recalcitrant suspect with a night stick, an exploit that drew compliments from the magistrate and the *New York Times*. He and his wife, Mollie Feiner (whom he married on 18 February 1923 and with whom he had a son), interrupted a confectionery store robbery near their Brooklyn home in 1926 as they returned from celebrating their wedding anniversary. Ruditsky overpowered one robber and seized his gun, then handed the firearm to Mollie, telling her to guard the culprit until the police arrived. Meanwhile, Ruditsky chased down a second robber, who had fled the premises.

In 1924, when he became a detective, Ruditsky was teamed with Detective Johnny Broderick as part of the police department's "gangster-industrial squad." In 1928 he and another detective disguised themselves as patrons in a Turkish bathhouse on Second Street, an underworld hangout, in order to apprehend the celebrated "poison ivy" gang. Later he arrested the notorious "pear buttons" outfit from the West Side. Much to the approval of newspaper readers, Ruditsky and Broderick tangled with such major underworld figures as Jack "Legs" Diamond and Arthur "Dutch Schultz" Flegenheimer. At various times in his career, Ruditsky arrested Benjamin "Bugsy" Siegel and Abe "Kid Twist" Reles, both of whom would later be part of New York's infamous "Murder, Inc." Posturing as fearless, Ruditsky testified at the 1950 crime hearings held by Senator Estes Kefauver that he had been "threatened a thousand times . . . , but I got around them pretty good . . . ; nobody got back at me."

Ruditsky retired from the New York Police Department in 1941. During World War II, he rejoined the U.S. Army, serving in a unit assigned to guard prisoners of war in Africa. He suffered wounds from shrapnel in 1943. While in the armed forces, he completed writing "Angel's Corner," his memoirs about his police era exploits.

At the end of the war, Ruditsky moved to the Los Angeles area, where he operated a small liquor store, a bar and restaurant called Sherry's, and a private detective firm. These business ventures brought him into contact with entertainment figures, law enforcement officials, and individuals linked with the underworld. At one time, he asked Frank Costello, New York gambling entrepreneur, to help him obtain a certain line of liquor. In 1949, gangster Mickey Cohen, a regular at Sherry's, was gunned down outside the establishment in an assassination attempt. Ruditsky's private detective agency also collected on bad debts owed various Las Vegas casinos. His clients included Bugsy Siegel, who owned the celebrated Flamingo and discussed with Ruditsky underworld financing of the casino. After Siegel was assassinated in 1947, Ruditsky offered Los Angeles police officers his theories about the killing. Much to his embarrassment, his observations were then leaked to syndicated columnist Westbrook Pegler, who made much of the fact that Ruditsky, once a squeaky clean New York cop, had tried to collect on bad debts for Siegel. In 1950, at the televised Kefauver hearings, Ruditsky tried to distance himself from any suggestion that he had improper ties to the underworld.

As a private detective, Ruditsky frequently became involved in questionable activities. In 1954, for example, baseball hero Joe DiMaggio, then involved in divorce proceedings with Marilyn Monroe, hired Ruditsky's firm to uncover embarrassing intelligence on the film star. With DiMaggio and Frank Sinatra on the scene, Ruditsky and a cameraman broke into an apartment where they believed Monroe was secreted with a lover. Much to their embarrassment, however, they discovered a horrified woman, not Monroe, sleeping alone. The legendary "Wrong Door Raid" became the subject of Hollywood gossip and an embarrassing exposé in the September 1955 issue of *Confidential* magazine. In 1957 a state legislative committee looked into the Wrong Door Raid as part of its investigation of the Hollywood gutter press. Shortly thereafter, the matter was again aired when the California attorney general brought a criminal libel suit against *Confidential*. Ruditsky, suffering from heart problems, was spared from testifying before the legislative committee, but the unfavorable publicity generated by the case and the discovery that his detective firm lacked a state license sullied his reputation. Embarrassed, Ruditsky explained that "private detective work is a dirty, filthy, rotten business." Reggie Darryl, his second wife, died in 1957.

By the late 1950s Ruditsky's literary efforts had helped salvage his self-esteem. After a decade of negotiations, he worked out an agreement to televise his unpublished memoirs. In 1959 NBC premiered "The Lawless Years," a thirty-minute weekly series based on Ruditsky's "Angel's Corner." Ruditsky himself served as technical adviser to the series, which won considerable praise for its attention to detail. "The Lawless Years" ran during the summer seasons of 1959 and 1961 before being canceled. It inspired an even more successful rival, ABC's "The Untouchables," which was based on Eliot Ness's exploits against the Chicago underworld during the 1920s and 1930s. At least partially vindicated, Ruditsky died in Los Angeles. His career, based on daring and self-promotion, underscored the close ties that often existed in the twentieth century between law enforcement, the criminal underworld, and the media and entertainment fields.

• Ruditsky's testimony before the Kefauver Committee is in U.S. Senate, *Hearings before the Special Committee to Investigate Organized Crime in Interstate Commerce*, 82d Cong., 2d sess., pt. 10. Also see the *New York Times*, 15 Aug. 1923, and 22 Feb. 1926, for press accounts of his career as a police officer. For accounts of the Wrong Door Raid, see Anthony Summers, *Goddess: The Secret Lives of Marilyn Monroe* (1985), and Kitty Kelley, *His Way: The Unauthorized Biography of Frank Sinatra* (1986). Obituaries are in the *New York Times*, 19 Oct. 1962, and the *Washington Post*, 20 Oct. 1962.

WILLIAM HOWARD MOORE

RUDKIN, Margaret Fogarty (14 Sept. 1897–1 June 1967), bakery executive, was born in New York City, the daughter of Joseph Fogarty, a trucker, and Margaret Healey. She attended public schools, and on graduating from high school, she was hired as a bookkeeper at a bank in Flushing, Queens. She left the bank after four years to join the brokerage firm of McClure, Jones & Company in New York City as a "customer's woman" (account service representative), a position she held for four years. In 1923 she married Henry Albert Rudkin, one of the partners in the firm. The couple continued to live in New York City until 1929, when, with the money Henry Rudkin had made on Wall Street, they built a mansion on a 125-acre estate in Fairfield County, Connecticut, that they named "Pepperidge Farm."

With the onset of the depression in 1929, however, Margaret Rudkin's life as a conventional young society wife came to an end. The severe economic decline compelled them to be frugal. Then in 1931 Henry Rudkin was incapacitated for a time as a result of an injury incurred playing polo. Early in 1937 one of the Rudkins' three sons, Mark, was afflicted with asthma. An allergist posed two alternatives: either the boy should be sent to live in the dry, warm climate of the Southwest, or his diet should be altered to replace store-bought bread with bread baked at home, free of the additives used in commercial baking that he suspected were aggravating the boy's condition. Because their financial exigencies made it impossible for the family to move across the country, Margaret Rudkin tried her hand at breadmaking. Later she would recall that her first loaf of stone-ground whole-wheat bread was "hard as rock and about one inch high." Trial and error led to loaves not only better in flavor, texture, and appearance but also healthy for her son to eat.

At the allergist's request, Rudkin baked bread for his other patients, and she was prevailed upon by neighbors to supply them as well. By the summer of 1937 Rudkin set herself up as a commercial baker. A grocery store in Fairfield took delivery of her first batch of loaves at wholesale. As regular orders came in, Rudkin's kitchen could no longer accommodate a commercial operation, and an abandoned stable on the estate was converted to her needs. It was only natural to identify the estate in the brand name that Rudkin adopted: Pepperidge Farm.

Rudkin soon entered the New York City market, selling her bread to a famous specialty food store, Charles & Co. During this initial expansion of her business—a period in which many new enterprises fail—Rudkin was helped by a quantity of free publicity. An article in a November 1937 issue of the *New York Journal and American* announcing her bread was one in a series of articles in newspapers and magazines featuring the product and praising its wholesomeness. Rudkin's breakthrough to the national market came in 1939, when Benjamin Sonnenberg, a well-known public relations man, contrived to have Pepperidge Farm featured in a *Reader's Digest* article, "Bread, de Luxe," thereby introducing the brand to readers all over North America. Orders began to pour in from every part of the United States and Canada, and sales soon surpassed 50,000 loaves a week.

Rudkin insisted on using fresh ingredients, including butter and whole milk, and refused to use the shortenings, yeast foods (dough conditioners that cut rising time), and other additives common in commercial baking. Mixed in small batches, the dough was kneaded and cut by hand. The cooked loaves were wrapped by machine, initially without slicing. Though she believed that bread should properly be cut in the home just before eating, Rudkin did eventually, and with reluctance, adopt bread-slicing machines. As her business grew, Rudkin had to obtain ever-larger quantities of raw ingredients. She traveled to Minneapolis to secure a supply of wheat that satisfied her exacting specifications and contracted with several gristmills to grind it into flour. Because of the expense of the ingredients and Rudkin's labor-intensive production method, Pepperidge Farm bread was twice as expensive as comparable commercial breads. Rudkin succeeded nonetheless, because the homestyle flavor and texture of her product, unusual at the time, caught the public imagination.

Rudkin first began to expand her product line by adding to it pound cake and melba toast. Since her bread contained no preservatives, company policy dictated that it remain on store shelves for no longer than two days. Consequently, large quantities of unsold bread were returned to her plants for disposal each day. Rudkin's solution to the problems this posed revealed both her business acumen and her housewife's ingenuity. The stale bread was turned into poultry stuffing, and the company quickly became one of the country's leading stuffing manufacturers. As sales increased, Rudkin opened more plants. The company grew into a major national firm, while Pepperidge Farm became one of the iconic American brand names of the 1950s. Rudkin's image also became familiar. As "Maggie" Rudkin, she appeared in a series of calculatedly homespun television commercials throughout the decade.

By 1960 Pepperidge Farm was the largest independent bakery in the United States, with sales in excess of $32 million, profits of $1.3 million, and 1,000 employees, most of them women. As president, Rudkin took a hand in all aspects of production, while her husband managed the firm's finances and marketing. But the couple was now ready to relinquish family ownership. The Campbell Soup Company acquired the Pepperidge Farm brand for $28 million worth of Campbell stock, and Margaret became a director of the parent company. As an autonomous unit within the Campbell conglomerate, Pepperidge Farm remained under the Rudkins' management.

In 1962 their son William Rudkin replaced his mother as president, and Margaret Rudkin in turn replaced her husband as chair of the company's board. The *Margaret Rudkin Pepperidge Farm Cookbook*, which was published in 1963, included with the recipes a fair amount of autobiographical material. Although it sold very well at the time, its bestseller status did not make it a lasting classic. In 1966 Rudkin was diagnosed with breast cancer and resigned from the company. At the time of her death in New Haven, Connecticut, the Pepperidge Farm Division of Campbell had achieved annual sales of some $50 million.

Rudkin achieved extraordinary success in business during a period of unparalleled social conformity in American life, when the great majority of women were restricted to the role of homemaker. That she did so without appearing to defy social convention is largely owed to her success in a field traditionally defined in the United States as feminine—baking—and to her cultivation of a public image that always emphasized her domesticity.

• No personal or corporate papers are available. For contemporary accounts of her life and career, see "Mrs. Rudkin of Pepperidge," *Time*, 14 July 1947; "Champion of the Old Fashioned, *Time*, 21 Mar. 1960; John Bainbridge, "Striking a Blow for Grandma," *New Yorker*, 22 May 1948; "Mrs. Rudkin Revisited," *New Yorker*, 16 Nov. 1963; "Through the Mill to Success," *American Home*, Apr. 1951; W. B. Hartley, "Story of Pepperidge Bread: 5000 Loaves a Week," *Coronet*, Aug. 1953; and *Current Biography* (1959). An obituary is in the *New York Times*, 2 June 1967.

JOHN INGHAM

RUDOLPH, Wilma (23 June 1940–12 Nov. 1994), track and field athlete, was born Wilma Glodean Rudolph in St. Bethlehem, Tennessee, the daughter of Edward Rudolph, a railroad porter, and Blanche (maiden name unknown), a domestic. Born nearly two months premature and weighing only four-and-a-half pounds, Wilma was a sickly child who contracted both double pneumonia and scarlet fever, which resulted in her left leg being partially paralyzed. Her doctors doubted that she would ever regain the use of her leg. Undaunted, Wilma's mother made a ninety-mile bus trip once a week with her to Nashville, Tennessee, so she could receive heat, water, and massage treatments. At age five she began wearing a heavy steel brace and corrective shoes to help straighten her leg. After years of physical therapy, at age twelve she was finally able to move about without her leg brace.

When she entered a racially segregated high school in Clarksville, Tennessee, Rudolph tried out for the basketball team and, in recognition of her abilities, made the all-state team four times. As an outstanding athlete she came to the attention of Ed Temple, the premier women's track coach at Tennessee State University. Though Rudolph was still in high school, Temple invited her to spend the summer with other track athletes at the university training camp. In 1956 she participated in the national Amateur Athletic Union track and field competition, winning the 75-yard and 100-yard events as well as anchoring the winning relay team. Encouraged by her coach, she traveled with the Tennessee State team to the tryouts for the 1956 Olympic Games in Melbourne, Australia. At sixteen Rudolph became the youngest member of the U.S. women's track and field team. Though she did not make the Olympic finals in the 200-meter event, she and her team won a bronze medal in the 400-meter relay event.

Rudolph returned home to complete her last two years of high school and looked forward to going to college. However, in her senior year of high school she became pregnant and gave birth to a daughter. Her boyfriend wanted to marry her, but Rudolph was unwilling to give up her fledgling track career. Her daughter was sent to live with a married older sister in St. Louis. In 1957 Rudolph enrolled at Tennessee State on a track scholarship and continued to train for the 1960 Olympic Games in Rome, Italy.

During the 1960 Olympics, temperatures in Rome hovered around 100 degrees. Rudolph contended not only with the weather, but with an ankle injury she suffered the day before the first race. Despite her impairment she won three gold medals: one in the 100-meter event, setting a world record with a finishing time of 11.0 seconds; another in the 200-meter dash with a time of 23.2 seconds; and her third as anchor of the women's 400-meter relay team. She thus became the first American woman to win three gold medals in a single Olympics.

In 1961 Rudolph competed in the previously all-male Millrose Games, tying her own world record in the 60-yard dash with a time of 6.9 seconds. She also became the first woman to compete in the heralded New York Athletic Club meet, the Los Angeles Times Games, and the Penn Relays. That year she received the Sullivan Award as the nation's top amateur athlete.

In 1962 Rudolph was awarded the coveted Babe Didrikson Zaharias Award as the most outstanding female athlete in the world. That same year she competed in a meet against the Soviet Union held at Stanford University. She won the 100-meter dash and overcame a 40-yard deficit to win the women's 400-meter relay. When Rudolph recalled the race she said: "That was it. I knew it. The crowd in the stadium was on its feet, giving me a standing ovation, and I knew what time it was. Time to retire, with a sweet taste."

After retiring from competition, Rudolph returned to college and graduated from Tennessee State University in 1963 with a degree in education. She first took a job teaching second grade and coaching basketball. She coached track for a brief time at DePauw University in Greencastle, Indiana. Over the next several years she worked in a variety of positions as a goodwill ambassador to French West Africa, a radio show co-host, an administrative assistant at the University of California at Los Angeles, and an executive for a hospital in Nashville. In 1982 Rudolph established the Wilma Rudolph Foundation, a nonprofit organization dedicated to educating and inspiring underprivileged children. In so doing she said, "If I have anything to leave, the foundation is my legacy."

In 1961 Rudolph had married William Ward, but the marriage dissolved the next year. In 1963 she married Robert Eldridge, who was the father of her first child. They would have one more daughter and two sons before they divorced in 1976.

In July 1994, while giving a speech, Rudolph fainted. Diagnosed with brain cancer, she died at her home in Brentwood, Tennessee. Overcoming physical challenges and racial barriers, Rudolph became a world-class athlete whose legacy inspired successive generations. In an earlier interview she remarked, "I just want to be remembered as a hard-working lady with certain beliefs."

• Rudolph wrote an autobiography, *Wilma* (1977). Articles about her include William C. Rhoden, "The End of a Winding Road," *New York Times*, 19 Nov. 1994; Tenley-Ann Jackson, "Olympic Mind Power," *Essence*, July 1984; and Margaret Bernstein, "That Championship Season," *Essence*, July 1984. Also see "Wilma Rudolph" in Michael Davis, *Black American Women in Olympic Track and Field* (1992). An obituary is in the *New York Times*, 13 Nov. 1994.

GAYNOL LANGS

RUEF, Abraham (2 Sept. 1864–29 Feb. 1936), politician, was born in San Francisco, the son of Meyer Ruef, a successful merchant and real estate developer, and Adele Heruch. Both parents were French-born and Jewish. In 1883, at age eighteen, Ruef graduated with high honors from the University of California; three years later he graduated from Hastings College of Law (San Francisco).

Ruef began to practice law and quickly emerged as the leading Republican in the Latin Quarter, a working-class neighborhood of French-, Italian-, and Spanish-speaking residents. In 1901 he formed a broadly based Republican Primary League in an unsuccessful effort to supplant city Republican leaders. In the same year San Francisco witnessed a major strike, as waterfront unions shut down the port in support of a strike by teamsters. Police protected strikebreakers, causing some unionists to create the Union Labor Party (ULP) to win control of city hall.

Ruef's law practice and his Republican Primary League both included unionists; he persuaded one of them, Eugene Schmitz, president of the Musicians' Union, to seek the ULP mayoral nomination. Despite opposition from some union leaders, Schmitz won both nomination and election. Ruef became known as the real power in the Schmitz administration. He was named attorney for the mayor's office and was soon accepting large retainers from companies dealing with the city. Schmitz won reelection in 1903; in both 1901 and 1903, however, the ULP won only a handful of other offices. An aggressive open-shop drive united labor behind the ULP in 1905, resulting in a third term for Schmitz and a sweep of all other major offices.

Fremont Older, editor of the *Bulletin*, began early to accuse Ruef and Schmitz of corruption but offered little evidence. Some dismissed his charges as antilabor or anti-Semitic. After 1905 Older stepped up his efforts and gained financial support from James D. Phelan and Rudolph Spreckels, prominent businessmen. The newly elected ULP city supervisors proved so receptive to bribes that Ruef, perhaps to insulate the ULP from scandal, began to act as middleman.

After the 1906 earthquake, Francis J. Heney and William J. Burns, federal officials known for finding and prosecuting corruption, joined Older's efforts. For the "graft prosecution," indictment of the bribers was always the highest priority; they offered immunity to ULP politicians in return for testimony against Ruef and offered immunity to Ruef for testimony against corporate officials. Ruef refused and accused the prosecution of suborning perjury. Indicted four times between November 1906 and May 1907 on some eighty-five charges, and convicted in 1908, Ruef appealed unsuccessfully and in 1911 entered San Quentin penitentiary to begin a fourteen-year sentence. The prosecution produced many indictments and several convictions, but only Ruef served time in prison.

Older, however, became convinced that the prosecution had mistreated Ruef; his campaign to secure Ruef's release included publishing Ruef's memoirs. Ruef was paroled in 1915 and pardoned in 1920. Disbarred, he turned to real estate and prospered for a time, but his business failed in the 1930s, and Ruef died bankrupt, in San Francisco. He never married.

The graft prosecution painted Ruef as a corrupt boss and the ULP as his political machine, a judgment little changed by early historians. Recent historians have argued convincingly that Ruef was more a twentieth-century influence peddler than a nineteenth-century party boss and have shown that the ULP was a genuine labor party rather than Ruef's personal political machine.

• Ruef's memoirs, entitled *The Road I Traveled*, appeared in the San Francisco *Bulletin*, 21 May–5 Sept. 1912; records of the graft prosecution are at the Bancroft Library, University of California, Berkeley. The classic account of the ULP and the graft prosecution is Walton Bean, *Boss Ruef's San Francisco* (1952); a similar treatment appears in George Mowry, *The California Progressives* (1951). Revisionist accounts include James P. Walsh, "Abe Ruef Was No Boss," *California Historical Quarterly* 51 (1972): 3–16; Steven P. Erie, "The Development of Class and Ethnic Politics in San Francisco, 1870–1910" (Ph.D. diss., UCLA, 1975); Jules Tygiel, "'Where Unionism Holds Undisputed Sway': A Reappraisal of San Francisco's Union Labor Party," *California History* 62 (1983): 196–215; William Issel and Robert W. Cherny, *San Francisco, 1865–1932* (1986); Michael Kazin, *Barons of Labor* (1987). For obituaries, see the *New York Times* and *San Francisco Chronicle*, 1 Mar. 1936.

ROBERT W. CHERNY

RUFFIN, Edmund (5 Jan. 1794–17 June 1865), agricultural reformer and southern nationalist, was born in Prince George County, Virginia, the son of James River planter George Ruffin and Jane Lucas. As a consequence of the early demise of his parents and the absence of siblings near his own age, Ruffin grew up in an atmosphere of emotional isolation. He became a voracious reader, digesting, for example, all of Shakespeare's plays before reaching the age of eleven. He also developed a fierce sense of independence and a determination to control his own destiny. During these formative years Ruffin was profoundly influenced by Thomas Cocke, who became his legal guardian following the death of his father in 1810 and remained his closest friend for the next thirty years. Ruffin enrolled in the College of William and Mary shortly before his father's death but withdrew after little more than a year of study. During his brief residence in Williamsburg, he formed an amorous attachment to a local belle, Susan Hutchings Travis, whom he married in 1813. After six months' service as a militia private during the War of 1812, Ruffin returned home to claim his inheritance, a 1,600-acre farm at Coggin's Point on the south side of the James River, bequeathed to him by his grandfather. There, in company with the bride who would bear him eleven children within a span of eighteen years, Ruffin embarked upon a career as a gentleman-farmer.

When the depleted lands of his Coggin's Point property—later named "Beechwood"—proved unresponsive to traditional ameliorative practices, such as those suggested by fellow Virginian John Taylor of Caroline (1753–1824), Ruffin discovered a possible explanation in Sir Humphry Davy's treatise on agricultural chemistry. Suspecting that the soils of Tidewater Virginia suffered from excessive acidity, which negated the fertilizing effect of noncalcareous manures, Ruffin, in 1818, inaugurated an elaborate series of experiments with marl, a shell-like deposit rich in calcium carbonate that neutralized soil acidity and thus facilitated the rejuvenation of sterile land. When these experiments proved immediately successful, he set out to publicize his findings, first in a paper to his county agricultural society; then, in 1821, in a piece prepared for John S. Skinner's pioneering journal, the *American Farmer;* and finally in a 242-page book entitled *An Essay on Calcareous Manures* (1832). The thesis propounded in that celebrated work, that soil fertility was a dynamic condition subject to change as a result of organic action, earned for Ruffin a reputation as the father of soil chemistry in the United States.

Never really enamored of the practical side of farming, Ruffin gradually abandoned the active management of his property and turned to journalism as a means of alleviating the agricultural depression then afflicting his native state. From 1833 to 1842 he was occupied primarily with the publication of his distinguished journal, the *Farmers' Register,* first at "Shellbanks," a new homesite on his Coggin's Point estate, and later at Petersburg, to which city he moved in 1835. Conceived as a vehicle through which agriculturists could exchange information on innovative farming practices, this periodical maintained an unrivaled standard of excellence until the editor's tirades against the banking establishment led to its premature demise in December 1842. After conducting an agricultural survey of South Carolina in 1843 at the request of Governor James H. Hammond, Ruffin again returned to active farming with the acquisition of a new tract—appropriately named "Marlbourne"—situated on the banks of the Pamunkey River, about fifteen miles northeast of Richmond. Here, during the next decade, he proved once again that his progressive theories could yield efficacious results. Although he was increasingly occupied with politics during the 1850s, Ruffin continued to analyze agricultural resources during his extensive southern travels and to publish articles based on his observations. He also helped revive the long-dormant Virginia State Agriculture Society in 1852 and was four times elected president of that body. Although historians dispute the degree to which Ruffin was successful in persuading fellow agriculturists to implement his theories, there is little doubt that he influenced many to change their thinking about agrarian problems.

In the mid-1850s Ruffin turned his proselytizing zeal from agriculture to politics. Like others of his class, he had long displayed an interest in politics and statecraft. But only once did he hold political office. Elected in 1823 to a four-year term in the state senate, he soon became disenchanted and resigned his seat before the end of his term. Strongly opinionated, frequently irascible, contemptuous of democracy, and deficient in oratorical skills, Ruffin recognized that he could influence public policies most effectively from a position behind the scenes—through personal contacts and the power of his pen. It was the abolitionist onslaught against slavery, however, that engendered in Ruffin an all-consuming interest in political affairs and ultimately converted him into the quintessential southern nationalist. Sufficiently moderate in 1831 to have interceded vigorously on behalf of a black wrongfully accused of complicity in the Nat Turner revolt, Ruffin had moved fifteen years later to an implacable proslavery position. A substantial slaveholder himself—family holdings numbered more than 200 in 1860—he vociferously defended the institution on historical, racial, and economic grounds. Convinced that slavery was the indispensable cornerstone of southern society and that it could not be preserved within the existing union, he became an outspoken advocate of southern independence.

Although Ruffin's secessionist stance had crystallized at least as early as 1850, it was not until the last four years of the antebellum period, following his retirement from farming and the division of his property among his surviving children, that his crusade for disunion became most intense. Wherever he traveled—at Virginia summer resorts; at the Southern Commercial Convention in Montgomery, Alabama; in hotel lobbies from Washington, D.C., to Charleston, South Carolina; on steamboats and in railroad cars—Ruffin preached the message that southern rights could be preserved only through secession and the creation of a separate nation. Even more significant were his voluminous writings. These included two lengthy pamphlets, "The Political Economy of Slavery" and "African Colonization Unveiled," both published in 1858; an article, "Consequences of Abolition Agitation," which was serialized in *De Bow's Review* (1857), and another in *The South* (1858), calling for the removal, through enslavement or forced exile, of the bulk of the free black population in Virginia; a 426-page political novel entitled *Anticipations of the Future* (1860), which was inspired by John Brown's (1800–1859) raid on Harpers Ferry; and dozens of newspaper pieces, many printed as editorials in the Charleston *Mercury*.

Despite these exertions, Ruffin had little influence in actually effecting secession. Certainly his voice was not heeded in Virginia. Moreover, his prolific writings attracted little notice from the general public, and his attempt in 1858, with the assistance of Alabama fire-eater William L. Yancey, to mobilize public opinion behind secession through a League of United Southerners proved ineffectual. Still, he remained active and highly visible, albeit most often as an observer. Following the abortive raid on Harpers Ferry, he enlisted in the corps of cadets of the Virginia Military Institute for one day so that he might witness the execution of John Brown. Shortly thereafter, he dispatched pikes, seized from the Brown conspirators, to the governors of each slave state, with the request that they be displayed as a "sample of the favors designed for us by our Northern Brethren."

As events moved toward a climax in the winter of 1860–1861, Ruffin was on hand to witness the act of secession in both South Carolina and Florida. Disgusted by the inaction of what he termed the "submissionist" Virginia Convention, he departed for Charleston on the eve of Lincoln's inauguration, vowing to remain an exile from his native state until it seceded and joined the Confederacy. There, on 12 April 1861, the aging Ruffin was accorded the honor of firing the first cannon shot against Fort Sumter from the Iron Battery on Morris Island. Although the question of who fired the first shot at Sumter remains controversial, Ruffin's first-shot distinction was recognized by many contemporary observers on both sides and did not, as some have argued, emanate from the Lost Cause mythology. Elevated to the status of a popular hero in the South, Ruffin returned to Virginia, where he rejoined his South Carolina unit, the Palmetto Guard, and again performed symbolic military service—this time in the Manassas campaign.

For a time, the fiery old Virginian continued to indulge his propensity to witness at firsthand the exciting events unfolding around him, but eventually physical infirmities and wartime tribulations began to take their toll. The family farms, Marlbourne and Beechwood, were overrun during General George B. McClellan's (1826–1885) Peninsular campaign, and the latter was systematically pillaged by Federal troops. Compelled by these circumstances to seek refuge elsewhere, the increasingly embittered Ruffin finally settled at "Redmoor," a modest farm in Amelia County, situated about thirty-five miles west of Richmond. Despite the deteriorating fortunes of the Confederacy, he remained steadfast in his devotion to the cause of southern independence until that dream was shattered by Robert E. Lee's surrender at nearby Appomattox on 9 April 1865.

After the fall of the Confederacy, Ruffin no longer had any reason to live. Deeply affected by the suicide twenty-five years before of Thomas Cocke, his former guardian and confidant, Ruffin had, for some time, contemplated a like course of action. Although precipitated by the outcome of the war, Ruffin's decision to take his own life was the product of many factors: debilitating physical ailments, the tragic deaths of thirteen members of his immediate family over a span of two decades, the decimation of his estate, and the fear that he might become both a political and pecuniary burden to the surviving members of his family. After two months of methodical preparation, he executed the act of self-destruction by shooting himself in the mouth with a silver-mounted musket shortly after noon on Saturday, 17 June 1865. Thus did Ruffin, long frustrated by his inability to exercise significant influence over the agricultural and political destinies of the South, finally, in his last moments on earth, assume command of his own destiny.

• Letters, papers, and account books relating to Ruffin are in the Virginia State Library, Richmond; the University of Virginia Library, Charlottesville; and the Southern Historical Collection of the University of North Carolina, Chapel Hill. His manuscript diary (1856–1865) is in the Library of Congress. The latter has been edited by William K. Scarborough and published in three volumes as *The Diary of Edmund Ruffin* (1972–1989). Other recently published Ruffin writings include *Incidents of My Life: Edmund Ruffin's Autobiographical Essays*, ed. David F. Allmendinger, Jr. (1990), and *Agriculture, Geology, and Society in Antebellum South Carolina: The Private Diary of Edmund Ruffin, 1843*, ed. William M. Mathew (1992). J. Carlyle Sitterson has edited the most scholarly edition of *An Essay on Calcareous Manures* (1961). Biographies are Avery O. Craven, *Edmund Ruffin, Southerner: A Study in Secession* (1932; repr. 1966), and Betty L. Mitchell, *Edmund Ruffin: A Biography* (1981). Allmendinger, *Ruffin: Family and Reform in the Old South* (1990), provides the fullest coverage of Ruffin's family and early life, and the most sophisticated analysis of his agricultural reform efforts is in Mathew, *Edmund Ruffin and the Crisis of Slavery in the Old South: The Failure of Agricultural Reform* (1988). On the controversy surrounding the date of Ruffin's suicide, see Allmendinger and Scarborough, "The Days Ruffin Died," *Virginia Magazine of History and Biography* 97 (1989): 75–96. See also Drew Gilpin Faust, *A Sacred Circle: The Dilemma of the Intellectual in the Old South, 1840–1860* (1977), and Eric H. Walther, *The Fire-Eaters* (1992).

WILLIAM K. SCARBOROUGH

RUFFIN, George Lewis (16 Dec. 1834–20 Nov. 1886), lawyer and municipal judge, was born in Richmond, Virginia, the son of George W. Ruffin and Nancy Lewis. His free black parents' strong desire for an education for their eight children and Virginia's restrictions on teaching African Americans led them to abandon their meager property in Virginia and move to Boston in 1853.

Ruffin attended Boston public schools, where he distinguished himself as a scholar. At Chapman Hall

School he began his long association with the Republican party that led to his lifetime public commitment to equal rights and racial uplift. In 1858 he married Josephine St. Pierre of Boston, a union that produced five children.

Ruffin's first protest occurred when he left Boston shortly after his marriage and moved with his wife to Liverpool, England, to escape American racism after the *Scott v. Sandford* decision (1857; also known as the *Dred Scott Case*), a ruling that Ruffin believed irreversibly eroded black status. The couple returned to Boston about six months later. Ruffin worked as a barber while keeping his books close by. He met and worked with some of the leading abolitionists of the day, including Frederick Douglass and William Lloyd Garrison. He later associated with the young editor T. Thomas Fortune and the historian, politician, and activist George Washington Williams. Physically unfit for military service during the Civil War because of his poor eyesight, he and Josephine worked with the Massachusetts Home Guard and further contributed to the war effort by mending and making clothes at Twelfth Baptist Church for the Sanitary Commission.

In the 1860s Ruffin emerged as a leading black activist on the national level. In 1863 he wrote a review for the *Anglo-African*, the leading African-American journal of the time, that pointed out several shortcomings in William Wells Brown's race history, *The Black Man, His Antecedents, His Achievements* (1863). He also attended his first National Negro Convention at Syracuse (1864), supported Abraham Lincoln's 1864 reelection, pushed for African-American suffrage, and was elected one of the secretaries at the 1865 National Negro Convention in Boston. After that convention Ruffin began reading law at the Boston firm of Jewel and Gaston.

Seeking a more formal legal education, Ruffin entered Harvard University Law School (which did not then require a bachelor's degree) in 1868. During his first month at Harvard white students proposed a resolution to exclude him from the student assembly—and all other rights—because of his color. After successfully debating the students and defeating the resolution, Ruffin completed the three-year program in one year and received his LL.B. in 1869, the first African American to earn a university law degree. After graduation, he was admitted to the bar of the Supreme Judicial Court of Massachusetts on 18 September 1869.

Ruffin then immediately joined Harvey Jewell's law firm. He specialized in criminal law and developed a prosperous practice that included both white and African-American clients. He was an active Republican, and his party loyalty and strong organizing skills, especially in Boston's Ninth Ward, led to his election to the Massachusetts State Legislature in 1869 and reelection in 1870. In the state house, Ruffin focused much of his attention on the violence directed toward African Americans in the South. His political star rose when, as a delegate to the 1871 state Republican convention at Worcester, he made a rousing nomination speech for former Union general Benjamin F. Butler

for governor. Ruffin continued his political activities through the 1870s, winning a seat on the Boston Common Council (1876 and 1877), the first African American elected to that body.

In addition to his legal work, Ruffin remained active in the local and national racial uplift movements. He frequently helped African-American lawyers, such as George Washington Williams, by vouching for their character when they applied for admission to the bar. At Frederick Douglass's request, he wrote the introduction to the 1881 revision of Douglass's *Life and Times of Frederick Douglass*. Several years later Ruffin came to Douglass's aid when the latter's marriage to a white woman caused a raging controversy throughout the movement. In "A Look Forward" (*A.M.E. Church Review*, July 1885), Ruffin not only supported Douglass but also declared that intermarriage was the inevitable solution to the race problem.

Ruffin's career reached its pinnacle in 1883 when Governor Benjamin F. Butler nominated him to a municipal court judgeship for Charlestown. Although he was not Butler's first choice—newly converted Democrat Edward Walker, son of abolitionist David Walker, held that honor—Ruffin was the leading Republican prospect for the job. The Republican Executive Council of the state legislature unanimously confirmed him on 7 November 1883, and Butler himself administered the oath of office. Ruffin thus became the first African American to hold a judicial appointment higher than magistrate in the North. Ruffin served honorably on the bench until his death. In 1883 he was also appointed consul resident in Boston for the Dominican Republic.

In spite of his politics and party loyalty, Ruffin never avoided controversy or altered his organizing efforts in his community. While remaining a Republican, he participated in the first meeting of the Massachusetts Colored League, an organization urging African Americans to vote as independents, reflecting growing black disaffection with the Republicans. He also served as first president of the Wendell Phillips Club of Boston, as president of the Banneker Literary Club of Boston, and for twelve years as superintendent and a key officer of the historic Twelfth Baptist Church of Boston.

Ruffin died in Boston of Bright's disease after a lengthy illness. Because of his generous contributions to charities and racial uplift causes, he died poor.

Ruffin's standing among both contemporaries and succeeding generations is evident in the honors they bestowed on him. By 1900 civic and professional clubs bearing his name sprang up in the nation as far west as Cincinnati, Ohio, in memory of his political, legal, and civic contributions. His epitaph read "He did his duty bravely, and not one trust betrayed."

• The George Lewis Ruffin Papers are at the Moorland-Spingarn Research Center, Howard University. His published writings appear in the *A.M.E. Church Review* (1885), the *Anglo-African* (1863), and the introduction to Frederick Douglass's 1881 revision of *The Life and Times of Frederick Doug-*

lass. Good secondary sources include biographical sketches in Philip Foner and George Walker, *Proceedings of the Black National and State Conventions, 1865–1900* (1986–); Charles S. Brown, "The Genesis of the Negro Lawyer in New England," *Negro History Bulletin* 22 (May 1959): 171–77; William T. Davis, *Bench and Bar of the Commonwealth of Massachusetts,* vol. 2 (1974); Walter J. Leonard, *Black Lawyers: Training and Results, Then and Now* (1977); Fitzhugh L. Styles, *Negroes and the Law* (1937); and James Horton and Lois Horton, *Black Bostonians* (1979). His education at Harvard and his judicial career are chronicled in J. Clay Smith, *Emancipation: The Making of the Black Lawyer, 1844–1944* (1993); William J. Simmons, *Men of Mark* (1887); Paul Finkelman, *Race, Law, and American History, 1700–1990: The African-American Experience,* vol. 10: *African-Americans and the Legal Profession in Historical Perspective* (1992); Emory L. West, "Harvard's Black Graduates," *Harvard Bulletin,* May 1972; and W. Sollors and T. Underwood, eds., *Variety of Black Experience at Harvard* (1986).

JOHNIE D. SMITH

RUFFIN, Josephine St. Pierre (31 Aug. 1842–13 Mar. 1924), editor and woman's club organizer, was born in Boston, Massachusetts, the daughter of Eliza Matilda Menhenick of Cornwall, England, and John St. Pierre, a clothing seller whose father was a French immigrant from Martinique. Though Josephine's complexion was very light, public schools in Boston were closed to people of color until 1855, so she received her early education at nearby Salem and Charlestown. Later she attended Boston's Bowdoin School and took two years of private tutoring in New York. In 1858 she married George Lewis Ruffin, who made his living as a barber but later became a prominent Boston legislator and judge. The marriage produced five children.

Because of the slavery issue in the United States, Ruffin and her family moved briefly to Liverpool, England, in 1858 but soon returned to Boston to fight for civil rights when the Civil War began. Even at her young age, Ruffin was beginning to demonstrate her organizational and leadership skills. Despite the demands of raising a family, she was soon busy recruiting soldiers for the war effort and working for the U.S. Sanitary Commission. She also worked with other charitable groups, such as the Boston Kansas Relief Association, which helped freed slaves who migrated west, and the Massachusetts School Suffrage Association.

In 1890 Ruffin used what little was left of her husband's resources (he died in 1886 nearly destitute because he gave much of his money to charitable and civil rights work) to embark on a new adventure. With her family's help, she founded the *Woman's Era,* a monthly magazine devoted almost exclusively to issues affecting African-American women. The publication covered society news but also dealt with more serious social issues like abolition, suffrage, and living conditions in the cities. Though the articles were written by a staff, Ruffin acted as editor, layout person, and editorial writer—she even became her own advertising executive. Besides editing and publishing her own magazine, she supplemented her income in 1891 by acting as editor in chief of the *Boston Courant,* a black weekly newspaper. She gave up this work, though, in 1893 to devote more time to the *Era,* and she also joined the New England Women's Press Association in 1893. Though the *Woman's Era* gave Ruffin a decent living for several years, it suffered from insufficient advertising revenue, as did most of the African-American periodical press of the time. Also the *Woman's Era* catered to the elite African-American society of Boston, and its $1-per-year subscription price was more than most ordinary African-American women could afford. The last issue was dated January 1897.

Ruffin's work as an editor and her friendship with many influential people aroused in her an interest in the field for which she is best remembered. In 1894, influenced by Julia Ward Howe and others, she organized with her friend, Maria Baldwin, and her daughter, Florida Ruffin Ridley, the Woman's Era Club. Using the *Woman's Era* as its official publication, the club devoted itself to the education of young African-American women and to charitable causes. The Woman's Era Club became so successful under Ruffin's leadership that it grew in 1896 from a sixty-member Boston club into the National Association of Colored Women, with thousands of members. Ruffin tried to gain more support from the white women's clubs by joining the Massachusetts State Federation of Women's Clubs, and she also joined the all-white General Federation of Women's Clubs and was asked to serve on its executive committee. Not realizing that she was president of a black club, the federation had accepted her membership. When she arrived at the biennial convention in Milwaukee in 1900, however, the situation was quite different. What happened there was one of the defining moments of Josephine Ruffin's career and one of the most unfortunate incidents in the history of the women's club movement. Southern delegates were outraged that an "octoroon" wanted to become a member of the General Federation, and they insisted that the membership remain white. The executive board of the federation claimed that she had violated the rules by not revealing that the Woman's Era Club was a black club. The federation was fearful of losing southern members, and despite protests from Ruffin's supporters, it refused to recognize her organization or seat her as a delegate to a black club, although it was willing to seat her as a member of the two white clubs to which she already belonged, the New England Women's Press Association and the Massachusetts State Federation of Women's Clubs. Never one to compromise her principles, however, Ruffin refused its offer.

Ruffin remained president of the Woman's Era Club until 1903, but her activities in it gradually began to dwindle, although her involvement in the community remained strong. Among other organizations to which she gave her time were the Association for the Promotion of Child Training in the South and the American Mount Coffee School Association, which helped raise funds for a school in Liberia. She was also instrumental in establishing the Boston chapter of the National Association for the Advancement of Colored People, of which she remained a member for many years.

Advanced age did not stop Josephine Ruffin from giving her time and energy to worthy causes. Her daughter, Florida Ridley, recalled that Ruffin attended the "Women's Day" celebration in Boston when she was seventy-nine, and, at the age of eighty-two, she took a taxi on a stormy night to attend a meeting of the League of Women for Community Service. Less than a month later she died of nephritis at her home in Boston.

• The Ruffin family papers are at the Amistad Research Center, Tulane University. Incomplete files of the *Woman's Era* are in the Moorland-Spingarn Research Center at Howard University and at the Boston Public Library. Hallie Quinn Brown, *Homespun Heroines and Other Women of Distinction* (1926), contains a brief sketch on Ruffin, with comments by Florida Ruffin Ridley concerning her mother's activities in later years. For a discussion of the *Women's Era*, the best sources are Penelope Bullock, *The Afro-American Periodical Press, 1838–1909* (1981), and the article by Rodger Streitmatter, in *A Living of Words: American Women in Print Culture*, ed. Susan Albertine (1995), which also discusses the Woman's Era Club. See also Charles H. Wesley's study, *The History of the National Association of Colored Women's Clubs* (1984), which includes a detailed account of the history of the Woman's Era Club. For women's clubs in general, consult Mary I. Wood, *The History of the General Federation of Women's Clubs* (1912), which describes the Milwaukee convention and its aftermath. A brief summary of the Milwaukee incident is in Rayford W. Logan, *The Betrayal of the Negro from Rutherford B. Hayes to Woodrow Wilson* (1965).

ROGER A. SCHUPPERT

RUFFIN, Thomas (17 Nov. 1787–15 Jan. 1870), planter and judge, was born in King and Queen County, Virginia, the son of Sterling Ruffin, a planter, and Alice Roane, who was the first cousin of Spencer Roane, one of the leading figures of early Virginia jurisprudence. Thomas Ruffin was also a relative of the later southern firebrand, Edmund Ruffin, whose home he visited on occasion, despite their political differences.

Within a short time of Ruffin's birth his father moved the family to North Carolina, where Ruffin went to school before entering the College of New Jersey (now Princeton University), from which he graduated in 1805. After graduation he began the study of law in the offices of David Robertson, a Petersburg, Virginia, lawyer. One of his most prominent classmates in the law office was Winfield Scott, later ranking general of the Union army at the outbreak of the Civil War. Ruffin finished his legal studies in North Carolina under Judge A. D. Murphey and was admitted to the state bar in 1808.

Ruffin married Annie M. Kirkland in December 1809. She was barely sixteen years old; they had fourteen children. At the end of the Civil War four of the children were still living at home, as he wrote to President Andrew Johnson in his petition for a pardon. There were two unmarried daughters, one son who

was almost forty-eight and had been blind for thirty years, and one son Ruffin described as "decrepit having lost a limb near the hip." In addition he claimed a "large number of grand-children, who are orphans and infants and mostly dependent" on him.

Although Ruffin was a leading judge in the years before the war, he was also a very successful planter and agricultural reformer. From 1854 to 1860 Ruffin served as president of the state agricultural society, an association committed to promoting the interests of scientific agriculture and of the planting class. Ruffin owned more than one hundred slaves who labored on his two plantations, one in Rockingham and one in Alamance County, at the outbreak of the war. He was one of the wealthier slaveholding judges in the South. Ruffin also served for a short time in the late 1820s as the president of the State Bank of North Carolina in order to oversee its stabilization amid threats of forfeiture of its charter, and for many years he was a trustee of the University of North Carolina. A deeply religious man, Ruffin served as a delegate to the General Convention of the Episcopal Church on various occasions before the war.

Politically, Ruffin was not a particularly active figure in North Carolina. He served in 1816 in the state legislature, and in the presidential election of 1824 he was an elector on the William Crawford ticket. In his youth he was deeply committed to Jeffersonian Republicanism, but he displayed no heady desire to devote himself to politics—rather it was the law that absorbed his public career. The major exception came with the secession crisis when he joined many of the older southern Unionists at the Washington peace conference in 1861. With the failure of the "Old Gentlemen's Convention" Ruffin joined the secession movement and voted in favor of the withdrawal of North Carolina. Although he was not particularly active under the Confederacy, except as one of the commissioners of the Sinking Fund of his state, he did throw his emotions into the fray. In an 1862 letter to one of his sons, for instance, he referred to northerners as "demons" and urged his son to "harass them day and night, and make them wish themselves back in their infernal regions of abolition" and urged further that he "never . . . give up *the cause*—never, never; but resist 'the Devils' to the bitter end."

When the end of the Civil War came, however, Ruffin urged a son to avoid involvement with the Ku Klux Klan because it was a movement "against Law and the Civil Power of Government." Ruffin was a man whose whole life had been committed to the cause of law and the order and the stability that law provided. It was as a judge that he made his mark, and after the failure to establish independence on behalf of slavery, a system to which he was profoundly committed, he returned to his reverence for the law.

Ruffin served on the North Carolina Supreme Court from 1829 to 1852; he was chief justice from 1833 to 1852. Ruffin returned to the court in December 1858 and served until August 1859. He participated in nearly 1,500 cases on both the legal and the equitable side of the court's jurisdiction. With such a prolific output it is difficult to single out areas of the law of the greatest significance to Ruffin. Many of his most often cited and most important cases involved slavery but by no means all. Two cases, for example, have often been noted, *Hoke v. Henderson* (1833) and *Raleigh and Gaston R. R. Co. v. Davis* (1837). The first case maintained that the holder of an office possessed an "estate" in that office of which he could not be divested without the abolition of the office itself—a position rejected by many courts. In declaring the state law that divested the estate unconstitutional, Ruffin noted that "public liberty requires that private property should be protected even from the government itself." Ruffin relied here, as he did on numerous occasions, not on legal precedents but on what he called "general principles," even though those principles did not point in only one unavoidable direction.

Like Roger Brooke Taney in *Charles River Bridge v. Warren Bridge* (U.S. Supreme Court, 1837), Ruffin tried to balance the rights of private property and the claims of the public. The second case concerned public claims involving questions of "takings" jurisprudence and held that the legislature could condemn property, such as a railroad, for the purposes of an internal improvement, without providing for a jury trial to assess the money to be paid to the property owner. This flowed from the notion of a "right inherent in society" to take private property, and this notion he found in the "laws of nature and nations."

But it was in the area of slave law that Ruffin is most remembered and often cited. In these cases he also often relied on "general principles," or natural law rather than on precedent. Two frequently cited cases are *State v. Mann* (1829) and *Ponton v. Wilmington Railroad* (1858). *Ponton* concerned the liability for injuries suffered by a hired-out slave when the injury resulted from the conduct of a so-called "fellow servant."

State v. Mann involved the criminal liability of a hirer, who was seen as the temporary owner, for violence inflicted on the slave. Ruffin ruled him not liable on the ground that the "power of the master" must be "absolute" in order to render the "submission of the slave perfect"; nonetheless, in *State v. Hoover* (1839) he qualified the absolute power with the observation that the master "must not kill." Harriet Beecher Stowe praised *Mann* for its lack of "dissimulation" even while it upheld a brutish social system.

Ruffin, a slaveholding planter from one of the least industrialized states of the Old South, has little of legal significance to say to the world of modern corporate America. There is little of the law of corporate personality, agency, or labor relations in his judging that was not developed better by judges in states such as Massachusetts or New York. But Ruffin does provide one of the most brilliant illustrations of a world that has passed and with it the legal problems it generated—a republican, agrarian, slaveowning world controlled by small to middling farmers. He died in Hillsboro (now Hillsborough), North Carolina.

• A superb and indispensable collection of letters and other documents is J. G. DeRoulhac Hamilton, ed., *The Papers of Thomas Ruffin* (4 vols., 1918–1920). The papers ought to be supplemented with the voluminous judicial record left by Ruffin, which can be followed in the *North Carolina Reports* (which includes both law and equity decisions) from vol. 13 to vol. 57. Letters from and references to Ruffin are in the collection of other judges, especially North Carolina judges; an example is the reference to Ruffin's presence at the deathbed of Judge William Gaston in 1844 in the William Gaston Papers, Southern Historical Collection, University of North Carolina, Chapel Hill. Two articles on Ruffin are available: Patrick S. Brady, "Slavery, Race, and the Criminal Law in Antebellum North Carolina: A Reconsideration of the Thomas Ruffin Court," *North Carolina Central Law Journal* 10 (1978): 248–60; and Julius Yanuck, "Thomas Ruffin and North Carolina Slave Law," *Journal of Southern History* 21 (1955): 456–75. Ruffin's involvement in the 1861 peace effort can be followed in Robert Gray Gunderson, *Old Gentlemen's Convention: The Washington Peace Conference of 1861* (1961).

THOMAS D. MORRIS

RUFFING, Red (3 May 1904–17 Feb. 1986), baseball player, was born Charles Herbert Ruffing in Granville, Illinois, the son of John Ruffing, a German-born mine foreman, and Frances (maiden name unknown). "Red," as he was always known, began working as a miner at thirteen after only a grade-school education; he learned early the necessity of dedicated "hard work." He observed: "I wasn't too fond of school. My dad was the mine boss, and coal was in my blood. . . . I was tall . . . strong . . . eager to work."

After hours he played for his father's baseball team, mostly as an outfielder, and showed considerable hitting ability. However, when he was sixteen a mine accident in which his left foot was caught between colliding coal cars necessitated amputation of four toes and deprived him of running speed. He turned to pitching and soon was signed by Danville of the Three I League. He spent only two years in the minors and joined the Boston Red Sox in 1924. The Red Sox struggled, and Ruffing twice led his league in defeats, his worst season being a 10–25 won-lost record in 1928. Seemingly, Ruffing would never rise above mediocrity. Yet true to his work ethic, he jogged regularly every day. In one stretch he lost twelve successive games by just one run. At that point the Red Sox surprised him with a $500 raise because management liked "the way you keep hustling." After the club unsuccessfully tried to shift him to the outfield, Ruffing was traded to the New York Yankees in 1930 for journeyman outfielder Cedric Durst and $50,000; it was a move that saved his pitching career. Later, Ruffing pointed to two decisive "steps" in his life: (1) his emergence from the mines; and (2) his trade from Boston to New York. By then, at 6′1½″, he weighed 205 pounds.

With the Yankees Ruffing vaulted from mediocrity to stardom, aided by the greatest hitters in the game: Babe Ruth, Lou Gehrig, Joe DiMaggio, and catcher Bill Dickey, Ruffing's roommate for many years, with whom he developed a "perfect understanding." Dickey regarded Ruffing as the best pitcher he ever caught. Ruffing's fortunes reached their peak when he won twenty or twenty-one games each season from 1936 through 1939 and the Yankees won four consecutive world championships. His best year was 1938 when he had a 21–7 record with a 3.32 earned run average. Overall, Ruffing won seven of nine World Series decisions, with his most noteworthy game being against the St. Louis Cardinals in 1942 in which he retired 23 consecutive batters and had a no-hitter for 7⅓ innings. The *Sporting News* named him to its All-Star Major League teams from 1937 through 1939.

Ruffing also developed his youthful talent as a hitter, compiling a .269 career batting average, surpassing .300 in eight seasons, and a career total 36 home runs. His home run total ranked him third among all major league pitchers. A dependable pinch hitter, he made 58 pinch hits, ranking second among hurlers. He taunted young pitchers to work harder, especially on their hitting. "Don't you want to contribute something more than four outs to your club?" he charged them. When other pitchers complained of sore arms, he told them about the constant throbbing in his right shoulder and the persistent pain from his partially amputated foot.

Two years (1943–1945) in military service with the U.S. Army Air Force deprived him of the chance to win 300 games. The Yankees released him in 1946 after he suffered a broken kneecap. His last active season (1947) saw him with the Chicago White Sox. From 1951 through 1959 he scouted for the Cleveland Indians. He demanded running from young pitchers every day: "The most important thing for a pitcher is to get his legs in shape. . . . Get the legs strong and the arm will come around." Also, he advised them, even when not pitching, to be intensely observant from the bench: "Study good pitchers . . . pick up pointers. . . . Make each minute count." He stressed control: "Keep in shape and know where each pitch is going. It pays off." Recalling his early days of adversity with the Red Sox, he told them: "Don't get discouraged. Stay in there and give your best, no matter what happens." He served as pitching coach with the fledgling New York Mets in 1962, his last major league position.

Recognition of his dedication and achievements came in 1967 when he was voted into the National Baseball Hall of Fame. At that time he lived in retirement in a suburb of Cleveland, but he suffered a stroke in 1973 that confined him to a wheelchair. During his active career his habit of retiring at ten o'clock each night earned him the nickname "Granpa Ruffing," and he subsisted largely on a low-fat fish and vegetable diet. "The guy who stays in shape lasts the longest," he asserted, pointing to his 23-year baseball career. He compiled 273 victories with 225 defeats for a .548 winning percentage, ranking him twenty-seventh in career wins among all major league pitchers. Such pitching contemporaries as Carl Hubbell (253), Bob Feller (266), Lefty Gomez (189), Bucky Walters (198), and Paul Derringer (223), the best of that generation, had fewer career victories. Sportswriters Martin Appel and

Burt Goldblatt described Ruffing as "the complete professional . . . a proud, rugged competitor, who commanded respect on and off the field . . . something of a symbol of Yankee success." Although he struggled in his early major league career with Boston, his later years with New York, combined with his overall dedication to the sport, brought him to the Hall of Fame. He married Pauline Mulholland in 1934 and fathered one son. He died in Mayfield Heights, Ohio.

Ruffing expressed his gratitude to the game by saying: "It took me out of the coal mines." His devotion to baseball accomplished the rest.

• The Ruffing files are located at the Hall of Fame in Cooperstown, New York, and the *Sporting News* in St. Louis. No authoritative biography exists, but his career is outlined in Dave Anderson, "Ruffing Is Named to Baseball Hall of Fame in Special Run-off Election," *New York Times*, 17 Feb. 1967; "Rickey, Ruffing, and Waner Inducted into Hall of Fame," *New York Times*, 25 July 1967; Hal Lebovitz, "'Granpa' Gets New Lease on Life with Kids, Cleveland Coach Urges Hurlers to 'Work, Study,'" *Sporting News*, 7 Mar. 1951; and Russell Schneider, "I Will Let My Record Do My Speaking, Declares Ruffing," *Sporting News*, 21 Jan. 1967, and "Ruffing Gains Shrine in 'Last of Ninth,'" *Sporting News*, 4 Mar. 1967. See also Martin Appel and Burt Goldblatt, *Baseball's Best: The Hall of Fame Gallery* (1977); David L. Porter, ed., *Biographical Dictionary of American Sports: Baseball* (1987); Rick Wolff, ed., *The Baseball Encyclopedia*, 8th ed. (1990); Lowell Reidenbaugh, *Cooperstown: Where Baseball Legends Live Forever* (1983); and John Thorn and Pete Palmer, eds., *Total Baseball*, 3d ed. (1993). Obituaries are in the *New York Times*, 20 Feb. 1986, and the *Sporting News*, 3 Mar. 1986.

WILLIAM J. MILLER

RUFFNER, William Henry (11 Feb. 1824–24 Nov. 1908), educational reformer, clergyman, and geologist, was born in Lexington, Virginia, the son of Henry Ruffner, an educator and clergyman, and Sarah Lyle. Ruffner spent much of his childhood on the campus of Washington College in Lexington, where his father was president and where he earned a bachelor's degree (1842) and a master's degree (1845). The elder Ruffner, a Presbyterian minister and an outspoken opponent of slavery, stimulated his son's lifelong interest in religion and the education of African Americans.

Managing family-owned salt mines in Kanawha County (1842–1843) began young Ruffner's involvement with geology. He prepared for a career in the ministry at Union Theological Seminary (1845–1846) and Princeton Theological Seminary (1846–1847). After two years of traveling, preaching, and distributing Bibles in the valley of Virginia, he served as chaplain of the University of Virginia (1849–1851), where he studied moral philosophy with William Holmes McGuffey, author of the widely used school readers. In 1852 Ruffner was ordained a Presbyterian minister and appointed pastor of the Seventh Presbyterian Church of Philadelphia, where he served on the board of directors of the African Colonization Society.

Chronic throat problems cut his active ministry short in 1853, and Ruffner returned to Virginia for a quiet life of scientific farming, geological surveying,

and occasional preaching. He resided first in Rockingham County and then near Lexington with Harriet
Ann Gray, whom he had married in 1850, and their
four children. Cultivating a circle of academic friends
at Washington College, Virginia Military Institute,
and the University of Virginia, Ruffner built a reputation as a consummate moderate. He was opposed to
forced abolition but in favor of schooling and gradual
emancipation for African Americans; he was opposed
to secession but, with the outbreak of the Civil War in
1861, strongly supportive of his region.

During Reconstruction, Ruffner's conciliatory
views enabled him to play a key role in the return to
power of conservative whites. As a trustee of Washington College (1865–1876), Ruffner helped recruit Robert E. Lee as its president. Lee soon joined other
friends of Ruffner's in the Educational Association of
Virginia, a group of college and university educators
committed to building a viable state school system.
Members of the association lobbied successfully to
keep an integrated school clause out of the state constitution that was adopted in 1869. The following year
they persuaded the legislature to elect Ruffner state superintendent of schools. To Virginia's higher education elite, Ruffner seemed to hold the perfect credentials for steering a course between reactionary whites
who viewed public education as a social threat and African Americans and radical whites who wanted racially mixed schools.

What Ruffner lacked, as he readily admitted, were
teaching experience and knowledge of the "details of
public school systems." Moreover, he had concluded
in the early days of Reconstruction that a state school
system would be impractical for Virginia. When Congress made the establishment of such a system a condition for readmission to the Union, however, Ruffner
and other influential whites resolved to design the system themselves rather than leave the planning to others. Given thirty days by the legislature to draw up a
proposal, Ruffner turned to the work of his father,
who had devised a statewide school plan during the
1840s. He also consulted his friends and associates, including Lee, McGuffey, and Barnas Sears, general
agent for the Peabody Education Fund in the South.

The plan Ruffner submitted to the legislature in
1870 was a variation of the common school model
adopted in the North and West before the war. He
tried to head off criticism by stipulating separate
schools for whites and blacks and by earmarking local
school taxes for the district where they were levied.
Yet the plan involved one of the highest degrees of
centralized control in the nation, for it gave the state
superintendent and state board of education a wide
range of responsibilities—from selecting textbooks to
appointing county superintendents and local trustees.
The Virginia legislature adopted Ruffner's plan, and
Sears promoted it in other southern states as an example of what conservative whites could accomplish if
they regained control over public education.

During his tenure as state superintendent (1870–
1882), Ruffner found himself constantly defending the
system he was building. In newspaper columns, the
Education Journal of Virginia, and his *Annual Reports*
to the legislature, he took on a variety of critics. To
those who objected to the cost of public education in a
state devastated by war, Ruffner portrayed schooling
as an investment—the best way to help Virginia rebuild. To those who predicted public education would
be "secularized" education, Ruffner replied that the
schools would teach nonsectarian Christian principles.
To those who resurrected the "pauper school" image
that had stigmatized tax-supported education before
the war, Ruffner preached a doctrine of equality before the Lord as well as the law. Critics who opposed
the system because it offered schooling to African
Americans heard Ruffner counter that formal education would make blacks "more intelligent, more moral, more industrious" and less inclined toward "that
contemptible ambition to associate with white people." Ruffner viewed schooling for African Americans
as a means of social control; he advocated "education
of the Hampton [Institute] type" for black students in
Virginia's public schools.

The system Ruffner built weathered the political
storms of the 1870s. Although he and the state board
of education had to relinquish most of their control
over textbooks and local appointments, Virginia's
school system became one of the more successful in
the South as measured by enrollment and expenditures. Ruffner himself, however, lost his base of support in the legislature during a dispute over state revenue. He resigned in 1882.

After returning for a short time to farming and geological surveying, Ruffner was appointed the first
president of the State Female Normal School at Farmville (1884–1887). Health problems once again forced
his retirement, and he devoted his remaining years to
geological work, religious studies, and the completion
of his father's "Early History of Washington College"
(*Washington and Lee Historical Papers*, no. 1 [1890]).
He died in Asheville, North Carolina, where he had
relocated to increase his involvement with Presbyterian church conferences.

William Henry Ruffner's role in Virginia education
was part of the return to power of the "redeemers"—
the white aristocracy that dominated the antebellum
South. Ruffner's belief that African Americans should
go to school, a progressive view before the war, ironically helped justify an education system designed to
keep blacks in their place after the war. Working to
reassure whites about public education, he won support for the state system but set the stage for *Plessy v.
Ferguson* (1896) and the spread of de jure segregation
into all walks of life.

• Ruffner's papers are in the Historical Foundation Archives, Montreat, N.C. Although old and relatively uncritical, accounts of Ruffner and his work include C. Chilton
Pearson, "William Henry Ruffner: Reconstruction Statesman of Virginia," in two parts, *South Atlantic Quarterly* 20
(Jan. 1921): 25–32 and (Apr. 1921): 137–51; Cornelius J.

Heatwole, *A History of Education in Virginia* (1916); and Charles W. Dabney, *Universal Education in the South* (1936). An obituary is in the *Asheville* (N.C.) *Gazette*, 25 Nov. 1908.

JOSEPH W. NEWMAN

RUGER, Thomas Howard (2 Apr. 1833–3 June 1907), soldier, was born in Lima, New York, the son of Thomas Jefferson Ruger, an Episcopal minister, and Maria Hutchins. The family moved to Janesville, Wisconsin, when Ruger was eleven. He was appointed to the U.S. Military Academy in 1850 and graduated in 1854 ranked number three in his class. He was commissioned a brevet second lieutenant and assigned to the Corps of Engineers, with whom he was posted to duty on the approaches to New Orleans, Louisiana. Ruger, however, preferred a civilian life, and he resigned his commission on 1 April 1855. He returned to Janesville, where he studied law and was admitted to the bar in 1856. In 1857 he married Helen Lydia Moore; they had two children.

When the Civil War broke out, Ruger was named engineer in chief of the volunteer forces in Wisconsin. He desired active service, however, and was commissioned lieutenant colonel of the Third Wisconsin. Ruger shouldered the responsibility of training the regiment. According to the regimental historian, "Few regiments in the service had more thorough drill in the system of tactics and manual of arms." Within two months Ruger was promoted to colonel of the regiment. During the fall of 1861 and spring of 1862 he participated in operations in Maryland and the Shenandoah Valley, where he saw action at the battle of Winchester. One of his officers wrote afterward, "All were anxious to know how he would conduct his regiment in its trying situation, and all were astonished at his determined bravery and coolness." Ruger's regiment was subsequently attached to Nathanial Banks's army corps of John Pope's Army of Virginia. It participated in the Union defeat at the battle of Cedar Mountain and suffered heavy losses. Following the defeat at Second Manassas, Ruger participated in the Maryland campaign as part of the Twelfth Army Corps. At Antietam, on 17 September 1862, his regiment was heavily engaged and suffered two hundred casualties, including Ruger, who was slightly wounded. Ruger's performance at Antietam earned him promotion to brigadier general of volunteers on 29 November 1862 and assignment to command of an infantry brigade in the Twelfth Corps. At Chancellorsville Ruger performed ably in some of the bloodiest fighting of that battle. During the battle of Gettysburg, Ruger was temporarily in command of the First Division, Twelfth Corps. His command was posted on Culp's Hill and saw sharp fighting on the second and third day of battle. A month after the battle, Ruger's regular division commander, General Alpheus S. Williams, wrote to his daughter: "General Ruger . . . is one of my especial favorites—commander of the third brigade. He is as modest as a girl but of the most thorough and sterling character." On 15 August 1863 Ruger was ordered with ten regiments to New York City to help suppress the draft riots.

In October 1863 the Eleventh and Twelfth corps were detached and sent to the western theater and consolidated to form the Twentieth Corps. Ruger retained command of his old brigade. He was assigned to duty guarding the Nashville and Chattanooga Railroad at Tullahoma, Tennessee, until April 1864 then joined William T. Sherman's army in its campaign to take Atlanta. Ruger saw action in the battles of Resaca, New Hope Church, Kulp House, and Peach Tree Creek and in numerous skirmishes and minor affairs in between these general actions. On 15 November 1864 he was promoted to command of the Second Division in the Twenty-third Corps of General George H. Thomas's army. Ruger participated in the Union victory at Franklin on 30 November 1864, and his service was such that he was rewarded with a promotion to brevet major general of volunteers. Following this battle Ruger organized the First Division, Twenty-third Corps, which in February 1865 he accompanied to North Carolina, where it participated in the final phase of Sherman's campaign that led to Joseph E. Johnston's surrender.

Following the end of the war, Ruger was assigned to command of the District of North Carolina, where he remained until September 1866. In the reorganization of the regular army, Ruger was appointed colonel of the Thirty-third Infantry. He held various posts in the Reconstruction South, including provisional governor of Georgia and command of the Department of the South. Applying the law firmly and fairly, his principal accomplishment during Reconstruction was maintaining order while not making the presence of U.S. troops oppressive or seeming to support the policies of the radicals, a delicate diplomatic task. He was selected as superintendent of the U.S. Military Academy in 1871 and served in that position until 1876, when he resumed his duties as commander of the Department of the South. During the controversial governor's election of 1876 in South Carolina, Ruger executed his duties so tactfully and skillfully that he earned praise from all parties involved.

In 1879 Ruger was posted to the frontier and placed in command of Fort Assiniboine, Montana. Following six years of service in Montana, Ruger was ordered to command the U.S. Army Infantry and Cavalry School at Fort Leavenworth, Kansas. On 19 March 1886 he was promoted to brigadier general in the regular army and subsequently assigned to command the Department of Dakota, where he checked a disturbance on the Crow Indian Reservation in Montana in the fall of 1887. In 1891 Ruger was placed in command of the Division of the Pacific. He was retired in 1897 and spent two years touring Europe with his family. He made his home in Stamford, Connecticut, and lived a quiet life until his death there.

The historian of the Third Wisconsin left a description of Ruger that succinctly captured the man and the soldier: "He was constantly on duty. Careful, regular in habits, temperate, he was always in excellent health, and endured whatever hardships the service exacted without apparent fatigue or any sign of irritability or impatience. . . . He never did anything for show or to attract attention or make mere newspaper reputation. To do every assigned duty, do it well, obey orders, to require like fidelity of subordinates, these were his cardinal rules."

• Ruger's battle reports and some official correspondence can be found in U.S. Department of War, *The War of the Rebellion: A Compilation of the Official Records of the Union and Confederate Armies* (128 vols., 1880–1901). For a good description of Ruger, see Edwin E. Bryant, *History of the Third Regiment of Wisconsin Veteran Volunteer Infantry 1861–1865* (1891). Additional information about Ruger's military service can be found in G. W. Cullum, *Biographical Register of United States Military Academy*, vol. 2 (1891), and William H. Powell, *Officers of the Army and the Navy Who Served in the Civil War* (1892).

D. SCOTT HARTWIG

RUGG, Arthur Prentice (20 Aug. 1862–12 June 1938), lawyer and judge, was born in Sterling, a small town in Worcester County, Massachusetts, the son of Prentice Mason Rugg and Cynthia Ross, farmers. He attended Amherst College (A.B., 1883) and Boston University Law School (LL.B. 1886), and was admitted to the bar in Massachusetts in 1886. Returning to Sterling, Rugg worked hard in the general practice of law for the next twenty years. While at John R. Thayer's firm, shortly after named Thayer and Rugg, he also served as moderator of the local town meeting; later he was Worcester city solicitor, a member of the Common Council, and an assistant district attorney. He was named associate justice of the Massachusetts Supreme Judicial Court in 1906 and chief justice in 1911, a position he held until his death. He married Florence May Belcher in 1889; they had four children.

Rugg's words at an address delivered at Amherst College's centennial in 1921 are an epitome of his own career. Lawyers, he said, must have a "character, strong and above reproach, the imperious incentive to unremitting industry which springs from the pinch of necessity, and intellectual ability of no mean order." He began, as a friend once observed, by walking "five miles every morning to take the 6:00 train to Worcester"; he ended by working as chief justice to within one week of his death, having spoken for the court in almost 3,000 carefully drafted opinions. Toil, thrift, earnestness, and religious devotion were the traits that marked out Rugg for his contemporaries.

Collegiality was to Rugg a virtue, but only as part of a larger aim: the clear and plain declaration of what the law is. His successor as chief justice emphasized that among all Rugg's opinions, only four were written in dissent. For Rugg, during his lifetime notable advances were made in plain pleading, married women's property acts, employers' liability acts, workmen's compensation, and the growing and proper use of police powers (the ability of state and local governments to regulate noise, pollution, and real estate uses). Through his opinions, Chief Justice Rugg played a

shaping role in these and many more areas, interpreting and upholding novel legislation concerning workers, banks, zoning, and administrative law. His opinions on common law were similarly influential, some beyond Massachusetts.

Rugg's care in composition and his hard-won and commanding knowledge of the law cannot be conveyed through brief examples. Among his many opinions that repay reading is *Old Dominion Copper Mining and Smelting Co. v. Bigelow* (1909), which confirms a stock promoter's liability for a secret profit to the corporation he assisted to organize (an opinion written in the face of a Supreme Court decision holding the contrary), with its exacting treatment of the facts and compelling analysis of the law in the several states, of federal law and of English precedent, and finally of the public policy ground for the holding. In *Smith v. New England Aircraft Co.* (1930), Rugg examined in fascinating detail an infant industry, whether an airport's monoplanes and biplanes were a legal nuisance to a country neighbor on his luxurious estate, and if legislative regulations on flight were valid. Finally, in *Baker v. Libbie* (1912), Rugg offered a concise review of authors' rights to their letters, beginning with Alexander Pope and concluding with Mary Baker Eddy. The legal puzzle was whether Eddy's estate could enjoin publication and sale of her letters; Rugg answered yes on publication and no on sale, and his legal reasoning remains vivid.

Rugg was a dedicated Unitarian and a member of various Worcester clubs. Although his friends remarked on Rugg's "extreme reticence," he was also affable and friendly, particularly to young advocates before his court. While the public addresses he gave could sometimes be tedious, falling into a compendium of received ideas, he could also be moving, as in his spare recounting of President Calvin Coolidge's life in a memorial delivered to both houses of Congress. Coolidge was a close friend of Rugg's; they shared qualities of character as well as mutual respect, in Rugg's words, for "the compelling power of the State." Rugg died in Sterling.

• Rugg's opinions as justice appear in volumes 193 through 300 of the *Massachusetts Reports*. His occasional writings, including publications in learned journals, are collected mostly in the Boston Athenaeum. "A Famous Colonial Litigation: The Case between Richard Sherman and Capt. Robert Keayne, 1642," *American Antiquarian Society Proceedings*, 1921, pp. 217–50, Rugg's analysis of a "tort for the conversion of an ordinary white sow," is characteristic, and without a trace of humor. *Arthur Prentice Rugg . . . A Memorial* (1939) contains Rugg's addresses, including a tercentenary history of the Commonwealth's legislature, as well as remarks by friends and colleagues.

THOMAS A. REED

RUGG, Harold Ordway (17 Jan. 1886–17 May 1960), educator, was born in Fitchburg, Massachusetts, the son of Edward F. Rugg, a carpenter, and Merion Abbie Davidson. Rugg entered Dartmouth College in

1904 and received a B.S. in civil engineering (1908) and a C.E. from the Thayer School of Civil Engineering (1909).

Rugg worked briefly as a civil engineer in Illinois in the summer of 1909. He then taught engineering at James Milliken University in Decatur, where he met his first wife, Bertha Miller, whom he married in 1912; the couple had two adopted children. After two years at Milliken, Rugg left to enroll at the University of Illinois in a doctoral program in education. He received his Ph.D. in education in February 1915, having already been hired in January 1915 as an instructor at the University of Chicago, where he stayed until 1920, and where he was promoted to assistant and then associate professor. During his years at Chicago, Rugg wrote widely on educational psychology, educational administration, statistics for teachers, and curriculum, the area for which he would be best known. He coauthored a study of school history texts in 1914 and two books on the school mathematics program in 1917 and 1919.

During World War I Rugg also worked briefly in Washington, D.C., as a member of the Committee on Classification of Personnel of the U.S. Army. He came into contact with a diverse group of intellectuals, and his interactions with them prompted his idea of teaching the social sciences in an integrated manner, organizing the subjects around a common theme. In 1920 Rugg accepted an offer to serve as educational psychologist at the Lincoln School, an experimental school affiliated with Teachers College in New York City. During Rugg's first years at the Lincoln School, he voraciously read contemporary social science research and theory and formed a team to aid him in writing the integrated social studies materials he had first envisioned in Chicago. In 1921–1922 Rugg began writing materials and distributing them himself to schools throughout the country. Using the contacts he had established while teaching the Teachers College's foundations of education course, Rugg was soon sending published materials, called *The Social Science Pamphlets*, to schools as fast as he could write them.

Rugg's growing prominence in education is evidenced by his appointment as editor of the 1923 National Society for the Study of Education (NSSE) yearbook, the topic of which was social studies in the elementary and secondary school. Rugg demonstrated boundless energy, but some colleagues were concerned by his ever-changing interests. John Hockett, a former student and colleague, noted in 1974, "Rugg's enthusiasms were strong, but not always permanent."

From 1922 to 1929 Rugg coauthored three books, authored two works, edited and was the largest contributor to two NSSE yearbooks, and wrote at least fifteen other major pieces. His main thrust, however, was the writing and rewriting of *The Social Science Pamphlets*. The pamphlets were purchased and published by Ginn in a six-volume edition for use in grades 7–9 that began in 1929 and was published until 1945. At its peak, it is estimated that the series was used by over 5 million youngsters. Rugg's was the first

social studies textbook series ever developed for school use; indeed, it was the first series of any curricular discipline developed for school use. The books brought Rugg fame and enmity, the latter from business groups and so-called patriotic organizations, like the American Legion and the Daughters of the American Revolution.

In 1939 the series was attacked by writers from the American Legion, the New York State Economic Council, the National Association of Manufacturers, and the Advertising Federation of America for being un-American, communistic, socialistic, and unfair in its portrayal of advertising and American business. Rugg questioned whether there was true equality of justice, housing, employment, and opportunity for all American citizens, which incited right-wing zealots and so-called patriots. Rugg and his writings were accused of being subversive, and school districts around the country were pressured to ban Rugg's books; one even burned them (Bradner, Ohio).

Despite written and personal appeals from such educators and social scientists as William Ogburn, Arthur Schlesinger, Sr., Robert Lynd, Carleton Washburne, and Franz Boas, Rugg's books were discontinued in district after district during the period from 1940 to 1943. Sales dropped to a low of $21,000 from a high of $289,000, and Ginn ceased publication in 1945. Rugg went from being "the most influential and prolific textbook writer in the history of American education to a virtual outcast from American elementary classrooms" (Blanshard, p. 92).

Rugg was divorced from his first wife in 1930, and that same year he married Louise Krueger; they had one child. Krueger was the coauthor of his elementary social studies series, which appeared in 1939 but never sold well because of the controversy surrounding the junior high series. Rugg and Krueger were divorced in 1946. In 1947 he married Elizabeth May Howe Page; they had no children.

Though the textbook controversy was personally and financially draining, Rugg remained active in various aspects of education. His book *Now Is the Moment* (1943) is both a formula for a postwar society and a last retort to his textbook critics. The book also develops some of the social reconstructionist views that had characterized his nontextbook writing during the period from 1920 to 1940, taking the position that the school and community should work together to change society for the betterment of all. Much of Rugg's work appeared in *Frontiers of Democracy* (1934–1943), a progressive education journal, the last issues of which he edited. *Frontiers* often took a left-wing social reconstructionist stance on school and societal problems. Rugg began writing about the new field of teacher education shortly before his retirement from Teachers College in 1951. He saw teacher education as crucial to real creativity and demanded that teachers be leaders in society. As early as 1935 he had taught a course called "Arts in Education and Life," and during his last years at the college his interest in the subject of creativity became paramount to Rugg, culminating in the posthumous publication of *Imagination* (1963), in which Rugg attempted to explain the spark of creativity that inspired artistic acts.

Rugg died in Woodstock, New York. In remembering Rugg, education philosopher F. Ernest Johnson asserted, "It is doubtful if any American educator, working at the classroom level, has done more than Harold Rugg to make the best of our traditions live in the minds and hearts of youth" (Johnson, p. 176).

• Rugg's papers have not been made available. According to his widow, he kept few papers and instead heavily marked his books with notes. His personal library, with these notes, is intact in Woodstock, N.Y. Rugg authored a semiautobiographical work, *That Men May Understand* (1941), while in the midst of his textbook controversies. There is no major published biography of Rugg, but he is discussed in Peter Carbone, Jr., "The Social and Educational Thought of Harold Rugg" (Ph.D. diss., Harvard Univ., 1967). A revised version of the dissertation was published by Duke University Press as *The Social and Educational Thought of Harold Rugg* (1977). A number of other dissertations focus on Rugg's work: Elmer A. Winters, "Harold Rugg and Education for Social Reform" (Ph.D. diss., Univ. of Wisconsin, 1968); Albert Malatesta, "Harold Rugg's Theory of Creative Self-Expression and its Development and Importance to Education and Living" (Ph.D. diss., Boston Univ., 1973); Murry R. Nelson, "Building a Science of Society: The Social Studies and Harold R. Rugg" (Ph.D. diss., Stanford Univ., 1975), which provides annotations of more than twenty-five of Rugg's most notable books, chapters, and articles; Virginia S. Wilson, "Harold Rugg's Social and Educational Philosophy as Reflected in His Textbook Series, Man and His Changing Society" (Ph.D. diss., Duke Univ., 1975); John J. Schwartz, Jr., "The Work of Harold Rugg and the Question of Objectivity" (Ph.D. diss., Univ. of Rochester, 1978); Marion C. Schipper, "The Rugg Textbook Controversy: A Study in the Relationship Between Popular Political Thinking and Educational Material" (Ph.D. diss., New York Univ., 1979); and Donald W. Robinson, "Patriotism and Economic Control: The Censure of Harold Rugg" (Ph.D. diss., Rutgers Univ., 1983). The Ginn controversy is discussed in Paul Blanshard, *The Right to Read* (1955). Also informative is F. Ernest Johnson, "Harold O. Rugg, 1886–1960," *Educational Theory* 10, no. 3 (1960): 176–81. An obituary is in the *New York Times*, 18 May 1960.

MURRY NELSON

RUGGLES, Carl (11 Mar. 1876–24 Oct. 1971), composer, was born Charles Sprague Ruggles in Marion, Massachusetts, the son of Nathaniel Sprague Ruggles and Josephine Hodge. He was descended from a New England family of seafarers and whalers. At age six, Ruggles constructed a violin from a cigar box and strings in order to accompany his mother, who was an amateur singer. His parents soon after gave him a real violin and lessons with George Hill, a bandmaster from New Bedford. By the time he was nine, Ruggles was entertaining visitors to Cape Cod, including President Grover Cleveland and his wife. As a teenager, Ruggles played in local theaters, attended concerts of the Boston Symphony Orchestra, and began to play chamber music with orchestra members.

Although Ruggles originally moved to Boston to study shipbuilding, by 1900 he was working for the music publishing firm of F. H. Gilson in Boston. He also wrote music criticism for the *Belmont Tribune* and the *Watertown Tribune* in 1902–1903. During this period, he studied violin with Felix Winternitz, theory with Josef Claus, and composition with Harvard professors John Knowles Paine and Walter Spaulding in 1903. Ruggles performed some of his own songs with BSO pianist Alfred de Voto, but he destroyed most of these early vocal pieces. Only two of these works remain, and copies are housed in the Library of Congress. Throughout his career, Ruggles revised his works many times, left some unfinished, and destroyed pieces he did not like, leaving only the early sketches.

In Boston, Ruggles studied English literature with Barrett Wendell and continued his composition study with Paine at Harvard (1903–1907). During this period, Ruggles gave lectures on modern music to local music clubs, emphasizing the achievements of Richard Wagner and the French composers César Franck, Vincent d'Indy, and Claude Debussy. In his own works, he began to transcend both the impressionism of Debussy and the chromaticism of Wagner to find a completely dissonant idiom. It was also in the first decade of the twentieth century that he abandoned his Yankee family name of Charles Sprague to call himself Carl Ruggles.

Ruggles left Boston in 1907 to teach at the Mar d'Mar School of Music in Winona, Minnesota, where he founded a symphony orchestra. Ruggles conducted a number of performances of operas in concert versions in Winona and began working on his own opera, *The Sunken Bell* (1912–1923). After a labor of eleven years, he eventually left the piece unfinished and destroyed all but the early sketches. While living in Winona, he met and married Charlotte Snell, a singer who often performed with the symphony.

In 1917 Ruggles moved to New York City, where he hoped to generate interest in *The Sunken Bell* at the Metropolitan Opera. While he continued to compose, he gave composition lessons, received some support from a private patron, and worked at the Rand School of Social Science, where he founded an orchestra and directed the chorus until 1921.

Ruggles's first mature published work was the song "Toys," composed in 1919 for the fourth birthday of his son, Micah, and published in 1920. In New York, Ruggles became associated with modernist Edgard Varèse, with whom he organized the International Composers' Guild of the Pan American Association of Composers, which offered concerts and rehearsals of new music. Ruggles saw first performances of some of his important early works under Guild auspices, including *Angels*, for muted brass instruments (1922); "Toys" (1923); *Vox clamans in deserto*, for soprano and small orchestra, with texts by Robert Browning, Meltzer, and Walt Whitman (1924); *Men and Mountains*, for orchestra (1924); and *Portals*, for string orchestra (1926). This was perhaps the most productive period in Ruggles's compositional career.

In the late 1920s Ruggles began to concentrate almost exclusively on composing, holding only one more teaching position, at the University of Miami from 1938 to 1943. He worked to develop an individual dissonant style. Although he knew and respected the work of the nontonal and twelve-tone Viennese School composers, he did not follow their models precisely. He sometimes developed his own formulas, such as avoiding repetition of a note in a melody until at least seven to ten other notes had sounded. This absence of melodic repetition leaves the listener without a strong sense of tonal center, and this was often Ruggles's goal. He cared less about public understanding or appreciation of his work than about meeting his own standard of experimental and creative excellence.

Henry Cowell selected *Men and Mountains* for the first issue (1927) of his *New Music Edition*, where he also published *Portals*. Published in journal form, *NME* was designed to bring to Cowell's colleagues, if not to a larger public, works that would not otherwise be published because of their difficulty or their experimental nature. Composer Charles Ives learned of Ruggles's work through *New Music Edition*, and he and Ruggles developed a lasting friendship. They shared a common New England heritage, an interest in nineteenth-century American poets, and a commitment to stylistic independence, irrespective of audience or critical responses to dissonance. In 1932 *New Music Edition* published Ives's *Lincoln the Great Commoner*, and Ruggles, who had taken up painting, designed the cover.

Ruggles did not compose for a popular audience, and his musical accomplishments often went unrecognized except by his colleagues. For example, his best-known orchestral piece, *Sun Treader* (1926–1931), was performed in Paris on 25 February 1932 under the baton of Nicolas Slonimsky, published by Cowell in *NME* in 1934, and performed at the International Society for Contemporary Music Festival in Barcelona in 1936. Ruggles himself did not hear the piece until 1965, when it was recorded, and *Sun Treader*, now regarded as one of his most important works, was not performed publicly in the United States until 1966, when Bowdoin College sponsored a two-day festival of Ruggles's music.

In the late 1930s and 1940s Ruggles composed *Evocations* for piano and *Organum* for orchestra. Both works were revised several times. By this time, he was again receiving help from a patron, Harriet Miller, whose support freed him to compose on a full-time basis. He composed "Exaltation," a hymn tune, as a memorial to his wife in 1958. He spent the last decades of his life revising earlier works and painting in the abstract expressionist style to which he had become attracted in the mid-1930s.

Like his colleague Ives, Ruggles was honored for his contributions to American music late in his career. He received an award from the National Association of Composers and Conductors in 1953. Ives nominated him to the National Institute of Arts and Letters, to which he was elected in 1954. Ruggles received a Brandeis University Creative Arts Award in 1964 and the Koussevitzky International Recording Award in 1966. On the occasion of his eighty-fifth birthday in 1961, the state of Vermont, where Ruggles had lived since the 1920s, celebrated "Carl Ruggles Day." The two-day Bowdoin College festival in 1966 recognized his compositional legacy. He was noted for his musical individuality, a trait that was especially important early in the twentieth century when American composers were searching for their own styles, distinct from European models. Ruggles died in Bennington, Vermont. In 1980 the Buffalo Philharmonic under Michael Tilson Thomas recorded Ruggles's complete works on the CBS Masterworks label.

• Two dissertations have brought to light information on particular aspects of Ruggles's life: see T. E. Peterson, "The Music of Carl Ruggles" (Univ. of Washington, 1967) and J. Saecker, "Carl Ruggles in Winona" (Winona State College, 1967). More recently, the unitary nature of Ruggles's individual approach to art and music was discussed in N. Archabal, "Carl Ruggles: Composer and Painter" (Ph.D. diss., Univ. of Minnesota, 1975). See also Paul Rosenfeld, *An Hour with American Music* (1929); Henry Cowell, *New Musical Resources* (1930, repr. 1969); Charles Seeger, "Carl Ruggles," *Musical Quarterly* (Oct. 1932), reprinted in Henry Cowell, ed., *American Composers on American Music* (1933; repr. 1962); L. Harrison, *About Carl Ruggles* (1946); John Kirkpatrick, "The Evolution of Carl Ruggles: A Chronicle Largely in His Own Words," *Perspectives of New Music* (1968); J. Tenney, "The Chronological Development of Carl Ruggles' Melodic Style," *Perspectives of New Music* (1977); M. J. Ziffrin, "Angels—Two Views," *The Music Review* (1968) and "Interesting Lies and Curious Truths about Carl Ruggles," *College Music Symposium* (1979); Virgil Thomson, "Ruggles," *American Music Since 1910* (1971); and H. Gleason and W. Becker, "Carl Ruggles," in *Twentieth Century American Composers*, Music Literature Outlines series, 4 (1981).

BARBARA L. TISCHLER

RUGGLES, David (15 Mar. 1810–26 Dec. 1849), abolitionist and journalist, was born in Norwich, Connecticut, the son of David Ruggles and Nancy (maiden name unknown), both free blacks. Educated at the Sabbath School for the Poor, he moved to New York City at the age of seventeen. In 1829 he opened a grocery, selling goods of "excellent quality" but no "spirituous liquors." He later served as an officer in the New York City Temperance Union.

In 1833 Ruggles sharpened his speaking skills as an agent for the *Emancipator and Journal of Public Morals*, the organ of the American Anti-Slavery Society. He attacked colonization and spoke in support of the black national convention movement and the newly established Phoenix Society, organized to nurture black education. The society sponsored the Phoenix High School for Colored Youth, which by 1837 employed thirteen teachers.

With Henry Highland Garnet, Ruggles organized the Garrison Literary and Benevolent Association, named after famed abolitionist William Lloyd Garrison, which sponsored a reading room. In 1834 he opened the first known African-American–owned bookshop, which served the abolitionist and black community. An antiabolitionist mob destroyed the store, however, in 1835.

Ruggles became well known to white abolitionists through his numerous articles in the *Emancipator*. In 1834 he published his first pamphlet, the anticolonization satire, *Extinguisher, Extinguished . . . or David M. Reese, M.D. "Used Up."* He expanded his abolitionist arguments in 1835 in *The Abrogation of the Seventh Commandment by the American Churches*. Published by Ruggles's own press, another African-American first, the pamphlet stood proslavery arguments that the abolition of slavery would lead to interracial sex on their heads. He charged slaveowners with violating the Seventh Commandment by forcing slave women to surrender "to their unbridled lusts," thus offending "every principle of feminine sensibility and Christian morals." In this appeal to the emerging northern feminist movement, Ruggles beseeched northern women to shun their southern white sisters who brought their slaves north "while on a summer tour." Those same women, he thundered, passively allowed their husbands to father children in the slave quarter or used as domestics "the spurious offspring of their own husbands brothers and sons." He found these actions of southern white women "inexcusably criminal" and demanded that northern women close their churches to them. Angelina Grimké used Ruggles's arguments in a speech before the Anti-Slavery Convention of American Women held in New York City in 1837.

In 1835 Ruggles founded and headed the New York Committee of Vigilance, which sought to shield the growing number of fugitive slaves from recapture and protect free blacks from kidnapping. Cooperating with white abolitionists Lewis Tappan and Isaac T. Hopper, Ruggles and other black leaders were daring conductors on the Underground Railroad and harbored nearly 1,000 blacks, including Frederick Douglass, before transferring them farther north to safety. A fearless activist, he raised funds for the committee, served writs against slave catchers, and directly confronted suspected kidnappers. In frequent columns for the *Colored American*, he exposed kidnapping incidents on railroads. In 1839 he published the *Slaveholders Directory*, which identified the names and addresses of politicians, lawyers, and police in New York City who "lend themselves to kidnapping." His bold efforts often led to his arrest and imprisonment, which contributed to his failing health and eyesight.

Between 1838 and 1841 Ruggles published five issues of the *Mirror of Liberty*, the first African-American magazine. Circulated widely throughout the East, Midwest, and the South, the magazine reported on the activities of the Committee of Vigilance, kidnappings and related court cases, antislavery speeches, and the activities of black organizations. Despite its irregular appearances, its publication was a significant achievement. In 1844 Ruggles attempted unsuccessfully to establish a second magazine, entitled the *Genius of Free-*

dom. In 1838 he attacked colonization once more in *An Antidote for a Poisonous Combination*.

Ruggles's antislavery zeal caused a fractious dispute with Samuel Eli Cornish in 1838. Without the permission of editor Cornish, Ruggles published the accusation in the *Colored American* that John Russell, a local black and landlord of a home for African-American seamen, trafficked in slaves. Russell successfully sued Ruggles and the newspaper for libel, and Cornish blamed Ruggles for the subsequent upheaval that split the black community. By 1839, stung by the divisive battle with Cornish, accused of mishandling funds by the Committee of Vigilance, and suffering from poor health and near blindness, Ruggles moved to Northhampton, Massachusetts. There Lydia Maria Child and the Northhampton Association of Education and Industry gave him succor in the 1840s while he continued his activities on the Underground Railroad. In 1841 he showed his old grit when he pioneered protest against segregation on public transit by refusing to leave his seat in a New Bedford, Massachusetts, railroad car.

Beset by illness and weary of failed cures, Ruggles in the 1840s tried successfully the water-cure treatments made famous by Vincent Priessnitz of Austrian Silesia. In Northhampton, Ruggles overcame his poor health and built a prosperous practice as a doctor of hydropathy. In 1846, with the help of the Northhampton Association, he refurbished an old watermill and opened the first establishment devoted to water cures in the United States. Using "cutaneous electricity" treatments, Ruggles became nationally known. He assisted a variety of patients, from the wife of a southern slave owner to William Lloyd Garrison and Sojourner Truth. He died in Northhampton from a severe bowel inflammation. As an abolitionist, journalist, and physician, Ruggles gave selflessly to help others.

• The most complete collection of Ruggles's writings is in C. Peter Ripley et al., eds., *The Black Abolitionist Papers* (1981–1983), microfilm. Excerpts are available in Ripley, *Black Abolitionist Papers*, vol. 3 (1991), and in Dorothy B. Porter, ed., *Early Negro Writing, 1760–1837* (1971). Basic data about Ruggles is available in Porter, "David Ruggles, An Apostle of Human Rights," *Journal of Negro History* 28 (1943): 23–50, and "David Ruggles, 1810–1849: Hydropathic Pioneer," *Journal of the National Medical Association* 48 (1957): 67–72, 130–34.

GRAHAM RUSSELL HODGES

RUGGLES, Samuel Bulkley (11 Apr. 1800–28 Aug. 1881), lawyer, land developer, and economist, was born in New Milford, Connecticut, the son of Philo Ruggles, a lawyer, and Ellen Bulkley. The family moved to Poughkeepsie, New York, around 1804. Samuel was educated at the Poughkeepsie Academy and Yale College, graduating with the class of 1814. He studied law in his father's office and was admitted to the bar in 1821, setting up practice in New York City. There in 1822 he married Mary R. Rathbone, daughter of a prominent merchant; decades later her inheritance from her father helped the Ruggles family through difficult financial times. Samuel and Mary Ruggles had two sons and one daughter; after 1839 they lived in a house he had built on fashionable Union Square. Ruggles made many friends among New York's "Knickerbocker" patricians and the leaders of the Whig party of New York City and state. Like most of their social circle, the Ruggleses were devout Episcopalians.

During the 1830s and 1840s Ruggles's principal business was real estate development, by which he helped shape the growing city of New York. He purchased several large tracts between 19th and 24th Streets, had the land leveled with millions of loads of gravel, and built and sold hundreds of houses. In the center of this development Ruggles laid out Gramercy Park (1831), which he reserved in perpetuity to the owners of the surrounding lots. He also laid out Lexington Avenue and helped establish Union Square (1833–1834). Ruggles hoped that these "free glorious open spaces" would "bless the city forever."

Ruggles wholeheartedly supported the Whig program of "internal improvements" to increase the wealth of the city, state, and nation. He was a founding director and comptroller of the New York & Erie Railway Company, chartered in 1832 to build a line between the Hudson River and the Great Lakes. Ruggles later helped promote other railroads, such as the Panama Railroad across the isthmus, but he is best remembered for promoting and conducting the enlargement of the Erie Canal. Elected to the New York State Assembly in 1837 as a Whig, Ruggles was appointed chairman of the committee that oversaw state finances. Ruggles prepared a *Report on the Finances and Internal Improvements of the State of New-York* (1838), which argued brilliantly that the state could responsibly borrow many millions of dollars to enlarge the canal system, repaying the loans from tolls on the traffic to and from the fast-growing middle western states. Democrats furiously denounced the Ruggles report as recommending an unpayable $40 million debt. Newly elected Whig governor William H. Seward appointed Ruggles a canal commissioner in 1839, and Ruggles supervised the initial enlargement of the Erie Canal until the resurgent Democrats passed the "Stop Law" of 1842. By the time canal enlargement was resumed in the later 1840s, Ruggles's optimistic projections of canal traffic growth were fully confirmed.

Ruggles was "land-poor"; his real estate investments had always depended on loans secured by mortgages. In the later 1840s he constructed several large warehouses on the Brooklyn waterfront, but the proceeds from rent were inadequate. Ruggles became insolvent in 1851, and he was obliged to resume his law practice in order to pay his many debts. However, civic duties increasingly occupied his attention. In 1848 he led in organizing the new Astor Library, endowed by the will of John Jacob Astor. After 1859 he was an active member of the powerful New York Chamber of Commerce and became its lobbyist for canal improvements and international monetary cooperation.

As a trustee of Columbia College from 1836 until his death, Ruggles led repeated efforts to transform the small college into a university, despite frequent opposition from less imaginative trustees. In 1854 Ruggles broadmindedly urged the appointment of Wolcott Gibbs, a Unitarian, as professor of chemistry. After much public controversy, the Columbia board of trustees declined to appoint Gibbs, by all indications because of his religion. In 1858 the trustees rejected Ruggles's proposal for full-fledged postgraduate schools in letters and science but approved a law school, which Ruggles worked hard to develop; he also helped foster the new medical school (1859) and school of mines (1863). In 1876 Ruggles arranged the appointment of John W. Burgess as professor of history, political science, and international law. Four years later Ruggles persuaded the trustees to approve Burgess's proposal for an advanced school of political science, the beginning of graduate instruction at Columbia.

Ruggles became much involved in international discussions on monetary policy. In 1863 Secretary of State William H. Seward appointed him delegate to the Fifth International Statistical Congress in Berlin, which proposed common international standards of values and weights for gold coins, to be tied to the French gold franc. Ruggles vigorously promoted this proposal, as well as international use of the metric system of weights and measures. As a delegate to the international monetary conference in Paris in 1867, Ruggles helped develop the plan for a uniform metric gold standard. After this conference and another at The Hague in 1869, Ruggles lobbied Congress to support an international gold standard. Ultimately, a modified national gold standard was enacted in 1873, but Ruggles opposed the growing interest in bimetallism—the use of gold and silver as international currency at a fixed ratio.

Ruggles remarked after the Berlin conference that "statistics are the very eyes of the statesman, enabling him to survey and scan with clear but comprehensive vision, the whole structure and economy of the body politic—to adjust, in finest harmony all its varied functions." Ruggles, an old Whig and now a Republican, continued to believe in essential government regulation of the economy. It was said that Ruggles himself "could evoke from dry columns of statistics profound lessons of political economy and philosophy." Far better than most people of his time, Ruggles understood (however imperfectly) the role of economics in national development and international relations. He died in Fire Island, New York.

Ruggles's energy and enthusiasm, his consistency of vision and persistence of effort, made him a successful advocate for several of the great undertakings of his age, including the development of Manhattan Island, the extension of canals and railroads, the foundation of graduate education, and international cooperation in monetary policy.

• The main body of Ruggles's surviving papers is at the New York Public Library, Rare Books and Manuscripts Division.

Ruggles's published writings took the form of pamphlets or government reports; an extensive bibliography is in Franklin B. Dexter, *Biographical Sketches of the Graduates of Yale College*, vol. 6 (1912). A full biography is Daniel G. B. Thompson, *Ruggles of New York: A Life of Samuel B. Ruggles* (1946). Much of Ruggles's life between 1848 and 1875 is recounted in the diary of his son-in-law, *Diary of George Templeton Strong*, ed. Allan Nevins and Milton H. Thomas (4 vols., 1952).

JAMES FOLTS

RUGGLES, Timothy (20 Oct. 1711–4 Aug. 1795), Loyalist lawyer, soldier, and judge, was born in Rochester, Massachusetts, the son of the Reverend Timothy Ruggles and Mary White. His father hoped he would become a minister, but he preferred the law. He was sworn into the bar at Plymouth in 1733, the year after he graduated from Harvard College. Ruggles soon ranked with the elder James Otis (1702–1778) at the top of the South Shore bar. "His reasoning powers and his legal information placed him among the most able advocates of that day; but his manners were coarse, rough, and offensive; his wit was brilliant, but harsh and unpleasant" (Samuel L. Knapp, *Biographical Sketches* [1821], p. 332). Ruggles briefly represented Rochester in the house of representatives in 1736 before moving to Sandwich, the hometown of his wife, Bathsheba Bourne Newcomb, a wealthy widow he married that same year. They managed a tavern and two shops she inherited, while he served six terms in the assembly between 1739 and 1752 for his new residence. In 1753 they moved to Hardwick, a frontier town in Worcester County. Ruggles became one of the county's leading men, served repeated terms in the General Court, including a year (1762) as Speaker of the house, and was elevated to the county court of common pleas in 1757. He became its chief justice in 1762 and was a most imposing presence. The *Boston Evening Post* on 13 February 1775 commented that Ruggles "could sit upon the Bench, and with . . . heavy lowering Brows and harsh thundering Voice, sway the whole bench of Justices, Jurors and all." John Adams (1735–1826) spoke of his "genius and . . . resolution" along with his "disagreeable" behavior but concluded that Ruggles's "grandeur" was owing to "the boldness and strength of his thoughts and expressions, his strict honor, conscious superiority, [and] contempt of meanness" (John Adams, *Works*, vol. 2 [1851–1856], pp. 67, 90, 180).

Ruggles made a considerable career for himself as a soldier as well as on the bench and in the legislature. In 1755 he raised a regiment for the Crown Point campaign led by Sir William Johnson, in which he served as third in command. He is reputed to have said to Johnson, after the campaign failed and Colonel Ephraim Williams died in an ambush, "General, I hope the damnable blunders you have made this day may be sanctified unto you for your spiritual and everlasting good." In 1757 Ruggles joined fellow Massachusetts legislator Israel Williams in commanding a futile relief expedition to the beleaguered Fort William Henry. The next year he was promoted from colonel to brigadier general and commanded the right wing of General James Abercromby's army in its disastrous attack on Fort Ticonderoga. In 1759 he raised provincial troops for General Jeffrey Amherst's army and in 1760 was second in command of a division in the Montreal campaign.

Ruggles was a staunch supporter of Massachusetts governors Francis Bernard and Thomas Hutchinson in the General Court. His opinion of the election of James Otis the younger (1725–1783) to the assembly in 1761 sums up his position, "Out of this election will arise a d——d faction, which will shake this province to its foundations" (Adams, *Works*, vol. 10, p. 248). Ruggles was one of three Massachusetts delegates to the Stamp Act Congress of 1765 and was chosen by one vote to preside over the delegates. However, he refused to sign a petition to the Crown expressing the sense of the body that Americans had the sole right to tax themselves. After opining that only the colonial legislatures, as legally constituted bodies, had the power to do so, he suddenly returned to Massachusetts, leaving his colleagues stunned and without a chair. The Massachusetts Assembly, which was willing to assert the colonies' exclusive right of taxation, reprimanded him publicly, entered the fact in its published journals, and refused him the right to print a reply. Ruggles's defense appeared in the *Boston Post-Boy* on 5 May 1766. He denied that the Stamp Act Congress represented the general sense of the colonists, as five colonies sent no delegates, three did not empower their envoys to sign anything, and other representatives were not chosen by the local legislatures.

Ruggles stood firmly at the side of the British administration and kept his bailiwick of Hardwick on the Loyalist side until 1771, when a severely divided community refused to be represented. He cast the assembly's sole vote against nonimportation in 1768 and was one of seventeen representatives who voted that year to rescind the "Circular Letter," in which Massachusetts invited the other colonies to concert with its defense of liberty and opposition to the British soldiers' arrival in Boston. Ruggles thus figured prominently in a 1768 Paul Revere engraving of the seventeen, titled *A Warm Place—Hell* (Colonial Society of Massachusetts, *Publications* 25 [1923]: 48–49).

The American Revolution severely divided the Ruggles family. As Timothy Ruggles rode out of Hardwick, on one of the splendid horses he loved to raise, to serve on the Mandamus Council appointed solely by the Crown in 1774, his brother Benjamin warned him that, if he left, he could never return alive. Soon thereafter, Timothy's mansion was plundered and his best horse poisoned. His three sons followed him as a Loyalist; his wife and four daughters remained in Hardwick and supported the revolutionaries. The elder Ruggleses were a notoriously quarrelsome couple, but their problems paled beside those of a daughter, Bathsheba: although probably insane, she was executed for murdering her husband, Joshua Spooner, in 1778.

Ruggles never ceased his often solitary efforts on behalf of the Loyalist cause. With Thomas Gilbert of Freetown, he raised three hundred men to temporarily resist the revolutionary organization and the terrorism against Loyalists that arose in the wake of the 1774 Coercive Acts. That October he offered to raise a Loyalist corps in Boston. In December he proposed to join together "such loyal subjects to the King, as dare to assert their right to Freedom, in all respects consistent with the Laws of the Land, against such Rebellious . . . ones . . . , as under pretext of being Friends to Liberty, are frequently committing the most enormous outrages upon the Persons and Properties of . . . His Majesty's peaceable Subjects, who for want of knowing who to call upon . . . fall into the hands of Banditti, whose Cruelties surpass those of Savages" (*Boston News-Letter*, 29 Dec. 1774). This call to arms and association gives a good idea of Ruggles's pugnacity.

Ruggles was frustrated by the unwillingness of British general Thomas Gage to heed his advice or avail himself of a Loyalist regiment. After he retired to Halifax with his sons when the British evacuated Boston in March 1776, he returned that June with General William Howe's forces to New York, where he commanded the garrison on Staten Island. Again his recruiting efforts met with scorn, so he refused further service. He ultimately received £5,000 of the £20,000 he claimed in losses from the British government along with a pension of £200 per year. In 1783 he occupied a tract of ten thousand acres in Wilmot, Nova Scotia, "as fine a country as I ever saw in my life, capable of vast improvement." He died there, a "brave, worthy old man, who at three score and ten [began] the world anew with as much activity as if he were but one score and ten," according to fellow exile Edward Winslow.

An extraordinary jurist, soldier, and leader of men, Ruggles exemplified the fate of wealthy American provincials who refused to repudiate the government under which their careers and estates had flourished. Ruggles stood out from his fellow Loyalists in Massachusetts, most of whom simply gave up the ghost and escaped to British lines in Boston and thence to England and Canada. Given his associates' inability to fight a revolution on their own terms and the British unwillingness to use American troops, Ruggles remains a neglected symbol of a lost cause.

• Clifford K. Shipton's sketch of Ruggles in *Sibley's Harvard Graduates: Biographical Sketches of Those Who Attended Harvard College*, vol. 9 (1956), is one of the highlights of that compendium. Shipton pieced together much of Ruggles's career from primary sources in the Massachusetts Archives and the *Journal of the House of Representatives of Massachusetts Bay* for the years he served. W. O. Raymond, ed., *The Winslow Papers* (1901), has much information on Ruggles's years in Canada. Edmund S. Morgan and Helen M. Morgan, *The Stamp Act Crisis: Prologue to Revolution* (1953), is the best source for Ruggles's controversial role there.

WILLIAM PENCAK

RUKEYSER, Merryle Stanley (3 Jan. 1897–21 Dec. 1988), financial columnist and lecturer, was born in Chicago, Illinois, the son of Isaac Rukeyser and Pauline Solomon. Rukeyser grew up in Manhattan, New York, and graduated from Townsend Harris High School at the age of sixteen. He began his newspaper career at the age of seventeen while attending Columbia University. During the summers of 1914 and 1915, he worked as a reporter for the *Reporter Rockaway News*, Far Rockaway, New York, a New York weekly. From 1915 to 1917 he served as assistant sports editor and correspondent at the *Morning Telegraph* in Manhattan, enabling him to pay his tuition.

Upon graduating with a bachelor of literature degree in journalism from Columbia in 1917, he worked for the *New York Tribune* until 1923. In 1920 he became financial and business editor at the age of 23; he served as financial editor of the *New York Evening Journal* from 1923 to 1926. After he received his M.A. in economics at Columbia in 1925, Rukeyser was hired in 1927 by William Randolph Hearst to write a financial column for the *New York Evening Journal* and International News Service. Hearst wanted him to "humanize and simplify" financial news coverage for the general reader.

In 1930 he married Berenice Helene Simon; they had four sons, all of whom, like their father, pursued careers in business and journalism.

Rukeyser served as editorial writer for Hearst Newspapers from 1931 to 1952. In 1958 he began writing his column, "Everybody's Money," which was eventually syndicated in close to 200 newspapers. While pursuing his journalism career, Rukeyser taught at the School of Journalism at Columbia University from 1918 to 1935. He also acted as president of the Alumni Association of the School of Journalism from 1924 to 1927.

In addition to the many financial columns Rukeyser wrote, he also authored nine books. As a result of his financial columns, he received 30,000 questions from readers in over three years asking for advice on financial matters. Through these questions he became very aware of the concerns of the small investor. His first book, *The Common Sense of Money and Investments* (1924), was published when he was twenty-seven years old and a mere four years after the Nineteenth Amendment (granting woman suffrage) was ratified. Rukeyser presents an enlightened view of women for that era, stating that "despite the demonstration of the obvious by capable women bank officials and bond sellers, the traditional investment advisor continues to associate women with imbeciles and minors." Later he states, "Sex should be no factor in selecting investments." In his second book, though titled *Financial Advice to a Young Man* (1927), he addresses both young men and women on how best to plan their careers. Rukeyser continued to publish books of financial advice through the 1950s, including *Investment and Speculation* (1930), *The Diary of a Prudent Investor* (1937), and *Financial Security in a Changing World* (1940).

The Attack on Our Free Choice: A Forthright Appraisal of the State of Our Nation: Sensible Government Regulation vs. Unbridled Regimentation (1963) was written one year after he stepped down as president of the Board of Education in New Rochelle, New York. During his two years as president of the school board (1960–1962), a judge ruled that members of the 1930 board had gerrymandered the school districts so that one particular district would be attended predominantly by African-American children and later boards had not acted to desegregate. The board was ordered to present to the court a plan for desegregation.

Merryle Rukeyser denied that the schools were purposefully segregated. Schools at the elementary level were simply neighborhood schools: "I feel that the board has acted lawfully. We have drawn no racial, color or religious lines." Despite appeals to the federal Circuit Court of Appeals and later to the Supreme Court, the decision was upheld. On 9 April 1962 Rukeyser and three other members resigned from the board because they were not in agreement with the policies or tactics of the other five members.

This incident received a good deal of media attention and had a profound effect on Rukeyser. In the introduction to *Attack on Our Free Choice* he refers to it as an "irrelevancy." He disparages the media and warns that people are not always in control of the image they create. Increasing government regulation and control and media manipulation of facts serve to infringe on the individual's rights. Rukeyser asserted that it is in the best interest of the individual to seek education and self-discipline and to be in control of his or her own economic destiny.

In the 1960s, Rukeyser wrote *The Kennedy Recession* (1963), about the economy and financial markets. He disputed the theory that budget deficits help an economy to prosper, and he advocated tax reform, not tax cuts, as a means to stimulate the economy. In 1964 Berenice Simon Rukeyser died in New York. Rukeyser married Marjorie Ballin Leffler in 1965.

During his career, Rukeyser contributed numerous articles on investments to national magazines, including *The Executive*, *The Nation's Business*, *Forbes*, and *World's Work*. At one time he was a commentator for the Mutual Broadcasting System and appeared as a guest on television and radio programs, including "America's Town Meeting of the Air," "Meet the Press," and "The Open Mind." He acted as a business consultant and advised corporations on making their annual reports more comprehensible to shareholders.

Rukeyser continued to lecture at least once a year until a year before his death in White Plains, New York. His son Louis said, "He called [these lectures] his annual senility test, to see if he could deliver a one-hour lecture on economics without notes." The senior Rukeyser was a favorite guest on his son Louis's "Wall Street Week," his last appearance being in November 1987. In an article published in June 1987 in *Money* magazine titled "Sages of Wall Street," Merryle Rukeyser advised investors just as he did in the 1920s and 1930s. He advocated careful selection and monitoring of one's investments, diversification to cushion mistakes, and the patience to ride out market fluctuations: "Successful investors know themselves and do their own thinking. . . . They find a good investment and let it pay off."

• Rukeyser's correspondence from 1924 to 1926 is at the American Jewish Historical Society, Waltham, Mass. Other books by Rukeyser are *The Doctor and His Investments* (1931); *Life Insurance Property: The Hallmark of Personal Progress* (1958); and *Collective Bargaining: The Power to Destroy* (1968). For more information on the New Rochelle segregation ruling, see the *New York Times*, 25 Jan. 1961 and 1 June 1961. Obituaries are in the *New York Times*, 22 Dec. 1988 and the *Chicago Tribune*, 23 Dec. 1988.

MARY FRANCES GROSCH

RUKEYSER, Muriel (15 Dec. 1913–12 Feb. 1980), poet, author, and social activist, was born in New York City, the daughter of Lawrence B. Rukeyser, a construction supplies businessman, and Myra Lyons, a bookkeeper. While her adult life was intense and eventful, her childhood was quiet, affluent, and sheltered. She was educated at Manhattan's School of Ethical Culture; the Fieldston school, from which she graduated in 1930; Vassar College, which she left in 1932 without graduating; and Columbia University. At Vassar, where her classmates included Elizabeth Bishop and Mary McCarthy, she founded the undergraduate leftist journal *Student Review*. She also attended the Roosevelt School of Aviation in order to learn to fly, a process celebrated in the long title poem of her first book of poetry, *Theory of Flight* (1935).

Rukeyser was a prolific writer, producing, in addition to her nineteen volumes of poetry, numerous translations, scripts, children's books, a novel, and three biographies. Her poetry is impressive for its sheer bulk and variety but recognized still more for its personal intensity and social awareness. Rukeyser began early to travel, to write, and to immerse herself in political issues. At nineteen she was arrested for interviewing black reporters at the Scottsboro trials in Alabama; she caught typhoid fever in jail. At twenty-two she published *Theory of Flight*, which won the Yale Younger Poets Award and which established her vision of the poet as prophet and leader. In 1936 she investigated and reported on silicosis among the miners at Gauley Bridge, West Virginia. Later that year the British journal *Life and Letters Today* sent her to report on the Anti-Fascist Olympics in Barcelona. While she was there, the Spanish Civil War broke out, and Rukeyser worked with the Spanish Medical Bureau; she later lobbied in the United States for the loyalists. In the books that followed, between 1938 and 1945, these experiences and others found their way into the poems. *U.S. 1*, which treated the exploitation of mine workers as well as Rukeyser's Spanish experience, appeared in 1938; *A Turning Wind*, in 1939; *The Soul and Body of John Brown*, in 1940; *Wake Island*, in 1942; and *Beast in View*, in 1944.

In 1945 Rukeyser moved to California to teach at the California Labor School. In the same year she married painter Glyn Collins, but they divorced after two months. Two years later she had an illegitimate son and was subsequently disowned by her family, an experience she wrote about in her poetry. During this period Rukeyser published *The Green Wave* (1948), *Orpheus* (1949), and *Selected Poems* (1951). In 1954 she moved back to New York to accept a position at Sarah Lawrence College, where one of her students was Alice Walker. Walker later wrote that Rukeyser "taught by the courage of her own life" (*In Search of Our Mothers' Gardens* [1983]). The books of poems kept coming: *Chain Lightning* (1955), *The Body of Waking* (1958), *Sun Stone* (1961), *Poems, 1935–1961* (1961), *The Speed of Darkness* (1968), and *Breaking Out* (1973).

Rukeyser's activism was undiminished in her later years. In 1972 she flew to Hanoi to protest American involvement in the Vietnam War, and she was arrested in Washington, D.C., during a peace demonstration. In 1974, as president of American PEN, she traveled to South Korea to plead for the life of imprisoned poet Kim Chi-Ha. This last experience inspired *The Gates* (1976), the last separate book of her poems published in her lifetime. *The Collected Poems* appeared in 1977.

Rukeyser was influenced early by the formal techniques as well as by the politics of W. H. Auden, but the celebratory expansiveness of her poetry, as well as its long lines and rhetorical rhythms, often invites comparisons with Walt Whitman. The Whitmanian influence became more pronounced in the 1960s, when she began to write a more highly charged and personal free verse. She wrote about her failed marriage, her disinheritance, and her son's exile in Canada during the Vietnam War, using language still thought by many to be unsuitable for poetry. This confessional and often feminist poetry influenced younger women poets such as Anne Sexton and Adrienne Rich, both of whom acknowledged a debt to Rukeyser. Rukeyser can be seen as emblematic of the mid-century urge to strip away, to narrow the gap between experience and artifact, and to write an unmediated poetry.

Rukeyser's critical reception, like her own work, has been uneven. It is generally felt that her poetic voice, which tended toward sloganeering in the early work, became more sophisticated in her later work; her images, less at the service of didactic ends, became more complex and surreal; and her style moved from the rhetorical to the colloquial. Randall Jarrell, reviewing *The Green Wave*, regretted her rhetoric and emotionalism. Other critics found her work loose and unfocused. Rukeyser trusted emotional intensity rather than technique to create poetic effect; the sheer quantity of her writing suggests both that intensity and an impatience with revision—perhaps, too, the absence of self-doubt that would prompt revision.

Her death was little noted by scholars, and her work has seldom been included on syllabi of mid- to late twentieth-century American poetry. Nevertheless, Rukeyser continues to be read as a powerful poet of the political and the personal, a poet, as Jascha Kessler called her, "in the very front line, a . . . spokespoet

perhaps, speaking up loudly for freedom in the world."

Rukeyser also wrote several volumes of prose, including *The Life of Poetry* (1949), the novel *The Orgy* (1966), and children's books such as *Come Back Paul* (1955), *I Go Out* (1961), *Bubbles* (1967), and *Mazes* (1967). She wrote biographies of Wendell Willkie and Thomas Hariot and *Willard Gibbs: American Genius* (1942), which was nominated for a Pulitzer Prize. Her translations include the work of Octavio Paz, Gunnar Ekelöf, and Bertolt Brecht.

Rukeyser died in Greenwich Village.

• Virginia R. Terris, "Muriel Rukeyser: A Retrospective," *American Poetry Review* 3, no. 3 (May/June 1974): 10–15, traces Rukeyser's movement from the social to the personal, as well as her effort in both poetry and biography to explore a meeting ground for science and poetry. Shortly before Rukeyser's death, her friend Louise Bernikow wrote a celebratory article, "Muriel at 65: Still Ahead of Her Time," *Ms.*, Jan. 1979, pp. 14–16. Other articles appearing during Rukeyser's lifetime include Kenneth Rexroth, *American Poetry in the Twentieth Century* (1971), pp. 123–24; Randall Jarrell, *Poetry and the Age* (1953), pp. 163–66; M. L. Rosenthal, "Muriel Rukeyser: The Longer Poems," in *New Directions in Prose and Poetry*, ed. James Laughlin (1953), pp. 201–29; and Robert Coles, "Muriel Rukeyser's *The Gates*," *American Poetry Review* 7, no. 3 (May–June 1978): 15. Of more recent articles, especially interesting are Adrienne Rich, "Beginners," *Kenyon Review* 15, no. 3 (Summer 1993): 12–19; and Suzanne Gardinier, "A World That Will Hold All the People: On Muriel Rukeyser," *Kenyon Review* 14, no. 3 (Summer 1992): 88–105. A special Rukeyser issue of *Poetry East* was published in 1985. Louise Kertesz, *The Poetic Vision of Muriel Rukeyser* (1980), is a book-length study that is particularly helpful in tracing Rukeyser's roots in Hart Crane, Auden, and Whitman; it offers a full bibliography. An obituary is in the *New York Times*, 13 Feb. 1980.

JEFFREY GRAY

RUMFORD, Count. *See* Thompson, Benjamin.

RUML, Beardsley (5 Nov. 1894–18 Apr. 1960), social scientist, was born in Cedar Rapids, Iowa, the son of Wentzle Ruml, a physician, and Salome Beardsley, the superintendent of the Cedar Rapids hospital. A graduate of Dartmouth College in 1915, Ruml earned a Ph.D. in psychology and education from the University of Chicago in 1917. Also in 1917 he married Lois Treadwell; they had three children.

Ruml's major interests were government, business, and education, whose relations he sought to rationalize through the methods of social science. From 1917 to 1918 he was an instructor in applied psychology at the Carnegie Institute of Technology. In 1918 he was co-director of the trade test division of the U.S. Army, where he helped to devise intelligence and aptitude tests for American soldiers in World War I. He later employed the statistical techniques used in these tests to measure social deviance. In these projects Ruml viewed society as composed of groups whose traits could be measured and ranked on a scale of normality and deviance.

At the end of the war Ruml joined a company to advise industry on personnel matters and in 1921 became an assistant to the president of the Carnegie Corporation. In 1922 he became director of the Laura Spelman Rockefeller Memorial Fund, whose resources he granted for fellowships in the social sciences. During his years with the fund (1922–1929), he began to see society as a constantly changing panoply of interactions. No longer could society be divided according to disciplinary specialties; all these phenomena converged and interacted in specific locations, such as a "city" or a "region." In order to solve social problems, then, it was necessary to "integrate" the social sciences.

From 1929 to 1931 Ruml served as a trustee of the Spelman Fund and as an assistant to Arthur Woods, chair of President Herbert Hoover's Emergency Committee for Unemployment. Ruml proposed the "domestic allotment" system, whereby domestic food processors would pay farmers an enhanced "tariff" price, and farmers would sell only a specified amount of their crops in the domestic market. A version of his system was incorporated into the Agricultural Adjustment Act of 1933. In 1931 University of Chicago president Robert M. Hutchins appointed Ruml dean of the Division of Social Sciences and charged him to integrate the social sciences. However, the professors refused to be integrated, and in 1934 Ruml resigned to become treasurer of R. H. Macy & Company, rising to become chairman in 1945 and director in 1951. He also served as a director of the New York Federal Reserve Bank (1937–1947) and participated in the Bretton Woods Conference (1944) that established the post–World War II international monetary system.

In 1939 President Franklin D. Roosevelt appointed Ruml an "adviser" to the National Resources Planning Board. Ruml had served since 1935 in a similar capacity on the National Resources Committee. He urged detailed studies of consumer income and spending, which, he believed, held the key to prosperity. Like many "Keynesian" economists, Ruml advocated "compensatory" government fiscal policies, but he differed from many by focusing on tax policy. He favored low tax rates, which in boom times would encourage high production and high employment and would generate sufficient revenues to balance the budget and retire the debt. In slack times the lower rates would reduce tax payments and stimulate recovery. Ruml believed businesspeople ought to favor a "compensatory" policy that guaranteed low tax rates.

In the summer of 1942 Ruml gained national attention by proposing to a Senate committee that the United States collect income taxes through a withholding system. From his perspective as a high-salaried treasurer of Macy's, it seemed that young executives who left lucrative jobs for military service would be stuck with large tax bills and military salaries insufficient to pay them. Thus he proposed to "forgive" the previous year's taxes, making up the revenue by immediately collecting on the current year's taxes. Opponents charged that this would mean a windfall of tax forgive-

ness to the 385,000 wealthiest Americans, who owed half the tax bill that would be forgiven. This Ruml privately and unashamedly conceded. Still, he argued no Americans would collect their "bonuses" until they died and any loss to the Treasury would be spread over many years and could be made up by changes in the tax code. In 1943 Congress adopted the withholding system.

In 1942 Ruml helped form the Committee for Economic Development, a private nonprofit association intended to assist businesspeople in planning for reconversion to a peacetime economy and to recommend policies to sustain high levels of production and employment. Drawing upon the regulatory experiences of the New Deal and the war but hoping to avoid their conflicts and uncertainties, Ruml looked for ways to coordinate and balance a plurality of rule-making agencies. Business should strive for monopoly power by providing better goods and services, but government should never allow them to achieve monopoly. Customers should shun businesses that did not follow the rules. Ruml was ambivalent about the role of labor in a pluralistic society, once arguing that full employment guaranteed worker security better than collective bargaining. He later acknowledged the prospect of continued labor-management conflict until a "new pluralism" placed the labor union alongside family, church, state, and business as a legitimate rule-making institution. He continued to believe that a healthy economy and free society depended upon widespread purchasing power. In 1953 he proposed separating the federal budget into an "expense" budget for regular outlays and a "capital" budget for projects that would bring a return to the government. This latter budget he would fund by borrowing in private capital markets, which in turn would reduce taxes and stimulate consumer spending. Congress did not adopt his proposal.

Because he assumed that American society would always be in flux, Ruml called for less emphasis on vocational education and more on a liberal education that prepared students for diverse and unexpected challenges. In *Memo to a College Trustee* (1959) he turned his attention to strengthening liberal arts colleges and especially to raising faculty salaries. He recommended that colleges increase enrollments and class sizes and allocate tuition revenues and the savings generated by curriculum reform to higher salaries. He saw the major obstacles to such reforms in the departmental structure and a faculty culture that defined education as an "artistic or public-service" activity. To overcome faculty resistance, he recommended a Council for Educational Policy and Program that would contain faculty and administrative representatives and would be acknowledged by both as authoritative.

Ruml died the following year in Danbury, Connecticut. Had he lived another decade he would have seen his objectives achieved not by his prescriptions but by the unprecedented prosperity of the 1960s.

Like all serious and thoughtful Americans who adopted a pluralist analysis, Ruml wrestled with the problem of finding common loyalties and acknowledged authorities. He proposed to solve the problems of pluralism by identifying institutions that played complementary roles and earned their legitimacy by carrying out clearly understood functions in honest and predictable ways. Ruml was the main link between economists and businesspeople. His attempt to apply formulas from the social sciences, such as Keynesian economics, to social problems and to formulate policies through boards, councils, and committees that combined various business, governmental, academic, and philanthropic interests placed him in the tradition of "corporate liberalism," which emerged as the consensus view of centrist politicians and social thinkers in the postwar era. Ruml imagined that such an approach would produce not utopian progress but stability and security. For him, diversity worked best in a society that was "constantly changing and yet, in a strange but real sense, through continuity, . . . always . . . the same."

• Ruml's papers are at the University of Chicago. His early assumptions about social science are included in *The Reliability of Mental Tests in the Division of an Academic Group* (1917). His major writings on economics and education include "The Business Man's Interest in National Fiscal Policy," *Advanced Management* 4 (1939): 122–25; *Government, Business and Values* (1943); and *Tomorrow's Business* (1945). An extensive profile is Alva Johnson, "The National Idea Man," *New Yorker*, 10 Feb. (pp. 28–35), 17 Feb. (pp. 26–34), and 24 Feb. (pp. 30–41) 1945. His role in the further development of the social sciences is discussed in Barry Karl, *Charles E. Merriam and the Study of Politics* (1974). "The Reminiscences of Milburn Lincoln Wilson" (1973), in the Oral History Collection of Columbia University, discusses Ruml's further contributions to social science thinking and his specific contribution to farm policy. Robert M. Collins, *The Business Response to Keynes* (1981), and Herbert Stein, *The Fiscal Revolution in America* (1969), discuss his role in the New Deal. His advocacy of the withholding tax is discussed in *Current Biography* (1943) and in Patrick D. Reagan, "The Withholding Tax, Beardsley Ruml, and Modern American Policy," *Prologue* 24 (1992): 19–31. Obituaries are in the *New York Times*, 19 and 20 Apr. 1960.

GEORGE MCJIMSEY

RUMMEL, Joseph Francis (14 Oct. 1876–8 Nov. 1964), Roman Catholic clergyman and social leader, was born in Steinmauern, Baden, Germany, the son of Gustave Rummel and Teresa Bollweber. The family immigrated in 1882 to New York City, where the elder Rummel, initially a shoemaker, worked as a rent collector for a brewery with large property holdings. Young Rummel became a naturalized U.S. citizen on 2 February 1888. He attended St. Boniface Elementary School, where classes were still taught in German, and later St. Anselm's College in Manchester, New Hampshire, from which he received a B.A. in 1896. He studied at St. Joseph Seminary in Yonkers, New York, and the North American College in Rome, Italy, from which he received his S.T.D. in 1903.

Rummel was ordained to the priesthood in Rome on 24 May 1902. He spent his early priestly years in pastoral work and administration in the Archdiocese of New York at St. Joseph Parish in New York City (1903–1907), St. Peter's Parish in Kingston (1907–1915), St. Anthony Parish in the Bronx (1915–1924), and St. Joseph of the Holy Family in Harlem (1924–1928). He took an early interest in social problems and first gained national prominence through postwar relief efforts, serving as executive secretary of the German Relief Committee (1923–1924) and president of the local Society for the Prevention of Cruelty to Children.

Rummel was consecrated bishop of Omaha, Nebraska, in New York City on 29 May 1928. In Omaha, he directed the rapid expansion of parishes, schools, and other diocesan institutions and encouraged the formation of rural ministry and greater lay participation in diocesan life. He also hosted the Sixth National Eucharistic Congress (1930) and the National Council of Catholic Charities convention (1932) to foster wider participation in church life and to serve as a public affirmation of the Catholic community's presence in Nebraska.

Rummel was appointed archbishop of New Orleans on 9 March 1935. Father Joseph Vath, future bishop of Birmingham, Alabama, later recalled, "There was a sense that we needed leadership. . . . [Rummel] took the city by storm." Rummel guided a period of rapid growth as the number of local Catholics increased almost 75 percent to 630,000 by 1962. More than 680 building projects were completed, and forty-eight new parishes were established. With the help of a major fundraising drive—the Youth Progress Program (1945)—he guided an expansion program for Catholic education that included more than seventy new school buildings. The number of elementary and secondary school children rose from 40,000 to 85,000. Social service facilities and programs were likewise expanded.

During Rummel's tenure in Louisiana, the Diocese of Baton Rouge was carved from the archdiocese on 20 July 1961. Archdiocesan policies, procedures, and practices had been updated through a diocesan synod in June 1949. He was a strong advocate of increased lay involvement in Louisiana church life, promoting the establishment of many local units of national organizations, such as the Confraternity of Christian Doctrine (1935), the Archdiocesan Council of Catholic Women (1936), and the Catholic Youth Organization (1936). In 1938 he hosted the Eighth National Eucharistic Congress, the first such congress to be held in the South. Rummel's influence reached beyond Louisiana. He served on numerous national Catholic boards and committees, including as episcopal chair of the Catholic Committee on Refugees (1936–1947) and on the board of trustees of the National Catholic Community Services—U.S. (1940–1944).

Rummel encouraged local clergy to educate their parishioners in social justice issues and consistently supported their efforts to implement social programs. He sponsored the first Catholic Conference on Industrial Problems held in the South to promote better understanding between capital and labor in the light of Catholic teachings and to foster industrial peace (8–10 Apr. 1940). Rummel vigorously and publicly opposed Louisiana's right-to-work laws. He actively supported the efforts of Louisiana agricultural workers to organize in the 1950s, and he supported the unsuccessful 1953 sugar-cane workers strike. He exhorted generous, self-sacrificing service to one's country in his 7–8 December 1941 pastoral letter "The Nation at War" and encouraged wholehearted Catholic support of the war effort. After World War II he encouraged equally generous support for relief efforts, worked for a temporary extension of rent control, and established a local resettlement bureau to assist (and sometimes resettle) more than 33,000 displaced persons who entered the United States via New Orleans between 1949 and 1952.

Rummel labored patiently for more than a quarter-century to create a community atmosphere conducive to full racial equality and to foster the growth of church organizations, facilities, and activities among African-American Catholics and, eventually, to achieve integration of Catholic parishes, schools, organizations, and institutions. In 1939, at Rummel's urging, Xavier University in New Orleans began a Catholic Action School for blacks to address social, economic, and moral issues and barriers facing the African-American community; more than 250 attended the first sessions. In 1951 he established the archdiocese's first secondary school for black youth—St. Augustine High School—where numerous national and local black leaders were educated. On 15 March 1953 his pastoral letter "Blessed Are the Peacemakers" ordered the desegregation of all Catholic parish activities and organizations. He suspended all Catholic services at Jesuit Bend mission (1955–1958) after an African-American priest was prevented from celebrating Mass there. In his pastoral letter of 11 February 1956 he declared racial segregation morally wrong and sinful. Rummel was also influential in preparing and gaining support for the 1958 U.S. Catholic bishops' statement condemning racism. On 27 March 1962, working closely with Archbishop John Cody and key clergy advisers, he ordered all Catholic schools within the archdiocese desegregated, leading to international news stories of confrontations with vocal segregationists and a self-proclaimed Association of Catholic laymen.

Rummel turned over administration of the Archdiocese of New Orleans to Cody on 1 June 1962. He died two years later in New Orleans. Close associate Joseph Vath later observed that, although Rummel was considered a hard man and a tough administrator, he was "a real German; like the famous German poet, Goethe, [he had] a lot of sentimentality in him. He loved everything human." In an April 1960 memorandum, his close associate, the historian and journalist Roger Baudier, wrote of Rummel's striking accomplishments, both spiritual and material, noting, "Even in the face of provocation and frustration and disappointment, he has never lost his calm dignity. He has never been recriminating. . . . This was abundantly clear at the time of the Right-to-Work Law before the legislature, when many prominent Catholic laymen openly attacked the archbishop, and during the more recent racial flare-ups when opposition was even more bitter."

• The main sources of information on Rummel are the Joseph Francis Rummel Papers, the Roger Baudier Collection, and taped interviews with Monsignor Charles J. Plauche and Bishop Joseph G. Vath of Birmingham, 30 Aug. and 11 Oct. 1980, in the archives of the Archdiocese of New Orleans. Local Catholic newspapers in New York, Omaha, and New Orleans contain detailed information on Rummel's views, programs, and activities; see, in particular, *Catholic Action of the South*, 14 and 21 Mar. and 16 May 1935; 27 July 1939; 4 Apr. 1940; 29 July 1943; 14 May 1953; and 20 May 1960; and the *New Orleans Clarion Herald*, 12 Nov. 1964. See also Thomas Becnel, *Labor, Church, and the Sugar Establishment: Louisiana 1887–1976* (1980), and Philip A. Grant, Jr., "Archbishop Joseph F. Rummel and the 1962 New Orleans Desegregation Crisis," *Records of the American Catholic Historical Society of Philadelphia* 91 (Mar.–Dec. 1980), pp. 59–66. An obituary is in the *New York Times*, 9 Nov. 1964.

CHARLES E. NOLAN

RUMSEY, Charles Cary (29 Aug. 1879–21 Sept. 1922), sculptor and polo player, was born in Buffalo, New York, the son of Laurence Dana Rumsey, a tanning and railroad businessman, and Jennie Cary. From 1893 to 1895 Rumsey apprenticed with American expatriate sculptor Paul Bartlett in Paris, France. While enrolled at Harvard from 1898 to 1902, Rumsey studied sculpture at the School of the Boston Museum of Fine Arts under Bela Lyon Pratt. His first publicly exhibited work was a sculpture of an Indian at the 1901 Pan-American Exposition in Buffalo.

After graduating in 1902, Rumsey returned to Paris, took classes at the Julian and Colarossi Academies, and studied under sculptor Emmanuel Frémiet, who specialized in equestrian sculpture. Rumsey moved to New York in 1906 and, with his traditional *beaux-arts* training, earned a reputation as a talented animal sculptor. His studies of horses, dogs, and buffalo depicted the animals' various stages of activity, such as attacking, stretching, or running. His careful modeling of the subject always conveyed his Rodin-like touch and the malleability of the original sculpting medium, which was usually clay, wax, or plaster.

By 1908 Rumsey began exhibiting widely and winning awards for his small animal bronzes and occasional human figures. Throughout his career he participated in numerous exhibitions with the Architectural League of New York, the Art Institute of Chicago, and the Albright Art Gallery in Buffalo. Rumsey's first solo exhibition was at the Sculptor's Gallery in New York City in 1917.

Rumsey's first major commission, which he started in 1909, was for Arden House, the home of railroad baron Edward H. Harriman in Rockland County, New York. The commission included a large limestone relief of an Indian hunting a buffalo for the Music Room's mantlepiece, a large bronze fountain for the outside terrace, a caricature study of Arden's chief architect Thomas Hastings, and two hound andirons. Just after Harriman died in 1910, Rumsey married his patron's daughter Mary. They had three children.

An avid rider and polo player throughout his life, Rumsey played on every U.S. team in international cup matches from 1913 to 1921, and in his last year he was ranked an eight-goal player. His polo activities also provided him with several horse portrait commissions for American horsemen such as Thomas Hitchcock, August Belmont, and Harry Payne Whitney.

In 1913 Rumsey participated in the landmark Armory Exhibition, of which his wife had been a monetary contributor. Rumsey showed three works, including his "Three Graces Fountain" and a study of Indians hunting buffalo for his "Manhattan Bridge Frieze," completed in 1916. The frieze for the bridge, also designed by Thomas Hastings, is six feet high and forty feet long. The poses are similar to the Arden relief, yet the style is more abstract and flatters to convey the scene to spectators far below or beyond the actual bridge.

At the 1915 Panama-Pacific Exposition, Rumsey won a bronze medal for his sculpture of Francisco Pizarro, the sixteenth-century Spanish explorer of South America. His nineteen-foot-tall, Renaissance-type equestrian portrait depicts the explorer in full armor, sitting atop a squat, stocky horse similar to what the conquistadors preferred. Cast in bronze twice, one version was placed in the town square of Trujillo, Spain, the birthplace of Pizarro, and the other was placed in the Plaza des Armas in Lima, Peru.

Rumsey joined the U.S. Army in 1917, during World War I, serving in France and reaching the rank of captain of cavalry. His sculpture after the war was influenced by modern trends toward monumentalism and abstraction, as exemplified in his sculpture, "The Pagan" (1921). Similar in style to French sculptor Aristide Maillol's classically influenced nudes, "Pagan" (also known as "Pagan Kin") is a large female reclining nude with rotund appendages and abstracted facial features. Rumsey, a member of the Architectural League of New York, sued the organization when they threatened to remove "Pagan" from an exhibition of their members' work at the Metropolitan Museum of Art. Jury members criticized the work as "lewd," "obscene," and "brutal," and there were rumors that it represented a Bolshevist woman. The League opted to include the sculpture, which a New York Times reporter described as "a study of brawn and fat, bulging muscles, obtuse angles, lumpy curves, with thick outward layers of flesh in rolls and creases" (22 Mar. 1921).

In 1921 Rumsey received a commission for friezes in the Rice Memorial Stadium, Pelham Bay, New York. Installed around 1928, the friezes consist of extremely stiff and muscular male athletes competing in various events such as hurdles, swimming, and running, inspired by ancient Greek reliefs.

By the beginning of the 1920s Rumsey displayed interest in the emerging Art Deco style, with its stream-lined shapes and industrially-inspired geometric forms. Completed in 1922, Rumsey's last major work, "Victory," is a highly stylized presentation of the Greek goddess, made of deeply recessed limestone relief. It decorates a memorial for Jewish soldiers and sailors who died in World War I and was placed in Zion Park, Brooklyn, New York. The female figure's rounded and full torso is shown frontal, but the legs and head are turned to the side for a severe profile. The stiff, flat lines of the wings are repeated in the figure's wind-blown hair and drapery, resembling the Art Deco treatments of other sculptures of the same time, such as those by Lee Lawrie and John Storrs. The New York Society of Architects gave "Victory" a special posthumous gold medal of honor in 1923.

Rumsey's death in an automobile accident on Long Island prematurely ended his active polo and artistic careers. His earlier *beaux-arts* style animal and mythical work quickly lost favor as abstract trends dominated much of the mid-twentieth-century sculptural styles. Although he was an early practitioner of the Art Deco style, his work was soon overshadowed by other artists from that era such as Lawrie, Leo Friedlander, and Hermon Atkins MacNeil.

In 1927 the Société Nationale des Beaux-Arts in Paris held a retrospective of Rumsey's work. The Burchfield-Penney Art Center of Buffalo State College held a retrospective in 1983 to commemorate the opening of a permanent display of his work in the Rumsey Gallery.

• The personal papers of Charles Cary Rumsey are in the archives of the Burchfield-Penney Art Center of Buffalo State College. In conjunction with their 1983 retrospective, they published the catalog *Charles Cary Rumsey, 1872–1922.* See also Patricia Janis Broder *Bronzes of the American West* (1973); Beatrice Gilman Proske, *Brookgreen Gardens Sculpture* (1968); Marjorie Brown, *Arden House* (1976); W. H. Glover, "The Sculptor of 'The Centaur,'" *Niagara Frontier* (Winter 1953); and Arsène Alexandre, "Charles Cary Rumsey," *La Renaissance de l'Art Français et des Industries de Luxe,* June 1927. For his polo career, see Newell Bent, *American Polo* (1929). An obituary is in the *New York Times,* 21 Sept. 1922.

CHARLES RUMSEY, JR.
N. ELIZABETH SCHLATTER

RUMSEY, James (Mar. 1743–21 Dec. 1792), inventor, first appeared on the historical scene in 1784. Almost nothing is known about his life before then, except that he was born at Bohemia Manor in Cecil County, Maryland, the son of Anna Cowman and Edward Rumsey, modestly successful farmers. It is not clear what sort of formal education he received, if any, or what he did during the revolutionary war. Mary Morrow became his wife sometime before 1784; she survived him. They raised two daughters and one son. The eldest daughter was apparently born to Rumsey and an unnamed first wife.

By 1784 Rumsey was living along the Potomac River in Bath, Virginia (now Berkeley Springs, W.Va.). Some years before he had left Baltimore for Sleepy

Creek, Maryland, where he formed a grist milling partnership with George Michael Bedinger. When that enterprise did not prosper Rumsey moved to Bath and began a new milling and boardinghouse partnership with Robert Throgmorton. Rumsey's life changed when George Washington passed through town on one of his trips west. Rumsey used his considerable charm to great advantage and contracted with Washington to erect several small buildings in Bath. Despite running late and over cost, Rumsey mollified the general and was made, at Washington's behest, superintendent of the Potomac Canal Company in the summer of 1785.

Rumsey resigned from his post a year later to pursue a career as an inventor. Though more of an entrepreneur than a mechanic, Rumsey knew a good deal about smithing and milling, and, equally as important, he had a talent for applying scientific principles to engineering tasks—principles that he learned more by observation and trial and error experimentation than by reading texts.

In October 1784 the Virginia legislature granted Rumsey a patent for a mechanical boat that moved against the current without using a sail. Apparently Rumsey was already a partner with James McMechen, who had applied to the Continental Congress the year before for a land grant as a reward for inventing a mechanically powered boat. What, exactly, Rumsey and McMechen had in mind remains a mystery. The best evidence suggests that they were working on a boat that would go upstream as the flow of water downstream turned a wheel connected to poles that struck the river bed and pushed the vessel more quickly in the opposite direction. Virginia granted Rumsey a ten-year monopoly; Maryland and Pennsylvania soon followed. Congress did not issue patents, but it was amenable to making a land grant, if Rumsey could construct a full-scale working model. He never did, years of hard work notwithstanding. Therefore he received no real estate windfall from Congress and his state patents meant little, given the limited feasibility of his design and his turn to steam as a motive force.

When Rumsey switched to steam he encountered trouble from three sources: financial, technical, and competitive. Of his two rivals for patents, Englehart Cruse proved less nettlesome than John Fitch. From 1785 to 1791 Fitch battled Rumsey over who had first contemplated using steam for navigation, then over who could secure the most patents, and, finally, over who could make the first operable vessel. Recriminations filled the air; disputes over facts and dates raged. Rumsey claimed to have thought of using steam in 1784, well before Fitch. Although he did not stage a public trial of any steamboat until December 1787, near Shepherdstown, Virginia (now W.Va.), Rumsey also insisted that he had made a successful private run in the spring of 1786. He and Fitch never put aside their differences, and through their bitter rivalry they helped bring an end to the patchwork state patent system, which was replaced by the first federal patent act in 1790.

Under that federal act both men received patents for their steam engine designs on the same date: 26 August 1791. Rumsey, who was less monomaniacal than Fitch and probably possessed a greater genius, received four additional patents for various applications of steam power and another for a type of water turbine. His steam engine designs for grist and saw milling were, in the long run, probably more important than his steamboat experiments. Despite two successful runs on the Potomac in December 1787, Rumsey's steamboat had not lasted long. Rather than use steam power to move paddles, the arrangement adopted by Fitch, Rumsey applied steam in a form of jet propulsion by designing a cylinder that drew water into a pipe and then pushed it out the stern at a greater velocity. Furthermore, instead of using a large kettle boiler, Rumsey devised a tubular system. He could use his Watt-type, single-acting engine to generate greater pressure, but not enough to drive his boat more than four or five miles per hour. Even at that speed the soldered joints would not hold, and Rumsey's boat enjoyed no commercial success.

Rumsey had appeared before the American Philosophical Society in the spring of 1788. Impressed by his ideas, some of its members, including Benjamin Franklin, organized the Rumseian Society to finance Rumsey's steamboat experiments. Funded by the society, Rumsey left for England, hoping to find even more backers and a solution to his technical problems. Besides, Fitch had secured monopolies for all forms of steam navigation in five states, most notably Virginia and Pennsylvania, giving him an advantage that Rumsey could not counter before the passage of federal patent law, which superseded all state grants.

Rumsey never returned home. Except for brief trips to France (where he met an admiring Thomas Jefferson) and Ireland, Rumsey spent his time in England. He obtained English patents for a steam-powered boat, and both steam- and water-driven mill machinery, but he did not garner the financing he needed. Nor could he escape the technical problems associated with his tubular boiler and jet propulsion. Failing to strike an acceptable bargain with James Watt and Matthew Boulton in 1788, he spent four years searching for other prospective partners. With money from the Rumseian Society and a few English investors, he oversaw the construction of *The Columbian Maid*. On 20 December 1792, as the date of the *Maid*'s trial run neared, Rumsey suffered a massive stroke in London; he died the next day. His *Columbian Maid* steamed successfully up the Thames early in 1793 but ultimately met the same fate as its Potomac predecessor. A monument commemorating Rumsey was erected in Shepherdstown in 1915. Rumsey's body presumably remains in the unmarked grave of St. Margaret's Church cemetery, Westminster, where his English friends buried him.

While enmeshed in his contest with Fitch, Rumsey warned that inventors must learn to endure "the heavy abuse and bitter scoffs of ill-natured ignorance." With himself in mind, he lamented that the man of genius would be ridiculed as an "impostor," even a "madman," and his motives would be impugned as "knavish" (*Short Treatise*, p. 3). If so, then Fitch actually had more cause for complaint than Rumsey. Rumsey never had enough money and was stymied time and again by mechanical breakdowns; still, he did attract investors and found mechanics who were capable of following his specifications. Although Robert Fulton and other steamboat pioneers of the next generation would not follow Rumsey's technical lead, they tapped into the same entrepreneurial and expansionistic urges of the new nation.

• Sources for Rumsey's career as an inventor are found in James A. Padgett, ed., "Letters of James Rumsey," *Maryland Historical Magazine* 32 (1937): 10–28, 136–55, and 271–85, which were drawn from papers in the Library of Congress, and "Letters of James Rumsey, Inventor of the Steamboat," *William and Mary Quarterly*, 1st ser., 24 (Jan. 1916): 154–74, 24 (Apr. 1916): 239–51, and 25 (July 1916): 121–34, assembled from collections at the Virginia State Library. Rumsey's *A Short Treatise on the Application of Steam* (1788) prompted a retort by Englehart Cruse, *The Projector Detected* (1788), and John Fitch, *The Original Steam-Boat Supported* (1788). Brother-in-law and business partner Joseph Barnes quickly came to Rumsey's defense in *Remarks on John Fitch's Reply to James Rumsey's Pamphlet* (1788). Rumsey laid out some of his design ideas in *The Explanations, and Annexed Plates, of the Following Improvements in Mechanics* (1788). Ella May Turner, *James Rumsey: Pioneer in Steam Navigation* (1930), includes long excerpts from many of the sources listed above. Turner insisted that Rumsey had the idea for steam navigation well before Fitch, and that Rumsey's public trial in December 1787 was far more significant than anything done by Fitch before 1790. H. A. Gosnell reached a similar conclusion in "The First American Steamboat: James Rumsey Its Inventor, Not John Fitch," *Virginia Magazine of History and Biography* 40 (1932): 14–22 and 124–32. Frank D. Prager reviewed the Fitch-Rumsey dispute in "The Steamboat Pioneers before the Founding Fathers" and "The Steamboat Interference, 1787–1793" in the *Patent Office Society Journal* 37 (1955): 486–522 and 40 (1958): 611–43. James Thomas Flexner, *Steamboats Come True* (1944; repr. 1978, 1992) remains the best overall account. More recent insights are offered in Edwin T. Layton, "James Rumsey: Pioneer Technologist," and Brooke Hindle, "James Rumsey and the Rise of Steamboating in the United States," both in *West Virginia History* 48 (1989): 7–32 and 33–42.

NEIL L. YORK

RUMSEY, Mary Harriman (17 Nov. 1881–18 Dec. 1934), social reformer and consumer activist, was born Mary Williamson Harriman in New York City, the daughter of Edward Henry Harriman, a railroad financier, and Mary Williamson Averell. She enjoyed a comfortable childhood that included private schooling and vacations at her family's ranches in the West, living most of the year in New York City and at "Arden," the family's country estate in Ramapo Hills, New Jersey. A buoyant and animated personality who mixed intensity with humor, Mary maintained a close relationship with her father, who shared with her his plans for railroad expansion as he acquired the Union Pacific and Southern Pacific railroad systems.

Despite these privileges, Mary developed a keen social conscience. In 1898, when she traveled with her father and sister on a special train to inspect the Union Pacific system, she came into contact with a large swath of American life outside her privileged milieu. She later wrote that from an early age she "began to realize that competition was injuring some" and "dreamed of a time when there would be more cooperation, not only among the people themselves but also between the government and the people" (*New York Times*, 19 Dec. 1934).

After hearing Professor Vida Scudder of Wellesley appeal to young people to work in poor immigrant neighborhoods, Mary and her friend Nathalie Henderson led eighty-five New York debutantes in 1901 to form the Junior League for the Promotion of Settlement Movements (later the Junior League of New York) to promote voluntarism as a means of expressing the idea that "privilege carried with it a responsibility to the community" (*New York Times*, 12 Mar. 1961). Mary and her friends at Barnard College raised $1,500 at a benefit for the College Settlement House on Rivington Street and worked with children at the settlement. The Junior League rose to national stature and has continued to provide upper middle class women with opportunities to engage in social service.

Although wealthy young women did not usually attend college, Mary's activism led her to enter Barnard College, graduating in biology and sociology in 1905. Her biology studies led to such a strong enthusiasm for eugenics that her classmates nicknamed her "Eugenia." Her ties with Barnard remained strong: she served as a trustee from 1911 until her death. After her father's death in 1909, she successfully managed the family's dairy herd at Arden while pursuing her interest in eugenics by experimenting with cattle breeding. She encouraged her mother's philanthropic activism, particularly her financing of the Eugenics Records Office in Cold Spring Harbor, Long Island. In 1910 she married Charles Cary Rumsey, a Harvard graduate and sculptor from Buffalo who had been employed in the redecoration of Arden; they had three children. Mary continued her interest in cattle breeding at one of their three family homes—a farm near Middleburg, Virginia.

During World War I Rumsey supported the war effort by serving in many defense and welfare organizations, especially the Community Councils of the United States Council for National Defense. After the war she kept the community councils alive in greater New York City, fostering their ability to promote parks, playgrounds, and swimming pools, to use schools as community centers, to improve housing conditions and transit facilities, and to lower public utility charges. Believing the local community was the most fundamental unit of democratic government, Rumsey also took an active part in the creation of commodity, community, and consumers' cooperatives such as the Eastern Livestock Cooperative Marketing Association and the American Farm Foundation. Her commitment to cooperation was deepened by reading *The National*

Being (1916) by the Irish poet and social reformer George Russell.

After her husband died in an automobile accident in 1922, Rumsey shifted her political loyalties to the Democratic party. She and her brother Averell (later a U.S. ambassador to the Soviet Union and a governor of New York) supported Alfred E. Smith's campaign for the presidency. During Franklin D. Roosevelt's terms as governor of New York, she became a close friend of Eleanor Roosevelt. After Roosevelt's election as president, he appointed Rumsey as the chair of the Consumers' Advisory Board of the National Recovery Administration in June 1933. On that occasion she explained that her father's era had been "a building age, when competition was the order of the day." But the present need "is not for a competitive but for a cooperative economic system" (*New York Times Magazine*, 6 Aug. 1933). She also defended positive government: "New ideas have come into being and the people are beginning to realize that government exists for their benefit, that it concerns itself with their well-being and that they can turn to it for assistance and help." Under Rumsey's leadership, the Consumers' Advisory Board protected cooperatives from price discrimination; within the board, in 1933 she formed the Bureau of Economic Education under Paul H. Douglas, a professor of economics at the University of Chicago. That same year Roosevelt subsequently appointed her as head of the Consumers' Division of the National Emergency Council. In Washington, D.C., Rumsey lived with Frances Perkins, who was the secretary of labor and the first woman cabinet member.

An expert horsewoman, Rumsey often won blue ribbons and was a frequent rider to hounds. Her sudden death in Washington was caused by pneumonia contracted during her recovery from broken bones incurred in a fall during a fox hunt. Eleanor Roosevelt and Perkins attended her funeral and escorted her body to the cemetery at Arden, New York, where she was buried next to her parents.

• Correspondence about Rumsey's cooperative ventures is in the Leland Olds Papers, Franklin D. Roosevelt Library, Hyde Park, N.Y.; correspondence about her activities in the National Emergency Council is in the National Archives, Washington, D.C.; and correspondence from 1934 is in the Sue Shelton White Papers, Schlesinger Library, Radcliffe College. For background on Rumsey's family life, see Persia Campbell, *Mary Williamson Harriman* (1960). See also two articles in the *New York Times*: S. J. Woolf, "Champion of the Consumer Speaks Out," 6 Aug. 1933; and Rhoda Aderer, "Junior League Will Mark 60th Anniversary in Big Time of Social Work," 12 Mar. 1961. The most complete account of her work in Washington is in Persia Campbell, *Consumer Representation in the New Deal* (1940). See also Sue Whelton White, "The County Consumer Councils and Their Service," *National Consumer News*, 25 Aug. 1935. A detailed obituary is in the *New York Times*, 19 Dec. 1934.

KATHRYN KISH SKLAR

RUNKLE, John Daniel (11 Oct. 1822–8 July 1902), mathematician and educator, was born at Root, a farming community in Montgomery County, New York,

the son of Daniel Runkle and Sara Gordon, farmers. The name Runkle goes back to castle Runkle near Limburg in West Germany. Runkle worked on the farm, educating himself as best he could, especially in mathematics. He taught at Onondaga Academy for three years, until 1847, when he had the opportunity to enter the newly founded Lawrence Scientific School at Harvard University. There he studied under the Harvard mathematician Benjamin Peirce, graduating in 1851 with a B.S. and an honorary master's degree. Through Peirce he then joined the recently established American Nautical Almanac Office in Cambridge, where he met several mathematically trained men, such as Simon Newcomb and Asaph Hall, both astronomers. Runkle became well acquainted with the Boston-Cambridge scientific circle and remained, in some form or other, in contact with the Almanac Office until 1884. In 1857 he was elected a fellow of the American Academy of Arts and Sciences. From 1858 to 1861 he edited *The Mathematician Monthly*, which, despite some outstanding collaborators such as Peirce and Newcomb, expired at the beginning of the Civil War.

In 1869 Runkle received a Ph.D. from Hamilton University and in 1871 an LL.D. from Wesleyan University. By this time he had found a new interest by supporting William Barton Rogers, who had come from Virginia to Boston in 1851, in his plans for an independent polytechnical school. Engineering education had, until this time, only been part of the curriculum of some schools, as for instance the U.S. Military Academy at West Point, or the Lawrence School. In 1861 a charter was obtained for a corporation for a school, Massachusetts Institute of Technology. Its secretary was Runkle, who in April 1862 notified Rogers that he had been elected president. In February 1865 MIT started classes; among them was a course in applied mathematics. The school soon obtained its new building on land reclaimed from Back Bay. This Rogers Building was the home of the so-called "Boston Tech" until 1916, when MIT moved to a new building in Cambridge, also on made land.

Runkle remained the right-hand man of Rogers, whom from 1870 to 1878 he replaced as president. Among his many achievements, apart from weathering the financial crisis of 1873, were the institution of laboratory instruction, first in mining and metallurgy; the creation of shop instruction, professional summer schools, and field excursions, such as one in 1871 to Colorado and Utah; and the admission of women students. The shop instruction was influenced by Russian methods that Runkle had admired at the Philadelphia Exhibition of 1876 and was recognized by a citation from the Moscow Technical School in 1878.

After a two-year absence, spent mostly in travel abroad, Runkle returned to MIT in 1880 and devoted much of his time to the teaching of mathematics. His *Technical and Industrial Education Abroad* appeared in 1881.

For Runkle, with his applied training at the Almanac Office, mathematics was subject to be taught primarily as an applied science, and he was known for his stimulating classes. A robust, venerable, and bearded figure, in skullcap, Runkle supplemented his lectures with quick questioning and good blackboard drawing. For many years, he, together with William Watson and George Osborne, were the only mathematics teachers at MIT.

Runkle resigned in 1901 and was succeeded as head of the mathematics section by Harry W. Tyler, who encouraged research while maintaining the excellent teaching traditions established by Runkle.

In 1851 Runkle had married Sarah William Hodges, who died childless in 1856. In 1862 he married Catherine Robbins Bird; they had six children. The family lived from 1870 to 1897 in Brookline, Massachusetts, where Runkle was active in civil affairs. They then moved to Cambridge. There exists a J. D. Runkle School in Brookline. Runkle died in South West Harbor, Maine.

• The MIT Archives possess manuscript material concerning Runkle. Biographical accounts include G. Dana, "John D. Runkle," *Proceedings of the Brookline Historical Society for 1953*, pp. 11–14; Benjamin van Doren Fisher, *The Runkle Family* (1899); Samuel Cate Prescott, *When MIT Was "Boston Tech," 1861–1916* (1954); and Harry Walter Tyler, *John Daniel Runkle, 1822–1902: A Memorial* (1902). For general background, see Robert V. Bruce, *The Launching of Modern American Science, 1846–1876* (1987).

DIRK JAN STRUIK

RUNYON, Damon (4 Oct. 1880–10 Dec. 1946), journalist and short-story writer, was born Alfred Damon Runyan in Manhattan, Kansas, the son of Alfred Lee Runyan, a printer and newspaper publisher, and Elizabeth Damon. In 1887 the family moved to the frontier mining town of Pueblo, Colorado, where Runyon's father worked as a typesetter for the local newspaper, the *Pueblo Chieftain*. Runyon's mother died the following year, and thereafter the boy divided his time between school and running in the streets with other tough kids. His irresponsible, alcoholic father was indifferent to his son's being a messenger in Pueblo's red-light district. Expelled from school in 1893, he ran errands for local papers and in 1895 became a reporter—as Alfred Damon Runyon—for the *Pueblo Evening Press* and then the *Evening Post*. A printer's error in his first byline caused his last name to be misspelled "Runyon." When the Spanish-American War began, Runyon enlisted—though underage, 5'6", with 5½ B shoes—in the Thirteenth Minnesota Volunteers. He served in Manila, in the Philippines, in 1898–1899 and wrote for two local periodicals and the *Chieftain* back home. He returned to Pueblo with lies about his participation in the battle of Manila, about being wounded twice, and about training troops in China.

Runyon partly wasted his next several years in binge drinking, sporadic newspaper work in Pueblo and elsewhere, and perhaps traveling and "jungling" with hoboes, until he got a job on the *Denver Post* (1905–1906) and—after a brief stint with the *San Francisco Post*—on the *Rocky Mountain News* back in Denver (1906). He covered business, crime, sports, and political events. He began to publish poetry and short stories, mainly about barroom and barracks life, in national periodicals such as *Collier's, Harper's Weekly, Lippincott's, McClure's, Metropolitan, Munsey's,* and *Reader Magazine.* Late in 1910 he moved to New York City and early the following year began writing sports columns—as Damon Runyon—for William Randolph Hearst's *New York American.*

His anecdotal coverage of the New York Giants' spring training in Texas in 1911 catapulted Runyon to fame. Later that year he married Ellen Egan, a former *Rocky Mountain News* society editor. The couple had two children. He published two books of Kiplingesque poems—*The Tents of Trouble: Ballads of the Wanderbund and Other Verse* (1911) and *Rhymes of the Firing Line* (1912); they concern, respectively, western misfits and cynical soldiers. From 1913 Runyon was featured as a humorist in the *American*, and in 1914 he also started a daily column in it called "Th' Mornin's Mornin'," comprising short-short stories, verse, and news items. His accounts of General John Joseph Pershing's pursuit of Pancho Villa in Mexico were syndicated by Hearst newspapers in 1916. In September 1918 Runyon went to Europe as a war correspondent. In 1919 the *American* began to carry "A Tale of Two Fists," Runyon's biographical series about Jack Dempsey, his friend from Colorado days.

In the 1920s Runyon habitually spent whole nights on Broadway nattily dressed, drinking coffee (upwards of forty cups a day), talking with cronies, and gambling. Home after dawn, he wrote, often moodily. He neglected his wife, and they separated in 1924. In addition to doggerel and quasi-editorials, his columns included more rehearsals for short fiction—featuring baseball players, racetrack bookies, boxers, chorus girls, con men, gamblers and gangsters, loan sharks, policemen, society swells, touts, westerners, and others. One of his closest friends was the notorious criminal Arnold Rothstein. More legitimate ones included the columnists Arthur "Bugs" Baer, Gene Fowler, Walter Winchell, and the war hero Eddie Rickenbacker. Runyon's manner as well as his matter, however, was unique. Notable are his observant, play-it-safe narrators and their use of Runyonese "slanguage" and the first-person, historical present tense. For example, "The Brain Goes Home" begins thus: "One night The Brain [Rothstein] is walking me up and down Broadway in front of Mindy's Restaurant [based on Lindy's], and speaking of this and that, when along comes . . . " By this time, he commanded up to $5,000 per story. He started his Broadway stories with "Romance of the Roaring Forties" (July 1929, *Cosmopolitan*—starring columnist "Waldo Winchester"), and assembled one collection in *Guys and Dolls* (1931) and another in *Blue Plate Special* (1932).

Runyon sold many of his characters and plot sequences to the movies—eventually totaling seventeen—for ever-mounting fees. The most famous movies from his fiction are *Lady for a Day* (1933), based on

"Madame La Gimp" (*Guys and Dolls*), and *Little Miss Marker* (1934), making Shirley Temple famous and based on "Little Miss Marker" (*Blue Plate Special*). In 1934 Runyon took the first of several trips to Hollywood to work on the *Marker* film script. In 1935 he published *Money from Home*, his third story collection, and cowrote the Broadway hit *A Slight Case of Murder* with Howard Lindsay. Before his next book of stories, *Take It Easy* (1938), he had reached such heights of popularity that many of his innumerable columns were assembled as follows: *My Old Man* (1939), containing pronouncements of a shrewd, kindly father figure; *My Wife Ethel* (also 1939), with the blue-collar Joe Turp writing about his witty, manipulative wife; and *Short Takes* (1946, including parts of *My Old Man*), laced with antiestablishment cynicism.

In 1932, a year after his wife Ellen died, Runyon married Patrice Amati del Grande. His friend Jimmy Walker, mayor of New York, presided at the ceremony. Once again, however, work interfered with marriage and during World War II Runyon and his wife split up. (She divorced him in June 1946.) They had no children. Early in 1944 Runyon began a brave, unsuccessful battle with throat cancer. Thereafter, he wrote irregularly but did assemble a final collection of stories, mostly bitter, called *Runyon à la Carte* (1944). After desperate surgery, he could not speak and used pad and pencil to communicate. He died in New York City. A few days after his death Winchell broadcast a few sentimental words about him and appealed for funds to establish a Runyon Memorial Fund to fight cancer. Money poured in from all quarters. Milton Berle put on a telethon and raised $1 million in a single night. The fund grew into the Walter Winchell–Damon Runyon Memorial Cancer Fund.

Runyon was one of the most skillful reporters who ever lived. Some of his practices, such as the acceptance of gifts and betting tips from the people he covered, were condemned by journalists who followed him, but they were common in the journalism of his day. He seized upon the essential and dramatized it with humor, sometimes rollicking but more often bitter. His short stories, often grotesquely plotted, tingle with life and resonate with credible dialogue, highlighted by slang, odd syntax, and surprising turns; further, their message teases the reader in identifying with the doltish and the downtrodden, and often suggests that if the respectable rich and famous switched places with the sordid and the criminal, little would be different in this troubled country.

• Runyon's extant letters are mostly in the libraries at the University of California at Berkeley and at Temple University in Philadelphia. Several of his manuscripts are available at the New York Public Library. He (over)estimated his complete production at 90 million words. Damon Runyon, Jr., *Father's Footsteps* (1954), describes painful family relationships. Jimmy Breslin, *Damon Runyon* (1991), is a well-researched but unannotated and unindexed biography, with irrelevant anecdotes and fictional scenes and dialogue. John Mosedale, *The Men Who Invented Broadway: Damon Runyon, Walter Winchell and Their World* (1981), places Runyon and Winchell in the 1920s, 1930s, and 1940s. H. L. Mencken, *The American Language: An Inquiry into the Development of English in the United States*, 4th ed. (1936), suppl. 1 (1945), and suppl. 2 (1948), all mention Runyon as a word coiner. Norris W. Yates, *The American Humorist: Conscience of the Twentieth Century* (1964), praises Runyon for sympathizing with powerless Americans numbed by big business, government, labor unions, militarism, and the national debt. Jean Wagner, *Runyonese: The Mind and Craft of Damon Runyon* (1966), and Patricia Ward D'Itri, *Damon Runyon* (1982), are substantial critical studies of Runyon as philosopher and stylist. Abe Laufe, *Broadway's Greatest Musicals* (1969), discusses Abe Burrows's 1950 reworking of Runyon's *Guys and Dolls* for the stage. An obituary, with a portrait, is in the *New York Times*, 11 Dec. 1946.

ROBERT L. GALE

RUPP, Adolph Frederick (2 Sept. 1901–10 Dec. 1977), basketball coach, was born in Halstead, Kansas, the son of Henry Rupp and Ann Lichti, farmers. Among the first generation of coaches who shaped the modern game of basketball, Rupp absorbed the values of hard work and discipline from life on a Kansas farm and from his father, who died when he was nine. Rupp attended the University of Kansas, where he played basketball for the legendary coach Forest C. "Phog" Allen. Rupp did not have a distinguished playing career at Kansas, but he learned the game from one of its first great coaches. Rupp graduated in 1923 and launched his coaching career at the high school in Burr Oaks, Kansas. Between 1925 and 1930 he coached high school basketball in Freeport, Illinois, where he compiled an impressive winning record of 80 percent. Rupp married Esther Schmidt (year unknown); they had one child.

The turning point in Rupp's career came in 1930 when the University of Kentucky hired him to replace John Mauer, who left Kentucky for a coaching position at Miami University of Ohio. When Rupp began his college coaching career, basketball was a low-scoring game that stressed a deliberate style of play. Rupp favored a game that encouraged the fast-break offense and supported rules changes that increased the tempo of the game. For example, Rupp advocated the elimination of the center jump after every basket and the adoption of the rule requiring the offensive team to bring the ball across the half-court line in ten seconds. He quickly realized that a successful coach needed to recruit effectively and maintain good relations with the press. Rupp had the knack of fashioning an amusing anecdote, and his superstitions were legend. He always coached in a brown suit, which earned him the sobriquet the "Man in the Brown Suit."

Rupp enjoyed immediate success at Kentucky, where he was fortunate to have inherited three All-Americans, Ellis Johnson, Forrest "Aggie" Sale, and Carey Spicer. In his first two seasons in the Southern Conference, Kentucky's combined record was 30 and 5. After the 1931–1932 season Kentucky joined the Southeastern Conference (SEC). Kentucky was the SEC champion in the conference's first season and would continue to dominate the conference for the remainder of Rupp's career. In the 1934–1935 season Kentucky earned national attention when it played New York University in a Madison Square Garden college basketball doubleheader. Leroy "Cowboy" Edwards, who played only one year for Kentucky before joining the professional Oshkosh (Wisc.) All-Stars, led the Wildcats into this contest. In an extremely physical game, Kentucky lost 23–22 but had taken a big step toward establishing a national reputation. The game, with its rough play under the basket, also contributed to the momentum for the three-second rule adopted in 1936.

While Rupp favored interregional play, initially he enjoyed less success against midwestern and northeastern rivals than against Southeastern Conference schools. Notre Dame, for example, defeated the Kentucky Wildcats in their first seven meetings. It was not until the early 1940s that Kentucky established itself as a national power. Between the 1943–1944 and 1953–1954 seasons Kentucky set the standard for collegiate basketball success nationally. Rupp's teams won ten conference championships, one National Invitational Tournament, and three National Collegiate Athletic Association tournaments. One of Rupp's teams during this period, nicknamed the "Fabulous Five," won two NCAA titles (1947–1948, 1948–1949), and its starting five played on the 1948 U.S. Olympic basketball team, which included two three-time All-Americans, Ralph Beard and Alex Groza.

Rupp possessed a presence that earned him the title the "Baron of Bluegrass." As a coach he was a strict disciplinarian and a fierce competitor. He said of himself, "I know I have plenty of enemies but I'd rather be the most hated winning coach in the country than the most popular losing one." His primary objective was to win basketball games, and in forty-two years at Kentucky he won 876 games against only 190 defeats, more than any other NCAA Division One coach. During his career Kentucky won twenty-seven Southeastern Conference titles, one National Invitational Tournament, and four National Collegiate Athletic Association tournaments.

Along with its triumphs Rupp's coaching career also included scandal and controversy. In 1951 law enforcement authorities identified thirty-three players who took money from gamblers to control the outcome of almost ninety intercollegiate games. Five Kentucky players, including Beard and Groza, admitted taking money, and, as a result, Kentucky was among the schools prohibited by the Southeastern Conference and the NCAA from playing any intercollegiate games during the 1952–1953 season. While the National Basketball Association permanently banned Groza and Beard, Herman L. Donovan, president of the University of Kentucky, held that Rupp violated no rules and bore no responsibility for the conduct of his players.

A quirk in the NCAA selection process and the basketball scandals may have robbed Kentucky of additional NCAA titles. Although Kentucky won the SEC championship in 1949–1950, at this time a conference title did not bring an automatic invitation to the NCAA tournament. In this year North Carolina State received the district bid so that Kentucky lost its chance for its third straight title. The Wildcats won their third NCAA title in 1951, lost in the NCAA Eastern Regional finals in 1952, and in 1952–1953 just practiced and played intrasquad games.

The following year Kentucky won 30–0 but rejected an NCAA invitation when the NCAA declared that three stars, Cliff Hagen, Frank Ramsey, and Lou Tsioropolous, were ineligible to play in the postseason tournament. Although the players had not lost any regular season eligibility because of the suspension, by attending classes they had acquired enough hours to graduate so that the NCAA considered them graduate students by tournament time. The NCAA tournament champion in 1954 was La Salle, a team that Kentucky beat by thirteen points during the regular season.

Rupp coached nineteen years after the 1952–1953 suspension, and his teams continued to win almost 80 percent of their games. Despite this level of success, which would have been the envy of most coaches, Rupp was unable to duplicate the success of the middle part of his career. While he was able to win numerous conference titles, Rupp managed to win only one more NCAA national title, in 1958. That year Kentucky's team, dubbed the "Fiddlin' Five," featured Johnny Cox, Adrian Smith, and Vernon Hatton. Although this team was not as talented as some of Rupp's earlier teams, the members played well together and defeated Seattle University, which fielded the gifted Elgin Baylor, by a score of 84–72.

One of the explanations for Kentucky's failure in postseason tournament play after 1958 was Rupp's reluctance to recruit African-American basketball players who changed the style of play in the 1960s. Ironically, the most dramatic illustration of the significance of the African-American presence in college basketball came in 1966, the last time Rupp took a team to the championship game of the NCAA tournament. This squad, nicknamed "Rupp's Runts," did not have a black player. Outstanding teamwork and the excellent shooting of Louis Dampier and Pat Riley made this a group of overachievers. In the final game Kentucky met Don Haskin's unheralded Texas Western Miners (now the University of Texas at El Paso), which started five black players, a first in NCAA title history. Under normal conditions a final game between an all-white and an all-black team would have drawn great attention, but 1966 also began an extremely militant phase of the civil rights struggle in the United States with its appeal for black power. Given this background to the match-up, the game seemed almost anticlimactic, especially when Texas Western quickly established its superiority and cruised to a 72–65 victory. If there were any basketball experts who doubted the importance of recruiting black talent, this game most likely dispelled their doubts. Nonetheless, in his last six years at Kentucky, the only black athlete to play for Rupp was Tom Payne, who played one varsity season for Kentucky in 1970–1971.

After suffering through a 13–13 record in 1966–1967, Rupp's only season without a winning record, he concluded his coaching career with five twenty-plus victory seasons. In Rupp's last season, 1971–1972, Kentucky won the Southeastern Conference for the twenty-seventh time, and Kentucky students, fans, and friends embarked on a statewide campaign to change the mandatory retirement age of seventy to extend Rupp's career. Rupp supported these efforts and said that university administrators "can leave me with my team or . . . take me to the Lexington cemetery." He and his supporters failed to achieve their goal, and Kentucky selected one of Rupp's assistants, Joe B. Hall, to succeed him.

When Rupp died in Lexington he had already become a legend in basketball and in his state. He loved his adopted state, which paid homage to him by flying its flags at half-staff and declaring a day of mourning. Rupp made no apologies for his fierce desire to win and the tough discipline he imposed on his players to achieve his goals. Rupp was the prototype of the coach who prevailed in the fiercely competitive arena of college basketball. He said, "I knew when I came here that the only way I could be successful would be to go out and win these basketball games." He built a tradition at Kentucky that made the university and winning basketball synonymous.

• Burt Nelli, *The Winning Tradition: A History of Kentucky Wildcat Basketball* (1984), is the best source on Rupp. Neil D. Isaacs, *All the Moves: A History of College Basketball* (1975), also is useful. Dan Issel, *Parting Shots* (1985), provides interesting anecdotes. Charles Rosen, *Scandals of 51: How the Gamblers Almost Killed College Basketball* (1978), and Stanley D. Cohen, *The Game They Played* (1977), provide good overviews of the college basketball scandal, including material on Kentucky. See also Joe Gergen, *The Final Four* (1987). Sam Goldaper, "Adolph F. Rupp Dies: Tribute for Renowned Coach Scheduled Tonight," *New York Times*, 12 Dec. 1977, provides reaction to Rupp's death.

ADOLPH H. GRUNDMAN

RUPPERT, Jacob (5 Aug. 1867–13 Jan. 1939), brewer and baseball club owner, was born in New York City, the son of Jacob Ruppert, a brewer, and Anna Gillig. His paternal grandfather was a brewer from Bavaria and after coming to the United States became in 1851 the owner of the Turtle Bay Brewery, which became the basis for the extensive family brewing business. Born to wealth, Ruppert attended the Columbia Grammar School and passed entrance examinations for the School of Mines at Columbia University but did not enroll there. He later turned down an opportunity to attend the U.S. Military Academy at West Point. On the request of his parents, he entered the brewing business at age nineteen and began the ritual process of career advancement. Starting as a barrel washer, Ruppert moved upward through several positions and after four years became general superintendent while his father was on an extended overseas trip. The position became permanent, and within a few years he was a vice president.

In 1886 Ruppert joined the New York National Guard and served as a private until 1889. He was then appointed to the staff of Governor David B. Hill as aide de camp and promoted to colonel. He continued as senior aide to Governor Roswell P. Flower. He retained the nickname "Colonel" throughout the remainder of his life.

In 1898 Ruppert was named the Tammany Hall candidate for the U.S. House of Representatives from the Fifteenth Congressional District. He was elected to office as a Democrat from a Republican district and served four terms, from the Fifty-sixth through the Fifty-ninth Congresses (1899–1907). In 1907 he returned to New York and the family brewing business and was instrumental in expanding output, becoming one of the most respected brewers in the United States. In 1911 he was elected president of the U.S. Brewers Association; he served in this capacity until 1914. He would be elected to this position fifteen more times, the final time in 1938.

As Ruppert looked to diversify his investments he turned to real estate, the stock market, and baseball. In 1903 he was involved in negotiations to buy the New York Giants of the National League, and in 1912 he was approached by the Chicago Whales of the Federal League. Neither situation developed, but in 1914 he was approached with a solicitation to buy the New York Yankees of the American League. A week later he was introduced to Colonel Tillinghast L'Hommedieu Huston, who became Ruppert's partner in the purchase. After considerable negotiation and some difficulties, which led to the intervention of American League president Ban Johnson, the deal to purchase the Yankees was consummated for $450,000, or $225,000 per man.

Without a home ballpark—the Yankees played in the Polo Grounds, the Giants' home park—or any star players, the Yankees needed major revamping, which Ruppert engineered. While he added a number of talented players, Ruppert made three key personnel acquisitions: the 1918 hiring of Miller Huggins from the St. Louis Cardinals as manager, a decision that angered Huston, who was in Europe at the time; the 1919 purchase of Babe Ruth from the Boston Red Sox for $100,000 and a $350,000 loan to Red Sox owner Harry Frazee; and the 1920 hiring of Ed Barrow from the Red Sox, who as general manager presided over the building of the Yankee dynasty that would last for the next several decades.

In 1921 the Yankees won their first American League pennant; shortly thereafter the Giants forced the Yankees out of the Polo Grounds. A new ballpark, Yankee Stadium, was thus constructed on land owned by Ruppert. Located across the Harlem River from the Polo Grounds, the stadium opened in 1923 at a cost of $2.5 million. After repeated disagreements between Huston and Ruppert, meanwhile, Huston sold his half-share of the Yankees to Ruppert for $1.2 million in the winter of 1922, although announcement of the transaction did not come until May 1923, a month after the opening of the new stadium. At the time of

Ruppert's death the Yankees were valued at $7 million.

A perfectionist by nature, Ruppert demanded excellence from his players. He did not interfere with the day-to-day operations of the ball club, leaving that to his manager and general manager, but he personally conducted contract negotiations with his players. Under his leadership the Yankees built a formidable farm system, with Ruppert owning several minor league franchises. He also designed the Yankee pinstripe uniforms, in the hope that they would make Babe Ruth look thinner, and was among the first to endorse uniform numbers for players. During Ruppert's ownership the Yankees won ten American League and seven World Series championships.

Ruppert was deeply involved in the changing power structure of baseball in 1919 and 1920. He was instrumental in the hiring of Judge Kenesaw Mountain Landis as the first baseball commissioner, a move designed to reduce the power of Ban Johnson. Johnson and Ruppert had battled in the New York courts over Ruppert's purchase of Carl Mays in 1919 from the Red Sox while Mays was under suspension. Johnson voided the deal, and Ruppert successfully fought the decision in court. This led to Johnson's involvement in forcing the Yankees out of the Polo Grounds and his threats to confiscate the Yankee franchise from Ruppert. Ruppert contended that these events necessitated the hiring of Landis as much as did the Black Sox Scandal. In turn Landis broke the power of Johnson as American League president.

In addition to brewing and baseball, Ruppert invested heavily in real estate in New York City and added to his fortune during the worst years of the Great Depression. Ruppert took advantage of low prices to add a number of New York City real estate gems to his collection. His real estate holdings at the time of his death were estimated at $30 million. Among his other interests Ruppert was involved in a number of Catholic service organizations and was a member of several yacht and athletic clubs. He also collected art, rare books, jade, and Chinese porcelain; raised St. Bernards and Boston terriers for show; owned a racing stable; and had the largest collection of small monkeys in the world. He served as president of Astoria Silk Mills and was a director of the Alaska Industrial Company, the Yorkville Bank, and the Casualty Insurance Company of America. In 1933 Ruppert sponsored Admiral Richard Evelyn Byrd's second Antarctic expedition.

A lifelong bachelor, Ruppert died in his apartment in New York City. Babe Ruth was one of the last people who spoke to him before Ruppert slipped into a coma. Ruppert was a significant figure in New York City as a businessman, sportsman, and politician. As owner of the New York Yankees he built a baseball dynasty that dominated the game through and beyond his lifetime. He was a power figure in baseball's ruling circles and is regarded as one of the "new style" owners who made his money before entering the game rather than as a result of the game. The most significant of Ruppert's accomplishments, however, were the acquisition of Babe Ruth, who became a cultural icon in New York, and the construction of Yankee Stadium.

• The most useful source on Ruppert is the clipping file maintained by the archives of the *Sporting News* in St. Louis, Mo., which includes articles from both the *New York Times* and the *Sporting News*. There is also a clipping file at the National Baseball Library in Cooperstown, N.Y. Materials on Ruppert are also in Robert Creamer, *The Babe* (1974); Frank Graham, *The New York Yankees* (1943); Claire Hodgson Ruth, *The Babe and I* (1959); David Quentin Voigt, *American Baseball*, vol. 2: *From the Commissioners to Continental Expansion* (1969); and Tom Meany, *The Magnificent Yankees*, rev. ed. (1957) and *The Yankees: The Four Fabulous Eras of Baseball's Most Famous Team*, rev. ed. (1980). An obituary is in the *New York Times*, 14 Jan. 1939.

RICHARD C. CREPEAU

RUSBY, Henry Hurd (26 Apr. 1855–18 Nov. 1940), pharmacognosist and botanical explorer, was born in Franklin, New Jersey, the son of John Rusby, a country storekeeper and a farmer, and Abigail Holmes. John Rusby was an ardent abolitionist who maintained a station on the Underground Railroad, with young Henry helping to pass provisions to escaping slaves. Henry acquired an interest in plants at an early age from his mother, and a village schoolteacher encouraged his interest in botanical collecting. Rusby studied at the Massachusetts State Normal School and the Centenary Collegiate Institute (N.J.) and then taught for several years in country schools in Massachusetts and New Jersey. He also undertook the first of his botanical explorations, a field trip to the Southwest, to study the flora of the region in 1880, under the auspices of the Smithsonian Institution.

In 1882 Rusby entered the College of Physicians and Surgeons in New York City, transferring the following year to the University Medical College of New York University. His medical studies were financed in part by the sale of his extensive herbarium to Parke, Davis and Company. He was employed by that pharmaceutical firm as a botanist and pharmacognosist after he obtained his medical degree in 1884.

Parke, Davis and Company sent Rusby to Bolivia in 1885 to procure a supply of coca leaves, the local anesthetic properties of cocaine (derived from coca) having just been discovered. The supply of coca leaves that he collected was lost during a revolution in Colombia, but Rusby decided not to return home. Instead he organized a botanical expedition across South America in 1886 and emerged from the jungle at the end of the year with 45,000 specimens representing 4,000 species, many of them previously unknown to botanists. His adventures on this trip are recorded in his *Jungle Memories* (1933).

In 1887 Rusby married Margaretta Saunier Hanna, with whom he had three children. Two years later he was appointed professor of materia medica (and soon thereafter botany and physiology as well) at the New York College of Pharmacy, which became affiliated with Columbia University in 1904. Rusby served as dean of the college from 1901 to 1930, remaining on the faculty until his retirement in 1932. He also served as professor of materia medica at the Bellevue Hospital and New York University Medical College from 1897 to 1902.

Over the years Rusby made several more trips to Latin America. He surveyed Mexican forests for rubber supplies after a new source of rubber was discovered there in 1909 and searched for new sources of quinine in Colombia in 1916. Rusby's last trip was made in 1921–1922 under the sponsorship of the pharmaceutical firm H. K. Mulford; poor health forced him to return ahead of the rest of the party. His explorations contributed about 1,000 new species to the known flora of the regions that he covered.

As an educator, Rusby was at the forefront of the campaign to raise entrance standards for schools of pharmacy. He was the coauthor, with A. Richard Bliss, Jr., and Charles Ballard, of an important textbook, *The Properties and Uses of Drugs* (1930).

Rusby's concern about the adulteration of drugs led him to serve on the revision committees of the *United States Pharmacopoeia* and the *National Formulary* and to consult part time as a specialist in pharmacognosy for the Bureau of Chemistry of the Department of Agriculture from 1907 to 1916. The bureau, led by Harvey Wiley, was charged with the enforcement of the 1906 Pure Food and Drugs Act, and Rusby was assigned to inspect the drugs arriving at the Port of New York. In 1911 Wiley's opponents stimulated a congressional investigation of the bureau chief for supposed misappropriation of funds. Wiley and Rusby were charged with conspiring to pay the latter more than he was entitled to by law, but they were both acquitted.

Several other controversies involving commercial products in some way earned Rusby the criticism of the American Medical Association. Although there is no evidence that he was acting on financial motives in any of these instances, and in at least one case his name and picture appear to have been misused in an advertisement for a particular product, Rusby's reputation no doubt suffered from these affairs.

However, Rusby's contributions to the pharmaceutical field were recognized. He was elected president of the American Pharmaceutical Association in 1909, and he received the prestigious Remington Medal in 1923 and the Hanbury Memorial Medal in 1929. He died in Sarasota, Florida. His botanical explorations and publications were responsible for bringing to light many new species and their properties, and his strong commitment to high standards for drug quality and for pharmaceutical education contributed to improvements in these areas.

• The Kremers Reference Files in the F. B. Power Pharmaceutical Library, University of Wisconsin, Madison, contain a small amount of manuscript material related to Rusby and his research on plants, in addition to copies of many of his publications. For a selected bibliography of his works, in addition to biographical information, see Susan Rossi-Wilcox, "Henry Hurd Rusby: A Biographical Sketch and Selectively Annotated Bibliography," *Harvard Papers in Botany* 4 (1993): 1–30. Useful biographical references include Curt Wimmer, *The College of Pharmacy of the City of New York* (1929), and George Bender, "Henry Hurd Rusby: Scientific Explorer, Societal Crusader, Scholastic Innovator," *Pharmacy in History* 23 (1981): 71–85. On the controversies in which Rusby became involved, see Rossi-Wilcox, "Henry Hurd Rusby's Alleged 'Commercial Ventures,'" *Pharmacy in History* 37 (1955): 87–93, and Charles Jackson, "The Ergot Controversy: Prologue to the 1938 Food, Drug, and Cosmetic Act," *Journal of the History of Medicine and Allied Sciences* 23 (1968): 248–57.

JOHN PARASCANDOLA

RUSH, Benjamin (4 Jan. 1746–19 Apr. 1813), physician, professor of chemistry and of medicine, and social reformer, was born in Byberry Township, Pennsylvania, thirteen miles northeast of Philadelphia, the son of John Rush, a farmer and gunsmith, and Susanna Hall Harvey. John Rush died when Benjamin was five years old. His mother ran a grocery store to support the family. She sent Benjamin at age eight to live with an uncle by marriage, the Reverend Dr. Samuel Finley, in Nottingham, Maryland. Finley, a pastor and headmaster of an academy there, saw to it that Benjamin received an education. Rush entered the College of New Jersey (now Princeton) in 1759. There Rush received the A.B. degree in 1760 at age fourteen. On returning to Philadelphia, Rush came into contact with some of the most prominent American physicians of the time. From 1761 to 1766 Rush apprenticed under John Redman and attended the first lectures of John Morgan and William Shippen at the newly founded College of Philadelphia. During these years Rush also began his lifelong habit of regularly making entries in his *Commonplace Book*, including notes that later afforded the only written eyewitness account of the 1762 yellow fever epidemic in Philadelphia.

In 1766, at Redman's urging, Rush left British North America to continue his medical education at the University of Edinburgh, then one of the most renowned medical schools in Europe. At Edinburgh Rush attended lectures of eminent scholars such as the chemist Joseph Black and the celebrated anatomist Alexander Monro *secundus*. More important, Rush became the disciple and friend of the highly respected William Cullen, who profoundly influenced Rush's theoretical approach to medicine. Meanwhile, back in Philadelphia, Rush was elected to the American Philosophical Society; he would eventually serve as its vice president. Rush brought his chemistry training to bear on his thesis, "On the Digestion of Food in the Stomach" (1768), written in classical Latin and based in part on self-experimentation. After receiving his medical degree in 1768, Rush spent several months training at St. Thomas's Hospital in London. Residence there also afforded Rush the opportunity to attend dissections by William Hunter and to see Benjamin Franklin, who was then in London. Franklin persuaded Rush to take, and partially financed, a trip to France early in 1769, where he met French physicians, scientists, and literati.

Having studied medicine for nine years, on returning to Philadelphia in the summer of 1769 Rush immediately began his practice. Because he had few contacts among the well-to-do, at first he treated mainly the poor. Fortunately, Redman had encouraged him to prepare for a faculty opening in Philadelphia while still in Edinburgh. On 1 August the College of Philadelphia appointed him professor of chemistry, the first native-born American to hold such a position. The following year, Rush published *A Syllabus of a Course of Lectures on Chemistry*, the first American text on chemistry.

In January 1776 Rush, aged thirty, married Julia Stockton of Princeton, aged seventeen. Rush had known Julia and her father Richard, a judge and future co-signer of the Declaration of Independence, since his adolescence. Their marriage lasted until Rush's death.

On 20 July 1776 the constitutional convention of Pennsylvania voted to send a less conservative delegation, which included Rush, to represent Pennsylvania in Congress. On 22 July Rush took his seat in the Second Continental Congress and on 2 August signed the Declaration of Independence. Rush soon also was sitting on the medical care committee. He lost his seat in February 1777 but was commissioned surgeon general of the Middle Department of the Continental army in April.

It was not long before Rush became outraged at the disorganization and corruption plaguing army hospitals. Not one to suffer incompetence quietly, Rush repeatedly expressed his dissatisfaction with the situation to his superiors and later to their superiors and to Congress. Finally, as the result of events stemming from an unsigned letter to Governor Patrick Henry of Virginia that General George Washington attributed to Rush and considered evidence of disloyalty, in late January 1778 Congress accepted Rush's resignation from the army.

Disillusioned, Rush soon resumed his practice and professorship in Philadelphia. He now turned his attention almost exclusively to medicine. In 1780 he began lecturing at the new University of the State of Pennsylvania. From 1784 until his death Rush served as surgeon to the Pennsylvania Hospital, assuming responsibility in 1787 for its insane patients. There he began advocating changes to humanize psychiatric treatment.

In 1786, to provide medical care for the poor, Rush set up the Philadelphia Dispensary, the first such institution in the United States and likely modeled on dispensaries that Rush had seen in London. Committed to high standards of medical practice, Rush also helped start the College of Physicians of Philadelphia in 1787.

Rush had not entirely lost his taste for state and national politics, however. In 1787 Rush was elected to the Pennsylvania ratifying convention for the new federal Constitution, and he and James Wilson led the movement for adoption. Two years later the same two men mounted a successful campaign to make over the Pennsylvania constitution, the last time that Rush engaged in state or national politics.

In 1789 the trustees of the College of Philadelphia elected Rush professor of theory and practice of medicine. After the college merged with the University of the State of Pennsylvania in 1791 to become the University of Pennsylvania, Rush held the chair of the Institutes of Medicine and Clinical Practice. In 1796 he assumed the chair of Theory and Practice of Medicine.

The conceptual foundation of Rush's medical practice drew on Cullen's system and that of John Brown, who had studied under Cullen with Rush in Edinburgh. Whereas traditional medical doctrine had based diagnosis and treatment largely on changes in balance among the bodily humors, Cullen emphasized nervous energy and stimulation of the nervous system. Brown believed disease to be caused by either excessive or inadequate nervous stimulation. Thus, excess stimulation required therapeutic depletion by purging, puking, or bloodletting, whereas a deficit called for stimulation from diet or brandy.

Rush reduced Brown's bipolar etiology to a single cause. "I will say there is but one disease in the world," he later announced. "The proximate cause of disease is irregular convulsive or wrong action in the system affected" ("Lectures on the Practice of Physic," mss., vol. 1, no. 31 [1796], library of University of Pennsylvania). Rush's unitary theory of disease held that the "excited" nervous state characterizing all life had only two forms: healthy and morbid. For Rush, morbid excitement from convulsive action in the blood vessels, which caused symptoms ranging from fever to insanity, required immediate depletion to restore the body's balance.

Rush's therapeutic theories would soon be severely tested. The yellow fever epidemic of 1793 in Philadelphia struck harder than any of the six such epidemics before it. From early August until November, between 4,000 and 5,000 residents of Philadelphia, or about one-tenth of the population, died from it.

As the epidemic worsened, Rush grew desperate. Nothing he tried seemed to work. Then, in late August, Rush happened to reread a 1744 manuscript written by John Mitchell, a Scots physician who had experienced the 1741 yellow fever epidemic in Virginia and who urged strong purges for even the weakest patients. Rush accordingly began "depletion" treatments consisting of heavy doses of purgatives complemented with bloodletting and applications of cold water. Believing that American diseases were more virulent than those in the Old World and thus justified more dramatic interventions, Rush bled some patients two and three times in a single day, often removing more than a pint of blood per treatment. Some physicians and historians later referred to Rush's regimen as "heroic" therapy.

Rush found his system highly effective, especially when employed early. "At no period of the disease did I lose more than one in twenty of those whom I saw on the first day, and attended regularly through every stage of the fever" (*An Account of the Bilious Remitting Yellow Fever, as It Appeared in the City of Philadelphia, in the Year 1793* [1794]). Twice during the epidemic Rush himself fell ill with fever, which he treated with bloodletting and purgatives and from which he recovered quickly.

When the epidemic lifted, stories of Rush's untiring devotion to his patients, while other physicians were fleeing the city, made him a popular hero. Yet a few lay persons and a number of Rush's professional colleagues accused him of applying his therapy indiscriminately and excessively. The newspaper editor William Cobbett later called Rush's practice "one of those great discoveries which have contributed to the depopulation of the earth" (*The Rush-Light*, 28 Feb. 1800). Rush's continued use of his therapy in later yellow fever epidemics excited such antagonism between him and the College of Physicians that he resigned from the body and nearly left Philadelphia for New York.

Rush also made a number of professional enemies during bitter debates within Philadelphia's medical ranks when he defended unpopular theories on the origins and transmission of the disease. Rush's insistence, for instance, that yellow fever arose from putrid matter left in the open rather than from contagion angered many proud Philadelphians.

As Rush continued practicing, teaching, advocating social reforms, and writing after the yellow fever epidemic, his renown grew even faster. From 1797 to 1813 Rush served as treasurer of the U.S. Mint. His interest in the medical relationship between mind and body prompted publication of *Medical Inquiries and Observations upon the Diseases of the Mind* in 1812, one of the first important American works on psychiatry, which was reprinted four times by 1835.

In the spring of 1813 Rush fell ill with a fever and died five days later in his home in Philadelphia. A firm believer to the last in his therapeutic approach, Rush had himself bled twice during his final illness. His friends Thomas Jefferson and John Adams, among others, eulogized him. His wife, three daughters, and six sons survived him. (His four other children had died in infancy.)

Writing prolifically over nearly half a century, Rush was the first American physician to become widely known at home and abroad. More than any other physician, Rush established the reputation of Philadelphia as a center for medical training. Moreover, by challenging the complex nosology of the day (Cullen distinguished among nearly 1,400 diseases), Rush moved medicine toward diagnoses and treatment regimens that were more comprehensible and manageable. He also encouraged the use of hypotheses in medicine (although he showed considerably less rigor about testing them experimentally). His drive to understand mental illness and render the treatment of mental patients more humane earned Rush the title "father of American psychiatry."

Rush's stature elevated the study of medicine in the United States. His position as educator gave him far-reaching influence in the American medical profession. Rush's son James later maintained that in forty-four years of teaching his father had instructed some 3,000 public and private medical students. These students carried Rush's ideas throughout the country. Rush was also one of the first to promote the study of veterinary medicine in North America.

Rush the politician was active mainly in three areas. A member of the Continental Congress, he unequivocally supported independence from Britain. He worked to see that the United States and Pennsylvania both adopted liberal constitutions. Rush helped found and govern Dickinson College (1783) in Carlisle and Franklin and Marshall College (1787) in Lancaster, Pennsylvania. He campaigned to make public schools free, broaden education for women, and create a school system culminating in a national university.

Rush's professional and political prominence—among his friends he numbered Jefferson, John Adams, Franklin, Thomas Paine, and Patrick Henry—no doubt brought attention to his social reforms. His lifelong stance against slavery, including his participation in and later presidency of the Pennsylvania Society for Promoting the Abolition of Slavery, helped free many slaves. Rush also deemed public punishments, then common, to be counterproductive, and he proposed private confinement, labor, solitude, and religious instruction for criminals. His outspoken opposition to capital punishment figured in the decision of the Pennsylvania legislature to abolish the death penalty for all crimes other than first-degree murder. For his advocacy of temperance in the use of "spirituous liquors," Rush became known as the "instaurator" of the American temperance movement.

By the late nineteenth century, harsh views of Rush as benighted bloodletter and enemy of Washington were giving way to favorable reappraisals of the contributions of the "American Sydenham" to medicine and politics. It is now clear, for example, that Rush did not originate "heroic" therapy so much as passionately advocate aggressive treatments that had prevailed elsewhere for centuries. Indeed, it is no doubt Rush's very contradictions—"polished yet contentious; a nonconformist and a conservative; a good observer but a poor reasoner; religious and materialist" (George Corner, "The Character of Benjamin Rush," *Western Journal of Surgery, Obstetrics and Gynecology* 56, no. 3 [1948])—that assure him so prominent a place in the American pantheon.

• Manuscripts of Rush's voluminous writings may be found at the Historical Society of Pennsylvania, the College of Physicians of Philadelphia, the Ridgway Library in Philadelphia (founded by Rush's son James), and the Library of Congress. Rush collected what he saw as his most important writings in *Medical Inquiries and Observations* (4 vols., 1805). For an idea of Rush's pedagogy, see *Sixteen Introductory Lectures* (1811). George W. Corner has edited Rush's *Travels through Life*, which Rush intended for his children and not for publication, and his commonplace books in *The Autobiography of Benja-*

min Rush (1948), which includes appendices on Rush's medical theories and his offspring.

Two edited collections of Rush's works also deserve attention: Letters, ed. Lyman H. Butterfield (2 vols., 1951), and *The Selected Writings of Benjamin Rush*, ed. Dagobert D. Runes (1947). A thorough compilation of works by and about Rush can be found in the earliest full biography, Nathan G. Goodman, *Benjamin Rush: Physician and Citizen 1746–1813* (1934), and the more recent Claire G. Fox et al., *Benjamin Rush, M.D.: A Bibliographic Guide* (1996).

Among the most important secondary sources is the authoritative biography by Carl Alfred Lanning Binger, *Revolutionary Doctor: Benjamin Rush, 1746–1813* (1966). Specialized portraits are available in Harry Gehman Good, *Benjamin Rush and His Services to American Education* (1918), and Donald J. D'Elia, *Benjamin Rush, Philosopher of the American Revolution* (1974). For assessments of Rush's progressive views on mental illness, see Richard Harrison Shryock, "The Psychiatry of Benjamin Rush," *American Journal of Psychiatry* 101 (1945): 429–32, and E. T. Carlson and M. M. Simpson, "The Definition of Mental Illness: Benjamin Rush (1746–1813)," *American Journal of Psychiatry* 121 (1964): 209–14.

Finally, two articles that examine changes in historiographic interpretations of Rush's life and practice are Shryock, "The Medical Reputation of Benjamin Rush: Contrasts over Two Centuries," *Bulletin of the History of Medicine* 45, no. 6 (Nov.–Dec. 1971): 507–52, and Robert B. Sullivan, "Sanguine Practices: A Historical and Historiographical Reconsideration of Heroic Therapy in the Age of Rush," *Bulletin of the History of Medicine* 68, no. 2 (June 1994): 211–34.

ROBERT B. SULLIVAN

RUSH, James (15 Mar. 1786–26 May 1869), physician, was born in Philadelphia, Pennsylvania, the son of Benjamin Rush, a prominent physician and signer of the Declaration of Independence, and Julia Stockton, daughter of Richard Stockton, a New Jersey lawyer and also a signer of the Declaration. James Rush graduated from the College of New Jersey (later Princeton) in 1805. He received his medical education at the University of Pennsylvania Medical School and graduated with an M.D. degree in 1809. He then went to Edinburgh and London for additional medical studies but spent as much time in the study of philosophy.

Rush returned to Philadelphia in 1811 and began his medical career as a general practitioner, also serving as a preceptor for medical students. After Benjamin Rush's death in 1813 James Rush read his father's written lectures on the institutes and practice of medicine at the University of Pennsylvania Medical School, but he discontinued the practice in 1816 when only his private students attended the sessions. Rush blamed his failure to keep and attract students on the university and its "aristocratic tyranny."

In 1819 Rush married Phoebe Ann Ridgway, the daughter of Jacob Ridgway, a wealthy Philadelphia Quaker merchant. She became a leader in Philadelphia society, and Rush was personable and well-to-do; the childless couple spent much time in social activities and travel until Phoebe's death in 1857.

In spite of his father's reputation, his own training, and his social standing, Rush never occupied a teaching position at any of the medical schools in Philadelphia. In 1826 he was considered for the position of professor of the theory and practice of physic at the Jefferson Medical College, but the board of trustees accepted another physician for the post. On 1 November 1831 Rush and his brother William were appointed professor and adjunct professor, respectively, of the theory and practice of medicine by the Jefferson Medical College. No doubt James Rush remembered the earlier snub, and they both declined the offer. In 1827 Rush accepted membership in the American Philosophical Society but resigned ten days later when he was informed that a physician with whom he had personal differences was also elected.

After ten years as a general practitioner, Rush began to devote more of his time to the pursuit of various avocations—the life of Napolean, ancient Egyptian history and African-American history—in addition to his writing and scientific interests. In 1827 he published *The Philosophy of the Human Voice*, which at the time was said to be the most advanced medical study of the human voice; it included a detailed exposition of elocution. Of little interest to the modern reader, in the age of grandiose oratory it was a popular book and went through six editions by 1867. In 1834 Rush published *Hamlet, a Dramatic Prelude in Five Acts*, which one librarian said was "not to be confused with a play of similar title by another author." During his student days in Scotland and England and his formative years in the medical profession, and perhaps influenced by the work of his father in psychiatry, Rush had developed an interest in psychology. With the death of his wife in 1857, he withdrew from society and returned to his earlier study of the human mind. In 1865 he published the two-volume *Brief Outline of an Analysis of the Human Intellect*, a learned and original but circumlocutory and difficult work, of interest as an early American contribution to the study of psychology as an objective science. His last book, *Rhymes of Contrast on Wisdom and Folly* (1869), was an attack on the morality of the younger generation.

Rush died in his Philadelphia home, embittered and solitary. He left an estate valued at over $1 million to the Library Company of Philadelphia to establish the Ridgway Branch in honor of his wife's family. His will made the bequest contingent on many eccentric conditions. Every decade for fifty years the Library would publish 500 copies of each of his books, to be sold at cost; there were to be no cushioned seats for lounging readers; the Library would not contain everyday novels, mind-tainting reviews, controversial politics, scribblings of poetry and prose, biographies of unknown persons, nor daily newspapers. The library was designed to house 400,000 books. The plans included a memorial apartment to contain furniture, art works, and personal effects belonging to the Rush household, and the will decreed that the apartment was not be exposed to "vulgar curiosity." The Library Company was glad to accept the money but not the stipulations; after years of litigation the library was completed in 1877, and the following year the directors of the Library Company accepted the building.

The books of the Logan Library and the Library Company, and those donated by Rush, formed the Ridgway collection. The bodies of James Rush and his wife were placed in a crypt on the east side of the building.

The library was a gloomy edifice, poorly designed for its intended purpose. Because of its location and physical arrangement, few members of the Library Company used it as a lending library. Its collection of rare books was used primarily for research, and books for circulation were relocated to other facilities. In 1966 the Library Company built a new home for the collection, and the Ridgway Library building was converted into a community center.

It is difficult to assess Rush's contributions to the medical profession. Most modern writers have labeled Rush a "gloomy," "melancholy," and "cantankerous" person, which clouds an unbiased examination. E. Digby Baltzell, a modern sociologist and historian of Philadelphia society, claimed that Rush would not have been included in the *Dictionary of American Biography* had it not been for his "distinguished ancestry and extreme wealth." J. Thomas Scharf and Thompson Westcott, chroniclers of Philadelphia history, writing in the 1880s, referred to Rush as having "achieved a high reputation as a physician," and the *Philadelphia Ledger*'s obituary noted that his death ended a "long and estimable life."

• Rush's activities appear in the context of nineteenth-century Philadelphia history in Burton A. Konkle, *Standard History of the Medical Profession of Philadelphia* (1977); J. Thomas Scharf and Thompson Westcott, *History of Philadelphia, 1609–1884*, vol. 2; Frederick B. Wagner, *Thomas Jefferson University: Tradition and Heritage* (1989); and John F. Watson, *Annals of Philadelphia and Pennsylvania in the Olden Times* (1905). He is also mentioned briefly in E. Digby Baltzell, *Puritan Boston and Quaker Philadelphia* (1979), p. 354; and Whitfield J. Bell, Jr., *The Colonial Physician and Other Essays* (1977), pp. 227–29.

SAM ALEWITZ

RUSH, Richard (29 Aug. 1780–30 July 1859), statesman and diplomat, was born in Philadelphia, Pennsylvania, the son of Benjamin Rush, a physician and signer of the Declaration of Independence, and Julia Stockton. Rush graduated from the College of New Jersey (now Princeton University) in 1797, the youngest in his class. He then read law with William Lewis, a leading figure in Philadelphia legal circles, and was admitted to the bar in 1800. He soon built a thriving practice, gaining special recognition in 1808 for his successful defense of William Duane, editor of the *Aurora*, against the charge that he had libeled Governor Thomas McKean. In 1807 he made his first public appearance, delivering a powerful speech denouncing the attack on the USS *Chesapeake* by the British warship *Leopard*. In 1809 he married Catherine Elizabeth Murray. They had eleven children.

After a brief stint as attorney general of Pennsylvania, Rush accepted federal appointment as comptroller of the treasury in November 1811. He rapidly developed close relations with Secretary of the Treasury Albert Gallatin, President James Madison, and other leading Republicans. Soon he began to write unsigned editorials for the administration organ, the *National Intelligencer*. His Fourth of July oration at the Capitol in 1812, justifying the declaration of war against England, stressed the impressment issue (the forcible British seizure of crewmen on American ships) and the need to confirm national independence. One sentence captures the essence of his lifelong view of Great Britain: "From no other nation are we in danger the same way; for, with no other nation have we the same affinities, but, on the contrary, numerous points of repulsion that interpose as our guard."

In February 1814 President Madison offered Rush a choice between the offices of secretary of the treasury and attorney general, and Rush chose the latter. While attorney general, he edited, with the assistance of Joseph Story, a five-volume compendium entitled *The Laws of the United States* (1815) and wrote a lengthy essay, *American Jurisprudence* (1815), that described the American system of law as morally superior to all others. During this period, he became increasingly close to President Madison, and he was in the president's entourage during the battle of Bladensburg and Madison's flight from the capital.

In 1817, upon James Monroe's succession to the presidency, Rush became acting secretary of state, pending the return of John Quincy Adams from Europe. As acting secretary, he signed the Rush-Bagot agreement to limit naval armaments on the Great Lakes with the British minister, Charles Bagot, on 28 April 1817.

Appointed minister to Great Britain on 31 October 1817, Rush arrived in London in December and was received by the prince regent in February 1818. During his seven and a half years in Britain, his tactful and patrician manner ensured his welcome. His memoirs include numerous accounts of dinners with grandees and conversations with such men as Thomas Erskine, Henry Brougham, and Alexander Baring. However, he remained a nationalistic American, convinced of the superiority of his country and sensitive to British condescension toward it. He believed that, being grounded on aristocratic principles and avid for commerce, Britain would always follow policies basically hostile to the United States. His ability to mask such beliefs from the British with whom he dealt was a remarkable accomplishment.

In 1818 Secretary of State Adams directed Rush and Gallatin, then minister to France, to seek negotiations with the British on a broad range of subjects. After lengthy negotiations, a convention was signed on 20 October. Although it failed to settle the issues of impressment and American access to trade with the British West Indies, the convention extended for ten years the commercial convention of 1815, which ensured that the U.S. merchant marine would dominate the direct trade between Britain and the United States; arranged for arbitration of U.S. claims to compensation for slaves carried away during the War of 1812; and settled, to American advantage, the dispute over the rights of New England fishermen to ply their trade in the waters off the coast of British North America. On the Canadian-American boundary, the negotiators compromised by drawing the boundary from the Lake of the Woods along the forty-ninth parallel as far as the Rocky Mountains but leaving the Oregon Territory open to settlement by both nations. This, the most important Anglo-American settlement between 1815 and 1842, won unanimous Senate approval.

In 1819 Rush firmly and effectively presented to Lord Castlereagh, the British foreign secretary, the defense of Andrew Jackson's execution of two British subjects captured during his incursion into Spanish Florida. But Rush's greatest test came in 1823. The preceding year, despite British opposition, the European powers had authorized France to invade Spain in order to restore the full powers of the reactionary monarch Ferdinand VII. After the French invasion in the summer of 1823, reports spread that French forces might next be sent to Spanish America to suppress the colonial revolts against Spain. In August, George Canning, Castlereagh's successor as foreign secretary, proposed to Rush that they join in a formal warning against such action. Rush was strongly tempted to agree, but he suspected that Canning's motives were short-range and commercial. As the price of a joint declaration, therefore, he insisted that Britain extend diplomatic recognition to at least one of the rebellious Latin American countries. Since, for political reasons, Canning could not agree to this, the discussions ended in September. The foreign secretary turned, successfully, to unilateral negotiations with the French, and Rush reported developments to Washington, where his dispatches powerfully influenced deliberations leading to the Monroe Doctrine in December.

In May 1825 Rush left his London post to serve as secretary of the treasury in the administration of John Quincy Adams. As secretary, he strongly supported the "American System," which to him meant a nationalistic economy integrating and balancing the interests of agriculture, commerce, and industry. He favored internal improvements and support for manufacturing. He endorsed a protective tariff, stressing the "home market" argument, but he had no apparent role in framing the Tariff of Abominations of 1828, a protectionist measure that became an important electoral issue. In that year, he was vice presidential candidate on the Adams ticket and published pamphlets in an unsuccessful attempt to defeat Andrew Jackson. Alone among members of the cabinet, he supported Adams's decision, similar to that of Adams's father in 1801, not to attend the inauguration of his successor.

After Rush left office, leaders of the Anti-Masonic party asked him to be their candidate for the presidency in 1832. He issued several public letters denouncing the Masons but, despite Adams's urging, declined to run; he preferred to support Henry Clay, who, however, refused to renounce the Masons, and Adams, who had no stomach for another presidential race. Within a few years, Rush shifted to the Democratic party. Although he had learned of the usefulness of the Bank of the United States to the government while at the Treasury, he supported President Jackson's attack upon that institution and remained a Democrat for the rest of his life.

In 1835 Jackson appointed Rush and General Benjamin Chew Howard as commissioners to settle a boundary dispute between Michigan and Ohio; the endeavor failed. In July 1836 Jackson again sought Rush's assistance, this time to procure the release of funds bequeathed to the United States in 1829 by a wealthy Englishman, James Smithson, which were tied up in Britain's Court of Chancery. Smithson had requested that his fortune be used "to found at Washington, under the name of the Smithsonian Institution, an establishment for the increase and diffusion of knowledge among men." After long negotiations in London, Rush won a favorable settlement in 1838, converted the securities into specie, and with £104,500 ($508,000) in gold returned to the United States, where he took a leading part in discussions over the appropriate use of this windfall. He was substantially responsible for the formation of the Smithsonian Institution in 1846 and remained a Smithsonian regent until his death.

After several years of retirement, Rush accepted an appointment by President James Polk as minister to France in March 1847. In Paris, he quickly recognized the almost universal opposition to the regime of King Louis-Philippe but failed to anticipate the revolution of February 1848. When it occurred, however, he extended recognition to the new republican government without waiting for authorization, a course later endorsed by the administration. Rush watched with dismay the radicalism and political chaos that followed, the growing importance of Louis-Napoléon, and his election to the presidency in December.

In October 1849, recalled from office by the new Whig administration, Rush entered his final retirement. He became deeply concerned over the rising threat to the Union, placing the blame primarily on antislavery agitators, and in 1856 voted for James Buchanan. He died at his brother's home in Philadelphia.

Rush can best be described as an able lieutenant rather than a creative statesman. Aside from his vice presidential candidacy in 1828, he never ran for public office. However, he was not unwilling to take on responsibility, as was shown during his discussions with Canning in 1823 and by his unauthorized recognition of the French republic in 1848. In all of the offices he held, Rush proved diligent, capable, judicious, and, when necessary, firm. He rarely engaged in open controversy, one notable exception being in 1825 when he and the always quarrelsome John Randolph engaged in a fiery public argument following Randolph's statement that Rush's appointment to the Treasury was the worst since Caligula made his horse a consul. Never, while serving as a diplomat, did he show a loss of temper. Tall, lean, and almost bald since his youth, Rush presented a physical appearance appropriate to his manner, and his personality—friendly, even tempered, usually grave but sometimes gently witty—also suited his role.

• The Rush Family Papers are held at the Princeton University Library, and the Richard Rush Papers are at the Historical Society of Pennsylvania in Philadelphia. Rush's official correspondence is in the National Archives. His works include *Memoranda of a Residence at the Court of London* (2 vols., 1833, 1845), written with the avowed purpose of smoothing controversies between Great Britain and the United States, and *Occasional Productions, Political, Diplomatic, and Miscellaneous* (1860), which includes an acerbic essay, originally published anonymously in 1827 in the *National Intelligencer*, describing George Canning as "of all British statesmen, the least disposed to do us justice" and a lengthy account of Rush's service in France. The only biography is J. H. Powell, *Richard Rush: Republican Diplomat, 1780–1859* (1942). For Rush's service in London, see Bradford Perkins, *Castlereagh and Adams: England and the United States, 1812–1823* (1964). His activities at the Treasury Department are mentioned in Mary W. H. Hargreaves, *The Presidency of John Quincy Adams* (1985).

BRADFORD PERKINS

RUSH, William (4 July 1756–17 Jan. 1833), sculptor and arts administrator, was born in Philadelphia, Pennsylvania, the son of Joseph Rush, a ship carpenter, and Rebecca Lincoln. At that time, Philadelphia was the seat of the colonial government and a principal shipbuilding and mercantile center. Rush showed an early ability at carving and drawing. As a teenager he served a three-year apprenticeship to Edward Cutbush, a carver from London, and soon made better figureheads than his teacher. Probably by 1774 he had his own ship-carving business. On 9 September 1777, soon after the outbreak of the Revolution, Rush joined the American cause and was commissioned an ensign in the Fourth Regiment of Foot of Lieutenant Colonel Wills's Philadelphia militia. Little else is known of his service. He married Martha Simpson Wallace on 14 December 1780; they had ten children. The eldest, John, became a ship carver and joined his father in business.

For the next thirty years William Rush carved figureheads and ship ornaments for merchant ships, especially those of Stephen Girard. He usually carved American subjects: Indians; heroes such as George Washington or Benjamin Franklin (1706–1790); historical figures such as Sir Walter Raleigh or Captain John Smith (1580–1631); and, for Girard, portraits of French philosophers including Voltaire. Rush's figureheads were much admired in American and foreign ports for their masterful carving and poses. By the time of the Grand Federal Procession on 4 July 1788 (celebrating both the anniversary of the Declaration of Independence and the ratification of the Constitution), Rush was a leader in his profession. For the procession he designed and executed the elaborate "federal car," which represented the contribution of the carvers and gilders. When Congress established the U.S. Navy on 27 March 1794, Rush was chosen to design and execute symbolic figureheads and other carvings for the six frigates to be built in Philadelphia and other ports.

The subjects he chose—Goddess of Liberty, Hercules, and the Washington eagle, for example—testify to the ideals of the young republic and his own patriotism.

On 29 December 1794 Rush joined a group of forty artists, including Charles Willson Peale, to organize an art academy, later called the Columbianum, a forerunner of the Pennsylvania Academy of the Fine Arts. Its purpose was to collect old master paintings and casts of antique statuary, establish classes, and hold art exhibitions, but the group was short lived. In 1801 Rush carved missing mastodon bones for a skeleton at Peale's natural history museum. On 16 October 1801 Rush was elected to the Common Council, serving on it or the Select Council until 1826. In 1805 he helped found the Pennsylvania Academy of the Fine Arts and served as a director until his death.

The Embargo Act of 1807 virtually ended the shipbuilding industry in Philadelphia, and Rush turned to other interests: creating sculpture for commission and exhibition, civic functions, and arts organizations. In 1808 he carved his first architectural statues, *Comedy* and *Tragedy*, for the Chestnut Street Theatre (Philadelphia Museum of Art). Rush served on the city council's Watering Committee, which, in response to the earlier yellow fever epidemics, built a waterworks at Philadelphia's Centre Square. In 1809 he carved one of his most notable works, *Allegory of the Schuylkill River*, a fountain of a woman and bittern for the waterworks grounds (pine head, Pennsylvania Academy of the Fine Arts; bronze cast of figure, on loan to Philadelphia Museum of Art). The critics of the day appreciated its elegant ornamental effect within the city and thought the female figure well executed.

The Society of Artists elected William Rush its first president in 1810 and the following year appointed him professor of sculpture. In 1811 he began exhibiting sculpture at the Pennsylvania Academy, which in March 1812 elected him academician, placing his name first on a list that included painters Thomas Sully, Benjamin West (1738–1820), and John Singleton Copley. In 1813 Rush assisted and supervised the academy's first class using live models. In 1812–1813 he produced a series of portrait busts in terracotta, including political leader Samuel Morris; physicians Caspar Wistar (1761–1818), Philip Physick, and his second cousin Benjamin Rush; and botanist Carolus Linnaeus. Like his contemporaries, including Jean-Antoine Houdon, Rush modeled his busts in clay, fired them, and then exhibited them to attract orders for plaster casts.

Rush was one of the earliest American sculptors to create busts of soldiers, statemen, and scientists for the libraries of middle-class gentlemen. His portraits were made from life or from memory. In 1815 he carved his most ambitious portrait, a full-length figure of George Washington (Independence Hall). All his wooden sculptures were painted white to simulate antique marble sculptures, anticipating the neoclassical style that was soon to prevail in America. Throughout Philadelphia Rush continued to produce commissions of crucifixes, angels, and eagles for churches, figures of the virtues for Masonic Hall, decorations for bridges, and designs for city parks.

In the 1820s he was on the city council committee that oversaw the waterworks expansion at Fairmount on the Schuylkill, and he and his son carved figures, *Allegory of the Schuylkill River in Its Improved State* and *Allegory of the Waterworks* (Fairmount Park Commission), for the millhouse entrances. In 1824 he was a founding member of the Franklin Institute. When the marquis de Lafayette visited Philadelphia on his grand tour, Rush was on the city council committee to organize activities. His figures *Wisdom* and *Justice* (on loan to Pennsylvania Academy) decorated the Grand Civic Arch erected for the occasion, and he produced a terracotta likeness of the general (Pennsylvania Academy). In 1825 Rush was awarded honorary membership in New York's American Academy of the Fine Arts.

Rush's masterpiece, his 1822 self-portrait (Pennsylvania Academy), sums up his life and career. His noble head emerges from a pine knot that serves as neck and shoulders; however, the work is not carved in wood, but modeled in clay. This switch from wood carving to modeling in clay is an important indication of Rush's transition from wood carver to sculptor, something most contemporary wood carvers did not accomplish. William Rush never went abroad for study or travel and rarely left Philadelphia, but he emerged as an extremely gifted craftsman and self-taught artist whose career flourished as a ship carver and then as a sculptor in a critical period in America's history. He died in Philadelphia.

• The best biography on William Rush, from which much of this material is drawn, is Linda Bantel, "William Rush, Esq.," in *William Rush, American Sculptor*, (1982). The book includes a revised genealogy by Susan James-Gadzinski. It updates the previous major study on Rush, Henri Marceau, *William Rush 1756–1833: The First American Sculptor* (1937). See also John F. Watson, *Annals of Philadelphia and Pennsylvania, in the Olden Time* (1830; repr. 1887, 1905); William Dunlap, *A History of the Rise and Progress of the Arts of Design in the United States* (1834; repr. 1969); Charles Henry Hart, "William Rush Sculptor and William Rush Publicist," *Pennsylvania Magazine of History and Biography* 31 (1907): 381–82; Pauline A. Pinckney, *American Figureheads and Their Carvers* (1940); and Wayne Craven, *Sculpture in America* (1968; repr. 1984). An obituary is in the *Philadelphia Gazette*, 18 Jan. 1833.

SUSAN JAMES-GADZINSKI

RUSHING, Jimmy (26 Aug. 1903–8 June 1972), singer and composer, was born James Andrew Rushing in Oklahoma City, the son of musical parents who ran a family luncheonette business. In addition to his mother and brother, who were singers, his father played trumpet well enough to be in the Oklahoma City Knights of Pythias Marching Band. A relative, Wesley Manning, resident pianist in a "gaming house," taught young Jimmy the basics of piano playing. The youngster even managed to pick up enough violin technique to claim that instrument as well. In fact, he first

thought of singing more as a hobby than as a profession. After finishing Douglas High School in Oklahoma City in 1921, Rushing attended Wilberforce University in southwestern Ohio for two years, where he participated in the school's outstanding choral program. In addition to a native intelligence and sophistication, he was a thoughtful and trained musician, one of the few professional band or cabaret singers of his era who could read music fluently.

Rushing was blessed with a remarkably accurate ear and a uniquely focused voice, a sound that could cut through a tangled band texture yet still project a pathos ideally suited for the blues. His vocal range was exceptionally wide (two octaves), and within that baritone-plus-tenor territory he exercised precise control. For this reason alone it is a pity that what one hears in many of his recorded performances, especially with bands, is limited to the high end of his tenor range. (For instance, the 1938 recording with the Basie band of "Sent for You Yesterday" winds through a narrow band of only about six notes.)

While only twenty, Rushing was singing professionally in California (on occasion to the accompaniment of Jelly Roll Morton), at the Jump Steady Club and at the Quality Club on Los Angeles's legendary South Central Avenue. But he returned to his hometown in 1925 to help his family run the luncheonette service for over a year. His next professional engagement was a tour with the Billy King Review, followed by brief stints with the traveling bands of Jay McShann and Andy Kirk.

Bassist Walter Page led the band for the King show. Rushing's association with him led to appearances for two years with the Blue Devils band, also led by Page. It was during this tenure that he first met and played with pianist William Basie, who, subsequently as the "Count," would play a dominant role in his career. When Basie and Page abandoned the Blue Devils to join the Bennie Moten band in Kansas City in 1929, Rushing went with them. He recalled frequently how the Moten band provided a new and exciting musical experience for him because of its unique rhythmic vitality, a quality he described as sounding "like a train a-comin'." His affiliation with that ensemble lasted until just after Moten's death in 1935. (Buster Moten kept the band working for a brief time following his brother's sudden death.)

The big turn toward success in Rushing's career began when he joined the new Basie Band in Kansas City. Consisting of no more than seven to eight pieces when it began its inaugural run at the Reno Club in 1935, the Basie group so prospered during its first two years that Basie could add personnel to bring the band into conformity with the norm that was developing in the country. A recording session for the band in 1937 ("One O'Clock Jump") lists thirteen players, including Basie. Rushing was featured singer with Basie until 1948 and even after that appeared frequently with the band as a guest singer until 1950, and sporadically even into the 1960s. He was one of the few real blues artists who occupied a headliner-vocalist role in the band world of the 1930s and 1940s, most organizations opting for straight ballad and/or "novelty" singers of a more pop-commercial persuasion. Rushing had begun his own professional life singing music of more pop-ballad orientation. He nonetheless claimed his first and greatest influences to have been Bessie Smith and Mamie Smith, dating back to their appearance at a theater in Oklahoma City in 1923.

Rushing's identity is dominated by his long association with the Basie Band, although after 1950 he enjoyed the success of an established solo entertainer. For two years he fronted, as singer, his own small band in the Savoy Ballroom in Harlem. Following that he made solo appearances throughout the United States and Canada, sometimes accompanying himself, at other times accompanied by a pianist or small instrumental group. European tours presented a new and especially lucrative performance source for American jazz artists following World War II, and Rushing made three. He first toured as a solo act, then as featured singer with the Benny Goodman band for the Brussels World's Fair in 1958, and as featured singer with a band led by trumpeter Buck Clayton in 1959.

Rushing was a popular participant at the jazz festivals in this country—mostly summer outdoor affairs that took root during the late 1950s—until ill health forced him into virtual retirement during the final year of his life. His later tours with groups covered a broad array of jazz styles. They included one with Harry James, another with the Benny Goodman Sextet, and in 1964 a tour to Japan and Australia with Eddie Condon. Back in New York in 1965, he filled an extended contract at the Half-Note, returning there during the early 1970s on a permanent weekends-only schedule, this capped by one brief string of performances in Toronto during early 1971. He died in New York, never having married.

This ebullient rotund figure, an original Mr. Five-by-Five, was one of the great blues singers of the first half of this century. With such artists as Bessie Smith, Joe Williams, Jack Teagarden, Billie Holiday, and later Ray Charles, he brought that genre into the mainstream of jazz, to become a national commodity cutting across the race lines that had confined it until the Great Depression.

• Of his own recorded work Rushing once told Nat Hentoff in a *Down Beat* interview that among his favorites were "I Want a Little Girl," "Take Me Back Baby," and "Mean and Evil," all with the Basie Band. Perhaps the best-known recording, and still readily available in the Smithsonian *Big Band Jazz* collection, is "Sent for You Yesterday." But this recording has him singing only two short blues choruses, the remainder an admirable collection of instrumental solos by other members of the band (Basie, Earl Warren, Herschel Evans, and Harry "Sweets" Edison), so not much of Rushing is heard. More thorough introductions to his artistry can be heard on singles such as "How Long Blues" (Vanguard), and "Gee Baby, Ain't I Good to You" (in a Columbia Records album titled *Cat Meets Chick*), and in other Basie oldies, such as the 1946 "Good Morning Blues" (Decca 1446) or the 1942

"I'm Gonna Move to the Outskirts of Town" (Columbia 3660).

The revealing interview of Rushing reported by Hentoff appeared in *Down Beat*, 6 Mar. 1957. The most informative discussion of principal details in his career can be found in Gunther Schuller's *The Swing Era* (1989), a less extensive coverage in Martin Williams's *Jazz Heritage* (1985); also see *Black Perspective in Music* (Spring 1974). A collection of blues songs, *Jimmy Rushing Sings the Blues*, composed by Rushing (with such illustrious cocomposers as Basie, Edison, Eddie Durham, and Tab Smith) was published in 1941.

WILLIAM THOMSON

RUSIE, Amos Wilson (30 May 1871–6 Dec. 1942), baseball player, was born in Mooresville, Indiana. The names of his parents are not known. Rusie grew up in central Indiana, where he played baseball, as he later recalled to an interviewer, "from the time I was able to toddle." While playing for a city league team in Indianapolis, the strapping 6'1" right-hander attracted the attention of the Indianapolis Hoosiers of the National League. Although he was primarily an outfielder, the Hoosiers decided to put his rifle arm to use by turning him into a pitcher. He made his professional pitching debut in 1889, a few days shy of his eighteenth birthday. His overall performance during his rookie year was less than impressive, as he won only 12 games and surrendered on average more than five earned runs per game. Nonetheless, when the Hoosiers folded after the 1889 season, the New York Giants were sufficiently impressed that they included Rusie with a number of other players whose contracts they purchased from the defunct club.

In New York, Rusie blossomed almost overnight into one of the league's top pitchers. Dubbed the "Hoosier Thunderbolt" on account of his blazing fastball, Rusie reportedly hurled the ball with such force that his catcher kept a piece of lead hidden in his glove to deaden the impact. His repertoire of pitches also included a hard-breaking curve that Rusie claimed to throw with only slightly less velocity than his fastball. From 1890 to 1894 Rusie averaged more than 32 wins a season and led the National League in strikeouts four times. An admiring John McGraw, who was then a member of the Baltimore Orioles, summed up the reason for Rusie's success when he quipped, "You can't hit 'em if you can't see 'em."

Rusie was feared not only for his speed but also for his wildness. In 1894 a stray pitch knocked Baltimore's Hughie Jennings out cold, leaving him dazed for days afterward. He led the league in walks every year between 1890 and 1894, setting a modern-day record for most bases-on-balls issued during a single season with 218 in 1893.

The 1893 season was the first to be played under the new rules that moved the pitcher five feet further from home plate, to a distance of 60'6". Team owners agreed to make the adjustment in the hopes of injecting more offense into the game and boosting fan interest. The new distance frustrated some pitchers, but Rusie took the change in stride. In 1893 he won 33 games while establishing modern-day marks for games started (52) and games completed (50). The following year he turned in an even more remarkable performance. The 1894 season saw National League hitters run wild, batting a collective .309 and knocking in close to six earned runs a game. Rusie, however, remained as overpowering as ever. He carried the Giants to a league championship on the strength of his pitching arm, winning 36 games during the regular season and two more in the postseason Temple Cup series. His league-leading earned run average of 2.78 was nearly a full run lower than his next closest competitor.

While Rusie had no trouble cowing opposing hitters, he was less successful in his confrontations with management off the field. He stayed with New York during the Brotherhood and Association Wars of 1890 and 1891. The Giants rewarded him handsomely for his loyalty, paying Rusie a salary of $6,200 for the 1891 season. After the demise of the Players League in 1890 and the merger of the National League with the American Association in 1891, however, team owners returned to the restrictive labor practices of the previous decade. Beginning in 1892 the owners resumed enforcing the notorious reserve clause, which bound a player indefinitely to the team that owned his contract. They also slashed salaries, placing a cap of $2,400 on player earnings by 1894. Rusie accepted the cut in pay, but he rebelled at the end of the 1895 season when the owner of the Giants, the imperious Andrew Freedman, fined him $200 for disciplinary reasons. Rusie charged that the fine was nothing more than a weakly disguised attempt at forcing him to swallow an additional salary reduction. Rusie sat out the entire 1896 season in protest. He also took his grievances to federal court, suing for damages and challenging the legality of the reserve clause. Before the case could go to trial, however, Freedman's fellow magnates intervened and negotiated a settlement. Rusie dropped the lawsuit and rejoined the Giants. In return, the other owners paid him a reported $5,000 as compensation for his lost income and legal expenses. While the outcome could be considered a limited victory for Rusie, the league owners still won the war. The reserve rule went untested, and clubs continued to exercise near dictatorial control over their players.

Rusie's one-year layoff had no appreciable effect on his skills. He enjoyed one of his finest seasons in 1897, winning 28 games and once again posting the best earned run average in the National League. A year later, however, Rusie injured his shoulder while making a snap throw on a pickoff attempt at first base. With his effectiveness diminished, Rusie retired after the 1898 season rather than agree to another salary cut at the hands of owner Freedman. He tried to return to baseball in 1901, pitching for the Cincinnati Reds, but his comeback lasted only three games. At the age of thirty, Rusie gave up the game for good.

Following his retirement Rusie worked in a variety of blue-collar jobs before settling in Washington state with his wife, Mary Smith, whom he had married in 1890; the couple had one daughter. He worked in Seattle as a steamfitter from 1911 until 1921, when John McGraw lured him back to New York by offering him a job as assistant superintendent at the Polo Grounds. In 1929 Rusie resigned his position and returned to Washington due to health problems. He purchased a five-acre chicken ranch near Seattle, where he remained until his death.

The premature close to his career probably prevented Rusie from attaining the enduring stature of some of the other early pitching stars like Cy Young and Kid Nichols. Nonetheless, he deserves to be remembered as one of the most dominating and durable pitchers of the 1890s. His peers certainly rated him highly. In the 1940s Clark Griffith ranked him as second only to Walter Johnson in terms of overall pitching greatness. During the course of his nine-year career, Rusie won 246 games and finished an astonishing 92 percent of his 427 starts. His single-season records for games started and completed in 1893 will almost certainly never be eclipsed so long as teams continue the practice established in the twentieth century of relying on four- or five-man pitching rotations and large relief staffs.

Rusie was also perhaps the first sports figure to capture the imagination of New York City. At the height of his popularity, a New York vaudeville team included a skit about him in their act, street vendors hawked a 25-cent pamphlet touting his pitching secrets, and a hotel bar named a cocktail after him. Final and more lasting recognition came in 1977, when the Veterans Committee elected Rusie to the National Baseball Hall of Fame.

• Brief accounts of Rusie's life and career are in many baseball reference books, such as Mike Shatzkin, ed., *The Ballplayers* (1990), and John Thorn and Pete Palmer, eds., *Total Baseball* (1989). James D. Hardy, Jr., *The New York Giants Base Ball Club* (1996), also provides information on Rusie's career in the context of the early history of the Giants organization. An interview in the Seattle *Sunday Times*, 9 June 1929, supplies Rusie's own recollections of his playing days, while a 1943 newspaper article reprinted in *From Cobb to Catfish*, ed. John Kuenster (1975), contains Clark Griffith's reminiscences about Rusie. Obituaries are in the *New York Times* and the *New York Herald Tribune*, both 7 Dec. 1942.

JEFF SEIKEN

RUSK, Dean (9 Feb. 1909–20 Dec. 1994), U.S. secretary of state, was born David Dean Rusk in rural Cherokee County, Georgia, the son of Robert Hugh Rusk, a former Presbyterian minister, small farmer, and schoolteacher, and Frances Clotfelter, a former schoolteacher. During his early boyhood, Rusk's family moved to Atlanta, where his father became a mail carrier. Rusk graduated from Boys' High School in Atlanta in 1925. He worked for two years as a general helper in a law office to earn money for his college education. In 1927 he entered Davidson College in Davidson, North Carolina, where he was elected to Phi Beta Kappa and graduated magna cum laude in 1931 with a bachelor of arts degree. He then attended Oxford University as a Rhodes Scholar, earning a master of arts degree in politics, economics, and philosophy in 1934.

His experience at Oxford had a formative impact on Rusk's subsequent view of the world. By the conclusion of his studies, Japan had invaded Manchuria, and Germany had withdrawn from the League of Nations and the Geneva Disarmament Conference. While at Oxford Rusk studied in Berlin, witnessing Adolf Hitler's rise and the turmoil in the streets as the Nazis consolidated power. In his memoirs, *As I Saw It* (1990), he described formal debates at Oxford on whether the British would fight for king and country. Rusk observed how overwhelming pacifist sentiment in Britain contributed to permitting Hitler a free hand in Europe and caused many Germans, including Hitler, to believe the British would not fight. The conclusion Rusk reached was that failing to check German aggression, Britain would later have to go to war to protect itself.

After returning from Oxford, Rusk became associate professor of government and dean of faculty at Mills College in Oakland, California. Concurrently, from 1937 to 1940, he studied international law at the University of California at Berkeley. In 1937 he married Virginia Wynifred Foisie, a former student and faculty member at Mills. They had three children.

An Army Reserve officer, Rusk was called to active duty in 1940 as an infantry captain, cutting short his law studies. Just prior to Pearl Harbor, because of his knowledge of the British empire, he was transferred to military intelligence and sent to the War Department. In 1943, promoted to major, he requested overseas duty and was sent to the China-Burma-India (CBI) theater to join General Joseph Stilwell's staff. There, after earning Stilwell's confidence, he was eventually appointed deputy chief of staff for war plans (G-3) and promoted to colonel. Upon his recall to Washington in June 1945, he served as assistant chief of the Operations Division of the War Department General Staff. Rusk's experiences with the Far East in World War II only served to reinforce impressions drawn from his earlier sojourn at Oxford "that if aggression is allowed to gather momentum, it can continue to build and lead to general war."

After his discharge in February 1946, Rusk joined the State Department at the invitation of newly appointed secretary of state George C. Marshall, who was familiar with his work in CBI and on the General Staff. At the State Department Rusk was appointed assistant chief of the Division of International Security Affairs and in the summer of 1946 went on to serve as special assistant to the secretary of war until March 1947, when he returned to the State Department as director of the Office of Special Political Affairs. In the spring of 1949 he was appointed deputy under secretary of state, remaining in that position only until March 1950, when he assumed duties as assistant secretary of state for Far Eastern affairs. At this time he became a dedicated anti-Communist and advocate of the containment policy in Asia while many at the State Department had a European focus. Indeed, he pushed for greater U.S. attention to Asia, and with his international outlook, he played a key role in formulating U.S. policy. When North Korean Communists invaded South Korea in June 1950, Rusk, believing both the Soviets and Communist China complicit, advised intervention and hardened his advocacy of containment based on the World War II lesson that aggression should not be rewarded.

Rusk left the State Department in 1952 to become head of the Rockefeller Foundation, directing the spending of more than $247 million to promote "the well-being of mankind throughout the World." During his tenure, which lasted until 1960, the foundation greatly expanded support of agricultural, public health, and social science programs in the underdeveloped nations of the third world, which he believed were "a time bomb for the entire human race."

In 1961 President-elect John F. Kennedy nominated Rusk as the new secretary of state, and Rusk was sworn in on 21 January. According to Arthur M. Schlesinger, Jr., in *A Thousand Days* (1965), Kennedy chose Rusk over more well-known candidates because he "wanted to be his own Secretary of State." Others agreed, and Rusk's own philosophy supported the concept of the secretary of state as adviser and the president as maker of foreign policy.

The new secretary was immediately confronted by crises all over the world: Communist rebels in Laos, the independence of South Vietnam threatened, friction between the United States and Cuba, strife in the Congo, and the need to strengthen the North Atlantic Treaty Organization (NATO). Rusk advocated "quiet diplomacy," preferring to work through trained professionals rather than through summitry. He became deeply involved in the hot and cold American relations with the Soviet Union, helping engineer the first arms control accords with Moscow and serving as foreign policy adviser to President Kennedy during the Bay of Pigs incident, the confrontation over Berlin, and the Cuban missile crisis. He later wrote that, after having essentially been excluded from the decision process, he had been too deferential when the fledgling Kennedy administration began reviewing plans for the Cuban invasion by failing to express his serious misgivings that the scheme would work.

With regard to the burgeoning situation in Vietnam, Rusk at first hoped to limit the role of the State Department, leaving the conflict there to the Department of Defense as essentially a military problem. However, by 1963 the U.S. advisory role had expanded, and Rusk became concerned about the ability of Ngo Dinh Diem to govern South Vietnam. Throughout 1963 Rusk, sensing Diem's isolation from the people of South Vietnam and his inability or unwillingness to stop the government's repression of the Buddhists, became increasingly vocal in his demands that Diem initiate serious reforms or be removed from office. He cabled Ambassador Henry Cabot Lodge in Saigon that Diem should be given every encouragement to rid himself of elements hostile to reform, but if he remained recalcitrant, the United States should "face the possibility that Diem himself cannot be preserved." Rusk's recollection was that, despite his and the president's desire not to support a coup, Kennedy instructed Lodge that the United States would not attempt to thwart a coup. Subsequently, Diem was toppled by a coup and assassinated.

Rusk had been skeptical in the beginning about whether the United States should become militarily involved in the conflict, but he quickly became a more and more visible proponent of a hard-line approach to Vietnam. Taking a Cold Warrior position, he strongly advocated the use of military force to prevent Communist expansion. William Bundy, assistant secretary of state for Far Eastern affairs, wrote that Rusk "concluded that to walk away from an American commitment, to temporize in our actions to meet it, to do anything short of all we possibly could, would pose the gravest possible danger to world peace." Rusk believed that if the United States failed to make a stand in Vietnam, it would be perceived as weak, thus inviting further Communist aggression. In Rusk's eyes, the United States had a commitment to South Vietnam that it could not break without risking a larger war with China or Russia. Rusk saw the Vietnam conflict in Cold War terms, as a clear case of Communist aggression, orchestrated by the People's Republic of China and supported by the Soviet Union. At a press conference in October 1967, he justified the U.S. presence in Southeast Asia as necessary to protect the region from the future threat of "a billion Chinese. . . . armed with nuclear weapons."

As President Lyndon B. Johnson's closest adviser, Rusk pressed consistently for more troop commitments and more bombing, meanwhile opposing negotiations with Hanoi. Unlike Secretary of Defense Robert S. McNamara and his successor, Clark Clifford, Rusk never wavered in his support of American policies in Vietnam and became the administration's chief spokesperson for Johnson's Vietnam War policy. Staunchly defending Johnson's policy in Vietnam in front of a Senate Foreign Relations Committee headed by Senator J. William Fulbright (D.-Ark.), who had broken with the administration policy, Rusk cited the appeasement of the Nazis at Munich as justification for U.S. involvement in Southeast Asia.

Thomas J. Schoenbaum wrote that Rusk "made himself the rock against which crashed the successive waves of dissent" and was "widely regarded as the chief hawk in the aerie of Vietnam advisers." The secretary of state increasingly came to be reviled by antiwar protestors, who mobbed his appearances, shouting insults. It eventually became so bad that he rarely spoke to groups outside Washington for fear of provoking such protests.

Despite the increasing strength of the antiwar movement, Rusk urged President Johnson to stay with the war, remaining one of the most vocal proponents of a hard line toward Hanoi. The situation in Vietnam changed drastically in February 1968, when the Communists launched their Tet Offensive. The ferocity of the widespread combat stunned the Johnson administration, which had been making claims about progress in the war. A shaken Johnson announced that he would not run for reelection and immediately instituted a policy of de-escalation, declaring his desire to enter into negotiations with the North Vietnamese. Hanoi accepted Johnson's offer with the provision that initial meetings deal only with the conditions required for a total bombing halt. Rusk apparently felt that such talks were not in the best interests of the United States. When the talks began in Paris in May 1968, Rusk played little part in them.

Rusk left office with the end of the Johnson administration in January 1969. That year he was awarded the Medal of Freedom. He never wavered from his defense of U.S. policies in Vietnam. When asked at a news conference shortly before he left office, he quickly responded, "What went wrong was a persistent and determined attempt by the authorities in Hanoi to take over South Vietnam by force." In interviews in later years and in his memoirs, he recanted a bit and said that he had made two mistakes about the Vietnam War: underestimating the tenacity of the North Vietnamese and overestimating the patience of the American people.

Because he had become so closely associated in the public mind with the Johnson administration policy in Vietnam, Rusk paid a price of sorts upon leaving office, when most prestigious universities refused to even consider him for a faculty appointment. According to Schoenbaum, "Not only did he have difficulty finding work, but many people, including many former friends, despised him." Ultimately, in 1970 Rusk accepted a teaching post as Sibley Professor of International Law at the University of Georgia in Athens. Rusk retired from teaching in 1984. He died at his home in Athens, Georgia.

With the exception of Cordell Hull, secretary of state for President Franklin D. Roosevelt in the 1930s and 1940s, Rusk held the job longer than any predecessor—a total of eight years. James Chace of the Carnegie Endowment for International Peace probably described him best when he wrote in 1988 in the *New York Times Book Review* that Rusk was "a good man—loyal, intelligent, and self-sacrificing—who was marked by a fatal lack of imagination and who came to bear the onus for perhaps the most tragic failure of American foreign policy in this century, the waging of the Vietnam War."

• Rusk's role in the Kennedy administration is addressed in David Halberstam, *The Best and Brightest* (1972). His entire career as secretary of state is covered in Thomas J. Schoenbaum, *Waging Peace and War: Dean Rusk in the Truman, Kennedy and Johnson Years* (1988), and Warren I. Cohen, *Dean Rusk* (1980).

JAMES H. WILLBANKS
ARTHUR T. FRAME

RUSK, Jeremiah McClain (17 June 1830–21 Nov. 1893), congressman, governor, and U.S. secretary of agriculture, was born in Deerfield Township, Morgan

County, Ohio, the son of Daniel Rusk and Jane Faulkner, farmers. He attended the common school at Deerfield for a time, but his father's death in 1846 forced him to drop out at the age of sixteen to run the family farm. Young Rusk also engaged in other occupations, including stagecoach driver, railroad section hand and construction crew foreman, and cooper. In 1849 he married Mary Martin; they had two children. In 1853 Rusk left Ohio for Viroqua in Bad Axe (now Vernon) County, Wisconsin. There his versatility enabled him to acquire in rapid order a farmstead, a threshing business, a hotel, a stagecoach line, and, in the 1870s, a bank. His first wife died in January 1856, and in December 1856 he married Elizabeth M. Johnson. They had four children, two of whom died in infancy.

Rusk's real vocation, however, was politics. His daring capture of a horse thief shortly after his arrival in Wisconsin earned him local notoriety and election as county sheriff in 1855 and then county coroner in 1857. In 1861 Rusk won election to the state assembly on the Republican ticket. In September 1862 he resigned to join the Union army as a major in the Twenty-fifth Wisconsin Volunteer Infantry, a regiment he had helped recruit. Serving in General William T. Sherman's command throughout the war, Rusk and the Twenty-fifth saw action in the Vicksburg siege, the Meridian campaign in Mississippi, and the march through Georgia and the Carolinas in 1864–1865. He exhibited "conspicuous gallantry" at the Salkehatchie River in South Carolina near the war's close and was brevetted brigadier general.

After the war Rusk returned to Wisconsin and public life. In November 1865 he was elected state comptroller, a position he held until the office was abolished in 1870. From 1871 to 1877 he served three terms in the U.S. House of Representatives from Wisconsin's Sixth and (after 1873) Seventh Congressional Districts. His service on the House Committees on Agriculture and Invalid Pensions gained him national recognition as a spokesman for American farmers and Union war veterans.

Rusk proved influential in the Republican National Convention in Chicago in 1880 during the deadlock among supporters of a third term for Ulysses S. Grant and those favoring James G. Blaine and John Sherman. Even before the convention Rusk favored nomination of dark horse James A. Garfield, a friend from his Ohio youth, and he probably engineered Wisconsin's switch to Garfield at the end of the thirty-fifth ballot, starting the rush that resulted in Garfield's nomination on the thirty-sixth. Garfield offered Rusk appointment as chargé d'affaires to Paraguay and Uruguay, which he refused. He also turned down appointments as ambassador to Denmark and as head of the Bureau of Engraving and Printing. He instead turned his interest to state politics. Endorsed by Senator Philetus Sawyer, the boss of Wisconsin Republican politics, Rusk became the GOP nominee for governor in 1881. He won the election and took office in January 1882.

Though initially perceived as merely a tool of the Sawyer machine, Rusk emerged as a popular governor who exercised his own judgment and commanded considerable respect from the party rank and file. In office he became the principal advocate for the state's agricultural interests. He lobbied successfully for agricultural experimentation and education and the expansion of inspection procedures to protect against the spread of infectious diseases among livestock. A decorated war veteran and former commander of the state Grand Army of the Republic, the governor shrewdly portrayed himself as the friend of veterans, often attending public events with an entourage of seventeen disabled ex-soldiers popularly called "the maimed heroes." As a skilled practitioner of coalition politics, Rusk built a loyal following among veterans, farmers, small-town businesspeople, and, until 1886, laborers. Reelected in 1884 and 1886, "Uncle Jerry," as he was commonly known, became a dominant figure in the state's political landscape in the 1880s.

Two particular events reflected Governor Rusk's independence and generally confirmed his popularity among Wisconsin voters. In the winter of 1882 the Chicago, Portage, and Superior Railroad failed, leaving 1,700 construction workers stranded near Superior Junction without pay, food, or lodging. The men grew unruly, threatening to destroy the bridges they had built. When property owners in the vicinity appealed to the governor for troops, he replied humanely that the men "want bread not bayonets." Rusk sent supplies and transportation and persuaded the workmen to leave their wage claims in his hands. The governor subsequently arranged for another company, the Omaha Line, to take over the defunct concern, its land grant, and its outstanding debts, including the payment of back wages.

Rusk responded less charitably, though no less in line with public opinion, to labor disturbances in Milwaukee. In the spring of 1886 Milwaukee labor, like organized labor nationally, was agitating for an eight-hour workday. Union leaders in Milwaukee called a general strike for 1 May, the day national organizers had set for such a demonstration. Several thousand Milwaukee workers left their jobs. Responding to appeals from local officials, Rusk deployed seventeen militia companies to Milwaukee and personally joined them to oversee operations. On 5 May rioting broke out near the Illinois Steel Company in Bay View, and the militia, directed by the governor to use deadly force if necessary, fired into the crowd. Four workers and bystanders were killed, and several others were wounded seriously. Rusk's intervention, the day after the Haymarket Square riot and massacre in Chicago, made him a national hero and a presumptive presidential candidate in 1888.

As Wisconsin's favorite son, Rusk made an unsuccessful bid for the presidential nomination at the Republican National Convention in 1888. The following year successful candidate Benjamin Harrison appointed him to the newly established cabinet position of secretary of agriculture.

In his cabinet post, Rusk established the credibility and direction of the department, ultimately winning the president's praise that he had enlarged "the measure of the man" desired for this post (Casson, p. 2). Emphasizing the practical application of science to agriculture, the secretary helped disseminate laboratory research results via the *Farmer's Bulletin* and other publications. Rusk also promoted the expansion of foreign markets. For example, he secured regulatory legislation to offset restrictions imposed by some European nations on imports on the grounds that American livestock and meat products were unhealthy. The Meat Inspection Act of 1891 and consequent eradication of pleuropneumonia and other livestock diseases led several European countries to revoke their prohibitions. Rusk also advocated inspection and quality grading of all food products for domestic as well as foreign consumption. Such initiatives foreshadowed expansion of the department's regulatory functions in the twentieth century.

Rusk retired from politics in March 1893 and died eight months later in Viroqua. Wisconsin history recalls Rusk as a popular governor largely responsible for preserving Republican party unity. This enabled the party to dominate state politics in the 1880s in the face of intraparty friction and major political challenges from a revived Democracy and various third party contenders. In posthumous tribute to his former cabinet member, Harrison described Rusk as a self-educated, self-made man who "like [Abraham] Lincoln, . . . multiplied small chances, and on a hard and barren youth builded a great life" (Casson, p. 19).

• Rusk's papers are in the State Historical Society of Wisconsin in Madison. Henry Casson, *"Uncle Jerry," Life of General Jeremiah M. Rusk* (1895), though uncritical, remains an important source. More recent critical assessments are George H. Wood, "A Diamond in the Rough—A Study of the Administration of Governor Jeremiah McClain Rusk 1882–1889" (M.A. thesis, Univ. of Wisconsin, Madison, 1970); and Robert C. Nesbit, *Urbanization and Industrialization, 1873–1893* (1985), vol. 3 of *The History of Wisconsin*, ed. William Fletcher Thompson. Obituaries are in the *New York Times* and the *Madison Democrat*, 22 Nov. 1893.

JAMES B. POTTS

RUSS, John Dennison (1 Sept. 1801–1 Mar. 1881), educator of the blind, social reformer, and physician, was born in what is now Essex (then part of Ipswich), Essex County, Massachusetts, the son of Parker Russ, a physician, and Elizabeth Cogswell. He graduated from Yale College in 1823 and soon afterward went to Brunswick, Maine, where he studied medicine with Dr. John D. Wells, a member of the faculty of medicine at Bowdoin College (Russ did not enroll at Bowdoin, however). He studied further in Baltimore and Boston and in 1825 received the M.D. degree from Yale Medical School. During 1825 and 1826 Russ was in Europe where he served in several hospitals. After his return to the United States he practiced medicine in New York City.

The movement of Greek independence from the Turks became an important issue for Russ. He went to Europe again in 1827 to assist with food transportation, medical supplies, and hospital services. He was an associate of Dr. Samuel Gridley Howe of Boston who had similar interests in Greece and who later was involved with the education of the blind. Poor health forced Russ's return in the spring of 1830 to New York City, where he resumed the practice of medicine.

Russ became interested in the medical condition of the inflammation of the eyeball (ophthalmia) as it appeared among poor children, a result of the ophthalmia epidemic in New York City. He also became involved with the instruction of the blind and with two other colleagues, Samuel Akerly and Samuel Wood, established the New York Institution for the Blind (later called the New York Institution for the Education of the Blind), chartered by the state in 1831. He was the first teacher at its opening in 1832. In addition to his post as teacher-principal, he became one of the managers (trustees) and served as recording secretary during 1833–1834. Poor health forced him to leave the school in 1835, and he traveled to Europe for recuperation.

After returning home, Russ became involved with several social agencies, among them the Prison Association of New York, the New York Juvenile Asylum, and the New York City Board of Education. He served as superintendent of the Juvenile Asylum from 1853 to 1858. This institution later became the Children's Village of Dobbs Ferry, New York. Further work with the education of the blind included the development of a phonetic alphabet and adjusting Braille for use in the United States.

Russ was a joint author with Nathaniel Niles of *Medical Statistics; or, A Comparative View of the Mortality in New York, Philadelphia, Baltimore and Boston* (1827). He also wrote *Letter Music, or Musical Tones Expressed by Letters* (1879). He was married twice, first to Mrs. Eliza Phipps Jenkins, a widow who died in 1860, and second, in 1872, to Elsie Birdsell. His only children were those he adopted, the children of his first wife. His last years were spent in Pompton, New Jersey, where he died. He was buried in his birthplace, Essex, Massachusetts.

• A small amount of information about John Russ in his years at Yale College is found in the archives of the Yale University Library. *General Catalogue of Bowdoin College and the Medical School of Maine* (1950) contains the academic credentials and career data of Dr. John Wells, of the faculty of medicine, with whom Russ studied in 1823. Laura E. Richards, *Samuel Gridley Howe* (1935), and Harold Schwartz, *Samuel Gridley Howe: Social Reformer, 1801–1876* (1956), make brief references to work of Russ during the revolution in Greece, where Russ was associated with Howe. *The Yearbook of the New York Institute for the Education of the Blind: 100th Year* (1932) gives rosters of the officials at the institute, and Russ is listed, with dates, as teacher-principal, manager, and recording secretary. William B. Waite, *A Manhattan Landmark: The New York Institution for the Blind* (1944), makes a reference to Russ as the first teacher there. A notice in the *New York Eve-*

ning Post, 15 Dec. 1832, mentions Russ as the teacher in the recently opened institution for the blind. Charles H. Haswell, *Reminiscences of an Octogenarian of the City of New York* (1897), cites the work of Russ in the incorporation of the New York Juvenile Asylum. *Obituary Record of Graduates of Yale University, 1880–1890* (1890) contains information on the high points of his life.

RICHARD G. DURNIN

RUSSELL, Annie (12 Jan. 1864–16 Jan. 1936), actress, was born in Liverpool, England, the daughter of Joseph Russell, an Irish civil engineer, and Jane Mount. When Annie was five, the family moved to Montreal, Canada, where Joseph Russell soon died. The family's subsequent financial troubles took Annie to the stage. In 1872 she appeared in Rose Eytinge's touring production of *Miss Moulton* at the Montreal Academy of Music.

Russell debuted in New York seven years later, in John H. Haverly's juvenile company of *HMS Pinafore* at the Lyceum Theatre. She stayed with the company for two years, continuing to play children's roles, including Eva in *Uncle Tom's Cabin*, then accompanied her brother Tommy on a tour with E. A. McDowell's Repertoire Company. In 1881 she returned to New York, where she auditioned for the title role in *Esmerelda*. William Gillette, who had adapted the Frances Hodgson-Burnett story, was casting the play and at first dismissed Russell because of her youth. When she returned to the theater in a long gown and wearing her hair up, he did not recognize her, and she won the role. *Esmerelda* opened at the Madison Square Theatre on 29 October 1881, giving Russell her first big break. She made the most of it, playing the role nearly 900 times—350 of these in New York, followed by a year's tour throughout the country. In 1884, in Albany, New York, she married Eugene Wiley Presbrey, variously referred to as an artist and the stage manager for the tour.

Russell's reputation established, she undertook the title role in the well-received *Hazel Kirke*, then returned to the Madison Square Theatre, now managed by A. M. Palmer. There she starred in a number of now-forgotten hits, including *Broken Hearts* (1885), *Engaged* (1886), and *Elaine* (1887), an especially popular Russell vehicle. "It was a most complete and harmonious, a most poetic yet real performance" (Strang, p. 91).

Russell's marriage faltered during the run of *Captain Swift* in 1889, and so did her health. She became seriously ill, and rumors about her "brute of a husband" contributed to public sympathy. She did not begin to recover until two years later, when she traveled to Italy on $3,000 from a benefit thrown for her at Palmer's Theatre. In 1894, finally in full health, she appeared as Margery Sylvester in Sydney Grundy's *The New Woman*, which opened 12 November 1894 at Wallack's theater. While sick, Russell had thought a great deal about her craft, and her acting was even simpler and more "natural" than it had been before she fell ill.

In 1895 Russell did three shows with Nat Goodwin, then appeared with Sol Smith Russell in *A Bachelor's Romance*. And in 1896 she appeared at Hoyt's Theatre in New York as the title character in Bret Harte's *Sue*. It was an enormous hit for Russell. She then gave another memorable performance as Rose Primrose in *Dangerfield, '95*, which Charles Frohman brought to London in 1898. She also played *Sue* in London and garnered extremely favorable responses in both shows. Even *Dangerfield, '95*, a curtain raiser, drew London audiences, who simply came to see Russell; her naturalness led them to dub her "the Duse of the English-speaking stage." In 1898 Russell returned to the United States, where her popularity continued until her retirement. Her divorce from Gene Presbrey having been finalized in 1897, she married an English actor, Oswald Yorke, in 1904 and continued to act until 1918.

Throughout Russell's career, she had yearned for more challenging roles, rather than the fresh young heroines in which she seemed entrenched. Over the next two decades she tried to expand her repertoire, with some success. Notable Russell performances during this time include the title role in *Major Barbara* (Court Theatre, London, 28 Nov. 1905), Puck in *A Midsummer Night's Dream* (in a revival that opened the New Astor Theatre in New York in Sept. 1906), and three productions by the Annie Russell Old English Comedy Company in 1912: *She Stoops to Conquer*, *Much Ado about Nothing*, and *The Rivals*, with Russell in the leading roles. Russell's last professional performance was as Madame La Grange in Bayard Veiller's thriller, *The Thirteenth Chair*, on 19 January 1918, at the Belasco Theatre, Washington, D.C. Tired of the theater and exhausted from her war work for the Red Cross, the Salvation Army, and French war orphans, she gave up acting for over a decade.

Still, Russell's departure from the professional stage was a working retirement. Her friend Mary Louise Curtis Bok (Mrs. Edward Bok) donated $100,000 to build the Annie Russell Theatre at Rollins College in Winter Park, Florida. There Russell trained college actors and occasionally stepped out of retirement to reprise well-known roles (*In a Balcony* in 1932, then Madame La Grange in *The Thirteenth Chair* and Mrs. Malaprop in *The Rivals*, both in 1933).

Known for her beautiful voice and her wistful charm as fresh young ingenues, Russell's career was torn, as so many actresses' are, by the need to make a living and the desire for satisfying roles. She found the young characters she played to be uninteresting, yet she consistently accepted the roles in which she was easily typecast. She did pursue opportunities to play more substantial roles, including Beatrice, Lady Teazle, and Mrs. Hardcastle, but these proved less financially rewarding than the "Annigenues" she scorned. At the end of her life, Russell found teaching as an outlet for expressing the ideals that she found difficult to translate to the professional stage. She died in Winter Park and was buried at Short Hills, New Jersey. She had no children from either marriage.

• The most abundant sources for information on Russell are the Billy Rose Theatre Collection, New York Public Library for the Performing Arts, Lincoln Center, and the Harvard Theatre Collection. For her own remarks on the theater, see articles in the *Ladies' Home Journal*, "What It Really Means to Be an Actress," Jan. 1909, pp. 11, 49; "As the Player Sees the Playgoer," Nov. 1912, p. 16; and "The Tired Business Man at the Theater," Mar. 1914, p. 56. For personal sketches from the turn of the century, see Gustav Kobbe, *Famous Actors and Actresses and Their Homes* (1903), and Lewis Strang, *Famous Actresses of the Day in America* (1899). An obituary is in the *New York Times*, 17 Jan. 1936.

CYNTHIA M. GENDRICH

RUSSELL, Benjamin (13 Sept. 1761–4 Jan. 1845), printer, newspaper editor, and politician, was born in Boston, Massachusetts, the son of John Russell, a mason. By his fourteenth year he had learned the rudiments of typesetting by working around Isaiah Thomas's Boston printing house. Benjamin's career as a newspaperman was determined, in part, by his boyish curiosity when he followed British troops marching toward what turned out to be the battle of Concord on 19 April 1775. But British forces closed off travel between Boston and the outlying areas, preventing him from returning home.

After three months as an errand boy for Continental soldiers quartered in Harvard Yard, Russell encountered his father, who at first greeted him warmly, then gave him a thrashing and sent him to Worcester. There he was apprenticed to Thomas, who by then was publishing his *Massachusetts Spy*. After a night of imbibing to celebrate Thomas's reading of the Declaration of Independence in Worcester, Russell, who was only fifteen, awoke to find he had enlisted in the army. Thomas, unwilling to lose his apprentice, pleaded successfully that the lad had not reached the legal age of sixteen for enlisting. In 1780, however, when Thomas was conscripted by the Continental army, he hired Russell to be his substitute, a custom that was both common and permissible.

Joining the army at West Point, New York, Russell fought in no battles during his six months' service; the real violence he encountered while serving as a member of the guard during the execution of Major John André for treason. He then returned to Thomas's printing house and negotiated an early release from his apprenticeship at age nineteen. While working for Thomas as a journeyman printer for two more years, Russell married Esther Rice of Worcester in September 1783. They had three children.

Late in 1783 Russell began the process of starting a newspaper in his native Boston, eventually publishing the first issue of the *Massachusetts Centinel and the Republican Journal* on 24 March 1784 in partnership with William Warden. Published on Wednesdays and Saturdays, the newspaper predictably carried a motto: "Uninfluenced by Party, We Aim to Be Just." In 1785, when the Massachusetts legislature levied a short-lived six pence per insertion tax on advertisements (an "insertion" would run for six issues), the *Centinel* favored that tax while other newspapers were angrily recalling the British taxation of the press and the Stamp Act riots of 1765. In March 1786 the death of Warden made Russell the *Centinel*'s sole proprietor.

Russell amended the name to the *Massachusetts Centinel* late in 1786 and to the *Columbian Centinel* in 1790. Historian Frank W. Scott termed the *Centinel* "the most enterprising and influential newspaper in Massachusetts." Like other leading printer-journalists of the time, Russell rose from the hardscrabble lot of an apprentice printer to substantial wealth by energetic joining of organizations and involvement in civic activities. Even so, he evidently thought of himself as a "mechanic" or working-class artisan. He cultivated close ties with both merchants and mechanics, cofounding the Massachusetts Charitable Mechanics Association in 1795 and, from 1808 to 1819, serving as its president.

Russell became known as an able publisher and editor, as well as something of a typographic innovator whose newspaper had a far livelier appearance than most. Woodcut cartoons or illustrations and other typographical devices frequently attracted readers and enlivened the *Centinel*.

Russell's newspaper favored a well-ordered society run by the deserving. Quite predictably, it denounced Shays's Rebellion in 1784. Russell robustly supported adoption of the Constitution, mobilizing support among Boston's mechanics to influence the Massachusetts Ratifying Convention in 1788. An article attributed jointly to Paul Revere and Russell asserted that an antifederalist victory over the Constitution would result in a loss of jobs. Using the *Centinel* as their pulpit, in January 1788 they urged artisans to support the approval of the Constitution "without any conditions, pretended amendments, or alterations whatever."

When that ratification was complete, Russell wrote and published poetry to celebrate his state's contribution to the Union. His taste for the dramatic also could be seen in his allegory that celebrated President George Washington's inauguration in 1789. It began, "Just *launched* on the *Ocean of Empire*, the Ship COLUMBIA, GEORGE WASHINGTON, Commander, which, after being thirteen years in *dock*, is at length well *manned*, and in very good condition."

In such a viciously partisan era, it was hard to find moderate or judicious language in either the great majority of the newspapers favoring the Constitution or the antifederalist newspapers opposing it. Strident political name-calling was not all Russell and his newspaper would supply for the Federalists. He even printed, gratis, laws and official documents of the United States, evidently fearing that the new nation could not afford to pay for that vital service. President Washington, however, learned of this and ordered that Russell be paid the $7,000 the government owed him; it, by Washington's estimation, was a "debt of honor."

During the administration of John Adams, Russell's *Columbian Centinel* supported the Federalists zealously, including the Sedition Act of 1798, which in effect made criticism of the national government a crime. The *Centinel* thus ignored the First Amendment's protection of speech and press. On 5 October 1798 the *Centinel* declared, "Whatever American is a friend of the present Administration of the American Government is undoubtedly a true republican, a true Patriot . . . Whatever American opposes the Administration is an Anarchist, a Jacobin and a Traitor." The *Centinel* later cheered the Sedition Act prosecution of Vermont congressman Matthew Lyon, who had earlier published his own antiadministration paper, the *Scourge of the Aristocracy*.

The election of President Thomas Jefferson was greeted with dismay in the *Centinel*, with Russell publishing a suggested epitaph for the Federalist party in March 1801: "YESTERDAY EXPIRED, Deeply Regretted by MILLIONS of grateful Americans, and by *all* GOOD MEN, The FEDERAL ADMINISTRATION of the GOVERNMENT of the *United States*."

As the Federalist party waned in the early years of the nineteenth century, so did the influence of the *Centinel*, although echoes of its columns lingered. In 1811, when drawing a *Centinel* map of a proposed Massachusetts congressional district that took on a strange outline in order to protect a Republican, the artist Gilbert Stuart added some claws and said it looked like a salamander. Russell is said to have dubbed the creature a "gerrymander," making fun of Massachusetts governor Elbridge Gerry.

Ironically, during the War of 1812, the *Centinel* may well have benefited from the 1801 expiration of the Sedition Act, which was used to punish foes of the Federalists. Russell opposed the "useless and unnecessary war" as a "waste of blood and property," a subtle opposition to the government that could have met the elastic definition of "sedition" in 1798 and 1799.

After the death of his first wife, Russell married Guest Campbell, in 1803. Russell retired from journalism in 1828, selling his paper to lawyer Joseph T. Adams and a former apprentice, Thomas Hudson. This provided more time for Russell's civic pursuits. He was an alderman and member of the Common Council from 1817 to 1821 and from 1822 to 1826 before leaving the *Centinel*. After his retirement he served from 1829 to 1832. He also was a member of the Massachusetts House of Representatives from 1805 to 1821 and was elected as a senator from Suffolk County in 1825 and as representative for Boston from 1828 to 1835. Russell was a member of the Executive Council of Massachusetts in 1836 and 1837.

• Russell evidently left few private papers, so the outlines of his career are best found in the *Centinel*, for the forty-four years he was publisher, and in Joseph T. Buckingham, *Specimens of Newspaper Literature*, vol. 2 (1852). Other useful accounts are in Robert Allen Rutland, *The Ordeal of the Constitution* (1966); James Morton Smith, *Freedom's Fetters: The Alien and Sedition Laws and American Civil Liberties* (1956); and Jeffery A. Smith, *Printers and Press Freedom: The Ideology of Early American Journalism* (1988). Old but still useful accounts include Frank Luther Mott, *American Journalism*, 3d ed. (1962); Alfred McClung Lee, *The Daily Newspaper in America* (1937); and Frederic Hudson, *Journalism in the United States from 1690 to 1872* (1873).

DWIGHT L. TEETER, JR.

RUSSELL, Chambers (4 July 1713–24 Nov. 1766), judge and legislator, was born in Charlestown, Massachusetts, the son of Daniel Russell, a merchant and landowner and longtime member of the provincial council, and Rebecca Chambers. Russell's grandfather, Charles Chambers, also a councillor and a judge of the Middlesex County Inferior Court of Common Pleas, provided for his early education at Cambridge Latin School. Russell received his A.B. at Harvard in 1731 and his M.A. there in 1734. He married Mary Wainwright, daughter of Francis and Mary Dudley Wainwright of Boston, on 2 April 1738. The couple had no children.

Russell settled in Concord on lands inherited from his grandfather and in 1740 was elected as the town's representative to the General Court. In the same year, apparently as a reward for his legislative support, Governor Jonathan Belcher appointed him a justice of the peace for Middlesex County. Russell then moved to Charlestown, which he represented in the General Court in 1744 and 1745.

In 1746 Russell was appointed by the king to succeed Robert Auchmuty as judge of the royal vice admiralty court for Massachusetts, New Hampshire, and Rhode Island. Auchmuty had fallen into disfavor with Boston's merchants because of his calls for strict enforcement of the Acts of Trade and Navigation, British customs laws that were within the jurisdiction of his court. Despite his mercantile family connections, Russell soon acquired his own reputation for strict enforcement and his place in the provincial establishment. In 1747 he was appointed to the Middlesex County Inferior Court of Common Pleas by Governor William Shirley, and in 1752 he took his seat on the Superior Court of Judicature, the highest court in the province.

Russell's judicial positions did not deter him from further legislative service. Having moved back to Concord, he was elected to represent that town in the General Court from 1750 until 1753. Leading a successful effort to create the town of Lincoln out of parts of Concord and adjacent towns in 1754, he served the new town as moderator and held its seat in the General Court in nearly every year from 1754 through 1765. He was elected to the council in 1759 and 1760. In his legislative capacity, Russell was a loyal supporter of the positions of the royal governors against local political opposition.

Despite his provincial judicial and legislative offices, Russell continued to sit as judge of the vice admiralty court, though Rhode Island was eliminated from his commission by the Crown in 1758. This multiple officeholding seems extreme even by eighteenth-century standards, and it did engender contemporary criticism. It has been suggested by the historian M. H. Smith that Governor Shirley appointed Russell to the superior court so that he would be in a position to prevent the use of the common-law writ of prohibition to block customs enforcement actions brought before him in the vice admiralty court. In fact, Russell was sensitive to his dual position and recused himself when the superior court considered such challenges to his actions.

As the political tensions between Great Britain and the colonies, which were to lead to revolution, began to mount in the early 1760s, Russell found himself in the center of controversy. He was one of the justices of the superior court who rejected the arguments of patriot lawyer James Otis on behalf of Boston's merchants and ruled that general warrants, called writs of assistance, could issue to colonial customs officers. As vice admiralty judge, he was also involved in the decision of several highly visible cases involving the continuing skirmishing between the merchants and the customs establishment. In the Stamp Act crisis of 1765, Russell was one of the superior court justices who refused to grant the petition of Massachusetts that the courts be open for business despite the absence of stamped paper. After being listed in the radical press as one of a group of legislators who had supported the Stamp Act, he was not returned to the General Court in the 1766 election. John Adams called him one of "the original Conspirators against the Public Liberty, [a] Conspiracy . . . first regularly formed, and begun to be executed, in 1763 or 4" (Adams, *Diary*, 6 Mar. 1774).

In the fall of 1766 Russell sailed for England. The revolutionary pamphleteers opined that his purpose was to obtain Crown salaries for the judges of the superior court that would replace salaries appropriated annually by the Massachusetts General Court. More likely, he went to pursue a recently submitted petition in which he had sought a fixed salary as vice admiralty judge. In his petition, he had noted that the existing system of compensation by the fees received from forfeitures for violations of the customs laws created an inappropriate incentive for unjust condemnation of vessels and goods. His true purpose remains unclear, because he became ill and died shortly after his arrival in England. His extensive estate consisted of land in Lincoln, Boston, and other towns; five slaves for whose care he sought to provide in his will; and substantial personal property, including a large library.

Russell was widely respected even by many of his political opponents as a public-spirited man who conducted the public business in his charge with fairness and dispatch. Though not formally trained as a lawyer, he was learned in the law. His library contained numerous law books, and Jonathan Sewall, a leading Boston lawyer and later a vice admiralty judge, studied law with him. Known as a genial host, he exhibited kindness to family, friends, servants, and slaves throughout his life. At his death he was widely praised for those attributes in obituaries and in a eulogy delivered by Chief Justice Thomas Hutchinson at the opening of the March 1767 term of the superior court. The *Boston Post-Boy* described him as "avoiding, with a scrupulous Conscientiousness, whatever might have the most remote possible Tendency to warp or bias his Judgment, and always giving the surest Evidence of his unalterable Intention and Endeavour, to make the Rule of Right, the governing Principle of all his Actions" (19 Jan. 1767).

• A few papers relating to Russell's vice admiralty judgeship are found in the Massachusetts Vice Admiralty records and papers, Massachusetts State Archives. His work on the Superior Court is documented in the Massachusetts Superior Court records and files, 1752–1766, and also in the Massachusetts State Archives. For published court papers and contemporary materials concerning his cases, see Dorothy S. Towle, ed., *Records of the Vice Admiralty Court of Rhode Island, 1716–1752* (1936; repr. 1975), pp. 414–513, and Samuel Quincy, ed., *Reports of Cases Argued and Adjudged in the Superior Court of Judicature . . . between 1761 and 1772* (1865), where Hutchinson's eulogy appears at pp. 232–33. The best account of Russell's life is in Clifford K. Shipton, *Sibley's Harvard Graduates*, vol. 9 (1956), pp. 81–87. Other details appear in Peter E. Russell, *His Majesty's Judges: Provincial Society and the Superior Court in Massachusetts, 1692–1774* (1990), pp. 195–99, and M. H. Smith, *The Writs of Assistance Case* (1978), pp. 86–94. For obituaries, see *Boston Post-Boy*, 19 Jan. 1767 (quoted in Shipton, pp. 83, 84); *Boston Evening Post*, 19 Jan. 1767 (quoted in Smith, p. 88); and the *Massachusetts Gazette*, 15 Jan. 1767.

L. KINVIN WROTH

RUSSELL, Charles Edward (25 Sept. 1860–23 Apr. 1941), journalist and reformer, was born in Davenport, Iowa, the son of Edward Russell, a newspaper editor, and Lydia Rutledge. Russell was graduated from St. Johnsbury Academy in Vermont in 1881, after which he returned to Davenport to work at his father's newspaper. In 1884 he married Abby Osborne Rust, whom he had met while in Vermont. The couple had one son. Russell's father was a crusading editor and abolitionist, and Russell was introduced to reform ideas in his early days in journalism.

From 1884 to 1886 Russell worked as a reporter and editor at newspapers in Minneapolis and Detroit. In 1886 he went to New York City, where he worked for the next fourteen years at the largest circulating newspapers in America. He worked first as a reporter at the *New York Herald* (1886–1891), then became an editor at Joseph Pulitzer's *New York World* (1892–1896) and William Randolph Hearst's *New York Journal* (1896–1899). Russell's most extensive reporting took place at the *Herald*, where he was described as one of the ten best reporters in America. After years of reporting on both national and local issues—including capital punishment, race conditions in the South, slum conditions in New York City, and labor disturbances in the Pennsylvania coalfields—Russell wrote in his autobiography *Bare Hands and Stone Walls* (1933) that "the only education I ever had that amounted to anything was when I was a police reporter on the East Side of New York." Russell was impressed by the terrible poverty he saw in this immigrant quarter of Manhattan, and the experience led him eventually to question the system of private capital that he felt was responsible for creating this slum.

In 1894 Russell left reporting to become the city editor of the *New York World*, which at that time had the largest circulation of any newspaper in the world. Russell so liked this job that he once commented in another memoir that "the best job on earth is that of city editor of a New York daily. Other employments are but rubbish in comparison" (*These Shifting Scenes* [1914]). Russell left the *World* to become the chief editor for the *New York Journal* in 1897, a time when the American press was embroiled in the sensationalist period known as "yellow journalism." In 1901 Russell moved to Chicago to become publisher of Hearst's new paper, the *American*.

Russell left daily journalism in 1902 when his wife died and he suffered what seemed to be a nervous breakdown. He took a year off, then returned to journalism in 1904 when he accepted a magazine reporting assignment that led to his first important book, *The Greatest Trust in the World* (1905)—a critical examination of the methods of the meatpacking industry. This book, which appeared first in serial fashion in a national magazine, *Everybody's*, also plunged Russell into a journalistic reform movement known as "muckraking" as he joined with, among others, Lincoln Steffens, Ida Tarbell, and Upton Sinclair to write about a variety of problems caused by the excesses of industrialism.

For the next ten years Russell was among the most prolific, versatile, and best known of these investigative journalists. One national magazine dubbed him "chief of the muckrakers." Writing with clarity and a controlled passion, Russell produced dozens of articles in mass circulation national magazines, such as *Cosmopolitan*, *Everybody's*, *Hampton's*, and *Pearson's*. He wrote about railroad stock manipulations, slum landlords, legislative graft, election fraud, race relations, and prison conditions. His most controversial writing was about Trinity Church, America's wealthiest church, which he accused of being the biggest slum landlord in New York City. Soon after Russell's articles, the church sold or fixed up many of its worst buildings. Russell also received national attention for his articles about prison conditions in various states and about financial irregularities in the railroad industry. His work had considerable effect on federal regulation of the rails and on reform of prison conditions. Although muckraking had died down by 1912, Russell continued his exposé-writing until the start of World War I, writing, for example, about pressure brought to bear on magazines that continued to write articles critical of business practices.

In 1909, the year he married Theresa Hirschl of Chicago, he also joined with Oswald Garrison Villard and William E. Walling to help found the National Association for the Advancement of Colored People. His interest in this issue began in his youth when his father was nearly hanged in Iowa because he opposed slavery. Russell especially saw the need for the NAACP after race riots occurred in Springfield, Illinois, in 1908. After the NAACP was formed, Russell often wrote eloquently about racial equality, and he served on the NAACP board of directors until his death.

Russell's newspaper and magazine journalism led him increasingly to believe that capitalism was flawed and that a cabal of financial interests controlled the American economy. When a magazine sent him around the world to investigate social conditions he returned as a critic of an unfettered marketplace, which he described in *The Uprising of the Many* (1905). In 1908 he declared for socialism (*Why I Am a Socialist*) and joined the Socialist party. Russell then lectured widely, always advocating a gradualist and democratic brand of socialism and arguing for government takeover of major utilities and key industries. He was the Socialist party candidate for governor of New York in 1910 and 1912, for mayor of New York City in 1913, and for the U.S. Senate in 1914; he lost all three elections by wide margins.

In 1916 he was one of three candidates considered for the Socialist party's presidential nomination. Russell split with his party over the First World War, joining a faction that became known as "prowar socialists." Russell, who had traveled widely in Europe for many years, supported the war because he believed that Germany presented a threat to democratic values. "A victory for German imperialism would mean the defeat and annihilation of democracy and freedom," Russell wrote (*Bare Hands and Stone Walls*). Russell aided his country in various ways, first doing minor diplomatic chores in the Netherlands and then, when America entered the war, working officially in Great Britain as America's chief publicist on behalf of the war effort. In 1917 he was formally expelled from the Socialist party because he accepted President Woodrow Wilson's invitation to join a delegation that visited Russia in an attempt to convince that nation to stay in the war against Germany.

After the war Russell remained active in various movements, writing on behalf of Filipino independence, Irish separatism, and Zionism. He also wrote and spoke against using animals for medical research. But writing was his continued passion and between 1922 and 1931 he wrote five biographies. In 1927 he received the Pulitzer Prize for his biography, *The American Orchestra and Theodore Thomas* (1927), which provided a detailed look at the first conductor of the American Orchestra. The book culminated Russell's lifelong interest in the arts. Another of his biographies was about his close friend Julia Marlowe, an American actress, and he also wrote three volumes of poetry. Russell died in Washington, D.C.

Although he was a prolific writer (thirty-one books and dozens of magazine articles), Russell is not as well remembered as many of his muckraking colleagues. Nonetheless he was one of the most famous, respected, and widely read journalists of his time, writing on more topics than any of the other muckraking journalists. Russell disliked capitalism but believed that the solution to industrialism's problems would come gradually, through reform and not through social revolution. He believed that the journalism of exposé to which he contributed had aided considerably in bringing about important social reforms.

• Russell's papers, including unpublished diaries from the war years, are in the Library of Congress. His other important books include *Lawless Wealth: The Origin of Some Great American Fortunes* (1908), *Business: The Heart of the Nation*, and *Stories of the Great Railroads* (both 1911). The most comprehensive analysis of his journalism is Robert Miraldi, "Charles Edward Russell: Chief of the Muckrakers," *Journalism Monographs* 150 (Apr. 1995): 1–27. A broader look at his work is found in Donald H. Bragaw, "Soldier of the Common Good: The Life and Career of Charles Edward Russell" (Ph.D. diss., Syracuse Univ., 1970), which includes the most complete bibliography of his work. His ideology is discussed in David Chalmers, *The Social and Political Ideas of the Muckrakers* (1964). An obituary is in the *New York Times*, 24 Apr. 1941.

ROBERT MIRALDI

RUSSELL, Charles Marion (19 Mar. 1864–24 Oct. 1926), artist and author, was born in St. Louis, Missouri, the son of Charles Silas Russell, a wealthy businessman, and Mary Elizabeth Mead. As a child, Russell always preferred modeling in clay, drawing, and playing hooky. In 1879 his parents sent him to a military academy in New Jersey, but after a year they relented and allowed him to realize his dream of becoming a cowboy. He moved to the Judith Basin in Montana, where he tended sheep (1880), did chores for a hunter and trapper (1881–1882), and sketched western activities and scenery in his spare time. After a visit back in St. Louis for a month in 1882, he returned to the Great Northwest as a horse wrangler and cow puncher for several Montana cattlemen (1882–1893), but he continued to sketch and paint as much as he could.

In 1886 Russell sent his first significant oil painting to a St. Louis exhibit. The following year he gained international fame by chance when he executed a hasty but eloquent watercolor on a two-by-four-inch piece of collar-box cardboard, depicting a half-starved steer menaced by coyotes during Montana's bitter winter of 1886–1887. He sent it instead of a written report to the herd owner, and the picture was made into hundreds of thousands of postcards as a worldwide Montana weather and cattle news item. Later in 1887 his popularity increased when a Chicago company lithographed "The Cowboy Artist," a montage of seven different paintings done on the same canvas, depicting various scenes from cowboy life. Russell spent six months in 1888 in Alberta, Canada, as an artist-guest of the Blood Indians there. Even after gaining added fame with his *Studies in Western Life* (1890), a portfolio of twenty-one fine color pictures, Russell kept on painting only in a haphazard way, in saloons and elsewhere. Finally, following one last cattle run in 1893, to Chicago, where he held an exhibit, Russell bid goodbye to the cowboy life forever. He began to work full-time as an artist in Great Falls, Montana, and then in Cascade, where he married Nancy Cooper in 1896.

Life with Nancy was a complete change for Russell, age thirty-two. Fifteen years his junior, she persuaded him in 1897 to move back to Great Falls, where she kept him away from his drinking cronies, and busy at painting and clay modeling. He began publishing short stories (1897), published his second portfolio, entitled *Pen Sketches* (1899), and let Nancy handle his business affairs. On her advice, Russell charged much

more per painting than his habitual, ridiculously low fee of $25. He often went to New York with her, first in 1903, the same year he modeled *Smoking Up*, which became his first bronze statue. Nancy encouraged him to open a summer cabin at Lake McDonald, Montana, in 1906 as a haven for fellow artists and writers. With her help, he arranged numerous one-man shows and other exhibits, including shows in Brooklyn in 1907, Seattle in 1909, New York in 1911, and London in 1914, and others later. He began illustrating books by such eastern authors as Emerson Hough, Theodore Roosevelt (1858–1919), and Owen Wister. In 1921 he sold a painting for $10,000, and in 1926 he contracted to execute a pair of murals in a Los Angeles millionaire's mansion for a mind-boggling $30,000.

During his last few years, Russell found some satisfaction in international acclaim and yet became increasingly melancholy. He used to say of his wife, "She lives for tomorrow, an' I live for yesterday." His artistic productions gradually evolved into subtle laments for the vanished Old West. This muted sorrow is also evident in his three books of prose—*Rawhide Rawlins Stories* (1921), *More Rawhides* (1925), and a posthumously issued classic sadly called *Trails Plowed Under* (1927). These varied fictional and nonfictional works, often presented by folksy narrators, have the virtues of verisimilitude, suspense, and humor. The fictional pieces feature hardworking, fun-loving, occasionally vicious hunters and cattlemen, and also Indians, usually noble and loyal, if crafty, but almost never cruel. Russell's essays concern range life, ranches, whiskey, the "Injun" temperament, and horses—his favorite animal, man's best friend, and one worthy of his enduring love.

Nancy inordinately relished her husband's late-life friendships with Hollywood personalities and therefore expressed a desire for a lavish residence in Pasadena, California. Charlie of course agreed, and construction on "Trail's End" soon started; but it was never to be his home. The tired artist had been plagued for years with sciatic rheumatism. Goiter surgery in the summer of 1926 weakened his heart, and soon thereafter he died in Great Falls.

Russell's short stories and essays capture the spirit of the Old West and its pioneering people. His statues are vigorous, dramatic, and eloquent. But it is almost entirely through his paintings that this self-taught artist will live. In them, he records his youthful experiences as a cowboy, portrays the activities of North Plains Indians, and authentically depicts events of outstanding importance in the history of American frontier exploration, pioneering, and settlement.

• Karl Yost and Frederic G. Renner, *A Bibliography of the Published Works of Charles M. Russell* (1971), lists Russell's written work. The following present detailed biographical information: Ramon F. Adams and Homer E. Britzman, *Charles M. Russell: The Cowboy Artist, a Biography* (1948), an early effort; Austin Russell, *C.M.R.: Charles M. Russell, Cowboy Artist, a Biography* (1957), a loving and informative tribute by the subject's nephew; and Frank Bird Linderman, *Recollections of Charley Russell*, ed. H. G. Merriam (1963), reminiscences of a personal friend. The following are analytical and critical: Robert L. Gale, *Charles Marion Russell* (1979), includes an analysis of Russell's short stories, semiautobiographical anecdotes, and essays; Brian W. Dippie, in *"Paper Talk": Charlie Russell's American West* (1979), collects and reproduces Russell's illustrated letters, poems, and Christmas greetings to his numerous friends; Ginger Renner, *A Limitless Sky: The Work of Charles M. Russell in the Collection of the Rockwell Museum, Corning, New York* (1986), discusses a significant collection; Dippie's *Looking at Russell* (1987), critically analyzes Russell's art and explains the evolution of his moods; Peter H. Hassrick, *Charles M. Russell* (1989), contains stunning reproductions of Russell's pictorial art as well as expert commentary and a useful chronology; and Peggy and Harold Samuels, Joan Samuels, and Daniel Fabian, *Techniques of the Artists of the American West* (1990), includes a brilliant study of Russell's untutored, spontaneous, captivating technique. See also *Persimmon Hill* 11 (Summer/Fall 1982), a double issue devoted exclusively to Russell.

ROBERT L. GALE

RUSSELL, Charles Taze (16 Feb. 1852–31 Oct. 1916), founder of the Watch Tower Bible and Tract Society, was born in Allegheny (now a part of Pittsburgh), Pennsylvania, the son of Joseph Lytle Russell, a haberdasher, and Ann Eliza Birney. He joined his father in business at age eleven and three years later withdrew from public school. He was raised in a pious Scotch-Irish Presbyterian home, but doubts about eternal punishment and biblical authority caused him first to join a more liberal Congregational church and then briefly to leave the church altogether. In 1869 an Adventist minister restored his faith in the Scriptures, and Russell began to study the Bible with a small group, which a few years later chose him as its pastor.

While he never joined an Adventist congregation, several Adventists shaped his theology. From George Storrs he learned that immortality was not intrinsic to human life but rather a conditional gift given only to the obedient. Accordingly Russell often emphasized that the damned did not suffer eternal torment, only simple annihilation. Russell also learned from Storrs that those who died without the opportunity to believe in Christ would be resurrected at the end of time and given a chance to believe and live in a paradise on earth forever.

Initially Russell was dubious of attempts to discern from the Bible the year of Christ's return; however, he found the intricate calculations of Nelson H. Barbour of Rochester, New York, persuasive. From 1876 to 1878 he provided financial backing for a magazine that he jointly edited with Barbour. Both Barbour and Russell adopted the view that the Bible promised the return of Christ's spiritual presence rather than his bodily reappearance. They believed this had begun in 1874 and that God's kingdom would come into full control over the earth in 1914. In 1879 Russell broke with Barbour, charging that Barbour had abandoned the teaching that Jesus had paid the ransom price for all humanity. That same year Russell began publishing *Zion's Watch Tower and Herald of Christ's Presence* (from 1908 to 1930 the *Watch Tower and Herald of Christ's Presence* and since 1939 the *Watchtower Announcing Jehovah's Kingdom*), which he edited for the rest of his life.

As head of an independent movement, Russell continued to refine his theology. He rejected the doctrine of the Trinity and accepted Jehovah as the personal name of God. But the basic eschatology outlined by Barbour and a commitment to the authority of the Bible and the harmony of its different parts remained constant throughout his career.

While he always maintained a refined, middle-class appearance, Russell strongly condemned existing churches for becoming too worldly, too much like "social clubs." He believed true Christian teaching had become fragmented among different denominations that were more interested in supporting their costly buildings and maintaining their creeds than promoting the truth. He also saw the conflicts caused by industrialization and nationalism as evidence that the world was in decline and the millennium was near. Russell believed that Christians seeking to convert the world were misguided because God was not planning to save the world in the present age. Instead he was electing a special group of 144,000 who would form the church, the body of Christ. The rest of the world would not be saved until God's kingdom was established.

In 1879 Russell married Maria Frances Ackley; they had no children. The following year he began to establish congregations among his readers in other cities modeled after the one in Pittsburgh. In 1884 he organized the Watch Tower Bible and Tract Society, which he headed until his death. Supporters of this society were known variously as Russellites, Millennial Dawnists, Bible Students, and after 1931 as Jehovah's Witnesses. In 1886 he published the first volume of *Millennial Dawn*, later retitled *Studies in the Scriptures*. By his death almost 5 million copies of this volume had been distributed. Russell traveled extensively to preach, journeying to Britain and Europe as well as throughout the United States and Canada. In 1909 he relocated the headquarters of the society from Pittsburgh, Pennsylvania, to a more prominent location in Brooklyn, New York. In 1914 his sermons were syndicated in almost 2,000 newspapers, and his "Photo-Drama of Creation" presented his view of world history from the creation to the millennium to audiences of more than 9 million around the world.

Throughout his career Russell remained ambivalent about the centralization of his movement and his own authority. He directed each local congregation to elect its own leader and engage in its own study of the Bible. Russell claimed no special revelation. He believed that the Bible was the only authority and anyone could learn the truth by diligently studying it. Yet, he also believed that his own *Studies in the Scriptures* was simply the Bible topically arranged and that it was better to study them than the Scriptures themselves. He also assigned traveling preachers to encourage uniformity in belief and practice among the congregations.

Several public controversies marred Russell's career, most notably his divorce and his promotion of "Miracle Wheat." Maria Russell assisted her husband's work through both her writing and public speaking. Russell, however, appears to have showed little appreciation and to have had a more conservative vision of a woman's role. Furthermore, when they married they had agreed not to consummate their union. While Russell appears to have been comfortable with this, Maria Russell appears to have come to resent it. These differences resulted in their separation in 1897 and a bitter divorce trial in 1906. In 1911 Russell was again in court, this time suing the *Brooklyn Daily Eagle* for its lampooning of the Miracle Wheat marketed by Russell. He believed that this unusually productive strain of wheat was evidence that the earthly paradise would soon be restored. Russell lost both trials, and his public reputation suffered.

As 1914 approached, Russell became more guarded in his claims about what would happen in that year. Undaunted by the fact that he and his followers did not experience the rapture that year, he regarded the advent of World War I as confirmation of biblical prophecies and predicted that the final battle of Armageddon and the rapture of the church would take place in 1918. Despite his declining health, his followers were greatly shocked when he died while traveling between speaking engagements on a train in Pampa, Texas, and thus did not live to experience the rapture. It fell to Russell's successor, Joseph Franklin Rutherford, to guide the movement through this turbulent time and to strengthen and centralize the organization.

The Watch Tower Bible and Tract Society survived Russell's death and became an enduring and controversial presence throughout the world. While it continued to respect his central role in organizing the society and to accept much of his teaching, its developing knowledge of religious truth led it to dismiss certain of his teachings as incorrect and to deemphasize his role. A much smaller group of Bible Students who broke with the larger society continued to revere his teachings and publish his works.

• Jerry Bergman, *Jehovah's Witnesses and Kindred Groups: A Historical Compendium and Bibliography* (1984), provides the most complete list of Russell's writings. M. James Penton, *Apocalypse Delayed: The Story of Jehovah's Witnesses* (1985), provides a useful history of Russell's career. Melvin D. Curry, *Jehovah's Witnesses: The Millenarian World of the Watch Tower* (1992), connects Russell to industrial America and studies his millennial thought. The leadership of the Watch Tower Bible and Tract Society gives its view of Russell's career in *Jehovah's Witnesses: Proclaimers of God's Kingdom* (1993). There is an obituary in the *New York Times*, 1 Nov. 1916.

DAVID R. BAINS

RUSSELL, Clayton (1910–1981), minister and political activist, was born in Los Angeles, California. Primarily educated in Los Angeles area schools, Russell also studied theology in Copenhagen, Denmark, in the early 1930s at the nation's International College. Russell later remarked that his experiences studying abroad profoundly influenced his thinking about the plight of fellow African Americans in the United States. Foremost among his overseas memories was a visit to prewar Germany, where the Los Angeles cleric witnessed firsthand the rise of Adolph Hitler's Nationalist Socialist (Nazi) party and its racist ideology. The eventual Nazi political triumph in Germany made him keenly aware of what a German victory in the Second World War would mean for American blacks.

In 1936 Russell took over the pastorate of Los Angeles's People's Independent Church. This church, which had emanated in 1915 from the black community's more conservative and powerful First African Methodist Episcopal Church, became known for its outreach programs for poor and disenfranchised blacks. Within a year into Russell's tenure, the People's Independent Church had become the most popular church in Los Angeles's black community. Spurred on by Russell's charisma and exceptional organizational skills, parishioners of the People's Independent Church confronted the problems of the Great Depression with unusual zeal. Under his direction, the church set up a medical outreach service for the poor, a free employment service, a staffed youth center, a college scholarship program, and a homeless shelter for neglected young men.

With the outbreak of the Second World War, Russell expanded his efforts to galvanize and organize the city's black community, with particular emphasis on getting the community behind the Allied war effort. Using his popular radio show (he was the first African American in Los Angeles to have his own radio program) as a bully pulpit, Russell organized the Negro Victory Committee, whose dual purpose was to defeat fascism abroad and racism at home. To those ends, Russell led several large-scale protests against defense industry companies that continued to refuse to hire blacks despite their desperate need for defense workers. So successful were these protests that they caught the attention and open political support of both President Franklin Roosevelt and California governor Culbert Olsen.

After helping to open Los Angeles's massive defense industries to previously neglected minority groups, in 1944 Russell led another successful protest campaign that culminated in black and Latino men being allowed to work as streetcar conductors for the city's large urban railway system.

While continuing to work on opening up jobs for minorities, Russell labored tirelessly to desegregate the city's schools. A strong proponent of education, he feverishly worked to convince local school board authorities that the city's continued practice of educational segregation was both un-American and harmful to all concerned. Within the black community, Russell openly encouraged the study of science and mathematics.

Another of Russell's lifetime goals was to make the black community as self-sufficient as possible. To that end he planned and created the nation's first black-owned cooperative market system. Opened on 11 April 1942, the Negro Victory Market played an important role in aiding black war workers and their families. Although it closed when the Second World War ended, the Negro Victory Market served as testament to the strong will and organizational skills of Russell and his followers.

Following the war, Russell continued his work to forward the cause of civil rights. In addition, in 1953 he founded the Church of Divine Guidance. Although his death was not highly publicized outside the black community of Los Angeles, his legacy of black self-sufficiency, the opening of defense jobs for women and minorities, and the desegregation of the nation's largest school system remain a living testament to those who believe that one individual can make a difference.

• Unfortunately, little has been written about Clayton Russell and his contributions to black America. The most notable exception is E. Frederick Anderson, *The Development of Leadership and Organization Building in the Black Community of Los Angeles, 1900 through World War 2* (1982). In addition, consult Arthur C. Verge, *Paradise Transformed: Los Angeles during the Second World War* (1993).

ARTHUR C. VERGE

RUSSELL, David Allen (10 Dec. 1820–19 Sept. 1864), soldier, was born in Salem, Washington County, New York, the son of David Abel Russell, a lawyer, and Alida Lansing. His father, a Whig, served as a representative from New York in Congress from 1835 to 1841. During his father's last year in Congress Russell received an appointment to West Point. He graduated in 1845, thirty-eighth in his class of forty-one, and was appointed a brevet second lieutenant in the First U.S. Infantry. His first posting was on the frontier at Fort Scott, Kansas, from 1845 to 1846. During the war with Mexico, from 1847 to 1848 he served with the Fourth U.S. Infantry. He participated in several minor engagements against Mexican irregulars and in the general engagement at Cerro Gordo. His behavior in these combats earned him a brevet to first lieutenant on 15 August 1847. Following the war his service was routine. He served garrison duty in East Pascagoula, Mississippi, in 1848, then was on recruiting duty until 1850. From 1850 to 1855 he served in garrisons at Fort Mackinac, Michigan; Fort Columbus, New York; Fort Vancouver, Washington; Fort Steilacoom, Washington; Fort Jones and Fort Dalles, Oregon; and Fort Yakima, Washington. On 22 June 1854 he was promoted to captain in the Fourth Infantry. During 1855 and 1856 he participated in operations against the Yakima Indians, taking part in the action at Tap-pin-ish River (6–8 Oct. 1855). After these operations Russell served garrison duty at Fort Walla Walla, Washington; Fort Yamhill, Oregon; and Camp Sumner, California.

At the outbreak of the Civil War, Russell returned from California and served in the preparation of the defenses of Washington, D.C., from November 1861 to January 1862. During this time he managed to secure command of the Seventh Massachusetts Volunteer Infantry and was commissioned as its colonel on 31 January 1862. Russell and his regiment accompanied the Army of the Potomac on the Peninsula campaign in the spring of 1862. His regiment was lightly engaged at Williamsburg on 5 May, and more severely at Seven Pines (31 May–1 June) and the Seven Days Battles (25 June–1 July). Following the Union defeat at Second Manassas (28–30 Aug.), Russell's regiment accompanied the Army of the Potomac during the Maryland campaign but did not participate in the various combats that ensued. On 29 November 1862 Russell was promoted to brigadier general of volunteers and assigned to command of the Third Brigade, First Division, Sixth Corps. Russell's brigade was only lightly engaged in the battle of Fredericksburg (13 Dec. 1862), but it saw heavy action during the Chancellorsville campaign near Salem Church on 4 May 1863. During the battle of Gettysburg (1–3 July 1863), Russell's command was held in reserve and saw little action. On 7 November 1863, at Rappahannock Station, Virginia, Russell, then in temporary command of the First Division, Sixth Corps, planned and executed a brilliantly successful assault against Confederate troops of General Jubal Early, capturing 1,303 officers and men, eight battle flags, and several pieces of artillery. General Horatio Wright, commanding the Sixth Corps, reported, "To General Russell is due the credit of leading his troops gallantly to the attack, and of carrying the first entrenched positions of importance during the war on the first assault." General George G. Meade, commanding the Army of the Potomac, permitted Russell to personally take the trophies his division had captured and present them to the War Department in Washington.

During Ulysses S. Grant's Overland campaign in the spring of 1864, Russell participated in nearly constant combat from the Battle of the Wilderness to Petersburg. When Sixth Corps commander, General John Sedgwick, was killed at Spotsylvania, Russell succeeded to permanent command of the First Division, which he led very ably throughout the remainder of the campaign. In July 1864 the Sixth Corps was withdrawn from the Petersburg lines and sent north to Washington, D.C., to confront Confederate forces under Jubal Early, who had threatened the capital. The Union forces, under the command of General Philip Sheridan, pursued Early to the Shenandoah Valley. On 19 September 1864 Early's and Sheridan's forces confronted one another at Winchester, Virginia. At a critical moment in the hard fought battle, Russell's division was ordered to mount a counterattack. According to the Sixth Corps commander, General Wright, who resumed command after Sedgwick's death, the attack proved to be "the turning point in the conflict." Russell personally accompanied the assault troops and during the advance received a serious wound in the left breast. He refused to leave the field, and moments later a shell fragment struck him, passing through his heart and killing him instantly. Philip Sheridan wrote of Russell: "Russell's death oppressed us all with sadness and me in particular. In the early days of my army life, he was my captain and friend, and I was deeply indebted to him for sound advice and good example. But for the inestimable services he had just performed and sealed with his life, so it can be inferred how keenly I felt his loss." Horatio Wright, in a fitting summary to Russell's life, wrote that Russell was "an officer whose merits were not measured by his rank, whose zeal never outran his discretion, whose abilities were never unequal to the occasion, a man tenderly just to his friends and heartily generous to his foes."

Russell was buried in Salem, New York. He never married.

• For a thorough biography of Russell see A. D. Slade, *That Sterling Soldier: The Life of David A. Russell* (1995). There is also a brief biography in New York Monuments Commission, *New York at Gettysburg*, vol. 3 (1902), and in New York Monuments Commission, *Dedication of the New York Auxiliary State Monument on the Battlefield of Gettysburg* (1926). A complete record of his military career is in George Washington Cullum, *Biographical Register of the Officers and Graduates of the United States Military Academy*, vol. 2 (1879). Russell's Civil War reports and some of his official correspondence were published in U.S. War Department, *War of the Rebellion: A Compilation of the Official Records of the Union and Confederate Armies* (128 vols., 1880–1901). Also see N. V. Hutchinson, *History of the Seventh Massachusetts Volunteer Infantry in the War of the Rebellion* (1890). A description and illustration of his death at Winchester can be found in James E. Taylor, *With Sheridan up the Shenandoah Valley in 1864: Leaves from a Special Artist's Sketchbook and Diary* (1989). An obituary is in the *Albany (N.Y.) Evening Journal*, 26 Sept. 1864.

D. SCOTT HARTWIG

RUSSELL, Elbert (25 Aug. 1871–21 Sept. 1951), educator, Quaker minister, and religious writer, was born near Friendsville, Tennessee, the son of William Russell, a teacher and Quaker minister, and Eliza Sanders. William Russell was an idealist who had moved from Indiana to East Tennessee to help rebuild the small Quaker communities there after the Civil War. He and his wife both died in 1879, and Elbert Russell spent the rest of his childhood with his grandparents in West Newton, Indiana. In 1890 he entered Earlham College, the Quaker school in Richmond, Indiana, graduating with honors in 1894 and remaining as governor of the men's dormitory. In 1895 he married an Earlham classmate, Liuetta Cox.

That same year Russell, despite a complete lack of training, became Earlham's professor of Bible. Over the next twenty years, Russell became the most embattled figure in American Quakerism. Earlham was affiliated with Gurneyite Friends, who between 1870 and 1890 had passed through a revolution. Accounting for about 75 percent of all American Friends, they had experienced a wave of revivals and had given up most of their peculiarities, embracing pastors and music. Many were tied to the interdenominational Holiness movement and were sympathetic to what would later be known as fundamentalism. Earlham had established its biblical department to meet the growing Quaker demand for pastoral ministers.

Russell, however, was not a fundamentalist. His sympathies instead were with the young Friends like Rufus M. Jones who melded a respect for Quaker tradition with a modernist theological outlook and an interest in critical study of the Bible. Russell, especially after two years of graduate study at the University of Chicago (1901–1903), became the best-known proponent of Higher Critical methods of scriptural scholarship. He especially urged the need for a progressive understanding of the Bible, arguing that as a result of modern scriptural scholarship, Christians understood the Bible better than previous generations and thus needed to be open to new interpretations. Russell was also an outspoken critic of the revivalism that had become popular among many Friends, arguing that it produced only fleeting effects. Russell's abilities as a teacher and preacher won him many followers, but he also became the target of Friends with fundamentalist sympathies, who charged him with heresy and "unsoundness." His offenses, in their eyes, included questioning the authority of the Bible and the divinity of Christ, charges that he fervently denied, and doubting the reality of the devil, which he admitted but saw as a nonessential issue. From 1903 to 1915 his critics kept up a constant campaign to force Earlham to fire Russell, a campaign that never succeeded. Instead, when Russell did resign his Earlham position in the spring of 1915, it was because of fierce disagreements with Earlham's president, Robert L. Kelly, whom Russell accused of eroding the college's Quaker character.

After leaving Earlham, Russell studied from 1915 to 1917 at Johns Hopkins University, using this work to obtain his doctorate from the University of Chicago in 1919. He then became the director of the Woolman School, a private Quaker secondary school on the campus of Swarthmore College outside Philadelphia. He also remained active in Quaker affairs, playing a leading role in Quaker opposition to World War I and in the Five Years Meeting of Gurneyite Friends, serving as a delegate to the World Conference of Friends in 1920, and helping to found a short-lived journal of liberal Quaker thought, *The Quaker*, in 1921. He continued to be a leader of the opposition to fundamentalist Friends, who were attempting to purge modernists from administrative and teaching posts. In 1924–1925 Russell traveled in England and Germany, lecturing on peace, Quakerism, and religion.

In 1926 Russell went to Duke University, which was just beginning operation in Durham, North Carolina, as professor of biblical instruction. In 1928 he was appointed dean of the Duke Divinity School, a position he held until his retirement in 1941. Under his leadership, Duke became an outstanding center of Methodist scholarship and ministerial training. Although Duke was a Methodist school, Russell remained a Friend and active in Quaker affairs. In 1927 he traveled to Nicaragua for the American Friends Service Committee and the Fellowship of Reconciliation on a goodwill mission. He also continued to speak and write extensively on Quaker doctrine and history. His magisterial *History of Quakerism*, for two generations the best one-volume treatment available, was published in 1942. After retiring, Russell moved to St. Petersburg, Florida, where he lived until his death there.

• Russell's papers are in the Friends Collection at Earlham College. They include considerable material cut from his published autobiography, *Elbert Russell, Quaker* (1956). Russell's other important books include *The Parables of Jesus* (1909); *Jesus of Nazareth in the Light of Today* (1909); *The Message of the Fourth Gospel* (1931); *Book of Chapel Talks* (1935); and *The Separation after a Century* (1938). For Russell's importance to Friends, see Thomas D. Hamm, *The Transformation of American Quakerism: Orthodox Friends, 1800–1907* (1988). An obituary is in the *American Friend*, 11 Oct. 1951.

THOMAS D. HAMM

RUSSELL, Harry Luman (12 Mar. 1866–Apr. 11, 1954), bacteriologist and university administrator, was born in Poynette, Wisconsin, the son of E. Fred Russell, a physician, and Lucinda Estella Waldron. In many ways the career of Harry L. Russell recapitulated the history of science in modern America. In 1890, as a young University of Wisconsin graduate in biology, he followed the path of many hundreds of other budding professionals in seeking advanced training in Europe. His field, the "hot" new science of bacteriology, led him to the laboratories of the masters, Robert Koch and Louis Pasteur, and afterward to the Zoological Station in Naples. There, following Koch's early lead, he did researches aimed at raising bacteriology to the status of a fully developed independent discipline. To his mind the new field deserved to be more than just an adjunct of medicine, and the remainder of his research career would be dedicated to that pursuit.

As a finish to his preparation for that career, Russell chose not to take a Ph.D. in Europe but to join the increasing number of his compatriots who would pursue it at home. The institution he chose was America's model research university, Johns Hopkins; and his major professor, its exemplar, William Henry Welch. Under Welch, Russell did a study of plant bacteriology that was not only pathbreaking but earned him America's first Ph.D. in general bacteriology.

As a beginning professional, Russell remained at the forefront of major new trends. His first job, in 1892, was an assistant professorship at another pacesetting institution, the University of Chicago, then being created with John D. Rockefeller's money and William R. Harper's leadership. There Russell also shared in the work of applying science to solve pressing problems of public health, an enterprise important in its own right but one that also finally enabled American science to fulfill its long-offered promise of practical usefulness. His contribution, more representative than significant, was a study of the threat to Mississippi River cities from typhoid organisms discharged into the Illinois River from Chicago (he proved there was none).

In 1893 he married H. May Delaney (they had one child) and began a work that would bring him national recognition. That year he returned to the University of Wisconsin to take a post as bacteriologist to its agricultural experiment station. It was a move that would put him at the center of another science-driven transformation of American life, the scientific revolution in agriculture. Owing to the showering of federal government support in the Morrill, Hatch, and (in 1906) Adams Acts, a handful of "cow colleges," such as those at Cornell, Illinois, Pennsylvania State, and Wisconsin, were emerging as leading research institutions.

The opportunity was tailor-made for Russell, and in fourteen years of experiment-station work he molded the emerging field of agricultural bacteriology and showed its value to economic development. A pioneer in using tuberculin to diagnose bovine tuberculosis, he eventually convinced state dairymen to eradicate the disease from Wisconsin herds. With chemist Stephen M. Babcock he solved the age-old mystery of cheese curing and, in the process, discovered a new way to manufacture cheese (cold-curing), which established Wisconsin as the industry's national leader. He developed bacteria-resistant crops, provided a scientific basis to the nation's canning industry, and helped convert Americans to pasteurized milk.

Thus, when he succeeded William A. Henry as agriculture college dean in 1907, he brought a conviction that basic research was the key not just to solving farmers' practical problems but also to unloosing the full productive potential of American agriculture. That faith, along with impressive skills at administration, enabled Russell in his twenty-three years as dean to build his college into one of the nation's great research institutions (and at the same time aid the enthronement of the university—not the government agency— at the center of American scientific research). At his instigation Wisconsin's college of agriculture added a host of new departments, all grounded in the research ideal. Among them were agricultural genetics, biochemistry, entomology, plant pathology, and wildlife management (giving the great ecologist Aldo Leopold a base of operations). Such was the quality of Russell's leadership that on his retirement in 1930, his college counted more members in the National Academy of Sciences than all the rest of the university combined.

But Russell did not retire to rest. That same year he became first director of the Wisconsin Alumni Research Foundation (WARF), a novel undertaking in the patent management area, and in 1932 married a second time, to Susanna Cocroft Headington. As the vigorous salesman of biochemist Harry Steenbock's discovery of the nutritional possibilities of ultraviolet radiation (it offered an artificial source of vitamin D), Russell brought to the Foundation leadership talents critical to the success of that pioneering venture in enabling research—via patent royalties—to pay its own way. By the end of World War II the WARF idea had surpassed its founders' hopes: its endowment—$12.5 million by 1947—had not only sustained Wisconsin research in the midst of severe economic depression but had lifted it, by the mid-1930s, to a top ranking among the nation's universities.

By the time of his death in Madison, Wisconsin, Harry L. Russell was recognized nationally as a science administrator and a man who had made large contributions to the research standing of his university and the economic welfare of his state. But his career had broader significance. As much as any American of his day, Russell stood as both barometer and instigator of the nation's conversion from a rural-commercial country into the world's preeminent scientific state.

• Russell's papers, comprising professional correspondence, scientific publications, and several travel journals (one from a fact-finding trip to Asia for the Rockefeller International Education Board), are housed at the Division of Archives of the University of Wisconsin in Madison. Russell's leadership as college dean is summarized in Merle Curti and Vernon Carstenson, *The University of Wisconsin: A History, 1848–1925* (2 vols., 1949), and in more detail in Wilbur H. Glover, *Farm and College: The College of Agriculture of the University of Wisconsin, a History* (1952). For a full-scale biography, see Edward H. Beardsley, *Harry L. Russell and Agricultural Science at Wisconsin* (1969).

EDWARD H. BEARDSLEY

RUSSELL, Henrietta. *See* Hovey, Henrietta.

RUSSELL, Henry Norris (25 Oct. 1877–18 Feb. 1957), astronomer, was born in Oyster Bay, New York, the son of Alexander Gatherer Russell, a Presbyterian minister, and Eliza Hoxie Norris. After several years in an Oyster Bay Dames' school, Russell lived with his maternal aunt in Princeton, New Jersey, in order to enter Princeton Preparatory School in 1890 and Princeton in 1893. Russell quickly distinguished himself at Princeton as an abnormally serious undergraduate. Avoiding much of the social life by living with his aunt, his classmates voted him their most awkward colleague at graduation in 1897, even though he earned highest honors and was affectionately listed in the class record as "Our Star."

Russell was a student of the astronomer Charles A. Young and of the mathematician Henry B. Fine, and he was torn between a career in astronomy and one in mathematics. His Princeton Ph.D. dissertation (1900), "The General Perturbations of the Major Axis of Eros Caused by the Action of Mars," was a combination of those interests, but it also is an early example of Russell's ability to search out and enter into hot new areas of research. Indeed, dating even from his graduate years Russell deftly ferreted out unexplored yet fruitful research topics, often at the same time as others. Hence it is not unusual to see Russell listed as co-discoverer in the astronomical literature. The Hertzsprung-Russell Diagram is one example, as is the Vogt-Russell theorem and Russell-Saunders Coupling; only the last example, however, was the result of collaboration.

Russell spent nearly his entire professional life at Princeton. After a year as a postdoctoral scholar at Cambridge University, where he attended George Darwin's lectures on orbit theory and dynamics, Russell spent almost two years as Carnegie Institution Research Associate at the Cambridge University Observatory, developing one of the first photographic parallax programs. Hired as instructor at Princeton in 1905, Russell set about reducing his trigonometric parallax data. To account for all possible systematic effects, as well as test a theory of stellar evolution he had been harboring, Russell obtained photometric and spectroscopic data for his stars from E. C. Pickering, director of the Harvard College Observatory. As he was analyzing these masses of data, Russell began to realize that for most of his stars, there was a definite correlation between intrinsic brightness, as derived from his parallax measurements, and gross spectral classification type. Although he first recognized this correlation in early 1909, he did not tell Pickering about it until September, and he did not begin to discuss it publicly until 1910. In the interim he conducted an exhaustive search for systematic effects.

What Russell had co-discovered, independently of the Dane Ejnar Hertzsprung, was that two classes of red stars existed; soon they both called the more common class dwarfs, for stars on the order of the Sun, and giants, for the rarer class of stars of vastly greater luminosity and volume, though not of significantly greater mass. In addition, though the giants were all approximately the same intrinsic brightness, the dwarfs varied in brightness according to color.

Between 1909 and 1913, when Russell could have presented his results in diagrammatic form, as Hertzsprung did in 1911 and 1912, he did not do so. Instead, Russell highlighted what his discovery meant for how stars lived and died; he thus revived a theory of stellar evolution developed by Norman Lockyer and August Ritter in the late nineteenth century. The Lockyer/Ritter theory, as revived by Russell, envisioned stars as beginning their lives as cool, vastly extended giants. Gravitational contraction caused them to heat up to a point where densities were reached that caused them to deviate from the perfect gas laws. From that point on, they would continue to contract, but instead of heating they would cool to extinction.

What made Russell's treatment distinct from that of Hertzsprung's, or from the majority of astronomers of his day, was that Russell collected and analyzed data only in pursuit of particular problems. The typical astronomer of Russell's day, especially in the United States, was a data collector and compiler. Russell, like his mentors Young and Darwin, thought that there was a more effective way to do astronomy. As Russell matured, becoming full professor in the short span of six years, then director of the observatory in 1912 and chairman soon after of Princeton's two-man department, his views became known through his actions as well as his rhetoric. The promotional efforts of his first prominent graduate student, Harlow Shapley, who became a staff member at George Ellery Hale's Mount Wilson Observatory in southern California, established a link that would change Russell's life.

Just before the United States entered World War I, Hale came to know Russell through Shapley and then through membership on the National Academy of Sciences panels concerned with both the mobilization of scientists for war and the needs of American science. Finding that they thought alike, in contrast to senior astronomers like Pickering, who with the majority of astronomers pushed mainly for the support of routine cartographic observations, Hale asked Russell to state his views formally to the academy. His remarks, published after the war as "Some Problems in Sidereal Astronomy," left little doubt about Russell's view of astronomical research: "The main object of astronomy, as of all science, is not the collection of facts, but the development, on the basis of collected facts, of satisfactory theories regarding the nature, mutual relations, and probable history and evolution of the objects of study" (*Popular Astronomy* 28 [1919]: 212).

Russell's scientific career can best be understood in this manner. How he approached what became the HR Diagram as well as the motives underlying his development of techniques for calculating the orbits of all forms of binary stellar systems, and of quick and efficient means for determining the masses of the stars—all early activities—clearly were stimulated by his strong desire to get away from the mere taking of data to the analysis and exploitation of those data. He said as much when applying to Woodrow Wilson in 1905 for the Princeton position. Russell saw American observatories as producers of a vast amount of photographic data, "but there are not more than half-a-dozen men in the country who are familiar with the modern ways of measuring them, and of reducing the result to a useful form" (Russell to Wilson, 6 Apr. 1905, in Arthur Link et al., eds., *The Papers of Woodrow Wilson*, vol. 16 [1976], p. 81).

Russell continued this blueprint after the war when he was invited by Hale to be a Carnegie Research Associate at Mount Wilson. From 1921 until the United States entered World War II, Russell spent several months each year helping Hale's spectroscopic staff exploit the vast stores of astrophysical data they had accumulated over the years. Coincidentally upon his appointment, Russell became highly excited by the appearance of a series of papers by the Calcuttan Megnad Saha on ionization equilibrium in stellar atmospheres. Using Bohr theory and Nernst's chemical heat balance theorem, Saha was able for the first time to show, on the basis of physical theory, that the spectral classification sequence adopted by astronomers was in fact a temperature sequence and that temperature and pressure were the primary factors influencing the appearance of a typical stellar spectrum. The abundances of the elements in the stellar atmosphere played only a small role, far less than the influence of the physical state of the medium. Russell saw that Saha's work had an immediate and far-ranging application at just the place he was now invited to by Hale. Hale had wanted Russell to help his staff learn how to incorporate modern physical theory into their work. Armed with Saha's perspective, Russell did just that. In the first decade of his associateship, Russell refined Saha's theory and embarked on a program of analyzing line spectra not only for its astrophysical use, but as a means of delving into the structure of matter. As he told a professional audience, Saha's work had galvanized physics and astronomy into one body. Combining forces, he said, "It is not too bold to hope that, within a few years, science may find itself in possession of a rational theory of stellar spectra, and, at the same time, of much additional knowledge concerning the constitution of atoms" ("The Properties of Matter as Illustrated by the Stars," *Publication of the Astronomical Society of the Pacific* 33 [1921]: 280).

By 1924 Russell had published more than a dozen papers extending Saha's work and by the end of his first decade at Mount Wilson had developed a full-blown quantitative analysis of the abundances of the elements in the solar atmosphere. He lectured often at Mount Wilson and greatly impressed those on the staff whose work, long performed in isolation, was now becoming fully integrated with theoretical astrophysics. In July 1923 veteran Mount Wilson laboratory spectroscopist A. S. King reported to Hale about Russell's recent visit:

Henry Norris Russell arrived, "sailed in high," and (to continue the disrespectful comparison) with plenty of oil in his crankcase. The talking became a solo and continued unabated during his stay. He gave us three or four talks a week on spectral series applied to atomic structure (King to Hale, 22 July 1923, Hale papers).

Both Hale and Russell were insatiable workers, both shared the same hyperactive enthusiasm for astronomy, and both suffered frequent breakdowns from overwork or nervous exhaustion. Unlike Hale, Russell never sought higher office beyond Princeton, though he was courted for the directorships of far larger observatories at Harvard and Yale and reluctantly accepted various society obligations from time to time. Nor did Russell wish to enlarge his department at Princeton, preferring frequent faculty exchanges to building a local empire. Russell became convinced that he was most effective at direct action, which he managed by forming numerous ad hoc networks of physical laboratory and observatory personnel to attack such diverse problems as a complete term analysis, description, and evaluation of the line structure of complex spectra to the organization and analysis of masses of eclipsing binary data. His influence at Mount Wilson was matched by his role in helping his former student Shapley modernize programs at the venerable and entrenched Harvard College Observatory. After he became director in 1921, Shapley immediately put Russell on his visiting committee to help redirect efforts in what Russell regarded as "a land of settled habits" (Russell to Shapley, 31 Jan. 1920, Russell papers).

Much of Russell's influence derived from his tireless efforts at popularization. From 1900 to around 1943, Russell wrote a column for *Scientific American* that quickly became a platform for promoting progress in astronomy. In his hundreds of columns over the years, Russell rarely if ever used his venue to take sides in the many debates of the day. Rather he worked hard to explain all sides and to assure his readers that differing views in science were not evidence of weakness or divisiveness, but of the robustness of the discipline. Thus, even though privately Russell often said nasty things about Percival Lowell's claims for an advanced civilization on Mars, publicly the claims were never derided but always discussed on the face of the evidence, with alternatives provided and limitations identified. Russell paid salutary and sympathetic attention to the efforts of the observatories he favored, which was any place where anything at all useful, in his opinion, was being accomplished. Russell similarly used his two-volume textbook, *Astronomy* (1926, 1927), coauthored by his departmental colleagues R. S. Dugan and J. Q. Stewart, as a means not only to disseminate astronomical information but also to stimulate growth in modern astrophysics.

Russell was a devout and thoughtful Christian thinker. Son, grandson, and brother of liberal (though Old School–trained) Presbyterian ministers, he was very much in step with the legacy of James McCosh, who from his installation in 1868 as Princeton's president fought to establish what was then called the College of New Jersey as a first-rate national institution. Russell continued in the spirit of McCosh by lecturing frequently to students and the lay public, both from the pulpit and from the campus lectern, on the relationship of science and religion, especially how the former might inform the latter by revealing unity of design in nature. He was also a liberalizing influence on campus, arguing in the 1920s for the abolishment of mandatory chapel attendance by undergraduates. Russell thought it was wasted effort to preach to a captive, unwilling audience.

Russell was very much a family man, to the extent that he often preferred working at his ancestral home on the border of campus. He had married Lucy May Cole in 1908, and they had four children, living comfortably after 1921 on Russell's comparatively high faculty salary, his generous Carnegie stipends, and family investments. Russell's influence in the astronomical community was such that his family became well known. He constantly reported in some detail on their progress in his professional correspondence, and they often accompanied him in his travels west, usually spending summers as guests of the Lowell Observatory while Russell moved on to Mount Wilson. Russell died in Princeton.

• Russell's papers, including correspondence, manuscripts, and working notes, are in the Firestone Library, Manuscripts Division, Princeton University. There is a microfilm edition of the correspondence. Large collections of his correspondence can also be found in the George Ellery Hale Papers, microfilm edition. A. G. Davis Philip and David DeVorkin, eds., *In Memory of Henry Norris Russell*, Proceedings of IAU Symposium No. 80, Dudley Observatory Report No. 13 (1977), contains papers by historians and astronomers who were colleagues and students of Russell as well as an extensive bibliography and a reprinted autobiographical reminiscence. DeVorkin, "Henry Norris Russell," *Scientific American* 260 (May 1989): 126–33, serves to identify the range of his scientific contributions. An obituary is by Harlow Shapley, "Henry Norris Russell," National Academy of Sciences, *Biographical Memoirs* 32 (1958): 353–78.

DAVID H. DEVORKIN

RUSSELL, Irwin (3 June 1853–23 Dec. 1879), poet, was born in Port Gibson, Mississippi, the son of William McNab Russell, a physician, and Elizabeth Allen, a teacher at the Port Gibson Female College. His family moved to St. Louis in 1853, after he had survived a bout of yellow fever, but, sympathizing with the Confederate cause, returned to Port Gibson when the Civil War began. Frail as a child, he was not allowed by his overly protective mother to participate in boisterous outdoor play. Thus isolated from other children, he compensated by becoming introspective and building his imagination. Russell developed a love of books from his mother. He read John Milton at age six; later he grew to love the poetry of Robert Burns.

After attending local schools in Port Gibson, Russell went to what is now St. Louis University, where one of his favorite subjects was mathematics. Completing his formal education with distinction, he graduated in 1869. Returning to Port Gibson, Russell read law in the office of Judge L. N. Baldwin. Restlessness often led him to stray from his studies. While on impulsive trips to New Orleans and Texas, he stayed at places such as sailors' boardinghouses before hardships and ill health drove him home. Developing a penchant for drink that would lead to chronic alcoholism, Russell could be headstrong and gloomy, but he also revealed a side given to kindness and a love of poetry and fun. Erratic but brilliant, he was admitted to the bar in 1872 at the age of nineteen by a special act of the Mississippi legislature.

Though he worked as a lawyer until the late 1870s, Russell did not find the practice of law suited to his disposition. Given his love of literature, he was improvising verses to his own banjo accompaniment by 1867. His signed poems were published in national magazines such as *Scribner's Monthly* from 1871 until his death. Becoming active in local social life, he joined the Port Gibson Thespian Society, for which he wrote a play entitled "Everybody's Business; or, Slightly Mistaken." The play, now lost, was never produced because of an outbreak of yellow fever in the summer of 1878. Serving as his father's assistant, Russell worked day and night to help the ill and the dying among his fellow townspeople. The woman he loved, Dora Donald, died in the epidemic.

Russell had won national recognition when *Scribner's Monthly* published his "Uncle Cap Interviewed" in January 1876. This was the first of many dialect poems in which he reported the songs and stories of black life around him. In his masterpiece, "Christmas Night in the Quarters," which appeared in *Scribner's* in January 1878, Russell portrays the jubilant atmosphere of Christmas night in the black quarters of a large plantation.

Even though Russell was not the first postwar poet to write about the lives of black people, he was the period's most significant writer of black dialect verse. Writers such as Sherwood Bonner, Thomas Dunn English, and Sidney and Clifford Lanier anticipated Russell's use of black dialect in poetry, but they lacked what he possessed—a spontaneity and spark of genius that gave to his work a feeling of sharing intimately the emotions of the people he described. This feeling overcame any shortcomings in the transcription of black dialect.

Though physically and emotionally weakened by his work in the yellow fever epidemic, Russell moved to New York in December 1878, hoping to further his literary career. Encouraged by Robert Underwood Johnson and Richard Watson Gilder of the staff of *Scribner's Monthly,* he was featured regularly in the "Bric-A-Brac" section of the magazine, writing principally in black dialect. His pieces were often embellished with illustrations of his characters. His success was short-lived, however. Illness and homesickness, coupled with bouts of heavy drinking, plunged him into depression. Johnson and Henry C. Bunner, the editor of *Puck* magazine, tried to take care of Russell, but he eventually fled from his friends. Penniless, he managed to work his way to New Orleans as a coal heaver on a steamer. His father had died while Russell was in New York, and his mother had subsequently moved to California. Alone (he had never married), refusing to ask for help from his friends in Port Gibson, Russell worked briefly for the *New Orleans Times.* He died of exposure and pneumonia in a cheap boardinghouse in New Orleans.

Collected by Charles C. Marble, Russell's work was published in a small volume titled *Poems* in 1888. Impressed by Russell's verse, Joel Chandler Harris provided an introduction in which he cited Russell as having drawn by far the most accurate and artistic portrait of southern blacks. An expanded volume of Russell's verse, illustrated with drawings from *Scribner's Monthly,* was published in 1917, again with an introduction by Harris.

Russell's position as the most significant poet of black dialect of the post–Civil War period was enhanced by the praise liberally bestowed on him by Thomas Nelson Page and, especially, Joel Chandler Harris. For many of his contemporaries, Russell captured the mind and spirit of a race that was seemingly inscrutable to his predecessors. It was this inner sense rather than the use of dialect or specific circumstances that made Russell a true progenitor of southern writers such as Page and Harris.

• Bibliographical materials on Russell can be found in Laura D. S. Harrell, "A Bibliography of Irwin Russell, with a Biographical Sketch," *Journal of Mississippi History* 8 (1946): 3–23, and Harriet R. Holman, "Irwin Russell (1853–1879)," in *A Bibliographical Guide to the Study of Southern Literature,* ed. Louis D. Rubin, Jr. (1969). For biographical information, see Charles C. Marble, "Irwin Russell," *The Critic,* n.s., 10 (1888): 199–200; William Malone Baskervill, *Southern Writers: Biographical and Critical Studies* (2 vols., 1897); Alfred Allen Kern, "Biographical Notes on Irwin Russell, *Texas Review* 2 (1916): 140–49; and John S. Kendall, "Irwin Russell in New Orleans," *Louisiana Historical Quarterly* 14 (1931): 321–45. An obituary is in the *New Orleans Times,* 24 Dec. 1879.

L. MOODY SIMMS, JR.

RUSSELL, Israel Cook (10 Dec. 1852–1 May 1906), geologist, was born near Garrattsville, New York, the son of Barnabas Russell and Louisa Sherman Cook. When Russell was twelve, the family moved to Plainfield, New Jersey. He attended Rural High School in Clinton, New York, and Hasbrook Institute in Jersey City. He then entered the University of the City of New York and received a B.S. and the degree of civil engineer in 1872. He took postgraduate courses at the School of Mines of Columbia University.

Russell wanted to join the 1874 U.S. expedition to New Zealand and Kerguelen Island to observe the transit of Venus. When he found that the only available opening was as a photographer, he took a brief course in that field from astronomer Lewis Morris Rutherfurd and was appointed photographer for the expedition. On its conclusion he continued around the world. His first scientific papers were about New Zealand, including aspects of its geology, the giant birds, and New Zealand flax. On his return in 1875 he received an M.S. from the University of the City of New York and became assistant professor at the School of Mines of Columbia University for two years. In 1878, as assistant to geologist John James Stevenson, he participated in the final year of the U.S. Geographical Surveys West of the One Hundredth Meridian, usually called the Wheeler Survey for its leader, First Lieutenant George Montague Wheeler. Stevenson and Russell explored the geology of the New Mexico region.

Russell traveled in Europe during 1879, and on his return in 1880 he became assistant geologist with the newly established U.S. Geological Survey (USGS). He was assigned to work under Grove Karl Gilbert in the Great Basin region, beginning with the area of Pleistocene Lake Bonneville. In his second year, as a designated geologist, he was assigned to independent work on the geologic history of the desert basins in Nevada, Oregon, and parts of California. Following his four years in that region, he wrote a classic account, *Geological History of Lake Lahontan, a Quaternary Lake of Northwestern Nevada* (1885). He later expressed his enthusiasm for "the vast arid regions of the southwest" where "the features of the naked land are fully revealed beneath a cloudless sky." He said that such exposures had created the field of physiography, the description of land forms that is now called geomorphology. Russell's reports for the USGS established his reputation as a careful observer.

After four years of work in the western United States, Russell was assigned by the USGS to map the Paleozoic formations in the southern Appalachian Mountains and then the geology of the area of the Newark formation in New Jersey and adjacent areas.

In 1886 he married Julia Augusta Olmstead; they had four children.

Russell especially enjoyed exploration of spectacular geology. He obtained permission from the USGS to accompany an expedition in 1889 by the U.S. Coast and Geodetic Survey, which was intended to determine the eastern boundary of northern Alaska with Canada. He traveled up the Yukon River and, with three local miners, crossed 2,500 miles of wilderness to the Lynn Canal near Juneau. He returned to Alaska during the next two summers and explored Mount St. Elias and Yakutat Bay, under the joint auspices of the USGS and the National Geographic Society, with continued travel assistance from the Coast and Geodetic Survey. Colleagues commented on his boundless energy and resourcefulness in the field. Storm-bound and alone on Mount St. Elias, he survived by digging into a snowdrift where he stayed for three days until the weather cleared. He published a number of papers on glaciers and other aspects of Alaska, in both scientific journals and popular magazines. He introduced the term "piedmont" in glacial terminology to describe broad expanses of sheet ice, which had left major characteristic features in various regions of North America during Pleistocene advances of glaciation.

In 1892 Russell became professor of geology at the University of Michigan, holding that position until his death. His courses were primarily for undergraduate students. He continued fieldwork for the USGS during summers, working in Nevada, Idaho, Washington, Oregon, and the Mono Valley in California. Some of his work was directed particularly to water supplies and their potential for irrigation. At the request of the National Geographic Society he visited the islands of Martinique and St. Vincent in the West Indies to observe the eruptions of Mount Pelée and La Soufrière in 1902. He also studied the geology of Michigan, including work for the state survey in 1904 and 1905 in the northern peninsula. To the city of Ann Arbor he donated his time studying and advising on the water supply.

Russell completed many scientific reports, including long ones for the USGS, richly illustrated with his own photographs. He also wrote five books that were intended for students of geography and geology but that were also well accepted by laymen. These included *Lakes of North America* (1895), *Glaciers of North America* (1897), *Volcanoes of North America* (1897), *Rivers of North America* (1898), and *North America* (1904). He was a member of a number of scientific societies and was president of the Geological Society of America at the time of his death in Ann Arbor, Michigan.

Not one who developed broad theories in his field, Russell is most noted as a knowledgeable geologic explorer, one who described effectively the remote places that he reached.

• In addition to his books, Russell wrote about 100 scientific and popular papers, including "Quaternary History of Mono Valley, California" for the eighth report of the U.S. Geological Survey (1889) and *The Newark System* (Bulletin 85 of the U.S. Geological Survey, 1892). His accounts of glaciers in Alaska and volcanic eruptions in the West Indies were published in *National Geographic*; see, for example, "An Expedition to Mount Saint Elias, Alaska," 3 (1891): 53–194; "Height and Position of Mount Saint Elias," 3 (1892): 231–37; "Report to the National Geographic Society on the Recent Volcanic Eruptions in the West Indies," 13 (1902): 267–85; and "Volcanic Eruptions on Martinique and Saint Vincent," 13 (1902): 415–36. Russell also published articles in other popular magazines such as *Overland Monthly, Century, Popular Science Monthly*, and *Scribner's*. Biographies of Russell are by Warren P. Lombard and Martin L. D'Ooge in *Science* 24 (1906): 426–31; by G. K. Gilbert in the *Journal of Geology* 14 (1906): 662–67; and by Bailey Willis in the *Bulletin of Geological Society of America* 18 (1907): 582–92, with bibliography. An obituary is in the *Detroit Free Press*, 2 May 1906.

ELIZABETH NOBLE SHOR

RUSSELL, James Earl (1 July 1864–4 Nov. 1945), college dean, was born in Hamden, New York, the son of Charles Russell and Sarah McFarlane, farmers. Russell attended the Delaware Academy in Delhi, New York, and received his A.B. from Cornell University in 1887. After graduating from Cornell, Russell taught secondary school and, beginning in 1890, served as principal of the Cascadilla School, a preparatory school in Ithaca, New York. In 1893 Russell resigned the principalship of the Cascadilla School and traveled to Germany for advanced academic study. There he pursued work in pedagogy, philosophy, and psychology at the Universities of Jena and Leipzig, receiving a Ph.D. from the latter institution in 1894. Concurrent with his academic work abroad, Russell served as European commissioner of the regents of the University of the State of New York and as European agent for the U.S. Bureau of Education. In those capacities he studied and reported on the state of European education. In 1895 Russell returned to the United States conversant in the "science of education" and, while aware that the autocratic spirit of German education was ill suited to public schooling in a democracy, was impressed with the high level of academic and professional training German teachers received, as well as the distinction afforded pedagogy as a subject of study in the German university.

Following his return to the United States, Russell began an appointment as professor of philosophy and pedagogy in the College of Liberal Arts at the University of Colorado at Boulder. While there, he focused primarily on establishing a program for the professional education of secondary teachers and recruiting prospective teachers to the university for training. In 1897 Russell left the University of Colorado to begin an appointment offered to him on the recommendation of Benjamin Ide Wheeler, a noted classicist with whom Russell had studied at Cornell, to head the Department of Psychology and Methods of Teaching at Teachers College in New York City. Teachers College, attended predominantly by women, was established in 1887 by Grace Hoadley Dodge, an evangelical Protestant reformer, and Nicholas Murray Butler, an aspiring academic administrator and public leader. A small yet diverse institution, the college was a hybrid of the different social and educational reform goals and interests that Dodge and Butler had introduced.

Russell joined the faculty of Teachers College at a critical moment in its history. The president of the college had resigned the previous spring, and the college trustees' search for a new administrative head had been unsuccessful. The institution's relationship with Columbia University, with which it had formed an alliance in 1893, was also at risk of being dissolved. Russell quickly won the confidence of the trustees for his insight into the problems confronting the college, and he was instrumental in easing Teachers College through these crises and in suggesting ways to negotiate a new contract with Columbia. The contract, ratified in 1897, stipulated that Teachers College be made a full-ranking professional school of the university and, in keeping with the earlier contract of 1893, that it remain financially independent of Columbia. In connection with the negotiation of this new agreement, Russell was named dean of Teachers College, effective January 1898.

It was in this capacity that Russell made his mark as a highly skilled academic administrator. While technically a dean of the university, Russell functioned—given Teachers College's semiautonomous relationship with Columbia University—more nearly in the role of a college president. In charge of his own physical plant, able to draw on the resources of an independent board of trustees, and responsible, notwithstanding certain university policies, for shaping the college's curricular goals and aims, Russell managed Teachers College firmly, purposefully, and with a keen sensitivity to the educational needs of a growing industrial and class-stratified society. Over the course of his career, Russell transformed Teachers College. It grew from a small college for teachers into a graduate institution internationally renowned for training educational and social leaders. Russell's administrative strategy hinged on recruiting a first-class faculty of men and women, enlarging and modernizing the college's classroom and research facilities, advancing the institution's admissions standards, and building on the broad set of goals that had shaped Teachers College from the time of its founding.

Intent on placing the study of education on the same plane in the university as the study of law, medicine, and engineering, Russell encouraged the development of a "systematized body of [educational] knowledge" based on scientific research and investigation and the practical application of educational theories and ideals. Like other prominent educators and academic administrators of the period, Russell was committed to building a well ordered, "meritocratic" system of secondary and postsecondary education that would serve the needs of a mass student population and guarantee the selection and training of an elite corps of educational leaders. Eager to distinguish Teachers College

as a first-rate institution and in accord with goals defined by the college's two previous administrations, Russell distanced the college from the training of rank and file teachers and guided its development toward the preparation of leaders. In 1899 Russell outlined what he believed competent leadership in teaching rested on—namely a strong academic and cultural foundation, scholarly expertise specifically directed toward instructional goals, professional knowledge drawn from philosophy, psychology, and the history of education, and learned teaching technique.

Not constrained by any need to follow one particular vision, Russell's concept of education embraced the complex needs of an industrial and commercial society. He capitalized on Teachers College's divergent pattern of growth and pushed its expansion into specialized areas of professional service that lay outside public schooling. In particular, Russell emphasized developing advanced professional programs of study for women in fields such as public health nursing, nursing education, and the household arts and sciences. Russell thus positioned Teachers College to tap into the growing market for women's professional training, particularly for training in professions like teaching and nursing, which affirmed rather than countered women's traditional social roles.

Teachers College grew at a phenomenal rate under Russell's administration, significantly outpacing the growth and development of other prominent schools and university departments of education across the country. When Russell took office in 1898 Teachers College owned two buildings adjacent to Columbia University, enrolled fewer than 200 students (who were matriculating at a level roughly equivalent to the freshman and sophomore years in college), and had operating expenses of less than $250,000 annually and no endowment. By 1927, when Russell resigned, the college held classes and conducted research in seventeen buildings both on and off its Morningside Heights campus. It supported three research institutes—the International Institute, the Institute of Child Welfare Research, and the Institute of Child Development—enrolled 5,333 students (many of whom were college graduates), expended $2.7 million on annual operating costs, and had investments and funds totaling close to $6 million. By the end of Russell's administration it was possible to pursue advanced training and research in an array of specialized studies, including kindergarten education, elementary and secondary teaching, rural education, comparative education, physical training, music and art education, school administration, nutrition and health education, and nursing supervision and administration.

Outside of his duties as dean of Teachers College, Russell developed an interest in cattle breeding, an avocation he pursued for nearly forty years on his farm near Peekskill, New York, and in later years on property he owned near Lawrenceville, New Jersey.

Active in a number of professional organizations and associations, Russell was president of the Boy Scouts National Committee on Education (1916–

1935), president of the American Association for Adult Education (1926–1929), chair of the Organizing Committee of the Federal Advisory Committee on Education (1929), a member of the New Jersey State Board of Health (1932–1940), and a member of the New Jersey Milk Control Board (1933–1934).

Russell was married twice. In 1899 he married Agnes Fletcher, with whom he had four children, including William Fletcher Russell, who succeeded his father as dean of Teachers College in 1927. In 1929, two years after his first wife's death, Russell married Alice Forman Wyckoff. He died at his home in Trenton, New Jersey.

A highly skilled and aggressive college administrator, Russell easily ranked among the best of the academic executives of his generation. Professionally active in an era of enormous growth and change in higher learning, Russell's importance as a college dean is best understood in relation to contemporary reform efforts to order and systematize learning in America, and, more pointedly, to centralize and codify professional practices and training in select educational institutions.

• The primary source for Russell's administrative career is the James Earl Russell Papers in Special Collections, Milbank Memorial Library, Teachers College, Columbia University. The TCana Collection, which includes official records and publications related to Teachers College and several volumes of newspaper clippings, is also in the Milbank Library. Additional manuscript material may be found in the President Papers, Central Files, Columbia University. Important works by Russell include "The Function of the University in the Training of Teachers," *Columbia University Quarterly* 1 (Sept. 1899): 323–42; *German Higher Schools* (1907); "Democracy and Education: Equal Opportunity for All," National Education Association, *Addresses and Proceedings* (1908): 155–58; *The Trend in American Education* (1922); *Founding Teachers College* (1937); "Education in Colorado Thirty-five Years Ago," *Teachers Journal and Abstract* 5 (Nov. 1930): 507–12; and *Heredity in Dairy Cattle* (1944). The best biographical account of Russell's early life and professional career is Kenneth H. Toepfer, "James Earl Russell and the Rise of Teachers College, 1897–1915" (Ph.D. diss., Columbia Univ., 1966). See also Lawrence A. Cremin et al., *A History of Teachers College, Columbia University* (1954); [anon.], "Anniversary Dinner in Honor of James Earl Russell," *Teachers College Record* 24 (May 1923): 280–313; memorial tributes to Russell in *Teachers College Record* 47 (Feb. 1946): 285–95; and Geraldine Joncich Clifford, *The Sane Positivist* (1968). Obituaries are in the *New York Times*, 5 Nov. 1945, and *Adult Education Journal* 5 (Jan. 1946): 56–57.

BETTE WENECK

RUSSELL, James Solomon (20 Dec. 1857–28 Mar. 1935), educator and priest, was born on the Hendrick Estate in Mecklenburg County near Palmer Springs, Virginia. His father, Solomon, and his mother, Araminta (maiden name unknown), both lived as slaves on adjoining properties, with the North Carolina state line between them. With the ambiguity of slave status following Abraham Lincoln's Emancipation Proclamation in 1863, the largely illiterate black people were left wondering how they might survive. After share-cropping during and following the war, in 1868 Solomon rented a nearby plot with his brother as partner. They raised a good crop of corn and $80 worth of tobacco. Then the brothers' barn burned and the Russells, with son James, ten years old, were destitute again. In spite of their poverty, Araminta insisted that her son learn to read, and even in the absence of public schools for blacks, James's fortunes improved.

A plantation overseer, Thomas Wade, allowed James to ride behind him on his rounds and to ask questions. An elderly woman with only a second-grade education also coached him in reading and writing for fifty cents per month. In 1870 white lay missionaries John E. P. Wright and Mack Duggar started a Sunday school for black children, and in the same year a private school for blacks was opened by Armisted Miller. By 1873 young Russell had established himself as an excellent student and at sixteen was superintendent of the Wright-Duggar Sunday School. The state of Virginia opened a school for blacks that Russell attended when not required for farm work. Then he went as a boarding student to Hampton Institute for a year, but he could not return in 1875 because of family obligations. He received a teaching certificate from Brunswick County, and after teaching two years near his home, he returned to Hampton for another year.

At this point a benefactor entered his life. Patti Hicks Buford, the wife of a prominent lawyer in the county, was just beginning what would become her life's work—a school for black children and later a hospital for black patients (the first one in Virginia, according to her obituary in a 1901 Richmond paper). Russell so captivated her that in due course she gave him $50 and told him to visit the Episcopal bishop, Francis M. Whittle, to discuss furthering his education. Because the Diocese of Virginia had never had a black postulant and the seminary at Alexandria was not to desegregate for nearly another hundred years, Whittle's solution was to form the Bishop Payne Divinity School, an all-black institution in Petersburg, with Russell as its first matriculant.

Russell developed a fast friendship with the Reverend Giles Buckner Cooke, rector of St. Stephen's parish in Petersburg, principal of its school for black students, and a former major on the staff of Robert E. Lee. This extraordinary man tutored him during what would normally have been his college and seminary years. Russell became well known as a speaker. In 1882, the year that he was ordained a deacon in the Protestant Episcopal church, he made such a moving appeal at the diocesan convention for missionary work among blacks that he was voted a horse, saddle, bridle, and $300. Thereafter, "Ida" was the all-purpose animal who delivered him to his missions, hauled bricks for campus construction, and later pulled the water wagon at Saint Paul's School.

Also in 1882 Russell married Virginia Morgan, an accomplished organist and graduate of Cooke's St. Stephen's School. Together they started a church and Sunday school in Lawrenceville, Virginia, and opened one mission after another in surrounding towns; she taught when she was not delivering their five children.

With his lofty title, the archdeacon for colored work for southern Virginia, and his dignified humility, Russell was able to coexist with the white half of the population. In 1888 he opened Saint Paul's Normal and Industrial School in Lawrenceville, which in 1969 became a four-year college. He held the title of principal until 1929, when he was succeeded by his son James Alvin Russell. Russell's business acumen was remarkable. He bought the first electric generator in the community and soon was selling electricity to neighboring businesses. He acquired an ice machine; henceforth, when the Southern Railway's passenger trains stopped at nearby Emporia, they loaded 100-pound ice blocks from the school's wagon. His reputation for reliability was such that when he bought the school's first piece of land, 3.1 acres for $1,000, he was not required to pay down any cash. All that was required was a promissory note cosigned by Virginia Russell. The next year he bought "the Hill," which became the center of the campus. In 1921 Russell sold enough timber to cover the entire cumulative cost of the land. He continued buying and trading land until, at the time of his death, the college owned 1,600 acres, many of these purchased with the disapprobation of Bishop Whittle, who felt that land speculation was inappropriate for an Episcopal priest.

In 1904 Russell borrowed the idea of an annual farmer's conference, originally conceived by Booker T. Washington, his friend and contemporary at Hampton Institute. In two years, attendance at the conference had grown to 2,000. Experts were brought in to urge the planting of food as well as cash crops. Russell lost no opportunity to preach his philosophy—own your land, keep out of debt, add rooms to your house, pay your poll tax, and vote. All of these concepts were anathema to many hostile whites. Saint Paul's became the biggest business in Brunswick County. Practically all surgery for blacks in the area was performed in the school's infirmary. Ninety percent of the black teachers in the county were Saint Paul's graduates.

During Russell's active career of over a half century, the Episcopal church's principal medium of evangelistic communication was a little magazine called the *Spirit of Missions*. Russell's reports in it were powerful appeals. He began making regular trips to New York, Boston, and Philadelphia. He attracted the interest of well-known individuals—Francis L. Stetson, George Foster Peabody, J. Pierpont Morgan, and Charles Comfort Tiffany. Before World War I he had become the best-known black priest in the Episcopal church. When the Diocese of Arkansas was seeking a suffragan bishop for work among blacks, Russell was elected by the House of Bishops, but he declined. When North Carolina offered the same opportunity, he declined once more. Had he accepted he would have been the first black bishop in the Episcopal church in the United States, but Russell was convinced that he had found in his school the place in which he could be of greatest use to God and humanity. Three thousand people attended his funeral, including three dozen vested clergy. His great magnetism, force, energy, judgment, and dedication carried him to remarkable success. He died in Lawrenceville and was buried near the campus of the school he founded.

Russell's charity and compassion, combined with astute business acumen, won him such admiration among whites and blacks that the churches, businesses, and schools of the area remained at peace at a time when crosses were burned in many other parts of the South.

• Most of the material about Russell can be found in Lawrenceville, Va., where he spent his adult life after 1882. The Saint Paul's College Library has the best collection of his letters and papers, but some important material remains in the hands of his numerous descendants. The Archives of the Episcopal Church in Austin, Tex., has files of publications that cover aspects of his career. By far the most important source is his autobiography, *Adventure in Faith* (posthumous ed., 1936). Almost as important is Frances Ashton Thurman, "History of Saint Paul's College" (Ph.D. thesis, Howard Univ., 1978). Also worth consulting is Arthur Ben Chitty's monograph, *Miracle Worker of Southside Virginia* (1982), which includes some material not found in the earlier works. An obituary is in the *New York Times*, 29 Mar. 1935.

ARTHUR BEN CHITTY

RUSSELL, Jane Anne (9 Feb. 1911–12 Mar. 1967), endocrinologist, was born near Los Angeles, California, the daughter of Josiah Howard Russell, a rancher and deputy sheriff, and Mary Ann Phillips. She completed her early education in the public school system of Long Beach and received a B.A. from the University of California at Berkeley in 1932, graduating first in her class. During her first year as a graduate student at Berkeley she worked as a technician in the biochemistry department, and from 1934 to 1937 she worked as an assistant in the university's Institute of Experimental Biology.

At the institute, Russell experimented with the pituitary hormones to see how they affected carbohydrate metabolism, the process by which the body produces glucose to fuel the muscles. Her most important discovery was that an unidentified pituitary secretion could maintain sufficient amounts of glucose, both in the bloodstream and in the form of glycogen, the complex molecule in which glucose is stored in muscle tissue, during periods of carbohydrate deprivation. In 1936, as a research associate in pharmacology at Washington University in St. Louis, Missouri, she collaborated with Gerty and Carl Cori, co-winners of the 1947 Nobel Prize in physiology or medicine for their work in carbohydrate metabolism. During Russell's stay in St. Louis, the Coris discovered glucose-1-phosphate, or the "Cori ester," the first of two compounds into which glycogen breaks down before becoming glucose. She received a Ph.S. from Berkeley in Biochemistry in 1937.

Russell remained at the institute for an additional year as a Porter Fellow of the American Physiological Society. In 1938 she received a fellowship from the

National Research Council to continue her investigation into the ways in which hormones regulate carbohydrate metabolism at the Yale University School of Medicine. In 1940 she married a colleague, Alfred Ellis Wilhelmi; they had no children. The next year she was offered a full-time position at Yale as an instructor of physiological chemistry. While at Yale she identified the substance secreted by the pituitary that regulates carbohydrate levels as somatotropin, or growth hormone. Because of this and other discoveries, she was presented with the prestigious Ciba Award for hormonal studies in 1946, appointed to a National Institutes of Health study section on arthritis and rheumatism in 1949, and elected vice president of the Endocrine Society in 1950. Despite these honors, she never rose above the level of instructor at Yale because the university enforced strictly its rules against nepotism; as long as Yale employed Wilhelmi as a professor, it would never elevate Russell to the position. Accordingly, in 1950 the couple moved to Atlanta, Georgia, to accept positions at Emory University's Department of Biochemistry, he as professor and department chair and she as assistant professor.

While at Emory, Russell began to follow a new line of inquiry, that of the role of somatotropin as a regulator of nitrogen metabolism, the process by which the body forms amino acids into proteins. One result of this research was her theory, which later won wide support, that somatotropin plays an important role in preventing the decomposition of structural proteins such as collagen, an essential component of bone, tendon, ligament, and skin, and keratin, an essential part of hair and nails. She also devoted much of her time and energy to public and scientific organizations, particularly after her promotion to associate professor in 1953. From 1955 to 1958 she served on the National Research Council committee that evaluated postdoctoral fellowships. From 1958 to 1964 she held a position on the National Science Board. In 1958 she was elected to the editorial board of the American Physiological Society and in 1962 became a section editor for metabolism and endocrinology for the *American Journal of Physiology*. She received recognition for her research activity and professional involvement in the form of two awards and a promotion: in 1961 she was named the Woman of the Year in Professions in Atlanta and shared the Upjohn Award of the Endocrine Society with her husband, and in 1965 Emory made her a full professor. She developed breast cancer in 1962 and spent the last five years of her life in pain. She died in Atlanta. A posthumous honor was conferred on her by Emory with the establishment of the Jane Russell Wilhelmi Memorial Lecture Series in 1976.

Russell's contribution to science consisted of her work on hormones and the regulatory role they play in carbohydrate and nitrogen metabolism. Her seventy-plus publications demonstrate the complex interrelationships that exist between the human endocrine system and the processes the body employs to maintain and energize itself.

• Russell's papers, including a list of her publications and a biographical outline, are in the Special Collections Department of the Robert W. Woodruff Library at Emory University. Some of her personal letters are in the Manuscript Division, Bancroft Library, University of California at Berkeley. A brief biography is C. N. H. Long, "In Memoriam: Jane A. Russell," *Endocrinology* (Oct. 1967): 689–92. An obituary is in the *New York Times*, 14 Mar. 1967.

CHARLES W. CAREY, JR.

RUSSELL, Jonathan (27 Feb. 1771–17 Feb. 1832), diplomat and politician, was born in Providence, Rhode Island, the son of Jonathan Russell, Sr., a merchant, and Abigail Russell. He graduated from Rhode Island College (later Brown University) in 1791 and studied law, but he declined legal practice in favor of commercial pursuits. He married Sylvia Ammidon in 1794; they had four children. Russell became active in state Republican politics and published several pamphlets, including a Fourth of July speech, *An Oration* (1800), which went through twenty editions; and *The Whole Truth* (1808), written on behalf of James Madison's presidential candidacy. Madison subsequently appointed Russell secretary to the American legation at Paris in 1810; following the resignation of John Armstrong, Russell succeeded him as chargé d'affaires. Although considering himself a Francophile, he deplored Napoleon's underhanded treatment of American shipping as intolerable and issued numerous diplomatic protests. Soon after Joel Barlow was named minister to replace him and on 27 July 1811, Russell transferred to London as chargé.

In England, Russell proved himself to be an ardent nationalist. He strenuously opposed the Orders in Council and argued to suspend American grain shipments to the Spanish peninsula, which sustained Lord Wellington's army. In light of British inflexibility, he also advocated war against Great Britain. When war was declared in June 1812, Russell took particular pleasure in delivering the diplomatic note to the British government. He continued in London during the war years as chargé and also functioned as the agent for American prisoners. In 1813 the U.S. government authorized Russell to conclude an armistice with Lord Castlereagh contingent upon suspension of the Orders and impressment of American mariners. When these negotiations failed, Russell became one of five commissioners appointed to pursue a peace treaty. Arriving at Ghent, Belgium, he quickly became embroiled in a contretemps with John Quincy Adams over free navigation of the Mississippi River in exchange for rights in the northeastern fishing areas. However, Russell also expressed great empathy for the western-oriented policies of Henry Clay, who subsequently became his friend and mentor. Russell's overall role in the negotiations was relatively minor, and they successfully concluded on 24 December 1814.

After the war Russell was dispatched to Stockholm where he served as minister to the kingdom of Sweden and Norway. He attempted to resolve longstanding claims against the Swedish government for its seizure of American cargoes during the Napoleonic wars. Russell pressed his case forcefully, but Swedish intransigence delayed a settlement until after his recall by President James Madison in 1818. Russell's work was carried on and eventually completed by the chargé, Christopher Hughes.

Russell's first wife died in 1811, and he married Lydia Smith in April 1817; they had four children. After returning from Europe he settled in Mendon, Massachusetts, where his interest in politics was reawakened. In 1820 Russell gained election to the General Court, a constitutional convention, and to the U.S. House of Representatives. He served as chairman of the Committee of Foreign Relations and as partisan supporter of House Speaker Clay's presidential aspirations, but his own machinations proved Russell's undoing. In a bid to embarrass another presidential aspirant, John Quincy Adams, Russell circulated a forged letter suggesting that during the Ghent negotiations Adams was willing to concede Mississippi navigation to the British, positing him as the foe of western interests. However, Adams deftly responded by publishing the original document, and he enlisted the press in a successful bid to derail Russell's career. The phrase "to jonathanrussell" someone (publicly destroy him) entered the political lexicon. Russell returned to Mendon and served one term in the state legislature before retiring from public life. Though weakened by a series of strokes, in 1828 he became a vocal proponent of Andrew Jackson's candidacy, authoring a series of letters and newspaper articles. He died in Mendon.

Russell was a gifted writer, an ardent patriot, and a competent diplomat; however, he could also be scheming, ambitious, and quick to criticize others in a vitriolic fashion. As his squabble with Adams suggests, Russell allowed partisanship and personal antipathy to overrule common sense, bringing an end to a promising political career.

• Russell's official correspondence is in Record Group 84, Foreign Service Posts, Secretary of State, National Archives. Major collections of personal letters are at the Hay Library, Brown University, and the Massachusetts Historical Society. Other materials are in the Joseph Pitcairn Letters, Cincinnati Historical Society, and the William Crawford Papers, Perkins Library, Duke University. See also "Letters of Jonathan Russell, 1801–1827," *Massachusetts Historical Society Proceedings* 44 (1914): 293–310; and "Journal of Jonathan Russell," *Massachusetts Historical Society Proceedings* 51 (1918): 369–498. The only biographical study is Twila M. Linville, "The Public Life of Jonathan Russell" (Ph.D. diss., Kent State Univ., 1971). See also Norman E. Saul, "Jonathan Russell, the President Adams, and Europe in 1810," *American Neptune* 30, No. 4 (1970): 279–93; and Lawrence S. Kaplan, "Jonathan Russell and the Capture of the Guerriere," *William and Mary Quarterly* 24, No. 2 (1967): 284–87. For insight into his diplomatic career, see Clifford L. Egan, *Neither Peace Nor War: Franco-American Relations, 1803–1812* (1983); Fred L. Engleman, *The Peace of Christmas Eve* (1962); and Brynjolf J. Hovde, *Diplomatic Relations of the United States and Sweden* (1921). An obituary is in the *Boston Daily Advertiser*, 20 Feb. 1832.

JOHN C. FREDRIKSEN

RUSSELL, Joseph (8 Oct. 1719–16 Oct. 1804), merchant, shipowner, and manufacturer, was born in Dartmouth, Massachusetts, the son of Joseph Russell II and Mary Tucker, farmers. Russell was raised in an early Dartmouth Quaker family and appears to have been an exemplary Quaker. In 1744 he married Judith Howland, whose family dated back to the earliest Quaker converts in Dartmouth. The couple had eleven children.

Russell's business career reflected the intersections of religion, commerce, and manufacturing characteristic of the late colonial and early national periods. As early as the 1750s, Russell had a number of ships engaged in trade with the West Indies. In 1750 he had begun to manufacture spermaceti candles. By 1765, the owner of shares in four sloops and two brigs, Russell characteristically spread the risks of enterprise among family members and other Quakers, including his brother William Russell and fellow Quakers from the town of Dartmouth, William and Caleb Tallman. His principal factor in London after 1770 was his eldest son, Barnabas, who was also involved in his father's West Indies trade.

In 1765 Russell sold a portion of his farm in southeastern Massachusetts to Joseph Rotch, a Nantucket merchant looking for an alternative site for his whaling operations. The land shortly thereafter became the village of Bedford and subsequently was incorporated as the town of New Bedford in 1787. Russell and Rotch were examples of the symbiotic relationship between religion and commerce common among eighteenth-century members of the Society of Friends. Originally part of the town of Dartmouth, Russell's land seemed ideally suited for the development of industries related to whaling. The possibilities of the harbor and Russell's previous activities probably attracted Rotch; at the time of his purchase, he probably was aware that Russell already had four sloops engaged in whaling as well as the spermaceti candle factory. In 1769 Rotch became a partner in Russell's factory and, in the process, obtained an ascendant position in prerevolutionary American whaling. Rotch's investments in Russell's candle factory vertically integrated the whaling industry in its two most important centers, New Bedford and Nantucket. Carried along by Rotch's development of both the whaling industry and New Bedford, Russell benefited by converting his land into new capital assets, whalers, and oil works. His initial sale to Rotch netted £4,000, and the development of New Bedford further helped to increase the prices of his real estate.

Despite the family tradition of Quakerism, Russell and his family were heavily involved in revolutionary activities. The Revolution posed profound debates among Quakers over the peace testimony, and its ultimate acceptance as a prerequisite for membership in the meeting generally led most members to a position of neutrality. Russell, however, declared his sentiments openly, naming one of his vessels *No Duty on Tea* and reportedly investing heavily in Continental paper currency. During the Revolution, New Bedford became an alternative to the more heavily blockaded ports of Boston and Providence and was known as a haven for prizes captured from the British. In retribution, the British raided New Bedford in September 1778 and destroyed over seventy vessels, as well as warehouses, shipyards, and ropewalks. Russell lost a sloop, a barn, and the candle factory. Three of the four New Bedford residents shot and killed during the raid were apprentices or employees of his, and all three died of their wounds in his home.

Despite the destruction of his sloop and oil works, Russell emerged from the war in good financial shape. In 1785 he was able to weather the postwar depression and then invest in new, more efficient ships. After the war, competition for sperm whales in the Atlantic and trade restrictions by European nations led to declining earnings in the industry. In response, Russell with his sons Barnabas and Gilbert financed the construction of the *Rebecca*. Designed by George Claghorn, the architect of the *Constitution*, the *Rebecca* at a 175-ton burden was nearly three times the capacity of Russell's prerevolutionary ships. Its size was illustrative of new economies of scale that facilitated the exploitation of distant whaling grounds and, along with the residence of its owners, was a harbinger of the shift of the center of American whaling from Nantucket to New Bedford during the nineteenth century. One of the first whalers to round Cape Horn for the Pacific and return, the *Rebecca* went down on its homeward passage in 1803. The loss poignantly symbolized the closing of Russell's business career, coming shortly before his death in New Bedford.

According to his grandson Daniel Ricketson, Russell, like most Quakers, persisted in wearing long coats, knee breeches, and buckled shoes after they had become unfashionable. Other commentators also noted his integrity, industry, and prudence. A devout Quaker, he donated land for the site of the New Bedford Meeting House in 1785. At his death, his real and personal estate totaled £6,400.

Credited with the founding of New Bedford, Russell illustrates the shifts in economic focus of southeastern Massachusetts during the early national period. He ranked behind Joseph and William Rotch, revolutionary New Bedford's most important figures; but his land sales and subsequent investments in ships, candle factories, and oilworks were significant. He was at the center of the postrevolutionary developments that led to New Bedford's domination of whaling during the first half of the nineteenth century and, with his descendants, provided the economic basis for its subsequent development as a textile and fishing center.

• An occasional deed or invoice as well as ship registers may be found in the Old Dartmouth Historical Society at the Whaling Museum, New Bedford, Mass., but there is little primary material directly relevant to Russell. The major sources on Russell are Daniel Ricketson, *The History of New Bedford, Bristol County, Mass.* (1858); Leonard Bolles Ellis, *History of New Bedford and Its Vicinity, 1602–1892* (1892); Zephaniah W. Pease, *History of New Bedford* (3 vols., 1918);

and Barrett Beard Russell, "Descendants of John Russell of Dartmouth, Massachusetts," *New England Historical and Genealogical Register* 58 (1904): 364–71. For more recent descriptions of the early economic and social history of the region, see Edward Byers, *The Nation of Nantucket* (1987); and A. Sue Friday, "The Quaker Origins of New Bedford, 1765–1815" (Ph.D. diss., Boston Univ., 1991).

JONATHAN M. CHU

RUSSELL, Lillian (4 Dec. 1861–6 June 1922), entertainer, actress, and singer, was born Helen Louise Leonard in Clinton, Iowa, to a well-to-do family. Her father, Charles E. Leonard, was the publisher of the local newspaper, the *Clinton Herald*, and her mother, Cynthia Howland Van Name, was an early and ardent feminist. Her family moved to Chicago in 1865, and she attended local schools, completing her formal education at the Park Institute, a finishing school. However, as she later recalled, her most significant education occurred at home: "Our family was a musical one. We sang and danced and played, and all my sisters had exceptionally fine voices, which were carefully trained." Her parents subsequently divorced after separating in 1877, and, with her mother and sisters, she moved to New York City. Within a short time, she secured a chorus part in Edward E. Rice's production of Gilbert and Sullivan's *H.M.S. Pinafore* at the Brooklyn Academy of Music. As she later recalled, "I travelled as a chorus girl in Mr. E. E. Rice's *Pinafore* company and was royally proud of my salary, because it was the first money I had ever earned. And how I worked. There was not a day that season that I was not hard at work acquiring voice technique and stage deportment" (Young, p. 995). Considering an opera career, she took voice lessons from Leopold Damrosch but to her mother's disappointment chose the popular stage as her venue. Impresario Tony Pastor engaged her as a singer in 1879, renaming her Lillian Russell. She made her debut for Pastor on 22 November 1880, billed as "Lillian Russell, the English Ballad Singer, a Vision of Loveliness and a Voice of Gold." Her voice and great personal charm helped Russell score personal successes in Pastor's travesties of *Olivette* and *The Pirates of Penzance*. She worked under Pastor's management until 1893, appearing in a variety of opéra bouffe productions. Her performance in Pastor's travesty of Gilbert and Sullivan's *Patience* led to her employment in the Bijou Theater production of the original show in 1881.

Having made a name for herself in the United States, Russell spent the years from 1883 through 1885 in England, where she appeared in a few successful productions, including *Spirit of the Times* (1883) and *Polly; or, The Pet of the Regiment* (1884), which brought her triumphantly back to New York. While in New York under Pastor's management, Russell was offered $20,000 a year by manager Rudolf Aronson to appear at New York's fabled Casino, where she scored some of her greatest successes. These included her performances in *The Princess Nicotine* (1893) and *An American Beauty* (1896), the latter title supplying an epithet often used to describe Russell, who was also known to the public as "Airy Fairy Lillian." During this time Russell became close friends with the legendary Diamond Jim Brady, a high-rolling fixture of the Gilded Age's high society. Although their relationship was apparently platonic, they both gained in celebrity by their association with one another. Russell's charm, beauty, and hourglass figure perfectly suited the fashions of the era, and her friendship with the extravagant Brady, another icon of the period, captured the imagination of the American public who followed their escapades with rabid interest. Brady and Russell gave lavish parties, wore eye-popping jewelry, lived in the very finest homes with lavish furnishings and one-of-a-kind art works, and entertained the most celebrated figures of the day, and all of this was reported in daily newspapers for a public that simply could not get enough of lives that seemed to epitomize the Gay Nineties.

Over the years, critics debated the talents of Russell. Most acknowledged her unequaled popularity with her audience, but some were less certain of her true abilities as a vocalist. As biographer Parker Morrell noted, "Her voice while never rich, was at least a clear, full-throated, lyric soprano of true pitch and impressive quality." Perhaps her vocal prowess was insignificant because she became for the members of her audience a larger-than-life and singular image who perfectly suited their tastes for glamour and beauty and for whom they had considerable affection. As Ella McKenzie wrote in 1909: "All the world loves a beautiful woman. It doesn't make any difference who she is, or where she is, if a beautiful woman appears, she will attract the admiration of those who happen to see her. . . . It is this fact more than any other that accounts for the never ending popularity of Lillian Russell. Other stars may shine for a while—possibly a long while at that—but they go again, while Lillian shines on forever" (Young, p. 993). Beginning in the 1890s Russell struggled with weight problems that threatened her reputation as a beauty, and still her career continued unabated. She made a transition from operetta to burlesque by joining comedians Joe Weber and Lew Fields, who had previously worked closely with Russell's rival, Fay Templeton, in 1898. In an 1899 Weber and Fields show Russell introduced her most famous song, "Come Down, My Evenin' Star," which she subsequently recorded. Despite the inadequacies of the recording techniques of the time, Russell's recorded voice has a pleasant, pseudo-operatic quality but hardly suggests the impact her vocalizing apparently had on audiences at the peak of her fame. Russell continued with Weber and Fields in revues such as *Fiddle-dee-dee* (1900) and *Whoop-dee-doo* (1903) until 1904, when they disbanded their company. She next appeared in *Lady Teazle* (1904), a musical version of *The School for Scandal*.

On 2 October 1905 Russell made her debut in vaudeville at Proctor's Twenty-third Street Theatre for a salary of $100,000 for a 33-week engagement. Diamond Jim Brady bought a box for Russell's entire run. The *New York Sun* critic, Acton Davies, wrote of her appearance, "Songs may come and songs may go, but age cannot wither nor variety custom stale Miss Russell. She is the same old Lillian, and her voice is the same old voice" (3 Oct. 1905). She remained in vaudeville until 1907, when she attempted two non-musical productions, *Butterfly* (1907) and *Wildfire* (1908). She was moderately well received in these productions but soon returned to vaudeville, where she could command enormous salaries and maintain complete control over her performance.

In 1912 Russell made a successful comeback on the musical stage with Weber and Fields in *Hokey-Pokey*, costarring Templeton and George Beban. Russell returned to vaudeville periodically, and when she played New York's Palace Theatre in 1915, *Variety* wrote, "What matters how she sings or why she sings, she's Lillian Russell, and there's only one." Russell's vaudeville act evoked the Gay Nineties, and she always included "Come Down, My Evenin' Star," a nostalgic favorite with audiences. She played another celebrated engagement at the Palace in 1918, leading *Variety*'s Sime Silverman to call her a "feminine freak of loveliness," and critic Alan Dale noted that she "is one of the very, very few women who never needed advertising."

In 1915 Russell made her only movie appearance in a World Film production of her 1908 play, *Wildfire*, costarring Lionel Barrymore. The film was only a minor success, and since she was still able to command huge salaries on the stage, Russell saw little reason to return to the screen.

Improbably enough, Russell became involved in politics in the last years of her life, encouraged by her fourth husband, Alexander P. Moore. Russell had previously been married to Harry Braham from 1880 to 1883, and their union produced a son who died in infancy, with each parent blaming the other for his tragic death. Russell was next married to showman Edward Solomon from 1884 to 1893, and their marriage produced a daughter. Following her 1886 separation from Solomon (with an annulment granted in 1893), Russell married John Haley Augustin Chatterton (known in the theatrical profession as Signor Don Giovanni Perigini) in 1894, but this marriage ended in divorce four years later. Moore, who Russell married in 1912, was a staunch Republican who encouraged Russell's political interests. She worked vigorously to sell war bonds during World War I and encouraged other stars to join the effort. In 1922 President Warren G. Harding asked her to investigate immigration issues for his administration. Her appointment by Harding was particularly pleasing, since there were occasional public scandals in Russell's life, some involving romantic interludes following the breakups of her first two marriages as well as broken contracts, but despite all this, as one obituary noted, Russell "left a trail of affection wherever she passed."

In 1922 Russell suffered a fall while traveling on a transatlantic liner returning to the United States from Europe. Complications arose, and she died in Pittsburgh, Pennsylvania, after ten days of illness. In 1940 20th Century–Fox produced a highly fictional motion picture about Russell's life titled *Lillian Russell*, with Alice Faye in the title role. As a result of the popularity of that film, Russell's name has remained synonymous with the Gilded Age stage of the 1890s.

• Archival materials are available at the Billy Rose Theatre Collection at the New York Public Library for the Performing Arts, Lincoln Center, and in the Harvard Theatre Collection. Russell provides some vivid views on life as an actress in her article "Is the Stage a Perilous Place for the Young Girl?" *Theatre*, Jan. 1916, p. 22. For additional information on Russell, see Albert Auster, "Chamber of Diamonds and Delight: Actresses, Suffragists, and Feminists in the American Theater, 1890–1920" (Ph.D. diss., State Univ. of New York, Stony Brook, 1981); Djuna Barnes, *Interviews*, ed. Alyce Barry (1985); De Witt Bodeen, *Ladies of the Footlights* (1937); James Brough, *Miss Lillian Russell: A Novel Memoir* (1978); John Burke, *Duet in Diamonds: The Flamboyant Saga of Lillian Russell and Diamond Jim Brady in America's Gilded Age* (1972); "Lillian Russell: Her Path to Fame," *Literary Digest*, 24 June 1922, pp. 40–41; Ella McKenzie, "Lillian Russell To-day," *Greek Book Album*, Feb. 1909, pp. 358–60; Parker Morrell, *Lillian Russell: The Era of Plush* (1940); Lois Rather, *Two Lilies in America: Lillian Russell and Lillie Langtry* (1973); and William C. Young, *Famous Actors and Actresses of the American Stage* (1975). Burke and Rather provide the most complete accounts of Russell's life, while Auster offers useful accountings of Russell's stage credits. An obituary is in the *New York Times*, 6 June 1922.

JAMES FISHER

RUSSELL, Luis Carl (6 Aug. 1902–11 Dec. 1963), jazz bandleader, arranger, and pianist, was born in Careening Cay in Bocas Del Toro Province, Panama, the son of Felix Alexander Russell, a pianist and music teacher who taught him several instruments. In 1917 he played piano accompanying silent films and the next year moved to Colon, where he played in the Casino Club with a small dance band. Nothing is known of Russell's mother except that in 1919 she and her daughter accompanied him to New Orleans after he had won $3,000 in a lottery. Once settled, he studied jazz piano with Steve Lewis and in the fall of 1921 worked at the Cadillac Club in Arnold De Pass's band, where he first met clarinetist Albert Nicholas. In 1923 he played with Nicholas's six-piece jazz band at Tom Anderson's Cabaret, and when the clarinetist left for Chicago in May 1924 to replace Buster Bailey in King Oliver's Creole Jazz Band, Russell was given temporary leadership of the group. Later in the year, after Nicholas had returned, he too went north to work with Doc Cooke's Orchestra at the Dreamland Ballroom, but by 1925 he was reunited with Nicholas in King Oliver's newly formed Dixie Syncopators at the Plantation Café.

A sideman on all of the Dixie Syncopators' recordings between March 1926 and April 1927, Russell debuted as a leader at the beginning of this period when he took his Hot Six, with cornetist George Mitchell and some Oliver sidemen, including Nicholas, trombonist Kid Ory, and tenor saxman Barney Bigard, into the Vocalion studios to record two numbers in definitive New Orleans "hot dance" style. This coupling was followed in November 1926 by four titles on the OKeh label under the name of Luis Russell's Heebie Jeebie Stompers, another six-piece group drawn from Oliver's working band, this time including cornetist Bob Shoffner, trombonist Preston Jackson, and reedmen Darnell Howard and Bigard. In March 1927, after the Plantation was bombed in a gang war, Russell went with Oliver on a tour through Milwaukee, Detroit, St. Louis, and New York, where in May the band played two weeks at the Savoy Ballroom. When Oliver ran out of bookings the men dispersed, with Russell leaving in September 1927 to join drummer George Howe's band at the Nest Club. The next month Howe was fired by the management for repeatedly falling asleep on the bandstand, and Russell was appointed leader, a position he maintained through the following year.

After Howe's dismissal Russell brought in New Orleans drummer Paul Barbarin and replaced the trumpeter and trombonist, respectively, with Louis Metcalf, a Louis Armstrong devotee, and J. C. Higginbotham, who was then playing in the lusty, broad-toned manner of Kid Ory. By the end of the summer of 1929 Russell had added Nicholas and bassist Pops Foster and replaced Metcalf with Henry "Red" Allen, an even better Armstrong-influenced New Orleanian. Unlike any other northern-based orchestra of the time, the Russell band now had five New Orleans musicians in its ranks, as well as the brilliant solo talents he already had in Higginbotham and alto saxophonist Charlie Holmes, himself a disciple of Sidney Bechet. With a personnel so deeply immersed in New Orleans–style polyphony, blues timbre, and rhythm, Russell had a band that was truly one of a kind.

In 1929 and 1930 the group played at a number of New York venues, including the Savoy Ballroom, the Saratoga Club, and Connie's Inn, as well as touring theaters as a backup band for Louis Armstrong. During this period Russell's orchestra also recorded fourteen titles that remain definitive examples of early big-band jazz. They also recorded, in whole or in part, under the names of Armstrong, Allen, and Higginbotham, and as accompanists to blues singers Victoria Spivey and Addie "Sweet Pease" Spivey. Between 1931 and 1934 the Russell band continued to tour, while also playing residencies at Connie's Inn, the Arcadia Ballroom, and the Empire Ballroom, where cornetist Rex Stewart briefly joined the band as featured soloist. The records of 1934 indicate a total abandonment of the 1929–1930 New Orleans–based orchestral style, with its emphasis on polyphonic ensembles and loosely swinging rhythm, and instead display an attempt to come closer to the more heavily arranged patterns of other contemporary dance bands. Russell encouraged tenor saxman Bingie Madison to contribute his own arrangements to the band's library, and these rather tricky and virtuosic charts reflect the more mechanical but highly popular styles of the Casa Loma and Jimmie Lunceford orchestras, a far cry from the free and jubilant swing of only a few years before. In effect, this was a move toward the commercialism that would characterize the band's playing for the remainder of its days.

In September 1935 Armstrong's manager, Joe Glaser, decided that Russell's band would be the ideal setting for his star trumpeter and singer, who had recently returned from a long European tour and was ready to front a permanent band of his own. On 1 October, with very little rehearsal time, Armstrong and Russell opened at Connie's Inn, and from that time through early 1943 the Russell band, once on a level with McKinney's Cotton Pickers and the orchestras of Fletcher Henderson and Duke Ellington, functioned as a mere backdrop to Armstrong. The records of the early period indicate a drastic change in the Russell sound, as Armstrong had an inexplicable liking for the syrupy saxophones and clipped-brass-section phrasing of Guy Lombardo and no doubt asked Russell to follow that example. Additionally, because he was so confident of his ability to capture and maintain his audiences' attention all by himself, Armstrong seemingly expressed little interest in such niceties of orchestral performance as uniform intonation and sectional precision. Russell's and Madison's arrangements were designed to showcase Armstrong's solos and vocals, and it was undoubtedly Glaser, as much as Armstrong, who dictated this musical policy. But, as leader, Armstrong ultimately must be held responsible for the shoddiness of the band's performance standards at this time. Presumably, Russell and Madison did the best they could under existing stylistic restrictions and with the popular and novelty song material they were obliged to arrange, but because of the pedestrian nature of their work the records of this period are valued not for the band's contributions but for Armstrong's brilliance as a performer. However, the band does begin to rise to the occasion by May 1936, when it recorded "Swing That Music," with Foster's prominent bass and effective riffing by the horn sections, and "Mahogany Hall Stomp" in a competent version that nevertheless demands comparison with the far superior Armstrong/Russell collaboration on the same number from March 1929.

By 1935 only a handful of the original Russell bandsmen were still present, but in the summer of 1937 Allen, Higginbotham, and Nicholas returned, and in late 1938 Barbarin was replaced by Sid Catlett, one of the finest of all swing drummers, whose subtle but strong propulsion added a valuable rhythmic impact that was lacking in the more rigid playing of his predecessor. However, even by mid-1937 the band was performing up to standard, and the arrangements were beginning to reflect the influence of Fletcher Henderson. According to Nicholas, who solos to advantage on the spirited "I've Got a Heart Full of Rhythm," the band played even better in person than it did on record, which by this time was already quite an improvement over what it had been doing in 1935. Recording dates in 1939 and 1940 indicate that the band was being allowed more liberties than earlier, and there are a number of excellent performances that survive, such as the sessions that produced remakes of some of Armstrong's late 1920s classics.

However, after his departure from Armstrong, in 1944 Russell formed another totally different orchestra that opened at the Savoy and in 1945 and 1946 recorded several commercial sessions for the Manor and Apollo labels that bear no stylistic relation to his previous work. He divided his time between touring and appearing at New York–based theaters and ballrooms, but unfortunately the band had no major soloists, and its arrangements possessed neither distinction nor originality. With little prospect for continued work for his band, in 1948 Russell retired from full-time music and opened a candy and stationery store in Brooklyn, at the same time leading small bands for occasional jobs, managing the Town Hill nightclub, and teaching piano and organ. During the 1950s he married concert singer Carline Ray. Russell's last years were spent teaching, and he also worked as a chauffeur for the president of Yeshiva University. He died in New York City.

In the words of Gunther Schuller, Russell "was a gifted composer and a constantly explorative arranger," but Albert McCarthy believes that "compared with the McKinney or Henderson bands, Russell's offered little in the way of innovatory scoring." McCarthy quite rightly points out that the main virtues of the original band lay not in its arrangements but in its swinging rhythm section and its inspired, inventive soloists. If the arrangements that Russell churned out for Armstrong in the 1930s and for his own band in the mid-1940s constituted the only evidence of his writing extant, then estimations of his talent would not be so different. But, to his credit, early in his career he wisely sensed his limitations as a pianist and rarely took solos. What little we do hear of him reflects a stiff and awkward touch and a decidedly unswinging sense of time. Russell was at his best when writing for his own orchestra in a style shaped by his musical experiences in the 1920s in New Orleans and Chicago, but by the time the swing era was in full gear he had already passed his prime. He should more properly be remembered for his accomplishments in 1929–1930 than for his subsequent activities with Armstrong and beyond.

• The most careful analysis of the Russell orchestra's work is in Gunther Schuller, *The Swing Era* (1989). Information on his early career is in Walter C. Allen and Brian Rust, *King Oliver* (1987), while Albert McCarthy, *Big Band Jazz* (1974), discusses both his work with Oliver and his own orchestras with admirable objectivity. More personal views of Russell and his band are in Pops Foster, *The Autobiography of Pops Foster: New Orleans Jazzman* (1971), as told to Tom Stoddard, and Whitney Balliett, "The Blues Is a Slow Story (Henry "Red" Allen)" in his *American Musicians* (1986). Max Jones and John Chilton, *Louis: The Louis Armstrong Story* (1971), instructively contrasts the authors' appraisal of the band's merits during the Armstrong period, with recollections of some of the sidemen, but James Lincoln Collier, *Louis Armstrong: An American Genius* (1983), presents a highly controversial picture of Armstrong's relationship with Joe Glaser that many find distasteful and demeaning. In preparing the album notes for Columbia's *Luis Russell and his Louisiana Swing Orchestra* (1974), Frank Driggs added considerable biographical data based on interviews with former bandsmen and Russell's widow, concert singer Carline Ray Russell, who also provided him with rare documents. Complete discographical listings are in Brian Rust, *Jazz Records, 1897–1942* (1982), and Walter Bruyninckx, *Swing Discography, 1920–1988* (12 vols., 1989).

JACK SOHMER

RUSSELL, Pee Wee (27 Mar. 1906–15 Feb. 1969), musician and composer, was born Charles Ellsworth Russell in St. Louis, Missouri, the son of Charles Ellsworth Russell, Sr., a store and club manager, and Ella Ballard. Ellsworth, as he was known at home, grew up in Muskogee, Oklahoma, and in 1918 heard Alcide "Yellow" Nunez, a clarinetist with the Louisiana Five, a New Orleans jazz band. This exposure prompted the youth to ask his parents for a clarinet. The boy's first professional job as a musician was in the summer of 1919. While still in high school he became addicted to alcohol, an event that had a major influence throughout his life.

Ellsworth was offered a job with a jazz band on a riverboat. Because of family opposition, he sneaked out to play but was discovered by his father. As a result, he was sent to school at the Western Military Academy in Alton, Illinois, which he attended in 1920–1921. The youth subsequently joined Herbert Berger's Orchestra, which played in both the United States and Mexico during 1922–1923. At this time Ellsworth began to be called Pee Wee because his slight build contrasted with the size of other band members.

In 1924 Russell went with the legendary Peck Kelley. With his extensive experience, he had by this time developed into an excellent dance band musician. The following year, Russell joined Frankie Trumbauer in a band that included Bix Beiderbecke. Bix and Russell became close friends, and both liked the music of Debussy, Stravinsky, and Eastwood Lane. In fact, Russell once cited Beiderbecke as his greatest musical influence.

The clarinetist joined Loring "Red" Nichols in New York City early in 1927 and worked with him periodically into the 1930s. Russell's playing became increasingly individualistic, and by the summer of 1929, he had developed a recognizable and unique jazz style that included such factors as "bent notes" and a gravelly, breathy tone. In the early 1930s Russell performed with Paul Specht, Cass Hagan, and Don Voorhees. Following the opening of the club the Famous Door in March 1935, the clarinetist went with the house band led by Louis Prima. Later he left Prima and joined the group that played for the opening of Nick's club in 1937.

By this time, Russell was highly regarded by jazz fans and producers. He was also achieving national fame as a result of coverage in *Life* magazine. In the

summer of 1938 Russell had his own first recording session, and during this time the famous *"Life* Goes to a Party" photo-essay was produced together with the well-known St. Regis Jam Session hosted by Alistair Cooke.

When Bobby Hackett's band at Nick's broke up, Bud Freeman formed another group, including Russell, to perform there. This was the Summa Cum Laude Orchestra, which first recorded in July 1939. The following year this group disbanded, but through the early 1940s Russell was busy performing at Jimmy Ryan's club, Nick's, and the Carnegie and Town Hall concerts and working with Eddie Condon and other well-known exponents of the Chicago School of Dixieland Jazz. Early in 1942 Russell met Mary Chaloff, a sometime model. They were married in 1943. Mary was very protective of her husband despite what was at times a difficult marriage. They had no children.

Russell's popularity continued to increase, and in 1942, 1943, and 1944 he won first place in the *Down Beat* magazine Readers' Poll for the clarinet category. Following World War II, however, musical tastes began to change. Chicago Dixieland became boring for some listeners, though in 1945 Condon opened his own nightclub in New York's Greenwich Village.

In 1948 Russell was back at Nick's for a last time with Billy Butterfield's band, but by this time Condon's had become Russell's home base. In this same year he first played with impresario George Wein (later the organizer of the Newport Jazz Festival), who had a great impact on the remainder of the clarinetist's career.

However, Russell's alcoholism and other health problems began to catch up with him, and New Year's Eve, 1950, he collapsed on the bandstand in San Francisco and was put in a hospital charity ward. National press coverage of his condition resulted in benefit concerts. He recovered after being near death.

By the early 1950s, Russell managed to shed his reputation as exclusively a Dixieland player, became more "mainstream" musically, and with Mary's help reduced his consumption of alcohol. He performed in Hackett's band at the opening of the 1954 Newport Jazz Festival and during the mid-1950s, with the help of Wein and Mary, began what was perhaps the most successful segment of his life. Toward the end of 1959, Russell was made a member of the American Society of Composers, Authors, and Publishers, thus recognizing his ability as a composer. He played extensively at jazz festivals and rid himself of his image as a kind of "musical clown," which had typecast him for decades, especially during his work with Condon.

In 1964 Pee Wee won the *Down Beat* Critics' Poll for clarinet and was third in 1965 and 1966. At this time Mary motivated him to paint in order to keep busy during his semiretirement. Within a year he had completed sixty abstract works. In the spring of 1967, Mary's stomach pains, earlier diagnosed as ulcers, were found to be a result of pancreatic cancer. She died on 7 June 1967. Without Mary, Russell's life was virtually meaningless. His musical and artistic success was due in part to her influence, and after her death he ceased painting, though continuing to play. In 1968 he won the *Down Beat* International Critics' Poll and the Readers' Poll for the first time since 1944. On 20 January 1969 he performed with Wein's Newport All-Stars at Washington's Sheraton Park Hotel for one of Richard Nixon's inaugural balls.

Two weeks later, on 9 February, Russell was admitted to an Alexandria, Virginia, hospital with rapidly failing health. He died from cerebral edema and cirrhosis of the liver. He was memorialized by a tribute in the *Congressional Record* presented by Representative Seymour Halpern of New York and later was inducted into the *Down Beat* Hall of Fame.

Russell, while noted for his at times introverted behavior and a playing style that made some listeners question his ability as a musician, was nevertheless a master of his instrument and a great improviser. His skill and adaptability are illustrated by his performances with Beiderbecke in the 1920s and with Thelonious Monk in the 1960s and recordings with Coleman Hawkins in 1929 and 1961 "mainstream" style.

• By far the best source for information about Russell is Robert Hilbert's *Pee Wee Russell: The Life of a Jazzman* (1993). Hilbert's *Pee Wee Speaks: A Discography of Pee Wee Russell* (1992), in collaboration with David Niven, is an essential adjunct to the 1993 volume. Gunther Schuller's *The Swing Era: The Development of Jazz, 1930–1945* (1989) contains an outstanding musical analysis of Russell's style. Additional analysis is in Whitney Balliett's "P. W. Russell, Poet," in *The Sound of Surprise: 46 Pieces in Jazz* (1959). See also Balliett's "Even His Feet Look Sad," in *American Musicians: 56 Portraits in Jazz* (1986). Roger D. Kinkle, *The Complete Encyclopedia of Popular Music and Jazz, 1900–1950* (1974), contains a short biographical sketch as well as a brief discography. *Jazz: The Rough Guide* (1995) and Leonard Feather's *The New Encyclopedia of the History of Jazz* (1960), *The Encyclopedia of Jazz in the Sixties* (1966), and *The Encyclopedia of Jazz in the Seventies* (1976) also provide information.

Russell is shown briefly in Jean Bach's Academy Award nominee film *A Great Day in Harlem: A Historic Gathering of Jazz Greats* (1995). Obituaries are in the *New York Times*, 16 Feb. 1969, and *International Musician*, Mar. 1969.

BARRETT G. POTTER

RUSSELL, Richard Brevard, Jr. (2 Nov. 1897–21 Jan. 1971), senator and political leader, was born in Winder, Georgia, the son of Richard Brevard Russell, a lawyer and judge, and Blandina Dillard. Russell was educated at Gordon Military Institute and at the University of Georgia, where he received a law degree in 1918. After serving only about two months in the navy at the end of World War I in late 1918, he returned to practice law with his father in Winder.

Politics, however, was Russell's chief interest. In 1920, at age twenty-three, he was elected as a Democrat to the Georgia General Assembly. He served there for ten years, his last two terms as Speaker of the house. Elected governor in 1930, he emphasized improving education and building state highways.

The death of Senator William J. Harris in April 1932 opened the way for Russell to run for the U.S.

Senate. He was easily elected in November 1932 for the term ending in 1936 and took office on 10 January 1933. Except in 1936, when he defeated Eugene Talmadge, Russell never again had an opponent for his Senate seat.

Russell's rapid rise to political leadership was due to his friendly, outgoing personality, his identification with popular issues, his organizational and speaking skills, his honesty and fairness, and his ability to reconcile rival groups.

Russell was appointed to the Naval Affairs, Immigration, Manufactures, and Appropriations committees. He was on the important Appropriations Committee until his death, serving as chairman from 1969 to 1971. In 1947 he moved from Naval Affairs to the newly formed Armed Services Committee, serving as chairman from 1951 to 1953 and from 1955 to 1969, during the Korean and Vietnam wars. Much of Russell's growing power in the Senate came from his leadership of the Appropriations and Armed Services committees. He fought legislation that would liberalize immigration and opposed admitting large numbers of refugees after World War II. He believed in the superiority of Anglo-Saxon culture and feared that immigrants from Latin America and Asia would weaken that culture.

The welfare of farmers was one of Russell's chief interests. He favored high price supports for major crops and worked for larger appropriations for the Farm Security Administration and the Farmers Home Administration in the 1930s and 1940s. Both of these agencies sought to provide cheap credit for poor farmers. He also favored land and water conservation. Russell was the father of the school-lunch program, and he gave early support to the food stamp program.

By the late 1940s Russell had emerged as one of the most powerful senators in Washington. Besides serving on two of the most influential committees, he was a member of the seven-man Democratic Policy Committee and the Democratic Steering Committee. He spoke sparingly on the Senate floor, preferring to work behind the scenes, where his strong personality, integrity, wisdom, fairness, and ability to work out compromises influenced his colleagues. As President Richard Nixon wrote years later in *In the Arena* (1990), "No one surpassed [Russell] in his capacity to influence his colleagues and the course of events."

Although Russell began his career in Washington as a New Dealer, he became deeply disturbed when elements of his party began pressing for civil rights legislation. A firm believer in white supremacy and racial segregation, he opposed special laws designed to protect the rights of black Americans. By the late 1940s Russell had become the leader of the Southern Caucus, a group of southern senators who resisted civil rights legislation. This group so opposed President Harry Truman's advocacy of civil rights that Russell permitted his name to be placed in nomination for president against Truman at the 1948 Democratic convention. While some southerners bolted to the Dixiecrat party after Truman's nomination, Russell, a loyal

Democrat, reluctantly supported Truman. Russell made a strong bid for the Democratic presidential nomination in 1952, but he failed to get much support outside the South. Nonetheless, Russell and the Southern Caucus were able to block effective civil rights legislation until 1964 and 1965. No one was more responsible for holding up civil rights legislation for two decades than the senator from Georgia.

Russell gained wide national attention in 1951 when he headed the special Senate committee to investigate President Truman's dismissal that April of General Douglas MacArthur as commander of United Nations forces in Korea. By conducting a fair and impartial hearing, Russell defused this emotionally charged issue. During the hearings one reporter called him the "most powerful man in the Senate." Russell later served on the commission that in 1964 investigated the 1963 assassination of President John F. Kennedy.

As chairman of the Armed Services Committee Russell favored a strong military establishment. He fought successfully for large defense appropriations and vigorously supported the development of high-tech weapons. Russell believed that the nation's military defenses should be so strong that no country would dare attack the United States. Some observers believed that he was the most knowledgeable authority on national defense and military matters in Congress. Russell did not believe that the United States should act as a world policeman, and he at first strongly opposed U.S. military involvement in Vietnam. Once committed, however, he urged President Lyndon Johnson to use massive military power to achieve victory. Russell also believed that foreign aid was wasteful and ineffective and never voted for a foreign aid bill after 1952.

Although Russell enjoyed great power during his 38-year service in the Senate, the nation's mood gradually shifted to positions that he could not support. Besides fighting civil rights, he opposed most of President Johnson's Great Society programs. It was Russell's inability to accept the principle of racial equality, however, that kept him from achieving true national greatness. Nevertheless, he left many positive achievements in the fields of agriculture, defense, foreign affairs, and social programs such as the school lunch program. He was a vigorous defender of the Senate as an institution, which he said was "the last protection and bulwark of the rights of the American people." Senator Margaret Chase Smith called him "one of the rare few giants of the Senate." His colleagues honored him in a special way when in 1972 they named the Russell Senate Office Building for him.

A strong nationalist and patriot, Russell spent two-thirds of his life in public service. A member of the Methodist church, he never married. He died in Washington during his seventh term in the Senate.

• The Russell papers are located in the Richard B. Russell Library at the University of Georgia in Athens. They contain material on Russell's personal life, his early political career, and his years in the Senate. Much material on Russell's Sen-

ate career is in the Johnson papers at the Lyndon B. Johnson Library in Austin, Tex. The fullest account of Russell's life and service is in Gilbert C. Fite, *Richard B. Russell, Senator from Georgia* (1991). For a detailed account of Russell's fight against civil rights, see David D. Potenziani, "Look to the Past: Richard B. Russell and the Defense of Southern White Supremacy" (Ph.D. diss., Univ. of Georgia, 1981). Karen K. Kelly, "Richard B. Russell: Democrat from Georgia" (Ph.D. diss., Univ. of North Carolina–Chapel Hill, 1979), contains especially valuable material on the Russell family background. "Richard B. Russell, Georgia Giant" is the title of a three-part manuscript by the Cox Broadcasting Company, Atlanta, Ga., written in 1970 to accompany a video documentary on Russell's life and career; in it he answers many questions about his personal and political life and gives his views on numerous public issues. An obituary is in the *Atlanta Constitution*, 22 Jan. 1971.

GILBERT C. FITE

RUSSELL, Rosalind (4 June 1908–28 Nov. 1976), actress, was born in Waterbury, Connecticut, the daughter of James Edward Russell, a lawyer, and Clara McKnight, a former teacher. Her parents, who were devout Catholics, educated her in the parochial school system, first at St. Margaret's Grammar School and Notre Dame Academy in Waterbury and then at Marymount College in Tarrytown, New York. Like her parents, Russell remained a practicing Catholic throughout her life. She saw no conflict between her religion and her career. Her desire to act resulted in her leaving Marymount in 1928 after her sophomore year and enrolling at the American Academy of Dramatic Arts, from which she graduated in 1929. Before making her Broadway debut a year later in *Garrick Gaieties*, she gained valuable experience working in stock companies in Greenwich, Connecticut, and Saranac Lake, New York. Eager to return to Broadway, she had the misfortune of appearing in one play that closed after its dress rehearsal and another that ran a mere eight performances. Undaunted, Russell found employment on the "subway circuit," performing in the boroughs of Brooklyn and the Bronx and in nearby towns like Newark that were accessible by subway and rail. In 1934 a talent scout from Universal Pictures saw her performance in *The Second Man* in Newark and offered her a contract at $750 a week. Having no prospects in New York, she headed to California.

When Universal did not know what to do with a 5′6½″ actress with a flair for sophisticated comedy, Russell feigned unhappiness with Los Angeles to get out of her contract and went to MGM, making her film debut in *Evelyn Prentice* (1934). Her competition at MGM—Joan Crawford, Jean Harlow, Myrna Loy, Luise Rainer, and Greta Garbo—precluded her appearing in major roles. When Columbia Pictures offered her the lead in the movie version to George Kelly's Pulitzer Prize–winning play, *Craig's Wife* (1936), she was grateful for the opportunity to play a dramatic part. Another such opportunity arose in 1937 when she played Olivia in the melodrama *Night Must Fall*, which was followed by two years of unmemorable roles. When she learned that MGM was planning the film version of Claire Booth Luce's *The Women* (1939), she persuaded George Cukor to test her for the role of the gossip monger Sylvia, despite his preference for Ilka Chase. The test convinced Cukor, and Russell made Sylvia a less odious character than she might have been otherwise. Her role in *The Women* brought her back to Columbia for *His Girl Friday* (1940), although she was not the studio's first choice. Yet her performance as Hildy Johnson in Howard Hawks's classic screwball comedy was the first in a series of comedic roles in Columbia films in which she perfected her timing and created a persona whose sophisticated exterior never completely concealed the earthy and tender woman within. Russell's ability to suggest the tension between a proper facade and an uninhibited nature led to her playing characters such as the wife in *This Thing Called Love* (1941), who champions platonic relationships until she discovers that passion is preferable; the budding writer in *My Sister Eileen* (1942), who learns that life, not books, is the basis of literature (for this role she won an Oscar nomination); and careerists like the literary agent in *What a Woman!* (1943), the psychiatrist in *She Wouldn't Say Yes* (1945), the judge in *Tell It to the Judge* (1949), and the college dean in *A Woman of Distinction* (1950), all of whom were women of formidable intelligence. Unfortunately, the scripts catered to moviegoers who expected women to favor marriage over a career.

Eager to do drama as well as comedy, Russell appeared in *Roughly Speaking* (1945), which required her to age over a forty-year period; *Sister Kenny* (1946), which earned her another Oscar nomination for her portrayal of the Australian nurse who pioneered a treatment for polio; *The Guilt of Janet Ames* (1947), as a World War II widow who cannot forgive the men whose lives her husband saved; and the film version of Eugene O'Neill's *Mourning Becomes Electra* (1947), for which she received her third Oscar nomination. Despite critical praise for her acting in dramatic roles, the public preferred her in comedies.

In 1951 Russell, feeling the urge to return to the stage, starred in the touring production of *Bell, Book and Candle*. When *My Sister Eileen* was transformed into the Broadway musical *Wonderful Town* (1953), with a score by Leonard Bernstein, Russell was chosen to play the same role that she did in the 1942 movie. Despite her limited vocal range, she won ecstatic notices. Her next and final stage appearance was in *Auntie Mame*, an even bigger hit that put her on the cover of *Life* (12 Nov. 1956) and two years later became the basis of the movie with which she will always be identified and which brought her a fourth Oscar nomination. The other films she made during the last two decades of her life were mostly undistinguished except for *Picnic* (1955) and *Gypsy* (1962). Neither drew heavily on her comedic talent; instead, she emphasized the coarseness of the characters—a sexually frustrated teacher and a tyrannical stage mother, respectively.

Her private life was exemplary. Her marriage to producer Frederick Brisson in 1941, which produced one child and lasted until Russell's death, was much happier than most unions in the film community. While other stars gained publicity for their humanitarian and philanthropic efforts, few did as much or were honored for their efforts as regularly as Russell. In 1964 Canisius College in Buffalo awarded her the St. Peter Canisius Medal; the University of Portland granted her an honorary degree in 1966; and the Academy of Motion Picture Arts and Sciences voted her the Jean Hersholt Humanitarian Award in 1973. Although she did not live to witness its construction, she would have considered the Rosalind Russell Medical Research Center of the University of California in San Francisco the highlight of her career. The last fifteen years of her life were beset by tragedy. Breast cancer, resulting in two mastectomies, and rheumatoid arthritis led to her death in Beverly Hills.

"Life is a banquet," Auntie Mame explained to her timid and humorless secretary. Russell used that line as the title of her posthumously published autobiography. Mame's philosophy was essentially Russell's, except that Russell's banquet was not an orgy of self-indulgence but an elegant dinner party where the guests were impeccably dressed and well spoken. Russell's best films (*The Women, His Girl Friday, This Thing Called Love, My Sister Eileen, A Woman of Distinction, Auntie Mame*) reflect her belief that a zest for life cannot be divorced from style and wit.

• A clippings file on Russell is at the Margaret Herrick Library in the Center for Motion Picture Study in Beverly Hills, Calif. The chief source for Russell's life is her autobiography; written in collaboration with Chris Chase, *Life Is a Banquet* (1977) was published the year after her death. An interview with Russell appears in Roy Newquist, *Showcase* (1966), 387–401. The obituary in the *New York Times*, 29 Nov. 1976, gives her age as sixty-three. No birth date is mentioned in *Life Is a Banquet*, and publicity releases claim it was 4 June 1913. Actually, she was born five years earlier.

BERNARD F. DICK

RUSSELL, Sol Smith (15 June 1848–28 Apr. 1902), actor, was born Solomon Smith Russell in Brunswick, Missouri, the son of Charles Elmer Russell, a storekeeper, and Louisa Mathews, the daughter of a music teacher. He was named for Solomon Smith, his uncle by marriage and a leading theatrical manager of the time. The young Russell showed an interest in the theater, putting on shows with friends and becoming a class clown, but his parents opposed this attraction. His uncle Sol Smith, however, allowed him to see his work and visit backstage. The child lived with his parents in Missouri and Illinois but left home to join the Union army as a drummer boy during the Civil War. He left the army in 1862, then joined a theater company in Cairo, Illinois, and slowly began to learn his craft. For six dollars a week, from which the young actor paid three dollars and a half for board while living in the theater, he soon emerged as a young man of disparate talents: he could drum in the orchestra, sing comic songs, and—because of his youth and delicacy—he could also play female roles. All the while he watched his colleagues closely, studying scripts and reading widely.

He wandered the Midwest, by the end of the war winning a minor provincial reputation. By 1865 he was playing major support in Nashville to Maggie Mitchell, Laura Keene, and others of similar rank. The next year he appeared in Ben DeBar's Theatre in St. Louis. He began to gravitate to the East, appearing in a stock company in Philadelphia in 1867, along with James E. Murdock, a major star of the time. Russell toured New England giving monologues and in 1868 toured with the Berger family. In 1869 he married Louisa Berger in Detroit; she died, childless, two years later and Russell, then on the road in the South, could not attend her funeral. In 1876 he married Alice M. Adams, with whom he had two children.

In 1871 he appeared for the first time in New York City, at Lina Edwin's Theatre. Three years later he was a substantial hit in New York in *The Wandering Minstrel*. He next appeared in Augustin Daly's company for almost a year, then rejoined the Berger family. The leader, Fred Berger, became Russell's personal manager, and together they tried to establish Russell as a legitimate actor. Audiences and critics, however, perceived him as an entertainer, not a dramatic artist. Roles such as Tom Dilloway in *Edgewood Folks or Connecticut Country Life* in 1880 gave him little opportunity to show his skills and talents, although they were usually successful at the box office. After touring in *Edgewood Folks* for four years, Russell joined the Boston Museum Company in an attempt to secure a more legitimate success. By 1887 Russell had grown discouraged and considered retiring from the stage to enter business with his father-in-law, publishing books for boys. Edward Kidder, who was to become Russell's "official dramatist," offered him one of his scripts, *Bewitched*, with which Russell scored success sufficient to keep him in the theatrical profession. Another script by Kidder, *A Poor Relation*, was written with Russell and was equally successful, as was the subsequent *Peaceful Valley*.

After some twenty years of stage experience, Russell had risen to legitimate stardom with his peculiar and original style, one based on realistic American types with whom audiences identified. Many of his vehicles have long since disappeared from the stage: *Felix McKusick*, *Pa*, *The Tale of a Coat*, *Peaceful Valley*, *April Weather*, *Uncle Dick*, *The Honorable John Grigsby*, and *A Bachelor's Romance*. Better-known roles included Dr. Pangloss in the then-popular *The Heir at Law* and Fighting Bob Acres in *The Rivals*. For the 1897–1898 season he essayed Petruchio in *The Taming of the Shrew* but soon realized he had extended himself too far and dropped the show.

He appeared in *The Honorable John Grigsby* in Chicago, but illness on 18 December 1899 forced him to cancel his performance. He reappeared in a revival of *A Poor Relation* a week later, but the play soon closed, and Russell retired to regain his health. After a lingering illness, the nature of which is unknown, he died in Washington, D.C.

Russell never achieved the first level of success in New York, but he often outdrew far more famous actors on the road, doing one-night stands. New York critics considered Russell's scripts out of date and hopelessly naive, but they objected more to his vehicles than to him. Playwright Kidder claimed, "Sol Smith Russell's smile was as near to human sunshine as anyone's smile can be," calling it quaint, genial, captivating, and winning. Others described him as tall and slight in appearance, deliberate in action, and with a dry, crackling comedic manner. His appeal was likened to that of the great French actor Coquelin, and he earned the affection and respect of provincial, less-sophisticated audiences through his offstage activities as well as his acting. No hint of scandal ever touched his name, and his strong sense of dignity ensured his wide appeal to a populace suspicious of the theater. Russell enjoyed both poker and wine on occasion, but his public esteem never suffered from either. Above all, Russell proved to America that the theater could be a relatively harmless diversion, an entertainment without moral danger.

• See Charles Bazaldua for Russell material in special collections: the Harvard Theatre Collection, The Players, and private collections. Much of the material cited by Bazaldua now resides in the Western Historical Manuscript Collection at the University of Missouri, Columbia. These include forty-one folders of clippings, correspondence, and scrapbooks; a personal diary kept for 1867–1868; and an outline of his life by his wife. The most detailed and well-researched source for Russell remains Bazaldua's "'Going to the People': The Career of Sol Smith Russell" (Ph.D. diss., Univ. of Missouri, 1975). John Bouvé Clapp and Edwin Francis Edgett include a biographical essay on Russell in *Players of the Present*, vol. 1 (1901). Bazaldua also cites several substantial articles about Russell: Charles H. Day, "On the Road with Sol Smith Russell," *New York Dramatic Mirror*, Christmas 1899, pp. 28–29; Edward E. Kidder, "The Sol Smith Russell Plays," *Greenbook*, Sept. 1911, pp. 620–23; Bertha K. Mason, "Sol Smith Russell: Actor from Jacksonville," *Journal of the Illinois State Historical Society* 45 (Spring 1952): 23–29; and George H. Payne, "The Personal Side of America's Greatest Actor," *Saturday Evening Post*, 29 Oct. 1898, pp. 281–82. A biographical series of articles by Tom Kenney, "Sol Smith Russell: America's Greatest Comic Actor," appeared in the Brunswick (Mo.) *Brunswicker*, 29 Aug., 5 Sept., 19 Sept., 26 Sept., 3 Oct., and 10 Oct. 1991. Obituaries are in the *Philadelphia Record*, the *Boston Herald*, the *Boston Journal*, and the *Boston Globe*, all 29 Apr. 1902, as well as the *New York Dramatic Mirror*, 3 May 1902.

STEPHEN M. ARCHER

RUSSELL, William Eustis (6 Jan. 1857–16 July 1896), lawyer and governor of Massachusetts, was born in Cambridge, Massachusetts, the son of Charles Theodore Russell, a prominent attorney and local politician, and Sarah Elizabeth Ballister. Russell graduated from Harvard College in 1877. An avid horseman and athlete, he served as class secretary, performed for the Hasty Pudding Club, and distinguished himself as the most ardent Democrat at Harvard by campaigning for Samuel Tilden in the then solidly Republican school. He inherited his politics from his father, a Whig turned Democrat who was mayor of Cambridge during the Civil War. In 1879 Russell graduated at the head of his class at Boston University Law School, earning the school's first summa cum laude degree. He was admitted to the Suffolk bar in 1880 and joined the family firm of Russell and Russell in Boston. First elected to the Cambridge Common Council in 1881 through a write-in campaign run by friends, Russell was elected the following year to the higher-level board of aldermen. Narrowly elected alderman again in 1883, he led opposition to the mayor and became mayor himself in 1884 on a reform ticket. In 1885 he married Margaret Manning Swan; they had three children.

In his first year in office, Russell cleared the previous year's unpaid bills, balanced the budget, financed the city's floating debt, and managed to cut taxes, creating his "pay as you go" slogan. Russell was reelected three times, twice without opposition. Although he opposed Prohibition, Russell strictly enforced the measure in Cambridge when the city used its local option to turn dry. In addition, he supported civil service and sided against workers in a local transit strike, making Irish Democrats somewhat suspicious of him. However, his mayoral success quickly made him a rising star in the state Democratic party, especially after his tireless campaigning for Grover Cleveland in the 1884 and 1888 presidential elections. Russell turned down a nomination for U.S. representative in 1886 but became the party's gubernatorial candidate in 1888. The Democrats created a coalition of older Democrats, immigrants, workers, and Mugwump refugees from the Republican party to seek victory in the heavily Republican state.

Russell campaigned vigorously but lost his first gubernatorial election by a large margin. He cut the margin greatly in his second attempt in 1889 and was elected in 1890 as only the third Democratic governor of Massachusetts since the Civil War. He campaigned on the issue of tariff reform, telling workers that tariffs only hurt working men and, in the long run, business. Known for his unadorned yet riveting speeches and extensive campaigning in both small towns and cities, Russell did not seem out of place with Brahmins or playing pool with Irish laborers. One of only two Democrats elected to statewide office, Russell never had a Democratic majority in the state legislature nor in the influential Governor's Council, an elected body that held most of the state's appointment powers. The office of governor was weak, frustrating many of Russell's reform ideas, and he agitated unsuccessfully for lessening the powers of the council and numerous state commissions. He saved his influence for a few strategic vetoes, all sustained, and important election and labor reform legislation, including a widely emulated law to regulate sweatshops and a reduction in hours for state employees to nine hours a day and for women and children to fifty-eight hours a week from sixty. Also during his tenure, the poll tax was abolished, campaign finance reforms were passed, and employers were prohibited from forbidding unions and from using out-of-state police as strikebreakers. He encouraged metropolitan cooperation to provide water, sewer, and rapid transit services and created a Metropolitan Park Commission. He was reelected twice, the only Democratic governor to accomplish such a feat in thirty years.

Increased financial pressures led Russell to announce that he would not run for reelection in 1893. Critics protested it was because he was afraid to lose, which was the expected outcome of the election. He spent the time after his term building up his practice and authoring articles to increase his national prominence.

Russell had been mentioned as a presidential candidate both in 1892, when it was unsure if Cleveland would run again, and 1896, but the rise of the silver Democrats deprived him of a chance at the executive mansion. Russell refused to lead a third party based on the gold standard, because he hoped the Democrats would not enthrone silver on their platform and a third party had a slim chance to win. His last public speech was on 9 July 1896 at the Chicago Democratic convention, where his championing of "sound money" met with little support. William Jennings Bryan's riveting "Cross of Gold" speech immediately following his completely overshadowed Russell. Feeling the party had conspired with the Populists to throw aside its principles for political expediency, Russell left the convention early in disgust. Fatigued, he returned home before taking a fishing trip to the Little Pabos River near St. Adelaide, Quebec, where his companions discovered him dead in his bed. The local coroner pronounced the cause of death to be heart disease, although the widespread Victorian sentimentality was that he died of a broken heart over his betrayal by the party.

Russell's death at such an early age brings up the question of whether he would have been able to maintain his reputation as one of the brightest lights of the party. He prided himself in upholding democracy, claiming he was only a Democrat because he felt the party represented both the people and democratic principles. His devotion to equality appeared genuine and not the product of political expediency. He once admonished a friend for not greeting their hotel waitress when they met her on the beach. Whether he would have stayed to fight the influence of those with whom he disagreed or would have fled to a third party or to the Republicans will not be discovered, leaving in place a reputation as a true public servant, competent, shrewd, and devoted to democratic principles.

• Russell's papers, including fourteen scrapbooks of press clippings on his political career, at the Massachusetts Historical Society pertain largely to his public life and contain few personal letters or effects. Russell's brother, C. T. Russell, Jr., published the *Speeches and Addresses of William E. Russell* (1894). Major articles authored by Russell include "Jefferson and His Party Today," *Forum*, July 1896, pp. 513–24, and "The Issues of 1896: A Democratic View," *Century Magazine*, Nov. 1895, pp. 73–77. The most comprehensive published information about Russell is in Geoffrey Blodgett, *The Gentle Reformers: Massachusetts Democrats in the Cleveland Era* (1966); a memorial oration by Charles Eliot Norton reprinted in *Sons of the Pioneers*, ed. Samuel A. Eliot (1908); and a memoir by Charles Carroll Everett in *Publications of the Colonial Society of Massachusetts, December 1897*, vol. 5 (1902). See also Michael E. Hennessy, *Four Decades of Massachusetts Politics, 1890–1935* (1935). Obituaries are in the *Boston Evening Herald*, 16 July 1896; the *Boston Daily Globe*, 16 and 17 July 1896; and the *Boston Morning Herald* and *Boston Daily Advertiser*, both 17 July 1896.

DOLLY SMITH WILSON

RUSSWURM, John Brown (1 Oct. 1799–9 June 1851), journalist and first nonwhite governor of Maryland in Liberia Colony, West Africa, was born in Port Antonio, Jamaica, the son of John Russwurm, a white American merchant, and an unidentified Jamaican black woman. As a boy known only as John Brown, Russwurm was sent to Canada for an education by his father. After his father's settlement in Maine and marriage in 1813 to a white New England widow with children, he entered the new family at his stepmother's insistence. John Brown thereupon assumed his father's surname and remained with his stepmother even after the senior Russwurm's death in 1815. His schooling continued at home and, later, at preparatory institutes such as the North Yarmouth Academy in Maine. He made a short, unhappy visit to Jamaica and returned to Portland, Maine, to begin collegiate study. Thrown on his own after just one year because of his sponsor's inability to continue support, young Russwurm took a succession of brief teaching jobs at African free schools in Philadelphia, New York, and Boston.

Russwurm entered Bowdoin College in Brunswick, Maine, in September 1824 and soon evinced an interest in books by joining the Athenean Society, a campus literary group. He graduated two years later with a B.A. Asked to give a commencement oration, he titled his speech, "The Condition and Prospects of Hayti." He claimed that Haitians, having overthrown French rule, exemplified the truth that "it is the irresistible course of events that all men, who have been deprived of their liberty, shall recover this previous portion of their indefeasible inheritance." That a young man partially of African descent had graduated from college, the second or third nonwhite to do so in the United States, and had spoken so eloquently of freedom garnered attention from several newspapers and journals, which published extracts of his remarks. Bowdoin College awarded Russwurm an honorary master of arts degree in 1829.

As a college student Russwurm entertained the idea of emigrating to Haiti, but, diploma in hand, he went to New York City and, with Samuel E. Cornish, a Presbyterian minister, began publishing *Freedom's Journal*, the first black newspaper in the United States. The editors declared in the inaugural issue, on 16 March 1827, that they wanted to disseminate useful knowledge of every kind among an estimated 500,000 free persons of color, to bring about their moral, religious, civil, and literary improvement, and, most important of all, to plead their cause, including their civil rights, to the public. They emphasized the value of ed-

ucation and self-help. Although they vowed that the journal would not become the advocate of any partial views either in politics or in religion, it spoke clearly for the abolition of slavery in the United States and opposed the budding movement to colonize freed blacks in Africa. Weekly issues carried a variety of material: poetry, letters of explorers and others in Africa, information on the status of slaves in slaveholding states, legislation pending or passed in states that affected blacks, notices of job openings, and personal news such as marriages and obituaries. Advertisements for adult education classes appeared frequently and even Russwurm appealed for subscribers to attend an evening school in lower New York where he taught reading, writing, arithmetic, English grammar, and geography. Agents in twelve states as well as in Canada, Haiti, and England sold subscriptions, but total circulation figures can only be guessed as several hundred copies. Six months after the newspaper's beginning Cornish resigned as an editor, ostensibly in order to return to the ministry and to promote free black schools, but more likely because he disagreed with Russwurm's new views on African colonization. Russwurm was becoming convinced that blacks could not achieve equality with whites in the United States and that emigration to Africa was their best hope. In one of his last editorials, he wrote that "the universal emancipation so ardently desired by us & by all our friends, can never take place, unless some door is opened whereby the emancipated may be removed as fast as they drop their galling chains, to some other land besides the free states." The final issue of the journal appeared on 28 March 1829, whereupon, two months later, Cornish resumed its editorship under a new title, *The Rights of All*. His vigorous denunciation of the colonization movement in fact represented the majority view among slaves and free blacks.

That fall Russwurm sailed for Monrovia, capital of the colony of Liberia, which had been established in 1822 by the American Colonization Society, a national group that favored the voluntary repatriation of blacks to Africa as a solution to accelerating racial problems. He assumed editorship of the foundering, government-controlled *Liberia Herald* in 1830, became the official government printer by virtue of his appointment as colonial secretary, undertook the supervision of public education, and engaged in trade. In 1833 he married Sarah E. McGill, daughter of George R. McGill, a Baltimorean who had emigrated to Liberia six years earlier and was then acting colonial agent for the society. The couple had five children, including an adopted son. Russwurm's tenure in the public affairs of Liberia was characterized by controversy over freedom of the press and his close links with unpopular colonial officials. The colonists wanted the *Herald* to be independently run, which it could not be, they believed, if the editor were a government employee. Russwurm was removed from his editorship and from other posts in 1835.

Of equal importance historically to his role in pioneering the American black press is Russwurm's fifteen-year career as the governor of Maryland in Liberia, a colony founded in 1834 at Cape Palmas, 200 miles south of Monrovia, by the Maryland State Colonization Society. This organization was originally a state auxiliary of the American Colonization Society, but its leaders, disappointed by the disparate views among supporters from northern and southern states, by the slow pace of emigration, and by poor management in Monrovia, created a settlement of their own to which primarily freed Maryland blacks would emigrate. It was heavily subsidized by annual grants from the Maryland legislature. The first two governors of the colony, both whites, were overcome by ill health during their brief stays on the West African coast. The society's board of managers in Baltimore therefore concluded that it must appoint a nonwhite who was already acclimated to Africa and familiar with the governance of a settlement and who not only could survive but develop in the colonists a sense of autonomy and an expectation of self-government. Russwurm received his appointment in September 1836 and, proceeding immediately to Cape Palmas, found a small town called Harper, a few outlying farms, a mission of the American Board of Commissioners for Foreign Missions, and a population of about 200 immigrants. Over the next ten years, the governor created a currency system, improved business procedures, and adopted a legal code. He attempted to smooth relations with neighboring African groups but, having mixed success, enlarged the militia and encouraged the American African Squadron, whose goal was the suppression of the slave trade, to visit along the coast as a display of support. He worked to stimulate agriculture, both by the colonists on their own farms and by the enlargement of the public farm on which he planted a nursery and experimented with various crops. He oversaw numerous public improvements and the addition of territory to the colony.

Russwurm's judicious application of the colony's constitution and ordinances, political preeminence over the often fractious settlers, and ability to govern well with decreasing supervision of the board in Baltimore coincided with a mounting demand among the colonists in the late 1840s that Maryland in Liberia either be granted independence or that it seek annexation to the newly created Republic of Liberia. The governor himself seems not to have taken a stand, possibly because of his disappointment with the current generation of colonists, whom he characterized as still too unenlightened to accomplish much. Furthermore he was in ill health and suffered from ulcerations on his foot, which may have been related to gout. In spite of these factors and the sudden death of his adopted son, Russwurm continued to direct the colony, and even on the day of his own death, he attended to a portion of his official duties before succumbing to multiple ailments at the government house in Cape Palmas.

The citizens lauded Russwurm as statesman, philanthropist, and Christian. They named an island off Cape Palmas and a township after him. Back in Baltimore, members of the board recalled his visit to the United States in 1848, when he not only exhibited an excellent and courteous bearing but confirmed that he was an educated and accomplished gentleman. They spoke of his faithful service and how he had vindicated their belief in "the perfect fitness of his race for the most important political positions in Africa." They ordered the construction of a marble obelisk with suitable inscriptions over his grave at Cape Palmas. The board's high estimate was reinforced by his stepmother in a laudatory letter in which she characterized him as a literary man whose family and library were to him the world. By the time of Russwurm's death, the settlement numbered nearly a thousand inhabitants and owned a strip of coastline stretching northward more than a hundred miles.

Russwurm sometimes likened himself to Moses, leader of the Israelites, in trying to push his people ahead; indeed, under his administration a colony of former American slaves achieved a large degree of self-government. He proved capable of handling difficulties with settlers, with adjacent Africans, and with white missionaries. His physical and executive perseverance gave the settlement the benefit of stability until it could consider viable alternatives to its dependent relationship with the Maryland State Colonization Society. The survival of the colony, now known as Maryland County in the Republic of Liberia, is attributable principally to the success of Russwurm's governorship.

• A critical biography of Russwurm has yet to be published because of the paucity of sources about his personal life and career. Bowdoin College in Brunswick, Maine, holds about 900 items, many of them of a secondary nature, in its special collections and also has copies of Russwurm material from the Tennessee State Library and Archives, Nashville. *Freedom's Journal* is available either bound or on microfilm in numerous libraries. Primary sources for a study of Russwurm's career as governor of the Maryland colony are available in the Maryland State Colonization Society Papers and in other writings at the Maryland Historical Society, in the American Colonization Society Papers at the Library of Congress, in the African Squadron Papers (particularly from Matthew Perry's cruise in the 1840s) at the National Archives, and in the American Board of Commissioners for Foreign Missions Papers at Houghton Library, Harvard College.

There are short biographical sketches of Russwurm in standard reference works, but the sole monograph dealing at any length with his governorship is Penelope Campbell, *Maryland in Africa, the Maryland State Colonization Society 1831–1857* (1971). A short biography designed for children is Mary Sagarin, *John Brown Russwurm, the Story of Freedom's Journal* (1970). Articles dealing with particular aspects of Russwurm's early life are Philip S. Foner's commencement address, "John Browne [sic] Russwurm, a Document," in *Journal of Negro History* 54 (Oct. 1969): 393–97; Lerone Bennett, Jr.,'s comparison of the importance of Russwurm and Cornish in "Founders of the Black Press," *Ebony* 42 (Feb. 1987): 96ff.; and Momo K. Rogers's discussion of his editorship of the *Liberia Herald* in "The Liberian Press: An Analysis," *Journalism Quarterly* 63 (Summer 1986): 275–81. A scholarly treatment of Russwurm's place in American journalism is Frankie Hutton, *The Early Black Press in America, 1827 to 1860* (1993).

PENELOPE CAMPBELL

RUST, John Daniel (6 Sept. 1892–20 Jan. 1954), inventor, was born near Necessity, Texas, the son of Benjamin Daniel Rust and Susan Minerva Burnett, farmers. As a boy Rust picked cotton and thought about inventing a mechanical picker. After high school he attended Western College in Artesia, New Mexico. He dropped out after a year of study. At the age of twenty-one he began work as a migrant farm hand in Texas, Oklahoma, New Mexico, and Kansas until 1917. Rust became interested in socialism and joined the Milton Colony, a utopian, cooperative coal-mining town in Oklahoma. During World War I he served in the army at Camp Stanley, Texas. After the war he completed a correspondence course in automotive engineering and mechanical drawing. This training enabled Rust to gain employment in 1922 as a designer with the Marriage Thresher Company in Wichita, Kansas, and later with the Gleaner Combine Company in Independence, Missouri. Rust married Faye Pinkston in 1924; they had two children, one of whom died in infancy.

In 1924, while employed by the Gleaner Combine Company, Rust began work on a mechanical cotton picker. At first he used barbed and serrated spindles to twist the fiber from the bolls as the implement passed between the rows, but the spindles failed to extract enough cotton to merit commercial production. Rust did not solve the problem of mechanical picking until the spring of 1927, when he remembered that his grandmother had moistened the spindles of her spinning wheel to make the cotton adhere. He wetted a nail into which he spun a handful of cotton, and the technique worked. He then returned to Texas and settled in Weatherford, where he began designing a mechanical picker that used the principle of moistened, smooth spindles. Rust patented his first cotton picker on 27 January 1928 and completed a test model that year with the aid of his brother Mack, who had a degree in mechanical engineering from the University of Texas.

Although financing always proved difficult because investors insisted on an interest in the project, and Rust only wanted investment capital with no strings attached, in 1930 Rust gained the financial support of the Llano Cooperative Community in Louisiana and attracted enough attention to obtain the sponsorship of investor Wallace A. Clemmons. This financial aid enabled Rust to develop a machine that picked a bale during a test day near Waco, Texas, in 1931. On 31 August 1936 Rust demonstrated an improved cotton picker at the Delta Experiment Station near Stoneville, Mississippi, which picked 400 pounds—four-fifths of a bale—in an hour, or approximately fifty times more than an average fieldworker. In 1937 his machine picked thirteen bales during a demonstration near Gilliam, Louisiana. Although further improvements were needed, Rust's machine had proved the feasibility of mechanical cotton harvesting. Having divorced in 1927, Rust married Thelma Ford in 1933; they had no children.

Rust, however, feared that a mechanical cotton picker would cause great social dislocation because landowners would no longer need sharecroppers, tenants, or migrant workers to harvest their cotton crop. Millions of people, he feared, would be forced from the land and onto the unemployment rolls. Although Rust wanted his machine to improve southern agriculture by reducing the labor required to pick cotton, he did not want his implement to cause massive unemployment. Accordingly, Rust had attempted to design a machine that small-scale farmers could afford and to market it with restrictions. He planned to lease rather than sell his cotton picker to farmers who agreed to pay minimum wages, maintain maximum hours for their workers, and abolish child labor. Although these ideas show Rust's strong belief in the obligation of an inventor to society, they ultimately proved impractical because of the cultural traditions and economic needs of southern farmers. Rust hoped that eventually farm cooperatives would purchase his cotton picker to save both labor and money, but inadequate financing, organizational problems, and racial divisions prevented the development of a strong cooperative movement in the South.

During the late 1930s financing problems continued to plague Rust, and his machine remained in the developmental phase with no prospect for commercial production. World War II finally forced him to end his work because he could not acquire needed materials. In 1940 Rust sold his tools to help pay his debts, but he continued to work on improvements and redesigned his cotton picker in 1943. While in Washington, D.C., the next year to file for patents on his improvements, the Allis-Chalmers Manufacturing Company offered to build his machine. Rust granted the company a license and accepted a position as a consulting engineer. In 1944 Allis-Chalmers began to manufacture his implement. Rust continued to improve his cotton picker and moved to Pine Bluff, Arkansas in 1949, where Ben Pearson, Inc. began to manufacture his machine. He also chartered the John Rust Company, which sold stock to enable Rust to continue improving his cotton picker, and he used his earnings from licensing fees to repay two dollars for each dollar that others had invested in his past work.

By the time of his death in Pine Bluff, Rust had patented thirty-six inventions and had eleven patents pending that related to mechanical cotton picking. During the late 1950s the J. I. Case and Massey-Ferguson companies manufactured the Rust cotton picker. By 1975 the cotton harvest had been essentially mechanized in the United States. Rust contributed to that technological achievement by proving that mechanical cotton picking was possible. His inventions helped revolutionize southern agriculture by decreasing the need for millions of fieldworkers each year, by helping to eliminate the sharecropping system, and by removing the last obstacle to the complete mechanization of cotton farming.

• John Rust describes his work in "The Origin and Development of the Cotton Picker," *Western Tennessee Historical Society Papers* 7 (1953): 38–56. The most thorough treatment of

Rust is "Mr. Little Ol' Rust," *Fortune* 46 (1952): 150–52, 197–205. James H. Street, *The New Revolution in the Cotton Economy: Mechanization and Its Consequences* (1957), provides an important overview of cotton harvesting technology. For later developments in cotton farming, see R. Douglas Hurt, *Agricultural Technology in the Twentieth Century* (1992). An obituary is in the *New York Times*, 22 Jan. 1954.

R. DOUGLAS HURT

RUSTIN, Bayard (17 Mar. 1912–24 Aug. 1987), civil rights leader and political activist, was born in West Chester, Pennsylvania, the illegitimate son of an immigrant from the British West Indies. Raised by his maternal grandparents (his grandfather was a caterer), Rustin was educated in the local public schools. He first experienced racial discrimination as a member of his high school football team when he was denied service at a restaurant in Media, Pennsylvania. After high school, he worked at odd jobs, traveled widely, and studied at Wilberforce University in Ohio, Cheney State Teachers College in Pennsylvania, and the City College of New York, never earning a formal degree.

As a young man, Rustin joined the Young Communist League, believing at the time that Communists "seemed the only people who had civil rights at heart." As a Quaker and pacifist, however, his beliefs conflicted with party policy. When Communists demanded U.S. participation in World War II in June 1941 after the German invasion of Russia, Rustin broke with the party. Thereafter he devoted himself to the antiwar and civil rights movements. In 1941 he became field secretary for the Congress of Racial Equality (CORE) and race relations director for the Fellowship of Reconciliation, a nondenominational group founded by the radical pacifist Abraham J. Muste to promote the nonviolent resolution of world problems.

Rustin soon allied with A. Philip Randolph, president of the Brotherhood of Sleeping Car Porters and an advocate of civil rights for African Americans. Rustin organized young people to participate in Randolph's 1941 March on Washington Movement, an effort to pressure President Franklin D. Roosevelt to ban racial discrimination in employment. When Randolph postponed the scheduled mass protest march because the president established a Fair Employment Practices Committee, Rustin accused the civil rights leader of compromising his principles.

Rustin paid dearly for maintaining his own principles, serving twenty-eight months in a federal prison for refusing to register for the draft. After the war, he continued to promote pacifism and civil rights. In 1947 he participated in the first "freedom ride" (the Journey of Reconciliation) sponsored by CORE, an effort to desegregate interstate bus travel. As a result, a court in North Carolina convicted Rustin of violating the state's Jim Crow laws and sentenced him to labor on a prison chain gang. He also served as executive director of the War Registers League (1953–1955), an indication of his hesitancy to devote himself solely to civil rights. By the early 1950s, however, Rustin drew closer to Randolph and other African American civil rights advocates.

Although Rustin remained committed to the use of nonviolent civil disobedience, he increasingly stressed the need for African Americans to build alliances with white reformers, especially with progressive elements in the labor movement. As the civil rights movement intensified in the late 1950s, the importance of Rustin's role heightened. Randolph sent him to Montgomery, Alabama, in 1955 to aid Martin Luther King, Jr., in organizing a boycott against the city's segregated buses. For the next five years, Rustin worked closely with King, tutoring him in how to organize mass nonviolent demonstrations and also in the importance of building alliances with progressive white reformers. Rustin favored an interracial coalition of poor people because he believed that the achievement of civil rights alone would not lift the mass of African Americans from poverty. Yet until segregation collapsed, he concentrated on the struggle for civil rights. In 1960 Rustin organized civil rights protests at both the Republican and Democratic national conventions. Later he organized the most massive and effective civil rights demonstration in history—the August 1963 March on Washington. More than 250,000 people gathered at the nation's capital to endorse civil rights legislation and to listen to Martin Luther King's "I Have a Dream" speech. The march illustrated Rustin's commitment "to build, through means that are democratic and nonviolent, a just society . . . in which men of all races . . . need not fear each other." In 1964 Rustin organized an equally successful one-day boycott of the New York City public schools in order to speed the process of integration.

The civil rights bill of 1964 and the voting rights act of 1965 ended one phase of Rustin's career. Success split the civil rights movement. One element, consisting mostly of younger African Americans, gloried in "black power" and suggested that violent action might be necessary. Rustin insisted that civil disobedience had not failed and that the time had arrived to move from protest to politics. He argued in 1965 that since civil rights legislation had failed to end poverty for African Americans, the movement should turn to coalition politics and join with trade unionists and white liberals to erect a more generous welfare state. Rustin's refusal to endorse "black power" and to reject white political allies caused militant African Americans to condemn him as an "oreo," a black cracker with a white filling. In response, Rustin drew closer to his white allies. During the 1968 New York City teachers' strike, he supported the cause of the United Federation of Teachers against the demands of African-American militants who sought community control of the schools. Rustin forged firm links with the American Federation of Labor and Congress of Industrial Organizations and with the Jewish American community. Because of his support for the state of Israel and his commitment to multiracialism, Rustin was honored by the American Jewish Committee in 1978 for "illustrious leadership in the cause of racial justice, world peace and human understanding."

From 1964 until his death, Rustin served as executive director of the A. Philip Randolph Institute, which sought to amalgamate the civil rights and labor movements. Only by working with labor, liberal, religious, and reformist business groups, Rustin asserted, could African Americans achieve improved economic and social conditions. Rustin wrote a series of books and pamphlets in defense of a multiracial civil rights movement and a social democratic welfare state, including *Black Studies: Myths and Realities* (1969), *Down the Line* (1971), and *Strategies for Freedom: The Changing Patterns of Black Protest* (1976). Only a few months before his death, Rustin admitted publicly in an interview published in the *Village Voice* that he was a homosexual. He had previously hidden his sexual orientation because public knowledge of it as well as his youthful Communism might have ended his influence as a reformer. Rustin died in New York City.

Rustin was a leading exemplar of the African American–Jewish American, civil rights movement–labor movement coalition that did so much to demolish segregation and to build the American welfare state. Moreover, he used nonviolent civil disobedience to mount extremely effective multiracial mass protests.

• There is no single collection of Rustin's papers. Much material on him may be found in the records of the A. Philip Randolph Institute in the Library of Congress and in the Congress of Racial Equality Papers at the State Historical Society of Wisconsin. There is also no biography of Rustin. His contributions to the civil rights movement and to political coalition building can be followed best in Paula F. Pfeffer, *A. Philip Randolph, Pioneer of the Civil Rights Movement* (1990), and David J. Garrow, *Bearing the Cross: Martin Luther King, Jr., and the Southern Christian Leadership Conference* (1988). Obituaries are in the *New York Times*, 25 Aug. 1987; *Jet*, 7 Sept. 1987; *New Leader*, 7 Sept. 1987; and the *New Republic*, 28 Sept. 1987.

MELVYN DUBOFSKY

RUTH, Babe (6 Feb. 1895–16 Aug. 1948), baseball player, was born George Herman Ruth in Baltimore, Maryland, the eldest son of George Herman Ruth and Kate Schamberger. Ruth's birth date is taken from the official certificate, although he mistakenly believed the date to be 7 February 1894. Six of his siblings died in infancy, with only Ruth and his younger sister, Mary Margaret ("Mamie"), surviving to adulthood. Ruth was born at his paternal grandfather's home at 216 Emory Street near the city's seedy waterfront district, where his parents operated a combination grocery store and saloon. Because his poorly educated German-American parents worked long hours earning less than $20 a week, Ruth was a neglected child. He spent much of his early childhood in the saloon and in the streets, becoming a swearing, stealing, truant boy.

In 1902 Ruth's frustrated parents committed their seven-year-old son to the St. Mary's Industrial School for Boys as an incorrigible. A combined orphanage, boarding school, and detention center for adjudicated delinquents, St. Mary's was operated by the Xaverian Brothers, a lay branch of the Jesuit order of the Roman Catholic church. Ruth spent eight years at the school, occasionally returning home, but always being returned because of his chronic truancy. After his mother's death in 1912, Ruth received no family visitors before his discharge from St. Mary's at age 19.

The St. Mary's experience provided the fun-loving Ruth with much-needed discipline but left him unsophisticated and with little interest in academic subjects. He learned the shirtmaking trade and became a nominal Roman Catholic. The school's disciplinary mentor, Brother Matthias, became a father figure to him, Ruth's own father, from whom he was estranged, having died in 1918. Brother Matthias encouraged Ruth's passionate interest in baseball. Naturally gifted and left-handed, he became the school's best pitcher and hitter. In 1913, as a muscular, 6'2", 150-pound youth, the 18-year-old starred as pitcher and catcher and batted an impressive .537 in interscholastic competition.

The following year Ruth's baseball prowess attracted the attention of Brother Gilbert, the athletic director of Mount St. Joseph's School, who advised Jack Dunn, the owner of the Baltimore Orioles of the International League, of Ruth's promise. After scouting Ruth, Dunn agreed to become his legal guardian and signed him to a $600 contract. With the Orioles, the 19-year-old Ruth acquired his nickname "Babe" by which legions of fans were to know him. But his stint with the Orioles was brief. His pitching virtuosity, as well as a shortage of player talent among established major league teams caused by raids of the rival Federal League, hastened Ruth's rise to the major leagues. And when competition from the Federal League's Baltimore franchise threatened to bankrupt the Orioles, owner Dunn sold Ruth and two other players to the Boston Red Sox of the American League (AL) for $16,000 and the cancellation of some debts. Thus, after compiling an 11–7 won-lost pitching record with the Orioles, Ruth became a major league pitcher in 1914.

Although Ruth's lack of sophistication as a fledgling major leaguer astonished his Boston teammates, he pitched and won his first game against the Cleveland Indians. He spent five weeks with the Red Sox, compiling a 2–1 record, and received a $2,500 contract. In August 1914 the Red Sox sent him to Providence of the International League for further seasoning. His 11–2 pitching helped Providence win the league pennant. Ruth then joined the Red Sox and in October 1914 married Helen Woodford, the 18-year-old waitress whom he courted during his brief Boston stint.

Given a $3,500 contract for the 1915 season, Ruth quickly established himself as a star pitcher. Playing under Bill "Rough" Carrigan, whom he regarded as his ablest manager, Ruth improved his curveball and learned to exploit the weaknesses of rival batters. Pitching regularly, he posted an 18–8 won-lost record with an ERA of 2.44 and batted a lusty .315 with four home runs. The Red Sox won the AL pennant, and the team's World Series victory over the Philadelphia Phillies netted him an additional $3,750. The following year Ruth's 23–12 pitching mark, which included a league-leading nine shutouts and 1.75 ERA, helped the Red Sox repeat as world champions against the Brooklyn Dodgers. Although the Red Sox faltered in 1917, Ruth's 24–13 won-lost record and his team-leading .325 batting average justified his $5,000 salary. In 1918 wartime restrictions shortened the major league season, and military drafts thinned the ranks of players. As a married man, Ruth was not inducted into military service, and Boston manager Ed Barrow called on him to play in the outfield as well as pitch in order to capitalize on his formidable hitting ability. As a pitcher, Ruth responded with a 13–7 record and as a batter tied for the league lead with 11 home runs. The Red Sox won the AL pennant and defeated the Chicago Cubs in the World Series. Ruth pitched two shutouts, establishing a record total of scoreless innings pitched in World Series competition that lasted until 1961.

The 1918 season marked the turning point in his career. Although he was a dominant left-handed pitcher, his prodigious batting skills diverted him to full-time play as an outfielder. The transformation came in 1919 after Ruth signed a three-year contract at $10,000 a year. During that season Ruth pitched rarely after July and posted a seasonal 9–5 (2.97 ERA) record, but performing regularly as an outfielder he batted .322 and set a major league record by hitting 29 homers while also leading the AL in runs scored (103) and runs batted in (112). A superb fielder, he also led AL outfielders in fielding average and assists (26). The astonishing metamorphosis ended his brilliant pitching career, with the 24-year-old Ruth having compiled an 89–46 won-lost record with a 2.28 ERA and 3–0 World Series record compiled over six seasons. Had he continued to pitch, he might well have ranked among the game's greatest pitchers, but as the game's home run king his fame would be unmatched by any player.

Ruth, the hero of Red Sox fans, became the most coveted player in the game. At the close of the 1919 season, the financially hard-pressed Boston owner, Harry Frazee, chose to sell Ruth to the highest bidder. Having previously sold players to the New York Yankees, Frazee accepted an offer in January 1920 from the millionaire Yankee owners, Jacob Ruppert and Tillinghast l'H. Huston. Ruth was sold to the Yankees for $125,000 and a $350,000 personal loan to Frazee from Ruppert, the highest sum paid for a ballplayer to that time. News of the sale electrified the baseball world, and Ruth's presence in the New York City newspaper and, later, radio center greatly enhanced his prestige. As a Yankee, Ruth quickly became the game's most storied and photographed player, and New York sportswriters vied with one another in touting the Babe and bestowing such nicknames as the "Bambino" and "the Sultan of Swat" on the 25-year-old slugger.

Ruth was ill-prepared for the avalanche of publicity that cast him as a celebrity. Unsophisticated and un-disciplined, he occasionally exhibited temperamental outbursts on the field. Off the field his already legendary living habits included a prodigious appetite for food, beer, womanizing, and lavish spending. But he was also generous, charitable, and genuinely fond of people, especially children. A natural showman, he hit .376 in 1920 and established yet another home run record by slugging 54. His hitting attracted record crowds to Yankee games, and fans elsewhere clamored for news of his exploits. The nation's "Ruthomania" deflected attention in 1920 from newspaper discoveries of the Black Sox scandal involving the 1919 World Series, which had seriously threatened professional baseball's image. Ruth's home run–hitting transformed baseball's style of play from the low-scoring, "scientific" game, with its emphasis on pitching and defense, to the explosive, "big bang" style that continues in part to this day.

In 1921 Ruth set another home run record, with his 59 leading the Yankees to their first of three consecutive American League championships, which marked the beginning of a long era of Yankee domination in major league baseball. Nevertheless, the Yankees lost to the New York Giants in the World Series matchups of 1921 and 1922. Ruth's poor hitting substantially contributed to the 1922 defeat, ending a blighted season for him. Early that season he was suspended for having defied Baseball Commissioner Kenesaw Mountain Landis's edict against playing postseason exhibition games. Ruth missed the first six weeks of the season, costing the Yankees an estimated $100,000 in gate receipts and depriving him of the AL home run crown.

The repentant Ruth atoned for his misdeeds the following season. In 1923 the Yankees occupied the newly constructed Yankee Stadium. Dubbed "the House That Ruth Built," the new edifice attracted a capacity opening day crowd of 60,000, which was delighted when Ruth hit the park's first home run. Thereafter, in what he always regarded as his finest year, Ruth batted .393 with 41 home runs, drawing a record 170 bases on balls and reaching base on half of all his plate appearances. In the 1923 World Series against the Giants, Ruth batted .368 with three home runs in leading the Yankees to their first world championtionship.

Ruth added to his towering reputation by leading the AL in batting (.378) and home runs (46) in 1924. As the highest-paid player in baseball, he surpassed his $52,000 salary with earnings from postseason play and endorsements. Such was his popularity that in 1924 he autographed an estimated 10,000 baseballs and 2,000 bats. But his lavish spending from 1920 through 1925 cost him an estimated $250,000 in fines, legal fees, gambling losses, and abortive business investments. On one occasion he admitted to losing a $1,000 bank note. Moreover, excessive eating and drinking made him overweight and contributed to his poor performance in 1925. In the spring of that year Ruth shed 21 pounds in as many days and later developed a serious medical problem described by sportswriters as "the big bellyache." Reports even circulated that he had died, and the condition, described as an intestinal abscess, required an operation and a seven-week hospital stay. Returning to action, Ruth proved ineffective and defiant of manager Miller Huggins. For breaking a curfew rule, Huggins fined Ruth a record $5,000. Ruth's .290 batting average and 25 home runs in 1925 caused some observers to pronounce his career finished.

But it was a measure of his magnetism that he transcended the crisis. Apologizing to the press and the fans, the contrite Ruth promised to reform. His finances were entrusted to Christy Walsh who administered his off-the-field appearances and instituted an annuity fund to manage his earnings. Now estranged from his wife, Helen, Ruth's current companion, the former actress and divorcée Claire Merritt Hodgson, stabilized his personal life. After Helen died in a 1929 house fire, Ruth married Hodgson and adopted her daughter, Julia. The Ruths brought up Julia with Ruth's adopted daughter, Dorothy, in a stable family environment. To keep his burgeoning body in shape, Ruth annually engaged Arthur McGovern, a physical training specialist, for off-season training.

Ruth's determined efforts enabled him to refurbish his tarnished image with splendid performances. In 1926 he regained the AL home run title and retained it for six straight seasons. His return to form delighted fans, and his income from salary and appearances reached $200,000 in 1926. He attained a new level of greatness in 1927 by hitting 60 homers, a season mark that endured for 34 years. His offensive performance in 1927 had him singlehandedly surpassing the home run production of 12 of the other 15 major league teams. That season a record 2.24 million fans thronged Yankee Stadium to see the Ruth-led team that some have judged the greatest of all major league clubs. In the 1927 World Series some 50 radio stations described the Yankees' victory over the Pittsburgh Pirates to the nation's fans. Ruth's performance earned him a two-year contract for $70,000 annually, and he responded by winning home run titles in 1928 (54) and 1929 (46). For these feats and his consistent drawing power, the 35-year-old Ruth received a two-year contract for $80,000 a year. It was the highest sum paid to a ballplayer until the post–World War II era. Ruth honored his reward by winning his final home run titles in 1930 (49) and 1931 (tied at 46 with Lou Gehrig).

By 1932 the Great Depression diminished baseball revenues. Nevertheless, the burly, aging Ruth still commanded a $75,000 salary, plus a percentage of receipts from spring training games. With the big slugger hitting .341 and pounding 41 home runs, the Yankees won their first AL pennant since 1928. In the 1932 World Series Ruth hit his famous "called shot" home run against the Chicago Cubs at Wrigley Field, reputedly pointing to the bleachers before hitting a towering drive. A lively debate persists over the authenticity of that deliberate, dramatic blow, which Ruth himself came to believe.

The aging Ruth played his last season with the Yankees in 1934 and hit his seven hundredth home run that year. Although his skills were eroding, his popularity continued. In 1933 his dramatic home run in the first major league All-Star game delighted the crowd and radio listeners, insuring a victory for the AL team.

In October 1934 Ruth headed a visiting team of major league all-stars that toured Japan and drew large crowds to exhibition games. Japanese fans lionized him, and the nation has continued to celebrate an annual Babe Ruth Day.

On returning to the United States, Ruth learned that his career with the Yankees was over. He had hoped to manage the Yankees, but owner Ruppert offered only a minor league post. Ruth spurned the offer, saying, "I've always been a big leaguer." When no other major league team offered him a managerial position, the Yankees arranged a deal that enabled him to join the Boston Braves as assistant manager for no monetary consideration. But Ruth soon learned that the Boston team's financially straitened owner only hoped to exploit his popularity. Anticlimactically, the 40-year-old Babe retired after appearing in 28 games. Although batting only .181, Ruth showed flashes of his old élan by homering on opening day and by blasting three long home runs in a May game at Pittsburgh. On 2 June 1935 Ruth quit the Braves and waited the next several years for a managerial opportunity that never came his way. He briefly served as first base coach for the Brooklyn Dodgers in 1938 but resigned at the end of the season. Major league baseball, it seemed, reserved no place for its greatest star.

Ruth's popularity with the fans endured. In his heyday, no American, not even Presidents Warren G. Harding, Calvin Coolidge, or Herbert Hoover, matched his public appeal or gained such wide recognition. He was the most acclaimed athlete in an era when spectator sports enthralled Americans. The era's most versatile baseball player, the gifted young pitcher had become the game's greatest slugger. His 2,873 lifetime hits included 1,356 for extra bases, including 714 home runs, a total unsurpassed until 1974. Moreover, no player ever matched his career home run percentage (8.5 percent) or his record total of 2,056 bases on balls. Nor was any player as celebrated. Performing in New York, the nation's newspaper center, enhanced his visibility, as did his extensive radio and newsreel coverage. Ruth's presence on and off the field continually attracted hero-worshipers who were drawn by the legends that surrounded him. His dramatic home runs had transformed the game's style of play, but Ruth's personality, physical appearance, love of the game and of people, and even foibles magnified his appeal. Thus, when the National Baseball Hall of Fame at Cooperstown, New York, opened in 1939, Ruth stood among the first five players enshrined. In 1941 Ruth portrayed himself in a popular Hollywood film, *The Pride of the Yankees*, honoring his critically ill teammate Lou Gehrig. In 1948 Hollywood produced a mediocre, highly fictionalized version of Ruth's life, *The Babe Ruth Story*, starring William Bendix. A more colorful and explicit biographical film, *The Babe*, starring John Goodman, was released to middling reviews and box office returns in 1992.

In his last years Ruth continued to draw large crowds wherever he went. He was frequently involved in charitable causes, including his beloved St. Mary's Industrial School for Boys. During World War II, his presence boosted sales of war bonds.

Ruth was 52 years old in 1947 when he underwent surgery for the throat cancer that would take his life. That year a Babe Ruth Day was celebrated in all parks of Organized Baseball by order of Baseball Commissioner A. B. Chandler. On 13 June 1948 Ruth made his final appearance at Yankee Stadium as part of commemoration ceremonies recalling the twenty-fifth anniversary of "the House That Ruth Built." Returning to Memorial Hospital in New York, he died there two months later. His body lay in state at the rotunda of Yankee Stadium, and an estimated 200,000 fans passed by his bier. His burial was at the Gate of Heaven Cemetery near New York City, and an estimated 100,000 watched his cortege pass by. His survivors included his second wife and two daughters.

But Babe Ruth's legend transcended his death. Indeed, in 1974, the year Henry Aaron surpassed his record of 714 homers, several biographies of Ruth appeared. Most fans continue to think of Ruth as the greatest player in the game's history.

• Useful source material on Ruth's career can be found at the Baseball Library at Cooperstown, N.Y., where a dozen volumes of scrapbooks are housed along with the official files of the New York Yankees for the period. Other primary sources include Ruth's autobiography, Babe Ruth and Bob Considine, *The Babe Ruth Story* (1948), and two biographical works by family members, including Mrs. Babe Ruth with Bill Slocum, *The Babe and I* (1959), and Dorothy Ruth Pirone, *My Dad: The Babe* (1988). Important works by sportswriters who knew Ruth include Dan Daniel and H. G. Salsinger, *The Real Babe Ruth* (1963), and Tom Meany, *Babe Ruth: The Big Moments of the Big Fella* (1947). Other works by those close to Ruth at various points in his career include Waite Hoyt, *Babe Ruth As I Knew Him* (1948), and Louis J. Leisman, *I Was with Babe Ruth at St. Mary's* (1956).

No American baseball player has been the subject of more biographies than Babe Ruth. Among some thirty, the best work is Marshall Smelser's scholarly *The Life That Ruth Built* (1975). The best popular work is Robert W. Creamer, *Babe: The Legend Comes to Life* (1974). An important assemblage of photos covering Ruth's life is the compilation by Lawrence S. Ritter and Mark Rucker, *The Babe: A Life in Pictures* (1988). Among many popular biographies worth reading are Ken Sobol, *Babe Ruth and the American Dream* (1974); Ed "Dutch" Doyle, *The Only One* (1974); and Kal Wagenheim, *Babe Ruth: His Life and Legend* (1974). Ruth's career can also be traced through various team histories, with John Mosedale's *The Greatest of All: The 1927 New York Yankees* (1974) being worthy of attention.

For Ruth's place in the general history of major league baseball, see David Q. Voigt, *American Baseball: From the Commissioners to Continental Expansion* (1983). The records of Ruth's performances as a major league pitcher and hitter can be found in John Thorn and Pete Palmer, eds., *Total Baseball* (1991).

DAVID QUENTIN VOIGT

RUTHERFORD, Griffith (1721?–10 Aug. 1805), revolutionary war militia officer and politician, was born in Ireland, the son of John Rutherford and Elizabeth Griffith. Details of Rutherford's background and personal life are sketchy and based largely on family tradition. Like many other Scotch-Irish, the Rutherfords emigrated from Ireland to Pennsylvania. The parents died en route to America in 1721, and relatives in Pennsylvania adopted the infant boy.

In the early 1750s Rutherford moved to North Carolina and settled in Rowan County, in the extreme western section of the province. As a surveyor, Rutherford quickly assumed a position of importance in the rapidly growing backcountry. In 1754 he acquired 656 acres on Grant Creek near Salisbury, the principal settlement and trade center in the area. That same year Rutherford married Elizabeth Graham, the daughter of his neighbor James Graham. They had ten children.

During the 1760s political and military duties consumed more of Rutherford's time. By 1760 he served as captain of the militia company from his section of Rowan County. In 1766 he was elected to the lower house of the North Carolina Assembly, and he represented Rowan County through 1775. From 1767 to 1769 he was county sheriff.

Rutherford weathered the North Carolina Regulator movement of 1768–1771 with his political prestige intact. Regulators in Rowan County challenged the legality of fees collected by county officers, which included Rutherford in his capacity as surveyor. In a conciliatory gesture he and other officers offered to return any excessive fees that they had accumulated. During the decisive May 1771 campaign against the Regulators, Rutherford demonstrated tactical insight when he dissuaded militia general Hugh Waddell from engaging a superior Regulator force.

Rutherford became a conspicuous military and political leader during the American Revolution. Rowan County elected him to the Provincial Congress of 1775. In September the Provincial Congress appointed him colonel of the Rowan County minutemen, and he became a member of the committee of safety for the Salisbury district. In late 1775 he led his regiment to the South Carolina backcountry and helped patriot militia forces in that province quell a Loyalist uprising in the Snow campaign. When six military districts were formed in North Carolina the following April, the Provincial Congress named Rutherford brigadier general of Salisbury district, an area that encompassed the western frontier.

That spring, when the Cherokee attacked white frontier settlements, Rutherford proposed that both the Carolinas and Virginia launch a punitive campaign. If "the Frunters, of Each of them Provances" were to combine forces, said Rutherford, he had "no Doubt of a Finel Destruction of the Cherroce Nation." Between July and September 1776 he recruited and led a force of nearly 2,000 men into the middle and valley Cherokee settlements in the westernmost part of the Carolinas. In coordination with the South Carolina militia under the command of Major Andrew Williamson, he destroyed thirty-six Cherokee towns. The surviving Cherokee fled across the Blue Ridge Mountains and ceased to be a major threat to the Carolinas. A remarkable military success, the campaign formed the basis of Rutherford's reputation as an officer. He lost only three men of his immediate command.

For the duration of the revolutionary war, Rutherford alternated between political and military duties. He represented Rowan County in the North Carolina Senate from 1777 to 1786, with the exception of a two-year hiatus, 1781–1782. A rough, untutored man, Rutherford naturally associated with the so-called Radicals, a group of planters who favored a strong state legislature and resisted attempts to strengthen the governor's powers. This faction, according to one opponent, appealed to the "lower class of people."

When the focus of the war shifted to the South, Rutherford spent more time in active military duty. In early 1779 he led 800 men to assist Continental general Benjamin Lincoln in a failed campaign against the British in Georgia. In June 1780 Rutherford raised more than 1,000 militia to counter 1,300 Loyalists camped at Ramsour's Mill in Lincoln County, where they awaited a British invasion. On 20 June troops under Rutherford's overall command overwhelmed the Loyalists, but he did not arrive until the battle was over. The patriot victory at Ramsour's Mill frustrated British hopes of utilizing Loyalists to subjugate North Carolina.

Rutherford led a militia brigade at the battle of Camden on 16 August 1780, and he was wounded and captured by British cavalry in the pursuit following the rout. The British first held Rutherford prisoner at Charleston, but he was eventually transferred to St. Augustine, where he was confined until his parole on 22 June 1781.

On his return to North Carolina, Rutherford collected more than 1,000 militia and launched a concerted effort to eradicate the Loyalist strongholds in southeastern North Carolina. In a well-executed campaign, Rutherford's force routed an army of 600 Loyalists at Raft Swamp and virtually ended organized Loyalist resistance. His force next laid siege to the British garrison at Wilmington. After the British evacuation on 14 November, Rutherford and his militia briefly occupied the town. The conclusion of the successful operation was marred by his failure to control the troops, who looted and plundered Wilmington.

At the close of the war, Rutherford continued his service in the senate, where he remained aligned with the Radicals. Noted as a ruthless officer during the conflict, he recommended no leniency toward Loyalists, whom he considered "imps of hell." As a delegate to the state convention at Hillsborough in 1788, he voted with the anti-Federalist majority not to ratify the Constitution. Rowan County did not elect him to the subsequent convention in 1789, which approved the new federal government.

Like other prominent North Carolinians, Rutherford speculated in western lands. His ability as a surveyor again served him well, and by 1790 he had amassed between 12,000 and 20,000 acres. Two years later he moved to Sumner County in what is now Tennessee, where he continued his political career. Elected to the first territorial legislature in the area south of the Ohio River, which convened in 1794, Rutherford was appointed by President George Washington to serve on the five-member legislative council. The legislature unanimously voted him president of the council.

Rutherford died at his home in Sumner County. Both of his adopted states named counties in his honor. The principal military leader in revolutionary North Carolina, Rutherford was instrumental in eliminating Indian and Loyalist threats to the state government. His political career followed the pattern of the self-made frontier planter who identified himself with the interests of smaller farmers.

• There is no major collection of Rutherford's papers. His revolutionary war correspondence is in Walter Clark, ed., *The State Records of North Carolina*, vols. 11–26 (1895–1906). Jerry C. Cashion has presented a detailed biographical sketch in the fifth volume of *Dictionary of North Carolina Biography*, ed. William S. Powell (1994). The Cherokee campaign is covered thoroughly in Robert L. Ganyard, "Threat from the West: North Carolina and the Cherokee, 1776–1778," *North Carolina Historical Review* 45 (1968): 47–66. For a firsthand account of the 1781 campaign, see "General Joseph Graham's Narrative of the Revolutionary War in North Carolina in 1780 and 1781," in *The Papers of Archibald D. Murphey*, ed. William Henry Hoyt, vol. 2 (1914). Some evidence of Rutherford's political style and details of his career in Tennessee are in Thomas P. Abernethy, *From Frontier to Plantation in Tennessee: A Study in Frontier Democracy* (1932).

GREGORY D. MASSEY

RUTHERFORD, Joseph Franklin (8 Nov. 1869–8 Jan. 1942), lawyer and religious leader, was born in Morgan County, Missouri, the son of James Calvin Rutherford and Lenore Strickland, farmers. Experiencing both near poverty and hard work, Rutherford came to value education. He borrowed money and went away to school, where he learned shorthand. After studying law under Judge E. L. Edwards and serving as the official reporter of the Court of the Fourteenth Judicial Circuit of Missouri, he passed the Missouri state bar examination in 1892. Beginning private law practice in Booneville, Missouri, he soon joined the firm of Draffen and White. While practicing law he served four times as a special judge in the Eighth Judicial Circuit Court; this experience was the basis for the title "Judge" given to him later by many of his followers. In 1896 he campaigned for William Jennings Bryan.

Although his family appears to have been Baptist, Rutherford had little interest in religion until he read three of Charles Taze Russell's books in 1894. About 1900 he met Russell, who later encouraged him to write a book that was published in 1906 as *Man's Salvation from a Lawyer's Viewpoint*, describing his new religious beliefs. That same year he was baptized into Russell's International Bible Students movement. The following year he became a full-time "pilgrim," as workers in the movement were known, accompanying Russell as a lecturer, lecturing on his own, and serving as legal counsel. In 1909 he moved to New York, becoming a member of the New York bar and joining the staff of the People's Pulpit Association, one of the legal corporations of the International Bible Students. He subsequently defended cases involving Russell and the Bible Students and in 1910 began traveling internationally to promote the organization.

By the time of Russell's death in 1916 Rutherford had become a member of the boards of the People's Pulpit Association of New York and the Watch Tower Bible and Tract Society of Pennsylvania, the parent corporation of the movement. Through a series of controversial moves and aided by his knowledge of the society's legal affairs, he became president of the movement's corporations in 1917, positions he held until his death. He quickly removed dissenters from the boards. Although about 4,000 members left the movement because of his actions, some establishing alternative organizations, internal opposition had largely died out by 1923.

Upon becoming president, Rutherford commissioned a compilation of Russell's commentaries on Ezekiel and Revelation, which was published as *The Finished Mystery* in 1917. Because the book attacked Catholics, Protestants, and civil government, it was banned in Canada the following year. In the United States the clergy led an outcry against the society. Furthermore, Rutherford's condemnation of U.S. participation in World War I and recommendation that the Bible Students refuse to cooperate with the military led to conflict with the U.S. government, which seized the society's business records. In 1918 he and six other board members were arrested and convicted of violating the Espionage Act, the government arguing that *The Finished Mystery*, the magazines the *Bible Student's Monthly* and the *Watch Tower*, and letters to conscientious objectors were evidence of a conspiracy to hinder the U.S. war effort. They were held in prison in Atlanta for nine months until U.S. Supreme Court justice Louis Brandeis ordered their release on bail in March 1919. Later the appeals court reversed their convictions, and in May 1920 the government withdrew its case. During Rutherford's incarceration, the Bible Students sold their tabernacle and closed their headquarters (called "Bethel") in Brooklyn, reestablishing offices in Pittsburgh. Rutherford was reelected to the presidency in 1919 while still in prison and on his release moved the headquarters back to Bethel; persecution, however, had reduced membership from approximately 17,000 to 4,000.

Rutherford soon shifted the Bible Students' emphasis from character building, as it had been under Russell, to preaching, calling on believers to "advertize, advertize, advertize the King and his kingdom." He began in 1919 publication of a new magazine, *Golden Age* (later called *Consolation* and then *Awake!*), intended for nonbelievers and distributed from house to house. In 1920 individual members began reporting their evangelistic activities to the Brooklyn headquarters. Also expanding the Bible Students organization internationally, by 1921 Rutherford oversaw eighteen foreign branch offices.

Continually seeking new ways to promote his organization, between 1922 and 1928 Rutherford turned annual conventions into publicity events by passing resolutions condemning organizations or groups such as the League of Nations and the clergy as being parts of Satan's organization, which was opposed to the true government of Jehovah. Using the new medium of radio, in 1924 he established station WBBR on Staten Island and smaller stations elsewhere and broadcast sermons on many stations throughout the United States. In 1926 he razed the existing building and constructed a nine-story residence and office building at Bethel. Five years later Rutherford announced that the Bible Students would henceforth be known as Jehovah's Witnesses.

Meanwhile, Rutherford established absolute authority over his organization. In 1917 he gained control of its business affairs and in 1925 established authority over doctrine by overriding the editorial committee. In 1932 he replaced the congregationally elected elders with Service Committees, also congregationally elected, but in 1938 he made all officers appointees of the Watch Tower Society. Rutherford accompanied the development of this "Theocratic Society" with emphasis on separation from the world, declaring in 1935 that it was unfaithful to Jehovah to salute any earthly emblem, including flags, or stand for national anthems. He opposed observance of "pagan" customs such as Christmas and birthday parties and— for a time—prohibited congregational hymn singing. He further urged Witnesses to withdraw from most secular contacts and activities such as unions, lodges, Parent-Teacher Associations, Boy Scouts and Girl Scouts, purchase of government bonds, voting, and holding of public office.

This separate theocracy grew in part out of the doctrinal changes Rutherford brought into the organization. In addition to dropping Russell's teachings of sabbath observance, the gathering of the Jews to Palestine, and numerological theories of the great pyramid, Rutherford emphasized 1914 as the year in which war in heaven began and Satan was confined to earth. The year 1925 was to be "the completion of all things." "Millions Now Living Will Never Die" became Rutherford's slogan, proclaimed from billboards, barn posters, and newspaper advertisements. In 1927 he stated that Russell was not the "wise and faithful servant" of Matthew 25:45, as had been believed. Two years later he told his followers that obedience to the Watch Tower Society took primacy over allegiance to government. With the number of Jehovah's Witnesses approaching 144,000, originally thought to be the biblically ordained maximum number of members, in 1932 Rutherford introduced the concept of a "Jonadab" class, members who would participate in the destruction of Babylon and inherit the new earth while the 144,000 would go to heaven.

Believing that the Witnesses were the only true Israel, Rutherford through his writing and preaching castigated "the unholy alliance of big business and big politicians supported by big preachers." Protests from both Protestants and Catholics led many radio stations to drop Rutherford's broadcasts, and in 1937 he withdrew from the air. Nonetheless, Rutherford carried his message through the short recorded messages that Witnesses carried house to house to play on their portable phonographs and through his many tracts and books that appeared almost annually. Among his books were *Millions Now Living Will Never Die* (1920), which asserted that the world began to end in 1914; *The Harp of God* (1921), an interpretive overview of the Bible; *Government* (1928), an argument that 1914 began a series of steps toward the setting up of Jehovah's government on earth; and *Religion* (1940), which contrasted the word of God with religion, the latter being an instrument of the devil.

Although little is known about Rutherford's personal life, he appears to have been estranged from his wife, Mary (maiden name and date of marriage unknown), with whom he had one child, shortly after becoming president of the Watch Tower Society. It is also reported by several sources, including Olin R. Moyle—who brought a libel suit against the society in 1943—and James Penton, that Rutherford was an alcoholic, a situation that sometimes made it difficult for him to address conventions. Rutherford died at "Beth Sarim," a mansion near San Diego, California, that he had built in 1929 for the use of resurrected Old Testament princes but in which he lived for the last decade of his life, apparently with little objection from society members. Nathan Homer Knorr succeeded Rutherford as president of the Watch Tower Society, which had 115,240 "peak publishers" in 1942.

• Personal recollections of Rutherford appear in A. H. Macmillan, *Faith on the March* (1957). Biographical information may be found in books on Jehovah's Witnesses. Marley Cole, *Jehovah's Witnesses: The New World Society* (1955), and Timothy White, *A People for His Name: A History of Jehovah's Witnesses and an Evaluation* (1968), provide a Jehovah's Witness perspective. A Catholic viewpoint appears in William J. Whalen, *Armageddon around the Corner: A Report of Jehovah's Witnesses* (1962). Scholarly works include Herbert Hewitt Stroup, *The Jehovah's Witnesses* (1945); Alan Rogerson, *Millions Now Living Will Never Die: A Study of Jehovah's Witnesses* (1969); James A. Beckford, *The Trumpet of Prophecy: A Sociological Study of Jehovah's Witnesses* (1975); Heather Botting and Gary Botting, *The Orwellian World of Jehovah's Witnesses* (1984); and M. James Penton, *Apocalypse Delayed: The Story of Jehovah's Witnesses* (1985). An obituary is in the *New York Times*, 11 Jan. 1942.

GARY LAND

RUTHERFORD, Leonard C. (c. 1900–c. 1950), country music fiddler and composer, was born in Corbin, Kentucky, the son of Henry Rutherford, a restaurant owner. His mother's name is unknown. He was reared in the nearby town of Somerset. When Rutherford was only thirteen or fourteen, he began to work for Dick Burnett, a blind banjoist, guitarist, and singer who was traveling around the southern Kentucky area performing old-time music. Burnett, born in 1883 in Monticello, Kentucky, was a driller in the local oil fields until 1907, when he was shot and blinded in a robbery. After that, Burnett had won fame as a "busker" (a traveling musician who played on street corners and courthouse lawns) and was well known in the area when he asked Rutherford's family if he could take the boy along as a guide and apprentice musician. They agreed, and the team of Burnett and Rutherford was born, a duo that would remain intact for some thirty-five years.

Burnett, who had learned "rudiments" of music from old religious songbooks like *The Southern Harmony*, taught Rutherford to play the fiddle in the smooth "long bow" style that was becoming fashionable in the South. The younger musician quickly adapted to his style and soon became a superb back-up fiddler, an expert at playing the traditional fiddle tunes of south-central Kentucky. Throughout the 1920s and 1930s the pair traveled from West Virginia to Florida, playing schoolhouse shows, fiddling contests, dances, and at coal mining camps. In November 1926 they traveled to Atlanta, Georgia, to record in the Columbia studios there, the first of some two dozen sides they would record; the songs included several that over the years became classics of southern string band music, including "Lost John," "Little Stream of Whiskey," "Pearl Bryan," and their bestseller, "I'll Be with You When the Roses Bloom Again." At later sessions (Apr. and Nov. 1927 and Oct. 1928), they added classics like "Ladies on the Steamboat" and "Willie Moore."

Though the pair continued to travel together, after 1929 each recorded separately with other partners. Rutherford found a new guitarist and singer in John Foster, from Elgin, Tennessee, and recorded extensively with him for the Gennett Company. Their recordings included the popular prison song "Six Months Ain't Long" and the first recording of the lyric "There's More Pretty Girls Than One" (both Jan. 1929). The recording activity for both, however, ceased in late 1930, and for the next two decades they continued to travel and eke out a living where they could. Rutherford began to develop serious health problems, eventually being diagnosed as suffering from epilepsy. His seizures became more and more frequent and were complicated by his fondness for drinking. One morning in the early 1950s he was found alongside a road near Burnside, Kentucky, dead from such a seizure. He was buried at Somerset.

Though Rutherford only recorded eight fiddle solos (in addition to the sides on which he backed up singing), they are considered masterpieces of Kentucky fiddle styles. Historian Guthrie Meade has commented that he was "an unsurpassed master" when it came to instrumentals. Most of his old records remained in print on LPs through the 1960s and 1970s. One of Rutherford's pupils who had absorbed his style was Clyde Davenport, from the Monticello area, who traveled widely in the 1980s and won a National Heritage Fellowship, given to the nation's premier traditional musicians. Through him and others, Rutherford and Burnett's distinctive central Kentucky folk music style was preserved in a national venue.

• The best detailed account of Rutherford's life is an extensive interview with his partner Dick Burnett: Charles K. Wolfe, "Man of Constant Sorrow: Richard Burnett's Story," pts. 1 and 2, *Old Time Music*, no. 9 (Summer 1973): 6–9; and no. 10 (Autumn 1973): 5–9. A discography of the Burnett-Rutherford recordings is in the brochure notes to the Rounder LP *Ramblin' Reckless Hobo* (Rounder 1004).

CHARLES K. WOLFE

RUTHERFORD, Mildred Lewis (16 July 1851–15 Aug. 1928), southern educator, was born in Athens, Georgia, the daughter of William R. Rutherford and Laura Rootes Cobb. Her father, a professor of mathematics at the University of Georgia, was also a slaveholder and master of a plantation in Crawford County, Georgia, at which the family spent part of each year. One of Rutherford's uncles, Howell Cobb, was a cabinet member in the administration of James Buchanan. Howell Cobb and his brother, T. R. R. Cobb, both held the rank of general in the army of the Confederate States of America.

In 1859 Rutherford matriculated at the Lucy Cobb Institute in Athens, Georgia. The school, founded the previous year by T. R. R. Cobb and named in honor of his daughter, was designed to provide a proper education for southern women. The Civil War, which disrupted Rutherford's education, became the central event in her life and subsequent career. As an impressionable child, she, along with her sisters, assisted her mother in work with the Soldiers' Aid Society. The young girls rolled bandages and packed food for the Confederate army.

Two major themes dominated Rutherford's career: commitment to the education of young women and devotion to the values and history of the Old South. Following graduation from Lucy Cobb in 1868, she taught private classes to girls in Athens. In 1875 Rutherford accepted a teaching position in the public schools of Atlanta, Georgia. Five years later, she returned to her home and alma mater to serve as principal of the Lucy Cobb Institute. For the next four decades, Rutherford served the institution as principal (1880–1895), coprincipal with her sister Mary Ann Rutherford (1895–1907), president (1917–1922), and director (1925–1926).

Rutherford was determined that Lucy Cobb alumnae be proper ladies and devoted southern patriots. To achieve the former, she established strict rules of conduct regarding dress and deportment. To accomplish the latter, she fashioned a curriculum, particularly in English and history, which emphasized the significance of the South in the life of the nation. Although Rutherford wrote a number of books on literature, she considered her most significant to be *The South in Literature and History* (1907). In it she insists that the

northern publishing and critical establishment purposely ignored southern authors, many of whom she deemed the peers of more celebrated northern writers. Rutherford's promotion of southern literature apparently succeeded, for by the early twentieth century, the institute claimed to attract students "from Texas to Massachusetts . . . from Florida to Minnesota."

Despite her long and intimate identification with the Lucy Cobb Institute, the driving force in Rutherford's life was undoubtedly her devotion to the cause of the Old South, especially its cultural and political contributions to the life of the nation. She held a series of local, state, and national offices in the United Daughters of the Confederacy (UDC), an organization dedicated to preserving the memory of the Civil War and its heroes. In 1890 Rutherford was one of the founding members and the first president of the Athens, Georgia, chapter of the UDC, holding that post until 1928. Between 1899 and 1902, she was historian general and president of the Georgia division of the organization and historian general and honorary president of the national UDC.

Rutherford was an indefatigable pamphleteer and public speaker in defense of the southern cause. Her more colorful pamphlets include *What the South May Claim; or Where the South Leads* (1916?), *Truths of History* (1920?), and *The South Must Have Her Rightful Place in History* (1923). In both her writing and speaking, Rutherford's arguments seldom varied. She maintained that, although the South produced a significant number of innovators in science, literature, and agriculture, the North refused to acknowledge the contributions of the region. The Civil War, she insisted, was a war of northern aggression rather than southern rebellion. Furthermore, she contended that the institution of slavery, rather than demoralizing blacks and whites alike, had produced obedient, contented black workers and a white leadership of great wisdom and skill, as the preponderance of southern presidents indicated.

A physically imposing woman, Rutherford wore long skirts and upswept hair long after the fashion for both had ceased. She always sported an abundant corsage when she spoke, insisting that this enhanced her performance. Accounts of her speaking indicate that she possessed a dramatic delivery and occasionally even wore costumes.

In addition to her work with the Lucy Cobb Institute and the cause of the Old South, Rutherford was an active member of the Young Women's Christian Association, serving on its national board from 1910 until her death. The University of Georgia honored her literary achievements in 1923 by conferring upon her an honorary doctorate of literature. Rutherford spent the last years of her life concerned about the fate of Lucy Cobb Institute, which suffered from declining enrollment. Despite her work on behalf of the school, the institute closed within several years of her death in Athens, Georgia. She never married.

• The Mildred Lewis Rutherford Papers are in the Hargrett Rare Book and Manuscript Library of the University of Georgia. These include seventy scrapbooks of clippings that Rutherford compiled while historian general of the Georgia chapter of the UDC. The library also houses Rutherford's numerous publications, some of which include *English Authors* (1890), *American Authors* (1894), *French Authors* (1906), *Georgia: The Empire State of the South* (1914?), *The Civilization of the Old South* (1918), and *The History of the Stone Mountain Memorial* (1924). The Hargrett Library also contains issues of the local newspapers, *Athens Daily Herald* and *Athens Banner-Herald*, which are excellent sources for Rutherford's activities. There are two biographies: Virginia Clare, *Thunder and Stars: The Life of Mildred Rutherford* (1941); and Margaret Anne Womack, "Mildred Lewis Rutherford, Exponent of Southern Culture" (M.A. thesis, Univ. of Georgia, 1946). The former, a mawkish treatment of her life, is of limited use to the historian. The latter, however, contains an apparently accurate chronology and an extensive bibliography. For additional information concerning Rutherford, see Margaret A. Moss, "Miss Millie Rutherford, Southerner," *Georgia Review* 7 (Spring 1953): 56–66.

CAROLYN TERRY BASHAW

RUTHERFURD, Lewis Morris (25 Nov. 1816–30 May 1892), astrophysicist, was born at Morrisania, New York, a residential section of the south Bronx, the son of Robert Walter Rutherfurd and Sabina Morris. While a student at Williams College (B.A., 1834), Rutherfurd helped Professor Ebenezer Emmons prepare demonstrations for his lectures on natural philosophy and chemistry, and he was able to take good advantage of the scientific apparatus recently obtained with $4,000 raised by alumni. Graduating at a time when science was not widely regarded as a promising career, Rutherfurd went to Auburn, New York, to study law with William Seward. He was admitted to the bar in 1837 and spent the next twelve years practicing law in New York City.

Rutherfurd married Margaret Stuyvesant Chanler, who also came from a prominent and wealthy family, in 1841, and they eventually had seven children. The family went abroad in 1849, touring England, France, Germany, and Italy and seeking spas where Margaret might regain her health. Rutherfurd—who took with him a microscope objective made by Charles A. Spencer of Canastota, New York, and a spy glass by Henry Fitz of New York City—used the occasion to get to know the leading European instrument makers. G. B. Amici in Florence shared some of his insights regarding achromatic microscope lenses. N. J. Lerebours in Paris, however, refused to show Rutherfurd his optical shop.

Returning to New York in 1856, Rutherfurd resumed his law practice. His main interest, however, was in the new techniques of astronomical photography and spectroscopy. His work helped make spectroscopy a basic element of astrophysics, and it helped photography gain acceptance as an important astronomical research technology. This scientific work brought Rutherfurd numerous honors, including election as a founding member of the National Academy of Sciences and as a foreign associate of the Royal Astronomical Society, as well as the Rumford Medal of the American Academy of Arts and Sciences.

Rutherfurd built an observatory in the garden of his house in New York City and furnished it with an 11¼-inch equatorial refracting telescope, one of the larger telescopes then in use in the United States. Henry Fitz, America's first successful commercial telescope maker, provided the mount. Rutherfurd, with advice from Fitz, figured the achromatic objective. Rutherfurd's first project was to take astronomical photographs like those recently made by John H. Whipple and George P. Bond at the Harvard College Observatory. Using the new wet collodion plates, Rutherfurd recorded images of the moon, Jupiter, Saturn, stars as faint as fifth magnitude, and the sun showing spots and faculae.

In 1865 Rutherfurd acquired a second 11¼-inch objective, this one focused for photographic rather than for visual observations. With this he obtained spectacular photographs of the moon, similar to those captured by Henry Draper, another New York amateur astronomer. Copies of these photographs were distributed to astronomers around the world and widely praised. Rutherfurd also photographed the Pleiades and Praesepe. The best pictures showed stars as faint as ninth magnitude—at least two magnitudes fainter than anyone previously had been able to reach. In 1870, believing that photography had advanced to the point at which it could be used for astrometry, Rutherfurd designed and built a series of micrometers for measuring the linear and the angular distance from one star to another. One he used himself; the U.S. Coast Survey used the other to evaluate the reliability of photography for solar observations. The results were sufficiently positive that the commission in charge of American observations of the transit of Venus of 1874 decided to photograph this important but infrequent astronomical event and to use Rutherfurd-type micrometers to measure the position of Venus as it moved across the face of the sun.

With his third refracting telescope—a 13-inch visual achromat with a "corrector" lens that would focus the light for the photographic rays—Rutherfurd took many fine photographs of the sun. This telescope was made in Rutherfurd's house in 1868, and the work was done by Henry Fitz, Jr., under Rutherfurd's supervision.

Largely because of the introduction of spectroscopy, astronomy underwent a major revolution during the second half of the nineteenth century. No longer concerned simply with the positions and motions of celestial bodies, astronomers began to investigate their physical properties. Rutherfurd took up spectroscopy soon after R. W. Bunsen and G. R. Kirchhoff's 1859 announcement that the positions of the emission and absorption lines were uniquely defined by the constituent elements. Attaching a simple one-prism spectroscope to his telescope, Rutherfurd found that he could classify stellar spectra and correlate them with other stellar characteristics. He also found that the spectroscope could be used to test the color correction of a lens. As spectroscopes were not yet commercially available in the United States, Rutherfurd made some instruments from scratch and assembled others from parts supplied by local opticians and mechanics. Wishing to increase the dispersion, to see more spectral details, he experimented with compound prisms, with hollow glass prisms filled with carbon bisulphide, and with a six-prism spectroscope in which the prisms could be adjusted for angle of minimum deviation.

Early spectroscopists were well aware that diffraction gratings produce normal spectra—that is, ones in which the relative distance between one spectral line and another remains constant. Prisms, however, do not, and so prismatic spectra cannot be easily compared with one another. As he was eager to observe diffraction spectra, and as diffraction gratings were not commercially available in the United States (or widely available in Europe), Rutherfurd began in 1863 to design and build his own ruling engine, a machine that produced diffraction gratings by ruling closely spaced parallel lines on a piece of glass or metal. By 1872 he was able to make gratings that were sufficiently regular for scientific work. Over the course of the next decade, Rutherfurd gave gratings to dozens of scientists around the world. Rutherfurd's first gratings were small—some were 0.64 inches (1.63 cm) wide by 1.08 inches (2.74 cm) long, with 1,500 lines per inch—but they ranked with the best to be had. By 1877 Rutherfurd, with the assistance of Daniel Chapman, was ruling gratings about 1.7 inches (4.3 cm) square, with spacings up to 17,296 lines per inch. Following Rutherfurd's pioneering work, Henry A. Rowland was able, in the early 1880s, to design and build an even better ruling engine.

Rutherfurd's two main interests came together in his photographs of the solar spectrum. As early as 1864 he was getting pictures of the prismatic spectrum that were warmly admired by scientists in Europe as well as the United States. In the 1870s Rutherfurd used his diffraction gratings to photograph the normal spectrum of the sun. His finest map, over ten feet long, was a composite of twenty-eight separate pictures taken with different exposures.

As Rutherfurd's health deteriorated, his active involvement in astronomy decreased. He gave his 13-inch telescope and photographic micrometer to Columbia University (of which he had long been a trustee) in 1883 and donated his astronomical photographs to the same institution in 1890. These resources enabled John K. Rees, Harold Jacoby, and Frank Schlesinger to continue the investigations Rutherfurd had begun. Rutherfurd died at "Tranquility," the country homestead that had been in his family for more than 150 years.

• Information on Rutherfurd and his work can be found in Deborah Jean Warner, "Lewis M. Rutherfurd: Pioneer Astronomical Photographer and Spectroscopist," *Technology and Culture*, 12 (April 1971): 190–216; and Owen Gingerich, ed., *Astrophysics and Twentieth-Century Astronomy to 1950: Part A* (1984), especially A. J. Meadows, "The Origins of As-

trophysics," pp. 3–15, and John Lankford, "The Impact of Photography on Astronomy," pp. 16–39. Rutherfurd's publications include "Observations during the Lunar Eclipse, September 12, 1848," *American Journal of Science* 6 (1848): 435–37; "Astronomical Observations with the Spectroscope," *American Journal of Science* 35 (1863): 71–77; "Letter on Companion to Sirius, Stellar Spectra and the Spectroscope," *American Journal of Science* 35 (1863): 407–9, "Observations on Stellar Spectra," *American Journal of Science* 36 (1863): 154–57; "Astronomical Photography," *American Journal of Science*, 39 (1865): 2–7; "On the Construction of the Spectroscope," *American Journal of Science* 39 (1865): 129–32; "On the Stability of the Collodion Film," *Anthony's Photographic Bulletin*, 4 (1873): 52–55; "Astronomical Photography," *British Journal of Photography* 22 (1875): 630–31; and "A Glass Circle for the Measurement of Angles," *American Journal of Science* 12 (1876): 112–13.

DEBORAH JEAN WARNER

RUTLEDGE, Archibald (23 Oct. 1883–15 Sept. 1973), educator and writer, was born in McClellanville, South Carolina, the son of Henry Middleton Rutledge, an army colonel, and Margaret Hamilton. His family played a key role in South Carolina politics during the eighteenth century. Rutledge spent his childhood on his family plantation and was known as an avid reader of literature. At the age of thirteen, he was enrolled at Charleston's Porter Military Academy. He graduated as class salutatorian four years later. In 1904 he received his B.S. from Union College in Schenectady, New York, and started his career as an English teacher at Mercersburg Academy in Mercersburg, Pennsylvania. In 1905 he became the chairman of the English department and held that position for more than thirty-two years.

Despite his long teaching career, Rutledge was also a versatile and prolific writer who published more than eighty volumes of prose and poetry on such subjects as wildlife, history, and life on a plantation in the South. His first book, *Under the Pines*, appeared in 1907, and he married Florence Hart at the end of the same year. They would have three children. *The Banners of the Coast* (1908) was his first book of poetry; his second, *New Poems*, did not appear until 1917. Rutledge did not receive substantial recognition until his *Tom and I on the Old Plantation*, a memoir, was published in 1918. This autobiographical account of his first twenty years at his home on the Hampton Plantation was highly praised for its genuine picture of the southern landscape and its touching description of the joy and bond shared by the author, his brother, Tom, and their black servant-companion, Prince. As he indicated in the book, Rutledge wrote the book with the wish to preserve the best of those years, which were "crowded with happy memories, with incidents and adventures, tragic, pathetic, and humorous."

Following the success of this book, Rutledge seemed to make a fresh start in his writing career. He published nearly twenty books in prose and poetry during the 1920s and 1930s, his most productive years. In such prose works as *Old Plantation Days* (1921), *Plantation Game Trails* (1921), *Days Off in*

Dixie (1924), *Heart of the South* (1924), *Life's Extras* (1928), and *My Colonel and His Lady* (1937), Rutledge presented fascinating images of life in the South, from hunting in the southern woods and fishing along the southern coast to customs and traditions on the southern plantations. Although less in quantity, his poetry contributed more to his popularity as a leading southern writer. Both his *Collected Poems* (1925), the first full collection of his poems, and *Veiled Eros* (1933) won rave reviews for their insightful representation of and passionate love for the unique qualities of southern life. In 1934 he was chosen by legislative action to be the first poet laureate of South Carolina, an honor that he held for the rest of his life, but the year was marred by the death of his wife. Three years later he married Alice Lucas, a childhood sweetheart, with whom he had no children.

Rutledge retired from teaching in 1937. After an absence of forty-four years, he returned to Hampton Plantation, his family estate in McClellanville, South Carolina, in 1939. The estate had been in his family for more than two hundred years. At the time of his return, though, the mansion and the vast plantation had been deserted for years, surrounded by what Rutledge later described as "a lush of grass and briars." Despite the warning from many friends that it would be foolish to reclaim the property, Rutledge decided to restore Hampton Plantation and its gardens to original magnificence. He recorded this huge project, as well as his fond memories of the plantation's long history, in his *Home by the River* (1941). Written in an autobiographical form, the book depicts Rutledge's close attachment to Hampton Plantation. In the book he claimed never to have left the plantation of his own "free will" but because "the rural plantation son had urgent need of the disciplines of education and contact with civilization." The book also celebrates the romantic, picturesque, and delightful life of the plantation with detailed descriptions of its glamour, entertainment, and culture. Many consider this book Rutledge's masterpiece because it fully displays his remarkable descriptive powers and his extraordinary knowledge of the history and life in the South.

With a steady output of prose and poetry, Rutledge enhanced his reputation in the next three decades as one of the prominent writers in the South. Among his better-known works during the second part of his career were *Love's Meaning* (1943), *God's Children* (1947), *Brimming Tide, and Other Poems* (1954), and *I Hear America Singing* (1970). He won special recognition from his peers and readers in 1958 when he was called on by the Library of Congress to record his poems for the National Archives. Seventy-five of his poems were recorded.

While race is not a primary concern in Rutledge's work, he wrote frequently and passionately about his close longtime friend, Prince. The way in which he wrote of blacks might be unacceptable to modern-day readers, yet he revealed in *God's Children* a deep appreciation for blacks' contribution to America, asserting that "the strength and beauty and glory of our country . . . have been in part due to a race originating in the Dark Continent, long held in slavery and now free to work out its own destiny."

During his long career as an educator and writer, Rutledge received more than twenty honorary degrees and more than thirty medals for his writing, including the John Burroughs Medal for nature writing. Apart from his many books, he also contributed more than one thousand articles and poems to various periodicals, his work was included in various literary anthologies, and more than sixty of his poems were set to music. When he died in McClellanville, Rutledge had been working on *In His Land*, an autobiography. Although most of his work has been out of print since his death, Rutledge is still remembered for his portrayal of the people and the natural world of the South.

• Rutledge's manuscript materials are in the South Caroliniana Library at the University of South Carolina. *Deep River: The Complete Poems of Archibald Rutledge*, 2d ed. (1966) is the most complete collection of his poems. It contains more than nine hundred poems written throughout his career. *We Called Him Flintlock* (1974), a memoir written by his son, Irving Rutledge, is a valuable source of information about Rutledge's life and career. A chapter entitled "The Poet: Archibald Rutledge (1883–1973)" in *Hidden Glory: The Life and Times of Hampton Plantation, Legend of the South Santee* (1983) by Mary B. Wheeler and Genon H. Neblett provides a full assessment of Rutledge. George B. Evans offers a brief sketch in his *Men Who Shot* (1983) and *George Bird Evans Introduces* (1990). Virginia Ravenel's "South Carolina's Poet Laureate," *Sandlapper*, Oct. 1968, pp. 47–51, and Rob Wegner's "Flintlock: A Dixie Deerslayer," *Deer and Deer Hunting*, June 1990, pp. 23–44, are also useful. For his prose works see Jim Casada's *Hunting and Home in the Southern Heartland: The Best of Archibald Rutledge* (1992), the first of a projected trilogy that contains selections of Rutledge's most famous descriptions of adventure and nature.

AIPING ZHANG

RUTLEDGE, Edward (23 Nov. 1749–23 Jan. 1800), signer of the Declaration of Independence and governor of South Carolina, was born in Christ Church Parish, South Carolina, the son of John Rutledge, a physician and planter, and Sarah Hext. He studied law with his elder brother, John Rutledge, and later at the Middle Temple in London. Admitted to practice in English courtrooms in 1772, he returned home the following January. The next year, indulging the lowcountry elite's penchant for endogamy, Rutledge married Henrietta Middleton, daughter of Henry Middleton, a prominent planter and political figure. The couple had three children, one of whom died in infancy. Rutledge rose to the pinnacle of Charleston's legal community in partnership with Charles Cotesworth Pinckney, who likewise married a Middleton. He eventually held some forty slaves at his Winton County plantation and fifteen more in Charleston.

Amidst the growing imperial crisis, Rutledge took a firm stand for American rights within the British Empire. In 1773 he successfully argued, in the case of a printer charged with contempt, that South Carolina's council was simply an advisory body and not an upper house of the legislature that might presume to jail citizens. Selected with his brother and father-in-law to represent South Carolina in the First Continental Congress in 1774, Rutledge was subsequently elected to the Second Continental Congress and to the first and second provincial congresses (1775–1776). Though taken by his fellows in Congress to be less conservative than John Rutledge, he was similarly slow to surrender hopes of reconciliation. He initially tried to balance his reluctance to concede ground on colonial rights, his wish to avoid irreversible provocation of Britain, and the interests of the lowcountry elite as staple growers and slaveholders. He worked unsuccessfully to stop the shipment of American products to any foreign port, so that the burdens of nonexportation would be more equally shared between the South, which sent its staples chiefly to Britain, and the North, which enjoyed a broader international trade. Rutledge also wished to have African Americans purged from the Continental army.

By late 1775 Rutledge was prepared more actively to contemplate separation. He had been particularly alarmed by the promise of the royal governor of Virginia to emancipate slaves who would take up arms for the British. "I would now wish to fight it fairly out," he declared, "and either establish a Connection consistent with the Principles of Liberty and placed on a permanent Basis, or have nothing more to do with them. The latter I think most likely to be the case" (Haw, "The Rutledges, the Continental Congress, and Independence," p. 244). Yet in June 1776, as Congress moved toward actually declaring independence, Rutledge worked to slow the process, insisting that first a more substantial confederation should be constructed among the rebelling states and alliances secured with foreign nations. As late as 28 June 1776 he was still suggesting he opposed a Declaration of Independence, feeling perhaps hemmed in by South Carolina's seeming coolness toward the cause. Only on 2 July did Rutledge, acknowledging the need for unanimity, commit himself and his state. He became the youngest signer of the Declaration of Independence, having led the efforts to delete from it Thomas Jefferson's rather strained attempt to blame the sins of the slave trade on the British monarchy.

Like many among the patriot elite, Rutledge did not wish independence to be accompanied by any very extensive restructuring of authority within the United States. Dreading New England's "levelling Principles," he declared himself "resolved to vest the Congress with no more Power than what is absolutely necessary . . . for I am confident if surrendered into the Hands of others a most pernicious use will be made of it" (Haw, "The Rutledges, the Continental Congress, and Independence," p. 248). His sort of conservatism dictated that a strong executive, on the other hand, be established in individual states: "A pure Democracy may possibly do when patriotism is the ruling Passion, but when a State abounds in rascals (as is the case with too many at this day) you must suppress a little of that Popular Spirit" (Smith, vol. 5, p. 538). Rutledge

served in Congress through the end of 1776, sitting on the committee that drafted the Articles of Confederation and on the first Board of War.

Returning to South Carolina, Rutledge sat in the general assembly from 1776 to 1780. In the same years he served in an artillery company of the state militia and saw action at Beaufort, South Carolina, in 1779. Captured the next year during the British siege of Charleston, he was held prisoner at St. Augustine through the middle of 1781. In 1782 he resumed his place in the general assembly and held on to it for the next thirteen years. Rutledge authored a bill providing for the confiscation of Loyalist property and afterward invested in several appropriated plantations. He clearly did not wish any reshuffling of property or power extending beyond the lowcountry elite, however, and opposed moving the capital to Columbia, important debtors' and paper money legislation, and mandatory rotation of office. While leery of a strong central government, by the mid-1780s he saw the need for a national authority vigorous enough to protect the overseas trade, upon which his state and his class depended. Rutledge supported the ratification of the federal Constitution at the 1788 state convention.

Though Rutledge and his partner Pinckney headed a powerful faction within South Carolina and helped set their state's course in national politics, Rutledge's own allegiances remained unsteady through much of the 1790s. Counted as a Federalist, he was devoted to George Washington, who permitted him considerable influence over federal appointments and eventually proffered him a seat on the U.S. Supreme Court which Rutledge declined. His displeasure with British interference with American trade and the growing political and commercial clout of émigré English merchants in Charleston estranged him from both northern Federalists and Carolina Anglophiles. The 1795 Jay Treaty so enraged Rutledge that, according to his second wife, Mary Shubrick Eveleigh (whom he had married in 1792 after the death earlier that year of Henrietta Middleton), the Carolina grandee taught his son to sing the "Marseillaise," the revolutionary anthem of England's mortal enemy France. By 1796 Rutledge was heading a mongrel slate of presidential electors pledged to Jefferson and Thomas Pinckney (Charles C. Pinckney's brother), the vice presidential candidate on the opposing ticket. With no separate balloting for vice president, Rutledge vainly hoped that the southern Federalist Pinckney might by this maneuver garner the most votes in the electoral college and, thus, the presidency.

Rutledge's Francophilia withered with France's depredations on American shipping, the insults it offered to Charles C. Pinckney, and Rutledge's growing conviction that revolutionary ideas were infecting South Carolina slaves. Elevated to the state senate in 1796, he was elected governor by the legislature two years later. Having warmed to the John Adams administration, he once again stood as a standard-bearer of southern Federalism. Some said it was news of Washington's death that occasioned the apoplexy that felled Rutledge in Charleston before the end of his term.

Rutledge was a formidable political personality in his own day, and some two hundred years later the play *1776* (first produced on Broadway in 1969 and filmed in 1972) ensured that he remained among the better known of the Carolina patriots who resisted the more radical implications of the revolution that they helped to make.

• A collection of Edward Rutledge Papers is at the South Caroliniana Library, University of South Carolina, Columbia. Some of Rutledge's correspondence has been published in Paul H. Smith, ed., *Letters of Delegates to Congress, 1774–1789*, vols. 1–5 (1976–1979). See also James Haw, *Founding Brothers: John and Edward Rutledge* (1997). Haw, "The Rutledges, the Continental Congress, and Independence," *South Carolina Historical Magazine* 94 (1993): 232–51, covers the years 1774–1776 well. In addition see Richard B. Clow, "Edward Rutledge of South Carolina, 1749–1800: Unproclaimed Statesman" (Ph.D. diss., Univ. of Georgia, 1976). Useful detail is in Walter Edgar and N. Louise Bailey, *Biographical Directory of the South Carolina House of Representatives*, vol. 2 (1977). Rutledge's career after 1776 is treated in Jerome Nadelhaft, *The Disorders of War: The Revolution in South Carolina* (1981); Lisle Rose, *Prologue to Democracy: The Federalists in the South, 1789–1800* (1968); George Rogers, Jr., *Evolution of a Federalist: William Loughton Smith of Charleston (1758–1812)* (1962); and Stanley Elkins and Eric McKitrick, *The Age of Federalism: The Early American Republic, 1788–1800* (1993).

PATRICK G. WILLIAMS

RUTLEDGE, John (1739–18 July 1800), lawyer and statesman, was born in or near Charleston, South Carolina, the son of John Rutledge, a physician, and Sarah Hext, a wealthy heiress who was only fifteen years old at Rutledge's birth. His early education was in Charleston, where he read law with one of the leading members of the Charleston bar, James Parsons, before being enrolled in the Middle Temple in London on 11 October 1754. Admitted to the English bar on 9 February 1760, he soon returned to South Carolina. The voters of Christ Church parish promptly elected him to the Commons House of Assembly in 1761, and he continued to represent that area in the local legislature for the remainder of the colonial period. During his first term the house was embroiled in the "Gadsden election controversy" with the royal governor over its right to judge the qualifications of its own members. Rutledge became chairman of the committee on privileges and elections, which vigorously upheld the powers of the representatives of the people. Meanwhile, his private practice as an attorney was flourishing, and he soon became one of the two or three best-paid lawyers in the province. He also operated several plantations and acquired at least 30,000 acres in various grants. These activities may help to explain why his committee work in the Commons House usually put him in the second, rather than the first, rank of leaders. Nevertheless, his colleagues chose him for important assignments. In 1765 the Commons House sent him and two others to the Stamp Act Congress in New York, where Rutledge served as chairman of the committee that drew up a memorial to the House of Lords protesting taxation of Americans by Parliament. In 1763 he married Elizabeth Grimké; they had ten children.

With the outbreak of the Revolution, Rutledge assumed larger roles on both the local and national scenes. Believing that the representative bodies of the American legislatures constituted the basis for legitimate government in the colonies, Rutledge consistently championed their rights and privileges. Ultimately, the unwillingness of British authorities to acknowledge these rights convinced him that independence was justifiable and inevitable, but he arrived at this conclusion slowly and reluctantly. In July 1774 a popular meeting in Charleston elected him as one of the South Carolina delegates to the First Continental Congress. There, Rutledge, who proved to be one of its more conservative members, unsuccessfully supported the plan of union with Great Britain proposed by Joseph Galloway of Pennsylvania. Rutledge also insisted that the proposed continental nonimportation-nonexportation association be modified so that South Carolina could continue to send rice to Great Britain. Although the other colonies acquiesced to prevent a threatened walkout by most of the South Carolina delegation, this provision provoked controversy in Charleston because indigo growers believed that they deserved equal treatment. But Rutledge was elected to the Second Provincial Congress, which met in November 1775, and by it to the Second Continental Congress. There, he drafted Congress's official advice to New Hampshire and South Carolina recommending that they should, "by a full and free representation," adopt such forms of government "as will best produce the happiness of the people." Rutledge accordingly returned to South Carolina, where he helped to write the constitution of 1776, by which the provincial congress transformed itself into the General Assembly of the state. That body then elected him president. Under the colonial government, the president of the council had been the acting executive in the absence of the governor and lieutenant governor, and the constitution of 1776 was designed to facilitate the preservation of order until the dispute with Great Britain could be resolved. As president of South Carolina, Rutledge presided over the successful defense of Charleston against a British naval attack on 28 June 1776.

Immediately thereafter, the Declaration of Independence made necessary the adoption of a new and more permanent state constitution, and the General Assembly drew up a document that deprived the Anglican church of its privileged position and the governor of his veto; the new constitution also provided for the popular election of the upper house, which had hitherto been elected by the lower. But when the legislature presented the constitution to Rutledge on 5 March 1778, he refused to approve it. It was, he maintained, excessively democratic and unnecessary, for "democratic power" was "arbitrary, severe and destructive" and "accommodation" with Great Britain was still "as desirable as it ever was" (Ramsay, vol. 1, pp. 136–137). He then resigned as president. After some confusion, the legislature elected Rawlins Lowndes, who approved the new constitution.

In 1779, however, the legislature again turned to Rutledge, and he accepted the governorship. When British troops under General Augustine Prevost moved northward from Georgia toward Charleston, Rutledge, who had been granted dictatorial powers during the emergency, made vigorous efforts to augment and rally local forces, but the strain showed. When guards caught several men supposedly deserting to the British, Rutledge ordered them summarily hanged. And when Prevost demanded that Charleston surrender, Rutledge offered to capitulate, provided that the inhabitants might be allowed to remain neutral for the remainder of the war. Controversial at the time, this proposal still puzzles historians. Prevost demanded unconditional surrender but shortly thereafter withdrew to prevent being trapped by Continental forces under General Benjamin Lincoln. In 1780 a larger British expedition under Sir Henry Clinton attacked South Carolina. The legislature once again granted Rutledge power to do whatever might be "judged expedient and necessary" for the safety of the state, but this time it added "except taking the life of a citizen without legal trial," and he again tried to rally the defenders. But Clinton's force was too powerful. Rutledge and part of his council escaped before Lincoln surrendered the city and more than 5,000 troops on 12 May. A Continental army officer who encountered Rutledge shortly thereafter in Camden, South Carolina, noted that he was under heavy criticism from all sides for failing to make a stronger personal commitment to the defense of Charleston. Nevertheless, Rutledge became the de facto revolutionary government of South Carolina for the next two years. He went to Philadelphia and lobbied Congress for reinforcements; he appointed Thomas Sumter, Francis Marion, and Andrew Pickens (each from one of the three major areas of the state) brigadier generals in the South Carolina militia, and he coordinated their activities. After they and another Continental army under General Nathanael Greene had cleared the British from the interior of South Carolina, Rutledge also issued a series of proclamations designed to prevent plundering, restore order, and establish the terms under which Loyalists would be readmitted to citizenship. Calling the legislature to meet at Jacksonborough, a little town near British-occupied Charleston, Rutledge opened the session on 15 January 1782 with a vehement speech suggesting that the assembly confiscate the estates of the most conspicuous Loyalists. The legislature complied and thereby undoubtedly forestalled much—but not all—vigilante justice.

Rutledge's subsequent political career, though distinguished, was somewhat anticlimactic. While serving as a member of Congress from 1782 to 1784, he turned down a congressional appointment as minister to the Netherlands. Back in the state legislature for the 1784–1785 session, he became embroiled in a controversy with a tavern-keeper, William Thompson, who took umbrage at Rutledge's hauteur and attacked him in newspaper polemics that called into question the assumptions undergirding government by a social and economic elite. Rutledge in turn received support from his colleagues in the state house of representatives which briefly imprisoned Thompson for contempt on the grounds that he had insulted one of its members. In 1784 Rutledge became the senior judge in the court of chancery, where he presided until 1790. But because decisions were announced collectively, Rutledge's part in them cannot be ascertained.

His role in the four-man South Carolina delegation to the Constitutional Convention of 1787 was more conspicuous and important. He was a member of the committee that brought in the Connecticut Compromise over representation, and he served as chairman of the Committee of Detail, which compiled the first draft of the Constitution. Rutledge also made a number of suggestions from the floor of the convention. Among them was the stipulation, subsequently adopted, that federal law and treaties be the "supreme law of the several States and of their citizens." But he was unsuccessful in advocating property qualifications for federal office, wealth as well as population as the basis for state representation in Congress, and indirect election of representatives by the legislatures rather than the people of the states. He was also an outspoken defender of South Carolinians' right to own and import slaves. The slave trade, he asserted, had nothing to do with "Religion and humanity"; it was purely a matter of economic interest. Having protected this interest by demanding and obtaining a guarantee that Congress could not interfere with the slave trade before 1808, Rutledge returned home and voted for the Constitution in the South Carolina ratifying convention of 1788.

After Congress established the Supreme Court pursuant to the Constitution, President George Washington named Rutledge as the senior associate justice. His chief duty at the time was to ride the southern circuit in 1790. The inconveniences of this travel undoubtedly contributed to his decision to resign in February 1791 and become chief justice of the South Carolina Court of Common Pleas. One of the more notable cases to come before him in that capacity involved a slave who had purchased another slave's freedom but whose master claimed ownership of both women on the grounds that his property had merely acquired another piece of property. In this, as in several other recorded instances, Rutledge's sense of fair play crossed racial lines, and he was undoubtedly aware that South Carolinians traditionally allowed slaves considerable autonomy in controlling their own property. Thus his charge to the jury enabled it to find in favor of the slave without leaving the courtroom. By 1795 Rutledge had changed his mind about the Supreme Court, and when John Jay resigned as chief justice to assume the governorship of New York, Rutledge asked for the job. On 1 July 1795 Washington notified him of his appointment. On 16 July, however, Rutledge participated in a public meeting held in Charleston to protest the Jay Treaty, which had been negotiated between the United States and Great Britain several months earlier. Considering it a bad bargain for the United States and for South Carolina, Rutledge denounced it in a long speech, and senators who supported the agreement retaliated by refusing to confirm his nomination as chief justice.

Rutledge's rejection as chief justice closed his public career. His wife died in 1792; her loss affected him deeply. Rumors of his mental instability circulated while his nomination was being considered, and on the day after Christmas 1795 Rutledge unsuccessfully attempted suicide. Five years as a virtual recluse followed before his death in Charleston. In his prime Rutledge was a man of great vigor. He spoke rapidly, wrote a kind of shorthand, and had a volatile temper. At the time of the federal convention, an observer described him as "imperious." More pragmatic and decisive than theoretical and contemplative, he was always a champion of South Carolina. His nationalism, on the other hand, tended to be conditional. No doubt the conflict between the Carolinians' commitment to slavery and the hostility of many other Americans to it circumscribed his thought and his allegiance. But among South Carolinians Rutledge was a giant.

• No unified collection of Rutledge's papers survives, but there is a considerable body of material scattered through the Papers of the Continental Congress at the National Archives, the John Rutledge, Jr., Papers at Duke University, the Nathanael Greene Papers at both the William L. Clements Library, Ann Arbor, Mich., and the Library of Congress. The Benjamin Lincoln Papers in the Massachusetts Historical Society reveal Rutledge's efforts to defend South Carolina in 1779–1780, and the South Carolina Historical Society holds an important Rutledge account book covering the years from 1761 to 1779. The Charleston Library Society also has a number of items from the years 1780 to 1782. The most significant published sources can be found in Robert W. Gibbes, *Documentary History of the American Revolution* (3 vols., 1853–1857; repr. 1972), and Maeva Marcus et al., *The Documentary History of the Supreme Court of the United States, 1789–1800* (1985–), as well as the journals of the other official bodies of which Rutledge was a member. David Ramsay, *History of the Revolution of South-Carolina, from the British Province to an Independent State* (2 vols., 1785), provides a remarkably judicious assessment of both Rutledge and the Revolution by a contemporary. The only full-scale biography, Richard Barry, *Mr. Rutledge of South Carolina* (1942), suffers from the author's fascination with dictators and is totally unreliable. Robert W. Barnwell, Jr., "Rutledge, 'The Dictator,'" *Journal of Southern History* 7 (1941): 215–24, is more judicious. Reasonably comprehensive biographical articles are Henry Flanders, *The Lives and Times of the Chief Justices of the Supreme Court of the United States*, vol. 1 (1858), which contains errors as well as information unavailable elsewhere, and Leon Friedman, "John Rutledge," in Friedman and Fred L. Israel, *The Justices of the United States Supreme Court 1789–1969*, vol. 1 (1969).

ROBERT M. WEIR

RUTLEDGE, Wiley Blount, Jr. (20 July 1894–10 Sept. 1949), associate justice of the U.S. Supreme Court, was born in Cloverport, Kentucky, the son of Wiley B. Rutledge, Sr., a Baptist minister, and Mary Louise Wigginton. As a young man, he survived a prolonged battle with tuberculosis, a disease that had killed his mother when he was nine years of age. He attended the preparatory department of Marysville College before transferring to the University of Wisconsin, from which he received a B.A. in 1914. He then taught high school in Indiana while attending the Indiana University Law School. Trying to do both broke his health, and in 1915 he entered a tuberculosis sanitarium in Asheville, North Carolina. In 1917 he married Annabel Person, his teacher of Greek from Marysville College. They had three children. He and Annabel moved to Albuquerque, New Mexico, where they hoped the air would cure his lungs. Rutledge taught high school in Albuquerque, and in 1920 he enrolled at the University of Colorado Law School. Working his way through by teaching school, he received his degree in 1922. He joined the University of Colorado Law School faculty in 1924. He later served as law school dean at Washington University in St. Louis, Missouri, and then at the State University of Iowa.

Rutledge was a staunch supporter of President Franklin D. Roosevelt's New Deal policies and thought that Supreme Court decisions striking them down were wrongly decided. When Roosevelt proposed his Court-packing plan in 1937, Rutledge supported it. Opposition to the bill in Iowa, where Rutledge was dean of the university's law school, was strong. When asked by Roosevelt's aides if he would testify in favor of the bill, Rutledge assented. He called the university president to offer his resignation, since it was rumored that Rutledge's testimony would lead the Republican state legislature to defeat a bill restoring faculty salaries that had been cut during the depression. The university president encouraged him not to resign and to speak his mind. While the administration ultimately called no witnesses, Rutledge's willingness to support Roosevelt had made an impression.

Rutledge was first seriously considered for a U.S. Supreme Court appointment in 1938, when he lost out to Felix Frankfurter. Rutledge instead received the consolation prize of a seat on the prestigious U.S. Court of Appeals for the District of Columbia. His position as a circuit judge in Washington, D.C., did not deprive him of his geographic status as a "westerner," and he continued to appear on short lists for Supreme Court appointments. President Roosevelt's desire to appoint someone from west of the Mississippi came behind other considerations until finally, in 1943, Rutledge was named as the last of Roosevelt's eight Court appointments.

On the Court, Justice Rutledge favored an expansive reading of individual constitutional rights. He was the only other member of the Court to join Justice Frank Murphy's dissenting opinion in *Adamson v. California* (1947), arguing that due process rights enforceable against the states under the Fourteenth Amendment not only included the protections under the first eight amendments of the Bill of Rights but also encompassed other violations of "fundamental standards" of criminal procedure. In the area of the commerce power, Rutledge wrote majority opinions for the Court eleven times, upholding the federal government's expansive post–New Deal regulatory power.

Rutledge's own favorites of his Supreme Court opinions were his dissents in *Everson v. Board of Education* (1947) and *In re Yamashita* (1946). In *Everson*, the majority upheld a New Jersey school district's policy of providing transportation to students who attended both public and parochial schools. Rutledge found the statute to be a dangerous breach in the wall separating church and state. Joined by three of his colleagues, Rutledge argued that the history of the framing of the First Amendment supported the idea that the Constitution forbade any state appropriations to aid or support religion. He was an advocate of the "preferred positions" doctrine, arguing in *Everson* and in his majority opinion in *Thomas v. Collins* (1945) that "the preferred place given in our scheme to the great democratic freedoms secured by the First Amendment gives them 'a sanctity and a sanction not permitting dubious intrusions.'"

Rutledge was a voice ahead of his time on the issue of gender-based equality. His dissent in *Goesart v. Cleary* (1948) argued that a state law that prohibited women from working as barmaids unless the bar was owned by the woman's father or husband was unconstitutional. The majority saw no constitutional infirmity in banning women from barroom employment in order to protect their moral character. The Supreme Court would not reverse this line of analysis until the 1970s.

In *Korematsu v. United States* (1944), Rutledge joined the Court's majority opinion upholding the exclusion of Japanese Americans from the West Coast. Although the decision was a great blow to civil liberties, Rutledge's position in *Korematsu* was consistent with his view that the nation faced Armageddon during World War II and that unqualified support of the war effort was needed.

In spite of his devotion to the war effort, Rutledge's tolerance of government action had limits. In *In re Yamashita* (1946), the Court majority dismissed the constitutional challenge of a Japanese general prosecuted by the United States for violations of the law of war due to the acts of his soldiers. Rutledge, in dissent, argued that Fifth Amendment protections applied. Quoting Thomas Paine, Rutledge admonished the Court, stating, "He that would make his own liberty secure must guard even his enemy from oppression; for if he violates this duty he establishes a precedent that will reach himself."

Although Rutledge had an impact on the Court, that impact was limited by the shortness of his tenure. After six years of service, Rutledge suffered a cerebral hemorrhage and died in York, Maine. His death followed by less than two months the death of Justice Murphy, with whom Rutledge had often dissented. Rutledge was replaced by Sherman Minton. As these liberal voices were replaced by more conservative Harry S. Truman appointees, the Court took a more conservative turn.

• In addition to his judicial opinions, Rutledge published a short book, *A Declaration of Legal Faith* (1946), and various articles and essays. Bibliographies of his judicial opinions and other writings are in *Iowa Law Review* 50 (1950): 693, and *Indiana Law Journal* 25 (1950): 560. Fowler V. Harper, *Justice Rutledge and the Bright Constellation* (1965), focuses principally on Rutledge's years on the U.S. Supreme Court. A biographical essay on Rutledge is in Leon Friedman and Fred L. Israel, eds., *The Justices of the United States Supreme Court, 1789–1969: Their Lives and Major Opinions*, vol. 4 (1969). The most insightful writing on Rutledge is published in law reviews. His impact on civil liberties is effectively analyzed in Landon G. Rockwell, "Justice Rutledge on Civil Liberties," *Yale Law Journal* 59 (1949). Helpful on Rutledge's commerce power opinions is Lester E. Mosher, "Mr. Justice Rutledge's Philosophy of the Commerce Clause," *New York University Law Review* 27 (1952). A useful work on the Court during Rutledge's tenure is C. Herman Pritchett, *The Roosevelt Court: A Study in Judicial Politics and Values, 1937–1947* (1948). Many articles and tributes were written in honor of Rutledge following his death. Of particular interest is Irving Brandt, "Mr. Justice Rutledge—The Man," *Iowa Law Review* 35 (1950).

MARY L. DUDZIAK

RUXTON, George Augustus Frederick (24 July 1821–29 Aug. 1848), soldier, adventurer, and author, was born in Eynsham Hall, Oxfordshire, England, the son of John Ruxton, an army surgeon, and Anna Maria Hay. On 14 July 1835 Ruxton became a cadet at the Royal Military Academy, Sandhurst. After about two years at the academy, Ruxton was apparently expelled and subsequently traveled to Spain, where he participated for a time in that country's civil war as a cornet of lancers in the British Auxiliary Legion, a unit serving with forces loyal to Queen Isabella II. For his distinguished actions at the Battle of the Bridge of Belascoain, 29 April–1 May 1839, the queen of Spain awarded Ruxton the Cross of the First Class of the National Military Order of San Fernando.

Ruxton returned to England in 1839 and on 2 August of that year was commissioned a lieutenant in the Ceylon Rifle Corps. A month later, however, he was serving as ensign in the Eighty-ninth Foot. Ruxton saw duty in Ireland in 1840–1841 before joining the service corps of the Eighty-ninth in upper Canada on 8 July 1841. Ruxton was back in England on a leave of absence during the winter of 1842–1843, starting again for Canada on 23 May 1843 and arriving at Montreal on 12 July 1843. Two months later, Ruxton "requested permission to retire from the army by the sale of his commission." He subsequently had a change of heart about leaving the army, yet despite his attempt to halt the process, Ruxton's resignation was accepted on 6 October 1843.

Ruxton spent the winter of 1843–1844 hunting in Upper Canada. He returned to England in 1844 and that same year embarked on trips to both North and South Africa. He made his South Africa excursion (1844–1845) with the intention of traversing the continent from Walvis Bay on the west coast to the Sofala settlement on the east. Thwarted in his efforts to travel into the interior by the intrigues of local traders and a missionary at Walvis Bay, Ruxton was forced to abandon the expedition. Upon his arrival back in England, Ruxton asked the British government to help fund a second attempt at crossing South Africa, but growing tired of bureaucratic delays, he set sail on 2 July 1846 for a tour of Mexico and the western United States. War had erupted between the United States and Mexico two months earlier.

Exactly why Ruxton traveled to Mexico at this time is unclear. Ruxton himself confused the matter when he wrote that "It is hardly necessary to explain the cause of my visiting Mexico in such an unsettled period; and I fear that circumstances will prevent my gratifying the curiosity of the reader, should he feel any on that point" (preface to *Adventures in Mexico and the Rocky Mountains*). Yet it is known that Ruxton, at one point on his journey, acted in the capacity of a commercial agent with the charge of overseeing the interests of British merchants then in Mexico. Besides any diplomatic duties, however, it was probably the promise of adventure and exploration, more than anything else, that motivated the young Englishman. An old theory that Ruxton was a British spy is no longer given credence by scholars.

Ruxton landed at Vera Cruz, on the Gulf of Mexico, and traveled inland to Mexico City, then north to Zacatecas, Durango, Chihuahua, and El Paso del Norte (present-day Ciudad Juárez, Mexico). At Valverde, a campsite on the Chihuahua Trail approximately 180 miles north of El Paso, Ruxton encountered the advance of an army of Missouri volunteers under Colonel Alexander W. Doniphan, who was about to begin his now-famous march to Chihuahua. Here also were encamped hundreds of wagons belonging to overland merchants (some British) bound for Chihuahua, to whom Ruxton delivered a circular from the Chihuahua governor stating the conditions upon which foreign traders would be allowed into that Mexican state.

Ruxton arrived in Santa Fe, New Mexico, on 23 December 1846. After a few days he set out again, traveling north to Taos, then up the San Luis Valley and over the Sangre de Cristo Range of Colorado, eventually reaching the small adobe trading post of Pueblo (present-day Pueblo, Colorado) on the Arkansas River. He spent the remaining winter months hunting and exploring near Pueblo, along Fountain and Ruxton creeks (the latter named for the Englishman) in the vicinity of Pikes Peak; and in South Park.

On 30 April 1847 Ruxton departed Pueblo, traveling east down the Arkansas to Bent's Fort, another Indian trading post, where he joined a government wagon train bound for Fort Leavenworth on the Missouri River. Ruxton's party arrived at that place in early June, whence Ruxton traveled to St. Louis, Chicago, and New York. By the middle of August he was back in England. That same year Ruxton published his first book, *Adventures in Mexico and the Rocky Mountains*, which recounted his many interesting experiences of 1846–1847 and also provided detailed observations on the people and places he encountered on his journey.

Also while in England at this time Ruxton wrote his second and last book, a novel of the American mountain men titled *Life in the Far West*. It first appeared serially in *Blackwood's Edinburgh Magazine* beginning in June 1848 and was published in book form in 1849. *Life in the Far West* has had a tremendous influence on both historians of the fur trade and later novelists. It is considered the best contemporary source for the life and manners of the famed mountain men and is particularly noteworthy for its profuse employment of the mountain man vernacular. Ruxton himself claimed of his novel that "It is *no fiction*. There is no incident in it which has not actually occurred, nor one character who is not well known in the Rocky Mountains." A common error committed by those who have consulted Ruxton, however, is to associate his mountain man characterizations (which resulted from his personal observations of 1846–1847) with fur trappers and traders of an earlier period.

Suffering off and on from a spinal injury he had received while in Colorado in 1847, Ruxton set out again for the American West in 1848. He arrived in St. Louis on 14 August 1848, where he contracted dysentery and died unexpectedly. Lewis Garrard, who traveled a part of the Santa Fe Trail with Ruxton in 1847, described him in his *Wah-To-Yah, and the Taos Trail* (1850) as "a quiet, good-looking man, with a handsome moustache. He conversed well, but sparingly, speaking little of himself. . . . He was a true gentleman, and his loss is much to be deplored."

Although he lived a short but exciting life filled with numerous adventures in different parts of the world, it is Ruxton's detailed writing of life in the nineteenth-century American West and Mexico found in his two books, one a factual narrative and the other a novel, that remain his lasting contributions to American history and literature.

• The only known collection of Ruxton papers is in the Everett D. Graff Collection of Western Americana at the Newberry Library, Chicago, Illinois. This collection includes Ruxton manuscripts, family letters, a few Ruxton sketches, and also a copy of a rare published pamphlet written by Ruxton titled *The Oregon Question* (1846). Many of Ruxton's papers and notes compiled during his travels in Mexico and the western United States were destroyed after they became soaked with water during a crossing of Pawnee Fork on the Santa Fe Trail near present-day Larned, Kansas, in 1847. The best treatment of Ruxton's life is LeRoy R. Hafen, ed., *Ruxton of the Rockies* (1950). This volume reproduces much of the autobiographical manuscript material now in the Newberry Library and also portions of Ruxton's *Adventures in Mexico and the Rocky Mountains*. The best modern printing of *Adventures in Mexico and the Rocky Mountains* is the Rio Grande Press edition (1973). This edition contains a useful bibliography of works by and about Ruxton prepared by

Crawford R. Buell. A contemporary review of *Adventures* is found in the *American Review*, March 1848, pp. 307–18. For a modern printing of *Life in the Far West*, the University of Oklahoma Press edition edited by LeRoy R. Hafen (1951) is recommended. A modern literary assessment of Ruxton is Neal Lambert, *George Frederick Ruxton* (1974).

MARK L. GARDNER

RUZICKA, Rudolph (29 June 1883–20 July 1978), artist, typographer, and author, was born in Kourim in central Bohemia, the son of Václav Ruzicka, a tailor, and Josefa Reichman. Accompanying his parents to the United States in 1894, he settled in Chicago, where he completed seven grades of public school in three years while at the same time learning to speak English. He then left in 1897 to begin an apprenticeship at the Franklin Engraving Company, where he learned to engrave on wood and to work a Washington hand press. In subsequent employment in other firms, Ruzicka learned the electrotype and photogravure processes while studying art at Hull-House and the Art Institute of Chicago.

In 1903 Ruzicka moved to New York City, where he worked first for the American Bank Note Company as an illustrator and then for the advertising firm of Caulkins & Holden. There he was fortunate in having an employer interested in the graphic arts who encouraged his staff to develop their talents. Ruzicka began engraving his own designs on wood, inspired by the work of Auguste Lepère in France, and around 1905 he attended classes at the Art Students League.

Ruzicka met D. B. Updike, founder of the Merrymount Press, in 1907, which led to a lifelong friendship as well as a significant number of commissions for illustrations. The best known of these are the wood engravings Ruzicka produced for the annual Merrymount Press keepsakes from 1912 to 1942, which Philip Hofer described as "the most distinguished series of architectural and similar views that has ever been published in America."

After a trip to Italy to make the illustrations for Mrs. Charles MacVeagh's *Fountains of Papal Rome* (1915), Ruzicka went to Prague, where in 1914 he married Filomena Srpová; they had two children.

By 1917 Ruzicka had produced a sufficient body of work to merit his first major exhibition, held at the Newark Museum. In the catalog essay William M. Ivins described Ruzicka and his work:

The first thing that impresses one in Ruzicka's prints is their workmanlike competency, a quality which considered with his notable common sense, creates the feeling that the artist who made them knows not only his business but his own mind. Having found himself, and in so doing having acquired simplicity of thought, he is content to make his designs directly and calmly, without resort to forcing or over emphasis, confiding fully in the telling power of terse veracity.

Subsequent exhibitions were accorded Ruzicka by the American Art Galleries in 1921; the Architectural League in 1935, at which he was awarded the gold medal of the American Institute of Graphic Arts; the Grolier Club in 1948; the Boston Public Library in 1951; and the Century association in 1977.

During an active career that spanned three quarters of a century, Ruzicka produced a notable oeuvre. Beginning with single prints of subjects around New York City, he participated in the 1908 publication *A Portfolio of Prints*, followed by two books in collaboration with Walter P. Eaton, *New York: A Series of Wood Engravings in Colour* (1915) and *Newark: A Series of Engravings on Wood* (1917). He was involved in about 130 jobs with the Merrymount Press, ranging from bookplates to illustrations for important books, such as the Limited Editions Club publication of *The Fables of La Fontaine*, published in 1930. In addition to designing a great many books, Ruzicka also designed three typefaces: "Fairfield" in 1940, "Fairfield Medium" in 1948, and "Primer" in 1951, all for the Mergenthaler Linotype Company. His portfolio of ten *Studies in Type Design* was published by Dartmouth College Library in 1968.

Ruzicka's design work was not limited to books and typography. Following his move to Concord, Massachusetts, in 1948 and to Boston in 1953, Ruzicka worked for numerous learned societies, redesigning their seals and letterheads. In 1961 he redesigned the Harvard diplomas. He also designed medals, including the Emerson-Thoreau Medal for the American Academy of Arts and Sciences and the John F. Kennedy Medal for the Massachusetts Historical Society.

Ruzicka's writings include *Thomas Bewick, Engraver* (1943) and collaboration on books about other designers and printers, including Updike, William A. Dwiggins, Fred Anthoensen, and John Howard Benson. Active right to the end of a long life, Ruzicka died at Hanover, New Hampshire, where he had moved in 1962.

Those who remember Ruzicka have spoken of him as a quiet, modest, amiable man. Updike wrote that we could all learn from Ruzicka "not merely the technique of engraving, but (incidentally) the technique of good manners and admire a man whose work shows that he possesses the rarest of all possessions—himself." Philip Hofer observed, on the occasion of Ruzicka's receiving the Gold Medal of the American Institute of Graphic Arts, that "Ruzicka, the artist and craftsman, is only a fraction of Ruzicka the Scholar, the Humanist, and the Man."

• The archives of the Merrymount Press at the Henry E. Huntington Library in San Marino, Calif., include information on the work Ruzicka did with that firm. Letters received by Ruzicka from D. B. Updike are in the Houghton Library, Harvard University. His correspondence with Walter Muir Whitehill is at the Massachusetts Historical Society in Boston. The most complete account of Ruzicka's life and work is *Speaking Reminiscently* (1986), a series of recollections recorded and edited by Edward Connery Lathem. The 1917 and 1948 exhibitions were accompanied by catalogs with essays by William M. Ivins and Walter Muir Whitehill, respectively. *The Colophon, Part Five* (1931) includes an article on

Ruzicka's book illustrations with a bibliography by W. A. Kittredge. An obituary is in the *Proceedings of the Massachusetts Historical Society* 90 (1978): 143–45.

ELTON W. HALL

RYAN, Abram Joseph (5 Feb. 1838–22 Apr. 1886), Catholic priest and poet, was the son of Matthew Ryan and Mary Coughlin, who came to the United States from Ireland sometime during the decade after 1828. They lived in Norfolk, Virginia, for a short while, then moved to Hagerstown, Maryland. A variety of dates have been given for Ryan's birth, and claims to his birthplace have been made for Norfolk and several towns in Ireland. Yet certain church records, the baptismal certificate in Hagerstown, and an 1859 letter in which he states his age as twenty-one, all seem to substantiate that Abram Ryan was born on 5 February 1838, in Hagerstown.

Not long after Abram's birth the Ryans moved to St. Louis, Missouri, where their daughter Ellenor was received into the community of the Sisters of St. Joseph of Carondelet. Young Abram was educated at the Christian Brothers' School in St. Louis and then studied theology at Niagara University. He interrupted his studies at Niagara to enter the Vincentian novitiate at Germantown, Pennsylvania, in 1854. He took his solemn vows in 1856. After completing his theological studies he taught for a time at Niagara University and at the diocesan seminary in Cape Girardeau, Missouri.

In September 1862 Father Ryan joined the Confederate army as a chaplain. A fellow priest later described him during this period as "a person of commanding presence, dark, with the Eagle look of the Indian, his black hair thrown back from a noble brow." While tending the wounded on the battlefield and hearing the confessions of the dying, Father Ryan revealed uncommon physical courage and is even said to have seized a musket on occasion and fought alongside his companions. Throughout the war years Father Ryan showed by his actions that he rarely thought of himself and that he had no fear of death. For example, he gave comfort to the victims of a smallpox epidemic at Gratiot Prison in New Orleans after the chaplain had abandoned his post. While in that city, Father Ryan also demonstrated that his convictions about the justness of the Confederate cause could sometimes override his general humanitarian feelings. When summoned before the notorious Union general Benjamin Butler (1818–1893) to answer a charge that he had refused to bury a dead soldier because he was a Yankee, Father Ryan defended himself by saying: "Why, I was never asked to bury him and never refused. The fact is, General, it would give me great pleasure to bury the whole lot of you."

By undertaking tasks that nobody else would attempt, Father Ryan endeared himself to many suffering war victims. However, he served the Confederacy even more effectively with the pen when he gave vent to an "uncontrollable divine impulse to sing the emotions of his soul." The final defeat of the Confederate army, and his own grief at the loss of a younger brother in battle, inspired him to write such verses as "In Memory of My Brother," "In Memoriam—David J. Ryan, C.S.A.," "The Conquered Banner," and "The Sword of Robert E. Lee." These were followed by "The Lost Cause," "March of the Deathless Dead," and similar lyrics.

The duty of the southern poet was, Father Ryan felt, to keep alive the memory of the Confederacy. His best and most popular poem, "The Conquered Banner," first appeared in the *Freeman's Journal* of New York on 19 May 1866 over the pen name of "Moina." Composed to the measures of a Gregorian hymn, one of its stanzas entreats:

> Furl that Banner, for 'tis weary;
> Round its staff 'tis drooping dreary;
>   Furl it, fold it, it is best;
> For there's not a man to wave it,
> And there's not a sword to save it,
> And there's not one left to lave it
> In the blood which heroes gave it;
>   Furl it, hide it—let it rest!

Regarding this poem, Father Ryan later observed: "In expressing my own emotions at the time, I echoed the unuttered feelings of the Southern people; and so 'The Conquered Banner' became the requiem of the Lost Cause."

After Appomattox, Father Ryan resided for a time near Jefferson Davis's home, "Beauvoir," in the vicinity of Biloxi, Mississippi. He was posted for a few years as a curate at St. Patrick's Church in Augusta, Georgia. There he edited the short-lived *Pacificator* and, later, with the aid of John Quinn, the *Banner of the South*. Though ill health forced Father Ryan to give up the *Banner*, he later edited a Catholic weekly, the *Star*, while serving as a pastor in New Orleans. A popular lecturer wherever he went, he remained on the move. At various times during the postwar years he was stationed in Biloxi, Mississippi; in Nashville, Knoxville, and Clarksville, Tennessee; in Macon, Georgia; and, for the longest consecutive period, in Mobile, Alabama, where he was pastor of St. Mary's Church from 1870 to 1883. He also toured frequently in the United States and Canada in efforts to raise funds for the relief of southern widows and orphans.

Father Ryan's devotion to the South was intense, and he long refused to accept the results of the war. His indignation at efforts to reconstruct the South frequently found expression in such verses as "The Land We Love." He remained unreconcilable until 1878, when the yellow fever epidemic of that year brought physicians, nurses, and money from the North. Touched by the North's generosity, he surrendered his sectional prejudice in "Reunited."

Father Ryan had no high regard for his verses, and he disliked calling them poems. Only after persistent urging by Hannis Taylor did he permit them to appear in book form. His *Father Ryan's Poems* was published in 1879, followed the next year by *Poems: Patriotic, Religious, Miscellaneous*. Many of the verses in these volumes were household favorites, and several of them were set to music and used extensively in southern schools.

In 1882 Father Ryan published *A Crown for Our Queen*, a volume of beautifully written devotional verse. His last literary project was a life of Christ, to which he devoted a great deal of time and labor but did not complete. He died while on retreat at a Franciscan monastery in Louisville, Kentucky. Although Ryan was only forty-eight years old at the time of his death, his health was broken, and he had prematurely aged. Mourned throughout the South, he was buried in Mobile, where a monument was erected to his memory with dimes given by southern school children. Having brought comfort to countless southerners sore with the sorrow of defeat, Father Ryan had become the recognized poet of the Confederacy.

• Obituaries containing biographical information on Father Ryan are in the Louisville *Courier-Journal* and the Mobile *Daily Register*, 23 Apr. 1886; and Young E. Allison, "How Father Ryan Died," *Southern Bivouac*, n.s., 2 (Aug. 1886): 167–77. A memoir by John Moran is in the twelfth edition of Father Ryan's *Poems* (1888). Other useful sources are F. V. N. Painter, *Poets of the South* (1903), pp. 103–18, and *Poets of Virginia* (1907), pp. 217–21; H. J. Heagney, "Recollections of Father Ryan," *Catholic World* 126 (Jan. 1928): 497–504; Howard Meriwether Lovett, "Father Ryan of the South," *Commonweal* 10 (18 Sept. 1929): 503–4; William T. Wynn, ed., *Southern Literature* (1932), pp. 505–6; Jay B. Hubbell, *The South in American Literature, 1607–1900* (1954), pp. 477–9; L. Moody Simms, Jr., "Father Abram Joseph Ryan: Poet of the Lost Cause," *Lincoln Herald* 73 (Spring 1971): 3–7.

L. MOODY SIMMS, JR.

RYAN, Cornelius (5 June 1920–23 Nov. 1974), journalist and author, was born Cornelius John Ryan in Dublin, Ireland, the son of John Joseph Ryan and Amelia Clohisey. His grandfather Cornelius Ryan was a journalist, and Ryan noted that "Both their vocations rubbed off on me. As did their names." He grew up in Dublin, graduating from the Synge Street Christian Brothers School, and then entered the Royal Irish Academy of Music to study the violin. At age sixteen Ryan had mastered the violin, graduated from the last of his formal schooling, and started his own orchestra, the HiLo, which played in Dublin and at nearby country inns. He was stagestruck at this time and took to hanging around the Abbey Theatre; he even submitted some plays, all of which were "emphatically" turned down.

His father secured the eighteen-year-old Ryan a position as junior secretary to Garfield Weston, the "biscuit magnate" and a member of Parliament, and Ryan relocated to London. He worked for Weston from 1940 to 1941, yet he knew that he wanted to write and in 1941 got a job as a copy boy for the Reuters News Agency. He later became a reporter. By 1943 he had moved on to the London *Daily Telegraph*, working as a war correspondent, and at age twenty-four he witnessed the D-day invasion of Normandy. Ryan later remarked, "I was too horrified and too young then to

fully appreciate what I saw." But the experience drove him to learn more, reading books and talking to many people. Fifteen years later this enthusiasm would result in *The Longest Day: June 6, 1944* (1959). Ryan also covered the progress of General George S. Patton's Third Army as it drove through France and into the heart of Germany. Following the fall of Berlin, Ryan covered the war in the Pacific.

After the Japanese surrendered in August 1945, Ryan opened the Tokyo bureau of the London *Daily Telegraph*. From 1946 to 1947 he worked as the newspaper's Middle East bureau chief in Jerusalem. The busy Ryan was also a stringer for *Time* and *Life* magazines as well as the *St. Louis Post-Dispatch*. Late in 1947 he moved to New York City as a contributing editor for *Time*. During these years Ryan reported on key stories such as the 1948 atomic bomb tests on the Bikini Atoll in the Pacific and the Arab-Israeli war of the same year. By 1949 Ryan had taken a new job at "Newsweek," a television program, as a reporter. In 1950 he moved on to *Collier's* magazine as an associate editor. That same year he became a U.S. citizen and married Kathryn Ann Morgan, an editor and author. The couple would have two children.

Although working continuously as a reporter, Ryan was also writing books. His first book, *Star-Spangled Mikado* (1948), coauthored with Frank Kelly, was inspired by his postwar experiences in Tokyo. He and Kelly also wrote *MacArthur: Man of Action* (1950). Ryan edited two books on space: *Across the Space Frontier* (1952), by Joseph Kaplan and others; and Wernher Von Braun's *Conquest of the Moon* (1953). *One Minute To Ditch!* (1957) was a book of his own short stories, which Ryan said, "failed to bang the gong." Fame would finally come in 1959 with the publication of *The Longest Day*.

After a trip to Normandy on the fifth anniversary of D-day, Ryan had again become fascinated with the invasion and decided to write a history of it. While continuing to work at *Collier's*, he began researching the event in depth. *Collier's* closed in 1956, and Ryan was not only out of a job, but was also $20,000 in debt. Fortunately, *Reader's Digest* came to the rescue with financial backing. Ryan would work for *Reader's Digest* in a variety of capacities, from staff reporter to roving reporter, for the rest of his life.

All of the magazine's resources were employed to gather the masses of information required and to advertise for interviews of anyone who had participated in the invasion. Ryan went through 283 works on the invasion and interviewed 700 individuals, including American, British, Canadian, German, and French. He ended up with forty-eight drawers of files and a riveting account of the invasion told by a variety of participants, from Madame Angèle Levrault, the French school mistress, to German Naval Lieutenant Commander Heinrich Hoffmann, to American Ranger Sergeant Regis McCloskey. Ryan's minute description of The Wait, The Night, and The Day electrified his readers. The subject was historical fact, but the book read like a novel with a wide cast of characters, excitement, pathos, heroism, barbarity, and even humor. As Ryan states in the foreword, the book is "not a military history. It is a story of people: the men of the Allied forces, the enemy they fought and the civilians who were caught up in the bloody confusion of D Day."

The Longest Day was an immediate success and resulted in financial stability for Ryan, who bought a home in Ridgefield, Connecticut, where he would live and work for the remainder of his life. The book was bought by 20th Century–Fox, and Ryan wrote the screenplay of the film that was nominated for an Academy Award for best picture in 1962.

Ryan's next book took six years to write. For *The Last Battle* (1966), which is about the fall of Berlin, Ryan followed his usual method of meticulous research and interviewing participants. He accumulated sixty-four drawers of files and was the first American in more than forty years to be allowed access to Russian documents. The book, told largely through eyewitness accounts, details the last twenty-one days of the Thousand Year Reich. Ryan shows how the decision of a minor British official affected Operation Rankin, which divided Germany into a pie and gave Russia the piece that contained the plum, Berlin. The book reached number nine on the annual bestseller list.

By 1970 Ryan was deep into research for his next book *A Bridge Too Far*, the story of the failed Allied invasion of Arnhem during World War II, when he was diagnosed with cancer. The book was to occupy him for seven years, but the final four years became a race between the book and the progress of Ryan's prostate cancer. He would later say, "*Bridge* is keeping me alive."

The book is an account of the disastrous Operation Market-Garden, the Allied code name for the drive through Holland to capture the Arnhem bridge and use it as a springboard across the Rhine into Germany. Told with his usual attention to detail, Ryan's book is based on interviews of participants, from German Field Marshal Gerd Von Rundstedt and General Dwight D. Eisenhower to American pilots and cheering Dutch civilians. According to reviewer Melvin Maddocks, "In its sense of inevitable doom Ryan's account reads like a Greek tragedy—written by a meticulous police reporter" (*Time*, 13 Sept. 1974).

Ryan finished the book on 27 October 1974. When it was published the following fall, Ryan led a publicity tour to the battlegrounds in Holland. Weeks later he died at Memorial Sloan-Kettering Hospital in New York City. At that time the book was second on the nonfiction bestseller list. It would be made into a successful film in 1977. Ryan had planned a five-volume history of the European theater, but completed only three of the volumes. He explained, "The spirit is willing, but the flesh has called a halt."

His posthumous book *A Private Battle* (1979), written with Kathryn Ryan, is based on the secret tapes and notebooks in which Ryan recorded his four-and-a-half-year struggle with cancer. Kathryn integrated Ryan's material with her own reflections, producing an account of a family's struggle with a terminal illness. However tragic the subject matter, the book also celebrates a life. One section in particular shows Ryan, desperately ill yet standing erect, receiving the French Legion of Honor from the French ambassador to the United States, Jacques Kosciusko-Morizet, on 8 July 1973. In his speech the ambassador referred to a poll taken in France to see who were the best-read authors. Ryan was in the top five.

Ryan always saw himself as a reporter; in fact, it was his wish to have the simple legend "reporter" engraved on his tombstone. However, it was as the author of books about World War II that he became famous. Although *The Longest Day*, *The Last Battle*, and *A Bridge Too Far* are histories, they read like novels. Employing the journalist's technique for immediacy, Ryan made historical fact come alive, and with his "snapshots" of individuals involved in the events, he gave history a human touch. Walt Whitman's statement, "Underneath all I swear nothing is good to me now that ignores individuals," was pinned on Ryan's office wall. As Ryan wrote in *A Private Battle*, "there can be no understanding of war or disease without knowledge of what the individuals involved endured." Although Ryan's academic credentials ended with a parchment from the Royal Irish Academy of Music, he accomplished the detailed research of a scholar for his books. Some criticized Ryan for going too far into the minutia of the events surrounding his subjects. Ryan countered with, "I'm a reporter . . . I know how to combine a vast amount of material into a dramatic context. There is no reason for history to be dull." The fact that ten million hardcover copies of *The Longest Day* and *The Last Battle* were published in twenty languages attests to the popular appeal of his work. Ryan also knew how to put humanity into history and was, according to Maddocks, "the conscientious Herodotus of World War II."

• The Cornelius Ryan Memorial Collection of World War II papers, including his research files, correspondence, and working library, are at Ohio University in Athens, Ohio. Also in the collection are 166 audio recordings of interviews done by Ryan, including those of Generals Eisenhower and Bernard Law Montgomery. For a general biographical article see Henry Boylan, *A Dictionary of Irish Biography* (1988). See also Jerome Beatty, Jr., "The Author," *Saturday Review*, 26 Mar. 1966, p. 31. The article "Through Their Eyes," *Reader's Digest*, June 1994, pp. 7–8, provides information on the involvement of *Reader's Digest* in *The Longest Day* project. See extended reviews of *The Last Battle* by David Schoebrun, "The Red Tape Road to Berlin," *Saturday Review*, 26 Mar. 1966, pp. 30–32, and Melvin Maddocks, "Review of *A Bridge Too Far*," *Time*, 23 Sept. 1974, pp. 95–96. For a study of *A Private Battle*, see Anne Hawkins, "Two Pathographies: A Study of Illness and Literature," *Journal of Medicine and Philosophy* 9 (Aug. 1984): 231–51. Extended obituaries are in the *Irish Times*, the *Boston Globe*, and the *New York Times*, all 25 Nov. 1974.

MARCIA B. DINNEEN

RYAN, Edward George (13 Nov. 1810–19 Oct. 1880), jurist, was born near Enfield, County Meath, Ireland, the son of Edward Ryan and Abby Keogh. In Ireland he was educated at Clongowes (or Clongoes or Clougones) Wood College from 1820 to 1827. For the next two years Ryan studied law in Ireland. In 1830 he immigrated to New York City and supported himself by teaching and clerical work while preparing for the New York bar, to which he was admitted on 13 May 1836. Later that year he moved to Chicago, where he continued practicing law. In 1839 he became the editor of the *Tribune*, a Democratic newspaper, but it ceased publication two years later. From 1840 through early 1841 Ryan also served as a prosecuting attorney for Cook County, Illinois. On 4 March 1841 he was appointed state's attorney for the Seventh Judicial Circuit of Illinois. Ryan married Mary Graham in 1842 and moved to Racine, Wisconsin, where he practiced law until 1848. The first constitutional convention of the territory was held in 1846, to which Ryan was a delegate. As such, he sat on the committees on banking, the judiciary, and education (which he served as chair). Ryan also served as a delegate to the Democratic party's national convention in Baltimore in 1848. In December of that same year Ryan relocated to Milwaukee, where he continued in private practice as a partner with James G. Jenkins and Matthew H. Carpenter.

Ryan's first wife died in July 1847. In 1850 he married Carolyn Willard Pierce of Newburyport, Massachusetts. The couple had at least three children.

Ryan had a number of high-profile cases, including the 1853 impeachment trial of Wisconsin circuit judge Levi Hubbell, the first such proceeding in Wisconsin's history. Ryan was retained on behalf of the prosecution, but Judge Hubbell was acquitted. In another significant case, Ryan represented the Missouri owner of a fugitive slave who had been arrested in Wisconsin and then illegally released (*In re Booth*, 3 Wisc. Rep. I [1854]). Several such cases arose in the 1840s and 1850s concerning the constitutionality of state "personal liberty" laws, which set higher standards than federal law for those hunting fugitive slaves in free states. Ryan's opponent challenged the constitutionality of the fugitive slave law and asserted the right of a state to release a person being held under a federal law that a state deemed unconstitutional. While Ryan lost in the state venue, the U.S. Supreme Court later reversed the decision (*U.S. v. Booth*, 21 Howard's Reports 506). In another politically-charged case, Ryan represented Republican gubernatorial candidate Coles Bashford, who had lost to the Democratic candidate William A. Barstow amid charges of fraudulent elections in 1855. In this instance Ryan's representation before the Wisconsin Supreme Court was successful, and Bashford was seated as governor. A lifelong Democrat, Ryan replied to criticism of his representation of the Republican Bashford: "I am not aware that I have any general retainer from the Democratic Party. If to keep with my party all principle must be sacrificed, . . . then the party may go" (Lewis, p. 105).

In 1862 Ryan was called upon by a Democratic state convention to draft an address to the people of Wisconsin concerning his party's attitude toward the Civil War. The resulting "Ryan Address" condemned the secession of the southern states, while warning the federal government to restrain its war effort to constitutionally legitimate ends, specifically the restoration of the Union, rather than abolition of slavery. Following a very active private practice Ryan was appointed city attorney of Milwaukee from 1870 to 1872. In June 1874 he was appointed chief justice of the Wisconsin Supreme Court to fill the unexpired term of Luther S. Dixon, who had resigned. In April 1875 Ryan stood unopposed for election to a six-year term as chief justice. His first opinion, which ran to some eighty-five pages, was one of his weightiest. In *Attorney General v. Railroad Companies* (35 Wisc. Rep. 425 [1874]), Chief Justice Ryan issued writs of injunction against the Chicago & Northwestern and the Chicago, Milwaukee & St. Paul railway companies, prohibiting their continued violation of legislatively mandated passenger and freight rates. The railroads had challenged the authority of the state to so legislate but failed completely in their arguments before the state supreme court.

Ryan died in Madison before the expiration of his first full elected term on the Supreme Court. In political life and in practice and on the bench, Ryan faced and addressed the most pressing issues of his day, from fugitive slave laws to the Civil War to the rapidly expanding power of the railroads.

• For information on Ryan's career, see John R. Berryman, *History of the Bench and Bar of Wisconsin*, vol. 1 (1898); William Draper Lewis, ed., *Great American Lawyers*, vol. 6 (1909); P. M. Reed, *The Bench and Bar of Wisconsin* (1882); and G. E. Roe, *Selected Opinions of Luther S. Dixon and Edward G. Ryan* (1907). Obituaries are in the *Milwaukee Daily Sentinel*, 20 Oct. 1880, and "Death of Mr. Chief Justice Ryan," 50 Wis. 23.

BARRY T. RYAN

RYAN, Harris Joseph (8 Jan. 1866–3 July 1934), engineering educator, was born at Matamoras, Pennsylvania, the son of Charles Ryan, a banker and farmer, and Louisa Collier. Receiving a chemistry set from his father at an early age inspired him to embark on a technical career. Ryan attended Baltimore City College for the 1880–1881 academic year, followed by two years at Lebanon Valley College before he entered Cornell University. There he was able to work closely with William Anthony, a physics professor involved in establishing electrical standards. Ryan and his classmates helped Anthony build the equipment and facilities for studying electricity at Cornell, including a large tangent galvanometer that long remained a landmark on the campus; Ryan was marked as showing exceptional promise. He graduated in 1887 with a degree in mechanical engineering—Cornell had not yet developed a separate electrical engineering program.

With two partners, Ryan formed the Western Engineering Company in Lincoln, Nebraska, but this business venture struggled. Within a year Ryan was back in Ithaca, where he accepted a position at Cornell as instructor in electrical engineering, a post first offered to him immediately after his graduation. He remained in academia for the rest of his career. Ryan married Katherine K. Fortenbaugh on 12 September 1888; they had no children. After a year, Ryan was promoted to assistant professor of electrical engineering.

On a field trip as an undergraduate Ryan had visited the New York City works of pioneer electrical engineer Frank Sprague, who talked to the students about the possibilities of long-distance transmission of electrical power at high voltages. Many years later Ryan recollected that this conversation "started me out in life with a never-ending enthusiasm for the study of high voltage phenomenon." The first evidence of Ryan's interest came in 1890 with publication of his first professional paper in *Transactions of the American Institute of Electrical Engineers*. It described how Sprague's idea might work, became a classic, and was translated into eight European languages. Ryan then sought to turn his ideas into reality, in 1893 constructing an oil-immersed transformer to operate at 30,000 volts. This was a very high voltage for the time, and it burned out on the first trial. A subsequent unit with air insulation proved more successful, and in 1899 Ryan rebuilt that device to operate at 90,000 volts. Another paper in 1904 demonstrated that the fear of some engineers—that high-voltage transmission of electricity might face a technical limit of 40,000 volts—was not correct.

The field of electrical engineering was a very exciting place to be in the 1890s; alternating current emerged as the preferred system, and projects like the transmission plant at Niagara Falls were opened. Ryan stood at the center of his field. Cornell recognized this by promoting him to associate professor in 1892, and to full professor and head of the department in 1895. During these years he established a longtime connection to the leading American professional organization for the field, the American Institute of Electrical Engineers (AIEE). He joined the group in 1887, served as manager from 1893 to 1896, and as vice president from 1896 to 1898. He published most of his papers in the organization's journals and was elected president (1923–1924).

In 1905 Ryan left Cornell to become head of the department of electrical engineering at Stanford University. Part of Stanford's appeal was its proximity to the challenging electrical developments on the West Coast. California's electric utilities were developing long-distance transmission of electricity to the state's rapidly growing cities from hydroelectric generating plants in the mountains. Ryan helped to solve the problems facing such systems, especially by developing a high-voltage wattmeter which accurately measured current losses from high tension wires. He also became an expert on corona, a phenomenon in which energy losses from high-tension wires produced a visible glow surrounding the wire. Ryan also used cathode-ray tubes to produce measuring devices for ob-

serving high-voltage circuits, bringing some of the first such tubes to the United States from Germany.

In 1913 Stanford opened a high-voltage laboratory for Ryan and the electrical engineering department, enabling him to study insulation and insulators. The Pacific Gas and Electric and Southern California Edison companies formally began supporting this work in 1920, and Ryan and his colleagues conducted research leading to the development of the insulators that carried 220,000-volt lines from Pitt River to Vaca (near San Francisco) and from Big Creek to Blue Bell near Los Angeles. Their success inspired a substantial expansion of the laboratory in 1926, underwritten by the state's leading electrical utilities. The electrical equipment installed, among the largest in the world, included enormous transformers capable of generating electric sparks of 2.1 million volts for testing equipment. Also in the laboratory was an experimental high-voltage power line for testing apparatus. The facility was named for Ryan.

Ryan's service to society did not stop with work in his laboratory. From 1909 to 1923 he served on the board of consulting engineers for the Los Angeles Municipal Bureau of Power and Light, paying special attention to the development of hydroelectric generating equipment along the Owens Aqueduct. During World War I he headed a research group at California Institute of Technology for the National Research Council, studying the application of high-speed sound waves to submarine detection. After he retired from Stanford in 1931 he continued to consult on the development of the 275,000-volt transmission lines from Boulder Dam to Los Angeles.

Ryan, however, called himself a "faculty man," conveying his deep commitment to teaching. His students rose to many important positions in electrical equipment manufacturing firms and in utility companies. A number of students from Japan studied with him, leading to an invitation in 1933 for Ryan to lecture at the Iwadare Foundation of the Institute of Electrical Engineers in Japan. This was the first such invitation to an American scientist or engineer, but ill health forced Ryan to cancel his visit.

Recognition came to Ryan in other ways. He was elected to the National Academy of Sciences in 1920, and in 1925 he received the AIEE's Edison Medal "for his contributions to the science and the art of high-tension transmission of power." After his retirement he remained curious about electrical ideas; he was studying electric hearing aids at the time of his death in Palo Alto—he was hard of hearing. But the most enduring images are of the electrical engineer working in his laboratory at Stanford, surrounded by huge electrical apparatus, leading an obituary writer to describe Ryan as a "modern Thor."

• Archival records relating to Ryan deposited in the Stanford University Archives include his personal papers (Harris J. Ryan Papers, SC 25) and material in the School of Engineering Records (SC 165). He published more than eighty professional papers, many of them in the *Transactions of the Ameri-*

can Institute of Electrical Engineers, the most important being "Transformers," 7 (1889–1890): 1–29; "The Cathode Ray Alternating-Current Wave Indicator," 22 (1903): 593; and "The Conductivity of the Atmosphere at High Voltages," 23 (1904): 101–34; see also his presidential address, 43 (June 1924): 740–44, and the announcement of his Edison Medal in the *Journal of the American Institute of Electrical Engineers* 45 (Oct. 1926): 1043–44. Information on the high-voltage laboratory at Stanford is in "High Voltage Laboratory," *Stanford Alumnus* 15 (Dec. 1913): 140–42; and "Two Million Man-Made Volts," *Stanford Illustrated Review* 28 (Oct. 1926): 14–17. The best biography is W. F. Durand, National Academy of Sciences, *Biographical Memoirs* 19 (1938): 285–306. Additional information on Ryan's research is in Thomas P. Hughes, *Networks of Power: Electrification in Western Society, 1880–1930* (1983). Obituaries are in *Electrical Engineering* 53 (Aug. 1934): 1240, and the *New York Times*, 6 July 1934.

BRUCE E. SEELY

RYAN, Jack (1926–13 Aug. 1991), inventor, was born in New York City, the son of well-to-do parents. Their names are unknown, but his father was a contractor. Ryan attended Yale University, graduating from Yale's School of Engineering with a B.S. in 1948. He then relocated to Los Angeles, California, to work for the Raytheon Company. Raytheon's "Lab 16" (later the Missile and Radar Division) began working on Defense Department contracts in 1950, creating missiles for use during the Korean War. Ryan assisted in the design of the Sparrow (air-to-air) and Hawk (surface-to-air) missiles.

In 1955 Ryan was contacted by Elliot Handler, who, with his wife Ruth, had founded Mattel, Inc., in 1944. Handler wanted Ryan's high-tech expertise and offered him the position of vice president of research and development. Ryan did not accept immediately, and Handler's offer eventually included the promise of payment to Ryan of a royalty for each patent obtained by his design group. Ryan was swayed, and Mattel gained this "wildly eccentric, Yale-educated electrical engineer whose sexual indiscretions, extravagant parties, and sometimes autocratic management style would shake the company from within" (Lord, p. 24). As the research and development vice president, he was in a position to turn toy ideas into realities, and he did so with great success.

The product with which Ryan is most widely associated is the biggest hit in toy history to date: the Barbie doll. Obituaries credited Ryan with inventing the doll, but that is erroneous. The idea for the doll came from Ruth Handler, who noticed that her daughter, Barbie (the Handlers also had a son named Ken), preferred playing with adult-looking paper dolls to playing with baby dolls. The three-dimensional doll that most caught Barbie Handler's attention was a teenage-looking, fashionable "Lilli" doll she and her mother found in Switzerland. (Lilli was a svelte and sexy creation of German cartoonist Reinhard Beuthien and was made into a doll in 1955.) When Ryan was leaving California for a trip to Tokyo to locate manufacturers for a few of his electronic inventions, Ruth Handler gave him a Lilli doll with instructions to find a manufacturer to copy it. Ryan left Tokyo after three weeks, leaving colleague Frank Nakamura with the task of locating a manufacturer, and returned to California. There he began the task of modifying the doll's joints and finding artists to soften the doll's rather harsh-looking facial features.

In 1959, after the creative input of many at Mattel under the guidance of Ruth Handler, the Japanese-made Barbie was ready for her debut at the Toy Fair in New York City. Response was lukewarm—buyers thought that girls wanted to pretend to be mommies and that their real mommies would never buy a doll with breasts. After a few months, however, children noticed the Barbie doll, and it began to sell briskly. The popularity of the doll grew enormously in the following decades. By 1968 Barbie fan clubs boasted 1.5 million members, more than the Girl Scouts and Boy Scouts combined. In 1991 a Mattel study indicated that 95 percent of girls three to eleven years old owned at least one Barbie doll, and the doll's sales reached the $1 billion mark in 1992. The *International Directory of Company Histories* has dubbed Barbie the "best-selling toy of all time" (vol. 7, p. 304). A large portion of the doll's financial success surely is due to the constant updating of Barbie's image. Each year, new dolls, clothes, and accessories go on the market (up to 50 different dolls and 250 accessories per year during the 1980s). And in a 1990s role reversal, live fashion models are made up in Barbie's image to display the season's newest Barbie clothes. In the last few years of the twentieth century, Barbie was more popular than ever and showed no signs of decline. Whether the doll is a positive or negative influence on female self-esteem and body ideal is the subject of much controversy, but it was Ruth Handler who conceived Barbie's image rather than Jack Ryan.

Ryan contributed his technical inventiveness to the ongoing success of Barbie during his years at Mattel. For instance, in 1967 he designed and patented Twist 'N Turn Barbie's complex and realistic joint system, considered a "feat of engineering . . . a marvel" (Lord, p. 86). And he led the design of approximately thirty-five bestselling toys, including Hot Wheels cars (1968)—of Mattel toys, second in sales only to Barbie. Chatty Cathy (1960), the first talking doll; Major Matt Mason; and the Thingmaker series (1960s), which included Incredible Edibles, Creepy Crawlers, Fun Flowers, and Fright Factory, also have been well loved by many American children, both boys and girls, in the last half of the twentieth century. Ryan held more than 1,000 patents and worked for several years as a self-employed consultant to Mattel.

In 1962 Ryan bought a Bel-Air, California, mansion previously owned by Warner Baxter, a star of the silent screen. Ryan, a millionaire from his patent royalties, remodeled the mansion to look like a medieval castle and fitted it out with mechanical gizmos of his own invention. He provided free housing for several students of the University of California–Los Angeles in exchange for twelve hours of unpaid labor on the mansion per week. He and his wife Barbara (maiden name unknown) became society host and hostess, throwing more than 150 parties and charity events a year, often accommodating up to 1,000 guests at a time. He often wore outlandish outfits to his own parties—"fantasy costumes for his fantasy life" (Lord, p. 24)—lived a swinging lifestyle, and often kept mistresses at the mansion. His unpredictable ways occasionally cost him friends; he was not shy with opinions around his professional equals at Mattel and submitted subordinates to his sometimes humiliating whims.

Ryan was married five times; few details are known. His fourth wife, whom he wed in 1975, was the celebrity Zsa Zsa Gabor; they were divorced in 1976 after seven months of marriage. His fifth was Magda (maiden name unknown). He had two daughters. Ryan's health was poor toward the end of his life, as he suffered a heart attack and underwent bypass surgery before having a massive stroke in 1989. The stroke caused severe debilitation in his final years, and he died at his home in Los Angeles.

• Biographical information on Ryan is scarce. For overviews of the companies with which he was associated, see the *International Directory of Company Histories*, vol. 2, ed. Lisa Mirabile (1990), for the Raytheon Company, and vol. 7, ed. Paula Kepos (1993), for Mattel, Inc. The latter, p. 304, includes the story of Ruth Handler's idea for Barbie, as does Ruth Handler with Jacqueline Shannon, *Dream Doll: The Ruth Handler Story* (1994). A detailed study of the Barbie doll is M. G. Lord's entertaining and well-researched *Forever Barbie: The Unauthorized Biography of a Real Doll* (1994), which contains several colorful anecdotes involving Ryan and explains his role in Barbie's development. Lucinda Ebersole and Richard Peabody, eds., *Mondo Barbie* (1993), collects stories and poems centering on the theme of Barbie as a cultural icon. See also Robert Goldsborough, "Billion-Dollar Barbie, the Biggest Hit with Kids," *Advertising Age* 59 (9 Nov. 1988): 22. Obituaries are in the *Los Angeles Times*, 19 Aug. 1991, and the *New York Times*, 21 Aug. 1991.

BETH A. SNOWBERGER

RYAN, John Augustine (25 May 1869–16 Sept. 1945), Roman Catholic priest, theologian, and reformer, was born in Vermillion, Minnesota, the son of William Ryan and Maria Elizabeth Luby, farmers. His theological, moral, and social roots were planted in a rich soil of Irish Catholic devotionalism and American prairie populism. During his youth, the call for political and economic change on the part of reformers like Patrick Ford of the *Irish World* and agrarian organizations like the Farmers' Alliance, as well as devotional sources such as the sermons of the Reverend Thomas N. Burke, heightened Ryan's moral consciousness.

Beginning his formal education in ungraded public schools, the sensitive youth was transferred to a parochial institution and eventually decided to prepare for the diocesan priesthood. In 1887 he entered St. Thomas (later St. Paul) Seminary in Minnesota. There Ryan refined his understanding of the social question. Exposure especially to incipient Catholic social teaching like Pope Leo XIII's encyclical *Rerum Novarum* convinced him that the American national character was in need of moral renovation. The writings of Bishop John Lancaster Spalding, more than those of any other American Catholic, at the same time stimulated the young seminarian's awareness of the sympathy between Catholic social teaching and economic democracy. Ryan came to see democracy as the political economy in which Americans could best develop as co-creators with God of a just society. He opposed conservative Catholic resistance to social reforms like minimum wage laws and regulation of child labor and began to make his views public in letters to the editors of regional periodicals.

After his ordination to the priesthood in 1898, Ryan served the parish of Belle Creek for a summer, the only pastoral service of his career. Archbishop John Ireland had other plans for the young priest, arranging for Ryan to pursue theological studies at the Catholic University of America in Washington, D.C. Ryan received a bachelor's degree in sacred theology in 1899, a licentiate in sacred theology the next year, and a doctorate in sacred theology in 1906. Ryan's thesis was quickly published as *A Living Wage: Its Ethical and Economic Aspects* (1906), a book that set the standard for American Catholic social thought in the twentieth century. In his introduction, economist Richard T. Ely, a Protestant, recognized that Ryan's social theology represented the most serious American attempt at a neoscholastic reconciliation with the modern marketplace. Arguing man's natural right to a decent standard of living, Ryan particularly attended to the great divorce between modern economic practices and moral rules. Happiness in an unregulated capitalist market was measured in terms of the self-interested attainment of material goods rather than the social attainment of a humane common good. In later essays—for example, "From Christian to Pagan Industrial Ethics," in *Declining Liberty and Other Values* (1927)—Ryan traced the change in values back through the Enlightenment to the Protestant Reformation, noting the Christian turn from a culture wherein economics was a branch of ethics concerned for the right rule of the social household to the separation of economics from ethics. The turn reflected the larger Reformation misinterpretation of God's rule as concerned for the salvation of the individual soul rather than for the well-being of the whole creation. Ryan believed that the gospel of God's rule was not a matter of right belief alone but encompassed the righting of modern life gone the wrong way of material narcissism.

Ryan taught at St. Paul Seminary for thirteen years, beginning in 1902. Students described him as serious and cool though good-natured outside of class. Despite his dry classroom demeanor, his vital interest in social debate steered him toward a public career. He worked with organizations such as the National Consumers' League and the National Conference of Charities and Corrections, pressed state legislatures to pass protective legislation for women and children, and issued comprehensive reform platforms, including demands for the eight-hour day, progressive taxation, a minimum wage, public housing, public ownership of utilities, and old-age, unemployment, and health insurance.

In 1915 Ryan moved to Catholic University. Initially associate professor of political science, he later served as associate professor of theology (1916), full professor of theology (1917), and, by 1919, dean of the School of Sacred Sciences. In between life in the classroom and in the public forum, he established himself as the premier American interpreter of Catholic social teaching. He published *Distributive Justice: The Right and Wrong of Our Present Distribution of Wealth* in 1916 and the next year established—and for five years edited—*Catholic Charities Review*. He drew up the Bishops' Program for Social Reconstruction in 1919 and lectured at the Catholic Summer Schools of Social Action. In his work in the Social Action Department of the National Catholic Welfare Conference, Ryan encouraged capital and labor to recognize their mutual dependence. He remained in the public eye through the 1920s as a member of the national board of the American Civil Liberties Union and as an opponent of Prohibition, as well as an advocate of the reforms to which he had long been devoted.

But Ryan also acquired a certain notoriety after the publication in 1922 of *The State and the Church*, written with Moorhouse F. X. Millar. It is interesting to note that, while his neoscholastic interpretation of natural law theory enabled him to be progressive in economic thought, his application of natural law to church-state issues seemed a static and anachronistic symptom of an antimodernist lack of confidence in the American democratic spirit. Instead of attending to an extensive body of American Catholic literature on the Constitution's religion clause as unfolding a higher truth in the natural order, he denied that the principles of religious liberty and the separation of church and state reflected divine will and dared hope for a time when a Catholic majority might rewrite the American Constitution so as to unify church and state under the banner of the Roman Catholic church, allowing it to guide the nation toward the civil end of social justice. These much-publicized writings outraged many Protestants and during the 1928 presidential campaign helped fuel the anti-Catholic polemics of opponents of Democratic candidate Al Smith.

Pope Pius XI elevated Ryan to monsignor in 1933. Ryan's denunciations of poor working conditions, child labor, and the lack of insurance and pension plans for workers had long anticipated the type of public policy that would characterize Franklin Roosevelt's democratic welfare state. The president's recognition of the congruence between the monsignor's social and moral vision and New Deal policies was expressed by the appointment of Ryan to the Industrial Appeals Board of the National Recovery Administration in July 1934 and his role as an adviser to several other agencies. He gave the benediction at Roosevelt's second and fourth inaugurations.

Catholic University's adoption of a mandatory retirement age of seventy brought Ryan's academic career to a close in 1939, but he remained active on the

National Catholic Welfare Council until his death in St. Paul, Minnesota. Decades later, John A. Ryan's social imagination remained one of the wellsprings of Catholic social theology in the United States. The legacies of *A Living Wage* and *Distributive Justice* were manifest in the 1986 American Catholic bishops' pastoral letter *Economic Justice for All*. Ryan presented a model of a church that steps outside the sanctuary for the sake of justice, realizing that God makes holy in Christ even the marketplace. His attempt to reconcile a new scholasticism and American egalitarianism fixed the Catholic presence within a continuing national debate over the nature and structure of social justice.

• Ryan's collected papers are at the Catholic University of America in Washington, D.C. His autobiography, *Social Doctrine in Action* (1941), is a compilation of articles, speeches, and remembrance of his work for social justice. Other works include *The Church and Socialism* (1919), *Social Reconstruction* (1920), *The Church and Labor* (1920), *A Catechism of the Social Question* (1921), *The Questions of the Day* (1931), *A Better Economic Order* (1933), and *Seven Troubled Years* (1937). The most comprehensive biography is Francis L. Broderick, *The Right Reverend New Dealer: John A. Ryan* (1963), but see also Patrick Gearty, *The Economic Thought of Monsignor John A. Ryan* (1953), George G. Higgins, "The Underconsumption Theory in the Writings of Monsignor John A. Ryan" (M.A. thesis, Catholic Univ., 1942), and, on Ryan's understanding of church-state relations, Rebecca Kasper, "The Development of Interpretative Method in the Tradition of American Catholic Church-State Theory" (Ph.D. diss., Marquette Univ., 1993).

DOMINIC SCIBILIA
REBECCA KASPER

RYAN, Robert (11 Nov. 1909–11 July 1973), actor, was born Robert Bushnell Ryan in Chicago, Illinois, the son of Timothy Ryan, a shipbuilder, and Mabel Bushnell. The son of Irish immigrants, Timothy Ryan founded his own contracting company, which prospered during the early part of the century. He expected his son to take over the business one day, but Robert had other intentions.

Ryan majored in dramatic literature at Dartmouth College, with aspirations of becoming a playwright and journalist. By the time he graduated in 1931, the depression had swept the country. Unable to land a newspaper post, he took a succession of odd jobs over the next six years, including steel salesman, loan collector, school supplies superintendent, bodyguard, photographer's model, and miner. After participating in an amateur theater production, Ryan switched career goals. Determined to become a movie star, he headed to California in the summer of 1938.

Ryan studied acting at the Max Reinhardt Workshop for a year, taking part in several of the school's productions. He made his professional theater debut in 1939 in the musical *Too Many Husbands*. His performance impressed a talent scout from Paramount Pictures. The studio signed him to a contract but did not give him an opportunity to blossom as an actor. Also in 1939 Ryan married Jessica Cadwalader, an actress and novelist, with whom he had three children.

He made his film debut as a boxer in *Golden Gloves* (1940), in which he had only one line of dialogue. He played bit roles in three additional films for Paramount, and then his contract was dropped.

Reasoning that his talents might be better suited to the stage than to films, Ryan worked the summer stock circuit on the East Coast. Playwright Clifford Odets saw him in one such production and cast him in his new play, *Clash by Night* (1941), which had a short run on Broadway. The production drew poor box office receipts, but Ryan received good notices and landed another movie contract, with RKO. Unlike his Paramount experience, RKO gave Ryan ample opportunity to prove himself—casting him in six features in 1943 alone. Most of his early films were mediocre, low-budget entries, but he was honing his craft and would soon emerge as a capable leading man.

Ryan was away from movie audiences for two years due to a stint in the Marine Corps. Shortly after his release in 1945, he took on the controversial role of an anti-Semitic bully in *Crossfire* (1947). His performance was widely praised, and he was nominated for a best supporting actor Oscar. The attention he attracted for *Crossfire* proved to be a double-edged sword. The film gained him recognition as a first-rate actor, but it also limited the roles he would be offered in the future. Ryan was so convincing as the murderous racist that he was never fully able to shake his bad-guy image. In a 1960 interview he lamented, "I've played more heroes than villains . . . But most people seem to remember only the heels." Subsequent roles in *Act of Violence* (1949) and *The Racket* (1951) further cemented his nefarious screen image.

Whether playing saints or sinners, Ryan so invested his characters with humanity that even his "heavies" were often sympathetic. Director Samuel Fuller observed that Ryan had "a charismatic gift for making you like the bastard he played, because he understood what made that bastard tick—and he made the audience understand" (Jarlett, p. 39).

After being released from his RKO contract in 1952, Ryan worked as a free agent and was rarely short of film offers. In choosing his vehicles he was more concerned with the film's message than its commercial prospects. He sought varied roles that would allow him to grow as an actor. His most memorable films include *The Set-Up* (1949), *The Naked Spur* (1953), *The Tall Men* (1955), *God's Little Acre* (1958), *Billy Budd* (1962), *The Dirty Dozen* (1967), *The Professionals* (1966), *The Wild Bunch* (1969), and *The Iceman Cometh* (1973).

Ryan returned to the legitimate theater on occasion throughout his career, often performing at minimum salary. The lure of the footlights and the challenge of performing Shakespeare or Eugene O'Neill were more important to him than financial gain. He starred in productions of *Coriolanus* (1954), *Antony and Cleopatra* (1960), *Mr. President* (1962), *The Front Page* (1968), and *Long Day's Journey into Night* (1971) in the United States as well as in British productions of *Othello* and *Long Day's Journey into Night* in 1971. He was a cofounder of the Theatre Group at the University of California at Los Angeles.

Throughout his life Ryan struggled with a feeling that he ought to be doing something more valuable to society than acting. In a posthumous tribute, his friend and colleague John Houseman wrote, "Throughout his long and distinguished career as a film and stage star, he was deeply and passionately concerned with social and political problems." An outspoken Democrat and committed activist, Ryan once said he was interested in "just about all organizations working for better race relations and disarmament." He held posts with the National Committee for a Sane Nuclear Policy, the United World Federalists, and the American Civil Liberties Union.

Dissatisfied with the educational system in California, in 1951 Ryan and his wife started their own school, the Oakwood Elementary School. From its humble beginnings in their backyard, the school evolved to be rated among the country's best. The Ryans' marriage was regarded as one of Hollywood's most solid partnerships. Fourteen months after his wife's death, Ryan died in New York City.

Ryan appeared in more than seventy films, many of them westerns or crime dramas. Often these were low-budget, hastily and inexpensively made, but Ryan never let the quality of the picture compromise the integrity of his performance. *New York Times* critic Charles Champlin wrote, "It would . . . be hard to think of another major American actor who had so often lent dignity and the sureness of great craft to inferior material" (12 July 1973). Although he never quite achieved superstardom, Ryan worked steadily and garnered commendatory reviews consistently. The passage of time has not diminished his reputation as one of cinema's best bad guys.

• The most comprehensive source is Franklin Jarlett, *Robert Ryan: A Biography and Critical Filmography* (1990). Actor Harold J. Kennedy's autobiography, *No Pickle, No Performance* (1978), includes a chapter on his friendship with Ryan. Chapters on Ryan also can be found in James Robert Parish, *The Tough Guys* (1976), and Ian Cameron and Elizabeth Cameron, *The Heavies* (1967). Jeanne Stein profiled Ryan for *Films in Review* in Jan. 1968 ("Robert Ryan: Unlike Most Handsome Actors He Was Willing to Be a Heavy"). *Films and Filming* printed "Acts of Birth," an extensive interview with the actor, in Mar. 1971. Other notable articles include Patricia Bosworth, "Ryan: In Search of Action," *New York Times*, 1 June 1969; Sue Chambers, "Robert Ryan—Heavy and Hero," *Milwaukee Journal*, 13 Jan. 1963; John Cutts, "Robert Ryan: Villain Extraordinary," *Films and Filming*, July 1961, p. 5; Glenn Loney, "In the Words of Robert Ryan," *Cue*, 11 Jan. 1970, p. 10–11; Mary Murphy, "Robert Ryan—A New Life on Borrowed Time," *Los Angeles Times*, 5 Sept. 1972; "Robert Ryan—Hero and Heel," *Coronet*, Jan. 1960, p. 16; John L. Scott, "Good or Bad; Robert Ryan Plays Either," *Los Angeles Times*, 10 Aug. 1947; and Jesse Zunser, "Stratford: Ryan, Hepburn, et al," *Cue*, 30 July 1960, p. 8–9. Obituaries are in *Boxoffice*, 16 July 1973; *Daily Variety, Hollywood Reporter*, and the *New York Times*, all 12 July 1973; and *Time*, 23 July 1973.

BRENDA SCOTT ROYCE

RYAN, Thomas Fortune (17 Oct. 1851–23 Nov. 1928), financier, was born near Lovingston, Virginia, the son of George Ryan, a farmer, and his wife, whose maiden name was Fortune. He became an orphan at age fourteen and worked for three years as a farm laborer in Reconstruction-era Virginia before going to Baltimore, Maryland, the closest large city, to search for work. Taking a job as an errand boy for John S. Barry, a dry goods merchant, he remained with Barry's firm for four years, during which he worked hard and was given several promotions.

Impressed by Ryan's energy and intelligence—and his obvious desire to make his middle name a reality—Barry encouraged him to migrate north to New York City in 1872 and try for a career on Wall Street, a nineteenth-century breeding ground for many self-made men. Ryan promptly landed a job as a messenger in a brokerage firm, soon became a broker's assistant, and with Barry's backing opened his own brokerage firm with two partners in late 1873, the same year he married Barry's daughter Ida. In 1874 the new firm of Lee, Ryan and Warren purchased a seat on the New York Stock Exchange, and during the next decade it grew in importance and wealth as Ryan himself rose in prominence.

A major key to Ryan's success was his acute political savvy. Quickly realizing that New York was controlled by the Democratic machine of Tammany Hall, he had become a Tammany supporter soon after his arrival in the city; he soon became a Tammany committeeman and a major financial contributor to the machine. He also learned to work quietly behind the scenes, doing and receiving political favors, and he made contacts that proved useful in business.

When "street railways"—streetcars—were proposed for Manhattan in 1883, Ryan quickly organized a paper entity that he named the New York Cable Railroad and bid against entrepreneurs Jacob Sharp and William C. Whitney to gain control of the franchise for a line running along Broadway between Union Square and the Battery. To get the franchise, all three men offered bribes to aldermen on the city council, but Sharp's $500,000 in cash exceeded the offerings of Ryan and Whitney, and the franchise was awarded to him.

Refusing to give up, Ryan persuaded Whitney and another entrepreneur, Peter A. B. Widener, to combine their financial resources with Ryan's, form a syndicate, and gain control of the franchise. Led by Ryan, the syndicate pursued the fight in 1884 by bringing legal action again Sharp for alleged improprieties in his financial dealings, which resulted in an investigation by the New York State legislature. In an attempt to stop the inquiry from going further, Sharp sold his shares to the syndicate, but the investigation went on anyway. Initially, all parties were losers: The franchise was annulled, and Sharp was convicted of bribery and sentenced to four years in prison; a ruined man, he died as his lawyers were preparing an appeal.

Ryan and the syndicate fought the annulment in the courts, and in 1886 the annulment was declared un-constitutional. They then organized the Metropolitan Traction Company (MTC) as the holding company for the various companies that had been joined together to form the syndicate; the MTC is believed to have been the first holding company in the United States. Ryan and the syndicate went on to form the Metropolitan Street Railway Company, which began construction on the Broadway streetcar lines, in 1893. During the next decade the syndicate extended their properties, acquiring other streetcar line franchises through a combination of bribery and purchase at illegally manipulated low rates. By 1900 the Metropolitan Street Railway Company controlled nearly all the streetcar lines in New York City.

In 1902, however, longtime manipulation and artificial inflation of Metropolitan stock prices by Ryan and the syndicate threatened to finally derail the system. Ryan shrewdly turned for assistance to Jacob H. Schiff, a partner in the brokerage firm of Kuhn, Loeb & Company. Together Ryan and Schiff reorganized and refinanced Metropolitan, creating the Metropolitan Securities Company.

Another crisis loomed in 1905, as the Metropolitan found itself in competition for ridership with New York's popular new subway system, which had been financed by August Belmont through his Interborough Rapid Transit Company. Ryan used various tactics, initially innocuous but ultimately threatening, to persuade Belmont to merge his company with the Metropolitan. When Belmont refused and sought to extend his subway franchise, Ryan countered by submitting his own for the franchise. In so doing he proposed creating a single transportation system for the entire city by issuing transfers that patrons could use on both streetcars and subways.

To create support for his proposal, Ryan hired a publicity agent, Lemuel E. Quigg. Ryan's efforts succeeded in securing Belmont's agreement to a merger, and later in 1905 the two transportation systems were united into the Interborough-Metropolitan Company. Its financial underpinnings were shaky, however, and Ryan, aware of this, quietly withdrew from the company in 1906. A year later it went into receivership, and further investigation, including a congressional inquiry, revealed that the $35 million raised by Ryan in a special municipal bond issue had been misappropriated. The assumption, of course, was that much of it had enriched other Ryan enterprises, which by then included the American Tobacco Company, but there was no hard evidence and Ryan was not prosecuted.

By now Ryan had made the fortune he had dreamed of as a youth. At the time of the Metropolitan collapse his wealth was estimated to be at least $50 million, which he had garnered through substantial holdings in banking and industry, including coal mines and railroads, as well as various public utilities. By the early twentieth century he had acquired controlling interests in more than thirty corporations. He thus suffered only a minor setback when the U.S. Supreme Court ordered in 1911 that the American Tobacco Company as then constituted be dissolved because it had established a monopoly of the tobacco industry. Investigations of other, more lucrative Ryan enterprises, especially his vast holdings in the banking industry—the consequence of a series of mergers that began with Ryan and Whitney's acquisition of the State Trust Company in 1898 and ended twelve years and several transactions later with Ryan controlling the Guaranty Trust Company—were usually never pursued beyond the preliminary stage.

A rare exception occurred in 1900, when the *New York World* newspaper published a copy of a quashed state report on violations of banking laws—specifically, the misappropriation of trust funds—by the Ryan syndicate and called for tighter regulation. The state legislature responded by calling for the merger of two separate Ryan-owned banks, the State Trust and the Morton Trust, which made government oversight more feasible but in fact further improved Ryan's financial position.

Other major Ryan ventures in the early 1900s included the founding of the National Bank of Commerce and the acquisition of the Seaboard Air Line Railroad, which he seized underhandedly from its founder, John Skelton Williams. Ryan also moved into the insurance industry during this period, gaining control of the Washington Life Insurance Company in 1904, the year that his syndicate partner Whitney died. Ryan was now officially in sole control of the syndicate, though in reality he had been the de facto head for years.

In 1905 Ryan bought the controlling interest in the Equitable Life Assurance Society, a deal that put him at loggerheads with the financier E. H. Harriman, who had also sought to buy the stock. Privately, Harriman complained that Ryan was ill suited to run the company, a sentiment shared by other Wall Street scions of an older moneyed class who looked down on the onetime Virginia country boy as unscrupulous, without honor, and decidedly not a gentleman. No one dared criticize him too openly, however, for Ryan was a powerful man with powerful friends.

Ryan's greatest talent may have been his ability to use the system to his advantage, appointing as trustees of his various operations people of unimpeachable character. They lent their names and their prestige, presumably in exchange for private favors from Ryan, while never challenging his authority, although on paper they were given the power to act independently. Former president Grover Cleveland was one such prominent appointee; another was Paul Morton, who had served as secretary of the navy in the cabinet of President Theodore Roosevelt.

Ryan's ventures were not confined to the United States. At the invitation of King Leopold of Belgium, Ryan organized a syndicate, the Société Internationale Forestière et Minière du Congo—known for short as Forminière—in the decade before the outbreak of World War I to develop the natural resources of the Belgian Congo. After deciding that rubber production would not be profitable, Ryan organized diamond-, gold-, and copper-mining operations in the Congo. At his death he was said to be the largest individual owner of Congo diamond mines. Ryan's African venture drew wide publicity back in the United States, and he openly discussed his goals for the Congo—which included, he said, not only its material development but its moral and social improvement—with reporters from popular periodicals of the day.

Ryan remained an important figure in the Democratic party throughout his life, and his influence was a factor at national party conventions. He attended the 1904 and 1912 conventions as a delegate from Virginia, where he maintained a residence. He undoubtedly helped secure the 1904 presidential nomination for Alton B. Parker of New York, a strong supporter of the gold standard, over party leader and silver advocate William Jennings Bryan. At the 1912 convention in Baltimore, the still-powerful Bryan, fearful that delegate Ryan and his associates would derail Bryan's efforts to secure the nomination for Woodrow Wilson, forced the convention to adopt a resolution declaring that it opposed the nomination of any candidate who represented the special interests of Ryan, August Belmont, and J. P. Morgan, who collectively symbolized the power of Wall Street and big business.

Ryan's primary residence was a block-long domicile on Fifth Avenue in New York City; it included both a mansion and an extensive private garden, and it housed Ryan's priceless collection of Limoges enameled porcelain as well as other art objects. Ryan's first wife, with whom he had five sons, died in 1917, on his sixty-sixth birthday; twelve days later he married a widow, Mary Townsend Lord Cuyler. During their lifetimes and under the terms of their wills, Ryan and his first wife donated a total of nearly $20 million to the Roman Catholic church. Ryan died in New York City, leaving an estate valued at more than $200 million.

• Ryan's entry in *Who Was Who in America*, vol. 1 (1943), a reprint of the entry in the 1928–1929 edition of *Who's Who*, contains basic factual information about his life and career; contemporary secondary sources have to be relied on for further data. Ryan's own account of his most controversial insurance company acquisition is "Why I Bought the Equitable," *North American Review*, Aug. 1913. For accounts of various aspects of Ryan's activities, see W. N. Amory, *The Truth about Metropolitan*, 2d ed. (1906); the series by Burton Jesse Hendrick, "Great American Fortunes and Their Making: Street-Railway Financiers," in *McClure's*, Nov. and Dec. 1907 and Jan. 1908; Hendrick, *The Age of Big Business: A Chronicle of the Captains of Industry* (1919); Harry James Carman, *The Street Surface Railway Franchises of New York City* (1919); Henry Rogers Seager and Charles Adams Gulick, *Trust and Corporation Problems* (1929); and Isaac Frederick Marcosson, *An African Adventure* (1921). Obituaries are in the *New York Times* and the *Baltimore Sun*, both 24 Nov. 1928.

ANN T. KEENE

RYAN, Tommy (31 Mar. 1870–3 Aug. 1948), boxer, was born Joseph Youngs in Redwood, New York, near the Canadian border, the son of Joseph Youngs, a glassblower, and Betsy Stratton. Little is known about his early life. After leaving home he worked in Michigan as a lumberjack. Assuming his pseudonym, he had his earliest fights in the Midwest from 1887 to 1893. During this period unpadded gloves were typically used, and the combatants frequently fought until one of them could not continue. These fights often occurred under unusual conditions; for instance, Ryan fought Mike Dunn in an icehouse, and he knocked out Martin Shaughnessy in 46 rounds in a bonfire-lighted ring pitched on the shore of Lake St. Clair in Michigan.

Having won 26 of his first 30 fights, Ryan finally made a name for himself by knocking out Con Doyle in 28 rounds in Shelby, Indiana, in 1891 and Billy Needham in 76 rounds in Minneapolis in 1892. These victories made him the foremost challenger for the welterweight championship for which the weight limit was then 142 pounds, held by Mysterious Billy Smith. They fought for the title in Minneapolis on 26 July 1894 under Marquis of Queensberry rules—with three-minute rounds and padded gloves worn—and Ryan won decisively on points after 20 rounds of vicious battling.

At about 5′8″ tall, Ryan possessed a rather slender physique and used a wide repertoire of blows, especially a very effective left jab. He was nimble and avoided the punches of his opponents by quick footwork and movements of the head. His punches were sharp, but his many knockout victories were almost always the result of many blows instead of a devastating few. He was a good strategist who depended on intelligent planning and proper conditioning; only on rare occasions did he fight recklessly.

In 1895 Ryan twice defended his welterweight title successfully, first against Nonpareil Jack Dempsey and later against Smith, both fights occurring at Coney Island in Brooklyn. Dempsey was suffering from tuberculosis, and Ryan won easily in three rounds because of his opponent's poor physical condition. Smith was badly beaten, and the police intervened in the 18th round to save him from further punishment.

On 2 March 1896 Ryan suffered the first setback of his career at the hands of Kid McCoy at Maspeth, Long Island, New York, in a nontitle fight. McCoy, who had been a sparring partner of Ryan, had left Ryan's employment with bad feelings because of the relentless punishment that Ryan meted out. Taking his opponent too lightly, Ryan entered the ring about 15 pounds lighter than McCoy and much less well trained than usual. After several close rounds, McCoy took charge and handed Ryan a bad beating, finally knocking him out in the 15th round. A famous but apocryphal story holds that McCoy persuaded Ryan to fight him, and underrate the seriousness of their fight, by claiming that he was ill and needed money and by wearing makeup to simulate a sickly pallor.

Ryan successfully defended his welterweight title four more times: against Smith at Maspeth and Billy Payne in Syracuse, New York, both in 1896; Australian Tom Tracy in Syracuse in 1897; and Tommy West in New York City in 1898. In his clash with Smith, who was a very tough and dirty fighter, Ryan was fouled several times before his opponent was disqualified in the ninth round.

After defeating West, Ryan gave up the welterweight title and campaigned as a middleweight. He gained general recognition as champion of the heavier division by defeating Jack Bonner, Dick O'Brien, Jack Moffatt, and others. On 18 September 1899 he defended his claim successfully at Coney Island against Frank Craig, a well-known black fighter who used the sobriquet "The Harlem Coffee Cooler." On 4 March 1901 he won a difficult defense against Tommy West at Louisville, Kentucky, the fight being stopped by the referee in the 17th round to save West. Ryan made two more successful middleweight defenses in 1902, on 24 June against Johnny Gorman in London, England, and on 15 September against Kid Carter in Fort Erie, Ontario, Canada.

Although he continued to be active in 1903 and 1904 and made a brief comeback in 1907, Ryan lost interest in holding his title and tried unsuccessfully to bestow it on an appointed successor, Hugo Kelly. He had already taught the young James J. Jeffries the use of the left jab and the crouch and showed more interest in teaching the sport to others than in fighting more. In 1903 he seconded James J. Corbett in his final fight with Jeffries, in which he is thought to have been the first to administer oxygen to a fighter between rounds. Finally, without having announced retirement or losing his title in the ring, he opened a gymnasium in Syracuse, New York, where he had lived since reaching the peak of his career.

A bright, affable, intelligent man, Ryan is credited along with with Corbett and Joe Choynski with making clever boxing, defensive skills, conditioning, and strategy into standard elements of the sport. His appearance and demeanor helped counteract the old negative image of boxers. Although he had three managers, most notably Charles E. "Parson" Davies and Captain James Westcott, he also seems to have handled most of his own business affairs. Despite his long career in the ring, Ryan retired unmarked. His final record of 104 fights included only three official defeats, the knockout loss to McCoy, a six-round decision loss to McCoy in 1900, and a loss by foul to George Green in 1901. He knocked out 68 opponents and won most of his other fights either by official decision or by the unofficial verdict of newspapermen.

Ryan moved to California in 1920, where he enjoyed married life with his wife Annie (maiden name unknown) and dealt successfully in real estate, owned homes and a ranch, and indulged his favorite pastime of gardening. Except for losing sight in one eye owing to an accident in his home, he was in good health nearly to the end of his life. His death in Los Angeles was caused by heart failure. He was elected to the International Boxing Hall of Fame in 1991.

• Ryan's record is available in Herbert G. Goldman, ed., *The Ring 1986–87 Record Book and Boxing Encyclopedia* (1987). Articles published in *The Ring* provide most of the available information, especially the following: "In Class by Himself,"

Oct. 1948; "Irony of Fate," Aug. 1934; George T. Pardy, "When Welters Waged Wild Fistic War," Nov. 1934; Jack Curley, "Memoirs of a Promotor, Part Two," May 1930; Charles T. Mathison, "Tommy Ryan Ridicules Trickery of Kid McCoy," Sept. 1925; and Mathison, "Freak Fights in Modern Ring History," July 1924. A good source of information on Ryan's rivalry with Kid McCoy is Robert Cantwell, *The Real McCoy: The Life and Times of Norman Selby* (1971). The *Philadelphia Item* contains contemporary accounts of Ryan's major fights. Ryan's obituary is in the *New York Times*, 4 Aug. 1948.

Luckett V. Davis

RYAN, Walter D'Arcy (17 Apr. 1870–14 Mar. 1934), illuminating engineer, was born in Kentville, Nova Scotia, Canada, the son of James William Ryan and Josephine Rafuse. After attending St. Mary's College in Halifax, Memramcook College in Memramcook, New Brunswick, and the Royal School of Calvary in Quebec, Ryan finished his studies at the Massachusetts Institute of Technology, where he exhibited exceptional talent in engineering. Upon graduation, Ryan took a job as student engineer with the Thomson-Houston Electric Company in their Lynn, Massachusetts, works. Rising rapidly, in 1896 he became superintendent of test men in what was then the West Lynn Works of the General Electric Company, designing and building railway motors and electrical machines. In 1899 he became a commercial engineer and established the world's first laboratory focused on illuminating engineering. In 1903 Ryan was given the title of illuminating engineer, the first electrical engineer ever to be so named. His remaining professional life was spent directing the illuminating engineering laboratory he created at the General Electric plant at Schenectady, New York. He married Alice Brady in 1897; they had two children.

Displaying energy and persuasiveness, Ryan propelled change in the field of lighting by emphasizing both the technical aspects of the lightsource and the context in which it was to be used. He distinguished illumination from lighting, or producing light for light's sake, by defining illumination as putting a desired amount and kind of light on a specific object. Such a seemingly straightforward task quickly developed into a broad and complex movement, with technical, aesthetic, professional, and commercial ramifications. Ryan influenced three fundamental aspects of this development. First, thinking of lighting as less a series of lightsources than a spectrum of effects, he helped spur the concept of lighting as an item of consumption and not merely a homogeneous object of mass production. In this way, Ryan helped change General Electric from a company that manufactured lightbulbs to one that sold lighting. Second, Ryan emphasized illuminating engineering as a unique professional service uniting lamp and globe manufacturers, architects, and electrical engineers among others. Supporting this cause, he became a charter member of the Illuminating Engineering Society of 1906. And finally, Ryan insisted on engaging and not intimidating the public. While he was the first to be given the title of

illuminating engineer, he was also the first to regret its formality, preferring to think in terms of light improvement.

Ryan's work in linking the science and art of illumination began with the study of light distribution and the development of globes and reflectors. In 1902 he provided the first graphs depicting the localized intensity and distribution of candle power emitted by various lamps on city streets. Ryan emphasized the development of light sources and lamp standards that were designed in accordance to the size and function of the street. The simultaneous refinement of luminous arc lamps by C. A. B. Halvorson, Jr., helped enable "white way" lighting to be established for the first time in New Haven, Connecticut, in 1911. Ryan went on to design, in 1916, installations in Los Angeles and San Francisco, California, among other cities. In San Francisco, the city's main commercial thoroughfare, Market Street, was renamed "The Path of Gold" after the golden glow given from specially colored globes. With the design assistance of J. W. Gosling, Ryan customized the design of lighting standards for the Path of Gold as well as for the "triangle district," the location of numerous retail stores, and Chinatown, where he emphasized Asian motifs as a means to reinforce that district's special character.

Broadening his specialty to include all aspects of exterior illumination, Ryan made his next major contribution with the introduction of elaborate flood lighting. He illuminated Niagara Falls using a scintillator, or a battery of searchlights, for thirty consecutive nights in 1907. In 1908 the Singer Building of 1906 in New York City became the first building to be fully illuminated on the exterior. In 1912 the Buffalo General Electric Building became one of the first buildings with electric light as an integral part of its interior and exterior design, a feature that would become standard in skyscrapers and most commercial buildings in the 1920s and 1930s. In 1927 Ryan modified the basic floodlight and developed a "light gun" designed to project specific images such as signs or drawings a distance of up to five miles.

Ryan's practical and artistic skills reached their fullest expression at the Panama-Pacific International Exposition of 1915 in San Francisco, where he worked closely with electrical engineers, architects, and color consultants to create a tour de force. The exposition was the first to have a unified color scheme and a system of floodlighting, in contrast to previous fairs' use of outline lighting along the edges of buildings and an occasional spotlight. The design of the fair as a series of courts rather than individual buildings unified the fair overall but allowed for an unprecedented demonstration of lighting's diverse and evocative nature in individual settings. Rising in the center, a 432-foot central Tower of Jewels, entirely covered in novagems, or reflecting crystals, hung from the building's exterior so that they moved in the breeze and captured light. Even more ambitious, Ryan orchestrated a complicated series of projected light performances, or scintillator drills, using a bank of forty-eight searchlights, each thirty-six inches in diameter and equipped with variable filters to change their color. The searchlights typically used clouds or fog cover as a background, but if the sky was too clear, the wheels of a stationary locomotive would turn to create clouds of artificial smoke. Seeing effects as spectacular as the aurora borealis, the official historian of the fair noted that "people poured out by the thousands to witness them, stood thrilled and speechless until the splendor faded, and turned away with sighs." Ryan's last project was as chief of exterior illumination for the Chicago Century of Progress Exposition in 1933. Said by some to dwarf previous expositions' lighting, it was really just a continuation of techniques initiated earlier by Ryan with the addition of some new materials such as neon.

Ryan became a consulting engineer for GE's illuminating engineering laboratory in 1932. By that time, the principles of illumination he had helped establish were widely practiced. Although Ryan never worked alone or was sole originator, he was a central figure in shaping the application of light and defining modern illumination as an integral part of our cultural landscape. Ryan laid the foundation for using light in a scientifically and aesthetically pleasing manner, a feat that only a few future illuminators, such as Matthew Luckiesh, can claim to have matched or exceeded. Ryan's wife having died, in 1909 he married Catherine Haskins, with whom he had three daughters and a son. He died at his home in Schenectady, New York.

• Original sources document the life of Ryan and the profession of illuminating engineering. Ryan's publications include, on street lighting, "Street Illumination and Units of Light," *Electrical Review* 40, no. 2 (11 Jan. 1902): 37–38, "Luminous and Flame Arcs versus Open and Enclosed Carbon Arcs for Street Illumination," *General Electric Review* 14, no. 6 (June 1911): 269–79; on flood lighting, "Spectacular Illumination: A Story without Words," *General Electric Review* 17, no. 3 (Mar. 1914): 329–36, "The Lighting of the Buffalo General Electric Company's Building," *Transactions of the Illuminating Engineering Society* 7 (1912): 597–615; and on exposition lighting, "Building Exterior, Exposition and Pageant Lighting," *Illuminating Engineering Practice* (1917): 547–56, "Lighting the Exposition," *Architectural Forum* 59 (July 1933): 47–50. On the inception of illuminating engineering, see his *Light and Illuminating Engineering* (1903), and Samuel G. Hibben, "The Society's First Year," *Transactions of the Illuminating Engineering Society* 51, no. 1 (Jan. 1956): 145–50. Obituaries are in *Transactions of the Illuminating Engineering Society* 29, no. 4 (Apr. 1934): 238–39; *General Electric Monogram* (Apr. 1934): 15; and the *New York Times*, 15 Mar. 1934.

E. G. Daves Rossell

RYDER, Albert Pinkham (19 Mar. 1847–28 Mar. 1917), artist, was born in New Bedford, Massachusetts, the son of Elizabeth Cobb and Alexander Gage Ryder, a laborer turned customs official turned merchant. Ryder attended grammar school. He manifested an early interest in art and took lessons from a part-time painter, John Sherman. By 1870 Ryder had settled in New York City, where he received criticism from William Edgar Marshall, whose work consisted of somewhat naive realistic portraits and fantasies in a romantic manner. After initially having been denied admission to the National Academy of Design, he was registered there as a student from 1870 to 1873 and 1874 to 1875.

Ryder soon joined a circle of avant-garde artists who studied at the academy—J. Alden Weir, George de Forest Brush, Abbott Thayer, and Helena de Kay among them. He and some of his companions gathered around the Scot Daniel Cottier, a dealer of European and American fine and decorative arts who maintained homes in London, Paris, and New York, and his associate and eventual successor, James S. Inglis. Cottier and Inglis would become Ryder's supporters and dealers as well as his friends. Ryder shared a studio with, and later for a few years in the 1880s, lived in the same building as, some of the members of this group of artists. And he followed their example in joining the recently founded American Art Association—soon renamed the Society of American Artists—which presented exhibitions from 1877 to 1887. Ryder also occasionally exhibited at the National Academy of Design.

Ryder's works of the 1870s and early 1880s, such as *The Pasture* (North Carolina Museum of Art, Raleigh), revealed a genuine interest in the mostly pastoral, romantic-naturalist painting of the French School of Barbizon and its vigorous offshoot, the School of The Hague—most particularly, carefully observed effects of lighting and atmosphere that were stressed in order to heighten the poetry of fields and meadows as well as marines. Occasional sunsets echo the European artists' fascination with the mysterious and suggestive half-lights of dusk. But Ryder's works are characterized by a more vigorous and looser brushstroke, a bolder use of hues, stronger light-dark contrasts, and a more arbitrary structure. His technique, altogether more naive—albeit artfully so—was all at once fuzzier in its atmospheric suggestions, more translucent in the rendering of surfaces, and often linear to the point of bluntness in delimiting forms. Ryder's poetic message, more rugged, more exalted, and more challenging to the viewer's imagination than that of the schools of Barbizon and The Hague, is distinctly American.

Ryder spent one month in Europe in 1877, mostly in London, but also in Amsterdam, where he visited the Rijksmuseum. In 1882 he traveled to England, France, Spain, Tangier, Italy, Switzerland, and Germany and returned to London briefly in 1887 and 1896. He was influenced by works of Rembrandt, whose layering of glazes of varying translucency Ryder was to emulate to add an aura of mystery to his subsequent works. During the 1882 trip, he visited the London studio of one of the most imaginative members of the Dutch romantic-naturalist of the School of The Hague, Matthew Maris, whose gently whimsical linearism, stainlike application of paint, dreamlike vision, and near-magical quality must have affected him. Furthermore, even before the second trip, in 1879, a critic justly likened him to the Frenchman Adolphe Monticelli, another imaginative romantic-naturalist, whose work, characterized by an aura of mystery and suggestiveness and executed in multicolored pearly strokes eerily emerging from a softly glowing haze, he may well have already known. It is also likely that Ryder's increasing inclination toward "synthetism," to use the appellation the French symbolists were later to coin for one of their own stylistic initiatives—specifically the practice of creating somewhat flat linear patterns delimiting fairly uniform luminescent areas—owes something to the harbingers of such tendencies evinced by Whistler as early as the 1870s in such works as the *Nocturnes*.

Ryder evolved what has been called his imaginary manner in the 1880s. Increasingly, the simplifications and abbreviations of his compositions, the occasionally flattened design, the bold use of contrasts foreshadow the synthetist mode of the symbolists. And for his subjects he now turned wholeheartedly to the world of imagination. For all his borrowings from earlier and recent European trends, Ryder's work, in the course of those years, was characterized by profound originality in form and content. *Moonlight*, of the early to middle 1880s (Metropolitan Museum of Art, New York City), ranks as one of the most powerful. The dark lustrous silhouettes of the sails and foreshortened hull constitute a simple, nearly uniform design that detaches itself from the vaporous, luminescent areas of the white foam and the moonlit sky. In *Siegfried and the Rhine Maidens* (c. 1888–1891; National Gallery of Art, Washington, D.C.), through an equally bold process of abbreviation and simplification, the curving banks of the river and the highlight over its surface, the bending path, the twisted limbs of the trees and their foliage, the streams of clouds—in some ways the figures themselves—all become striplike entities that seem to respond to, and amplify, the dialogue between Siegfried and the nymphs with baroque vigor. In both works the opposition between the shimmering light and the deep shadow, no less than the blurring effects due to the loose brushstrokes, set the subject in a dreamlike atmosphere. In both, motion seems to have been slowed to a somnambulistic crawl, and the phantasms of imagination seem to have displaced physical reality. As Ryder himself put it, "imitation is not inspiration, and inspiration only can give birth to a work of art." The artist, furthermore, "has only to remain true to his dream."

Ryder's dream could be sparked by a reminiscence or a current event or drawn from literature as an inspiration. Whatever its source, the original idea evolved simultaneously with the design and underwent profound metamorphoses in the process. The painting *Constance*, executed from the middle 1880s to the middle 1890s and later (Museum of Fine Arts, Boston), showed a resigned woman lying down in a drifting boat. Undoubtedly inspired by Chaucer's "The Man of Lawes Tale," it became in the course of such a development a poignant evocation of the isolation of the individual in the grandest romantic tradition.

Ryder's work contains numerous other literary allusions: to the Bible, to the works of Shakespeare, Poe, Heine, La Fontaine, Tennyson, and even to his own endearingly basic and robust poetry. Such allusions, however, are but accompaniments to the complex play of associations that would arise even in the mind of the spectator who did not recognize the literary connection. Indeed, *The Toilers of the Sea* (c. 1883–1884; Metropolitan Museum of Art, New York City), inspired by Victor Hugo's novel, and *Moonlight (Moonlight at Sea)* of the early 1890s (National Museum of American Art, Smithsonian Institution, Washington, D.C.) both represent a sailboat fighting waves in the moonlight. They are evocative of the human struggle with destiny, and, in varying degree, of alternating hope and despair, endurance and resignation, dreams of success and fears of failure—the allusion to the novel merely contributing a degree of specificity to the play of associations conveyed by the picture.

Ultimately, Ryder's works reflect the deep religious convictions instilled by what must have been a strongly Protestant upbringing: a serene moonlight dominates the most dramatic sea scenes as if to suggest ultimate redemption; while the reddish glow surrounding the moon in *Macbeth and the Witches*, of the middle 1890s and later (The Phillips Collection, Washington, D.C.), suggests momentous wrath. Divine providence and justice seem ever-present in Ryder's visionary world.

In all cases, the suggestiveness of line and color, the stress on a play of associations, the aura of mystery, and the essential subjectivity of Ryder's mature manner are typical of romantic symbolism. The element of synthetism, whenever it occurs, brings the artist closer to full-blown symbolism.

By the late 1880s, Ryder seems to have become less creative. From that time on, rather than creating new pictures, he retouched old ones with ever greater persistence. The artist had acquired the reputation of being a recluse. A confirmed bachelor, he kept house quite casually and led a solitary life in a succession of modest New York apartments. But he had old friends whom he greatly enjoyed seeing, particularly Helena de Kay Gilder—whose brother, a literary and art critic of the *New York Times*, had done much to promote the artist—J. Alden Weir, and the sculptor Olin L. Warner. An older artist, the painter Robert Loftin Newman, also became a close friend, as did important collectors of his work, Dr. and Mrs. Albert T. Sanden. Around 1896 he met his neighbors, Charles and Louise Fitzpatrick, who took care of him when his health began to fail in 1915. He was hospitalized for three months that year and then lived in boardinghouses. He died in a house in Elmhurst, New York, on Long Island, into which the Fitzpatricks had moved.

Ryder had been appreciated by a small but expanding group of collectors since the 1880s. He was often near destitution, but his works appreciated in value in his lifetime. In 1902 he was elected associate member, and in 1906 member, of the National Academy of Design. He received a handsome tribute from a younger generation of artists in 1913, when ten of his works were selected for New York's avant-garde Armory Show, which a group of them had organized that year.

A memorial retrospective exhibition of Ryder's work was presented at the Metropolitan Museum of Art in 1918. Arthur B. Davies, Marsden Hartley, and Jackson Pollock, among several other major twentieth-century American artists, all considered him to have had a profound influence on them.

• The National Museum of American Art, Smithsonian Institution, Washington, D.C., has the largest holdings of Ryder's pictures, while New York's Metropolitan Museum of Art and the Brooklyn Museum also possess impressive collections. Aware of the importance of the artist in the development of American art, many other museums in the United States have successfully vied for examples of his works: the National Gallery of Art, Washington, D.C., the Cleveland Museum of Art, and the Phillips Collection, Washington, D.C., among them. The most complete study of the artist is William Innes Homer and Lloyd Goodrich, *Albert Pinkham Ryder: Painter of Dreams* (1989). It contains a comprehensive bibliography, and the chronological list of works is essential to whoever attempts to isolate Ryder's creations from innumerable forgeries. A section by Conservator Sheldon Keck, "Albert Pinkham Ryder: His Technical Procedures," is devoted to the artist's technique and the conservation problems caused by his innovative but untested methods. Elizabeth Broun, *Albert Pinkham Ryder* (1989), is an interesting critical study. It includes a catalogue raisonné by Eleanor L. Jones, Matthew J. Drutt, and Sheri L. Bernstein of the works presented in the exhibition *Albert Pinkham Ryder*, National Museum of American Art, 6 Apr.–29 July 1990, and the Brooklyn Museum, 14 Sept. 1990–8 Jan. 1991. Its bibliography contains a list of unpublished sources. The catalog of a small exhibition at the Washburn Gallery, New York, *Albert Pinkham Ryder, the Descendants* (1989), adds to our understanding of Ryder's impact. Homer's and Brown's books are reviewed by Henri Dorra, "*Albert Pinkham Ryder* by William I. Homer and *Albert Pinkham Ryder* by Elizabeth Broun," *The Burlington Magazine*, Aug. 1990, pp. 583–84. Homer, "National Museum of American Art, Smithsonian Institution, Washington, D.C. [. . .]," *Art Journal* 50 (Spring 1991): 86–90, is an important review of the 1989 exhibition in that institution.

HENRI DORRA

RYDER, Chauncey Foster (29 Feb. 1868–18 May 1949), artist, was born in Danbury, Connecticut, the son of Benjamin Franklin Ryder, an inventor, and Josephine Hull. By 1874, for unknown reasons, his family had moved to New Haven, Connecticut. His Quaker parents always encouraged the quiet, thoughtful Ryder to draw. His father's influence on him was profound. Ryder conceded, "No true artist ever existed" without his father's kind of dream. "[He] had in him those qualities that make the real artist. An unquenchable and dominating vision. That creative faculty that is called invention." Ryder inherited the same qualities.

Facts about Ryder's early years are sketchy. For unknown reasons he moved to Illinois in 1890, and in 1891 he married Mary Keith Dole in Chicago. They adopted three daughters. From 1892 to 1898 Ryder worked during the day as an accountant for a bank, took evening art classes at the Art Institute of Chicago, and drew book illustrations for publishing companies.

In 1900 Ryder's artistic proficiency was awarded with the distinguished Academy Prize, a highly sought-after scholarship to attend the Académie Julian in Paris.

In 1901 Ryder and his wife left Chicago for Paris. They lived in poverty while Ryder studied at the Académie Julian until 1907. In 1902 the couple moved to Etaples, France, where Ryder worked with the successful painter Max Bohm. The 1904 Paris Salon catalog incorrectly lists Bohm as Ryder's teacher. Ryder's fascination with the natural environment grew in Etaples, and his canvases from this period combine fine academic figural work with a more abstracted construction of landscapes.

While Ryder was in France, he exhibited at the Salon (his first work, *Les Amies*, was hung in 1903), at the Société des Artistes Français in the principal London and Glasgow exhibitions, and at the international exposition in Antwerp. Before he left Paris, Ryder agreed to let art dealer William Macbeth of New York become his agent, and because of Macbeth's promotional efforts all of Ryder's paintings shown by Macbeth received instant acclaim and were sold quickly.

Ryder returned to New York City in 1907, a distinguished oil painter and watercolorist known for putting on canvas what he saw and felt in a luminous, contemporary manner. Combining abstract and academic realism into a unique style, Ryder transcribed enduring qualities found in nature's four seasons by blending simple form and minimal lines with a harmonious use of color into recognizable brushwork uniquely his own. Using both a brush and a palette knife, the reclusive, unassuming Ryder created robust, lucid, expansive visual images of majestic mountain ranges, sweeping landscapes, or rugged, often desolate-looking hillsides. His well-constructed, solid paintings of France, Italy, Scotland, the British Isles, and New England utilize broad, melodic color masses and an economy of line to give the appearance of immense, restful space; distance; and atmosphere. Sidney C. Woodward wrote in 1922, "Ryder . . . sensed the right proportion between the real and the unreal, between detail and vagueness. . . . There is no disturbing note." William Howe Downes identified Ryder in the *Evening Transcript* (2 Feb. 1919) as "a very genuine and original painter, one of those men who, without troubling himself much about style, attains style because he has something to say and goes about it by the straightest route. . . . He does not repeat himself."

Ryder received numerous awards, including medals at the Paris Salon, the San Francisco Pan-Pacific Exposition, and the National Academy of Design. He was given many one-man exhibitions because he painted well the poetry and grandeur he found in barren trees, rolling hillsides, babbling brooks, windswept fields, approaching storms, and desolate roads. He gravitated to and identified with an aloof, isolated, distant mountain (*Under the Mountain*, Harmsen Collection), a lonely beach (*Cape Porpoise*, Corcoran Gallery of Art), or a remote town shadowed by dark clouds (*Over There*, Brockton Art Museum).

By 1915 the retiring, modest Ryder was famous for his oils, drypoints, drawings, watercolors, lithographs, and etchings of far-off, desolate landscapes. During his life more than seventy museums owned Ryder's work, including the Metropolitan Museum of Art, the Corcoran Gallery of Art, the National Gallery, the Art Institute of Chicago, the Brooklyn Museum, the Smithsonian Institution, the Bibliotheque Nationale in Paris, the British Museum, and the Victoria and Albert Museum in London.

Although Ryder did not like to teach, he had many followers who emulated his style. He was a revered member of the National Academy; the Allied Artists of America; the Salmagundi Club; the National Arts Club; the New York Water Color Society and the American Water Color Society; the Society of Etchers in Brooklyn, Chicago, and Philadelphia; and the Print Makers Society of California.

Ryder's personality and subject matter were similar. Both were unpretentious, yet recognizable and consistently original. Ryder was proper and dignified and derived deep satisfaction from art. He died in Wilton, New Hampshire. Art historian Ronald G. Pisano astutely observed that Ryder will be remembered "as being the artist who . . . successfully translated the American landscape into 20th-century terms."

• See "50th Ryder Reunion, Descendants of Colonel Stephen Ryder and Betsey Nichols, His Wife, Held at the Old Homestead, 'The Sycamores,' Pearch Lake, Town of Southeast Putnam County, New York State," with Chauncey F. Ryder, "An Approach to Art," 4–5 July 1937, in files at the Danbury Scott–Fanton Museum, Danbury, Conn. For correspondence and exhibitions, see Archives of American Art, Washington, D.C., microfilm rolls N106 (clippings and reproductions from the New York Public Library), NMc11, NMc44 (Macbeth files), P78 (Pa. Academy of Fine Arts records), and D195 (Sidney C. Woodward Papers). For Ryder's evolving style, see Ronald G. Pisano, "Chauncey Foster Ryder, Peace and Plenty," *American Art Antiques*, Sept.–Oct. 1978, pp. 76–83. For memberships and awards, see exhibition catalog *Chauncey F. Ryder, N.A., 1868–1949*, Pierce Galleries, Hingham, Mass. (1973). For reappreciation, see Patricia Pierce, "Chauncey F. Ryder, American Expressionist," *Antiques News*, 12 Jan. 1972, p. 3. For etchings and drypoint critique, see Leila Mechlin, "Drypoints and Lithographs on View at the Smithsonian," *Sunday Star* (Washington, D.C.), 6 Mar. 1927. For obituaries, see *Journal American* (N.Y.), 19 May 1949, and the *Boston Herald*, 19 May 1949.

PATRICIA JOBE PIERCE

RYLAND, Robert (14 Mar. 1805–23 Apr. 1899), educator and Baptist minister, was born in King and Queen County, Virginia, the son of Josiah Ryland and Catharine Peachey, farmers. When the elder Ryland divided up his land to give to each of his sons, Robert requested money from his father instead, so that he could pursue an education. Ryland enrolled at Humanity Hall Academy in Hanover County, Virginia, one of the growing number of schools established by Baptist educators to prepare local Baptist boys for entrance to college. From there he went directly to Columbian

College (now George Washington University) in Washington, D.C., where he graduated with the A.B., probably in 1826.

After graduation Ryland entered the ministry and became pastor at a small Baptist parish in Lynchburg, Virginia. He obtained his A.M. from Columbian in 1829. Meanwhile, he met and married Josephine Norvell in 1830; they had four children who survived to adulthood. After the death of his first wife in 1846, Ryland married Elizabeth Presley Thornton of Caroline County in 1848; they had three children.

Although his tiny church was flourishing, Ryland left Lynchburg in 1832 to move to Richmond because the Virginia Baptist Education Society had asked him to take charge of the newly established Virginia Baptist Seminary, which was to provide for the recruitment and training of competent Baptist ministers. When the school opened Ryland acted not only as president of the institution but also as its sole teacher and administrator, whose duties included the care and maintenance of the 220-acre farm on which the school was located. Members of the education society had decided that a program of manual labor on the farm, combined with academic study, would teach students the value of manual labor and responsibility as well as reduce school expenses. The work was never popular with students; Ryland eventually convinced the society that the concept was a failure.

Ryland was concerned primarily with providing a proper education for his students. He insisted on hiring a highly competent faculty and on presenting a challenging curriculum, with particular emphasis on the "fundamentals" of language, mathematics, history, and rhetoric. He pushed his students to develop strong habits of thinking and study and took to quizzing them on spelling and grammar at mealtimes. In 1835 he took advantage of the opportunity to further his own education by accepting a one-year post as chaplain at the University of Virginia.

By 1838, in an effort to improve the institution's financial situation, the education society applied for a charter of incorporation from the state of Virginia; the general assembly enacted this charter for the newly named Richmond College on 4 March 1840. Ryland remained on as president. To obtain this charter from the state, Richmond College became an institution of liberal arts, dropping compulsory theological instruction from the curriculum. Ryland wholeheartedly supported this move, maintaining that above all else Baptist churches should require their ministers to be learned. Education, Ryland concluded, constituted "the radical distinction between the civilized and the savage." Therefore, it was "the duty of everyone, first to cultivate his own mind, and then to help others in the same important object" (Ryland, *The Virginia Baptist Education Society*, p. 9).

Money remained a major concern for the new college, which faced difficult years in the 1840s. Ryland was untiring in his appeals to the citizens of Richmond, publicizing the college's past achievements and plans for the future. Under Ryland's leadership the college experienced much growth in the 1850s, both in number of students and in endowment.

In addition to his duties as president of Richmond College, Ryland became the first pastor of the First African Baptist Church in Richmond in 1841. Ryland was already overworked but agreed to take charge of the church because "he felt that all the ministers of Christ . . . were called on to put forth new efforts to evangelize the people of color" (Taylor, p. 353). Ryland used the pulpit to educate his congregation on the precepts of Christianity, seeking to replace their "superstitions" with Christian "doctrine." Himself a slaveholder, Ryland was at least once accused of using his position to promote abolitionism, but the local Baptist newspaper assured readers that Ryland spoke "favorably" of the institution of slavery. He served as pastor of the First African Baptist Church until 1865, when he insisted that his newly emancipated congregation would prefer a member of their own race to serve as their preacher.

During the Civil War Richmond College closed down. Federal troops occupied buildings, causing damage and delaying the reopening of the institution until 1866. While the college was closed Ryland spent much of his time ministering to the men in army camps and hospitals around Richmond. When it reopened, he tendered his letter of resignation, believing others would be more qualified to rebuild the college.

In 1867 Ryland assisted in opening the National Theological School (later known as Virginia Union University) in Richmond for the recruitment and training of black ministers. After only a year, however, Ryland moved to Shelbyville, Kentucky, to serve as president of the Shelbyville Female College there. Ryland had been among the first Baptists to take an interest in women's education, supporting as early as 1844 the establishment of a Baptist school for the education of females. After his tenure at Shelbyville, he moved around Kentucky, serving as president at female schools in Lexington and Newcastle and serving as pastor of various county or village churches. From 1893 to 1897 he was chaplain at the Southwest Virginia Institute at Bristol. He died two years later in Lexington, Kentucky.

Ryland's commitment to providing and directing quality higher education to a growing number and variety of students lasted the whole of his adult life. He also remained dedicated to his preaching but was never overzealous. He was widely respected by contemporaries and has remained well regarded for his devotion to his faith and his unending labor in the promotion of educational opportunity.

• Ryland's papers are located at the Virginia Baptist Historical Society, University of Richmond. The collection contains Ryland's published works, including numerous pamphlets, sermons, and addresses, as well as some personal letters and correspondence related to the administration of the seminary and Richmond College. Published works include *The Virginia Baptist Education Society: The Society, the Seminary, the College—an Address* (1891), which describes his activities as

president of the seminary and the college; *Lectures on the Apocalypse* (1857); *A Scripture Catechism for the Instruction of Children and Servants* (1848); and *Baptism for the Remission of Sins* (1836). Biographical sketches are available in George Braxton Taylor, *Virginia Baptist Ministers*, 4th ser. (1913); and Woodford Hackley, *Faces on the Wall: Brief Sketches of the Men and Women Whose Portraits and Busts Were on the Campus of the University of Richmond in 1955* (1955).

Reuben Alley, *History of the University of Richmond, 1830–1971* (1977), contains numerous references to Ryland, as does Alley, *A History of Baptists in Virginia* (1973), and Garnett Ryland, *The Baptists of Virginia, 1699–1926* (1955). Several articles by W. Harrison Daniel offer detailed accounts of the early years of Richmond College, including Ryland's role. See, for instance, "The Genesis of Richmond College, 1843–1860," *Virginia Magazine of History and Biography* 83 (1975): 131–49, and "The Virginia Baptist Seminary, 1832–1842," part 1, *Virginia Baptist Register* 9 (1970): 387–406.

MOLLY M. WOOD

RYSKIND, Morrie (20 Oct. 1895–24 Aug. 1985), librettist and screenwriter, was born in Brooklyn, New York, the son of Russian immigrants Abraham Ryskind, a cigar store operator, and Ida Etelson. Ryskind graduated from Townsend Harris Hall and went on to Columbia College, where his classmates included Lorenz Hart and Herman Mankiewicz. He was expelled from Columbia in 1917, only a short time before graduation, as a result of some verses satirizing university president Nicholas Murray Butler (or, as another source has it, for not learning to swim, a college requirement). While at college, he was a frequent contributor to "The Conning Tower," Franklin P. Adams's column in the *New York Tribune*, which specialized in light verse, quips, and amusing anecdotes. He also wrote frequently for two campus publications. He and Ira Gershwin occasionally wrote lyrics together for "The Conning Tower," and Ryskind was part of a circle surrounding Ira. The friendship with Ira and, later, with George Gershwin eventually led to their working together on several musicals. In 1921 Ryskind published a book of light verse, *Unaccustomed as I Am*.

Ryskind began his career in the theater by writing the lyrics to a song for Nora Bayes. He had been making his living as a journalist (he was a reporter for the *New York World* until 1921) with comic verse as his specialty. Ryskind drifted to the *New York Times* and soon began writing on the theater for drama editor George S. Kaufman. He devised skits for a 1922 show entitled *The Forty-Niners* (other contributors included Heywood Broun, Howard Dietz, Marc Connelly, Dorothy Parker, Robert Benchley, Ring Lardner, Franklin P. Adams, and Robert E. Sherwood, with the overall direction by Howard Lindsay). In 1925 Lorenz Hart asked him to write for the first edition of a revue called *Garrick Gaieties*, with lyrics mostly by Hart and music mostly by Richard Rodgers. Ryskind wrote two of the sketches for the show, one called "Mr. and Mrs." satirizing Calvin Coolidge and the other satirizing William Jennings

Bryan. The following year, Ryskind, the Gershwins, and others wrote parts of another revue, *Americana*.

Kaufman accepted some help from Ryskind in 1925 on his vehicle for the Marx Brothers, *Cocoanuts*, with music by Irving Berlin (in 1929 Kaufman and Ryskind wrote the screenplay for the film). In 1927 Ryskind and Dietz (still another college friend) wrote book and lyrics for *Merry-Go-Round*, which starred Libby Holman. The following year, Kaufman and Ryskind were librettists for a Marx Brothers show, *Animal Crackers* (the screenplay was later written by Ryskind alone).

Ryskind met and married Mary House in 1929, with Groucho Marx as best man. The Ryskinds had two children. The year of his marriage Ryskind also wrote lyrics for a show called *Ned Wayburn's Gambols*.

In 1927 George and Ira Gershwin and George S. Kaufman had worked on a satire on war, *Strike Up the Band*. However, the text was considered too sharply critical of the United States, and the musical died before arriving on Broadway. Ryskind was called in to make the satire more palatable; his alterations included a switch in the product (from cheese to chocolate) over which the United States and Switzerland go to war, and, to increase the element of fantasy, he made the war take place in a dream of the American manufacturer. *Strike Up the Band* achieved some success; starring Bobby Clark, it ran on Broadway for 191 performances. Ryskind was represented on Broadway in 1931 by two shows: *The Gang's All Here*, for which his colibrettists were Russel Crouse and Oscar Hammerstein II, and *Of Thee I Sing*. For the latter, a satire on American politics, George and Ira Gershwin wrote music and lyrics, and Kaufman and Ryskind the libretto. Ira Gershwin, Kaufman, and Ryskind were awarded a Pulitzer Prize for the show, the first time a musical had been so honored (George Gershwin did not receive a prize, since the Pulitzer committee felt the award was for literature, not music). The show added at least one word to the American political vocabulary—"Throttlebottom," the name given to a nearly anonymous, bumbling vice president. The Gershwins, Kaufman, and Ryskind wrote still another satire, *Let 'Em Eat Cake*, a sequel to *Of Thee I Sing*, in 1933. Ira Gershwin remarked of it, "If *Strike Up the Band* was a satire on War, and *Of Thee I Sing* one on Politics, *Let 'Em Eat Cake* was a satire on Practically Everything." Ryskind worked one last time with the Gershwins, on a musical called *Pardon My English* (1933), but when the producers introduced changes in the script, Ryskind had his name removed from it. The musical was unsuccessful. Next, Kaufman and Ryskind in 1934–1935 worked on a nonmusical satire (although there was one song for which Ryskind wrote the lyric); the play was a spoof of the New Deal and of the men who administered it. Even with Jack Benny as star, *Bring on the Girls* closed before reaching Broadway.

Almost all the rest of Ryskind's scripts were written for the screen, although he did return to Broadway to work with Irving Berlin on *Louisiana Purchase* in 1940 and to direct *The Lady Comes Across* in 1942. There also is a strong possibility that he wrote the book for a 1946 musical, *Nelly Bly*, with music by Jimmy Van Heusen.

In Hollywood, Ryskind began with Marx Brothers scripts—*A Night at the Opera* (1935) was especially notable—and was later nominated for Academy Awards for his screenplays for *My Man Godfrey* (1936) and *Stage Door* (1937). Other screenplays included *Palmy Days* (1931, with story by Eddie Cantor), *Ceiling Zero* (1935), *Room Service* (1938), *Man About Town* (1939), *Penny Serenade* (1941), *Claudia* (1943), and *It's in the Bag* (1945). The only film on which Kurt Weill and Ira Gershwin collaborated was *Where Do We Go from Here?* (1945), with a script by Ryskind.

Ryskind's politics turned more and more to the right during his Hollywood years, in part, he said, because Franklin D. Roosevelt ran for a third presidential term, an act that Ryskind believed was a threat to American democracy. In an appearance before the House Committee on Un-American Activities in 1947 he spoke of Communists in the Screen Writers Guild and felt that his testimony resulted in his being barred from work. Later, he published in the *Freeman* a parody of Kipling's "Fuzzy-Wuzzy," part of which read:

"So here's to you, Joe McCarthy, you're a swell
A-meri-can;
You're a terror to the traitors an' a first-class fightin'
man;
Oh, bless him for the enemies he's made!"

Ryskind's writing was now about politics, and he was an original director and writer for the *National Review*; he wrote for the Los Angeles Times Syndicate for eleven years and then for the *Los Angeles Herald Examiner*. He retired in 1978. He died in Crystal City, Virginia.

Ryskind is remembered primarily for the changes he and George S. Kaufman brought to the American musical. They expected to revolutionize the musical stage with their plot for *Of Thee I Sing*, in part because of its analysis of contemporary politics. But their work went even further with its tight integration of book, lyrics, and music. Ryskind's contribution to the American musical stage will be remembered for his biting satire on American politics.

• No biography of Ryskind has been published, but biographies of people he worked with frequently have extensive references to him. The best of these, in large part because the information is based on interviews with him, are *Fascinating Rhythm: The Collaboration of George and Ira Gershwin*, by Deena Rosenberg (1991), and Malcolm Goldstein's *George S. Kaufman, His Life, His Theatre* (1979). Howard Dietz knew Ryskind and makes helpful references to him in *Dancing in the Dark: An Autobiography* (1974). Howard Teichman offers some insight in *George S. Kaufman, an Intimate Portrait* (1972); also helpful is Ira Gershwin's *Lyrics on Several Occasions* (1973). The *New York Times* obituary, 25 Aug. 1985, gives a good outline of Ryskind's life and work.

JULIAN MATES

S

SAARINEN, Aline Bernstein (25 Mar. 1914–13 July 1972), art critic and historian, was born in New York City, the daughter of Allen Bernstein, an investment counselor, and Irma Lewyn. Both parents were amateur painters. Aline graduated from Vassar College as a member of Phi Beta Kappa in 1935. That same year she married Joseph H. Louchheim, a public welfare administrator; they had two children. Aline Louchheim received a master's degree in architectural history from New York University in 1939. During World War II she worked in governmental service.

Her first position in the arts was as a contributing essayist for the *Art News*, where she was hired in 1944 and promoted to managing editor in 1946. She wrote and edited articles concerning a wide range of contemporary issues, including painting, exhibitions, architectural projects, and the decorative arts. Aline Louchheim was known for her willingness to express firm and sometimes controversial, but well-supported, opinions and arguments.

In 1947 she moved to the *New York Times* as an associate art editor and associate art critic. She remained at these posts until 1959, at which time she left the newspaper. She had divorced Joseph Lochheim in 1951. Three years later she met Eero Saarinen, a prominent architect, and the two were married in 1954; they had one child. During her years of marriage to Eero Saarinen and just after his death in 1961, she worked to promote his architectural firm by continuing to write about him for various periodicals and by acting as editor of *Eero Saarinen on His Work* (1962), in which the architect gives statements on his building designs.

In 1958 Aline Saarinen's book titled *The Proud Possessors* was published, describing her research into the history of art collecting with a focus on the major collectors in the United States. She surveyed the interests, tastes, and collecting patterns of this country's most influential art buyers, including J. P. Morgan, Isabella Stewart Gardner, the Havemeyers, and the Rockefellers. Moreover, she analyzed the nature of each collection in depth, shedding light on the extraordinary contributions the collectors made in supporting American artists as well as bringing into the country important works by artists from all over the world. In the process of this survey, Saarinen drew original and daring conclusions about the psychology and nature of collecting and patterns of taste in Western culture. The book was both well-received by critics and commercially successful.

In 1962 Saarinen began her career as a personality in a new medium—television. As a television art critic, she continued her commitment to art education with careful and discerning commentary on art and archi-

tecture. She believed firmly in art as an important part of life and felt that it would enrich the lives of all those who came to learn about it. Her commentaries have been characterized as combining scholarly knowledge with a relaxed and easily understood presentation well suited to the broad audience of television.

Saarinen also appeared on the "Today" show and hosted an audience question-oriented talk show called "For Women Only," on which she dealt with a wide range of women's issues from civil rights to health. A year and a half before her death Saarinen was named the chief of the National Broadcasting Company's Paris news bureau, making her the first woman to hold that post. She died in 1972 from the effects of a brain tumor.

Saarinen received countless awards and honors for her contributions to the arts during her lifetime. She was also the recipient of numerous journalistic and academic awards, and President Lyndon B. Johnson offered her the position of ambassador to Finland. Saarinen made a significant contribution to the world of art and art criticism. Her success in bringing issues of art and life to the public audience are evidence of her commitment to education and understanding. As an assertive, intelligent woman, she was also a pioneer in breaking down gender barriers in the male-dominated fields of art, history, and the media.

• Saarinen's papers are at the Archives of American Art, Washington, D.C. Her published works include *The Proud Possessors: The Lives, Times and Tastes of Some Adventurous American Art Collectors* (1958), and *Jacob Lawrence* (1960). See also *New York Times Biographical Edition* 5, no. 3 (15 July 1972).

KENNIE LUPTON

SAARINEN, Eero (20 Aug. 1910–1 Sept. 1961), architect, was born in Kirkkonummi, Finland, the son of Eliel Saarinen, an architect, and Loja Gesellius, a sculptor, weaver, and photographer. Born into an artistic family, Saarinen was sketching and modeling from an early age. When he was twelve he won the first of many design awards, including first place in a matchstick design contest. Having moved with his family to Michigan in 1923, he returned to Europe to study sculpture at the Académie de la Grande Chaumière in Paris from 1929 to 1930. Saarinen began a four-year program at the School for Fine Arts of Yale University in 1931. He graduated in 1934 as the Charles and Margaret Ormrod Matcham Fellow, having complete his course work in just three years. Returning to Finland, in 1935 Saarinen joined the firm of Jare Eklund, where the young architect became better acquainted with the International style including the work of fellow Finn Alvaro Alto. In 1936 Saarinen settled back in the United States, first working as a draftsman in New York and then as a professor at Cranbrook Academy of Art in Michigan, where his father served as head of the program of architecture. At this time he joined his father's architectural firm with F. Robert Swanson, and the three worked closely together on a number of projects.

During the next four years Saarinen lived and worked at Cranbrook. In 1939 he married Lily Swann, a sculptor and native of New York; they had two children. He joined with another member of the staff at Cranbrook, Charles Eames, in developing chair designs using molded plywood techniques. Their entry won first prize in the Organic Design in Home Furnishings Competition of 1941 sponsored by the Museum of Modern Art in New York. The pieces that the two created were emblematic of their awareness and adoption of the utilitarian approach to design principles being promoted at the Bauhaus. Father and son collaborated on a number of projects before and during the Second World War, including the Berkshire Music Center (1938) in Tanglewood, Massachusetts; the Smithsonian Institution Art Gallery (1939) in Washington, D.C.; and the A. C. Weymouth House (1941–1942) in Fort Wayne, Indiana. By the end of World War II, during which he served with the Office of Strategic Studies in Washington, D.C., Eero Saarinen had assumed major responsibility in the Saarinen architectural firm from his aging father. By this time, however, the two were working in very different manners. Eero was heir to a different set of masters—Le Corbusier, Walter Gropius, and Frank Lloyd Wright—and a sense of the aesthetics of the industrial age. The younger Saarinen was by necessity affected by the new age of mass production, standardization, and machine efficiency in the twentieth century. This background moved him to design paths divergent from his father. When in 1948 the two separately entered a competition for the design of the Jefferson Expansion Memorial in St. Louis, it was Eero Saarinen who won first prize for his design of an arch of stainless steel that stretched 590 feet into the sky.

In designing the memorial, which was executed in the years 1959–1964 to a slightly redesigned height of 630 feet, Saarinen sought to create a structure of both timeless dignity and particular relevance to its own time. Of the design Saarinen said, "Lofty, dynamic, of permanent significance, the arch could be a proper visual center and focus for the park and, as 'The Gateway to the West', it could symbolize the spirit of the whole Memorial" (Saarinen, p. 22). Further consideration was given to the design of the area surrounding the arch, so that the river and the banks on both sides would reflect the overall spirit carried by the arch.

In winning the Jefferson Memorial competition, Saarinen unequivocally announced his arrival as a major force in international architecture. Following his father's death in 1950 Saarinen opened his own architectural firm, and for the next decade he received numerous important commissions. Among the first of these was the design of a Technical Center for General Motors in Warren, Michigan, a project with a then-unprecedented total budget of $100 million. Saarinen's work with General Motors had actually begun the previous decade in partnership with his father, and shortly before his father's death the enormous task was entrusted entirely to him. The enormous complex was completed in 1956 in conjunction with the firm of Smith, Hinchman & Grylls. The design features water fountains created by the sculptor Alexander Calder throughout the grounds. The buildings occupy more than a third of a nearly 1,000-acre plateau on which parklands, forests, and lakes surround and intermingle with the buildings.

Saarinen's design for the technical center was influenced by modernist architect Mies van der Rohe's design in its use of polished steel and dark glass to create direct lines and firm, sharp angles. Saarinen himself has acknowledged this debt, but he also stated that the buildings were descendent from the midwestern factories built by Albert Kahn. Although the rectilinear solidity of the General Motors complex seems removed from Saarinen's Jefferson Memorial and many of his later designs, it shares with all of his work the goal of creating structures that related directly to the nature of their purpose in both spirit and function. "General Motors," he said in 1961, "is a metal-working industry; it is a precision industry; it is a mass-production industry. All these things should, in a sense, be expressed in the architecture of its technical center" (Saarinen, p. 24). In 1953 Eero was divorced his from his first wife, Lily. In 1954 he married Aline B. Louchheim, an artist and writer on art and history; the two had one child.

During the next decade Saarinen created structures for a wide variety of purposes and clients. One of the first of these, underway while the General Motors complex was being constructed, was the Kresge Auditorium and Interdenominational Chapel (1950–1955) of the Massachusetts Institute of Technology (MIT) in Cambridge. The chapel's design reflects a radically different appearance than the buildings for General Motors. The domed roof of thin-shell concrete supported by a framework of glass and metal prefigured the structures of the late 1950s and 1960s for which Saarinen is best known. The exterior appearance of the auditorium, a bold design when it was created, was determined by both practical concerns and a desire for sculptural expression.

In the chapel Saarinen was faced with the unique task of creating an environment conducive to prayer but not determined by any one religion; as the chapel was nondenominational, the program called for a universally spiritual space. In one of his most creative solutions Saarinen employed dual natural light sources, one above the altar and one reflected up from the moat that surrounds the chapel. The exterior of the auditorium generated, like so many of Saarinen's designs, a great deal of criticism, both positive and negative. Saarinen's own reaction is indicative of his constant efforts to reassess and learn from his own previous work. While pleased with the interior of the auditorium and the chapel, in 1960 he spoke of what he perceived to be a failure to effectively synthesize the exterior with the surrounding environment. In light of these feelings, Saarinen sought to incorporate what he had learned from experience into a future overall court plan at MIT. (These plans were interrupted in 1961 by his death.)

Other commissions during the final decade of Saarinen's life included work for numerous universities including Drake University, the University of Chicago, Vassar College, the University of Pennsylvania, and his alma mater, Yale. Saarinen also executed civic and governmental structures. The most well known of these included the Milwaukee County War Memorial and the U.S. Embassy and Chancellery in Oslo. Additional designs were completed for important commercial concerns, such as IBM, Bell Telephone, and one of his most important designs, the Trans World Airlines terminal at Idlewild (later John F. Kennedy) Airport in New York City.

In addressing the TWA terminal Saarinen was faced, as always, with the task of creating a structure that derived from and simultaneously reflected the purpose for which it was intended. Saarinen also sought to make the centrally located terminal blend harmoniously with the surrounding landscape and provide a distinctive and "dramatic accent" (Saarinen, p. 60). Furthermore, he wanted to incorporate both the sensation and anticipatory excitement of travel into the design. Once again, he looked back to his MIT design, and he decided in contrast that he would seek a lighter, less gravity-bound building. Composed essentially of four intersecting barrel vaults, the TWA terminal was the product of exhaustive studies, schemes, and models. The resulting building was a dramatically expressive form reflecting Saarinen's goal of a structure characterized by spontaneous energy and a rigorous mathematical precision of harmonious relationships. Again, this work by Saarinen has created a large body of critical literature, but the inventiveness of Saarinen's approach has been little debated.

In 1958 Saarinen turned his attention to another design related to air travel, John Foster Dulles International Airport outside of Washington, D.C., in Chantilly, Virginia. The particular challenge in this case was to design the first airport in the world for strictly jet airplane traffic. Saarinen recognized that the movement of enormous number of passengers in a convenient and efficient manner was a necessity far beyond issues of aesthetics. He grappled with the changing needs of an industrial society that had evolved exponentially even since the beginning of his career. He and his assistants diligently researched the project, visiting numerous airports and engaging in technological research. Eventually, a unique system of "mobile lounges" that shuttled passengers to and from terminal and planes was developed. This was the key to Dulles's adaptability, allowing the structure to efficiently accommodate a greater number of gates and passengers as traffic grew. The final design of Dulles airport has been generally acknowledged to be Saarinen's

masterpiece, and he himself said, "I think this airport is the best thing I have done" (Saarinen, p. 96).

Saarinen died during brain surgery in Ann Arbor, Michigan. At this time he had a number of projects underway that were completed posthumously, including the construction of Dulles airport in 1963 and the Gateway Arch in 1964. Also among these was the Columbia Broadcasting System building in Manhattan, one of his few urban designs. In 1962 he was posthumously awarded the gold medal of the American Institute of Architects, the most prestigious recognition of its kind.

Saarinen died at the height of his architectural power. Given the constant growth and evolution in his innovative designs, many have concluded that he would have continued to create structures that continued to challenge and redefine the boundaries of modern architecture. Active in a number of city planning projects, including an ambitious design for Detroit, it has been further suggested that Saarinen would have been a vital participant in the urban development projects that have become widespread in the years after his death. Saarinen, who worked for most of his life in the United States, was one of this century's most innovative architects. He sought to unite the forms of the modernist tradition to which he was heir with a desire to create structures that would form a harmonious whole with the landscape that surrounded them. He also attempted to bring into form the essential spirit and character of the structures he created. Saarinen was a pioneer, not only in the aesthetics of architecture, but also in developing technologically advanced solutions to the many practical issues that faced him on his extensive commissions. His legacy of ingenuity and integrity in the field of architecture has been influential to subsequent generations.

• *Eero Saarinen on His Work* (1962) contains statements by Saarinen on a selection of buildings from 1947 to 1964 and was edited by his wife, Aline Saarinen. Among the best biographies of the architect is Allan Temko's *Eero Saarinen* (1962). For more information on Saarinen, see Rupert Spade, *Eero Saarinen* (1971); Robert A. Kuhner, *Eero Saarinen, His Life, His Work* (1975); and William Bainter O'Neal, *Eero Saarinen: A Bibliography* (1963). An obituary is in the *New York Times*, 3 July 1950.

KENNIE LUPTON

SAARINEN, Eliel (20 Aug. 1873–1 July 1950), architect, was born Gottlieb Eliel Saarinen in Rantasalmi, Finland, the son of Juho Saarinen, a pastor, and Selma Broms. Saarinen's youth was spent in the forests and open plains of rural Finland and the Ingermanland region of Russia. In school he studied sciences and languages and by his early teens had developed an interest in the arts. During breaks from school he frequented the Hermitage Museum in St. Petersburg and later referred to it as his "Mecca." Eventually he was enrolled in art school at Tammersfors, Finland, where his first interest was landscape painting and watercolors. Later he also took design courses and enrolled in the Polytechnical Institute in Helsinki, Finland.

In 1896 Saarinen joined with two classmates, Armas Lindgren and Herman Gesellius, to create an architectural firm. They did not wait long for success; in 1897, the year Saarinen graduated from architectural school, the new firm was awarded a major commission, the Tallberg apartments in Helsinki (1897). Business grew steadily, and as a team they designed numerous churches, factories, libraries, and office buildings, notably the Pohjola Insurance Company (1899–1900) in Helsinki, at numerous locations throughout Finland. The Finnish Pavilion for the 1900 Exposition in Paris (1899–1900), the project that established the firm's reputation, was built during this period. An important lesson for Saarinen during this era was his recognition of the notion of total design. His work began to take on new meaning as he struggled to create a harmonious whole by combining the architectural structure with the interior design, which was expressed through the furniture, the textiles, and in some cases the dishes designed for a specific structure. This concept of overall environmental design would prove to be one of the defining features of Saarinen's career.

In 1902 Saarinen, Gesellius, and Lindgren completed the construction of "Hvitträsk," a studio-home situated on a spectacular lake (Hvitträsk) surrounded by dense forest north of Helsinki. The architects lived and worked at Hvitträsk with their families. In 1904 Saarinen married Loja Gesellius, Herman's sister and a sculptor, weaver, and photographer; the couple would have two children, one of whom, Eero Saarinen, would become an outstanding member of the second generation of modern American architects. The partnership between Saarinen, Gesellius, and Lindgren dissolved in 1905, but Saarinen remained partners with Gesellius alone until 1907. The Saarinens remained at Hvitträsk until their relocation to the United States.

One of Saarinen, Gesellius, and Lindgren's most important creations was the Helsinki Railway Station, which remains a landmark in Finnish architecture. The firm was awarded the commission in 1904 based on their design, which eventually was completed by Saarinen alone, at least through 1910. The challenge of the railway station was essentially a modern one—to express the new modes and speed of transportation for ever-growing numbers of passengers in an aesthetically satisfying yet functional structure. Saarinen's solution to the problem was one that rejected many of the traditions of stations he had seen while traveling in Europe to research his task. He renounced the traditions of nineteenth-century eclecticism (and its successor, the national romantic style of Finland that he had helped to establish) by designing a clean-lined vertical tower surrounded by strongly proportioned horizontal masses. Construction on the Helsinki Railway Station was finished in 1914. Greeted with enormous international acclaim, it established Saarinen's reputation both as an architect and as a civic planner.

Between 1907 and 1923, Saarinen became an important member of the European art and design community. Professionally, he was engaged in an ever-increasing number of architectural and civic projects, both private and public. As a city planner, Saarinen was compelled by the political and social ideas of the English utopian socialists as well as the artistic and technical concepts of Austrian Camillo Sitte. Combining medieval and baroque organizational principles into designs with strong central axes and formal waterways, he created town plans for Canberra (1912) and greater Helsinki (1910–1918) among other locales during this period; with the exception of portions of the Mukkiniemi-Haaga design (1910–1915) for Helsinki, however, none were realized. Later in his career, Saarinen would use his city plans to form the basis for his 1943 manifesto on urban planning, *The City: Its Growth, Its Decay, Its Future*. Socially, at this time, he and his wife met and entertained numerous important artists and literary figures, including Maxim Gorky, Gustav Mahler, and art historian Julius Meier-Graefe.

In 1922 Saarinen placed second in the famed competition to design the Chicago Tribune Building; though never built, his drawings influenced later architects of skyscrapers in New York and Chicago. Encouraged by his new-found fame in the United States and affected by postwar depression in his native Finland, Saarinen chose to immigrate. By the fall of 1923 the Saarinens had settled in Ann Arbor, Michigan, where he took a faculty position at the University of Michigan. Over the next few years he became deeply engaged in his new educational tasks as well as in designing development plans for the Flint Civic Center (1937–1944) and the Detroit Cure Center (1938–1951), both in Michigan. Most importantly, however, he began, in 1925, to plan what would be his landmark achievement in the United States, a series of structures for the Cranbrook Foundation in Bloomfield Hills, Michigan (a Detroit suburb). These would include his own residence (1928–1929), the Cranbrook School for Boys (1924–1930), the Kingswood School for Girls (1929–1930), the Cranbrook Institute of Sciences (1931–1933), and the Cranbrook Museum and Library (1940–1943). Together these complexes form his definitive statement on the harmonious synthesis of architecture and interior design with the environment that surrounds them. The unprecedented unity of forms that Saarinen sought to establish at Bloomfield Hills can be seen as an extension of his long-held interest in civic planning. Here, and in many other commissions in the years to come, Saarinen worked cooperatively with designers to integrate interior and exterior, just as the architecture was to become joined with the environment. Participants in many of these projects included Loja Saarinen, an accomplished weaver, and the Swedish sculptor Carl Milles.

For the next two decades, until his death in Bloomfield Hills, Saarinen continued to be active in architecture and design. Eero Saarinen joined with him in the late 1930s to create the firm Saarinen, Swanson and Saarinen. Important collaborative commissions for the two included the Berkshire Music Center (1938) in Tanglewood, Massachusetts; the Crow Island School (1939–1940) in Winnetka, Illinois, with Perkins,

Wheeler and Will; and the First Christian Church of Columbus, Indiana (1939–1940). Eliel Saarinen also served as president of the Cranbrook Academy of Art (1932–1942) and as the head of its architecture program. He committed enormous time and energy to his role as an educator at Cranbrook, exerting a lasting influence on a new generation of artists and designers, including F. Robert Swanson, Charles and Ray Eames, and Harry Bertoia.

Apart from constant supervision of his firm's architectural projects, Saarinen sat on the juries of numerous design and architecture competitions and lectured on art and architecture before European as well as American audiences. In 1935 he was elected to the chairmanship of the American Institute of Architects' City and Regional Planning Committee. His models and designs were featured in numerous exhibitions, both national and international, and many of these exhibitions also featured his wife's work. He received numerous honorary doctorates as well as architecture and design awards on three continents, and in 1947 he was awarded the Gold Medal by the American Institute of Architects.

Eliel Saarinen was a contemporary of Frank Lloyd Wright and a member of the first generation of architects whose structures reflected profound changes in the materials, forms, and purposes of architecture as required by a rapidly modernizing world. Though neither as instrumental as Wright nor as innovative as his son Eero, Saarinen made substantial contributions to the field of international architecture, particularly in his designs of the Helsinki Railroad Station and the Chicago Tribune Building. Significantly, he was the first to turn the world's attention to the art and architecture of his native Finland, thus laying the foundation for the extraordinary influence later Finnish architects and artists such as Alvaro Alto would have on twentieth-century design. Known also as a theorist, Saarinen's influential ideas about total design were articulated vividly in the classroom and in written expositions of theory—most notably *Search for Form in Art and Architecture* (1985), first published as *Search for Form* (1948)—as well as in structures and drawings. His innovations in urban design maintained their relevance long after their formulation. More than fifty years of work established a legacy that spanned many facets of creativity.

• For more information on Saarinen see Albert Christ-Janer, *Eliel Saarinen: Finnish-American Architect and Educator* (1979), and note in particular the book's introduction written by Eero Saarinen. See also Lamia Doumato, *Eliel Saarinen, 1873–1950* (1980), and Marika Hausen, *Eliel Saarinen: Projects, 1896–1923* (1990). Cranbrook Academy of Art has published a number of works on Saarinen's role in the design of that institution; among the most comprehensive is Eliel Saarinen's *Saarinen Door: Eliel Saarinen, Architect and Designer at Cranbrook* (1963). An obituary is in the *New York Times*, 3 July 1950.

KENNIE LUPTON

SABATH, Adolph Joachim (4 Apr. 1866–6 Nov. 1952), U.S. congressman, was born in Zabori, Bohemia, the son of Joachim Sabath, a butcher, and Barbara Eissenschimmel. The Sabaths were a Jewish family in an overwhelmingly Catholic town. Adolph earned enough money by working as a store clerk to immigrate to the United States by himself at age fifteen. After settling in Chicago, he worked at a variety of jobs, including as a real estate agent selling property to immigrants. Sabath decided to become a lawyer. In 1885 he graduated from Bryant and Stratton Business College, and in 1891 he received an LL.B. from Lake Forest University. That same year he was admitted to the bar.

Sabath's interest in law and his desire to reform the corrupt practices of the city's aldermen led him first into local Chicago politics and ultimately into national politics. In 1895 he was appointed justice of the peace by reform governor John Peter Altgeld, and in 1897 he became a police magistrate. From 1896 until 1944 Sabath was a delegate to every Democratic National Convention. In 1906, after ten years as a local magistrate, he was elected as a Democrat to the U.S. House of Representatives for the Fifth District in Chicago. It was the first of his twenty-four consecutive elections to the House. One of Sabath's first appointments was to the Immigration and Naturalization Committee.

Immigration became the most consistent and important issue of Sabath's long congressional career. In his maiden speech, given in December 1907, he praised immigration, and he never tired of trying to hold the door open for any who might desire to make the United States home. He led the fight against restrictive literacy test immigration bills in 1913 and again in 1916–1917. In 1913 Sabath led the successful fight to keep Congress from overriding President Woodrow Wilson's veto. The same scenario replayed itself in 1916–1917, but (this time) he was unable to stem the anti-immigration tide as Congress overrode the president's veto. In 1917 Sabath married Mae Ruth Fuerst. They had no children.

Sabath championed numerous other issues, causes, and candidates that were important to urban liberals of his day. An enthusiastic supporter of Democratic president Wilson, Sabath favored woman suffrage, cast his vote in favor of Wilson's April 1917 request for a declaration of war, became an ardent supporter of the League of Nations in 1919, and voted for a constitutional amendment to eliminate child labor. During the conservative 1920s, he unsuccessfully opposed Prohibition and immigration restriction, and he sought to heal relations between the United States and the Soviet Union.

Given Sabath's keen interest in immigration issues, he was predictably troubled by efforts in Congress in the 1920s to enact restrictive immigration legislation—first a temporary bill in 1921 that severely curtailed immigration, then, a permanent measure in 1924 that deliberately skewed allowable immigration to favor northern and western Europeans over southern and eastern Europeans. During the House debate over the

1924 bill, Sabath sharply attacked its eugenic assumptions:

The obvious purpose of this discrimination, however much it may be disavowed, is the unfounded anthropological theory that the nations which are favored are the progeny of fictitious and hitherto unsuspected Nordic ancestors, while those discriminated against are not classified as belonging to that mythical ancestral stock. No scientific evidence worthy of consideration was introduced to substantiate this pseudoscientific proposition. (*Congressional Record*, 68th Cong., 1st sess., 1924, vol. 65, pt. 6, p. 5578)

With the onset of the Great Depression of the 1930s, Sabath turned his attention to other, more pressing problems. Highly critical of Republican president Herbert Hoover, he wholeheartedly supported the presidential candidacy of Franklin Delano Roosevelt in 1932. When Roosevelt won, Sabath became one of the New Deal's staunchest congressional supporters. "In Franklin Roosevelt," Sabbath said, "I found a true leader of the people, one with the people, the exponent of the common man, and I fought with all my strength for his ideals and for his legislative recommendations" (*Congressional Record*, 79th Cong., 2d sess., 1946, vol. 92, pt. 3, p. 3571).

Throughout the 1930s, Sabath enthusiastically supported almost all of the major relief and reform measures favored by Roosevelt, particularly the Social Security Act, the Wagner Labor Relations Act, the formation of the Securities and Exchange Commission, and the Federal Deposit Insurance Corporation. Under the seniority system, Sabath became the chairman of the powerful Rules Committee in 1939. By this time opposition (within Congress) to the New Deal had grown so powerful that Sabath used the power of his chairmanship principally to block conservative legislation.

As the international situation deteriorated in the late 1930s, Sabath changed from a nonmilitaristic outlook to supporting a U.S. preparedness effort. Warned by friends and relatives in his homeland, he began speaking out on the dangers of Adolf Hitler and fascism. He supported a repeal of the ban on arming ships, the arms embargo, and the Lend-Lease Act of 1941. After the United States entered the world conflict in December 1941, Sabath proposed a national lottery as a means of paying for the war effort. As the war came to an end, he supported the formation of the United Nations, the World Court, the International Monetary Fund, and the World Bank.

In the postwar era, Sabath continued to fight for humanitarian and civil libertarian principles. Accordingly, in 1945 he renewed an earlier fight to defund the House Un-American Activities Committee, and in 1948 he urged Congress and President Harry Truman to support the foundation of a Jewish homeland in Palestine. He also unsuccessfully fought against the constitutional amendment to limit the president's tenure to two terms. He generally supported Truman's attempts to implement the Fair Deal program of labor reform, civil rights, public housing, medical care, and agricultural subsidies.

In 1952, at age eighty-six, Sabath ran for reelection but became ill during the campaign and was hospitalized. He won the election despite his illness. Two days after election to his twenty-fourth consecutive term, he died at the Bethesda Naval Hospital, Bethesda, Maryland.

• Sabath's papers are at the American Jewish Archives in Cincinnati, Ohio. For the best synopsis of his legislative record, see two articles by Burton A. Boxerman, "Adolph Joachim Sabath in Congress: The Early Years, 1907–1932," *Journal of the Illinois State Historical Society* 66 (Autumn 1973): 327–40, and "Adolph Joachim Sabath in Congress: The Roosevelt and Truman Years," *Journal of the Illinois State Historical Society* 66 (Winter 1973): 428–43. An older source that gives more detail about his personal and professional life is John R. Beal, "Adolph J. Sabath: 'Dean of the House,'" in *Public Men in and out of Office*, ed. John Thomas Salter (1946). For some insight into how his colleagues on both sides of the political aisle felt about him, see *Memorial Services Held in the House of Representatives of the United States, Together with Remarks Presented in Eulogy of Adolph Joachim Sabath, Late a Representative from Illinois* (1953). Obituaries are in the *New York Times*, 7 Nov. 1952, and *Time* and *Newsweek*, both 17 Nov. 1952.

MARK N. MORRIS

SABIN, Albert Bruce (26 Aug. 1906–3 Mar. 1993), physician, scientist, and research immunologist, was born near Bialystok, Russia (now Poland), the son of Jacob Sabin and Tillie Krugman, silk weavers. Sabin immigrated with his family to the United States in 1919, settling first in Patterson, New Jersey. His collegiate career began with the study of dentistry at New York University, but William H. Park, his professor in bacteriology, soon convinced him to shift to medicine. Sabin entered the College of Medicine at New York University in 1927 and received an M.D. in 1931. While attending medical school he began his research activity as a research associate in the Department of Bacteriology at NYU and published some ten papers on pneumonia in leading medical journals. During this period he developed a rapid typing method that became the standard for testing the pneumonia bacterium. He obtained his U.S. citizenship in 1930.

Following graduation, Sabin served as house physician at Bellevue Hospital, New York City. In that year there was a major polio epidemic in that city, and Sabin was recruited by his old mentor, William Park, to assist in the ongoing polio research work, the field in which he would eventually make his greatest contributions to medicine. In 1934 he was awarded a National Research Council fellowship, and he joined the staff at the Lister Institute of Preventive Medicine in London. On his return to the United States at the end of 1935, he became a member of the research staff of the Rockefeller Institute for Medical Research in New York City, where he continued his investigative work on polio and other viral diseases. In 1936 Sabin, working with Peter Olitsky, became the first to successfully cultivate the polio virus in vitro.

In 1939 Sabin left New York to join the research staff of the Children's Hospital Research Foundation at the University of Cincinnati as fellow and associate professor of pediatrics at the College of Medicine of the University of Cincinnati. This dual appointment afforded him the opportunity to combine research studies with a hospital unit and his own patient group, enabling him to correlate laboratory and clinical findings. He rose to the rank of professor of research pediatrics in 1946, Distinguished Service Professor in 1960, and finally to Emeritus Distinguished Service Professor in 1971. During the first two years in Cincinnati, Sabin published a seminal paper titled "Natural History of Poliomyelitis," which proved crucial for the ultimate discovery of its prevention.

Having focused his research on infectious diseases (particularly immunity to viruses, the nature of inherited resistance to viruses, and the behavior of viruses in the central nervous system), Sabin was made a member of the U.S. Army Epidemiological Board's Commission on Virus and Rickettsial Diseases at the onset of World War II. In 1943 he became an officer in the Army Medical Corps, attached to the Preventive Medicine Division of the surgeon general's office; he eventually rose to the rank of lieutenant colonel. In that capacity he carried out research on encephalitis, sandfly fever, and dengue fever, and was sent on special missions to Egypt, Palestine, Sicily, Okinawa, and the Philippines.

At the end of the war Sabin returned to the University of Cincinnati and to the Children's Hospital Research Foundation, where his primary research focus turned again to poliomyelitis. Polio epidemics in this country and abroad were frequent and severe. Because of his previous research endeavors and his wartime experiences with a variety of viral diseases, according to John R. Paul in his *A History of Poliomyelitis*, "few people in the early 1950s had more experience in trials in man of both killed and live virus vaccines in a number of infections than Albert Sabin." One of the few researchers that rivaled Sabin was Jonas Salk, head of a virus research laboratory at the University of Pennsylvania. Salk and his group directed their efforts toward the development of a formalin inactivated polio vaccine, a procedure first successfully demonstrated in monkeys by Isabel Morgan in 1951. By 1953 Salk had developed an inactivated virus vaccine for use in humans.

Sabin, on the other hand, was convinced that the killed-virus approach could not protect humans as effectively as a live, attenuated virus vaccine. At a meeting of the National Foundation for Infantile Paralysis in Hershey, Pennsylvania, in January 1953, Salk reported his findings and petitioned the NFIP for permission to begin field testing his new vaccine. Sabin spoke out in opposition to the killed-virus vaccine, urging prolonged testing before the release of the vaccine for general human use. In October 1953 Sabin served as witness at a congressional committee hearing, reasserting his doubts about the safety of the Salk vaccine. In spite of his opposition, Sabin learned that the NFIP fully supported Salk's vaccine, and field testing on a small group of human volunteers began in 1954. By 1955 the tests proved successful; Salk's vaccine became available for inoculation of the general public.

This was a bitter disappointment for Sabin, who remained convinced that a live, oral vaccine was the preferred immunization route for the prevention of polio. He had isolated poliovirus clones and had demonstrated that they multiplied in the intestinal tracts of chimpanzees without causing paralysis of the central nervous system in the animals. In spite of the NFIP's success with the Salk vaccine, the foundation remained interested in Sabin's work and continued to promote his research with a live, attenuated vaccine. By 1954 he had developed a vaccine, a weakened live strain of all three types of polio virus to be ingested on a sugar cube. Sabin had successfully used it in a few human subjects of which he was the first. He had presented his findings and arguments at the New York meeting of the Immunization Committee of the National Foundation of Infantile Paralysis/March of Dimes in December 1954. Between 1954 and 1957 extensive studies were carried out on the mode of action of these attenuated strains of poliovirus on volunteers at the Federal Reformatory in Chillicothe, Ohio. From 1957 to 1959 cooperative studies were undertaken in the United States, Mexico, Holland, the Soviet Union, Malaysia, and Czechoslovakia. Because of the success of these field trials, a major trial involving six million children and adults was undertaken in the USSR in 1959. The success of these trials led the Soviet government to accept the vaccine for general use. During the first six months of 1960, the vaccine was given to some seventy-seven million persons under the age of twenty-one in the Soviet Union.

The first field trials in the United States were undertaken on 24 April 1960 in Cincinnati, Ohio. Some 20,000 persons were administered the free immunization—a sugar cube soaked with the cherry-flavored vaccine. Other field trials followed in the United States. By June 1961, the American Medical Association recommended mass inoculation of the oral vaccine for the entire U.S. population as soon as enough vaccine was available. In August 1961 the United States Public Health Service approved the oral vaccine for use in the United States. On "Sabin Sundays" between 1962 and 1964 over 100 million persons in the United States were administered the free vaccine. In his rivalry with Salk, Sabin lost the race to be the first to introduce a polio vaccine; but ultimately Sabin prevailed. By the mid-1960s the Sabin vaccine had superseded the Salk vaccine as the preferred polio immunization throughout most of the world. By the end of the twentieth century, all pediatric immunization protocols recommended the use of the Sabin vaccine as the immunization of choice; the Salk vaccine was used only in a few medical conditions in which the use of a live vaccine is contraindicated.

In recognition of his achievements, Sabin received 120 honors and citations from around the world, including the Legion of Merit, U.S. Army (1945); the Robert Koch Medal of the Koch Foundation, West Germany (1963); Order of Merit of Bavaria (1964); Liceaga Gold Medal, Mexico (1964); Albert Lasker Clinical Medicine Research Award (1965); Grand Cross of Argentina (1967); Order of the Sacred Treasure of Japan (1968); Royal Society of Health Gold Medal, England (1969); U.S. National Medal of Science (1970); Distinguished Civilian Service Medal, U.S. Army (1973); and the United States Medal of Liberty (1986).

Following his retirement from the University of Cincinnati in 1970, Sabin served as president of the Weizmann Institute of Science in Israel (1970–1972), consultant to the National Cancer Institute of the U.S. Public Health Service (1974), Distinguished Professor of Biomedicine at the College of Medicine of the University of South Carolina (1974–1982), and consultant at the Fogarty International Center for Advanced Studies in the Health Sciences of the National Institutes of Health in Washington, D.C. (1984–1986). Although he had suffered an ascending spinal paralyzing illness in 1983, he had partially recovered. However, progressive heart failure led to increasing disability and forced complete retirement in 1988. He died of heart failure in Washington, D.C.

Sabin was married three times. In 1935 he married Sylvia Tregillus, with whom he had two daughters; she died in 1966. A second, brief marriage to Jane B. Warner in 1970 ended in divorce in 1971. In 1972 he married Heloisa Dunshee de Branchis; they had no children. He described himself as a political independent whose leisure time interests included symphonic music and travel. Historian John R. Paul observed that "no man has contributed so much effective information—and so continuously over so many years—to so many aspects of poliomyelitis, as Sabin."

• The Cincinnati Medical Heritage Center is the repository of the Sabin Archives, which includes five hours of oral history videotapes and copies of his curriculum vita, as well as his awards, medals, and honorary diplomas. John R. Paul, *A History of Poliomyelitis* (1971), contains a large section devoted to Sabin and his work. Short biographies can be found in *Who's Who in America* (1986–1987) and in Cecil Roth and Geoffrey Wigoder, eds., *Encyclopedia Judaica* (1971). An obituary is in the *New York Times*, 4 Mar. 1993.

STANLEY L. BLOCK

SABIN, Ellen Clara (29 Nov. 1850–2 Feb. 1949), educator and college president, was born in Sun Prairie, Wisconsin, the daughter of Samuel H. Sabin and Adelia Bordine, farmers. As a young child Sabin moved with her family to a farm in Windsor, Wisconsin, where she attended the district school. In 1866 she entered the University of Wisconsin. Although she did not graduate, Sabin began teaching at a country school near Sun Prairie while still a student herself. Believing in the importance of parental involvement, she often invited parents to participate in the geography lesson when they arrived with their children in the morning. Her use of parental participation in daily lessons re-

sulted in an invitation to present this successful teaching approach at the state teachers' convention. This recognition led to a teaching position in the Sun Prairie Grade School in 1868. The next year Sabin moved to Madison, Wisconsin, to teach seventh grade and within a year became principal of the Fourth Ward School. She left that position in 1872 to accompany her family in their move to Oregon.

Hoping to provide educational opportunities for his children, Samuel Sabin settled his family in Eugene, Oregon, the rumored site of the future state university. Since only a "dilapidated building in a sea of mud" served as the district school, Sabin established her own school in 1872 and enrolled thirty students in the first year. Her abilities as an educator came to the attention of Oregon officials when she addressed the state teachers' convention about her teaching methods. Sabin declined an offer to become state superintendent of schools in 1873, feeling that she was not ready for the responsibility. She accepted instead a teaching position in the Old North School of Portland and became its principal a year later. Identifying dirt and discipline as two of the major problems at the school, Sabin cultivated the cooperation and loyalty of students, families, and businesses in her efforts to deal with these concerns. She substituted whipping as the chief means of punishment with a large, black book in which she recorded student infractions. After the second offense, Sabin contacted parents, counting on them to participate in disciplining the child. She referred to her black book when employers sought prospective workers among her former students, thus encouraging students to keep their names out of the book. Following a year's leave of absence to travel in Europe, Sabin agreed in 1887 to become superintendent of the Portland schools, the first woman to hold such a job in a large, urban school system.

In June 1890 Sabin accepted the offer of the Downer College Board of Trustees to become president of their small school in Fox Lake, Wisconsin. Although the move meant a large reduction in Sabin's salary, Downer trustees agreed to her request that they "back her plans and in no way hamper her." When school officials merged the struggling Downer College with Milwaukee College in 1897, Sabin became president of Milwaukee-Downer College, a position she held until her retirement in 1921.

Despite having earned her reputation in elementary education, Sabin played a pivotal role in promoting women's higher education in Milwaukee. Emphasizing the importance of liberal arts training, she noted in her 1920 commencement address that she had constantly fostered "sound academic studies" and that she "would allow nothing to impair the cultural disciplines of the languages, literature, social sciences, pure science and philosophy." She was, nevertheless, determined not to create "recluses or bluestockings," but instead to train Downer students to take their places at the head of homes and to be self-supporting if necessary. Sabin also incorporated into the curriculum "concepts of utility and service to the broader civic community." Under her leadership the Downer curriculum developed courses in home economics, occupational therapy, and nursing as well as the traditional liberal arts.

During her term as Downer College president and in her retirement years, Sabin was active in numerous organizations, including the National Council of Education, the General Federation of Women's Clubs, and the Association of Collegiate Alumnae (predecessor to the American Association of University Women). In 1929 the Wisconsin State Branch of the AAUW established a fellowship fund in her honor. She was also a member of the Wisconsin State Board of Education from 1919 to 1923. A staunch Republican, she served in the Milwaukee County League of Women Voters and the Women's Club of Wisconsin. After her retirement, Sabin lived briefly in Milwaukee, Lake Mills, Wisconsin, and finally moved to Madison, Wisconsin, to live with her sister. Sabin died in Madison and was buried in Windsor, Wisconsin.

• Sabin's papers are part of the Milwaukee-Downer College Papers 1852–1964, which are housed at the Milwaukee Area Research Center, Golda Meir Library, University of Wisconsin-Milwaukee. For additional biographical information see Grace N. Kieckhefer, *Milwaukee-Downer College History, 1851–1951* (1950; located in the Milwaukee-Downer Papers); Walter Peterson, "Ellen Sabin: Educator," *Historical Messenger* 26 (Mar. 1970): 24; Neita Oviatt Friend, "Ellen Clara Sabin and My Years at Downer," *Wisconsin Magazine of History* 59 (Spring 1976): 179–91; Estelle Pau on Lau, *Ellen C. Sabin: Proponent of Higher Education for Women* (1978); Virginia Palmer, ed., "Faithfully Yours, Ellen C. Sabin," *Wisconsin Magazine of History* 67 (Autumn 1983): 17–41; Janice M. Leone, "The Mission of Women's Colleges in an Era of Cultural Revolution, 1890–1930" (Ph.D. diss., The Ohio State Univ., 1989). Obituaries are in the *Milwaukee Journal*, 2 Feb. 1949, and the *Chicago Tribune* and the *New York Times*, 3 Feb. 1949.

JANICE M. LEONE

SABIN, Florence Rena (9 Nov. 1871–3 Oct. 1953), physician and medical researcher, was born in Central City, Colorado, the second of two daughters of George K. Sabin, a mining engineer, and Serena Miner. Both parents had migrated west from Vermont in the 1860s. Florence's sister, Mary, remembered a happy childhood full of parental warmth and independent exploration, but Florence's home life was disrupted when her mother died of puerperal fever after giving birth to a son, who lived only a few months. Unable to care for the girls himself, their father boarded them at a private Episcopal school in Denver. Fortunately, the following year the sisters were sent to live with their uncle Albert in Chicago, where Florence stayed for the next four years. A teacher and lover of music, nature, and good reading, this warm and urbane New Englander gave her the security and encouragement she had lost upon her mother's death. His influence remained with her throughout her life. Long after Sabin had received her medical degree, a quotation sent by her uncle remained pinned over her desk in the laboratory. It

read, "Jehovah never did a finer thing than when he turned Adam and Eve out of the Garden of Eden and said, 'Children, get busy!'"

Sabin had always intended to become a musician, but when an overfrank fellow student at the Vermont Academy, a preparatory school for girls that she attended as a teen, told her she would never amount to more than an ordinary pianist, she gave up the instrument in favor of academic studies. In 1889 she entered Smith College, which her sister also attended, where she excelled academically, particularly in science. By 1890 the prestigious women's colleges had begun the ambitious recruitment of women faculty with advanced degrees, and they provided an excellent education, especially to those who sought scientific training. Sabin joined the Colloquium, a group of twenty-five students who met for weekly discussion with the science professors, but she remained a shy loner in college. Acutely conscious of her plain looks, she seems never to have anticipated marriage and a family for herself. Indeed, her papers bear no evidence of any romantic interest during college or later.

In 1892 medical school was still the most logical choice for a woman like Sabin, whose serious interest in the biological sciences was matched by an equally sober desire for a useful career. The Ph.D. was only just beginning to become more accessible to women, and careers in full-time laboratory research—even for men—were largely a thing of the future.

Vassar's resident physician, a graduate of the Woman's Medical College of the New York Infirmary, urged Sabin to apply to Johns Hopkins, which was about to admit its first class, with women accepted on the same basis as men. Sabin's father and sister were unwilling to make the financial sacrifices necessary for medical school, however, and after graduation Sabin taught school for three years until she had accumulated the funds to enter Johns Hopkins in 1896. She became one of fourteen women in a class of forty-five.

Women still had to prove themselves at Hopkins, and most of them knew it. An outstanding student, Sabin ranked third in her class and, along with Dorothy Reed Mendenhall, won a coveted internship under William Osler at Johns Hopkins Hospital in 1900. But the year was a difficult one. Unlike Mendenhall, who relished defending herself, Sabin shrunk from the occasional hazing and gradually came to believe that she was unsuited for clinical practice. After a few months, she complained to her sister, "I don't seem to work well under pressure. I need a calm and placid atmosphere. . . . I never get time to do research" (Bleumel, p. 46).

Sabin's internship year was the last that she spent in full-time clinical medicine. Her originality, accuracy, and skill in the laboratory had attracted the attention of several faculty members, especially Franklin P. Mall, probably the greatest American anatomist and the most outstanding scientist at Hopkins. A product of the great German university tradition in scientific medicine, Mall displayed a passionate commitment to the pursuit of science for its own sake and to the importance of stimulating students to independent investigation. Many found Mall cold and unapproachable, but born researchers like Sabin were inspired. While still a medical student under his guidance, she had become the first to construct a three-dimensional model of the brain stem of a newborn. This early work was published as *An Atlas of the Medulla and Midbrain* in 1901 and was widely used as a textbook thereafter.

Although Sabin's early promise made her a likely candidate for a teaching position, the Hopkins faculty proved reluctant to hire a woman. In 1902 the Baltimore feminist community managed to secure Sabin a research fellowship from the Naples Table Association, an organization dedicated to promoting scientific research by women. After the publication of two outstanding papers, however, Sabin's talent could no longer be ignored, and a year later she became the first woman faculty member at Johns Hopkins, an assistant in the Department of Anatomy.

For the next twenty-three years Sabin distinguished herself as a researcher in embryology and histology. Her most important work was in the origins of blood cells and the lymphatics. She demonstrated that they formed directly from the veins in the embryo, discrediting an older theory claiming that they originated from tissue. She is also credited with popularizing the important technique of supra vital staining. She was an inspiring teacher with a keen eye for the gifted student. But the young scientists she worked with most closely were all men. Supportive of other women physicians, she never managed to attract a woman to follow in her footsteps. Perhaps the increasing numbers of educated women in the twentieth century seeking to balance marriage and a career found her an inappropriate role model. Sabin practiced a quiet, good-natured brand of feminism but always remained unwilling to make her gender an issue. "Women," she once remarked, "get exactly what they deserve in this world and needn't think they are discriminated against; they can have whatever they are willing to work for" (Bleumel, p. 44).

Sabin remained reluctant to recognize sex bias even when it affected her own career. In 1917 the death of Franklin Mall left the chair of the anatomy department vacant. To the shock of almost everyone, Sabin was passed over for promotion in favor of Lewis Weed, one of her former students. When friends threatened to protest, she was hastily appointed professor of histology, the first full-time woman professor on the faculty. Throughout this incident she kept her own counsel, remaining at Hopkins for another seven years. Only in 1925 did she leave her beloved alma mater, when Simon Flexner enticed her to join the Rockefeller Institute as head of a section on cellular immunology, the first woman to receive a full membership. Probably no early twentieth-century institution better defined modern scientific medical professionalization than the New York–based institute, which focused its resources on experimental work in chemistry, biology, pathology, bacteriology, physiology, pharmacology, and experimental surgery. That same year Sabin became the first woman elected to the National Academy of Sciences, as only a year before she had become the first woman president of the American Association of Anatomists.

Sabin's thirteen years in New York were happy and productive, but in 1938 the Rockefeller Institute began to enforce its retirement policy. At sixty-seven, Sabin returned to her native state of Colorado to live with her sister Mary. For a number of years thereafter, she kept up a vigorous scientific correspondence and traveled east frequently to serve on the numerous national advisory boards to which she was appointed. In 1944 she embarked on the third and perhaps most dramatic phase of her career, when Governor John Vivian invited her to serve on Colorado's Post-War Planning Committee as an adviser on health. Her biographer believes that Sabin was expected to be a "do nothing" appointee whose personal reputation was intended to bring prestige to the office. But Sabin took her new post seriously.

Sabin had been introduced to issues of public health through her warm relationships with a number of Baltimore women physicians, including Lillian Welsh and Mary Sherwood, resident physicians at Goucher College and the Bryn Mawr School for Girls, respectively, and Kate Campbell Hurd (Kate Campbell Hurd-Mead) and Alice Hall, graduates of the Woman's Medical College of Pennsylvania and founders of the Evening Dispensary for Working Women and Girls. There Sherwood, Welsh, and a number of women physicians from Hopkins, including Sabin and Elizabeth Hurdon, a surgical protégé of gynecologist Howard A. Kelly, donated their time. From 1891 to 1910, when it closed, the dispensary remained an exemplary women's institution, which practiced social medicine with compassionate determination.

In Colorado, Sabin began her new task by launching a vigorous investigation of the state's health. The committee's findings were a shock: Colorado's health program, she discovered, was plagued by insufficient funds, a poorly trained staff, and inadequate legislation. For the next seven years Sabin, who became known throughout the state as the "little doctor," gathered facts, made speeches, hounded legislators, wrote articles, and charmed physician colleagues and state officials. In addition, she helped draft a series of health laws known as the Sabin Program. In 1947 she took on the additional burden of chairing the interim Board of Health and Hospitals of Denver, a post she held until 1951.

When she died in Denver, Florence Sabin was probably the most well known American woman scientist of her era. Yet she remained very much a token woman among medical scientists, unwilling to recognize the extent to which cultural prejudices tainted the scientific institutions that she cherished. Ironically, she ended her career performing the quintessential task assigned to the woman physician in the late nineteenth and early twentieth centuries. Unknowingly, she fulfilled a role Elizabeth Blackwell had often described as best suited to her medical sisters, that of "occupying a role which men cannot fully occupy, and exercising an influence which men cannot wield at all" ("On the Education of Women Physicians," 1860, Blackwell MSS, Library of Congress). Sabin's statue stands in the U.S. Capitol.

• Florence Sabin's papers, including professional and personal correspondence, can be found at the American Philosophical Society Library in Philadelphia and the Sophia Smith Collection, Smith College. A summary of her scientific contributions is in Philip D. McMaster and Michael Heidelberger, "Florence Rena Sabin," *Biographical Memoirs of the National Academy of Sciences*, 34 (1960), which also contains a bibliography of her published work. Sabin is also the author of *Franklin P. Mall: The Story of a Mind* (1934). The best biography is Elinor Bleumel, *Florence Sabin: Colorado Woman of the Century* (1959). Also helpful are Genevieve Parkhurst, "Dr. Sabin, Scientist: Winner of Pictorial Review's Achievement Award," *Pictorial Review*, Jan. 1930, p. 2; Katherine Best and Katherine Hillyer, "Colorado's Little Doctor," *Coronet*, Mar. 1949, pp. 99–103; Edna Yost, *American Women of Science* (1943); Vincent T. Andriole, "Florence Rena Sabin—Teacher, Scientist, Citizen," *Journal of the History of Medicine and Allied Sciences* 14 (July 1959): 320–50; Lawrence Kubie, "Florence Rena Sabin, 1871–1953," *Perspectives in Biology and Medicine* 4 (Spring 1961): 306–15; Mary Kay Phelan, *The Story of Dr. Florence Sabin: Probing the Unknown* (1969); and John H. Talbott, *A Biographical History of Medicine* (1970). Other interesting perspectives can be found in George W. Corner, *A History of the Rockefeller Institute, 1901–1953* (1964); Margaret Rossiter, *Women Scientists in America* (1982); Regina Morantz-Sanchez, *Sympathy and Science: Women Physicians in American Medicine* (1985); Penina Migdal Glazer and Miriam Slater, *Unequal Colleagues: The Entrance of Women into the Professions, 1890–1940* (1987). An obituary appears in the *New York Times*, 4 Oct. 1953.

REGINA MORANTZ-SANCHEZ

SABIN, Joseph (6 Dec. 1821–5 June 1881), bibliographer and bookseller, was born in Braunston, Northamptonshire, near Oxford, England, the son of Joseph Sabin and Mary Shirley. He studied in the common schools in Oxford but did not attend a university. At age fourteen he was apprenticed to Oxford book dealer Charles Richards, who taught him bookbinding but transferred him to sales when his bibliophilic interests began to emerge. Thus immersed in books and prints, Sabin grew to be effective with customers and was promoted to general manager, a position that allowed him to buy books. His increasing responsibilities included the preparation of library sale catalogs, which drew him into the art of bibliographic description. In 1842 he left Richards to form a partnership as a bookseller and auctioneer with a man named Winterborne, whose father was an architect and builder in Oxford and whose sister, Mary Ann, Sabin married in 1844. They had two children.

In 1848 Sabin sold his business and sailed with his family to New York. He soon moved to Philadelphia, where he worked in the publishing house of George S. Appleton and introduced to the United States the use of full and half calf and morocco bindings. He cataloged for Cooley & Kesse, a firm later acquired by Ly-

man & Rawdon, for whom Sabin cataloged the principally theological collection of Dr. Samuel Farmar Jarvis, reported to be the finest library auctioned in the United States up to that time. A dispute in 1851 over compensation for the Jarvis catalog evidenced Sabin's pride in his accomplishments and resulted in his departure for Bangs, Brother & Company in New York. He cataloged the library of Edwin Brush Corwin (1856), one of the earliest such collections to consist almost entirely of Americana material and likely the source of Sabin's interest in publications pertaining to America. In 1856 Sabin launched his own business as a book and antique dealer in New York. Having limited success, he returned to Philadelphia in 1857 and opened a store there. Initially he thrived, but since much of his trade was with southerners, he lost many customers with the onset of the Civil War. He returned to New York in 1861, leaving behind a corps of disgruntled creditors.

Sabin continued to put together other important catalogs, including those describing the libraries of actor William Evans Burton, whose principally theatrical collection of more than 12,000 volumes was Sabin's first New York sale, fully launching his career (1860); John Allan, whose collection included John Eliot's "Indian Bible," the first sold at auction in the United States (1864); Colonel Brantz Mayer, attorney, author, and a founder of the Maryland Historical Society (1870); John A. Rice, a Chicago hotelier whose library was one of the "most profitable" sold "in the United States up to that time" (1870); William Menzies, a wealthy Scot whose holdings included imprints of Johann Gutenberg, Johann Fust and Peter Schöffer, William Caxton, and Wynkyn de Worde (1876); and E. George Squier (1876), whose materials on Latin America were acquired by historian Hubert Howe Bancroft, who later sold them to the University of California at Berkeley. Such catalogs became a staple of Sabin's business enterprises and, although only twenty-one of them appear in his *Dictionary*, he reputedly compiled more than 150.

In 1861 Sabin and H. A. Jennings established an auction house as J. Sabin and Company on East Fourth Street near Broadway and Lafayette Place. Continued financial problems drove Sabin out of business until 1864, when he was established successfully on Nassau Street. Brayton Ives, a contemporary collector, recalled Sabin's shop as an important gathering place for bibliophiles attracted both by the latest arrivals from London and by Sabin's infectious enthusiasm for Americana. His crowning effort as an auctioneer was to conduct the first three sales of the library of George Brinley, a wealthy landowner and farmer from Hartford. Brinley's holdings, regarded as the most imaginative and complete collection of contemporary Americana, included a Gutenberg Bible, which Sabin sold less than two months before he died.

Sabin's greatest achievement was to compile *A Dictionary of Books Relating to America, from Its Discovery to the Present Time* (29 vols., 1868—1936), also known as *Bibliotheca Americana*, covering books, pamphlets, and periodicals in every language issued between 1500 and 1800. With a bibliographical description of its alphabetically arranged items, this work became the cornerstone of retrospective bibliography pertaining to North America. Eventually it identified 106,413 publications but, with variant editions and titles, actually cited more than 250,000 separately published items. Sabin began this work in 1856 and issued the first volume in 1868, noting in his prospectus that had the "magnitude and extreme difficulty" of the task been apparent at the outset, he might never have made the attempt. Yet he recorded that he was moved by a "deep sense of its importance" and a "strong partiality for bibliographical pursuits." Twelve volumes were published before his death and one more, already compiled, appeared soon thereafter.

The *Dictionary* lay dormant for a number of years but, with the growth and maturity of American historical teaching and research, the significance of Sabin's contribution came to be more widely appreciated. Funds from the Carnegie Corporation facilitated the completion of the *Dictionary* more than fifty years after Sabin's death under the auspices of the Bibliographical Society of America and the editorial direction of Wilberforce Eames and R. W. G. Vail.

Sabin worked on his *Dictionary* while helping his sons, Frank and Joseph, reprint rare Americana, manage an auction house, and publish the *American Bibliopolist* (1869—1877), a monthly for bibliophiles. He died in Brooklyn. His affection for Americana and appreciation of his customers made Sabin one of the premier booksellers of his era, and his *Dictionary* remains a lasting contribution to American historical and literary scholarship.

• Materials pertaining to Joseph Sabin are contained in introductions to the catalogs he compiled, collections of which are held by the Library of Congress and the New York Public Library. The principal biographical sources are Gary Dennis Jensen, "Joseph Sabin and His *Dictionary of Books Relating to America*" (Ph.D. diss., George Washington Univ., 1980); Frederick R. Goff, "Joseph Sabin, Bibliographer (1821–1881)," *Inter-American Review of Bibliography* 12 (1962): 39–53; Randolph G. Adams, "A Goodly Company of American Book Collectors," in *Bookman's Holiday: Notes and Studies Written and Gathered in Tribute to Harry Miller Lydenberg*, ed. Deoch Fulton (1943), pp. 29–32; and W. L. Andrews, "Joseph Sabin," *Bookman* 1 (1895): 381–83. See also references to Sabin in Donald C. Dickinson, *Dictionary of American Book Collectors* (1986). Obituaries are in the *New York Times*, 6 June 1881, and *Publishers' Weekly*, 11 June 1881.

JOHN MARK TUCKER

SABIN, Pauline Morton (23 Apr. 1887–27 Dec. 1955), Prohibition repeal leader and Republican party official, was born in Chicago, Illinois, the daughter of Paul Morton, a railroad executive, and Charlotte Goodridge. At the age of sixteen Pauline accompanied her father to Washington, D.C., when he served as secretary of the navy from 1904 to 1905. Her father was also one of the Morton Salt heirs, and when he died Pauline inherited several million dollars. Her education included private schooling both in Chicago and in Washington before she made her debut into society.

In 1907 Pauline Morton married James Hopkins Smith, Jr., a well-to-do New York yachtsman. They had two sons before divorcing in 1914. She then owned an interior decorating business. In 1916 she married Charles Hamilton Sabin, president of Guaranty Trust Company. They mingled with society's upper class, dividing their time between a house in New York City and an estate at Southampton, Long Island, where Pauline Sabin held extravagant lawn parties. They had no children.

Although Charles was a Democrat, Pauline remained loyal to her Republican upbringing. Increasingly active in politics, she first became a member of the Suffolk County Republican Committee in 1919. By 1920 she joined the Republican party's state executive committee, and within a year she helped to found the Women's National Republican Club. As the club's president from 1921 to 1926, she recruited thousands of new members, raised funds, and gained recognition for her excellent organizational abilities. Selected to be New York's first woman representative on the Republican National Committee in 1923, Sabin was the committee's national convention delegate in 1924 and 1928. During the presidential elections of 1920, 1924, and 1928, she mobilized women's support for the Republican presidential candidates.

In the early 1920s Sabin advocated Prohibition, stating that "it would help" her sons and that she "thought a world without liquor would be a beautiful world." Toward the mid-1920s, however, she realized that Prohibition had not been effective. She saw a rising population of bootleggers and hypocritical politicians, who condemned alcohol consumption in public while drinking in private. Instead of protecting teenagers, Prohibition had actually enticed many toward alcohol consumption. In 1929 she publicly resigned as a Republican national committeewoman to work to reverse the Eighteenth Amendment. Since the Republican party officially backed the ban on liquor, she explained, her affiliation with the party would interfere with her drive to change the law.

Following her resignation, Sabin received a tremendous outpouring of support. Although Prohibition repeal groups were already in existence, in May 1929 she formed a new association. As the dynamic head of the nonpartisan Women's Organization for National Prohibition Reform (WONPR), Sabin attracted many prominent women, including Mrs. R. Stuyvesant Pierrepont, Mrs. Pierre S. du Pont, and Mrs. Coffin Van Rensselaer, to serve as its leaders. She sought out women who would be effective workers by spending countless hours scouring volunteer lists for model citizens involved in the welfare of their communities. The WONPR received publicity that could have had an adverse effect since the women were shedding the respectability of the "dry" image for the impropriety of a female being a "wet." But Sabin's method of bringing in leaders of high standing encouraged people to take a stand on their side of the issue.

In constant rivalry with the Woman's Christian Temperance Union (WCTU), Sabin employed tactics that had successfully drawn women to the WCTU. Besides its leadership and primarily independent state organizations, the WONPR reinforced the idea of home protection by stressing that Prohibition had not done what it had promised. Prohibition had not eliminated alcohol but had made the problem dramatically worse. The WONPR leaders constantly made comparisons in membership figures, claiming that at its height their organization had 1.5 million members—at least triple that of the WCTU. Under Sabin the grassroots organization outshone in militancy and membership its allied Association against the Prohibition Amendment (AAPA), a male group.

As national chairwoman of the WONPR, Sabin energized the organization through her charismatic appeal. She appeared before congressional committees, lobbied intensely, and made sure that the cause was made public. In 1932, when the WONPR moved the campaign southward, Sabin's Charleston, South Carolina, plantation home became the opportune spot for committee meetings, luncheons, and lawn parties to appeal for southern support. Sabin then went to Atlanta, where she was the subject of a write-up on the social page of the *Atlanta Constitution*, which drew many new members. When the WONPR backed Franklin D. Roosevelt and the Democratic repeal platform in the 1932 election, Sabin's picture appeared on the cover of *Time* magazine. With the ratification of the repeal amendment in December 1933, the WONPR dissolved immediately.

Sabin's interests returned to Republican politics. A fight for personal liberty and opposition to Roosevelt's policies led her to join the American Liberty League. Appointed to the league's seventeen-member executive committee, she thought women would show as much enthusiasm for the league as they had for the WONPR. Because of a lack of membership, the women's section lasted for only a year, but Sabin remained on the executive committee during the 1930s. She campaigned for Fiorello La Guardia's bid for mayor in 1933 and for Alfred Landon in 1936. She was widowed in 1933, and in 1936 she married Dwight F. Davis, former secretary of war and donor of the Davis Cup tennis trophy. They had no children. In 1940 she became the director of Volunteer Special Services for the American Red Cross. Once again proving an effective leader, she organized the various Red Cross duties and raised the number of families aided from under 100,000 to more than 4 million. She resigned her post following a policy dispute in 1943. That year she returned to Washington, where she became a consultant on the White House interior decoration renovation for President Harry Truman. She died in Washington, D.C.

Sabin's elevated social status won her many influential friends, but it was always her charismatic personality that drew people to her. Her contribution in reversing the Eighteenth Amendment was enormous. Despite her organization's affiliation with the AAPA, the association her husband was aligned with, Sabin maintained independence from it. Her dynamic leadership taught women how to be effective politically by gaining knowledge. In turn, the women proved to be vital components in convincing the American public to change their thinking about Prohibition. Sabin was the driving spirit behind the organization.

• Sabin left no papers. Her work with the WONPR is in its files at the Pierre S. du Pont Papers at Eleutherian Mills Historical Library. The archives of the American Red Cross contain information on her volunteer work. Most published material is on her activities with the WONPR, including S. J. Woolf, "A Woman Crusader for the Wet Cause," *New York Times Magazine*, 8 May 1932, pp. 7, 21; "Prohibition: Ladies at Roslyn," *Time*, 18 July 1932, pp. 8–10; "Mrs. Sabin: Arch-Enemy of Drys Is Zealous Crusader," *Newsweek*, 8 July 1933, p. 15; Grace C. Root, *Women and Repeal: The Story of the Women's Organization for National Prohibition Reform* (1934); David E. Kyvig, "Women against Prohibition," *American Quarterly*, Fall 1976, pp. 465–82; Nancy F. Cott, "Across the Great Divide," in *One Woman, One Vote: Rediscovering the Woman Suffrage Movement*, ed. Marjorie Spruill Wheeler (1995); and Kenneth D. Rose, *American Women and the Repeal of Prohibition* (1996). Obituaries are in the *New York Times*, 29 Dec. 1955, and the *Washington Post*, 28 Dec. 1955.

MARILYN ELIZABETH PERRY

SABINE, Wallace Clement Ware (13 June 1868–10 Jan. 1919), physicist, was born in Richwood, Ohio, the son of Hylas Sabine, a lawyer, and Anna Ware. Sabine attended Ohio State University, where he received his B.A. in 1886. After graduating, he moved to Cambridge, Massachusetts, where he pursued graduate studies in physics at Harvard University. He received his M.A. in 1888 and remained at Harvard to teach physics to undergraduates. In 1895 he was promoted to assistant professor, and in 1905 to full professor, even though he never presented himself as a candidate for the Ph.D. He served as dean of the Harvard Graduate School of Applied Science from its establishment in 1906 until 1915, when the school was dissolved in a short-lived merger between Harvard and the Massachusetts Institute of Technology.

Although his earliest researches concerned spectral analysis and electricity, Sabine is best known for his work in architectural acoustics. In 1895 Harvard president Charles Eliot assigned him the task of correcting the faulty acoustics of a lecture room in the university's new Fogg Art Museum. Sabine turned this assignment into a general and rigorous investigation of the behavior of sound in rooms, a subject that had received little scientific attention prior to his efforts.

Sabine was a fastidious experimenter. He carried out his acoustic experiments on rooms in the middle of the night, as Cambridge was too noisy during the day for accurate measurements. His technique was simple; a tank of compressed air was employed to sound an organ pipe. After shutting off the air supply, Sabine would listen to the residual sound, or reverberation, until it was no longer audible. A chronograph recorded this interval, the reverberation time, to hundredths of a second.

By measuring the reverberation time in numerous rooms on the Harvard campus and in Cambridge and Boston, Sabine was able to quantify the sound-absorbing properties of various architectural materials and objects such as wood, plaster, glass, and carpets. From this data, he developed a mathematical formula that related the reverberation time of a room with the room's volume and the sound-absorbing power of the materials that formed its interior. Sabine's formula could be applied to the design of a room not yet built, to predict and then manipulate its acoustical quality. The formula was first applied to the design of Symphony Hall in Boston. Sabine worked with the architect Charles McKim, of McKim, Mead and White, to create a room that would possess the same reverberation time as the acoustically successful Leipzig Gewandhaus. Sabine published an account of this work in 1900 in the *American Architect and Building News* and *Engineering Record*.

After the success of his work with McKim, Mead and White was established, Sabine's advice was sought by numerous other architects. He both advised on the design of new buildings and recommended how to improve the acoustics of extant structures. Projects included the New Theatre of Carrère and Hastings, and Cram, Goodhue and Ferguson's St. Thomas's Church, both in New York City. Ralph Adams Cram introduced Sabine to the ceramic tile manufacturer Raphael Guastavino, and Cram's hope that the two would collaborate to develop new sound-absorbing building materials was fulfilled when Sabine and Guastavino jointly patented "Rumford" tile (1914) and its successor, "Akoustolith" (1916). Sabine was paid a substantial fee for his contribution, and he also received royalty payments as the tiles were employed in numerous chapels, synagogues, banks, and offices by architects who sought to combine traditional masonry construction with untraditionally high levels of sound absorption.

In addition to consulting for architects, Sabine continued to carry out laboratory research in the years before World War I. In his initial investigation, he had utilized just one organ pipe. Sabine later expanded this work to measure the absorption of sound by materials at numerous frequencies spanning several octaves. He also mapped the interference patterns set up by sound waves in rooms, and he studied the subjectivity of human evaluation of the acoustical quality of rooms for music.

The events of World War I interrupted Sabine's work on the acoustics of rooms. Invited to present lectures on architectural acoustics at the Sorbonne, in 1916 Sabine traveled to France with his wife, Jane Downes Kelly Sabine, M.D., whom he had married in 1900, and their two daughters. While in Europe, the Sabines joined the Rockefeller War Relief Commission. Sabine spent several months inspecting facilities for tubercular patients, and his wife supervised the ac-

commodation in Switzerland of Belgian refugee children. Upon completion of his lecture series in May 1917, Sabine remained in Europe to advise the French, British, and Italian governments on topics ranging from acoustic detection of enemy guns and submarines to aerial photography and bombardment. After Sabine returned to the United States in the fall of 1917, his experience with military aeronautics led to his appointment as director of the Department of Technical Information of the Bureau of Aircraft Production. While continuing to teach at Harvard, Sabine additionally served on the National Advisory Committee for Aeronautics.

Sabine had been severely ill while abroad, and his health suffered from the workload to which he subjected himself in 1918. He neglected a kidney infection and postponed surgery until after the Armistice. The operation failed to restore Sabine's health, and he died in Boston shortly after the New Year.

At the time of his death, Sabine had been planning to resume his acoustical studies. A philanthropist, Colonel George Fabyan, was constructing a specially designed laboratory for Sabine on his country estate, "Riverbank," located outside of Chicago, and Sabine had intended to supervise work there while continuing to teach at Harvard. Sabine never occupied the facility, but his cousin Paul Sabine, also a Harvard-trained physicist, was appointed director, and the program of research that Wallace Sabine had intended to carry out was established there in 1919.

The Riverbank Laboratory, and the field of architectural acoustics in general, flourished in the 1920s, as a growing number of scientists and engineers developed the work that Sabine had begun in 1895. The Acoustical Society of America was founded in 1929 by those who considered Wallace Sabine to be the founder of their profession, and they identified Sabine's reverberation equation as the scientific basis of their work.

Holding himself to impractically high standards, Wallace Sabine published little throughout his career. When he did choose to publish, the results of his research often appeared in architectural and engineering journals, as he preferred to offer his work directly to the audience that would find it of immediate practical value. Aspects of that published research in architectural acoustics, including his reverberation equation, continue to be employed today. Sabine's legacy is additionally located in the structures upon which he consulted, as buildings like Symphony Hall continue to serve the listening public.

• Sabine's research notebooks on acoustics are located in the Harvard University Archives. His extant professional correspondence is kept at the Riverbank Acoustical Laboratories of the Illinois Institute of Technology in Geneva, Illinois. Copies of this correspondence are available at the Harvard Archives. Sabine's scientific papers on acoustics are reproduced in his *Collected Papers on Acoustics* (1922; repr. 1992). William Dana Orcutt's biography, *Wallace Clement Sabine: A Portrait in Achievement* (1933), was apparently commissioned by Sabine's widow. While perhaps overly laudatory, the book is still an accurate account of the scientist's life and work. For a more concise account, see the obituary written by Sabine's Harvard colleague Edwin Hall in the *Scientific Memoir Series of the National Academy of Sciences*, vol. 21 (1926), pp. 1–19; this volume is sometimes cataloged as *Biographical Memoirs of the National Academy of Sciences*, vol. 11.

More recently, the acoustician Leo Beranek has written several articles describing Sabine's work, including "The Notebooks of Wallace C. Sabine," *Journal of the Acoustical Society of America* 61 (Mar. 1977): 629–39, and "Wallace Clement Sabine and Acoustics," *Physics Today*, Feb. 1985, pp. 44–51. Beranek and John Kopec discuss Sabine's professional correspondence in "Wallace C. Sabine, Acoustical Consultant," *Journal of the Acoustical Society of America* 69 (Jan. 1981): 1–16, and Fred W. Kranz's "Early History of Riverbank Acoustical Laboratory," *Journal of the Acoustical Society of America* 49 (Feb. 1971): 381–84, describes the laboratory that was built for Sabine shortly before his death. For an analysis of the cultural significance of Sabine's work, see Emily Thompson's doctoral dissertation, "'Mysteries of the Acoustic': Architectural Acoustics in America, 1800–1932" (Princeton Univ., 1992).

EMILY THOMPSON

SACAGAWEA (c. 1786/1788?–20 Dec. 1812?), the Shoshone (Snake) interpreter of the Lewis and Clark expedition, was born in a northern Shoshone village in what is today Idaho; it is likely that she was a member of the Agaiduka, or Salmon Eater, band of the Shoshone tribe. Around 1800, while her tribe was engaged in a hunting or war expedition east of their home territory in the Three Forks area of the Missouri River (Montana), she was captured along with several others, most likely by the Hidatsa from the Knife River village of Metaharta (North Dakota). Sacagawea was twelve to fourteen years old at the time of her capture. By 1804 she (and another girl) had been sold or gambled away and had become the property and wives of Toussaint Charbonneau, a French-Canadian trader and trapper.

In the winter of 1804–1805, Captains Meriwether Lewis and William Clark wintered at Fort Mandan on the Missouri River in what is today North Dakota, where they encountered Charbonneau and Sacagawea. Lewis and Clark had embarked from St. Louis in 1804 on an exploratory cross-country journey initiated by President Thomas Jefferson. Before leaving Fort Mandan in April 1805 to continue their westward journey, Lewis and Clark hired Charbonneau as an interpreter, requesting that he bring one of his Shoshone wives with him. Charbonneau brought Sacagawea, who had given birth to their son, Jean Baptiste, on 11 February 1805 at the fort; the infant became the youngest member of the expedition.

Sacagawea's role as expedition guide has been greatly exaggerated; unfamiliar with most of the terrain through which the expedition traveled, she could not have directed the expedition to the Pacific Ocean. Sacagawea's geographical knowledge was limited to the region near her homeland in the Three Forks area of the upper Missouri River; here she recognized landmarks and provided some direction to Lewis and Clark.

While it is not likely that Sacagawea acted as the expedition "guide," her services certainly contributed to the success of the expedition. She served as an interpreter, collected wild foods, and on occasion pointed out landmarks and possible routes (such as the Bozeman Pass on the return trip); she even saved valuable instruments and records from being lost overboard in a storm when the expedition was traveling on the Missouri River. Clark was particularly impressed by Sacagawea's service and strength, and he nicknamed her "Janey" in his expedition journals. He also became attached to Sacagawea's son, Jean Baptiste, and assumed responsibility for the education of this boy, whom he fondly nicknamed "Pomp." It is possible that the success of the expedition hinged on Sacagawea's presence as an emissary and liaison. In August 1805, west of the Continental Divide in present-day Lemhi County, Idaho, she was unexpectedly reunited with her brother Cameahwait. He had become Shoshone band chief during her many years of absence and provided the expedition with horses and guides to continue the journey across the Bitterroot Mountains and through the Salmon River country to the navigable waters of the Clearwater and Columbia rivers. Clark's journals also present conclusive evidence that her presence as a woman with an infant served as a sign that the intentions of the "Corps of Discovery" were peaceful.

Sacagawea, Toussaint Charbonneau, and their son parted from the expedition at Fort Mandan, their starting point, on 17 August 1806. Charbonneau was paid $533.13. Sacagawea was an unofficial member of the expedition and received no monetary compensation. Little is known of her life after the expedition. Historical records, however, suggest that Charbonneau, Sacagawea, and Jean Baptiste went east to St. Louis, Missouri, around 1810 to accept Captain Clark's offer to provide them with 320 acres of land and additional pay and to finance the education of their son. Apparently city life did not agree with Toussaint Charbonneau, and he and Sacagawea left St. Louis to return to the plains country of the upper Missouri to work for Manuel Lisa, a successful Missouri Fur Company trader. It is assumed that the young Jean Baptiste Charbonneau remained in St. Louis to begin his education under Clark's patronage. Most historians believe that Sacagawea died at Fort Manuel (Manuel Lisa's post) on the Missouri River in what is today South Dakota on 20 December 1812; their evidence is based on three recorded accounts that suggest this as the date of her death. One account is that of Henry Brackenridge of Pittsburgh who recorded in his journal on 2 April 1811 that a wife of Charbonneau who had accompanied Lewis and Clark to the Pacific was on board a trading boat with him in the vicinity of Fort Manuel. His journal entry indicates that she was ill and wanted to return to her people. Over a year later, on 20 December 1812, John Luttig, head clerk of the Fort Manuel trading post, wrote in his journal: "This Evening the Wife of Charbonneau a Snake Squaw, died of a putrid fever she was a good and the best Woman in the fort, aged about 25 years she left a fine infant girl." Finally, somewhere between 1825 and 1828 Clark wrote "dead" next to Sacagawea's name (listed as Se-car ja we au) on the cover of his cash or accounting book, along with the known whereabouts of the other members of the expedition.

Other accounts provide an alternate view. Shoshone, Comanche, Mandan/Hidatsa, Gros Ventres, and other oral traditions maintain that Sacagawea lived to be an old woman (ninety-six to ninety-eight years old) and died on 9 April 1884. According to these oral traditions, Sacagawea (Bird Woman in Hidatsa or Boat Pusher in Shoshone), also known as Porivo (Chief Woman), Wadze Wipe (Lost Woman), and Bo-i-naiv (Grass Woman), left Charbonneau (perhaps around 1810) and wandered from tribe to tribe in what is now Kansas and Oklahoma, finally settling with the Comanche, among whom she married and had children. Upon the death of her husband, who was called Jerk Meat, she traveled up the Missouri River in search of her own people. Reunited with her son, Jean Baptiste (now Baptiste), and an adopted nephew whom she named Bazil, she helped her Wind River Shoshone people in their transition to life on their newly created reservation. Venerated by her tribe, she was buried on the Wyoming reservation in 1884. Tribal historians argue that Charbonneau had at least two Shoshone wives and that Brackenridge and Luttig (who never named Sacagawea) misidentified the correct wife; they also contend that Clark's information about Sacagawea's whereabouts as recorded on the cover of his account book was inaccurate. The works of Charles Eastman (Sioux) and Grace Hebard, while somewhat inconsistent and subjective, provide evidence to support this position. As has been indicated, written records do not support this theory, which is based on oral tradition. Most historians hold that Eastman, Hebard, and others either mistakenly identified Bazil's mother as Sacagawea, falsely created a counterfeit Sacagawea, or greatly embellished on Indian oral history.

Sacagawea has become an appealing figure in the history of the American West, and she continues to capture the romantic imagination of both the Indian and non-Indian American. It has been said that there are more monuments, memorials, rivers, lakes, and mountain areas named for her than for any other American woman. Novelists, poets, historians, anthropologists, and feminists have resurrected, created, and immortalized the mystique of Sacagawea. Legend mixed with fact has shrouded this extraordinary woman's life in myth and mystery. Differing accounts of her role in the Lewis and Clark expedition and the date of her death remain contested and may never be resolved to the satisfaction of all. Controversies aside, Sacagawea emerges as a courageous, determined, and admirable Indian woman in her own right.

• Sacagawea's name here follows the now-accepted spelling, though Sacajawea and Sakakawea are commonly used; the meaning and spellings of her name also are a matter of dispute. For evidence of Sacagawea's role as provided in the original journals of Lewis and Clark, see Reuben Gold Thwaites, ed., *Original Journals of the Lewis and Clark Expedition 1804–06*, vols. 1–7 (1904–1905); Gary Molton's most recent edition, *The Journals of the Lewis and Clark Expedition*, vols. 1–6 (1983); and Donald Jackson, *Letters of the Lewis and Clark Expedition with Related Documents, 1783–1854*, 2d ed., (1978). For documentary evidence of Sacagawea's death in 1812, see Henry M. Brackenridge, *Views of Louisiana Together with a Journal of a Voyage up the Missouri River, in 1811* (1814), p. 202; John Luttig, *Journal of a Fur-Trading Expedition on the Upper Missouri, 1812–1813*, ed. Stella Drum (1920), p. 106; and *Autograph Manuscript Account Book of Captain William Clark* (1825–1828) in the Newberry Library Graff Collection, Chicago, Ill. For accounts that many historians find inconsistent, but that many Native Americans believe include the true story of Sacagawea, see Grace Raymond Hebard, *Sacajawea* (1933), and Charles Eastman, manuscript on final burial place of Sacajawea, U.S. Department of the Interior, Office of Indian Affairs, 2 Mar. 1925. For tightly argued and informative current articles refuting Hebard's and Eastman's work, see Irving W. Anderson, "Probing the Riddle of the Bird Woman," *Montana* 23, no. 4 (1973): 2–17, and his "A Charbonneau Family Portrait," *The American West* 17, no. 2 (1980): 4–13. The most balanced and scholarly work on Sacagawea's life remains Harold Howard, *Sacajawea* (1971).

SALLY MCBETH

SACCO, Nicola (22 Apr. 1891–23 Aug. 1927), and **Bartolomeo Vanzetti** (11 June 1888–23 Aug. 1927), Italian anarchists convicted of murder in the celebrated Sacco-Vanzetti trial, were born, respectively, in Torremaggiore, Italy, and Villafalletto, Italy. Sacco was the son of Michele Sacco, a peasant landowner and merchant, and Angela Mosmacotelli. (Sacco's given name was Ferdinando; he adopted the name Nicola in 1917 to honor an older brother who had died.) Vanzetti was the son of Giovan Battista Vanzetti, a peasant landowner, and Giovanna Nivello. Both Sacco and Vanzetti emigrated to the United States in 1908. Sacco found steady work as an edge-trimmer in shoe factories in Milford and Stoughton, Massachusetts. He married Rosina Zambelli in 1912; they had two children, the second born during Sacco's imprisonment. Vanzetti, whose lonely private life was mitigated by the pleasure he found in books, endured long periods of unemployment or toiled at menial jobs before becoming a fish peddler in the spring of 1919. What Sacco and Vanzetti shared in common during these years was a deep commitment to anarchism.

Traditionally depicted by supporters as "philosophical anarchists" (defined by writer John Dos Passos as "an anarchist who shaves daily, has good manners and is guaranteed not to act on his beliefs"), Sacco and Vanzetti in reality were militant disciples of Luigi Galleani, an anarchist who advocated revolutionary violence, including bombing and assassination. Neither Sacco nor Vanzetti had been radicalized in Italy. Only after experiencing and observing the hardships and inequities of working-class life in America did they become receptive to the criticism of capitalism and the state propagated in Galleani's *Cronaca Sovversiva*, an anarchist newspaper described by its editor as "a rag of a paper that lives on crusts and bits of bread, with the support and pennies of five thousand beggars." Between 1912 and 1917 Sacco and Vanzetti both engaged in fundraising for the anarchist movement and occasional strike agitation. After the U.S. Congress passed the military conscription act in May 1917, they were among some sixty Italian anarchists who followed Galleani's recommendation and fled to Mexico rather than register for the draft. Their purpose was not merely to avoid military service or imprisonment for draft resistance; they wanted to remain at liberty so they could join the revolution they expected to erupt in Italy in the wake of the March revolution in Russia. When revolution failed to spread and exile became wearisome, they reentered the United States, Sacco resuming work as an edge-trimmer in Stoughton and Vanzetti selling fish in Plymouth. By now, however, the government's antiradical campaign was intensifying, and Italian anarchists ranked at the top of the enemy list. Because of its antiwar stance, *Cronaca Sovversiva* was suppressed in July 1918, and Galleani and eight of his closest associates were deported on 24 June 1919. Most of the remaining Galleanisti sought to survive repression by becoming inactive or going underground. However, some sixty militants—including many who had gone to Mexico—considered themselves engaged in a class war that required retaliation. For three years they waged an intermittent campaign of terrorism directed at politicians, judges, and other federal and local officials involved in political repression. Chief among the dozen or more terrorist acts the Galleanisti committed were the bombing of Attorney General A. Mitchell Palmer's home on 2 June 1919 and the Wall Street explosion of 16 September 1920.

Sacco and Vanzetti were marginally involved in the bomb conspiracy, although their precise roles have not been determined. This fact explains much about their activities and behavior on the night of their arrest, 5 May 1920. Two days earlier they had learned that Andrea Salsedo had plunged to his death from the Bureau of Investigation offices on Park Row in New York. Salsedo was an anarchist to whose Brooklyn print shop federal agents had traced a revolutionary leaflet found at Palmer's bombed house. The anarchists knew that Salsedo had been held incommunicado for several weeks and repeatedly beaten. So when Palmer announced to the press that Salsedo and his comrade Roberto Elia had made important disclosures concerning the bomb plot of 2 June 1919, the Galleanisti realized that the attorney general was not making an idle boast. It was now imperative that they go deeper underground and get rid of incriminating evidence. Thus on the evening of their arrest, Sacco and Vanzetti may have been transferring Italian anarchist literature—including a bomb manual innocuously titled *La salute è in voi* (Health is in you)—to a safe place; or, more likely, they may have been hiding dynamite. Both men were carrying pistols and ammunition when arrested, and during their interrogation—initially about their radical activities, not payroll robbery and murders—they told lies and gave contradictory statements to the police. This behavior constituted "consciousness of guilt" to the authorities.

The trap that ensnared Sacco and Vanzetti had been set by Michael Stewart, the police chief of Bridgewater, Massachusetts, who had been assisting the Justice Department in rounding up Italian anarchists for deportation. When one of them, Ferrucio Coacci, failed to report for deportation at the east Boston immigration station on 15 April 1920—the same day of the payroll robbery at the Slater & Morrill shoe factory in South Braintree, Massachusetts, in which a guard and paymaster were killed—Stewart concluded that the robbery and murders must have been committed by Coacci and his comrades, among whom were Sacco, Vanzetti, Riccardo Orciani, and Mario Buda. Stewart also believed them responsible for a botched holdup of a shoe factory in Bridgewater the previous Christmas Eve. Justice Department agents in Boston believed the South Braintree crime had been committed by professionals, but since Sacco and Vanzetti were listed in their files as "radicals to be watched" and known comrades of the bomber Carlo Valdinoci, whose dismembered body had been found at Palmer's house, a murder conviction presented an effective way of eliminating them. The Justice Department subsequently furnished prosecuting authorities with information about Sacco and Vanzetti's radical activities, placed a spy in a cell adjacent to Sacco's, and infiltrated one or more informants into the Sacco-Vanzetti defense committee.

Of the five suspects, Coacci was deported, Orciani was released because he had strong alibis for the days both crimes were committed, and Buda disappeared to plot revenge (the Wall Street explosion) for the indictment of the remaining two anarchists, Sacco and Vanzetti. Because the evidence linking him to South Braintree was weak, Vanzetti was tried first for the lesser crime at Bridgewater (Sacco's alibi for that day was solid) so that he would go before the second jury as a convicted felon. Held in Plymouth from 22 June to 1 July 1920, Vanzetti's trial was a travesty. The presiding magistrate, Webster Thayer, despised foreigners and considered anarchism "cognate with the crime." The prosecutor was Frederick G. Katzmann, a cunning and unscrupulous district attorney willing to suborn perjury and manipulate and withhold evidence to obtain a conviction. Vanzetti's attorney, John Vahey, who became Katzmann's law partner in 1924, performed so poorly that he was suspected of collusion with the prosecution. The testimony of more than twenty witnesses who had seen Vanzetti selling eels on the day of the Bridgewater crime was discounted because the individuals were all Italians. Prosecution witnesses—typified by a newsboy who caught a glimpse of a perpetrator and "knew by the way he ran he was a foreigner"—were believed. Found guilty, Vanzetti was condemned by Judge Thayer to serve twelve to fifteen years in prison.

The trial of Sacco and Vanzetti for the South Braintree murders was held in Dedham from 31 May to 14 July 1921. The atmosphere in court was transfused with the nativist and reactionary sentiments still pervading American society in the wake of the Red Scare. District Attorney Katzmann was able, therefore, to try Sacco and Vanzetti not only for murder but, in effect, for being anarchists, atheists, foreigners, and draft dodgers. Judge Thayer, repeating his role as presiding magistrate, had no objection to Katzmann's interjecting such extraneous and inflammatory information, despite its prejudicial effect on the jury. Nor did he interfere with Katzmann's coaching and cajoling of prosecution witnesses to obtain descriptions of the shooting and of the perpetrators that were remarkably more detailed and incriminating than those they had provided to Pinkerton investigators more than a year earlier. With defense witnesses, especially Italians, Katzmann was patronizing and disdainful, implying that they were lying to defend their compatriots. Several witnesses whose testimony would have helped the defendants were never called to testify or brought to the attention of the defense. Katzmann's handling of the alleged murder weapons and ballistics evidence was likewise unethical. The prosecution's chief expert, Captain William Proctor of the state police, did not believe that Sacco's Colt .32-caliber automatic had fired the bullet that killed the guard. (The remaining five bullets taken from the two bodies could not have been fired from the guns found on Sacco and Vanzetti.) Nevertheless, by prearrangement with Katzmann, Proctor testified when asked about the bullet in question that "it is consistent with having been fired from that gun," meaning any Colt .32-caliber automatic, not Sacco's weapon. Katzmann also knew that the .38-caliber revolver found on Vanzetti at the time of his arrest could not have been taken from the slain guard, as the prosecution claimed. The guard's weapon was a .32-caliber revolver with a different serial number—evidence withheld from the defense. Katzmann's manipulation of evidence may even have included substituting a test bullet fired from Sacco's gun for the real fatal bullet.

Outmatched by Katzmann in the courtroom, defense attorney Fred Moore, a radical lawyer previously involved with Industrial Workers of the World cases, sought to demonstrate that the proceedings against Sacco and Vanzetti were politically motivated, the result of collusion between local and federal authorities seeking to suppress Italian anarchists. Moore's strategy generated widespread publicity and support for Sacco and Vanzetti but failed to thwart the prosecution. The weight of evidence—the weapons, ballistic tests, and eyewitness testimony—and the issue of consciousness of guilt (independently stressed by Judge Thayer in his instructions to the jury) as well as the prejudice Katzmann had evoked against the accused combined to ensure a guilty verdict on 14 July 1921.

A six-year struggle to save Sacco and Vanzetti followed the trial. Countless observers worldwide were convinced that political intolerance and racial bigotry had condemned two men whose only offense was that of being foreigners, atheists, and anarchists. Edmund Wilson, like many others, believed that the case "re-vealed the whole anatomy of American life, with all its classes, professions, and points of view and all their relations, and it raised almost every fundamental question of our political and social system." This perception was reinforced by the dignity and courage Sacco and Vanzetti displayed throughout their ordeal. That such men were capable of common murder struck many as inconceivable. Sacco and Vanzetti defenders eventually included radicals, trade unionists, intellectuals, liberals, and even some conservatives, such as Boston lawyer William G. Thompson, who replaced Moore as chief defense counsel in 1924, and Harvard law professor and future Supreme Court justice Felix Frankfurter. Arrayed against them were the upholders of traditional conservative values and institutions associated with patriotism, religion, and capitalism. They were intransigent in their belief that the American system of justice could do no wrong and that the two subversives were guilty as charged, had been fairly tried, and deserved the maximum penalty.

But the fate of Sacco and Vanzetti was not decided in the arena of public opinion. Eight motions for a new trial—in accordance with Massachusetts law—were submitted to Judge Thayer. Several pertained to perjured testimony by prosecution witnesses and to collusion between local police and Justice Department agents. Another addressed a jailhouse confession by a convicted bank robber, Celestino Madieros, who claimed he and other members of the Morelli gang of professional criminals had committed the South Braintree holdup and murders. Still another was based on comments Judge Thayer himself had made after rejecting a previous motion, namely, "Did you see what I did with those anarchistic bastards the other day? I guess that will hold them for a while." Each motion was denied. Finally, after the Massachusetts Supreme Court ruled that no errors of law or abuses of discretion had been committed, Judge Thayer sentenced Sacco and Vanzetti to death on 9 April 1927. In the face of mounting criticism of the legal proceedings and the impending death sentence, Governor Alvan T. Fuller appointed a committee on 1 June headed by A. Lawrence Lowell, president of Harvard University, to review the case and advise him on the issue of clemency. The Lowell committee ignored exculpatory evidence the defense had discovered since the trial while validating the prosecution's every step. Even Judge Thayer's remarks about "those anarchistic bastards," although deemed a "grave breach of decorum," did not cause the committee concern. Reporting its findings to Governor Fuller on 27 July, the Lowell Committee declared that the trial and appeals process "on the whole" had been fair and advised against clemency. Governor Fuller followed the committee's recommendation, and in the face of worldwide protest and demonstrations, Sacco and Vanzetti were electrocuted at Charlestown State Prison on 23 August 1927.

The Sacco-Vanzetti case was an international cause célèbre in the 1920s and still remains one of the most controversial legal proceedings in modern history. Decades after they were sentenced to death, Sacco and

Vanzetti still have their partisan defenders and accusers. Historians of the case, manifesting the same biases, continue to disagree. Some pronounce Sacco definitely and Vanzetti possibly guilty on the evidence of ballistics tests and rumors attributed to a few Italian anarchists. Others contend that both men were innocent victims of a frame-up, based on the prosecution's collusion with federal authorities, suppression of evidence, and manipulation of ballistics tests. Preoccupation with guilt or innocence has resulted in the neglect of more important dimensions of the case such as the atmosphere in which the trial and appeals took place, the conduct of the officials involved, and the broader implications of the proceedings for American society. Even Sacco and Vanzetti themselves—their personalities, ideas, and writings—have not received sufficient attention from historians, although recent work establishing their revolutionary credentials represents a significant step in that direction. Thus the Sacco-Vanzetti case will probably remain, in the words of attorney Herbert B. Ehrmann, "the case that will not die."

• A wealth of original sources is available to scholars, including *The Sacco-Vanzetti Case: Transcript of the Record of the Trial of Nicola Sacco and Bartolomeo Vanzetti in the Courts of Massachusetts and Subsequent Proceedings, 1920–1927* (6 vols., 1928–1929); *The Sacco-Vanzetti Case Papers*, microfilm (23 reels, 1986); the Aldino Felicani Sacco-Vanzetti Collection, Boston Public Library; the Herbert H. Ehrmann Papers, Harvard Law Library; the Massachusetts State Police Sacco-Vanzetti Files, Massachusetts State Archives; and the Department of Justice/FBI Sacco-Vanzetti Files, National Archives, Washington, D.C. The most influential book written about the trial, amounting to a devastating critique of Judge Thayer and the prosecution, is Felix Frankfurter, *The Case of Sacco and Vanzetti: A Critical Analysis for Lawyers and Laymen* (1927). The principal works written during the 1930s and 1940s, asserting the innocence of the accused and the unfairness of the legal proceedings, are Osmond K. Fraenkel, *The Sacco-Vanzetti Case* (1931), and Louis G. Joughin and Edmund M. Morgan, *The Legacy of Sacco and Vanzetti* (1948). The first book to argue that Sacco and Vanzetti were guilty and fairly tried was Robert H. Montgomery, *Sacco-Vanzetti: The Murder and the Myth* (1960). An important work that posits a split-guilt thesis (Sacco guilty, Vanzetti innocent) is Francis Russell, *Tragedy in Dedham: The Story of the Sacco-Vanzetti Case* (1962). Russell subsequently asserted Vanzetti's guilt in numerous articles and in *Sacco and Vanzetti: The Case Resolved* (1986). Seriously critical of Russell is William Young and David E. Kaiser, *Postmortem: New Evidence in the Case of Sacco and Vanzetti* (1985), which argues on the basis of new evidence pertaining to ballistics testing and the alleged murder weapons that Sacco and Vanzetti were innocent men framed by the prosecution. The most thorough and well-balanced study of the case, written by a former member of the defense team, is Herbert B. Ehrmann, *The Case That Will Not Die: Commonwealth vs. Sacco and Vanzetti* (1969). Indispensable for an understanding of the Italian anarchist movement to which Sacco and Vanzetti devoted their lives is Paul Avrich, *Sacco and Vanzetti: The Anarchist Background* (1991). Letters written by the condemned men to relatives and friends have been collected in Marion D. Frankfurter and Gardner Jackson, eds., *The Letters of Sacco and Vanzetti* (1928; 1960), and Bartolomeo Vanzetti, *Non piangete la mia morte* (1962).

NUNZIO PERNICONE

SACHS, Bernard (2 Feb. 1858–8 Feb. 1944), pediatric neurologist, was born in Baltimore, Maryland, the son of Joseph Sachs, a teacher and boardingschool owner, and Sophia Baer. Sachs's parents, who were Bavarian Jews, emigrated to Philadelphia in 1847, at a time of much revolutionary unrest in Europe. By 1859 the family had moved to New York. Sachs's father sold the school when his health failed and moved the family back in 1867 to Germany, where he died two years later. Sachs's mother died of diabetes three years after the family had returned in 1869 to New York. Here Sachs was raised by an aunt.

At the age of two, Sachs fell eighteen feet from an open porch and suffered a depressed skull fracture. He wore a leaden skull cap that was devised and fitted to his head by a Professor Detmold, "as though he had a premonition that the little boy was some day to devote himself to diseases of the brain . . . Fortunately I escaped without any serious injury—no epilepsy, and I hope, with a normal mental capacity," Sachs later recalled in his autobiography. He entered the Sachs Collegiate Institute, which his brother Julius had opened in New York in 1870, and profited much from his fraternal mentor. He attended Harvard from 1874 to 1878, concentrating first on liberal arts, then increasingly on science, receiving an A.B. The famous psychology professor William James, who was half-blind, employed Sachs to read to him daily a chapter of German psychologist Wilhelm Wundt's just published *Grundzüge der Physiologischen Psychologie*. Sach's thesis, a comparative study of vertebrate limbs, won him the Bowdoin Prize; he was an honor student and won election to Phi Beta Kappa. Bent on a medical career, he went off to study with the great names in Europe: first at the University of Strassburg (Strasbourg), with the chemist Felix Hoppe-Seyler, the anatomist Wilhelm Waldeyer, the physiologist Friedrich Leopold Golts, and the clinician Adolf Kussmaul; there, he received his medical degree in 1882. He then studied pathology, neurology, and psychiatry with Carl Westphal and Rudolf Virchow in Berlin, Theodor Meynert and Sigmund Freud in Vienna, Jean Martin Charcot in Paris, and John Hughlings Jackson in London. During those years neurology had begun to break off as a speciality from psychiatry and internal medicine as a result of recent anatomical and physiological discoveries about the nervous system.

By the time he returned to New York in 1884, Sachs's focus on neurology, or neuropsychiatry, had been established. His bilingual upbringing enabled him to translate the convoluted German textbook *Psychiatrie* by Theodor Meynert into readable English. As an assistant of Isaac Adler, Sachs came upon his first two cases of "amaurotic idiocy," the pediatric condition that later was to make his fame. In 1885 he began work with the neurologist Edward Constan Seguin in New York, the son of French pediatric neurologist Edouard Seguin, at the Polyclinic Hospital, the Montefiore Home, and the Mt. Sinai and Bellevue Hospitals. At Mount Sinai he organized the first neurological service in 1900.

In addition to being one of the first members of the American Neurological Association and twice its president, Sachs also served twice as president of the New York Neurological Society. In 1931 he was elected president of the First International Congress of Neurology in Berne and president of the New York Academy of Medicine. He served as director of Child Neurology at the New York Academy of Medicine from 1933; of Child Neurology at the New York Neurological Institute from 1932 to 1942; and of the Child Neurology Research Fund, which was established by the Friedman Foundation in 1936. An ardent historian and bibliophile, he cofounded in 1898 the Charaka Club to cater to those interests. Its prominent members included Charles Loomis Dana, Silas Weir Mitchell, William Osler, Surgeon General John Shaw Billings, George L. Walton, and Harvey Cushing.

In 1887 Sachs published the paper that inaugurated a series on what was later called "amaurotic family idiocy." In it, he pointed out that the existing knowledge of cerebral pathology in patients with mental derangement was still limited to cerebral syphilis. He presented as evidence an infant who was blind, unable to speak, generally retarded, and with a "cherry red spot" in the retina, as noticed by Dr. Hermann Joseph Knapp, the associated ophthalmologist. The autopsy and microscopic examination of the brain, performed by Sachs, showed narrow cerebral convolutions that contained ballooned cortical nerve cells. After publishing several more articles on the subject, he discovered that Warren Tay, an English ophthalmologist, had also in 1881 written about the case of an infant with a "brownish-red" circular spot in its retinal macula. The condition consequently later received the eponym "Tay-Sachs disease." Sachs produced a total of 194 publications, mostly on nervous disease in children. These included the first textbook on this subject in 1895, *A Treatise on the Nervous Diseases of Children for Physicians and Students*, as well as a severely critical paper, "The False Claims of Psychoanalysis," published in the *American Journal of Psychiatry* in 1933. He also left an autobiography.

In 1887 Sachs married Bettina R. Stein of Frankfurt; they had two children. After her death in 1940, he married Rosetta Kaskel in 1941, at the age of 83. A great supporter of charitable causes, such as the Mt. Sinai Hospital, Sachs was also an expert in the fine arts and a consultant and personal physician to collector Benjamin Altman, who was associated with the Metropolitan Museum in New York. Though full of ambition and pride, he also combined "gaiety with goodness, wisdom with tolerance," according to his son-in-law. He died in New York. Sachs's name remains forever associated with the inception of child neurology.

• Sachs's first paper on amaurotic family idiocy, "On Arrested Cerebral Development, with Special Reference to Its Cortical Pathology," appeared in *Journal of Nervous and Mental Disease* 14 (1887): 541–53. He provides an extensive microscopic analysis, "On Amaurotic Family Idiocy. A Disease Chiefly of the Gray Matter of the Central Nervous System," in the same journal, 3 (1903): 1–30. His autobiography, *Barney Sachs, 1858–1944*, was privately printed in 1949. Biographies of Sachs include those by W. Haymaker in *The Founders of Neurology*, ed. Haymaker and Schiller (1970); by D. A. Stumpf in *The Founders of Child Neurology*, ed. Stephen Ashwal (1990); and his obituary by Louis Hausman in *Archives of Neurology and Psychiatry* 51 (May 1944): 481–86.

FRANCIS SCHILLER

SACHS, Hanns (10 Jan. 1881–10 Jan. 1947), psychoanalyst, was born in Vienna, Austria, the son of Samuel Sachs, a lawyer, and Heimine Heller. Sachs grew up in a home dominated by artistic and literary concerns. He graduated from the Gymnasium in 1899 and had qualified to practice law by 1904. That year he also first read Austrian psychologist Sigmund Freud's *The Interpretation of Dreams* and subsequently attended, with Freud's permission, Freud's Saturday night lectures at the University of Vienna. In 1909 Sachs decided to join Freud and his small group in Vienna, but even as a member of the Vienna Psychoanalytic Society, he continued to practice law. In 1912 Sachs, along with Otto Rank, became a founding editor of the influential journal *Imago*, which was designed to specialize in "applications" of psychoanalytic thinking to nonmedical subjects of a humanistic interest, such as literature, art, and the general knowledge of psychology.

At the outset of World War I Sachs was one of the few of Freud's intimates to remain in Vienna. After a bout of tuberculosis forced Sachs to spend two years recovering in Switzerland, he decided in 1919 to abandon law and commit himself entirely to psychoanalysis. Freud, who preferred his disciples to give up their previous careers, was pleased when Sachs wanted to practice analysis full time. Sachs's undiluted support also would be conducive to bringing Freud more students in the future. Soon after Sachs began to analyze patients in Zurich, he was invited in 1920 to become a training analyst at the new Psychoanalytic Institute being founded in Berlin by Karl Abraham and Max Eitingon.

Sachs continued to typify, no matter where he lived, the qualities and talents of a bon vivant of old Vienna. Full of a seemingly endless stock of the best Jewish humor, he used jokes clinically—as did Freud—to illustrate human dilemmas. Sachs was both loquacious and optimistic; he loved good food, wine, and beautiful women, and enjoyed spending time in cafés. Although almost none of Sachs's younger analytic colleagues ever knew about it, he was briefly and unhappily married (date unknown) to Emmy Pisco, who attended Freud's lectures along with Sachs. The marriage was childless. Sachs was known as a charming, carefree bachelor with multiple women in his life.

In spite of his lack of previous clinical experience, Sachs immediately became a prominent training analyst in Berlin. Among his analysands who later became famous as analysts themselves were Franz Alexander, Ella Sharpe, Erich Fromm, Karen Horney, and Gregory Zilboorg; Sachs also analyzed prominent academic psychologists such as Yale's John Dollard and Harvard's Edwin Boring. Sachs always stressed the significance of the intuitive element in analysis, especially in contrast to what he viewed as the heavy-handed German scientific emphasis on the advantages of looking on psychoanalysis as a laboratory experiment. In the 1920s little authoritative work existed on the issue of therapeutic technique, and Sachs proceeded to lecture widely on the subject. Along with Rank, Sachs was a defender of the lay, nonmedical practice of analysis, and he always remained committed to the use of psychoanalytic understanding in the realms of literature and art.

In Berlin Sachs was an avid moviegoer. Along with Abraham, Sachs became in 1925 an adviser to the director of the psychoanalytic movie *The Secrets of the Soul*, although Freud himself had a rooted objection to the whole project. Abraham and Sachs nevertheless wielded special stature within the movement as members, along with Rank, Eitingon, Ernest Jones, and Sandor Ferenczi, of a secret committee that was designed by Freud to forward the cause of psychoanalysis after the pre–World War I losses of Carl Jung, Alfred Adler, and Wilhelm Stekel. As such, Sachs was among the first to receive a cherished ring from Freud, marking him as a specially chosen bearer of Freud's message. Sachs, however, had no particular talent for or interest in the political sides of the psychoanalytic movement and, even though Freud had taken a great personal interest in him, could never bring himself to pay much attention to matters of an organizational nature.

Psychoanalysis became the absolute center of Sachs's life, "the only thing" he "could live by." In his consulting room in Berlin the analytic couch was placed so that the analysand faced a bust of Freud standing on a high pedestal. Despite Sachs's apparently easygoing ways, when difficulties arose between Freud and Rank, Sachs was able to drop his friend Rank entirely. Sachs once described with unashamed religious imagery what he thought the purpose of a didactic training analysis was: "Religions have always demanded a trial period, a novitiate, of those among their devotees who desired to give their entire life into the service of the supermundane and the supernatural, those, in other words, who were to become monks or priests. . . . It can be seen that analysis needs something corresponding to the novitiate of the Church." More a prophet than a scientist, Sachs proceeded to treat psychoanalysis as a revealed religion.

Sachs always insisted on the importance of nourishing the positive aspect of the patient's relationship with the analyst and deemphasizing possible negative feelings. His penchant for treating each patient as an exception did not suit him to the needs of an increasingly bureaucratized movement. Partly because of the rise of the Nazis, but also because of his own solitary ways, Sachs accepted an invitation to help found the Psychoanalytic Institute in Boston, Massachusetts, in 1932.

In Boston Sachs was a desperately needed training analyst, and he had been guaranteed, before he agreed to resettle there, eight analytic patients a day. Although Sachs analyzed the famous neurologist Stanley Cobb, who founded the first psychiatric department at a U.S. general hospital, and obtained a teaching appointment at Harvard Medical School, he did not at all approve of the committee-style decision making insisted on by the new Boston institute itself. Modeling himself on Freud, Sachs would accept on the spot a candidate for training and afterward simply notify the Psychoanalytic Institute. Despite his independent ways, Sachs succeeded in living in luxury in the beautiful, old Back Bay section of town.

Once Hitler came to power Sachs felt obliged to help his old friends and relatives (including his former wife) escape from Europe. The catastrophe of Nazism, combined with his own bad health (anginal attacks and abdominal troubles), left Sachs more skeptical and gloomier than he had ever seemed to anyone before. He was also disappointed in his failure to make disciples of several prominent patients. He died in Boston.

Sachs's most outstanding single piece of writing was his touching memoir, *Freud: Master and Friend* (1944). It is a beautifully evocative portrait of Freud's character, as seen by someone whose adoring love for his master remained unquestioned and intact. The book contains interesting details about Freud's work habits, along with information concerning some of his characteristic idiosyncrasies; it has become one of the most continuously cited sources about Freud for historians and students of culture. Whatever the work may have lacked in objectivity was made up for in Sachs's poetic command of the language. (His American friends were astounded at the contrast between Sachs's labored spoken English and his complete facility with the written word.)

On a July 1939 visit to London shortly before Freud died, Sachs received Freud's permission to move *Imago* to the United States. Sachs commented of that London meeting: "fundamentally he remained as remote as when I first met him in the lecture hall." Sachs's remark about the distance that remained after having known Freud for over thirty years is as telling about himself as about Freud; Sachs's longings and the frustrations he was willing to accept were ideally suited to Freud's own particular needs. Freud had a high degree of disdain and suspiciousness about what would become of his life's work in the New World; but he revealed his confidence in Sachs personally in his final words when they parted in London: "I know that I have at least *one* friend in America."

• In addition to *Freud: Master and Friend*, Sachs published a book on *Caligula* (1932), and two collections of his essays, *The Creative Unconscious: Studies in the Psychoanalysis of Art* (1942) and *Masks of Love and Life: The Philosophical Basis of Psychoanalysis* (1948). He coauthored with Otto Rank *The Significance of Psychoanalysis for the Mental Sciences*, Nervous Mental Disorder Monograph, no. 23 (1915). Fritz Moellenhoff wrote an article about Sachs subtitled "The Creative Unconscious" in *Psychoanalytic Pioneers*, ed. Franz Alexander et al. (1966), pp. 180–99. An obituary is in the *New York Times*, 11 Jan. 1947.

PAUL ROAZEN

SACHS, Julius (6 July 1849–2 Feb. 1934), educator, was born in Baltimore, Maryland, the son of Joseph Sachs and Sophia Baer. He attended Columbia University, where he earned an A.B. in 1867 and an A.M. in 1871. From 1867 to 1871 Sachs studied at several German universities (Rostock, Göttingen, Berlin, and Würzburg) and earned a Ph.D. in philosophy from Rostock in 1871. Following graduation Sachs served for one year (1871–1872) as classical master at Callisen's School in New York City. In 1872, in a deliberate effort to raise the standards of secondary education, he opened the Dr. J. Sachs Collegiate Institute School for Boys and served as its principal for the next thirty-two years (1872–1904). In 1891 he opened the Dr. J. Sachs School for Girls and also served as its principal until 1904. Both schools had a widespread influence on the standards and the methods of the emerging American secondary school. The schools also became training schools for teachers. In 1874 he married Rosa Goldman; they had two children.

In 1900 Sachs was offered a position at Teachers College, Columbia University, which he did not immediately accept because his "relations with valued associates and warm friends" made it difficult to sever connections with his schools on such short notice. When in 1902 Sachs was again offered a position at Teachers College, he wrote asking "that the department assigned to me rank fully with any other of the departments at Teachers College and that if intrusted with the charge of it, I hold the position as full Professor and member of the faculty." He was appointed professor and head of the college's program in secondary education and served in that capacity until his retirement in 1917. When Sachs became a professor, fewer than 20 percent of all American youth were attending high school. Sachs became a pioneer in the field of secondary education, bringing to his position long years of experience as a secondary schoolteacher and administrator. He believed in single-sex schools and even wrote that he felt that boys needed more male teachers, especially in the early grades. Many of the pupils in the Sachs schools became leaders in all aspects of American society.

Throughout his career Sachs continued his scholarly studies. He belonged to a number of scholarly and professional organizations and served as president of the Schoolmasters Association of New York (1889), Middle States Association of Colleges and Secondary Schools (1898), American Philological Association (1891), and the New York Society of the Archeological Institute of America (1900–1903). He was the secondary school representative to the College Entrance Examination Board from 1900 to 1907. He contributed to the proceedings and journals of many learned organizations, such as the History Teachers Association and the New England Modern Language Association, and

to professional journals such as the *School Review*. Even after retirement, Sachs lectured often at New York's Metropolitan Museum of Art.

In his book *The American Secondary School and Some of Its Problems* (1912), Sachs examined "the vigorous and unrestricted growth rootward and upward . . . that have made definition of the present purposes and functions of the Secondary School a matter of difficulty." He discussed the American public high school, the private secondary school, the continuation/vocational school, and education policy of the secondary school. In a discussion of teaching methods in the German gymnasium, the French lycée, and the English public school, Sachs observed that it was "the high order of efficiency in their teachers, rather than the nature of their curricula, that imparts distinction to them, and it is the quality in the teacher, professional ability and exactness in information, toward which our efforts must be directed." Upgrading the quality of teachers and teaching remained the continual focus of Sachs's life. He stressed teachers' learning the content of the disciplines, the sequencing of curriculum, improved lecture-discussion methods, and classroom management and control.

Sachs retired from the Teachers College faculty in 1917. On the occasion of their fiftieth wedding anniversary in June 1924, Dr. and Mrs. Sachs established a $20,000 endowment fund to support an annual prize for studies of secondary education. After their deaths, the endowment was renamed the Julius and Rosa Sachs Memorial Lectures in Secondary Education, and the prestigious lecture series continues to this day at Teachers College. Sachs died at his home in New York City. The obituary in the *New York Times* observed: "As an educator, Dr. Sachs was distinguished by his forward vision, his cordiality toward new ideas and his lack of hesitation in advocating modern methods. These traits, with his personality and ability, placed him in the very first rank of his contemporaries."

At a time when the American high school was a fledgling institution, Sachs exercised considerable influence in determining its evolution. As head of the secondary education program at Teachers College, then the premier institution of teacher education, he helped formulate the nature and direction of secondary education in the United States. He also was a member of the Latin Sub-Committee that produced the highly influential Committee of Ten Report (1893) and was a representative to the College Entrance Examination Board in its formative years.

• Sachs's only major publication, *The American Secondary School and Some of Its Problems*, contains an appendix titled, "Outlines for the Teaching of Certain Subject Groups in the Secondary School Course," including English, history, Latin and Greek, and German and French. The outlines are for teaching courses to new teachers, and they provide insight into Sachs's ideas about content and methods. A brief account of the memorial service held at Teachers College is contained in the *Teachers College Record*, Mar. 1934. An obituary is in the *New York Times*, 3 Feb. 1934.

A. HARRY PASSOW

SACHS, Leonard David (7 Aug. 1897–27 Oct. 1942), basketball coach, was born in Chicago, Illinois. Little is known of his parents and early childhood, but he graduated from Carl Schurz High School in Chicago as class president in 1914. Sachs distinguished himself in athletics, earning eleven varsity letters. After high school, he played basketball for the Cleveland Naval Reserve team during World War I. He also helped the Illinois Athletic Club team win the Amateur Athletic Union championship in 1918 with a record of thirty-two wins and one loss. The following year he entered the American College of Physical Education.

He simultaneously pursued his education and a coaching career by assuming duties in football and basketball at Wendell Phillips High School in Chicago's Black Belt. In 1921 he accepted a position as basketball coach at Marshall High School in Chicago, and he completed his physical education degree program two years later. He earned a degree from Loyola University of Chicago in 1933. He embarked on a professional football odyssey from 1920 until 1926 in the fledgling National Football League. He played end for the Chicago Cardinals for three years, followed by stints with the Milwaukee Badgers (1923–1924) and Hammond Pros (1924–1925). He returned to the Cardinals in 1925 and ended his playing days with a road team, the Louisville Colonels, as a player-coach in 1926.

Sachs's success at high school coaching led to his hiring as the head college basketball coach at Loyola of Chicago in 1923. He later took on responsibilities as track coach and athletic director. In nineteen years at Loyola, Sachs's basketball teams compiled an outstanding 224–129 won-lost record, including winning streaks of thirty-two (1927–1929) and twenty games (1939). The 1929 contingent was Loyola's first nationally ranked squad. The 1939 team advanced to the championship game of the National Invitational Tournament, the premier basketball spectacle of the time, before losing to an undefeated Long Island University team. Known as a defensive strategist, Sachs developed a 2-2-1 zone defense, a fast-break offense, and an innovative use of a tall center, resulting in a rule change to disallow goal tending. He tutored a number of All-America basketball players during his years at Loyola, including Charles Murphy (1930), Marvin Colen (1937), Michael Novak (1938–1939), and Wilbert Kautz (1939).

Throughout much of his tenure at Loyola, Sachs continued to coach football at Phillips High School during the fall. It was at Phillips that he complained of chest pains and collapsed on the field as he sought a physician's diagnosis. A resuscitation squad was unable to revive him, the victim of a heart attack.

Sachs left a wife, Vera Blair (date of marriage unknown), and one child. Loyola colleagues and officials eulogized him as a molder of men, a Catholic gentleman, and a true friend. In 1961 he was elected to the Basketball Hall of Fame as an innovative and successful coach, and in 1964 the Helms Athletic Foundation named him a member of its hall of fame.

• In the absence of a biography, personal papers, or autobiographical writings, information on Sachs is relatively spotty. Carl Schurz High School in Chicago maintains yearbooks and school records from Sachs's era, and the Loyola University archives contain a relevant file and yearbooks. His career is touched on in Zander Hollander, ed., *The Modern Encyclopedia of Basketball* (1979); the National Collegiate Athletic Association's *NCAA Basketball's Finest* (1991); Ronald L. Mendell, *Who's Who in Basketball* (1973); and Sandy Padwe, *Basketball's Hall of Fame* (1970). Also see the Loyola sports media guide, 1964–1965. An obituary is in the *Chicago Tribune*, 28 Oct. 1942.

GERALD R. GEMS

SACHS, Paul Joseph (24 Nov. 1878–17 Feb. 1965), museum director, teacher, and art collector, was born in New York City, the son of Samuel Sachs, a partner in the firm of Goldman, Sachs & Co., and Louisa Goldman. The family was part of the close-knit German-Jewish community in New York City. Paul Sachs attended the Sachs School in New York, a preparatory school operated by his uncle. He was attracted to art from his youth. In his memoirs he recounted how his bedroom became a gallery of prints and photographs and that he secretly harbored artistic aspirations. Although he soon determined that he lacked artistic talent, the study of the fine arts became the driving force of his life. At eighteen he took a trip with his father to Europe, where he saw many works of art. He entered Harvard in 1896, where he studied art under Charles Herbert Moore and Martin Mower who, he later recalled, "more than any other man taught me how to see." Moore urged him to continue on at Harvard in fine arts after his graduation with an A.B. in 1900 but, at the insistence of his father, he reluctantly returned to New York and entered the family banking business.

From 1900 to 1915 Sachs led two lives, one as a Wall Street banker and respected member of the New York business community and the other as an amateur art collector and connoisseur. He married Meta Pollack in 1904; they had three children. Every spare moment not devoted to business and his family, he spent visiting art dealers, collectors, and museums in New York City and acquiring works of art. During these years he made several gifts to Harvard's Fogg Art Museum, directed by his mentor Moore.

In 1912 Sachs's interest and generosity came to the attention of the new director of the Fogg, Edward Waldo Forbes, who invited him to join the Fogg's Visiting Committee. In 1913 Sachs became the committee's chair and demonstrated considerable effectiveness in using his New York connections and influence to obtain objects for the Fogg. Forbes, impressed by Sachs's competence, energy, and devotion to the fine arts, offered him the assistant directorship of the Fogg Art Museum in 1915.

Sachs accepted without hesitation, retired from the banking firm, and moved his family to Cambridge. He purchased "Shady Hill," the former home of famed Harvard fine arts professor Charles Eliot Norton. Despite his Jewish origins and "outsider" status, Sachs rapidly established himself as an active participant in

Boston's Brahmin culture. Shady Hill became the center of an active fine arts community in Cambridge, as Sachs used his home both as a classroom and as a place to entertain visiting dignitaries from the museum world. During World War I he was in the Ambulance Service of the American Red Cross, serving in France in 1918.

From 1915 until his retirement in 1948, Sachs built an international reputation as a collector and educator but most of all as a museum director. His friends and connections spanned continents, and he influenced a generation of students who went on to shape museum practice in the United States.

Sachs's devotion was first and foremost to the Fogg Art Museum. During the first decade of his partnership with Forbes, the two men succeeded in building a new structure for the museum, which opened in 1927. Besides much more space for the collection, the new building had classrooms and a conservation laboratory. In their tireless efforts on behalf of their alma mater, the "heavenly twins," as Sachs's close associate Agnes Mongan described them, raised money during the 1920s not only to build the museum but also to construct the Harvard Business School.

Central to Sachs's and Forbes's mission was the development of a world-class art collection. In the space of a decade Sachs created an internationally renowned collection of master drawings whose quality attested to his connoisseurship. His drawing collection was bequeathed to Harvard at his death. Through his infectious zeal, other donors and collectors, including Felix Warburg, Grenville Winthrop, and Maurice Wertheim, also gave generously to the Fogg.

In 1917 Sachs accepted the position of assistant professor at Harvard, becoming associate professor in 1922 and full professor in 1927. Teaching went hand-in-hand with administration throughout his tenure. He taught courses in eighteenth- and nineteenth-century drawings and prints until his retirement. His most popular course, however, was Museum Work and Museum Problems, which he established in 1922 to address the practical issues of museum management. He taught this unique course annually to a small group of graduate students as an informal and interactive seminar both in his home and in the Fogg Museum.

It was in the museum course that Sachs extended his influence as museum director and made his greatest mark. In a time when the museum movement in the United States was developing at a rapid pace, institutions were struggling to develop professional leadership and define operating principles. Through the museum course, Sachs worked tirelessly to instruct students in his model of ideal museum management and in principles of connoisseurship. He insisted on the highest standards of quality and on collecting only the best in all fields.

His ideal museum director was part art expert, part scholar, and most of all an effective mediator among the many factions that make up the museum world. His early years in New York had taught him to understand and respect the symbiotic relationships that exist among collectors, dealers, museum personnel, and scholars. He instructed his students in such knowledge and in the practical skills of becoming a museum administrator.

Students described Sachs as a "one-man employment agency," so effective was he in placing them in key museum positions around the country. In 1929 he recommended his most famous protégé, Alfred H. Barr, as first director of the Museum of Modern Art. From his post as founding member of MOMA's board of trustees, Sachs guided his former student in the establishment of America's first museum of modern art. Other students also became directors and curators in major institutions, among them the Museum of Fine Arts, Boston; the Metropolitan Museum of Art; the National Gallery, Washington D.C.; and numerous urban museums around the country. Sachs himself served on boards of trustees of a number of these institutions and played an active role in the American Association of Museums (president, 1932).

During World War II Sachs was a member of the American Commission for the Protection and Salvage of Historic and Artistic Monuments and devoted his time to protecting works of art in occupied countries. He received the French Legion of Honor, and in 1965 a gallery of the Museum of Modern Art devoted to drawings and prints was named in his honor. He died in Cambridge.

• Sachs's paperrs are in the Archives of the Fogg Museum, Harvard University Art Museums, Cambridge, Mass. See the Columbia Oral History Project, N.Y., for a transcribed interview with Sachs conducted by Saul Bennison (including letters and commentary). His publications include *Drawings in the Fogg Museum of Art* (1940), coauthored with Agnes Mongan; *The Pocket Book of Great Drawings* (1951); and *Modern Prints and Drawings* (1954). For information on his art collection, see *Memorial Exhibition: Works of Art from the Collection of Paul J. Sachs (1878–1965)* (1965). For information on his work as associate director of the Fogg Art Museum see *Harvard's Art Museums: 100 Years of Collecting* (1996). For his relationship to several of his famous students, see Nicholas Fox Weber, *Patron Saints: Five Rebels Who Opened Up America to a New Art, 1928–1943* (1992).

SALLY ANNE DUNCAN

SACHSE, Julius Friedrich (22 Nov. 1842–14 Nov. 1919), antiquarian, historian, and photographer, was born in Philadelphia, the son of Johann Heinrich Friedrich Sachse, an artist and designer, and Julianna D. W. Bühler. Julius F. Sachse attended public schools and the Lutheran Academy but had no university education; he was largely a self-educated man. Sachse's early business career was as a merchant of men's clothing accessories and a manufacturer of men's silk shirts. His achievements in shirtmaking were recognized at international trade fairs.

Having attained a secure financial position before the age of fifty, Sachse retired from his business interests to devote himself to historical pursuits. He focused his historical research on Pennsylvania German studies (for which he is best remembered) and Masonic studies. He was one of the founders of the Pennsylvania German Society in 1891, an officer from that time until his death, and the leading figure in the society's extensive publication program. Elected the first treasurer of the society, he held that office for twenty-three years before voluntarily retiring. He then became the society's president for one term (1913–1914), and served on its executive committee from 1914 until his death.

Sachse contributed eleven monographs to the informative series of published proceedings of the Pennsylvania German Society, beginning with his initial volume, "The Fatherland," in the multivolume *Narrative and Critical History of Pennsylvania: The German Influence in Its Settlement and Development* (1897–1929). He also provided the profuse illustrations—photographs, facsimiles, and drawings—that graced all of the society's publications. After his retirement from business, Sachse had become a proficient photographer, often selling his photos to leading Philadelphia publishers and periodicals, such as the *Ladies' Home Journal*. For a time he edited the *American Journal of Photography*.

Sachse collected extensively in the United States and abroad, developing a knack for finding rare imprints and manuscripts, either those of Pennsylvania German provenance or European materials of relevance to Pennsylvania history. His collection was especially focused on the German sects and dissenters—the Ephrata Society and its parent, the Dunkers (later known as the Church of the Brethren); the communitarian group, often called the Society of the Woman in the Wilderness, led by Johannes Kelpius; the Mennonites; and the keenly religious but individualistic Separatists of colonial Pennsylvania. Most of his Ephrata materials were secured in 1916 by the Seventh Day Baptist church, with headquarters in Plainfield, New Jersey; in 1982 this material was permanently loaned to the Pennsylvania State Archives in Harrisburg.

The best known of Sachse's work is his trilogy, *The German Pietists of Provincial Pennsylvania, 1694–1708* (1895); *The German Sectarians of Pennsylvania, 1708–1742* (1899); and *The German Sectarians of Pennsylvania, 1742–1800* (1901). Because these lavishly illustrated books were limited to 350 numbered copies, they continue to command high prices on the antiquarian market. Sachse also wrote a biography, *Justus Falckner, Mystic and Scholar* (1903), and edited the *Diarium of Magister Johannes Kelpius* (1917). Long considered to be the definitive works on their subjects, Sachse's books are credited with initiating interest in Pennsylvania German history. Because of Sachse's taste for the legendary, modern scholarship has raised questions about the documentary basis for Sachse's books, as well as their interpretation. Despite these caveats, Sachse's diligence in acquiring rare materials and his eloquence in portraying these little-known dissenters remain worthy of praise. Something of

Sachse's approach is revealed in the first lines of his 1899 volume on the German Sectarians:

Ephrata! Of all the words and names in the vocabulary of Pennsylvania none embraces so much of what is mystical and legendary as the word Ephrata, when it is used to denote the old monastic community which once flourished in the valley of the Cocalico in Lancaster County, and whose members lived according to the esoteric teachings, practised the mystic rites, and sought for both physical and spiritual regeneration and perfection according to the secret ritual as taught by the ascetic philosophers of old.

Although the Pennsylvania German subjects were of primary interest to Sachse, he also studied Masonry in the United States and Europe, developing for this purpose a wide international correspondence. He became the librarian and curator of the Grand Lodge of the Free and Accepted Masons of Pennsylvania (1906–1919) and was a member of several Philadelphia-area lodges. Of his many publications on this subject, Sachse's *Benjamin Franklin as a Freemason* (1906) received the most attention.

Sachse was elected to the American Philosophical Society in 1895, publishing in this connection a paper entitled "Horologuim Achaz." A member of numerous historical societies, he was one of the founders of the Pennsylvania Federation of Historical Societies in 1905, serving in its leading offices thereafter.

Sachse married Emma Caroline Lange of Philadelphia in 1864; they had five children. His friend and collaborator on Pennsylvania German Society projects, Henry M. M. Richards, wrote in his obituary:

Dr. Sachse may, very properly, be called a 'self-made' man. . . . He was a fine example of the strong mind in a strong body, which, with his active temperament, made him a person of unremitting industry, patient and painstaking in research, especially in the procuring of original matter. As an annalist, biographer, compiler and collector, and as a practical illustrator, along the lines of the specialities of his study and research, he was unsurpassed and has left behind him voluminous and striking evidences of his faithful, comprehensive labors in his chosen field of investigations.

• There are many references to Sachse's work and publications in Homer Tope Rosenberger, *The Pennsylvania Germans, 1891–1965 . . . Seventy-Fifth Anniversary Volume of the Pennsylvania German Society* (1966). Corlis F. Randolph, *Seventh Day Baptists in Europe and America*, vol. 2 (1910), refers often to Sachse. A succinct biographical notice is contained in Albert N. Rogers, *Seventh Day Baptists in Europe and America*, vol. 3 (1972). Information on Sachse's valuable Ephrata collection is found in Don A. Sanford, *A Choosing People: The History of the Seventh Day Baptists* (1992). Detailed information on Sachse's life and publications is found in several obituaries; these include Henry M. M. Richards, *Proceedings of the Pennsylvania German Society* 31 (1920 [1925]): 40–46; Corlis F. Randolph, the Seventh Day Baptist Church *Sabbath Recorder*, 15 Mar. 1920; and the Philadelphia *Public Ledger*, 16 Nov. 1919.

DONALD F. DURNBAUGH

SACK, Israel (15 Sept 1883–4 May 1959), antiques dealer, was born in Kovna (now Kaunas), Lithuania, the son of Abraham Zak. His mother's name is unknown. Under Russian rule Lithuanian Jews suffered from religious, political, and economic intolerance, and Sack's prosperous merchant family was no exception. Sack recalled that in 1894, the year Nicholas II became czar, "the position of the Jewish people began to get worse," and he resolved that when he was old enough he would go to America.

In order to work toward this goal Sack determined to equip himself with a universally necessary skill. He left school at age fourteen and, believing that "tools speak a universal language," apprenticed himself to a cabinetmaker. In two years he had mastered the trade and begun to take in piecework to earn money for his emigration. When he was eighteen, after a conscription notice arrived from the Russian army, he contracted with a local agent to join a group of emigrants who were to be smuggled into Germany. As part of the plan, the group was to remain hidden in a locked barn for the night, but before the night was over, Russian soldiers discovered the hideaway; while they broke in on one side of the barn, Sack dug his way out under another. A series of strangers helped him to continue his escape, which ended with his safe arrival in London. He found cabinet work there and in Birmingham, enabling him to save the $31 required for steerage passage to America.

Upon his arrival in Boston on 15 November 1903, Sack found a job working for a cabinetmaker who, he later recalled, both repaired antiques and "concocted" them from old wood. In 1905 Sack set up his own cabinetmaking shop and was soon fully employed repairing, buying, and selling old pieces. His shop was on Charles Street, Boston's antiques mecca, first at No. 85 and later also next door at No. 89. In 1910 he married Ann Goodman, with whom he would have four children.

From the beginning Sack was a great admirer of American furniture, particularly, he later reminisced, "furniture . . . that was made for important people. . . . I never had anything against ordinary people, usual people; only they don't interest me! I started to deal in the things that belonged to the most important families in America. Naturally I had the most important things and I sold to the most important people." Among the eminent Boston collectors who were his clients were artist Dwight Blaney and lawyer Eugene Bolles; the latter's large group of early New England furniture formed a cornerstone of the Metropolitan Museum's American Wing, opened in 1924. In 1923, after industrialist Henry Ford bought the Wayside Inn—a colonial building in Sudbury, Massachusetts, made famous by poet Henry Wadsworth Longfellow's 1863 collection *Tales of a Wayside Inn*—he asked Sack to furnish the entire place. "He didn't ask me what, where, or how much," reported Sack, who in two weeks furnished the inn with "the best."

Sack's fame spread, and during the 1920s he helped to form a number of private collections, including those of Henry Francis du Pont, founder of the Winterthur Museum, and Miss Ima Hogg, whose home, "Bayou Bend," is now part of the Houston Museum of Fine Arts. He was also a leader in encouraging and helping to create museum collections of American furniture, among them those of the William Rockhill Nelson Gallery in Kansas City, the Detroit Institute of Arts, and the Art Institute of Chicago. During this decade he established, in addition, the I. Sack Cabinet Hardware Company in Boston to produce reproduction furniture hardware and replacement parts for furniture and clocks. He opened the King Hooper Shop on Chestnut Street in Boston to offer a decorating service and textiles, ceramics, and other accessories, and he bought the King Hooper mansion in Marblehead, Massachusetts, filling it with a selection of choice American furniture. In 1927 he opened a branch of his antiques business on Madison Avenue in New York City.

Unfortunately all of this activity put a strain on the firm's finances, and the ensuing depression years were dismal for the business. Debts forced a sale of inventory in January 1932 at the New York auction house American Art Association–Anderson Galleries, and sales lagged. In 1934 Sack closed his Boston shop and centered his business in New York. His sons Harold and Albert joined the firm in the early 1930s, only to leave again with the onset of World War II. They and their younger brother, Robert, returned to the business in the 1950s. By that time Sack's health had begun to deteriorate. He died in Brookline, Massachusetts.

Israel Sack was part of a small but influential group of collectors, scholars, and dealers who, in the first quarter of the twentieth century, began to see the relatively simple forms and understated ornament of American furniture as an expression of a uniquely American artistry. Because high-style European furniture of the same period achieved greatness in an exactly opposite manner—through elaborate form and ornament—Sack and the other promoters of American furniture were breaking new ground. The major components of the American style that Sack discerned were explained in *Fine Points of Furniture: Early American*, written by Albert Sack and first published in 1950: line, form, and proportion were preeminent; decoration was subordinate. An impressive provenance, or historical association, while always desirable, could not make up for deficiencies in these major design areas. In providing a format in which each type of object was illustrated and discussed so that the reader could see the differences among examples designated good, better, and best, Albert Sack codified his father's aesthetic approach to American furniture. It was the first book to provide a practical guide to connoisseurship in the field, and it shaped the aesthetics of a generation.

Although Israel Sack's enthusiasm had always been directed toward the chase and the capture of fine pieces and not the pursuit of wealth—or even, necessarily, the practice of sound business principles—he conveyed his knowledge of both the practical and the artistic aspects of American furniture to his sons with passion and clarity. As the prestige of American antiques rose in the years after World War II, the firm continued to specialize in high-style American furniture, perpetuating and expanding Israel Sack's legacy and putting the business on a sound financial footing. In addition, his sons passed along in tangible form their father's gift of appreciation and understanding of American furniture through gifts to museums, research grants, and educational exhibitions. In 1996 the Winterthur Museum honored Israel Sack by presenting its seventh Henry Francis du Pont Award posthumously to him and to his three sons, for having "dedicated themselves to the connoisseurship, preservation, and collecting of American furniture."

• "The Reminiscences of Mr. Israel Sack" (Oct. 1953) are in the Oral History Section of the Ford Motor Company Archives, Dearborn, Mich. For additional biographical information see Harold Sack with Max Wilk, *American Treasure Hunt: The Legacy of Israel Sack* (1986), and Helen Harris, "Israel Sack: An American Awakening," *Town and Country*, Feb. 1982. For more on his impact see American Art Association–Anderson Galleries, Inc., *100 Important American Antiques* (1932) and *The Israel Sack Collections of American Antiques* (sales brochure, 1928). An obituary is in the *New York Times*, 5 May 1959.

ELIZABETH STILLINGER

SACKLER, Arthur Mitchell (22 Aug. 1913–26 May 1987), research psychiatrist, art collector, and philanthropist, was born in Brooklyn, New York, the son of Isaac Sackler and Sophie (maiden name unknown). In the 1930s Sackler simultaneously studied medicine at New York University (NYU) and art history at NYU and the Cooper Union Art Institute. To fund his medical studies, he joined the William Douglas MacAdams medical advertising agency. Sackler earned his B.S. from NYU in 1933 and his M.D. from NYU in 1937. In 1935 he married Else Jorgensen; they had two children.

After receiving his medical degree, Sackler worked as a physician and pediatrician at New York's Lincoln Hospital until 1939 and as a resident psychiatrist at Creedmoor State Hospital on Long Island from 1944 to 1946. Following a divorce, he married Marietta Lutze in 1949; they had two children. Also in 1949 he became the director of research at Creedmoor Institute of Psychobiological Studies, a position that he held until 1954. As a medical researcher, Sackler performed pioneering work in biological psychiatry and the chemical causes of illness. With his two physician brothers and other collaborators, he eventually published more than 140 research papers on neuroendocrinology, psychiatry, and experimental medicine. He also served as the associate chair of the 1950 First International Congress of Psychiatry's international committee for research. Sackler was the first to use ultrasound for medical diagnosis and to identify histamine as a hormone. He also developed sex steroids and other biochemotherapies and called attention to the importance of cell receptor sites. He coauthored *Great Physiodynamic Therapies* (1956) and was the editor in chief of the *Journal of Clinical and Experimental Psychopathology* from 1950 to 1962. Sackler chaired the International Task Force on World Health Manpower for the World Health Organization beginning in 1969 and the National Committee to Save Our Schools' Health from 1971 to 1972.

Combining his practice of medicine with an acute business sense, Sackler began buying stocks in pharmaceutical companies, which became the foundation of his fortune. In 1947 he bought the MacAdams advertising agency, and in the 1950s he entered the vastly profitable medical publishing field. He became the chair of the board of Medical Press Incorporated in 1954 and the president of Physicians News Service Incorporated in 1955. In 1960 Sackler began publishing the *Medical Tribune*, a biweekly newspaper for doctors that expanded into an international publishing organization with publications in ten languages and offices in eleven countries. By the time of his death, Sackler's fortune was estimated by *Forbes* magazine at more than $175 million.

Sackler's dedication to medicine and to medical publishing was complemented by his dedication to art collecting. He began collecting art in the mid-1940s, concentrating on pre- and early Renaissance and French impressionist and postimpressionist paintings. In 1950 he began to acquire what became the world's largest and most important private collection of ancient Chinese art. Sackler gave much of his art away, asserting that "great art doesn't belong to anybody. Never did. Never will" (*Washington Post*, 27 May 1987). Throughout the 1960s and early 1970s he was a member of the advisory council of the Columbia University Department of Art History and Archaeology. Museums and galleries bear his name at the Metropolitan Museum of Art, Princeton University, Harvard University, the Smithsonian Institution, and Beijing University, among other institutions. Particularly notable are the Sackler Wing of the Metropolitan Museum of Art, which opened in 1978 and which houses the ancient Egyptian Temple of Dendur, and the Smithsonian's Sackler Gallery, a museum of Asian and Near Eastern art built through Sackler's gift of 1,000 objects and his contribution of $4 million (the museum opened in Washington, D.C., four months after his death). Sackler's generosity prompted Thomas Lawton, the director of the Smithsonian's Freer Gallery of Art, to call him "a modern Medici" (Dongjing, p. vi).

Sackler explained his parallel interests as two sides of the same coin: "Science is a discipline pursued with passion; art is a passion pursued with discipline." He preferred to purchase entire collections rather than individual pieces, stating, "I collect as a biologist. To really understand a civilization, a society, you must have a large enough corpus of data. You can't know twentieth-century art by looking only at Picassos and Henry Moores" (*New York Times*, 27 May 1987).

Sackler also made many philanthropic contributions to the sciences, beginning in 1958 when he founded the Laboratories for Therapeutic Research, a nonprofit basic research center at the Brooklyn College of Pharmacy of Long Island University. He endowed the Sackler Institute of Graduate Biomedical Science at New York University, the Sackler Center for Health Communications at Tufts University in Philadelphia, the Sackler Sciences Center at Clark University in Worcester, Massachusetts, and the Sackler School of Medicine at Tel Aviv University in Israel. Beginning in 1983 he sponsored Chinese doctors and interpreters to study in the United States and sent American experts to China to train hospital managerial and administrative staff. In 1986 he was instrumental in forging an agreement for the contraceptive company G. D. Searle to make its technological knowledge and trademark available to China.

Following his divorce from his second wife, Sackler married Jill Lesley Tully; they had no children. He died in New York City.

• For information on Sackler's career and his contributions to the art world, see "Arthur Sackler: Art, Discipline, Passion, Science," *Economist* 304 (26 Sept. 1987): 37–38; Chen Dongjing, "A Modern Medici Benefits China," *Beijing Review* 30 (20 July 1987): vi–vii; and Yang Yuli, "U.S. Doctor's Generosity to China," *Beijing Review* 34 (13 May 1991): 32–34. Obituaries are in the *New York Times* and the *Washington Post*, both 27 May 1987; *Smithsonian* 18 (Oct. 1987): 10; and *Apollo* 126 (Oct. 1987): 303.

CHRISTINE KEINER

SACKLER, Howard Oliver (19 Dec. 1929–14 Oct. 1982), dramatist, director, and screenwriter, was born in New York City, the son of Martin Sackler, a real estate agent, and Ida Rapaport. Sackler spent most of his youth in Florida before returning as a young man to the city of his birth. He wrote his first screenplays while he attended Brooklyn College, from which he received his B.A. in 1950. One of these early scripts, *Desert Padre*, was filmed in 1950 by another young artist, Stanley Kubrick, at the beginning of his own career. Grants from the Rockefeller and Littauer foundations allowed Sackler to complete two more early screenplays for Kubrick, *Killer's Kiss* (1952) and *Fear and Desire* (1953).

In 1953 Sackler founded what quickly became one of the most highly regarded labels in the recording industry, Caedmon Records. Sackler's tenure as Caedmon's production director lasted until 1968; during these years he resided almost entirely in London. In an interview with Lewis Funke shortly after his retirement from Caedmon, Sackler revealed how much his experience in the recording industry affected the development of his art: "One can't learn about plays by reading them nearly as well as one can by getting inside them, conducting them, directing them" (Funke, p. 56).

In part because of the insights he gained directing for Caedmon Records, success came early to Sackler as a playwright. He won the Maxwell Anderson Award for verse drama in 1954 for his first one-act play, *Uriel Acosta*, and he won the Sergel Award in 1959 for his next short work, *The Yellow Loves* (produced in 1962). Sackler married Greta Lynn Lungren in 1963; they had two children. *A Few Enquiries*, an anthology of four one-act plays that were produced in 1965 and published in 1970, and *The Pastime of Monsieur Robert*, a full-length play produced in 1966, established Sackler as one of this country's leading young playwrights.

Sackler found fame as a mature dramatist with his second full-length work, *The Great White Hope*. This play won for its author both a large popular audience and what is known as the triple crown of drama prizes for the 1968-1969 season: the Antoinette Perry (Tony) award, the New York Drama Critics Circle award, and the Pulitzer Prize. Like many of his plays, *The Great White Hope* grew out of Sackler's lifelong interest in poetry and history. It was written in four-beat lines, a verse form that Sackler thought best captured the syncopated speech of the American vernacular. As for the play's central protagonist, Sackler had long wanted to stage the life of Jack Johnson, the turn-of-the-century boxer who became this country's first black heavyweight boxing champion. Sackler saw in Johnson's story the raw materials for a uniquely American tragedy. "Specifically," he told Funke, "what drew me to *Great White Hope* was not that it dealt with elements in the black and white struggle but that it dealt with a man who, following his personal bent, ran into the taboos and the obstacles of a black man" (Funke, p. 41). The play was first produced at the Arena Stage in Washington, D.C., before opening on Broadway in October 1968. Two years later it was made into a feature film starring its original stage leads, James Earl Jones and Jane Alexander.

Nothing Sackler was to write later achieved the success of *The Great White Hope*. *Semmelweiss* (1977), another historical drama in the mold of *The Great White Hope*, was produced in Buffalo, New York, but it never reached Broadway because of conflicts over casting and re-writing. *Goodbye Fidel* (1980) made it to Broadway, but was poorly received by critics and met with a short, disappointing run. Sackler turned most of his creative energies to screenwriting during the 1970s. He collaborated on scripts for *Bugsy* (1973), *Jaws II* (1976), *Gray Lady Down* (1978), and *Saint Jack* (1979). At age fifty-two he died suddenly of pulmonary thrombosis on the island of Ibiza, off the Mediterranean coast of Spain, where he had made his home during the final fifteen years of his life.

Though Sackler is best known for his work for the stage and screen, he was also a talented poet who acknowledged W. H. Auden and T. S. Eliot as lifelong influences. His poems were published in the *Hudson Review*, *Poetry*, *Commentary*, and *New Directions Annual*. In 1954 a collection of his poetry was published under the title *Want My Shepherd*. But Sackler's talents were by no means confined to the pen. He was an accomplished stage director, and he had even tried his hand at directing for television in a well-regarded NBC special, *Shakespeare: Soul of an Age* (1964).

What is most notable about Howard Sackler is the variety of his accomplishments. He was simultaneously a gifted poet, playwright, and stage and television director. But his chief artistic and cultural legacy is most likely the ambitious project he engineered early in his career for Caedmon Records. With Sackler at its helm, Caedmon issued more than 200 masterfully directed recordings of classics of world drama. Because Sackler saw his mission at Caedmon to be making these works more publicly accessible, he put to use many of the period's best-known actors, including Rex Harrison, Albert Finney, Jessica Tandy, and Paul Scofield. At Caedmon Records, Sackler was instrumental in creating a new modern audience, not just for the masterpieces he chose to record, but for drama as a whole.

• Howard Sackler's manuscripts are at the Humanities Research Center at the University of Texas, Austin. See Lewis Funke, *Playwrights Talk about Writing: 12 Interviews with Lewis Funke* (1975), pp. 39–67, for Sackler's fullest comments about his own life and art. Laudatory reviews of *The Great White Hope* are numerous; especially thoughtful negative ones are in *Harper's*, Jan. 1969, and the *New Republic*, 26 Oct. 1968. Obituaries are in the *New York Times*, 15 Oct. 1982, the *Washington Post*, 16 Oct. 1982, and *The Times* (London), 18 Oct. 1982.

KEVIN R. RAHIMZADEH

SADLER, Harley (4 Sept. 1892–14 Oct. 1954), tent show actor-manager, oilman, and Texas legislator, was born near Pleasant Plains, Arkansas, the son of Junius E. and Lula T. Sadler. Junius, after several years of marginally successful farming, settled down to the life of a general merchant in Stamford, Texas, where Harley first demonstrated the interest in show business that was to dominate his life. With no training beyond participation in high school plays and the town band, he left home before graduation to join a small carnival as a musician.

In the next few years, the fledgling actor appeared in repertoire in Fort Worth and Waco; barnstormed to the West Coast; failed in Chicago variety theaters; played on tab(leau) shows, which featured girls and gags, a medicine show, and a Mississippi riverboat; and appeared with Rentfrow's Jolly Pathfinders, a tent show, for twenty-six weeks in Texas City. At the age of twenty-two, Sadler joined Roy E. Fox's Popular Players as second comedian, doubling on baritone horn in the street band; not long after he became first comedian. In 1917 he married Willie Louise "Billie" Massengale, from Cameron, Texas. The couple joined Brunk's No. 2 tent show, with Sadler serving as principal comedian and stage director; his wife soon joined him onstage.

Sadler managed Brunk's No. 2 show while Glen Brunk served in the army during World War I. After Brunk's return, Sadler entered into a partnership with the Brunk Brothers' organization, becoming manager and equal owner of Brunk's No. 3. His company proved an immediate success. "I really believe that Sadler would do business on the Sahara Desert," a correspondent wrote to *Billboard*. In 1922 Sadler bought out the Brunk's interest and became owner/manager/principal comedian of "Harley Sadler's Own Show."

Like most tent shows, this was a family affair: Billie, in addition to functioning as business manager, became the leading lady; Gloria, the Sadlers' only child, performed at intermission as soon as she could walk onstage; Harley's mother-in-law worked backstage; his brother-in-law was boss canvasman; Ferd, his brother, served as advance man, and Ferd's wife sold tickets in the box office; numerous nieces and nephews spent summer vacations working on their uncle's show. As the show prospered, Sadler became a favorite son of the sixty-odd communities in west Texas and eastern New Mexico that he visited on a biennial basis. His popularity, both onstage and off, was phenomenal, based in part on an incredible memory for names, faces, and local events, but even more on a sympathetic understanding of the people who comprised his audience. Generosity with both his talent and money cemented this popularity.

He remained prosperous and generous until the coming of the Great Depression. Then, in 1931, instead of cutting back as most companies were doing, he purchased an enormous tent that seated 2,500 spectators, and he enlarged his company to over fifty people. He quickly found that his audience could no longer afford the price of admission. An attempt to manage a circus proved financially disastrous, as did a Texas centennial pageant called *The Siege of the Alamo*. His substantial holdings, said to be over $1 million, rapidly melted away. Rather than declare bankruptcy, he sold off his investments, paid what bills he could, and promised eventual payment of those outstanding. Taking over a tiny tent show playing in the Rio Grande Valley, he served as leading actor, emcee, drummer, boss canvasman, and truck driver; by 1938 he had returned to a state of solvency, managing to pay off $25,000 in debts.

Around 1940, with tent show audiences lured away by air conditioned movie houses and drive-in theaters, Sadler branched out to become an independent oil operator. As with most wildcatters, he enjoyed occasional periods of feasting interrupted by prolonged stretches of famine. He continued to operate a much-reduced tent show until the death of his daughter in 1941, when he sold his tent and retired from show business. This retirement was short-lived; Sadler remained intermittently active on the stage until a farewell tour in partnership with Joe McKennon in 1947.

In 1941 Sadler entered state politics and was elected to the Texas House of Representatives from the Sweetwater district. He proved to be an honest, compassionate, and diligent—if somewhat naive—legislator. "There has never been a milder, more sincere sort of man in the Legislature than Harley Sadler, within the memory of the old-timers of the press corps," wrote Raymond Brooks in the *Austin American*. Having served three terms in the house, he rejected suggestions that he run for the U.S. House or the governorship of Texas and instead lost a race for the Texas Senate over the issue of a tax exemption for tractor gas used on farms and ranches. In 1950 he moved to Abilene, where he was again elected to the Texas House. Two years later he ran unopposed for a seat in the state senate; he was serving this term when he died while emceeing an amateur talent show in Avoca, Texas.

Tent shows, an often-overlooked theatrical form, provided entertainment for small town America during the late nineteenth and early twentieth centuries. Offering full-length plays and variety acts during the intermissions, they were headlined by the *New York Times* in 1927 as "Bigger than Broadway." This article estimated that while annual attendance at "legitimate" theater was 48 million, the tent shows played to a total audience more than twice that size. Harley Sadler's tent show was in its time the most successful and largest of the many hundreds of traveling "rag op'ries" that brought family entertainment to thousands of isolated villages all over the United States.

• Archival materials are found in the Southwest Collection of Texas Tech University and at The National Society for the Preservation of Tent, Folk and Repertoire Theatre in Mount Pleasant, Iowa. Sadler's life is chronicled in Clifford Ashby and Suzanne DePauw May, *Trouping through Texas: Harley Sadler and His Tent Show* (1982). See also Clifford Ashby, "Folk Theatre in a Tent," *Natural History*, Mar. 1983, pp. 6–20, and William L. Slout, *Theatre in a Tent* (1972).

CLIFFORD ASHBY

SAFFIN, John (22 Nov. 1626–18 Jul. 1710), jurist and merchant, was born in Exeter, Devonshire, England, the son of Simon Saffin and Grace Garrett. While Saffin's later public life is well documented, other details are vague and incomplete. Around 1634 the family immigrated to Scituate, Massachusetts, where Saffin became a student at Charles Chauncy's (1592–1672) school. He did not attend college, but employment by Foster and Hoar in Boston apparently provided his legal training. His mercantile interests perhaps led to his election to the board of selectmen (the chief administrative authority of the town) in 1653, but in 1654 and for the next few years he was engaged in commercial activities in Virginia. He was back in Plymouth by December 1658, at which time he married Martha Willett, daughter of Thomas Willett, who later became the first mayor of New York City. They had eight children. For the next three decades he lived in Boston, where his wife died in a smallpox epidemic in 1678. Saffin's second wife was Elizabeth, the widow of Peter Lidgett, whom he married in June 1680. She died in 1687, childless, and Saffin moved to New Bristol, Massachusetts (now in Rhode Island), in 1688. That November, he married Rebecca Lee.

Saffin's economic, social, and governmental position came through his mercantile interests, realty, and slave trading. He was a member of a committee of the General Court (the colonial legislature) charged with drafting a governmental charter in 1686. He was also the last Speaker of the colonial House of Representatives in 1686 and the first judge of probate in the Inferior Court of Common Pleas when the county of Bristol was formed in 1692. Saffin was elected councilor annually from 1693 to 1699, continuing to serve as judge until 1702. He was named judge of the Supreme Court at Plymouth on 1 August 1701, but his councilorship in Bristol in 1703 was vetoed by Governor Joseph Dudley, principally because of a lawsuit between Saffin and his servant Adam that had come before the supreme court in 1702. In 1694 Saffin had signed a document agreeing to free Adam seven years later. But he then turned Adam over to Thomas Shepherd of Bristol, and Shepherd bound him out to John Wilkins. Adam called for his freedom in 1701, but Saffin threatened to maintain his slave status by exiling him from the province. The records of this case are among the earliest abolition documents on record.

Saffin's only published prose, *A Brief and Candid Answer*, (1701) argued against a tract by Judge Samuel Sewall, *The Selling of Joseph* (1700), which likened the slave trade to the biblical Joseph's being sold by his brethren. Saffin tried to refute Sewall's argument by Scripture and by alleging that God had ordained a hierarchy of all peoples, "some to be born Slaves, and so to remain during their lives." Saffin's bigotry and economic thinking show in his distinction between "men" and "Negroes," whose character he described as "Cowardly," "Prone to Revenge," "Libidinous, Deceitful, False and Rude," and in his argument that, should slaves be set free, owners would lose the money spent to purchase them.

Aside from fugitive printings and *A Brief and Candid Answer*, all of Saffin's writing is recorded in a holograph commonplace book of 198 pages (some original pages are missing), which includes biographical notes, letters, religious thoughts and maxims, medicinal cures, memoranda from his reading or of events (some of the foregoing being copied from such sources as Sir Philip Sidney's *Arcadia*), and poems. The poems are not entered in chronological order, and a few are given in two versions. The fifty-five poems include a range of types: the elegy, epitaph, love lyric, verse letter, epithalamion, encomium, satire, character, acrostic, anagram, as well as occasional and "society" verse. These are supplemented by "The Negroes Character" (the eight-line poem referred to above) and a tombstone epitaph for his son Thomas. (The tombstone reproduces arms, partially from Saffin of Somersetshire, "three crescents jessant as many etoiles, impaling a lion rampant.") The poetry employs public and private themes, including domestic life; generally it employs the heroic couplet in a plain style. Saffin died in Bristol, Massachusetts.

• There is no principal repository of Saffin's papers. *A Brief and Candid Answer* (1701) is reprinted in George H. Moore, *Notes on the History of Slavery in Massachusetts* (1866; repr. 1968), Appendix C, pp. 251–56; *A True and Particular Narrative* (1701), Saffin's version of the lawsuit with his servant, which originally appeared annexed to *A Brief and Candid Answer*, is reprinted in *Publications of the Colonial Society of Massachusetts* 1 (1895): 103–12.

Saffin's manuscript commonplace book is in the Rhode Island Historical Society, Providence, and has been edited by Caroline Hazard, *John Saffin, His Book (1665–1708): A Collection of Various Matters of Divinity, Law, & State Affairs Epitomiz'd Both in Verse and Prose* (1928). Poetic selections are given in Harrison T. Meserole, ed., *Seventeenth-Century American Poetry* (1968), and Kenneth Silverman, ed., *Colonial American Poetry* (1968).

Discussions of Saffin's writings appear in Harold S. Jantz, *The First Century of the New England Verse* (1944; repr. 1962, 1974); Alyce E. Sands, "John Saffin: Seventeenth-Century American Citizen and Poet" (Ph.D. diss., Penn. State Univ., 1965); Kathryn Zabelle Derounian, "'Mutuall Sweet Content': The Love Poetry of John Saffin," in *Puritan Poets and Poetics*, ed. Peter White (1985); and Lawrence W. Towner, "The Sewall-Saffin Dialogue on Slavery," *William and Mary Quarterly* 21 (1964): 40–52.

JOHN T. SHAWCROSS

SAFFORD, James Merrill (13 Aug. 1822–3 July 1907), geologist, was born in Zanesville, Ohio, the son of Henry Safford, a physician, and Patience Van Horne. Safford entered Ohio University in Athens, Ohio, from the public schools of Zanesville. He received the B.S. in 1844 and the A.M. in 1846. He then entered Yale University where he spent two years. In 1847 he reportedly was living in Benjamin Silliman's laboratory at Yale. Yale later granted him an honorary Ph.D. in 1866, one of the earliest American doctorates in geology. He also received an M.D. at the University of Nashville in 1872, apparently earned through on-the-job study while at Cumberland University during the post–Civil War years.

In 1848 Safford joined the faculty of Cumberland University in Lebanon, Tennessee, as professor of "Chemistry, Mineralogy, Geology, etc.," and natural history. He remained at Cumberland, variously titled as professor of natural history, chemistry, and geology; professor of natural science; or professor of physical science, until 1873. The university closed, however, between 1862 and 1866 because of the Civil War, so Safford operated his farm, taught languages at the preparatory school level, and engaged in oil and gas prospecting. He married Catherine K. Howard Owen, widow of Benjamin R. Owen, a former trustee of Cumberland University, in 1853. She had three children, and they had two daughters.

In 1873 Safford became professor of chemistry in the medical department of the University of Nashville. This proprietary school, owned by the faculty, contracted its services to the university. Safford may have purchased the position from his predecessor, John Berrien Linsley, an old acquaintance. In 1874 Nashville's chemistry department was merged with that of Vanderbilt University, but Safford retained his position until the departments were separated in 1895. He then resumed his position at the University of Nashville for two years. In 1875 he was appointed a half-time professor of geology and natural history in the newly organized literary department of Vanderbilt University, retaining his position in the proprietary medical college until 1895. From 1865 to 1900 he was dean of the pharmaceutical department and was in charge of the School of Chemistry for the 1885–1886 academic year. When he retired from both the academic and pharmaceutical departments of Vanderbilt and became a professor emeritus in 1900, he was the last active member of the original faculty of Vanderbilt University. He was Tennessee state geologist and mineralogist while on leave from Cumberland University between 1854 and 1860 and, after the survey was suspended during the Civil War, from 1871 to 1899. He was a member of the Tennessee State Board of Health from its founding in 1866 to 1896 and was vice president for much of his tenure. He was a judge in Group I, including mines and ores, at the Centennial Exposition in Philadelphia in 1876. He also was a judge at the Cotton Exposition in Atlanta in 1882 and at the Louisville Exposition in 1883. He was chief of the Department of Geology Minerals and Mining at the Tennessee Centennial Exposition in Nashville in 1896–1897.

Safford contributed to general geology, geologic mapping, economic geology, paleontology, and geology related to public health and agriculture. He was an important college-level instructor and administrator. His reputation rests primarily on his pioneering description of Tennessee's geologic rock column and in the geologic mapping of Tennessee. He began field studies for this work when much of the state remained a wilderness, requiring him to "live off the country"; much of it had to be carried out on foot and with only a compass and a pocket level. The first comprehensive study of the state's geology, Safford's work became the basis for all subsequent research. He published fifty-three works, including three consultant reports. In 1858 he first recognized a probable island, eighty to ninety miles in diameter, existing in the Paleozoic seas at the state's center. This feature, which became known as the Nashville Dome, is one of the major structural elements of the North American continent. His *Geology of Tennessee* (1869) includes the first colored geologic map of Tennessee and a comprehensive description of the sequence of rocks exposed in the state. It clearly recognized the use of fossils in correlating rock layers.

Safford also described the geology of each Tennessee county, with county maps, in *Introduction to the Resources of Tennessee* (1874), edited by J. B. Killebrew and assisted by Safford. *The Elementary Geology of Tennessee* (1876), with Killebrew as coauthor, is an updated and more comprehensive version of his earlier *Geology of Tennessee*. In 1884 Safford wrote *Physicogeographical and Agricultural Features of the States of Tennessee (and Kentucky)*, which was included in the reports of the *Tenth Census of the United States*, along with a *Report on the Cotton Production in the United States*. He published an improved *Geological Map of Tennessee* in 1888 and followed with later editions. Safford and Killebrew also coauthored *The Elements of the Geology of Tennessee* (1900), a textbook adopted by the state legislature for use in the public schools. He wrote several bulletins on water supply problems, including a report on the public water supply of the city of Memphis.

Safford was a member of the American Association for the Advancement of Science and was a founding member of the Geological Society of America. He died in Dallas, Texas.

• Basic sources of information include Leonard Alberstadt, *From Top to Bottom: A Small Science Department's 120-Year Struggle to Develop and Survive at Vanderbilt University (1875–1995)* (1995); Samuel M. Bain, "Southern Contributions to Natural History," *Journal of the Tennessee Academy of Science* 3, no. 2 (1928): 25–32, and no. 3 (1928): 27–31; Winstead Payne Boone, *A History of Cumberland University, Lebanon, Tennessee* (1935); J. T. McGill, "James M. Safford," *Transactions of the Tennessee Academy of Science* 2 (1917): 48–54; George P. Merrill, "Contributions to the History of American Geology," *Report of the U.S. National Museum under the Direction of the Smithsonian Institution, for the Year Ending June 30, 1904* (1906), pp. 189–733; William S. Speer, *Sketches of Prominent Tennesseans, Containing Biographies and Records of Many of the Families Who Have Attained Prominence in Tennessee* (1888); Richard G. Stearnes, "James Merrill Safford," *Earth Science History* 4 (1985): 38–48; and John J. Stevenson, "Memoir of James Merrill Safford," *Bulletin of the Geological Society of America* 19 (1909): 522–27.

RALPH L. LANGENHEIM, JR.

SAFFORD, Mary Jane (31 Dec. 1834–8 Dec. 1891), Civil War nurse and physician, was born in Hyde Park, Vermont, the daughter of Joseph Warren Safford and Diantha Little, farmers. Mary had three older brothers and one or two sisters. In 1837 or 1838 the entire family moved to the frontier town of Crete, Illinois, in Will County, on the Indiana border about thirty miles south of Chicago. Mary, an unusually intelligent child, received some education at home under the tutelage of her mother. To further her education, Mary was sent to Canada, probably near Montreal, during the early 1840s. There she learned French, needlework, and German. According to contemporary documents, she then undertook further educational travels in the United States and the West Indies before returning to Illinois to live. Her father died when Mary was fourteen, and her mother died the following year. She subsequently lived with one of her brothers, Alfred Boardman Safford, who had prepared for a legal career but became a successful businessman.

In 1854 Alfred began work as a banker in Shawneetown, Illinois, near the Ohio River, and there Mary joined him. She proceeded to open and teach a public school. Despite local opposition to the "Safford Ragged School" (Perrin, p. 56c), stemming from the town's divided allegiances between northern and southern political factions, virtually all the local children attended, and, in time, the school proved the foundation of Shawneetown's system of public education. In 1858 bank business led Alfred and Mary to relocate in Cairo, Illinois, at the confluence of the Ohio and Mississippi rivers. It has been recorded that she and her brother founded a free school in Cairo before the outbreak of the Civil War.

The outbreak of the Civil War in 1861 changed the course of Mary's life. In April Cairo became the base camp for the Union's Army of the West, under the leadership of General Ulysses S. Grant, formerly a merchant from Galena, Illinois. The Saffords knew Grant as well as Abraham Lincoln, who had left Illinois for the presidency only two months earlier. With permission from Grant, Mary began to bring food and relief supplies to the encamped soldiers, who had been suffering from exposure, illness, and malnutrition even before they commenced fighting. The soldiers dubbed her the "Angel of Cairo" for her efforts.

By June Mary Ann Bickerdyke of Galesburg, Illinois, had arrived in Cairo and joined with Mary Safford in an entirely volunteer effort to improve health conditions for the army. Together, and with the help of Eliza Porter, the relief efforts expanded beyond personal distribution of food and supplies to the opening of a hospital with a kitchen and the use of supplies shipped south by train from Chicago. Bickerdyke took charge of this enterprise, and Safford assisted her.

Grant's first major contest with the Confederacy came at the battle of Belmont, on the west bank of the Mississippi River, in November 1861. Medical historian Linus P. Brockett wrote that on the morning after the conflict, Safford ventured "early on the field, fearlessly penetrating far into the enemies' lines, with her handkerchief tied upon a little stick, waving above her head as a flag of truce,—ministering to the wounded" (Brockett and Vaughan, p. 358). Boats brought the wounded back to Cairo, where they received care from Safford and the other unofficial army nurses, supported with supplies from the new U.S. Sanitary Commission, organized the previous month. After the battle of Fort Donelson in Kentucky during the winter of 1862, Safford again helped Bickerdyke tend the wounded aboard the *City of Memphis*, a steamboat converted to a floating hospital. At the battle of Shiloh, April 1862, Safford nursed the wounded aboard the hospital ship *Hazel Dell*.

Under the strain of her nursing service in the battle of Shiloh, Safford's health broke down in early 1862. She therefore undertook an extensive world tour that lasted five years. The ostensible reason for this trip was to regain her health, and she did have an operation on her back in Paris for an injury sustained while caring for the wounded. But she reportedly also became involved in nursing the wounded in Austria during the Austro-Prussian War of 1866 and in Italy during the war leading to Italian unification, and she spent time abroad helping Norwegian girls who wanted to emigrate to the United States (Brockett and Vaughan, p. 360).

Upon her return to the United States, probably late in 1866, Safford enrolled in the New York Medical College for Women, founded in 1863. She completed a three-year curriculum that included training in homeopathic medicine, obstetrics, and diseases of women. She graduated in 1869 and returned to Europe, this time to the University of Vienna, for additional medical training. She also spent time in Breslau, Prussia.

She is credited with having performed the first ovariotomy by a woman physician during this second extended sojourn abroad, and she made the acquaintance of James Jackson Putnam, a Bostonian and pioneer in developing the medical specialty of neurology.

Following her return to the United States in about 1872, Safford lived in Chicago, where she had a medical practice, and married James Blake, with whom she moved to Boston in 1873. In Boston she joined the faculty of the newly opened Boston University School of Medicine as a professor of diseases of women and was admitted to membership in the Massachusetts Homeopathic Medical Society in the same year.

Also in 1873 she joined the faculty of the Boston University School of Medicine. Boston and the Homeopathic Society distinguished themselves from orthodox medical practice by their adherence to the philosophy of homeopathy, that is, the belief that small, specially prepared doses of a substance that produces symptoms of illness in a healthy person will cure a sick person exhibiting the same symptoms. Safford shared and practiced this medical philosophy.

In 1879 Safford's title changed to professor of gynecology. The subjects she taught included the study of normal and abnormal menstruation, normal and abnormal ovarian function, diseases of the uterus, diseases of the breasts, and hysteria. Under the name Mary Blake, she published a book on pregnancy titled *Pre-Natal Influence* in 1874. She also took a leading role in advocating exercise for women's health and stressed the importance of hygiene, environment, and climate to good health. She advocated dress reform, preferring wide, flat-heeled shoes herself, and worked to improve conditions for working women and girls in Boston. In 1875 she became a member of the Boston School Committee, and in 1884, under the name Mary Safford, she cooperated with Mary E. Allen, superintendent of a ladies' and children's gymnasium, in publishing a book titled *Health and Strength for Girls*.

In 1880 Mary Safford resumed use of her maiden name, and James Blake disappeared from the record of her life. In 1887 her health again failed, and she retired to Florida, where her brother Anson P. K. Safford, an entrepreneur and former governor of the Arizona Territory, had founded the new city of Tarpon Springs. She is said to have taken with her two daughters she adopted in Boston, but this has yet to be verified. In Tarpon Springs she resumed her medical practice but died soon after of typhoid fever. Her brother Anson died a week later of the same cause. Mary Safford is buried in a family plot in Cycadia Cemetery, Tarpon Springs.

Mary Safford, teacher, Civil War nurse, and women's physician, was at the forefront in the effort to improve wartime medical treatment, in the struggle for women's rights, and in the emergence of the new medical field of gynecology. Not a publicist in these causes, she taught by example both in and out of the classroom and insisted that "women should stand shoulder to shoulder with their brothers" (Stoughton, p. 29), which she did.

• Most of the existing sources about Safford, fragmentary and conflicting, are located in the Tarpon Springs Historical Society in Florida. Material on her medical schooling includes an annual announcement of the New York Medical College for Women (1867) and the annual announcements of the Boston University School of Medicine, which may be found in the archives of Boston University. At the Francis A. Countway Library in Cambridge may be found Safford's certificate of membership in the Massachusetts Homeopathic Society and a handwritten letter from her to James Jackson Putnam, M.D., 16 Apr. 1871. A family genealogy, Edward S. Safford, "The Saffords in America" (1923), is in the Library of Congress and the New York State Library in Albany. The best overviews of her life include an obituary in the Vermont *News and Citizen*, 24 Dec. 1891, and L. P. Brockett and Mary C. Vaughan, *Woman's Work in the Civil War* (1867). Other pre–Civil War sources include William Henry Perrin, ed., *History of Alexander, Union and Pulaski Counties, Ill.* (1883). Short and frequently conflicting accounts of her Civil War experiences may be found in a number of books on the war, including Nina Brown Baker, *Cyclone in Calico: The Story of Mary Ann Bickerdyke* (1952); Mary A. Livermore, *My Story of the War* (1887); Mrs. A. H. Hoge, *The Boys in Blue* (1867); and Agatha Young, *Women and the Crisis* (1959). An extremely inaccurate biography of Safford appears in Frances Willard and Mary H. Livermore, eds., *A Woman of the Century* (1893). Sources about Mary Safford's retirement in Tarpon Springs include Gertrude K. Stoughton, *Tarpon Springs, Florida: The Early Years* (1975).

SARAH H. GORDON

SAFFORD, Truman Henry (6 Jan. 1836–13 June 1901), astronomer and mathematician, was born in Royalton, Vermont, the son of Truman Hopson Safford, a farmer, and Louisa Parker, who, prior to her marriage, was a teacher. A sickly child, Safford was unable to attend school regularly and instead studied privately from the books in the family library. As early as the age of two he had learned the alphabet, and by the age of six he had exhibited the ability to carry out involved mathematical calculations, mentally and on paper, with surprising rapidity and accuracy. On the occasion of one test of his skills, for example, he reportedly squared the number 365,365,365,365,365,365 correctly in about one minute.

When he was only ten years old Safford honed his calculational talents by computing an almanac for Bradford, Vermont, and the following year, in 1847, he worked up almanacs for the cities of Bradford, Cincinnati, Philadelphia, and Boston. Also in 1847 he came to the attention of Harvard College president Edward Everett and to Benjamin Peirce, Harvard's Perkins Professor of Mathematics and Astronomy. These men took a personal interest in the boy, and his family moved to Cambridge so that the two Harvard officials could supervise young Safford's preparatory education. Safford joined Harvard's class of 1854 as a junior in 1853 and went on to graduate with honors. He also served briefly as a calculator under Peirce's supervision at the office of the American Ephemeris and Nautical Almanac, which was located in Cambridge from

1849 to 1866. In 1860 Safford married Elizabeth Marshall Bradbury, with whom he had six children.

With the successful completion of his college work, Safford immediately took a position on the staff of the Harvard Observatory, then under the directorship of William C. Bond. In 1863 he was promoted to assistant observer and, following the death in 1865 of succeeding director George P. Bond, he served as acting director for about one year. During his twelve years at the Harvard Observatory, Safford gradually made a name for himself in astronomical circles, owing particularly to his work on the orbital motion of Sirius. For many years prior to Safford's work, astronomers had suspected that Sirius actually formed part of a binary star system, two stars held in mutual orbit about a common center of gravity, where one star was too faint to be visible. In 1861, by combining the results of previous studies with his own calculations of a different aspect (the declination as opposed to the right ascension) of the assumed orbital motion, Safford succeeded in accurately predicting the position of the companion star, which was actually observed through an eighteen-inch refracting telescope by Alvan Clark in 1862. In addition to this important work, Safford also compiled a *Catalogue of Standard Polar and Clock Stars for the Reduction of Observations in Right Ascensions*, which appeared as part one of the fourth volume of the *Annals of Harvard Observatory* in 1863, and he edited the fifth volume of the *Annals* (1867), which George P. Bond had begun. Safford's early researches earned him election as a fellow of Boston's American Academy of Arts and Sciences in 1861 and as an associate of the Royal Astronomical Society in 1866.

In 1866 Safford left Cambridge to take up the first directorship of the Dearborn Observatory in Chicago. This position also entailed a professorship of astronomy at the institution, which was then called the University of Chicago (closed in 1886). While in Chicago, Safford not only undertook the observation and study of nebulae but also participated in the Astronomische Gesellschaft's internationally coordinated star-mapping project. Unfortunately, Chicago's great fire of 1871 deprived Safford of his livelihood; the observatory depended on private funding, which could no longer be spared for the support of astronomical pursuits.

From 1871 to 1876 Safford earned his living in the government's employ as a participant in Lieutenant George M. Wheeler's expedition to draw up topographical maps for the region of the United States west of the hundredth meridian and as a consultant to various government scientific bureaus. In 1876 Safford once again found a secure and permanent job, this time as Field Memorial Professor of Astronomy at Williams College in Williamstown, Massachusetts.

The return to academia brought with it much-increased teaching obligations as well as the responsibility for maintaining a certain level of research activity. Responding to a survey conducted by Florian Cajori and published in 1890, Safford outlined the commitments of his post: "I teach mathematics about five to nine hours weekly, astronomy three to fifteen hours weekly; and, this term, am teaching algebra. In addition, I have certain duties connected with the observatory, and a requirement of the founder of my professorship, viz., I have to contribute to the advancement of astronomical science" (Cajori, p. 347).

Safford apparently succeeded in both aspects of his mission. He took a great interest in students and their development, as Harold Jacoby's poignant anecdote about his relationship with Safford illustrates: while on a visit to the Columbia College observatory in New York City in 1884, Safford "found there a stripling engaged in testing a level. The youngster noticed a kindly face appearing in the doorway; conversation began about the level—and from that day on, no year has passed without the interchange of friendly visits between Safford and the writer of these words" (p. 23). Likewise, Safford devoted himself to building up the Williams College observatory and to pursuing his own astronomical work. Of particular note, he studied stars in the vicinity of Polaris and published a catalog in 1884 of the mean right ascensions of 133 such stars.

In 1898 Safford suffered a paralytic stroke that effectively ended his career. He died in Newark, New Jersey. Although not an astronomer of the first rank, Safford made solid contributions to the field, especially in the areas of star positions, proper motions, and orbits.

• Safford's most notable scientific works include "On the Proper Motion of Sirius in Declination," *Monthly Notices of the Royal Astronomical Society* 22 (1861–1862): 145–48, *Right Ascensions of 505 Stars Determined with the East Transit Circle at the Observatory of Harvard College*, vol. 4, pt. 2, *Annals of Harvard Observatory* (1878), and "Mean Right Ascensions of 133 Stars Near the North Pole, Observed in 1882 and 1883, at the Field Memorial Observatory of Williams College," *Proceedings of the American Academy of Arts and Sciences* 19 (1884): 324–52. For biographical accounts of Safford, consult Harold Jacoby, "Truman Henry Safford," *Science* 14 (1901): 22–24; Arthur Searle, "Truman Henry Safford," *Proceedings of the American Academy of Arts and Sciences* 37 (1901–1902): 654–56; and *Monthly Notices of the Royal Astronomical Society* 62 (1902): 247–48. Safford's activities during his twelve years at the Harvard Observatory are documented in Solon L. Bailey, *The History and Work of Harvard Observatory: 1839–1927* (1931). Safford's responses to Florian Cajori's survey on mathematics instruction at American institutions shed much light on the latter part of his career and may be found in Cajori's *The Teaching and History of Mathematics in the United States* (1890). An obituary is in the *New York Times*, 14 June 1901.

KAREN HUNGER PARSHALL

SAGE, Henry Williams (31 Jan. 1814–18 Sept. 1897), merchant, lumberman, and college benefactor, was born in Middletown, Connecticut, the son of Charles Sage, a merchant, and Sally Williams. When he was two years old Sage's family moved to Bristol, Connecticut, where he attended the local academy. In 1827, following the lead of several relatives, his father moved the family again, this time to Ithaca, New York, where he struggled to establish himself in the dry-goods business. Eager to rise above the poverty into which the family was slipping, young Sage sought a professional career. In June 1830 he began the study of medicine with Austin Church in Ithaca. Forced to abandon his studies after a few months because of poor eyesight, in 1832 he entered into business with his maternal uncles as a clerk with the firm of Williams & Brothers. Sage remained with his uncles for five years, becoming experienced in every aspect of their shipping business.

Financial success became increasingly important to Sage as his role of family provider escalated (his father, returning home from a trip to Texas—where he had hoped to earn fees for settling colonists—was killed by Native Americans following a shipwreck off the coast of Florida). Establishing his own firm in early 1837 in partnership with Joseph E. Shaw, the two subsequently purchased the Williams brothers' operation, which included canalboats. The business grew despite hardships brought on by the panic of 1837, and in 1839 a fateful connection was forged—Sage purchased an interest in an Albany, New York, lumbermill owned by his uncles.

Utilizing a series of short-term partnerships, Sage expanded his involvement in the lumber business. While he also continued to deal in other commodities such as pork, flour, and coal, he correctly viewed the ever-expanding timber industry as a potential source of immense wealth. Having achieved some degree of business success, Sage married Susan Linn in 1830; they had two sons. Well educated for that time, his new wife may have influenced his later efforts on behalf of women's higher education. In 1847 Sage was elected to the New York State Assembly as a Whig, where he served one term, which included a stint on the Committee on Canals. Elected village trustee of Ithaca in the spring of 1848, he repudiated his party's nomination of proslavery Zachary Taylor and even drifted to the Democrats before settling on membership in the new Republican party. Defeated in an 1849 reelection bid, he never again held public office.

Having purchased a small lumbermill in Ithaca in 1853, Sage then expanded his lumbering operations into Canada the next year. He purchased a large tract of timberland on Lake Simcoe (located north of Toronto, Ontario), where he founded (along with new partner William Grant) the village of Bell Ewart. Constructing a large, steam-driven lumbermill on the site (which was supplied by contracted timber as well as timber from land owned by Sage), the operation proved immensely successful. Sage moved his family to Brooklyn, New York, in 1857 to supervise a New York City lumberyard (which, as the eastern terminus of the water route leading to Buffalo, was important to both retail and wholesale trade).

Still in search of opportunities, Sage entered into a partnership in 1864 with Albany lumberman John McGraw and opened a sawmill in Wenona (later West Bay City), Michigan, the following year. The newly opened territory proved highly lucrative; it allowed Sage to sell his interest in the Canadian operation in 1869. From its base in the Saginaw River Valley, the partnership expanded its holdings throughout the east-central portion of Michigan's Lower Peninsula.

Although the timber supplies became depleted by the mid-1880s, Sage successfully shifted his focus to land speculation, holding by 1893 vast acreages in Wisconsin, Minnesota, Alabama, Mississippi, and Washington Territory in addition to land in Michigan.

Having achieved the wealth and success in the business world that he so desperately craved, Sage turned his attentions to the fields of philanthropy and education. He contributed toward a library and churches in West Bay City and soon gave larger gifts to the newly established Cornell University. As early as 1865 Sage had counseled Ezra Cornell, the university's founder, regarding the location of timberlands that formed a large portion of the university's early endowment. While attending the opening ceremonies of the university with his partner (and Cornell trustee) McGraw, Sage was so moved by the speech of President Andrew D. White that he turned to McGraw and said, "John, we are scoundrels to stand here doing nothing while these men are killing themselves to establish this university." By 1870 Sage was a member of the board of trustees himself; after Cornell's death in 1874 he was chosen chairman of the board (with the concurrent duties of managing the university's timberland endowment). Both Cornell and White were intent on making their institution coeducational; Sage greatly facilitated this development with his donation of Sage College—a separate dormatory for women complete with lecture rooms—which opened in 1874. He also donated a chapel (dedicated in June 1875), the library building, endowed professorial chairs of ethics and philosophy, and gave generously to the campus museum of archaeology. Yale Divinity School also benefited from his largess; Sage established the Lyman Beecher Lectures on Preaching at that institution in 1871.

Cornell University also benefited from Sage's business acumen. His astute management of the endowment timberlands prevented their premature sale during a period of depressed prices and ultimately resulted in a huge endowment for the university. His managerial skills as chairman of the board of trustees proved valuable, particularly after founder Cornell's death and after White's acceptance of an overseas diplomatic post in 1879 (which he assumed without resigning as president of Cornell). Having relocated back to Ithaca in 1880, Sage died there at his home (which was subsequently donated by his sons to the university for use as an infirmary) and was buried in the Sage Chapel on the School's campus.

Henry Williams Sage belongs solidly in the tradition of the self-made nineteenth-century businessman who, after rising from poverty and achieving great wealth, felt obligated to return a portion of that wealth to his community. While Sage's work in the lumbering industry, however profitable, might draw the ire of this century's environmental movement, his notable contributions to the growth and development of Cornell University are beyond reproof.

• The papers of Henry Williams Sage are split between the Cornell University Archives in Ithaca, N.Y., and the DeWitt

Historical Society of Tompkins County, N.Y. Important current scholarship on Sage is Anita Shafer Goodstein, *Biography of a Businessman: Henry Williams Sage, 1814–1898* (1962). Most histories of Cornell provide insight into Sage's role with the university; the best in this regard is Morris Bishop, *Early Cornell: 1865–1900* (1962). An excellent overview of Sage and the rather complex timberland transactions that occurred in the early history of Cornell University is provided in Paul W. Gates, *Wisconsin Pine Lands of Cornell University* (1943). An obituary is in the *Albany Journal*, 18 Sept. 1897, and in the *Brooklyn Eagle* and *New York Tribune*, both 19 Sept. 1897.

EDWARD L. LACH, JR.

SAGE, Margaret Olivia Slocum (8 Sept. 1828–4 Nov. 1918), teacher and philanthropist, was born in Syracuse, New York, the daughter of Joseph Slocum, a successful merchant and state assemblyman, and Margaret Jermain. Olivia, as she was known to family and close friends, was reared in comfortable circumstances and received her early education in Syracuse.

At the age of eighteen Olivia set out to enroll at the then nine-year-old Mount Holyoke Female Seminary founded by Mary Lyon. Falling ill in Troy, New York, where an uncle resided, she ended up studying instead with another of the great women educators of the mid-nineteenth century, Emma Willard, whose Troy Female Seminary (now called the Emma Willard School) imbued a generation of women with a sense of social responsibility. Leaving the seminary in 1847, Olivia moved to Philadelphia, where she taught French and geometry at the Chestnut Street Seminary. After only two years, ill health forced her to resign, although she continued to teach sporadically over the next twenty years in Syracuse and elsewhere.

Olivia Slocum did not marry until the age of forty-one. In 1869 she became the second wife of financier Russell Sage, whose first wife had been a close school friend of Olivia. She joined him in New York City, where earlier in the decade he had established himself on Wall Street. They maintained a house on Fifth Avenue as well as homes in Lawrence and Sag Harbor, both on Long Island. Although they had no children, Olivia was close to her two nephews and generously contributed to children's organizations.

After her marriage Sage began to move more confidently within a group of wealthy and leisured friends. She was able to span two social worlds, linking the very rich to middle-class reformers. Well into her sixties and seventies she was working at her charitable endeavors virtually full time; she taught occasionally in settlement houses and mission societies, involved herself in such issues as women's education and animal well-being, and wrote occasional articles on women's social obligations. A visitor once compared her study in her Fifth Avenue home to the office of a busy newspaper editor; it was cluttered with clipping files, journal articles, annual reports, and correspondence.

The Sages lived relatively simply despite their vast wealth, and their marriage seems more intimate and loving than popular journalistic portrayals of a cold and aloof Russell Sage would have allowed. Fond references to her husband abound in Sage's letters. The couple seems to have shared many interests, from opera and theater (although they were not "first-nighters," as Russell Sage once said) to the quiet pleasures of their summer homes. Russell Sage himself was involved in some of the educational and charitable endeavors that attracted his wife's concern.

Much of Sage's charitable work was concentrated in New York City, and her concerns evolved as women redefined their public role. During the 1870s and 1880s she was a mainstay of the women's boards of Presbyterian home and foreign mission societies and of the Women's Auxiliary Board of New York University. As early as 1879, and for the next twenty-five years, she served as vice president of New York Women's Hospital, overseeing the hospital's day-to-day financial matters. Although she was a member of a Dutch Reformed congregation and generous to her own Collegiate Church of St. Nicholas, she was remarkably ecumenical in her religious gifts. She gave to Presbyterian and Methodist churches, black congregations, and Catholic schools and convents. She sought to propagate strong Christian morality through support of foreign and domestic missions, the Women's Christian Temperance Union, various tent meetings, Bible societies, and the American Sunday School Union. She was a major benefactor of Young Men's Christian Associations and Young Women's Christian Associations across the country. Sage also pursued a lifelong interest in the well-being of animals, supporting the American Society for the Prevention of Cruelty to Animals and donating money for the purchase of an animal ambulance and horse-drinking fountains in New York City. Her efforts to protect birds led to the purchase of Marsh Island in Louisiana as a bird sanctuary. Vocational schools, women's colleges, and major universities, organizations to aid working women, emergency relief campaigns, even city agencies including the New York City Fire Department and Parks Department, all benefited from her contributions. By the 1910s she had become a national figure, an important backer of the movement for woman suffrage and a symbol of women's advancement. In 1916 her donation of $500,000 led to the founding of Russell Sage College under the auspices of the Emma Willard School and on that school's former campus in Troy, New York.

The Russell Sage Foundation marked both the culmination of Sage's charity and the beginning of the modern philanthropic foundation. She established the foundation in 1907 with $10 million of the estimated $70 million fortune left to her by her husband when he died in 1906. Advised by Robert de Forest, a prominent attorney and president of the New York Charity Organization Society, Sage charged the foundation "to improve social and living conditions in the United States." It was a major step toward creating a more "scientific philanthropy," the term used by the creators of new foundations to distinguish their efforts from traditional charitable work.

The foundation embarked quickly on a program to eradicate tuberculosis, the dreaded "white plague" of the slums. The staff members were concerned with the health and hygiene of children, with playgrounds and open spaces for recreation. They were troubled by the conditions confronting young working women in the garment trade and other factory settings. The foundation's first major research effort resulted in the famous "Pittsburgh Survey," completed in 1914, an early attempt to explore the ills afflicting an entire city. The survey served as the paradigm for thousands of similar efforts in the 1910s and 1920s as towns and cities used rudimentary survey methods to measure social problems. In its first ten years the foundation published dozens of books and hundreds of pamphlets that helped the public learn about public health improvements, educational reform, and working conditions.

In the eleven years before her death in New York City, Margaret Olivia Sage gave away $35 million. She bequeathed another $36 million in her will, only $5 million of which went to the foundation. However, it was the foundation that would be her most enduring legacy. At its founding, it was immediately heralded in a leading social work journal as a "new force" in Western civilization. Indeed the foundation was new, antedating such general-purpose foundations as the Rockefeller Foundation and the Carnegie Corporation. In its efforts to link social research, popular education, and reform it embodied the ethos of Progressive Era reform. Its creation placed Sage among the pioneers of twentieth-century philanthropy.

• The bulk of the surviving papers of Margaret Olivia Sage as well as the archives of the Russell Sage Foundation are at the Rockefeller Archive Center, Pocantico Hills, N.Y. Small holdings of Sage's papers are at the Emma Willard School and Russell Sage College. Sage wrote about her interests in "Opportunities and Responsibilities of Leisured Women," *North American Review* 181 (Nov. 1905): 712–21. Her adviser, Robert W. de Forest, memorialized her in "Margaret Olivia Sage, Philanthropist," *The Survey* 41 (1918): 151.

JAMES ALLEN SMITH
MELISSA A. SMITH

SAGE, Russell (4 Aug. 1816–22 July 1906), financier, was born in Oneida County, New York, the son of Elisha Sage, Jr., and Prudence Risley, farmers. Sage had little formal schooling and during his youth developed a lifelong interest in horses as a business and a hobby. At the age of twelve Sage left home and served as an apprentice in his brother Henry's grocery store in Troy, New York. There he worked hard and learned the skill of horse trading. By bargaining fiercely, he eventually earned a substantial profit and started making loans to friends and people whom he met while traveling on the sailing ships down the Hudson River to New York. He soon learned that making money through money was easier and more lucrative than through manual labor. By the time he was twenty-one, he had become a successful grocer and moneylender. In 1840 he married Marie-Henrie Winne, the daughter of a wealthy local lumberman. That same year he

was appointed to the Troy Common Council. In 1844 he became treasurer of Rensselaer County and a year later was elected alderman of Troy. He attended the 1848 Whig National Convention and served two terms in Congress as a Whig, beginning in 1853.

Although Sage was probably less corrupt than his colleagues, his terms in Congress enabled him to promote legislation that resulted in greater profits for his business interests, particularly railroads and the Pacific Railroad. After leaving Congress in 1857, he became a speculator in railroads and a director or president of several lines, including the Milwaukee and St. Paul, Iowa Central, Missouri Pacific, Union Pacific, Wabash, and Texas & Pacific. In 1863 he moved to New York City, where he continued his career as banker and speculator in the stock market. After his wife's death in 1867, Sage concentrated even more on his money-making activities. In 1869 he was arrested for violation of New York State's usury laws. He had lent $230,000 at 7 percent, the legal maximum; however, at the end of a loan period, he had extended the loan for a month at an additional 1 percent interest. He pled guilty and was sentenced to a fine and jail sentence, but the jail sentence was later waived. That year he married Margaret Olivia Slocum, who was twelve years his junior.

In 1881 Sage and Jay Gould, another railroad financier and tycoon, outwitted William H. Vanderbilt in their attempts to control Western Union. In 1883 Sage began to focus his attention on the Missouri Pacific Railroad and Western Union, both successful money-making enterprises for him. In the panic of 1884 his stock manipulations and financial dealings failed him, and he lost over $7 million. This experience made him more shrewd, and he never again lost in banking or on the market. In 1891 a man to whom he had refused a loan came to his office demanding $1 million. When Sage attempted to leave, the man set off a satchel of dynamite, killing himself and Sage's secretary and slightly wounding Sage. A clerk, William Laidlaw, sued Sage for compensation for his injuries, claiming that Sage had used him as a shield. After lengthy trials, Sage was exonerated, although public sentiment had been with Laidlaw.

Sage wrote very little, but the titles of two of his articles for the (New York) *Independent* give some evidence of his character. In "The Injustice of Vacations" (2 June 1904), Sage claims never to have taken a vacation during the eighty-eight years of his career and considers the "vacation habit" invalid. In the other article, "Wealth—A Decree of Justice" (1 May 1902), he asserts that "intelligence, industry, honesty and thrift produce wealth, and those who possess such qualities are best fitted for its custody."

When Sage died in Lawrence, New York, his fortune was estimated at between $63 million and $100 million. He left small sums to family members and the remaining fortune to his wife. Margaret Sage set up the Russell Sage Foundation for the improvement of social and living conditions, one of the largest philanthropies of the time. Curiously, Sage is best known for this foundation, in which he had no direct interest. He is credited with devising in 1872 the system of "puts and calls" on the stock exchange—the options to buy or sell at a given price within a set period of time—which became one of the major sources of his fortune. Known as the "king of 'puts and calls'," he was a giant in his time and perhaps more honest than most of the financiers of the day. He lived unostentatiously, concentrating his life on his banking. In an article in *World's Work*, Lindsay Denison wrote that Sage "has been the skinflint of the great Yankee nation" (June 1905). He was well known and widely feared for his business acumen. He left no children, and his fame lives on through the foundation set up by his widow.

• A few of Sage's letters are at the State Historical Society of Wisconsin. The only biography of Sage is Paul Sarnoff, *Russell Sage, the Money King* (1965), a popular rendering, which includes an extensive bibliography. Henry Whittemore, *History of the Sage and Slocum Families of England and America* (1900), gives some family background. Brief biographies are included in Franklyn Hobbs, *Twelve Good Men & True* (1909), and Henry Clews, *Fifty Years in Wall Street* (1908). See also Lindsay Denison, "Russell Sage: A Man of Dollars—The Story of a Life Devoted Solely to the Chill Satisfaction of Making Money for Its Own Sake," *World's Work* 10 (1905): 6298–301, and Jane Remson, "Russell Sage: Yankee," *New England Quarterly* 11 (Mar. 1938): 4–28. An obituary is in the *New York Times*, 23 July 1906.

GEORGE M. JENKS

SAINT. See also the spelling *St.*

SAINT-ANGE DE BELLERIVE, Louis Groston de (c. 1700–27 Dec. 1774), French colonial commandant, was born at Montreal, New France (present-day Canada), the son of Robert Groston de Saint-Ange and Marguerite Crevier. In 1720 Saint-Ange moved with his family to Fort Saint-Joseph, near present-day Niles, Michigan. In 1723 Saint-Ange, who had evidently been commissioned cadet in the French service, accompanied Étienne de Veniard de Bourgmond on an expedition to Fort Orléans, a French outpost 280 miles above the mouth of the Missouri River. Saint-Ange continued to serve in the Missouri Valley until 1736. During his thirteen-year tour of duty along the Missouri River, Saint-Ange commanded numerous diplomatic and military missions, resulting in his eventual promotion to the rank of ensign. In 1736 he served as acting commandant of Fort Orléans.

On 29 June 1736 and again on 15 October 1736 Jean-Baptiste Le Moyne de Bienville, governor of Louisiana, recommended that the colonial ministry appoint Saint-Ange to replace Jean-Baptiste Bissot, sieur de Vincennes, as commandant of the Wabash post. Bienville also recommended that Saint-Ange be promoted to either lieutenant or half-pay lieutenant. Saint-Ange assumed Vincennes's duties—with the rank of half-pay lieutenant—on 8 May 1737, although he was not formally named to the post until 22 June 1737.

Saint-Ange served as commandant at Vincennes until 1764. He was promoted to the rank of half-pay captain c. 1 September 1738. He did not achieve the rank of captain until c. 1758, despite universally glowing recommendations of his superior officers. In 1758, for example, Governor Louis Billouart de Kerlérec noted that Saint-Ange, who had served in the garrison "since childhood," was an "excellent officer for this country, and particularly for the Indians, whom he leads . . . as he pleases. A man of great probity, a zealous servant of the king, having always considered it beneath his dignity to engage in commerce. He is thus impoverished." Saint-Ange's slow rise through the ranks reflected the marginal status of the frontier district, which, in the mid-1750s, numbered only eighty settlers. The settlers initially engaged in trade with the local Indians, but, succumbing to pressure from Saint-Ange, many of them gradually turned to farming—with only modest success.

Having avoided most of the fighting in the Ohio Valley during the French and Indian War, Saint-Ange gained notoriety after 10 June 1764, when he became commandant of the Illinois district. He successfully avoided French entanglement in the so-called Pontiac's Uprising, and on 10 October 1765 he transferred possession of Illinois's main military installation, Fort de Chartres, to British military representatives. Saint-Ange then led the migration of French settlers from the east bank of the Mississippi, which had been ceded to Great Britain by the 1763 Treaty of Paris, to west-bank settlements in present-day Missouri—territory that had been ceded to Spain, but which at the time remained under French control. Establishing his headquarters and the French garrison at the recently established settlement of St. Louis, Saint-Ange served as commandant of present-day Missouri after the arrival of Spanish troops in 1767. In 1771 he formally transferred control of the Missouri country to the Spaniard Pedro Piernas, but Saint-Ange remained an adviser to the Spanish military until his death at St. Louis.

Though characterized by some historians as a historical personage of no real significance, Saint-Ange was largely responsible for the peaceful transfer of upper Louisiana to British and Spanish rule. By avoiding entanglements with Pontiac, Saint-Ange also doomed the 1763 Indian uprising to failure. Finally, he helped coordinate the migration of hundreds of Frenchmen responsible for the early settlement of Missouri.

• Works touching upon various facets of his career include Marc de Villiers du Terrage, *Les Dernières Années de la Louisiane Française* (1904); Carl A. Brasseaux, trans. and ed., *A Comparative View of French Louisiana, 1699 and 1762: The Journals of Pierre Le Moyne d'Iberville and Jean-Jacques-Blaise d'Abbadie* (1979); Gilbert J. Garraghan, "Fort Orleans of the Missoury," *Missouri Historical Review* 35 (1940–1941): 373–84; Louis Houck, *A History of Missouri* (3 vols., 1908); W. B. Douglas, "The Sieurs de St. Ange," Illinois State Historical Society, *Transactions* 14 (1909): 135–46; W. O. Collet, ed., "Will of St. Ange de Bellerive," *Magazine of Western History* 2 (1885): 60–65.

CARL A. BRASSEAUX

SAINT-CASTIN, Baron de (1652–1707), French officer and Abenaki Indian leader, was born Jean-Vincent D'abbadie at Saint-Castin in southwestern France near the Pyrenees Mountains, the son of Jean-Jacques D'abbadie de Saint-Castin and Isabeau de Béarn-Bonasse. The D'abbadies were a minor noble family that has been traced back to the early 1300s, while Jean-Vincent's mother was a direct descendant of Louis VIII of France. Louis XIV conferred the title of baron de Saint-Castin on Jean-Jacques in 1654. Little is known about Jean-Vincent's childhood except that his mother died of the plague in 1652, and his father died ten years later. The first record of Jean-Vincent is his enrollment at age thirteen as an ensign in the Carignan-Salières regiment being transported to Canada in 1665. This youthful endeavor was not unique for the second son of a lesser noble who probably chafed under the control of the second baron de Saint-Castin, his brother only two years older.

Although his regiment participated in the marquis de Tracy's 1666 campaign against the Iroquois, historical records do not mention Jean-Vincent until July 1670 as an ensign with Captain Andigné de Grandfontaine's expedition to Penobscot Bay. The colony of Acadia had been restored to France at the Treaty of Breda in 1667, and its new governor, Grandfontaine, took possession of the old French fort at Pentagoet. During the next four years, Jean-Vincent became familiar with the Abenaki Indians in the vicinity of the Penobscot River. In 1674 Pentagoet was surrendered to Dutch and English pirates, resulting in the capture, torture, and eventual escape of Jean-Vincent. After spending several days with friends among the local Indians, he traveled cross-country to Quebec to report these events to Governor Louis de Buade, comte de Frontenac. Impressed by the young officer, Frontenac instructed him to use his influence to secure the support of the Indians of Acadia for the French king. Earlier in the year, at age twenty-two, he had become the third baron de Saint-Castin after the death of his brother in France. However, when he returned to Pentagoet, Saint-Castin abandoned most indications of his role as a French noble and officer, began living and trading with the nearby Indians, and was eventually adopted by them as a kinsman.

The outbreak of King Philip's War in southern New England benefited Saint-Castin's endeavors when, in 1676, several unprovoked English atrocities against various Abenaki bands drew these Indians into the conflict. The Abenakis retaliated with a series of devastating attacks that forced the English to abandon many of their more advanced settlements, much to the delight of Saint-Castin's French superiors. Stung by these losses, the English unsuccessfully sought a truce in 1677 and ultimately agreed to humiliating terms to gain peace in 1678. English and French colonial officials seeking to explain the surprising success of these Indians attributed much credit to the young Frenchman living among them. Saint-Castin's actual role in these events was limited, but the wartime situation enabled him to gradually increase his influence among the Abenakis. During or shortly after King Philip's War, he enhanced his position by marrying Pidianske (Marie-Mathilde), the daughter of Madokawando, principal chief of the Abenakis in the Penobscot area. This union, according to Abenaki traditions, was later confirmed in a Catholic ceremony conducted by Father Jacques Bigot, the Jesuit missionary to the Abenakis, in 1684 at Pentagoet. They had seven children.

Following King Philip's War, an uneasy decade of peace was punctuated by frequent Abenaki complaints concerning unpaid annual quitrents for their land, nets blocking fish runs, and wandering cattle trampling Abenaki cornfields. These issues were primarily the concern of Abenakis in western Maine, but the English assumed the complaints were incited by Saint-Castin. English officials sought to gain influence over him during the 1680s with varying combinations of favorable trade, economic incentives, and offers of land before ultimately resorting to threats and intimidation. In 1687 Saint-Castin and a group of Abenaki warriors accompanied French governor Jacques-René de Brisay Denonville's expedition against the Iroquois, and while Saint-Castin was away, Massachusetts soldiers raided his dwellings at Pentagoet. This incident, as well as a series of escalating mutual retaliations over Abenaki crops damaged by settlers' cattle, led in 1688 to open hostilities, including an Abenaki attack on North Falmouth led by Saint-Castin. This conflict, known on the Maine frontier as Casteen's War, was encompassed by King William's War (1689–1697). Saint-Castin participated in the Franco-Indian expedition against Casco in 1690 and played the major role in capturing Fort Pemequid in 1696. Throughout the war Saint-Castin led Abenaki raids against frontier settlements. He provided timely warning of English plans to attack Quebec in 1690 and avoided an English assassination effort in 1692.

Saint-Castin spent most of his life living with the Abenakis, and his actions and decisions were always in the Abenakis' best interest, often causing frustration among French officials. English assumptions about Saint-Castin's control over the Abenakis were exaggerated, but he was well respected by the Abenakis and greatly facilitated Franco-Abenaki communication and cooperation. His status as a French baron choosing to live as an Indian and his marriage to an Indian "princess" provided ample material for romantic legends, and he ultimately became one of the most famous figures in the history and folklore of colonial Maine.

In 1701 Saint-Castin returned to France to confront several legal actions against his lands and titles that had emerged during his long absence, only to become enmeshed in a long frustrating series of legal maneuvers and political chicanery. The renewal of Anglo-French warfare eventually prompted the French court to intervene in an effort to speed his return to Acadia. However, an exhausted Saint-Castin died near his birthplace in Pau, southwestern France.

• French primary sources are in the Public Archives of Canada and Reuben G. Thwaites, ed., *The Jesuit Relations and Allied Documents, 1610–1792* (1896–1902). English sources have been published in James P. Baxter, *Documentary History of the State of Maine* (24 vols., 1889–1916), and *Collections of the Massachusetts Historical Society* (1792–1871). Recent works on Franco-English-Abenaki relations during this period include Alvin Morrison, "Dawnland Decisions: Seventeenth-Century Wabanaki Leaders and Their Responses to the Differential Contact Stimuli in the Overlap Area of New France and New England" (Ph.D. diss., State Univ. of New York, 1974); Kenneth M. Morrison, *The Embattled Northeast: The Elusive Ideal of Alliance in Abenaki-Euramerican Relations* (1984); John G. Reid, *Acadia, Maine, and New Scotland: Marginal Colonies in the Seventeenth Century* (1981) and P.-André Sévigny, *Les Abénaquis: Habitat et migrations* (1976). Saint-Castin is the focus of Pierre Daviault, *Le baron de Saint-Castin, chef abénaquis* (1939); Robert Le Blant, *Une figure légendaire de l'histoire acadienne: le baron de Saint-Castin* (1934); Gorham Munson, "St. Castin: A Legend Revisited," *Dalhousie Review* 45 (1965–1966): 338–60; and Paul Chasse, "The D'abbadie de Saint-Castin and the Abenakis of Maine in the Seventeenth Century," *Proceedings of the French Colonial Historical Society* 10 (1984): 59–73.

DAVID L. GHERE

SAINT-DENIS, Louis Juchereau de (17 Sept. 1676–11 June 1744), French colonial explorer and commandant, was born at Quebec, New France, the son of Nicolas Juchereau de Saint-Denis and Marie-Thérèse Giffard. Saint-Denis's early life is veiled in obscurity. He accompanied his cousin Pierre Le Moyne d'Iberville to the Gulf Coast in 1700 and remained at Biloxi's Fort Maurepas after Iberville's return to France. Saint-Denis subsequently explored the region between the Red and Ouachita rivers before assuming command of Fort du Mississippi, in present-day Plaquemines Parish, Louisiana, sometime in late 1702 or early 1703. From 1703 until the fort's closure in 1707, Saint-Denis reportedly devoted much time and energy to exploring the lower Mississippi River valley, including trading forays into modern-day Texas. From 1707 to 1713 Saint-Denis temporarily retired from the royal service, establishing a *habitation* along Bayou Saint John (in present-day New Orleans) and evidently engaging in trade with local Indians.

Governor Antoine Laumet, alias Lamothe Cadillac, recalled Saint-Denis to active duty in 1713 as part of Cadillac's effort to establish trade between Louisiana and New Spain. After organizing a trading expedition, Saint-Denis, whom Cadillac had invested with the brevet rank of captain, and his men ascended the Red River to an island, near present-day Natchitoches, Louisiana, where he established a base of operations. From this outpost, which he named St. Jean-Baptiste des Natchitoches, Saint-Denis and a few handpicked men ventured into present-day Texas, where he engaged in trade with the Hasinai. The Frenchmen subsequently made their way to San Juan Bautista, arriving at the Spanish outpost near modern-day Piedras Negras, Mexico, in July 1714. Having arrived without Spanish authorization, Saint-Denis and his men were arrested and detained. While the commandant, Diego

Ramón, awaited orders regarding the disposition of the smugglers, Saint-Denis courted Ramón's granddaughter, Emmanuela Sanchez-Navarro. Saint-Denis's romantic overtures, however, were cut short when he was moved to a Mexico City prison. Having ascertained that his Spanish captors were now interested in establishing a defensive perimeter closer to French Louisiana, Saint-Denis offered to lead Spanish missionaries and soldiers into Texas for the purpose of establishing missions and presidios. Saint-Denis's offer appears to have been motivated by three considerations: first, he hoped to end his confinement; second, he evidently wished to ingratiate himself with colonial administrators capable of making the decision to permit trade with Louisiana; third, the proposed Spanish installations would actually facilitate French trade—either legal or illegal—with New Spain. Spanish authorities readily accepted Saint-Denis's proposal.

After embarking on his new mission, Saint-Denis stopped at San Juan Bautista sometime in late 1715 or early 1716 and married Emmanuela; the couple would have seven children. Leaving his new bride behind, Saint-Denis helped his Spanish companions establish four installations in present-day Texas. The Spaniards then released Saint-Denis by midsummer 1716.

Following his release, Saint-Denis traveled to Mobile, Louisiana's capital, where he arrived in August 1716. Despite his recent imprisonment by Spanish authorities, Saint-Denis immediately set about organizing a smuggling expedition to the Rio Grande valley. Upon arrival at San Juan Bautista, Saint-Denis's contraband was seized by Commandant Ramón. The Frenchman then traveled to Mexico City in an effort to secure the release of his goods, but, once again, his encounter with New Spain authorities only resulted in his imprisonment. Saint-Denis was eventually released, evidently through the efforts of the Ramón family, and though he was permitted to sell his contraband, he was warned never to return to Texas.

Saint-Denis arrived at Natchitoches in February 1719. He soon saw active duty in the border war between French Louisiana and Spanish Florida, leading fifty Pascagoula Indian warriors in the defense of Dauphin Island in August 1719. Saint-Denis's services were rewarded with an appointment as lieutenant in the Louisiana garrison on 3 March 1720. On 1 July 1720 the Company of the Indies, the colony's new proprietary company, appointed Saint-Denis commandant of the Cane River area (Natchitoches), and on 12 December 1720 the Crown awarded Saint-Denis the Cross of Saint Louis for meritorious career service to the Crown.

On 21 October 1723 Saint-Denis was discharged from the royal service, but he remained commandant of the Natchitoches district, a position he held in April 1730. In 1731 Saint-Denis repulsed a Natchez Indian assault against Fort Saint-Jean-Baptiste des Natchitoches.

Saint-Denis's appointment as commandant of the Natchitoches district lapsed with the retrocession of Louisiana from the Company of the Indies to the

French monarchy in 1731. Governor Jean-Baptiste Le Moyne de Bienville of Louisiana consequently urged the Crown, on 24 April 1734, to issue Saint-Denis a royal commission as commandant of Natchitoches. The royal appointment was forthcoming on 18 July 1734.

Saint-Denis's twilight years were largely uneventful. In 1741 he was compelled to settle a 18,361-*livre* debt to the Company of the Indies. This financial setback, coupled with his gradually declining health, prompted Saint-Denis to formally request permission to retire on 10 January 1743. Saint-Denis's letter to the minister also contained a request that he, his family, and his slaves be given permission to settle in Spanish territory and that two of his sons be given military appointments in Louisiana's French colonial garrison. The French colonial minister responded on 13 January 1744 that Saint-Denis could retire but only after Louisiana's governor had found a suitable replacement. The minister then directed Louisiana's governor to procrastinate in the search for a replacement to ensure that Saint-Denis would remain in the French colonial service. Saint-Denis died five months later at Natchitoches.

Although Saint-Denis was only a local commandant, his activities on the southwestern Louisiana frontier transcended regional boundaries. His smuggling activities and his competent administration of the Natchitoches post forced New Spain to respond to threatened French encroachment into traditionally Spanish territory. Spanish settlement of Texas was the direct result.

• As with most early borderlands figures, there is little secondary literature dealing directly with Saint-Denis's career. Ross Phares, *Cavalier in the Wilderness: The Story of the Explorer and Trader Louis Juchereau de St. Denis* (1952), a full-length biography. Katherine Bridges and Winston De Ville, "Natchitoches and the Trail to the Rio Grande: Two Early Eighteenth-Century Accounts by the Sieur Derbanne," *Louisiana History* 8 (1967): 241–42, sheds additional light on Saint-Denis's forays into Texas. André Penicaut, *Fleur de Lys and Calumet: Being the Pénicaut Narrative of French Adventure in Louisiana*, trans. and ed. Richebourg G. McWilliams (1953), provides an entertaining but often unreliable account of many of Saint-Denis's exploits.

CARL A. BRASSEAUX

SAINT-GAUDENS, Augustus (1 Mar. 1848–3 Aug. 1907), sculptor and educator, was born Augustus Louis Saint-Gaudens in Dublin, Ireland, the son of Bernard Paul Ernest Saint-Gaudens, a French-born shoemaker, and Mary McGuiness, a native of Ireland. The family emigrated to the United States in the fall of 1848, sailing first for Boston, Massachusetts, but moving to New York City a month or so after arriving. Sometime after his brother Louis's birth Augustus's middle name was dropped. Augustus attended public schools in New York until the age of thirteen when his father apprenticed him to a cameo cutter named Avet. He characterized this three-year period as "a miserable slavery" (*Reminiscences*, vol. 1, pp. 38–39). However,

it was a slavery that was somewhat ameliorated by his evenings at the art school of the Cooper Institute (now the Cooper Union). He wrote that while there he studied with Daniel Huntington and Emanuel Leutze. After leaving Avet he was employed by another cameo cutter, Jules LeBrethon, who gave him his first instruction in modeling. He enrolled in evening drawing classes at the National Academy of Design, then on the corner of Twenty-third Street and Park Avenue, next door to his father's shoe store. The defining moment of his youth came in 1867, when his father offered him the opportunity to go to Paris to visit the International Exposition.

Arriving in what was then the capital of the international art world, the young and ambitious sculptor-to-be began his formal training at the Petite École while awaiting admission to the École des Beaux-Arts. In the afternoons he worked to earn his living as a cameo cutter. The following year he was accepted into the atelier of François Jouffroy. Acceptance by a professor at the École was a necessary requirement for matriculation, and Jouffroy was one of its most distinguished teachers. Saint-Gaudens's French schooling was not only technical but included courses in architecture, descriptive geometry, history, anatomy, and perspective. Undoubtedly his fluency in the French language facilitated his acceptance at both schools and eased his absorption of the curriculum. The three years he spent in Paris coincided with the final years of the Second Empire, a period of extensive city planning and massive building by Georges-Eugène Haussmann under the auspices of Napoleon III. Haussmann's works changed the face of Paris and were pivotal influences in the career of Saint-Gaudens. In 1870, impelled by the advent of the Franco-Prussian War, the sculptor left for the comparative safety of Rome. There he spent most of the next five years carving cameos, copying sculpture to order for foreigners, and creating his first life-size work of art, *Hiawatha* (1872, marble 1874–1875). While in Rome he received his first important commission, *Silence* (1874, marble) for the new Masonic Lodge on Twenty-third Street in New York (now in the Tomkins Memorial Chapel of the Masonic Home, Utica, N.Y.). He also met and fell in love with his future wife, Augusta Fisher Homer.

Following his mother's death, Saint-Gaudens returned to New York in 1875. He looked for work that would enable him to marry. After much diligent petitioning and with the recommendation of John Quincy Adams Ward, the Farragut Monument Committee of New York engaged the young sculptor to create a monument honoring the first admiral of the U.S. Navy. With the contract for the *Farragut Monument* and other projects in hand, he was able to convince the Homers that he was capable of supporting their daughter. In 1877, just eleven days after signing the *Farragut* contract, Saint-Gaudens and Homer were married and left for Paris.

In 1878 Saint-Gaudens's friends, the architects Stanford White and Charles Follen McKim, came to visit. The sculptor invited White to stay on, and they began their first collaboration, on the pedestal and environment for the *Farragut*, in the French capital. After White returned to New York the architectural firm of McKim, Mead and White was formed. Meanwhile, Saint-Gaudens exhibited the plaster of the *Farragut Monument* at the Salon of 1880 along with relief medallions of his friends, Dr. Henry Shiff and artists William Gedney Bunce, George W. Maynard, Francis Davis Millet, and William Picknell. He was awarded an honorable mention. After the *Farragut* was successfully cast in bronze by Adolphe Gruet in Paris in 1880, the sculptor and his wife departed for America. Augusta went to her parents' home in Boston to await the birth of their first child. Augustus proceeded to New York City to finalize the arrangements for the installation of the monument and to complete other work. After the birth of their son, Homer, in the fall of 1880, mother and son joined Saint-Gaudens in New York.

The *Farragut* was unveiled in Madison Square Park in New York on 25 May 1881. It became a lightning rod for many artists and critics who understood its creation to be the beginning of an American Renaissance. The dynamic bronze, a striding figure of Farragut, was set upon a bluestone exedra carved with the figures of Loyalty and Courage. It was placed in an enclosure of trees, shrubbery, and grass on the west side of Madison Square Park facing Fifth Avenue at a great distance from the curb. Visitors approached it on a graceful bluestone path shaped like an hourglass. Saint-Gaudens and White created an environment that was intended to encourage visitors to enter and rest upon its seat and view the passing parade. It was unparalleled in American sculpture. The entire ambience was so remarkable that some critics of the period suggested that sculpture should never be held to a lesser standard. Today other nineteenth-century models to which it can be compared still exist in the same park. They are essentially static figures set upon square or rectangular pedestals that have little or no relation to the space around them. Unfortunately, Saint-Gaudens and White's environment for the *Farragut* was destroyed early in the twentieth century. Following the widening of Fifth Avenue and the consequent destruction of its entranceway, the monument was removed to the north end of the park and placed upon a new granite pedestal. The new pedestal was a copy of the original bluestone, which had deteriorated. Neither setting, base, nor original coloration of bronze remain (the original base is now on exhibition at the Saint-Gaudens National Historic Site).

The *Farragut Monument* proved an important catalyst for the sculptor's career. On the basis of the success of this work, Saint-Gaudens received three other major commissions for Civil War monuments: *The Standing Lincoln* (1887, Lincoln Park, Chicago), the *Shaw Memorial* (1897, Boston Common), and the *Logan Monument* (1897, Michigan Avenue, Chicago). *The Standing Lincoln* is a heroic and masterful representation of a thoughtful sixteenth president who has just risen from his seat. Saint-Gaudens's bronze image is surrounded and framed by a massive granite exedra

designed by Stanford White. The entire work is placed in Lincoln Park but is shielded from the rest of the park by trees and shrubbery on the north and by Lake Michigan on the east. Fortunately, the setting planned by Saint-Gaudens and White remains as it was originally intended, a fitting monument to its subject and creators. The *Shaw Memorial* was executed with McKim. It is a history painting in bronze and a unique synthesis of a traditional equestrian statue with the reliefs frequently placed on the pedestals of such works. Situated opposite the Boston State House at the edge of Boston Common, it, too, movingly honors its subject, a white colonel and his black regiment. The Fifty-fourth Massachusetts was the first black regiment recruited in the North during the Civil War. The *Shaw Memorial* integrated both art and setting in an unparalleled and enduring tribute to the Union. The *Logan Monument* was designed by Saint-Gaudens in collaboration with White. It memorializes Union general John A. Logan who later, as a congressman, was instrumental in the passage of the Fifteenth Amendment to the Constitution, which extends the right to vote to all citizens regardless of race, creed, or previous servitude. The majestic monument is framed by the firmament and located at the summit of an architecturally created hill that overlooks a premier street of the Windy City. It was Saint-Gaudens's first formal equestrian monument.

Other major monuments created by Saint-Gaudens and White were *The Puritan*, *Diana*, and the Adams memorial. Chester W. Chapin, president of the Boston and Albany Railroad and a friend of the sculptor, commissioned *The Puritan* (1887, Springfield, Mass.) to commemorate his ancestor Deacon Samuel Chapin, one of the founders of Springfield. It became a paradigm for American images of a Puritan. Stanford White commissioned *Diana* (1891, 1893, Philadelphia Museum of Art) for Madison Square Garden to decorate his new palace of entertainment. It was executed by Saint-Gaudens as a "labor of love." The originally gilded, nude figure was the subject of much scandalized commentary, but the citizens of New York eventually considered it a landmark. It was Saint-Gaudens's only major work for which no contract was written. One of the models for *Diana* and the smaller bronze casts created from it was Davida J. Clark, who became the sculptor's mistress. They had a son who was the subject of the 1892 relief, *Novy* (plaster, Saint-Gaudens National Historic Site). The historian and scion of two presidents, Henry Adams, commissioned the Adams memorial (1886–1891, Rock Creek Cemetery, Washington, D.C.) to honor the memory of his wife, Marian Hooper, after her death in December 1886. Adams chose Saint-Gaudens to execute the memorial because of his close friendship and association with John La Farge, an older, revered colleague and frequent promoter of the sculptor. It is one of the most complete and successful environments that the artist and his collaborator White created. It is Saint-Gaudens's chef d'oeuvre.

Saint-Gaudens and McKim again worked together to create the gilded bronze equestrian monument and pink granite base that was the sculptor's final major work. *General Sherman Led by Victory* was installed on Fifth Avenue and Fifty-ninth Street in New York City on Memorial Day 1903 (and later moved slightly north of its original location to make way for a subway). The Chamber of Commerce of the State of New York and the citizens of New York City commissioned it after Sherman's death in 1891. Saint-Gaudens had executed a dynamic bust of the general in 1887. It evidently pleased Sherman and from their interaction at the sittings they had become friends. As a result the family specifically requested that Saint-Gaudens be chosen to execute the memorial, as that was the general's wish. When the monument was completed there was great difficulty in finding an appropriate site for the colossal group, but it was acclaimed both in the United States and abroad. A full-page article in the *New-York Tribune* (31 May 1903) compared it favorably with the greatest equestrian statues of all times.

The major monuments of Augustus Saint-Gaudens were pivotal in creating a climate in the United States in which art was no longer considered derivative of European models. They were unique in expressing American symbols and ideals integrated with a mastery of European technical facility. In the last two decades of the nineteenth century, Saint-Gaudens, White, and McKim collaborated in the creation of eight major environments that forever changed the course of art in America. They ushered in an era in which artists no longer needed to travel to Europe to receive an art education. Although American artists continued to study abroad, American training was now considered on a par with its European precedents. It was a time when artists like Saint-Gaudens returned to America to teach at the Art Students League, in their own studios, and elsewhere. They brought back the techniques and influences that they had absorbed abroad.

Saint-Gaudens was also the first American master of relief portraiture. At the time when he sculpted the *Bust of Sherman* he also created the first of his delicately drawn relief portraits of *Robert Louis Stevenson* (1887–1888). Relief portraits of friends and acquaintances became an increasingly important activity for him. During his first trip to Europe he was overwhelmed by the beauty of the Renaissance reliefs that he saw and from which he occasionally made casts during his Roman sojourn. When he returned to the United States he wondered aloud to John La Farge whether he should attempt a similar project. La Farge responded that he did not know why he should not (*Reminiscences*, vol. 1, p. 162). In the late 1870s and early 1880s he made his first trials in this mode of representation.

Saint-Gaudens's reliefs profoundly influenced his students and followers. They were so subtly drawn that one might not realize that just a decade or so earlier, the typical manner of representing such a subject was simply to bisect the image and set it upon a blank ground. In 1898 the sculptor exhibited an unprece-

dented fifteen works at the Exposition Nationale des Beaux-Arts, among which were *Amor Caritas*, a relief; *Bust of Sherman*; the tondo relief portrait of *Robert Louis Stevenson*; and the third version of the *Shaw Memorial*, an unusual fusion of relief and three-dimensional sculpture. His works were warmly received. The Société Nationale, at which he exhibited, was the more avant-garde of the main exhibition venues in Paris. It was undoubtedly through the intercession of Auguste Rodin, president of the jury of that salon, that Saint-Gaudens was permitted to exhibit such a large number of works in a separately designated area. He was not only well received critically, but the director of the Luxembourg Museum purchased *Amor Caritas* and several of his relief portraits for his museum, and he was awarded the Legion of Honor. Honored at home and abroad, Saint-Gaudens effectively established his international reputation as the preeminent American sculptor of the nineteenth century.

Saint-Gaudens will be remembered and revered not only as an artist but as one of the most accessible and supportive teachers of any of his contemporaries. He taught at the Art Students League in New York until leaving for Paris in 1897. He employed many of his students in his ateliers in New York and Cornish, New Hampshire, and was most encouraging to female as well as male students at a time when female sculptors were more ignored than recognized. In 1900 he was diagnosed with cancer and immediately returned to New York from Paris. Nevertheless, he continued working and exhibiting for more than seven years, until his death at the age of fifty-nine. During these last years he also revived the art of coinage for the United States with the active support of President Theodore Roosevelt. Saint-Gaudens's wife formalized his legacy by creating a place of exhibition and dissemination of information about the artist at their home, "Aspet." It was later given to the nation and is now known as the Saint-Gaudens National Historic Site in Cornish, New Hampshire.

The reputation of the sculptor has ebbed and flowed with the passage of time and changes in taste. After the publication of *The Reminiscences of Augustus Saint-Gaudens*, edited and amplified by his son Homer in 1913, interest in the sculptor's work seemed to fade. This was in part due to the introduction of new ideas about painting and sculpture that began to dominate the American scene. Thirty-five years later a small exhibition of his work at the Century Club in New York on the occasion of the one-hundredth anniversary of the artist's birth and a doctoral dissertation the following year by Margaret Bouton, "The Early Works of Augustus Saint-Gaudens" (Radcliffe College, 1949), were the only notable exceptions to this apparent decline. In 1969, however, an exhibition of his reliefs by the Smithsonian Institution and a biography by Louise Hall Tharp seemed to stimulate interest in the sculptor. New opportunities to reevaluate the work of Saint-Gaudens and his collaborators McKim and White and their place in the history of American and world art are now beginning to emerge.

• Much of the documentary evidence that survived two fires at Cornish was given to the Baker Library of Dartmouth University in Hanover, N.H., in 1969. It now resides in the Saint-Gaudens Collection at that library and is also available on microfilm. Other archival information can be found at the Saint-Gaudens National Historic Site in Cornish, N.H., the New-York Historical Society Library, the Boston Athenaeum, the Massachusetts Historical Society, the Chicago Historical Society, and the Library of Congress. Among recent studies of Saint-Gaudens are the National Portrait Gallery–Smithsonian Institution, *AVGVSTVS SAINT-GAVDENS: The Portrait Reliefs* (1969), organized by the director, Marvin Sadik, with a catalog prepared by John Dryfhout and Beverly Cox; and Louise Hall Tharp, *Saint-Gaudens and the Gilded-Era* (1969), a biography. Also see Lois Goldreich Marcus, "The *Shaw Memorial* by Augustus Saint-Gaudens: A History Painting in Bronze," *Winterthur Portfolio* 14, no. 1 (Spring 1979): 1–23. This was followed by her "Studies in Nineteenth-century American Sculpture: Augustus Saint-Gaudens" (Ph.D. diss., City Univ. of New York, 1979), also available on microfilm, in which the sculptor's working methods are systematically detailed for the first time, his major works identified, their metamorphoses detailed, their sources identified, and his work placed in an international context, and her "Augustus Saint-Gaudens: The Sculptor of the American Renaissance," *Arts Magazine* 54, no. 3 (Nov. 1979): 144–48. See also Dryfhout, *The Work of Augustus Saint-Gaudens* (1982), a catalogue raisonné; Kathryn Greenthal, *Augustus Saint-Gaudens: Master Sculptor* (1985), which accompanied a Metropolitan Museum of Art exhibition; and Burke Wilkinson, *Uncommon Clay: The Life and Work of Augustus Saint-Gaudens* (1985).

LOIS GOLDREICH MARCUS

SAINT INNOCENT. *See* Veniaminov, Ivan.

SAINT MARY MAGDALEN, Sister. *See* Healy, Eliza.

SAINT-MÉMIN, Charles Balthazar Julien Févret de (12 Mar. 1770–23 June 1852), artist and museum director, was born in Dijon, France, the son of Bénigne-Charles Févret de Saint-Mémin, a lawyer, and Marie-Victoire de Motmans. His father was a member of the Burgundian nobility; his maternal grandfather, a wealthy sugarcane planter in the Caribbean colony of Saint-Domingue and solicitor general of the sovereign council of Port-au-Prince. Saint-Mémin was privately educated in Dijon. In 1784 his parents enrolled him in the royal military academy in Paris. After graduation in 1788 he was appointed to the palace guard of Louis XVI. His military career ended abruptly when the guard was disbanded in 1789 at the beginning of the French Revolution. After the nobility was abolished in 1790, Saint-Mémin and his parents and two sisters fled to Switzerland.

Saint-Mémin's American career as portraitist and engraver began after he, his father, and the family valet, Pierre Mourgeon, left Switzerland in 1793 for the French colony of Saint-Domingue, hoping to reclaim their French citizenship. In New York City, however, they encountered thousands of French refugees who were fleeing the revolution in Saint-Domingue. They therefore settled in New York, where they met John

R. Livingston, brother of chancellor Robert R. Livingston, who invited them to live at his home. Impressed by a landscape drawing that Saint-Mémin made, Livingston encouraged him to learn the techniques of engraving and, according to Philippe Guignard, "introduced him to the public library, so that he could acquire the basic principles of engraving from the Encyclopedia [ed. Diderot and d'Alembert]. He mastered them quickly. He was endowed with a thoughtful nature, and had an extraordinary aptitude for the sciences, a remarkable manual dexterity, and an enduring perseverance" (Dexter, p. 8). Saint-Mémin probably had been taught drawing at the military academy and may have attended classes at a drawing school in Dijon. His earliest work, dated 1788, was a watercolor of a scene in Dijon.

Saint-Mémin established himself as an engraver in New York in 1795. This led in 1796 to the more profitable career of profile portraitist, for which he is best known. He formed a partnership with Thomas Bluget de Valdenuit, who like Saint-Mémin came to the United States in 1793 during the French Revolution. While Valdenuit made the large, almost life-size black-and-white chalk drawings (on beige paper that was first coated with a pink wash), Saint-Mémin made the 2¼-inch round engravings. Saint-Mémin commented many years later that the portraits were "drawn by means of the Physionotrace and engraved by the *roulette*, in the manner of those with which [Gilles-Louis] Chrétien, Quenneday [Edme Quenedey] and others, flooded France at the end of the 18th century" (letter to M. Sauvageot, 7 Dec. 1849, quoted in Norfleet, p. 64); the "physionotrace" (physiognotrace) was an "automatic" drawing instrument by which an artist copied the view through an eyepiece, and the roulette was a tool for making random dots in an engraving that produced darkened tones when printed. During less than a year with Saint-Mémin, Valdenuit made about sixty large profile portraits, most of which Saint-Mémin engraved. Their sitters were from prominent New York families and from the French émigré community and included Robert Livingston and Theodosia Burr, daughter of Aaron Burr.

In September 1797 Valdenuit returned to France to claim an inheritance. (Saint-Mémin and Valdenuit had made 145 portraits in New York, an average of more than 70 a year.) Saint-Mémin then became the primary user of the physiognotrace, finishing several orders begun under the partnership with Valdenuit and making about sixty new portraits. Louis Lemet, also a French émigré, became his assistant. In 1798 he and his father were joined by his mother and his sister Adélaïde, who left Switzerland for New York in January. The family moved to Burlington, New Jersey, fifteen miles from Philadelphia. Here they spent nearly all of their remaining years in the United States.

Saint-Mémin moved his portrait business to Philadelphia. From the fall or winter of 1798–1799 through the early spring of 1803, he made about 270 portraits there. He publicized his work in newspapers, stating in one advertisement that "the original portrait, plate and twelve impressions, shall be delivered for the moderate price of twenty five dollars for gentlemen, and thirty five dollars for ladies; the portrait without engraving, may be had for 8 dollars" (Philadelphia *Aurora*, 22 Dec. 1801–11 Mar. 1802), prices that Saint-Mémin maintained throughout his career. His drawings are noted for their immediacy and their almost photographic truthfulness.

Because Philadelphia was the capital of the United States from 1790 to 1800, many of Saint-Mémin's sitters were prominent Americans, including John Adams (Metropolitan Museum of Art), Speaker of the House of Representatives Jonathan Dayton (unlocated), and Supreme Court justice James Iredell (privately owned in North Carolina). Others were from the large French émigré community in the city. During this period the Saint-Mémin family initiated a series of legal maneuvers to try to prove that they were not subject to the French laws governing émigrés and the confiscation of property, in order to return to Dijon. Their efforts were not immediately successful.

The artist's father died in 1802 on a trip to Saint-Domingue to examine his wife's sugarcane plantation. Saint-Mémin worked in several southern cities during the next six years, the length of his stay in each depending on how many sitters he could attract. His mother and sister remained in Burlington, where he returned during the hot summer months to engrave the copperplates, print the engravings, and prepare the materials he needed for the next trip. In 1803 and 1804 he was in Baltimore and Washington (and possibly Annapolis). He spent most of 1805 in Washington, with perhaps a short stay in nearby Alexandria, Virginia. Some of his best-known sitters were drawn in Washington. One of these was President Thomas Jefferson (Worcester Art Museum), who sat for Saint-Mémin in 1804. In Washington Saint-Mémin also made the profiles of Meriwether Lewis (Missouri Historical Society) and of eight American Indians who came to the city after the Lewis and Clark exploration of the Louisiana Purchase of 1803. These portraits of Osage, Mandan, and Delaware individuals are among his most striking images.

In 1806 and 1807 Saint-Mémin divided his time between Baltimore and Washington, and then went to Richmond, where he worked from the summer of 1807 until the spring of 1808. He timed his arrival to coincide with the treason trial of Aaron Burr, which attracted large numbers of spectators. His visit to Richmond was very successful; he made more than 120 portraits. The following winter, he was in Charleston, South Carolina.

In 1810 Saint-Mémin went back to France but, still unsure of the political climate, returned to New York two years later. He continued to support himself as an artist but gave up profile portraiture and the detailed work of engraving. Instead he became a painter of landscapes and portraits; however, no examples are known today.

Saint-Mémin and his mother and sister returned permanently to France in 1814, after Napoleon's abdi-

cation and the restoration of the Bourbon monarchy. When he left the United States, he destroyed the physiognotrace and renounced the American citizenship that he had acquired.

Saint-Mémin and his family regained their property in Dijon. In 1817 he was appointed director (*conservateur*) of the Dijon Museum, a position he held for the rest of his life. As a museum official, he played a major role in the preservation of a number of important Gothic monuments and works of art in Burgundy. He remained proud of his American work, citing the engravings as evidence of his artistic abilities when his qualifications to be director of the museum were challenged. The letter that he sent with some of his engravings to his friend "Monsieur Sauvageot" in 1849 provides the most eloquent description of his American career: "The creation of my little engravings is so much my own work that I was obliged to be at the same time draughtsman and engraver, builder of pantograph, physionotrace and small-sized press, manufacturer of *roulettes* and other instruments necessary to engraving, brayer of my ink, and, furthermore, my own printer." Saint-Mémin died in Dijon.

Between 1796 and 1810 Saint-Mémin made about 900 head and shoulder profile portraits and engraved about 90 percent of them. His work also includes some watercolor portraits and landscapes. The portraits are unique in American art in quality and accuracy, and they are significant both for the importance of many of the sitters and as an indication of the growing interest in portraits among the middle class.

• Most of Saint-Mémin's surviving papers concern his years as director of the museum and are at the Archives Municipales, Dijon. Others are in the De Juigné Collection, Bibliothèque Municipale, Dijon, and the Saint-Mémin file, Musée de Dijon, France, as well as the Department of Prints, Metropolitan Museum of Art, New York. Many of the artist's portrait drawings are owned by descendants of his sitters; others are in the collections of numerous American museums. The major collections of the artist's engravings are in the Corcoran Gallery of Art, Washington, D.C.; the National Portrait Gallery, Washington, D.C.; and the Bibliothèque Nationale, Paris. A short biography by his friend Philippe Guignard, *Notice historique sur la vie et les travaux de M. Févret de Saint-Mémin* (1853), was translated as the introduction to Elias Dexter, *The St.-Mémin Collection of Portraits; Consisting of Seven Hundred and Sixty Medallion Portraits, Principally of Distinguished Americans* (1862). The most recent study of his work, with a catalogue raisonné, is Ellen G. Miles, *Saint-Mémin and the Neoclassical Profile Portrait in America* (1994). The only other study of his work in English is Fillmore Norfleet, *Saint-Mémin in Virginia: Portraits and Biographies* (1942). Recent monographs in French include the exhibition catalog by Pierre Quarré, *Charles-Balthazar-Julien Févret de Saint-Mémin* (Musée de Dijon, 1965), and Madeleine Hérard, "Contribution à l'étude de l'émigration de Charles-Balthazar-Julien Févret de Saint-Mémin aux États-Unis de 1793 à 1814," *Mémoires de l'Académie des Sciences, Arts et Belles-Lettres de Dijon* 117 (1963–1965): 129–76. Shorter articles about aspects of his work include Howard C. Rice, Jr., "An Album of Saint-Mémin Portraits," *Princeton University Library Chronicle* 13, no. 1 (Autumn 1951): 23–31; Quarré, "Un document sur la vie Dijonnaise au XVIIIᵉ siècle: Une lettre de Bénigne-Charles Févret de Saint-Mémin" *Annales de Bourgogne* 38 (1966): 42–45; Quarré, "Le voyage de Bénigne-Charles Févret de Saint-Mémin et de son fils de Fribourg à New York en 1793," *Mémoires de l'Académie des Sciences, Arts et Belles-Lettres de Dijon* 121 (1970–1972): 159–81; Warren J. Wolfe, "A Trip Down the Hudson in 1793: The Journal of Févret de Saint-Mémin," *American Society Legion of Honor Magazine* 48 (1977): 73–86; Miles, "Saint-Mémin, Valdenuit, Lemet: Federal Profiles," in *American Portrait Prints: Proceedings of the Tenth Annual American Print Conference*, ed. Wendy Wick Reaves (1984), pp. 1–29; Miles, "Saint-Mémin in the South, 1803–1809," *Southern Quarterly* 25, no. 1 (Fall 1986): 22–39; and Miles, "Saint-Mémin's Portraits of American Indians, 1804–1807," *American Art Journal* 20, no. 4 (1988): 2–33.

ELLEN G. MILES

SAKEL, Manfred Joshua (6 June 1900–3 Dec. 1957), psychiatrist, was born in Nadvornaya, Bukovina, then part of the Austro-Hungarian monarchy (now Ukraine), the son of Mayer Sakel, a rabbi, said to be descended from the famous twelfth-century physician-philosopher Maimonides, and Judith Golde Friedman. To study, Manfred went to Brno, capital of the Austrian province Moravia, now in the Czech Republic, then to the University of Vienna, where he earned his M.D. in 1925. After working as an assistant physician he left Vienna for Berlin to become a research fellow in 1925 and later chief psychiatrist at the private Lichterfelde Hospital. After the ascendance of Hitler in Germany he returned to Vienna in 1933 as a neuropsychiatrist with the university clinic.

In 1936 Sakel immigrated to New York thanks to an invitation from the state commissioner of mental hygiene, Frederick Parsons. By then Sakel had not only published a number of articles on the treatment of drug addiction but had also caused a stir in international psychiatric circles with his insulin shock treatment for "schizophrenia," the term coined by Eugen Bleuler of Switzerland to characterize the split mind. In the 1930s all kinds of madness were increasingly considered to have a somatic basis and thus thought to respond favorably to biophysically based therapeutic agents. Before the discovery of penicillin, Julius Wagner-Jauregg's First World War suggestion to treat tertiary (i.e., cerebral) syphilis, or general paresis, with malaria fever became widely accepted. It was under his successor, Otto Poetzl in Vienna, that in 1933 Sakel first achieved success by injecting insulin to alleviate the psychotic excitement of addicts during drug withdrawal treatment. He did so by lowering their level of consciousness to the point of coma. Insulin, the pancreatic hormone, had begun to be used in the treatment of diabetes mellitus in the 1920s. An overdose to lower the blood sugar (causing hypoglycemia) was known to reduce cerebral function to the point of coma or "shock." Madness had always been seen as a kind of mental overexcitement, hence some drastic, even punishing, methods—driving the Devil out with Beelzebub, as it were—had been in use for centuries. Sakel's original physiologic line of thought had been that "vagotonic" insulin would be useful by counteracting the "sympathicotonic" overreaction manifested in mental states of excitement.

After 1933 insulin shock treatment made Sakel's name known worldwide. Perhaps the most famous among many patients who underwent hypoglycemic shocks was the schizophrenic dancing genius Vaslav Nijinsky, whom Sakel treated in Switzerland with transient success. Sakel's method, however, yielded only fairly satisfactory and inconsistent results particularly in the early stages of schizophrenia. In addition to coma, the hormone often also produced epileptic seizures. Moreover, the practice required extensive and costly attention by a supervising staff. After insulin, other physical methods to treat schizophrenia soon followed, such as Meduna's metrazol (1935) and Cerletti and Bini's electrical convulsion treatment (1937), in addition to sectioning the frontal lobes of the brain (1937). Sakel's method remained more popular in Europe than in the United States. It altogether lost its appeal in the 1950s with the advent of antipsychotic drugs such as the phenothiazines, for example, chlorpromazine (Thorazine).

Except for the devotion to his professional calling and to charity Sakel led a rather lonely life. Self-centered, he was not popular among his colleagues and did not seek academic appointments. In the United States he trained the staff at the Rockland State Hospital and worked at the Worcester State Hospital in Massachusetts and Bellevue Hospital in New York City. He remained unmarried. He died in New York City of a heart attack, having had one eleven years earlier. Although hardly used nowadays, Sakel's insulin shock treatment remains an outstanding landmark in the history of psychiatry as an attempt to overcome a profound mental disorder by biophysical means.

• Biographical sources about Sakel are sparse. An interesting recent reference to his person and his method is in Peter Ostwald, *Vaslav Nijinsky: A Leap into Madness* (1991). For sources on hypoglycemic shock treatment, see Manfred Sakel, "Schizophreniebehandlung mittels Insulin-Hypoglykämie sowie hypoglykämischer Schocks," *Wiener medizinische Wochenschrift* 84 (1934) and 85 (1935); D. Ewen Cameron and R. G. Hoskins, "Experiences in the Insulin-Hypoglycemia Treatment of Schizophrenia," *Journal of the American Medical Association* 109 (1937): 1246–49; and Charles A. Rymer et al., "The Hypoglycemia Treatment of Schizophrenia," *Journal of the American Medical Association* 109 (1937): 1249–51. Obituaries are in the *American Journal of Psychiatry* 115 (1958): 287–88, the *British Medical Journal* (1957): 1439–40, and *Lancet* 273 (14 Dec. 1957): 1235.

FRANCIS SCHILLER

SALAZAR, Ruben (3 Mar. 1928–29 Aug. 1970), newspaper reporter and columnist, was born in Ciudad Juárez, Mexico, the son of Salvador Salazar and Luz Chávez. At eight months of age he and his parents moved to El Paso, Texas, where he became a naturalized citizen. In 1954 Salazar graduated with a degree in journalism from the University of Texas at El Paso, then known as Texas Western College. His experiences on the campus newspaper, *El Burro*, led to a career as one of the first Latino reporters to work for the mainstream press, the first Latino foreign correspondent, and the first Latino columnist.

He began his professional journalism career in 1955 at the *El Paso Herald-Post* where he covered the police and Juárez beats and earned a reputation as a hard-hitting, streetwise reporter. In his first investigative role, Salazar posed as a drunk and spent twenty-five hours in El Paso's city jail. He then wrote an exposé—"25 Hours in Jail—I Lived in a Chamber of Horrors"—of filthy jail conditions and disclosed how drugs were being smuggled to prisoners. He later worked at the *Santa Rosa (Calif.) Press-Democrat*, the *San Francisco News* and the former *Los Angeles Herald-Express*.

In 1959 Salazar joined the *Los Angeles Times*, where he covered the Mexican-American community, which had largely been ignored by the media. His stories about injustices against Mexican Americans and other minorities and working for better understanding among all racial groups proved to be the hallmark of his career. Salazar married Sally Robane in 1960; they had three children. In 1963 he won a State Medal Award for best local news coverage in California for his six-part series "Spanish-Speaking Angelenos: A Culture in Search of a Name." The series examined Latino problems of substandard education, high dropout rates, and lack of political power. In 1965 Salazar became a *Los Angeles Times* correspondent in the Dominican Republic, where he covered the revolutionary outbreak, crawling over barricades to talk to members of both sides of the warring groups. From 1965 to 1968 he was with the paper's bureau in Saigon, where he narrowly missed being caught in the blast of a bomb at Da Nang. In 1968 he took charge of the *Times* Mexico City bureau later that year, covering Central America, the Caribbean, Cuba, and Mexico, where he was an eyewitness to the mass shooting of students by soldiers during the 1968 uprisings.

In 1969 the *Times* brought Salazar back to Los Angeles where he began writing news stories and a weekly column about Mexican Americans, whom he characterized as the "forgotten community." In the four years that Salazar had been out of the country, East Los Angeles had become a hotbed of protest by activists who were now calling themselves Chicanos instead of Mexican Americans. Thousands of students had staged walkouts at area high schools, demanding more Chicano teachers and improved facilities. During the height of the Chicano movement, Salazar wrote about the educational alienation of Chicanos, urban problems, and the tensions between Mexican Americans and African Americans.

In April 1970 Salazar left the *Times* to become news director for the Spanish-language television station KMEX, where he again specialized in the Los Angeles Mexican-American community. He continued writing a column for the *Times*. According to Ruben Martinez, editor at Pacific News Service, up to this point Salazar's writings had been "thoughtful, nuanced distillations of Mexican-American culture for the white reader of the *Times*." But with the advent of Chicano militancy, his topics and tone of writing shifted. In his final columns for the *Times*, he assumed an advocacy role. Though no revolutionary, Salazar's writings became impassioned pleas for cross-cultural and cross-generational understanding. He called upon whites to listen to the needs of Chicano students. In addition, Salazar did some of his most hard-hitting reporting on law enforcement. Salazar and his KMEX colleague William Restrepo began a major investigation into widespread allegations that police and sheriff's deputies had beaten residents and planted evidence when making arrests.

On 29 August 1970 Salazar, Restrepo, and a cameraman were covering a Chicano civil rights demonstration in Laguna Park (now Ruben Salazar Park), which erupted into a riot when deputies, responding to reports of looting at a nearby liquor store, were hit by rocks and bottles. According to Restrepo, he and Salazar went into the Silver Dollar Cafe on Whittier Boulevard in East Los Angeles to use the bathroom and to grab a quick beer. What happened next is disputed to this day. A sheriff's deputy fired a 10-inch tear gas projectile inside, striking the 42-year-old Salazar in the head and killing him instantly.

His death made him a martyr of the Chicano/Latino civil rights movement, and questions remain as to whether he was the victim of a tragic accident or was assassinated. According to Charlie Erickson, the founder of Hispanic Link, a Latino news service, Salazar was the victim of a political assassination. He said Salazar told him before his death that he was under surveillance and was being followed by undercover law enforcement officers. A coroner's inquest concluded that Salazar's death was accidental. However, four years after he died, the county paid Salazar's family $700,000 for negligence without admitting wrongdoing. No one was ever prosecuted.

The significance of his work was twofold. First, as a *Times* reporter and columnist he was *la voz* for *la Raza*, the voice for his people, the most articulate spokesperson for Chicano concerns to the Anglo community. He once said of himself: "Someone must advocate a community that has been forgotten." Second, as a news director for KMEX, he gave militants access to the airwaves, providing Mexican Americans information that could lead to their politicization or even radicalization. For Chicanos, writes Professor Edward J. Escobar, Salazar became a hero—"a martyr who died for the cause of Chicano liberation and a symbol for those who fought ongoing repression."

• Ruben Salazar, *Border Correspondent: Selected Writings, 1955–1970*, ed. Mario T. Garcia (1995), a compilation of Salazar's writing over a fifteen-year career that ended with his column at the *Times*, is the most complete assessment of Salazar's life and work. See also Edward J. Escobar, "The Dialectics of Repression: The Los Angeles Police Department and the Chicano Movement, 1968–71," *The Journal of American History* 79 (1993): 1483–514, and the *Los Angeles Times*, 31 Aug. 1970, 1 Sept. 1970, 2 Sept. 1970, and 26 Aug. 1995, on the controversy surrounding Salazar's death. Enrique Lopez,

"Ruben Salazar Death Silences a Leading Voice of Reason," *Regeneracion* 1 (1970): 5, addresses Salazar's impact as America's first prominent Mexican-American journalist.

ANTHONY R. FELLOW

SALCEDO, Manuel María de (3 Apr. 1776–3 Apr. 1813), governor of Spanish Texas, was born in Malaga, Spain, the son of Manuel Juan de Salcedo, the last governor of Spanish Louisiana, and Francisca de Quiroga y Manso. Manuel María attended the Royal Seminary of Nobles until age seventeen. He then became a lieutenant in the command of his father, an infantry colonel. When their father was appointed governor, Manuel and his brother Francisco were also assigned to Louisiana. In 1800 Salcedo married María Guadalupe Prietto y la Ronde, a native New Orleanian of Spanish-French ancestry. He served as a boundary commissioner that same year, when Spain agreed to transfer Louisiana to Napoleon Bonaparte.

On 24 April 1807, while he was a captain of the Infantry Battalion of the Canary Islands, the Council of the Indies appointed Salcedo governor of Texas. He took the oath of office in Cádiz on 1 May 1807 but did not begin his new duties for more than a year. In the spring of 1808 he toured the central United States with his wife and their small daughter and only child, Mariquita. In Natchitoches, Louisiana, he obtained intelligence on conditions in New Spain (Mexico). Rumors that a Napoleonic emissary planned to revolutionize New Spain caused him to leave quickly for Texas. On 7 November 1808 he arrived in San Antonio de Béxar, the villa that grew into the city of San Antonio. Now a colonel, Salcedo became the youngest governor Texas has ever had.

As chief executive, Salcedo was only third in command in the colonial hierarchy in Texas. His immediate superior was his friend Antonio Cordero, deputy commandant general in the provinces of Coahuila and Texas. Cordero worked under the new governor's uncle, Nemesio Salcedo, commandant general of the Interior Provinces.

On 22 January 1809 the Supreme Central Governing Junta of Spain decreed, in the name of Ferdinand VII, that each Spanish colony should elect a deputy, or member, to sit on the Junta. Salcedo wrote a detailed report on the needs of Texas to Miguel de Lardizábal, the elected representative of the Interior Provinces. Whether the report ever reached Lardizábal is unknown. Salcedo maintained in the report that the government of Spain paid too little attention to Texas.

Salcedo typified the Spanish colonial bureaucracy by involving himself in the minutiae of his administration. He sometimes changed the mail schedule to coordinate more effectively the arrivals and departures of the couriers. He also occasionally intervened in ecclesiastical affairs in an effort to keep praiseworthy clerics in the province.

In May 1809 Governor Salcedo objected to Nemesio's instructions to close the Texas frontier to U.S. Army deserters because it was nearly impossible to police the entire border. He recommended instead a repopulation program allowing local authorities to create new settlements in strategic areas. In the spring of 1810 the commandant general gave Hispanic Texas administrators discretionary powers in handling local problems. That summer Salcedo went to Washington, D.C., to confer with President James Madison about the Neutral Ground, a demilitarized zone that had been created in 1805 on the Louisiana-Texas border after France ceded Louisiana to the United States in 1803. Since the boundary was not clearly defined, military commanders on both sides of the border were concerned with bandits, the movement of contraband, and unauthorized settlers. Madison wanted the U.S. Army in Louisiana to cooperate with Hispanic officials.

In late November 1810 the viceroy of New Spain, Francisco Javier de Venegas, sent an urgent communiqué: insurrection leader Father Miguel Hidalgo and two confederates might invade Texas on their way to the United States. He asked Hispanic Texans to apprehend the rebels. Salcedo wrote to Félix Calleja, commander of the vice-regal forces, informing him of Texas's defenseless position, and in an edict stated, "It may be justly feared that the revolutionary leaders may have some partisans here, although I do not believe that any such perfidious monster can be found among us because of the loyalty of the inhabitants of this province" (Webb, p. 359).

The governor sent his wife and daughter to East Texas for safety early in 1811. Speculation on their whereabouts intensified public anxiety. On 2 January Salcedo assembled the 300 troops of the Béxar (San Antonio) garrison in the military plaza. He announced that soon they would proceed to the Rio Grande to defend the province more effectively. He urged Texans to support the royalist cause and angrily denied rumors that he planned to abandon them to revolutionists and Indians. Juan Bautista de las Casas, a retired militia captain, led the local opposition to Salcedo's administration and with his confederates arrested the governor and his military staff before dawn on 22 January.

On 1 March 1811 opponents of the revolution formed a junta that pledged fidelity to King Ferdinand VII and promised to restore legitimate authority in Texas. Emissaries from the junta helped Salcedo escape from the hacienda where he was imprisoned. Loyalist troops captured the rebel Pedro de Aranda and obtained maps showing the route of Hidalgo's forces, and on 21 March they captured a sizable part of the rebel "Army of America," including the high command.

On 26 April 1811 Nemesio Salcedo appointed a military tribunal, with Manuel María Salcedo as president, to prosecute the revolutionaries. On 29 July, after pronouncing the death sentence, the military board turned Father Miguel Hidalgo y Costilla over to an ecclesiastical court, which defrocked him according to canon law. Manuel Salcedo acted as a witness for the state, which executed Hidalgo on 30 July.

Salcedo, who had to enforce the law where people had seen him dragged through the streets in chains, thought his office had lost prestige in the las Casas upheaval. He therefore requested an inquiry by a military board into the events surrounding that disaster. He returned to Béxar on 11 September 1811 but refused to perform regular duties. Nemesio Salcedo declined to commission an inquiry. He argued that the fact that higher authorities had allowed Governor Salcedo to return to Texas proved they trusted him. Manuel Salcedo resumed his full responsibilities on 15 December 1811.

In November 1812 Salcedo invited Republican army leaders to discuss a truce. In exchange for allowing Anglo-American filibusters to leave Texas, he demanded that Mexicans in the Republican army surrender to Spanish authorities. The truce ended futilely on 23 November. After suffering heavy casualties, Salcedo and Governor Herrera of Nuevo León withdrew in February 1813 to San Antonio de Béxar. They made their final stand near San Antonio. The rebels defeated Salcedo's troops on 19 March 1813 at the battle of Salado, also known as the battle of Rosillo. They executed Salcedo on 3 April 1813. Months later, on 28 August, Father José Dario Zambrano buried him in the San Fernando Church.

Like the Tories in eighteenth-century North America, who had been steadfast toward George III, Salcedo exemplified an anachronistic form of patriotism. He did not imagine that his nemesis, Father Miguel Hidalgo, would be immortalized as Mexico's greatest patriot.

• "Texas Archives, Nacogdoches: Transcripts," in the Edward E. Ayer Manuscript Collection at the Texas State Library in Austin, contains transcripts of documents relating to the province of Texas (1729–1843). Félix D. Almaráz, Jr., *Tragic Cavalier: Governor Manuel Salcedo of Texas, 1808–1813* (1971), is a good introduction to Salcedo's career. See also Almaráz's "The Administration of Manuel Maria de Salcedo of Texas: 1808–1813" (Ph.D. diss., Univ. of New Mexico, 1969). Nettie Lee Benson, "A Governor's Report on Texas in 1809," *Southwestern Historical Quarterly* 71 (Apr. 1968), has excerpts from Salcedo's report to Miguel de Lardizábal, deputy-elect to the Spanish Cortes. A copy of Salcedo's report to Lardizábal is in the National Archives of Mexico City. Walter Prescott Webb, ed., "Texas Collection: Christmas and New Year in Texas," *Southwestern Historical Quarterly* 44 (Jan. 1941): 357–79, discusses the governor's efforts to keep up traditions during the Hidalgo insurrection.

DIANNE JENNINGS WALKER

SALISBURY, Edward Elbridge (6 Apr. 1814–5 Feb. 1901), Orientalist, was born in Boston, Massachusetts, the son of Josiah Salisbury, a merchant and clergyman, and Abby Breese. He received his preliminary education at home from his father and later at the Boston Latin School and graduated from Yale in 1832. He remained for the next four years in New Haven, studying Hebrew and theology in preparation for a career as a minister. Under the influence of his teacher Josiah Gibbs, he became interested in comparative philology.

In 1836 he married Abigail Salisbury Phillips, and having come into a considerable sum of money he and his wife set out on a voyage to Europe. At Oxford, Horace Hayman Wilson encouraged him to study Sanskrit, at that time virtually unknown in America. After six months studying art in Italy, in 1837 Salisbury went to Paris, where he studied Arabic with A. I. Sylvestre De Sacy and Garcin de Tassy. Later he went to Berlin to study Sanskrit and the nascent discipline of linguistics with Franz Bopp. The Salisburys' only child was born in Europe. After his return to America in 1841, Salisbury was appointed professor of Arabic and Sanskrit at Yale, the first such appointment in the United States. In 1842 he returned to Europe for further study of Sanskrit in Bonn with Christian Lassen and in Paris with Eugène Burnouf.

Returning to Yale in 1843, Salisbury inaugurated the first formal academic program in Oriental languages, literatures, and history in the United States, including the Semitic languages of the Near East, ancient and modern, and Sanskrit (*An Inaugural Discourse on Arabic and Sanskrit Literature* [1844]). By 1845 he offered graduate study, "provided a sufficient number present themselves to form a class." He served without salary and committed his own resources to the purchase of Arabic, Turkish, and Persian manuscripts and books to begin a Near Eastern library. Through contacts with American missionaries in the Near and Far East he rapidly built a large research collection of Oriental materials, the first of its kind in America.

Salisbury was a founder of the American Oriental Society (1842), thereafter the principal professional organization for scholars of Oriental studies in the United States. He served as corresponding secretary and editor of its *Journal* from 1846 to 1863 and as president of the society from 1863 to 1866 and 1873 to 1880, being an active member of the society for sixty years in all. He contributed to the first volume of the *Journal* (1849) the first American publication in the field of cuneiform studies ("On the Identification of the Signs of the Persian Cuneiform Alphabet") and a wide-ranging survey of contemporaneous progress in Oriental studies that illustrates his breadth of interest. He paid for the acquisition of typefonts in Oriental scripts and for the publication costs of the early volumes of the *Journal* and solicited or wrote a substantial portion of the content. Largely through his initiatives, the American Oriental Society and American scholarship opened contacts with their European counterparts, and Salisbury encouraged promising students to continue study in Europe. He was also a founder of the Classical Section of the American Oriental Society (1869), which later became the American Philological Association. His interest in the contemporary Orient led him in 1852 to open relations with the Syrian Academy of Sciences, then at Beirut, with a view to improving knowledge of Arabic in America and to bringing Western education to the subjects of the Ottoman Empire.

Salisbury's major publications in Arabic and Islamic studies, all in the Society's *Journal*, included "Translation of Two Unpublished Arabic Documents Relating to the Doctrines of the Isma ilis and Other Bāṭinian Sects, with an Introduction and Notes" (1851), "Translation of an Unpublished Arabic Risā-lah" (1853), "On the Science of Muslim Tradition" (1859), "Materials for the History of the Muhammadan Doctrine of Predestination and Free Will" (1863), and "The Book of Suleiman's First Ripe Fruit, Disclosing the Mysteries of the Nuṣairian Religion" (1864). These works were characterized by a thorough command of the Arabic language and of contemporaneous European scholarship. Although for the most part translations, summaries, and discussion of the work of others, Salisbury's studies laid the foundation for Oriental scholarship in America by demonstrating that mastery of languages, current scholarship, accuracy, and good judgment were the prerequisites of sound original research. His last publication in this area was "On Some of the Relations between Islam and Christianity" (*New Englander*, Oct. 1876), also published separately (1876).

In his twelve years as professor of Sanskrit, Salisbury had only two students, as by his own account he was not suited to be a teacher. These were the classicist and linguist James Hadley and William Dwight Whitney, who became one of the ablest Sanskritists of his time. In Salisbury's own words, "Their quickness of perception and unerring exactness of acquisition soon made it evident that the teacher and the taught must change places" (*Journal of the American Oriental Society* 19 [1897]: 13). With characteristic generosity and self-effacement, Salisbury resigned his professorship in Sanskrit in Whitney's favor, endowing the chair from his own resources (1853–1854). He increased the endowment in 1869 when Harvard attempted to draw Whitney to its own faculty. Salisbury himself declined a professorship in Arabic at Harvard the same year, at which time the graduate program at Yale was established in a more systematic form.

In 1847 Salisbury published an essay in the *Journal* on the origins of Buddhism, largely inspired by Burnouf's work; this was the first scholarly study of Buddhism published in the United States. Salisbury also wrote a study of the Nestorian inscription of Singan-fu, China (1852), on a Phoenician inscription from Sidon (1855), and on Mesopotamian cylinder seals (1855), as well as numerous other essays and reviews on various oriental subjects ranging from Syria to Japan.

Salisbury's artistic interests were manifest in his substantial support of the Yale Art Gallery and in his lecture "Principles of Domestic Taste" (*New Englander*, Apr. 1877, also published separately). His first wife died in 1869, and in 1871 he married Evelyn McCurdy; he and his second wife had no children. In his later years he devoted most of his energies to genealogical research; his failing eyesight left him dependent on his wife for reading. He published *Mr. William Diodate* (1876); "The Griswold Family of Connecti-

cut" (*Magazine of American History* [1884]); *Family Memorials* (2 vols. [1885]), about his own family and that of his first wife; *Family Histories and Genealogies* (7 vols. [1892]), concerning the family of his second wife; *Pedigrees of Newdigate* (n.d.); and *In Memory of Hon. Charles Johnson McCurdy* (1891). Throughout his life he continued his benefactions to Yale. In 1850 he endowed another professorship, first held by the geologist James Dwight Dana, and he contributed funds for buildings, including the library and divinity school, and for library collections, which he further enhanced by donating his own outstanding collection of Arabic books and manuscripts in 1870. He died in New Haven, Connecticut.

Salisbury was a modest, generous-minded man who E. W. Hopkins said in his memorial address was characterized by "a gentle dignity and antique stately courtliness." He inspired reverence and affection throughout the American Orientalist community, as well as in European scholarly circles. His career marks the beginning of professional Orientalist scholarship in America. He saw the need to train a generation of American scholars in the philological methods being pioneered in Europe. Beyond the study of individual languages, such as Arabic and Sanskrit, which very few Americans of his time could read, he advocated the importance of linguistics as a tool for understanding both languages and language itself and encouraged his students to train themselves in its methods. His interest in the contemporary Near East and in Semitic languages beyond the narrow focus of early nineteenth-century American biblical studies set him apart from his contemporaries; he had few imitators in American colleges and universities for nearly fifty years after his initial appointment. He was regarded in his own time as a key figure in the transition from the American college to the American university and was considered the first American university professor. He was a member of the Société Asiatique (Paris), the Deutsche Orient-Gesellschaft, the American Antiquarian Society, the Connecticut Academy of Arts and Sciences, and the Imperial Academy of Sciences and Belles Lettres (Constantinople).

Salisbury's most lasting achievement was to put the American Oriental Society on a sound footing to serve both as a forum for disseminating knowledge of the non-European world in America and for presenting American scholarship to the world at large. His own research set high standards that proved to be auspicious beginnings for Sanskrit, Arabic, and Islamic studies and for Semitics in the United States.

• Salisbury's scholarly and family papers are in the Yale University Manuscripts and Archives, Sterling Memorial Library, Yale University. Additional material is in the files of the American Oriental Society, New Haven. Autobiographical sketches are in [Edward E. Salisbury, ed.], *Biographical Memoranda Respecting All Who Ever Were Members of the Class of 1832 in Yale College* (1880), pp. 235–38; Salisbury, *Family-Memorials*, vol. 1 (1885), pp. 98–100; F. Edgerton, "A Letter of Salisbury," *Journal of the American Oriental Society* 64 (1944): 58–61. A partial bibliography of his publications is in *Journal of the American Oriental Society* 21 (1902): 34–35. A description of Salisbury's early academic programs at Yale was given by T. D. Seymour, *American Journal of Philology* 15, no. 59 (1894): 274–75. Salisbury's study of Buddhism is discussed in Thomas A. Tweed, *The American Encounter with Buddhism, 1844–1912: Victorian Culture and the Limits of Dissent* (1982), and his place in American scholarship in Louise L. Stevenson, *Scholarly Means to Evangelical Ends: The New Haven Scholars and the Transformation of Higher Learning in America, 1830–1890* (1986). Biographical sketches and memoirs include *Obituary Record of the Graduates of Yale University 1900–1910* (1910), pp. 10–12; E. W. Hopkins, "Memorial Address in Honor of Professor Salisbury," in *India Old and New*, ed. Hopkins (1901), pp. 3–19, and in abridgement as "In Memoriam," *Journal of the American Oriental Society* 22 (1901): 1–6; A. P. Stokes, *Memorials of Eminent Yale Men*, vol. 1 (1914), p. 366; and an obituary in *New Haven Register*, 5 Feb. 1901.

BENJAMIN R. FOSTER

SALISBURY, Harrison Evans (14 Nov. 1908–5 July 1993), journalist and historian, was born in Minneapolis, Minnesota, the son of Percy Pritchard Salisbury, a bag-factory executive, and Georgianna Evans, a writer. In 1925 Salisbury enrolled at the University of Minnesota and became a cub reporter for the campus newspaper. He left school for brief periods in 1928 and in 1929 to earn money as a *Minnesota Journal* reporter. In January 1930, when briefly suspended from the university for smoking in the library vestibule, he was hired by the United Press (UP) as a correspondent in St. Paul. Later in 1930 he received a B.A. and also covered the trial of Chicago crime boss Al Capone. Salisbury was transferred to the UP's Chicago bureau in 1931. In 1933 he married Mary Jane Hollis; the couple had two children. He was assigned to the UP bureau in Washington, D.C., in 1934, and when his pay was frozen after he joined a newspaper guild, he freelanced and published under pen names in *Coronet*, *Ken*, and *Newsweek*, among other periodicals.

In 1940 Salisbury was sent to the foreign desk of the UP's New York City office. In 1943 he transferred to London, without his family, to be bureau manager of the UP office there. He reported events in World War II in England, North Africa, and the Middle East. From January to September 1944 he was in Moscow and then returned to New York to be foreign news editor of the UP. He wrote his first book, *Russia on the Way* (1946), a bland comparison of the United States and war-fatigued Russia. However, he soon grew so unsettled personally and professionally that late in 1948 he entered a psychiatric clinic.

Upon his discharge early in 1949 he was hired by the *New York Times* to became correspondent in its Moscow bureau, a position that had been unstaffed for eighteen months. The fact that his dispatches were censored by Soviet authorities remained unknown in the United States and caused his rivals to claim that he was soft on communism. In 1950 he and his wife were divorced. By the time Salisbury left Moscow in 1954 and returned to New York as a *Times* staff member, he was an expert on the Soviet Union. His fourteen arti-

cles on Kremlin policies and Joseph Stalin's crimes gained him a 1955 Pulitzer Prize for international reporting. Salisbury described his prize-winning material as "hard-rock observations of reality as I had seen it in Russia from the Neva to the Amur, from the Lena to the Volga, a detailed reconstruction of Stalin's terror, an overview of Russia's real life . . . after nearly forty years of Bolshevism" (*A Journey for Our Times: A Memoir*, pp. 469–70). He included commentary on drunkenness, banality, bureaucracy, and absence of ideas, goods, and services. In 1957 Salisbury received the George Polk Memorial Award for excellence in foreign reporting for his coverage of events in Iron Curtain countries. He later won additional honors. In 1960 he filed ominous dispatches on racism in Birmingham, Alabama. City officials sued him and the *Times* for libel; they won in 1964, but lost on appeal. In 1961–1962 he revisited Russia and traveled into Mongolia and along the Sino-Soviet border.

From 1962 to 1964 Salisbury was director of national correspondence for the *Times*, where he worked to augment coverage of religion and the arts. He married the writer Charlotte Young Rand in 1964; they had no children. He was assistant managing editor of the *Times* from 1964 to 1972. Accompanied by his wife, he was sent to China and countries bordering it in 1966. The trip, during which he traveled 30,000 miles, resulted in a series of dispatches, partly revised as his book *Orbit of China* (1967), in which he discusses Chinese history and traditions, includes personal observations on Hongkong, Thailand, Laos, Burma, India, Sakkim, Mongolia, Russia, and Japan, and comments on poverty, opium, and international politics.

During the Vietnam War Salisbury was the first American reporter allowed to visit Hanoi, from which he filed electrifying dispatches—journalistic coups, one and all—in December 1966 and January 1967. He reviled President Lyndon B. Johnson and his administration for defining as surgical bombings what amounted to the slaughter of civilians. His *Behind the Lines—Hanoi, December 23, 1966–January 7, 1967* (1967) recasts these dispatches in book form (later events proved his optimistic trust of the enemy to be unfounded). In 1970 Salisbury initiated and became the first editor of the "Op-Ed" page (*op*posite the *edi*torial page) of the *Times*, a forum for regular columnists and guest contributors to air their views. In 1972 he was appointed associate editor of the *Times*, the year before he reached the age of obligatory retirement.

From this point until his death, Salisbury wrote eleven more books and edited three others, including Andrei Sakharov's appeal for peaceful coexistence titled *Sakharov Speaks* (1974). Salisbury appeared on television as guest host of "Behind the Lines" in the fall of 1974. *Esquire* commissioned him to write a series of essays that became "Travels through America" in 1975 and the book *Travels around America* a year later.

In 1988 Salisbury revisited China to investigate the May–June 1987 fire in Manchuria's Greater Hinggan

Forest, which he wrote about in *The Great Black Dragon Fire: A Chinese Inferno* (1989), his account of the catastrophe costing China three million acres of timber valued at $4 billion. Salisbury happened to be in Beijing's Tiananmen Square in June 1989 making a television documentary and reported the experience in his rushed *Tiananmen Diary: Thirteen Days in June* (1989), a less than first-hand account, since he had left Beijing before the Chinese army attack on dissident students.

Salisbury's many books may be divided into those on the Soviet Union, on China and Vietnam, on American topics, and two autobiographies. Most likely to endure are his major studies of Russia and China. *American in Russia* (1955) details his experiences and observations during his years from 1949 to 1954 as a reporter in Russia. It is so balanced that he was denounced by some reviewers as pro-Soviet and by others as reactionary. In *To Moscow—and Beyond: A Reporter's Narrative* (1960) he considers current cultural trends in the Soviet Union and suggests that Russian life improved under Nikita Khrushchev. *A New Russia?* (1962) reflects Salisbury's optimism with respect to liberalizing events in a Russia in flux but also his concern over Sino-Soviet border unrest, and his 625-page bestseller, *The 900 Days: The Siege of Leningrad* (1969), describes the German-Russian World War II standoff from August 1941 to January 1944. It was banned in Russia as pro-Nazi and critical of Soviet politics, praised as an "epic" by author C. P. Snow in the *London Times*, but criticized by some reviewers as cluttered with digressions. Salisbury's *Black Night, White Snow: Russia's Revolutions, 1905–1917* (1978) explains the political, economic, social, and intellectual developments causing Russia's upheavals. This lively 746-page account, well researched and exhaustively documented, emphasizes Nicholas II and Nikolai Lenin.

Salisbury had great faith in China, which he once called "the world's most talented nation." He followed *Orbit of China* with *War between Russia and China* (1969), in which he expresses fear of a Sino-Soviet clash, hope that the United States might prevent it, and worry about Taiwan. His book *To Peking—and Beyond: A Report on the New Asia* (1973) discusses Chinese problems and foreign policy and is mainly valuable because Salisbury was able to interview Chou En-lai, Sihanouk, Kim Il Soong, and other Asian leaders. To prepare to write *The Long March: The Untold Story* (1985), an account of Mao Zedong's heroic 6,000-mile, three-year retreat from Chiang Kai-shek's forces, Salisbury and his wife made a comparable trek for four months in 1984 by jeep, minivan, mule, and on foot. Along the way he interviewed old survivors of Mao's march and younger military and political officials. His last book, *The New Emperors: China in the Era of Mao and Deng* (1991), dedicated to the youth of China, is a well-researched analysis of China's post-1949 rulers, partly based on interviews.

Ever versatile, Harrison Salisbury wrote one novel cast in Leningrad (1962) and another based on Aleksandr Solzhenitsyn's life (1975). He also published a collection of controversial Op-Ed columns (1973) and freelanced for many magazines. While his wife was at the wheel of their automobile, driving with him outside Providence, Rhode Island, Salisbury suffered a heart attack and died at once. He is regarded as one of the most distinguished newsmen of the twentieth century. Without fear or favor, resourceful and seemingly tireless, he reported what he saw, attacked falsehood and prejudice in the seats of power, and did so in often contentious prose. His abiding hope lay in American ingenuity and the democratic imagination.

• Most of Salisbury's voluminous papers and related materials are at Columbia University. Others are in libraries at Iowa State University, Ames; the University of Michigan; and Yale. Detailed sources of personal information are his candid autobiographies—*A Journey for Our Times: A Memoir* (1983) and *A Time of Change: A Reporter's Tale of Our Time* (1988). Minor works include *The Shook-up Generation* (1958), about American youth gangs and violence; *Moscow Journal—The End of Stalin* (1961), about Soviet unrest just before and after 1953; *The Key to Moscow* (1963), a guidebook; *Russia* (1965), about Soviet Union evolution to world-power status; *The Many Americas Shall Be One* (1971), about America's continuing socio-political problems; *Russia in Revolution, 1900–1930* (1979), a word-and-picture chronicle; and *China: 100 Years of Revolution* (1983), a popular history. Opinions concerning Salisbury by two distinguished newspaper men who knew him well are in Gay Talese, *The Kingdom and the Power* (1969), and Turner Catledge, *My Life and The Times* (1971). Salisbury's accounts of Siberian prison camps and the death of Stalin are reprinted in Karen Rothmyer, *Winning Pulitzers: The Stories Behind Some of the Best News Coverage of Our Time* (1991). Obituaries are in the *Chicago Tribune*, the *Los Angeles Times*, the *New York Times*, and the *Washington Post*, all 7 July 1993.

ROBERT L. GALE

SALISBURY, Rollin D. (17 Aug. 1858–15 Aug. 1922), geologist and educator, was born in Spring Prairie, Wisconsin, the son of Daniel Salisbury and Lucinda Bryant, farmers. The boy helped on the farm and attended a nearby country school until he was sixteen. He then completed the four-year course of the state normal school in Whitewater, Wisconsin, in three years, taught school for a year, and entered Beloit College in 1878. There he became acquainted with professor Thomas Chrowder Chamberlin, with whom he was associated for the rest of his life.

After receiving a Ph.B. in 1881, Salisbury was employed by the U.S. Geological Survey (USGS) to work with Chamberlin, who had become head of its new division of glacial geology. He and Chamberlin published their observations, "On the Driftless Area of the Upper Mississippi Valley" (USGS, *Sixth Annual Report* [1885], pp. 199–322).

In 1883 Salisbury was instructor of geology and biology at Beloit College, where he received an M.A. and advanced to professor of geology in 1884. In Europe during the summer of 1887 he traced an extensive but previously unrecognized glacial moraine from Denmark to Russia, then spent the 1887–1888 school year at the University of Heidelberg, Germany, studying mineralogy and petrography with Karl Harry Ferdinand Rosenbusch. Salisbury returned to Beloit College until 1891, when he accepted a position as professor of geology at the University of Wisconsin (in Madison), where Chamberlin was president.

When Chamberlin went to the newly founded University of Chicago in 1892 to organize its geology department, he employed Salisbury as professor of geographic geology. Salisbury assisted Chamberlin extensively in the administration of the department, was dean of the university colleges from 1894 to 1896, and then dean of its Ogden Graduate School of Science from 1899 until his death.

Chamberlin and Salisbury wrote a classic work, simply called *Geology* (3 vols., 1904–1906), which took ten years to complete. The three volumes, *Geologic Processes and Their Results*, *Earth History: Genesis—Paleozoic*, and *Earth History: Mesozoic and Cenozoic*, became the standard textbook of American geology for many years.

In 1903 the University of Chicago established a geography department, the first graduate department in that field in the United States. As its head, Salisbury hired several professors, and he began a program of field instruction distinct from field trips in geology, "directed toward problems of life response, especially human response, to physical earth conditions," according to his biographer William D. Pattison (p. 107). Salisbury himself said, "Knowledge of present resources and conditions, and of their bearing on the life and activities of the future, is vital to the welfare of mankind" (quoted in Pattison, p. 109). He wrote the textbooks *Physiography* (in three editions, 1907, 1909, and 1919), *Elements of Geography* (with H. H. Barrows and W. S. Tower, 1912), and *Modern Geography* (with Barrows and Tower, 1913). He stepped down as head of the geography department to take over the geology department when Chamberlin retired in 1919.

In summers from 1891 to 1915 Salisbury pursued studies of glacial geology in New Jersey, at the request of the state's geologist, John C. Smock. His biographer Rollin T. Chamberlin said this was "mapping the glacial drift of the State with a detail and accuracy not theretofore attempted by any State survey." Salisbury recognized that at least two, and possibly three, ages of glacial drift were found in the state. This agreed with Thomas Chamberlin's theory, from his earlier geological survey of Wisconsin, that there had been two distinct periods of glaciation, but the concept had not thus far been extended to New Jersey. Salisbury also identified some unusual gravel terraces as having resulted from glacial ice that had stagnated, leaving pitted surfaces, and he carefully described kame terraces, which are mounds resulting from stream deposits beneath melting glaciers. With graduate student George N. Knapp, Salisbury concluded that certain unusual yellow gravel deposits in New Jersey had most probably formed as buried gravels without contact by air. These were all new concepts in glacial geology. Salisbury published his findings in three volumes of the *Reports of the State Geologist of New Jersey* ("The Physical Geography of New Jersey," vol. 4 [1895]; "The Glacial Geology of New Jersey," vol. 5 [1902]; and "The Quaternary Formations of Southern New Jersey," vol. 8 [1917]) and in several scientific papers.

In 1895 Salisbury accompanied the relief expedition to Greenland that was to transport U.S. Navy lieutenant Robert Edwin Peary and his party home from two years of exploration. There Salisbury first observed existing glaciers and moraines in valleys and along steep sea cliffs. In addition to his published papers on them, he was noted for "masterful teaching of glacier phenomena ever after."

Salisbury wrote *Outlines of Geologic History* with Bailey Willis (1910). He had editorial responsibilities with the *Journal of Geology*, especially in landform subjects, from its founding at the University of Chicago in 1893, and he was its editor from 1918 until his death. He was a founder of the American Association of Geographers in 1904 and its president in 1912.

Salisbury was considered an excellent teacher, who emphasized clear writing. His geological observations were carefully detailed. Some of the students in his geography department went on to make contributions in environmental awareness. Salisbury never married. He died in Chicago.

• Salisbury's archival records are chiefly in the Department of Special Collections at the University of Chicago Library; some records about his early years are in the Beloit College Archives. In addition to the works cited above, he wrote about ninety scientific papers, including "Distinct Glacial Epochs and the Criteria for Their Recognition," *Journal of Geology* 1 (1893): 61–84, and "Salient Points Concerning the Glacial Geology of North Greenland," *Journal of Geology* 4 (1896): 769–810. The primary biography is by Thomas C. Chamberlin's son, geologist Rollin T. Chamberlin, "Memorial of Rollin D. Salisbury," *Bulletin of Geological Society of America* 42 (1931): 126–38, with bibliography. D. Jerome Fisher, *The Seventy Years of the Department of Geology, University of Chicago* (1963), contains background and anecdotes on the department and on Salisbury himself. An analysis of Salisbury's role in geography is William D. Pattison, "*Rollin D. Salisbury, 1858–1922*," in *Geographers: Biobibliographical Studies*, vol. 6, ed. T. W. Freeman (1982). An obituary is in the *New York Times*, 17 Aug. 1922.

ELIZABETH NOBLE SHOR

SALK, Jonas Edward (28 Oct. 1914–23 June 1995), physician and virologist, was born in New York City, the son of Orthodox Jewish-Polish immigrants Daniel B. Salk, a garment worker, and Dora "Dolly" Press. Salk's early years were spent in a tenement in East Harlem and later in the Bronx, where he attended grade school. A voracious reader, he won entry at age twelve to the elite Townsend Harris High School, and after graduating at fifteen, he in 1930 entered City College. Although he initially considered becoming a lawyer, at City College he decided that science was more fascinating than law and resolved to become a doctor.

Salk graduated with a bachelor's degree in science in 1934 and entered the New York University School of Medicine. There he was named to the elite medical society Alpha Omega Alpha. Other students regarded him as a quiet, hard worker, but not as brilliant; his later fame would surprise them. In 1935 he took a year's leave of absence to study biochemistry at New York University. That year resulted in his first published paper, a laboratory study of streptococcal bacteria.

On the frontier of medicine at that time was the study of viruses, the tiniest known form of "life" deserving of the word. In his last year, Salk met a researcher who would have a profound impact on his career, Thomas Francis, Jr., the chair of bacteriology at the New York University School of Medicine. Together they studied ways to develop an influenza virus that could be killed yet still stimulate the production of antibodies—the molecular soldiers of the bodily immune system that defend against infections. Francis's work was unorthodox; at that time few virologists believed that killed-virus vaccines would ever prove effective. But if they did, they would offer a distinct advantage: they would not risk triggering a full-blown illness in inoculated persons, like that suffered by the children injected with the failed polio vaccines of the 1930s.

The day after Salk received his M.D. in June 1939, he married Donna Lindsay, a social worker, with whom he had three sons. In March 1940, while continuing to work with Francis, Salk entered a two-year medical internship at Mount Sinai Hospital in New York City. In December 1941 the nation entered the Second World War. Several months later Salk received a National Research Council Fellowship and joined Francis at the University of Michigan, where the latter had moved, and together they developed a vaccine against an old military foe: influenza. Their killed-virus vaccine defied virological dogma by generating as many antibodies as a natural influenza infection. The vaccine was eventually injected into millions of soldiers. Salk also served as acting director of the U.S. Army Influenza Commission.

Such early success whetted Salk's appetite for more. After several years at Michigan, he was eager to escape from Francis's shadow and run his own laboratory. His big break came in October 1947, when he moved to the then-uncelebrated University of Pittsburgh School of Medicine. With a $12,500 grant from the Sarah Mellon Scaife Foundation, he assembled his lab in the basement of Municipal Hospital.

In 1949, at the request of the National Foundation for Infantile Paralysis, that the ambitious young laboratory chief began to research a more ominous threat, the polio virus, or poliomyelitis, a viral infection common among children, a very small percentage of whom were paralyzed, suffered shortness of breath, and in many cases died. In the popular imagination the most fearful image of polio was that of a paralyzed child who, unable to breathe on its own, was placed on its back inside a mechanical "iron lung," to remain there until death. The efforts of a few physicians who had tested polio vaccines in the 1930s had ended in disaster when several inoculated children died. Salk first sought to determine how many types of polio virus existed. Previous research by others suggested there

were three types, but a definitive answer was essential to ensure that any future vaccine conferred complete protection. Salk agreed to undertake the long, tedious "virus typing" study, using monkeys exposed to polio virus. The creatures were expensive and difficult to work with. An alternative was to grow the virus in test-tube cultures; however, in the 1930s Albert Sabin and a colleague at the Rockefeller Institute had concluded that polio virus could be grown only in cultures of animal or human nerve tissue. That meant Salk would need thousands of monkeys to have enough nervous tissue for the virus typing project.

Being a newcomer to polio research, Salk felt insecure and was eager for acceptance by veterans such as Sabin. Ironically, he began to display a touchy side to his personality that complicated his relationships with his peers, particularly Sabin, who served on the National Foundation virus-typing committee. Sabin once remarked, "Now, Dr. Salk, you should know better than to ask a question like that." Salk felt like he had been "kicked in the teeth." Eventually he "went ahead and did what I pleased and ignored the committee" (Carter, pp. 81–82).

In 1948 John F. Enders, Thomas H. Weller, and Frederick C. Robbins succeeded in growing polio virus in non-nervous human embryonic tissue. Their achievement helped speed Salk's virus-typing project. Using their method, he grew polio virus in monkey kidney tissue in test tubes. A single monkey kidney yielded 200 tubes of virus. After placing an unknown polio virus into a test tube, where the virus multiplied, he dropped blood from a human or monkey that contained antibodies for one type of polio virus into the tube. If the virus died, then its type was identified. Salk would finish his viral typing study in 1952 and conclude, as generally expected, that there were only three types of polio virus.

Enders's achievement was also a crucial step toward a safe polio vaccine. Nervous-tissue cultures, the only medium in which scientists had previously thought they could grow polio virus, offered little hope for a vaccine. Stray nervous tissue might slip into the vaccine and cause a fatal allergic reaction in the brain. Now the Enders technique offered a way to mass-produce polio virus without using either risky nervous tissue or costly, scarce primates. The next logical goal was a polio vaccine, containing killed or weakened (attenuated) viruses that would generate enough antibodies in inoculated persons to protect them against full-blown infections.

In the late 1940s and early 1950s, several other researchers were working toward a vaccine. Isabel Morgan and Howard A. Howe injected killed viruses into monkeys and chimpanzees, who thereafter were immunized against polio. David Bodian showed that gamma globulin injections into monkeys protected them against paralytic polio. William McDowell Hammon injected tens of thousands of children with gamma globulin shots, which supposedly provided several weeks of immunity during polio epidemics. In March 1951 Hilary Koprowski startled polio researchers when he reported that he had orally fed live polio virus to two adults and twenty children, all of whom developed antibodies to polio and suffered no ill effects.

How then, did Salk, a youthful researcher at a relatively undistinguished university who was best known for his work on influenza, and who was finishing a virus-typing study that yielded an unsurprising result, emerge from behind to develop the first successful vaccine? One factor was his personal relationship with National Foundation president D. Basil O'Connor, a rich lawyer and former confidante of the late U.S. president (and polio victim) Franklin Delano Roosevelt. Salk and O'Connor grew close on a transatlantic voyage on the *Queen Mary* in 1951, while returning from a polio conference in Copenhagen, Denmark. O'Connor, who was almost sixty, was impressed by the much younger man's dinner-table repartee and by his kindness to O'Connor's favorite daughter, Bettyann, an adult polio victim who had accompanied her father on the voyage. As the descendant of working-class Irish-Catholic immigrants, O'Connor appreciated Salk's urge to rise above modest roots: "In some ways he reminds you of a girl who's never been in a bar before . . . Before that ship landed, I knew that he was a young man to keep an eye on . . . [He was] overcoming the same obstacles that faced anybody who was not Anglo-Saxon, not Protestant, not the child of wealthy or educated parents" (Gould, p. 129). Eventually O'Connor threw the National Foundation's support behind Salk's effort to develop a killed-virus vaccine. The timing was appropriate: in 1952 the number of polio cases reached an all-time U.S. record of almost 58,000 of which more than 3,000 were fatal.

In Salk's Viral Research Laboratory at the University of Pittsburgh, he killed or "inactivated" polio viruses by exposing them to formaldehyde for a few weeks. He injected the killed viruses into monkeys, who then developed antibodies to the virus. Salk refined his virus-killing technique to ensure that the viruses remained barely potent enough to generate enough antibodies but not so strong that they could cause paralytic polio or death. After thoroughly soaking viruses in formaldehyde, he calculated that there was only a one-in-a-trillion chance that a batch contained a single live virus.

Human tests followed. Salk injected his killed-virus vaccine into himself, his family, and members of his lab, later explaining: "You wouldn't do unto others that which you wouldn't do unto yourself " (Smith, p. 136). In 1952 he secretly conducted vaccinations on residents of two Pennsylvania institutions, the Polk State School and the D. T. Watson Home for Crippled Children. The former was a home for retarded males, including children. At that time, researchers felt freer to use socially disadvantaged persons, such as the retarded and prisoners, as medical guinea pigs. Still, Salk acknowledged, "When you inoculate children with a polio vaccine, you don't sleep well for two or three months." The injected children developed abundant antibodies against polio, and none fell ill. "It was

the thrill of my life," Salk later recalled (Carter, p. 140).

Salk reported the results of vaccine tests on 161 persons in the 28 March 1953 *Journal of the American Medical Association*. The news media preceded its publication with reported rumors that a polio vaccine would soon be available. Salk feared that the public would expect too much too soon; further research was needed to ensure that his vaccine was safe. Approaching O'Connor, Salk offered to deliver a nationwide radio broadcast explaining the status of vaccine development. O'Connor agreed and arranged for Salk's appearance on the CBS radio network broadcast on 26 March 1953, on a show titled "The Scientist Speaks for Himself." Speaking publicly two days before his scientific article was scheduled to appear, Salk violated scientific decorum and gained "a lasting reputation in the scientific community as a publicity seeker," in the words of one polio historian (Smith, p. 187).

Salk's fiercest and most distinguished opponent, Sabin, who was trying to develop a live-virus vaccine, claimed the Salk vaccine was "insufficiently tested for mass trial, potentially unsafe, of undetermined potency, and of undetermined stability" (Gould, p. 144).

The National Foundation nevertheless scheduled national field tests of Salk's vaccine for 1954, to be supervised by Francis, and Salk started inoculating children on 23 February 1954 at Arsenal Elementary School in Pittsburgh. Nationwide, the entire $7.5 million national trial involved more than 300,000 doctors, nurses, public health officials, teachers, school principals and nonprofessional volunteers. More than 400,000 children were injected with the vaccine, while a group of similar size received placebos and another group was observed but not injected. Francis and his team used computers to record and analyze data.

Francis announced the results of the national trial on 12 April 1955 at Ann Arbor, Michigan, in front of television and movie cameras, 150 reporters, and hundreds of doctors and scientists. The vaccine, he said, was effective, powerful, and safe. A wave of joy swept the nation. Shoppers in stores listened to the Francis speech over radio loudspeakers; church bells were rung. On 23 April, President Dwight Eisenhower gave Salk a citation "for his extraordinary achievement" in the White House Rose Garden.

As it turned out, the celebrations were premature. Batches of viral vaccine from Cutter Laboratories, a firm in Berkeley, California, had not completely eliminated live polio virus. The bad batches were eventually linked to 204 polio infections; most victims were paralyzed and eleven died. On 7 May 1955 the U.S. surgeon general temporarily stopped the injections. Salk claimed the laboratory had failed to follow his precise instructions for killing the virus. At a bitter emergency meeting, Enders warned Salk that a larger catastrophe loomed: "Every batch has live virus in it," Enders charged. Salk later recalled, "This was the first and only time in my life that I felt suicidal" (Gould, p. 154). The tragedy inspired accusations that the National Foundation or the pharmaceutical industry had moved too quickly to vaccinate the nation's children. Safety standards for vaccine manufacture were tightened, then mass inoculations were resumed.

The magnitude of Salk's triumph soon became clear. The number of cases of paralytic polio fell from 13.9 per 100,000 in 1954 to 0.5 in 1961. To many ordinary Americans, Salk became a revered figure and a symbol of the wonderful potential of science. In an opinion poll, he was ranked for significance between Mahatma Gandhi and Winston Churchill among modern figures. He was bombarded by media inquiries, and Hollywood filmmakers offered to make a movie about his life. By Salk's account, the publicity made him uncomfortable. He asked the media, without success, to refer to the achievement as the "Pitt vaccine" (for Pittsburgh) rather than "Salk vaccine." The media's tendency to focus on lone scientific heroes, not on the obscure legions on whose shoulders they stand, kept Salk in the limelight. Other scientists resented his good fortune. In later years, Sabin would dismiss Salk's work as "pure kitchen chemistry. Salk didn't discover anything" (*New York Times*, 24 June 1995). Others apparently agreed: the 1954 Nobel Prize in medicine-physiology went to Enders, Robbins, and Weller, not to Salk. Nor was Salk ever elected to the National Academy of Sciences or the American Philosophical Society. Salk lamented: "The worst tragedy that could have befallen me was my success" (quoted in Carter, p. 2).

Meanwhile, Sabin continued developing and testing his live-virus vaccine, which could be swallowed. Although it caused an extremely small number of cases of full-blown polio, by the mid-1960s Sabin's vaccine had eliminated Salk's as the inoculation of choice in the United States. The Salk vaccine continued to be used in Canada and several other countries. Medical experts would debate the relative merits of the two vaccines for decades to come.

Salk's fame persisted, however, and he began to expand his intellectual horizons. An enthusiast of the popular philosophical writings of Kahlil Gibran, Salk hoped to unite with others to discuss philosophy, art, and other creative endeavors. He met the famed physicists Robert Oppenheimer and Leo Szilard, who advised him to start his own intellectual center. The result was the opening, in 1963, of the Salk Institute for Biological Studies in the La Jolla coastal section of San Diego, California. Built on land donated by the city, with funds from the March of Dimes, the facility was designed in a stark, modernistic style by architect Louis Kahn. Salk served as director. In time the institute became a leading research institution in such fields as neuroscience and molecular biology and attracted a number of Nobel laureates. Unfortunately for Salk, some of the institute scientists treated him as their intellectual inferior.

After polio, Salk investigated the role of the immune system in cancer and multiple sclerosis. He also tried during the late 1980s to develop a vaccine that would protect persons infected by the human immunodeficiency virus (HIV) from developing full-blown acquired immune deficiency syndrome or AIDS, a fatal illness that swept the world starting in the late 1970s. In 1990 the Food and Drug Administration authorized nationwide tests of Salk's AIDS vaccine, but its efficacy was disputed. Salk and his colleagues claimed the vaccine markedly slowed the growth of HIV in infected volunteers, but the medical community as a whole remained lukewarm about the so-called vaccine for the rest of his life.

Salk and his wife divorced in 1968, and in 1970 he married the painter Francoise Gilot, a former mistress of artist Pablo Picasso. They had no children. Salk, who also painted, wrote poetry and expressed his literary ambitions in a series of philosophical books. *Anatomy of Reality— Merging of Intuition and Reason* (1983) optimistically suggested that humanity is undergoing a "major transformation" into a vaguely defined higher state via social "error-correcting mechanisms" akin to enzymes that correct chemical errors on the genetic code. Other nonmedical writings included *Man Unfolding* (1972), *The Survival of the Wisest* (1973), and *How Like an Angel* (1975). The ecologist S. P. R. Charter scorned *World Population and Human Values: A New Reality* (1981), coauthored by Salk and his son Jonathan, as a "pamphlet" that was "pallid and mechanistic" ("Jonas Salk Tackles the Meaning of Life," *Los Angeles Times*, San Diego County edition, 6 July 1983).

During his career Salk received many honorary degrees and awards, including the Lasker Award from the American Public Health Association in 1956, the Bruce Memorial Award from the American College of Physicians in 1958, the Jawaharlal Nehru Award for International Understanding in 1975, and the Congressional Gold Medal and Presidential Medal of Freedom, both in 1977. He died in San Diego.

Salk developed the first safe and effective vaccine against polio, thereby rescuing hundreds of thousands from lifetimes of suffering, paralysis, and death. To an admiring public, he symbolized science at its noblest. To his detractors in the scientific community, he was a capable but unremarkable researcher whose achievement was the inevitable outcome of work by others. His career epitomized the rewards and risks that scientists face in an age of what has been called "science by press conference," when mass media often champion "heroes" rather than depict the complex, collaborative nature of scientific research.

• The Jonas Salk Papers are at the University of California at San Diego Library. Detailed analyses of Salk's career include Richard Carter, *Breakthrough: The Saga of Jonas Salk* (1966), and Jane S. Smith, *Patenting the Sun: Polio and the Salk Vaccine* (1990). Smith observes that the rapid success of the polio vaccine spawned unrealistic public expectations about the potential of biomedical science in general. An insider's view of polio research is John R. Paul, M.D., *A History of Poliomyelitis* (1971). Regarding the importance of O'Connor to Salk's career, see Tony Gould, *A Summer Plague: Polio and Its Survivors* (1995). Gould also discusses ethical debates over the use of children and other vulnerable groups in early polio inoculations. Allan M. Brandt, in his "Polio, Politics, Publicity, and Duplicity: Ethical Aspects in the Development of the Salk Vaccine," *International Journal of Health Services* (1978), observes that the Salk vaccine emerged during the Cold War between the United States and Soviet Union and "became a perfect cause for an age in which ideology was suspect . . . [It] was viewed as a triumph of the American system." An obituary is on the front page of the *New York Times*, 24 June 1995; in a *New York Times* op-ed piece of 4 July 1995, Daniel S. Greenberg laments that with Salk's death "we have run out of scientific folk heroes."

KEAY DAVIDSON

SALMON, Daniel Elmer (23 July 1850–30 Aug. 1914), veterinarian, was born in Mount Olive, New Jersey, the son of Daniel Landon Salmon and Eleanor Flock, farmers. He attended the Mount Olive district school, the nearby Chester Institute, and Eastman Business College before entering Cornell University in 1868 with its first class. There he studied with James Law, who had come to Cornell from Edinburgh, Scotland, as the first professor of veterinary science. Because Cornell lacked clinical facilities, Salmon spent the last six months of his four-year course at the famed Alfort Veterinary School in Paris. He received a bachelor's degree in veterinary science from Cornell in 1872. That same year he married Mary Thompson Corning and opened a private veterinary practice in Newark, New Jersey. Salmon moved to Asheville, North Carolina, for health reasons in 1875. Cornell University awarded him their first doctor of veterinary medicine degree in 1876.

Veterinarians who were trained in science, like Salmon, were rare in the United States in the 1870s. When Congress appropriated $10,000 to the Department of Agriculture for the study of animal disease, Salmon became one of the first scientifically-trained veterinarians hired to study swine diseases. In 1879 he joined James Law in an effort to control contagious pleuro-pneumonia of cattle for the state of New York. That fall, another commission from the Department of Agriculture sent him south to study Texas cattle fever. Salmon's government work helped him develop methods for regional disease eradication and gave him a reputation for quality scientific investigations. In 1880 he began an independent study of fowl cholera and developed a method for diluting pathogenic organisms and injecting them into healthy chickens to create immunity to the disease. This was among the earliest scientific work on immunity done in the United States.

In 1884 the Department of Agriculture opened a permanent Bureau of Animal Industry for the scientific control of animal disease. Salmon became its first director and held the position until 1905. The first significant, well-funded laboratory for research into animal infectious diseases in the country, the BAI preceded the establishment of similar laboratories devoted to human infectious disease by several years. As its director, Salmon immediately became the country's most influential veterinarian. He staffed his laboratory with other Cornell graduates, Frederick L. Kilborne, Theobald Smith, Cooper Curtice, and Veranus A. Moore.

Under his guidance, they became the country's foremost veterinary scientists. While Salmon was director, BAI scientists eradicated contagious pleuro-pneumonia of cattle from the United States, identified the protozoal agent and tick vector of Texas Cattle Fever, established the Federal Meat Inspection Service, reduced the death rates of exported animals by addressing the cruel conditions animals suffered aboard ship, kept imported animal diseases out of the country, improved dairy sanitation, and published reams of scientific findings about livestock and poultry diseases.

Salmon's position as director of the BAI often placed him at the center of controversy. Before Congress gave the BAI authority to enforce quarantines and pay for slaughtered livestock, animal growers criticized the bureau's effectiveness and complained about the cost of disease control. An acrimonious dispute over the cause and control of hog cholera added to the criticism. Salmon and Theobald Smith held the view that there were two distinct but similar bacterial diseases, hog cholera and swine plague, opposing several respected veterinarians who thought them identical. Many midwest animal growers sided with the BAI's primary opponent, Dr. Frank S. Billings, who claimed he could develop an antiserum to eradicate hog cholera. Billings's antiserum failed, and in 1888 a panel of outside scientists quelled the scientific debate when they concurred with Salmon and Smith. But as long as diseases like hog cholera caused losses to farmers, criticism of Salmon and the BAI persisted. Two BAI scientists, Emile de Schweinitz and Marion Dorset, developed a successful antiserum to hog cholera in 1903 when they discovered it was a viral disease, not a bacterial one. Despite the criticism that plagued the bureau, Salmon retained the confidence of Congress. By 1901 the BAI budget had reached nearly $1 million, almost a third of the entire Department of Agriculture's appropriation.

Eventually, the political relations of the bureau proved too much for Salmon. After several successful defenses against anti-vivisectionists, he succumbed to the pressure of the meat-packing scandal precipitated by the publication of Upton Sinclair's *The Jungle*. Salmon was charged with profiting from the sale of meat inspection labels. Although the government exonerated him of wrongdoing, President Theodore Roosevelt asked for his resignation, and he left the directorship of the BAI in September 1905.

In the summer of 1906, Salmon investigated the deaths of livestock exposed to smoke from a copper smelter at Anaconda, Montana. He testified in federal court for farmers suing Washoe Copper Company and the Anaconda Copper Mining Company, arguing that the animals had died of chronic arsenic poisoning from grazing on grass contaminated by smelter smoke. His toxicology findings, published in nine installments in the *American Veterinary Review* (1911–1912), are among the earliest scientific articles on the effects of smelter smoke on the environment.

Salmon had a major influence on veterinary education. In 1892 he opened the National Veterinary College in Washington, D.C., to provide scientific training for meat inspectors and veterinarians hired by the bureau. The two-year evening college, which had no formal affiliation with the Department of Agriculture, nevertheless drew most of its faculty from the BAI staff. It closed in 1896 after granting fifty diplomas. Although short-lived, it succeeded in bringing attention to the limitations of the country's veterinary schools. At Salmon's urging, the Civil Service Commission enhanced requirements for veterinary inspectors, making a D.V.M. degree and an examination necessary by 1894. Because the Federal Meat Inspection Service was a major source of employment for veterinarians, it encouraged overall improvements in the quality of veterinary education. In 1906 the government of Uruguay asked Salmon to organize a veterinary college in Montevideo. He approved the faculty, designed the buildings, and by 1913 had created one of the finest veterinary schools in South America.

Salmon's contemporaries felt, however, that this faithful civil servant and skilled administrator had never regained his spirit after suffering his country's "ingratitude" in 1905. He returned from South America in 1913 in poor health and died a year later in Butte, Montana, where he had managed a plant that manufactured hog cholera serum. Salmon had married Agnes Christina Dewhurst in 1904, after the 1902 death of his first wife.

Salmon served his profession as president of the American Veterinary Medical Association, president of the American Public Health Association (1891), and fellow of the American Association for the Advancement of Science. In 1900 bacteriologists renamed the group of bacteria containing *Bacillus cholerasuis*, the organism he isolated in 1885, the *Salmonella*, in his honor. As the most powerful veterinarian in the United States for twenty years, Salmon, through the Bureau of Animal Industry, had rescued the livestock industry from rampant infectious disease and had established the scientific foundation for disease control that helped create modern veterinary medicine.

• Most of Salmon's writings are in the annual reports and bulletins of the U.S. Department of Agriculture, Bureau of Animal Industry. RG 17 at the U.S. National Archives holds the papers of the Bureau of Animal Industry. Salmon gives his own account of the bureau's accomplishments and biographical data in *The United States Bureau of Animal Industry at the Close of the Nineteenth Century 1884–1900* (1901). See also U. G. Houck, *The Bureau of Animal Industry of the United States Department of Agriculture* (1924), and O. H. V. Stalheim and W. M. Moulton, "Veterinary Medicine in the United States Department of Agriculture," in *100 Years of Animal Health, 1884–1994*, ed. Vivian Wiser et al. (1987), pp. 19–62. Stalheim discusses his contributions to veterinary education in "Daniel Elmer Salmon, the National Veterinary College, and Veterinary Education," *Journal of the American Veterinary Medical Association* 182 (1983): 33–36. His work in immunology is treated in Steven M. Niemi, "D. E. Salmon and the First Bacterin," *Modern Veterinary Practice* 62, no. 18 (1981): 913–17. Fredric L. Quivik recounts his work on smelter smoke in "Conflict in the Science of Environmental Impact: The Anaconda Smelter Smoke Cases, 1902–1910," a paper presented at the American Society for Environmental History's biennial meeting, Mar. 1995. An obituary is in *American Veterinary Review* 46 (1914): 93–96.

PATRICIA PECK GOSSEL

SALMON, Thomas William (6 Jan. 1876–13 Aug. 1927), psychiatrist and reformer, was born in Lansingburgh (now Troy), New York, the son of Thomas Henry Salmon, a physician, and Annie E. Frost. Salmon, whose father had immigrated from England in 1860, went to the local public school and graduated from the Lansingburgh Academy in 1894. He taught school at Pleasant Valley, New York, until 1895 and then attended Albany Medical College for the next four years. In 1899 he received an M.D. from Albany Medical College and, that same year, married Helen Potter Ashley; they had six children.

In 1900 Salmon started his professional career with a struggling practice as a general practitioner in Brewster, New York. He soon had to look for additional sources of income and, from October 1901 to 1903, served as bacteriologist at the Willard (N.Y.) State Hospital, where he was employed by the state health department to investigate an epidemic of diphtheria. Salmon's careful study of diphtheria carriers, *Report of Epidemic of Diphtheria* (1905), was among the earliest recorded and was widely circulated. He also developed an interest in psychiatry after coming into close contact with Willard staff physician William L. Russell, among the leading figures in psychiatry at the time.

Salmon joined the staff of the U.S. Public Health Service on 29 October 1903, as commanding assistant surgeon in the U.S. Marine Hospital Service (now the Public Health Service). In 1905 Salmon was assigned as psychiatrist to the immigration station at New York's Ellis Island. Shocked by the living conditions of the insane immigrants awaiting deportation, he repeatedly applied to his superiors for improved facilities. The Public Health Service did not take this criticism kindly, and after a short suspension from duty, Salmon was stationed at the Marine Hospital in Chelsea, Massachusetts, from 1907 until 1911, when he returned to the question of mentally ill immigrants. His support for a restrictive immigration policy resulted in his appointment as chief medical examiner of the New York State Board of Alienists in 1911, on leave of absence from the U.S. Public Health Service. This work on foreign-born mental patients in state hospitals eventually led to the introduction of restrictive clauses in New York State immigration legislation.

Salmon's research on immigrants shared the prejudices current at the time. He received wide recognition for it and, by 1912, ranked among the leading research-oriented psychiatrists. Between 1912 and 1914, with a continued leave of absence from the U.S. Public Health Service, Salmon conducted, for the National Committee for Mental Hygiene (an organization for improving conditions among the institutionalized mentally ill), a series of studies on the incidence of mental illness and the dual system of state and local care of the insane. In January 1915 Salmon resigned from the U.S. Public Health Service and joined the staff of the Rockefeller Foundation, which "lent" him on a continuing basis to the National Committee for Mental Hygiene, for which he served as (first) medical director until his resignation in January 1922. Between 1915 and 1917 Salmon directed most of the committee's surveys of the institutionalized population and mental institutions in over thirty states and recommended eliminating the mixed system of state and county care, building new institutions, and introducing new methods of treatment. He also helped to establish several experimental psychiatric clinics, such as the Psychopathic Laboratory at the Sing Sing Prison in Ossining, New York. These clinics sought to explore the relationship of mental illness to delinquency and crime. This move was part of Salmon's attempt to go beyond the context of the institutionalized mentally ill and to merge psychiatry with broader remedial and educational efforts to promote social adjustment.

Salmon made his largest contribution to psychiatry during World War I. He enlisted in the army, was appointed chief consultant in psychiatry in the American Expeditionary Force, and developed a system of mental-health screening for military recruits, which was responsible for the rejection of more than 72,000 men as unfit for service on psychiatric grounds. He also instituted so-called "neuropsychiatric units" to treat cases of "shell-shock," or war neuroses. In addition, he arranged for those sailors and soldiers who were sent back to the United States as mental cases to receive proper treatment and later saw to their rehabilitation and adjustment once they were back home. Altogether, the psychiatric approach to the mental impact of trench warfare was highly successful. After retiring from the army in 1919, Salmon was awarded the Distinguished Service medal and placed on the reserve list with the rank of a brigadier general.

After the war, Salmon made a lasting contribution to the child guidance movement by helping the Commonwealth Fund establish professional help for children with emotional or social problems. In November 1920 he wrote a lengthy proposal recommending that the fund undertake a study of juvenile delinquency, and the fund's directors were sufficiently impressed to call a conference for March 1921 at Lakewood, New Jersey, to consider it. Salmon shaped the conference's report, which in the main copied his original plan and rationale. Crime, the report argued, "has its root deeply planted in childhood" with delinquency shadowing more children's lives than "some of the most prevalent and serious diseases." As a first step toward preventing delinquency, the report recommended that schools be provided with "carefully prepared case-histories," to inform teachers and authorities of the "present scientific conception of disorders of conduct and their treatment."

In November 1921 the Commonwealth Fund's board adopted a five-year "Program for the Prevention of Juvenile Delinquency." The first of its kind, according to historian Sol Cohen, and better financed and more comprehensive than any later large-scale attempts to deal with juvenile problem behavior, the program had three general objectives: to show how professional help for problem children works; to train suitable personnel, such as psychiatric social workers or visiting teachers; and to conduct psychiatric research leading to "a thorough understanding of the complete make-up, mental and physical, of the child tending toward delinquency." The fund provided appropriations for a "traveling psychiatric field service" in order to demonstrate the usefulness of such child psychiatric clinics to the juvenile courts in dealing with problem children. The mobile child psychiatric clinics introduced the concept of a child guidance clinic into common usage. Salmon and psychiatrist Victor Vance Anderson served on the Joint Committee for the Prevention of Delinquency that the fund established to coordinate the various enterprises under the program. Having inaugurated his mission, Salmon withdrew from the joint committee in June 1922, following his resignation as medical director of the National Committee in January 1922.

During 1920–1921, Salmon had worked for two competing foundations, receiving his salary as medical director from the Rockefeller Foundation and, at the same time, advising the Commonwealth Fund in selecting a proper field of philanthropy. He left the staff of the Rockefeller Foundation in July 1921 to become a professor of psychiatry at Columbia University. As a professor, Salmon felt it necessary to enter into private practice, which led him to withdraw from the fund's program. In the last part of his career, Salmon concentrated on the development of psychiatry as a profession. He remained at Columbia University until his death. He was active also as a consulting psychiatrist at the New York Presbyterian Hospital from 1922 until his death. In 1923–1924 he served as president of the American Psychiatric Association and was responsible for making the New York Psychiatric Institute an integral part of the Columbia Medical Center.

Salmon had a crucial role in establishing professional help for the mentally ill, criminals, and problem children. His concern about the dangers of unrestricted immigration, delinquency, and unadjusted behavior led him in the words of psychiatrist Frankwood Williams (in an obituary speech given at the New York Academy of Medicine on 11 October 1927), to influence "the course of medicine and psychiatry in America." Salmon died in a sailing accident on Long Island Sound, New York.

• The Thomas William Salmon Papers, Department of Psychiatry, History of Psychiatry Section, New York Hospital–Cornell Medical Center, N.Y., contain biographical material and are especially informative on all aspects of his professional work. The records of the National Committee of Mental Hygiene, Rockefeller Foundation Archives, Rockefeller Archive Center, Pocantico Hills, North Tarrytown, N.Y., document Salmon's work for this committee. Biographical accounts include Earl D. Bond, with Paul O. Komora, *Thomas W. Salmon, Psychiatrist* (1950), and Margo Horn, "Thomas William Salmon," in *Biographical Dictionary of Social Welfare in America*, ed. Walter J. Trattner (1986). Main parts of his career are also treated by Norman Dain, *Clifford W. Beers: Advocate for the Insane* (1980), and Gerald N. Grob, *Mental Illness and American Society, 1875–1940* (1983). Bibliographies of Salmon's writings are in Bond (1950) and in M. Thérèse de Bermingham, comp., "Thomas William Salmon, M.D.: A Bibliography of His Writings," *Mental Hygiene* 12 (1928): 114–18. Obituaries are in the *Medical Journal and Record* 126 (1927): 317; the *Journal of the American Medical Association* 89 (1927): 709; and *Mental Hygiene* 11 (1927): 673.

KARL TILMAN WINKLER

SALM-SALM, Agnes Elisabeth Winona Leclercq Joy (25 Dec. 1844–21 Dec. 1912), princess, adventurer, and wartime humanitarian, was born in Swanton, Vermont (or southern Canada), the daughter of William Leclercq Joy, a farmer, and his second wife, Julia Willard. Salm-Salm always remained secretive about her youth, thereby feeding romantic rumors about her age, ancestry, and past. After spending some time in Cuba, as she asserted in her autobiography, she arrived in Washington, D.C., in the fall of 1861, a vivacious, pretty young woman. There she attracted the attentions of Prince Felix zu Salm-Salm, the adventurous younger son of an old aristocratic German family. After serving in the Prussian and Austrian armies the prince had left Europe to escape his debts and to seek employment in the American Civil War.

Without the consent of his family to an obvious mésalliance, Felix and Agnes were married on 30 August 1862. The energetic bride immediately took charge of her husband's career and succeeded in obtaining his appointment as colonel in the Eighth, later the Sixty-eighth, New York Infantry Regiment and eventually his commission as brigadier general. Spirited and adventuresome but soon taking interest in the plight of wounded soldiers, Agnes accompanied her husband on his tours of duty in Virginia, Alabama, and Georgia, where Felix Salm-Salm was appointed military governor of Atlanta in 1865.

Seeking further military honors, Felix Salm-Salm left in February 1866 to join the staff of Archduke Maximilian of Austria, who had become emperor of Mexico. The princess again followed him, soon to witness the collapse of the imperial government. In the weeks after the fall of Querétaro in May 1867, Agnes used every effort to mediate between the doomed emperor and his staff and the republican generals, personally persuading Benito Juárez to postpone Maximilian's trial. Together with her husband, who shared the emperor's captivity, she made plans for Maximilian's escape, trying to bribe officers of the republican army. When their schemes were discovered, Agnes was exiled to San Luis Potosí, where Juárez refused her desperate pleas for Maximilian's life but promised that her husband would be spared. In January 1868 Agnes joined her husband in Europe. She did not return to the United States for more than three decades.

After a brief meeting with the Salm family, the couple proceeded to Vienna in February. Although the prince failed to draw the attention he expected as a close companion of Maximilian's final days, Agnes was graciously received by the Archduchess Sophie, Maximilian's mother, and granted an annual pension for her valiant efforts on behalf of the unfortunate emperor. Felix Salm-Salm subsequently obtained a commission as major in a Prussian Regiment of Guards stationed at Koblenz. At the outbreak of the Franco-Prussian conflict in summer 1870, Agnes again accompanied her husband to war, this time securing permission to join a medical unit attached to the Prussian First Army. In the ensuing months, she exerted herself to the utmost in caring for the wounded and consoling the dying, assisting in operations, supervising the kitchen staff, and organizing hospital supplies. After the cease-fire, Agnes returned to private life, receiving thanks and an imperial decoration for her charitable work.

Salm-Salm's husband, however, had been killed in battle, and her personal situation proved difficult. Since she had no means—nor the Salm family the intention—to pay the prince's old debts, she felt compelled to repudiate her husband's inheritance. Much to the family's dismay but with characteristic initiative, she appealed to the German emperor for help, which was granted, thus enabling her to establish herself independently at Bonn. Although at times toying with plans to work in a hospital or even to enter a convent—an idea she abandoned after an audience with Pope Pius IX—she spent the next years traveling in Europe and writing her memoirs.

In 1876 Salm-Salm married Charles Heneage, the younger son of a respectable Lincolnshire family and a minor British diplomat with literary ambitions. However, the couple separated, and Agnes, childless from both marriages, continued to live in retirement in Germany as Princess Salm-Salm. She made headlines again in 1899, when she visited the United States to present the survivors of her husband's old regiment with the flags of their Civil War unit. The Boer War tempted her to resume her army relief work, but its brief duration prevented her from doing so.

Salm-Salm spent her last years mostly at Karlsruhe and nearby Herrenalb at a residence she named "Minnehaha." When she died at Karlsruhe, newspapers in Europe and the United States as well as novelists and playwrights later remembered her as the somewhat enigmatic, courageous, and warmhearted woman who had managed to play an active role in three wars on two continents. She shares a grave in the old cemetery in Bonn with Louise Runkel, an associate during the Franco-Prussian War who had remained her confidante.

• The private Salm-Salm Archives at Isselburg-Anholt do not provide access to the family correspondence to researchers interested in Agnes Salm-Salm, asserting that there is no material pertaining to her in their manuscript holdings. Thus her autobiography remains the main source for her life: *Zehn Jahre aus meinem Leben, 1862 bis 1872* (3 vols., 1875), published in English as *Ten Years of My Life* (London, 1876; Detroit, 1877). The events in Mexico are described by Felix Salm-Salm, *Queretaro* (2 vols., 1868), in English as *My Diary in Mexico in 1867* (2 vols., 1868), with an appendix by Agnes Salm-Salm. A scholarly work that includes photographs of Agnes and Felix Salm-Salm is Konrad Ratz, *Maximilian in Querétaro* (1991). For her family see James Richard Joy, *Thomas Joy and His Descendants* (1900). She plays a minor role in Franz Werfel's drama *Juarez und Maximilian* (1924) and features prominently in a number of novels and adventure stories, all based on her autobiography, among which the less sensational is Juliana von Stockhausen, *Wilder Lorbeer* (1964), with a new French edition titled *Agnes de Salm-Salm* (1982) that includes a reproduction of her portrait painted by Franz Xaver Winterhalter. Among the numerous newspapers in Europe and the United States that carried her obituary is the *Times* (London), 24 Dec. 1912.

MARIE-LUISE FRINGS

SALOMON, Haym (c. 1740–6 Jan. 1785), New York financier and patriot, was apparently born in Lissa, Poland, of Jewish parents. He traveled widely in his youth, becoming fluent in most European languages and acquiring considerable business skills before coming to the colonies. Despite the tradition that he left Poland in 1772 at the time of the first partition, he may have migrated as early as 1764 or perhaps as late as 1776. Most likely, he arrived in New York City shortly before the outbreak of the Revolution and soon established himself as a successful commission merchant. While there is no evidence of his participation in prerevolutionary political affairs, he immediately cast his lot with the patriots once hostilities began. Warmly recommended by Leonard Gansevoort, the Albany patriot, as a strong supporter of the American cause, Salomon, in June 1776, offered his services as sutler to the American forces under General Philip Schuyler in northern New York. He returned to New York City shortly before its capture by the British in September 1776.

Salomon's decision to remain in New York during the British occupation put him at considerable risk. His known political sympathies and recent services to Schuyler's army would naturally have targeted him for suspicion. The British arrested him along with other suspected American agents after a fire destroyed much of the city. He was confined for a time in the notorious Provost prison but was released and paroled to General Heister, the Hessian commander, who needed someone fluent in German and skilled in business to assist in his commissary operations. Besides working for the Hessians, Salomon did business on his own account, and over the next two years he achieved a considerable measure of prosperity. In July 1777 he married Rachel Franks, the fifteen-year-old daughter of Moses B. Franks. During this period Salomon led a secret life that would have sent him straight to the gallows if he had been discovered. He used his contacts with the Hessians to encourage defections among the officers, conversing with them in German to keep the British in the dark. He also provided American and French prisoners with money and helped them to escape. When the British finally discovered what he had been doing, he narrowly avoided arrest and fled the

city in August 1778, leaving behind his wife and infant son.

Salomon reached Philadelphia two weeks later, and he immediately petitioned Congress for some employment. He recounted his services in New York and reported that he had arrived penniless, having left behind several thousand pounds sterling when he fled. His petition was referred to the Board of War and apparently forgotten along with hundreds of similar requests. So Salomon had to start over again in Philadelphia on his own, gradually rebuilding his business as a commission merchant. He managed somehow to get his wife and child to Philadelphia and for the next three years lived in comparative obscurity. By 1781 he had become one of Philadelphia's leading dealers in bills of exchange. These were the eighteenth-century equivalent of modern checks; they enabled persons having funds available in other places to raise money for local use. Salomon's numerous advertisements in Philadelphia newspapers indicate that he specialized in foreign bills, an expertise, along with his fluency in French, that led the French armed forces in America to use him to sell their bills. The Spanish agent in Philadelphia also used his services, making him the leading broker in foreign bills in the city.

His work for the French most likely brought Salomon to the attention of Robert Morris, newly appointed by the Continental Congress as superintendent of finance. Morris needed a highly skilled and reliable broker to help him sell the bills, which he drew against funds on deposit for the United States in France, Holland, and Spain. In June 1781 Salomon became the principal bill broker for Morris, who selected him from more than twenty other bill brokers in the city. Large amounts of money were needed in 1781 to finance the Yorktown campaign, and Morris relied almost completely on Salomon to market the bills that he issued. Great skill was needed in managing these sales, because flooding the market too quickly would have driven down the value of the bills and undermined the credit of the government. Morris would issue the bills directly to Salomon, who would then sell them by endorsement to the actual buyer. The proceeds of the sale would be credited to Salomon's own account and then transferred by him to Morris and the government. These brokerage arrangements, which were common at the time, later gave rise to the myth that Salomon advanced vast sums of his own money to the United States. The funds transferred to the government belonged to the government and only passed through his hands.

Salomon became even more important to Morris after the victory at Yorktown. The financial condition of the country worsened in 1782, and Salomon was repeatedly called upon to help market government bills. His services were so important that in July 1782 Morris authorized him to advertise that he was the government's official broker. By now he had acquired a reputation for generosity, freely advancing money to members of Congress who needed financial help to continue with their public work. He was the major contributor to the first synagogue built in Philadelphia and served as treasurer of the short-lived Travelers Aid Society, the first organized Jewish charity in the United States. Nor did he forget his family in Poland from whom he had been cut off during the Revolution. He renewed relations with them after the war, sending substantial sums of money for their support.

Salomon died in Philadelphia after a lingering illness generally attributed to his imprisonment by the British. His death was financially disastrous for his widow and four young children. Most of his assets were in government notes and securities that had to be discounted at ruinous rates in settling the estate. When all his debts had been paid, nothing remained for his family in the final accounting. Posthumous bankruptcy was not uncommon in the postrevolutionary period, but it had special irony for one who had done so much to uphold the public credit during the war years. But he died rich in public esteem. The report of his death in the *Pennsylvania Packet* of 11 January 1785 describes him as "an eminent broker . . . remarkable for his skill and integrity in his profession, and for his generous and humane deportment." The myths and fabrications that sprang up about Salomon after his death were not needed to embellish his real contributions to his adopted country. A committed patriot who risked his life for the Revolution in New York, he helped to shape the financial sinews that made military victory possible.

• Unpublished material can be found in the Oppenheim Papers and Haym Salomon Collection of the American Jewish Historical Society in Waltham, Mass., and in the collections of the American Jewish Archives in Cincinnati, Ohio. Secondary sources on Salomon should be used selectively and with caution. Unsubstantiated claims by his descendants and outright fabrications about his life and career have added a heavy layer of myth to the historical record. Serious scholarly work on Salomon did not begin until the 1931 publication of Max J. Kohler's pamphlet, *Haym Salomon, the Patriot Broker of the Revolution, His Real Achievements and Their Exaggeration.* A special caveat is in order for the biography by Charles E. Russell, *Haym Salomon and the Revolution* (1930), which repeats all the myths and fabrications found in earlier accounts. Historically reliable treatments of Salomon can be found in Laurens R. Schwartz, *Jews and the American Revolution* (1987); Samuel Rezneck, *Unrecognized Patriots: Jews in the American Revolution* (1975); and Jacob R. Marcus, *United States Jewry, 1776–1985* (4 vols., 1989–1993), vol. 1 of which contains a useful bibliography. Salomon's arrival in the colonies is discussed by Isaac Rivkind in "Early American Hebrew Documents," *Publications of the American Jewish Historical Society* 34 (1937): 51–74, which suggests that he may have left Poland in 1767 after a fire destroyed most of Lissa, and by Harold Korn in "Receipt Book of Judah and Moses M. Hays, Commencing January 12, 1763, and Ending July 18, 1776," *Publications of the American Jewish Historical Society* 28 (1922): 223–29, which places him in New York as early as 1764.

EDGAR J. MCMANUS

SALT, Waldo (18 Oct. 1914–7 Mar. 1987), screenwriter, was born in Chicago, Illinois, the son of William Haslem Salt, a British-born business executive, and Wini-

fred Porter. After graduating from Stanford University in 1934, Salt taught drama and music for a year at Menlo School and Junior College, in Menlo Park, California. In 1936 he was hired as a junior writer by Metro-Goldwyn-Mayer, the Hollywood film studio, to work in the unit headed by producer Joseph L. Mankiewicz.

After uncredited contributions to the dialogue of films such as *Double Wedding* (1937) and *The Adventures of Huckleberry Finn* (1938), Salt earned his first screenwriting credit with the romantic drama *The Shopworn Angel* (1938), starring James Stewart as a naive soldier who marries a cynical Broadway star. Salt's tenure at MGM included *The Philadelphia Story* (1940, uncredited co-writer) and *The Wild Man of Borneo* (1941, co-written with John McClain), a comedy about a man who redeems himself for the love of his daughter. Salt left the studio in 1943 to work as a civilian consultant during World War II for U.S. Army films and was a writer/director for the Office of War Information, Overseas Film Bureau, until 1945. Participating in the Hollywood studios' war effort, Salt wrote two films during this period, *Tonight We Raid Calais* (1943, Twentieth Century-Fox), a spy drama about a British agent in occupied France, and *Mr. Winkle Goes to War* (1944, Columbia, sharing credit with George Corey and Louis Solomon), a comedy-drama about a middle-aged bank clerk who joins the army and becomes a hero. Once the war was over, Salt returned to his profession full time under a contract with RKO, for which he wrote *Rachel and the Stranger* (1948), a romantic pioneer drama starring Loretta Young and William Holden. Salt also wrote the lyrics for the songs in the film.

Salt's career as a studio contract writer was disrupted in 1947 when the House Committee on Un-American Activities (HUAC) subpoenaed Salt, along with eighteen other Hollywood screenwriters, actors, and directors, to testify before Congress on their alleged membership in and connections to the Communist party. The first ten of those "unfriendly witnesses," known as the "Hollywood Ten," refused to testify about their political affiliations and were later tried and convicted of contempt of Congress. The HUAC hearings of 1947 marked the beginning of widespread blacklisting in the American film industry. Even though Salt himself was not called to the stand at this point—the hearings were canceled after the Ten's refusal to testify—the writer's contract with RKO was not renewed. Blacklisted by the major Hollywood studios, Salt wrote for independent producer Harold Hecht a swashbuckling adventure film, *The Flame and the Arrow* (1950), starring Burt Lancaster as a revolutionary peasant in medieval Italy. Hired by director Joseph Losey, Salt wrote dialogue for the remake of Fritz Lang's classic murder drama *M.*

When HUAC resumed its hearings, Salt was called to the witness stand on 13 April 1951. Under the provisions of the Fifth Amendment, the writer refused to testify about his membership in the Communist party (which he later acknowledged in an affidavit to the committee in 1963) or to identify other party members in the Hollywood creative community. Like other blacklisted Hollywood writers, Salt was thereafter unable to make a living under his own name. During the 1950s Salt's film and television work was either uncredited, like his screen story for Hecht's *The Crimson Pirate* (1952), or, in television, identified by the use of pseudonyms: "M. L. Davenport," "Mel Davenport," "Arthur Behrstock," and "Felix Van Lieu." Salt wrote regularly for the British television series "The Adventures of Robin Hood," "The Buccaneers," "The Sword of Freedom," and "The Highwayman," produced by Sapphire Films. For Screen Gems, the television branch of Columbia Pictures, he wrote episodes of "Espionage," "Ivanhoe," and "Stakeout." With singer and composer Earl Robinson, Salt, writing under his own name, completed a folk opera, *Sandhog*, about the plight of Irish construction workers in New York. It opened in an off-Broadway production in 1954.

In 1963 Salt's affidavit to the television networks and to HUAC enabled him to break the blacklist. A year before, however, Hecht had hired him again to co-write, under his own name, scripts for three films, the historical drama *Taras Bulba* (1962), the romantic comedy *The Wild and the Wonderful* (1963), and the action thriller *Flight from Ashiya* (1964). Salt's reputation as a writer was firmly established a few years later with his screen version of *Midnight Cowboy* (1969), adapted from the James Leo Herlihy novel of life in the New York underworld of prostitution. The film won Academy Awards for best picture, best director (John Schlesinger), and best adapted screenplay. This landmark work was the first of three collaborations between Salt and producer Jerome Hellman.

The Gang That Couldn't Shoot Straight (1971) was an adaptation by Salt of a novel by Jimmy Breslin that dealt in dark comic undertones with the New York mafia. New York was again prominent in Salt's following project, *Serpico* (1973), as a quintessential urban jungle where an honest policeman is defeated by corrupt officials. Based on the novel by Peter Maas about a real undercover policeman, the film earned Salt and co-writer Norman Wexler an Academy Award nomination. *The Day of the Locust* (1975), Hellman and Salt's second collaboration, was an adaptation of Nathanael West's grim view of the 1930s Hollywood establishment and its fringes.

Salt's last produced work and his third collaboration with Hellman was *Coming Home* (1978), directed by Hal Ashby. It recounts the love affair between the wife of an officer serving in Vietnam and a paraplegic veteran who becomes an antiwar activist and the catalyst for the heroine's personal and political transformation. The film offered a grim view of the emotional ravages of war. Salt shared an Academy Award for best original screenplay with Nancy Dowd and Robert C. Jones.

Parallel to screenwriting activities in his later years, Salt was involved in teaching and mentoring, at New York University School of the Arts (1977–1985) and

the Sundance Film Institute, Utah (1981–1986). In 1986 the Writers Guild of America distinguished Salt with its prestigious Laurel Award. Salt was married four times: in 1939 to Ambur Dana, whom he divorced; in 1942 to Mary Davenport, with whom he had two daughters and whom he divorced in 1968, the same year he married artist Gladys Schwartz; she died in 1980; and in 1983 to poet Eve Merriam, from whom he was legally separated at his death in Los Angeles.

Salt's writing career encompassed more than forty years of the American film industry—from the midthirties to the early eighties—and was marked by success and failure, blacklisting and recognition. He worked during the peak of the studio era as a contract writer, was caught in the economic and political upheavals that shook Hollywood in the fifties, and reemerged a decade later as an independent and valuable player. In his writings Salt displayed a remarkable consistency of themes and narrative patterns: willful, strong, sometimes alienated and even innocent characters are transformed by their principled response to social or political upheaval, seeking new values in a changing world.

• Waldo Salt's personal and professional papers were donated by his family to the University of California, Los Angeles. Held at the Arts Library, Special Collections, the papers comprise film and television scripts, a wide variety of projects (some unfinished or unproduced), plus abundant script-related research materials. Maria Elena de las Carreras, "The Waldo Salt Papers," *UCLA Librarian*, Spring–Summer 1991, pp. 13–18, offers a detailed account of the collection's contents. The two most complete assessments of Salt's life and career are in *Contemporary Authors* (1984) and the *Dictionary of Literary Biography* (1986). The HUAC period is covered in John Cogley, *Report on Blacklisting* (1956), and Larry Ceplair and Steven Englund, *The Inquisition in Hollywood: Politics in the Film Community, 1930–1960* (1979). Salt's testimony on 13 Apr. 1951 is transcribed in *Hearings before the Committee on Un-American Activities, House of Representatives, Eighty-second Congress. First Session, "Communist Infiltration of Hollywood"* (1951), pp. 259–74. Obituaries are in the *New York Times*, 9 Mar. 1987, and the *Los Angeles Times*, the *Los Angeles Examiner*, and the *Washington Post*, all 10 Mar. 1987.

MARÍA ELENA DE LAS CARRERAS-KUNTZ

SALTER, William Mackintire (30 Jan. 1853–18 July 1931), lecturer and author, was born in Burlington, Iowa, the son of William Salter, a clergyman, and Mary Ann Mackintire. William's father was one of the first Congregationalist ministers in Iowa and served the same church in Burlington for sixty-eight years. Encouraged to pursue studies, William began reading Latin at the age of ten, Greek at twelve, and entered Knox College in Galesburg, Illinois, at fourteen. His young, questing mind noted difficulties and inconsistencies in traditionally accepted religious doctrines. This skepticism regarding orthodoxy became a basic characteristic in his own spiritual life and in the wider contours of his subsequent career. In a speech delivered at his college graduation in 1871, Salter questioned whether orthodoxy was necessary for a professing Christian, and while studying at Yale Divinity School during the next two years he grew less and less certain about accepted doctrines.

After receiving a master's degree from Knox in 1874, Salter attended Harvard Divinity School, earning a bachelor of divinity degree in 1876 in the hope of becoming a minister within the wide latitudes of the Unitarian ministry. He won the Parker Fellowship at Harvard, enabling him to study at the University of Göttingen, but poor health forced him to return from Germany in 1877. Working as a shepherd in Colorado until 1879 to recover his strength, Salter found time to formulate his personal beliefs in some detail. By that time he had concluded that there was no solid basis for any distinctively Christian affirmations, and so he abandoned the pretense of claiming the name. He expressed this generally liberated position in pamphlet form, *On a Foundation for Religion* (1879), which subsequently became well known and widely read.

Salter's independent conclusion about religion received additional backing when he met Felix Adler, founder of the Ethical Cultural Society (ECS), in 1879. Adler encouraged the young freethinker to continue his intellectual development under the society's auspices in New York. Salter moved to the metropolis in 1881, affiliated with the society, and rounded off his studies at Columbia University through 1882. He quickly became a noted exponent of a religion of social service, based not on theological arguments but rather on simple humanistic affirmations. The act of doing good for humanity was, in his view, far more important than wasting energy on disputes over obtuse, intangible concepts. His ideas fit so well with his new institutional home that Adler once said that Salter was "one of the crown jewels of Ethical Culture." In 1883 the young advocate traveled west and founded the Chicago branch of ECS. He served there as a lecturer (equivalent to clergy but chary of the title) until 1892 and again from 1897 to 1907. In the interim he served the ECS in Philadelphia in the same capacity. Between 1907 and 1913 he was adjunct professor (specializing in Nietzsche) in the philosophy department of the University of Chicago. Thereafter he spent years of retirement in New York and New Hampshire. In 1885 he had married Mary Sherwin Gibbens of Cambridge, Massachusetts. They had a daughter who died in infancy, and later they adopted a son.

In his zeal for practical religious action Salter espoused a number of liberal causes and urgent social issues. He advocated reforms in a variety of areas because he genuinely believed that it was possible to achieve a more just and humane society. Early in his ministry he tackled the problems of urban poverty, child labor, racism, and unemployment. He defended those convicted in the Haymarket labor organizing incident of 1886 and pioneered such welfare innovations as settlement houses, visiting nurses, and free legal aid for the poor. Woman suffrage, family nurture, and ethical guidance in public schools also received his backing. In other crusades Salter criticized imperialism in the Philippines, charging that America was becoming as despotic as Russia by embodying a new militarism. Later he attracted notoriety by expressing pro-German and anti-British sympathies during World War I. As a strong defender of ECS he lectured on its philosophical basis and practical aims, its roots in Judaism, and the general appeal of ethical considerations. In 1905 he also prepared a liturgical collection for use in Chicago titled *Moral Aspiration in Song*. For Salter morality was religion, and its ideal elements were clues to meaning in life. Such an orientation found tangible outlets in humane, benevolent concerns. His usefulness as a lecturer and consultant continued for two decades after formal employment as he continually appealed to conscience and altruism as motivations for benevolent service. He died at his summer home in Silver Lake, New Hampshire.

• Many of Salter's essay manuscripts are located at the Ethical Culture Society headquarters in New York City; other correspondence, lecture notes, and clippings are housed at Knox College in Galesburg, Ill. His books are *Ethical Religion* (1889), *First Steps in Philosophy* (1892), *Anarchy or Government?* (1895), and *Nietzsche the Thinker* (1917). An obituary is in the *New York Times*, 19 July 1931.

HENRY WARNER BOWDEN

SALTONSTALL, Dudley (8 Sept. 1738–1796), naval officer, was born in New London, Connecticut, the son of Gurdon Saltonstall, a prominent citizen of Connecticut and a general of the militia, and Rebecca Winthrop, a descendent of one of the early founding families of Massachusetts Bay. Dudley Saltonstall was a direct descendant of Richard Saltonstall, one of the founders of the Massachusetts Bay Company. His grandfather Gurdon Saltonstall, born in Haverhill, Massachusetts, took the pulpit in New London, Connecticut, and began the Connecticut branch of the Saltonstall family; he later became governor of Connecticut. In 1765 Dudley Saltonstall married Frances Babcock of nearby Westerly, Rhode Island; the couple had seven children.

Living in the New London–Norwich area on the Thames River, Saltonstall went to sea at a fairly early age. He probably engaged in the West Indies trade as did most seafarers from this region. During the French and Indian War he went to sea as a privateer.

At the outbreak of the Revolution, Saltonstall joined the patriot cause. His sister Elizabeth had married Silas Deane, a prominent Connecticut politician who served in the Continental Congress. Deane served on the naval committee of the Congress, and thanks to his lobbying efforts Saltonstall was commissioned a captain in the Continental navy on 27 November 1775 and given command of the ship *Alfred*.

On 17 February 1776 Saltonstall, in command of the *Alfred*, sailed with seven other Continental vessels under the command of Commodore Esek Hopkins, who was ordered to sweep the coast of the southern colonies. But instead Hopkins took his squadron to the Bahamas, where they captured Nassau. On the homeward voyage to Providence, Hopkins's squadron fought a battle with the HMS *Glasgow*. To the great embarrassment of Hopkins and his captains, the *Glasgow* escaped. Several courts-martial followed the incident. Saltonstall was summoned to Philadelphia to appear before a congressional committee but was exonerated of all charges.

After the *Glasgow* affair Saltonstall was given command of the Continental frigate *Trumbull* being built at Chatham, Connecticut, on the Connecticut River. Although completed in 1777, the *Trumbull* did not get to sea until 1779. The frigate's deep draft made it impossible to get it across the shallows at the entrance to the river. Saltonstall, in the meantime, did go to sea in another vessel, also named the *Trumbull*, which was probably a ten-gun ship fitted out by the state of Connecticut. On 12 April 1777 Saltonstall's *Trumbull* captured two British transports off the Virginia Capes.

Due to a paucity of ships Saltonstall did not get another command until the summer of 1779. In mid-June of that year a British force under the command of General Francis McLean occupied the Bagaduce Peninsula on Penobscot Bay, Maine. Alarmed by the British movement, the Massachusetts General Court organized a force to expel the invasion. To aid in the effort the Continental Congress sent a naval force under Saltonstall's command. In command of the frigate *Warren*, he had nineteen armed vessels and twenty transports. His orders were to escort the fleet to Penobscot Bay and help expel the British.

Saltonstall's fleet left Boston on 19 July and arrived off Bagaduce on 25 July. News of the American operation had reached the British long before, allowing McLean time to prepare his defenses. Saltonstall and the militia commander, General Solomon Lovell, fell into a bitter dispute. Lovell insisted that Saltonstall attack and destroy the British warships anchored close to the fort. Saltonstall refused. After many days of argument Lovell told Saltonstall, "The alternative now remains, to destroy the ships or raise the siege." Saltonstall replied, "I am not going to risk my shipping in that damned hole."

Finally on 13 August Saltonstall agreed to attack. Because of the American delay the British command in New York had time enough to dispatch a squadron to assist McLean. On the morning of 13 August the squadron sailed into Penobscot Bay. A disaster resulted. For the most part the American captains had no notion of how to act in concert, and it became a situation of every man for himself. Some American vessels tried to escape but failed and were captured. Others were blown up by their crews to prevent capture, including the *Warren*. Although every American vessel was lost, many soldiers and seamen managed to escape and trudge overland back to Boston, Saltonstall among them. News of the disaster arrived in Boston before the survivors, and investigations and courts-martial followed. Saltonstall was tried on board the frigate *Deane* in Boston harbor. The court found him to be the officer responsible for the defeat, and on 27 December 1779 he was dismissed from the service.

Saltonstall returned to New London. For the remainder of the war he engaged in privateering activities. In 1781 he commanded the letter of marque *Minerva*. In 1782 he served on a committee to assess the damage done to New London and Groton by a British raid. After the Revolution Saltonstall apparently renewed his West Indian trading ventures. He died, day and month uncertain, at Mole Saint Nicholas, Hispaniola.

• The best collection of naval papers from the time of Saltonstall's service is published in the multivolume *Naval Documents of the American Revolution*, Naval Historical Center, Washington, D.C. (1964–). See also Gardner W. Allen, *A Naval History of the American Revolution* (2 vols., 1913); William M. Fowler, Jr., *Rebels under Sail: The American Navy in the Revolution* (1976) and "Disaster in Penobscot Bay," *Harvard Magazine* 81 (1979): 26–31; and James Leamon, *Revolution Downeast* (1993).

WILLIAM M. FOWLER, JR.

SALTONSTALL, Gurdon (27 Mar. 1666–20 Sept. 1724), Congregational minister and colonial governor (1707–1724), was born in Haverhill, Massachusetts, to a politically prominent family, the son of Nathaniel Saltonstall, a leader in civil and military affairs, and Elizabeth Ward. After receiving his B.A. (1684) and M.A. (1687) from Harvard College, he moved to New London, Connecticut, which had been without a pastor for four years, where he began to preach in the winter of 1687. He was formally ordained on 25 November 1691, and continued his ministry until late 1707, when, upon the death of his close friend, Governor Fitz-John Winthrop, he became the only ordained minister elected governor of an American colony.

Saltonstall's unique political ascendancy was the product not only of widely recognized personal and ministerial capacities (he was chosen to give the 1697 election sermon, published as *A Sermon Preached before the General Assembly of the Colony of Connecticut*), but also of his public and widely appreciated assistance to Governor Winthrop. As a secretary and agent for the oft-absent governor, Saltonstall functioned both as his personal confidant and as an indispensable conduit between Winthrop and colony officials. In his own right, Saltonstall served on various commissions that dealt with boundary and ecclesiastical difficulties. A further factor in his election as governor was his traditional political and social philosophy, which favored the generally popular seventeenth-century Connecticut status quo: a charter government that allowed the colony to pursue a quasi-independent direction within a secured British empire, and a deference to established social and religious authority within the colony that placed a premium on order and stability.

As governor, Saltonstall was vigorous in his actions to bring Connecticut more fully into the British military effort against the nearby French and the Indians in Queen Anne's War (1702–1713), a successful effort that resulted in a period of greater security, and also in an enlarged colony debt. He was also instrumental in the convening of the colonial conference that enacted the Saybrook Platform (1708), an agreement that would affect Connecticut religion for several generations. Intended both as a reform of church discipline and a strengthening of the clergy's authority, the platform established a more Presbyterian structure creating county consociations to oversee the various congregations, an arrangement intended to ensure religious uniformity and doctrinal purity. Saltonstall helped found Yale College (1701), and his active interest enhanced the development of the school and influenced its move from Saybrook to New Haven in 1716.

Saltonstall's insistence on proper respect for established authority helped to lead him, along with his mentor, Winthrop, into a long-running feud with James Fitch, a populist-style Norwich political leader and land speculator. Involving personal conflict as well as struggles over political power and economic development, these disputes often merged with political strife between the two houses of the colony's legislature. While the specific issues contested between the two houses included local judicial appointments and title to Indian lands, Saltonstall was convinced that the underlying conflict was the same in both cases; at stake, he believed, was the necessity for deference to established authority, the only guarantor of social stability and order. The alternative, in his view, was a society turned upside down, undermined by personal ambition, faction, and irregular, incendiary appeals to the populace.

A revered and popular governor, Saltonstall died while serving in office. Sensitive to any apparent challenge to the standing order both before and during his governorship, Saltonstall was the principal and the most visible proponent of that order during the first quarter of the eighteenth century. Quick to lecture the recalcitrant lower house of the General Assembly about the respective prerogatives and responsibilities of the two houses of Connecticut's assembly, Saltonstall was dismayed by the lower house's increasing lack of deference to the governor and the assistants and to the traditional political and social order. Saltonstall's conservative vision of Connecticut's polity continued to play a normative role in the colony's political life and discourse after his death. Yet, ironically, Saltonstall's victory over Fitch and his particular brand and Yankee individualism, a discordant note seemingly echoed in the efforts of the lower house, was a victory that was more immediate than ultimately lasting. The stirrings of a more democratic and individualistic order, a Yankee order, were not to be so easily deflected.

He was married three times: to Jerusha Richards (d. 1697), with whom he had five children; Elizabeth Rosewell (d. 1710), five children; and Mary Whittingham (d. 1730), the widow of William Clarke of Boston.

• Saltonstall manuscripts can be found in the Connecticut Archives at the Connecticut State Library and the Saltonstall papers at the Connecticut Historical Society, both in Hartford. The Massachusetts Historical Society in Boston houses related materials in the Winthrop family papers, many of which are published in the society's *Proceedings* and *Collections*. For his term as governor see J. Hammond Trumbull and Charles J. Hoadley, eds., *Public Records of the Colony of Connecticut*, vols. 5 and 6 (1850–1890). Biographical information is available in John L. Sibley and Clifford K. Shipton, *Biographical Sketches of Those Who Attended Harvard College*, vol. 3 (1873–1975); and James M. Poteet, "The Lordly Prelate: Gurdon Saltonstall against His Times," *New England Quarterly* 53 (1980): 483–507. Saltonstall's ministerial career is covered in Frances M. Caulkins, *History of New London, Connecticut* (1852); his relationship with Fitz-John Winthrop is noticed in Richard S. Dunn, *Puritans and Yankees: the Winthrop Dynasty of New England, 1630–1717* (1962); and his place in early eighteenth-century Connecticut history is explored in Richard L. Bushman, *From Puritan to Yankee: Character and the Social Order in Connecticut, 1690–1765* (1967). Additional general information may be found in Robert J. Taylor, *Colonial Connecticut, a History* (1979).

THOMAS W. JODZIEWICZ

SALTONSTALL, Leverett (1 Sept. 1892–17 June 1979), Massachusetts governor and U.S. senator, was born in Chestnut Hill, Massachusetts, the son of Richard Middlecott Saltonstall, an attorney, and Eleanor Brooks. Both parents came from wealthy and established families that had been in Massachusetts since 1630. After graduating from Harvard College (like nine generations of his family before him) in 1914, Saltonstall took his law degree at Harvard Law School in 1917. While still a law student, he married Alice Wesselhoeft on 27 June 1916; they had six children. Following two years as a first lieutenant in the field artillery during World War I, including a six-month tour in France, he returned to Boston, was admitted to the Massachusetts bar, and entered into law practice with his uncle, Endicott Saltonstall, in the firm of Gaston, Snow, Saltonstall, and Hunt. Saltonstall won his first elected office in 1920, that of alderman in the town of Newton, a position he held until 1922; simultaneously he served as assistant district attorney for Middlesex County. In 1922 he was elected to the lower house of the General Court, the state legislature of Massachusetts, where he served for fourteen years, the final eight as Speaker. In the legislature he carved out a mixed record, frequently opposing organized labor but supporting such measures as old age pensions, mothers' aid, unemployment insurance, and a minimum wage. He gave up his legislative seat in 1936 to run, unsuccessfully, for lieutenant governor.

Saltonstall's next attempt to win higher office resulted in a stunning upset victory over former Boston mayor James Michael Curley in the 1938 Massachusetts gubernatorial race. He was a popular governor, presiding over a 90-percent reduction in the state deficit and winning easy reelection in 1940 and 1942, despite strong support in the state for the Democratic president, Franklin D. Roosevelt. Highly respected by his fellow governors, Saltonstall served as chairman of both the New England Governors' Conference (1939–1944) and the National Governors' Conference (1944). In 1944 he opted to run for the U.S. Senate and outdistanced his Democratic opponent by almost 600,000 votes to win the seat vacated by Henry Cabot Lodge, Jr., who had resigned to enter the military.

Reelected to the Senate three times (in 1948, 1954, and 1960), Saltonstall was an unspectacular but effective legislator—influential more in the bill-drafting process and in conference committees (he had a particular knack for framing acceptable compromise language) than on the Senate floor. He conscientiously tended and actively advocated the interests of his constituents (for example, he was a leading opponent of construction of the St. Lawrence Seaway, which allowed Great Lakes ports to compete with those in the Northeast) and brought considerable federal largesse to Massachusetts. His commitment to civil liberties was strong and steady as well; in 1954 he was the only member of the Republican Senate leadership to vote for the motion to censure Senator Joseph R. McCarthy. Throughout his twenty-two year Senate career, he served on powerful committees: Appropriations; Armed Services, including membership on its elite CIA Subcommittee; and Small Business. Because of turnover in Senate membership, by the early 1950s he ranked among the most senior Republicans on these key committees.

It is somewhat misleading to think of Saltonstall in terms of the important party leadership posts that he held in the Senate—GOP senate whip from 1949 to 1957 and chair of the Republican Senate Conference from 1957 until his retirement ten years later. A consistent internationalist, he was neither liberal nor conservative on domestic issues; the degree of his loyalty on party-line votes placed him somewhere near the middle of the Republican pack. As a middle-of-the-roader, he commanded the respect of his colleagues but had no real following. Rather, his elevation to leadership posts reflected compromises reached by those who sought to balance power between the two ideological wings of a deeply divided party. The way in which GOP conservatives smoothly engineered his replacement as whip in 1957 (by Everett Dirksen) was testimony to his lack of any real base of support. It was never a possibility that Saltonstall would become floor leader, as had so many others in both parties who had served as whip.

Saltonstall could certainly have been reelected in 1966, but instead he chose not to seek renomination—in part, to cooperate with the Massachusetts Republican leadership's desire to open a Senate seat for the state's black attorney general, Edward Brooke. Upon leaving the Senate in January 1967, Saltonstall retired to the life of a gentleman farmer in Dover, Massachusetts, where he lived until his death.

A quintessential Boston Brahmin, Saltonstall had the social status, wealth, and long career of public service that made him a prototype of the "patrician" American politician. If he left no lasting monument in the form of legislation bearing his name, neither was there ever a hint of corruption in his record. Always cooperative for what he perceived as the greater good, he was a rarity in politics—retiring after a forty-year career with virtually no political enemies.

• Saltonstall's papers are available at the Massachusetts Historical Society in Boston; in addition, a small collection of his letters is located at Boston University. Lengthy oral histories by Saltonstall are to be found in the Dwight D. Eisenhower Project at Columbia University and at the John F. Kennedy Library; briefer oral histories are available at the Library of Congress, Lyndon B. Johnson Library, Princeton University, and Mississippi State University (John C. Stennis Project). There has been no scholarly biography of Saltonstall, but his memoirs, *Salty: Recollections of a Yankee in Politics*, were published in 1976.

GARY W. REICHARD

SALTONSTALL, Richard (1610–29 Apr. 1694), colonial magistrate, was baptized 1 October 1610 at Woodsome, Almondbury, Yorkshire, England, the son of Richard Saltonstall and Grace Kaye, daughter of Robert Kaye. His father was the nephew of Sir Richard Saltonstall, lord mayor of London. A committed Puritan and an original patentee and assistant of the Massachusetts Bay Company, Saltonstall's father crossed to Massachusetts with his family in 1630. He helped found the town of Watertown, Massachusetts, but was so dismayed by the primitive conditions of the settlement that he returned to England in 1631. The family had not sold its English land, and the younger Richard was to divide his time between England and Massachusetts. In 1631 he returned with his father to England where he studied law and, in 1633, married Muriel Gurdon, daughter of Brampton Gurdon of Suffolk; they would have six children.

In 1635 Saltonstall, with his wife and child, went back to America and helped found the town of Ipswich. He settled in Ipswich as magistrate, becoming an important property owner and proprietor of its only grist mill. He served the central government of Massachusetts as assistant, 1637–1649, 1664, and 1680–1682, and kept the magistrate's court in Ipswich, Newbury, and on the Piscataqua in what is now New Hampshire. He also served in the military, and as alternate commissioner of the New England Confederacy in 1644 and substitute agent of the colony in 1660.

In the 1640s Saltonstall joined Nathaniel Ward and other dissidents who had settled in and around Ipswich in opposition to the rule of Governor John Winthrop, who complained of him in his *Journal*. Committed to a new society in America, Saltonstall was not willing to allow it to acquire the trappings of arbitrary government that had been left behind in England. He wrote, but never published, a treatise condemning the proposed Life Council, on which magistrates were to be elected for life terms by the General Court. In 1643 Saltonstall, with other prominent Ipswich men, hinted to Winthrop that Ipswich might stay neutral if Winthrop led the colony into war on behalf of one of the rival French governors of Acadia. In 1645 he petitioned the New England Confederacy against giving aid to either one of the French claimants. In 1645 he protested against the slave trade and supported Dr.

Robert Child and Samuel Maverick, who were sent back to England for protesting the requirement of membership in the established Puritan church as a prerequisite for voting and officeholding.

Between 1649 and 1663, the period from the beginning of Oliver Cromwell's rule until Charles II's abandonment of any support of the English Puritans, Saltonstall lived in England. He served Cromwell as commissioner of the High Court of Justice to repress the enemies of the Commonwealth (1650) and as trustee for settling sequestered estates in Scotland (1654). He returned to Massachusetts in 1663 and remained there until 1672. During this sojourn he showed his commitment to the Puritan ideal by giving £50 to Edward Whalley and William Goffe, who had condemned Charles I to death in 1649, and £450 to Harvard College. Yet after the Restoration New Englanders were less outspoken than they had been in the days of Puritan ascendancy in the 1640s, and Saltonstall did not speak out publicly on matters of policy. Between 1672 and 1680 he returned to England to manage the family property. He was in Massachusetts between 1680 and 1686 but went back to England in 1686 and died at Hulme, Lancaster.

Sympathetic to the Puritan commonwealth in Massachusetts, Saltonstall had the resources to return to a more cosmopolitan and comfortable life in England. His descendants, beginning with his grandson Gurdon Saltonstall, governor of Connecticut, have served New England in public positions ever since.

• The Saltonstall papers at the Massachusetts Historical Society in Boston contain manuscript material by Richard Saltonstall. Saltonstall's descendant Leverett Saltonstall wrote *Ancestry and Descendants of Sir Richard Saltonstall* (1897), which reprints letters and records the activities of the Saltonstalls in England and America. Saltonstall appears in the public records of Massachusetts Bay, both in Nathaniel B. Shurtleff, ed., *Records of the Governor and Company of Massachusetts Bay*, and John Noble, ed., *Records of the Court of Assistants*. The best edition of Winthrop's journal is James Savage, ed., *The History of New England* (1853; repr. 1972).

MARY RHINELANDER MCCARL

SALTUS, Edgar Evertson (8 Oct. 1855–31 July 1921), writer, was born in New York City, the son of Francis Henry Saltus and Eliza Howe Evertson, both of Dutch descent. Edgar Saltus was privately educated, and upon graduation from St. Paul's School in New Hampshire he entered Yale for one year, then returned briefly a year later. He then went abroad, studying in Paris, Heidelberg, and Munich, before returning to New York City to pursue a law degree at Columbia University, where he received an LL.B. in 1880.

Independently wealthy and therefore relieved of the necessity to earn a living, Saltus turned his attention to literature and philosophy. Small in stature, he cultivated a distinguished appearance, dressing elegantly and sporting a waxed mustache. Only a pronounced stutter belied the persona of a self-assured man of letters. Saltus's first book, *Balzac*, a biography, was published in 1884 to generally favorable reviews. His next work, *The Philosophy of Disenchantment*, a sympathetic study of the pessimistic philosopher Schopenhauer, appeared a year later. In 1886 he published *The Anatomy of Negation*, a study of antitheistic philosophies.

Saltus's first novel, *Mr. Incoul's Misadventure*, was published in 1887, and in the next seven years he published six more novels: *The Truth about Tristrem Varick* (1888), *The Pace That Kills* (1889), *A Transaction in Hearts* (1889), *Mary Magdalen* (1891), *Madam Sapphira* (1893), and *Enthralled* (1894). A volume of short stories, *A Transient Guest, and Other Episodes*, was published in 1889. During this time Saltus also published two essay collections, *Love and Lore* (1890) and *Imperial Purple* (1892), a series of essays on imperial Rome.

Nearly all of Saltus's early fiction focused on New York society and had melodramatic and often bizarre plots; concision and stylistic elegance were usually sacrificed to florid overwriting and lurid detail. As Oscar Wilde once commented, "In the work of Edgar Saltus, passion struggles with grammar on every page."

For nearly a decade, beginning in 1894, Saltus worked as a hack writer, publishing virtually nothing under his own name. In the late 1890s he was employed by P. F. Collier & Son, publishers of popular multivolume series; he is believed to have compiled Collier's *The Lovers of the World* (n.d.) and *The Great Battles of All Nations* (2 vols., 1899), and to have been a major contributor to the publisher's Nations of the World series.

Saltus's return to fiction writing was marked by the publication in 1903 of a short-story collection, *Purple and Fine Women*, and in the next decade he published four more novels: *The Perfume of Eros* (1905), *Vanity Square* (1906), *Daughters of the Rich* (1909), and *The Monster* (1912). Like his earlier fiction, these works were sensational, often bizarre, and pessimistic in outlook; many critics found them flawed by weak characterization. During this period Saltus also published three nonfiction works: the essay collections *The Pomps of Satan* (1904) and *Historia Amoris* (1906), and a history of religions called *The Lords of the Ghostland* (1907).

Saltus suffered from ill health in the last decade of his life and published no books between 1913 and 1919, the year that his novel *The Paliser Case* appeared. A year later he published a history of Russia called *The Imperial Orgy*. Three of his works were published posthumously: *The Ghost Girl* (1922), a novel; *The Uplands of Dream* (1925), a collection of essays and poetry; and *Poppies and Mandragora* (1926), poetry coauthored by his third wife.

Saltus was married three times. His first wife was Helen Sturgis Read, whom he married in 1883; they were divorced a decade later. In 1895 he married his second wife, Elsie Welsh Smith, from whom he separated shortly afterward; the couple had a daughter. Saltus married his third wife, Marie Giles, in 1911. Marie Giles Saltus converted her husband to theosophy, and its influence can be seen in his later writings.

Saltus died at his home in New York City and was buried at Sleepy Hollow Cemetery in Tarrytown, New York, in the same plot as his wife's dog. In the years following his death, several American critics who had been sympathetic to Saltus during his lifetime, most notably Carl Van Vechten, tried to resurrect an interest in his work but to little avail. Saltus is considered a curious footnote in American literary history.

• Two book-length biographies of Saltus have been written. Marie Giles Saltus, *Edgar Saltus: The Man*, appeared in 1925, but it has scant information on Saltus's early years, and its factual accuracy has been questioned by literary scholars. A more reliable account is Claire Sprague's brief biography *Edgar Saltus* (1968). Biographical information about Saltus is included in *Yale Seventy-seven: Their Lives and Letters* (1892). For a sympathetic evaluation of Saltus's work, see Carl Van Vechten, *The Merry-Go-Round* (1918), and Benjamin De Casseres, "Edgar Saltus," in *Forty Immortals* (1926). A more objective assessment is Eric L. McKitrick's "A Pinch of Saltus," in the *New York Review of Books*, 5 Nov. 1970. Generous excerpts of reviews and other critical assessments of Saltus's work written between 1887 and 1978 are included in *Twentieth-Century Literary Criticism*, vol. 8 (1982). An obituary is in the *New York Times*, 2 Aug. 1921.

ANN T. KEENE

SALTUS, J. Sanford (9 Mar. 1854–23 June 1922), art patron and numismatist, was born John Sanford Saltus in New Haven, Connecticut, the son of Theodore Saltus, a merchant and ironmaster, and Elizabeth Sanford. The vast family fortune was made by Saltus's grandfather, the merchant Francis Saltus, who established an ironworks in upstate New York that pioneered rifled steel cannon. When Francis Saltus died in 1854, Theodore Saltus was his executor; litigation over the estate lasted into the 1890s.

Always sickly and something of a hypochondriac, Saltus was educated at home. He trained as a painter at the Art Students League and also studied at the École des Beaux-Arts in Paris. His haphazard education comes out in his atrocious spelling. In 1888, in Stratford, Connecticut, he married Medora S. Hubbell, the daughter of O. S. Hubbell; she is described as a painter of "rare talent." The couple had no children.

Saltus had a penchant for the odd and romantic; he was fascinated by subjects such as the fate of Louis XVII, Joan of Arc, the Confederacy, gypsies, and zombies. He wrote several books of travel sketches, a book on animals in Shakespeare, and one on Louis XVII, *Mystery of a Royal House* (1900). Saltus argued that Eleazar Williams of Green Bay, Wisconsin, had a very strong claim to be Louis XVII; after looking through Saltus's book, the reader can understand better Mark Twain's satire of the king and the duke in *Huckleberry Finn*. Saltus's best work is the *Statues of New York* (1923), written with Walter Tisné and published posthumously.

Saltus became a member of the American Numismatic Society in November 1892. Saltus and George F. Kunz, the president of Tiffany's, pushed the society to issue numerous medals, some executed by great artists like Victor D. Brenner and Adolph A. Weinman. Saltus's donations to the society gave it one of the best collections of orders and decorations in the world. Saltus donated to the society three of the rarest American coins: the strawberry leaf cent of 1793, the Confederate half dollar, and the Saint-Gaudens extremely high relief double eagle of 1907.

Around 1906 Saltus was one of the "Gang of Four"—the others were Archer Huntington, Daniel Parish, and E. T. Newell—who took control of the society and moved it to its own building on 155th Street next to Huntington's Hispanic Society of America. Like all juntas, they quarreled among themselves. When Newell fired Bauman Belden, the society's secretary, in 1916, Saltus resigned from the council. Newell placated him, and Saltus became a councillor for life in 1917. Saltus then had the society resume its extensive program of issuing medals; seventeen were issued between 1917 and 1922.

In 1915 Saltus paid $35,000 to set up a statue of Joan of Arc, sculpted by Anna Vaughn Hyatt, on Riverside Drive in New York City. Copies of the statue were given to the Cathedral of St. John the Divine, to New Orleans, to Winchester Cathedral in England, and to Paris, Domrémy, Blois, Rouen, and Orléans.

No fewer than three societies give medals named after Saltus: the American Numismatic Society, for medallic art; the British Numismatic Society, for numismatic scholarship; and the Art Students League. Saltus is portrayed in a plaque by Victor D. Brenner of 1900; on a medal executed by Jonathan M. Swanson commemorating Saltus's presidency of the New York Numismatic Club; and in an oil painting by Eugène Boulet-Cyprien.

Saltus withdrew somewhat from public life after his wife's death in 1906; thereafter he lived in hotels, often in Paris, Nice, and London. He suffered a grotesque death. He had gone to London to be installed as president of the British Numismatic Society, when he was found dead in his hotel room. The coroner suggested that Saltus had been cleaning coins using potassium cyanide; he had a glass of the poison and a glass of mineral water side by side (some accounts say the second glass contained ginger ale); in a macabre accident he drank the wrong glass. A telegram addressed to him was found after his death that said, "Letters received. Great surprise and honour. Am happy but not well, and will go to sanatorium. Let us remain true friends for the present. There is no one but you. Be cheerful and hold your own.—Love, Estelle." This lady was Estelle Campbell, the widow of the civil engineer Robert James Campbell and daughter of the New York surrogate judge John Harvey Vincent Arnold. It is possible that the death was no accident and that Saltus committed suicide after she refused his proposal of marriage. Saltus left an estate worth more than $3.5 million, of which the bulk was stock in New York banks. Estelle Campbell inherited $500,000 and his jewelry.

Saltus was modest with a sly sense of humor and sound aesthetic judgment. He was a worthy Maecenas for some of America's finest medallists and sculptors. Despite his love of monarchies and pageantry, Saltus had a great fund of good sense, writing from Paris in October 1911 after the second Morocco crisis:

Things are more quiet than they were a short time ago, but still wa[r] may break out at any moment. If it does I think it will be the most bitter war of modern times. I think the trouble is this. It[']s time war came, human nature requires it. Europe needs it, so if a war can[']t be made for a just cause, it[']s sure to come for an unjust one. That's the danger, the evil of a country that is to [sic] long at peace has to face, as is shown by the teachings of history and our collection of "War Medals."

• The North Country History Center of the State University of New York at Plattsburgh has papers relating to Saltus's grandfather Francis and the Saltus ironworks among the records of the Peru Steel and Iron Company. Numerous letters of Saltus to Bauman Belden and others (1910–1922) are preserved in the archives of the American Numismatic Society. The family background is covered by Ethel Saltus Ludington (who inherited $577,003 from Saltus) in *Ludington-Saltus Records* (1925). The best biography of Saltus is William Francklyn Paris, *J. Sanford Saltus* (1922), which was printed separately and also appeared as a chapter of Paris's *Personalities in American Art* (1930). Another biographical sketch is "J. Sanford Saltus: A Remembrance," Edward Alexander Parsons, *Louisiana Historical Society Quarterly* 5 (Oct. 1922): 493–98. Howard L. Adelson, *The American Numismatic Society 1858–1958* (1958), provides a workmanlike history of the ANS, its medals, and Saltus's role, but at one point he gives the wrong year (1906; the correct year is 1916) for Saltus's resignation from council. Both the *New York Times*, 25, 26, and 29 June 1922, 22 July 1922, 8 Aug. 1922, and 19 May 1923, and *The Times* (London), 26 and 28 June 1922, 30 Dec. 1922, have useful information about his macabre death by poisoning and the settlement of his estate; the *New York Times*, 4 Jan. 1901, tells about the lengthy litigation over his grandfather's estate. An obituary is in the *Numismatist*, Aug. 1922.

JOHN M. KLEEBERG

SAMAROFF, Olga (8 Aug. 1882–17 May 1948), pianist and teacher, was born Lucie Mary Olga Agnes Hickenlooper in San Antonio, Texas, the daughter of Carlos Hickenlooper, an auditor, and Jane Loening. At the time of her birth, her father was an army officer stationed in San Antonio. When she was six, she was taken to Houston to live with her mother and grandmother and later moved to Galveston.

Olga's first piano teacher was Lucie Palmer, her maternal grandmother, who was married to George Loening and after his death to Lorenzo Grunewald. At the age of three, Olga was able to improvise melodies at the piano. Although the convention of the time dictated that she should undertake a concert career only if marriage was not a possibility, her talent was quickly recognized. She auditioned before composer Edward MacDowell, pianist Vladimir de Pachmann, and piano manufacturer William Steinway. They unanimously agreed that she should study in Europe, the prescribed destination of most musicians who wished to become successful.

In 1894, accompanied by her grandmother, who sacrificed her teaching profession to travel with her, Olga embarked on a five-year effort to attend the Paris Conservatory. After some private study with Antoine Marmontel and Ludovic Breitner, she won a scholarship for entrance to the conservatory in 1896 and was placed in the class of Elie Delaborde. Fighting his conviction that "Americans are not meant to be musicians," she acquired the self-discipline for intensive work with him.

After Paris, Olga and her grandmother moved to Berlin for further study and better musical and living conditions. Her teachers there were Ernst Jedliczka and Ernest Hutcheson. It was here in 1900 that she elected matrimony over a career by marrying Boris Loutzky, a Russian inventor and civil engineer employed by the Russian embassy in Berlin. During the marriage, Olga's contact with musical life was severely curtailed. The marriage was finally annulled in 1904.

Having the opportunity to choose between a teaching career in St. Louis, where her family had moved, and a concert career, Olga engaged the services of New York concert manager Henry Wolfsohn. Although extremely reluctant to recommend a concert career without European press reviews, which she could not provide for financial reasons, he finally suggested that she hire an orchestra, give a Carnegie Hall concert, and adopt a foreign name. She chose the name Samaroff, after one of her remote ancestors, with the understanding that she would continue to promote her American heritage. The New York Symphony Orchestra under Walter Damrosch was engaged for the evening of 18 January 1905, with Schumann's Concerto in A Minor and Liszt's Concerto in E-Flat on the program. The reviews were mixed, but Wolfsohn was able to extract a sufficient number of favorable statements for publicity.

After several local concerts, Samaroff was engaged by Boston manager Charles A. Ellis, one of the most prominent concert managers of the time, to play the C Minor Sonata for Piano and Cello by Saint-Saens in Boston with one of the members of the Boston Symphony Quartet. Critic Philip Hale's review of this successful concert helped earn her an engagement to play with the orchestra the following season. Samaroff's solo concert career debut took place in London in May 1905, followed shortly thereafter by a second recital, which received excellent reviews. Her appearance with the Boston Symphony took place in April 1906, following which Ellis offered to become her manager. The ensuing relationship earned her concerts throughout the United States at $500 to $600 a concert as well as a few concerts abroad. She was managed by Ellis until 1911.

On 24 April 1911 Olga Samaroff married Leopold Stokowski, who was conductor of the Cincinnati Symphony Orchestra at that time. Her concert career was curtailed for a short time, owing both to the marriage and to the birth of their daughter on 23 December 1921. They were divorced in 1923. After her divorce she made her home in New York City, while maintaining a summer home in Seal Harbor, Maine, which was to become the site of many gatherings of well-known musicians and of her students, with whom she developed close personal relationships. She often bought concert clothing for her students and would frequently welcome her students into her apartment. Her students were also invited to "Haus Hirth" near Ober- and Untergrainau in the Bavarian Alps, built by Walther Hirth and used for the purpose of intellectual and artistic gatherings.

In 1925 a series of incidents drastically altered Samaroff's career. An accidental fall caused a torn ligament in her arm, thus putting an end to her concert engagements for a year. Shortly thereafter she was offered a position as music critic for the *New York Evening Post*, a position she held for two years. Also in 1925 she was asked to teach in the new Juilliard Graduate School of Music, joining a faculty that consisted of Ernest Hutcheson, Alexander Siloti, Josef and Rosina Lhevinne, Carl Friedberg, and James Friskin. Her pupils included Joseph Battista, William Kapell, Eugene List, and Rosalyn Tureck. She taught at Juilliard until her death.

In 1929 Samaroff began to teach as head of the piano department at the Philadelphia Conservatory of Music after the death of director Hendrik Ezerman. She taught there one day a week concurrently with her duties at Juilliard. Her interest in the Philadelphia Conservatory reflected her desire to train teachers of music as well as performing artists.

Although her arm had eventually healed, Samaroff's widening interest in pursuing many musical activities, coupled with a lack of true enthusiasm for concert life, caused her to turn down offers of new concert engagements. In 1928 she established the Schubert Memorial, a scholarship fund to promote worthy young musicians. Through the efforts of competitions sponsored by the National Federation of Music Clubs, the endeavor became a national success. In 1931 she also founded the Musician's Emergency Fund of New York to assist depression-era musicians.

Samaroff also developed the Layman's Music Course in order to reach a wider audience. Designed for "the young of all ages," these classes were held first at the New York Junior League and Steinway Hall and eventually found a permanent home at the David Mannes Music School. The course was later given in such other cities as Washington, D.C., and Philadelphia, and Samaroff presented it on radio and television. The course led to the publication of three of her books: *The Layman's Music Book* (1935), a textbook for the course that was expanded in 1947 and called *The Listener's Music Book*; *The Magic World of Music* (1936), a book on music for children; and *A Musical Manual* (1937), which contained material on various elements of music for the layperson. She also published her autobiography, *An American Musician's Story* (1939).

Samaroff was a frequent guest lecturer at many universities, including Yale, Harvard, and Columbia. In 1936, probably as a result of her Layman's Music

Course activities, she represented the United States at Prague for the first International Congress of Music Education, organized by the Society for International Music Education. In May 1938 she was selected to serve on an international piano jury for the Concours Eugène Ysaÿe in Brussels, organized by Queen Elisabeth of Belgium. She also received the Order of the Crown of Belgium.

Olga Samaroff died of a heart attack in New York City. After her death, several of her students contributed $5,000 toward the establishment of the Olga Samaroff Foundation, which was used to create a home in New York City for music students. Although she trained as a concert pianist and concertized quite actively, she is remembered mostly as a teacher and educator. The recording industry was in its infancy during the years she made records, but she recorded often, primarily for the Victor Talking Machine Company, and strongly believed in the importance of recordings as educational tools. Her many activities in fundraising, teaching, lecturing, and writing beyond the concert stage are a testament to her belief in the importance of music in everyone's life.

• In addition to her works mentioned above, see Samaroff's "The Performer as Critic," in *Music and Criticism: A Symposium*, ed. Richard F. French (1948), in which she asks for informed and fair criticism. For a chronicle of her life, career, and theories of music education, see Donna Pucciani, "Olga Samaroff, 1882–1948: American Musician and Educator" (Ph.D. diss., New York Univ., 1979). For her experiences as the first female music critic in New York City, see Donna Kline, "Olga Samaroff Stokowski: Music Critic," *Journal of the American Liszt Society* 32 (July–Dec. 1992): 52–60. For her legacy as a piano teacher, see Geoffrey McGillen, "The Teaching and Artistic Legacy of Olga Samaroff Stokowski" (Ph.D. diss., Ball State Univ., 1988). Obituaries are in *Musical America*, June 1948; *Etude*, Sept. 1948; and the *New York Times*, 18 May 1948.

RICHARD R. HIHN

SAMPLE, Paul Starrett (14 Sept. 1896–26 Feb. 1974), painter, was born in Louisville, Kentucky, the son of Wilbur Stevenson Sample, a civil engineer, and Effie Averill Madden. Because of his father's profession, Sample and his family moved frequently. In 1911 the family settled in Glencoe, Illinois. Sample graduated from New Trier high school and matriculated at Dartmouth College in 1916. When the United States entered World War I Sample joined the U.S. Merchant Marine. Following the war he returned to Dartmouth College. In 1921, shortly after he graduated, Sample became ill with tuberculosis and was treated at Saranac Lake, New York. In 1923, while under treatment, Sample began to study drawing and painting from the noted painter Jonas Lie, whose wife also was being treated for tuberculosis at Saranac Lake. When he was pronounced cured in early 1925 Sample studied art briefly in New York; in June he moved to California.

Sample resumed his art studies at the Otis Art Institute in Los Angeles. In 1926 he left school, determined to be an artist. In September 1926 he began a part-time job teaching drawing at the University of Southern California; within ten years he was chairman of the art department. On 1 December 1928 Sample married Sylvia Howland of Vermont, whom he had met when both were tuberculosis patients; they had one child. Until he left California he spent a part of each summer painting in Vermont.

During the 1930s many American painters turned their attention to America—her land, her cities, and her people. This movement, American Scene painting, comprised two groups: the Social Realists, who painted life in the American cities, frequently focusing on the problems of urban life, and the Regionalists, who painted both the glories and the harsh realities of the rural landscape. An important figure in American scene painting, Sample was one of the moving forces behind a group of Los Angeles painters that included Barse Miller and Millard Sheets. By 1932 he was president of the California Art Club. Sample's social realist paintings such as *Unemployment* (1931) are among the early West Coast scenes of urban life in the American Scene movement. Sample studied mural painting with Siqueiros and later participated in the New Deal mural projects, painting two post office murals (Redondo Beach, Calif.; Apponaug, R.I.) for the Section of Painting and Sculpture of the U.S. Treasury Department. In late 1934 *Time* magazine proclaimed Sample as one of America's most important living painters. On view at private and public galleries, his work was featured in the art press as well as in popular magazines, including *Life* and *Fortune*.

In 1938 Sample left California and accepted the position of artist-in-residence at Dartmouth College, where he remained until his retirement in 1962. In 1941 Sample, his wife, and their son, Tim, moved permanently to Norwich, Vermont. During World War II Sample served as an artist-correspondent for *Life* magazine. His painting assignments included a training mission on an aircraft carrier in the North Atlantic, two weeks in a submarine on patrol in the Pacific Ocean, and accompanying the troops in the invasion of Leyte Gulf in the Philippines.

Following the war Sample continued to be active on the art scene, lecturing and serving on the juries of exhibitions at major museums, including the Metropolitan Museum of Art, the Corcoran Gallery, the Carnegie Museum, and the National Academy of Design. His honors included election to the National Academy of Design and awards from the Pennsylvania Academy of the Fine Arts, the National Academy of Design, and others. He was a member of the American Watercolor Society, the Century Club, and the Lotos Club. Sample's paintings are in many public collections including the Metropolitan Museum, the Museum of Fine Arts in Boston, and the Art Institute of Chicago. Although representational painting was generally out of favor after mid-century, Sample's work was in demand. Much of the work was commissioned: portraits, magazine illustrations, and murals, including projects for the Brevoort Hotel in New York in 1955; for the Massachusetts Mutual Life Insurance Compa-

ny in Springfield, Massachusetts, in 1965; and for the National Life Insurance Company in Montpelier, Vermont, in 1961. During the 1960s he was also commissioned by NASA to document a Saturn rocket launch, and a year before his death he completed a work for the Environmental Protection Agency.

Sample's theory about painting was stated in 1939: "The most important thing for painters is to paint . . . and let others discuss and analyze." His family, friends, and his many interests, including music, fishing, and hunting, were grist for his artistic mill. Sample's paintings changed during the 1940s. During the 1930s much of his focus had been on genre scenes, and quite often the figures and their activities dominated the landscape, as in *Janitor's Holiday* (1936). With the passage of time Sample shifted his focus from human activities to the landscape. Sample's landscapes were not exact representations but rather his vision of the landscape and man's relationship to nature. He loved the variety of the New England seasons, especially late autumn and winter when the trees were bare; as a result, he acquired the reputation of being a New England painter. Perhaps his most familiar work is *Maple Sugaring* (1944), which appeared in *Britannica Junior* and was also used as a logo by a major producer of Vermont maple syrup. In the 1950s his subject matter remained the same, but his style changed, becoming looser and flatter, but he did not abandon representation or his disciplined compositions.

Gradually Sample's name slipped into relative obscurity. Perhaps his position at Dartmouth College was responsible for this. Had he remained in a major art center such as Los Angeles or New York, he would have stayed in the public eye and in contact with the art press and thus received the accolades he deserved. Nevertheless his paintings continued to be popular with private collectors, who purchased for pleasure rather than investment. Always dignified and reserved, Sample was not daunted by lack of public acclaim, and he continued to paint even to the day of his death. He died at a hospital in Hanover, New Hampshire, after suffering a heart attack at his home in Norwich, Vermont.

Accompanying the emergence of Photorealism as an important art movement in the last quarter of the twentieth century was a revival of interest in the painters of the 1930s. In 1984 Sample's "Regionalist" work was exhibited at the Lowe Art Museum at the University of Miami in Coral Gables. This was followed by a major retrospective of his work at the Hood Museum of Dartmouth College in 1988. With the reevaluation of American Scene painting Sample's position in the history of American Art has been assured.

• Many of Sample's papers and oral interviews with the artist are in the Archives of American Art, Washington, D.C. Dartmouth College also has a large collection of material on and by Sample. There is material about him and his work in the records of the galleries that represented him: Ferargil Galleries (before 1942), AAA Galleries (Associated American Artists—1941–1957), and Milch Galleries (1957–1967) in New York City; Vose Galleries in Boston; and Capricorn

Galleries in Bethesda, Md. The Hood Museum catalog, *Paul Sample, Painter of the American Scene* (1988), contains an extended chronology of the artist's life as well as an analysis and appreciation of his work. His work prior to 1949 is discussed in *Paul Sample, Ivy League Regionalist* (1984), the catalog of the exhibition at the University of Miami. See also John Condit, "Paul Sample" (M.A. thesis, Columbia Univ., 1954), and Paula F. Glick, "The Mural Paintings of Paul Sample" (M.A. thesis, George Washington Univ., 1981). An obituary is in the *New York Times*, 27 Feb. 1974.

PAULA GLICK

SAMPSON, Deborah (17 Dec. 1760–29 Apr. 1827), revolutionary heroine and public speaker, was born in Plympton, Massachusetts, the daughter of Jonathan Sampson and Deborah Bradford, farmers. Born into a family that claimed a distinguished lineage from the days of the early Pilgrims in Massachusetts, Sampson endured a painful and impoverished childhood. Her father died when Deborah was five. She lived with an elderly female relative for three years and with a pastor's widow for two more years before she was bound out as a servant to the family of Jeremiah Thomas in Middleborough, Massachusetts. Sampson thrived during the period of her indenture, learning manual skills and her letters. She became literate enough to teach school for a period of six months after she became free from her indenture in 1779. To this point in her life, little distinguished her from her fellows other than her physical strength. She was five feet seven inches, and observers commented on her sturdy physique.

A more headstrong and even reckless aspect to Sampson's nature appeared during the year 1782. Inspired by the events of the American Revolution, she dressed in men's clothing and enlisted in the Massachusetts militia forces under the assumed name of Timothy Thayer. Caught soon afterward and exposed as a woman masquerading in men's clothes, she was forced to yield the bounty money that was customarily paid to enlistees during that period of the revolutionary war. Unhindered by this initial setback, and rejecting a suitor who was favored by her mother, Sampson dressed in men's clothing once again and on 20 May 1782 enlisted in the Fourth Massachusetts Regiment in Uxbridge, Massachusetts, under the assumed name of Robert Shurtlieff (given variously in other sources as Shirtliff, Shurtleff, or Shirtlief). Mustered in Worcester, Massachusetts, on 23 May 1782, she marched southward to West Point, New York, as a member of the Continental army.

Sampson saw considerable action during her year and a half in the American forces (20 May 1782–23 Oct. 1783). She took part in a battle against American Loyalists near Tarrytown, New York, where she was wounded in the thigh. Treated by a French surgeon in the American army, she extracted a musket ball from her thigh rather than have her gender discovered. Around this same time she suffered the indignity of having the First Baptist Church of Middleborough,

Massachusetts, sever its connections with her, citing her "verry loose and unchristian like" behavior.

Sampson continued to serve in the Continental army. She saw action near Fort Edward in upstate New York and then was transferred to serve in Philadelphia. She contracted malignant fever while she was in that city and was treated by Doctor Barnabas Binney, who was probably the first soldier or doctor to uncover her sexual identity (and who maintained her secret). After she recovered from the fever, Sampson went with the Eleventh Massachusetts Regiment on a land surveying expedition toward the Ohio River. She became ill once again while en route and went to Baltimore rather than continue on the expedition. Returning soon afterward to West Point, she was on a boat that capsized and lost the diary of her soldiering in the water. She was discharged by General Henry Knox at West Point on 23 October 1783. She took a boat to New York City and another one to Providence, Rhode Island, and finally walked home from Providence to Stoughton, Massachusetts, thus ending a remarkable period of her life.

For a time Sampson posed as a man, assuming the name of Ephraim Sampson, but in 1784 she married Benjamin Gannett. The couple had three children and, on a small farm in Sharon, Massachusetts, lived a routine family life that was aggravated by mild poverty and by Sampson's illnesses. She may also have suffered from her war wounds. In 1792 she petitioned the Massachusetts General Court for a pension based on her service in the Massachusetts regiments. She eventually received £34 as back pay. She told her wartime stories to Herman Mann, who wrote and published *The Female Review: or, Memoirs of an American Young Lady* (1797), which related her experiences in vivid imagery and fanciful hyperbole. In 1802 she stepped forward as a speaker to audiences in New England and New York. Wearing a blue and white uniform and armed with a musket, she related how she had "burst the tyrant bounds which held my sex in awe."

Continuing to experience financial difficulties, Sampson asked for help from her friend and neighbor in Canton, Massachusetts, Paul Revere. The silversmith and former dispatch rider wrote letters in her behalf and may have given generously from his own purse in her support. Following her petitions and the exhortations of Revere, Sampson was placed on the pension list of the United States in 1805 (retroactive to 1803). The remainder of her life was uneventful. She died in Sharon. Her husband applied to Congress for further financial assistance, claiming that as a war widower he deserved special consideration. He died before 7 July 1838, when the U.S. Congress approved an "Act for the relief of the heirs of Deborah Gannett, a soldier of the Revolution, deceased" (the money went to the three children).

Sampson's wartime service was both sensational and remarkable. The activities of this American "Joan of Arc" were in many ways more extraordinary than the heroics of persons such as Betsy Ross and Molly Pitcher. First, Sampson's military service was reasonably well documented; second, she took obvious pride and pleasure in both her service and in the manner of her disguise; and third, she attracted the attention of a revolutionary notable, Revere. Even in her own day, a Massachusetts newspaper marveled at the story of a "lively, comely young nymph, nineteen years of age, dressed in man's apparel," serving in the armies of the revolutionary cause (Davis, p. 322). As was the case with many heroes and heroines of the Revolution, Deborah Sampson Gannett's name faded from the public memory by the mid-nineteenth century, but her story was rediscovered and related by many historians during the feminist-conscious period of the 1960s, 1970s, and 1980s.

• A manuscript collection relating to Sampson is in the public library of Sharon, Mass. Primary sources include Sampson's *An Address Delivered in 1802 in Various Towns in Massachusetts, Rhode Island and New York* (1905) and James Adams Vinton, ed., *The Female Review—Life of Deborah Sampson* (1866). Her war records are presented in Julia Ward Stickley, "The Records of Deborah Sampson Gannett, Woman Soldier of the Revolution," *Prologue* 4 (1972): 233–41. Her life and career have been chronicled in numerous articles and books, notably Elizabeth Evans, *Weathering the Storm: Women of the American Revolution* (1975); Vera O. Laska, "*Remember the Ladies*": *Outstanding Women of the American Revolution* (1976); Curtis Carroll Davis, "A 'Gallantress' Gets Her Due: The Earliest Published Notice of Deborah Sampson," *Proceedings of the American Antiquarian Society* 91, no. 2 (1981): 319–23; and Kathleen Doyle, "'Private Robert Shurtleff': An Unusual Revolutionary War Soldier," *American History Illustrated* 23, no. 6 (1988): 30–31. Sampson's connection with Revere is mentioned in Esther Forbes, *Paul Revere & the World He Lived In* (1942).

SAMUEL WILLARD CROMPTON

SAMPSON, Edith Spurlock (13 Oct. 1901–8 Oct. 1979), lawyer and judge, was born in Pittsburgh, Pennsylvania, the daughter of Louis Spurlock, the manager of a cleaning and dyeing business, and Elizabeth A. McGruder. She came from a poor black family. Her resourceful mother had managed, by weaving and selling hat frames and switches, to earn enough money to buy a home. Financial necessity forced her to interrupt her grade school education to go to work, but eventually she was able to return and to graduate from Peabody High School in Pittsburgh. After high school she was employed by Associated Charities, a group that made it possible for her to attend the New York School of Social Work. While there she received the highest grade in a criminology course, which prompted Professor George W. Kirchwey of Columbia University School of Law to encourage her to study law. This she did as a night student at John Marshall Law School in Chicago (1922–1925). She ranked highest of ninety-five students in a class on jurisprudence, which earned her a commendation from Dean Edward T. Lee.

In 1925 she took and failed the Illinois State Bar examination. She later said that was the best thing that could have happened to her because it cured her overconfidence and made her settle down and work harder. She returned to her studies and in 1927 became the first woman to earn a master of laws degree from the Graduate Law School at Loyola University. She passed the bar exam in 1927. For a time, she also took courses at the University of Chicago School of Social Service Administration.

During law school Sampson had been employed by the YWCA and the Illinois Children Home and Aid Society. In 1925 she began eighteen years of association with the Juvenile Court of Cook County, Illinois. She was eventually appointed a probation officer and served as a referee from 1930 to 1940. Since 1924 she had maintained a law office on the south side of Chicago, specializing in criminal law and domestic relations; her clients were predominantly black. She was admitted to practice before the U.S. Supreme Court in 1934.

In 1949 Sampson was invited to participate in a world tour as one of twenty-six American civic, cultural, labor, and welfare leaders involved in the Round-the-World Town Meeting. She participated in debates on political questions and met leaders of the countries she visited. She saw her role as countering Moscow radio's propaganda about the status of black Americans. In answer to a heckler in India she said, "I would rather be a Negro in America than a citizen in any other land." When the organization was made permanent as the World Town Hall Seminar, she was chosen by the other members as its president.

President Harry S. Truman named Sampson an alternate U.S. delegate to the fifth regular session of the United Nations General Assembly in August 1950. She was the first member of her race to be an official U.S. representative to the United Nations. Some suggested her appointment was an effort to refute Soviet propaganda about the condition of blacks in the United States, but she said, "I would be glad to refute such propaganda. There are pitfalls for our race in this country, but they are not as bad as the Kremlin would like to picture them." She was assigned to UN Committee Three, on social, humanitarian, and cultural issues, where she lobbied for the United Nations to continue supporting work in the social welfare field. She was also assigned to deal with a complaint that the Soviet Union had not carried out complete repatriation of its POWs. President Truman reappointed her as an alternate delegate for the 1952 session of the United Nations General Assembly.

Sampson served as an assistant Cook County state's attorney, then as assistant corporate counsel for the City of Chicago (1955–1962). In 1962 she became an associate judge for the Municipal Court of Chicago. When the court system was reorganized in 1964, she became an associate judge for the Circuit Court of Cook County and held that position until her retirement in 1978. As a judge she dealt mostly with cases involving housing issues.

Throughout her life, Sampson was active in a wide variety of organizations. She was a board member of the Chicago Council on Foreign Relations, of the UN Association of Chicago and the U.S. Commission for

UNESCO. She was a member of the U.S. Citizens Commission on NATO, the National Council of Negro Women, and a host of other organizations. She served as a guest lecturer for the State Department, urging that the objectives of the UN charter be carried out and that the United States use its abundant resources "for building a people's front against aggression and for world development."

Sampson's first marriage, to Rufus Sampson, a field agent for Tuskegee Institute in Alabama, ended in divorce, but she retained his name throughout the rest of her life. After she married Joseph E. Clayton, a lawyer, in 1934, they shared a practice until his death in 1957. She had no children of her own but helped to rear several nieces and nephews. Sampson died in Chicago.

• Sampson's papers are in the Special Collection, Arthur and Elizabeth Schlesinger Library on the History of Women in America, Radcliffe College. She is listed in numerous biographical reference works. Upon her appointment as a delegate to the United Nations in 1950, articles about her appeared in *Look*, *Time*, *Scholastic*, the *Christian Science Monitor*, and the *New York Times*, among other periodicals. Obituaries are in the *Chicago Sun-Times*, 10 Oct. 1979, and the *New York Times*, 11 Oct. 1979.

REBECCA S. SHOEMAKER

SAMPSON, William (27 Jan. 1764–28 Dec. 1836), New York lawyer and legal reformer, was born in Londonderry, Ireland, the son of Rev. Arthur Sampson, a Church of Ireland clergyman, and Anne Wilson. After a spartan childhood, during which he was raised by a maiden aunt, he joined the Irish Volunteers and read law at Trinity College, Dublin. He then fulfilled the requirements of the London Inns of Court and was admitted to the Irish bar. In 1790 he returned to Belfast and married Grace Clarke, by whom he had three children. Although, as he wrote later in his *Memoirs*, his personal interest "lay decidedly with the court party, rather than the people," from 1792 he became a regular contributor to the Belfast United Irish newspaper, the *Northern Star*, and a pamphleteer with a gift for satire. Sampson later claimed he was a reformer, not a revolutionary, and that he was never privy to United Irish secrets, knowing nothing about links with the French until he read of them in the newspapers. Certainly he played an open role in politics until 1798, mainly as defense counsel in the trials of many Defenders and United Irishmen in the North. But his friend Valentine Lawless, Lord Cloncurry, recalled how in 1796, on their return from dinner with the Duke of Leinster, Sampson "illustrated the reckless character of his zeal" by scattering political pamphlets in the camp of the Kildare militia. His claim not to have been sworn into the United Irishmen is difficult to believe.

Following the arrest of the United Irish Executive in March 1798, Sampson, dressed in women's clothes, fled to Whitehaven in England with his servant-cum-chaperone. Legend has it he was arrested after being seen shaving in his petticoats. Taken back to Dublin, he was imprisoned for many months but was never brought to trial. Because of ill health and the influence of friends, Sampson was not sent to Fort George in Scotland with the other United Irish leaders but was allowed in November 1798 to emigrate to Portugal. From there he was forcibly removed to France, where he spent four disillusioned years writing the first part of his memoirs before going to Hamburg. From there, hoping to obtain permission to return to Ireland from the new Foxite ministry, he returned to England but was arrested. On 12 May 1806 he sailed, at government expense, to New York. Like his friend Thomas Addis Emmet (1764–1827), Sampson received privileged treatment from the New York bar and obtained a license to practice law within one month of his arrival. By assiduously enlarging his social contacts, and by sheer determination, he advanced his career and gained a reputation as an eloquent counsel and an accurate court reporter. He finally persuaded his wife and children to leave Ireland and settle with him in New York in 1810.

Sampson's reputation in the United States rests primarily on his advocacy of common law reform in America. The abolition of the common law and its replacement by a written code of simply-written laws were the reform goals of many anglophobic British and Irish Jacobins who emigrated to the United States at this time. William Duane (1760–1835) and others had failed in their attempts to abolish the common law in Pennsylvania during Thomas Jefferson's presidency. Sampson's conversion to this program began in 1810 when he unsuccessfully defended the New York cordwainers, who were prosecuted for conspiracy under the common law when they went on strike. He believed that the common law was incompatible with America's democratic pretensions. In 1823 he delivered an address to the New-York Historical Society (*Discourse on the Common Law*) in which he destroyed the historical arguments for the common law and asserted that all laws should be placed on a rational footing. According to Sampson, laws should be based on the principles of "natural reason, universal justice, and present convenience," and all court decisions ought to be published, for the benefit and understanding of the public.

Sampson's program was aimed at reforming the law from within, but his 1823 address, which was published the following year, caused great controversy. For two years he corresponded with leading jurists on the issue, but the first stages of the dropsy that would eventually kill him gradually wore him down. The agitation subsided with the victory of the Jacksonians, who sought to democratize the legal system rather than reform the law.

Throughout his career in New York and in Washington, D.C. (1825–1830), Sampson promoted the interests of his fellow-Irish exiles. In 1813 he was instrumental in clarifying the law so that priests could not be forced to disclose the secrets of the confessional in the courts. In 1824 he helped prosecute Orangemen (anti-Catholic Protestants) who had attacked Catholic Irish in Greenwich Village, New York, and in 1831 he defended Catholic Irish who were accused of rioting in Philadelphia. He died in New York City. He is chiefly remembered as an Irish patriot who worked tirelessly for the benefit of his less-fortunate fellow immigrants.

• The main source for Sampson's life up to 1807 is his *Memoirs of William Sampson* (1807; 2d, enlarged ed. 1817). A third, shorter edition was published in London in 1832. His letters to his wife from July 1806 to 1831 are in the Library of Congress. Sampson's most important pamphlets include *A Faithful Report of the Trial of Hurdy Gurdy* (1794), *Trial of the Journeymen Cordwainers* (1810), *The Catholic Question in America* (1813), *Anniversary Discourse on the Common Law before the Historical Society of New York* (1824), and *Sampson's Discourse, and Correspondence with Various Learned Jurists, upon the History of the Law* (1826). There is no modern biography of Sampson, but his daughter's eulogy on him forms the basis of R. R. Madden, *The United Irishmen, Their Lives and Times*, 2d ser., vol. 2 (1843), pp. 335–88. See also Charles C. Beale, *William Sampson: Lawyer and Stenographer* (1907), and Edward J. McGuire, "William Sampson," *Journal of the American Irish Historical Society* 15 (1916): 342–58. Sampson's role as a legal reformer is best analyzed in Maxwell Bloomfield, "William Sampson and the Codifiers: The Roots of American Legal Reform, 1820–1830," *American Journal of Legal History* 11 (1967): 234–52.

MICHAEL DUREY

SAMPSON, William Thomas (9 Feb. 1840–6 May 1902), naval officer, was born in Palmyra, New York, the son of James Sampson, a day laborer, and Hannah Walker. An excellent student, Sampson did not have the means to attend college but in 1857 received an appointment to the U.S. Naval Academy from Congressman Edwin Barbour Morgan. Sampson ranked first in his class for three consecutive years and graduated in 1861. As a passed midshipman he was assigned to duty at the Washington Navy Yard, after which he reported to the sloop *Pocahontas*, then patrolling the Potomac River and Chesapeake Bay for Confederate raiders. That summer Sampson was reassigned to the frigate *Potomac*, which served in the Gulf of Mexico.

The following year Sampson was promoted to lieutenant and was appointed an instructor at the naval academy, which was functioning in temporary facilities in Newport, Rhode Island. After nearly two years there, Sampson returned to sea as executive officer of the monitor *Patapsco* of the South Atlantic Blockading Squadron. In January 1865 the ship was sunk by a mine off Charleston, South Carolina. Several dozen men died, but Sampson, who was standing on the top of a gun turret when the explosion occurred, survived without serious injury. In 1863 he married Margaret Sexton Aldrich; they had four children before she died in 1878. Four years later Sampson married Elizabeth Susan Burling; they had two children.

Following the Civil War Sampson served on the steam frigate *Colorado* on the European Station. Promoted to lieutenant commander in 1866, he returned to the United States in 1867 to begin a four-year tour teaching in the Department of Natural Philosophy (later the Department of Physics and Chemistry) at the naval academy, which was once again in Annapolis. After three years at sea, serving first as executive officer of the screw sloop *Congress* on the European Station and then as commander of the gunboat *Alert*, Sampson returned to the naval academy (1874–1878) to head the Department of Physics and Chemistry. Sampson, who believed strongly in the possible military applications of modern technology, endeavored to see that naval cadets received a thorough grounding in the scientific principles on which technology was based. He also encouraged the research interests of a young member of the department, Albert Michelson, who would become the first American to win the Nobel Prize. A superb lecturer, Sampson was particularly interested in astronomy and joined a special expedition to Wyoming to observe a solar eclipse. The expedition's findings led to valuable revisions of navigational charts.

Sampson next returned to sea duty on the Asiatic Station, where he commanded the screw gunboat *Swatara* (1879–1881). He then had three assignments ashore: assistant superintendent of the Naval Observatory in Washington, D.C. (1882–1884), inspector of ordnance at the Torpedo Station in Newport, Rhode Island (1884–1886), and superintendent of the naval academy (1886–1890). His goals at the naval academy were to modernize the curriculum and physical plant, to improve cadet retention, and to eliminate hazing. He did not accomplish all of these goals, but retention did improve while hazing declined. The aptitude for service grade that was inaugurated during his term as superintendent became an important part of the evaluation process for naval academy cadets.

Promoted to captain in 1889 or 1890, Sampson in 1890 received command of the protected cruiser *San Francisco*. He next became inspector of ordnance at the Washington Navy Yard for a year, after which he moved up to head the Bureau of Ordnance (1893–1897), one of the navy's most important administrative positions. As bureau chief, Sampson attempted to acquire superior steel for use as armor plate, recommended that electricity be installed to turn the gun turrets on new battleships and cruisers, and insisted that industrial suppliers such as Du Pont sell to the navy high-quality matériel instead of the marginally adequate supplies several had often delivered in the past.

Late in 1896 Sampson was appointed to a special board established to formulate plans in the event of war with Spain. He then commanded the navy's newest battleship, the *Iowa*, before chairing the board of inquiry established in 1898 to investigate the sinking of the *Maine*. Once the board's work was concluded late in March, Sampson was promoted to acting rear admiral and given the navy's most prestigious post afloat, command of the North Atlantic Squadron. In getting this appointment Sampson was jumped over a dozen senior officers, many of whom felt resentment at being bypassed. The austere Sampson did not make any effort to mend fences with the aggrieved officers but concentrated on his duty: preparing for the war with Spain that now seemed imminent. Sampson's orders from the Navy Department were to blockade Cuba once war began and prevent a Spanish force under Admiral Pascual Cervera y Topete from reaching the island.

American leadership was found wanting at almost all levels. Cervera, who commanded a half-dozen decrepit ships that had been in the Cape Verde Islands when war broke out, eluded American patrol vessels in the Caribbean and made port at Santiago de Cuba. After detaching some ships to monitor naval activity at Havana, Sampson steamed with his force to San Juan, Puerto Rico, skeptical of initial reports that Cervera had reached Cuban waters. Once Sampson ascertained that Cervera's squadron was not at San Juan, he followed Navy Department orders to return to Key West and recoal. At Key West he also conferred with his principal subordinate, Commodore Winfield Scott Schley, who had independently commanded the Flying Squadron off the East Coast of the United States before coming under Sampson's authority in Cuban waters, ordering Schley to reconnoiter the ports of Cienfuegos and Santiago and to blockade the enemy when he located the Spanish force. New information soon convinced Sampson that Cervera was more likely to be at Santiago, and he notified Schley by fast dispatch boat to proceed there. Schley, for reasons never satisfactorily resolved, did not arrive off Santiago until 28 May. Sampson reached Santiago with the North Atlantic Squadron on 1 June and, employing ships from both forces, strengthened and reorganized the blockade that Schley had finally instituted. He detached ships as necessary to recoal at the newly established American base at Guantanamo, Cuba, and next arranged to escort transports carrying army ground forces to beaches near the port of Daiquiri, about fifteen miles east of Santiago. Army general William Shafter, who had command of ground operations in Cuba, wanted Sampson to brave the Spanish minefields at the entrance to Santiago harbor in order to bombard Spanish fortifications and facilitate Shafter's own operations. Under orders not to unduly risk his ships, Sampson demurred, aware that to confront Cervera's squadron in Santiago's inner harbor his ships would first have to steam in single file through a narrow, winding channel protected both by shore batteries and electrically detonated mines. No combined army-navy operations had occurred since the Civil War, making it necessary for Sampson and Shafter to relearn this difficult art. The brevity of the Spanish-American War did not allow sufficient time, and disagreements between Sampson and Shafter continued. Sampson simply refused to enter Santiago's inner harbor until Shafter had first neutralized Spanish shore defenses.

On 3 July Sampson steamed away from Santiago in his flagship, the armored cruiser *New York*, to confer with Shafter, who was ill and unable to visit him. Sampson did not name an interim commander. Just as the *New York* was about to disappear beyond the horizon, lookouts spotted the smoke from Cervera's squadron preparing to leave the harbor at Santiago. A battle appeared imminent. Sampson immediately ordered the *New York*'s skipper to turn back, but by the time the cruiser reached the scene, Sampson's other ships had left Cervera's force in ruins. No American ships had been lost or even severely damaged. The *New York* could only fire a few shots at an already disabled Spanish vessel.

The war's biggest battle now ensued when Sampson sent the Navy Department a message (prepared by a staff officer) saying, "The fleet under my command offers the nation as a Fourth of July present the whole of Cervera's fleet." Noting the resemblance between Sampson's cable and William T. Sherman's 1864 message to Abraham Lincoln informing the president that Savannah, Georgia, had fallen to Union forces, the press commented on Sampson's boastful tone and began to question the extent of Sampson's contributions to the victory. Many papers wondered whether Schley, the senior officer present, did not deserve credit for the resounding victory. Others, however, supported Sampson, contending that his well-conceived blockade and organization of the North Atlantic Squadron allowed it to fight so effectively when Cervera made his desperate attempt to escape. Some criticized, too, Schley's performance before the battle and his maneuvers during it. The navy's officer corps was similarly polarized. Meanwhile, still refusing to risk his ships in the minefields, Sampson tried to placate Shafter by ordering a small force of cruisers and battleships to bombard the city of Santiago from positions outside the harbor on 10 and 11 July. Sampson was prepared to continue shelling Santiago, but ground fighting was nearing a conclusion, and on 16 July Shafter informed Sampson that the Spanish had accepted American terms. The surrender documents were signed the following day.

Both Sampson and Schley were soon promoted to rear admiral on the permanent (as opposed to temporary wartime) list of ranks, but the Navy Department exacerbated matters by posting Sampson just ahead of Schley on the seniority list, a reversal of their prewar standings. Since Congress had to approve the promotions, more wrangling erupted there, with Schley's partisans scoring many points before the promotions were confirmed in 1899. Sampson continued in command of the North Atlantic Squadron, but rapidly failing health (symptoms of which had begun to appear two years before) led him to request assignment ashore in 1899. Old friends like Alfred Thayer Mahan were shocked by his loss of vigor. He turned down the presidency of the Massachusetts Institute of Technology in the hope he could remain on active duty until he reached the mandatory retirement age in 1902. He was named commandant of the Boston Navy Yard, a post that was not considered demanding. However, the decline in his health forced him to leave Boston in September 1901 to rest at Lake Sunapee, a New Hampshire resort, and when a court of inquiry convened that same month at Schley's request to go over Schley's own leadership during the Santiago campaign, Sampson was too ill to appear before it. He was wasting physically and was also apparently the victim of what his physicians described as a "certain form of aphasia," a disease that often manifests itself in a diminishing capacity to use and understand words. The court found Schley's decisions wanting in several instances. However, an unprecedented minority report issued by the court's president, Admiral George Dewey, differed in many key details and insisted that credit for the victory at Santiago belonged to Schley, since he was the senior officer present during the battle. The conflicting reports only added to the furor in the navy and in the press. Sampson died in Washington, D.C., and was buried at Arlington National Cemetery.

During his forty years of service, Sampson distinguished himself on numerous occasions: with personal bravery during the Civil War, through the reforms he introduced at the naval academy, and through his efforts to keep the navy abreast of technological changes and prepared for war. The American victory at Santiago was as overwhelming as Dewey's earlier triumph at Manila Bay. However, Sampson's absence from the scene of battle and the resulting dispute with Schley long obscured the facts of the battle itself and embarrassed the principals and the service as a whole.

• Sampson's own papers were destroyed by his widow, but official correspondence survives in a collection of Sampson materials at the U.S. Naval Academy and in RG 45, RG 405, which contains his correspondence from his years at the naval academy, and RG 313, Records of the Naval Operating Forces, at the National Archives. Otherwise, the best sources for study of Sampson are Joseph G. Dawson III, "William T. Sampson: Progressive Technologist as Naval Commander," in *Admirals of the New Steel Navy: Makers of the American Naval Tradition, 1880–1930*, ed. James C. Bradford (1990); and Richard S. West, Jr., *Admirals of American Empire* (1948). The chapter on Sampson in Alfred Thayer Mahan, *Retrospect and Prospect* (1902), is also of interest. More about Sampson is in studies of his peers such as Edwin A. Falk, *Fighting Bob Evans* (1931); Robert Seager II, *Alfred Thayer Mahan* (1977); and Paolo E. Coletta, *Admiral Bradley A. Fiske and the American Navy* (1979). Two good sources about his role in the Spanish-American War are W. A. M. Goode, *With Sampson through the War* (1899), and David F. Trask, *The War with Spain in 1898* (1981). Jack Sweetman, *The U.S. Naval Academy* (1979), helps put Sampson's contributions to the naval academy in perspective. An obituary is in the *New York Times*, 7 May 1902.

LLOYD J. GRAYBAR

SAMPTER, Jessie Ethel (22 Mar. 1883–11 Nov. 1938), Zionist poet and educator, was born in New York City, the daughter of Rudolph Sampter, a lawyer, and Virginia Kohlberg. Her mother came from a traditional German-Jewish household, and her father, the son of East European Jewish immigrants, was an atheist affiliated with the Ethical Culture Society. Her father was a strong and supportive influence, reading and encouraging Sampter's early writing.

Sampter was schooled at home because her parents thought her too frail to attend school. Her father died of pneumonia when she was twelve, an event from which her mother never quite recovered. The next year Sampter was stricken by polio, which left her bedridden for many months. She spent her convalescence writing poems and stories and sending them to children's magazines, winning not only publication, but prizes.

Sampter described herself as self-educated. This education included trips and extended visits to Europe led by her mother, who often sought out literary sites and people such as the English playwright Israel Zangwill. In New York Sampter was friendly with other young writers such as Mary Antin, whose autobiography, *The Promised Land*, was the story of Jewish assimilation in America. Antin and Sampter often met with Josephine Lazarus, a mentor for both of them, and the sister of poet Emma Lazarus. Sampter dedicated her first major publication, "The Great Adventure," to Josephine Lazarus. This nineteen-chapter prose-poem, greatly influenced by Walt Whitman, was described by Sampter as a biblical "affirmation of self-faith."

Spiritual seeking led Sampter away from the atheistic ethical cultural background to Jewish Reform temples, Orthodox synagogues, and the Unitarian church. Through friends at the Unitarian church, she was introduced to Henrietta Szold, the founder of Hadassah, the Women's Zionist Organization. Szold became one of Sampter's great teachers, welcoming her into her home and sharing the customs and holidays of traditional Jewish life. Szold's teachings, combined with instruction from Mordecai Kaplan in discussion groups on Jewish law and history, brought Sampter the spiritual and political community that she was looking for.

In July 1914, convinced that the community should be rooted in a national Jewish homeland, Sampter opened the School of Zionism and taught weekly classes in club leadership, public speaking, and Zionism. She also added her literary talents to the movement with the manual *Course in Zionism* (1916), which sold well and later ran second and third editions.

Sampter's passion for Zionism was one that aimed for a peaceful solution to the conflict in Palestine. She was against a system of racial apartheid and instead envisioned a neighborly, two-state solution with the Arabs. Palestine was to be a model nation embodying, as she called it, the "dream of a regenerate humanity." To this end she wrote a pacifist, Zionist tract in the spiritual manner of the prophets called *Book of the Nations* (1917). Exhausted from the completion of the book and dismayed by the continued fighting of World War I, she sank into a deep depression.

Although still plagued by physical weakness and depression, Sampter was able to publish an optimistic collection of poems, *The Coming of Peace* (1919), and the joyful *Around the Year in Rhymes for the Jewish Child* (1919). The affirmation of hope present in these works found even greater expression that autumn in her decision to move to Palestine, despite concerns over her health voiced by her sister.

Sampter arrived in Palestine in 1919 amid the turbulence of Arab riots and an uncharacteristic blizzard and stayed with Leah Berlin, a friend introduced to her by Szold. She immediately became involved in the lives of the persecuted underclass of Yemenite Jews by holding evening classes for young Yemenite working women whom she saw as doubly victims of racial prejudice and gendered oppression within the family. With Alexander Dushkin, she organized a Hebraic Scout movement where Jewish practices replaced military ones.

After a long visit to her sister in America in 1922, she returned to Palestine and adopted a three-year-old girl named Tamar. Sampter never married. She and Tamar soon moved from urban Jerusalem to the orange groves of rural Rehoboth, where two years later Sampter built a house. Her work with the Yemenite community in Rehoboth focused on organizing and running a kindergarten, which was often in desperate need of funds. Letters to friends in America brought the fiscal relief that the state would not supply.

From the beginning of her stay in Palestine, Sampter had been writing articles on the Zionist experience that were published in the magazine *New Palestine*. During a trip to the Emek, her journalistic reports to *New Palestine* become poetic portraits of the people, settlements, and problems of the pioneers, tourists, and religious sects inhabiting the region. Her editor at the magazine accepted the pieces as experimental reportage. Sampter then collected the fifteen pieces in a volume, *The Emek, or the Valley of the Children* (1927), which sold out its first edition.

The Arab riots of 1929 in Jerusalem and the Hebron brought Palestinian unrest to a head. Sampter's anger mostly focused on the British administration that had forbidden the Jews to carry guns in defense, yet did nothing to protect them from violence and death. The British "divide and rule" policy was successful to the extent that Sampter lost her earlier romanticized view of the Arabs and of the entire conflict. However, Sampter remained true to hopes for a peaceful Palestine and continued to advocate a Jewish policy of nonretaliation against the Arabs.

At age fifty Sampter took the final step toward the fulfillment of a life's work in the realm of collective education and labor: she sold her house in Rehoboth and used the money to join the kibbutz at Givat Brenner. On the kibbutz Sampter taught Hebrew, held discussion groups for young people, and continued her writing.

With funds raised in America, Sampter founded a rest home on the kibbutz for aging workmen and pioneers as well as for herself and Leah Berlin. In August 1938 Sampter was diagnosed with malaria; she died in November and was buried on the kibbutz. In her last months she was still writing. She completed a novel begun in 1922; wrote essays on living on the kibbutz called "Collective," which were never found; and recorded her final thoughts on Arab-Jewish life in a work titled "Unity."

• Other works of Sampter's span many different genres. *The Seekers* (1910) is described as documenting an "experiment in collective thinking." The 1916 manual *Course in Zionism* was greatly expanded in its second edition and retitled *Guide to Zionism* (1920), and the third edition became *Modern Palestine, a Symposium* (1933) and included writings by Albert Einstein, Henrietta Szold, and others. *The Last Candles* (1918) and *Candle Drill for Hanukka* (1922) are two short plays. *Ingathering* (1934) is a series of four poems forming an abbreviated history of the immigration to Palestine and of the pioneers. A broad collection of her verse, "the salvage of thirty years of expression in poetry," is in *Brand Plucked from the Fire* (1937). Translations of children's poetry by the revered Hebrew poet Bialik make up *Far over the Sea* (1939). A spiritual biography, *In the Beginning*, was published in three volumes in 1953. Other unpublished autobiographical novels include "Hester Lynn," describing her childhood, and "The Speaking Heart," an account of her first years in Palestine. Bertha Badt-Strauss wrote *White Fire* (1956), the biography of Jessie Ethel Sampter. An obituary is in the *New York Times*, 26 Nov. 1938.

AMY FEINSTEIN

SAMUEL, Maurice (8 Feb. 1895–4 May 1972), author and radio host, was born in Macin, Romania, the son of Isaac Samuel, a shoemaker, and Fanny Acker. In 1900 his family left their native country and settled in Paris, where he learned French, the first of the many languages he mastered and later translated into English (Yiddish, Hebrew, German, Russian). A couple of years later the family moved again, this time permanently, to Manchester, England, where Samuel began and completed his formal education. From the outset he proved to be a brilliant, diligent, and competitive student. He won several prizes in high school and a scholarship for three years to the University of Manchester, which in his time had many faculty members who had achieved world renown. The most famous was physicist and Nobel laureate Ernest Rutherford. Also at Manchester was chemist Chaim Weizmann, who later became a leading Zionist and the first president of the state of Israel. (Many years later Samuel was credited with helping Weizmann write his autobiography, *Trial and Error* [1949].)

In 1914, at the outbreak of World War I, Samuel found himself in Paris, where he witnessed with deep disgust the assassination of the Socialist leader Jean Jaurès and the hysteria of mobs of patriotic French who demanded that their army march on Berlin. Samuel, who had publicly identified himself early in life as a socialist and pacifist, had very mixed feelings about volunteering for or being drafted to serve in the British army, which was engaged in what he considered an imperialist and immoral war. Before the end of 1914 he decided, against his father's strong objections but with his mother's support, to emigrate to the United States, which he hoped would be immune to the war fever that had seized Europe. Three years later, however, Samuel, still not an American citizen, was drafted into the U.S. Army and sent with its expeditionary forces to France, where his linguistic skills qualified him for work with the intelligence service. He served until the Armistice of November 1918. In 1919, while awaiting demobilization, he was invited to serve on the Morgenthau Commission, created by the U.S. Congress to investigate the deplorable and deteriorating conditions of East European Jewry in the wake of the Bolshevik Revolution in Russia in 1917 and the achievement of independence by Poland after the disintegration of the czarist empire. The painful experience of witnessing the plight of Jews in Eastern Europe subsequently influenced Samuel to convert to activist Zionism.

On his return to the United States in 1921, Samuel was naturalized as an American citizen. His oath of allegiance marked perhaps the most important commitment of his life. More than forty years later, in his autobiography *Little Did I Know* (1963), Samuel said, "I would like to write a long essay on my relation to America, the country without which there would hardly be a Jewish people today and therefore no Jewish homeland."

Between 1922 and 1929 Samuel was employed by the Zionist Organization of America as a lecturer and propagandist. An individualist and the very opposite of an "organization man," he resigned this salaried post in 1929 to risk becoming a freelance writer and lecturer. Without becoming bestsellers, his books secured him a loyal following, and he lectured successfully throughout the United States and Canada as well as British-mandated Palestine, independent Israel, and South Africa. His books had a symbiotic relationship with his lectures, and large parts of them were composed in trains, ships, planes, and hotels during his extensive travels. Of his books, critic Robert Alter has written: "For more than three decades, Maurice Samuel was a kind of one-man educational movement in American Jewish life. Anyone with even a passing interest in the East-European milieu, Yiddish and Hebrew literature, Zionism, the future of American Jewry, the nature of antisemitism, the role of Judaism in the West, is likely to have read at least one of Samuel's books." Ludwig Lewisohn described him as "perhaps the ablest Jewish intellectual of his time."

The advent of radio broadcasting vastly extended the reach of his voice; Samuel was asked by the Jewish Theological Seminary of America to host a regular Sunday morning program called "The Eternal Light," the subject of which was the Bible considered as literature. His interlocutor in discussions of incidents, themes, and personalities of the Bible was most often the American poet, critic, anthologist, and professor of English at Columbia University Mark Van Doren. Two books based on transcriptions of these weekly conversations were published after Samuel's death. His own *Certain People of the Book* (1955) also was derived from these radio broadcasts.

Of his more than twenty-five books, the longest lasting in print was probably *The World of Sholom Aleichem* (1943), which combined translation and interpretive commentary on the work of the humorist, whom the popular press had dubbed "the Yiddish Mark Twain." (When the two men were introduced to each other in New York, Mark Twain graciously turned the description into a neat compliment by calling himself "the American Sholom Aleichem.") Ronald Sanders wrote that "Maurice Samuel is, to my mind, the only writer who ever turned the mental processes of the translator into the stuff of literature in its own right. The only way writers like Sholom Aleichem could be properly rendered into English, it occurred to him, was by a technique of explanatory paraphrase that would ultimately shed light upon the entire culture that had produced it." Samuel was sufficiently encouraged by the reception of his book on Aleichem to apply the same method to the work of another great Yiddish writer, J. L. Peretz, in *The Prince of the Ghetto* (1948).

In 1944 Samuel published the most readable short history of Zionism before the establishment of the state of Israel, *Harvest in the Desert*, and in 1947 he published a well-received historical novel about Machiavelli, *Web of Lucifer*. Samuel also produced several polemical works, the most notable an attack on the historian Arnold Toynbee, *The Professor and the Fossil* (1956). In 1966 he published his most interesting book on anti-Semitism, *Blood Accusation*, a detailed account of the trial of a Russian Jew in Kiev in 1911, which was also the subject of Bernard Malamud's novel *The Fixer* (1967).

Twice married, Samuel had three children. He died in New York City.

• Excerpts from Samuel's various works, as well as hitherto uncollected journalism, literary essays (on Marcel Proust, Thomas Mann, James Joyce, and Saul Bellow), verse, and travel impressions contributed to such periodicals as *Commentary*, *Midstream*, the *Menorah Journal*, and the *New Palestine* have been gathered into a volume entitled *The Worlds of Maurice Samuel*, ed. Milton Hindus (1977). Information on Samuel also can be found in two volumes by S. Liptzin, *Generation of Decision* (1958) and *The Jew in American Literature* (1966).

MILTON HINDUS

SANBORN, Franklin Benjamin (15 Dec. 1831–24 Feb. 1917), author and social activist, was born in Hampton Falls, New Hampshire, the son of Aaron Sanborn and Lydia Leavitt, farmers. Sanborn was educated at Harvard College from 1852 to 1855. Those years also saw two events that would have a profound effect on him. The first was his ill-fated marriage on 23 August 1854 to Ariana Smith Walker, who had encouraged Sanborn to pursue a formal education. Already gravely ill, she died only eight days after the wedding. The second event was a ten-minute meeting with Ralph Waldo Emerson in Concord, Massachusetts, in July 1853. In late 1854 Emerson offered Sanborn the position of schoolmaster at the small private school in Concord where the children of the Emersons and other distinguished citizens of the town and its literary community would be his students. That association, in turn, formed the basis of his literary career as biographer and editor of Amos Bronson Alcott, Emerson, Theodore Parker, Henry David Thoreau, and other authors associated with American Transcendentalism.

Sanborn was interested in abolitionist politics from an early age, and once settled in Concord he became actively involved in the organized abolitionist movement, developing acquaintances with leaders such as William Lloyd Garrison, Samuel Gridley Howe, Parker, and Wendell Phillips and serving on committees for the colonization and defense of Kansas. These associations led to Sanborn's meeting John Brown (1800–1859) in late 1856 and to his involvement in Brown's plot to capture the federal arsenal at Harpers Ferry, Virginia. Sanborn became a member of Brown's "secret six," members of the Massachusetts Kansas Committee engaged in raising financing for Brown's abolitionist activities. When Brown's attempt to capture the Harpers Ferry arsenal failed on 18 October 1859, Sanborn's role came under the scrutiny of southern senators investigating Brown's raid, which led to an attempt by federal marshals to capture Sanborn in Concord on 3 April 1860 and return him to Washington, D.C., to testify about his part in the affair. Sanborn was rescued by the townspeople of Concord, and the U.S. Senate warrant for his arrest was eventually declared illegal by the Massachusetts Supreme Court. Sanborn remained devoted to Brown's memory for the rest of his life, and he published a biography of him, *Life and Letters of John Brown, Liberator of Kansas, and Martyr of Virginia*, in 1885. In 1862 Sanborn married Louisa Augusta Leavitt, his cousin; they had three children.

With the end of the Civil War, Sanborn's enormous philanthropic energies were applied to a variety of social concerns. In 1865 he was appointed by Governor John A. Andrew as secretary of the Massachusetts Board of Charities. That year he also assisted in organizing the American Social Science Association, serving as one of its secretaries until 1868 and, beginning in 1873, as sole chief secretary. He also served as an officer of the National Prison Association and the National Conference of Charities, both of which he also helped found. In 1866–1867 Sanborn called the meeting from which grew the Massachusetts Infant Asylum, and he was instrumental in founding the Clarke Institution for the education of the deaf. Sanborn served as the first secretary of the Board of State Charities from 1863 to 1868 and as chairman from 1874 to 1876. In 1878 he reorganized the whole system of state charities in Massachusetts and was appointed inspector of charities in 1879, serving in that post until 1888. This wide-ranging experience, an expertise in the care of the insane, and his abiding interest in social science resulted in Sanborn's being appointed a special lecturer on that subject at Cornell University from 1885 to 1888.

Sanborn was a newspaperman of some note, serving as editor of the abolitionist *Boston Commonwealth* in 1863 and enjoying a long association with the *Springfield Republican* (from 1856 to 1914) that included a stint as resident editor (1868–1872). But he is best remembered as one who shared and chronicled the lives of the Transcendentalists of Concord. His most significant contributions in this vein are *Henry D. Thoreau*

(1882); *A. Bronson Alcott: His Life and Philosophy* (1893), which he wrote with William Torrey Harris; *The Personality of Thoreau* (1901); *Ralph Waldo Emerson* (1901); *The Personality of Emerson* (1903); *Bronson Alcott at Alcott House, England, and Fruitlands, New England* (1908); and *The Life of Henry D. Thoreau* (1917). Sanborn was also a literary editor, notably of Thoreau, but his editions of *The Familiar Letters of Henry David Thoreau* (1894); *Poems of Nature*, which he edited with Henry S. Salt; and *Walden* (1909) are generally discredited today because of Sanborn's practice of rewriting Thoreau's work to suit his taste. In 1879 Sanborn, Alcott, Ednah Dow Cheney, Emerson, and Harris founded the Concord School of Philosophy, a summer school devoted to teaching the ideas of the Transcendentalists. One of the first and most lasting fruits of that venture was the still valuable collection, *The Genius and Character of Emerson* (1885). Sanborn died at the home of his son, Francis Bachiler Sanborn, in Westfield, New Jersey, and was buried in Concord.

• Sanborn's manuscripts were widely scattered after his death, but the largest collections are located at the Concord Free Public Library, the American Antiquarian Society, the Houghton Library of Harvard University, and the Boston Public Library. Information on locations of other holdings can be found in John W. Clarkson, "An Annotated Checklist of the Letters of F. B. Sanborn (1831–1917)" (Ph.D. diss., Columbia Univ., 1971). The best listing of Sanborn's published work is John W. Clarkson's "A Bibliography of Franklin Benjamin Sanborn," *PBSA* 60 (1st quarter 1966): 73–85. Sanborn's autobiography is *Recollections of Seventy Years* (1909). Kenneth Walter Cameron has compiled numerous autobiographical and biographical sources for Sanborn; see especially "Some Memorabilia of Franklin Benjamin Sanborn," *ESQ* no. 16 (3d quarter 1959): 23–30, and *Transcendental Youth and Age: Chapters in Biography and Autobiography by Franklin Benjamin Sanborn* (1981). The best available biography is Benjamin Blakely Hickock, "The Political and Literary Careers of F. B. Sanborn" (Ph.D. diss., Michigan State Univ., 1953).

ROBERT E. BURKHOLDER

SANCHEZ, George Isidore (4 Oct. 1906–5 Apr. 1972), educator and civil rights leader, was born in Albuquerque, New Mexico Territory, the son of Telesfor Sanchez, a miner, and Juliana Sanchez. According to Sanchez's correspondence, both parents descended from colonial settlers. The family's financial situation varied with the economy, and in 1913 the family moved to Jerome, Arizona, where the mining industry was booming. For the first year or two, Sanchez attended boarding school in Prescott, Arizona, until a school was opened for miners' children in Jerome. Sanchez's remembrances of his school days in Jerome were happy ones; he often referred to his teachers and his education as "A-One."

During high school Sanchez played cornet in the band. When times were hard, his father moonlighted by running a poker game in a saloon. Sanchez stated, "We children got our spending money by gathering and selling discarded (some not very discarded!) copper and brass from trash dumps and abandoned mines. We also, on Sunday mornings, would fish coins and even bills through the cracks of the board-walks with a piece of gum on a yardstick. We loved those drunks! With that bonanza and what I earned at a grocery store sorting out rotten potatoes, eggs, fruit, and vegetables, I bought a cornet to take the free music instruction offered at school" (letter to Harold Alford, 30 Dec. 1971, Benson Latin American Collection). Later he and his brother organized a dance band. The money from the band and that which Sanchez earned as "Kid Feliz," boxing at 112 pounds, helped the family through the times when the mines were not profitable. By Sanchez's senior year the mines were in trouble, so the family moved back to Albuquerque, where Sanchez graduated from high school in 1923.

By this time the depression had already come to New Mexico. Sanchez wanted to go to college but could not afford to go full time, so shortly before his seventeenth birthday he accepted a position as teacher and principal at Yrrisarri, a rancheria about forty-five miles east of Albuquerque. He continued teaching at the elementary level and serving as principal and supervisor of various rural schools while attending the University of New Mexico, where he studied with Loyd S. Tireman. When he graduated in 1930, Sanchez was offered a General Education Board (GEB) Fellowship to pursue his master's degree in educational psychology (with a minor in Spanish) at the University of Texas with Herschel T. Manuel. His master's thesis, "A Study of Spanish-Speaking Children on Repeated Tests" (1931), began his research into the misuse of tests for placement and segregation of Spanish-speaking children. This research would lead to his recognition as the early authority on discrimination of Mexican-American children through testing, not only for segregation but also for placement in special education classes. He was called as an expert witness in many court cases concerning the abuse of such testing.

While completing his master's degree at the University of Texas and an Ed.D. in educational administration at the University of California, Berkeley, as a GEB fellow (1934), Sanchez continued his association with the GEB as its director of the New Mexico State Department of Education's Division of Information and Statistics. In 1934–1935 he was president of the New Mexico Teachers' Association, leading the successful fight for equalization of state school funding between rural and urban areas.

In 1935 Sanchez left his position with the state department of education and became a research associate for the Julius Rosenwald Fund (1935–1937). He conducted surveys of rural education in Mexico, the South, and New Mexico for the fund; this research resulted in the book *Mexico: A Revolution by Education* (1936), which for many years remained the definitive text on education in Mexico. In 1937–1938 he was director of the Institutio Pedagogico Nacional in Caracas, Venezuela. From 1938 to 1940 he was a research associate and assistant professor, directing a Carnegie

Foundation grant by surveying rural education in Taos County, New Mexico. Sanchez's book, *Forgotten People: A Study of New Mexicans* (1940), is based on this research. He also wrote *The Development of Higher Education in Mexico* (1944).

Sanchez would have remained in New Mexico if his opportunity for a tenured position at the University of New Mexico had been realized. However, he believed that because he had made many powerful political enemies during the school finance reform battle, the promise of a tenured position was withdrawn. By the time that he was told that the position was no longer available to him, he had received an offer from the University of Texas in Austin for a tenured, full professorship. In 1940 he moved to Austin, was elected president of the League of United Latin American Citizens (LULAC), and published *Forgotten People*. He remained on the faculty of the University of Texas until his death (with the exception of his service as a consultant during World War II to the Inter-American Affairs Foundation and the U.S. Office of Civil Defense). At the University of Texas he served as chairman of the Department of History and Philosophy of Education (1951–1959) and as professor of Latin-American studies (1940–1972).

Sanchez's work with the Carnegie Foundation, the GEB, and the Julius Rosenwald Fund provided him with the reputation that led to his development of the American Council on Spanish-Speaking People (1951–1959) with funding from the Marshall Trust—funding that was recommended by Roger Baldwin, president of the American Civil Liberties Union and a board member of the Marshall Trust. Through this organization, Sanchez helped fund and promote awareness of discriminatory practices.

In 1984 Sanchez's contributions to the civil rights of Mexican Americans were recognized by the University of California at Berkeley School of Law, which dedicated a retrospective to his contributions to laws affecting Mexican Americans. His work on laws and court cases was extensive during his Texas years. An agreed judgment in the *Delgado v. Gracy et al.* (1948) case resulted in the Texas State Board of Education issuing a policy statement against discrimination of Spanish-speaking students in the public schools. The board acknowledged that the decision came about "as a direct result of the *Delgado* case, and after presentation of arguments by Gus Garcia and George I. Sanchez" ("Illegality of Segregation of Spanish-speaking Children Recognized by Texas State Board of Education," Benson Latin American Collection). Carlos Cadena, Garcia, and Sanchez were primarily responsible for the successful ruling in *Hernandez v. Texas* (1954), the first case concerning Mexican-American rights to be decided by the U.S. Supreme Court. This case concerned discrimination in jury selection. Over a 25-year period, no Mexican American had been selected to participate in the jury process in Jackson County, Texas. Garcia was the primary attorney in the case, and he used Sanchez's "class apart" theory to argue his case—that the Mexican Americans in Jackson County were treated as a "class apart" because of their Spanish surnames. Cadena, a former law partner of Garcia, had assisted Sanchez with the research for this theory, and he and Garcia were the principle attorneys before the Supreme Court. In the decision, Chief Justice Earl Warren, commenting on the obvious climate of discrimination in Jackson County, pointed out that one of the original trial attorneys, John J. Herrera, had found two outhouses behind the courthouse where the trial was being held; instead of being designated "Men," the "Anglo" outhouse had no marking; however, the other outhouse for men was clearly designated "Colored Men" with "Hombres Aqui" (Men Here) written beneath it in Spanish.

In case after case, attorneys turned to Sanchez for advice and called him as an expert witness when discrimination occurred. Mexican American Legal Defense and Education Fund (MALDEF) attorneys were writing him for advice shortly before his death. He advised pioneer civil rights attorneys Cadena, James De Anda, Garcia, and A. L. Wirin in cases in Bastrop, Odem, Driskell, Edna, and Mathis, Texas. Each case built on the *Delgado* judgment and the previous court decisions until a body of law existed that could be used as precedent in future cases. Also, precedents were established that could be referred to by attorneys when questioning the actions of local school board and city officials. The existence of this body of law was beneficial in changing and preventing discriminatory practices.

Sanchez's prestige is illustrated by his service on many national boards, including the Migrant Children's Fund, John F. Kennedy's Citizen's Committee of 50 on the New Frontier Policy in the Americas, the National Council on Agricultural Life and Labor, the Peace Corps National Advisory Committee, and the Progressive Education Association in Albuquerque, New Mexico. He also served on the boards of the Southwestern Council of Spanish-Speaking People (1945–1950) and of the San Jose Experimental School, and as a consultant to the Navajo Tribal Council; the *Nation's Schools*; the Institute of Ethnic Affairs; the Texas State Department of Education; the Texas Good Neighbor Commission; the United Nations Educational, Scientific, and Cultural Organization (UNESCO); the Bureau of Indian Affairs of the U.S. Department of the Interior; the U.S. Department of Civil Defense; and the Bureau of Intelligence and Research of the U.S. Department of State and the U.S. Office of Education. Sanchez died in Austin.

In addition to the retrospective in his honor, Sanchez's contributions have been recognized by the naming of schools after him in Texas and California, the designation of a room named after him at the U.S. Office of Education in Washington, D.C., and a $100,000 endowed George I. Sanchez Centennial Professorship in Liberal Arts in the College of Education at the University of Texas at Austin. In May 1995 the College of Education at the University of Texas was dedicated in his honor, becoming the George I. Sanchez College of Education.

• The majority of materials concerning Sanchez are in the Benson Latin American Collection at the University of Texas at Austin. The Rockefeller Archive Center in Pocantico Hills, N.Y., has papers concerning his association with the General Education Board. Sanchez's other books include: *The People: A Study of the Navajos* (1948); *Concerning Segregation of Spanish-Speaking Children in the Public Schools* (1951); *Arithmetic in Maya* (1961); *The Development of Education in Venezuela* (1963); and *Mexico* (1965). Other informative sources are Thomas P. Carter and Roberto Segura, *Mexican Americans in School: A Decade of Change* (1979); John R. Chávez, *The Lost Land: The Chicano Image of the Southwest* (1984); David Montejano, *Anglos and Mexicans in the Making of Texas, 1836–1986* (1987); Americo Paredes, ed., *Humanidad: Essays in Honor of George I. Sanchez* (1977); Guadalupe San Miguel, *Let All of Them Take Heed: Mexican Americans and the Campaign for Educational Equity in Texas, 1910–1981* (1987); Steven Schlossman, "Self-Evident Remedy? George I. Sanchez, Segregation, and Enduring Dilemmas in Bilingual Education," *Teachers College Record* 84 (Summer 1983): 871–907; Martha Tevis, "George I. Sanchez," in *Lives in Education: A Narrative of People and Ideas*, 2d ed., ed. L. Glenn Smith et al. (1994); and Tom Wiley, *Public School Education in New Mexico* (1965). See also chap. 3, "George I. Sanchez in New Mexico," of Lynne Marie Getz's *Schools of Their Own* (1997).

MARTHA TEVIS

SANDBURG, Carl (6 Jan. 1878–22 July 1967), poet, writer, and folk musician, was born Carl August Sandburg in Galesburg, Illinois, the son of August Sandburg, a railroad blacksmith's helper, and Clara Mathilda Anderson. His parents were hardworking Swedish immigrants who had met when August Sandburg was working on the Chicago, Burlington and Quincy Railroad in Galesburg and Clara Mathilda Anderson, who had traveled on her own to the new world, was employed as a hotel maid in Bushnell, Illinois. The frugal couple instilled in their seven children the necessity of hard work and education, as well as a reverence for the American dream. When Carl Sandburg entered first grade, he Americanized his Swedish name, thereafter signing his school papers and his early work as a poet, orator, and journalist "Charles A. Sandburg."

Officially ending his public school education after eighth grade, Sandburg worked in his hometown shining shoes, delivering milk and newspapers, and performing other odd jobs. His thirst for travel and adventure, supported by a railroad pass borrowed from his father, led in 1896 to his first significant journey, a trip to Chicago, the city he later covered as a reporter and celebrated as a poet. In 1897 Sandburg became one of thousands of American hoboes stowing away atop and inside railroad boxcars, working their way west by train through Iowa, Missouri, Kansas, Nebraska, and Colorado in search of jobs.

After a few months Sandburg returned to Galesburg for a brief, restless stint as a housepainter before enlisting in Company C of the Sixth Infantry Regiment of the Illinois Volunteers for service in the Spanish-American War. He was assigned to duty in Puerto Rico from July until late August 1898. In October

1898, although he lacked a high school diploma, Sandburg's status as a war veteran qualified him for admission with free tuition to Lombard College in his hometown. He also received a conditional appointment to the U.S. Military Academy in 1899. He traveled to West Point to take the entrance examinations but failed the required mathematics and grammar tests. He returned to Galesburg to study at Lombard until May 1902.

He left college without a degree but with a new appetite for reading and writing poetry, encouraged by his first significant mentor, economist and poet Philip Green Wright, a Lombard professor who later taught at Harvard. An amateur publisher, Wright used a small handpress in his cellar to produce four leaflets by Charles A. Sandburg: *In Reckless Ecstasy* (1904), *Incidentals* (1907), *The Plaint of a Rose* (1908), and *Joseffy* (1910), a promotional profile commissioned by a popular magician and inventor. The other three booklets contained short essays, aphorisms, and poems after the fashion of Sandburg's favorite writers at that time: Walt Whitman, Ralph Waldo Emerson, Rudyard Kipling, Robert Browning, and Elbert Hubbard.

Chronically infected with wanderlust, Sandburg roamed the country after his departure from college, supporting himself by selling Underwood and Underwood stereoscopic pictures and giving an occasional lecture on Whitman, George Bernard Shaw, or Abraham Lincoln. When he ran out of money, he hopped a freight train and "rode the rods," a feat that left him stranded for ten days in the Allegheny County Jail in Pittsburgh, Pennsylvania, in 1902 because he could not pay the requisite train fare.

From 1902 through late 1907 Sandburg wrote for minor journals in Chicago and tried to launch a career on the Lyceum and traveling Chautauqua lecture circuits, specializing in orations on Whitman, Lincoln, Shaw, and the ideals of socialism. Emblazoned on the 1907 advertisement for his lecture on Walt Whitman titled "An American Vagabond" were the words "Books are but empty nothings compared with living, pulsing men and women. Life is stranger and greater than anything ever written about it."

His fiery intensity as an orator won the attention of Wisconsin Social-Democratic party leader Winfield P. Gaylord, who recruited Sandburg to become a party organizer. From 1907 until 1912 Sandburg campaigned vigorously throughout Wisconsin for social democracy, writing for newspapers and journals, organizing workers, making stump speeches, and in 1910 serving as secretary to Emil Seidel, the first socialist mayor of Milwaukee. At Social-Democratic party headquarters in Milwaukee in December 1907 Sandburg met Lilian Steichen, a young Socialist and schoolteacher, a Phi Beta Kappa graduate of the University of Chicago (1904), and the younger sister of painter and photographer Eduard (later Edward) Steichen, who had already won wide recognition in New York and Paris.

During the first six months of 1908, Lilian Steichen and Charles Sandburg corresponded, he from the out-posts of Wisconsin and she from Princeton, Illinois, where she was teaching. They fell in love and were married in 1908 in Milwaukee. They had three children. Because his wife encouraged Sandburg to reclaim his christened name, he became once and for all Carl Sandburg.

In his spare time during the Milwaukee years, Sandburg wrote poems replete with such rugged, unorthodox free verse and such unconventionally realistic subject matter that he himself could not even be sure they were poetry. He continually experimented with poetic images of the working men, women, and children whose harrowing problems he confronted daily in the Milwaukee municipal office. Always the passionate advocate of social justice and equality, Sandburg gradually became disenchanted with Social-Democratic party politics in Milwaukee because of the ever-widening gap between reality and the ideal. In 1912 he moved his family to Chicago, where he went to work on the staff of the socialist *Chicago Evening World*. Later he worked for other Chicago journals, including the Scripps daily tabloid, the *Day Book*, simultaneously writing occasional articles for the *International Socialist Review*, usually under pseudonyms. Both of these journals and a handful of others also published his poetry.

Otherwise Sandburg received no significant affirmation as a poet until Harriet Monroe, founder and editor of the landmark Chicago journal *Poetry: A Magazine of Verse*, accepted six of his poems for publication in the March 1914 issue. In effect, his career as a poet was launched, and he stepped into the stimulating company of poets and writers such as Vachel Lindsay, Edgar Lee Masters, Theodore Dreiser, Floyd Dell, and Eunice Tietjens, who inhabited the modest *Poetry* offices. From Europe, Ezra Pound, associate editor of *Poetry*, wrote letters of advice and encouragement to Sandburg, and Masters and Dreiser urged him to collect his poems in a book. Another *Poetry* associate editor, Alice Corbin Henderson, persuaded young editor and book salesman Alfred Harcourt to read Sandburg's manuscript for Henry Holt and Company, who published Sandburg's *Chicago Poems* in 1916.

This first volume of poetry articulated his lifelong themes. From the beginning, Sandburg the poet gave a powerful voice to the "people—the mob—the crowd—the mass" (p. 172). He championed the cause of "the Poor, millions of the Poor, patient and toiling; more patient than crags, tides, and stars; innumerable, patient as the darkness of night" (p. 6). He was quickly established as the poet of the American people, pleading their cause; reciting their songs, stories, and proverbs; celebrating their spirit and their vernacular; and commemorating the watershed experiences of their shared national life.

His second volume of poetry, *Cornhuskers*, was published by Henry Holt in 1918, but in 1919 Sandburg moved with Alfred Harcourt to the new company he had founded, Harcourt, Brace & Howe, which published collections of poems titled *Smoke and Steel*

(1920); *Good Morning, America* (1928); *The People, Yes* (1936), an epic, book-length poem about the depression; and *Complete Poems* (1950), for which Sandburg was awarded the Pulitzer Prize in poetry.

Sandburg moved as restlessly through literary forms as he did through the American landscape, also distinguishing himself as a journalist at the *Chicago Daily News*. He covered World War I in Europe for the Newspaper Enterprise Association, and the articles he wrote as a syndicated columnist during World War II were collected in *Home Front Memo* in 1943. Between wars he investigated the American scene, covering politics, crime, business, and civil rights. His farsighted investigative reportage of racial strife in Chicago for the *Chicago Daily News* resulted in *The Chicago Race Riots, July 1919*, published in 1919.

The poet of the American vernacular was not only a tough, gregarious reporter but a rollicking folk musician who accompanied himself somewhat crudely on the guitar while he sang American folk songs in his mellifluous baritone. He interspersed his songs with poems and commentary, and audiences across the country so loved Sandburg the showman that until the end of his life he was in great demand as a consummate platform entertainer. He had collected folk songs since his hobo days, interviewing people in his travels across the country over many years and setting down the lyrics and the notations in his pocket notebooks. He gave many of these songs their first publication in *The American Songbag* in 1927.

Sandburg was also a devoted and tender family man. Before World War I he had begun inventing zany, sometimes poignant American fairy tales for his children. Two events influenced him to develop those stories into a book: the First World War and the ensuing economic, political, and racial strife left him profoundly disillusioned, and then his eldest daughter was diagnosed with epilepsy, for which there was as yet no seizure-suppressing medication. From that global and personal misery sprang a delightful series of storybooks for young people: *Rootabaga Stories* (1922), *Rootabaga Pigeons* (1923), *Rootabaga Country* (1929), and *Potato Face* (1930). Sandburg also wrote two books of poems for children: *Early Moon* (1930) and *Wind Song* (1960).

The popularity of the *Rootabaga* books prompted Alfred Harcourt to suggest that Sandburg write a juvenile biography of Abraham Lincoln, whose life had fascinated Sandburg since his boyhood in Illinois, Lincoln's home state. Eagerly setting to work on the proposed short book for young people, Sandburg soon became engrossed in thousands of Lincoln's papers scattered throughout the country, most still in the hands of private individuals. His growing absorption in the Lincoln research quickly convinced Sandburg that he should write a full-fledged biography that would evoke not only Lincoln the tragic hero but the national spirit his life and death embodied.

With the appearance of the massive, two-volume *Abraham Lincoln: The Prairie Years* (1926), Sandburg the poet was superseded by Sandburg the biographer, who made a small fortune from these bestselling books. He immediately set to work on a four-volume sequel, *Abraham Lincoln: The War Years*, which dominated his creative life until its completion in 1939. He received the Pulitzer Prize in history for *The War Years*.

In 1943 the most famous troubadour poet and Lincoln biographer in the United States was ready for another new challenge. He signed a lucrative contract with Metro-Goldwyn-Mayer studios in Hollywood to write an epic, multigenerational American novel that would be converted into a motion picture. The movie was never made, but the novel, *Remembrance Rock*, published in 1948, was a popular if not a critical success.

Sandburg was awarded the American Academy of Arts and Letters gold medal in biography and history in 1952, one of numerous honors and awards, and settled down to finish writing his memoirs at "Connemara," the beautiful 245-acre farm in Flat Rock, North Carolina, that he had purchased in 1945. By that time his wife had begun to breed champion dairy goats that needed wider grazing lands and a more temperate winter climate than their home on the dunes of Lake Michigan afforded. In 1953 Sandburg published *Always the Young Strangers*, the lyrical, autobiographical account of the first twenty years of his life. He was a much-honored American icon by then, an elder statesman who freely spoke his mind on contemporary issues and enjoyed the adulation of an international audience.

Sandburg set aside work on the second volume of his autobiography, *Ever the Winds of Chance* (posthumously published in 1983) to collaborate with his world-famous brother-in-law, Edward Steichen, on an unprecedented photographic exhibition, *The Family of Man* (1955). The work included 503 pictures gathered by Steichen from sixty-eight countries to serve as a "mirror of the essential oneness of mankind throughout the world." In an era of Cold War and McCarthyism, this was a bold and courageous affirmation of the ideal of global community, as well as, for both Sandburg and Steichen, a culmination of the work of their lives. Steichen, then director of the Department of Photography for the Museum of Modern Art in New York, wrote the introduction to the exhibition catalog, which sold more than 5 million copies by the mid-1990s, and Sandburg wrote the prologue, recapitulating the themes that had animated his work for more than half a century. He celebrated the universal "toil, struggle, blood and dreams, among lovers . . . workers, loafers, fighters, players, gamblers . . . landlords and the landless, the loved and the unloved, the brutal and the compassionate—one big family hugging close to the ball of Earth for its life and being."

In 1959 Sandburg gave a Lincoln Day address before a joint session of Congress and later in the year traveled with Steichen on a State Department tour to open *The Family of Man* exhibition in the Soviet Union. He lived in Hollywood during much of 1960, working as George Stevens's creative consultant on

The Greatest Story Ever Told, and he published his last book of poetry, *Honey and Salt*, in 1963. The next year he received the Presidential Medal of Freedom. To the end of his life, accolades continued to pour in, and he took special pride in the more than half a dozen public schools named in his honor.

Sandburg sized himself up in the preface to *Complete Poems*:

All my life I have been trying to learn to read, to see and hear, and to write. At sixty-five I began my first novel, and the five years lacking a month I took to finish it, I was still traveling, still a seeker. . . . It could be, in the grace of God, I shall live to be eighty-nine, as did [the Japanese poet] Hokusai, and speaking my farewell to earthly scenes, I might paraphrase: "If God had let me live five years longer I should have been a writer."

Considered garrulous, sentimental, and dated by some, and powerful, original, and timeless by others, Sandburg spoke to and for the American century in which he lived and did his work. At the Carl Sandburg Memorial Ceremony on the steps of the Lincoln Memorial on 17 September 1967, nearly two months after Sandburg's death at Connemara, poet Archibald MacLeish told President Lyndon B. Johnson, Chief Justice Earl Warren, and thousands of Sandburg's fellow Americans that "with Sandburg it is the body of the work that weighs, the sum of it, a whole quite literally greater than the total of its parts. . . . Sandburg had a *subject*—and the subject was belief in man."

• The Carl Sandburg Collection at the University of Illinois Library in Urbana-Champaign is the major repository of Sandburg's papers. Smaller collections of Sandburg papers exist at Connemara, the Carl Sandburg Home National Historic Site, now a national park, in Flat Rock, N.C. Other important Sandburg manuscript collections are housed at the University of Virginia and Knox College in Galesburg, Ill. Other major published works by Sandburg include *Abe Lincoln Grows Up* (1928); *Harvest Poems* (1960); *Lincoln Collector: The Story of Oliver R. Barrett's Great Private Collection*, with Oliver R. Barrett (1949); *Mary Lincoln: Wife and Widow*, with Paul Angle (1932); *The Sandburg Range* (1957); and *Steichen the Photographer* (1929). Sandburg's daughters and granddaughter produced helpful editions of his work, as well as memoirs. See Margaret Sandburg, ed., *Breathing Tokens* (1978), for previously unpublished poems, and *The Poet and the Dream Girl: The Love Letters of Lilian Steichen and Carl Sandburg* (1987); Helga Sandburg, *A Great and Glorious Romance* (1978), *Sweet Music: A Book of Family Reminiscence and Song*, with a preface by Carl Sandburg (1963), and " . . . Where Love Begins" (1989); and Paula Steichen, *My Connemara* (1969), and "Hyacinths and Biscuits," in *Carl Sandburg Home Handbook 117* (1982). Two important editions of Sandburg's letters are *Carl Sandburg, Philip Green Wright and the Asgard Press*, comp. Joan St. C. Crane (1975), and *The Letters of Carl Sandburg*, ed. Herbert Mitgang (1968). A comprehensive biography is Penelope Niven, *Carl Sandburg: A Biography* (1991). Other biographical studies include North Callahan, *Carl Sandburg, Lincoln of Our Literature* (1970); Richard Crowder, *Carl Sandburg* (1964); Gregory d'Alessio, *Old Troubadour* (1987); Karl Detzer, *Carl Sandburg: A Study in Personality and Background* (1941); Hazel Durnell, *The America of Carl Sandburg* (1966); and Harry Golden, *Carl Sandburg* (1961; repr. 1988). For an analysis of Sandburg's controversial political journalism and poetry, consult Phillip Yanella, *The Other Carl Sandburg* (1996). Additional unpublished or uncollected Sandburg poems have been gathered in George Hendrick and Willene Hendrick, eds., *Carl Sandburg: Billy Sunday and Other Poems* (1993) and *Carl Sandburg: Selected Poems* (1996). For a collection of Sandburg's film criticism, see Dale and Doug Fetherling, eds., *Carl Sandburg at the Movies: A Poet in the Silent Era, 1920–1927* (1985). For Carl Sandburg on Broadway, consult Norman Corwin, *The World of Carl Sandburg* (1961).

PENELOPE NIVEN

SANDE, Earle (13 Nov. 1898–20 Aug. 1968), thoroughbred jockey, was born in Groton, South Dakota, the son of John C. Sande, a railway maintenance worker. His mother's name is unknown. After spending his earliest years in Groton, nine-year-old Sande moved with his family to a farm near American Falls, Idaho, where he received a public education into his high school years. Growing up on a farm, he came to know a great deal about the behavior, care, and riding of horses. At age 12 he bought his own pony, and when he left school five years later he quickly found work as a racetrack exercise boy.

Just before World War I, horse racing in the American West was still a rough-and-tumble activity. Such an open, fluid setting gave Sande many chances to ride in competition at state and county fairs and even on the dirt streets of rural towns from Idaho to Arizona. He reputedly was a likable youth, and older riders helped him hone his skills and tactics.

By age 18 Sande was ready to step up to a tougher competitive level. At first he rode at the Fair Grounds in New Orleans, bringing home his first feature race winner, Prince S, in early 1918. During that racing year he won on 22 percent of his mounts (158 victories in 707 races), a better-than-average winning ratio for the time but still well below what he would achieve. Later that season he guided Billy Kelly to a win in the Columbus Handicap at Laurel Park near Baltimore.

Sande made himself known throughout racing in 1920. He signed to ride for Sam Hildreth, the leading U.S. trainer of thoroughbreds five times over an eight-year span (1909–1911 and 1916–1917). Sande was aboard Sir Barton—the first of all Triple Crown winners the previous year—in the winner's circle at the Saratoga Handicap. He also rode the great Man o'War to victories in major stakes and handicap races in that three-year-old's undefeated season. By then many observers agreed that jockeys Johnny Loftus and Clarence Kummer were among his only peers.

Sande continued his association with Hildreth through 1924, often wearing the Roncocas Stable silks of oilman Harry Sinclair; during each of those years Hildreth was the sport's top money-winning trainer. Sande's biggest victory came that spring with Grey Lag in the Belmont Stakes, his first of five career Belmont winners. Sande's 1921 winning percentage was a phenomenal 33 percent (112 wins), a standard unchallenged in the twentieth century. Of all his mounts that year, he finished first, second, or third on more than

70 percent of them. At age 22 he was widely recognized as thoroughbred racing's preeminent jockey. Sometime during this period Sande married Marion Casey, who died in 1927; they had no children.

The year 1922 was good for Sande, but 1923 was his finest. Not only was he the leading jockey in America with 28 percent of his mounts winners, but he rode the purse-winning leader of the year, Zev, to a longshot victory on a muddy track at Churchill Downs in the Kentucky Derby and to a win in the Belmont Stakes. Overall, Zev triumphed in 12 of 14 starts, while Sande for the year rode 39 stakes and handicap winners.

Appropriate to his roughhouse apprentice years, Sande was a strong, aggressive rider whose nickname among racetrackers was the "Handy Guy." He never hesitated to use the whip to goad his mounts to the maximum, and he was a master tactician and an intense competitor.

In 1924, leaving Hildreth to sign on with owner Joseph Widener, Sande won another Belmont Stakes aboard Mad Play. At New York's Saratoga Park in August, however, he was trampled in a five-horse spill, suffering career-threatening injuries. Yet despite dire predictions he recovered to win the 1925 Kentucky Derby on Flying Ebony. Two years later he guided yet another Belmont victor in Chance Shot. Then, shortly after the Belmont, he was set down by the stewards for using rough tactics, and his suspension may have caused him to fall victim to the jockey's nemesis: inability to "make the weight." Too heavy to find quality mounts, he remained suspended for part of 1928 and effectively retired at age 30 in 1929.

Everything changed in 1930 when Sande was matched with the horse of a lifetime, Gallant Fox. Sande won nine major races on the great three-year-old, which, after Sir Barton, became only the second Triple Crown winner. Besides the Kentucky Derby and the Belmont Stakes, Gallant Fox's victory in the Preakness (the second "crown") at Pimlico marked Sande's first and only triumph in that event.

In 1931 Sande's riding victories dwindled to fewer than half his peak seasons' totals, and he retired from racing. A year later he married Marion Kummer; childless, they divorced in 1945. With his jockey's earnings, Sande put together his own stable and acted as his own trainer, but the venture was short-lived. He next became an independent trainer, contracting with an occasional owner of prominence such as John Hay Whitney. As a thoroughbred conditioner, Sande met with enough success to be honored in 1938 with the New York Turf Writers Training Award. That was his high point; from then on his fortunes gradually but steadily declined until he gave up training altogether by the late 1940s.

Separated entirely from thoroughbred racing for the first time since his teens, Sande attempted a new career as a professional singer. Although he was capable enough to perform in vaudeville and to have his own radio broadcast for a brief while on NBC, he never found any greater success.

In 1953 Sande made a quixotic attempt to come back as a jockey. He had 10 mounts, but only one winner—at Jamaica Park in Queens, New York—before giving up the futile gesture. Broke now after poor real estate investments, he became a hanger-on at major New York metropolitan tracks, but, increasingly bad-tempered and erratic, he steadily withdrew into a solitary life. Friends paid his expenses to travel to Jacksonville, Oregon, to live with his father. He died in Jacksonville.

Sande is widely accepted as one of the most outstanding jockeys in U.S. thoroughbred racing history. During an injury-interrupted career that lasted barely a decade, he rode 968 winners and achieved the remarkable statistical marks of a career-victory average of 26.4 percent and a 60.9 percent average for in-the-money finishers. In 1955 he was elected to the Jockey's Hall of Fame and to the National Museum of Racing's Hall of Fame. His finest mounts were some of the greatest ever: Sir Barton, Man o'War, and Gallant Fox.

• Biographical and career information on Sande is surprisingly difficult to come by. He is discussed in a major entry in David L. Porter, ed., *Biographical Dictionary of American Sports: Outdoor Sports* (1988). Contemporary news articles worth consulting are in the *New York Times*, Apr.–June 1930. An obituary is in the *New York Times*, 21 Aug. 1968.

ROBERT MIRANDON

SANDEMAN, Robert (29 Apr. 1718–2 Apr. 1771), founder of the Sandemanian churches in New England, was born in Perth, Scotland, the son of David Sandeman and Margaret Ramsay. His father was a wealthy linen merchant and magistrate. Around 1734 Robert enrolled at the University of Edinburgh, where he intended to become either a minister in the national Church of Scotland or a medical doctor.

At Edinburgh Sandeman met John Glas, founder and leader of the Glassite sect. In the 1720s, Glas, a minister in the Church of Scotland at Tealing (near Dundee), had concluded that the concept of a national church contradicted the teaching of Scripture. In 1725 nearly one hundred members of his congregation agreed to follow Glas's teaching and establish their faith on Scripture alone. Glas and his followers were soon deemed a threat to the social and ecclesiastical order of Scotland, and following the publication of his views, he was suspended (1728) and deposed (1730) by the Church of Scotland. As a fervent restorationist—one who seeks to reform the Christian faith by restoring New Testament teachings and practices of the church—Glas not only advocated congregational independency and the separation of the church from the state, but he also promoted a return to the early church's practice of weekly communion, believer's baptism by immersion, and footwashing. When Glas visited Edinburgh in 1734 to form a "Glassite" meetinghouse, he found an enthusiastic convert in Sandeman.

After completing two terms at the university, Sandeman returned to Perth as an apprentice in the weaving business. From 1736 to 1744 he and his brother William manufactured linen. In 1737 he married Glas's eldest daughter, Katherine. After his election to the office of elder in the Perth Glassite church in 1744, Sandeman withdrew from the weaving business and devoted his energies to the church.

For a quarter of a century, beginning in the mid-1750s, Sandeman greatly assisted in the expansion of Glassite congregations. His aggressive and controversial ways overshadowed the amiable manner of his father-in-law, and gradually Sandeman became the movement's leader. In 1757 he published *Letters on Theron and Aspasio*, his major theological treatise and a work that thrust the small and insignificant Glassites into public view. Earlier, Sandeman had carried on a private correspondence with Evangelical Anglican clergyman James Hervey over Hervey's theological views expressed in *Dialogue between Theron and Aspasio* (1755). Sandeman's *Letters* was a public rejoinder to Hervey's Calvinism, particularly Hervey's defense of the doctrine of the "imputed righteousness" of Christ. This doctrine, first expressed by Martin Luther, developed by Philip Melancthon, and taken up by virtually all of the major Protestant reformers, held that God's justifying righteousness was imputed to the sinner by God through the merits of Christ's righteousness. Sandeman argued otherwise, attacked the doctrine as unscriptural, and insisted that faith alone, not a divine transaction, ensured salvation. Sandeman advanced an intellectualist view of faith, which he defined as a simple assent to scriptural testimony about Christ. His convictions put him squarely at odds with the writings of Jonathan Edwards, whose views on evangelical repentance and the role of the affections were popular among evangelicals on both sides of the Atlantic. Sandeman thus rejected the evangelical conception of an emotional, heartfelt conversion experience as a necessary precondition to salvation.

In 1760 Sandeman's *Letters* were published in America. The book gained favor with a few New England ministers, including two Connecticut clergymen, David Judson of Newtown and Ebenezer White of Danbury. Disillusioned with the theological factionalism and spiritual torpor then prevalent among Congregationalists, Judson, White, and several other clergy found in Sandeman's writings a tonic for Congregationalism's ills. A correspondence ensued with Sandeman, who, encouraged by the reception of his views, embarked for the colonies. He arrived in Boston in the fall of 1764, accompanied by James Cargill, a Dunkeld (Scotland) Elder.

Sandeman itinerated up and down the Atlantic coast, preaching wherever he could find an audience—in taverns, public houses, and Separatist churches. While he attracted sizeable crowds, they tended to be more curious than convinced of his message. But Sandeman persisted, even when threatened with violence. On 14 December 1764 a Portsmouth, New Hampshire, mob broke the windows of a meetinghouse where Sandeman was preaching and gave him four days to leave. Leave he did, but by the following May Portsmouth Sandemanians (as Glassites were called in America) established a church. In 1765, when the Stamp Act was issued, Sandeman and his Portsmouth followers became even more unpopular when they expressed their loyalty to the British Crown. They proclaimed that Scriptures explicitly taught the duty of citizens to support those in political authority over them. Their views, however, enjoined a passive rather than active loyalty; that is, Sandemanians recognized England's authority, but they refused to actively support Britain's efforts to quash the rising independence movement. During the Revolution, however, such distinctions meant little, as in 1777 when several Sandemanians were ordered out of New Haven for expressing Loyalist sentiments.

Sandeman and his followers encountered opposition not only to their political and theological views, but their ecclesiastical practices were often ridiculed. As restorationists the Sandemanians reintroduced the primitive church practices of footwashing, the love feast, and the kiss of peace, for which they were derisively dubbed "Kissites." Samuel Finley, Presbyterian minister and president of the College of New Jersey, typified a common sentiment among the established clergy in noting that Sandeman was "an instrument of Satan to divide the Church."

In the fall of 1766 Sandeman settled permanently in Danbury, Connecticut. As in previous settings, he was met by resistance from town authorities. In 1770 a Danbury judge ordered Sandeman and a cohort arrested and fined £40 each because they ignored an order issued four weeks earlier to leave town as "strangers and undesirable persons." Sandeman pled his case, the sentence was never executed, and he continued to minister to a congregation that became the largest, most influential, and longest lasting in New England.

During his tenure in America, Sandeman gave himself wholly to missionary work and to establishing Sandemanian congregations. He had no family obligations (his wife died childless in 1746), nor did he need to work, for his followers shared their possessions with him. By the time he died, in Danbury, churches were formed in Taunton, Massachusetts, Portsmouth, New Hampshire, and Danbury and Newtown, Connecticut. In the 1770s groups of followers worshiped regularly in New Haven, Providence, and Boston.

In several respects Sandeman's convictions anticipated developments that recast America's religious landscape in the quarter century after his death. His views on the separation of church and state, shared by Baptists (who otherwise opposed him) and other religious dissenters, achieved a legal status in the U.S. Constitution. Sandeman also indirectly influenced the restorationist ideas of Alexander Campbell, founder of the Disciples of Christ. While Campbell rejected much of Sandeman's theology, during his student year at the University of Glasgow (1808–1809), he was attracted to Sandeman's ecclesiology as mediated by the Haldane brothers. Not surprisingly, when Campbell visited the Sandemanians of Danbury in the 1840s, the church transferred to the Disciples.

• The primary collections of Sandemanian material are in the Dundee University Library (MS 9); the Massachusetts Historical Society has the Sandeman-Barrell Papers, a volume of correspondence between Sandeman and Nathaniel Barrell, a prominent Portsmouth merchant, member of New Hampshire's Governor's Council, and ardent Sandemanian. The Stiles Collection at Yale University contains letters about Sandeman, written between 1764 and 1769, by twelve clergymen. Sandeman's other works include *An Epistolary Correspondence between S. P. and R. S.* (1760), letters between Samuel Pike (a London dissident) and Sandeman; *An Essay on Preaching* (1763); *Some Thoughts on Christianity* (1764); *Discourses on Passages of Scripture: With Essays and Letters* (1857); Daniel Macintosh, ed., *Letters in Correspondence by Robert Sandeman, John Glas, and Their Contemporaries* (1851); and James Morison, ed., *Supplementary Volume of Letters and Other Documents by John Glas, Robert Sandeman and Their Contemporaries* (1865).

For thoughts by his American contemporaries, see Samuel Langdon, *An Impartial Examination of Mr. Robert Sandeman's Letters on Theron and Aspasio* (1765); and Franklin B. Dexter, *The Literary Diary of Ezra Stiles* (3 vols. 1901). Williston Walker, "The Sandemanians of New England," *Annual Report of the American Historical Association, 1901* (1902), remains the standard treatment of Sandeman in America, but also see Jean F. Hankins, "A Different Kind of Loyalist: The Sandemanians of New England during the Revolutionary War," *New England Quarterly* 60 (June 1987): 223–49, for a recent interpretation of Sandeman's political views. Lynn McMillon, *Restoration Roots* (1983), charts the rise of the Sandemanians and their impact on America.

DAVID W. KLING

SANDERS, Daniel Clarke (3 May 1768–18 Oct. 1850), Congregational clergyman and educator, was born in Sturbridge, Massachusetts, the son of Michael Sanders and Azubah Clarke. His father died in 1773. Sanders was probably the first member of his family to attend college. Aided by scholarships and loans, he worked his way through Harvard University and graduated Phi Beta Kappa in 1788.

Heavily in debt, Sanders taught in a grammar school in Cambridge while studying theology under the direction of Rev. Thomas Prentiss of Medfield. In 1790 he was licensed to preach by the Dedham Association. In 1794 he was ordained as a pastor in Vergennes, Vermont, where in 1792 he had married Nancy Fitch, the daughter of Dr. Jabez Fitch.

In August 1799 he was invited to preach in Burlington, where he was elected secretary of the corporation of the university, which had been chartered in 1791. He opened a preparatory school in the college house, and in January 1800 he was appointed a trustee of the University of Vermont. In October he was chosen to be its first president.

During the university's first six years Sanders was its sole instructor, overseer of the physical plant, solicitor of legislative funds, and principal fundraiser. He personally directed the studies of all the classes, a task that took eight and often ten hours a day. He was also general supervisor over the management of lands and funds and even cut some of the tall pines on the college property with his own hands. In addition, he preached regularly to the only religious society in the town from 1799 to 1807. In 1807 there were forty-seven students enrolled, and he was aided by a tutor and two years later by a professor of mathematics and natural philosophy and a teacher of anatomy and surgery. By 1809 the foundations of a library were laid and a public building, 4 stories high and 160 feet long, had been completed, with chapel, lecture rooms, and rooms for students.

When President Sanders opened the University of Vermont in 1800, he personified the institution: he literally combined the administration, faculty, and staff into his own image. As in most American colleges of that period, Sanders as president was spokesman to the various constituencies—the town, the business community, and state legislators—and he set the tone of instruction on which the university's reputation in academic circles would eventually be based. Later he had assistants, but he did not delegate administrative work. Thus he exemplified a style of university leadership that prevailed during the nineteenth century.

Under Sanders's leadership the only religious requirement for admission to the university was proof of a "good moral character." In 1808 Sanders reported that there were sixty-one "paying" students when tuition was only $12 a year. His salary of $600 was augmented by an additional $400 paid by the parish of Burlington. The students increased from four the first year to over fifty in 1813, when the university was in serious financial difficulty because the War of 1812 had disrupted its operations.

Two years after the beginning of the War of 1812, the board of trustees suspended instruction and leased the main university building to the government for use as barracks for U.S. Army soldiers. In the summer of 1813 the army commandeered the 48-room building as an arsenal and posted a guard. The troops invaded the college grounds, broke down Sanders's fences, trampled his grain and corn, and smashed his pumpkins against the college steps. They rioted through the college halls, breaking into rooms when students were away and stealing property. The federal government finally settled the claims of the university for rental and damage to its building from occupancy by troops and paid $5,600 in compensation to the closed and now debt-ridden institution.

As students departed for other colleges or found work, the trustees dismissed President Sanders and the faculty without explaining whether or not they were to return later. At this time Sanders was experiencing a series of tragic misfortunes. His wife was a victim of occasional attacks of insanity, and five of his eight children had recently died in an epidemic. Moreover, his book, *A History of the Indian Wars with the First Settlers of the United States, Particularly in New England*, published anonymously in Montpelier in 1812, had aroused harsh criticism from Rev. John Hough, professor of divinity at Middlebury College, because of its criticisms of colonial cruelty and bigotry toward the natives. This book, which made an important contribution to the study of early colonial history, was one of the first works to express some sympathy for Native Americans. Sanders's theological opponents did not share his sympathy. Hough, in particular, attacked Sanders for maligning the venerable fathers of New England in suggesting that "orthodox creeds do not always sanctify the heart and conduct" and accused Sanders of "the most barefaced and mischievous heresy." This edition is scarce because Sanders destroyed most of the books after the controversy. In 1814 Sanders was unemployed without adequate financial resources.

From 1815 to 1829 Sanders was pastor of the First Congregational Church in Medfield, Massachusetts, where his parents and grandparents had been born and where he had preached his first sermon. During the fourteen years of his pastorate in Medfield he became well known as an eloquent speaker, and he left over thirty published discourses. In 1820 and 1821 he was a member of the Massachusetts Constitutional Convention, and he represented the Medfield district in the Massachusetts house from 1833 to 1836. Opposed to theological controversies, he tried unsuccessfully to guide his church through a tumultuous period. After the Calvinists seceded, he refused to remain with the Unitarians and resigned his pastorate in 1829. He outlived his long-ailing wife and two of his three remaining children and died in Medfield.

• The manuscript "Autobiography of Daniel Clarke Sanders, D.D., First President of the University of Vermont" is in the possession of Nancy Wolcott of Scituate, Mass.; a photocopy and two typescript copies are in the Wilbur Library, University of Vermont Archives. Also noteworthy are Jeffrey D. Marshall, "Building the Foundation, 1791–1824–The First President, Daniel Clarke Sanders," in *Universitas Viridis Montis: An Exhibition of Documents and Artifacts Telling the Story of the University of Vermont, 1791–1991* (1991); P. Jeffrey Potash, "Years of Trial: Religion, Money, War, Fire, and the Competition with Middlebury," in *The University of Vermont: The First Two Hundred Years*, ed. Robert V. Daniels (1991); and Julian Ira Lindsay, *Tradition Looks Forward: The University of Vermont, A History, 1791–1904* (1954). Most of the pictures taken of Sanders were destroyed by fire. There is, however, an official portrait in oil by James Sanford Ellsworth painted about 1835 at Medfield, Mass., hanging in Memorial Lounge, Waterman Building, University of Vermont, which is reproduced in Lindsay's history.

S. ALEXANDER RIPPA

SANDERS, George (3 July 1906–24 Apr. 1972), actor, was born in St. Petersburg, Russia, the second son of Henry Sanders, a Russian industrial manager of English descent, and Margaret Kolbe, daughter of an Estonian industrialist of Scottish descent. The family moved to England during World War I and remained there after the Bolsheviks seized power in Russia. George and his older brother, Tom, were educated at Dunhurst Preparatory School, Bedales School in Hampshire, and Brighton College in Sussex. Sanders acted, boxed, and won academic prizes at school but left, he said, with "a sense of utter worthlessness and the conviction that I was too stupid to cope with life." One biographer has argued that the snobbery and hostility Sanders encountered as a foreign-born schoolboy and his own deep embarrassment at his family's financially straitened circumstances explain both his notorious stinginess in later life and the feelings of inadequacy that he never overcame and that influenced important career decisions.

After college, Sanders worked briefly for a textile company. In 1926 he went to Argentina as a representative of the British and American Tobacco Company. After four years there he was expelled for fighting a duel over a woman. Back in London, he drifted into acting, making his first stage appearance in the revue *Ballyhoo* in 1932. After a spell in radio plays and a supporting role as a Regency rake in Noël Coward's *Conversation Piece*, he secured his first leading stage role as a young airman in *Further Outlook* (1935), which brought him good reviews. A small supporting part in *The Man Who Could Work Miracles* (1936) launched his film career, and he signed a long-term contract with British and Dominion Films. When that studio's assets were acquired by 20th Century-Fox, Sanders made a highly successful Hollywood debut as the icily villainous aristocratic cad Lord Everett Stacy in the historical epic *Lloyd's of London* (1936). Sanders thereafter became the supreme exemplar of a now largely obsolete film type. The contemptuous curl of the lip, the sardonic lift of the eyebrow, the wicked twinkle in the eye, the purring drawl of the voice, Sanders mastered all of these mannerisms and blended them to create a unique gallery of suave swine.

Notable among his roles were the arrogantly charming Jack Favell in *Rebecca* (1940), the ruthless misogynist painter Charles Strickland in *The Moon and Sixpence* (1942), Oscar Wilde's epigrammatic Lord Henry Wotton in *The Picture of Dorian Gray* (1945), the heartless womanizer Georges Duroy in *The Private Affairs of Bel Ami* (1947), and the witty and cynical English King Charles II in *Forever Amber* (1947). In such roles he etched himself permanently into collective cinematic memory. But in a career spanning 111 films, he played many other parts.

During the 1940s Sanders appeared in a number of major films by leading directors. In addition to *Rebecca*, he played a leading role for Alfred Hitchcock in *Foreign Correspondent* (1940). He appeared in Fritz Lang's *Man Hunt* (1941), Jean Renoir's *This Land Is Mine* (1943), and a trio of elegant melodramas for Douglas Sirk: *Summer Storm* (1944), *A Scandal in Paris* (1946), and *Lured* (1947). Sanders is also fondly remembered as the debonair man-about-town hero of two RKO "B" movie series, *The Saint* (five films) and *The Falcon*. After four films as the Falcon, he passed the role on to his brother, Tom Conway, whom Sanders had helped launch on a motion picture career. A high point of Sanders's acting life came when he won the Academy Award for best supporting actor for his performance as the mordant theater critic Addison De Witt in *All about Eve* (1950). Sanders, however, claimed to see little of value in his work, observing with characteristic tongue in cheek: "If I have accidentally given brilliant performances on the screen this was entirely due to circumstances beyond my control." In fact, he was a thorough professional, as fellow actors and actresses have testified. Despite his success, he detested Hollywood, writing in his diary of "the rackets, the bullshit, the sham."

During the 1950s Sanders was often cast in costume epics not geared to his acting strengths. He recorded several albums of songs in the mid-1950s but missed the chance to take over the starring male role in the stage version of *South Pacific* on Broadway because of characteristic fears about his vocal inadequacy. But there was a welcome return to the vintage cad in *Death of a Scoundrel* (1956) and Fritz Lang's *While the City Sleeps* (1956). In the late 1950s, he returned to live in Europe, and although he worked steadily, only a few of his films, notably *A Shot in the Dark* (1964) and *The Quiller Memorandum* (1966), were memorable. After the mid-1960s, he was mainly confined to pedestrian horror and suspense films, culminating in *Psychomania* (1972). His distinctive voice, however, was heard to memorable effect as Shere Khan, the tiger, in Walt Disney Pictures' animated *Jungle Book* (1967).

Outside of films, the 1960s proved a disastrous decade for him in many ways. He became involved in a catastrophic business venture to make and sell sausages in England. When the company, called CAD-CO, collapsed in 1964, leaving massive debts, Sanders went bankrupt and was severely criticized by a government inquiry. The death in 1967 of his third wife, Benita Hume, meant the end of a marriage that had provided stability and happiness. There was a troubled final relationship with writer Helga Moray, the loss of his beloved Majorcan home, and finally a series of strokes that made it increasingly difficult for him to work. Work always had enabled him to keep his inner demons at bay, and that bulwark was now lost. In 1972 he committed suicide in a Barcelona hotel, taking an overdose of Nembutal and leaving a note reading: "Dear world, I am leaving because I am bored. I feel I have lived long enough. I am leaving you with your worries in this sweet cesspool. Good luck."

Sanders always sought to convey the impression in interviews and in his autobiography, *Memoirs of a Professional Cad* (1960), that he was the same offscreen as on. But in a revealing and sympathetic biography, *George Sanders: An Exhausted Life* (1990), Richard VanderBeets, drawing on Sanders's letters and diaries and on memories of his relatives, paints a very different picture. Although Sanders was a civilized and accomplished man, widely read, fluent in German and Spanish, a sketch artist, and a good singer with a rich baritone voice, his aloof, self-confident, acid-tongued public image was a mask. It concealed a complex, chronically insecure, reclusive figure who suffered bouts of depression and underwent twenty years of psychoanalysis.

Sanders kept his private life discreet but had love affairs with several of Hollywood's leading ladies including Gene Tierney, Dolores Del Rio, Hedy Lamarr, and Lucille Ball. He was married four times, first to the actress Susan Larson (real name, Elsie Poole), whom he married in 1940 and divorced in 1947. In 1949 he married the actress Zsa Zsa Gabor; they divorced in 1954. Five years later he married the actress Benita Hume, widow of Ronald Colman. After her death in 1967, he married Magda Gabor, Zsa Zsa's sister, in 1970; they were divorced in 1971. Sanders's best performances, of which there are a commendably large number, continue to give enormous pleasure and remain an object lesson in how to convey—without apparent effort—polish, poise, and wicked wit.

• There is an account of Sanders's film career in Tony Thomas's *Cads and Cavaliers* (1973). A longtime friend, actor Brian Aherne, published a collection of letters to him from George Sanders and Benita Hume under the title *A Dreadful Man* (1979). Zsa Zsa Gabor recorded her memories of Sanders in her autobiography, *One Lifetime Is Not Enough* (1991).

JEFFREY RICHARDS

SANDERS, George Nicholas (27 Feb. 1812–12 Aug. 1873), political booster and Confederate agent, was born in Lexington, Kentucky, the son of Lewis Sanders, a breeder of horses, and Ann Nicholas. Sanders's maternal grandfather was Colonel George Nicholas, who had proposed the celebrated Kentucky Resolutions of 1798 in opposition to the Federalists' Alien and Sedition Acts. As a youth, Sanders worked with his father raising and selling Kentucky thoroughbreds. He first spoke politically during a November 1843 mass meeting at Ghent, Kentucky, held in support of Texas annexation. He used this opportunity to begin a dialogue with various contenders for the Democratic presidential nomination to discover attitudes on the Texas issue, and he soon became acquainted with the rough and tumble world of political promotion and lobbying. In 1846 Sanders used his lobbying skills to calm Democratic critics after it was rumored that he had earned a huge commission as the agent of the Hudson's Bay Company, seeking claims adjustments during the settlement of the Oregon country question. During the next few years he acted as an agent in a series of curious business arrangements, ranging from highly speculative Chicago real estate transactions to the provision of weapons to the French revolutionists of 1848.

In the early 1850s Sanders became an impassioned leader of the Young America movement. This enthusiastic faction within the Democratic party copied its name from Giuseppe Mazzini's Young Italy movement. Intrinsic in the movement was the belief that the worldwide balance of power was destined to shift from the old decrepit nations of Europe to the vibrant young Western republics emerging through revolutionary movements. Finding kinship with revolutionists everywhere, this group advanced a platform that called for free trade, the expansion of foreign markets, the development of a subsidized merchant marine, and the direct annexation of Mexican territory or other

Latin American filibustering exploits. Believing Illinois senator Stephen A. Douglas to be the candidate most likely to support such an aggressive program, Sanders began to publish the *United States Magazine and Review* (later called the *Democratic Review*) in 1851 as a party organ that endorsed the Young America platform and promoted the political aspirations of Douglas. The mean-spirited tone of articles written to hurt the political fortunes of Douglas's rivals (described as "Old Fogies" and "vile toads") had the opposite effect of injuring Douglas's chance for the 1852 Democratic presidential nomination, and the Sanders-Douglas friendship was damaged by the fiasco.

The Pierce administration appointed Sanders as consul to London to serve with U.S. minister James Buchanan. Without waiting for official confirmation by the Senate, Sanders assumed the responsibilities of U.S. consul from 1853 to 1854. In London, the new consul's home became a gathering place for European radicals and revolutionaries, and at various times visitors included Lajos Kossuth, Giuseppe Garibaldi, Alexandre-Auguste Ledru-Rollin, Aleksandr Ivanovich Herzen, and Mazzini. Despite the complacency of British diplomats, who held that Sanders was "too stupid to do any mischief," the unorthodox new American consul quickly became embroiled in several embarrassing episodes. Besides inciting discussion of the Ostend Manifesto question among other American diplomats in Europe, Sanders openly endorsed parties encouraging the assassination of Napoleon III and made unauthorized promises of American financial aid to European revolutionaries. The Senate never did confirm his appointment as consul at London, so Sanders returned to the United States. In 1857 President Buchanan nominated him to the more lucrative position of navy agent at New York, and the Senate ratified the appointment.

Sanders spent most of the Civil War as a Confederate agent in Canada and in Europe, hoping to negotiate foreign loans and striving to develop creative means of breaking the Union blockade of southern ports. He and his wife, Anna Reid, who edited a New York literary journal, worked tirelessly to win the release of a son, Lewis Sanders, who eventually died in a Union prison camp. In 1864 Sanders was one of the southern commissioners appointed to meet with Union delegates at the ineffectual Niagara Peace Conference that was organized by Horace Greeley. Upon Abraham Lincoln's assassination, Sanders was initially considered to be a conspirator, and the government announced a $25,000 reward calling for his arrest. Most of Sanders's private papers were seized and examined to determine his role in the Lincoln conspiracy, but after finding none, the authorities dropped the call for his arrest.

At the end of the American Civil War, Sanders spent several years living in Europe. He continued to associate with those who fought for liberty, and many European revolutionaries sought his counsel. In 1871, during the Paris Commune, French radicals feted him at the hôtel de ville, and it was rumored that he occa-

sionally appeared along the barricades. Shortly after returning to the United States, Sanders died in New York City. Known primarily in the United States as a political gadfly often allied to dubious schemes, Sanders won admiration and a greater sense of support among a younger generation of European radicals and revolutionists.

• Sanders's papers are housed in the Library of Congress. See also Merle E. Curti, "Young America," *American Historical Review* 32 (Oct. 1926): 34–55; Curti, "George N. Sanders, Patriot of the Fifties," *South Atlantic Quarterly* 27 (Jan. 1928): 79–87; Meriwether Stuart, "Operation Sanders," *Virginia Magazine of History and Biography* 81 (1973): 157–99; David B. Danbom, "The Young America Movement," *Journal of the Illinois State Historical Society* 67 (June 1974): 294–306; George Fort Milton, *The Eve of Conflict* (1934); Frank Lawrence Owsley, *King Cotton Diplomacy* (1959); and Edward C. Kirkland, *The Peacemakers of 1864* (1927). Obituaries are in *Harper's Magazine*, Oct. 1873, p. 794; and the *New York Times*, 13 Aug. 1873.

JUNIUS P. RODRIGUEZ

SANDERS, Harland David (9 Sept. 1890–16 Dec. 1980), restaurateur, was born near Henryville, Indiana, the son of Wilbert Sanders and Margaret Dunlevy, poor farmers. Sanders had an abbreviated childhood. His father died when Sanders was five years old and this forced his mother to supplement the family income through occasional factory work. Beginning at age seven she left Sanders in charge of his two siblings, sometimes for days at a time. He began working at age ten and his formal schooling ended during the seventh grade. Sanders left home when he was twelve years old, although he remained close to his family.

For most of the next thirty years Sanders drifted from job to job. In 1906 he lied about his age and joined the army. He was posted to Cuba where, his true age still undiscovered, he was honorably discharged after four months service. Returning to the United States, Sanders became a railroad man, working his way up from sectionhand to fireman in less than two years. While working out of Jasper, Alabama, in 1908 he met and married Josephine King. They had three children.

Shortly after the birth of their second child Sanders began correspondence courses in law. In 1915 the family moved to Little Rock so he could practice in the Justice of the Peace Courts, where admission to the bar was not required. His legal career ended when a courtroom fistfight with a client over a fee ruined his practice. Sanders next worked in rapid secession as a railroad sectionhand, insurance salesman, ferryboat operator, acetylene lamp maker, and tire salesman. From 1925 to 1929 he ran a service station.

Unemployed because of drought and the depression, Sanders rebounded in 1930 when he was offered proprietorship of a Shell station in North Corbin, Kentucky. The Sanders family prospered there. His station sat beside U.S. 25, one of the main north-south routes in the eastern United States. He worked it hard. Sanders began cooking lunch for hungry travelers shortly after the station opened, and the cafe was an immediate success. He added a motel in the mid-1930s and gained national recognition in 1939 when Duncan Hines gave him a favorable mention in his *Adventurers in Good Eating* guidebook.

While his cafe and motel business was expanding, Sanders became involved in several unsuccessful ventures and served for a time as a Works Progress Administration district supervisor. Sanders was active in a large number of civic and business groups. Although not exceptionally wealthy, he gave heavily to charity, especially those that aided children and alcoholics.

Sanders's personal life was strained until 1949. His only son died in 1930 and his relationship with Josephine and their two daughters was uneasy, although it improved after the Sanderses divorced in 1947. Sanders married Claudia Ledington in 1949. They were a well-matched couple. Ledington had worked for Sanders since 1932 and by the end of the depression had risen to become a trusted manager. With her solid business sense and unperturbable nature she helped counterbalance his sometimes impulsive actions and quick temper.

A perfectionist in the kitchen, Sanders constantly tinkered with his recipes and cooking techniques. In 1939 he discovered that the newly developed pressure cooker could cut cooking time for chicken from thirty minutes to seven without any loss of taste or texture. In 1952, after more than a decade of adjustments, he settled on the famous mixture of "eleven herbs and spices" that gave his chicken its distinctive flavor. In 1954 he began licensing his recipe when he granted a friend in Salt Lake City the right to sell "Colonel Sanders' Kentucky Fried Chicken."

Sanders began to develop his "Colonel Sanders" persona in 1949 after he received his second honorary Kentucky Colonel's Commission. Exactly why he did so is unknown, but it was a role he clearly relished. The Colonel's public image of gracious hospitality and down-home charm clashed somewhat with his personal reputation for fierce independence and quick and sometimes violent temper. In the early 1930s, for example, a disagreement with a business competitor escalated into a shootout among several people that left one person dead, and throughout much of his career his explosively profane outbursts kept most of the help in his various ventures on edge.

Sanders's rise to national prominence began in 1955 when he discovered Interstate 75 would bypass his restaurant and motel. Believing that "you'll rust out quicker 'n you'll wear out," instead of retiring, the 65-year-old Sanders sold the business and began looking for another profitable way to occupy his time. Convinced that his chicken recipe was better than most, Sanders loaded his white Cadillac with seasonings and pressure cookers, and began traveling the country looking for restaurateurs willing to add Kentucky Fried Chicken to their menus. He charged a royalty of four cents per chicken and hoped to make most of his money from seasoning sales. By 1960 the Colonel had signed up over 200 restaurants in the United States and Canada; by 1963 the number had grown to over 600, and prospective licensees now came to his Shelbyville home.

This rapid growth left Sanders rich but exhausted and unable to adequately oversee his operations. For these reasons he sold most of his business to John Y. Brown, Jr., and Jack Massey in 1964. He received $2 million and an annual salary of $40,000. Once retired from the active management of the company he devoted a substantial portion of his time and fortune to charity.

The new owners transformed the Colonel into the company's living symbol. Sanders began appearing regularly on talk shows, in magazines, and later in commercials. Until shortly before his death, he frequently logged over 250,000 miles a year attending public relations events. Always a bit of a showman, Sanders reveled in the opportunity to "do a little Coloneling," as he called his appearances. A 1976 poll identified him as the second most recognized personality in the world.

Much of Sanders's appeal came from his candidness. When, for example, his gravy recipe was changed, he loudly denounced it as "slop." His insistence on uniformly high quality and vocal protest when he failed to find it both inspired and terrorized franchisees.

As an entrepreneur Sanders was remarkably successful. Although he was not active in developing the franchise system that made Kentucky Fried Chicken one of the pioneers of the fast food and franchise industries, he developed the original product, marketed it masterfully, and guarded its quality with zeal. In his later years as spokesperson, the Colonel achieved the status of icon of American popular culture both in the United States and abroad. He died in Louisville, Kentucky.

• Very few of Sanders's personal papers survive; however, artifacts and other information about Sanders can be found at the Colonel Harland Sanders Museum located at KFC International Headquarters, Louisville, Ky. The best source on Sanders's life is John Pearce, *The Colonel: The Captivating Biography of the Dynamic Founder of a Fast-Food Empire* (1982). Sanders's autobiography, *Life as I Have Known It Has Been Finger Lickin' Good* (1976), is the only other extensive treatment of his life. Many brief accounts of Sanders's life can be found in the popular press, but most contain conflicting or inaccurate information. The best brief treatment of Sanders's life and career is William Whitworth, "Profiles: Kentucky Fried," *New Yorker*, 14 Feb. 1970, pp. 40–46ff. A concise summary of the Colonel's life can be found in an unexpected source: *Contemporary Authors*, vol. 114. An obituary is in the *New York Times*, 17 Dec. 1980.

THOMAS S. DICKE

SANDERSON, Ezra Dwight (25 Sept. 1878–27 Sept. 1944), rural sociologist and entomologist, was born in Clio, Michigan, the son of John Phillip Sanderson, a Congregational minister, and Alice Gertrude Wright. Signing his name E. Dwight in his early adult years, Sanderson later dropped the initial. He graduated from the Michigan Agricultural College with a bachelor of science degree in 1897. A second B.S. degree was earned in 1898 at Cornell University's College of Agriculture with a specialization in entomology. From 1915 to 1918 he was a graduate student in sociology at the University of Chicago, receiving the Ph.D. degree in 1921. In 1899 he married Anna Cecilia Blandford, a rural schoolteacher who had been raised on a Maryland farm; they had one child.

Sanderson achieved eminence in two distinct fields, first in economic entomology and then in rural sociology. He held a number of positions in economic entomology. In 1898 he was assistant state entomologist at the Agricultural College of Maryland and from 1898 to 1902 served as entomologist at the Delaware Agricultural Experiment Station and professor of zoology at Delaware College. In 1902 he moved to Texas, becoming state entomologist and professor of entomology at the Texas Agricultural and Mechanical College, positions he held to 1904. Then he became entomologist for New Hampshire and professor of zoology at New Hampshire College (1904–1910).

The majority of Sanderson's nearly sixty scientific and technical publications in entomology dealt with the life history, habits, and means of control of insects injurious to crops. He was also interested in the effect of temperature upon insect life. He had a guiding role in work that resulted in the Federal Insecticide Act of 1910 to standardize and properly label insecticides. Sanderson was one of the founders of the *Journal of Economic Entomology*. In 1910 he was elected president of the American Association of Economic Entomologists.

A move into agricultural college administration started a transition from entomologist to rural sociologist. Starting in 1907 Sanderson also served as director of the New Hampshire Agricultural Experiment Station. He then moved to West Virginia University, where he was dean of the College of Agriculture from 1910 to 1915 and from 1912, concurrently, director of the Agricultural Experiment Station. He was dean of a land-grant college at a time when the county agricultural extension agent system was spreading because of passage of the Smith-Lever Act in 1914. Sanderson later stated that attempting to work out a satisfactory basis of local organization for the new extension work in West Virginia brought him face to face with the problem of rural organization. He found, however, little scientific knowledge available about the rural community. The interest stimulated through this personal experience led Sanderson, at age thirty-seven, to start graduate work in sociology.

Before his Ph.D. dissertation was completed, Sanderson was appointed in 1918 to head and get underway a department of rural social organization (renamed rural sociology in 1939) in the College of Agriculture at Cornell University. He held the post for twenty-five years, until retirement in 1943. Under his leadership the department, believed to be the first of its kind, gained wide recognition for its research, extension, and graduate training programs. Sanderson

was committed to building a body of scientific knowledge about rural society. But the objective of the research was to advance the welfare of rural people. The title of his text *Rural Sociology and Rural Social Organization*, published in 1942 near the end of his career, suggested the distinction Sanderson made between rural sociology as a science and rural social organization as the art of applying science to the solution of human problems.

Sanderson applied the appreciation and knowledge of scientific methods gained from his training and experience in entomology to his social research. Believing that the first step in scientific analysis was to describe and classify phenomena, he chose social groups as his special area of study and within this area concentrated on rural locality groups. His *The Rural Community: The Natural History of a Sociological Group* (1932), a comparative analysis of communities in different regions of the world at different times and an expansion of his doctoral dissertation, is perhaps his most enduring work. This book and his eight field investigations of New York locality groups were aimed at securing "a knowledge of the forces and principles which influence the formation, persistence, and decline of various types of rural locality groups." Sanderson's second most important area of research emphasis was on developing the sociology of the family. The entomological background was reflected in the comprehensive categories for describing and classifying groups that he and his students developed ("Group Description," *Social Forces*, Mar. 1938; "A Preliminary Group Classification Based on Structure," *Social Forces*, Dec. 1938). Such group description and classification was expected to bring out differences in behavior associated with differences in structure.

Sanderson's first book in sociology, *The Farmer and His Community* (1922), was intended for use by rural leaders working to improve country life. *Research Memorandum on Rural Life in the Depression* (1937) was one monograph in a series sponsored by the Social Science Research Council to stimulate study of the social aspects of the Great Depression. His *Rural Community Organization* (with R. A. Polson, 1939) was a text but also suitable for rural professional leaders. His *Leadership for Rural Life* (1940) was addressed to problems of local leadership. The outstanding application of Sanderson's research was the use of his rural locality group studies in New York State's rural school centralization plan starting in the mid-1930s. He urged that new schools be located in village and town centers, which were the foci of emerging dominant communities.

Sanderson was a founder and first secretary of the American Country Life Association in 1919 and was its president in 1938. When a special rural section was organized on 1 July 1934 within the Federal Emergency Relief Administration's Division of Research and Statistics, Sanderson went to Washington, D.C., for six months as the first coordinator of rural research. In 1935 Secretary of State Cordell Hull appointed him as a delegate for the United States to the Twelfth Congress of the International Institute of Sociology held in Belgium. He was a member of nearly every national policy, planning, and advisory committee in rural sociology for twenty-five years. He was elected first president of the Rural Sociological Society for 1938 when it was organized and was elected president of the American Sociological Association for 1942.

Sanderson entered his second professional career, rural sociology, when the field was in its early stages. For twenty-five years, he was a major contributor to its development. After his death, Sanderson was characterized by Carl C. Taylor, a distinguished contemporary, as "one of the most scientific sociologists of all time" (*Rural Sociology* [1946]: 14). His systematic long-term work in rural locality groups, especially the rural community, is a part of the core literature of rural sociology.

Dwight Sanderson died in Ithaca, New York, less than a year after retiring.

• Sanderson's papers are in the Department of Manuscripts and University Archives, Cornell University Libraries; Albert R. Mann's correspondence with and about Sanderson is among Mann's papers in the same location. Sanderson's books in entomology were *Insects Injurious to Staple Crops* (1902); *Insect Pests of Farm, Garden and Orchard* (1912; rev. eds., 1921 and 1931); *Elementary Entomology*, with C. F. Jackson (1912); and *School Entomology*, with L. M. Peairs (1917). A complete listing of his publications may be found in *A Bibliography of Ezra Dwight Sanderson to September 25, 1943*, printed for private circulation. *Rural Sociology* 11 (Mar. 1946) is a memorial number with five articles about Sanderson and his work; they are "Dwight Sanderson, Rural Social Builder," by W. A. Anderson; "Dwight Sanderson, Social Scientist," by Carl. C. Taylor; "Group Classification: Dwight Sanderson's Contribution," by Howard W. Beers and John H. Kolb; "The Family," by Robert G. Foster; and "The Concept of the Community," by Douglas Ensminger and Robert A. Polson. For obituaries see *American Sociological Review* 9 (Dec. 1944); *Necrology of the Faculty of Cornell University, 1944–45*; Ithaca (N.Y.) *Journal*, 27 Sept. 1944; *Journal of Economic Entomology* 37 (Dec. 1944); and *Rural Sociology* 9 (Dec. 1944).

OLAF F. LARSON

SANDOW, Eugen (2 Apr. 1867–14 Oct. 1925), physical culturist, was born Friedrich Wilhelm Müller in Königsberg, East Prussia (later Kaliningrad, Russia), the son of merchants whose full names are unknown. His childhood is shrouded in mystery, but during the late 1880s Sandow immigrated to Brussels to escape Prussian military service and to pursue a performing career. A less reliable account records that he attended the University of Göttingen and later studied anatomy in Brussels. He did, however, benefit in Brussels from the tutelage of the legendary Professor Attila (Louis Durlacher), who fostered Sandow's physical development by impressing upon him the importance of lifting heavy weights. In Amsterdam he drew attention to his tremendous strength by breaking novelty weightlifting machines in the city's cafes. His equally awesome physique later attracted the attention of artists in search of models. But Sandow built his reputation as a strongman by pitting his strength against such notables of the period as Charles Sampson, "Cyclops" (pseudonym for Frank Bienkowski), and Henry "Hercules" McCann. His match against McCann in 1890 was closely regulated and served as a basis for all subsequent weightlifting competitions.

Having thus established his credentials as one of the world's foremost strongmen, Sandow became a showman. His strength feats included breaking chains with his biceps and wire cables with his chest, human lifting, bent pressing, and tests of leg and abdomen strength on the Roman Chair. Sandow also set many weightlifting records and flaunted his physique, for which he was lionized by London's high society. In 1893 he visited the United States for the Columbian Exposition in Chicago, where his talents were exploited by the promotional genius of Florenz Ziegfeld, Jr. Through his daring physical displays Sandow became, with Ziegfeld's help, a symbol of strength, masculinity, and sexual potency. Realizing the immense commercial appeal of this formula, Sandow and Ziegfeld toured throughout the United States for several years as the Trocadero Company. At Thomas Edison's motion picture studio in West Orange, New Jersey, Sandow's physique was captured for posterity on a primitive device called the Kinetoscope, which utilized a new celluloid film developed by George Eastman. Dr. Dudley A. Sargent, physical educator and anthropometrist at Harvard University, examined Sandow and was so impressed by his strength, speed, and proportions that he pronounced him to be "the most wonderful specimen of man I have ever seen." Sandow earned more than $250,000, and his name became a household word. Lest wealth and adulation lead him to conceit, reality set in for Sandow in 1894 at a San Francisco exhibition, where an elderly lion named "Commodore" refused to allow the world's strongest human to conquer the king of beasts. After his momentous tour Sandow's magnificent body turned against him; his weight dropped from 210 to 112 pounds, and he was exhausted from overwork.

Upon recuperating, Sandow began pursuing the less taxing goal of helping others develop their bodies. In 1897 he opened an Institute of Physical Culture in London. Soon there were nearly two dozen Sandow Institutes in Great Britain, and he used his fame to promote various fitness-oriented publications, exercise devices, and health foods. Falling squarely within the spirit of the times for self-improvement and muscular Christianity (in which the moral tone of Christianity in the Victorian era was combined with the secular values of Darwinism to produce an overtly masculine culture that emphasized the worth of the human body and fitness), Sandow's business ventures received an added boost from the mood of anxiety stemming from the number of British youth declared unfit for service in the Boer War. There was also an anthropometry craze among late Victorians, leading the natural history director at the British Museum to choose Sandow to represent the Caucasian race in a body cast. A more significant contribution was the great bodybuilding contest he staged before an audience of 15,000 in London's Albert Hall in September 1901. What set this event apart from previous shows was that well-developed physiques, rather than one's ability to hoist heavy weights, received top billing. Though it remained a stepchild, bodybuilding began to attain a separate identity from weightlifting under Sandow's tutelage. The great competition staged by Sandow at his prime was a tour de force, and its effect was enhanced by a similar extravaganza held by Bernarr Macfadden in America shortly afterward.

From 1901 to 1905 Sandow traveled to many different countries, including Australia, New Zealand, China, Japan, and India, among others, where he continued his efforts on behalf of good health and fitness. Though no less interested in money and glory, he helped inspire a generation keenly interested in moral and muscular improvement. Both American writer Jack London and President Theodore Roosevelt were influenced by him. In the physical culture field Afrikaner Tromp van Diggelen, Indian K. V. Iyer, and American promoters Alan Calvert and Earle Liederman were indebted to Sandow. He also took an interest in women's fitness, developing a health corset and an indoor exercise contraption called the "Symmetrion." Sandow's final undertaking was his Curative Institute, an urban alternative to the sanitaria so much in vogue among the neurasthenic upper classes. Based on the holistic principle that a healthy body is more resistant to breakdown, it boasted a success rate of 96 percent among patients showing improvement. His most important book, *Life Is Movement* (1919), was written amidst the manpower stresses of World War I. Though it addresses the pressing issues of military preparedness and national survival, it is an idealistic manual for the conduct of life. Glowing testimonials for Sandow came from such celebrities as Arthur Conan Doyle, who believed that "few men have done more for England than he." But Sandow's greatest accolade came from his appointment in 1911 as "Professor Scientific and Physical Culture" to King George V.

Unfortunately Sandow's private life was less idyllic. Show business life and marital infidelities led to an estrangement from his wife Blanche Brookes, whom he had married in 1894, and to his two daughters. The circumstances surrounding his death have remained obscure, and his grave site at Putney Vale near London has been totally neglected by his family. Yet he was an inspiration to millions who sought physical improvement. Sandow exemplified his business motto, "Amicus Humani Generis."

• There are no known manuscripts or correspondence files on Sandow. The Sandow Scrap Book is in the Todd-McLean Collection at the University of Texas at Austin. His publications include *Sandow on Physical Training*, ed. G. Mercer Adam (1894); *The Construction and Reconstruction of the Human Body* (1907); *Strength and How to Obtain It* (1897); and *Sandow's Magazine of Physical Culture* (1898–1907). A thorough biographical treatment is David Chapman, *Sandow the Magnificent, Eugen Sandow and the Beginnings of Bodybuilding* (1994). Other useful accounts are Leo Gaudreau, *Anvils,* *Horseshoes and Cannons, The History of Strongmen*, vol. 2 (1978); David Webster, *Barbells and Beefcake* (1979) and *The Iron Game, an Illustrated History of Weight-lifting* (1976); and Terry Todd, "The Day Sargent Examined Sandow," *Strength & Health* 33 (June 1965): 55, 61–64. Also see Gerard Nisivoccia's *Sandow, the Mighty Monarch of Muscle* (1947). Obituaries are in the *New York Times* and *The Times* (London), both 15 Oct. 1925.

JOHN D. FAIR

SANDOZ, Mari (11 May 1896–10 Mar. 1966), novelist and historian, was born in Sheridan County, Nebraska, the daughter of Jules Ami Sandoz and Mary Elizabeth Fehr, Swiss immigrant homesteaders. Sandoz grew up in an impoverished household, ruled by her violent-tempered father. The family led a painful existence, but Mari later realized that growing up in that place and time gave her poignant writing material. Living near an old Indian and trapper crossing on the Niobrara River, not far from two Indian reservations, she learned the area's history and also the art of storytelling from the old friends of her father who stopped to exchange tales of their experiences with him. She also learned of the recent disappearance of the Indians' way of life as settlers established their own civilization in the region.

When Sandoz was fourteen the family moved into the Sandhills southeast of the Niobrara. Treeless, stark, and wild, the hills frightened and fascinated Mari. Both the Niobrara neighborhood and the Sandhills became settings for her writing.

Mari spoke the Swiss German of her mother until she began to attend country school at the age of nine. Then she quickly learned English. She soon was writing her own stories; the first was published on the children's page in an Omaha newspaper when she was eleven.

She graduated from country elementary school at seventeen and began to teach in nearby rural schools. In 1914 she married Wray Macumber, a neighboring rancher, but in 1919 divorced him and moved to Lincoln, 400 miles away. She expunged any reference to her marriage from her correspondence, although she wrote under her married name of Marie Macumber until 1929.

From 1919 to 1935 Sandoz taught, attended business college, held a variety of other jobs, and managed to enroll at the University of Nebraska despite her lack of a high school diploma. She also wrote continuously but with almost no national recognition.

In 1930 Sandoz and her friend Eleanor Hinman took a 3,000-mile trip to the Rosebud and Pine Ridge reservations, the Little Big Horn and Rosebud battlefields in Montana, and the sites of other important Indian battles. By interviewing several ancient veterans of the Indian wars, they gained information white historians had not known. Until that time Sandoz had focused her writing on white subjects, but after this trip she experimented with Indian material, told from an Indian point of view.

In 1935 *Old Jules*, her biography of her father, won the $5,000 Atlantic Monthly Press Prize for nonfiction, after having been rejected by thirteen publishers. From then on, she dedicated herself to writing and research.

Sandoz moved from Lincoln to Denver in 1940 in order to use the research facilities there but also to escape harassment by Lincoln residents angered by her 1939 novel *Capital City*, which many believed denigrated their city. In 1943, after her biography of the Oglala Sioux war chief Crazy Horse was published, she moved to New York. She was drawn to the fine western research repositories there, but she also reluctantly recognized that she could work more efficiently with eastern publishers if she lived in New York. Although she professed to hate the city and was often in the West for long periods doing research or lecturing, she remained a New York resident until her death.

Sandoz's mercurial father, his experiences as a settler in an untamed country, and her own life as a child on a frontier were the most important influences on her life and determined the direction of her writing. Her earliest goal was to write fiction, and she was always concerned about style, but she eventually viewed herself primarily as a historian. Sandoz wrote a number of novels and taught summer-session novel writing courses at the University of Wisconsin (1947–1953, 1955–1956), but her reputation is based primarily on her six-book Great Plains Series as well as *Love Song to the Plains* (1961), *These Were the Sioux* (1961), and *The Battle of the Little Bighorn* (1966). Her works illustrate her belief in the significance of the Great Plains in American geography and history. They also reveal her great love for the natural world she grew up in, especially the Niobrara River and the Sandhills.

Sandoz was a teacher and moralist; her novels generally reflect her worldview. Her use of allegory in several works—*Slogum House* (1937), *Capital City* (1939), *The Tom-Walker* (1947), and *Winter Thunder* (1959)—met with varying degrees of popularity with readers and critics. These books generally reflect her concern with twentieth-century aspects of human greed, fascism, war, and the treatment of contemporary Native Americans.

Sandoz's histories are based on meticulous research, often from esoteric sources, but because she chose to write them as narratives, they read like fiction and thus have drawn criticism from some historians. Nevertheless, writers interested in the West often have relied on her material. Recent researchers in fields as diverse as western American history, sociology, and criminal justice have verified the authenticity of much of her work.

• Mari Sandoz's correspondence for the years 1926–1966 is in the Sandoz Collection, University of Nebraska Archives, Love Library, Lincoln, Nebraska. Sandoz kept letters received and carbons of her replies. Smaller collections are also at Syracuse University, University of Wyoming, and Chadron State College (Nebraska). The Sandoz Family Corporation holds unpublished manuscripts and family records at the home of Caroline Sandoz Pifer, Gordon, Nebraska. Sandoz's letters are collected in Helen Winter Stauffer, ed., *Letters of Mari Sandoz, 1928–1966* (1992). The only full-length biography is Helen Winter Stauffer, *Mari Sandoz: Story Catcher of the Plains* (1982). See also *Mari Sandoz* in the Western Writers of America series (1984). Caroline Sandoz Pifer, *The Making of an Author: Mari Sandoz* (3 vols., 1972, 1982, 1984) uses family recollections and Sandoz's letters from the early 1920s to 1932.

Dorothy Nott Switzer, "Mari Sandoz' Lincoln Years: A Personal Recollection," *Prairie Schooner* (Summer 1971), and Bruce Nicoll, "Mari Sandoz: Nebraska Loner," *American West* (Spring 1965), give personal recollections of the author.

Mari Sandoz, *Hostiles and Friendlies*, ed. Virginia Faulkner (1959), includes considerable autobiographical information, as does Sandoz, "Outpost in New York," *Prairie Schooner* (Summer 1963).

Unpublished manuscripts, housed in the Sandoz Collection, include Judith Louise McDonald, "Antaeus of the Running Water: A Biographical Study of the Western Nebraska Years of Mari Sandoz, 1906–1922" (1972), and Barbara W. Rippey, "Mari Sandoz: Novelist as Historian" (1989). A useful videotape is "Song of the Plains" (a biography of Mari Sandoz) KNTV, Lincoln (1978). An obituary is in the *New York Times*, 11 Mar. 1966.

HELEN WINTER STAUFFER

SANDS, Benjamin Franklin (11 Feb. 1812–30 June 1883), naval officer, was born in Baltimore, Maryland, the son of Benjamin Norris Sands and Rebecca Hook. The family soon moved to Louisville, Kentucky, where Benjamin received his schooling until 1827, when he was sent to Washington, D.C., to complete his studies. A year later, on 1 April 1828, Sands was appointed a midshipman in the U.S. Navy from Kentucky. His first sea duty was aboard the sloop *Vandalia* of the Brazil Squadron, followed in 1832 by a West Indies cruise aboard the *St. Louis*. Sands was commissioned as passed midshipman in 1834. He married Henrietta Maria French two years later; the couple had eight children. From 1836 to 1841 Sands was given coast survey duty, during which time, in 1840, he was promoted to lieutenant. Following two years of sea duty aboard the *Columbia* from 1842 to 1844, he worked in the Bureau of Charts and Instruments at the Naval Observatory in Washington until 1847. As executive officer of the *Washington* in 1847 he saw limited service during the war with Mexico. In June of that year the *Washington* was attached to Commodore Matthew C. Perry's squadron operating off Campeche and Yucatan. On 16 June 1847 Perry brought his ships up to the Grijalva River, and Sands was among the landing force that routed the Mexicans at Fort Iturbide and occupied the city of Villahermosa during this, Perry's second Tabasco Expedition. Afterward, as executive officer and commander of the *Porpoise*, Sands was engaged in the suppression of the slave trade off the coast of Africa. He returned to coast survey duties in 1851 and continued that work until 1858. Promotion to commander came in 1855. Sands's important survey and hydrographic work resulted in his inventing a device for deep-sea sounding. In 1858 he became head of the Naval Bureau of Construction, followed by more survey duty aboard the survey steamer *Active*.

In April 1861 Sands was part of the naval expedition sent to Norfolk, Virginia, to evacuate Federal forces at the navy yard there. He supervised the burning of ships and warehouses to prevent them from falling into the hands of the Confederates. Because Secretary of the Navy Gideon Welles was suspicious of officers from Border States, Sands spent the next several months aboard the *Active* on survey duty on the Pacific coast. When finally convinced of Sands's loyalty to the United States, Welles authorized his promotion to captain in July 1862 and had him assigned to more meaningful service. In October 1862 Sands became senior officer of the blockade of the Cape Fear River and Wilmington, North Carolina, aboard the steam sloop *Dacotah*. He stayed with that inadequate vessel for more than a year, then transferred to the superior sidewheel steamer *Fort Jackson*. Sands originated the practice of using an additional outer line of blockaders, but he was frustrated at what seemed a near-impossible task—enforcing the blockade—and complained to his superior officer that he lacked the necessary ships to make it a "close blockade." Swift blockade runners took advantage of their superior speed and darkness to evade capture. As Sands observed, "There was great rivalry in shrewdness, in skill and in daring between the blockaders and the runners of the blockade" (*From Reefer to Rear-Admiral*, p. 246). Nevertheless, in just over a year Sands's division succeeded in capturing a total of fifty-three enemy vessels and blockade-runners. It also staged a successful raid on a saltworks near Wilmington and engaged enemy forces ashore on other occasions. While commanding the *Fort Jackson*, Sands participated in the joint army-navy attacks on Fort Fisher on 24–25 December 1864 and 13–15 January 1865. He next commanded a division of the West Gulf Blockading Squadron on the Texas coast. On 2 June 1865 Sands accepted the surrender of Galveston, and three days later his forces occupied the city.

From 1867 until his retirement in 1874, Sands served as head of the Naval Observatory. He was promoted to commodore in 1866 and to rear admiral in 1871. He died at his residence in Washington.

Sands's distinguished naval career spanned some forty-three years. He was completely devoted to duty, and his health suffered as a result. During the many months he spent on blockade duty, Sands acknowledged, he never once enjoyed a complete night's rest.

• The Benjamin F. Sands folder is in RG 45 (Naval Records Collection), National Archives. Sands's official Civil War correspondence is in *The Official Records of the Union and Confederate Navies in the War of the Rebellion*, ser. 1, vols. 8, 9, 10, and 11 (30 vols., 1894–1922). His prewar and Civil War careers are covered in his autobiography, *From Reefer to Rear-Admiral: Reminiscences and Journal Jottings of Nearly Half a Century of Naval Life* (1899). See also Lewis Hamersly, *The Records of Living Officers of the U.S. Navy and Marine Corps* (1870). An obituary is in the *Washington Evening Star*, 2 July 1883.

NORMAN C. DELANEY

SANDS, David (4 Oct. 1745–4 June 1818), Quaker preacher, was born in Cow Neck, Long Island, New York, the son of Nathaniel Sands and Mercy (maiden name unknown), farmers. Sands's Presbyterian parents moved about 1759 to a farm near Cornwall, Orange County, New York. Self-taught, he left home in 1765 to teach school and later kept a store in Cornwall. In deep religious anxiety he found reassurance in the home of Quakers Edward and Phebe Hallock, who introduced him to Nine Partners Meeting across the Hudson River, of which he became a member. He married their daughter Clementina in November 1771 and lived thereafter in a house next to his parents. At the homes of his wife's kin and later on visits everywhere he refused to be served by slaves. Speaking in meeting and in a worship group in his home, he was "recorded as a Minister" and began a career as one of the itinerant "public Friends" by whom the growing network of meetings was sustained. In 1775 with a fellow member of his meeting he visited nineteen meetings and home worship groups in Rhode Island and on Cape Cod, staying in the home of merchant Moses Brown. His wife kept their store and four children in his absence. When the revolutionary war began she sometimes had to feed up to fifty patriot soldiers in their home.

Sands's next mission lasted thirty-one months, from 1777 to 1779, involving many crossings of military lines. From the home of William Rotch, a Quaker, on neutral Nantucket Island, he circled four times to strengthen the Quaker settlements in Rhode Island, Salem and Lynn in Massachusetts, the New Hampshire coast, and Maine, returning by way of inland New Hampshire and central Massachusetts. The Kennebec Valley meetings in Fairfield, Vassalboro, Winthrop, and Durham, all in Maine, arose largely from his visits to newly settled Friends and non-Quakers. Sands's intensely Christ-centered gospel, new for Quakers, was later carried to the Midwest by Robert and John Henry Douglas and by Sybil Jones, all from the Kennebec Valley, who thus made the influence of the Kennebec Valley Meetings dominant among evangelical Friends across America. Sands felt God laid his mission "as a cross" upon his desire to be home to support his message of submission to God and conscience there. After his return he felt called to two missions to Friends in Philadelphia, Pennsylvania, where he made a stark prophecy of judgment weeks before yellow fever broke out in the grim 1793 epidemic.

In July 1794 Sands's meeting endorsed his inner call to preach in Europe but his sailing was delayed a year by a night shipwreck off Marblehead, Massachusetts. Meanwhile he revisited meetings in eastern New England, traveling with Martha Routh, newly come from England. Landing at Liverpool, England, after a stormy voyage, he spent months visiting meetings twice a day, and often many homes within each, in Lancashire, Yorkshire, and Durham, staying in Quaker leaders' homes. He never spoke unless he felt led by the Spirit.

Sands began to study Dutch and German before attending the London Yearly Meeting, whence he sailed to Germany and went overland to Hamburg with Quaker leaders William Savery, George Dillwyn, and William Farrer. He found Moravians and other fellow spirits in Hanover and Pyrmont, which became the German Quaker center. They met and traveled on with Ludwig Seebohm, the father of Quaker writer Benjamin Seebohm, to hold worship meetings in Potsdam, Berlin, Magdeburg, Minden, and other cities with sympathetic groups of a hundred or more. In 1797 he went to Amsterdam, Rotterdam, and other Dutch cities, but found few Quaker families remaining from William Penn's visit a century earlier. As an American Quaker, Sands was able to go through French-occupied Flanders and to Paris and Lyons to visit at Congenies a French spiritual sect that became affiliated with the Friends. On his return via Dunkirk he had to be smuggled ashore in England by a fishing boat.

After a summer in which he visited meetings across southern England and Wales, Sands crossed alone to Ireland, where he was involved in doctrinal controversies. He opposed Abraham Shackleton, leader of the Quaker school at Ballitore, who cast doubt on the inerrancy of Scripture, as had Tom Paine, against whom Sands had argued while in Paris. Furthermore, Sands accused Hannah Barnard, a member of his own Nine Partners Meeting who was welcomed at Ballitore in 1799, of Deism and Jacobin sympathies because she denied that a loving God could have commanded Joshua to exterminate the Amalekites and that salvation depended on the Atonement, a cornerstone of faith for Sands and leading English Quakers. Referring to these conflicts, William Rathbone reported in *A Narrative of Events . . . in Ireland* (1804) that six "weighty" elders among Irish Friends had objected when Sands praised his own humility, accused individual Quakers—Shackleton and Barnard—of doctrinal "infidelity," prayed during worship for George III (whom Sands had visited), and justified capital punishment and war. The elders were censured and resigned, and after much debate, a move in the Ireland Yearly Meeting to refuse Sands a Quaker certificate of approval on his departure was rejected.

Sands continued to minister in England until 1805. After his return home he made a final trip through New England. At the request of the New York Yearly Meeting, Sands and the "quietist" Elias Hicks visited new meetings in Ontario whose members had emigrated there as Loyalists after the American Revolution. Sands died at Cornwall. Although he strengthened many meetings, he exacerbated the division of Quakers over evangelical doctrines, which led in 1828 to the Hicksite-Orthodox separation.

• *The Journal of the Life and Gospel Labors of David Sands* (1848), heavily edited by his daughter Catharine Ring and by Edward Pease, includes letters by and to Sands. See also Jonathan Evans, *A Journal of the Life . . . of William Savery* (1837), for a description of his travels and encounters with Sands. On Sands in England, see *Records and Recollections of James Jenkins*, ed. J. William Frost (1984). Rufus Jones's *The Quakers in the American Colonies* (1911), *The Later Periods of Quakerism* (2 vols., 1921), and *The Society of Friends in Kennebec County* (1892) remain the most cordial secondary sources.

HUGH BARBOUR

SANDS, Diana (23 Aug. 1934–21 Sept. 1973), actor, was born Diana Patricia Sands in the Bronx, New York, the daughter of Rudolph Thomas Sands, a carpenter, and Shirley Walker, a milliner. Sands spent her childhood in suburban Elmsford, New York, but returned to Manhattan to attend the High School for the Performing Arts. She graduated in 1952 and made her film debut as a bar girl in the film *Caribbean Gold* (1952).

Sands soon discovered that few paying jobs were offered to black actresses, and the roles that did exist were degrading or one-dimensional. Rather than submit to a career of maid and mammy parts, Sands worked days as a keypunch operator for Con Edison and acted on the off-Broadway stage, extending her dramatic range with traditionally white roles in *An Evening with Will Shakespeare* (1953), *The World of Sholom Aleichem* (1953), and *Major Barbara* (1954).

Sands joined the Pantomime Art Theatre in 1955. By 1956 she was working fairly regularly off-Broadway, in *The Man with the Golden Arm* (1956), *A Land beyond the River* (1957), *The Egg and I* (1958), and in the films *Four Boys and A Gun* (1957) and *The Garment Jungle* (1957). In 1959 she made her Broadway debut as the idealistic student, Beneatha Younger, in Lorraine Hansberry's *A Raisin in the Sun* (1959). Her performance in the play won her the Outer Circle Critics' Award for best supporting actress and the Variety Critics' Award as most promising young actress, and when the film version was released in 1961, she added an International Artist Award to her collection.

Sands returned to off-Broadway for the revues *Another Evening with Harry Stoones* (1961) and *Brecht on Brecht* (1962). Her work in *Tiger Tiger Burning Bright* (1962) brought her a Theater World Award, and her performance in *Living Premise* (1963) won an Obie (Off-Broadway Theatre Award). She began to pick up good television parts as well. She was nominated for an Emmy Award for her work in the series "East Side, West Side" (1963) and the next year won the award for the special *Beyond the Blues* (1964).

She filmed the slight *Ensign Pulver* (1964) before being cast in James Baldwin's explosive *Blues for Mister Charlie* (1964). The play, which *Time* magazine described as telling "every white man how much every Negro hates him" (5 June 1964), cast Sands as a woman whose lover had been killed by a white man. Her climactic monologue was termed "an unparalleled tour de force" by the *New York Times* (10 May 1964), and she was nominated for a Tony Award as best supporting actress. The same year she married Lucien Happersberger, James Baldwin's manager. The couple were divorced in 1967 and had no children.

Sands was next cast opposite Alan Alda in the romantic comedy *The Owl and the Pussycat* (1965), in a part originally written for a white actress. The color-blind casting was controversial in some quarters (*New York Times* critic Martin Gottfried continued to complain about it five years later), but most audiences found the pairing pleasant and unremarkable. A critic for *Ebony* magazine wrote that the show proved "how attractive and natural interracial casting can seem when it is handled casually." The show was a hit, with rave reviews for both actors and a Tony nomination as best actress for Sands. "This is the first Broadway show in which I was cast as a person rather than a racial type," she said at the time. "I love it."

When Sands finished the London production of *The Owl and the Pussycat*, she spent a year playing in repertory around the United States. In an eleven-month period during 1967 she performed in *Macbeth* at Spelman College in Atlanta, *Caesar and Cleopatra* at Theater Atlanta in Georgia, *Antony and Cleopatra* at Macarthur Park in Los Angeles, and *Phaedra* at the Theatre of the Living Arts in Philadelphia. She capped the year of classics with *Saint Joan* at Lincoln Center in New York. Her Joan of Arc was widely praised, and *New York Times* critic Clive Barnes noted that "the fact that she is colored adds a quite fortuitous yet theatrically not irrelevant forcefulness to her rebellion and subsequent persecution" (5 Jan. 1968).

While Sands enjoyed playing the classics, she resented the fact that she had had to prove her abilities in regional theater. "Most white actresses who have been received as I have been received on Broadway and television would not have to go into repertory; they wouldn't have time," she told *Look* magazine. "I had no choice but to go to repertory if I wanted to do roles that offer me some kind of challenge, besides racial roles." She continued to speak out on the lack of "uptown" black roles and to push for color-blind casting for other black actors. "It has to become the rule, not the exception," she told Mel Gussow. "If it only works for me, that means I'm the freak. I don't want to be somebody's token" (*New York Times*, 31 Dec. 1967).

She found a strong role in Hal Ashby's *The Landlord* (1970), as the slum-dweller who has an affair (and a child) with Beau Bridges's fair-haired title character. The *New York Times* deemed the satiric film a "brilliant piece of cinema craftsmanship" and called Sands "as fine an actress as we have with us today, filling the screen with a warmth that haunts and sorrow that manages again and again to induce chills" (30 Sept. 1973).

Despite the good notices, an award from the Black Academy of Arts and Letters, and a recurring role in the popular television series "Julia," Sands worked less than she wished, often taking roles in regional theater and summer stock. After filming the forgettable *Doctors' Wives* (1971), she opened the Diana Sands Sitting Service, a forty-employee child care agency. Not long after, she and actor/director Ossie Davis cofounded Third World Cinema, a film production company dedicated to showcasing black artists and experiences.

Sands appeared in *Georgia, Georgia* (1972), *Willie Dynamite* (1973), and *Honeybaby, Honeybaby* (1974) for Third World and was scheduled in 1973 to star with James Earl Jones in *Claudine*, the love story of a welfare mother and a sanitation worker. However, shortly before filming began in July, Sands was diagnosed with cancer. Two months later she died in New York City.

Sands is remembered for her talent and for her contribution to integration and acceptance of blacks in theater and on film. Ossie Davis wrote, "The stage was not only good to Diana, it was good for Diana. . . . Out there she became what America is not yet prepared to let black women be within their private lives: invulnerable, inviolate, invincible!" Her final project, *Claudine*, released in 1974 with Diahann Carroll in the lead, finally presented what Sands often said was missing in American cinema: a black female as a real woman and romantic lead.

• Clippings on Sands can be found in the Billy Rose Theatre Collection at the New York Public Library for the Performing Arts, Lincoln Center. A biographical essay is in Delia Reyes, *Black Women in American: An Historical Encyclopedia* (1993). Excellent profiles include those in the *New York Times*, 10 May 1964 and 31 Dec. 1967; "Diana Sands: Notes on a Broadway Pussycat," *Look*, 9 Feb. 1965; and "The Passion of Diana Sands," *Look*, 9 Jan. 1968. An obituary is in the *New York Times*, 23 Sept. 1973.

DIANA MOORE

SANDYS, George (2 Mar. 1578–4 Mar. 1644), writer and official of colonial Virginia, was born at Bishopthorp near York, England, the son of Edwin Sandys, the archbishop of York, and his second wife, Cicely Wil(s)ford. Sandys entered Oxford University as a gentleman-commoner at the age of eleven in 1589, then at eighteen went to the Middle Temple, London. He remained at the Inns of Court only a year or two. Before the age of twenty-one, he married Elizabeth Norton of Ripon. The exact date of the family-arranged marriage is unknown, but it had ended, although it was never formally dissolved, by 1606. The couple had no children.

In 1610 Sandys began extensive travels to France, Constantinople, Egypt, Palestine, Phoenicia, Malta, and Italy. In 1615 he published *A Relation of a Journey Begun An: Dom: 1610. Four Books Containing a Description of the Turkish Empire, of Egypt, of the Holy Land, of the Remote Parts of Italy, and Islands Adjoining* in four books; it was reprinted eight times before 1700. Sandys's work was used as a sourcebook by Francis Bacon, Sir Thomas Browne, Robert Burton, Abraham Cowley, Thomas Fuller, Ben Jonson, and John Milton and earned a significant place in the tradition of travel literature.

Sandys accepted an appointment in 1621 as the first treasurer of the Virginia colony and arrived at Jamestown in October of that year. His four-year tenure as treasurer and director of industry for the colony seems to have been successful. He led a raid on Indians involved in the 1622 massacre, cultivated his own acreage, sponsored iron and glass manufacture, and built the first water mill in America. But Michael Drayton's poem "To Master George Sandys, Treasurer for the English Colony in Virginia" may indicate where his true interests lay:

> And, worthy George, by industry and use,
> Let's see what lines *Virginia* will produce;
> Go on with Ovid, as you have begun,
> With the first five books; let your numbers run
> Glib as the former, so shall it live long,
> And do much honor to the English tongue.

Sandys brought his translation of five books of Ovid's *Metamorphosis* with him to Virginia and completed the remaining ten books during his years at Jamestown. The translation was first published in England in 1616, followed by an expanded edition in 1632. This is the publication that his biographer Richard Beale Davis hails as "the first belletristic product of British America." Sandys's commentaries "made the 1632 edition and its reprint in 1640 one of the well-known and influential books of the century." It was apparently used by both John Milton and John Keats.

His years in Virginia provided Sandys with details from the New World to buttress Ovid's description of Old World fantasies and marvels. In rendering Ovid's account of yokels turned into frogs, Sandys comments: "These depopulated a City in *France*, and now not a little infest *Virginia* in Summer: called Pohatans hounds by the *English*, of their continuall yelping. And as they croake and ride one upon another in shallow plashes: so Pesants baule and gamball at their meetings; soused in liquor, as frogs in the water" (Sandys's Ovid, book 6, p. 117).

Sandys uses Ovid's reference to weasels to add: "I have seene a Beast, which the *Indians* call a *Possoun*, that hath two flaps beneath her belly, which she can shut and open at pleasure: within which, when affrighted, she receives her broode, and runnes away with them: whereupon, by a like mistake, it was supposed at first by some of the *English* that they reenter'd her belly" (book 9, p. 179).

After his return to England in 1625, Sandys served as a Gentleman of King Charles I's Privy Council and an agent for the Virginia colony, where he continued to own property. He published several scriptural paraphrases in verse between 1636 and 1641 and wrote three surviving original poems, "Deo Opt. Max.," "A Dream," and "Hymn to the Redeemer." These lines from "Deo Opt. Max." demonstrate the flexible couplet usually employed by Sandys:

Thou [God] sav'dst me from the bloody massacres
Of faithless Indians; from their treach'rous wars.
From raging fevers; from the sultry breath
Of tainted air, which cloy'd the joys of death.
Preserv'd from swallowing seas, when tow'ring waves
Mix'd with the clouds, and open'd their deep graves.
(Hooker, vol. 2, p. 406)

Sandys's versification represents an important step toward the development of the heroic couplet in John Dryden and Alexander Pope's time.

"Here is a poet-adventurer," Davis concludes. "Forthright, honest, quick-tempered, resourceful, shrewdly analytical, he is individual evidence that England could give of her best in laying the foundations of the world she was to dominate two centuries later" (p. 18). Sandys probably died at Boxley Abbey, his last residence, in Kent, England.

• The R. B. Davis Papers in the Alderman Library, University of Virginia, contain many documents relating to Sandys. The first full-length study of Sandys, by Richard Beale Davis, *George Sandys: Poet-Adventurer* (1955), establishes many facts about his life and work through the use of records in England, including those of his previously unknown marriage. Davis's article, "America in George Sandys' Ovid," appears in Davis, *Literature and Society in Early Virginia, 1608–1840* (1973) and in the *William and Mary Quarterly*, 3d ser., 4 (July 1947).

Richard Hooker edited *The Poetical Works of George Sandys*, 2 vols. (1872; repr., 1968), excluding the Ovid translation but including Sandys's translation of Hugh Grotius's *Christ's Passion*, a five-act tragedy with annotations by Sandys, and also including the tunes written by Henry Lawes for twenty-three of Sandys's paraphrased psalms (Hooker, vol. 2, appendix, n.p.). Numerous articles and several books have been written about Sandys, most often about his Ovid, his travel book, and his versification. Ruth Wallerstein, "The Development of the Rhetoric and Metre of the Heroic Couplet, Especially in 1625–1645," *PMLA* 50 (Mar. 1935): 166–209, is a pioneering study of Sandys's influence on later poets.

DORA JEAN ASHE

SANFORD, Edmund Clark (10 Nov. 1859–22 Nov. 1924), college president and research psychologist, was born in Oakland, California, the son of Edmund P. Sanford, a druggist, and Jennie E. Clark. Sanford earned an A.B. at the University of California in Berkeley in 1883. After a year of teaching at Oahu College in Honolulu, he enrolled at Johns Hopkins University in Baltimore and earned a Ph.D. in experimental psychology in 1888. During his years in Baltimore he came under the influence of G. Stanley Hall, professor of psychology and one of the discipline's founders. Sanford would remain close to Hall for the rest of his life.

Sanford taught at Johns Hopkins for one year (1888) before joining the faculty of Clark University in Worcester, Massachusetts. Hall, who had just been named Clark's first president, hired Sanford as director of the laboratory of experimental psychology. Sanford's lifelong affiliation with Clark would culminate in his being named president of the newly established Clark College in 1909. In 1901 Sanford married Florence Bartling; they had no children.

Sanford's major contribution to teaching was his creation of a laboratory manual for experimental psychology courses, the first in the English language. Called *A Course in Experimental Psychology I: Sensation and Perception* (1898), the manual contained 239 practice experiments, designed to acquaint the student with basic laboratory procedures in the experimental study of sensory and perceptual processes. At a time when psychology as a scientific discipline was just establishing its identity, the manual helped to regularize the training of a generation of research psychologists. Although the book was supplanted by Cornell University professor E. B. Titchener's more elaborate four-volume set of manuals after the turn of the century, Titchener acknowledged the importance of Sanford's work. According to Titchener, Sanford's manual had "high historical importance, as the first manual of experimental psychology; it has exerted, and still exerts, a wide influence, as the gateway through which American students are introduced to laboratory work; and it is a monument of accurate erudition" (*Memorial*, p. 28).

One section of the manual concerned apparatus and featured numerous pieces that were created or significantly improved by Sanford. His best-known invention was the Sanford Vernier Chronoscope, which was used for reaction-time research. Developed in 1890, the chronoscope combined the functions of several pieces of equipment (for presenting the stimulus, for the response by the subject, and for timing the interval between stimulus and response) into one device. Because of its simplicity, ease of operation, and minimal cost, the chronoscope became a standard piece of laboratory equipment until the 1930s. Sanford also deserves credit for pioneering one of experimental psychology's most famous procedures: maze-learning in rats. To investigate the rat's "home-finding" tendencies, Sanford in 1898 suggested building a rat-sized replica of England's famous hedge maze at Hampton Court. The idea was carried through, and it resulted in a series of investigations on the topic by Sanford's student Willard Small in 1900 and established a procedure that continues to be widely used.

Although Sanford's 77-item bibliography contains little original research, he was active in promoting the research efforts of his students and adept at writing coherent summaries and reviews of existing research. He established and edited a series of twenty-three published studies from the Clark laboratory, called collectively the Clark University Minor Studies. Published between 1898 and 1924, these studies covered a variety of topics in experimental psychology, including perception, learning, memory, and thinking.

Sanford contributed to the development of psychology as a profession through his work in the American Psychological Association and as an editor of a major journal. A charter member of the APA (founded by Hall in 1892), he served as its secretary-treasurer in 1895 and as an elected member of the powerful six-person council from 1896 to 1899. In 1902 Sanford was elected the association's eleventh president. His 1902 presidential address, "Psychology and Physics," warned research psychologists against the tendency to model their new science exclusively on physics, which he worried would lead to a strict mechanistic and materialistic psychology. He suggested that psychology should borrow some of its metaphors from evolutionary biology rather than from mechanistic physics. In 1908 he was a member of the Seashore Committee, the first APA committee to address the broad question of how the psychology curriculum should be structured. With Hall and Titchener, Sanford edited the *American Journal of Psychology* for most of his Clark years. The journal had been established by Hall in 1887 as the first psychology journal published in the United States. Sanford was responsible for recommending one-third of the journal content and for most of the routine activities that resulted in the journal's production.

Clark College merged with Clark University upon Hall's retirement in 1920, eliminating Sanford's position as college president in the process. Sanford then returned to the university's faculty after a sabbatical in 1920–1921. He remained there until a month before his planned retirement, when he suffered a fatal heart attack while en route to Wellesley College to deliver a talk. He died in Boston.

• Sanford's papers, including copies of a number of talks, some lecture notes, and some correspondence, are in the Clark University Archives. The archives at Cornell University has an especially large number of Sanford letters in its E. B. Titchener Papers. Clark University published a *Memorial* to Sanford in 1925; it includes a complete bibliography; testimonials from former students; obituaries by Titchener, Mary Whiton Calkins of Wellesley, and William H. Burnham of Clark; and a biographical sketch by Sanford's sister, Martha L. Sanford. The most complete recent assessment of Sanford's life and work is C. James Goodwin, "In Hall's Shadow: Edmund Clark Sanford (1859–1924)," *Journal of the History of the Behavioral Sciences* 23 (1987): 153–68. An obituary is in the *Boston Post*, 23 Nov. 1924.

C. JAMES GOODWIN

SANFORD, Edward Terry (23 July 1865–8 Mar. 1930), jurist, was born in Knoxville, Tennessee, the son of Edward Jackson Sanford, a highly successful lumber and wholesale drug merchant, and Emma Chavannes. He received his A.B. and Ph.B. in 1883 from the University of Tennessee, where he graduated at the head of his class and was elected to Phi Beta Kappa. He earned a second A.B. two years later at Harvard, where his election as Class Day orator presaged many future requests for his eloquence at such ceremonial occasions. After a year in Europe devoted to study and travel, Sanford returned to Harvard Law School in 1886. There he served on the inaugural editorial board of the *Law Review* and received his LL.B. in 1889. Admitted to the bar in 1888, he returned after graduation to his hometown, where he practiced law until 1907, earning a reputation as a skillful and powerful advocate. In 1891 he married Lutie Mallory Woodruff. They had two daughters.

Sanford was named special assistant to the U.S. attorney general for the prosecution of the Fertilizer Trust in 1905, which led to his appointment as assistant attorney general two years later. He returned to Tennessee in 1908, when President Theodore Roosevelt nominated him to sit as the sole federal district judge for both the eastern and middle districts of his native state. Despite a deliberate, meticulous nature that disposed him to ruminate over opinions longer than many litigants would have liked, Sanford won the respect of the bar and the public for his diligence, patience, impartiality, scrupulous propriety, and compassion. His tenure on the lower bench ended in 1923 when, with the vigorous recommendation of Chief Justice William Howard Taft, he became President Warren G. Harding's fourth appointment to the Supreme Court.

On the Court, Sanford was esteemed for his urbanity, erudition, genial disposition, and courtly manners. He was, as Justice Oliver Wendell Holmes put it, "born to charm." During his seven-year tenure he delivered 130 opinions of the Court, many of them in such technical areas as admiralty, taxation, bankruptcy, and patent law. His learned opinion in the *Pocket Veto Case* (1929) provided the definitive interpretation of the constitutional provision making a bill not returned by the president within ten days law "unless the Congress by their Adjournment prevent its Return." Where federal and state economic regulation were concerned, Sanford was among the more receptive members of the Taft Court. He supported federal control of both stockyards and grain exchanges in *Tagg Bros. & Moorhead v. U.S.* (1930) and *Chicago Board of Trade v. Olsen* (1923). He voted to uphold residential zoning in *Euclid v. Ambler Realty Co.* (1926), and he joined Taft's opinion dissenting from the Court's invalidation of the minimum wage in *Adkins v. Children's Hospital* (1923). He would break with Taft in *Tyson & Bro. v. Banton* (1927), dissenting from the majority opinion striking down a statute limiting resale prices of theater tickets. Yet though his sentiments on matters of economic regulation often placed him in the minority, his respect for precedent prompted him to join or concur specially in subsequent opinions dealing with issues on which his views had earlier not prevailed.

On the civil rights front, Sanford would join the majority in *Meyer v. Nebraska* (1923), *Pierce v. Society of Sisters* (1925), and *Farrington v. Tokushige* (1927), the trilogy of cases shielding Catholics and immigrants from nativist school regulations and recognizing noneconomic rights protected by the Fourteenth Amendment's due process clause. His record in cases involving the rights of African Americans, however, was mixed. He joined the majority in *Moore v. Dempsey* (1923), reversing the conviction of black defendants at a trial dominated by a mob, and voted to invalidate the Texas all-white Democratic primary in *Nixon v. Herndon* (1927). Yet he voted to uphold segregated public education in *Gong Lum v. Rice* (1927) and wrote the opinion sustaining racially restrictive real estate covenants in *Corrigan v. Buckley* (1926).

Sanford is best remembered for his First Amendment opinions. In both *Gitlow v. New York* (1925) and *Whitney v. California* (1927) he sustained state authority to punish advocacy of the violent overthrow of government. The "bad tendency" of such speech placed it outside the amendment's protections. "The State cannot reasonably be required to measure the danger from every such utterance in the nice balance of a jeweler's scale," he wrote in *Gitlow*. The authorities might extinguish a revolutionary "spark without waiting until it has enkindled the flame or blazed into the conflagration." Yet *Gitlow* laid the groundwork for more speech-protective decisions in the future, by explicitly committing the Court for the first time to the view that the First Amendment's prohibitions applied to state governments through the Fourteenth Amendment. Sanford wrote the opinion overturning the state criminal syndicalism conviction of a member of the Industrial Workers of the World in *Fiske v. Kansas* (1927), and in 1929 dissented from the denial of American citizenship to Rosika Schwimmer, a pacifist who would not promise to bear arms in the nation's defense.

Sanford was involved in numerous civic, professional, and charitable activities. He was a charter member of the Knoxville General Hospital's Board of Governors, served as vice president of the American Bar Association and the Tennessee Historical Society, and was president of the Tennessee Bar Association (1904–1905). Chief among the passions of this impressively cultured man was education. The recipient of honorary degrees from the University of Cincinnati (1908) and Harvard (1924), he taught law at the University of Tennessee from 1897 to 1916 and served on its board of trustees for twenty-six years (1897–1923). He was a charter member and chairman of the board of George Peabody College for Teachers, on which he remained until his death.

En route to Justice Holmes's eighty-ninth birthday celebration in Washington, Sanford stopped at the dentist for a tooth extraction. Immediately thereafter he collapsed, the victim of fatal uremic poisoning. Chief Justice Taft coincidentally expired later that same day. As his moderate career on the Court had stood in Taft's shadow, so too news of Sanford's death would be eclipsed by the passing of his friend and sponsor.

• A small collection of Sanford's papers is in the University of Tennessee Library in Knoxville. On Sanford's life before his appointment to the Supreme Court, see Stanley A. Cook, "Path to the High Bench: The Pre-Supreme Court Career of Justice Edward Terry Sanford" (Ph.D. diss., Univ. of Tennessee, 1977), and John W. Green, "Some Judges of the United States District Court of Tennessee (1878–1939)," *Tennessee Law Review* 18 (Apr. 1944). Lewis L. Laska, "Mr. Justice Sanford and the Fourteenth Amendment," *Tennessee Historical Quarterly* 33, no. 15 (1974), Allan E. Ragan, "Mr. Justice Sanford," *Eastern Tennessee Historical Society Publications* 15 (Summer 1943), and James A. Fowler, "Mr. Justice Edward Terry Sanford," *American Bar Association Journal* 17 (Apr. 1931), also provide useful if brief overviews of Sanford's life and career. An obituary is in the *New York Times*, 9 Mar. 1930.

BARRY CUSHMAN

SANFORD, Henry Shelton (15 June 1823–21 May 1891), diplomat and businessman, was born in Woodbury, Connecticut, the son of Nehemiah Curtis Sanford, a merchant and manufacturer, and Nancy Bateman Shelton. The elder Sanford's prosperous mercantile ventures enabled Henry to attend the Episcopal Academy in Cheshire, Connecticut, from which he graduated in 1839, and Washington College in Hartford, from which he withdrew for reasons of health during his sophomore year in 1840. Sanford spent much of the ensuing eight years traveling and studying in Europe, where he learned several languages and earned a doctor of laws degree from the University of Heidelberg in 1849.

During his European wanderings, Sanford decided upon a career in the diplomatic service. After temporary stints as an attaché and secretary in the American legations in St. Petersburg and Berlin in 1847 and 1848, he served as permanent secretary to William C. Rives, the U.S. minister to France from 1849 to 1853, and as chargé d'affaires from mid-1853 through early 1854 following Rives's resignation. Over the remainder of the 1850s Sanford, an aspiring diplomat, prosecuted a private claim against Venezuela over the expulsion of guano miners from Aves Island in the Caribbean, twice traveled to Latin America as an agent for the Honduras Interoceanic Railway Company and the Panama Railroad Company, and unsuccessfully solicited diplomatic appointments from the Buchanan administration.

Sanford's campaign for a significant diplomatic position came to fruition in March 1861 with his appointment as U.S. minister resident to Belgium. Never an active participant in either Whig or Republican politics, his appointment resulted from the influence of his uncles Edward N. Shelton and Philo S. Shelton with New York politico Thurlow Weed, U.S. Senator Truman Smith, and Secretary of State William H. Seward. Sanford ably represented U.S. interests in Brussels over the ensuing eight years, but his most significant work involved countering Confederate operations in Europe. He initiated a broad-ranging secret service network against Southern agents in England and France. In 1861 his use of private detectives and coordination of the espionage work of U.S. consuls obtained important intelligence on Confederate shipbuilding and contraband shipments and established the framework for subsequent northern efforts. Thereafter, U.S. consuls Freeman H. Morse in London, Thomas Haines Dudley in Liverpool, and John Bigelow in Paris employed similar tactics to help block Confederate shipbuilding schemes. Sanford's attempts at sabotaging ships laden with Confederate materiel threatened relations with Great Britain and were less prescient. Together with the unfavorable publicity his secret service work occasioned in the British press and the objections of U.S. minister Charles Francis Adams to Sanford's interference in Great Britain, these attempts led Secretary of State Seward to replace him as the Union espionage coordinator in late 1861.

Sanford assumed similar pan-European responsibilities in the purchase of munitions and other war materiel. From October 1861 through January 1862, he controlled a fund of $1 million and oversaw Union procurement. Seeking simultaneously to deny the Confederates supplies and to provide useful materials to the North, Sanford approved nearly $300,000 in arms purchases by U.S. agents and personally secured another 125,000 arms and 400 tons of saltpeter. Together with these contracts came unsubstantiated charges of corruption that dogged Sanford to the grave. The peripatetic minister complemented these secret service and purchasing assignments with persistent attempts to disseminate Union propaganda through influential European newspapers and to carry Lincoln's ill-advised and abortive offer of a northern command to Giuseppe Garibaldi in September 1861. Sanford's years in Brussels were highlighted by his marriage in 1864 to Gertrude Ellen du Puy of Philadelphia. Drawing primarily upon Henry's inheritance, the Sanfords established a lavish household in Brussels and had seven children over the next fourteen years.

Sanford's tenure in Belgium ended with the inauguration of the Grant administration in 1869. Through the remainder of his life, he sought "an opportunity to *do* something to gain a solid reputation" (Fry, p. 86). The results of this quest were mixed. Beginning in 1868, he invested heavily in the New South. These investments included renting a sea-island cotton plantation in South Carolina (1868–1870), purchasing a sugar plantation in Louisiana (1869), and buying 12,547 acres of raw land in central Florida (1870). Endeavoring to develop and sell the Florida acreage, Sanford founded the town bearing his name, financed a hotel and several other businesses, and experimented extensively in citrus cultivation. This experimentation, particularly at his Belair Grove, substantially furthered citrus growing in the United States and led historians to laud Sanford as the "founder" of the modern Florida citrus industry (Fry, p. x). All of these southern speculations proved disastrous financially. Although the causes were complex, Sanford's inattention was critical. He and his family continued to live extravagantly at least half of each year in Brussels, which exacerbated their increasing insolvency.

Sanford's final grasp at fame and renewed fortune came with the promotion of Leopold II's projects in the Congo Basin. Flattered by the cunning monarch's personal attention, convinced that the United States would profit from the king's assurances of free trade in Central Africa, and hopeful of personal financial rehabilitation, Sanford was primarily responsible for convincing the Arthur administration to extend formal diplomatic recognition to the Association Internationale du Congo (AIC) in March 1884. He thereafter served as an associate U.S. delegate to the Berlin West African Conference of 1884–1885. Sanford steered the American delegation toward public positions that simultaneously aided the AIC and promoted neutrality and free trade in the Congo Basin. Privately, he played a central role in the negotiations leading to French and Portuguese recognition of AIC territorial claims. Following the conference, Sanford organized the Sanford Exploring Expedition, the first trading company on the Upper Congo; but the envisioned returns never materialized and he lost heavily in still another speculative venture. Sanford completed his African involvements by serving as a member of the American delegation to the Brussels Anti–Slavery Conference in 1889-1890.

Sanford's African involvements concluded his public life. He died in Healing Springs, Virginia, having failed to attain the significance or the prominence he sought. Still, he had been an active and important Union diplomat, the central figure in the evolution of United States policies toward the Congo during the 1880s, and the most important single contributor to Florida's late nineteenth-century citrus industry.

• Sanford's personal papers are housed in the Sanford Memorial Library, Sanford, Fla. For his diplomatic career, essential is U.S. diplomatic correspondence, Record Group 59, in the National Archives. The only comprehensive biography and complete list of sources is Joseph A. Fry, *Henry S. Sanford: Diplomacy and Business in Nineteenth Century America* (1982). On Sanford's Civil War diplomacy, see also Harriet C. Owsley, "Henry Shelton Sanford and Federal Surveillance Abroad, 1861–1865," *Mississippi Valley Historical Review* 48 (1961): 211–28, and Neil F. Sanders, "Henry Shelton Sanford in England, April–November, 1861: A Reappraisal," *Lincoln Herald* 77 (Summer 1975): 87–95. On Sanford's New South investments, see especially Richard J. Amundson, "The Florida Land and Colonization Company," *Florida Historical Quarterly* 44 (1966): 153–68, and "Oakley Plantation: A Post–Civil War Venture in Louisiana Sugar," *Louisiana History* 9 (1968): 21–42. On the Congo, see Lyle E. Meyer, "Henry S. Sanford and the Congo: A Reassessment," *African Historical Studies* 4 (1971): 19–39, and James L. Roark, "American Expansionism vs. European Imperialism: Henry S. Sanford and the Congo Episode, 1883–1885," *Mid-America* 60 (1978): 21–33. An obituary is in the *New York Times*, 23 May 1891.

JOSEPH A. FRY

SANFORD, Maria Louise (19 Dec. 1836–21 Apr. 1920), professor and public lecturer, was born in Saybrook, Connecticut, the daughter of Henry E. Sanford, a shoemaker, and Mary Clark. Early indebtedness that her father repaid over many years taught Sanford the importance of responsibility and kept the family close to poverty. Her own account nonetheless, was of a happy and secure childhood in a Congregational household that read the Bible and worked for community betterment. An unusually able student, she completed local schooling at the Meriden Academy and then asked her father to provide, instead of a marriage portion, the money to attend the New Britain Normal School. She graduated with honors in 1855 and began teaching in Gilead, Connecticut.

Self-conscious and self-critical, Sanford initially found teaching very difficult and had intermittent bouts of depression during her early years of teaching. Nonetheless she was able to draw her students to their subjects and was delighted when a visiting county superintendent told her, "I have been watching your children all the afternoon. You said nothing. Each one seemed to be doing exactly as he wanted to do, and each one wanted to do right." For her entire teaching career Sanford took special pride in the independence

and commitment she could instill in her students, particularly those who were slower or who had a reputation for being difficult. Various family members lived with her as she moved from school to school. She eventually settled for several years in New Haven, where she was briefly engaged to a theological student at Yale. When that relationship ended, she devoted herself to a course of self-study in history and literature, although never novels, which she thought were frivolous and without moral value.

Sanford's reputation as an exceptional teacher led the superintendent from Parkersville, Pennsylvania, to visit her classroom. She was gone the day of his visit, caring for a member of her family, but had left a schedule of work for her pupils; the impressed superintendent found the classroom running smoothly without supervision. Sanford accepted in 1867 his offer of a position in West Chester, Pennsylvania, where she impressed local Quakers with her teaching ability. Shortly after an unsuccessful bid to become county superintendent of schools, she accepted an offer from Swarthmore College, where she taught history and moral economy from 1869 to 1879. By this time she had also developed a reputation as a public speaker at the short-term training institutes for teachers that were held on weekends and in the summer. Taking advantage of women's increasing acceptance as public lecturers, she also spoke before mixed audiences of men and women on cultural topics. Sanford's exceptional visibility and success as a lecturer resulted partly from her strong, well-modulated voice and her poised demeanor in her standard black dress decorated with only a white ruff at the collar. Fond of reciting long poems and prose passages, Sanford also presented public lectures on a range of topics, which inevitably included a message about human character. Most famous was her talk on "The Value of Moral Power in the Classroom."

The mutual attraction between Sanford and Swarthmore president Edward Magill, who was already married, seems to have led to her decision to resign from the college. Her few educational credentials and a reluctance of other colleges to hire women for their faculties complicated her search for another position. In 1880 she arranged an interview with W. W. Folwell, then president of the University of Minnesota, while they both were participating in the lecture and self-study programs held each summer in Chautauqua, New York. He hired her that year as assistant professor of English to teach rhetoric and elocution. She earned $1,200 her first year. Sanford's classes were well attended and their content moved beyond rhetoric and elocution to include the study of literature, history, and art history. She also spent considerable time coaching debate teams and judging oratorical contests. She was a popular teacher at the university but also faced some difficult times, as when she was nearly forced to resign over the issue of taking money for tutoring students; her salary was later reduced by the board of regents.

Sanford again established a regional reputation at teachers' institutes in the Dakotas, Iowa, and Minnesota. She taught summer school and pioneered in what eventually became an official university extension program. The topics of her lectures were resonant with progressive public opinion at the turn of the century. Active in local organizations, she promoted the point of view and the projects of such groups as the Woman's Christian Temperance Union, the Minneapolis Business and Professional Women's Club, and the Minneapolis Improvement League (an affiliate of the National Federation of Women's Clubs). Concerned about women's health and working conditions, she was a belated, but eventually solid, supporter of the woman suffrage movement.

In 1909 she retired from the University of Minnesota with a $1,500 Carnegie pension. She continued to travel across the country to address women's clubs, teachers' associations, and alumni groups. In Atlanta in 1910 she participated in the dedication of the First Congregational Church, the largest black church in the city, and that event launched her into a new series of lectures on behalf of people of color throughout the South and East. A few years later she became interested in the circumstances of Blackfeet Indian children at a reservation at Browning, Montana, where she helped stem a trachoma outbreak and worked to get federal money for a school. Now in her seventies, she persisted in lecturing at the university and on tours across the country, activities that were dutifully recounted in the *Minnesota Alumni Weekly*. These tours were obviously invigorating for the indomitable lecturer, who spoke in country churches as well as major city civic centers. They also provided money to pay off a debt that she carried for nearly thirty years, retiring it a little at a time from her earnings. Abstemious in her personal habits, she had been at times naive about financial schemes of friends and students and inevitably generous to both family and friends, who often stayed with her for extended periods. By 1916 the debt was repaid. The following year she received an honorary doctorate from Carleton College, where her former student, now dean of women, observed that Sanford "influenced great numbers by her truth and moved them by her eloquence." Local tributes accrued as she continued her vigorous lecture schedule; these included the naming of the Maria L. Sanford School in Minneapolis, Sanford Hall dormitory for women at the university, and the Sanford Fellowships for girls by the State Federation of Women's Clubs.

Sanford's final public triumph was an address made in Washington, D.C., to the Daughters of the American Revolution, which included a well-known apostrophe to the flag. Although she was frail, her words rang through the hall, and she received a standing ovation. Two days later she died peacefully in her sleep at the home of her host, Senator Knute Nelson, in Washington, D.C. Her grave is in the Mount Vernon Cemetery near Philadelphia. When her statue was placed in the Capitol in 1958 as one of the two Minnesota representatives, she was only the second woman to be so honored.

Teaching, lecturing, and living interlocked for this rather private woman whose entire life was devoted primarily to public concerns. Friendly to many people, Sanford apparently had few intimates. A cordial correspondence with Magill continued over the years, but she did not accept his offer of marriage in her later years, after his wife had died. She tried to live the moral, dedicated, hardworking life that she advocated in her public speeches, and her constancy accounts in part for the vivid memories and staunch loyalty of students, audiences, and colleagues in reform.

• Sanford's correspondence and personal memorabilia are primarily at the Minnesota Historical Society; additional correspondence and manuscripts are in the Sanford and other administrative collections in the University of Minnesota Archives. Helen Whitney's biography, *Maria Sanford* (1922), reflects the thoughtful assessment of a close associate and includes a short autobiographical account of Sanford's childhood. Maude S. Shapiro, "A Rhetorical Critical Analysis of Lecturing of Maria Louise Sanford" (Ph.D. diss., Univ. of Minnesota, 1959), provides a thorough account of the range and content of Sanford's public lectures. Additional personal information and testimonials are in U.S. Congress, *Acceptance of the Statue of Maria L. Sanford Presented by the State of Minnesota*. 86th Cong., 1960. A more recent analysis of her academic career is found in Geraldine Joncich Clifford, "'Best Loved' . . . and Besieged: Maria Louise Sanford, 1836–1920," in *Lone Voyagers: Academic Women in Coeducational Universities, 1870–1937*, ed. G. J. Clifford (1989).

SALLY GREGORY KOHLSTEDT

SANGER, Charles Robert (31 Aug. 1860–25 Feb. 1912), chemist, was born in Boston, Massachusetts, the son of George Partridge Sanger, a lawyer, judge, and editor, and Elizabeth Sherburne Thompson. He entered Harvard College in 1877 and graduated with an A.B. in 1881. For the next year he remained at Harvard, carrying on chemical research under Henry B. Hill. Having received an A.M. in 1882, Sanger went to Germany for a year of study in Munich, and later in Bonn, where he met distinguished organic chemist Richard Anschütz. On his return home he completed his Ph.D. studies under Hill. His doctoral dissertation was on pyromucic acid (2-furoic acid) and its derivatives. Sanger continued as Hill's research assistant until 1886, when he was appointed professor of chemistry at the U.S. Naval Academy in Annapolis, Maryland. That same year he married Almira Starkweather Horswell; they had three children.

During his stay in Annapolis, Sanger published his important paper "The Quantitative Determination of Arsenic by the Berzelius-Marsh Process, especially as Applied to the Analysis of Wallpaper and Fabrics" (*American Chemical Journal* 13 [1891]: 431–53). Hitherto, quantitative measurements of arsenic could be obtained only when large amounts were present. In such cases, the arsenic, reduced to elemental form, could be weighed. But arsenic poisoning could result from quantities of the element too small to be weighed. Sanger showed how the arsenic deposit obtained in the

Berzelius-Marsh analysis could be compared visually with deposits obtained from known amounts of arsenic. His meticulous work led to a procedure by which arsenic quantities as small as 0.0007 milligrams in wallpaper samples could be measured.

Sanger left Annapolis in 1892 to become Eliot Professor of Chemistry at Washington University in St. Louis, Missouri. But by 1899 he had returned to Harvard, as an assistant professor. His mentor Hill now ailing, Sanger gave the course in qualitative analytical chemistry previously taught by Hill. Sanger also initiated a course in industrial chemistry. After Hill's death in February 1903, Sanger was promoted to full professor and made director of the chemistry laboratory, a position he held for the rest of his life. In 1902–1903 he was vice president of the Northeast Section of the American Chemical Society. A fellow of the American Academy of Arts and Sciences, he served as the editor of its *Proceedings* for 1909–1910. After the death of his wife in 1905, in 1910 he had married Eleanor Whitney Davis.

Sanger is best known for his work on arsenic poisoning of people exposed to arsenic-containing wallpaper, carpets, and other house furnishings. Using his improved analytical methods, he showed that arsenic levels found in human tissues and excreta were directly correlated with exposure to arsenic-containing materials. The transfer of arsenic from wallpaper to human beings was a further mystery. While removal of the wallpaper resulted in disappearance of toxic symptoms, painting over the wallpaper did not. The source of toxicity was arsine (arsenic hydride), an extremely toxic gas formed on reduction of the small amounts of nonvolatile arsenates present in wallpaper. He thus confirmed the discovery by the Italian chemist Gosio that mold growing on an arsenic-containing substrate generated an arsenical gas. The arsine-forming fungus could live even on the painted surface, its cells reaching into the underlying wallpaper.

The formation of arsine was also the key reaction in the analytical method for detecting arsenic. The arsenates were reduced by hydrogen or other inorganic reducing agents to arsine gas. In the Berzelius-Marsh method, the arsine was passed through a heated tube, where it was decomposed to elemental arsenic and hydrogen. Impingement of the heated arsenic-containing molecules on a cool glass or porcelain surface left a dark spot, or mirror. Sanger, by precise control of the conditions of analysis and by the use of reference standards containing known amounts of arsenic, had been able to correlate the spot size with the amount of arsenic in the original sample. Later he applied the same rigorous controls to the Gutzeit method, in which the arsine produces a spot through passage through silver nitrate-impregnated paper. Sanger further improved the Gutzeit method by substituting mercuric chloride for silver nitrate as the oxidant for arsine. Thus improved, the Gutzeit method became a reliable, sensitive method in arsenic analysis.

Sanger's last researches dealt with the preparation and properties of pyrosulfuryl chloride and chlorosul-fonic acid; the reaction of sulfur trioxide on silicon tetrachloride; and the detection of fluorine. He died in Cambridge, Massachusetts, where he had spent most of his professional career.

• Biographical accounts include those by C. L. Jackson in the *Proceedings of the American Academy of Arts and Sciences* 48 (1912–1913): 813–22; and by S. J. Kopperl in *American Chemists and Chemical Engineers*, ed. W. D. Miles (1976), p. 423. An obituary is in the *New York Times*, 26 Feb. 1912.

CHARLES H. FUCHSMAN

SANGER, Margaret (14 Sept. 1879–6 Sept. 1966), birth control advocate, was born Margaret Higgins in Corning, New York, to Michael Hennessey Higgins, an Irish-born free thinker who eked out a meager living as a stonemason, and Anne Purcell, a hard-working, devoutly Roman Catholic Irish-American. Deeply influenced by her father's iconoclasm, Margaret, one of eleven children, was also haunted by her mother's premature death, which she attributed to the rigors of frequent childbirth and poverty. Determined to escape a similar fate, Margaret Higgins, supported by her two older sisters, attended Claverack College and Hudson River Institute before enrolling in White Plains Hospital as a nurse probationer in 1900. She was a practical nurse in the women's ward working toward her registered nursing degree when her 1902 marriage to architect William Sanger ended her formal training. Though plagued by a recurring tubercular condition, she bore three children and settled down to a quiet life in Westchester, New York. In 1911, however, in an effort to salvage their troubled marriage, the Sangers abandoned the suburbs for a new life in New York City.

The radical activism and bohemian culture that permeated New York in the prewar years created a formative educational environment for Margaret Sanger. "Our living-room," she recalled in her autobiography, "became a gathering place where liberals, anarchists, socialists and IWW's could meet." Exposed to modernist notions of political, social, and personal revolution, Sanger discovered the ideological justifications and practical outlets for her rebelliousness and unconventionality. She joined the Women's Committee of the New York Socialist party and participated in several labor actions undertaken by the Industrial Workers of the World, including the notable 1912 strike of textile workers at Lawrence, Massachusetts. Sanger's emerging feminist/Socialist interests, coupled with her nursing background, led in 1912 to an invitation to write "What Every Girl Should Know," a column on female sexuality and social hygiene for the New York *Call*. The series quickly drew the attention of postal authorities, which in 1913 banned her article on venereal disease as obscene.

Sanger's general interest in sex education and women's health soon focused on family limitation. Returning to work as a visiting nurse among the immigrants of New York City's Lower East Side, she saw graphic examples of the toll taken by frequent childbirth, miscarriage, and self-induced abortion. With access to contraceptive information prohibited on grounds of obscenity by the 1873 federal Comstock law and a host of state laws, Sanger realized that poor women did not have the same freedom from the physical hardships, fear, and dependency inherent in unwanted pregnancy as did those radical middle-class women who were espousing sexual liberation. Awakened to the connection between contraception and working-class empowerment by anarchist/feminist Emma Goldman, Sanger became convinced that liberating women from the risk of unwanted pregnancy would effect fundamental social change. With older feminists espousing family limitation through sexual abstinence and Socialists unwilling to be distracted by a fight for birth control, Sanger launched her own campaign, challenging governmental censorship of contraceptive information by embarking on a series of law-defying confrontational actions designed to force birth control into the center of public debate.

In March 1914 Sanger began publishing *The Woman Rebel*, a radical feminist monthly that advocated militant action and the right of every woman to be "absolute mistress of her own body." The educational, economic, and political equality espoused by most feminists were irrelevant, Sanger declared, unless women first had the means to avoid the burden of unwanted pregnancies. Only birth control, a term coined in *The Woman Rebel*, would free women from the tyranny of uncontrolled childbirth. Although she did little more than espouse birth control in *The Woman Rebel*, postal authorities suppressed five of its seven issues. Sanger defied the authorities by continuing publication while preparing her next salvo against the obscenity laws: *Family Limitation*, a sixteen-page pamphlet containing the most precise evaluations and graphic descriptions of various contraceptive methods then available to American women. In August 1914 Margaret Sanger was indicted for violating postal obscenity laws in *The Woman Rebel*. Unwilling to risk imprisonment, she jumped bail in October and, using the alias "Bertha Watson," set sail for England via Canada. En route she ordered the release of *Family Limitation*. A few weeks later William Sanger was tricked into providing a copy of the pamphlet to an operative of antivice crusader Anthony Comstock and went to jail for thirty days. This escalated interest in birth control as a civil liberties issue.

Margaret Sanger spent much of her 1914 exile in England, where contact with British neo-Malthusianists helped refine her socioeconomic justifications for birth control. She was also profoundly influenced by the liberation theories of British sexual theorist Havelock Ellis. Under his tutelage she formulated a new rationale that would liberate women not just by making sexual intercourse safe, but also pleasurable. It would, in effect, free women from the inequality of sexual experience.

In these years Sanger also set about ordering her personal life in accordance with her belief in sexual freedom and the empowerment of women. Her abrupt 1914 departure effectively ended her already rocky marriage to William Sanger, and she embarked on a series of romantic liaisons with men, including Havelock Ellis and H. G. Wells. In 1922 she married wealthy oil producer James Noah H. Slee, but it was a marriage on her own terms. Though fond of Slee, she accepted his proposal only after he agreed to accept her demand for personal autonomy. He also promised to provide support for the birth control movement. The marriage, successful in its own way, lasted until Slee's death in 1943.

Sanger returned to New York in October 1915 anxious to capitalize on the publicity surrounding William Sanger's trial by facing her own charges for publishing *The Woman Rebel*. Her campaign to focus media attention and generate favorable public support received an unexpected boost from the wave of sympathetic publicity that followed the sudden death on 6 November of Sanger's five-year-old daughter, Peggy. Unwilling to grant the bereaved mother and her cause further press coverage, the government decided not to prosecute. Margaret Sanger then undertook a nationwide lecture tour, a journey marked by volatile confrontations with local authorities and several arrests.

Near the end of the tour, Sanger decided to shift her strategy from defying censorship laws to challenging the prohibition on the distribution of contraceptive services. Seeking to replicate the Dutch system of medically supervised clinics she had observed in 1914, Sanger opened the nation's first birth control clinic, in Brooklyn, on 16 October 1916. Nine days later police raided the clinic arresting Sanger and her coworkers. Tried and convicted, she served thirty days in prison. Sanger appealed, but her conviction was upheld. Nevertheless, the state appellate court's 1918 decision interpreted the prohibitory statute broadly enough to allow physicians to prescribe birth control to women when medically indicated. The decision provided Sanger with the legal basis for establishing a birth control distribution system of doctor-staffed clinics. Equally significant for Sanger was the expanding circle of wealthy women who volunteered their time and money in support of birth control.

With her talent for keeping the birth control controversy in the public eye, Sanger prepared a 1917 silent film entitled "Birth Control," which was quickly confiscated by New York authorities. Undaunted, she continued to provoke authorities by promoting birth control publicly. While audiences, disarmed by her delicacy and personal charm, applauded her frankness and courage, opponents, particularly Catholic groups, persisted in efforts to ban her from speaking. Such clumsy attempts usually backfired. "I see immense advantages in being gagged," Sanger noted in a 1929 speech at Boston's Ford Hall. "It silences me but it makes millions of others talk about me and the cause in which I live."

With the collapse of the radical left after World War I, Sanger, who had grown increasingly disillusioned by the lack of interest of Socialists and feminists, abandoned her radical/Socialist stance and sought to broaden the movement's base of support. In 1917 she had begun promoting birth control as a medical and socio-economic issue in a new monthly, the *Birth Control Review*. In 1921 she founded the American Birth Control League, which aimed at cultivating mainstream respectability. Sanger also tried to enlist the support of the liberal wing of the scientific eugenics movement, championing birth control for those with genetically transmitted mental or physical defects, and even supporting forced sterilization for the mentally incompetent. While she did not advocate efforts to limit population growth solely on the basis of class, ethnicity, or race, and refused to encourage positive eugenics for white, native-born, middle and upper classes, Sanger's reputation was permanently tainted by the growing prominence of race-based eugenics.

Critical to Sanger's efforts was the support of the medical community. In Holland in 1914 she had been introduced to the occlusive diaphragm. She now argued that the proper use of these devices required medically skilled and individualized instruction. In 1923 she opened the Birth Control Clinical Research Bureau (later renamed the Margaret Sanger Research Bureau), staffed by female physicians who provided an array of gynecological and contraceptive services. The bureau kept extensive patient records, compiled statistics tracking the effectiveness of contraceptives on women's health, and became the model for a nationwide system of doctor-staffed clinics. In 1929 Sanger formed the National Committee on Federal Legislation for Birth Control to lobby for legislation granting doctors exclusive right to disseminate contraceptives. Nevertheless, most doctors remained hostile to Sanger's efforts. Even those who supported birth control distrusted her, a nonprofessional with a feminist focus and a history of militant action. For her part, Sanger resisted their efforts to take control of her clinic and her movement. It was not until 1937 that the American Medical Association endorsed birth control.

Despite Sanger's success in cultivating public support, powerful opposition from the Catholic Church helped insure the failure of her legislative work, along with her efforts to secure government funding for birth control as a public health measure. She did win a judicial victory in 1936 when the U.S. Court of Appeals in *U.S. v. One Package of Japanese Pessaries* ruled that physicians were exempted from the ban on the importation of birth control materials. This decision effectively legalized the distribution of birth control for medical use, though the prohibition on importing contraceptive devices for personal use was not lifted until 1971.

In courting an alliance with establishment forces, Margaret Sanger provided the birth control movement with the financial support and social rationale needed to battle significant opposition. Yet her pragmatic approach also led to a subtle but steady change in the direction of the movement. As the number and influence of conservative supporters increased, Sanger's initial focus on women's personal autonomy and empowerment was subordinated to an emphasis on selective

population control and the maintenance of traditional middle-class values. She was forced to resign as president of the American Birth Control League in 1928. The movement's new leaders viewed Sanger's militant tactics and persistently feminist focus as a liability. When in 1939 the American Birth Control League and Sanger's Birth Control Clinical Research Bureau were reorganized into the Birth Control Federation of America, Sanger's role became largely honorific. Even the term "birth control" was deemed too aggressively radical by the new leadership. In 1942 the Birth Control Federation of America became the Planned Parenthood Federation of America. Tired and disillusioned, Sanger retired to her home in Tucson, Arizona.

From the start, Sanger recognized overpopulation as a critical global issue. During the 1920s and 1930s, she organized international conferences and lectured on birth control throughout Europe and Asia. Her 1936 tour of India, which included a widely reported debate with Mahatma Gandhi, helped launch the Indian birth control movement. Sanger also cultivated an extensive worldwide network through the London-based Birth Control International Information Centre, which she cofounded in 1930 with British activist Edith How-Martyn. However, the pronatalist policies of the rising fascist regimes in Europe and Japan impeded their work, and by 1937 they had resigned from the center.

The post–World War II alarm over population growth and its relationship to economic development and social stability, particularly in the Third World, propelled Sanger back onto the world stage as chief propagandist for the revival and expansion of an international birth control movement. Among her first goals was the resuscitation of the Japanese movement, which she had helped mobilize during her 1922 visit. Although she was barred from entering occupied Japan in 1950, a steep hike in the Japanese birth rate created a new consensus on birth control, and in 1954 Sanger was invited to address the Japanese Diet, the first American woman to be so honored.

Sanger's primary goal after 1946 was to establish an international organization. In 1952 she joined other international family planning advocates in founding the International Planned Parenthood Federation (IPPF). Sanger played a critical role in organizing the founding conference in Bombay, cajoling an impressive array of world figures to lend their support. While her IPPF colleagues often were annoyed with her tendency toward imperiousness and unilateral action, they elected her their first president. Though in her seventies and increasingly frail, Sanger nevertheless tried to direct the growth of the infant organization to reflect her unwavering conviction that by reducing the number of unwanted children, birth control would facilitate more efficient allocation of economic and social resources. As president she opposed all efforts to broaden the IPPF's mission beyond the dissemination of birth control. She also resisted efforts to impose mandatory, government-controlled measures that ignored the needs and requirements of women. When Sanger relinquished the presidency in 1959, the IPPF, with twenty-six member nations, was the largest private international organization devoted to promoting family planning.

Throughout these years, Sanger persisted in her pursuit of a simpler, less costly, more effective female contraceptive. In 1925 she arranged for the American manufacture of the spring-form diaphragms she had been smuggling in from Europe. In subsequent years she fostered research projects to develop spermicidal jellies and foam powders, and finally hormonal contraceptives. Vindication for her persistence came in the 1950s after she helped secure the funds that enabled Gregory Pincus to develop the first effective anovulant contraceptive: the birth control pill.

Margaret Sanger died in Tucson, one year after the Supreme Court affirmed the right of married couples to use birth control, a right extended to unmarried couples in 1972.

• The two largest collections of Sanger's papers are in the Library of Congress and the Sophia Smith Collection of Smith College. The Sophia Smith collection also holds the records of the Birth Control Clinical Research Bureau and the Planned Parenthood Federation of America. The Houghton Library at Harvard University houses the records of the American Birth Control League, while Harvard's Countway Library of Medicine houses the correspondence of several of Sanger's medical colleagues. The records of the International Planned Parenthood Federation are in the Population Centre at the University of Cardiff. A comprehensive microfilm edition of Sanger's papers, prepared under the direction of Esther Katz, and four volumes of selected letters, edited by Katz, are scheduled for publication. Sanger's published works include two autobiographies: *My Fight for Birth Control* (1931) and *Margaret Sanger: An Autobiography* (1938). Her other books are *Women and the New Race* (1920), *The Pivot of Civilization* (1922), *Happiness in Marriage* (1926), *Motherhood in Bondage* (1928), and two compilations of her articles, *What Every Girl Should Know* (1916) and *What Every Mother Should Know* (1914). Gloria and Ronald Moore, *Margaret Sanger and the Birth Control Movement: A Bibliography*, (1986), is a bibliography of materials relating to Sanger. The best and most comprehensive scholarly biography of Sanger is Ellen Chesler, *A Woman of Valor: Margaret Sanger and the Birth Control Movement in America* (1992). Less satisfying though informative is Lawrence Lader's uncritical, *The Margaret Sanger Story and the Fight for Birth Control* (1955), written with Sanger's assistance. David Kennedy, *Birth Control in America: The Career of Margaret Sanger* (1970), is a largely negative account of Sanger's public life to 1938. See also the treatments of Sanger included in Margaret Forster, *Significant Sisters: The Grassroots of Active Feminism, 1839–1939* (1986); Linda Gordon, *Woman's Body, Woman's Right: A Social History of Birth Control in America* (1976); and James Reed, *From Public Vice to Private Virtue: The Birth Control Movement and American Society since 1830* (1978). An obituary is in *New York Times*, 7 Sept. 1966.

ESTHER KATZ

SANKEY, Ira David (28 Aug. 1840–14 Aug. 1908), singing evangelist and gospel songwriter, was born in Edinburg, Lawrence County, Pennsylvania, the son of David Sankey and Mary Leeper. Sankey's father was a Pennsylvania state representative, collector of internal revenue, member of the State Board of Equalization, and newspaper editor. During Sankey's childhood his father also farmed in West Central Pennsylvania, near the Ohio border. The family attended King's Chapel near Western Reserve Harbor, where Sankey was converted during revival meetings in 1856. In 1857, when Sankey's father accepted the presidency of a local bank, the family moved to New Castle, Pennsylvania, where Sankey joined the New Castle Methodist Church. By 1860 he was Sunday school superintendent and choir director.

Encouraged by songwriter Philip Phillips and especially by William Bradbury, author of such well-known gospel songs as "Just as I Am," "The Solid Rock," and "Even Me," Sankey began singing solos at local gatherings and devoting his energies to helping others express their religious feelings through music. He gradually won a local reputation that brought him invitations to sing at Sunday school conventions and political rallies in western Pennsylvania and neighboring towns in eastern Ohio. Sankey worked at a bank until the spring of 1861, when President Abraham Lincoln issued a call for soldiers, and he enlisted in the Union army. When his term expired, Sankey secured a position in the Internal Revenue Department and in 1863 married Fanny V. Edwards, daughter of a Pennsylvania state senator and a member of his New Castle Methodist choir. The couple had two children. Together Sankey and his wife traveled in an expanding network of revivals and churches in Pennsylvania and nearby states.

When a branch of the Young Men's Christian Association opened in New Castle in 1867, Sankey became an enthusiastic supporter. He served first as secretary, then as president. In 1870 the local organization sent him as their delegate to the International Convention of the YMCA in Indianapolis. The event became a watershed in Sankey's life, for in Indianapolis he met Dwight L. Moody, another tireless promoter of the YMCA. Moody already had a national reputation as a Sunday school worker and urban evangelist in Chicago. In Indianapolis, Moody heard Sankey sing and impulsively invited him to give up his job and move to Chicago to assist in Moody's various enterprises. Sankey acquiesced, and until Moody's death in 1899 he was an indispensable part of Moody's evangelism efforts. The two first won wide acclaim during a visit to Great Britain from 1873 to 1875.

Sankey became the model for the host of musicians who have accompanied every major revivalist since Moody. He set the poetry of others to simple music, often drawing heavily on popular tunes and rhythms. Occasionally Sankey wrote his own words, but more often he popularized the works of others. He used story songs like "The Ninety and Nine" with considerable effect. His gospel songs were always easy to learn and sing, and he used them effectively to enhance Moody's messages and involve the audience in participation. He did important work as a compiler and editor, collecting the songs he and other gospel singers used and issuing them in cheap editions for use in revival services. His *Sacred Songs and Solos* (1873) and *Gospel Hymns Nos. 1–6* (1875–1891) sold by the hundreds of thousands. Sankey assigned the royalties to a cause Moody deeply cherished: the various schools in Moody's hometown of Northfield, Massachusetts.

Through the many networks provided by Moody, Sankey associated with many of the men and women who gave turn-of-the-century popular Protestantism its musical idiom, among them Fanny Crosby, Robert Lowry, Philip P. Bliss, James McGranahan, and George C. Stebbins. In the 1880s the Sankeys bought a house in Northfield that they used especially during the Northfield conferences. They had another residence in Brooklyn, where they joined the Lafayette Avenue Presbyterian Church, of which Theodore Cuyler was pastor. Failing strength during the 1890s forced Sankey to curtail his schedule and to leave some of the singing in Moody's campaigns to others. His health declined rapidly after 1903, when glaucoma caused his eyesight to deteriorate. Sankey died at his home in Brooklyn.

Generally credited with being the first of the revival choristers, Sankey left a strong imprint on popular evangelism. His songbooks were widely used in the United States, Great Britain, and Canada and helped keep his legacy of simple gospel songs alive.

• For more information, see Ira Sankey, *My Life and the Story of the Gospel Hymns* (1906), and Sandra Sizer, *Gospel Hymns and Social Religion* (1978).

EDITH L. BLUMHOFER

SANTAYANA, George (16 Dec. 1863–26 Sept. 1952), philosopher and writer, was born in Madrid, Spain, the son of Agustín Ruiz de Santayana, a Spanish diplomat, and Josefina Sturgis (formerly Josefina Borrás y Carbonell), the daughter of a Spanish diplomat. His mother had previously married a Boston merchant, George Sturgis, who died in 1857. Santayana was christened Jorge Agustín Nicolás, but his half sister Susana insisted that his name not be the Spanish Jorge, but George, after her father. A permanent resident of Spain only during 1863–1872, he retained his Spanish citizenship throughout his life and frequently returned to visit family and to write.

In 1869 Santayana's mother left Spain, fulfilling a pledge to her first husband to raise their children in Boston. In 1872 Santayana's father brought George to Boston and after a few months returned alone to Spain. The separation between father and mother was permanent. In Boston, Santayana attended a kindergarten to learn English. He later completed his B.A. and Ph.D. at Harvard College (1882–1889), including eighteen months of study in Germany. Santayana regularly corresponded with his father, and after his first year at Harvard, Santayana lived with or visited him in Spain for portions of each year until his father's death in 1893.

Santayana's juvenilia include *Un matrimonio* (A married couple), the poem of an eight-year-old describing the trip of a newly married couple who meet the queen of Spain; a poetic parody of the *Aeneid*; "A Short History of the Class of '82"; and "Lines on Leaving the Bedford St. Schoolhouse." At Harvard he was active as a member of eleven organizations, including the *Lampoon* (largely as a cartoonist), the *Harvard Monthly* (a founding member), the Philosophical Club (president), and the Hasty Pudding.

Several scholars have concluded that Santayana led an active homosexual life from his student days on, but their evidence is drawn largely from allusions in Santayana's early poetry (McCormick, pp. 49–52) and supported by the known homosexual and bisexual orientations of several of Santayana's friends and associates. Santayana never married, and he provides no clear indication of his sexual preferences. Attraction to both women and men seems evident in his correspondence. The one documented comment about his homosexuality was made when he was sixty-five. Following a discussion of A. E. Housman's poetry and homosexuality, Santayana remarked, "I think I must have been that way in my Harvard days—although I was unconscious of it at the time" (Cory, *Santayana*, p. 40).

As a faculty member at Harvard University (1889–1912), Santayana was hesitant about academic life from the start. His father had hoped he would return to Spain either to pursue a diplomatic career or to become an architect. Although Santayana chose scholarship and teaching, he continued at first to live more as a student. He found faculty meetings, committees, and governance structures largely empty, their discussions mostly partisan heat over false issues, and the general corporate and businesslike adaptation of universities not conducive to intellectual curiosity, development, and growth. In a letter to a friend in 1892, Santayana expressed the hope that his academic life would be "resolutely unconventional" and noted that he could only be a professor *per accidens*, saying, "I would rather beg than be one essentially" (letter to H. W. Abbot, 15 Feb. 1892).

Santayana, along with William James and Josiah Royce, was a central figure in an era now called Classical American Philosophy. He became a popular teacher, and his students included poets (Conrad Aiken, T. S. Eliot, Robert Frost, Wallace Stevens), journalists and writers (Walter Lippmann, Max Eastman, Van Wyck Brooks), professors (Samuel Eliot Morison, Harry Austryn Wolfson), a Supreme Court justice (Felix Frankfurter), many diplomats (including his friend Bronson Cutting), and a university president (James B. Conant).

In 1893 Santayana underwent a change of heart. He gradually altered his mode of living and eventually began to plan for his early retirement. Three events preceded what he called his *metanoia*: the unexpected death of a young student, witnessing his father's death, and the marriage of his sister Susana. Santayana's reflections on these events led to a festive conclusion: "Cultivate imagination, love it, give it endless forms, but do not let it deceive you. Enjoy the world, travel over it, and learn its ways, but do not let it hold you. . . . To possess things and persons in idea is the only pure good to be got out of them; to possess them physically or legally is a burden and a snare" (*Persons and Places*, pp. 427–28). For Santayana, this conclusion was liberating; it was the ancient wisdom that acceptance of the tragic leads to a lyrical release.

Naturalism and the lyrical cry of human imagination became the focal points of Santayana's life and thought, and they set him apart from his colleagues in the Harvard philosophy department. His naturalism had its historical roots in Aristotle and Benedictus de Spinoza and its contemporary background in James's pragmatism and Royce's idealism. But the focus on and celebration of creative imagination in all human endeavors (particularly in art, philosophy, religion, literature, and science) is one of Santayana's major contributions to American thought.

The beginning of Santayana's philosophical career was "resolutely unconventional." His first book was *Sonnets and Other Verses* (1894), a book of poems, not philosophy. And until the turn of the century, much of his intellectual life was directed toward the writing of verse and drama. He was a principal figure in making modernism possible, although he cannot be considered a modernist in poetry or literature. His naturalism and emphasis on constructive imagination influenced both Eliot and Stevens: Eliot's notion of the "objective correlative" is drawn from Santayana, and Stevens follows Santayana in his refined naturalism by incorporating both Platonism and Christianity without any nostalgia for God or dogma.

Santayana also had a major effect in transforming the American literary canon. He was among the Harvard intellectuals who helped displace the dominant canon of Henry Wadsworth Longfellow, James Russell Lowell, John Greenleaf Whittier, Oliver Wendell Holmes, and William Cullen Bryant. Santayana's essay "The Genteel Tradition in American Philosophy" (presented to the Philosophical Union of the University of California in 1911) greatly affected Van Wyck Brooks's *America's Coming-of-Age* (1915), a book that set the tone for modernism. Brooks drew directly on Santayana's essay, adapting Santayana's idea of two Americas to fit his notion of an American split between highbrow and lowbrow culture.

By the turn of the century Santayana's philosophical interests exceeded his poetical ones, but he never abandoned poetry. The trench warfare and casualties of World War I inspired some of his most moving work: "A Premonition: Cambridge, October, 1913"; "The Undergraduate Killed in Battle: Oxford, 1915"; "Sonnet: Oxford, 1916"; and "The Darkest Hour: Oxford, 1917." Throughout his life, even near death, he would recite long fragments of Horace, Racine, Leopardi, and others.

His philosophical writings during his Harvard years extended the development of his pragmatic naturalism and his literary interests. *The Sense of Beauty* (1896) remains a primary source for the study of aesthetics. Philip Blair Rice wrote in the foreword to the 1955

Modern Library edition, "To say that aesthetic theory in America reached maturity with *The Sense of Beauty* is in no way an overstatement." In the introduction to the 1988 critical edition, Arthur Danto notes that Santayana brings "beauty down to earth" by treating it as a subject for science and giving it a central role in human conduct, in contrast to the preceding intellectualist tradition of aesthetics. In *Interpretations of Poetry and Religion* (1900) Santayana develops his view that religion and poetry are celebrations of life, but if either is taken for science, that art of life is lost along with the beauty of poetry and religion. The impact of Santayana's view was significant, and Henry James (after reading *Interpretations of Poetry and Religion*) wrote that he would "crawl across London" if need be to meet Santayana.

The five books of *The Life of Reason: or the Phases of Human Progress* (1905–1906) marked Santayana as a major force in the philosophy of the new century. This work became almost canonical for naturalists such as Woodbridge, Edman, Randall, Erskine, Cohen, and Lamont. A survey of the religions, societies, arts, and sciences of the Western world, *The Life of Reason* deciphers intellectual policies consistent with reasonable action. From this work comes the often-quoted warning to those who do not remember the past: they are condemned to repeat it (*Reason in Common Sense*, p. 284). Morris R. Cohen noted that it "is the only comprehensive, carefully articulated, philosophy of life and civilization which has been produced on these shores" (*American Thought*, p. 311).

Three Philosophical Poets (1910)—Santayana's analysis of Lucretius, Dante, and Johann Wolfgang von Goethe—unites his philosophical and poetic interests. According to John McCormick, one of Santayana's biographers, it is "a classical work and one of the few written in America to be genuinely comparative in conception and execution, for its absence of national bias and its intellectual, linguistic, and aesthetic range" (p. 193).

Santayana announced his retirement in May 1911, but Harvard president Abbott Lawrence Lowell asked him to wait and agreed to give Santayana as much free time as he needed. After he initially assented, the resolve to retire overtook Santayana's sense of obligation to Harvard. His mother had died, leaving him a small inheritance. The legacy plus the steady income from publications made retirement easier, and Santayana arranged for his half brother to manage his finances. Hence, in January 1912, at forty-eight, Santayana was free to write, free to travel, free to choose his residence and country, and free from the constraints of university regimen and expectations.

During World War I he resided first in London and then primarily at Oxford and Cambridge. After that, his principal locales were Paris, Madrid, Ávila, the Riviera, Florence, Cortina d'Ampezzo, and Rome. Harvard attempted to bring Santayana back as a professor as early as 1917 and as late as 1929 offered him the Norton Chair in Poetry, one of Harvard's most respected faculty positions. In 1931 he turned down an invitation from Brown University, and Harvard later tempted him to accept for only a term a newly established honorary post, the William James Lecturer in Philosophy. But Santayana never returned to America. In 1932 he delivered two public addresses celebrating the tricentennial of the births of Spinoza and John Locke: "Ultimate Religion," presented in The Hague, and "Locke and the Frontiers of Common Sense," presented to the Royal Society of Literature in London.

Becoming a full-time writer led to remarkable productivity. In retirement, Santayana published sixteen works, including *Winds of Doctrine* (1913), *Character and Opinion in the United States* (1920), *Scepticism and Animal Faith* (1923), the four books of *The Realms of Being* (1927, 1930, 1938, 1940), *The Last Puritan* (1935), *The Idea of Christ in the Gospels* (1946), and *Dominations and Powers* (1951). Santayana appeared on the cover of *Time* on 3 February 1936 in conjunction with his bestselling novel, *The Last Puritan*. The novel and his 1944 autobiography, *Persons and Places*, were each for several months at the top of the Book-of-the-Month Club selections.

In *Character and Opinion in the United States*, Santayana offers his principal reasons for leaving the United States. The English emphasis on social cooperation and personal integrity are corrupted in America so that "[y]ou must wave, you must cheer, you must push with the irresistible crowd; otherwise you will feel like a traitor, a soulless outcast, a deserted ship high and dry on the shore" (p. 211).

Santayana's mature philosophical naturalism is introduced in *Scepticism and Animal Faith*. With Spanish irony Santayana structured the book after René Descartes's *Meditations* while arriving at the opposite conclusion. Genuine doubt ends in a meaningless "solipsism of the present moment," and philosophy must begin in medias res with an instinctive, arational belief in the natural world. This natural belief Santayana called "animal faith." By focusing on animal action Santayana displaced privileged mentalistic accounts with his pragmatic naturalism. This challenge to American and English philosophy is carried forward in his four-volume *Realms of Being*, which focuses on distinguishable characteristics of our knowledge of the world: matter, essence, spirit, and truth. Santayana's antifoundationalism, pragmatic naturalism, emphasis on the spiritual life, and view of the philosophy of literature anticipated many developments in philosophy and literary criticism that occurred in the latter half of the twentieth century and served as a challenge to the more humanistic naturalism of John Dewey.

The Last Puritan, Santayana's only novel, was an international success that was favorably compared with Goethe's *Wilhelm Meister*, Walter Pater's *Marius*, and Thomas Mann's *The Magic Mountain*. Essentially, it is about the life and early death of an American youth, Oliver Alden, who is sadly restricted by his puritanism. Santayana draws a sharp contrast with the European Mario, who delights in all matters without a narrow moralism.

In October 1941, having failed in his efforts to leave Rome before World War II, Santayana entered the Clinica delle Piccola Compagna di Maria, a hospital clinic run by an order of Catholic nuns, where he lived until his death eleven years later. He is buried in the Panteon de la Obra Pia espanola in Rome's Campo Verano cemetery.

The fear that Santayana's autobiography would be lost or destroyed during World War II led Scribner's, the publisher, to conspire with the U.S. Department of State, the Vatican, and the Spanish government to bring the manuscript of the first part (*Persons and Places*) out of Rome sub rosa, despite the Italian government's refusal to allow any mail to the United States. The manuscript for the second part (*The Middle Span*, 1945) also was conveyed surreptitiously to New York. The third part (*My Host the World*, 1953) was published after Santayana's death.

Throughout Santayana's life he displayed both intellectual and financial generosity. In 1937, when Bertrand Russell was unable to find a teaching post in the United States or England, Santayana provided significant financial support, although their philosophical and political outlooks conflicted. Both his financial and his personal generosity are reflected in his correspondence, which provides some of the greatest insights into his person and intellect. Lionel Trilling said he could think of no collection of letters comparable in their sustained quality except those of Keats.

There is no question that Santayana was politically conservative; in short, he believed that freedom derived from order and not order from freedom. Hence, he developed many criticisms of democratic liberalism that began with his youthful assessments of his father's political inclinations and ended with *Dominations and Powers*. He viewed human behavior as natural, an outgrowth of material heritage and environment, and as subject to the "authority of things." Believing that suffering is the worst feature of human life, he focused more on the dilemmas of individuals than on broader social inequalities. This focus and his institutional pragmatism (a view that all institutions, including governments, are inextricably rooted in their culture and background) partially explain why Santayana held that particular views of social inequality could not be transferred easily from one culture to another. His hesitancy in the area of social justice led to criticism from American philosophers, including John Dewey and Sidney Hook, but his consistent "Latin" perspective caused him to look with considerable suspicion toward Anglo-Saxon outlooks forcing their way on other cultures.

Santayana played a towering role in classical American philosophy, the equal of Dewey and James; as an American literary figure his total production is matched perhaps only by Ralph Waldo Emerson. His early retirement left him without graduate students and colleagues to advance his philosophical and literary work, and his influence and reputation waned following his death. The centennial celebrations of Santayana's birth refocused attention on his philosophy, and Hilary Putnam later remarked, "If there has been less attention paid to Santayana's philosophy than to that of Royce or Peirce, this is in large part because his philosophical mood and philosophical intuitions were actually ahead of his time. In many ways he anticipated some of the dominant trends of American philosophy of the present day" ("Santayana Restored" [1985], Massachusetts Institute of Technology brochure for *The Works of George Santayana*).

Santayana presents a remarkable synthesis of European and American thought. His Hispanic heritage, shaded by his sense of being an outsider in America, captures much of the apprehension and concern that are apparent as Americans find their milieus fragmented. His naturalism and emphasis on constructive imagination were harbingers of important intellectual turns on both sides of the Atlantic. He was a naturalist before naturalism grew popular; he accepted multiple perfections before multiculturalism became an issue; he thought of philosophy as literature before it became a theme in American and European scholarly circles; and he managed to naturalize Platonism, update Aristotle, fight off idealisms, and provide a striking and sensitive account of the spiritual life without being a religious believer.

• Major collections of Santayana's papers are at Harvard University, Columbia University, the University of Texas, and the University of Waterloo (Canada). A sampling of letters is in *The Letters of George Santayana*, ed. Daniel Cory (1955), and *Santayana: The Later Years, a Portrait with Letters*, ed. Cory (1963). Works of Santayana not mentioned in the text include *Egotism in German Philosophy* (1915), *Soliloquies in England and Later Soliloquies* (1922), *Dialogues in Limbo* (1926), *Platonism and the Spiritual Life* (1927), *The Genteel Tradition at Bay* (1931), and *Some Turns of Thought in Modern Philosophy* (1933). *George Santayana: A Bibliographical Checklist, 1880–1980* (1982) is a comprehensive bibliography compiled by Herman J. Saatkamp, Jr., and John Jones. MIT Press is publishing a twenty-volume critical edition of *The Works of George Santayana* with Saatkamp (general editor) and William G. Holzberger (textual editor) that includes Santayana's published volumes and some unpublished material: *Persons and Places*, vol. 1 (1986); *The Sense of Beauty: Being the Outlines of Aesthetic Theory*, vol. 2 (1988); *Interpretations of Poetry and Religion*, vol. 3 (1990); and *The Last Puritan*, vol. 4 (1994). Essays and previously unpublished material may also be found in *George Santayana's America*, comp. James Ballowe (1967); *Santayana on America*, ed. Richard C. Lyon (1968); *Physical Order and Moral Liberty*, ed. John Lachs and Shirley Lachs (1969); and *The Complete Poems of George Santayana*, ed. Holzberger (1979). *Overheard in Seville: Bulletin of the Santayana Society*, ed. Angus Kerr-Larson and Saatkamp, publishes critical essays, previously unpublished material, and updated bibliographical information. Biographies include John McCormick, *George Santayana: A Biography* (1987); Bruno Lind, *Vagabond Scholar* (1962); and George W. Howgate, *George Santayana* (1938). David Carter, *George Santayana* (1992), is a children's book in the Chelsea House Hispanics of Achievement series. Scholarly accounts of Santayana's thought include Jacques Duron, *La Pensée de George Santayana: Santayana en Amérique* (1950); Irving Singer, *Santayana's Aesthetics* (1957); Alonso Gamo, *Un español en el mundo: Santayana, poesia y poética* (1966); Willard Arnett, *Santayana and the Sense of Beauty* (1955); Timothy Sprigge,

Santayana: An Examination of His Philosophy (1974); Lois Hughson, *Thresholds of Reality: George Santayana and Modernist Poetics* (1977); John Lachs, *George Santayana* (1988); Anthony Woodward, *Living in the Eternal* (1988); Nynfa Bosco, *Invito al pensiero di George Santayana* (1989); Pedro García Martin, *El sustrato abulense de Jorge Santayana* (1989); and Henry Samuel Levinson, *Santayana, Pragmatism, and the Spiritual Life* (1992). Critical essays on Santayana are in Paul Arthur Schilpp, ed., *The Philosophy of George Santayana* (1940); John Lachs, ed., *Animal Faith and Spiritual Life* (1967); *Southern Journal of Philosophy: Special Issue on Santayana* (Summer 1972); and Kenneth M. Price and Robert C. Leitz, eds., *Critical Essays on George Santayana* (1991). Obituaries are in *Time*, 6 Oct. 1952, and *Indice*, 15 Oct. 1952.

HERMAN J. SAATKAMP, JR.

SAPERSTEIN, Abe (4 July 1902–15 Mar. 1966), basketball promoter, was born Abraham Michael Saperstein in London, England, the son of Louis Saperstein, a tailor, and Anna (maiden name unknown). The Polish-Jewish family migrated to Chicago in 1907, settling in Ravenswood, a rough North Side German-Irish neighborhood.

Despite his diminutive size (5'3"), Saperstein earned fifteen letters at Lake View High School in wrestling, baseball, track, and lightweight basketball before attending the University of Illinois from 1922 to 1923. He worked for Schiller Florists (1920–1925), and for $5 a game he was player-coach of the semipro Chicago Reds, winner of the 1921 Interpark and Intercity basketball championships. In 1925 former Negro League pitcher George Walter Ball of the Chicago American Giants hired Saperstein for $250 a month to coach his all-black basketball team representing the American Legion's Giles Post. Whites had often financed African-American baseball teams before the 1920s, but not as managers; for basketball, the situation was brand-new. The team became known as the Savoy Big Five because they played at the new Savoy Ballroom twice a week before dances or on nights when no dance was scheduled.

In 1926 Saperstein began booking the team around Chicago on off-nights; the following year, when the ballroom became a skating rink, his club began touring as Saperstein's New York Globetrotters (renamed the Harlem Globetrotters in 1931) to suggest well-traveled, sophisticated African-Americans. However, the first notable African-American barnstorming team was not the Globetrotters, but the black-owned New York Renaissance (Rens), recognized as one of the best basketball teams in the United States.

The Globetrotters' first game was on 7 January 1927 in Hinkley, Illinois, about fifty miles west of Chicago. They were paid $75, of which Saperstein took 28 percent as owner, coach, promoter, sole substitute, and chauffeur. They most often played in small midwestern towns, using high school gyms, armories, social halls, and even a drained swimming pool, traveling in an old Model T Ford. Conditions on the road were difficult because of racial prejudice, and the Globetrotters had a hard time getting adequate food and shelter, despite Saperstein's efforts.

The Globetrotters won 101 games, losing only six, during their first year. Their won-lost record was 196–26 over the next two years. Overall, during the depression, the Globetrotters won 90 percent of the 150 to 175 games they played each year, mostly against local teams.

Since the Trotters were too good for their competition, Saperstein encouraged players to employ razzle-dazzle, probably conceived in the 1920s by New York's Original Celtics, for entertainment and to gain bookings and relieve the fans' boredom in uncompetitive games. The practice started with a pregame circle that included slick ballhandling, passes off knees and elbows, behind the back, between the legs, and sleights of hand. After some years the song "Sweet Georgia Brown" was added as accompaniment. In the 1940s fancy dribbling, trick shooting, and comedy routines during games were added to promote ticket sales, for the players' own amusement, and to save physical wear and tear.

In 1934 Saperstein married Sylvia Franklin. They had two children.

In 1939, on the basis of their 148–13 record, the Globetrotters were invited to the first professional world basketball tournament in Chicago. It became an annual affair, lasting through the 1946 season and attracting twelve to sixteen of the nation's best black and white professional teams. Games at Chicago Stadium drew capacity crowds of 20,000 at a time when professional basketball was still considered a minor sport. The Globetrotters placed third in 1939, losing to the Harlem Rens, the eventual champion. In 1940 the Globetrotters went 159–8 and were invited back, winning the tournament over George Halas's Chicago Bruins of the National Basketball League (NBL). This marked the height of their success in straight basketball, and purportedly it was their first profitable year.

Saperstein was active in Negro baseball as a partner in the Birmingham Black Barons, as owner of the Minneapolis–St. Paul Gophers, and as a leading midwestern booking agent for the Negro American League and touring teams. Several black owners in the Negro National League, particularly Cumberland Posey of the Homestead Grays, himself a booking agent, opposed Saperstein, identifying him in 1941 as "a symbol of those who are attempting to edge into professional Negro athletics and to eventually control them." However, Saperstein was on cordial terms with Effa Manley of the Newark Eagles, who respected his business acumen. Furthermore, veteran players like Ed "Double Duty" Radcliffe remember Saperstein's contributions as positive because he provided jobs.

Saperstein is credited with discovering several great basketball talents. In 1942 he took Goose Tatum from his St. Paul baseball team and made him a Globetrotter. With huge hands and 84″ arm span, Tatum was an outstanding showman with an uncannily accurate hook shot who became the team's leading draw. In 1947 Saperstein signed Marques Haynes, a 1946 Langston University graduate, who became known as the world's greatest dribbler. His third find was Meadowlark Lemon, who joined the team in 1954.

At mid-century the Globetrotters were the single most famous professional basketball team and the greatest gate attraction in the United States. They were good enough to beat the NBL champion Minneapolis Lakers in seriously played exhibition games in 1948 and 1949. In 1950 Saperstein organized a world series of basketball, a national tour against college All-America players, which the Globetrotters won 11 games to 7. The series lasted through 1962, with the Trotters winning each year.

In 1950 the year-old National Basketball Association (NBA) became racially integrated. Owners, however, were reluctant to hire black players, mostly because of racial prejudice, but also because of their dependence on Saperstein, whose Globetrotters were a big attraction at NBA doubleheaders; they did not want to challenge his near monopoly on black talent. Duquesne's Chuck Cooper, the first African-American in the NBA, signed with the Celtics for no more money than that offered by the Trotters, with whom he briefly toured. Saperstein later sold the contract of Nat "Sweetwater" Clifton, who wanted to play in the NBA, to the New York Knicks. Clifton made $10,000 with the Trotters, well above the NBA average, but not an unusual salary for the team's top players. Despite integration, many important African-American athletes played for the Globetrotters in the 1950s, including Wilt Chamberlain who in 1958 skipped his senior year at the University of Kansas to join the team. A few, like Connie Hawkins, found the clowning to be demeaning because of its pandering to racial stereotypes of African-Americans as lazy and mischievous. However, most players respected Saperstein for the opportunities he offered.

The Trotters had become so popular that they operated three traveling teams in the early 1950s. Two movies were made about them, *The Harlem Globetrotters* (1951), starring Thomas Gomez as Saperstein, and *Go, Man, Go* (1954), a history of the team starring Dane Clark, as Saperstein, and Sidney Poitier. The films portrayed Saperstein as a racially sensitive, albeit patronizing, individual who was concerned about the welfare of his players. In 1948 the Globetrotters made their first trip to Europe, where they played annually after 1950. In 1951 a game in Berlin was attended by 75,000, still the largest crowd in basketball history. One year later they made their first round-the-world tour to serve as goodwill ambassadors for the U.S. State Department.

Despite the team's popularity, however, they could not escape racism. They played separate games for white and black audiences in the South and had to sleep in people's homes because they usually could not stay in hotels; if they did stay, they were barred from dining rooms. In the 1950s Alabama, Mississippi, and Georgia were dropped from the schedule until African-American spectators were allowed into arenas, albeit in segregated sections.

Saperstein anticipated that his influence with the NBA would get him a West Coast franchise, but in 1960 the choice Los Angeles site was given to the Minneapolis Lakers, who moved west. One year later a disappointed Saperstein established a rival American Basketball League (ABL) with himself as commissioner and owner of the Chicago franchise. He also had financial interests in five of the eight clubs. The ABL introduced the 30-second clock and the three-point shot. However, the league was unable to overcome poor attendance, less capable players, bickering owners, and undercapitalized, badly managed franchises. Saperstein often scheduled the Globetrotters to play at ABL games to bring in spectators. The ABL lasted a year and a half and cost him $1.5 million.

The Globetrotters won 4,233 games, losing 260, and tying once during their first twenty-five years. However, by the 1950s, they rarely played competitive matches. They went undefeated during Saperstein's last five years, mainly against white teams such as the Washington Generals, who worked for Saperstein. By 1966 the team had traveled 5 million air miles. After Saperstein's death the Globetrotters were sold for $3.7 million.

Saperstein died in Chicago, his lifelong hometown. While he had his critics, he probably did more than any other white entrepreneur to showcase African-American talent in team sports in the era of segregation. In addition to his interests in African-American sports, he held stock in baseball owner Bill Veeck's Cleveland Indians and St. Louis Browns of the American League and in Eddie Gottlieb's Philadelphia Warriors of the NBA. Saperstein was elected to the Basketball Hall of Fame in 1970.

• For information on Saperstein's career, see the Saperstein File, National Basketball Hall of Fame. Material on Saperstein and the Globetrotters can be found in David Zinkoff, *Around the World with the Harlem Globetrotters* (1953); George Vecsey, *The Harlem Globetrotters* (1971); *Harlem Globetrotters 1976: 50th Anniversary Issue* (1975); and Chuck Menville, *The Harlem Globetrotters: Fifty Years of Fun and Games* (1978). For the Globetrotters' role in professional basketball, see Robert W. Peterson, *Cages to Jump Shots: Pro Basketball's Early Years* (1990). Saperstein's work in baseball is discussed in James Overmyer, *Effa Manley and the Newark Eagles* (1993). For obituaries, see the *New York Times, Chicago Daily News,* and *Chicago Tribune,* 16 Mar. 1966.

STEVEN A. RIESS

SAPIR, Edward (26 Jan. 1884–4 Feb. 1939), linguist and anthropologist, was born in the Prussian town of Lauenberg, Pomerania (now Lebork, Poland), the son of Jacob David Sapir, a cantor, and Eva Seagal. Sapir's first language was Yiddish, though he undoubtedly also acquired some knowledge of German in childhood; he read Hebrew with his father from the age of seven or eight. Sapir's father was not particularly orthodox in his practice of Judaism, focusing on liturgical music over theology. His lifelong, though unfulfilled, ambition was to sing in the Berlin Opera.

The Sapir family emigrated to North America by way of Liverpool, England, where Edward attended kindergarten. Jacob Sapir obtained a position as cantor in Richmond, Virginia, in 1890. The family fortunes declined, however, after Edward's younger brother Max died of typhoid and Jacob was dismissed by his congregation. Jacob held a series of brief positions until the family settled on the Lower East Side of New York City when Edward was ten. Much of the family's livelihood during his early years was provided by Eva Sapir's small notions shop. Jacob and Eva Sapir were divorced sometime after 1910.

At the age of fourteen Sapir was awarded a prestigious Pulitzer scholarship designed to identify the brightest of New York City's immigrant children; instead of four years at the prestigious Horace Mann High School, Sapir chose to attend the local Peter Stuyvesant High School and reserved the scholarship to finance his undergraduate education at Columbia University and to supplement his mother's income.

Sapir entered Columbia in 1901; he obtained his B.A. in German in 1904, completing the four-year program in three years. His M.A. in German was awarded in 1905. Two additional years of coursework in Germanics and anthropology led to fieldwork and the study of several American Indian languages, and he received his Ph.D. in 1909.

From the start Sapir excelled at languages. Columbia had no independent department of linguistics, but the program in German was about equally divided between literature and linguistics. Sapir was sidetracked from Germanic philology (now usually called Indo-European linguistics) when he began to work with anthropologist Franz Boas on preserving the endangered languages of the American Indians. The urgency of this challenge inspired him to change disciplines and to apply the methods of philology to the unwritten languages of aboriginal North America. Although all of Boas's students were encouraged to include language within the scope of their fieldwork, Sapir was the only one with formal training in linguistics. Indeed, Boas himself was a self-taught practical linguist, with little interest in theory. Almost single-handedly, Boas revolutionized North American anthropology, bringing it within the professional academic model of German graduate education.

Although Sapir's master's thesis in German was on Herder's theory of the origin of language, he included Eskimo examples that undoubtedly were drawn from Boas's fieldwork data and argued for the functional equivalence of all languages, including those of so-called primitive peoples. Although the theoretical basis of his anthropology was articulated in this thesis, Sapir's apprenticeship as a linguist in anthropology began with his first fieldwork in the summer of 1905. After extensive work on field material collected by Boas, his mentor sent Sapir to Yakima Reservation in Washington to study Wasco and Wishram Chinook. The following summer he worked with Takelma on the Siletz Reservation in Oregon; his dissertation three years later was a grammar of Takelma. In his spare time, he worked on Chasta Costa, an unrelated language. Through Boas, this research was supported by the Bureau of American Ethnology, the U.S. government's official anthropological organization.

In 1907–1908 Sapir held a research fellowship at the University of California, Berkeley, where Boas's first Columbia Ph.D., Alfred Kroeber, was building a research and teaching program around mapping the ethnological and linguistic diversity of the state of California. Sapir did fieldwork on the Central, Southern, and Northern dialects of Yana. He also worked briefly on Kato, in collaboration with his California colleague, Pliny Earle Goddard.

From 1908 to 1910 Sapir held a Harrison fellowship at the University of Pennsylvania, where university teaching of anthropology was based in the affiliated museum. He carried out brief fieldwork with Catawba in collaboration with his colleague Frank Speck, a fellow Boas student. In the summer of 1909, Sapir began fieldwork with Ute on the Uintah Reservation in Utah. The University of Pennsylvania, however, declined to support his proposed long-term research project on Ute language and culture. In 1910 Sapir studied Southern Paiute, a closely related language, in Philadelphia; his primary informant was Tony Tillohash, a student from the Carlisle Indian School. He also worked briefly on Hopi with another Carlisle student. Sapir's method of linguistic description, based on the intuitions of native speakers for their languages, crystallized in the work with Tillohash; his grammar of Southern Paiute remains the exemplar of this approach. In 1910 he married Florence Delson; they had three children.

The same year, through the auspices of Boas, Sapir was appointed chief ethnologist of the newly created Division of Anthropology of the Geological Survey of Canada, within the Department of Mines, a position he was to hold for fifteen years. At the age of twenty-six he was in a position to develop a program of research, publication, and museum display on a national scale. Almost immediately he initiated his own fieldwork among the Nootka of Vancouver Island. Characteristically, while in Alberni, British Columbia, he also worked on Comox. Although Sapir intended a long-term commitment to Nootka linguistics, his only further fieldwork was in the winter of 1913–1914.

Sapir's administrative responsibilities increasingly tied him to Ottawa. In the summer of 1911 he explored the languages of northeastern Canada, working briefly in Ontario and Quebec with Mohawk, Seneca, Tutelo, Delaware, Abenaki, Malecite, Micmac, and Montagnais (Cree). Sapir was able to pursue his interests in West Coast languages when Indian delegations came to Ottawa; he worked on Chilcat Tlingit in 1914, Nass River in 1915, Kootenay, Nass River, Thompson River, Lillooet, Shuswap, and Okanagan in 1916, and Skidegate Haida and Tsimshian in 1920.

In the summer of 1915, at Kroeber's request, Sapir returned to California to work with Ishi, the last survivor of the Yahi, a tribe of the Yana. Sapir was the only linguist who knew much about this language family;

he used his knowledge of dialects studied in 1907–1908 to extract a grammar from this so-called wild Indian in the months before Ishi's death from tuberculosis. This was Boasian salvage linguistics at its most extreme.

In spite of cutbacks in funding during the First World War, Sapir managed one more stretch of new fieldwork. He spent the summer of 1922 on the Sarcee Reserve in Morley, Alberta. He added two more languages to his repertoire at Camp Red Cloud in Pennsylvania: Ingalik and Kutchin of the Canadian far North.

Sapir's ultimate goal was to produce a grammar, texts, and a dictionary for each of the languages on which he had collected extensive data; much of this data, however, remained unpublished at the time of his death. But at the same time this immense fieldwork experience allowed Sapir to turn to comparative problems in American Indian linguistics. His training in Indo-European linguistics allowed him to reconstruct the historical relationships of languages and to infer the culture history of their speakers. The methodology was laid out in *Time Perspective in Aboriginal America: A Study in Method* (1916). Sapir argued that the study of sound change in language would provide more precise historical information than any other part of culture; the folklore elements analyzed by Boas on the Northwest Coast would not distinguish between the effects of borrowing or diffusion and prior historical relationship with subsequent diversification. This monograph showed anthropologists studying culture why they could not ignore evidence from linguistics.

The classification of American Indian language families had not been particularly useful to anthropology in reconstructing culture history. The standard was the 55-unit classification of Major John Wesley Powell, director of the Bureau of American Ethnology, in 1891. Because neither Powell nor most of his staff was trained in linguistics, they were able to identify only the most superficial of linguistic relationships. By 1921 Sapir had reduced this diversity to twenty-three stocks that most linguists would acknowledge as demonstrated by the fieldwork of the previous two decades; much of this work was done by Sapir himself. For example, he demonstrated the unity of Uto-Aztecan, linked Athbascan to Haida and Tlingit, connected Wiyot and Yurok in California to Algonquian, and set out the evidence for Hokan and Penutian as defined by Kroeber and Roland Dixon in California. Simultaneously, he proposed a further dramatic consolidation of language families north of Mexico into only six superstocks: Eskimo-Aleut, Algonquian-Ritwan, Na-dene, Penutian, Hokan-Siouan, and Aztec-Tanoan. In spite of Sapir's warning that further work was needed, his anthropological colleagues eagerly adopted the six-unit classification as their standard for reconstructing culture history. The best-known form of Sapir's classification appeared in 1929, but its essential outlines were complete in the 1921 version.

During the later Ottawa years, Sapir's interests began to move toward psychology and belles-lettres. He wrote and published poetry and literary criticism (as did several of his fellow Boasians, particularly Ruth Benedict), composed music, and explored new work in psychoanalysis. World War I seemed to demonstrate the costs of modern civilization, calling into question Sapir's belief that science was an international ideal transcending local politics. The later Ottawa years were saddened by the mental and physical illness of his first wife, who died in 1924. Sapir began to rethink his theory of culture, placing increasing emphasis on symbolic and expressive aspects of cultural form and upon the relationship of culture and the individual. His only book, *Language* (1921), brought his fascination with linguistic form across the world's languages to a general audience. From about 1917 on, Sapir's narrowly linguistic work was increasingly set in the background.

Sapir had long regretted that he did not teach during his Canadian period because no Canadian university offered anthropology at that time. In 1925 he was called to the University of Chicago as the superstar who would revitalize anthropology and allow it to attain autonomy from sociology (which happened in 1929). Chicago was already the home of a broadly interdisciplinary social science, largely supported by the Rockefeller Foundation. Sapir quickly became a spokesperson for this interdisciplinary work, serving as a personal and theoretical link between sociology and psychology/psychiatry. His collaboration with interactional psychiatrist Harry Stack Sullivan and political scientist Harold D. Lasswell set the tone for the annual Social Science Research Council conferences in Hanover, New Hampshire. As the only anthropologist at most of the conferences, Sapir refused the role of purveyor of the exotic or primitive in favor of rethinking the role of the individual in culture along lines suggested by the life histories used by clinical psychologists. He dissolved the boundaries between primitive and civilized, adopting the Chicago school of sociology version of fieldwork in contemporary American society (itself adopted in great part from an earlier generation of anthropologists). In 1926 Sapir married Jean McClenaghan; they had two sons.

In 1931 Sapir was appointed to a Sterling Professorship at Yale University with Rockefeller Foundation funding for a seminar of international students to study the impact of culture on personality in their own cultures. This project was based in the broad interdisciplinary research program of the Yale Institute for Human Relations. Sapir's relations with the Institute deteriorated rapidly, in part because of anti-Semitism, but he continued to have enormous influence in the interdisciplinary conference circuit outside Yale. For example, he and Sullivan made an abortive proposal to the National Research Council to train Yale anthropology students in psychology so that they could study personality cross-culturally.

At Yale, for the first time in his career, Sapir had a chance to work with colleagues trained in linguistics. He had been a founding member of the Linguistic Society of America in 1925 but had little connection to linguists in the Chicago years. Several of his anthropology graduate students from Chicago moved to New Haven with him, constituting the core of what Hymes and Fought have called "the first Yale school of linguistics," including Morris Swadesh, Mary Haas, Stanley Newman, George Trager, Benjamin Whorf, Carl Voegelin, and Charles Hockett. During these years Sapir developed his concept of the phoneme and its "psychological reality" for speakers of a language and illustrated what a process-oriented grammar would look like. The so-called Sapir-Whorf hypothesis explored the relation of habitual thought to grammatical categories, although neither Sapir nor his student Benjamin Whorf espoused it in its deterministic form. Along with Leonard Bloomfield, Sapir cemented the applicability of the methods used in Indo-European studies to the study of unwritten languages.

While teaching at the Linguistic Society of America's Summer Institute of Linguistics at Ann Arbor in 1937, Sapir had his first heart attack. Ill health plagued his sabbatical in 1937–1938, and he died two years later, after attempting to return to teaching at Yale. He was president of the American Anthropological Association at the time of his death.

Sapir did not leave a formal school, either in linguistics or in anthropology. No single one of his students pursued the range of disciplines and interests that characterized his own career. But he set a standard for the integration of linguistics, anthropology, and the humanities that persisted in the late twentieth century, evidenced by the ongoing publication of his collected works in sixteen volumes by Mouton de Gruyter of Berlin, under the general editorship of his third son Philip. Sapir's uncompleted book *The Psychology of Culture*, reconstructed from students' class notes, established him as the foremost Boasian theoretician of society, culture, and the individual. In the 1940s and 1950s, linguistics turned toward behaviorism under the influence of Leonard Bloomfield and his students and away from the study of American Indian languages, resulting in a temporary eclipse of Sapir's mentalistic and symbolic theory of culture. North American linguistics since the 1960s, however, has returned to the view of Sapir as a "genius," whose intuitions about linguistic form are at the core of humanistic linguistics. The personality and culture school associated with Ruth Benedict and Margaret Mead has waned, leaving Sapir's theory of the complex, variable relationship of culture and the individual of considerable contemporary relevance.

• Some excerpts from Sapir's work are in David Mandelbaum, ed., *Selected Writings of Edward Sapir* (1949). A useful source is Dell Hymes and John Fought, "American Structuralism," in *Current Trends in Linguistics 10: Historiography of Linguistics*, ed. T. A. Sebeok (1975). See also Regna Darnell, *Edward Sapir: Linguist, Anthropologist, Humanist* (1990); Judith T. Irvine, *The Psychology of Culture (Edward Sapir)* (1994); and Konrad Koerner, ed., *Edward Sapir: Appraisals of His Life and Work* (1984).

REGNA DARNELL

SAPPINGTON, John (15 May 1776–7 Sept. 1856), physician, was born in Maryland, the son of Mark Brown Sappington, a physician, and Rebecca Boyce. Early in John's life his family emigrated to Nashville, Tennessee, where he studied medicine under his father. About 1800 John moved to Franklin, Tennessee, where he practiced medicine alone. In 1804 he married Jane Breathitt; they had nine children. To complete his education Sappington visited Philadelphia, Pennsylvania, where he studied in 1814–1815 a course of medicine and received his M.D. from the University of Pennsylvania. Returning to Franklin, Sappington remained there until 1817, when he located in Howard County, Missouri. In 1819 he crossed the Missouri River and settled in Saline County, Missouri.

Sappington became the champion of quinine, an alkaloid obtained from Peruvian bark, in 1820, for the treatment of malaria. Quinine was first produced in the United States in Philadelphia in 1823. In 1832, Sappington began to manufacture his own remedy for malaria, called "Sappington's Anti-Fever Pills." They contained one grain of quinine, three-fourths of a grain of liquorice, and one-fourth of a grain of myrrh, with oil of sassafras to improve the odor. He asserted, however, that the active ingredient in the pills was solely the quinine. To distribute the remedy widely, he employed twenty-five or thirty agents who, mainly in the Midwest, successfully sold the pills formed from hundreds of pounds of quinine delivered to him by steamboat at Arrow Rock, Missouri.

In promoting quinine, Sappington rejected the bleeding of patients for the treatment of malaria resorted to by many of the doctors of his day. As a consequence he partook of modern medical practice.

In 1844 Sappington wrote *The Theory and Treatment of Fevers* (1844). Published by the author at Arrow Rock, it was probably the first medical book issued west of the Mississippi River. Ferdinando Stith, a physician and a classmate of Sappington at the University of Pennsylvania, revised and corrected the work for an edition that was also published in 1844.

In addition to chapters on malaria, yellow fever, scarlet fever, and measles, the book treated "Of Children Infantum; or, The Puking and Purging of Children; with Some Other Conditions of the System, Peculiar to Children Attributed to Teething and Worms." In chapter six, "Of Intermittent, or Ague and Fever," Sappington remarked:

We believe it is now universally admitted, that low, marshy lands, and all those countries or situations where the surface of the earth is such as to retain the waters that fall on it . . . are ever fruitful sources of that condition of atmosphere which generates in the human subject the types of fever called intermitting and remitting fevers [malaria]. (p. 92)

Therein, Sappington recognized the importance of low and swampy ground as well as stagnant waters to the prevalence of malaria. Of course, he did not, as did

no one else in the early nineteenth century, realize that mosquitoes transmitted the dreaded disease.

In his book Sappington indicated his departure from the standard practice of his time. He cautioned against the depletive measures, including blood-letting, of many physicians, particularly Benjamin Rush, thus rejecting the heroic therapy of the early nineteenth century.

Sappington's book did not experience the popularity of his pills. He published 16,000 volumes with the intent to distribute 9,000 in Missouri and 7,000 east of the Mississippi River. His agents for the pills made the books available, and some bookshops carried the text in the major towns and cities. Still, the work did not sell well even at the nominal price of twenty-five cents a copy.

Sappington, however, made many friends. Some prominent ones were Andrew Jackson, Thomas Hart Benton, and Brigadier General Thomas Adam Smith. Certainly, too, he won the friendship of the large majority of the victims of malaria who took his pills.

Lasting fame escaped Sappington. Known for his pills in his day, he was soon forgotten by the descendants of those he saved from malaria. He died at his home, "Fox Castle," near Arrow Rock, Missouri.

• The State Historical Society in Columbia, Mo., holds a collection of manuscripts, including letters, of Sappington. The Missouri Historical Society in St. Louis has the manuscript of his *The Theory and Treatment of Fevers* (1844). For an informative monograph on Sappington, see Thomas B. Hall, "John Sappington," *Missouri Historical Review* 24 (Jan. 1930): 177–99. A more recent study is Thomas B. Hall, Jr., and Thomas B. Hall, III, *Dr. John Sappington of Saline County, Missouri, 1776–1856* (1975), a pamphlet that includes portraits.

KEITH L. MILLER

SARGENT, Charles Sprague (24 Apr. 1841–22 Mar. 1927), botanist and administrator, was born in Boston, Massachusetts, the son of Ignatius Sargent, a distinguished merchant in the East India trade, and Henrietta Gray. Of a well-to-do family background (he was third cousin to the artist John Singer Sargent), Charles Sprague Sargent was privately educated in Boston (mostly at Epes Sargent Dixwell's school) and graduated from Harvard University in 1862, having studied classics. His academic career was undistinguished; he completed his Harvard education eighty-eighth in a class of ninety. In 1863 he enlisted in the army as an aide-de-camp, earning the rank of second lieutenant on the staff of the Department of the Gulf. Following discharge from the service in August 1865, with the rank of brevet major, Sargent left for a three-year tour of Europe and returned in 1868.

Shortly after returning to the United States Sargent received and accepted an offer of appointment to the directorship of the Harvard Botanical Garden and a professorship of horticulture, positions that he held between 1872 and 1873. On 24 November 1873 he took on the directorship of Harvard's newly established Arnold Arboretum, and in 1879 he assumed the official title of Arnold Professor of Arboriculture. Giving up the position only when he fell ill in 1927, Sargent was best known as a guiding force of the arboretum, helping to make it one of the leading institutions in American botanical science, and a driving force in the establishment of forestry research and in the establishment of national parks and forests.

Sargent had not had much early formal training in the botanical sciences, though he had an interest in horticulture and dendrology, which had been fashionable pastimes for well-to-do Bostonians. It was only after he became director of the Arnold Arboretum that he became an authority in arboriculture and dendrology, especially of the native trees of North America. With his growing knowledge of arboriculture and with the help of generous endowments that he secured from his numerous wealthy friends and his own personal finances Sargent built up the arboretum from its original 150 acres of "worn-out farm" to 250 acres of a sprawling world-class facility. Sargent designed the arboretum with the help of noted landscape architect Frederick Law Olmstead, who was then planning the Boston park system. In addition to building the garden, Sargent contributed personal resources to the Arnold herbarium and especially to the Arnold library, which began from his personal collection that he had donated.

In addition to building and directing the Arnold Arboretum, Sargent was a moving force behind forestry research and conservation, then vitally important countrywide. In 1879 he embarked on a government-sponsored program to survey national forests. The project took some five years and earned Sargent a reputation in forestry research. His efforts were published as part of the Tenth Census of 1890. This expertise later aided him in his conservation efforts. Between 1882 and 1883 he was a member of the group that surveyed the glaciers of Montana as part of the Northern Pacific Transcontinental Survey; in 1884 he served as chair of a committee to investigate policy on the Adirondack forests of New York. He strongly supported the creation of national parks and forests and was instrumental in helping to preserve millions of acres of native forests. His work also helped to create the Bureau of Forestry, which was appended to the U.S. Department of Agriculture; as a result in 1896 he became chair of a committee appointed by the National Academy of Sciences to set policy on native forests.

Sargent's scientific contributions were primarily composed of descriptive botanical studies, especially on the trees of North America. Between 1891 and 1902 he produced the massive *Silva of North America*, illustrated with 740 plates in fourteen quarto volumes. Revised in 1922, the work became the authoritative source on North American trees. In 1905 he completed his *Manual of North American Trees*. He additionally edited the *Journal of the Arnold Arboretum* and the *Garden and Forest*, a popular journal that was instrumental in raising consciousness about forestry conservation.

In pursuit of his botanical studies, Sargent traveled widely to collect specimens that could be grown in New England and also took note of landscape designs, gardens, and horticultural practices around the world. In 1894 he published *Forest Flora of Japan*. Sargent shared much of his own knowledge and botanical specimens with noted international establishments, like those at Kew Gardens, Edinburgh, and Paris, and returned favors by hosting noted botanists at his home estate. Many of the trees and plants gracing North American sites were species introduced with the help of Sargent. After 1900 Sargent's own research centered on study of the complex genus *Crataegus* (hawthorne); he described more than 700 species, some of which he introduced into cultivation.

Noted honors given to Sargent included fellowship to the American Academy of Arts and Sciences, membership in the National Academy of Sciences, the American Philosophical Society, and foreign member of the Linnaean Society of London, in addition to other international organization memberships. He also received several awards from noted horticultural societies for his work in introducing and cultivating new varieties.

In 1873 Sargent had married Mary Allen Robeson (the daughter of Andrew Robeson), a charming Boston socialite. The Sargents had five children. By contemporary accounts Sargent appears to have been a quiet and somewhat conservative individual who was methodical in his work habits but pursued his interests with enthusiasm. He died at his home estate of "Holm Lea" in Brookline, Massachusetts, which was a spectacular example of the sort of arboreal landscape that he had helped create.

• Sargent's correspondence and other materials are located at the Arnold Arboretum Libraries and the University Archives at Harvard University. The most comprehensive historical treatment of Sargent and the Arnold Arboretum is S. B. Sutton, *Charles Sprague Sargent and the Arnold Arboretum* (1970). See also William Trelease, "Charles Sprague Sargent," *Biographical Memoirs* (National Academy of Sciences) 12–13 (1929–1930): 247–70; and Alfred Rehder, "Charles Sprague Sargent," *Journal of the Arnold Arboretum* 8 (1927): 68–86. See also the entry on Sargent in Harry Baker Humphrey, *Makers of North American Botany* (1961). Obituaries appear in *Journal of Forestry* 25 (1927): 513–14, and *Proceedings of the Linnaean Society of London* 119 (1926–1927): 96–98.

VASSILIKI BETTY SMOCOVITIS

SARGENT, Dudley Allen (28 Sept. 1849–21 July 1924), physical educator and physician, was born in Belfast, Maine, the son of Benjamin Sargent, a spar-maker and ship's carpenter, and Caroline Jane Rogers. Sargent was seven years old when his father died. He quit school at thirteen and worked as a carpenter, a seaman, and a circus gymnast. He graduated from Bowdoin College with an A.B. in 1875 and received his medical degree from Yale Medical School in 1878. Sargent unsuccessfully sought a position as a college faculty member in physical training. In 1878 he went to New York City and opened his own private gymnasium, the Hygienic Institute and School of Physical Culture.

A year later, Dudley Sargent accepted the positions of assistant professor of physical training at Harvard and director of the college's new Hemenway Gymnasium. Thus began his forty-year tenure at Harvard and his professional career, in which, according to R. Tait McKenzie, he "influenced physical education more than any other man of his time . . . in the spreading abroad of the sound gospel of physical education" (p. 7).

At this time physical education was virtually an unknown subject in most colleges and, if it did exist, was an elective taught by an ex–prize fighter, a gymnast, or a janitor. Sargent induced students to come to the gymnasium by giving each one a medical examination of the heart and lungs, obtaining a family history, and conducting a physical examination consisting of forty anthropometric measurements and several strength tests. From these data he prepared an individual prescription of exercises designed to develop the major muscle groups of the body. Sargent invented a number of exercise machines and modified others, such as the chest pulley weights, to make them adjustable to even the weakest student. With a handbook of instructions to guide him, each student then worked out on his own and could return in six months or so for another examination to measure his progress and possibly receive a different prescription. Sargent's exercises, along with the introduction of German and Swedish gymnastics in the mid-1880s, marked the real beginning of college physical education programs and were still in common use until after 1900.

Sargent's most significant contribution to the profession of physical education was in the preparation of teachers. Teacher preparation before 1880 was limited to the German Turnverein Seminary and one or two small private schools. In 1881 Sargent began a one-year course for prospective teachers, which was the genesis of his Sargent School of Physical Education in Cambridge. Men were originally admitted but few came, so it became a school for women only. Here Sargent became a leader in freeing women from Victorian customs. He opposed corsets and long skirts and advocated the divided skirt or bloomers and middy blouse in the gymnasium. His female students performed on the parallel bars and horse; used the Swedish apparatus and did gymnastics; scaled a twelve-foot wall as a team event; used wands, dumbbells, and Indian clubs; climbed ropes and ladders; and ran and jumped in track events. The women also learned to play tennis, field hockey, archery, basketball, indoor baseball, and fencing. The opening of the Sargent summer camp in 1913 in Peterboro, New Hampshire, considerably enhanced the curriculum with a variety of outdoor recreational activities and water sports. In 1903 Sargent established a three-year training program for the diploma.

Closely allied with the Sargent School was the Harvard Summer School of Physical Education, which Sargent started in 1887. This was initiated to provide in-service training in theory and practice for both men and women, and it soon became a magnet for teachers and students from all over the country. At a time when German and Swedish gymnasts were locked in a "Battle of the Systems," Sargent did not take sides but taught both; nor did he exclusively promote his own exercises. At both his own school and the Harvard Summer School he provided a broad curriculum that included German gymnastics taught by George Brosius and Swedish gymnastics taught by Hartvig Nissen. Constance Applebee came from England in 1901 to introduce field hockey to college women at the Harvard Summer School.

Sargent's schools offered a wide variety of theory courses as well, conducted by distinguished physicians from Boston and the Harvard Medical School. Prominent physical educators such as R. Tait McKenzie, Fred E. Leonard, George Meylan, and Edward M. Hartwell also served as instructors. Although Harvard allowed Sargent the use of Hemenway Gymnasium for the summer courses and collected a good share of the income, the college administration never officially recognized the school or granted any credit for the courses.

By 1920 the Sargent School had graduated 3,008 students—compared to 6,648 from all 28 other teacher training institutions combined—nearly one-third of the total number of graduates. Between 1887 and 1918 the summer school enrolled 4,469 students, who came from every state in the Union. The impact of these individuals on the professionalization of physical education in schools and colleges was incalculable.

In 1882 Harvard became the first college to appoint a faculty athletic committee to provide some control over intercollegiate competition. Sargent was one member of a three-man committee, which aroused fierce opposition when it banned football competition for the 1885 season because of rough play and fighting. Sargent was unjustly accused of being an opponent of football, when in fact he only wanted to eliminate its excesses.

The football ban cost Sargent dearly. When President Charles Eliot and the fellows of Harvard College recommended him for a full professorship in 1889, the Board of Overseers, composed of alumni, in a most unusual move rejected the proposal. Sargent lost his cherished faculty status, and his only title thereafter was director of Hemenway Gymnasium. This action also kept him from any further involvement in intercollegiate athletics.

Sargent not only worked to encourage physical activity for all college students, male and female, but also for everyone—young and old, working class, the handicapped, and all strata of society. His book *Health, Strength, and Power* (1904) was a comprehensive handbook of health and exercise for the masses. He also contributed eight articles for popular magazines. He was truly "the apostle of exercise for everybody," as described in a *New York Times* editorial (23 July 1924).

Dudley Sargent took positions of leadership in all the major professional organizations. He served five years (1890, 1892–1893, 1899–1901) as president of the American Association for the Advancement of Physical Education (which has since become the American Alliance for Health, Physical Education, Recreation, and Dance). In 1899 he was president of the Society of College Gymnasium Directors (now the National Association for Physical Education in Higher Education), and in 1904 he was a founding member of the distinguished Academy of Physical Education. Sargent also took an active interest in several health societies, the most important of which was his presidency of the Health Education League in 1905.

The professional activities of Sargent completely eclipsed his personal and social life. He planned more than he could achieve, and his good friend McKenzie recalled that "he always gave me the impression of being a tired man." He married Ella Frazier Ledyard in 1881, and they had one child, Ledyard, who succeeded his father as director of the Sargent School and edited his father's autobiography. But Sargent and his wife separated after a few years. The separation was friendly, and the family maintained contact until Sargent's death, which occurred at his beloved camp in Peterboro, New Hampshire.

Sargent's influence was felt in all phases of the teaching of physical education—teacher training, curriculum, tests and measurements, apparatus and gymnasium construction, and athletics. He labored relentlessly through his writings and speeches to give the subject of physical education respectability in the college curriculum and to achieve faculty status for its teachers. He challenged the Victorian tradition of the "fainting female" and campaigned for freedom of dress and the right for vigorous activity for girls and women. He fought for sane control of intercollegiate athletics and the elimination of the abuses. He adhered steadfastly to his belief that "the grand aim of all muscular activity from an educational point of view is to improve conduct and develop character."

• The archives at Harvard University have some of Sargent's papers and letters, but a larger collection of papers and unpublished articles once located at the Sargent School of Physical Education in Cambridge have apparently disappeared. The school is now part of Boston University. The only comprehensive account of Sargent's life and work is Bruce L. Bennett, "The Life and Contributions of Dudley Allen Sargent, M.D., and His Contributions to Physical Education" (Ph.D. diss., Univ. of Michigan, 1947). This reference lists all of his extensive writings, published and unpublished. Sargent's *Physical Education* (1906) is a collection of speeches and articles for the profession. A personal narrative of his life and views may be found in Ledyard Sargent, ed., *Dudley Allen Sargent: An Autobiography* (1927), but it does have some serious omissions.

The scholarly first historian of physical education, Fred E. Leonard, makes an appraisal of Sargent in his *Pioneers of Modern Physical Training* (1919). Sargent's good friend R. Tait McKenzie evaluates his work in the *Journal of Health and Physical Education* 2 (Nov. 1931): 6–7. A fine and detailed description of the Harvard Summer School by its former secretary is provided by Clarence B. Van Wyck, "The Harvard Summer School of Physical Education," *Research Quarterly* 13 (1942): 403–31. The article on Sargent in the

Dictionary of American Biography, vol. 16 (1943), pp. 355–56, deserves mention because it was written by George Meylan, a close personal friend of his. A summary of his professional achievements is given in Bennett, "Contributions of Dr. Sargent to Physical Education," *Research Quarterly* 19 (1948): 77–92. At the time of his death, Sargent was the subject of an editorial in the *New York Times*, 23 July 1924.

BRUCE L. BENNETT

SARGENT, Epes (27 Sept. 1813–30 Dec. 1880), author and editor, was born in Gloucester, Massachusetts, the son of Epes Sargent, a shipmaster, and Hannah Dane Coffin. In 1818 the family moved to Boston, where the father became a merchant before returning to the sea. Young Sargent attended the Boston Latin School from 1823 until 1829, during which time he interrupted his studies to accompany his father on a voyage to St. Petersburg, Russia. It is said, but evidently cannot be confirmed, that Sargent then briefly enrolled at Harvard.

He soon demonstrated great versatility and productivity as a writer. Not long after Samuel Griswold Goodrich began his popular "Peter Parley" series of books for children in 1827, Sargent wrote some of the books, as did Nathaniel Hawthorne, among many others. Goodrich used so many editorial assistants, however, that it is impossible to identify all the authors of the more than one hundred volumes. Sargent's first mature publication was a poem titled "A Sea-Piece," issued in *Illustrations of the Athenaeum Gallery of Paintings* (1830). Poetry remained perhaps his favorite form of expression. Sargent did editorial work in the early 1830s for the *Boston Daily Advertiser* and then the *Boston Daily Atlas*. He worked in Washington, D.C., as the *Atlas* correspondent during much of the period 1837–1839. He wrote several dramas, notably *The Bride of Genoa* (1837) and *Velasco* (1839), both produced at the Tremont Theatre in Boston. The latter starred actress Ellen Tree, with whom gossip in rival newspapers associated Sargent. Copies of his other plays are not extant.

In 1839 Sargent moved to New York City, where that year and into the next he edited the *Evening Signal*, worked with Park Benjamin on the editorial staff of the *New World*, and was associate editor of George Pope Morris's *New York Mirror*. Because of his knowledge of federal politics, Sargent was able to write *The Life and Public Services of Henry Clay* (1842), which Clay called the best of several biographies of him. Sargent founded his short-lived *Sargent's New Monthly Magazine of Literature, Fashion and the Fine Arts* in 1843. Meanwhile, he was placing more of his own writings in various periodicals. He edited the first seven volumes of *The Modern Standard Drama: A Collection of the Most Popular Acting Plays, with Critical Remarks . . .* (1846–1848). In 1847 he returned to Boston to edit the *Transcript*, until 1853. In 1848 he married Elizabeth W. Weld. The couple had no children.

Even while continuing his editorial work, Sargent contributed to periodicals, did some lecturing, and wrote poetry. Some of his verse appeared in Goodrich's annual gift-book *Token*, which he had helped edit in 1833. In 1847 he assembled his *Songs of the Sea, with Other Poems*. Some of the poems in it resulted from a voyage he took to Cuba; one, "A Life on the Ocean Wave," became one of the most memorable sea poems ever written, especially when it was set to music in 1838 by Henry Russell. Its first stanza is the following:

> A life on the ocean wave,
> A home on the rolling deep,
> Where the scattered waters rave,
> And the winds their revels keep.

"Sunrise at Sea" has these fine lines: "How reverently calm the ocean lay / At the bright birth of that celestial day!" In "A Summer Noon at Sea" the poet notes that "Our vessel lies . . . / As [if] she were moored to her dark shadow." In "Rockall" he expresses a longing for the sort of faith that enables the rock to face the fury of the sea. The genuine charm of Sargent's poetry lies in its unforced rhythms, its easy, natural rhymes, and its picturesque imagery.

Sargent compiled two nonfictional narrative books stemming from his love of the sea: *American Adventure by Land and Sea* (1841) and *Arctic Adventure by Land and Sea* (1857). He also wrote two novels: *Fleetwood; or, The Stain of Birth* (1845) and *Peculiar, a Tale of the Great Transition* (1864). Back in 1837 or so, he had become interested in mesmerism. Studying the subject avidly, he became convinced of the credibility of clairvoyance and thought-reading. As editor of the *Transcript*, he publicized an alleged spirit-rapping event that occurred in 1848 in Hydesville, east of Rochester, New York. Later in his career he wrote *Planchette; or, The Despair of Science . . .* (1869), *The Proof Palpable of Immortality* (1875), and *The Scientific Basis of Spiritualism* (1880).

It is for his other publications, however, that Sargent is now best known. Over the years, he wrote or edited streams of textbooks and school readers. Numerous individual books appeared under the following rubrics: Sargent's Standard Series of Speakers (1852–1857), Sargent's Standard Series of Readers (1854–1856), Sargent's Standard Series of Spellers (1856–1864), Sargent's Standard Series of Primers (1857–1861), Sargent's Standard Series of Readers, Part II (1860–1867), Sargent's Standard Intermediate Readers (1865–1867), and New American Series of Readers (coauthored, 1871). He also adapted or coauthored miscellaneous textbooks as late as 1873. Though in competition with the more famous McGuffey Readers, Sargent's school books, at least thirty-one in number, were popular for several decades and gave the busy man considerable income.

Sargent was much respected in his day as a gifted writer. Edgar Allan Poe discusses him in an 1846 review that was part of "The Literati of New York City," praising his poetry and his play *Velasco*, regarding him as apt in burlesque and satire, and esteeming him as a man of "industry, talent and tact." Sargent died in Boston.

• Most of Sargent's voluminous and widely scattered papers are at the Boston Public Library, the Walter Hampden–Edwin Booth Theatre Collection and Library in New York City, the Houghton Library at Harvard, the Historical Society of Pennsylvania, the Pierpont Morgan Library in New York City, the New York Society Library, and the University of Virginia library. Sargent's extensive bibliography is presented in Jacob Blanck et al., eds., *Bibliography of American Literature* 7 (1983): 338–62. Frank Luther Mott, *A History of American Magazines, 1741–1850* (1938; repr., 1957), traces Sargent's associations with the *New York Mirror*, *Sargent's New Monthly Magazine*, *Godey's Lady's Book*, the *New-York Magazine*, and the *Democratic Review*. Merle M. Hoover, *Park Benjamin: Poet & Editor* (1948), treats Sargent's professional association with Benjamin. Daniel Roselle, *Samuel Griswold Goodrich, Creator of Peter Parley: A Study of His Life and Work* (1968), discusses the probable degree of Sargent's aid to Goodrich. Dwight Thomas and David K. Jackson, *The Poe Log: A Documentary Life of Edgar Allan Poe, 1809–1849* (1987), details Sargent's relationship with Poe. Joseph Flibbert, "Poetry in the Mainstream," in *America and the Sea: A Literary History*, ed. Haskell Springer (1995), pp. 109–26, discusses Sargent's "A Life on the Ocean Wave" and "Rockall." In a review in the *Boston Daily Advertiser*, 10 Mar. 1869, William James criticizes *Planchette* for overreliance on cases discussed by others. Obituaries are in the *Boston Transcript*, 31 Dec. 1880, and the *New York Times*, 1 Jan. 1881.

ROBERT L. GALE

SARGENT, Henry (Nov. 1770–21 Feb. 1845), painter and art advocate, was baptized 25 November 1770 in Gloucester, Massachusetts, the son of Daniel Sargent, a prominent merchant, and Mary Turner. As a boy he attended Dummer Academy in South Byfield, Massachusetts, where he was taught basic Latin and Greek. Between 1776 and 1779 the family moved from Newburyport to Boston, and Sargent received further instruction (to what extent is unclear) in Boston schools.

After a stint in the counting room of the merchant prince Thomas Handasyd Perkins and a further apprenticeship until the age of nineteen or twenty in his father's business, Sargent decided to pursue a career in painting. His earliest experiments included a landscape he painted on the back wall of the summer house of the family's Boston residence and the head of a sea nymph on one of his father's ships. He used a room in the family home as his atelier, where he painted portraits and copied works by various masters. He progressed quickly, and in 1790 the visiting painter John Trumbull praised highly Sargent's copy of John Singleton Copley's *Watson and the Shark* (Museum of Fine Arts, Boston). Encouraged by friends and carrying letters of introduction penned by Trumbull, Sargent departed for London in 1793 to study with the American painter Benjamin West. While there he was also kindly received by the expatriate Copley, who in 1763 had painted a portrait of Sargent's mother. Sargent remained in England for four years, despite great expense and his feeling, conveyed in a letter to a friend dated 27 March 1795, that "painting is very dull here" due to the effects of war (quoted in Addison, p. 280).

The ongoing war between Britain and France also prevented Sargent's study on the Continent, and in

1797 he returned to Boston, where he spent two years deeply discouraged by the apathy toward the arts in the United States. Perhaps looking for a change of career, in 1799 he joined the recently formed Boston Light Infantry, captained by his brother Daniel. On 1 October 1804 he was promoted to lieutenant and later served as captain of the company, from 31 March 1807 until his resignation in 1815. Two days after his promotion to captain, Sargent married Hannah Welles, daughter of Samuel and Isabella Pratt Welles, in Boston. They had four children, two of whom lived to adulthood.

During the War of 1812, when British attack in the Boston area was expected, Sargent in 1814 was appointed assistant adjutant-general, and his company prepared defenses at Fort Strong in Boston Harbor. Sargent was named aide-de-camp, with the rank of colonel, to Governor Caleb Strong on 31 May 1815. He also served in the state legislature in 1812 and 1815–1817 but eventually withdrew from public service due to deafness purportedly caused by a cannon blast. He then devoted his time once again to painting and to dabbling in mechanics.

Sargent is perhaps best known as the painter of *The Dinner Party* and *The Tea Party* (both at the Museum of Fine Arts, Boston). Both were made as exhibition pictures and were advertised for view by the public in the 1820s for a fee of 25 cents (see, for example, the *New York Evening Post*, 16 Oct. 1821). Their owner, the painter David L. Brown, took them on tour to cities that included New York, Philadelphia, Montreal, and Salem as well as Boston itself. *The Dinner Party* portrays a group of men seated around a long table after a formal daytime dinner. The painting may be a group portrait, but if so, the sitters have not been convincingly identified. The tastefully decorated interior, probably that of Sargent's own home, provides insight into the appointments of an upper-class Boston dwelling of the early decades of the nineteenth century. *The Tea Party* may also show the interior of Sargent's home at 10 Franklin Place; it depicts a large gathering of elegantly dressed ladies and gentlemen in a pair of Empire drawing rooms.

These paintings, as well as other larger historical and biblical scenes that Sargent painted for public display, such as *The Landing of the Pilgrims* (c. 1818–1825, Pilgrim Society, Plymouth, Mass.) and *Christ Crucified* (c. 1802, unlocated, for the Church of the Holy Cross, Boston), were well received by audiences and critics. "We feel confidence in asserting, that few if any living Artists can paint two interiors more perfectly than the two by Mr. Sargent," an anonymous enthusiast wrote in the *Columbian Centinel* (8 May 1824), lauding the "minute fidelity" with which Sargent portrayed the physical world. His portraits were similarly praised for their "spirit and exactness." Among his sitters were General Benjamin Lincoln, Jeremy Belknap, and John Clarke (all in the Massachusetts Historical Society, Boston). Sargent's popularity with American audiences seems to have been due in large part to his precise painting style, which (to

quote the same *Columbian Centinel* writer) emphasized "magical" illusionism over flashy brushwork.

Sargent was granted an honorary A.M. from Harvard in 1826 and in 1840 was made an honorary member of the National Academy of Design in New York. As well as producing many works that were popular during his lifetime—*Christ's Entrance into Jerusalem* (c. 1817, unlocated) sold for the astonishing sum of $3,000—Sargent was active in developing Boston's art institutions. He was a founder and the first vice president of the Boston Artists' Association and became its president in 1843 upon the death of Washington Allston. His support of younger artists was made apparent in his generous donation of a collection of plaster casts to the association; at the time, drawing from the antique was deemed crucial to an artist's development, but rarely were statues and casts available to most art students. Sargent's further connections to the American art scene are evident in his friend William Dunlap's book *A History of the Rise and Progress of the Arts of Design in the United States*, originally published in 1834, in which he is presented as a benevolent gossip, a font of information about the personal and professional lives of many of his contemporaries.

It is probably as an advocate of American art and artists that Sargent made his greatest contributions; his support of local talent, especially through his work with the Boston Artists' Association, came at a time when Old Master copies were considered the height of good taste by American collectors generally and by the Boston Athenaeum specifically. Sargent's desire to help find new artistic markets and venues of display helped foster the growth of both artists and art institutions in the United States. He died in Boston.

• Letters and documents pertaining to Sargent can be found at the Essex Institute, Salem, Mass.; the Massachusetts Historical Society, Boston; the Historical Society of Pennsylvania, Philadelphia; the American Antiquarian Society, Worcester, Mass.; and the Archives of American Art, Washington, D.C. William Dunlap, *A History of the Rise and Progress of the Arts of Design in the United States* (2 vols., 1834), is the source from which subsequent biographers most often derive their information; these later works include Henry T. Tuckerman, *Book of the Artists* (1867), and, to some degree, Frank W. Bayley's entry in Emma W. Sargent, *Epes Sargent of Gloucester and His Descendants* (1923), which provides the best information on Henry Sargent's family history. Dorinda Evans, *Benjamin West and His American Students* (1980), explores Sargent's early artistic development. A glimpse into Sargent's exhibition practices is provided in Robert F. Perkins, *The Boston Athenaeum Exhibition Index, 1827–1874* (1980), and Mabel Munson Swan, *The Athenaeum Gallery 1827–1873: The Boston Athenaeum as an Early Patron of Art* (1940). Sargent's role in the Boston art community in the last years of his life is documented in the two volumes of the *Journal of the Proceedings of the Boston Artists' Association* at the Department of Rare Books and Manuscripts of the Boston Public Library and is discussed in Leah Lipton, "The Boston Artists' Association, 1841–1851," *American Art Journal* 15 (Autumn 1983): 45–57. For a discussion of Sargent's two best known paintings, see Jane C. Nylander, "Henry Sargent's *Dinner Party* and *Tea Party*," *Magazine Antiques* 121 (May 1982): 1172–83. Criticism of Sargent's paintings is included in Samuel Lorenzo Knapp (pseudonym, Ignatius Loyola Robertson), *Sketches of Public Characters, Drawn from the Living and the Dead* (1830); John Neal, *Randolph* (1823); and the *North American Review*, May 1815 and January 1817.

CARMA R. GORMAN

SARGENT, Irene Jesse (20 Feb. 1852–14 Sept. 1932), teacher and art critic, was born in Auburn, New York, the youngest daughter of Rufus Sargent, a manufacturer, and Phebe (maiden name unknown). Privately educated as a child, Sargent moved from Auburn to Boston with her parents when she was in her early twenties and thereafter claimed that city as her birthplace. Though no record of her formal education survives, she apparently studied music at the Boston Conservatory. She later studied the history of art and architecture at the University of Paris and in Rome as well as with Charles Eliot Norton at Harvard University. A self-described littérateur, she traveled widely in Europe from the 1880s to the time of World War I. Fluent in five languages, she wrote in, taught, and translated them in a wide range of subjects relating to the history of art and music. She was a commanding public speaker. She devoted her life to her career and never married.

After some years of private-school teaching in central New York, in 1895 Sargent began a distinguished 37-year career at Syracuse University, originally as an instructor in French. By 1901 her title was "Lecturer in Italian and on the History of Fine Arts," and by 1908 she was a full professor. Though she continued to teach the history of art, ornamentation, and Italian literature, her courses in the history of architecture brought the greatest honors. In 1926 she was the second woman in the history of the American Institute of Architects and Allied Arts to receive honorary membership for "a lifetime of outstanding contributions to architecture and its allied arts."

Concurrently with her career in university teaching, Sargent established herself as an author and critic. She helped to found and contributed many articles to Gustav Stickley's monthly magazine, the *Craftsman*, in which she did more, perhaps, than any other American writer to introduce and disseminate the ideas and values of the Arts and Crafts movement in the United States. The movement sought to foster a return to a handcraft ethic in architecture and the decorative arts not only on aesthetic grounds but also as a means of social reform. Representing a reaction against the machine ethic of the Industrial Age and the dehumanizing conditions of factory life, the Arts and Crafts movement sought to dissolve the distinction between art and craft. In 1901 she wrote every article for the first three numbers of the *Craftsman*. Each of these issues was devoted to a single subject: William Morris, John Ruskin, and the history of medieval crafts guilds. In subsequent issues she contributed reviews, translations, original poetry, and such historical and critical articles as "Robert Owen and Factory Reform," "The Gothic Revival," "The History and Design of Textiles," "[Henry H. Richardson's] Trinity Church, Bos-

ton, as a Monument of American Art," "Color, an Expression of Modern Life," and "The Silversmith's Art in the Middle Ages." She wrote a pioneering series on American art potters and potteries, including such figures as Charles Binns of Alfred University, Mary Louise McLaughlin of the Rookwood Pottery, and Thomas S. Nickerson of the Merrimac Pottery. She wrote extensively of the decorative arts in articles such as "The Life and History of a Design," which examined the use of the lotus as a motif, and "A Minor French Salon," in which she illustrated the works of the French glass designers René Lalique and Emil Gaillard. In all, she contributed eighty-four articles to the *Craftsman* in over three years. When Stickley moved his headquarters from Syracuse to New York City in 1905, Sargent, who had come to differ with him over editorial policy and who did not want to move to New York, severed her relationship with the *Craftsman*.

In 1903 Stickley had sponsored a major Arts and Crafts exhibition in Syracuse, organized by Sargent and Theodore Hanford Pond, a leading art educator and designer-craftsman. The exhibition reflected Sargent's well-articulated theoretical foundations for the movement. Its broad and enlightened scope featured "works by leading American Arts and Crafts designers, Native American weaving and basketry, school exhibits, and European examples."

Soon after breaking with the *Craftsman*, Sargent became a contributing editor to *Keystone* magazine, a journal of the watch, jewelry, and optical trades, published in Philadelphia. Her affiliation gave the magazine a new emphasis on historical articles relating to finely crafted decorative objects and on criticism of contemporary crafts. She contributed sixty-six articles to the magazine in the next twenty-five years. The profusely illustrated essays dealt with historical and contemporary silver, jewelry, ceramics, and glass, and their outstanding creators. She was a champion of women artists of her time and especially of her colleague, the ceramist Adelaide Alsop Robineau. In her time, no other American writer on the visual arts produced so extensive a body of publications characterized by great learning, high intelligence, sharp critical acumen, and dignified elegance of expression.

At Syracuse University, Sargent became a legend in her own time. Having apparently lost whatever remained of her private income with the onset of the Great Depression and with no surviving family, she taught until the last. She died in Syracuse and was buried in the Syracuse University plot for indigent professors.

• There is no known collection of Sargent's papers. Most of Sargent's work is in the *Craftsman* 1–8 (1901–1905) and *Keystone* 26–57 (1905–1930). See also Cleota Reed, "Irene Sargent: A Comprehensive Bibliography of Her Published Writings," *Courier* 18, no. 1 (Spring 1981): 9–25. Obituaries are in the *Syracuse Herald*, 14 Sept. 1932, and the Syracuse *Post Standard*, 15 Sept. 1932.

CLEOTA REED

SARGENT, John Singer (12 Jan. 1856–15 Apr. 1925), painter, was born in Florence, Italy, the son of Fitz-William Sargent, a surgeon, and Mary Newbold Singer. Though born in Italy and raised abroad, Sargent considered himself American. Sargent's parents were from Pennsylvania, and his paternal line included Epes Sargent of Gloucester, Massachusetts, whose portrait was painted by John Singleton Copley. Sargent's early education consisted of a patchwork of tutors and short periods of attendance at local schools in Austria, Italy, England, and France. Recognizing her young son's skill, Sargent's mother, who herself painted in watercolor, taught him to use this demanding medium. A childhood friend, Violet Paget (pseudonym Vernon Lee), suggested in her 1927 essay, "J.S.S.: In Memoriam," that Sargent's painting gift came from his mother, who, she wrote, was invariably "painting, painting, painting away, always an open paint-box in front of her, through all the forty years I knew her" (Charteris, p. 235). Sargent's cousins Emma Worcester Sargent and Charles Sprague Sargent noted in their 1923 history of the Sargent family that Mary Sargent instructed her son that he "might begin as many sketches each day as he liked, but that one of them must be finished" (p. 86). His mother's instruction served as the basis for Sargent's lifetime of disciplined, artistic production.

Sargent received more formal artistic education at the Accademia delle Belle Arti in Florence. By the age of eighteen Sargent and his family were firmly committed to his pursuit of a career as an artist. In Paris he enrolled at the École des Beaux-Arts, where he remained for three years, finishing his studies there in 1877. He made his first trip to the United States in 1876 in order to claim his American citizenship. With his mother and sister he visited the Centennial Exposition, traveled widely in the United States, and then returned to Paris to resume his professional studies. In 1874, concurrent with his academic training and probably more important to his future career, Sargent entered the teaching studio of Émile Auguste Carolus-Duran, a portrait painter and muralist of French and Spanish descent. There he met American artist James Carroll Beckwith, with whom he shared a studio in Paris. In 1877 the two young artists assisted Carolus-Duran with his ceiling decorations for the Palais du Luxembourg. With this experience of large-scale decorative work, Sargent established the foundation for his own later important mural commissions in Boston. In addition, Sargent's association with Carolus-Duran enabled him to gain access to Parisian patrons and to begin to build his reputation as a painter of portraits. Between 1877 and 1879 Sargent exhibited several works at the Salon, and in 1879 his portrait of Carolus-Duran (Sterling and Francine Clark Art Institute, Williamstown, Mass.) received an honorable mention.

Sargent confirmed his talent with several subject pictures, including *Fumée d'Ambre Gris* (1880, Sterling and Francine Clark Art Institute) and *El Jaleo* (1882, Isabella Stewart Gardner Museum, Boston), both of which were exhibited at the Salon and received considerable critical praise. One critic wrote in the *Gazette des Beaux-Arts* of *El Jaleo*, a large-scale oil painting of a Spanish dancer and musicians in a dusky interior, that it "reveals the most remarkable qualities of observation and invention" (Downes, p. 129). *El Jaleo* builds on Sargent's study of seventeenth-century Spanish painter Diego Velasquez, whose works he had copied at the Prado Museum in Madrid in 1879 at the suggestion of Carolus-Duran. Sargent followed the success of his dramatic *El Jaleo* with a portrait of Virginie Gautreau (Madame Pierre Gautreau) begun in 1883 and completed and exhibited at the Salon in 1884 (Metropolitan Museum of Art). The portrait, exhibited under the title *Madame X*, did not receive the kind of positive attention *El Jaleo* had. In fact, it caused a scandal: both Sargent's skill and his subject's renowned beauty were criticized as being superficial. In 1915, after three decades of hanging prominently in the artist's studio, the controversial portrait was chosen by Sargent as his entry in the Panama-Pacific International Exposition in San Francisco. Shortly after that exhibition he sold it to the Metropolitan Museum of Art, noting that he considered the painting one of his finest works.

Sargent's experience in Paris was discouraging and might have proven disastrous for his career had he not had good friends in London, including American author Henry James, whom Sargent met in 1884 and who helped Sargent establish himself in England. In 1886 Sargent left Paris for London and the United States. James's review of Sargent's work was published in *Harper's New Monthly Magazine* in October 1887. The essay included biographical data as well as descriptions of and responses to Sargent's major works to date, including *El Jaleo*, his innovative Venetian subject pictures, as well as his portraits of Carolus-Duran, Virginie Gautreau, the Boit children (1882, Museum of Fine Arts, Boston), and Charlotte Louise Burckhardt (1882, Metropolitan Museum of Art), which received James's highest praise. James concluded, "Mr. Sargent is so young, in spite of the place allotted to him in these pages, so often a record of long careers and uncontested triumphs, that, in spite also of the admirable works he has already produced, his future is the most valuable thing he has to show" (p. 691). James's critical yet complimentary essay, published in a popular American periodical, enhanced Sargent's reputation in the United States. Upon the occasion of James's seventieth birthday Sargent was commissioned to paint the author's portrait, which now hangs in the National Portrait Gallery in London. Sargent and James remained friends until James's death in 1916.

In 1886 Sargent rented James McNeill Whistler's former studio on Tite Street in London. Sargent met Whistler in 1881, and although the two artists were never particularly close socially or artistically, Sargent respected Whistler's work and in 1892 recommended Whistler as a contributor to the murals proposed for the Boston Public Library. Sargent is consistently linked to his American contemporaries Whistler and

Mary Cassatt because, like them, he spent much of his professional career in Europe, the implication being that he, like them, withdrew from mid- and late nineteenth-century America in favor of Europe. However, Sargent was born and educated abroad and therefore could not withdraw to Europe; rather he remained where he had been raised and traveled regularly to the United States to carry out commissions and to visit family and friends.

After moving to London Sargent began to receive many important portrait commissions from American and English patrons. During his 1887–1888 trip to the United States he painted Elizabeth Allen Marquand (1887, Art Museum, Princeton University), Mrs. Edward D. Boit (1888, Museum of Fine Arts, Boston), and Mrs. Adrien Iselin (1888, National Gallery of Art). Sargent's portraits were greeted with praise, but the praise was not unqualified. One observer wrote with mock horror or delight in the *Art Amateur* (Apr. 1888) that "Boston propriety has not yet got over the start Mr. John D. [*sic*] Sargent's exhibition of portraits at the St. Botolph Club gave it. . . . Not, of course that there were any nudities . . . but the spirit and style of the painter were so audacious, reckless and unconventional! He actually presented people in attitudes and costumes that were never seen in serious, costly portraits before." The author's comments suggest that Sargent's style was not entirely familiar to or embraced by his audience. His style was unconventional, and it both puzzled and pleased audiences because of the "attitudes" in which he presented his sitters. A particularly compelling work of this trip was his portrait of wealthy Boston art collector and trendsetter Isabella Stewart Gardner (1888, Isabella Stewart Gardner Museum, Boston). Henry James had introduced Gardner to Sargent when she visited London in 1886. Their meeting resulted in a commission that Sargent carried out at Gardner's home in Boston. The full-length portrait, in which Gardner directly engages her viewers from a position of authority, was a test of the artist's patience, as it went through eight renderings before Gardner accepted the ninth and final version. Gardner remained an important patron, purchasing *El Jaleo* for the Spanish court of her mansion on Fenway Park in Boston, as well as ten watercolors and six smaller oils.

While active as a portrait painter, Sargent's subjects also included landscape and genre. One of Sargent's most important works from the 1880s was a subject picture titled *Carnation, Lily, Lily, Rose* (1885–1886, Tate Gallery, London). The image, a depiction of two children lighting Chinese lanterns at dusk in a garden, was painted over a two-year period in the garden at "Farnham House" at Broadway, an artists' colony in the English Cotswolds. It is a large-scale work and was painted entirely outdoors. One of Sargent's early biographers, William Howe Downes, quotes a letter from Edwin Austin Abbey to Charles Parsons in which Abbey describes the painting as being "seven feet by five" and writes that "as the effect only lasts about twenty minutes a day—just after sunset—the picture does not get on very fast" (Downes, p. 24). Sargent exhibited

Carnation, Lily, Lily, Rose at the Royal Academy in 1887. It was acquired for the Tate Gallery that year and, according to Downes, was the first of Sargent's paintings to be purchased by a public institution. Painting outdoors, or *en plein air*, was a popular practice among the French impressionists, particularly Claude Monet. Sargent met Monet in 1876 and painted with him in 1887, an event recorded in Sargent's image titled *Claude Monet Painting at the Edge of a Wood* (Tate Gallery). Sargent is credited by one biographer, Charles Merrill Mount, with bringing impressionism to England. Over several seasons spent at Broadway, Sargent painted a number of masterful *plein air* works, including *St. Martin's Summer* (1888, private collection), *Violet Fishing* (1889, Ormond family), and *Paul Helleu Sketching with His Wife* (1889, Brooklyn Museum). Paintings such as these from the mid- and late 1880s led observers to place Sargent among the American impressionists. The classification may indeed be appropriate for these works but does not characterize Sargent's oeuvre.

In 1890 Sargent and Abbey were asked to contribute murals to the new Boston Public Library designed by the architectural firm of McKim, Mead and White. Both artists accepted the commission. Sargent's work was to be installed on the vaulted ceiling of the hall outside the special collections library. His subject was to have been Spanish literature, but after returning from a trip to the Near East in the winter of 1890–1891 he changed his subject to religious history. He did not conceive of the mural cycle as a chronological history of world religions but rather as a complex composition examining aspects of religious thought. Sargent returned to his London studio to sketch out ideas for his figures and paint the final canvases. The paintings were then shipped to the United States and installed by craftsmen who finished the architectural details and gilding with the canvases in place. Sargent's first section was installed in 1895, followed by three more in 1903, 1916, and 1919. The murals were well-received by contemporary critics, with the exception of his 1919 panel, "Synagogue," which the Boston Jewish community criticized for what it perceived as a negative interpretation of Judaism.

While at work on the project for the Boston Public Library, Sargent continued to receive numerous portrait commissions, including one from President Theodore Roosevelt completed in 1903 (White House Collection), as well as two additional mural commissions, from the Museum of Fine Arts in Boston (1916–1921) and from the Widener Memorial Library at Harvard University (1922). During World War I the British government commissioned Sargent to produce a work in honor of the joint effort of the British and Americans. Sargent traveled in 1918 to the western front, where he painted a number of watercolors of the soldiers and the landscape (Imperial War Museum, London). Based on his experience at the western front, he painted his almost life-sized work *Gassed* to fulfill his commission (1919, Imperial War Museum). Also at this time he painted a large-scale portrait of British officers for the National Portrait Gallery.

In addition to placing himself in the public eye, Sargent's American murals gave him the opportunity he needed to break away from the restrictive and demanding routine of commissioned portraiture. Flattering the sitter had become drudgery, and in 1907 he wrote Mrs. Daniel Sargent Curtis (a relative) that he "made a vow not to do any more portraits" and "shall soon be a free man." Exceptions to his vow included portraits of President Woodrow Wilson (1917, National Gallery of Ireland) and John D. Rockefeller (1917, Kykurt, Tarrytown, N.Y.).

Having a secure income from the murals enabled Sargent to concentrate on other subjects and media, most notably watercolor. Watercolor played a central role in the last twenty years of Sargent's life. His subjects, taken from his travels across Europe, the Near East, and North America, were familiar to his American and British audiences from their own travels or literary and historical sources; the audience and the artist shared knowledge of the places painted. It has been suggested that Sargent painted in watercolor only on holidays as an escape from portraits and murals; however, Sargent exhibited and sold his watercolors regularly and paid careful attention to the details of their subject, execution, and public display. The first major exhibition of Sargent's watercolors was held at Knoedler's Gallery in New York in 1909. It consisted of approximately eighty-six watercolors of subjects ranging from Venice to Bedouins. Sargent preferred that they be sold as a group to a public institution rather than as individual images to private collectors, and the Brooklyn Museum complied, purchasing eighty-three of the watercolors for its collection. Following Brooklyn's example, in 1912 the Museum of Fine Arts in Boston purchased forty-five watercolors, including images of Carrara and the Simplon Pass; in 1915 the Metropolitan Museum purchased ten, including Italian and Spanish subjects, and in 1950 was given approximately 200 more by the artist's younger sister Violet (Mrs. Francis Ormond); and in 1917 the Worcester Museum purchased eleven, including images of Florida. With such consistent public patronage Sargent could support himself with work of his own choosing.

Sargent never married and after his death in London was survived by his younger sisters, Emily and Violet. His two sisters inherited their brother's work and arranged for it to be dispersed among American institutions.

As Henry James noted in his 1887 essay, John Singer Sargent achieved high standing at a young age. He continued to prove himself throughout his career by exhibiting regularly at the Royal Academy and the National Academy of Design in New York (becoming a full member of each in 1897), in the American sections of international expositions, at the Union League in New York and at London's Grosvenor Gallery and Carfax Gallery. In 1907 he was recommended for a knighthood by Britain's King Edward VII but declined as he was unwilling to give up his U.S. citizenship. He was awarded in 1909 both the Order of Merit from France and the Order of Leopold from Belgium. At the height of his career Sargent was immensely popular both professionally and socially. He was not, however, without critics, beginning with the exhibition of *Madame X* and continuing into the twentieth century. Art critic Roger Fry, for example, was a vocal critic of what he perceived to be Sargent's conservatism in an era of great artistic and cultural change. Indeed, the advent of modernism eventually led to a decline in Sargent's standing. After his death his murals and portraits began to lose their public appeal. The murals were dismissed as vacant, and he was criticized as lacking the talent for such decorative work; his portraits were described as both technically and intellectually superficial. Yet Sargent was still recognized as an important American artist. He brought American art to an international audience and helped strengthen the American patronage of native artists. Sargent's life and work have again become the subject of active scholarship as demonstrated by the abundance of publications and exhibitions that investigate his artistic production.

• Sargent's papers consist primarily of correspondence located in the Archives of American Art and in the files of his correspondents, such as the Curtis family in the Boston Athenaeum and Vernon Lee in the Special Collections Library of Colby College, Waterville, Maine. Sargent has been the subject of a number of biographies, including William Howe Downes, *John S. Sargent: His Life and Work* (1925); Evan Charteris, *John Sargent* (1927); Charles Merrill Mount, *John Singer Sargent: A Biography* (1955); and Stanley Olson, *John Singer Sargent: His Portrait* (1986). In addition to Henry James's article, "John S. Sargent," *Harper's New Monthly Magazine*, Oct. 1887, many contemporary reviews and accounts of Sargent and his work may be found in Robert H. Getscher and Paul G. Marks, *James McNeill Whistler and John Singer Sargent: Two Annotated Bibliographies* (1986). Monographs on Sargent's art include Richard Ormond, *John Singer Sargent: Paintings, Drawings, Watercolors* (1970); Carter Ratcliff, *John Singer Sargent* (1982); and Trevor Fairbrother, *John Singer Sargent* (1994). Sargent's art has generated important scholarship by individuals such as Margaretta M. Lovell, *A Visitable Past: Views of Venice by American Artists, 1860–1915* (1989), and in exhibition catalogs such as Patricia Hills, ed., *John Singer Sargent* (1986); Mary Crawford Volk, ed., *John Singer Sargent's El Jaleo* (1992); Theodore Stebbins Jr., ed., *The Lure of Italy: American Artists and the Italian Experience, 1760–1914* (1992); and Marc Simpson, ed., *Uncanny Spectacle: The Public Career of the Young John Singer Sargent* (1997). Museums holding significant collections of Sargent's watercolors have compiled rich catalogs of their holdings, including Susan Strickler, ed., *American Traditions in Watercolor: The Worcester Art Museum Collection* (1987); Metropolitan Museum of Art, *American Watercolors from the Metropolitan Museum of Art*, with commentaries by Stephen Rubin (1991); and Sue Welsh Reed and Carol Troyen, *Awash in Color: Homer, Sargent and the Great American Watercolor* (1993). Among the doctoral dissertations that focus on different aspects of Sargent's work are M. Elizabeth Boone, "Vistas de Espana: American Views of Art and Life in Spain, 1860–1898" (City Univ. of New York Graduate Center, 1995); Kathleen L. Butler, "Tradition and Discovery: The Watercolors of John Singer Sargent" (Univ. of California, Berkeley, 1994); and Derrick Cartwright, "Reading Rooms: Interpreting the American Public Library Mural, 1890–1930 (Univ. of Michigan, Ann Arbor, 1994).

KATHLEEN L. BUTLER

SARGENT, Winthrop (1 May 1753–3 Jan. 1820), soldier, territorial administrator, and author, was born in Gloucester, Massachusetts, the son of Winthrop Sargent, a shipping trade merchant, and Judith Sanders. Winthrop attended Harvard, from which he was nearly expelled for his part in the violent student disorders of 1770. Upon his graduation in 1771, he served as naval merchant at Gloucester until the outbreak of armed hostilities with Britain in 1775. He joined General Henry Knox's artillery regiment, serving with distinction and earning the brevet rank of major.

After the signing of the Treaty of Paris, Congress appointed Sargent surveyor of the Northwest Territory, where he worked on the Seven Ranges. In 1786 Sargent became connected to the Ohio Company of the United States, a group of revolutionary war veterans and speculators seeking to develop land north of the Ohio River in southeastern Ohio. That year he served on the committee in Boston that drafted a plan for the company and was subsequently elected secretary. Of the nine shareholders, he emerged by August 1787 with the most shares, more than 25 percent of the company's holdings. The following summer he reached Marietta, where he played a valuable part in planning the burgeoning colony. Sargent served as secretary of the Ohio Territory for a decade. Governor Arthur St. Clair was frequently absent for prolonged periods, and during these phases Sargent assumed the executive reins with the force of principle and attention to duty characteristic of his public service. In early 1789 Sargent married Rowena Tupper, who died in 1790 after the difficult birth of a son who did not long survive.

As St. Clair's adjutant and secretary, Sargent was wounded twice during the autumn 1791 expedition against the Miami and the consequent ghastly defeat of the American military force at Fort Recovery, roughly twenty-four miles from Greenville, Ohio. In this military debacle, Native Americans from at least seven tribes attacked two regular U.S. Army regiments and several smaller, poorly organized militia units. His diary accounts, like virtually all of his journal entries, letters, official reports, and directives, are cogent, informative, well crafted, and sometimes even luminiferous. For instance, the diary entry of 4 November 1791 begins: "Moderate north-west wind, serene atmosphere and unclouded sky; but the fortunes of this day have been as the cruelest tempest to the interests of the country and this army, and will blacken a full page in the future annals of America. The troops have all been defeated, and though it is impossible at this time to ascertain our loss, yet there can be no manner of doubt that more than one-half of the army are either killed or wounded." Sargent's narrative account of the incident and its aftermath manifests Caesar-like dramatic eloquence: "In this desperate situation of affairs, when even hope, that last consolation of the wretched, had failed the army, . . . the General [St. Clair] took the resolution of abandoning his camp and attempting a retreat. There was a mere possibility that some of the troops might be brought off, though it could not be counted on among the probabilities. But there was no alternative." Sargent, acting governor in late 1791 and 1792, organized the remaining forces to repel subsequent attacks at Fort Recovery, Fort Jefferson, Fort Hamilton, and Fort Washington (now Cincinnati). Serving again as adjutant and secretary under Governor St. Clair, Sargent also performed active service in the so-called Indian War of 1794–1795.

On 7 October 1798 the U.S. Congress officially organized the territory of Mississippi, which included what became a part of the Louisiana territory, annexed in 1803, and the present state of Alabama. Colonel Sargent resigned his Ohio position and accepted President John Adams's prompt offer to be the first governor of the new territory. Sargent followed Adams's broad governmental, Federalist philosophy when he instituted his policies in the newly formed territory.

Congress and the president extended U.S. sovereignty into this region in the hope of securing the frontier in the Southwest against European interests, those of Spain most immediately. Sargent believed that, to assure this goal, American legal and governmental institutions had to be enforced in this remote area. To this end, he instituted the territory's first American codified laws. Under the Organic Act of the Mississippi Territory, the governor had extensive powers, which he used to organize the territory into counties and to select militia officers, local county officials, and all territorial county judges. Since communication and transportation between Washington and the Mississippi area proved slow and arduous, Sargent's substantial exercise of gubernatorial power proved necessary, but it was seldom appreciated by the local population.

In 1798 Sargent's code initially comprised nine sections, and he expanded it before long to nearly four dozen. The code established the territory's first American-based court system and governmental apparatus. Local response to Sargent's strict judicial system was almost universally negative. The territorial people wanted more say in the court system and in the appointment of militia officers than the Sargent-developed code allowed. Widespread local dissatisfaction also surfaced over his system of fees on previously lightly taxed or untaxed items, such as liquor licenses, marriage licenses, and divorces. His statutes furthermore established unpopular procedures to seize lands as payment for debts and frauds.

Sargent attempted thus to regulate public behavior, develop the territorial treasury, and control the militia because he recognized the need to establish and maintain order in an environment that, if an insurrection should occur, could lead to unwelcome European interference. Moreover, a codified system of fees and taxes would fund development of roadways, bridges, ferries, and schools. Although much of the legal, governmental, and fiscal structure of Sargent's code remained in place for years, in 1800 the code was formally abolished. In 1798 he married Mary McIntosh Williams; they had two sons. When Thomas Jefferson became the third president, he replaced the highly unpopular Sargent with a governor of Jeffersonian Republican party principles who was less rebarbative to the people of the territory.

Sargent retired from public life in the early nineteenth century. He lived and wrote on the Natchez plantations, "Pine Grove" and "Belmont," of his wealthy second spouse. Sargent died on a northbound steamboat near New Orleans.

The playing of the fountain of honor is sometimes erratic. Neither Sargent's cathectic personality nor the steel of his character has received due praise. Nor have literary and intellectual historians as yet devoted sufficient attention to the capacious intellect to which Sargent's wide-ranging writings serve as ample attestation. An original member of the Society of the Cincinnati, Sargent was also elected to the American Philosophical Society, the American Academy of Arts and Sciences, and the Massachusetts Historical Society. With Benjamin S. Barton, Sargent wrote *Papers Relevant to Certain American Antiquities* (1796). As an Ohio surveyor and then secretary, he performed admirably. As territorial governor, he performed solid administrative work and established the first court system for the Mississippi Territory that served as the precedent for several later revisions.

• Sargent papers are in the Massachusetts Historical Society (Boston); the Ohio Historical Society (Columbus); and the Historical Society of Pennsylvania. Biographical information is in "Indiana American Revolution Bicentennial Commission Collection," *Indiana History Bulletin* 50, no. 12 (1973): 139–44; Winthrop Sargent, *Early Sargents of New England* (1922); E. W. Sargent and C. S. Sargent, *Epes Sargent of Gloucester and His Descendants* (1923); B. H. Pershing, "Winthrop Sargent," *Ohio Archeology and History Quarterly* 35 (Oct. 1926); and Pershing, "Winthrop Sargent: A Builder of the Old Northwest" (Ph.D. diss., Univ. of Chicago, 1927). See also "Diary of Colonel Winthrop Sargent during the Campaign of MDCCXCI," *Ohio Archeology and History Quarterly* 33 (July 1924); A. B. Hulbert, ed., *The Records of the Original Proceedings of the Ohio Company* (2 vols., 1917); Dunbar Rowland, ed., *The Mississippi Territorial Archives, 1798–1803* (1905); William H. Smith, ed., *The St. Clair Papers* (2 vols., 1882); John D. W. Guice, "The Cement of Society: Law in the Mississippi Territory," *Gulf Coast Historical Review* 1, no. 2 (1986): 76–99, which primarily discusses Sargent's code; John Wunder, "American Law and Order Comes to Mississippi Territory: The Making of Sargent's Code, 1798–1800," *Journal of Mississippi History* 38, no. 2 (1976): 131–55, which also examines the development of Sargent's codified laws; Williams S. Coker and Jack D. L. Holmes, "Daniel Clark's Letter on the Mississippi Territory," *Journal of Mississippi History* 32, no. 2 (1970): 153–69; Theodore Chase, "Harvard Student Disorders in 1770," *New England Quarterly* 61, no. 1 (1988): 25–54 *American State Papers, Miscellaneous*, vol. 1 (1834); Winthrop Sargent's own *Papers in Relation to the Official Conduct of Governor Sargent* (1801); *Political Intolerance* (1801), papers attacking Jefferson's judgment in removing Sargent, likely written by Sargent himself; and Rowland, *History of Mississippi* (2 vols., 1925).

JAMES J. KIRSCHKE

SARNOFF, David (27 Feb. 1891–12 Dec. 1971), media executive, was born in Uzlian in the Russian province of Minsk, the son of Abraham Sarnoff, a trader and house painter, and Leah Privin, a seamstress. When David was five, his father left for the United States and he was sent to live with an uncle. When his father sent money for his passage five years later, David rejoined the family and traveled to Canada in steerage, landing in Montreal and entering the United States by train in 1900. The Sarnoffs settled in the Lower East Side of New York City, and David entered school but also helped support the family by running errands for a local butcher, delivering newspapers, and singing soprano in a synagogue. He also studied at the Educational Alliance, quickly learning English. When he was fifteen his father died, and David left school for good; while he later received many honorary degrees, his formal education ended with eighth grade.

Sarnoff's intention in 1906 was to seek a job at a newspaper. However, he was misdirected upon entering the *New York Herald* Building and ended up in the office of the Commercial Cable Company, where he was given a job delivering cables and cleaning up the office. He quit this job after a few months, but his fascination with telegraphy had begun, and he soon found a position as an office boy with the British-owned American Marconi Wireless Telegraph Company. Sarnoff quickly rose through the ranks of the small office, becoming a wireless operator and being sent to company stations in Nantucket and Brooklyn and aboard ships. His distinctive "fist" on the telegraph key became known for its speed and accuracy. Sarnoff also struck up a lasting friendship with Guglielmo Marconi, the inventor of the wireless telegraph and founder of the company.

Sarnoff's first taste of fame was the result of the *Titanic* disaster in April 1912. As the manager of Marconi's station atop the Wanamaker Department Store, he received news of the accident and relayed it to the press. Subsequent claims that he was the sole operator in the station, that he stayed until the list of all survivors was complete, and that the Wanamaker station was in direct contact with the ships on the scene are all dubious, but Sarnoff handled the story effectively. However, the need for adequate radio equipment was clearly demonstrated by the *Titanic*'s inability to reach ships close at hand, resulting in much loss of life. Congress's decision to require radio equipment on all large ocean-going vessels resulted in the growth of American Marconi and Sarnoff's own success.

Despite taking an intensive course in electrical engineering, Sarnoff soon decided that he would never make an outstanding engineer and so chose to go into management, where, incidentally, the money was better. He continued to rise through the ranks of American Marconi, promoted to radio inspector, assistant chief engineer, and then contract manager, in which position he evaluated new inventions and services for the company. In 1917, at the age of twenty-six, Sarnoff became Marconi's commercial manager. That year he married Lisette Hernant, the daughter of French Jews recently arrived in the Bronx; the couple had three sons.

Sarnoff requested a commission in the U.S. Navy during World War I but did not receive it—the result, in his opinion, of anti-Semitism. Instead, he spent the war supplying navy forces with radio equipment and communications advice. After the war, the navy was anxious to put radio communications in American hands and encouraged British Marconi to sell its stock in American Marconi to General Electric (GE). In November 1919, American Marconi was absorbed by a new company called the Radio Corporation of America (RCA). In order to consolidate patents and license agreements, GE transferred large amounts of RCA stock to Westinghouse, American Telephone and Telegraph (AT&T), and United Fruit. In exchange, RCA gained control of all major radio patents, nearly giving it a monopoly on communication systems in the United States.

Sarnoff, who became a commercial manager at RCA, wrote a long memo in 1920 detailing the current state of radio and reiterating an idea he claimed to have originally suggested to Marconi executives in 1915. The memo ran in part: "I have in mind a plan of development that would make radio a household utility in the same sense as a piano or phonograph. The idea is to bring music into the home by wireless." Since the 1915 copy of this memo has never been recovered, Sarnoff's reputation for prescience in this area is unsupported, but the "radio music box" memo became a legend in the communications business nevertheless. And his suggestion was insightful: between 1922 and 1924, RCA's radio sales amounted to $83 million. Sarnoff also wanted RCA to move into broadcasting, and in 1921 he arranged to air a boxing match between Jack Dempsey and Georges Carpentier to an audience of 300,000, giving them a taste of what radio would be like. In 1922 Sarnoff wrote to the president of GE to recommend that the company create a broadcasting network to provide news and entertainment to the whole country, and RCA created a central broadcasting organization through which it could feed programs to interconnected radio stations by 1926. This became the National Broadcasting Company (NBC), the first radio chain in the country. Sarnoff envisioned radio as a public service, and he pushed for high-quality programming like Dr. Walter Damrosch's weekly "Music Appreciation Hour," which featured classics, and the Metropolitan Opera. Sarnoff was particularly proud of bringing Italian conductor Arturo Toscanini to conduct the newly created NBC Orchestra on the air in 1937. However, he was realistic about what the public wanted to listen to, commenting that "a lot of people would rather listen to swing than Toscanini. Of course we have a certain responsibility for creating programs,

but basically we're the delivery boys" (*New York Times*, 13 Dec. 1971).

In the late 1920s, Sarnoff oversaw RCA's expansion into new markets as he rose to become a member of the board and, in 1928, an executive vice president. Three years earlier, RCA had acquired the Victor Talking Machine Company and had begun manufacturing radios and phonographs in the same set. In 1928 Sarnoff and Joseph P. Kennedy arranged the creation of Radio-Keith-Orpheum (RKO), a movie production company. The next year, another new company was formed in cooperation with General Motors to manufacture radios for cars.

Sarnoff became the president of RCA in 1930. Two years later, in the midst of the depression, the government brought an antimonopoly suit against RCA that forced GE, Westinghouse, and AT&T to divest themselves of their stock in the company. The suit left RCA with $18 million in debts, but also with manufacturing plants, broadcasting stations, and two radio networks. It also allowed Sarnoff to have complete control of RCA.

With radio clearly a success, Sarnoff turned his attention elsewhere. As early as 1923 he had announced confidently that "television . . . will come to pass in the future." During the 1930s, despite RCA's debt burden, he pushed for huge and costly research programs. Sarnoff liked to visit RCA's development labs in Camden, New Jersey, where Russian scientist Vladimir Zworykin was working on television technology. He went not only to watch the work but to give the impression that he was ready to roll up his sleeves and pitch in. Sarnoff pushed hard for RCA's early development of television as he was convinced that it would make radio obsolete, and he had the privilege of conducting the first public television broadcast in April 1939 at the New York World's Fair. Speaking from the RCA Pavilion on the fair's Avenue of Progress, Sarnoff said, "It is with a feeling of humbleness that I come to this moment of announcing the birth of a new art so important in its implications that it is bound to affect all society."

During World War II, Sarnoff got a taste of the glory that had eluded him in World War I. Having been commissioned as a lieutenant colonel in 1924 and promoted to full colonel in 1931, he was called to active duty to coordinate D-Day communications for the Allies in Europe. This gave him the chance to work with General Dwight D. Eisenhower and to meet Winston Churchill and other political leaders. Sarnoff remained in Europe to restore the communications system in France, spurred on by the rumor that he was being considered for a promotion, and he did not leave active duty until he had received the rank of brigadier general in 1944. Sarnoff preferred the title of general for the rest of his life.

NBC had begun commercial television broadcasting in 1941, and upon Sarnoff's return to civilian life he began trying to convince radio stations to follow—a move that seemed expensive and risky at the time. However, as the postwar TV market boomed, RCA earned back its $50 million investment in research in just three years. Sarnoff then became obsessed with the development of color television, gambling millions of dollars on its success and very nearly losing. The difficulty lay in creating a set that was "compatible"— able to receive black-and-white as well as color images. In 1950 the Federal Communications Commission approved a rival, noncompatible system developed by Columbia Broadcasting System, but it reversed itself and adopted RCA's compatible system three years later. Sarnoff had spent $150 million to come out ahead, but the investment proved worthwhile.

In the last two decades of his life, Sarnoff continued to push RCA's production of new technologies and expansion in new areas. Unfortunately, RCA's product development was plagued by numerous patent lawsuits in the 1940s and 1950s, creating rifts between Sarnoff and engineers with whom he had once been close friends. In the 1960s he tended to his image, commissioning a biography from his cousin Eugene Lyons. Lyons's final draft included some hints at Sarnoff's frequent infidelities and occasional business failures, so Sarnoff rewrote the book himself and destroyed all copies of the author's own work before it was published in 1966. He also began putting his papers in order, creating the David Sarnoff Library at RCA's labs in Princeton, New Jersey, and publishing a collection of his speeches and writings, *Looking Ahead* (1968). In 1966, the sixtieth anniversary of his first work in communications, Sarnoff retired as the chief executive officer of RCA, and his son Robert replaced him. However, Sarnoff remained as the board chairman and continued to be involved in RCA's affairs, occasionally coming into conflict with his son.

In the summer of 1968, Sarnoff became ill; a mastoid infection spread to his nervous system, and he never fully recovered. He died in New York City. At his death, RCA was grossing more than $3 billion annually and had sixty-four manufacturing plants in the United States and abroad. While he had profoundly influenced the course of radio and television in the United States, Sarnoff had also alienated many old friends by constantly attending to the needs of RCA over the needs of all participants in the field, and his marriage and family life had been largely neglected in favor of his work. However, he had seen his dearest dreams for radio and then color television come true as a result of his own hard work and determination. His ability to see the practical applications of new technologies made him successful, and while he himself did not invent new technologies, his knowledge and ambition were the driving force behind the development of electronic media in the United States.

• Sarnoff's papers are in the David Sarnoff Library in Princeton, N.J. Published writings by Sarnoff include *Pioneering in Television: Prophesy and Fulfillment* (1945) and *The Fabulous Future: America in 1980, as Seen by David Sarnoff and Others* (1956). Books about Sarnoff include the RCA Department of Information, *Biographical Sketch of David Sarnoff* (1959); John Tebbel, *David Sarnoff* (1963); Carl Dreher, *Sarnoff: An American Success* (1977), written by an RCA engineer; and

Kenneth Bilby, *The General: David Sarnoff and the Rise of the Communications Industry* (1986), a book by a close associate of Sarnoff. For accounts of Sarnoff's role in the development of the communications industry, see Eric Barnouw, *A History of Broadcasting in the United States* (3 vols., 1966–1970); Robert Sobel, *RCA* (1986); and Tom Lewis, *Empire of the Air: The Men Who Made Radio* (1991). For a skeptical assessment of the 1915 date for the "radio music box" memo, see Louise M. Benjamin, "In Search of the Sarnoff 'Radio Music Box' Memo," *Journal of Broadcasting and Electronic Media* (Summer 1993). Obituaries are in the *New York Times*, 13 Dec. 1971; *Broadcasting*, 20 Dec. 1971; *Electronic News*, 20 Dec. 1971; and the *Journal of the Society of Motion Picture and Television Engineers* (Feb. 1972).

BETHANY NEUBAUER

SAROYAN, William (31 Aug. 1908–18 May 1981), writer, was born in Fresno, California, the son of Armenak Saroyan, a writer and Presbyterian minister, and Takoohi Saroyan. He was the youngest of four children born to Armenian immigrants who fled from Bitlis in eastern Turkey to avoid persecution under the Ottoman empire. Although Saroyan was born in the United States and rarely visited Armenia, he thought of himself not as an American, but as an Armenian-American, and his fiction, essays, memoirs, and plays were among the earliest expressions of a specifically ethnic voice in American literature. The Armenian identity, he believed, was a matter of personality and culture rather than geography and politics.

Until the late nineteenth century, when the great wave of Armenian massacres began, the rulers of the Islamic Ottoman empire tolerated their Christian Armenian subjects as "people of the book" or as *rayahs* (sheep), who should be protected. At the same time, however, considerable social, economic, and political restraints were enforced. An Armenian legacy from that experience was a distrust of authority. That distrust, emerging throughout Saroyan's work, also gives his books a place in that libertarian and antiauthoritarian tradition in American literature extending from Walt Whitman and Henry David Thoreau to the present.

Saroyan's father died in 1911, and Takoohi Saroyan, unable both to work and to care for her family, sent her four children to an orphanage in Oakland, California. This event so disturbed Saroyan that, despite the generally autobiographical and confessional nature of his work, he did not mention it in print until he published *The Bicycle Rider in Beverly Hills* in 1952, two years after his mother's death. The family was reunited in 1916, and Saroyan lived with them in Fresno until 1925, when he moved to San Francisco. He left school at age fifteen and never graduated from high school or attended college.

Except for a brief and dispiriting visit to New York in 1928–1929, Saroyan spent most of the late 1920s and early 1930s in San Francisco trying to succeed as a writer. Aside from a couple of sketches and a few poems, however, he was not able to place any of his work until 1933, when several pieces appeared in a Boston-based Armenian periodical, *Hairenik*, to which he became a frequent contributor. *Hairenik* was published for a small, well-defined audience, however, and Saroyan wanted wider recognition. Under the pseudonym Sirak Goryan, which he had earlier used in *Hairenik*, he sent copies of his recently published fiction to Edward J. O'Brien, who edited an annual selection of what he considered the best short stories of the preceding year. O'Brien chose one of Saroyan's stories, "The Broken Wheel," for the next volume, *The Best American Stories of 1934*.

Saroyan also sent copies of the *Hairenik* stories to Whit Burnett and Martha Foley, editors of *Story*, a prestigious magazine publishing the work of writers such as William Carlos Williams and William Faulkner. Burnett and Foley liked Saroyan's stories and asked for more. He had been working on a novel (never published, although the manuscript still exists) entitled "Trapeze over the Universe." Strongly indebted to James Joyce and the stream-of-consciousness technique, the novel provided Saroyan with material that he reworked into "The Daring Young Man on the Flying Trapeze," which Burnett and Foley accepted for their magazine and published in 1934. The story won the O. Henry Award the same year in a special category: the short-short story. Republished later that year by Random House as the title piece in a collection of Saroyan's short fiction and sketches, the story deals with a young writer unable to support himself in the economically depressed America of the 1930s. Rather than despair, he adopts a jaunty, whimsical attitude; he has no interest in social reform or in revenge against the economic system that oppresses him, and if his strategy does not save him materially (in fact, at the end of the story he literally starves to death), it saves him spiritually, uncorrupted by anger or hate. Like the song "Brother, Can You Spare a Dime?" and the film *The Gold Diggers of 1933*, Saroyan's story is an important representation of the popular culture of the depression era.

"The Daring Young Man on the Flying Trapeze" immediately made Saroyan a popular writer. The collection for which it became the title piece became a bestseller, going through five printings in its first two years, and his fiction began to appear in such popular magazines as *Story*, *Harper's*, *Scribner's*, and *Atlantic Monthly*. Another story written at this time, "Seventy Thousand Assyrians," proved more characteristic of his future work, however. A long, meandering account by an Armenian who once rejected his heritage but who, in the course of his narrative, finds compelling reasons to accept it, the piece was loosely modeled on stories by Sherwood Anderson. "Seventy Thousand Assyrians" is a successful and widely reprinted example of that expressionist current in American literature extending from Whitman and Mark Twain to Gertrude Stein and Anderson and in turn to Faulkner, Henry Miller (1891–1980), Thomas Wolfe, Jack Kerouac, and many others. Essentially the goal in expressionist writing is not the objectively crafted poetry and fiction associated, for example, with Edgar Allen Poe, but, rather, the direct expression of the author's or narrator's feelings and convictions. The self that emerges from an account of this sort may in turn be considered representative of a particular nationality, race, or ethnic group; in this manner, Whitman found authority to speak for Americans generally and Saroyan found authority to speak for the Armenian diaspora.

Saroyan said that he was never particularly attracted to "the short story form, as such." What he wanted was "a form or formlessness which would permit me to write"—a means, that is, of expressing himself fully on a given subject. The result as developed in "Seventy Thousand Assyrians" was effectively a new genre, half essay and half story (with roots in Anderson's digressive, rambling narratives), which was in turn a model for Kerouac. Saroyan did not, however, limit himself to this kind of fiction; he also published, for example, fables, parodies, and short anecdotal pieces, but he wrote particularly well when he made the narrator the real subject of the story.

Much of Saroyan's best short fiction can be found in his second and third books, *Inhale and Exhale* and *Three Times Three* (both published in 1936), and in the stories based on his memories of his boyhood in Fresno and published in *My Name Is Aram* (1940). Toward the end of his life he worked on a series of stories concerning a family named Basmadjian; collected in the posthumous volume, *Madness in the Family* (1988), these belong among his best. So does the title story in *The Assyrian* (1950). Much of his other short fiction and most of his novels seem hastily and indifferently written, however; indeed, he insisted that between 1934 and 1939 he had written an average of 100 stories per year.

In the late 1930s Saroyan began writing plays. *My Heart's in the Highlands* and *The Time of Your Life* (both produced in 1939) were enthusiastically received on Broadway, and *Love's Old Sweet Song* (1940) and *The Beautiful People* (1941) had successful runs. *The Time of Your Life* was awarded a Pulitzer Prize in 1940, but Saroyan rejected it on the grounds that art should not be patronized by wealth. *Across the Board on Tomorrow Morning* (1942) and its successors, however, pleased neither New York audiences nor most critics, and Saroyan's Broadway career dissolved rapidly. He left a series of plays, the best of which is *The Time of Your Life*, which define a new sensibility in the American theater.

Like "The Daring Young Man on the Flying Trapeze," Saroyan's plays responded to political and economic crises with that jaunty, whimsical, and sentimental sensibility that one of his critics labeled Saroyanesque. Unlike playwrights who simply wished to entertain or divert, or those who, like Clifford Odets, proposed politically committed solutions to the world's problems, Saroyan preached withdrawal into the self. The wildly eccentric individuals in *My Heart's in the Highlands* and the social drifters patronizing Nick's Saloon in *The Time of Your Life* are victims of impersonal political and economic forces. Although Saroyan himself was among the most notoriously ambitious writers of his generation, his heroes and heroines were generally "little people" whose solution to the problems of the day was not to worry—or at least to stay clear of any authority with designs on their lives.

Given Saroyan's suspicion of people in charge, it is not surprising that he rejected the Pulitzer Prize. He had much to gain from his refusal, for the rejection surely brought more publicity than acceptance would have. Further complicating the matter, he accepted the New York Drama Critics Circle Award for the same play. Nonetheless, rejecting the Pulitzer gave him the opportunity to make widely reported statements about the need for art to be free of authority.

On this occasion, Saroyan was clearly the popular victor, but he was less successful in his next battles. Difficulties with Metro-Goldwyn-Mayer were in part responsible for his most popular book, *The Human Comedy* (1943), but he was not allowed to direct the film version, nor was it made as he wanted. Finally, his much-publicized problems with the U.S. government, first over military service and then income taxes, ended altogether in defeat.

The Human Comedy, set in a small American town during the Second World War, was originally written as a scenario for MGM, and Saroyan understood that the terms of the agreement gave him the right to direct it. Louis B. Mayer, the head of the studio, disagreed; not only was Clarence Brown assigned as director, but the scenario was rewritten by Howard Estabrook. Saroyan tried to get his original scenario published, but when the editor Robert Giroux saw it, he realized that it might succeed if rewritten as a novel. Saroyan followed the suggestion, and the result was the book for which he is best known. The novel's greatest weakness is its idyllic and unrealistic vision of small-town America, a vision owing more perhaps to MGM movies, such as the popular Andy Hardy series, than to Saroyan himself. Nonetheless, the author's characteristic resistance to all authorities (ranging here from an imperiously intellectual lecturer to the Washington officials who were conducting the war) makes the book quite different from the brazenly patriotic film (Mayer's favorite), which celebrates the submissive or conformist personality (exemplified by Van Johnson in the role of the good soldier) that Saroyan would never have admired.

Saroyan tried unsuccessfully to avoid military service and wrote a novel, *The Adventures of Wesley Jackson*, critical of military service. The book was harshly criticized, however, for by the time it was published in 1946, Saroyan's complaints seemed jejune and childish as reports arrived from Auschwitz and Belsen. Saroyan served in the U.S. Army from 1943 to 1945, first stationed in the United States but, later, in 1944–1945, in Great Britain.

In the remaining twenty-five years of his career, Saroyan published novels, plays, short-story collections, children's books, memoirs, and miscellaneous works, but he never regained his earlier popularity. In part that may be attributed to a postwar academic and critical establishment hostile to expressionist writing, but the conservative political and social nature of the period may have had its effect as well. By the late 1950s, when Kerouac and other beat writers initiated another wave of expressionist writing in American literature, Saroyan had become, at best, an "elder statesman."

Personally as well as professionally, Saroyan's life after the war was marked by tragedies and disappointments, including a period of creative sterility in the late 1940s. In 1943 he had married Carol Marcus, but the marriage ended in divorce in 1949; they were remarried in 1951 and divorced the following year. Gambling losses in 1949 totaled $50,000, and the Internal Revenue Service claimed tens of thousands of dollars against his income for unpaid taxes. During his final years he had little contact with his two children.

Among his last works, Saroyan's memoirs in particular deserve more attention than they have received. Although such books as *Here Comes There Goes You Know Who* (1961), *Letters from 74 rue Taitbout* (1969), and *Days of Life and Death and Escape to the Moon* (1970) are in part indifferently written, at their best they reveal the power available to writers who ignore formal conventions and make their language the directly expressive medium of personal feelings and convictions. The books are also important as further investigations of Saroyan's Armenian heritage.

In 1961 he purchased an apartment in Paris and two years later purchased two neighboring houses in Fresno, one as a home and the second as a place in which to store possessions. His final years were divided between these two cities. He died in Fresno.

• Saroyan's letters and manuscripts are housed in the William Saroyan Collection at the Humanities Research Center in Austin, Tex., and in the Bancroft Library at the University of California in Berkeley. In addition to the titles mentioned above, his memoirs include *After Thirty Years: The Daring Young Man on the Flying Trapeze* (1964), *Births* (1983), *Chance Meetings* (1978), *My Kind of Crazy, Wonderful People: 17 Stories and a Play* (1966), *Not Dying* (1963), *Obituaries* (1979), *Places Where I've Done Time* (1972), *Short Drive, Sweet Chariot* (1966), *Sons Come and Go, Mothers Hang in Forever* (1976), and *The Twin Adventures* (1950). For primary and secondary bibliographies, see David Kherdian, *A Bibliography of William Saroyan: 1934–1964* (1965), and Elizabeth C. Foard, *William Saroyan: A Reference Guide* (1989). See also Lawrence Lee and Barry Gifford, *Saroyan: A Biography* (1984), supplemented by Leo Hamalian, ed., *William Saroyan: The Man and the Writer Remembered* (1987), and Aram Saroyan, *Last Rites: The Death of William Saroyan* (1982) and *William Saroyan* (1983).

EDWARD HALSEY FOSTER

SARPY, Peter A. (3 Nov. 1805–4 Jan. 1865), fur trader and western entrepreneur, was born Pierre Sylvester Grégoire Sarpy in St. Louis, Missouri, the son of Grégoire Berold Sarpy, a merchant and fur trader, and Pelagie L'Abadie, who had ties of blood and marriage with the family of Pierre Chouteau, Jr. Because of the economic and social prominence of his family, Sarpy enjoyed the best of educational opportunities, but furs were dominant in the family's life, and he went into the fur trade as did his brothers, John B. Sarpy and Thomas Lestang Sarpy. Thomas was sent to work for the American Fur Company at a post located on the Cheyenne River at the mouth of Rapid Creek, in present-day western South Dakota. He was killed early in 1832 by the explosion of a keg of gunpowder set off by the spark of a candle. John spent most of his time in St. Louis, employed first in the firm of Berthold & Chouteau, the promoters of the Missouri Fur Company, and later in association with the American Fur Company. The Western Department of the American Fur Company underwent a number of organizational and name changes in the late 1820s and 1830s, and after 1838 the business was legally known as Pierre Chouteau, Jr., and Company. For the most part the public continued to know it as the American Fur Company, and writers often refer to it as Chouteau's American Fur Company. At the time of his death in 1857, John Sarpy's share in the company amounted to 26 percent.

The exact date for Peter Sarpy's entry into the country west of the Missouri River is unknown; it may have been as early as 1823. Records indicate he was shipping furs to Pierre Chouteau in 1830 and 1831, and in 1832, on the orders of his employer, John P. Cabanné, the agent of the American Fur Company at Council Bluffs, he executed the arrest of P. N. Leclerc, whose keelboat was taking trade goods up the Missouri River as well as annuities due to the Indians. The excuse given by Cabanné and Sarpy for their seizure of persons and property was to search for whiskey, but since Leclerc had valid permits for the small amount of whiskey aboard, the protests in Washington were sharp against the overgrown monopoly of the American Fur Company. The order banning Cabanné and Sarpy from Indian country proved very temporary.

Sarpy came to have charge of the post at Bellevue, strategically located just north of the junction of the Platte and Missouri rivers, which commanded the traffic of both rivers, and close by the Council Bluffs Indian Agency, which also permitted a large business with the Oto, Omaha, and Pawnee tribes as well as with whites. Across the river, on the Iowa side, was the post of St. Mary. Soon Sarpy became one of the best-known persons in the trade, trusted by both Pierre Chouteau and the Indians, who called him the White Chief.

In 1836, with his company providing cash and credit, Sarpy entered into a partnership with Henry Fraeb to tap the trade of the Rocky Mountain area. Along the South Platte River, the two established a post, named Fort Jackson, in present Colorado. It was one of four posts on the river within an area less than twenty miles square and like the others did more business in buffalo robes than in beaver skins. Bent, St. Vrain & Company eliminated Fraeb and Sarpy's competition by buying Fort Jackson in 1838, and Sarpy returned to the Bellevue post.

Whether Sarpy returned as owner or as an agent of Chouteau's American Fur Company is unclear. The fur and robe packs that his traders in the Dakotas and Nebraska collected went down to the St. Louis warehouses of Chouteau, and, as long as his brother John lived, he seems to have had unrivaled credit with the firm. In addition to the Indian tribes of the area, he supplied army units, explorers, and the overland migrants, including the Mormons trekking to Utah and the gold seekers of 1849. He augmented his profits by providing blacksmiths and carpenters and by establishing ferrying services over the Missouri, Elkhorn, and Loup rivers, and at St. Mary he set up a post store and newspaper.

Well versed in the native languages, Sarpy played a major role in negotiating the land cessions made by the Omaha and Oto tribes to the U.S. government in 1854. The next year he was made quartermaster for a regiment of Nebraska volunteers to join with the Omaha in repelling the Sioux. In recognition of his various activities and contributions, including participation in the laying out of the towns of Bellevue and Decatur, the Nebraska legislature named Sarpy County for him.

In 1862 Sarpy moved from Bellevue to Plattsmouth, Nebraska, where he established a steam flouring mill and where he died, without direct descendants, and where he was buried. Later his body was returned to St. Louis and interred in Calvary Cemetery. His Indian wife of many years (from around 1834 or later), Nicomi, originally the spouse of army surgeon John Gayle, remained in the Plattsmouth area, provided by Sarpy with a $200 annuity, grudgingly paid by the St. Louis relatives who inherited his considerable property in Nebraska, Iowa, and St. Louis.

In the pursuit of his business enterprises, Sarpy spared no one, but he had a kind heart, and the stories of his hospitality were legion as were those of his fondness for fast horses, fine hunting dogs, and liquor. The German artist and naturalist H. Balduin Möllhausen noticed that he was "the most complete specimen of the backwoodsman" he had ever seen. He felt enclosed by the world of the city, and his occasional visits to St. Louis lasted no more than four weeks. Sarpy was the epitome of those fearless, free-spirited men who pushed out into the far frontier for the purpose of carrying on their trade. In so doing they carried America west with them.

• The Nebraska Historical Society has a painting of Sarpy as well as copies of T. B. Cuming's 1855 letters appointing him quartermaster general, and the Missouri Historical Society, St. Louis, contains records of his estate. Records of the Bureau of Indian Affairs, National Archives, RG 75, St. Louis Superintendency, Roll 750, frames 149–167, 322, 336, 405, 569, document beyond question Sarpy's participation in the Leclerc affair. John E. Wickman's biography in *The Mountain Men and the Fur Trade of the Far West*, vol. 4, ed. LeRoy R. Hafen (10 vols., 1965–1972), is the best overall sketch of his life. LeRoy R. Hafen, "Fort Jackson and the Early Fur Trade on the South Platte," *Colorado Magazine* 5 (1928): 9–17, chronicles Sarpy's two years in that region and identifies Ione, Colorado, as the location of the fort. The Presbyterian missionary Samuel Allis captures the flavor of the Bellevue area and notes Sarpy's fondness for liquor in "Forty Years among the Indians on the Eastern Borders of Nebraska," *Nebraska State Historical Society Transactions* 2: 133–66.

MARY LEE SPENCE

SARTAIN, Emily (17 Mar. 1841–17 June 1927), art educator and painter/printmaker, was born in Philadelphia, Pennsylvania, the daughter of John Sartain, a mezzotint engraver, and Susannah Longmate Swaine. Sartain, one of two daughters and five sons, grew up in a family in which her father trained her brothers as professional artists. Socially prominent Unitarians and Associationists, her parents encouraged her to attend Philadelphia Normal School for Girls. When she began to teach public school upon graduation in 1858, she joined a predominantly female profession.

In August 1862 Sartain joined her father for a year-long "grand tour" of Europe, during which she decided to become an artist. Early in 1864 she began engraving lessons with her father while she studied drawing with Christian Schussele. After her second trip to Europe in the summer of 1868, Sartain began her formal, intensive years of study at the Pennsylvania Academy of the Fine Arts. As leader among the female students, Sartain was the first to sign the petition to establish training in drawing from nude models.

Sartain produced her first large mezzotint, *Christ Walking on the Sea*, after Henry Richter, in 1865. It was published by Bradley & Company of Philadelphia, which published plates by many of the Sartains. Over the next three years she produced *Christ Raising Jairus' Daughter* after Theodore von Holst, *A Night on the Sea of Galilee* after Charles Francois Jalabert, *Our New Baby* after Stephen J. Ferris, *President Lincoln and Son* after the well-known photograph by Anthony Berger, of Mathew Brady's studio, and a portrait of family friend Ralph Waldo Emerson, after a painting by his son, William Furness. She also accepted commissions to engrave smaller portraits as illustrations for books and periodicals.

Soon she was renowned for her skill and "rapidity . . . a marked characteristic of her execution" (*Beecher's Illustrated Magazine*, July 1871). By 1871 she had saved enough to finance a trip to Europe with Mary Cassatt to further her studies. They settled in Parma, Italy, for the winter, Sartain renting a studio and hiring models to practice drawing and painting from life. In the spring Sartain visited Florence on her way to Paris.

For the next three years Sartain studied with history painter Evariste Vital Luminais, taking occasional trips to the French countryside and to London and making one long trip to Philadelphia in the summer of 1873. By 1874 she was sending paintings home to be exhibited at Earle's Gallery in Philadelphia. Two paintings, *La Pièce de Conviction* (*The Reproof*) and her portrait of Madeleine del Sarte were accepted in the Paris Salon in 1875.

When Sartain finally returned to Philadelphia in October 1875, she set up her studio as a portrait pain-ter and mezzotint engraver. She began to show her work in important East Coast exhibitions, including at the National Academy, the Pennsylvania Academy of the Fine Arts, and in both the Art Department and Women's Pavilion of the U.S. Centennial Exposition in Philadelphia. Her *La Pièce de Conviction* (*The Reproof*) was the only painting by a woman that won a medal at the centennial. It also was the only painting by an American woman reproduced in wood engraving in Edward Strahan's (Earl Shinn) *Masterpieces of the Centennial International Exhibition* (1876–1877). In 1895 at the Cotton States and International Exposition in Atlanta she received a diploma for her large etchings.

Active professionally but not able to support herself financially by her painting and engraving, Sartain went to work in 1881 as art editor for *Our Continent* magazine. She remained at *Our Continent* until early May 1883, when she spent several months in Europe celebrating her latest entry in the Paris Salon, her portrait of her sister-in-law Marie Sartain, which had won the Mary Smith Prize at the Pennsylvania Academy.

In 1886 Sartain became principal of the Philadelphia School of Design for Women, one of the most important professional positions then available to women. Single and responsible for her aging parents, she took them to live with her in her apartment at the school. Sartain instituted the first life drawing class at the school and modernized its philosophy and its curriculum of art training. As a leader in art education, Sartain was appointed chairman of the Woman's Art Committee for the Pennsylvania State Building at the 1893 World's Columbian Exposition in Chicago. She also served as chairman of the Art Committee for the World's Congress Upon the Progress of Women at the Art Institute of Chicago in May 1893, delivering an address, "The Progress of Women in Industrial Art Education." Before the International Congress of Women at its July 1899 meeting in London she gave a speech called "Art in Its Various Branches for Women." One of two official delegates representing the U.S. government at the International Congress for Art Education, Drawing, and Art Applied to Industry in Paris in 1900, she was selected to write the official report. Later she addressed the convention of the Eastern Art Teachers' Association in Philadelphia on the results of the 1900 International Congress on drawing. As a member of the congress's Permanent International Committee, she participated in the 1904 congress in Berne.

Sartain was a founder, in 1877, of the New Century Club of Philadelphia and, in 1897, of the Plastic Club of Philadelphia. Inspired by the success of the Women's Pavilion at the U.S. Centennial, the New Century Club promoted women in science, literature, and art. The Plastic Club, still active in the late twentieth century, provided support and camaraderie for women artists through their clubhouse, exhibitions, lectures, and classes. She was also a member of the Contemporary Club, Philadelphia, the Ladies' Art Association, New York, the Browning Society, the Art Union of

Philadelphia, and the Three Arts Club of Philadelphia. From 1888 until 1891 she served as one of several directors from the 29th Section of the Philadelphia City Schools and worked on behalf of women graduates of the public schools in the Alumnae Association of the Girls' High and Normal Schools of Philadelphia.

Sartain remained with the school until her retirement thirty-three years later. Each year until 1914, when she got caught in the war zone, she spent summers in Europe. In 1915 she began to spend summers in San Diego, California, where she retired in 1919. She was visiting Philadelphia, on her way to Europe, when she died.

Sartain's ideas and work on behalf of achieving equitable training and opportunities for professional women artists were progressive. Her sensitivity to the needs of women artists had evolved gradually from her own desire to be a professional artist through her experiences and observations as she patterned herself, ironically, after the professional artist closest to her, her father. Early in her training she had helped to win access for women to the life drawing class. As principal of the Philadelphia School of Design for Women, Sartain inspired several generations of female art students. By insisting that "commercial" and "fine" art students receive the same rigorous training, she developed an innovative curriculum that brought increased respect and professional opportunities to its graduates. Sartain facilitated the transition from the mid-nineteenth-century world of her artist-father, in which there were only a few professional women artists, to the modern era of the early twentieth century, when tens of thousands of women practiced art as professionals.

• Sartain's letters home during her 1862–1863 and 1871–1875 trips to Europe are in Moore College of Art (Philadelphia School of Design for Women), Philadelphia. Thomas Eakins's letters to her are in the Pennsylvania Academy of the Fine Arts, Philadelphia. Small numbers of her prints are in the Library of Congress, Pennsylvania Academy, Moore College of Art, the National Portrait Gallery, and the New York Public Library. The Historical Society of Pennsylvania and the Philadelphia Museum of Art each own one mezzotint. Sartain describes her ideas on art education in "'The Pioneer in Industrial Art Education,' an Address Delivered at The Art Club of Philadelphia, February 21, 1890." Many of her letters are published in Nancy Mowll Mathews, *Cassatt and Her Circle: Selected Letters* (1984). Phyllis Peet, "The Emergence of American Women Printmakers in the Late Nineteenth Century" (Ph.D. diss., UCLA, 1987), is the most thorough source. For descriptions of Sartain's printmaking career, see Phyllis Peet, "Emily Sartain, America's First Woman Mezzotint Engraver," *Imprint* 9 (Autumn 1984): 19–26, and Ellen Goodman, "Emily Sartain: Her Career," *Arts Magazine* 61 (May 1987): 61–65. Phyllis Peet, "The Art Education of Emily Sartain," *Woman's Art Journal* 11 (Spring/Summer 1990): 9–15, interprets the importance of her art education. An obituary is in the *New York Times*, 19 June 1927.

PHYLLIS PEET

SARTAIN, John (24 Oct. 1808–25 Oct. 1897), entrepreneurial engraver and publisher, was born in London, England, the son of John Sartain, a shoemaker, and Ann Burgess. Before Sartain was eight years old, his father died, and by age twelve he was working as an assistant to a theatrical pyrotechnist and scene painter. At fourteen he received an inheritance from his grandmother and apprenticed himself to the engraver John Swaine. Fortunate in being asked to complete the engravings for William Ottley's *Most Eminent Masters of the Early Florentine School* (1826), he received a virtual education in the arts through his access to Ottley's extensive collection of paintings, prints, and illustrated books. As a connoisseur, publisher, and art dealer, Ottley offered introductions to the elite of the London art world. From 1827 to 1828 Sartain became a pupil of Henry Richter. He studied miniature painting and became a master of the art of mezzotint, the skill that would establish his career. He studied briefly with the landscapist John Varley and by 1829 opened his own engraving studio in London. Despite commissions from notable individuals and the publisher Rudolph Ackermann, in 1830 Sartain married and decided to immigrate to the United States with his new wife, Susannah Longmate Swaine, daughter of John Swaine. (The couple had eight children.) On 31 August 1830 they arrived in Philadelphia with letters of introduction, one of which was addressed to the publisher Henry C. Carey.

Sartain's London credentials and his ability to translate images sensitively into a graphic medium where they could be more widely disseminated to the public placed him in great demand with Philadelphia artists and publishers. His expertise with mezzotint engraving was unique and the rich pictorial effects of light, shadow, and texture he created attracted the attention of Thomas Sully, who provided Sartain with a commission to engrave his 1829 portrait of Bishop William White and encouraged Sartain to remain in the city. Cephas B. Childs, engraver, publisher, and co-owner of Philadelphia's first important lithographic firm, Childs and Inman, commissioned Sartain to produce highly finished and expensive prints to supplement his firm's less costly engravings and lithographs. Portrait engraving remained a staple of Sartain's career, but in the late 1840s, partly in response to the newly invented medium of photography, his romantic style and elite subjects yielded to greater realism, stressing character and the specifics of individual appearance. Known for his superior eye in selecting real yet flattering and dynamic images, he produced hundreds of portraits of America's diverse cultural, business, and political leaders during the 1840s and 1850s. Among his most notable portrait engravings were U.S. president *Martin Van Buren* (1837) after Henry Inman, author *Henry Wadsworth Longfellow* (1860) after Thomas Buchanan Reed, activist Seminole Indian chief *Osceola* (1838) after George Catlin, and American artist and inventor *Samuel F. B. Morse* after a daguerreotype by Matthew Brady.

Intent on technical excellence, Sartain trained his own printer and eventually owned his own press. In 1838 he won a silver medal from the Franklin Institute in Philadelphia for the quality of his work, and in 1880 his "Brief Sketch of the History and Practice of Engraving" was published in their journal. Resourceful in both the business and creative aspects of his art, he adapted the mezzotint process to mass production to facilitate larger editions by employing a mixed method of engraving, etching, and aquatint.

The 1840s marked the beginning of his many productive years in the flourishing periodical industry. He supplied a large number of plates for publications such as *The Casket, Gentleman's Magazine, Eclectic Magazine of Foreign Literature, Science and Art, Godey's Lady's Magazine,* and *Graham's Magazine of Literature and Art.* From 1842 to 1844 he was part owner of *Campbell's Foreign Semi-Monthly,* and in 1849 he established *Sartain's Union Magazine of Literature and Art.* Publishing Henry Wadsworth Longfellow, Edgar Allan Poe, and other writers, he wrote art criticism and established reviews of the annual exhibitions of the Pennsylvania Academy of the Fine Arts. The misappropriation of profits by his financial partner, William Sloanaker, caused the magazine's demise in 1852, leaving Sartain with substantial debts. Between 1832 and 1855, gift books formed an important segment of his work. These genteel, sentimental keepsakes with their fine engravings and elaborate decorative covers were expensive to produce but popular and profitable. Sartain's technical excellence, ease as a copyist, and extensive collection of European books and engravings as a visual resource provided him with a competitive advantage in providing publishers with timely and impressive illustrations. Sartain also served as both editor and engraver of *The American Gallery of Art* (1848), a publication he designed to "record works of American artists for Europeans."

Sartain also produced individual framing prints in various formats. From 1840 to 1872 he executed elaborate prints for the Apollo Association, the American Art-Union, and the Art-Union of Philadelphia. Among these were Christian Schussele's *Men of Progress: American Inventors* and Peter Frederick Rothermel's *Battle of Gettysburg.*

A self-made man who continually sought to improve himself, Sartain's humanitarian perspective drew him to the temperance and abolition movements as well as the utopian philosophy of the French social theorist Charles Fourier, who advocated dividing society into agriculturally based units called phalanges. These small communities took responsibility for the welfare of their individual members while emphasizing teamwork and the importance of adapting society to meet human needs. Sartain's active involvement with Fourierism included his presidency of the Philadelphia Union of Associationists (1850) and his membership in the North American Phalanx located in Red Bank, New Jersey. Sartain's many contributions to the local, national, and international art communities were clearly linked to his utopian convictions that art had

the power to touch all men's souls and improve society.

As an academician of the Pennsylvania Academy of the Fine Arts for twenty-three years (1855–1877), he served in various roles and was instrumental in establishing permanent and professional instruction at the academy. Active in the Artists Fund Society, the National Art Association, the American Art-Union, and the Art-Union of Philadelphia, he also served as chief of the Art Bureau for the 1876 Centennial Exhibition and as a member of the U.S. Sanitary Commission. He participated in international art affairs, received international honors, and was chief of the American Art Bureau for the 1887 London Exposition. During his later years, he served as a director and vice president of the Philadelphia School of Design for Women (later the Moore College of Art), where his daughter Emily was principal.

John Sartain died in Philadelphia. He was a proud and energetic man whose prodigious graphic output has been estimated at 1,500 plates. He occasionally practiced oil and miniature painting, photography, and architectural design. An example of the latter, his monument to Washington and Lafayette (1869), stands in Monument Cemetery, Philadelphia, where he is buried.

• Sartain's personal and business papers and the largest collection of his prints, are in the Harriet Sartain Collection, Historical Society of Pennsylvania, Philadelphia. Additional papers are in the Archives of the Pennsylvania Academy of the Fine Arts and the Moore College of Art library. Sartain's personal print collection belongs to the Philadelphia Museum of Art. Useful printed sources by Sartain are *The Annals of the Sartain Tribe, 1557–1886* (1886) and *Reminiscences of a Very Old Man, 1808–1897* (1899). William Sartain's "Autobiography" is an informative manuscript owned by the Philadelphia Museum of Art. See "Sartain Family Papers, 1795–1944," Archives of American Art, for selections from these materials and additional miscellaneous sources. A useful assessment of Sartain, including a discussion of his political and social attitudes, is Ann Katharine Martinez, "The Life and Career of John Sartain (1808–1897), A Nineteenth Century Printmaker" (Ph.D. diss., George Washington Univ., 1986). It has an extensive bibliography and lists his gift book publications. For additional references to Sartain, see Thomas Sully's "Journal" (typescript) in the New York Public Library and "Papers of the North American Phalanx," Monmouth County Historical Society. An obituary is in the *Philadelphia Public Ledger,* 26 Oct. 1897.

CAROL EATON SOLTIS

SARTON, George Alfred Léon (31 Aug. 1884–22 Mar. 1956), historian of science, was born in Ghent, Belgium, the only child of Alfred Sarton, a chief engineer and administrator with the Belgian State Railroads, and Léonie Van Halmé. His mother died when he was one year old; his childhood was comfortably bourgeois but isolated and lonely. After dabbling with a literary career and the history of the theater, Sarton abandoned philosophy in favor of the sciences, earning a B.Sc. in chemistry in 1906 and graduating with a D.Sc. in mathematics in 1911 from the University of

Ghent. Indicative of his developing historical interests, he wrote his doctoral dissertation on the principles of Newtonian mechanics. In 1911 he married Eleanor Mabel Elwes, an English artist and designer seven years his senior. They settled in Wondelgem, Belgium, near Ghent. They had one surviving child, the poet and novelist May Sarton.

Influenced by Auguste Comte, Henri Poincaré, Paul Tannery, and Herbert Spencer, Sarton soon turned to the "mission" that constituted his life's work: the creation of a scholarly discipline for the history of science. Recruiting a distinguished, international editorial board, in 1912 he launched *Isis*, "a review devoted to the history of science." The first volume appeared in 1913, and *Isis* quickly became the preeminent journal in the field.

World War I disrupted Sarton's life and plans. Following the German invasion of Belgium in August 1914, Sarton buried his scholarly papers in his garden and fled to London, an impoverished refugee. He emigrated to the United States in 1915 with $50 (he later said $100) in his pocket. He became a naturalized citizen in 1924, but throughout his life he retained his Gallic accent and the aura of an émigré.

Circumstances forced Sarton to invent his own professional career. After teaching briefly at the University of Illinois and George Washington University, Sarton was drawn to Harvard University by Lawrence J. Henderson, a professor of biochemistry and amateur historian of science. Sarton secured a lectureship in the history of science at Harvard from 1916 to 1918. Renewed annually from 1920, the appointment was unpaid at first and later brought only a small stipend; Sarton taught at Harvard mainly in exchange for quarters in Widener Library. Initially he gave a single semester course annually, complementing Henderson's history of science offering.

In 1918 Sarton wangled a full-time appointment as research associate at the Carnegie Institution of Washington, D.C., with life tenure coming a year later. He remained in Cambridge, Massachusetts, but the full-time salary from the Carnegie Institution, supplemented by what his wife earned teaching and designing clothing, sustained him and his family and provided funds for books, travel, a secretary, and, later, two research assistants.

Sarton retrieved his papers in Belgium in 1919 and returned to Massachusetts, fixed in the notion of organizing an independent scholarly discipline for the history of science. Given the undeveloped state of the field at the beginning of the twentieth century, Sarton proceeded to write annotated general surveys and to create bibliographic and other tools and reference aids. The foremost product of his industry remains his monumental *Introduction to the History of Science* (3 vols. in 5 parts, 1927–1948). While Sarton's goal was a complete chronological survey, the *Introduction*, more than 4,000 pages long, covers only the period through the fourteenth century. The work is a justly acclaimed resource, encyclopedic and rich in esoteric information, but it lacks thematic unity in that it documents

science on a world scale in arbitrary fifty-year intervals. The bulk of his magnum opus surveys the medieval period, and Sarton perforce became a leading medievalist, winning the highest publication award of the Medieval Academy of America in 1949.

After a hiatus caused by World War I, Sarton resumed publication of *Isis* in 1919. The History of Science Society, organized in 1924 with Sarton as a charter member, began underwriting *Isis* as its official organ in 1926. Through 1952 Sarton edited forty-three volumes of *Isis*, regularly meeting publication deficits, once more than $1,700, out of his own pocket; the History of Science Society assumed full responsibility for *Isis* only in 1941. In addition to serving as editor of *Isis*, Sarton held the position of honorary president of the History of Science Society from 1938 until his death. He participated actively in society affairs, and in 1955 was the first recipient of the society's Sarton Medal, its most prestigious award, conferred on distinguished historians of science for exceptional life achievement and service to the profession.

To further strengthen the study of the history of science, Sarton compiled seventy-nine critical bibliographies that appeared in *Isis*; his own contribution amounted to about 100,000 notes. In 1936 he founded the companion monograph series, *Osiris*, of which he then edited eleven volumes. Thousands of cross-references tie together *Isis*, *Osiris*, and Sarton's *Introduction*. In 1952 he issued *Horus*, a bibliographic and institutional guide to the field. Late in life he began another survey, *History of Science*, based on his Harvard lectures; only two of the projected eight volumes appeared (one posthumously), and they surveyed only Greek science in antiquity.

Influenced by H. G. Wells, Bernard Shaw, and the Fabians, Sarton rejected Marxism in favor of utopian socialist philosophies. He held liberal beliefs in the unity of knowledge, in universal brotherhood, and in the equality of men and women. He looked to Comte as the father of the history of science and viewed the subject as the cumulative record of positive knowledge. Such positions led him to downplay the role of scientific revolutions, but they helped him envision the history of science as the capstone of an even more grand "new humanism," bridging science and the traditional humanities. In gathering information, he undertook prodigious feats of scholarly labor with phenomenal industry and diligence. He was an autodidact as a historian, and he worked almost exclusively with printed sources and not original manuscripts. Some thought him the most learned scholar of his time.

Based on the principle of the unity of science, Sarton's work possesses remarkable ecumenical and multicultural emphases. Fluent in many languages, he was ahead of his time in emphasizing comparative studies of science in different civilizations, and he was among the first historians to trace scientific developments in India, China, and Japan. He was especially appreciative of Islamic science, learning Arabic in middle age to facilitate his researches.

Sarton largely ignored both materialist and idealist trends affecting the history of science in the 1930s. Rather, he focused on amassing the hard facts of the development of science in history. To the consternation of some, he strictly separated the history of science from the history of technology and from the history of medicine, and he had a low opinion of the philosophy of science. Regarding the Western tradition, he likewise played down scientific developments prior to the Greeks.

Sarton was a founding member of the International Committee for the History of Science, and from 1950 to 1956 he served as president of the succeeding International Union of the History of Science. He held memberships in more than forty learned societies worldwide and received seven honorary degrees. After his death friends established the George Sarton Memorial Fund, an endowment that presently underwrites the annual Sarton Lecture before the American Association for the Advancement of Science.

With no administrative or committee duties and a light teaching load, Sarton never fully integrated himself into university life at Harvard, even though in 1940 J. B. Conant finally appointed the 56-year-old Sarton tenured professor of the history of science. Sarton's course expanded to a four-semester cycle, and its popularity increased in the 1940s. In 1949 Sarton retired from the Carnegie Institution, which, to his dismay, then dropped the history of science as a research focus. He retired from Harvard in 1951. Although his Institute for the History of Science never materialized, the Harvard department he left behind remained a center for the study of the history of science.

Fastidious and methodical, Sarton maintained an almost obsessive passion for order and control, and he affected an inability to handle mundane matters. He was good-humored but exact and demanding in his scholarly standards. He distinguished "enthusiasts" from "jobholders," doubtless including himself among the former. Classical music and his record collection provided the main diversion from his scholarly labors. In a commemorative poem written in 1956, May Sarton evoked her father, saying, "He worked as poets work, for love."

As the founding father of the modern scholarly discipline of the history of science, Sarton left an ambiguous legacy. Despite all his labors, his influence remained limited and his importance obscured by later developments within the field. He was a lone scholar who trained only two Ph.D.s, produced no real disciples, and established no Sartonian research school. Sarton was a phenomenal doer but not a great thinker. His approach was as a self-described "naturalist," cataloging the vast and largely virgin landscape of the history of science. Sarton wistfully envisioned his great labors as a "means to an end." But he never produced his hoped-for intellectual synthesis, and he left little theoretical imprint on the field. Furthermore, even before the 1950s practitioners rejected his Whiggish, nineteenth-century-style positivism. In the end, his impact paled before others, like Alexandre Koyré and

Thomas S. Kuhn, who exercised a more profound intellectual influence on the history of science and established problems and techniques for research.

Sarton's wife passed away in 1950. Lonely and disappointed, Sarton died at his home in Cambridge, Massachusetts.

• Thousands of letters to and from Sarton are cataloged and held in the Houghton Library of Harvard University. An additional 500 to 1,000 are uncataloged at the Carnegie Institution of Washington, D.C. Paul van Oye, *George Sarton: De Mens en zijn Werk uit Brieven aan Vrienden en Kennissen* (1965), offers a selection of letters with European correspondents. In addition to autobiographical remarks scattered throughout his works, see Sarton's "The History of Science in the Carnegie Institution," *Osiris* 9 (1950): 624–38, and "Reminiscences of a Pioneer," *Osiris* 11 (1954): 108–18. May Sarton, *I Knew a Phoenix* (1959; repr., 1969), evokes the first stages of her father's life and work; see also her "An Informal Portrait of George Sarton," *Texas Quarterly* (Autumn 1962): 101–12. The George Sarton Memorial Issue of *Isis* 48 (1957): 281–350, remains an important resource that includes a complete bibliography of Sarton's fifteen books and more than 300 articles and occasional pieces. Several of Sarton's essays are reprinted in Dorothy Stimson, *Sarton on the History of Science* (1962). Additional vignettes, biographical data, and leads on other collections of Sarton's papers can be found in *Isis* 66 (1975): 443–82, and in "Sarton, Science, and History: The Sarton Centennial Issue," *Isis* 75 (1984): 6–62. Sarton's annual reports appearing in the *Yearbook* of the Carnegie Institution from 1919 through 1949 document the development of his work.

Arnold Thackray and Robert K. Merton collaborated on both the Sarton entry in the *Dictionary of Scientific Biography*, vol. 12 (1975); and "On Discipline-Building: The Paradoxes of George Sarton," *Isis* 63 (1972): 673–95. In addition, Merton has added an insightful "Recollections and Reflections," as new prefatory material to a reprint of Sarton's *The History of Science and the New Humanism* (1988). See also J. Murdoch, "George Sarton and the Formation of the History of Science," in *Belgium and Europe: Proceedings of the International Francqui-Colloquium*, ed. G. Verbeke (1981).

JAMES E. McCLELLAN III

SARTON, May (3 May 1912–16 July 1995), poet and novelist, was born Eléanore Marie Sarton in Wondelgem, Belgium, the daughter of George Sarton, a noted historian of science, and Eleanor Mabel Elwes, an English portrait painter and designer. Sarton moved with her parents to England, and in 1916 the family immigrated to the United States. All three became naturalized Americans in 1924, by which time Sarton's name had been Americanized to Eleanor May. An only child (a younger brother died in infancy), May felt extremely close to her artistic and sensitive mother. She had a more difficult relationship with her father, whom she once described as "a fiery scholar of enormous magnitude. . . . My father was very much not a father, not human, not a husband, but a child, a brilliant child." She deeply resented his frequently harsh criticism of her behavior.

Sarton attended Shady Hill School in Cambridge, Massachusetts, an open-air school that encouraged creative and intellectual development. Her experiences there, particularly her relationship with several remarkable female teachers, greatly influenced both her life and her writing. Her novel *The Magnificent Spinster* (1985), for instance, is a tribute to several of the women who taught there. After graduating from Cambridge High and Latin in 1929, Sarton left home to become an actress in Eva Le Galliene's Civic Repertory Theater rather than attending college. When that theater disbanded in 1933, the young actress formed her own Apprentice Theater, forgoing any serious devotion to a strictly literary career until her company failed in 1935.

Although she avoided college (her parents had intended for her to go to Vassar), Sarton read voraciously and had begun writing poetry early in life. Her first published poems (five sonnets) appeared in *Poetry* magazine in 1929; likewise, a volume of her poems, *Encounter in April*, was published in 1937. Poetry (sonnets, short lyrics, and free verse with images of landscape, weather, art, and music) continued as her preferred genre throughout her life, but she could write it only when inspired by what she referred to as her "Muse." Sarton filled the intervals by teaching (including a three-year stint between 1949 and 1952 as a freshman composition instructor at Harvard and another from 1960 to 1964 as a creative writing teacher at Wellesley), writing novels, and keeping journals. She was not a diarist, however, in the traditional sense of the word because she wrote a journal only when she hoped to publish it. In all of her work Sarton treated the recurring themes of solitude, the conflict between marriage and women's freedom, relationships among women, and aging.

Sarton's first novel, *The Single Hound* (1938), was about an aspiring poet and represents the first of many novels about the artistic life. *The Bridge of Years* was published in 1946, followed by four or more novels per decade through the 1970s. *Anger* appeared in 1982. *Faithful Are the Wounds* (1955) probably received the greatest single recognition, perhaps because its protagonist was a man and the subject matter McCarthyism; certainly it differed from her usual themes. Although widely read, Sarton's novels received little attention from scholars and literary critics, primarily because she wrote to explore her own feelings and was not always careful with style. Carolyn G. Heilbrun wrote in the introduction to the 1974 Norton edition of Sarton's *Mrs. Stevens Hears the Mermaids Singing*, "Sarton has not escaped the fate of the readable, to be disdained by the unreadable." Although ignored by the literary establishment, Sarton's reputation grew among feminists as they read and discussed her work. She recognized this popularity and once told an interviewer, "People pass my books on to their friends; it's a network." Sheila Ballantyne, writing for the *New York Times Book Review* in 1982, said in a review of *Anger*, "It is clear that May Sarton's best work, whatever its form, will endure well beyond the influence of particular reviews or current tastes. For in it she is an example: a seeker after truth with a kind of awesome

energy for renewal, an ardent explorer of life's important questions."

Hailed by feminists but poorly rewarded by critics, Sarton jeopardized her chances for general recognition with the publication of *Mrs. Stevens Hears the Mermaids Singing* in 1965. In this novel about the difficulties of the female writer, she shocked the literary world and many of her dedicated readers by presenting a protagonist who was openly bisexual. Her agent advised against publication, and her publisher, Norton, would not advertise the book; this so angered Sarton that she bought a full-page ad for herself in the *New York Times*. Sarton apparently lost two jobs in 1965 after revealing that she was a lesbian, "but, as with so much in her life, she had no regrets" (*New York Times*, 18 July 1995). Indeed, she went on to speak openly of her sexual preferences in her journals. These revelations damaged her universal reputation but made her a heroine to many feminists.

In spite of critical neglect, Sarton continued to produce approximately one book per year, claiming it was a financial necessity to do so because "my books don't sell." Nevertheless, she received huge amounts of mail from fans, particularly in response to the journals and memoirs *I Knew a Phoenix* (1959), *A Plant Dreaming Deep* (1968), *Journal of a Solitude* (1973), and *At Seventy* (1984). Although she resented this burden of correspondence, Sarton was touched by the reader response to her work and, until her 1987 heart attack, answered each letter herself. In a 1977 interview she said, "I answer every letter, and lives just pour into mine. I write about fifty letters a week." She admitted, "These letters are what keep me going. They're better than a good review."

Plagued by illness, Sarton wrote *Recovering* in 1980 about her mastectomy and *After the Stroke* in 1988. She also discussed her frequent bouts of depression in the journals. In each case, her greatest distress seemed to focus on the time these illnesses stole from her work.

Although she had no inclination to marry and usually lived alone (for a long time in New Hampshire and, in her last years, in Maine), Sarton had many friendships. Her writing schedule usually tied her up for three hours each morning; she found it unproductive to write for longer periods. This gave her time to entertain, and she claimed that from May through September 1976 she "had somebody for a meal every other day." She also maintained friendships through frequent correspondence. She wrote to and occasionally saw Virginia Woolf, whom she greatly admired, and later wrote the poem "Letter from Chicago" in her memory, saying, "I send you love forward into the past." Sarton exchanged long letters with various other writers, including poet Louise Bogan, in which they carried on discussions about their art. In "My Sisters, O My Sisters," Sarton aligns herself with other female authors, calling them, "We who are writing women and strange monsters." She felt women were treated badly by male critics and, when she was seventy, said of her own career, "I can't imagine another writer who appeals to so many people in such depth . . . but whom the literary establishment regards as having no value. Ask [Robert] Penn Warren. Ask any of the people who are the establishment and you'll get 'Who's May Sarton?'" The fact that many did know her name, however, is attested to by the fellowships and honorary doctorates the author received, although the honor she claimed touched her most was the Unitarian "Ministry to Women" Award she received in 1981.

Sarton died in York, Maine. She once wrote in a letter to Bogan, "I like best to think of poetry as a long life with the best at the end," and this describes her rise to fame. An interviewer for *Publishers Weekly* called Sarton's literary recognition "one of the most interesting and long-overdue." In a career spanning sixty years and encompassing more than forty volumes of poetry and prose, Sarton grew gradually from an unknown to a respected and unique artist of her craft.

• A number of Sarton's papers were purchased in the late 1970s by the New York Public Library and comprise part of the Berg collection. For a fairly comprehensive bibliography of primary works see Earl G. Ingersoll, ed., *Conversations with May Sarton* (1991). Some of her works not already mentioned are the volumes of poetry *Inner Landscapes* (1939), *The Lion and the Rose* (1948), *The Land of Silence* (1953), *In Time Like Aire* (1957), *A Private Mythology* (1966), and *Collected Poems, 1930–1973* (1974). Sarton's novels include *Shadow of a Man* (1950), *A Shower of Summer Days* (1952), *The Small Room* (1961), *Joanna and Ulysses* (1963), *As We Are Now* (1973), and *A Reckoning* (1978). She also wrote a play, *The Underground River* (1947), and several books for children. Useful secondary sources include Warren French, ed., *May Sarton Revisited* (1989); and selections from Sandra M. Gilbert and Susan Gubar, eds., *The Norton Anthology of Literature by Women* (1985). An obituary appears in the *New York Times*, 18 July 1995.

ELAINE FREDERICKSEN

SASSACUS (d. June 1637), paramount chief of the Pequot Indians, was the successor to Tatobem, though it is unlikely that they were father and son. His mother's name is unknown. The Pequots' core territory lay between the lower Thames and Mystic rivers of today's Connecticut, and they laid claims beyond it through tributaries in the Connecticut Valley. They also disputed right to lands and peoples between themselves and the Narragansett Indians. As materials are wanting for specific treatment of Sassacus's life, the assumption must be made that actions and policies recorded or inferred about the Pequot tribe reflected his leadership during the period 1634–1637. This seems to have continued the policies of his predecessor, Tatobem.

The historical record of the Pequots focuses on their trade with European colonials and on the wars ensuing from their rejection of clientage to either Dutch or English colonies. They were much affected also by relations to the east with the Narragansetts under Chief Miantonomo and to the west with the Mohegans under Chief Uncas, who claimed the hereditary right to be the Pequot head. Birth was an important qualification,

but not the only one; paramount chiefs were chosen by the tribe from otherwise qualified men.

Tatobem had driven Uncas and others of the same family into the Narragansett country. Then Tatobem tried to monopolize trade at the Dutch trading post on the upper Connecticut. He killed some interlopers seeking access to the Dutch post, in retaliation for which the Dutch launched an attack that killed Tatobem and some of his men.

In 1634 Sassacus became chief. He immediately tried to resume European trade relations but with Massachusetts Bay instead of New Netherland. He sent an embassy to Boston with offers of gifts in exchange for trade. The embassy was favorably received, but its treaty document has disappeared. Governor John Winthrop, Sr., substituted an ostensible description stating that the Pequots were willing to cede their claims to the Connecticut Valley, and the embassy presented a small present of wampum to the Bostonians, with a promise of two bushels more. This did not satisfy Winthrop, who demanded large sums of wampum tribute annually and obedience to Massachusetts's orders, even to enforcing them on Pequot tributary Indians—in short, to accept status as subjected clients. Subsequent events demonstrated that the Pequots did not agree to these terms, though Winthrop later invoked their "violation" as reasons for war. There was genuine agreement on one point in 1634: the Pequots requested mediation for peace with the Narragansetts, and this was done immediately.

Relations with "the English" became confused when English colonials split into independent polities with contradictory demands. In 1634 and afterward, several towns broke away from Massachusetts's rule to found Connecticut, whose leaders wanted to acquire Pequot territory. Massachusetts's leaders decided to preempt the issue. In 1636 they concocted an excuse that captains John Stone and John Oldham had been killed by Pequots—neither had—and sent soldiers under John Endecott to subject the tribe. Endecott botched his campaign, which resulted only in precipitating the Pequots into open hostility and persistent attacks on an English fort at the mouth of the Connecticut River.

Surrounded by enemies, Sassacus proposed to the Narragansetts a united front against the English but met rebuff. Meanwhile Connecticut's leaders evicted Sequasson, a local chief, from his lands in the upper Connecticut Valley. He appealed to Sassacus for help, and Pequot warriors responded by killing nine people at Wetherfield, Connecticut. This event substantiated rumors of Pequot belligerence spread by Sassacus's enemy, the Mohegan chief Uncas, who hoped to manipulate the colonials to increase his own power. Connecticut declared war against the Pequots and dispatched troops to the English fort at the river's mouth. In Boston, John Winthrop, Sr., concluded that English colonists must regard all Indians "as a common enimie" (Salisbury, p. 221).

Though Massachusetts's leaders were alarmed by the prospect of Connecticut acquiring "rights of conquest" over Pequot lands desired by themselves, Boston's plans were delayed by a heresy hunt against antinomians, so Massachusetts's troops did not march until Connecticut began hostilities and struck a decisive blow.

Still another party involved against the Pequots was the Saybrook Company of noblemen represented by Captain John Underhill with a company of men who joined Connecticut's Captain John Mason. Their combined force was advised and assisted by allied Narragansetts and Roger Williams, whose plea for mercy for the Pequots was disregarded. Being informed that Pequot noncombatants—women, children, and old men—had taken refuge in a stockaded village on the Mystic River while Sassacus's warriors awaited attack in the Pequot main stockade of Weinshauks, Mason and Underhill determined to attack the noncombatants. They attacked the undefended Mystic village in a predawn raid, set fire to it, and killed some 300 to 700 persons who tried to flee. Protests from the allied Narragansetts were brushed aside.

From their fort five miles distant, Sassacus's warriors rushed to the scene but arrived too late to prevent the slaughter of their kin. When they tried to take revenge, they were fought off by the Narragansetts and Massachusetts's late-arriving troops. The massacre decisively destroyed Pequot power though more of their people were taken captive or killed in subsequent smaller-scale massacres. For a long time, Connecticut and Massachusetts squabbled over rights of conquest over lands and captives. Sassacus escaped and fled west to solicit refuge and help from the Mohawk tribe. Hearsay evidence (there is no other kind) states that he took the Pequot tribal treasury of wampum and that the Mohawks killed him and seized it.

The Pequot War is often regarded as a portent for future relations of New Englanders with Indians, though Rhode Islanders followed a different course. The war determined much of the territory of the state of Connecticut.

• John Winthrop, Sr., *The History of New England*, ed. James Savage (1825), must be consulted because it is the only document available for some data, but it cannot be trusted without confirmation. Roger Williams supplements it in *The Correspondence of Roger Williams*, ed. Glenn W. La Fantasie (2 vols., 1988). Other Rhode Island materials are in *The Publications of the Narragansett Club*, vol. 4 (1874). A convincing argument that the Pequots were indigenous to their region is made by Alfred A. Cave, "The Pequot Invasion of Southern New England: A Reassessment of the Evidence," *New England Quarterly* 62, no. 1 (Mar. 1989): 27–44. The attack on the Pequot village is described best by commanders John Mason and John Underhill, whose accounts are in *The History of the Pequot War*, ed. Charles Orr (1897). John W. De Forest, *History of the Indians of Connecticut from the Earliest Known Period to 1850* (1851), is well intentioned but uncritical of the source propaganda tracts. Such acceptance has also misled Alden T. Vaughan, *New England Frontier* (1965). Connecticut's aggressive expansionism is portrayed in Richard S. Dunn, *Puritans and Yankees: The Winthrop Dynasty of New England, 1630–1717* (1962). Detailed analysis of Puritan source texts, and disclosure of their discrepancies and contradictions, is in Francis Jennings, *The Invasion of America* (1975). Jennings also traces the competition between Connecticut and Massachusetts. The most detailed description of intertribal relations, with the effect on them of colonial policies, is in Neal Salisbury, *Manitou and Providence* (1982). An excellent concise account by Wilcomb E. Washburn, "Seventeenth-Century Indian Wars," is in *Northeast*, vol. 15 of *Handbook of North American Indians*, gen. ed. W. C. Sturtevant (1978), pp. 89–100.

FRANCIS JENNINGS

SATHERLEY, Uncle Art (19 Oct. 1889–10 Feb. 1986), recording industry executive, was born Arthur Edward Satherley in Bristol, Somerset, England. His parents' names are not known, but it is known that his father was a clergyman. After leaving school, Satherley first joined the Royal Somerset Yeomanry, then got a job testing tires by riding motorcycles around England. Nursing a fascination for cowboy folklore, Satherley went to Montreal, Canada, in 1913, then journeyed to Chicago and Milwaukee.

Satherley took a job grading lumber at the Wisconsin Chair Company in Port Washington, Wisconsin, and then transferred to their Grafton plant as a bookkeeper. Later, he went to New London, Wisconsin, to work for a plant that manufactured the High Boy phonograph for the Thomas Edison Company. Edison bought the plant in 1915 or 1916, and Satherley worked in the office as an assistant to Edison. After a year and a half, Satherley was asked to return to the Grafton Chair Company, which was devoting a plant to record production. Satherley learned record manufacturing techniques but was not involved in talent acquisition or recording at that time.

Satherley later went on the road for Paramount Records (the label started by Grafton) as a salesman. He recognized a market niche in the recording of blues and jazz music, and his success in this field led to him being appointed manager of the company's eastern seaboard operation, from Boston to the Florida Keys. Satherley was also in charge of the company's New York studio, and he later recalled that his first sessions were with pop artists such as Ben Selvin. The first big seller he produced was "My Lord's Gonna Move This Wicked Race" by the Norfolk Jubilee Quartet.

Satherley left Paramount to join the QRS label, a company then known primarily for its piano rolls. He quickly became disenchanted with QRS and in 1928 moved on to Plaza Records, which specialized in rural field recordings that were sold under different imprints to chain stores. Plaza was eventually absorbed into the American Record Corporation (ARC), and Satherley became a roving A & R (artists and repertoire) person for ARC. He would travel with a store of wax discs, which were insulated in felt and had to be rushed back to New York for processing immediately after a recording session to avoid heat damage. Satherley usually tried to persuade his bestselling performers to record in New York or Chicago, but field recordings were the only viable way of recording many artists on his roster. An article published in the *Saturday*

Evening Post in 1944 describes Satherley's routine and provides a snapshot description of field recording techniques:

Because much of the hillbilly talent is employed in farming or ranching, Satherley must seek out his talent in the bayous, the canebrakes, the cotton plantations, the tobacco regions. Every spring, he departs from his home in Los Angeles with a complete portable recording outfit—a set of six microphones, pickups, turntables, a truck load of blank discs, and he follows a trail from Dallas to Amarillo, Tulsa, Oklahoma City, Houston, San Antonio, Beaumont, working through New Orleans, around to Shreveport, up into Birmingham, Nashville, and Columbia. He makes about 400 recordings on each tour. . . . When word spreads that "Uncle Art" has arrived in a Southern town, dozens of folk will come trooping in from the mountains to attend the "recordin' jamboree." . . . When Satherley is told that there is somebody in an out-of-the-way place who has a very original ballad . . . he will pack his recording equipment into suitcases and head to regions where no city shoes have ever trod before. . . . He journeys 70,000 miles during a typical year.

ARC Records was bought by the Columbia Broadcasting System (CBS) in December 1938, and from 1938 until 1952 Satherley worked for Columbia Records and its OKeh Records subsidiary. Among the artists that Satherley recorded for Columbia were cowboy stars Gene Autry, Roy Rogers, Tex Ritter, and the Sons of the Pioneers; country singers Johnny Bond, Al Dexter, Jimmy Dickens, Roy Acuff, George Morgan, and Marty Robbins; Western Swing bands the Hoosier Hotshots and Bob Wills and His Texas Playboys; and bluegrass pioneer Bill Monroe. Many of the artists reflected Satherley's personal interest in folk and ballad forms, and, in particular, his fascination with the West. He also continued to record blues, and his recordings included work by Memphis Minnie and Roosevelt Sykes.

Satherley's peak years were in the late 1930s and early 1940s, climaxing with the multimillion-seller "Pistol Packin' Mama" by Al Dexter, an artist Satherley had discovered in Texas on one of his field trips. His fascination with the pure forms of American folk music, which he always related back to his love of English folk forms, meant that he was ill equipped to handle the commercialization of country music in the years immediately after the Second World War. In 1951 Columbia Records divided responsibility for its country division between Satherley and his one-time assistant, Don Law, another Englishman whom he had hired from the Dallas branch of ARC. Satherley, still based in Los Angeles, was given the territory from El Paso west, and Law, the territory from El Paso east. Law had the commercial savvy to sign honky-tonk singers Lefty Frizzell and Carl Smith, while Satherley's signings did comparatively little business. In May 1952 Satherley was dismissed. Among his last signings was Marty Robbins, who, under Law's tute-

lage, became one of Columbia Records' bestselling country artists of the 1950s and 1960s.

Satherley continued to work in the recording business for a while as a music publisher and consultant, but he eventually retired to run a motel in Savannah, Georgia. Forced out of the motel business by impending bankruptcy, Satherley returned to California around 1962. In May 1963 he was hired as a night watchman at Abbott Scientific Products, and he remained with the company until February 1975. He was inducted into the Country Music Hall of Fame in October 1971. Satherley retired to his Fountain Valley home in the greater Los Angeles area, where he died.

Together with Ralph Peer and Frank Walker, Satherley did much to bring many forms of American folk music onto record. In addition to his work with country artists, Satherley also recorded Tex-Mex conjunto music, polka bands, Cajun music, French-Canadian music, and other localized forms. He frequently expressed concerns about the dilution of pure forms of folk expression, particularly in country music.

• An extensive interview with Satherley conducted by Ed Kahn in June and July 1969 is on file at the John Edwards Memorial Library. Some of the correspondence between Satherley and various members of the Country Music Association is on file at the Country Music Foundation in Nashville. See also Maurice Zolotow, "Hillbilly Boom," *Saturday Evening Post*, 12 Feb. 1944.

COLIN ESCOTT

SATTERLEE, Henry Yates (11 Jan. 1843–22 Feb. 1908), first bishop of the Episcopal diocese of Washington, D.C., was born in New York City, the son of Edward Satterlee, a cultivated man of leisure, and Jane Anna Yates. His parents, members of influential families, gave Satterlee a broad-ranging education, including European travel, while inculcating him with a strong sense of civic duty. Educated initially in Albany, New York, where his family moved when he was an infant, and then in New York City, where his family returned in 1856, he completed his liberal arts studies at Columbia College in 1863. He attended the General Theological Seminary of the Episcopal Church in New York City to prepare for the ordained ministry, completing the bachelor of divinity program in 1865. He was appointed assistant to the rector of Zion Church, Wappinger Falls, New York, where in 1875 he was elected rector. He married Jane Lawrence Churchill in 1866; they had two children.

In 1882 Satterlee was called to be rector of Calvary Church in Manhattan. Influenced by the "social Christianity" developed by the Church of England in urban centers, the Episcopal church, concentrated in eastern urban regions of the United States, pioneered in promoting social ministries through parish programs. Calvary Church, finding that its members were moving uptown, decided to establish a ministry among the immigrants moving into the parish bounds. During his distinguished career there, Satterlee developed a multifaceted social program for the area, converting Calvary into an "institutional church," an ecclesiastically based settlement house that provided employment assistance, nursing care, recreational facilities, and a community meeting place. He extended his work to the physically and socially blighted East Side, establishing Galilee Mission in that area. He also helped organize the Parochial Mission Society to promote and coordinate social ministry endeavors among the Episcopal parishes in New York City. Satterlee's mission activities widened even further when he was appointed to the Board of Managers of the Domestic and Foreign Mission Society of the Episcopal Church (1883). For many years he served as liaison between the board and dissident Mexican Christians who were attempting to form an episcopally organized Protestant church in their land.

In 1893 Satterlee was elected bishop of the newly formed diocese of Washington, D.C., encompassing the nation's capital and the contiguous counties in Maryland. It was formed to relieve the burdens of the bishop of Maryland but also to provide a visible Episcopal church presence in the nation's capital. From the outset Satterlee sought to develop a diocesan ministry that would have an impact on national affairs. He was a strong advocate of the separation of church and state, but his understanding of separation was that the church should not seek favors or privileges from the government. He assumed that the United States was a Christian nation and that church and governmental leaders should work together to promote national piety, morality, and welfare. He invited political figures, including presidents, to participate in religious functions that would benefit national life, and he expected national leaders to participate in religious affairs, thus setting a good moral example for the nation. In 1898 he began plans for the construction of a "national cathedral" that would be a symbol of the Christian basis of American life and serve the nation as well as the Episcopal church. Much of Satterlee's energies for the remainder of his career were devoted to the construction of the National Cathedral of St. Peter and St. Paul, which took ninety-three years to complete; it was dedicated in 1991.

Satterlee continued to promote social ministries in the church while serving as bishop of Washington. He was particularly concerned for the welfare of the Native Americans, whose cause he championed among government authorities, and for the African Americans, who were receiving scant support in the nation. He served on the board and as instructor at King Hall, a clergy training center for African Americans affiliated with Howard University.

Satterlee was an apologist for Anglican "churchmanship." His books enjoyed wide popularity within the Episcopal church during his lifetime. In 1895 he published *A Creedless Gospel and the Gospel Creed*. In it he attacked the prevailing idolization of "progress," which he saw as committed to improvement of the material conditions of life in contrast to the Christian ideal based on divinely revealed truths of service. The occasion for the publication was the holding of the World's Parliament of Religions during the 1893 World's Columbian Exposition that celebrated the progress of civilization, which Satterlee believed threatened revealed religious ideals. In 1899 he published *New Testament Churchmanship and the Principles upon Which It Was Founded*, an apologetic for Anglican "churchmanship," contrasting it with other denominational traditions. Satterlee shared with Episcopalians of his day a deep interest in church unity. However, as one who espoused the catholic tradition of the Anglican communion, his view of a reunited church was essentially the consolidation of churches on Anglican principles. Satterlee died in Washington, D.C.

Satterlee embodied the ideals and ambitions of the social Christian movement of his age. As a church leader in the nation's capital with ready access to national leaders, he was seen by his contemporaries as an effective representative of the churches in their social concerns.

• The Satterlee papers are in the Archives of the National Cathedral of St. Peter and St. Paul, Washington, D.C. His papers relating to the Domestic and Foreign Mission Society are in the Episcopal church's national archives in Austin, Tex. Charles Henry Brent has written the official biography of Satterlee, *A Master Builder: Being the Life and Letters of Henry Yates Satterlee, First Bishop of Washington* (1916).

FRANK SUGENO

SAUER, Carl Ortwin (24 Dec. 1889–18 July 1975), geographer, was born in Warrenton, Missouri, the son of German-born William Albert Sauer and Rosetta J. Vosholl. As a boy he was sent to study for five years in southern Germany. In 1908 he graduated from Central Wesleyan College (now defunct), where his father taught French and music and served as the school's botanist. The elder Sauer, a student of geography and history who insisted on the close relationship of those two disciplines, most likely had a significant influence on his son's interest and outlook. Carl Sauer studied geology at Northwestern University briefly and then enrolled at the University of Chicago to study geography. There he came under the influence of geologist Rollin D. Salisbury and plant ecologist H. C. Cowles. Sauer received his Ph.D. in 1915 with a dissertation on the geography of the Ozark highlands—a study of regional, cultural geography—that received high acclaim and was published in 1920 (*Geographical Society of Chicago Bulletin*, no. 7).

Sauer had worked in 1912–1913 as a map editor at Rand McNally Company in Chicago and then in 1913–1914 as an instructor at the Massachusetts State Normal School in Salem. He married Loren Schowengerdt in 1913; they had a son and a daughter. In 1915 he joined the Department of Geology and Geography at the University of Michigan as an instructor; within seven years he was a full professor. While at Michigan, he was drawn into matters relating to public policy and played a major role in the establishment of the Michigan Land Economic Survey in 1922. His experience in the cutover pine lands of the northern part of the state also aroused his initial recognition of the ecological danger signs that would increasingly concern him in later life.

In 1923 Sauer became a professor of geography at the University of California, Berkeley, where for the next thirty-one years, he was chair of the Department of Geography. In those years he gave shape to what was perhaps the most distinctive school of geography in the United States. After stepping down as chair in 1954, he taught at Berkeley for another three years and thereafter accepted temporary lecturing appointments, typically at institutions where his former students were now employed.

Shortly after his arrival at Berkeley, Sauer launched field studies in Baja, California, and northwestern Mexico, which he continued through the 1940s. Initially, he was interested in the contemporary landscape of northwestern Mexico, but his focus soon shifted to the early Spanish exploration of this region and then to the prehistoric Indian cultures of northwestern Mexico. In these studies Sauer emphasized the close association of his department with other departments, especially anthropology and history. Out of this cooperative effort developed the so-called "Berkeley School" of Latin American studies, whose major vehicle for publication was the *Ibero-American* monographic series, published by the University of California Press.

From his work in Mexico, Sauer cultivated a growing interest in the antiquity of humanity's first arrival in the Americas, which he contended was much earlier than traditional archaeology had accepted, that is, ten to twenty thousand years ago. This engendered controversy among archaeologists and anthropologists, and no consensus has yet emerged to support the view that humans were in the New World before twenty thousand years ago. Sauer also insisted on the antiquity of fire as a human tool, arguing that no group of humans could have entered the Americas without it. He suggested that fire provided humans with a way of experimenting with possible food sources such as roots, stems, and buds, which would otherwise have been indigestible. And he held that most grasslands were the products of fires, both natural and man-set.

For Sauer, geography was, as he put it in his Bowman Memorial Lecture (1952), the "meeting of natural and cultural history." He asserted, for instance, that lakes and streams would have provided the necessary protein base for the earliest sedentary populations, and that freshwater fishing folk may well have been responsible for the original domestication of plants. Sauer's proposition that southeastern Asia was "the cradle of earliest agriculture," has been confirmed in much subsequent archaeological research.

The history of exploration also attracted Sauer's attention. In "The Road to Cibola" (*Ibero-American* 3 [1932]), *The Early Spanish Main* (1966), *Northern Mists* (1968), and *Sixteenth-century North America* (1971) he sought to recount the history of the early European explorations and to reconstruct past environ-

ments, as well as the life of Native Americans and the impact of Europeans on both.

Sauer's interest in Native American history and his sympathy and admiration for the Indians were manifested in his school text *Man in Nature: America before the Days of the White Man* (1939; repr. 1975). A supporter of the American Indian movement, Sauer was on the advisory board of the *Indian Historian* from its inception in 1964.

Sauer published twenty-one books and more than ninety papers and articles. In an early essay, "The Morphology of Landscape" (*University of California Publications* 2 [1925]: 19–53), he "largely demolished the environmental determinism [then] prominent in American geography," as James J. Parsons observes (*Geographic Review* 68 [Jan. 1976]). Parsons goes on to describe this work as Sauer's "most influential and widely quoted paper" and "a landmark definition of geography and its place within the larger field of human inquiry" (p. 87).

Sauer was an extremely disciplined scholar, who apparently never took a vacation and spent most of his summers in the field (usually with his students). Widely read and possessing an exceptional memory, he could discourse in depth on a broad range of subjects—whether historical, botanical, archaeological, anthropological, or biological. He did not rely on research assistants but rather on his own labors in the field and the archive. He also eschewed duplicating machines and calculators. He remained alert and active until his death at age eighty-five; in the last decade of his life, he finished four books and some nine articles.

In the classroom, as Dan Stanislawski asserts, Sauer was "an eloquent lecturer," but he was not a popular teacher with all students because he "rejected the proposition that a teacher was obligated to pour knowledge into students while they were comfortably unaware—a method that may result in saturated sponges but hardly artesian wells of inspiration" ("Carl Ortwin Sauer, 1889–1975," *Journal of Geography* 84 [Dec. 1975]: 548–54). He expected his students to learn by their own efforts. A few days before he died, Sauer summed up simply what he felt he had contributed to education: "I tried to encourage students to keep on thinking."

Sauer did not limit his energies to the field and the classroom. In the 1920s with the Michigan Land Economic Survey and in the 1930s as a consultant with the Soil Conservation Service (which he was instrumental in establishing), he was involved with public policy and the problems of resource depletion. Indeed, Sauer, who became increasingly critical of modern man's exploitation of natural resources, helped to organize a conference at Princeton, New Jersey, in June 1955 that addressed this issue. The conference, according to Alfred W. Crosby ("The Past and the Present of Environmental History," *American Historical Review* 100 [Oct. 1996]: 1177–89), may be seen as the "scientific debut" of the "new environmentalism." The proceedings resulted in an influential anthology, *Man's Role in*

Changing the Face of the Earth (ed. William L. Thomas [1956]). Appropriately, the book was dedicated to George Perkins Marsh, the nineteenth-century naturalist who had issued an early warning about man's destructive impact on the globe.

Sauer's other public or semi-public functions included positions on the advisory councils of the Office of Naval Research (Geography Branch), the Air University at Montgomery, Alabama, the President's Science Advisory Board, the Social Science Research Council, the Conservation Foundation, and the Rockefeller Foundation. He also spent thirty years on the John Simon Guggenheim Memorial Foundation's selection committee.

Recognized as one of the most distinguished American geographers of his time, Sauer was awarded the Charles P. Daly Medal of the American Geographic Society (1940), the Vega Medal of the Swedish Society of Anthropology and Geography (1957), the Alexander Von Humboldt Centennial Medal of the Berlin Geographic Society (1959), and the Victoria Medal of the Royal Geographic Society (1975). In 1974 he received a special award from the Association of American Geographers for "a lifetime of exceptional achievement as a scholar of geography." Sauer died in Berkeley, California.

• A collection of Sauer's correspondence and other material is in the Bancroft Library of the University of California, Berkeley. Other letters of his may be found in the Edward Louis Papers, University of Washington Library, Seattle; and in the Martson Bates Collection at the Bentley Historical Society Library, University of Michigan, Ann Arbor. The best summaries of Sauer's career and thinking are the article by James J. Parsons cited above and his "Berkeley: The Later Sauer Years," *Annals of the Association of American Geographers* 69 (Mar. 1979): 9–15. John Leighly, "Carl Ortwin Sauer," *Annals of the Association of American Geographers* 66 (Sept. 1976): 337–48, contains a list of his publications. Many of the essays in Martin S. Kenzer, ed., *Carl O. Sauer: A Tribute* (1987), are important for understanding Sauer's intellectual heritage and development. For Latin American studies at Berkeley, see Robert C. West, "A Berkeley Perspective on the Study of Latin American Geography in the United States and Canada," in *Studying Latin America: Essays in Honor of Preston E. James*, ed. David J. Robinson (1980), pp. 135–75. Obituaries are in the *Geographic Review* 141 (Nov. 1975): 516–17, and the *New York Times*, 21 July 1975.

RICHARD HARMOND
THOMAS J. CURRAN

SAUGRAIN DE VIGNI, Antoine François (17 Feb. 1763–18 or 19 May 1820), naturalist, mineralogist, surgeon, and physician, was born in Paris, France, the son of Antoine Claude Saugrain, a bookseller, and Marie Brunet. Little is known of Saugrain's education other than through a 1787 letter of introduction to Benjamin Franklin. Saugrain's brother-in-law, Joseph Guillotin, wrote "He has lived since early childhood, in the medical schools, under my observation in the amphitheaters, laboratories, etc., and as young as he is, he has taken, for a number of years, not only my lessons, but also courses in anatomy, surgery, chemis-

try, natural history [and] physics." Saugrain practiced surgery in New Orleans, in the territory of Louisiana, from 1783 to 1786. He returned to Paris in 1786, gathered books and a "cabinet of physical science" filled with chemical balances, assorted mirrors, barometers, aerometers, thermometers, batteries, and "electrical machines," and crossed the Atlantic once more under the employ of Count Bernardo de Galvez, Viceroy of Mexico, for whom he pursued explorations in mining.

Saugrain traveled throughout the United States in 1787–1788. While in Pittsburgh, Pennsylvania, during the winter of 1787, Saugrain experimented to determine the kinds of wood that yielded the "largest quantity and best quality of potash," concluding that cornstalks yielded the largest amount. On exploration of many local mines, he identified iron, lead, copper, and silver mines on both sides of the Ohio River. On 19 March 1788 Saugrain was attacked by American Indians as he journeyed down the Ohio River to Louisville, Kentucky. All but one of his companions was killed, and Saugrain escaped with gunshot wounds to his neck and hand, the latter of which left him "with the loss of perfect use" of his index finger. While recuperating at Fort Pitt, Louisville, he analyzed mineral specimens brought to him from several mines on Silver Creek, and among other naturalist pursuits, he discovered a resin from the sweet gum tree, which the locals named after him. On examining the large number of salt springs from Kentucky to Pennsylvania, Saugrain concluded that "all this country has been covered by the water of seas or has been a lake." Saugrain described the details of his travels to the French writer Jacques Pierre Brissot de Warville, who recorded them in his 1788 *Nouveau Voyage en Septentrionale Amerique.*

After a brief return trip to France in 1789, Saugrain joined a party of French settlers from Lyons and Paris bound for Ohio. This group founded the settlement of Gallipolis, Ohio, on 20 October 1790. Saugrain opened an inn in this community, where, in the back room, he pursued electrical and chemical experiments and made barometers, thermometers, and phosphorous matches, all of which "found a ready sale." Although Saugrain gained local renown for his electrochemical demonstrations and matches, many, as one countryman later recounted, deemed his work to be magical, "too near resemblance of the black art" (Dandridge, p. 204) for others to seriously pursue. In March 1793 Saugrain married Genevieve Rosalie Michau; they had six children. Saugrain left Ohio, arriving in Lexington, Kentucky, in 1796–1797. While in Kentucky he engineered the local manufacturing of bar iron and iron shot. Late in 1797 Saugrain was invited to settle in St. Louis, the capital of Upper Louisiana. After acquiring land at nearby St. Charles, Saugrain moved his family there in 1799–1800. On his arrival, Saugrain took up practice as the only physician in St. Louis and was also appointed as surgeon of the Spanish Army post. Following the cession of Upper Louisiana to the United States, President Thomas Jefferson appointed Saugrain surgeon of the American army post in St. Louis in 1805, a position he held until his resignation in 1811.

Saugrain gained considerable respect for his successful inoculations against smallpox. During Saugrain's early years, general preventative measures against smallpox included prayers, fasting, quarantines, and travel bans. By 1800, many New England physicians were using British physician Edward Jenner's preventative method of vaccinating patients with matter taken from infected lesions of sufferers of cowpox. This exposure to a related disease appeared to protect against contracting smallpox. As historian Samuel Dicks reported, Saugrain had previously administered smallpox inoculations to "a great many people" while living in Ohio (p. 18). By 1809 he had introduced the less virulent but equally effective cowpox vaccine to the people of St. Louis. He made this vaccine available to all physicians and "intelligent persons" living some distance from his residential practice and offered vaccinations gratis to "Persons in indigent circumstances, paupers and Indians" (Dicks, p. 23). The success achieved by Saugrain and many others with the use of vaccination prompted the U.S. Congress to establish the National Vaccine Agency in 1813. Saugrain continued to practice medicine in St. Louis until he died.

Saugrain has become known as the "First Scientist of the Mississippi Valley" and the first to introduce smallpox vaccine west of the Mississippi River. His career, as Dicks noted, "reflects the important role played by the French in the development of . . . the Mississippi Valley" (p. 27).

• Saugrain's papers are in the Saugrain-Michau Collection, Missouri Historical Society, St. Louis, Mo. Saugrain recorded his early experiments in *Recueil d'Observations Physiques* (1786) and *Observations Physiques* (1786–1787). His account entitled *Dr. Saugrain's Relation of his Voyage down the Ohio River from Pittsburgh to the Falls in 1788*, first published in 1876, later appeared in *Proceedings of the American Antiquarian Society* (1897): 369–80; and *Dr. Saugrain's Notebooks*, also first published in 1876, appeared in *Proceedings of the American Antiquarian Society* 19 (1903): 221–38. Biographical accounts include William Vincent Byar, *The First Scientist of the Mississippi Valley: A Memoir of the Life and Work of Doctor Antoine Saugrain* (c. 1902); N. P. Dandridge, "Antoine Francois Saugrain (De Vigni.) The First Scientist of the Mississippi Valley," *Ohio Archives and Historical Society Publications* 15 (1906): 192–206; H. Foure Seler, *L'Odyssee americaine d'une famille française: Le Docteur Antoine Saugrain* (1936); and Samuel E. Dicks, "Antoine Saugrain (1763–1820): A French Scientist of the American Frontier," *Emporia State Research Studies* 25 (1976): 5–27.

PHILIP K. WILSON

SAULSBURY, Eli (29 Dec. 1817–22 Mar. 1893), U.S. senator, was born in Mispillion Hundred, Delaware, the son of William Saulsbury, a farmer and sheriff of Kent County, and Margaret Smith. Eli attended Dickinson College in Carlisle, Pennsylvania, where for a time he ranked first in his class, though he left without finishing a degree. Returning to his family's land, Saulsbury worked as a teacher and surveyor. He then studied law in the office of his younger brother Willard Saulsbury in Georgetown, Delaware, where Eli was admitted to the bar in 1857, when he was nearly forty. He established a practice at Dover, the state capital.

Saulsbury had meanwhile begun to take part in politics, along with Willard, his older brother Gove Saulsbury, and Willard's brother-in-law James Ponder. The Saulsburys acquired a powerful position in the Democratic party of downstate Delaware equivalent to the role played by the Bayard family in New Castle County. Eli represented Mispillion twice in the state legislature during the early 1850s. By the late 1850s he and Gove were running the *Dover Delawarean*, which became the family's organ. A Douglas Democrat during the 1860–1861 crisis, Saulsbury wrote his state's legislative resolution condemning secession. A delegate to the 1864 convention that nominated George B. McClellan, Saulsbury always defended the Delaware Democracy's wartime stance of adhering to the Union but of condemning the Abraham Lincoln administration's war effort and its "outrageous" use of the military to guarantee this Border State's loyalty. "Where is the law we did not obey? Where is the requisition by the Government for men and money that we did not meet?" he retorted when a Senate Republican in 1878 questioned Delaware's war record. "We were cut off by [Chesapeake] Bay from the Southern States," Saulsbury added. "We knew that our interest was to remain in the Union" (*Congressional Record*, 46th Cong., 2d sess., pp. 1423–25).

Willard, considered the most talented brother, had held one of Delaware's Senate seats since 1859, but by the end of his second term in 1871 the youngest Saulsbury's notorious alcohol problems were embarrassing the state. In a strange contest that had the trappings of a family quarrel, the Delaware legislature elected Eli, a faithful Methodist known for his diligence, over Gove to replace the scandalously negligent Willard.

Through most of his three Senate terms, Eli was overshadowed in national Democratic politics by his senior colleague, Thomas F. Bayard, but Saulsbury did exert influence among Senate Democrats. He earned a reputation as a conscientious legislator, a frequent, sometimes long-winded participant in Senate debate, as well as a reliable partisan. Sharing the hostility of his downstate Delaware constituents toward an active federal government in general and Republican measures to secure black rights in particular, Saulsbury in January 1872 made his first important speech for the reenfranchisement of ex-Confederates and against the Civil Rights Bill. He often assailed Reconstruction as an "odious" turn toward "centralization" and Republican governance as the height of "extravagance" and "corruption." Some of his targets took umbrage at such rhetoric. In its obituary, the Republican *New York Times* (23 Mar. 1893) dismissed Saulsbury as "a chronic scold."

Saulsbury's legal knowledge and painstaking methods proved an asset in his lengthy service on the Senate Committee on Privileges and Elections. Only once in his eighteen years in the Senate did a Democratic majority afford him an opportunity to chair this panel, during the Forty-sixth Congress, 1879–1881. The Delawarean handled this role with the usual level of partisanship: his committee attempted without success to remove Louisiana's William P. Kellogg, one of the last "carpetbag" senators, but the panel exonerated Kansas's John J. Ingalls, a fervent Republican partisan, of having obtained his seat through bribery. Saulsbury also held a seat on the politically sensitive Committee on Post Offices and Post Roads.

In 1888 a former student in Saulsbury's law office, James L. Wolcott, challenged his mentor's reelection. The ensuing split among Delaware Democrats enabled Republicans to capture the state legislature and elect Anthony Higgins the first Republican senator in Delaware history. Saulsbury retired to Dover, where he died. He never married. Tall and gaunt, with a green broadcloth coat that a colleague felt fit him "like a nightgown on a bedpost" (*New York Times*, 23 Mar. 1893), Saulsbury fit well in the Gilded Age Senate, which was full of picturesque characters.

• The Saulsbury papers at the Morris Library, University of Delaware, contain political correspondence from Saulsbury. Sketches are in John Thomas Scharf, *History of Delaware* (1888), and Henry C. Conrad, *History of the State of Delaware* (1908). Harold B. Hancock, *Delaware during the Civil War* (1961), Hancock's chapters in *Delaware: A History of the First State*, ed. H. Clay Reed (1947), and Richard O. Curry, ed., *Radicalism, Racism, and Party Realignment: The Border States during Reconstruction* (1969), place the Saulsbury family within Delaware politics. The *Every Evening and Wilmington Daily Commercial*, 22–23 Mar. 1893, offers an obituary and an assessment.

ALAN LESSOFF

SAULSBURY, Willard (2 June 1820–6 Apr. 1892), U.S. senator, was born in Mispillion Hundred, Kent County, Delaware, the son of William Saulsbury and Margaret Smith. After first attending Delaware College in Newark, he completed his undergraduate degree at Dickinson College in Carlisle, Pennsylvania. After graduation, he studied law under James L. Bartol of Maryland, later a chief justice of that state, and Martin W. Bates, later a U.S. senator from Delaware. Saulsbury was admitted to the bar of Delaware in 1845 and began practicing law in Georgetown, in Sussex County. Appointed Delaware attorney general in 1850, he held the office until 1855. Saulsbury, who enjoyed a fine reputation as an orator and lawyer, was active in the state Democratic party, and in 1856 he was elected as a delegate to the national Democratic convention at Cincinnati. There he lent his support to James Buchanan, who became the presidential candidate. In 1859 the state legislature elected Saulsbury to the U.S. Senate, where he served until 1871.

He began his term in the Senate in the midst of the secession crisis. Although from a long line of slaveholders, Saulsbury strongly opposed secession. In a speech that would gain him much notoriety in his home state and throughout the Union, the senator announced on 5 December 1860 that "my state having been the first to adopt the Constitution will be the last to . . . lead to the separation of . . . this glorious Union" (*Congressional Globe*, 36th Cong., 2d sess., p. 14). During this period, Saulsbury maintained that the Union could be restored through peaceful means. If South Carolina and other seceding states refused to return to the Union, thought Saulsbury, then perhaps a new Union should be formed, one that excluded the extreme proslavery states of the deep South as well as the extreme antislavery states of New England. Saulsbury's scheme of a "central confederacy" never came to fruition, and once the Civil War broke out he supported the Union but remained firmly opposed to Abraham Lincoln's war policy. As a Peace Democrat (or "Copperhead"), Saulsbury denounced the president and other Republicans for supporting conscription and undermining civil liberties. In early 1862 he defended Jesse D. Bright, a senator from Indiana, when Republicans in the Senate expelled him for disloyalty. He was particularly distressed by interference at Delaware polling places by Federal troops. On 27 January 1863 Saulsbury delivered a scathing speech in the Senate in which he attacked Lincoln as a "tyrant." His speech led to an unsuccessful motion to expel him from the Senate. In 1864 he served as a delegate to the Democratic National Convention in Chicago, which nominated George B. McClellan for president and called for an immediate cease-fire.

Saulsbury was opposed to all measures for emancipation and equal rights for black Americans. When officials from Delaware proposed a plan for compensated, gradual emancipation in the state, he denounced the measure as a form of "negro equality" and proclaimed, "The United States of America . . . shall be the white man's home; and not only the white man's home, but the white man shall govern, and the nigger never shall be his equal" (*Congressional Globe*, 37th Cong., 2d sess., pp. 1923–24). Saulsbury also delivered a long speech against the Thirteenth Amendment, which abolished slavery, and he proposed a substitute amendment upholding slaveholding rights and denying citizenship to anyone of African descent. After reelection in 1865, he continued to defend white supremacy, taking firm stands against both the Fourteenth and Fifteenth Amendments.

During his two terms, he served on the committees on commerce, mining, patents, and pensions. He was defeated for reelection in 1871 when he was opposed by his brother Eli and another brother, Gove, who had just completed a term as governor. Willard eventually supported the candidacy of Eli, who won the election. Two years later, Saulsbury was appointed chancellor of Delaware by Governor James Ponder, his brother-in-law. He served as chancellor until his death. Throughout his career, Saulsbury was considered an intelligent, industrious lawyer. He could be overly confrontational in his manner, however, and it was this trait that led him to constant feuding with the Bayards, the most powerful political family in Delaware. Saulsbury also was known as a heavy drinker. His speech against Lincoln given in January 1863 was probably delivered under the influence of alcohol, and it was rumored that Ponder appointed Saulsbury to the position of chancellor on the condition that he abstain from drinking.

In 1850 Saulsbury had married Annie Milby Ponder. They had one daughter and two sons. One of their sons, John P. Saulsbury, became secretary of state of Delaware, and the other son, Willard Saulsbury, Jr., became a U.S. senator. Saulsbury died at his home in Dover, Delaware. Although he has been remembered mostly as a forceful opponent of Lincoln and the cause of equal rights, he should also be considered one of the leading legal minds of Delaware in the nineteenth century.

• There is no collection of Saulsbury's papers, although some material concerning him may be found in the papers of his son Willard Saulsbury, Jr., at the University of Delaware. Harold Bell Hancock, *Delaware during the Civil War: A Political History* (1961), contains much information on Saulsbury's activities in the years immediately preceding and during the Civil War. Also helpful are Henry C. Conrad, *History of the State of Delaware* (3 vols., 1908), and Walter A. Powell, *A History of Delaware* (1928). For Saulsbury's activities within the Democratic party, see Jean H. Baker, *Affairs of Party: The Political Culture of Northern Democrats in the Mid-Nineteenth Century* (1983), and Roy F. Nichols, *The Disruption of American Democracy* (1948). Obituaries are in the *Wilmington (Del.) Daily Commercial* and *Every Evening*, both 6 Apr. 1892.

MICHAEL VORENBERG

SAUNDERS, Clarence (Dec. 1881–14 Oct. 1953), merchant and entrepreneur, was born in Amherst County, Virginia, the son of a tobacco farmer; his parents' names are not known. Saunders grew up in Clarksville, Tennessee, and his educational background was quite limited; he attended school for four years before going to work at age fourteen as a clerk at a grocery store. After working briefly in Alabama and Tennessee, Saunders returned to Clarksville and, by age eighteen, took a sales job for a wholesale grocery company. In Memphis, Tennessee, while still in his twenties, he organized a retail food chain called United Stores, which he sold after a few years.

In 1916, after a brief stint as a wholesaler on his own, Saunders began to create a name for himself on the national scene when he developed what is believed to be the first modern supermarket. In September of that year the first store, which was named King Piggly Wiggly, opened its doors in Memphis. When asked by a business associate in Memphis why he had chosen the name Piggly Wiggly, Saunders replied, "So people would ask me what you just did" (*New Yorker*, 6 June 1959, p. 131). The self-service market revolutionized the grocery business. Serving as a departure from the traditional store in which customers would have to line up at counters to receive their groceries from a clerk. At Saunders' store, the clerks and counters were gone, replaced by aisles of individually packaged groceries with price tags attached to them. The customers would gather their purchases in baskets and pay as they went out.

By the end of 1919 nine Piggly Wiggly stores were in operation. They prospered so well that by the fall of 1922 the chain consisted of over 1,200 stores in twenty-nine states. Only around 650 of the stores were owned by Saunders; the remainder were independently owned, but the owners paid royalties to the corporation for the right to use its method of operation, which Saunders had patented in October 1917.

The success of Piggly Wiggly Stores, Inc. soon led to the acceptance of its shares on the New York Stock Exchange. After six months on the exchange, Piggly Wiggly stock earned a reputation as a dependable, albeit unsensational, dividend-paying commodity. However, in November 1922 that reputation began to diminish when several small companies that had used the name Piggly Wiggly in running grocery stores in New York, New Jersey, and Connecticut failed. When these stores went under, certain stock market operators seized the opportunity for a bear raid. They believed that if more of these individual stores were failing, they could convince the uninformed public that the parent corporation was in trouble as well. These operators began selling short, forcing the price of the stock down from $50 a share to $39.

Saunders, not one to go down without a fight, vowed to the press that he would "beat the Wall Street professionals at their own game" (*New Yorker*, 6 June 1959, p. 132), despite the fact that he was a Wall Street novice himself, never having owned a single share of stock prior to Piggly Wiggly's listing on the New York Stock Exchange. He bought 30,000 shares, thereby increasing the market price of the stock from $39 to $77 a share. The price eventually reached $124 a share; however, the exchange declared that a "corner" existed. Saunders had to take delivery of all the stock he had contracted to buy, but after receiving all of his shares, the price of the stock fell again. Saunders lost $10 million and was deposed as president of Piggly Wiggly.

Saunders's earlier marriage to Carolyn Walker, which produced three children, began to crumble; it ended in divorce in 1928. His unfinished $1 million mansion, being built out of a pinkish-yellow marble on a 160-acre estate on the outskirts of Memphis, was seized by the city and transformed into a museum. Undaunted by these personal and professional setbacks, Saunders gathered up what personal assets he could from the collapse of his empire, borrowed some money, and, in 1929, started another large retail grocery chain. This group of stores, known as "Clarence Saunders, Sole Owner of My Name," grew into a $60 million a year business until Saunders was bankrupted during the depression.

Next, Saunders began tinkering with the idea of an automatic, electrically operated type of retail grocery store. Named the Keedoozle, which was derived from the words "Key Does All," it was a mechanized store in which the customer selected merchandise by placing a "key" into a slot beside the desired item and pushing a button. This would perforate a tape inside the key. When finished shopping, the customer would hand the perforated tape to a clerk who would run it through a machine that added up the bill. Additionally, every item ordered would tumble down from bins and come out together on conveyor belts. "It's by far the biggest thing that ever came along in the grocery business," Saunders told *Newsweek* (26 Nov. 1945). "It can't miss."

In 1937 Saunders's first attempt at the Keedoozle concept failed due to mechanical difficulties; a plan to revive the idea in 1945 was delayed for several years. Finally, in August 1948 an improved Keedoozle was unveiled. Although Saunders sold twelve franchises, the automatic devices proved too complicated and too expensive to compete with the lesser costs of normal grocery stores. Saunders ended the Keedoozle experiment in 1949.

Saunders made one final attempt at a comeback in 1953. He had designs for another mechanical grocery store, the Foodelectric, which would put him "back in the $1 million class within a year" (*New York Times*, 15 Oct. 1953). However, plans to put the Foodelectric into operation were delayed by an illness. Saunders died in Memphis, survived by his second wife, Patricia Bomburg, their one child, and the three children from his previous marriage.

An article in the *New Yorker* (6 June 1959) remembered Saunders as having "most of the standard traits of the flamboyant American promoter—suspect generosity, a knack for attracting publicity, love of ostentation, and so on." The article acknowledged his less well-known virtues, such as a colorful speaking and writing style and an unwitting flair for comedy. However, the article continued, "like so many great men before him, he had a weakness, a tragic flaw. It was that he insisted on thinking of himself as a hick, a boob, and a sucker, and, in doing so, he sometimes became all three."

• For biographical profiles of Saunders, see *Newsweek*, 26 Nov. 1945, 30 Aug. 1948, and 19 Oct. 1953; the *New Yorker*, 6 June 1959; *Time*, 8 July 1936, and 30 Aug. 1948; *Business Week*, 24 Nov. 1934, and 15 Apr. 1939; the *St. Louis Post-Dispatch*, 12 June 1967; and *Food Topics*, June 1967. An obituary is in the *New York Times*, 15 Oct. 1953.

FRANCESCO L. NEPA

SAUNDERS, Prince (?–Feb. 1839), author and colonizationist, was born in either Lebanon, Connecticut, or Thetford, Vermont, the son of Cuff Saunders and Phyllis (maiden name unknown). Although the exact date of Prince Saunders's birth remains unknown, he was baptized on 25 July 1784 in Lebanon and received his early schooling in Thetford. He taught at a black school in Colchester, Connecticut, and later studied at Moor's Charity School at Dartmouth College in 1807 and 1808. President John Wheelock (1754–1817) of Dartmouth recommended Saunders as instructor at Boston's African School in late 1808. By 1811 Saunders was secretary of the African Masonic Society and had founded the Belles Lettres Society, a literary group. He also taught at the African Baptist Church in Boston, founded by Thomas Paul. He was engaged to one daughter of emigrationist and sea captain Paul Cuffe. Although the engagement ended for unknown reasons, his acquaintance with Cuffe undoubtedly awakened Saunders to Pan-Africanism and the black colonization movement.

In 1815 Saunders and Thomas Paul traveled to London as delegates to the Masonic Lodge of Africans. Saunders met with many influential British people, including abolitionist leaders William Wilberforce and Thomas Clarkson. As a result of these meetings, Saunders focused his interest on Haiti, the first black republic in the Western Hemisphere. He shared the British abolitionists' desire to anglicize Haiti. In 1816 he made his first visit to Haiti, where King Henri Christophe greeted him enthusiastically. Saunders introduced the concept of vaccination by vaccinating Christophe's children, and he introduced the Lancastrian system of education. Adopted by many schools in the United States, including the African Free Schools, the system used student monitors to assist teachers and emphasized learning by rote. Saunders then returned to England, where he published his first work, *Haytian Papers* (1816), a collection of Haitian civic laws governing agriculture, commerce, the police, and politics. In December 1816 he traveled again to Haiti. Christophe accused him of publishing *Haytian Papers* without permission and dismissed him as an adviser. Saunders was allowed, however, to continue his work in schools and medicine until 1818, when he sailed to Boston. There he published a second edition of his book.

Living in Philadelphia in 1818, Saunders served as a lay reader for Absalom Jones's St. Thomas's African Episcopal Church. He joined the Pennsylvania Abolition Society and promoted colonization to the Caribbean, especially Haiti. Although it had been supported earlier by black leaders, by 1818 colonization had become intensely unpopular among blacks. James Forten and Richard Allen both denounced colonization as a trick of the newly organized American Colonization Society. Generally African-American and white abolitionists regarded the society as an organization seeking to protect slavery and counteract antislavery. Saunders persisted in his views, however, publishing in 1818 two pamphlets: *An Address Delivered . . . before the Pennsylvania Augustine Society for Education of People of Color* and *A Memoir Presented to the American Convention for Promoting the Abolition of Slavery.*

Saunders settled in Haiti in 1820. He took with him letters from Philadelphia alleging the desire of thousands of free blacks to emigrate to Haiti. Saunders convinced Christophe to supply a ship and $25,000 to initiate colonization. As the agreement neared completion, however, a coup displaced Christophe, who then committed suicide. Saunders was left penniless and friendless. Newly installed President John Pierre Boyer received Saunders politely but refused to guarantee support for the former ally of Christophe. Despite Boyer's expressed desire to promote greater democracy in Haiti, Saunders became disillusioned and feared that Boyer's approach (he abolished universal education established by Christophe) would cause the downfall of black Haiti. Convinced of Boyer's inability to rule effectively, he lobbied the British and Russian governments to intervene to replace Boyer.

Saunders's disaffection with Haiti's government did not lessen his zeal for emigration to Haiti. It is doubtful that he played a key role in Haitian politics, although a claim has been made that he was Boyer's attorney general. There is no evidence to support this claim in Haitian records, however. Saunders lived in Haiti until his death in Port-au-Prince.

Saunders's position on colonization continued from the Pan-Africanism of Paul Cuffe and the Sierra Leone settlers in the late eighteenth century to the black hostility in the United States toward colonization after 1817. His efforts to create a Pan-African nationalism, of which his involvement with Haitian politics was an exceptional example, became politically unpopular in later years, but he should be recognized for his remarkable abilities as an educator, abolitionist, writer, and public speaker.

• For primary references on Saunders, see Earl Leslie Griggs and Thomas Clarkson, eds., *Henri Christophe and Thomas Clarkson: A Correspondence* (1952; repr. 1968). For information on Saunders's career, see Franck Bayard, "Prince Saunders," in *Dictionary of American Negro Biography* (1982), and Arthur D. White, "Prince Saunders: An Instance of Social Mobility among Antebellum New England Blacks," *Journal of Negro History* 55 (1975): 526–35.

GRAHAM RUSSELL HODGES

SAUNDERS, Romulus Mitchell (3 Mar. 1791–21 Apr. 1867), U.S. congressman and diplomat, was born in Caswell County, North Carolina, the son of William Saunders, a landowner, and Hannah Mitchell. After the death of his mother, he moved with his father and brother to Sumner County, Tennessee. Following his father's death in 1803, he returned to North Carolina to live with his uncle James Saunders. He enrolled in the University of North Carolina in 1809 but was expelled along with two other students for firing a pistol and for throwing a stone at a member of the faculty. He studied law in Tennessee under Hugh Lawson White, received his license in 1812, and settled in Milton, the seat of Caswell County. In 1812 he married Rebecca Peine Carter; they had five children. She died in 1821. Two years later he married Anna Hayes Johnson; they had six children.

Thanks in part to the influence of his uncle, who had served as Caswell County's first state senator, Saunders rose rapidly in politics. He was elected to the House of Commons in 1815 and to the state senate in 1816. He returned to the lower house in 1818 and served as Speaker in 1819 and 1820. During his tenure in the assembly, he was an advocate of publicly financed internal improvements and of reform in the state's undemocratic constitution. In 1821 he won

election to the U.S. House of Representatives, where he remained until 1827. He supported William H. Crawford for the presidency in 1824 and cast his vote for him when the election was decided in the House. He opposed the administration of John Quincy Adams and supported Andrew Jackson for the presidency in 1828.

During the 1830s Saunders was a leading figure in the Democratic party. As a delegate to the Baltimore Convention of May 1832, he rallied southerners behind the vice presidential candidacy of Martin Van Buren. In June 1834 he established the *Raleigh Standard* as the official organ of the North Carolina party and hired its first editor. He played an active role in the proceedings of the Baltimore Convention of May 1835 and helped Van Buren carry North Carolina in the presidential election of 1836.

In 1833 Saunders was appointed to a commission to adjudicate claims by American citizens for depredations arising out of the Napoleonic wars. Saunders's service on the commission won him respect and esteem as a jurist. However, his decision to retain the state office of attorney general, to which he had been elected in 1828, generated considerable controversy since it seemed to violate a state law against dual office-holding. In 1834 the general assembly passed a resolution declaring the attorney general's office vacant, and Saunders resigned under protest. At the next session, the Democrats elected him to the superior court.

Although Saunders, like most southern Democrats, was a fiscal conservative in national politics, his progressive views on state-financed internal improvements were at variance with those of many in the North Carolina party, whose strength lay primarily in the tax-conscious plantation counties of the East. As the Democratic candidate for governor in 1840, he adopted an ambiguous position, claiming to favor a "judicious and economical system" of state development while opposing "those extravagant projects, which must end in failure." That equivocal stance satisfied neither wing of the party and contributed to his defeat.

Saunders returned to the U.S. Congress in 1841, where he distinguished himself for his intense partisanship. As one Democrat acidly remarked, "His highest ambition seems to be to engage and bluster in party polemics" (Paul, p. 86). By now a disciple of John C. Calhoun, he sought his party's nomination for the U.S. Senate in 1842. When the Democratic caucus gave the nomination to former senator Bedford Brown, a Van Buren loyalist, Saunders took his case directly to the floor of the general assembly and, with considerable Whig support, nearly succeeded in winning the election. Both candidates eventually withdrew, and the Democrats elected William H. Haywood, Jr. Public attacks by Saunders on the "wire-workers in Washington City" and his defiance of the caucus aroused resentment within his party. Van Buren characterized him as a politician who "thought no man in North Carolina capable of filling office but himself" (Paul, p. 87). Nonetheless, Saunders remained popular in his own district and won reelection to the U.S. House of Representatives in 1843.

As a delegate to the Democratic National Convention of 1844, Saunders served as floor manager for the faction opposed to Van Buren's nomination. He called the convention to order before the time set for its official opening and engineered the nomination of Hendrick Wright as presiding officer. He then successfully moved for the adoption of the rule requiring a two-thirds majority for nomination. This rule eventually led to the nomination of James K. Polk and played a crucial role in Democratic national conventions until 1936.

In February 1846 Saunders was appointed minister to Spain with instructions to negotiate for the purchase of Cuba. His rough-hewn personality was not well suited for such a sensitive diplomatic endeavor, and he succeeded only in alienating the Spanish government. He resigned his office in May 1849 and returned to Raleigh, where he had lived since the early 1830s. Elected to the House of Commons in 1850, he played an important role in reconciling his party to the North Carolina Railroad, an east-west trunk line that had been chartered by the previous legislature with a state subsidy of $2 million. Reelected in 1852, he championed the extension of the North Carolina Railroad eastward to the Atlantic Ocean and westward through the mountains.

Despite his legislative accomplishments, Saunders's ambition for the U.S. Senate again placed him at loggerheads with his party in 1852. Once more refusing to abide by the decision of the party caucus, he received enough votes to prevent the election of James C. Dobbin, the official nominee. With the support of the Whigs, Saunders subsequently won election to the superior court, but the legislature adjourned without electing a U.S. senator. Saunders remained on the bench until the end of the Civil War. He died in Raleigh.

Saunders's most important contribution as a statesman lay in his steering the North Carolina Democratic party in a progressive direction on the issue of internal improvements. In national politics he is significant primarily for his role in depriving Van Buren of the presidential nomination in 1844. A leader of the North Carolina Democracy during its formative years, his insatiable ambition for office eventually deprived him of influence within his party.

• Saunders did not leave a substantial number of personal papers. The largest collection can be found in the Walter Clark Manuscripts, North Carolina Division of Archives and History. These letters, which provide valuable information about state and national politics during the 1820s, are published in Albert R. Newsome, ed., "Letters of Romulus M. Saunders to Bartlett Yancy, 1821–1828," *North Carolina Historical Review* 8 (1931): 427–62. Other letters by Saunders are in J. G. de Roulhac Hamilton, ed., *The Papers of Thomas Ruffin* (4 vols., 1918–1920); and Henry T. Shanks, ed., *The Papers of Willie Person Mangum* (5 vols., 1950–1956). The most detailed secondary account is the biographical sketch by Samuel A. Ashe in *Biographical History of North Carolina*, ed.

Ashe et al., vol. 3 (1905). For Saunders's role in the Democratic National Convention of 1844, see James C. N. Paul, *Rift in the Democracy* (1951). For his role as a leader of the progressive wing of the North Carolina Democratic party, see Thomas E. Jeffrey, "Internal Improvements and Political Parties in Antebellum North Carolina, 1836–1860," *North Carolina Historical Review* 55 (1978): 111–56. An obituary is in the *Raleigh Sentinel*, 22 Apr. 1867.

THOMAS E. JEFFREY

SAUNDERS, Stuart Thomas (16 July 1909–8 Feb. 1987), lawyer and railroad executive, was born in McDowall, West Virginia, the son of William Hamett Saunders and Lucy Smith, farmers. His childhood was spent on a dairy farm outside Roanoke, Virginia. After graduating from Roanoke College in Salem, Virginia, in 1930 and from Harvard Law School in 1934, he spent five years practicing law outside Washington, D.C. Then, in 1939, he married Dorothy Davidson, with whom he had four children, and took a job as assistant general solicitor with the Norfolk & Western Railroad. He became its executive vice president in 1956, and two years later he succeeded Robert H. Smith as its president.

Saunders left the company's daily operations to others and concentrated on the larger problems of finance, relations with connecting railways, political chores, and public affairs. One of his first actions as president was to dieselize his railroad, scrapping all its coal-burning steam engines despite the fact that his was the largest coal hauler in the country. Saunders surprised everyone within a year when the N&W took over the competing Virginian Railway, which had long been allied with the New York Central, while his own company was controlled behind the scenes by the Central's hated rival, the Pennsylvania Railroad. Alfred Perlman, the Central's president, who was involved in merger talks with the Pennsylvania, viewed the merger of Saunders's two coal roads in 1959 as an inappropriate expansion by the Pennsylvania. Saunders gained labor's support for his merger, however, by promising union leaders that all labor savings would come through attrition.

Saunders then turned to a possible merger between his company and the Wabash and Nickle Plate roads in the Midwest. Both were profitable and could route export traffic to the N&W's Norfolk port, but to make the merger work the Pennsylvania would have to sell the N&W a road that connected the merger candidates. During the negotiations, however, Saunders was tapped to replace James M. Symes as chairman and chief executive officer on the Pennsylvania Railroad on 1 October 1963. A Democrat on a staunchly Republican road, and a man who did not rise through the technical and operating end of the company, Saunders was an unusual choice. He took over a road that had fallen on hard times; its net profits were shrinking, its traffic base was eroding, and its physical condition had begun to deteriorate. The line desperately needed someone to improve its physical condition. Instead, it chose a man determined to diversify outside the rail business.

Saunders saw his first chance when the Justice Department ruled that the Pennsylvania dominated the N&W and would have to sell its investment in it before the agency would allow the N&W's merger with the Wabash and Nickle Plate. Saunders sold off the Pennsylvania's N&W holdings and used the money to purchase the Buckeye Pipeline; some real estate development companies in Florida, Texas, and California; and a small airline, Executive Jet Aviation.

The Pennsylvania Railroad's decline forced it to merge with the equally strapped New York Central. Important figures in New York and Pennsylvania opposed the union, fearing that the new company would no longer serve their states' interests. Saunders campaigned relentlessly in both states, winning endorsements from important regional political figures and from the Kennedy administration. He quelled labor suspicions by guaranteeing the jobs of all workers who were with the roads on 20 May 1964. He eliminated Justice Department opposition by bowing to Robert F. Kennedy's pressure to include the bankrupt New Haven & Hartford Railroad in the merger. Perhaps Saunders's most important contribution to the merger was to bring pressure on Pennsylvania's Democratic gubernatorial candidate, Milton Shapp, who opposed the merger because he feared Republican New York railroad interests were making a grab for Pennsylvania's railway. Saunders worked a deal whereby Shapp received a large campaign contribution from the Democratic National Committee in return for dropping his opposition.

The merger was consummated on 1 February 1968, and Saunders became the Penn Central's chairman and CEO, while Perlman took the jobs of president and chief operating officer. The two men did not get along from the start, and the two weakened railways, saddled with the bankrupt New Haven, were in immediate financial trouble. Saunders had allowed his chief financial officer on the Pennsylvania Railroad to engage in "imaginative accounting," and after the merger the new company discovered it was in worse financial shape than originally thought. The Penn Central continued to doctor its books to deceive its bankers, whose loans it desperately needed. Dividends were paid regularly with borrowed funds, and by the first quarter of 1970 the Penn Central was losing $1 million a day. Bankers and board members finally realized the road's severe problems, and on 8 June the Penn Central directors fired Saunders, Perlman, and their chief financial officer. Two weeks later the Penn Central became the nation's biggest bankruptcy ever.

Saunders was called before the Securities Exchange Commission, Congress, and the Interstate Commerce Commission to testify in investigations of the Penn Central debacle, and in 1975 he and other former Penn Central officials signed a consent decree on charges of dereliction of duty, falsifying financial statements, and issuing misleading proxy information. Saunders paid an undisclosed fine. He spent his last years as a securi-ties consultant on coal resources and transportation in Richmond, Virginia, where he died.

• The surviving Pennsylvania Railroad papers are at the Eleutherian Mills Historical Library, Wilmington, Del. The best general accounts of the Penn Central affair are Joseph Daughen and Peter Binzen, *The Wreck of the Penn Central* (1971); Stephen Salsbury, *No Way to Run a Railroad: The Untold Story of the Penn Central Crisis* (1982); Robert Sobel, *The Fallen Colossus* (1977); and Richard Saunders, *The Railroad Mergers and the Coming of Conrail* (1978). For Saunders's testimony see Robert Bedingfield, "$12.6 Million Settlement Proposed in Pennsy Suits," *New York Times*, 4 Sept. 1975; Felix Belair, Jr., "Ex-Pennsy Head Consents to Restrictions by S.E.C.," *New York Times*, 30 July 1974; and U.S. Congress, Senate, Committee on Commerce, *The Penn Central and Other Railroads*, 92d Cong., 2d sess., 1973. An obituary is in the *New York Times*, 9 Feb. 1987.

JAMES A. WARD

SAUTER, Eddie (2 Dec. 1914–21 Apr. 1981), arranger/composer and trumpeter, was born Edward Ernest Sauter in Brooklyn, New York. His parents' names are not known. After studies at Columbia University and the Juilliard School of Music in the early 1930s, Sauter began playing trumpet and mellophone with local bands. He first came to prominence in 1935 as sideman and arranger with Red Norvo's orchestra. During his three-year tenure with that band, Sauter made most of the arrangements for Mildred Bailey's recordings, both with Norvo and under her own leadership. In 1939 Sauter was hired by Benny Goodman as staff arranger, producing some of his most notable work, not only pieces like "Clarinet à la King" and "Hour of Parting," but superior arrangements for Helen Forrest and Peggy Lee, like "The Man I Love," "How Deep Is the Ocean," and "My Old Flame." After Goodman disbanded his orchestra in 1943, Sauter worked for Artie Shaw ("The Maid with the Flaccid Air" and "Summertime," both extended compositions recorded on 12-inch discs that were very unusual at the time), Tommy Dorsey, Woody Herman, and later, in 1946, Ray McKinley.

In 1952 Sauter joined forces with Bill Finnegan, a former arranger for Glenn Miller, to form the Sauter-Finnegan band, which attained considerable popular and commercial success for a few years—largely, to the dismay of many jazz fans, because it eschewed all jazz improvisation, used many classical instruments (oboe, English horn, harp, and recorder), and flirted openly with quotations and obvious allusions to classical repertory. When the band's success faded and it fell upon financially hard days, Sauter and Finnegan were unwilling to compromise or cater to commercial pressures and so disbanded their orchestra. Sauter turned to the Broadway theater for work but because of its "commercial" restrictions, it was not a field in which he could exercise his true creativity. In 1957 Sauter succeeded Kurt Edelhagen as leader of the famous jazz orchestra of the Südwestfunk radio in Baden-Baden, Germany. After 1959, returning to the United States but with no permanent position and no financial security, Sauter was driven to work again as a freelance writer for Broadway, films, and television, producing, among other things, a number of jazz-oriented jingles, and also devoting himself increasingly to composing classical chamber music for various instrumental ensembles. In the 1960s he worked on several occasions with tenor saxophonist Stan Getz, writing for him string-orchestra arrangements ("Focus," 1961) and compositions ("Tanglewood Concerto," 1966).

Many of Sauter's compositions and arrangements remain unknown or even unperformed. His greatest contributions to jazz were undoubtedly made during his years with Norvo and Goodman. But even there, while the former deeply appreciated Sauter's skill in making a relatively small band sound big and full, admiring as well his ingenious use of dynamics, instrumental timbres and counterpoint, Goodman was often worried about what he regarded as Sauter's "too modern" and "too explorative" arrangements, rejecting many of them outright and personally modifying others. Although widely appreciated and admired by musicians, Sauter's work received little public recognition during the Goodman and Shaw years. His only period of public success came during the mid-1950s, when pieces like the "Doodletown Fifers," "Eddie and the Witch Doctor," and "Midnight Sleigh Ride" (the latter based on the Troika from Prokofiev's *Lieutenant Kijé*), were recorded by the Sauter-Finnegan band.

Sauter was often driven by circumstances to do lightweight commercial work, and there, ever the idealist, he found the implicit restrictions to real creativity unendurable. But his best work shows an extraordinary inventiveness, and what was at the time an unprecedented skill in the use of thematic and motivic materials, a mastery of instrumental/harmonic voicing and coloring, and, finally, an ingenious talent for modulation. Initially influenced by Duke Ellington, Sauter had already developed in his twenties a highly personal style that affected arranging and composition in jazz in subsequent decades, particularly the work of Gil Evans.

In the end Sauter never received the public recognition that many musicians feel he should have because arrangers in general always work behind the scenes and their achievements are rarely considered important or appreciated by the general public and because much of his writing was too "sophisticated," too "advanced" for its time; it was often rejected and misunderstood even by his colleagues, peers, and employers (Goodman, for example). It should be remembered that jazz, even in its Swing Era heyday, was always under various pressures to commercialize and to pursue mass public success, temptations that very few band leaders were able to resist.

• In addition to the titles mentioned above, some of Sauter's best work can be heard on "A Porter's Love Song," "Remember," "I Would Do Anything for You" (all recorded by Norvo), and "How High the Moon," "Superman," "Darn That Dream," and "When the Sun Comes Out" (recorded by Goodman). Although there is hardly any substantial literature on Sauter, a fine tribute to him titled "Coda: Eddie Sauter" is in *Jazz Forum* 71 (1981). Much of Sauter's best work with Norvo and Goodman is also discussed in Gunther Schuller, *The Swing Era* (1989).

GUNTHER SCHULLER

SAUVEUR, Albert (21 June 1863–26 Jan. 1939), metallurgist and university professor, was born in Louvain, Belgium, the son of Lambert Sauveur and Hortense Franquin. His father was a professor of Latin and Greek at the University of Louvain and authored several books. His parents immigrated to the United States in the 1880s, but Albert joined them only after completing his studies at Athénée Royale in Belgium and the École des Mines in Liege (1881–1886). He then enrolled as an advanced student at the Massachusetts Institute of Technology, wrote a thesis on copper smelting, and graduated in 1889 with a degree in mining and metallurgy. In 1891 he married Mary Prince Jones of Spencer, Massachusetts; they had three children.

Sauveur's first job was with the Pennsylvania Steel Company at Steelton, Pennsylvania, doing chemical analyses. He found that steel men preferred to be guided by experience and tolerated metallurgists only for routine testing. "I was kept in constant danger of occupational starvation," Sauveur remembered, so he sat in the lab and read every metallurgy book he could find. Disillusioned, Sauveur moved to the South Chicago Works of Illinois Steel in 1891, where the superintendent supported his desire to investigate the internal structure of steel. In this endeavor, Sauveur was assisted by Henry Marion Howe, whom he had encountered at MIT. Howe pointed Sauveur to the work of Europeans who, in the mid-1880s, began studying the physical structure of steel with a microscope. With Howe's introduction, Sauveur established a close relationship with one pioneer, Floris Osmond. After acquiring a microscope, Sauveur introduced metallography (the microscopic study of the structure of metals) to the United States.

In 1893 Sauveur presented his first paper, "The Microstructure of Iron and Steel," to the Engineering Congress at the World's Columbian Exposition in Chicago. In it he argued that the strength of steel depended largely on grain size (i.e., its internal structure), which in turn depended on the temperature of the metal when worked. Translated into French, German, and Russian, this paper led to modifications in procedures of rolling steel. Another paper in 1896, "Microstructure of Steel and Current Theories of Hardening," built on these insights into the importance of grain size and became a landmark in heat treating, the technique of controlling temperature to achieve improved hardness and strength. That same year, Sauveur became perhaps the first investigator to use X rays to probe metal structures. By then, the number of visitors to the South Chicago laboratory testified to Sauveur's growing reputation in metallurgy.

The steel industry's traditional assumptions about science were deeply entrenched, however, and in 1897 a new manager closed the South Chicago laboratory. His numerous letters to industrial firms failed to bring employment offers, so Sauveur opened the Boston Testing Laboratory. His real intent was to advance metallography. In 1898 he launched and edited *The Metallographist*, a quarterly journal that published papers and talks, conference summaries, and biographical sketches of key people. At first Sauveur wrote many articles but this was a time of rapid development in metallography, and the journal soon attracted solid contributors. Sauveur also started a book publishing company, whose list included Howe's noted textbook *Iron, Steel, and Other Alloys* (1903). Even so, the journal struggled financially; monthly publication and a name change to *Iron and Steel Magazine* in 1904 did not help. The journal ceased publication in 1906, just as the testing lab had closed the year before. But metallography was now accepted—ten steel companies adopted microscopic analysis between 1896 and 1901—and Sauveur was recognized as a leading metallurgical scientist.

That reputation brought Sauveur a lecturer's position at Harvard in 1899, where he remained for forty years, advancing to assistant professor in 1901, to professor in 1905, and to Gordon McKay Professor of Metallurgy in 1924. In 1935 he became professor emeritus. Metallurgist Cyril Stanley Smith argued that Sauveur produced little original research after joining Harvard, but he made numerous other contributions. He was a fine and clear lecturer who also prepared important teaching tools. These included a popular seventeen-part correspondence course in metallurgy developed with H. M. Boylston in 1904, a laboratory manual in 1908, and in 1912 a textbook that remained in print through four editions. He also designed a professional microscope and published more than 150 papers.

Sauveur was equally active in professional organizations. He helped organize the American Society for Steel Testing, later the American Society for Metals. He was vice president of the American Institute of Mining Engineers (AIME) from 1910 to 1912 and chaired its iron and steel section from 1913 to 1915. In 1916–1917 he served on the John Fritz Medal board. During 1917–1919 he joined the American Aviation Commission and spent twenty months in France, working on aircraft engines and consulting for the French Ministry of Munitions. He also wrote two short books in 1915 branding Germany the aggressor in World War I.

After the war Sauveur continued to consult for several corporations using special steels. He was a member of numerous professional organizations, including the American Philosophical Society, the American Academy of Arts and Sciences, the British Iron and Steel Institute, Sigma Xi, and the engineering honorary Tau Beta Pi. Later he was elected an honorary member of both AIME and the American Society for Metals. He also was a member of the Society of Engineers of the Liege School, Société de l'Industrie Na-

tionale (France), and the Société des Ingénieurs de France.

Numerous awards and honors came Sauveur's way in recognition of his position as the "Dean of American metallographers" (Daly, p. 121). He was an American delegate to the Pan-American Scientific Congress in Lima in 1924, the same year he was invited to deliver the inaugural Henry Marion Howe Lecture in metallurgy to AIME. Similar opportunities came in 1929, when he delivered the Henry de Mille Lecture to the American Society for Steel Testing, and in 1938, when he was the Marburg Lecturer of the American Society for Testing Materials. He was awarded the Elliott Cresson Medal from the Franklin Institute in 1919 and its Franklin Medal posthumously. The British Iron and Steel Institute presented him its Bessemer Medal in 1924, while the American Society for Metals honored him with the first Albert Sauveur Achievement Medal in 1934. He also was elected *officier* of the Legion of Honneur, *officier* L'Académie (France), and *officier* of the Order of Leopold (Belgium). Finally, he was elected to the U.S. National Academy of Sciences in 1927.

Sauveur's contributions to metallurgy were numerous. He was superb with a microscope and at interpreting results, and he played a pivotal role in the introduction of metallography to American metallurgists and to industry. He also advanced understanding of heat treating steel. Sauveur continued publishing as professor emeritus, including a delightful book in 1935 titled *Metallurgical Dialogue* that adopted a Socratic style to convey the history and a basic understanding of metallurgy. But perhaps most important, throughout his career he was an urbane, cosmopolitan colleague, "a man who was truly and thoroughly civilized" (Daly, p. 125). He died in Boston.

• A file of material at Harvard College Library includes clippings from newspapers and journals, a list of papers, and other items on Sauveur. Perhaps the best biographical sketch of Sauveur is Reginald Daly, "Albert Sauveur," *Memoirs of the National Academy of Sciences* 22 (1943): 121–33, which includes a list of his publications. This essay rests heavily on Sauveur's own autobiography, *Metallurgical Reminiscences* (1937; repr. 1981). An assessment of his role within metallurgy can be found in the entry by Cyril Stanley Smith in the *Dictionary of Scientific Biography*, vol. 12, ed. Charles C. Gillespie (1975), pp. 126–27. Other sources of information include tributes from Herbert M. Boylston, "Albert Sauveur," *Mining and Metallurgy* 20 (Mar. 1939): 181; "Albert Sauveur, 1863–1939," *Metals and Alloys* 10 (Feb. 1939): 64; Lionel A. Marks, "Albert Sauveur," *Journal of Applied Physics* 8 (Mar. 1937): 160–62; and *Iron Age* 143 (15 June 1939): 39. His groundbreaking paper delivered at the Columbian Exposition was published as "The Microstructure of Steel," *Transactions of American Institute of Mining Engineers* 22 (1893): 546–90; other works by Sauveur not mentioned above are *Laboratory Experiments in Metallurgy* (1908), *The Metallography and Heat Treatment of Iron and Steel* (1912; repr. 1916, 1926, and 1935), *Germany and the European War* (1914), and *Germany's Holy War* (1915). His *Metallurgical Dialogue* was reprinted in 1981 by the ASM.

BRUCE E. SEELY

SAVAGE, Augusta (29 Feb. 1892–27 Mar. 1962), sculptor, was born Augusta Christine Fells in Green Cove Springs, near Jacksonville, Florida, the daughter of Edward Fells, a Methodist minister and laborer, and Cornelia Murphy. As a child, Fells molded small ducks and other animals from the local clay. Concerned that his daughter was "fashioning graven images," her father "almost whipped all the art out of me" (quoted in Bearden and Henderson, p. 168).

At age fifteen Fells married John T. Moore; the couple had a daughter. Moore died a short while later, and around 1915 Augusta Moore married James T. Savage, a carpenter. They had no children and were divorced in the early 1920s. She then moved to West Palm Beach, where her parents had relocated in 1915.

Augusta Savage returned to school, and her skills in clay modeling caught the attention of the school principal, who gave her a job teaching modeling to her fellow students. She briefly attended the State Normal and Industrial School in Tallahassee (now Florida A&M), but she soon returned to West Palm Beach. In 1919 county fair official George Graham Currie, amused by her sculptures of ducks and other creatures, gave Savage a booth at the fair over the objections of others. Her figures were a success with visitors, and she won a ribbon for most original exhibit.

Currie commissioned a portrait bust of himself (c. 1919, location unknown) and encouraged her to go to New York. Instead, Savage moved to Jacksonville, Florida, planning to work as portraitist of the African-American community. She left for New York City in 1921 with a letter of introduction from Currie to noted sculptor Solon Borglum, who declined to take her as a student. Still, impressed with her life and work, Borglum recommended her to the Cooper Union, where she was admitted in October 1921.

At the Cooper Union Savage studied with the portrait sculptor George T. Brewster. By 1922, however, Savage ran short of money when her job as an apartment caretaker was terminated. The Cooper Union Advisory Council, impressed with her work, supplied her with funds to cover her living expenses. Savage completed the four-year course of study at the Cooper Union in three years.

Reading in art history at the 135th Street branch of the New York Public Library, Savage came to the attention of librarian Sadie Peterson. Peterson persuaded the friends of the library to commission a bust of W. E. B. Du Bois (1923, Schomburg Center, missing since 1960) from Savage. Savage soon received other commissions, including one for Marcus Garvey (c. 1923–1930, private collection). At this time Savage met Garvey's associate, the lawyer Robert L. Poston. Savage and Poston married in 1923, but Poston died returning from Liberia four months after the marriage.

In 1923 Savage applied to study at the school of fine arts at the Palace of Fontainebleau under a program sponsored by the French government. Before Savage's application was complete, her application fee was returned and she was rejected. Savage enlisted the aid of Alfred W. Martin, leader of the Ethical Culture Society, who learned that Savage had been rejected because she was black and the other students might feel uncomfortable in her presence. Savage's rejection soon became a *cause célèbre* and attracted front-page stories in the New York papers and support from a range of well-known figures including the noted Columbia University anthropologist Franz Boas.

Pleading her own case in the press, Savage's letter to the *New York World*, headlined "Augusta Savage on Negro Ideals," appeared on 20 May 1923. In this eloquent appeal for equality in the art world, Savage queried: "how am I to compete with other American artists if I am not to be given the same opportunity." She concluded with "But we do want—and we have a right to seek—the chance to prove that we are men and women with powers and possibilities similar to those of other men and women." Hermon MacNeil, president of the National Sculpture Society, after unsuccessfully interceding on Savage's behalf, invited her to study with him that summer at his studio.

For the next several years Savage exhibited regularly at the Harmon Foundation, which had been created by the white businessman-philanthropist William E. Harmon to promote black art. She also exhibited at the Sesquicentennial Exposition in Philadelphia (1926) and the 135th Street branch of New York Public Library.

Gamin (1929, Schomburg Center) is a typical work of this period. The bust portrays a street-smart youth modeled on her nephew, and it is considered a landmark in the portrayal of African-American subjects by African-American artists. The popular success of *Gamin* brought Savage to the attention of Eugene Kinckle Jones of the National Urban League and others, who succeeded in getting Savage a Julius Rosenwald Fellowship for two consecutive years. The African-American community supplemented the scholarships with money raised in parties in Harlem and Greenwich Village and from groups across the country.

Arriving in Paris in 1929, Savage studied at the Académie de la Grande Chaumière with Félix Beauneteaux. The following year she exhibited at the Grand Palais and won citations at the Salons d'Automne et de Printemps. While in Europe Savage also briefly studied with the portrait sculptor Charles Despiau and traveled through France, Belgium, and Germany with the help of a Carnegie Foundation grant.

Returning to New York in late 1931, Savage exhibited at the Argent Gallery and the Anderson Art Galleries, both in New York City. Some critics felt her work suffered from her European studies. James A. Porter, in *Modern Negro Art* (1943, p. 128) noted that she "set aside her own convictions to learn technics and to carve subjects that communicate a certain *joie de vivre*—but which also happen to be trivial." Among her works from this period are *Terpsichore at Rest* (1932, private collection), which depicts a reclining nude female, and *Bust of a Woman* (1934, location unknown), a work in white marble that is reminiscent of the work of Auguste Rodin.

Savage received portrait commissions from prominent figures such as James Weldon Johnson and the radio personality Major Edward Bowes. Her portrait of the entertainer Ted Upshure (1934, location unknown) resulted in her becoming the first black artist elected to the National Association of Women Painters and Sculptors. Opening her own school in New York, the Savage Studio of Arts and Crafts, she attracted a number of young artists including William Artis.

In 1936 Savage became an assistant supervisor for the WPA's Federal Art Project (FAP) and in 1937 the director of the influential Harlem Community Art Center, one of the most successful of the FAP community art centers. Among the artists she assisted there were Jacob Lawrence, Elton C. Fax, and Gwendolyn Knight (Savage completed a bust of Knight in 1934, private collection).

In 1939 Savage received a commission for the New York World's Fair. Choosing to celebrate African-American music, Savage created *Lift Every Voice and Sing* (also known as *The Harp*). Inspired by the Rosamond and James Weldon Johnson song of the same title, the large (16′) painted plaster sculpture depicted a choir in the form of a giant harp. Popular with fair-goers, countless miniature reproductions and postcards of the work were sold. At the close of the fair Savage lacked the funds to store the work or have it cast in metal, and it was destroyed. Savage's portrait of Johnson, by then head of the NAACP (1939, Schomburg Center), completed in the same year, is a powerful portrayal of the NAACP leader. This same year Savage opened her own gallery, the Salon of Contemporary Negro Art, in Harlem. Though exhibiting the work of a number of prominent artists, including Lois Mailou Jones and Meta Warrick Fuller, the gallery closed within a few months. Planning a nine-city tour of her works in 1940, Savage opened her exhibition in Chicago to large crowds but few sales, and the expense of shipping the works back to New York forced many to be abandoned or destroyed. Today only a small portion of Savage's works can be located.

James A. Porter has noted that "Because Miss Savage has been so unsparing of her time and strengths in the cause of art education, she has lost valuable hours that otherwise would have been devoted to her own creative efforts" (*Modern Negro Art*, 1943, p. 128). However, one of her last works, *The Pugilist* (1943, Schomburg Center), a half-length depiction of a proudly defiant boxer, is a fine example of her expression of character.

After 1945 Savage effectively retired from the art world, living in Saugerties, New York. She taught art to children, wrote children's stories and mysteries (none published), and worked at odd jobs including that of assistant to a mushroom grower. Her own artistic production ceased. In failing health, Savage returned to live with her daughter in New York City, where she died.

• Much of Savage's work has been lost and is only documented in photographs. The largest collection of her work is held by the New York Public Library (Schomburg Center for Research in Black Culture). Other examples are in the collections of Howard University, Washington, D.C.; Yale University; and the DuSable Museum of African American Heritage, Chicago. Primary source material on Savage's career on the Federal Art Project may be found at the Archives of American Art, Smithsonian Institution. Additional materials are in the collections of the Julius Rosenwald Fund Archives, Fisk University. An important biographical source is Romare Bearden and Harry Henderson, "Augusta Savage," in *A History of African-American Artists from 1792 to the Present* (1993). Elton C. Fax (a student and associate of Savage's), "Augusta Savage," in *The Dictionary of American Negro Biography* (1982), pp. 542–43, is a valuable reference. See also Reginia A. Perry, "Augusta Savage" in *Free Within Ourselves: African-American Artists in the Collection of the National Museum of American Art* (1992); "Augusta Savage: An Autobiography," in *Crisis* 36 (Aug. 1929): 269; Eric D. Walrond, "Florida Girl Shows Amazing Gift for Sculpture" (unidentified clipping, c. 1923 located in Savage's file at the National Museum of American Art/National Portrait Gallery Library, Smithsonian Institution); and Charlotte Streifer Rubinstein, *American Women Artists from Early Indian Times to the Present* (1982). See the exhibition catalogs, Catherine Bernard, *Afro-American Artists in Paris: 1919–1939* (Hunter College, 1989), and *Augusta Savage and the Art Schools of Harlem* (New York Public Library, 1988). Obituaries are in the *New York Times* and the *New York Herald-Tribune*, both 27 Mar. 1962.

MARTIN R. KALFATOVIC

SAVAGE, Edward (26 Nov. 1761–6 July 1817), artist and museum proprietor, was born in Princeton, Massachusetts, the son of Seth Savage and Lydia Craige, occupations unknown. Savage, a self-taught artist, may have worked first as a goldsmith. His earliest paintings include a naively proportioned group portrait of his parents, grandfather, and siblings (c. 1779, Worcester Art Museum), copies of portraits by Boston colonial artist John Singleton Copley, a full-length portrait of Abraham Whipple, a Rhode Island sea captain (1786, U.S. Naval Academy, Annapolis), and miniatures of himself and his fiancée, Sarah Seaver (c. 1791, Worcester Art Museum).

In 1789 Savage offered to paint George Washington's likeness for Harvard College. The sittings took place in New York City in the winter of 1789–1790. While finishing the portrait (Harvard University Portrait Collection), Savage began *The Washington Family* (National Gallery of Art), a large group portrait of George and Martha Washington, their grandchildren, Eleanor Parke Custis and George Washington Parke Custis, and an unidentified black servant. The painting has become his best-known work. In 1791, leaving the group portrait unfinished, he went to London, where he engraved his own images of Washington and General Henry Knox, the American secretary of war, and studied painting by copying two of Benjamin West's most popular works, *William Penn's Treaty with the Indians* and *Cupid Stung by a Bee*. Returning to Massachusetts in 1794, he placed on view his "Columbian Exhibition of Pictures and Prints" at Franklin

Hall in Boston (*Massachusetts Mercury*, 27 May, 1 Aug. 1794), including his 130-by-20-foot panorama of London (unlocated). In 1794 he married Sarah Seaver in Boston; they had eight children.

By the summer of 1795 Savage was in Philadelphia, where he exhibited his painting of London, the first panorama seen in that city. He completed *The Washington Family* and placed it with a "large collection of ancient and modern Paintings and Prints" in his new Columbian Gallery, which he opened on Washington's birthday, 1796 (*Gazette of the United States*, 20 Feb. 1796). He worked successfully as a painter and engraver in Philadelphia until 1801 and exhibited the panorama in New York City (1797) and Charleston, South Carolina (1798), where he also painted portraits. He opened a new exhibition gallery in Philadelphia in 1800 that included works by "several of the first masters in Europe, together with some original American Historical Paintings" (*Aurora*, 4 Apr. 1800). To complete his own paintings and engravings during these years, Savage relied considerably on the assistance of John Wesley Jarvis, his apprentice from about 1796 to 1801, and David Edwin, a skilled engraver who emigrated from England in 1797. They and others later claimed that their talents added significantly to the quality of Savage's work.

In 1801, after visiting Baltimore and perhaps Washington, Savage moved to New York City, where he reopened his Columbian Gallery at the Pantheon at 80 Greenwich Street. There he exhibited over two hundred paintings, prints, and sculptures by himself and others. His own work included *Columbus's First Landing in the New World*, which was "the size of life," and engravings of "The Washington Family, Liberty, Columbus, Etna, Vesuvius, a large whole length of Washington . . . and many other Prints," which were for sale (*Mercantile Advertiser*, 18 Nov. 1801). In 1802 Savage acquired the collection of "Natural History and Curiosities" of the American Museum, founded by the Tammany Society in 1791, naming the newly combined institution the Columbian Gallery of Painting and City Museum. He advertised that "the Museum will be arranged, agreeably to the ideas of Sir Hans Sloane, and with the addition of a number of Paintings, and other interesting articles, will form a complete source of amusement for every class, particularly the amateurs of Arts and Sciences" (*Daily Advertiser*, 10 June 1802). Among its exhibits over the next two years were a large painting of the mastodon skeleton that Charles Willson Peale had unearthed in 1801, apparatuses for demonstrating electrical experiments, life-sized wax figures by John Christian Rauschner, and a collection of preserved animals and plants from Cayenne, South America. In the summer of 1803 Savage offered profile portraits made with a mechanical copying device called a physiognotrace, advertising the same attraction in Boston that autumn (*Columbian Centinel*, 14 Sept.; *New England Palladium*, 23 Sept. and 11 Oct. 1803). He leased the rotunda of the Pantheon to the fledgling American Academy of Fine Arts in 1803–1805 for the display of its collection of casts of

antique statues and moved the museum to 166 Greenwich Street. During these years he continued to work on his own scenes of American historical events, including an eight-by-eleven-foot painting of the signing of the Declaration of Independence. Charles Bird King and Ethan Allen Greenwood were his apprentices during these years.

In the summer of 1806 Savage made a sketching trip through New Jersey and New York. The views that he drew, primarily of waterfalls (Worcester Art Museum and the Rush Rhees Library, University of Rochester), may have been intended for a series of engraved landscape views that he planned to publish. He made a second sketching trip in the summer and autumn of 1807 in New England, New York, Pennsylvania, and Virginia, with similar results. By this time his wife and children had moved back to Princeton, Massachusetts. He, too, returned to Massachusetts permanently, probably in 1810, the year he also painted portraits briefly in Baltimore (*American, and Commercial Daily Advertiser*, 19 Mar. 1810). In 1812 Savage opened the New York Museum in Boylston Hall, Boston. After he died at his farm in Princeton, his obituary in the Boston *Columbian Centinel* (12 July 1817), described him as "proprietor of the New York Museum, lately exhibited in this town—and an eminent painter and engraver."

As one of the first American proprietors of a museum, Savage was less successful than his contemporary Charles Willson Peale. In addition, many of his paintings were never completed or have not survived, making an assessment of his work difficult. But his ambitions were considerable and his achievements admirable. Savage was one of a number of American artists in the early republic who recognized the commercial value of paintings and prints of contemporary events and public figures, as well as the popularity of public exhibitions.

• The inventory of Savage's museum in Boston with that of his property in Princeton and his administrator's accounts are in the Worcester County Probate Records, series A, no. 52130. The earliest essay on Savage is William Dunlap's negative comment on his personality and reliance on other artists *A History of the Rise and Progress of the Arts of Design in the United States* (2 vols., 1834), vol. 1, p. 321, and vol. 2, pp. 75–76. Recent biographies are Harold E. Dickson, "The Great Savage," in *John Wesley Jarvis, American Painter; 1780–1840* (1949), and Louisa Dresser, "Edward Savage, 1761–1817," *Art in America* 40 (Autumn 1952): 155–212, which lists his known work. Rita Gottesman reproduced a review of his New York museum in "New York's First Major Art Show," *New-York Historical Society Quarterly* 43 (July 1959): 288–305. Savage's advertisements are published in Alfred Coxe Prime, *The Arts and Crafts in Philadelphia, Maryland and South Carolina*, vol. 2, *1786–1800* (1933), pp. 33–34, and in Gottesman, *The Arts and Crafts in New York, 1777–1799* (1954), p. 18, and *The Arts and Crafts in New York, 1800–1804* (1965), pp. 25–26, 29–37, 60–62, 68–69, 89, 91, 407, 426–27, and 448–50. More recent comments on his activities are found in Dresser, "Studies in the Portraiture of New England," *Apollo*, n.s., 94, no. 118 (1971): 477–80; Wendy Wick, *George Washington, an American Icon* (1982), pp. 43–44, and 122–24; Lillian B. Miller et al., *The Selected Papers of Charles Willson Peale and His Family*, vol. 2 (1988), pp. 113–14, 744, 913, 932, and 934; Carrie J. Rebora, "The American Academy of the Fine Arts, New York, 1802–1842" (Ph.D. diss., City Univ. of New York, 1990); and Susan E. Strickler, ed., *American Traditions in Watercolor: The Worcester Art Museum Collection* (1987), pp. 68–69 and 217–20. Some advertisements are cited through the generosity of the Museum of Early Southern Decorative Arts, Winston-Salem, N.C., and Peter Benes, Concord, Mass.

ELLEN G. MILES

SAVAGE, Henry Wilson (21 Mar. 1859–29 Nov. 1927), real estate entrepreneur and theatrical manager, was born in New Durham, New Hampshire, the son of Captain M. Henry Savage and Betsey Woodhouse. He graduated from Harvard University in 1880 with an A.B. degree and entered the field of real estate. For fifteen years he built up a thriving real-estate business before he switched careers almost accidentally. In 1894 Savage built the Castle Square Theatre in Boston as an investment. The following year the manager of a light opera troupe deserted his company, and the desperate performers turned to Savage for assistance. Savage took over the operation and began his managerial career on 6 May 1895 with his company presenting light opera in English. The Castle Square Opera Company soon gained a large following and a reputation for high-quality musical productions offered at reasonable prices. Savage arranged extensive nationwide tours for his company, and eventually it branched out to Romantic opera and grand opera, presenting *The Bohemian Girl*, *Faust*, *Der Freischütz*, *Lohengrin*, *Tannhäuser*, *Die Meistersinger*, and *Romeo and Juliet*. All the operas were presented in English, an uncommon practice at that time and a distinctive feature of the Savage productions. In the fall of 1900 he presented a well-received series of operas in English at the Metropolitan Opera House in New York. By 1900, in addition to the standard repertory, Savage was producing original musicals in Chicago, New York, and Boston. *The Sultan of Sulu* (Alfred G. Walthall, composer; 1902), *The Prince of Pilsen* (Gustav Luders; 1903), and *The Sho-Gun* (Luders; 1904) all debuted in Chicago at the Studebaker Theatre. Meanwhile, in the East he inaugurated *The Yankee Consul* (Alfred Robyn) and *Peggy from Paris* (William Lorraine) both in 1903, and *Woodland* (Luders) a year later. For over twenty-five years, through the Henry Savage Grand Opera Company and other organizations, Savage produced a remarkable list of productions, several of which were especially noteworthy. In 1904 Savage gave Richard Wagner's *Parsifal* its first production in English. In 1906 Savage produced the splendid and sumptuous American premiere of Giacomo Puccini's *Madame Butterfly*, also in English. He followed that in 1911 with a production of Puccini's *The Girl of the Golden West*. Perhaps the highlight of Savage's career occurred in 1907, when he secured the American rights to produce *The Merry Widow*, an operetta by the Austro-Hungarian composer Franz Lehár. That presentation enjoyed a phenom-

enal success, running in New York and in touring companies for several years and spawning a rage not only for its beautiful waltz music but for auxiliary items of fashion as well. In 1910 his production of *Everywoman*, an updated morality play by Walter Browne with music by George Chadwick, gained surprising popularity. His production of *Have a Heart* in 1917 united Jerome Kern's music with lyrics by P. G. Wodehouse and a book by Guy Bolton. Kern also produced the music for *Head over Heels* the following year. Other significant musical productions included *King Dodo* (Luders; 1902), *Sari* (Emmerich Kalman; 1914), *See-Saw* (Louis Hirsch; 1919), *Lady Billy* (Harold Levey; 1920), *The Clinging Vine* (Levey; 1922), and *Lollipop* (Vincent Youmans; 1924).

Although most of his attention was given to opera and musical comedy, Savage also produced several notable nonmusical plays. Chicago journalist George Ade had mimicked Gilbert and Sullivan in writing the librettos for *The Sultan of Sulu* and *The Sho-Gun*, and in 1903 and 1904 Savage successfully produced Ade's comedies of small-town life, *The County Chairman* and *The College Widow*. In 1908 Savage put on *The Devil*, starring George Arliss, which introduced the Hungarian dramatist Ferenc Molnár to American audiences. Other notable nonmusicals included the 1911 farce *Excuse Me*, by Rupert Hughes, and the 1920 comedy *Shavings*, by Pauline Phelps and Marion Short. Savage's last production was *Lass o' Laughter*, a comedy by Edith Carter and Nan Marriott Watson, in 1925.

Savage was best remembered, in the words of the *New York Times*, as "the first impresario to present grand opera in English," and Edward Ellsworth Hipsher, in his book on American opera, called Savage "the most successful American champion which Opera in English has known." His productions were invariably tasteful, sometimes lavish, and always assembled with a businesslike efficiency that sometimes overshadowed their aesthetic elegance. Savage also represented the very antithesis of the star system, for instead of engaging expensive star performers and building his productions around them, he created balanced productions, often using youthful performers who went on to star with other opera companies. Savage was president of his own firm, Henry W. Savage, Incorporated. He served as director of the National Theatrical Producing Managers for many years and was the president of that organization from 1907 to 1909. He had married Alice Louise Batcheler in 1889; they had two children. After Savage began producing in New York, he lived in Ridgefield, New Jersey. In his later years he wintered at Jensen, Florida, and he died in Boston.

• Clippings, programs, letters, and other documents and information are available at the Theatre Collection at Harvard University and in the Billy Rose Theatre Collection at the New York Public Library for the Performing Arts. Henry Edward Krehbiel, *Chapters of Opera* (1979), and Edward

Ellsworth Hipsher, *American Opera and Its Composers* (1934; repr. 1978), mention Savage. An obituary is in the *New York Times*, 30 Nov. 1927.

ROGER A. HALL

SAVAGE, John Lucian (25 Dec. 1879–28 Dec. 1967), civil engineer, was born near Cooksville, Wisconsin, the son of Edwin Parker Savage and Mary Therese Stebbins, farmers. As a boy he worked on neighboring farms and earned enough to pay board and tuition for the first two years at the Hillside Home (High) School near Spring Green, where he became something of a Latin scholar. After his money ran out he transferred to nearby Madison High School and graduated in 1899. He then matriculated at the University of Wisconsin and worked during the summers as a draftsman for the Geological Survey of Wisconsin and as a surveyor for the U.S. Geological Survey. He received a B.S. in civil engineering in 1903 and was about to begin teaching at Purdue University when he was offered a position as an engineering aide with the newly formed U.S. Reclamation Service.

Savage joined the service's Idaho Division and assisted in the design of a number of irrigation-related structures. He was promoted to assistant engineer in 1903 and became the division's engineer in charge of design and construction in 1905. In 1908 he joined the Boise-based consulting engineering firm of Andrew J. Wiley, with whom he had worked on several projects and who specialized in the design and construction of private irrigation and hydroelectric projects in Idaho. Savage spent much of his time in the field inspecting and consulting on a variety of hydraulic construction projects involving dams, power plants, and irrigation canals. Although private engineering proved to be lucrative employment, he yearned to participate in much larger design projects than Wiley's firm could handle. In 1916 he returned to the Reclamation Service and was assigned to the newly organized Office of the Chief Engineer in Denver, Colorado, as the engineer in charge of civil engineering design. Two years later he married Jessie Burdick Sexsmith; they had no children.

In 1924 Savage was made chief designing engineer, a position that gave him responsibility for all of the renamed Bureau of Reclamation's civil, electrical, and mechanical engineering design. In this capacity he designed dams, canals, and other irrigation-related structures throughout eleven western states, the most impressive projects being Hoover, Grand Coulee, Parker, and Shasta dams. Because the first three were respectively the highest, widest, and deepest dams in the world at the time of their construction, Savage and his design team developed trial-load analysis for determining actual versus theoretical stresses in arched dams as well as models for determining concrete deterioration, land subsidence, and increased seismicity caused by the weight of a mammoth dam. Much of this work was performed by the bureau's Technical Engineering Analysis and Laboratory Division, which was organized by Savage.

His greatest accomplishment was the design of Hoover Dam, the supreme engineering feat of its day. Designed to control the unpredictable and disastrous flooding of the Colorado River, the project called for erecting at Black Canyon an arched concrete structure 1,244 feet long at the crest and 726 feet high, more than twice the height of the highest dam in the world. Because of its height, he had to devise new methods for shaping abutment excavations. Because of its volume, he had to devise a method that would prevent almost 4.5 million cubic yards of concrete from cracking as it expanded and contracted during the curing process, which under normal conditions would have taken over 100 years. Savage designed a chilled-water piping system that was imbedded in the pour forms, developed a pouring schedule by which the individual sections were poured in a modified checkerboard pattern, and devised a finishing process whereby all the sections were grouted together after the concrete had cured. The result was a crack-free structure ready for operation in 1935 after only four years of construction. Savage's innovations in pouring and curing massive volumes of concrete became standard procedure for large-scale concrete construction projects throughout the world. Only slightly less challenging were the Colorado River's Parker Dam, completed in 1938 after its foundation was extended 253 feet below the river bed; Washington's Grand Coulee Dam, completed in 1942 after massive grouting was required to treat the shear zones in more than ten million cubic yards of concrete; and California's Shasta Dam, the world's second biggest dam in terms of height and volume at the time of its completion in 1944 after concrete-filled trenches and deep cutoff shafts were constructed to treat fault zones.

Savage retired in 1945 but continued to serve the bureau as its chief consulting engineer. He also became an independent consultant and participated in post–World War II reconstruction by providing design and construction advice to nineteen foreign governments. In 1950, ten years after his first wife had died, he married Olga Lacher Miner; they had no children. He retired from his consulting business in 1953 to Englewood, Colorado, where he died.

Savage served as American vice president of the International Commission on Large Dams of the World Power Conference from 1937 to 1939 and from 1946 to 1947 and as a member of the Point Four Program's International Development Advisory Board from 1951 to 1953. He was awarded the Colorado Engineering Council's Gold Medal in 1937, the John Fritz Gold Medal in 1945, the American Concrete Institute's Henry C. Turner Gold Medal in 1946, the Western Society of Engineers' Washington Award in 1949, and the U.S. Department of Interior's Gold Medal in 1950. He was made a life member of the American Society of Civil Engineers in 1942 and was elected to the National Academy of Sciences in 1949, the Reclamation Hall of Fame in 1950, and the Popular Mechanics Hall of Fame in 1952.

Because of the number, size, and cost of the hydraulic structures he designed, Savage acquired the sobriquets "Jack Dam" and the first "billion dollar American engineer." The forty major dams that he designed for the American West provided that region with irrigation and power and greatly stimulated the growth and development of its economy and population.

• Savage's papers are in the University of Wyoming's American Heritage Center. A biography is Abel Wolman and W. H. Lyles, "John Lucian Savage," National Academy of Sciences, *Biographical Memoirs* 49 (1978): 225–38. Obituaries are in the *New York Times*, 29 Dec. 1967, *Time*, 5 Jan. 1968, and *Newsweek*, 8 Jan. 1968.

CHARLES W. CAREY, JR.

SAVAGE, Minot Judson (10 June 1841–22 May 1918), Unitarian minister, was born in Norridgewock, Maine, the son of James Lambert Savage and Anne Swett Stinson, farmers. Raised under the religious influences of Calvinism and Methodist revivalism, he wrestled with the question of his salvation in his early years. "From my earliest thought on the subject, I grew up in the unquestioning belief that I must experience a 'change of heart,' or I could have no hope of salvation in the future world." Although he experienced what he felt at the time was a conversion experience, he was later wracked with doubts about its validity. "At last, I gave it up, thinking I had done all I could, and that perhaps the experience was genuine." On this basis he joined the Congregational church: "I stood by and heard the creed read, almost no part of which did I understand." Even so, Savage prepared for the ministry, graduating from Bangor Theological Seminary in 1864. He married Ella Godfrey Dodge that year, and four children were born to their marriage.

After serving as a home missionary in California (1864–1867), Savage held Congregational pastorates in Framingham, Massachusetts (1867–1869), and Hannibal, Missouri (1869–1872), but endured "pain [which] sometimes came to be almost unbearable" as he struggled with his religious beliefs in the light of the theory of evolution. His struggle eventuated in his conversion to Unitarianism in 1872. In Unitarianism he found a denomination that accorded well with his speculative bent of mind and deep interest in science and its implications for religion. He served as pastor of the Third Unitarian Church of Chicago (1873–1874), forming there a deep friendship with Robert Collyer, who was then minister of the Unity Church. Savage then served as minister of the Church of the Unity in Boston (1874–1896), where as Maxwell Savage reported, "he preached to thronging congregations and his sermons were printed every week and circulated in thousands all over the world." He was an impressive pulpit orator, who, through rigorous preparation, was able to deliver his sermons without a manuscript or notes. He was also influential in denominational affairs, serving on the Council of the National Conference of Unitarian Churches and the American Unitari-

an Association Board of Directors. In 1896 he joined Collyer as his associate at the Church of the Messiah in New York, where he served until 1906. During his New York ministry, Savage suffered from increasingly frequent attacks of vertigo, and a collapse in health forced his retirement in 1906. He died in Boston.

Savage's principal theological concern was to reconcile religion with the modern scientific worldview. He believed that "when there passes any great change over the scientific thought of men, there must of necessity go along with it a corresponding change in theological thought and religious feeling." He made one of the first and most thorough attempts to develop an optimistic religious interpretation from the theory of evolution, and in *The Religion of Evolution* (1876) he urged that his readers look beyond the conflict of science and religion to see how "science has exalted our concept of God, of the universe, of the nature of man and the grandeur of human destiny." Savage argued that, ironically, "religion has been an unspeakable gainer by being defeated in its conflicts with science," since it had been forced continually to enlarge its conception of the nature of the universe and of humanity.

Savage conceived the "God of evolution" as "the hidden life and secret force of this unfolding universe," and he explained salvation as "coming into perfect accord with the whole life and movement of things." In his version of optimistic evolutionary progress, Savage argued that Christianity itself was the product of evolutionary forces and that the religious life could be understood only in terms of a never-ending process of growth. While "the popular forms and creeds and institutions may be outgrown, and replaced by better, the essential spirit and life of Christianity will become more and more the essence and spirit of evolution itself." Such reformulations of familiar Christian concepts answered the need of his age, whose capacity for belief had been threatened, but whose desire for belief remained intense.

• Savage's theology was spelled out in a series of books, including *The Religion of Evolution* (1876), *The Morals of Evolution* (1880), *Belief in God* (1881), and *Life Beyond Death* (1899). His account of his early religious experience is contained in the initial chapters of *My Creed* (1887). Biographical information can be found in Maxwell Savage, "Minot Judson Savage," in *Heralds of a Liberal Faith*, vol. 4, ed. Samuel A. Eliot (1952); and David Robinson, *The Unitarians and the Universalists* (1985).

DAVID M. ROBINSON

SAVAGE, Thomas Staughton (7 June 1804–29 Dec. 1880), Episcopal clergyman, missionary, and physician, was born in Middletown (now Cromwell), Connecticut, the son of Josiah Savage, a ship owner and trader, and Mary Roberts. He was raised a Congregationalist in a wealthy family and attended Yale College, from which he graduated in 1825. He received his M.D. from the Yale Medical School in 1833 and then traveled extensively throughout the United States. Savage then entered the Virginia Theological

Seminary, Alexandria, from which he graduated in 1836. He was ordained deacon on 17 July 1836 and priest on 23 October 1836.

The missionary spirit within the Episcopal church was awakened in 1820–1821 with the organization of the Domestic and Foreign Missionary Society of the Protestant Episcopal Church. The missionary spirit created a sense of responsibility to carry the gospel to the destitute millions of Africa. In 1835 three students at Virginia Seminary, after much prayerful consultation, decided to devote their lives to the African mission. These three were Launcelot Byrd Minor, John Payne, later the first bishop of Liberia, and Savage. Savage had been appointed as missionary to Persia to assist Horatio Southgate, but he decided later that because of the dangers of the African climate his medical skills would be more valuable there than in Persia. Accordingly he sailed for Africa on 1 November 1836 and reached Cape Palmas, Liberia, on 25 December 1836. So deep was his interest in this work that as he stepped on the deck he exclaimed, "I am going home." The secretary of the foreign board of the Domestic and Foreign Missionary Society wrote Savage a letter that provided "the design of the Mission to Cape Palmas," which became the charter for Episcopal missionary work in Africa. He was instructed to explore the country and ascertain the character of the natives and their reaction to religion: "In making personal excursions into the country, you may become an exploring Missionary" (Dunn, p. 52). He was to study the language of the natives and their dialects, "with a view to their gradual reduction to a written tongue." He was to plan the establishment of a high school that would not only inculcate knowledge and habits of industry, but would also provide religious and school teachers for the Africans. As a physician he was to heal the sick, but first he was to be a faithful dispenser of the word of God and God's holy sacraments. "You are to make this a primary object, and your medical services must be subordinate or rather auxiliary to it" (Dunn, p. 53). Above all Savage was to be a Christian missionary who would form a visible Church of Christ, a congregation of faithful people, under the ordinances of the Church. "The great aim of your mission is toward the native African. You are to establish a mission which seeks nothing less than the Christianizing of Africa . . . the redemption of Africa" (Dunn, pp. 52, 55).

Upon his arrival at Cape Palmas, Savage began to work with James Madison Thompson and his wife, Elizabeth Mars Johnson Thompson, a black couple who had gone to Liberia in 1833. In March 1837 Savage moved the mission from Cape Palmas to a new location, named Mt. Vaughan, where he preached every Sunday. He explored extensively in accordance with the instructions of the foreign secretary, and his health gave way. On 30 April 1838 he returned to the United States. In June 1838 he married Susan Metcalf in Fredericksburg, Virginia. They returned to Africa and reached Cape Palmas on 23 January 1839, but Susan Savage died three months later, "the first of that heroic band who died that Africa might live" (Good-

win, vol. 2, p. 302). In 1842 Maria Chapin joined the mission, and in June 1842 she and Savage married. She died in December 1842. In June 1843 Savage returned to the United States to recuperate; on 18 May 1844 he and four other missionaries sailed for Liberia. In December 1844 he married Elizabeth Rutherford of Providence, Rhode Island, one of the four missionaries he had journeyed with. They had no children. Savage worked at Fishtown, Liberia, in 1845–1846 and resigned the mission work in December 1846.

While in Africa, Savage studied the skulls and bones of an unknown animal that was later determined to be the gorilla. Back in the United States, he published about this animal in the *Boston Journal of Natural History* (Dec. 1847, Apr. 1843, Jan. 1844). He also published scientific articles in 1850 in the *Proceedings* of the Academy of Natural Sciences of Philadelphia.

From 1 October 1848 until late 1849, Savage was rector of St. James Church, Livingston, Alabama. On 1 December 1849 he became rector of Trinity Church, Pass Christian, Mississippi, and served there until 1857. From 1857 to 1868 he lived in Pass Christian and served at different times as rector of Trinity Church, rector of Trinity Female School, principal of a military school, and associate principal of the female school. In 1869 he was named associate secretary of the foreign committee of the Board of Missions of the Episcopal church. When the board was reorganized he retired, and from 1871 until his death he served the Church of the Ascension, Rhinecliff, Dutchess County, New York. Savage died at Rhinecliff.

• There is no collection of Savage's papers. His life and work is discussed rather completely in William Archer Rutherfoord Goodwin, *History of the Theological Seminary in Virginia and Its Historical Background* (2 vols., 1923, 1924), and in E. F. Hening, *History of the African Mission of the Protestant Episcopal Church in the United States, with Memoirs of Deceased Missionaries, and Notices of Native Customs* (1850). D. Elwood Dunn, *A History of the Episcopal Church in Liberia, 1821–1980* (1992), also treats Savage rather completely. Another helpful study is Artley Beeber Parson, "The Beginning of the Church in Liberia," *Historical Magazine of the Protestant Episcopal Church* 7 (June 1938): 154–77.

DONALD S. ARMENTROUT

SAVERY, William (1722–May 1787), cabinetmaker, is known today almost entirely through his furniture and through isolated historical references. Nothing is known of his parents, birth, or boyhood, although he probably moved to Philadelphia in 1740. Relatively recent discovery of a 1741 receipt issued to John Wister and signed by Savery acknowledging payment "for the use of My Master Salomon Fussel [*sic*] & me" (Winterthur Museum, John Wister Receipt Book, 1736–1745) documents Savery's apprenticeship. Given Savery's date of birth, he probably remained apprenticed until about 1742. Little is known about Solomon Fussell, who was a turner, or Savery's training under him. Fussell's account book describes production of turned chairs, suggesting that Savery was probably trained as a turner. His name appears as a member of the Fellowship Fire Company in 1745. Records of the Society of Friends note his marriage to Mary Peters in Philadelphia in 1746; they had eleven children. In 1750 Savery described himself as "Chair-maker in Second Street" in a newspaper notice. His public offices included appointment as assessor of some central wards of Philadelphia in 1754 and as tax agent and collector for guardians of the poor in 1767. Monthly Meeting records list Savery's burial on 28 May 1787.

Savery's name first came to public notice in 1913, when Luke Vincent Lockwood published both a walnut Chippendale-style dressing table and the printed Savery label applied to its upper drawer in his pioneering study *Colonial Furniture in America* (2d ed.). Five years later R. T. Haines Halsey supplied biographical information in "William Savery, the Colonial Cabinet-maker and His Furniture." More important, Halsey attributed several elaborate high chests and dressing tables in the Palmer Collection at the Metropolitan Museum of Art to Savery. Savery's reputation continued to grow as other researchers followed Halsey's lead and expanded the body of furniture believed to have been made by him.

The revised understanding of Savery as a furniture maker of more modest achievements, which characterizes his place in history, began in the work of William Macphearson Hornor, Jr. ("William Savery, Chair-maker and Joiner," *Philadelphia Museum Bulletin* [Feb. 1928]: 14–20, and *Blue Book, Philadelphia Furniture: William Penn to George Washington* [1953]). Through illustration of several labeled chairs and documented references to other furniture forms, Hornor demonstrates that Savery's work focused on fabrication of simpler, more utilitarian objects as well as routine furniture repair. Savery produced many inexpensive, turned slat-back chairs made of maple and having rush seats, which exemplify the practice of making these furniture forms in urban settings. In comparison, he made fewer ornamented case pieces, such as walnut chests of drawers, carved Chippendale-style chairs, and the Wharton family mahogany high chest (Philadelphia Museum of Art), which have received so much attention.

Since publication of these early studies, cabinetmakers such as Thomas Affleck and Benjamin Randolph and carvers James Reynolds and the partnership of Nicholas Bernard and Martin Jugiez have replaced Savery as the principal exemplars of the distinctive and acclaimed Philadelphia school of furniture making in the Chippendale style. When General John Cadwalader ordered furniture for his Philadelphia mansion in 1770–1772, for example, he commissioned Affleck and Randolph for important mahogany parlor furniture. Savery billed Cadwalader for making walnut chests and chairs destined for bedrooms and a pine cupboard and tables for the kitchen. Savery's shop burned on 30 January 1772 while he executed the Cadwalader work. Despite the loss, which newspapers noted was considerable, his billing dates suggest he was back in business by July.

Scholarly interest in Savery's life and work has shifted to its value as representative of broader consumer tastes and craft practices. Ongoing research has brought to light the approximately twenty-five pieces of furniture bearing one of Savery's six known printed labels. Further details about his training and patrons contribute to an evolving biography of Savery as a competent and successful, if not leading, furniture maker in colonial Philadelphia.

One of the printed labels Savery used, and perhaps the earliest chronologically, states that he made "all sorts of rush bottomed chairs," like those described in Fussell's account book. However, more elaborate and expensive Savery chairs survive. They incorporate stylishly carved cabriole legs, cased seat rails, and pierced splats, pointing to craft skills beyond turning, namely joinery and carving. Savery changed his labels to advertise "all sorts of chairs and joiner's work" and his address from the shop "at the Sign of the Chair" to the "Sign of the Chest of Drawers, Coffin, and Chair," suggesting his more diversified shop skills and broader product line as his career advanced. The several chests and other pieces of case furniture bearing Savery labels attest further to his range of woodworking skills. Because manuscript evidence suggests that Savery never operated a large shop or trained many apprentices, it is likely that he personally possessed these varied skills. Thus, he exemplifies a talented and resourceful generalist in an urban craft community that increasingly depended on specialized skills and training. Like Fussell before him (who began trading in textiles in his later years), Savery expanded his own skills from turnery to joinery and cabinetmaking. Savery's life and work demonstrates the flexibility and responsiveness evident in colonial American craft practices in contrast to their more regulated English and European counterparts.

• Incidental information about Savery's life and career appears in Records of the Philadelphia Monthly Meeting in the collection of the Pennsylvania Historical Society. Solomon Fussell's account book survives in the Stephen Collins Papers in the Library of Congress. R. T. Haines Halsey's "William Savery, the Colonial Cabinet-maker and His Furniture," *Bulletin of the Metropolitan Museum of Art* (Dec. 1918): 254–67, the first notable treatment of Savery's life, takes much of its information from A. H. Savery and F. R. Taylor, *General, and Brief Biography of the Savery Family of Philadelphia* (1911). A modern biographical work appears as the short entry "William Savery" by Beatrice B. Garvan in *Philadelphia: Three Centuries of American Art* (1976), pp. 50–51. A valuable discussion of Savery's furniture making is in Benno M. Forman, "Delaware Valley 'Crookt Foot' and Slat-Back Chairs: The Fussell-Savery Connection," *Winterthur Portfolio* (Spring 1980): 41–64. See also Alfred Coxe Prime, *The Arts and Crafts in Philadelphia, Maryland, and South Carolina* (1929; repr. 1969); and Nicholas B. Wainwright, *Colonial Grandeur in Philadelphia: The House and Furniture of General John Cadwalader* (1964).

PHILIP D. ZIMMERMAN

SAVITCH, Jessica (1 Feb. 1948–23 Oct. 1983), journalist, was born Jessica Beth Savitch in Kennett Square, Pennsylvania, the daughter of David Savitch, a clothing merchant, and Florence Spadoni, a registered nurse. The eldest of the couple's three daughters, Savitch attributed her interest in journalism to her father, who insisted that dinner-table conversation be focused on current events and issues. His death, when Savitch was twelve years old, would be the first of several tragedies shaping her life. The changed financial situation of the family forced Florence Savitch to return to nursing and was a major factor years later in Savitch's decision to attend Ithaca College, the least expensive of the schools she wanted to attend. She completed a degree in communications in 1968.

Savitch noted in her 1981 autobiography, *Anchorwoman*, that at Ithaca College she faced the first of many barriers to entering a male-dominated field. When she applied for a position with the campus radio station, the faculty adviser, "with a grin," told her that "there's no place for broads in broadcasting." After complaining to the college's administration she was given a position, only to be fired immediately. She failed to turn off the station's transmitter after sign-off, one of her duties that the station manager "conveniently" neglected to tell her. Nevertheless, she worked as a disc jockey for WBBF-AM in nearby Rochester; known as "the Honeybee," she was a local celebrity. She also worked as a model and as an on-camera commercial announcer—the Dodge Girl—and acquired a reputation for daredevil stunts. Once, for example, she jumped over a new Dodge car on horseback.

Joan Showalter, the personnel director for CBS and the woman whom Savitch called her mentor, hired Savitch in September 1968 as an administrative assistant. While working at WCBS radio, Savitch met Charles Osgood and Ed Bradley, both of whom gave her encouragement, support, and advice for breaking into television news broadcasting. She applied for news positions all over the country, but only the Houston CBS affiliate, KHOU-TV, responded with an interview and ultimately a job offer. During her two years in Houston, 1970–1972, Savitch was general assignment reporter and weekend anchor. The station's cameramen were reluctant to work with her until she proved herself by covering gruesome murders and dangerous situations. She was burned when a derailed tank car exploded.

The Texas gubernatorial race of 1972 brought Savitch national exposure, and in November of that year she was hired by KYW-TV in Philadelphia, the fourth largest market in the country. Though she performed well as weekend anchor, she was never permitted to substitute for vacationing prime-time nightly news anchors—a privilege accorded her male predecessors. Savitch tried to break her five-year contract; unsuccessful, she began to champion the entry of women into the Philadelphia police force. Refuting the argument that women were not strong enough to do police work, Savitch completed the training course with first-class male recruits. Savitch's involvement with the Philadelphia police also broke another barrier. She did a five-part series on rape, which was viewed by legislatures in Pennsylvania, New Jersey, and Delaware and

was instrumental in changing laws concerning the treatment of victims and the prosecution of rapists. "Rape: The Ultimate Violation" also won the 1974 Clarion Award from Women in Communications, Inc.

At the end of her contract with KYW-TV in 1977 Savitch joined NBC News. Although the three major networks were interested in hiring women with her experience, NBC's Don Meaney gave her the best offer: Washington correspondent for the Senate and anchor on "Sunday Night News" and "Update." She covered events such as the passage of the Humphrey-Hawkins bill, the Bert Lance affair, and the Panama Canal debate. In 1979 Savitch was chosen to do the NBC magazine show "Prime Time Sunday," but her real breakthrough came in 1980 when she was assigned to be podium correspondent at both of the national conventions and anchor the House and gubernatorial desk on election night.

At this time, according to *Anchorwoman*, Savitch felt she needed some "balance" in her life: "to combine a fully satisfying personal life with a successful career." In 1974 she had been briefly engaged to Ron Kershaw; in January 1980 she married Philadelphia advertising executive Melvin Korn. Unable to strike that elusive balance, however, the couple divorced before the end of that year. In March 1981 she married Donald Rollie Payne, a Washington, D.C., gynecologist. Four months later Savitch had a miscarriage, and in August of that year Payne committed suicide after discovering he had incurable cancer.

Savitch asked to be transferred to NBC's New York City bureau. In 1982 she turned down the anchor position for NBC's "Sunrise" program. She suffered from severe ulcers. However, by 1983 Savitch seemed to be pulling her life and her career back together. She signed a new contract with NBC, and the network assigned her to cover the 1984 elections. However, on the evening of 23 October, during a heavy rainstorm, the car in which she was riding with Martin Fishbein, vice president and assistant general manager of the *New York Post*, went off the road in New Hope, Pennsylvania, and overturned in the Delaware Canal. Both Savitch and Fishbein drowned.

During her lifetime Savitch garnered many awards and honors, including four Emmys and the Alfred I. DuPont–Columbia University Award. She was also elected to serve on the Ithaca College board of trustees. A scholarship fund was created at Ithaca College in her memory, but Savitch's effort to establish women's credibility in newscasting is perhaps her most significant legacy. Her mentor Joan Showalter urged her to dispel the myths that trail professional women—that they are prima donnas, that they will not help one another, and that they are all surface and no substance. In her autobiography Savitch noted that she was "stunned" when a reporter asked her what it felt like to be a leader in the women's movement. "It was never my intention," she wrote, "to lead *any* movement. I had merely set out to be a television journalist, and in the process I became an inadvertent pioneer and was given the unrequested mantle of role model."

• Savitch's autobiography, *Anchorwoman*, and the entry in the 1983 *Current Biography Yearbook* are the most detailed treatments of her life. See also Gwenda Blair, *Almost Golden: Jessica Savitch and the Selling of Television News* (1989), and Alanna Nash, *Golden Girl: The Story of Jessica Savitch* (1988). An obituary is in the *New York Times*, 25 Oct. 1983.

JUDITH E. FUNSTON

SAWYER, Caroline M. (10 Dec. 1812–19 May 1894), author and editor, was born Caroline Mehitable Fisher in Newton, Massachusetts, the daughter of Jesse Fisher and Anna Kenrick. Her father, of whom little is known, died sometime during her childhood. Sawyer was educated at home by her maternal uncle, Enoch Kenrick, for ten years; her education exceeded that of most women of her time. She learned to recite from the Bible, to read Shakespeare and Plutarch, and to compose poetry, all before she reached her teens. She also acquired proficiency in French and German. After her father's death, she was raised in the home of her grandfather, John Kenrick, a prominent member of his community and an abolitionist.

She married Thomas Jefferson Sawyer in 1831 and took up residence in New York City, where her husband worked as a Universalist church minister and teacher of theology. Sawyer worked with her husband and devoted herself to the life of a minister's wife, finding time, in spite of the demands that came with a husband and seven children, to write. Much of her writing deals with affirming Christian virtue and reflects her firm belief in Universalist doctrine.

Sawyer wrote a great deal in the course of her life. Before her marriage she published poetry under the name of "Marpessa," but after her marriage she contributed stories, poems, and essays to journals such as the *Christian Messenger*, the *Universalist Union* (she directed its "Youth's Department" from 1840 to 1845), the *Democratic Review*, *Graham's Magazine*, the *Knickerbocker Magazine*, and the *New Yorker*.

Sawyer's first book, *The Merchant's Widow, and Other Tales* (1841), was a great success; its first edition of a thousand copies sold out in ten days. She states in the preface that she aims in these tales "not to show the deformity of vice, but to hold up virtue in its most attractive colors." The volume is a collection of short sentimental pieces, two of which ("Unequal Marriage" and "Lonely Burial") recount events to which she was "an actual, and deeply-moved spectator," and which show that "the romance of life is indeed stranger than that of fiction!" One of the fictional tales, "The Merchant's Widow," is devoted to portraying "the evils too frequently resulting from the present injudicious system of fashionable female education." The story, which argues for the importance of both an intellectual and a practical education for women, tells of a woman born and raised in the South whose training in "useful domestic skills" is neglected, left to the black slaves in her father's household. Later her lack of practical domestic training in the face of unexpected poverty leaves her unable to cope with the challenges of running a household and dealing with the needs of a family. The book was reviewed in the *New Yorker* as a work of "the gentle teachings of an earnest and holy spirit" that leaves a "deep and salutary impression" on the reader. Another critic called it "a source of instruction and of serene enjoyment."

Sawyer published a four-volume collection of her stories for children titled *The Juvenile Library* in 1845 and "The Poetry of the Hebrew Tradition" in 1847. She edited and contributed poems to *The Rose of Sharon*, an annual gift book publication, from 1850 to 1858. She also edited the *Memoir of Mrs. Julia H. Scott; With Her Poems* in 1853 and the *Ladies' Repository*, a Universalist monthly distributed in the Boston area, from 1861 to 1864. Sawyer continued writing until very near the end of her life. Her poem "The Narcissus" (1894) is said to be the last thing she wrote.

Sawyer was considered by her contemporaries to be a talented and well-educated writer and editor, but she was apparently best known for her prolific and polished skill as a poet. Her poems, as a rule, are short, predictable in diction and imagery, and memorable for their even rhythm and rhyme scheme. Her contemporaries referred to her poetry as "inspired thought" captured in a "scholarly finish." Sawyer's work as a whole testifies to her use of literary skills as a vehicle for moral instruction. Her writing reflects a combination of sentiment, virtue, and practicality dedicated to the betterment of society and, as such, is a very good example of writing within the traditional sphere of women's writing in the nineteenth century. She clearly saw the access to the public realm that her literary skills afforded her as an opportunity to be active in upholding spiritual and moral good.

Sawyer died at her home in Somerville, Massachusetts.

• See Richard Eddy, *The Life of Thomas J. Sawyer, and of Caroline M. Sawyer* (1900), for an extensive biographical account.

KATHLEEN MOORE

SAWYER, Lemuel, Jr. (1777–9 Jan. 1852), congressman and author, was born in Camden County, North Carolina, the son of Lemuel Sawyer, Sr., a planter and merchant, and Mary Taylor. His father was prominent in local and state affairs, serving as sheriff and representing his county in both the provincial congress and the general assembly. After attending the local schools, young Sawyer studied at the Flatbush Academy on Long Island from 1793 to 1796. He spent a portion of 1796 in Philadelphia as a visitor in the home of his brother-in-law Congressman Dempsey Burgess. There he dabbled in the study of mathematics at the University of Pennsylvania and acquired a lifelong habit of extravagant living.

In 1797 Sawyer returned to North Carolina as heir to a dilapidated farm and several slaves. The rural life proved dull, and in 1799 he enrolled at the University of North Carolina. His stay was brief. At age twenty-three he was elected the youngest member of the state house of commons. He served without note in the general assemblies of 1800 and 1801. An ardent Jeffersonian, he was a presidential elector in 1804. Also in 1804 he was admitted to the bar, but the legal profession was never his vocation, rather it was the stage for a career in politics. Between 1807 and 1829 he represented his coastal district in eight Congresses: the Tenth, Eleventh, Twelfth, Fifteenth, Sixteenth, Seventeenth, Nineteenth, and Twentieth. There was a hiatus in his service from 1813 to 1817, when he did not seek office, and from 1823 to 1825 because he was defeated in the election of 1822. He enjoyed the fame of office and Washington, D.C., society and probably would have remained in Congress indefinitely had his district not retired him in the election of 1828.

Sawyer was a Jeffersonian Democrat early in his career and a Jacksonian Democrat later. Referring to Thomas Jefferson's first inauguration, he said, "That glorious event affords a greater subject for joy and congratulations than the capture of Cornwallis, for by one our liberty was declared and by the other restored" (*Raleigh Register and Gazette*, 17 Dec. 1804). He supported the purchase of Louisiana and the embargo and gained a reputation as a War Hawk despite his opposition to expanding the army and navy prior to hostilities. Presidents James Madison and James Monroe enjoyed his backing, but his strict constructionist views led him to object to legislation extending federal authority. Curiously, because of his eclectic intellectual interests, Sawyer did support government expenditures for scientific exploration. In December 1825 he encouraged Congress to provide funds for a western expedition that included exploration of the Northwest coast. He believed that geological, geographic, and hydrographic surveys would promote commercial development.

Sawyer's congressional career, though long, was undistinguished at best. He seldom spoke or offered legislation and, because of poor health, was rarely in attendance in the later sessions of his tenure. His conduct was eccentric and erratic, and his comments were usually colorful. An opponent of government spending, on one occasion Sawyer said that he wished there could be stationed at the door of the Treasury "an angel with a flaming sword, to prohibit entrance to all who had not a pass from the Genius of Economy . . . countersigned by the hand of justice" (*Annals of Congress*, 15th Cong., 1st sess., Dec. 1817, p. 469). In opposing naval expenditures, Sawyer denounced commanders "who feasted in their cabins like bashaws, with bands of music to entertain them . . . and twenty or thirty men employed for no other purpose than to fiddle and pipe to the crew" (*Annals of Congress*, 10th Cong., 2d sess., Jan. 1809, p. 1057). His dislike for Washington and the legislative hall in which Congress met led him to propose removal of the capital to Philadelphia. After indicting the unhealthful Washington climate, he implied that "this Hall . . . this elegant building" might have contributed to his recent severe

illness and concluded that "the place ought to be destroyed and annihilated, and if it were as opulent as Babylon I would have the ploughshare run over it" (*Annals of Congress*, 10th Cong., 1st sess., Feb. 1808, p. 1583).

It is ironic that Sawyer acted in most instances to protect the federal treasury, for in his personal life he was improvident and profligate. He wavered between extravagance and penury his entire adult life and suffered extreme poverty in his dotage, having ravaged the estate of his wealthy third wife. For a while in Washington, he relied on the "card-playing abilities of a friend, whom he staked for petty losses and from whom he gained ample winnings" (Walser, p. xx). These winnings were quickly spent, for Sawyer admitted being reckless with money.

Sawyer read widely and considered himself a member of the literati. In addition to three lost works, he wrote two plays, a biography, a revealing autobiography, and several essays on scientific subjects. In 1824 he published his best-known work, *Blackbeard*, a four-act comedy that alternates between melodrama and farce. *Blackbeard* is the first play by a North Carolinian about North Carolina scenes and characters. Because of its financial success, Sawyer quickly produced *The Wreck of Honor* (1824), a bawdy tale of seduction and murder set in Napoleonic France. Neither play has much literary merit, and only *Blackbeard* was even staged, having a brief run in New York. His *Biography of John Randolph of Roanoke* (1844), which portrays its subject in most unflattering terms, was a poorly organized, poorly written literary disaster. But Sawyer was no more scathing in his characterization of Randolph than he was of himself in the *Auto-Biography of Lemuel Sawyer* (1844). One of the most self-damaging works in American letters, the book reveals Sawyer as venal, selfish, and immoral.

Sawyer married three times, but no offspring survived infancy. In 1810 he wed Sarah Snowden, daughter of a wealthy Camden County planter. Two years later she died in childbirth while Sawyer, who had abandoned her, enjoyed the pleasures of Norfolk, Virginia. In 1820, after a three-day courtship, he married sixteen-year-old Camilla Wertz of Washington, D.C., probably to quiet his political foes who had accurately noted his association with a notorious prostitute. This wife died in January 1826. In 1828 Sawyer married to repair his financial fortunes. His third wife was a well-to-do widow, Diana Rapalye Fisher of Brooklyn, New York. Their courtship lasted three weeks; the marriage was a prelude to lavish living and financial ruin.

Having dissipated his wife's holdings, Sawyer experienced poverty, unemployment, and unhappiness. In 1850 he was appointed to a minor departmental clerkship in Washington and held this post until his death there. He was buried in an unmarked grave in the family cemetery in Camden County.

It is difficult to explain Sawyer's electoral successes. He was a negligent, ineffective legislator but was popularly elected numerous times. Perhaps his political attainments were a commentary on North Carolina electoral practices rather than on the man. His literary legacy, aside from *Blackbeard*, is hardly remembered; its place as the first drama by a North Carolinian is all that renders it memorable.

• The primary materials on Sawyer are scattered, consisting of county records, the *Annals of Congress*, the *Raleigh Register and Gazette*, and the *Auto-Biography of Lemuel Sawyer* (1844). A short, perceptive biographical sketch may be found in Jesse F. Pugh, *Three Hundred Years Along the Pasquotank* (1957), pp. 132–38. For a consideration of Sawyer's literary work see Richard Walser, *Literary North Carolina* (1986), and his introduction to the 1952 edition of *Blackbeard*.

MAX R. WILLIAMS

SAWYER, Philetus (22 Sept. 1816–29 Mar. 1900), lumber merchant and U.S. senator, was born in Whiting, Vermont, the son of Ephraim Sawyer, a farmer and blacksmith, and Mary Parks. When Philetus was an infant, his family migrated across Lake Champlain to Crown Point, New York. The fifth of ten children in a struggling family, Sawyer acquired such cursory schooling that political opponents later gibed him unmercifully for his awkward writing and speaking. As a teenager, he worked in a Crown Point sawmill, which he then rented and operated on his own before he turned twenty-one. In 1841 Sawyer married Melvina Hadley, a neighbor. Three of the couple's five children survived to adulthood.

As timber around Lake Champlain diminished, Sawyer in 1846 used $2,200 he had saved to purchase farmland in Rosendale, Wisconsin. Three years later he sold this farm at a profit, which he used to enter the Oshkosh lumber trade. By 1853 he owned a sawmill and was a partner in a firm of lumber dealers. By the end of the Civil War, P. Sawyer & Son, the partnership Sawyer formed with his son Edgar, milled more than 6 million feet of lumber and lath per year and operated a 230-ton steamboat that plied Lake Winnebago. To secure a niche in the Chicago market, the Sawyers joined with William O. Goodman, who in 1878 married Sawyer's daughter Erna, and William's brother James Goodman to form the Sawyer Goodman Company. This firm built a network of pinelands, sawmills, and lumberyards that spread from Michigan to Nebraska.

Sawyer made much of his fortune, which reached between $4 million and $5 million, from shrewd land deals. Dressed in lumberjack's clothes and accompanied by skilled foresters, Sawyer hiked through Wisconsin forests to evaluate land worth little at the time because it stood far from transportation. Careful and patient, he might wait decades for the market to reach his timber, if he did not construct the sawmills, booms, and river improvements himself. In part to gain access to massive tracts of Wisconsin timberland reserved for railroad land grants, Sawyer in the late 1870s joined in founding the Chicago, St. Paul, Minneapolis & Omaha Railroad, the so-called Omaha line, which operated more than 1,000 miles of track through the upper Midwest. Sawyer associated himself with Frederick Weyerhaeuser's Mississippi River

Logging Company, invested in banks in Oshkosh, Fond du Lac, and Milwaukee, operated a farm machinery factory, and even came to hold 200,000 acres of Texas ranch land.

The dependence of the lumber trade on state and federal infrastructure, land, and tax policies drew Sawyer into politics. Service as an alderman (1858–1859, 1862–1863), state assemblyman (1857, 1861), and Oshkosh mayor (1863–1864, 2 terms) culminated in election to Congress in 1864. The first Republican to hold a traditional Democratic seat, Sawyer won four straight reelections, a lengthy stint by Gilded Age standards. On Reconstruction and civil rights, Sawyer voted with the Radicals, but nearly all his House activity concerned internal improvements. Aware of his inadequacy as an orator, Sawyer confined floor remarks to terse explanations of spending items and concentrated on committee work. From his seat on the Commerce Committee, Sawyer came to manage the River and Harbors Bill, which he used to underwrite navigation projects along the Great Lakes and upper Mississippi Valley. The lumberman/politician grew so adept at "logrolling" members' projects that some contemporaries mistakenly believed that this expression arose to describe his methods. Eschewing public recognition for influence, Sawyer acquired a high standing among House Republicans. As Speaker Schuyler Colfax remarked, Sawyer quietly did so many favors for colleagues "that whatever he wants goes" (Thomson, p. 275).

After retiring from Congress in 1875, Sawyer, in characteristic strong language, disclaimed any desire to seek office again. in 1880, however, the prospect of a Republican rival, Elisha Keyes, gaining a U.S. Senate seat persuaded Sawyer to run himself. An overwhelming victory confirmed Sawyer as Wisconsin's most powerful Republican. During the 1880s the central Wisconsin businessman reinforced his statewide position through his famed "triumvirate" with attorney John C. Spooner from Hudson in western Wisconsin (who joined Sawyer in the Senate in 1885) and utilities executive Henry C. Payne of Milwaukee.

Over two Senate terms, Sawyer exhibited the same qualities that had brought him success in the House. He kept his hand in internal improvements as chair of the Railroad Committee and as a member of the Commerce Committee. As chair of the Committee of the Post Offices and Post Roads during his second term, he managed such political currency as postmaster confirmations and railroad mail contracts. His expediting of hundreds of veterans' pension bills made him a favorite of the Grand Army of the Republic. While Sawyer went entire sessions without making floor remarks, only about a dozen of more than 2,000 bills he reported failed to pass. Of 5,000 nominations Sawyer managed, the Senate rejected not one. In line with prevailing standards regarding public sector support for enterprise, Sawyer rarely hesitated to push measures that obviously benefited his business interests. One controversial example was his long campaign to speed timber cutting on Wisconsin's Menominee Indian Reservation.

In 1890 disaffection among German voters over the allegedly nativist Bennett education law sent Wisconsin Republicans to an unprecedented defeat. To strengthen their weak hold on Madison, Democrats sued five former Republican state treasurers for interest they had pocketed on public funds deposited in banks with Republican connections. Though technically unlawful, this practice had been openly tolerated for decades. Sawyer, bondsman for two of the ex-treasurers, now stood responsible for $160,000. While the millionaire senator could afford this, he was so angered by what he saw as a vindictive attack that he tore up a will containing a large bequest for the University of Wisconsin. In this atmosphere, Sawyer committed an act that tarnished his reputation. In a private meeting in a Milwaukee hotel in September 1891 he offered Robert M. La Follette, Sr., then an ex-congressman practicing law, a retainer that La Follette, whose brother-in-law was a judge in the state treasury case, interpreted as a bribe. After the affair made the papers, Sawyer and his circle feuded with La Follette, thereby deepening the nascent split between regular and reform Republicans that eventually made La Follette a national figure.

A widower since 1888, Sawyer left the Senate in 1893 and returned to Oshkosh, where his philanthropy and genial character had earned him repute as the town's "Grand Old Man." He died at home. Richard N. Current, Sawyer's distinguished biographer, describes a stubby, rough figure with sharp blue eyes, kindly but willful in disposition, who, even after he had gained wealth and power, would sit whittling on the curbstones of Oshkosh as he talked business and politics with townspeople. He was almost the image of the resourceful New Englander determined to make what he could from the Wisconsin forests.

• The Sawyer papers in the Oshkosh Public Museum pertain mostly to family matters. Though moralistic in places, Richard N. Current, *Pine Logs and Politics: A Life of Philetus Sawyer, 1816–1900* (1950), is thorough and graceful in style. Robert M. La Follette, *La Follette's Autobiography* (1913), contains a deft critical portrait, while A. M. Thomson, *A Political History of Wisconsin*, 2d ed. (1902), offers a sympathetic view. Robert B. Fries, *Empire in Pine: The Story of Lumbering in Wisconsin, 1830–1900* (1951), places Sawyer's lumber activities in context. Chaps. 23–25 of Robert C. Nesbit and William F. Thompson, *Wisconsin: A History*, 2d ed. (1989), succinctly recreate Sawyer's political environment. Dorothy Ganfield Fowler, *John Coit Spooner: Defender of Presidents* (1961), discusses Sawyer from the perspective of his most important political ally. An obituary is in the *Milwaukee Sentinel*, 30 Mar. 1900.

ALAN LESSOFF

SAWYER, Ruth (5 Aug. 1880–3 June 1970), children's writer and lecturer, was born in Boston, Massachusetts, the daughter of Francis Milton Sawyer, an importer, and Ethelinda (or Ethalinda) Smith. Sawyer was raised in New York City's Upper East Side, and the family passed their summers in Maine. Both places provided the settings for many of Sawyer's works. The death of her prosperous father when Sawyer was fourteen shook the family's financial security and sent them to live solely in Maine for about a year, but the family returned to New York City, where Sawyer finished her secondary education.

After her graduation Sawyer attended Garland Kindergarten Training School in Boston. She then went to Cuba, where she helped organize kindergartens. For this work she earned a scholarship to Columbia University, where she majored in folklore and storytelling and graduated with a B.S. in education in 1904. During and after her education, Sawyer volunteered as a storyteller at various missions, libraries, and schools and wrote for the *New York Sun*. In 1905 and in 1907 the *Sun* sent her to Ireland to write features; while there, she traveled, met many traditional storytellers, and collected stories. After her return to the United States, she began her career as a professional storyteller with the New York Public Lecture Bureau in 1908, and she instituted the storytelling program in the New York Public Library.

In 1911 Sawyer married Albert C. Durand, an ophthalmologist, though she retained her birth name in her professional life. The couple moved to Ithaca, New York, and had two children. While her children grew, Sawyer continued her work as a storyteller and saw her first novel, *The Primrose Ring*, published in 1915. This work, like her other novels geared toward an adult audience, has been forgotten for the most part; most were victims of formulaic plots in which kind heroines succeed because of virtue and hard work.

Sawyer's reputation lies in her writings for children. Although her earliest children's books have not generally enjoyed lasting popularity, *This Way to Christmas* (1916) has endured as a seasonal favorite. This work features a boy called David (named after Sawyer's own son), who, while his parents are on a trip, stays with his former nurse (modeled on Sawyer's own childhood nurse) and meets people of various occupations and backgrounds who tell him Christmas stories from their native lands.

Sawyer's career took a favorable turn in the 1930s. She traveled to Spain to collect folktales in 1931–1932, and this experience inspired her writing. From this trip and a chance acquaintance with a Spanish boy, she produced *Toño Antonio* (1934), the story of a poor boy who takes his goats to Málaga to sell their milk and has various adventures along the way before returning home. The same trip also inspired Sawyer's *Picture Tales from Spain* (1936).

Her experiences at home, like her experiences abroad, proved to be fruitful material. Sawyer's life as a young girl in New York inspired two autobiographical novels. The first, *Roller Skates* (1936), is set in the 1890s; this work features Lucinda Wyman, aged ten and "so everlastingly full of life," who stays in New York City with the Misses Peters while her parents are abroad. Free to skate wherever she wishes, Lucinda meets and makes friends with people of diverse backgrounds and ages. Because of its frank treatment of death, some controversy arose over the book when it appeared, but the work earned the Newbery Medal in 1937. The sequel to this novel, *The Year of Jubilo* (1940), continues the story of the Wyman family after Mr. Wyman's death.

Sawyer also wrote about the art of storytelling itself. The book *The Way of the Storyteller* (1942) gives advice to those who wish to practice this art and offers eleven stories that can be told or read by anyone old enough to read. This work includes a bibliography of sources for potential storytellers, and the revised edition (1962) has two added chapters and a newer bibliography. This book became a standard reference for storytellers.

Many books, short stories, and other writings followed. In addition, Sawyer also wrote a book of poetry, *A Child's Year-Book* (1917), as well as two plays, and she continued to deliver lectures and tell stories to many audiences.

Throughout her career, Sawyer worked with many illustrators, including Maurice Sendak, who illustrated her children's book *Maggie Rose, Her Birthday Christmas* (1952). In 1945 Sawyer's *The Christmas Anna Angel* (1944), illustrated by Kate Seredy, was named a Caldecott Honor Book. Later Sawyer worked with her son-in-law Robert McCloskey on *Journey Cake, Ho!* (1953), which also received the Caldecott Honor, in 1954.

Sawyer's body of work as a whole earned her additional honors. The Ruth Sawyer Collection of rare children's books was established by the College of Sainte Catherine in St. Paul, Minnesota, in 1958. In 1965 she was honored with both the Regina Medal (the Catholic Library Association) and the Laura Ingalls Wilder Medal (the American Library Association). A storytelling festival in her honor was held in Provincetown, Massachusetts, also in 1965.

Sawyer continued her work long after she and her husband moved from Ithaca to Maine, then to Florida, then to Massachusetts, after Durand's retirement in 1946. Finally they settled in Hancock, Maine. In 1967 Albert Durand died. Three years later, Ruth Sawyer died in Lexington, Massachusetts. She left a vast body of work that enriched the lives of countless children and proved that the art of storytelling is ageless.

• Sawyer's manuscripts are at the College of Sainte Catherine Library, St. Paul, Minn. Her other works for children include *The Tale of the Enchanted Bunnies* (1923), *Old Con and Patrick* (1946), *A Cottage for Betsy* (1954), and *The Enchanted Schoolhouse* (1958). Her other Christmas books include *The Long Christmas* (1941), *The Year of the Christmas Dragon* (1960), and *Joy to the World: Christmas Legends* (1966). Her novels for adults include *Seven Miles to Arden* (1916), *Leerie* (1920), and *Folkhouse: The Autobiography of a Home* (1932). Some of Sawyer's short stories can be found in *Doctor Danny* (1918). Recordings include *Ruth Sawyer: Storyteller* (1965). A complete bibliography of Sawyer's works is in Virginia Haviland, *Ruth Sawyer* (1965), a book-length monograph. An additional source is an article by Sawyer's daughter Margaret Durand McCloskey, "Our Fair Lady!" *Horn Book*, Oct. 1965, pp. 481–86. See also Beryl Robinson, "To Ruth Sawyer," *Horn Book*, Oct. 1965, pp. 478–80, and Beryl Robinson, "Ruth Sawyer," *Horn Book*, Aug. 1970, pp. 347, 431. An obituary is in the *New York Times*, 6 June 1970.

SHARON V. STENZEL

SAWYER, Wilbur Augustus (7 Aug. 1879–12 Nov. 1951), public health administrator and medical researcher, was born in Appleton, Wisconsin, the son of Wesley Caleb Sawyer, a university professor, and Minnie Edmea Birge. He moved with his family to Oshkosh in 1882 and to Stockton, California, in 1888. He matriculated in 1898 at the University of California at Berkeley but transferred the next year to Harvard University, where he received an A.B. and an M.D. in 1902 and 1906, respectively. After completing a two-year internship at Boston's Massachusetts General Hospital, he returned to the University of California, where he worked as a medical examiner until 1911. In that year he married Margaret Henderson, with whom he had four children. In 1914 he became a lecturer in hygiene and preventive medicine in the University of California's medical school, and in 1916 he was promoted to clinical professor. He also became affiliated with the state board of health in 1910 as director of its hygienic laboratory and was elevated to secretary and executive officer of the board in 1915.

During World War I Sawyer joined the U.S. Army Medical Corps as a captain. Assigned to the surgeon general's office and the Inter-Departmental Social Hygiene Board while also serving as acting general secretary of the American Social Hygiene Association, he worked chiefly to prevent the spread of venereal diseases among U.S. servicemen in stateside training camps. In 1919 he moved to New York City and became a director of the Rockefeller Foundation's International Health Board (IHB). He spent the next five years in Australia overseeing a campaign against the spread of hookworm disease and serving as a public health adviser to the Australian ministry of health. In 1924 he returned to New York as director of IHB's Public Health Laboratory Service, which provided laboratory support for other IHB public health endeavors.

Sawyer is best remembered for the role he played in the development of a vaccine against yellow fever, at the time one of the greatest threats to international public health. In 1926 he became a member of the foundation's West Africa Yellow Fever Commission, whose findings confirmed that the disease is caused by a virus, that rhesus monkeys contract the virus and could therefore be used for laboratory testing, and that African and South American yellow fever are epidemiologically the same. In 1928, the year after he became associate director of the renamed International Health Division (IHD), he was also appointed director of its Yellow Fever Laboratory. He immediately set out to develop a vaccine for the untreatable disease, and in 1929 he contracted a mild case of yellow fever. In 1931 Sawyer, Wray D. M. Lloyd, and Stuart F. Kitchen produced a vaccine by combining an attentuated virus developed in white mice by Max Theiler, an IHD researcher, with human immune serum, but the scarcity of such serum permitted the production of only enough vaccine to inoculate researchers. That same year Sawyer modified the mouse-protection test developed by Theiler to determine an individual's immunity to yellow fever and then implemented a program to use the test to map the disease's global distribution.

Appointed IHD's director in 1935, Sawyer continued to participate in the laboratory's work, which resulted in Theiler's development two years later of 17D, a strain of yellow fever that thrives on nervous tissue and that can be used without modification as a vaccine because it is virulent enough to induce immunity in humans yet gentle enough to prevent them from contracting the disease. When the foundation decided to provide yellow fever vaccine free of charge to American military personnel during World War II, Sawyer decided unilaterally to inoculate the troops with a combination of 17D and human serum (to prevent encephalitis), despite reports from Brazil that many of those immunized with this combination developed hepatitis, and despite Theiler's insistence that 17D could be produced so that it did not cause encephalitis. After eighty-four military recipients died from serum hepatitis, Sawyer was criticized vehemently both for the decision itself and for making it without due consultation. This criticism marred his reputation as an otherwise brilliant and devoted public health official and haunted him for the rest of his life. It also likely prevented him from sharing Theiler's 1951 Nobel Prize for developing a yellow fever vaccine.

During World War II Sawyer supervised the work of several military and civil commissions related to the control of tropical diseases. He also organized and directed the Rockefeller Foundation Health Commission as a branch of IHD in order to prevent a major European epidemic of typhus, a deadly louse-borne disease that thrives in the unsanitary and chaotic conditions of war. Immediately following the Allied occupation of Naples, Italy, in 1943, Sawyer organized a team to delouse the city's entire population via the first widespread application of dichlorodiphenyltrichloroethane, or DDT. Because the team's efforts completely halted an incipient epidemic, by the war's end virtually all refugees streaming into Allied-occupied territories were being deloused with DDT, thus preventing typhus from becoming a significant health threat to the Allies.

In 1944 Sawyer retired from IHD and joined the United Nations Relief and Rehabilitation Administration. As its director of health, he implemented a project that greatly reduced Sardinia's mosquito population, thus ridding it of malaria, by spraying the entire island with DDT. In 1947 he retired to Berkeley, California, where he died.

Sawyer was president of the New York Society of Tropical Medicine from 1934 to 1935, the American Academy of Tropical Medicine from 1936 to 1937,

and the American Society of Tropical Medicine from 1943 to 1944. He also served as chairman of the U.S. Public Health Service's national advisory health council in 1940 and secretary general of the International Congress of Tropical Medicine and Malaria in 1948. He was awarded knighthood in Norway's Order of St. Olaf in 1926, the League of Nations' Leon Bernard Prize in 1939, grand officialdom in Cuba's Order of Carlos Finlay in 1940, and the American Foundation of Tropical Medicine's Richard B. Strong Medal in 1949.

As a researcher and administrator Sawyer contributed to the advance of international public health by developing and implementing protective measures against a number of deadly social and tropical diseases.

• Sawyer's papers are in the archives of Rockefeller University and the Rockefeller Foundation. His contributions are discussed in Greer Williams, *The Plague Killers* (1969), and George K. Strode, ed., *Yellow Fever* (1951). An obituary is in the *New York Times*, 13 Nov. 1951.

CHARLES W. CAREY, JR.

SAX, Karl (2 Nov. 1892–8 Oct. 1973), botanist and geneticist, was born in Spokane, Washington, the son of William L. Sax and Minnie A. Morgan, pioneer farmers. Sax's father was a well-known local figure who involved himself in politics, business, and education and became mayor of Colville, Washington; his mother was an artist with a lifelong interest in botany. Sax's interest in plants, genetics, and agriculture developed early as a result of family influence and his fondness for the Washington environment, a rich agricultural state. Following schooling in Colville, he entered Washington State College in 1912 to major in agriculture. While there, he came under the influence of wheat breeder Edward Gaines, who encouraged him to pursue graduate study. He also met and married his teacher of cytology, Dr. Hally Jolivette, in 1915; they would have three sons. In 1916 she accepted an offer of an instructorship at Wellesley College. Having obtained a B.S. in agriculture, Sax followed her to the East Coast. He enrolled in the doctoral program at Harvard's Bussey Institution Graduate School of Applied Biology, where he worked with the noted quantitative agricultural geneticist Edward Murray East. He received an M.S. in agricultural genetics in 1917 but left for military service shortly thereafter. During 1917–1918 he served as private in the U.S. Army, becoming discharged as second lieutenant in the coastal artillery.

Appointed instructor in the Department of Genetics at the University of California, Berkeley, the following year, Sax collaborated with Berkeley geneticist E. B. Babcock on the latter's genetic studies of the genus *Crepis*. In 1920 he left Berkeley for a research appointment at Riverbank Laboratories in Geneva, Illinois, where he began to work on wheat genetics, but left shortly to take an appointment as research biologist at the Maine Agricultural Experiment Station in Orono.

He continued his graduate research at the Bussey Institution, receiving a D.Sc. in agricultural genetics in 1922. He left Orono in 1928 to begin what would be a long-term association with Harvard University by accepting a faculty appointment at the Bussey. He was promoted to full professor in 1936. In that same year the Bussey Institution was dissolved because President A. Laurence Lowell of Harvard had decided that applied biology was not of sufficient interest to his university. As a result, Sax moved to the Biological Laboratories in Cambridge, where he taught cytology. After the death of his former Bussey mentor, East, Sax taught genetics. In 1946 he was appointed acting director of the Arnold Arboretum. He became the third director of the arboretum in 1947 and held this position until 1954, when his administrative appointment was terminated by Harvard.

Sax's lengthy research career was also characterized by a diversity of interests that fall roughly into three areas: cytogenetics, horticulture and plant breeding, and demography. Although his early background and interests were in horticulture and plant breeding, Sax slowly turned to theoretical cytogenetics as his work in the practical breeding of new horticultural varieties demanded understanding of chromosome behavior. The first and second areas of his work thus overlapped greatly. His first paper, published only in 1916 in *Bulletin of the Torrey Botanical Club*, was a detailed study of the chromosomal behavior during fertilization in *Fritillaria pudica*. While working on the cytology of fertilization, Sax grew to recognize the importance and utility of chromosomes as taxonomic tools. By the early 1920s this interest led to his research on the bread wheats, in which, using cytogenetic methods, Sax showed that the polyploid nature of bread wheat indicated that it was a hybrid of an ancestral species that had undergone chromosome doubling after hybridization. Japanese geneticists were independently deriving a similar understanding, and Sax has traditionally shared in the credit given with Hitashi Kihara and Te Tsu Sakamura for this pioneering work in understanding mechanisms of polyploidy in wheat.

In the early 1930s Sax's work in cytogenetics led him to become embroiled in a much-publicized debate with the British cytogeneticist C. D. Darlington over the exact cytogenetic mechanism of crossing over (Darlington's views were since held to be more correct). From this interest there followed the line of work that occupied him during the middle years of his life and led him to be called the "father of radiation cytology" and the leader of a generation of geneticists called the "chromosome busters." While working on a project with Edgar Anderson at the Missouri Botanic Garden, Sax recognized that the genus *Tradescantia* made a superb study organism for following the effects of chromosome breakage, especially following radiation. In 1938 he introduced the field of radiation cytology with a paper titled "Chromosome Aberrations Induced by X-rays," which demonstrated that radiation could induce major genetic changes by affecting chromosomal rearrangements. After numerous experi-

ments, Sax was the first to show that the effects of radiation on chromosomes were a function of both dosage and the mitotic or cellular reproductive stage at which the tissues were irradiated. In addition to theoretical concerns, Sax continued his attempts to find improved horticultural varieties. As a result of his efforts, new varieties of ornamental trees and shrubs of apples, crabapples, magnolias, and forsythias were introduced. Among the new varieties was a cherry, the result of a cross between *Prunus subhirtella* and *P. apetela*, which he named after his wife 'Hally Jolivette'; another new variety of forsythia that he bred earned him a certificate of merit from the Royal Horticultural Society of England. Along with the new varieties he introduced were numerous new horticultural techniques that became of value to nursery workers. One variety of *Forsythia* bred originally by Sax and grown by a nurseryman was eventually given the name 'Karl Sax.'

Sax considered his interest in human demography, his third area of research, a hobby; but his contributions to this field were so important that Sax properly deserves a place as a researcher, publicist, and leading reformer in efforts to raise social awareness of growing human populations and the need for population control through contraceptive technology. Sax's scientific and public involvement with respect to modern science increasingly occupied him in his later years. In 1955 he published *Standing Room Only: The Challenge to Overpopulation*, on the consequences of uncontrolled human population growth. This book and other public efforts to support contraception met with strong opposition, especially from Catholic groups in Massachusetts. In the 1950s and 1960s Sax actively fought these Catholic groups when he and Planned Parenthood sought to abolish restrictive birth control laws in Massachusetts.

Through both his publications and his widespread lecture tours, Sax was one of the few scientists to point out both the dangers of irresponsible scientific research and the dangers of irresponsible political interference in scientific research. He was one of the first scientists to draw attention to the threat against free science by the policies dictated by Trofim Lysenko and his "Lysenkoism" in the Soviet Union and to raise a call of alarm on behalf of Soviet geneticists like N. I. Vavilov and N. V. Timofeev-Ressovsky, who had suffered under political oppression.

In the 1950s Sax became involved in one of the most celebrated scandals in the history of Harvard University. As director of the arboretum, he protested the university's proposal to transfer its resources (books, specimens, and funds) to Cambridge. Harvard administrators believed that the consolidation of resources would help mend the botanical divisions and conflicts for which Harvard botany was renowned. Sax believed it would lead to the demise of the Arnold Arboretum and horticultural practice at Harvard (Sax had similarly deplored the dissolution of the Bussey). The danger also existed that such a consolidation of botanical resources could also lead to the engulfment of botany by the more inclusive rubric of "biology," if botany were forced to consolidate with zoology. Sax enlisted the aid of wealthy backers of the Arnold Arboretum (The Friends of the Arnold Arboretum) to file a suit against the Harvard Corporation, arguing that the resources of the Arnold had been purchased through private donations and were exempt from university control. As a result of his involvement in this suit while still director, Sax's administrative appointment was abruptly terminated in 1954. He continued to be a professor of biology at Cambridge until 1959.

Though Sax was a much-admired and well-respected director and Harvard colleague, his legal entanglement with Harvard effectively ruined many of his personal and professional interactions with his colleagues; many of his opponents continued to hold personal animosities until Sax's death. Nonetheless, Sax continued to distinguish himself for his research efforts within his three areas of scientific expertise and earned a well-deserved international reputation.

The list of honors and awards bestowed on Sax was long. Among these were election in 1941 to the National Academy of Sciences and the American Academy of Arts and Sciences. He served as president of the Genetics Society of America in 1958, and he was an active member of the Botanical Society of America (winning a certificate of merit in 1956), the American Genetics Association, the American Society of Horticultural Science, and the Radiation Research Society. He served as president of the Massachusetts chapter of the Planned Parenthood League in 1958; he was a member of the Population Association of America and the American Academy of Political and Social Sciences. For his horticultural efforts, he received the Jackson Dawson Memorial Medal of the Massachusetts Horticultural Society in 1959, and in 1961 he received the Norman J. Coleman Award of the American Association of Nurserymen. He served as lecturer of the American Institute of Biological Science and Sigma Xi and was Lowell Lecturer.

In 1959 he retired and moved to Media, Pennsylvania, where he continued his breeding experiments on his son's estate. As visiting professor and lecturer he continued to travel extensively. In 1961 he received a Guggenheim Fellowship, which he held at Oxford University; in 1962 he was resident collaborator at Brookhaven National Laboratory. He visited and taught at the University of Florida, the University of Tennessee, and Yale University. His winters were often spent at the University of Georgia. His wife continued to be his lifelong coworker and critic who accompanied him on his travels and continued her collaborative research with him until the end; many of his articles were coauthored with her. He died in Media, Pennsylvania, just one month short of his eighty-first birthday.

• Sax's administrative files, including his correspondence, are located with the Record of the Directors at the Arnold Arboretum, Harvard University. The collection also includes twenty volumes of his notebooks, mainly on his horticultural

research at the Arnold. The most complete biographical essay is Carl P. Swanson and Norman H. Giles, "Karl Sax," *National Academy of Sciences, Biographical Memoirs* 57 (1987): 373–97. See also Alan Conger, "Karl Sax, 1892–1973," *Radiation Research* 53 (1974): 557–58; Richard A. Howard, "Karl Sax, 1892–1973," *Journal of the Arnold Arboretum* 55 (1974): 333–43. An obituary is in the *New York Times*, 9 Oct. 1973.

VASSILIKI BETTY SMOCOVITIS

SAY, Benjamin (28 Aug. 1755–23 Apr. 1813), physician, was born in Philadelphia, Pennsylvania, the son of Thomas Say, an apothecary and physician, and Rebekah Atkinson Budd. He received his early education at Friends' schools. One account of his life indicates that he was a "free" or "fighting Quaker," one of a small group of Quakers who supported the American Revolution. However, records are not clear as to whether he actually fought in the war. Say married Anne (or Ann) Bonsall, a granddaughter of botanist John Bartram, in 1776. The couple had two daughters and two sons, one of whom was the famed entomologist Thomas Say.

While some accounts have Say graduating from medical school at the University of Pennsylvania in 1780, existing records do not support this claim. After his marriage Say began studying the preparation of drugs and medicines; presumably he studied under his father. He began his medical practice in Philadelphia, and at the same time he also ran an apothecary shop. In 1783 Say's home was near that of noted physician Benjamin Rush, between Arch and Race Streets, and he later moved to 64 South Street. His medical practice (which included the administration of small pox vaccinations) was reportedly both extensive and lucrative.

Say had interests other than medicine. While Fitch was building his steamboat, Say not only subscribed liberally for its construction but also persuaded others (including his father) to contribute toward it. He also helped raise money to build a more powerful steam engine when it was found that the original engine lacked sufficient power. Say was on the boat during several of its trial runs on the Delaware River.

Say served as one of the first junior fellows of the College of Physicians of Philadelphia; his name appears on the original constitution of the college, dated 2 January 1787, and he also held the post of college treasurer between 1791 and 1809. One of his most interesting associations was with the Humane Society of Philadelphia. Founded in 1780 and incorporated in 1793, the society sought to prevent sudden death from a variety of causes, including drowning, suffocation, burning, and shock (from drinking cold water on a hot day). An incorporator of the society in 1793 and its president in 1799, Say and his fellow members sought to take a proactive role in the prevention of needless deaths. To that end, by 1799 the society had set up eighteen lifesaving devices along the Delaware and Schuylkill Rivers. Equipped with drags, hooks, nets, and medicines, the devices represented the society's most visible attempt to reach its goal of "re-activating those who apparently died." In a further effort to improve society, Say often spoke out against the intemperate use of distilled spiritous liquors as well as the general practice of smoking and chewing tobacco.

Public service led to public office for Say; a state senator from 1799 to 1800, he also served in the United States House of Representatives for portions of two terms between 1808 and 1811. As an outgrowth of his interest in horticulture, he helped organize the Company for the Improvement of the Vine in 1802 and served as its first president. Say was also a member of the Pennsylvania prison society and was an active abolitionist.

Say's literary achievements were minimal. He wrote an account of his father's career and mystical beliefs, "Short Contemplation of the Extraordinary Life and Writings of Thomas Say" in 1796. Although he is alleged to have written a medical treatise, "Spasmotic Affections of the Eye," in 1792, no extant copy has been located.

In 1793 Say's wife died shortly after he lost one of his daughters. In 1795 Say married Miriam Moore, with whom he had three children. At the time of his death in Philadelphia, he was considered one of the city's richest individuals.

While largely forgotten today, Say combined a successful medical career with contributions in numerous other fields of endeavor. He is an example (albeit a minor one) of the multitalented individuals who contributed so much to eighteenth-century American society.

• While no collection of Say's papers in known to exist, his manuscript ledgers from 1796 to 1804 are held at the College of Physicians of Philadelphia, while his account books from 1785 to 1803 are at the Historical Society of Pennsylvania. Secondary sources on his life and career include Howard Atwood Kelley and Walter L. Burrage, *American Medical Biographies* (1920), and Harry B. Weiss and Grace M. Ziegler, *Thomas Say, Early American Naturalist* (1931). An obituary is in *Poulson's American Daily Advertiser*, 24 Apr. 1813.

DAVID Y. COOPER
EDWARD L. LACH, JR.

SAY, Thomas (27 June 1787–10 Oct. 1834), naturalist and explorer, was born in Philadelphia, Pennsylvania, the son of Benjamin Say, a physician, and Ann Bonsall, granddaughter of the botanist John Bartram. Say's great-uncle, William Bartram, and Bartram's friend and neighbor, the ornithologist Alexander Wilson, inspired Say to study nature. Another strong influence was Charles Willson Peale, whose famous museum, located in the State House (Independence Hall), was an important study source of insect and shell specimens for the budding naturalist. In 1799 Say entered Westtown, a Quaker boarding school, where he stayed for three years.

From 1802 until 1812 Say assisted his father in an apothecary business. Toward the end of this time he entered into partnership in an apothecary with John Speakman, but the venture failed due to a lack of business acumen. During this time, at his father's suggestion, Say studied at the University of Pennsylvania

Medical School, more than likely taking courses with Dr. Say's colleagues Caspar Wistar and Benjamin Rush. The title "doctor" given in later years to Thomas Say probably resulted from these years of study.

In 1812 Say and six friends founded the Academy of Natural Sciences of Philadelphia (ANSP), whose object was "the advancement and diffusion of useful, liberal, human knowledge" (*Minutes of the ANSP*, 25 Jan. 1812). Named curator of the new institution and serving as editor of the academy's *Journal*, Say devoted himself exclusively to the study of natural science, abandoning his unsuccessful profession as an apothecary and neglecting his health in his single-minded devotion to science. He frequently slept at the academy beneath a tent made by draping a sheet over a horse skeleton and was assiduous in helping other aspiring naturalists.

During the fall of 1814 Say enlisted for several months as a dragoon in the First Troop Philadelphia City Cavalry in the War of 1812. He was stationed at Mount Bull at the head of Chesapeake Bay helping to monitor enemy movements.

Say's life as an explorer began in 1817 when he traveled with his patron, the wealthy Scottish geologist and social reformer William Maclure, to Georgia's coastal islands and to Spanish-controlled Florida. During 1819–1820 Say, employed as zoologist, accompanied a government-sponsored expedition to the West: Major Stephen Harriman Long's expedition to the Rocky Mountains. On this journey, Say named and described for science many birds, mammals, reptiles, insects, and shells. He also studied the manners and habits of Native Americans and was deeply sympathetic to the symbiotic relationship between native peoples and wildlife.

Say was named a curator of the American Philosophical Society in 1821 and professor of natural history, including geology, at the University of Pennsylvania in 1822.

In 1823 Say, as zoologist and "antiquary" (paleontologist), accompanied Major Long on a second western exploration, the expedition to St. Peter's (Minn.) River. On this journey—as far north as the Lake of the Woods in Canada and across the northern part of Lake Superior—Say collected enough insect specimens to truly represent North America in his *American Entomology, or Descriptions of the Insects of North America* (3 vols., 1824–1828). The first part was published in Philadelphia in 1824 with illustrations by Titian Peale, Hugh Bridport, Charles Alexandre Lesueur, and William Wood. Boston's *North American Review* (July 1825) affirmed the prominence that Say had by this time achieved as a naturalist: "No person, who has paid any attention to the advancement of science in this country for the last ten years can be ignorant of the doings and movements of Mr. Say, or of his particular devotedness to the subjects of which he has treated in this volume."

In 1825 the course of Say's life took a dramatic change when he accompanied William Maclure—traveling by a keelboat dubbed "the boatload of knowledge" because of the famous scientists aboard—to visit Robert Owen's "utopian" community of New Harmony, Indiana. Because Say was completely dependent on Maclure's patronage for his livelihood, and because Maclure wanted him to stay in New Harmony to set up a school for the teaching of science, Say would remain in New Harmony for the rest of his life except for a trip with Maclure to Mexico in 1827–1828 and a short visit to Philadelphia in 1833. Unfortunately, his morale and eventually his health suffered from the isolation he felt away from his colleagues and cut-off from the collections and libraries of the East.

In 1827 Say married Lucy Way Sistare, thirteen years his junior; they had no children. Lucy, whose drawing teacher during the winter of 1824 in Philadelphia had been John James Audubon, made exquisite renderings of the shells discussed in her husband's pioneering book, *American Conchology* (7 pts., 1830–1836). The first six parts of the book were printed (partly by the Says) on a handpress in New Harmony, with the plates hand-colored by Lucy.

Worn out by ill health due in part to stomach, liver, and intestinal problems as well as the onslaught of typhoid fever, Say died in New Harmony.

Say established the sciences of entomology (insects) and conchology (shells) in the United States, for which he has been called the "father of American descriptive zoology." Say's two pioneering works, *American Entomology* and *American Conchology*, were the first books on these subjects published in America. He named approximately 1,500 new North American insects for science, setting the stage for the future study and control of such disease carriers as the American dog tick, the principal vector of Rocky Mountain fever in the central and eastern United States, and a mosquito species found to carry malaria.

Say's groundwork in identifying notorious crop predators has been of long-term economic importance. Say was the first to describe the chinch bug, which is injurious to corn, wheat, and sorghum; the Colorado potato beetle, which attacks potato and tomato plants; the grape leafhopper, which affects grape yield; the green stinkbug, which spoils harvest quality in soybeans; the peach tree borer, which weakens and kills peach, almond, and apricot trees; the walkingstick, which strips leaves of deciduous trees; and the Hessian fly, once a cause of serious wheat crop losses.

Fellow entomologists praised Say's invertebrate descriptions. In 1840 the German entomologist Wilhelm Ferdinand Erichson wrote in his *Genera et Species Staphylinorum* that "in brevity I see that no one excels the American Say, who published descriptions so concise that they hardly go beyond the extent of a diagnosis, nevertheless, so clear that you will hardly ever find doubtful a form exhibited by him."

Say also described and classified more than twenty-five mollusks that proved to have medical significance, although he was unaware of this factor at the time. Among them is the North American freshwater mollusk *Pomatiopsis lapidaria*, a potential transmitter of the disease schistosomiasis, and a snail, *Helisoma*

bicarinatus, named by Say in a pioneering article on conchology for William Nicholson's *British Encyclopedia* (1816), which carries a cattle disease. The mollusk responsible for transmitting trichobilharzia to poultry, *Physa gyrina*, was also first identified by Say.

One of Say's most innovative contributions to the advancement of science appeared in his article of 1818 on fossil shells for Benjamin Silliman's *American Journal of Science and Arts*, in which he pointed out the uses of the fossil record in dating rock strata. At the time this concept was imperfectly understood, even in Europe.

The animals Say named and scientifically described include such western species as the coyote, the plains gray wolf, and the swift (kit) fox. Among birds he described on the first Long expedition are the band-tailed pigeon, the orange-crowned warbler, the burrowing owl, and the lazuli bunting.

Say made detailed studies of Native-American customs, beliefs, health, and diet and compiled vocabularies of languages he encountered. A considerable portion of the published accounts of both Long expeditions was taken from Say's notes on native peoples, in addition to his notes on American fauna.

A prolific writer, Say's articles on diverse zoological subjects appeared in the earliest issues of the foremost scientific periodicals of his time. Aside from the numerous papers he wrote on insects, crustaceans, amphibians, and mammals for the *Journal of the Academy of Natural Sciences of Philadelphia* from its founding in 1817 until his death, his work appeared in volume 1 of the *Transactions of the American Philosophical Society* (n.s.) in 1818; the first volume of Silliman's *American Journal of Science and Arts* (1818); the first number of John Godman's *Western Quarterly Reporter* (1823); the first issue of *Contributions of the Maclurian Lyceum* (1827); and posthumously, volume 1 of the *Boston Journal of Natural History* (1835). During his years in New Harmony Say wrote continuously for the *Disseminator of Useful Knowledge*, a newspaper he edited.

Say has been immortalized by his colleagues, who named several species in his honor: Say's phoebe (*Sayornis saya*) by Charles Lucien Bonaparte (the genus *Sayornis* was established later by W. G. Gray); Say's squirrel (*Sciurus sayi*) by John James Audubon and John Bachman; Say's blister beetle (*Pomphopoea sayi*) by John Lawrence LeConte; Say's lettered olive (*Oliva sayi*), a shell, by Edmund Ravenel; and a daddy-long-legs (*Eumesosoma sayi*) by James C. Cokendolpher, the last as recently as 1980.

Perhaps most significant to the history of the early republic is the fact that Say devoted his life to establishing the authority of American scientists to name and describe their own flora and fauna, instead of sending specimens to Europe as they had previously done. He was held in esteem by European naturalists, with whom he exchanged knowledge and collections. In 1818 Say was elected to the prestigious Société Philomatique of Paris and, in 1830, to the Linnean Society of London.

Say's role as one of the earliest scientific participants in western exploration not only established him as one of the first professional zoologists but contributed significantly to American history and self-knowledge. The credit and respect he brought to American scientists laid the foundation for their future authority in world natural science.

• Say's letters may be found in the libraries of the Academy of Natural Sciences and the American Philosophical Society, both in Philadelphia; Haverford College Library's Quaker Collection; the Library of Congress; Harvard University's Museum of Comparative Zoology Library and Houghton Library; the Workingmen's Institute Library in New Harmony, Ind.; and the manuscript department of the Filson Club, Louisville, Ky. Say's collected works on conchology are in W. G. Binney, *The Complete Writings of Thomas Say on the Conchology of the United States* (1858). His works on entomology can be found in John L. LeConte's two-volume collection, *The Complete Writings of Thomas Say on the Entomology of North America* (1859). Say's papers on paleontology were reprinted in the *Bulletins of American Paleontology* 1, no. 5, with an introduction by G. D. Harris in 1896. There are two Say biographies, Harry B. Weiss and Grace M. Ziegler, *Thomas Say, Early American Naturalist* (1931), and Patricia Tyson Stroud, *Thomas Say: New World Naturalist* (1992).

PATRICIA TYSON STROUD

SAYENQUERAGHTA (1707?–1786?), Seneca leader and diplomat, was born probably in Ganundasaga near present-day Geneva, New York, the son of Cayenquaraghta, a Seneca chief killed during one of the frontier clashes between France and England. His mother's name is unknown. Variant spellings and translations of his name include Kaien?kwaahton, Kayenquarachton, Smoke, Smoke Vanishes, Old Smoke, Old King, the Seneca King, and the King of Kanadesaga.

If he was born in 1707, as tradition has it, Sayenqueraghta experienced major political and diplomatic changes in his lifetime. During his youth the Senecas were still divided in their allegiances between the French and the British, a schism reflected by the action of many western Senecas who backed the French in the Seven Years' War. Throughout his career there were not only wars, but also constant pressure from the colonies for more Native-American land cessions. His first public appearance in connection with the long-standing problem of the British desire for lands reportedly took place in 1754 at the Treaty of Philadelphia, where he signed as one of the participating Senecas. Four years later at Easton, he identified himself as a Seneca war captain during negotiations with the British, who sought peace with the Six Nations and their neighbors. In 1759 he demonstrated his loyalty to the British by joining an expedition against the French fort at Niagara.

Toward the end of 1764 he agreed to act as protector for Samuel Kirkland, a young missionary from Connecticut who wished to preach among the Iroquois. The minister's journal refers to Sayenqueraghta as his "adopted Father." When Kirkland's life was threatened because a death had occurred in the lodge where he was living, Sayenqueraghta made an impassioned speech to the council defending the young minister.

After the death of the Seneca principal leader, Sagechsadon, Sayenqueraghta apparently became the leading chief. In this capacity he journeyed to Johnson Hall for negotiations with Sir William Johnson, superintendent of Indian affairs, and signed an agreement ending the participation of the Senecas in the French and Indian War. Next to his name on the document dated 3 April 1764 is a turtle totem, representing his clan. In 1768 he was an active participant in negotiations at Fort Stanwix that resulted in the establishment of a boundary line between the colonies and the Native Americans along Britain's northern and western frontiers. He again conferred with Johnson in 1771, and in 1774, during the last summer of Johnson's life, he made three speeches to Johnson outlining the needs of the Iroquois. Shortly after the superintendent died in July, he arranged for a private conference with the new superintendent, Guy Johnson. Early the following year Guy Johnson gave Sayenqueraghta presents, and he returned the favor with the presentation of a historic belt of wampum, signifying his approval of Johnson as the new superintendent.

At the outbreak of the American Revolution he was one of Britain's most loyal Iroquois allies. According to tradition, this venerable Seneca sachem was seventy years old at the time. An experienced military leader with a reputation as a bold warrior, he participated in a number of bitter campaigns, including the battle of Oriskany (1777), the invasion of the Wyoming Valley in Pennsylvania (1778), the resistance against John Sullivan's invasion of the Iroquois homelands (1779), and other devastating raids against the New York and Pennsylvania frontiers. His lifelong faithfulness and service to the British cause had led him to believe that his homelands would be protected by the king. Unfortunately, in the Peace of Paris ending the war in 1783, no such assistance was forthcoming. He and his people already had been forced from their homes at Ganundasaga. In the summer of 1780, Sayenqueraghta, his wife, and their eleven children relocated farther west in a settlement on Smoke's Creek, a tributary of Buffalo Creek, near present-day Buffalo, New York. A captive named Benjamin Gilbert reported that Sayenqueraghta's daughter adopted the young man and his sister, and they were treated well by all the members of the family. Although the exact date is not certain, his death was reported by Seneca leader Cornplanter when he journeyed to Fort Harmar on the Ohio for a conference in 1789.

A respected diplomat as well as a persuasive orator, Sayenqueraghta participated in treaty conferences from the 1750s until the 1770s. Although his health forced him to travel on horseback by the outbreak of war in 1775, he remained sufficiently influential to become the leading war chief of the Senecas during the Revolution. An indefatigable traveler and firm defender of his homeland, he did not wish to see Seneca lands lost. No effort was too great for him to exert in rallying and leading Seneca warriors and others in attempts to protect their families and homes. At the same time he was a sensitive and generous host, both to resident missionaries and to frightened captives. It is no wonder that General Frederick Haldimand, who had sent him a pair of pistols as a gift during the war, celebrated Sayenqueraghta as "by many degrees the most leading and the man of most consequence and influence in the Six Nations" (quoted in Graymont, p. 159).

• The only biographical sketch of Sayenqueraghta is a nineteenth-century pamphlet, George S. Conover, *Sayenqueraghta, King of the Senecas* (1885). There are scattered references to him in revolutionary war manuscript collections, especially in the Daniel Claus Papers at the Public Archives of Canada in Ottawa and the Lyman S. Draper Collections at the State Historical Society of Wisconsin. Some attention is given to Sayenqueraghta in Barbara Graymont, *The Iroquois in the American Revolution* (1972); Isabel Kelsay, *Joseph Brant, 1743–1807: Man of Two Worlds* (1984); and Francis Jennings and William N. Fenton, eds., *The History and Culture of Iroquois Diplomacy: An Interdisciplinary Guide to the Treaties of the Six Nations and Their League* (1985).

JAMES H. O'DONNELL III

SAYLES, John (9 Mar. 1825–22 May 1897), lawyer and author, was born in Ithaca, New York, the son of Welcome Sayles, a physician, and Harriett Elizabeth Sergeant of Massachusetts. Sayles became a schoolteacher in New York State when he was fifteen years old and later taught school in Georgia and in his eventual destination, Texas. He attended college in New York between school terms and in 1845 received a B.A. from Hamilton College. In that year he moved to Brenham, Texas, where he read law while continuing as a teacher. In 1846 Sayles was admitted to the Texas bar, and in 1849 he joined the practice of local lawyer and planter Barry Gillespie. He married Gillespie's daughter, Mary Elizabeth Gillespie, in 1849. The couple had three daughters and three sons.

From 1853 to 1855 Sayles was a member of the Texas legislature. Sayles's law partnership with B. H. Bassett, Sayles & Bassett, was formed in 1856 and continued to 1886; it was among the most successful firms in Texas. While continuing to practice law Sayles served on the law faculty of Baylor University, apparently the first law school in Texas, from 1857 to 1860. During the Civil War Sayles served under Confederate general J. Bankhead Magruder, reaching the rank of brigadier general of the Texas militia. Sayles rejoined the law faculty at Baylor in 1867 after military service. He moved to Abilene, Texas, in 1886 and established the firm of Sayles and Sayles in partnership with his son Henry.

A capable and successful lawyer, Sayles was also an enormously fruitful writer of practical legal treatises, especially expounding on the laws of Texas. His first book, *A Treatise on Practice of the District and Supreme Courts of the State of Texas* (1858), comprised some of his lectures at Baylor. In time it extended through three editions, proving its day-to-day usefulness to practicing attorneys in Texas.

Sayles's volume for local officials, *A Treatise on the Civil Jurisdiction of Justices of the Peace* (1867), had a life of four editions, the last entitled *Sayles' Guide for Justices* (1894). From his Baylor lectures he also assembled a specialized work, *A Treatise on the Principles of Pleading in Civil Actions in the Courts of Texas* (1872). Between 1882 and 1893 Sayles used this latter work as the basis of three additional books on criminal and civil procedure: *The Rules of Pleading and Practice in the Courts of Record in the State of Texas* (written with his law partner, B. H. Bassett); *Revised Statutes of the State of Texas Relating to Organization, Jurisdiction and Practice of the District and County Courts* (written with his son, Henry Sayles); and *Precedents and Rules of Pleading in Civil Actions in the Court and District Courts of Texas*.

Sayles published various other major works for practitioners, including *The Probate Laws of Texas* (1871) and *A Manual of the Laws of Business* (1876). With his son Henry he wrote *Early Laws of Texas* (1888) and *A Treatise on the Laws of Texas Relating to Real Estate* (1891–1892). In 1888 Sayles published the third edition of his volume *The Constitutions of the State of Texas*, the first of what he intended to be a four-volume magnum opus about the constitution and statutes of his state (earlier editions had appeared in 1872 and 1884). The second volume in the series was *The Annotated Statutes, Civil and Criminal, of the State of Texas . . . Supplement for 1889* (1889), and the third was *Sayles' Annotated Civil Statutes of the State of Texas* (2 parts), published in 1897. The intended fourth volume, a treatise on the criminal statutes of Texas, was never published. Sayles also published a work entitled *The Masonic Jurisprudence of Texas* (1879), stemming from his position as one-time grand master of Masons in his home state. Sayles died in Abilene, Texas.

Sayles's prolific writing undoubtedly shaped the jurisprudence of Texas. For decades lawyers, judges, and lawmakers in his adopted state looked to his works for guidance on practical matters ranging from simple ministerial acts by justices of the peace to the fashioning of appellate precedent. His teaching at Baylor University influenced a generation of Texas practitioners. Sayles's scholarship helped unify legal practice in all corners of an expansive frontier state.

• Sayles is discussed in J. D. Lynch, *The Bench and Bar of Texas* (1885). An obituary is in the *Dallas Morning News*, 30 May 1897.

FRANCIS HELMINSKI

SAYPOL, Irving (3 Sept. 1905–30 June 1977), lawyer and judge, was born on Manhattan's Lower East Side in New York City, the son of Louis Saypol, a building contractor, and Minnie Michakin. After attending public schools in the city, Saypol enrolled at St. Lawrence University in Canton, New York. In 1925 he married Adele Kaplan, whom he met while taking night classes at Brooklyn Law School; they had three children. Before Saypol received his LL.B. in 1927 and was admitted to the bar in 1928, the couple operated a court-reporting and messenger service, primarily for lawyers. Saypol was politically ambitious even at twenty-two, causing some of his later critics to speculate that his first position as assistant corporation counsel in the Law Department of New York City was gained through his connections with the Tammany political machine. Saypol served in this post from 1929 to 1934, at which time he established a private practice in the city. In 1945 he was appointed chief assistant U.S. attorney for the Southern District of New York, an achievement Saypol sentimentally referred to as "the proudest moment in my parents' life" (*New York Times*, 1 July 1977).

Four years later, after being named U.S. attorney for the same district, Saypol began to make a name for himself in highly publicized cases involving alleged Communists. As the chief prosecutor for federal cases in Manhattan, Saypol rose to prominence in the midst of Cold War tensions and anti-Communist crusading. The prosecution of Communists both in the courts and testimony before the House Un-American Activities Committee helped to bolster Saypol's career.

The first of Saypol's Communist trials led to the conviction of eleven defendants accused of conspiring to overthrow the government. The Supreme Court affirmed their convictions (*Dennis v. United States* [1951]), and Saypol was credited with helping to limit the growth and activities of the American Communist party during the early 1950s.

Less than a year later Saypol found himself supervising the government case against Alger Hiss, a former State Department official. According to author Alistair Cooke, Hiss was a man "who was judged in one decade for what he was said to have done in another" (p. 3). Accused by Whittaker Chambers, a self-described spy messenger who claimed to have accepted papers from Hiss in 1937 and 1938, Hiss appeared before the House Un-American Activities Committee to deny those accusations in August 1948. Because the statute of limitations had expired on Hiss's alleged activities, he was indicted on charges of perjury. The first trial against Hiss resulted in a hung jury, but in July 1949 he was convicted in a second trial and sentenced to five years. Despite the fact that Justice Felix Frankfurter and Governor Adlai Stevenson had appeared as character witnesses at Hiss's first trial, his conviction was upheld on appeal to the highest court.

In 1950, after inviting Roy M. Cohn to be his assistant in national security cases, Saypol successfully prosecuted Abraham Brothman, a chemical engineer who was charged, along with his boss Harry Gold, of conspiring to obstruct justice by lying to a grand jury in 1947. With Gold and admitted Communist messenger Elizabeth Bentley as the chief witnesses for the prosecution, the judge sentenced Brothman to seven years, another victory for Saypol, who was simultaneously preparing the case of his career: the trial of Ethel and Julius Rosenberg on charges of conspiracy to commit espionage.

Saypol's previous courtroom battles were merely precursors to the prosecution of the Rosenbergs, a case he handled zealously. Not only were the couple accused of having divulged atomic secrets to the Soviets, but they also reportedly engaged Ethel's brother David Greenglass and his wife Ruth, who would act as witnesses for the prosecution, in espionage. Like Hiss, the Rosenbergs adamantly maintained their innocence throughout the trial, but slowly Saypol was able to construct a riveting tale for the jury and the public, involving the Greenglasses, who received and transmitted information about the atomic bomb project in Los Alamos, New Mexico; two of Julius Rosenberg's former college classmates, Morton Sobell and Max Elitcher, who were also involved in the spy ring; Soviet vice consul Anatoli Yakovlev, who supposedly sent Harry Gold to Albuquerque to retrieve atomic information from Greenglass; and Klaus Fuchs, a British atomic scientist with connections to Gold. On 29 March 1951 both the Rosenbergs and Sobell were found guilty, and in April the Rosenbergs were sentenced to die in the electric chair. In June 1953, after numerous appeals, interventions for clemency by Pope Pius XII, and brief stays of execution granted by Judge Learned Hand and Justice William Douglas, the Rosenbergs' clemency plea was rejected and they were executed.

Saypol appeared to maintain an even hand throughout the case, commenting, "The conviction of defendants in a criminal case is no occasion for exultation. The conviction of these defendants is an occasion for sober reflection." His critics, however, accused him of shrewdly influencing the jury by insinuating that the Rosenbergs' Communist party membership was the motive for their acts. Saypol was also accused of joining forces with the trial judge in an effort to convince the Justice Department to push for the death penalty for both Julius and Ethel Rosenberg, despite the government's lack of evidence against Ethel.

Although historians widely believe that the Rosenbergs were guilty of something, it is not clear that they were active Soviet agents, and their sentence was perceived as severe, given that their self-confessed Communist counterparts escaped with their lives after testifying against the couple. Furthermore, their refusal to confess despite a pending execution left many convinced that the significance of their transgressions had been overstated for political purposes. Nonetheless, Saypol was hailed by *Time* magazine as the "Number One legal hunter of top Communists," and in 1952, less than a year after the Rosenberg verdict, he was elected to the bench of the New York State Supreme Court, which carried with it the highest salary of any judge in the United States.

On the bench, Saypol was forbidding in manner and unyielding in his sense of propriety—he fined a female lawyer in 1964 for wearing a hat he deemed "grotesque." Such a pronouncement was ironic; only thirteen years earlier he had been rebuked for a pun involving the words "rushing" and "Russian" by a judge who admonished Saypol to "restrain your desire to be another Milton Berle" (Wexley, p. 213). Saypol also held Harlem congressman Adam Clayton Powell in contempt of court in 1966 for refusing to pay a libel judgment against him, calling Powell "his own worst enemy" (Weeks, p. 8).

Saypol was a strong advocate for what he perceived to be just causes. He ruled in a 1971 police officers' dispute that the city had a binding contract with the Patrolmen's Benevolent Association and that consequently it must pay 27,000 police officers a retroactive pay increase. He led fundraising campaigns for both the United Jewish Appeal and the Federal Division of the Salvation Army Drive earlier in his career.

In 1976 Saypol was indicted on bribery charges that alleged he gave the best assignments to lawyers who agreed to route $20,000 worth of business to one of his children, an appraiser. Although the case was dismissed, Saypol was devastated, causing his friend Roy Cohn to remark, "He was never the same after that happened." Saypol is considered by some a hero for winning a conviction for one of the most serious crimes ever committed against the United States, and seen by others as a persecutor of innocent citizens. Nevertheless his talents at the bench and at the bar were undisputed, and throughout his career he was often commended for his ability to "mix street talk with Latin" in an effort to get his point across in the courtroom. Saypol died at his home in New York.

• Elements of Saypol's career, particularly the prosecutions of the Rosenberg and Brothman cases, are discussed in John Wexley, *The Judgment of Julius and Ethel Rosenberg* (1955). For more information on the Rosenberg trials see Walter Schneir and Miriam Schneir, *Invitation to an Inquest* (1965), and Ronald Radosh and Joyce Milton, *The Rosenberg File: A Search for the Truth* (1983). For facts surrounding the prosecution of Alger Hiss see Allen Weinstein, *Perjury: The Hiss-Chambers Case* (1978), and Alistair Cooke, *A Generation on Trial* (1950). For Saypol's involvement with Adam Clayton Powell see Kent M. Weeks, *Adam Clayton Powell and the Supreme Court* (1971). Saypol is also mentioned in various *New York Times* articles preceding and following the Rosenbergs' conviction on 29 Mar. 1951. His obituary appears in the *New York Times*, 1 July 1977.

DONNA GREAR PARKER

SAYRE, John Nevin (4 Feb. 1884–13 Sept. 1977), peace organization executive and editor, was born near Bethlehem, Pennsylvania, the son of Robert H. Sayre, general manager of the Bethlehem Iron Works and founder of the Sayre Mining and Manufacturing Company in Alabama, and Martha Finley Nevin, daughter of the president of Franklin and Marshall College, Lancaster, Pennsylvania. Sayre graduated from Princeton University in 1907 and Union Theological Seminary in New York in 1910. In June 1910 he married Helen Augustus Bangs, who died a year later during Sayre's further study at Episcopal Theological School, Cambridge, Massachusetts. Ordained a minister in the Protestant Episcopal church in 1911, Sayre officiated when his brother Francis B. Sayre married President Woodrow Wilson's daughter Jessie at the White House. He taught for a year at Princeton and in 1913 became an instructor in New Testament at Boone University, Wuchong, China. He returned to teach at Princeton but left in 1915 to go to Christ Church, Suffern, New York, serving as its minister and becoming rector in 1916.

During World War I Sayre became an outspoken pacifist, joining the Fellowship of Reconciliation (FOR) and working actively in the National Civil Liberties Bureau (the forerunner of the American Civil Liberties Union [ACLU]), where he assisted its principal founder, Roger Baldwin, and Norman Thomas in defending conscientious objectors against the atrocities being inflicted on them and others in military prisons. His family tie to Woodrow Wilson gave him important access to the president. On 2 December 1918 he went to the White House to ask President Wilson to intervene. On 6 December the secretary of war ordered that the harsh punishment of all prisoners in military prisons must end. In September 1918 when two periodicals, the *World Tomorrow* and *The Nation*, were denied the use of the mails for alleged violation of the espionage laws, Sayre again went to the White House, this time bringing banned issues with him. President Wilson overruled the postmaster general and ordered restoration of mailing privileges for both publications.

In 1919 Sayre resigned as rector of Christ Church to help found Brookwood Labor College in Katonah, New York. In 1922 and 1923 he served as editor of the *World Tomorrow*, sponsored by the FOR. In February 1922 he married Kathleen Whitaker, with whom he had three children. Sayre not only worked on the staff of the pacifist FOR during the postwar years but also organized and became the first chairman of the Committee on Militarism in Education, to oppose compulsory military training and Reserve Officer Training Corps in civilian colleges. When U.S. marines were fighting in Nicaragua, he organized and led a peace mission to Central America in 1927 in an unsuccessful effort to see the guerrilla leader, Augusto Sandino. Subsequently he was influential in stopping the marines' bombing of Nicaraguan villages and ending the war by visiting an international conference in Havana and persuading U.S. delegates, especially Dwight Morrow, to endorse his message to the State Department and U.S. senators.

In 1930 Sayre was urged by Hubert Brown, the chief of the U.S. Bureau of Efficiency, to accept the post of governor of the Virgin Islands, but Sayre turned it down to remain in peace work. He successfully fought the efforts of U.S. communists to infiltrate the FOR in 1933 by persuading its membership to reject a minority effort to endorse international class warfare. In 1934 he became its executive secretary for a year, later serving as co-secretary with A. J. Muste from 1941 to 1946, and from 1940 to 1946 as editor of *Fellowship*, the successor to the *World Tomorrow*.

Sayre worked actively for U.S. recognition of the Soviet Union beginning in 1930 and, prior to World War II, organized church and labor leaders in Europe into Embassies of Reconciliation to prevent World War II. They traveled to the United States and other countries attempting to persuade their leaders to hold a peace conference. In 1939 he organized the Episcopal Pacifist Fellowship and soon thereafter arranged for Baptist, Lutheran, Presbyterian, and other similar pacifist groups to organize and affiliate with the FOR. During World War II Sayre devoted himself to aiding European war resisters, Jews, pastors, and others who were persecuted or imprisoned by the Nazis. He began a War Victims Fund, aided individuals who rescued people from concentration camps, and maintained contact with FOR members throughout Europe. He visited Japanese Americans in American concentration camps and raised money for their release and resettlement.

In 1946 he became the international secretary of the FOR and assumed the important task of trying to rebuild a postwar international religious pacifist movement. When he went to Japan in 1949, he was received by the emperor and empress and also by General Douglas MacArthur, who had worked with Sayre's brother Francis when the latter was governor general of the Philippines; but he accepted no help from the occupation authorities in establishing a pacifist group in Japan. In 1953 he persuaded Philippine president Elpidio Quirino to pardon all 105 Japanese prisoners sentenced to death and to permit their return to Japan.

Until he suffered a stroke in 1967, Sayre climbed mountains and walked for miles, both for pleasure and for peace. He walked some five miles in the hot sun at age eighty-two in a Rockland County, New York, demonstration against the war in Vietnam.

Sayre lived much of his adult life in Rockland County, New York, and died in South Nyack. Nationally and internationally he was one of the major figures in the pacifist movement. He lived simply, contributing much of his inherited wealth not only to the peace movement but to saving the lives of thousands of individuals. Sayre's philosophy of life was Christian pacifism, developed while teaching at Princeton from 1914 to 1915. He wrote, "It was crystal clear to me that Jesus had been an unequivocal pacifist, that for himself, his disciples and his nation, he had totally repudiated war. From that moment on, and throughout the rest of my life, I felt sure of this conclusion and have never doubted it." He remained a thorough pacifist through both world wars and the Korean and Vietnam wars; though too old to be conscripted, he publicly announced his refusal to register for the World War II draft in order to identify with the non-registrants. When Sayre died, Roger Baldwin of the ACLU wrote, "Nevin Sayre was a determined pacifist. . . . He never seemed discouraged; he had faith in his work and an almost saintly devotion to his mission."

• John Nevin Sayre's papers are in the Swarthmore College Peace Collection, Swarthmore, Pa. The most complete biography, written by John M. Swomley, appeared in four articles in *Fellowship* magazine in Nov. 1977, June 1978, Jan.–Feb. 1979, and Nov. 1979. See also Nancy L. Roberts, *American Peace Writers, Editors, and Periodicals* (1991), and Harold Josephson, ed., *Biographical Dictionary of Modern Peace Leaders* (1985). An obituary is in the *New York Times*, 16 Sept. 1977.

JOHN M. SWOMLEY

SAYRE, Lewis Albert (29 Feb. 1820–21 Sept. 1900), orthopedic surgeon, was born in Bottle Hill, New Jersey, the son of Archibald Sayre and Martha Sayer, farmers. After completing his secondary education at Wantage Seminary in Deckertown, New Jersey, he went to Lexington, Kentucky, to live with his uncle while attending Transylvania University. In 1839 he received an A.B. and moved to New York City, where he became a medical apprentice to Dr. David Green and a student at the College of Physicians and Surgeons. He developed an interest in physical deformities and wrote a thesis on spinal irritation, which drew the attention of surgeons around the country following its publication in the *Western Journal of Medicine and Surgery* in 1842.

Sayre received an M.D. that same year and remained at the college as a prosector. In this position he assisted Willard Parker, the college's professor of surgery, by preparing cadavers for demonstration to and dissection by Parker's students. Also in 1842 he opened a private surgical practice that in time became one of the largest in the city. In 1851 he married Eliza Ann Hall; they had four children. He left the college in 1853 to join the surgical staff at New York's Bellevue Hospital, where in 1854 he became the first American to successfully remove part of the hip bone from a patient afflicted with a diseased hip joint. In 1859 he also became a surgeon at Charity Hospital.

In 1860 Sayre joined a group of physicians that petitioned the city's Commissioners of Public Charities and Correction to establish and affiliate a medical college with Bellevue Hospital. When the college opened its doors the next year he was appointed professor of orthopedic surgery, thereby becoming the first person to occupy such a chair in the United States. He continued to experiment with the surgical treatment of bone deformities, especially spinal disorders, and eventually became an international authority on the subject. He invented a number of devices for correcting such deformities, two of which deserve special mention. The Sayre method for treating lateral spinal curvature involved outfitting the patient in a Sayre's jacket, an upper body cast made from plaster of Paris, which also proved to be highly effective when prescribed for patients who suffered from a number of other abnormal curvatures or diseases of the vertebrae. The club-foot shoe, a device that corrected congenital foot disorders, revolutionized the treatment of such conditions following its publicization in *A Practical Manual on the Treatment of Club Foot* (1869).

In 1871 Sayre acquired an international reputation while demonstrating his methods on a lecture tour of England, Norway, and Sweden. He continued to perform surgery at Bellevue and Charity hospitals until 1873, after which he served as a consulting surgeon to both institutions while continuing to practice privately, teach, and write *Lectures on Orthopaedic Surgery and Diseases of the Joints* (1876) and *Spinal Diseases and Spinal Curvature* (1877). In 1877, while attending a meeting in Manchester, England, as a delegate of the American Medical Association, he was invited to give a series of lectures at a number of British hospitals, which he did before returning to the United States. In 1898 he retired from the college (he was succeeded by his son Reginald Hall Sayre) and spent the remaining years of his life as consulting surgeon for Saint Elizabeths Hospital, the Northwestern Dispensary, and the Home of Incurables.

Sayre served as surgeon general of the New York Militia from 1845 to 1861 and resident physician of New York City from 1860 to 1866. In the latter capacity he issued reports to the board of health, persuading it to address the deplorable sanitary conditions that prevailed in the city's poor neighborhoods. He also argued in favor of universal vaccination, demonstrated the infectious nature of cholera, and drew up stringent health regulations for the city's port to prevent the importation of communicable diseases. He also invented several nonorthopedic devices, such as the serotal clamp for use in lung surgery and an improved tracheotomy tube.

Sayre played an important role in forming the New York Pathological Society and the New York Academy of Medicine and served as president of the American Medical Association in 1880. Largely as a result of his urging, two years later the association began publishing the *Journal of the American Medical Association*. He was elected to honorary membership in the British and Norwegian medical societies and in 1872 he was made a knight in Sweden's Order of Wasa. He died in New York City.

Sayre was an international pioneer in the development of orthopedic surgery. His many inventions and methods for treating deformities coupled with his ability to teach these methods to two generations of medical students qualifies him for consideration as the "father of American orthopedic surgery" (Shands, p. 22).

• Sayre's papers are located in the New York Academy of Medicine Library in New York City. A biography is Alfred R. Shands, "Lewis Albert Sayre: The First Professor of Orthopaedic Surgery in the United States (1820–1900)," *Current Practices in Orthopaedic Surgery* 4 (1969): 22–42. An obituary is in the *New York Times*, 22 Sept. 1900.

CHARLES W. CAREY, JR.

SAYRE, Robert Heysham (13 Oct. 1824–5 Jan. 1907), civil engineer and railroad executive, was born in Columbia County, Pennsylvania, the son of William H. Sayre and Eliza Kent. His father was employed by the Lehigh Coal and Navigation Company, which had built and was operating the Lehigh Canal from Mauch Chunk (now Jim Thorpe) to Easton, Pennsylvania. Robert attended public schools in Mauch Chunk and for a time studied civil engineering under James Nowlin, a mathematician. Most of his training in engineering, however, came from on-the-job experience. In 1840 he helped to enlarge the Morris Canal in New Jersey and in 1843 began working for the Lehigh Coal and Navigation Company under his father's direction. Sayre was active in building the company's Switchback Railroad, a pioneer road carrying coal by gravity from Summit Hill to Mauch Chunk, and the inclined plane or "back track" by which the empty cars were returned to the mines. "Alias Back Track" was the way he signed a letter to a friend in 1845. The company gave him the responsibility for building, maintaining, and operating all of its railroads and inclined planes in and about the mines.

In 1852 Asa Packer, a wealthy merchant of Mauch Chunk and shipper of coal, began constructing the Lehigh Valley Railroad and hired Sayre as chief engineer. Sayre supervised the building of the main line from Mauch Chunk to Easton. When the line was completed the Lehigh Valley became one of the major coal-carrying roads from the anthracite districts of eastern Pennsylvania to Philadelphia and, within a few years, other eastern cities. From 1855 Sayre was superintendent of all operations and in 1856 moved from Mauch Chunk to what was soon to be the Borough of South Bethlehem (now part of the city of Bethlehem, Pa.). He was one of Packer's closest associates, and until his resignation as superintendent in 1882 he supervised all construction and operations, including the acquisition and building of feeder lines and the Musconetcong tunnel in New Jersey, which enabled the road to gain access to tidewater opposite New York City. Sayre promoted the introduction of iron bridges to replace wooden ones and the use of steel instead of iron for rails. His interest in railroads, especially the Lehigh Valley road, governed his entire professional life. In later years, from 1885 to 1898, he served as second vice president of the Lehigh Valley Railroad even though other concerns demanded most of his energies.

From the time the main line of the Lehigh Valley Railroad was completed, Sayre sat on the board of all of Packer's main business and philanthropic enterprises. One of these was the Bethlehem Iron Company. Sayre was instrumental in 1860 in bringing John Fritz, ironmaster at the Cambria Iron Company, to Bethlehem. Fritz's genius, benefiting from encouragement given and restraints imposed by Sayre, was largely responsible for the success of Bethlehem Iron. Another enterprise was Lehigh University, which Packer founded in 1865. Sayre maintained a general oversight of the construction, maintenance, and operation of the university. In 1868 he gave Lehigh University an astronomical observatory.

Frequently Sayre worked in cooperation with Elisha P. Wilbur, Packer's nephew and right-hand man in financial matters. Wilbur built his mansion a few rods north of Sayre's. Both were, like Packer, Episcopalian in religion and actively promoted their church in South Bethlehem and elsewhere.

Packer died on 17 May 1879, leaving his possessions to the control of a trust known as the Asa Packer Estate. A five-man board governed the estate, which operated the Lehigh Valley Railroad and administered various bequests, including $1.5 million in Lehigh Valley Railroad stock for Lehigh University. Sayre was chairman of the estate, and Wilbur was its secretary. The two men retained these positions until they died.

In 1882 Sayre made a decision that he later regretted. Troubled by disagreements with Packer's son Harry Eldred Packer, Sayre resigned as superintendent and chief engineer of the Lehigh Valley Railroad and accepted the positions of president and chief engineer of the South Pennsylvania Railroad Company, a concern financed by William K. Vanderbilt and others who were determined to build a line that would end the near monopoly in cross-state travel of the Pennsylvania Railroad. As chief engineer of the South Pennsylvania Railroad Sayre constructed the seven tunnels that, approximately fifty years later, became part of the Pennsylvania Turnpike. He also found himself involved with railroad politics and finances in uncongenial ways. "The whole work has been delayed for want of practical men, and men of broad ideas," he wrote in a memorandum attached to his diaries for 1883. "I never again want to be associated with so grasping narrow a set."

The line of the South Pennsylvania Railroad was never completed. However, before operations ceased on 30 November 1885, Sayre left the company, and early in 1886 he accepted an appointment as general manager of the Bethlehem Iron Company, a position he held until 1897. During his tenure as general manager, Bethlehem Iron changed its principal focus from the manufacture of rails to the forging of guns and armor plate for the U.S. Navy and ships of other countries, and it grew to become second in the nation, behind the Carnegie Steel Company, in the manufacture of heavy forgings.

In 1897 Sayre was elected president of the board of trustees of Lehigh University, a position formerly held only by Episcopalian bishops. The university was in financial trouble. Sayre and Wilbur helped it with personal gifts and loans and used the Asa Packer Estate to return it to financial health. In the process, in 1899 they sold the Lehigh Valley Railroad to Drexel and Company, the Philadelphia agent for J. Pierpont Morgan.

For recreation Sayre played cards, collected coins, fished, and, more rarely, hunted. In 1867 he was one of a party shooting buffalo on western plains near Fort Kearny. In later life he traveled extensively in North America, Europe, and lands bordering the Mediterranean. He liked card games such as whist, cribbage, and euchre and once kept track of a series of one thousand games of euchre he and a friend had played against opponents. Over the years he built up a large library that included rare volumes.

By the turn of the century Sayre was reducing the extent of his activities. He resigned as a director of the Bethlehem Steel Company, formerly Bethlehem Iron, at the time of its sale to Charles M. Schwab in 1901. Sayre's memberships on governing boards in 1901 reflect the scope of his later interests. In addition to his positions with the Asa Packer Estate and Lehigh University, he was on the boards of four coal companies, two iron and steel companies, two hospitals, two institutions for the care of children, and one each of concerns in wood carving, gold dredging, banking, railroading, real estate, and education.

He died at his home in South Bethlehem. Sayre had been married four times. His first marriage was to Mary Evelyn Smith in 1845; they had nine children before she died in 1869. In 1871 he married Mary Bradford, widow of Richard Brodhead; they did not have children. She died in 1877. Sayre wed his third wife, Helen Augusta Packer, widow of Rollin H. Rathbun, in 1879; they also had no children, though she was pregnant at her death a year later. He was married a fourth and final time, in 1882, to Martha Finley Nevin, daughter of Reverend John W. Nevin of Mercersburg, Pennsylvania; they had three children.

Sayre was not an entrepreneur, if by that term is meant an imaginative and resourceful founder of new enterprises. His importance lies rather in an ability to spot excellence in others and, opportunity appearing, make their undertakings successful. Chief among these undertakings were the Lehigh Valley Railroad, the Bethlehem Iron (Steel) Company, Lehigh University, and some less well known institutions in Lehigh Valley, Pennsylvania. The value of these to the nation at the time of his death is a fair measure of his standing in American history.

• For the last fifty-six years of his life Sayre kept a diary in which he wrote briefly at the end of almost every day about events important to him and to the enterprises with which he was associated. These diaries are housed in the library of the Canal Museum in Easton, Pa., and have been the subject of a short book by the director of the museum, Lance Metz, and Frank Whelan, *The Diaries of Robert Heysham Sayre* (1990). No other biographical account exists. Much additional information can be found in the Joseph Wharton Papers, housed in the Friends Historical Library, Swarthmore College, and the archives of the Lucy Packer Linderman Library, Lehigh University, which also has copies of the annual reports of the Lehigh Valley Railroad and the records of the Asa Packer Estate. Volumes that include descriptions of Sayre's various activities are *Bethlehem of Pennsylvania: The Golden Years* (1976); and W. Ross Yates, *Joseph Wharton: Quaker Industrial Pioneer* (1987) and *Lehigh University: A History of Education in Engineering, Business and the Human Condition* (1992).

W. ROSS YATES

SBARBORO, Andrea (26 Nov. 1839–28 Feb. 1923), wine producer and banker, was born in Acero, Italy, near Genoa, the son of Stefano Sbarboro, a farmer, and Maria (maiden name unknown). In 1844 the Sbarboros and their nine children emigrated to New York City, where Andrea was a street peddler of toys from the age of eight. His mother, a strong Catholic, did not allow Andrea to attend public schools because they offered no religious instruction; thus, he received little formal education. He learned to write from a neighbor who gave evening lessons and later received additional instruction in an Italian-American school.

The life of this poor immigrant boy who became a successful businessman in many enterprises resembles a Horatio Alger story. At age thirteen, he left home to join his oldest brother, Bartolomeo, in San Francisco. Working in his brother's grocery store, a booming business during the gold rush prosperity of the 1850s, he soon became the bookkeeper, then a partner. In 1861 he married Maria Dondero, the sister of newspaper editor Carlo Dondero, a prominent member of San Francisco's Italian community. After her death, Sbarboro married Romilda Botto, whom he met during a year-long visit to Italy, in 1872; they had five children. By 1873 he was sole owner of the grocery and food import business and began investing his profits in land. Between 1875 and 1890 he developed and managed several mutual building and loan associations in the San Francisco area, having been a founding member of the first mutual benefit society formed by Italian immigrants in the city, La Società Italiana di Mutua Beneficenza (1858).

In 1881 Sbarboro organized the Italian Swiss Colony winery (originally the Italian Swiss Agricultural Association), the enterprise for which he is best known. Although the winery was originally designed as a cooperative, the employees preferred higher wages to ownership shares. The first years were marked by a number of crises relating to crop disasters and falling grape prices, but then it achieved amazing success, becoming the second largest wine producer in the state and the largest dry wine producer in the nation. Colony wines won medals throughout the world. The first integrated winery in California, it grew and fermented its own grapes and marketed its own wine. As secretary of the board of directors, Sbarboro was the driving force of the winery operation until 1913. The sales office was in San Francisco; the winery and vineyards were eighty miles away, in Asti (Sonoma County), where the Sbarboros had a second home.

Sbarboro organized another cooperative venture in 1896, the Sanitary Reduction Works, a garbage service that provided employment for many Italian immigrants at the turn of the century. The company was purchased by the city of San Francisco in 1910. In 1899 Sbarboro founded the Italian-American Bank, the second bank to be located in San Francisco's Italian district. Although its stated purpose was to provide banking services to working-class immigrants, the bank soon moved into the financial district, becoming more "American." These enterprises—the winery, the garbage service, and the bank—were all highly successful and were eventually purchased by larger corporations. Sbarboro was a talented entrepreneur whose professed object was not to accumulate money but to "win success" for his projects. Respected by his peers, in the early part of the twentieth century Sbarboro presided over the California Manufacturers and Producers Association (forerunner of the State Chamber of Commerce) and the California Grape Growers Association and was vice president of the American Wine Growers Association.

Sbarboro was also a social activist, combining a desire to help fellow citizens, especially Italians, with his entrepreneurial drive. Concerned with many of the major issues of the early 1900s, he was most outspoken against the temperance movement, lobbying Congress, making speeches, and writing pamphlets arguing that drinking wine leads to a lower incidence of alcoholism, as evidenced in European wine-drinking countries. He was instrumental in establishing the California Grape Protective Association in 1908 to foster anti-Prohibition views, but he and the association were unable to prevent the passage of a constitutional amendment in 1919 prohibiting the sale of alcoholic beverages, including wine. During Prohibition, the winery survived by selling grapes and crushing them for individuals who made wine for home use and by making and marketing nonalcoholic grape juice, plus making sacramental wine for churches. Sbarboro's other reform activities included testifying before the California legislature about the need to protect consumers from fraudulent savings and loan institutions and establishing a school to teach English to Italian immigrants.

Although Sbarboro became a Freemason and was a founding member and officer of an Italian-language lodge established in 1871, he nevertheless supported the Catholic church in San Francisco. He served on a commission to develop a new city charter in 1902 and on the Relief and Reconstruction Committee after the 1906 earthquake. Sbarboro was often urged to run for political office, but he refused, writing in his memoirs that he did not want to take time away from his many business enterprises. His life was the embodiment of his philosophy that "every moment of a man's life is of great importance." He died in San Francisco.

Sbarboro's historical significance springs from the interaction between an exceptional man and his setting. Arriving in San Francisco during the early economic development of the Italian community, he used his personality and drive to bridge the gap between the immigrant and American communities. Described in a 1911 history of Sonoma County as "one of the most engaging and striking personalities of the Pacific Coast" (Gregory, p. 377), Sbarboro was recognized as an outstanding citizen and in 1904 was awarded the Knight of the Gold Crown of Italy, the highest honor the Italian government bestowed on immigrants who made outstanding contributions to their communities. One obituary warmly praised him as "a striking example of a self-made man . . . who all his life . . . had given of his time and money for the betterment of the Italian people both in America and Italy." Some historians, however, have questioned this glowing view of Sbarboro, suggesting that his business success came from his personality and public relations ability rather than from a solid business sense; others have criticized him for what was perceived as his racist opposition to Asian workers in the vineyards.

• Sbarboro's unpublished memoirs, "Life of Andrea Sbarboro: Reminiscences of an Italian American Pioneer" (1911), are on microfilm at Bancroft Library, University of California, Berkeley, which also houses two of his antitemperance pamphlets, "Wine as a Remedy for the Evil of Intemperance" (1906) and "The Fight for True Temperance" (1908), and some of his letters in the George C. Pardee Papers. Some Italian Swiss Colony records are at the California Historical Society Library, San Francisco. See also Edmund A. Rossi, "Italian Swiss Colony and the Wine Industry," Regional Oral History Office, Bancroft Library (1971), and Frank Norris, *Italian Swiss Colony* (no. 12 in the series *The Vine in Early California*, 1955). Sbarboro is discussed in many accounts of the Italian community in San Francisco; see, for example, Sebastian Fichera, "The Meaning of Community: A History of the Italians of San Francisco" (Ph.D. diss., UCLA, 1981); Rose Scherini, *The Italian American Community of San Francisco* (1980); Deanna Paoli Gumina, *The Italians of San Francisco, 1850–1930* (1978); and Andrew F. Rolle, *The Immigrant Upraised* (1968). Articles primarily about Sbarboro include Gumina, "Andrea Sbarboro, Founder of Italian Swiss Colony Wine Company," *Italian Americana* 2, no. 1 (1975): 1–17; M. B. Levick, "Interesting Westerners: A Man with Three Thousand Monuments," *Sunset* 30 (1913): 93; and Carlo Dondero, "Asti, Sonoma County: An Italian-Swiss Agricultural Colony—And What It Has Grown To," *Out West* 17, no. 2 (1902): 251–65. Sbarboro's leadership in the wine industry is described in Hans Palmer, "Italian Immigration and the Development of California Agriculture" (Ph.D. diss., Univ. of California, Berkeley, 1965), 251–84, and Tom Gregory, *History of Sonoma County* (1911), pp. 376–77. On his role in banking, see Joseph Giovinco, "Democracy in Banking: The Bank of Italy and California's Italians," *California Historical Society Quarterly* 47, no. 3 (1968): 195–218. On his involvement with the Catholic church, see Alessandro Baccari, Jr., Vincenza Scarpaci, and Gabriel Zavattaro, *Saints Peter and Paul Church: The Chronicles of "the Italian Cathedral" of the West, 1884–1984* (1985), pp. 17, 57, 62, 77–78. Obituaries are in the *San Francisco Examiner* and the *San Francisco Call and Post*, 1 Mar. 1923.

ROSE D. SCHERINI

SCALA, Francis (1820?–18 Apr. 1903), military band leader, was born Francisco Maria Scala in or near Naples, Italy. Nothing is known of his parentage other than that his family was apparently well-to-do. Francis attended the musical college in Naples, majoring in clarinet performance. When he was about twenty-one years old the American frigate *Brandywine* anchored in the Bay of Naples for some months. Scala was one of thirteen young Italian men who enlisted in the U.S. Navy in the summer of 1841, Scala being ranked as a third-class musician. The voyage to the United States in the spring of 1842 found Scala so seasick that at times he could not play his clarinet. On 21 July 1842 he obtained his discharge in Norfolk and turned down an offer of the leadership of the band at Fort Monroe, Virginia; the sight of the seawater surrounding the fort was too much for his stomach. Instead, he enlisted on 22 August 1842 in the Marine Corps, which had a "band" of ten or twelve players—nominally fifers and drummers but actually encompassing other instruments. On 22 May 1843 Scala was promoted to fife major.

On 4 March 1851 Scala became a citizen of the United States. It was apparently about that same time that he was promoted from principal musician to leader of the Marine Band, which under his direction was improving in its personnel and technique. (The Marine Corps has given the date as 9 Sept. 1855, but an official letter of 19 Nov. 1855 puts the date earlier by four years, soon after his becoming a U.S. citizen.) He seems to have been the first person to be made leader. Arrangements of music played by the band at this time—some of them now in the Scala Collection at the Library of Congress—show the group's adaptation to the band instrumentation coming into use during this period, especially in the brass and reed choirs. These arrangements included a work for solo clarinet and band. Among the works by Scala are a funeral march for Abraham Lincoln; inaugural marches for Presidents James Buchanan, Lincoln, and Ulysses S. Grant; and a Brightest Eye Quickstep. The band generally performed for parades and for various social functions. In 1860 Scala directed the band in the "Miserere" from Verdi's *Il Trovatore* during a visit of the Prince of Wales (later Edward VII) to Mount Vernon.

Scala credited Harriet Lane, President Buchanan's niece and official hostess at the White House during his administration, with helping the Marine Band to become formally recognized; she often used the band for White House events. The *Washington Times* (26 Apr. 1903) quoted Scala as saying that

Miss Lane was the lady of the White House in this Administration, and she was fond of social life. The Band thus had plenty to do. It was at the White House several times a week. I asked Miss Lane to have something done to have the band enlarged and she appealed to the President with success. This was the beginning of the Marine Band as it is today. It was doubled in strength and all kinds of instruments were added to it.

This is no doubt the organization specified when Abraham Lincoln in July 1861 (four months after Buchanan's departure) signed an act "legalizing" the Marine Band, something that had not previously been done. The leader was designated "Principal Musician" and he was to have a drum major and thirty musicians. The rank of fife major was abolished.

Despite the fact that Scala was widely credited with great improvements in the makeup, performance, and general functioning of the band, he came to be blamed by a few members of the group for unspecified failures—apparently matters of personality and methods of leadership. Scala put it that a "clique" formed against him. The problem was seen by those responsible for the band as serious enough that in the fall of 1871 Scala was given the choice of demotion from leader to first-class musician or resignation from the band. Scala took resignation, effective on 13 December 1871. After that he apparently was no longer active in music to any extent. It is unclear how he made his living after leaving the band.

Scala had married soon after he settled in Washington, D.C., a marriage that apparently ended with the death of his first wife; there were two daughters from this marriage. In 1862 he married Olivia Otavia Arth; the marriage produced eleven children.

From the time of his resignation, he lived quietly in Washington, D.C., where he died. The Marine Band played at his burial service.

• The Scala Collection at the Music Division of the Library of Congress includes a collection of music from the library of the Marine Band: manuscript and printed parts numbering 608 items, with a few full and piano-conductor scores. The most informative single source on Scala is David M. Ingalls, "Francis Scala: Leader of the Marine Band from 1855–1871 (master's thesis, Catholic Univ., 1955). Musical themes from some of Scala's works are included. Another pertinent work is P. J. LeClair, "The Band Music in the Francis Scala Collection: Music Played by the Marine Band at the Time of the Civil War (Ph.D. diss., Catholic Univ., 1973). A third helpful dissertation is Kenneth W. Carpenter, "History of the United States Marine Band" (Ph.D. diss., Univ. of Iowa, 1970), which is available in several forms through University Microfilms, Ann Arbor, Mich. The Scala obituary in the *Washington Times*, 26 Apr. 1903, contains copious quotations from Scala regarding his contacts with the various presidents from Tyler to Grant. It also includes his remark that to him the most brilliant of the many pieces and arrangements he wrote for the band was the inaugural march he wrote for President Grant (1869).

WILLIAM LICHTENWANGER

SCALES, Alfred Moore (26 Nov. 1827–9 Feb. 1892), Confederate general and state governor, was born at his father's plantation, "Ingleside," in Rockingham County, North Carolina, the son of Dr. Robert Henry Scales and Jane Watt Bethell. Scales was educated at the Caldwell Institute in Greensboro and attended the University of North Carolina in Chapel Hill in 1845–1846. Following his college year, on a visit to relatives in Louisiana, Scales married Margaret Smith. Unfortunately, the marriage, which produced no children, failed quickly, and they were divorced by 1851. When Scales returned home he taught in the local schools and served briefly as a trustee of Caldwell Institute in 1849. He began to read law with Judge Thomas Settle and finished with Judge William H. Battle. Upon being admitted to the bar in 1851, Scales opened his practice in Madison, North Carolina. A lifelong Presbyterian, Scales was an elder of the Madison Presbyterian Church.

In 1852 he began a four-decade political career as a Democrat by being elected county solicitor and representative to the state House of Commons. He served a second term in the state legislature in 1856–1857, in which he was chairman of the Finance Committee. Although he was in a congressional district with a Whig majority, Scales chose to run for the House of Representatives. Defeated in his first attempt, he won election to the Thirty-fifth Congress of 1857–1859. When he was not reelected he became clerk and master of the equity court in his county. In the 1860 presidential campaign he was an elector for John C. Breckinridge.

A moderate secessionist, Scales, as a candidate for the state constitutional convention in February 1861, engaged in a series of debates with Thomas Settle,

Jr., the pro-Union candidate. Historian R. D. W. Connor wrote of the joint debate that "perhaps in no county in the State were the two prevailing views of the political situation better represented." The narrow defeat of Scales was nullified when the convention did not convene because Union candidates won a majority of the electoral vote.

Opinion was reversed in the state by the attack on Fort Sumter, and on 3 May 1861 Scales enlisted in the Rockingham Guards as a private and was elected captain of the company on the same day. The unit was mustered into Confederate service in June as Company H of the Thirteenth North Carolina Regiment under the command of Colonel William Dorsey Pender. The regiment became acclimated to military life with garrison duty on the James River in the fall, and Scales was promoted to colonel on 11 October 1861 when Pender became the brigade commander. The Thirteenth North Carolina first came under fire in the Peninsular campaign in 1862 at Williamsburg and then was heavily engaged in the battles of Seven Pines and the Seven Days. Scales was cited by General Samuel Garland as "conspicuous for his fine bearing." At a crucial point in the struggle near Cold Harbor when the regiment wavered from a surprise Union attack, Scales rallied his troops by advancing with the colors in hand, "restoring confidence and keeping his men in position." Brave and always exhibiting calmness of judgment under fire, Scales rapidly developed into a superb field officer with a natural instinct for combat leadership. The regiment again was fully involved in the Maryland campaign at South Mountain and Antietam and closed out the year at Fredericksburg. During General Thomas J. Jackson's flank attack at Chancellorsville on 2 May 1863, the Thirteenth was cited by Pender as "models in duty, courage, and daring." In the evening, with the regiment in the vanguard, Scales was severely wounded in the thigh, and Pender wrote, "I was deprived of as gallant a man as is to be found in the service."

When Pender became the division commander he strongly endorsed the promotion of Scales to brigadier general, which Scales received on 13 June 1863. Two weeks later, on 1 July 1863 as Scales led his brigade up Seminary Ridge, dislodging and routing the Union forces who fled through Gettysburg, he was again seriously wounded by shrapnel. The brigade, shattered by the heavy fighting, lost all but one of its field officers. In 1864 Scales's brilliant combat record continued through the Wilderness, Spotsylvania Court House, Cold Harbor, and Petersburg, but when the surrender came he was on convalescent leave at home. Scales believed that true soldiers are "prompt to guard and defend the life and honor of the Nation" and that "when done they are the best conservators of the peace."

In 1863, while recovering from his second wound, Scales married Katherine Henderson. They adopted Scales's niece. When the war ended he settled in the Rockingham County seat, Wentworth, to practice law, remaining there until 1874, when he moved to Greensboro to join his brother Junius I. Scales in a law partnership. That same year he was elected to the U.S. Congress, where he served five consecutive terms from 1875 to 1884. In the later sessions he chaired the Committee on Indian Affairs. On 30 December 1884, after he had been nominated for governor and handily elected, he resigned from Congress. During his term as governor, 1885–1889, the state saw significant railroad construction. Scales secured increased expenditures on public education, and the state agricultural and engineering college was founded. His 1887 commencement address at Wilson Collegiate Institute on women's rights is well ahead of his time for the region.

Scales retired from public life in 1889 to Greensboro, where he was elected president of the Piedmont Bank. An elder in the First Presbyterian Church, Scales became the first layman selected moderator of the state synod. He died in Greensboro.

• The North Carolina State Archives has the personal correspondence and gubernatorial papers of Scales. His military reports and citations by his commanders for his battlefield heroism are published in *The War of the Rebellion: A Compilation of the Official Records of the Union and Confederate Armies* (128 vols., 1880–1901), and the *Congressional Record* contains his speeches in Congress. For biographical sketches see Robert D. W. Connor, *Address on Alfred Moore Scales* (1907); Charles D. Rodenbough, ed., *The Heritage of Rockingham County* (1983); Jerome Dowd, *Sketches of Prominent Living North Carolinians* (1888); and Bettie Caldwell, ed., *Founders and Builders of Greensboro, 1808–1908* (1925). The history of the Thirteenth North Carolina Regiment is in Weymouth T. Jordan, Jr., ed., *North Carolina Troops, 1861–1865: A Roster*, vol. 5 (1975). His obituary is in the Raleigh *News and Observer*, 10 Feb. 1892.

LINDLEY S. BUTLER

SCAMMELL, Alexander (27 Mar. 1747–6 Oct. 1781), schoolmaster, military officer, and surveyor, was born in Mendon (now Milford), Massachusetts, the son of Samuel Leslie Scammell, a physician, and Jane Libbey. His parents had emigrated from Portsmouth, England. His father, who died in 1753, had asked the town's Congregational minister, Amariah Frost, to prepare Alexander for Harvard. Scammell successfully matriculated at Harvard in 1765, where he held the Hollis and Browne scholarships, waited on dining hall tables, and taught school during intersessions but nevertheless found it difficult to finance his education. He briefly left the college during a student protest his junior year but soon thereafter was readmitted. At his graduation in 1769, he delivered a commencement oration in Greek and received an award for scholarly merit. Harvard also awarded him an M.A. three years later.

Following graduation Scammell became a schoolmaster in several Massachusetts and New Hampshire communities. During his vacations he often worked with his cousin Thomas Scammell, surveyor of the King's Woods in North America. He also conducted surveying, exploring, and mapmaking on a private basis in several parts of New England. These occupations were evidently viewed as impermanent, since Scammell commenced legal studies in 1773 in Durham, New Hampshire.

Increasing imperial tensions diverted Scammell's aspirations to a legal career. In 1774 he became involved in antiroyal activities in New Hampshire, among which was the seizure of gunpowder and small arms from Fort William and Mary. After the outbreak of the American Revolution, the provincial congresses of both Massachusetts and New Hampshire simultaneously commissioned him a major in their militias. Scammell served in this rank in the American regiments besieging Boston, and there, on the recommendation of General George Washington, the Congress in Philadelphia in late 1775 commissioned him a brigade major in the Continental army.

After the British evacuation of Boston in March 1776, Major Scammell participated in several military actions. He was part of the New Hampshire contingents under General John Sullivan (his former legal mentor) dispatched to upstate New York to assist the American withdrawal from Canada in the spring of 1776. Later that year he was promoted to colonel and commander of the Third New Hampshire Regiment. Shortly afterward he took part in the battles of Long Island and Trenton and, in January 1777, Princeton. Colonel Scammell participated in the unsuccessful defense of Fort Ticonderoga against General John Burgoyne's invading army, and he was later wounded commanding his regiment in the fighting near Saratoga. Following his recovery, Congress (5 Jan. 1778) appointed him adjutant general of the Continental army, to succeed Timothy Pickering, and in this important capacity Scammell served with the American troops at Valley Forge. The following June General Washington ordered him to arrest the untrustworthy General Charles Lee for insubordination at the battle of Monmouth Court House. Colonel Scammell spent most of the next sixteen months handling routine administrative duties, though on 2 October 1780 he was delegated by Washington to conduct the execution of British major John André for espionage. A few months later he helped put down a mutiny among Continental army troops stationed in New Jersey, who were rebelling against the lack of adequate supplies from Congress and the failure to receive their pay.

By the beginning of 1781 Colonel Scammell had returned to the field, once again as commander of the Third New Hampshire Regiment, then, after the Third dissolved, of the First New Hampshire Regiment. He led this unit with distinction in several military actions early that year against British forces in the vicinity of New York City. Afterward he obtained Washington's permission to raise a light infantry corp drawn from Continental army and militia regiments. This newly created force was part of the Franco-American army that moved from New Jersey to Virginia seeking to trap enemy forces commanded by Lord Cornwallis in the South. Illness obliged Scammell to relinquish his command before the completion of the march. However, by the end of September the colonel had recovered and was given command of a new corps facing British and Hessian troops now cornered on the York Peninsula.

On 1 October 1781 Colonel Scammell, as officer of the day, decided to reconnoiter some recently evacuated enemy positions near Yorktown. In doing so, however, he advanced too far forward and found himself surrounded by hostile cavalry. In the process of surrendering to these dragoons, he was unexpectedly shot by one of his captors. The mortally wounded colonel was returned to American lines the following day. He died in Williamsburg and was buried in the Governor's Palace grounds there. Scammell never married, though he held a long courtship with Abigail "Nabby" Bishop.

• Important manuscript materials relating to the life and career of Scammell are in the Harvard University Archives, the Massachusetts Historical Society, and the New Hampshire Historical Society. William F. Goodwin offers some fascinating primary source insights into Scammell's personality in his article, "Colonel Alexander Scammell and His Letters, 1768 to 1781, Including His 'Love Letters' to Miss Nabby Bishop," *Historical Magazine*, 2d ser., 8 (1870): 129–46. Another worthwhile view of his character is in an April 1770 letter from Scammell to his mother published in Massachusetts Historical Society, *Proceedings*, 2d ser., 52 (1919): 145–46. Other relevant printed primary source materials relating to Scammell are Otis G. Hammond, *Letters and Papers of Major-General John Sullivan, Continental Army*, vol. 1 (1930), vol. 2 (1931), and John C. Fitzpatrick, ed., *The Writings of George Washington from the Original Manuscript Sources . . .* , vol. 23 (1937). The best description of Scammell's career to date is a thirteen-page essay by Clifford K. Shipton in *Biographical Sketches of Those Who Attended Harvard College in the Classes 1768–1771*, vol. 17 (1975). Charles Coffin includes a lengthier biographical essay in his book, *The Lives and Services of Major General John Thomas, Colonel Thomas Knowlton, Colonel Alexander Scammell, Major General Henry Dearborn* (1845), but this work is incomplete as well as quite outdated. Secondary sources relating to Scammell's family and his prerevolutionary career include Thomas Baldwin, ed., *Vital Records of Milford Massachusetts to 1850* (1917); Adin Ballou, *History of Milford, Worcester County, Massachusetts, from Its First Settlement to 1881* (1882); and Everett S. Stackpole, *History of the Town of Durham New Hampshire* (1913).

SHELDON S. COHEN

SCAMMON, Jonathan Young (27 July 1812–17 March 1890), lawyer, banker, and civic promoter, was born in Whitefield, Maine, the son of Eliakim Scammon and Joanna Young, farmers. As a boy he lost two fingers on his left hand, an injury that diverted his attentions away from farming and toward a profession. Scammon attended Maine Wesleyan Seminary, Lincoln Academy, and then Waterville (now Colby) College. Abandoning his studies at Waterville after only one year because of financial difficulties, Scammon went to Hallowell to read law at age nineteen and was licensed to practice in 1835.

Believing there were more opportunities in the burgeoning frontier settlements, Scammon headed west, arriving in Chicago on a lake steamer. It was an inauspicious introduction: the steamer had weathered a frightful storm during its passage, and Chicago looked like a dismal, muddy swamp. After receiving such a cold welcome, Scammon planned to head south, but just as he was to leave he was offered a temporary position as a deputy for the clerk of the circuit court. Scammon did an exemplary job and was offered the position permanently. To make the job more inviting, Scammon was permitted to use part of the office, which was carefully separated from official space by an imaginary wall, for his own law practice. In 1837 Scammon married Mary Ann Haven Dearborn of Bath, Maine; the couple had one son. That same year he was appointed attorney for the Illinois State Bank, a public institution as the state constitution prohibited the chartering of private banks.

Over the next three decades, Scammon served in a host of local judicial offices: judge of probate, clerk of the circuit court, clerk of the county commissioners' court, recorder of deeds, notary public, bank commissioner, and, most prominently, as reporter for the Illinois Supreme Court, from 1839 to 1845, during which time he prepared four volumes of excellent reports. He also maintained his private practice throughout his life with several different partners.

In addition to his success at the bar, Scammon was soon prominent in a variety of commercial and civic activities. In 1836 he helped found the Chicago Marine and Fire Insurance Company, which also received deposits and lent money, though it was explicitly prohibited from issuing bank notes. Nevertheless, when Jackson's Specie Circular created a financial crisis, Scammon's company issued certificates of deposit for $100 to $500, redeemable on demand. This action mitigated the crisis, and the certificates circulated at par for several years. More importantly, Scammon provided the model for fellow Chicagoan George Smith's Wisconsin Marine and Fire Insurance Company, which created identical extralegal money—redeemable certificates of deposit, but in small denominations of one to five dollars—that became a critical financial innovation for the economic development of the region over the next fifteen years.

Scammon also recognized the importance railroads would eventually play in Chicago's development. In 1839 he mapped out the route for Chicago's first rail link to the Mississippi with the help of William Ogden. The depression of 1839 forced a decade delay, however, and when construction began in 1847, there was so little faith in the railroad's future that Scammon had to borrow in his own name to carry the Galena and Chicago Union to completion. Scammon was also instrumental in bringing the first eastern connection into Chicago after he recovered a critical charter controlling a right-of-way, which permitted continuation of the Michigan Central from Michigan City to the Illinois line.

Scammon was also deeply interested in public education. In 1840 he was appointed a school inspector, later serving as secretary for the Board of Education from 1841 to 1843. After joining the Board of Education, he also served as president from 1845 to 1848 during a particularly critical period. Chicago had rejected free public schools in a referendum in 1836, and the inspectors had for a time closed the utterly inadequate schools. When the board built a fine school building in 1844, however, they were greeted with wide criticism. Scammon responded by running for city council on an education platform. Winning by the largest margin ever at that time, he chaired a Committee on Schools, writing the laws and regulations for public schools and successfully pushing through a commitment for the rapid construction of quality free schools.

Along with his business ventures and educational concerns, Scammon developed a love for newspapers as well. He launched the *Chicago Journal* in 1844 and later helped establish the *Chicago Republican* in 1865. Unfortunately, the latter was forced to cease publication because of the great fire of 1871. Consequently, when the *Tribune* abandoned its long-standing support of the Republican party, Scammon founded the *Inter Ocean*, declaring it would be "Republican in everything, Independent in nothing." It would also be the first newspaper in Chicago to use color illustrations in Sunday editions.

The final arena in which Scammon played a critical role was the world of banking. Though he himself had introduced extralegal money with redeemable deposit certificates in 1837, he came to hate such money issued by George Smith and others. Scammon was thus instrumental in writing a new state constitution in 1848 which permitted private bank charters. He also helped draft the Illinois Free Banking Law, and when it was adopted by referendum in 1851, he secured the first charter for the Marine Bank. When the law proved ineffective in eliminating extralegal certificates, Scammon helped revise the statute in 1853. Then, as a state senator in 1861, he again strengthened the banking laws, and in 1864 he established a second bank, Mechanics National.

In addition to this remarkable array of professional activities, Scammon played a major role as founder, major supporter, and president of various local organizations, including the Chicago Historical Society, the Chicago Academy of Sciences, the Hahnemann Medical College and Hospital, the old University of Chicago, and the Chicago Astronomical Society, for which he funded the Dearborn Observatory. Named for his first wife, who died in 1857, the observatory housed the country's largest refractory telescope. Scammon also helped organize the Inter-State Industrial Exposition, which ran successfully for eighteen years until Chicago hosted its great World's Columbia Exposition in 1893. In 1867 he married Maria Sheldon Wright of Delaware County, New York.

When the great fire of 1871 leveled much of Chicago, Scammon, true to his role as leading civic booster, was among the first to announce he was breaking ground to rebuild having already fully rented his store and office block. But the fire cost him millions, and he lost millions more during the collapse of 1873, never recovering his financial standing.

A devout Swedenborgian and long prominent in activities of the New Jerusalem Church, Scammon had a remarkably broad impact on the history of early Chicago. In addition to playing a key role in the development of Chicago as a railroad center, he also helped to shape Illinois banking and Chicago's public school system, while simultaneously fostering vigorous local journalism and creating a vibrant web of civic organizations. Scammon died in his Hyde Park home, Fernwood Villa, on the south side of Chicago.

• For information about Scammon's life, see T. W. Goodspeed, *The University of Chicago Biographical Sketches*, vol. 2 (1925), and William H. Bushnell, "Biographical Sketches of Some of the Early Settlers of the City of Chicago," *Fergus Historical Series* 2, no. 6 (1876): 19–31. Robin L. Einhorn, *Property Rules: Political Economy in Chicago, 1833–1872* (1991), is also a valuable source. Obituaries are in the *Chicago Daily Tribune* and the *Chicago Times*, both 18 Mar. 1890, and the *Chicago Daily News*, 17 Mar. 1890.

FRED CARSTENSEN

SCARBOROUGH, Dorothy (27 Jan. 1878–7 Nov. 1935), novelist and folklorist, was born Emily Dorothy Scarborough near Flora, an extinct village near Mount Carmel, Texas, the daughter of John B. Scarborough and Mary Adelaide Ellison. Her father, a Confederate veteran, taught school while studying law. Becoming a successful lawyer and district judge, he moved the family west to Sweetwater before settling in Waco so that his children could receive good educations. He became a trustee of Baylor University, the leading Baptist school in the state.

Young Dorothy attended Waco's public schools and took courses at Baylor, where she graduated with a bachelor's degree in 1896. Granted a Burleson Fellowship at Baylor for graduate study, she received her master's degree in 1899, writing a thesis titled "Some Aspects of Modern Fiction." After teaching in various Texas public schools and touring Europe during the summer of 1904, she became an instructor at Baylor, teaching the first journalism classes offered in Texas. In addition, she taught a Sunday school class at Waco's First Baptist Church.

From 1906 to 1910 Scarborough attended summer classes at the University of Chicago. During 1910–1911 she studied at Oxford University in England. She took another leave from Baylor during the 1915–1916 academic year to complete her doctorate at Columbia University in New York. Her dissertation, "The Supernatural in Modern English Fiction," was published promptly by G. P. Putnam and Sons and long remained the standard work in the field. Subsequently she edited *The Best Psychic Stories* (1920), *Famous Modern Ghost Stories* (1921), and *Humorous Ghost Stories* (1921). Resigning from Baylor, she took a teaching position at Columbia; she became a lecturer in 1918, an assistant professor in 1922, and an associate professor in 1931. Folklorist Roark Bradford and novelists Carson McCullers, Tess Slesinger, and Myron Brinig were among her students. She remained at Columbia until her untimely death in New York City; the cause was attributed to "la grippe."

Scarborough was a prolific writer. Her first book was a volume of poetry, *Fugitive Verses* (1912). Although she never published another volume of poetry, individual poems occur in many of her novels. Her interest in folklore began in her Texas years when she was a charter member of the Texas Folklore Society, serving as its president in 1916. Her specialty was folk songs, which she featured prominently in all her novels and writings. An early group of essays defying easy classification, *From a Southern Porch* (1919), contains folk songs as well as reflections on southern life before the age of air conditioning.

As a novelist, Scarborough began the "cotton trilogy," a series of novels intended to depict southern agricultural life in the age of the boll weevil. *In the Land of Cotton* (1923) included perhaps the finest paean ever penned to cotton's way of life. Set in Texas, her novels retain important elements from the previous century's local color school, including the unconscious racism typical of the South's white intellectuals. Although a southern liberal on race issues, she accepted racial stereotyping seemingly without question. Politically, she was a Republican (unusual for the daughter of a Confederate veteran) and served on the McLennan County committee while at Baylor.

Her Texas novel, *The Wind* (1925), published anonymously, depicted the effects of the West Texas environment on a delicate southern woman. The song "Bury Me Not on the Lone Prairie" served as the book's leitmotif. Made into a motion picture starring Lillian Gish, it aroused considerable resentment from West Texas boosters. Scarborough addressed the problems of southern women in *Impatient Griselda* (1927), which featured an unwanted pregnancy. The second volume of the "cotton trilogy," *Can't Get a Red Bird* (1929), despite its title suggestive of crossed loves, was really her plea for planters and farmers to unite and reform the South's agriculture. *Woman's Viewpoint* magazine in 1926 published serially "The Unfair Sex," the most complete exposition of her commitment to women's rights. She had to file a lawsuit concerning payment for this piece, and it was never published in book form. *The Stretch-berry Smile* (1932) completed the "cotton trilogy," although cotton had become less important to her than education and women's rights.

Scarborough's most enduring work was in the area of southern folk songs. *On the Trail of Negro Folk-Songs* (1925) not only presented the results of her research but also described in often charming detail how she located her sources and coaxed songs from often unwilling performers. For her work on the blues, she interviewed W. C. Handy. Her memoir, *A Song Catcher in the Southern Mountains: American Folksongs of British Ancestry* (1937), was completed after her death and was published posthumously.

Although there were hints of an early romance, "Dottie," as her family called her, never married. Petite and feisty, she tried to blend southern norms and national standards. On the one hand, she remained faithful to her religiously conservative Southern Baptist upbringing and made her New York apartment a mecca for southerners. On the other hand, she embraced the liberation of women, echoing in her novels the triumph of modernization over traditionalism. She never considered returning to the South to teach. Her novels show her to be a regionalist with a national perspective.

• Scarborough's papers, housed at Baylor University, were subjected to the family's expurgating. She has been the subject of a number of master's theses done at Baylor. James W. Neatherlin, "Dorothy Scarborough: Form and Milieu in the Work of a Texas Writer" (Ph.D. diss., Univ. of Iowa, 1973), is the most comprehensive treatment to date. A useful introduction to her life is Ann F. Crawford and Crystal S. Ragsdale, "I Have Books I Must Write: Dorothy Scarborough," in *Women in Texas: Their Lives, Their Experiences, Their Accomplishments* (1983). Another standard reference is "Dorothy Scarborough," in *Handbook of Texas*, vol. 2 (1952). For the beginnings of a modern assessment, see Sylvia Grider, "Women's Networking in Researching the Biography of Dorothy Scarborough," *Southern Folklore* 47 (1990): 77–83. An obituary is in the *New York Times*, 8 Nov. 1935.

MICHAEL B. DOUGAN

SCARBOROUGH, Lee Rutland (4 July 1870–10 Apr. 1945), seminary president and clergyman, was born in Colfax, Louisiana, the son of George W. Scarborough, a farmer and Baptist minister, and Martha Elizabeth Rutland. In 1874 his family relocated from Colfax to McLennan County, Texas, near Waco. A second move in 1878 took the family to an isolated area in Jones County in West Texas. He was educated in log schoolhouses in McLennan and Jones counties, and he worked sporadically as a cowboy between 1878 and 1886.

From his early youth Scarborough exhibited talent as a student. Impressed by the skill of a local lawyer during a murder trial in Anson, Texas, he resolved to become an attorney. In January 1888 he left home for Baylor University. He graduated in 1892 with a B.A. and made plans to study law at Yale University. During a three-year interim between studies at Baylor and Yale he worked as a book agent, taught at Baylor, and was the principal of the high school in Mexia, Texas. He moved to New Haven in 1895 and began a pre-law program. He earned Phi Beta Kappa honors and was awarded an A.B. in 1896.

Scarborough had been raised in a strict religious home, and his mother hoped he would train for the ministry. Though baptized at age fourteen, he considered his conversion premature and was not an active church member. In 1887 he responded to a Presbyterian evangelist's call to repentance and experienced the emotional reconciliation typical of evangelical conversion. He remained active in church affairs thereafter, was baptized again in 1889, and evidently led a fervidly spiritual life until, while at Yale, he reported a calling to the ministry. He returned to Texas, where he was ordained to the ministry and took a position as the pastor of the First Baptist Church in Cameron. He served in this capacity for five years, taking a one-year leave in 1899 to attend the Southern Baptist Theological Seminary in Louisville, Kentucky. He intended to complete a degree but returned home in 1900 after his brother, a law officer in Arizona, was killed by train robbers. The year in Louisville was Scarborough's only formal theological training and his last formal education of any kind. In 1900 Scarborough married Mary Parker "Neppie" Warren; they had six children.

In 1901 Scarborough was called to the pastorate of the First Baptist Church in Abilene, Texas, a position he held until 1908. As at Cameron he was a successful pastor, emphasizing evangelism and demonstrating an ability to win converts. The church at Abilene had a membership of fewer than 500 when Scarborough arrived; within seven years membership had grown to more than 1,200. Scarborough's talent for evangelism led to his selection in 1908 as a professor of evangelism at the recently established Southwestern Baptist Theological Seminary in Waco.

Southwestern was founded in 1905 as Baylor Theological Seminary, but the two schools separated in 1908. After much consideration and a painful separation from the congregation in Abilene, Scarborough joined the seminary faculty. From 1908 to 1910 he labored primarily as a fundraiser, procuring the money to relocate the institution to its present campus at Fort Worth, Texas. The remainder of his career was divided between his duties as a professor and administrator at the seminary and his larger role as a denominational leader.

Scarborough's experience as a fundraiser was instrumental in his appointment as the director of the Seventy-five Million Campaign, a pledge drive undertaken by Southern Baptists in 1919. Through his efforts, the denomination exceeded its goal of $75 million in pledges, to be collected over the following five years. More than $92 million was pledged, but less than $59 million was actually collected, owing to economic difficulties in the South after 1920. An enduring result of the campaign was the establishment of a centralized agency for disbursement of funds, which evolved into the modern Southern Baptist denominational structure.

From 1914 until his retirement in 1942, Scarborough filled dual roles at Southwestern as both the president of the seminary and a professor of evangelism. As a professor he produced a series of textbooks on evangelism to be used in seminary courses. The most noteworthy of these are *With Christ after the Lost* (1919), *Endued to Win* (1922), and *How Jesus Won Men* (1926). All of Scarborough's works viewed the biblical account of Jesus' ministry as a model for contemporary evangelism. Scarborough also wrote a history of Southwestern titled *A Modern School of the Prophets* (1939).

During his twenty-seven years as the president of Southwestern, Scarborough emphasized evangelism and missions. He was a frequent revival speaker and attended countless denominational meetings, both lo-

cal and national. In a variety of elected or appointed offices, Scarborough helped shape Southern Baptist organizations and traditions. He was a member of the committee that drafted the 1925 statement of faith, "The Baptist Faith and Message," and his leadership was instrumental in rebuffing the criticisms of the fundamentalist J. Frank Norris, who opposed modernism and denominational centralization. Along with Edgar Young Mullins, then the president of the Southern Baptist Theological Seminary, Scarborough staunchly opposed the extremist positions of what he termed "Norrisism." Mullins and Scarborough both ignored the denomination's anti-evolution resolution of 1926.

Scarborough helped build Southwestern Seminary. His books formed an important part of its curriculum, and his leadership helped secure the funding for many of its buildings. During the later years of his presidency, the institution struggled with financial deficits, but it eventually recovered and prospered, growing into one of the largest seminaries in the world.

The Texas Baptist subculture of which Southwestern was so integral a part promoted an imperialist view of missions, a conservative theology, and a defense of entrenched racism and patriarchy. Scarborough reflected that culture, but he left two enduring legacies in Southwestern Seminary and the denominational structures of the Southern Baptist Convention. He died in Amarillo, Texas.

• Scarborough's papers are housed at Southwestern Baptist Theological Seminary in Fort Worth, Tex. The L. R. Scarborough Collection contains approximately 900 files. Glenn Thomas Carson, "Lee Rutland Scarborough: Architect of a New Denominationalism within the Southern Baptist Convention" (Ph.D. diss., Southwestern Baptist Theological Seminary, 1992), and Michael Mark Hawley, "A Critical Examination of Lee Rutland Scarborough's Concept of Evangelism" (Ph.D. diss., New Orleans Baptist Theological Seminary, 1992), are helpful. Harvey Eugene Dana, *Lee Rutland Scarborough: A Life of Service* (1945), is informative but eulogistic. Additional information can be found in H. Leon McBeth, *The Baptist Heritage* (1987), and Robert A. Baker, *Tell the Generations Following: A History of Southwestern Baptist Theological Seminary, 1908–1983* (1983). For a study of the social and cultural milieu, especially with respect to conservative social positions and twentieth-century developments in Southern Baptist history, see John Lee Eighmy, *Churches in Cultural Captivity* (1972), Charles R. Wilson, *Baptized in Blood: The Religion of the Lost Cause, 1865–1920* (1980), and Bill J. Leonard, *God's Last and Only Hope: The Fragmentation of the Southern Baptist Convention* (1990).

LEE SWAFFORD BURCHFIELD

SCARLETT, William (3 Oct. 1883–28 Mar. 1973), Episcopal clergyman, was born William Joseph Scarlett in Columbus, Ohio, the son of William Scarlett, a manufacturer of lodge and organization regalia, and Myrna Siebert. In early life he was influenced by Washington Gladden, a minister of the Congregational church in Columbus, and by the writings of Walter Rauschenbusch. After early education in the public schools of Columbus, Scarlett entered Harvard College and was graduated in 1905. Undecided between medicine and theology, he spent a year on a ranch in western Nebraska "punching cows." Regarded as a man of religious bent, he was called on to conduct religious services for the ranchers. This experience led him back to theology, and he was graduated from the Episcopal Theological School in Cambridge, Massachusetts, in 1909. While in theological school he had attended some classes at Harvard in the new field of Christian ethics. Following ordination on 2 June at St. John's Chapel in Cambridge, he served as an assistant in St. George's Church in New York City, helping to establish a mission on the Lower East Side.

In 1911 the bishop of Arizona called Scarlett to be dean of Trinity Cathedral in Phoenix, then a small parish in the capital city of the Territory of Arizona. In Phoenix he began to establish a reputation as a preacher and pastor and, also, as one who cared for the poor and dispossessed. When local cooks and waiters went on strike and tensions ran high, Scarlett attempted to mediate but discovered that the issues demanded governmental attention. In this situation and others he became known in Arizona as one clergyman who did not fear the power of the copper mining companies.

When in 1917 the owners of a number of copper mines herded several hundred striking miners from their homes in Bisbee and attempted to deport them out of Arizona, Scarlett was one of few clergymen willing to take a stand on the matter. He called on the Department of Justice to investigate, and the young Felix Frankfurter was sent from Washington. Scarlett and the future Supreme Court justice became firm friends. The matter was finally settled, not to everyone's satisfaction, but copper was once again produced to meet the needs of the United States at war.

After turning down calls to other parishes, Scarlett accepted a call to be dean of Christ Church Cathedral in St. Louis, Missouri. He held his first service in St. Louis on 7 May 1922. Christ Church Cathedral was the oldest Episcopal congregation west of the Mississippi. It is a downtown church, attracting and ministering to people from the whole metropolitan area. During his eight years as dean Scarlett strengthened the congregation's ministry to all persons, and many non-Episcopalians looked to it for leadership.

When Ferdinand Isserman, a young rabbi from Canada, arrived in St. Louis to take charge of a local Jewish congregation, he was advised to seek out Scarlett. The two became friends and in 1932 formed the Social Justice Commission to deal with local conflicts by providing an unbiased third party to serve a mediating function and to furnish a face-saving way to ease tension. The commission was useful in reducing tension during a dispute over milk prices and later in a threatened strike by streetcar employees. The commission also mediated a dispute between mine owners and the Progressive Mine Workers in Illinois.

When in 1929 Bishop Frederick Foote Johnson of Missouri became ill and could no longer provide the leadership the diocese demanded, he called for the election of a bishop coadjutor. The convention of the diocese acted with alacrity and elected Scarlett on its first ballot. Consecrated on 6 May 1930, Scarlett set out to rebuild the work of the diocese, particularly in its outreach. Commenting on Scarlett's election, the *Christian Century* magazine called it "another argument for episcopacy." Scarlett succeeded Johnson as bishop of Missouri on 8 November 1933.

Entering the House of Bishops Scarlett soon became its conscience, calling attention to "man's inhumanity to man." A longtime member of the General Convention Commission on Marriage and Divorce, he labored for years to relax the Episcopal church's position on marriage after divorce. Finally, in 1946, the General convention did make the marriage of divorced persons possible. Scarlett's role in this decision was manifested when he and the bishop of Chicago came to an agreement on the text of the amended canon.

In 1940 Scarlett encouraged the General Convention to correspond with a commission in the Church of England, chaired by Archbishop Temple, to work on plans for reconstruction following the end of World War II. The convention set up the Joint Commission on Social Reconstruction, with Scarlett as its chairman. The commission reported in 1943 and again in 1946 and 1949 with printed books, each time calling for more attention to civil rights and social justice.

Scarlett's interests extended beyond Sunday worship and social justice into ecumenism, and the doors of Christ Church Cathedral were open to all. An interdenominational celebration of the Holy Communion was held there when such services were frowned on by many hard-core Episcopalians. He resisted these protests and strongly supported efforts to establish some sort of intercommunion with Presbyterians. Learning that St. Louis Presbyterians were interested in opening a hospital, Scarlett encouraged them instead to join in the operation of St. Luke's Episcopal Hospital, thus strengthening its basis of support. The result was St. Luke's Episcopal-Presbyterian Hospital, a collaboration that led the way to other health and welfare projects in the St. Louis metropolitan area. Scarlett was also an early member of the Urban League of St. Louis, serving as its president for several years.

The Walker Trusts for mission work and the Thompson Fund for religious and charitable purposes, two major endowment funds of the Episcopal church in Missouri, grew out of Scarlett's relationship with business and professional men.

In 1941 Scarlett had married Leah Van Riper Oliver, a widow whom he had known for several years. By 1950 Scarlett had begun to tire, so he called for the selection of a successor. Arthur Lichtenberger was consecrated as bishop coadjutor on 5 April 1951 and succeeded as bishop of Missouri on 1 November 1952. In retirement the Scarletts had hoped to remain in St. Louis, where they had many roots, but her illness interfered, and they moved to Castine, Maine, near one of her sons. (She died in 1965.) However, before the move, Scarlett was able to serve as president of the St. Louis Ministerial Alliance and to write occasionally on social issues. He also conducted "quiet days" for the clergy and provided counseling. At the age of eighty Scarlett toured Israel with Rabbi Isserman.

At the time of Scarlett's death at Boston Hospital, the media often referred to him as a social reformer, listing his many activities on social issues. But he would have rejected that description. For Scarlett the gospel was social. It was as a spiritual leader that he was known in the Episcopal church. His views on social issues were an extension of his faith, a faith that he successfully communicated to his parishioners. His sermons, books and prayers, and reports to the General Convention were all based on his understanding of God's will for mankind.

• Scarlett's papers are in the archives of the Diocese of Missouri, St. Louis; in the archives of the Episcopal Church, Austin, Tex.; and in the Niebuhr papers in the Library of Congress. Scarlett's attempt at an autobiography, "The Road Taken; or, A Parson's Tale," is an unpublished manuscript and is located in the Scarlett papers in the Episcopal Church Archives, Austin, Tex. Scarlett's published works include the two reports of the Joint Commission on Social Reconstruction to the General Convention of the Episcopal Church that he edited, *Toward a Better World for All People* (1946), and its companion paperback edition, *Christianity Takes a Stand* (1946), and *Christian Demands for Social Justice* (1949). He also edited two little books of prayers and devotions, *In His Presence* (1917) and *To Will One Thing* (1948). Scarlett wrote the "Exposition of Jonah" for *the Interpreter's Bible* (1956), and he edited a selection of sermons by Phillips Brooks that was published in 1949. References to Scarlett's work are found in the journals of the conventions of the Diocese of Missouri; in the Archives of the Diocese of Missouri, St. Louis; in various issues of the *Spirit of Missions* and *Forth* magazines; and in James W. Byrkit, *Forging the Copper Collar: Arizona's Labor-Management War of 1901–1921* (1982), Richard Wightman Fox, *Reinhold Niebuhr: A Biography* (1985), William G. Chrystal, ed., *Young Reinhold Niebuhr* (1977), and Charles F. Rehkopf, "The Episcopate of William Scarlett," Missouri Historical Society *Bulletin* 20 (Apr. 1964): 193–217. An obituary is in the *New York Times*, 29 Mar. 1973.

CHARLES F. REHKOPF

SCAROUADY (fl. 1750–1758), Oneida leader also known as Skaroyady, Monachatoocha, or Half-King, was the successor of Tanacharison (also known as Half-King) as the principal spokesman of the Mingoes, the name given to those members of the Iroquois confederation who had moved westward and settled among the Shawnees and Delawares in the Ohio country. Nothing is known of his early life. This land was claimed by the Iroquois confederacy of New York, and Scarouady was believed by early observers to represent it and was called a "half-king" or "viceroy." In fact, the Mingoes did not regard themselves as under the control of the Iroquois confederacy but established an independent council fire on the Ohio with the Delawares and Shawnees.

When Tanacharison died in 1754, Scarouady succeeded him as the leader of the pro-British faction of the Ohio Indians and continued to regard the French territorial ambitions as the greater danger to the Ohio Indians. He represented the Ohio Indians in discus-

sions with Virginia and Pennsylvania at Winchester and Carlisle in 1753. He supported George Washington in his effort to force the French from the Ohio region and opposed the Delawares' principal chief Shingas's pro-French faction during the French and Indian War. Washington's defeat at Fort Necessity undermined Scarouady's prestige and forced him to flee. Afterward, in October 1754, he took a message from the Wyoming Delawares to colonial officials in Philadelphia, offering an alliance with the British. However, Governor Robert Morris declined the offer and thus drove the majority of Delawares over to the French.

Scarouady continued to warn British officials of the impending war. In a message to colonial officials he declared, "We pray . . . the people of Pennsylvania not to leave us in the lurch, but to supply us with necessaries to enable us to fight the French" (Wallace, p. 73). Again, his appeal was rejected. On 8 November 1754 Scarouady, who was speaking for the pro-British Delawares, addressed the Pennsylvania Assembly and pointed out that there were about 300 Delaware warriors in the Wyoming Valley and that he had been sent by these Indians to seek a formal military alliance. Scarouady bluntly told the solons, "Brethren, I must deal plain wth. you & tell you if you will not fight, with us, we will go somewhere else. We never can, nor ever will put up [with] yt. Affront. If we cannot be safe where we are we will go somewhere else for Protection & take care of our selves" (Wallace, p. 73). Still the Pennsylvanians refused to provide arms or money that would have allowed Scarouady's followers to resist the French.

Although his life was threatened because of his pro-British views, Scarouady continued to work for peace between the British and the Delawares, and between 19 April and 23 April 1755 he took part in a peace conference held at Israel Pemberton's home. In spite of the rejection of his offer of an alliance by colonial officials, Scarouady and a force of about 50 Delawares joined British major general Edward Braddock's campaign to drive the French from the Ohio region. But as Scarouady commented, Braddock "looked upon us as dogs, and would never hear anything what was said to him" (Weslager, p. 223). On 9 July 1755 Scarouady was with the British at the Battle of the Wilderness, when 1,850 British regulars and colonial militia were defeated by French and Indians. Forced to flee with the retreating British, he served as a Six Nations' messenger on the Susquehanna River, where he continued to support the British; however, his influence waned following the British defeat. He appears to have died before 26 August 1758, when his wife presented his pipe to the governor of Pennsylvania. Her name and the number of their children, if any, are unknown.

• The official colonial accounts of Scarouady's role in the French and Indian War are in the *Pennsylvania Colonial Records* (16 vols., 1852–1853). Recent material on Scarouady can be found in C. A. Weslager, *The Delaware Indians: A History* (1972), Anthony F. C. Wallace, *King of the Delaware: Teedyuscung, 1700–1763* (1949), and Michael N. McConnell, *A*

Country Between (1992). An older sketch is given in Chester Hale Sipe, *Indian Chiefs of Pennsylvania* (1927). See also Francis Jennings, *Empire of Fortune* (1988).

PAUL F. LAMBERT

SCARRY, Richard McClure (5 June 1919–30 Apr. 1994), author and illustrator, was born in Boston, Massachusetts, the son of John James Scarry, owner of a small chain of department stores, and Barbara McClure. Raised in Boston, Scarry (rhymes with "carry") struggled through five years of high school and, because he did not have enough credits, was unable to get into a college. In 1938, after a short stint at the Boston Business School, he enrolled at the Boston School for Fine Arts, affiliated with the Museum of Fine Arts, to study drawing and painting. Scarry also attended the Archipenko Art School in Woodstock, New York, and the Eliot O'Hara Watercolor School in Gooserocks Beach, Maine.

World War II interrupted his education, and Scarry left the Boston School of Fine Arts in 1941. Drafted as a radio repairman, he soon secured a place at an officer candidate school. Scarry spent five years in the army, serving as an art director for the Morale Services Section, where he drew maps and designed graphics for troop entertainment, information, and education. He served in North Africa, Italy, and France, advancing to the rank of captain.

After the war Scarry moved to New York City, intending to pursue a career as a freelance commercial artist. In 1946 he completed illustrations for a children's book by Joan Hubbard titled *The Boss of the Barnyard*, published by Golden Press. From this point he had steady work illustrating a number of other authors' books, until he decided to write and illustrate his own.

During this period Scarry met Patricia "Patsy" Murphy from Vancouver, British Columbia, also an author of children's books. They married in 1949, two weeks after they met at a party. Days after this meeting, he proposed by sending her a telegram with these words: "Must move grand piano. Heavy. Come immediately." The Scarrys lived on a farm in Ridgefield, Connecticut, and collaborated on several books, including *Danny Beaver's Secret* (1953). In 1953 their only child, Richard McClure "Huck" Scarry II, was born. He, too, became a successful author and illustrator of children's books. The family moved to Westport, Connecticut. In 1968 they made their final move to Gstaad, Switzerland.

As an illustrator-author, Scarry published more than 250 books, which have been translated into thirty different languages. These books range from counting and alphabet primers, to picture books about manners and daily life, to pop-up books. Altogether, his books sold over 100 million copies. In 1989 *Publishers Weekly* compiled a list of fifty of the bestselling children's books of all time, which included eight books by Scarry.

Scarry's first book as both author and illustrator was *The Great Big Car and Truck Book* (1951), full of the bright, detailed illustrations characteristic of his work. It was in 1963 that he first achieved commercial success with the publication of *Richard Scarry's Best Word Book Ever*. Still in print, it has sold more than four million copies. The book depicts more than 1,400 objects, labeled and commented upon, and an assortment of droll animals, all engaged in a variety of human activities, who help define the words.

The animals in Scarry's books are always cheerful and energetic, and each has a distinct personality. Some animals are favorites and tend to reappear in different books. Scarry was particularly fond of Lowly Worm who, wearing his Tyrolean plaid hat, "can often be found in some obscure corner of a complicated drawing" (Mehegan, *Boston Globe*, 4 May 1994). When asked why he used animals instead of people in his illustrations, Scarry said, "I use animals rather than humans firstly because they're more fun and it's easier to distinguish one character from another if one is a rabbit and the other is a cat than if both are boys" (quoted in Moss, p. 182). Scarry also said that he found children of all races would identify more readily with an animal than with a child of a different race or color.

Other extremely popular Scarry books include *Busy, Busy World* (1965), which is set in all the famous cities of the world and filled with adventure and Scarry's usual slapstick humor. An animated TV series based on this book began airing on Showtime, a cable channel, in 1994. Richard Scarry's *What Do People Do All Day* (1968) shows his "people" working at a variety of jobs. Particularly effective is a two-page cutaway view of an ocean liner, from bridge to engine room, showing all sorts of activities. It is this mass of detail and movement that has such a strong appeal to children, who have been known to spend "unnaturally long periods of time" poring over the illustrations (Lanes, p. 123). Although his target audience was between two and ten, Scarry noted that "I see babies looking at the pictures, even if they're holding the book upside down. And plenty of teenagers, too, sneak back to my books when they think no one is looking" (quoted in Chelminski, p. 106).

Although children love his books, Scarry's work has been criticized by adults. Some think his illustrations show too much violence. But Scarry defended his position: "It's not true violence, it's fun. I have cars pile up and people get into trouble . . . The only thing that really suffers is dignity" (quoted in Chelminski, pp. 106, 109). An example would be Sergeant Murphy (a dog) about to collide with a birthday cake. Other critics see his work as using sexual stereotypes. He responded to this criticism by drawing his animals to indicate gender in their clothing and including more female characters in "male" occupations, such as Flossie the policewoman.

His mystery series, which began with *The Great Pie Robbery* (1969), was particularly successful. *Richard Scarry's Great Steamboat Mystery* (1975) earned him a Mystery Writers of America Edgar Allan Poe special award in 1976.

Adaptations of Scarry's work include the talking books *What Do People Do All Day and Other Stories* (1978) and *What Do People Do All Day and Great Big Schoolhouse* (1979), both read by Carol Channing. Computer software was developed in 1985 for *Richard Scarry's Best Electronic Work Book Ever!*

Scarry died in Gstaad, Switzerland. Described by *Boston Globe* critic David Mehegan as a "writer who had a direct wire to children's hearts" (4 May 1994), Scarry himself felt that it was a "precious thing to be communicating to children, helping them discover the gift of language and thought. I'm happy to be doing it" (quoted in "Scarry Good," p. 116). Summing up Scarry's work, Clay Reynolds, critic and father, writes: "Through his multifarious menagerie, Scarry demonstrates that all people, big and little, make mistakes and have accidents, that the world is a sort of funny, crazy, zany, and confusing place, that there really is no such thing as a disaster when there is love and understanding, and, most importantly, that there is humor and wisdom in human folly" (pp. 285–86).

• A collection of Scarry's works is included in the Kerlan Collection at the University of Minnesota. For a complete listing of Scarry's work as illustrator alone and as author-illustrator, see Laura Standley Berger, ed., *Twentieth-Century Children's Writers*, 4th ed. (1995). For biographical and critical information, see Bobbie Burch Lemontt, "Richard Scarry," *American Writers for Children Since 1960: Poets, Illustrators, and Nonfiction Authors* (1987). Additional information on Scarry's career is in Selma G. Lanes, *Down the Rabbit Hole: Adventures and Misadventures in the Realm of Children's Literature* (1971), and Lee Kingman et al., comps., *Illustrators of Children's Books, 1957–1966* (1968). General information on Scarry, including an interview, is in Rudi Chelminski, "Pages: This is the House the Menagerie of Richard Scarry Built," *People Weekly*, 15 Oct. 1979, pp. 105–10. For a critical article of Scarry's work see Clay Reynolds, "The Book That Scarry Built: Being Part a Discourse on the Importance of the Role of Children in Children's Literature," *Studies in American Humor* 5 (Winter 1986–1987): 280–86. See also Elaine Moss, "Richard Scarry," *Children's Literature Review* 3 (1978): 181–87. An article assessing Scarry's influence on children's literature is David Mehegan, "Richard Scarry Wrote His Way into Children's Hearts," *Boston Globe*, 4 May 1994. Another assessment is "Scarry Good," *People Weekly*, 16 May 1994, p. 116. Detailed obituaries are in the *Boston Globe*, 4 May 1994, and the *New York Times*, 3 May 1994.

MARCIA B. DINNEEN

SCATCHARD, George (19 Mar. 1892–10 Dec. 1973), physical chemist, was born in the village of Oneonta, New York, the son of Elmer Ellsworth Scatchard and Fanny Lavinia Harmer. Taught to read at home at an early age, Scatchard began school in the third grade at the Oneonta Normal School and attended there through high school. Entering Amherst College in 1909, he majored in chemistry and graduated in 1913. In that year he began graduate work at Columbia University in organic chemistry with a minor in physiological chemistry. He finished his Ph.D. dissertation in 1916 and remained at Columbia until 1918 as an assistant to Alexander Smith, studying the vapor pressure of very dry ammonium chloride and, from 1917, doing research on gas masks for the war. Drafted in 1918, Scatchard entered the army as a first lieutenant in the Sanitary Corps and was sent to France, where he worked at the Sorbonne with Victor Grignard on the detection of low concentrations of mustard gas.

On his return to the United States early in 1919, he received a National Research Council (NRC) fellowship, but he chose instead to accept a teaching position as associate professor at Amherst. While there, Scatchard studied the vapor pressure of sucrose (table sugar) solutions and the inversion of sucrose (the breakdown of sucrose into two simpler sugars, glucose and fructose) in concentrated solutions.

In 1923 he went to the Massachusetts Institute of Technology (MIT) on an NRC fellowship and in 1924 joined the faculty as an assistant professor of physical chemistry. He became associate professor in 1926 and married Willian Watson Beaumont, whom he had met at Columbia, in 1928. They had no children. A Guggenheim fellowship in 1931–1932 was spent mostly writing and studying with Peter Debye in Leipzig, Germany. He became full professor at MIT in 1937.

At MIT, Scatchard continued the study of the thermodynamics of solutions of electrolytes, proteins, and other colloids. In his autobiography, he says that his major contribution to the exciting developments being made in the physical chemistry of solutions and reaction rates during the 1920s was "the meticulous survey of the assumptions underlying the various treatments and the definition of ideal solutions in terms of mole fraction [the ratio of the number of a particular kind of molecule to the total number of molecules present] instead of volume concentration."

Scatchard's interest in protein solutions arose from discussions with Edwin Cohn, a physical chemist at the Harvard Medical School, whom Scatchard had known since their undergraduate years at Amherst. These talks concerned the applicability of the Debye-Hückel theory (dealing with the effect that the electrical charges on ions have on the properties of solutions) to protein solutions. Although he and Cohn shared this interest and were in close contact, they never collaborated on a joint paper, but Scatchard's colleagues used Cohn's experimental data to check their theoretical results, and Cohn's colleagues used these results as a guide in their experimentation. One of Scatchard's purposes in this work was to show that proteins were, in fact, very large molecules, rather than aggregations of smaller ones.

During the Second World War Scatchard worked with Cohn on the fractionation of blood plasma proteins. Albumin is needed to counteract the effects of shock, which it does by drawing water from body tissues into the bloodstream, thus increasing the blood volume. This effect depends on the osmotic pressure of the albumin solution; Scatchard, together with A. C. Batchelder and A. Brown, measured the osmotic pressure of bovine serum albumin over a wide range of pH values and albumin concentrations in such a way that the interactions between the protein and electrolytes in the solution could be evaluated and the molecular weight of the protein determined. His studies of the binding of small molecules and ions to serum albumin were fundamental to the development of a way to stabilize the protein at elevated temperatures, thus allowing it to be heated to destroy the hepatitis virus. He continued work in this area after the war.

Scatchard was also acting director of the Physical Chemistry Laboratory at MIT from 1943 to 1945 and a scientific adviser to Harold Urey at Columbia University for the Manhattan Project. He spent part of each week in New York, working on the thermodynamics of the fluorocarbon systems used in the separation of uranium isotopes by gaseous diffusion. In 1946 he was for six months in Berlin, Germany, where, besides being scientific adviser to the deputy military governor, he was chief of the Research Control Branch of the Office of Military Government. After the war, he became a consultant to the Oak Ridge National Laboratory in Tennessee, where he and his wife would spend part of the summer.

Although much of Scatchard's work involved making very precise measurements (of temperature or conductivity, for example) he was not interested in measurement techniques per se. He is quoted as saying that his apparatus was "a box where a lot of things go on inside that I really don't care about as long as I can get the numbers that come out" (Scheinberg, p. viii).

He enjoyed walking and hiking in what spare time he had, and he had a deep love of music. He and his wife, a member of the music department at Smith College, were devoted patrons of the Boston Symphony, attending most of the weekly performances during the concert season.

A member of the American Chemical Society, Scatchard received the Theodore W. Richards Medal in 1954 and the Kendall Company Award in colloid chemistry in 1962. He was elected a member of the National Academy of Sciences in 1946 and also belonged to the American Association for the Advancement of Science, the New York Academy of Sciences, the American Academy of Arts and Sciences, Alpha Chi Sigma (the chemistry fraternity), and Sigma Xi (the scientific research fraternity). In 1951 he was a Sigma Xi national lecturer. Although he retired in 1957, he continued to write and direct research until a few years before his death in Cambridge, Massachusetts.

• Scatchard's papers are in the MIT archives. Two sets of his course lectures, "Equilibrium in Solutions" and "Surface and Colloid Chemistry," were published posthumously as G. Scatchard, *Equilibrium in Solutions: Surface and Colloid Chemistry* (1976). This volume also contains his "Autobiographical Note," in which he comments briefly on each of his 165 papers, and a biographical sketch by I. Herbert Scheinberg as an introduction. Additional autobiographical material is contained in Scatchard's Kendall Award talk, "Half a Century as a Part-time Colloid Chemist," printed in K. J. Mysels et al., eds., *Twenty Years of Colloid and Surface Chemistry: The Kendall Award Addresses* (1973). Articles appearing in *Chemical and Engineering News*, 24 May 1954, pp. 2098–99, and 2 Apr. 1962, p. 100, when he received the Richards Medal and the Kendall Award, are short but informative. There is a complete bibliography in J. T. Edsall and W. H. Stockmayer, "George Scatchard," National Academy of Sciences, *Biographical Memoirs* 52 (1980): 335–77. An obituary is in the *New York Times*, 15 Dec. 1973.

RUSSELL F. TRIMBLE

SCHABINGER, Arthur August (6 Aug. 1889–13 Oct. 1972), college basketball coach and sports administrator, was born in Sabetha, Kansas, the son of Karl Augustus Schabinger and Johanna Pohl. Schabinger's father died before the boy was three years old, after which the family moved to Emporia, Kansas. Schabinger graduated from Lewis Academy (since defunct), where he played basketball, football, and baseball, and ran track. At the College of Emporia he again participated in four sports. He played baseball, led the team in batting, and served as captain in 1911. In basketball he twice won all-state honors as a guard. On the track team he raced at 440 yards and in the relays. But his greatest success came in football. Three years in a row he was chosen as quarterback on the all-Kansas Conference team, and he was renowned as an excellent passer before Notre Dame quarterback Charles "Gus" Dorais popularized that offensive skill in a 1913 game against Army.

After graduating from Emporia in 1912, Schabinger, known by now as "Schabie," enrolled at Springfield College in Massachusetts for graduate training in coaching. He played baseball and football, helped as a student coach in both sports, and received a degree in 1915. Fans of Springfield football long remembered his eighty-yard touchdown run against Army in 1914.

Schabinger returned to Kansas to become director of athletics and coach of all sports at Ottawa University. Over a span of five years, interrupted by his infantry service in World War I, his teams established an enviable record in football, track, and basketball. His track teams lost only one dual meet at home during his tenure and twice finished second in state meets. His football squads always ranked high, and his basketball teams won one state championship, finished second twice, third once, and fourth once in a seventeen-team conference.

Schabinger was married to Gladys Miriam Johnson of Waverly, Kansas; they had three children. In 1920 he moved back to Emporia to join the athletic staff at the Kansas State Normal School (now Emporia State University), where he assisted football coach H. W. Hargiss (his own coach at the College of Emporia); Schabinger also directed the basketball and baseball teams. He began to build a reputation for getting the most out of whatever talent was on his teams, but after two years he left to become athletic director and basketball coach at Creighton University in Omaha at an annual salary of $5,000.

Schabinger assumed control of a successful, if modest, basketball program. In his first year, 1922–1923, he guided Creighton to the North Central Conference championship, a feat the team repeated three times in the next four years by using an innovative, fast-break offense. He moved Creighton to the Missouri Valley Conference (MVC) for the 1928–1929 season. During a stretch of seven seasons the Bluejays won the MVC title once outright (1931–1932), were co-champions twice (1929–1930 and 1934–1935), and tri-champions in 1930–1931. His overall won-lost record at Creighton was 163–66 (.712).

Throughout his coaching career Schabinger was an original thinker who constantly worked to improve the game of basketball. Early on, Creighton added intersectional games to its schedule against such opponents as Marquette, Indiana, Iowa, Notre Dame, and Kentucky. Creighton became the first college basketball team to fly to distant games. Schabinger was also instrumental in organizing the National Association of Basketball Coaches (NABC), which he led as president in 1931–1932.

After the 1934–1935 season he resigned at Creighton and moved to Chicago to work for a major sporting goods firm. He participated in the research, development, and promotion of a molded basketball that performed with improved consistency over previous equipment because it had no laces or panels.

In 1936 basketball became an Olympic sport, and the U.S. Olympic Committee chose Schabinger to direct the intercollegiate tournament to select the team. The Americans won the gold medal at Berlin, beginning a streak of consecutive U.S. victories that lasted until 1972.

Schabinger entered the Army Air Corps during World War II and was assigned to Special Services where he learned the educational potential of motion pictures. After the war he founded the Official Sports Film Service, a company sanctioned by several athletic governing bodies to produce films in English and several other languages that would teach consistent interpretation and application of playing rules. He also officiated at games and served on the NABC rules committee. Before his retirement in 1956, he conducted coaching and officiating clinics across the country.

The Naismith Memorial Basketball Hall of Fame recognized Schabinger's contributions to the game by inducting him in 1961 as a basketball pioneer. He died in Atlanta.

• Although no biography has been published, there are clipping files on Schabinger at the Basketball Hall of Fame and at the William Allen White Library, Emporia State University.
STEVEN P. GIETSCHIER

SCHAEFER, Walter V. (10 Dec. 1904–15 June 1986), lawyer, judge, and professor, was born in Grand Rapids, Michigan, the son of Henry Schaefer and Martha Erck. Walter's parents died when he was still very young, and consequently he was raised by his two aunts in Green Bay, Wisconsin. Moving to Chicago to attend college in the early 1920s, Schaefer unwittingly established ties to the state of Illinois that would eventually lead to a career as a notable jurist. By 1928 he

had earned a B.A. in philosophy and a law degree from the University of Chicago. Describing his academic career a few years later, Schaefer labeled himself as "just a pretty good student; no world beater," who might have done better had he not "devoted so much time to baseball and tennis," a characteristic description from a modest man who in fact was both an excellent law student and a fine athlete who helped the university tennis team garner the Big Ten Championship two years in a row.

After being admitted to the bar in 1928, Schaefer worked briefly as a statutory draftsman for the Legislative Reference Bureau in Springfield, Illinois, before becoming an associate at Tolman, Sexton, & Chandler in Chicago. From 1929 to 1934 Schaefer established firm ties to the state of Illinois while simultaneously struggling through the depression. In 1931, quite fortuitously, Schaefer and another young lawyer, Albert E. Jenner, Jr., persuaded the Chicago Bar Association to form a Younger Members Committee on Amendment of the Law. Tremendously successful, the Younger Members movement soon extended beyond the borders of Chicago, and by 1933 Schaefer was helping to organize the Junior Bar Conference of the American Bar Association in Milwaukee.

As members of the Young Lawyers Committee, Schaefer and Jenner drafted and helped enact several bills. Schaefer is most well known during this period for his efforts in preparing the Illinois Civil Practice Act, which instituted a contemporary pleading and practice statute in place of common law. In 1929 the Chicago Bar Association finally called for a committee to replace the outdated common law pleading system with a modern pleading and practice statute. Although not officially members of the drafting committee, Schaefer and Jenner—as members of the Young Lawyers organization—volunteered for the task of comparing the final document of 1931 against every section, paragraph, and line of the Illinois Revised Statutes of 1929. While the undertaking appeared to be both a tedious and thankless job, both men were unmarried and ambitious, and their sense that the task would serve to propel their careers proved accurate. By January 1934 the act had taken effect.

Meanwhile, a senior partner in Schaefer's firm became secretary to a federal committee charged with establishing Rules of Civil Procedure in the federal courts. Schaefer was invited to work with the committee as a reporter. He abandoned that task in 1934, joining the Agriculture Adjustment Administration in Washington, D.C., as a litigation lawyer. Within a year or so, however, Schaefer returned to Chicago for a two-year stint in the legal department of the Reconstruction Finance Corporation, where he met his future wife, Marguerite "Margo" Moreland Goff. Then, just as Chicago was emerging from the depression, Schaefer secured a job as assistant corporation counsel for the city of Chicago. Serving as head of the organization's land division, Schaefer helped rebuild the city during a time when land acquisition and construction were crucial for economic revitalization, a feat that earned him the praise of both the mayor and the Chicago City Council.

In 1940 Schaefer married Goff; the couple had two children, and Schaefer also helped raise two of Margo's sons by a previous marriage. For the next eleven years Schaefer taught at Northwestern University School of Law, where a former student and colleague commented that "he could teach almost any course and when one looks at the law school catalogues of the time, it appears that over the years he came close to doing that" (Rahl, p. 700). Not only did Schaefer pour an exorbitant amount of energy into his instruction, but he once jokingly commented that "getting ready to teach a class is like preparing for an appellate argument" (Rahl, p. 701). In addition to his skills as a teacher, which he characteristically downplayed by striving to play the role of an "instructor in the background," Schaefer also served as an able mentor for many of his younger colleagues. Speaking of his generosity in this respect, one young colleague later remarked that Schaefer "unostentatiously did those things for young faculty members that senior members should, but do not always, do" (Allen, p. 693).

The decline in enrollment during World War II forced the university to relieve Schaefer of his duties from 1942 to 1943, when he served as a referee in bankruptcy courts. He was a fixture in Northwestern's legal community until 1948 when he took a leave of absence to serve as a legal assistant to Adlai Stevenson, who was running for governor of Illinois. Schaefer helped Stevenson, a longshot, win the governorship and served Stevenson as a top aide until 1951, when Stevenson appointed him to the Illinois Supreme Court. According to one colleague, the relationship between Stevenson and Schaefer was one of mutual respect "that paid its biggest dividend for the public interest generally, and for the legal world in particular, in 1951" (McGowan, p. 680).

Schaefer was reelected to the Illinois Supreme Court until he retired in 1976, and his opinions and judicial wisdom served as a model for other state courts and judges; he was often referred to as the "thinking member of the court" (*New York Times*, 17 June 1986). When, during the 1960s, a bank stock scandal reached to the state's highest court, Schaefer's moral presence did a great deal to repair the institution's integrity. Speaking of Schaefer's sense of right, Robert L. Stern, a partner in a Chicago firm, went so far as to say, "If you wanted to name one outstanding judge in Illinois, in the state courts at least, he's the only one" (*New York Times*, 17 June 1986). Schaefer not only authored opinions on a wide variety of issues, but by the end of his reign on the court he was considered one of the nation's most well known and influential appellate jurists, prompting Supreme Court justice William Brennan to comment that "he possessed in the highest degree deep and perceptive insights into the larger function of law in our turbulent and rapidly changing society" (Brennan, p. 677). Serving twice as chief justice of the court, Schaefer's approach was ethical, practical, and unsentimental, with his judgments revealing "an almost biblical pragmatism: by their fruits you shall know them, not by their vocal adherence to the conventional morality" (Allen, p. 692). Awarded the American Bar Association Gold Medal in 1969, Schaefer joined the ranks of Oliver Wendell Holmes and Arthur T. Vanderbilt. Retiring from the bench in 1976, he continued to practice law in Chicago and to lecture at the University of Chicago, Harvard, Northwestern, and New York University. Schaefer died in Lake Forest Hospital in Michigan.

Schaefer once remarked to his friend the Honorable Roger J. Traynor, "There are no simple villains and no pure heroes either. There is only time. Time longer than our lifetimes." Realizing his own limitations as a jurist, Schaefer remained to the end a modest man, despite his many accomplishments. In addition to his wisdom on the bench, he was also a man intent on generosity in both his personal and professional life, prompting a former student and colleague to say that Schaefer "has gone further than anyone I know toward converting the practice of kindness into a fine art" (Allen, p. 693). Still, in a century often devoid of legal heroes or heroines, Schaefer's three rules of "fairness, fairness, and fairness" (*Chicago Tribune*, 17 June 1986) made his career, according to Justice Brennan, "living proof of Justice Holmes's confident assertions that it is possible 'in the law, as elsewhere, to live greatly'" (*New York Times*, 17 June 1986).

• Walter Schaefer was the author of three books, including *The Suspect and Society: Criminal Procedure and Converging Constitutional Doctrines* (1967), *Courts and the Common Places of Federalism* (1959), and *Illinois Civil Practice Act, Annotated* (1934). He also wrote numerous articles and book reviews; a full listing appears in the Dec. 1989 edition of the *Northwestern University Law Review*, which was dedicated to Schaefer and also contains a biographical résumé. For more specific biographical and personal information concerning Schaefer's reputation as a teacher, colleague, jurist, and friend, see tributes by William J. Brennan, Jr., Carl McGowan, Roger J. Traynor, Francis A. Allen, Albert E. Jenner, Jr., James A. Rahl, Daniel P. Ward, all in the *Northwestern University Law Review* (Dec. 1989): 677–705. Obituaries are in the *New York Times* and the *Chicago Tribune*, both 17 June 1986.

DONNA GREAR PARKER

SCHAFF, Philip (1 Jan. 1819–20 Oct. 1893), theologian, biblical scholar, and church historian, was born Philipp Schaf (or Schaaf) in Chur, Switzerland, the illegitimate son of Philipp Sha(a)f, a carpenter, and Anna Louis Schindler, who came from a large farming family. (He changed the spelling of his name sometime around 1847, a few years after his arrival in the United States.) Schaff was born into poverty and obscurity as well as illegitimacy in the Swiss mountain canton of Graubündten. His father died before his first birthday, and his mother was ordered to leave Chur because of the scandal. Thus left as a ward of the city, he was reared in an orphanage. Having grown up without parents or siblings, in later life Schaff would never meet a stranger, male or female, and he would always yearn for an extended family.

In the local schools Schaff became well known for his brilliance, but at the age of fifteen he suffered the humiliation of being dismissed from school—and Chur—after he and some of his classmates were caught committing what was then called "the secret sin" (masturbation). None of Schaff's own writings refer to this incident or to his illegitimacy, and there is no direct indication as to when he learned that his parents were not married.

The kindness of the Reverend Paul Kind of Chur resulted in Schaff's removal in 1834 to a boarding school at Kornthal, Württemberg, a pietist settlement founded the year Schaff was born. Kornthal would become Schaff's "spiritual birthplace" and the main source of his particular kind of warm evangelical pietism. It was at Kornthal, Schaff later recalled, that he experienced the internal change, or spiritual conversion, that became the driving force of his life forever after. Confirmed in the Lutheran church, the young pietist dedicated himself to the ministry of the church. After eight months at the boarding school, Schaff entered the Stuttgart Gymnasium, where for two years he studied classical literature and German poetry.

Schaff matriculated at the University of Tübingen in 1837, at a time when great theological and intellectual changes were taking place in German centers of higher education. New Lutheranism, rationalism, and the school of mediation all vied for his attention, and each contributed to his thinking, but the school of mediation most appealed to him, as he completely identified with its evangelical and conciliatory approach to theology and history. Schaff began theological studies under the most famous German scholars of the century. The great New Testament scholar F. C. Baur introduced Schaff to the idea of historical development in the Scriptures, an approach that became central to his particular understanding of church history. The mediationists C. F. Schmid and J. A. Dorner meanwhile drew him into their inner circle.

After two years at Tübingen, Schaff spent his third year of theological study divided between Halle and Berlin. At Halle his favorite professor was another mediationist, F. A. G. Tholuck. Later, in Berlin, he studied under E. W. Hengstenberg, F. W. J. Schelling, and Augustus Neander, the latter becoming his special mentor in church history. In the intellectual and religious circles of Berlin Schaff was first exposed to the concept that became the essence of his ecumenical viewpoint, "evangelical catholicism," a synthesis of the Protestant emphasis on the gospel and the historical tradition of Catholicism, through which Christians retain their corporate connection to the early church and thus to the body of Christ. In 1841 Schaff published his first book, *Die Sünde wider den heiligen Geist* (The sin against the Holy Spirit), passed his comprehensive examinations, and received his theological degree. The next fourteen months were spent on a Grand Tour of Europe as private tutor to a well-to-do family.

In the fall of 1842, at the University of Berlin, Schaff commenced his lifelong career as a privatdocent—though he had no idea at the time that it would be spent almost entirely in the United States. The following year, by chance, he became the second choice of a search committee from a small and struggling German Reformed seminary in Mercersburg, Pennsylvania. Schaff accepted their offer with mixed emotions but never regretted it. Following his ordination on 12 April 1844, he spent six weeks of orientation in England, where he met several prominent religious leaders, among them E. B. Pusey of Tractarian fame. Fifteen weeks later, on 28 July, Schaff made the following entry in his diary: "I see this morning, for the first time, my future homeland." On 12 August he was given a royal welcome to Mercersburg and the seminary. That evening he enjoyed his first meal on campus, in the home of his only colleague, John W. Nevin. A few months later, in late October, Schaff delivered the traditional inaugural address, entitled "The Principle of Protestantism." Within a year this address, which viewed the Reformation as a historical outgrowth of the best of the medieval Roman church, had been expanded, published, and become the source of great dissension within the German Reformed church. A conservative element in the church attacked Schaff for espousing liberal, Catholic views, and as a result he was tried for heresy. Although he was completely vindicated, in 1846 Schaff was put on trial again, this time for his views on the concept of the "middle state," whereby individuals not exposed to Jesus Christ and the salvation story in their earthly lives owing to circumstance of birth are given an opportunity to respond to them before entering heaven or hell. He was found innocent in this instance as well. It would be the last trial in the German Reformed tradition.

One happy experience of his trial years was that in December 1845 Schaff married Mary Elizabeth Schley of Frederick City, Maryland. Their union lasted until his death and produced eight children, five of whom, unfortunately, died in a variety of tragic situations.

During the two decades that Schaff taught at Mercersburg, he and Nevin, through numerous publications, developed what came to be known as the Mercersburg Theology, in which the history of Christianity and intellectual developments in Christian scholarship were treated seriously. Schaff's *What Is Church History?* (1846) and *History of the Apostolic Church* (1853) along with the journals he edited, the *Mercersburg Review* and *Der Deutsche Kirchenfreund*, set forth the themes identified with the Mercersburg school, themes associated with "historical churchliness." During this period Schaff also made major contributions to liturgical reform within his denomination. He published a catechism, edited a hymnbook, and was chairman of the committee that produced a new liturgy for the German Reformed church.

The first of Schaff's fourteen visits back to Europe took place between 1853 and 1854 and resulted in one of his most important publications. An excellent illustration of that illusive process known as Americanization, *America: A Sketch of the Political, Social and Religious Character of the United States of America* (1855) reflected Schaff's growing belief that the fulfillment of the Reformation would be realized in America, where the best of the Protestant and Catholic traditions would be united in a singleness of purpose in a new age of evangelical ecumenicity. Within two years Schaff published his parallel volume, *Germany, Its Universities, Theology, and Religion* (1857), which introduced the leading scholars and academic institutions of Germany to America. Interestingly, especially given its title, *Germany* was the first work that Schaff wrote entirely in English.

During his second trip back to Europe in 1865 Schaff became a perceptive interpreter of the Civil War for European audiences, and his lectures were published as *Der Bürgerkrieg und das Christliche Leben in Nord-Amerika* (1866). Also during this trip Schaff decided to move from the "retired" village of Mercersburg to a metropolitan area with the kind of research libraries he needed for his numerous writing projects. His official resignation letter was penned in Europe in September 1865. Since the fall of 1863 he had been on a two-year leave of absence in New York City. Returning from Europe he made New York his permanent residence.

Schaff began what would be a thirty-year career in New York as secretary of the New York Sabbath Committee, holding the post from 1864 to 1870. In addition, he quickly became involved in numerous editing and translating projects, such as the twenty-five volumes of J. P. Lange's *Commentaries on the Holy Scripture*. Also at this time Schaff's long-term relationship with the Evangelical Alliance, the world's most prominent interdenominational agency, began, and he was the primary reason for the alliance's successful world meeting held in New York on 2–12 October 1873. Necessitating four years of work on Schaff's part, including four trips to Europe, the meeting represented the first large-scale, formal gathering of international religious figures in the United States, and the crowds it generated were greater than those at *any* previous religious or political event in New York. To that time it was the most ecumenical moment of the nineteenth century and, Schaff believed, a first fruit of the coming age of evangelical catholicism.

After lecturing at various New York seminaries for several years, in 1870 Schaff accepted an invitation to join the faculty of Union Theological Seminary. He would hold four different academic chairs during his 23-year career at Union, the last appropriately being in church history, awarded in 1887. Also in 1870 he joined the Presbyterian Church in the U.S.A., another Reformed tradition and the one with which Union was then associated.

Schaff's tenure at Union was marked by extraordinary productivity in various areas. In 1870 he began his fifteen-year relationship with the Church of England–authorized American Committee of Bible Revision, serving from the outset as president. Of all his scholarly endeavors, this project took more of his time and energy than any other. The monumental ecumenical effort, completed in 1885, resulted in the Revised Version (of the King James Bible), one of the finest translations in the modern period.

Schaff's scholarly pursuits also continued apace, and he completed his two best-known works while at Union. His still useful three-volume set of *The Creeds of Christendom* appeared in 1877, and between 1882 and 1892 he published his multivolume *History of the Christian Church*.

Schaff also continued to travel abroad, one trip in 1877 resulting in the popular book *Through Bible Lands* (1878). His travels took him to major university centers in Europe, where he was able to reunite with some of his closest friends, including Swiss poetess Meta Heusser and her two daughters, as well as to Scotland, where he visited his dearest female friend, Sarah Borthwick.

Schaff's last years at Union were marked by several major contributions. In both his speeches and his writings, he called for critical revisions to the creeds of the Presbyterian church, and in 1893 he became the great defender of the biblical orthodoxy of Old Testament scholar Charles A. Briggs in the most famous heresy trial of the nineteenth century, after which Union broke its denominational ties to the Presbyterian church and became the most influential interdenominational seminary in the United States. It is appropriate that, at Schaff's death, Briggs inherited the mantle of ecumenicity from his friend and colleague.

Schaff's most significant act late in his career was the founding, in 1888, of the American Society of Church History, whose pursuit of ecumenism, scholarship, and service to the Christian church mirrored Schaff's own lifelong goals. This diverse body of interdenominational scholars continues to nurture ecumenical and scholarly interests today. As president of the society until his death, Schaff made sure that ecumenism was fostered in every way possible. One of his ecumenical goals for the society, the publication of a series of denominational histories, was eventually realized in the thirteen-volume American Church History series (1893–1897).

In September 1893 Schaff participated in the unprecedented World's Parliament of Religions held in Chicago as part of the World's Columbian Exposition. His address, "The Reunion of Christendom," was a clarion call for what was now his lifelong belief that *all* Christian bodies should reunite. In very poor health at the time, Schaff risked his life to attend the meeting, and he died the following month at his home in New York City.

Schaff often described himself as "a Swiss by birth, a German by education, and an American by choice." Certainly his various identities were crucial to his development as an international Christian scholar and bridge builder between Europe and the United States. His scholarly writings, his efforts at Bible revision, and his founding of the American Society of Church History have all remained as living monuments to his name. His defense of academic freedom in his own trials as well as those of C. A. Briggs made its indelible mark in academic and religious circles. His vision of an age of evangelical catholicism and his related work on behalf of Christian as well as church union were all part of the prelude to the burgeoning ecumenical movement of the twentieth century.

• The most important archival materials, including Schaff's letters, manuscripts, and personal papers, are housed in the Burke Library, Union Theological Seminary, and in the Philip Schaff Library and the Evangelical and Reformed Historical Society at the Lancaster Theological Seminary. The most complete studies of his life and thought, including complete and current bibliographies, are David Schaff, *The Life of Philip Schaff* (1897); George H. Shriver, *Philip Schaff: Christian Scholar and Ecumenical Prophet* (1987); and Klaus Penzel, ed., *Philip Schaff, Historian and Ambassador of the Universal Church: Selected Writings* (1991). See also Penzel, *The Private Life of Philip Schaff* (1995), a pamphlet published by Union Theological Seminary; Henry W. Bowden, *Church History in the Age of Science* (1971); Bowden, ed., *A Century of Church History: The Legacy of Philip Schaff* (1988); Robert T. Handy, *A History of Union Theological Seminary in New York* (1987); James H. Nichols, *Romanticism in American Theology: Nevin and Schaff at Mercersburg* (1961); George W. Richards, *History of the Theological Seminary of the Evangelical and Reformed Church at Lancaster* (1952); Shriver, ed., *American Religious Heretics* (1966); and Charles Yrigoyen and George Bricker, eds., *Reformed and Catholic: Selected Historical and Theological Writings of Philip Schaff* (1979).

GEORGE H. SHRIVER

SCHAMBERG, Jay Frank (6 Nov. 1870–30 Mar. 1934), physician, was born in Philadelphia, Pennsylvania, the son of Gustav Schamberg, a merchant, and Emma Frank. After attending public grammar schools in Philadelphia, he succeeded in winning a place at Central High School, a distinguished secondary school that awarded the bachelor's degree. At the age of eighteen, he matriculated in the medical department of the University of Pennsylvania, receiving his M.D. degree in 1892. He then won a coveted internship at the Hospital of the University of Pennsylvania. Eighteen months later, he was off to Europe for a postgraduate tour of famous medical centers. Louis A. Duhring, professor of dermatology at the University of Pennsylvania, had suggested that Schamberg study under Ferdinand Hebra in Vienna and Paul Gerson Unna in Hamburg. He also visited skin clinics in Paris and London.

Schamberg returned to Philadelphia in 1894 to enter general practice until he felt confident enough to be a full-time specialist. Schamberg assisted Duhring in the dermatology clinic at the Hospital of the University of Pennsylvania, serving as his assistant and quizmaster. The students of the era remembered the young physician as an enthusiastic teacher. Based on what he learned from this assignment, Schamberg wrote his first book, *Compend of Diseases of the Skin* (1898), which went through nine editions, the last appearing in 1934.

During this period Schamberg was also interested in infectious diseases. He received an appointment to the Municipal Hospital, which was crowded with patients afflicted with a wide assortment of contagious dis-

eases. Philadelphia then was the second largest city in the United States and an important port for European immigrants. During a smallpox epidemic, Schamberg had the opportunity to study more than five thousand patients with this viral disease. This led to his textbook *Acute Contagious Disease* (1905), written with William M. Welsh; a second edition appeared in 1928. He wrote two other textbooks—*Diseases of the Skin and Eruptive Fevers* (1908, 1911, 1915, 1921), and *Treatment of Syphilis* (1932), written with Carroll Wright.

By 1901 Schamberg had earned the reputation to enter full-time specialty practice. In the same year he published his observations on "a peculiar progressive pigmentary disease of the skin," now known as Schamberg's disease. The condition, which he had observed for four years, "begins as pin-head reddish puncta or dots forming irregular patches, which slowly extend by the formation of new lesions upon the periphery. The puncta in the course of time disappear, leaving behind, brownish-yellow or reddish-brown pigmentation, which slowly fades" ("A Peculiar Progressive Pigmentary Disease of the Skin," *British Journal of Dermatology* 13 [1901]: 1–3).

Schamberg was also interested in parasitic diseases. There had been periodic outbreaks of severe itching among the dockworkers in Philadelphia, but in 1909 it became a frightening epidemic. First the crew on traction magnate P. A. B. Widener's steam yacht became afflicted, and then guests at a fashionable hotel also came down with the itch. Philadelphians feared that a new contagious disease had descended on them. The U.S. Public Health Service sent Joseph Goldberger, who would later find the cause of pellagra, to investigate. Within forty-eight hours he and Schamberg found the cause of grain itch to be a mite, *Pediculoides ventricosus*.

Widener was so grateful that he later agreed to fund the Dermatological Research Institute, which was founded in 1912 in the basement of the Philadelphia Polyclinic. Its initial research was directed toward psoriasis, a disease from which Widener suffered, but with the onset of World War I, priorities were redirected toward finding a treatment for syphilis. Germany was the only source of arsphenamine, the standard treatment at the time, and little remained in America. Schamberg, George Raiziss, and John Kolmer were able to synthesize neoarsphenamine in only nine months. So large was the demand for this drug that the Institute made over half a million dollars in profit. This money was kept for research at the renamed Research Institute of Cutaneous Medicine, later a part of Temple University. Abbott Laboratories successfully assumed production of the drug in 1922. After Schamberg's death, Temple redirected the Institute funds to the Institute of Public Health and Preventive Medicine.

In the 1920s Schamberg became intrigued with gold therapy and introduced this treatment for lupus erythematosus. He was also responsible for developing an antiseptic, mercuriphen, a mercury-phenol agent.

In 1912, when the controversy over whether vaccination should be required reached great heights, Schamberg succeeded in keeping smallpox vaccination compulsory in Pennsylvania. The following year he became one of the founders of the Jewish Society for the Sanitary Improvement of Palestine, an organization formed to combat malaria and other infectious diseases.

Schamberg's teaching began at the University of Pennsylvania in 1898 with his appointment as lecturer on infectious eruptive diseases. He soon became professor of dermatology at the Philadelphia Polyclinic, later merged with the Graduate School of Medicine of the University of Pennsylvania. He held the dermatology chairs at Temple University School of Medicine (1910–1918) and at Jefferson Medical College (1918–1920). With the full development of the Graduate School of Medicine after World War I, Schamberg accepted a professorship of dermatology; later he was also appointed vice dean.

Schamberg built an international reputation, holding membership in six foreign dermatological societies. He was one of the founders and a president of the Philadelphia Dermatological Society (1900). In the American Medical Association, he served in the house of delegates (1904) and was chairman of the Section on Dermatology (1928–1929). He was elected to membership in the American Dermatological Association (1903), serving as president (1920–1921). He was also appointed in 1927 to the editorial board of the *Archives of Dermatology and Syphilology*, the leading publication of the era. In 1931 he was president of the Philadelphia County Medical Society.

Schamberg married Mae Bamberger of New York on 11 October 1905. They had two children.

While often aloof and presenting a patrician appearance, with pince-nez on a black ribbon and spats, Schamberg was an erudite clinician who was meticulous in his research. His discussions at the Philadelphia Dermatological Society and at national meetings were highly informative. He had superb organizational skills and was dedicated to his chosen profession of dermatology. His legacy includes four scientific books and more than one hundred papers.

• Many of Schamberg's papers may be found in the Library of the College of Physicians of Philadelphia. Biographical details can be obtained from a reminiscence written by his son, Ira Leo Schamberg and Aaron Lichtin, "Jay Frank Schamberg: A Pioneer in Dermatologic Research and Chemotherapy," *Archives of Dermatology* 73 (1956): 493–500. See also Frederick Weidman, "Memoir of Dr. Jay Frank Schamberg," *Transactions and Studies of the College of Physicians of Philadelphia*, 4th ser. (1934): 12–14, and Carroll Wright and William Pusey, "Jay Frank Schamberg," *Archives of Dermatology and Syphilology* 29 (1934): 901–3.

LAWRENCE CHARLES PARISH

SCHARY, Dore (31 Aug. 1905–7 July 1980), film producer, screenwriter, and director, was born Isidore Schary in Newark, New Jersey, the son of Herman Hugo Schary and Belle Drachler. His Russian-born parents operated a successful kosher catering business and banquet facility, but a venture into hotel ownership during the mid-1920s caused them to go bankrupt. At the age of fourteen, Schary left Newark's Central High School after an argument with a teacher. He worked at various jobs until he returned to Central High School five years later to complete the high school course in ten months.

Beginning in 1925, Schary worked for three summers as a drama counselor at a Young Men's Hebrew Association camp at Lake Tiorati, New York. He also helped organize theatrical productions at Catskill Mountain resort hotels. During the winter months he worked as a chinaware salesman, a newspaper proofreader, and a publicity manager for Admiral Richard E. Byrd's Newark appearance. In 1928 Schary joined Stuart Walker's stock company in Cincinnati, Ohio, as a stage manager and bit part actor but was fired after two weeks for punching a fellow actor who had supposedly made homosexual advances. After playing small parts in a touring company and in the Broadway production of *The Last Mile*, he returned to organizing amateur theatricals. In his spare time he wrote plays and tried to sell them to Broadway producers. In March 1932 he married Miriam Svet, who shared his middle-class, northern New Jersey, Jewish background. They had three children.

In December 1932 Schary was hired as a screenwriter for Columbia Pictures and moved to Hollywood. His first screenplay credits were *Fury of the Jungle* (1934), *The Most Precious Thing in Life* (1934), and *Fog* (1934). He was fired by Columbia after less than a year when he objected to a salary cut. For the next eight years, he freelanced at various motion picture studios, writing screenplays for *Chinatown Squad* (1935), *Her Master's Voice* (1936), and *The Girl from Scotland Yard* (1937), among others. He gained wider recognition when he and co-writer Eleanore Griffin won an Academy Award for best original story for *Boys Town* (1938), a fictionalized account of the Nebraska school for wayward youths run by Father Edward Flanagan. Schary's original story for *Edison the Man* (1940) was also nominated for an Academy Award.

In 1941 Schary approached Metro-Goldwyn-Mayer (MGM) Pictures chief Louis B. Mayer for permission to write and direct a low-budget screen version of Paul Gallico's anti-Nazi short story *Joe Smith, American*. During his conversation with Mayer, Schary explained how the quality and profitability of low budget pictures could be enhanced with more imaginative storytelling and the effective use of young creative talent. Instead of letting Schary direct the film, Mayer appointed him executive in charge of MGM's "B" Picture division. Most notable among the films Schary made for this division are *Journey for Margaret* (1942), the story of a homeless survivor of London's blitz bombing; *Lassie Come Home* (1943), a tale of a young boy whose poverty-stricken family must sell his beloved collie; and *Bataan* (1943), a realistic World War II action story.

In November 1943 Schary, an active Democrat and staunch supporter of Franklin D. Roosevelt, resigned from MGM after being denied permission to film a screenplay he had written with Sinclair Lewis called *Storm in the West*, which the studio considered sympathetic to leftist ideas. Schary described it as "the story of Hitler, Churchill, Mussolini, and the United States as an American Western epic" (*Heyday*, p. 129). He quickly found employment with Vanguard Productions, newly founded by independent producer David O. Selznick to handle his secondary projects. Schary stayed with Sleznick for three years, producing *I'll Be Seeing You* (1944), a love story about an ex-convict and a shell-shocked veteran; *Till the End of Time* (1946), a drama about servicemen readjusting to civilian life; *The Spiral Staircase* (1946), a suspense thriller; *The Bachelor and the Bobby-Soxer* (1947), in which a dashing playboy must cope with a lovestruck adolescent, and *The Farmer's Daughter* (1947), a story about a down-to-earth Swedish-American housekeeper who runs for Congress.

From January 1947 to June 1948, the tall, bespectacled Schary was executive vice president in charge of production at Radio-Keith-Orpheum (RKO) Pictures. In October 1947, as RKO production head, Schary testified before the U.S. House Un-American Activities Committee and forcefully defended his right to hire suspected Communists. He later compromised his position and accepted "blacklisting" when it became film industry policy. During Schary's brief tenure at RKO, the studio produced many well-received films, including the anti-Semitism drama *Crossfire* (1947) and *The Boy with Green Hair* (1948), a fable about a war orphan who becomes an outcast when his hair changes color; *Fort Apache* (1948), a western about a rigid commander of a frontier outpost and *The Set-Up* (1949), about a boxer who refuses to take a dive.

Unwilling to deal with interference from RKO's new owner, businessman Howard Hughes, Schary returned to MGM in the summer of 1948 as head of production under Louis B. Mayer. (He later replaced Mayer as studio chief in 1951.) Unlike Mayer, who frequently used bluster and threats to get his way, the smooth-mannered, articulate Schary used affability and ingratiation. He increased the number of films made by the large but sluggish MGM and gave more attention to topical, realistic stories. "Films must provoke thought as well as entertain." They must educate and inform *as they entertain*, Schary said (*Films in Review*, Aug–Sept. 1954, p. 326). He took little interest in musicals, one of MGM's strongest suits, and left their development almost entirely to producers Arthur Freed, Joseph Pasternak, and Jack Cummings.

During Schary's tenure as head of MGM, the studio made more than 250 films. Schary personally supervised production on twelve films, most notably *Battleground* (1949), *The Next Voice You Hear* (1950), *Bad day at Black Rock* (1955), *The Blackboard Jungle* (1955), and *The Swan* (1956).

In November 1956 Schary was abruptly fired as head of MGM. Various reasons have been given for his ouster: declining profits, a change in management personnel at Loew's Inc. (MGM's parent company), his penchant for serious "message films" that were rarely great box office draws, his time-consuming outside activities (he was heavily involved in Adlai Stevenson's 1952 and 1956 presidential campaigns), and his slowness in utilizing technological innovations, such as the wide screen. Also, Schary did not develop new star performers of the first rank and failed to recognize the full potential of MGM contract players such as Elizabeth Taylor and Grace Kelly.

After leaving MGM Schary moved to New York City and wrote the hit play *Sunrise at Campobello* (1958), the story of Franklin D. Roosevelt's battle with polio. Schary was a close friend of Eleanor Roosevelt, who was consulted about the play's accuracy. Continuing on Broadway, Schary directed and produced Leonard Spigelgass's comedy *A Majority of One* (1959) and Meredith Willson's musical *The Unsinkable Molly Brown* (1960). In the film world, Schary produced and wrote the screenplays for *Lonelyhearts* (1958) and a movie version of *Sunrise at Campobello* (1960). He likewise produced, wrote, and directed *Act One* (1963), a screen biography of playwright Moss Hart. From 1963 to 1969, Schary served as national chairman of the Anti-Defamation League of B'Nai B'rith. In 1970 Mayor John V. Lindsay appointed him New York City's first commissioner of cultural affairs. Schary died at his home in New York City.

• Schary's personal papers are at the University of Wisconsin, Madison. His autobiography is *Heyday* (1979). For a memoir of his childhood and his parents' catering business, see *For Special Occasions* (1962). Schary contributed a detailed autobiographical chapter to Bernard Rosenberg and Harry Silverstein's *The Real Tinsel* (1970). See also Schary and Charles Palmer, *Case History of a Movie* (1950), about the making of *The Next Voice You Hear*; Schary, "Censorship and Stereotypes," *Saturday Review*, 30 Apr. 1949, pp. 9–10; Schary, "Executive Responsibility," *Films in Review*, Aug–Sept. 1954, pp. 321–26; Schary, "Hollywood's Public Relations," *Films in Review*, Dec. 1955, pp. 500–502; Sam Boal, "Plan for Hollywood—By Schary," *New York Times Magazine*, 6 Feb. 1949, pp. 16, 26–27; "Schary, The Messenger," *Newsweek*, 29 May 1950, pp. 82–83; and "Schary Keeps Ideas and People on the Track," *Business Week*, 15 Aug. 1953, pp. 78–85. An obituary is in the *New York Times*, 8 July 1980.

MARY C. KALFATOVIC

SCHECHTER, Mathilde Roth (16 Dec. 1857–28 Aug. 1924), founder of the Woman's League for Conservative Judaism and the wife of Solomon Schechter, was born in Guttentag, a small town in Silesia, and orphaned at an early age. Little is known about her parents or family background. Having grown up in the Jewish home for orphans in Breslau, she was educated in local schools and attended the Breslau Teacher's Seminary. Home to a thriving Jewish community, Breslau was also the site of the Jewish Theological Seminary, an eminent scholarly and rabbinical institution. After teaching in Breslau for a number of years, she moved to England to study at Queens College London and to "read in the treasures of the British Museum, the National Gallery and the endless private collections." Not long after arriving she met Solomon Schechter, a Jewish scholar who later discovered in a Cairo synagogue the large cache of ancient Jewish manuscripts that came to be known as the Cairo Geniza.

The couple were married in June 1887, and their home soon became the meeting place for London's young intellectual Jewish elite. Mathilde Schechter's hospitality was legendary, a reputation she maintained when the Schechters moved to Cambridge and later to the United States. In this regard her life resembled the celebrated early nineteenth-century German-Jewish salonists Rahel Varnhagen and Henrietta Herz, except that Schechter had a stronger Jewish identity and was greatly involved in her religious community. While her husband taught at Cambridge and traveled around Europe and the Middle East collecting manuscripts, she brought up their three children, edited the works of local scholars, and engaged in various literary pursuits, including a translation of the Jewish poet Heinrich Heine. She also edited almost everything that her famous husband wrote and is primarily responsible for the expressive style of his English essays.

The Schechter family immigrated to the United States in 1902, when Solomon Schechter was appointed president of the Jewish Theological Seminary of America in New York City. The Schechter home again became an intellectual center for a diverse group of people. Longtime friend Henrietta Szold, in writing to Frank Schechter in 1924, described the Schechter home and ". . . those full vivid days when she [Mathilde Schechter] and your father and your house were a stimulating, creative center, in whose genial warmth we—so many, many of us—basked and were transformed."

In New York, Mathilde Schechter pursued serious interests outside the home. On the Lower East Side, she established a Jewish vocational school for girls that not only prepared young women for the world of work but also helped strengthen their Jewish identity. Her musical talent and her interest in congregational singing (at that time an innovation in Conservative synagogues) led to the organization of the Society for Ancient Hebrew Melodies as well as the publication of a hymn book titled *Kol Renna—Hebrew Hymnal for School and Home*.

The most significant achievement of her public career, however, was the establishment in 1918 of the Women's League of the United Synagogue of America. The United Synagogue, organized by Solomon Schechter a few years before his death in 1915, was designed to include all types of synagogues, but, in fact, it essentially marked the beginning of the Conservative movement in America. The establishment of the Women's League was a way for Mathilde Schechter to pay tribute to her husband, and she hoped that the Women's League would not duplicate the functions of

other women's organizations within the Jewish community. "We wish to serve the cause of Judaism", she said, "by strengthening the bond of unity among Jewish women and by learning to appreciate everything fine in Jewish life and literature." The Women's League for Conservative Judaism (as it is now called) was at first a constituent body of the United Synagogue, but Schechter strongly advocated the autonomy of the Women's League, lest the organization "be swallowed into the United Synagogue entirely." The Women's League, whose sisterhoods were within the synagogue, expanded quickly; within a few years there were some thirty-four affiliates all over the country.

One of the first projects of the Women's League was the establishment of the Student House located in the neighborhood of Columbia University. The house, which opened in the fall of 1918, served as a center for Jewish students as well as for Jewish soldiers and sailors on leave, a place to meet, eat, rest, and study. The concept of a student house epitomized Mathilde Schechter's caretaking personality and fulfilled an important function as a recreational and cultural center before the existence of the B'nai B'rith Hillel university system.

Speaking on Mother's Day 1919 at Mordecai Kaplan's Jewish Center in New York, Schechter stressed the "absolute unselfishness and utter forgiveness of mother-love," at the same time emphasizing the need for Jewish women to retain a sense of their individual identities apart from their maternal role. She believed strongly in the power of Judaism to soothe and to comfort. The Mitzvot (commandments) and especially the rituals were, she said, "the song of our soul's communion with God." Defending the very idea of ritual, she eloquently stated her belief that "a living religion needs the spirit and the redblooded warmth of forms, forms tenderly kissed into life by the spirit." She died a few years later in New York City.

Mathilde Schechter exemplifies the difficulties of learning about the wives of famous men, frequently women of talent, who are overshadowed by their well-known spouses. Like so many women of her day, her energy was expended primarily in the private sphere, and thus the task of reconstructing her life is difficult. Living in an age when domesticity was the ideal for women, she was a multifaceted individual, creative both in her home and in the public arena. As an organizational person, she developed herself fully, in line with the traditional women's roles of her era yet stretching them in new and creative ways. Indeed, despite the fact that she was intent on creating a life rather than building an empire, she founded what became one of the largest Jewish women's organizations in the United States.

• The papers of Mathilde Schechter are found scattered throughout Solomon's Schechter's papers at the Jewish Theological Seminary. Some of her speeches, including "A Task for Jewish Women," which originally appeared in 1918, have been reprinted by the Women's League for Conservative Judaism, based in New York City. A biographical study is Mel

Scult, "The Baale Boste Reconsidered: The Life of Mathilde Roth Schechter (M.R.S.)," *Modern Judaism* 7 (Feb. 1987): 1–27.

MEL SCULT

SCHECHTER, Solomon (7 Dec. 1850?–19 Nov. 1915), Judaica scholar and seminary president, was born in Focsani, Romania, the son of Isaac Schechter, a ritual slaughterer, and Chaya Rachel (maiden name unknown). The trajectory of Schechter's life mirrored the movement of Jews and Judaism from Eastern Europe to the West, a process that resulted in new syntheses of tradition and modernity in Jewish life and thought. Born into a Hasidic family, Schechter received a traditional Jewish education, including study in a series of yeshivot (Talmudic academies). It was in such an academy in Lvov (Lemberg), headed by Rabbi Joseph Nathanson, a noted rabbinic scholar, that he first encountered Haskalah, the movement for a Jewish Enlightenment. This included advocacy of greater contact between Jews and European culture, integration and emancipation for the Jews, and the revitalization and modernization of Judaism and Jewish culture through the study of Hebrew and the creation of a new Hebrew literature.

After a brief, arranged marriage failed, possibly the casualty of the clash between Schechter's modernizing aspirations and the world view of Eastern European Orthodoxy, in 1875 Schechter journeyed to Vienna to attend the Bet Hamidrash, a rabbinical seminary. This school represented a deviation from a traditional yeshiva in that despite its religious traditionalism in terms of Jewish praxis and the makeup of its faculty, the scholars were trained as well in Wissenschaft des Judentums (the science of Judaism), in which Jewish classical texts were studied critically and historically for the purpose of reconstructing rabbinic texts based on collation of manuscripts and the like. This methodology, heavily influenced by German academic historicism, was regarded with suspicion and often outright opposition by more traditional rabbinic scholars.

Schechter acquired not only the epistemology and methodology of the science of Judaism but also role models in the personages of his teachers, especially Isaac Hirsch Weiss and Meir Friedmann. Beyond their considerable erudition and scholarship, these men epitomized the model of scholars at both the yeshiva and the modern seminary or university, that is, in the worlds of tradition and modernity. In 1879 Schechter received rabbinic ordination from Weiss and Friedmann. It was also in Vienna that he experienced general education—in the formal sense—for the first time, at the University of Vienna.

Schechter's desire to continue to study simultaneously in both Jewish and general European educational environments led him to Berlin, where he attended the University of Berlin as well as the Hochschule für die Wissenschaft des Judentums (College for the science of Judaism). Schechter's choice of this school of Jewish studies is striking, considering that its founder was Abraham Geiger, the leading Reform rabbi in nineteenth-century Germany as well as a formidable scholar of rabbinics. Throughout his life Schechter held no brief for Reform Judaism, regarding it as assimilationist in bent.

Schechter's earliest writings—dating from Vienna and Berlin—reveal aspects of style and emphasis that characterized his later, better-known writings. His first two publications, published anonymously in the Hebrew journal *HaShahar* in 1876 and 1877, were sharply worded anti-Hasidic satires, then a popular Jewish Enlightenment genre. His wish for anonymity was no doubt due to his Hasidic family background. Years later he returned to the subject of Hasidism, a movement emphasizing pietism as well as Talmudic erudition, this time more affirmatively. He often maintained that the spirituality of Hasidism and of Eastern European Jewry in general stood as a useful counterpoint to the assimilated, rationalistic Judaism of the West.

In 1881 Schechter also contributed to a liberal Viennese newspaper on the subject of anti-Semitic ethnographic stereotypes of Jewish practices. Despite his expectations for progress in general and for Judaism in particular in the emancipated West, Schechter spent his life vigorously opposing what he viewed as the intellectual and cultural anti-Semitism of the so-called enlightened West. He rejected biblical criticism, terming it higher anti-Semitism, and insisted that Jews needed to write their own modern studies of the Bible rather than allow their texts, and their self-image, to be determined by non-Jewish, anti-Jewish scholars.

In Berlin Schechter met Claude Montefiore, scion of the distinguished Anglo-Jewish family, who hired Schechter to tutor him upon Montefiore's return to Britain; this position would enable Schechter to research Jewish manuscripts at Oxford and the British Museum, and he moved to London in 1882. Five years later he married Mathilde Roth; they would have three children.

Schechter spent twenty years in England, during which he came into prominence as one of the foremost Judaica scholars in the world. In 1890 he was appointed lecturer in Talmudics at Cambridge University, and in 1892 he became reader in rabbinics at the same university, a position he held until 1902. Concurrently, he became the first professor of Hebrew at University College, London, beginning in 1899.

His writings were of two types. On the one hand, he wrote traditional critical editions of texts such as *Massekhet Avot D'Rabbi Natan* (Tractate of the fathers according to Rabbi Nathan, 1887), which appeared in Hebrew, as did his introduction and commentary. On the other, he increasingly wrote in his adopted language, English, in a style intended to reach the educated layperson. These writings, later collected in the three-volume series *Studies in Judaism* (1896, 1908, 1924), consisted of essays on a variety of topics drawn from the literary and historical traditions of Jewry, everything from depictions of children in Jewish literature to the memoirs of a Jewish woman from seventeenth-century Germany.

In many of his English-language publications, including *Some Aspects of Rabbinic Theology* (1909), a collection of lectures delivered in 1895 in Philadelphia, Schechter sought to make rabbinic thought accessible to a broad reading public. He did this by adopting Western terms, such as "theology," and using them to communicate Jewish categories of religious thought, such as repentance, the importance of God's commandments, and the like. Writing for non-Jews as well, he maintained that Judaism had a theology that preceded Christianity and that deserved serious scrutiny. These essays reflected his desire to introduce rabbinic, or postbiblical, Judaism—from a Jewish perspective—to the Western world and thus counter Christian polemics against rabbinic Judaism by allowing the Talmudic sages to speak for themselves. His popular writings also mirror Schechter's desire to play the role of a public intellectual or a kind of rabbi in the realm of contemporary Jewish affairs. Thus in "Four Epistles to the Jews of England," four essays published in 1900, he criticized the Anglo-Jewish community for its assimilation in both religious and social terms, decrying its adoption of fashionable trends in theology rather than striving to retain authentic Jewish categories of meaning.

Schechter's greatest scholarly coup occurred in 1897, when he journeyed to Cairo and researched what has come to be known as the Cairo Geniza, a horde of manuscripts and incunabula dating from the late Second Temple to modern times that had been ritually set aside in an attic of the synagogue in Old Cairo. This treasure trove of essential source material incalculably influenced the direction and shape of the study of ancient and medieval Jewish culture and community. Earlier, in 1896, Schechter had achieved international renown for identifying what was known as the Ben Sira fragment, which he had received from two English students. The only known piece of the Hebrew original of this apocryphal work, the Ben Sira fragment dates from two centuries before the Common Era. In conjunction with his popular writings, the Ben Sira fragment and the Geniza made Schechter the best-known Judaica scholar of his day, especially in the English-speaking world. Yet in spite of his fame, Schechter was increasingly frustrated: shut out of a coveted fellowship to one of the Cambridge colleges because he was Jewish, powerless in isolated Cambridge to provide a vibrant Jewish lifestyle and education for his young children, and as a foreigner playing no leadership role in the Anglo-Jewish elite (though he dominated, through the sheer force of his personality, a circle of Jews of a literary and intellectual bent called the Wanderers).

By the turn of the century the Jewish Theological Seminary in New York City, which had been founded in 1886 to train modern, traditional rabbis, had fallen on difficult times; a dynamic figure was needed to revitalize the school. Possessing the scholarly credentials, the religious piety, and the fame, style, and desire to reach both Eastern European immigrants and more westernized Jews, Schechter quickly emerged as the leading candidate. He accepted the task in the hope that he could build a traditional yet modern Judaism in a city that was emerging as a major center of Jewish life. As president of the seminary from 1902 until his death, Schechter reshaped the institution. He created a new curriculum and insisted that entering rabbinical students be college graduates, thus ensuring their ability to be conversant in general as well as Jewish affairs. He also hired other European-trained faculty with the aim of making the seminary the center for academic Judaica scholarship. Moreover, under his leadership the seminary came to be seen as the center of the nascent Conservative movement, which ultimately came to predominate among American Jewry between the two world wars.

The creation of the Conservative movement reflected Schechter's ambivalence about the phenomenon of denominationalism that came to dominate modern Judaism in institutional and ideological terms. As a pious Eastern European Jew, Schechter believed deeply in a traditional Judaism both in its theology and praxis and in its vision of an all-embracing Jewish community. Yet the emerging Jewish communities of the West were increasingly Balkanized, riven by differences wrought by acculturation, assimilation, and manifold immigrant populations. In perhaps his most famous phrase, Schechter used the term "Catholic Israel" to suggest the power of the Jewish people to live out, and thereby continually renew, the texts and traditions of the Jewish past. In his view, God's revealed texts became actualized through the interpretations and ritual instincts of both rabbis and Jewish communities. Schechter rarely addressed how his vision of history might be implemented given the fragmentation of Jewish communities and theologies, but he was loath to part with his vision of a "Catholic," or united, Israel. So too he became an advocate of Zionism, seeing the creation of a physical and spiritual center for world Jewry as a unifying force in Jewish life and as a countering force to assimilation and anti-Semitism.

Schechter's thought reveals a man who continued to wrestle with the conflicting categories implicit in tradition and modernity. Enthusiastic about American democracy, he nonetheless decried the substitution of secularism for religious faith and civilization, and he believed that Judaism definitively constituted the latter. As such he rejected reformist attempts to reduce Judaism to a universalistic ethos articulated as a "mission" focused on a social gospel. He embraced Judaism as a faith, with a history and tradition, but argued that it also embodied an evolutionary quality. Indeed, the history of "Schechter's seminary," as the Jewish Theological Seminary came to be known, is a reflection of his ability to seize the vital center in Jewish life, against Reform on his left and Orthodoxy on his right. He hoped that the seminary would serve as a unifying force in Jewish life in America, but he did not hesitate to criticize Reform for its assimilationism and Orthodoxy for its rigidity and inability to adapt to new realities. He worked tirelessly to place seminary graduates in pulpits, thereby developing rabbinic alumni as a coherent body through which a "Conservative" Judaism could be promulgated. He sought to create a teachers course for the training of Jewish educators (it became the Teachers' Institute in 1909), and he promoted the construction of model schools.

Schechter's creation in 1913 of the United Synagogue, an assemblage of synagogues loyal to the Conservative approach in matters theological and practical, was an indication of his increasing awareness of the need to broaden the seminary's base of support. The organization's hierarchical model, borrowed from the United Kingdom's Jewish community framework, placed the seminary and its scholarly leadership ostensibly at the helm of the rabbis, the congregations, and by extension, the entire American Jewish community. Ironically, although the Conservative movement was the most American of the three Jewish denominations in sociohistorical terms, given the American proclivity for religious eclecticism and congregationalism, the United Synagogue's rigidly scholastic and stratified institutional structure was the least American.

At the time of his death in New York City, Schechter's vision of the future was somber, having been chastened by domestic as well as foreign developments. American Jewry lacked the will and the vision to create a vibrant Jewish culture, and religious Jewry had become increasingly factionalized. The outbreak of World War I in 1914 tragically confirmed Schechter's abiding suspicion of European jingoistic nationalism. Yet his impact on American Jewry was palpable. Schechter's writings and the seminary and its affiliates offered American Jewry a center ground and the beginnings of a high culture rooted in traditional texts but also well versed in modern methods of scholarship. In addition, Schechter helped to legitimize the modern rabbi and scholar as a public figure as well as a religious leader, albeit in the bewildering freedom of American religious pluralism and factionalism.

• Schechter's papers are in the Archives of the Library of the Jewish Theological Seminary of America, New York City. There are several collections of Schechter correspondence: Frank I. Schechter, "Schechteriana," *Menorah Journal* 8 (1922); Meir Ben Horin, "Solomon Schechter to Judge Mayer Sulzberger," *Jewish Social Studies* 25 (1963): 249–86, 27 (1965): 75–102, and 30 (1968): 262–71; Abraham Millgram and Emma Erlich, eds., "Nine Letters from Solomon Schechter to Henrietta Szold," *Conservative Judaism* 32 (Winter 1979) and (Summer 1979); and Joshua B. Stein, ed., *Lieber Freund: The Letters of Claude Goldsmid Montefiore to Solomon Schechter 1885–1902* (1988). A collection of his commencement addresses and other writings is *Seminary Addresses and Other Papers* (1915). More specialized treatments, drawn from Schechter's Geniza research, include *Saadyana: Geniza Fragments of R. Saadya Gaon and Others* (1902) and *Documents of Jewish Sectaries* (1910). A full-length biography is Norman Bentwich, *Solomon Schechter: A Biography* (1938). Briefer treatments include Bernard Mandelbaum, *The Wisdom of Solomon Schechter* (1963); Gerson D. Cohen, "On the Eightieth Anniversary of Solomon Schechter's Arrival in the United States," *Proceedings of the Rabbinical Assembly* 44 (1982); and Seymour Siegel, "Solomon Schechter: His Contribution to Modern Jewish Thought," *Proceedings of the*

Rabbinical Assembly 39 (1977). A bibliography of Schechter's writings is Adolph Oko, *Solomon Schechter: A Bibliography* (1938).

DAVID B. STARR

SCHEELE, Leonard A. (25 July 1907–8 Jan. 1993), physician and public health officer, was born in Fort Wayne, Indiana, the son of Martin F. Scheele and Minnie Vogely. Scheele attended public grade schools and Fort Wayne's Central High School, then entered the University of Michigan in Ann Arbor, graduating in 1931 with a B.A. Scheele then spent four years at Wayne State University School of Medicine in Detroit, receiving his M.D. in 1934. Early in his medical education, Scheele became interested in public health, and he took an opportunity to spend his fourth year of medical school as an intern at the United States Marine Hospital in Chicago, which was operated by the U.S. Public Health Service (PHS). He married Francis K. McCormick in 1929; they had three children.

In July 1934 Scheele was commissioned as a medical officer in the PHS. He spent his first two years with the nation's health agency as a quarantine officer, serving one year in San Francisco and one in Honolulu. In 1936 he was assigned to the Maryland State Health Department for one year, during which he served as the health officer of Queen Anne's County, Maryland.

After this Scheele became involved in an increasingly important function of the PHS, medical research. He spent two years, beginning in 1937, as a cancer research fellow at Memorial Hospital in New York City. After this period of intense training, Scheele was assigned in 1939 to the National Cancer Institute (NCI) on the new campus of PHS's National Institute of Health (NIH) in Bethesda, Maryland. With NCI, Scheele served as officer in charge of the new National Cancer Control Program, coordinating a pioneering nationwide effort to examine systematically the epidemiology of cancer and the effects of various cancer treatments.

World War II brought an abrupt halt to Scheele's cancer investigations. The day after the attack on Pearl Harbor, he was assigned to the Medical Division of the Office of Civilian Defense. From early 1942 through January 1943 he worked in Washington, D.C., as chief of that agency's Field Casualty Section, preparing for the possibility that major military engagements might take place on American soil. The war did not come to Scheele, but in January 1943 Scheele went to war when PHS lent him to the Medical Department of the U.S. Army. The army soon sent him to the European theater, where he served with honor in a variety of important posts, including a stint on General Dwight Eisenhower's planning staff in London during 1944 and another under General Lucius Clay as a medical consultant to the Allied Control Council, which governed Berlin after the German surrender. Most of Scheele's work in Europe centered on public health planning for the control of epidemic diseases among civilian populations. He received several military decorations for his efforts, including the American Typhus Medal, the Legion of Merit, the Croix de Guerre with Palm (France), and Commenda nell'Ordine dei SS. Maurizio e Lazzaro (Italy).

In September 1945 Scheele returned to the United States and resumed his career with the PHS as assistant director of the National Cancer Institute. In July 1947 Surgeon General Thomas Parran promoted him to assistant surgeon general, associate director of NIH, and director of NCI. Six months later, on 12 February 1948, President Harry S. Truman nominated Scheele to replace Parran. The Senate quickly confirmed the nomination, and on 6 April 1948 Scheele became the seventh surgeon general.

Scheele served in this post for seven years under Presidents Truman and Eisenhower. In marked contrast to his predecessor, who had clear ties with the Democratic party, Scheele attempted to take an apolitical approach to the position. Most significantly, he excused himself from harsh debates about "socialized medicine" (the American Medical Association's term for national health insurance) that made news in the late 1940s and early 1950s. His decision to remove himself—and, by extension, PHS—from political discussions of broad federal health policy had important consequences. Rather than engaging in controversies over federal involvement in health care delivery, Scheele helped to forge a path for PHS that proved popular with almost every postwar political faction, building PHS into the world's leading source of support for medical research. During his term as surgeon general, the annual NIH budget increased from $37 million to almost $100 million, and the *I* of NIH was officially made plural ("Institutes"), in recognition of several new research facilities built on the Bethesda campus. The increased budget also supported investigations at other research institutions across the country.

Scheele is perhaps best remembered, however, for his actions during several weeks in the spring of 1955. On 12 April 1955, amid great media fanfare, he advised his superior, Secretary of Health, Education, and Welfare Oveta Culp Hobby, to license six pharmaceutical companies to distribute Jonas Salk's polio vaccine. At the time many of Salk's numerous critics in the scientific community accused Scheele and Hobby of acting prematurely, influenced by the public enthusiasm for Salk's work. At 3:00 A.M. on 27 April Scheele was awakened by a call from agitated PHS subordinates who had received reports that six vaccinated children had come down with paralytic polio less than a week after receiving their first shot of Salk's vaccine. All had been injected with material prepared by Cutter Company. Later that morning Scheele conferred with several national experts, and, less than eight hours after he had received the initial call, he telephoned Cutter, requesting that the company cease distribution of polio vaccine. Cutter complied, and on 7 May Scheele sent a similar message to the other five companies engaged in the preparation and distribution of polio vaccine. After several weeks of intense investigation, these companies instituted improved quality-

control measures but not soon enough to prevent tragedy: 204 people were eventually determined to have been afflicted by cases of polio that could be linked to faulty vaccine; three-quarters of these suffered from paralysis, and eleven died.

In August 1956 Scheele retired from federal service to become senior vice president of Warner-Lambert Pharmaceutical Company, where he worked until retiring in 1968. He returned briefly to federal service in 1962, when President John F. Kennedy called on him to assist in negotiations with Cuba over prisoners captured in the ill-fated Bay of Pigs invasion. Scheele helped to oversee the delivery of $60 million worth of medical supplies and baby food to Cuba in exchange for the prisoners' release.

Scheele died in Washington, D.C. He stands as a significant figure in the history of American public health and medical research administration.

• Records from Scheele's tenure as surgeon general are at the National Library of Medicine, History of Medicine Division, Bethesda, Md. Short biographical accounts appear in *Public Health Reports* 63 (9 Apr. 1948): 469–70; and *American Journal of Public Health* 38 (Mar. 1948): 462, and (May 1948): 750. Information on Scheele's early career and his initial years as surgeon general are treated in Ralph-Chester Williams, *The United States Public Health Service, 1798–1950* (1951), pp. 486–88. Historical examinations of polio in America noting Scheele's actions with regard to Salk's polio vaccine include Aaron E. Klein, *Trial by Fury: The Polio Vaccine Controversy* (1972), pp. 111–26; Jane S. Smith, *Patenting the Sun: Polio and the Salk Vaccine* (1990), pp. 350–67; and Tony Gould, *A Summer Plague: Polio and Its Survivors* (1995), pp. 153–56. Fitzhugh Mullan gives Scheele's term as surgeon general more balanced attention in *Plagues and Politics: The Story of the United States Public Health Service* (1989), pp. 128–34. An obituary covering Scheele's entire career is in *Journal of the American Medical Association* 270 (8 Dec. 1993): 2749.

JON M. HARKNESS

SCHELLENBERG, Theodore Roosevelt (24 Feb. 1903–14 Jan. 1970), archivist, was born in Harvey County, Kansas, the son of Abraham Schellenberg and Sarah Schroeder, farmers. The family had moved to Kansas as part of the large German Mennonite immigration there, and Abraham Schellenberg later served as director of the national Mennonite Brethren Publishing House. After briefly attending Tabor College, Schellenberg was graduated Phi Beta Kappa from the University of Kansas in 1928, and he received an M.A. in history there in 1930. He earned a Ph.D. in history from the University of Pennsylvania in 1934. He married Alma Groening in 1929; they had two children.

Schellenberg worked in 1934–1935 for the Joint Committee on Materials for Research of the American Council of Learned Societies and the Social Sciences Research Council, helping to write a pioneering report on the use of microfilm for the preservation of historical records. He was also a historian for the National Park Service before joining the staff of the newly established National Archives as a deputy records examiner in 1935. He spent most of the remainder of his career at the National Archives, rising through the ranks to serve as director of archival management from 1950 to 1962 and then as assistant archivist of the United States before his retirement in 1963.

Schellenberg's principal contribution to archival theory and practice came in the area of appraisal, the process of deciding which records have sufficient long-term historical or research value to warrant permanent preservation in the archives and which records may be discarded. This problem was particularly acute for the National Archives, which faced the twin dilemmas of assembling the archivally valuable records of the nation for the first time while also addressing the problems of the bulk and duplication inherent in modern bureaucratic records. Schellenberg led a team of archivists who tried to identify all of the records produced by government agencies and then to develop and apply standards for determining which of those records to retain. The principles for making these decisions he later codified in his writings, which became the core of archival theory within the National Archives and indeed for the entire archives profession in the United States.

Schellenberg's first compilation of archival appraisal theory, *Appraisal of Modern Public Records*, was published as a National Archives staff circular in 1956. His full-length volume, *Modern Archives: Principles and Techniques* (1956), remained the basic textbook for a generation of American archivists. All records were to be evaluated, he wrote, according to their "evidential" and "informational" values. The former value consisted of the evidence that the records contained of the existence, organization, and operations of government agencies—the core legal, fiscal, and administrative records that established an entity's existence and functions. The latter consisted of the information that those records contained (perhaps unintentionally) about persons, events, and activities—information that would make the records useful to historians and other subsequent researchers. The principles Schellenberg outlined for assessing those values in records and making selection and acquisition decisions on the basis of them eventually guided the practice of all American archivists who dealt with twentieth-century records—those of private individuals and institutions as well as government agencies. His second major text, *The Management of Archives* (1965), further extended this reach by seeking to describe the different but complementary practices of archivists, librarians, and curators of private papers. The principles that Schellenberg established were emulated worldwide: his writings were read internationally and were translated into German, Hebrew, Portuguese, and Spanish.

As an archival teacher Schellenberg had a seminal influence on the development of the modern archives profession. In 1953 he developed an extensive in-house training program for the National Archives, and in retirement he offered short courses and institutes around the country. From 1957 to 1963 he was a principal teacher in the program of archival training at American University, virtually the only professional education of its kind in the United States at the time. He also lectured abroad, especially in Latin America, Australia, and New Zealand. His teaching and consulting work in the latter two places in the 1950s served as central events in the organization of the archives profession in those countries. He died in Washington, D.C.

Schellenberg was a key figure in the "founding generation" of American professional archivists. Although his sometimes prickly personality kept him from higher positions within the National Archives and from elected office in professional societies, he nevertheless became internationally renowned as an author, teacher, and theoretician of archives work. Schellenberg's archival writings still constitute an established "orthodoxy" of archival theory and practice, acknowledged for their important role, even as more recent archival theorists seek to extend beyond them.

• Schellenberg's personal and professional papers are in the Kansas State Historical Society. There is no complete biography of him, but see the several memoirs written by American and international colleagues in "In Memoriam: Theodore R. Schellenberg (1903–1970)," *American Archivist* 33 (Apr. 1970): 190–202; this also contains a complete bibliography of his writings. A useful interpretive essay on his role in the history of the American archival profession is Jane R. Smith, "Theodore R. Schellenberg: Americanizer and Popularizer," *American Archivist* 44 (Fall 1981): 313–26. An obituary is in the *Washington Post*, 22 Jan. 1970.

JAMES M. O'TOOLE

SCHELLING, Ernest Henry (26 July 1876–8 Dec. 1939), pianist, composer, and conductor, was born in Belvidere, New Jersey, the son of Felix Emmanuel Schelling, a physician and musician from St. Gall, Switzerland, and the English-born Rose White Wilkes of Philadelphia. Schelling's early musical studies were under the strict training of his gifted father. Ernest's public debut at age four at the Philadelphia Academy of Music was hailed by a review in the *Sunday Transcript* (8 Mar. 1880). At seven, already trilingual in English, French, and German, he was enrolled in the Paris Conservatoire—the youngest applicant ever—and assigned to Chopin's pupil, Georges Mathias.

Schelling's studies continued in central Europe with leading pedagogues: Isidor Philipp, Dionys Pruckner (student of Franz Liszt), Percy Goetschius (theory), Theodor Leschetizky, Karl Heinrich Barth, Moritz Moszkowski, and Hans Huber (organ and composition). At age ten he played for Brahms. Studying music, languages, and literature so strenuously and concertizing throughout Europe from age twelve to eighteen damaged his health (neuritis in his arms and hands) and jeopardized his future. Later he credited his last master, Ignace Jan Paderewski, for practice methods and techniques that enabled him to make the transition from child prodigy to mature artist. They remained lifelong friends.

In 1900 Schelling became court musician to the Grand Duke Johann-Albrecht of Mecklenburg-

Schwerin, whose wife Princess Elizabeth of Saxe-Weimar-Eisenach, the sister of the emperor, had studied with Liszt. In 1903–1904 he undertook an international tour and was among the first American-born artists to concertize in Latin America. Playing 186 concerts in eighteen months, Schelling made his North American debut as a mature artist on 24–25 February 1904 with the Boston Symphony under Wilhelm Gericke, fulfilling the artistic promise of the former child prodigy. It was through Paderewski, in Boston, that Schelling met Lucie How Draper, whom he married in 1905. They had no children.

Schelling's virtuosity as a pianist extended to composition, which began to develop at age three, with "Mon Premier Pas," op. 1. In 1907 his "Suite fantastique pour piano et orchestre," op. 7, premiered in Amsterdam with Willem Mengelberg conducting the Concertgebouw and the composer at the piano. (He would often lead from the piano, a feat popular with the public.) His success as a composer and performer continued to attract international attention with "Impressions from an Artist's Life, Symphonic Variations for Orchestra and Piano" (1915) and Concerto for Violin and Orchestra (1916). Both premiered with the Boston Symphony under Karl Muck. "Impressions" was the first American work to figure on a Toscanini program. Schelling's compositions were performed by orchestras with himself and other leading soloists, including Paderewski, who requested that Schelling write "a short Barcarolle" for his repertoire. This resulted in "Nocturne à Raguse" (1924), which Paderewski played seventy-eight times in one season and also recorded for the Victor label. "Theme and Variations" (1904) had already been dedicated to Paderewski.

An event of deep significance to Schelling was his military service during World War I. Completing officers' training at Fort Myer, Virginia, he enlisted in April 1917 on the day the United States declared war. He served first as a captain and then as a major with the American Expeditionary Force and was assigned to the Intelligence Branch of the general staff. Judged "a brilliant intelligence officer" and praised publicly for his "discipline, duty and devotion to his country," Schelling maintained an active status in the Military Intelligence Reserve throughout his life. He was also an early and active member of the International Entente against the Third International to combat communism. He received the Distinguished Service Medal (U.S.), Légion d'Honneur (France), and Polonia Restituta (Poland).

Schelling's war service inspired his most dramatic composition, "A Victory Ball, Fantasy for Orchestra" (1923), after the poem by Alfred Noyes and premiered by Leopold Stokowski with the Philadelphia Orchestra. He dedicated it "To the Memory of an American Soldier."

Schelling was active in numerous public enterprises. His social conscience and generosity were expressed in the performances he organized for needy colleagues. As first president (1929–1939) of the Ed-

ward MacDowell Artists' Colony in Peterborough, New Hampshire, he promoted its expansion and funding, and in 1932 he and his wife founded the Musicians' Emergency Fund, Inc. Schelling's international reputation as pianist, composer, and innovator led to his inclusion in a group of prominent citizens who met in 1936 with President Franklin D. Roosevelt to dramatize the need for a cabinet post of secretariat of fine arts. (The position never materialized.)

Schelling had already anticipated the need to cultivate an audience to assure the future of the symphony orchestra. "Music means culture," he said. "Culture means refinement. Refinement means good citizenship . . . Upon the intelligent listener . . . rests the responsibility." In 1924 he established his celebrated Children's and Young People's Concerts with the New York Philharmonic-Symphony Orchestra. Over the first four years children became acquainted with more than 100 orchestral works from composers ranging from Bach to Stravinsky. A series of five to fifteen performances per season at Carnegie Hall for an audience whose ages varied from five to the teenage years, the Children's and Young People's Concerts became a national fixture and under Schelling's direction they expanded to cities across the nation, from Boston to San Francisco. One hundred and eighty-seven concerts in New York City were carried nationally by the Columbia Broadcasting System beginning in 1930. Schelling gave demonstration concerts in the Netherlands in 1936. With the outbreak of World War II in 1939, the series in London was postponed. Schelling's first wife died in 1938, and the following year he married Helen Huntington Marshall, a young New Yorker dedicated to his work. They had no children.

Novelist and pianist John Erskine called Schelling "the musical god-father of America's younger generation." At the time of Schelling's death he was planning a book of his "Spoken Notes" to the audience, illustrated from his famous collection of 5,000 large-format, hand-colored glass lantern slides used at these concerts. He longed to concentrate again on composing and intended to write his memoirs. He died suddenly in New York City and was mourned by a host of friends and admirers. A thousand people attended his funeral.

Schelling was a composer with a keen, inventive mind. He had the power to sustain the gradual unfolding of ideas to build dramatic climaxes. By the logic of broadly arched voice, leading over suspended harmonies, often with ostinato figuration in counterpoint, Schelling created modern sonorities within the framework of late Romantic harmony. He used all the means at his disposal—both orchestrally and pianistically—and his works show great skill, colorful rhetoric, and brilliant virtuosity, originality, and expressiveness.

• The Ernest Schelling Archives of some forty file drawers and 300 pounds of press clippings are located at the International Piano Archives of the University of Maryland at College Park. Otherwise the New York Philharmonic-Symphony Orchestra, Lincoln Center, holds materials relating to the Children's and Young People's Concerts. See also Thomas H. Hill, "Ernest Schelling (1876–1939): His Life and Contributions to Music Education through Educational Concerts" (Ph.D. diss., Catholic Univ. of America, 1970). Obituaries are in most major newspapers, 9 Dec. 1939.

MARY LOUISE BOEHM

SCHENCK, Ferdinand Schureman (6 Aug. 1845– 6 Apr. 1925), minister and professor, was born in Plattekill, Ulster County, New York, the son of Martin Luther Schenck, a minister, and Abigail Van der Veer. As a child Ferdinand lived in Plattekill, New York; Fort Plain, New York; and Rocky Hill, New Jersey, while his father served parishes in these towns.

Schenck received his A.B. from the College of New Jersey in 1865 and his LL.B. from Albany Law School in 1867. He practiced law for two years and then enrolled in New Brunswick Theological Seminary, where he earned a divinity degree in 1872. He was ordained as a minister in the Reformed Church in America (RCA) and served four parishes in New York State: Clarkstown in West Nyack from 1872 to 1877; Montgomery from 1877 to 1890; Hudson from 1890 to 1897; and University Heights Collegiate in the Bronx from 1897 to 1899. He married Ellie Haring in 1874; they had five children.

Schenck was elected president of the RCA's General Synod in 1892, and in 1899 the General Synod elected him as professor of practical theology at New Brunswick Theological Seminary. He taught preaching, worship, education, English Bible, pastoral counseling, administration, church government, and missions.

Schenck was notable for his achievements as an author, pastor, and teacher, but also for his distinctive voice in his denomination. While his career path was similar to those of his peers, his ideas were not. The RCA was a conservative denomination with churches located primarily in the small towns of Michigan, Illinois, Iowa, New York, and New Jersey. Most of its members, even the numerous Dutch immigrants, had achieved financial stability and middle-class respectability. When confronted with the poverty and labor conflict of the early twentieth century, many RCA pastors suggested that poor people should become Christians, work hard, and live morally, and that affluent people should be charitable to the poor.

A Christian movement known as the Social Gospel proposed a more systematic approach, suggesting that these individualistic solutions would never make society more equitable. Leaders of the Social Gospel, such as Walter Rauschenbusch, Washington Gladden, Frank Mason North, and Charles Stelzle, encouraged churches and individuals to live out their religious convictions by working for social justice and trying to prevent poverty rather than simply ameliorate it.

Studies of the Social Gospel have never linked Schenck to the movement, but the catalog description of his courses at New Brunswick Seminary illustrates Schenck's interest in social problems and the church's role in solving them. The church administration course examined the work of institutional churches, settlements, and rescue missions. Students in the English Bible course studied its social principles. Topics in the sociology course included the classification of social forces and conditions, industrial and wealth problems, the church and the masses, and the social mission of the church. Students gained firsthand knowledge of social problems by investigating them in the city of New Brunswick.

The ideas of the Social Gospel are also evident in two of Schenck's books, *The Ten Commandments and the Lord's Prayer* (1902) and *The Sociology of the Bible* (1909). The source of Schenck's passion for the social dimension of the gospel is unclear. Other Social Gospel leaders cited pastoral encounters with poverty or labor conflict as transforming events, but Schenck said nothing about his background. He did not cite sources in his writings, so it is difficult to discern which authors shaped his thinking.

Whatever the source of his vision, it is clear that Schenck saw the dark side of American progress and prosperity. Along with the luxurious palaces of the wealthy, observed Schenck, stood crowded tenement houses. Behind the abundance of factory-produced goods were adults and children who worked long hours for little pay.

Troubled by the injustice and inequity he saw around him, Schenck studied the sociology of the Bible to discern principles that could be applied to contemporary society. He believed that Hebrew society offered a good model of justice and equity. The Hebrews cared for the poor and strangers among them. Land laws limited the proliferation of large estates at the expense of the poor.

These Biblical principles encouraged charity and personal responsibility, but they also emphasized the need for justice. Schenck wrote in *Modern Practical Theology* (1903) that "religious emotions and sentiments of charity, propriety, and self-denial cannot atone for the absence of justice in dealings and of high regard for the rights of other" (pp. 226–27). Schenck criticized Christians who claimed to love God but in business took advantage of others. He insisted that poverty did not result simply from individual laziness or immorality but from the unfair division of resources in American society.

Schenck also called for structural changes in the social order. While many pastors chastised drunkards and prostitutes, Schenck criticized those who profited from these vices by manufacturing and selling alcohol or renting to saloon and brothel owners. He encouraged good will between laborers and capitalists but he recognized that good will could not always overcome human sinfulness and that laws must protect the rights of labor and restrict the power of capital.

Schenck insisted that churches and Christians do more than simply encourage conversion and morality. In *The Sociology of the Bible* he criticized the church for neglecting its social responsibility: "She fixes her attention so much upon the future life that she neglects the present life; so much upon individual salvation from sin against God, that she neglects social salvation from sins against brothers; so much upon God's forgiveness of sin that she neglects social duties" (p. 405). Schenck envisioned the church as a powerful force that would help establish the kingdom of God in the community and the world.

Despite Schenck's thoughtful and persuasive application of biblical themes to contemporary social problems, his work had minimal impact in the RCA. His peers praised his preaching and his pastoral gifts but said nothing about his social consciousness. One of his students, peace and justice advocate A. J. Muste, recalled only that he had learned some preaching tips from Schenck, even though Schenck may have been writing *The Sociology of the Bible* while Muste was his student.

Schenck was part of a denomination that usually supported the status quo, but he challenged the church to enlarge its vision and live out the gospel by seeking justice for all God's people. His words were not easy for his peers, or their descendants, to hear, but he raised questions about the church's social consciousness that remained relevant long after his time. Schenck retired in 1924 and died in White Plains, New York.

• A small file of Schenck's papers is in the Archives of the Reformed Church in America at New Brunswick Theological Seminary. Some of his other books include *Modern Practical Theology* (1903), *Christian Evidences and Ethics* (1910), *The Apostles' Creed in the Twentieth Century* (1918), and *A Guide to the Stars* (1922). An obituary is in the *Christian Intelligencer*, 15 Apr. 1925.

LYNN WINKELS JAPINGA

SCHENCK, Joseph M. (25 Dec. 1877–22 Oct. 1961), motion picture executive, was born in Rybinsk, Volga, Russia. (His parents' names are unknown.) Schenck and his younger brother, Nicholas Schenck, came to the United States in 1892. Little is known of their early years. We do know that they grew up poor in New York City and left school early to help support the family. Schenck looked for a time to be fashioning a career in pharmacy, but in his teens he was lured by the bright lights of show business. Success did not come quickly. He labored mightily before he was able to find his show business niche in the nascent amusement park business in 1908. He and his brother would go on to build Palisades Park across the Hudson River from New York City.

From this base Joe and Nick Schenck moved into the big-time vaudeville industry with the Marcus Loew organization. While Nick Schenck remained with Loew's to become the ultimate corporate executive (as head of Loew's and later its production unit, MGM), Joe Schenck took a far riskier route, starting an independent movie company, and by the end of the 1910s he had relocated to Hollywood. To the public in the 1920s Joe Schenck ranked as the ultimate "star maker," the man who discovered Constance, Natalie,

and Norma Talmadge, Roscoe "Fatty" Arbuckle, and Buster Keaton.

Joe Schenck married Norma Talmadge in 1917, while Keaton married Natalie Talmadge, and through the 1920s the Schenck-Keaton-Talmadge "extended family" ranked atop the Hollywood pantheon of celebrity and power. In time, Schenck and Talmadge found that careers and marriage did not mix, and they were secretly divorced in 1929. Thereafter, through the studio era, Joe Schenck played the role of the bachelor in Hollywood, rumored to have had affairs with stars from Merle Oberon to Marilyn Monroe.

Because many of the films he produced for his stable of stars during the 1920s were distributed through United Artists, in 1924 Joe Schenck took charge of United Artists' corporate fortunes. Quickly—by signing top stars and producers—he was able to refashion the then floundering company and mold it into one of Hollywood's most powerful corporate entities. As the head of United Artists, he helped create the Academy of Motion Picture Arts and Sciences and was at the head of the committee that initiated the Oscar ceremony.

For pure economic power, his brother had much more economic might. Nick became Joe's angel; from his office high atop the Loew's State Theatre building on Times Square, he helped his older brother when needed. During the Great Depression, Joe twice called on Nick. In 1933, tired of bickering with the founding partners of United Artists, Nick Schenck backed Joe's new production company, Twentieth Century Pictures. When in 1935 an ailing Fox Film Company sought new management, Nick again put up the monies to create Twentieth Century-Fox with Joe Schenck in charge.

Darryl F. Zanuck, Twentieth Century-Fox's outspoken, flamboyant head of motion picture production, got the bulk of the publicity, but Hollywood insiders knew Joe Schenck made all of the important decisions at Fox. Schenck signed up the stars, coordinated worldwide film distribution, and ran Twentieth Century-Fox's chain of more than 700 theaters.

Through the 1930s Joe Schenck and all of the other movie company heads paid bribes to Willie Bioff of the International Alliance of Stage and Theatrical Employees and Moving Picture Operators to prevent the Bioff-controlled union from proceeding with a threatened shutdown of their movie houses. In time government authorities, as part of ongoing investigations of racketeering and gangsterism, caught on to the bribes and convicted Bioff. One movie mogul had to go to jail as part of that judgment, and Joe Schenck took the fall. Convicted of perjury, he spent four months and five days in a federal prison in Danbury, Connecticut; in 1945 he was pardoned and cleared on all charges by President Harry Truman.

Both Schenck brothers probably would have gone on to become beloved figures had they retired in the late 1940s. Instead, they hung on until the changing economic climate of the 1950s made their methods of nearly thirty years obsolete. The *Paramount* case forced the studios to sell their theaters, and Hollywood diversified because it no longer possessed a vertically integrated advantage. In time, in separate corporate power struggles, both Schencks lost their vaunted positions. Nick Schenck retired. Joe Schenck never did, returning to independent production.

Ever the deal maker, during the 1950s Schenck and longtime pal Mike Todd signed up a wide-screen process, named it Todd-AO, and produced *Oklahoma!* (1955) and a number of other top-drawer films. Yet at the end, age finally slowed Schenck, and he died in Hollywood a bitter old man, living at the edge of an industry he had helped create.

• There are no papers for Joseph M. Schenck. For a scholarly examination of his years at United Artists, see Tino Balio, *United Artists: The Company Built by the Stars* (1976). For his role in the founding and workings of Twentieth Century-Fox, see Mel Gussow, *Don't Say Yes until I Finish Talking: The Biography of Darryl F. Zanuck* (1971), and Aubrey Solomon, *Twentieth Century-Fox: A Corporate and Financial History* (1988). To understand the changing nature of the motion picture industry, see Douglas Gomery, *The Hollywood Studio System* (1986). Joe Schenck is still best remembered as a star maker, and this is chronicled in Fred Lawrence Guiles, *Norma Jean: The Life of Marilyn Monroe* (1969), and Anita Loos, *The Talmadge Girls: A Memoir* (1978). A front-page obituary is in the *New York Times*, 23 Oct. 1961.

DOUGLAS GOMERY

SCHENCK, Nicholas Michael (14 Nov. 1881–3 Mar. 1969), motion picture executive, was born in Rybinsk, Volga, Russia, the son of Hyman Schenck, a laborer, and Elizabeth (maiden name unknown). In 1892 Schenck came to the United States, where he received an elementary school education in New York City until he was forced to leave school to help support his family. His first business success came in 1908 when he and his brother, Joseph M. Schenck, entered the amusement park business in New York City. In time the brothers acquired Palisades Amusement Park in Fort Lee, New Jersey, just across the Hudson from Manhattan. Through that venture Schenck met Marcus Loew, president of a growing chain of vaudeville and movie theaters. Within only a brief time Schenck became Loew's, Inc.'s chief assistant.

Schenck first married sometime between 1910 and 1920 (first wife's name unknown). He was married again in 1927, this time to Pansy Wilcox, with whom he had three daughters.

During Schenck's early years at Loew's Theatrical Enterprises the company steadily expanded until it owned some 400 movie theaters throughout the eastern United States. In 1924 Loew's gained controlling interest in the Goldwyn Company and in Louis B. Mayer Pictures; the three film production studios were merged by Loew's, always the controlling company, into Metro-Goldwyn-Mayer (MGM), the most famous moviemaking enterprise in the world.

Known by all as "the General," Schenck took over from Marcus Loew in 1927. For almost three decades, until 1955, Schenck ran a tight corporate empire from his office high atop the Loew's State Theater building in Times Square. A trusted team of assistants, many of whom remained loyal to him during his entire tenure, skillfully executed his every order. Louis B. Mayer, head of production at MGM's Hollywood studios, was far more famous among the moviegoing public, but Mayer made no important decisions without first "checking with New York"—that is, with Schenck.

Loew's, Inc.'s fiscally conservative business practices continued to produce profits during the Great Depression. By 1935 the Loew's movie empire, with some 200 lavish picture palaces, stood at the top of the international film industry. Its methods of film production, distribution, and exhibition reflected Schenck's conservative business philosophy. For example, MGM created only top drawer feature films, which were the greatest money makers, while it distributed short subjects and newsreels made by others.

In Culver City, California, a suburb of Los Angeles, Schenck's movie factory had twenty-seven sound stages on nearly 200 acres. MGM's laboratories could process 100,000 feet of film each day, and its property rooms contained more than 15,000 items to be used in movie after movie. Sound studios in Paris, Barcelona, and Rome dubbed films into more than one dozen languages. Offices ranging from Hong Kong to Cape Town distributed MGM's films to virtually every country in the world. And Loew's theaters offered audiences the best in movie house entertainment, from Times Square to downtown Los Angeles.

MGM used a variety of stars to realize enormous profits. During the 1930s MGM presented jungle adventures (the *Tarzan* series), slapstick comedies (Stan Laurel and Oliver Hardy in *Sons of the Desert*, for example), and the burlesque satire of the Marx Brothers (*A Night at the Opera*, *A Day at the Races*, and more). Schenck also took some risks. During the 1940s MGM pioneered the lavish, Technicolor musical. *Meet Me in St. Louis*, with Judy Garland, *Easter Parade*, starring Fred Astaire, and the innovative *On the Town*, codirected and starring Gene Kelly, were expensive to make but skillfully used all of the talents on the lot as well as the latest moviemaking technology. At the same time, MGM made and distributed such dependable, low-budget movies as the Dr. Kildare and Hardy family series. *Our Gang* comedy shorts made millions, while during the 1940s the studio developed the popular *Tom and Jerry* cartoon series. MGM never created its own newsreels; instead Schenck subcontracted them from the giant newspaper organization of his friend William Randolph Hearst.

Schenck would have become a Hollywood legend had he chosen to retire before 1950. But he decided to hang on, and in the 1950s the changing economic climate made obsolete the methods he had employed for nearly a half-century. Loew's under Schenck began losing money, and in 1955 he resigned as president. By 1956 he had lost his power and severed all ties with Loew's after a fierce stockholder's proxy fight.

Schenck retired a bitter man and died in Miami Beach, Florida.

• There are no known Nicholas Schenck papers; neither are there any published writings. The obituary in *Variety*, 5 Mar. 1969, gives a comprehensive biography. Dore Schary, *Heyday* (1979), tells what it was like to work for Schenck, whereas Lillian Ross, *Picture* (1952), profiles the making of MGM's *The Red Badge of Courage* and Schenck's key role in the production. Bosley Crowther, *The Lion's Share* (1957), remains the best history of the Loew's/MGM empire. Douglas Gomery, *The Hollywood Studio System* (1986), a business history of the American motion picture industry, describes the changing role and status of Schenck's corporate colossus.

DOUGLAS GOMERY

SCHENCK, Robert Cumming (4 Oct. 1809–23 Mar. 1890), congressman and diplomat, was born in Franklin, Warren County, Ohio, the son of General William Cortenus Schenck, a pioneer land speculator, and Elizabeth Rogers. After graduating from Ohio's Miami College (now Miami University) in 1827, he remained there for three years teaching French and Latin. He then studied law in the office of Thomas Corwin, who took the young man under his wing. In 1834 Schenck married Rennelche Smith; they had six children, three of whom survived infancy.

Schenck (pronounced Skenk) followed Corwin into the Whig party. Defeated in his first campaign for the Ohio legislature, Schenck won election in 1841 and was immediately chosen to be his party's floor leader in the general assembly. In his two terms he advocated state-sponsored internal improvements and vigorously opposed Democratic schemes to restrict banking and to gerrymander the state's districts.

In 1843 Schenck was elected to the first of four consecutive terms as U.S. congressman from Ohio's Third District. In Washington he became friendly with leading Whigs such as Daniel Webster and John Quincy Adams, who appreciated Schenck's assistance in combating the "Gag Rule," by which southern congressmen attempted to suppress antislavery petitions. He also opposed the Mexican War and the spread of slavery, though not the institution of slavery itself.

Political battles lost their zest for Schenck after the death of his wife on 5 November 1849. Seeking a change of scene, he asked for a diplomatic assignment and in March 1851 was appointed envoy extraordinary and minister plenipotentiary to Brazil, a post he would hold until October 1853. In Brazil, Schenck succeeded in persuading Emperor Dom Pedro to denounce (but not to end) the African slave trade but failed to secure free navigation on the Amazon River. Collateral negotiations with the Argentine Confederation produced a treaty that opened the Río de la Plata to U.S. commerce, but commercial treaties negotiated with Uruguay and Paraguay failed to be ratified.

Schenck returned to the United States to find his Whig party in disarray. Turning from politics to business, he became president of the Fort Wayne and Western Railroad. Not even the formation of the Republican party could tempt him to return to public life, largely because of his personal dislike of its first presidential candidate, John C. Frémont. By 1859 he was finally in the Republican fold and was, so he claimed, among the first to advocate Abraham Lincoln for president.

On the outbreak of the Civil War, Lincoln appointed Schenck brigadier general of volunteers, dating from 17 May 1861. On 17 June 1861 his command stumbled into an embarrassing railroad ambush at Vienna, Virginia, but he redeemed his reputation at First Manassas with a tenacious defensive stand that helped slow the advance of the victorious Confederates. This was followed by service as a brigade and then corps commander in western Virginia, where he fought in the Shenandoah Valley campaigns and at Cross Keys (8–9 June 1862). His active military career was ended by a Confederate bullet that shattered his right wrist at Second Manassas. Promoted to major general as of 30 August 1862, he was assigned to command the Middle Department, consisting of Maryland and Delaware. A high-handed administrator with little patience for either Confederate sympathizers or civil liberties, he jailed political opponents, censored newspapers, and barred antiwar voters from the polls. He resigned from the army on 5 December 1863 to take the seat in Congress he had won in November 1863 in a gratifying victory over his Dayton neighbor, the arch Copperhead, Clement Vallandigham.

In his four congressional terms, Schenck stood in the vanguard of the Radical wing of the Republican party, opposing both Lincoln and Andrew Johnson for their perceived moderation on the issues of war and Reconstruction. His radicalism can be seen by the titles of two of his most influential congressional speeches: "No Compromise with Treason" (11 Apr. 1864) and "Rebels Should Not Rule" (8 May 1866). As chairman of the Military Affairs Committee during the war, he pressed for a more rigorous conscription bill. In the immediate postwar years, as chairman of the Ways and Means Committee, he helped put a stop to Treasury secretary Hugh McCulloch's policy of currency contraction and committed the government to the goal of specie resumption.

Schenck particularly shone in debate, where his no-nonsense, self-assured manner won the admiration of colleagues such as James G. Blaine, who regarded him as "an intellectual marvel." According to Blaine, Schenck's "perceptions were keen, his analysis was extraordinarily rapid, his power of expression remarkable. On his feet . . . he had no equal in the House" (*Twenty Years of Congress*, vol. 1, p. 499). Schenck's congressional service was abruptly terminated with his narrow defeat in the election of 1870 by Democrat Lewis D. Campbell. Bitter over his rejection by the voters, he angrily declared to his friend James A. Garfield that henceforth he intended to work "for one Schenck—a particular friend of mine—not for the great, stupid, exacting public!" (Schenck to Garfield, 29 Oct. 1870, Garfield Papers, Library of Congress).

On 22 December 1870 Schenck resigned from Congress to become U.S. minister to Great Britain. Before leaving for England, he took part in the negotiations leading to the Treaty of Washington, which settled the *Alabama* claims and other Anglo-American disputes arising out of the Civil War. His five-year tenure at the Court of St. James was both a social success, highlighted by his introduction of the American game of draw poker into English drawing rooms, and a diplomatic one, especially through his efforts that kept the Treaty of Washington from being derailed.

These achievements, however, were clouded by Schenck's involvement in the affair of the Emma Mine, a Utah silver mine of which Schenck was a director and whose stock he recommended to English investors. The failure of the mine led to charges of corruption against Schenck, who resigned his post on 17 February 1876. A congressional investigation cleared Schenck of fraud but not of impropriety, for which he was formally censured by the House in July 1876, effectively ending his public career. He spent the remainder of his life as a lawyer in Washington, D.C., where he died.

• Although a substantial collection (9 linear feet) of Schenck papers is available at Miami University Library, Oxford, Ohio, no modern biography of Schenck has yet been published. Two useful unpublished studies are Epiphanie Clara Kokkinou, "The Political Career of Robert Cumming Schenck" (M.A. thesis, Miami Univ., Ohio, 1955); and James R. Therry, "The Life of General Robert Cumming Schenck" (Ph.D. diss., Georgetown Univ., 1968). For a contemporary view, see Howard Carroll, *Twelve Americans . . .* (1883). Schenck's diplomatic career is discussed in Allan Peskin and Donald Ramos, "An Ohio Yankee at Dom Pedro's Court," *Americas* 38 (Apr. 1982): 497–514; and Martha Chapman Guilford, "The Diplomatic Career of Robert C. Schenck in England, 1871–1876" (M.A. thesis, George Washington Univ., 1950). For the Emma Mine investigation, see U.S. House, 44th Cong., 1st sess., H. Rept. 579 (1876). Schenck's notorious manual for the game of poker was published as *Draw: Rules for Playing Poker* (1880).

ALLAN PESKIN

SCHERESCHEWSKY, Samuel Isaac Joseph (6 May 1831–15 Oct. 1906), Episcopal bishop and translator, was born in Tauroggen, Russian Lithuania, the son of Samuel Joseph Schereschewsky and Rosa Salvatha. His father was of the Ashkenazic and his mother of the Sephardic Jews. Both of his parents, about whom little is known, died when he was a boy, and he was raised by a half brother and his wife, who wanted him to become a rabbi. From about 1846 to 1850 he studied at the rabbinical schools at Krazi and Zhitomir, Russia. From 1852 to 1854 he studied at the University of Breslau, Germany. At Zhitomir and Breslau his interest in Christianity was aroused by missionaries of the London Society for Promoting Christianity among the Jews, but it probably was his study of a Hebrew translation of the New Testament that convinced him that Jesus had fulfilled the messianic prophecies of the Hebrew Bible (or Old Testament).

To learn more about Jews who had become Christians, Schereschewsky came to the United States in 1854, and at a Passover meal with a group of Christian Jews in the spring of 1855 he said, "I can no longer deny my Lord. I will follow Him without the camp" (quoted in Muller, p. 32). Convinced that immersion was the proper mode of baptism, he was immersed by a Baptist minister. Later he joined the Presbyterian church and from December 1855 to February 1858 studied for the ministry at the Western Theological Seminary in Allegheny, Pennsylvania. While there he became friends with Theodore B. Lyman, rector of Trinity Episcopal Church in Pittsburgh; he also began to question Calvinist theology and Presbyterian polity, and this led him to join the Episcopal church. He then studied at the General Theological Seminary in New York City (1858–1859). While there, after a visit to the seminary by William Jones Boone, the first missionary bishop of China, Schereschewsky decided to "devote his whole life to the China Mission" and to translate the Bible into Chinese. Boone ordained him deacon on 7 July 1859, and on 13 July he and three others sailed for China. On 28 October 1860 Bishop Boone ordained him priest.

Schereschewsky's missionary strategy was twofold: translation and education. He had a natural ability for languages and soon after his arrival began translating the Bible and the Book of Common Prayer into Mandarin, the vernacular used by the majority of Chinese. He married Susan Mary Waring, a teacher from St. Anne's Church, Brooklyn, in 1868; they had two children. In 1872 his translations of the New Testament and the Book of Common Prayer into Mandarin were published, and that of the Old Testament was published in 1874. From 1 July 1875 to 20 April 1878 Schereschewsky traveled in the United States. During that period, on 19 July 1875, he was naturalized as a U.S. citizen.

Bishop Boone had died on 17 July 1864 and was replaced as missionary bishop of China and Japan by Channing Moore Williams. Williams relinquished the China part of his jurisdiction on 23 October 1874, and on the same day the House of Bishops changed the China jurisdiction to missionary bishop of Shanghai, having episcopal jurisdiction in China. The House of Bishops elected Schereschewsky to this position on 29 October 1875, but having no ambition other than to pursue his translation work, he declined. Reelected by the House of Bishops on 13 October 1876, he accepted and was consecrated at Grace Church, New York City, on 31 October 1877 by Bishop Benjamin Bosworth Smith of Kentucky. On his return to China he attended the second Lambeth Conference (2–27 July 1878) and began working to establish a college. In February 1879 he purchased thirteen acres of land known as Jessfield Farm, situated on Soochow Creek, five miles from Shanghai. He decided to call the college St. John's, and the cornerstone was laid on 14 April 1879. It later became St. John's University. Schereschewsky Hall, erected in 1894, commemorates him.

Schereschewsky came down with a high fever, probably as a result of severe sunstroke or thermic fever, on 12 August 1881 and almost died. When he recovered he was almost completely paralyzed and unable to speak clearly. He resigned as bishop on 30 September 1883 and determined to spend the rest of his life translating, though he could write only by pressing the keys of a typewriter with one finger on one hand. In 1897 he went to Tokyo, where he died. His greatest contributions were his translations of Christian writings for the Chinese. In 1881 his translation of the Book of Common Prayer into Easy Wenli was published. The American Bible Society published his Mandarin Reference Bible in 1908.

• Some of Schereschewsky's papers are in the Archives of the Episcopal Church, Austin, Tex., and in the American Bible Society Archives, New York City. The major study of his life and work is James Arthur Muller, *Apostle of China: Samuel Isaac Joseph Schereschewsky, 1831–1906* (1937). A helpful brief study is Massey H. Shepherd, Jr., *Schereschewsky of China* (1962). Other studies that treat Schereschewsky's work are Kenneth S. Latourette, *A History of Christian Missions in China* (1929); Arthur R. Gray and Arthur M. Sherman, *The Story of the Church in China* (1913); and three pamphlets published by the Episcopal church, *An Historical Sketch of the China Mission* (1893), *Letters, Documents, etc., in the Matter of Episcopal Jurisdiction in China* (1907), and *The Bishops of the American Church Mission in China* (1908).

DONALD S. ARMENTROUT

SCHERMAN, Harry (1 Feb. 1887–12 Nov. 1969), publisher, was born in Montreal, Canada, the son of Jacob Scherman, a laborer, and Katharine Harris, both of whom were Jewish. In 1889 the family moved to Philadelphia. In 1893 the father deserted his family and returned to his native England. Living in poverty in a boardinghouse with his hard-working mother, Scherman attended Central High School in Philadelphia, where fellow classmates included Alexander Woollcott and Ed Wynn. By freelancing for city newspapers, Scherman supported himself and was able to graduate in 1905. He attended the Wharton School of Finance at the University of Pennsylvania on a scholarship, did not like his classes, and dropped out, but in 1906 he enrolled in the university's law school. Not relishing the prospects of a law career, he turned in 1907 to journalism in New York City, where he wrote news items about books, politics, the city, social life, and the theater for the weekly *American Hebrew*. He tried unavailingly to write short stories and plays but did place other items in New York and Philadelphia newspapers and wrote advertising copy with considerable success. In 1912 he freelanced as an advertisement writer. He saved enough money not only to travel widely in the United States but also to try, once again unsuccessfully, to become a creative writer.

Scherman returned to New York in 1912 and worked for the advertising agency of Ruthrauff & Ryan, where he prepared booklets, circulars, and direct mail letters. In 1914 he got a job in the mail-order department of the J. Walter Thompson agency. That same year he married Bernardine Kielty, with whom he was to have two children. His wife taught in an orphanage in Pleasantville, Westchester County, north of New York City. Through Westchester social contacts Scherman met the publishing brothers Charles and Albert Boni. When in 1916 the Bonis showed Scherman a dummy of the first book in their projected Little Leather Library, an edition of *Romeo and Juliet*, he immediately saw the possibility of big profits. He knew that a tobacco company wrapped miniature Shakespeare texts in cigarette packs; so he proposed appealing to the Whitman Candy Company to include tiny books in candy boxes. Scherman, in partnership with the Bonis, contracted with Whitman to provide a thousand copies, at ten cents each, for each of fifteen plays by Shakespeare. He resigned from the Thompson firm, lured a copywriter named Maxwell Sackheim away as well, and with the Bonis and Sackheim obtained a contract with the Woolworth chain to distribute what eventually amounted to 25 million Little Leather Library books. Scherman and Sackheim purchased the concern from the Bonis (who then joined in forming the Boni and Liveright publishing firm), sold their books by mail order, and in 1920 also created their own advertising agency. In addition, they tried a book-of-the-week club—fifty-two classics for five dollars per annum—but this venture soon collapsed. In 1925 Scherman and his partner, having cumulative sales of 48 million Little Leather Library books, experienced financial difficulties and sold their inventory of 300,000 copies to the *Literary Digest*'s owners, who gave them as premiums to new subscribers.

Next, Scherman conceived an idea that revolutionized book-buying in the United States. It was the Book-of-the-Month Club, organized as a corporation, with Robert K. Haas (later a Random House vice president) as president, and with capital of $40,000, a quarter of which was Scherman's. Scherman and Haas hired five literary experts—Heywood Broun, Henry Seidel Canby, Dorothy Canfield Fisher, Christopher Morley, and William Allen White—to judge and choose books that were then offered for sale by mail on a monthly basis to a list of customers. Scherman advertised in national magazines for subscribers, and in April 1926 the first selection was sent to 4,750 club members. By year's end, the list had grown to 46,539, and the club enjoyed net sales of $503,000. Scherman's income that year was just over $92,000. In 1927 sales reached $1.5 million, and a year later membership reached 100,000. Growth was steady even through the depression. Scherman served as the president of the corporation from 1931 to 1950. During this period he wrote three books on economics, inflation, and democracy: *The Promises Men Live By: A New Approach to Economics* (1938), *The Real Danger in Our Gold* (1940), and *The Last Best Hope of Earth* (1942). A few months after World War II ended, membership in the Book-of-the-Month Club reached a high of 918,000, then dropped, but rose to one million by 1969. In 1947 shares in the corporation were first offered to the public. Scherman and his family, however, retained a majority interest and grew very wealthy.

From the start, Scherman maintained amiable relations with the American Booksellers Association and was therefore slow to sell club choices at reduced prices. But when the club was secure enough for him to do so, he began to include premiums with the purchase of a certain number of selections. Surprisingly, perhaps, bookstore sales were never hurt by club sales, which meant that Scherman's company encouraged reading in general. In 1950 he became chairman of the board, a position he retained until his death. The club continued to thrive impressively under his imaginative and innovative leadership. Over the years, it inspired numerous competing organizations, most of which failed, with the Literary Guild being a significant exception. The criticism that the Book-of-the-Month Club has been neither highbrow nor lowbrow, yet dictatorial, is manifestly unfair, since selections in Scherman's day included works by Pearl Buck, Ellen Glasgow, Ernest Hemingway, Sinclair Lewis, Thomas Mann, George Santayana, William Shirer, Sigrid Undset, and Thornton Wilder, among numerous other superb authors.

A man of charitable instincts, Scherman befriended Jewish refugees from Nazi Germany and helped struggling members of the arts, partly through his association, as a director, with the MacDowell Colony, the New Hampshire retreat for writers and composers. Always addicted to his work, he greatly relished his speaking acquaintance with most of the thousand-person workforce at Book-of-the-Month Club headquarters. He was at his Manhattan office regularly until ten days before his death in New York City.

• Scherman's part in the formation and evolution of the Book-of-the-Month Club is presented in Charles Lee, *The Hidden Public: The Story of the Book-of-the-Month Club* (1958). Scherman's career in publishing is detailed in John Tebbel, *Between Covers: The Rise and Transformation of American Book Publishing* (1987). Obituaries are in the *New York Times*, 13 Nov. 1969, and *Publishers Weekly*, 24 Nov. 1969.

ROBERT L. GALE

SCHICK, Béla (16 July 1877–6 Dec. 1967), pediatrician and allergist, was born in Boglar, Hungary, the son of Jacob Schick, a grain merchant, and Johanna (or Joanna) Pichler. Although the family home was in Graz, Austria, Béla was born prematurely at the Hungarian home of a maternal uncle, a physician whose care saved the infant's life.

Schick graduated in 1895 from the Staatsgymnasium in Graz, where he was an excellent student, shy and bookish. In 1900 he received an M.D. from Karl Franz University, also in Graz. The faculty members who most impressed Schick were Friedrich Kraus (internal medicine), who taught that illness was a condition of the whole organism, not of single organs; and Theodor Escherich (pediatrics), who focused Schick's interest on diseases of children.

Schick spent the fall and winter of 1900–1901 in the Medical Division of the Austro-Hungarian Army at Komarno. On returning to Graz, he began work as Escherich's assistant alongside Clemens von Pirquet, who was to be a longtime collaborator.

In 1902, when Escherich moved to the University of Vienna, he took Schick and von Pirquet with him. For Schick the move involved considerable financial strain. For eighteen months he received no salary and had to survive on the fifty kronen per month sent him by his parents. He lived in uncomfortable quarters, skimped on food, and undertook private instruction of foreign students to help pay his bills.

In 1903 Schick published his first paper (on cerebral hypertrophy in infants). It was followed shortly by papers on diphtheria and scarlet fever, two dreaded diseases of young children.

Schick and von Pirquet also studied "serum sickness," a response of the immune system to foreign substances. Their monograph, *Die Serumkrankheit* (1905), which established allergy as a definable human illness, remained a standard reference work for many years. The authors expained that first exposure to a foreign substance may take many days to produce the allergic reaction, as the body takes time to prepare chemical defenses against the invading substance, whereas, on later exposure, the body, already prepared, responds rapidly, producing the same reaction in a few hours.

In the next few years Schick collaborated further with von Pirquet in studies on allergy, and with Escherich on scarlet fever. By 1908, however, Schick was already actively studying the skin reaction to diphtheria toxin as an indicator of susceptibility to that disease. The disease was widespread, and fatal in 5 to 10 percent of all cases, usually by strangulation as the disease membrane in the throat cut off the air passage.

Schick's work on diphtheria culminated in 1913 in the famous paper describing what has since become known as the "Schick test," which made it possible to distinguish between the large numbers of children who were already immune to the disease and those who were not. This development was important because large-scale administration, by injection, of horse serum containing diphtheria antitoxin to protect exposed children was unmanageable, costly, and dangerous, with the serum often producing its own undesirable reactions. But, as Schick pointed out, most adults are immune, and most infants retain for about a year the immunity acquired from their mothers. Even in the more vulnerable age groups of young children, over half were immune. The Schick test, using minute, precisely measured dosages of the toxin and a suitably designed needle, minimized the possibility of adverse side reactions, while providing a rapid means of determining who was susceptible, and who therefore needed the antitoxin-bearing serum. Since the test meant that protection could be provided in advance of diphtheria outbreaks, it was well received by physicians.

Although Schick was not called to active military duty during World War I, he did assume the added medical work of other pediatricians who had been sent to the front. During the war and immediate postwar period Schick was concerned with the care of newborn children and nursing mothers. He counseled against hurrying "overdue" births, and, with von Pirquet, he advocated using sugar supplements to the infant diet to promote early weight gain. He was appointed professor extraordinarius (adjunct professor) of children's diseases at the University of Vienna, in 1918. Despite his world renown, his Jewish parentage precluded his receiving the title of full professor in Austria.

Responding to an offer from Mount Sinai Hospital of New York City to become director of its Pediatric Department, Schick visited the United States early in 1923. The hospital offered him research facilities and financial support on a scale unimaginable in postwar Vienna. During his visit he was widely feted, and he received requests for lectures from many universities and medical societies. He delivered the Cutter Lecture at Harvard Medical School on "Prevention and Control of Diphtheria." At the New York Academy of Medicine he gave the prestigious Harvey Lecture. When, after returning to Vienna, he decided to emigrate to the United States, his visa application was supported by many prominent American medical authorities. He landed in New York in September 1923, to assume the position as chief pediatrician at Mount Sinai Hospital. In 1925 Schick married Catharine Carrie Fries, a New York lawyer; the couple had no children.

In New York, Schick combined his continuing pediatric studies with engagement in large public health campaigns. Under his leadership the Schick test became part of public school programs throughout the United States and was administered to millions of children. Those who lacked immunity were given antitoxin inoculations. The incidence of diphtheria declined almost to zero.

Schick advanced the status of pediatric medicine by helping found the American Academy of Pediatrics in 1930. In *Child Care Today* (1932), coauthored with William Rosenson, he emphasized the primary importance of love for the child. On sex education for children, his rule was "no secrets and no emphasis." He opposed corporal punishment.

From 1928 until his retirement, Schick wrote extensively on childhood. A form of stridor in infant breathing is now known as "Schick's sign," indicative of tuberculosis. His 1939 article on "Common Forms of Childhood Tuberculosis" (*Medical Clinics of North America* 23 [May 1939]: 645–60) is considered a classic. Schick also stressed the similarity of allergy and immunity, both involving the body's chemical reaction to foreign substances.

In 1938 Schick received the Addington Gold Medal, a British award "for the most valuable discoveries for the relief of pain and suffering of humanity," and the Gold Medal of the New York Academy of Medicine, as a "benefactor of mankind." In 1954 Schick received the John Howland Medal of the American Pediatric Society.

Basically a nonpolitical person, Schick saw governments in terms of their impact on child care. He applauded the Russian establishment of a network of childcare institutions, and the efforts of the Mexican government to bring health care to Indian communities where 70 percent of all children died before the age of ten. He helped the Russian War Relief, and served until 1948 as editor of *American Review of Soviet Medicine*. During World War II over thirty of Schick's close family members died in German extermination camps.

After retiring from Mount Sinai Hospital in 1942, Schick continued as a consultant pediatrician, while maintaining a private practice at an office filled with toys and games for child patients. Schick was not affluent; he often accepted patients whose families could pay little or nothing.

After World War II Schick, noting that many patients did not respond well to the new antibiotics, became an early proponent of the use of gamma-globulin for protection against infection. In November 1967, while on a cruise to South America, Schick became ill with pleurisy. Rushed to New York, he died in Mount Sinai Hospital, where he had spent much of his professional life.

• A biography by Antoni Gronowicz, *Béla Schick and the World of Children* (1954), is a useful source of information about Schick's life and career. Other sources include an editorial in the *Journal of the American Medical Association* 203 (1 Jan. 1968): 44; and an obituary by H. L. Hodes, "Béla Schick, 1877–1967," in *Pediatrics* 41, no. 2 (1968): 379–81. A front-page newspaper obituary is in the *New York Times*, 7 Dec. 1967.

CHARLES H. FUCHSMAN

SCHIFF, Dorothy (11 Mar. 1903–30 Aug. 1989), publisher and author, was born in New York City, the daughter of Mortimer Leo Schiff, an investment banker, and Adele Neustadt. Born into a wealthy Republican family, she received her early education at the Brearley School in New York City from 1912 to 1920 and entered Byrn Mawr College in 1920. Her grades were so low that she was asked to leave after one year.

Before taking control of the *New York Post* at age thirty-six, Schiff, who remained a lifelong philanthropist, actively supported many social issues. Deeply concerned about the effects of the depression upon Americans, among her many civic causes she numbered the Ellis Island Investigating Committee (1934), the Social Service Committee of Bellevue Hospital (1937–1939), and the New York City Board of Child Welfare (1937–1939). She served also as secretary-treasurer of the New York Joint Committee for the Ratification of the Child Labor Amendment (1937–1939) and as a member of the Board of Directors of the Henry Street Settlement (1934–1938). Mt. Sinai Hospital (1934–1938), the Women's Trade Union League of New York (1939), the National Association for the Advancement of Colored People, and the women's division of the Democratic State Committee of New York were also beneficiaries of her time and efforts. In 1942, when she took control of the *New York Post*, she stopped her committee work to avoid conflict of interest charges. Throughout her life, however, she maintained both personal and professional commitments to social welfare programs and the Democratic party.

For forty-one years Schiff owned and published the oldest continuously published newspaper in the United States. During her long tenure she occupied the positions of director (1939); vice president and treasurer (1939–1942); and president, publisher, and owner (1943–1976). Founded by Alexander Hamilton in 1801, the newspaper initially endorsed Hamilton's conservative politics. Over time, however, the paper shifted to a more independent stance, and with Schiff's assumption of the reins, it gained a more liberal reputation. Although she had no experience in running a large newspaper and despite her rivals' absolute belief in her failure, Schiff had an innate ability to define what the working people of New York City wanted. She changed the newspaper's format to a tabloid form with more human interest stories, scandal, gossip, comics, and columns. Indeed, the *Post* became known for its extravagant use of columnists, supporting as many as fifty in the late 1940s. Listed among the more famous columnists were Langston Hughes, Sylvia Porter, Drew Pearson, Elsa Maxwell, Eleanor Roosevelt, Jackie Robinson, and Edmund Wilson. Between 1951 and 1958, Schiff, referred to by her staff merely as "Dolly," penned her own outspoken column titled "Publisher's Letter," subsequently called "Dear Reader." Later, in a personal interview in *Contemporary Authors* (vol. 121), when asked why she gave up her column in 1958, she remarked that "it was fun for a while, but I got into so much trouble with it." In 1945 she acquired the *Bronx Home News*, a daily newspaper that merged with the *Post* in 1948. Her continued championing of liberal causes ensured a loyal readership among the working-class population to whom the publication was directed. In 1962, as the editor in chief, Schiff demonstrated potent business acumen and tenacious survival instinct while managing to survive a three-month New York newspaper union strike that threatened her with bankruptcy. Withdrawing from the New York Publisher's Association, she recommenced her newspaper under the terms of an old contract while agreeing to abide by any future financial settlement. Schiff could not, however, maintain her iron grip. In the early 1970s the price of the *Post* increased three times, which resulted in a large readership loss and increased financial woes. As a result, to the amazement of the public and her staff, in 1976 the newspaper was sold to Australian publisher magnate Rupert Murdoch, known for notorious news items highlighting sex and violence. The negotiations were kept so quiet, in fact, that it took the *Post*'s rival, the *New York Times*, to break the story of the $31 million sale. Later, when asked about the *Post* under Murdoch's management, Schiff responded, "I'm entertained by it, but I deplore the sharp turn to the right." Although the sale met with severe public criticism, the *New York Post* remains the longest-running daily newspaper in the United States and, outlasting two rivals, the only afternoon paper in New York City.

Under Schiff, the *Post* became known as the champion of liberal causes. In conflict with her wealthy Jewish banking family's staunch Republican stance, Schiff came to admire and support liberal policies and candidates. She promoted in particular the New Deal politics of Democrat Franklin D. Roosevelt despite the majority of rival newspaper publishers who opposed him. Indeed, she made a point of assigning reporters to cover liberal causes. One of Schiff's business aims was to make the *Post* the exclusive publication of her readers. To accomplish this, she attempted to summarize articles and columns from other publications, making it unnecessary for her readers to purchase additional newspapers and magazines.

Schiff had a turbulent personal life, living through a total of four marriages. Speculation credits her multiple marriages to a poor-little-rich-girl complex: despite the overabundance of material goods, she searched for the love denied by her parents. Shortly after her society debut, she married Richard Hall, an investment broker, in 1923; they had two children. Hall, it is rumored, considered her Jewish lineage a social handicap. She divorced him in 1932 after her parents died, leaving her the sole stockholder of the *New York Post* and independently wealthy. That same year she married George Backer, a political adviser and writer who was publisher and president of the *New York Post* from 1932 until 1942, when he resigned because of illness. This marriage lasted eleven years and ended in divorce; the couple had one child. Theodore Olin Thackrey, an editor at the *New York Post*, and Schiff were married in 1943, and this childless marriage was dissolved in 1949. Her final marriage to Rudolf Sonneborn, an oil executive, which also ended in divorce and produced no children, lasted from 1953 until 1974.

Schiff's life was certainly not without color. Many considered her a rebel. She defied her parents in 1923 by marrying her first husband. She became associated with the Algonquin Round Table, a group consisting of such luminaries as George S. Kaufman, Harpo Marx, Dorothy Parker, and Robert Benchley who met regularly at the New York Algonquin Hotel. In 1976 Jeffrey Potter's *Men, Money and Magic: The Story of Dorothy Schiff*, which focuses on Schiff's marriages, brought to light the story of a close friendship with the late president, Franklin D. Roosevelt. This was followed by a *New York Times* front-page headline on 27 May 1976 purporting an affair between Schiff and Roosevelt—"Dorothy Schiff Says She Had an Affair with Roosevelt"—which she vehemently denied. Although Schiff initially cooperated with Potter and at first found the book "entertaining," after she had to bear the ensuing uproar, she came to refer to the publication as "that awful book." Schiff claimed friendship with both Franklin and Eleanor Roosevelt.

When Schiff assumed leadership of the *Post*, she became the first woman newspaper publisher in New York City. She was decorated with the Légion d'Honneur by France and was a member of the American Association of Newspaper Editors, the Washington Press Club, and the League of Women Voters. She was the founding member of New York Post Foundation (also known as the Pisces Foundation). Often referred to as an eccentric, Schiff, it was rumored, feared sinking into poverty. She would often plead lack of funds and supposedly never gave a compliment to a staff member out of fear of being asked for a raise. Although she would never give free newspapers to *Post* personnel, she was admired by her staff and well respected in the business community. In her typical rebellious manner, Schiff refused treatment for the cancer that took her life. She died at her home in New York City.

• Biographical information on Schiff is in Peter Benjaminson, *Death in the Afternoon: America's Newspaper Giants Struggle for Survival* (1984), which details Schiff's career at the *New York Post*, particularly her determination to keep it financially afloat. Jeffrey Potter, *Men, Money and Magic: The Story of Dorothy Schiff* (1976), focuses on Schiff's four marriages and her lovers and highlights her relationship with Franklin D. Roosevelt. A *New York Times* article on 27 May 1976 entangles Schiff and Roosevelt in an affair. *Contemporary Authors*, vol. 121 (1987), details Schiff's personal and business life and provides anecdotal information as well as a lively personal interview with Jean W. Ross in which Schiff's career, liberal politics, and relationships with President Roosevelt and Rupert Murdoch are explored. An obituary is in the *New York Times*, 31 Aug. 1989.

M. CASEY DIANA

SCHIFF, Jacob Henry (10 Jan. 1847–25 Sept. 1920), banker and philanthropist, was born in Frankfurt, Germany, the son of Moses Schiff, a merchant, and Clara Niederhofheim. Schiff attended Jewish schools in Frankfurt until the age of fourteen, then embarked on a business apprenticeship before entering the banking firm of a brother-in-law. In 1865, armed with letters of reference, he emigrated to the United States, where he joined the brokerage firm of Frank & Gans (New York City) as a clerk. A year later he formed, with Henry Budge and Leo Lehman, the partnership of Budge, Schiff & Company. In 1870 Schiff became a naturalized U.S. citizen.

The great expansion of the American railroad system after the Civil War required capital from abroad. Schiff's extensive contacts in Germany and elsewhere on the Continent made him a valuable bond merchant there for railroads in need of capital. He spent much of his time as a Budge, Schiff partner in Europe negotiating the sale of railroad bonds for, among others, the St. Louis and Southeastern Railway, which was being built by General James H. Wilson and Edward F. Winslow, and the Northern Pacific Railway of James J. Hill.

The Franco-Prussian War (1870–1871), the German occupation of France, and the payment of a large indemnity by France to Germany combined to throw the European financial world into tumult in the early 1870s and to temporarily dry up this source both of capital for American railroads and of business for Budge, Schiff. Schiff returned to the United States in 1872 and with his partners liquidated the firm. After some time in Germany, Schiff again returned to the United States as a partner in the New York banking firm of Kuhn, Loeb & Company, which he joined on 1 January 1875. He remained a partner in the firm until his death. In 1875 he also married Therese Loeb; their union produced two children.

Kuhn, Loeb & Company was interested mainly in U.S. Government obligations and in railroad bonds. Before long, the energetic Schiff was the principal spokesman for the firm, particularly in its contacts with European banks and investors. When the last of the original partners in the firm, Solomon Loeb, went into semiretirement in 1885, Schiff was, at thirty-eight clearly the head of the firm.

Under Schiff's leadership, Kuhn, Loeb & Company quickly rose to become (with that of J. P. Morgan) one of the two leading investment banking firms in the United States by the turn of the century. The activities of the firm involved Schiff in the financing, reorganization, and direction (as the member of several boards of directors) of many of the leading American railroads in the late nineteenth and early twentieth centuries. Among those in which Schiff was intimately involved were the Pennsylvania, Great Northern, Illinois Central, and Union Pacific railroads.

By the turn of the century two men—James J. Hill and Edward H. Harriman—together with their associated railroads, had emerged as the principal rivals in that industry. Their rivalry was such that it was impossible to remain on close terms with both. By 1900, Schiff and his firm had parted with Hill to form a close relationship with Harriman and his enterprises. Although Schiff and Harriman had known each other for some time, their close relationship originated with Kuhn, Loeb & Company's successful reorganization of the Union Pacific Railway in 1896. The competition between Hill and Harriman now broadened to include Morgan and Schiff as the principal bankers for the respective antagonists. Besides numerous smaller lines, the Hill-Morgan interests controlled the Great Northern and Northern Pacific railways, the Harriman-Schiff group the Union Pacific and Southern Pacific lines.

In 1901 Schiff learned that the Hill-Morgan group was purchasing stock in the Chicago, Burlington & Quincy Railroad, generally referred to as the Burlington line. Control of this railroad by Hill would seriously jeopardize the "heartland" of Harriman's operations. To protect the Union Pacific, the Harriman-Schiff group purchased a sizable block of Northern Pacific stock so that they might have a voice in decisions with respect to operations of the Burlington. This precipitated a struggle for control of the Northern Pacific, which in 1901 resulted in the creation of a gigantic holding company, the Northern Securities Company, through which the competing parties sought to protect their respective interests and end the struggle between them. This organization, however, was attacked for its ability to virtually monopolize transportation in the northwestern United States and was prosecuted successfully by President Theodore Roosevelt's administration in its first action under the Sherman Antitrust Law.

Through the balance of his life, Schiff was interested, to some extent at least, in the financing of virtually every major American railroad. Beginning in the 1890s, however, an increasing share of his time was occupied with nonbanking matters. Of particular concern for him was the plight of Jews in Eastern Europe, especially in Rumania and Russia, who lived under conditions fraught with official restrictions and both official and unofficial persecution. These conditions, together with other factors, began to trigger a massive immigration of East European Jewry into the United States beginning in the early 1880s.

As the flow of their East European co-religionists into the United States swelled to a flood, the older, mostly German, Jewish-American community faced a dilemma. Many of the new arrivals were destitute and unable—because of religious restrictions, language difficulties, and lack of training—to immediately become self-sufficient. This created strains on Jewish charitable organizations and threatened to promote a backlash against Jews, in general. Moreover, it was apparent that immigration could be a solution for only a small percentage of the Jews living in Rumania and Russia. Accordingly, Schiff and other American Jewish leaders sought ways to apply pressure on the governments of those countries to ease the living conditions of Jews, and to enlist the assistance of the United States Government, when possible, in those efforts.

As a wealthy and influential banker, and a Republican, Schiff was well known in Washington to the GOP administrations of Theodore Roosevelt and William Howard Taft, and he later cultivated a close relationship with the Democratic administration of Woodrow Wilson. By such contacts, Schiff and other Jewish leaders like Oscar Straus and Simon Wolf were able to generate protests from the U.S. government to the governments of Rumania and Russia in the late nineteenth and early twentieth centuries in response to the persecution of Jews in those countries. These actions laid the foundation of the American Jewish foreign policy lobby and also of a growing conviction that the human rights of peoples elsewhere in the world ought to be a legitimate concern of American foreign policy.

Schiff's efforts to aid East European Jewry went beyond such diplomatic pressures, however. When war broke out between Russia and Japan in 1904, Schiff quickly mobilized American financial support behind Japan in the hope that a Russian defeat would lead to the overthrow of the hated czarist government. At the same time, he worked tirelessly to bar the Russian government from access to the American financial market. Schiff also underwrote a revolutionary propaganda campaign among Russian prisoners-of-war held by the Japanese. Four Japanese war bond issues, totaling $180 million in face value, were underwritten in the United States by Schiff's syndicate, and the participation of American bankers was probably of critical importance, too, in obtaining for Japan the support of bankers in England and on the European Continent. Japan's access to foreign financing was crucial to that nation's success in the war against Russia.

Schiff's prominence in Japan's wartime finance gave him the reputation in the United States as "Japan's banker." Actually, his interest in East Asia dated back to the late nineteenth century. In 1872 he had tried unsuccessfully to obtain for Budge, Schiff & Company (and for Wilson and Winslow) a share of the underwriting of a Japanese government bond issue. Also, in the 1890s Schiff had been a party to equally abortive attempts, again with James H. Wilson, to float loans for China. After the Russo-Japanese War, Schiff was involved in the ill-fated attempt of E. H. Harriman to gain control of the South Manchurian Railway as a segment of his proposed "round-the-world" transportation network.

Schiff's concern over the concentration of Russian-Jewish immigrants in the eastern port cities of the United States, and the possible demands for restricted immigration that might result, led Schiff to attempt to deflect such immigration into the interior of the country. The Galveston Movement matched prospective Russian-Jewish immigrants with communities in the interior of the United States. Between 1907 and 1914 it brought approximately 10,000 such immigrants to the United States through Galveston, Texas, from whence they quickly were dispersed by train to the cooperating communities inland. These immigrants, together with relatives and friends who followed them, created sizable Jewish communities in many towns and cities in the Midwest and Plains states.

In addition to his banking and humanitarian pursuits, Schiff's philanthropic contributions were significant. In the long list of those contributions several stand out as evidence of Schiff's support for education and the arts: the Harvard Union, the Harvard Semitic Museum, the underwriting of archaeological expeditions in Jerusalem, and contributions to the Semitic collections of the New York Public Library and the Library of Congress, to name only a few. Schiff died in New York City.

• Schiff's papers were accidentally destroyed in a fire, but fortunately they were not burned until after Cyrus Adler had made extensive copies and notes of the correspondence for the biography he was writing. Those copies and notes are available in the American Jewish Archives, Hebrew Union College, Cincinnati, but contain little on his early banking career. The James H. Wilson Papers in the Delaware Historical Society, Wilmington, contain Schiff letters to Wilson from the Budge, Schiff & Company days. Letters relating to a number of Schiff's diplomatic and humanitarian activities may also be found in several collections accessioned in the Library of the American Jewish Historical Society at Brandeis University. Adler's biography, *Jacob H. Schiff: His Life and Letters* (2 vols., 1928), remains the only book-length study of Schiff's life. Details of Schiff's efforts in behalf of East European Jews, including the Galveston Movement, can be found in Gary Dean Best, *To Free a People: American Jewish Leaders and the Jewish Problem in Eastern Europe, 1890–1914* (1982). A front-page obituary and related articles are in the *New York Times*, 26 Sept. 1920.

GARY DEAN BEST

SCHIFF, Leonard Isaac (29 Mar. 1915–19 Jan. 1971), physicist and academic statesman, was born in Fall River, Massachusetts, the son of Edward Schiff, the owner of a department store, and Mathilda Brodsky, a gifted pianist and composer. Both families were of Lithuanian Jewish descent, the father coming from a long line of rabbinical scholars. Schiff was a prodigy who was already well versed in calculus when he entered Ohio State University at the age of fourteen in 1929. He also had considerable musical talent; he was and remained a fine clarinetist, and he liked to remark in later life that he knew three languages: English, mathematics, and music. Young as he was, he joined many student activities, becoming captain of the university shooting team. He also adopted early on an active Christian faith, to which he held firmly throughout his life while remaining conscious of and close to his Jewish heritage.

Schiff was drawn to physics by the young Welsh physicist Llewellyn Thomas, who had recently come to Ohio State from Cambridge after his discovery of the relativistic Thomas precession in atomic theory. Schiff obtained a B.S. in 1933 and an M.S. in 1934, as part of which he wrote, with Thomas, an elegant paper on the quantum theory of metallic reflection, published in *Physical Review* in 1935. Proceeding to Massachusetts Institute of Technology, he obtained a doctorate in 1937 for work with P. M. Morse on quantum scattering theory. He then spent three years at the University of California at Berkeley with J. Robert Oppenheimer. Oppenheimer's Berkeley, as Schiff later said, was "a Mecca for theoretical physicists." There, by example and the master's cryptic utterance, they were urged to learn all the physics of the time and stay close to experiment. In everything except the habit of talking in riddles this was to become Schiff's style.

In 1940 Schiff was appointed assistant professor of physics at the University of Pennsylvania, marrying in 1941 Frances Ballard, with whom he had two children, and settling into a career. Soon he did an unheard-of thing. Though more than busy with teaching and research, he told his department chairman that he had some free time and could help with administrative chores. A year later he inherited the chair. The pattern repeated when he moved to Stanford University in 1947. There he became chairman of physics in 1948 and held that position for eighteen years, of which the first ten at least were unremitted triumph. His influence rapidly widening, he became one of the most powerful figures in the university and the "obvious" man to put on innumerable national and international committees. Not least of his services to Stanford was his skill, as first chairman of his faculty senate, in guiding the university through the chaos of the late 1960s.

Among Schiff's qualities as an academic statesman were clarity, fairness, attention to detail, and, above all, his stature as a human being. He was a man of exceptional (sometimes frightening) integrity, loved and revered far beyond the confines of the academic world. As one young colleague put it, "I always thought I had a special relationship with Schiff until I discovered that everyone else did too." The same unqualified admiration remains in many memories. Schiff's immense moral authority had one serious drawback: in becoming too indispensable, he left behind him a leadership vacuum.

As a physicist, Schiff is remembered for important work on nuclear structure and general relativity, and for his classic textbook, *Quantum Mechanics*, from which generations of students learned this subject. The text, first published in 1949, went through three editions with major revisions and improvements in the second (1955) and third (1968). He began in nuclear physics under Morse a few years after James Chadwick had discovered (c. 1932) that the atomic nucleus contains not only protons, but a new semistable uncharged particle, the neutron. Schiff soon devised clever calculational techniques for treating the "strong forces" between these nuclear components, and after Hideo Yukawa had hypothesized a new particle, the meson, as carrier of the force, Schiff investigated with Willis Lamb the effects of "exchange currents" in the nucleus, i.e., the additional electromagnetic currents resulting from the flow of charged mesons back and forth between the nucleons.

During World War II Schiff worked on engineering problems—submarine steering, radar detectors, helium purity in blimps—in the physics department of the University of Pennsylvania. This diversion was a gain. When he came to Stanford in 1947, the most original mind in the physics department was the engineer-physicist W. W. Hansen, who had just invented the linear electron accelerator. Construction was starting on the first 180-foot-long accelerator, and Schiff contributed a series of vital, still unpublished, memoranda on the formidable mathematical problems of accelerator design. After Hansen's death in 1949, he rallied the devastated team with another memorandum (also unpublished), outlining with extraordinary insight the entire future research program of the accelerator. One insight was that the accelerator could be used to determine charge distribution in atomic nuclei. An electron accelerator is in effect a very fine electron microscope. Electrons moving rapidly enough to have wavelengths comparable with the dimensions of the atomic nucleus can explore the charge distribution, "much as lower energy electrons are now used to explore charge distributions in molecules and crystals" (Technical Report of the Stanford Univ. Microwave Laboratory, no. 102, Nov. 1949, p. 15).

Over the next decade, the program Schiff had sketched was brilliantly executed by Robert Hofstadter, whom Schiff brought to Stanford from Pennsylvania. Far from having sharp boundaries, atomic nuclei were shown to comprise a uniform core surrounded by a region of progressively decreasing proton density. Other studies, also foreseen by Schiff, included electron scattering from single protons, neutrons, and deuterons. In all this work Schiff, with his students and younger colleagues, was essential, developing many classic calculational methods in theoretical nuclear physics. One could even fairly ask whether he might have shared the Nobel Prize awarded to Hofstadter in 1961. That he did not may be because good theoretical work was done elsewhere, especially by L. R. B. Elton in London and H. Feshbach at MIT, but it probably is also a reflection of Schiff's self-effacing style.

In 1958 Schiff began to turn his attention to gravity. His first paper in this field ingeniously combined gravitational and nuclear physics to argue against an intriguing speculation by P. Morrison and T. Gold that the gravitational force between matter and antimatter is repulsive rather than attractive. Schiff's argument was quite persuasive; however, the question continues to be open to legitimate debate. His next paper, written in 1959, analyzed the significance of experimental tests of Albert Einstein's general theory of relativity. Schiff argued that the standard tests proved much less than was commonly thought, especially the famous light deflection experiment performed by Arthur Stanley Eddington and others in 1919. Worse, he gave convincing reasons for believing that, owing to the minuteness of the deviations from Newtonian theory, no experimentally feasible refinement of the standard tests would yield any useful information.

It was an exquisite irony that a month or so after having reached this gloomy conclusion Schiff managed to think of two entirely new tests of Einstein's theory, based on observation of gyroscopes in orbit around the Earth. The first test measures in effect the distortion of space-time due to the mass of the Earth. The second, which theoretically is even more profound, measures the "dragging of the inertial frame" caused by the rotation of the Earth with respect to the rest of the universe. The paper announcing this impressive result appeared in *Physical Review Letters* on 1 March 1960.

Schiff's knowledge of gyroscope technology from his work on submarines in World War II was one factor behind this idea. Discussions with Stanford physicist William Fairbank and aeronautical and astronautical scientist Robert Cannon led in 1963 to a proposal to the National Aeronautics and Space Administration to begin research into the many new technologies required to perform the experiment that became known as Gravity Probe B. (Gravity Probe A was a suborbital clock experiment launched in 1976.) The arduous research effort resulted in 1984 in a two-stage flight program, led by B. W. Parkinson, J. P. Turneaure, and the present writer, with the final expected satellite launch in October 2000. Meanwhile, in no small part through Schiff's influence, experimental gravitation became a field of major importance and a constant challenge to the ingenuity of physicists.

To be at once a statesman, a distinguished teacher, and an effective research scientist, Schiff needed (and had) great rapidity of mind and intensely disciplined work habits. Though he had been a prodigy, his best research came in his thirties and forties, at the height of his administrative career. For eleven years after his first paper on the gyroscope he continued in full vigor

and apparently perfect health, publishing significant work in both gravitational and nuclear physics, and toward the end he was moving into another field ideal to his talents, theoretical astrophysics. Interestingly, for all his admiration for Oppenheimer, his hero was the nineteenth-century English physicist Lord Rayleigh. More than once he announced his intention of writing after his retirement a biography of Rayleigh. This was not to be. Very abruptly he collapsed and died on the Stanford campus of a congenital heart defect of which he but none of his colleagues was aware.

• Schiff's papers are in Stanford University's library, except for private materials in the possession of Mrs. Schiff. Schiff coedited with Robert Hofstadter *Nuclear Structure* (1964). A short biography by F. Bloch in National Academy of Sciences, *Biographical Memoirs* 54 (1983): 301–23, idealizes the history of the Stanford physics department. See P. Galison et al., "Controlling the Monster: Stanford and the Growth of Physics Research," in *Big Science: The Growth of Large-Scale Research*, ed. P. Galison and B. Hevly (1992). A valuable picture of Schiff and his work is contained in J. D. Walecka, "A Tribute to Leonard Schiff—Teacher, Scientist, and Statesman," *Schiff Memorial Lecture* (17 Apr. 1991). An account of the origin of the gyroscope experiment is in C. W. F. Everitt, "The Stanford Relativity Gyroscope Experiment (A): History and Overview," in *Near Zero: New Frontiers of Physics*, ed. J. D. Fairbank et al. (1988), pp. 587–639. An obituary is in *Physics Today*, 24 July 1971.

C. W. F. EVERITT

SCHILLER, A. Arthur (7 Sept. 1902–10 July 1977), professor of law at Columbia University and leading American authority on Roman law, was born in San Francisco, California, the son of George Marcus Schiller and Bertha Kohn. He studied at the University of California in Berkeley, where he received in 1924 a bachelor's degree in arts and in 1926 an M.A. in Coptic and a doctorate in law. From then on he was associated with the Law School of Columbia University in New York, beginning as a law fellow in 1926, advancing to lecturer in 1928, assistant professor in 1930, associate professor in 1937, and full professor in 1949. He spent the 1929–1930 academic year studying Egyptology and Roman law in Munich and in 1932 received a second law doctorate at Columbia. During the Second World War he taught at the U.S. Navy School of Training in International Administration and later trained Peace Corps volunteers for various countries in Africa. In 1926 he married Irma H. Coblentz. She died in 1946, and in 1947 he married Erna Kaske, with whom he had two children.

His earliest scholarly interest was in Coptic law, about which he published his first three articles, as well as his Columbia doctoral dissertation, *Ten Coptic Legal Texts and Coptic Law* (1932). He maintained this interest throughout his life, and it was the subject of about a fifth of his nearly one hundred publications.

Soon after his arrival at Columbia he was asked, unexpectedly, to teach a course in Roman law. This became the center of his scholarly activities from then on. It was facilitated by the collection of Roman law books in the Columbia University Law Library, which he built to be the fullest in the United States, and for which he devised a classification system. An early interest in substantive law—the relations of slaves and their owners and of freedmen and their patrons in the sphere of commercial law—soon gave way to a concentration on the legal sources of Roman law. He devoted his studies to the role of custom in classical Roman law, to interpretation in Roman and Anglo-American law, and to jurists' law. His major work in this field is the magisterial *Roman Law: Mechanisms of Development* (1978). The book compiles excerpts in English translation from ancient sources both legal and nonlegal on the sources, development, and general characterization (though not at all on the substance) of classical Roman law. Each text is followed by extensive summaries of research in all the major western European languages, providing a guide through the scholarly controversies on the issues treated in the book. The texts had formed the core of his annual course in Roman law at the law school.

Schiller was also interested in legal papyrology, in particular in the evidence Greek papyri from Egypt could offer on the legal activity of the Roman emperors. The most important of these studies is his large legal commentary to the rescripts of the emperor Septimius Severus contained on a Columbia University papyrus, published alongside that of William L. Westermann in *Apokrimata: Decisions of Septimius Severus on Legal Matters* (1954). Schiller devoted several other studies to the obscure *Sententiae et Epistulae Hadriani*, long considered worthless. He intended to rehabilitate it and prove it a genuine report of the emperor's oral legal activity by using computer-assisted vocabulary studies long before computer-readable texts and computer-assisted research became common among textual scholars. The project was left incomplete at his death.

Schiller was also a recognized authority on military law and on various modern non-European legal systems. His textbook *Military Law* went through four editions from 1941 to 1968. He also published *Adat Law in Indonesia* (1948), with E. A. Hoebel, and *The Formation of Federal Indonesia, 1945–1949* (1955). In 1965 he founded at Columbia University the Institute of African Law, the first of its kind in the United States. As a legal consultant to the United Nations he helped draft the constitution of Eritrea.

Schiller was an unusually careful scholar, so scrupulously fair in representing the views of others that he understated his own positions. Conscious of being the only productive native-born American scholar of his day in the field of Roman law, he entitled a collection of his articles *An American Experience in Roman Law* (1971). He believed it his responsibility to assist Jewish scholars fleeing Nazi persecution in Europe.

Schiller received three Guggenheim Fellowships and a Rockefeller Fellowship; was a member of the Institute for Advanced Study in Princeton, New Jersey, of the Accademia Nazionale dei Lincei in Italy, and of the Council on Foreign Relations; as well as of a large number of scholarly associations. His favorite was the informal Ancient Civilization Group in New York. Upon retiring from Columbia University in 1971 he moved to Oneonta, New York, where he died.

Schiller's importance lies primarily in his having been the sole representative of Roman legal scholarship in his generation in the United States. This cannot, however, be said to have generated much further study in Roman law in the United States, for though thousands of students attended his courses in Roman law over the years, only two continued to write doctoral dissertations in Roman law under his direction, and both made their homes in Israel thereafter. Of more lasting effect was his pioneering work in organizing study and library resources of foreign legal systems outside the Anglo-American and European legal traditions.

• Some of Schiller's papers on unfinished studies are deposited at the Columbia University Law School Library. A list of his publications and a full appreciation appear in Roger S. Bagnall and William V. Harris, eds., *Studies in Roman Law in Memory of A. Arthur Schiller* (1986). An obituary notice is in the *New York Times*, 12 July 1977.

RANON KATZOFF

SCHILLINGER, Joseph (31 Aug. 1895–23 Mar. 1943), music theorist, composer, and teacher of composition, was born in Kharkov, Ukraine, the son of Moses Schillinger, a prosperous businessman of Jewish descent, and Anna Gielgur. His principal studies from 1914 to 1918 were in musical composition and conducting at the St. Petersburg Imperial Conservatory of Music, where he earned the highest prize, a gold medal. Schillinger was mostly autodidactic in mathematics, physics, acoustics, several languages, history, and many other subjects. From 1918 to 1922 he held important administrative, conducting (Ukrainian State Symphony Orchestra), composing, and musical teaching positions at the State Academy of Music in Kharkov and elsewhere in the Ukraine. From 1922 until 1928, when he left the Soviet Union, Schillinger held important teaching positions in both Moscow and Leningrad (St. Petersburg). In 1925 he was composer for the State Academic Theatre of Drama in Leningrad. He was later dean of the Ukraine's State Academy of Music. In 1927 he recorded folk songs of the ethnic groups in Georgian S.S.R. He organized the first jazz orchestra concert in the U.S.S.R., which was held on 28 April 1927 in Moscow. Most of his musical compositions were written between 1914 and 1931, including *March of the Orient*, for orchestra, Op. 11 (1924; performed by the Cleveland Orchestra, 1927); *L'Excentriade*, for piano, Op. 14 (1924); Sonata-Rhapsody, for piano, Op. 17 (1925); Two Vocalises, for voice and piano, Op. 18 (1928); Symphonic Rhapsody, *October*, for large orchestra, Op. 19 (1927; performed by the Philadelphia Orchestra under Leopold Stokowski), selected by the State Committee as the best work composed in the first ten years of existence of the Soviet Union; *Dance Suite*, for violoncello solo,

Op. 20 (1928); *North-Russian Symphony*, for large orchestra, Op. 22 (1930); and a ballet, *The People and the Prophet* (1931). His compositions reflected a chromatic, conservative modern style with an eclectic Russian influence.

In 1930 Schillinger came to the United States at the invitation of the American Society for Cultural Relations with Russia to lecture on contemporary Russian music. He decided to stay and settled in New York City, where he taught music, mathematics, art history, and his own theory of rhythmic design at the New School of Social Research and New York University from 1932 to 1933, and Teachers College, Columbia University, from 1932 to 1936. He became an American citizen in 1936. While still in Russia he had married Russian actress Olga Mikhailovna Goldberg; when he immigrated to the United States the marriage was simply dissolved. In 1938 he married Frances Rosenfeld Singer. There were no children from either marriage.

Schillinger experimented extensively with complex rhythms that were realized on the Rhythmicon (the earliest electronic rhythm instrument, with seventeen keys that were able to produce complex rhythms separately and simultaneously) constructed by Leon Theremin to specifications by Henry Cowell. His compositions in this area included the *First Airphonic Suite*, for theremin and orchestra, Op. 21 (1929; Theremin was the soloist in the first performance); *Bury Me, Bury Me Wind*, for voice, theremin, and piano, Op. 23 (1930); and other pieces for theremin and piano. Schillinger's early training led him to formulate principles of art in scientific and mathematical terms. *The Mathematical Basis of the Arts* (1948; repr. 1976) elaborates his theories of art and music. His "system" of music theory and composition was the basis for a course of study he used for private pupils, many of whom were composers and arrangers of commercial and film music. Among his better-known students were Tommy Dorsey, Benny Goodman, Oscar Levant, Vernon Duke (Vladimir Dukelsky), Leith Stevens, Red Norvo, Paul Lavalle, Lyn Murray, Carmine Coppola, George Gershwin, and Glenn Miller. Gershwin employed Schillinger techniques in composing the Variations on "I Got Rhythm" and in composing and orchestrating his folk opera, *Porgy and Bess*; Miller's theme song, "Moonlight Serenade," was composed for a Schillinger lesson. Many of Schillinger's lectures and writings in the United States were concerned with performance and production of music by electronic instruments, which he believed would eventually displace traditional instruments. *The Schillinger System of Musical Composition* (1941; 4th ed., repr. 1977) has been widely used for instruction in music theory. His other writings that manifest his theories of music in greater detail are *Kaleidophone: New Resources of Melody and Harmony* (1940; repr. 1976) and *Encyclopedia of Rhythm* (1966; repr. 1976). Schillinger died in New York City of cancer.

• There are collections of Schillinger's art and musical works in the holdings of the New York Public Library for the Performing Arts, Lincoln Center; the Fleischer Collection of the Philadelphia Free Library; the Smithsonian Institution, Washington, D.C.; the Columbia University Library, New York; the Museum of Modern Art, New York; and the University of Wyoming. Biographical treatments include Vernon Duke, "Gershwin, Schillinger, Dukelsky: Some Reminiscences," *Musical Quarterly* 33, no. 1 (1947): 102–15, and Frances Schillinger, *Joseph Schillinger: A Memoir* (1949; repr. 1976), by the composer's wife. A memorial issue of *Music News* 39, no. 3 (1947), was devoted to articles by Nicolas Slonimsky et al. on Schillinger's life, theories, and influence on film music. Critical discussions of Schillinger's musical theories include Sidney Cowell and Henry Cowell, "The Schillinger Case: Charting the Musical Range," *Modern Music* 39, no. 3 (1946): 226–28; E. Carter, "The Schillinger Case: Fallacy of the Mechanistic Approach," *Modern Music* 23, no. 3 (1946): 228–30; James M. Burk, "Schillinger's Double Equal Temperament System," in *The Psychology and Acoustics of Music: A Collection of Papers*, ed. Edward Asmus (1979), pp. 33–73; Daniel S. Augestine, "Four Theories of Music in the United States, 1900–1950: Cowell, Yasser, Partch, Schillinger" (Ph.D. diss., Univ. of Texas, Austin, 1979); and Paul Nauert, "Theory and Practice in 'Porgy and Bess': The Gershwin-Schillinger Connection," *Musical Quarterly* 78, no. 1 (1994): 9–33. Obituaries are in the *New York Times*, 24 Mar. 1943, with a portrait, and *Etude*, May 1943.

JAMES M. BURK

SCHILT, Jan (3 Feb. 1894–9 Jan. 1982), astronomer, was born in Gouda, the Netherlands, the son of Arie Johannes Schilt and Marrigie Klazina de Jong. He completed his undergraduate training at the University of Utrecht in 1915 and served in the Royal Dutch Army during World War I. He earned his Ph.D. in astronomy from the University of Groningen in 1924, serving as an assistant astronomer at the Leyden Observatory in the Netherlands while completing his degree (1922–1925). Working with J. H. Oort, he published a monograph on linear velocity of particular types of stars. Schilt received a gold medal from the Bachiene Institute in the Netherlands in 1924. In his work at both Groningen and at the Leyden Observatory, he studied under J. C. Kapteyn, the founder of statistical astronomy.

In 1925 Schilt married Joanna Timmer; they had one child. After their marriage Schilt and his wife moved to the United States, where he served as a fellow at the Mount Wilson, California, observatory. While there he published papers on the statistical properties of galactic Cepheids having periods longer than one year and on the short-period variable star RV Canum Venaticorum. In 1926 he received an appointment at Yale University, where he was an instructor and assistant professor through 1931. At Yale he worked closely with Frank Schlesinger, who had established some twenty-five years earlier the proper technique for parallax measurement by photography using long-focus telescopes. In 1931 Schilt joined the faculty of Columbia University.

Schilt's work at Columbia gained him international fame. He helped clarify the motions of stars in the galaxy and invented the Schilt Photometer, which by measuring the brightness of stars aids in calculating their distance from the earth. The photometer, which Schilt had first developed while working at Leyden in 1924, remained in use for decades. He had further developed it while at Yale and then received permission from Schlesinger to take it to Columbia to determine the photographic magnitudes of stars. He developed a brass frame with silk threads to provide X and Y coordinates to overlay glass photographic plates. Taking photographs on Eastman glass plates, Schilt exposed the plates for ten minutes, using comparison plates and comparison stars to generate the measurements for previously unmeasured stars and developing multiple plates to provide verified data. Rather than using plates that overlapped to establish reference points (a procedure he rejected because of irregularities in the plates), he established zero points to set relative positions by using nearby reference stars from the Gottingen Actinometry. He detailed the procedure in a report published in the *Transactions of the Astronomical Observatory of Yale University* in 1933.

In 1935 Schilt helped demonstrate that each star in the Pleiades cluster moves independently of other stars in the group. In 1936 he was named Rutherford Professor and chairman of the Department of Astronomy at Columbia; he was also named director of the Rutherford Observatory, most likely the same year. He served as director of the Yale-Columbia Southern Station in Johannesburg, South Africa, and in Canberra, Australia. In 1937 Schilt and his research assistant Sarah J. Hill published a tabular presentation of the photographic magnitude of 6,902 stars in a particular zone of the sky. In 1938 they supplemented that work with a similar measurement of another 7,280 stars. Schilt's careful work in the measurement of stellar magnitudes using a number of correction factors for background radiation and interference, together with his fame for developing the photometer, established his international reputation as a specialist on the use of photographic results to determine both star brightness and distance.

In the 1940s Schilt worked on the problem of measuring the total matter in the universe, recalculating the Oort limit, which can be used to determine the amount of matter in the universe not condensed into stars. Throughout the 1950s he was respected as an expert on the problem of clarifying parallax measurements of distance, and he was often cited in works dealing with the size, structure, and motion of the Milky Way Galaxy.

Schilt remained chair of the Department of Astronomy at Columbia until his retirement in 1962, after which he continued to actively engage in academic administrative work. He also remained Rutherford Professor Emeritus after retirement. He died in Englewood, New Jersey.

• Schilt's papers are at the Columbia University Rare Book and Manuscript Library. An obituary is in the *New York Times*, 12 Jan. 1982.

RODNEY P. CARLISLE

SCHINDLER, Rudolph Michael (5 Sept. 1887–22 Aug. 1953), architect, was born in Vienna, Austria, the son of Rudolf Schindler, who operated an import business, and Maria Francija Hertl. He studied architecture at Vienna's Royal Technical Institute (1906–1911) and at the Academy of Fine Arts (1910–1913). At the academy he studied under Otto Wagner, and he was much influenced by the vigorous and highly original designs of the Vienna Secessionists Josef Hoffmann, Joseph Olbrich, and Adolf Loos. While he was completing his studies he worked as a designer/draftsman in the Vienna office of Mayr & Mayer. For this firm he designed the five-story Clubhouse for Actors (1912), constructed in the old section of Vienna. Schindler's 1912–1913 thesis project for the academy, a crematorium and chapel, posed, in a disquieting and unusual fashion, a seven-story building hidden below a high cantilevered reinforced concrete roof.

As was true with many other young European designers of these years, Schindler was tremendously impressed with the presentation of Frank Lloyd Wright's designs in his famed Berlin Wasmuth portfolio, published in 1910–1911. Stimulated by this publication, and by the earlier example of both his father's and Adolf Loos's travels to the United States, he obtained a position in 1914 with the Chicago firm of Ottenheimer, Stern & Reichert. From 1914 through early 1918 he was active as a designer for this firm and entered a number of local competitions. He also produced a small group of fascinating figurative drawings and posters in the manner of the Vienna painter Egon Schiele.

With America's entry into the First World War, Schindler's position as an Austrian citizen made life difficult for him. He finally prevailed upon Frank Lloyd Wright to employ him, and he worked on a number of Wright's projects, including the Imperial Hotel in Tokyo and the Aline Barnsdall house in Los Angeles. Wright sent him to Los Angeles to supervise the construction of the Barnsdall house, and after its completion in 1921 he established his own practice there. In 1919, before moving to California, Schindler had married Sophie Pauline Gibling, a teacher of music and advocate of social reform. Their house became a gathering place for young intellectuals and designers. The couple had one son.

His first important design was his own concrete lift-slab house built on Kings Road in Hollywood (1921–1972). This house not only entailed an innovative structure and an intense unity of indoors and out, but was a provocative assertion of how two families could live and share space together: in this case the Schindler's, and the engineer Clyde Chase and his family. This was followed by such masterpieces as the Newport Beach house for Dr. Philip M. Lovell (1922–1926). In this famed design Schindler miniaturized the theme of his thesis project, producing a series of stucco boxes that lay below and within, or project outside, a set of five upright concrete frames.

Though he returned from time to time to the use of concrete, almost all of his residential designs of the

1920s and later utilized the stucco-sheathed wood frame, so typical of the California scene. He delighted in the use of commonplace structures, materials, and methods of construction, not only in his buildings but in the hundreds of pieces of furniture that he designed. In the mid- to late-1920s he collaborated with Richard J. Neutra and the urban planner Carol Arnovici of the Architectural Group for Industry and Commerce on designs for a number of large-scale buildings, including an entry (by Neutra and Schindler) in the 1926 international competition for the League of Nations building.

Though he was considered a modernist, Schindler's work never easily fitted into the accepted dictums of the International Style Modern. His designs were affected by European movements such as the Dutch de Stijl, which he combined with elements derived from Wright, and by his earlier experiences in Vienna. "The architect has finally discovered the medium of his art: space," wrote Schindler in his 1912 "Manifesto" (published privately). Complex space, and particularly vertical space, was his lifelong concern in the modest budget houses he designed from the 1920s on. Many of these houses, such as the Wolfe house at Avalon (1928) and the Van Patten house in Los Angeles (1934–1935), were posed theatrically on steep hillside locations. The theatrics of their exterior forms was equaled by their complex, picturesque interior landscapes.

Though Schindler was intensely interested in group housing, as is illustrated by his Pueblo Ribera Court in La Jolla (1923) and his hillside Falk Apartments in Los Angeles (1939), he did not receive many such commissions. Nor did he obtain commissions for public buildings or large commercial structures.

His designs after the Second World War became even more complex, with regard to his use of structure, his use of old and new materials, and, above all, in the way he articulated interior spaces. The involved sense of disorder in such late designs as the Bethleham Baptist Church in Los Angeles (1944), the Janson house in the Hollywood Hills (1949), or the Tischler house in Westwood (1949–1950) anticipated many facets of contemporary Post Modernism and Deconstructivist architecture.

• The architectural drawings and other papers of Schindler are housed in the Architectural Drawing Collection of the University Art Museum, University of California, Santa Barbara. A listing of his published writings, together with a list of his most important built and unbuilt projects, is in David Gebhard's biography, *Schindler* (1980). Other writings on the architect are Esther McCoy, *Five California Architects* (1960) and *Vienna to Los Angeles: Two Journeys* (1979); Hans Hollein, "Rudolf M. Schindler," *Bau* (Vienna) 21, no. 4 (1966): 67–87; and August Sarnitz, *R. M. Schindler* (1986).

DAVID GEBHARD

SCHIOTZ, Fredrik Axel (15 June 1901–24 Feb. 1989), Lutheran pastor, mission executive, and church president, was born in Chicago, Illinois, the son of Norwegian immigrants Jacob Schiotz, a sailor and later a cab-inetmaker, and Stina Akerholt. He graduated from St. Olaf College in 1924 with an A.B. After teaching high school in Ladysmith, Wisconsin (1924–1926), he studied theology at Luther Seminary in St. Paul, Minnesota, earning a B.Th. and an M.Th. In 1928 he married Dagny Aasen; they had three children. He was ordained in 1930 by the Norwegian Lutheran Church of America.

After serving parishes in Duluth and Moorhead, Minnesota, Schiotz was appointed executive secretary of the Student Service Commission of the American Lutheran Conference (1938–1945). Following a brief return to the parish ministry in Brooklyn, New York (1945–1948), he became director of the Commission on Younger Churches and Orphaned Missions of the National Lutheran Council (1948–1954), and from 1952 to 1954 he also directed the Department of World Missions for the Lutheran World Federation in Geneva, Switzerland.

In 1954 Schiotz was elected president of the Evangelical Lutheran Church. His quiet but persuasive diplomacy enabled him to encourage that conservative body to join the World Council of Churches and to pursue negotiations leading to the merger in 1960 of Lutherans of Norwegian, German, and Danish heritage to form The American Lutheran Church (TALC), with 2.5 million members. He served as president of this body from 1961 to 1971 and was president emeritus from 1971 until 1989. He was also a member of the central committee of the World Council of Churches (1962–1971) and president of the Lutheran World Federation (1963–1970). In 1968 King Olaf V of Norway named him Commander with Star of the Order of St. Olav.

Schiotz's wide-ranging career in the church led from a parish pastorate to the presidency of a world organization representing 70 million Lutherans in more than 100 countries. His ecumenical world view grew out of a youthful interest in missions that matured through a year of service as a traveling secretary for the Student Volunteer Movement for Foreign Missions while he was a seminary student and ultimately led to membership on its board of directors (1948–1954). His distinctive contribution to world missions was made in the years immediately following World War II. During the war, home country support for the work of German, Danish, and Norwegian mission societies in Africa, Asia, Palestine, Indonesia, and New Guinea was cut off. Through the Lutheran World Federation, he directed a program of support for these orphaned missions, saving their properties from confiscation after the war and assisting them in achieving status as independent, indigenous Lutheran churches.

Although Schiotz was known for his irenic qualities of patience and tact, he did not hesitate to take firm stands on major issues that faced the church. He was active in the civil rights movement in the 1960s and publicly attacked housing discrimination in Minneapolis, Minnesota. Although he was a conservative theologian, he strongly resisted the efforts of ultraconservatives in his church to impose a fundamentalist interpretation of the Scriptures. He commended the initiation of formal ecumenical dialog with the Roman Catholic church in 1965. After his retirement in 1971, he taught and lectured on ecumenism in Lutheran colleges and seminaries. His successor as president of The American Lutheran Church, David W. Preus, described him as "a man of simple faith" who nevertheless led his church unafraid into a technologically complicated age. Schiotz died in Minneapolis.

• Schiotz's papers are in the archives of the Evangelical Lutheran Church in America, Chicago, Ill. See also his autobiography, *One Man's Story* (1980).

RICHARD W. SOLBERG

SCHIPPERS, Thomas (9 Mar. 1930–16 Dec. 1977), conductor, was born in Kalamazoo, Michigan, the son of Peter Schippers, a businessman, and Anna Nanninga. Although his parents were not musical, they began his formal musical training with piano lessons when he was age four, and two years later he played in public for the first time. At eight, he left the family's local Dutch Reformed church to become the organ accompanist for the boys' choir at the local Episcopal church, and that same year he began playing the piano regularly on a local radio station.

Schippers was precocious academically as well as musically and graduated from high school at age thirteen. A year later, in 1944, he enrolled as an organ major at the Curtis Institute in Philadelphia, where he became the first student to complete the four-year course in two years. After studying at the Juilliard School in New York City during the 1946–1947 academic year, he enrolled for a semester at Yale, where he attended philosophy classes and studied composition with Paul Hindemith.

Schippers then returned to Philadelphia, where he studied piano and composition under Olga Samaroff and also audited a conducting class at the Berkshire Music Center in Tanglewood, Massachusetts, in the summer of 1948. Later that year, after being named one of six finalists in the Philadelphia Orchestra's Young Conductor Competition, he moved to New York City, where he became a church organist and opera coach. When Schippers accompanied one of his pupils to an audition for Gian Carlo Menotti's first full-length opera, *The Consul*, the composer was so impressed with the young pianist that he hired him on the spot as musical supervisor of the company.

Schippers's conducting career was launched in 1950, when the company conductor became ill during the premiere run of *The Consul* and Schippers stepped in to replace him. During the early 1950s he made guest appearances as the conductor of major American orchestras, including the Philadelphia Orchestra, the Boston Symphony, and the New York Philharmonic. He also conducted the music for the movie version of Menotti's *The Medium*; for the premiere of *Amahl and the Night Visitors*, which Menotti wrote for television (both 1951); and for other Menotti works, including the premiere of *The Saint of Bleecker Street* (1954).

Good reviews of Schippers's performances led to increasingly important engagements. During the 1953–1954 season he conducted several productions at the New York City Opera; at the end of the season he toured Europe and conducted at several leading opera houses, including La Scala in Milan. A year later Schippers became a regular conductor at the Metropolitan Opera, debuting in a production of Donizetti's *Don Pasquale*. In the course of his career, Schippers mastered an operatic repertory of eighty-three works.

Continuing his close association with Menotti, Schippers and the composer founded the Spoleto Festival of Two Worlds in Italy in 1958. It became an annual summer event and drew talent in the performing arts from all over the world. Schippers became the festival's resident conductor of both concerts and elaborately staged operas. In the late summer of 1959, following that year's Spoleto Festival, Schippers went on tour with Leonard Bernstein and the New York Philharmonic in the Soviet Union and led the orchestra in several performances.

In the fall of 1960, Schippers became the first American to conduct an opening-night performance (a production of Verdi's *Nabucco*) at the Metropolitan Opera. His career now securely launched, Schippers went on to regular appearances at the Met, at the New York Philharmonic, and on concert and operatic stages throughout the world during the 1960s. Highlights of that decade included his appearance on opening night, 16 September 1966, of the Met's new opera house at Lincoln Center as the conductor of the world premiere of Samuel Barber's *Antony and Cleopatra*. He also appeared from time to time on the concert stage in the dual roles of pianist and conductor of several ensembles, including the New York Philharmonic. Reviews of his conducting performances were generally favorable and even enthusiastic, although occasionally critics complained of a youthful brashness and impetuosity that did not seem to diminish over the years.

In the fall of 1970, Schippers was named to succeed Max Rudolf as director of the Cincinnati Symphony. In his seven years there, Schippers strengthened the orchestra's reputation as a major music-making ensemble. While serving in that post, he continued as a principal conductor at the Met and La Scala, and from 1972 until his death he was also a professor of music at the Cincinnati Conservatory.

Schippers was married in 1965 to Elaine Lane Phipps, and the couple maintained homes in New York City and, after 1970, in Cincinnati. Not long after her death from cancer in 1973, Schippers was also stricken with the disease, and as his condition grew worse he was forced to withdraw gradually from his heretofore hectic schedule. He died in New York City.

• Biographical information on Schippers is limited. See entries on Schippers in *Current Biography Yearbook 1970*, *Current Biography Yearbook 1978*, and *Who Was Who in America*, vol. 7 (1981). An obituary is in the *New York Times*, 17 Dec. 1977.

ANN T. KEENE

SCHIRMER, Gustav (19 Sept. 1829–6 Aug. 1893), music publisher, was born in Königsee, Germany, the son of Ernst Rudolph Schirmer, a builder of pianos, and Wilhelmine Dünkler, daughter of the burgomaster of Saalfeld. The family immigrated to America in 1840, sailing from Hamburg on 23 August and arriving in New York City on 8 October. Gustav attended school there for the next three years until, at age fifteen, he entered into a brief apprenticeship with a local cabinetmaker.

After a period of employment with Scharfenberg & Luis, a music store, Schirmer joined the New York City music dealership Kerksieg & Breusing in 1853–1854. An energetic and ambitious worker, he rose in responsibility at Kerksieg & Breusing, attaining the position of manager in 1854. Schirmer and colleague Bernard Beer purchased the business in 1861 and operated as Beer & Schirmer. After Schirmer bought out Beer's interest in 1866, the firm became G. Schirmer, Music Publishers, Importers and Dealers. That same year Schirmer married Mary Fairchild; they had seven children.

Schirmer brought to the publishing trade a unique combination of keen business acumen and passionate musical sensitivity. He inherited the keyboard skills that had developed as a result of his father's piano manufacturing concern, and he was a dedicated avocational pianist all his life. His native interest in music played an important role in building his American publishing company. Given his Teutonic heritage it is perhaps not surprising that he cultivated strong ties with publishers and dealers in important German musical centers; at the same time, he also had strong ties with vendors in capitals throughout Central Europe, Italy, and Great Britain.

Schirmer's personal ties did not extend merely to other businessmen. Schirmer was on close personal terms with a number of European composers active during the second half of the nineteenth century, including Franz Liszt (whom Schirmer met through his wife) and Peter Illytch Tchaikovsky. During his visit to New York in connection with the opening of Carnegie Hall in 1891, Tchaikovsky made the following journal entry: "We went to see the Brooklyn Bridge. From there we went on to see Schirmer, who owns the largest music business in America; the warehouse—especially the engraving plant—resemble Jurgenson's in many respects." Schirmer was also one of Richard Wagner's financial supporters, leading to the construction of the composer's custom-designed theatre in Bayreuth where the landmark music dramas were produced.

Schirmer initially operated out of the original Kerkseig & Breusing storefront at 701 Broadway. By 1880, however, business had grown to the point where larger quarters were required, and a new structure was built at 35 Union Square, where the company remained until 1910. In 1891 Schirmer started a printing and engraving plant, originally on West Sixteenth Street (it later moved to Woodside in the New York City borough of Queens). Schirmer died in Eisenach, Germany.

It is undeniable that important historical forces contributed to the success of Schirmer's business. The last half of the nineteenth century witnessed enormous growth in American industry; the resulting industrial revolution gave birth to a new moneyed class that longed for the cultural amenities of the European capitals. Schirmer, with his commercial acuity, musical sensibility, and abounding energy, was uniquely positioned to funnel the musical materials of Europe to an eager American clientele. His legacy lived on long after his death—his printing and engraving plant operated well into the 1980s, long after most American music publishers had ceased doing their own printing.

• Articles on the centennial of Schirmer's birth appeared in *Musical Courier*, 14 Sept. 1929; *Musical America*, Sept. 1929; and *Music Trade Indicator*, Sept. 1929. The Schirmer publishing house is chronicled in S. Craft, "G. Schirmer: the Music Publishing Experience," *AB Bookman's Weekly*, 12 Dec. 1983, p. 4155; and in Paul Henry Lang, "Portrait of a Publishing House," in *One Hundred Years of Music in America*, ed. Lang (1961; repr. 1985). Obituaries are in the *New York Tribune*, 8 Aug. 1893; *Signale für die Musikalische Welt*, Sept. 1893; and the *Metronome*, Sept. 1893.

CHRISTINE HOFFMAN

SCHLATTER, Michael (14 July 1716–31 Oct. 1790), German Reformed clergyman, was born in St. Gall, Switzerland, the son of Paulus Schlatter, a bookkeeper, and Magdalena Zollikofer. His paternal grandfather, also named Michael (1648–1714), had been a prominent churchman. After attending the local Gymnasium, Schlatter studied theology with Professor Bartholome Wegelin of St. Gall. Later, he went to the Netherlands where he enrolled at the University of Leiden and possibly also at Helmstedt. Upon his return to St. Gall and completion of his studies with Wegelin, he was ordained in 1739.

Schlatter served briefly as a tutor in the Netherlands and then began his ministry as a vicar in Thurgau, Switzerland. In 1745, he became the Sunday evening preacher in Linsebühl, near St. Gall. Possibly because of the accusation that he had fathered an illegitimate child, he left Switzerland and went to Heidelberg where he became aware of the need for clergymen to serve the German Reformed people in America. He volunteered and was accepted by Dutch Reformed officials who had begun to assist them. They instructed him to visit, report on, and coordinate the scattered congregations.

Schlatter arrived in Philadelphia in September 1746 and immediately began to implement his commission. He promptly visited congregations in the interior of New Jersey, Pennsylvania, Maryland, and Virginia and sent his observations to his superiors, noting that forty-six congregations could be combined into sixteen charges. In 1747, he organized four ministers and twenty-eight elders into a coetus, an administrative body subordinate to the church in the Netherlands. All the while, he attempted to serve as regularly as possible the Philadelphia, Germantown, and other neighboring congregations.

In 1751, the coetus sent Schlatter back to Europe to report on the condition of the churches in America and to obtain additional support. His expedition was successful. Dutch churchmen returned Schlatter to America in the next year with increased financial subsidies, 700 Bibles, and six recently ordained ministers.

When Schlatter returned, he expected to resume his position of leadership but found this impossible. His frequent absences, use of unfamiliar liturgical forms, the rumors of his earlier indiscretion, as well as competition from a newly arrived German Reformed clergyman, created problems in the Philadelphia congregation and led to his dismissal from the congregation and the coetus.

Under the circumstances, Schlatter determined to concentrate on education. In 1754, he accepted an appointment by the Society for the Propagation of the Knowledge of God among the Germans, a group of prominent Londoners who coordinated English, Scottish, and Dutch contributions, as superintendent of its charity schools in Pennsylvania. Despite the good intentions of the contributors and the administrator, the project encountered strong opposition. Many German settlers resented the society's implication that they were poor and ignorant. Some charged that the schools' purposes were to Anglicize the Germans and to bring them into the Church of England. Consequently, Schlatter succeeded in founding fewer than a dozen schools, and these disbanded within a few years. He resigned his position in 1756.

The most significant phase of Schlatter's life was over, though he was only forty. During the French and Indian War, he served as a chaplain in the British army and accompanied the Royal American Infantry to Louisbourg in 1757. During the American Revolution, he refused to report for duty with British forces and supported the rebels instead, for which the British imprisoned him in 1777, sacked his house at Chestnut Hill, and burned his papers. He spent the rest of his life quietly on his farm, performing many weddings and preaching only occasionally.

It is likely that Schlatter died at his Chestnut Hill home. His wife Maria Henrica Schleidorn, daughter of a prominent New York and Philadelphia merchant, whom Schlatter married in 1747, had died earlier. Of their nine children, five daughters and one son survived their father.

Although Schlatter's career had numerous dimensions, his major achievement was the organization of the German Reformed Church in Pennsylvania and the adjacent provinces. During his relatively short period of leadership, he initiated the transformation of widely separated congregations in numerous German settlements into a cohesive denomination that provided spiritual nurture and ethnic identity for its members well beyond his lifetime.

• Schlatter's "True History of the Real Condition of the Destitute Congregations in Pennsylvania" was published in Dutch in 1751 and in German in 1752. Excerpts are included in Henry Harbaugh's biography, *The Life of Rev. Michael Schlatter with a Full Account of His Travels and Labors among the Germans* (1857). Portions of Schlatter's diary, edited by William J. Hinke, have been published in *The Journal of the Presbyterian Historical Society*, vol. 3 (1905). Several of Schlatter's letters to ministers and congregations are in the Harbaugh Collection, Eden Theological Seminary, Webster Groves, Missouri. Portions of Schlatter's correspondence and journal are included in *Minutes and Letters of the Coetus of the German Reformed Congregations in Pennsylvania, 1747–1792* ed. W. J. Hinke (1903), pp. 32–132. For brief sketches of Schlatter's life and work, see Hinke, *Ministers of the German Reformed Congregations in Pennsylvania and Other Colonies in the Eighteenth Century* (1951), pp. 37–47; Charles H. Glatfelter, *Pastors and People: German Lutheran and Reformed Churches in the Pennsylvania Field, 1717–1793*, vol. 1 (1980), pp. 117–19; and Marti Pritzker-Erlich, "Michael Schlatter (1716–1790): A Man-In-Between," in the *Yearbook of German-American Studies* 20 (1986): 83–95. M. Pritzker-Ehrlich, *Michael Schlatter von St. Gallen (1716–1790): Eine biographische Untersuchung zur schweizerischen Amerika-Auswanderung des 18. Jahrhunderts* (1981), is the most accurate and complete account of Schlatter.

JOHN B. FRANTZ

SCHLESINGER, Arthur Meier, Sr. (27 Feb. 1888–30 Oct. 1965), historian, was born in Xenia, Ohio, the son of Bernhard Schlesinger, a dry goods proprietor, and Katherine Feurie. In 1910 he graduated from Ohio State University with a B.A. degree in American history and political science. Afterward he entered graduate school at Columbia University. There he studied American history, mainly under William A. Dunning and Herbert L. Osgood, who directed his doctoral dissertation, *The Colonial Merchants and the American Revolution* (1917). Schlesinger returned to Ohio State in 1912 as an instructor of history; he remained there until 1919, during which time he completed his dissertation. In this important study, Schlesinger showed that merchants in different colonies responded differently at different times to the Revolution and that only a few remained indifferent to the momentous events swirling about them. In September 1914 Schlesinger married Elizabeth Bancroft, a fellow student at Ohio State. They had three sons, and Arthur Meier Schlesinger, Jr., would also become a prominent American historian.

In 1919 Schlesinger went to the University of Iowa, where he stayed for the next five years. While at Iowa he began teaching what was probably the first course in the social and cultural history of the United States in an American college or university. In doing this Schlesinger broke away from the long traditions of political, military, and diplomatic history, the main emphasis on the teaching and writing of American history at that time. Schlesinger thought that this conventional history was irrelevant to the experiences of someone like himself as the son of a German father and an Austrian mother from a small town in Ohio. History encountered in school and college at that time was narrowly Anglo-Saxon, which, as he later wrote seemed "snobbish and exclusive." Why, he wondered, did the history books portray England as the only mother country? Why leave to popular writers the way ordinary people lived? "I could not help feeling," he wrote later, "there was something wanting in a history that skipped so much that seemed to me important." At Columbia Schlesinger had been influenced by historians such as James Harvey Robinson, James T. Shotwell, and Charles A. Beard, who broadened traditional history with the inclusion of social, economic, and intellectual matters in their work.

When Schlesinger returned to teach at Ohio State, he had to wait seven years before he was allowed to teach "less orthodox aspects of American history." But upon his arrival at Iowa as head of the history department, he introduced a course entitled "New Viewpoints," and a few years later he began his new course on the social and cultural history of the United States. Seeking to deal with "the totality of man's experience in the past," Schlesinger widened his break with traditional history with the publication in 1922 of his *New Viewpoints in American History*, an influential book for some time to come. In so doing Schlesinger intended to show the social side of history and to bring hitherto neglected forces such as immigration, the role of women, intellectual history, and urban history into the mainstream of American history.

Expanding his ideas about social history, Schlesinger and Homer C. Hockett, a colleague at Ohio State, collaborated on *The Political and Social History of the United States* (1925). This was a textbook on American history that, according to Schlesinger, "departed from the customary pattern by giving the political story a social and cultural context." But more was needed for social history to achieve academic standing. Schlesinger believed there had to be a cooperative effort by professional historians to describe "the formation and growth of civilization in the United States"—an effort "in which the diverse actions and passions of men and women could be conceived" not "separately and independently of one another but as an integral and integrated part of American life." Hence Schlesinger and Dixon Ryan Fox, then a Columbia University historian, started the *History of the American Life* series in 1923. They planned ten volumes in three years, but it finished with thirteen volumes over twenty-one years, from 1927 to 1948. According to Schlesinger, the intent of the series was to "free American history from its traditional servitude to party struggles, war and diplomacy, and to show that it properly included all the varied interests of the people."

Schlesinger's own volume, the eighth to be published in the series, appeared in 1933. *The Rise of the City, 1878–1898* covered a period that historians had neglected except for its political history. "It was only as my examination of the sources proceeded," wrote Schlesinger, "that I realized that this space of years marked the emergence of urban centers as the dominant force in American civilization pulsating to the very fingertips of the whole land." With that as the key, noted Schlesinger, "the diverse social and cultural developments fell into an intelligible pattern."

In 1924 Schlesinger accepted a position at Harvard University. In 1928 he became chairman of the Department of History, and he remained in this capacity until 1931. He then was Francis Lee Higginson Professor of History from 1931 to 1954, when he retired. Schlesinger's appointment at Harvard represented a triumph for his style of history, as well as a recognition by the history "establishment" of what he was doing. Despite receiving discouragement and advice from such historians as Carl Becker and Charles A. Beard to stop expending their time on other people's manuscripts and to give up their *History of American Life* series, Schlesinger and Fox continued with it "sustained by the faith that the undertaking would redirect the future course of American historical research and instruction." They were rewarded for their efforts when the American Historical Association paid the series the then unusual honor of devoting a general session to an appraisal of the enterprise at its 1936 annual meeting. The verdict was forthright approval, with the session speakers stressing the value of the series in "leavening the historical lump."

While at Harvard Schlesinger directed sixty-four doctoral dissertations in social and intellectual history, with three others at Radcliffe College. As John Higham, not himself of Harvard, wrote in the *American Historical Review* in 1951, they comprised "a sizable share of the best Ph.D.'s in United States History," and together they had made probably "the most impressive contribution" in the social and intellectual field. Some of them, such as Merle Curti, Carl Bridenbaugh, and Oscar Handlin, eventually became almost as prominent and influential historians as Schlesinger.

Schlesinger believed that "the authoring of books constitutes the highest function of the historian," and he remained a productive scholar until his death in Cambridge, Massachusetts. He published *Paths to the Present* (1949) and *The American as Reformer* (1950), both of which consist of his essays; his son Arthur edited a posthumous group of his essays, published as *Nothing Stands Still* (1969). Schlesinger also wrote *Learning How to Behave* (1946), an examination of American etiquette books; *Prelude to Independence: The Newspaper War on Britain, 1764–1776* (1957); and his informative memoirs, *In Retrospect: The History of a Historian* (1963).

In addition to his teaching, writing, and directing of graduate students, Schlesinger served on the advisory committee for the Pulitzer Prize in American history and cofounded both the Social Science Research Council in 1924 and the *New England Quarterly* in 1928. He also assisted in the establishment of the Institute of Early American History and Culture and the restoration of Colonial Williamsburg, and he served as president of the American Historical Association in 1942.

Schlesinger was one of the most influential and prominent American historians in his time. His importance in the teaching and writing of American history is his loosening of American history from a sole emphasis on "politically important" subject matter.

According to his son Arthur, Schlesinger raised social history "from the status of sheer antiquarianism and impressionistic description to the status of a general historical discipline," and at the time of his retirement he could note that American social history "was now firmly established in colleges and universities. The battle was won."

• In addition to his autobiography, several accounts are useful in learning about Schlesinger. An Oral History memoir and eight boxes of documents and letters are at the Oral History Archives, Columbia University. See also Arthur M. Schlesinger, Jr.'s introduction to *Nothing Stands Still* (1969).

VINCENT P. DESANTIS

SCHLESINGER, Benjamin (25 Dec. 1876–6 June 1932), labor leader, was born in Krakai, Lithuania, the son of Rabbi Nechemiah Schlesinger and Judith Schlesinger. (His surname is his mother's maiden name, as, at some point, his father began to use it for himself; his father's original surname is unknown.) Schlesinger came from a poor family and was educated in the local cheder (Hebrew school). Orphaned by the time he was twelve, he left his hometown in late 1891 to join his brother in Chicago. Shortly after his arrival he found work in a garment factory and rose from floor boy to skilled cloakmaker. Known as a socialist and follower of Daniel De Leon, Schlesinger became active in the Chicago cloakmakers union. In the mid-1890s he moved to New York City to work as a journalist for the Socialist Labor Party's Yiddish daily, the *Abendblatt*, and, after a political disagreement with the SLP, the *Jewish Daily Forward*, thus beginning a pattern that would repeatedly lead him back and forth between journalism and trade union activism and between New York City and Chicago. By 1902 he had moved back to Chicago to be business manager of his old cloakmakers' union, which had become local 5 of the newly founded International Ladies Garment Workers Union (ILGWU). At the center of a revitalized clothing workers' movement in Chicago, Schlesinger became the first manager of the joint executive board of the Chicago garment workers unions and was international president of the ILGWU in 1903–1904.

Schlesinger returned to journalism after his first tenure as president of the ILGWU and became business manager of the *Jewish Daily Forward* from 1907 to 1912. While in New York he also managed the New York Cloak Joint Board. He returned to the presidency of the ILGWU in 1914. During the early years of this second presidency Schlesinger helped negotiate a compromise settlement during a large-scale strike of cloakmakers in 1916, which preserved most of the gains won by the union in the "Protocols of Peace" of 1910. His stature as a skillful negotiator and union leader continued to increase worldwide, and he served as a member of the General Executive Board of the International Clothing Workers Federation from 1919 to 1923. He visited Europe once, in 1920, met Lenin and came back with renewed enthusiasm for the new economic order of Soviet Russia. In the United States he advocated the organization of cooperative clothing factories. In 1923 he resigned his union offices amid a factional struggle between communists and socialists in the ILGWU. After three years as the manager of the Chicago office of the *Jewish Daily Forward* (1923–1926) he returned to the union, first as executive secretary in 1926 and then as president, beginning in 1929. Schlesinger's last years were marred by his struggle against tuberculosis and by the onset of the depression that left his union in grave financial and organizational difficulty. He was reelected in May 1932 in a symbolic vote of confidence but succumbed to his lifelong illness a month later in Colorado Springs, Colorado. He was survived by his wife, the former Ray Schanhous, and three children.

A self-taught intellectual and writer and an energetic leader, Schlesinger was an important figure among the first generation of immigrant labor leaders from Eastern and Central Europe. Rooted in the secular socialist culture of Yiddish-speaking immigrants, he was also well read in American history and politics. Through most of his life he advocated the integration of the garment workers into the mainstream of American unionism and American culture. To fellow unionists and employers alike he was known to be a melancholic and difficult man to get along with. Schlesinger's energy and dictatorial temperament also masked an inability to set clear priorities and forcefully lead when factional struggles threatened to break apart the union. But his experience as a journalist and organizer also made him highly conscious of the need for positive public relations for his union's cause. Although not a great orator, he knew how to mobilize the press and the support of the community of workers and wealthy backers such as Julius Rosenwald or Felix Warburg. Good publicity work, thorough preparation, and persistence made him a much respected and successful bargainer. As president of the ILGWU, he was known to favor reconciliation of the diverse factions within the union and integration into the mainstream politics of the American Federation of Labor.

• Schlesinger's papers are located in the ILGWU Archives, New York City. The most detailed and reliable biographical sketch can be found in Melech Epstein, *Profiles of Eleven* (1965). See also Wilfred Carsel, *A History of the Chicago Ladies' Garment Workers Union* (1940); David Dubinsky and A. H. Raskin, *David Dubinsky: A Life with Labor* (1977); Melech Epstein, *Jewish Labor in the USA: 1914–1952*, vol. 2 (1952); and Benjamin Stoler, *Tailor's Progress: The Story of a Famous Union and the Men Who Made It* (1944). An obituary is in the *New York Times*, 7 June 1932.

DOROTHEE SCHNEIDER

SCHLESINGER, Frank (11 May 1871–10 July 1943), astronomer, was born in New York City, the son of William Joseph Schlesinger and Mary Wagner, immigrants from Silesia. Despite financial hardships, particularly after his father's death in 1880, Schlesinger attended the public schools of New York City and then entered the College of the City of New York, graduating with a B.S. in 1890. For the next six years he worked as a surveyor, first with the Title and Guarantee Trust Company and then for the city of New York. In 1894 he also became a special student in astronomy at Columbia University. By 1896 his academic talents had secured for him a fellowship that enabled him to pursue graduate work full time.

Schlesinger devoted his career to measuring the position, proper motion, and parallaxes of stars using images on photographic plates. John A. Whipple had taken the first photograph of a star (other than the sun) at the Harvard College Observatory in 1850, but for many years thereafter star positions were determined by more traditional visual observation. For his doctoral dissertation, Schlesinger measured positions of stars in the Praesepe cluster, using photographic plates taken by pioneering amateur astronomer Lewis M. Rutherfurd. After receiving his Ph.D. from Columbia in 1898, Schlesinger spent the summer at the Yerkes Observatory in Williams Bay, Wisconsin, and then was appointed observer-in-charge at the New International Latitude Station at Ukiah, California. During his years in Ukiah, he met Eva Hirsch, whom he married in 1900; they had one child.

In 1903 Schlesinger returned to Yerkes on a fellowship from the Carnegie Institution of Washington. During his two years there, he made his first important contribution to astronomy, developing both observational techniques and methods of data reduction that greatly advanced photographic studies of stellar parallax. The parallax of a star is the angle at the star subtended by the radius of the earth's orbit and can be used to compute stellar distances. Schlesinger's methods were widely adopted by other astronomers.

Schlesinger's success at Yerkes led to his appointment in 1905 as director of Pittsburgh's Allegheny Observatory. When he arrived there, the observatory had a new reflecting telescope and plans for a new refractor. Refractors were usually built for visual observations, with the addition of special apparatus or adjustments for photographic work. After considerable correspondence with other astronomers and consultation with the committee that governed the Allegheny Observatory, Schlesinger's preference for photographic rather than visual observation prevailed, and the lenses on the new Thaw refractor were figured for photography, with a correcting lens for visual observations. When the instrument was completed in 1914, he immediately set out on a systematic and successful photographic study of stellar parallaxes.

Schlesinger spent some months of 1918 as an aeronautical engineer with the U.S. Signal Corps, in charge of airplane instruments. When World War I ended, he resumed his research and from 1919 to 1922 also undertook the duties of the president of the American Astronomical Society. In 1920 he accepted the position of director of the Yale University Observatory. At Yale, he set out on an ambitious program of cataloging the positions and proper motions of stars shown on photographic plates, seeking to cover much of the sky. For this work, he used photographs taken at the Allegheny Observatory, at Yale, and at a new refracting telescope built by Yale and Columbia University in Johannesberg, South Africa. He paid careful attention to the cameras being used, techniques of observation, and the design of machines for measuring star positions. He also used computing equipment at the Watson Astronomical Laboratory of Columbia University to speed data reduction. The actual work of measuring plates and preparing data for publication was done by a staff of women at Yale, who were directed by Ida Barney. Volume four of the *Transactions of the Yale University Observatory*, published in 1925, contained the first results, the positions and proper motions for 8,359 stars between declinations −50° and +55°. The program continued long past Schlesinger's death, with observations published into the 1980s. Although the photographs did not cover the entire sky, the catalogs represent a substantial contribution to modern astrometry.

Schlesinger also used the new telescope in South Africa to extend his work on stellar parallaxes. At the same time, he extended Edward C. Pickering's catalog of the positions, magnitudes, and spectral classes of all stars of magnitude 6.5 or brighter. To this information, he added proper motions, radial velocities, and other relevant data as available. This *Catalogue of Bright Stars*, first published in 1930, has seen several editions. Jenkins's edition of 1940, produced more efficiently than the first edition and therefore more up-to-date, proved of great use.

Schlesinger also influenced the development of science through his active participation in societies. A faithful member and officer of the American Astronomical Society, he was also elected to the American Philosophical Society in 1912 and the National Academy of Sciences in 1916. He was active in G. E. Hale's International Solar Union and attended meetings of the International Astronomical Union from its first in 1919 through 1935, serving as its president from 1932 to 1935. On a less formal basis, Schlesinger was the organizer of the Neighbor's, a gathering of astronomers from the eastern part of the United States that began shortly after he came to Yale. Members met three or four times a year at the Yale Observatory to discuss their research and other professional matters. Schlesinger preferred to restrict these meetings to men, despite the objections of some other observatory directors and the importance of women to his own research program.

After the death of his first wife in 1928, Schlesinger married in 1929 Katherine Bell Rawling Wilcox. They had no children. Schlesinger's health began to fail in the late 1930s, and he retired from Yale in 1941. He died at his summer home in Old Lyme, Connecticut.

• Schlesinger's papers are in the Manuscripts and Archives division of Yale University's Sterling Memorial Library. There is also considerable Schlesinger correspondence in the papers of other astronomers, particularly those of Harlow Shapley at Harvard and Henry Norris Russell at Princeton. For biographical information, see Dirk Brouwer, "Frank Schlesinger: 1871–1943," National Academy of Sciences, *Biographical Memoirs* 24 (1947): 105–44. On the Thaw refractor, see John Lankford, "Photography and the Long-Focus Visual Refractor: Three American Case Studies, 1885–1914," *Journal for the History of Astronomy* 14 (1983): 77–91. On Schlesinger's years at Yale, see Dorrit Hoffleit, "Astronomy at Yale 1701–1968," Connecticut Academy of Arts and Sciences, *Memoirs* 23 (1992). For an overview of astrometry that includes a discussion of the Yale catalogs, see Heinrich Eichhorn, *Astronomy of Star Positions* (1974). On some of Schlesinger's contributions to instrumentation, see Louis F. Drummeter, Jr., "Notes on the Blink-Comparator," *Rittenhouse* 6 (1991): 11–19.

PEGGY ALDRICH KIDWELL

SCHLESINGER, Hermann Irving (11 Oct. 1882–3 Oct. 1960), inorganic chemist, was born in Minneapolis, Minnesota, the son of Louis Schlesinger, the owner of a woodworking factory, and Emily Stern. When Schlesinger was six, the family moved to Chicago. There he attended a grammar school established by the German-American community before entering the public school system in 1896. A talented high school teacher inspired him to choose chemistry as a career. In 1900 he enrolled in the University of Chicago and received a bachelor's degree in 1903 and a doctorate in chemistry in 1905. For the next two years he studied with eminent German chemists in Berlin and Strasbourg. In 1907 he returned to the University of Chicago to teach general chemistry and inorganic preparations. In 1910 he married Edna Simpson, whose family included the paleontologist George Gaylord Simpson; the couple had two children.

At Chicago, Schlesinger rose through the professorial ranks, becoming full professor in 1922, at which time Julius Stieglitz, the department chairman, named him secretary of the department. When Stieglitz retired in 1933, Schlesinger became the executive secretary, and because no one was appointed chairman until 1946, the department's full administrative duties fell on him during the difficult times of the depression and World War II. He became professor emeritus in 1948.

An outstanding teacher, Schlesinger taught the major proportion of general chemistry courses for four decades. His graduate students considered him one of the best teachers in the country. He was the author of two popular textbooks: *General Chemistry* (1925) and *Laboratory Manual of General Chemistry* (1926). In its fourth edition, the former was still in use in the 1950s. A pioneer in visual aids, he produced and directed from 1933 some of the earliest educational films. High schools and colleges throughout the country used the films to enrich their chemistry courses.

Despite the heavy load of both teaching and administration, Schlesinger developed an extensive research program on the nonmetallic element boron. This work introduced a new chemistry important to both pure science and the commercial synthesis of many biomedical substances. His research with boron began in 1929 when German chemist Alfred Stock discovered several hydrogen compounds of boron. These boron hydrides do not have enough electrons to form a stable electronic structure, and no one had proposed a satisfactory

bonding scheme for them. This puzzle concerning bonding and the limited supply available for study of these unusual compounds drew Schlesinger into boron hydride research. Between 1931 and 1938 he and his Ph.D. student Anton Burg explored the compounds' chemistry and devised an efficient electric discharge method for the synthesis of boron hydrides from hydrogen and boron halides. They also developed preparation methods for metal borohydrides, such as aluminum borohydride, and for double metal hydrides.

Together with another doctoral student, the 1979 Nobel Prize winner Herbert C. Brown, Schlesinger coauthored many papers during the 1940s and 1950s on a more productive method of synthesis for boron hydrides and the discovery of versatile alkali metal hydrides. On attempting to purify their preparation of sodium borohydride by dissolving it in acetone solvent, they recognized that the ketone had been reduced to an alcohol. Further research disclosed that the alkali metal borohydrides were unexcelled reducing agents for several organic functional groups. The best hydride reducing agent proved to be a double metal hydride, lithium aluminum hydride, discovered by Schlesinger, Albert Finholt, and A. C. Bond in 1945. This hydride and the alkali metal borohydrides offered an ideal way to obtain desired functional groups in organic synthesis. By 1960 more than 1,700 papers had been published worldwide on lithium aluminum hydride alone and its uses in providing high-yield reductions of organic compounds. The hydride was extensively used not only in fundamental research but commercially in the preparation of vitamins, hormones, and many pharmaceuticals. The Schlesinger-Brown method for the preparation of sodium borohydride also became an industrial process, the complex hydride having many uses as a specific agent in the synthesis of vitamins, antibiotics, flavors, and fine chemicals. Sodium borohydride was essential to pharmaceutical manufacturers faced with incomplete catalytic hydrogenation of the carbonyl group. They could now obtain 100 percent reduction by using the borohydride after the initial reaction. The metal hydrides were much more specific and selective in the reduction of organic functional groups than other reducing agents. They could carry out reductions of groups ordinarily troublesome, for example, the carboxyl group to the hydroxyl and the cyanide group to the amino, and they did this without reducing groups in the molecule that chemists wanted to preserve. These characteristics made the hydrides essential to many industrial and pharmaceutical operations. Schlesinger and his associates held many patents on a variety of complex hydrides.

During World War II Schlesinger led an active research group investigating the military potential of boron hydrides. The Chicago group fulfilled the Signal Corps's desire for a portable generator of hydrogen gas in order to lift radio antennas by balloon to altitudes where they were useful. Knowing that the alkali metal hydrides generated a large amount of hydrogen on hydrolysis, the Schlesinger group developed a practical method of producing hydrogen from sodium borohydride in a portable unit suitable for use on the battlefield.

In the postwar years Schlesinger was sponsored by the Office of Naval Research and the Naval Research Laboratory to explore the use of boron hydrides as jet and rocket fuels. A classified defense research program in the 1950s also tested the Schlesinger-Brown synthetic method for boron hydrides as part of a billion-dollar effort to create fuels. The program ended in failure, however, when boron fuels did not fulfill theoretical predictions of high performance. Some boron hydrides did become ingredients in solid propellants, but they were eclipsed by other substances.

Widespread recognition of Schlesinger's achievements came in the postwar era. In 1948 the National Academy of Sciences elected him to membership. In the 1950s he was twice nominated for the Nobel Prize. In 1959 he received both the highest honor in American chemistry, the Priestley Medal of the American Chemical Society, and the U.S. Navy's top civilian medal, the Distinguished Public Service Award. He was also actively involved in two major interests outside chemistry. Throughout his life he participated in the family business started by his father, a fine woodworking firm that specialized in architectural paneling and furnishings, and his interest in literature led to an active membership in the Chicago Literary Club. He died in Chicago.

Schlesinger's research on boron hydrides provided a basis for most subsequent American research in the field and also for the large-scale production of borohydrides and mixed metal hydrides. His discovery of the reducing power of these substances transformed chemists' methods for reducing functional groups and became essential to organic synthesis and industrial chemistry.

• The University of Chicago Archives has a biographical file and other material relating to Schlesinger. There are two brief, unsigned articles in the *Chemical and Engineering News*, 21 Feb. 1949, p. 496, and 13 Apr. 1959, p. 104. Herbert C. Brown discusses some of his mentor's research in *Boranes in Organic Chemistry* (1972). See Jon A. Zubieta and Jerold J. Zuckerman, "Inorganic Chemistry: The Past 100 Years," *Chemical and Engineering News*, 6 Apr. 1976, esp. pp. 66–68, for his contributions to boron chemistry. See also Andrew Dequasie, *The Green Flame* (1991), and the *New York Times*, 7 Apr. 1959, p. 19, on boron hydrides as jet and rocket fuels. An obituary is in the *New York Times*, 4 Oct. 1960.

ALBERT B. COSTA

SCHLEY, Winfield Scott (9 Oct. 1839–2 Oct. 1911), naval officer, was born in Richfields, Maryland, the son of John Schley and Georgianna Virginia McClure, prosperous farmers. Following the death of Schley's mother in 1848, the family moved into the nearby town of Frederick. Schley attended school there and at St. John's College in Annapolis before gaining an appointment to the U.S. Naval Academy in 1856. An affable and natural leader, Schley graduated in 1860,

eighteenth in a class of twenty-five, and was assigned to the frigate *Niagara* as a passed midshipman. By the time the ship had completed a voyage to Japan, China, and various ports in Africa, the Civil War had begun. Without hesitation Schley took the oath of loyalty required of officers. He remained on the *Niagara* when it went on blockade duty off Charleston, South Carolina.

In the summer of 1862 Schley was promoted to lieutenant and transferred to the steam gunboat *Winona* as executive officer. His action in reporting the ship's commander as medically unfit was upheld by the senior naval officer in the Mobile area. Schley was next named acting commander of the screw sloop *Monongahela*, then with David Farragut's West Gulf Squadron near Port Hudson, Louisiana, on the Mississippi. When Farragut bombarded Port Hudson, Schley had orders to shell a Confederate fortress in the area. In the dense smoke Schley failed to see a flag signal ordering him to withdraw, and he continued firing until the post's guns were silenced. When he reported his success, Farragut publicly responded that he had ignored orders. In the privacy of his flag cabin, however, Farragut offered Schley a drink and praised his aggressive leadership.

In March 1863 Schley was transferred to the sloop *Richmond*, after which he served for three months at the ordnance factory of the Washington Navy Yard. The same year he married Annie Rebecca Franklin; the couple had three children. Schley returned to sea in 1864 as executive officer of the *Wateree*, a small, uncomfortable ship intended for service on rivers. During Schley's two years aboard, the *Wateree* spent most of its time cruising the Pacific, mainly in the area of Panama. In 1866 he was promoted to lieutenant commander and assigned to the naval academy as a member of the Department of Discipline. The following year he moved over to the Department of Modern Languages to teach Spanish.

Following his tour at Annapolis, Schley became executive officer of the *Benicia* (1869–1872), a new steam sloop attached to the Asiatic Squadron. In the aftermath of an 1871 incident in which Korean forts fired on American ships, Schley participated in a large landing party that in retaliation seized and then demolished a Korean fortress. He was proud of his part in avenging an insult to the American flag. Schley's next assignments were at the naval academy, where he headed the Department of Modern Languages (1872–1875), and command of the screw steamer *Essex* (1875–1879). He reported to Boston in 1880 to head the Second District of the Lighthouse Board. He had oversight of all lighthouses, ship lights, and buoys within an area bounded by Newburyport, Massachusetts, on the north and Newport, Rhode Island, on the south.

In 1884 Schley was offered command of an expedition, made up entirely of volunteer personnel, charged with attempting the rescue of a group of polar explorers, led by army lieutenant Adolphus Greely, that had set out for Lady Franklin Bay in 1881. The party had subsequently been reported missing, but after some months word was received that survivors were still alive. Schley secured the services of five officers experienced in the Arctic and ice pilots and departed for Baffin Bay in the spring of 1884 in three ships that had been made ready for the rigors of Arctic service. When his expedition reached Portsmouth, New Hampshire, with Greely and the few other survivors early in August, Schley was hailed as a national hero. President Chester Alan Arthur greeted the party in New York City and personally informed Schley of his next assignment: duty in the Navy Department as chief of the Bureau of Equipment and Recruiting. To his responsibilities was added oversight of the Bureau of Provisions and Clothing. In his combined positions Schley paid special attention to upgrading the quality of life for enlisted men. He introduced several changes, including professional training for new navy cooks and the acquisition of better-quality clothing for both officers and men.

Having been promoted to commander in 1874 and to captain in 1888, Schley took command of the new cruiser *Baltimore* in 1889, his first experience on a steel-clad ship. Schley captained the cruiser in European waters and then took the ship to South America as tensions began to run high during a civil war in Chile. Insurgents, who had recently captured the important port of Valparaiso, resented the *Baltimore*'s presence, feeling that U.S. ships had provided aid to government forces on several occasions. Anxious for his men to have liberty after several months at sea, Schley asked local authorities if his men could safely have shore leave. They could, he was told. More than a hundred men went ashore on 16 October 1891, and many of them were attacked, and two were killed. Schley disregarded advice from junior officers to fire on Valparaiso in retaliation. Instead, he saw to the safety of his injured and imprisoned crew members and established a three-man court of inquiry to gather information as soon as possible. The court ascertained that while some Chileans had tried to help the Americans, others, notably the police, had offered no aid. In December Schley received orders to steam for San Francisco, where another inquiry upheld Schley's actions and the findings of his own investigation. The U.S. government then successfully demanded an apology from Chile and an indemnity to be distributed among the injured members of *Baltimore*'s crew and the families of the two deceased men. Although Schley might well have erred in allowing his men liberty, his restraint thereafter had helped keep the Valparaiso incident from escalating into the war many jingoes would have liked to see.

Between 1892 and 1898 Schley had two tours with the Lighthouse Board (1892–1895 and 1897–1898), the second in Washington as its elected chairman, and one tour at sea commanding the armored cruiser *New York* (1895–1897). Schley was promoted to commodore in February 1898 and six weeks later received command of the Flying Squadron, a newly created force of some half-dozen ships assigned to cover the Atlantic seaboard between the Chesapeake Bay and Delaware Bay in the event of war between Spain and the United States. Schley's record of capable and resourceful leadership earned him this command over a dozen officers senior to him.

War began in late April. Schley's force remained at Hampton Roads until mid-May, when it was ascertained that Spanish warships had arrived in the West Indies and posed no threat to the eastern seaboard. Schley was ordered to lead the Flying Squadron to Key West, where he would be under the command of Admiral William T. Sampson, who had graduated from Annapolis a year later than Schley but who, as an acting rear admiral, now outranked him. Sampson ordered Schley to blockade Cienfuegos on the southern coast of Cuba instead of Havana as the Navy Department had previously instructed him. A flurry of communications between Schley and the Navy Department and between Schley and Sampson failed to clarify whether Schley should proceed first to Cienfuegos or to Santiago, another Cuban port where Admiral Pascual Cervera y Topete's Spanish squadron might put in. Schley had to send messages to his superiors by dispatch boat to Jamaica or some other neutral location, after which they would be cabled to the appropriate recipient, and replies came by the same time-consuming method. Acting on information he had independently received, Schley believed the reports that Cervera was at Santiago were erroneous and decided to head back to Key West to recoal before establishing a blockade. Calm seas enabled him to recoal at sea. The Flying Squadron arrived at Santiago on the night of 28 May to discover that Cervera's ships were already inside the fortified harbor, which was protected by shore batteries and minefields and which could only be entered through a narrow, winding channel that large warships would have to enter in single file.

The next morning Schley, who temporarily shifted his flag from the cruiser *Brooklyn* to the *Massachusetts*, reconnoitered the area with the *Massachusetts* and two additional battleships, purposely approaching close enough to land to draw Spanish fire. This enabled him to locate the Spanish batteries and determine the size of their guns. Although several of his officers advised him to close the range and return the enemy fire, Schley had orders from the Navy Department not to risk his ships by entering into action against enemy land guns. Cervera did not venture forth from the harbor. When Sampson reached the scene with the North Atlantic Squadron on 1 June, he expressed no disapproval of any of the decisions Schley had made during the previous days. This, however, did not mean tacit approval, as Schley believed, for in reality Sampson's view was that Schley's possible neglect of orders in recoaling before proceeding to Santiago warranted the attention of the Navy Department and that in the meantime he should reserve comment. Sampson continued the blockade, placing his flagship, the *New York*, near one end of the semicircular formation and Schley's flagship, the *Brooklyn*, at the opposite end.

For weeks the blockade continued while U.S. Army troops, who had landed to the east, closed in on Santiago. On 3 July Sampson headed east in his flagship to confer with General William Shafter, the commander of ground operations. Four other ships, including a battleship and two cruisers, had also left their stations to recoal. Aware that the U.S. forces seemed weaker than usual, Cervera steamed forth to reach the open seas. He seemingly intended to ram the *Brooklyn* with his own flagship. The Spanish flagship drew heavy fire and turned away from the *Brooklyn*, which maneuvered erratically before taking station in the American line of battle. One by one the Spanish ships were disabled, while Sampson, informed by a lookout that a battle was about to commence, ordered his flagship back to the scene. By the time Sampson reached the edge of the combat zone, the firing had stopped.

Partisans of Sampson and Schley quickly commenced a public debate over which officer deserved credit for the victory and whether Schley had acted properly prior to and during the battle. Much of the acrimony initially centered on Schley's orders to have the *Brooklyn* turn sharply away from the enemy to evade Cervera's apparent effort to ram it. However, Schley never clearly explained the reasons for his decision, which struck some officers as cowardly. Other captains emphasized his poor seamanship in ordering the unexpected maneuver, which nearly caused other American ships to collide. Although they initially acted cordially toward each other, Sampson and Schley grew bitter as the dispute gained intensity and brought under scrutiny as well Schley's slowness in reaching Santiago in the first place. The press, which generally favored Schley, made much of the dispute, and some of Schley's backers even charged that his assignment to command the distant South Atlantic Station (1899–1901) was an effort to exile him. His promotion to rear admiral did not ease matters. When the naval academy adopted a new text that lauded Sampson and criticized him, Schley requested a court of inquiry that convened in September 1901, only a month before he reached the navy's mandatory retirement age.

The court criticized some of the decisions Schley had made and, while it praised his coolness under fire, failed to grant him the recognition he sought for the victory at Santiago. Admiral George Dewey, a longtime friend, filed a minority report supporting Schley, who appealed the court's verdict to President Theodore Roosevelt. The president, who hoped to bring the embarrassing dispute to an end, declined to reverse the court's decision but did throw out all references to events prior to the actual battle. The battle itself, Roosevelt concluded in an effort to avoid taking sides, had developed in such a manner that decisions made by the captains of the individual ships had determined the outcome. Younger naval officers long remembered the controversy as unfortunate. Schley, who retired in Washington, D.C., restated his position in his memoirs. He died on a visit to New York City.

Schley had a long and worthy career during a time of remarkable change in the U.S. Navy. His principal contributions were his leadership of the Greely relief expedition and a concern for enlisted personnel not shown by all officers of his generation. Instead of enjoying acclaim for the victory at Santiago that would have been a fitting cap to his career, he found himself embittered by the controversy that began almost as soon as the last of Cervera's ships had struck its colors. Schley's actions before and during the engagement could hardly have been examined more closely had the result been a U.S. defeat rather than an overwhelming victory.

• Schley failed to leave behind a collection of papers, but various letters he wrote in an official capacity are in RG 45 and RG 313 at the National Archives and at the Nimitz Library, U.S. Naval Academy. Schley did write two accounts of his service, Winfield Scott Schley and J. R. Soley, *The Rescue of Greely* (1885), and his memoir, *Forty-five Years under the Flag* (1904). Edgar Stanton Maclay, *A History of the United States Navy* (3 vols., 1901), is the work that so angered Schley. The best scholarly work on Schley is the extended essay by Harold D. Langley, "Winfield Scott Schley: The Confident Commander," in *Admirals of the New Steel Navy: Makers of the American Naval Tradition, 1880–1930*, ed. James C. Bradford (1990). George Edward Graham, *Schley and Santiago* (1902), is an account by a reporter who was on Schley's flagship during the engagement. Bradford, ed., *Crucible of Empire: The Spanish-American War and Its Aftermath* (1993), is a helpful collection of essays. Also useful are Richard S. West, Jr., *Admirals of American Empire* (1948); Walter R. Herrick, Jr., *The American Naval Revolution* (1966); and Joyce Goldberg, *The "Baltimore" Affair* (1986). The last offers insight into the Chilean version of the riots in Valparaiso. An obituary is in the *New York Times*, 3 Oct. 1911.

LLOYD J. GRAYBAR

SCHLOSS, Oscar Menderson (20 June 1882–13 Oct. 1952), physician and pediatrician, was born in Cincinnati, Ohio, the son of Hugo Schloss and Aurelia Menderson. He received an S.B. in 1902 from Alabama Polytechnic Institute and an M.D. in 1905 from Johns Hopkins Medical School. He married Rowena Farmer in October 1912; they had one son.

Schloss interned from 1905 to 1907 at the King's County Hospital, Brooklyn, New York, and spent another year at New York Nursery and Child's Hospital. From 1908 to 1922 he managed a busy career in New York City, encompassing pediatric practice, teaching at Bellevue Medical College and at Columbia and Cornell Medical Schools, and research in a number of institutions that opened their doors to him: Bellevue Hospital, New York Nursery and Child's Hospital, the Department of Biological Chemistry at Columbia, and the Department of Pathology at St. Luke's Hospital in New York. Schloss was appointed professor of pediatrics at Cornell Medical College in 1919. In 1921 he left to become professor of pediatrics at Harvard Medical School and physician in chief of the Infant's and Children's Hospital in Boston, Massachusetts, but he returned to the professorship at Cornell in 1923. The stock market crash of 1929 caused a delay in implementing the development of the projected New York Hospital–Cornell Medical College complex as well as his plans for a modern Children's Clinic, which he had envisioned as a model for the teaching of outpatient pediatrics. In 1934 he resigned his professorship of pediatrics for financial reasons; he then accepted a part-time professorship at Cornell Medical College until he reached retirement age.

In 1912, in one of Schloss's greatest contributions to modern medicine, he reported "A Case of Allergy to Common Foods" (*American Journal of Diseases of Children* 3:361), the case of an eight-year-old boy who developed hives on ingestion of eggs, almonds, and oatmeal. Schloss demonstrated that skin inoculation of these foodstuffs produced an immediate swelling at the site of inoculation. Furthermore, the reactions were produced only by the protein constituents he extracted from these foods. These experiments supplied the basis for the use of skin testing with allergens as a diagnostic measure in medical practice.

Schloss's second major contribution was his recognition of the chemical imbalance in infants with diarrheal diseases and his further demonstration of the role of a pathologically high acidity level in the infant's blood in dehydration accompanying infantile diarrhea. In one of his most elegant papers, "Intestinal Intoxication in Infants; the Importance of Impaired Renal Function" (*American Journal of Diseases of Children* 15[1918]: 165), he not only gave the basis for understanding the source of some of the disorders in infants with impaired renal function, but also taught physicians to think of the role of chemical imbalances in sick infants. At the 1915 meeting of the American Pediatric Society, Schloss gave a report on allergy to common foods as a follow-up to his first observations, published three years earlier. He made skin inoculations and discovered several cases of egg sensitivity. In one case of sensitivity to milk and in one to oats, he succeeded in passive transfer of sensitivity with the patient's serum to a normal individual. He also described several cases in which eczema was relieved by elimination of offending foods and a few cases that demonstrated similar results in asthma. This paper was an extremely important milestone in the study of human allergy. At the 1923 meeting of the American Pediatric Society, Schloss described cases of cow's milk allergy in nutritional disorders of infants. He and his co-workers demonstrated circulating antibodies that reacted with an antigen to cause a precipitate (precipitins) in eight of ninety-eight sickly infants; this study was also a significant advance in the understanding of the mechanisms underlying the genesis of allergy.

Schloss in 1930 strongly argued against the ancient idea that sudden death in an infant may be caused by an enlarged thymus, pointing out that "proof is entirely lacking" and drawing on observations made in 1927 that the size of the thymus is directly related to the child's state of nutrition, being large in cases of sudden death merely because there had been no preceding period of malnutrition. Schloss was also ahead of his time in arguing that infants with an "enlarged" thymus should not be treated, as they commonly were, by X-ray to reduce the size of the thymus. Studies more than two decades later would prove that X-radiation of the area of the thymus could, and did, lead to cancer of the thyroid years later and that, furthermore, the concept of "thymic death" was a myth.

In his presidential address at the 1933 meeting of the American Pediatric Society, "Recent Advances in Terms of Equilibrium," Schloss pointed out that great improvements in techniques, particularly quantitative chemical measurements, had led to impressive advances in our understanding of chemical aberrations in pediatric diseases, which in turn would lead to a clearer understanding of the processes involved in the maintenance of health and disease.

Schloss's clinical and laboratory studies reveal an impressive breadth of interests, and his concern for the health of the whole child was balanced by his expertise in laboratory medicine. Harry Gordon, a former student and personal friend, wrote that "in retrospect it is difficult to understand how he could have been so productive scientifically during his early professional career when his livelihood depended entirely on the private practice he was building." Gordon also described Schloss's "unfailing gentleness and courtesy, a sternly critical attitude in the study of disease, high standards of excellence, scholarliness, and a refusal to confuse shadow with substance" and noted that "the most important part of his teaching was not in formal lectures but rather in the example he set: gentleness toward all patients and parents, whether from slum or mansion." Schloss died in Southold, New York.

Although he spent almost all his professional life in New York, Schloss never lost the southern accent and courteous deference he had acquired in his early life in Alabama. He attracted a large number of brilliant young investigators to the Cornell Medical School pediatric department. The breadth and depth of his scholarship was unexcelled by that of any other pediatrician of his time. He stands as one of the giants in the field of pediatrics.

• Among Schloss's most significant papers are, in *American Journal of Diseases of Children*, "A Case of Allergy to Common Foods" 3 (1912): 361; "The Occurrence of Acidosis with Severe Diarrhea" 13 (1917): 218, with R. Stetson; and "Intestinal Intoxication in Infants: The Importance of Impaired Renal Function" 15 (1918): 165–69. Harry H. Gordon wrote a detailed biographical sketch in *Pediatric Profiles*, ed. B. S. Veeder (1957). See also L. Emmett Holt, Jr., "Oscar Menderson Schloss," *Archives of Pediatrics* 70 (1953): 151. Harold K. Faber and Rustin McIntosh, *History of the American Pediatric Society* (1966) and Clement A. Smith, *The Children's Hospital of Boston* (1983), contain many references.

THOMAS E. CONE, JR.

SCHMIDT, Arthur Paul (1 Apr. 1846–5 May 1921), music publisher, was born in Altona, Germany, a suburb of Hamburg. Little is known about either his parents or his early life. He emigrated to the United States at age nineteen, arriving in New York City on 16 January 1866. He went to Boston, Massachusetts, and lived there the remainder of his life, becoming a naturalized citizen on 23 May 1871. His first position was as a clerk in the retail department of the G. D. Russell & Co. music publishing house, where he worked for ten years. In 1868 he married Helene Philippine Suck, sister of the cellist August P. F. Suck; their only child, a daughter, died in 1911.

In October 1876 Schmidt established his own business as a retailer and importer of foreign music, including the popular Litolff Edition. He registered his first copyright on 26 March 1877, a choral composition by the Boston organist S. B. Whitney. Initially Schmidt's publications were heavily slanted toward European compositions, but within a few years his catalog began to include works by New England composers, ushering in a thirty-year career of encouragement for American musicians. Often referred to as "the pioneer publisher of American music," Schmidt was the first to issue symphonic and chamber music scores by native American composers. The primary supporter of the Boston Group, he brought out major works by Amy Beach, Arthur Bird, George W. Chadwick, Henry Hadley, John Knowles Paine, and Horatio Parker, as well as almost the entire body of compositions by Arthur Foote. He became Edward MacDowell's American publisher in 1899.

Schmidt's first orchestral work, Paine's Symphony no. 2, "Im Frühling," was published in 1880 in conjunction with the August Cranz firm of Hamburg. In 1888 Schmidt published Chadwick's Symphony no. 2, op. 21, which was the first symphonic score by an American composer to be issued by an American publisher. Schmidt was unique among American publishers of the period for committing time and money to large symphonic and chamber-music scores, the expense of which he acknowledged was far greater than any expectation of profit.

In 1889 Schmidt sold his retail business in Boston to Miles and Thompson and expanded his publishing operations into Europe. He engaged the Kistner firm of Leipzig to act as his European agent, enabling him to gain international copyright protection for his American publications. He developed a Leipzig catalog of over 500 titles, primarily piano and chamber-music works, although several large American orchestral scores, including MacDowell's First Orchestral Suite, op. 42, and Beach's "Gaelic" Symphony, had their first publication in Leipzig. The rights to Schmidt's European catalog were bought by B. Schott's Söhne of Mainz in 1910.

Schmidt's efforts to promote American composers also extended to England. Beginning in 1899 and continuing through 1910 he signed contracts with several London publishers that gave them the English rights for numerous songs and some piano and choral works. Schmidt had a branch in New York from 1894 to 1937 and was a partner in the Boston firm of Charles W. Homeyer & Co. from 1899 to 1912.

At the height of his career, Schmidt's Boston catalog consisted of more than 15,000 original titles by American and European composers, whom he cultivated through prolific correspondence and a personal interest in their welfare. He was known as a meticulous editor who exercised tight control over his publications to insure that they met his high standards for accuracy and detail. He had a reputation as a man of strong principles and astute business sense, whose desire to publish works of serious musical value was balanced with an overriding concern for what would sell.

After Schmidt's retirement in 1916, three longtime employees, Harry B. Crosby, Florence J. Emery, and Henry R. Austin, took over the firm, focusing primarily on educational publications. The Arthur P. Schmidt Co. was sold to Summy-Birchard in 1959. Although the bulk of Schmidt's publications were in small forms—for piano, voice, chorus, and chamber works—it is the large orchestral works by American composers for which he is best remembered. Schmidt died in Boston.

• The Arthur P. Schmidt Archives in the Music Division of the Library of Congress include the original manuscripts from which the music was printed, correspondence, and business records. Contemporary sources include William Arms Fisher, *One Hundred and Fifty Years of Music Publishing in the United States* (1933); Christine M. Ayars, *Contributions to the Art of Music in America by the Music Industries of Boston, 1640 to 1936* (1937; repr., 1969); and Harry Dichter and Elliott Shapiro, *Handbook of Early American Sheet Music* (1941; repr., 1977). Wilma Reid Cipolla's "Marketing the American Song in Edwardian London," *American Music* 8, no. 1 (Spring 1990): 84–94, describes Schmidt's expansion into English music publishing. Adrienne Fried Block, "Arthur P. Schmidt, Music Publisher and Champion of American Women Composers" in *The Musical Woman II* (1984–1985), notes the firm's legacy in publishing the works of Beach, Daniels, Branscombe, Bauer, and other women composers. Cipolla's "A. P. Schmidt: The Publisher and His American Composers," in *Vistas of American Music: Essays and Compositions in Honor of William K. Kearns* (1998), analyzes the extent to which American composers were represented in Schmidt's published catalogs. Obituaries are in the *Boston Evening Transcript*, 6 May 1921; the *Boston Herald*, 7 May 1921; *Musical America*, 14 and 28 May 1921; and *Daily Telegraph* (London), 24 June 1921.

WILMA REID CIPOLLA

SCHMIDT, Friedrich August (3 Jan. 1837–15 May 1928), Lutheran church leader, was born in Leutenberg, Thuringia, Germany, the son of Martin Schmidt and Helena Wirth. Schmidt came as a young child to St. Louis, Missouri. After graduating from Concordia Theological Seminary in St. Louis in 1857, he served until 1861 as the pastor of Missouri Synod Lutheran congregations in Eden, New York, and Baltimore, Maryland. In 1858 he married Caroline Sophia Allwardt; they had eight children.

Active at first in the Missouri Synod, Schmidt became a member of the Norwegian Synod in 1861, when he joined the faculty at Luther College. This school, begun at Halfway Creek, Wisconsin, and moved in 1862 to Decorah, Iowa, was established for ministerial students who left St. Louis at the outbreak of the Civil War. Missouri Synod Lutherans tended to sympathize with the southern view of slavery, while most Norwegian Lutherans settled above the Mason-Dixon Line and regarded slavery as unjust. While at Luther College, Schmidt and its first president, Laur. (Peter Laurentius) Larsen, defended the view also held by C. F. W. Walther, the leader of the Missouri Synod, that on the basis of the Scriptures the institution of slavery (as distinguished from its abuses) should not be condemned, because it was not a sin "in itself" but an evil, a consequence of sin. They did so in the face of criticisms from the theological faculty in Christiania (now Oslo), Norway, and against the sentiments of lay leaders in their own church, who were opposed to slavery as practiced in the South, were not impressed by the pastors' distinction between evil and sin, and wanted to declare slavery a sin. Gradually Schmidt and his colleague won support for the view that slavery is not condemned by the Scriptures, but because of its abuse, Christians out of love should work to abolish it. Their theological influence lessened the Norwegian Synod's dependence on leaders in Norway while at the same time distinguishing church teaching from a simple endorsement of the political views found in American culture.

In 1872 the Missouri Synod and the Norwegian Synod joined with two other synods to form the Synodical Conference. Walther was elected its first president and Schmidt its first secretary. Schmidt had been a member of Walther's congregation and his respected student at Concordia Seminary, and from 1872 to 1876 Schmidt served with Walther on the Concordia faculty as the Norwegian Synod's professor. During earlier controversies Schmidt ardently defended the Missourian position affirming predestination. In 1879, however, he objected publicly to the formulation Walther offered at the 1877 meeting of the Western District of the Missouri Synod. Walther's emphasis on God's unconditioned election of some and only some to salvation seemed to Schmidt to divert people's attention away from the hope of the gospel toward speculation about the hidden, inscrutable will of God. Schmidt wanted not to deny the priority of grace, which predestination sought to uphold, but to emphasize the centrality of faith. For him "particular election" (God's choice of specific individuals) was based on God's foreknowledge of the faith of believers, a position rejected by Walther and his associates.

As the controversy intensified, Schmidt, who from 1876 to 1886 served as a professor at the Norwegian Synod's newly established Luther Seminary (Madison, Wisc.), was joined by theologians from the Ohio Synod. The clergy in the Western District warned of "synergism," the view that salvation depends on the cooperation of humans with divine grace. Since synergism was in their minds associated with Roman Catholicism and incompatible with the Lutheran teaching of justification by grace through faith, they were in effect accusing those who disagreed of being un-Lutheran. Their opponents, including Schmidt, emphasized the importance of faith and warned of a "Calvin-ist" understanding of irresistible grace, in effect also accusing those who disagreed of being un-Lutheran. Each side considered the teachings of the other dangerous, and each claimed the support of Martin Luther, the Lutheran Confessions, and the Scriptures.

The reasons for Schmidt's shift from defending to opposing Walther's position on predestination remain unclear. At the time Schmidt was annoyed at not being elected professor at Concordia Seminary, but he denied that this disappointment motivated any change in his loyalty. His own explanation was that in the 1877 report regarding Walther's presentation he recognized for the first time a new principle at work—that, without respect to their faith, God before creation predestines some individuals to salvation—and felt compelled to speak out against its dangers. Schmidt at first expressed his reservations privately. Indeed, only after the position Schmidt favored had been severely attacked in the Western District in 1879 did he bring his controversy with Walther into the open. Whatever the motivation, Schmidt, Walther, and others who participated in the disputes of the 1880s all expected a high degree of doctrinal uniformity and were quick to find fault with those who disagreed.

In 1882 the Synodical Conference declined to seat Schmidt, an official delegate from the Norwegian Synod. It labeled his views heretical and said it could not recognize him as a "brother in Christ." Considering Schmidt's rejection a repudiation of the group that elected him, the Norwegian Synod in 1883 withdrew from the Synodical Conference. Its withdrawal constituted an important step toward the eventual isolation of the Lutheran Church–Missouri Synod from the rest of American Lutheranism. Schmidt supported the decision, hoping it would bring an end to controversy. However, the disputes continued within his own Norwegian Synod and ultimately produced a split. In 1886 the anti-Missourians within that synod established the Lutheran Seminary in Northfield, Minnesota, with Schmidt as one of its two professors. In 1887 he and Peter Andreas Rasmussen helped organize the Anti-Missourian Brotherhood. It attracted about one-third of the Norwegian Synod but was short-lived. In 1888 Schmidt served on a joint committee that worked out a doctrinal settlement between the brotherhood and two other Lutheran groups, paving the way for the formation in 1890 of the United Norwegian Lutheran Church of America. From 1890 to 1893 Schmidt taught at Augsburg Seminary (Minneapolis, Minn.) and from 1893 to 1912 at the newly established United Norwegian Church Seminary (in Minneapolis until 1902 and thereafter in St. Paul, Minn.).

Schmidt figured prominently in another controversy about predestination between 1908 and 1912, but by this time the climate had changed. Relations with the Missouri Synod were not at issue, and the positions of Schmidt's opponents had softened. In the eyes of many younger pastors he was merely rehearsing old arguments when he accused others of "Calvinism." In 1912, the year that he retired, a formal agreement, ironed out in Madison, Wisconsin, allowed and affirmed, within certain limits, two different approaches to predestination, one emphasizing God's electing will and the other emphasizing the individual's response to grace. The Madison Agreement permitted Schmidt's United Norwegian Lutheran church to join in 1917 with the Norwegian Synod and Hauge's Synod (named in honor of Norway's pietist lay leader, Hans Nielsen Hauge) to form the Norwegian Lutheran Church of America. This merged group, whose name changed in 1946 to the Evangelical Lutheran church, comprised over 92 percent of the Norwegian Lutherans in the United States.

Contemporaries described Schmidt as "learned." Four times (1861, 1876, 1886, and 1893) his colleagues turned to him to help begin a new school. A good teacher and a lucid writer who was adept at drafting position papers on theological topics, he knew well the writings of the Reformation and the seventeenth-century Lutheran dogmaticians and used them effectively as sources for his arguments. Fidelity to tradition rather than creativity was the earmark of his thought. During his teaching career he edited several German and Norwegian Lutheran periodicals, including the *Lutheran Watchman* (1866–1867), *Altes and Neues* (1880–1885), *Lutherske Vidnesbyrd* (1882–1890), *Luthersk Kirkeblad* (1890–1895), and *Der Sprechsaal* (1901–1903).

As an educator and church leader, he helped shape the outlook of Norwegian-American immigrants. In response to religious freedom and the absence of coercive ecclesiastical authority, they at first stressed the importance of orthodox teaching. After that approach led to schisms and the vilification of opponents, their sense of cultural, ethnic, and religious ties inclined them toward a more inclusive ecclesiastical community. Although not a perfect embodiment of this transition, Schmidt did move from division-creating controversy to serving on committees that formulated agreements and paved the way for mergers.

Schmidt's significance as a theologian lies less in the views he defended than in the seriousness with which he engaged in theological debate. By fostering an intense, public discussion of theology, he helped create among the immigrant Lutheran communities an indigenous intellectual tradition. Schmidt's teaching—perhaps inadvertently—opened Norwegian Lutherans to certain aspects of American culture, especially its stress on human freedom and on diversity. Simultaneously, a thorough grounding in the classical traditions of the denomination prevented him and those influenced by his teaching from abandoning their distinctive religious heritage as they adjusted to life in this new cultural setting.

Schmidt died in Minneapolis, Minnesota.

• The Norwegian-American Historical Association at St. Olaf College in Northfield, Minn., has five folders of Schmidt correspondence (641 letters), one folder of clippings, and a box of articles and reports. The Luther College Archives at Preus Library in Decorah, Iowa, has approximately sixty-five letters in RG 2, 11, and 15, some from Schmidt to Laur. Larsen and Herman Amberg Preus, the leader of the Norwegian Synod, and others to and from the Norwegian Synod. Also in its collection are the records (about eight linear feet) of the Norwegian Synod, 1853 to 1912, which include minutes, reports, and correspondence. The Concordia Historical Institute in St. Louis, Mo., has a biographical file on Schmidt that includes clippings, letters, pictures, and a handwritten autobiographical sketch.

In addition to his many journal articles, Schmidt's writings include *Naadevalgsstriden* (1881), *Intuitu fidei* (1895), and *Sandhed og Frihed* (1914). A detailed analysis of Schmidt's role in the predestination controversies is in Hans R. Haug, "The Predestination Controversy in the Lutheran Church in North America" (Ph.D. diss., Temple Univ., 1967). A more general history of the developments in which Schmidt participated is in E. Clifford Nelson and Eugene Fevold, *The Lutheran Church among Norwegian-Americans: A History of the Evangelical Lutheran Church* (2 vols., 1960), and Nelson, *The Lutherans in North America* (1975). J. Magnus Rohne, *Norwegian Lutheranism up to 1872* (1926), discusses the early years of Schmidt's career. An assessment of Schmidt's theological outlook is Leigh D. Jordahl, "Centennial Article: F. A. Schmidt," *Luther Theological Seminary Review* 8 (Nov. 1969): 19–27. Obituaries are in the *Minneapolis Morning Tribune*, 17 May 1928, and the *Lutheran Church Herald*, 29 May 1928, p. 679. Schmidt's portrait is on the cover of the latter periodical.

DARRELL JODOCK

SCHMIDT, Karl Patterson (19 June 1890–26 Sept. 1957), herpetologist, was born in Lake Forest, Illinois, the son of George Washington Schmidt, a professor, and Margaret Patterson. His mother's keen interest in natural history, especially botany, was an early influence on his childhood. When Schmidt was about five years old he spent a year in Europe, where he acquired fluency in German. He enjoyed camping in northern Wisconsin with his father during three summers. He attended Lake Forest Academy and in 1906 entered Lake Forest College, where his father taught German and literature. After one year he left college to work on a family-owned farm in Stanley, Wisconsin, for six years, helping to establish a dairy farm. There he developed a keen interest in natural history. He kept notes on variations in the woodland plant *Trillium*, and he systematically recorded weather data. He also took correspondence courses from the University of California.

Among his professors at Lake Forest College was naturalist James George Needham, who became a professor at Cornell University in 1907. Needham urged the young man to return to college. So in 1913 Schmidt entered Cornell, where his first interest was invertebrate paleontology. He made several geologic field trips, including one to Santo Domingo during his senior year. On his way home from that trip in 1916 he visited the American Museum of Natural History in New York, where he met its associate curator of herpetology, Mary Cynthia Dickerson. She gave him a temporary job unpacking a large collection of amphibians and reptiles collected by Herbert Lang in the Congo area of Africa, and she persuaded him to finish college. Schmidt received an A.B. from Cornell in 1917 and became an assistant in the division of reptiles and amphibians at the American Museum of Natural History, first under Dickerson and from 1919 under Gladwyn Kingsley Noble. He wrote his first scientific papers while at the American Museum, beginning with two that described reptiles from the Congo collection. From this work began his lifelong interest in zoogeography, the distribution of animals.

In 1919 Schmidt married Margaret Wightman, who immediately accompanied him on an expedition to Puerto Rico to collect specimens for the New York Academy of Sciences. The couple had two sons.

In 1922 Schmidt became assistant curator of reptiles in the newly established division of reptiles and amphibians at the Field Museum of Natural History in Chicago, Illinois. He was appointed curator of reptiles in 1937 and, in 1941, chief curator of zoology, a post he held until his retirement in 1955. Schmidt contributed to the design of exhibits at the museum and to its educational programs. From 1943 he was also a lecturer in zoology at the University of Chicago.

At the Chicago museum Schmidt participated in many collecting expeditions: Central America (1923); Brazil, Argentina, Uruguay, and Chile (1926); Panama, the Galápagos Islands, and South Pacific islands (1928–1929); Guatemala (1933–1934); Peru (1939); New Zealand (1949); Israel (1953); and many trips within the United States and northern Mexico. Because of his own broad interests, said his biographer D. Dwight Davis, "the collections he brought home were likely to include almost anything pertaining to natural history" (Davis, p. 190). They certainly increased his museum's collections in herpetology enormously. His most detailed research was on coral snakes, beginning in 1925 and continuing for many years. He published a number of papers on this group but did not complete the intended monograph.

Schmidt's fluency in German led to his translating Richard Hesse's *Tiergeographie auf oekologischer Grundlage* (1924), which, with Hesse's permission, he then revised with Warder Clyde Allee as the highly regarded *Ecological Animal Geography* (1937). With D. Dwight Davis he wrote *Field Book of Snakes of the United States and Canada* (1941). He was also a coauthor of the widely used textbook *Principles of Animal Ecology* (1949), with W. C. Allee, Alfred E. Emerson, Orlando Park, and Thomas Park.

Schmidt accepted a number of editorial responsibilities. From 1926 until his death he was editor of the amphibian and reptile section of *Biological Abstracts*. From 1937 to 1949 he was herpetological editor of *Copeia*, the journal of the American Society of Ichthyologists and Herpetologists. From 1941 to 1955 he edited the zoological publications of the Chicago Natural History Museum. He also was herpetological editor for *American Midland Naturalist* for many years and a department editor of the *Encyclopaedia Britannica*. He translated several long scientific publications from German, making them available to colleagues. From 1953 he was a useful participant of an international committee to establish uniform usage in terminology of zoological nomenclature.

Schmidt was president of the American Society of Ichthyologists and Herpetologists from 1942 to 1946 and president of the Society for the Study of Evolution in 1954. He was elected to the National Academy of Sciences in 1956.

A competent taxonomist, Schmidt named twelve genera and more than two hundred species. He presented information on the geographical distribution, ecology, and variations of reptiles and amphibians throughout the world. He accumulated an extensive library in herpetology, which he gave to the Field Museum. Colleagues acknowledged him as a sincere and earnest person, with a contagious enthusiasm for life and knowledge. "His love of nature amounted almost to reverence," said D. Dwight Davis, who also noted his keen interest in conversing with young people.

Schmidt died in Chicago from a bite by the extremely poisonous snake boomslang from Africa, a young specimen from the Lincoln Park Zoo that he had been asked to identify. He ignored his own advice to others of the danger of a bite by that kind of snake, kept notes of his reactions but, because he thought that a juvenile snake was not likely to be highly poisonous, took no antitoxin, and died the next day.

• Schmidt published about 200 papers on herpetology from many regions of the world. In addition to the books cited above, he wrote *A Check List of North American Amphibians and Reptiles*, 6th ed. (1953), and *Amphibia* (1959), with Robert F. Inger. Biographies include Alfred E. Emerson, "K. P. Schmidt—Herpetologist, Ecologist, Zoogeographer," *Science* 127 (1958): 1162–63, and D. Dwight Davis, "Karl Patterson Schmidt: 1890–1957," *Copeia*, no. 3 (1959): 189–92. A volume-length tribute to Schmidt was published in honor of his sixty-fifth birthday in *Fieldiana: Zoology* 37 (1955); it includes a brief biography.

ELIZABETH NOBLE SHOR

SCHMUCKER, Beale Melanchthon (26 Aug. 1827–15 Oct. 1888), Lutheran clergyman, was born in Gettysburg, Pennsylvania, the son of Samuel Simon Schmucker, a professor of theology and founder of Gettysburg Lutheran Seminary, and Mary Catherine Steenbergen, mother of thirteen children. Of the nine children who survived to maturity, Beale Schmucker was one of three brothers who entered the Lutheran ministry. He studied at Gettysburg Seminary under the tutelage of his father and the Reverend Charles Philip Krauth. He formed a lifelong friendship with Professor Krauth's son, Charles Porterfield, and the conservative bent of this gifted theologian strongly influenced his own theological development. Upon graduation from the seminary in 1847 he became pastor of a church in Martinsburg, West Virginia. He later served parishes in Allentown, Easton, Reading, and Pottstown, Pennsylvania. While a pastor at Allentown in 1860, he married Christianna M. Pretz; they had two sons.

During the years preceding and following the Civil War, Schmucker found himself in the midst of a doctrinal struggle that sharply divided the Lutheran church. One segment, known as American Lutherans and headed for nearly a quarter of a century by his father Samuel, sought amalgamation with American culture and some sort of working union with other Protestant denominations. The other body, known as the "Old Lutherans," wanted to preserve their ties to the German heritage and to retain a sharply defined Lutheran identity based upon a strict adherence to its liturgical and confessional heritage. Beale Schmucker was inclined by conviction to side with the latter group. For a time, he held these conservative views in abeyance out of personal affection and concern for his father. However, when the conflict had reached its crisis and a new seminary was established at Philadelphia in direct opposition to the one his father had founded in Gettysburg, he made his position clear by assisting in its founding and serving on its first board of directors. After the "Old Lutherans" broke with the General Synod in 1866 and formed the General Council, he took a leading role in the council's affairs.

From his early years, he had developed a great love of books, and his literary output was significant. In 1870 he received the degree of Doctor of Divinity from the University of Pennsylvania, specializing in the study of Lutheran liturgics and worship. The Lutheran historian Adolf Spaeth noted that he was the most prominent of all writers in North America in this field and that "even in Germany few scholars were his equal in exact knowledge of liturgical matters, and perhaps none his superiors." This expertise enabled him to make vital contributions to the compilation of the *Church Book*, which was later utilized for worship in the congregations of the General Council. His efforts, more than the work of any other single individual, made possible the publication in 1888 of a liturgy and hymnal called the *Common Service*, which after modification in 1919 under the title of the *Common Service Book* became the primary guide for worship in the majority of Lutheran churches in this country until 1958. These books of worship represent the principal and abiding contribution of Schmucker. His keen liturgical scholarship and a goodly portion of his energies went into their preparation. He was still engaged in the final revision of the *Common Service* when he died in Pottstown, Pennsylvania.

• The Beale M. Schmucker papers are in the library of the Lutheran Theological Seminary in Philadelphia. The most adequate and concise summary of his life and theological contributions is in Adolph Spaeth's "Memorial of Beale Melanchthon Schmucker, D.D.," *Lutheran Church Review* 8 (1889), with some additional materials in the *Encyclopedia of the Lutheran Church* (1965), and in *American Lutheran Biographies* (1890). Special aspects of his career are found in Abdel Ross Wentz, *Pioneer in Christian Unity* (1967); Luke Schmucker, *The Schmucker Family and the Lutheran Church* (1937); and Edward T. Horn, "The Lutheran Sources of the Common Service," *Lutheran Quarterly Review* 21 (Apr. 1891).

PAUL P. KUENNING

SCHMUCKER, Samuel Simon (28 Feb. 1799–26 July 1873), minister and theologian, was born in Hagerstown, Maryland, the son of John George Schmucker, a Lutheran clergyman, and Elizabeth Gross. Raised in the pious environment of a church parsonage, Schmucker received instruction as a young man both from his father and from his father's mentor in theology, Justus H. C. Helmuth, and as a consequence he chose to enter the Lutheran ministry. He attended the University of Pennsylvania between 1814 and 1816; after teaching for a year at the York County Academy, he enrolled at Princeton Theological Seminary in 1818. He graduated from Princeton in 1820 and was licensed to serve as pastor of a cluster of congregations in the vicinity of New Market, Virginia—the only parish position he was to hold. Ordained in 1821, he remained at New Market until 1826. Schmucker married three times: in 1821 to Elenora Geiger, who died in 1823; in 1825 to Mary Catherine Steenbergen, who died in 1848; and in 1849 to Esther M. Wagner. He had one child by his first wife, and twelve children by his second.

Schmucker's most lasting contributions to American life were in the area of theological education and in the fostering of cooperation among the major Protestant denominations. He believed strongly in the necessity of establishing schools to train candidates for the ministry; he was instrumental in founding both Gettysburg Theological Seminary in 1825 and the school that became Pennsylvania (later Gettysburg) College in 1832. After leaving New Market, he served as a professor at Gettysburg Seminary until his retirement in 1864, and briefly as president (1832–1834).

Schmucker's *Elements of Popular Theology* (1834) was the first English-language systematic theology published by a Lutheran in the United States. His pioneering *Fraternal Appeal to the American Churches* (1838) anticipated ecumenical trends that became popular in the mid-twentieth century. Although he respected the juridical independence of the various denominational traditions, Schmucker believed that Protestants should consider a noncompetitive approach to Christian mission and conceive a basic creed on which they all could agree. These ideas strongly influenced the creation of the Evangelical Alliance, which was formed at a gathering in London, which Schmucker attended, in 1846.

Schmucker had a profound effect, moreover, on the growth and development of Lutheranism in America. He played a major role in the formation of the General Synod, the church body that encompassed nearly two-thirds of all Lutheran congregations in the United States in 1860, and he served as its president from 1828 until 1845. In works such as *The American Lutheran Church* (1851) and *The Lutheran Manual of Scriptural Principles* (1855), he discussed how Lutherans should relate to the cultural and religious milieu of their day by adopting a stance that was not only loyal to the sixteenth-century European heritage of their denomination but also compatible with American evangelical Protestantism. Schmucker believed, for example, that religious faith needed to be more practical than intellectual, and he stressed ethics and activism over dogma and theological analysis. While justification by divine grace alone—the central tenet of Lutheranism—remained at the core of his theology, he also emphasized the importance of living out the implications of one's faith through tangible acts of service—the Christian doctrine of sanctification. As a consequence, Schmucker accepted both the revivalism and the optimistic millennialism common among evangelical Protestants in the early nineteenth century. These beliefs further led him to argue that American Lutherans did not need to affirm literally every tenet of the Augsburg Confession of 1530 (the denomination's traditional creed) as long as they followed the essential doctrines of Christianity that were contained in the Bible.

Despite Schmucker's efforts to strengthen Lutheranism in this way, his approach ultimately failed to persuade the majority of his fellow church members. While the flood of German immigrants that began in the 1840s dramatically increased the size of Lutheranism in the United States and buoyed his hopes, the narrow doctrinal conservatism to which many of those settlers adhered ultimately undermined the assimilationist model Schmucker championed. While his followers sought to adapt Lutheranism to the democratic mold of American culture, his "Old Lutheran" opponents demanded strict observance of Reformation-era confessional standards. Mounting opposition to Schmucker's theories eventually inspired traditionalists in the General Synod to create a new church body, the General Council, in 1867. Sectional divisions within the nation and the coming of the Civil War also led Lutherans in the South to form their own denomination, the United Synod, in 1863. Still residing in Gettysburg at the time of his death, Schmucker lived long enough to see his ideas widely repudiated within American Lutheranism.

Despite the controversial nature of his views, Schmucker was the preeminent leader of his denomination before the Civil War and helped bring Lutheranism into the mainstream of American Protestant evangelicalism in the nineteenth century. Although not accepted during his lifetime, his desire to foster harmony not simply among Lutherans but among all Protestants provided a vision of Christian unity that achieved broad acceptance in the United States a century after his death.

• Schmucker's papers are at the Gettysburg College Archives and at the Lutheran Theological Seminary Archives in Gettysburg, Pennsylvania. Basic information about Schmucker and his career is in Peter Anstadt, *Life and Times of Rev. S. S. Schmucker* (1896), and in Luke Schmucker, *The Schmucker Family and the Lutheran Church in America* (1937). Abdel R. Wentz, *Pioneer in Christian Unity: Samuel Simon Schmucker* (1967), is a modern account of Schmucker's life. For a recent scholarly assessment of Schmucker's impact on nineteenth-century American Lutheranism, see Paul P. Kuenning, *The Rise and Fall of American Lutheran Pietism: The Rejection of an Activist Heritage* (1988). See also Vergilius T. A. Fern, *The Crisis in American Lutheran Theology: A Study of the Issue Between American Lutheranism and Old Lutheranism* (1927).

GARDINER H. SHATTUCK, JR.

SCHNABEL, Artur (17 Apr. 1882–15 Aug. 1951), pianist, teacher and composer, was born in the tiny town of Lipnik, Poland (then a part of Austrian Silesia), the son of Isidor Schnabel, a textile businessman, and Ernestine Labin. He began piano lessons at age six, after effortlessly imitating his elder sister's playing. He progressed rapidly and was sent to Vienna in 1889 at age seven to play for Professor Hans Schmidt at the Vienna Conservatory. Schmidt immediately accepted the boy as a private pupil, and the Schnabel family moved to Vienna.

After two years with Schmidt, Artur began studies with the great pedagogue Theodor Leschetizky, who had studied with Carl Czerny (a pupil of Beethoven). Schnabel studied technique with Leschetizky's wife, Annette Essipoff, until the couple's divorce in 1892. He also studied music theory with Eusebius Mandyczewski, who was then editing a forty-volume edition of the collected works of Franz Schubert. Mandyczewski had a great influence on Schnabel and introduced him to Brahms, who quickly became the boy's hero. Schnabel visited Brahms's home, participated in informal evenings of chamber music with Brahms present, and—when he was twelve or thirteen—joined the composer on several of his weekly excursions to the hilly woods near Vienna.

Schnabel made his official Vienna debut on 12 February 1897, in a recital at Bösendorfer Hall. He completed his studies with Leschetizky the following year, moved to Berlin, and made his debut there on 10 October 1898. He toured Norway as a sonata partner with the great German violinist Willy Burmester and also concentrated on composing. In 1899 he won a young composers' competition and embarked on the first of a series of concert tours with the contralto Theresa Behr, whom he married in 1905. They had two sons. In 1901 he performed the world premiere of his own piano concerto with the Berlin Philharmonic under the direction of Josef Rebicek in a privately sponsored concert. Although the concerto was coolly received, Schnabel continued to compose for the rest of his life. Among his compositions were three symphonies, five string quartets, and a piano sonata—thorny atonal works in the tradition of Arnold Schoenberg.

Schnabel had a keen interest in chamber music throughout his life. In 1902 he formed a very successful trio with the violinist Alfred Wittenberg and the cellist Anton Hekking, which lasted for three seasons. He formed another trio with the violinist Carl Flesch and the cellist Jean Gerardy in 1910, which lasted until 1914 when Hugo Becker replaced Gerardy. Flesch and Schnabel remained recital partners for the next two decades.

Schnabel's solo career progressed as well. In 1903 he gave several performances with the Berlin Philharmonic under the great Artur Nikisch, including the

Brahms B-flat major piano concerto at the Gewandhaus in Leipzig and the Brahms D minor piano concerto in Berlin, and he made his London debut in February 1904 with Hans Richter and the Halle Orchestra. He toured Russia in 1911, making both recital and concerto appearances, including a performance of Liszt's E-flat major concerto with Willem Mengelberg conducting. Later that year in Hamburg he gave his first all-Beethoven recital—a format for which he eventually became famous. He made his U.S. debut in 1921 but was not particularly well received. In 1924 he accepted an appointment at the Berlin Hochschule für Musik to teach piano master classes.

His real breakthough came in 1927, Beethoven's centennial year, when he gave his first complete cycle of the Beethoven piano sonatas in seven programs in Berlin. He then embarked on a tour of Amsterdam, Leningrad, Milan, Rome, London, Vienna, and Scandinavia, performing Beethoven everywhere he went. The next year was Schubert's centennial, so he similarly programmed Schubert's piano music, which was then relatively unknown, in his recitals and accompanied his wife in programs of Schubert lieder. The tours brought him much attention, and Serge Koussevitzky invited him to return to the United States in 1930 to participate in the Boston Symphony Orchestra's Brahms Festival in Boston and New York City. His performances of the two Brahms piano concertos in those concerts were a great success.

Up to that point Schnabel had steadfastly refused to record (although he did make some Ampico piano rolls in 1921). Then in 1931 he finally agreed to appear before the microphone on the condition that he could record all of the Beethoven sonatas and concertos, a feat that had never been done before and one that forever linked his name to Beethoven. He completed the project for His Master's Voice (HMV) in 1935. Among his other recordings are the two Brahms concertos, five of the Mozart concertos, a selection of Schubert works (including some lieder with his wife), and various other works by Bach, Dvořák, Schumann, and Weber. Although his technique was not always perfect ("You'll never be a pianist. You are a musician," Leschetizky once told him), his interpretations, especially of Beethoven, are legendary. He stands as one of the primary exponents of the German school of piano playing, which advocated an intellectual approach to music making and eschewed virtuosity for virtuosity's sake.

Schnabel, a Jew, gave his last concert in Nazi Germany in 1933 and gave up his home in Berlin shortly thereafter. Following a period of exile he settled in the United States, where he obtained citizenship. He published his own edition of the Beethoven sonatas in 1935. In 1946, after World War II, he toured England, France, Belgium, Holland, and Italy. He suffered a heart attack in 1948, and his health then deteriorated rapidly. He died in Axenstein, Switzerland. Among his many pupils were Clifford Curzon, Rudolf Firkusny, Leon Fleisher, Claude Frank, Eileen Joyce, Lili Kraus, and Ruth Slenczynska.

• Schnabel's writings include his editions of the complete Beethoven piano sonatas (1935) and (coedited by the violinist Carl Flesch) the complete Mozart sonatas for violin and piano (1912), and three books based on his lectures: *Reflections on Music* (1934), *Music and the Line of Most Resistance* (1942), and *My Life and Music* (1961). A number of his compositions were published by Simrock, Dreililien, Boosey & Hawks, and others, and some have been recorded. Virtually all of his commercial recordings as a pianist, as well as several live performances, have been issued on compact disc by Arabesque, EMI, Music & Arts, and Pearl. A great deal has been written about Schnabel, including Cesar Saerchinger, *Artur Schnabel* (1957), the official biography; Konrad Wolff, *The Teaching of Artur Schnabel* (1972); Doris Sossner, "Revisiting Artur Schnabel" (Ph.D. diss., Univ. of California, San Diego, 1986); B. Brubaker, "Contemplating Schnabel," *Piano Quarterly*, no. 154 (Summer 1991): 35–36; and Samuel Lipman, "Beethoven and the Pianists," *Commentary* 97 (1994): 46ff. *Piano Quarterly* devoted a complete issue to Schnabel (no. 84, Winter 1973–1974) that included reminiscences by his students, a bibliography, a discography (which is more thorough than the one in Saerchinger's biography), and a list of his compositions.

JOHN ANTHONY MALTESE

SCHNEERSOHN, Joseph Isaac (21 June 1880–28 Jan. 1950), sixth rebbe (leader) of the Lubavitch-Chabad Chasidic movement, was born in Lubavitch, Belorussia, the only son of Rabbi Shalom Dovber Schneersohn, the fifth rebbe, and the latter's first cousin, the Rebbetzin Shterna Sarah Schneersohn. In 1897 he married his second cousin Nechamah Dinah Schneersohn; they had three daughters.

Joseph Isaac grew up in Lubavitch in an atmosphere of rabbinic scholarship, contemplative prayer, chasidic melodies, and Chabad teachings, the last of which function as a mystical commentary on the Bible and Talmud. From the age of eighteen he worked closely with his father in communal activities. When the latter died on 21 March 1920, Rabbi Joseph Isaac succeeded him as the sixth Lubavitcher rebbe, now based in Rostov-on-Don. For the rest of his life he had two overlapping aims: the spread of the teachings of Chabad and the preservation of traditional Judaism in a changing world. Expressing the first aim, in 1921 he founded the Chabad Torah Academy in Warsaw, which was a center of traditional Jewish life. In Russia, however, his efforts were limited by political realities to the preservation of Judaism.

At this point in the revolution, the Communists, aided by the *Yevsektsiya*, the Jewish section of the Communist party, were actively suppressing the expression of all religions but particularly Judaism. By 1922 most major rabbinic leaders had left Russia. As a result, Rabbi Joseph Isaac saw himself as the religious head of all Soviet Jews. At a secret meeting held in Moscow in 1922, he selected nine men who would be responsible for different regions of the USSR. From Rostov he directed operations in the setting up of clandestine religious schools, sent roving emissaries to encourage communities to maintain religious institutions, and succeeded in marshaling the forces of many non-Chabad rabbis in the USSR to help in this task, which was financed by the American Jewish Joint Distribution Committee. In May 1927 Rabbi Joseph Isaac was arrested for his leadership of underground religious activities. Thanks to diplomatic intervention the threatened death sentence was commuted first to exile to the remote city of Castrama and then to full release on 12 July (which happened, that year, to be 12 Tammuz in the Hebrew calendar). For the Lubavitch followers this date—also the Hebrew date of Rabbi Joseph Isaac's birthday—became a chasidic festival. In October he left the USSR for Riga, Latvia.

Rabbi Joseph Isaac saw the spirituality of Chabad teaching as the key to preserving traditional Judaism in the modern West. In 1924 he had set up the Agudas Chasidei Chabad (Union of Followers of Chabad) in the United States and Canada, maintaining contact with members through encyclical letters and mimeographed discourses of chasidic thought. In 1929, after visiting the Holy Land, he traveled to the United States, where he visited Jewish communities in New York City, Philadelphia, Baltimore, Chicago, Milwaukee, Detroit, St. Louis, and Springfield, Massachusetts. In July 1930 he met with President Herbert Hoover in Washington, D.C., and thanked him for granting freedom to Jews in the United States and for the positive interest shown by the American government in Jewish affairs abroad. After returning to Riga he sent personal emissaries back to the United States; they traveled from city to city on speakers' tours, strengthening the work of Agudas Chasidei Chabad, which was directed by Rabbi Israel Jacobson (1896–1975).

In 1934 Rabbi Joseph Isaac moved from Riga to Warsaw and later to Otwock, where he created the journal *Hatamim* to spread Chabad chasidic ideals. He also established a Chabad women's group and published chasidic teachings in Yiddish (rather than Hebrew); these teachings were specially aimed at women because he believed that chasidic women would become a knowledgeable and inspired task force for the strengthening of Judaism. In 1938 he established a Chabad women's group in New York City.

In March 1940 Rabbi Joseph Isaac emigrated to the United States, settling in Brooklyn. He subsequently attempted to help other rabbis, such as Rabbi Abraham Alter, the rebbe of Ger, as well as a number of his own followers to escape from Europe. In 1941 he met Eleanor Roosevelt at the White House in an attempt to win freedom for Rabbi Ben Zion Halberstam, the rebbe of Bobov, who despite efforts on his behalf later died in the Holocaust. Rabbi Joseph Isaac had arrived in New York in a wheelchair. He nonetheless was able to create and lead a dedicated activist team, which included his son-in-law and future successor, Rabbi Menachem M. Schneerson, the husband of Chaya Mushka; another son-in-law, Rabbi Samarius Gurary; and powerful figures such as Rabbi H. M. Hodakov. Together they established a number of educational and publishing organizations.

From his headquarters at 770 Eastern Parkway in Crown Heights, Brooklyn, Rabbi Joseph Isaac ran a network of schools in the eastern states, the Midwest, and Montreal, Canada, as well as a variety of outreach activities. Roving emissaries with the goal of promulgating traditional Jewish observance and education were sent as far as Los Angeles, which became a base for educational work on the West Coast. Activities abroad also continued. In 1941 Agudas Chasidei Chabad was set up in Palestine. Although he was critical of the secularism of the Zionists, during the Israeli War of Independence Rabbi Joseph Isaac wrote an open letter to his followers in which he expressed support for the Jewish war effort, saying, "Our souls are bound with their souls" (*Collected Letters*, vol. 9, p. 428). In 1948 he founded a Chabad village for refugees from Russia at Safaria (later Kfar Chabad), near Tel Aviv. As soon as possible after the war, he also set up a Lubavitch Talmudic Academy in Europe; initially based in Poking, Germany, it subsequently moved to Brunoys, Paris. Emissaries from there traveled to Britain and other countries. His final area of outreach activity concerned the Jews of North Africa, efforts that later led to the establishment of Jewish schools in Morocco.

When Rabbi Joseph Isaac said, "America is not different," he meant that the full extent of traditional Jewish spirituality could be expressed in a modern context. This included, in his view, the ideals of contemplative prayer, study of mystical teachings, and chasidic melody. He saw the history of the twentieth century as expressing the last stages before the advent of the Messiah. Thus *Bosi LeGani* ("I Have Come into My Garden"), the most famous of his chasidic discourses, presents a spiritual account of the history of the world. The goal of Creation, he wrote, is that the Divine Presence should dwell in the "lower world," together with physical human beings, as in the Garden of Eden. Because of sin the Divine Presence departed, but through the process of history and the spiritual service of each individual it eventually will return permanently to the rebuilt Temple in Jerusalem for the benefit of all humanity.

Rabbi Joseph Isaac faced opposition from both the orthodox Jewish opponents of Chasidism and the proponents of westernized forms of Judaism. Despite this resistance, his work laid the foundation for the subsequent expansion of Chabad-Lubavitch into a global movement. Rabbi Joseph Isaac died in Brooklyn. His funeral was attended by 3,000 people.

• Rabbi Joseph Isaac's papers are housed in the Lubavitch Library in Crown Heights, Brooklyn. His mystical discourses are collected in Hebrew and Yiddish under the general title *Book of Discourses* (13 vols., 1944–1986); translations include *On Learning Chassidus* and *On the Teachings of Chassidus*, both trans. Z. Posner (1959); *Chassidic Discourses*, trans. S. Weinberg (1986); and *Bosi LeGani*, ed. Uri Kaploun (1990). Another genre of his published teachings comprises "Talks." Those from Poland in the 1930s are translated by U. Kaploun in *Likkutei Dibburim* (1988); those from the years 1940–1945 are as yet untranslated but are available in the Yiddish *Book of Talks* (6 vols., 1957–1967). He also wrote an interesting tract on education, *Principles of Education and Guidance*, trans. Y. E. Danziger (1990). His historical writings include *Lubavitcher Rabbi's Memoirs*, trans. N. Mindel (1956), and *The "Tzemach Tzedek" and the Haskalah Movement*, trans. Z. Posner (1969). His letters have been collected in the as yet untranslated *Collected Letters*, ed. S. B. Levin (13 vols., 1982–1993). Many of his sayings are collected in Rabbi M. M. Schneerson, *Hayom Yom . . . "From Day to Day"*, trans. Y. M. Kagan (1988). The Lubavitch-Chabad branch of Chasidism has generated a large amount of primary and secondary source material. See the bibliography in Naftali Loewenthal, *Communicating the Infinite: The Emergence of the Habad School* (1990). Works focusing on Rabbi Joseph Isaac include, in Hebrew, two important books by S. D. Levin, chief librarian of the Lubavitch Library in Brooklyn: *History of Chabad in the United States 1900–1950* (1988) and *History of Chabad in the U.S.S.R. 1917–1950* (1989). David E. Fishman, "Preserving Tradition in the Land of Revolution: The Religious Leadership of Soviet Jewry, 1917–1930," in *The Uses of Tradition: Jewish Continuity in the Modern Era*, ed. Jack Wertheimer (1992), gives an informative account and discussion of his activities in the USSR. Ada Rapoport-Albert discusses his use of historical writing in "Hagiography with Footnotes: Edifying Tales and the Writing of History in Hasidism," in *Essays in Jewish Historiography, beiheft 27 of History and Theory* (1988). Gershon Greenberg has written on Rabbi Joseph Isaac's response to the Holocaust in articles such as "An Actual Messianic Response during the Holocaust: Mahane Israel-Lubavitch," in *Bearing Witness 1939–1989*, ed. Alan Berger (1991).

NAFTALI LOEWENTHAL

SCHNEERSON, Menachem Mendel (18 Apr. 1902–12 June 1994), was born in Nikolayev, Ukraine, the son of Levi Yitzchak Schneerson, a rabbi, and Chana Yanovsky. He played a unique role in American Jewish history of the second half of the twentieth century as the seventh "rebbe" (spiritual leader) of the Lubavitcher Hasidim also known as "Chabad," a group of ultra-Orthodox Jews who maintain allegiance to the Eastern European Hasidic movement founded in the eighteenth century. Under Schneerson's leadership, after the Nazi and Bolshevik atrocities destroyed the world within which they had lived for centuries, Lubavitchers adapted themselves to the United States, where they built a self-sufficient, vibrant community. At the same time, Schneerson oversaw something of a revolution: he formed this group, relics in the eyes of more assimilated Jewish and non-Jewish Americans, into a highly successful movement that overflowed the boundaries of Orthodox Judaism, reached out to Jews across the religious spectrum, and exerted a powerful influence on Jewish life and on politics in the United States and worldwide.

Named for his ancestor, the third Lubavitcher rebbe, Schneerson followed his family's calling to rigorous studies of the Jewish religious tradition. He was recognized as a prodigy and was ordained as a rabbi at the age of seventeen. In 1923, after meeting his cousin Rabbi Yosef Yitzchak Schneersohn, the sixth Lubavitcher rebbe, he became active in Chabad, which was facing persecution from Soviet authorities. In 1928 he married Chaya Mushka (or Moussia) Schneersohn, Rebbe Schneersohn's daughter.

In 1933 the couple moved to Berlin, where Schneerson studied mathematics and science at the University of Berlin until the Nazi seizure of power in 1933, when they moved to Paris to continue his studies at the Sorbonne. At the same time he directed religious activities, served as contributing editor of Chabad's scholarly journal, and served as the rebbe's private secretary. In June 1941 the Schneersons arrived in New York to join the rebbe and a small community of Lubavitchers who had recently escaped Europe. Schneerson was appointed by his father-in-law to lead Chabad's educational arm, its social service organization, and its publishing firm. When the elder man died in January 1950, Lubavitch leaders selected Schneerson over his older brother-in-law to succeed him as rebbe. He assumed the title on the first anniversary of his predecessor's death. Schneerson settled in Crown Heights, Brooklyn, with his wife and only left metropolitan New York for a few day trips to the Catskills in the late fifties. From Chabad headquarters at 777 Eastern Parkway, he presided over the expansion of what became one of the most visible and vigorous movements in contemporary Judaism.

When Schneerson became rebbe, the future of American Orthodox Judaism did not seem promising. American Jews were increasingly integrated into the mainstream culture, and Jewish religion and culture played a diminishing role in their lives. Schneerson, however, made it his mission and that of his followers to fight assimilation. In the fifties he founded the Lubavitch Women's Organization and the Lubavitch Youth Organization. In the sixties he directed the establishment of Chabad Houses, outreach centers near college campuses that reached tens of thousands of non-Orthodox Jews. Schneerson's emphasis was on Jewish education and community. He sent his emissaries to the streets of American cities, where Chabad "mitzvah" (good deed) tanks cruised, looking for American Jews to bring back into the fold. Chabad emissaries led prayers; distributed religious pamphlets, books, and religious objects; organized open Sabbath dinners, religious services, and holiday celebrations; and advertised their ideas in the mainstream press and on New York City subways. In 1978 they led a menorah-lighting ceremony on the White House lawn, and in the following years they organized menorah lightings at public events and in public places in cities nationwide, even at professional football games. Schneerson's talks were broadcast globally and printed in pamphlets on a regular basis, and the Chabad publishing firm, Kehot Publication Society, claimed to be the largest publisher of Jewish books in the world. Schneerson led Chabad into controversial American debates, like court battles over the separation between church and state. Chabad became involved in social service programs and humanitarian aid worldwide. Many non-Orthodox Jews looked to Schneerson as a leader, often showing their support by donating money.

Owing to a high birthrate and an influx of new members, the Lubavitchers swelled to about 200,000 worldwide in 1990, with many more supporters, making them by far the largest of all Hasidic sects. In the same year the annual budget was approximately $100 million, and Chabad was organized across six continents. As the Soviet Union fell apart in the late eighties and early nineties, Chabad, which had long operated underground in that country, forcefully took advantage of the situation by establishing Jewish institutions and reviving Orthodox Jewish observances.

Like Schneerson, many of his followers lived in Crown Heights, which in 1950 had been predominately non-Lubavitcher Jewish. As many residents left for the suburbs, Crown Heights became increasingly a black neighborhood, and tensions grew. After severe rioting in 1969, Schneerson refused to move his community because, he said, "People living in a neighborhood are responsible for one another . . . and cannot just run away" (Schneerson, p. 160). The situation was again ignited on 19 August 1991, when a car traveling with the rebbe's entourage went out of control, killing eight-year-old Gavin Cato and wounding his cousin, both of whom were black. The incident was followed by four days of rioting by blacks and the murder of Yankel Rosenbaum, a visiting Australian Lubavitcher. The events reverberated far beyond Crown Heights, grabbing national headlines and affecting the political landscape of New York State.

Because of the deference that some ultra-Orthodox Israeli politicians paid to Schneerson, his political influence extended to Israel, where he had numerous followers whose votes he controlled. Schneerson used this power to pursue ideological ends. Under Schneerson, the Lubavitchers became major supporters of a controversial amendment to the Israeli Law of Return that sought unsuccessfully to narrow the definition of who is a Jew, excluding those who had converted under Conservative and Reform rabbis. This provoked a fury among many American Jews who considered themselves Conservative and Reform. Schneerson took another position that split Jews in America and in Israel when he rejected compromise with Israel's neighbors that would exchange territories occupied by Israel for peace. The fundamental questions of Jewish identity and "land for peace" brought him into the tempest of international politics, where he remained a controversial figure as the Middle East peace process gathered momentum in the early 1990s.

In an interview with Israel Shenker of the *New York Times*, Schneerson said, "I have never given any reason for a cult of personality, . . . and I do all in my power to dissuade them from making it that" (*New York Times*, 27 Mar. 1972). He nevertheless increasingly became the center of such a cult, which, in later years at least, he did little to discourage. Because of the Lubavitch movement's long tradition of messianism, the great reverence his followers had for him, the ways in which they interpreted recent historical events, and the fact that the childless rebbe made no provisions for a successor, many Lubavitchers became convinced that he was the Messiah foretold in Jewish tradition.

The rebbe, paralyzed by a stroke in his last years, was in no position to disagree.

When Schneerson died in New York City, some still expected him to announce his messianic identity. Rabbi Shmuel Spritzer, a leader of the Lubavitch Youth Organization, said before the burial ceremony: "We are certain that he will now be resurrected. . . . The revelation will come at any moment" (*New York Times*, 13 June 1994). Subsequently, Lubavitch leaders were openly divided over the issue of messianism, which some believed would split the movement.

For the Lubavitchers, Schneerson was a holy man in a way that the vast majority of Americans would find difficult to comprehend. He was one of the most imposing figures in the resurgence of ultra-Orthodox Judaism in the United States and abroad. By combining allegiance to his tradition with mastery of modern public relations, his influence extended far beyond the confines of ultra-Orthodox Judaism. Other Hasidic groups criticized the Lubavitchers for compromising too much with the modern world. Many non-Hasidic American Jews considered them fanatics, even a cult. Yet the eminent American and Israeli politicians who attended his funeral, the Lubavitcher reactions to his death, his posthumous Congressional Gold Medal, and most of all the movement he left behind indicate that Schneerson achieved a position unparalleled for an American rabbi.

• For a general introduction to Schneerson and a selected bibliography of his work see Menachem Mendel Schneerson, *Toward a Meaningful Life*, adapted by Simon Jacobson (1995). Edward Hoffman, *Despite All Odds: The Story of Lubavitch* (1991), is an overview of the movement. Lis Harris, *Holy Days: The World of a Hasidic Family* (1985), is about life among the Lubavitchers, and her three-part article, "Holy Days," *New Yorker*, 16, 23, and 30 Sept. 1985, provides an excellent introduction to Schneerson and his movement. For Schneerson in a broad historical context see Edward S. Shapiro, *A Time for Healing: American Jewry since World War II* (1992). For an introduction to Jewish history see Robert M. Seltzer, *Jewish People, Jewish Thought: The Jewish Experience in History* (1980). See also Jerome R. Mintz, *Hasidic People: A Place in the New World* (1992). An obituary is in the *New York Times*, 13 June 1994.

DANIEL N. MOSES

SCHNEIDER, Alexander (21 Oct. 1908–2 Feb. 1993), violinist and conductor, was born Abram Sznejder at Vilna in Russian Lithuania, the son of Izhok Sznejder, a locksmith, and Chasia (maiden name unknown). Because of unsettled conditions during and following World War I, Abram Sznejder never attended school in Vilna. He learned Yiddish and Russian at home. From age five he had a violin and was supposed to practice four hours a day, but he seldom did. At thirteen he was playing with a pianist in a movie theater. At fifteen he was studying violin with Ilya Malkin, a pupil of Leopold Auer, and playing in the Vilna opera orchestra. In 1924 he went to Frankfurt, Germany, where his elder brother Mischa played cello. There he studied with violinist Adolf Rebner and played in the

Frankfurt Symphony Orchestra and at a sanatorium. By the fall of 1927 the young violinist was concertmaster of a symphony orchestra in the free city of Saarbrücken, having changed his name to Alexander Schneider to satisfy the need for a German personality. In 1929 he became concertmaster of the Norddeutscher Rundfunk, the radio orchestra in Hamburg.

Conditions in Germany were worsening with the rise of the Nazis, so it was with relief that in May 1932 Schneider became second violinist of the Budapest String Quartet, in which his brother Mischa had been cellist for two years. Tours in the United States, Australia, and the Dutch East Indies were highly successful. Thus began an association with the quartet that lasted for thirty-three years; from 1944 to 1954 Schneider occasionally filled in when the regular second violinist was ill. From the time Schneider joined the quartet, the results were extremely successful in terms of attendance and critical acclaim, less so monetarily because of the low fees the quartet was paid and the expenses of constant travel.

In the fall of 1938 the quartet played its first three concerts at the Library of Congress in Washington, D.C., beginning an association that lasted for twenty-four years. There the group laid down their personal instruments and took up four of the five Stradivaris—three violins, a viola, and a cello—given to the library by Gertrude Clarke Whittall. The Whittall Foundation paid the quartet to play at the library: a fall season, a spring season, and usually a special concert on 18 December, the death date of Antonio Stradivari.

With the spring season of 1944 Schneider left the Budapest Quartet. He was tired of being, as he only half-jokingly put it, "the world's greatest second violinist." He wanted to be free to engage in all kinds of musical activities. Nonquartet activities were impossible with the quartet's strenuous schedule and were forbidden under its strict rules limiting the four players to their roles in the ensemble. He had already been playing privately with harpsichordist Ralph Kirkpatrick, and in 1944 they began touring, playing a repertoire of eighteenth-century violin and harpsichord music. Schneider soon formed the Albeneri Trio with cellist Benar Heifetz and pianist Erich Itor Kahn; the group's name was derived from the first syllables of their respective given names. In 1948 Schneider formed the New York Quartet with violist Milton Katims, cellist Frank Miller, and pianist Mieczyslaw Horszowski.

In his next venture Schneider performed the six Bach unaccompanied violin suites. In 1950 he was responsible for Pablo Casals's coming out of his self-imposed retirement at age seventy-four to play a principal role in the first Casals Festival at Prades in French Catalonia. The festival continued every summer for several years, but Schneider resigned from it after the 1952 festival for musical and political reasons. In 1949 he formed a string quartet, in which he played first violin, to record all eighty-three of Joseph Haydn's string quartets. The sponsor was the Haydn Society, which unfortunately ran out of funds before the project was completed. In 1945 Schneider received the Elizabeth Sprague Coolidge Medal for outstanding services to chamber music. He was active as a teacher from time to time, was especially concerned with seminars and concerts for young performers, and acted as adviser to the Paul Fromm foundation, which sponsored concerts by chamber groups.

With the death of Jac Gorodetzky, Schneider's second successor in the Budapest Quartet, Schneider was persuaded in 1955 to return to the quartet as second violinist. He did so with the understanding that the number of annual concerts would be reduced—they had numbered as high as 125 a season—and that he would be allowed to continue, insofar as time permitted, his other playing and teaching activities. The quartet was together again and reached its highest peak of perfection. "Refreshingly new is a vigor and drive that seemed not there before," stated the *Washington Post* on 23 March 1956; "Everyone is a year older but the Quartet seems more than a few years younger." This new peak lasted until the early 1960s, when first violinist Roisman ran into problems with tone and intonation. Schneider stayed with the quartet through its final performances in a recording session at CBS Records in January 1965. He remained active as a teacher and as a performer with various groups. He helped found the Mostly Mozart Festival in New York. Even in his eighties he arranged concerts at the New School of Social Research in New York. On a number of Christmas Eves he conducted concerts by high school musicians at Carnegie Hall.

Schneider was twice married and twice divorced. At London in 1935 he was married to Gerda Benfey; they were separated in 1937 but not divorced until after Schneider came to the United States and went to Las Vegas. At New York in 1954 he was married to the actress Geraldine Page, from whom he was divorced in 1957. From 1948 to 1951 Schneider lived at his Beekman Place apartment in New York with the photographer Margaret Bourke-White. No children are known to have resulted from any of these relationships. Schneider died in New York City.

According to Michael Steinberg in the *New Grove Dictionary of American Music* (vol. 4, p. 157), Schneider was "a thoroughly musical, but not always subtle, player, whose performances convey infectious enthusiasm and ebullience. Into his 70s he was one of the most unquenchably energetic figures in the public musical life of the USA."

• The chief source of information on Alexander Schneider's life and works is his autobiography, *A Musical Life*, unpublished but privately printed in several copies. Some of the information found there is reported in Nat Brandt, *Con Brio: Four Russians Called the Budapest String Quartet* (1993). Allan Kozinn's obituary in the *New York Times*, 4 Feb. 1993, describes some of the high spots in Schneider's life.

WILLIAM LICHTENWANGER

SCHNEIDER, Herbert Wallace (16 Mar. 1892–15 Oct. 1984), philosopher, educator, and public administrator, was born in Berea, Ohio, the son of Frederick

William Schneider, a Methodist minister and vice president of Baldwin-Wallace College, and Marie Severinghaus. Schneider received his B.A. from Columbia College in 1915. He went on to study with Frederick J. A. Woodbridge, John Coss, and W. T. Bush and received his doctorate in 1917 with a dissertation under John Dewey, published in 1920 as *Science and Social Progress: A Philosophical Introduction to Moral Science*. In 1921 he married Caroline Catherine Smith. At Columbia he taught philosophy and religion.

When the philosophy department under the leadership of Dewey and Woodbridge enlarged the curriculum, Schneider was entrusted with putting together the Contemporary Civilization two-year course, which soon became a model of education in the humanities. He joined the editors of the *Journal of Philosophy* in the early 1920s and by 1926 assumed the responsibility for a philosophy of religion course. He was the prime mover in founding the *Review of Religion* in 1936, which became part of an effort to start an interdepartmental doctoral program in religious studies. He was similarly instrumental in launching the *Journal of the History of Philosophy* in 1963.

Schneider's wider interest in philosophy and in culture won him a prominent place in international scholarly affairs. Aside from his publishing his own books, he edited works by such thinkers as Thomas Hobbes, Adam Smith, Samuel Johnson, Thomas Jefferson, Benjamin Franklin, and John Stuart Mill; he also initiated the bibliographical work on John Dewey in 1929, reissued with a revised edition in 1939. In 1926 he went to Italy to study the newly founded Fascist state. The outcome was the first study of this political experiment, *Making the Fascist State* (1928; repr. 1968), followed by other monographs and articles, including *Making Fascists* (with S. B. Clough, 1929).

Reaching back to seventeenth-century America to trace the earliest roots of intellectual life, Schneider wrote *The Puritan Mind* (1930; repr. 1930, 1931, 1958), a careful study on how past and present interact in interpretations. It signaled the beginning of a strong interest in the history of religion in colonial America that was to continue throughout his career. With Horace Friess, he published *Religion in Various Cultures* (1932). In 1938 he published his *Meditations in Season: On the Elements of Christian Philosophy*, and in 1939 he wrote a pamphlet, *Natural Religion*. In 1942 he edited, with George Lawton, *A Prophet and a Pilgrim: Being the Incredible History of Thomas Lake Harris and Laurence Oliphant*, dealing with religious cults in California. Also in 1942, his first marriage having ended, he married Grenofore Westphal; they had three sons.

At the suggestion of John Coss, Schneider began work on his *History of American Philosophy*, which was published in 1946. He maintained that intellectual life in America had a start of its own in the colonial period. Thinkers of that period worked selectively with the traditions of Europe and in relation to problems of their own in their new environment. The vitality of philosophy in America emerged as reinterpretations

of these borrowings. It was not until the end of the nineteenth century that universities presented philosophy as a separate field of inquiry. In a second edition he added discussions on critical realism, pragmatism, and naturalism (a philosophical position that excludes dualisms and absolute discontinuities; relies on the continuity of the scientific method as the only intellectually trustworthy criticism of experience; and views all subject matters of inquiry as being in principle intelligible, their regularities discoverable, and their respective theories subject to constant revision).

Schneider was elected president of the American Philosophical Association in 1948. From 1953 to 1956 he served as head of the UNESCO Division of International Cultural Cooperation in Paris. In this position he promoted conferences and exchanges of scholars, founded the International Association for the History of Religions, and started the International Bibliography of Philosophy. Upon his return to the United States, he published *Three Dimensions of Public Morality* (1956) based on the Mahlon Powell Foundation Lectures at Indiana University. Invited in 1957 to start the Claremont Graduate School as its first dean, Schneider moved to Claremont, California, where he also directed the Blaisdell Institute for Advanced Study in World Cultures and Religions from 1957 to 1963.

Morals for Mankind was published in 1960, a mature work continuing ideas that originated in seminars in ethics and politics he conducted with Dewey. Schneider argued for the need to establish a global and cooperative framework in support of shared values and activities to meet the emerging worldwide common concerns in religious, community, cultural, and educational affairs.

Published as *Ways of Being: Elements of Analytic Ontology*, Schneider's Woodbridge lectures at Columbia in 1962 discussed metaphysics. Continuing Dewey's naturalism, Schneider developed an ontology to explore the ways of "how" real things are and are viewed in their natural settings rather than in whole systems. He discussed three such ways of being—natural, cultural, and formal—each with its own features, and each requiring distinct yet continuous modes of investigation. Schneider called this approach "objective relativism."

Schneider retired in 1957 and died in Claremont, California. He contributed significantly to the philosophy of humanistic naturalism in ethics, political philosophy, metaphysics, and religion.

• Schneider's personal papers and library were donated to Southern Illinois University and became part of its extensive collections in American philosophy. Articles on Schneider's views on religion, political thought, and philosophy have appeared in diverse journals in the United States and other countries. His activities and place in the development of the Department of Philosophy at Columbia University are discussed by John Herman Randall, Jr., and Horace Friess in *A History of the Faculty of Philosophy, Columbia University*, ed. Jacques Barzun (1957). Biographical and bibliographical essays compiled by Craig Walton and John P. Anton, eds., are in *Philosophy and the Civilizing Arts: Essays Presented to Herbert W. Schneider on His Eightieth Birthday* (1974). See also Andrew J. Reck, *The New American Philosophers* (1968), and John E. Smith, "Herbert Schneider on the History of American Philosophy," *Journal of the History of Philosophy* 25, no. 1 (Jan. 1987): 169–77. An obituary is in the *New York Times*, 15 Oct. 1984.

JOHN P. ANTON

SCHNEIDERMAN, Rose (6 Apr. 1882–11 Aug. 1972), labor organizer and trade union official, was born in Saven, Poland, the daughter of Adolph Samuel Schneiderman, a tailor, and Deborah Rothman, a seamstress. Schneiderman grew up in a poor, Orthodox Jewish family that unlike most stressed the importance of education for their daughters as well as for their sons. She entered a local Hebrew school at age four and went on to public school two years later. In 1890, seeking to escape the poverty and religious persecution that most Jews faced in what was then Russian Poland, the Schneidermans immigrated to the United States. Like countless other Eastern European immigrants, the family made their home on the Lower East Side of New York City. Only two years later, Adolph Schneiderman suddenly died. Rose, the oldest, was ten years old at the time, and her mother was left a widow with three young children to support, with a fourth child due any moment.

Once her baby was weaned, Deborah Schneiderman found work in a factory making fur capes, placing her three older children in a Hebrew orphanage. Although Rose only spent a year in the orphanage, her brothers would spend several years there. When she returned home, Schneiderman managed to combine schoolwork with looking after her baby sister as their mother continued to work long hours at the fur cape factory. When her mother was laid off in 1895, Schneiderman went to work in a local department store. She was thirteen years old and had managed to complete the ninth grade.

Schneiderman found her first job through the United Hebrew Charities. Her mother approved, not only because now her daughter was the primary wage earner in the family, but also because retail work was seen as far more respectable than factory work. However, the wages were far less. Working sixty-four hours a week, Schneiderman earned $2.16. After three years she was making only $2.75 a week. Hearing about a job sewing linings for men's caps, Schneiderman entered factory work and was soon making $6 a week though the hours were still long. Like most garment workers, she was expected to furnish her own needles and thread as well as her own sewing machine. In 1902 Schneiderman, her mother, and younger sister spent a year in Montreal, living with more prosperous relatives. Schneiderman found work in a cap factory there; but her mother could not find a job, and so the three returned to New York within a year. But while living in Montreal, Schneiderman became friends with the Kellert family. Devout Socialists, the Kellerts opened Schneiderman's eyes to the world of politics

and the necessity of trade unionism for exploited workers such as herself.

When she returned to the same cap factory in New York, she became good friends with Bessie Braut, a new coworker who was an anarchist. Together the two women set about organizing their workplace. By January 1903 Schneiderman and her fellow women capmakers were organized into Local 23 of the United Cloth Hat and Cap Makers' Union. She was elected the local's first secretary and a delegate to the New York City Central Labor Union. In early 1905 the Cap Makers' Union went out on strike for thirteen weeks, demanding higher wages and better working conditions. Schneiderman, not yet twenty-three years old, honed her abilities as an organizer and as a speaker during the strike, leading meetings and walking the picket line. Only four feet nine inches tall, with flaming red hair, she was a commanding presence within the labor movement.

Although her union had assisted in the organization of her shop, Schneiderman was well aware of how difficult it was to get women involved in an ambivalent trade union movement. At that time, much of organized labor was dominated by men, despite the fact that women were an increasing part of the total labor force, particularly in the textile and garment industries. In part because their wages were lower as they were confined to the less skilled parts of production and because they were seen as only temporary workers before marriage, women were frequently dismissed by trade unions at the turn of the century.

When she was approached during the 1905 strike by the Women's Trade Union League (WTUL), Schneiderman sensed that this group might be able to effect necessary changes. Formed in 1903 as a cross-class alliance of working-class women trade unionists and middle- and upper-class women supporters, soon called the "allies," the WTUL sought to organize women workers into existing but generally male-dominated trade unions. At first she was hesitant about the WTUL, for she could not understand why wealthy women would be interested in the labor movement. But after the New York WTUL provided helpful publicity during the 1905 capmakers' strike, Schneiderman was swayed by the possibilities of a cross-class effort aimed at addressing the needs of women workers. In 1906 she was elected vice president of the New York branch of the WTUL, and in 1908, with the financial assistance of one of the allies, Schneiderman left her job in the cap factory and worked as an organizer for the WTUL while taking night classes at the Rand School of Social Science.

In 1909, after a brief strike, Schneiderman organized women white-goods workers into Local 62 of the International Ladies Garment Workers' Union (ILGWU). Later that same year she was one of the most effective leaders of a much larger strike of women garment makers in New York, called the "Uprising of the Thirty Thousand." By the time the strike ended in 1910, Schneiderman had left school and was organizing full time for the WTUL in addition to serving as president of Local 62. Women garment workers faced horrendous conditions in the city's hundreds of sweatshops. In 1911, when a fire broke out in one such nonunion shop, the Triangle Shirtwaist factory, 146 women died because the company routinely kept the factory doors locked, supposedly to prevent employee theft but also to stop union organizers from entering the shop. Schneiderman would remember this tragedy for the rest of her life, seeing it as the ultimate justification for the organization of women.

At the same time, she increasingly came to see the need for women to have the vote. In 1912 she went to work for the National American Woman Suffrage Association, speaking across the country to women such as herself, explaining how suffrage would give working-class women yet another weapon to fight the harsh conditions of their labor. After one year, however, Schneiderman returned to labor organizing, leading ILGWU Local 62 in a general strike. Frequently frustrated by what she saw as a lack of true understanding of the needs of immigrant working women among the well-to-do allies of the WTUL, Schneiderman worked as an organizer for the ILGWU until 1917. But here, too, she experienced another kind of frustration. While most of the union's members were women, most of the leaders were men, often disinterested in what Schneiderman had to say. Despite the class and ethnic differences, she found it easier to achieve her goal—the organization of working-class women—through the WTUL rather than through the male-dominated trade union movement. She returned to the league in 1917 and was elected president of the New York branch the following year, serving until 1949. She was elected president of the National WTUL in 1926, holding that position until 1950, when the league itself disbanded.

As WTUL president on the local and national level, Schneiderman channeled much of her energy toward legislation to protect women workers, especially laws regarding maximum hours and minimum wages. In 1920 she ran for the U.S. Senate on the New York Farmer-Labor ticket and lost. Long a Socialist, she turned away from radical politics during the politically conservative 1920s. Her growing friendship with Eleanor Roosevelt brought Schneiderman into Democratic state politics, and she often discussed the needs of labor with Franklin Roosevelt during his years as governor of New York. Once president, Roosevelt appointed Schneiderman in 1933 to the National Recovery Administration (NRA), part of his New Deal attempt to end the Great Depression. She was the only woman appointed to the NRA Advisory Board, which set industrywide codes of production, wages, and prices. When the NRA was found unconstitutional in 1935, Schneiderman returned to New York, focusing on her duties as WTUL president. There she helped organize hotel workers and laundry workers and successfully lobbied the New York state assembly for an eight-hour day and a minimum wage. Although she always preferred the more active role of labor organizer,

Schneiderman served as secretary of labor for the state of New York from 1937 to 1943.

Although the National WTUL closed down in 1950, the New York branch remained active until 1955, as did Rose Schneiderman. When that organization, which she had belonged to for fifty years, ceased to exist, she retired. She never married and died in New York City's Jewish Home and Hospital for the Aged. Before entering the home in 1967, she spent her last few years writing her autobiography, *All for One* (1967), which focuses not so much on her personal accomplishments as on the collective efforts of many involved in labor organizing. Yet she personally dedicated her life to the women's trade union movement in the hopes of improving working conditions for all.

• Schneiderman's papers are at the Taminent Library, New York University, which also has the papers of the New York Women's Trade Union League. See also the papers of the National Women's Trade Union League, held by the Library of Congress and the Schlesinger Library, Radcliffe College. The papers of the WTUL are also on a microfilm series, *The Papers of the Women's Trade Union League and Its Principal Leaders* (1981). Schneiderman's autobiography, *All for One* (1967), is a most useful source. Also helpful is a biographical portrait by Alice Kessler-Harris, "Rose Schneiderman," in *Labor Leaders in America*, ed. Warren Van Tine and Melvyn Dubofsky (1987), pp. 160–84. Annelise Orleck examines the life and work of Schneiderman, along with that of her cohorts Fannia Cohn, Pauline Newman, and Clara Lemlich Shavelson, in *Common Sense and a Little Fire: Women and Working-Class Politics in the United States, 1900–1965* (1995). On the New York and National WTUL, in which Schneiderman played key roles, see Nancy Schrom Dye, *As Equals and As Sisters: Feminism, the Labor Movement, and the Women's Trade Union League of New York* (1980), and Robin Miller Jacoby, *The British and American Women's Trade Union Leagues, 1890–1925: A Case Study of Feminism and Class* (1994). An obituary is in the *New York Times*, 12 Aug. 1972.

KATHLEEN BANKS NUTTER

SCHOEBEL, Elmer (8 Sept. 1896–14 Dec. 1970), jazz pianist, composer, and arranger, was born in East St. Louis, Illinois. When he was a boy, his family moved to Champaign, Illinois, where he learned the piano and played in movie houses by the age of fourteen. From 1912 to 1917 he worked as a pianist for touring vaudeville shows and then served as a soldier in the First World War. In 1920 Schoebel traveled to Chicago with the 20th Century Jazz Band and settled in that city.

Schoebel, a formally trained musician, was one of the few white jazz pianists in Chicago who could read and write music. His skills gained him work as a songwriter, arranger, and pianist with many pickup bands, and in 1922 the cornetist Paul Mares hired Schoebel for a group that would play at the Friars' Inn nightclub. Mares, the clarinetist Leon Rappolo, the trombonist George Brunies, and the bassist Arnold Loyecano were New Orleans players and masters of the popular new "Dixieland" style; they quickly tutored Schoebel, the saxophonist Jack Pettis, the drummer

Frank Snyder, and the banjoist Louis Black in that style. Loyecano recalled, "I was a good [music] reader and so was Elmer, and we sort of helped the others when they needed it" (Hentoff and Shapiro, p. 82). Billed as the Friars' Society Orchestra, the band played in a colorful, gangland-run nightclub milieu that epitomized the Jazz Age. The band made recordings in 1922 and 1923, and in the second year it renamed itself the New Orleans Rhythm Kings (NORK). Appearing months before the Joe "King" Oliver band's historic "race records," the NORK disks gave jazz aficionados and the national audience their first exposure to the blues inflections and complex ensemble improvisation that became the hallmarks of the classic jazz tradition. Young white players in Chicago, in particular, flocked to the Friars' Inn to hear the famous group. Despite his talents, Schoebel never became a major force in the band (which was dominated by Mares and Rapollo), and on recordings his piano playing is almost inaudible. Mel Stitzel took his place as the NORK pianist in 1923, just before the group disbanded.

Schoebel then led his own group at the Midway Gardens from 1924 to 1925, a band that featured some former NORK members as well as the local teenage clarinetist Benny Goodman. Later in 1925 he traveled to New York with the Isham Jones Orchestra, one of the most popular jazz groups in the nation, but the following year he returned to Chicago to work for bandleaders Louis Panico and Art Kassel. In 1927 he again led a band, appearing on WGEJ radio in Chicago, and in 1929 he fronted his own Elmer Schoebel Friars' Society Orchestra. During this busy time, Schoebel began to compose popular songs that were often used for jazz improvisation, including "Bugle Call Rag," "Farewell Blues," "House of David Blues," "Nobody's Sweetheart," "Prince of Wails," and "Spanish Shawl." He also became one of jazz's earliest arrangers. Chicago publishers employed him to transcribe recordings by King Oliver, Jelly Roll Morton, and others for print arrangements. A long-term relationship with the Melrose Brothers Music Company resulted.

During the Great Depression, Schoebel dabbled in electrical engineering, inventing the "tunematic" radio and attempting to manufacture the device. In 1935 he moved to New York and became the chief musical arranger for Warner Brothers' music publishing office. This work corresponded with the new popularity of big-band swing, and Schoebel's compositions and arrangements became increasingly accomplished and complex. After World War II, he returned to piano playing and toured in the early 1950s with the Conrad Janis and Tommy Lyman groups. In 1956 Schoebel moved to St. Petersburg, Florida, where he performed occasionally with the Blue Rhythm Rebels and Arnie Mossler's Suncoaters. His last performance was with the Mossler group two days before his death in Pinellas Park, near St. Petersburg. He was survived by his wife, Esther A. Schoebel, a daughter, and four grandchildren.

Schoebel's lack of recordings and his low profile as a performer belie the significance of his career as representative of many facets of the world of early jazz. His early work with the New Orleans Rhythm Kings indicated how quickly midwestern whites embraced the Dixieland sound and how jazz easily became an avocation for members of the white middle class. Schoebel's growth as an arranger demonstrated the rapid adaptation of jazz to written notation and the sheet music industry. His revived performing career in Florida in the 1950s and 1960s reflected jazz's new vigor as nostalgic entertainment for the Sun Belt's growing elderly population, as well as for many other listeners in that region.

• A discography of Schoebel's recordings is in Brian Rust, *Jazz Records, 1897–1942*, 4th ed., vol. 2 (1978). The New Orleans Rhythm Kings are discussed in Nat Hentoff and Nat Shapiro, *Hear Me Talkin' to Ya* (1955); Martin Williams, "N.O.R.K.," in *Jazz Masters of New Orleans*, rev. ed. (1978); and James Lincoln Collier, *Benny Goodman and the Swing Era* (1989). An obituary is in the *St. Petersburg Times*, 15 Dec. 1970.

BURTON W. PERETTI

SCHOENBERG, Arnold (13 Sept. 1874–13 July 1951), composer and musical theorist, was born Arnold Franz Walter Schönberg in Vienna, Austria, the son of Samuel Schönberg, the proprietor of a shoe shop, and Pauline Nachod. He received his primary and secondary schooling in Vienna. He began violin lessons at age eight and was soon composing little violin duets. He progressed from violin to viola and then to the cello and began playing in quartets and other string ensembles. He next started to compose string quartets, having learned the rudiments of sonata from articles in an encyclopedia. The death of his father at the end of 1890 forced Schoenberg to leave secondary school to begin work as a clerk in a bank, a job he soon hated. In 1893 the talented composer and conductor Alexander von Zemlinsky began conducting an amateur orchestra in which Schoenberg played cello. Zemlinsky, only about three years older than Schoenberg, soon became a close friend and was Schoenberg's only instructor in composition. Schoenberg quit the bank in 1895, announcing that he intended to make his career in music. He converted from Judaism to Protestantism in 1898.

Schoenberg earned a meager living over the next few years conducting amateur choruses and doing hackwork for music publishers such as scoring other composers' operettas and making piano arrangements of their orchestral works. In 1899 he completed his first major composition, a string sextet titled *Verklärte Nacht* (Transfigured night). This work, greatly influenced by the music of Richard Wagner, was first performed in Vienna in 1902. In 1900–1901 Schoenberg was chiefly at work on a huge cantata, *Gurrelieder* (Songs of Gurre), which called for five vocal soloists, a speaker, four choirs, and an immense orchestra. He completed the orchestration of this music in 1911, and its first performance in Vienna in 1913 was one of his few popular successes.

Schoenberg married Zemlinsky's sister, Mathilde, in October 1901; they had two children. In December of that year they moved to Berlin, where Schoenberg became the musical director of a popular cabaret. In 1902 he secured a position teaching composition at the Stern Conservatory in Berlin, on the recommendation of well-established composer Richard Strauss. Strauss's encouragement also led him to compose a large-scale symphonic poem, *Pelleas und Melisande*, in 1903. In July of that year Schoenberg and his family returned to Vienna. He taught composition for a year in a short-lived music school and in 1904 began giving private lessons in composition. Among his first students were Anton von Webern and Alban Berg, both of whom became distinguished composers and lifelong friends and disciples of Schoenberg. Schoenberg found that he liked teaching; it was an important part of his activities thereafter. In 1905 he completed the string quartet that he formally declared to be his first quartet, and in 1906 he produced his Chamber Symphony no. 1. In about 1907 he began to paint in oils, chiefly abstract human faces and figures. His activity in this field continued until about 1911. He was not a great artist, but his paintings are of sufficient interest to be reexamined occasionally.

All of Schoenberg's music before 1908 was basically tonal in nature; that is, it made use of the diatonic scale traditional in Western classical music. In 1908 Schoenberg abandoned tonality in favor of atonality, the treatment of all the tones of the chromatic scale as being musically equal to one another. The result of this practice was music often much more dissonant and complex than heretofore. This in turn led to frequent incomprehension or outright hostility on the part of audiences long accustomed to tonal music. Thus began the alienation of much of the musical public from the music of Schoenberg and his followers, which persisted during his lifetime and long after. The first important example of Schoenberg's new phase was the Second String Quartet of 1908, which caused an uproarious outburst of catcalls, jeers, and whistling on door-keys at its premier in December of that year. Most of the newspaper reviews denounced Schoenberg and his quartet; one claimed that "it sounded like a convocation of cats" (MacDonald, p. 1). From that time onward the sensitive composer was both defensive and belligerent about all of his creations. He produced several important works in his new style in 1909, including the Five Orchestral Pieces, Opus 16, and the surrealistic monodrama *Erwartung*.

In 1911 Schoenberg completed and published the first edition of *Harmonielehre* (Treatise on harmony), a large textbook on the history and theory of harmonic practice, still a standard work on the subject. In September of that year he and his family again moved to Berlin, hoping to improve their economic situation. There he again lectured at the Stern Conservatory and took on a number of old and new private composition students. In 1912 he completed *Pierrot Lunaire*, a chamber work for five musicians and a female reciter who is required to speak in precise musical pitches

(called *sprechtstimme* or "speech song"). This music, depicting the bizarre adventures of Pierrot the clown by the light of an omnipresent moon, was both one of the most controversial and one of the most frequently performed of his works.

During 1912–1915 Schoenberg was becoming increasingly well known beyond Austria and Germany, and he traveled to music centers such as Prague, Amsterdam, St. Petersburg, and London to conduct his own works. In the summer of 1915 he and his family returned to Vienna when he was ordered to report for a medical examination for military service in World War I. He was called up in December of that year and served in a noncombatant regiment in Austria until October 1916, when he was released. His health declined at this time, and he began to suffer the asthma attacks that plagued him for the rest of his life. He was called up again in September 1917, only to be discharged as physically unfit in December.

Partly because of the upheavals of World War I and partly on account of the difficulties of earning a living during the war years, Schoenberg composed little music from 1913 to 1920. However, he was also seeking a new method of composing at this time. He seems to have worked out the basic idea of the method by 1921. This invention of Schoenberg's was the twelve-tone system or serial method of composition in which every theme, harmony, or accompaniment in a specific musical work is based on a particular arrangement (or row) of the twelve tones or notes of the chromatic scale. This arrangement remains unaltered throughout the composition. The composer must select his row before he begins the actual work of composing. Schoenberg always insisted that his twelve-tone system was only a method of composition and that, far from constricting his musical inspirations, it allowed them to flow freely. The musical results, not the method employed, were the important thing. "I can't say it often enough," he once wrote, "my works are twelve-note *compositions*, not *twelve-note* compositions" (MacDonald, p. 88). He used the twelve-tone method in whole or in part in most of the music he wrote from about 1921 to the end of his life. Notable examples of such compositions are the Five Piano Pieces, Opus 23 (1923); the Serenade, Opus 24 (1923); the Wind Quintet (1924); the Third String Quartet (1927); the Variations for Orchestra, Opus 31 (1928); and the opera *Moses und Aron* (1932). The twelve-tone method had a profound influence on composers of classical music into the late twentieth century.

Mathilde Schoenberg died in October 1923. In August 1924 Arnold married Gertrude Kolisch, the sister of one of his composition pupils, violinist Rudolf Kolisch. This second marriage produced three children. In 1926 Schoenberg moved once more to Berlin, where he had been appointed head of the master class for advanced students of composition at the Prussian Academy of Arts. This position was not only one of considerable prestige but also one that allowed him to live more affluently than at any other time in his life and gave him ample free time for composition, travel, lecturing, and conducting. The only drawback was that the climate of Berlin adversely affected his health.

This happy period came to a sudden end with the takeover of Germany by Adolf Hitler and his Nazi party in January 1933. Not only was Schoenberg of entirely Jewish ancestry, but his atonal and twelve-tone music was anathema to Nazi ideas of musical correctness. He and his family fled to Paris on 17 May of that year, and in July, partly from a renewed conviction and partly as a symbol of protest, he returned to Judaism. In October he agreed to accept a teaching position at the Malkin Conservatory of Music in Boston. He sailed from France on 25 October.

Schoenberg was disappointed both with the Malkin Conservatory and with Boston. The school was small and the students few and ill prepared. The New England winter severely taxed his already poor health. In the autumn of 1934 he moved to Los Angeles, seeking a better climate.

In the spring of 1935 Schoenberg lectured at the University of Southern California. Working with his usual dogged determination, he gradually mastered the English language. In the autumn of 1936 he became a professor of music at the University of California in Los Angeles. He held this position until 1944, when he reached the mandatory retirement age of seventy. He proved to be a popular teacher at UCLA, giving courses ranging from lectures on elementary counterpoint to graduate seminars in composition and theory. He never, either at UCLA or earlier, pushed his advanced composition students to write atonal or twelve-tone music, though they could if they so desired. He did not have any American students who became as well known as Alban Berg and Anton Webern, but some did go on to respected careers as composers and professors, notably Earl Kim and Leon Kirchner. Schoenberg had a brief friendship with popular American composer George Gershwin, which ended with Gershwin's death in 1937; the two respected each other as both men and musicians. Schoenberg and his wife became American citizens on 11 April 1941.

Schoenberg composed a number of important works during his American years, including the Violin Concerto (1936); the Fourth String Quartet (1936); the Second Chamber Symphony (1939; begun in 1906); the *Ode to Napoleon Buonaparte* (1942), an ironic work that by implication was an attack on all dictators, especially Hitler; and the Piano Concerto (1942). All of them, with the exception of the chamber symphony, were twelve-tone compositions. Because of his brief tenure at UCLA, his pension was small, and he was therefore obliged to once again take private pupils and deliver occasional lectures, despite his declining health. He suffered a near-fatal heart attack on 2 August 1946. However, on 20 August he began a string trio, which he completed a month later. This work, by his own testimony, reflected the experience of the heart attack. Though he was a semi-invalid for the remaining five years of his life, he did manage to compose one more striking work in 1947: *A Survivor from Warsaw*, scored for speaker, male chorus, and orchestra. In this piece, lasting about seven minutes, he conveyed the essence of his personal reaction to the horrors of the Jewish Holocaust. Always superstitious, Schoenberg had a fear of dying on Friday the thirteenth; the final irony of his life was that he did indeed do so, at home in Los Angeles.

Schoenberg's lengthy residence in the United States seems to have had little obvious influence on his music, but he himself influenced the American musical scene through his students in California. However, his ideas and his music affected in a much broader and more profound sense several generations of composers in both America and Europe. His place as one of the great innovators in twentieth-century classical music is secure. However, he always wanted something more: the popular acceptance of his music. "There is nothing I long for more intensely," he wrote in 1947, "than to be taken for a better sort of Tchaikovsky—for heaven's sake: a bit better, but really that's all. Or if anything more, than that people should know my tunes and whistle them" (Stuckenschmidt, p. 484). His works have not achieved this kind of success. Only a few of his early compositions are heard at all frequently either in concerts or on recordings. His music remains more cited than performed, more respected than loved.

• Some of Schoenberg's musical manuscripts are in the Music Division of the Library of Congress, Washington, D.C. The bulk of his musical and nonmusical manuscripts and other memorabilia were as of 1997 in the hands of the Schoenberg family, pending final deposit in an archive. His principal books, besides *Harmonielehre* (published in a complete English translation in 1978 as *Theory of Harmony*), are *Models for Beginners in Composition* (1942); *Style and Idea*, ed. Dika Newlin (1950); and *Structural Functions of Harmony* (1954). The most lengthy and detailed biography in English is H. H. Stuckenschmidt, *Schoenberg: His Life, World and Work*, trans. Humphrey Searle (1977). Two good, brief biographies are Willi Reich, *Schoenberg: A Critical Biography*, trans. Leo Black (1971), and Malcolm MacDonald, *Schoenberg* (1976). See also Charles Rosen, *Arnold Schoenberg* (1975), and Alexander L. Ringer, *Arnold Schoenberg: The Composer as Jew* (1990). For the most recent scholarly studies of Schoenberg and his disciples, see the *Journal of the Arnold Schoenberg Institute* (1976–). For complete lists of his compositions and full bibliographies of writings by and about Schoenberg, see the article on him in H. Wiley Hitchcock and Stanley Sadie, eds., *The New Grove Dictionary of American Music* (4 vols., 1986).

JOHN E. LITTLE

SCHOENBRUN, David Franz (15 Mar. 1915–23 May 1988), broadcast journalist, was born in New York City, the son of Max Schoenbrun, a traveling jewelry salesman, and Lucy Cassirer. Schoenbrun's career in news began in large part because of his fluency in foreign languages. After graduating from New York City College in 1934, he worked as a high school teacher of French and Spanish. He also worked as a labor relations adjuster, as an editor of a trade newsletter for the Dress Manufacturers Association, and as a freelance writer. In 1942 he worked for the Office of War Information doing propaganda analysis on the western European news desk.

Schoenbrun joined the U.S. Army in 1943 and was sent to Algiers, where he directed the Allied Forces newsroom and did a weekly radio commentary (in French and English) for United Nations radio. He covered major battles in France and Germany, and after being discharged in 1945 he remained in Paris to manage a bureau there for the Overseas News Agency. Edward R. Murrow heard his wartime and postwar reports and hired him to run the CBS News Paris Bureau in 1947. A colleague, Fred W. Friendly, said in Schoenbrun's obituary in the *New York Times*, "There were people who were more handsome. There were people with more charisma, and people who better understood the chemistry of television. But nobody ever covered Paris and Charles de Gaulle as well as he did."

Another colleague, Don Hewitt, recalled that Schoenbrun's office at 33 Champs Élysées and his apartment on avenue Bosquet at rue Cognac-Jay became well known, "a stopping off place for everybody who was anybody who was coming to Paris." De Gaulle was slow to warm to most Americans, but gradually he came to have a good working relationship with the CBS bureau chief. Schoenbrun quickly established a solid reputation in covering France, which included trips to cover French colonial problems in Algeria and French Indochina. He occasionally returned to the United States for special coverage of events such as elections, but he did not permanently return from Paris until 1961, when he replaced Howard K. Smith in the dual role of top Washington correspondent and bureau chief. The shuffle did not work. He had to catch up because his contacts in the new John F. Kennedy administration were not as deep or developed as those of some of his colleagues in the Washington bureau. He also was frequently at odds with producers in New York because he demanded more time for the bureau's reports.

Network officials grudgingly gave Schoenbrun a Sunday noontime slot for a half-hour news analysis and interview program. This took on added significance on 28 October 1962 when Radio Moscow said that Soviet missiles in Cuba would be withdrawn, effectively ending the Cuban Missile Crisis. Schoenbrun and his staff, with just minutes to airtime, learned of the news, scrapped all plans, brought in guests and film, and ad-libbed the program. He was speaking on the air via a phone link with Marvin Kalb, the Moscow correspondent. Kalb was speaking of the grim faces and muted tones that greeted the news in Moscow. Schoenbrun saw an emergency signal flashing and quickly took a break. He picked up the studio phone and heard the voice of Pierre Salinger, the presidential press secretary. Salinger said he was in an Oval Office meeting and that it was far too dangerous to stress a Soviet defeat; Soviet premier Nikita Khrushchev might be so angered and humiliated that he would change his mind about withdrawing the missiles. Schoenbrun got back on the air and on the phone with

Kalb and quickly redirected the conversation along the lines of "a victory for peace and all mankind." Schoenbrun later wrote about the "powerful national impact" and the "unprecedented break with television procedures, one that raised troubling ethical and political problems."

By 1963 Schoenbrun and then CBS News president Dick Salant were at odds. Salant wanted to end Schoenbrun's Sunday program and instead give him some undefined role on the "CBS Evening News," then expanding from fifteen to thirty minutes. Schoenbrun was too committed to long-form analysis and commentary to accept the arrangement, eventually reaching a contract settlement and leaving CBS. He then took a series of part-time and freelance jobs, all to fulfill his desire for commentary/analysis and his passion for travel. He served as a correspondent for ABC News and Metromedia from 1963 to 1979 and as an analyst for Independent Network News from 1980 until his death. He also served as narrator and reporter for documentaries on public television, and he wrote occasional articles for *Parade* magazine. Schoenbrun also was a senior lecturer in international affairs at Columbia University starting in 1967, a year later joining the New School for Social Research and working there for the next two decades. In addition, he did charity work for the United Jewish Appeal and had frequent public speaking engagements. In the last two years of his life he served as historian for the New York Friars Club.

David Schoenbrun's historical significance is as both historian and journalist. He was the conduit through which many Americans learned of postwar France. He not only interviewed world leaders; he counseled them, as he did with Franklin D. Roosevelt, Dwight D. Eisenhower, John F. Kennedy, British prime minister Winston Churchill, and French president Charles de Gaulle.

Schoenbrun also was one of the earliest voices against Western intervention in Indochina. He first interviewed Ho Chi Minh in 1946 in a Paris coffee shop, and Ho warned him that war with France would break out. In 1954 he was the only American to report from the fortress of Dienbienphu just before its fall. In 1961 he warned President Kennedy about getting involved in Vietnam; in 1967 he was the first American broadcast correspondent to get into North Vietnam, and he freelanced that report for ABC.

Schoenbrun won Overseas Press Club honors for distinguished reporting in 1951, 1953, and 1956. In 1958 the same group honored him for the best book on foreign affairs, *As France Goes* (1957). The French government in 1948 awarded him the Croix de Guerre and in 1952 named him a chevalier of the Legion of Honor. His colleagues recall his dedication to the best reporting and his keen analytical sense.

Schoenbrun had married Dorothy Scher in 1938. Their only child, Lucy, was born in Paris in 1947. Lucy and her husband, Robert Szekely, frequently accompanied Schoenbrun in his later years on reporting trips to Israel. He died in New York City. David Schoenbrun will be remembered as one of "Edward R.

Murrow's boys," the crew of CBS radio and television correspondents who set ethical and journalistic standards for the developing forms of broadcast news.

• Some of the best sources concerning Schoenbrun are his own writings. He developed an interest in French history and wrote several books about prominent events in France, including *The Three Lives of Charles de Gaulle* (1966), *Triumph in Paris: The Exploits of Benjamin Franklin* (1976), and *Soldiers of the Night: The Story of the French Resistance* (1980). His daughter and son-in-law collaborated with him on *The New Israelis* (1973). Schoenbrun also wrote *America Inside Out* (1984), a series of personal and historical reflections; *Vietnam: How We Got In, How to Get Out* (1968), an early call for U.S. withdrawal; and *On and Off the Air* (1989), an informal history of CBS News, published shortly after his death. Schoenbrun's colleagues John Corporan and Marvin Scott, his agent Richard Leibner, and his widow were interviewed for this essay. An obituary is in the *New York Times*, 24 May 1988.

MARK D. HARMON

SCHOENHEIMER, Rudolph (10 May 1898–11 Sept. 1941), biochemist, was born in Berlin, Germany, the son of Hugo Schoenheimer, a gynecologist, and Gertrude Edel. After receiving his early education in local schools, Schoenheimer graduated from the Real Gymnasium in Berlin in 1916. He was immediately drafted into the German army and spent two years fighting on the western front. On discharge from the army at the end of the First World War, he began the study of medicine at the University of Berlin, where he received his M.D. in 1922.

After graduating Schoenheimer remained in academic medicine and served as resident pathologist at the Moabit Hospital in Berlin, studying the production of atherosclerosis by administering cholesterol to animals. Schoenheimer advanced his biological and physiological knowledge, with the aid of a Rockefeller Foundation fellowship, through three years of study at the University of Leipzig under Karl Thomas, a biochemist interested in elucidating metabolic pathways. At Leipzig, he continued his studies on the role of cholesterol in the production of atherosclerosis.

While at Leipzig, Schoenheimer made an important contribution by developing a unique procedure for synthesizing peptides. Schoenheimer left Leipzig and spent eighteen months in the laboratory of Peter Rona to fill in gaps in his knowledge of physiology and biochemistry. In 1926 he joined the famed pathologist Ludwig Aschoff on the faculty of the University of Freiburg, with the rank of docent (assistant professor). Schoenheimer spent 1930–1931 in the United States as the Douglas Smith Fellow at the University of Chicago. Following his fellowship, Schoenheimer returned to the University of Freiburg, where he became head of the Department of Pathological Chemistry. In his new position at Freiburg, Schoenheimer continued his work on the mechanism by which the body handles cholesterol and demonstrated that the body's cholesterol exists in a dynamic state, continuously undergoing degradation and synthesis.

In April 1933, after gaining control of the German government, Adolf Hitler's Nazi regime issued an edict ordering the dismissal of all Jewish faculty members in German universities. Hearing of Schoenheimer's plight, Professor Hans T. Clark immediately offered him an assistant professorship at Columbia University in New York. In 1937 Schoenheimer married Salome Glucksohn, a zoologist who had earned a Ph.D. at the University of Freiburg. She continued her scientific work after they emigrated to the United States. They had no children.

At Columbia Schoenheimer, along with Walter M. Sperry, continued his work on the metabolism of cholesterol and made other important contributions to research on atherosclerosis, such as developing a technique for measuring trace amounts of cholesterol in blood, serum, and plasma.

Harold Urey's successful concentration of heavy hydrogen in 1934 was the stimulus for Schoenheimer's most significant research. Urey's deuterium provided a means of labeling metabolic intermediates without changing their chemical properties. Such labeled compounds were ideal substances for following metabolic pathways. Working in Urey's laboratory with David Rittenberg, Schoenheimer developed methods for synthesizing lipid compounds labeled with deuterium (linseed oil hydrogenated with the label deuterium), then studied the fate of the compounds in experimental animals. Before this study, it had been believed that animals used fats directly from freshly ingested foods, drawing on fat stores only during starvation. Schoenheimer's experiments demonstrated that, even during starvation, fatty acids were stored in the depots of the body. Schoenheimer and Rittenberg also fed heavy water (deuterium oxide, or D_2O) to rats and found that heavy hydrogen showed up in various compounds, thus revealing the active use of water in metabolic processes. These experiments were the first demonstration of the dynamic transfer of water in metabolic processes.

Urey's concentration of the heavy isotope of nitrogen, N-15, in ammonia led to Schoenheimer's study of protein metabolism. Schoenheimer and Rittenberg synthesized amino acids containing the isotope N-15 as well as some doubly labeled with N-15 and deuterium. After feeding these substances to the animals and analyzing their distribution in the body, Schoenheimer concluded that body proteins are in a highly dynamic state, being continuously degraded and synthesized. These experiments debunked the hypothesis that the body proteins existed in a static state. From Schoenheimer's and Rittenberg's experiments, the concept of the body's "metabolic pool" emerged, for their data indicated that body tissues are continuously drawing chemical substances from the pool as well as placing substances into it.

Schoenheimer's and Rittenberg's methods of using stable isotopes to follow metabolic pathways in vivo and in vitro began a revolution in biochemistry. During the 1940s their discovery led to techniques in following enzyme reactions with stable isotopes when the radioactive isotopes C-14, tritium, I131, Sulfur 35, and P-32 became available.

Despite his revolutionary work in biochemistry, Schoenheimer suffered from depression, which some speculate may have stemmed from his experiences during the First World War in Europe and the treatment of the Jews by the Nazis. Schoenheimer also was separated from his wife, which apparently exacerbated his depression. These factors, as well as others perhaps not made public, led to Schoenheimer's suicide by poisoning at his home in Yonkers.

Although his career came to a tragic and premature end, Schoenheimer was responsible for major breakthroughs, in the early to mid-twentieth century, in the field of biochemistry. Through the use of his isotope-labeling techniques, biochemists were able to work out the various metabolic pathways of the body, resulting in significant biochemical advances in the latter half of the twentieth century.

• There is a curriculum vitae and personal biography in the Archives and Special Collections at Columbia University. For summaries of his work and its significance, see, by Schoenheimer and David Rittenberg, "The Application of Isotopes to the Study of Intermediary Metabolism," *Science* 87 (1938): 221–26; and "Deuterium as an Indicator in the Study of Intermediary Metabolism," *Science* 82 (1936): 156–57. A short biographical sketch is DeWitt Stetten, Jr., "Rudi," *Perspectives in Biological Medicine* 25 (Spring 1982): 354–68. Important studies on the significance of his work include Robert E. Kohler, Jr., "Rudolph Schoenheimer, Isotope Tracers and Biochemistry in the 1930s," *Historical Studies of Physical Sciences* 8 (1977): 257–98; Sarah Ratner, "The Dynamic State of Body Proteins," *Origins of Modern Biochemistry: A Retrospect on Proteins, Annals of the New York Academy of Sciences* 235 (31 May 1979); and David Nachmansohn, *German Jewish Pioneers in Science 1900–1933* (1979), pp. 357–60. Obituaries are in *Science* 94 (1941): 2449–50; and *Nature* 149 (1942): 15–16.

DAVID Y. COOPER
MICHELLE E. OSBORN

SCHOEPPEL, Andrew Frank (23 Nov. 1894–21 Jan. 1962), U.S. senator, was born in Barton County, Kansas, the son of George J. Schoeppel, a farmer and grain dealer, and Anna Filip. He was raised in Ness County in west-central Kansas, where he attended local schools. He enrolled in the University of Kansas (1916–1918), leaving to serve in the Naval Aviation Reserve Corps during World War I. He completed his education at the University of Nebraska, graduating with an LL.B. in 1922. While attending Nebraska, Schoeppel played end on the Cornhusker football team that upset Notre Dame and the famous Four Horsemen, and he received All-American recognition. He married Marie Thomsen in 1924; they had no children.

In 1923 Schoeppel began practicing law in Ness City, Kansas, and almost immediately entered local politics, serving variously as city solicitor, county attorney, city councilman, and mayor. He also enjoyed a good reputation as a high school football and basketball official. Appointed chair in 1939 of the State of

Kansas Corporation Commission, an important state regulatory body, he soon gained a reputation as a defender of corporate interests. He resigned from that position in 1942 to run for governor, and after winning a close three-way election in the Republican primary he defeated his Democratic opponent by 75,000 votes. In 1944 he won reelection by an unprecedented 230,000 votes. His four years as governor were devoid of major policy initiatives although marked by several controversies. His decision to permit the first executions since the state legislature reinstituted the death penalty in 1935 stirred public debate, as did his pardon of an embezzler whose bond fraud schemes cost the state nearly a half-million dollars. In 1945 he became involved in a much-publicized dispute with federal liquor enforcement authorities, who charged him with failing to enforce the state's prohibition law. Following federal seizure of large quantities of illegal liquor and a subsequent grand jury report censuring him and other state officials for inaction, Schoeppel set in motion the eventual repeal of the law by requesting that the legislature conduct its own investigation.

Schoeppel reentered law practice in Wichita in 1947, but the following year he won election to the U.S. Senate seat held for thirty years by the popular but aging (eighty-three) Arthur Capper. Schoeppel angered many Kansans by announcing his intent to run against Capper in the 1948 Republican primary election, and an extremely bitter intraparty fight loomed, threatening to splinter the party. At the last moment the frail and exhausted Capper announced his retirement, and Schoeppel easily won the Senate seat. He took to the Senate staunchly conservative, isolationist views, early on advocating American withdrawal from the United Nations. Although he voted for membership in the North Atlantic Treaty Organization in 1949, Schoeppel subsequently voted against legislation authorizing the deployment of American troops in Europe and the shipment of arms to the alliance. In 1952 he enthusiastically supported the presidential candidacy of the conservative Ohioan Robert A. Taft and suffered deep disappointment when Dwight D. Eisenhower won the nomination. His enthusiasm for Eisenhower's administration remained tepid at best as Schoeppel firmly aligned himself with the party's conservative wing. He routinely voted against foreign aid bills and abandoned Eisenhower to support the controversial constitutional amendment sponsored by fellow Republican John W. Bricker of Ohio, which would have greatly constricted presidential discretion in the conduct of foreign policy. His partisan criticism of Harry S. Truman's secretary of state, Dean Acheson, was matched by an equal disdain for Eisenhower's top diplomat, John Foster Dulles.

Schoeppel's conservatism extended with equal fervor to domestic policy. Adamantly opposed to the liberal domestic programs proposed by President Truman, he once remarked that he could see little "magic" in federal domestic spending programs but "a lot of monkey business." Schoeppel voted to override Truman's veto of the Internal Security Control Act (McCarran Act) of 1950 and was an enthusiastic supporter of the anticommunist crusade of Joseph R. McCarthy. Throughout his career he worked to cut federal expenditures and routinely opposed tax increases. His public statements and Senate votes earned him a reputation as a foe of organized labor.

As a farm belt senator, however, Schoeppel endorsed federal farm support programs and devoted much of his Senate career to serving the interests of Kansas agriculture. He frequently referred to himself as "a friend of the American farmer" and based his successful reelection campaigns in 1954 and 1960 upon his behind-the-scenes role in helping secure commodity price supports, direct subsidies, and trade policies favorable to Kansas farmers. Schoeppel also continued to be recognized as a friend of Kansas pipeline, oil, and natural gas interests. Because the law firm of which he was a senior partner specialized in serving corporate clients engaged in insurance, real estate, oil and gas, and manufacturing, and because of allegations regarding his intervention with the Kansas Corporation Commission on behalf of major gas and pipeline companies during his governorship, former Republican governor and 1936 presidential nominee Alf Landon became an outspoken critic of Schoeppel, contending that the senator was "an errand boy for the big utilities, big pipeline companies and oil companies."

Such criticisms notwithstanding, Schoeppel enjoyed a widespread popularity with Kansas voters. At the same time, he was considered by his Senate peers to be a consummate "Senate insider" who understood the traditions and customs of the nation's most exclusive club and who held the respect and friendship of many senators on both sides of the aisle. Blessed with an engaging personality, he was well known as a talented orator on the campaign circuit, yet he spoke only rarely on the Senate floor, preferring to do much of his work in committee sessions and in cloakroom negotiations. No major legislation bears his name, although he was frequently closely associated with farm legislation. A longtime member of Rotary and a thirty-third-degree Mason, he was also active in the affairs of several bar associations, the American Legion, and the Chamber of Commerce. He died at Bethesda Naval Hospital in Bethesda, Maryland.

• Schoeppel's gubernatorial and senatorial papers are deposited in the Kansas State Historical Society in Topeka. See David C. Boles, "Andrew Frank Schoeppel, Governor of Kansas, 1943–1947" (master's thesis, Kansas State Univ., 1967). See also Donald R. McCoy, *Landon of Kansas* (1966); *New York Times Magazine*, 7 Nov. 1954, p. 9ff; *Life* 21 June 1954, p. 133; *Time*, 23 Aug. 1954, p. 10; *U.S. News and World Report*, 12 Apr. 1957, pp. 132–37; and *Congressional Directory* (1961), p. 53. An obituary is in the *New York Times*, 29 Feb. 1962. The *Congressional Record*, 13 Mar. 1962, pp. 3957–77, contains eulogies and several reprinted obituaries from Kansas newspapers.

RICHARD O. DAVIES

SCHOFIELD, John McAllister (29 Sept. 1831–4 Mar. 1906), soldier, was born in Gerry, New York, the son of James Schofield, a Baptist clergyman, and Caroline McAllister. After moving to Illinois in 1843, the family settled in Freeport. Young Schofield surveyed land in northern Wisconsin and taught a district school before entering the U.S. Military Academy in 1849. Dismissed for withholding information about improper cadet behavior, he secured reinstatement through the influence of U.S. senator Stephen Douglas of Illinois and graduated in 1853, ranked seventh out of fifty-two. Schofield later reflected that what he "needed to learn was not so much how to command as how to obey."

Between 1853 and 1855 Schofield served at Fort Moultrie, South Carolina, and in Florida as second lieutenant, First Artillery. Promoted to first lieutenant and assigned to the Military Academy, he taught natural and experimental philosophy from 1855 to 1860, when he secured a leave of absence to become professor of physics at Washington University in St. Louis. In 1857 Schofield married Harriet Bartlett; they had five children. Schofield's wife died in 1888, and in 1891 he married Georgia Kilbourne. This marriage produced one child.

Schofield returned to military service during the Civil War. Responding to President Abraham Lincoln's call for volunteers, he became major, First Missouri. As adjutant general and chief of staff for Brigadier General Nathaniel Lyon, Schofield assisted efforts to keep Missouri in the Union and behaved gallantly in the defeat at Wilson's Creek, 10 August 1861, that left Lyon dead and jeopardized Federal control over southwestern Missouri.

Thanks in part to Missouri friends, Schofield was nominated brigadier general of volunteers and assigned to command the Missouri Enrolled Militia in November 1861. Raising and equipping this force, authorized only for state defense, occupied Schofield until April 1862. A factional dispute in Missouri between "radicals," desiring immediate emancipation and punitive military actions, and "conservatives," seeking gradual emancipation and military restraint, complicated Schofield's position. More problems arose from Confederate incursions across the border with Arkansas. Given command of the "Army of the Frontier," Schofield campaigned in southwestern Missouri and Arkansas from October 1862 to April 1863. Although he had kept Missouri relatively quiet and supplied needed troops for the Vicksburg campaign, radicals defeated his nomination as major general of volunteers in January 1863, a rank he eventually attained in March.

Briefly given command of the Third Division, Fourteenth Army Corps, Army of the Cumberland, at Murfreesboro, Tennessee, Schofield returned to the political fracas in Missouri as department commander in May 1863. Lincoln, who liked Schofield, counseled, "If both factions, or neither, shall abuse you, you will probably be about right." Contending with calls for retaliatory raids into Missouri following William C. Quantrill's guerrilla attack on Lawrence, Kansas, in August was perhaps the most difficult of many challenges. In January 1864 he was ordered to Chattanooga.

Assuming command of the Department and Army of the Ohio in February 1864, Schofield parried Confederate forces near Knoxville until joining Major General William T. Sherman for the Atlanta campaign. Schofield's army performed well through the battles that ended with Atlanta's fall on 2 September. Soon after the "March to the Sea" began, Sherman granted Schofield's wish to support the Army of the Cumberland under Major General George H. Thomas, defending Tennessee. Schofield's command alone severely checked the Confederates at the battle of Franklin, 30 November, and, as part of Thomas's concentrated force, inflicted a crushing blow at the battle of Nashville, 15–16 December. Thomas's procrastination nearly had resulted in Schofield's elevation to command, a circumstance that provoked harsh allegations concerning Schofield's ambition.

Seeking additional active operations, Schofield volunteered for duty in the East and was transferred with the Twenty-third Army Corps to the Cape Fear River, North Carolina, in January 1865, arriving in February. As head of the Department of North Carolina, he engineered the capture of Wilmington, drove inland, and united with Sherman's army at Goldsboro on 23 March. Schofield accompanied Sherman to surrender talks with General Joseph E. Johnston and drafted the final capitulation convention on 26 April. By then he was brigadier general, U.S. Army, for his victory at Franklin.

Schofield remained in North Carolina until summoned in June to discuss a special mission to eliminate the French-sponsored government in Mexico. Schofield eventually spent six months in France and facilitated the desired French withdrawal. Back in the United States, he oversaw Reconstruction measures in West Virginia and Virginia as commander of the Department of the Potomac and then solely in Virginia as commander of the First Military District. Citing a need for educated appointees to hold local offices, he worked against measures that excluded former Confederates and gave preference to freedmen. Deemed a suitable compromise figure between Radical Republicans and conservatives embroiled in the impeachment of President Andrew Johnson, Schofield accepted nomination as secretary of war to replace embattled Edwin M. Stanton. During his ten-month tenure, 1 June 1868-12 March 1869, Schofield participated meaningfully in cabinet deliberations.

Promoted to major general at the start of Ulysses S. Grant's presidency, Schofield took command of the Department of the Missouri. In 1870 he was transferred to the Division of the Pacific. A mission to the Hawaiian Islands in early 1873, which led to a recommendation to purchase Pearl Harbor, highlighted a period primarily devoted to railroad and American Indian concerns. At Sherman's request, Schofield served as superintendent of the Military Academy from September 1876 to January 1881. A controversy over the expulsion of Johnson C. Whittaker, a black cadet allegedly assaulted by white classmates, prompted Schofield's departure for a European tour and other division commands.

The death of Lieutenant General Philip H. Sheridan in 1888 brought Schofield to command of the army, a position he held until mandatory retirement on 29 September 1895. His tenure was marked by the last major Indian uprising at Wounded Knee and periodic labor strife. Personally, Schofield maintained an unusually harmonious relationship with President Grover Cleveland and was gratified by congressional action granting him the rank of lieutenant general. Schofield published a memoir in 1897 and died at St. Augustine, Florida. Described by contemporaries as "sensible" and "fair-minded" as well as "artful" and "shrewd," Schofield had talent, ambition, and a network of friends to sustain him through an extraordinary career.

• Schofield's papers at the Library of Congress form the principal manuscript collection. Other useful collections are the papers of William T. Sherman and Andrew Johnson, Library of Congress, and William Henry Seward, Rush Rhees Library, University of Rochester, Rochester, N.Y. The Hiram Barney Collection at the Huntington Library, San Marino, Calif., holds several dozen insightful letters from Sherman to Schofield between 1864 and 1891. Schofield's *Forty-Six Years in the Army* (1897), a detailed but overly defensive effort, is the only book-length treatment of his entire career. James L. McDonough, *Schofield: Union General in the Civil War and Reconstruction* (1972), draws heavily on printed sources, including Jacob D. Cox, *Atlanta* (1882) and *The March to the Sea: Franklin and Nashville* (1886). As Schofield's trusted subordinate commander, Cox brings a participant's perspective. Albert Castel, *Decision in the West: The Atlanta Campaign of 1864* (1992), assesses Schofield from greater distance.

The War of the Rebellion: A Compilation of the Official Records of the Union and Confederate Armies (128 vols., 1880–1901) is indispensable for Schofield's Civil War service. Also valuable are Roy P. Basler, ed., *The Collected Works of Abraham Lincoln* (1953–1955); and John Y. Simon, ed., *The Papers of Ulysses S. Grant* (1967). Nuggets are found in Theodore Calvin Pease and James G. Randall, ed., *The Diary of Orville Hickman Browning* (2 vols., 1925, 1933); Howard K. Beale, ed., *The Diary of Edward Bates, 1859–1866* (1933); and Beale, ed., *The Diary of Gideon Welles: Secretary of the Navy under Lincoln and Johnson* (3 vols., 1960). George W. Cullum, *Biographical Register of the Officers and Graduates of the U.S. Military Academy*, 3d ed. (1891); and Francis B. Heitman, *Historical Register and Dictionary of the United States Army* (1903), outline Schofield's military career. The *New York Times* and the *Saint Louis Globe-Democrat*, 5 Mar. 1906, have informative obituaries.

WILLIAM M. FERRARO

SCHOFIELD, Martha (1 Feb. 1839–1 Feb. 1916), educator and school founder, was born in Newtown, Pennsylvania, the daughter of Oliver Schofield and Mary Jackson, farmers. Reared as a Quaker and an abolitionist, from early adolescence Schofield was in the company of social reformers, including Susan B. Anthony, William Lloyd Garrison, and Lucretia Mott, many of whom became lifelong friends. Liberal Quakerism, abolitionism, and women's rights deeply affected her life's work, though in spiritual matters she drew from many sources, particularly Christian Science. Her education included common school in Newtown and the Friends' School in Byberry, Pennsylvania.

Schofield began teaching in private schools in New York state at age eighteen. In 1861 she took over as the only teacher at the Bethany School, a Quaker-sponsored institution for black children in Philadelphia, where she remained for two terms. After serving as a volunteer in a Philadelphia military hospital in 1863, she taught for one year in a common school in that city and attended sessions of the teachers' institute, the only professional training she ever received.

Although not in robust health as a young woman, Schofield sought a position as a teacher among the freed slaves in the South in 1863. In October 1865 the Pennsylvania Freedmen's Relief Association of Philadelphia (PFRA) commissioned her to open a school and provide relief to the freed people on Wadmelaw Island, one of the South Carolina Sea Islands near Charleston. In the next two years she taught in four other schools in the Sea Islands and in Charleston and then in 1868 was assigned to Aiken, South Carolina, where she remained the rest of her life. In 1870 she bought land in Aiken and, with the assistance of the Bureau of Refugees, Freedmen, and Abandoned Lands, built a schoolhouse on it in 1871, the first permanent structure of what became known as the Schofield Normal and Industrial School.

Schofield's purchase of land and the construction of the school corresponded with the demise of PFRA and of the Freedmen's Bureau. In the previous two years, PFRA had been able to provide only partial support, as dwindling northern interest in the freed people forced it and many other voluntary freedmen's aid societies to discontinue their work. The Germantown Friends' Aid Association picked up a portion of the moral and pecuniary support for Schofield's school, but virtually from the beginning of the work in Aiken, she shouldered the responsibility of raising funds for the school.

Despite perpetual financial hardship and harsh social and political opposition from southern whites, Schofield expanded her institution, focusing primarily on teacher training. By the mid-1870s the school included primary and secondary schooling through the tenth grade. The economic pressures on southern blacks were so great, however, that few could afford even the minimal fees or the time to complete all ten grades. The school did not graduate any students until 1885; many moved into teaching positions as soon as they had mastered the rudiments themselves. She assisted a few in transferring to Lincoln University in Pennsylvania or Hampton Institute in Virginia for more advanced training.

Initially the school emphasized a simplified classical curriculum, stressing reading, writing, arithmetic, rudimentary geography, history, and literature, along with religious and character education. To the classical curriculum Schofield added courses in physiology to improve the health of southern blacks. Within a few years, however, Schofield shifted her emphasis from the classical curriculum to a more practical, vocational curriculum patterned after the work of Samuel Chapman Armstrong at Hampton Normal and Industrial Institute. In 1880 she opened a printshop and offered training for printers; over the next decade she added cobbling, farming, carpentry, and harness making for men and the "housekeeping arts" for women. No student could complete the academic course of study without mastering a manual skill; similarly, all students in the industrial curriculum were expected to gain basic competence in academic skills. The products of the school's shops and farms were sold locally or consumed by the students and faculty.

Schofield Normal and Industrial School gained a reputation in the region for high-quality workmanship, and much of the white opposition to the school withered in the 1890s. Simultaneously, the shift to an industrial curriculum earned the school the support of northern philanthropists. Although the school was never on fully secure financial footing during Schofield's life, its industrial curriculum won more wealthy benefactors than it had enjoyed earlier. Yet despite the industrial curriculum, teacher education remained its primary contribution to South Carolina. Its teachers were in great demand to supply the black schools of the region, and in 1908 the state recognized the quality of its program by accepting the school's students for licensure without examination. Schofield Normal and Industrial School became one of the most noteworthy elementary and secondary industrial schools for southern African Americans in the half century after emancipation.

Like Armstrong and his protégé, Booker T. Washington, Schofield was convinced that industrial education would result in economic power and social acceptance for southern blacks and that political power and improved race relations would eventually follow. Yet unlike Armstrong, whose advocacy of industrial education arose from his conviction of the racial inferiority of African Americans, Schofield, who was white, embraced the doctrine of industrial education out of her belief that northern and federal abandonment of the freed people demanded new tactics to achieve racial equality. She remained a staunch advocate of the freed people rather than a spokesperson for an industrialized South. Schofield's activism on behalf of African Americans was echoed by her support of woman suffrage, and women's-rights advocates cited her work as evidence of the potential power of women.

Schofield relinquished control of her school in 1912 but lived out the remainder of her life on its grounds, advising students and speaking in favor of the reform causes she had long embraced. She died in Aiken. She had never married. Her school was eventually adopted by the Aiken public school system.

• Schofield's letters and journals, along with papers related to the Schofield Normal and Industrial School and its board of trustees, are housed in the Friends' Historical Library, Swarthmore College; she published no books or articles. Katherine Smedley, *Martha Schofield and the Re-education of the South, 1839–1916* (1987), is a scholarly biography. Matilda A. Evans, *Martha Schofield: Pioneer Negro Educator* (1916), written by a former student and close personal friend, provides a less objective, more intimate, and laudatory account. Regarding her women's rights stand, see Smedley, "Martha Schofield and the Rights of Women," *South Carolina Historical Magazine* 85 (1984): 195–210.

RONALD E. BUTCHART

SCHOLANDER, Per Fredrik Thorkelsson (29 Nov. 1905–13 June 1980), physiologist, was born in Örebro, Sweden, the son of Thorkel F. Scholander, a civil engineer, and Agnete Faye-Hansen, a Norwegian-born professional pianist. The boy took an early interest in music and, especially, natural history. The family moved to Kristiania (later Oslo), Norway, where he attended local schools. He entered the University of Oslo for medical studies and received an M.D. in 1932.

While a college student, Scholander became interested in lichens by noticing fruiting bodies on some of them while walking among hardwood trees. He sought information from professor of botany Bernt Lynge, who gave Scholander the opportunity to serve as botanist on three scientific expeditions to Greenland and Spitsbergen during the summers of 1930 to 1932. Scholander made significant plant collections and published with Lynge on lichens. He continued at the University of Oslo for graduate study in botany and received his Ph.D. in 1934, with a dissertation on higher plants of Spitsbergen.

On the arctic trips Scholander became interested in the ability of seals to dive to great depths without suffering from nitrogen narcosis as do humans. While on a research fellowship at the Physiological Institute of the University of Oslo, he developed equipment to record the respiratory metabolism of diving animals. His early work on diving animals was published as "Experimental Investigations on the Respiratory Function in Diving Mammals and Birds" (*Hvalrådets Skrifter* 22 [1940]: 1–131).

In 1939 Scholander received a Rockefeller Foundation Fellowship to conduct research at Swarthmore College in Pennsylvania, where physiologist Laurence Irving was doing research on diving physiology. Scholander just managed to leave Norway before World War II prevented him from accepting the fellowship.

In 1943 Irving and Scholander both joined the U.S. Army Air Force, the latter as captain, advancing to major in 1946. During the war, Scholander tested survival equipment personally and provided improvements that were adopted by the military on sleeping bags under blizzard conditions and life rafts during storms in the Aleutian Islands. Without military authorization, he parachuted to rescue three downed flyers in Alaska, which almost led to a court-martial. But in 1945 he received a Soldiers' Medal for Valor. That same year, by means of his military service, he became a U.S. citizen.

In 1946 Irving and Scholander set up the Arctic Research Laboratory at Point Barrow, Alaska, with support from the U.S. Navy. There they conducted physiological studies on arctic mammals and birds to determine the relationship between external temperature and metabolic rate. In 1949 Scholander became a research fellow at Harvard University, at the invitation of Albert Baird Hastings, professor of biological chemistry. In 1951 Scholander married Susan Irving (daughter of Laurence); they had no children. From 1952 to 1955 he was a physiologist at Woods Hole Oceanographic Institution in Massachusetts. In 1955 he accepted an invitation to be director of the new Institute of Zoophysiology and professor at the University of Oslo.

In 1958 Scholander became professor of physiology at Scripps Institution of Oceanography of the University of California, with the added title in 1963 of director of the Physiological Research Laboratory that he had just established there. He had obtained funds in 1962 from the National Science Foundation for a research building at the institution (later named for him) and a 133-foot research ship, which he named *Alpha Helix*. His concept of the ship was a floating laboratory, with facilities primarily for physiological studies. When the program began in 1966, expeditions were scheduled to stay at remote locations for long periods of time, with shorter visits by scientists from many countries, selected by a national advisory committee. Over six years, the ship spent time at the Great Barrier Reef off Australia; a jungle location 1,200 miles up the Amazon River; the Bering Sea; New Guinea; the Galápagos Islands; and Antarctica. Scholander participated in many of these trips. His direction of the program ended in 1972, but it continued under a committee of the University-National Oceanographic Laboratory System for another eight years. Reports required from each participating scientist resulted in many volumes of studies, including the physiology of some land mammals, details of the life of the chambered nautilus, and much more.

Scholander's primary interest was in the survival of organisms under extreme conditions. He was especially adept at devising micro-techniques for measuring precisely the composition and interchange of gases within a living system. While at Point Barrow, in addition to measuring very small samples of gas in animals, he tried the technique on air bubbles in ice and suggested that air trapped in glaciers would contain a record of the composition of earlier atmosphere ("Gases in Icebergs," *Science* 123 [1956]: 104–5, with J. W. Kanwisher and D. C. Nutt). An instrument that he developed at Harvard measured the oxygen consumption of single cells during division, a technique not previously accomplished. At Woods Hole he created a device to analyze very small samples of gases in the swim bladders of fishes, to determine how oxygen and nitrogen in these structures are secreted against deep-sea pressures. His studies extended to human metabolism, and while at Oslo and later he used body-temperature measurements to compare the adaptability on cold nights in the open of such native peoples as Lapps, Australian aborigines, and Alacaluf natives of southern Chile with that of his volunteer Norwegian students.

At Scripps Institution of Oceanography he continued his varied interests. In investigating the diving capability of marine animals, he found that seals have a differential vascular control that reduces the supply of blood and oxygen to the muscles during diving, and that the heart slows to a few beats each minute in a dive. In studies of plants he concluded that suction and the cohesive force of water were mainly responsible for the rise of sap into the tops of the tallest trees, and he worked out an explanation of osmosis in the salt interchange in the roots of mangroves that grow in seawater. His researches continued long after he reached emeritus status in 1973.

Scholander was a stimulating scientist, who interested many others in pursuing questions of survival and adaptability of animals and plants. His wife noted (in his autobiography) that "he enjoyed his students as sparring partners, from which they benefited as much as he, and they frequently became his coauthors." He was elected to the National Academy of Sciences in 1961 and received the Fridtjof Nansen Prize of Norway in 1979. He died in La Jolla, California.

• Scholander's archival papers and the records of the Physiological Research Laboratory are in the archives of Scripps Institution of Oceanography (Univ. of California, San Diego). Among his roughly 190 scientific papers are three he published with Vladimir Walters, Raymond Hock, and Laurence Irving on body insulation, heat regulation, and adaptation to cold of arctic and tropical mammals and birds in *Biological Bulletin* 99 (1950): 225–71. His papers on measuring gases in ice include "Radio-carbon Age and Oxygen-18 Content of Greenland Icebergs," *Meddelelser om Grönland* 165 (1962): 1–26. He published on sap in plants in "Reverse Osmosis and Sap Pressure in Vascular Plants," *Science* 150 (1965): 384, and in several other papers. With Harold Theodore Hammel he published the monograph *Osmosis and Tensile Solvent* (1976). Scholander wrote "Rhapsody in Science," *Annual Reviews of Physiology* 40 (1978): 1–17, about himself and completed a lively autobiographical manuscript that was published posthumously, with a bibliography, as *Enjoying a Life in Science* (1990). A biographical account by Knut Schmidt-Nielsen in National Academy of Sciences, *Biographical Memoirs* 56 (1987): 386–412, includes a bibliography. Susan Irving Scholander provided helpful information to the author.

ELIZABETH NOBLE SHOR

SCHOLLAR, Ludmilla (15 Mar. 1888–10 July 1978), ballet dancer and teacher, was born Liudmila Frantsevna Shollar in Saint Petersburg, Russia; nothing is known about her parents or early childhood. Trained at the Imperial Theater School in Saint Petersburg, she graduated into the Maryinsky Ballet there in 1906. As a student she trained under master teacher Enrico Cecchetti and choreographer-teacher Michel Fokine. While still a student, she was chosen by Vaslav Nijinsky to be his partner for his graduation performance of *The Prince Gardener*, a pas de deux arranged for them by Klavdia Kulichevska.

Schollar enjoyed telling a story about that performance when at the very end of the ballet a small accident happened. In the process of supporting Schollar in a pirouette, Nijinsky cut his hand on the trimming of her bodice. "I looked down at my tutu," Schollar said in an interview published in *Dance Magazine* (Apr. 1979), "and it was covered with blood." The interviewer went on to note that "Nijinsky's mother was very upset about this incident and felt it was a bad omen for the beginning of his career."

Schollar was one of the original members of the first company of Serge Diaghilev's Ballets Russes. She appeared in the company's first public performances in Paris on 18 May 1909, dancing in three of Fokine's ballets: *Le Pavillon d'Armide*, the *Polovtsian Dances* from *Prince Igor*, and *Le Festin*. In 1910 she also danced in the original western European productions of Fokine's *Le Carnaval* in Paris, where she performed Estrella in a cast that included Tamara Karsavina as Columbine, Nijinsky as Harlequin, and Cecchetti as Pantalon. She also performed in *Petrouchka* in Paris in 1911 and with Karsavina in the premiere of Nijinsky's controversial ballet *Jeux* in Paris in 1913.

Schollar remained with the company, performing in both the London and Paris seasons, until 1914, when she returned to Saint Petersburg for four months of training as a war nurse. During World War I she served as a Russian army nurse and was wounded seriously in the arm. For her bravery in service she was awarded the Saint George medal.

From 1917 to 1921 she performed at the Maryinsky Theater while still appearing as a guest artist with the Diaghilev company. A member of Diaghilev's company from 1921 to 1925, she appeared in the first western European production of the choreographer Marius Petipa's *Sleeping Beauty* in London in November 1921. That year Schollar married Anatole Vilzak, a fellow graduate of the Imperial Theater School and a member of the Ballets Russes. Vilzak's proposal was, "Would you do a pas de deux with me forever?" Prior to her marriage to Vilzak, which was childless, Schollar had been married to an officer, Count Vorontzoff, with whom she had a daughter.

Schollar and Vilzak collaborated to restage a one-act *Swan Lake* for Diaghilev in 1922. They clashed with Diaghilev in 1925 when they spoke out on behalf of the company's underpaid corps de ballet, and a furious Diaghilev dismissed them from the company. Following a season with the company of Ida Rubinstein in 1928, in which Vilzak created roles in Bronislava Nijinska's *La Bien-Aimée* and *Boléro*, Schollar and her husband formed their own company with Karsavina. In 1930 they briefly joined the State Opera House in Riga, Latvia.

Schollar began her second career, that of a ballet teacher, in 1936 when she retired from the stage and she and Vilzak came to New York to serve as teachers in George Balanchine's new School of American

Ballet. By 1940 Schollar and Vilzak had their own school in New York, which they ran until 1946. Gifted as teachers, they taught jointly at a succession of schools, including the Ballet Russe de Monte Carlo (1949–1951), the American Ballet Theatre School (1951–1963), and the Washington School of Ballet (1963–1965). In 1965 Schollar and Vilzak arrived in San Francisco by boat via the Panama Canal to take over teaching company classes for the San Francisco Ballet, where Schollar continued to teach until her retirement in 1978.

Schollar's classes strongly reflected her training from Cecchetti in her quick footwork, while her graceful *port de bras* (arm and upper-body movement) revealed the influence of Fokine. Schollar's students included some of the leading names of twentieth-century classical ballet: Svetlana Beriosova, Irina Baronova, Tamara Toumanova, Alicia Alonso, Diana Adams, Nora Kaye, Alexandra Danilova, Maria Tallchief, Ruthanna Boris, Lucia Chase, Jerome Robbins, Michael Kidd, Frederic Franklin, and Paul Draper.

As a dancer Schollar was noted for her elevation (ability to jump high), which she used to great effect in airborne roles such as Myrtha in *Giselle*, the Polovtsian Girl in *Prince Igor*, and in *Les Sylphides*. She was also a gifted mime and character dancer. As a teacher she schooled generations of American dancers in these technical and dramatic traditions of the Maryinsky Theater and the Russian Imperial Ballet. She died in San Francisco.

• The most complete information about Schollar is contained in Marian Horosko's two-part article, "Teachers in the Russian Tradition," *Dance Magazine*, Apr. 1979, pp. 67–82. Part one traces the careers of Schollar and Vilzak, and part two details the Sugar Plum Fairy variation from *The Nutcracker* as taught by Schollar. See also Lynn Garafola's *Diaghilev's Ballets Russes* (1989), Barbara Newman's interview with Vilzak about his career and teaching with Schollar in *Striking a Balance: Dancers Talk about Dancing* (1982), pp. 13–21, and Jack Anderson's *Dance* (1974), pp. 72–73, which has a brief mention of Schollar and a photo. Obituaries are in the *San Francisco Examiner*, 14 July 1978, and the *New York Times*, 16 July 1978.

JANICE ROSS

SCHOLTE, H. P. (25 Sept. 1805–25 Aug. 1868), Reformed cleric, journalist, and founder of the Pella, Iowa, Dutch colony, was born Hendrik Pieter Scholte in Amsterdam, the Netherlands, the son of Jan Hendrik Scholte, a sugar box factory owner, and Johanna Dorothea Roelofsz. The Scholte family for generations operated sugar refineries in Amsterdam, and young Hendrik, called "H. P.," was destined to carry on the business tradition. Religiously, the family members were "outsiders" who belonged to a pietistic German Lutheran congregation rather than the national Dutch Reformed church, headed by the monarchy. The death of his father, grandfather, only brother, and mother, all within six years (1821–1827), freed Scholte to use his inheritance to enroll as a theology student at

Leiden University. In 1832 he married Sara Maria Brandt. They would have five children before her death in 1844.

Scholte became a leader of the antirationalist, theological-philosophical movement known as the Dutch *Reveil* (Revival), which aimed to restore traditional teachings in the increasingly modernistic Reformed church. The religious and government authorities moved against the dissenting churches for their open challenge to the established order. Police broke up the "unauthorized" worship services, fined clerics, and generally harassed the *kleine luyden* (little people) who flocked to the powerful preaching services. Scholte and a half-dozen associates withdrew under duress from the Reformed church in the Secession of 1834, and within a decade these Seceders laid plans to leave the Netherlands. An economic depression, a cholera epidemic, and especially a potato crop blight in the mid-1840s pushed the already ostracized Seceders to the decision to emigrate. "There must be a change in the running of affairs," Scholte sadly wrote to King Willem II early in 1846, "or the Netherlands is lost." God's judgment will soon fall in Holland and indeed all of Europe, Scholte prophesied in his journal *De Reformatie*, because of Constantinianism and spiritual apostasy.

Within weeks, a message from God—"Go out of her, my people"—convinced "the Dominie," as Scholte was affectionately called, to lead his followers to the United States for religious freedom and economic opportunity. Although his fellow Seceder Albertus C. Van Raalte had already decided to relocate in Michigan, Scholte's group of 900 ended up in Iowa. This was the beginning of a mass Dutch emigration to the United States.

Scholte departed in early 1847 with his second wife, Mareah Hendrika Elisabeth Kranz, whom he had married in 1845, and three surviving children from his first marriage. The cultural and refined Mareah was hardly pioneer material; she always described herself as a "stranger in a strange land." Their only child died three days after birth.

Scholte named his colony "Pella" after the classical Macedonian "city of refuge" where the Christians fled upon the Roman destruction of Jerusalem in A.D. 70. The Dominie used his family fortune and the combined funds of his emigration association members to purchase 18,000 acres of government land in Lake Prairie Township, Marion County, Iowa, which were then distributed by lot and sold on credit to the colonists. The Dutch enclave on the rich and rolling Iowa prairie thrived beyond all expectations and within twenty years, with a population of 2,000, was a "beehive ready for swarming." Pella inspired other colonies in northwest Iowa, Kansas, and Nebraska.

For the first decade the Dominie dominated the colony. As an American neighbor aptly noted, he was the Hollanders' "prophet, priest, and king." He served as minister, editor of the English-language *Pella Gazette*, lawyer, notary public, real estate developer, agent of the New York Life Insurance Company, justice of the peace, school inspector, major ex officio, and local political leader. He founded "The Christian Church at Pella," an independent congregation that he served without pay. Scholte was also an energetic capitalist. Besides owning almost one-third of the land in and around the town of Pella, his investments in local industries included a brick kiln, a steam flour mill, a limestone quarry, and the Pella National Bank. In 1853 he was also a benefactor and founding trustee of the local college, now Central University. These "secular" activities by the Dominie inevitably drew criticism from the pious but stubbornly independent Dutch folk.

The early political views of the Pella leader were decidedly Whiggish. Scholte idolized Henry Clay and shared his positive views of government economic programs and his concern that abolition agitation jeopardized the Union. Scholte failed in a bid for nomination as state senator in 1852 but served as a delegate at large and vice president of the 1860 Republican National Convention in Chicago.

In 1864 President Abraham Lincoln appointed him U.S. minister to Austria, but the Senate refused to confirm the nomination because Scholte was not a native-born American. This was not the first sting of nativism. In the mid-1850s Scholte had been so castigated personally by Know Nothing nativists and temperance forces for opposing a state prohibition amendment that he had joined the Democratic party from 1854 until 1859. After being elected a delegate to the 1859 Democratic State Convention, however, Scholte suddenly appeared at the Republican convention, announced his conversion, and joined the party. In the 1860 presidential election, despite Scholte's strongest editorials in the *Gazette*, the Pella colonists remained staunchly Democratic, choosing Stephen Douglas over Lincoln. Despite the charges of his nativist enemies, Scholte failed to drive Pella citizens to the polls "like cattle to the slaughter" (*Pella Gazette*, 21 Aug. 1856). Indeed, they had some years earlier already repudiated his leadership in church and state. The city had incorporated in 1855 to limit his control, and in 1856 dissenters from his Christian church formed a Dutch Reformed church and affiliated with the Michigan branch of that denomination led by Van Raalte.

Scholte filled his remaining years in millennial religious speculations, but no one was listening. The disillusioned leader died virtually alone in Pella. Nevertheless, the versatile and energetic Scholte had contributed in a critical way to the economic, political, and intellectual life of Pella and the state of Iowa. The colony's success was his monument.

• Scholte's papers are in the Central College Archives. For Scholte's writings, see the *Pella Gazette* (1855–1860); "First Voice from Pella," in Jacob Van Der Zee, "The Coming of the Hollanders to Iowa," *Iowa Journal of History and Politics* 9 (1911): 528–74; and "Second Voice from Pella," in Robert P. Swierenga, ed., "A Place of Refuge," *Annals of Iowa* 39 (Summer 1968): 321–57. There is no biography, but a superb assessment of his religious thought and background in the

Netherlands is Lubbertus Oostendorp, *H. P. Scholte, Leader of the Secession of 1834 and Founder of Pella* (1964). General accounts of Scholte and the Pella colony are in Van Der Zee, *The Hollanders of Iowa* (1912); Jacob van Hinte, *Netherlanders in America: A Study of Emigration and Settlement in the 19th and 20th Centuries in the United States of America*, ed. Swierenga, trans. Adriaan de Wit (1985); and Henry Lucas, *Netherlanders in America: Dutch Immigration to the United States and Canada 1789–1950* (1955; repr. 1989). Scholte's political career is documented in Swierenga, "The Ethnic Voter and First Lincoln Election," *Civil War History* 11 (Mar. 1965): 27–43.

ROBERT P. SWIERENGA

SCHOLZ, Jackson Volney (15 Mar. 1897–26 Oct. 1986), Olympic Games track and field champion, was born in Buchanan, Michigan, the son of S. B. Scholz, M.D., the medical director of the Pennsylvania Mutual Life Insurance Company. His mother's name and occupation are unknown. Scholz participated in track and field athletics at Soldan High School in St. Louis, Missouri, graduated in 1916, and entered the University of Missouri where he ran world record times for 50 yards (5.2 seconds), 70 yards (7.2 seconds), and 75 yards (7.6 seconds); he also ran world class times for 100 yards (9.6 seconds) and 220 yards (21.6 seconds). He left the university to serve in the First World War as a U.S. Navy pilot in Pensacola, Florida.

After the war Scholz returned to school, received a bachelor's degree in journalism from Missouri, and resumed his athletic training, this time wearing the uniform of the famous New York Athletic Club. The 5′6″, 130-pound Scholz made the Olympic team in 1920, and in Antwerp he finished fourth in the 100-meter dash and collected a gold medal and a world record in the 400-meter relay. On 5 September 1920, in Stockholm, he tied the world record for 100 meters: 10.5 seconds. At the 1924 Olympic Games in Paris, Scholz received a measure of athletic immortality by finishing second in the 100 meters, inches behind Englishman Harold M. Abrahams, both timed in 10.6 seconds.

The 27-year-old Scholz reached his peak as an athlete in 1924, winning the Olympic gold at 200 meters (21.6 seconds), equaling the record. Grantland Rice described the race as one of stirring drama. "The greyhound Scholz," wrote Rice, "won the race in the last stride by less than the width of a human body." Four years later, Scholz again was at the Olympics, finishing a strong fourth place in the Amsterdam 200-meter dash. The last year of his long-running career (1929), Scholz ran a brilliant 20.9-second 200-meter dash. He began a longer career as a sports fiction writer after having earned two gold medals and one silver medal in Olympic Games competition.

Multiple Olympic sprint champion, Charles Paddock, said of his teammate, "Scholz would float along watching his opponents and seeking a weakness would drive for the string, passing men who under ordinary conditions possessed as much speed as himself."

Olympic trainer Jake Weber said of Scholz: "He would run inches behind an opponent and at the precise moment of weakness, he would drive forward and win the race with his famous 'shrug' finish." An author of thirty-one sports novels for children, Scholz also wrote for *Collier's*, *Liberty*, and *Boys' Life*. He married Phyllis June Rahner in 1935. They had no children, and after spending many years on a Doylestown, Pennsylvania, farm, both of them retired to Delray Beach, Florida. Scholz once again gained international notoriety in 1983 with a series of irreverent remarks about his alleged conduct in the film *Chariots of Fire*. Scholz died in Delray Beach.

• Adam R. Hornbuckle learned much about J. V. Scholz from the University of Missouri Alumni Association. No full biography of Scholz has been published. For information mostly about his track career, see Bill Mallon and Ian Buchanan, *Quest for Gold* (1984), p. 341; Cordner Nelson, *Track and Field: The Great Ones* (1970), p. 205; David Wallechinsky, *The Complete Book of the Olympics* (1992), p. 15; and Jake Weber, *Training Olympic Champions* (1951), pp. 8–9. Charles W. Paddock's two books are delightful; *Track and Field* (1938), and *The Fastest Human* (1932), both contain anecdotes on Scholz. Obituaries appear in the *Los Angeles Times*, 29 Oct. 1986; the *New York Times* and the *Atlanta Constitution*, both 30 Oct. 1986; and the *Washington Post*, 1 Nov. 1986.

JOHN A. LUCAS

SCHOMBURG, Arthur Alfonso (24 Jan. 1874–10 June 1938), historian, bibliophile, and curator, was born Arturo Alfonso Schomburg in San Juan, Puerto Rico, the son of Mary Joseph, an unwed midwife or laundress who had been born free in 1837 on St. Croix, Virgin Islands. Some sources claim that his father was Carlos Federico Schomburg, a German-born émigré merchant, but in a reply to a questionnaire from E. Franklin Frazier for his *The Negro Family in the United States* (1939), Schomburg himself named Carlos as his grandfather; he stated that his father was Carlos's son, unnamed, born in 1839, and also a merchant (Ortiz, p. 21).

Details of Schomburg's education are also sparse. He wrote that while living with his maternal grandfather, Nicholas Joseph, on St. Thomas, he attended the College of St. Thomas, a secondary school, but there is no documentation. Schomburg knew French, and his writings in Spanish are both grammatically correct and eloquent. His lack of formal education ate away at him all his life, and it was surely one of the spurs to his untiring search for information and his efforts to make the results widely known. The familiar anecdote that his quest was inspired by a teacher who told him that Negroes have no history may be apocryphal; however, he belonged to a club of young people who studied history, and he was acquainted with cigar makers, the most educated workers of the time. Strong supporters of independence for Cuba and Puerto Rico, then colonies of Spain, these tobacco workers provided lessons in history and nationalism for children and adults outside the factory.

Schomburg moved to New York City on 17 April 1891. He lived among the tobacco workers and participated in their meetings, fundraising, and publication activities. José Martí, the Cuban patriot, as well as Ramón Betances and J. Julio Henna, Puerto Rican heroes of the independence movement, inspired his activism and scholarly bent. Martí, in New York from 1881 to 1895, founded the Cuban Revolutionary Party in January 1892; in August its newspaper, *Patria*, published Schomburg's first article, a description of Las Dos Antillas, a political club Schomburg had co-founded earlier that year. He served as the club's secretary for four years. Club members cooperated with other interracial groups committed to independence for Cuba and Puerto Rico. Still a teenager, Schomburg worked as an elevator operator, bellhop, printer, and porter. He taught Spanish in the night school where he learned English. In this busy year he also managed to visit New Orleans, where he was impressed both by the "joyous and sad" spirituals he heard in a Baptist church, and by the beautiful women he saw (Sinnette, pp. 21–22). On his return Schomburg, an exceptionally social and fraternal man, joined a Masonic lodge, El Sol de Cuba #38, founded by Cuban and Puerto Rican exiles in 1881. English-speaking blacks were encouraged to join, and Schomburg translated the proceedings into English. He began acquiring and organizing the lodge's papers, books, correspondence, and photographs. He was elected master in 1911. The lodge, by then mostly black, changed its name to Prince Hall, after the first black Mason in the United States.

This name change may be seen as emblematic of Schomburg's expanded interests, a change which had been occurring over the preceding fifteen years. In 1895 he married Elizabeth Hatcher, an African American from Staunton, Virginia, and began to use the English form of his name. Three children had been born by 1900, when his wife died. The middle name of one child was Guarionex, a pen name Schomburg sometimes used on letters to editors (1903–1905), after a legendary Carib hero who struggled against the Spanish invaders.

Around 1895 cracks began to appear in the unity of the exiled revolutionary groups. Martí's death in battle in 1895, and the Spanish-American War of 1898, which put Cuba, Puerto Rico, and the Philippines under the control of the United States, effectively ended the revolutionary efforts of the exiles. Schomburg now turned his attention to the state of black America, realizing that his future was here, among people of color. His second marriage, to Elizabeth Morrow Taylor of Williamsburg, North Carolina, lasted from 1902 until 1909, when she died, leaving two children. As he visited his children, who were being raised by maternal relatives in the South, Schomburg encountered full-blown racism.

Schomburg worked as a clerk and messenger for Pryor, Mellis and Harris, a law firm, from 1901 to 1906. On 1 February 1906 he took a job with the Bankers Trust Company on Wall Street, where he remained for twenty-three years. He rose from messenger to supervisor of the bank's foreign mailing section. His knowledge of French and Spanish, his exceptional memory, and his attention to detail were valuable qualities. But Schomburg's real work was not on Wall Street; it was wherever he found others equally impassioned to prove that black people did indeed have an international history of accomplishment that stretched past slavery days to Africa. In April 1911 Schomburg was one of five founders of the Negro Society for Historical Research, an outgrowth of the Men's Sunday Club, which he had joined in 1905. The others were John E. Bruce, a journalist whose pen name was Bruce Grit; David Bryant Fulton, a sleeping-car porter and journalist who wrote as Jack Thorne; W. Wesley Weekes, a musician; and Ernest Braxton, an artist. The society aimed "to show that the Negro race has a history that antedates that of the proud Anglo-Saxon race"; they planned "to collect useful historical data relating to the Negro race, books written by or about Negroes, rare pictures of prominent men and women . . . letters . . . African curios of native manufacture" (Sinnette, p. 43). It acquired members in Europe, the Americas, the Caribbean, and Africa, including the vice president of Liberia, James Dossen, Edward Blyden of Sierra Leone, and Mojola Agbebe of Nigeria—which must have gratified Schomburg, a Pan-Africanist.

Schomburg, activist and expansive in outlook, generously made available to those in his wide network his private library, acquired with a limited budget. He had already begun to carry out the society's mission of collecting historical documents. At about this time he married Elizabeth Green, his third wife. By 1916 their household was filled with three young children and Schomburg's growing library.

"Racial Integrity," a paper Schomburg read before a summer class of teachers in July 1913 at Cheney Institute in Pennsylvania, called for the establishment in colleges of chairs of Negro history. He said, "We have chairs of almost everything, and believe we lack nothing, but we sadly need a chair of Negro history. . . . We need the historian and philosopher to give us, with trenchant pen, the story of our forefathers . . . the background for our future" (Schomburg, "Racial Integrity," pp. 17, 19). His idea was realized more than fifty years later, when courses in black history were begun at colleges and universities.

The American Negro Academy, founded in Washington, D.C., in 1897 and limited to forty members, elected Schomburg to membership in 1914. Schomburg became the academy's fifth president (1920–1929). The group held annual conventions, encouraged publication of scholarly works, and urged members to acquire books and manuscripts by and about people of African descent. At the 1915 convention, Schomburg's paper, "The Economic Contribution by the Negro to America," brought to the academy's attention the theme that had always engaged him: that people of African origin, wherever they were in the world, had made significant but unrecognized contributions in all fields to white society. Schomburg's research, writings, and talks about Haitians and blacks of European, Central, and South American

birth broadened the perspective of the academy's members.

In 1918 Schomburg was elected grand secretary of the Prince Hall Grand Lodge of the State of New York, a position that required frequent travel and attention to many organizational activities, including planning a new temple. He was still able to mount a week-long exhibition at the Carleton Street YMCA in Brooklyn in August, in conjunction with the Negro Library Association. On view were rare books, manuscripts, engravings, paintings, and sculpture, as well as African art lent by a private collector. Robert Goldwater (*Primitivism in Modern Art* [1967], p. 275) noted only one earlier exhibition, in New York in 1909, where African art was displayed as art, not as ethnographic curiosities.

By 1925 Schomburg had formed a library of nearly 4,000 books and pamphlets and about 1,000 manuscripts and prints, which he wished to make widely available, especially if it "may mean inspiration for the youth of my race" (Sinnette, p. 141). With a grant of $10,000 from the Carnegie Corporation in 1926, the New York Public Library purchased the collection and housed it in its 135th Street Library. Among its rarest items were Benjamin Banneker's almanacs (1792–1796) and manuscripts by Paul Lawrence Dunbar and Toussaint L'Ouverture. In the center of Harlem during the peak years of the Harlem Renaissance, the library became a site for many intellectual and cultural events. Lectures, art exhibitions, and concerts filled the branch's calendar, and the speakers included the leading personalities of the day. Schomburg's most influential essay, "The Negro Digs Up His Past," appeared first in *Survey Graphic* (Mar. 1925) and in Alain Locke's *The New Negro* (1925) and was often reprinted. Schomburg called for rigorous historical research, not "a pathetically over-corrective, ridiculously over-laudatory . . . apologetics turned into biography." He wrote, "History must restore what slavery took away"; he concluded, "There is no doubt that here is a field full of the most intriguing and inspiring possibilities." Yet half a century passed before his collection was recognized as a treasure house and received funding for renovation and new construction.

Considering that Schomburg made only one trip to Europe, in the summer of 1926, the extent and rarity of the collection is amazing. He made agents and scouts of friends who lived or traveled abroad: Langston Hughes, James Weldon Johnson, and the artist Albert Smith were among those given "assignments" or lists of desiderata. His correspondence with other book collectors and dealers was voluminous and nearly worldwide. In 1927 Schomburg received the Harmon Foundation Bronze Medal and $100 for his nationally significant contribution to education.

After the sale of his collection Schomburg began to spend more time at the 135th Street Library. When he retired from Bankers Trust at the end of 1929, he planned to devote his time to research and to travel to Spain again. Even before his retirement, however, Charles S. Johnson, former editor of *Opportunity*, the journal of the National Urban League, and now chairman of the social science department of Fisk University in Nashville, Tennessee, invited him to build Fisk's Negro Collection. Both Johnson and Louis Shores, the new librarian, had received Schomburg's guidance in New York. From November 1930 until the end of 1931 Schomburg was the curator of that collection, acquiring 4,524 books out of a total of 4,630. Shores wrote Sinnette that Schomburg's "bibliographic memory was spectacular." Schomburg also initiated discussions and seminars and was active in preservation efforts, but funding ended, and he returned to New York to accept his final position as curator in charge of his own collection, serving from January 1932 until his death in Brooklyn.

Money was short because of the Great Depression, but Schomburg managed to add outstanding items to the New York collection, including the long-sought *Ad Catholicum* of Juan Latino (1573) and a folio of engravings by Patrick Reason, a nineteenth-century black artist. The marble-and-bronze sculpture of Ira Aldridge as Othello, which often serves as the graphic symbol of the Schomburg Center, was bought in 1934, with assistance from a fellow bibliophile, Arthur B. Spingarn. Donations from authors, artists, and Schomburg's many friends further enriched the collection, as did purchases paid for by Schomburg himself.

The acquisition of Schomburg's collection by the New York Public Library vindicated his forty-year search for the evidence of black history. He was gratified that it would be freely available to all. A teenage immigrant without influential family, formal education, or ample funds, consigned to a segregated world, he nevertheless amassed a collection of inestimable value. Schomburg was "a man who built his own monument," said one eulogist. From his core of 5,000 items, the Schomburg Center for Research in Black Culture would grow to 5 million items and become the world's most important repository in the field. Schomburg's name is also commemorated in a street in San Juan, Puerto Rico, an elementary school in the Bronx, and a housing complex in Harlem.

• A large collection of Schomburg's papers is at the Schomburg Center for Research in Black Culture of the New York Public Library, along with extensive clipping files about him; the *Kaiser Index to Selected Black Resources 1948–1986* (1992) cites many articles about him. Schomburg's 1913 speech, "Racial Integrity," was reprinted as a pamphlet by Black Classics Press (n.d.). For a nearly complete bibliography of Schomburg's writings, see Betty Kaplan Gubert and Richard Newman, *Nine Decades of Scholarship: A Bibliography of the Writings 1892–1983 of the Staff of the Schomburg Center for Research in Black Culture* (1986). A full-length biography, Elinor Des Verney Sinnette, *Arthur Alfonso Schomburg: Black Bibliophile and Collector* (1989), is of exceptional importance for understanding Schomburg and his library. See also a biographical essay in English and Spanish by Victoria Ortiz in *The Legacy of Arthur Alfonso Schomburg: A Celebration of the Past, a Vision for the Future* (1986), an exhibition catalog with a checklist of more than 350 items, a chronology, and photographs. An obituary is in the *New York Times*, 11 June 1938.

BETTY KAPLAN GUBERT

SCHOOLCRAFT, Henry Rowe (28 Mar. 1793–10 Dec. 1864), author, ethnologist, and Indian agent, was born on a farmstead on Black Creek, near Albany, New York, the son of Lawrence Schoolcraft, a farmer and glass manufacturer, and Margaret Anne Barbara Rowe. He attended school and received tutoring in Latin in Hamilton, New York, where his father served as justice of the peace. After the family moved to Vernon, New York, in 1808, he held responsible positions in the construction and management of glass factories in New York, New Hampshire, and Vermont, often in business with his father. Although for a time he had the stimulating intellectual influence of an older mentor, a professor at Middlebury College, Vermont, Schoolcraft never attended classes. He acquired a library of scientific books and performed experiments in chemistry and mineralogy. Despite his recognized competence, he achieved only temporary success in glass manufacturing.

After declaring bankruptcy in 1817, Schoolcraft traveled west into Arkansas, investigating mining and smelting operations. His adventures led to his first significant publication, *A View of the Lead Mines of Missouri* (1819). He secured an assignment as mineralogist on the first American expedition through the upper Great Lakes in 1820 headed by Lewis Cass, governor of Michigan Territory. In the spring of 1821 Schoolcraft brought out *Narrative Journal of Travels in the Northwestern Regions of the United States* and returned to the Midwest, serving in August 1821 as secretary to a treaty council in Chicago for acquisition of Potawatomi and Ottawa land in southwestern Michigan. His 1821 experiences were described in *Travels in the Central Portions of the Mississippi Valley* (1825).

Schoolcraft commenced a nineteen-year career in the federal Indian service in 1822 when he was appointed the first Indian agent at Sault Ste. Marie, Michigan. In 1823 he married Jane Johnston, twenty-two-year-old daughter of trader John Johnston, whose wife, Oshawguscodawayqua, came from a respected Ojibwa family in LaPointe, Wisconsin. Educated by her father, Jane had spent the winter of 1809–1810 with relatives at the family estate in Ireland and in London. Henry and Jane had two children who survived to adulthood.

With the aid of his Ojibwa-Irish wife and her family, including her seven siblings, Schoolcraft embarked on a pioneer study of Ojibwa language and oral literature. After publishing individual ethnological and literary papers, he presented the first collection of Indian myths and legends for American readers in a popular two-volume work, *Algic Researches* (1839). In the introduction he set forth his views on Indian history and the characteristics of Indian people. His work brought him into contact with philologist Albert Gallatin and other members of meetings of the American Ethnological Society and the New-York Historical Society as well as European scholars.

As Indian agent for the Ojibwas, Schoolcraft conducted a delegation to the first government-sponsored intertribal council in the Midwest, held at Prairie du Chien, Wisconsin, in 1825. The purpose of the council was to draw up a treaty that would end regional warfare, particularly the long-standing hostilities between the Sioux and the Ojibwas. He was also present for the signing of two follow-up treaties in Wisconsin in 1826 and 1827 with bands not present at Prairie du Chien. Prominent in Michigan public affairs, he was appointed judge of Chippewa County when it was created in 1827. As elected delegate to the territorial council, he attended four sessions in Detroit between 1828 and 1831. During the winter of 1830–1831, he experienced religious revelations that culminated in his joining the Presbyterian church in Detroit in March 1831. Schoolcraft henceforth devoted himself to the causes of temperance and conversion of Indians, whom he now regarded as inferior pagans deserving compassion. His changed attitude toward Indian people permanently estranged him from his wife.

During the summer of 1831, Schoolcraft investigated the continuing Sioux-Ojibwa boundary dispute in the Minnesota-Wisconsin district, then led the well-known expedition to the head of the Mississippi River, reported in *Narrative of an Expedition through the Upper Mississippi to Itasca Lake . . . in 1832* (1834). With the closing of the Sault Ste. Marie agency in 1832, he was transferred to the agency at Mackinac Island in 1833. As commissioner representing the federal government, he secured Ottawa and Ojibwa lands in the eastern Upper Peninsula and northwestern Lower Peninsula of Michigan through terms of a treaty signed in Washington on 28 March 1836. Following this success he was appointed superintendent of the Michigan Indian Agency in July 1836. He subsequently negotiated four treaties with Ojibwa bands for the surrender of reservation lands in southeastern Michigan. Spending winters in Detroit, he was an active member of the Michigan Historical Society, which he had established in 1828. He also served as regent of the reincorporated University of Michigan from 1837 to 1841.

An ardent Democrat, Schoolcraft unsuccessfully opposed the Whigs headed by American Fur Company leaders in the election of 1840. He was dismissed from the Indian service in April 1841, a month after a circular letter was issued forbidding Indian departmental personnel from engaging in partisan political activity. At the time he was already under investigation for mishandling funds and for giving jobs in the Indian service to eight members of the Johnston and Schoolcraft families.

Unable to secure backing for his publishing ideas in New York City, Schoolcraft determined to seek support abroad, sailing for England in April 1842. The children were boarded in Albany, while his wife went to live at her sister's home in Canada. Jane Schoolcraft died in May 1842, her frail health weakened by addic-tion to laudanum, an opiate probably prescribed for whooping cough in 1836. Returning to New York in October 1842, Schoolcraft began lecturing, using the New-York Historical Society as a base for career promotion.

In 1843 the Treasury Department instituted a civil suit against him for misappropriation of government funds, seeking repayment of more than $16,000. The trial, held in Detroit, Michigan, resulted in a judgment against Schoolcraft in July 1844 for $9,965.23, essentially the amount of two payments for alleged losses in the Indian trade made a week before he left office, one of $8,200 to the Johnson estate, which he administered, and the second to his brother James. He finally settled his accounts with the government in 1850.

In 1845 Schoolcraft conducted a state-sponsored census of New York Indians that is reported in *Notes on the Iroquois* (1846). Expanding his ideas for enumerating Indians, he next lobbied in Washington for a bill, passed in March 1847, to conduct a national Indian census ostensibly to provide the basis for future government legislation. In 1847 he married Mary Howard, a plantation-reared South Carolinian who promoted his career but alienated his children. Employed again by the Bureau of Indian Affairs from 1847 to 1857, he brought out the six-volume *Historical and Statistical Information Respecting the . . . Indian Tribes of the United States* (1851–1857), a miscellany of articles and data covering selected Indian tribes and archaeological investigations that included Captain Seth Eastman's exceptional lithographs. Though uneven in quality, the impressive volumes remain a standard reference work. Concurrently Schoolcraft published his *Personal Memoirs* (1851), including fictitious autobiographical information as well as a number of reprints and popularized versions of earlier works.

Paralytic attacks, which had commenced in 1828, confined him to his home by 1857 and led to his death in Washington, D.C.

• The principal correspondence of Henry Rowe Schoolcraft is in Record Group 75 of the National Archives. Personal papers are held by the following repositories: Library of Congress; Burton Historical Collections, Detroit Public Library; New-York Historical Society; Huntington Library, San Marino, Calif.; DeWitt Historical Society of Tompkins County, Ithaca, N.Y.; Minnesota Historical Society, St. Paul; and Missouri Historical Society, St. Louis. A biography of Schoolcraft is Richard G. Bremer, *Indian Agent and Wilderness Scholar: The Life of Henry Rowe Schoolcraft* (1987). Other accounts of his life are in Robert E. Bieder, *Science Encounters the Indian, 1820–1880* (1986), and Chase S. Osborn and Stellanova Osborn, *Schoolcraft-Longfellow-Hiawatha* (1942), which includes a bibliography of Schoolcraft's works.

HELEN HORNBECK TANNER

SCHORER, Mark (17 May 1908–11 Aug. 1977), professor of English and man of letters, was born in Sauk City, Wisconsin, the son of William Carl Schorer, a manufacturer, and Anna Walser. His education was mainly at the University of Wisconsin, from which he received an A.B. in 1929, a Ph.D. in 1936, and a Litt.D. in 1962. He was also an A.M., Harvard, 1929–1930. On 15 August 1936 he married Ruth Page, with whom he had two children.

Schorer taught as an English instructor at Dartmouth from 1936 to 1937 and at Harvard from 1937 to 1945. In the fall of 1945 he joined the English department of the University of California at Berkeley as an associate professor; in 1946 he was appointed full professor. From 1960 to 1965 he served as chairman of the English department, and he retired in 1973.

From 1948 on, he was a fellow in the School of Letters in Bloomington, Indiana. He was a Fulbright fellow in Italy in 1952–1953, 1964; a fellow at the Center for Advanced Study in the Behavioral Sciences in Palo Alto, California, 1958–1959; a Bollingen fellow in 1960; a Guggenheim fellow in 1941, 1942, 1948–1949, and 1973–1974; a Rockefeller fellow at Bellagio, Italy, in 1974; and a senior fellow in the National Endowment for the Humanities in 1974–1975. Schorer won the Commonwealth Club Gold Medal Award in 1961 and the Distinguished Service Citation from the Wisconsin Academy of Sciences, Arts and Letters in 1969. He was a member of the Academy of Arts and Sciences, the executive council of the Modern Language Association from 1962 to 1966, and the board of directors of the American Council of Learned Societies from 1970 to 1972.

As a teacher, Schorer was exemplary at every level, from introductory undergraduate courses to the directing of dissertations; he was one of the most sought-after graduate instructors on the Berkeley faculty. He was an extremely gifted lecturer, relaxed, witty, informative. Although he wrote out his lectures, which accounts for some of their grace and charm, he was able to deliver them not as if he were reading from a text, but as if he were talking to his audience. His lectures on modern British literature were attended by hundreds of students and had to be given in the largest auditorium on campus (seating capacity of 1,200). He had to limit the numbers in his graduate seminars in prose fiction, which were always oversubscribed.

As a man of letters, Schorer was an immensely creative novelist, short-story writer, biographer, scholar, and literary critic. His four novels, *A House Too Old* (1935), *The Hermit Place* (1941), *The Wars of Love* (1954), and *Pieces of Life* (1977), were notable for their complexities and ironies and for the power and grace of their literary style. His many short stories were first published in the *New Yorker* and other national journals. Most of them were "*New Yorker*-style" stories for the simple reason that Schorer was one of the writers who created that particular, and now well-known, genre marked by wit, irony, concision, obliqueness, and astringency. Some thirty-two of these stories were collected and published in *The State of Mind* (1947).

Schorer's principal piece of scholarship was *William Blake: The Politics of Vision* (1946), which originally had been his Ph.D. dissertation at Wisconsin. It was a major contribution to Blake scholarship, which had begun to flourish around the middle of the century.

Schorer's massive *Sinclair Lewis: An American Life* (1961), the result of nine years of painstaking research, constitutes the definitive biography of the novelist, who, like Schorer, was born in the Midwest (not in Sauk City, Wis., but in Sauk Center, Minn.).

Schorer was probably best known as a leading literary critic of his time. Many of his critical essays were collected in *The World We Imagine* (1968). His single most famous essay, "Technique as Discovery" (1948), was translated into several foreign languages and, along with other Schorer critical essays, was made the center of discussion at a College English Association seminar held in 1968. He was greatly interested in D. H. Lawrence, wrote many essays and reviews about him, and edited the published facsimile of the manuscript of *Sons and Lovers* (1977).

Schorer was a man of great vitality and charm with hosts of friends in both the United States and Europe. He and his wife delighted in entertaining and did so copiously. Indeed, being invited to a Schorer dinner party was as if to be swept into the opening chapter of *Tender Is the Night* to attend a party presided over by Dick and Nicole Diver. Schorer was also a valiant man and met his approaching death in a hospital in Oakland, California, with his customary wit and grace. Thus in his last work, which he was able to see in print before he died, he had quoted from Ralph Waldo Emerson: " 'Twill soon be dark / Up! mind thine own aim, and / God speed the mark!"

• The Mark Schorer Papers are in the Bancroft Library, University of California, Berkeley.

JOHN HENRY RALEIGH

SCHOTT, Charles Anthony (7 Aug. 1826–31 July 1901), geophysicist, was born in Mannheim, Germany, the son of Anton Carl Schott, a merchant, and Anna Maria Hoffman. Schott graduated as a civil engineer after six years at the Technische Hochschule, Karlsruhe. The revolution of 1848, in which he briefly participated, and poor career prospects caused him to emigrate that year to the United States. In December 1848 he joined the U.S. Coast Survey, continuing in its service until his death. In 1854 Schott married Theresa Gildermeister; after her death he married her sister Bertha Gildermeister. Schott had one child by the first marriage and four by the second.

The heyday of the Coast Survey (later Coast and Geodetic Survey) coincided with Schott's years of service. Until the coming of the Geological Survey, it was the premier scientific agency of the government. During the middle decades of the nineteenth century, the Coast Survey was the largest employer of physical scientists and mathematicians in the United States. Beyond its role in high-precision geodetic surveying (taking into account the earth's actual shape) of the land area of the nation, it surveyed the coastline, actively studied terrestrial magnetism and the tides, and made occasional forays into astronomy, meteorology, and other scientific areas. It represented a consequential application of classical (that is, Newtonian) physics to the service of commerce and national expansion. Because of the high quality of its products, the survey was well regarded internationally during the last century.

Schott was clearly very well trained both in the physical sciences and in mathematics. Before the age of electronic computers, the calculations involved in the survey were arduous, if not tedious, often requiring great ingenuity in devising short cuts and methods of approximation. But Schott's importance to the survey far transcended his industry and cleverness in computing. On him, more than any other person, depended the precision and the theoretical sophistication of the survey's work. Beyond the actual computations of the data to produce maps, charts, and other products, Schott reviewed the instruments, the observational techniques, and the very data brought back to Washington at the end of each surveying season. He appraised new magnetic devices, base-bar apparatuses, and recording devices such as tidal gauges. When theoretical issues like isostasy (the equilibrium of the earth's crust) possibly impinged on the operations, it was Schott who handled the issue.

Appraising Schott's specific role is awkward. The survey was a team effort; individual contributions were not always clearly delineated. Schott played his role within the process behind the scenes. Details of his participation remain largely buried in unpublished and unstudied documents in the records of the Coast and Geodetic Survey. Yet, Schott also published many articles and official reports and was held in esteem by knowledgeable contemporaries. Before the work of John F. Hayford, Schott was the leading geodesist of the survey. His work on the great post–Civil War triangulation across the continent was a high point in the older style of determining the figure (i.e., true shape) of the earth. The results of the Mexican War and the spread of settlement between the Mississippi and the Pacific Ocean necessitated the expansion of the Coast Survey from its original geodetic surveying along the Atlantic and Gulf coasts. Linked to the geodetic arc from Maine to Florida was a transcontinental arc from New York to San Francisco. This would link also with a Pacific Coast arc and, later, with an arc from Canada to the Gulf. Schott had primary responsibility for maintaining uniform standards and for the completion of the calculations connecting the field observations into one coherent system.

Like others in the agency, Schott was greatly interested in terrestrial magnetism, producing several studies on the subject. When the French Academy of Science awarded him its Wilde Prize in 1898, it was for nearly fifty years of collecting and reducing data, devising new apparatus, and studying such phenomena as the aurora borealis and sunspots for their relations to the earth's magnetism. In his day, Schott was also known for contributing to meteorology. His memorialist, the meteorologist Cleveland Abbe, lists in Schott's bibliography many works on the relations of meteorology and geodesy as well as "a long series of volumes on the climate of America." Many of these are mathematical reductions of field data gathered by survey personnel and others.

In addition to the lack of study of the large body of unpublished examples of his work, Schott is little known and perhaps underappreciated because of the nature of his activities and their relation to the historiographic concerns of contemporary historians. His was neither a life of spectacular discoveries in field and laboratory nor a life devoted to generating new conceptual structures. Schott was largely engaged in the elaboration and extension of the Newtonian world view to this planet. Both great skill and erudition were required for what was a group effort on an international scale. Schott is historically interesting not only for the specifics of his career but also as an exemplar of a style of science (not the literal content) ubiquitous in the modern industrial world. Increasingly human societies depend on the systems devised and kept operating by the intellectual and cultural successors of the Schotts of the nineteenth century.

• The best source for Schott's career are the records of the survey in RG 23 of the U.S. National Archives. They are described in N. Reingold, comp., Preliminary Inventory No. 105 of the National Archives (1958); Schott's reports are in entry 45 (Computing Division Reports) and entry 83 (Geodetic Reports) of the inventory. Cleveland Abbe's memoir of Schott, National Academy of Sciences, *Biographical Memoirs* 8 (1915): 87–133, has a good bibliography of his published works.

NATHAN REINGOLD

SCHREIBER, Frederick Charles (13 Jan. 1895–15 Jan. 1985), organist, conductor, and teacher, was born in Vienna, Austria, the son of Charles Robert Darwin Schreiber, a doctor, and Anna (maiden name unknown). Both parents were musicians who delighted in playing piano, and they provided countless hours of musical enrichment for Frederick and his sister Ella. In this way Schreiber learned to appreciate the classical repertoire. Schreiber began formal study of the piano at age eight and wrote his first composition when he was just ten years old. He attended the Humanistic High School in Vienna, the Vienna University, and the State Academy of Music, studying composition, conducting, piano, and violoncello.

During World War I Schreiber served in the Austrian army. He married Lucy Erenreich in 1920. They had no children. In 1924 Schreiber was appointed choirmaster and organist at the Dorotheenkirche in Vienna. From 1927 to 1938 he served as a professor of composition, orchestration, and theory at the Vienna Conservatory of Music.

Fleeing the Nazis, the Schreibers left their homeland in 1938 and came to the United States. In 1939 they settled permanently in New York City and became American citizens six years later. From 1939 until 1958 Schreiber acted as choirmaster and organist of the Reformed Protestant Church on East Sixty-eighth Street. He served as organist and music director at the Broadway Presbyterian Church from 1958 until his retirement in 1972.

Schreiber continued to teach and compose until his death, leaving over 800 compositions. An extremely modest man, he never flaunted himself or his music, but a considerable number of his works, when entered in competitions, won prizes and citations. Between 1945 and 1956 he received ten first prizes in international competitions. Among these, *Sinfonietta* was chosen, in 1948, from among 110 entries in a contest sponsored by the Musical Fund Society of Philadelphia. The following season the premiere was given by the Philadelphia Orchestra under Eugene Ormandy. In 1954 his Concerto Grosso won the Chicago Symphony contest and was premiered by Fritz Reiner and the Chicago Symphony. In Europe Schreiber's orchestral works have been played by the Vienna Philharmonic and the Vienna Symphony and at the Salzburg Festival. Among the conductors who have performed Schreiber's works are Paul Gaston, Leon Barzin, George Szell, Joseph Kripps, and Fritz Litschauer.

Most of the prizes Schreiber won were awarded for choral works on religious texts, submitted in contests sponsored by the American Guild of Organists, of which he was a member, the Presbyterian church, and choral societies throughout the United States. During Schreiber's 33-year tenure as organist and choirmaster in New York City he provided music for over 1,500 church services. His attitude and work method harked back to baroque times. The music he composed or arranged for each service was often used just once and then laid aside. Like Johann Sebastian Bach, Schreiber left behind several hundred religious works—anthems, oratorios, original compositions, and arrangements for one to four voices with organ or piano accompaniment—all superbly crafted and imbued with a joyful spirit.

Most of Schreiber's music was written in a late romantic, polyphonic style reminiscent of the works of Richard Strauss and Gustav Mahler. His music sprang from a happy frame of mind yet was also ardent and uplifting. In his later works Schreiber reached an unusual technical freedom and power of expression. Schreiber was a member of the American Society of Composers, Authors and Publishers. Among his publishers was the H. W. Gray Co., Inc., New York. His compositions include nine symphonies and other orchestral works; concertos for piano, violin, cello, and other instruments; *The Beatitudes* for chorus and symphony orchestra (1950); six sonatas, four trios, seven quartets, and two quintets; sacred choral music; organ and piano works; and many lieder. He died in New York.

Schreiber made a major contribution to the literature of sacred choral and organ works. As a master craftsman, endowed with a fine poetic sense, he chose to write in a style reminiscent of Mahler. During Schreiber's long life the style became anachronistic, but his compositions attained an unusual perfection and expressive power.

• The bulk of Schreiber's manuscripts and papers is located in the music library at Lincoln Center in New York. Biographical information and discussion of his music can be found in program booklets of the Philadelphia Orchestra (1949–1950), the Chicago Symphony (1954), and Westminster Choir (1956). A partial listing of works is given in "Dizionario della Musica e del Musicisti," vol. 7 (1988).

KEES KOOPER

SCHREMBS, Joseph (12 Mar. 1866–2 Nov. 1945), Roman Catholic archbishop, was born in Wurzelhofen near Regensburg, Bavaria, the son of George Schrembs, a blacksmith, and Mary Gess. His youthful experience as a singer in the celebrated boys' choir of the Regensburg cathedral gave him a lifelong love for, and expertise in, liturgical music. At the age of eleven, he immigrated to America to study at St. Vincent's Archabbey in Latrobe, Pennsylvania, where his older brother, Ignatius, was a monk. After five years at the monastery school and two years as a teacher in a parochial school in Louisville, Kentucky, he was accepted as a candidate for the priesthood by Bishop Henry J. Richter of Grand Rapids, Michigan. Richter sent Schrembs to study at the Grande Séminaire in Montreal, where he added a facility in French to his knowledge of German and English. He returned to Grand Rapids for his ordination on 29 June 1889, and successively served as the pastor of two parishes and then as vicar general of the diocese. In 1911 he was appointed auxiliary bishop of Grand Rapids and later that same year was installed as the first bishop of the newly created diocese of Toledo, Ohio.

Schrembs organized the new diocese and set in motion a complete system for its administration. Although there were as yet no paved highways in northwestern Ohio, he made his first tour of the sixteen county diocese in a new motor car presented to him by the priests. He then divided the diocese into four deaneries, established thirteen parishes, opened thirty-three schools, ordained over sixty priests, and recruited an additional five religious communities to work in the diocese.

During World War I, Schrembs was one of the four bishops of the administrative committee of the National Catholic War Council established by Cardinal James Gibbons of Baltimore to coordinate Catholic relief efforts. After the war the bishops of the United States decided to make this organization a permanent one and changed its name to the National Catholic Welfare Council (NCWC). Schrembs was then named to the seven-member administrative committee of the new council.

On 16 June 1921 Schrembs was appointed the fifth bishop of the neighboring diocese of Cleveland, Ohio. The immigration of Catholics from eastern and southern Europe to Cleveland and the migration of the descendants of earlier Irish and German immigrants from the inner city to the suburbs prompted Schrembs to establish fifty-nine new parishes, many of them for designated ethnic groups. He also built a new seminary, established Ursuline College and Notre Dame

College, initiated a Sisters' College to promote the certification of all teachers, established new secondary and elementary schools, and enhanced church music both by encouraging the wider use of approved hymnals and manuals of Gregorian Chant and also by composing new music for worship.

On 25 February 1922 the Vatican suppressed the National Catholic Welfare Council at the request of two influential American cardinals, William O'Connell of Boston and Dennis Dougherty of Philadelphia, and of a few other bishops who felt that this national organization interfered with their autonomy in their own local dioceses. The administrative committee of the NCWC delegated Schrembs to make a personal appeal in Rome to save the council. Through his skillful lobbying of Vatican officials and several constructive meetings with Pope Pius XI, Schrembs succeeded in getting the suppression reversed. In order to save some face, the Vatican requested that a substitute for the term "council" be found for the organization's title. The term "conference" was selected, much against the wishes of Cardinal O'Connell who preferred a less significant term such as "committee." This National Catholic Welfare Conference continued to serve as the standing secretariat of the American bishops until it was reorganized as the National Conference of Catholic Bishops in 1966.

Perhaps the principal fumble in Schrembs's career was his initial support of the controversial "radio priest," Father Charles E. Coughlin of Royal Oak, Michigan. His support of Coughlin was expressed not only in private comments but also in favorable comments from the pulpit, on the radio, and in the diocesan newspaper. Schrembs's own effective use of the radio in Cleveland and his friendship with Coughlin's bishop, Michael J. Gallagher of Detroit, seems to have prompted his support. Although he eventually ceased these favorable comments because of Coughlin's strident anti-Semitism and extremely violent attacks on President Franklin D. Roosevelt, lingering doubts about his judgment diminished his influence.

On 25 March 1939 the newly elected Pope Pius XII conferred upon Schrembs the personal title of archbishop in recognition of his services both to his own diocese and to the universal church. Schrembs died in Cleveland. His recognition of the value of consensus and cooperation among the American bishops enabled him to play a crucial role in rescuing the National Catholic Welfare Conference.

• The bulk of Schrembs's personal and official papers are preserved in the Archives of the Diocese of Cleveland. Michael J. Hynes, *The History of the Diocese of Cleveland* (1953), contains a comprehensive account of Schrembs's life and work. See also Lawrence A. Mossing, *History of the Diocese of Toledo: General History Prior To and After Its Establishment in 1910* (1983), for an account of the earlier period of Schrembs's life.

M. EDMUND HUSSEY

SCHROEDER, Rudolph William (14 Aug. 1886–29 Dec. 1952), aviation and flight safety pioneer, was born in Chicago, Illinois, the son of John August Schroeder and Nora Ann Reidy. Little is known of his early life beyond the facts that he attended Crane Technical High School in Chicago and that his father died before Schroeder completed school. He then went to work in a garage as an automobile mechanic. One of the other mechanics, Otto Brodie, learned to fly an airplane, and Schroeder became his mechanic about 1910. For several years, Schroeder toured the country, working with a number of early aviators.

In 1916 he became a private in the aviation section of the Army Signal Corps. Rising from that rank to major in four years, Schroeder also achieved a number of significant firsts. He initiated, developed, and personally tested parachute flares and airplane lights for night landings. In 1919 he suggested antiknock fuel for high-compression and supercharged engines—something industry later developed. He played a major role in the development of the controllable pitch propeller, a gasoline flowmeter for aircraft, and other flight equipment. Reportedly, he tested the first turn indicator for airplanes and recommended the instruments for flying in poor visibility that the Army Air Corps later adopted, also helping in other ways to establish instrument flying in the army.

As chief test pilot of the Engineering Division at McCook Field in Ohio in 1919 and 1920, the tall, gangly major perversely known as "Shorty" set several altitude records. His organization was seeking to solve the problems involved in high-altitude flight and to develop improved equipment so that this would be possible. On 6 September 1919 Schroeder took Lieutenant George A. Elfrey up as a passenger in a Le Pere-Liberty 400 biplane with an open cockpit, equipped with a Moss turbosupercharger. Flying to 28,500 feet, they set a two-person altitude record. The two men rose to 30,900 feet on 24 September and to 31,821 on 4 October of that year.

Then on 27 February 1920 Schroeder went up alone in the Le Pere to go even higher. He wore the warmest flying suit available at the time and took an automatic oxygen system supposed to last three hours plus a manually controlled reserve tank. However, the automatic oxygen system broke down at 18,000 feet, and he had to switch on the reserve tank. At a temperature of −67 degrees Fahrenheit, and with the exhaust from the engine pouring carbon monoxide over his head, the reserve tank gave out after he passed 33,000 feet. Gasping for breath, he tore his mask and goggles off. In the carbon monoxide, he tried to steer the aircraft into a spiral but instead went into a dive as he passed out. He was unconscious for five miles but revived in time to pull out of the dive at about 2,000 feet. His eyes were cut from ice fragments that had formed beneath his eyelids, but he managed to land the biplane despite the damage his body had suffered from the carbon monoxide poisoning, cold, and rapid descent. Two barographs showed that he had reached 33,143 feet, easily surpassing the world record. He left the service that year, and his record did not last much longer. Nevertheless, in 1945 the army awarded him the Distinguished Flying Cross for his high-altitude achievements.

Not much information is available about Schroeder's personal life. He married Lillian (maiden name unknown) before the First World War, and the couple adopted a son. Following a divorce, in 1934 he wed Janet T. Carr, and they had a daughter; but this marriage suffered the same fate as his first.

In 1920 Schroeder became the chief of the airplane division in the Underwriter Laboratories, a post he held until 1925. Perhaps influenced by his own near accident in setting his altitude record, he began the process of setting safety standards for aviation. He continued this activity in 1933, when he became chief of the Air Commerce Bureau's Air Line Inspection Service. With the motto "There is no place for heroes in flying" (*Time*, 12 Jan. 1953), he developed a new technique for determining the causes of aviation accidents and thereby preventing their recurrence. After a mishap, he gathered remains of the aircraft and data on the flight from witnesses all along its path. Then he attempted to reconstruct what had gone wrong, using that determination to develop procedures and regulations to make flying increasingly safe.

Schroeder established such a solid reputation that in 1937, when United Air Lines was having reservations cancelled following a series of mishaps, the airline called Schroeder to be its manager of operations. His safety campaign there succeeded in making United's operations less hazardous, and he became vice president in charge of safety. In 1941 he suffered a stroke and was forced to retire in 1942.

Schroeder had helped design the trimotor Ford airplane right after he left the army, and in 1925 he became chief of Ford Motor Company's new airline, Ford Air Transport, obtaining in the process the first contract pilot's license. In 1928 he helped organize the Curtiss Flying Service, becoming manager of Curtiss Field near Glenview, Illinois, the next year. In 1930 he directed the National Air Races there, and in 1931 he managed the *Chicago Tribune*'s air show.

Following his stroke, Schroeder lived for more than a decade as something of an invalid before becoming critically ill at the age of sixty-six on Christmas Day while opening gifts at his home. He died four days later at Hines Veterans Hospital in Maywood, Illinois, near Chicago. Besides his contributions to flight safety and his transitory altitude record, Schroeder deserves credit for his altitude research, which paved the way for the subsequent development of superchargers, oxygen systems, and other equipment used on airliners and military aircraft up to and during World War II. Without these developments, bombardment and pursuit operations so critical to the Army Air Corps in operations against Germany and Japan would have been impossible.

• Biographical information on Schroeder is limited, but incomplete material is available in W. B. Courtney, "Under His Wing," *Collier's*, 13 Nov. 1937, pp. 21, 82–84. Roger E. Bilstein, *Flight Patterns* (1983), and Maurer Maurer, *Aviation in the U.S. Army, 1919–1939* (1987), cover the events surrounding his altitude research and records. Frank J. Taylor, *High Horizons . . . The United Airlines Story* (1951), briefly treats his career with United. An obituary is in the *New York Times*, 30 Dec. 1952.

J. D. HUNLEY

SCHROEDER, Theodore (17 Sept. 1864–10 Feb. 1953), lawyer and author, was born on a farm near Horicon, Wisconsin, the son of Theodor Schroeder, a miller, and Barbara (maiden name unknown). His mother, a Catholic, was disowned by her family when she married his Lutheran father, who had left Germany after the revolution of 1848. Already predisposed against religion by his mother's experience, Schroeder became a freethinker as a young man after reading the works of Robert Ingersoll. Schroeder attended the University of Wisconsin, where he received a civil engineering degree in 1886 and a law degree in 1889. While traveling through Utah on one of his many trips to the West, Schroeder was so deeply affected by the persecution of Mormons that he decided to begin his legal career in Utah. He later wrote that he wanted to defend the "downtrodden" Mormons "even as my mother had once a need for such a defender" against her religiously intolerant family. Schroeder established a financially succesful legal practice in Salt Lake City, and in 1891 he married Mary Parkinson. They had one daughter.

Schroeder's sympathy for the Mormons did not last long. Soon after moving to Salt Lake City, he concluded that "the Mormons were quite capable of even more bitter persecution of apostates than that which was being inflicted upon them." His extensive reading of Mormon texts convinced him that Mormonism was rooted in psychosexual problems. Schroeder began to write anti-Mormon polemics, including a pamphlet claiming that Joseph Smith, the founder of Mormonism, had been guilty of "sexual excesses" and of illegally "procuring the commission of abortions." This pamphlet prompted a prosecution against Schroeder for mailing obscene literature. Although the grand jury did not return an indictment, the prosecution alerted Schroeder to free speech issues and led him to oppose on constitutional grounds any regulation of alleged obscenity.

Schroeder became actively involved in the defense of free speech following the deaths of his wife in 1896 and his daughter in 1901. He moved to New York City in late 1901, originally to participate in what became the successful effort to prevent Brigham Roberts, a Mormon polygamist elected in Utah, from taking his seat in the U.S. House of Representatives. Schroeder remained in New York, where he "met every variety of radicals of that time" and "debated with them in open forums." Schroeder joined some of these radicals in the Free Speech League, which from its founding in 1902 until World War I was the only organization in the United States that supported free speech for all viewpoints. Schroeder's major collaborators in the league included Lincoln Steffens, the prominent "muckraking" journalist; Emma Goldman, the infamous anarchist; Margaret Sanger, the birth control activist; and Gilbert E. Roe, a New York lawyer who had been Schroeder's law school classmate and the law partner of Senator Robert M. La Follette. In 1908 Schroeder began living with Nancy Sankey-Jones, an active feminist. The couple, who remained together until her death in 1950, had no children. By living carefully on the money he had saved from his legal practice in Utah, Schroeder was able to serve without remuneration as the principal administrator of the league and to write prolifically about free speech.

In his work for the Free Speech League, Schroeder provided legal advice and financial assistance to defend free speech in court. He publicized disputes over free speech, corresponded and lobbied with public officials, testified before government commissions, and lectured at scholarly and professional conferences. Schroeder coordinated the meetings and activities of the league's small board of directors and cooperated with the local free speech leagues that emerged throughout the country in response to particular controversies. He never conditioned his assistance on the ideology of the speaker, and he repeatedly criticized others for defending free speech only for views they shared. Refusing efforts by several other organizations to affiliate with the Free Speech League, he insisted that the league must maintain its independence in order to convince the public that "it has a genuine interest in free speech quite distinct from the person or doctrine of those whom it seeks to help." Schroeder regarded his numerous articles on free speech, many of which became part of his most important book, *"Obscene" Literature and Constitutional Law* (1911), as contributions to the work of the Free Speech League. He emphasized throughout his writings and even in the league's articles of incorporation that speech should not be penalized on the basis of speculation about "the prospective psychological tendency of an idea upon a hypothetical future reader."

Schroeder continued his free speech activities during World War I, when federal prosecutors used the Espionage Act of 1917 to convict opponents of American intervention for their antiwar speech. The repression of dissenting speech during and after the war led Roger Baldwin and others to form the American Civil Liberties Union (ACLU). Having had no prior experience with free speech issues, Baldwin and his colleagues initially relied on Schroeder. But the ACLU quickly superseded Schroeder and the Free Speech League as the major defender of free speech. Schroeder reacted to this development with equanimity, probably because he had increasingly shifted his interests to psychology. He became a frequent contributor to the *Psychoanalytic Review*, a journal cofounded by William Alanson White, the eminent psychiatrist who was Schroeder's analyst in 1914–1915. Yet Schroeder remained interested in the subject of free speech, and on several occasions through the mid-1920s he tried unsuccessfully to convince Roger Baldwin that censorship of alleged obscenity, as well as repression of political dissent, raised free speech issues.

In 1916 H. L. Mencken described Schroeder as having "done more for free expression in America than any other." Schroeder's writings, which were widely reviewed, influenced major prewar scholars, including Ernst Freund, Roscoe Pound, and E. A. Ross. For the last thirty years of his life, however, Schroeder lived quietly in Cos Cob, Connecticut, where he died. His major contributions as a free speech scholar and activist are largely forgotten. Only in recent years have some scholars rediscovered his importance.

• Schroeder's papers are located in the Southern Illinois University Library. His major work was *"Obscene" Literature and Constitutional Law* (1911). The 1972 reprinted edition of this work contains an excellent analytical introduction by Jerold Auerbach. *Free Speech for Radicals* (enlarged ed., 1916) is the other major collection of Schroeder's essays. R. McCoy, ed., *Theodore Schroeder: A Cold Enthusiast* (1973), available at the Southern Illinois University Library, is an indispensable guide to Schroeder's publications. It consists largely of a lengthy annotated bibliography of works by and about Schroeder and a summary of the contents of the ninety-one boxes that comprise the Schroeder papers. Hutchins Hapgood, *A Cold Enthusiast* (1913), provides a vivid portrait of Schroeder by a contemporary journalist. The most comprehensive treatment of Schroeder's life and work is David Brudnoy, "Liberty's Bugler: The Seven Ages of Theodore Schroeder" (Ph.D. diss., Brandeis Univ., 1971). For analysis of Schroeder's scholarly contributions, see Mark A. Graber, *Transforming Free Speech: The Ambiguous Legacy of Civil Libertarianism* (1991), and David M. Rabban, *Free Speech in Its Forgotten Years* (1997), which also describes Schroeder's work as a free speech activist.

DAVID M. RABBAN

SCHROEDER, William J. (14 Feb. 1932–14 Aug. 1986), longest-surviving recipient of the Jarvik-7 artificial heart, was born in Jasper, Indiana, the son of Alois Schroeder, an insurance salesman, and Lorena Miller. Schroeder, like his mother and father, grew up in the small Indiana town of Jasper with a deeply ingrained loyalty to family and community. Schroeder was popular and well liked in high school for his humor and energy. The caption under his 1950 Jasper High School yearbook read: "A sense of humor and wit to enliven the bluest of days." His drive and energy, which earned him the nickname "Bull," served him well when he was presented with the opportunity to be the second recipient of the Jarvik-7 artificial heart.

Schroeder enlisted in the U.S. Air Force in 1950 after graduating from high school. After basic training, he returned to Jasper to marry Margaret Huff in 1952. His first assignment was as a cook at Fort Bragg, North Carolina. Over the next fourteen years, he was assigned to bases in South Carolina, Newfoundland, Saudi Arabia, Texas, and Michigan. During that time, he and his wife had six children. In Michigan he was a sergeant working a high-stress job as an air traffic controller. He returned to Jasper in 1966, when his mother died and his father became disabled.

Back in Jasper, Schroeder got a federal job at the U.S. Naval Weapons Support Center in Crane, Indiana. He started working on the assembly line and was soon promoted to quality assurance supervisor. He worked long hours and earned a reputation as a leader. He was active in the federal employees union and became a powerful negotiator. He also managed a Little League team and was active in the Knights of Columbus. He was known as being stubborn, tenacious, and unstoppable.

Schroeder's health began to decline in the early 1980s. He developed diabetes, smoked two packs of cigarettes a day, and was slightly overweight. In 1982 he had a small heart attack, and in January 1983 a second, more damaging one. In March 1983 he had heart bypass surgery; he did not recover well, and his health continued to decline. By March 1984 it was clear that he would not fully recover. Meanwhile, organ transplants were becoming more common, and one patient had already received a completely artificial organ. Barney Clark had been the first patient to receive the Jarvik-7 artificial heart two years earlier, and artificial hearts were routinely being used to maintain patients waiting for human heart transplants. In October 1984 Schroeder was told by his doctors that his condition was imminently terminal, but that an artificial heart might be an option. In November 1984 the Schroeder family met with William DeVries, the surgeon who had installed the first Jarvik-7 into Barney Clark. DeVries and other doctors decided that Schroeder would be the next recipient of the artificial heart.

On 25 November 1984, at Humana Hospital in Louisville, Kentucky, Schroeder received a Jarvik-7 artificial heart in place of his own dying heart. The media paid close attention to his story even before the operation. Just days before, the Schroeder family saw themselves on the front page of the *New York Times*, and Schroeder told the press, "I feel like I've got ten years left right now." His reputation with the press as a home-town hero was also growing. Two weeks after the operation, he took a phone call from President Ronald Reagan; he told the president that he had not received his Social Security check and that he was "just getting a runaround" (*Time*, 24 Dec. 1984). Two Social Security officials appeared the next day at the hospital and handed Schroeder a check.

The next day, Schroeder suffered a stroke, a common complication in Jarvik-7 heart recipients. This was the first in a constant series of complications. Although he recovered enough to move out of the hospital and into a nearby apartment, he suffered another stroke. He again recovered enough to visit Jasper and take a fishing trip with the inventor of his new heart, Robert Jarvik. He and his wife celebrated their thirty-third wedding anniversary in Louisville.

In November 1985 Schroeder suffered a devastating stroke. He lingered in a semiconscious state for seven months, until the family agreed to disconnect the artificial heart from the machine that kept it pumping. At Schroeder's death, DeVries said, "Through his bravery, much was learned that will contribute to advanc-ing this project from the experimental to the therapeutic stage."

Schroeder was chosen as a recipient of the artificial heart not just because he was sick enough to need it, but because he had a strong will to live and the strength to fight. His will to survive and his desire to live a productive life gave him 620 days with a permanent, artificial heart, and Schroeder and his family became folk heroes to the nation as the media followed his story. He was a subject of research for the doctors involved, as well as an admired friend. The Jarvik-7 was used on only one more human patient, Murray Haydon, as a permanent heart, but was used into the 1990s to "bridge" patients until a human heart became available for transplant.

• Reports on William Schroeder's death are in *Time*, 18 Aug. 1986, p. 58, and *Newsweek*, 18 Aug. 1986, p. 47, which included a short discussion of Schroeder's death and the implications for artificial hearts. The Schroeder story was featured in *People*, 16 Dec. 1985. *Time* and *Newsweek*, both 4 Mar. 1985, provide updates on the Schroeder story. *U.S. News and World Report* and *Time*, both 10 Dec. 1984, updates Schroeder's condition soon after the transplant. The Schroeder Family and Martha Barnette, *The Bill Schroeder Story* (1987), is a comprehensive account of Schroeder's life, family, and ordeal with the artificial heart.

BETH MARTIN

SCHUCHERT, Charles (3 July 1858–20 Nov. 1942), paleontologist, was born in Cincinnati, Ohio, the son of Philip Schuchert, a cabinetmaker, and Agatha Muller. His parents were impoverished German immigrants and Charles, the eldest of six children, was forced to leave school at the age of thirteen to help his father establish a tiny furniture business. In 1877, after fire struck the factory and his father suffered a breakdown, Schuchert rebuilt the business and became the family provider.

As a child, Schuchert had pursued a hobby of fossil collecting and, through self-guided reading, had taught himself to identify the abundant brachiopods (fossil shellfish) that he found near his home. After leaving school, Schuchert took night classes in lithography and became interested in its application to scientific illustration and analysis. In 1878 he began to attend meetings of the Cincinnati Society of Natural History, where he became friends with E. O. Ulrich, curator of the society's collections. Schuchert introduced Ulrich to lithography and convinced him to seek remunerative work preparing lithographic illustrations for state geological surveys. In 1884, after fire had struck the furniture factory again, Ulrich convinced Schuchert to become his paid assistant.

Schuchert spent the next three years preparing specimens and producing scientific lithographs with Ulrich. In 1888 his work and his collection (which eventually numbered over 10,000 specimens) came to the attention of New York state geologist James Hall, who hired him to assist in the production of volume 8 of *Paleontology of New York* (1889–1891). As Hall's assistant, Schuchert was exposed to the larger geological problems of stratigraphy, mountain building, and the relation of fossil evolution to earth history, and he began to develop contacts in the professional geological community.

In 1893 Schuchert became an assistant paleontologist at the U.S. Geological Survey. One year later, he became assistant curator of invertebrate paleontology at the U.S. National Museum in Washington, D.C. While at the museum, Schuchert participated in numerous international collecting expeditions and became an expert in global geology and its relation to the distribution of fossil species. In 1904 Schuchert accepted a position at Yale University, where he would achieve his greatest level of scientific accomplishment and professional leadership. From 1904 to 1925, he served simultaneously as curator of geological collections for the Peabody Museum, professor of paleontology at Yale University, and professor of historical geology at the Sheffield Scientific School. He also served stints as chairman of the Department of Geology, acting dean of the Yale Graduate School, member of the Governing Board of the Sheffield Scientific School, and trustee of the Peabody Museum.

By the time he joined the Yale faculty, Schuchert was widely recognized as a leading brachiopod expert. His pamphlet, *Directions for Collecting and Preparing Fossils* (1895), had become a curatorial standard. The demands of teaching, however, led Schuchert into the area for which he ultimately became most famous: paleogeography. Having never taken a college course himself, Schuchert was vexed by the difficulty of conveying to students the massive amount of geological detail needed to understand the distribution of fossil species in relation to earth history. To solve this problem, he began to compile maps that illustrated the distribution of fossils with respect to global structure and stratigraphy. These maps became increasingly synthetic: ultimately, the data of geology and paleontology were used to reconstruct the limits of land and sea in each succeeding geological period.

Compilation of his paleogeographic maps led Schuchert to write his magnum opus, the three-volume *Historical Geology of North America* (1935–1943). The maps also led to his involvement in the debate over continental drift. In the 1910s and 1920s Schuchert had been active in the search for an explanation of the distribution of similar fossil forms in widely distant locales. When continental drift was proposed as a solution to this problem, however, Schuchert opposed it because the distribution of marine invertebrates did not appear to be consistent with the radical changes in climatic patterns implied by continental drift. Together with Stanford geologist Bailey Willis, Schuchert developed the alternative concept of isthmian links: narrow land connections that could explain the observed paleontological similarities without causing major climatic disturbances. Schuchert's solution was widely accepted by American geologists, until the continental drift debate was reopened by geophysical evidence in the late 1950s.

Schuchert's life was devoted to scientific work. Although he never married, he had a longtime female assistant, Clara M. LeVene, who attended to both personal and scientific matters. LeVene coauthored several books and articles, including the great bibliographic catalog *Brachiopoda* (1929). Perhaps reflecting his own life story, Schuchert believed that science advanced primarily by laborious empirical work: leaps of insight were useless without the careful observation needed to prove or disprove them. When he died in New Haven, Schuchert was still at work on the final volumes of his *Historical Geology* (vol. 2 was published posthumously in 1943; vol. 3 was never finished).

Schuchert was a leading figure in American science, having forged a scientific career based entirely on self-education and apprenticeship. In addition to his research, he served as the first president of the Paleontological Society, in 1910, president of the Geological Society of America in 1922, and vice president of the American Association for the Advancement of Science in 1927. He was a member of the National Academy of Science, an editor of the *American Journal of Science*, and he received numerous scientific awards and medals. His legacy is recalled annually by the Geological Society of America Schuchert Medal for contributions to paleontology.

Ironically, the organizations that Schuchert presided over helped to consolidate the professionalization of American science that excluded the self-taught man. Schuchert's biography thus highlights the tremendous changes that occurred in American science near the turn of the century. Schuchert began his career as an apprentice and ended it teaching in a Ph.D.-granting institution. He was one of the last professional scientists in the United States with no formal training in any scientific field.

• Schuchert's personal papers, in the Yale University Archives, Manuscript Collections, contain Schuchert's copious correspondence and provide one of the best available collections of historical materials on American geology in the early twentieth century. Letters from Schuchert are also in the Bailey Willis Collection at the Huntington Library, San Marino, Calif. Schuchert published over 200 scientific articles, memorials, and book reviews, mostly in the areas of invertebrate paleontology, stratigraphy, and paleogeography. Among his numerous books that have not already been mentioned are *Synopsis of American Fossil Brachiopoda* (1897), *Paleogeography of North America* (1910), *Textbook of Historical Geology* (1915), *A Textbook of Geology* (1924), *The Earth and Its Rhythms* (1927), *Outlines of Historical Geology* (1931), and *O. C. Marsh, Pioneer in Paleontology* (1940). A brief view of Schuchert is given in Curt Teichert, "From Karpinsky to Schindewolf—Memories of Some Great Paleontologists," *Journal of Paleontology* 50 (1976): 1–12. Schuchert's role in the continental drift debate is briefly discussed in Naomi Oreskes, "The Rejection of Continental Drift," *Historical Studies in the Physical and Biological Sciences* 18 (1988): 311–48. Malcolm Weiss gives an account of Ulrich's later resentment of Schuchert's professional success in "Geological Society of America Election of 1921: Attack of Candidacy of Charles Schuchert for the Presidency," *Earth Sciences History* 11 (1992): 90–102. Obituaries are by Carl O. Dunbar, *Pro-*

ceedings of the Geological Society of America, Annual Report (1942): 217–40, which includes a complete bibliography, and by Adolpf Knopf, National Academy of Sciences Biographical Memoirs 27 (1952): 363–37, which includes a list of other important obituaries.

NAOMI ORESKES

SCHULTZ, Dutch (6 Aug. 1902–24 Oct. 1935), gangster and underworld entrepreneur, was born Arthur Flegenheimer in the Bronx, New York City, the son of Herman Flegenheimer, a glazier and baker, and Emma Neu. Before the boy completed the sixth grade, his father either deserted the family or died. Arthur's mother then took in laundry to support the family, and he quit school to sell newspapers, run errands, and work as an office boy, printer's apprentice, and roofer. While he proudly retained his roofers' union card as evidence of his working-class respectability, he was pulled into the gang world of the Bronx slums. In 1919 he was convicted on a burglary charge and was sent to a reformatory for fifteen months. This police record, plus his cultivation of a reputation as a hardened tough, led to his calling himself Dutch Schultz, the name of a well-known former street brawler in the area.

After several years of odd jobs and brushes with the law, Schultz became a partner in an illegal Bronx saloon in 1928. Newspaper reporters sensationalized the bootlegging wars and assorted violence that soon flared between the gangs of Schultz, Jack "Legs" Diamond, and the exceptionally reckless Vincent "Mad Dog" Coll. Schultz hired a small army of gunmen that protected his beer trucks and destroyed or hijacked those of his competitors. He also succeeded in purchasing police protection by generous backing of New York political figures. By the early 1930s Schultz was the most powerful bootlegger in the Bronx and upper Manhattan.

Journalists and law enforcement officials sometimes drew comparisons between Schultz and such celebrated gangsters as Al Capone of Chicago. Indeed, in 1939 Schultz's attorney, J. Richard "Dixie" Davis, remembered him as cultivating gangster slang and that "the girls" thought he looked like "Bing Crosby with his nose bashed in." Despite his reputation for outbursts of calculated violence, Schultz was a mousy and frequently secretive individual. Although he was widely feared, few in the underworld seem to have had any affection for him. His frugality, especially in the purchase of apparel, became legendary. "Only a sucker," Schultz told New York Times reporter Meyer Berger in 1935, "will pay $15 or $20 for a silk shirt." Berger observed that the drab gangster had the appearance of an "ill-dressed vagrant." Sometime in the mid-1930s Schultz entered into a common-law marriage with Frances Maxwell, who bore him two children.

Schultz's real genius lay in his sense of business and political leverage. Assembled during the beer wars of earlier years, his gang directed its energies in other directions by the early 1930s. Schultz's operatives used threats of violence to muscle their way into food servicing unions; once in control, they embezzled union funds and extorted "protection" money from the restaurants. The organization's links to Tammany leader James J. Hines (who in turn exercised considerable control over the police) neutralized appeals to law enforcement by either unions or restaurants.

The ties to Hines apparently were critical to Schultz's dramatic takeover of large portions of the black-run Harlem policy game. Commonly called "numbers," these gambling operations appealed to many people, mostly poor, and employed as many as 15,000 street runners, or "collectors." The Harlem numbers racket was in some chaos at the time, the result of a series of reform exposés as well as rapid growth during the depression. In early 1932 the Schultz organization began to threaten black policy bankers with violence and then to squeeze them from control of the lucrative racket. Resistance seemed useless because of Schultz's payoffs to Hines. Soon the Harlem numbers were dominated by the Schultz combination, which prosecutors later estimated grossed as much as $20 million annually.

As part of a long-term campaign aimed at industrial racketeering in New York, U.S. Attorney Thomas E. Dewey in 1933 initiated an income tax investigation of Schultz. While the investigation proceeded, Schultz went into hiding for more than a year. By 1935, however, he had surrendered and was tried twice, once in Syracuse and once in the village of Malone, New York. In Syracuse, Schultz and his attorney won a hung jury; in Malone, he was acquitted after a whirlwind public relations effort possibly influenced the jury.

Schultz's acquittal, however, did not mark the end of his ordeal. Dewey's office continued a broad-gauged investigation into the restaurant and numbers rackets and into Schultz's evasion of New York state taxes. Meanwhile, underworld rivals, apparently counting on Schultz's conviction, moved in on his holdings in New York City. Alarmed, Schultz retaliated against deserters from his ranks and allegedly planned to assassinate Dewey. In the midst of a major underworld power struggle, Schultz and two subordinates were gunned down in a Newark, New Jersey, saloon. Delirious and ranting, Schultz died in a Newark hospital the following day.

Although the subsequent corruption trial of Hines and Dixie Davis's writings provided substantial information on Schultz's work as an underworld entrepreneur, the details behind his killing remain clouded. Ultimately, gunman Charles Workman served twenty-three years in prison for the shooting, but he revealed little about his motives. In the 1960s and 1970s some writers speculated that Charles "Lucky" Luciano, putative leader of a secret Sicilian-dominated criminal cartel, had ordered Schultz's killing. A number of later motion picture films, including The Cotton Club (1984) and Billy Bathgate (1991), also present a highly mythologized portrait of Schultz's career.

• In *Kill the Dutchman! The Story of Dutch Schultz* (1971), veteran reporter Paul Sann advanced the argument that Schultz was murdered because he ran afoul of an Italian-American criminal cartel. Thomas E. Dewey, *Twenty against the Underworld* (1974), and Richard Norton Smith, *Thomas E. Dewey and His Times* (1982), are especially useful on the prosecutor's investigation of Schultz's underworld operations. J. Richard "Dixie" Davis wrote "Things I Couldn't Tell Till Now," a colorful but not entirely reliable series of articles for *Collier's* in 1939. See also the *New York Times*, 24, 26, and 29 Oct. 1935.

WILLIAM HOWARD MOORE

SCHULTZ, Henry (4 Sept. 1893–26 Nov. 1938), economist and econometrician, was born in Szarkowsczyzna, county of Disna, Vilna Province, in then Russian Poland, the son of Sam Schultz, a picture framer, and Rebecca Kissin. In 1907 his family immigrated to the United States, settling in New York City's Lower East Side. The family was poor, and Schultz worked evenings while he went to school. He received an A.B. from the College of the City of New York in 1916. He then undertook graduate studies in economics at Columbia University, where he was deeply influenced by the teaching of Henry L. Moore and his pioneering research on the empirical estimation of economic models of the demand for goods. He also attended courses taught by Professors Edwin Seligman, Wesley Clair Mitchell, H. Parker Willis, and John Dewey. His studies were interrupted in 1917 by World War I. He saw combat with the 316th Machine Gun Battalion in France and was wounded in action while serving in the Meuse-Argonne offensive. He left the army with the rank of sergeant. He then served briefly with the War Trade Board in 1918 as a statistician. He was awarded an army scholarship that enabled him to spend the spring and summer terms of the academic year 1919 at the London School of Economics and Political Science and at the Galton Laboratory of Eugenic Research at the University of London, England. During this time he attended the lectures of Edwin Canaan on economic theory, of Graham Wallas on political theory, of Hobhouse on philosophy, and of Arthur L. Bowley and Karl Pearson on statistics. Upon his return to the United States, he served as a statistician with the U.S. Bureau of the Census (1919–1920) in Washington, D.C.

Schultz married Bertha Alice Greenstein in 1920; they had two children. From 1922 to 1926 he held several posts in Washington, D.C., including an appointment at the Institute of Economics at the Brookings Institution (1922–1924). He served as director of statistical research at the Children's Bureau of the U.S. Department of Labor (1924–1926). His final position in Washington was as an economist with the U.S. Tariff Commission (1926). He completed his Ph.D. at Columbia in 1925 under the supervision of Henry L. Moore, whose own work on estimating demand functions was an inspiration to Schultz. Comments received from Professors Isador Lubin, Frederick C. Mills, and Wesley Clair Mitchell are also acknowledged in his dissertation, "The Statistical Law of Demand as Illustrated by the Demand for Sugar," which was published in two parts in the *Journal of Political Economy* in 1925.

In 1926 Schultz received an appointment at the University of Chicago, where he developed a large research program motivated by his earlier studies and those of his mentor Henry Moore. Starting with his 1925 study of sugar, he estimated the demand for numerous agricultural commodities where supply was volatile but demand was stable. In this way, he solved an econometric "identification problem" that plagued previous studies that used price and consumption data to identify the market demand for products and separate out supply response from demand response.

In executing his research program, Schultz united three previously disconnected branches of knowledge: (a) the theory of consumer demand; (b) the statistical theory of regression and time series analysis; and (c) the empirical analysis of economic data. The culmination of his research was the publication of *The Theory and Measurement of Demand* (1938), in which he analyzes the three branches. One appendix from the book was published as a separate textbook on correlation analysis. His synthesis was unprecedented at the time it appeared and is still widely regarded as a model of rigorous empirical research in economics guided by theory.

The application of rigorous models and methods to analyze economic data was the most original aspect of Schultz's work. While he produced few new theoretical results, his syntheses of economic and statistical theory were important catalysts for contemporary scholarship on the pure theory of consumer demand and on economic statistics. His studies of the classical theory of consumer demand were elegant, precise, and far ranging. He synthesized the analyses of August Cournot, Leon Walras, and Vilfredo Pareto. A close follower of contemporary developments in the theory of consumer demand by John Hicks and R. G. D. Allen, he was responsible (along with Hicks) for disseminating an important and highly original paper on consumer theory by the Russian economist and statistician Eugene Slutsky, published in Italian in 1915, that had languished in obscurity. He also synthesized known methods in time series analysis and regression analysis that he found useful in estimating his models for market demand. In all of his research, he was at the frontier of economic and statistical knowledge although he rarely innovated in methodology.

Schultz also played a pivotal role in fostering the development and dissemination of rigorous empirical methodology in economics. At Chicago he trained a cadre of students and research assistants in modern econometric research methods. Noteworthy students and research assistants on the Schultz project at Chicago were Nobel laureates Milton Friedman, George Stigler, and Paul Samuelson (the latter as an undergraduate). The founder of modern labor economics, H. G. Lewis, was a Schultz student and research assistant as were Jacob Mosak and Martin Bronfenbrenner. His influence on Chicago was so strong that he carried the day in having the Frieden hand calculator—the tool in trade of the empirical economist of the day—carved into stone as the official emblem of the economics department in the Social Science building constructed in 1929.

Schultz was one of the founders of the Econometric Society, a highly influential international body of scholars devoted to the application of mathematical and statistical tools to the study of economic problems. A major lectureship in that society was established in his honor. The study of consumer demand along the lines pioneered by Schultz is still considered the most rigorous form of empirical research by the Econometric Society. He was also active in the Cowles Commission, which was founded to foster the application of mathematical and statistical methods to the study of economic problems.

Both organizations were responsible for promoting the development of formal methods of empirical and theoretical analysis in economics, and both shaped the way modern economics is practiced today. Through his students, his writings, and the organizations he founded and nourished, Schultz fostered the widespread use of formal mathematical and statistical methods in economic research.

Schultz, his wife, and his two daughters were killed in an automobile accident near San Diego, California. At the time of his death, he was exploring plans for estimating supply response to prices in agricultural markets to supplement his research on consumer response to price.

• Schultz was the author of scores of articles, including "Elasticity of Demand and the Coefficient of Correlation," *Quarterly Journal of Economics* 38 (Nov. 1923): 169–71; "An Extension of the Method of Moments," *Journal of the American Statistical Association* 20, no. 149 (June 1925): 242–44; "Cost of Production, Supply and Demand, and the Tariff," *Journal of Farm Economics* 9, no. 2 (Apr. 1927): 192–209; "Mathematical Economics and the Quantitative Method," *Journal of Political Economy* 35, no. 5 (Oct. 1927): 702–6; "Rational Economics," *American Economic Review* 18, no. 4 (Dec. 1928): 643–48; "Marginal Productivity and the General Pricing Process," *Journal of Political Economy* 37, no. 5 (Oct. 1929): 505–51; and "A Misunderstanding in Index-Number Theory: The True Konüs Condition on Cost-of-Living Index Numbers and Its Limitations," *Econometrica* 7, no. 1 (Jan. 1939): 1–9. Information on Schultz is in Oscar Lange et al., eds., *Studies in Mathematical Economics and Econometrics in Memory of Henry Schultz* (1942), and Harold Hotelling, "The Work of Henry Schultz," *Econometrica* (Apr. 1939).

JAMES J. HECKMAN

SCHULTZ, Jack (7 May 1904–29 Apr. 1971), geneticist, was born in Astoria, New York, the son of Morris Schultz, a merchant, and Bessie Krones. Raised on Long Island, Schultz attended the public schools in Astoria and received religious training in the community Jewish schools. Despite some financial problems, his father managed to send him and his brothers to college as well as finance some of Schultz's graduate studies. At Columbia University during his first two years,

Schultz enjoyed New York life: the theater, art, literature, and music. It was not until his junior year that Schultz became interested in planning his career. His decision to study medicine was diverted by his spending of his tuition money to purchase books and concert tickets. To improve his financial condition, he answered a bulletin board advertisement seeking someone to do menial work in the laboratory of Thomas Hunt Morgan, the world famous geneticist. This job drew Schultz to the now legendary "Fly Room" in the Department of Zoology at Columbia University. Morgan soon recognized Schultz's abilities, for he quickly learned the procedures and became a helpful laboratory assistant. Money from this job and some family support allowed Schultz to enroll as a graduate student and study directly under Morgan. He received his B.S. from Columbia in 1924. For the years 1925–1927 he served as a teaching fellow in the zoology department at Columbia. In 1925 he became a university scholar, and in 1927–1928 he was appointed a National Research Council fellow. In 1925 he obtained his master's degree and in 1929 his Ph.D. For his doctoral thesis he studied the *Minute* reaction in flies, which was initiated by a mutation that produced *Minutes: Drosophila*, characterized by short bristles on the flies' bodies. Schultz demonstrated that, although the *Minute* class reaction resulted from changes at many loci on the chromosome, these alterations produced the same somatic effect. In 1925 Helen Redfield came to work in Morgan's laboratory at Columbia, and since her work overlapped with Schultz's, they began a collaboration and in 1926 were married. They had two children.

While at Columbia, Schultz also worked with Selig Hecht, a physicist interested in optics, on a study on the biophysics of vision, which resulted in an early analysis of the adaptive spectra of the eye pigments. This work showed that the eye pigments were metabolically related, a result that was later confirmed and refined by Boris Ephrussi, George Beadle, and Edward L. Tatum.

Schultz and his wife moved to Pasadena, California, in 1928, when Morgan and his group moved to the California Institute of Technology (Caltech). At Caltech Schultz worked with C. B. Bridges, Theodosius Dobyzhanski, David G. Catcheside, and others to study the genetics of *Drosophilia*, especially the mechanism that controls growth and the effects of suppressor genes. With Bridges, Schultz in 1932 discovered specific suppressor genes whose relevance in the control of gene action was not recognized until much later, when the chemistry of the gene was better understood. This work led to Schultz's interest in determining the chemical composition of genes that controlled these processes.

To further study this problem, in 1937 Schultz, who had some background in biophysics as well as in genetics, went to work with Torbjörn Caspersson in Stockholm, Sweden, who had developed a microspectrophotometer capable of studying the spectral properties of genetic substances. Schultz and Caspersson found a relationship between the two forms of nucleic acids. The nucleolus contained large amounts of pentose nucleic acids (RNA), while the chromosomes were composed of deoxypentose nucleic acids (DNA). During growth the cytoplasm contained more pentose nucleic acid than the resting cell. This work suggested the mechanism of gene action.

After two years in Sweden as a Rockefeller fellow, Schultz returned to the United States and set about finding support to obtain the expensive equipment he had learned to use in Sweden. During these uncertain years he spent twelve months as a visiting professor at the University of Missouri, and periods at Caltech and the Marine Biological Laboratory at Woods Hole, Massachusetts. This hectic period of Schultz's life ended in 1943, when he joined the Institute for Cancer Research of the Lankenau Hospital in Philadelphia.

At the institute Schultz began working on the chemistry of human chromosomes with Patricia St. Laurence. A significant contribution of Schultz was his study of the giant chromosome *Rhynchosciara*, where they found certain bands of the gene increased their DNA in the process of "puffing," the stage in which the genes become active and synthesize RNA. This novel discovery led to an understanding of the relationship between compacted and extended chromosome regions. The compacted regions were relatively inactive, while extended chromosome regions are active and produce RNA messengers that direct protein synthesis. Schultz was willing to talk about many of these projects privately as well as in public, but he was unwilling to write about his ideas because he lacked definitive proof. Thus much of Schultz's work has been lost.

Schultz made an effort to visit frequently the laboratories of the investigators at the Institute for Cancer Research to keep himself abreast of the work in progress. This awareness of the status of the projects at the institute resulted in Schultz having a great influence on the direction of science there. His awareness of the progress of science in general also allowed him to play a significant role in bringing distinguished scientists to the institute, such as Theodore Hansch and Beatrice Minz.

Although Schultz was never director of the Institute for Cancer Research, he played a prominent role in determining its scientific direction.

Through Dale Coman, professor of pathology at the University of Pennsylvania, Schultz recommended David Hungerford, an expert on the study of chromosomes, to Peter Nowell. This recommendation resulted in the discovery of the Philadelphia chromosome.

Schultz retired in 1969. For the remainder of his life he studied *Drosophilia* chromosomes with Kenneth Tartof and Francis Ashton using the electron microscope. In the last few years of his life he developed angina pectoris, which restricted his activities. He died in Philadelphia.

• Most of Schultz's papers are at the American Philosophical Society. A few are preserved in the archives of the Institute for Cancer Research in Philadelphia. Biographies include National Academy of Sciences, *Biographical Memoirs* 47 (1975): 393–422; *Genetics* 68 (1971): 97–98; and *Genetics* 81 (1975): 1–7. An obituary is in the *New York Times*, 1 May 1971.

DAVID Y. COOPER

SCHULTZ, Sigrid Lillian (5 Jan. 1893–15 Mar. 1980), foreign correspondent, was born in Chicago, Illinois, the daughter of Herman Schultz, a portrait painter, and Hedwig Jaskewitz. When Sigrid was born the Schultzes were visiting Chicago because her father had been commissioned to paint the mayor's official portrait for the 1893 World's Fair. They stayed for seven years before returning to Europe because he had been commissioned to paint a royal portrait.

Herman Schultz had studios in several cities, including Paris, where the family was based. After Sigrid's graduation from the Sorbonne in 1914, she and her mother traveled to the Berlin studio, a popular gathering place where conversation invariably turned to politics. Sigrid's exposure to those conversations shaped her interests, and the contacts she made through her father's work proved invaluable later. Caught in Berlin when World War I began, they stayed for the duration of the war because her parents' ill health ruled out travel. Schultz spent her time studying history and international law at Berlin University and teaching French and English mainly to wealthy Jewish families.

When the war ended in 1919, Schultz got a job working for Richard Henry Little of the *Chicago Tribune*. Serving as Little's interpreter, Schultz learned her journalism skills on the job, translating interviews, deciphering cables, and typing letters. On her own, she became an expert on military strategy and armaments. Well-educated, multilingual, and well-connected, she was a valuable resource though the *Tribune* editors were slow to see it. They took her first stories on a freelance basis, and she told friends that they only began to take her seriously when she risked her life to cover the frequent street battles and riots in postwar Germany.

The editors were not the only ones slow to take Schultz seriously. The first woman to serve as a foreign correspondent in Europe, Schultz had no problems developing personal rapport with sources from all walks of life, from royalty to peasants, but German officials did not know what to do with women correspondents. In 1924 she was elected to the board of directors of Berlin's Foreign Press Association, and officials were forced to take her seriously. As a result of her presence women were soon invited to all functions.

In 1925 Parke Brown was appointed as the Berlin bureau chief, but by the end of the year *Tribune* publisher Colonel Robert R. McCormick had transferred Brown to Rome and appointed Schultz correspondent in chief for Central Europe. She held the job until 1941 and was the first woman to head a foreign bureau for a major American newspaper. She and McCormick respected each other, and he supported her work, even though her views on Germany varied greatly from his own.

Schultz did not like the Nazis, but that did not keep her from entertaining them. Having discovered that Herman Göring had decent table manners, she regularly included him on her guest list. Over good food, Göring provided information and insights on Nazi thinking that was invaluable to the correspondents gathered around the table.

Schultz came to be known by Nazi officials as "that dragon from Chicago." She interviewed Hitler three times and he is reported to have come to dislike her so much that he refused to deal with any women correspondents. Always on her guard, Schultz managed to foil various Nazi attempts to entrap and expel her. She was among the first to warn of the threat the Germans posed to world peace. In her dispatches, she covered the rise of the Nazis, the progress of German rearmament, and the details of Nazi persecution of the Jews.

The depth of Schultz's coverage became clear only after the war when the *Tribune* revealed that she was "John Dickson," the author of a series of articles published in 1938 and 1939—"The Truth about Nazi Germany." As Dickson she also wrote predicting a nonaggression pact between the Nazis and the Russians—nearly two months before the pact itself shocked the world. She traveled to Denmark to transmit the Dickson stories free of German censors. From 1938 to 1940 she also served as the Mutual Broadcasting Service correspondent in Berlin.

A respected journalist, Schultz was nonetheless a writer who needed an editor. In *20th Century Journey*, volume two: *The Nightmare Years 1930–1940* (1984), William Shirer wrote that Schultz knew more than anyone about what was going on behind the scenes in Nazi Germany, but he also noted that his friend seemed to have "no feeling for the American language."

In 1941 Schultz left Germany and traveled to the United States lecturing on the situation in Europe. Dismayed to find Americans romanticizing the Germans, she spent two years writing *Germany Will Try It Again* (1944), which forecast Hitler's attempts to conquer Europe. She returned to Europe in 1944 as a war correspondent for the *Tribune*, Mutual Broadcasting, and *McCall's* magazine. She covered the entry of Allied troops into Germany and was one of the first correspondents to enter the Buchenwald concentration camp. In 1945 she quit working for the *Tribune* but continued to report for Mutual and *McCall's*. She covered the Nuremberg war crimes trials and for several years worked as a correspondent in Bonn.

Schultz retired to Connecticut and continued to write, but obsessed by Germany she lost her audience in a postwar world where Germans were allies. A founder of the Overseas Press Association, she served as a member of its board of governors. Interviewed for an oral history project of the American Jewish Committee, she revealed that she had helped Jews escape from Nazi Germany. When she died in Westport, Connecticut, she was working on a history of German anti-Semitism. Schultz never married and had no children.

The first woman to win a post as a foreign correspondent in Europe and the first to head a foreign bureau for a major American newspaper, Schultz believed women had a place in journalism but should earn their opportunities. An indefatigable reporter, she earned the respect of her peers covering Germany during a difficult period. Known variously as "the dragon from Chicago" and "Hitler's greatest enemy," Schultz managed to stay in Germany and report on the Nazis while many male reporters were forced out, their health and nerves shattered.

• Schultz edited the *Overseas Press Club Cookbook* (1962), and her contributions to that work, which supplements recipes with stories about entertaining Nazi officials, are interesting. Her entry in the Overseas Press Club of America's *I Can Tell It Now*, ed. David Brown and W. Richard Bruner (1964), tells of the last days of Hitler's life. Biographies of Schultz appear in Julia Edward, *Women of the World* (1988); in Lilya Wagner, *Women War Correspondents of World War II* (1989); and in Barbara Belford, *Brilliant Bylines: A Biographical Anthology of Notable Newspaperwomen in America* (1986).

CATHERINE CASSARA

SCHULZ, Adolph George (19 Apr. 1883–14 Apr. 1951), college football player, coach, and administrator, was born in Fort Wayne, Indiana, the son of Adolph F. Schulz, a physician, and Sophia Seidensticker. Schulz, nicknamed "Germany" when he reached college, played guard on the Fort Wayne High School team for four years and developed strength while working part-time in steel mills. The 6'4" and over 200-pound Schulz came to the attention of Coach Fielding H. Yost at the University of Michigan, who learned of Schulz's quickness, speed, and prowess as a blocker. In 1904 Schulz joined the famous Michigan "point-a-minute" team, which starting in 1902 under Coach Yost was undefeated in 34 games and scored 1,739 points in those contests while giving up only 18 points. On the 1904 team Schulz played guard for the first seven games and was moved to center for the game against the University of Wisconsin. Center proved to be his natural position, and he was a consensus All-American center in 1907. He was an All-Western regional selection in 1905, 1907, and 1908.

Schulz became a dominating two-way player and is credited with introducing a number of innovations. He developed a spiral pass from center that eventually replaced the end-over-end pass. The direct spiral pass by the snapper meant that the backfield could move with the ball more quickly and the defense had less time to react to where the ball was snapped. On defense, Schulz took a stand-up position five yards behind the line of scrimmage where he could react to the developing offensive play and move toward the ball carrier while using his strong arms and legs to fight off blockers. This position introduced the concept of the middle linebacker as the key defensive position to stop the run. Schulz also introduced the practice of the roving or pulling center who aided the tackles or ends in a double-team block in order to break a back loose on an outside run. In Yost's aggressive offensive and varied formations the center was a key blocking position, and because of his large hands Schulz could snap the ball with one hand and use his other arm to begin his blocking. As Yost said, "He led the interference on offense and could open holes no ball carrier could miss." Schulz was second in a long line of brilliant All-American centers at Michigan, but he was by far the most sensational and legendary. He served as captain of the 1908 Michigan team.

The Schulz legend was built around his reputation as one of Yost's famous "iron men." In his four years of play at Michigan Schulz missed only 10 minutes of competition. Those came in 1908 in the last game of his collegiate career against the University of Pennsylvania. Schulz suffered a torn hip muscle after putting on an incredible one-man show of tackling and breaking up blocking interference. In the *Detroit Free Press* (8 Nov. 1908), sportswriter E. A. Batchelor stated, "The last of the old guard was injured. The sole remnant of the former band of football players which had made Michigan famous for years had taken the count for the first time." Schulz was the last member of Yost's "point-a-minute" teams, which dominated football in the West from 1901 to 1905. After the 1905 season Michigan left the Western Conference and played as an independent, scheduling significantly fewer season games and taking on such national powerhouses as Pennsylvania, Syracuse, and Vanderbilt. In the four years Schulz played, the football team's record was 32–4–1, and in his final two years Michigan made the transition from regional dominance to being a nationally prominent school in football.

Schulz left Michigan before graduation and took a job at General Electric in Madison, Wisconsin. Between 1911 and 1924 Schulz held coaching positions at five different schools, enjoying little job security during a period in which athletic departments frequently changed staffs. He served as a line coach under University of Wisconsin head coach John R. Richards in the 1911 season and under William J. Juneau in the 1912 season. The 1912 Wisconsin team was undefeated with a 7–0–0 record and claimed a Western Conference championship. In 1913 Yost called Schulz back to Michigan as a line coach, a position he held through the 1915 season. In 1916 Schulz became the athletic director at Kansas State Agricultural College and served as line coach under Zora G. Clevenger. In 1920 and 1921 Schulz held the position of athletic director at Tulane University. From 1921 through 1924 he was a contributing editor to the *Athletic Journal*, the first national professional journal for coaches and administrators. In the September 1921 issue Schulz published an article titled "How to Play Center."

Schulz's last college position came in 1922 as director of athletics at the University of Detroit. In December 1922 he was appointed head football coach, replacing Jimmy Duffy. Schulz was aided by assistant coach Judge William H. Heston of the recorder's court in Detroit, formerly an All-American halfback and Schulz's teammate at the University of Michigan. Schulz's coaching record in the 1923 season at the University of Detroit was 5–2–2, and Duffy was returned to his head coaching position in 1924.

While serving as athletic director at Detroit, in 1922 Schulz began work part-time as an insurance adjuster in the Detroit office of the Medical Protective Society of Fort Wayne. After he left the University of Detroit, Schulz lived in Detroit with his wife Emilie, worked in the insurance business, and was an organizer of American Legion baseball. Less than two weeks before his death, Schulz was selected for the Associated Press all-time All-American team, and he was a charter member of the Helms Athletic Foundation College Football Hall of Fame in 1951. In 1954 Grantland Rice chose Schulz as his center on an all-time college football team.

In spite of his imposing physique and punishing field presence, Schulz was an affable, easygoing individual who enjoyed the admiration of his University of Michigan teammates. They called him "Germany," a nickname he continued to use the rest of his life. He was also known for his sportsmanship and clean, hard play. He was a sharp critic of two-platoon football. In February 1951 he underwent an operation for a malignant ulcer of the stomach, a condition that resulted in his death in Detroit.

• No collection of Schulz's personal papers exists. The University of Michigan Alumni Records Office has a clipping file. The best source of information on Schulz's playing career at Michigan is the *Detroit Free Press*, especially the columns and game reports of E. A. Batchelor. Information can also be found in Allison Danzig, *The History of American Football: Its Great Teams, Players, and Coaches* (1956); John D. McCallum, *Big Ten Football since 1895* (1976); and Will Perry, *The Wolverines: A Story of Michigan Football* (1974). An obituary is in the *Detroit Free Press*, 15 Apr. 1951.

DOUGLAS A. NOVERR

SCHUMAN, William Howard (4 Aug. 1910–15 Feb. 1992), composer, educator, and administrator, was born in New York City, the son of Samuel Schuman, an executive of a printing company, and Ray Heilbrunn. He attended the public schools in New York. He took violin lessons as a youngster but showed no special proficiency. In high school he formed a jazz band. He also tried his hand at writing musical shows and popular songs, though he knew almost nothing about composition or musical theory. One of his collaborators, Frank Loesser, was to become a famous writer of songs and musical shows, and together they wrote Loesser's first published song, but it was not a success. In 1928 Schuman enrolled at the New York University School of Commerce. In 1930 he was persuaded by his sister to attend a concert by the New York Philharmonic, conducted by Arturo Toscanini. The performance was a revelation to young Schuman, and he immediately decided that he wanted to become a composer of classical music. He abandoned the

School of Commerce and signed up for courses first in harmony and later in counterpoint at the Malkin Conservatory, a small music school in New York City. By 1933 he had entered Teachers' College at Columbia University, so that he might support himself as a teacher of music while he established himself as a composer. After his graduation in 1935, he persuaded the president of Sarah Lawrence College in Bronxville, New York, to give him a job. He proved to be a popular and innovative teacher at Sarah Lawrence, remaining there until 1945. He married Francis Prince in 1936; they had two children.

Schuman composed his first symphony in 1935. The work was rejected for a prize given by Columbia University. He sought the advice of the successful American composer Roy Harris, then teaching at the Juilliard School of Music in New York City. Schuman studied with Harris, first at Juilliard in 1936 and then privately at Harris's home until 1938. He wrote a second symphony in 1937 that did win a prize. The prize jury included the influential American composer Aaron Copland, who was impressed with the music and wrote favorably about Schuman in the journal *Modern Music* in 1938. After actually hearing the symphony performed in public in New York and on a radio concert later that year, Copland recommended the work to Serge Koussevitzky, the famed conductor of the Boston Symphony Orchestra. Koussevitzky conducted the Second Symphony in Boston in 1939; though the piece proved unpopular with both audiences and critics, the conductor became an enthusiastic champion of Schuman's music. Koussevitzky conducted the first performances of Schuman's *American Festival Overture* in October 1939 and of the Third Symphony in October 1941. The latter, dedicated to Koussevitzky, was a great success with audiences and critics alike, won Schuman the first award ever given by the New York Critics' Circle, and proved to be his most enduringly popular composition. Schuman was to write seven more symphonies during his lifetime. Though best known for his orchestral music, he wrote in most of the usual categories of classical music, including many choral works (his cantata *A Free Song* in 1943 won the first Pulitzer Prize ever given for a musical composition); chamber music; and an opera, *The Mighty Casey* (1953), inspired by Ernest Lawrence Thayer's well-known poem *Casey at the Bat*, in which the composer gave expression to his lifelong love of baseball.

In June 1945 Schuman left Sarah Lawrence College to become director of publications at the important New York music publishing firm of G. Schirmer, Inc. However, he had scarcely begun his new job when several members of the board of directors of the Juilliard School of Music asked him to consider becoming president of that institution. At first reluctant, he finally accepted the position as of 1 October 1945, with the understanding that he was to have full authority to carry out educational reforms and changes that he believed necessary. He also continued with Schirmer as a consultant on publications until 1952.

Schuman brought sweeping changes to Juilliard. In 1946 he merged the Institute of Musical Art (founded by Frank Damrosch in 1905) and the Juilliard Graduate School (established in 1923), which had coexisted with much autonomy under the same organization since 1926, into a single, truly unified entity. He brought many talented younger musicians to the faculty, including choral conductor Robert Shaw, orchestral conductor Thor Johnson, and composers Vincent Persichetti and Peter Mennin (who would succeed Schuman as president of Juilliard). He founded in 1946 the Juilliard String Quartet, whose members were to teach at the school but were allowed to spend most of their time rehearsing, performing, and touring. The ensemble became one of the most successful and long-lived quartets in musical history. It performed much contemporary music as well as the traditional string quartet literature.

Schuman's most significant innovation at Juilliard was the revision of the curriculum. He insisted that the institution be more than a musical trade school, as so many conservatories were at that time. He added liberal arts courses to the traditional musical course of study. Beyond this, he replaced the standard courses in the theory and history of music with a program of study in what he called "literature and materials of music." The basic aim of the program was to give the student not only the technical ability to perform music of all types and from all historical periods but also an intelligent comprehension of how the music was constructed and how it fit into the long history of the art form. This aim was to be accomplished primarily through the analysis and performance of many specific works chosen to illustrate the evolution of music over the centuries. Moreover, Schuman and his colleagues insisted that the program must be tailored to the needs and background of each student rather than simply set forth in a standard series of courses and hours required to obtain a degree. The Juilliard program became highly influential and was widely adopted in whole or in part in conservatories and college and university music departments throughout the United States.

As president of Juilliard, Schuman participated in the preliminary discussions and planning for the projected Lincoln Center for the Performing Arts in New York City beginning in 1955. By early 1957 he had persuaded the school's board of directors to agree to ultimately move it into the center. Later that year he became Juilliard's representative on the newly formed Lincoln Center Council. By 1958 plans were being drawn for a new and greatly enlarged Juilliard School as an integral part of the Lincoln Center complex. As it turned out, construction delays were to postpone the opening of the new school until 1969.

In September 1961 Schuman was chosen president of Lincoln Center, effective 1 January 1962. By the time he took office, the New York Philharmonic Orchestra, the Metropolitan Opera, and the Juilliard School were firmly committed to participation in Lincoln Center. The New York Public Library was substantially committed to building a library and museum of the performing arts, a repertory drama theater was in the planning stage, and it was hoped that the New York City Ballet and the New York City Opera would soon come into the center. During Schuman's term of office, Philharmonic Hall (later Avery Fisher Hall) was completed and opened in 1962, the New York State Theater in 1964, the Library and Museum of the Performing Arts in 1965, and the new Metropolitan Opera House in 1966.

Schuman's primary interests and efforts as president of Lincoln Center lay in educational activities and musical presentations rather than in the financing and building of the complex. He initiated a popular and successful program of outreach to the public schools of New York City and vicinity. He also tirelessly advocated the creation of new constituent organizations within the center for the presentation of artistic motion pictures and of chamber music. The film program began during his tenure of office; the Chamber Music Society came into being after his departure. He also led the parent organization of Lincoln Center into the sponsorship of extensive presentations of artistic programs above and beyond what the member organizations such as the Metropolitan Opera and the New York Philharmonic were already carrying out, including participation in the New York World's Fair of 1964–1965 and the presentation of elaborate summer festivals in 1967 and 1968. Unfortunately, these activities, together with increasing difficulties in raising new funds, resulted in mounting deficits that threatened Lincoln Center with bankruptcy. This in turn led the center's executive committee and board of trustees to demand and secure drastic cuts in the operating budget. In early December 1968 Schuman announced his resignation from the presidency.

By careful allocation of his time, Schuman had remained amazingly active as a composer during his presidencies of the Juilliard School and of Lincoln Center and he remained so until the mid-1980s, when increasing ill health gradually curtailed his activities. He died in New York City.

William Schuman's presidency of Lincoln Center was a somewhat mixed record of considerable accomplishment followed by ultimate disappointment and defeat. However, he had long since proved his ability as an innovative administrator in turning the Juilliard School into one of the great musical educational institutions of the world. He would probably most wish to be remembered as an important American composer, and he was beyond doubt, along with contemporaries such as Aaron Copland and Walter Piston, one of the most significant figures in American classical music from the late 1930s until the mid-1980s.

• Schuman's papers are in the Music Division of the New York Public Library for the Performing Arts, Lincoln Center, and his music manuscripts are in the Music Division of the Library of Congress. A book-length biography and analysis of Schuman's music is Flora Rheta Schreiber and Vincent Persichetti, *William Schuman* (1954), it is not only quite brief but obviously covers only the first half of his life. Bruce Saylor's biographical article in the *New Grove Dictionary of Amer-*ican Music*, vol. 4 (1986) includes a brief sketch of his life together with a list of his compositions through 1985. George Martin, *The Damrosch Dynasty: America's First Family of Music* (1983), discusses the early history of the Juilliard School of Music. Harriet Gay, *The Juilliard String Quartet* (1974), notes briefly Schuman's role in the creation of that ensemble. *The Juilliard Report on Teaching the Literature and Materials of Music* (1953), analyzes in detail Schuman's most significant educational innovation and includes an introduction by him. Edgar B. Young, *Lincoln Center: The Building of an Institution* (1980), deals with the creation of Lincoln Center and the early years of its operation. A brief obituary of Schuman is in the *New York Times*, 16 Feb. 1992.

JOHN E. LITTLE

SCHUMANN-HEINK, Ernestine (15 June 1861–17 Nov. 1936), opera singer, was born in Lieben, near Prague, in what was then Austro-Hungary, the daughter of Hans Röessler, an officer in the Austrian army, and Charlotte Goldman, a singer. When she was three years old, her father was transferred to Verona, Italy. Her family remained there until the outbreak of war between Austria and Italy in 1866, when she and her mother were sent back to Prague. After the war her father was transferred to a post near Krakow, where she was placed in the St. Andreas Convent as a day scholar. Army pay was poor, and in later years she would describe the struggles of her mother to make ends meet and how she herself secretly did odd jobs for a circus to get some extra food.

The family returned to Prague, and Ernestine was placed in the Ursuline Convent, where the Mother Superior noted her exceptional voice and predicted that she would become a great actress or singer. Lessons were arranged with a former prima donna from Paris, but a short time later her father was again transferred, this time to Graz in southern Austria. Here she finally received the vocal training that she needed from another former opera singer, Marietta von Leclair, the daughter of an officer in her father's regiment.

After three years of study she had her first opportunity to sing publicly when Marie Wilt, a famous soprano, came to Graz to participate in a performance of Beethoven's Ninth Symphony. Ernestine was given the alto part in the performance and was paid the equivalent of six dollars for her work. She was befriended by the daughter of a senior officer and assisted to make the trip to Vienna for an audition with the director of the Vienna Opera, who dismissed her as having no future in opera because of her homeliness. However, she was more successful in obtaining an engagement with the Dresden Royal Opera, where she made her debut as Azucena in Verdi's *Il Trovatore* on 13 October 1878.

During this period she met Ernest Heink, secretary of the Royal Opera, and married him. Since they had not obtained the prior permission of the director of the opera, both were summarily dismissed. This difficult situation was resolved when a friendly critic recommended her to the visiting director of the Hamburg Opera. She was accepted for that company in 1883, and her husband obtained a job with the local customs house. She attracted the attention of Hans von Bülow, one of the preeminent conductors of the day, who engaged her to sing the solo role in Brahms's Alto Rhapsody at an important festival in Hamburg. The composer himself was present and at the end of the performance joined conductor and soloist on stage for a memorable joint bow.

After this accomplishment von Bülow took a special interest in the young artist, who was struggling to support her family on a pitifully inadequate salary. She had already had three children with Heink, who lost his customs house position and had gone back alone to his native Saxony. She was pregnant with her fourth child when von Bülow invited her to sing in a Mozart cycle. Upon learning her condition he refused to let her participate, but she continued her work at the opera until a few hours before the new baby arrived. Made desperate by the addition of one more mouth to feed, she tried to throw herself and her children in front of a train but was saved by the terrified plea of her little daughter to take them home.

Her big break came when the leading contralto of the Hamburg Opera quarreled with the director, and she was given the opportunity to take her place in a performance of Bizet's *Carmen* conducted by Gustav Mahler. Her triumph in this performance was followed by equal success as Fidès in Meyerbeer's *Le Prophète* and Ortrud in Wagner's *Lohengrin*, and with these three big roles her position as a major artist was firmly established. Having divorced Heink, she married Paul Schumann, a singing actor and manager of Hamburg's Thalia Theater. His son from his first marriage became an integral part of her growing family (which eventually included three more children).

Her repertory at Hamburg included three Verdi roles, Amneris in *Aida*, Ulrica in *Ballo in maschera*, and Dame Quickly in the first German performance of *Falstaff*. She even sang Katisha in a production of Gilbert and Sullivan's *The Mikado*. Gifted with a vocal range of almost three octaves, she also had impressive acting ability.

In 1887 Schumann-Heink made her Berlin debut at the Kroll Opera House, again as Azucena in Verdi's *Il Trovatore*, and for the next nine years she sang in a number of major German houses, as well as in concerts and recitals. One of her favorite lieder composers was Brahms, who often attended both her opera performances—especially when she was singing Carmen—and her recitals. He was particularly pleased with her interpretations of his Sapphic Ode and Lullaby and told her that she sang them better than anyone else.

As her international reputation grew, she performed in London for the first time in 1892 in Wagner's *Ring* cycle under Mahler and was a fixture at the Bayreuth Festival from 1896 to 1914, where she was particularly noted for her Erda in *Das Rheingold*. In 1898 she accepted an offer from Maurice Grau, general manager of the Metropolitan Opera in New York City, to join that company, although she had just signed a new ten-year contract with the Berlin Opera.

Buying out the Berlin contract, Schumann-Heink made her American debut in Chicago, Illinois, on 7 November in her familiar role of Ortrud in *Lohengrin*. Despite being near the end of one more pregnancy, she enjoyed another spectacular triumph. She made her house debut at the Metropolitan Opera on 9 January 1899, again as Ortrud, but she remained on the company's roster only until 1903, leaving out of loyalty to Grau when he retired. She returned at intervals, singing seventeen roles in fourteen scattered seasons until her final performance as Erda at age seventy.

In 1904 she appeared in the operetta *Love's Lottery*. The next year she suffered a breakdown and went to Germany to recuperate but returned to the United States the following season with a full schedule of performances. She created the role of Clytemnestra in the world premiere of Richard Strauss's *Salome* in Dresden in 1909.

The death of her husband brought fresh tragedy to her life, but the most difficult period for her came with the outbreak of World War I. In 1915 her first son, August, insisted on returning to Germany, where he joined the submarine service and was lost in a U-boat attack. A second son, Hans, died of typhoid in the same year, and her other four boys, including her stepson Walter, joined the American forces. All four returned safely at the war's end.

Schumann-Heink had taken out her naturalization papers in 1905, shortly after which she married George Rapp, Jr., a Chicago lawyer. They separated in 1911 and were divorced three years later.

When the United States entered the war she devoted her talents to the American cause, singing for the men in the training camps and at rallies. She became immensely popular among war veterans and was made an honorary officer of the American Legion.

As the years passed, her homeliness gave way to a serene older beauty. She had grown stout, and the total effect of her appearance became that of an amiable grandmother. She was affectionately known as Mother Schumann-Heink and reveled in the role. Although her opera days were behind her, she still sang some of the songs for which she was famous, especially Brahms's Lullaby, and during the last years of her life it became a tradition to play her recording of "Silent Night" on the radio just before midnight on Christmas Eve.

In 1935 she conquered a new medium by carrying off the acting honors as Nino Martini's vocal teacher in the film *Here's to Romance*. MGM promptly signed her to a three-year contract, but no new vehicle had been found for her when she died a year later in her last home in the hills above Hollywood, California. Her beloved veterans paid her their final tribute at the American Legion Hall on Highland Avenue in Hollywood.

Music critic Henry Pleasants notes that it was Madame Schumann-Heink's distinction to win the affection of an enormous public extending far beyond the usual coterie of habitual opera and concertgoers. She was well aware of this affection and used it to urge her own strong sense of family values and moral conduct upon her public, suggesting that the proper role for women was that of mother and deploring such habits as smoking by young women. However, at the end of her memoirs she observed with pride that the mainspring of her life had been her concentration on her art, and her parting advice to young singers was "know what you want to do—then do it."

• Mary Lawton's biography, *Schumann-Heink: The Last of the Titans* (1928), which is told in the first person and in Madame Schumann-Heink's own inimitable style of speaking, is essentially the subject's own memoir. Henry Pleasants, *The Great Singers: From the Dawn of Opera to Caruso, Callas and Pavarotti* (1981), contains an authoritative commentary on her personality and art. A concise summary of her career is in David Hamilton, ed., *The Metropolitan Opera Encyclopedia* (1987). See also Joseph L. Howard, *Madame Ernestine Schumann-Heink: Her Life and Times* (1990), and Shirlee Emmans, "Ernestine Schumann-Heink," *The National Association of Teachers of Singing Bulletin* 40, no. 4 (Mar.–Apr. 1984): 29–33, and 40, no. 5 (May–June 1984): 25–27. An interesting interview from the final period of her life that concerns her brief film career is Adela Rogers St. Johns, "Schumann-Heink—Why Is She Neglected?" *Photoplay*, Oct. 1936. An obituary is in the *New York Times*, 18 Nov. 1936.

ALBERT O. WEISSBERG

SCHUMPETER, Joseph Alois Julius (8 Feb. 1883–8 Jan. 1950), economist, was born in Triesch, Moravia, Austro-Hungarian Empire (in what is now the Czech Republic), the only child of Joseph Schumpeter, a cloth factory owner, and Johanna Grüner. Schumpeter's father died when he was only four. His mother remarried, to Sigismund von Kéler, a high-ranking military officer and member of the aristocracy. Because of his stepfather's position, Schumpeter was admitted to the Theresianum Gymnasium, a famous preparatory school for the children of the aristocracy. There he received an excellent classical education and is supposed to have developed his agreeable, political nature.

Schumpeter enrolled in 1901 at the University of Vienna to study economics and graduated in 1906 with a doctor of law degree. Economics at Vienna was then under the strong influence of the recently retired founder of the Austrian School of economics, Carl Menger. Although Schumpeter studied extensively many subjects, he was most influenced by some leading theoretical economists of the day, Eugen von Böhm-Bawerk, Friedrich von Wieser, and Eugen von Philoppovich.

In 1906 Schumpeter published his first major paper, "On the Mathematical Method in Theoretical Economics" (*Zeitschrift für Volkswirtschaft, Sozialpolitik und Verwaltung* 15 [1906]: 30–49). After receiving his doctorate later that year, he began to travel in Europe. While studying in England he met and married Gladys Ricarde Seaver, a daughter of an official of the Church of England; they had no children. He then went to work for an Italian law firm in Egypt but continued to pursue his desire to become an economist.

Schumpeter returned to Vienna in 1908 and submitted his first book, *The Nature and Essence of Theoretical Economics*, to the University of Vienna as his *Habilitationsschrift*, or requirement to become a privatdozent, the first step in the Austrian academic hierarchy, a nonsalaried position that allowed him to lecture at the university. He was the youngest economist ever to be given this position in Austria. In the fall of 1909 Schumpeter was made an associate professor at the University of Czernowitz, becoming the youngest economist in Austria to be awarded that position as well. Two years later he was made a full professor of political economy at the University of Graz, again the youngest Austrian to have ever achieved this rank.

During his early career Schumpeter produced a remarkable number of important books and articles on economic theory. Possibly his most innovative work, *The Theory of Economic Development*, appeared in 1912. His *Economic Doctrine and Method: An Historical Sketch* was published in 1914. It was a truly remarkable accomplishment to write two path-breaking theoretical books and a history of economic theory all before the age of thirty. Schumpeter had a theory that a scholar's third decade of life held the greatest potential for creativity, a theory that his own career substantiates.

Schumpeter was a highly ambitious man with many interests outside economics, including horses and the architecture of French cathedrals. His ambition is best illustrated by his famous lament: "Early in life I had three ambitions: to be the greatest economist in the world, the greatest horseman in Austria, and the best lover in Vienna. Well, in one of those goals I have failed" (Swedberg, p. 12). He did not participate in World War I but did become immersed in politics and unsuccessfully sought a position in the Austro-Hungarian Empire. He did receive a position in the German Socialization Commission in 1918. Curiously, although Schumpeter was considered a proponent of capitalism and conservatism, he signed the final report of the commission, which contained some socialist measures.

Schumpeter was appointed minister of finance in the newly formed socialist-led coalition government of Austria after the war. His capitalist credentials and socialist sympathies combined with his academic standing (both of his famous teachers, von Wieser and Böhm-Bawerk, had also served as important ministers in the empire) to make him a natural candidate for the position. His policy positions, which made him unpopular within the government, combined with the general economic turmoil after the war, caused his quick dismissal.

On his departure, the government granted Schumpeter a valuable concession to establish a public banking corporation. In 1921 he completed an agreement with the small, privately owned Biedermann Bank that made him the president with a large salary and some stock ownership in exchange for his banking license. Schumpeter used his credit at the bank to make investments and substantial profits until 1923, when Austria was hit by a severe economic crisis. He lost all of his investments and his position as chair, but he still had big debts and owed back taxes to the government.

In 1925 Arthur Spiethoff, an old friend, arranged for him to become professor of public finance at the University of Bonn. Having divorced his first wife in 1920, in 1925 Schumpeter married Anna Reisinger, who was twenty years his junior. His happiness was soon shattered by the deaths of his mother, wife, and child all within one year of marrying his beloved "Annie." Although not a religious man, Schumpeter continued to honor and worship Annie and his mother in a spiritual manner for the rest of his life. For several years he remained deeply depressed by the loss of his family and by the difficulties involved in paying off his debts. He produced little academic work and failed to complete his proposed book on monetary economics (manuscript published posthumously as *The Nature of Money* [1970]). One exception to this unproductive malaise was "The Instability of Capitalism," published in 1928 in the *Economic Journal*, in which he developed his thesis that capitalism would falter because of political and ideological factors. This theme would become the hallmark of his monumental *Capitalism, Socialism, and Democracy* (1942), his most celebrated contribution to social science.

In 1932 Schumpeter accepted a position at Harvard University and emigrated to the United States, never to return to Austria. After this complete break with his depressing past, Schumpeter soon became admired as a teacher and highly respected colleague. He was assigned the tasks of teaching the renowned F. W. Taussig's graduate class in economic theory and developing a course in mathematical economics that would help make Harvard a world-class department. Given that Harvard would later become a hotbed of Keynesian economics, it is ironic that this new arrival from Europe was one of the first and foremost academic critics of Keynes's *General Theory*.

Schumpeter married Elizabeth Boody, a Radcliffe economist, in 1937. She cared for his emotional and material needs and contributed greatly to his comeback as an economic theorist. She was largely responsible for finishing his monumental *History of Economic Analysis* (1954) after his unexpected death at "Windy Hill," her old country home in Teconic, Connecticut, where she and Schumpeter had spent a great deal of time. The couple had no children.

Schumpeter's ambitious *Business Cycles: A Theoretical, Historical and Statistical Analysis of the Capitalist Process* (2 vols., 1939), was intended as a sequel to his highly acclaimed *The Theory of Economic Development* but met with a less-than-enthusiastic reception. The monumental nature of this study, which included extensive theoretical, historical, and statistical work, placed it beyond the full comprehension of most economists. Its length, combined with the rising tide of Keynesian economics, put it beyond the interests of the profession as well. Colleagues, however, could readily comprehend and respect the amount of effort and scholarly seriousness that went into the project.

The surprising success of *Capitalism, Socialism, and Democracy* (1942) soon displaced the disappointment of *Business Cycles*. Published as an extension of *Business Cycles*, it contained the missing political and sociological factors that explained why the capitalist business cycle was no longer behaving according to theory during the Great Depression. The institutions of capitalism were in a transition from what Schumpeter called "competitive capitalism" to what he labeled "trustified capitalism." He reintroduced the important role that entrepreneurship plays in economic development with his famous idea of "creative destruction," in which entrepreneurs are constantly, although not evenly, introducing a gale of innovations that disrupts the theoretical stationary state of the economy and produces the business cycle. His distinction between invention (the product of inventors) and innovation (the product of entrepreneurs that involves marketing and mundane changes such as altering the production process to reduce cost) explains both why the entrepreneur is so important in economic development and why entrepreneurs make profits and inventors typically do not. Entrepreneurs depend on the existence of a social ideology that makes it possible to fulfill their crucial role. Trustified capitalism makes people bureaucratic, anticapitalistic, and less entrepreneurial. The change in ideology—not a failure of capitalistic vitality—is the basis for Schumpeter's famous prediction of the rise of socialism.

Schumpeter's final grand contribution to economic thought, his massive *History of Economic Analysis*, demonstrates his almost unique ability to understand the entire breadth of economic thought in all of its complexity and detail. His insightful commentary has raised issues of bias and eccentricity, such as his calling into question the contributions of Adam Smith, whom he believed was neither insightful nor an original thinker, but most of these controversial insights have either been confirmed by subsequent scholarship or stem from the general equilibrium bias of the "Schumpeterian system," a complex theoretical model, first introduced in *The Theory of Economic Development*, for understanding society and economic processes.

In spite of Schumpeter's controversial claims and idiosyncratic personal and professional life, he ranks as one of the greatest economists and social theorists of all time. There is no explicit Schumpeterian school of economics; he is admired by members of all schools of economics but fully embraced by none. Instead he attempted to form a three-way bridge among the economic theorists (Menger, Jevons, and Walras), the empiricists (German historical school and American institutionalism), and the new methodologies of neoclassical economics (mathematical economics and econometrics). Moreover, his contributions transcend the traditional borders of economics and are admired by sociologists, political scientists, and historians.

A great economic theorist and methodologist, Schumpeter was a model of scientific endeavor—swift with criticism and shy with answers—who demonstrated an unsurpassed breadth and impressive depth of knowledge and insights. He contributed greatly to change in economics by adopting (though sometimes rejecting) new methods and subject matter and then transmitting them to his colleagues. He shocked the profession with his evaluation of the contributions of Adam Smith and David Ricardo and showed that progress in economics was not linear. His reintroduction of the important role of the entrepreneur showed economists the dangers of remaining in a professional vacuum and emphasized that progress in the economy was also not automatic.

Schumpeter dealt with the battle between capitalism and socialism, the most important debate of modern times, in a persuasive, innovative, and nonpolitical manner. He found that the socialization of capitalism was not only feasible but likely, because Western intellectuals were undermining the ideological foundations of entrepreneurship, and capitalistic efficiency was concentrating production into what was approaching the rationalized socialist firm. Although he was not directly involved in the Socialist Calculation Debate that was raging in the profession and did not believe that pure socialism was possible, Schumpeter's high scholarly standing probably tipped the balance of opinion in favor of predicting the rise of socialism. However, he also concluded that capitalism was more efficient and provided the clues for the ultimate resolution of that battle. Schumpeter's writings are still one of the best sources of economic knowledge for both novice and expert alike and will no doubt continue to be a source of scientific inspiration and progress in economic thought.

Schumpeter was an inspiring teacher as well as a creative and driven scholar. His student, Nobel laureate Paul Samuelson found him brilliant and stimulating and noted that Schumpeter taught a host of students who would later become the leaders of American economics. Schumpeter received many awards and accolades toward the end of his life, recognizing his lifetime contributions to economics. He was a founder of the Econometric Society in 1930 and served as its vice president in 1938–1939 and president in 1940. He was made president of the American Economic Association in 1948. Just before his death, he was elected the first president of the International Economic Association (1949).

• Schumpeter's papers are in the Pusey Library at Harvard University. Collections of his articles and other publications include *Ten Great Economists: From Marx to Keynes* (1951), *Imperialism and the Social Classes* (1951), *Essays*, ed. Richard V. Clemence (1951), and *The Economics and Sociology of Capitalism* (1991). Bibliographies of his publications include Michael I. Stevenson, *Joseph Alois Schumpeter: A Bibliography, 1905–1984* (1985), and Massimo M. Augello, *Joseph Alois Schumpeter: A Reference Guide* (1990). The numerous biographical, critical, and retrospective writings on Schumpeter include Seymour E. Harris, ed., *Schumpeter: Social Scientist* (1951); Arthur Smithies, "Memorial: Joseph Alois Schumpeter, 1883–1950," *American Economic Review* 40 (1950): 628–48; Arthur Spiethoff, "Josef Schumpeter: In Memoriam,"

Kyklos 3 (1949): 289–93; Gottfried Haberler, "Joseph Alois Schumpeter: 1883–1950," *Quarterly Journal of Economics* 64 (1950): 333–72; Arnold Heertje, ed., *Schumpeter's Vision: Capitalism, Socialism, and Democracy After Forty Years* (1981); Helmut Frisch, ed., *Schumpeterian Economics* (1982); Robert Loring Allen, *Opening Doors: The Life and Work of Joseph Schumpeter* (2 vols., 1991); Eduard März, *Joseph Schumpeter: Scholar, Teacher and Politician* (1991); Richard Swedberg, *Schumpeter: A Biography* (1991); and Wolfgang F. Stopler, *Joseph Alois Schumpeter: The Public Life of a Private Man* (1994). For further theoretical assessment, see Heertje, "Joseph Alois Schumpeter," in *The New Palgrave: A Dictionary of Economics*, vol. 4, ed. John Eatwell et al. (1987), and John Cunningham Wood, ed., *Joseph A. Schumpeter: Critical Assessments* (4 vols., 1991).

MARK THORNTON

SCHURMAN, Jacob Gould (22 May 1854–12 Aug. 1942), scholar and diplomat, was born on a farm near Freetown, Prince Edward Island, Canada, the son of Robert Schurman and Lydia Gouldrup, farmers. Schurman's great-grandfather William Schurman, a Tory, acquired wealth in New Rochelle, New York, and with his family was exiled to Nova Scotia in 1783, moving to Prince Edward Island the following year. Family wealth had dissipated by the time of Schurman's birth, and he grew up poor.

Schurman received an elementary education at a district school and left his family's farm at the age of thirteen to clerk in a country store. In 1870 he used savings to attend high school for a year, studying Latin, Greek, and algebra and winning a scholarship to Prince of Wales College at Charlottetown, Prince Edward Island. In the fall of 1873 Schurman transferred to Acadia College in Nova Scotia, a school established to train Baptist ministers. He studied English history and literature, the classics, religion, chemistry, and physics. He won the Canadian Gilchrist scholarship in 1875, which provided for three years of university study in Great Britain.

Schurman, at first, had problems reconciling his fundamentalist Baptist religious views with the cosmopolitan intellectual climate at the University of London. James Martineau's philosophy lectures helped him over this intellectual hurdle, and Martineau observed that Schurman's intellect was "animated not simply by speculative interest, but by an earnest love of truth as a sacred object of human quest" (Maynard, p. 10). Schurman later described Martineau as the "champion and defender of spiritual faith" (DeAngelis, p. 9). Schurman received a B.A. in 1877, graduating with highest honors in philosophy and political science, and continued to study philosophy at the University of Edinburgh, receiving his Sc.D. in the spring of 1878.

Schurman's academic achievements helped him win the prestigious Hibbert Travelling Fellowship in Mental and Moral Philosophy, supporting two years of study on the Continent. He attended the University of Heidelberg to learn German and "to extend and deepen" his "knowledge of German thought, science, and culture" (DeAngelis, p. 10). He focused on Kant,

Goethe, and Dürer and spent the following year at the Universities of Berlin and Göttingen, where he met leading German philosophers. He also befriended Andrew D. White, the American minister to Germany, who was on leave as president of Cornell University.

For two years beginning in the fall of 1880, Schurman taught logic, English literature, and political economy at Acadia College, summered near libraries in Baltimore, Maryland, and Cambridge, Massachusetts, and during this period published *Kantian Ethics and the Ethics of Evolution* (1881). This book established his reputation as a thoughtful scholar in the first English-language critique of Kant's work. From 1882 to 1886 he taught English literature and metaphysics at Dalhousie College, Halifax, Nova Scotia. In 1884 he married Barbara Forrest Munro; seven of their children survived to adulthood. His wife's father, who was a New York publisher, endowed a chair of metaphysics at Dalhousie for Schurman.

Appointed Sage Professor of Philosophy at Cornell University in 1886, Schurman became dean of the newly created Sage School of Philosophy in 1890 and president of the university two years later. During these years he published *The Ethical Import of Darwinism* (1888), *Belief in God, Its Origin, Nature, and Basis* (1890), and *Agnosticism and Religion* (1896). These books, the first scholarly and the latter two compilations of popular lectures, took issue with the Social Darwinism of Herbert Spencer, arguing that it denied free will and individual moral responsibility. He was also the founding editor (1892–1905) of the *Philosophical Review*, the first national philosophical journal. Modern philosophers still read Kant and Spencer but ignore Schurman because he was not an original thinker. During Schurman's 28-year tenure as president, the university expanded dramatically—the faculty grew from less than 150 to 847, enrollment increased from 1,600 to 7,000, academic offerings multiplied, and a modern campus infrastructure was created.

Schurman, who became a naturalized U.S. citizen in 1892, actively involved himself in public affairs. A conservative Republican, he often spoke and wrote about public issues, openly opposing annexation of the Philippine Islands in 1898. Early the next year, President William McKinley appointed him president of the first U.S. commission to the Philippines. His suggestion that only one Protestant denomination be allowed to proselytize in the islands to provide Filipinos a clear choice between Catholicism and Protestantism caused controversy. Schurman's time in the Philippines reinforced his anti-imperialist convictions. Although he publicly supported administration policies to retain the islands, he later advocated Philippine independence in *Philippine Affairs, a Retrospect and Outlook, an Address* (1902) because his experiences in the islands convinced him that imperialism was incompatible with democratic principles.

In 1912 Schurman supported President William Howard Taft's unsuccessful reelection campaign and was rewarded with a brief appointment as U.S. minister to Greece and Montenegro (1912–1913). He ac-

complished little as minister, although he soon published *The Balkan Wars, 1912–13* (1914), a book that went through three editions. He championed Charles Evans Hughes's unsuccessful presidential bid in 1916 and campaigned for Warren G. Harding in 1920. Schurman, a member of the internationalist wing of the Republican party, favored ratification of the Treaty of Versailles with mild reservations to limit American obligations to enforce the treaty unless first approved by the Senate.

Schurman retired from Cornell in 1920, and the next year Hughes secured Schurman's appointment as U.S. minister to China. Schurman witnessed an extremely turbulent period in Sino-American relations. He initially focused on protecting American treaty rights under the unequal treaty system that had grown up in the nineteenth century, granting extraterritorial rights to westerners in China and western control of Chinese tariffs. Schurman traveled extensively in China, making an unprecedented visit to all twenty American consulates in the country. He gradually recognized the growing power of Chinese nationalism and sought to channel it into a path acceptable to Americans. As concern increased about the influence of Bolshevism in China, Schurman publicly lectured the Chinese people on the benefits of American-style democracy. Convinced that the West would ultimately have to surrender its privileged position in China and end the unequal treaty system, he advised his government to ignore the many calls from American business interests (and occasionally from American missionaries and educators too) to intervene militarily in Chinese internal affairs. While Schurman never developed a clear understanding of Chinese nationalism, nonetheless he served as an able emissary during a confusing and often vexatious period and possibly prevented direct military intervention by the West.

President Calvin Coolidge rewarded Schurman for his work in China by appointing him ambassador to Germany in 1925. In his new position, Schurman hoped to renew the "old relations of cordial friendship between the American and German peoples" (Maynard, p. 149). His mastery of the German language and knowledge of German culture made him an ideal emissary. He maintained excellent relations with German officials and helped reestablish academic ties between German and American universities. Schurman advised his government that the 1924 Dawes Plan—placing German reparation payments on a long-term payment plan, providing for the Reichsbank's reorganization under Allied supervision, and arranging substantial private loans from American bankers to promote German industrial recovery—needed to be revised to scale down the German reparations demanded by the Allies. He predicted that a German economic collapse would likely result in a Fascist dictatorship. Schurman's attempts to improve relations with Germany were cut short by the Great Depression; his diplomatic career ended in 1930.

In retirement, Schurman continued to lecture and to travel widely. He became alarmed by Adolph Hitler's repressive and aggressive policies and in 1938 publicly favored American rearmament. By 1940 he became convinced that the United States would have to confront Germany in Europe, although he did not believe that American interests in China warranted a military confrontation with Japan in the Far East. Schurman died in New York City nine months after the Japanese attack on Pearl Harbor.

• Schurman's papers are located at Cornell University, Ithaca, N.Y. The National Archives, Washington, D.C., contains official records relating to his government service, especially RG 59, Records of the Department of State, and RG 84, Records of the Foreign Service Posts of the United States. Schurman wrote numerous books and articles on academic topics and public issues. The most comprehensive bibliography of his writings is in Richard DeAngelis, "Jacob Gould Schurman and American Policy toward China, 1921–1925," (Ph.D. diss., St. John's Univ., 1975), which is an excellent account of Schurman's years in China. Kenneth P. Davis, "The Diplomatic Career of Jacob Gould Schurman" (Ph.D. diss., Univ. of Virginia, 1975), examines Schurman's diplomatic career, while Moser Maynard, "Jacob Gould Schurman: Scholar, Political Activist, and Ambassador of Good Will, 1892–1942" (Ph.D. diss., Univ. of Santa Barbara, 1976), provides a broader perspective. See also Kenneth E. Hendrickson, Jr., "Reluctant Expansionist—Jacob Gould Schurman and the Philippine Question," *Pacific Historical Review* 36 (1967): 405–21. An excellent obituary is in the *New York Times*, 13 Aug. 1942.

DAVID L. WILSON

SCHURZ, Carl (2 Mar. 1829–19 May 1906), Civil War general, U.S. senator, and secretary of the interior, was born in Liblar near Cologne, the son of Christian Schurz, a teacher and small businessman, and Marianne Jüssen. He was educated at the Marcellen Gymnasium in Cologne and at the University of Bonn, where he was strongly influenced by Professor Gottfried Kinkel, a convinced German nationalist and democrat. During the Revolution of 1848 Schurz joined Kinkel in agitating for radical democratic and republican reforms. His participation in an ill-conceived attempt to seize the arsenal at Siegburg caused him to flee to the Palatinate, where he joined the revolutionary forces. Commissioned a lieutenant, he took part in engagements at Übstadt and Bruchsal and was almost captured by the Prussians in besieged Rastatt. In danger of punishment for treason, he managed to escape through a sewer and reach safety in France.

Schurz did not stay abroad for long. Anxious to free Kinkel, who had been captured and condemned to life imprisonment, he returned to Germany using a false passport, secured financial aid through Mrs. Kinkel, and succeeded in rescuing the professor from a jail in Spandau by bribing a guard. Lowering Kinkel from the roof, he fled with the freed prisoner to Mecklenburg and then to Great Britain, a feat that made him famous.

After spending two years as a teacher and journalist in France and England, Schurz immigrated to the United States, arriving in 1852. Also in 1852 he married Margarethe Meyer, a wealthy Hamburg heiress;

they would have five children. Helped financially by his marriage, he settled first in Philadelphia to engage in business. In 1856 he moved to Watertown, Wisconsin, a town with a large German population, where he was active in real estate and journalism. His principal occupation, however, was politics, and since he was an opponent of slavery, he joined the Republican party. He had become fluent in English, was an excellent speaker, and was much sought after by the party to win over other German Americans. So effectively did he campaign for the antislavery cause in two languages that in 1857, before he had even completed his naturalization, he was nominated for lieutenant governor. Because of nativist influence, he, unlike other Republicans, lost. But he remained loyal to the party, even in 1859 when he failed in his efforts to obtain the gubernatorial nomination. Lecturing throughout the North and taking up the law to recoup financial losses incurred during the panic of 1857, he made a name for himself and in 1860 became the chairman of the Wisconsin delegation to the Republican National Convention in Chicago.

In Chicago, Schurz first favored William H. Seward but then switched to Abraham Lincoln, whom he had come to appreciate in the 1858 campaign. Elected to the Republican National Committee, he organized a campaign centered on ethnic groups. He himself wooed the Germans, and Lincoln was convinced that this effort made a decisive contribution to the Republican victory. Schurz's reward was an appointment as minister to Spain.

Before Schurz could leave for Madrid, the Civil War broke out. Delaying his departure, he was active in raising several German cavalry regiments and succeeded in establishing close relations with the president. Once in Spain, he came to the conclusion that only an active emancipation policy could prevent European powers from intervening in the Civil War, and he so advised the administration.

Schurz returned to the United States early in 1862 and was appointed a brigadier general. He performed well at Second Manassas (Bull Run) and was promoted to major general. But he then had the misfortune of being blamed for the disaster that befell the heavily German Eleventh Corps at Chancellorsville, although he had warned his superiors of the dangerous position of the army's right wing. At Gettysburg, Schurz and the Eleventh Corps were again criticized for their repulse on the first day, and even their gallant stand on Cemetery Hill could not restore their prestige. Finally, when Schurz was ordered to the Chattanooga theater, Joseph Hooker falsely accused him of tardiness at Wauhatchie. Schurz asked for and received a court of inquiry, which vindicated him, but when the corps was reorganized he became a supernumerary and was given command of a camp of instruction near Nashville. In the fall of 1864 he campaigned for Lincoln's reelection. He finished the war as General Henry W. Slocum's chief of staff in North Carolina.

The assassination of Lincoln was a severe blow for Schurz. Although he had at times annoyed the president with his never-ending advice, he enjoyed Lincoln's trust and early appreciated the Great Emancipator's stature. His contacts with Andrew Johnson were entirely different. At first he hoped to maintain friendly relations with the new president, but ultimately he was unable to do so. After a tour of inspection in the South in the summer of 1865 Schurz reported that Johnson's Reconstruction policies were resulting in atrocities against blacks and Unionists. A complete break between Johnson and Schurz followed. In a long report that was printed by Congress, Schurz provided a campaign document for the radical Republicans and became an outspoken critic of the administration.

In the meantime, Schurz had again turned to journalism. He first served as the Washington correspondent of the New York *Tribune*, then accepted a position with the Detroit *Post*, and then in 1867 moved to St. Louis, where he became editor and part-owner of the influential *Westliche Post*. He traveled to Germany, had an interview with Bismarck, and was more and more identified as the principal spokesman for the Germans in America.

Schurz's position as an ethnic leader contributed to his election as temporary chairman and keynote speaker of the 1868 Republican National Convention in Chicago, which nominated Ulysses S. Grant. After campaigning successfully for the Republicans' presidential ticket, he secured election to the Senate from his new home state of Missouri and took office in 1869.

Schurz's senatorial term was one of the high points of his career. Considered the "Dutch" senator, he served as a spokesman for German Americans, whose interests he sought to uphold. His telling orations and well-turned phrases—as he said, "My country right or wrong; if right to be kept right; and if wrong, to be set right"—were widely quoted. Although he was elected as a Republican, Schurz soon broke with the administration. Differences over civil service reform, the annexation of the Dominican Republic, southern policies, and patronage in Missouri eventually led Schurz to become one of the initiators of the Liberal Republican movement. His breach with the administration caused a lessening of his radical commitment; eager to conciliate the South, he even voted against the Ku Klux Act and other radical measures.

With great confidence the Liberal Republicans met in Cincinnati in 1872 with Schurz as presiding officer. After adopting a platform condemning the corruption of the administration and its southern policy, advocating civil service reform, and straddling the tariff issue, they nominated Horace Greeley. Schurz had been outmaneuvered; from his point of view Greeley's choice was a disaster. A temperance advocate and protectionist, the editor was unpopular with Germans and free-traders. In spite of his misgivings, Schurz eventually supported Greeley, who was also endorsed by the Democrats. The campaign exposed Schurz to savage attacks, particularly in the acerbic cartoons of Thomas Nast, and ended in a complete defeat for the Liberals.

The Liberal debacle also foreshadowed Schurz's own defeat. His advocacy of reenfranchising former Missouri Confederates helped lead to the election of a Democratic legislature, which in 1875 denied him reelection to the Senate. As revelations of corruption during Grant's second term underscored the necessity for political reform, Schurz was among the main speakers at a clean government conference held in New York City in 1876. The Republicans' nomination of Rutherford B. Hayes, who came complete with reform credentials, seemed to satisfy the conference's demands, and Schurz lent Hayes his support. His reward when Hayes became president was an appointment as secretary of the interior.

In his new position Schurz introduced civil service rules within his department, set in motion a policy of conservation of natural resources (especially forests), and cleaned up corruption in the Indian Bureau. His continuation of the practice of large-scale removals of various Native-American nations to large reservations, particularly the forcible resettlement of the Poncas in the Indian Territory, subjected him to criticism, but, in the end, he reversed himself and inaugurated a more equitable policy. His protection of the Indian Bureau from an attempted War Department takeover was also a boon to Native Americans, whose treatment by the army left much to be desired.

At the end of his term Schurz moved to New York City to assume the editorship of the New York *Evening Post* in conjunction with E. L. Godkin and Horace White. Using the paper to further his favorite causes, such as civil service reform, he also made it a mouthpiece for tolerance, particularly in the face of the growing anti-Semitic movement in Europe, which he deplored. But in 1883 he fell out with Godkin, who condemned a telegraphers' strike, while he maintained his perspective while dealing with the workers. Forced to resign, for a while he experienced great financial difficulties. Eventually, however, he succeeded in reversing his fortunes by lecturing, writing, and serving as the American representative of the Hamburg-American steamship company.

In the meantime, Schurz had again become politically active. After supporting James A. Garfield in 1880, in 1884, a typical Mugwump, he refused to endorse the Republican ticket headed by James G. Blaine, whom he considered a corruptionist, and campaigned for the Democrat, Grover Cleveland. His main political interest during these years, however, was civil service reform. He was active in the National Civil Service Reform League, of which he became president in 1892, and he pursued an independent course, supporting either Democrats or Republicans (for local or national office), depending on their position concerning the reforms he advocated. Concerned about inflation, he supported William McKinley in 1896 but turned against the McKinley administration after the outbreak of the Spanish-American War and the annexation of overseas territories. A mainstay of the anti-imperialist movement, he collaborated with Andrew Carnegie and others in demanding that the United States return to its anticolonial past. He was so strongly opposed to the annexation of territory that he supported William Jennings Bryan in 1900 and Alton B. Parker in 1904 against his former ally Theodore Roosevelt (1858–1919). But he also resumed his former advocacy of black rights and became friends with Booker T. Washington.

Schurz's later years were taken up with literary endeavors. In 1887 he published a two-volume biography of Henry Clay, a work still readable. Essays on Lincoln, Charles Sumner, and the South kept him busy, as did editorial work for *Harper's Weekly*, but his main effort was devoted to the completion of his *Reminiscences*, a three-volume enterprise that appeared in book form after his death. Characteristically, he wrote the first volume, dealing with his European adventures, in German and the other two, covering his American career, in English. The third volume, unfinished at the time of his death, was completed by William A. Dunning and Frederic Bancroft.

Schurz's wife died in 1876. Although Schurz never remarried, he became intimate with Fanny Chapman, the model for Sybil in Henry B. Adams's novel *Democracy*. He died in New York City.

Schurz's greatest contribution was his role as an ethnic leader. As a model for German Americans, he advanced the notion that the United States could be a melting pot while newcomers still retained some of their ethnic characteristics. Let his countrymen learn English, he advised, yet retain their mother tongue. The most prominent German American of the nineteenth century, the tall, red-bearded Schurz also deserves to be remembered for his fight against slavery, his advocacy of conservation, and his contribution to the integration of his compatriots into American life.

• The Carl Schurz Papers are located in the Library of Congress, which now also houses a private collection of Schurz materials donated by Mrs. Arthur R. Hogue of Bloomington, Ind. Additional Schurz papers may be found in the State Historical Society of Missouri, the National Archives, the New York Public Library, the Watertown (Wis.) Historical Society, and the State Historical Society of Wisconsin. The Schurz-Chapman correspondence is at the University of Münster. *Speeches, Correspondence, and Political Papers of Carl Schurz* (3 vols., 1913) was edited by Frederic Bancroft, and Joseph Schafer translated and edited *Intimate Letters of Carl Schurz, 1841–1869* (1928). The most recent biography is Hans L. Trefousse, *Carl Schurz: A Biography* (1982); older works of value are Claude M. Fuess, *Carl Schurz, Reformer, 1829–1906* (1932), and Chester V. Easum, *The Americanization of Carl Schurz* (1929). A convenient bilingual reproduction of parts of *Reminiscences* and some other documents, with excellent illustrations, is Rüdiger Wersich, ed., *Carl Schurz, Revolutionary and Statesman* (1979).

HANS L. TREFOUSSE

SCHURZ, Margarethe Meyer (27 Aug. 1833–15 Mar. 1876), kindergarten teacher and advocate, was born in Hamburg, Germany, the daughter of Heinrich Meyer, an affluent Jewish businessman (her mother's name is unknown). With other politically liberal Jews and Christians, her family sponsored various educational and cultural activities. She trained in Hamburg in the

1840s as a kindergarten teacher under Friedrich Froebel, originator of the kindergarten, who praised her understanding of his lectures.

Meyer left Germany in 1852 to live in London with her ailing sister Bertha Meyer Ronge, who was married to Johann Ronge, a radical German Catholic dissident. Meyer taught at the kindergarten the Ronges had founded, the first in England. Johann Ronge introduced her to another young German expatriate, Carl Schurz, a university-educated, Christian "freethinker" who had been exiled for his involvement in the revolution of 1848, the failure of which caused an exodus of political liberals from Germany. Schurz was immediately struck by Meyer's intelligence and beauty and wrote later in the first volume of his *Reminiscences* that he admired her "curly hair . . . and large, dark, truthful eyes." Despite the Meyers' concern over how the penurious Schurz could support their daughter, the two were married on 6 July 1852.

Shortly after her marriage, Margarethe Schurz emigrated with her husband to New York. The couple settled near German friends in Philadelphia, where their first child was born in 1853. Margarethe Schurz, unlike her husband, never became fully accustomed to America and spent a period of convalescence in England, where a second daughter was born. In 1856 the Schurzes moved to Watertown, Wisconsin, where Carl Schurz had relatives.

In November 1856 Margarethe Schurz started a small kindergarten in her home in Watertown. Six children, including Schurz's three-year-old daughter, attended this first German-speaking kindergarten in the United States, which Schurz soon moved to a small building in downtown Watertown. Schurz employed methods she had learned directly from Froebel, including the sequence of educational materials and arts and crafts activities such as wooden blocks and paper cutting that he called "gifts" and "occupations." She also taught the children the German games and songs Froebel used to enhance children's learning and social development. Though she stopped teaching when she moved with her husband to Milwaukee in 1859, Schurz's relatives continued the program in Watertown for a number of years.

Margarethe Schurz continued advocating Froebelian kindergartens while she followed her husband's advancing career as a public speaker and liberal Republican politician. During a trip to Boston in 1859 she met the American Transcendentalist and educator Elizabeth Peabody, to whom she sent a copy of the introduction to Froebel's *The Education of Man*. Impressed by the comportment of the Schurzes' daughter, which Margarethe Schurz attributed to kindergarten education, Peabody began a private kindergarten in Boston in 1860, the first English-speaking kindergarten in the United States.

Margarethe Schurz moved frequently during the 1860s and 1870s because of her husband's changing political fortunes and events of the Civil War period. A close friend of Abraham Lincoln, Carl Schurz served as minister to Spain and as a brigadier general in the

Union army. Margarethe visited her husband at the front and on one occasion carried a letter from her husband to the White House to read to Lincoln. In 1869 she moved to Washington, D.C., when Carl Schurz became a senator from Missouri; after one term in the Senate he was nominated in 1876 to be secretary of the interior under Rutherford B. Hayes. Though supportive of her husband's political efforts, Margarethe missed her family and friends in Europe, and her health continued to be fragile. She died in New York from complications following the birth of a fifth child.

Capable and intelligent, Margarethe Meyer Schurz was unable in her relatively brief life to develop her potential as an educator. Her commitment to Froebelianism, in part as a means of fostering German culture in the United States, and her adherence to Froebel's original methods exemplified the first generation of German-trained kindergartners in America. Though she did not become actively involved in the efforts to modernize the kindergarten and adapt it to American life, her contacts with liberal American politicians and educators advanced awareness of the kindergarten in the United States.

• The Carl Schurz Papers are in the Library of Congress. There is also a collection of Schurz family papers at the Watertown Historical Society in Wisconsin. Correspondence to Margarethe Schurz can be found in both collections. She is also mentioned in her husband's writings, particularly his *Reminiscences of Carl Schurz* (3 vols., 1907–1908) and in Joseph Schafer, ed., *Intimate Letters of Carl Schurz, 1841–1869* (1928). A biography is Hannah Werwath Swart, *Margarethe Meyer Schurz* (1967). Her kindergarten work is discussed in Johann and Bertha Ronge, *A Practical Guide to the English Kindergarten* (1874); Elizabeth Peabody, "The Origin and Growth of the Kindergarten," *Education* 2 (May–June 1882): 507–27; Nina C. Vandewalker, *The Kindergarten in American Education* (1908); Elizabeth Jenkins, "How the Kindergarten Found Its Way to America," *Wisconsin Magazine of History* 19 (Sept. 1930): 48–62; Agnes Snyder, *Dauntless Women in Childhood Education, 1856–1931* (1972); and Michael Steven Shapiro, *Child's Garden: The Kindergarten Movement from Froebel to Dewey* (1983).

BARBARA BEATTY

SCHUSCHNIGG, Kurt Alois Josef Johann von (14 Dec. 1897–18 Nov. 1977), Austrian statesman and American university professor, was born at Riva del Garda, South Tirol, Austria, the son of Artur Viktor Schuschnigg, a general in the imperial army, and Anna Wopfner. Early life in garrisons and school led Schuschnigg to emphasize duty, propriety, and rectitude as well as to value Austria's traditional Catholic culture. He received rigorous schooling at Stella Matutina, a Jesuit academy in Vorarlberg. After frontline service from 1915 to 1918 and a year-long imprisonment in Italy, Schuschnigg studied at Freiburg and then, despite a personal preference for the liberal arts, completed a degree in law at the University of Innsbruck in 1922. He began his career in Innsbruck, his mother's hometown, and in 1924 he married Hermine Masera, with whom he had one son. "Herma" died in 1936. In 1927 he took a seat in the *Nationalrat*, the

lower house of the federal parliament, where he soon won notice as a diligent and intense protagonist for the conservative cause. During this period he also wrote about constitutional law and founded and led the small, pro-Catholic *Ostmärkische Sturmscharen*, one of the military-political formations that threatened to disrupt the republic's political life.

For six years Schuschnigg held posts in Austria's federal cabinet, including minister of justice early in 1932, minister of education in 1933, chancellor and concomitantly foreign and defense minister following the murder of Engelbert Dollfuss during an abortive coup by Austrian Nazis late in July 1934. He played a major role in the drafting of the quasi-authoritarian "corporative" constitution, which was partially inspired by the papal encyclical *Quadragesimo Anno* (1931) and was put into effect following a brief civil war and the dissolution of the Social Democratic party in mid-February 1934.

As chancellor, Schuschnigg faced enormous economic and political challenges and stood on a very narrow political base, primarily the church, the government-sponsored Fatherland Front, and the fascistic *Heimwehr*. He depended on Benito Mussolini's government for defense against Adolf Hitler's Germany and its proponents within Austria, a relationship with which Schuschnigg himself, given his devotion to the ideal of German culture, was uncomfortable.

After Mussolini's rapprochement with Germany early in 1936, the chancellor found himself largely bereft of outside support, thus virtually forced to agree to the corrosive terms of the "gentlemen's agreement" reached with the German government in July 1936. A monarchist at heart, Schuschnigg may have considered a Habsburg restoration during the following months, but international opposition prevented such a step. In 1937 he published *Dreimal Österreich* (*My Austria* [1938]), a memoir designed to foster patriotism.

By early 1938 Austria's economic and political isolation, combined with Germany's dynamism, left the country vulnerable to Hitler's appeal and pressure. Emotionally badgered at the famous meeting with the Nazi leader at Berchtesgaden on 12 February, Schuschnigg consented to damaging concessions that led to virulent Nazi agitation. He attempted to counter the Nazis by calling for a plebiscite on the question of Austria's independence as a "Christian" and "German" state.

In response to this challenge, Hitler orchestrated the invasion of Austria and annexed the country to Germany. In one of Schuschnigg's most controversial decisions, one that he defended vigorously for the rest of his life, he gave way without ordering armed resistance to German forces. In one of his most celebrated expressions, he concluded his farewell address, broadcast nationwide on 11 March, with the words, "God protect Austria!"

Schuschnigg spent the next seven years as a prisoner. German authorities eventually allowed his second wife, Vera Fugger, Countess von Czernin-Chudenitz, to whom he was married by proxy in June 1938, to live with him and permitted him to read almost anything he wanted to. Thus, at the end of the war Schuschnigg was, although emaciated, intellectually very much alive. During this period he also had a daughter.

After the war a penniless Schuschnigg, sensing himself unwelcome in the reemerging Austrian republic, took up residence in Italy and began giving lectures and publishing articles about both prewar events and postwar issues. In 1946 his memoir about the end of Austria and his years of imprisonment, *Ein Requiem in Rot-Weiss-Rot*, which was soon translated into English (as *Austrian Requiem* in the United States [1946]), French, and Italian, gained him widespread attention and sympathy. An invitation followed for Schuschnigg to give a series of lectures in the United States early in 1947.

Despite some protests against his governmental policies and the cancellation of an address at Temple University (*New York Times*, 11 Feb. and 22 Mar. 1947), the overall success of the highly publicized trip prompted Schuschnigg to return later in 1947 to give more lectures and to seek employment, "to live a quiet life [as] just another displaced person" (*New York Times*, 8 Sept. 1947). He won appointment, effective mid-1948, to the faculty of St. Louis University, a Jesuit school with which he could feel an affinity. On his birthday in 1956 he became a U.S. citizen.

A full professor of political science and international law, Schuschnigg also offered courses in modern European history prior to 1918. He gave guest lectures throughout the country. In his teaching and public addresses he tried to avoid discussions of the 1930s and often dealt with current events. Over the years he received honorary doctorates from several small colleges in the Midwest, and upon retirement in 1967 he received his own university's prestigious Fleur-de-Lis award. One colleague described him as "courtly in manner, tolerant in controversy, profound in knowledge and dynamic in presentation" (Hopfgartner, p. 283).

Schuschnigg published regularly during the 1950s. He wrote a number of articles, reviews, and reminiscences for American and European journals and newspapers, most notably the journal *Social Order*. His major scholarly book, *International Law: An Introduction to the Law of Peace*, appeared in 1959. In it he contended that

the rediscovery of universal International Law with the Charter of the UN, the near-universality of our contemporary international organization, with its bearing on world opinion, . . . despite all drawbacks and shortcomings, justifies the statement that the last decade shows the greatest progress ever made in the history of International Law. (p. 430)

In the Smith History Lecture, which he delivered in 1959 at the University of St. Thomas (Houston, Tex.) and published under the title of *Central Europe: Past Adventure, Present Labor, Future Vision*, Schuschnigg lamented the passing of the Habsburg empire, which despite its foibles was, in his view, "a nearer approach to our contemporary ideas of supranational arrangements than any of its successors" (p. 27). He looked forward to a post–Cold War rebirth of Central Europe based on its "history, geography, and civilization" (p. 32). In this lecture, as well as in other settings, he also praised the contributions of Christian Humanism to European civilization (pp. 33–34).

As the 1950s progressed, Schuschnigg's involvement with his homeland grew. A steady stream of Austrians called on him, including Chancellor Julius Raab. He also remained in contact with Otto von Habsburg and praised the House of Austria for its "truly European spirit" in a brief prologue he wrote for Maria Rita Cancio's book about Queen María Christina of Spain (1956). From 1956 he acted as honorary trade representative for Austria in the Midwest. In 1957 he visited Austria to address a university convocation in Salzburg. Thereafter he returned regularly to give lectures, to vacation, and to attend the Salzburg Festival. His wife died in 1959.

Upon his retirement early in 1967, Schuschnigg, abjuring political activity and noting that his stay in the United States had broadened his outlook, moved to Mutters, a village near Innsbruck, where for over ten years he lived modestly in rented rooms. There he completed his final book, *Im Kampf gegen Hitler: Die Uberwindung der Anschlussidee* (1969) (*The Brutal Takeover* [1971]). He continued to give lectures and wrote a series of articles for *Die Furche*, including reflections on an extended journey to South America in 1972. In interviews he defended his key governmental decisions in the 1930s for having made it possible for Austria to be seen as Hitler's victim rather than as an eager accomplice. He died in Mutters.

A man stunned by the collapse of the world of his youth and by the threat of social revolution, Schuschnigg played a fateful role during the 1930s and remained marked by that experience, even during his years as a model citizen of the United States. One might wish that he had been more broad-minded and flexible earlier in life, but he was principled and consistent. On both sides of the Atlantic, he was known as a formal, almost austere, but polite intellectual, albeit one excoriated by the political left for his linkage with "clerico-fascism." As Walter Laqueur wrote in a review of *The Brutal Takeover* for the *Economist* (239 [5 June 1971]: 56), "It seems likely that posterity will treat him more leniently than many of his contemporaries do."

• Schuschnigg deposited papers from his American sojourn at St. Louis University, but by the time they reached a permanent home in the library archives, parts of the collection seem to have been misplaced. An appraisal of the collection and a list of Schuschnigg's writings are in Robert Stanley Gerlich, "Kurt von Schuschnigg and the Austrian Authoritarian Experiment, 1934–1938: Historical Perspectives and the American Archives" (Ph.D. diss., St. Louis Univ., 1987). The family retains a collection of Schuschnigg's letters, and a private collection in St. Louis contains material relating to Schuschnigg's American period. State archives in

Vienna as well as those of the Institute for Contemporary History and of the Austrian Resistance (the *Dokumentationsararchiv*) contain much material about Schuschnigg before 1945. Schuschnigg figures prominently in the extensive historical literature about Austria in the 1930s. A sympathetic biography that deals with the American period and also provides a valuable bibliography is Anton Hopfgartner, *Kurt Schuschnigg: Ein Mann gegen Hitler* (1989). Obituaries are in the *New York Times*, the *Presse* (Vienna), and the *St. Louis Post-Dispatch*, all 19 Nov. 1977, with a follow-up on 20 Nov. in the latter paper.

C. EARL EDMONDSON

SCHUSSELE, Christian (16 Apr. 1824–21 Aug. 1879), painter, was born in Guebviller, Alsace, France. Uncertainty in regard to his birthdate and the spelling of his name have characterized accounts of this artist. Both 1824 and 1826 have appeared, and "Schuessele" is apparently the original spelling of the artist's name and how he typically signed his works. However, since the late nineteenth century, "Schussele" has become the usual spelling. According to an 1888 questionnaire completed by Cecilia Schussele (his wife), the artist was born in 1824, he spelled his name "Schussele," and he pronounced it in a French, not German, manner.

Little is known of Schussele's parentage other than that his father was a baker. In 1841 Schussele settled in Strasbourg to learn lithography (it is unclear whether he studied at the Strasbourg Academy or apprenticed in a commercial lithographer's shop). Two years later he moved to Paris to study at the École des Beaux-Arts. He trained under Paul Delaroche, Godefroy Englemann, Franz Graf, and Adolphe Yvon. After a commission to prepare chromolithographs of the paintings at Versailles was abruptly terminated by the 1848 revolution, Schussele emigrated to Philadelphia. There he married Cecilia Muringer, a Philadelphian he had met in Strasbourg and the daughter of a lithographer, Caspar Muringer.

In Philadelphia the artist produced chromolithographs and designed illustrations to be engraved. His work appeared in journals such as *Graham's Magazine* and *Sartain's Union Magazine of Literature and Art* and in gift books like *The Iris*. Schussele executed and exhibited his first oil paintings in 1851, including *Lager Beer Saloon* (LaSalle University Art Museum) and *The Artist's Recreation* (unlocated). The former appeared at the Franklin Institute, where it received First Premium, and the latter formed part of the annual exhibition of the Pennsylvania Academy of the Fine Arts. At the following year's academy exhibition, his *Clear the Track* (Physician's Planning Service Corporation, N.Y.) was well received. In 1854 the Art Union of Philadelphia published a John Sartain engraving of the popular work. Throughout Schussele's career, large engravings of his works were published.

Along with genre painting, Schussele favored history painting, a form of art highly regarded in midcentury Philadelphia. History paintings depicted significant human events and actions (real and imaginary) not only drawn from history but also from mythology, literature, and the Bible. Schussele's best-known history pictures include *Andrew Jackson before Judge Hall, 1815* (1859; Thomas Gilcrease Institution of American History and Art, Tulsa, Okla.; the Pennsylvania Academy of the Fine Arts owns a study for this work); *Hetty Reading the Scriptures to the Indians* (1860; private collection); *The Power of the Gospel: Zeisberger Preaching to the Indians* (1862; Moravian Archives, Bethlehem, Pa.); *King Solomon and the Iron Worker* (1863, Museum of American Art, Pennsylvania Academy of the Fine Arts); and *Franklin Appearing before the Privy Council* (1867; Henry E. Huntington Library and Art Gallery, San Marino, Calif.). Two of his most widely known works combine the grandeur of history painting with the realism of portraiture: *Men of Progress* (1862; National Portrait Gallery, Smithsonian Institution) and *Washington Irving and His Literary Friends* (1863; Sleepy Hollow Restorations, Tarrytown, N.Y.). These compositions depict idealized gatherings of prominent American scientists and writers. Both works became well known through engravings; as a print, *Men of Progress* carried the subtitle *American Inventors*.

The artist enjoyed success until stricken with palsy of the right hand in 1863, causing him to seek a cure in Europe. Returning to Philadelphia in 1868, Schussele was unanimously elected the first professor of drawing and painting at the Pennsylvania Academy. He held this position the remaining eleven years of his life. During his tenure as professor, Schussele oversaw a traditional European academic approach and curriculum that featured drawing from plaster casts of antique sculpture before progressing to rendering live models.

Active in the Philadelphia art world, Schussele served as president of the Artists' Fund Society, treasurer of the Philadelphia Graphic Club, a member of the exhibition and instruction committees of the Pennsylvania Academy of the Fine Arts, and president of its Council of Pennsylvania Academicians. Through these activities and by the quality of his paintings and the character of his professorship at the Pennsylvania Academy of the Fine Arts, Schussele embodied and promoted the academic art tradition in the United States. He died in Merchantville, New Jersey.

• Accounts of Schussele's art and life include George W. Dewey, "C. Schuessele," *Sartain's Union Magazine of Literature and Art* 10 (June 1852): 462–63; George H. Johnston, *A Memorial Sermon to Christian Schussele, for Eleven Years Professor of Drawing and Painting in the Pennsylvania Academy of the Fine Arts, Philadelphia* (1879); Bernard E. Michel, "Christian Schussele: Portrayer of America," *Transactions of the Moravian Historical Society* 20, part 2 (1965): 249–67; and Ronald Onorato, "The Context of the Pennsylvania Academy: Thomas Eakins' Assistantship to Christian Schuessele," *Arts Magazine* 53 (May 1979): 121–25. See also "Christian Schussele" in the Artists' Files of the New York Public Library.

MARK THISTLETHWAITE

SCHUSTER, Max Lincoln (2 Mar. 1897–20 Dec. 1970), publisher, was born Max Schuster in Kalusz, Austria, the son of Barnet Schuster and Minnie Stieglitz, both of whom were American citizens. The family returned to the United States when Max was seven weeks old. The Schusters lived in New York City and ran a stationery and cigar store in Harlem. They later moved to the Washington Heights neighborhood of upper Manhattan, where Max attended public school. In high school he became so interested in Abraham Lincoln that he took Lincoln as his middle name. His helping his father sell newspapers sparked an interest in journalism, which increased when he worked for the *New York Evening World* as a copy boy. At age sixteen, he enrolled in the Pulitzer School of Journalism at Columbia University. He edited a radical school magazine titled the *Challenge*, wrote articles for periodicals, and was a college correspondent for the *Boston Evening Transcript*. After graduating from Columbia in 1917, he became a reporter for the Washington, D.C., bureau of the New Republic News Service, which was to become the United Press. During World War I he remained in Washington, first as chief of the publication section of the Bureau of War Risk Insurance, in the Treasury Department. Later he was publicity director for Liberty Loans and then Victory Loans of the U.S. Navy. He wrote pamphlets urging military personnel to buy such bonds.

After the war, Schuster returned to New York, taught briefly at Columbia, handled advertisements for the Motor and Equipment Manufacturers Association, and edited its trade magazine. In 1921 he met Richard L. Simon, who was selling pianos and whose office was in the same building as Schuster's. The two men discussed the French writer Romain Rolland, a copy of whose *Jean-Christophe* was on Schuster's desk. Thus began a professional friendship of great consequence in the publishing world. Simon was soon employed by the publishers Boni & Liveright, while Schuster continued in his same work; but they enjoyed lunches together and in 1923 decided to form a publishing house. In January 1924 they pooled $4,000 and opened an office for business. Their first publication, in April, was *The Cross Word Puzzle Book*. It sold a half million copies by year's end, grossed almost $400,000, and netted Simon & Schuster $100,000. During the following decade, 1.5 million copies of its subsequent series of crossword puzzle books were sold, making possible the initially haphazard expansion of the innovative firm.

During their first year, the partners hired the dynamic Leon Shimkin, destined to become later president of Simon & Schuster. Simon's admiration for the Little Blue Books, booklets mail-ordered from E. Haldeman-Julius of Girard, Kansas, led to a joint venture with Haldeman-Julius to reissue several Little Blue Books on philosophy by Will Durant, a Columbia professor. Schuster then persuaded Durant to revise and combine them into *The Story of Philosophy: The Lives and Opinions of the Greater Philosophers*; Simon & Schuster sold upwards of half a million copies

in the year of publication, 1926. A succession of profitable books followed, including *Trader Horn: Being the Life and Works of Alfred Aloysius Horn* (1927), Ernest Dimnet's *The Art of Thinking* (1928), Felix Salten's *Bambi* (1928), Robert Ripley's *Believe It or Not!* (1929), and Laurence Stallings's *The First World War: A Photographic History* (1933). In 1931 Schuster published *Men of Art* and followed it with books on men of mathematics, music, science, and wealth. The first—and best—of numerous Simon & Schuster "How to . . ." books appeared in 1936: Dale Carnegie's *How to Win Friends and Influence People*, which eventually sold over 6 million copies. Schuster and his colleagues were well aware of the commercial payoff of first deciding on an idea for a potential bestseller and then seeking out the author to write it. Dozens of other "How to" books followed Dale Carnegie's, explaining how to become a good dancer, buy real estate, develop a good memory, fight mental depression, make sound investments, make out an income tax form, play checkers or golf or tennis better, raise a dog, read a book, start housekeeping, stop worrying, succeed in business without really trying, think straight, write a play, and so on.

In 1939 Schuster and Simon, together with Shimkin, by then their hard-driving partner, joined Robert de Graff to create Pocket Books, Inc., which began flooding a receptive market with small, cheap paperbacks. Schuster himself compiled and annotated over the years the contents of *A Treasury of the World's Great Letters, from Ancient Days to Our Own Time* . . . ; published in 1940, it was an instant hit, followed a year later by *A Second Treasury* . . . , assembled by two of Schuster's colleagues. He also directed the publication of home-library books, anthologies, Inner Sanctum Mysteries, Little Golden Books for children, and Giant Golden Books—all aggressively marketed. Amid that activity, Schuster married Ray Haskell in 1940; the couple did not have children.

In 1944 Field Enterprises, led by the department-store millionaire Marshall Field III, bought Pocket Books and Simon & Schuster, with Schuster and Simon remaining to alternate as president and chairman of the board. In 1957 Simon resigned because of illness, and Shimkin and Schuster repurchased Simon & Schuster for $1 million from Field's estate, held it jointly, and functioned as joint chief executive officers. In 1966 Schuster sold his half interest to Shimkin for $2 million and planned to become an independent editor, scholar, and author.

From 1924 through 1966, the years when Schuster played an active role in the firm, Simon & Schuster had fifteen novels and sixty-one nonfiction works on the annual bestseller lists. After retiring, Schuster devoted much of his free time to civic affairs and to his several clubs. In 1968 he and his wife formed an editing and publishing partnership, which lasted only two years, ending with his death (in New York City). Schuster's uncanny entrepreneurial skill helped turn American publishing away from an elite profession and into big business.

• Kenneth C. Davis, *Two-Bit Culture: The Paperbacking of America* (1984), and John Tebbel, *Between Covers: The Rise and Transformation of American Book Publishing* (1987), summarize Schuster's career. Alice Payne Hackett and James Henry Burke, *80 Years of Best Sellers: 1895–1975* (1977), lists Simon & Schuster's numerous bestsellers over the years. Obituaries are in the *New York Times*, 21 Dec. 1970, and *Publishers Weekly*, 4 Jan. 1971.

ROBERT L. GALE

SCHUTZ, Alfred (13 Apr. 1899–20 May 1959), philosopher and social scientist, was born in Vienna, Austria, the son of Alfred Schutz and Johanna Fialla. His father died before Schutz was born, and his mother then married Schutz's uncle, Otto Schutz, a bank executive. In adolescence he became passionately interested in music, literature, and art. He was drafted at age eighteen after graduating from the Esterhazy Gymnasium and fought on the Italian front in World War I. Upon his discharge, he studied law at the University of Vienna under Hans Kelsen and economics under Ludwig von Mises. He received his LL.D. in international law and became executive secretary of the Austrian Banker's Association in 1921. In 1929 he joined the private bank of Reitler and Company, where he stayed until his retirement in 1958. Schutz and Ilse Heim were married in 1926, and they had two children.

In addition to his full-time job, Schutz devoted most of his evenings to theoretical aspects of human action and relationships in the broad sense of the social sciences. He was quite taken initially with the theories of German sociologist and political economist Max Weber but found Weber's methodological self-understanding inadequate. Schutz turned to Henri-Louis Bergson's philosophy of inner duration and the changing attitudes of action, imagination, dream, and theory. Felix Kaufmann then led him to study the phenomenologist Edmund Husserl. Schutz came to consider himself a close follower of Husserl and visited him frequently during the 1930s.

Schutz's thought crystallized in *Der sinnhafte Aufbau der sozialen Welt* (The Meaningful Structure of the Social World, 1932). This masterpiece investigates how action and thereby other matters can become meaningful through being projected and then interpreted in relation to causes and purposes. It goes on to investigate how the self relates to others, namely consociates, who understand and act upon one another directly, and contemporaries, who do so indirectly; and how the living are able to understand but not act upon predecessors while they act upon but cannot understand successors. Finally, it is concerned with how the socio-historical cultural world can be scientifically investigated. Schutz refined and extended this position in his later work.

After the German invasion in 1938, Schutz immigrated with his wife, children, and later, parents via Paris to New York, where Reitler and Company had transferred its headquarters. He was Jewish and, although not religious, never considered living in Austria again. His friends in the United States consisted of other émigrés, such as Aron Gurwitsch and Herbert Spiegelberg, and American students of Husserl, including Dorion Cairns and Marvin Farber, with whom he founded the journal *Philosophy and Phenomenological Research* in 1940.

Schutz continued his studies, fitting insights of American social science and philosophy into the position developed in Vienna. This position is, in Husserlian terms, constitutive phenomenology of the cultural sciences. He emphasized interpretive sociology and marginal utility economics but also included archaeology, ethnology, history, legal theory, linguistics, political science, and psychology among others as sciences concerned with human actions, groups, motivations, objects, persons, and worlds. His theories begin with familiar matters of everyday life and include working, fantasizing, dreaming, and finally theorizing in philosophy as well as science. Although Husserl grounded meaningfulness in consciousness as it presents itself in a nonworldly or transcendental manner, Schutz searched for foundations in philosophical anthropology.

During his last twenty years, Schutz taught part time on the graduate faculty of the New School for Social Research and continued to be, as Husserl had said, a business executive by day and a phenomenologist by night. He studied, taught, and wrote about social science, intersubjectivity, language, literature, music, race relations, reality, relevance, and technology. He died in New York City.

Schutz published dozens of articles and reviews, but his major international influence began with four posthumous volumes of *Collected Papers* (1962, 1964, 1966, 1996). An English translation of his *Sinnhafte Aufbau*, titled *The Phenomenology of the Social World*, appeared in 1967 followed by editions of more than a dozen previously unpublished manuscripts. He left outlines during his last year that guided Thomas Luckmann in completing a final statement in two volumes, *The Structures of the Life-World* (1973, 1983). Schutz's work has been translated into Chinese, English, Danish, Dutch, French, German, Hungarian, Italian, Japanese, Polish, Portuguese, Serbo-Croatian, Spanish, and Swedish.

Schutz's work is studied and taught around the world, primarily in philosophy and sociology but also in communicology, economics, education, ethnology, history, geography, management, political science, psychology, religion, and urban planning. His influence stems from the clarity of his expression and his exemplary employment of phenomenological methods as well as the scope, concreteness, and relevance of his analyses.

• Schutz's papers are in the Beinecke Library at Yale University, and copies are in the Sozialwissenschaftliches Archiv at the Universität Konstanz and at the Center for Advanced Research in Phenomenology, Inc., at Florida Atlantic University. For a listing of *Nachlass* as well as a primary and secondary bibliography, see Manuel Martin Algarra, *Materiales para el Estudio de Alfred Schutz* (1991). His correspondence with Gurwitsch, *Philosophers in Exile: The Correspondence of Alfred*

Schutz and Aron Gurwitsch, 1939–1959, ed. Richard Grathoff, trans. J. Claude Evans (1989), illuminates the productive period of his years at the New School. In addition to those works mentioned in the text, Schutz wrote *Life Forms and Meaning Structure*, trans. Helmut R. Wagner (1982). A biography is Wagner, *Alfred Schutz: An Intellectual Biography* (1983). See also Lester Embree, ed., *Alfred Schutz's "Sociological Aspects of Literature": Text Construction and Complementary Essays* (1996), and Embree, ed., *Worldly Phenomenology: The Continuing Influence of Alfred Schutz on North American Human Science* (1988).

LESTER EMBREE

SCHUYLER, Catherine Van Rensselaer (4 Nov. 1734–7 Mar. 1803), revolutionary-era hostess, was born in Claverack, New York, the daughter of Johannes Van Rensselaer, a prominent Dutch landowner, and Engeltia (or Engeltie) Livingston. Her mother died in 1747, and her father then married Gertrude Van Cortlandt. Little detailed evidence of Catherine's education survives, but her contemporaries indicated that she read widely. Guests at her home and dinner table recorded that she discussed morality, poetry, religion, and politics. As was common among the landed families of New York, she was thoroughly trained in the arts of housewifery. She spoke French as well as English and read the Bible in Dutch. As a child she attended the Dutch Reformed church. When she reached her late teens she engaged in an active social life; she was admired for her beauty and vivacious personality and was called the "Morning Star." Among her admirers was Philip Schuyler, who courted the "sweet Kitty V. R." for two years before their marriage in 1755. The marriage was an important social and economic alliance for the two families.

At the time of the marriage Philip Schuyler was serving in the British army so Catherine went to live with his aunt. Later she moved in with Philip's widowed mother Cornelia Schuyler, who ran the family estates and businesses. In the early years of her marriage, Catherine widened her social circle while helping to run the households in which she lived. She also gave birth to her first two children. In 1757 she nursed wounded soldiers whom Philip brought to his family home after the battle of Ticonderoga.

When his mother died in 1762 Philip received his inheritance, and he and Catherine set up their own home. Catherine herself was a wealthy heiress and brought an interest in her father's estate to her marriage; this money financed the building of a new home, the Schuyler mansion in Albany, New York. While Philip was in Europe in 1761 and 1762, Catherine supervised the building of the home, and Philip furnished it on his return to Albany. Catherine's primary responsibility throughout her adult life was the running of the household. She had fifteen children, eight of whom survived to adulthood. She managed the family estates in Albany and Saratoga during Philip's frequent absences. Philip wrote to her with advice on estate matters and about the children's schooling, but he left household management totally in her hands. Catherine Schuyler had a reputation as an ex-

cellent housewife; she made clothing for family, servants, and slaves, and she supervised preserving, weaving, soap making, candle dipping, and dairying. She nursed her family when ill, even traveling to New York City in the winter of 1759 to care for Philip when he had an attack of gout. She frequently entertained guests, including family, prominent politicians, businessmen, foreign tourists, and Indian ambassadors. Guests were usually flattering in their appraisal of her hospitality, though François-Jean, marquis de Chastellux, found her of serious disposition and somewhat rude. In general her health was good, but she was quite ill during and after several of her pregnancies. She led a varied and active social life, attending parties, dinners, dances, and plays. She and Philip blended into both English and Dutch cultural life. They attended the Episcopalian church. She was well known for her charitable works as befitted a woman of her status. As a prominent figure in New York society, she was often asked to use her influence to help friends and acquaintances, especially when Philip was away.

Catherine Schuyler viewed the successful marriages of her children as one of her important responsibilities, and she was usually closely involved in their choice of a spouse. However, she had not met Alexander Hamilton before his engagement to her daughter Elizabeth (known as Eliza) in 1780. Their marriage received her approval because Philip convinced her of the suitability of the match. Her daughter Angelica's elopement with John Barker Church in 1777 angered her to such an extent that she refused at first to meet with the couple. She objected to Church's inferior social position and to her daughter's willful disobedience. Catherine was finally reconciled to the marriage through the intercession of her parents.

During the revolutionary war Catherine Schuyler continued to run the household and to entertain important visitors, even General John Burgoyne after his surrender at Saratoga. She suffered difficulties during the war, such as food shortages and vandalism. She was deeply resentful of the attacks on her husband's military performance and of his court-martial. Her most famous revolutionary experience, immortalized in the 1852 painting by Emanuel Leutze, probably never happened. Tradition would have it that as the British marched down the Hudson River, Catherine headed north from Albany to save the contents of the family's house in Saratoga. After leaving Albany she encountered a crowd that was fleeing from the British and that encouraged her to turn back. Her response was that "the General's wife must not be afraid," and she continued on to Saratoga. After her arrival at her home, on her husband's orders, she burned the wheat field so that the grain would not fall into the hands of the British. There is no contemporary record of this incident; in fact, General Burgoyne reported that before he burned Schuyler's house the estate was intact. The only fact in the tale is that Catherine did go to Saratoga and did save many of the family belongings, but her trip occurred several months before the British arrived. The dramatic wheat field story first appeared in print in 1846 and was told to the historian Elizabeth Ellet by Catherine's youngest daughter Catharine Van Rensselaer Cochrane. The tale is typical of the romantic legends formulated in the mid-nineteenth century about revolutionary-era women and was probably the product of distorted family memories created from accounts of Catherine's bravery and patriotism during the Revolution. Leutze's painting turned family memory into national legend.

After the war Catherine and Philip Schuyler were active in Washington's political and social circle, where her daughter Eliza Hamilton was a brilliant hostess. Catherine's activities lessened as she aged, and her last years were spent visiting with her children and grandchildren and entertaining family friends and Philip's associates. Her marriage remained close and loving. Philip's confidence in her abilities and his reliance on her judgment is illustrated by his will, which left her the income from his estates and the power to alter his bequests as she saw fit. However, she died suddenly of a stroke in Albany a year before her husband, leaving him deeply saddened at the loss of the affection and friendship they had shared for nearly a half-century.

Catherine Schuyler's life was primarily concerned with family and household matters. Her birth and marriage assured her a life of economic comfort, but she worked diligently at household management. Her husband's career introduced her to the prominent political events and personalities of the revolutionary era, and she won renown as a hostess, wife, and mother.

• None of Catherine Schuyler's papers are known to have survived. Several accounts of her life were written in the nineteenth century, including Elizabeth F. Ellet, *The Eminent and Heroic Women of America* (1846), and Mary Gay Humphreys, *Catherine Schuyler* (1897). Don Gerlach, *Philip Schuyler and the American Revolution in New York* (1964) and *Proud Patriot: Philip Schuyler and the War of Independence* (1987), include information on Catherine, as does Michael Quick, "A Bicentennial Gift: *Mrs. Schuyler Burning Her Wheat Fields on the Approach of the British* by Emanuel Leutze," *Los Angeles County Museum of Art Bulletin* 23 (1977): 26–35. A portrait of Catherine Schuyler painted by Thomas McIlworth, c. 1762–1767, is in the New-York Historical Society.

ALLIDA SHUMAN MCKINLEY

SCHUYLER, Eugene (26 Feb. 1840–16 July 1890), diplomat and scholar, was born in Ithaca, New York, the son of George Washington Schuyler, a well-known state official and author, and Matilda Scribner, a half sister of the publisher Charles Scribner. A brilliant student, Eugene entered Yale College at the age of fifteen and graduated in 1859; remaining two years longer to study languages and philosophy, he received his Ph.D. in 1861. Studying law at Columbia University, he graduated in 1863 and practiced in New York.

While a fledgling lawyer, Schuyler studied Russian and in 1867 published a translation of Ivan Turgenev's *Fathers and Sons*. The next year he edited John A. Porter's *Selections from the Kalevala*, a Finnish epic. Ap-

pointed American consul in Moscow in 1867, he continued his studies of Russia and its language. While assigned to Moscow he made a trip to the lower reaches of the Ural River. His fluency in Russian and his social background opened the doors of Russian society much more than would have been normal for an American consul or diplomat of the time.

Losing his Moscow post after the Ulysses S. Grant administration took office in 1869, he was appointed consul to the less important post at Revel. The new American minister to the Russian court at St. Petersburg, Andrew G. Curtin, a former governor of Pennsylvania, however, appointed Schuyler secretary of legation because of his knowledge of the country and language.

While assigned to St. Petersburg, Schuyler made an extensive trip to the newly conquered territories of Russian Central Asia in 1873. His detailed report on the administration of the area was critical of Russian military rule, with references to corruption, torture, and slavery. Later in the year the Department of State published the report, which, despite its unfavorable tone, was well received within Russian government circles because it gave officials a clearer picture of the situation than had been forthcoming from their own occupying forces.

Schuyler was appointed consul general and secretary of legation to Constantinople in 1876, the same year in which he published his two-volume *Notes on a Journey in Russian Tukistan, Khokand, Bukhara and Kuldja*. Arriving in Constantinople, American missionaries prevailed on him to investigate stories of the massacre of Bulgarian Christians by Turkish irregular troops, the *bashi-bazouks*. Along with an American correspondent, Januarius MacGahan, he visited the subdued countryside and found massive evidence of Turkish brutality, which became known as the Bulgarian horrors. His preliminary report to the American minister in Constantinople became public almost immediately, before being received in Washington. It supported the sensational accounts of MacGahan in the European and American press. Schuyler's report also gave credence to those in Great Britain opposed to their country's support of Turkey in the Balkans and was influential in reversing that policy.

Schuyler's reports on events in Bulgaria and his assistance to the Russians in drafting a constitution for a proposed autonomous Bulgaria resulted in an unofficial Turkish protest; he was recalled in July 1878 and assigned to Birmingham as consul but shortly after was appointed consul general in Rome. In July 1877 he married Gertrude Wallace King, daughter of Charles King, a president of Columbia College.

Schuyler returned to Eastern Europe in 1880 as the first U.S. diplomatic agent to Romania, then a principality. When Romania became a kingdom in 1881 he was named minister. His official residence was moved to Athens in 1882 and his diplomatic responsibilities were extended to include Greece and the newly independent Serbia. He negotiated a commercial treaty and a consular convention with Serbia, both signed 14 October 1881.

In 1884 the legation in Athens was closed for budgetary reasons and Schuyler returned to the United States. He lectured at Johns Hopkins and Cornell and wrote *Peter the Great* (2 vols., 1884), as well as magazine articles. He lived in Alassio, Italy, from 1886 to 1889, at which time he was proposed for assistant secretary of state by Secretary of State James G. Blaine. However, the nomination was withdrawn because of opposition within the Senate's committee on foreign relations, in part the result of Schuyler's frank comments on the actions of former secretary of state Elihu Washburn in his book *American Diplomacy and the Furtherance of Commerce* (1886). Instead he was assigned to Cairo as agent and consul general in 1889 but, succumbing to a weak heart and an attack of malaria, died in Venice, Italy. Schuyler was the preeminent diplomat and authority on Eastern Europe at a time when U.S. diplomatic and consular services were poorly served by appointees who owed their posts to political patronage.

• Examples of Schuyler's writings can be found in *Eugene Schuyler: Selected Essays, with a Memoir by Evelyn Schuyler Schaeffer* (1901); see also his *Report on Central Asia*, Foreign Relations of the United States Series, no. 524 (10 Mar. 1874), and *Report on Conditions in Bulgaria*, Foreign Relations of the United States Series, no. 106 (21 Nov. 1876). Additional information is in *Obituary Records of Graduates of Yale University, 1800–1900* (1900), and G. W. Schuyler, *Colonial New York* (2 vols., 1885). An obituary is in the *New York Tribune*, 19 July 1890.

CHARLES STUART KENNEDY

SCHUYLER, George Samuel (25 Feb. 1895–31 Aug. 1977), journalist, was born in Providence, Rhode Island, the son of George Francis Schuyler and Eliza Jane Fischer. Both of his parents were cooks; his father worked at a hotel. He grew up in Syracuse, New York, in a racially integrated community; as far as Schuyler knew, he was not the descendant of slaves. Although he left high school before finishing, Schuyler grew up reading the classics.

Schuyler joined the U.S. Army at seventeen and wrote for the *Service*, a weekly read by the military. Serving in the segregated military, he saw the racial situation as never before. Schuyler served two stints in the army, rising to the rank of first lieutenant. His first stint lasted three years. After several months of civilian life, in November 1915 he signed up for four more years, but the war ended three years later, and, according to Schuyler's autobiography, he was among the first to be discharged.

In 1923 Schuyler took a position on the staff of the African-American socialist monthly, the *Messenger*. It was here that he wrote his column "Shafts and Darts: A Page of Columny and Satire." Schuyler believed that too many black publications were solemn and serious, and he lampooned fads of the day. In 1926 Schuyler became managing editor of the *Messenger*. He stayed with this magazine until its demise in 1928.

Also in 1923, Schuyler began writing a column for the *Pittsburgh Courier*, which had the second highest circulation among black newspapers. This was the beginning of a relationship that would last throughout Schuyler's career. In 1925 he embarked on an eight-month tour of the South for the *Courier* and wrote about his observations, and in August 1926 he began writing *Courier* editorials. In 1928 Schuyler married Josephine Cogdell; they had one daughter, who also became a journalist. (On their marriage certificate, Schuyler's wife is cited as Josephine Lewis, but in his autobiography Schuyler refers to her as Josephine Cogdell. Sources are unclear, but it is likely that she had been married before, that Lewis had been her married name, and that Cogdell was her maiden name, or vice versa.)

While on the *Courier* staff, Schuyler contributed articles to other publications, such as the *American Mercury*, *Negro Digest*, the *Nation*, *Reader's Digest*, and the *Crisis*, the NAACP publication. In these pieces his topics included his position against a separate state for blacks, how a long war would help the African American, and "Negroes Reject Communism." In 1931, while still working for the *Courier*, Schuyler's satirical novel, *Black No More*, was published. He received critical acclaim for this work, which told the story of a black man who invented a chemical process that would change a person from black to white overnight.

That same year, Schuyler served as correspondent to Liberia for the *New York Evening Post*; his tour included Senegal and Sierra Leone. In his autobiography, *Black and Conservative*, published in 1966, he said it was the first time a black person had served as foreign correspondent for an important metropolitan newspaper. What Schuyler learned on his assignment became a novel, *Slaves Today* (1931; repr. 1969), in which he discussed forced labor on the west coast of Africa. Later the *Courier* would send Schuyler to Latin America and the West Indies.

Also in 1931, Schuyler attacked the popular "Amos 'n' Andy" radio program, which featured two white men, Freeman Gosden and Charles Correll, who played black roles and poked fun at blacks. The *Courier* was not amused. It said black pride was at stake and launched a campaign to solicit one million signatures in an effort to get the Federal Radio Commission to ban the program from the airwaves. Other goals of the protest included a suit against Gosden and Correll; a call for 5,000 black ministers to preach against the program on a single day; and a nationwide radio broadcast protesting "Amos 'n' Andy." The *Courier* did not attain any of its goals, but it did claim to have received nearly three quarters of a million signatures, and the protest did have a beneficial side effect; it taught whites that all blacks were not like Amos 'n' Andy. According to Melvin Ely's book, *The Adventures of Amos 'n' Andy* (1991), large and small white newspapers reported the *Courier*'s complaints as very short wire-service items. Ely further reported that some papers discussed the protest in editorials "almost as varied as white listeners' views of Amos 'n' Andy itself." In 1951, when the NAACP protested the "Amos 'n' Andy" television program, Schuyler attacked the civil rights organization for being mum about other "more offensive productions."

When World War II began in Europe, Schuyler spoke out against U.S. involvement. He saw little sense in blacks helping to give Europeans something that African Americans did not have at home—freedom. And he dared question whether the United States was treating blacks any better than Germany was treating Jews. On 3 January 1942, nearly one month after the bombing of Pearl Harbor, Schuyler used his "Views and Reviews" column in the *Courier* to set the tone for others he would write during the war:

Courier readers need not look here for any essays on patriotism and loyalty. . . . All the talk about fighting for democracy, freedom and the American Way is just so much blather as long as pigment separates an American citizen from the enjoyment of all the rights, privileges and duties of citizenship.

The *Courier* and the rest of the black press would use their pages to push for the rights Schuyler talked about in what became known as the "Double V" campaign. One "V" was for victory over the Axis powers; the second "V" was for victory over racism at home. And while he supported the war in the paper's more conservative editorials, he would question that support in his column. Former *Courier* reporter Frank Bolden described Schuyler as an iconoclast and the white establishment's archenemy. "Whatever the white people wanted he was against," Bolden said in an interview. "He could stick 'em with a pen and he did it."

Because of the columns he wrote, the FBI called Schuyler pro-Japanese. Although the FBI investigated the entire black press during the war, Schuyler was singled out for his unflinching criticism of the racial practices of the United States and its allies. But he was also critical of Communists, who he felt were just using black people to get a foothold in the United States. In his autobiography he refers to his anticommunist columns as his most significant.

From 1944 to 1960 Schuyler edited the New York edition of the *Courier*. After stepping down as editor, he remained in New York and continued to write about race problems and to attack communism. Schuyler believed that much of the civil rights movement, with its sit-ins and street protests, was communist-inspired. These views put him in direct opposition to large segments of the American black community. This conflict came to a head in 1964, when Schuyler wrote a column saying that Martin Luther King, Jr., did not deserve the Nobel Peace Prize. The *Courier* refused to print the column, but the conservative Manchester *Union Leader* did. As a result of his criticism of King, the *Crisis* denounced Schuyler. He stopped writing the *Courier*'s editorials, although he continued to write book reviews and his column for the paper and to contribute articles to conservative publications. Schuyler moved to the right as he recog-

nized what he thought were moves by Communists to use African Americans for their own purposes. And while he knew that blacks faced racism in the United States, he often noted that they were treated better in America than anywhere else. So Schuyler refused to sit by silently while Communists proselytized the black masses. He used his column to speak out. He died in New York City.

Schuyler's greatest contribution came in the editorials and columns he wrote for the *Pittsburgh Courier* during World War II. Those columns and editorials challenged the treatment of people of color in the United States and in the armed forces and even questioned the attitudes and practices of America's allies at a time when it was not popular to do so. His comments were colorful, witty, biting, and often filled with sarcasm. As editorial writer for one of the two largest black newspapers in the country, Schuyler had a pronounced effect on how African Americans viewed the war. Schuyler's criticism and that of the rest of the black press helped to set the stage for the desegregation of the military services.

• Schuyler's papers are housed at the Schomburg Center for Research in Black Culture, the New York Public Library. Schuyler's other books include *Racial Intermarriage in the United States* (1929) and *The Communist Conspiracy against the Negro* (1947). Michael W. Peplow wrote *George S. Schuyler* (1980), a biography. Edward Welch interviewed former *Courier* reporter Frank Bolden on 28 Feb. 1986. See also Theodore Kornweibel, Jr., *No Crystal Stair* (1975), and Harold Cruse, *The Crisis of the Negro Intellectual* (1967).

EDWARD M. WELCH, JR.

SCHUYLER, Louisa Lee (26 Oct. 1837–10 Oct. 1926), leader of Civil War relief and philanthropist, was born in New York City, the daughter of George Lee Schuyler, an engineer and attorney, and Eliza Hamilton. Her father was the grandson of Philip Schuyler, a revolutionary war general; her mother was the granddaughter of Alexander Hamilton (1755–1804). Louisa and her brother and sister were brought up both in New York City and on an estate near Dobbs Ferry on the Hudson River. Educated by private tutors, the wealthy family traveled to Europe and spent their summers in such fashionable places as Newport, Rhode Island.

Schuyler's parents, both of whom were involved in the Children's Aid Society of New York, introduced their children early to the world of elite charity. Louisa first participated in that world as a volunteer teacher for the aid society just before the outbreak of the Civil War. When the war started, Eliza Hamilton Schuyler was among the "gentlewomen" whose call founded the Woman's Central Association of Relief (WCAR), the organization that became first the impetus and then the major auxiliary of the United States Sanitary Commission.

Virtually from the beginning, 24-year-old Louisa Schuyler played a major role in the WCAR's growth as the first centralized, quasi-public organization for the relief of soldiers from around the North. As the chair of the committee of correspondence and part of the group of upper-class reformers who sought to reestablish wartime relief on a national scale, Schuyler helped organize a huge bureaucracy, maintaining contact with associate managers in communities throughout the North, supervising publications about the WCAR's work, and scheduling lecturers to spread the message of centralization and order. Although women were celebrated for their wartime sacrifices as nurses, it was in the more mundane work on the homefront that they made their greatest impact on the war and in turn on national efforts to feed, clothe, transport, and heal the soldiers. Under the WCAR's—and Schuyler's—watchful if distant supervision, thousands of women in communities throughout the North organized local societies, sewed for the soldiers, packed boxes of food, and picked lint for bandages. Schuyler herself quickly became known for her efficiency and method, skills that were considered characteristic of corporate, rather than charitable, organizations. The "ultimate end" of the Sanitary Commission, insisted one of its reports, "is neither humanity nor charity. It is to economise for the National service the life and strength of the National soldier." In sharp contrast to the benevolent style of her mother's generation, Schuyler explicitly took on the goal of creating a national system of relief that would combat what she saw as the obstacles of "religious feeling, localism, and sentimentalism" and was herself praised for her business sense.

The end of the war found Schuyler exhausted and near collapse. After issuing various orders to her friend Angelina Post about how to organize (and censor) the Sanitary Commission archives, Schuyler left the country for several years of recuperation in Europe. When she returned in 1871, she initiated plans for a new organization, one that would, in style as well as many of its leaders, closely resemble the Sanitary Commission. Along with her sister Georgina, with whom she shared an apartment after their parents' deaths, she eagerly enlisted her old Sanitary Commission colleagues in the new State Charities Aid Association (SCAA), an organization designed as an elite, civilian watchdog over the public poorhouses and asylums throughout New York State.

The stated purposes and the personnel of the State Charities Aid Association reflected all that the Sanitary Commission—and Louisa Lee Schuyler—stood for; it represented the "best people" in the community, advocated experts' intervention between government and the people, and called for a businesslike efficiency in the running of public institutions. The list of officers and associate managers included such notable Civil War relief workers as Frederick Law Olmsted, Ellen Collins, Jane Woolsey and Abby Woolsey, Henry Bellows, and Josephine Shaw Lowell. Schuyler's particular interests in the organization were the establishment of Bellevue Hospital training school for nurses (in 1872), the first to achieve high standards for such training, and the care of the mentally ill, a campaign that resulted in an 1890 law mandating that

mentally ill persons be removed from poorhouses and placed in state institutions.

Until the end of her life, Schuyler used her wealth and connections in a range of philanthropic endeavors in New York. Bringing together a coalition of groups that worked with blind children, she founded the National Committee for the Prevention of Blindness in 1915; she also served on the first board of trustees of the Russell Sage Foundation (established with $10-million endowment by Margaret Olivia Slocum Sage in 1907). Yet Schuyler's major organizational contribution remained her work in the Civil War. In the diary that she kept briefly in the early 1870s, she noted that "Anything I may write about [my postwar] work can never interest me as one or two pages about the war would." For her, wartime imperatives of efficiency, nationalization, and militarylike order were the major elements in the changes of a philanthropy for which she wished to be known. Louisa Lee Schuyler died in Highland Falls, New York

• There is no major biography of Louisa Lee Schuyler, nor is there a central collection of her correspondence. Her most important writings and documents can be found in the mountainous papers of the United States Sanitary Commission at the New York Public Library, the *Bulletins* of the USSC, and the *Reports* of the WCAR. Important, if scattered, sources can also be found at the New-York Historical Society and the Manuscript Division of the Library of Congress (which file also includes a picture of Schuyler). Biographical information is in Robert D. Cross, "Louisa Lee Schuyler," in *Notable American Women*, ed. Edward James and Janet Wilson James, vol. 3 (1971), and Cross, "The Philanthropic Contribution of Louisa Lee Schuyler," *Social Service Review*, Sept. 1961, pp. 290–301. See also *Louisa Lee Schuyler* (National Committee for the Prevention of Blindness, 1927); her pamphlet, *Forty-Three Years Ago* (SCAA, 1915); and L. P. Brockett and Mary Vaughan, *Woman's Work in the Civil War* (1867).

LORI D. GINZBERG

SCHUYLER, Margarita (Jan. 1701–Aug. 1782), political and military adviser, was born in Albany, New York, the daughter of Johannes Schuyler, a soldier and diplomat, and Elizabeth Staats Wendell. Her paternal grandfather had settled north of Albany on the Hudson River during the seventeenth century, and the family soon began to play an important role in colonial politics. One of Margarita's uncles was acting governor of New York, and her father served as British envoy to Canada and mayor of Albany. Margarita, her father's favorite child, spent her childhood studying politics, military tactics, and Indian affairs under his tutelage. In 1729 she married her cousin Philip Schuyler, a soldier and heir to the Schuyler estate, "The Flatts," which was situated on the Hudson between Troy and Albany, New York.

Once married, Schuyler combined her zeal for politics with entertaining and made the Flatts the center of the social and political life of the region. Schuyler hosted "every officer of distinction throughout North America" and advised them on the most effective methods in frontier warfare (Baxter, p. 47). Under the influence of her father, Schuyler became a proponent of anti-French military schemes, discussing with military leaders the most effective means of transportation in the isolated North as well as the appropriate uniforms and tactics for soldiers. While her husband was on active duty during the French and Indian Wars, Schuyler housed more than 100 men, including a company of British soldiers, and ran a military hospital at the Flatts.

As an expert on Indian tribes in northern New York, Schuyler's value to political and military authorities, traders, and merchants was enhanced through her friendships with Indian leaders and her knowledge of many languages. She was fluent in Mohawk, could understand several other Indian languages, and was proficient in English, Dutch, French, and German. Schuyler and her husband advocated and eventually secured the appointment of the first superintendent of Indian affairs in the region.

Although Schuyler was a friend and adviser to officers as distinguished as Jeffrey Amherst, John Bradstreet, and Thomas Gage, she considered George A. Howe her "favorite pupil." At their daily breakfast meetings, Schuyler advised Howe on reforms in the areas of dress, equipment, and military tactics. At her urging, Howe instituted a ban on all displays of gold and scarlet on uniforms, shortened coats and muskets for better agility in the woods, blackened gun barrels to camouflage weapons, and demanded that soldiers wear leggings to protect themselves from insects and vegetation. When Howe was killed at Ticonderoga in 1758, Schuyler wept bitterly. Earlier that year her husband had died.

By all accounts, Schuyler and her husband had had a happy marriage, though he was often away from home or in ill health. The Schuylers had no children of their own, yet they took an active role in the rearing of numerous nieces and nephews, who referred to Margarita as "Aunt Schuyler." In spite of their numerous commitments at home, the Schuylers traveled to New York City at least once a year in the early years of their marriage to see family and mingle with other prominent families, including the Livingstons, the Rensselears, and the De Lanceys. At home, as a devout member of "the Dutch church," Schuyler took special care to provide a Christian upbringing to the family's slaves and to Indians, besides running the largest household in the region. Devastated by her husband's death, Schuyler suffered a nervous breakdown for two years afterward, until she was roused by the news of the taking of Oswego by the French.

Though known as a friend of the army, Schuyler lived under a constant threat of violence from the French and often had her own goods seized for the war effort. When the Flatts was destroyed by fire in 1763, Bradstreet "considered that his men were in the King's service in rebuilding Mrs. Schuyler's house" (Baxter, p. 21). Though always loyal to England, Schuyler resisted affiliating herself with Tory politics and always hoped for a reconciliation between the two countries. While she personally regretted the signing of the Dec-

laration of Independence, she maintained good relations with family members on both sides of the revolutionary war. She died on her estate, just north of Albany. Her life illustrates how influential colonial women could be in political and military affairs.

• In the absence of an extant collection of her papers, researchers may contact the Schuyler Mansion Historic Site, 32 Catherine Street, Albany, N.Y. 12202, for information on the Schuyler family artifacts. The most comprehensive account of her life is in the sentimental Anne M. Grant, *Memoirs of an American Lady* (2 vols., 1808; repr. 1846). Grant's treatment of Schuyler was later revised in Katharine Schuyler Baxter, *A Godchild of Washington* (1897); George W. Schuyler, *Colonial New York: Philip Schuyler and His Family* (2 vols., 1885); and Mary V. Terhune, *More Colonial Households and Their Histories* (1899). Another Schuyler family history with information on Margarita Schuyler is Montgomery Schuyler, *The Schuyler Family* (1926). Two histories of the colony of N.Y. that mention Schuyler's activities are E. B. O'Callaghan, *Documents Relating to the Colonial History of the State of New York*, vols. 4 (1854), 5, and 9 (1855); and Peter Wraxall, *An Abridgement of the Indian Affairs . . . in the Colony of New York, from the Year 1678 to the Year 1751*, ed. Charles H. McIlwain (1915; repr. 1968). Unfortunately more recent works on colonial N.Y. include little on the activities of Schuyler women. For information on the estate and artifacts, see Anna K. Cunningham, *Schuyler Mansion: A Critical Catalogue of the Furnishings and Decorations* (1955).

SHERYL A. KUJAWA

SCHUYLER, Peter (17 Sept. 1657–19 Feb. 1724), Indian trader and merchant, was born in Albany (then called Beverwyck), New Netherland, the son of Philip Pieterse Schuyler, a successful Indian trader, and Margarita Van Slichtenhorst, the daughter of Brant Aerts Van Slichtenhorst, director of Rensselaerswyck. It is unclear what formal schooling Peter Schuyler had, but living at his father's home and trading center, "The Flatts," he learned enough about the Iroquois, including their language, to become one of only three European colonial New Yorkers trusted by them. Called "Quidor" by those unable to pronounce his given name, he derived much of his influence in the province from his special relationship with the Indians. While Schuyler was alive, no governor could negotiate with the Five Nations without him.

Schuyler's base was Albany. In 1686 he and his brother-in-law Robert Livingston procured a charter for Albany from Governor Thomas Dongan. Through this incorporation Schuyler became Albany's first mayor, a position he held until 1694. During Leisler's Rebellion, New York's civil disturbance that resulted when James II fled the English throne in 1688 thus leaving the governorships of royal colonies in doubt, Schuyler, with Indian help, kept Albany from falling to the Leislerians. He and the rest of Albany's merchant elite understood that good relations with the Indians were the key to peace and wealth. Leislerian militancy jeopardized both.

The peaceful coexistence and trade that Schuyler would have preferred was shattered in the 1690s as relations between the English and the French deteriorated. During these years Schuyler skillfully managed both war and business. In 1690 he joined Connecticut's Fitz-John Winthrop in an abortive campaign against Quebec. In 1691, at Laprarie, Canada, he led a war party of colonists and Indians against the French, but this engagement ended indecisively. Two years later he led a force of colonists and Indians against the French and Indian marauders who had attacked the Mohawk castles. Schuyler's task was to win the support or at least the neutrality of the Iroquois and other Indian groups in New York as the French and their Jesuit missionaries tried to do the same. The need for a formal body to deal with the Indians was recognized in 1696 when Governor Benjamin Fletcher appointed the first commissioners of Indian affairs. Schuyler held a permanent place on this board.

Peter Schuyler seems to have been genuinely concerned for the Indians and the price they paid for French encroachments. In 1710 he and four Mohawks journeyed to England where, amid great pomp, they asked Queen Anne to support the conquest of Canada. That same year he and a small group of New Yorkers persuaded the Onondagas to allow them to destroy a French blockhouse, thereby ending French threats to that area. Schuyler, rising to the rank of major, eventually took charge of New York's frontier defenses.

Security was one facet of Indian policy; commerce was another. New York's Indian fur trade centered in Albany. During the 1680s most of Albany's furs came from the west, but the killing of beavers and increasing warfare with the French forced changes in the 1690s. The legacy of King William's War (1688–1697) was a shift of the trade north, which meant greater peaceful interaction with the French. In the wake of the Treaty of Ryswick, which ended hostilities, New York's governor, the earl of Bellomont, sent Schuyler and the Dutch Reformed minister Godfrey Dellius to Montreal to alert the French authorities of the new peace and arrange an exchange of prisoners. They used their time there also to establish connections with French merchants and thus begin a Montreal-Albany trading connection that would supply furs to New York. The success of this trade route generated considerable ill will among other colonists as New Yorkers declined to unite against the French in Queen Anne's War. As late as 1720 Schuyler refused to interfere in this trade.

While Schuyler spent considerable energy in military engagements and diplomatic negotiations, he was also a businessman, often in partnership with Robert Livingston. In the early 1690s they operated a shipping line that sailed between Albany and New York City. They also were part owners in larger oceangoing ventures, some of which skirted the law by trading with the French. In 1698 they won the lucrative contract to victual royal troops in Albany.

Schuyler's close connections with the Indians helped his business and also gave him inside influence in the scramble for Indian lands. While it is unclear exactly how much land Schuyler owned, in 1683 he acquired holdings along the Mohawk River and in 1694 had a one-seventh right to the Saratoga patent.

Had it gone through, his partnership in the 1697 Dellius patent, which granted its four principals two miles on each side of the Mohawk River for fifty miles or 537,000 acres, would have made him one of the major landowners in the region. Unfortunately for Schuyler, Governor Benjamin Fletcher's grant was voided by his successor, the earl of Bellomont. Schuyler managed to resign from the partnership before his reputation with the Indians as one concerned with their welfare and the integrity of their lands was undermined. He would later be a patentee of the Schenectady grant given by Lord Cornbury.

Schuyler's Indian expertise and his position and wealth also brought him political office. In 1691 he was named to the provincial council in the spot reserved for Albany. While he attended relatively few meetings, he remained there until 1721, when Governor William Burnet dismissed him. At least twice, in 1709 and 1719, he was senior councillor and thus became acting governor in the absence of the governor and lieutenant governor.

Schuyler was twice married, both times to women of prominent Albany Dutch families. His first marriage, in 1681 or 1682, was to Engeltie Van Schaick, with whom he had four children, but only a daughter survived. In 1691, after his first wife's death, he married Maria Van Rensselaer, daughter of Jeremiah Van Rensselaer, with whom he had four children. Schuyler died in New York, probably in Albany.

Schuyler was an example of the new breed of New Yorker who was able to work with both English and Dutch, European and Native American, smoothing ethnic tensions and reaping a fortune for himself and his family in the process.

• Some of Peter Schuyler's papers are housed in the Syracuse University Library. E. B. O'Callaghan and Berthold Fernow, eds., *Documents Relative to the Colonial History of the State of New York* (1853–1887), contains multiple references to him in his various public capacities. Personal information on Schuyler comes from Bayard Tuckerman, *Life of General Philip Schuyler, 1733–1804* (1905), and Cynthia A. Kierner, *Traders and Gentlefolk: The Livingstons of New York, 1675–1790* (1992). His relationship with the Indians is discussed in Allen W. Trelease, *Indian Affairs in Colonial New York: The Seventeenth Century* (1960); Thomas Elliot Norton, *The Fur Trade in Colonial New York, 1686–1776* (1974); and Daniel K. Richter, "War and Culture: The Iroquois Experience," *William and Mary Quarterly*, 3d ser., 40 (1983): 528–59. Schuyler's land transactions are noted in Patricia U. Bonomi, *A Factious People: Politics and Society in Colonial New York* (1971); Donna Merwick, *Possessing Albany, 1630–1710: The Dutch and English Experiences* (1990); and Thomas E. Burke, Jr., "Leisler's Rebellion at Schenectady, New York, 1689–1710," *New York History* 70 (1989): 405–30. His business dealings are explored in Lawrence H. Leder, *Robert Livingston, 1654–1728, and the Politics of Colonial New York* (1961).

JESSICA KROSS

SCHUYLER, Philip John (10 Nov. 1733–18 Nov. 1804), soldier and statesman, was born in Albany, New York, the son of John Schuyler, a merchant-landowner, alderman, and Indian commissioner, and Cornelia

Van Cortlandt. His father died in 1741, and Philip was reared in the Dutch tradition by his mother (daughter of the first lord of Cortlandt Manor), his grandfather Johannes (1668–1747), and Aunt Margaretta Schuyler. During 1748–1751 he studied with the Reverend Peter Stouppe of the New Rochelle French Protestant Church, where he learned French and became proficient in mathematics. At New Rochelle he began to suffer attacks of "rheumatic gout," probably a form of rheumatism and pleurisy, which would repeatedly interrupt his military and political careers. His formal studies were supplemented by practical experience in estate management and commerce. In Albany and New York he moved in family and political circles of the provincial gentry; and although appearing carefree and good humored, he soon proved to be ambitious and enterprising.

During the Anglo-French struggle for North America (1754–1763), Schuyler's cousin, Lieutenant Governor James DeLancey, commissioned him to raise and command a company in William Johnson's expedition to Lake George. On 7 September 1755 he married Catharine Van Rensselaer. (They were to have fifteen children, eight of whom survived childbirth or infancy. One daughter became the wife of Alexander Hamilton; another, the wife of Stephen Van Rensselaer, the last patroon.) Returning to the field, Schuyler escorted French prisoners to Albany and then worked in the commissariat, which brought him into the profitable friendship of Colonel John Bradstreet, deputy quartermaster general for British forces in New York. His connection with Bradstreet gave him training in provisioning armies, a valuable asset for his revolutionary war responsibilities.

In 1756–1758 Schuyler served on the Albany city council, the beginning of a political career that, with his growing landed interests, propelled him to election as provincial assemblyman in 1768. Meantime his connection with Bradstreet took him to England in 1761–1762 to settle quartermaster accounts with the war office. During his travels, which included a visit to Ireland, he became interested in canal construction—an enterprise that led him to promote similar projects north and west of Albany in the 1790s. Returning to New York, he developed lands at Saratoga (now Schuylerville) and "Cortlandt Manor," inherited from his parents and his uncle Philip Schuyler. With Bradstreet, he acquired thousands of acres in the Mohawk Valley. Concentrating on his Saratoga estate, Schuyler rented farmland and hired help to operate grist and saw mills; he built the province's first water-driven flax mill. Fishing and lumbering brought him contacts with merchants along the Hudson River and in the West Indies to whom he shipped produce in his own schooner and several sloops.

Elected to the New York Assembly in 1768, Schuyler joined the partisan struggle between the Livingstons and the DeLanceys over which faction might better manage protests against British attempts at regulating and taxing the colonies. Although Schuyler did not condone radical violence, he was regarded as a troublemaker by Lieutenant Governor Cadwallader Colden, who in 1775 thought he "wish'd to bring this Colony into all the dangerous & extravagant Schemes which Disgrace too many of the Sister Colonies." Refusing to allow as effective a criticism of British policies as Schuyler sought, the DeLanceys finally forced him to choose a colonial loyalty over fealty to the empire.

Pleading illness for declining election to the First Continental Congress, and failing to move the New York Assembly to consider its proceedings, he attended a revolutionary convention, which chose him a delegate to the Second Continental Congress. On 15 June 1775 he was named one of four major generals under George Washington; assigned to the Northern Department, he proceeded to recruit and provision an army for the invasion of Canada—the principal campaign of 1775. Before launching the invasion he negotiated with the Six Nations for their neutrality, but illness forced him to give field command to Brigadier General Richard Montgomery, who captured Montreal and proceeded to Quebec. Schuyler's skillful handling of the commissariat was of considerable help to Montgomery, but after the failure to take Quebec in December 1775 the American army was forced to retreat. This and the army's sufferings discredited Schuyler with New Englanders, many of whom were hostile to his support of New York's claims to the "Hampshire Grants" (later Vermont) and to his strict military discipline. Yankee and Yorker animus was aggravated in 1776 by Schuyler's quarrels with General David Wooster and General Horatio Gates over their jurisdictions within the Northern Department.

At Valcour Bay (Lake Champlain) on 11 October 1776 Sir Guy Carleton destroyed a fleet that Schuyler had built with the help of Benedict Arnold, but the British invasion was later checked, leaving Schuyler time to reconstitute his army and prepare for the campaign of 1777. But his relations with Congress became so strained that in March 1777 he left the army to explain and defend his position before Congress. While others were exculpated from any blame for the reverses in Canada, he was annoyed that his own conduct was questioned, and he resented rumors of his mismanagement of the army and Congress's dismissal of Samuel Stringer as Northern Department surgeon without any explanation. Congress rebuked Schuyler for his protestations, and New Englanders maneuvered to assign Gates to Ticonderoga with orders that seemed to make him Schuyler's successor, but Schuyler cleared himself of rumored fiscal malfeasance and was ordered to resume command of the Northern Army.

Gates declined to serve as his subordinate and conspired with Schuyler's enemies in Congress to replace him—an opportunity that arose when General John Burgoyne's invasion from Canada forced Schuyler to retreat. He tried to raise the forces needed to stop Burgoyne and managed to impede Burgoyne's army by obstructing its line of march and by scorched-earth tactics. He sent Arnold to relieve Fort Stanwix, thus wrecking a second prong of the British invasion in the Mohawk Valley.

Alarmed by the loss of Ticonderoga and rumors of Schuyler's incompetence and disloyalty, Congress ordered him to headquarters and sent Gates to supersede him, partly on the premise that Gates would better be able to raise New England militia to defeat Burgoyne. The militia proved no more cooperative with Gates than they had with Schuyler. Burgoyne was finally defeated by Continental troops after Schuyler laid the groundwork for the British surrender at the battle of Saratoga. There Schuyler suffered substantial losses when the British destroyed his country estate.

For the remainder of the war Schuyler proved to be an unswerving patriot. At his insistence he was finally court-martialed in October 1778 and acquitted with the highest honor of the charge of neglect of duty. After resigning his commission he remained on the Board of Indian Commissioners of the Northern Department until 1785, advising Washington concerning enemy movements on the New York frontiers and the 1779 Sullivan-Clinton campaign against the Iroquois. In 1779–1780 he was again elected to Congress, where he urged reforms of the currency system and chaired a committee assigned to Washington's headquarters for reorganizing staff departments, raising men and supplies for effective cooperation with French allied forces. His constant surveillance of the northern and western frontiers enabled him to supply state and Continental officials with vital information for their defense efforts and for the repulsion of enemy incursions like that of Major Christopher Carleton in October 1780. So substantial was his intelligence service, his pacification of the Oneida and Tuscarora, and his support of the superintendent of finance and quartermaster general that the British tried to put him out of action. By January 1782 at least three parties were sent from Canada to capture or kill him; one raided his Albany house on 7 August 1781, but he cleverly eluded them.

Schuyler was a state senator in 1780–1784, 1786–1790, and 1792–1797; state surveyor general in 1781–1784; member of the New York Council of Appointment (which shared the governor's appointive powers) in 1786–1787, 1788–1789, 1790–1791, and 1794–1795; and U.S. senator in 1789–1791 and 1797–1798. In addition he served as a regent of the University of the State of New York in 1784–1804. An advocate of enlarging powers of the central government and fair treatment of the state's creditors, he favored New York's surrender of its claims to Vermont territory and to the west. He opposed Governor George Clinton's junto for advocating a state impost and retention of all power in the hands of the legislature, giving none to Congress. As member of the Council of Appointment, he led Federalist opposition to Clinton's patronage system, and he supported the movement that culminated in the establishment of the Constitution of 1787. He counseled Federalists in their campaign to ratify the Constitution, and as the first U.S. senator from New York he assisted in preparing Alexander Hamilton's financial program and championing its passage. His and Hamilton's private talks with George Beckwith, agent for the governor-general of Canada, influenced foreign policy by assuring British officials that Federalists favored Anglo-American rapprochement in opposition to Jefferson's and Madison's proposals to exclude Britain from commercial reciprocity for its failure to make a commercial treaty with the United States. An ardent Federalist, Schuyler remained hostile to France even when President John Adams insisted on negotiating a settlement of the undeclared naval war of 1798–1800. Schuyler was defeated for reelection as U.S. senator in 1791 by partisans of Aaron Burr—a political rivalry that ultimately led to Hamilton's fatal duel with Burr. He then worked to stop Governor George Clinton's bid for reelection. Failing in that until 1795, he fought the Clintonians at every successive election. Again a state senator in 1792–1797, he promoted penal law and prison reforms, state aid to education, a general road bill for the whole state, and loans to the inland lock and navigation companies. As a member of the state university regents he pushed through the incorporation of Union College of Schenectady, subscribed funds for its support, and participated in the regents' incorporation of and assistance to various academies.

Schuyler's investments in government securities, bank stock, and land were coupled with his public-spirited pioneering in the Western and Northern Inland Lock and Navigation Companies. After guiding their incorporation by the state legislature in 1792 to improve the commerce and economy of both state and nation, he served as their president until he died; he directed much of the field work himself. The western company improved the navigation of the Mohawk River and then became part of the larger project of the Erie Canal. The northern company's efforts to improve connections between Albany and Lake Champlain were less successful, but it pioneered the work of the Champlain Canal.

Between 1775 and 1790 Schuyler's household included between nine and twenty-seven slaves who were divided between his Albany and Saratoga residences. He purchased four in 1797; but, as none were mentioned in his will, it appears that by 1803 all had been freed or sold. Although not quite six feet tall, his presence was commanding, his temper ardent. His austere manner, impeccable dress, and deportment struck many as arrogant and overbearing. But his manners were warm and gentlemanly, and his proud carriage was tempered by kindness and courtesy. He inspired trust in friends and intimates, but disquietude in enemies and those less familiar with him. He died in Albany.

For thirty years there was little public business in which Schuyler had not taken some part or contributed some aid or influence. His statue stands at the entrance of the Albany City Hall.

• Schuyler's papers are in the New York Public Library, the New York State Library, the Library of Congress, and the

New-York Historical Society. Some of these are printed in Edmund C. Burnett, ed., *Letters of Members of the Continental Congress* (8 vols., 1921–1936); Peter Force, ed., *American Archives* (9 vols., 1837–1853); *The Writings of George Washington*, ed. John C. Fitzpatrick (37 vols., 1931–1940); *The Correspondence and Public Papers of John Jay*, ed. Henry P. Johnston (4 vols., 1890–1893); and *The Papers of Alexander Hamilton*, ed. Harold C. Syrett et al. (27 vols., 1961–1987). Biographies include Benson J. Lossing, *The Life and Times of Philip Schuyler* (2 vols., 1860–1873); Bayard Tuckerman, *The Life of General Philip Schuyler* (1903); Don R. Gerlach, *Philip Schuyler and the American Revolution in New York, 1733–1777* (1964), and *Proud Patriot: Philip Schuyler and the War of Independence, 1775–1783* (1987). Related monographs of significance are Broadus Mitchell, *Alexander Hamilton* (2 vols., 1957–1962); Alfred E. Young, *The Democratic Republicans of New York: The Origins, 1763–1797* (1960); John R. Elting, *The Battles of Saratoga* (1977); Don R. Gerlach, *Twenty Years of the "Promotion of Literature": The Regents of the University of the State of New York, 1784–1804* (1974); George W. Schuyler, *Colonial New York: Philip Schuyler and His Family* (2 vols., 1885); and George Dangerfield, *Chancellor Robert R. Livingston of New York, 1746–1813* (1960).

DON R. GERLACH

SCHUYLER, Robert Livingston (26 Feb. 1883–15 Aug. 1966), historian, was born in New York City, the son of Montgomery Schuyler, a prominent journalist and critic of architecture, and Katherine Beeckman Livingston, a talented amateur singer and artist. Schuyler's parents emphasized the importance of a liberal education; perhaps as a result of this their young son became both a gifted violinist and an adept student. He maintained his interest in music throughout his years at Columbia College, where he played in an orchestra, but ultimately he chose a career as a scholar.

Schuyler enrolled at Columbia in 1899 during a period of formative intellectual ferment in the disciplines of history and political science. His prominent teachers included John W. Burgess, who founded the college's Faculty of Political Science; Herbert L. Osgood; and James Harvey Robinson. His interest in constitutional history, inspired by these influential historians, led him to enroll there as a graduate student after receiving his B.A. in 1903. While he worked toward his master's degree he reported for the *New York Times*; he earned his degree in 1904 and became an instructor of history at Yale University in 1906 while he pursued his doctorate. His years at Yale were busy ones. In 1907 he married Sara Keller Brooks; they had one daughter. In 1909 he completed his dissertation, published that year as *The Transition in Illinois from British to American Government*, and received his Ph.D. in history from Columbia.

While at Yale Schuyler developed a friendship with senior historian George Burton Adams. Later in life his admiration for Adams led him to revise and expand one of the older scholar's most notable works, *A Constitutional History of England* (1934). Schuyler revealed in this carefully edited publication not only his respect for Adams but his own modesty as a historian: "Retouched portraits are rarely satisfactory, and I have neither the temerity nor the inclination to attempt the

reconstruction of a master's work." Schuyler's deep admiration for the medieval historian Frederic William Maitland and other great British historians similarly reflected on Schuyler's own qualities as a scholar. He wrote, "A mind as acute as Maitland's and historically conditioned as his was, could not fail to be constantly concerned with the meanings of words, with ambiguities in their meanings, with changes that have come over their meanings in the course of time." Schuyler was a cautious historian who resisted flamboyant generalization and who, like Maitland, tried hard to place the events of the past in their contemporary context.

Throughout his career Schuyler attempted to convey this respect for historical context to his students, particularly to his graduate students. He became a lecturer in history at Columbia in 1910 and an assistant professor one year later. During his next two years at Columbia he compiled the college's syllabus in American history (1913) and, with the help of Carlton J. H. Hayes, in modern European history (1912). By 1919 he had been promoted to associate professor. In 1924 he became a full professor of history and continued throughout his career to set high standards for his students' historical scholarship. In the later part of his career he taught the historiography course required of all graduate students, insisting on careful examination of documentary sources, detailed analysis of secondary material, and vigilance in separating contemporary assumptions from historical interpretation.

Schuyler had a rich life outside as well as inside the classroom. In 1918 he became a first lieutenant in the Twenty-second Engineers, New York National Guard, a commission he held for three years. More pertinent to his professorial career, he was editor of the *Political Science Quarterly* from 1919 to 1921, of *Columbia Studies in History, Economics and Public Law* from 1923 to 1929 and from 1944 to 1958, and of the *American Historical Review* from 1936 to 1941. He also wrote numerous book reviews for the *New York Times* throughout his career. Finally, he maintained a serious commitment to historical research, publishing scholarly articles and books. In *The Constitution of the United States* (1923) his grounding in the history of the British empire enabled him to reject the prevailing nationalistic interpretation of the American colonists' rebellion against Britain and to view events in the thirteen colonies in the context of an evolving legal relationship between England and its colonial possessions. His *Parliament and the British Empire* (1929) and *The Fall of the Old Colonial System* (1945) perhaps best reflect his enduring interest in the relationship between Britain's constitutional system and its empire and in how this empire actually worked.

After becoming Gouverneur Morris Professor of History at Columbia in 1942, Schuyler continued to publish, to teach, and to lecture. In 1948 he was a principal speaker at Dwight D. Eisenhower's inauguration as president of Columbia. In the year of his retirement he gave the presidential address at the annual dinner of the American Historical Association, speaking about his hero, Maitland, and titling the lecture "The Historical Spirit Incarnate." For his own students Schuyler seemed to set an example similar to the one set by Maitland before him. One of his students later paid tribute to his "critical acumen in appraising historical evidence, his clarity in formulating persuasive arguments, unmarred by the advocate's special pleading, and his skill as a literary craftsman." As a historian and a teacher Schuyler was modest and cautious, but he was never dull.

After retiring from Columbia Schuyler taught briefly at the University of Denver and at Hobart College and continued his historical research. He also became editor of the second supplement of the *Dictionary of American Biography* (1958). When he was nearly eighty years old he edited and published selections of Maitland's work. He died in Rochester, New York.

• Schuyler did not leave a collection of personal papers, but three manuscript collections contain material relevant to his career as a historian: the papers of Nicholas Murray Butler, president of Columbia during part of Schuyler's career, at the Columbia University Libraries; the records of the American Historical Association, in the Manuscript Division, Library of Congress, which contain material related to Schuyler's years as editor of the *American Historical Review*; and the papers of Josiah Tucker at the Columbia University Libraries, which contain correspondence and writings collected by Schuyler for his biography of Tucker, *Josiah Tucker: A Selection from His Economic and Political Writings* (1931). Photocopies of some originals from the Tucker papers are held at Yale University and at the British Museum. For further primary sources concerning Schuyler's career see the *New York Times*, 20 Oct. 1907; 8 July 1914; and 17 July 1914. Relevant secondary sources include Lionel Trilling, "The Van Amringe and Keppel Eras," in *A History of Columbia College on Morningside*, ed. Dwight C. Miner (1954); Richard Hofstadter, "The Department of History," in *A History of the Faculty of Political Science, Columbia University*, ed. R. Gordon Hoxie et al. (1955); and Herman Ausubel et al., *Some Modern Historians of Britain: Essays in Honor of Robert Livingston Schuyler* (1957). Obituaries are in the *New York Times*, 16 Aug. 1966, and the *American Historical Review* 72 (Jan. 1967): 803.

EMILY B. HILL

SCHWAB, Charles Michael (18 Feb. 1862–18 Sept. 1939), steel executive, was born in Williamsburg, Pennsylvania, the son of John Schwab and Pauline Farabaugh. His father was a weaver and in 1874 moved to the village of Loretto on the crest of the Allegheny Mountains and purchased a livery stable. At Loretto, Charles attended St. Francis College (then a Catholic secondary school). His secular studies included the humanities, bookkeeping, surveying, and engineering. From an early age he was active, curious, ambitious, and gregarious—a natural showman. "I can do something else yet," he is reported as saying at the conclusion of entertaining friends with songs, jokes, somersaults, and magic tricks. The words sum up the way he lived.

In 1879, at the age of seventeen, without having taken his degree, Schwab began life on his own at Braddock, Pennsylvania, the site of Andrew Carnegie's Edgar Thomson Steel Works. The center of the nation's iron and steel industry had in midcentury moved from southeastern Pennsylvania to the trans-Appalachian bituminous coal regions, with a hub at Pittsburgh. Braddock was a few miles from Pittsburgh. There Schwab clerked in a store for a few months, until William R. "Captain Bill" Jones, superintendent of the Thomson works, offered him a job. Schwab became a rodman on a surveying crew and started learning everything he could about the manufacture of steel. In 1883 he married Emma Eurania "Rana" Dinkey, a marriage that lasted a lifetime. They had no children. The newly wedded Schwab made himself useful to Jones, who brought him to the attention of Carnegie. In 1886 Carnegie sent Schwab to Europe to study steel making as a preliminary to becoming superintendent of the Homestead Works at Homestead, Pennsylvania. When Jones was killed in an industrial accident, Carnegie appointed Schwab to replace him at Thomson, thereby making him, at age twenty-seven, head of the largest steelworks in the United States.

By the time Schwab became superintendent at Thomson, Carnegie was semiretired. His "boys," as Carnegie called his chief lieutenants, managed his enterprises. Schwab was one of these, along with Henry Clay Frick and John G. A. Leishman, but unlike them, as time went by he grew in Carnegie's esteem. In 1892 the Homestead Works experienced one of the most savage strikes the American steel industry had ever known. Carnegie sent in Schwab to restore normal relations, which he did successfully. In 1893–1894 and again several years later, Schwab ran interference for Carnegie against allegations of wrongdoing in supplying the U.S. Navy with armor plate for warships. The mutual regard of the two men deepened. In 1897 Carnegie made Schwab president of his consolidated enterprises, the Carnegie Steel Company.

From 1900 to 1903 Schwab gained national recognition for putting together and heading the United States Steel Corporation. Many were talking about a need for integration in the steel industry, but little had as yet been done. At a dinner at Delmonico's in New York City on 12 December 1900, attended by the financier John Pierpont Morgan and many of the industry's leaders, Schwab outlined a plan for purchasing and integrating a large number of concerns specializing in mining, smelting, and manufacturing basic steel products. He subsequently received Morgan's support in financing the venture and Carnegie's agreement to sell. In April 1901 Schwab became president of U.S. Steel, the nation's first billion-dollar corporation. In creating it, however, he had passed over a number of companies, among them the small and prosperous Bethlehem Steel Company in the borough of South Bethlehem, Pennsylvania. Bethlehem Steel had been Carnegie's competitor in making armor plate for the navy. It was known to be up for sale, but it could not have been included in U.S. Steel without interfering with the competitive bidding that Congress required. Leaving Bethlehem Steel out of U.S. Steel made the company available for someone else. Schwab took Bethlehem Steel off the market by purchasing it. He immediately resold it to a syndicate controlled by Morgan.

As president of U.S. Steel, Schwab relished his prestige. Formation of the corporation had also made him extremely wealthy, and he indulged "a passion for owning the biggest and the best," as his biographer put it (Hessen, p. 133). In 1901 he began building an ornate mansion covering an entire block at Seventy-second Street and Riverside Drive in New York City. On a trip to Europe in 1901–1902 he spent lavishly, gambled for high stakes at Monte Carlo, and in general displayed an opulence that he had repressed during his years under Carnegie's control. The puritanical Carnegie was furious; his criticism deeply wounded Schwab, whose enemies called for his resignation. But Schwab had also been chafing under restraints imposed by the corporation's board of directors. As luck would have it, an opportunity to "do something else yet" was in the making.

A group of financiers was contemplating a merger of seven shipbuilding and outfitting facilities with the idea of pooling their resources to transform marginal or deficit operations into a profitable enterprise. They needed a supplier of steel and approached Schwab, who repurchased the Bethlehem Steel Company from the Morgan syndicate and sold it to the new concern, called the United States Shipbuilding Company. In the process he took advantage of a superior bargaining position to demand conditions that in the event of financial difficulties would put him in possession of the undertaking. The financial difficulties occurred, bankruptcy followed, and the attendant publicity disclosed Schwab's clever dealings. On 4 August 1903 he submitted his resignation from the presidency of U.S. Steel. A year later he found himself the owner of the United States Shipbuilding Company, whose future looked bleak. It was reorganized and in December 1904 became the Bethlehem Steel Corporation.

Now began what some have called Schwab's greatest work. He moved to South Bethlehem and announced his intention for the Bethlehem company to become "the greatest steel plant in the world." He introduced a bonus system and chose his "boys" from among the younger echelons of management, giving one in particular, Lehigh University graduate Eugene G. Grace, power similar to that which Schwab had exercised under Carnegie. He refused to allow the corporation to pay dividends on its stock and put his own fortune to work in modernizing, diversifying, and expanding so that Bethlehem Steel might control the eastern markets. He brought in ore from Chile and purchased several other companies for Bethlehem Steel. Especially, he took a chance on a new form of wide-flanged beam invented by Henry Grey, "the beam that made the skyscraper possible," as it was later termed. From 1904 to 1916 the company's sales rose from $10 million to $230 million.

Schwab bought a house in South Bethlehem and contributed to civic and cultural life with great effi-ciency and showmanship. He became a trustee of Lehigh University, salvaged and supported the Bethlehem Bach Choir, took a leading role in consolidating in 1917 the boroughs of Bethlehem and South Bethlehem into the city of Bethlehem, and did much more. The press warmed to him. High points in his popularity occurred during the war years. First, in 1914 he arranged for a British order for submarines to be manufactured in the United States but assembled in Montreal to circumvent the government's stand on neutrality. Then, in 1918 he accepted from President Woodrow Wilson an appointment as the head of the Emergency Fleet Corporation, charged with overseeing increases of the nation's troop and cargo ships.

In the postwar years Schwab lived in semiretirement; Grace did the active work of managing Bethlehem Steel. Schwab was often at "Immergrun" (Evergreen), a home he built at Loretto. From 1927 to 1932 he was the principal spokesman for the American steel industry in his capacity as president of the Iron and Steel Institute. Over the years he received many honors. He continued to live lavishly but gave millions to charitable projects and loaned large sums to friends who never paid him back. However, the acumen he had shown in making steel deserted him when he invested outside the industry. He died insolvent in New York City.

Schwab's career began in the early years of the American steel industry and carried over into its maturity. He enjoyed an immense talent for leadership in management, meaning, in his words, "management in its broadest aspects which includes, in addition to the proper handling of men, machines, materials and money, the underlying position and trend of the industry in its relation to the whole economic structure. I mean also business statesmanship" (Grace, p. 37). He was the first to give operational meaning to the concept of the integrated corporation by forming the U.S. Steel Corporation; he then supplied a second example, Bethlehem Steel. Schwab's career reflects a time when individuals could shape large organizations rather than be shaped by them.

• Robert Hessen, *Steel Titan: The Life of Charles M. Schwab* (1975), contains the most complete assessment. The book has no bibliographical section, although a fairly complete bibliography may be gleaned from Hessen's many notes, with one exception: after Hessen wrote, the Bethlehem Steel Corporation closed the Schwab Memorial Library and distributed its papers to the Hagley Museum, Wilmington, Del., which holds the fourteen-page manuscript by Sidney B. Whipple, "Notes on Mr. Schwab's Life," on Schwab's early years in Braddock, and other papers. Scrapbooks, diaries, World War I–era papers, and photographs were distributed to the Canal Museum, Easton, Pa. Limited collections of Schwab papers are also contained in the Pattee Library, Pennsylvania State University; National Archives (Emergency Fleet Corporation), Library of Congress; and the Corporate Records Division, Baker Library, Harvard University. Many letters also exist in the collected papers of Schwab's correspondents, including the Andrew Carnegie Papers, Library of Congress; Carnegie papers, New York Public Library; Jacob H. Schiff Papers, American Jewish Archives, Cincinnati; and George

W. Perkins Papers, Columbia University. See also Eugene G. Grace, *Charles M. Schwab* (1947), for an excellent summary of Schwab's personality. Many biographies and histories centering on the American steel industry deal with aspects of Schwab's life. See especially Joseph Frazier Wall, *Andrew Carnegie* (1970), on Schwab's years under the titan, and W. Ross Yates, ed., *Bethlehem of Pennsylvania: The Golden Years* (1976), on the sale of Bethlehem Steel and Schwab's civic activities in Bethlehem and South Bethlehem.

W. ROSS YATES

SCHWARTZ, Arthur (25 Nov. 1900–4 Sept. 1984), songwriter and producer, was born in Brooklyn, New York, the son of Solomon S. Schwartz, a lawyer, and Dora Grossman. As a boy Schwartz showed instinctual musical talent; by the age of fourteen he was working professionally as a piano player at silent cinemas. His father, however, forbade him from formally studying music, demanding that he pursue a career in law.

Schwartz attended New York University, where he was elected to Phi Beta Kappa and received a B.A. in English in 1920. He took only one music course while in college, but he wrote several marches and fight songs that were performed by the school band. Schwartz received an M.A. in literature from Columbia University in 1921 and a J.D. from the Columbia law school in 1924. He supported himself during these years as a high school English teacher and as a summer camp counselor. Around 1922, while working at a boys' camp in upstate New York, Schwartz met Lorenz Hart, also a member of the staff. Hart, though still unknown as a lyricist, had committed himself to a songwriting career. He befriended Schwartz and encouraged him to persevere as a composer. Later that year Schwartz published his first song, "Baltimore, Maryland, You're the Only Doctor for Me." Hart remained a lifelong influence and confidant.

Determined to accede to his father's wishes, Schwartz opened a law office in 1924. But he could not resist his attraction to music. While still a member of the bar, he began composing songs and scores for theatrical revues, including *Grand Street Follies* (1926) and *The New Yorkers* (1927). In 1928 he decided to close his law practice and pursue a career as a composer. That same year he began a long and fruitful partnership with the lyricist Howard Dietz. Their first joint effort was a Broadway revue, *The Little Show* (1929), and the two became long-term, though irregular, collaborators.

Halfway between the anthological stringing together of acts that characterized vaudeville and the narrative musicals of the "legitimate" stage, the revue offered audiences a series of song-and-dance skits built around a unifying theme, rather than a developing story. Dietz and Schwartz, as the team became known, emerged as masters of this form. Their score for *The Band Wagon* (1931), which was produced by Max Gordon and which starred Fred and Adele Astaire, is widely regarded as among the finest examples of the genre. The team followed up with *Flying Colors* (1932), another hit revue. Some songs from their re-

vue period that have survived as standards include "I Guess I'll Have to Change My Plans" (1929), "Dancing in the Dark" (1931), and "Louisiana Hayride" (1932).

In 1934 Dietz and Schwartz scored *Revenge with Music*, their first "book" (narrative) musical, which is an adaptation of a Spanish-language novel by Pedro de Alarcón, *El Sombrero de Tres Picos (The Three-Cornered Hat)*. "You and the Night and the Music" was among the hit songs from the production. *Between the Devil*, a comedy about a bigamist with one wife in England and another in France, opened in 1937 and includes the song "I See Your Face before Me." With the 1938 premiere of *Virginia*, written with Albert Stillman, Schwartz found himself with two hits running concurrently on Broadway. Schwartz also collaborated with Dorothy Fields on *Stars in Your Eyes*, a 1939 musical satire about Hollywood.

Schwartz spent the years during World War II working in Hollywood, collaborating with Dietz and other lyricists, including Frank Loesser and Leo Robin. He expanded his work from songwriting to composing complete musical scores for feature films such as *Navy Blues* (1941) and *Thank Your Lucky Stars* (1943). His legal background and business savvy allowed him to advance to the position of film producer. His two notable productions, both musicals, were *Cover Girl* (1944) and *Night and Day* (1946), the latter a biography of Cole Porter.

Returning to Broadway in 1946, Schwartz collaborated with Ira Gershwin on *Park Avenue* (1946). Working once again with Dietz, he scored three new stage musicals: *Inside U.S.A.* (1948), a revival of the otherwise dormant revue form; *The Gay Life* (1961), an adaptation of a Viennese bedroom farce; and *Jennie* (1963), based on the life of the actress Laurette Taylor. But perhaps Schwartz's greatest stage success, both artistically and commercially, was the score to *A Tree Grows in Brooklyn* (1951), written with Fields. "Make the Man Love Me," a ballad from the show, became a Broadway standard.

Schwartz had been composing for radio since 1934, when he served as musical director for the weekly series "The Gibson Family." Among his television credits were the scores for "American Jubilee," one of the first publicly broadcast television programs, which originated from the New York World's Fair (NBC, 1940); "Surprise for Santa" (CBS, 1948), the first ninety-minute TV special; and the score for a dramatic production of "A Bell for Adano" (CBS, 1956).

Throughout his career, Schwartz was lauded by critics for the urbane, sophisticated, yet effortless and unpretentious quality of his melodies. Alec Wilder observed in *American Popular Song* (1972) that none of Schwartz's songs "concern themselves with anything but the American musical atmosphere of the time. Schwartz never looked over his shoulder at Europe or operetta or the concert hall" (p. 313). In the *New York Times*, Benjamin Welles, reviewing the previous Broadway season, noted "a tremendous freshness, a boundless variety of musical expression" in Schwartz's songs (7 July 1940).

Schwartz married Katherine Carrington, an actress, in 1934; they had one child. His first wife having died in 1954, Schwartz married Mary O'Hagan; they also had one child. Schwartz was a member of the board of directors of the American Society of Composers and Performers from 1958 to 1983 and served as president of the League of New York Theatres from 1951 to 1954. He died in Kintnerville, Pennsylvania.

• An interview by Gene Lees appears in "The Distinctive Style of Arthur Schwartz," *High Fidelity* (Sept. 1976), pp. 20–22. Other articles are in the *New York Times*, 7 July 1940, pp. 1–2, and the *Los Angeles Times*, 17 Oct. 1976, p. 76. Also see Stanley Green, *The World of Musical Comedy* (1960, repr. 1980). A record album of Schwartz singing his own works, *From the Pen of Arthur Schwartz*, was released by RCA Victor in 1976.

DAVID MARC

SCHWARTZ, Delmore (8 Dec. 1913–11 July 1966), writer, was born in Brooklyn, New York, the son of Harry Schwartz, a real estate developer, and Rose Nathanson. Both parents were Jewish immigrants to the United States from Rumania. Schwartz studied philosophy at the University of Wisconsin and at New York University, where he received the B.A. in 1935. He was a graduate student in philosophy at Harvard from 1935 to 1937, although he received no advanced degrees. He returned to Harvard in 1940 as an instructor in English, rising to the rank of assistant professor in 1947. He also taught at Syracuse University at the end of his career (1962–1965). His marriage to Gertrude Buckman in 1938 ended in divorce in 1944; his second marriage in 1949 to Elizabeth Pollet was over by 1955, although the couple was never legally divorced. He had no children with either of his wives. He is the basis for the character of Humboldt, an erratic genius full of a self-destructive irony and wit, in Saul Bellow's novel *Humboldt's Gift* (1975), and he appears in the poems of John Berryman and Robert Lowell as a brilliant but doomed poet.

Schwartz's first book, *In Dreams Begin Responsibilities*, was published in 1938 at New Directions by James Laughlin, with whom he had a lifelong association. This was essentially a collection of lyric poetry, but it also included a verse play, "Coriolanus and His Mother," inspired by Shakespeare's *Coriolanus*, with interpolated prose commentaries by Aristotle, Marx, Freud, and Beethoven. The title of the book comes from a sensational short story about his parents' courtship that appeared in the first issue of *Partisan Review* in 1937. Schwartz was only twenty-five at the time of publication, and leading literary critics greeted the book with astonishment. In a letter, Allen Tate said, "I want to tell you that your poetic style is beyond any doubt the first real innovation that we've had since Eliot and Pound."

Schwartz was never again to publish a book of poems that was as successful as *In Dreams Begin Respon-*

sibilities, and he suffered throughout his life from a sense of the decline of his poetic powers. He quickly became a spokesman for the urban, alienated, immigrant-born, Marxist-oriented depression generation. Irving Howe spoke of him as the "comedian of alienation." His public, declamatory style—often in blank verse—as well as his social and political concerns led James Laughlin to call him "the American Auden." He was always a brilliant, witty conversationalist, full of wry, ironic humor, but his training and intensive reading in philosophy were evident in his poems. In the poem "In the naked bed, in Plato's cave," for example, Schwartz was preoccupied with his own insomnia as a symbol of the cultural anxiety of his times. The poem ends:

> O son of man, the ignorant night, the travail
> Of early morning, the mystery of beginning
> Again and again,
>   while History is unforgiven.

In "The Heavy Bear Who Goes with Me," perhaps his best-known poem, Schwartz wrestles with the unreconcilable dualism of mind and body.

> The heavy bear of his body is
> A caricature, a swollen shadow,
> A stupid clown of the spirit's motive,
> Perplexes and affronts with his own darkness,
> The secret life of belly and bone . . .

His later poetry was intensely concerned with his own identity, his immigrant origins, and the turbulent difficulties of his childhood and family life. *Shenandoah*, which appeared in 1941, was a long verse play about the rituals of naming a child, Shenandoah Fish being a substitute for Delmore Schwartz. *Genesis, Book I* (1943) was also a long, introspective poem not completely successful in integrating the personal and the public. *The World Is a Wedding*, a collection of autobiographical sketches and short stories published in 1948, revived interest in Schwartz's imaginative powers, although he never took his prose writing seriously. He considered himself primarily a lyric poet who had the misfortune seldom to write lyric poetry. *Vaudeville for a Princess and Other Poems* appeared in 1950, and *Summer Knowledge: New and Selected Poems, 1938–1958*, in 1959. That same year he won the Bollingen Prize in poetry for *Summer Knowledge*; he became the youngest winner of the award.

Schwartz was extremely interested in T. S. Eliot as a model for the modern poet. In the fall of 1949 he delivered a series of lectures on Eliot at the Gauss Seminar at Princeton University, but his projected book on Eliot was never published. Schwartz's importance as a literary critic has been underestimated. He was poetry editor for the *Partisan Review* from 1943 to 1955 and poetry editor for the *New Republic* from 1955 to 1957, and he wrote for the *Southern Review* and other leading literary journals of the period. His essays on John Dos Passos, Ernest Hemingway, William Faulkner, Thomas Hardy, Allen Tate, R. P. Blackmur, and others did a great deal to establish a fine, socially conscious sensibility for understanding their works. He was also a critic of popular culture and the movies.

Later in his life his manic-depressive style developed into full-fledged paranoia, with schizophrenic episodes. This was undoubtedly abetted by the overuse of sleeping pills, dexedrine, and alcohol. He died in squalid circumstances in the Columbia Hotel on West Forty-sixth Street in the Times Square area of New York City.

• Schwartz's papers are mostly in the American Literature Collection of the Beinecke Rare Book and Manuscript Library at Yale University, although there is also some material in the library of Syracuse University. The best available biography is James Atlas, *Delmore Schwartz: The Life of an American Poet* (1977), but this should be supplemented by the moving sketch by his friend William Barrett, "Delmore: A 30's Friendship and Beyond," *Commentary* 58 (Sept. 1974): 41–54, and also Barrett's previous essay, "The Truants: *Partisan Review* in the 40's," *Commentary* 57 (June 1974): 48–54. Schwartz's literary executor, Robert Phillips, has made available unpublished material in *The Ego Is Always at the Wheel: Bagatelles* (1986) and *Last & Lost Poems* (1989). He has also collected *Shenandoah and Other Verse Plays* (1992). In addition, Phillips has edited *Letters of Delmore Schwartz* (1984) and *Delmore Schwartz and James Laughlin: Selected Letters* (1993). Another valuable source of unpublished material is *Portrait of Delmore: Journals and Notes of Delmore Schwartz 1939–1959*, ed. Elizabeth Pollet, his second wife (1986). Schwartz's literary criticism is reprinted in *Selected Essays of Delmore Schwartz*, ed. Donald A. Dike and David H. Zucker (1970). Eight stories are collected in *In Dreams Begin Responsibilities and Other Stories*, ed. James Atlas (1978). The only critical book, aside from Atlas's biography, is by Richard McDougall in the Twayne United States Authors Series #243 (1974).

MAURICE CHARNEY

SCHWARTZ, Maurice (18 June 1890–10 May 1960), Yiddish producer, director, and actor, was born Avrom Moishe Schwartz in Sedikov, Ukraine, the son of Isaac Schwartz and Rose Bernholtz. As a child he sang in a choir, wishing to grow up to be either a cantor or an orchestra leader, despite the fact that his destitute Jewish family had no theater background. Maurice's uncle loved the theater, however, and would often take Maurice to see plays starring such renowned actors as Tomashefsky and David Kessler; young Maurice also admired such silent screen stars as Charlie Chaplin, Ruth Draper, and Bert Williams.

In 1901 Maurice immigrated with his family to the United States, where he attended New York's Lower East Side public schools. At age fourteen he became president of the Delancy Street Dramatic Club and moved to Baltimore to act in plays for producer Leo Largman for nine dollars a week. He then moved to Chicago to perform in Ellis Glickman's productions. In 1906 Morris Morrison, a producer in Philadelphia, gave Schwartz his first chance as an actor and director. Finally, in 1912 Schwartz's childhood idol, David Kessler, brought him back to New York to the Second Avenue theaters. In 1914 he married Anna Bordofsky. Schwartz continued to perform for seven years in

Kessler's company until he founded the Yiddish Art Theatre in 1918.

The Schwartz theater was a family operation from the start. Schwartz's wife worked in the box office, his brother was the manager, and Schwartz himself performed, directed, and even applied the actors' makeup at times. As the only repertory theater in the country, the Schwartz theater's philosophy differed sharply from that of the Broadway houses. Schwartz disliked the traditional star system, arguing "We play as a unit and we take our curtain calls as a unit . . . drama should always be greater than its interpreters." Despite this sentiment some of his illustrious ensemble, including Paul Muni and Edward G. Robinson, would go on to stardom elsewhere, while others achieved a different sort of fame. (Stella Adler, for example, became a pioneering acting teacher.) Occasionally, Schwartz worked with the members of another renowned Yiddish theater troupe, the Artef, which included Jules Dassin and Sarah Silverberg.

In the 1920s Schwartz mounted Yiddish versions of classics like Gogol's *Inspector General* (1923) and new plays like *The Gold Diggers* (1927). Schwartz himself also appeared in *Yizhor* (1928), a silent film. That same year Schwartz moved the theater from Second Avenue to south of Union Square and then, in 1931, to midtown (at Forty-ninth Street and Broadway). The constant movements, he said, were caused by disagreements he had with theater owners.

The early days of the depression were difficult financially for the Yiddish Theatre. Schwartz performed in a Yiddish *Othello* (1929) and tried to lure audiences from Broadway with his English-speaking Shylock (in a 1930 anthology). Still, few of his plays, including *Chains* (1930) and *The New Man* (1932), did well. One, *The Wise Men of Chelem* (1933), was a lavish box-office failure. Only *Yoshe Kalb* (1933) was a hit, leading to a world tour of the play, another appearance for Schwartz in a Yiddish film, *Uncle Moses* (1933), and interest from Hollywood. In 1934 Schwartz signed a contract with MGM studios to act, write, and direct. No films resulted, however, and he returned to New York to stage *The Water Carrier* (1936) and *The Brothers Ashkenazi* (1937). The latter play, based on an I. J. Singer story, led to another world tour in 1938.

In 1939 Schwartz finally got to direct a film, *Tevya*, based on an Aleichem comedy. The $70,000 production, made in the Bronx, was well received (the *New York Times* called Schwartz "a priceless actor") and resulted in another call from Hollywood. But Schwartz's 1940 screen test, directed by George Sidney, neither excited the studio executives nor turned Schwartz into a "new Spencer Tracy." Schwartz returned to the theater and staged *Worlds Apart* in 1941; that same year he experienced anti-Semitism while he was touring when the government of Chili held up his visa because he was Jewish. World War II and the Holocaust deeply affected Schwartz, who addressed the issue in his 1942 work, *Hitler's Last Hour*, a prophetic depiction of the German dictator's demise. (Schwartz also appeared in the patriotic and pro-Soviet *Mission to Moscow*, a 1943 Hollywood film.)

After the war Schwartz and his wife adopted two Polish war orphans, while he restaged old hits like *Yoshe Kalb* (1946) and *Shylock and His Daughter* (1947), which was based on *The Merchant of Venice*. The *New York Times* called his performance in the latter play "one of his most eloquent portrayals," and once again it led Schwartz to Hollywood. But, this time, he closed his theater after thirty-one years and moved his family to Los Angeles, where he landed several film roles, including that of a Polynesian witch doctor in *Bird of Paradise* (1951). Schwartz also accepted smaller roles in *Salome* (1952) and *Slaves of Babylon* (1953).

Schwartz quickly tired of the Hollywood life, returning with his family to New York, where he attempted to reorganize the downtown Yiddish theater world with new financial backing. In 1955 he staged a Yiddish version of Moliere's *The Miser*, which flopped badly, and an English version of *The Grass Is Always Greener*, which fared somewhat better. His daughter, Fannie, appeared with him in *The Shepherd King*, and he made a rare TV appearance in *Lamp unto My Feet*, also in 1955. Soon after mounting a Yiddish version of *A Hole in the Head* (1958), which was not a hit, Schwartz realized his best days were behind him; it became one of his last productions. In 1960 Schwartz died in an Israeli hospital, near Tel Aviv. A massive Second Avenue memorial followed shortly thereafter.

Clearly, Schwartz was more than a prolific showman. His oeuvre included more than 150 productions of classic and modern plays, but, more importantly, Schwartz helped revolutionize contemporary theater by demonstrating the merits of the repertory and ensemble-player concepts. Culturally, Schwartz bravely brought what might be called a modern Jewish sensibility to a huge international audience, deflecting anti-Semitism along the way. Schwartz epitomized the creative and enterprising spirit of twentieth-century theater.

• Maurice Schwartz's papers are in the Jewish Division of the New York Public Library. Other memorabilia can be found at YIVO, the Institute for Jewish Research, also in New York. Schwartz himself occasionally wrote pieces in such publications as *The Jewish Forum*, including the article, "Appreciation for the Histrionic Heart," Feb. 1947. For biographical information, see Thomas Pryor, "Outside of Jericho," *New York Times*, 30 July 1939; "Maurice Schwartz, Actor," *Montreal (Canada) Gazette*, 9 June 1945; Stanley Garten, "A Great Artist with a Great Jewish Heart," *The Light*, 12, no. 12 (Aug. 1945); "All His World's the Stage," *New York Post*, 24 Aug. 1945; and Leon Crystal, "Maurice Schwartz," *Jewish Forum*, Feb. 1947. Also useful are "Home Becomes Actor's Stage," *New York Sun*, 12 Nov. 1947, and Barbara Berch Jamison, "From Second Avenue to Vine Street," *New York Times*, 6 Aug. 1950. For information concerning the Yiddish Theatre, see Nahma Sandow, *A World History of the Yiddish Theater* (1977), and Lulla Rosenfeld, *Bright Star of Exile: Jacob Adler and the Yiddish Theatre* (1977). An obituary is in the *New York Times*, 11 May 1960.

ERIC MONDER

SCHWARZMANN, Hermann Joseph (30 Apr. 1846–23 Sept. 1891), architect, was born in Munich, Germany, the son of Joseph Anton Schwarzmann, a decorative painter, and Wilhelmine Deutter. Schwarzmann's father enjoyed the patronage of King Ludwig I of Bavaria, and it was through that association that he obtained a scholarship to the Royal Military Academy. He graduated with honors and in 1865 entered an artillery regiment, serving the following year as a second lieutenant during the month-long Bavarian conflict with Prussia. Schwarzmann would likely have received some training in topographical drawing, mathematics, and engineering in the military academy and in the artillery, but details of his architectural education remain vague. An 1876 press account cited by John Maass recorded Schwarzmann's claim that he had studied architecture after the war of 1866. It is possible that he may have trained with his father, who had devised decorative schemes for buildings by architectural luminaries such as Heinrich Hübsch, Leo von Klenze, and Friedrich von Gärtner. Drawings by decorative painter George Herzog, who studied design in the elder Schwarzmann's studio in 1865–1867, show a remarkable graphic facility in drawing architectural subjects that may be an indication of what could be acquired there.

In August 1868 Schwarzmann resigned his commission and left Bavaria for the United States. His motives for emigrating are cloudy, but they may have paralleled those of Herzog, who followed early in the next decade: prospects at home may have seemed constrained relative to those offered in the expanding cities of the United States, where German work enjoyed a strong reputation. Schwarzmann found employment in Philadelphia, Pennsylvania, by April 1869 with the newly established Fairmount Park Commission. Fairmount Park had just grown from 200 acres to more than ten times that amount, extending northwest of the city center along the Schuylkill River and Wissahickon Creek. As junior assistant engineer, Schwarzmann performed extensive surveying work, planning and supervising the execution of roads, paths, and attendant small bridges. His duties at the park kept expanding as he demonstrated new abilities to his employers. When the head gardener left, Schwarzmann began studying books on the subject and soon showed a mastery for laying out planting schemes. In January 1870 he was promoted to senior assistant engineer. In 1871 he married Rose Marshall; they had no children. Promoted to chief engineer in 1872, he was entrusted with the design and alteration of park buildings as well, including a large dining room for Adolph Proskauer's restaurant (1871)—of Swiss style externally but painted in a Pompeian style within—and a small brick, iron, and glass art gallery (1872). That year the Fairmount Park commissioners demonstrated their confidence in him by choosing his plan for improving the eastern part of the park over one commissioned from the renowned landscape architecture firm of Olmsted & Vaux. Similarly, his landscape design was adopted in 1873 for the Philadelphia Zoological Garden, located in the western part of the park.

Even greater triumphs were to follow, for planning was already afoot for the Centennial Exhibition to be held in Fairmount Park in 1876. Schwarzmann visited the International Exposition in Vienna, Austria, in 1873 on behalf of the Fairmount Park Commission. Upon his return he laid out the grounds for this world's fair—covering 285 acres—and designed many of its major buildings, including the main permanent structure, the Art Building, which survives as Memorial Hall; Horticultural Hall, a large greenhouse with Moorish details; and the Judges' Pavilion, Women's Pavilion, German Pavilion, Pennsylvania Building, Photographic Hall, and some two dozen others.

After the centennial, Schwarzmann continued to do work at the park. He reworked a building for exhibiting pictures of Pompeii, which Schwarzmann accommodated in a matching style (1877). He also began to take private commissions, including improvements at Ridgway Park, a recreation spot with a restaurant and a music stand on Smith's Island in the Delaware River (1879). He formed a succession of short-lived partnerships, practicing architecture in 1876 with George R. Pohl and in 1877 with Hugo Kafka, who had worked with Schwarzmann on the centennial, and landscape architecture with Edward O. Schwagerl.

In 1878 Schwarzmann opened an architectural office in New York City. From 1881 to 1884 the firm was called Hermann J. Schwarzmann & Co. Working under him was Albert Buchman, who was his partner from 1885 to 1888. Schwarzmann's New York work reflected his German roots and his experience with recreational architecture. His best-known commissions were Koster & Bial's Summer Garden (1879), the Liederkranz Club House (1881, with William Kuhles, decorated by Herzog), and the Mercantile Exchange Building (1882), which was actually a privately owned loft building with a classically detailed cast-iron front that still stands on lower Broadway in Manhattan. He also designed private houses, still only sketchily known, some reportedly at Long Branch, New Jersey. Failing eyesight forced his retirement from active practice at about age forty, and he declined over the next five years. He died in New York City.

Schwarzmann's works and the styles he adopted are varied, but as an architect he is chiefly remembered for his work at the centennial, especially the design of Memorial Hall. This is a building of great monumentality, bearing a distinctly continental imprint. (Maass reported that it was adapted directly from a published French Prix de Rome design from 1867.) It ran somewhat outside the mainstream of American practice but provided a backdrop of cosmopolitanism and ceremony for the nation's international debut on the world stage in 1876.

Although Schwarzmann may have lacked the training of the leading American architects of that era—extended professional schooling abroad or a period of training with an established architect or designing builder—his skills, competence, conversance with modern European forms, and especially his discipline inspired a confidence among clients who may have been wary of excessive extravagance or independence. From his first years at Fairmount Park, Schwarzmann applied himself to the study of European publications and winningly demonstrated new proficiencies that accumulated in a career that blossomed quickly, unexpectedly, and briefly.

• Papers relating to Fairmount Park and the centennial can be found in the Philadelphia City Archives, the Historical Society of Pennsylvania, and the Fairmount Park Commission. Also see scrapbooks of newspaper clippings kept by Thompson Westcott in the 1870s and 1880s in the Historical Society of Pennsylvania. Schwarzmann's centennial account was published as "Report of the Chief Engineer of the Exhibition Grounds, and Architect of the Permanent Buildings and of Other Structures of the Centennial Board of Finance," in *International Exhibition, 1876: Report of the Director-General*, ed. A. T. Goshorn (1879). The most complete assessment of Schwarzmann's career remains John Maass, *The Glorious Enterprise: The Centennial Exhibition of 1876 and H. J. Schwarzmann, Architect-in-Chief* (1973). See also Martha Halpern, "Two Early Works by Hermann Schwarzmann," *Fairmount Park Historical Quarterly* 1, no. 4 (Fall 1984): 7–16; Sandra L. Tatman and Roger W. Moss, *Biographical Dictionary of Philadelphia Architects, 1700–1930* (1985); George E. Thomas, "Hermann J. Schwarzmann," in *Philadelphia Museum of Art: Three Centuries of American Art* (1976); Mark C. Luellen, "The Decorative Designs of George Herzog (1851–1920)," *Nineteenth Century* 12, nos. 3–4 (1993): 18–26; and Arnold Lewis and Keith Morgan, *American Victorian Architecture* (1975). An obituary is in *Architecture and Building* 15 (3 Oct. 1891): 163.

JEFFREY A. COHEN

SCHWATKA, Frederick (29 Sept. 1849–2 Nov. 1892), army officer and arctic explorer, was born in Galena, Illinois, the son of Frederick Schwatka, a cooper, and Amelia (maiden name unknown). At an early age he migrated with his family to Oregon. The lure of the frontier influenced Schwatka for the rest of his life. As a young man, he worked as a printer and attended Willamette University. In 1867 he obtained an appointment to the United States Military Academy at West Point. After graduating in 1871, he became a lieutenant in the Third United States Cavalry.

A contemporary of George A. Custer, Schwatka served at frontier posts in Nebraska and the region that would later form the states of Arizona, Wyoming, Montana, and the Dakotas. Chances for promotion were slim because most of his fellow officers outranked him in both seniority and combat experience. To escape the boredom of garrison duty, he studied law and medicine. Nebraska admitted him to the bar in 1875. He earned a medical degree from New York's Bellevue Hospital Medical College in 1876.

As the Indian campaigns subsided, Schwatka turned to the Arctic for new adventures. When he read about a proposed expedition to recover the records of the explorer Sir John Franklin, he decided to volunteer. The demise of Franklin and his men was an unsolved mystery.

In 1845 Franklin had sailed from England to discover the Northwest Passage. His two ships had entered the labyrinth of the Canadian arctic islands and vanished. After ten years of searching for the 129 lost men, both the British and the United States governments had refused to pay for further expeditions. The widowed Lady Franklin had sent her own expedition in 1857, which had reached the King William Island area. There they had found skeletons, relics, and one document stating that Franklin died on 11 June 1847, but no diaries or other records. The rescue effort had started with dozens of ships and hundreds of men but by 1871 had gradually dwindled to one obscure man, Charles Francis Hall. From 1860 to 1869 Hall, an American, and two Inuit (Eskimo) associates had continued the forlorn search for survivors among the Inuit settlements. Lady Franklin had failed to persuade Hall in 1871 to search again for the records before his planned North Pole expedition. Shortly thereafter, Hall died in North Greenland without completing either task.

Now Schwatka, the bold young cavalry officer, volunteered to accomplish the task that had frustrated the world's greatest explorers. Judge Charles Daly, president of the American Geographical Society, liked Schwatka's intelligence and vigor and appointed him the expedition leader. Other members included William H. Gilder, a *New York Herald* reporter; Henry Klutschak, a civil engineer; Frank Melms, a whaler; and Ebierbing (Joe), who had been Hall's trusted Inuit guide and translator. A whaling firm furnished the supplies and transportation. The entire expedition cost about $5,000; one of the greatest bargains in polar history!

Arriving in the Arctic in August 1878, the expedition landed on the northwestern coast of Hudson Bay. The explorers reached King William Island during the summer of 1879. They found skeletons and Franklin relics that Hall had not seen. A thorough search disclosed no further diaries or original records. Schwatka, like Hall, recorded Inuit accounts about the white men who had died there many years before.

The expedition encountered extremely cold temperatures (down to −69° F) on their winter return to Hudson Bay in 1880. Schwatka's explorations demonstrated that non-Inuits could travel successfully during the Arctic winter by using Inuit food and equipment. Their round trip of 3,124 miles established a new record for sledge travel. They made only minor geographical discoveries, but they collected valuable ethnological data and brought the open question of the Franklin records to a conclusion.

Upon returning to the United States, Gilder made Schwatka famous through articles in the *New York Herald* and a book about the search. The army also had promoted him to first lieutenant during his absence. Unfortunately, other expeditions soon replaced Schwatka in the headlines and the army bypassed him for the leadership of two new expeditions. Lieutenant Adolphus W. Greely led the expedition to Lady Franklin Bay, Ellesmere Island and Lieutenant Patrick H. Ray led the expedition at Barrow, Alaska. Schwatka secured a minor assignment to explore the upper Yukon River and gather information about Indian tribes.

Hopes for leading future military expeditions to the Arctic vanished with the tragic Greely Expedition (1881–1884) and George W. De Long's disastrous naval voyage (1879–1882). Each expedition lost a ship and many lives and generated politically embarrassing hearings. Congress refused to initiate further polar exploration. Returning to garrison duty did not appeal to Schwatka. He resigned his army commission in 1885.

The lure of travel and adventure continued to attract the ex-officer. In 1886 the *New York Times* sponsored Schwatka's new expedition to Alaska, but he made no significant discoveries. By 1889 he had concluded that other countries would assume leadership in arctic exploration, and he turned his attention to Mexico. In 1890 he led an expedition to Chihuahua and the cave-dwelling Tarahumari tribe and studied the resources of northern Mexico.

Schwatka died in Portland, Oregon, from an overdose of laudanum (opium). A physician stated that he had used the drug for several years. On the evening before his death he had dinner with a friend and discussed traveling to Mexico to make a large land transaction. After dinner he obtained laudanum from a druggist. A few hours later a policeman found him unconscious on a downtown street. He had never married.

History records Schwatka as the leader of the "Last Franklin Search Expedition." His other polar accomplishments included valuable ethnological work among the Inuit, successfully traveling in the arctic winter, and exploring in Alaska. Later explorers such as Admiral Robert E. Peary emulated Schwatka's expeditionary techniques. For examples, Schwatka had observed that cooking damaged the ability of fresh food to prevent scurvy, a fact that scientists confirmed decades later.

Although Schwatka was highly qualified physically and mentally, the army's promotion system stifled his military career in the small post–Civil War army. He lacked the requisite political connections to become the leader of the major army expeditions in the 1880s. Historians only can speculate how a dynamic, experienced leader such as Schwatka might have prevented the Greely Expedition's disaster. Ironically, the army promoted Greely to brigadier general two years after Schwatka resigned his commission.

• Schwatka's initial report appeared in the 1880 *American Geographical Society Journal* (vol. 12). Edouard A. Stackpole of the Marine Historical Association published Schwatka's narrative, *The Long Arctic Search*, in 1965. Schwatka's books include *Report of a Military Reconnaissance in Alaska in 1883* (1885), *Nimrod in the North* (1885), *Along Alaska's Great River* (1885), *A Summer in Alaska* (1893), *In the Land of Cave and Cliff Dwellers* (1893), and *The Children of the Cold* (1886). His articles include "Der arktische Skorbut und seine Heilmittel," *Deutsche Geographische Blätter*, vol. 4 (1881), pp. 162–74; "The Igloo of the Innuit," *Science*, vol. 2 (1883), pp. 182–

347; "The Great River of Alaska," *Century Magazine*, vol. 30 (1885), pp. 738–51, 819–29; and "The Next Polar Expedition," *North American Review* (1889), pp. 148–51. William H. Gilder, *Schwatka's Search* (1881), is the primary account of Schwatka's arctic expedition. Henry Klutschak published *Als Eskimo unter den Eskimos* in German in 1881. John E. Caswell, *Arctic Frontiers* (1956), provides the best historical analysis of his 1878–1880 expedition. Charles Lanman, *Farthest North* (1885), describes the frustrations that caused another young officer, like Schwatka, to volunteer for an arctic expedition. Schwatka's obituary is in the *New York Times*, 3 Nov. 1892.

TED HECKATHORN

SCHWEINITZ, Lewis David von (13 Feb. 1780–8 Feb. 1834), Moravian clergyman and botanist, was born in Bethlehem, Pennsylvania, the eldest son of Hans Christian Alexander von Schweinitz, belonging to the church and a baron from an ancient family in Silesia, and Anna Dorothea Elisabeth de Watteville, the daughter of Baron (later Bishop) John de Watteville and granddaughter of Nicolaus Ludwig, Count von Zinzendorf. It was chiefly due to the efforts of Zinzendorf and Watteville that the venerable Unitas Fratrum, more commonly known as the Moravian church, had been revived in the eighteenth century; and it was Zinzendorf who had founded Bethlehem, at the time of Lewis's birth a closed town where only Moravians lived in a communal manner, with most real property belonging to the church.

Though christened Ludwig, the boy grew up to sign his English letters Lewis and, while he used the less aristocratic "de" before his surname on his publications in Latin, he habitually signed his initials L.D.v.S. He began his education at age seven at Nazareth Hall, the Moravian boys' school—where one of the teachers, Samuel Kramsch, encouraged his interest in botany—and continued there until 1798, when he returned with his family to Europe.

At the Moravian Theological Seminary at Niesky, in Silesia, Schweinitz was greatly influenced by another teacher, Johann Baptista von Albertini, with whom he published in 1805 his first botanical contribution, a *Conspectus fungorum* of the region containing ninety-three species new to science. Since Albertini published little else, it has been speculated that Schweinitz wrote much of the text though listed as junior author; at any event, there is no doubt that the twelve plates of fungi that illustrate the book were drawn, engraved, and colored by him.

Schweinitz began to preach while still at Niesky and in 1807 was sent to be spiritual and temporal adviser to the single brethren at a nearby village; the following year he was sent in the same capacity to a village near Magdeburg. Having proved his pastoral ability, he was ordained a deacon the same year. In 1812 he married Louisa Amalia le Doux, who had been teaching in a Moravian school for girls and was the daughter of Huguenots living in Pomerania; they would have four children.

A month later the newlyweds set out for Salem, North Carolina, where Schweinitz was to be adminis-

trator of the church's Wachovia estate, a tract of some 90,000 acres. While their American ship, the *Minerva Smith*, was held up by a lawsuit at Kiel in the duchy of Holstein, Schweinitz made friends among the faculty of the university there; in 1817 it awarded him an honorary Ph.D. in recognition of the worth of the *Conspectus*. The trip was an adventurous one: they were bedeviled by privateers; the War of 1812 having begun, they were captured by a British war vessel but managed to escape; and finally they reached Newport, Rhode Island, only after weathering a hurricane.

The decade Schweinitz spent at Salem was one of his most productive, even though nearly all of one year during that period was taken up by his return to Germany, where in 1818 he was ordained a presbyter by his friend Albertini, now a bishop. In addition to his administrative work for the church in North Carolina, he accumulated an extensive herbarium, in part made possible by his constant travels throughout Wachovia. As a minister, he was called on to preach from time to time, and his executive skills brought him appointment as a trustee of the church's Salem Female Academy as well as a trustee of the secular University of North Carolina.

In North Carolina he was also in proximity with several fellow enthusiasts for botany—an unusual circumstance for most American botanists at the time—and he began corresponding with others. Elisha Mitchell was at Chapel Hill, where both botanized together as well as at Salem, and at Salem he had the companionship of his old teacher Kramsch and of Christian F. Dencke, who left a sizable herbarium to the academy.

Schweinitz had taken with him to Germany a list of 1,373 fungi of North Carolina with descriptions of those he believed to be new species and left it with his friend Christian Friedrich Schwägrichen, professor of natural history at Leipzig. Much to his surprise, this was published in 1822 as *Synopsis fungorum Carolinae Superioris* and was the first considerable work on American fungi. It, along with the earlier *Conspectus*, have earned for Schweinitz the sobriquet "Father of American Mycology." About 1820 he began to plan the publication of a cryptogamic flora of North America, to complement Frederick Pursh's phanerogamic *Flora* (1814), but was unsuccessful in enlisting the competent aid of others because no one else shared his level of knowledge. In 1821, just before his departure for new responsibilities at Bethlehem, he published in Raleigh, North Carolina, a pamphlet titled *Specimen florae Americae Septentrionalis cryptogamicae*, which was intended to be a sample of the proposed larger work. Despite his focus on cryptogams, he did not neglect the flowering plants, either in his collecting or in his writing. Two of his best shorter papers were on the genus *Viola* (*American Journal of Science and Arts* 5 [1822]: 48–81) and on the genus *Carex* (*Annals of the Lyceum of Natural History of New York* 1 [1824]: 62–71), both difficult genera in systematic botany because of their extreme complexity.

In Bethlehem Schweinitz was the pastor, principal of the school for girls, and "Proprietor of the Unity's property in Pennsylvania"—this last a job requiring great negotiating skill and sound judgment, for the considerable landed property still owned by the church was in the process of being sold off at a fair price to individuals. And in 1824–1825 he was again in Germany to attend the church's synod, where, in appreciation of his administrative work, he was ordained "senior civilis." He was the last to hold this ecclesiastical rank, midway between presbyter and bishop, the duties of which made him a kind of inspector general for the church. Appropriate to his analytical cast of mind, his sermons were described as "invariably practical, not argumentative—experimental, not speculative."

Schweinitz's single scientific work was published by the American Philosophical Society in its *Transactions* in 1832 as *Synopsis fungorum in America Boreali*; it covered 3,098 species. In all, it has been estimated that he published nearly 4,500 species of fungi, of which 1,533 were described as new; in the course of his work he also established ten new genera.

But by this time Schweinitz was ill; from the summer of 1830 to that of 1831 he was often confined to his room and became so depressed that he considered suicide. A trip to Indiana in his capacity of senior civilis did much to restore his spirits, but his health continued to worsen. Having complained for some time of a persistent cough, he may have been the victim of tuberculosis. He died in Bethlehem and was buried in the Moravian cemetery there.

Throughout his active botanical career Schweinitz had carried on a professional correspondence with nearly a hundred colleagues both at home and abroad, writing often in Latin to the Europeans, though he spoke and wrote German, English, and French. He had an extensive private library of botanical books and left a herbarium containing about 23,000 species, now preserved at the Academy of Natural Sciences of Philadelphia. Although botany was only his avocation, few others accomplished more in so short a space of time. His professional life was carried on by his four sons, all of whom entered the Moravian ministry, with two of them becoming bishops.

• There are Schweinitz papers in the Moravian Archives in both Salem and Bethlehem as well as in the Archiv der Brüder-Unitat in Herrnhut, Saxony. His scientific correspondence is scattered, the greatest single collection being his letters exchanged with John Torrey, which are at the New York Botanical Garden, published in *Memoirs of the Torrey Botanical Club* 16 (1921): 119–289. Other letters are at the Hunt Institute, the University of Michigan, and the Academy of Natural Sciences of Philadelphia, which also has a collection of his watercolors of plants. An English translation of his diary of the trip from Europe to Salem in 1812 appears in *Records of the Moravians in North Carolina* 7 (1947): 3021–43, and a translation of the journal he kept on his 1831 trip to Indiana appears in *Indiana Historical Society Publications* 8 (1927): 205–85.

The best single account of his scientific career is Donald P. Rogers, "L. D. de Schweinitz and Early American Mycology," *Mycologia* 69 (1977): 223–45. John Hendley Barnhart gives thumbnail biographical sketches of "The Botanical Cor-

respondents of Schweinitz" in *Bartonia* 16 (1934): 19–36; in the same issue, pp. 14–18, there is an article by Don M. Benedict on "Schweinitz' Botanical Library," which was sold to finance the publication of the anonymous "Sketch of the Life and Scientific Work of Lewis David von Schweinitz," *Journal of the Elisha Mitchell Scientific Society* 3 (1886): 9–25. In turn, this general consideration of his life was based on the memoir by Walter R. Johnson read before the Academy of Natural Sciences of Philadelphia in 1835 but had additional paragraphs contributed by his son, Bishop Edmund de Schweinitz.

CHARLES BOEWE

SCHWELLENBACH, Lewis Baxter (20 Sept. 1894–10 June 1948), judge and politician, was born in Superior, Wisconsin, the son of Francis W. Schwellenbach, a machinist, and Martha Baxter. In 1902 the family moved to Spokane, Washington, where Lewis attended the city's elementary schools. His father died in 1908, and Lewis, then only fourteen years old, helped support the family and finance his own education by selling newspapers, working on railroad construction, and harvesting wheat. While still a teenager he moved to Tacoma, Washington, where he completed his secondary education and came under the influence of a school debate team coach who steered the student toward an interest in law and politics.

After graduation from high school, Schwellenbach enrolled in the law department at the University of Washington in Seattle. He worked his way through the university, serving as an assistant instructor of law, the field in which he received his LL.B. in 1917. After graduation, Schwellenbach served as an army infantryman in France during World War I.

After the war, Schwellenbach returned to Seattle, where he was admitted to the Washington State bar in 1919. He practiced law between 1919 and 1935, first in association with a small local firm, then alone, and once again with partners. While practicing law, he also tried his hand unsuccessfully at the business of banking, brewing, and laundering.

Schwellenbach proved far more successful at politics and rapidly gained prominence in King County (Seattle) area Democratic party affairs, serving in 1924 as chair of the state party convention. In politics, he won a reputation as a populist friend of labor and a critic of business interests, especially banking and private utilities, attitudes that may have derived from the combined influence of his father, a William Jennings Bryan Democrat, and his own failures at private business. By the end of the 1920s, Schwellenbach had become an advocate of public ownership of utilities and a firm friend to trade unionists. Well respected locally, he served as president of the University of Washington Alumni Association (1928–1929) and as a member of the university's board of regents (1933).

In 1932 he entered the Democratic primary for governor of Washington and lost. Two years later, however, he ran as the Democratic party's candidate for the U.S. Senate on a platform demanding an end to poverty in Washington, an echo of Upton Sinclair's campaign for governor of California that same year as the candidate of EPIC (End Poverty in California). Elected to the Senate as part of a Democratic landslide, Schwellenbach became a leader among the newly elected Democratic senators and one of the most ardent New Dealers. He invariably supported President Franklin D. Roosevelt's proposed reforms, opposing the president only once, in 1940, on the issue of peacetime conscription. A diligent defender of the New Deal, he fought two of Roosevelt's most bitter enemies—Huey Long, the egoistical and idiosyncratic senator from Louisiana, and the Liberty League, a group of conservative Republicans and turncoat Democrats, which he dismissed as "leeches, rascals, and blood-sucking lawyers." During his tenure in the Senate he served on the Foreign Relations Committee, where he was an outspoken critic of Japanese expansion in East Asia and an advocate of economic sanctions and an embargo against Japan. He also served as a member of the La Follette subcommittee to investigate the abuse of the civil liberties of workers who were prevented from organizing or joining trade unions. During his first year as a senator he married Anne Duffy (30 Dec. 1935), the longtime confidential secretary at his Seattle law office. They did not have children. On 16 December 1940 he resigned from the Senate to accept an appointment as U.S. judge for the Eastern District of Washington, a position he held until 1944, when he became dean of the Gonzaga Law School in Spokane.

Following President Roosevelt's death in April 1945, his successor, Harry S. Truman, a former close colleague and friend of Schwellenbach when both were freshmen New Deal senators, asked Schwellenbach in May 1945 to serve as secretary of labor. Truman turned to Schwellenbach, because he had built a deserved reputation as a friend to organized labor and was much admired by Philip Murray, president of the Congress of Industrial Organizations (CIO), and other labor leaders. Schwellenbach fought attempts by conservative Republicans and southern Democrats to gut New Deal prolabor, prounion legislation and to weaken the National Labor Relations Board. He was an especially bitter critic of the Taft-Hartley Act, passed over a presidential veto in 1947, a law that diluted the prounion provisions of the 1935 National Labor Relations (Wagner) Act. Although an ally of the labor movement, he denounced labor radicalism, approving efforts by labor leaders to curb Communist influence in the organized labor movement and endorsing legislation to outlaw the Communist party.

Schwellenbach served as secretary of labor during an especially troublesome period, the post–World War II upheaval in industrial relations, which witnessed the most tumultuous wave of nationwide strikes ever in U.S. history. From 1945 through 1948 he found himself beset by labor conflicts in all the nation's major mass-production industries and its transportation sector, heading a department weakened by congressional attacks and budget cuts, and himself unable to resolve disputes to the satisfaction of labor leaders, business executives, and leading politicians. Frustrated by his impotence at settling industrial conflicts, primarily through his and his department's efforts at mediation and conciliation, Schwellenbach began to suffer severe heart problems, which grew progressively worse as the labor problem intensified. He finally succumbed to coronary disease while a patient at Walter Reed Army Medical Center in the nation's capital. Never a major national political figure, Schwellenbach typified the far western Democrats who, during the decades of the 1930s and 1940s, acted as ardent New Deal and Fair Deal reformers and who claimed that they represented the "common people."

• The Schwellenbach papers are in the Library of Congress. His role in the postwar labor upheaval can best be followed in R. Alton Lee, *Truman and Taft-Hartley: A Question of Mandate* (1966); Donald R. McCoy, *The Presidency of Harry S. Truman* (1984); and Alonzo Hamby, *Beyond the New Deal: Harry S Truman and American Liberalism* (1973). Obituaries are in the *New York Times*, 11 June 1948, and the *Nation*, 19 June 1948.

MELVYN DUBOFSKY

SCHWIMMER, Rosika (11 Sept. 1877–3 Aug. 1948), pacifist and feminist, was born in Budapest, Hungary, the daughter of Max Schwimmer, an experimental farmer who raised seed corn, produce, and horses, and Bertha Katscher. Schwimmer's upper-middle-class, secularized Jewish family had a history of involvement in progressive political and social movements.

Rosika Schwimmer grew up in the provincial cities of Temesvár (now Timisoara, Rumania) and Szabadka (now Subotica, Serbia), where she attended convent and public schools while also receiving private tutoring in music and languages. In 1895, when her father's business failed, Schwimmer was forced to take a job as a bookkeeper, a skill she had acquired during six months of commercial school. Schwimmer's career as a clerical employee in Budapest sparked her first successful political campaign in favor of the organization of women workers. In 1897 she founded the National Association of Women Office Workers, then the Hungarian Association of Working Women (1903), and, one year later, the Hungarian Council of Women. These organizations worked to improve the social, economic, and political status of women. Schwimmer's organizational leadership as well as her political articles in the German and Hungarian press established her reputation as a leading women's rights advocate.

In 1904 Schwimmer rose to prominence in the international women's movement when she was invited to address the International Council of Women and the International Women's Congress in Berlin. There she met Carrie Chapman Catt, president of the newly formed International Woman Suffrage Alliance, who recruited her as a participant in the battle for woman suffrage. Inspired by Catt, Schwimmer returned to Budapest to organize the Hungarian Feminist Association, which won suffrage for Hungary's women in 1920.

From 1904 until 1914 Schwimmer labored as a writer and organizer in Hungary. Her many political campaigns included not only woman suffrage, but also birth control, marriage reform, and abolition of child labor. She lectured throughout Europe, published a novel and short stories, and edited the Hungarian feminist journal *A Nö* (The Woman) from 1907 until 1928.

In 1911 Schwimmer married Paul Bédy, a journalist, but the couple divorced two years later. Schwimmer never remarried or had any children. Her life revolved around her political and social concerns, and with the onset of World War I, her energies were consumed by political campaigns and devotion to the pacifist cause.

In 1914 Schwimmer moved to London to fulfill her duties as press secretary of the International Woman Suffrage Alliance. The night that Britain entered World War I (4 Aug. 1914), Schwimmer drafted a proposal to convene a conference of neutral nations to settle the international conflict without war. Shortly thereafter she left for the United States, where she met with both President Woodrow Wilson and Secretary of State William Jennings Bryan, attempting to convince the United States to sponsor the neutral mediation conference. When Wilson declined, Schwimmer embarked on a nationwide lecture tour to rally public opinion for the pacifist cause as well as for woman suffrage. In 1915 Schwimmer joined Jane Addams in creating the Women's Peace party, with Addams as president and Schwimmer as international secretary. That same year, The Hague Congress of Women, at Schwimmer's suggestion, organized delegations to meet with the leaders of both neutral and belligerent nations and urge them to pursue peaceful mediation. Addams headed the delegation to the belligerents while Schwimmer led the delegation to the neutral countries.

When the United States refused to sponsor a mediation conference, Schwimmer set out to organize an unofficial international meeting. In November 1915 she convinced Henry Ford, the prominent automobile manufacturer, to sponsor a private peace conference to be held in Stockholm. With Schwimmer as an expert adviser, the American delegation sailed on the *Oscar II* and convened the Ford Neutral Mediation Conference on 8 February 1916. The Peace Ship expedition met with ridicule and criticism from the press from the time it left port. Unwilling to take the peace mission seriously, the American press portrayed the project as disorganized, reported internal squabbling among the delegates, and attacked Schwimmer as an ineffective leader. Ford departed midway through the voyage, complaining of illness. Many of the delegates openly attacked Schwimmer's strong leadership tactics and questioned her fiscal management. In the wake of attacks against her, Schwimmer resigned her position as adviser to the expedition. A determined and often uncompromising leader, Schwimmer had alienated many of the women delegates, and her public reputation had been severely damaged by the negative press accompanying the peace mission.

In 1918, after Hungary declared itself a republic, Schwimmer, who had remained in Europe after the conference, was appointed minister to Switzerland (Nov. 1918–Mar. 1919), an unusual diplomatic post for a woman of her generation. However, Schwimmer lost her position and was refused permission to leave Hungary after the republic was overthrown by Béla Kun's Communist regime. Menaced by the counterrevolutionary forces that in turn overthrew Kun, Schwimmer escaped to Vienna in 1920.

When she emigrated to the United States in 1921, Schwimmer found that she had become a notorious public figure. Press accounts and right-wing organizations charged her with a wide range of imagined misdeeds. She was called a German spy as well as a Bolshevik agent; she was accused of duping Henry Ford into sponsoring the Peace Ship and inciting his anti-Semitic hatred. Fueled by the 1920s right-wing backlash against feminists and pacifists as well as the xenophobia and anti-Semitism of the Red Scare, the attacks against Schwimmer effectively terminated her public career and alienated many of her colleagues in the pacifist and suffrage movements.

In 1928 Schwimmer's application for citizenship was denied in a Chicago federal district court because, as a pacifist, she refused to pledge to bear arms in defense of the country. In 1929 the U.S. Supreme Court upheld the decision, which was almost universally denounced by editorialists and commentators. The Supreme Court cited not only her refusal to bear arms (though the nation had never required persons of her sex or age to serve), but also her advocacy of world government and her profession as a "propagandist" as rendering her unfit for citizenship. Schwimmer remained in New York City as a resident alien for the rest of her life.

Schwimmer was never able to resume her career as a journalist and public speaker, but she continued to devote her energies to pacifist and feminist campaigns. With Mary Ritter Beard, she drafted a plan for the establishment of a World Center for Women's Archives. In 1937 she and her friend Lola Maverick Lloyd launched a Campaign for World Government, hoping to create a democratic federation of nations. That same year Schwimmer's devoted followers organized to present her with an unofficial World Peace Prize. She was nominated for the Nobel Peace Prize in 1948 but died that year in New York before an award recipient was named.

Schwimmer possessed a forceful personality that earned her both devoted followers and powerful detractors. Her fire and brilliant oratory were matched by a stubborn militancy that often alienated co-workers. Throughout her life and career, however, Schwimmer never wavered in her ideals, remaining forceful, determined, outspoken, and committed to realizing the goals of world peace and equality.

• The Schwimmer-Lloyd collection at the New York Public Library houses Schwimmer's personal papers as well as those of her friend and colleague Lola Maverick Lloyd. The collection includes correspondence, newspaper clippings, pamphlets, books, photographs, and other material reflecting Schwimmer's career. Some of Schwimmer's papers are included in the collections of other feminists and pacifists, including the Jane Addams, Emily Greene Balch, and Women's Peace Party Papers, Swarthmore College; the Louis P. Lochner and Julia Grace Wales Papers, Wisconsin State Historical Society; and the Lillian Wald and Carrie Chapman Catt Papers, New York Public Library. Additional material about Schwimmer can be found in the Bryan and Ford Expedition papers, Library of Congress, and the Ford Archives, Dearborn, Mich. See also the Schwimmer papers, Hoover Institution, Stanford University.

Little of Schwimmer's published work is available in English. In addition to her journalistic writings in the Hungarian and German press, she produced a Hungarian translation of Charlotte Perkins Gilman's *Women and Economics* in 1906. After her return to the United States in 1921, she found few publishers willing to accept her work, although she did publish a collection of Hungarian legends for children, *Tisza Tales* (1928). Schwimmer also authored the pamphlet *Union Now for Peace or War? The Danger in the Plan of Clarence Streit?* (1939) and coauthored *Chaos, War or a New World Order?* (1937) with Lola Maverick Lloyd.

A biographical sketch of Schwimmer can be found in *Rosika Schwimmer, World Patriot* (1937; rev. ed. 1947), a pamphlet authored by Schwimmer's friends and colleagues. See also Edith Wynner, *World Federal Government: Why? What? How?* (1954) and her article, "Out of the Trenches by Christmas," *Progressive*, Dec. 1965, pp. 30–33.

Secondary works that address Schwimmer's career include Mary Louise Degan, *History of the Woman's Peace Party* (1939); Jane Addams et al., *Women at The Hague* (1915); Keith Sward, *The Legend of Henry Ford* (1948); Burnet Hershey, *The Odyssey of Henry Ford and the Great Peace Ship* (1967); Anne Wiltsher, *Most Dangerous Women: Feminist Peace Campaigns of the Great War* (1985); Barbara J. Steinson, *American Women's Activism in World War I* (1982); Beth S. Wenger, "Radical Politics in a Reactionary Age: The Unmaking of Rosika Schwimmer, 1914–1930," *Journal of Women's History* 2 (Fall 1990): 66–99. The court briefs and reports from Schwimmer's citizenship case can be found in *U.S. v. Rosika Schwimmer*, 279 U.S. 644. An obituary is in the *New York Times*, 4 Aug. 1948.

BETH S. WENGER

SCHWINGER, Julian Seymour (12 Feb. 1918–16 July 1994), physicist, was born in New York City, the son of Benjamin Schwinger, a successful dress designer and manufacturer, and Belle Rosenfeld. He attended Townsend Harris High School and entered the College of the City of New York in 1934. While in high school he set about reading the *Encyclopaedia Britannica*, continuing until reaching the article on physics, which captured his interest; he next started to read Paul Dirac's masterpiece, *The Principles of Quantum Mechanics* (1930), which he mastered before entering college. Although his remarkable abilities were recognized, he neglected his formal studies and had academic difficulties. Through the efforts of Isidor I. Rabi, he transferred to Columbia University in 1936, where he received his A.B. in the same year. He then spent the year 1937–1938 at the University of Wisconsin, working with Gregory Breit and Eugene Wigner on a Tyndall traveling fellowship. Returning to Co-

lumbia, he was awarded his Ph.D. in 1939; his dissertation, "On the Magnetic Scattering of Neutrons," was written under Rabi's supervision.

Schwinger then worked with J. Robert Oppenheimer at the University of California at Berkeley as a National Research Council fellow (1939–1940) and as a research associate (1940–1941). He joined the faculty of Purdue University as an instructor (1941–1942) and assistant professor (1942–1943), before becoming involved in wartime work. He spent the summer of 1943 at the Metallurgical Laboratory of the University of Chicago. Finding the work on the atomic bomb not to his liking, he transferred to the Radiation Laboratory of the Massachusetts Institute of Technology (1943–1945) where he worked on radar with his mentor Rabi. He was an associate professor at Harvard (1945–1947) and became one of Harvard's youngest professors in 1947. He remained at Harvard until 1972, and from 1966 to 1972 he was the Higgins Professor of Physics. After retiring from Harvard, he was a professor of physics at the University of California at Los Angeles (1972–1980), and University Professor there from 1980 until his death.

Schwinger's research spanned a remarkable sixty-year period of virtually uninterrupted activity. At the age of sixteen he wrote his first (unpublished) paper on quantum electrodynamics, which contained an early version of the so-called interaction representation, later to be important in his Nobel Prize work, and commonly attributed to Dirac. The next year he published two papers in the *Physical Review*. It was this precocity that brought him to Rabi's attention in 1935. During that year he met the young Hans A. Bethe, who wrote Rabi that Schwinger's knowledge of quantum electrodynamics was equal to his own; Bethe predicted, "That Schwinger will develop into one of the world's foremost theoretical physicists if properly guided, i.e. if his curriculum is largely left to his own free choice." This advice was heeded, and by the time he received his A.B., Schwinger had already largely completed his dissertation. At Columbia his interests ranged over the general field of nuclear physics, and by 1937 he had eight substantial published papers, including joint work with Otto Halpern (1935), Lloyd Motz (1935), and Edward Teller (1937). Schwinger's work at Berkeley included joint papers with Oppenheimer (1939, 1941) on nuclear and meson theory, and a collaboration with William Rarita (1941). The latter contained the Rarita-Schwinger equation on the theory of particles with half-integral spin.

During the war and in the ensuing years, Schwinger was heavily involved with microwave transmission and radar theory. This encompassed work with Harold Levine on variational methods and Green's functions (1947–1950); a study with Nathan Marcuvitz on integral equations (1951); and a collaboration with David Saxon that eventually resulted in their jointly authored *Discontinuities in Wave Guides* (1968). Schwinger and Saxon became lifelong friends, with the delay in publication being largely due to Schwinger's involvement in other projects and his reluctance to participate in the preparation of the manuscripts. Schwinger's work in the late 1940s and 1950s also included his popular representation of angular momentum in quantum mechanics in terms of the oscillator creation and annihilation operators (not formally published until 1965).

Schwinger's postwar Harvard period began with his integral equation formulation of scattering theory with Bernard Lippmann—the so-called Lippmann-Schwinger equations—and variational principles for scattering, done with Walter Kohn. The first Shelter Island Conference (June 1947) focused his attention back on quantum electrodynamics. There immediately followed his celebrated series of papers, "Quantum Electrodynamics: I–III" (*Physical Review* 74 [1948]; 75 [1949]; and 76 [1949]). This was followed by the brief notes, "On the Green's Functions of Quantized Fields: I & II" (National Academy of Sciences, *Proceedings* 37 [1951]: 452–55, 455–59), and finally "The Theory of Quantized Fields: I–VI" (*Physical Review* 82 [1951]; 91 [1953]; 92 [1953]; 93 [1954]; and 94 [1954]). These contained the principal features of Schwinger's new approach to quantum electrodynamics that was the basis of his Nobel Prize work. The theory was developed in a less abstract form by Feynman, and it had been worked out in yet another approach by Tomonaga in wartime Japan. Many of the original papers were subsequently collected into a reprint volume, *Selected Papers on Quantum Electrodynamics* (1958), edited by Schwinger. The resulting theory is a blend of the approaches of Feynman, Schwinger, and Tomonaga, with important contributions and simplifications added by Freeman J. Dyson.

Schwinger's elaborate mathematical formalism was demanding, and one critic remarked, "Other people publish to show you how to do it, but Julian Schwinger publishes to show you that only he can do it." Later, much of Schwinger's analysis was replaced by the simpler intuitive formulation of Feynman. In 1983 Schwinger, referring to this, commented, "Like the silicon chip of more recent years the Feynman diagram was bringing computation to the masses." But Schwinger apparently regarded such methods more as a pedagogical expedient than as "real physics." Nevertheless, he had a high regard for Feynman's abilities, and in 1989 he characterized him as the "outstanding intuitionist of our age, and the prime example of someone who dared to follow the beat of a different drum." With the replacement of "intuitionist" with "formalist," the characterization is applicable to Schwinger himself. Schwinger's final contributions included the application of his field-theoretic methods to particle physics, the theory of matter (statistical mechanics), and general relativity.

Schwinger received many honors during his lifetime. He shared the 1965 Nobel Prize for Physics with Richard P. Feynman and Shinichiro Tomonaga. Other awards were the Charles L. Mayer Nature of Light Award (1948); the University Medal of Columbia University (1951); the first Albert Einstein Prize, shared with Kurt Gödel (1951); the National Medal of Science (1964); the Humboldt Award (1981); the Premio Citta di Castiglione di Sicilia Award and the Monie A. Ferst Award (both 1986). He was elected a member of the National Academy of Sciences (1949) and was the Gibbs Lecturer of the American Mathematical Society (1960).

In June 1947 Schwinger married Clarice Carrol; there were no children of their marriage. He remained productive and scientifically active, seeking harmony and perfection in his theories, until a few days before his death at his home in Los Angeles.

In person, Schwinger was a small man who was described as having an air of elegance and a taste for large, expensive cars. By nature, he preferred to work alone. His lectures were immaculately prepared and eloquently delivered (usually without notes), a virtuoso performance that challenged his audiences. Although he had about seventy doctoral students (mostly at Harvard), few former students were close to him, though almost all fondly remember his kindness, generosity, and gentle humor. Like Feynman, Schwinger always did his physics for himself, by himself, and in his own inimitable way. This habit, when combined with his penchant for perfection, made him reluctant to publish formal expositions of all his work; however, he wrote almost two hundred papers and several books. Fortunately, much of his unpublished work was presented in his lectures and became common knowledge in theoretical physics, often without its authorship or early discovery being properly acknowledged.

Schwinger usually employed his own technical terminology and developed his own approaches and techniques. During his Harvard years, when he was surrounded by numerous students—including three who became Nobel laureates—his methodology was learned and widely disseminated. However, as he became older and more isolated and the fashions in physics changed, fewer and fewer people understood or bothered to master his innovations. Consequently, much of his later work, in particular that contained in his three-volume treatise *Particles, Sources, and Fields* (1970, 1973, 1983), did not have the impact of his earlier contributions. Nevertheless, Schwinger was a prodigy, a consummate problem-solver, and a pioneer whose influence on the physics of his time was profound. Lloyd Motz, one of his early colleagues and co-workers at Columbia, said it best when he observed, "Schwinger was to physics what Mozart was to music."

• There is an extensive collection of Schwinger's papers in the library of the University of California at Los Angeles. A detailed tribute is Paul C. Martin and Sheldon L. Glashow, "Julian Schwinger: Prodigy, Problem Solver, and Pioneering Physicist," *Physics Today* 48 (Oct. 1995): 40–46. Schwinger's work on quantum electrodynamics is featured in Silvan S. Schweber, *QED and the Men Who Made It: Dyson, Feynman, Schwinger, and Tomonaga* (1994). An engaging insider's view of the creation of quantum electrodynamics and the personalities of Feynman and Schwinger is in Freeman Dyson, *Disturbing the Universe* (1979). Yee Jack Ng, ed., *Julian Schwinger: The Physicist, the Teacher, and the Man* (1996), contains commemorative papers by colleagues, a complete bibliography, and a list of his doctoral students. See also *Selected Papers of Julian Schwinger* (1979), and "Themes in Contemporary Physics: Essays in Honor of Julian Schwinger's 60th Birthday," in two issues of *Physica* 96A (1979). Schwinger wrote two reminiscences of his work that provide valuable insight into his thought: "Renormalization Theory of Quantum Electrodynamics—An Individual View," in *The Birth of Particle Physics*, edited by Laurie M. Brown and Lillian Hoddeson (1983), pp. 329–50; and "A Report on Quantum Electrodynamics," in *The Physicist's Conception of Nature*, edited by Jagdish Mehra (1973), pp. 413–29. The latter contains a noteworthy introduction to Schwinger's later "sourcery" reformulation of quantum electrodynamics. Schwinger wrote comparatively little of an expository or introductory character, but his *Einstein's Legacy: The Unity of Space and Time* (1986), based on his BBC television program "Understanding Space and Time," is an unusual example of his writing skill. Of special interest is his tribute to Feynman, "A Path to Quantum Electrodynamics," *Physics Today* 42 (Feb. 1989): 42–48. Obituaries are in the *New York Times*, 20 July 1994, the *Los Angeles Times*, 19 July 1994, and *Nature*, 25 Aug. 1994.

JOSEPH D. ZUND

SCIDMORE, Eliza Ruhamah (14 Oct. 1856–3 Nov. 1928), author and traveler, was born in Madison, Wisconsin, the daughter of George Bolles Scidmore and Eliza Catharine Sweeney, missionaries. Her parents' journeys to Japan and China served as inspiration for Scidmore's overseas travels in these areas, visits that resulted in nine travel narratives. Educated in private boarding schools and with one year at Oberlin College (1873–1874), Scidmore moved to Washington, D.C., and began a career in writing with letters about high society in the nation's capital that she published in the *New York Times* and the *St. Louis Globe-Democrat*. While Washington remained her permanent home, she journeyed to Alaska, Europe, and Asia (often staying for long periods of time) and wrote articles on travel and politics that appeared in numerous magazines, including *Harper's Weekly*, *Outlook*, *Century*, *World Today*, *Asia*, and *Cosmopolitan Magazine*. Her notes on Alaska were compiled to create her first book, *Alaska: Its Southern Coast and the Sitkan Archipelago* (1885).

In 1890 Scidmore joined the three-year-old National Geographic Society, and over the course of the next thirteen years she served as correspondence secretary, associate editor, foreign secretary, and first female member of the board of managers. Her publications in the society magazine were noteworthy, in part, because she used her own photographs, a hallmark also of her books.

Prolific and verbose, Scidmore published travel writing on subjects as diverse as Alaska, China, and Java. Part guidebook, part memoir, part documentary (with maps, photos, and sketches), her texts are distinctive in that they vividly recount her personal experiences as a tourist while including commentary on culture, politics, and history. In *As the Hague Ordains* (1907), she ventured into more overtly historical and political material by praising the Japanese treatment of prisoners of war during the Russo-Japanese war. Con-

sequently, this book endeared Scidmore to the Japanese and earned her a special decoration bestowed by the emperor of Japan. In an attempt to share her fondness for Japan with the American people, she worked on the project to bring Japanese cherry trees to Washington, D.C. Her ambassadorial interests also took her to the Eleventh and Thirteenth Oriental Congresses, international conferences at which scholars presented findings on linguistic, mythic, religious, and many other topics from studies of Asia and the Near East. Scidmore served as a secretary to the congress that convened in Rome in 1897 and traveled to Hamburg in 1902 as the delegate of the National Geographic Society; in Hamburg she gave a paper on the Nijurokuya Japanese Buddhist folk festival.

Scidmore's work has been praised by biographers for its aims to improve international relations through intercultural understanding. However, given her descriptions of the Chinese (whom she called the "yellow" people) as "the most incomprehensible, unfathomable, inscrutable, contradictory, logical, and illogical people on earth" (*China*, p. 5), she might better be called an "Orientalist" who reconfirms stereotypes of the Chinese as heathen and sinister. In her description of Singapore as a crossroads "where all who travel must stop and see what a marvel of a place British energy has raised from the jungle in less than half a century" (*Java*, p. 3), she celebrates British colonialism at the expense of its effects on the local peoples. Even though her work calls into question the equanimity implied in the title "ambassador" (by which she is often known), her focus on the East, its peoples, rituals, and myths, contributes to a canon of Orientalist literature that interestingly reflects on international relations between East and West at the turn of the century. Furthermore, the extensive depth and breadth of her writing is valuable as a historical record of perceptions by and about Americans traveling abroad.

In 1925 Scidmore made her home in Geneva, Switzerland, and died there. At the request of the Japanese government, her ashes were interred in Yokohama.

• Scidmore's other publications include *From East to West* (1890), *Jinrikisha Days in Japan* (1891), *Westward to the Far East* (1891), *Appleton's Guide-Book to Alaska and the Northwest Coast* (1893), *Java, the Garden of the East* (1897), *China, the Long-lived Empire* (1900), and *Winter India* (1903). Biographical information is sparse, but helpful entries are in Mabel Ward Cameron, *The Biographical Cyclopaedia of American Women*, vol. 1 (1924); Stanley J. Kunitz and Howard Haycraft, eds., *American Authors, 1600–1900* (1938); and Robert McHenry, ed., *Liberty's Women* (1980). Concerning her ancestry, consult Emily C. Hawley, *A Genealogical and Biographical Record of the Pioneer Thomas Scidmore* (1911). About her contribution to the cherry tree project, see Oliver Martin, "How the Japanese Cherry Trees Came to Washington," Chesapeake and Potomac Telephone Company, *Transmitter*, Apr. 1934. Obituaries are in the *New York Times*, 4 Nov. 1928, and the *Evening Star*, 3 Nov. 1928.

SUSIE LAN CASSEL

SCOBEE, Francis R. *See* Challenger Shuttle Crew.

SCOFIELD, Cyrus Ingerson (19 Aug. 1843–24 July 1921), churchman and editor of the Scofield Reference Bible, was born near Clinton, Michigan, the son of Elias Scofield and Abigail Goodrich, pioneer farmers and sawmill owner/operators. His mother died shortly after his birth, and he was raised by his stepmother. No information is available about his education. In 1861 Scofield joined the Confederacy in the Seventh Regiment, Company H, Tennessee Infantry. Apparently he had moved to Wilson County, east of Nashville, Tennessee, to be with his sister Laura, perhaps after his stepmother's death in 1859. After the expiration of his one-year enlistment, he was released from the service, and he dropped into obscurity until 1866, when he appeared in St. Louis, Missouri, doing case work in the law office of Sylvester Pappen, the husband of his oldest sister, Emeline. In the same year he married Leontene Cerré, the daughter of a prominent French family in St. Louis. In the late 1860s he settled in Atchison, Kansas, where he pursued a dual career in law and Republican politics. Admitted to the Kansas bar in 1869, he was elected to the lower house of the Kansas legislature in 1871 and 1872 and was U.S. attorney for the district of Kansas in 1873. For undisclosed reasons, though probably related to alcohol abuse, Scofield left his promising career and returned to St. Louis in 1879, leaving behind his wife, who secured a divorce decree in 1883, and two children.

Details of his life in the 1870s suggest a continual downward spiral of unpaid debts and criminal charges. In 1879, however, he experienced an evangelical conversion. Scofield quickly became assimilated into the religious milieu of St. Louis under the tutelage of James Hall Brookes, pastor of Walnut Street Presbyterian Church. Brookes was a dispensational premillennialist and a prominent figure in the Niagara Bible Conference movement, an annual summer conference that usually met in Niagara, New York, in reaction to certain cultural and religious liberalizing tendencies that questioned the literal integrity and historical accurateness of the Bible. Rooted in the thought of John Nelson Darby, an Englishman identified with the Plymouth Brethren movement (though in Scofield's experience the source was Brookes, who was influenced by religious and cultural factors in Southern Presbyterianism), dispensationalism is a theory of history (its beginnings and eventual outcome) that obtains its structure from the Bible. Between creation and a final cosmic judgment the Bible is perceived as elucidating at least three distinct eras or periods of time (though in Scofield's system there were seven eras): the Old Testament or Covenant of Law, the New Testament or Covenant of Grace, and a future earthly rule of Christ before the end of time. Dispensationalism was presented as a grid for synthesizing the entire Bible.

The zealous Scofield assisted in Dwight L. Moody's 1879 evangelistic campaign, joined the Pilgrim Congregational Church, and became acting secretary of the YMCA in St. Louis. In 1880 he organized and served as pastor of the Hyde Park Congregational Church, having been licensed by the St. Louis association of his denomination. On 22 October 1882 he was called as pastor of a small mission church founded by the American Home Missions Board for the Southwest, an agency of the denomination, in Dallas, Texas. He was subsequently ordained and installed in the First Congregational Church, Dallas, by the North Texas Congregational Association in October 1883. The church grew steadily from fourteen to over eight hundred members before he left in 1895. He married Hettie Hall von Wartz in 1883; they had one child.

In addition to establishing other churches and mission stations in the area, Scofield served as secretary of the American Home Missionary Society of Texas and Louisiana; founded the denominational Lake Charles College in Lake Charles, Louisiana, in 1890 and served as chairman of its board of trustees; organized the Central American Mission in 1890; and, also in 1890, began a correspondence course in the Bible. He wrote *Rightly Dividing the Word of Truth* (1888), which established him as a leading defender of dispensational premillennialism, and he became increasingly prominent in the embryonic transdenominational evangelical movement through his participation in the Niagara Bible Conference movement.

In 1895, following Moody's second evangelistic campaign in Dallas, Scofield was invited to serve as pastor of Moody's church, the Trinitarian Congregational Church of East Northfield, Massachusetts. In addition, he assumed the presidency of the Northfield Bible Training School, a layworkers institute. In 1902, the year after the inauguration of the Sea Cliff Bible Conference—an annual conference conceived by Scofield as the lineal successor of the Niagara Bible Conference that had ceased in 1899 upon the death of Brookes and because of internal dissension—he had the idea of preparing a Bible with explanatory notes defending the notions of a dispensational premillennial interpretation. Work on the project, which was an extension of his correspondence course, consumed several years. Scofield returned to the Dallas pastorate in 1903, though the reference Bible project required extended periods away from his pastoral duties. When the Scofield Reference Bible was finally published by Oxford University Press in 1909, it rapidly became the most widely received defense of dispensational premillennialism.

Basking in the popularity of his reference Bible, Scofield severed his largely absentee connection with the Dallas church in 1909, having in 1908, probably in reaction to perceived liberalism in the Congregational denomination, transferred his ministerial credentials to the Paris, Texas, Presbytery of the Presbyterian Church in the United States. He settled near New York City, where he operated a correspondence and extension school, the New York Night School of the Bible. In 1914 he founded the Philadelphia School of the Bible in Philadelphia, Pennsylvania (now Philadelphia College of Bible). During this period he edited the Tercentenary Edition of the Bible (1911) for Oxford University Press and in 1917 revised his reference Bible. Though enormously popular in the Bible conference circuit, he suffered from declining health. He died at his home in Douglaston, Long Island.

Scofield's influence on the evangelical fundamentalist movement of the early twentieth century was enormous. Not only did he contribute to the infrastructure of transdenominational (later nondenominational) evangelicalism by publishing the reference Bible (the most influential single publication in the movement) and by establishing several Bible training schools and a foreign mission, but his writings defined that segment of the movement known as dispensational premillennialism. Unfortunately, he was secretive about his past and not above distorting the facts of his shadowy years. He was intensely active in his work, which took its toll on both his families. His second wife appears to have been a loyal mate and friend, but he was never close to any of his children. He could incite loyalty, vision, and emulation by others, as attested by a movement that largely viewed his reference Bible as the centerpiece of its existence.

• Private correspondence from Scofield is sparse, though the following locations have material: the archives of Scofield Memorial Church (formerly the First Congregational Church), Dallas, Tex.; a private collection of letters in the Richard Seume Collection, Richmond, Va.; and copies of the Seume collection are available in the archives of the Dallas Theological Seminary, Dallas. There are two biographies: Joseph M. Canfield, *The Incredible Scofield and His Book* (1988), and Charles Gallaudet Trumbull, *The Life Story of C. I. Scofield* (1920). The latter is obliquely laudatory, lamentably biased, and inaccurate; the former provides considerable documentary evidence but is so negatively disposed that the interpretation is flawed. William A. BeVier prepared "A Biological Sketch of C. I. Scofield" (M.A. thesis, Southern Methodist Univ., 1960), but it is flawed by a lack of original research and a dependency on Trumbull. A synopsis of BeVier's work appears in published form as "C. I. Scofield: Dedicated and Determined," *Fundamentalist Journal* 2 (Oct. 1983): 37–39. Frank E. Gaebelein, *The Story of the Scofield Reference Bible, 1909–1959* (1959), is also valuable; see, in addition, Ernest R. Sandeen, *The Roots of Fundamentalism: British and American Millenarianism 1800–1930* (1970). Of other periodical literature the following are recommended: Lewis Sperry Chafer, "Dr. C. I. Scofield," *Bibliotheca Sacra* 103 (Jan. 1943): 4–6; Chafer, "Was C. I. Scofield a Modernist?," *Our Hope* 41 (Sept. 1934): 160–65; and Luther Rees, "Cyrus Ingerson Scofield," *Central American Mission Bulletin* 118 (15 Sept. 1921): 3–11. Other pertinent information is available in Eleanore W. Nichols, ed., *Congregational Year-Book* (1921). An obituary is in the *Dallas Morning News*, 28 Nov. 1921.

JOHN D. HANNAH

SCOPES, John Thomas (3 Aug. 1900–21 Oct. 1970), high school science teacher, was born in Paducah, Kentucky, the son of Thomas Scopes, a railroad machinist who had immigrated from England, and Mary Alva Brown. When the family moved from Paducah to Danville, Illinois, Scopes and his sisters experienced bigotry firsthand. They were ostracized as southerners who sounded different. They and two African-American students were seated separately from the rest of their class during school assemblies.

In most obvious ways, Scopes, nicknamed J. T., had a typical small-town childhood and adolescence: he attended Sunday school, played forward for the high school basketball team, and sneaked off with his buddies to buy liquor and see vaudeville shows during Prohibition. During summers, he worked as a railroad laborer to save money for college. He attended the University of Illinois and completed a bachelor of arts degree in 1924 from the University of Kentucky. In college he decided to study with the best teachers whatever subject matter they taught. He majored in law because he did not have enough credits in any other subject. He designed his own eclectic program of studies, including educational and child psychology, philosophy, social science, math, zoology, and chemistry. While he was enrolled there, a battle over whether evolution should be taught was fought at the University of Kentucky, in which university officials opposed the antievolutionists and won.

At age twenty-four, Scopes became a football coach and teacher of algebra, physics, and chemistry at Central High School in Dayton, Tennessee. Dayton was a "tranquil place," a typical mountain town, about forty miles from Chattanooga, where Scopes associated with a young crowd who went to dances at a local resort hotel. He knew everyone in town, boarded at the home of the hardware store owner, and attended church every Sunday.

In March 1925 the Tennessee legislature passed the Butler Act, a law making it a misdemeanor to teach evolution in the state's public schools. In April, when the principal became ill, Scopes substituted for him, teaching a biology class. The American Civil Liberties Union (ACLU) advertised in May that it would underwrite the expenses for a legal challenge to the Butler Act. School administrators in nearby Chattanooga had declined to take on the role of test case, but Dayton's business and civic leaders wanted to put their smaller town in the limelight. When, in response to their questions, Scopes confirmed that evolution was integral to the teaching of biology, he added that every teacher in the state had violated the law because they all used the same, state-adopted textbook that covered evolution. That book, Hunter's *Civic Biology*, had been in use since 1909. Civic leaders persuaded Scopes to be the defendant in a test case. He agreed though later in his autobiography wrote that he had felt trapped by these influential citizens: "If I had been a worldly-wise young man, I probably would have gone looking for a lawyer after getting trapped into testing the law."

Scopes was quickly arrested for teaching evolution, and the ACLU began to organize his defense. The case developed into a front-page story when William Jennings Bryan was named special prosecutor. Bryan, who had led the fundamentalist campaign against teaching of evolution in many southern Bible belt states, spoke in Nashville the evening before the vote was taken on Tennessee's Butler Act. Ironically, he was a native of Salem, Illinois, where the Scopes family had lived. Bryan and Scopes had attended the same high school in Salem, and Bryan had delivered the commencement speech for Scopes's graduating class. In another twist of fate Scopes's father had become a labor unionist and socialist as a result of the same railroad strikes of 1894 that had caused Clarence Darrow, Scopes's attorney, to abandon his lucrative practice as attorney for the railroads and begin the career that made him famous as defender of trade unionists. Bryan, a three-time Democratic presidential nominee, and Darrow, America's most famous defense lawyer, now squared off to argue fundamental issues of religion and free thought.

Scopes described himself as "merely the center of the storm." He accepted an offer from John R. Neal, who had taught constitutional law, to be his local defense counsel. Neal and several other law faculty at the University of Tennessee had lost their teaching positions over an earlier textbook conflict. Scopes also insisted that the ACLU accept Darrow's services, correctly predicting that at the trial he would need an attorney with courtroom skills, not just legal theories.

The local prosecutor in Dayton, Tennessee, indicted Scopes quickly so that the trial could get under way on 10 July. Publicity seemed more in evidence than did a concern for justice. Dayton began to look like a circus as fundamentalists, tourists, and hundreds of reporters overwhelmed the small community. H. L. Mencken, the writer and social critic for the *Baltimore Sun*, had named the case the "Monkey Trial," and he and other northern journalists mocked the "backward" Tennesseans. Bryan was assisted by his son and four local lawyers; Darrow and Neal were joined by two New York attorneys, Dudley Field Malone and Arthur Garfield Hays. The presiding judge, John T. Raulston, enabled the opposing sides to be as partisan as possible, permitting speech-making and appeals to the national audience. Although Darrow had represented clients without a fee upon their request, this was the first time that he offered his services voluntarily.

During the trial, Scopes stipulated in his brief that he had violated Tennessee's antievolution statute, and students testified that he had taught them about evolutionary theory. The legal issues were the rights of religious groups and government to decide what teachers could or could not teach. The ACLU sought a quick ruling so they could get the case to federal court to test the critical constitutional issue. Darrow wanted to defeat Bryan. Bryan pitted the Bible against the schoolroom, and Darrow argued that Americans could not legislate away the ideas they did not like or understand.

The jury found Scopes guilty on 21 July. His defense had clearly stated the principles of academic freedom, and Scopes announced to the court before his sentencing that "I feel that I have been convicted of violating an unjust statute. I will continue to oppose this law in any way I can. Any other action would be in violation of my ideals of academic freedom—that is, to

teach the truth as guaranteed in our Constitution—of personal and religious freedom." After the verdict, Judge Raulston fined him $100.

Scopes's case was not over, for the decision was appealed. The ACLU wanted other counsel to continue the case, but Scopes demanded that Darrow argue the appeal, which he did in June 1926. In *Scopes v. State* (17 Jan. 1927), the state's highest court asserted that the law was constitutional but reversed the case on judge's error. The court overturned the sentence on the grounds that the jury, not the judge, legally had to set the fine. Further, the supreme court recommended that the prosecutor drop the charges. Scopes had won his case on a technicality, and Tennessee no longer faced the prospect of having to defend the law's constitutionality in federal court. The statute remained on the books until it was repealed in 1967.

Following the trial, Scopes left his teaching job. He began graduate studies in geology at the University of Chicago, where he applied for a fellowship but was told by a university president who administered the fellowship that "he should take his atheistic marbles and play elsewhere." In 1927 Scopes took a job with the Gulf Oil Company. He worked in Venezuela for three years, when the company fired him because he refused to conduct an illegal survey. In February 1930 he married Mildred Walker, whose father had been a construction contractor in Venezuela; Scopes converted to Roman Catholicism for their marriage. They had two children. Although he pursued doctoral studies at the University of Chicago, he ran out of funds in 1932 before completing the degree, and he needed to work to support his children. In 1933 Scopes found another job as a surveyor with the United Gas Corporation. He worked in Texas and Louisiana until his retirement in 1964. He helped promote the 1960 film *Inherit the Wind*, which was based on his case.

In his autobiography of 1967, Scopes concluded that "my own life is a study in environment, heredity, and chance." He worried that he had been "just a warm body" that was needed for the trial. Yet, he served as a powerful symbol of academic freedom to generations of teachers. At the time of his death, in Shreveport, Louisiana, teachers in Tennessee still had to sign a pledge not to teach evolution and no federal court had ruled on the constitutionality of antievolution statutes. Long after the famous "Monkey Trial," state and local boards of education continued to fight battles over whether and how to teach evolution and "creationism" in public school classrooms.

• Scopes's autobiography, written with James Presley, is *Center of the Storm: Memoirs of John T. Scopes* (1967). S. N. Grebstein, *Monkey Trial: The State of Tennessee vs. John Thomas Scopes* (1960), and Ray Ginger, *Six Days or Forever? Tennessee v. John Thomas Scopes* (1958), provide further details. See also L. Sprague De Camp, *The Great Monkey Trial* (1968), and D. C. Ipsen, *Eye of the Whirlwind: The Story of John Scopes* (1973). An obituary is in the *New York Times*, 23 Oct. 1970.

KATHLEEN S. BROWN

SCOTT, Cecil Xavier (22 Nov. 1905–5 Jan. 1964), jazz clarinetist and saxophonist, was born in Springfield, Ohio, the son of a violinist. He started studying clarinet and music theory at age eleven and three years later, while in high school, played in a trio with his drum-playing older brother Lloyd and pianist Don Frye. By 1922 they had enlarged the group to seven pieces, and under Lloyd's leadership Scott's Symphonic Syncopators toured in and around Ohio until June 1924, when they began a four-month residency in Pittsburgh, later moving on to Harlem. The band spent all of 1925 working in Ohio and then went on tour again, adding trombonist Dicky Wells to the fold during a stop in Louisville, Kentucky. From 1926 through early 1927 they appeared at the 101 Club and the Capitol Palace in Harlem, worked as the relief band at the Savoy and Roseland ballrooms, and went on eastern and midwestern tours. On one of these, trumpeters Bill Coleman and Frankie Newton were hired in Lexington, Kentucky, thus bringing the solo potential of the band up to New York standards. Later in 1927 the Scotts played in Toronto, Buffalo, Pittsburgh, Detroit, and Ohio before taking up residency at the Savoy in December. While there, in addition to playing for nightly dancing, the newly dubbed Scott's Bright Boys participated in several of the ballroom's highly publicized "battles of the bands," contests that had them playing against such rivals as Duke Ellington, Fletcher Henderson, and Chick Webb.

In June 1929 Cecil Scott became the leader of the Bright Boys, and, in addition to playing at the Savoy, the now nine-piece band also appeared at the Renaissance Casino and toured for the first time under Cecil's leadership in June 1930. Scott affected a top hat on stage and sometimes performed jump splits off the piano and danced the Charleston while playing his tenor sax. Indeed, much of the Bright Boys' popularity seems to have stemmed from Scott's showmanship, but the band was also respected by fellow musicians for its ability to play hot, swinging arrangements. Besides Coleman, Newton, and Wells, some of the other young jazzmen who played with Scott between 1926 and 1932 were trumpeters Roy Eldridge and Joe Thomas and saxophonists Johnny Hodges and Chu Berry, but they do not appear on any of the band's records. After returning to the Savoy after a long midwestern tour, the men quit en masse when they learned that Scott had been cheating them out of money for months. According to Coleman, "we had such a promising future, and it all went down the drain because of Cecil's greediness" (*Trumpet Story*, p. 5). No longer with a band of his own, starting in the spring of 1932 Scott worked as a sideman with pianist Earle Howard at the Rose Danceland and with violinist/bassist Ellsworth Reynolds at the Renaissance and Lido ballrooms, occasionally finding work as a substitute in Henderson's band. Sometime in the early 1930s, to avoid being involved in a drunken rent party brawl, Scott jumped from the third-story window of a Harlem tenement, a fall that broke his ankle and ultimately led to the amputation of his right leg. After being fitted with an artificial limb, he concentrated on private teaching and after four years resumed his full-time career as before.

Scott joined a short-lived band that Henderson formed in November 1934, but he spent most of 1935–1936 with Vernon Andrade. From early 1936 through the spring of 1937 he worked in Teddy Hill's band but did not accompany the group on its celebrated tour of England and France in June or July 1937. After leaving Hill, Scott worked in Alberto Socarras's Latin band and perhaps others before forming his own group with trumpeter Henry Goodwin in 1943 for a residency at the Ubangi Club and relief work at the Zanzibar and the Savoy. Around 1944 he played with Hot Lips Page in Chicago and after returning to New York led a trio at Jimmy Ryan's with Frye and Baby Dodds. In the mid-1940s he and Dodds frequently played in Art Hodes's trio, and in January 1946, replacing Albert Nicholas, he joined Goodwin, George Lugg, Pops Foster, and Kaiser Marshall in Hodes's sextet. Between 1950 and 1952 Scott worked with drummer Henry "Chick" Morrison, and from 1953 he played in Jimmy McPartland's band and appeared regularly at Central Plaza, often in the company of Willie "The Lion" Smith, Max Kaminsky, Jimmy Archey, "Big Chief" Russell Moore, Jimmy Crawford, and Sonny Greer. He continued freelancing until his death in New York City. Married at age seventeen to a hometown girl (name unknown), the Scotts had thirteen children and three grandchildren by the mid-1940s, almost all of them living together in the couple's Harlem "railroad flat."

Although he played strong-toned tenor and baritone saxes throughout his career, Scott was known primarily for the pronounced throat growl he produced on clarinet. His earliest records, apart from some blues accompaniments to Clara Smith in 1924, were the two sessions he made with his own band in 1927 and 1929, but these are more notable for the solos of Wells and Coleman than they are for his own playing. Far more representative of his style are the many sides he made with pianist Clarence Williams between 1930 and 1937, including those by the Alabama Jug Band in 1934 and Willie Smith (The Lion) and His Cubs in 1935. Among the musicians Scott played with most frequently on the Williams series are trumpeter Ed Allen, tubaist Cyrus St. Clair, and drummer and washboard player Floyd "Fats" Casey, but occasional guests also included James P. Johnson, Ikey Robinson, Buster Bailey, and Russell Procope. Thanks largely to Scott's jovial and rhythmic style, the highly informal Williams records are recognized for their infectious, good-time, party ambience, and indeed this is the way they were marketed rather than as jazz records per se.

During this period Scott also recorded two sessions in 1935 with Henry "Red" Allen, two with Teddy Wilson and Billie Holiday in 1935 and 1937, three with Bob Howard in 1935, and two with Frankie Newton in 1937, as well as appearing on four sessions with Teddy Hill between 1936 and 1937. Scott did not record again until the mid-1940s, when he played on dates led by Rex Stewart, J. C. Higginbotham, Art Hodes, Dicky Wells, and Sandy Williams. However, the March 1946 Hodes session is the most instructive of them all because, unlike the other dates, this was performed by a regular working band, the one currently in residence at the Stuyvesant Casino. While Scott largely plays arranged parts on the saxophone for the other sessions, with Hodes he concentrates on clarinet, revealing a far more mature jazz style than he had in the thirties, a result of his forsaking the novelty growling affectation of his early career and substituting in its stead a more earnest, straightforward manner of playing. In 1953 and 1957 he recorded albums with Willie "The Lion" Smith in contexts that reunited him with Henry Goodwin and Pops Foster, and in November 1959, for the first time in thirty years, he recorded under his own name, leading a Williams-type group including Ed Allen, Don Frye, bassist Leonard Gaskin, and Floyd Casey. Scott's final recording was in August 1961 with a group backing singer Lucille Hegamin.

• The only historical accounts of the Scott brothers' orchestra and others in which Cecil Scott played are in Albert McCarthy, *Big Band Jazz* (1974), but valuable reminiscences of their experiences with him are in Dicky Wells, *The Night People: The Jazz Life of Dicky Wells*, as told to Stanley Dance (1971; repr. 1991), and Bill Coleman, *Trumpet Story* (1991). A very short appreciation and a partial interview with Scott taken in the mid-1940s are reprinted in Art Hodes, *Selections from the Gutter* (1977). For discographical information, see Tom Lord, *Clarence Williams* (1976); Brian Rust, *Jazz Records, 1897–1942* (1982); and Walter Bruyninckx, *Traditional Jazz Discography, 1897–1988* (6 vols.) and *Swing Discography, 1920–1988* (12 vols.), both published serially between 1985 and 1989. A brief career chronology is in John Chilton, *Who's Who of Jazz* (1985).

JACK SOHMER

SCOTT, Charles (c. Apr. 1739–22 Oct. 1813), revolutionary war general and governor of Kentucky, was born in what is now Powhatan County, Virginia, near Richmond, the son of Samuel Scott, a farmer. His mother's name is unknown.

Scott, orphaned in 1755 and placed under a guardian, ran away to join the Virginia regiment as a private under George Washington as the regiment was recouping from the Braddock defeat of 9 July 1755. On an army size roll of July 1756 Scott was described as "dark and swarthy with blk Hair & slim made" and five feet seven inches tall. During the Seven Years' War, Scott served in various garrison and detail duties on the Virginia-Pennsylvania frontier. In the Cherokee War (1759–1761), Scott accompanied the Virginia expedition into eastern Tennessee. There was no fighting. He left service as a captain.

Scott returned to Powhatan County to run the small farm he had inherited. He produced tobacco and flour. On 22 February 1762 he married Frances Sweeney; they had seven children.

At the outbreak of the revolutionary war in Virginia, Scott, who had raised a volunteer company, was made commander of the colony's troops. When forces were formally organized he served as lieutenant colonel and subsequently colonel of a regiment. He participated in the defeat of Governor Lord Dunmore's troops at Great Bridge on 9 December 1775 and in hounding him out of the colony. On 7 May 1776, Congress elected Scott colonel of the Fifth Virginia Regiment in the Continental line.

Scott had a major role at the first and second battles of Trenton on 26 December 1776 and on 2 January 1777. With the Continental army at Morristown during the winter and spring of 1777, Scott led his Virginia Continentals as light infantry in skirmishes. He insisted that his men fire low so that two British soldiers would have to assist a wounded comrade: "leg them damn 'em I say leg them!" Congress appointed Scott a brigadier general on 1 April 1777. He was in the thick of battle at Brandywine (11 Sept. 1777), Germantown (4 Oct. 1777), and Monmouth (28 June 1778). Although he retreated without good reason at Monmouth, Scott was a key accuser of General Charles Lee (1731–1782), resulting in Lee's court-martial and conviction. For the remainder of 1778 Scott commanded the new light infantry corps and Washington's intelligence operations.

In 1779 and 1780, Scott was in Virginia recruiting troops for the southern army and was also in charge of defending the state from British expeditions. He joined the army of General Benjamin Lincoln (1733–1810) at Charleston on 30 March 1780 as the city was under siege by the British. Lincoln's army surrendered on 12 May 1780, and Scott and other officers were interned as prisoners of war at Haddrell's Point, across from Charleston. He was paroled in March 1781 and exchanged for Lieutenant Colonel Lord Francis Rawdon in February 1782.

In early 1787, having sold his farm, Scott took his family to Kentucky and settled along the Kentucky River (near present-day Versailles). In the early years he had to fend off Indians and witnessed the scalping and killing of his son Samuel. Another son, Merritt, met the same fate in Josiah Harmar's Indian campaign of 1790. Scott was appointed major general of the Kentucky militia and served on the federal Board of War for Kentucky. He was a delegate to the Virginia House of Delegates from 1789 to 1791 and several times was a presidential elector (for the Democratic-Republicans).

Scott led futile Indian campaigns in April 1790 along the Scioto River and into the Wabash country in May 1791. In 1793 he again entered the field in conjunction with General Anthony Wayne's abortive Indian campaign into the Ohio country. The following year, again bringing his Kentucky militia to aid Wayne, Scott fought at the battle of Fallen Timbers, on 20 August 1794; his mounted troops became entangled in the woods and brush and contributed little to the victory.

Scott continued to look after his farm and acquired a reputation for being a heavy drinker. His wife died on 6 October 1804. On 25 July 1807 Scott married Judith Cary Bell Gist, the 57-year-old widow of Colonel Nathanael Gist, and moved to the 3,000-acre Gist plantation, "Canewood," in Clark County, Kentucky. Scott had achieved the status of country gentleman.

By 1808, patriotic fervor had mounted over Great Britain's violations of American neutral rights. The "Spirit of '76" became a rallying cry on the frontier. As Kentucky's highest ranking revolutionary officer and one of the last surviving revolutionary war generals, Scott emerged as the popular hero. He was elected governor in August 1808. Among his campaign aphorisms, the best known is, "The people, when they got wrong had to get damned wrong before they could get right."

Scott, assisted by his able and learned secretary of state, Jesse Bledsoe, vigorously performed his duties as governor. He exercised vetoes in the public interest of the state and attempted to quiet enthusiasm for war by advocating equanimity in the treatment of both France and Great Britain. Thanks to Bledsoe, Scott's speeches were extraordinarily eloquent. On 3 December 1811, in his annual commonwealth message, he warned, "We should ever bear in mind, that we have nothing so much to fear as from ourselves."

Nevertheless, Scott committed the Kentucky militia to go out of state and fight with General William Henry Harrison's army, first at Tippecanoe in November 1811 and then in an invasion of Canada. Scott greatly aided Harrison's military career. Scott implored President James Madison to employ Harrison in "a strong campaign against the northwestern Indians"; he also secured Harrison's appointment as brevet major general of the Kentucky militia.

After leaving the governorship in August 1812, Scott returned to his plantation. Of his children, noteworthy is the marriage of Martha to George M. Bibb, later U.S. senator and secretary of the treasury under President John Tyler. During his governorship, Scott slipped on the steps of the governor's mansion and afterward used crutches. He died at Canewood after a long illness.

• Scott's military and public papers are found in collections of revolutionary war officers (including the Washington papers, Library of Congress) and Virginia and Kentucky state archives. His own personal papers were destroyed by mice while in the possession of George M. Bibb. The University of Kentucky has a small collection of Scott material, and the Huntington Library has correspondence between Scott and two of his sons, Charles and Daniel. For the governorship, see Papers of the Governors–Charles Scott at the Kentucky Department for Libraries and Archives in Frankfort. The full treatment of Scott's life is Harry M. Ward, *Charles Scott and the "Spirit of '76"* (1988); in addition to notes, this work contains a bibliography of manuscript sources. An anecdotal account of Scott as governor is found in Colonel Orlando Brown, "The Governors of Kentucky," *Register of the Kentucky State Historical Society* 49 (1951): 93–112. Obituaries appear in the *Kentucky Gazette*, 26 Oct. 1813, and the *Niles' Weekly Register*, 25 Feb. 1815.

HARRY M. WARD

SCOTT, Charlotte Angas (8 June 1858–8 Nov. 1931), mathematician and educator, was born in Lincoln, England, the daughter of Caleb Scott and Eliza Ann Exley. Her father was pastor of the Congregational church in Lincoln and served as principal of the Lancashire Independent College (now the Congregational College) near Manchester. When Scott was a child, mathematical and logical games formed part of her home entertainment. Both gifted and diligent, she was privately tutored at home.

In 1876 Scott won a scholarship to Girton College, Cambridge. Geometry was her forte, and she helped found a club at Girton whose aim was to solve all mathematical problems that were brought before the group. From 1880 to 1888 a number of her problems and solutions first appeared in the *Educational Times* and then in *Mathematical Questions and Their Solutions from the "Educational Times."* In 1880 she was granted permission to take the Mathematical Tripos Examination, a fifty-hour ordeal spread over nine days endured by all students who sought an honors degree in mathematics from Cambridge. Scott finished equivalent to eighth place (bracketed with another mathematics student) and became the first woman to achieve first class honors on the Mathematical Tripos Examination. When the names of the examinees were read, a pause preceded the name of the Eighth Wrangler, and a large chorus of undergraduates who were aware of the results threw their hats in the air and shouted with glee "Scott of Girton! Scott of Girton!"

Because of her achievement on the Tripos examination, beginning in 1881 women were admitted to Cambridge examinations normally and not just by the courtesy of the male examiners. They were also allowed to have their names publicly announced. Women were not granted degrees from Cambridge University until 1948, but after 1881 women who were successful on the Tripos examinations were given certificates of achievement from the university.

Scott served as a resident lecturer at Girton (1880–1884), and during that period she studied modern algebra, Abelian functions, theory of numbers, theory of substitution, and theory of semi-invariants under the supervision of the renowned mathematician Arthur Cayley. Scott took external examinations and received two first class degrees from the University of London, a B.Sc. in 1882 and a D.Sc. in 1885.

Scott specialized in the analysis of the properties of algebraic curves of degree higher than two (plane curves that were neither linear nor conics). She worked in the field of algebraic geometry, in particular on problems involving the analysis of singularities of algebraic curves. Her text *An Introductory Account of Certain Modern Ideas and Methods in Plane Analytic Geometry* (1894) illustrated her geometric intuition and acumen. It integrated algebraic and geometric concepts and led diligent students to the frontiers of geometric research. In 1931 much of her work was generalized in B. L. van der Waerden's epoch-making text *Modern Algebra.*

Scott was the first British woman to receive a doctorate. The only European woman to precede her with a doctorate in mathematics was Russian mathematician Sofya Kovalevskaya. Scott remained a British citizen all her life, but in 1885 she accepted a position as head of the mathematics department at Bryn Mawr College in Pennsylvania, serving in that position for the next thirty-nine years. She was the only mathematician on its founding faculty of nine and was the first woman in the United States to hold a doctorate in mathematics. A dynamic teacher of undergraduates who was never tolerant of slipshod work or bluffing, Scott was patient with the slow and immature and believed in challenging students to their utmost and in broadening their horizons. She was well known for her no-nonsense style.

In 1891 Scott joined the New York Mathematical Society when it first opened its membership to those outside New York. The group was subsequently reorganized in 1894 into the American Mathematical Society (AMS). Scott was the first woman to serve on the AMS Council (1891–1894 and 1899–1902) and as a vice president (1905–1906). She was also a member of the London Mathematical Society, the Edinburgh Mathematical Society, the Deutsche Mathematiker-Vereinigung, and the Circolo Mathematico di Palermo and was an honorary member of the Amsterdam Mathematical Society.

Scott served as coeditor of the *American Journal of Mathematics* (1899–1926) with Abraham Cohen and Frank Morley. She traveled to England often and was the first American-based mathematician whose work was widely recognized in Europe. Her recognition and presence provided a link between the American and European mathematical communities. In 1900 she was one of seventeen American delegates to the World Congress of Mathematicians (WCM) in Paris and reported on the meeting to the membership of the AMS in its *Bulletin.* Her attendance at the WCM may well have influenced one young German woman who was also present, Emmy Noether, to change her field from the humanities to mathematics. Noether went on to become one of the foremost algebraists of the twentieth century.

In 1901 Scott was instrumental in founding the College Entrance Examination Board and served as its chief examiner in mathematics (1902–1903). In her position, she proved influential in setting directions in mathematics for the high school curriculum.

While at Bryn Mawr Scott supervised seven doctoral dissertations. She and her students exhaustively cataloged the possible arrangements of the singular points of various types of equations, locating and describing nodes, cusps, double tangents, and "inflexions." She urged students to distinguish carefully between proofs and examples, and her style of proof was the forerunner of the rigorous presentation that characterizes twentieth-century mathematics. Neither she nor any of her doctoral students married. During her tenure Bryn Mawr was surpassed only by the University of Chicago and Cornell University in the number of women granted doctoral degrees in mathematics.

In 1922 Scott was honored by the AMS and Bryn Mawr, who named their first endowed chair for her. The main address was given by British philosopher Alfred North Whitehead, who had turned down all other invitations while in the United States. Whitehead said of Scott that her life's work "is worth more to the world than many anxious efforts of diplomatists."

Scott's hearing deteriorated throughout her life, and she was frequently in delicate health. In 1906 she developed acute rheumatoid arthritis. In 1918 her house was struck by lightning, and the bolt passed through her. The incident slowed her down and caused some neurological damage. She retired from Bryn Mawr in 1924 and returned to Cambridge, England, a year later. In retirement she bet on the horses, took up golf, gardened, and developed a new strain of chrysanthemum. She died in Cambridge.

• Scott's papers are in the Canady Library archives at Bryn Mawr. For further biographical information see Patricia Kenschaft's articles in *A Century of Mathematics in America,* vol. 3 (1989), *Women in Mathematics: A Biobibliographic Sourcebook* (1987), and *College Mathematics Journal* 18 (Mar. 1987): 98–110. All of Kenschaft's articles contain extensive bibliographies on Scott. Two obituary notices worthy of mention are Francis S. Macaulay, "Dr. Charlotte Angas Scott," *Journal of the London Mathematical Society* 7 (1932): 230–40; and Isabel Maddison and Marguerite Lehr, "Charlotte Angas Scott: An Appreciation," *Bryn Mawr Alumnae Bulletin* 12 (1932): 9–12.

JAMES J. TATTERSALL

SCOTT, Colin Alexander (11 Feb. 1861–5 Apr. 1925), psychologist and educational reformer, was born in Ottawa, Ontario, Canada, the son of the Reverend Robert Scott and Isabel Laird. His father's work eventually led the family to move to New York City, where in 1876–1877 Scott entered the preparatory program of the College of the City of New York. He went on to Queen's University in Kingston, Ontario, where in 1885 he received the B.A. While an undergraduate, he married Helen McCall of Kingston; they had five children. In his early career he had difficulty choosing between teaching and painting as a profession. He studied at the Ontario Art School from 1885 to 1887 and continued to paint for pleasure throughout his life, exhibiting his work widely in the eastern United States. Though he had excelled in chemistry at Queen's University, his interest in philosophy and psychology eventually led him to graduate study at Clark University, a new institution with a strong focus on graduate education; he received a Ph.D. in psychology in 1896. Scott taught psychology at the Chicago Normal School from 1897 to 1901; at Miami University, Oxford, Ohio, from 1901 to 1902; at Tufts College from 1910 to 1911; and at the Boston Normal School from 1902 to 1910 and from 1911 to 1915. He was professor of education at Mount Holyoke College from 1915 to 1925, and he was also a member of the American Psychology Association.

Scott opposed the traditional approach to educating children through rote learning and stereotyped recitation, believing that children learned most effectively in small work groups of four or five students in which they were allowed to work out specific problems on their own. These classroom groups, although supervised by an instructor, were largely self-governed and set their own work standards and criteria by which to judge their efforts. He described this approach as "socialized teaching" and believed that it could be adapted for use with groups of all ages. His initial work with the group method of study was carried out with junior high school students and eventually involved elementary and high school students as well. He promoted this approach primarily through several publications that appeared in *Social Education Quarterly* in 1907–1908, as well as in his book *Social Education* (1908). His ideas gained momentum with the founding of a social education club by faculty members of Harvard University, Tufts College, and the Massachusetts Institute of Technology, along with some secondary teachers. Although the concept of social education was already a popular topic of discussion in higher education when he began writing professionally, Scott was a leading social education theorist and educational reformer whose ideas and applied work advanced the social education movement. Others later elaborated on his methods, using terms such as the "project method" and the "Dalton Plan" to describe a variety of popular education approaches in which students pursued their interests in small work groups of four to five pupils during part of the school day.

In the latter part of the twentieth century Scott's ideas about educating children continued to thrive in the form of cooperative learning models in education that were nearly identical to his original conception of socialized teaching. Cooperative learning models employ small group discussion among students, problem-solving techniques, and cooperative objectives, as well as guidance and mentoring by a teacher. These methods encourage student participation and promote learning.

During the last five years of his life Scott was the general supervisor of methods in the Springfield, Massachusetts, elementary and junior high schools, a position that involved collaborating with teachers and administrators and giving teachers individual instruction in applying his theories and methods in the classroom, with positive results. He employed objective tests of learning by which students themselves could assess their progress on a weekly basis. With the help of an instructor, students established learning goals and objectives and levels of mastery by which they were later able to judge the results of their group learning. His success in this innovative endeavor gained him national attention as an educational consultant and lecturer on educational reform.

After experiencing a severe episode of influenza while abroad when he was sixty-three, his health deteriorated, and Scott died suddenly the following year at the home of his daughter in Brookline, Massachusetts. He was working on a book about sex and art at the time of his death.

• Other publications by Scott appeared in the *Social Education Quarterly* (Mar. 1907–Jan. 1908). His doctoral thesis, "Old Age and Death," appeared in the *American Journal of Psychology* 8 (1896): 67–122. An obituary is in the *Springfield Daily Republican*, 7 Apr. 1925.

JOHN SCHIFANI

SCOTT, Dred (c. 1800–17 Sept. 1858), slave, was born of unknown parentage in Southampton County, Virginia, the property of plantation owner Peter Blow. After brief sojourns in Huntsville and Florence, Alabama, in 1830 the Blow family settled in St. Louis where, strapped for funds, Blow sold Scott to Dr. John Emerson. In 1833 Emerson's career as army surgeon took him, among other places, to Illinois and to what was then a part of Wisconsin Territory (now Minnesota). Scott accompanied him into these areas, one a free state and one a territory that had been declared free by the Northwest Ordinance of 1787 and the Missouri Compromise of 1820. In 1836 or 1837, while at Fort Snelling in Wisconsin Territory, Scott married Harriet Robinson, whose master, Major Lawrence Taliaferro, transferred her ownership to Emerson. Dred and Harriet Scott subsequently had two daughters. Posted in 1840 to the Seminole War in Florida, Emerson left his wife, Eliza Irene Sanford Emerson, and the slaves in St. Louis. Emerson returned the following year but died shortly thereafter.

The exact whereabouts of the Scotts for the next few years are uncertain, except that they were hired out to various people in St. Louis, a frequent experience for city-dwelling slaves. They seem also to have reestablished close relations with the Blow family, Dred's former owners.

On 6 April 1846 Dred and Harriet Scott sued Irene Emerson for freedom. *Dred Scott v. Irene Emerson* was filed in a Missouri state court under Missouri state law. (Two separate litigations were pursued. Since both entailed the same law and evidence, only Dred's advanced to conclusion; Harriet's suit was held in abeyance, under agreement that the determination in her husband's case would apply to hers.) Contrary to later widespread rumor, no political motivation attached to the institution of this suit; only when it reached the Missouri Supreme Court did it acquire the political overtones that made it so famous later. The suit was brought for one reason only: to secure freedom for Dred Scott and his family. Evidence suggests that Scott learned of his right to freedom from the white abolitionist lawyer Francis Butter Murdoch, recently moved to St. Louis from Alton, Illinois, where he had prosecuted criminal offenders in the Elijah P. Lovejoy riots and murders. Another possible instigator was the Reverend John R. Anderson, a former slave who was pastor of the Second African Baptist Church in St. Louis to which Harriet Scott belonged. Murdoch posted the necessary bonds and filed the legal papers that actually instituted the suit. Shortly thereafter, however, he moved to California.

Based on Missouri law and precedents, Scott's case for freedom seemed incontrovertible. Earlier Missouri Supreme Court decisions had emancipated a number of slaves whose travels had taken them to free states or territories. Indeed, one of those cases was strikingly similar to Scott's; that slave had also accompanied an army officer to the same military posts in Illinois and Wisconsin Territory as Dred Scott had done. Perhaps that explains why members of the Blow family so readily backed the slave's case when Murdoch left St. Louis. Indeed, even as the litigation dragged on beyond what had promised to be a very quick solution, they continued to provide necessary legal and financial support.

Unanticipated developments converted an open-and-shut freedom suit into a cause célèbre. In the trial on 30 June 1847, the court rejected one piece of vital evidence on a legal technicality—that it was hearsay evidence and therefore not admissible—and the slave's freedom had to await a second trial when that evidence could be properly introduced. It took almost three years, until 12 January 1850, before that trial took place, a delay caused by events over which none of the litigants had any control. With the earlier legal technicality corrected, the court unhesitatingly declared Dred Scott to be free.

But during the delay, money earned by the slaves had been held custodially by the local sheriff, to turn over to either the estate of the late John Emerson (which really meant to Irene Emerson, according to her husband's will) or the freed slaves, depending upon the outcome of the suit. Though not a large sum, those accrued wages made ownership of the slaves more worthwhile in 1850 than they had in 1847. Meanwhile, Irene Emerson had left St. Louis to marry Dr. Calvin Clifford Chaffee, a Massachusetts abolitionist, who was unaware of the litigation involving his wife. She left her St. Louis affairs in the hands of her businessman-brother, John F. A. Sanford, who had earlier been named executor of Dr. Emerson's estate. In Irene Emerson's name, then, and hoping to secure the accumulated Scott family wages, Sanford's attorneys appealed the freedom decision to the Missouri Supreme Court. But also during the delay, slavery had become a national issue of voluble divisiveness. In a singularly partisan 2-1 decision, which overturned long-standing "once free always free" judicial precedent—that once a slave resided in free territory with the knowledge and even tacit consent of the master, he or she became free by virtue of that residence and did not lose that freedom merely upon returning to a slave state—the Missouri Supreme Court on 22 March 1852 blatantly endorsed proslavery tenets, reversed the lower court, and remanded Dred Scott to slavery (*Dred Scott v. Irene Emerson*, 15 Missouri 576).

To clarify the "once free always free" doctrine based on freedom secured under the Northwest Ordinance of 1787 and the Missouri Compromise of 1820, friends of Scott instituted a new case in the federal courts, *Dred Scott v. John F. A. Sanford*. (Court records erroneously misspelled the name as "Sandford.") Though often in St. Louis, Sanford was a legal resident of New York. Scott as a citizen of Missouri suing Sanford thereby created a "diversity" case—that is, a citizen of one state suing a citizen of another state—which could litigate in the federal courts. But it also created a new issue when Sanford's attorneys claimed that Scott was not a citizen because he was "a negro of African descent" and therefore lacked the right to sue in the federal courts. Rather than deal with the matter on those jurisdictional grounds, the court found for Sanford, and the case was appealed to the Supreme Court of the United States.

There, nationally known legal figures argued the case: Montgomery Blair and George T. Curtis for Scott, and Reverdy Johnson and Henry S. Geyer for Sanford. The suit was argued twice, in February 1856 and in December 1856. Up to then virtually unknown, the case now aroused nationwide publicity and deep partisan interest. At first the Court exercised judicial restraint and thought cautiously to avoid controversial slavery matters. Prodded by pro-southern Chief Justice Roger B. Taney and associate justices James M. Wayne and Peter V. Daniel, and by antislavery associate justices John McLean and Benjamin R. Curtis, the Court decided to deal with those explosive issues.

The famous—or infamous—decision, which remanded Dred Scott to slavery, was pronounced on 6 March 1857 by Chief Justice Taney. Each of the concurring and dissenting justices rendered a separate opinion (*Dred Scott v. John F. A. Sanford*, 19 Howard 393). Extreme proslavery and extreme antislavery views were expressed. According to Taney's "Opinion of the Court," blacks were not considered citizens of the United States. Slaves were property protected by the Constitution, and any law prohibiting slavery in the territories (e.g., the Missouri Compromise) was unconstitutional. Regardless of prior free or slave condition, the status of a person entering into a slave state depended on the law of that state.

The decision triggered violent reaction in an already tense sectional-ridden atmosphere. Fearing that it pushed American law close to legalizing slavery throughout the entire country, antislavery forces mounted unprecedented assaults on the decision and on the majority members of the Court. Proslavery forces responded with equal fervor to defend their cause. The tragic result was to split a divided country even more and push it closer to civil war.

As to the slaves themselves, they remained in St. Louis throughout all this litigation, working at various jobs. Legally, however, they had become the property of Dr. Chaffee, Irene Emerson's second husband. Incredulously, though, he did not become aware of that consequence until just a week or two before the decision was announced, and his attorneys informed him that he could do nothing about that ownership until the litigation was concluded. Shortly after the Supreme Court announced its decision, the embarrassed Chaffee transferred his ownership to Taylor Blow in St. Louis—since by Missouri law a slave could be emancipated there only by a citizen of that state. Accordingly, on 27 May 1857 Blow executed the necessary documents to free the slaves. Scott lived only a year and a half longer, working most of that time as a porter in Barnum's Hotel in St. Louis. There he died of tuberculosis. His remains are interred in St. Louis.

• For the best-detailed account of the case's development and of Dred Scott himself, see Walter Ehrlich, *They Have No Rights: Dred Scott's Struggle for Freedom* (1979). Don E. Fehrenbacher's *The Dred Scott Case: Its Significance in American Law and Politics* (1978), which contains an exemplary analysis of the decision, examines that decision within the framework of the history of American slave litigation, as do William M. Wiecek, "Slavery and Abolition before the United States Supreme Court, 1820–1860," *Journal of American History* 65, no. 1 (1978): 34–59, and Harold M. Hyman and William M. Wiecek, *Equal Justice under Law: Constitutional Development, 1835–1875* (1982). See also David M. Potter, *The Impending Crisis, 1848–1861* (1976), and Paul Finkelman, *An Imperfect Union* (1981). The best brief account is Walter Ehrlich, "Dred Scott in History," *Westward* 1, no. 1 (1983): 5–10, reprinted in Robert J. Maddox, ed., *Annual Editions: American History*, 12th ed. (1993).

WALTER EHRLICH

SCOTT, Emmett Jay (13 Feb. 1873–12 Dec. 1957), educator and publicist, was born in Houston, Texas, the son of Horace Lacy Scott, a civil servant, and Emma Kyle. Scott attended Wiley College in Marshall, Texas, for three years but left college in 1890 for a career in journalism. Starting as a janitor and messenger for a white daily newspaper, the *Houston Post*, he worked his way up to become a reporter. In 1894 he became associate editor of a new black newspaper in Houston, the *Texas Freeman*. Soon he became the editor and built this newspaper into a leading voice in black journalism in its region. Initially, he tied his fortune to the state's preeminent black politician, Norris Cuney, and was his secretary for a while.

When Cuney retired, Scott turned to Booker T. Washington, founder of the Tuskegee Institute in Alabama. Scott greatly admired Washington, praising his 1895 "Atlanta Compromise" speech. Two years later, he invited Washington to speak in Houston. Scott handled the publicity and promotion so well that Washington hired him as his private secretary. When Scott moved to Tuskegee on 10 September 1897, he brought with him his wife, Eleonora Juanita Baker, daughter of a newspaper editor. They were married in April 1897 and eventually had five children.

From 1897 until Washington's death in November 1915, Scott was his closest adviser and friend. The two worked together so smoothly that determing which man authored a particular letter can be a challenge. As his top aide, Scott ran Tuskegee when Washington was away. Washington acknowledged that Scott made "himself invaluable not only to me personally, but to the institution" (Washington, *The Story of My Life and Work* [1901]). Scott developed and operated the "Tuskegee Machine," an elaborate apparatus by which Booker T. Washington controlled, influenced, and manipulated African-American leaders, press, and institutions. He also worked closely with Washington in founding the National Negro Business League in 1900. Washington was president of the league, but Scott, as secretary from 1900 to 1922, actually ran it. The two coauthored *Tuskegee and Its People* (1905). Scott served on the three-man American Commission to Liberia in 1909, the report of which led to an American protectorate over Liberia. In 1912 Tuskegee Institute's board made Scott the secretary of the school. When Washington died in 1915, Scott was a leading candidate to succeed him, but Robert R. Moton of Hampton was chosen instead. Scott remained as secretary. He and Lyman Beecher Stowe coauthored a highly laudatory biography, titled *Booker T. Washington* (1916). That year, Scott and others in the Tuskegean camp reconciled with Washington's rival and National Association for the Advancement of Colored People (NAACP) founder, W. E. B. Du Bois at the Amenia Conference on Long Island, New York.

The entrance of the United States into World War I gave Scott a chance to leave Tuskegee and end any rivalry with Moton. He became special assistant to the secretary of war and was in charge of affairs relating to African Americans. While in this post he wrote *Scott's Official History of the American Negro in the World War* (1919). He also wrote *Negro Migration during the War* (1920), under the auspices of the Carnegie Endowment for International Peace. Scott stayed in Washington after the war, becoming a top administrator at Howard University. From 1919 to 1932 he was the university's secretary-treasurer and business manager. He was the top black official until Howard's first black president, Mordecai Johnson, was appointed in 1926. The two clashed. Scott was reduced to secretary of the university but remained at Howard until he retired in 1938.

Meanwhile, he was active in business and politics. Among his business ventures in the African-American community were banking, insurance, and real estate. In politics, he was a staunch Republican. He served on an advisory committee for the 1924 Republican National Convention, specializing in black affairs. He was the assistant publicity director of the Republican National Committee from 1939 to 1942. In 1941 Scott went to work at the Sun Shipbuilding Company of Chester, Pennsylvania, at the request of the Republican party. The company president, John Pew, was a major funder of the party. Pew's company was nonunion. With Scott's help the company established Yard No. 4, staffed by African Americans supervised by Scott. When the war ended in 1945, Scott's yard was dismantled and Scott retired to Washington. From time to time he did some public relations work. He died in Washington, D.C.

• Scott's personal papers are in the Morris A. Soper Library of Morgan State University, Baltimore. His letters and other materials are also found among the Booker T. Washington Papers in the Library of Congress. Many of Scott's letters appear in print in the *Booker T. Washington Papers*, ed. Louis R. Harlan et al. (14 vol., 1972–1989). A detailed account of Scott's career is found in a 1971 M.A. thesis at the University of Maryland, James E. Waller, "Emmett Jay Scott: The Public Life of a Private Secretary." The most useful work for a study of Scott is Louis Harlan's two-part biography: *Booker T. Washington: The Making of a Black Leader, 1856–1901* (1972) and *Booker T. Washington: The Wizard of Tuskegee, 1901–1915* (1983). Other useful books are Rayford Logan's history, *Howard University* (1969), and August Meier's *Negro Thought in America, 1880–1915*. Obituaries are in the *Atlanta Daily World* and the *Washington Post*, both 13 Dec. 1957; the *Washington Afro-American* and the *New York Times*, both 14 Dec. 1957; and the national edition of the *Afro-American*, 21 Dec. 1957.

EDGAR ALLAN TOPPIN

SCOTT, Evelyn (17 Jan. 1893–3 Aug. 1963), writer, was born Elsie Dunn in Clarksville, Tennessee, the daughter of Seely Dunn, a railroad executive, and Maude Thomas. Because of her father's job the family lived in several different cities and towns in the South during her childhood; they settled in New Orleans when she was sixteen. She was raised to take her place in society as a privileged southern matron, but she began rebelling against her family's expectations as a teenager.

She was educated by private tutors and at the preparatory school of Sophie Newcomb College, the women's division of Tulane University, where she later studied art. She was an excellent student, read widely, and became a devotée of the avant-garde. Her parents' unhappy marriage undoubtedly fueled her resistance to their values, and that resistance erupted into outright revolt in December 1913, when she ran off to England with Frederick Creighton Wellman, the much older and married head of Tulane's School of Tropical Medicine. Assuming the names Evelyn Scott and Cyril Kay-Scott, the couple eluded searchers and eventually settled in a remote area of Brazil's Bahia province in the summer of 1914. That fall their son was born in Bahia, where the couple lived for five years with few conveniences. Although primitive living conditions and complications from childbirth permanently damaged Scott's health, she began writing poetry and criticism, and in 1919 she returned to the United States, determined to become a professional writer.

Settling in New York's Greenwich Village with her common-law husband and child, Scott prepared her first book, a collection of imagist poems. Titled *Precipitations*, it was published in 1920 to favorable reviews. During the next eleven years, the heyday of Scott's career, she published thirteen more books and a three-act play, and she contributed poetry and criticism to such leading literary publications as the *Egoist*, *Poetry*, and the *Dial*, occasionally using the pen name "Ernest Souza."

Scott's first novel, *The Narrow House*, was published in 1921 and made her a literary celebrity. Sinclair Lewis and H. L. Mencken, among others, hailed the work for its portrayal of an American family stifled by both conventional morality and self-centered idealism. Scott went on to create a trilogy by continuing the story of the same family in her novels *Narcissus* (1922) and *The Golden Door* (1925).

Escapade, a somewhat fictionalized autobiography in which she described her intellectual and emotional awakening during her years in Brazil, was published in 1923. Separating from her husband not long afterward, Scott adopted a nomadic existence during the remainder of the decade and into the early 1930s, living modestly in Bermuda, France, North Africa, and England. During this time her published works included another trilogy, comprising *Migrations* (1927), *The Wave* (1929), and *A Calendar of Sin* (1931).

Scott's second trilogy was a literary cavalcade that portrayed the development of American life from 1850 to 1914. She created hundreds of characters whose stories she interwove with events in the nation's history, employing techniques that ranged from conventional narrative to stream-of-consciousness interior monologues. Each volume was a critical success, but the second, *The Wave*, received the greatest praise and secured Scott's place as a major American writer of the decade. Many critics believe that *The Wave* is one of the best books ever written about the American Civil War.

Scott's prestige was so great at this time that a critical study that she wrote in 1929 of William Faulkner's *The Sound and the Fury* is credited with gaining Faulkner's art wider recognition and helping him to become an established writer. A year later she published a second volume of poetry, *The Winter Alone*, and in 1933 her novel *Eva Gay* appeared. Written with the assistance of a Guggenheim Fellowship, the novel was a fictionalized account of Scott's relationship with Cyril Kay-Scott, as well as her affair during the early 1920s with Owen Merton, a painter and the father of Thomas Merton.

Cyril Kay-Scott had secured a Mexican divorce from Evelyn in 1928, and around this time—the exact year is unknown—she married John Metcalfe, an English novelist. During the 1930s the couple lived first in the United States and then in Canada, and Scott published two more novels: *Breathe upon These Slain* (1934) and *Bread and a Sword* (1937). Both books examined the plight of the artist in an increasingly totalitarian world. Written from a libertarian viewpoint, their implicit rejection of communism earned Scott scorn from the left-leaning critical establishment. The general reading public found the novels unappealing.

By this time Scott's career had seen its most productive years, and though she continued to write poetry, fiction, and criticism, her output steadily decreased. Her reputation declined markedly during the 1930s, a consequence of both the political climate and general disaffection for the excesses of the previous decade. Her autobiography, *Background in Tennessee*, was published in 1937 but stirred only minor interest. The subject matter of her last published novel, *The Shadow of the Hawk*, had potentially broader appeal—it told the story of a man whose father was wrongly imprisoned for murder—but when the book appeared in 1941 it was barely noticed by critics or readers.

On the eve of World War II Scott moved to London to join her husband, who was stationed there as an officer in the Royal Air Force. They remained in England throughout the war, enduring the Blitz as well as poverty and ill health, and continued to live in reduced circumstances after the war ended. Hoping to resume their careers, they sought financial aid from private organizations, and in 1952 a grant from the Huntington Hartford Foundation enabled them to return to the United States. After a brief stay in California, they moved to New York City, where they settled in a cheap hotel.

In the last decade of her life, living with her husband in one room and struggling with the after-effects of a stroke that left her with temporary aphasia, Scott wrote two novels and two collections of poetry, one of them for children. However, none were published. She died in her sleep in her New York hotel room after returning there from a hospital stay. Her passing was little noted in the press, and the New York newspapers did not carry her obituary.

In recent years there has been renewed critical interest in Evelyn Scott as an innovative writer, a perceptive critic, and a female artist who defied convention to attain her goals.

• A collection of Scott's papers, including manuscripts and letters, is at the Humanities Research Center, University of Texas, Austin. Scott's autobiographical *Background in Tennessee* candidly describes the author's early years and her revolt against her genteel southern upbringing. A major biographical study is D. A. Callard's *"Pretty Good for a Woman": The Enigmas of Evelyn Scott* (1985). See also Mary E. Carrigg, "Escape from 'The Narrow House': The Autobiographies and Fiction of Evelyn Scott" (Ph.D. diss., Univ. of Wisconsin, 1978); and Robert L. Welker, "Evelyn Scott: A Literary Biography" (Ph.D. diss., Vanderbilt Univ., 1958). For a late twentieth-century critical assessment of Scott's work and its significance, see Peggy Bach, "Evelyn Scott: The Woman in the Foreground," *Southern Review* (Autumn 1982): 703–17.

ANN T. KEENE

SCOTT, Hazel Dorothy (11 June 1920–2 Oct. 1981), jazz pianist and singer, was born in Port of Spain, Trinidad, the daughter of R. Thomas Scott, an English professor, and Alma Long, a musician. The Scott family (Hazel, her parents, and her maternal grandmother) moved to the United States in 1924, settling in New York City's Harlem. A child prodigy, Hazel was reading by age three. By age four she was using both hands at the piano (playing by ear), and by age five she was improvising. Her first piano instructor was her mother. At age eight she was heard by Juilliard School of Music professor Paul Wagner, who explained that although she was too young to enter Juilliard formally, he would accept her as his pupil.

She made her debut at age thirteen, advertised as "Little Miss Hazel Scott, Child Wonder Pianist." The recital program announcement added, "Mrs. Alma Long Scott Presents . . . " In addition to being a piano teacher, her mother was a professional alto and tenor saxophonist who organized her own women's orchestra, American Creolians, now that she was sole breadwinner following Hazel's father's death. In her early teens Hazel played piano in her mother's group and doubled on trumpet, an instrument she soon abandoned.

Scott's first professional appearance was in 1935, when she performed with Count Basie and his orchestra at the Roseland Ballroom. Of the experience, she said, "It scared me to death. I had three footprints on my back—those of Lester Young, Jo Jones and Basie." According to all reports, the performance was a memorable one. Scott made her Broadway debut in 1938, appearing in the show *Sing Out the News*. The showstopper was the tune "Franklin D. Roosevelt Jones," as played by Hazel Scott, age eighteen. So successful was her performance that it consistently garnered rave reviews and her salary was instantly increased to $100 weekly.

Also during her eighteenth year, Scott organized her own short-lived band. She early mastered the classics but found it difficult to avoid altering the original score. In December 1940 she played Franz Liszt's *Second Hungarian Rhapsody* at Carnegie Hall. During the performance Scott began "swinging it." And as she often recalled, "The 'long hair' audience loved it." From that day forward, the distinguishing feature of her piano performances was quasi-jazz renditions of classical pieces. She played both jazz and classical music in concert, swung the classics, and mixed styles. As reported in *Time*, "Where others murder the classics, Hazel Scott merely commits arson. . . . She seems coolly determined to play legitimately, and, for a brief while, triumphs. But gradually it becomes apparent that evil forces are struggling within her for expression. . . . The reverse is also true: Into *Tea for Two* may creep a few bars of Debussy's *Clair de Lune*" (5 Oct. 1942, pp. 88 and 90).

Scott made her recording debut in 1939, on a date arranged by jazz journalist/critic/encyclopedist Leonard Feather. Publicized as "The Sextet of the Rhythm Club of London," the group was a racially mixed band that included three blacks of West Indian descent. In 1939 Scott was hired for a three-week fill-in engagement at the newly opened Cafe Society, Downtown, a Greenwich Village night club. When owner Barney Josephson (who loved pianists) heard her, he offered her "a job for life." She was so successful that when Josephson opened a new Cafe Society, Uptown (at East Fifty-eight Street), the star would be Hazel Scott.

There were occasional forays into other prosperous clubs, including Boston's Ritz-Carlton Hotel Roof and the New York City Paramount. Also in 1939 she did two performances at the New York World's Fair. The Hazel Scott/Cafe Society association, formed in 1939, lasted until 1943. Another side trip was to perform in the vaudeville-type show *Priorities of 1942* on Broadway. Of her piano performance, Brooks Atkinson wrote, "She was the most incandescent personality of anyone in the show. . . . There is not a dull spot in her number."

Between 1943 and 1945 Hazel appeared in five movies: *Something to Shout About, I Dood It, The Heat's On, Broadway Rhythm*, and *Rhapsody in Blue*. She shocked Hollywood by going on strike during the filming of *The Heat's On* because "black women extras weren't dressed properly." Filming was halted and was not resumed until the costumes were changed. She was permitted to appear in *Rhapsody in Blue* (her final film) simply because she was already under contract. In 1943 she received the Page One Award from the Newspaper Guild of New York. (In 1978 Scott was inducted into the Black Filmmakers Hall of Fame in celebration of Fifty Years of Black Music Achievement in Film.) By the late 1940s, all of Scott's performance contracts included a clause stating that she would not perform before segregated audiences.

Much has been written about Scott's marriage to the flamboyant congressman and minister Adam Clayton Powell, Jr. Always attracted to artists and the social elite, Powell frequented those places where such persons mingled. In addition, Scott had appeared frequently at various political rallies in New York City, including many for Powell as Harlem's congressional candidate. Soon the two were dining out, most often at "21" and the Stork Club. Powell was the first black elected to the New York City Council in 1941, and in 1944 he was elected to the U.S. House of Representatives, an office he was returned to in each subsequent election until 1970. Throughout his political career he maintained his position as pastor (inherited from his father in 1937) of Abyssinian Baptist Church in Harlem, one of the country's largest black congregations. Scott and Powell were married in August 1945 at Bethel African Methodist Episcopal Church in Stamford, Connecticut, shortly following a divorce from his first wife. Jazz impresario Barney Josephson hosted a reception in Manhattan at Cafe Society, where a host of celebrities were in attendance. The couple had one child.

In early October 1945 newspapers across the country carried the story, "Constitution Hall Ban on Hazel Scott." The Daughters of the American Revolution (owners of Constitution Hall) refused a concert permit to Scott. Though the ban stood, Powell asked President Harry S. Truman to intervene. Shortly following this incident, Scott was scheduled to appear at the National Press Club's annual dinner honoring the president. But she cancelled the engagement, citing as reasons that several members of the seven-member executive committee protested her appearance and that black journalists were being discriminated against.

Her marriage failing, Scott moved to Paris in 1957 with the intention of remaining for three weeks; their divorce became final in late 1960. Three months later, in 1961, she married a Swiss Italian, Ezio Bedin; this marriage was short-lived. Scott remained in Paris for ten years.

On her return to the United States, she spent three years on the West Coast, appearing in the television productions "The Bold Ones," "The Doctors," "Julia," and CBS's "Playhouse 90." Returning to New York City in 1970, she formed the Hazel Scott Trio (with changing personnel). Her last performance was at Kippy's, less than two months before her death in New York City.

• The most thorough coverage (though dated) of Scott is in *Current Biography* (1943). Updated and from the subject's perspective is a 1972 interview by Arthur Taylor that appears in his book *Notes and Tones: Musician-to-Musician Interviews* (1977). An informative article by Hollie I. West, also based on an interview, is in the *Washington Post*, 4 July 1970. As the second wife of a prominent politician, Scott, her life, many musical accomplishments, and political and artistic involvements are covered in Wil Haygood's biography of the congressman, *King of the Cats: The Life and Times of Adam Clayton Powell, Jr.* (1993). A tribute/obituary is in the *Washington Post*, 4 Oct. 1981.

D. ANTOINETTE HANDY

SCOTT, Hugh Doggett, Jr. (11 Nov. 1900–21 July 1994), politician, was born in Fredericksburg, Virginia, the son of Hugh Doggett Scott, Sr., and Jane Lee Lewis. Scott came from an established, Episcopalian family; he was born on an estate once owned by George Washington. After taking courses at the University of Pennsylvania, Scott earned a B.A. from Randolph-Macon College in 1919 and a law degree from the University of Virginia in 1922. That same year the state of Pennsylvania admitted him to the bar. He then opened a law practice in Philadelphia. In 1924 he married Marian Chase; they had one child.

Scott entered politics as a Republican. He served as assistant district attorney of the city of Philadelphia from 1926 to 1941. Voters in Reading, Pennsylvania, sent him to the U.S. House of Representatives in 1940. Reelected in 1942, Scott resigned to join the navy during World War II and eventually earned the rank of captain in the naval reserves. In 1947 Scott reclaimed his House seat and held it for the next twelve years. In 1958 Pennsylvanians elected him to the U.S. Senate. Scott won reelection three times, albeit by nail-biting margins.

Serving in politics during America's years as a superpower, Scott proved a flexible internationalist. He backed President Franklin D. Roosevelt's Lend-Lease Act (1941) to aid Great Britain and President Harry S. Truman's Marshall Plan and Greek-Turkish Aid Bill (1947) to contain the Soviet Union. Later he endorsed U.S. intervention in Vietnam under Presidents John F. Kennedy and Lyndon B. Johnson. When stalemate ensued, Scott proposed a unilateral American ceasefire and a negotiated peace.

On domestic issues, Scott emerged as a moderate, pragmatic Republican. Attuned to concerns of his urban, working-class, and African-American constituents, Scott favored many liberal policies of activist government: public housing, rent controls, and abolition of poll taxes. In 1957 he prevailed on President Dwight D. Eisenhower to support civil rights legislation. Scott also took more orthodox Republican positions. He supported lower taxes, voluntary price controls, and the allegedly antilabor Taft-Hartley Act (1947). He lambasted "big government" and "commie-coddling" Democrats during the presidential campaign of 1948.

In the 1960s Scott continued to balance his centrist outlook with party loyalty. He voted for the civil rights laws of 1964, 1965, and 1968. During the primary contest for the Republican presidential nomination in 1964, Scott backed the moderate governor of Pennsylvania, William Scranton, over the conservative senator from Arizona, Barry M. Goldwater. Goldwater's nomination dismayed Scott, but ever the partisan, he supported the GOP's national ticket. Four years later he endorsed the candidacy of New York's liberal governor, Nelson A. Rockefeller. When the GOP nominated former vice president Richard M. Nixon, Scott worked hard for his election.

In 1969 Scott defeated Howard Baker of Tennessee to succeed the late Everett M. Dirksen of Illinois as Senate minority leader. The triumph stemmed from Scott's seniority, not ideology; few Republican senators had compiled more liberal voting records. Scott's easygoing personality, protean beliefs, and partisan reputation won over many conservatives. "He did not conduct himself as an eastern establishment liberal," recalled one right-wing Republican. "First and foremost he was a Republican Senator and a loyal supporter of the president's program."

As the Republican minority leader, Scott blended independence with party loyalty. "I owed responsibilities," he remembered, "first to the voters of Pennsylvania who elected me; second to the Republican members of the Senate; and finally to the President as interpreter of his wishes." Refashioning Nixon's voting rights proposals, Scott coauthored the Voting Rights Act of 1970, which abolished literacy tests nationwide while keeping southern voting laws under the aegis of federal registrars. In 1969, however, Scott voted against the president's nomination of the conservative judge Clement F. Haynsworth, Jr., to the U.S. Supreme Court. A year later he backed the president's next nominee, G. Harrold Carswell, another conservative judge. (Scott later regretted his decision and denounced Carswell as a racist.) A Sinophile—he wrote a book on Chinese art—Scott endorsed Nixon's visit to the People's Republic of China in 1972. A year later he persuaded a reluctant president to sign a bill prohibiting American combat activities in Indochina.

Scott never lacked critics. Both liberal and conservative ideologues viewed his ever-changing positions as opportunism, not pragmatism. President Nixon found the minority leader's independent streak maddening. To others, his partisanship seemed outdated. Indeed, Nixon White House aide John Ehrlichman dismissed Scott as a "hack."

Scott handled the Watergate scandal of 1973–1974 with a mixture of partisanship and pragmatism. When questions about President Nixon's role first emerged on a national level, the minority leader initially and uncritically backed his president. The disclosure during Senate hearings in the summer of 1973 that Nixon's Oval Office conversations had been taped led Scott to demand full disclosure of the tapes, believing their release would exonerate Nixon of obstructing justice. When the tapes instead implicated the president, Scott informed Nixon that he could not survive impeachment proceedings. Two days later, on 9 August 1974, the president resigned.

Citing advanced age, Scott declined to seek reelection in 1976. Charges that he had received illicit contributions from Gulf Oil Company perhaps influenced his decision to retire. The Senate Ethics Committee ultimately cleared Scott of wrongdoing.

Out of office, Scott remained active, practicing law in Washington, D.C., from 1977 to 1987. Under President Jimmy Carter, Scott cochaired a committee to revise the Panama Canal treaties. In 1989 he served on another committee to commemorate the Senate's bicentennial. Otherwise, Scott passed time with his family. In 1987 Marian Scott died. Scott himself died in Falls Church, Virginia.

Scott's career spanned the rise and eclipse of the moderate/liberal wing of the GOP. Representing northeastern states with urban, working-class, and minority constituencies, Republicans like Scott moved the party toward internationalism in foreign policy and selective use of government power in domestic affairs. By the 1970s, however, the GOP's demographic base had shifted to the South and West, where voters proved skeptical of liberal/statist policies. Proponents of limited government, Presidents Ronald Reagan and George Bush led the party in a conservative direction.

• Scott's papers are housed in the Alderman Library at the University of Virginia. The transcript of a Scott interview with scholar A. James Reichley is at the Gerald R. Ford Library in Ann Arbor, Mich. Important sources include Scott's books, *How to Go into Politics* (1949), *The Golden Age of Chinese Art* (1967), *Come to the Party* (1968), *How to Run for Public Office and Win* (1968), *I've Been to the Party* (1976), and *The United States and China: A Report* (1976). Scott's relations with the Nixon and Ford administrations receive coverage in Reichley, *Conservatives in an Age of Change: The Nixon and Ford Administrations* (1981), John D. Ehrlichman, *Witness to Power: The Nixon Years* (1982), Stanley I. Kutler, *The Wars of Watergate: The Last Crisis of Richard Nixon* (1990), and H. R. Haldeman, *The Haldeman Diaries: Inside the Nixon White House* (1994). To place Scott within the context of the evolving Republican party, consult Nicol C. Rae, *The Decline and Fall of the Liberal Republicans: From 1952 to the Present* (1989), and Mary C. Brennan, *Turning Right in the Sixties: The Conservative Capture of the GOP* (1995). Obituaries are in the *New York Times* and the *Washington Post*, both on 23 July 1994.

DEAN J. KOTLOWSKI

SCOTT, Hugh Lenox (23 Sept. 1853–30 Apr. 1934), soldier and diplomat, was born in Danville, Kentucky, the son of William McKendry Scott, a Presbyterian minister, and Mary Elizabeth Hodge. After William Scott's death, the family moved, and Hugh Scott was reared in Princeton, New Jersey, attending Edgehill and Lawrenceville academies before graduating from the U.S. Military Academy in 1876. Until 1898 most of his service was on the frontier in the West, where he became a keen student of Indian customs and a leading expert on the Indian sign language. In 1880 he married Mary Merrill, daughter of General Lewis Merrill. The couple had five children.

Scott missed combat in the Spanish-American War, serving in frustration as a training camp adjutant in Tennessee while politically connected volunteers and junior men found their way to the fighting. He rose as the protégé of General Leonard Wood, serving as Wood's adjutant during the occupation of Cuba and military government of the Philippines. As governor of the Sulu Archipelago from 1903 to 1906, Scott saw action as a fighter and negotiator and gained considerable administrative experience. Subsequently, he served as superintendent of West Point (1906–1910) and as a unit commander in the Southwest, where he negotiated a series of Indian disputes ranging from land controversies to the return of Geronimo's Apaches to New Mexico.

Scott's star rose when Woodrow Wilson became president. His brother, William, was a distinguished paleontologist at Princeton who had supported Wilson in his intramural battles as college president. As one of his first acts, Wilson appointed Hugh Scott to the rank of brigadier and in 1914 named him chief of staff because he was one of the few army officers the president knew and trusted. Scott also possessed the requisite seniority, wide and varied experience, and good relations with all factions in the army.

Although Scott was not a profound military thinker or strategist, he was adept at implementing the ideas of others, and in matters that attracted his interest he could demonstrate originality and examine policy in detail. He preferred to work within bureaucratic channels, utilizing his familiarity with army routine and escaping fierce partisan opposition. He waged no bitter feuds with fellow officers and retained the confidence of the administration. Scott pressed for preparedness, worked to safeguard the general staff system from the efforts of Congress and others to reduce its size and function, and supervised the initial stages of U.S. involvement in World War I. He championed the creation of a nationally raised and controlled volunteer force, and when this cause failed, he became a leading advocate of conscription. John J. Pershing and Newton D. Baker, among others, credited Scott with laying the groundwork for the World War I draft.

During his tenure as chief of staff Scott became a leading player in U.S. diplomacy regarding the Mexican Revolution, having met Pancho Villa early in 1914. He was a key link between Wilson and Villa during 1914–1915. The president hoped to support a suitable leader for Mexico, and Scott and other figures in and out of government saw Villa, overtly pro-American and apparently amenable to direction, as a likely solution to Mexico's problems. Although Scott pressed Villa's cause, he accepted Wilson's 1915 decision to recognize Venustiano Carranza and lost contact with Villa, who turned against the United States in 1916, sparking the dispatch of the Pershing expedition. Scott's negotiating duties included several meetings on the Southwest border to solve problems ranging from treatment of prisoners by warring Mexican factions to threats against American lives and property. In December 1914–January 1915 he negotiated an end to fighting between Mexican units that had caused intense firing into the town of Naco, Arizona. In May 1916 in the midst of the crisis occasioned by the torpedoing of the *Sussex* by a German submarine, Scott rushed to El Paso–Juárez and negotiated with Mexico's minister of war and future president, Álvaro Obregón. This meeting won a breathing space that allowed the United States to deal with the *Sussex* crisis before Mexican relations flared up again. Scott's success as a negotiator stemmed from his patience, tolerance, diligence, and consistent efforts to avoid the spotlight.

Scott was nominally in charge of the army during the first six months after the United States entered World War I. He took a personal hand in laying the foundations for cooperation with Allied leaders, working for interservice cooperation, and selecting the commanders of the new American forces. He used his influence to prevent a repetition of the confused, politically based appointments of 1898 and to recommend Pershing as commander of the American Expeditionary Force. He also pushed for the annexation of the Virgin Islands and resisted Allied suggestions that the United States dispatch raw recruits piecemeal to France, where they might serve as replacements for the hard-pressed Allies.

Scott was less suited for overall supervision of the army war effort, however. His advancing age, habits forged in the smaller frontier army, and the enormity of the 1917 organizational task reduced his effectiveness, and he lacked the administrative ruthlessness demanded by the job. Most important, after the declaration of war, Scott served only seventy-six days in the War Department. From May until August 1917 he was a member of the ill-fated Elihu Root mission that sought to keep the Russian provisional government in the war. After Scott reached retirement age in 1917, he visited England and France as a military observer. In January 1918 he became commander of the Seventy-eighth Division in training at Camp Dix, New Jersey. This duty ended unhappily when the division was ordered overseas and Scott's age prevented his accompanying it.

Scott lived an active retirement in Princeton. From 1919 to 1929 he served on the Board of Indian Commissioners, and the group's annual inspection tours enabled him to continue his studies of Indians. He also wrote two articles about his Indian experiences and in 1928 published his memoirs, *Some Memories of a Soldier*. He devoted considerable effort to compiling a motion picture dictionary of the Indian sign language, but this project terminated in 1933, the victim of a rare New Deal economy measure. From 1923 until 1933 he also served as a member of the New Jersey Highway Commission. He died in Washington, D.C.

Hugh Scott's military career began shortly after the battle of Little Big Horn and ended after the battle of Château Thierry. In this span he made significant contributions to American history as a diplomat, soldier, and student of Native Americans.

• The Hugh Scott Papers in the Library of Congress include more than 200,000 items and are an invaluable source for U.S. diplomatic and military history during this period. Also valuable are the Scott papers at the U.S. Military Academy library. His career is detailed in James W. Harper, "Hugh Lenox Scott: Soldier Diplomat" (Ph.D. diss., Univ. of Virginia, 1968), and his diplomatic activities are studied in Harper, "Hugh Lenox Scott y la diplomacia de los Estados Unidos hacia la Revolucion Mexicana," *Historia Mexicana* 27 (Jan.–Mar. 1978): 427–45, and Harper, "The El Paso–Juarez Conference of 1916," *Arizona and the West* 20 (Autumn 1978): 231–44. Frederick Calhoun, *Power and Principle: Armed Intervention in Wilsonian Foreign Policy* (1986), explores the context of his diplomatic activities, as do Arthur S. Link, *Wilson: The Struggle for Neutrality, 1914–1915* (1960) and *Wilson: The New Freedom* (1956). For the military context, see Frank Vandiver, *Black Jack: The Life and Times of John J. Pershing* (2 vols., 1977); John W. Chambers, *To Raise an Army: The Draft Comes to America* (1987); Edward Coffman, *The War to End All Wars: The American Military Experience in World War I* (1968); and Peter Karsten, *The Military in America: From the Colonial Era to the Present* (1986).

JAMES W. HARPER

SCOTT, James (12 Feb. 1885–30 Aug. 1938), pianist, entertainer, and ragtime composer, was born James Sylvester Scott in Neosho, Newton County, Missouri, the son of James Scott and Molly Thomas, who had migrated to Missouri at the time of the Kansas exodus of African Americans from North Carolina between 1879 and 1881. Scott spent the greater part of his youth in the southwestern corner of Missouri, getting thirty formal lessons on the piano and musical notation from a local pianist, John Coleman, and from an unnamed Joplin physician. As his family was not rich, Scott taught himself much of what he needed to know on pianos in neighbors' homes, in public buildings, and in local music stores. In 1902 he moved to Carthage, Missouri, a community that thought of itself as the seat of culture, education, and refinement in Jasper County and the southwest.

Scott began his career in Carthage, where city alderman Charles R. Dumars, director of the Carthage Light Guard Band and owner of Dumars Music at 109 South Main Street, hired him to mind the store and to demonstrate pianos to prospective customers. Dumars published Scott's first two rags, "A Summer Breeze" and "The Fascinator—March and Two-Step," in 1903 and one year later Scott's "On the Pike," which recalled the commercial concession area of the Louisiana Purchase Exposition of 1904 in St. Louis. These early publications laid the foundation for his growing career as a composer.

Scott's influential career as a ragtime composer got its second major boost from the white St. Louis, Missouri, music publisher John Stillwell Stark, who in 1899 had published "Maple Leaf Rag" by Scott Joplin. Stark published Scott's best seller "Frog Legs Rag" in 1904 and for sixteen years thereafter turned out most of Scott's best works, although three other Missouri publishing companies also presented Scott's works to the ragtime public of parlor pianists and saloon entertainers.

Scott's piano music enlivened a wide variety of social and cultural occasions in small-town Missouri. Scott performed for many African-American gatherings in that terrifying time of lynchings and racial terror. He lent his keyboard skills to graduation ceremonies at the racially segregated Lincoln High School and at the black Chatauquas held in the region, and he became a mainstay performer of sacred music for the African Methodist Episcopal churches in the region. Scott organized an all-black wind ensemble that performed at political gatherings important to black civil rights and also organized the Carthage Jubilee Singers.

At the same time, however, Scott established himself in Carthage by buying a home "as an investment"; marrying Nora Johnson, a singer of sacred music, in 1906; and performing regularly at the nearby Lakeside Amusement Park. Several of his published waltzes and popular songs blend the gentle Victorian mood of turn-of-the-century Missouri with the more vital, energetic, and essentially cheerful sounds of the United States in the age of Theodore Roosevelt.

Ragtime's popularity waned in the late 1910s, and the zinc mining that had sustained prosperity in southwestern Missouri declined abruptly after World War I. Most of Scott's publishing career was behind him when he moved to Kansas City, Kansas, in the 1920s. For the next ten years he performed in three Kansas City vaudeville and movie theaters. He died of kidney failure and hardening of the arteries in Douglas Hospital in Kansas City, Missouri.

Scott published thirty-eight pieces during his lifetime, several of which—"Grace and Beauty" (1909), "Sunburst Rag" (1909), "Ragtime Oriole" (1911), and "Climax Rag" (1914)—are numbered among the classic compositions that define that turn-of-the-century genre of scored piano music. Scott's thirty rags, four waltzes, and four songs constitute what musicologist Scott Deveaux has called "one of the richest and most fully developed repertories of the ragtime era." He and Scott Joplin are generally considered to have been the "two greatest ragtime composers" of a literature further enriched by Tom Turpin, Artie Matthews, and Louis Chauvin. His rags, rooted in African-American culture, contributed to an instrumentally challenging musical genre that rejected the ugly racial stereotypes of the era's Coon Songs; his works also reflected the turn-of-the-century world of popular commercialized leisure-time merriment. His pianistically demanding scores document the composer's sparkling technique and the surging new democratic sensibilities caught and held in traditional nineteenth-century musical notation.

• Scott Deveaux and William Howland Kenney, eds., *The Music of James Scott* (1992), offers a complete collection of Scott's works as well as historical and musicological analysis. John Edward Hasse, *Ragtime: Its History, Composers, and Music* (1985), surveys the genre and Scott's place within it. See also John Higham, "The Reorientation of American Culture in the 1890s," in *Writing American History: Essays on Modern Scholarship*, ed. Higham (1970). Also useful are the *Carthage (Mo.) Evening Press*, 1903–1925, and the *Kansas City Call*, 1920–1938.

WILLIAM H. KENNEY III

SCOTT, James Wilmot (26 June 1849–14 Apr. 1895), newspaper editor and publisher, was born in Walworth County, Wisconsin, the son of David Wilmot and Mary Catherine Thompson. Like his father before him, David Scott was a country printer. Soon after the birth of James, he moved his family and business to Galena, Illinois. James learned the family trade as a typesetter for the *Galena Jeffersonian* and Republican values as a drummer boy in a Union recruitment brigade. Though a promising student, he left Beloit College after two years of study and moved to New York in 1868. He worked briefly there as a floriculturalist and wrote several articles for horticulture magazines. He relocated to Washington, D.C., in search of a government printing job, then began a newspaper in Prince Georges County, Maryland. In 1873 he sold his interest in that venture, returned to Galena to marry Carrie Green, and, with his father, began publication of the *Industrial Press*. He and his wife had one child who died in infancy.

In 1875 Scott permanently relocated to Chicago. He purchased an interest in the *National Hotel Reporter* with the hope of building it into a daily newspaper. When those prospects dimmed, he made several unsuccessful attempts to purchase a Chicago daily. In 1881 he organized the Chicago Herald stock company with several other ambitious young publishers. The *Herald*, a two-penny morning paper, struggled for a year until John R. Walsh, president of the Chicago National Bank and the Western News Company, bought the interests of Scott's associates. With firm financial backing and Scott's management, the *Herald* grew remarkably in size and circulation, and Scott quickly earned a reputation as one of Chicago's leading editors. Between 1886 and 1892 he served three years as president of the Press Club of Chicago, six terms as president of the American Newspaper Publishers Association, and six years as president of the United Press (UP).

A key to the *Herald*'s sudden rise was its connection to the UP. Scott and Walsh were instrumental figures behind the 1882 incorporation of the news-gathering organization, which provided wire service to newspapers excluded by the Associated Press (AP) and its allies. Within several years, the UP had absorbed most of the smaller press associations and established itself as the AP's chief rival. Scott rightly sensed that the future of the journalism business would be marked by competition between large, consolidated newspaper corporations. In 1890 he moved the Herald company into the evening newspaper market with the *Chicago Evening Post*. Soon afterward, he began to plot the purchase of the *Chicago Times*, which was realized early in 1895 with the first issues of the *Chicago Times-Herald*.

By 1892 Scott's reputation as a business manager brought an offer from Joseph Pulitzer to run the *New York World*. The salary offer was unprecedented—$100,000 a year for five years—nearly twice that of the highest-salaried executive in the United States. Scott declined Pulitzer's offer, claiming that the sum was not enough to leave Chicago, especially on the eve of the 1893 World's Fair. Scott had been a prime mover in the aggressive lobbying campaign that brought the fair to Chicago, and he served as a member of the fair's board of directors and chair of its press and printing committee. In these roles, Scott often served as a mediator between warring factions.

In politics, Scott performed a similar mediating role. The *Herald* began as a Republican paper but switched its support to Democratic candidate Grover Cleveland in 1884. Throughout, Scott's newspapers maintained a "Mugwump" orientation, limiting its crusades to tariff reduction and civil service reform. In its tone and content, the *Herald* generally avoided sensationalism and promoted its "high principles" and "cleanliness" to its intended middle-class audience. Only organized labor seemed to inspire Scott to hyperbole and invective; his last crusade as an editor was against the "anarchist" Pullman strikers and the "socialistic" Eugene Debs.

While visiting New York with his wife and niece in the spring of 1895, Scott was seized by a "sudden attack of apoplexy" and died at the age of forty-five. Friends praised his energy, loyalty, and good nature. Newspapers across the United States—United Press papers in particular—declared that the West had lost its greatest and "most progressive" journalist. Indeed, the trajectory of Scott's remarkable career—from a country printing press to the *Herald* building, with its twenty steam-powered presses—provides a case study of the enormous changes in American journalism in the late nineteenth century—changes in scale, scope, and organization that laid the groundwork for the newspaper chains and conglomerates of the twentieth century.

• John Moses and Joseph Kirkland, *History of Chicago* (1895), and John J. Flinn, *The Handbook of Chicago Biography* (1893), contain basic information on Scott's life. William H. Freeman, *The Press Club of Chicago: A History* (1894), devotes particular attention to his work on behalf of the 1893 World's Fair. On Scott and the United Press, see Richard Schwarzlose, *The Nation's Newsbrokers*, vol. 2 (1991), and, for the Associated Press viewpoint, Melville E. Stone, *Fifty Years a Journalist* (1921). On Chicago journalism in general, see David Paul Nord, "The Public Community: The Urbanization of Journalism in Chicago," *Journal of Urban History* 11 (1985): 411–41. An extensive obituary is in the *Chicago Times-Herald*, 15 Apr. 1895.

MARK G. SCHMELLER

SCOTT, John (c. 1632–1704), buccaneer, was born apparently in Ashford, Kent, England, the son of a bankrupt miller; neither his father's nor his mother's name is certain. In his long and colorful life, John Scott "of Long Island," as he was called, derived his past from the Scotts of Scot's Hall, Kent, a claim vehemently denied by that offended family. In his own account written in a petition to Charles II in 1661, Scott claimed that he had sabotaged Puritan forces by cutting loose the horses of a troop in London, for which action he was exiled to New England as an indentured servant. What seems certain is that he was bound to Emmanuel Downing in 1643 and then indentured to a Quaker, Lawrence Southwick, of Salem, in the Massachusetts Bay colony. Scott apparently ran away to sea in 1647 but was recaptured by his master by 1648. Again going to sea at the end of an indenture that was extended to 1652 in punishment for running away, Scott landed at Tortuga and became a buccaneer. He returned in 1654 to the mainland of North America at Long Island, whence his sobriquet among historians.

Scott quickly proved himself an avid litigator in Southampton and Setauket, Long Island, adding to his ill-gotten gains as a buccaneer a substantial landed property purchased from the Montauks, attested to by Governor Peter Stuyvesant in a description of Long Island. By 1657 he had become a freeman of Southampton and was appointed tax commissioner there. In 1658 Scott married Deborah Raynor in Southampton, Long Island; the couple had two children. In 1660 he returned to England where he became an agent of the speculators in the Atherton Company, who had designs on the Narragansett lands on the disputed Connecticut–Rhode Island border. While in England Scott probably saw his chance to suggest to England the possible conquest of New Netherland; he returned to America bearing a warning from the English to the Dutch. Sailing again to England, he was back on Long Island in 1663 as Connecticut began pressing its claims on the English towns of the island. Before Scott could realize his own ambition to rule Long Island for the English, an outraged Governor John Winthrop, Jr., had him arrested for contravening Connecticut's claims on the English towns.

Scott had led the expedition that forced Dutch cession of rights to Long Island towns and the Connecticut River valley. Escaping from jail just before the English conquest of New Netherland in 1664, Scott nonetheless refused to cooperate with Colonel Richard Nicolls, commander of the English forces. Instead, in a move that can only be interpreted as an attempt to further his own fortunes, he cast himself as a defender of the rights of New England's Puritans against the proprietary interests of the duke of York. His lands sequestered by Nicolls in 1665, Scott fled to Barbados. His wife Deborah divorced him on grounds of deser-

tion; she then married Charles Sturmey. Scott saw action against the Dutch in the Caribbean during the next two years, and as a result of his experiences there he composed his *History of the Coasts and Islands of America*, which was finally published in 1897–1898 as the *Description of Trinidad, Tobago, and Guiana*. In 1668 he was commissioned by Charles II to report on the fisheries at Newfoundland. In straitened financial circumstances, Scott decided instead to work for his former enemies until the Third Dutch War forced him in 1673 out of the Netherlands to London. Whether he worked as a spy for the English or the Dutch in France between 1675 and 1677 remains a matter of conjecture.

The most infamous episode in Scott's life was his attempt to implicate Samuel Pepys in the Popish Plot of 1678. Scott apparently cultivated ties to the duke of Buckingham, consistent with what he claimed was his pro-Royalist family past. Yet, at the same time, he carried on a romance with the widow of the regicide Sir Harry Vane, and during his time in the Netherlands he was considered to be a partisan of the Whigs and was protected by the Whig cabal. When Samuel Pepys's enemies, including Anthony Ashley Cooper, Lord Shaftesbury, tried to destroy him, they found in Scott a willing tool. Scott's testimony seemed to implicate Pepys in a scheme to sell naval secrets to the French. Pepys, for his part, believed that Scott was seeking revenge through his testimony since Pepys had ordered Scott's arrest on suspicion of having had a hand in the murder of the London magistrate Sir Edmund Berry Godfrey, the incident that began the Popish Plot.

When Pepys was released in June 1680 he vigorously pursued his vindication; by 1682 it was Scott who had to flee to France, wanted now for the murder of a hackney coachman in London. Finding his way from Zeeland to Montserrat, Scott was again in France by 1695. Contrary to earlier accounts he did not die in 1696 but after being pardoned arrived again in England, obtained the post of Speaker of the Assembly for Montserrat in 1698, and was council member for the Leeward Islands until his death at Bridgetown, Barbados.

Undoubtedly in part a victim of the tragedy of England's civil wars and the conspiratorial atmosphere of Restoration politics, Scott suffered even more from his own inability to direct his considerable talents with any degree of constancy and loyalty. His geographic description of Guiana made in the 1660s after he fled Long Island was equally as good as his shrewd knowledge of seventeenth-century colonial affairs that brought him to the attention of Shaftesbury and later, the Board of Trade. He recognized earlier than many the oncoming conflict with New Netherland; his linguistic abilities included Native American languages as well as French and Dutch. But both his personal and public career revealed an unbridled ambition curbed by few moral scruples. Flamboyant, fascinating, hated but found useful by contemporaries, he remained a roguish opportunist of the Restoration era to the end of his days in the Caribbean region where he had first made his ill fame and dubious fortune.

• The older, classic study of Scott is Wilbur Cortez Abbott, "Colonel John Scott of Long Island," in Abbott's *Conflicts with Oblivion* (1924; repr. 1969), pp. 281–386. This must be supplemented and in part corrected by Lilian T. Mowrer, *The Indomitable John Scott: Citizen of Long Island 1632–1704* (1960). Mowrer's heavily revisionist work brings to bear a valuable inventory of archival Dutch, French, and English sources that must be taken seriously, revising Scott's later career and death date. Her enthusiastic and romantic attempts at Scott's complete rehabilitation are, however, unconvincing.

A. G. ROEBER

SCOTT, John Adams (15 Sept. 1867–27 Oct. 1947), classical philologist, was born in Fletcher, McLean County, Illinois, the son of James Sterling Scott and Henrietta P. Sutton, farmers. Scott's father was sickly, and by the time Scott was thirteen he and his brother Walter Dill Scott had taken charge of the farm. There was no time for formal education, and the two boys were taught at home by their older sister Louise. So at an age when most boys were leaving high school, Scott began attending Illinois State Normal School, from which he graduated at the age of twenty in 1887. He proceeded to Northwestern University in Evanston, Illinois, and received his B.A. in 1891. He then taught Greek at the university's academy for two years while studying classics as a graduate student. In 1892 he married Matilda Jane Spring of Centralia, Illinois. The couple had one son and one daughter.

Scott proceeded to the prestigious classics program of the Johns Hopkins University, where he studied Greek, Latin, and Sanskrit. In 1897 he received his doctorate with a dissertation directed by Basil L. Gildersleeve, published as *A Comparative Study of Hesiod and Pindar* (1898).

In September 1897 Scott returned to Northwestern as an instructor and remained there until his retirement in 1938. He was promoted to professor in 1901 and became chairman of the Department of Classical Languages in 1904. In 1923 he was named John C. Shaffer Professor of Greek. Scott was associate editor of the *Classical Journal* from 1910 to 1933; president of the Classical Association of the Middle West and South from 1916 to 1917; president of the American Philological Association from 1918 to 1919; councillor of the American School for Classical Studies in Athens from 1926 to 1927; and Sather Professor of Greek at the University of California at Berkeley from 1920 to 1921.

The Sather Professor's duties include giving a series of lectures on classical literature. Scott's *Unity of Homer* (1921) was the first published Sather Lecture, initiating the most distinguished lecture series in American classics. (In 1930 he contributed a lecture, "The Poetic Structure of the Odyssey," to Oberlin College's prestigious *Martin Classical Lectures* [1 (1931): 97–124].) For Harvard classicist Sterling Dow, "Scott's *Unity of Homer* has been the most influential book in the whole Sather series" (1965). That judgment is an exaggeration. Scott's book was totally ignored in Europe, unlike Martin Nilsson's *Mycenaean Origin of Greek Mythology* (1932), and it did not shape the way English-speaking scholars view the development of Greek society and literature, as did E. R. Dodds's *The Greeks and the Irrational* (1951). It was, however, a very influential book in the United States.

The debate on whether *Iliad* and *Odyssey* had a single author, Homer, goes back to antiquity. Homeric analysis, arguing for multiple authorship for each poem, was initiated by the German scholar Friedrich August Wolf. Homeric analysis had been a hallmark of German scholarship during the nineteenth and early twentieth centuries. In the United States the defense of the unity of Homer was seen as a defense of Anglo-Saxon civilization against Teutonic *Kultur*. "In the battle of the Homericists Scott may be compared to General Pershing: the resources of the higher critics are beginning to show signs of exhaustion, for the tide is setting against the view of Homer which developed from the hypothesis of Wolf, and Scott has brought into action the forces of a young and vigorous, if somewhat inexperienced, national philology," wrote American Homericist Samuel E. Bassett. In 1965 Harvard's Sterling Dow was equally emphatic on the completeness of Scott's "victory": *The Unity of Homer* "did more than any other book to defeat, though it did not annihilate, those who believed the epics were a patchwork of different poems. . . . It was a magnificent achievement to have won the cause for Unitarianism a decade before Parry made it easy." "He devoted pages," E. R. Dodds objected, however, "to *minutiae . . .* which no modern analyst thinks important, while saying nothing at all about" major problems.

Scott's *Unity of Homer* is a superb polemic, witty, caustic, and sincere in turn. It followed a national revulsion against Germany that culminated in U.S. entry into World War I, but the work also needs to be seen in light of a systematic attempt to liberate American culture and scholarship from the dominance of Germany reflected in the scholarship of Paul Shorey, who edited *Classical Philology* at the University of Chicago.

Scott's attack on the German analysis of Homer was intimately linked with a repudiation of German higher criticism of the Bible. Scott was a convinced Presbyterian believer in the inerrancy of the Bible and published three books of lectures in defense of traditional Protestant Christianity under the aegis of the John C. Shaffer Foundation of Northwestern, which funded his chair. "Socrates and Christ" (1928) and "Luke, Greek Physician and Historian" (1930) were reprinted with two other essays in *We Would Know Jesus* (1936). All defended the sincerity of the text and the validity of the substance of the New Testament. In some cases, he was knocking at an open door. That Luke was a true historian in the ancient sense and the author of *Luke-Acts*, both propositions that had been denied by German higher critics, had both been defended before Scott by Adolph von Harnack and Eduard Meyer, the greatest German historians of ancient Christianity and the ancient world.

In recent publications on Homer it has become a commonplace to assert the irrelevance of the German Homeric analysis. Few who make the assertion acknowledge the important role in the acceptance of this attitude of a brilliant polemicist, John Adams Scott, whose hidden agenda was the defense of the Christian scriptures. Scott died in Augusta, Michigan.

• Scott's publications not mentioned above include a short book, *Homer and His Influence* (1925), for the popular series *Our Debt to Greece and Rome*. The research on which he based *The Unity of Homer* appeared in an estimated seventy articles, notes, and reviews. For evaluations of Scott's work, see Samuel E. Bassett, *American Journal of Philology* 43 (1922) 177–81; E. R. Dodds, in *Fifty Years of Classical Studies*, ed. Maurice Platnauer (1954); and Sterling Dow, *Fifty Years of Sathers* (1965). An obituary is in the *New York Times*, 28 Oct. 1947.

E. CHRISTIAN KOPFF

SCOTT, John Morin (1730?–14 Sept. 1784), lawyer and politician, was born in New York City, the son of John Scott, a New York merchant, and Marian Morin. Scott was educated at Yale College and received a B.A. in 1746 and an A.M. in 1749. He then began three years of legal training with William Smith, Sr. Around the time that he was admitted to the New York bar in 1752, Scott married Helena Rutgers, daughter of a Dutch merchant family; the couple had two children who survived to adulthood. Scott was most noted for being one of the "New York Triumvirate" of lawyer-politicians, along with William Livingston and William Smith, Jr. He was also a founder of the Sons of Liberty in New York. Writing after the American Revolution, the loyalist New York Supreme Court judge Thomas Jones, a political rival of Scott's, praised him as "honest, open, and generous, a good lawyer, a fluent speaker," and a man of honor and integrity, who was foolish enough to engage "himself in all the politics of the republican faction with the violence and acrimony of a madman. . . ." (E. F. DeLancey, ed., *History of New York during the Revolutionary War*, vol. 1 [1879] p. 5).

Politics in colonial New York were based on ties of family and religion. Scott, Smith, and Livingston, all Presbyterians educated at Yale, were among the first generation of lawyers trained in the colonies. As the Triumvirate, they assumed leadership of New York's Livingston-Presbyterian faction, in opposition to the colony's Anglican faction led by the DeLancey family. Scott, along with Smith and Livingston, first gained notoriety with the publication in 1752–1753 of the *Independent Reflector*, a series of essays arguing against the establishment of King's College (Columbia) under the control of the Anglican church. Inspired by the English Whig opposition writers John Trenchard and Thomas Gordon, they maintained that a nonsectarian college was needed to train the future leaders of New York's pluralistic society. When Lieutenant Governor James DeLancey succeeded in having King's College chartered under Anglican control, Scott prepared a bill for the New York Assembly calling for the establishment of a nonsectarian college. His arguments in support of the bill were published in the "Watch Tower" column in the *New-York Mercury* (1754–1755). That same year, Scott played a major role in the creation of the New-York Society Library, the colony's first public library, and served as its first treasurer. From 1756 to 1761 he held office as a New York City alderman. The climax of New York's political/sectarian struggle was reached in the late 1760s, when the Society for the Propagation of the Gospel pushed for the appointment of an Anglican bishop for America. Though the Triumvirate succeeded in stopping this move, the resulting acrimony helped cause Scott's defeat in his 1769 bid for a seat in the Assembly, amid charges that his opponent had resorted to bribery and strong-arm tactics.

Holding as they did top positions in the New York bar, Scott and the Triumvirate played a leading role in the judicial reform movements of the 1750s and 1760s. In cases brought before the New York Supreme Court, such as *Obriant v. Bryant* (1754) and especially *Forsey v. Cunningham* (1764), Scott helped establish the constitutional independence of the judiciary from the Crown and its officers. New York's chief justice, Daniel Horsmanden, supported Scott's position, later affirmed on appeal, that Lieutenant Governor Cadwallader Colden was not entitled by law to review the supreme court's minutes of the latter case. These decisions, widely covered in the press, escalated the level of political tension in the colony over the nature and limits of imperial power. Colden's attempt to control the judiciary and the legal profession became tied, in public opinion, with the Stamp Act and the British government's maneuvers to tighten control over the colonies. Scott, the most radical member of the Triumvirate, emerged as one of the leaders of the New York Sons of Liberty, and he became an early advocate of American independence. In the "Freeman" essays, appearing in *The New-York Gazette* in June 1765, he denounced the concept of virtual representation of the colonies in Parliament. Scott argued that if British and colonial interests could not be reconciled, "if the Welfare of the Mother Country, necessarily requires a Sacrifice of the most valuable natural Rights of the Colonies Their Right of making their own laws and Disposing of their own Property by Representatives of their own choosing . . . then the connection between them ought to cease" (6 June 1765). Scott hoped, however, that such extreme action would not be needed and that the colonists could secure all the rights due them under the British constitution. Despite his radicalism, Scott's interests as a landowner led him to support the suppression of the rural rent riots of 1766, causing the loyalist John Montresor to caustically remark that Scott and the urban Liberty Boys were "great opposers to these Rioters as they are of the opinion that No one is entitled to Riot but themselves" (*Montresor Journals*, 1 May 1766, New-York Historical Society Collections [1881], p. 363).

At the height of his legal career, from 1763 to 1765, Scott made 575 appearances before the supreme court. This bespoke a lucrative practice that enabled Scott to purchase extensive lands in Dutchess County, and to reside in elegance in his rural Manhattan home in what is now West Forty-third Street between Eighth and Ninth Avenues. John Adams commented in 1774 on the refinement of the home in contrast to Scott's less than exemplary manners as a host. After 1769 Scott was fully engaged in the revolutionary movement, working until 1771 on the successful defense of his Sons of Liberty colleague Alexander McDougall, in a celebrated political case of treasonable pamphleteering. The crisis between the colonies and the mother country put an end to the Triumvirate, as William Smith, Jr., broke with his associates and remained loyal to the king. Scott's radicalism helped deny him a seat in the First Continental Congress in 1774. In addition, he was one of the most active members of the revolutionary New York General Committee in 1775. During the revolutionary war, Scott served in the provincial congresses of New York, helping draft the New York State Constitution of 1777, and becoming a member of the state's Council of Safety, designed to root out all loyalist activity. Scott used his position to protect William Smith from arrest and deportation.

During the Revolution, Scott saw military service as a brigadier general at the battle of Long Island in 1776. He was defeated by George Clinton in his bid to become the state's first governor in 1777. Instead, Scott became New York Secretary of State in 1778, a position he held until his death. He also served in the Continental Congress from 1780 to 1783, and was in charge of the investigation of the boundary dispute between New York and Vermont. Scott died, probably of acute rheumatism, shortly after his return to New York City following the British evacuation. Though a secondary figure in the drama of the American Revolution, Scott's career as both lawyer and radical politician helped advance the political democratization of New York State.

• The bulk of Scott's law papers are located among the records of the New York Supreme Court in the County Clerk's Office, Manhattan. His surviving personal papers are scattered among several repositories, the most important of which are the New York Public Library, the New-York Historical Society, and the Pennsylvania Historical Society. Some of Scott's letters can also be found in the published volumes of *The Papers of William Livingston*, ed. Carl E. Prince et al. (1979–). The major study of Scott is Dorothy R. Dillon, *The New York Triumvirate: A Study of the Legal and Political Careers of William Livingston, John Morin Scott, William Smith, Jr.* (1949). Further information can be found in two articles by Milton M. Klein, "The Rise of the New York Bar: The Legal Career of William Livingston," *William and Mary Quarterly* 15 (1958): 334–58; and "Prelude to Revolution in New York: Jury Trials and Judicial Tenure," *William and Mary Quarterly* 17 (1960): 439–62. Biographical notices appear in F. B. Dexter, *Biographical Sketches of Graduates of Yale College*, vol. 2 (1896), and Maria S. B. Chance and Mary A. E. Smith, *Scott Family Letters* (1930). For background on colonial and revolutionary New York politics with assess-

ments of Scott's role, see Patricia U. Bonomi, *A Factious People: Politics and Society in Colonial New York* (1971), and Edward Countryman, *A People in Revolution: The American Revolution and Political Society in New York, 1760–1790* (1981).

MICHAEL KAPLAN

SCOTT, Kerr (17 Apr. 1896–16 Apr. 1958), governor of North Carolina and U.S. senator, was born William Kerr Scott in Haw River, North Carolina, the son of Robert Walter Scott, a prosperous dairy farmer and local politician, and Elizabeth Hughes. Scott received his B.S. in agriculture from North Carolina State College in 1917, a few weeks after the United States entered World War I. Eager to join the war effort, he served briefly as an emergency food production agent for the U.S. Department of Agriculture and in 1918 enlisted as a private in the army field artillery at Camp Taylor, Kentucky. Upon receiving his discharge in May 1919, Scott returned to Haw River, where he purchased a farm and married his childhood sweetheart, Mary Elizabeth White, a local schoolteacher. They had three children, the youngest of whom, Robert W. Scott, later served as governor of North Carolina (1969–1973).

In 1920 Scott accepted an appointment as Alamance County farm agent, a position he held for ten years. Chosen grand master of the North Carolina State Grange in 1930, he was an early advocate of rural electrification. In 1934 President Franklin D. Roosevelt appointed Scott regional director of the Farm Debt Adjustment Program of the Resettlement Administration. Traveling throughout the state, the cigar chomping, plain-spoken "Squire of Haw River" enjoyed rubbing elbows with his fellow farmers, many of whom he helped save from mortgage foreclosures. Able to speak their language and understand their concerns, he soon won the admiration of thousands of rural North Carolinians. This loyal constituency of "branch-head boys" proved invaluable to Scott when he announced his candidacy for state commissioner of agriculture in 1936. With the support of the farm vote and ample funding from the Democratic party organization, he registered an upset victory over incumbent William A. Graham.

As commissioner, Scott exposed the fraudulent business practices of the feed, fertilizer, and utility companies, earning the enmity of these powerful interests but further endearing himself to the farm folk. He also led the successful drive to rid North Carolina of Bang's disease and bovine tuberculosis, oversaw a complete reorganization of the department, and served with distinction on several national agricultural committees. In recognition of his efforts, the *Progressive Farmer* named him their "Man of the Year" for 1937. He easily won reelection in 1940 and 1944.

Scott shocked political observers in February 1948, when he resigned as commissioner to enter the Democratic gubernatorial primary. Given little chance against the political machine's anointed candidate, Charles M. Johnson, he nonetheless conducted an aggressive, hard-hitting campaign. Scott demanded that North Carolina's surplus funds, then sitting interest free in state banks, be invested and used to erase the "deficit in services to the people." He proposed a sweeping "Go Forward" program that pledged to build new schools and hospitals, promote education, and expand social welfare services. In particular, Scott called for the construction of a system of paved roads that would eliminate the "mud tax" on farmers. Though his opponent offered similar proposals, Scott's portrayal of himself as the "people's candidate," crusading against the "dictatorship" of the machine, resonated with voters. After finishing second in the first primary, he went on to win the nomination in the runoff. That November he handily defeated his Republican opponent, George M. Pritchard.

On 6 January 1949 Scott took the oath of office as North Carolina's first farmer-governor of the twentieth century. He quickly asked the legislature to approve a $200 million bond issue for the construction of secondary farm to market roads, then requested a $50 million bond issue—subsequently reduced to $25 million—to expand the public school system. Alarmed conservatives avowed that "the Wild Bull from Alamance" was out to bankrupt the state. Though even his advisers suggested compromise, Scott remained unyielding. He took to the radio waves, bringing his case directly to the people. In a ringing endorsement of the governor's program, North Carolinians approved both bond issues in a special referendum held on 4 June 1949. By the time Scott left office, the state had paved 14,810 miles of road and built 8,000 classrooms.

The governor achieved similar success in pressing for other Go Forward measures. His administration saw the installation of more than 31,000 rural telephones and the addition of 153,000 rural electrical connections. The legislature also appropriated funds for the construction of modern deep water port facilities in Wilmington and Morehead City, the improvement of various medical facilities, and the institution of a statewide health program for public school children. Fulfilling another campaign pledge, Scott won the right to invest the state's accumulated surplus. On the issue of civil rights, the governor's appointment of the first black to the State Board of Education led some North Carolinians to label him a racial liberal. However, his comments that blacks "did not want" integrated schools and, if allowed into professional courses of study, would enroll only "until the novelty wears off" indicate a more ambivalent stance.

In March 1949 Scott appointed renowned progressive Frank Porter Graham to fill a vacant seat in the U.S. Senate, an unexpected move that drew kudos from liberals throughout the country. The governor had overestimated the strength of liberalism in North Carolina, however. When the former University of North Carolina president went down to defeat in 1950, however, Scott's political stock also declined. The governor found the 1951 assembly far less willing to accept his reform proposals. Refusing to give any

quarter, he returned to the radio, hoping once again to mobilize the people behind him. This time his efforts were less successful. With urban and business interests intent on "holding the line," several of the administration's major initiatives, including conservation legislation, the establishment of a state minimum wage, and an attempt to repeal the Anti–Closed Shop Act, all died in committee.

Though his uncompromising activism had won him his share of enemies, Scott remained popular after leaving office in 1953. The next year he ran for the U.S. Senate, defeating incumbent Alton A. Lennon in the primary and Republican Paul C. West in the general election. As a member of the Agriculture and Public Works Committees, Scott remained involved in issues that had long concerned him. He proposed the establishment of a World Food Bank to distribute surplus agricultural products to countries in need and played a major role in framing legislation to finance the interstate highway network. In June 1955 he presented a resolution calling for a Tobacco Advisory Council to study the relationship between smoking and lung cancer. In the Senate, Scott remained a mild segregationist, though he never explicitly denounced the *Brown* decision. While home for Easter recess in 1958, Scott died in Burlington, North Carolina.

A tireless and effective advocate for the interests of rural North Carolinians, Scott challenged the state's long tradition of business-oriented government administered by wealthy lawyers. His Go Forward plan, heralded by the Raleigh *News and Observer* as "the most ambitious [program] ever taken into office by a North Carolina Governor," succeeded in bringing many poor and isolated farmers into the mainstream of twentieth-century America.

• Scott's personal and public papers are at the Department of Archives and History in Raleigh, N.C. Some of his correspondence and speeches have been published in David LeRoy Corbitt, ed., *Public Addresses, Letters, and Papers of William Kerr Scott, Governor of North Carolina, 1949–1953* (1957), which includes a biographical sketch by Robert W. Redwine. *Memorial Services Held in the Senate and House for William Kerr Scott* (1958) reprints obituaries from several N.C. newspapers as well as tributes from Scott's congressional colleagues. John W. Coon, "Kerr Scott, the 'Go Forward' Governor: His Origins, His Program, and the North Carolina General Assembly" (master's thesis, Univ. of North Carolina, Chapel Hill, 1968), provides a thorough analysis of Scott's policies and personality. Capus M. Waynick and John W. Harden, *North Carolina Roads and Their Builders* (2 vols., 1952, 1966), details the Scott administration's role in constructing the state's road system. Augustus M. Burns III and Julian M. Pleasants, *Frank Porter Graham and the 1950 Senate Race in North Carolina* (1990), examines Scott's controversial appointment of Graham and the fallout it precipitated in N.C. politics. Obituaries are in the *New York Times* and Raleigh *News and Observer*, 17 Apr. 1958.

THOMAS W. DEVINE

SCOTT, Leroy Martin (11 May 1875–21 July 1929), writer, was born in Fairmount, Indiana, the son of Eli J. Scott and Eleanor S. Reader. He attended high school in Fairmount and graduated in 1897 from Indiana University. His first jobs were on newspapers, initially in Louisiana on a paper owned by his brother, and then on the *Chicago Journal*. While working in Chicago, he lived at Hull-House, one of the earliest neighborhood settlement houses in America, founded by Jane Addams. In 1900 and 1901 he was an assistant editor for the monthly *Woman's Home Companion*, which was based in Springfield, Ohio, at the time.

In 1902 Robert Hunter, whom Scott had known at Hull-House, became head worker at the University Settlement, on the Lower East Side in New York, and called on Scott to become the salaried assistant head worker. In this position he assisted Hunter in a campaign to reform New York state's child-labor laws and served as a liaison with the public schools. When Hunter resigned in a disagreement with the settlement's supervisory board, Scott was placed temporarily in charge. He left the settlement in January 1904. In June 1904 he married a fellow settlement worker, Miriam Finn, a Russian immigrant who became a notable writer on child rearing. They had three children.

Scott embarked on a career as a freelance writer. He broke into print in *McClure's Magazine* late in 1904 with a short story and thereafter turned out a steady stream of stories, articles, and books. In 1905 he produced a string of articles for the *World's Work* and *American* magazines and published his first novel, *The Walking Delegate*, a tale of trade-union corruption and reform. The work received generally favorable reviews, although critics regarded the writing as crude.

Early in 1906 Scott and his wife joined a group of liberal and radical writers in organizing the A Club, a residence on lower Fifth Avenue in New York. Like his associates there, he was deeply interested in the Russian revolution of 1905. When writer Maxim Gorky came to New York in April 1905 to raise money for the revolution, Scott served as his press officer and had the thankless task of handling the fiasco that followed the revelation in the newspapers that Gorky was traveling with a woman who was not his wife.

Later in 1906 Scott and his wife went to Russia themselves, joining a news syndicate operated by William English Walling and Arthur Bullard, former associates at the University Settlement. Although the revolution had collapsed, Scott was able to place articles in several magazines, most notably *Everybody's* and *Outlook*. In 1910 he published a suspense novel set against the background of the 1905 revolution; a reviewer dismissed *The Shears of Destiny* as being of "slight importance but of undeniable cleverness" (*Outlook*, 10 Dec. 1910, p. 834).

On returning from Russia, Scott became involved with socialism. He and his wife lived for a time at Caritas, an island near Stamford, Connecticut, with James Graham Phelps Stokes, a leading "millionaire socialist," and his wife, Rose Pastor Stokes. Scott joined the board of the Intercollegiate Socialist Society, an organization designed to inform college students about socialism, and helped at a new socialist newspaper, the *New York Call*. He and his wife joined the Socialist Party of America, probably in 1908.

In 1912 Scott served on the staff of the *Masses*, a magazine of radical literature and art founded by Greenwich Village intellectuals. Although he occasionally penned short pieces for the magazine, he concentrated most on writing novels. *Counsel for the Defense* (1912), centering on the work of a woman lawyer, was well received, despite what was regarded as its overly elaborate plot. Subsequent efforts, such as *No. 13 Washington Square*, relied even more on twists of plot.

When the United States entered World War I in April 1917, Scott followed several American-born socialist intellectuals in leaving the Socialist Party of America because they considered the party's foreign-born leadership disloyal. Scott observed, "For a long time I have been sick of the Socialist Party" (letter to Stokes, 30 Apr. 1917, Stokes papers, Columbia University). Although several of his longtime associates became active in the war effort, Scott remained apolitical.

In this period Scott turned to writing novels dealing with crime and detection. The best known of these was *Mary Regan* (1918), about a woman criminal, which was adapted into a film. Of it, the socialist *Call* wrote, "'Mary Regan' has nothing whatever of importance to say. If Mr. Scott wants to or can afford to, we believe he can write literature instead of sublimated shilling shockers."

Scott was not swayed. He turned out similar works, such as *A Daughter of Two Worlds* (1919), *Children of the Whirlwind* (1921), and *The Heart of Katie O'Doone* (1925), none of which received better than mixed reviews. *The Trail of Glory* (1926) portrayed an amateur tennis champion and had the benefit of an introduction by such a champion, William T. Tilden II.

Scott was active in writers' organizations. In 1916 he and others briefly explored the possibility of creating a writers' union in the American Federation of Labor. In 1928 he was elected president of the Authors Guild, a branch of the Authors League of America. He drowned while apparently trying to swim across Chateaugay Lake, in upstate New York, and his body was recovered six days later.

Scott's career, both as a political activist and as a writer, was that of a secondary figure. In socialist and reform movements he served as a dependable lieutenant, even a hanger-on. As a writer he gave up the opportunity to create works of social significance in his desire to turn out many popular books. In her autobiography his friend Rose Pastor Stokes appraised Scott and his wife acutely: "They skirted the movement, yet seemed interested enough to be more actively in the work. Scott was very likeable, but he wrote cheap potboilers and never broke away from deadly work" (manuscript autobiography, Yale University).

• The University Settlement Papers, Social Welfare History Archives, University of Minnesota, contain information on the careers of Leroy Scott and Miriam Finn Scott; there is additional material in the James Graham Phelps Stokes Papers, Columbia University, and in the Rose Pastor Stokes Papers, Sterling Library, Yale University. Scott's other books include *To Him That Hath* (1907), *Cordelia the Magnificent* (1923), *Folly's Gold* (1926), and *The Living Dead Man* (1929). Scott's role in the Maxim Gorky affair is described in Ernest Poole, "Maxim Gorki in New York," *Slavonic and East European Review* 22 (1944): 77–83, and Arthur W. Thompson, "The Reception of Russian Revolutionary Leaders in America, 1904–1906," *American Quarterly* 18 (Fall 1966): 452–76. Scott is mentioned in passing in memoirs such as Ernest Poole, *The Bridge* (1940), and Max Eastman, *Love and Revolution* (1964). Brief reports of his death and the recovery of his body appeared in the *New York Times*, 22 and 28 July 1929.

JAMES BOYLAN

SCOTT, Orange (13 Feb. 1800–31 July 1847), Methodist Episcopal minister and abolitionist, was born in Brookfield, Vermont, the son of Samuel Scott, a poor day laborer, and Lucy Whitney. The family moved wherever Scott's father could find work, in Vermont and in Lower Canada (later Quebec). Because the large family needed what he could earn, young Orange had had only thirteen months of formal education by age twenty-one.

Scott knew almost nothing of Christianity until he was twenty and began to read the Bible and pray regularly. His conversion came at the first camp meeting he had ever attended, in Barre, Vermont, in September 1820. Almost immediately, he sensed a call to preach and became an active Methodist. In early 1821 he began to preach as an "exhorter" in the Methodist Episcopal church.

In 1822 Scott was received into membership "on trial," as a probationary minister under the supervision of more experienced clergy, by the New England Annual Conference of the Methodist Episcopal Church. After two years serving circuits, Scott was received in 1824 into "full connexion," as a voting member, by the conference. From 1822 to 1832 Scott served the Lyndon and Danville circuits in Vermont; Charlestown, Massachusetts; Lancaster, New Hampshire; and Springfield, Massachusetts. In 1826 he was ordained elder and married Amy Fletcher, who would die of tuberculosis in 1835, leaving Scott a widower with five children, the youngest being only five months old.

In 1830 Scott was appointed presiding elder of the Springfield (Mass.) District, an assignment he retained for three years. Here, as in his service as pastor, he was primarily an evangelist, conducting and preaching in revivals and camp meetings, always calling for conversions.

In 1833 Scott became aware that the national debate over slavery had now made its way into the Methodist Episcopal church. By 1834, after a period of voracious reading of earlier Methodist writers, including John Wesley himself, and William Lloyd Garrison and his *Liberator*, Scott became a radical, but nonviolent, abolitionist, opposed to temporizing and to colonization schemes. Through a number of articles decrying slavery and advocating abolitionism that appeared between 1834 and 1838 in *Zion's Herald*, the official paper of the New England Conference of the Methodist Episcopal Church, Scott became the leader of the conference's abolitionist faction. With an official decision to close the pages of that paper to debate over the issue of slavery, Scott wrote the important editorial "An Appeal to the Methodist Episcopal Church" in the sole number of the *Wesleyan Anti-Slavery Review* (1838).

In its 1835 annual meeting, the conference voiced its support of Scott's views by electing him as a member of its delegation, an abolitionist delegation, to the 1836 general conference. At that same 1835 annual conference, Scott was reappointed presiding elder, this time of the Providence (R.I.) District. In October 1835 he married Eliza Dearborn; they had two children.

At the Cincinnati, Ohio, general conference in 1836, the bishop's address called for ministers and people to "refrain from this agitating subject" (i.e., slavery). Scott nonetheless ringingly defended abolition to the conference.

Shortly after the general conference, Bishop Elijah Hedding presided at the 1836 New England Annual Conference and found a majority ignoring the bishops' "gag" order. He had to regain authority. By parliamentary maneuvering, he kept a conference antislavery committee from giving its report. And he made silence on the slavery issue a condition for reappointing Scott as presiding elder. Scott, who could not accept that condition, was then assigned to Lowell, Massachusetts.

The Lowell congregation responded by reviving and growing by a hundred members during the year and begging Scott to return. But he instead asked the 1837 annual conference for a relationship that retained conference membership but entailed no official assignment. He planned to be an agent for the American Anti-Slavery Society. The conference granted the request, but presiding bishop Beverly Waugh assigned Scott to a charge, anyway. When Scott's presiding elder overturned Waugh's decision by releasing Scott from pastoral duties, Scott successfully saw to the launching of several dozen chapters of the American Anti-Slavery Society all across New England, primarily among Methodists.

This work, as well as the bypassing of Waugh's authority, Scott's address in Cincinnati, Scott's articles in *Zion's Herald*, and his article in the *Wesleyan Anti-Slavery Review*, angered Hedding, the bishop presiding at the 1838 annual conference. Although Hedding charged Scott with insubordination and unbecoming conduct, the conference exonerated Scott. In a later four-hour exchange, Hedding lost his temper and his composure, producing an irreparable breach with Scott that the latter's efforts were unable to heal.

Scott resigned as agent for the American Anti-Slavery Society in 1839. Again, the New England Annual Conference elected him delegate to the general conference. He was also appointed to serve the Lowell, Massachusetts, congregation again but with misgivings on the part of the presiding bishop, who had only recently dropped charges of insubordination against him.

The 1840 general conference, at which Scott again led the abolitionist faction but to no avail, convinced Scott that his only choices were to live as a silenced abolitionist within a compromising denomination or to secede. Now believing that episcopal Methodism was wrong on both slavery and church government, he decided to secede.

Scott withdrew from the Methodist Episcopal church in November 1841 and revived plans to produce a weekly paper that would fortify Methodist radical abolitionists and those who believed that the Methodist bishops were more concerned with ecclesiastical power than with major ethical issues. From January to June 1840 Scott and Jotham Horton had published the weekly *American Wesleyan Observer* consistent with those purposes. They suspended publication hoping that the general conference would resolve both issues. But, as Scott saw it, the conference had shut any door of hope. With LaRoy Sunderland, Luther Lee, and Horton, Scott published the first issue of the weekly *True Wesleyan* on 7 January 1843. From 21 January 1843 until his death Scott was its sole editor, its proprietor, and its principal writer, with help from the other three. The paper carried articles, letters, and news sent in by abolitionists and those calling for curtailing episcopal authority. It became a major sounding board and rallying point for both causes, especially among episcopal Methodists, even after the secession of the Wesleyans later in 1843. By 1850 it was the official organ of the Wesleyan Methodist Connexion.

A preliminary convention of persons interested in forming a new Wesleyan denomination, free of slavery and of episcopacy, met at Andover, Massachusetts, in February 1843. Nine clergy and forty-three laypersons produced a *Discipline*, an authoritative collection of administrative, ethical, and doctrinal norms, and ordered a general convention to be held at the end of May in Utica, New York.

The Utica convention met as ordered, edited and ratified the *Discipline*, and arranged for leadership for the new Wesleyan Methodist Connexion. The majority of the membership of the Utica convention was Methodist Episcopal, but there was a scattering of abolitionists from eight other denominations. Only in its curtailing of centralization, in its insistence on lay participation in policy setting and decision making, and in its more explicit allegiance to the doctrine of entire sanctification did the new organization differ from episcopal Methodism.

The Utica convention elected Scott president, but when the new Wesleyan Methodist Connexion held its first general conference in 1844, he refused the presidency of the entire denomination. That general conference continued Scott as the editor of the *True Wesleyan* and made him book agent, the organization's principal permanent officer. He continued to write, but *The Grounds of Secession from the M. E. Church: Being an Examination of Her Connection with Slavery, and Also of Her Form of Government* (1846) proved to be his valedictory. The rigors of travel and unrelenting administration worsened his already poor health. He died in his Newark, New Jersey, home.

• Scott's autobiography, which focuses on the issues and events that led to his departure from the Methodist Episcopal church by quoting extensively from relevant documents on all sides, is included as pt. 1 of Lucius Matlock, *Life of Orange Scott* (1847; repr. 1971). Matlock's biography (pt. 2 of his work) is an important source. See also John McKivigan, *The War against Proslavery Religion* (1984), and Donald G. Mathews, *Slavery and Methodism: A Chapter in American Morality, 1780–1845* (1965).

PAUL MERRITT BASSETT

SCOTT, Randolph (23 Jan. 1898?–2 Mar. 1987), film actor, was born in Orange County, Virginia, the son of George Scott, a textile engineer, and Lucy Crane. Raised in Charlotte, North Carolina, Scott attended Georgia Tech and graduated from the University of North Carolina. Plans to join his father in the textile business proved short-lived, and Scott moved to southern California to pursue an acting career. After two years with the Pasadena Playhouse and an assortment of minor screen and stage roles in the late 1920s and early 1930s, he emerged from obscurity as the star of nine popular Paramount westerns based on novels by Zane Grey. Important parts followed in feature films, ranging from musical comedy (including two Fred Astaire–Ginger Rogers pictures) to major westerns and, after Pearl Harbor, to several war films. As his career began to take off in the mid-thirties, Scott married Marianna du Pont Somerville in 1936 and was divorced three years later. His marriage to Marie Patricia Stillman in 1944 proved permanent, and together they raised two children.

By the end of World War II, Scott was firmly established as a versatile screen performer, his tall, handsome looks and stolid but amiable manner easily adaptable to playing romantic comedy with Cary Grant and Irene Dunne in *My Favorite Wife* (1940) or frontier adventures with Tyrone Power and Henry Fonda in *Jesse James* (1939), Errol Flynn in *Virginia City* (1940), and John Wayne in *The Spoilers* (1942). In the postwar years Scott settled almost exclusively into the genre with which he is most identified. All but three of his forty-two postwar screen appearances were in westerns. Over the next decade and a half audiences could count on an average of five Randolph Scott westerns every two years, with as many as four per year in 1949, 1951, and 1955. For four consecutive years (1950–1953) Scott was ranked among the top ten motion picture box-office stars.

Scott collaborated on the production of nearly half of his postwar westerns with veteran producer Harry Joe Brown. In the latter half of the fifties they produced all but two of a series of taut, expertly crafted westerns starring Scott and directed by Budd Boetticher. The Boetticher-Scott westerns, particularly those scripted by Burt Kennedy—*Seven Men from Now* (1956), *The Tall T* (1957), *Ride Lonesome* (1959), *Comanche Station* (1960)—have since won the admiration of both European and American film scholars.

Scott's work with Boetticher might have been regarded as the capstone of a respectable career, but the actor was to go one better before retiring when he costarred with Joel McCrea in Sam Peckinpah's memorable *Ride the High Country* (1962). Cast against type as an embittered ex-lawman intent on stealing a gold shipment guarded by his old friend McCrea, Scott cuts an alternately menacing and poignant figure in contrast with McCrea's portrait of unswerving rectitude. *Ride the High Country* was ranked first by *Newsweek* on its annual ten-best film list and remains a much-admired film, owing in part to the engaging performances of its two veteran stars.

Scott was seldom inclined to discuss his films or acting career except to express gratitude for his steady success in a lucrative but unpredictable business. He also kept his celebrity status separate from his private life as a family man, avid golfer, faithful churchgoer, and astute investor—he was reputed to be one of Hollywood's wealthiest actors. Colleagues have testified to his exceedingly polite manner as well as to his unassuming attitude about his work. One frequently referenced anecdote tells of Scott on the set of one of his westerns blithely reading the *Wall Street Journal* during a key action sequence in which stuntmen roared by on a burning stagecoach. Scott remained virtually secluded from the public eye until his death at his Bel Air home.

• References to some of the scattered primary materials (mostly press clippings) on Scott can be found in the following biographical accounts: Jefferson Brim Crow III, *Randolph Scott: The Gentleman from Virginia* (1987), and John H. Lenihan, "The Western Heroism of Randolph Scott," in *Shooting Stars*, ed. Archie P. McDonald (1987). Lacking citations but containing a detailed filmography is Gene Ringgold, "Randolph Scott: Embodied Everyone's Idea of a Southern Gentleman," *Films in Review* 23 (1972): 605–32. See also Demetrius John (Jim) Kitses, *Horizons West* (1969), for a perceptive analysis of the Scott westerns directed by Budd Boetticher.

JOHN H. LENIHAN

SCOTT, Robert Kingston (8 July 1826–12 Aug. 1900), Union general and governor of South Carolina, was born in Armstrong County, Pennsylvania, the son of John Scott and Jane Hamilton, farmers. Scott was of Scottish ancestry and was raised in the Allegheny Valley north of Pittsburgh. He left home at the age of sixteen and attended Central College and then Sterling Medical College in Columbus, Ohio. In 1850, after practicing medicine for a few years in Ohio, he traveled overland to California to seek his fortune in the gold mines. Unsuccessful in mining, he visited Mexico and South America before settling in Henry County, Ohio, in 1851. In the mid-1850s he married Rebecca Jane Lowry and had two children. When some of his patients survived a cholera epidemic, he gained considerable prestige in the community, and his surgical practice thrived along with his investments in real estate and merchandising.

At the outbreak of the Civil War Scott was appointed a major with the responsibility of organizing the Sixty-eighth Ohio Infantry. He fought at Shiloh and in July 1862 was promoted to colonel. After serving under William T. Sherman on his famous march to the sea, Scott was commissioned as a brigadier general in April 1865 and, at war's end, was brevetted a major general that December. Over six feet tall and with an erect carriage, he seemed to have survived the war in perfect health. In actuality, his physical presence helped conceal the fact that he was addicted to opium as the result of a spinal injury suffered when, in late summer 1864, he fell off a train outside of Atlanta while a prisoner of war.

Scott returned to the South in January 1866, when he accepted the position of assistant commissioner of the Freedmen's Bureau for South Carolina, a post he held until the summer of 1868. He was appalled at the acts of white brutality against blacks attempting to assert their rights, and he soon came to believe that "the two races can only live together by the presence of a sufficient military force to protect them." His chief duties involved adjusting land disputes between whites and freedmen, particularly in the Sea Islands region that had been temporarily abandoned by local planters with the arrival of Union troops in the spring of 1862, and drafting and enforcing labor contracts between planters and their black field hands. He also set up camps and hospitals to provide supplies and medical relief to the destitute of both races. Although solicitous of the needs of the freedmen, Scott was an evenhanded commissioner who won the respect of conservative whites.

Responding to a draft from the Republican-controlled constitutional convention of 1867, Scott agreed to run for governor of South Carolina in 1868. He won handily and was reelected in 1870, serving as governor from July 1868 to November 1872. Scott's strongest support came from black voters, but the state's black politicians soon criticized him for not appointing more freedmen to office. His administration has gone down in history as one of the most corrupt of the so-called carpetbagger regimes during Reconstruction. Corruption was indeed rampant during his two terms in office, much of it centered on bribes, speculative manipulations, and kickback payments associated with state-funded railroad bonds and stock, especially that of the Blue Ridge Railroad Company and the Greenville and Columbia Railroad. Widespread fraud also characterized the dealings of the South Carolina Land Commission, a state agency created to purchase small parcels of land and resell them on easy credit terms to freedmen and poor whites.

Scott, the chief executive of the state, was certainly not faultless in this sorry record, and he was particularly remiss in placing too much trust in associates who served as intermediaries for the state in northern financial markets. Still, no hard evidence ever established that he personally benefited from the corruption or bribed the legislature as commonly charged. Inheriting a state government heavily in debt, he was unable to market state-backed securities at anything close to par because of the state's abysmal credit rating, in large part the result of a relentless Democratic campaign to undercut his administration by scaring off northern investors. He had no choice but to raise taxes and rely on short-term borrowing to meet the state's operating expenses and the costs of funding the state's first public school system for both races. Almost immediately after his reelection in 1870, he was faced with a terrorist campaign orchestrated by the Ku Klux Klan against Republicans and the largely black militia. After first trying to appease white conservatives by disarming most of the militia units that he had organized, Scott fully cooperated with federal authorities in suppressing the Klan under the provisions of the Enforcement Acts of 1870 and 1871. Still, the financial problems of his administration worsened, and though he fought off impeachment proceedings, he left office thoroughly discredited. As governor, he failed to bring financial stability to the state or to unite the warring radical and conservative factions within his party, but that failure was all but preordained by the fierce opposition of the state's traditional ruling class to a Republican government that supported a vital political role for the recently freed slaves. Moreover, many of these Democratic planters personally profited from the same corruption that they publicly decried during Scott's administration.

Scott was quite wealthy before he became governor, and after he left office he continued to live in Columbia, the state capital, to supervise his extensive real estate and moneylending operations in both South Carolina and Ohio. After the Democrats resumed power in 1876, they appointed a legislative committee to investigate the alleged financial wrongdoings of the outgoing Republicans. In November 1878 Scott was indicted for conspiracy to defraud the state. At that point, informed by his business friends that the charges would never be brought to trial if he permanently left the state, Scott returned to Ohio.

Scott's final years in his hometown of Napoleon, Ohio, were marred by his shooting to death a drugstore clerk, Walter G. Drury, whom he believed was responsible for encouraging his only son, Robert K. Scott, Jr., to take to alcohol. Scott was acquitted on a charge of accidental homicide. A year after suffering a stroke in 1899, he died in Napoleon.

• The Ohio Historical Society in Columbus has a large collection of Scott's private and military papers. His public papers as South Carolina governor are at the South Carolina Department of Archives and History in Columbia. There is no biography, but a sketch of his life can be found in J. M. Haag, ed., *The State of Ohio versus Robert K. Scott* (1882). For details of his career in South Carolina, see Martin Abbott, *The Freedmen's Bureau in South Carolina, 1865–1872* (1967), and Francis B. Simkins and Robert Hilliard Woody, *South Carolina during Reconstruction* (1932). The most positive treatment of his role as governor is in Richard Nelson Current, *Those Terrible Carpetbaggers* (1988). An obituary is in *State* (Columbia, S.C.), 15 Aug. 1900.

WILLIAM L. BARNEY

SCOTT, Walter (31 Oct. 1796–23 Apr. 1861), religious reformer, clergyman, and educator, was born in Moffat, Scotland, the son of John Scott, a music teacher, and Mary Innes. Young Scott's early training was in music, and he became a skilled flutist. He attended the University of Edinburgh, where he studied music but also considered preparation for the ministry. Following graduation in 1818, however, he accepted an invitation from an uncle, George Innes, to immigrate to America. After tutoring Latin for less than a year in Jamaica, Long Island, New York, the restless Scott traveled on foot to Pittsburgh, Pennsylvania.

Scott found a teaching position in a private academy operated by George Forrester, who quickly became one of the most significant religious influences in Scott's life. Forrester was a nominal Presbyterian lay minister for a congregation he had founded that met in the courthouse. Earlier Forrester had come under the influence of Robert Haldane and James Alexander Haldane, two wealthy Scottish laymen who began a reform movement in the 1790s to "restore" the worship and ritual practices of the early Christians to the Kirk of Scotland. The Haldane brothers, like other Protestant radical reformers, held that, over time, the beliefs and practices of the first Christians had been corrupted by state churches. The independent Pittsburgh congregation observed baptism by immersion and foot washing, held communion each Sunday, and members greeted each other with the holy kiss. These practices deeply impressed Scott, who began a period of intense biblical study, using the Greek New Testament. Scott's Calvinist upbringing had taught him to expect conversion after a long period of earnest searching. His study and Forrester's guidance led him toward accepting the truths revealed in the Bible that were supported by rational evidence rather than the mysterious, magical faith preached by revivalists who expected an emotional conversion. Scott found himself accepting restorationist ideas and asked Forrester to rebaptize him by immersion. After an unfortunate accident in which Forrester drowned while bathing in the Allegheny River, Scott assumed leadership of the congregation and the school.

During the winter of 1821–1822 in Pittsburgh, Scott met Alexander Campbell of Bethany, Virginia (now W.Va.), who was also a nominal Presbyterian reformer. They recognized in each other kindred spirits and developed a warm friendship that continued for forty years. Scott suggested the name *Christian Baptist* for a new periodical launched by Campbell that championed the cause of New Testament restorationism. In the first volume (1923) Scott began a series of articles, "On Teaching Christianity," that called for apostolic practices and standards for church membership. Also in 1823 Scott married Sara Whitsett. They had five children before Sara died in 1849.

In 1926 Scott relocated across the Ohio River to Steubenville, Ohio, to start an academy. That same year Campbell invited him to attend the annual meeting in Canfield, Ohio, of the Mahoning Baptist Association, which was already under Campbell's influence.

Scott, who was neither a Baptist nor an association member, was persuaded to become its evangelist the following year. The next three years formed one of the most significant chapters in Scott's life. By November 1827 he had worked out his key theological approach, which he outlined in a sermon preached in New Lisbon, Ohio, that month. The "restored gospel" he so eagerly sought was not based on emotional, subjective urgings of conversion stressed by churches growing out of the Second Great Awakening. Rather, the key to becoming a Christian was a simple, authoritative, and objective plan of salvation that over time had been lost or obscured by human traditions.

This "ancient gospel" consisted of six points, quickly reduced to a "five-finger exercise," that could easily be memorized. First came faith, accepting the belief that "Jesus is the Christ, the son of God." Scott called this truth the "golden oracle." Next came repentance for past sins, a logical extension of genuine faith. Third was baptism by immersion for the "remission" of sins, which symbolized a commitment to faith and repentance. Fourth came the fulfillment of God's promise through the release of penalty for sins, followed by points five and six, the gift of the Holy Spirit and eternal life. Gone was the "mercy seat" or "anxious bench" for those under conviction. Scott's converts received baptism without recounting a conversion experience, and they joined the church without a congregational vote. His direct, coherent approach spread like wildfire. Every rational person had the ability to hear the gospel message and the moral capability to respond. The Mahoning Association, whose membership was stagnant in 1826, increased in one year from 600 to 1,600 through Scott's efforts. Scott became widely known as a dynamic preacher who seldom missed an opportunity to spread the "ancient gospel." Over the next three decades he was credited with "converting" a thousand people each year. The combination of Scott's evangelical rationalism and Campbell's New Testament restorationism led to the dissolution of the Mahoning Association as an unscriptural and unwarranted church body in 1830. While Campbell stressed reforming the church and Scott emphasized evangelism, their cause became essentially the same. The demise of the Mahoning Baptist Association marks the formal beginning of the Campbellite movement and the Disciples of Christ.

Scott soon moved to Cincinnati, where he began publishing a monthly periodical, the *Christian Evangelist* (1832–1835 and 1838–1844). For several years in the 1830s and early 1840s he lived at Carthage, Ohio, and made extensive preaching tours to villages and towns in Ohio, Kentucky, Virginia, and Missouri. His interest in education also continued. The Ohio legislature appointed him a trustee for Miami University in Oxford, Ohio, in 1834, and he served until 1837. For one year, 1836–1837, he was also founder and president of Bacon College, named after Sir Francis Bacon, in Georgetown, Kentucky. In his inaugural address he extolled Lord Bacon as the "father of experimental

philosophy," and he applied Bacon's scientific method to an overall course of studies.

In 1844 Scott returned to Pittsburgh, Pennsylvania, where he pastored two congregations. He also published the *Protestant Unionist* (1844–1850), a weekly that advanced the union of all Christians on the basis of Scripture alone. In 1850 he married Annie B. Allen. They had one child before Annie died in 1854. Between 1850 and 1854 Scott was back in Kentucky as the principal of a small female academy in Covington. His final pastorate was in Maysville, Kentucky, on the Ohio River. In 1855 he married Eliza Sandige, a widow of modest wealth. They had no children. Scott died at the Sandige mansion in May's Lick, near Maysville.

In addition to his work as a preacher and editor, Scott wrote several small books. *A Discourse on the Holy Spirit* (1831) sets forth Scott's views on the inspiration of Scripture, and *The Gospel Restored* (1836) develops more fully the restored plan of salvation. *The Messiahship; or, The Great Demonstration* (1859) is an apologetic for "evidences of gospel truth" that Jesus is the Messiah and is Scott's largest, most closely reasoned book.

Scott died a loved and respected founder of the Disciples of Christ. His forty years of dedicated service as an evangelist, editor, and educator helped advance the theological ideas and doctrines central to the rapid growth of one of America's most original religious movements. His influence on shaping the early Restoration movement is second only to that of his longtime friend and colleague Campbell.

• Scott's personal notebook, brief autobiography, letters, printed sermons, church records, and a complete run of periodicals he edited are in the library at Lexington Theological Seminary, Lexington, Ky. Scott's published works not cited above include *Psalms, Hymns, and Spiritual Songs* (1834), which he produced with Alexander Campbell; *To Thnelion: The Union of Christians on Christian Principles* (1852); and *The Death of Christ* (1853). Full biographical treatments are Roscoe M. Pierson, ed., *The Autobiography of Walter Scott* (1952); William Baxter, *Life of Elder Walter Scott* (1874), which was later abridged by B. A. Abbott under the same title (1926); and Dwight E. Stevenson, *Walter Scott: Voice of the Golden Oracle* (1946). The best interpretive study is William A. Gerrard III, *A Biographical Study of Walter Scott: American Frontier Evangelist* (1992). See also Gerrard, "Walter Scott: Frontier Disciples Evangelist," *Lexington Theological Quarterly* 21 (Apr. 1986), and L. Edward Hicks, "Rational Religion in the Ohio Western Reserve (1827–1830): Walter Scott and the Restoration Appeal of Baptism for the Remission of Sin," *Restoration Quarterly* 34 (1992). Scott's role in the larger Restoration movement is treated in A. S. Hayden, *Early History of the Disciples in the Western Reserve, Ohio* (1876); Alonso W. Fortune, *The Disciples in Kentucky* (1932); and Winfred E. Garrison, *An American Religious Movement* (1945). His founding of Bacon College is discussed in Frank Gardner, "Walter Scott and Bacon College," *Christian Evangelist*, 25 Mar. 1937, and Dwight E. Stevenson, *The Bacon College Story* (1962).

DAVID B. ELLER

SCOTT, Walter Dill (1 May 1869–23 Sept. 1955), applied psychologist, was born in Cooksville, Illinois, the son of James Sterling Scott, a Nova Scotia–born farmer, and Henrietta Sutton, a teacher. Their oldest child, Mary Louise, taught Walter and three other siblings in a rural schoolhouse. Walter took over the management of the family farm for his ailing father. The health problems of his father and the rigors of farm labor later inspired his psychological interest in personal motivation.

In 1884 Scott entered Illinois State Normal University and after teaching in rural grade schools accepted a four-year scholarship to Northwestern in 1891. There he played on the varsity football team and paid his rent by tutoring and coaching children of wealthy families in numerous subjects and sports. Elected senior class president and member of Phi Beta Kappa, he contributed actively to undergraduate publications, the university settlement house, and the Young Men's Christian Association.

At Northwestern, Scott became a Presbyterian and an admirer of the Reverend Newell D. Hillis, who persuaded him to become a missionary to China. Scott also fell under the influence of the moral philosopher George A. Coe, who promoted the utility of knowledge in serving social improvement. Coe introduced Scott to William James's psychology and hypnotism. Another influence was his classmate and fiancée, Anna Marcy Miller; after graduation she prepared for graduate study in Germany while he prepared for China at McCormick Theological Seminary. As no call came from China at the time that he received his seminary degree in 1898, Scott made plans to study in Germany instead. He married Miller in 1898 just before the couple traveled to Halle, where she pursued a doctorate in literature. Scott began doctoral studies at nearby Leipzig in April 1899 with Wilhelm Wundt, the founder of modern laboratory psychology. The Scotts had two children.

Scott's dissertation, *Die Psychologie der Triebe historisch-kritisch betrachtet* (1900), was a "historical-critical" review of German contributions to the psychology of *Triebe*, which best translates as "impulses" but also connotes drives, instincts, or desires. It concludes with a favorable estimation of Wundt's idiosyncratic view of volitional mind. While most American psychologists had ignored Wundt's qualitative conceptions of "psychic causality" and impulses that originated in willed actions before evolving into involuntary movements, Scott researched their intellectual origins. When Northwestern hired him to develop a psychology laboratory in 1900, Scott spent a summer acquiring Wundt's methodology from the master's leading disciple in America, E. B. Titchener, who is most responsible for misinterpreting Wundt into the Anglo-American tradition of associationist psychology. Wundt rejected that tradition, however, and Scott's dissertation ignored it. Describing how Wundt's *Wille* was an evolutionary desire-power (*Begehrungsvermoegen*) that determined mentality and behavior, Scott noted that the master "felt obliged to abandon" any freedom for the will.

Scott's interest in a system that unified instinct, reflex, drives, and conscious choice as psych(olog)ically caused actions (that were reducible to volition, but not physiology) allowed him to explore new uses for scientific psychology before many of his contemporaries. American professional psychology was largely abandoning moral philosophical concern for individual agency at the turn of the century. Positivist leaders of the profession increasingly isolated demonstrable behaviors in the laboratory or measured mental abilities by comparing individuals' test scores with statistically aggregated norms. While the positivists believed their research would be useful to society, the earliest areas of application—in clinical counseling and special education—tended to bring psychologists into contact with subjects whose mentality and behavior were abnormal. Scott's psychology also moved away from a concern for moral agency. But his practical interest in motivating normal persons for social purposes and his Wundtian view of mind-body parallelism, which allowed the linkage of involuntary impulse with voluntary action, placed him outside the positivist mainstream.

Soon after becoming an instructor at Northwestern in 1900, Scott met Thomas Balmer, a persuasive business manager who was seeking scientific assistance and legitimacy for the field of advertising. Scott hesitated before agreeing to help; two better-known, positivist psychologists, Hugo Muensterberg and E. L. Thorndike, had previously rejected this request. Scott's paper "The Psychology of Involuntary Attention as Applied to Advertising" received the prolonged applause of an audience of businessmen at Chicago's Agate Club in December 1901. According to Scott, because "experimental science" was demonstrating the "close relation" of "feeling . . . to interest and desire," the advertiser "must be an artist . . . [whose] production will appeal to the sentiment as well as to the intellect of those who are to be influenced by it" (*Advertising Experience* 14 [1902], pp. 7–10). In arguing the limited effectiveness of rational persuasion, Scott redirected advertising toward the sensual impulses of consumers. Because he viewed all mental behavior as active and volitional, Scott regarded advertising as constructive and consensual motivation, akin to athletic coaching. During the next decade, he published three books and more than sixty articles on the techniques of suggestion in advertising, public speaking, and psychotherapy. He received disapproving comments from Titchener, the preeminent defender of "pure" psychology, and Scott's joint appointment in Northwestern's School of Commerce in 1909 did not enhance his scientific prestige.

After 1910 Scott's research interests shifted from motivating consumers as a generalized type to identifying those individuals who could best motivate workers or "sell" retail customers. Modifying the principles of Frederick W. Taylor, who had assumed the average worker to be rational in pursuit of maximal wages, Scott encouraged employers to appeal to nonrational instincts and habits as a means to increased productivity. In 1911 Scott published two books in which he analogized the workplace to the athletic field, advising managers to foster the spirit of constructive competition and teamwork as means to greater productivity. Employment managers' demands for proven methods for efficient personnel selection caused Scott to turn increasingly toward the positivist and more quantitative view of evolutionary mind, which was shaped by "individual [for Scott, 'personal'] differences" of inheritance and environment.

After 1914, Scott constructed rating scales that employers could use to evaluate personal qualities in job applicants. His inclination to link mind and motivation led him to adapt the scale to—and to originate the quantification of—personal qualities (e.g., "manner" and "conversational convincingness"). This can be seen both as a throwback to preprofessional faculty psychology and a forerunner of modern personality research. While Thorndike developed the scalar method to quantify a diversity of mental abilities, which challenged the current "pure" scientific conception of a monolithic "general intelligence," Scott's interest in rating personal qualities traced the outer boundary between professional respectability and charlatanry.

Scott's business research led to his appointment as the first American professor of applied psychology, at the Carnegie Institute of Technology in 1916. There Scott directed the Bureau of Salesmanship Research, one of the earliest business consortia within academia; implemented his Rating Scale for Selecting Salesmen; and devised early group tests of mental and personal qualities. These innovations led to his election to the executive council of the American Psychological Association in 1915 and membership on the editorial staff of the new *Journal of Applied Psychology* in 1917. His article in the first issue of this journal represents the first professional effort to validate a theoretical construct, "general intelligence," against an external criterion: in this case, employers' ratings of the same quality.

When the United States entered World War I, Scott hoped that APA president Robert M. Yerkes would encourage the military to adopt Scott's rating scale for use in officer selection. Yerkes, however, had a different vision of the role of the military psychologist, and Scott sought other means of access to the military. On Thorndike's recommendation, the Adjutant General's Office invited Scott to demonstrate the scale's efficiency in rationalizing personnel evaluations. Scott "sold" the method to numerous staff and line officers by adapting the criteria for rating officer candidates to their desiderata. His rating scale even proved useful to Yerkes and other mental testers, when Thorndike demonstrated the validity of the first mass intelligence test by corroborating recruit test performance with officers' estimations. Scott's contributions enabled the War Department to establish the civilian Committee on Classification of Personnel in the Army in August 1917.

Although officers appreciated the legitimacy that Scott's rating scale added to their judgments, the method proved unreliable and unsuited to rapid officer selection. Scott's primary wartime achievement was directing the innovation of more efficient personnel recordkeeping. Other CCPA members advanced the standardized testing of skill proficiency, which met army needs more readily and convincingly than either the personality or intelligence assessments. As Yerkes succeeded in establishing an alternative Psychology Division in the Surgeon General's Office, and as the CCPA did not include intelligence test results on recruit record cards until the war was almost over, the contributions of the new psychology to the military were far less than professional psychologists and the public have believed or social critics have feared.

A grateful War Department commissioned Scott as a colonel (the highest rank of any psychologist) in 1918 and conferred on him the Distinguished Service Medal in 1919. Although Yerkes and other colleagues did not received such honors, they gained greater publicity in the postwar era as the American public became fascinated by intelligence testing. Ironically, Scott became associated with the popular myth that the army had used "general intelligence" tests, while, within the profession itself, his pluralistic view of mental abilities became the dominant trend in psychological assessment.

The APA elected Scott its president for 1919. That same year he organized the Scott Company of psychological consultants to take advantage of his profession's new celebrity. His wartime and postwar collaboration with Robert Clothier produced *Personnel Management: Principles, Practices, and Point of View* (1923), which remained in print until 1979. Reflective of current welfare capitalist ideas, the textbook advanced a gestalt-like approach to workers as integrally related to their work and generalized, if not romanticized, a worker's desire for self-improvement that transcended the division of labor and mere financial gain.

Northwestern elected Scott president in 1920, which diverted him from further contributions to applied psychology. The Scott Company disbanded in 1923. As president, he endeavored to create an undergraduate department that would implement psychological methods for the admission, guidance, and placement of students. He also drew on his experience in salesmanship to link Northwestern and Chicago as an international nexus of education and commerce. A tireless fundraiser in the 1920s and during the Great Depression, Scott secured the construction of the university's North Side campus of professional schools.

Scott retired from Northwestern in 1939. Although his absence from professional activities precluded his participation in World War II psychology, his model of the wartime psychologist as civilian consultant was retained under the army's chief psychologist from 1941 to 1947, Walter V. Bingham, who had brought Scott to Carnegie Tech in 1916 and served as Scott's main assistant in the CCPA. During his later years, Scott served as chairperson of the editorial board of the *American People's Encyclopedia* and wrote biographies of some of Northwestern's greatest benefactors, including the school's founder, John Evans. Scott died in Evanston.

Scott held a progressive faith in the psychologist as an expert who could improve industrial capitalism by recognizing the importance of personal qualities in an increasingly impersonal society. He believed that the appeals of advertising to the impulses of consumers would humanize that field and that managerial attention to workers' nonfinancial desires would preserve worker dignity and the "instinct of craftsmanship" in the modern factory. Nevertheless he is responsible for helping construct a popular culture that regularly appeals to nonrational urges while suggesting conformism as the source of values (e.g., "Do You Want to Know What Others Think About You?" *American Magazine*, Nov. 1920, pp. 44–47, 98–99, 102). While Scott made no theoretical contributions to the new science of psychology, his interests in personal motivation and his practical-minded readiness to consult with business managers greatly accelerated the profession's development as an applied science: adherents of applied psychology began to dominate APA membership rolls after the 1940s.

• Scott's papers, which are in the Northwestern University Library, include a bibliography of his works, a copy of his dissertation, a 1949 autobiographical manuscript ("The Ancestry and Early Days of Walter Dill Scott"), and materials from his presidency and his involvement in both the CCPA and the Scott Company. The office papers of the CCPA are located in the Old Army Division of the National Archives; other collections that deal with Scott's World War I activities include the Walter V. Bingham Papers and the Leonard Ferguson Papers at Carnegie-Mellon University, the Grenville Clark Papers at Dartmouth College, the Robert M. Yerkes Papers at Yale University, and the papers of the Division of Psychology in the National Academy of Sciences. The Bingham collection contains Scott's apologia, "A History of the Committee of Classification of Personnel in the Army," of Sept. (?) 1917. A biography is Jacob Zarel Jacobson, *Scott of Northwestern: The Life Story of a Pioneer in Psychology and Education* (1951), which Scott helped write. Michael M. Sokal's bibliography in the *Dictionary of American Biography*, fifth supp., p. 612, should be consulted for important primary and secondary works. See also Daniel Kevles, "Testing the Army's Intelligence: Psychologists and the Military in World War I," *Journal of American History* 55 (1968): 565–81; Franz Samelson, "Putting Psychology on the Map: Ideology and Intelligence Testing, in *Psychology and Social Context*, ed. A. R. Buss (1979), pp. 103–68; and Richard T. von Mayrhauser, "The Triumph of Utility: The Forgotten Clash of American Psychologies in World War I" (Ph.D. diss., Univ. of Chicago, 1986). An obituary is in the *New York Times*, 25 Sept. 1955.

RICHARD T. VON MAYRHAUSER

SCOTT, Walter Edward (1870?–5 Jan. 1954), prospector and publicist, also known as "Death Valley Scotty," was born in Cynthiana, Kentucky, the son of a prosperous horse breeder. The names of his parents are not known. Dates suggested for his birth range from 1868 to 1876 (the date Scott himself claimed). At an early age Scott allegedly followed his older brother Warner to Nevada, where he was employed by a rancher, John Sparks. From there he went to Death Valley and reportedly drove a borax team at the Harmony Works in 1885. His subsequent job was as a sharpshooter and bronco rider for the Buffalo Bill Wild West Show toward the end of the 1880s; sources speculate that his talents as an entrepreneur and publicist stem from this period. While performing in New York City, he met a store clerk, Ella Josephine Millius, whom he married in 1900. The couple had one child.

After his marriage Scott quit his job with Buffalo Bill and moved with his wife to Death Valley, where gold had been discovered at Tonapah in 1900. Julian Gerard, vice president of New York's Knickerbocker Trust Company, provided Scott with a $1,500 grubstake in 1902. It is doubtful that Scott ever found any gold during his long career as a prospector; it is certain, however, that he quickly learned the art of public relations. After a period of time in Death Valley, Scott traveled by train to Philadelphia, where he reported to authorities that someone had stolen a sack with 120 pounds of gold from him, thereby earning national press attention for himself.

Scott's first large-scale public relations event involved another railroad trip. This time he arrived in Barstow, California, in June 1905 attired in his typical sombrero, blue shirt, and red tie. Here he arranged for a special locomotive and coach from the Santa Fe Railroad to take him and his party from Los Angeles to Chicago. For $5,500, which Scott apparently obtained from Burdon Gaylord, a New York and California mining promoter and operator, the railroad company agreed to provide him a train that would travel 106 miles per hour. Setting a speed record, Scott garnered widespread national attention for his trip on the Coyote Special. Newspapers called him "Death Valley Scotty, the cowboy miner, the mysterious Midas of the Desert" following his trip on 9 July 1905. The San Francisco Opera planned a melodrama starring Scott titled *Scotty, King of the Desert Mine*, which opened 26 March 1906. When the melodrama opened again in Los Angeles later in the year, Scott's role was played by an understudy, as Scott had been arrested for a shooting incident in Death Valley. During this decade, in addition to polishing his entrepreneurial skills, Scott found his real "gold mine" in Albert M. Johnson, president of the National Life Insurance Company. Johnson was happy to invest in Scott's schemes, releasing him from further prospecting.

In 1908 Scott took a party into Death Valley to see his alleged mine. The party consisted of Scott and his wife; Rol King, the owner of the Hollenbeck Bar; and Sidney Norman, a newspaperman. They traveled over the Wingate Pass into Death Valley. Norman implied that Scott engineered various "disasters" throughout the trip, such as staging armed attacks and providing them only brackish drinking water at the Eagle Borax Works, to prevent the party from reaching the mine. Scott mysteriously disappeared, leaving the party for seven days at Benne Wells, where the temperature reached 126 degrees during the day. King became ill, party members went for help, and all then left the area without ever seeing the mine.

In 1912 Scott claimed to have sold that same gold mine to a syndicate for $1 million. After the publicity from this announcement brought a suit from a creditor, Scott was arrested and subsequently confessed to a grand jury that the mine was in fact a fraud and that he was destitute. Scott faded from public view until the 1920s, when with Johnson's money he began building "Scotty's Castle" on land he purportedly owned in Death Valley. The castle contained lavish, handmade interior decorations, a music room, and eighteen fireplaces. Johnson had spent $2 million on its construction when the stock market crash of 1929 forced him to withdraw his support. On 4 February 1930 the Kansas City papers carried a story claiming that Scott's great wealth had been wiped out due to stock deals. Ever the creative publicist, Scott claimed that a "hidden gold mine" would return his wealth.

When a presidential proclamation created the Death Valley Monument on 11 February 1935, Scott was forced to tell Albert Johnson that he had never filed claim to the property. Thirteen days after Death Valley was made a national monument, however, the House of Representatives Land Committee approved a bill allowing Albert Johnson to buy 1,529 acres under and about Scotty's Castle for $1.25 per acre. Scott's name appears nowhere in this record.

In 1937, when Scott's wife sued him for a $2,500-per-month allowance, he was forced to testify in court that he had no personal assets. Julian Gerard sued Scott in 1940 on the basis of their 1902 contract and received seventeen worthless mining claims. After Johnson's death in 1948, Scott continued to live on the property and give tours of the estate. He was buried on the grounds following his death in Stovepipe Wells, California.

Walter Edward Scott managed to make a living for himself in the gold business without ever mining an ounce of ore. He is best remembered today for his ingenious creation and marketing of a persona that matched the public's image of the romance and myths surrounding those who prospected for gold.

• The California Room of the California State Library, Sacramento, has most of the publicized activities of Walter Edward Scott cataloged under "Characters; Eccentric." C. B. Glasscock, *Here's Death Valley* (1940), contains the most complete biographical account of Scott. Edwin Corle, *Desert Country* (1941), also contains useful information, particularly on the 1908 trip from Barstow to see the mine. Dane Coolidge, *Death Valley Prospectors* (1937), and Bourke Lee, *Death Valley Men* (1932), contain interesting views by contemporaries on Scott's activities. The Works Progress Administration's *Death Valley: A Guide* contains a good description of Scotty's Castle. See also the *New York Times*, 8 Jan. 1937, and *Newsweek*, 16 Jan. 1937, for further information on Scott's marriage. The *New York Times* obituary, 6 Jan. 1954, is not entirely reliable.

SUSAN E. GUNTER

SCOTT, William Alexander, II (29 Sept. 1902–7 Feb. 1934), newspaper publisher, was born in Edwards, Mississippi, the son of the Reverend William Alexander Scott, Sr., a Christian church minister and owner of a printing shop that produced church publications, and Emeline Southall, a typesetter who printed her husband's publications. Scott learned printing from his mother. At Jackson College in Mississippi (1920–1922) and at Morehouse College in Atlanta (1923–1925), he studied business and mathematics. He helped publish the Morehouse yearbook, was a quarterback on the football team, and with his older brother Aurelius became a champion debater. He left college without graduating.

After a year of teaching at Swift College in Knoxville, Tennessee, Scott began his business career in sales, advertising, and publishing. In 1927 in Jacksonville, Florida, he teamed with Aurelius to sell advertising for and to publish the *Jacksonville Negro Business Directory*, the first business listing to meet the needs of merchants catering to African Americans who migrated in the 1920s from farms to cities. In 1928 he published a similar directory for Atlanta's African-American businesses, printing it with equipment bought with a loan from an African-American bank. Scott planned to print a directory for Augusta when an Atlanta business executive persuaded him to publish a weekly newspaper. He decided that a newspaper could succeed financially if he made advertising rather than circulation his primary revenue source. Although Scott's banker warned him that there were not enough advertisers, Scott persisted, securing a loan with only his name.

The one African-American weekly in Atlanta, the *Independent*, was in decline, largely because its policies were linked to partisan politics. Scott was determined that his *Atlanta World* would be nonpartisan. From his first run (fewer than 2,000 copies) on 3 August 1928, Scott was sensitive to his market. He specialized in news about African-American religious, social, and educational activities, items that were systematically neglected by Atlanta's three white-owned dailies. The *World*'s news pages also contained national news of importance to African Americans. The newspaper's logo carried the words "Dixie's Standard Race Journal."

As Scott expanded his local advertising base and attracted national advertising, he followed the lead of successful big-city papers, sponsoring promotions. "Better Home Week" advertised "free prizes by the *World* and local advertisers" (1 Dec. 1931). He also offered advertisers free illustrations and layout and copy services. He sold the paper to white merchants, advertising the *World* as the way to reach Atlanta's "90,000 Negroes" (29 July 1932).

National advertising grew as Scott converted the paper from a weekly to a three-times-a-week paper and finally to a daily, and he built a syndicate consisting of three family-owned and dozens of affiliated weeklies and semi-weeklies. By 1930 he was publishing the *Atlanta World* twice a week and owned two other semi-weeklies, the *Birmingham World* and the *Memphis World*. Despite the onset of the depression, Scott, led on by what his family called his "dead reckoning," spent most of 1930 traveling and selling his plan to link African-American newspapers across the South.

On 1 January 1931 Scott launched his Scott Newspaper Syndicate, the first such independent venture by an African-American newspaper publisher. He created a financial base that enriched him and supported the expansion of the African-American press. Under cooperative agreements, members shared advertising revenue. The *World* kept income from national advertising in its national edition, which was shipped by train and inserted in the local weeklies or semi-weeklies. The local publishers kept revenue from local advertising and from local circulation sales. The syndicate's members also exchanged articles and news items.

Scott next aimed to make the *Atlanta World* into a daily. As a step toward that, in 1931 he hired as managing editor a Chicago journalist, Frank Marshall Davis, who helped him publish all three *World*s three times a week. From this time on Scott focused entirely on the business operation, delegating content to Davis and the printing of local and national editions to his younger brother Cornelius. On 14 March 1932 Scott unveiled a six-day daily; six weeks later he added the Saturday paper. Although the newspaper remained nonpartisan, Davis's editorials (usually written without Scott's knowledge) became a voice for criminal justice and civil rights. His first editorial criticized the state for "legal lynching" because it sentenced a disproportionate number of African Americans to the electric chair (14 Mar. 1932).

Because of his success and his aggressive, self-confident personality, Scott's four marriages made him a target of envy and controversy and may have contributed to his murder. Scott's first marriage in 1922 was to Lucile McAllister, daughter of a minister; they had two sons before they divorced in 1929. That same year Scott wed Mildred Jones of South Carolina, from whom he was separated within months. In 1932 Scott wed Ella Ramsay of Atlanta, a marriage that lasted about a year. On 21 October 1933 he secretly married Agnes Maddox, an Atlanta librarian, fueling rumors that he had not been divorced properly from his third wife. In January 1934 Scott was shot from behind at night as he parked his car in his garage. He survived surgery but developed peritonitis and died eight days after the shooting. On his deathbed, he reportedly named a suspect, his fourth wife's brother, who was exonerated after an inquest. No one was ever tried for Scott's murder.

The first African-American publisher of a chain of newspapers and the first African American since the Civil War to publish a daily newspaper, Scott overcame innumerable odds. At his funeral his banker observed, "To break down the barriers is the problem of every young Negro" (*Atlanta Daily World*, 11 Feb. 1934). At his death the *World* employed fifty full-time employees, including Cornelius Scott, who remained

as the publisher into the 1990s. The syndicate grew to include fifty minority-owned newspapers, including a Cherokee tribal weekly in Oklahoma. As the only African-American daily in the United States for twenty-four years, the *World* helped launch the careers of a generation of promising young black journalists. In 1976 *Jet Magazine* named Scott one of the nation's top 200 African Americans during the 200 years of American independence. In 1988 he was elected to the Howard University Hall of Fame for African-American journalists, and in 1996 he was inducted into the Georgia Newspaper Hall of Fame.

• Scattered papers and letters of Scott's belong to individual members of the Scott family, and others are located at the *Atlanta Daily World*. The best available primary sources are the issues of the *Atlanta World* (after 1932 the *Atlanta Daily World*) on microfilm, from 1928 to 1934. See also *Frank Marshall Davis: Livin' the Blues: Memoirs of a Black Journalist and Poet*, ed. John Edgar Tidwell (1992), and Leonard Ray Teel, "W. A. Scott and the *Atlanta World*," *American Journalism* 6, no. 3 (1989): 159-78. An obituary appears in the *Atlanta Constitution*, 8 Feb. 1934, and the *Atlanta Daily World*, 12 Feb. 1934.

LEONARD RAY TEEL

SCOTT, William Berryman (12 Feb. 1858–29 Mar. 1947), paleontologist, was born in Cincinnati, Ohio, the son of Mary Elizabeth Hodge and William McKendree Scott, a Presbyterian minister. Scott grew up in an environment suffused with Presbyterianism. His maternal grandfather was the leading Old School Presbyterian theologian, Charles Hodge, and his father, a graduate of Princeton Theological Seminary, taught at Northwestern (later McCormick) Theological Seminary. When Scott's father died in 1861, the family moved to Princeton to live with his mother's father, who was teaching at Princeton Theological Seminary.

Scott originally intended, not surprisingly, to become a minister. But at the College of New Jersey (later Princeton University), which he entered in 1873 at age of fifteen, Scott developed an interest in science, especially chemistry, psychology, and geology, the latter through a course from the famous Swiss geologist Arnold Guyot. Scott's future direction was determined when he and classmate and close friend Henry Fairfield Osborn convinced two faculty members that Princeton should copy Yale's example of sponsoring geological expeditions. Thus, after their graduation in 1877, Scott, Osborn, two faculty members, sixteen other students, and two cooks headed for Wyoming and Colorado. Scott spent the 1877–1878 academic year in graduate study at Princeton where he sided with paleontologist Edward D. Cope in his fierce feud with Othniel C. Marsh over the interpretation of fossil evidence. The following summer, Scott and Osborn went on a second Princeton expedition, which brought back important fossils that became the basis of Princeton's geological collection. These two expeditions launched Scott's and Osborn's scientific careers.

The Scottish president of the College of New Jersey, James McCosh, decided to strengthen his faculty by encouraging several of the brightest recent graduates, including Scott and Osborn, to pursue graduate study in Europe with a promised appointment to the Princeton faculty awaiting their return. In 1878 Scott went to England, where he attended Thomas H. Huxley's lectures in London and then studied embryology with Francis M. Balfour at Cambridge. The following year he went to Heidelberg to study under Carl Gegenbaur and wrote his Ph.D. dissertation on the embryology of the lamprey.

True to his word, in 1880 McCosh hired nine of "my bright young men," including Scott. Before offering Scott the position, McCosh wrote to him in Heidelberg to remind him that Princeton was a religious college and wanted to know how Scott's faith had withstood the European experience. Scott's response is not extant, but it apparently satisfied the president, and the newly minted Ph.D. was appointed assistant in geology for the 1880–1881 academic year. Promotions came rapidly as Scott became assistant professor in 1882 and in 1883 professor of geology, his rank for the next forty-seven years. He married Alice A. Post in December 1883 and settled in Princeton, where they raised seven children and lived the rest of their lives.

Although he initially taught a wide variety of science courses, he was able to concentrate on vertebrate paleontology as Princeton's staff became larger and more specialized. Scott energetically pursued fieldwork, going on eight more expeditions to the West. On the last trip, in 1893, he took John Bell Hatcher, a younger colleague. Realizing Hatcher's methodological superiority, Scott declared himself an amateur, went home, and never collected another fossil. Instead he spent much of the next four decades writing up the results of Hatcher's expeditions to the West and to Patagonia (1896–1899). Although Hatcher died in 1904, Scott continued to work on the Patagonian findings until 1932, producing fifteen volumes.

Not an innovator, Scott's greatest contributions to his field came from his work as a synthesizer and as a promoter of his field's academic welfare. He and Osborn were two of the dominant figures in paleontology in the 1890s and early 1900s. Scott remained at Princeton, and Osborn moved to Columbia, each creating leading paleontology graduate programs. As in his relationship with Hatcher, Scott continued to be willing to step aside for younger colleagues and to promote their work. When Princeton president Woodrow Wilson agreed in 1904 to create a geology department, Scott was named chairman, a position he held until his retirement in 1930. Scott taught only undergraduate courses and left graduate instruction to talented younger academics he recruited like William J. Sinclair. Scott built the department from three to thirteen members and made Princeton a center for the study of vertebrate paleontology.

Scott also became a national academic statesman, playing a leading role in several professional organizations. He served as president of the Paleontology Society in 1911, the Geological Society of America in 1925,

and the American Philosophical Society from 1918 to 1925.

Scott's main scholarly contribution was in increasing the base of knowledge rather than innovating. He was a workhorse who turned out more than 170 publications stretching over seventy years. The two series on Hatcher's expeditions were monumental. His *A History of Land Mammals in the Western Hemisphere* (1913) was his most significant single work. His publications showed careful attention to detail, and his strengths were description and taxonomy. Scott was not very interested in theory, and his essential views changed little after 1900. Although he rejected the position of his grandfather, Charles Hodge, one of the leading opponents of evolution, Scott never embraced Darwinism, first taking a neo-Lamarkian position and then withdrawing from the debate.

After retiring from his academic post at age seventy-two, Scott continued to write prodigiously, to the week of his death seventeen years later at age ninety. He finally finished the volumes on Hatcher's Patagonian expeditions in 1932 and published a second edition of his *A History of Land Mammals* in 1937. He directed a major project on the Oligocene mammalian fauna of the White River Group from 1936 to 1941. Then, already in his mid-eighties, he began a manuscript on the late Eocene Uinta fauna, which he worked on until two days before his death in Princeton.

Scott was a pioneer in the academic study of vertebrate paleontology whose original contributions ended by the turn of the century but who worked ceaselessly to shape and promote his discipline as it took its place in the emerging world of research universities.

• Scott's faculty file in the Seeley S. Mudd Manuscript Library of the Princeton University Archives provides plentiful biographical information. Fourteen boxes of Scott materials are in the main archives, and scattered materials are in the Woodrow Wilson Papers and other collections at Princeton. His autobiography, *Some Memoirs of a Paleontologist*, was published by Princeton University Press in 1939. But the original typescript in the Princeton archives is much more revealing. An obituary is in the *New York Times*, 30 Mar. 1947.

W. BRUCE LESLIE

SCOTT, Winfield (13 June 1786–29 May 1866), soldier, was born at "Laurel Branch," the family plantation near Petersburg, Virginia, the son of William Scott, a farmer, and Ann Mason. His father died when Scott was six and his mother when he was seventeen. He had two years of rudimentary education at a Quaker boarding school, and in 1804 he went to school in Richmond. He entered the College of William and Mary but left after a year to read law and was admitted to the bar in 1806. After the *Chesapeake* affair in 1807, Scott joined a volunteer cavalry unit in Virginia; his appetite whetted by this experience, he sought a commission as a captain in the army from President Thomas Jefferson, which he received effective 3 May 1808. He immediately recruited a company and was sent to New Orleans.

In New Orleans Scott was under the command of Brigadier General James Wilkinson, whom he had disliked ever since he heard Wilkinson's self-serving testimony at the trial of former U.S. vice president Aaron Burr in 1807. Scott thought Wilkinson had covered his own guilt and called him "a liar and a scoundrel." Scott was found guilty of disrespectful language at the resulting court-martial and was suspended from rank and pay for a year, which he spent reading military tactics. Scott was promoted to lieutenant colonel as of 6 July 1812 and became second in command of an artillery regiment as the War of 1812 began.

Scott was soon ordered to Lake Erie but became a prisoner of war just eight days after arrival. He was forced to retreat by overwhelming British forces at Queenston, and he and the other officers surrendered their commands when no rescue came from the American militia on the other side of the Niagara River. He had an understandable disdain for militia for the rest of his life. In November 1812 Scott was paroled, and in February 1813 he returned to his regiment a full colonel. As General Henry Dearborn's adjutant general, he set about putting the army in order and establishing a general staff, following a French manual. He led the invasion at Fort George on 27 May 1813 and broke his collarbone in the explosion of a magazine. Although injured, he pursued the British beyond Fort George but lost a chance (as he thought) to capture the entire British army in the area when he received orders to stop pursuit (*Memoirs*, vol. 1, p. 91).

Promoted to brigadier general and placed under Major General Jacob Brown, Scott established a camp of instruction near Buffalo, New York, with himself as drill sergeant. Forming his officers into squads, Scott instructed them endlessly in marching, deploying, and using the bayonet, and his officers then rigorously drilled the men. The effectiveness of Scott's training program was demonstrated at Chippewa on 5 July 1814. The British commander thought he was facing militia, but as Scott's disciplined and trained troops moved upon him, he is alleged to have said, "Those are regulars, by God!" The victory restored American morale; for the first time in the war, American regulars had met British regulars in roughly equal numbers and won. The success at Chippewa was followed by mixed success at Lundy's Lane. Scott heavily engaged the British in front while General Thomas S. Jesup conducted a successful flanking movement. The Americans did not have an adequate reserve, however, and both Scott and Brown were wounded. Brown ordered a retreat, and the battle ended with British control of the field, but tactically the battle was a draw, and American Soldiers had proved their ability to stand up to British regulars. Scott took no further active role in the war but received a gold medal from Congress and was promoted to brevet major general for his actions at Chippewa and Niagara. Moreover, his staff work for Dearborn and his training camp at Buffalo represented a new level of professionalism in the American army.

In 1817 Scott married Maria D. Mayo, the daughter of John Mayo, one of the richest men of Richmond, Virginia. The couple had seven children, two of whom died in infancy. Because of tensions, which arose from their different temperaments, and her desire to travel, his wife was often gone for long periods of time, and from 1838 to 1843 she and their four daughters were in Europe.

In his memoirs Scott is relatively brief about the years after the War of 1812, which were marked by notable achievement but also by controversy. In a private conversation in 1817, for example, Scott incurred the displeasure of Andrew Jackson, when he described one of Jackson's orders as mutinous. Further dispute developed in 1821, when Congress reduced the army. There would be only one major general, Brown, and two brigadiers, Edmund P. Gaines and Scott. The result was an acrimonious argument over seniority between the latter two, and in 1827, as Brown approached death, both officers violated army regulations by engaging in a pamphlet war over the seniority issue. When Brown died in 1828, President John Quincy Adams wisely appointed General Alexander Macomb, who was junior to both Gaines and Scott, as senior general.

In 1832 Scott was ordered west to deal with the Black Hawk War. Because of widespread cholera outbreaks that year, Scott studied the disease and treatment before he went. He was therefore prepared when the dread illness broke out on his troopships on the Great Lakes and won wide acclaim when he personally cared for some of the sick soldiers. He landed at Fort Dearborn (Chicago) as the epidemic appeared to be over and proceeded to Rock Island to negotiate a treaty with the Sac and Fox Indians. Cholera broke out again, however, and Scott wrote his famous cholera order, which required that drunken soldiers be forced to dig their own graves, for drunkenness led to cholera, Scott thought, and he saw no reason sober soldiers should perform the task (Henry Dodge Order Book, Iowa State Department of History and Archives). No sooner had Scott returned from the Black Hawk War than President Jackson called him to Washington to confer on the nullification crisis in South Carolina. Scott went south and unobtrusively inspected fortifications at Charleston, ordered their reinforcement, and went on to inspect other installations in Augusta and Savannah.

In 1836 Scott arrived in Florida, where he had been assigned to subdue the Seminole Indians after the Dade Massacre. Hampered by difficulties in manpower, transport, and supply, Scott's campaign was unsuccessful, and he was sent to Georgia to deal with Creek Indian uprisings. Accused of delay by General Jesup, Scott was called back to Washington by President Jackson to face a court of inquiry. Scott was vindicated by the court, which amounted to an offhand criticism of President Jackson for failing to support his general.

At this point Scott was assigned a series of duties that won him recognition as peacemaker. After the

Caroline incident in December 1837, President Martin Van Buren sent Scott to upper New York State to preserve U.S. neutrality by preventing American help to the Canadian rebels, for with most of the army in Florida, it was essential to keep the peace. He restored order without violence, holding public meetings to gather support, arresting American filibusterers, and blocking rebel efforts to transport arms and men across the international boundary. Scott was then sent south to superintend the removal of the Cherokee Indians under the Federal Removal Policy but was ordered back to the Canadian border to ensure continued enforcement of neutrality and to calm the boundary dispute between Maine and New Brunswick. Working with the governor of Maine and the lieutenant governor of New Brunswick, in 1839 Scott successfully persuaded both sides to withdraw troops from the disputed territory while the respective governments dealt with the boundary issue.

Scott's peacemaking activities along the northern boundary led to a movement to nominate him for the Whig candidacy for president in 1840. He was backed by party leaders in New York and Pennsylvania, who actually wanted William Henry Harrison but did not want to push Harrison too early. Scott apparently never understood he was being used, and he accepted his defeat gracefully. He was also mentioned for the Whig nomination in 1844, but Henry Clay was nominated without dissent.

Promptly after the outbreak of the Mexican War in 1846, President James K. Polk offered Scott, who had become general in chief on the death of General Macomb in 1841, supreme command of the enlarged army. Scott immediately plunged into planning, which upset the naïve president, who thought Scott should be off to the Rio Grande instead. When Scott submitted his plan for an attack on Veracruz to Secretary of War William L. Marcy, Marcy was convinced that Scott was the man to carry it out. However, by then Polk feared the potential political strength of two successful Whig generals, Scott and Zachary Taylor, either of whom might become popular enough to run for president. Polk and Senator Thomas Hart Benton cooked up a scheme to appoint Benton lieutenant general to command the expedition from Veracruz to Mexico City. The idea was abandoned in the face of strong objections from both parties, and on 23 November 1846 Scott was appointed to lead the Veracruz campaign. He landed below the city on 9 March 1847 and spent two weeks establishing his position, digging trenches, and constructing gun emplacements in order to mount a successful siege. Veracruz surrendered and was occupied on 29 March 1847.

Moving inland, Scott turned the Mexican army under Antonio López de Santa Anna at Cerro Gordo on 18 April and advanced to Jalapa, where he paused, concerned about short supply and the loss of seven regiments of volunteers at the end of their enlistments. However, Scott arrived at Puebla on 15 May, and in July he received desperately needed additional troops and money for the purchase of supplies. Scott then cut

his lines of communication with Veracruz and marched on Mexico City. This was a bold step, and in Britain the duke of Wellington was supposed to have remarked: "Scott is lost. He has been carried away by success. He can't take the city, and he can't fall back on his bases" (Eisenhower, *So Far from God*, p. 298).

Victory at Contreras opened the road to Mexico City. After a brief armistice, during which the Mexicans were to consider peace proposals but instead played for time, Scott resumed hostilities on 7 September 1847. Victories at Molino del Rey on 8 September and Chapultepec on 13 September forced the Mexican army to withdraw from Mexico City, and Scott entered on 14 September. In the face of civilian hostilities, Scott declared martial law over Mexican civilians and U.S. soldiers alike in order to prevent atrocities and placed the property of Mexican citizens under protection.

Then came news of the recall of Nicholas Trist, who was to negotiate a peace treaty, and Polk's order to Scott to resume the war. Justifiably concerned about the bloodshed and expense of potential guerrilla warfare and long occupation duty, Scott urged Trist to negotiate despite his recall. Trist agreed, and the Treaty of Guadalupe Hidalgo, which gave President Polk all he wanted, was signed 2 February 1848. Scott levied $3 million in taxes on those areas of Mexico he occupied and sent $100,000 back to the United States to be used for one of his favorite projects, an army "asylum."

Meanwhile some of the other generals, especially Gideon Pillow, whose motives were clearly vanity and ambition, exaggerated their exploits in letters to a New Orleans newspaper in a manner calculated to downgrade Scott. Indignant, Scott placed Pillow (who had been Polk's close friend, law partner, and political supporter) under arrest. Polk therefore relieved Scott on 13 January 1848 and ordered a court of inquiry. Pillow was charged with violating regulations by writing newspaper articles and exaggerating or falsifying his battle reports. Most of the testimony supported Scott, but the court cleared Pillow, and the president sustained the finding. Nevertheless, Scott eventually received the thanks of Congress, a gold medal, and promotion to brevet lieutenant general effective 29 March 1847 for the Mexican campaign.

Scott was mentioned for the Whig nomination in 1848, but General Taylor was elected president and died in 1850. The Whigs sought a military hero again in 1852, and the party mobilized for Scott's election. However, Scott remained quiet on the slavery question and had been slow in his support of the Compromise of 1850, which worried southern members of the Whig party. He accepted the platform, which included full support of the Compromise of 1850, including the Fugitive Slave Law, which worried many northern members of the party. Scott lost the election, carrying only four states, although the popular vote was not nearly so one-sided.

The successful Democratic candidate, Franklin Pierce, appointed Jefferson Davis as his secretary of war, and Davis and Scott soon quarreled, initially over reimbursements for official travel. Scott and Davis argued over other questions as well, but the underlying cause of their quarrels was longstanding defects in the command system, which led to a division between the line and staff of the army. Whereas the secretary of war controlled the staff, he had not customarily commanded the commanding general, whose duties were undefined by law. Davis sought to remedy that situation, and he had the law and Constitution on his side. Scott maintained that he did not have to follow the orders of the secretary of war except when they were given in the name of the president, but he lost the argument when the attorney general's opinion was that the orders of the secretary of war were always presumed to be issued under the authority of the president.

In the latter part of the 1850s, Scott devoted his attention to the establishment of a soldiers' home, a retired list, and increased pay for officers. He opposed the Mormon expedition in 1857, and in September 1859 he was sent to the Pacific Northwest on one last peace mission, successfully easing a boundary dispute between the United States and Great Britain over the island of San Juan.

Frightened by possible secession, Scott suggested in the fall of 1860 that the forts in the South be adequately garrisoned and renewed this appeal in December. During the Sumter crisis, Secretary of War John B. Floyd ignored Scott by directing military affairs without consulting the general in chief. However, when Buchanan reorganized his cabinet, he and the new secretary of war turned to Scott for advice, and Scott proposed to send 250 recruits and supplies to Fort Sumter. In January 1861 Scott assured Abraham Lincoln of his loyalty to the Union, and in February he took measures to insure the peaceful count of the ballots of the electoral college and proper security for the inauguration.

Scott had no desire to follow Virginia out of the Union and did his best to persuade Robert E. Lee to stay with the Union and to take command of the volunteer army. Scott sagely predicted a three-year war, a Union victory, and then prolonged need for federal power to control the defeated states. He thought Fort Sumter was vulnerable and advised that it be surrendered. He also proposed the famous Anaconda Plan, which required a blockade of the Atlantic and Gulf coasts, a thrust down the Mississippi, and a cordon along the border between North and South. Although this plan was rejected, it was a closer forecast of what actually happened than anyone else was able to make.

Scott desired to avoid precipitous action, but when Lincoln insisted on prompt suppression of rebellion, Scott appointed Irvin McDowell commander of the army around Washington and helped him plan the movement that ended in disaster at Manassas. McDowell was replaced by George B. McClellan, whose shamefully arrogant behavior toward his commander and disobedience of direct orders drove Scott to distraction. Scott was greatly offended and asked to be retired.

Scott went on the retired list 1 November 1861. Suffering from dropsy and vertigo, he sailed for Europe to join his wife, who was already in the mild climate of southern Europe because of a bronchial ailment. He spent the summer of 1862 at West Point and wrote his memoirs, which were published in 1864. After spending the winter of 1866 in New Orleans, Scott returned to West Point, where he died.

Ever ambitious, eager to grasp another honor, and jealous of his rank and fame, Scott was vain and dogmatic. He was always ready to write a letter when he took offense at some fancied insult. According to one of his biographers, he was generous and outgoing and possessed a "constitutional inability to nurse a grudge" (Elliott, p. 648). He was also an extremely effective commander, most notably in the Mexican War. Timothy Dwight Johnson, however, believes that Scott had a deep "streak of meanness and selfishness" and that his "ambition fed his arrogance and, in turn, his arrogance fed his ambition" (Johnson, pp. 4–5). This judgment is probably too harsh, for there is evidence that Scott could be forgiving and merciful. His concern for his soldiers, as in the cholera epidemic of 1832 or his desire for an asylum, went far beyond the normal obligation of a commanding general.

Scott, an Episcopalian, read the Bible often. He was well read and had a library of books on military subjects that was always with him. His reading was a mark of Scott's professionalism, as were his efforts to institutionalize such military skills as tactical training, camp sanitation, organization, and regularized procedure. Scott was responsible for much of the professionalization of the army between the War of 1812 and the Civil War, but his professionalism was limited by his narrow perspectives. His ideas were European in origin and did not fit frontier realities.

Scott never attained his cherished goal of the presidency, but he was not slow to express his views, opposing states' rights and believing that the slow extinction of slavery was inevitable. According to a public letter written in 1843, he thought abolitionism was injudicious, "but I am persuaded that it is a high moral obligation of masters and slaveholding States to employ all means, not incompatible with the safety of both colors, to meliorate slavery even to extermination" (*Memoirs*, vol. 2, p. 373).

• Many of Scott's personal papers were burned and the remainder scattered, but because of his official position, extensive correspondence may be found in the military records in the National Archives in Washington, D.C. Examples of Scott's contentious letter writing, which give some idea of what his superiors and subordinates had to tolerate when he was in a fit of pique, are in his *Abstract of a Correspondence with the Executive, Relative to the Rank and Command of Major-Generals Scott & Macomb* (1828) and *Letter to the Secretary of War, or, Review of the Controversy on a Question of Rank between Generals Scott and Gaines* (1827). Scott's other writings include a "Scheme for Restricting the Use of Ardent Spirits in the United States," (Philadelphia) *National Gazette*, 1821, and his widely circulated cholera order, both of which indicate his temperance proclivities. He also wrote numerous pamphlets arguing about courts-martial, rank, or politics, and his *General Regulations for the Army; or, Military Institutes* (1821) was revised by him in 1825 and 1835. In 1824 he published a manual of tactics, which was republished in 1825 and numerous times afterward as *Infantry Tactics; or, Rules for the Exercises and Manoeuvres of the Infantry of the U.S. Army*. His most notable publication was his rambling, vain, but informative *Memoirs of Lieut-General Scott, LL.D. Written by Himself* (1864).

Marcus J. Wright's biography, *General Scott* (1893), is not particularly penetrating or critical but is comprehensive and informative. For Scott's early career and his emphasis on professionalization, see the valuable work by Timothy Dwight Johnson, "Young Fuss and Feathers: Winfield Scott's Early Career, 1808–1841" (Ph.D. diss., Univ. of Alabama, 1989); but Charles Winslow Elliott's biography, *Winfield Scott: The Soldier and the Man* (1937; repr. 1979), is still the most complete and authoritative work.

For evaluations of Scott's military career, see the above mentioned works of Elliott and Johnson and the leading military histories, but see, also J. David Valaik, "The Wars of 1813 and 1846: The Leadership Factor," in *The American Military Tradition from Colonial Times to the Present*, ed. John M. Carroll and Colin F. Baxter (1993).

RICHARD E. BERINGER

SCOTTO, Charles (13 Mar. 1886–24 Oct. 1937), chef and founder of the American Culinary Federation, Inc., was born in Monte Carlo, Monaco. Little is known about Scotto's early life, though he was survived in 1937 by three brothers and three sisters. He attained at least an elementary education, and judging by his rapid rise in career, he probably was an exceptional student. Scotto served a lengthy apprenticeship in the pastry shop of the casino at Monte Carlo before moving to the Hotel Metropole in Brighton, England, in 1900. He completed his culinary apprenticeship at age twenty-one under Master Chef Georges Auguste Escoffier in Brighton. Scotto's relationship with the world-renowned Escoffier (called by the press the "Chef of Kings and the King of Chefs") was exceptionally close. Escoffier's biographers as well as the *New York Times* refer to Scotto as the master's "most beloved apprentice," and in his eighties Escoffier journeyed to New York to participate in Scotto's opening of the kitchens of the Hotel Pierre in 1930. After completing is apprenticeship, Scotto became *chef de cuisine* of the Ritz Carlton Restaurants aboard a number of palatial passenger ships of the Hamburg-America Line. He married Irma Marie Posch (date unknown); they had no children.

Immigrating to the United States in 1912, Scotto served in many fine establishments, from Philadelphia's Ritz-Carlton Hotel and the Hotel Sinton in Cincinnati to the Hotel Royal Ponciana in Palm Beach, Florida. He moved to New York about 1920, where he worked at the Knickerbocker Hotel. He oversaw the opening of the Hotel Ambassador's kitchens in 1924 and those of the Hotel Pierre in 1930, where he served as chef until his death, except for December 1933 to June 1935, when he became a partner in the Gigoux Brothers wholesale grocery company. Scotto's ability in the kitchen drew the attention of the New York press. The *Times* covered a 1925 Paris luncheon given in Scotto's honor by the Société des Cuisiniers de Paris as well as the dinner Scotto supervised for Chef Escoffier's visit to New York in 1926.

The rarefied culinary world honored Scotto with many of its highest awards. The Swiss Fraternity of Cuisine, the International Cooks Association, the Société des Cuisiniers de Paris, and other occupational groups presented diplomas of merit to Scotto, who also received a gold medal from the French Ministry of Public Health and a silver medal from the Ministry of Labor.

It was his service to the professionalization of his occupation for which Scotto is most justly remembered. Part of his education under Escoffier was in the rationalization of kitchen duties and in establishing methods of training future professionals. This removed the body of culinary knowledge from craft secrecy, giving it a scientific basis and beginning the process of professionalization. Scotto's technical proficiency, his unique position relative to the deified Escoffier, and the attention and awards he drew made him a leader within the American culinary world. Scotto took seriously his responsibility as a leader in his profession. He served as president for New York's Vatel Club, Inc., and the Chefs de Cuisine Association and as vice president for Société Culinaire Philanthropique, three mutual aid societies based on ethnicity and occupation that drew together in 1929 to form the American Culinary Federation (ACF), the first and largest professional culinary organization in the United States.

Breathing life into the ACF, with character and purpose so different from its parent organizations, while maintaining the financial strength of those parents during the worst days of the Great Depression was a difficult task, which Scotto and the ACF board of directors managed well. With Scotto as president, the ACF coordinated employment bureaus, established a magazine that disseminated the latest culinary information and member organization reports, attached to itself a number of other organizations in New York, Boston, and Chicago, and spoke for its members before the National Recovery Administration during the "Code of Fair Competition" hearings for the hotel industry in September 1933. Scotto's leadership and the respect in which he was held by American culinarians diminished organizational infighting and efficiently directed the organization's efforts to survive and to replace the mutual aid societies' representation of chef members.

As the depression eased, so did the fortunes of chefs, and the American Culinary Federation grew in response. When Charles Scotto died suddenly in Brooklyn after an operation, the ACF was well on its way to incorporating all chefs' organizations in the United States. His example and demeanor, his technical skills, and his adherence to Escoffier's system of kitchen rationalization gave both the impetus and specific direction to the course of professionalization among culinarians. Scotto was buried in Monte Carlo.

• Eugene Herbodeau and Paul Thalmann, *Georges Auguste Escoffier* (1955), contains a photograph of Scotto with Escoffier as well as a small biographical sketch of Scotto. The *New York Times* for 25 Aug. 1925, 26 Oct. 1926, 25 Oct. 1937, and 28 Oct. 1937 contains notices of Scotto's successes and his obituary and funeral notice. The American Culinary Federation's magazine, *The National Culinary Review*, for November and December 1937 contains Scotto's obituaries.

MARTIN T. OLLIFF

SCOVEL, Sylvester Henry (29 July 1869–11 Feb. 1905), newspaper correspondent, was born in Denny Station, Allegheny County, Pennsylvania, the son of the Reverend Sylvester Fithian Scovel, a Presbyterian minister, and Caroline Woodruff, an active churchwoman and member of the Presbyterian Board of Missions. In 1883 Reverend Scovel was named president of the University of Wooster in Ohio (now the College of Wooster). The younger Sylvester—who was known in all but the most formal contexts as Harry—entered Wooster's preparatory division, but his fondness for pranks and his avowed atheism persuaded his parents to let him quit school at age sixteen and go to work on a labor gang in Tennessee. He later finished his high school education at the Michigan Military Academy and in 1887 entered the University of Michigan, where he led a movement to break the domination of the fraternities in student politics.

Dropping out of the university after three semesters, Scovel pursued various occupations, including draftsman, insurance salesman, and promoter of a new, and ultimately unsuccessful, process for extracting fuel from bituminous slack. He performed with the First Cleveland Troop, a National Guard equestrian drill team also known as "McKinley's Own." In 1894 he became director of the Cleveland Athletic Club and wrote, produced, and starred in amateur musical productions. In the summer of 1895 Scovel made an impulsive decision to go to Cuba as a freelance foreign correspondent. He traveled with the insurgents in the Cuban countryside, became friendly with the nationalist leader General Máximo Gómez, and in January 1896 was arrested by the Spanish authorities on suspicion of being the semilegendary mercenary "El Inglesito," a popular hero who was probably a conflation of several foreign mercenaries attached to the rebel cause.

Joseph Pulitzer's *New York World* secured Scovel's release from prison and gave him a job. Scovel made a tour of western Cuba for the paper, collecting affidavits charging Spanish atrocities against the civilian population. Although *New York Herald* correspondent George Rea later asserted that Scovel had been duped by the exaggerated claims of the insurgents, Scovel's lengthy reports, which appeared periodically in the *World* from 27 May through November 1896, were the most factual accounts of the Cuban revolution published up to that time and proved influential in building sentiment in favor of American military intervention.

The *World* heavily promoted Scovel as "our intrepid correspondent," portraying him as a former cowboy and a revolutionary partisan. In reality, he cut a more modest figure. Using the aliases Harry Williams and Harry Brown, he traveled behind Spanish lines disguised as a dealer in scrap metal. Despite reports to the contrary, he never carried a gun. Scovel had excellent connections with the U.S. embassy in Havana and was used on occasion as a confidential channel of communication with the insurgents. This, combined with his influence on American public opinion, soon made him a target of loyalist death squads; his Cuban guide was murdered, and he narrowly escaped an assassination plot. Arrested on espionage charges in February 1897, he was treated as a hero by provincial jailers and had no difficulty smuggling out daily letters to the *World*. The arrest, meanwhile, had international repercussions; the U.S. Senate unanimously passed a resolution calling on the State Department to demand a guarantee of his safety from Spain, and Máximo Gómez took a Madrid correspondent, Luis Morote, hostage in retaliation.

Released in March 1897 through diplomatic pressure on Madrid, Scovel was banned from Cuba by the military governor, General Valeriano Weyler y Nicolau. During the spring and summer of 1897 he covered the Greco-Turkish war (traveling with Stephen Crane and his common-law wife Cora Howorth Stewart, known as Cora Taylor or Cora Crane) and the West Virginia coal strike, during which he displeased Pulitzer by writing favorably about the activities of socialist Eugene Debs. His next assignment was the Klondike gold rush. There he organized the dynamiting and reconstruction of the White Pass, which had been closed by mud slides, and with his bride of six weeks, the former Frances Cabanné of St. Louis, joined the procession of would-be prospectors on the trek over the mountains to Lake Bennett.

Weyler's declining fortunes made possible Scovel's return to Cuba in October. When the USS *Maine* exploded in Havana harbor on 15 February 1898, Scovel was on the scene within minutes and filed the first detailed report of the disaster. With the outbreak of the Spanish-American War, Scovel offered his services to Admiral William T. Sampson, who authorized him to form a naval spy ring, using the *World*'s journalistic activities as a cover. Scovel and other members of the ring mapped Spanish fortifications in Havana and Santiago de Cuba, placed undercover agents in the capital, and maintained contact with the insurgents through a series of surreptitious landings on Cuban beaches. During an expedition to a rebel stronghold in the mountains, he and Stephen Crane contracted a tropical fever, from which neither ever fully recovered.

As a result of his close association with the navy, Scovel became embroiled in feuding between Admiral Sampson and the commander of the army of invasion, General William Rufus Shafter. Tensions were exacerbated when the *World*'s staff collaborated on a controversial report, criticizing the conduct of the American general staff and the officers of New York's Seventy-first National Guard regiment. On 17 July 1898 a confrontation during the flag-raising ceremony marking the cessation of hostilities led to Scovel's arrest on a charge that he had physically attacked Shafter. Scovel maintained that the general had struck him first and that he returned the punch instinctively. His conduct was strongly defended by his journalistic colleagues; as a result, the charges were dropped, and he was reinstated by the *New York World*. Scovel, however, remained bitter that the William McKinley administration failed to clear his name and acknowledge his wartime services.

Scovel continued to report from Havana after 1898 but was primarily active as a plumbing contractor, importer, and automobile dealer. Reluctantly converted to the annexationist position, he hoped to become the first U.S. senator from Havana, but his political activities were curtailed by chronic malaria. He died in Havana after an operation for an abscess of the liver. The Scovels' only child had died in infancy.

As the most celebrated correspondent of the era of "yellow kid" journalism, Scovel was often singled out for attacks by rival newspapers. Erroneous and even ludicrous accounts of his career have at times been accepted at face value by chroniclers of the period. No one could deny that Scovel was hyperactive, hot-tempered, and often undisciplined in his personal and professional life. Recalling her husband and his close friend Stephen Crane, Scovel's widow later wrote to the poet John Berryman, "I don't think they had a moral between them but . . . they did have honesty, and bravery." On the whole, Scovel was a well-informed student of Cuban politics, and his personal political views (in contrast, at times, to the *World*'s) are best characterized by his credo, "moderate, always moderate." He held that economic development and a prosperous middle class must be the essential prerequisites of Cuban liberty. He supported the Spanish-American War but believed that the United States had squandered a unique opportunity to forge a constructive relationship with Cuban nationalists. He was critical, at one time or another, of the U.S. military occupation of the island, the Platt Amendment, the sugar lobby, and the fractious politics of the Cuban nationalist movement.

• Scovel's papers, including correspondence, the Cuban affidavits, and some photographs, are to be found at the Missouri Historical Society, St. Louis. An extensive clipping file, reflecting the now-forgotten controversies that made his career the subject of international debate, is included in the same collection. Also informative are letters by Frances Scovel Saportas to John Berryman, included among Berryman's papers at the University of Minnesota. Except for a few scattered newspaper articles, all of Scovel's published writings are in the *New York World* from Feb. 1896 through 1901. R. W. Stallman and E. R. Hagemann, *The War Dispatches of Stephen Crane* (1964), is an important source on the newspaper spy ring. (Scovel is the "closest friend" described in Crane's "War Fever" and appears as Sylvester Thorpe in an unfinished play.) The most complete account of Scovel's career is found in Joyce Milton, *The Yellow Kids: Foreign Correspondents in the Heyday of Yellow Journalism* (1989). Charles H. Brown, *The Correspondents' War: Journalists in the Spanish-American War* (1967), is a well-researched overview of the period, but its treatment of Scovel relies on factually questionable memoirs such as Ralph D. Paine's *Roads of Adventure* (1925).

JOYCE MILTON

SCOVELL, Melville Amasa (26 Feb. 1855–15 Aug. 1912), agricultural scientist, was born in Belvidere, New Jersey, the son of Nathan S. Scovell and Hannah Aller. When Scovell was young, his family moved to Chicago, then to a farm near Champaign, Illinois. Melville entered the Illinois Industrial University (later the University of Illinois), earning a B.S. in 1875 and an M.S. in 1877. In 1908 Scovell was formally awarded a Ph.D. for his earlier papers on methods of nitrogen determination. In 1880 Scovell married Nancy Davis; the couple was childless.

Scovell continued his career at the University of Illinois, rising to professor of agricultural chemistry by 1880. His first important research focused on methods for obtaining sugar from midwestern crops. In the early 1880s the U.S. government actively sought an alternative to the European domination of the sugar industry, and sorghum seemed to offer the solution. Scovell and a colleague, Henry Adam Weber, coauthored *Report on the Manufacture of Sugar, Syrup, and Glucose from Sorghum* (1881) and *The Northern Sugar Cane Manual* (1883), works based on their patent for clarifying sugar cane juices and manufacturing sugars from sorghum. The Champaign Sugar Works utilized Weber and Scovell's process, and in 1883–1884 Scovell managed the Kansas Sugar Company, a sorghum processing plant in Sterling, Kansas. In 1885 Scovell worked as a special agent for U.S. Department of Agriculture (USDA) sugar projects in Kansas and Louisiana. In the end, USDA policy favored the sugar cane industry over the sorghum industry.

Later in 1885 Scovell accepted a position as director of the newly created Kentucky Agricultural Experiment Station in Lexington. The station was not well funded, relying on proceeds gained through a fertilizer control program that Scovell administered as the official state chemist. Scovell's modifications in the Kjeldahl method of nitrogen determination in nitrates became a national standard. He was active also in the Association of Official Agricultural Chemists (AOAC), the national organization that sought to standardize experiment station practices and analytical procedures.

After 1887, when the Hatch Act appropriated federal funds to each of the state experiment stations, Scovell was able to broaden the Kentucky station's physical plant as well as its mission. Scovell's own research shifted to the goals of improving Kentucky's dairy herds and protecting consumers from adulterated food and dairy products. By inventing a milk-sampling tube and promoting the Babcock butterfat test as a reliable judge of a cow's economic value, Scovell sparked a greater interest in the quality of dairy cattle breeds. His 900-page report on dairy cows released at the Columbian World Exposition of 1893 brought the issue into the public arena. Scovell's work on food chemistry can be traced to 1880, and by 1898 he had helped secure a pure food law in Kentucky. Scovell was also active in the food standards committee of the AOAC, a group that joined the successful lobby for the national Food and Drugs Act of 1906.

Scovell's efforts as an institution-builder in Kentucky continued into the early twentieth century. For the Kentucky Agricultural Experiment Station, he helped establish experimental fields, experimental dairies, and funds for new buildings and laboratories. He was also instrumental in the foundation of the Kentucky State Fair and in promoting demonstration and extension projects that brought agricultural science to practicing farmers. At the time of his death, in Lexington, he had an additional post as dean of the agricultural college of the University of Kentucky.

Scovell's career reflects many issues common to agricultural scientists in the late nineteenth and early twentieth centuries. Though agricultural scientists first had to demonstrate the political and practical value of their work, their opportunities increased significantly after the passage of the Hatch Act. By the early twentieth century, Scovell's vision of regulation and standardization fit well within the reformist and professional climate of the Progressive Era. Perhaps his most lasting legacies lie in his promotion of scientific dairying and as an administrator of agricultural education in Kentucky.

• Dozens of Scovell's publications reporting results of his investigations of Kentucky's agricultural products survive, though they do not reveal much about his ideas or personality. The University of Kentucky Library has a large collection of manuscripts, business correspondence, and personal papers related to Scovell's work at the Kentucky Agricultural Experiment Station. Additional official correspondence is located in the Office of Experiment Stations records at the National Archives branch in College Park, Md. Scovell's work on the USDA's sugar projects and on food and drug legislation can be traced through the records of the Bureau of Agricultural and Industrial Chemistry at the National Archives and in the Harvey W. Wiley Papers at the Library of Congress. Little has been published about Scovell's career since a memorial essay appeared in the *Twenty-fifth Annual Report of the Kentucky Agricultural Experiment Station* (1912). His work on sorghum is mentioned in histories of the sugar industry, such as John Heitmann, *Modernization of the Louisiana Sugar Industry, 1830–1910* (1987). It also can be traced through the *Scientific American* and similar primary source material. Oscar E. Anderson, Jr., *The Health of a Nation* (1958), mentions Scovell both in the context of his sugar research and in the context of his work for pure food legislation. Obituaries are in the *Louisville (Ky.) Times* and the *Louisville Courier-Journal*, both 16 Aug. 1912.

MARK R. FINLAY

SCRANTON, George Whitfield (23 May 1811–24 Mar. 1861), iron manufacturer, was born in Mason, Connecticut, the son of Theophilus Scranton, owner of a stage coach line, and Elizabeth Warren. Family resources enabled George to acquire a common school education and to enroll at the Lees Academy in Madison, Connecticut. Scranton abandoned his schooling to join family members in Belvidere, New Jersey, where he began work as a teamster. Shortly, he took employment as a clerk in a local mercantile outlet where he eventually joined the owner, Judge John Kinney, as a partner. After several years in the business, in 1835 Scranton sold his interests to pursue farming. That same year Scranton married Jane Hiles of Belvidere; they had three children. In 1839 George and his brother, Selden T. Scranton, bought an iron furnace in Oxford, New Jersey, a move that would later facilitate his decision to engage in iron manufacturing in the Lackawanna Valley in northeastern Pennsylvania.

The explorations of Selden's father-in-law, William Henry, in the Lackawanna Valley convinced George Scranton of the possibilities of iron production in the region, given the local availability of anthracite coal, ores, and other essential natural resources. In 1840 the brothers moved to the future site of Scranton in the heart of the Lackawanna Valley. With $20,000 in capital they built a blast furnace to manufacture iron from which George intended to make nails. To accomplish this, he had to build a nail factory, a very expensive venture that he funded with money borrowed from his cousins Joseph and Erastus Scranton, then successful merchants in Georgia. Despite the initial enthusiasm, low-quality ores, shoddy nails, and almost insurmountable transportation costs reduced George and Selden Scranton to near bankruptcy.

Determined to survive, George persuaded the directors of the Buffalo, New York, and Erie Railroad that his operation could manufacture 12,000 tons of T-rails for the company's proposed line from Port Jervis on the Delaware River to Binghamton, just north of the Lackawanna Valley. In this effort Scranton relied on the aid of William Dodge, who had backed the Scranton ironworks and who was also a partner in the railroad company. As part of the agreement the railroad line provided $90,000 in capital to construct the rolling mill that would produce the T-rails.

Still Scranton faced a number of daunting obstacles before he could meet the demands of the contract. Neither George nor Selden actually knew much about the process of making iron T-rails, an activity dominated by British ironmakers. In fact, only the refusal of British suppliers, overburdened by their own market demands, to provide the rails had created the opportunity for the Scrantons. The ores and lime in the Lackawanna Valley, first identified by Henry, proved of such low quality that Scranton had to import these essential materials from other locations. Resolving the difficulties, they met the December 1848 deadline.

By 1853 Scranton's iron manufacturing had grown sufficiently for him to incorporate the Lackawanna Iron and Coal Company (LI&C), valued at $800,000. He secured this sum from three groups of investors. First, his own kinsmen and local entrepreneurial allies placed their financial resources at his disposal. Second, he persuaded New Yorkers, especially those tied to the Buffalo, New York, and Erie Railroad, to back his efforts. Finally, Scranton attracted capital from entrepreneurs in the small towns of northeastern Pennsylvania such as Montrose and Towanda. Their money and later migration to Scranton proved vital in sustaining the LI&C.

Scranton recognized the desperate need for inexpensive transportation. Beginning in 1850, with the support of New York money, he started two rail lines: the Ligget Gap from Scranton north to Great Bend, New York, where it connected with the Buffalo, New York, and Erie, and the Delaware and Cobb's Gap, which ran from Scranton to Stroudsburg on the Delaware River. The rail lines both opened up new markets and generated a steady demand for LI&C iron.

These lines merged to form one of the great anthracite railroads of the era, the Delaware, Lackawanna, and Western Railroad (DL&WRR). Scranton, who had served as an officer of both independent lines, assumed the presidency of the new corporation. This operation also depended on the Susquehanna and Cayuga Railroad (S&CRR), which extended his reach in New York state. As president of the S&CRR, Scranton held the means to deploy its resources to benefit his manufacturing activities. He also proposed and oversaw the construction of the Northumberland division of the DL&WRR, which aimed at expanding his markets in Pennsylvania.

These activities proved mutually beneficial. The LI&C owned considerable coal lands in the Lackawanna Valley, which supplied the company with energy for its iron-manufacturing operations. At the same time the LI&C relied on the DL&WRR to sell and haul its products to home heating and industrial markets on the East Coast and in upstate New York.

Keenly aware of the importance of political office to the fortunes of his operations, Scranton successfully pursued a congressional seat at the end of the 1850s. His political interests stretched back to his stay in New Jersey, where as a member of the Whig party and a colonel in the state militia, he served on the staff of the Whig governor. By the late 1850s he had joined the recently formed Republican party. As a member of the new party and an iron manufacturer acutely aware of the threat of British competition, Scranton entered the House of Representatives in 1858 as an ardent protectionist, a position he sustained throughout his first term. He carried this protectionist sentiment into a second term, unexpectedly ended by his early death of tuberculosis in Scranton.

Scranton's career contributed in two significant ways to the development of American industrial economy. His success in manufacturing iron T-rails broke the domination of American markets by British manufacturers. The ability of American producers to generate their own, far less expensive iron marked a milestone in the development of an autonomous industrial economy. The availability of cheap, high-quality iron helped spur the rapid expansion of the American railroad network, which fueled growth in various industries.

Scranton's activities also transformed the Lackawanna Valley from an agricultural frontier into a major industrial region. At its center stood the iron-manufacturing city of Scranton, the product of his efforts. Nonexistent in 1840, it reached almost 20,000 people by 1860, making it the third largest city in Pennsylvania and one of the state's major manufacturing communities.

• The bulk of the Scranton Family Papers is in the Edmund T. Lukens Collection in the Hagley Museum in Wilmington, Del. A smaller collection of family papers can be found in the Lackawanna Historical Society in Scranton. The best source for Scranton's life is Burton W. Folsom, *Urban Capitalists: Entrepreneurs and City Growth in Pennsylvania's Lackawanna and Lehigh Valleys, 1800–1920*, chaps. 1–3, and W. David Lewis, "The Early History of the Lackawanna Iron and Coal Company: A Case Study in Technological Adaptation," *Pennsylvania Magazine of History and Biography* 96 (1972): 424–68. Obituaries are in the *New York Times* and the *Scranton Republican*, both 25 Mar. 1861.

EDWARD J. DAVIES II

SCREWS, William Wallace (25 Feb. 1839–7 Aug. 1913), editor, was born in Jernigan, Alabama, the son of Benjamin Screws, a merchant and regional Whig party leader, and Mourning Drake. He was educated at the state-chartered male academy in Glennville but left school at age sixteen to work as a mercantile clerk. In January 1858 Screws moved to Montgomery to study law with the prominent firm of Thomas H. Watts, Thomas J. Judge, and J. F. Jackson. As he was not yet twenty-one, he had to be admitted to the bar in 1859 under special statute, remaining to practice with Watts, Judge & Jackson.

Like many former Whigs, Screws opposed secession in 1860–1861. Because of health problems that began about 1858, he was given a medical certificate exempting him from military service. When former Whig leader Henry W. Hilliard began raising a legion in mid-1862, however, Screws chose to ignore his infirmities and enlisted, gaining election to second lieutenant. Samuel G. Reid, editor of the *Montgomery Advertiser*, asked Screws to serve as a correspondent for the newspaper, and he began sending dispatches soon after the Alabamians arrived in Tennessee in July. Unfortunately for Screws, the *Advertiser* had just published an unflattering piece about Confederate general Braxton Bragg, which Bragg blamed on Thomas H. Watts, Screws's employer, who had become Confederate attorney general. Probably in retaliation against both the *Advertiser* and Watts, Bragg had Screws arrested in August and charged him with providing information on troop movements to the enemy through his newspaper dispatches. Reid protested, and Bragg released Screws after ten days. Hilliard's Legion garrisoned Cumberland Gap during the Confederate invasion of Kentucky in September 1862, then was stationed in East Tennessee from October 1862 until the region was abandoned in late 1863. When Screws's part of the legion was consolidated into the fifty-ninth Alabama Infantry, he was elected first lieutenant of Company G.

In late 1863 Screws went home on leave, reportedly because of health problems, and Watts, who had just been elected governor, asked Screws to become his private secretary. Screws held this position for the first couple of months of 1864 while Watts requested his official release from the army, but when officers of the Fifty-ninth Alabama insisted that Screws was needed with the regiment, the War Department refused to grant Watts's request. Screws rejoined his unit, which had been transferred to Virginia, just in time to be wounded at the battle of Drewry's Bluff in May 1864. He remained in Virginia through the siege of Petersburg, was captured at Sayler's Creek on 6 April 1865, and was imprisoned at Johnston's Island, Ohio, until June.

Screws apparently intended to return to his law practice, but Reid convinced him to take a position with the *Advertiser*. The paper's offices had been burned by Federal raiders in April 1865, and a military order forbidding publication was in force until July. When the *Advertiser* resumed publication on 20 July, Screws was on the staff. J. F. Gaines, Reid's partner, died that same night, and Reid soon expanded Screws's role with the paper. In November 1865 he sold Screws half-interest in the *Advertiser* and named him editor, a post Screws held for forty-eight years.

In April 1867 Screws married Emily Frances Holt, with whom he had four children. That same year Screws's brother B. H. joined the *Advertiser* staff and purchased half of Reid's remaining share, and in 1868 Screws bought out both his brother and Reid to become sole owner. He merged the *Advertiser* with the *Montgomery Mail* in 1871 and gained full control the following year after the death of the *Mail*'s proprietor. In 1885 Screws sold half of his interest to two associates but remained as president of the stock company they organized.

The *Advertiser* had traditionally been the state's leading Democratic newspaper, and with the Radical Republicans as the only alternative, Screws became a Democrat, albeit a Whig-influenced conservative one. His staunch opposition to Reconstruction policies won him favor among southern whites but also cost him the state printing contract in 1873 when the owner of the city's Radical paper used legislative action to take it from Screws. When the Democrats regained control of the state in 1874–1875, Screws turned his attention to plans to restore Alabama's credit, advocating aggressive retirement of the state debt. He was pro-railroad and championed civil improvements, hailing an 1885 water system as "the most important event in the history of Montgomery's progress as a city" (Muskat, p. 19). Screws also entered the political arena, winning two-year terms as Alabama secretary of state in 1878 and 1880. His editorial support of national Democratic candidates was rewarded when Grover Cleveland named him postmaster of Montgomery (1893–1897). By this time Screws was generally addressed as "Ma-

jor," the rank he held in the United Confederate Veterans.

Among the Democratic factions, Screws and the *Advertiser* were leaders of the conservative wing, voicing strong opposition to the Farmer's Alliance and the Populists. This stance led to several fierce battles in the 1890s against Populists and Populist-leaning Democrats. In the contentious 1890, 1892, and 1894 gubernatorial races, Screws aided Democrats Thomas G. Jones (1890 and 1892) and William C. Oates (1894) to narrow victories over Populist Reuben F. Kolb. But Screws's leading adversary became Birmingham industrialist and publisher Joseph F. Johnston, a Democrat with Populist ideas, including the free coinage of silver. Screws feared that Johnston's concept of a monopolistic combine to run the state coalfields would be the "knell of industrial freedom in Alabama" (*Montgomery Advertiser*, 21 Feb. 1896). With the *Advertiser*'s support, Oates had secured the party nomination over Johnston in 1894, but Screws was unable to block Johnston's election to the governorship in 1896 and 1898. Screws had announced his own candidacy for Congress in 1896 but pulled out of the race after state and national Democrats embraced neo-Populists Johnston and William Jennings Bryan.

Johnston labeled the *Advertiser* "Old Grandma" because of Screws's antireform conservatism, but Screws adopted the nickname, saying that his paper was proud to represent old-school wisdom and caution. He accused Johnston of corruption during his gubernatorial tenure and supported victorious opposition candidates during Johnston's bids for the Senate in 1900 and the governorship two years later. In 1913, however, with Johnston already holding a Senate seat and facing a challenge in 1914 from someone whom Screws distrusted, the aged editor admitted that his old foe had done a good job in Washington and gave him his endorsement. Neither man lived until the election, as Screws died on 7 August at his country home in Coosada, outside Montgomery. Johnston died the following day.

When writing of several Alabama newspapers in 1893, Screws pointed out what he valued in dailies, stating that the leading ones were "clean and chaste in sentiment, [and] devoted to the best interests of their state and country" (*Memorial Record of Ala.*, vol. 2, p. 235). The Montgomery editer could "Put the Screws On" (*Advertiser*, 22 Aug. 1913) carpetbaggers and political enemies when necessary, taking bold stands on certain issues and candidates, but he and his *Advertiser* were also Old Grandma, providing cautionary, conservative editorial leadership for the city and state for half a century.

• Screws's papers are at the Alabama Department of Archives and History in Montgomery. His wartime correspondence appeared in the *Montgomery Advertiser*, 1862–1865, and his editorial columns were in the same paper, 1865–1913. His article "Alabama Journalism," in *Memorial Record of Alabama*, vol. 2 (1893), pp. 158–235, contains a history of his tenure with the *Advertiser* to that point; the same volume has a biographical sketch, pp. 732–36. J. Cutler Andrews, *The*

South Reports the War (1970), discusses Screws's stint as a correspondent. Materials with information on the roles of Screws and the *Advertiser* in Alabama politics include Grace H. Gates, "An Epithet for the *Montgomery Advertiser,* or How 'Grandma' Got Her Name," *Alabama Review* 47 (Jan. 1994): 3–19; Beth T. Muskat, "The Last March: The Demise of the Black Militia in Alabama," *Alabama Review* 43 (Jan. 1990): 18–34; William W. Rogers, *The One-Gallused Rebellion: Agrarianism in Alabama, 1865–1896* (1970); Sheldon Hackney, *Populism to Progressivism in Alabama* (1969); Malcolm C. McMillan, *Constitutional Development in Alabama, 1798–1901: A Study in Politics, the Negro, and Sectionalism* (1955); Allen J. Going, *Bourbon Democracy in Alabama, 1874–1890* (1951); John B. Clark, *Populism in Alabama, 1874–1896* (1927); William W. Rogers, et al., *Alabama: The History of a Deep South State* (1994); Albert B. Moore, *History of Alabama* (1927, 1934); Thomas M. Owen, *History of Alabama and Dictionary of Alabama Biography* (1921); and Mark W. Summers, *The Press Gang: Newspapers and Politics, 1865–1878* (1994). Obituaries are in the *Montgomery Advertiser,* 8 Aug. 1913, and the *Confederate Veteran,* Oct. 1913.

FORD RISLEY

SCRIBNER, Arthur Hawley (15 Mar. 1859–3 July 1932), publisher, was born in New York City, the son of Charles Scribner, a publisher, and Emma Locke Blair. Charles Scribner founded Charles Scribner and Company in 1846. He designated two of his three sons, John Blair and Charles, as his heirs, and they assumed leadership of the company when their father died in 1871. In 1878 the firm's name was changed to Charles Scribner's Sons, but John died unexpectedly in January 1879 after a brief bout with pneumonia, and Charles became president.

In 1881, after graduating with honors from the College of New Jersey (now Princeton University), where he distinguished himself as both a student and an athlete, Arthur Hawley Scribner entered the firm. He was active in all phases of the business and became its vice president in 1903 when Charles Scribner's Sons was incorporated. Scribner's duties included responsibility for the house's physical plant. He was also president of the Scribner Realty Company (holder of the publishing house's real estate) and director of the New York Electrotyping Company. Three times during Scribner's lifetime, the company moved to larger and more modern facilities. It also built a large city manufacturing plant for printing, binding, and distributing its books. Scribner paid particular attention to the manufacturing aspects of the business—an avid bibliophile, he had a deep appreciation of books as aesthetic objects, and his personal library contained many rare editions—with the result that the books and magazines published under the Charles Scribner's Sons imprint were distinguished for their typography and design.

However, Scribner's duties were not confined to book production. In 1889 he pulled off a major coup for the publishing house when he made a hurried trip to Cairo, where he met Henry M. Stanley and obtained the contract for *In Darkest Africa,* in which Stanley described his search for David Livingstone. During the years the two brothers presided over the firm, Charles Scribner's Sons was one of the most in-

fluential publishing houses in the United States. Although Charles Scribner's Sons was committed to publishing the works of established authors, textbooks, reference books, and books on architecture and religion, it also was sensitive to changing trends in American culture and played a major role in shaping American literature of the twentieth century by promoting a new generation of writers. Both Arthur and Charles were involved in producing the *Dictionary of American Biography* (1928–1936) in conjunction with the American Council of Learned Societies; according to Charles Scribner's entry in the *Dictionary of American Biography,* both brothers "gave themselves wholeheartedly to the promotion of the work."

While Scribner was clearly committed to the making of fine books, he was equally devoted to his alma mater, Princeton University. He served on its graduate council as well as on the council of the Princeton University Press, which he and his brother Charles were instrumental in founding. He was the first graduate president of the Ivy Club and served as its president from 1927 to 1930; at the time of his death he was president of the Class of 1881. An Episcopalian, he was actively involved in the New York City Mission and Tract Society. He also belonged to various clubs, including the Grolier (serving as president from 1916 to 1920), the University, and the Century.

Scribner became president of Charles Scribner's Sons in 1930 on the death of his brother Charles, and he led the firm until he died of a heart attack in his sleep at his Mt. Kisco, New York, home. His estate went to his wife, Helen Culbertson Annan, whom he had married on 29 January 1900 (the couple had no children). He bequeathed $150,000 to Princeton, $5,000 to the New York City Mission and Tract Society, and $5,000 to the Skidmore School of Arts in Saratoga Springs, New York. These bequests reflected Scribner's lifelong commitment to education and philanthropic work.

The third son of the founder of Charles Scribner and Company, Scribner was throughout his life somewhat overshadowed by his older brothers. Nevertheless, he made real contributions to the publishing house, particularly in expanding and modernizing the firm as well as in overseeing the production of Scribner publications.

• The Charles Scribner's Sons Archive is located in the Department of Rare Books and Special Collections of Princeton University Libraries; the archive includes ledgers, business papers, and personal correspondence. Some of this material is included in John Delaney, ed., *The House of Scribner, 1846–1904* (1995), an illustrated chronicle published as a volume in the Documentary Series of the *Dictionary of Literary Biography.* An obituary appears in the *New York Times,* 3 July 1932.

JUDITH E. FUNSTON

SCRIBNER, Charles (21 Feb. 1821–26 Aug. 1871), publisher, was born in New York City, the son of Uriah Rogers Scribner, a successful merchant, and Betsey Hawley. Scribner attended New York University in 1837 and then moved to the College of New Jersey (now Princeton University), from which he graduated in 1840. After a physical breakdown forced him to abandon his law studies with a New York City attorney, he organized a publishing company with a local dry goods merchant, Isaac D. Baker, in 1846. Neither Baker nor Scribner had any background in the field, but they had the advantages of good literary judgment, solid financial backing, and an experienced assistant, Andrew C. Armstrong. They ensured themselves a core of regular sales from the start by buying out the stock of religious publisher John S. Taylor. Unlike most publishers of the day, they did not have a steady income from a printing plant, but this freed them from the necessity of maintaining a large list of British reprints simply to keep their presses busy; instead, they were able to concentrate on developing new authors, especially American ones. They had the luck to begin by publishing three enormously successful books by the historian J. T. Headley; together, these titles sold about 200,000 copies in the first two years. Two other very popular authors acquired during this period were journalist N. P. Willis, whose memoir, *People I Have Met*, had a huge sale in 1849, and Donald Grant Mitchell (writing as Ik Marvell), whose *Reveries of a Bachelor: A Book of the Heart* (1850) was a great success and continued to sell steadily for the next fifty years. In 1848 Scribner married Elizabeth Blair, the daughter of a wealthy railroad magnate; they had three sons, all of whom would devote their careers to the family firm.

In 1850, just as the publishing house was establishing itself, Baker died suddenly. Thereafter, Scribner continued the firm under his own name. A devout Presbyterian, he built a distinguished list of books by leading Presbyterian theologians. Among his most ambitious religious publications was the huge *Commentary on the Holy Scriptures* (25 vols., 1865–1880) by German scholar Johann Peter Lange, edited by Philip Schaff. It cost the firm nearly $100,000 to produce, but it proved to be an excellent investment, winning both scholarly acclaim and great commercial success. In a lighter vein, Scribner also took a chance on a book that had been turned down by two other houses, *Timothy Titcomb's Letters to Young People, Single or Married* by newspaper editor Josiah G. Holland. Published in 1858, it sold more than 100,000 copies, as did Holland's long poem *Bitter-Sweet* (also published that year) and several later volumes.

By 1857 Scribner was ready to move into the field of foreign reprints. He did so by buying the book division of Bangs & Co., an auction firm that was then one of the leading American importers of books from England. To launch his new venture, he formed a subsidiary—Scribner, Welford & Co.—taking as his partner Charles Welford, a young Britisher who had headed the book division under Bangs. The business grew rapidly, and in 1864 Welford moved to London to establish a branch office. As a result, Scribner's built a distinguished list of British reprints and European translations, including works by such giants as Theodor Mommsen and James Anthony Froude. Despite his success, however, Scribner continued to keep his company small. In 1855 the only staff members in the New York office besides Scribner were his brother Edward, Armstrong, and one other man. Armstrong gradually took charge of the company's business affairs and in 1864 became a full partner.

During this period several leading publishers had begun putting out their own magazines, and Scribner dreamed of surpassing them all with a magazine that would be, as he wrote privately, "different from any now published . . . handsomely illustrated, beautifully printed," with contributions from "the best authors of the day." His first effort, *Hours at Home* (1865–1870), did not achieve what he had hoped. Edited by a clergyman, the magazine exuded what historian Charles Madison called "a fog of piety" and failed to arouse much public interest. In 1870 Scribner learned that Holland, his most popular author, was considering starting his own magazine with a lawyer colleague, Roswell Smith. When Scribner offered to serve as their publisher, the two men accepted with alacrity. A new firm, Scribner and Company, was established for the purpose, and in November 1870 *Scribner's Monthly* published its first issue, using the subscription list from *Hours at Home*. The following month it absorbed *Putnam's Magazine* and *Riverside Magazine for Young People*. Scribner lived less than a year after the magazine was launched, but under Holland's editorship it became one of the leading journals of its day, notable for the handsomeness of its design, the quality and quantity of its illustrations, and the excellence of its writing; by 1879 it was selling more than 100,000 copies a month. In 1881 Scribner's son Charles sold it to the Century Company, where it was folded into the *Century Illustrated Monthly Magazine*, but he revived it four years later as *Scribner's Magazine*, and it flourished well into the twentieth century.

Scribner's health began to fail in 1871, and he died of typhoid in Lucerne, Switzerland, where he had traveled hoping for a cure. He was succeeded by his son John Blair, and on John's death in 1879, by his second son, Charles. By then the firm had taken the name under which it would operate from then on: Charles Scribner's Sons. Scribner lived in an era of personal publishing, when individual owner-managers chose their own books without either the guidance or interference of professional editorial staffs. Although most of his rivals entered the field with experience in printing or bookselling, Scribner brought only his own instinctive business acumen and literary taste. Yet with these he built one of the great publishing houses of his era, a firm that gave new opportunity to American writers and that continued to operate with distinction more than a century after his death.

• The fullest descriptions of Scribner's career appear in John Tebbel, *A History of Book Publishing in the United States*, vol. 1 (1972); Charles A. Madison, *Book Publishing in America* (1966), pp. 79, 89–91; "Charles Scribner's Sons: The History of a Publishing House, 1846–1894," *Scribner's Magazine*, Dec. 1894; J. C. Derby, *Fifty Years among Authors, Books and*

Publishers (1884); and a memoir by Scribner's great-grandson Charles, *In the Web of Ideas* (1993), pp. 187–90. *Scribner's Magazine* is also discussed in Algernon Tassin, *The Magazine in America* (1916), pp. 287–93, and Frank Luther Mott, *A History of American Magazines, 1865–1885* (1938). An obituary is in the *New York Times*, 28 Aug. 1871.

SANDRA OPDYCKE

SCRIBNER, Charles (18 Oct. 1854–19 Apr. 1930), publisher, was born in New York City, the second son of Charles Scribner, a publisher, and Emma Locke Blair. Charles attended a private school. He and his elder brother John Blair Scribner were designated heirs to Charles Scribner and Company, which their father founded in 1846. When their father died in 1871, John left the College of New Jersey (later Princeton University) without having graduated to manage the firm. In that same year Charles entered the College of New Jersey; upon his graduation with an A.B. degree in 1875 he joined his brother in managing the company. In 1878 the firm's name was changed to Charles Scribner's Sons. Shortly thereafter, in January 1879, John died unexpectedly of pneumonia and Charles became president. On 5 October 1882 Scribner married Louise Flagg, the daughter of the Reverend Jared Bradley Flagg; the couple had two children.

During the years of Scribner's tenure Charles Scribner's Sons expanded its scope to become the most comprehensive publisher in the country. The company sold *Scribner's Monthly* (renamed *The Century Illustrated Magazine*) and *St. Nicholas* to Century Company and, by terms of the contract, had to forswear periodical publication for five years. But in 1887 Scribner founded *Scribner's Magazine*, in which many significant works of American fiction, including those of Henry James and Edith Wharton, initially appeared in serial form and which numbered many prestigious American and European authors among its contributors. Scribner's ability to choose talented editors (Edward L. Burlingame and Robert Bridges) and art directors (August F. Jaccaci and Joseph H. Chapin) resulted in a publication that successfully competed with *Harper's* and *Century*, the top literary magazines of the day. In 1917 Charles Scribner's Sons took over the magazine *Architecture* from Forbes and Company, a venture that reflected Scribner's increasing interest in publishing architectural books.

Under Scribner's leadership the Scribner imprint set a precedent for publishing distinguished American and foreign authors. Scribner balanced fidelity to tradition with his encouragement of new writers. The Scribner list included such diverse writers as Henry James, Edith Wharton, George Washington Cable, Joel Chandler Harris, Frank R. Stockton, Francis Hodgson Burnett, Harold Frederic, Stark Young, Richard Harding Davis, Ernest Hemingway, Ring Lardner, Eugene Field, George Santayana, Theodore Roosevelt, Marjorie Kinnan Rawlings, Robert Louis Stevenson, George Meredith, Rudyard Kipling, J. M. Barrie, and John Galsworthy, many of whom considered Scribner a friend as well as their publisher. Collected editions of various authors were "labors of love," the most notable being the 24-volume "New York Edition" of Henry James (1906–1909). With frontispieces by the photographer Alvin Langdon Coburn, these volumes reflected Scribner's dedication to creating beautiful books. Also noteworthy was the publication in 1906–1907 of a four-volume edition of Cervantes's *The History of Don Quixote*, translated by Thomas Shelton and illustrated by Daniel Vierge.

Although Scribner possessed "peculiarly warm and enlightened literary sympathies," he was also recognized for his business acumen. He served as director of the National Park Bank, became its vice president in 1926, and oversaw its merger with Chase National Bank. He was strongly committed to higher education, serving on the board of trustees for Skidmore College for women, which was founded by Lucy Skidmore Scribner, John's widow. Throughout his lifetime he was also involved with Princeton University and was a founder in 1912 of the Princeton University Press, to which in addition to his time and expertise he donated land and buildings. He also served as president of the Princetonian Publishing Company, the corporate entity of the Princeton undergraduate newspaper, from 1910 (the year the articles of incorporation were filed) to 1926, and he guided the development of the Princeton University library.

As president of Charles Scribner's Sons, Scribner dedicated himself to his profession. He was one of the leaders of the fight for a law regulating international copyright and was present with William Appleton and Robert Underwood Johnson when President Benjamin Harrison signed the bill into law in 1891. He was also instrumental in founding the American Publishers' Association in 1900 and devoted considerable time to promoting the organization.

Although Charles Scribner's Sons was clearly a commercial enterprise, Scribner was keenly aware of his responsibility to the public. "He stands . . . as a symbol for whatever is most courteous, honorable, and fruitful of good in American endeavor," the citation noted when Princeton University gave him an honorary doctor of letters in 1925. Indicative of his "American endeavor" were Scribner's efforts, starting in 1927, to launch the publication of the *Dictionary of American Biography* in association with the American Council of Learned Societies. Both Charles and his brother Arthur Hawley Scribner avidly promoted the work and oversaw the design of its attractive, dignified format and the production of the first volumes.

Scribner remained president of the publishing house until 1928, at which time his brother Arthur became president. Scribner, however, served as chairman of the board from 1928 to his death in New York City from heart disease. An editorial in the *New York Times* on 21 April noted Scribner's "fine taste," "great personal charm," and "real public spirit." His funeral on 23 April drew more than 1,500 people, among whom were colleagues and fellow publishers, and he was memorialized in a ceremony at Skidmore College in Saratoga Springs. In recognition of his generosity to his alma mater, Princeton University paid special tribute to Scribner with a wreath of ivy cut from the walls of Nassau Hall, tied with orange and black ribbons, an honor bestowed on its most distinguished graduates and rarely given more than once in a decade.

During the years that he served as president, Scribner developed his father's firm into a major force in American magazine and book publishing. A family acquaintance, Royal Cortissoz, noted that under Scribner's leadership Charles Scribner's Sons became "the most comprehensive publishing business in the country." His encouragement and support of new writers was highly instrumental in shaping early twentieth-century American literature. At the time of his death, Charles Scribner's Sons was a prosperous and prestigious publishing house with its own press (established in 1908), a bookstore specializing in rare books, and a book importing firm (Scribner and Welford). The Scribner list included classics of American and European literature for adults and children, reference works, fiction by new authors, and periodicals. Although the success of Charles Scribner's Sons was the result of remarkable teamwork, Charles Scribner—a man who combined business acumen, artistic discrimination, and unstinting generosity—was the strongest voice behind an enterprise that shaped the course of American letters.

• The Charles Scribner's Sons Archive is located in the Department of Rare Books and Special Collections of Princeton University Libraries; the archive includes ledgers, business documents, personal correspondence, and diaries. Some of this material is included in John Delaney, ed., *The House of Scribner 1846–1904* (1995), an illustrated chronicle published as a volume in the Documentary Series of the *Dictionary of Literary Biography*. See also his grandson Charles Scribner's memoirs, *In the Company of Writers: A Life in Publishing* (1991). An obituary appears in the *New York Times*, 20 Apr. 1930.

JUDITH E. FUNSTON

SCRIBNER, Charles (26 Jan. 1890–11 Feb. 1952), publisher, was born in New York City, the son of Charles Scribner (1854–1930), a publisher, and Louise Flagg. When as a boy he displayed a flair for drawing, his parents kept art materials away from him, to discourage even the earliest inclination toward a career as a painter. After attending the exclusive St. Paul's School in Concord, New Hampshire, he enrolled in Princeton University, which he loved and from which he graduated in 1913. He began at once to work in the publishing company of Charles Scribner's Sons. This family firm, founded in New York City in 1846 by Scribner's grandfather, the first Charles Scribner, was called Scribner, Armstrong & Company until 1878, when it was taken over by two of the first Scribner's sons, John Blair and Charles Scribner. When John died in 1879, the second Charles Scribner became the dictatorial head of the company. His younger brother Arthur Hawley Scribner joined in 1881 and soon revealed skill in the art of book manufacturing.

Charles Scribner III started at ground level in the firm of which his father was then president. He first worked at the press, then handled advertising and distribution, and next was entrusted with editorial work. In 1915 he married Vera Gordon Bloodgood, who was the daughter of a Manhattan stockbroker and with whom he had two children. In 1917 Scribner was commissioned in the U.S. Army, saw duty in France as a first lieutenant in the Quartermaster Corps of the Remount Service, and after the armistice returned to employment at Scribners as its secretary. He commuted from his office in Manhattan to "Dew Hollow," his home in Far Hills, New Jersey, complete with tennis court, garden, stable, and horse pastures.

The decade of the 1920s was marked by a thrilling, often discomfiting combination of prosperity and irresponsibility, disillusionment and cynicism, creativity and chicanery, and intellectual and artistic ferment. The most important medium for expressing this was the written word. Scribners welcomed authors of many stripes, including—reluctantly at times—young, radical ones. This was so in large part because of Maxwell E. Perkins, advertising manager of Charles Scribner's Sons from 1910 to 1914, member of its editorial staff beginning in 1914, and without a doubt the finest editor in the history of American book publishing. He steadily argued in favor of providing opportunities for young talent. For example, in 1918 F. Scott Fitzgerald, destined to become the quintessential writer of the Roaring Twenties, sent Scribners the draft of a novel titled "The Romantic Egoist." Perkins saw possibilities in it, asked Fitzgerald to revise it, and showed the result to Scribner, who also admired it. Both men persuaded the senior editors to publish it as *This Side of Paradise* (1920). Scribner later was very tolerant and generous in handling the unstable Fitzgerald.

To a degree Scribner was in his father's shadow, and even that of his uncle Arthur, but nevertheless supported Perkins in many editorial decisions, some resulting in acceptance of works by newcomers such as Taylor Caldwell, Ernest Hemingway, Ring Lardner, and Thomas Wolfe. In 1926 Scribner was elevated to the position of vice president. In 1927 Arthur Scribner became president, succeeding his brother Charles, who thereafter officiated as chairman of the board until his death in 1930. Charles Scribner III was influential in the appointment that year of Alfred Sheppard Dashiell as editor of the staid *Scribner's Magazine*. With Scribner's approval, Dashiell quickly rejuvenated the magazine by accepting stories and nonfictional pieces not only by conservative authors, for example, James Truslow Adams and Joseph Conrad, but by progressives as well, including Clarence Darrow, John Dewey, Waldo Frank, Langston Hughes, and Lewis Mumford. The magazine ceased publication in 1939, three years after Dashiell quit editing it. Two heads of nations whom Scribner published and with whom he was on friendly personal terms were Winston Churchill and Herbert Hoover.

When Arthur Scribner died in 1932, Scribner became president of the publishing house. The depression hurt sales, but he fared comparatively well, not least when he put Marcia Davenport, Marjorie Kinnan Rawlings, and Stark Young, among other future bestsellers, under contract. Scribner saw to fruition two enduring series. Sponsored by the American Council of Learned Societies, the long-definitive *Dictionary of American Biography* appeared in twenty volumes (1928–1936), with ten supplements. The *Dictionary of American History* (6 vols., 1940), edited by J. T. Adams, was successful enough to be expanded later. *Atlas of American History* (1943) and *Album of American History, 1853–1893* (1946) were popular companions to the massive history. Scribner made the firm's impressive children's book department even better when he engaged Alice Dalgliesh as editor and recruited talented writers such as Marcia Brown, Genevieve Foster, Katherine Milhous, and Leo Politi. He solidified relations between British authors and his London office, which he visited annually for many years. Scribner helped make more attractive the Scribner Book Store, a Fifth Avenue landmark in the company building. A loyal Princeton alumnus like his father, Scribner served from 1940 to 1948 as president of the board of trustees at the Princeton University Press, which his father had founded in 1905 with an initial gift and improved later with gifts of land, a building, and an endowment.

The American publishing industry was in turmoil toward the end of World War II, with many mergers and takeovers occurring. In 1944 Scribner joined executives from the Curtis Publishing Company, the Book-of-the-Month Club, Harper's, Random House, and Little, Brown to buy Grosset & Dunlap for $2.25 million. Scribners itself, however, was not subject to the merger mania of the time. In his later years the company's head relished presiding over a family firm basking in a century of uninterrupted professional successes and did so with a combination of mellow humor and confidence.

Scribner loved horseback riding and was a member of the Essex Fox Hounds Hunt Club of Peapack, New Jersey. He also enjoyed membership in New York City's American Kennel Club, Grolier Club, Racquet and Tennis Club, and Westminster Kennel Club. He died in New York City. Sadly, he did not live to know that Hemingway dedicated *The Old Man and the Sea*, published later in 1952, "To Charlie Scribner and to Max Perkins."

The presidency of Scribners devolved on the heir of the next generation, the fourth Charles Scribner, to whose name was added "Jr." He downplayed the fiction and general nonfiction that his father had made the firm's hallmark in favor of predictably marketable special books and reference books.

• Scribner's papers, as part of much correspondence of the firm, are in the library at Princeton University. Charles Scribner, Jr., in both *In the Company of Writers: A Life in Publishing* (1990) and *In the Web of Ideas: The Education of a*

Publisher (1993), reminisces about his father; to the latter book he appended a history of the firm. Relating Scribner and his company to other publishing houses are Roger Burlingame, *Of Making Many Books: A Hundred Years of Reading, Writing and Publishing* (1946); Charles A. Madison, *Book Publishing in America* (1966); and John Tebbel, *Between Covers: The Rise and Transformation of Book Publishing in America* (1987). A. Scott Berg, *Max Perkins: Editor of Genius* (1978; repr. 1983), discusses Scribner illuminatingly. Scribner's treatment of three great novelist-friends is covered in Carlos Baker, *Ernest Hemingway: A Life Story* (1969); Matthew J. Bruccoli, *Some Sort of Epic Grandeur: The Life of F. Scott Fitzgerald* (1981); and David Herbert Donald, *Look Homeward: A Life of Thomas Wolfe* (1987). Whitney Darrow, *Princeton University Press* (1951), and Herbert S. Bailey, Jr., *Princeton University Press: Publishers for the World of Learning* (1958), briefly discuss Scribner's relationship to the Princeton University Press. An obituary is in the *New York Times*, 12 Feb. 1952.

ROBERT L. GALE

SCRIBNER, Charles, Jr. (13 July 1921–11 Nov. 1995), publisher, was born in Quogue, New York, the son of Charles Scribner (1890–1952), and Vera Bloodgood. His father was head of the family publishing firm, which was founded by the first Charles Scribner, Charles Jr.'s great-grandfather, in 1846. His mother purportedly did not share the Scribner enthusiasm for books. Her chief interest was horses—she rode and fox-hunted until she was in her seventies—but to her chagrin her only son was allergic to them. An older child, a daughter named Julia, had no such handicap, and Charlie—as he was called throughout his life—therefore grew up in the shadow of a favored, extroverted sibling. By all accounts his was a solitary, even lonely childhood on the family estate in Far Hills, New Jersey, and the uneasy relationship with his mother lasted until her death. Charlie, however, succeeded brilliantly as a student. At St. Paul's School, from which he graduated in 1939, his intellectual gifts were recognized and nurtured. At Princeton University—which the three previous Charles Scribners had also attended—he excelled in the classics and graduated summa cum laude. Scribner formed lifelong attachments and loyalties to both institutions, particularly to Princeton, where he served as a trustee and as president (the head of the board) of the university press.

The family publishing heritage marked Scribner from birth from following any other profession. He was thus obliged to forgo his first choice for a career, a life in the academy as a professor of classics at Princeton. World War II and service as an officer in the intelligence branch of the U.S. Navy delayed his entry in the business until 1946, when he was discharged and returned to New York City. At the time he joined his father at Charles Scribner's Sons, the company was still in the forefront of American publishing and enjoyed a cachet among authors and the reading public unmatched by almost any other publishing house. Under the legendary editor Maxwell Perkins, the house since the 1920s had been a bastion of American fiction and letters.

While nominally the advertising manager, Scribner was involved, as the heir apparent, in all areas of the business. But his father continued to rely mainly on Perkins, who until his death in 1947 remained in charge of the publishing program. Young Scribner was immune to Perkins's charm and influence, however, and disapproved of his power over the company and his father. Later in life, when Scribner was asked to describe Perkins, who was to his authors and much of the public the personification of the man of letters, he summed him up in one word: "Pickwickian."

Scribner's brief apprenticeship—two years as advertising manager and another two years as vice president of the company—ended in 1950 with the outbreak of the Korean War and his recall to active military service as a cryptanalyst in Washington. The sudden death of his father in 1952, however, led to an early discharge from the navy and his assumption of the presidency of the company. By his own admission, he was no more prepared, at age thirty, to head the house of Henry James, Edith Wharton, F. Scott Fitzgerald, Ernest Hemingway, and Thomas Wolfe than he was "to land on the moon."

He was still a young man, but Scribner soon settled into a pattern that varied little for the next thirty-five years. His world revolved around his apartment and the Racquet Club, both on Park Avenue, an estate in Far Hills, Princeton University, and, of course, his office in the Scribner Building, a landmark structure at 597 Fifth Avenue, which was built by an uncle, the architect Ernest Flagg. Scribner refused to use taxicabs, preferring to travel about the city by bus or subway—or better yet on foot. In the morning, he walked south on Park Avenue, then west on Forty-eight Street to Fifth Avenue. After work he walked up to Forty-ninth Street, then reversed exactly his morning route.

Scribner's routine guaranteed a measure of protection for this private, rather shy man, who was ill at ease among strangers. He much preferred the company of his family: his wife, the former Joan Sunderland, whom he married in 1949, and his three sons. Unlike his father, who had mixed easily with celebrity authors and glamorous figures from the entertainment world, the son found it difficult to accept that his name made him a celebrity. Thus he was both embarrassed and amazed when a Mexican customs inspector asked him, "Are you *the* Charles Scribner?" In general, he had little interest in travel and less interest in touring if there was any free time on business trips. He preferred to return to his hotel room and read. The hotel of choice was always part of a midpriced chain because, as he said, "There are no surprises." Scribner neither smoked nor drank, and he cared little about food. He astonished a reporter who was doing a feature on the favorite dishes of well-known people by solemnly, but truthfully, confiding to her that there was nothing better, to him, than a good boiled egg. And once when asked if he had any suggestions of what to serve at a luncheon for an editorial advisory board, he cheerily replied, "Let's have liver. Everyone likes liver."

Scribner's physical appearance complemented his routinized existence. He was never seen out of doors without a hat, even in summer, and he was often mistaken to be at least twenty years older than he was. This outward appearance, however, was misleading. He had not only read the Greeks and Romans; he emulated them. He believed in the precept "a sound mind in a healthy body" and kept himself in splendid physical condition by regular exercise, which included weight lifting, until well into his fifties. There were other contradictions as well. Throughout its history Scribners had had a reputation for paternalism, and Charles Scribner, Jr., continued that tradition by, for example, lending money at little or no interest to employees for down payments on houses. But he was never able to accept anyone who worked for him as a social equal. He therefore saw nothing wrong with telling a young woman who was leaving to attend law school that he was sorry to see her go because "Good help is so hard to find."

The Scribners had always believed that the family's social position, if not its reputation, was inextricably connected with the products of the publishing house—a conviction that book buyers were not just buying a book but a Scribner book. This attitude had left them open to the charge that publishing was a family hobby rather than the family business. But the earlier Scribners had surrounded themselves with strong editors whom they trusted and who also published great books. In following this custom, Charles Scribner, Sr., had been content to entrust the publishing program to Maxwell Perkins. His heir, however, was determined that no editor would have such authority. Finding that he had inherited a firm that was "top-heavy with novels," he set about to change the publishing program and the editorial process. As Scribner's characteristic inflexibility carried over into his management of the publishing house, he turned the company into an autocracy. Editorial independence was stifled.

Scribner's intellectual brilliance and patrician background would have been celebrated and ensured his continuing success in an earlier era of book publishing. But his takeover of Scribners in 1952 coincided with the beginnings of revolutionary changes in the old school, white, mainly Anglo-Saxon Protestant publishing world that was his birthright. In less than twenty years, minorities who had had little influence in the publishing world, in particular, women, blacks, and homosexuals, would become visible and powerful. Scribner was able, through a cultivated insularity, to avoid dealing socially with people not of his class or upbringing, but it was not possible to conduct business without them. In addition, many of the new publishers, editors, and agents were Jews, whom men such as Charles Scribner, Jr., disdained. Theirs might have been the drawing room, country club anti-Semitism of a particular social caste, but it was real, and no Jews worked for Scribners until the early 1960s.

Charles Scribner's abstemious nature and puritanical views paradoxically led to excesses of his own. He did not hesitate to delete what he thought was offensive in the letters and manuscripts of Ernest Hemingway that he edited for posthumous publication. His bowdlerization of the great prose master amused and amazed those employees who knew of Scribner's own mastery of profanity. Editorial and marketing meetings often degenerated into diatribes laced with expletives.

Scribner's scorn for popular publishing, which he dismissively called "ephemera," created serious problems for the editorial staff of the general trade book division, which largely lived on the successes of the past. While he publicly paid homage to Scribners' great literary tradition and continued to publish trade books, sometimes with great success, privately he spoke of agents as "vultures and parasites" and of most authors as greedy and avaricious. He refused to pay the large advances that had become necessary to attract important authors to the house and keep them there. Many authors who had their first success at Scribners were reluctant to leave, but they had little choice when other houses were willing to pay them significantly larger advances. One of the first to do so was James Jones, whose *From Here to Eternity*, *Some Came Running*, and *The Thin Red Line* had made millions for Scribners. Jones, the last important author put under contract by Maxwell Perkins, signed a million-dollar contract with a rival house, which was the beginning of a trend in the publishing industry. Later, the mystery writer P. D. James also bade a reluctant farewell to the company that had made her famous because Scribner declined to match a competing offer.

While Charles Scribner's personality and background precluded any interest in popular culture or the new fiction being produced in America, his dedication to what he called "the life of the mind" brought him great success in reference book publishing—an area that the firm came to dominate for almost two decades. Scribners had long been a publisher of reference works, but not on the scale that Charles Scribner, Jr., envisioned. Thus, beginning in the late 1960s, the firm began to bring out a list of works that not only were serious contributions to scholarship but were commercially successful and critically acclaimed as well. Many of these publications were of his own invention, most notably the sixteen-volume *Dictionary of Scientific Biography*, which grew out of Scribner's keen interest in, and understanding of, science. Although he was largely self-taught, his knowledge was both broad and deep, and several of his articles were published in leading scientific journals. He even devised the logo for the *Dictionary*, a design based on a thought experiment of the seventeenth-century Dutch mathematician Simon Stevin, which Scribner was fond of explicating. The next two decades saw the publication of dozens of similar titles, including the *Dictionary of the Middle Ages*, *Ancient Writers*, *British Writers*, *American Writers*, the *Dictionary of the History of Ideas*, and the *Dictionary of American History*.

Even with the success of the new additions to the Scribners reference list, the crown jewel remained the *Dictionary of American Biography*. This work had been a staple since the 1920s, but by the mid-1980s the original text had become dated and the many supplements had made it unwieldy. Its sponsor, the American Council of Learned Societies, thus decided to commission a completely new work. Scribner, following the advice of his literary adviser Jacques Barzun, shortsightedly refused, and the council moved the project to another publisher, which titled the work the *American National Biography*. The failure to seize the opportunity to redo *DAB* was the most telling sign that Scribner had lost control of his company.

In 1978 Scribner had merged the family firm with the debt-ridden Atheneum Publishers. Having naïvely trusted the executives who negotiated the arrangement, Scribner admitted that he barely glanced at the merger agreement and that, besides, he could not read a balance sheet. But then he found to his dismay that the Atheneum executives had been guaranteed full autonomy over their operations, including finances. The massive debt of the smaller company continued to grow until the new entity, the Scribner Book Companies, Inc., was faced with ruin. In 1984, after 140 years as a private, independent business, the company was sold to Macmillan for a fraction of its true worth. While the demise of Charles Scribner's Sons was a loss for American letters, it further enriched the Scribner family and the small number of stockholders. Within a year, the value of their Macmillan stock had increased fourfold, to more than $60 million.

In the frenzied financial world of the late 1980s and early 1990s, Scribners was passed from hand to hand as companies merged, became subsidiaries, or were bought out. Following the suicide of the Macmillan chairman, the British tycoon and embezzler Robert Maxwell, the company became part of Simon & Schuster, a subsidiary of Paramount Communications, which in turn became part of the multimedia giant Viacom. Charles Scribner's Sons is today simply Scribner, one of many imprints within a publishing conglomerate.

Charles Scribner, Jr., retired from publishing in 1986. But he remained true to his personal code. If he had any regrets about the decline of his once proud establishment, including the selling of the Scribner Building and the closing of the flagship Scribner Bookstore, a Fifth Avenue institution, he kept them to himself. In his retirement, he published two books of memoirs: *In the Company of Writers* (1991) and *In the Web of Ideas: The Education of a Publisher* (1993). He had earlier translated from the German and published a children's story called *The Devil's Bridge*—perhaps the inspiration for one of his favorite sayings, "We'll burn that bridge when we come to it." The autobiographical works are perfect reflections of the man. He is stingy with praise for his editors and colleagues; he rightly trumpets his considerable intellectual and scholarly contributions; and he vilifies those authors who left the company for more lucrative contracts elsewhere. But he never acknowledges the fact that his poor judgment in relying on unsuitable executives and advisers, his mistrust of people, and his ignorance of popular culture were the real reasons for the loss of his company.

After suffering for years from a degenerative nerve disease, Scribner died in Manhattan.

• The Charles Scribner's Sons archives are housed at Princeton University Library. Information in this entry was based on the Scribner memoirs cited above and the author's personal knowledge. An obituary appears in the *New York Times*, 13 Nov. 1995.

MARSHALL DE BRUHL

SCRIPPS, Ellen Browning (18 Oct. 1836–3 Aug. 1932), journalist and philanthropist, was born in London, England, the daughter of James Mogg Scripps, a bookbinder, and his second wife, Ellen Mary Saunders. After the death of his wife in 1841, James Mogg Scripps and their five children immigrated to the United States, eventually settling on a farm near Rushville, Illinois. In 1859 Scripps graduated from the Female Department of Knox College in Galesburg, Illinois. She worked briefly as a teacher and played an important role in raising the five children from her father's third marriage (to Julia Osborne). She was particularly close to the youngest of those children, Edward Willis Scripps. She never married.

In the late 1860s Scripps began her career in newspapers as a proofreader and later became a writer and reporter. She first worked at the *Detroit Tribune*, a newspaper managed by her elder brother James Edmund Scripps. In 1873 she joined James in the establishment of the *Detroit Evening News*. This paper was a pioneer in the field of small (four-page), cheap (two cents in an era when most papers cost five cents), and politically independent evening newspapers in the Midwest. The *Evening News* was at the forefront of change within the U.S. newspaper industry, and Ellen Scripps was an important part of that newspaper's great success in the 1870s and early 1880s.

One of the hallmarks of the *Evening News* was a condensed style, with interesting news provided in a brief space. Scripps was instrumental in developing the condensed style, producing a popular column of news and comment called "Miscellany," "Random Notes," "Matters and Things," or "Personal Paragraphs." Her brother Edward said that she had a good understanding not only of clear, crisp writing but of news that would interest readers.

By the 1870s Scripps had become an important figure in the Scripps family councils, in part because of her competence and also because she could reconcile the contentious personalities of her brothers James and George and her half-brother Edward. During this period, she was an advocate for and protector of Edward, who also worked at the family's Detroit newspaper. When Edward started the *Cleveland Press* in 1878, she sent him daily condensed news reports that helped in filling his paper and in attracting readers. She continued her writing and reporting until 1883, although the format she established had by then become a staple of the growing chain of Scripps family newspapers (in St. Louis and Cincinnati). Her columns of "Miscellany" and other topics became the inspiration for the Newspaper Enterprise Association, a news features service that Edward Scripps established in 1902.

Scripps avoided publicity but had great influence on the Scripps family newspaper business. She played an important role in the birth and growth of the first national newspaper chain developed by Edward Scripps between the 1890s and his death in 1926. She saved Edward from financial ruin on at least one occasion when he could not pay a note called in by their brother James and she provided the money that was needed. She sided with Edward in family financial disputes, notably the three-year battle (1900–1903) over the estate of brother George H. Scripps. Scripps invested in many of Edward's newspapers, both in the West and as part of the Scripps-McRae (later Scripps-Howard) newspaper chain in the Midwest. In the 1890s Scripps joined Edward in developing "Miramar," a large ranch near San Diego. She built her own home in La Jolla, California, in 1897 and lived there in great simplicity until her death.

In the last forty years of her life, Scripps became a philanthropist. Her extensive newspaper stock holdings and highly profitable investments in southern California real estate provided her with a sizable fortune. In 1906 she and Edward established the San Diego Marine Biological Association (later named the Scripps Institution of Oceanography at La Jolla). Scripps was also interested in educational institutions; with her sister Virginia, she helped to found the Bishop School for Girls in La Jolla. In 1925 she provided the funds to establish the Scripps College for Women. Opened in 1927, it joined Pomona College as the second of the projected Claremont colleges. Other major beneficiaries of Scripps's philanthropy included the Scripps Memorial Hospital in La Jolla (later named the Scripps Clinic and Research Foundation), the Scripps Metabolic Clinic, and the San Diego Zoo. A strong supporter of parks and outdoor recreation, Scripps donated funds for the development of Torrey Pines Park, gave a garden and park to the city of San Diego, and in 1917 became a director of the National Recreation Association.

When Scripps died in La Jolla, the leading newspaper industry trade journal *Editor & Publisher* lauded her contributions to American journalism, editorializing that "many women have contributed, directly and indirectly, to the development of the American press, but none more influentially and beneficently than Ellen Browning Scripps." The publication noted particularly her influence on Edward Scripps and reported that "she read business statements with uncommon powers of divination and [that] her opinion was regarded by all Scripps executives as clairvoyant." The *New York Times* recognized her, at the time of her death, as "one of the pioneers in modern American journalism."

• Ellen Browning Scripps's papers are at Scripps College. Additional letters are in the E. W. Scripps Correspondence in the Alden Library at Ohio University. Charles Preece, *E. W. and Ellen Browning Scripps: An Unmatched Pair* (1990), is a very useful source. See also Vance Trimble, *The Astonishing Mr. Scripps: The Turbulent Life of America's Penny Press Lord* (1992), Gilson Gardner, *Lusty Scripps: The Life of E. W. Scripps* (1932), and Negley Cochran, *E. W. Scripps* (1933). Obituaries are in *Editor & Publisher*, 6 Aug. 1932, and the *New York Times*, 4 Aug. 1932.

GERALD J. BALDASTY

SCRIPPS, E. W. (18 June 1854–12 Mar. 1926), journalist and publisher, was born Edward Willis Scripps near Rushville, Illinois, the son of James Moggs Scripps and Julia Osborne, farmers. As a youth, he was a voracious reader but left school at age fifteen to work full-time on his father's farm. Erratic in many things, Scripps sometimes signed his middle name "Wyllis"; both spellings were used by the family.

Scripps began his newspaper career as an office boy at the *Detroit Tribune* in 1872; a year later he joined the staff of the *Detroit Evening News*, a recently established newspaper owned by his older half-brother James Edmund Scripps. At his brother's paper, Scripps first worked in circulation, then began writing, and ultimately became city editor. His five years at the *Detroit Evening News* did much to shape his career and gave him ideas about how to produce a newspaper that was small, cheap, and politically independent. Both brothers sought the attention of working-class readers, unlike much of the established press of that time.

Impatient to create his own career independent of his half-brother, E. W. induced James to advance the capital to start the *Cleveland Press* in 1878. With E. W. Scripps as editor the *Press* sold for just a penny, was politically independent, refused to be deferential to local elites, and ardently advocated working-class interests. In the 1880s the paper provided ample and favorable coverage to working-class organizations, such as the Knights of Labor. The paper was enormously successful; in later years Scripps recounted that at Cleveland he learned that "it is not only profitable but pleasant and honorable to advocate the laboring class."

Two other attributes of the *Cleveland Press* would become hallmarks of Scripps's newspapers. First, it emphasized short articles. In his autobiography, Scripps wrote, "It was on the *Cleveland Press* that I learned from experience that everything else being equal, that paper sold the best which had the greatest number of individual separate items in it." Second, the paper operated on a proverbial shoestring—staffs were small, salaries low, hours long—and no opportunity for economizing was overlooked. Scripps's older half-sister Ellen Browning Scripps served as a key adviser during these years; she also provided many of the short, interesting articles that appeared in the *Press*.

Scripps was eager for new challenges; he disliked what he called the "slow pokey" chore of managing papers day to day. Rather, he wanted to establish new newspapers, while leaving others to handle the mundane managerial tasks. "I was always a man who hated details," he said. In 1880 Scripps started the *St. Louis Chronicle* with capital advanced by his half-brothers James and George. A year later he became involved with the *Cincinnati Penny Paper* (later called the *Post*), which James had just purchased.

In the 1880s Scripps pursued two goals. First, he wanted to become independent of his older brothers; by 1883 he had managed to obtain controlling interest in the Cincinnati and St. Louis newspapers. Second, he wanted to fashion a highly efficient newspaper chain, concentrating on centralization of management and news gathering. Both goals led to disputes with James and George, and by 1890 virtually all personal and business contact and civility between E. W. and James had ended. Throughout these disputes, E. W.'s key strengths were his own self-assurance and the support of his half-sister Ellen. Ellen's stock in the various Scripps family properties gave her the balance of power in family quarrels; she routinely sided with E. W. and protected him from foreclosure by James on at least two occasions. George joined E. W. in 1892, bringing control of the *Cleveland Press* to the Scripps-McRae newspapers.

In 1890, with control of newspapers in Cincinnati and St. Louis, Scripps began to create his own newspaper empire. He recruited an astute business partner, Milton A. McRae, to handle details that he loathed.

With McRae managing the Midwest papers throughout the 1890s, Scripps was free to pursue other goals. In 1890 he began to develop "Miramar," his ranch and estate near San Diego, where he lived for most of the next thirty years. In the 1890s Scripps's zeal for buying or starting newspapers continued. He became financially involved in the *San Diegan Sun* in 1892 and bought the *Los Angeles Record* in 1895 and the *San Francisco Report* in 1898. Enormous profits from the Cleveland and Cincinnati newspapers provided the dividends that financed Scripps's ranch development and additional newspaper acquisitions.

Hoping to expand his newspaper chain, Scripps returned to more active management in the late 1890s. He created an infrastructure for this by starting his own telegraph news services in the late 1890s (in 1907 these united to become the United Press Associations) to supply fast-breaking regional, national, and international news. In 1902 he established the Newspaper Enterprise Association to provide news features, photographs, illustrations, editorials, cartoons, and a variety of other materials. Dividing costs across Scripps's newspapers and other clients, these two services were able to produce large amounts of news cheaply.

Overall, Scripps established or purchased twenty-nine newspapers, including the *Cleveland Press* (established in 1878), the *St. Louis Chronicle* (1880), the *Cincinnati Post* (1881), the *San Francisco Daily News* (1903), the *Dallas Dispatch* (1906), the *Evansville Press* (1906), and the *Chicago Day Book* (1911).

All of the Scripps newspapers were strong advocates of working-class interests. They provided sympathetic coverage to a wide variety of labor-related issues: strikes, labor political organizations, union meetings, wage stagnation, and the cost of living. Scripps's papers favored the American Federation of Labor (led by Samuel Gompers) over more socialist-inclined labor groups, although they gave favorable coverage to Socialist Eugene V. Debs's campaigns for the presidency in the early twentieth century. Scripps flirted with socialism but usually called himself a Progressive or an independent Democrat. Under his direction, his newspapers provided vital support for several "progressive" politicians, including Robert M. La Follette, Woodrow Wilson, and Hiram Johnson.

By the late 1890s and early 1900s the Scripps newspapers were publicizing and supporting a wide array of Progressive reforms. The Scripps newspapers supported such proposals as the initiative process, referendum, recall, direct election of U.S. senators, government control over trusts and monopolies, and municipal ownership of utilities. This liberal emphasis reflected Scripps's dictum that "newspapers should be friends, advisers, advocates and even the special pleaders of the ninety-five percent of the population that were not rich nor powerful." He told one of his editors, "I would have every page and every article in the paper clearly show forth that you desire to be the advocate of the common people." At the time of his death, the leading newspaper industry journal *Editor & Publisher* called him a fighter for "the 'forgotten man,' the worker without the prestige of wealth, political or social position" (20 Mar. 1926).

Scripps's private life was often tumultuous. As a young man he was engaged in a series of unsatisfactory love affairs, and throughout much of his life he drank excessively. His marriage to Nackie Holtsinger in October 1885 brought a respite from some of this turmoil, but his autocratic personality eventually led to disputes with her and most of his children. He had few friends, suffered continually from nervous attacks, and was a lifelong hypochondriac. He loathed crowds and preferred living a fairly reclusive life at Miramar. He read voraciously and wrote extensively about journalism, science, and a host of other subjects. His interest in science led to his long friendship with biologist William Ritter and to the establishment (by Scripps and his sister Ellen) of the Marine Biological Station (now called the Scripps Institute of Oceanography).

In 1908 Scripps retired from the day-to-day supervision of his newspapers, turning management over to his two sons, James and John. John died in 1914, and serious disagreements between James and Scripps led to a break between father and son in 1920. That same year Scripps started the Science Service to explain scientific news in a popular form; he also returned to active control of his newspaper empire. In 1922 the elder Scripps retired again, creating the Scripps-Howard newspaper chain under the direction of his youngest son, Robert Paine Scripps, and Roy Howard. After 1922 Scripps became a peripatetic wanderer aboard his yacht, *Ohio*. He died on board his boat in Monrovia Bay, off the coast of Liberia, and was buried at sea.

Scripps was a pioneer in changing the way the newspaper industry operated. He demonstrated that non-local ownership and operation of newspapers could be economically efficient and highly profitable. At the beginning of his career, virtually all American newspapers were locally owned and operated; during his career he established the model of "group ownership" that would come to dominate the industry by the late twentieth century. Scripps believed that a chain (or group) of newspapers could be far more efficiently run than a series of independent newspapers; his desire to build a chain reflected his general approach to business. He asserted that "it is the duty of newspaper businessmen, as well as all businessmen, to make money."

• Scripps's papers, including his unpublished autobiography, are in the Alden Library at Ohio University in Athens. The most complete modern assessment of Scripps is Vance Trimble, *The Astonishing Mr. Scripps: The Turbulent Life of American's Penny Press Lord* (1992). Oliver Knight, *I Protest: Selected Disquisitions of E. W. Scripps* (1966), is an important source. See also Charles Preece, *Edward Willis and Ellen Browning Scripps, an Unmatched Pair: A Biography* (1990); Gilson Gardner, *Lusty Scripps: The Life of E. W. Scripps* (1932); Negley Cochran, *E. W. Scripps* (1933); Charles McCabe, *Damned Old Crank: A Self-Portrait of E. W. Scripps* (1951); and Milton A. McRae, *Forty Years in Newspaperdom: The Autobiography of a Newspaper Man* (1924).

GERALD J. BALDASTY

SCRIPPS, James Edmund (19 Mar. 1833–29 May 1906), journalist and publisher, was born in London, England, the son of James Moggs Scripps, a bookbinder, and Ellen Mary Saunders. When Scripps was eight years old his mother died; when he was eleven the family immigrated to the United States, settling on a farm near Rushville, Illinois.

At age twenty-two Scripps moved to Chicago and began to work as a newspaper reporter. In 1859 he lost his Chicago newspaper job and moved to Detroit, where he became commercial editor and soon news editor of the *Detroit Advertiser*. In 1861 he enlisted in the Union army; when his tour of duty ended in 1862, he returned to Detroit where he helped arrange the merger of two Republican-affiliated newspapers (the *Advertiser* and the *Tribune*) into the *Detroit Tribune*. He became a part owner of the new paper, serving first as its business manager and later as its managing editor. In 1862 he married Harriet J. Messinger; they had six children.

In 1873 fire destroyed Scripps's newspaper, and with the insurance money he set out to establish a newspaper that would be free from partisanship. In August 1873 the *Detroit Evening News* made its debut. It was a sharp contrast to the other newspapers of Detroit (and of the United States) of that era. It was inexpensive, selling for just two cents. It was small, running four pages reduced in size compared to the eight broadsheet pages ordinarily run by other papers. The *Evening News* specialized in condensed news items written in a lively fashion, in contrast to the often ponderous essays that crowded many newspaper columns. The paper consciously sought out a working-class audience instead of the more highbrow audiences sought by older papers. In an age of recurring partisan journalism, the little Scripps paper practiced independence from party. It was not devoid of advocacy, but chose to defend working-class interests broadly rather than any one party's interests. After a shaky start, the paper surged in popularity and profits.

The success of the *Detroit Evening News* accounts for Scripps's importance as a journalist. The paper was a pioneer in the development of cheap independent daily newspapers that grew in the Midwest in the 1870s and 1880s; moreover, its financial success demonstrated that a lucrative market existed for newspapers that avoided close links to political parties. Scripps and the *Detroit Evening News* thus represented a new model of American journalism, one that many publishers in the twentieth century tried to follow. The paper was a pioneer in printing *all* the news without bias or exception. In his manuscript autobiography, Edward Willis Scripps recalled the impact of his half brother's paper, saying that "so called respectable men in political offices who were doing wrong things, clergymen who had faults that unfitted them for church service or even decent society, professional men . . . who had depended upon the cloak of their respectability or position to cover a misdeed, and many other citizens, soon found out that, as far as the reporters of the *Evening News* were concerned, they were living in glass houses and they had no means of protecting themselves from public exposure."

The Scripps family newspapers, in which all the Scripps siblings were original stockholders from 1873, began to expand in the late 1870s to include the *Cleveland Press* in 1878, the *Buffalo Telegraph* in 1880, the *St. Louis Chronicle* in 1880, and the *Cincinnati Penny Paper* (later named the *Post*) in 1881. This was the first daily newspaper chain in the United States. All of these newspapers followed the general model established by the *Detroit Evening News*. The Cleveland and Cincinnati papers were enormously successful and, with the *Detroit Evening News*, produced very large dividends for members of the Scripps family.

Scripps's control over the newspapers outside of Detroit declined in the 1880s, primarily because of the efforts of his half brother Edward to establish his own business. By 1883 Edward had obtained a controlling interest in the Cincinnati and St. Louis papers. Sharp policy differences over Edward's desire to expand their holdings rapidly ended close relations between the two men in 1889. In 1892 Scripps's brother George shifted his allegiance to Edward, taking control of the *Cleveland Press* with him; this marked the beginning of the Scripps-McRae league of newspapers. James Scripps retained his base in the *Detroit Evening News*; a later effort to run a Chicago paper (the *Journal*) was a costly failure.

Part of Scripps's influence on American journalism undoubtedly stems from the success of Edward. Between the 1890s and World War I Edward established more than two dozen newspapers in the style of the *Detroit Evening News*, creating the largest newspaper of his era and the first national newspaper chain. He attributed his own great success to his half brother's view of journalism.

Scripps was avidly devoted to the betterment of Detroit. He was one of the original incorporators of the Detroit Museum of Art (later named the Detroit Institute of Art) and was a leading benefactor of that institution. Between 1890 and 1893 he built a Gothic-style church for the Reformed Episcopal denomination in Detroit. He served as a Detroit Park Commissioner from 1892 to 1894 and as a member of the Detroit Public Library Commission in 1900. He served one term in the Michigan state senate (1903–1904).

Shortly after Scripps died in Detroit, the Grand Rapids, Michigan, *Press* commented that "scores of papers have been established in every section of the country with the *Detroit Evening News* as a model. . . . Strict independence is the distinctive feature of modern journalism, and it is so largely because Mr. Scripps demonstrated that independent journalism is the most profitable journalism as well as the most satisfactory in other respects" (1 June 1906).

• Most of Scripps's papers are in the Detroit Public Library. Other papers are in the E. W. Scripps Correspondence, Alden Library, Ohio University, Athens, Ohio. William W. Lutz, *The News of Detroit: How a Newspaper and a City Grew Together* (1973), is an important source. Other sources, dealing primarily with E. W. Scripps, also provide substantial information on Scripps's life and work: Vance Trimble, *The Astonishing Mr. Scripps: The Turbulent Life of America's Penny Press Lord* (1992); Oliver Knight, *I Protest: Selected Disquisitions of E. W. Scripps* (1966); and Milton A. McRae, *Forty Years in Newspaperdom: The Autobiography of a Newspaper Man* (1924). An obituary is in the *New York Times*, 30 May 1906.

GERALD J. BALDASTY

SCRIPPS, Robert Paine (27 Oct. 1895–2 Mar. 1938), newspaper publisher, was born in San Diego, California, the son of Edward Willis Scripps, a newspaper publisher and founder of the modern newspaper chain, and Nackie Holtsinger. E. W. Scripps started the *Cleveland Press* in 1878 and by his death in 1926 owned more than fifty newspapers, United Press, Newspaper Enterprise Association, Scripps Science Service, and a newsreel service called ACME Pictures. He wanted to train his sons to take his place and manage the vast media empire. In 1908 he released his long-time partner and business associate, Milton McRae, from the position of general manager of Scripps-McRae Newspapers and inserted his eldest son, James G. Scripps, into that position. E. W. had trained James for the position and was now ready to train his younger children.

Robert Scripps's first job came at age fifteen when he was assigned to run his father's 2,000-acre ranch at Miramar, California. He was responsible for hiring, firing, and supervising a sizable crew, managing the day-to-day operations of the ranch, and making it profitable. In 1912, at age sixteen, he went to work as a circulation canvasser on the Scripps-owned *Philadelphia News-Post*. In 1913 he visited Europe to study municipal government. In January 1914, at eighteen, he took an editing job at the Scripps-owned *San Diego Sun*. He briefly attended Pomona College in California before moving on to brief stints with papers in Bakersfield and Eureka, California. In 1916 Scripps went to Hawaii, where he met author Jack London, who would become a lifelong friend. Scripps moved to Australia in the latter part of 1916 to travel and work for a newspaper to understand differences between the Australian and American press systems.

U.S. entry into World War I brought E. W. out of his nine-year "retirement." E. W. moved to Washington, D.C., where in May 1917 he set up an office and insisted that Robert help him lobby support for the administration of Woodrow Wilson and for the war effort. E. W. believed in the Wilson administration's policies, and he felt his influence would help win some battles on Capitol Hill. Shortly before he relocated, Robert Scripps married Margaret Culbertson, the daughter of a lumberman. In July, having approved of Robert's management of the Washington office, E. W. appointed him as editor in chief of Scripps-McRae. This sudden appointment of a younger sibling to a high administrative position so soon after E. W.'s seemingly impromptu emergence from retirement rankled James Scripps, who had been in command as chairman of the board of the company for nine years. This marked the beginning of several conflicts, ranging from editorial policies to employee management, between eldest son and father. Meanwhile, Robert Scripps plunged himself into the work. One of his first acts was to gather a small group of seasoned journalists in a back room of the Scripps-owned *Washington Daily News* and form an editorial board. This led to the beginning of the Washington news bureau and an expanded news service.

Between 1917 and 1920 the differences of opinion between E. W. and James over management of the chain became magnified. Incensed, James resigned from his father's empire. Taking with him several West Coast newspapers in which he was a majority stockholder, James founded the Scripps League of Newspapers. It was not a clean split, however. Depending on the newspaper, E. W. controlled between 10 percent and 45 percent of the stock, and because each paper was a corporation, James was able to take several papers in which E. W. had a nominal ownership. Neither E. W. nor James was sure who had controlling interest of the Scripps papers in Denver or Dallas, and E. W. was concerned that James might persuade other stockholders of various papers to join him. E. W. made attempts to bring James and his Scripps League back into Scripps-McRae, but James's untimely death in January 1921 and the subsequent decision of his widow, Josephine, to retain the papers made this difficult. E. W. pushed for immediate reorganization and dissolved the old company of Scripps-McRae. In November 1922 E. W. turned over complete control of the papers to Robert Scripps and United Press president Roy Howard and formed a new chain called Scripps-Howard. In the early 1920s Scripps-Howard was identified as one of the two largest newspaper chains, rivaling the Hearst Corporation.

Now fully responsible for the giant chain and its growing administrative chores, Robert Scripps appointed Roy Howard to head the business and editorial operations. When E. W. died in 1926, Scripps became sole trustee of the Scripps newspapers. He traveled across the country looking for papers to purchase and other expansion opportunities for the chain; Howard handled day-to-day management.

Under Scripps's direction, first as chairman and later as trustee, Scripps-Howard started or acquired newspapers in Birmingham, Alabama; Norfolk, Virginia; Fort Worth and El Paso, Texas; Washington, D.C.; Knoxville, Tennessee; Youngstown, Ohio; Indianapolis, Indiana; Baltimore, Maryland; Pittsburgh, Pennsylvania; Albuquerque, New Mexico; and New York City. Scripps-Howard also moved into radio, purchasing stations in Cincinnati, Ohio, and Knoxville and Memphis, Tennessee.

Scripps's reputation as leader was soon recognized beyond Scripps-Howard. In 1926 he was an American delegate to the first International Press Conference held in Geneva, Switzerland, under the auspices of the League of Nations. In 1930 a committee of British publishers honored him with a Walter Hines Page Fellowship, given to those who make outstanding contributions to journalism worldwide.

The depression of the 1930s led Scripps to become politically active. In 1931, appearing before a Senate conference on unemployment and industrial stabilization, he was one of the first representatives of big business to suggest shorter working hours and a wider distribution of wealth to solve the problems related to the depression. Although Scripps had strong political opinions, editorial policy was not dictated to Scripps-Howard papers, though they did generally support whatever position he was championing.

In 1933 Scripps and Howard successfully negotiated the terms of the first joint-operating agreement in the newspaper industry, involving the Scripps-Howard *Albuquerque Tribune* and the independently owned *Albuquerque Journal*. They attempted simultaneously to establish a similar agreement in San Diego but failed. The next joint-operating agreement was established in 1936 between the Scripps-Howard–owned *El Paso Herald-Post* and the independently owned *El Paso Times*; a later agreement was made between the Scripps paper and its competitor in Evansville, Indiana. These joint-operating agreements created an arrangement whereby the papers shared printing presses, production facilities, advertising sales, and circulation offices yet maintained editorial and news-gathering independence.

The establishment of joint-operating agreements has had a long-lasting effect on the newspaper industry, with competing papers in numerous cities, including Seattle, Tucson, Salt Lake City, Nashville, New Orleans, Honolulu, St. Louis, Detroit, Cincinnati, Knoxville, Pittsburgh, Columbus, San Francisco, and Atlanta, participating in such arrangements. The proliferation of these agreements led to passage of the Newspaper Preservation Act of 1970, which granted an antitrust exemption to newspapers. Since its inception, Scripps-Howard has had more newspapers under joint-operating agreements than any other chain in the United States.

Scripps's influence extended beyond the newspaper business. In 1936 the Treasury Department listened when he suggested an adjustment to the inheritance-tax system that would allow a payment plan in installments over a great number of years so that an estate might not be forced to liquidate to pay the tax.

Scripps died of a hemorrhage of the neck, later diagnosed as a varicose condition of the esophagus, while vacationing at Cabo San Lucas, Mexico, on his yacht *Novia Del Mar*. Howard assumed full responsibility for the chain, including trusteeship of the company on behalf of Scripps's six children.

Robert Scripps's most lasting legacy has been the establishment of joint-operating agreements. In a period when fierce competition forced many poorly managed newspapers to fold, these agreements helped ensure the survival of the Scripps-Howard chain and numerous other newspapers. It is an unexpected legacy given Scripps's attempts to distance himself from the chain's mundane business operations by immersing himself in editorial and expansion activities.

• For more information on Robert Paine Scripps, see the E. W. Scripps Papers, subseries 3.1, boxes 55 and 56, Ohio University, Athens; the Roy Howard Papers, boxes 72 and 75, Library of Congress; and the Roy Howard Archive, Indiana University School of Journalism, Bloomington. Also helpful are Vance H. Trimble, *Scripps-Howard Handbook* (1981) and *The Astonishing Mr. Scripps* (1992), and a contemporary view by Negley D. Cochran, *E. W. Scripps* (1933). An obituary is in the *New York Times*, 4 Mar. 1938.

EDWARD E. ADAMS

SCRIPPS, William Edmund (6 May 1882–12 June 1952), publisher and industrialist, was born in Detroit, Michigan, the son of James Edmund Scripps, the founder of the *Detroit Evening News*, and Harriet Josephine Messinger. After attending the Michigan Military Academy, he joined the *Detroit News* at age fourteen. It soon became apparent that his talents lay in the field of technology rather than journalism. He preferred to be among the printing presses and was interested in how things worked. In 1901 he married Nina Downey; they had three children.

Scripps was keenly interested in the then-new field of aviation and became an enthusiastic supporter. As airplanes grew in popularity he became the first owner of a private airplane in Michigan and even taught himself how to fly. Going a step further, he saw the tremendous potential of the airplane in business, and through his efforts the *Detroit News* became one of the first newspapers in the country to have airplane delivery where needed. In 1919 the *Detroit News* sponsored a Detroit–Atlantic City flight, and from 1922 to 1933 Scripps himself sponsored the National Air Races, which were held in Detroit.

Another new technology that caught Scripps's eye was radio broadcasting, then in its early years. In 1920, again seeing tremendous potential, he started the first radio station in Detroit, WWF, which was later renamed WWJ. It was also the first radio station owned by a newspaper, one of the first radio stations to realize the cultural and educational value of radio, and the first to broadcast election returns. It was also among the first stations to broadcast baseball games, giving listeners the thrill of play-by-play action right in their homes. Symphony concerts, courtesy of WWJ, also offered a chance to be part of the audience for those who were not able to attend in person. When television became possible, Scripps formed in 1947 WWJ-TV, the first television station in Detroit.

In 1929 Scripps became head of the *Detroit News* and president of the Detroit News Publishing Company, a post he held until his death. While he did not become the journalist his father might have wished him to become, he possessed the vision and foresight that kept the *Detroit News* a vehicle for making as well as reporting news. His enthusiastic acceptance, use, and promotion of technology played a major role in his success with the newspaper. Never losing his interest in how machines work, he started the Scripps Motor Company, of which he became president. The company manufactured gasoline-driven marine motor engines. He even tried his hand at a motor car company but was not successful.

In his later years Scripps developed new interests, among them conservation. On "Wildwood," his country estate located in Oakland County, Michigan, he raised award-winning livestock, the most famous being his Angus cattle. He also established a large game refuge on his property. Keenly aware of the need to protect forests and trees, he was also an advocate of reforestation.

A generous person, Scripps gave his personal art collection to the city of Detroit. His city residence was given, after his death, to the Roman Catholic Daughters of Divine Charity, who converted it into a residential school for girls. He also contributed to the Episcopal church of Detroit. He and his wife also designed a model country school in Oakland County, Michigan, which later became the model for country schools in other rural areas, and in 1941 he served as a member of the Seaway for Defense Committee, whose aim was to garner public support for the Great Lakes–St. Lawrence Seaway and Power Project.

Scripps's great strength lay in being on the cutting edge with revolutionary technologies: aviation, radio broadcasting, and television broadcasting. He possessed the ability to look ahead to the future, see the vast potential of each, and eagerly seize what each had to offer. As president of the Detroit News Publishing Company, he brought worldwide fame to the newspaper. He died at his country estate, located near Lake Orion, Michigan.

• William W. Lutz, *The News of Detroit* (1973), is a source of information about Scripps and his newspaper. Obituaries are in the *New York Times*, 13 June 1952, and in *Newsweek* and *Time*, both 23 June 1952.

BARBARA L. FLYNN

SCRIPTURE, Edward Wheeler (21 May 1864–31 July 1945), psychologist, phonetician, and speech therapist, was born in Mason, New Hampshire, the son of Orin Murray Scripture, a New York commodity trader, and Mary Frances Wheeler. After graduating from the College of the City of New York with an A.B. in 1884, Scripture studied at the universities of Berlin, Leipzig, and Zurich. The new experimental psychology then emerging from philosophy in Europe impressed him, as it did many other young Americans studying abroad. His 1891 Leipzig Ph.D. dissertation, which was directed by the influential psychologist Wilhelm Wundt, experimentally addressed the associative course of thought and won him a brief appointment at Clark University as fellow and assistant editor of university president G. Stanley Hall's *American Journal of Psychology*. In 1892 Yale University philosopher George Trumbull Ladd (whose interest in the new science had led to his *Elements of Physiological Psychology* [1887]) hired Scripture as instructor of experimental psychology. Once at Yale, Scripture almost immediately began issuing volumes of *Studies from the Yale Psychological Laboratory*. He formally became director of the Yale Psychological Laboratory in 1898 and was promoted to assistant professor in 1901. In 1890 he married May Kirk, a graduate of New York's Hunter College then studying vocal music in Germany; they had three children.

In his teaching of psychology at Yale, Scripture dismissed his teachers' and colleagues' (including Ladd's) continuing philosophical concerns and disparaged their scientific studies in order to emphasize extreme experimental exactness. His commitment to this cause of experimental precision carried the conviction of a convert, and he often spoke with his students in the German of the Leipzig laboratory. His research addressed such psychological phenomena as the localization of sound, the size-weight illusion, and the effect of rhythm on movement. Although his experiments seemed "more [like] telegraphy than psychology" to at least one well-known student (Carl E. Seashore), the apparatus Scripture designed for many of them soon found its way into many of his colleagues' laboratories.

At Yale, Scripture wrote two popular books, *Thinking, Feeling, Doing* (1895), for use by Chautauqua groups, and *The New Psychology* (1897), part of Havelock Ellis's London-based Contemporary Science Series. These books further illustrated Scripture's emphasis on experimental practice and harshly criticized many of his predecessors and such well-respected contemporaries as Ladd and Harvard's William James for the "endless speculation and flimsy guesswork" of

their "armchair psychology." These comments angered many colleagues—James called him "shallow, and a complete barbarian"—and others found even more despicable *Thinking, Feeling, Doing*'s ample plagiarism of a recent translation of one of Wundt's books by two Cornell professors, psychologist Edward B. Titchener and philosopher James E. Creighton. Scripture nevertheless remained active in the affairs of the American psychological community and (perhaps owing to his wife's influence) gradually began to focus his research on "the psychology of expression, especially by speech." His *Elements of Experimental Phonetics* (1902) introduced soon-to-be-standard methods and apparatus for experiments on speech, but Yale soon responded to its psychologists' continuing bickering by forcing Ladd's early retirement and firing Scripture in 1903.

One of the Carnegie Institution of Washington's earliest grants allowed Scripture to continue his research in Germany and Switzerland, where he produced *Researches in Experimental Phonetics: The Study of Speech Curves* (1906), which further defined that scientific speciality's emphasis on the physiology of speech production. He also lectured at Marburg, earned an M.D. from the University of Munich in 1906, and, after meeting Swiss psychiatrist and psychologist Carl Gustav Jung in Zurich, began claiming that his early experiments on thought had shown that association often involves unconscious ideas. He soon returned to New York, where he began addressing medical audiences on "psychanalysis," and by 1909 had become associate in psychiatry at Columbia University's College of Physicians and Surgeons and director of the Neurological Laboratory of the college's Vanderbilt Clinic. He also established a private practice in speech therapy with his wife, who had long sung professionally with the renowned choir of New York's St. Thomas Episcopal Church. His *Stuttering and Lisping* (1912; revised as *Stuttering, Lisping and Correction of Speech of the Deaf* [1923]) approached stuttering as a "typical psychoneurosis" to be treated both through modified psychoanalytic techniques and exercises designed to correct faulty speech patterns.

In 1913 May Kirk Scripture sued her husband for separation, claiming that he had abandoned her for Ethel King, his laboratory assistant. At about that time Scripture moved without his wife to London, where he continued his therapeutic and research work at the West End Hospital for Nervous Diseases and as honorary lecturer in phonetics at King's College. In 1923 he also became professor of experimental phonetics at the University of Vienna. The importance of his continuing connections to England waned until the mid-1930s, when he retired from his Austrian position and returned to London. His last published papers (in *Nature* in the late 1930s) give his address as the University of London Phonetics Laboratory. He died in Westbury on Tyne, a small town near Bristol, England.

Few late nineteenth-century American psychologists could be called modest; as such they readily tolerated their colleagues' arrogance when it accompanied actual achievement in science or philosophy. Many even endured (at least through 1914) the mendacity and extreme Germanophilia of Harvard's Danzig-born Hugo Münsterberg, whose psychological work they admired. But most disliked Scripture's chutzpah and shared James's and Seashore's opinion of him and his research; Münsterberg once called Scripture an experimentalist, but not a psychologist. Few mourned his departure from Yale, and twenty years later, even as his speech-therapy colleagues agreed that stuttering required a mix of treatments, they responded similarly when Vienna drew him from London. His personality thus limited his immediate influence, even in a field in which his legacy has lasted.

• In his autobiography (in *History of Psychology in Autobiography*, vol. 3, ed. Carl Murchison [1936], pp. 231–61), Scripture complained that he had been made "to suffer the fate of Socrates—all but the hemlock"—and mixed misremembered minutiae about his career with detailed explications of his experiments and extravagant claims for his scientific work. An almost complete bibliography of his writings appears in Carl Murchison, ed., *The Psychological Register*, vol. 3 (1932), pp. 436–40. Michael M. Sokal, "The Psychological Career of Edward Wheeler Scripture," in *Historiography of Modern Psychology: Aims, Resources, and Approaches*, ed. Josef Brožek and Ludwig J. Pongratz (1980), pp. 255–78, deals primarily with Scripture's pre-phonetic career within the context of the American psychological community. Mildred F. Berry, "Historical Vignettes of Leadership in Speech and Hearing: I. Speech Pathology: Edward Wheeler Scripture (1864–1945) [and] May Kirk Scripture (1865–1943)," *ASHA* 7 (1965): 8–9, provides some useful detail. Both the details and the context of Scripture's experimental studies of speech receive attention in W. J. Hardcastle, "Experimental Studies of Lingual Coarticulation," in *Towards a History of Phonetics*, ed. R. E. Asher and Eugénie J. A. Henderson (1981), pp. 50–56. Margaret Eldridge, *A History of the Treatment of Speech Disorders* (1968), emphasizes the significance of Scripture's approach to speech therapy for both America and Britain and portrays the difficulties he had in working with others in London.

MICHAEL M. SOKAL

SCUDDER, Horace Elisha (16 Oct. 1838–11 Jan. 1902), editor and author, was born in Boston, Massachusetts, the son of Charles Scudder, a well-to-do hardware and commission merchant, and Sarah Lathrop Coit. The family was active in the Congregational church. Scudder attended the Roxbury Latin School, the Boston Latin School, and then Williams College, edited the *Williams Quarterly*, and graduated in 1858. Suffering all his life from mysterious and intermittent deafness, which ruled out a career as a teacher or a clergyman, he went to New York City, where he tutored a rich Brooklyn couple's young son, read in Manhattan in his free time, published a few articles, and wrote *Seven Little People and Their Friends* (1862), which was pirated in England. In 1863 his father's death obligated him to return to Boston to head the Scudder household. The year 1864 was momentous. At his family's request he wrote and pub-

lished *The Life and Letters of David Coit Scudder* (1864)—David being his brother, who had accidentally drowned in 1862 while on missionary service in India. Scudder also published his second juvenile book, *Dream Children*, and an essay on William Blake in the *North American Review*. And he became literary adviser for the Boston publishers Hurd & Houghton.

In 1867 Henry Oscar Houghton, head of the firm, persuaded Scudder to establish and edit the *Riverside Magazine for Young People*, to be published by Hurd & Houghton. He made the magazine first-rate by including works by Jacob Abbott, Hans Christian Andersen (with whom he corresponded), Frank R. Stockton, and Sarah Orne Jewett, among others. It was absorbed by *Scribner's Magazine* in 1870. The well-to-do George Harrison Mifflin entered Houghton's firm in 1872. Scudder served as Houghton's partner during 1872–1875 but for the next three years devoted himself mainly to his own writing. In 1873 he married Grace Owen. The couple had two children. From 1875 to 1885 he wrote eight popular books for children about three generations of "the Bodley family." When he returned to the firm in 1878, it was Houghton, Osgood & Co., since Houghton had that year taken James R. Osgood as a senior partner. The relationship was not amicable and ended two years later, at which time the firm became Houghton, Mifflin & Co., with Scudder as its chief literary adviser and its trade department manager. He edited and annotated *American Poems* . . . (1879), featuring six major writers, *American Prose* . . . (1880), featuring eight major writers, and *The Children's Book* . . . (1881), collecting fables, fairy tales, Greek myths, nursery rhymes, and several new stories by Andersen. Scudder sought to balance his desire to accept for publication only the most moral and artistic writing and his awareness that what was published had to turn a profit.

In 1881 William Dean Howells resigned as editor of the *Atlantic Monthly*, which Houghton, Mifflin published, and Scudder hoped to become its editor. He was disappointed when Thomas Bailey Aldrich was chosen instead, but bided his time and remained incredibly busy. He declined a professorship at Williams and the post of literary editor of the *New York World*. His own personal work in the next several years was monumental. Among much else, he wrote a biography of Noah Webster (1882), two juvenile histories of the United States (1884, 1890), a biography of Bayard Taylor (1884, cowritten with Taylor's widow), and a biography of George Washington (1889), and he also edited the works of Henry Wadsworth Longfellow (1886) and William Makepeace Thackeray (1889). He minutely criticized manuscript submissions and offered exhaustive, and usually wise, suggestions. Houghton, Mifflin's amazing list to 1900 and just beyond was in large part owing to Scudder. The panic of 1893, which hurt other publishers, did no permanent damage to Houghton, Mifflin. After Houghton's death in 1895, Mifflin, who Scudder feared might be too commercially inclined, took charge.

In 1887 Scudder published his *Men and Letters: Essays in Characterization and Criticism.* A year later, he addressed a meeting in San Francisco of the National Teachers' Association and urged its members to inculcate in their pupils a patriotic, moral, and hence ennobling love of literature—all of which was the central concern of his *Men and Letters.* In 1890 Houghton accepted the resignation of Aldrich, who had not been diligent, and appointed Scudder as editor of the *Atlantic.* He also continued to be responsible for personally editing and annotating trade books as well, including the works of Robert Browning (1895), Henry David Thoreau (1895), John Greenleaf Whittier (1895), James Russell Lowell (1897), John Keats (1899), and Nathaniel Hawthorne (1901). He also accepted for publication in the *Atlantic* works by Gamaliel Bradford, John Jay Chapman, Henry James, Alfred Thayer Mahan, Theodore Roosevelt, George Santayana, Woodrow Wilson, and other significant writers. He also continued to write reviews and articles for the *Atlantic*—until his production totaled 185, more than that of any other contributor. Among numerous other authors whose works he reviewed may be named Edward Bellamy, George Washington Cable, Francis Marion Crawford, Henry Blake Fuller, Thomas Hardy, Helen Hunt Jackson, Anthony Trollope, Mrs. Humphrey Ward, and Mary E. Wilkins (later Freeman). Scudder's last book was a biography of Lowell (1901), which he completed shortly before dying of complications from chronic diabetes in Cambridge, Massachusetts.

Scudder, who modestly called himself a "literary workman," was important in the history of American letters for several reasons. His books for children, and those he edited by others, appealed to the innocent imagination of young readers cleanly and creatively. His biographies, most conspicuously that of Lowell, were landmarks built on solid research and an awareness of the history of the times. As educator, he helped create a love of home-grown, especially New England, fiction and poetry. And as editor, he encouraged the advance of realism but a realism that rises above documentary naturalism, develops shapely artistic form, and espouses helpful personal, social, and national ideals.

• Scudder's diaries and the bulk of his vast correspondence are at the Houghton Library, Harvard University. Many of his other papers are at the Buffalo and Erie County Public Library and at the New-York Historical Society and in libraries at the Boston Athenaeum; Columbia University; the University of Kansas; Trinity College, Hartford, Conn.; Washington University, St. Louis; and Yale University. Helen McMahon, in *Criticism of Fiction: A Study of Trends in the "Atlantic Monthly" 1857–1898* (1952), identifies 185 reviews and articles by Scudder in the *Atlantic* and quotes his comments on content, form, and social values of realistic fiction. Details of Scudder's publishing activities are presented in Ellen B. Ballou, *The Building of the House: Houghton Mifflin's Formative Years* (1970); John Tebbel, *Between Covers: The Rise and Transformation of Book Publishing in America* (1987); and Ellery Sedgwick, *The "Atlantic Monthly" 1857–1909: Yankee Humanism at High Tide and Ebb* (1994). An obituary is in the *Boston Transcript*, 13 Jan. 1902; another, by Thomas Wentworth Higginson, is in *Proceedings of the American Academy of Arts and Sciences* 37 (May 1902): 657–61.

ROBERT L. GALE

SCUDDER, Ida Sophia (9 Dec. 1870–24 May 1960), medical missionary and founder of the Vellore Medical College, was born in Ranipet, India, the daughter of John Scudder II, a medical missionary, and Sophia Weld. Scudder was born into the third generation of a missionary family that would eventually boast more than one thousand years of combined service abroad.

After experiencing the horror of a famine in India when she was eight years old, Scudder returned in 1878 with her family on furlough to the United States, where she was able to enjoy the peace of family life on a Nebraska farm. Six years later both her father and mother returned to India, leaving fourteen-year-old Ida in the care of her strict uncle, Henry Martyn Scudder of Chicago. When Henry himself left in 1887 for missionary duties in Japan, Ida was enrolled in D. L. Moody's Northfield Seminary for girls in Massachusetts. By this time, she had firmly resolved not to become another Scudder missionary.

When her mother fell ill in 1890, however, Scudder gladly returned to Asia to assist her parents. Shortly after her arrival in India, an experience reversed her previous resolve: in a single evening three different men knocked at the mission bungalow, each asking Scudder to come help his wife who was in the midst of a dangerously difficult delivery. Scudder's physician father could offer no help, because, according to Hindu religious tradition, a male outside the family was not even allowed to see the face of a married woman. All three women died in childbirth that night. Thrown into spiritual turmoil, Scudder recalled: "I shut myself in my room and thought about the condition of the Indian women." She concluded that she had come face to face with God and that she was being called to "help such women" (Jeffery, p. 27).

Scudder entered the Women's Medical College in Philadelphia, Pennsylvania, in 1895 and transferred to Cornell University's Medical School for the final year of her M.D. program in 1898, primarily for the broader clinical opportunities available in New York City. She graduated with an M.D. from Cornell in 1899.

Before returning to India to assist her father, Scudder was given the task of raising money for the construction of a hospital for the women and children of India. She succeeded beyond the desired $8,000 goal, having gained the support of a New York banker who donated $10,000 in memory of his wife, Mary Taber Schell.

Scudder bypassed the opportunity for a stateside internship, convinced that her father would be her best tutor. Unfortunately, John Scudder II died within five months of her arrival in India in 1900, leaving her with little practical experience and with a mostly rural populace distrustful of a woman doctor. Patients eventually sought her out, and soon the Schell Hospital, which opened in 1902 with a forty-bed capacity, was overcrowded.

To counteract the reluctance of rural folk to come to the hospital in Vellore for their basic medical needs, Scudder began in 1906 to establish a program of roadside clinics. The system worked much the way Methodist medical circuits had operated on the American frontier, first establishing a dispensary along a route, with the hopes of eventually setting up a resident nurse there to inculcate methods of preventive medicine. The cause of rural medicine became one of Scudder's lifelong passions.

With an overcrowded hospital and an ever-expanding rural case load, Scudder decided that the only way to meet the demand for medical care was to train Indian women to become doctors. She started a nursing school in 1909 in Vellore and in 1918 petitioned government officials in Madras to allow her to open a medical college for women. Leaders reluctantly agreed but cautioned her not to expect too much from women students. Scudder acted as the school's first principal and taught the course in anatomy. Her dream was vindicated when 100 percent of her first graduating class (1922) passed the Madras Presidency medical exam, several students receiving awards for highest marks (only 20 percent of the men had passed).

A new challenge arose in 1938 when the LMP (Licensed Medical Practitioner) degree offered by Vellore was abolished by the Indian government in an effort to strengthen national standards. Upgrading the Vellore degree would require more highly trained staff, as well as more beds, research facilities, and equipment. At the age of seventy, Scudder began a four-year tour of the United States to raise funds for this purpose. She created an international and interdenominational network of support called the Friends of Vellore, but in order to ensure the continued patronage of British and American Protestants, Scudder was finally compelled to allow male students to enter the college. Vellore Medical College eventually became affiliated with Madras University in 1950.

Scudder never married; by her admission, she was too dedicated to her work to have a family of her own. Her closest friend, Gertrude Dodd, moved in 1917 to Vellore, where she worked as an administrator for the college. The two lived and worked together until Dodd's death in 1942. Rarely sick, Scudder remained physically and professionally active until her death. She died at her hilltop home near Kodaikanal.

Scudder was effective and resolute as a doctor, teacher, hospital administrator, and fundraiser; but it was her faith, determination, and above all her allegiance to principle that set her apart from the rest of her peers. In remarks to her first graduating class in Vellore, she exhorted students with words descriptive of her own demeanor: "Face trials with a smile, with head erect and a calm exterior. If you are fighting for the right and for a true principle, be calm and sure and keep on until you win" (D. J. Scudder, p. 208). While most of the early biographical work done on Scudder verges on hagiography, her dedication to alleviating the suffering of others did, in fact, stem from a simple desire to imitate the compassion of Christ.

Throughout her career, Scudder was a staunch advocate for the medical needs of Indian women and was tireless in her pioneering efforts to bring the benefits of modern medicine to the villages and hamlets of South India.

• The Scudder papers, located in the Schlesinger Library of Radcliffe College, contain correspondence, diaries, and some material published for the Vellore Medical College. Interviews with Scudder in India resulted in two popularized, undocumented, and at times anecdotal, biographies, Mary Pauline Jeffery, *Ida Scudder of Vellore: The Life Story of Ida Sophia Scudder* (1951), and Dorothy Clarke Wilson, *Dr. Ida: The Story of Dr. Ida Scudder of Vellore* (1959; rev. ed., 1964). Another early popular account is Sheila Smith's two-part article "Doctor Ida," in the *Evangelical Christian* 55 (Sept. 1959): 384–413, and (Oct. 1959): 432–34, and 463–65. More recent attempts to interpret Scudder's work include Dorothy Jealous Scudder, *A Thousand Years in Thy Sight: The Story of the Scudder Missionaries to India* (1970); S. Immanuel David, "A Mission of Gentility: The Role of Women Missionaries in the American Arcot Mission, 1839–1938," *Indian Church History Review* 20 (1986): 143–52; and John J. Paul, "Religion and Medicine in South India: The Scudder Medical Missionaries and the Christian Medical College and Hospital, Vellore," *Fides et Historia* 22 (1990): 16–29. For brief overviews of Scudder's career, see Sally Knapp, *Women Doctors Today* (1947), pp. 65–68; Phillis Garlick, *Six Great Missionaries* (1955), pp. 148–76; and Sherwood Eddy, *Pathfinders of the World Missionary Crusade* (1945), pp. 128–39. An obituary is in the *New York Times*, 25 May 1960.

ROBERT STUART JUMONVILLE

SCUDDER, Janet (27 Oct. 1873–9 June 1940), sculptor, was born Netta Deweze Frazee Scudder in Terre Haute, Indiana, the daughter of William Hollingshead Scudder, a confectioner, and his first wife, whose name is unknown. Her mother died when Scudder was about five years old, and she was raised by her stepmother, Mary Sparks. She began drawing as a child, encouraged in her delight in form and color by her grandmother. After a public school education and Saturday drawing classes at the Rose Polytechnic Institute in Terre Haute, Scudder was sent by her father to the Cincinnati Art Academy, where she studied anatomy, drawing, and modeling and simplified her name to "Janet Scudder."

When her father died in 1890, her eldest brother supported her for a third year at the academy. In 1891 she went to Chicago, Illinois, to live with him, taking classes at the Art Institute and working at a factory as a wood carver. She was dismissed, however, because the craft union did not accept women. She was then hired by sculptor Lorado Taft as one of his assistants, enlarging from scale models works of sculpture for the 1893 World's Columbian Exposition. Under Taft she learned the basics of her art. Among her fellow assistants were Taft's sister, Zulime (or Zulh), and sculptor Bessie Potter Vonnoh.

Through Taft and a Terre Haute benefactor, Scudder received a commission to do a statue of *Justice* (later destroyed by fire) for the Illinois building at the exposition, and one titled *Nymph of the Wabash* for the Indiana building. The latter was eventually transferred to the Terre Haute Public Library. Her work received a bronze medal. Scudder's first sight of the fountain sculpture designed by another American sculptor, Frederick MacMonnies, for the Court of Honor at the exposition proved decisive for her career. It so delighted her that she made up her mind to study with Mac-Monnies at his studio in Paris.

Saving up some money, Scudder managed to leave for France in the fall of 1893, accompanied by Zulh Taft. Her determination finally overcame MacMonnies's well-known reluctance to take on students, and he set her to drawing from life—for the first time—and modeling in low relief, supplemented by additional drawing classes at the Vitti Academy and, at night, at Colarossi's Academy. Eventually she became a paid assistant, working with MacMonnies on, for example, the *Quadriga* sculpture now atop the arch in Grand Army Plaza in Brooklyn, New York.

In the summer of 1894, told by a jealous colleague that MacMonnies was displeased with her, Scudder returned to New York. Although she lived at first in great poverty, she refused her sister's invitation to make her home with her and, as she observed, take some "drab, hopeless job" as so many women did "from lack of courage and energy to cut out on their own" (Scudder, p. 123). By the end of her second year in New York she received a commission to design a seal for the New York Bar Association. Other work followed: architectural decorations and the portrait medallions that established her reputation.

By 1896 Scudder was able to go back to Paris, and she reestablished herself with MacMonnies, assured that he had regarded her as his ablest assistant. Through his recommendation, the French government purchased five of her portrait medallions. Others were acquired by the Numismatic Society in New York and the Library of Congress. For the next several years Scudder supported herself modeling urns and other cemetery pieces, until a trip to Italy provided another artistic revelation. In Florence she encountered the youthful, cherubic figures of Donatello and Verrocchio; in Naples and Pompeii she observed houses built around outdoor sculptures. Her realization that statuary could please, amuse, and decorate—not merely commemorate—changed her art. Returning to Paris, she began work on the first of her famous fountain sculptures, the *Frog Fountain*, an elfin child capering amid the spray.

Back in New York in 1899, Scudder met architect Stanford White, who bought a copy of the *Frog Fountain* for one of his clients; a second was eventually purchased by the Metropolitan Museum of Art. Another such piece, *The Fighting Boys*, was acquired by the Chicago Art Institute. Neither coy nor sentimental, the features of her realistic works were finely detailed, the masses broadly and freely treated. Thereafter, Scudder did garden pieces for the Rockefeller and McCormick families, among other wealthy patrons.

Apart from these private commissions, she achieved public success when her *Young Diana* won honorable mention at the Paris Salon of 1911.

In 1913 Scudder purchased a house at Ville d'Avray, outside Paris, and established a Saturday salon at which Gertrude Stein, Henry Adams, Mrs. Stanford White, and Mabel Dodge were among the frequent guests. She lived and worked there for the next twenty years, apart from a trip to China and Japan and visits to New York, where she maintained an apartment in Greenwich Village.

Returning to the United States at the start of World War I, Scudder worked to organize the Lafayette Fund for French war relief. By this time, also, she had become interested in women's rights and was active on the art committee of the National American Woman Suffrage Association. During the war she served in France with the YMCA and the Red Cross, later decorating recreation huts for demobilized French soldiers.

A member of the National Sculpture Society, Scudder became an associate of the National Academy of Design in 1920 and was created a chevalier of the French Legion of Honor in 1925. As the years went by, her sculpture became less exuberant, more reserved; at the same time, her childhood interest in color revived. Never giving up sculpture entirely, she began to paint, and in 1933 her oils were exhibited at the Macbeth Galleries in New York. She returned to her New York home in 1939 and died while on vacation in Rockport, Massachusetts.

• Examples of Scudder's sculpture are in the John Herron Museum in Indianapolis; the Chicago Art Institute; the Swope Art Museum in Terre Haute; and the Metropolitan Museum of Art. The best source for information about the artist is her autobiography, *Modeling My Life* (1925), an unaffected, lively account of the development of her career that reveals her passionate devotion to her art but is singularly devoid of exact dates. An article, untitled and unsigned, in the *International Studio* 39, nos. 81–88 (Feb. 1910), is a sympathetic description of her work, written by a contemporary critic. Obituaries are in the *New York Times*, 11 June 1940, and *Art Digest* 14, no. 24 (1 July 1940).

ELEANOR F. WEDGE

SCUDDER, John (3 Sept. 1793–13 Jan. 1855), first medical missionary from the United States, was born in Freehold, Monmouth County, New Jersey, the son of Joseph Scudder, a lawyer, and Maria Johnston. As a child Scudder often roamed the streets of Freehold gathering kindling for poor people. He earned a degree from the College of New Jersey (Princeton) in 1811. In 1813 he married Harriet Waterbury; they had thirteen children, three of whom died while very young.

After receiving a medical degree from the College of Physicians and Surgeons of the University of the State of New York in 1813, he practiced medicine in New York City. While attending to a patient in 1819, Scudder read a tract in the patients' anteroom titled *The Conversion of the World; or, The Claims of Six Hundred*

Millions, and the Duty of the Churches Respecting Them. This tract so influenced him that he soon offered himself to the American Board of Commissioners, which had been advertising for a person qualified as both an evangelist and a physician for work in Ceylon (now Sri Lanka). After the Classis of New York of the Reformed Church in America licensed him, he and his wife sailed from Boston on 8 June 1819, arriving in Calcutta, India, in October 1819. Scudder proceeded to Ceylon, where he opened a station at Panditeripo, Jaffna, in July 1820. In 1821 he was ordained in the Reformed Dutch church by a council of missionaries, which included a Congregationalist, a Baptist, and a Methodist.

Because Ceylon lay near the Indian subcontinent and because the Tamil language of southern India was the language of northern Ceylon, natural links joined the missionaries in these areas. In 1836 the board transferred Scudder and Rev. Myron Winslow from Ceylon to Madras (now Tamil Nadu), India. They were instructed to initiate the printing of tracts and scriptures in Tamil at the expense of the Bible and Tract Societies. During the first year of work, the societies printed 6 million pages, mostly translations from English. In addition to his involvement in this printing effort, Scudder conducted medical work and evangelistic tours. The rigors of itineration so weakened his health that Scudder was ordered to return to the United States.

Scudder and his wife spent the period from 1842 to 1846 in the United States, where he traveled extensively to make missionary addresses, many of which were published. He challenged children and urged parents to encourage their sons to pursue the Gospel ministry. In his book *The Redeemer's Last Command: A Voice from the East to the Young in a Series of Letters to the Children of the Reformed Protestant Dutch Church of North America* (1855), Scudder wrote to Christian mothers: "In the training of your children so solemnly consecrated to Christ, you should not inquire, how can my children be most comfortably provided for in the world, or how can they become most honorable in the sight of their fellow men, but in what situation can they bring most honor to Christ" (p. 11). In addition to children, Scudder addressed ministers, Sunday school teachers, and physicians. He urged theological students to pursue foreign missions with a sense of duty: "The fact is just this, unless you can show reasons why you should remain at home, the command settles your duty to go abroad" (*The Redeemer's Last Command*, p. 103).

After returning to India in March 1847, Scudder worked in Madura. In 1949 he again moved to Madras. In 1851 he and his son Henry Martyn established the Arcot mission near Madras. This work was assumed by the American Board in 1852, but it was passed to the Reformed church in 1857 when that body separated its mission efforts from the American Board.

Because of ill health, Scudder took a sea voyage in 1854, reaching the Cape of Good Hope in South Africa in November. Noting an improvement in his health, he arranged to return to India. However, before he could leave South Africa he died of a stroke in Wynberg.

During his thirty-five years of missionary service, Scudder contributed in direct and indirect ways to missions. He was a pioneer of the more settled work typical of nineteenth-century missions, conducting medical and evangelistic missions in three places over a lengthy period of time. Scudder also promoted missions in the United States, especially among young people. His own children and grandchildren contributed over a thousand years of mission work in India and elsewhere. The best known of Scudder's descendants, Ida Sophia Scudder, established a well-known medical facility at Vellore, India, including the Christian Medical School (1918). This school became a university in 1947.

Scudder's intensity and piety can be seen in the closing words of his book *The Redeemer's Last Command.* Scudder challenged wealthy Christians to earn money for Christ and contribute it for the work of missions: "Would that all of us who are engaged in the work of bringing back this revolted world to Christ, might so act, that in the day of final reckoning none from heathen lands shall be able to say to us, we are lost because you labored not—because you prayed not—because you contributed not, as you should have done, for our salvation" (p. 112).

• Harvard University's Houghton Library holds some of Scudder's correspondence in the Archives of the American Board of Commissioners for Foreign Missions. The library of New Brunswick Theological Seminary contains some Scudder family memorabilia. In addition to his dissertation, *An Inaugural Dissertation on the Diseases of Old Age, as Connected with a Plethoric State of the System* (1815), Scudder published several small booklets, including: *An Appeal to Christian Mothers in Behalf of the Heathen* (c. 1840); *Dr. Scudder's Tales for Little Readers about the Heathen* (c. 1849); *Grandpapa's Talk with His Little Mary about the Hindoos* (1859); *The Harvest Perishing for Want of Laborers: An Appeal to Christians Generally, to Pious Physicians, to Ministers, and to Pious Young Men* (n.d.); *Knocking at the Door: An Appeal to Youth, Letters from the East* (1833); *Letters to Sabbath-School Children on the Condition of the Heathen* (1843); and *Provision for Passing over Jordan* (c. 1846). Scudder published in the *Panoplist* and in its successor, the *Missionary Herald.* His life and work is treated briefly in Stephen Neill, *A History of Christian Missions* (1964). Fuller treatments are found in B. H. Badley, *Indian Missionary Directory and Memorial Volume*, 3d ed. (1886); A. M. Scudder, *A Brief Sketch of the Life and Work of Rev. John Scudder, M.D., His Wife and Descendants* (1912); and J. B. Waterbury, *Memoir of the Rev. John Scudder, M.D.* (1870). Another useful source on Scudder and his family is Dorothy Jealous Scudder, *A Thousand Years in Thy Sight: The Story of the Scudder Missionaries of India* (1984).

GARY J. BEKKER

SCUDDER, John Milton (8 Sept. 1829–17 Feb. 1894), physician and educator, was born in Harrison, Hamilton County, Ohio, the son of John Scudder, a cabinetmaker, and Matilda Marvin. John Scudder died when his son was eight years old, leaving his wife and three children with little inheritance. John Milton assumed the responsibility of helping the family by working in a button factory and educating himself. By the age of twelve he had saved enough money for college and enrolled in Miami University in Oxford, Ohio. After college, he too became a cabinetmaker and painter and later opened a general store in Harrison. In 1849 he married Jane Hannah; they had five children, of whom only two survived infancy. Scudder felt that the deaths of his three babies were the result of incompetent treatment and made the decision to forsake his present employment to study medicine.

In the nineteenth century alternative systems for the treatment of disease—notably botanic medicine, homeopathy, and eclectic medicine—were popular. Scudder chose to become an eclectic, which he later defined as "the right to choose or select from all other systems of medicine whatever they may deem true and best adapted to the relief and cure of the sick" (*Eclectic Practice of Medicine*, p. 8). He began by studying under Milton L. Thomas of Harrison, an eclectic preceptor, and subsequently enrolled in the Eclectic Medical Institute in Cincinnati, Ohio. Scudder proved to be a brilliant student and, upon graduating in 1856, was immediately appointed professor of general, special and pathological anatomy at the institute.

At the same time Scudder established a very successful and profitable medical practice in Cincinnati, taking on a number of partners to assist with caring for his large number of patients. The institute, meanwhile, was in decline—financially and administratively. Scudder, fearful for the school and the resulting damage to eclecticism itself, left his practice and set about to rescue the institute from failure. As head of the institute from 1861, he resolved its financial problems, revived the *Eclectic Medical Journal*, which he edited from 1861 to 1894, and wrote several new eclectic textbooks for his students. His textbooks covered a wide variety of subjects, including *A Practical Treatise on the Diseases of Women* (1857); *Materia Medica and Therapeutics*, with L. E. Jones (1860); and *Eclectic Practice of Medicine* (1864). His greatest contribution to eclecticism was *Specific Medication and Specific Medicines* (1870), in which he set forth the principles and practice of eclectic therapeutics. By 1902 the institute had graduated 3,743 medical students.

In addition to editing the *Eclectic Medical Journal*, Scudder published the monthly literary journal the *Eclectic* (1870–1871) and the short-lived *Family Journal of Health* (1860) for the laity.

Scudder also continued his teaching role. He held the chair of obstetrics and diseases of women and children from 1858 to 1860, the chair of pathology and principles and practice of medicine from 1860 to 1888, and the chair of physical diagnosis, hygiene, and electricity from 1883 to 1894. In 1887 his failing health caused him to give up the responsibilities of the chair of practice, although he continued to lecture on a variety of subjects, such as hygiene and specific and physical diagnosis, until his retirement.

After the death of his wife, Scudder married her sister, Mary Hannah, in 1861. They had five sons, three of whom became successful eclectic physicians. Although he was a member of the Swedenborgian church, his personal creed drew from the spirit of eclecticism: "I am surely not a sectarian protestant, or catholic, a theosophist, a mohammedan, or buddhist. I believe in the scriptures of all peoples, the religions of all peoples, in all the works for goodness of all peoples" (Felter, p. 239).

In 1894, hoping that a change of climate would improve his weakened condition, Scudder moved to Daytona, Florida, where he died shortly thereafter.

Scudder was a principal spokesman for one of the important medical sects of the nineteenth century. His voluminous writings were published in many editions and defined eclecticism for the medical community. While eclecticism was largely discredited after the 1910 Flexner Report, a national study evaluating the curriculum and teaching in American medical schools, Scudder remains an influential figure in the development of medical thought and practice.

• The Lloyd Library in Cincinnati, Ohio, the primary repository of documents relating to eclectic medicine, contains manuscripts (including correspondence and genealogies) of Scudder as well as the records of the Eclectic Medical Institute. Some of Scudder's numerous other works are *Principles of Medicine* (1867), *Diseases of Children* (1867), *Specific Diagnosis* (1874), *The Reproductive Organs and Venereal Diseases* (1874), and a popular work, *Domestic Medicine* (1865). All of these went through multiple editions and revisions, including title changes. Scudder also wrote several brief pamphlets on the history of eclecticism without publisher or date identified. Most biographical accounts have been based on Harvey Wickes Felter, *Biographies of John King, M.D., Andrew Jackson Howe, A.B., M.D., and John Milton Scudder, M.D.* (1912). Documentation of Scudder's years at the institute is in Felter, *History of the Eclectic Medical Institute, Cincinnati, Ohio, 1845–1902* (1902). More recent studies of Scudder include Cecil Striker, *Medical Portraits* (1963), and John Haller, *Medical Protestants* (1994). Obituaries are in *Eclectic Medical Journal* 55 (1895): 1–14, and the *Cincinnati Times-Star*, 19 Feb. 1894.

GLEN PIERCE JENKINS

SCUDDER, Samuel Hubbard (13 Apr. 1837–17 May 1911), entomologist, was born in Boston, Massachusetts, the son of Charles Scudder, a merchant, and Sarah Lathrop Coit. While at Williams College he began collecting butterflies, and by the time he graduated (B.A. 1857, A.M. 1860) he had determined to make entomology his career. He then studied under Louis Agassiz at Harvard's Lawrence Scientific School, earning a B.S. (1862) and serving as the first curator of insects in Agassiz's Museum of Comparative Zoology. He continued as Agassiz's assistant for two years following his graduation.

Throughout his career Scudder associated with scholarly institutions in Boston and Cambridge. At the Boston Society of Natural History (now the Museum of Science, Boston) he was recording secretary (1862–1870), librarian and custodian of collections (1864–

1870), vice president (1874–1880), and president (1880–1887). From 1870 to 1879 he held no salaried position. He was assistant librarian of Harvard University (1879–1882); editor of *Science* (1882–1885), and paleontologist with the U.S. Geological Survey (1886–1892). He helped found the Cambridge Entomological Club (1874), which met for many years in his specially constructed laboratory-study. He also helped found the Appalachian Club and contributed many articles to its journal. In 1874 he served as general secretary of the American Association for the Advancement of Science and in 1894 he was vice president.

In 1867 Scudder married Ethelinda Jane Blatchford, who died five years later. Their only son died in 1896, the year Scudder succumbed to a creeping paralysis that incapacitated him physically for years prior to his death in Cambridge.

Scudder achieved distinction for his taxonomic work on three different groups of insects: the Orthoptera, the Diurnal Lepidoptera, and fossil insects. Beginning with his first paper on the Orthoptera in 1861, Scudder quickly rose to leadership in this specialty. His *Catalogue of the Orthoptera of North America* (1868) served as the point of departure, and his *Alphabetical Index to North American Orthoptera Described in the Eighteenth and Nineteenth Centuries* (1901) summarized the state of knowledge up to the end of his career. At the time of Scudder's death, the renowned orthopterist J. A. G. Rehn declared that Scudder was "the greatest orthopterist America has produced" (*Entomological News*, July 1911, p. 289).

Scudder's contributions to the field of Diurnal Lepidoptera were equally important. By the 1870s he and William Henry Edwards were regarded as America's two leading Lepidopterists. Scudder's great work, *The Butterflies of the Eastern United States and Canada, with Special Reference to New England* (3 vols., 1888–1889), drew together thirty years of investigation. This beautifully illustrated work comprised elaborate accounts of each species, with taxonomic sections set off by charming essays on life histories, geographical distribution, protective coloring, and dimorphism. It was called perhaps "the finest work on any butterfly-fauna yet published" (T. D. A. Cockerell, *Science*, 15 Sept. 1911, p. 34). The nontechnical sections were later published as *Frail Children of the Air: Excursions into the World of Butterflies* (1895), one of Scudder's many popular books on butterflies. In the field of fossil insects, Scudder founded the discipline of American paleoentomology and he was for decades the main contributor to the subject. Two reference works mark his worldwide authority in this branch: *A Classed and Annotated Bibliography of Fossil Insects* (1890) and the *Index to the Known Fossil Insects of the World* (1891), both published by the U.S. Geological Survey. Scudder's descriptions, based on specimens from excavations at Florissant, Colorado, and Baden, Germany, marked a significant improvement over those of European paleoentomologists, who provided only brief summaries and then referred to type specimens in collections for details. Scudder's detailed descriptions, accompanied by precise line drawings, provided investigators who lacked access to type specimens with the detailed information they needed to evaluate specimens and classifications.

A person of broad erudition and a genius in the organization of knowledge, Scudder authored several path breaking reference works. His *Catalogue of Scientific Serials of all Countries, 1633–1876* (1879) simplified researchers' access to scientific literature, and his *Nomenclature Zoologicus* (2 vols., 1882, 1884) provided an indispensable reference to the scientific names of animals. His remarkable talents in the synthesizing of information, organization, writing and editing distinguished his tenure as Harvard librarian and as editor of *Science*. He also published some of the first scholarly reference works on the history of American entomology, most notably the *Entomological Correspondence of Thaddeus William Harris, M.D.* (1869), which made available the papers of America's pioneer agricultural entomologist.

Although Scudder collected frequently in the West and explored much of New England by foot, his contemporaries viewed him as a "closet naturalist." He demonstrated little concern for agricultural entomology and only passing interest in experimentation with breeding butterflies. He concerned himself primarily with the taxonomic arrangement of specimens which he collected or which he obtained from naturalists with government expeditions, or through purchase or exchange.

Scudder's taxonomy was precise, thorough, and exhaustive in bibliographic references. He could detect distinctions in specimens as fine as one 100th of an inch, which helped him achieve undisputed mastery in the accurate systematic recording of insect structure. In all he described 1,884 animal species, including 1,144 fossil insects, 630 Orthoptera, and 30 butterflies. Over seventy American butterflies are known by popular names he proposed.

Like other Agassiz students, Scudder initially opposed Darwinism, and even after accepting the principle of biological evolution, he retained the "essentialist" view that biological designations like species and genus represented indivisible units. He believed that generic designations should indicate differences between forms rather than relationships of biological descent. His essentialism, combined with his meticulous description and his indefatigable search for the earliest published descriptions of insects, made Scudder an avid "splitter" of genera and species. His radical splitting of butterfly genera based on minute distinctions in the genitalia produced consternation among his fellow lepidopterists. Scudder's genera have fallen in and out of favor with succeeding generations, with his insistence that priority belongs to the first describer of a species now universally accepted.

Scudder was the leading American entomological taxonomist of the nineteenth century. While Edwards surpassed him in breeding butterflies and in the study of polymorphism and evolution, Scudder laid the basis for the accurate taxonomy of American butterflies, cockroaches and crickets. He founded the field of American paleoentomology, and he produced reference works that are still essential to zoologists.

• Both the Boston Museum of Science, Boston, Mass., and the Museum of Comparative Zoology, Cambridge, Mass., have sizable collections of Scudder's papers and correspondence. Scudder's insect collection, which is very large and rich in type specimens, was originally donated to the Museum of Comparative Zoology but has since been transferred to the Academy of Natural Sciences of Philadelphia. The most complete account of Scudder's life is Alfred Goldsborough Mayor, "Samuel Hubbard Scudder, 1837–1911," National Academy of Sciences *Biographical Memoirs* 17 (1924), 81–104. The bibliography at the end of Mayor's memoir lists 791 works by Scudder. The majority of these are technical works on entomology, but there are a number of popular books and articles on butterflies, nature excursions, and other topics. Scudder's contributions to various scientific specialties are evaluated in obituaries by J. S. Kingsley et al., in *Psyche* 28 (Dec. 1911), 174–192. Scudder's work figures significantly in Sally Gregory Kohlstedt, "*Science*: The Struggle for Survival, 1880–1892," *Science* 20 (4 July 1980): 33–42. For an account of Scudder's early career, in particular his role in the evolution debate in America in the 1860s and 1870s, see W. Conner Sorensen, *Brethren of the Net: American Entomology, 1840–1880* (1995). An obituary is in the *Boston Transcript*, 17 May 1911.

W. CONNER SORENSEN

SCUDDER, Vida Dutton (15 Dec. 1861–9 Oct. 1954), social reformer, writer, and educator, was born Julia Vida Dutton Scudder in Madura, India, the daughter of David Coit Scudder, a Congregationalist missionary, and Harriet Louisa Dutton. Scudder moved to the United States as an infant, following the tragic drowning of her father. For the first few years of her life she lived with her mother and other relatives at the Dutton family home in Auburndale, Massachusetts. Scudder came from two well-established New England families—she was the niece of Horace Scudder, editor of the *Atlantic Monthly*, and Edward P. Dutton, a publisher. Growing up, Scudder spent several years traveling in Europe with her mother and aunt. Upon her return, she began attending Miss Sanger's school in Boston. She entered Boston's newly established Girls' Latin School in 1878 and earned her B.A. from Smith College in 1884.

Following her graduation from Smith, Scudder traveled to England to become one of the first women to study at Oxford University. At Oxford Scudder attended the last series of lectures by social critic John Ruskin. The lectures by Ruskin inspired Scudder to think critically about social stratification based on class. She realized her own privileged background and felt angered by the social divisions that she saw crystallizing within an increasingly industrialized society. Scudder's growing contempt for such divisions prompted her to begin participating in organized efforts to ameliorate social conditions, and she joined the Salvation Army while in England.

Scudder returned to Boston in 1885 and occupied herself with the activities of several newly organized women's organizations, including the Association of Collegiate Alumnae and the Saturday Morning Club in Boston. While these organizations helped Scudder create a network of professional contacts, they did not speak directly to the questions of social and moral responsibility that interested her. She turned to writing, and after completing a thesis on modern English poets she earned an M.A. from Smith College. In 1887 she accepted a position at Wellesley College to teach English literature.

During the fall of her first year at Wellesley, Scudder met with a small group of Smith alumnae to discuss the establishment of an American settlement house. The settlement idea, which had originated in England as a predominately male venture, appealed to Scudder's desire to work toward tempering class divisions. Settlement workers, mostly white and formally educated, moved into immigrant/working-class neighborhoods to offer cultural and social programs to members of the community. In an article for the *Andover Review*, "The Place of College Settlements" (Oct. 1892), Scudder wrote, "The amateur settlement expresses that pure and voluntary socialism which many of us feel holds our best and most permanent hope." Scudder believed that college-educated women, trained as both caretakers and intellectuals, had a primary role to play in the development of settlement houses.

By early 1889 Scudder and settlement-house organizers from Smith had expanded their informal association to include women from other colleges. The group opened the first successful American settlement house, located on Rivington Street in New York City, on 1 September 1889—Jane Addams and Ellen Gates Starr opened Hull-House in Chicago two weeks later. Founders of the Rivington Street settlement depended in large part on the financial support of other college-educated women. Such support enabled founders to organize formally into the College Settlements Association (CSA) in 1890. Membership in the CSA grew rapidly, and the organization opened two more settlement houses, Denison House in Boston and the College Settlement in Philadelphia, in 1892. By 1898 the CSA had more than 2,000 members nationwide.

During her tenure with the CSA, Scudder served on the CSA's electoral board and participated actively in the creation of programs at Denison House. She pushed members of the house to become involved with labor issues and in 1903 helped found the Women's Trade Union League. Although she never resided permanently at any of the CSA's houses—teaching duties at Wellesley and a commitment to living with her mother prevented her from doing so—Scudder served as one of the CSA's main spokespersons, publishing numerous articles on social reform and the role of the settlement house in American life.

By 1912 Scudder worried that her affiliation with socialism and other radical forms of politics would harm the CSA's reputation, and she resigned from the organization. Around that time Scudder had come under attack from members of the Wellesley community after having spoken out at a textile strike in Lawrence, Massachusetts. Since the late 1880s Scudder's politics had grown increasingly Leftist. She participated in such organizations as the Society of Christian Socialists, the Christian Social Union, the Episcopal Church Socialist League, and, later, the Intercollegiate Socialist League. In 1911 she joined the Socialist party.

Scudder grounded her socialist beliefs in a foundation of Christian doctrine and Christian faith. She joined the Society of the Companions of the Holy Cross (SCHC), a women's Episcopal organization practicing intercessory prayer, in 1889 and remained active until her death. She also published numerous books on the Catholic tradition. In *Socialism and Character* (1912) she argues for a spiritual and political union between Marxism and Catholicism.

Retiring from Wellesley in 1928, Scudder spent much of her later life writing. She continued to involve herself with church-related activities, and in the early 1930s she served as the first dean of the School of Christian Ethics, a three-week summer program run by the Church League for Industrial Democracy. In 1937 Scudder published the first volume of her autobiography, *On Journey*. She published the second volume, *My Quest for Reality*, in 1952.

Through her writing and organizational work, Scudder encouraged a new generation of middle-class women, college educated and professionally motivated, to bring about social change through settlement-house work and other forms of collective action. The effects of this work were long-lasting, and by the early twentieth century, women made up the majority of settlement workers in the United States. Privately, Scudder lived for thirty-five years with Florence Converse, whom she called her "Comrade and Companion." Scudder died at her home in Wellesley, Massachusetts.

• Collections of Scudder's papers are housed in the Wellesley College Archives; the archives of the Society of the Companions of the Holy Cross in South Byfield, Mass.; and the Sophia Smith Collection of the Smith College Library. Other archival sources include the Denison House Papers of the Arthur and Elizabeth Schlesinger Library, Radcliffe College, and the College Settlements Association Papers of the Sophia Smith Collection, Smith College Library. Some of Scudder's books not cited above include *The Witness of Denial* (1895); *The Life of the Spirit in Modern English Poets* (1895); *Social Ideals in English Letters* (1898); *Introduction to the Study of English Literature* (1901); *A Listener in Babel: Being a Series of Imaginary Conversations* (1903); *Saint Catherine of Siena as Seen in Her Letters* (1905); *The Disciple of a Saint* (1907); *Le Morte d'Arthur of Sir Thomas Malory and Its Sources* (1917); *The Church and the Hour: Reflections of a Socialist Churchwoman* (1917); *The Social Teachings of the Christian Year* (1921); *Brother John: A Tale of the First Franciscans* (1927); *The Franciscan Adventure* (1931); *The Privilege of Age: Essays Secular and Spiritual* (1939); and *Father Huntington* (1940). Some helpful secondary materials on Scudder are Theresa Corcoran, S.C., *Vida Dutton Scudder* (1982); Elizabeth Palmer Hutcheson Carrell, "Reflections in a Mirror: The Pro-

gressive Woman and the Settlement Experience" (Ph.D. diss., Univ. of Texas at Austin, 1981); and Arthur Mann, *Yankee Reformers in an Urban Age* (1954). For a discussion of Scudder at Wellesley, see Patricia Ann Palmieri, *In Adamless Eden: The Community of Women Faculty at Wellesley* (1995). An obituary is in the *New York Times*, 11 Oct. 1954.

MICHELLE A. SPINELLI

SCULL, John (23 July 1765–9 Feb. 1828), publisher and editor, was born in Reading, Pennsylvania, the son of Jasper Scull, a surveyor, and Mary Eyers. Jasper Scull, also a blacksmith, held civic offices. Of his nine children, John was the youngest of six born in his second marriage.

Little is known about John Scull's youth. His father died when he was ten, and Scull probably had scant means for whatever educational facilities the revolutionary war years afforded. He may have served a printing apprenticeship. Both Scull and his partner, Joseph Hall, were twenty-one when they issued the first number of the Pittsburgh *Gazette* on 29 July 1786. Hall died that November, and John Boyd became Scull's partner in December. Scull married Mary Irwin in 1786; they subsequently had three children. By 1787 Scull also published the Pittsburgh *Almanack* in a log building on Water Street, and he did job printing and sold textbooks, laws, and religious books. In August 1788 Boyd hanged himself from a tree on the hill later named for him, and Scull continued to publish the *Gazette* alone.

Scull is best known for founding the first newspaper west of the Allegheny Mountains. Previously, newspapers published generally only in or near Atlantic port cities. In 1786 Pittsburgh, more than 300 miles from Philadelphia over a route that could take up to twenty-four days travel, had thirty-six log buildings, one stone, and one frame, and six stores, according to some sources; Hugh Henry Brackenridge boasted in the first *Gazette* that the town had about 100 houses.

The hand press, bought from Andrew Brown, publisher of the Philadelphia *Federal Gazette*, took ten hours to produce 700 copies. In the first anniversary issue, Scull wrote of difficulties in producing the four-page weekly: "expense of paper at such a distance from mills," constant "wearing of our types, and our own labour," and "fluctuating and uncertain" public support. The worst problem was lack of "a speedy and certain mode of conveyance" because of unreliable carriers, and he urged subscribers to arrange for their own delivery.

Beginning in 1787, postal service alleviated distribution problems somewhat. On 19 July 1788 regular mail service began among Pittsburgh, Philadelphia, and the East, with William Tilton as postmaster. Scull succeeded Tilton on 5 January 1789 and served eight years as Pittsburgh's second postmaster. Until a mill began operation at Brownsville in 1797, paper had to be brought from the East over the mountains on pack horses or wagons, and scarcity led Scull to publish on military cartridge paper at times.

As late as 1797 Scull asserted that he and the *Gazette* were nonpartisan, and the paper, albeit supporting Federalist politics, seems to have been comparatively neutral until the late 1790s. After that, the paper's "neutrality" ended and Scull is known for scurrilous attacks on Brackenridge, a prominent Pittsburgh attorney, notable literary figure, and politician.

Nearly all accounts of the *Gazette*, beginning with the first history of American journalism published by Isaiah Thomas in 1810 while Scull still edited the paper, credit Brackenridge as the force behind its establishment and early years. Early *Gazette* numbers contained considerable writing by Brackenridge, who had moved to Pittsburgh in 1781 and gained a state legislative seat in 1786. However, Margaret P. Bothwell argues that Brackenridge planted and perpetuated the idea that he instigated the paper, and that Colonel John Irwin, a prominent longtime resident of the area and Scull's eventual father-in-law, was probably responsible for the paper's founding.

Whatever the Scull-Brackenridge relationship before Federalist and anti-Federalist groups formed, political differences led to permanent estrangement in the 1799 gubernatorial campaign. After winning the election, Thomas McKean appointed Brackenridge, a Democratic Republican, as a supreme court justice. Scull satirically asked Brackenridge's pardon for opposing McKean, addressing him: "To H. H. B.——e, Esq., President of the Jacobin Society, Professor of Chivalry, Privy Councillor to the Governor of Bantam, Poet Laureat to the Herald of Sedition, Biographer of the Insurgents, Auctioneer of Divinity, and Haberdasher of Pronouns, &c.&c." Brackenridge responded by establishing Scull's first competitor, the *Tree of Liberty*, edited by John Israel, on 16 August 1800. A newspaper war followed in which Scull repeatedly lashed out at Brackenridge. His account on 5 December 1800 of Brackenridge on a drunken spree through Washington and Allegheny counties is among the best-known newspaper attacks in U.S. journalism history. Brackenridge moved permanently to Carlisle in 1801, Scull won a libel suit against Israel in 1803, and the Democratic Republicans finally won Pittsburgh in 1803 in an election that left few Federalists in the state legislature.

Vituperative journalism was common at the time, but, except for this interim, and despite ensuing political controversies, the *Gazette* seems to have been comparatively staid. In addition to foreign and national news common in newspapers of the time, the *Gazette* provided western news for the East and eastern news for the West. Its columns provided glimpses of the early westward migration and the development of Pittsburgh and the West generally.

In 1816, after his son Edward died at age twenty-eight while serving as an army surgeon in New Orleans, Scull turned the *Gazette* over to his remaining son, John Irwin Scull, who in 1818 sold a half interest to Morgan Neville. In 1820 the partners sold the paper, ending the Scull family's involvement with it. In 1833 the *Gazette* became Pittsburgh's first daily under editor Neville Craig (1829–1841), who was the first to record the newspaper's history in his book, *The History of Pittsburgh* (1851).

Scull contributed substantially to Pittsburgh's development, serving at different times as editor, postmaster, city treasurer, trustee of the Western University of Pennsylvania, vice president of the Neptune Fire Company, and president of the Farmers and Mechanics Bank from its charter in 1814 until it closed in 1819. He moved around 1820 to a farm near Irwin in Westmoreland County, where he subsequently served as county commissioner and justice of the peace. He died on his farm.

• The Scull papers are in the Historical Society of Western Pennsylvania. A good source on the family and the first published work based on the Scull papers after they were deposited in the archives in 1962 is Margaret P. Bothwell, "The Sculls and Irwins, Pillars of Pennsylvania," *Western Pennsylvania Historical Magazine* 46, no. 1 (Jan. 1963): 57–77. In the absence of a biography of Scull, information about him can be found in histories of the *Gazette* and Pittsburgh. Among the most useful are J. Cutler Andrews, *Pittsburgh's Post-Gazette: "The First Newspaper West of the Alleghenies"* (1936), a book that grew out of his dissertation at Harvard University and relies heavily on content in the *Gazette*; Leland D. Baldwin, *Pittsburgh: The Story of a City* (1937); John Newton Boucher, ed., *A Century and a Half of Pittsburgh and Her People*, vol. 2 (1908); C. W. Dahlinger, *Pittsburgh: A Sketch of Its Early Social Life* (1916); Sarah H. Killikelly, *The History of Pittsburgh* (1906); and Reuben Gold Thwaites, "The Ohio Valley Press before the War of 1812–15," *Proceedings of the American Antiquarian Society*, n.s., 19 (1908–1909): 309–68. An item on microfilm is Virginia E. Luckhardt, "Notable Printers of Early Pittsburgh, Pennsylvania" (1949), in the American Antiquarian Society Library, Worcester, Mass. The author was assisted in the research for this article by Professor Patricia Dooley, University of Maine.

HAZEL DICKEN-GARCIA

SCULL, Robert Cooper (1917–1 Jan. 1986), art collector and patron and business executive, was born on the Lower East Side of New York City, the son of Mayo Scull, a tailor. His parents were Russian immigrants whose name, originally Sokolnikoff, was changed to Scull at Ellis Island. Upon his arrival in New York, his father took a job sewing and designing with the fashionable department store Bergdorf-Goodman. Eventually the Sculls moved to the Upper West Side, where Robert attended DeWitt Clinton High School for advanced students. Unfortunately, he was forced to drop out of high school because of the Great Depression, and it was another nine years before he actually earned his diploma. In order to help his family during those trying times, he refinished furniture, made and sold his own soap, and even hustled pool. He was motivated to complete high school because of his interest in business, but at the same time his grandfather was broadening his horizons by taking him to museums and to the opera. Scull became increasingly fascinated by art and began taking classes at the Art Students League, the Pratt Institute, and the Textile High School on a part-time basis. Meanwhile, he worked at a wide assortment of day jobs—artist's model, appliance repairman, and retail salesman—to pay the bills. Peter Wild, an artist for whom he occasionally modeled, gave him drawing lessons in return for his services, and in a short time Scull added commercial illustration to his résumé.

In 1943 Scull met Ethel Redner, a student at Parsons School of Design, whom he immediately nicknamed "Spike." After a whirlwind courtship of five months, they were married. The Sculls moved to a tiny apartment near the Museum of Modern Art (MoMA) and became members of the museum. To augment the cramped space of their tiny home they began to use its outdoor garden as a living room in which to entertain their guests. Scull became very interested in the works at MoMA and began to compile a wish list of paintings he would someday like to collect. Ethel supported and shared in his interest in art; even more importantly, she was partially responsible for his big financial break. When her father, Ben Redner, retired, he divided his taxi business between the husbands of his three daughters. With admirable business acumen, Scull took his small share of the cabs and used them as collateral to expand. In a very short period of time Scull's original eight cabs grew to 130. Even more significantly, the operating license, which had originally been free, skyrocketed in value—$22,500 by 1966—making Scull's enterprise, the Super Operating Company, worth several million dollars. Scull always had a flair for drama, and his drivers became known as Scull's Angels and were identified by the hot pink cupid emblazoned on their cabs. Off to a good start, Scull began to invest wisely in real estate, Broadway plays, and film companies, but his real claim to fame was his art collection.

Scull's first art purchase in the 1950s was an oil he believed to be by Maurice Utrillo. He paid $245 for the painting, and although it turned out to be a fake he managed to sell it later for a $45 profit. His early interest in postimpressionist painting and Renaissance bronzes faded as he became intrigued by the more contemporary abstract expressionists. As his business grew his collection expanded, and he became a sought-after guest at art auctions and openings. Dealers like Richard Bellamy began to court him; Bellamy was responsible for encouraging Scull to collect the pop art that later made him famous. Scull was fascinated by the pop artists and agreed to finance Bellamy's Green Gallery, while adding to his own collection works by Jasper Johns, Robert Rauschenberg, and James Rosenquist. His role as the primary patron of this influential gallery established him as a force in the New York art world.

Both Scull and his wife reveled in this elevated status and worked hard to cultivate their jet-setting image. The Sculls and their three sons split their time between a Fifth Avenue penthouse and a villa in fashionable East Hampton, Long Island. They threw huge parties in their posh apartment, which housed important works by Walter de Maria, Larry Poons, Rosenquist, and Robert Morris, as well as a cast sculpture of the Sculls themselves by George Segal and a silk screen of Ethel by Andy Warhol. Ethel, always perfectly coiffed and fashionably dressed, was a darling of the popular press, especially the paparazzi. A 1966 *New Yorker* magazine profile described Scull as "the man who is happening now." The couple was not without their detractors, however: in *The Pump House Gang* (1968), Tom Wolfe pointed an admonishing finger at the couple, whose meteoric rise to fame he thought came at the expense of the artists they patronized. They were accused of being ruthless social climbers who had used their art collecting to open social doors. Scull admitted the latter charge, but he saw himself in the role of the benevolent patron and was convinced that his generosity to young artists redeemed him from being a selfish profiteer. Indeed, many artists involved with Scull had mixed emotions, viewing him as a necessary evil. For example, de Maria created a piece for Scull called *Portrait of Dorian Grey* [*sic*], which involved a mirror made of sterling silver that steadily corroded. He required Scull to view himself in the mirror and make a photographic record of its (or his) deterioration.

Tensions came to a head in 1973 at the infamous Sotheby Parke–Bernet auction, later to be the subject of a documentary film by E. J. Vaughn. On the block were fifty works by important artists. The sale was widely publicized and well attended by a glittering cast of characters. It resulted in a stunning $2.2 million gavel total, and prices paid for works like Johns's *Double White Map* and *Painted Bronze* broke records for contemporary American art. The sale also brought up some pointed questions concerning the policies and practices of the art world. Some of the artists, like Rauschenberg, were outraged at the enormous sums fetched by their works and vowed to take legal action to receive percentages of the profit for future sales. Scull defended himself, saying that he had helped artists early in their careers and that he was doing the world a favor by giving these works exposure. In 1975, not long after the furor died down, the Sculls were divorced. Shortly thereafter, Scull sold his cabs, then quietly married a woman by the name of Stephanie and moved to a farm in Warren, Connecticut, removing himself from the public eye. He continued to collect art and to support young artists until his death in Warren.

• Information on Scull's early years is in the *Current Biography Yearbook* (1974). At the height of his career he was profiled in Jane Kramer, "The Man Who Is Happening Now," *New Yorker* 42 (1966). Information on the 1973 auction is in E. J. Vaughn's film, *America's Pop Collector: Robert C. Scull—Contemporary Art at Auction* (1974); and Baruch D. Kirschenbaum, "The Scull Auction and the Scull Film," *Art Journal* 39 (Fall 1979): 50–54. An obituary is in the *New York Times*, 3 Jan. 1986.

NORA C. KILBANE

SEABURY, Samuel (30 Nov. 1729–25 Feb. 1796), the first bishop of the Episcopal church in America, was born in Groton, Connecticut, the son of Samuel Seabury, a Congregational minister and later Anglican priest, and Abigail Mumford. In 1742 the family moved to Hempstead, Long Island. As a result of his father's conversion, young Samuel was raised in the Church of England. He graduated from Yale College in 1748 at the age of nineteen but was too young to be ordained a priest in the Church of England. While he waited for the canonical age of twenty-three, he served as a catechist under the direction of his father at Huntington, New York. He remained at Huntington for four years, and while there he studied medicine and theology under the tutelage of his father. Before there were medical schools in the United States, some clergy also practiced medicine. Clergy were viewed as physicians of the soul and the body. One reason for studying medicine was to be able to supplement his salary as a clergyman.

In August 1752 Seabury sailed for Scotland and spent over a year studying medicine at the University of Edinburgh. On 21 December 1753 he was ordained deacon at Fulham Palace by Bishop John Thomas and then two days later, on 23 December he was ordained priest by Bishop Richard Osbaldiston. In the spring of 1754, he left England and arrived in Philadelphia, Pennsylvania, on 22 May 1754. Several days later he began his work as a missionary of the Society for the Propagation of the Gospel (SPG) at Christ Church in New Brunswick, New Jersey.

Seabury served at Christ Church from 1754 until 1757, and while there he made several missionary visits to Cranbury and Readington, New Jersey, where he preached to large congregations. Since there were few Lutheran clergy in the area, he preached in Lutheran churches and baptized German Lutheran children. While he was in New Brunswick, he got involved in the controversy between the Presbyterians and Episcopalians over control of King's College in New York City. The Presbyterians wanted King's College to be nondenominational and the Episcopalians wanted it to be a Church of England institution. He and others published letters in the *New-York Mercury* under the title "Watch-Tower" attacking each other. This correspondence showed Seabury to be an avid defender of the Church of England and a leader among those who wrote against a "most renown Club of Scriblers," that is, the Presbyterians. While at New Brunswick he met Mary Hicks, the daughter of Edward Hicks of Staten Island, a wealthy landowner. Seabury married Hicks in October 1756; they had six children.

In January 1757 Seabury became the rector of a church in Jamaica, a section of New York City. He remained there until December 1766. In March 1767 he was inducted as the rector of St. Peter's Church in Westchester, New York, where he remained until 1776. While there he also served churches in Eastchester, New Rochelle, Yonkers, and the Manor of Pelham. The Westchester church had over 200 churchgoers but only 22 communicants. This illustrated to Seabury the desperate need for a bishop since only bishops could confirm, and only the confirmed could

be communicants. From then on he was a leading advocate for a resident episcopate in the American colonies. He believed not only that a bishop was needed to confirm and ordain, but also that a bishop was needed in order to combat the skepticism and violent sectarianism that threatened to undo the efforts of the Anglican missionaries. Anglicans considered all non-Anglicans sectarians and insisted that the one true church in the colonies was the Church of England which could trace its existence back to the apostolic period.

To address the issue of a bishop for the American colonies, the Episcopal clergy in the province of New York, and several others, met in a convention on 21 May 1766 in the home of Dr. Samuel Auchmuty, the rector of Trinity Church in New York City, and agreed to use "their joint Influence and Endeavours to obtain the Happiness of Bishops, to support the Church against the unreasonable Opposition given to it in the Colonies" (Mampoteng, p. 137). Seabury was chosen secretary of the group and served in that position until 21 May 1767. As secretary he wrote to the SPG conveying the concerns of the New York convention. This Episcopal propaganda provoked a controversy in the *New York Gazette* in which the Presbyterians opposed bishops in a column called "The American Whig." Seabury and others responded with "A Whip for the American Whig," and the Presbyterians retaliated with "A Kick for the Whipper." Anglicans insisted that bishops in the historic episcopate were essential to have a true church. Presbyterians and other Protestants feared that bishops would be temporal figures as in England and that they would work to have the Church of England the established church in the colonies.

As many of the American colonists began to support the cause of revolution and separation from England, Seabury showed himself to be an ardent supporter of the king and the Church of England. He insisted on loyalty to the crown since he had made that pledge in ordination. He could not conceive of a church that was not established and supported by the state. Shortly after the Boston Tea Party, 16 December 1773, a series of pamphlets began to appear defending the English Crown, written by "A. W. Farmer." The first one, published on 10 November 1774, was an attack on the Continental Congress. It was entitled "Free Thoughts on the Proceedings of the Continental Congress." Later it was learned that "A. W. Farmer" meant "A Westchester Farmer," that is, Seabury. He wrote three more pamphlets and incurred the bitter criticism of the Sons of Liberty. From then on Seabury was a marked man, and when the war broke out and the British forces took Long Island in September 1776, he fled behind enemy lines and joined the army of General William Howe, serving as a chaplain. Until June 1783 Seabury remained a refugee on Manhattan Island.

On 6 August 1782 William White, the rector of the United Parishes of St. Peter's and Christ Church, Philadelphia, and later the first bishop of Pennsylvania, published anonymously a pamphlet, *The Case of* the Episcopal Churches in the United States Considered, in which he proposed a plan for the organization of a national Episcopal church. Since there were no bishops in the United States, White proposed that as a temporary measure presbyters ordain presbyters until the episcopate could be secured. This horrified the few Connecticut clergy who had a High Church position, which insisted on the necessity of bishops in apostolic succession to ordain priests. Nevertheless, on 25 March 1783 ten clergy met in the home of the Reverend John Rutgers Marshall in Woodbury, Connecticut, to discuss The Case. Realizing the urgency of the situation, they decided to elect a bishop for Connecticut. They chose the Reverend Jeremiah Leaming, but he became ill and resigned. The clergy then chose Seabury, who had to go to England to be consecrated because there were no bishops in America to consecrate him.

Seabury arrived in London on 7 July 1783. The English bishops refused to consecrate him since the government of the state of Connecticut and the laity of the church had not participated in his selection; moreover, the consecration service included an oath of loyalty to King George III, which Seabury could not make since the United States was now independent. From 7 July 1783 until September 1784, Seabury tried to convince the English bishops to consecrate him but to no avail. He then decided to go to Scotland to seek consecration by the non-juring bishops, who were the successors of the eight English bishops who had refused to take the Oath of Allegiance to William and Mary because they had already taken an oath to King James II. Thus on 14 November 1784, in a room used as a chapel in the home of Bishop John Skinner in Aberdeen, Seabury was consecrated bishop of Connecticut by Robert Kilgour, bishop of Aberdeen and Primus, Authur Petrie, bishop of Ross and Murray, and Skinner, bishop coadjutor of Aberdeen. Some considered his consecration invalid since it was done in Aberdeen by schismatic bishops and not in England by English bishops.

Seabury returned to Connecticut on 20 June 1785 and exercised his episcopal ministry until his death. He opposed the way the General Convention of the church was organized as well as the lay representation in it, and thus he refused to attend its first meetings. He finally attended the second session of the 1789 general convention, which formally organized the Episcopal church in the United States. He served as the second presiding bishop from 5 October 1789 until 8 September 1792. During the remainder of his episcopate, Seabury visited parishes, confirmed new members, and ordained men to the diaconate and the priesthood. Seabury's greatest contribution was securing the episcopate for the Episcopal church in America. He died in New London, Connecticut.

• Seabury's papers are in the Archives of the Diocese of Connecticut, Hartford, and the Archives of the Episcopal Church in Austin, Tex. His major publications are *Discourses on Several Subjects* (2 vols., 1793), *Discourses on Several Important Subjects* (1798), and *Letters of a Westchester Farmer*, ed. Clarence H. Vance (1930). The major study of his life and work is Bruce E. Steiner, *Samuel Seabury, 1729–1796: A Study in the High Church Tradition* (1971). Older studies are Eben Edwards Beardsley, *Life and Correspondence of the Right Reverend Samuel Seabury, D.D.* (1882), John Norton, *The Life of the Rt. Rev. Samuel Seabury, D.D., Bishop of Connecticut* (1857), and William Jones Seabury, *Memoir of Bishop Seabury* (1908). A more popular study is Anne W. Rowthorn, *Samuel Seabury: A Bicentennial Biography* (1983). The *Historical Magazine of the Protestant Episcopal Church* 3 (Sept. 1934) was a "Bishop Seabury Sesqui-Centennial Number" and includes the following articles: Arthur Adams, "The Seabury Family," Charles Mampoteng, "Samuel Seabury, Presbyter," E. Clowes Chorley, "The Election and Consecration," John Skinner, "Consecration Sermon, 1784," and William A. Beardsley, "The Episcopate of Bishop Seabury."

DONALD S. ARMENTROUT

SEABURY, Samuel (9 June 1801–10 Oct. 1872), Episcopal clergyman and journalist, was born in New London, Connecticut, the son of Charles Seabury, a cleric, and Anne Saltonstall. The family moved to Setauket, Long Island, in 1814. Seabury's family, a long, established line of clerics, included a grandfather (and namesake) who was the first bishop of the Episcopal church in America. Charles Seabury, however, was a modest and uninspiring cleric, and his reduced economic circumstances markedly affected the education and early career of his son. Seabury's early formal education was limited to various village schools, and rather than being permitted to study the classical languages as a preparation for college, he was instead apprenticed to a furniture maker in New York City. This was a traumatic experience for Seabury, a "bleeding of self-pride," which he movingly recalled in his personal narrative written in 1831. His narrative includes descriptions of apprentice life and working-class religion and mores as seen through the eyes of a genteelly reared young man. His apprenticeship proved a failure, and he instead dedicated himself to the task of self-education, particularly in the classical languages. He received an honorary M.A. from Columbia College in 1826. Seabury was married three times: to Lydia Huntington Bill (1829–1834); to Hannah Amelia Jones (1835–1852); and to Mary Anna Jones (1854–1872). Altogether he had six children.

After running a private school associated with St. Ann's Episcopal Church in Brooklyn, Seabury entered the Episcopal ministry and was ordained deacon in 1826 and priest in 1828. His first pastoral charge was as a missionary on Long Island, where he organized a parish in what is now Astoria, Queens. He was then employed as a teacher at the innovative Flushing Institute founded by William Augustus Muhlenberg, which attempted to provide a classical education flexible enough for either the counting house or college. During his tenure there he published *The Study of the Classics on Christian Principles* (1831). In 1833 he became editor of the *Churchman*, a New York–based Episcopal weekly newspaper. In this position (1833–1849) he became one of the leading journalistic voices of the period and was a caustic critic of many of the religious and social trends of the time. Seabury and the *Churchman* were leading advocates of the high church understanding of the Episcopal church, with its concern for theological traditionalism and institutional order, and saw the church as an ark of refuge against both the subjectivism of evangelicalism and excesses of Jacksonianism. He regularly criticized revivalism, the temperance movement, abolitionism, and other movements that he claimed were products of a religious and social world that had lost its sense of intellectual authority.

Seabury was also an early and enthusiastic defender of the Oxford Movement's attempt to elevate the catholic heritage of Anglicanism. He was an active partisan in the controversies this movement provoked in America. During the mid-1840s he became an active participant in the debate over the trial of Benjamin T. Onderdonk, bishop of New York, whom he adamantly defended. Seabury argued that Onderdonk, who was brought to ecclesiastical trial on moral charges (and who was eventually suspended from his office), was in fact being attacked because of his support for the Oxford Movement. During these years he was an influential figure in the political machinations of the diocese of New York as leader of the party loyal to Onderdonk. In 1850 he narrowly missed being elected bishop.

During the late 1850s Seabury became involved in the debate over slavery and saw the forces of abolitionism reflecting a challenge to traditional religious order. For Seabury, abolitionism was a product of the modern morality of the nineteenth century and as such was at odds with both the teaching of scripture and Christian tradition. In early 1861 he published *American Slavery Distinguished from the Slavery of the English Theories*, which attacked abolitionist claims. The work was not well received and provoked controversy in both the religious and secular press.

In addition to his editorial duties Seabury was rector of the Church of the Annunciation in New York City (1838–1868) and was associated with General Theological Seminary in various ways. He was professor of evidences at the seminary from 1835 to 1838 and professor of biblical learning from 1862 to his death (in New York City). His views changed surprisingly little from the 1830s, and to his end Seabury continued to reflect the beliefs of his earlier high church theology. By the late 1860s he found himself out of step with the theological trends within his church. Although an early supporter of the Oxford Movement's concern to reclaim catholic theology, he was unsympathetic with the later movement of ritualism, or the concern to reintroduce advanced vestments and ceremonies into Episcopal worship.

• Seabury's other works include *The Joy of the Saints* (1844), *The Continuity of the Church of England* (1853), and *Discourses Illustrative of the Nature and Work of the Holy Spirit and Other Papers* (1874). Seabury's letters can be found in the Samuel Seabury correspondence in the General Theological Seminary Library, New York, and in the Seabury family papers in the New-York Historical Society. His personal narrative has been recently discovered and published, *Moneygripe's Apprentice* (1989), edited by R. B. Mullin, and the editor's introduction includes the most complete account of Seabury's life. Other biographical information can be found in S. R. Johnson, *A Discourse . . . in Memory of Samuel Seabury* (1873). His career and teachings are discussed in R. B. Mullin, *Episcopal Vision/American Reality* (1986).

ROBERT BRUCE MULLIN

SEAGER, Allan (5 Feb. 1906–10 May 1968), writer, was born John Braithwaite Allan Seager in Adrian, Michigan, the son of Arch Seager, a traveling salesman, and Emma Allan. When his father was transferred to Memphis in 1916, Seager hated being uprooted. He read voraciously as an escape and took up swimming to be by himself, but he won so many swimming events that he became popular and socially at ease. His mother died of cancer in 1925.

Seager enrolled at the University of Michigan, where he was a superb student, became an all-American swimmer, joined a fraternity, and was popular with coeds and other young drinkers. After graduating in 1930, he was a Rhodes scholar at Oriel College, Oxford University. An honor student, he rowed and swam in school events, partied often, vacationed on the Continent, and observed the British narrowly. After he was treated for tuberculosis at Saranac Lake, New York (1932–1933), he returned to Oriel (B.A., 1933). He stayed a third year, neglected his studies, and wrote two of his best short stories: "The Street" (*London Mercury*, Jan. 1934) and "This Town and Salamanca" (*Life and Letters*, May 1934). He became an editor at *Vanity Fair* (1934–1935), during which time he wrote thirteen short stories and was such a blasé man about New York City that he was happy to start teaching at the University of Michigan in 1935. From 1935 to 1939 he also earned thousands of dollars co-scripting *Scattergood Baines* radio shows for the Wrigley gum company. He bought a farm in Onsted, a little west of Adrian and Ann Arbor. Prevented by a tuberculosis-deflated lung from joining the armed forces, Seager continued teaching, helped his aging father on the farm, and wrote in his free time. In 1939 he married Barbara Watson; they had two children. *Equinox* (1943), his first novel, was popular, but sales stopped when the wartime paper shortage curtailed later printings. A friend from Michigan, the poet Theodore Roethke, persuaded Seager to teach with him at Bennington College in Vermont (1944–1945). One year was enough. The Seagers bought what became their permanent residence—a big Victorian house in Tecumseh, Michigan, between Adrian and Ann Arbor—and Seager returned to teach again at his alma mater. In 1948 his wife was diagnosed with multiple sclerosis. The following year his father died.

Seager continued to teach splendidly, advanced to top academic rank and great prestige, wrote steadily, and endured more misfortunes. Four novels followed *Equinox: The Inheritance* (1948), *Amos Berry* (1953),

Hilda Manning (1956), and *Death of Anger* (1960). None was a commercial success. A collection of his short stories—many of them written to pay for his wife's illness—is *The Old Man of the Mountain and Seventeen Other Stories* (1950). A sabbatical in France in 1956 resulted in *Memoirs of a Tourist*, his peppy, slightly abridged translation—the first in English—of *Mémoires d'un touriste* by Stendhal, whom Seager admired and resembled. Both writers enjoyed travel; were learned, observant, fluent in languages, and opinionated; and each commanded a powerful style. Seager could not find a publisher for *Memoirs* until 1962. Meanwhile, from 1959 on, his wife was often a helpless invalid. In 1960 he had an automobile accident, and his driver's license was suspended. In 1961, at a party following a writers' conference in Ann Arbor, he drank excessively, fell down some stairs, and shattered an arm. As self-therapy, he crafted a best-selling autobiography, *A Frieze of Girls: Memoirs as Fiction* (1964), and undertook a biography of Roethke, the prize-winning poet who had died in 1963. Three years later, while Seager was writing *The Glass House: The Life of Theodore Roethke*, his wife died. He married Joan Rambo in 1968 but died in Ann Arbor of lung cancer and a coronary blood clot seven weeks later.

Seager's varied writings reward careful reading. *The Glass House* (posthumously published in 1968) is a detailed, intimate, subjective analysis that received great critical acclaim. *Equinox*, perhaps his best novel, presents four main characters in New York in late 1939: a widowed war correspondent who has just quit Europe, his teenaged, convent-bred daughter, who develops incestuous feelings toward him; his nymphomaniacal ex-mistress; and a suavely villainous amateur psychologist. Its themes are the selfish use of others and the denial of responsibility. Its charged dialogue, effortless handling of point of view, and deftly sketched minor characters are captivating. In *The Inheritance*, Seager dramatizes a son's near-fatal attempt to refurbish and live up to his deceased hypocritical father's image. *Amos Berry* concerns the central character's divorce, his clever murder of a business rival, and the financial, psychological, and suicidal consequences of the killer's son witnessing the crime. *Hilda Manning*, a roman à clef featuring a sinfully beautiful woman, is an acrimonious sociological study of Seager's hometown of Onsted. *Death of Anger* shows grim doom descending on the husband of an attractive lesbian; he tries to escape her, fails, returns, and is admired by his uncomprehending friends and neighbors.

Of Seager's seventy or so short stories, many of which dramatize misunderstanding and have O. Henry endings, "This Town and Salamanca" and "The Old Man of the Mountain" are typically comical, ironic, and edgy. In the former story, a wanderer, eternally romantic in the eyes of his stick-at-home friends, returns to their town and seems not to mind its dreary reality. In the latter story, an old codger defends a cave on his Missouri property exploited by insensitive, history-perverting moviemakers and ignorant, thrill-seeking tourists. Driving them off with a menacing shotgun blast, he damns them all and "the whole twentieth century" for good measure. Was this the author's ultimate gesture? It seems tragic that Allan Seager did not recover from a disintegrating illness of body and spirit and live to impress in a more positive way those who survived him.

• The bulk of Seager's papers can be found in the Bancroft Library, University of California, Berkeley; the Newberry Library, Chicago; and the University of Michigan. Hugh Kenner, "The Insider," *Critique: Studies in Modern Fiction* 1 (Winter 1959): 3–15, praises Seager's syntax, dialogue, and handling of point of view. *Critique: Studies in Modern Fiction* 5 (Winter 1962–1963) is devoted entirely to Seager; four essays analyze and praise ingredients of Seager's style and discuss his profound disgust at contemporary American mechanization and the consequent lack of historical perspective and cultural accomplishment. The essays are Robert Bloom, "Allan Seager: Some Versions of Disengagement," pp. 4–26; Harvey Curtis Webster, "Seager as a Social Novelist," pp. 27–36; Allan Hanna, "The Muse of History: Allan Seager and the Criticism of Culture," pp. 37–61, which also provides a bibliography of Seager's works and of biographical and critical items about Seager; and R. W. Lid, "The Innocent Eye," pp. 62–74. In "The Greatest American Poet," *Atlantic Monthly*, Nov. 1968, pp. 53–58, James Dickey, calling Roethke the greatest, subjectively reviews Seager's *The Glass House*. Stephen E. Connelly, *Allan Seager* (1983), is a superb evaluative biography. An obituary is in the *New York Times*, 11 May 1968.

ROBERT L. GALE

SEAGRAVE, Gordon Stifler (18 Mar. 1897–28 Mar. 1965), physician, missionary, and writer, was born in Rangoon, Burma, the son of Albert Ernest Seagrave, a Baptist missionary, and Alice Haswell Vinton. After spending his early childhood in Burma, young Seagrave came to the United States at the age of twelve with his mother and three older sisters to attend preparatory school in Granville, Ohio. In 1914 he entered Denison University in Granville and three years later received an undergraduate degree in biology. Seagrave went on to the Johns Hopkins University Medical School, interrupting his education to serve in Europe with a medical unit from Hopkins during World War I.

A descendant of several generations of missionaries, Seagrave had long planned to enter the field himself. From an early age he also wanted to become a doctor, and in later years he often expressed the belief that missionaries should offer practical as well as spiritual assistance. In the fall of 1920, during his final years in medical school, he was admitted to the American Baptist Foreign Mission Society. Several weeks earlier he had married Marion Grace Morse, who became a full partner in his missionary work; they had five children.

After receiving his M.D. from Hopkins in 1921, Seagrave interned for a year at a children's hospital, the Garrett Sanitarium, and at Union Memorial Hospital in Baltimore. He departed for Rangoon in August 1922 to begin his career as a medical missionary. When the couple arrived in October, they were sent to

Namkham Hospital on the rugged northeastern frontier of Burma, only a few miles from the Chinese border; Seagrave had asked to be assigned to Namkham to replace a family friend who was retiring. The Seagraves discovered that the hospital was little more than a shanty.

Only temporarily overwhelmed by the task before them, the Seagraves rebuilt the structure and began attracting patients, both Burmese and Chinese from across the border. The hospital grew over the years into a twenty-two-building medical facility staffed by two additional doctors, eighteen nurses, and more than 100 assistants whom Seagrave trained.

Seagrave's hospital served as many as 6,000 patients a year, suffering from a variety of congenital ailments and tropical diseases; thousands more were treated by outreach units that traveled into the jungle. Seagrave also created a nursing school at the hospital that was accredited by the Burmese government, and nursing education remained a high priority for him during his many years in Namkham. To facilitate his practice, he learned two new languages, Shan and Burmese—he wrote a two-volume nursing textbook in Burmese—and he relearned Karen, which he had spoken as a child.

The Seagraves spent 1928 and 1929 in the United States. He attended postgraduate classes in medicine and surgery at Columbia University, and he and his wife raised funds for medical supplies for Namkham. A year later Seagrave launched an additional career as a writer with the publication of his first book, *Waste-Basket Surgery* (1930), an account of his experiences in Burma. Its sequel, *Tales of a Waste-Basket Surgeon*, appeared in 1938.

A year earlier Seagrave and his wife had concluded a second sabbatical year abroad, this time at the University of Vienna, where he studied surgery. Their return to Burma in the fall of 1937 followed the separation of that country from India by the British government and the granting of limited self-rule to Burma. Japan had also invaded China. Political unrest in the area around Namkham threatened Seagrave's practice, although he continued to serve as best he could; beginning in the fall of 1938 he also worked part time at a Chinese hospital across the border.

Namkham was near the newly constructed vital war-supply route known as the Burma Road, and Japanese bombing of the area had intensified by the summer of 1940. That fall Seagrave's wife and children were evacuated to the United States while he remained behind. During the next two years Seagrave worked with British authorities to bring medical assistance to several outposts in Burma, including a large hospital in Prome that he directed.

When General Joseph Stilwell assumed command of U.S. troops in the China-Burma-India theater in March 1942, Seagrave placed his facilities at the general's disposal and was commissioned a major in the U.S. Army Medical Corps. During the next few months Seagrave set up base hospitals behind the lines and treated hundreds of soldiers. In *Burma Surgeon*

(1943), his famous memoir, he recalled the conditions of hardship that prevailed. Working around the clock in temperatures that reached as high as 136° F, medical personnel had to make do with inadequate drugs and supplies, and hazardous conditions were the rule: during surgery on makeshift outdoor operating tables, for example, the duties of Seagrave and his staff included the painstaking removal of insects that frequently dropped into incisions from overhanging trees.

When Stilwell and his depleted forces were defeated by the Japanese and forced to begin their painful retreat through the Burmese jungle into India in May 1942, Seagrave and his staff accompanied the troops, giving aid and helping them forage for food. In recognition of his heroic efforts, Seagrave was awarded the Purple Heart and promoted to lieutenant colonel in August, following their arrival in India.

With the publication of *Burma Surgeon*, Seagrave became internationally famous; the book was not only a bestseller in the United States but was also widely read by Allied troops in a special military edition. After serving as an army medical officer in India, Seagrave returned to Burma with Allied troops in 1944 and aided them in retaking the country the following spring.

Following a six-month leave in the United States, during which he was reunited with his family, Seagrave returned to Burma early in 1946 as chief medical officer of the Shan States, which were under British military administration. This appointment also enabled him to oversee the rebuilding of his hospital at Namkham, which he decided to make nondenominational. Accordingly, he resigned amicably from the American Baptist Foreign Missionary Society in April 1946, but the society retained ownership of the hospital, which it leased henceforth to Seagrave for an annual fee of one dollar. That year Seagrave established the American Medical Center for Burma Frontier Areas (later renamed the American Medical Center for Burma) to bring aid to other remote regions of the country. Later that same year *Burma Surgeon Returns*, his account of the Allied recapture of Burma, was published.

During the postwar years Seagrave continued his medical practice in Burma, interrupting it in the fall of 1946 and again a year later to make fund-raising visits to the United States. His hard work and private financial support enabled him to continue his efforts as the political situation in Burma gradually deteriorated, but by 1950 a civil war between Karen and Kachin minorities threatened to bring those efforts to a halt. In August of that year Seagrave was arrested and forced to shut down his hospital. He was charged with treason for allegedly supporting Karen rebels and was taken to Rangoon. There he spent the next fifteen months alternately in jail and under house arrest before being sentenced to six years in prison in September 1951. Seagrave insisted on fighting the charges rather than having them dismissed on a technicality and was finally released in mid-November 1951. He returned to

Namkham and began rebuilding his hospital, which reopened in December 1952.

Seagrave remained at work in Namkham until his death there thirteen years later, a victim of chronic bouts with malaria and dysentery. His last book was another memoir, *My Hospital in the Hills* (1955). Seagrave received several awards for his work, including a commendation from President John F. Kennedy in 1961. His hospital in Namkham was nationalized by the Burmese government following his death.

• The major source of biographical information on Seagrave is his five volumes of memoirs. Additional material on Seagrave and his family is on file at the headquarters of the American Baptist Foreign Mission Society, Valley Forge, Pa., and at the American Baptist Historical Society, Rochester, N.Y. See also Sue Mayes Newhall's account of Seagrave's career, *The Devil in God's Old Man* (1969). For Seagrave's experiences in World War II, see Barbara Tuchman, *Stilwell and the American Experience in China* (1971). Seagrave's arrest is discussed in "Facts Surrounding the Trial of Gordon S. Seagrave in Burma," *U.S. State Department Bulletin*, 5 Feb. 1951. For his later years see Peter Kalischer, "He's Still the Burma Surgeon," *Collier's*, 30 Apr. 1954, pp. 34ff., and the account by his son Sterling Seagrave, "Burma Surgeon's Last Battle," *Saturday Evening Post*, 3 July 1965, pp. 38–40ff. An obituary is in the *New York Times*, 29 Mar. 1965.

ANN T. KEENE

SEALSFIELD, Charles (3 Mar. 1793–26 May 1864), Austrian-American writer, was born Carl Magnus Postl in Poppitz, Moravia, Austria (today Popice, Czech Republic), the son of Anton Postl and Juliane Rabl, farmers. One of eleven siblings in a farming family, Postl was able to receive a university-preparatory education only by declaring his intention of becoming a priest. He went to the Gymnasium in Znaim (today Znojmo, Czech Republic). He then studied Catholic theology in Prague (1808–1815) and took vows as a monk at the Order of the Kreuzherren in 1814. For a time he held an important position as secretary of the order. Philosophically and politically, Postl was influenced by the late enlightenment atmosphere of Prague and soon came into conflict with Austria's reactionary policies restricting political liberty and freedom of speech. Eventually, he broke his vows and escaped to the United States, probably with the aid of Freemasons. A warrant for Postl was put out at the request of the order, but the escapee was never apprehended. At some time after his arrival in the United States, he adopted the name of Charles Sealsfield. His true identity was only established after his death.

From 1823 until 1830, the naturalized Sealsfield lived in Louisiana, Pennsylvania, and New York. He claimed to be a clergyman, born in Pennsylvania, a biographical fiction he maintained for the rest of his life. His constant attempts to hide his original identity and obscure the actual course of his life make many biographical details difficult to establish. He may have owned a plantation in Louisiana, failed financially, and then taken up political and journalistic work for the exiled Joseph Bonaparte.

During a European tour in 1826–1827, Sealsfield prepared for publication his first two book-length works, political travelogues on the United States and on Austria, both of which appeared in 1828. These books show his strong interest in Jacksonianism (*The United States of North America as They Are in Their Political, Religious, and Social Relations* takes up some of the egalitarian and populist rhetoric of Andrew Jackson's election campaigns) and his rejection of reactionary European policies (*Austria As It Is: Or, Sketches of Continental Courts*, published anonymously, denounces absolutist styles of government as detrimental to sociocultural development). Also in the late 1820s he published sketches and short stories in English for American magazines while writing American reports for the important German publisher Cotta. His first novel, *Tokeah; or, the White Rose* (1829), combines an Indian story with Jacksonian politics by having the "General" (Jackson) triumph over the proud "Indian Chief" Tokeah. Although the book received favorable reviews, it was not as successful as the author had hoped, and this disappointment may have contributed to his move to Switzerland in 1830.

Sealsfield maintained his American identity after the move and, recognizing the great interest in fictional treatments of America, embarked on a series of German-language novels dealing with the westward movement of the United States, the American South, the relationship between the United States and Europe, and the relationship between the United States and Mexico. Scholars have variously emphasized either European or American characteristics in his works. Some have placed him in a German-Austrian Biedermeier tradition, owing to the eclectic and sometimes baroque style and imagery of his writing and his antiautocratic politics. Others have stressed his adherence to Jacksonian politics and their significance for the fictional presentation of the United States as a popular democracy. More recently, his affinity to early American writers has also been documented: Sealsfield borrowed material and actually lifted whole passages from early American authors such as Timothy Flint, James Kirke Paulding, and William Gilmore Simms.

Sealsfield's greatest significance as a writer, however, lies in his intercultural point of view. While he fully internalized the ideology, rhetoric, and political-literary atmosphere of the Jacksonian era, his work also contains a subversive, European perspective that undercuts and makes ironic the dominant discourse of his novels. The first-person narrator of the five novels making up the cycle *Lebensbilder aus der westlichen Hemisphäre* (*Life in the New World*), published between 1834 and 1837, for example, is a slaveholder who believes in American democracy, westward expansion, and the institution of slavery—an altogether characteristic representative of the Jacksonian era. By presenting this character as weak, fearful, and paranoid, however, Sealsfield is able to criticize slavery and a democratic ideology that has room for such an antidemocratic institution. Sealsfield's most famous novel, *Das Kajütenbuch* (1841), a story of Texas that extends to the whole continent of Latin America, is another comment on the validity of the American expansionist ideology of the nineteenth century. Practically all of Sealsfield's novels provide intercultural meeting grounds between Anglo-Saxon Americans on the one hand and various "ethnic" groups on the other. The resulting fictional confrontations of different cultural perspectives give his novels a literary sophistication that has brought them increasing critical recognition since the 1970s.

It is unclear why Sealsfield stopped writing in 1843, some twenty years before his death. In his correspondence, he vented his increasing frustration and anger with the political and economic development of the United States. As a series of unfinished works suggests, he found impossible a fictional reconciliation of what he considered the increasing internal contradictions within American culture, especially the rift between North and South and the rapid industrialization of the country. At about this time, however, Sealsfield achieved sudden and short-lived fame in the United States. His novels had had enormous success in German-speaking countries, and in 1843 *Blackwood's Magazine* began to publish pirated translations of his works without his knowledge. The attention given to an unknown American author by a leading British journal led Jonas Winchester's New World Press to translate what they called "genuine" American works into English—without paying royalties, of course. As Winchester's editions were cheap and distributed by mail, Sealsfield's works came to be widely known. The excitement over the discovery of a significant American author caused a lively discussion in the American press in 1844. Sealsfield was warmly appreciated by Henry Wadsworth Longfellow, who called him "our favorite," but he was scorned by Nathaniel Hawthorne and Edgar Allan Poe, who saw their one literary property, the "Americanness" of their writings, taken from them by Winchester's pirating enterprise, which they must have regarded as an intrusion into their creative domain.

Sealsfield embarked on a third prolonged stay in the United States between 1853 and 1858, living in New York, Philadelphia, and Louisiana. Finally, deeply disturbed by events foreshadowing the Civil War, he moved again to Switzerland, where he died in Solothurn.

• The major collection of Sealsfield's papers is located in the Zentralbibliothek, Solothurn, Switzerland. Important documents relating to Sealsfield's life, his works, and the reception of his works are collected in Eduard Castle, ed., *Das Geheimnis des großen Unbekannten: Charles Sealsfield–Carl Postl: Die Quellenschriften* (1943). The only full-length biography, deficient in many respects and somewhat influenced by National Socialist ideology, is Castle, *Der große Unbekannte: Das Leben von Charles Sealsfield (Karl Postl)* (1952). Castle, ed., *Der große Unbekannte: Das Leben von Charles Sealsfield (Karl Postl)—Briefe und Aktenstücke* (1955), contains many of the letters and other personal documents on which Castle's biog-

raphy is based. For an English-language summary of Sealsfield's life and achievement, see Walter Grünzweig, *Charles Sealsfield* (1985).

WALTER GRÜNZWEIG

SEAMAN, Elizabeth Cochrane. *See* Bly, Nellie.

SEAMAN, Valentine (2 Apr. 1773–July 1817), physician, surgeon, and public health advocate, was born at North Hempstead, Long Island, New York, the son of Willet Seaman, a merchant, and Martha Valentine. Seaman studied medicine with Nicholas Romayne in New York City, after which he worked in the city almshouse as a resident physician to gain further training. He graduated from the University of Pennsylvania with the M.D. degree in 1792. Upon graduation his inaugural dissertation, on the uses and clinical effects of opium, was published. It was dedicated to Adam Kuhn, professor of the practice of physic, and Benjamin Rush, professor of the Institutes of Clinical Medicine at the University of Pennsylvania.

Convinced that the mineral waters and spas of New York State had great medicinal value, in 1793 Seaman wrote on the therapeutic effects of the waters at Saratoga; in 1809 he wrote on the therapeutic effects of the waters at Boston. In 1794 he married Ann Ferris, with whom he had nine children.

In 1795 Seaman was a physician on the Health Committee of the City of New York, and that summer he published an account of the city's yellow fever epidemic. His report was similar to the Philadelphia reports on the yellow fever epidemic of 1793.

Seeing the need for more formal instruction for the midwives of New York City, in 1799 Seaman established a formal lecture series. This was followed in 1800 by his book *The Midwives Monitor*, the first instruction manual on midwifery published in the United States. It consisted of three sections: directions for the pregnant woman, management of natural birth, and explanation of when a physician's services are required. The *Monitor* gave concise instructions and advice to the pregnant woman about her pregnancy and how natural childbirth would be handled. It also detailed for the midwife the problems she could encounter with a patient in labor and when she should seek the consultation and services of a physician.

After William Jenner reported in 1799 on the beneficial effects of his smallpox vaccination, in 1800 Seaman, acutely aware of the importance of preventing the spread of smallpox in a large city, introduced the vaccination in New York. He believed so strongly in the public health aspects of vaccination that he even vaccinated his own son. By 1816 he reported that all children born in the New York Lying In Hospital were vaccinated against smallpox before they were discharged. That same year he published a discourse on vaccination and the kinepox inoculation.

In 1810 and 1811 Seaman, along with other physicians, founded a medical institution associated with Queen's College in New Brunswick, New Jersey. The institution closed after only three years, however, and neither its name nor the identities of the other physicians who were involved in it are known.

Seaman also worked in the surgical department of New York Hospital, and the first clinical lectures on surgery there were published by him in 1811; these included discussions of the remedies employed by surgeons in the department.

Seaman was an intellectual and progressive giant for his time. Slavery was anathema to him, and during his lifetime he sought the freedom of slaves and helped them obtain adequate medical care. A socially conscious physician who was acutely aware of the benefits of good public health measures to a large city, Seaman was cognizant of the need for vaccination, for implementing procedures to prevent outbreaks of yellow fever, for providing prenatal and delivery care to pregnant and laboring women, and for correcting social and racial injustices.

In the winter of 1815 Seaman developed an inflammation of the lungs that turned into tuberculosis and eventually led to his death in New York City.

• Seaman's 1792 inaugural dissertation is in the Historical Collection of the Library of the College of Physicians of Philadelphia; it is one among thousands of similar theses that are well preserved and fascinating reading. For additional information see the concise entry on Seaman in Howard Kelly and Walter Burrage, *American Medical Biography* (1920), p. 1028. An excellent summary on Seaman by D. O. Powell is in the *Dictionary of American Medical Biography*, vol. 2 (1984), p. 669.

W. ROBERT PENMAN

SEARES, Frederick Hanley (17 May 1873–20 July 1964), astronomer, was born on a farm near Cassopolis, Michigan, the son of Isaac Newton Seares, a land agent, and Ella Ardelia Swartwout. Isaac Seares and his family moved to Pasadena, California, in 1887, and Frederick Seares eventually enrolled at the University of California at Berkeley, where he studied astronomy under Armin O. Leuschner. Seares received a B.S. in 1895 and stayed on at Berkeley for one year as a fellow and two years as an instructor in astronomy. In 1896 Seares married Mabel Urmy, who later became editor of *California Southland* magazine. They had one son.

In 1899 Seares departed for Europe, where he continued his astronomical studies at the University of Berlin and at the Sorbonne in Paris. In 1901 he returned to the United States and obtained a position as professor of astronomy and director of the Laws Observatory at the University of Missouri in Columbia. During his time in Columbia, Seares studied variable stars and taught astronomy. His most noted student was Harlow Shapley, later his colleague and director of the Harvard Observatory.

Seares left Missouri in 1909 when George Ellery Hale, director of the Mount Wilson Observatory in California, offered him a position as a staff astronomer. A new 1.5-meter reflecting telescope just entering service on Mount Wilson was creating new opportunities for research at the observatory. The increased number of stars that could be resolved with the 1.5-meter and the planned 2.5-meter Hooker Telescope made Seares's expertise in photometry particularly important in the research at Mount Wilson. Seares was also placed in charge of the observatory's computers, who were, with few exceptions, college-educated women proficient in mathematics and physics.

On his arrival at Mount Wilson, Seares became involved in the photometric research plan proposed in 1906 by Dutch astronomer Jacobus C. Kapteyn. Using the 1.5-meter telescope, the Mount Wilson astronomers photographed 252 selected areas of the sky. The stars in these areas were then used as statistical samples for the study of all of the stars in the sky. One of the problems that Seares had to overcome was ensuring that the magnitudes of the faintest stars were measured correctly. He studied the photographic characteristics of the telescope and previous photometric standards of measurement and decided that the current methods of magnitude determination were inadequate for the selected area project.

Starting from scratch, Seares undertook the immense task of defining the proper methods and standards of in-focus photographic photometry. The entire process took nine years, and the results were published in 1930 as the *Mount Wilson Catalogue of Photographic Magnitudes in Selected Areas 1–139* by Seares, Kapteyn, and Pieter J. Van Rhijn, with the assistance of Mary Cross Joyner and Myrtle L. Richmond. This work set new standards for accuracy and faintness of stars measured and was hailed as an extraordinary technical accomplishment.

Another major photometric project that Seares undertook was a study of the magnitudes of the North Polar Sequence, a group of stars near the North Celestial Pole whose photographic magnitudes are used as standards for comparison with other stars in the sky. Stars near the North Pole are useful as standards as they can be observed year-round by astronomers in the northern hemisphere. With the large telescopes on Mount Wilson, Seares decided to extend the North Polar Sequence down to fainter stars than before. He painstakingly observed the stars in the sequence and obtained magnitudes for them. He then compared his values with those obtained at four other major observatories and made corrections to the magnitudes based on the various agreements between the different systems. Eventually, Seares obtained exact values of photographic magnitudes for more than 600 stars near the pole, and his system was adopted by the International Astronomical Union in 1932. With the aid of Frank E. Ross and Mary Cross Joyner, Seares extended his work to measurements of the magnitudes and colors of more than 2,200 stars near the North Celestial Pole, the results of which were published in 1941. Seares's work was highly respected by his colleagues, and in 1922 he was elected president of the Commission on Stellar Photometry of the new International Astronomical Union, a position he held for sixteen years.

Although photometry accounted for most of Seares's scientific work, he was also involved in other fields of investigation. These included studying the structure of the Milky Way based on star counts, the importance of star colors, attempts to measure the magnetic field of the sun, and determination of the masses of binary stars.

From 1904 to 1948 Mount Wilson Observatory issued its astronomers' published papers as *Contributions from the Mount Wilson [Solar] Observatory*. Even though these papers were published elsewhere, Hale felt the necessity of having a separate identity for his observatory's publications. As a consequence, he wanted to have one person take care of editing his staff's papers in order to provide some type of consistency. This became Seares's job, and he was highly praised by his colleagues in his ability to turn their work into polished scientific papers, in some cases practically rewriting them to do so. In 1927 Seares became a collaborating editor and in 1934, associate editor, of the *Astrophysical Journal*. In recognition of his administrative abilities, Walter S. Adams, Mount Wilson's second director, appointed Seares assistant director in 1925.

Seares's first wife died in 1940, and two years later he married his colleague, Mary Cross Joyner. They had no children. Also in 1940, Seares retired from Mount Wilson Observatory and was immediately appointed a research associate of the Carnegie Institution of Washington. In this capacity he continued to do research at the observatory for an additional five years. Seares ended his affiliation with Mount Wilson in 1945. He and his wife soon moved to Santa Barbara, California, then later to Honolulu, Hawaii, where Seares died.

Ironically, most of Seares's photometric work was soon surpassed by new technical developments. The introduction of photoelectric devices into photometry after World War II made most photographic photometry techniques obsolete. Although his techniques are no longer generally practiced, Seares deserves recognition for his contributions to the astronomy of his period.

• Seares's papers are in the Observatories of the Carnegie Institution of Washington Collection at the Huntington Library. A summary of Seares's achievements can be found in Alfred H. Joy, "The Award of the Bruce Gold Medal to Frederick Hanley Seares," *Publications of the Astronomical Society of the Pacific* 52 (1940): 69–79. Among the several obituaries that provide good summaries of Seares's life and work are Alfred H. Joy, "Frederick Hanley Seares, 1873–1964," National Academy of Sciences, *Biographical Memoirs* 39 (1967): 417–44, which contains a bibliography of Seares's writings; and those by R. O. Redman in *Quarterly Journal of the Royal Astronomical Society* 7 (1966): 75–79, and Horace W. Babcock in *American Philosophical Society Yearbook for 1967* (1968), pp. 145–48.

RONALD BRASHEAR

SEARING, Laura Catherine Redden (9 Feb. 1840–10 Aug. 1923), journalist and author, was born Laura Catherine Redden in Somerset County, Maryland, the daughter of Littleton James D. Redden and Wilhel-

mine Waller. The family soon moved to St. Louis, Missouri. When Laura was about eleven, she was stricken with cerebrospinal meningitis, which left her deaf and able to speak only in a tone she later described as "sepulchral, like a voice from the grave." She could, however, remember the specific sounds and general rhythms of spoken English. Because of her affliction, she developed a speech impediment. At the Missouri Institution for Deaf Mutes in St. Louis, she learned both signing and the manual alphabet but also developed the habit of communicating by pencil and paper with persons who did not understand these modes of communication. To outsiders she seemed deaf and dumb.

In 1857–1858 Laura Redden worked as the assistant editor of the *St. Louis Presbyterian* and in 1859 began to contribute prose and poetry to the *St. Louis Republican*. She wrote under the name "Howard Glyndon" to conceal her gender; many female writers adopted male pen names at this time to gain access to the male-dominated publishing world. In 1861 she wrote an article ridiculing Missouri's secessionist governor Claiborne Fox Jackson's repudiation of President Abraham Lincoln's call for 50,000 troops for the Union army. Editors of a St. Louis Confederate newspaper sought out Howard Glyndon, learned that Laura C. Redden was the writer's real name, and ridiculed a mere "school girl" for interfering in politics. Undeterred, she replied with "An Appeal from Judge to Jury," urging Missouri to side with the Union.

When the Civil War began, the *Republican* sent Redden to Washington, D.C., as a special correspondent. In 1861 she wrote "Belle Missouri" in reply to the rebel song "Maryland, My Maryland" and dedicated it to Missouri volunteers. Her poem was adopted as Missouri's war song. Her first extended publication, written as Howard Glyndon, was a 103-page pamphlet titled *Notable Men in "the House": A Series of Sketches of Prominent Men in the House of Representatives, Members of the Thirty-seventh Congress* (1862). She collected fifty-two of her war poems in *Idyls of Battle and Poems of the Rebellion* (1864), this time credited as "Howard Glyndon (Laura C. Redden)." In these and subsequent verses, loss of hearing caused her to overvalue basic rhythms, simple rhymes and rhyme schemes, and refrains. At the same time, the limitations of her education, as well as her notion of the taste of her reading public, led her to compose verse now regarded as sentimental and simplistic. For example, "Belle Missouri" begins "Arise and join the patriot train, / Belle Missouri! Belle Missouri! Four of its six stanzas begin with commands—"Arise," "Recall," and the like—while all six stanzas rhyme *a b a b a a a b*, the *a* rhymes of one stanza being "trust," "dust," "lust," "thrust," and "rust." The refrain "Belle Missouri! My Missouri!" appears in lines two, four, and eight of each stanza. Other war poems lament the dead ("Let us lay them [Gettysburg casualties] where they fell, / When their work was done so well!") and castigate the foe ("Couldst thou [Jefferson Davis] act this craven part, / Thus in hellish wisdom grow, / With no demon in thy heart?"). Her praise of Ulysses S. Grant includes these lines:

> Then he went gravely, earnestly to work,
>   And lo, a great sensation!
> For soon they found he was the only man,
>   With skill to serve the nation.

Redden sent Lincoln proof sheets of *Idyls of Battle* and welcomed his 29 August 1864 handwritten reply, stating that he found "these poems . . . all patriotic, and some very pretty."

From February 1865 until 1868 Redden served as foreign correspondent in Europe, mostly France and Italy, for the *Republican*, the *New York Times*, and the *New York Sun*. She also placed occasional pieces in several American magazines and studied French, German, Italian, and Spanish. While in Italy, she collected information concerning oranges and silkworms for the U.S. Agricultural Department, which published her "Culture of the Orange and Citron" in the *U.S. Department of Agriculture Report of 1867* (1868). Returning to New York, she worked for the *New York Mail* and the *New York Tribune*. She also continued to publish poems—about nature, made-up love relationships, pride, sorrow, loss, grief, weariness, and the like—in several periodicals, including *Harper's Weekly* and the *Atlantic Monthly*.

In 1871 Redden learned that the first articulation school in the United States had been established for deaf, dumb, and blind children at the Clark Institution in Northampton, Massachusetts. For two years she attended classes there. One of her teachers was Alexander Graham Bell, who corrected her chronic habit of speaking in a fast, falsetto voice while inhaling as well as exhaling. She followed Bell to Boston and continued classes with him there. Although she took instructions in lipreading in Mystic, Connecticut, she never mastered that technique. While in Mystic, she wrote "Silent Children," a series of articles for the *Mail* advocating speech instruction for deaf children in all schools. Then came *Sounds from the Secret Chambers* (1873). Most of the nearly 100 usually short poems are too singsong and saccharine to wear well. "Revocation," for example, begins "Come back! come back! for the light went out/When thine eyes looked away from my own!" and ends "for thee it [her heart] cries/Like a poor little frightened child!" At her best, Searing more acceptably extols her favorite flowers, trees, and birds, as in "An Idyl of the Early Spring."

In 1876 Laura Redden married Edward W. Searing, a New York lawyer; they had one child. Her popularity is indicated by the fact that gifts and congratulations came from writers Joaquin Miller, Bayard Taylor, and John Greenleaf Whittier, journalist-diplomat Whitelaw Reid, and the French National Chamber of Deputies. She retired from journalism, continued to compose verse, and taught deaf mutes. In 1886 she went to California to attend a convention of instructors of the deaf, decided for reasons of health to remain, and settled with her husband in Santa Cruz. Searing's last book was *El Dorado* (1897), written as Howard Glyndon. A representative poem in it is "The Hills of Santa Cruz," which, though marred by mixed metaphors for the hills—upright angels with Edenic outlines, blessed brows, "homesteads on their hearts," and laureled feet—is infused with sincere devotion to nature. During her final years she lived with her daughter in San Mateo, California, where she died.

• *Echoes of Other Days* (1921) is a complete edition of Searing's poems, with prefatory and biographical material prepared by her daughter, Elsa S. McGinn. Searing is mentioned in Mary Logan, *The Part Taken by Women in American History* (1921); J. Cutler Andrews, *The North Reports the Civil War* (1955); and M. L. Stein, *Under Fire: The Story of American War Correspondents* (1969). Obituaries are in the *San Mateo News*, 10 Aug. 1923, and the *San Francisco Chronicle*, 11 Aug. 1923.

ROBERT L. GALE

SEARS, Dick (26 Oct. 1861–8 Apr. 1943), tennis player, was born Richard Dudley Sears in Boston, Massachusetts, the son of Frederick Richard Sears, a trustee of the Sears family estate, and Albertina Homer Shelton. His grandfather, David Sears, amassed a fortune in shipping and real estate, permitting Sears to be raised in an elite wealthy family in Boston's exclusive Beacon Hill neighborhood. He attended J. P. Hopkinson's private school, and in 1879 he entered Harvard College.

In Nahant, Massachusetts, during the summer of either 1874 or 1875 (the exact year is unresolved), Sears's older half-brother, Frederick Sears, and his second cousin, Dr. James Dwight, played what they believed to be the first lawn tennis game in the United States. Coached by these individuals, Sears began playing lawn tennis around 1878. He won the Beacon Park Athletic Association tournament in 1880, defeating Edward Gray in the final. That September he accompanied Dwight to the advertised "United States championship" at the Staten Island (N.Y.) Baseball and Cricket Club where they competed in the doubles and lost in their second match.

In August 1881, during the first U.S. National Lawn Tennis Association (USNLTA) championship at the Newport (R.I.) Casino, Sears discovered other players invariably hit balls over the net's lowest point at its center. Thus he advanced to midcourt and consistently block-volleyed their shots from side to side. As a result he overcame all his opponents without dropping a set, defeating transplanted Englishman William Glyn in the final. Immediately afterwards, the Casino staged a "Ladies Cup" tourney to permit entries by players barred from the championship because they did not belong to member clubs of the USNLTA. John. J. Cairnes, an Irishman who came to America in 1880, defeated Sears decisively in the final, 4–6, 6–2, 6–1, 6–3.

In 1882 Sears won the Lenox (Mass.) Club open; the U.S. singles, defeating Clarence Clark in the championship match; and, with Dwight, the U.S. doubles crown. By this time he was punching his volleys and lobbing to forestall other volleyers.

In the fall of that year he lost the Harvard championship he had held for three years to Joe Clark, Clarence's brother. In 1883 he graduated from Harvard with a bachelor of arts degree; divided two singles contests with Joe Clark during team matches between Boston and Philadelphia clubs; won the Orange (N.J.) Lawn-Tennis Club spring open, downing Dwight in the process; and, in Newport, captured his third U.S. singles championship, again beating Dwight in the final, and, with him, took the doubles first prize.

Early in 1884 Sears joined Dwight for winter practice with English players on the French Riviera. During the Irish championships in Dublin, he lost in the fourth round to Herbert Lawford. At both Liverpool and Cheltenham he twice fell before Donald Stewart. A wrist injury scratched him from the Championship singles at Wimbledon and, in the doubles, the Dwight-Sears pair were routed and outclassed by twins Ernest and William Renshaw, the eventual champions. Before they departed for the United States, Willie Renshaw presented Sears with the Tate racket he used to win at Wimbledon. Sears was delighted, and he won his last eight U.S. titles with the racket.

During Sears and Dwight's European tour, and because of Sears's dominance in America, the USNLTA voted to debar singles champions from a U.S. "All-Comers" tournament, the winner of which would play the champion in a challenge round. Diminutive Howard Taylor won the 1884 All-Comers. Sears defeated him in the challenge match but lost a set, his first in national singles competition. This third victory gave Sears permanent possession of a trophy donated in 1882 for the first three-time champion.

After attending Harvard Medical College in 1884 and 1885, but not graduating, Sears won the initial Middle States championship singles, in which Cairnes entered but did not play; and the doubles with Joe Clark. Sears then successfully defended his singles title by defeating the left-handed Godfrey Brinley of Trinity College in the challenge round, and with Joe Clark he easily took the 1885 doubles event. That same year he edited Solomon C. F. Peile's book *Lawn Tennis as a Game of Skill*. Sears retained his singles championships in the 1886 and 1887 challenge rounds, turning back Livingston Beeckman (later governor of Rhode Island) and Harry Slocum, and permanently retired another trophy for three-time winners. In addition, playing with Dwight, he scored his fifth and sixth national doubles victories. Sears also served the USNLTA as its president in 1887 and 1888. A neck injury requiring surgery caused him to default the singles title to Slocum in 1888 and virtually ended his competitive career. His final triumph was the 1891 Tropical championship doubles in St. Augustine, Florida, during which he was paired with Ollie Campbell. That year he married Eleanor M. Cochrane, and the couple would have two children.

A slender, 5'9" righthander, Sears ruled early American competition by employing a precise, accurate all-court style and by repeatedly becoming the first to master new techniques and tactics. For example, he introduced to Americans the "Lawford," a hard-paced, exaggerated topspin forehand he had roughly copied from Lawford. During his career Sears set longstanding records for both most overall and most consecutive U.S. championships won, seven in singles and six in doubles; Bill Larned and Bill Tilden later tied the most nonconsecutive singles mark.

Turning to court tennis, Sears invented the reverse twist "railroad" service, adapted from his lawn tennis serve, and in 1892 he became the sport's first American amateur champion. He also played racquets at the Boston Athletic Association. In time, he entered into the family occupation of Sears family trustee. He died in Boston.

• Sears provided personal recollections in "The First National Championship," in U.S. Lawn Tennis Association, *Fifty Years of Lawn Tennis in the United States* (1931), pp. 21–29; and in "Lawn Tennis in America," in *The Badminton Library of Sports and Pastimes, Tennis: Lawn Tennis: Racquets: Fives* (1890), pp. 315–31. Henry W. Slocum, Jr., *Lawn Tennis in Our Own Country*, Part II (1890), pp. 105–207, covers in some detail the 1881–1887 period of Sears's play, including match-by-match summaries of his U.S. singles and doubles championship record. Bud Collins and Zander Hollander, eds., *Bud Collins Modern Encyclopedia of Modern Tennis*, 2nd ed. (1994), pp. 441–442, furnishes an overview of Sears's career. Bill Talbert with Pete Axthelm, *Tennis Observed* (1967), contains an evaluative sketch of Sears and records his U.S. singles championships scores. Obituaries are in the *New York Herald Tribune* and the *New York Times*, both 10 Apr. 1943; and S. Wallis Merrihew, "Lawn Tennis Loses Its First Champion," *American Lawn Tennis*, 20 May 1943, pp. 4–6.

FRANK V. PHELPS

SEARS, Edmund Hamilton (6 Apr. 1810–16 Jan. 1876), clergyman, author, and hymn writer, was born in Sandisfield, Massachusetts, the son of Joseph Hamilton and Lucy Smith, farmers. A shy and fragile boy, Sears soon found that the harsh realities of agricultural life prevented him from regularly attending school. At sixteen he briefly enrolled for several months at Westfield (Massachusetts) Academy, and a few years later he met the entrance requirements for Union College in Schenectady, New York. A diligent student, he completed his bachelor's degree in three years, graduating in 1834.

At an early age, Sears had shown an interest in poetry and writing sermons, and at Union his literary skills were recognized and encouraged. He helped edit the college newspaper and also won a prize for his verse. After graduating, Sears first began to read law in hopes of a legal career. An opportunity to teach at the Brattleboro (Vermont) Academy led him to study theology with Rev. Addison Brown, and Sears soon switched his vocational interests to the Christian ministry. He subsequently entered Harvard Divinity School and earned a theological degree in 1837. He then accepted an assignment with the American Unitarian Association and served two years as a missionary, preaching at various points near Toledo, Ohio. Upon returning to Massachusetts, he was invited to accept the pastorate of the Wayland Unitarian Church; there he was ordained on 20 February 1839. Later that year, Sears married Ellen Bacon of Barnstable, Massachusetts; they had three sons and a daughter.

Sears's soft voice, shyness, and weak physical condition prevented him from serving larger and more active churches, and he preferred the peaceful and meditative pace that country parishes provided. He pastored the Unitarian society in Lancaster from 1841 to 1847, when poor health forced him to resign. After retiring to a small farm at Wayland, he regained sufficient strength to serve the Wayland parish again, ministering to it for the next seventeen years.

Sears was proud of his New England heritage, which he traced to the Plymouth Colony in the 1630s. His genealogical research led to the publication of two works in 1857: *Pictures of the Olden Time as Shown in the Fortunes of a Family of Pilgrims* and *Genealogies and Biographical Sketches of the Ancestry and Descendants of Richard Sears*. He also wrote and published a local commemorative history, *The Town of Wayland in the Civil War of 1861–1865*.

While pastoring the Wayland society, Sears became widely known throughout New England for his religious books, devotional verse, and editorial work (in association with Rufus Ellis) for the Unitarian periodical *Monthly Religious Magazine* (1851–1871). His sermons and other writings are marked with a richly devotional and mystical quality, as well as poetic grace and beauty. Among Unitarian leaders of his era, Sears was a "conservative" who held that Christianity was divinely inspired and that Christ (although not a member of the Trinity) was its divinely appointed author. Yet his piety was also influenced by the Platonic idealism of the Concord Transcendentalists and by the eighteenth-century Swedish scientist and religious visionary Emanuel Swedenborg. His *Regeneration* (1853), for example, which was written at the request of the American Unitarian Association, reflects Swedenborg's stages of spiritual growth; namely, confession, putting one's external life in order, and forming a new internal will. *Athanasia; or, Foregleams of Immortality* (1858), examines the nature of the soul and the afterlife and was praised by English poet Elizabeth Barrett Browning for its deep spiritual insights.

Sears's last pastorate was in Weston, a neighboring town, where he served from 1866 until his death. While in Weston he published his most popular work, *The Fourth Gospel: The Heart of Christ* (1872), which was reprinted several times. This work presented a rational life of Christ but also stressed the spiritual nature of the Resurrection, the importance of religious experience, and the mystical quality of John's gospel. Sears is best remembered, however, as a writer of poetry and hymns, reflected in his last two books, *Sermons and Songs of the Christian Life* (1875) and *Life in Christ* (1877). He may be the only American poet to write two Christmas carols that continue to be reprinted and frequently sung by Christians everywhere: "It Came upon a Midnight Clear" (1850) and "Calm, on the Listening Ears of Night" (c. 1834).

An accidental fall from a tree in 1874 effectively ended his active pastoral work, although he continued to write. He died at his home in Weston.

• Basic biographical information on Sears may be found in *History of the Church in Weston* (1909), and Samuel A. Elliot, *Heralds of a Liberal Faith*, vol. 3 (1910). A more thorough account is Chandler Robins, "Memoir of Rev. Edmund Hamilton Sears," *Proceedings of the Massachusetts Historical Society* 18 (1891). See also Albert Christ-Janer et al., comps., *American Hymns Old and New* (2 vols., 1980); George W. Cooke, *Unitarianism in America* (1902); Conrad E. Wright, *The Liberal Christians* (1970); and Wright, *American Unitarianism, 1805–1865* (1989). Obituaries and tributes are in the *Unitarian Review* (Feb. 1876); the *Christian Register*, 22 and 29 Jan. 1872; and the *Boston Daily Advertiser*, 18 Jan. 1876.

DAVID B. ELLER

SEARS, Eleonora Randolph (28 Sept. 1881–26 Mar. 1968), athlete and sports patron, was born in Boston, Massachusetts, the daughter of Frederick Richard Sears, the heir to a shipping and real estate fortune and family trustee, and Eleonora Randolph Coolidge, a great-granddaughter of Thomas Jefferson. Raised in the Back Bay section of Boston, she received a private education at home and in Paris, where her grandfather Thomas Jefferson Coolidge served as minister to France. Eleonora, "an outstanding beauty . . . blue-eyed and blond" (Amory, *Proper Bostonians*, p. 348) and, in evening wear, "one of the best gowned women of America" (*New York Times*, 27 Mar. 1968), frequently dressed for daytime in casual, mannish clothes, often in riding hats, breeches, and boots, which shocked some women's groups as too bizarre. However, her wealth and status as an unassailable paragon of elite society enabled her, in her independent, outspoken, and fearless way, to pursue sports and other interests to her full satisfaction. Although many praised her as an idealist bent on advancing women's roles in sports, she totally disclaimed any such purpose and indicated she simply did what pleased her most.

"I began exercising the first time I fell out of my crib," Sears recalled (quoted in *New York Times*, 27 Mar. 1968). As a child she acquired her father's habit of daily brisk walks and sometimes accompanied him on 22-mile jaunts from their Beacon Street home to their summer residence in Pride's Crossing, Massachusetts. At the latter place she gained a fascination with horses, which led to a lifetime average of four hours on horseback daily and a devotion to equestrian sports. As an adult she was slender, agile, strong, and possessed of exceptional coordination, restless energy, stamina, and natural ability to quickly perceive and master the skills various sports required.

Sears's first notable athletic achievements occurred in Newport, Rhode Island, where she won lawn tennis club tournaments and, in 1904, swam 4½ miles against a strong current, from Bailey's Beach to Newport Beach. Her firsts or near firsts for women included driving an automobile and being ticketed for speeding; being taken undersea as a submarine passenger;

and, in 1910, being an airplane passenger, aloft for eleven minutes with British pilot Claude Grahame-White during an air show. Pre–World War I journalists linked her romantically with several society gentlemen, particularly Harold Sterling Vanderbilt, but she never married.

Sears featured an aggressive, right-handed, hard-hitting, all-court style of tennis. She first drew notice in tennis at a 1905 Newport invitation tournament by defeating former U.S. champion Marion Jones Farquhar before losing in the final round to Maud Barger-Wallach, a future champion. On the grass courts of the Merion Cricket Club in Haverford, Pennsylvania, Sears won the Pennsylvania and Eastern States women's singles championships in 1908, 1909, 1910, and 1918. In addition, she won the U.S. women's doubles titles in 1911 and 1915 with Hazel Hotchkiss Wightman and in 1916 and 1917 with Molla Bjurstedt. In U.S. singles play at Haverford and Forest Hills, New York, Sears competed fifteen times, from 1911 through 1929, and became an all-comers finalist in 1911, 1912, and 1916; a semifinalist in 1917; and a quarterfinalist in 1915 and 1918. After women's national rankings began in 1913, she placed sixth for 1914, tenth for 1915, ninth for 1916, and twelfth for 1918. At age fifty-seven, in 1939, with Sylvia Henrotin, she won the U.S. women's veterans championship (for players age forty-five and older). A frequent traveler abroad, Sears played in the 1922, 1923, and 1924 Championships in Wimbledon, London, England. While in Great Britain, she became acquainted with the Prince of Wales, the future king Edward VIII. When Edward visited America in 1924, Sears was his favorite dance partner.

Sears eventually turned from tennis to another racket sport, squash racquets. In 1918 she invaded the all-male Harvard Club and successfully demanded the right to play squash there. She also captured the first U.S. women's squash championship in 1928. Later she became president of the U.S. Women's Squash Racquets Association and captained a U.S. Wolfe-Noel Cup team that opposed a British team in England. At age fifty-eight she still reached the semifinals of the nationals and, at age seventy-two, still competed in the 1954 U.S. veterans' squash racquets championship.

Sears undertook several publicly noticed marathon walks, some to win wagers. Often she was paced by athletic males and usually was trailed by her automobile and watchful chauffeur. In March 1912 she walked 109¼ miles in 41½ hours, from Burlingame to Delmonte, California, before collapsing at the finish. In December 1925 she covered 47 miles in 10½ hours, from Providence, Rhode Island, to Boston; and the following year she traversed the same route in 9¾ hours. In April 1928 Sears marched 74 miles through rain in 16 hours, from the Newport Casino to her Beacon Street home, and two months later she went 42½ miles in 8½ hours, from Fontainbleau, France, to Paris. "It was fun," she said, "the traffic made it very exciting."

Some considered Sears eccentric for riding horses astride in men's breeches, or demanding entry into a men's polo game in 1909, or driving a fore-in-hand coach down New York City's Fifth Avenue in 1912 in order to win a bet. However, she was a serious, dedicated horsewoman who rode, bred, trained, and owned hunters, jumpers, steeplechasers, standard-breds, and thoroughbreds. The stables at Pride's Crossing were her greatest joy. Her horses, sometimes with Sears herself riding, won numerous blue ribbons at the National Horse Show in Madison Square Garden, New York City. She did not enter flat racing as an owner until 1954 when she purchased a bay yearling colt from the Aga Khan.

Other sports in which Sears engaged were many and varied. She raced speedboats and canoes and skippered a yacht that beat Alfred Vanderbilt's *Walthra*. A crack shot with rifle and pistol, she was a fine trapshooter. She also participated in baseball on Boston Common, field hockey, ice hockey, skating, boxing, and football with other girls, and even backgammon. A fine golfer, she once played forty-five holes in a day, but she found golf rounds too slow paced for her liking. Reputedly she won 240 trophies in all her various athletic endeavors. In addition, generous donations provided vital support to several sports, including the U.S. Olympic equestrian teams and the National Horse Show. After a 1961 air crash killed almost the entire U.S. figure skating team, her monetary gifts helped to rebuild a new team. Her voice and gifts of horses and money kept the Boston mounted police division from being abolished.

Sears lived her last five years in Palm Beach, Florida, where she died. She was posthumously elected to the National Lawn (later International) Tennis Hall of Fame in 1968, the Horseman's Hall of Fame in 1877, the International Women's Hall of Fame in 1984, the Show Jumping Hall of Fame in 1992, and the National Horse Show Foundation Hall of Fame.

• For insight on Sears's life and activities, see Cleveland Amory, "Bostonian Unique—Miss Sears," *Vogue*, 15 Feb. 1963, pp. 80–83, and Amory, *The Proper Bostonians* (1947), pp. 348–49. Brad Herzog, *The Sports 100: The One Hundred Most Important People in American Sports History* (1995), pp. 396–98, is also useful. Other references are Ralph Hickok, *A Who's Who of Sports Champions* (1995), pp. 709–10, and Frank G. Menke, *The Encyclopedia of Sports*, 3d rev. ed. (1963), pp. 1008–9. The *New York Times* published many news articles about Sears; consult the *New York Times Index to Proper Names*. Obituaries are in the *Boston Globe* and the *New York Times*, both 27 Mar. 1968.

FRANK V. PHELPS

SEARS, Isaac (c. 1730–28 Oct. 1786), revolutionary leader, was the son of Joshua Sears, an oyster catcher, and Mary Thacher. Sources vary on his place and date of birth, attributing the former to both West Brewster and Harwich, Massachusetts, on Cape Cod, and to Norwalk, Connecticut. Norwich, Connecticut (rather than Norwalk), is also given in one source as the place where he grew up. His date of birth appears as both 1729 and 1730.

What is certain is that Sears's parents were not well off and that in late youth he moved to New York City to improve his own fortunes. Strongly oriented toward the sea, he rose rapidly to command of a coastal trading vessel and was active in privateering during the Seven Years' War (1756–1763) between France and England. When the war ended he established himself as a merchant in New York, in the intercolonial trade rather than in transatlantic commerce. He married Sarah Drake, the daughter of a waterfront tavernkeeper in New York. With the marriage he abandoned his own family's four-generation tradition of Congregationalism and converted to his bride's Anglican faith, to which he adhered for the rest of his life. Eleven children resulted from the marriage.

Sears's adult life represents two strong trends within the American revolutionary movement. In personal and financial terms, he was assertively upwardly mobile. In political terms, he was intensely militant, always preferring direct action to debate.

As an aspiring merchant, with capital to invest from his privateering career, Sears was able to move into the lower levels of New York's merchant elite. He remained "Captain" Sears, however, rather than acquiring the more honorific title of "Mr." In the streets he became known as "King" Sears from his supposed ability to raise a mob at will. If this reputation had a basis in fact, it stemmed from the high regard in which he was held by the working sailors who frequented his father-in-law's bar. Sears was one of the founders of New York's organized Sons of Liberty, and he was one of ten men who traveled to New London, Connecticut, in December 1765 to negotiate a formal alliance between the New York group and its New England counterparts.

As a street leader, he participated in resistance to the Stamp Act (1765–1767) and the Townshend Acts (1767–1770) and in the increasing militance that followed the Boston Tea Party (1773–1775). He was a member of New York City's initial committee of correspondence and its subsequent Committees of Fifty-one, Sixty, and One Hundred, and he represented New York City in the first of four provincial congresses that drained power away from the royal government. In April 1775, just before the actual outbreak of war, he called on the city's populace to arm itself, "every man . . . with four-and-twenty rounds," and the city magistrates responded by arresting him. An uprising freed him, and when news of war arrived he led another crowd that seized the city's arsenal and distributed its contents "among the most active of the Citizens who formed themselves into a Voluntary Corps and assumed the Government of the City" (Becker, p. 193).

Thereafter, however, Sears's militance made the city too dangerous a place for him. He faced the possibility of kidnap by British agents, and the commander of HMS *Asia*, which was stationed in the harbor,

threatened to shell his house. Sears retreated to New England but remained active in New York affairs until the city and surrounding counties were invaded by British troops in the summer of 1776. Prior to the invasion he led New Englanders who came down to New York both to silence the city's Loyalist press and to force the submission of other Loyalists on Long Island.

Despite his militance, Sears did not win a permanent commission in the Continental army, and after 1776 he relocated to Boston, which had fallen under permanent American control after the British army evacuated it in March 1776. Returning to his first love, the sea, he organized a considerable fleet of privateers, thus pursuing both his personal lust for gain and his political desire for direct, militant action. He was also active in raising supplies for the American army, and he promoted efforts to stem rising wartime inflation through price controls and by direct action against "Jobbers, Monopolizers, and Torries." By the war's end he was very well off.

Returning to New York at the end of 1783, Sears established himself again as a popular leader, particularly on the issue of stringent punishment for former Loyalists. He served as one of the city's nine members of the state assembly in its first postwar session (Jan.–May 1784) and was elected again to the ninth session, which convened in January 1786. By then, however, he had embarked on the pioneering voyage of the *Empress of China* to the Orient. Contracting "fever" during the voyage, he died near the Chinese coast and was buried on an island in Canton Harbor.

• Not a man of words, Sears left few papers. The two best accounts of his life are Pauline Maier, "Isaac Sears and the Business of Revolution," in *The Old Revolutionaries: Political Lives in the Age of Samuel Adams* (1980), pp. 51–100; and Robert Jay Christen, "King Sears: Politician and Patriot in a Decade of Revolution" (Ph.D. diss., Columbia Univ., 1968). Sears appears as a major character in several accounts of the Revolution in New York: Carl Lotus Becker, *The History of Political Parties in the Province of New York, 1760–1776* (1909); Edward Countryman, *A People in Revolution: The American Revolution and Political Society in New York, 1760–1790* (1981); and Gary B. Nash, *The Urban Crucible: Social Change, Political Consciousness, and the Origins of the American Revolution* (1979). Maier's essay and Christen's dissertation list the full range of sources available on Sears.

EDWARD COUNTRYMAN

SEARS, Paul Bigelow (17 Dec. 1891–30 Apr. 1990), botanist, ecologist, and conservationist, was born in Bucyrus, Ohio, the son of Rufus Victor Sears, an attorney, and Sallie Jane Harris. He earned a B.S. (1913) in zoology and a B.A. (1914) in economics from Ohio Wesleyan University; an M.A. (1915) in botany from the University of Nebraska; and a Ph.D. (1922) in botany from the University of Chicago. His doctoral dissertation, "Variations in Cytology and Gross Morphology of *Taraxacum*," was published in the *Botanical Gazette* (April–June 1922). In 1917 he married Marjorie Lee McCutcheon; they had three children.

Sears started his teaching career as an instructor of botany at Ohio State University (1915–1919), although service in the U.S. Army (1917–January 1919) temporarily interrupted it. He next went to the University of Nebraska as an assistant and then associate professor of botany (1919–1927). He moved to the University of Oklahoma in Norman as a full professor and chairman of the department of botany (1927–1938). While on sabbatical, he was a research associate at Teachers College of Columbia University (1936–1938). He returned to his home state as professor of botany and chairman of the department at Oberlin College (1938–1950).

In 1950 Sears went to Yale University to assume the post of professor and chairman in the newly established Master of Science Conservation Program, the first of its kind in the United States. The program's purpose was to give to a limited number of qualified students, of varied vocational interests, the basic principles of natural and social science involved in conservation. Between 1953 and 1955 Sears was also chairman of the department of botany and the Yale Nature Preserve. Having reached the mandatory retirement age of sixty-eight, Sears left Yale in 1960. During the ensuing decade he was a visiting professor at several colleges and universities.

Over the course of his long career Sears published more than fifty research papers, some of them pioneering efforts. He wrote about fossil pollen, postglacial changes in vegetation and climate, the antiquity of maize, Pleistocene climate history, and the techniques by which borings in peat bogs throw light on vegetation of the past.

Sears was not satisfied, however, to limit himself to preparing technical papers for other scientists. He deemed it a responsibility of distinguished scientists to explain to the general public what they were trying to do in their work. Heeding his own call, Sears wrote a number of books for the general reader. Conservation and ecology were major interests of his and the subjects of many of his books. By making the American people scientifically literate, he hoped to advance the cause of conservation. "Only when people have learned to appreciate and cherish the landscape and its living cover," he wrote in *Wild Wealth*, "will they treat it with the care and respect it should have" (p. 4).

Sears's first book, *Deserts on the March* (1935; repr. 1947, 1959, 1964, 1980), dealt with the negative effects of the westward movement on the land. Americans had conquered a continent, wrote Sears, but in doing so they had "broken the gentle grip wherein nature holds and controls the forces which serve when restrained, destroy when unleashed." The unleashing of those forces resulted in floods, soil erosion, polluted waterways, and expansion of the desert in the West. Still, Sears was no pessimist and asserted that if suitable policies were adopted (such as rotating and diversifying crops), the land could be restored and the advancing desert turned back.

Deserts on the March was written after Sears had witnessed the tragic dust storms of the early 1930s during his tenure at the University of Oklahoma. Eloquent and wittily epigrammatic, the book earned Sears a Book-of-the-Month Club Fellowship Award (1937) and has been called his most successful work on conservation awareness.

His accomplishments as a scientist and conservationist earned Sears numerous awards. Among them were the Certificate of Merit, Botanical Society of America (1956); the Eminent Ecologist award, Ecological Society of America (1965); the Medal of the Garden Club of America (1963); the Louis Bromfield medal, Friends of the Land (1958); membership in the Ohio Conservation Hall of Fame (1979); and the Aldo Leopold Conservation Award, New Mexico Chapter of the Nature Conservancy (1984). His skill and success as a popularizer of science were recognized with the Richard Prentice Ettinger Medal (1963), awarded to writers or other individuals who have had "great influence in the dissemination of knowledge for the benefit of mankind, particularly in the public understanding of science."

Sears also held a number of offices in scientific organizations. He was president of the American Association for the Advancement of Science (1956), president of the American Society of Naturalists (1959), vice president (1943) and president (1948) of the Ecological Society of America, chairman of the board (1956–1959) and honorary president of the National Audubon Society, president of the Ohio Academy of Science (1949–1950), and trustee of the Pacific Botanical Garden (1963–1971). He was on the board of editors of *Daedalus* (1959–1969), and he was a member of the National Science Foundation Board (1958–1964).

Following his first wife's death in 1982, Sears married Marguerite Saxer in June 1983. He retired to Taos, New Mexico, where he was active on local boards and committees and was one of the founders of Project Discovery, a program in the schools which introduced children to the natural world. He died in Taos.

• A major collection of Sears's correspondence and other material is at Yale University. Oberlin College has papers relating to his tenure there, and correspondence is in the Records (1940–1962) of the Friends of the Land (Ohio), at the Ohio Historical Society (Columbus). In addition to works cited in the text, Sears wrote *This Is Our World* (1937, 1971), *Life and Environment* (1939), *Who Are These Americans* (1939, 1940), *This Useful World* (1941, with James Quillen and P. R. Hanna), *Charles Darwin: The Naturalist as A Cultural Force* (1950), *The Ecology of Man* (1957), *Where There Is Life* (1962, 1970), *The Living Landscape* (1966, an expanded version of *Where There Is Life*), *The Biology of the Living Landscape* (1964), *Lands beyond the Forest* (1969), and *Wild Wealth* (1971, with M. R. Becker and F. J. Poetker). The most complete account of Sears's career is Ronald L. Stuckey, "Paul Bigelow Sears (1891–1990): Eminent Scholar, Ecologist, and Conservationist," *Ohio Journal of Science*, 90 (1990): 186–90. See also Linda Joyce Forristal, "Paul Bigelow Sears," *The World and I* 3 (Feb. 1988): 199–203, based on an interview with Sears when he was ninety-six. An obituary is in the *Taos News*, 10 May 1990.

RICHARD HARMOND

SEARS, Richard Warren (7 Dec. 1864–28 Sept. 1914), businessman, was born in Stewartville, Minnesota, the son of James Warren Sears, a blacksmith, and Eliza Benton. Sears spent his childhood in several small Minnesota towns. He attended high school but never graduated. When he was fourteen his father bought a farm, but James Sears suffered from mental and physical illness and had to leave the operation of the farm to his son. Two years later his father died, and Richard became the family breadwinner.

Sears learned telegraphy, and the St. Paul and Duluth Railroad hired him to work as an agent at its North Branch, Minnesota, station. He was later employed as an auditor in the company's St. Paul office, but office work did not appeal to him. Sears secured a transfer to North Redwood, Minnesota, where he became manager of the town's railroad depot, a position that allowed him to trade with the locals and thereby add to his company salary.

Opportunity knocked for Sears in 1886, when a manufacturer shipped watches to a local merchant who did not order them, hoping the merchant would agree to sell them on a commission basis. The merchant refused, but Sears seized the opportunity and began reselling watches to other railroad agents, offering a money-back guarantee to agents whose credit was solid. He netted $5,000 within six months.

Sears abandoned his railroad career and moved to Minneapolis, where he established the R. W. Sears Watch Company in 1886. One year later he transferred his company headquarters to Chicago. By purchasing surplus watches, and selling them at cut-rate prices, Sears met the growing consumer demand for cheap manufactured goods.

Despite his success, Sears was a man divided between his entrepreneurial ambitions and his longing for the simple country life. In 1888 he retired to Iowa after selling his watch company to Alvah Curtis Roebuck, whom he had earlier hired to repair and assemble watches. Unable to remain inactive and settle into a quiet retirement, Sears invested in farm mortgages and started another watch company, which he also sold to Roebuck. Then, in 1891, Sears abandoned retirement entirely and formed a partnership with Roebuck that became Sears, Roebuck and Company.

Sears believed he could compete in the mail-order business, a market dominated by Montgomery Ward. Two decades earlier, Aaron Montgomery Ward had recognized that many Americans were dissatisfied with the high prices and limited selection of goods available in small-town stores. Ward cut costs by purchasing directly from manufacturers, passing the savings on to consumers. He also sold a great variety of goods; in 1884 his sales catalog listed 10,000 items. Ward overcame consumer reluctance to purchasing goods sight-unseen by promising "satisfaction guaranteed—or your money back." His marketing strategy worked; in 1889 Montgomery Ward reported sales of over $2 million. Ward's success attracted competitors, including Sears, who once pounded a Montgomery Ward catalog with his fist, declaring, "That's the game I want to get into—the biggest game in the United States today" (Asher, p. 21).

Sears entered "the biggest game" in a big way. He was an entrepreneurial daredevil who never took the time to evaluate risk carefully. During the economic depression of 1893 Sears plunged into debt to expand his operations. One year later he was publishing a 500-page catalog listing thousands of items. While the orders flowed into his Chicago office, he scurried across the country to find suppliers to meet the demand. He did, however, take time out in 1895 to marry Anna Lydia Meckstroth; they had four children.

Despite the increase in business, company liabilities exceeded assets. Roebuck worried about maintaining his financial solvency, and in 1895 he sold his interest to Sears, who then took on two new partners, businessmen Aaron Nusbaum and Nusbaum's brother-in-law Julius Rosenwald. Sears remained president of the company. (Disagreements over company policy led Sears and Rosenwald to buy out Nusbaum in 1901.) While Sears focused on the marketing, Rosenwald managed the rest of the company. During the next ten years, Sears, Roebuck enjoyed spectacular growth. In 1900 sales reached $10 million, and the company overtook Ward as the largest mail-order firm in the country.

This success derived partly from Richard Sears's imitation of methods pioneered by Ward. Sears competed with Ward on the basis of price, boasting that his was the "Cheapest Supply House on Earth." While Ward was the first to guarantee customer satisfaction, Sears described in detail what was covered and provided customers with certificates guaranteeing each purchase. Sears also matched Ward in variety; he told his customers that Sears, Roebuck sold "Everything you eat, wear, or use." His 1908 catalog contained over 100,000 items, including groceries and automobiles.

Although Sears imitated others, he displayed a knack for innovation that his competitors could not match. Sears experimented with rebates, sweepstakes, and pyramid schemes. He earned the trust of American farmers, ever suspicious of big-city businessmen, by allowing them to examine a product before paying for it. This "Send No Money" policy attracted customers who were reluctant to commit themselves to the purchase of goods they had never seen. Many mail-order customers felt intimidated by complicated order forms, so Sears simplified the ordering process by telling semiliterate farmers that they could write what they wanted in their own words.

It was Sears's flair for advertising that set his company apart from the competition. Contemporaries considered him a marketing genius. The investment banker Henry Goldman, for example, said of Sears, "I think he could sell a breath of air." Sears put great emphasis on advertising and placed no limits on the amount he was willing to spend promoting his products. By the turn of the century, he was one of the largest advertisers in America. Sears, who wrote his own copy, advertised nearly everywhere—in national magazines, big-city newspapers, literary journals, and in the publications of farm groups, churches, trade unions, and fraternal societies.

But it was the Sears, Roebuck catalog that served as his chief form of advertising. Having grown up in rural America, Sears understood farmers. His folksy prose made the businessman seem like a friendly neighbor who spoke their language. Sears was also a master of ballyhoo. He proclaimed, for example, that his inexpensive goods would "last forever" and were "the best in the world." Farmers welcomed the semiannual arrival of the Sears, Roebuck catalog, which became known as the "Farmer's Bible" and the "Nation's Wishbook." For many it was one of the only "books" they ever owned or read.

Sears did not always practice truth-in-advertising. Nineteenth-century businessmen operated in an unregulated environment. Deceptive business practices, including false or misleading advertising, were the norm. The principle of caveat emptor ("let the buyer beware") prevailed in retailing. Sears came to realize, however, that "honesty pays," especially in the competitive mail-order market. As consumers grew more sophisticated, Sears met their demand for both higher-quality products and truth-in-advertising. Other retailers followed his example, and eventually the old attitude of "the customer be damned" gave way to a new belief that "the customer is always right."

Sears's success threatened the interests of small-town merchants. They threw Sears catalogs on bonfires, spread rumors that Sears was black, urged newspaper editors not to accept his advertisements, and encouraged neighbors to "trade at home." Sears protected the privacy of his customers by shipping their orders in plain brown paper wrapping. In his catalog Sears portrayed himself as a friend of the consumer and an opponent of price-fixing monopolies, declaring that "We are Waging War against Combinations, Associations, Trusts and High Prices." Sears further enhanced his public image by hiring an army of letter-writers to communicate with his customers.

Sears's career was cut short by a general downturn in the economy. In 1907 the country experienced a severe business depression, and company sales dropped for the first time. Never one to slow down, however, Sears hoped to overcome the crisis by continuing to expand. Rosenwald disagreed; he favored organizational consolidation. Sears's closest associates sided with Rosenwald, arguing that Sears's old-style promotions were inappropriate now that the company had matured. Sears felt out of place, and on 21 November 1908 he resigned as president, citing "ill health the preceding five years." He was named chairman of the board of directors but soon resigned. After retirement, Sears sold his company stock for $10 million. He invested in several minor ventures involving lumber, railroads, typewriters, and farmland. Sears died in Waukesha, Wisconsin.

Sears's career is a study in irony. He began his marketing career as a huckster, yet ended up creating a company that maintained high ethical standards. Sears, the consummate risk-taker, built an institution that for over a half-century stood solid in the topsy-turvy world of retailing. He spent his life amassing a fortune but never slowed down long enough to enjoy it. Yet he exited gracefully once it became apparent that his swashbuckling sales tactics, so typical of the nineteenth century, had given way to the organizational imperatives of the twentieth century.

• Sears is arguably one of the most important figures in American business history, and his significance has not gone unnoticed by biographers and historians. One of his closest associates, Louis E. Asher (with Edith Heal), offers an anecdotal account of Sears's career in *Send No Money* (1942). For a more detailed and analytical look at the early history of Sears, Roebuck and Company, see Boris Emmet and John E. Jeuck, *Catalogues and Counters: A History of Sears, Roebuck, and Company* (1950), a definitive work. Emmet and Jeuck drew on Sears's papers, which are in the possession of Sears, Roebuck. More recent histories include Gordon L. Weil, *Sears, Roebuck, U.S.A.: The Great American Catalog Store and How It Grew* (1977), and Richard S. Tedlow, "Bringing the Mass Market Home: Sears, Montgomery Ward, and Their Newer Rivals," chap. 5 in his *New and Improved: The Story of Mass Marketing in America* (1990). For an account of the mail-order and retail wars between Sears and Ward, see Cecil C. Hoge, Sr., *The First Hundred Years Are the Toughest: What We Can Learn from the Century of Competition between Sears and Ward* (1988). Sketches of Sears himself have appeared in many magazine articles, including Brian McGinty, "Mr. Sears and Mr. Roebuck," *American History Illustrated* 21 (1986): 34–37, 48–49. Sears, Roebuck and Company has produced a short history, *Sears Yesterday and Today: A Brief History of the Origins and Development of Sears, Roebuck, and Co.* (1986). No discussion of Sears's career would be complete without mentioning works dealing with his catalog. Popular interest in the early editions has resulted in the publication of facsimile copies, including the 1993 reprint of the *1897 Sears, Roebuck Catalogue*, ed. Fred L. Israel. For a fascinating look at the changing lifestyle of Americans as reflected in the pages of the catalog, see David L. Cohn, *The Good Old Days: A History of American Morals and Manners as Seen through the Sears, Roebuck Catalogs, 1905 to the Present* (1940). Thomas J. Schlereth discusses how scholars have used the catalog to date artifacts and photographs in "Mail-Order Catalogs as Resources in American Culture Studies," *Prospects* 7 (1982): 141–61. The catalog even inspired the production of a full-length motion picture, *Mr. Sears' Catalogue* (1989). An obituary is in the Chicago *Daily Tribune*, 29 Sept. 1914.

JONATHAN J. BEAN

SEARS, Robert Richardson (31 Aug. 1908–22 May 1989), psychologist, was born in Palo Alto, California, the son of Jessie Brundage Sears, a professor and educational reformer, and Stella Louise Richardson. Sears grew up in comfortable surroundings. His first brush with scientific psychology came in the early 1920s when he was a subject for Stanford University psychologist Lewis M. Terman's Genetic Studies of Genius Project. Drawn first to the subjects of drama and literature, Sears majored in English at Stanford before switching to psychology in his senior year, because he and psychology major Pauline Kirkpatrick Snedden, had fallen in love. Terman made Sears his protégé.

Graduating in 1929, Sears took his doctoral studies with Clark L. Hull of Yale. Hull, then one of the rising stars of American behaviorism, was chiefly interested in rigid stimulus-response behavioral learning theories. Sears found Hull's work sterile and removed from the "real world of human emotions." His dissertation, a dutifully Hullian behavioristic study of reactions in a species of fish, left Sears cold. He married Snedden in 1932, right after receiving his Ph.D. Later she too won her Yale doctorate in psychology. They had two children.

In 1932 Sears became an instructor of psychology at the University of Illinois, where he taught a course in abnormal psychology. Exposed through this course to Sigmund Freud's work and to conceptions of Freudian psychodynamics, Sears discovered the "real-world" approach that he had found lacking in Hull's work. Over the next quarter century Sears established an experimental basis for Freudian psychodynamics and became one of the most original and sophisticated American Freudians. Using Freud's theories, Sears believed, one could account for relatively large units of behavior, such as love, anger, or frustration, rather than the much smaller units of behavior that Hull and other American behaviorists measured in their studies of learning. But Sears also criticized Freud, believing him to be mentalistic, too much of a clinician, and not enough of an experimental scientist. Only much later did Sears realize that, like Freud, he too had deployed mentalistic categories, which suggests the tenacity of positivistic behaviorist thinking among American psychologists—and scientists—then. Interested in providing empirical grounding for psychological theory, in being able to isolate variables, and in explaining how and why things happened, Sears believed that Freud's ideas could be tested experimentally and become the basis of theories about human nature. In this he departed from the standard versions of normative research that most American psychologists did; he was an important dissenter from his science's mainstream. At Illinois Sears tested Freud's theory of projection, that individuals without insight into themselves typically attributed their unpleasant characteristics to others. Using scales on which fraternity members rated themselves and others on such traits as stinginess, rowdiness, and obstinacy, Sears got exactly the results that Freud had predicted.

In 1936 Hull lured Sears to the reorganized Institute of Human Relations at Yale, where he and Hull soon drifted apart. Sears gravitated toward the younger faculty who despaired of the narrow and deterministic Hullian (and orthodox behaviorist) learning theories, which sought to explain the circumstances under which the organism behaved in response to new situations. Sears and his associates wanted to account for behavior of any kind in the immediate present, which included antecedent as well as current action—a much broader canvas on which to paint the many hues of human emotions as compared with behaviorist orthodoxy. Sears and his colleagues did a study that resulted in *Frustration and Aggression* (1939), a cooperative enterprise then so typical of the social sciences; Sears was the book's senior author. It was an intricate explanation of individual psychology in terms of the circumstances that led from frustration to aggression, using such foci as crime and adolescence. *Frustration and Aggression* was the first statement of the social learning school in dynamic social psychology, whose advocates insisted that culture and nature worked together to produce action.

In 1942 Sears changed his scientific identity again and became a child psychologist. Appointed director of the Iowa Child Welfare Research Station at the University of Iowa, the nation's first research institute in child psychology and development, Sears pared its research program down to work on theories of individual and group behavior. Developing a behavioristic science of personality that included child personality, he and his students produced important work that involved the use of children's doll play as a way of understanding their fantasies and emotions. In 1943 he published an important study for the Social Science Research Council in which he evaluated the available experimental evidence for Freudian psychodynamics in the extant literature. By relating Freud's work to contemporary concerns, Sears underlined the importance of social learning, as distinct from innate predisposition, for most Freudian mechanisms.

While at Iowa Sears began his largest contribution to science, a study of the effects of child-rearing practices on child personality and behavior, in which he and his associates concluded that the amount and kind of frustration and punishment the child received from the mother determined the child's dependent and aggressive drives, and that there were radical differences between how boys and girls learned these patterns of behavior, attributable to their mothers' notions of appropriate male and female behavior. Sears and his most important intellectual associate at Iowa, the German Gestalt psychologist Kurt Lewin, pioneered work in social psychology in mutually reinforcing ways. Lewin and his students stressed studies of group behavior, whereas Sears and his students worked on individual actions. While at Iowa Sears also promoted the field of child development by campaigning for mental health and reviving professional organizations.

In 1949 Sears left Iowa to become director of Harvard University's Laboratory of Human Development. The mother-child study was published during these otherwise unfruitful years. In 1953 he became head of psychology at Stanford, where Terman named Sears as his scientific executor on the Genetic Studies of Genius Project. After Terman's death in 1956, this became Sears's major scientific work. Under Sears's tutelage the genius project evolved into a study of the adjustment of persons of high intelligence to life's stresses and opportunities throughout the life cycle, thus becoming the first large-scale gerontology project as well as the first large longitudinal study of children in American social science.

At Stanford Sears was an important player in post–World War II academic entrepreneurship. He was a founding director of the famous Center for Advanced Study in the Behavioral Sciences, a model for postwar academic research institutes. As dean of Stanford's School of Humanities and Sciences from 1961 to 1970, he inaugurated demanding new requirements for appointment, tenure, and promotion which helped transform Stanford into a first-class national research university. Sears became David Starr Jordan Professor of Social Science in 1970 and retired as professor in 1978.

Blessed with a penetrating intellect and considerable creativity, Sears was one of the leading theoreticians of his science from the 1940s to the 1980s and was truly gifted at expressing his ideas. If he was famous for his outbursts of anger, he also showed great kindness to aspiring colleagues and much loyalty to friends. By all reports he was a stimulating lecturer and director of graduate work. He and his wife lived a close family life; she had her own career as a psychologist and educator. He died in Menlo Park, California.

• Sears's papers are in the Stanford University Archives, as are several interviews. Letters to and from Sears are in the faculty vertical files at the University of Iowa Archives, and in the Laura Spelman Rockefeller Memorial, the General Education Board, and the Rockefeller Foundation, Rockefeller Archive Center, in North Tarrytown, N.Y. There are interviews with Sears at the Archives for the History of American Psychology, University of Akron Libraries, and in the Milton J. E. Senn oral history interviews of child development and child guidance, located in the Historical Division, National Library of Medicine, Bethesda, Md.

Sears published approximately sixty articles and several monographs or books. Among his works not mentioned in the text are *Survey of Objective Studies of Psychoanalytic Concepts* (1943); "Some Child-Rearing Antecedents of Aggression and Dependency in Young Children," *Genetic Psychology Monographs* 47 (1953): 135–236; and, with Eleanor Maccoby, *Patterns of Child Rearing* (1957). Secondary literature on Sears is sparse, although his *Your Ancients Revisited: A History of Child Development* (1975), is an excellent beginning for any historian. Hamilton Cravens, *Before Head Start: The Iowa Station and America's Children* (1993), devotes a chapter to Sears as director of the Iowa Child Welfare Research Station and has many bibliographical leads. An obituary is in the *Stanford University Campus Report*, 24 May 1989.

HAMILTON CRAVENS

SEASHORE, Carl Emil (28 Jan. 1866–16 Oct. 1949), psychologist, was born Carl Emil Sjöstrand in Mörlunda, Sweden, the son of Gustaf Sjöstrand, a farmer and Lutheran lay preacher, and Emily Charlotta Borg. In 1869 the Sjöstrands moved to a farm in Boone County, Iowa, and anglicized their family name. His parents encouraged his musical interests (as a church organist) and educational aspirations, and in 1884 Seashore entered the preparatory department of Gustavus Adolphus College, which had long served the midwestern Swedish community. In 1891 he graduated as valedictorian with a B.A. and went to Yale to study philosophy with George Trumbull Ladd.

Although initially impressed by his teacher's scholarship, Seashore soon became disenchanted with Ladd's reliance on the authority of textbooks (including his own) and gradually redirected his attention toward the new experimental psychology then emerging at Yale and elsewhere. His first work in the psychology laboratory with Edward Wheeler Scripture seemed to Seashore more like telegraphy than a branch of mental philosophy. But he soon grew to appreciate both Scripture's emphasis on student initiative and the professional opportunities in American universities for psychologists with laboratory training. His 1895 Scripture-directed Ph.D. dissertation addressed important perceptual questions by examining "Illusions and Hallucinations in Normal Life" experimentally. He remained at Yale as an assistant for two years to sharpen his laboratory skills.

Seashore returned to the Midwest in 1897 as assistant professor at the State University of Iowa with charge of the psychological laboratory. He married Mary Roberta Holmes of Iowa City, Iowa, in 1900. The couple had four children (one son became a well-known psychologist, as did a grandson and two nephews). By 1902 Seashore was promoted to professor. Three years later he became head of the department of philosophy and psychology and in 1908 also became dean of the university's graduate college. He retired from these positions in 1937, at age seventy-one, but later served as dean pro tem during World War II. At Iowa, Seashore developed an influential career as one of the few leading American psychologists of his generation who was neither native-born nor the scion of an upper-middle-class family, and his psychological and administrative work helped to establish Iowa's significant place in both the psychological and educational communities of twentieth-century America.

From his initial appointment at Iowa, Seashore worked to enhance the role of the university's existing psychological laboratory. He thus developed courses that drilled undergraduates in the basics of psychology and experimental work, published the influential *Elementary Experiments in Psychology* (1908), and (for graduate students) emphasized the design and construction of instruments. For many years he regularly reviewed new laboratory apparatus in the *Psychological Bulletin* and, more important, built his department into one of the first large-scale midwestern graduate departments of psychology.

Like many of his contemporaries, Seashore wanted to apply his science, and (following Scripture) he wrote on the value of general psychological tests as early as 1901. He developed his most important contribution to psychology by building on his continuing interest in music and devising methods of measuring musical aptitude and talent. Like other early twentieth-century American psychologists, he broke down what he was studying into its sensory elements, which (for him) included the ability to distinguish differences in pitch, time, rhythm, loudness, and the like. In 1899 he began to publish articles in psychological journals on methods for testing such abilities, and by 1906 periodicals such as the *Musician*, *Musical Quarterly*, and *Etude* had asked him to describe his tests for their readers. Physicians, music schools, and psychological laboratories gradually adopted many components of his tests, and in 1919 Seashore published *The Psychology of Musical Talent* and issued phonograph records with standard tones so that these tests could be performed without special equipment. His 1937 book, *Psychology of Music*, brought together all of his previous studies, and in 1940 he issued (with several students) a revision of what had come to be called the Seashore Measures of Musical Talent.

As dean of the graduate college at Iowa, Seashore never hesitated applying his psychological ideas and using his position to direct university priorities toward areas in which he was interested. He was proud that his department of psychology worked closely with other university units, including the Child Welfare Research Station and Psychiatric Hospital, for which it operated a psychological clinic. He helped build strong programs in other scientific fields, and under his leadership the graduate college developed a well-deserved national reputation. Meanwhile, his interest in individual differences led to a serious concern with the development of gifted children, and through the 1920s he led a National Research Council project that urged school systems to section classes on the basis of tested ability.

Among his many memberships in professional organizations in psychology, education, and music, Seashore belonged to the American Psychological Association (for which he served as president in 1911) and the American Association for the Advancement of Science (for which he was vice president for the Section of Psychology in 1926–1927). As a former president of the American Psychological Association, he helped organize his science's contribution to the war effort in 1917, chairing the Committee on Acoustic Problems, which applied much of his earlier research to problems of submarine detection. After the war he was elected to the National Academy of Sciences and during the 1920–1921 academic year served in Washington, D.C., as resident chair of its Division of Anthropology and Psychology.

All Seashore did exhibited both firm confidence in his science and great pride in his career and his family. And while these traits at times limited his patience with points of view that did not mesh with his, almost all of his contemporaries in psychology and at the State University of Iowa admired his achievements and praised his warmth and generosity. He died in Lewiston, Idaho, while visiting a son.

• While the bulk of Seashore's personal and psychological papers remain undiscovered, professional papers relating to his administrative career may be found in many of the collections of administrative files at the University of Iowa Archives. Similarly, much of his correspondence with his psychological contemporaries may be found in the collections described in *A Guide to Manuscript Collections in the History of Psychology and Related Areas* (1982). Seashore's pride and confidence led him to write three autobiographies. While they overlap each other, each provides a different view of his life and career. The first, published in

History of Psychology in Autobiography, vol. 1 (1930), pp. 225–97, provides a general overview of his life and reveals much about his personality. *Pioneering in Psychology* (1942) appeared as vol. 70 of the University of Iowa series, Aims and Progress of Research, and deals most directly with his psychological work at the university. *Psychology and Life* (privately issued in 1964) rearranges and expands on material found in many of his published articles, including his first autobiography, and emphasizes his career as an educational administrator.

Two of Seashore's students compiled an annotated bibliography of his publications through 1926 for the "Seashore Commemorative Number" of *University of Iowa Studies in Psychology* (1928); more complete bibliographies are in *Pioneering in Psychology* and in the obituary by Walter R. Miles in National Academy of Sciences, *Biographical Memoirs* 29 (1956): 265–316. Other useful obituaries include Milton J. Metfessel, *Science* 111 (30 June 1950): 713–17; Joseph Tiffin, *Psychological Review* 57 (Jan. 1950): 1–2; and George D. Stoddard, *American Journal of Psychology* 63 (July 1950): 456–62.

MICHAEL M. SOKAL

SEATON, George (17 Apr. 1911–28 July 1979), film director, screenwriter, and producer, was born George Stenius in South Bend, Indiana, the son of Charles Stenius, a Swedish-born chef and restaurant manager, and Olga Berglund. In early childhood Seaton moved with his family to Detroit, where he attended public schools. He spent his junior year of high school at Phillips Exeter Academy in New Hampshire and then returned to Detroit to graduate from Central High School. Long interested in the theater, Seaton enrolled at a drama school run by actress/manager Jessie Bonstelle. Seaton also acted in Bonstelle's stock company productions at the Detroit Civic Theatre. After two years with Bonstelle, Seaton moved to New York City. Unsuccessful at finding work as an actor, he began submitting stories to magazines such as *True Confessions*, often using pseudonyms to disguise his prodigious output. When a story he had sent off under the name "George Seaton" (taken from a character in Philip Barry's play, *Holiday*) was accepted for publication, he took the name as his own. On a visit to Detroit in 1933, Seaton landed the lead role on the new radio show, "The Lone Ranger," produced at Detroit's WXYZ and broadcast on the Mutual Network. He left the program after eight months and returned to New York to pursue a career as a writer.

In late 1933 Seaton was hired as a $35-per-week staff writer by Metro-Goldwyn-Mayer Pictures and moved to Hollywood. On the train to California he encountered Phyllis Loughton, a stage manager with whom he had worked while at Bonstelle's stock company. Loughton was on her way to Hollywood to work at the Paramount Pictures talent department. Seaton married Loughton in 1936; they had two children. Seaton's first screen credit was the musical *Student Tour* (1934), starring Jimmy Durante. His next project, *The Winning Ticket* (1935), drew the attention of producer Irving Thalberg, who assigned Seaton and co-writer Robert Pirosh to write a vehicle for the Marx Brothers. After following the brothers on an eight-week vaudeville tour to better familiarize themselves with Marx-style humor, Seaton and Pirosh came up with a script for *A Day at the Races* (1937). The film was enormously popular, but Seaton was not interested in writing more "gag comedies." He turned down numerous offers for similar films in favor of working on the stageplay *But Not Goodbye*. The play was unsuccessfully produced on Broadway in 1944, and Seaton did no further writing for the theater.

Seaton began his 25-year association with producer William Perlberg when he wrote the romantic comedies *The Doctor Takes a Wife* (1940), starring Ray Milland and Loretta Young, and *This Thing Called Love* (1940), starring Rosalind Russell and Melvyn Douglas. Both films were produced by Perlberg for Columbia Pictures. In 1941 Seaton and Perlberg moved to 20th Century–Fox Pictures, for which they worked on numerous comedies and musicals, including *That Night in Rio* (1941), featuring Alice Faye and Don Ameche, *Coney Island* (1943), starring Betty Grable, and two Jack Benny vehicles—*Charley's Aunt* (1941), based on a play by Brandon Thomas, and *The Meanest Man in the World* (1943), based on a play by George M. Cohan. Seaton and Perlberg's first serious film was *The Song of Bernadette* (1943), starring Jennifer Jones. Based on a book by Franz Werfel and directed by Henry King, the film was a critical and box-office success and earned Seaton an Academy Award nomination for best screenplay.

After writing a film version of Maxwell Anderson's play *The Eve of St. Mark* (1944), directed by John M. Stahl, Seaton decided to start directing his screenplays. With the help of Perlberg, he convinced 20th Century–Fox chief Darryl F. Zanuck to let him both write and direct the musical *Billy Rose's Diamond Horseshoe* (1945), starring Betty Grable. The glossy show-business story was a substantial success, and Seaton never wrote another screenplay that he did not direct himself. Seaton was an advocate of the "auteur" approach to filmmaking, although he believed that a strong producer was needed to act as a tempering force and to handle financial matters.

Seaton's most celebrated effort is *The Miracle on 34th Street* (1947). Shot on location in New York City during the 1946 Christmas season, the film displayed Seaton's talent for blending fantasy and reality. He won the Academy Award for the film's screenplay, and the film was nominated for best picture. Seaton again injected whimsy into a realistic situation in *Apartment for Peggy* (1948). The popular comedy featured Edmund Gwenn, Jeanne Crain, and William Holden, who was one of Seaton's favorite actors. In *The Big Lift* (1950), Seaton combined a love story with documentary-like details about the Berlin airlift and shot the film on location in bomb-ravaged Germany.

In 1951 Seaton and Perlberg moved to Paramount Pictures, where they were given their own production unit, making Seaton coproducer as well as the writer and director of his films. "I direct in a calm way, he produced explosively," Seaton said of his relationship with Perlberg. "While a picture was shooting we had an arrangement by which he would be the 'heavy' and take off my shoulders the problems that annoy directors" (Simon, p. 524). Seaton's most noteworthy Paramount film is *The Country Girl* (1954). Seaton won an Academy Award for his adaptation of Clifford Odets's play, and his direction, which was also nominated for an Academy Award, elicited highly praised dramatic performances from Bing Crosby, Grace Kelly, and William Holden. Seaton also worked with Crosby on *Little Boy Lost* (1953). Seaton's other films for Paramount include *The Proud and the Profane* (1956), a romantic drama set in the South Pacific during the waning days of World War II starring William Holden and Deborah Kerr, and *Teacher's Pet* (1958), a popular comedy featuring Clark Gable. Seaton directed but did not write *The Pleasure of His Company* (1961), featuring Fred Astaire. The Perlberg-Seaton unit produced a number of films that Seaton did not write or direct. Most notable among these is *The Bridges at Toko-Ri* (1955), a Korean War drama directed by Mark Robson and starring William Holden and Grace Kelly.

Seaton's career declined in the 1960s with little-noticed films such as *The Counterfeit Traitor* (1962), an espionage story starring William Holden, and *36 Hours* (1965), a World War II drama featuring James Garner. His partnership with the ailing Perlberg was dissolved in 1965 (Perlberg died in 1968). Seaton returned to the stage to direct the unsuccessful Broadway comedy *Love in E Flat* (1967), written by Norman Krasna. He then directed, produced, and co-wrote for Universal Pictures *What's So Bad About Feeling Good?* (1968), a lackluster comedy featuring Mary Tyler Moore. He bounced back as the writer and director of the blockbuster *Airport* (1970), produced by Universal in conjunction with independent producer Ross Hunter with a screenplay that Seaton adapted from Arthur Hailey's bestselling novel. The great success of *Airport*, which featured a stellar cast that included Burt Lancaster, Helen Hayes, and Dean Martin, resulted in a spate of all-star "disaster" movies, most of which were inferior to Seaton's well-crafted effort. Seaton made only one more film, *Showdown* (1973), a western featuring Rock Hudson, which he directed and produced but did not write.

As a writer, Seaton is most noted for his skillful adaptations of stageplays and novels. Although not considered a director of the first rank, he is admired for his light touch with drama and for adding depth to comedies. Seaton was the president of the Academy of Motion Picture Arts and Sciences from June 1955 to May 1958. In 1962 he was given the academy's Jean Hersholt Humanitarian Award. He was also a trustee of Colonial Williamsburg and directed, from a script by Emmett Lavery, the 34-minute film, *Williamsburg: The Story of a Patriot* (1957), which was shown in the historic city for many years. Seaton died of cancer at his home in Beverly Hills, California.

• For further insight into Seaton's work see his articles, "Of Small Headaches," *New York Times*, 16 Apr. 1950, and "Letters to the Editor," *Saturday Review*, 25 Mar. 1950. A detailed overview of Seaton's career is Jerome S. Simon, "George Seaton Understands the Fundamental Needs of the Human Heart," *Films in Review*, Nov. 1971, pp. 521–40. An obituary is in the *New York Times*, 29 July 1979.

MARY C. KALFATOVIC

SEATON, William Winston (11 Jan. 1785–16 June 1866), journalist, was born at his family's stately homestead, "Chelsea," in King William County, Virginia, the son of Augustine Seaton and Mary Winston, Virginia gentry. Seaton was tutored at home before he attended Ogilvie's Academy in Richmond. At age seventeen he learned the printing trade in the offices of the *Virginia Patriot* in Richmond, becoming an assistant editor at age eighteen. Soon after, he moved to Petersburg, Virginia, where he edited the *Republican* for a short time.

Seaton moved to Raleigh, North Carolina, in 1806 to assist William Boylan with the printing of the *Minerva*. He left that newspaper in 1807 to become the editor of the *North Carolina Journal* in Halifax, North Carolina, where he remained for nearly two years. In January 1809 he returned to Raleigh to join the elder Joseph Gales in publishing the *Raleigh Register*, a Jeffersonian newspaper. In March 1809 he married Gales's daughter, Sarah Weston Gales, who was fluent in French and Spanish. Later, when he was an editor of the *National Intelligencer*, his wife often translated foreign documents that he used in the newspaper.

In 1812 Seaton joined his brother-in-law, the younger Joseph Gales, as associate editor and co-owner of the *National Intelligencer*, a tri-weekly newspaper in Washington, D.C. The *Intelligencer* was the unofficial "court paper" of Presidents Thomas Jefferson, James Madison, James Monroe, William Henry Harrison, and Millard Fillmore during its existence. As partners, Gales and Seaton supervised the most extensive printing operation in the United States for nearly five decades. The two were the exclusive reporters of the proceedings of Congress between 1812–1829 and were the official printers of Congress for nearly ten years between 1819 and 1829. They also received additional patronage from the federal government in the form of printing contracts.

Both men were known for their brief, dignified editorials, the authorship of which was often indistinguishable. However, their best work was their reporting of the daily proceedings of Congress, which they recorded in shorthand and published in the *Intelligencer*. Seaton covered the Senate, and usually sat next to the vice president, while Gales covered the House of Representatives, and sat next to the Speaker. Later, on authorization of Congress, Gales and Seaton compiled their reports with earlier ones dating to 1789 to publish a record of government that otherwise would have been lost to history. *The Annals of Congress* (42 vols., 1834–1856), covered congressional proceedings from 1789 to 1824; the *Register of Debates in Congress* (14 vols., 1825–1837), covered proceedings from 1824 to 1837; and a monumental series, *American State Papers*

(38 vols., 1832–1861), compiled major government documents prior to 1832.

The *National Intelligencer* became a daily on 1 January 1813; however, the tri-weekly edition was maintained as a separate publication. The *Intelligencer* supported Madison during the War of 1812. When British troops threatened to invade the capital in 1813, Gales and Seaton joined the local militia. Each partner supervised the newspaper on alternate days while the other stayed at camp, but the content of the paper suffered and friends urged them to resume full-time supervision. When the British burned Washington, D.C., in August 1814, the *National Intelligencer* lost much of its printing equipment, circulation lists, and bookkeeping records, although its building survived. The paper suspended publication until 31 August, when it appeared as a single sheet. Gales and Seaton suffered a great financial setback, but they refused to accept a donation of $30,000 raised by friends. The *Intelligencer* returned to its normal size on 26 September.

By 1818 Gales and Seaton owed the Bank of the United States $6,500 and were in debt to other creditors. However, the partners were unable to collect debts owed to them, which totaled nearly $100,000. The patronage provided by being elected the official printers of Congress in 1819 permitted them to pay creditors, but at a cost to the quality of the paper. On a typical day, at least two, and at times all four, pages were filled with government reports and announcements, and little else.

Seaton was aristocratic in taste, a Whig, a Freemason, and a Unitarian. While he believed Andrew Jackson was an honest man, he opposed his election as president because he saw Jackson as a crude frontiersman and an advocate of a low form of democracy. The *National Intelligencer* paid dearly for its opposition to Jackson. It lost its lucrative position as official printer of the Senate in 1827; lost the printing of the House in 1829; and lost its exclusive access to the proceedings of Congress, also in 1829. By the 1850s the *Intelligencer* was in decline. Besides mounting financial difficulties caused by lost patronage, the paper lost circulation because of its continued emphasis on government news, and the inability of its owners to adapt to the faster pace of journalism brought about by the telegraph. Once a leader, it had become stodgy. Seaton continued publishing the newspaper after Gales died in 1860, but by 1864, declining health and growing debt forced him to sell it.

A public servant as well, Seaton served as an alderman from 1819 to 1831 and as mayor of Washington from 1840 to 1850. He helped to develop the local educational system and led the movement for the construction of the Washington Monument. He was also active in creating the Smithsonian Institution and served as its treasurer from 1846 until his death. Although a staunch Unionist, he maintained that the government should not interfere with slavery and favored gradual emancipation, freeing his own slaves. He was also an official of the American Colonization

Society for many years. He died at his home in Washington, D.C.

• For a study of Seaton's career with the *Intelligencer*, see William E. Ames, *A History of the National Intelligencer* (1972). Also useful is Josephine Seaton, *William Winston Seaton of the National Intelligencer* (1871; repr. 1970), a loving memoir by his devoted daughter, but nevertheless a valuable resource. Culver H. Smith, *The Press, Politics, and Patronage: The American Government's Use of Newspapers, 1789–1875* (1977), examines the *Intelligencer's* role as a disseminator of government news. See also F. B. Marbut, *News from the Capital: The Story of Washington Reporting* (1971), and Donald A. Ritchie, *Press Gallery: Congress and the Washington Correspondents* (1991).

JOSEPH P. McKERNS

SEATTLE (1786?–7 June 1866), leader of the Coast Salish-speaking Duwamish tribe of east central Puget Sound, was born near present-day Seattle, Washington, the son of Schweabe, a Suquamish headman, and Scho-lit-za, who was reported to be a slave of Schweabe. This is a strong possibility since slavery was well established among natives of Puget Sound. Seattle's head was flattened in infancy to symbolize his aristocratic background. All sources claim that in his early years he lived west of present-day Seattle along Puget Sound in a Suquamish longhouse that was occupied by several families. His first wife, La-dai-la, was a Duwamish woman whose people lived in the present-day Seattle area. They had one child, Kick-is-om-lo, well known to early settlers as Princess Angeline. La-dai-la died young. Seattle's second wife was Oiahl, said to be a scolding woman. Their family comprised three girls, all of whom died in early childhood, and two boys, See-an-ump-kum (George) and Jim. Oiahl died in 1852.

Seattle lived in two worlds: that of the Indian and that of the white man. His first contact with whites occurred a quarter-century before his better-known meeting with them at his namesake city along the shores of Puget Sound. His early contacts were with traders of the Hudson's Bay Company post, Fort Nisqually, on southern Puget Sound not far from present-day Olympia, Washington. At that time his native society was marked by class distinctions of nobles, commoners, and slaves. Their subsistence was gained largely from the bountiful marine life of Puget Sound and the gift of the sacred cedar and other woods, roots, and berries from the shores, hills, and valleys of their homelands.

Before white settlement Seattle's people engaged in barter with other natives of Puget Sound, trading in items of wood, bone, and stone as well as in slaves. Unlike many slave masters Seattle was opposed to harsh treatment of slaves. Peaceful trading times were often interrupted by incursions into Puget Sound of fierce northern Indians who came down from British Columbia to plunder and to capture women and children to enslave. Closer to home, intertribal petty warfare was responsible for promoting Seattle into a leadership role among tidewater peoples in fights against natives of the Green and White rivers to the east of the early settlement of Seattle. Leadership traits that the chief exhibited in these conflicts led to his hegemony over lands near the Seattle settlement at the mouth of the Duwamish River, a Puget Sound effluent.

Seattle's friendliness to whites continued into the mid-nineteenth century as settlers discovered the natural advantages of Puget Sound. Among the chief's early friendships were those formed with white leaders Arthur Denny and Dr. David Maynard. Seattle had also formed an acquaintance with Washington's territorial governor and superintendent of Indian Affairs, Isaac I. Stevens. In January 1855 he again met Stevens and his delegation at the Point Elliott treaty council held near present-day Mukilteo, Washington, with tribesmen of the central Puget Sound.

As the council opened, Seattle sat at the front row with three other important chiefs: Patkanin of the Snoqualmies and allied tribes, Chow-its-hoot of the Lummis and allied tribes, and Goliah of the Skagits and allied tribes. U.S. government policy at the time was to incorporate tribes under individual leaders to facilitate the treaty-making process. Some indication of the importance of Seattle and these other leaders was the fact that over 2,000 Indians grouped under them were present in council.

Under the banner of a white flag signifying friendship with whites Seattle signed the document requesting Stevens to supply a physician to treat his people for their native diseases and maladies imported by whites. After presenting the flag to Stevens Seattle said, "Now by these we make friends and put away all bad feelings, if we ever had any." Seattle was also reported as saying in council, "We are friends of the Americans. All of the Indians are of the same mind. We look upon you as our father; we will never change our mind; as you have seen us we will always be the same. Now, now, do you send this paper of our hearts to the Great Father. That is all I have to say." Three years after the treaty signing Seattle told an Indian agent, "I am not a bad man; I want you to understand what I say: I do not drink rum . . . I am and always have been a friend to the whites . . . I do not steal, nor do any of my people."

Because of unhappiness with the treaty, certain Puget Sound "hostiles" joined by Yakima allies from east of the Cascade Mountains sought to physically prevent whites from occupying Indian lands. Seattle solidified his reputation as a friend of whites in 1856 by refusing to join the Indian faction that briefly besieged the infant white settlement in what became known as the "battle of Seattle." Not even the execution by white men (under an alien legal system) of Nisqually chief Leschi, who led his warriors against them, could persuade Seattle to abandon his friendship toward the newcomers.

With the end of the Indian wars (c. 1858) the hysteria marking the fledgling white Seattle community began to ease. Some indication that its local Duwamish Indians were no longer a threat is evidenced in cold statistics: there were approximately 1,200 Duwamish in 1780 as compared with only 162 at the time of the treaty. Seattle was aware of this declension as well as of encroachments of whites as numerous as "sands of the seashore."

Assured of their occupation of the area by treaty and victory in combat, whites could now lionize Chief Seattle. During the postwar period there was no paucity of written or spoken words lauding Chief Seattle. Typical was a flattering speech delivered on 29 October 1877 by Dr. Henry A. Smith. Playing to the hilt the picturesque oratory of native chiefs, Smith quoted Seattle as telling of a time "when our people covered the land as the waves of a wind-ruffled sea covers its shell-paved floor, but that time long since passed away with the greatness of tribes that are now but a mournful memory." With sadness but also offering assurance to whites that Indians no longer threatened the white community, Seattle said that his people were "ebbing away like a rapidly receding tide that will never return."

Despite his friendship with whites Seattle never lost his Indianness, even to the point of diplomatically defending Indian hostiles in their 1856–1857 fight with Americans in the infant white Seattle settlement. Speaking of these hostiles Seattle said, "It is the mean white men that are bad to them." He was also among the numerous Indian spokesmen who condemned the government's four-year delay in ratifying its treaties with Puget Sound chiefs. During this hiatus Seattle complained of the failure of government agents to deliver goods and services promised to his people as delineated in the treaties.

It is ironic that Seattle was given a Roman Catholic burial in his Suquamish birthplace, given the fundamental differences between whites and Indians in their views of religion and life in general. The chief did, however, express a commonality with white men about death: "Let him [the white man] be just and deal kindly with my people, for the dead are not powerless. Dead—I say? There is no death. Only a change of worlds."

Although monuments were created honoring the virtues of Seattle, perhaps a newspaperman at the eighteenth anniversary of the chief's death best expressed his legacy of friendship for those now occupying his former lands: "When the Seattles are no more, their chief will be remembered and revered for generations to come." An article in the *Seattle Post-Intelligencer*, 7 June 1866, attributed his death to the "fever and ague." Some sources, however, claim that he died of a heart attack.

• Eva G. Anderson, *Chief Seattle* (1944), is the most complete biography of the chief although it is written in fictionalized style. Clarence B. Bagley, "Chief Seattle and Angeline," *Washington Historical Quarterly* 22 (Oct. 1931): 243–75, deals more with Chief Seattle than with his daughter Angeline and is an important reference because she supplied information about her father that is not found in other sources. Edmond S. Meany, "Chief Patkanin," *Washington Historical Quarterly* 15 (July 1924): 187–98, provides interesting parallels between the Snoqualmie chief and Seattle. Murray Morgan,

Skid Road: An Informal Portrait of Seattle (1951), provides informal information about the early history of the city of Seattle with which its chief was familiar. Thomas W. Prosch, "Seattle and the Indians of Puget Sound," *Washington Historical Quarterly* 2 (July 1908): 303–8, gives information about Chief Seattle's contemporaries and disagrees with popular myths surrounding the chief. Robert H. Ruby and John A. Brown, *Indians of the Pacific Northwest* (1981), is a general history of the times in which Chief Seattle lived.

ROBERT H. RUBY

SEAWELL, Molly Elliot (12 Oct. 1860–15 Nov. 1916), novelist and short story writer, was born in Gloucester County, Virginia, the daughter of John Tyler Seawell, an attorney, and Frances Jackson. Her grandfather James Hoge Tyler was the Democratic governor of Virginia and the brother of President John Tyler. Although she spent a short period at boarding school, Seawell's school life was erratic, and much of her education took place in the library of the family plantation home, a former revolutionary war hospital called "The Shelter." Her parents kept an impressive library that included English classics and translations of Enlightenment philosophy. Reading Macaulay and Thackeray's favorable essays on the Roman Catholic church resulted in her conversion to Catholicism. In her *The Ladies Battle* (1911), Seawell reminisced that her early life "more nearly resembled the eighteenth than the nineteenth century." Upon the death of her father in her early twenties, she moved to Norfolk, Virginia, and then to Washington, D.C., where she supported her mother and sister through her writing. Eventually, Seawell became, in her words, "through literature alone, a householder, a property-owner, a taxpayer, and a regular employer of five people."

A number of Seawell's early articles and sketches appeared under various pseudonyms, including Vera Sapoukhyn. Her first successful publications, a series of stories set in Russia, appeared in *Lippincott's Magazine*. Although she used the pseudonym Foxcroft Davis to write political novels, Seawell, leery of criticism, never revealed some of her other names. An early novella, "Maid Marian" (1886), a satire on Knickerbocker New York society published in *Lippincott's*, was subsequently dramatized by Seawell and successfully presented on stage by Rosina Vokes. In 1889 her first novel, *Hale Weston*, later translated into German, achieved success. In 1896 she won a $3,000 prize in a *New York Herald* competition for her novella "The Sprightly Romance of Marsac."

After her successful 1890 short story "Little Jarvis," Seawell developed a reputation for juvenile literature. Selected from 2,000 entries, this tale of a patriotic midshipman won her a prize of $500 in a contest sponsored by the *Youth's Companion*. She went on from this success to write more naval stories, including the popular *Young Heroes of Our Navy* series (1891–1894) and "Quarter Deck and Fo'K'sl'e" (1895), using the technical knowledge of naval history and vessels that she acquired in childhood from an uncle who resigned from the U.S. Navy at the onset of the Civil War to support the Confederacy. The U.S. Naval Academy at Annapolis may have used her *Twelve Naval Captains* (1897) as a textbook.

Seawell is remembered as an antisuffragette. In 1891 her distinguished article in the *New York Critic*, "The Absence of the Creative Faculty in Woman," gained her national attention, being both praised and denigrated by writers in the United States and Europe. In 1911, by this time a popular author of six novels, she argued against woman suffrage in *The Ladies Battle*, dedicating the book to "those of my countrywomen who think for themselves." She maintained that granting women the right to vote would result in a "general revolution" and an "overturning of the social order." Although women, she argued, already "conduct the serious business of life," they lacked experience in making law and had no knowledge of commerce. A reply to Seawell, Adele Clark's *Facts vs. Fallacies*, was published by the Equal Suffrage League of Virginia in 1912.

Seawell wrote thirty-six books in all. Her more popular novels include *The History of the Lady Betty Stair* (1897), a historical romantic tale of Bourbon aristocrats in exile during the Napoleonic Wars; *Throckmorton* (1890), a romance set in post–Civil War Virginia; *A Virginia Cavalier* (1897), a biographical novel about George Washington; *The House of Egremont* (1900), set in late eighteenth-century England; and *The Whirl* (1909), which reveals Washington society's double standards.

For most of her life, Seawell wrote early in the day in the home she shared with her sister near Dupont Circle, otherwise known as Millionaires' Circle, in Washington, D.C. A socialite, she conducted a popular salon for writers and artists that included the painter William Glackens. She traveled abroad every year, using her journeys for inspiration. Seawell, who never married, died in Washington, D.C.

• See the *Diary of Molly Elliot Seawell 1900–1916* (1990). Information about Seawell can be found in E. F. Harkins and C. H. L. Johnston, *Little Pilgrimages among the Women Who Have Written Famous Books* (1901), which provides information on her childhood, daily life, and early works. The *Library of Southern Literature*, vol. 2 (1901), contains standard biographical information. See also Harkins, *Famous Authors (Women)* (1906). In addition to biographical information, *Twentieth Century Authors* (1942) provides a comprehensive list of Seawell's works.

M. CASEY DIANA

SEBASTIAN, Benjamin (c. 1745–Mar. 1834), jurist, was born in northern Virginia. Little is known of his ancestry or his upbringing prior to 1766, when he was ordained as an Anglican minister. Sebastian served for more than ten years as rector of St. Stephen's Church in Northumberland County, Virginia. His actions during the American Revolution also went unrecorded, but his three-year term as a soldier in the Virginia line earned him a military land warrant in Kentucky. Instead of returning to the clergy after the war, Sebastian chose to read law in preparation for a move to

Kentucky. The litigations created by overlapping land grants made Kentucky an inviting country for aspiring attorneys, and in 1784 Sebastian was among the earliest of pioneer lawyers.

In Kentucky Sebastian found much of the opportunity he desired. His legal practice thrived, and his prominence as an attorney soon connected him with the principal gentlemen in the Bluegrass region of the state. Along with friends and fellow lawyers, who included John Brown, Harry Innes, Caleb Wallace, and George Muter, Sebastian assumed a position of leadership in Kentucky's pre-statehood politics. In the conventions preceding Kentucky's separation from Virginia, Sebastian openly championed immediate statehood and vigorously asserted the claims of trans-Appalachian settlers for support from the new federal government. Sebastian was particularly determined to secure Kentuckians their right of navigation to the mouth of the Mississippi River, a right that the Spanish had not as yet granted and that the national government seemed all too ready to forfeit.

Behind the scenes Sebastian worked for these interests—and for his own. During the late 1780s he joined James Wilkinson in plotting to detach Kentucky from the United States. Just how much Sebastian knew about Wilkinson's secret dealings with Spanish officials in New Orleans has remained a mystery. Wilkinson repeatedly assured Spanish emissaries that Sebastian supported efforts to make Kentucky independent, but Sebastian may not have known the full extent of Wilkinson's promises, which entailed placing Kentucky under Spanish rule. Still, Sebastian clearly sympathized with Wilkinson's goal of obtaining shipping rights along the Mississippi River. He also seriously contemplated an offer to emigrate to Spanish Louisiana, an offer that included a substantial land grant in exchange for bringing settlers into the district. Eventually Sebastian accepted an annual pension that Wilkinson had convinced Spanish authorities to provide for influential Kentuckians.

With the attainment of statehood in 1792, secessionist impulses in Kentucky abated, though Sebastian maintained his correspondence with Spanish officials. Sebastian still hoped to receive a land grant, and he quietly continued to collect his annual payments from the Spanish Crown.

That year Sebastian settled into his new public responsibilities as one of three justices on Kentucky's highest court. Much of that court's business involved land litigation, a contentious field with which Sebastian was well acquainted. Those contentions peaked in 1795 in the wake of the high court's ruling in the case of *Kenton v. McConnell*. That decision, in which Sebastian and fellow justice George Muter comprised a 2 to 1 majority, threatened the land holdings of thousands of Kentuckians and sparked a legislative campaign to impeach the offending jurists. Because a two-thirds legislative majority was not obtained, Sebastian and Muter were allowed to continue in office.

That same year Spanish authorities entered into new negotiations with Sebastian. Emerging from Wilkinson's shadow, Sebastian traveled to Missouri and New Orleans to confer directly with Spanish officials about the future of the Ohio Valley. These negotiations broke off after the United States reached an agreement with Spain to open the Mississippi to American shipping.

Spanish intrigues persisted, however, with Sebastian having become a principal intermediary. In 1797 Sebastian approached his friends with offers from Spain to provide money and weapons to those who would effect Kentucky's separation from the United States. But while most of Kentucky's leaders remained opponents of Federalist rule, they were no longer prepared to secede from the federal union. Even after this rebuff, Sebastian returned to New Orleans in 1798 to conduct more talks and to receive another payment from his foreign benefactors.

Early in the nineteenth century Kentucky's Federalist minority used rumors of an ongoing "Spanish conspiracy" to accuse many of the state's Republican leaders of treason. In most cases, proof of a direct connection to the Spanish was hard to find, but Sebastian's trail was more easily recovered. His not so secretive travels together with the discovery of receipts for money from the Spanish led the Kentucky House of Representatives to appoint a committee to investigate Sebastian's conduct. Under increasing political pressure, Sebastian resigned from the bench in 1806; however, the move did not stop the legislative committee from issuing a unanimous verdict against the retired justice.

Following his resignation Sebastian retreated from public life. He moved to western Kentucky, where he operated a saw and grist mill and engaged in merchandising and land speculation. Often in financial difficulty, Sebastian was forced to ask for money from his former colleagues, not all of whom were as generous as he hoped. To the end of his life, however, he refused to implicate any of his friends in the "conspiracy" that brought him down. Sebastian had married a woman named Amelia (maiden name and year of marriage unknown), and the couple had five children. He died in Brandenburg, Kentucky.

• The Kentucky Library at Western Kentucky University holds a collection of Benjamin Sebastian papers. Other manuscript materials are widely scattered in the papers of Harry Innes at the Library of Congress, the papers of John Brown at the Filson Club in Louisville and the Kentucky Historical Society in Frankfort, and the Durrett collection at the University of Chicago. Elizabeth Warren, "Benjamin Sebastian and the Spanish Conspiracy," *Filson Club History Quarterly* 20 (Apr. 1946): 107–30, presents a brief summary of his career. For a careful dissection of Sebastian's role in the "Spanish Conspiracy," see Patricia Watlington, *The Partisan Spirit: Kentucky Politics, 1779–1792* (1972).

STEPHEN ARON

SECCOMB, John (25 Apr. 1708–29 Oct. 1792), Congregational minister and celebrated rhymester, was born in Medford, Massachusetts, the son of Hannah Willis and Peter Seccomb, a merchant. Seccomb attended Harvard College, where he was an unremarkable student who distinguished himself chiefly by his ability to write mock-heroic epics celebrating familiar and homely subjects. The best known of these concerned the college sweeper, Matthew Abdy. First published as "Father Abdy's Will" in the *Weekly Rehearsal* in January 1732, it enjoyed more than a century of popularity in both America and England, and a musical version was published as late as 1850.

Ministry offered a more stable vocation than rhyming, however, and in 1733, after some hesitation, Seccomb was ordained over the newly gathered church in Harvard, Massachusetts. His marriage that year to Mercy Williams, granddaughter of the controversial Puritan patriarch Solomon Stoddard and daughter of the Reverend William Williams, connected Seccomb to both power and wealth in the Massachusetts Congregational establishment. By popular account, his father-in-law's money subsidized the grand mansion Seccomb built for his bride as well as the couple's second home on a nearby island. The minister was a popular host to other local clergy and was well known for lavish entertainment. The manse was a popular local attraction for a century.

Neither Seccomb's relationship with his wife nor with his church was untroubled, however. The initial problems appear to have been largely personal. Tradition suggests that a youthful episode of infidelity with a servant girl, an offense for which Seccomb formally if somewhat ambiguously repented, caused his reputation to suffer, and some townspeople sought his dismissal. Theologically, at least, Seccomb was relatively liberal, supporting the Halfway Covenant of 1662, which altered strict church membership requirements, and agreeing to eliminate both written and verbal evidence of conversion. Both minister and congregation supported the Great Awakening during the 1740s and even hosted itinerant preacher George Whitefield in 1745. This "New Light" stance did little to enhance Seccomb's popularity with his ministerial colleagues in the local Marlborough Association, most of whose members were "Old Light" critics of the revival. For her part, Mercy Seccomb withstood her husband's various indiscretions and eccentricities, despite occasional public outbursts and a reputation for being somewhat odd herself. They had at least five children.

Seccomb's pastorate survived the Great Awakening, but in 1757, for reasons that remain unclear, he was dismissed from the Harvard pulpit. His new settlement, a frontier outpost in Chester, Nova Scotia, was a significant departure for any socially well-positioned minister and a radical change from the comfort and grand style of his earlier parish. For the next twenty years Seccomb supplied the pulpit of Mather's Congregational Church, named for the famous clerical dynasty of Boston. Like many ministerial families on the northern frontier, the Seccombs acquired land outside of town and eked out a marginal existence by farming as well as preaching. Nevertheless, their lives were difficult and spartan. Periodically Seccomb received charitable donations from the Provincial Assembly of Nova Scotia as well as supplies from his occasional trips to visit friends and preach in Boston.

With the outbreak of the American Revolution, the expatriate Seccomb preached publicly on behalf of a rebel victory, and he was promptly charged with promoting sedition and fined 500 pounds. Although he was forbidden to preach unless he recanted, no record that he ever did so exists. He continued to preach even after his formal retirement in 1784, presiding successfully over a lively, merged body of Congregationalists and Baptists. Disagreement over the proper requirement for church membership prevented Seccomb from formally uniting with his own flock, yet another departure from typical Congregational practice. Nevertheless, at his death in Chester, he was widely eulogized and hailed as the "father" of all the churches in the vicinity.

• Several of Seccomb's sermons and a brief diary are in the Nova Scotia Historical Society. A broadside edition and a partial bibliography of "Father Abdy's Will" are in the *Collections of the Massachusetts Historical Society*, vol. 75. The most complete biographical account is in Clifford K. Shipton, *Sibley's Harvard Graduates*, vol. 8 (1951).

ELIZABETH NORDBECK

SECCOMBE, Joseph (14 June 1706–15 Sept. 1760), minister and author, was born in Boston, Massachusetts, the son of John Seccombe, an innkeeper, and Mehitable Simmons. Despite the poverty of his parents, young Joseph distinguished himself as an intelligent youth with prospects for success in academia. His fellow members of the Old South Congregational Church of Boston supported the majority of his education, which extended from grammar school to Harvard. If the testimony Seccombe offered in his only published poem, a pastoral elegy titled "On the Death of the Reverend Benjamin Colman" (1747), is authentic, Colman served as an additional contributor to Seccombe's education. Assuming the identity of Tyro, "a young student at the Academy [Harvard]," Seccombe states that this young student was "supported there, by the Doctor's Influence and Bounty."

After graduating from Harvard with the class of 1731 (M.A. 1734), Seccombe embarked on a brief career as a missionary among the Native Americans of the Massachusetts Bay Colony. As a missionary, Seccombe, along with two others, was commissioned to teach the Native Americans to read the Bible in English, to write in English, and to learn the rudiments of math. This already onerous task became complicated by the fact that many of the Native Americans had already been converted to Catholicism by Jesuit priests. Seccombe and his compatriots were recalled to Boston and ordained on 12 December 1733. This ordination ceremony was attended by crowds of people who celebrated Seccombe and his colleagues as heroes returned from trials and tribulations among the natives. The Reverend Joseph Sewall, a grandson of Samuel Sewall, the diarist and judge at the Salem witch trials,

preached the ordination sermon. The events surrounding the mission of these three young ministers attracted much attention on both sides of the Atlantic. About Seccombe's involvement in particular, no less a figure than the English poet and hymnodist Isaac Watts was moved to comment: "I must own I know not what to say about his [Seccombe's] continuance, since he must contend at once with heathenism and popery."

By August 1737 Seccombe was ready to answer a call from a congregation in the New Hampshire town of Kingston. The following year he married Mary Thuriel; they had no children. Seccombe and his wife ministered successfully to the Kingston community for the rest of his life. His reputation, however, rests primarily upon his writings.

While Seccombe's principal biographer, Clifford K. Shipton, has remarked of Seccombe's "On the Death of Benjamin Colman" that "all that can be said for the author is that he had read English poetry" (Shipton, p. 94), the poem does not so much show a familiarity with "English poetry" as it does an affinity for the classical pastoral elegy, or more specifically for Vergil's fifth eclogue (on Daphnis). The fact that an American author would want to write a pastoral elegy in 1747, a time when this genre was virtually dead in Britain, is certainly remarkable. When one knows, moreover, that well over a dozen pastoral elegies were written by American authors on American subjects between the years 1725 and 1784, one must call this preoccupation truly worth investigating.

Some of Seccombe's expressions, such as "rustick Cotts," "Helconian [sic] streams," and "Rills divinely fair," are redolent of Vergilian pastoral. While the use of dialogue is common among Vergil's eclogues, the character's names who participate in Seccombe's dialogue are not common to pastoral. Neither do these names derive from English poetry. Tyro, for example, comes from the medieval Latin word for a beginner or novice in any given field; Tyro's identification as a "young student" is certainly appropriate. Not deriving from Latin but from early Renaissance Italian for a young and attractive shepherdess keeping sheep, "Pastorella" of Seccombe's poem does indeed serve as a shepherdess with a flock, perhaps a thin veneer for a pious spiritual adviser to certain members of Colman's "flock" of Congregationalists. While the name "Clericanor" is obviously a combination of clerk or churchman and singer, naming the poet-clergyman of the poem "Eusebius" calls up the father of Church history (c. the third and fourth centuries C.E.). This wide range of intellectual thought, from Vergilian and Renaissance pastoral to patristics, characterizes Seccombe's only extant poem and describes his better-known prose as well.

During his lifetime, Seccombe allowed seven of his sermons to appear in print, and an eighth was published two years after his death. It is noteworthy that of the eight homilies, only two, *A Plain and Brief Rehearsal of the Operations of Christ as God* (1740) and *Reflections on Hypocrisy* (n.d.), are clearly sermons. The remaining six prose tracts read more like "treatises" or nonfiction essays about how one can and should pursue a life of comfortable pleasure, for in Seccombe's view the "Ways of Pleasure and the Paths of Peace" lead to wisdom. One of those paths to wisdom is the use of the imagination, which was an unpopular notion during the first half of the eighteenth century. Viewing the imagination as largely a suspect faculty of the mind, the British poet Alexander Pope called it "dangerous." During the high point of the evangelistic Great Awakening—a time when enthusiasm, fueled by allegedly overactive imaginations, was causing quite a stir among the Colonial clergy—Seccombe wrote *Some Occasional Thoughts on the Influence of the Spirit with Seasonable Cautions against Mistakes and Abuses* (1742). Contrary to Jonathan Edwards—who insisted in many of his published works, especially *A Treatise Concerning the Religious Affections* (1746), that only a "sanctified" imagination, one constantly instructed by the gift of God's grace, could be relied upon—Seccombe contends in his tract that "the Divine Spirit, striving with man, would operate on the *Imagination*" (p. 9). Seccombe does not demand that the imagination be sanctified; rather, he goes on to declare the imagination to be a "very useful and powerful Faculty." He is clearly on the road toward a secular aesthetic, and his modest performance predicts the more ambitious exploration of the limits of imagination in America by such poets as Phillis Wheatley in her "On Imagination" (1773) and other poems.

In Seccombe's opinion, the best, most wholesome manner by which one may achieve peace and wisdom is to pursue the art of angling. Indeed, his most significant contribution to American culture resides in the fact that he is the first writer to celebrate in print the "virtues" of sport, especially those of fishing. While Seccombe scatters throughout his prose warm reflections on the leisure of sport, moving him at one point to say of recreation and exercise of the body that "the Soul . . . must have Suspensions from her more abstracted Pursuits," the tract *Business and Diversion Inoffensive to God, and Necessary for the Comfort and Support of Human Society . . . in the Fishing Season* (1743) most particularly develops Seccombe's thoughts on the value of angling. Quoting on the title page from Izaak Walton's *The Compleat Angler*, Seccombe places his essay within the tradition of sport writing. For the duration of this tract, the author appropriately adopts the name "Fluviatulis Piscator" (Fisher of the waterway). Not stopping with Walton, Seccombe quotes many other sources—from the Bible's Gospel of John ("Simon Peter saith unto them, I go a Fishing") to Thomas Burnet's *Sacred Theory of the Earth*—to prove his argument that fishing, even on Sundays, is "very friendly to Religion."

Along with allusions to these authors one can find within Seccombe's prose urbane and learned but unobtrusive references to such ancient figures as Jerome, Ambrose, Tertullian, Livy, and Herodotus, as well as to more recent thinkers such as Pierre de Charron and John Locke. During a period marked by a sharp decline in Puritan austerity despite the effects of the Great Awakening, the members of Seccombe's congregation and those among his readership apparently found his easy, cosmopolitan counsel regarding how one should make the best of leisure a delectable alternative. It is not difficult to grasp why those who knew of his work concerning "the good life"—a life in full accord with the auspices of an approving Deity—desired to place it before a wider readership. Indeed, Seccombe's life and career provide a valuable corrective to a somewhat jaundiced view of eighteenth-century American culture, a time punctuated by religious enthusiasm and severe social mores. For, unperturbed, we observe this gentleman minister trusting the aesthetic power of his imagination and taking up his fishing pole. Seccombe died in Kingston.

• Some material on Seccombe still in manuscript form is included among the Colman manuscripts housed by the Massachusetts Historical Society and in Sibley's Letters Received in the Harvard University Archives. Much of Seccombe's correspondence with such figures as Benjamin Colman is located in Colonial American newspapers such as the *Boston News-Letter*, the *New-England Weekly Journal*, and the *New Hampshire Gazette*, as well as in the *Proceedings of the Massachusetts Historical Society*. The most detailed biography is by Clifford K. Shipton in *Sibley's Harvard Graduates: Biographical Sketches of Those Who Attended Harvard College in the Classes 1731–1735*, vol. 9. Information is also available in William B. Sprague, *Annals of the Pulpit*, vol. 1 (1856), and James A. Levernier and Douglas R. Wilmes, eds., *American Writers before 1800: A Biographical and Critical Dictionary*, vol. 3 (1983).

JOHN C. SHIELDS

SEDDON, James Alexander (13 July 1815–19 Aug. 1880), congressman and Confederate secretary of war, was born in Fredericksburg, Stafford County, Virginia, the son of Thomas Seddon, a banker and merchant, and Susan Pearson. Spending much of his youth with an uncle, Seddon attended local academies and received private tutoring. His family's large library enabled him to pursue his interest in reading. He managed his father's properties in Virginia and studied law under Arthur A. Morison, a relative and local attorney. In 1834 Seddon spent nearly six months in Mississippi and Louisiana, where the climate helped his frail health. Thereafter he periodically returned to spend several winters in Louisiana, tending to his investments in sugar.

After returning to Virginia in 1834, Seddon enrolled in the law school of the University of Virginia, from which he graduated in 1835 with honors. His speaking ability earned him the campus honor of "first orator." In 1838 he began his practice in Richmond, where he associated with George W. Good. Their firm soon achieved a good reputation throughout the state. In 1845 Seddon married Sarah Bruce; they had nine children. Their mansion on Clay Street in Richmond, the scene of much social activity, later functioned as the White House of the Confederacy.

By 1840 Seddon was already interested in politics. An ardent follower of John C. Calhoun of South Carolina and a strong advocate of the theory of states' rights, he opposed the Whig party. Although not a delegate to the Democratic National Convention in Baltimore in 1844, he promoted the nomination of James K. Polk for president. That same year Seddon was elected to the U.S. House of Representatives, serving from 1845 to 1847. Because of his ill health and political disagreements with the local nominating convention, he did not seek a second term in 1846. Two years later he was again elected to the House, successfully running against John M. Botts and Charles C. Lee. In 1848 Seddon endorsed the presidential campaign of Democrat Lewis Cass of Michigan.

Seddon's second term in the House of Representatives lasted from 1849 to 1851. An active debater and forceful leader, he became known as a congressional defender of states' rights. He was a southern expansionist who favored the annexation of Texas and dreamed of Caribbean acquisitions. Even at this early date he secretly hoped for secession and the creation of a separate southern republic. An extremist, Seddon sided with the South on all positions relating to the Compromise of 1850 and scorned the final agreement as injurious to the South.

Upon retiring from Congress in 1851, Seddon returned to Virginia. He lived the life of a prosperous planter in Goochland County, where he acquired land and owned a moderate number of slaves. His new home, "Sabot Hill," a 26-room estate overlooking the James River, was the scene of many social events and private political conversations. But Seddon was never far removed from politics. As relations between North and South deteriorated in the turbulent 1850s, his views on southern nationalism deepened considerably. In 1856 he attended the Democratic National Convention in Cincinnati, but he refused the vice presidential nomination on the ticket headed by James Buchanan of Pennsylvania. He would have added geographical balance to the ticket and southern support. At that time, however, he was a planter and preferred a behind-the-scenes political life at home to a powerless office in Washington. Infrequently in the public arena in the 1850s, he nevertheless remained a powerful spokesman for southern interests.

During the secession crisis, Seddon joined former president John Tyler and other leaders as appointed commissioners to the Washington Peace Convention to try to resolve differences. Seddon assumed an active role in the deliberations. Placed on the Committee on Rules and Resolutions, he issued a minority report recommending amendments to the U.S. Constitution that had been introduced in the U.S. Senate by John J. Crittenden of Kentucky. Seddon included an additional article that expressly recognized the right of peaceful secession if a state wished to withdraw from the Union. In addition, he suggested partitioning power in the Senate between North and South. A secessionist spokesman, Seddon opposed the convention's final plan for compromise.

Attending the Spontaneous People's Convention, held in Virginia after the firing on Fort Sumter, Seddon addressed the gathering and strongly supported the secession of Virginia, which occurred on 17 April 1861. Seddon was delighted; his dream of an independent nation had at last been realized. He promised northern invaders "hospitable graves . . . six feet to each . . . and a few inches more to their leader, if he were taller" (*Daily Wilmington Herald*, 8 Mar. 1861). In June he was selected as a member of the Virginia delegation to the Confederate Provisional Congress in Montgomery, Alabama. In 1862 he unsuccessfully sought election to a seat in the Confederate House of Representatives that later convened in Richmond. This failure hurt him personally. Had his health permitted, he would have enlisted in the Confederate army to fight the war on the battlefields.

Upon the resignation of George Wythe Randolph, the Confederate secretary of war, in November 1862, President Jefferson Davis sought a capable replacement. Davis, who had long maintained close and friendly relations with Seddon, asked him to assume the position. Seddon accepted and entered the Davis cabinet on 20 November 1862. Devoted and intelligent, he brought certain strengths to his new post, including a sound knowledge of politics, administrative ability, numerous friends, and the trust of the president. On the other hand, Seddon lacked experience in military affairs. Moreover, a slightly neurotic, semi-invalid, and dyspeptic man, he was not in the best of health. In fact, his poor health gave him an emaciated and cadaverous appearance. But he commanded Davis's confidence, at least in the beginning.

As secretary of war, Seddon used tact in dealing with the egocentric Davis. Seddon, who entertained no political ambitions, concerned himself with recruiting, strategy, provisioning, and munitioning. The secretary delegated authority to his subordinates in the War Department, at first giving the assistant secretary, John A. Campbell, wide latitude and responsibilities. Seddon relied firmly on the Conscription Act, and the Confederate army attained its maximum strength in numbers during his time in office. His enforcement of conscription led to a disagreement with Governor Joseph E. Brown of Georgia, who claimed that the principle of state sovereignty prevented the general government from conscripting the citizens of any state. Seddon's relations with General Robert E. Lee were better. Working closely with Lee, Seddon encouraged him to take the offensive by invading the North, and the Gettysburg campaign in 1863 met with the secretary's approval. He also clearly saw the West as a vulnerable area for the Confederacy. He steadfastly refused to recognize African Americans as soldiers.

Seddon exerted considerable influence over President Davis until the fall of Vicksburg in 1863. Thereafter the tide was turning against the Confederacy. Seddon's military blunders cost him crucial support, and he procrastinated over bothersome administrative details. Some members of the Confederate Congress criticized his conduct. Growing pessimistic over the military situation by 1865 and hurt by the incessant attacks of his critics, he longed for the serenity of Sabot Hill. When conditions for the South worsened in early 1865, Virginia's delegates to the Confederate Congress requested that Davis shuffle and reorganize his cabinet in the hope of restoring public confidence. Although the Virginian was not singled out, a piqued Seddon immediately took their suggestion as a personal affront and an attack on his integrity. On 5 February 1865 he resigned his position, which he had held longer than any other Confederate secretary of war. He was replaced by John C. Breckinridge, former vice president of the United States. After denouncing the Confederate Congress for what he considered unconstitutional interference with his administration, Davis dispatched a cordial letter to Seddon praising him for his services.

Torn by despair and neuralgia, Seddon retired to his country estate in Virginia a broken man. For the next two months he watched the final collapse of the Confederacy. Its defeat absolutely crushed him. He never fully recovered from the debacle, blaming himself for its demise and seeing his life as a failure. He remained at Sabot Hill and took the oath of amnesty on 20 May. Three days later he was suddenly arrested by order of U.S. secretary of war Edwin M. Stanton and confined in Libby Prison. On 5 June Seddon arrived at Fort Pulaski, Georgia, where he was incarcerated with other former Confederate leaders. His imprisonment was a devastating experience that further contributed to his physical decline.

Released from prison in December 1865, when he took the oath of allegiance to the United States, Seddon returned to Sabot Hill. He attempted to rebuild his life and restore his property, some of which Union troops had burned in the Kilpatrick-Dahlgren raid to Richmond (1864). He engaged in agricultural activities associated with his plantations in Virginia and Louisiana and also resumed his law practice in Goochland County. Seddon did not write his memoirs and burned most of his papers to prevent their possible seizure by the Radical Republicans in the U.S. Congress. His health continued to deteriorate as the physical pain and mental anguish took their toll. He died at Sabot Hill in Virginia.

A Virginia aristocrat and fascinating conversationalist, Seddon was a man of dedication and will. He left his mark on southern history. Lee and Seddon were President Davis's most trusted military advisers, and the three men worked closely together. A former secretary of war during the administration of President Franklin Pierce, Davis controlled the southern armies and took a strong interest in the conduct of the War Department, scrutinizing Seddon's activities more than those of other cabinet officials. Seddon never publicly criticized this vigilance and always deferred to his superior. Still Seddon's influence with Davis was apparent. Seddon viewed the Civil War in large terms, emerging as a Confederate nationalist rather than as a proponent of narrow states' rights. Along with Judah P. Benjamin and Stephen R. Mallory, Seddon was one of the ablest men in Davis's cabinet.

• Seddon's papers are in the Seddon Family Papers at the Virginia Historical Society in Richmond. Some of his papers are in the Confederate States of America Papers at Duke University Library in Durham, N.C. The New-York Historical Society in New York City holds twenty-four items relating to Seddon and the Civil War. Others are in the manuscript collections of his contemporaries, including those of Jefferson Davis at the Mississippi Department of Archives and History in Jackson. Seddon's speeches are in the *Congressional Globe* from 1845 to 1847 and from 1849 to 1851. The major work on Seddon is Gerald F. J. O'Brien, "James A. Seddon: Statesman of the Old South" (Ph.D. diss., Univ. of Maryland, 1963). An article is Roy W. Curry, "James A. Seddon: A Southern Prototype," *Virginia Magazine of History and Biography* 63 (1955): 123–50. Material relating to Seddon is in Henry T. Shanks, *The Secession Movement in Virginia, 1847–1861* (1934); Charles H. Ambler, ed., "Correspondence of Robert M. T. Hunter, 1826–1876," in *Annual Report of the American Historical Association for the Year 1916* (1918); *The War of the Rebellion: A Compilation of the Official Records of the Union and Confederate Armies* (128 vols., 1880–1901); Paul D. Escott, *After Secession: Jefferson Davis and the Failure of Confederate Nationalism* (1978); Hudson Strode, *Jefferson Davis* (3 vols., 1955–1964); and Edward Younger, ed., *Inside the Confederate Government: The Diary of Robert Garlick Hill Kean* (1957). Obituaries are in the *New York Times* and the *Richmond Daily Dispatch*, 20 Aug. 1880.

LEONARD SCHLUP

SEDGWICK, Anne Douglas (28 Mar. 1873–19 July 1935), fiction writer, was born in Englewood, New Jersey, the daughter of George Stanley Sedgwick and Mary Douglas. She lived in New York City until age nine, when she accompanied her parents to England to live near relatives. Except for brief visits to the United States as an adult and two years of girlhood spent at her grandmother's home in Ohio, Sedgwick lived in England and France her entire life. When she was eighteen, she went with her family to Paris and studied drawing at the Académie Julian and under the French artist Amanjean. She married English author Basil de Sélincourt in 1908 and lived with him in Oxfordshire, England. They had no children. In 1931 she was elected to the National Institute of Arts and Letters.

Sedgwick published seventeen novels and two collections of short stories between 1898 and 1930. Her most notable works include the novels *Tante* (1911), *Adrienne Toner* (1922), and *The Little French Girl* (1924), which was popular in the United States and Europe. She also published two collections of short stories, *The Nest* (1912) and *Christmas Roses* (1920). *Dark Hester*, a novel published in 1929, was presented as a play in London in 1931. In part because of failing health and in part because her depictions of upper-middle-class social conventions had passed out of vogue, she stopped writing in 1930 after her last novel, *Philippa*, was published.

The international theme of the contrast between English society and American individualism or between English and French social conventions was the central concern of all of Sedgwick's fiction. Even though she lived in the United States for a shorter period than either Henry James or Edith Wharton, concludes Martin Day in the *History of American Literature* (1970), she upheld the sacredness of individualism against the enervating pull of European social conventions even more than they (pp. 253–54).

In an autobiographical sketch contributed to the *New York Times* (28 Jan. 1912), Sedgwick credited her emphasis on American traditions and preferences to her family life. Although she had always thought of herself as a painter rather than a writer, she began her literary career by telling long stories to her sisters. These stories then grew into novels, the first of which was a love story, *The Dull Miss Archinard* (1898). She stated that she tended to choose "funny Americans" for her characters because "any novelist interested in international contrasts and clashes will understand that these are the types who still embody the racy, primitive flavor (no, alas, they tell me fading) who give one one's telling opposition."

Louis Kronenberger, in a *New York Times* book review (31 Mar. 1929) of *Dark Hester*, celebrated Sedgwick's workmanship as "superb": "It is put together masterfully, symphonically . . . There is an economy, a smoothness, an effectiveness which would put most contemporary writers to shame. And there is a surface of realism which is pointed, exciting, direct; a psychology of situation, a command over manners, which amount to far more than technique." Yet he acknowledged that for the "extreme modernist" of his time, Sedgwick's work and themes were already outdated: "Her scheme of life has not in the most vital sense lasted into the present; and though she valiantly copes with the present, she seems to come a day too late. The manners which she, like Mrs. Wharton, has observed and understood so profoundly, are labels of a past generation; and though they still exist, fighting to the last ditch for survival, they have begun to assume a historical importance and to appear obsolescent."

Also of historical importance is a collection of Sedgwick's letters, dated from 1898 to 1935, posthumously compiled and edited by her husband in 1936. This collection gives a broad sense of Sedgwick's life and interests. Especially intriguing is her account of reading her contemporaries and near-contemporaries: Fyodor Dostoyevsky, Aldous Huxley, Henry and William James (with whom she corresponded), and Wharton. About Henry James, she wrote, "He is afraid of America. I don't know him at all (except one meeting when I thought him very dear), but he always seems to me, through his books, like a person who has always been too afraid of ugliness. I don't believe he has ever taken any risks in his life, or ever lived out dangerously into the world." About Wharton, "All that exquisite erudition dazes me; I don't suppose she is much older than I am, five or at most ten years—and yet what achievement!"

When Sedgwick traveled to Massachusetts and New York in 1902, she found that Americans supposed her to be typically English, yet she felt that in her temperament and point of view she was far more American than English. Shaped by the tastes and interests of Edwardian English society, she was especially fond of

philosophy, reading Josiah Royce, Thomas Hill Green, the neo-Hegelians, Plato, and, of course, William James—she felt her two visits with him to be the most valued experiences of her trips to America. Russian novelists—Tolstoy first and then Dostoyevsky—were her favorites, and Henry James, despite her criticism of "the decadent milieu he depicts so constantly," was her favorite American author.

Although her works tend to depict upper-middle-class society, neither Sedgwick nor her family could be considered well-to-do. She may have "slipped into professional writing almost by accident," as she describes in her 1912 *New York Times* autobiographical sketch, but throughout her career earning money for her writing was a primary concern, and her letters frequently describe depending on the next book to maintain her house and furnishings.

Although her writing has not been widely read since the early 1930s, Anne Douglas Sedgwick should be remembered as a woman who documented the styles and themes of her time during a period of rapid social changes.

Sedgwick died in Hampstead, England.

• A short biographical entry on Sedgwick and critiques of "Daffodils," in *Christmas Roses* (1920), and *Adrienne Toner* (1922) appears in Martin S. Day, *History of American Literature: From the Beginning to 1910* (1970). In addition to the works listed above, Sedgwick published *The Confounding of Camelia* (1899), *The Rescue* (1902), *Paths of Judgment* (1904), *The Shadow of Life* (1906), *A Fountain Sealed* (1907), *Amabel Channice* (1908), *Franklin Winslow Kane* (1910), *The Encounter* (1914), *A Childhood in Brittany 80 Years Ago* (1919), *The Third Window* (1920), and *The Old Countess* (1927). An obituary is in the *New York Times*, 22 July 1935.

MARGUERITE CULVER-JAMIESON

SEDGWICK, Catharine Maria (28 Dec. 1789–31 July 1867), author, was born in Stockbridge, Massachusetts, the daughter of Pamela Dwight and Theodore Sedgwick (1746–1813). Her father had worked his way up from poverty to fortune and respectability in the fields of law and politics. He served several terms in both the U.S. House of Representatives and the Senate and was chosen Speaker of the House during the administration of George Washington. A staunch Hamiltonian Federalist, he embodied the kind of aristocratic values that Catharine would rebel against with the rise of Jacksonian democracy. At the same time, his abolitionist sentiments helped foster her commitment to a variety of reforms, including antislavery, education reform, women's rights, and prison reform.

Catharine Sedgwick's childhood was spent mainly in the family mansion in Stockbridge, which remained her principal residence throughout her life. As a girl she also lived for short periods in Albany and Boston, as the family followed her father's political peregrinations. Though comfortable, her childhood was far from ideal: her mother suffered long bouts of depression, and her father was away for extended periods pursuing his political activities. Catharine's formal education was haphazard; she attended local district schools in Stockbridge and, briefly, two select schools for young women: Mrs. Bell's in Albany and Mr. Payne's in Boston. But her principal education came as a result of her position as a receptive daughter in an intellectual environment: her father often spent evenings reading to her from Shakespeare, Hume, Cervantes, and other classic authors.

In Stockbridge Catharine Sedgwick was exposed to the rigid Hopkinsian Calvinism of the Reverend Samuel West. It was largely in reaction to West's gloomy teachings that she wrote her first novel, *A New-England Tale* (1822), in which she sharply satirized Calvinism, endorsing such liberal religious tenets as God's benevolence and human perfectibility. The novel features a virtuous orphan, Jane Elton, who suffers at the hands of a grimly religious aunt but finally is rewarded with marriage and security. Although the novel outraged orthodox readers, it established Sedgwick as a skilled novelist of New England scenes and manners. She joined the Unitarian Society in New York in 1821.

Sedgwick's next novel, *Redwood* (1824), satirized aristocrats and endorsed humanitarian democracy. In the novel, the upper-class southerner Henry Redwood and his daughter Caroline have a carriage accident while traveling in Vermont and are invited by a farming family to stay with them. The vain and snobbish Caroline is taught a lesson in humility when a wealthy man intended for her chooses instead the lowly but kind Ellen Bruce, who turns out to be Henry Redwood's daughter from a youthful marriage to a servant. *Redwood* was reviewed enthusiastically and translated into five languages.

Sedgwick's growing reputation was consolidated with the publication of *Hope Leslie* (1827), the finest novel about Puritan times published before Hawthorne's *Scarlet Letter. Hope Leslie* describes a group of colonists in Springfield, Massachusetts, and their interactions with the Indians. Two of the colonists, Everell Fletcher and Faith Leslie, are taken captive by a Pequod tribe led by the sachem Mononotto. In a climactic scene, Fletcher is about to be killed by a tomahawk when the sachem's daughter, Magawisca, rescues him and loses her arm in the process. Faith Leslie remains among the Indians, one of whom she marries. Her sister, Hope, becomes the heroine of the second half of the novel, in which she rescues Magawisca, who has been unjustly imprisoned by the villainous Sir Philip Gardiner. *Hope Leslie* is Sedgwick's most interesting novel because of its spirited heroines, its tight narrative structure, and its daring treatment of miscegenation.

While Sedgwick was at work on her next novel, *Clarence*, she suffered tragedies in the death of her sister Elizabeth and the mental collapse of her brother Henry. By the late 1820s Sedgwick was spending part of each year with her brother Robert in New York and the rest in Lenox and Stockbridge with two other brothers and their families. When *Clarence* appeared in 1830, it was widely read, though today it seems one of her weakest efforts. It contains predictable devices

such as an attempted seduction, an abduction, and a conventionally happy ending. After writing a number of tales in the early 1830s, Sedgwick produced *The Linwoods* (1835), a revolutionary-war novel centering on the relationship between the Linwoods, a Tory family in New York, and the Lees, a Republican family in New England. In this novel Sedgwick continued her attacks on both aristocracy and Calvinism, extolling a new social order based on egalitarianism and liberal religion.

Her major novel-writing phase behind her, Sedgwick wrote a trilogy of didactic tales for laborers and children: *Home* (1835), *The Poor Rich Man and the Rich Poor Man* (1836), and *Live and Let Live* (1837). These didactic works, which championed domesticity and good manners, were Sedgwick's most popular books. Minimizing the complexities of urban poverty, they suggested that economic hardship could be compensated for by simple adherence to Christian values.

Sedgwick was an active member of the literary and artistic circles of New York and the Berkshires. She was a longtime friend of the poet William Cullen Bryant and the Shakespearean actress Fanny Kemble. Visitors to the Sedgwick home in Stockbridge included Herman Melville, Nathaniel Hawthorne, William Ellery Channing (1818–1901), Fredrika Bremer, and Washington Irving. In addition to a number of children's tales and a travel book, she produced one more novel, *Married or Single?* (1857). Although the novel was intended as a defense of staying single (reflecting Sedgwick's own situation), its heroine—like all of Sedgwick's other heroines—is happily married in the end. Sedgwick was notably ambivalent on women's issues. She drew high praise from Margaret Fuller as an example of the clearheaded, independent woman writer. She was capable of creating spirited heroines, and she denounced the common prejudice against "old maids." On the other hand, nowhere does Sedgwick question the conventional notion that marriage is the highest state for women. Indeed, while she never married, she consistently endorsed the institution of marriage in her writings.

By 1857 Sedgwick was the only surviving member of her immediate family. Her last book, *Memoir of Joseph Curtis* (1858), was a nonfictional sketch of a Massachusetts lawyer who is held up as a "model man" because of his moral rectitude. By the end of the Civil War her health was failing, and she moved into a niece's house outside Boston. She died there.

In her lifetime Sedgwick's fiction attracted considerable attention from the reading public and from such contemporaries as Ralph Waldo Emerson, Edgar Allan Poe, Irving, and Melville. Hawthorne called her "our most truthful novelist." She was among the first internationally known American writers. Although her reputation began to fade toward the end of her life, it was revived in the early 1950s, when Alexander Cowie featured her in *The Rise of the American Novel.* Scholars since Cowie have noted her faults—sentimentality, triteness, undeveloped characters—but also have brought attention to her very real strengths: the local-color realism of her New England vignettes; her daring treatment of miscegenation and liberal religion; and her occasional success, especially in *Hope Leslie*, in fashioning rounded heroines. Along with her contemporary, James Fenimore Cooper, Sedgwick was a pioneer in the use of American characters and settings in fiction. Her didactic works, emphasizing home and Christian values, were early examples of the domestic novel, a genre popularized in the 1850s by Susan Warner and Maria Susanna Cummins. Although Sedgwick's sales figures did not approach those of the latter authors, her fiction was, in general, better crafted.

• In addition to the works discussed in this article, Catharine Sedgwick's published writings include two collections of short stories, *Tales and Sketches* (1835), *Tales and Sketches: Second Series* (1844); the travel book *Letters from Abroad to Kindred at Home* (1841); and the children's books *The Travellers* (1825), *The Deformed Boy* (1826), *A Love-token for Children* (1838), *The Morals of Manners* (1846), *Facts and Fancies for School-day Reading* (1848), and *The Boy of Mount Rhigi* (1848).

A collection of Sedgwick's letters is at the Massachusetts Historical Society Library in Boston. An obituary by George William Curtis appeared in *Harper's New Monthly Magazine* 35 (Oct. 1867): 665. Her unfinished autobiography is included as part of *Life and Letters of Catharine Maria Sedgwick* (1871), edited by Mary Dewey. A chronology of her life and a set of annotated bibliographies can be found in Edward Halsey Foster, *Catharine Maria Sedgwick* (1974). See also Alexander Cowie, *The Rise of the American Novel* (1951); Richard Banus Gidez, "A Study of the Works of Catharine Maria Sedgwick" (Ph.D. diss., Ohio State Univ., 1958); David S. Reynolds, *Faith in Fiction: The Emergence of Religious Literature in America* (1981) and *Beneath the American Renaissance: The Subversive Imagination in the Age of Emerson and Melville* (1988); Adelheid Staehelin-Wackernagel, *The Puritan Settler in the American Novel before the Civil War* (1961); Sister Mary Michael Welsh, *Catharine Maria Sedgwick: Her Position in the Literature and Thought of Her Time Up to 1860* (1937); and Michael Davitt Bell, "History and Romance Convention in Catharine Sedgwick's *Hope Leslie*," *American Quarterly* 22 (Summer 1970): 213–21.

DAVID S. REYNOLDS

SEDGWICK, Ellery (27 Feb. 1872–21 Apr. 1960), magazine editor, was born in New York City, the son of Henrietta Ellery and Henry Dwight Sedgwick, a lawyer. After private boarding school, he graduated from the exclusive Groton School in Groton, Connecticut, in 1890, then from Harvard University in 1894. For the next two years Sedgwick taught Latin and English at Groton, then he briefly took up reporting for the *Worcester (Mass.) Gazette*. In 1896 he entered magazine journalism as an assistant editor at the *Youth's Companion*.

In 1900 Sedgwick moved to *Frank Leslie's Popular Monthly*, a national circulation leader, as editor. Here, from 1900 to 1906 Sedgwick began to develop his reputation as a discerning editor with an eye for wit, erudition, and humor. He published Stephen Crane, H. L. Mencken, and the feminist satirist Marietta Holley, as well as Sewell Ford, novelist and short-story writer; Samuel Merwin, a writer of popular fiction; and Frank R. Stockton, known for his 1882 short story "The Lady or the Tiger?"

Under Sedgwick the magazine (renamed *Leslie's Monthly* in 1904, the *American Illustrated Magazine* in 1905, and later that year, the *American*) offered distinguished coverage of public affairs. Although *Leslie's* was not really a muckraker like so many of its contemporaries, historian Louis Filler cites Sedgwick's significant impact on government legislation through his prominent publicizing of railroad safety violations in *Leslie's* pages in 1903.

The following year Sedgwick married Mabel Cabot; they had four children. He also worked as editor of *Appleton's Booklovers Magazine*, and after leaving the *American* in 1906 he was employed a year at *McClure's Magazine*, a muckraking leader, and then briefly as a book editor for D. Appleton and Company. After 1909 his chief focus was the *Atlantic Monthly*; he also edited briefly at *Living Age* (1919) and *House Beautiful* (1922).

Sedgwick bought the nationally prominent but down-on-its-luck *Atlantic* in 1908 for $50,000. With only about 10,000 subscribers and annually running about $5,000 in the red, the *Atlantic* needed fresh ideas and innovation. It got just this from Sedgwick, who found in the magazine the most absorbing challenge of his career. By 1921 his efforts, which included adding substantial political, economic, and social coverage, had attracted a modern generation of readers surpassing 100,000. In 1922 the *New York Times Book Review* stated, "There is no use arguing the question—the *Atlantic Monthly* is not the staid magazine that refreshed our grandfathers. It has grown lively during recent years."

Sedgwick gently masterminded the *Atlantic's* shift from its emphasis on belles lettres to more hard-hitting coverage of contemporary affairs. According to Frederick Lewis Allen, who worked with Sedgwick, the editor "resolved that the *Atlantic* should face the whole of life, its riddles, its adventures; the critical questions of the day, the problems of the human heart; and that no subject should be taboo if only it were discussed with urbanity." This editorial courage extended to religious topics, a noteworthy stance during the era of the sensational Scopes "monkey trial," in which religious fundamentalists attempted to quash the teaching of evolution. Sedgwick's many wellsprings of story ideas for the *Atlantic* included his daily perusal of newspapers such as the *New York Times* and the *Times* of London as well as his extensive correspondence and conversations with intellectuals, writers, and public officials. For advice on important editorial matters he also relied on a close circle of friends including Supreme Court justice Felix Frankfurter; international financier Thomas S. Lamont; Newton D. Baker, President Woodrow Wilson's secretary of war; and journalist Walter Lippmann.

Occasionally Sedgwick exercised vigorous editorial leadership on the day's most controversial issues. For instance, in 1927 he published articles that directly addressed the issue of the public's prejudice against presidential candidate Alfred E. Smith's Roman Catholicism. Under Sedgwick the *Atlantic* published other distinctive, influential pieces on contemporary social and political issues. These include Frankfurter's essay on the Nicola Sacco and Bartolomeo Vanzetti case (Mar. 1927) and Rear Admiral William S. Sims's sharp critique of the politics of navy promotions (Sept. 1935).

Sedgwick also preserved the *Atlantic*'s tradition of publishing strong literary fiction and poetry, making it the first American commercial magazine to publish an Ernest Hemingway short story ("Fifty Grand," July 1927).

Sedgwick also published writers such as H. G. Wells, Gertrude Stein, Jessamyn West, Eudora Welty, Louis Auchincloss, Randolph Bourne, and Robert Frost (although he once rejected some of Frost's verse with a note that stated, "We are sorry but at the moment the *Atlantic* has no place for vigorous verse"). Although some of Amy Lowell's poetry appeared in the *Atlantic*, the 1912–1925 correspondence between Sedgwick and the poet shows that the editor sometimes did not fully fathom the meaning or value of Lowell's work. As Ellery Sedgwick III observed, the editor was an "aesthetic conservative," while Lowell was the opposite.

In 1939 Sedgwick sold the *Atlantic* for a handsome profit; he maintained that he was not stepping down because of his split with his staff over his controversial support of General Francisco Franco during the Spanish Civil War. Thereafter he wrote book reviews and reminiscences. *The Happy Profession*, his 1946 autobiography, is a revealing account of his years at the *Atlantic*. For example, he wrote that "it has never occurred to me to change the colophon of the *Atlantic* to a distaff, and I have taken conscious pains that a preponderance of its contributors should be masculine." He added, "My friend [Edward] Bok [editor of *Ladies' Home Journal*] pointed out that I was sinning against the light of the cashbox, but I took comfort in the monthly comment of the historian, William Roscoe Thayer, who invariably commented: 'I see the men are still ahead in this month's *Atlantic*.'"

After Mabel Cabot Sedgwick died in 1937, Sedgwick married Isabel Marjorie Russell in 1939. They had no children. He spent his last years on a large estate in Beverly, Massachusetts, and he often lived in Washington, D.C., during the winters. He died in Washington.

• Sedgwick's papers are at the Massachusetts Historical Society in Boston. Information on Sedgwick can be found in Frederick Lewis Allen, "Sedgwick and the *Atlantic*," *Outlook and Independent*, 26 Dec. 1928, pp. 1406–8, 1417; Edward E. Chielens, ed., *American Literary Magazines: The Eighteenth and Nineteenth Centuries* (1986); Don E. Fehrenbacher, "Lincoln's Lost Love Letters," *American Heritage* 32 (1981): 70–80; Louis Filler, *Crusaders for American Liberalism* (1939); Gerald Gross, ed., *Editors on Editing* (1962); H. L. Mencken, *Letters of H. L. Mencken*, ed. Guy J. Forgue (1981); Ellery Sedgwick, ed., *Atlantic Harvest: Memoirs of the "Atlantic"* (1947); Ellery Sedgwick [III], *The "Atlantic Monthly," 1857–1909: Yankee Humanism at High Tide and Ebb* (1994); Ellery Sedgwick III, "'Fireworks': Amy Lowell and the *Atlantic Monthly*," *New England Quarterly* 51 (Dec. 1978): 489–508; Ellery Sedgwick III, "HLM, Ellery Sedgwick, and the First World War," *Menckeniana: A Quarterly Review* 68 (Winter 1978): 1–4; and Henry L. Shattuck, "Ellery Sedgwick," *Massachusetts Historical Society Proceedings 1957–60*, pp. 72, 395–96. Obituaries are in the *New York Times* and the *Boston Globe*, both 22 Apr. 1960, and the *Atlantic*, June 1960.

NANCY L. ROBERTS

SEDGWICK, John (13 Sept. 1813–9 May 1864), Union army general, was born in Cornwall Hollow in the Connecticut Berkshires, the son of Benjamin Sedgwick and Olive Collins, farmers. Sedgwick spent his boyhood on the family farm, received a portion of his early education at Sharon Academy, and taught in the rural schools. Sedgwick's grandfather served as an officer in the Revolution, a legacy that perhaps influenced young John to seek an appointment to the U.S. Military Academy. He graduated from West Point in 1837, finishing twenty-fourth in a class of fifty, and commenced a lifelong army career.

Lieutenant Sedgwick entered the artillery and saw duty in the Seminole War. He won brevet promotions to captain and major in Mexico in service under Generals Winfield Scott and Zachary Taylor. In 1855 Sedgwick left the artillery and became major of the newly authorized First Cavalry. He participated in various campaigns against the American Indians on the Plains, but in 1860, his career having stalled, Sedgwick considered retiring to his home in Cornwall Hollow. The rugged frontier army life had lost much of its charm for the 47-year-old bachelor.

The secession crisis persuaded Sedgwick to remain in the army. He was promoted to lieutenant colonel of the Second Cavalry in March, and later, when the ranking officers of the First Cavalry, Robert E. Lee and William J. Hardee, resigned to join the Confederacy, Sedgwick assumed command of his old unit. In June he journeyed to Washington and helped supervise the Washington defenses. A severe illness, perhaps cholera, prevented him from taking the field at Bull Run (Manassas) in July. In August the War Department finally assigned Sedgwick to command of an infantry brigade with the rank of brigadier general of volunteers.

Sedgwick owed his rising prominence to the new general in chief, Major General George B. McClellan (1826–1885). McClellan liked the genial, stocky, bearded officer, whose soldiers affectionately called him "Uncle John," and he appointed Sedgwick to divisional command in February 1862. Sedgwick shared McClellan's Democratic politics and repaid his superior's confidence with steadfast loyalty.

During the Peninsula Campaign in the spring of 1862, Sedgwick quickly distinguished himself as a combat leader assigned to the Second Corps of the Army of the Potomac. On 31 May, during a crisis at the battle of Fair Oaks, his division crossed an unstable bridge and rescued a portion of the army south of the Chickahominy River. Fire from his men felled the Confederate commander, General Joseph E. Johnston. Sedgwick's division fought with competence at Savage Station on 29 June and at White Oak Swamp and Glendale the following day. Sedgwick suffered two slight wounds at Glendale and the loss of his warhorse, Tom, but remained in the field. The army rewarded him for his performance on the Peninsula and at the Seven Days battles with a promotion to major general of volunteers to date from 4 July.

When McClellan again assumed command of the Union army around Washington, D.C., in September, he tapped Sedgwick to lead the newly designated Twelfth Corps. Sedgwick declined, however, retaining his divisional post. A few days later, at the battle of Antietam, he experienced the second worst day of his Civil War career. Obeying the orders of his impetuous corps commander, Major General Edwin V. Sumner, Sedgwick's division carelessly entered the West Woods at midmorning on 17 September and suffered more than 2,200 casualties in twenty minutes. Wounded in the leg, wrist, and shoulder, Sedgwick was carried unconscious from the field. He recuperated under the care of his sister in Cornwall Hollow and returned to the army at Falmouth, Virginia, on 22 December. He temporarily commanded the Second Corps and the Ninth Corps during the next six weeks.

In January 1863 Sedgwick's West Point classmate Major General Joseph Hooker assumed command of the Army of the Potomac and named Sedgwick to command the Sixth Corps. Sedgwick played an independent role during the Chancellorsville campaign, occupying Confederate forces at Fredericksburg while Hooker's main wing swept west around Lee's left flank. While Hooker experienced a bitter defeat at Chancellorsville, Sedgwick won a brilliant if minor victory at Fredericksburg on 3 May. He squandered his advantage, however, by moving west too slowly to strike Lee's rear while leaving a viable enemy in his own rear. The Confederates met Sedgwick's advance at Salem Church, repulsed stubborn Union assaults, and drove the Sixth Corps back across the Rappahannock River the following day. Hooker unfairly blamed Sedgwick for the campaign's failure, but Sedgwick's tentative performance did rob the Federals of a chance to redeem Hooker's own incompetent generalship.

As might be expected, Sedgwick shed no tears when Major General George G. Meade replaced Hooker as army commander in late June, although some observers thought Sedgwick coveted the position himself. Through no fault of its own, the Sixth Corps played a reserve role at the battle of Gettysburg, and Sedgwick could not distinguish himself in the army's greatest victory. Sedgwick led the pursuit of Lee following the battle, and his excessive caution reflected Meade's own leadership. During quiet periods in the fall of 1863, Meade trusted Sedgwick with army command while visiting Washington or conducting other business. Sedgwick presided over the successful operation at Rappahannock Station on 7 November and served

as a wing commander at the aborted Mine Run campaign later in the month.

Sedgwick's politics earned him no rewards. He employed McClellan's brother, Major Arthur McClellan, on his staff and promoted an effort to present "Little Mac" with a testimonial from the army in the fall of 1863. Secretary of War Edwin M. Stanton wanted Sedgwick removed from corps command in the winter of 1864, as he was not pleased with Sedgwick's support of McClellan or his Democratic politics, but Meade shielded his subordinate from such political maneuvers. Meade did agree to a scheme that would have placed Sedgwick at the head of Union forces in the Shenandoah Valley in the spring of 1864, but Abraham Lincoln opted to name a political figure, Major General Franz Sigel, to the post, sparing Uncle John for continued service with the Sixth Corps.

At the Wilderness, Sedgwick saw his right flank turned toward the end of the engagement, a potential disaster mitigated by the weakness of the Confederate attack, gathering darkness, and Sedgwick's own efforts to rally his men. The following night the armies moved toward Spotsylvania Court House, where on 8 May the Sixth Corps fought fiercely, and Sedgwick was struck by a spent ball. The next day a Confederate sharpshooter using a Whitworth rifle shot Sedgwick below the left eye, killing him almost instantly. Moments before his fatal wounding, Sedgwick reassured nervous infantrymen that the enemy "couldn't hit an elephant from that distance." Sedgwick was the highest ranking Union officer to be killed during the Civil War.

Ulysses S. Grant pronounced Sedgwick's demise to be a tragedy worse "than the loss of a whole division of troops," an odd statement based on Sedgwick's mediocre performance in the Wilderness. His men mourned the popular Sedgwick, whose generous issuance of favors to the troops, unpretentious demeanor, and personal bravery had earned him a tender spot in their hearts. Historians have generally shared this positive view. Bruce Catton characterized him as "solid, always cool and unruffled . . . [and] the canniest and most deeply beloved of the army's higher officers." Other writers describe him as "highly competent and steadfast." Sedgwick's modest military achievements, when added to his winning personality and combat death, account for such a lofty historical reputation. An enduring tradition at the U.S. Military Academy asserts that academically deficient cadets who twirl the rowels on the spurs of the Sedgwick monument after hours will excel on upcoming exams.

• The John Sedgwick Collection at the Cornwall Public Library in Cornwall, Conn., contains the largest accumulation of his papers. *Correspondence of John Sedgwick Major-General* (1902–1903), printed for Carl and Ellen Battelle Stoeckel, is the best published collection of the general's writing. Richard Elliott Winslow III, *General John Sedgwick, the Story of a Union Corps Commander* (1982), is the only full-length biography, but it concentrates almost exclusively on his Civil War career. Thomas W. Hyde, *Following the Greek Cross; or, Memories of the Sixth Army Corps* (1895; repr. 1988), contains much anecdotal material on Sedgwick. His Civil War record is documented in *The War of the Rebellion: A Compilation of the Official Records of the Union and Confederate Armies* (128 vols., 1880–1901). Sedgwick's chief of staff in the Sixth Corps, Colonel Martin T. McMahon, authored four useful articles about his superior, including the best account of Sedgwick's death, which appears in *Battles and Leaders of the Civil War*, vol. 4, ed. Robert U. Johnson and Clarence C. Buel (1888; repr. 1956).

A. WILSON GREENE

SEDGWICK, Theodore (9 May 1746–24 Jan. 1813), legislator and judge, was born in Hartford, Connecticut, the son of Benjamin Sedgwick, a storekeeper and farmer, and Ann Thompson. After moving the family to Cornwall, Connecticut, Sedgwick's father died in 1757, leaving Theodore to be raised in modest circumstances by his mother and older brother John, a farmer and tavernkeeper. Showing early promise, Theodore entered Yale in the winter of 1761–1762. Dismissed three years later for some unrecorded breach of college rules, he received his degree for his earlier work in 1772 as of 1765.

After a brief flirtation with a career in the ministry, Sedgwick studied law for a year in Great Barrington, Massachusetts. He opened a law office there and was admitted to the Massachusetts bar in 1766. Having moved to nearby Sheffield, Massachusetts, in 1767 and quickly prospering, in 1768 he married Elizabeth Mason. His wife died three years later of smallpox, said to have been contracted from her husband after he left quarantine for the disease. They had had no children. In 1774 Sedgwick married Pamela Dwight, daughter of Joseph Dwight and the former Abigail Williams, thus linking himself to two of the most influential families in western Massachusetts. The couple had ten children, of whom eight lived to maturity, among them Theodore Sedgwick, Jr., a Jacksonian politician, and Catherine Maria Sedgwick, a novelist.

Sedgwick commenced his public career in 1773 as author of the Sheffield Resolves, among the earliest declarations of grievances against Great Britain issued by a colonial town meeting. A year later he served as one of two Sheffield delegates to the Berkshire provincial congress, one of a number of such regional gatherings called to protest the abrogation of the Massachusetts Charter and the Intolerable Acts, and helped draft its resolutions, which called for the nonconsumption and nonimportation of British goods. Hoping, like most, to prevent a break with Britain, he later fully accepted independence when it came.

As major in the Continental army, Sedgwick served in the failed American invasion of Canada, following this tour with brief service at the battle of White Plains in 1776. Subsequently he acted only in civilian capacities. Between 1775 and 1778 he was a commissioner of supply for the northern department of the Continental army—purchasing, requisitioning, and shipping supplies to its forces.

As the war in New England wound down, Sedgwick turned back to state affairs. He was elected in 1780 as Sheffield's representative to the first state house of representatives under the new Massachusetts Constitution of 1780. Reelected annually through 1783, he was sent from Berkshire County to the state senate in 1784 and 1785. He resigned the next year, only again to accept election from 1787 through 1789 to the state house, serving as Speaker in 1788. In 1784 the Massachusetts legislature, or General Court, appointed Sedgwick chief of four commissioners to negotiate a settlement of the state's disputed border with New York State. Their efforts failing, the dispute was finally settled by the Confederation Congress in 1788. In opposing those who had championed a new state constitution that would, they believed, better protect the people's rights, and in representing as attorney the region's peaceable Loyalists, he began to be found most often on the side of property rights and "public order."

In 1785 Sedgwick returned to national service when he was elected by the General Court to a one-year term as one of five Massachusetts representatives to the Confederation Congress; he was returned for two additional terms beginning in 1787. Although a firm sectionalist, he nevertheless characterized himself, with typical sharpness of word, as "greatly pained at the stupid apathy of the united states" (Welch, p. 35). While favoring a national impost, he balked at amending the Articles of Confederation and opposed the Annapolis Convention of 1786. However, the outbreak in 1786 of Shays's Rebellion, in his own western Massachusetts, brought him to favor a strengthened national government.

In 1786 Sedgwick represented Stockbridge, to which his family had moved that year, in the Berkshire County convention that took a firm stand against the Shaysites. He raised a voluntary armed force in late 1786 and led it into a successful skirmish against the rebels. For his aggressive opposition, the Shaysites captured and briefly held Sedgwick and threatened to destroy his house. Yet he subsequently defended his attackers before the state supreme court and sought clemency for them after their conviction.

Elected from Stockbridge to the state ratifying convention in 1788, Sedgwick led the pro-Constitution forces from western Massachusetts. Coming to support a Bill of Rights as a just price for ratification, he sat on the convention committee that drafted the amendments introduced by Massachusetts into the First Federal Congress. Massachusetts narrowly approved the new constitution, 187–168.

After five closely contested elections in which no candidate received a required majority, Sedgwick was elected congressman from Hampshire and Berkshire counties to the First Federal Congress. For the next decade he led efforts to create a Federalist Party organization in western Massachusetts. A staunch, orthodox Federalist, he denounced Democratic-Republican societies as "illicit combinations" (Welch, p. 131) and championed appropriations to implement the Jay Treaty. He was so effective as Alexander Hamilton's chief lieutenant in the House that President George Washington offered him the Treasury secretaryship after Hamilton's resignation in 1795, an appointment that Sedgwick declined.

Elected in 1796 by the General Court to fill the Senate seat vacated by Caleb Strong, Sedgwick backed the presidential candidacy of John Adams. He supported the new president in his efforts to negotiate a solution to outstanding issues with France and, when these failed, urged defensive measures and a declaration of war against the continental power. Thus, when Adams named a peace mission to France in 1799, Sedgwick broke with the president, a break occasioned in part by Adams's rejection of Sedgwick's 1798 request for appointment to the Supreme Court vacancy caused by the death of Associate Justice James Wilson. Although Sedgwick acceded to the Convention of 1800, which brought a cessation of hostilities between France and the United States, Adams never forgave him for his attacks on the peace effort.

In the Senate, Sedgwick wrote an early draft of the Alien Friends Act and warmly backed the infamous Alien Enemies and Sedition Acts. Upon passage in 1798 of the Virginia Resolution, which condemned these measures, Sedgwick urged sending troops to Virginia's borders to intimidate the state into backing down. When his Senate term expired in 1799, Sedgwick was elected again to the House, where he became Speaker in the first fully partisan competition for that post. As Speaker he cast the tie-breaking vote for passage of the nation's first bankruptcy act in 1800.

Frustrated by his estrangement from Adams, Sedgwick spent most of his time as Speaker maneuvering to deny the president renomination and reelection. After joining with others in the unsuccessful promotion of Charles Cotesworth Pinckney's nomination as Federalist candidate in place of Adams, he worked privately to arrange that Pinckney, who was nominated to be vice president, receive more votes in the electoral college than Adams—an effort that split the party. After this endeavor failed, he backed Aaron Burr in the disputed election of 1800, in which the choice between Burr and Thomas Jefferson fell to the House of Representatives because of an electoral vote tie. In 1801, to Sedgwick's chagrin, he had to announce Jefferson's election from the Speaker's chair.

Increasingly alienated from politics and soured on the nation's future, Sedgwick refused to seek reelection to the House in 1800. Instead, he accepted appointment in 1802 as associate justice of the Massachusetts Supreme Judicial Court and served until his death. Sedgwick's claim to service on one of the nation's most illustrious benches owed as much to his eminence as attorney as to his political ideology and stature. As a lawyer, he is recalled chiefly for his successful defense in 1783 of Elizabeth Freeman (known as Mumbet) against efforts of the slavemaster from whom she had fled to reclaim her. Sedgwick based his case on the Massachusetts Constitution of 1780, which declared all men to be "born free and equal." He not only won the freedom of the woman who would become nurse to his children and die in his house, but, with others arguing similar cases by 1800, effectively

eradicated slavery in Massachusetts by denying constitutional protection to the reenslavement of runaways. While when in Congress he was the major force behind passage of the first fugitive slave law, which he justified as a legitimate protection of property, he also defended the rights of Quakers to petition for the abolition of slavery and was a member of the Pennsylvania Abolition Society from 1802 until his death.

On the bench, Sedgwick led efforts to reform court behavior and gain the publication (begun in 1805) of state court decisions. He failed, however, in an effort to overhaul the state's appellate structure and establish a separate court of equity. Embittered in 1806 by the appointment of Theophilus Parsons rather than himself to succeed Francis Dana as chief justice, Sedgwick gave up championing court reform.

His second wife died in 1807 after some years of mental instability, and Sedgwick married again in 1808, this time to Penelope Russell. The recipient of honorary doctorates from the College of New Jersey in Princeton (1799) and Harvard (1810), and an original trustee of Williams College, Sedgwick died in Boston.

A self-made man, among the most talented and influential, if most deeply conservative, Federalists of the first generation of national political leaders, Sedgwick was constant in his opposition to the democratization of politics and society brought on by the very Revolution and Constitution he had supported. Always controversial, often indiscreet, he went to his death, as did his party, believing that "the aristocracy of virtue is destroyed" (Welch, p. 240). Yet Sedgwick's stern elitism and regional particularism remained alive in New England's continuing contest with the slaveholding South and in the antislavery jurisprudence that he helped create.

• The Massachusetts Historical Society possesses the principal collection of Sedgwick papers, including those of both Theodore Sedgwick and his extensive family. Additional letters are located throughout the public papers of the many political figures, especially Federalists, with whom Sedgwick was in correspondence throughout his life. The fullest study of Sedgwick is Richard E. Welch, Jr., *Theodore Sedgwick, Federalist: A Political Portrait* (1965). For information on an important part of his judicial career, consult Welch's "The Parsons Sedgwick Feud and the Reform of the Massachusetts Judiciary," *Essex Institute Historical Collections* 92 (1956): 171–87. The political world in which Sedgwick moved is examined in James M. Banner, Jr., *To the Hartford Convention: The Federalists and the Origins of Party Politics in Massachusetts, 1789–1815* (1969). On Sedgwick's role in weakening slavery in Massachusetts, see Arthur Zilversmit, "Quok Walker, Mumbet, and the Abolition of Slavery in Massachusetts," *William and Mary Quarterly*, 3d ser., 25 (1968): 614–24, and Welch, "Mumbet and Judge Sedgwick," *Boston Bar Journal* 8 (1964): 12–19.

JAMES M. BANNER, JR.

SEDGWICK, Theodore (27 Jan. 1811–8 Dec. 1859), lawyer and legal theorist, was born in Albany, New York, the son of Theodore Sedgwick, Sr., a lawyer and author, and Susan Anne Livingston. After attending public schools in New York City and Stockbridge,

Massachusetts, he matriculated at Columbia University, from which he was graduated in 1829. He then studied law, for a time at Harvard and also as an attorney's apprentice, and in 1833 was admitted to the New York bar. That same year he was appointed as an attaché to Edward Livingston, U.S. ambassador to France. While in Paris Sedgwick met French statesman Alexis de Tocqueville, who became his close friend. After returning to New York in 1834, Sedgwick began to practice law. The following year he married Sarah Morgan Ashburner, whose family also was from Stockbridge; they would have seven children, three of whom died in infancy.

Sedgwick became active in politics as a conservative or National Democrat, and his "practical" approach to politics led him to take a moderate stand on slavery. He worked closely with legal reformer David Dudley Field, notably at the New York Constitutional Convention of 1846, the delegates of which voted to create a single court having general jurisdiction over both law and equity, to simplify judicial procedure, and to abolish the apprenticeship requirements for admission to the bar. Sedgwick wrote extensively on legal, judicial, and political subjects. A progressive in the Jeffersonian sense of the term, he nonetheless opposed some later democratic reforms, in particular, the popular election of judges, which he feared would inject partisanship into the judicial process. He also argued for certain checks on popular sovereignty, writing in *U.S. Magazine and Democratic Review* in 1843 that "the constitutional check" on tyranny and corruption "is the only one which people voluntarily assume, and is the only one known, that is based upon a liberal representation of the popular will." In addition, he served from 1848 to 1850 as the librarian of the Law Institution of the City of New York, the oldest subscription law library in New York City.

Sedgwick built a substantial legal practice in New York but was plagued by chronic ill health, and in 1850 he ceased to practice. He spent much of 1851–1852 traveling in Western Europe and then returned to New York, where he became president in 1852 of the recently established Association for the Exhibition of the Industry of all Nations, known informally as the Crystal Palace Association. The Crystal Palace Exhibition of 1853–1854, modeled after the London Exhibition of 1851, was the first international exposition (world's fair) held in the United States. Although it was a financial failure, the exposition helped New York City by attracting tourists and stimulating business, and it benefited the entire nation by symbolizing America's new place in the world, both industrially and politically.

Sedgwick's most important legal publication was *A Treatise on the Measure of Damages; or, An Inquiry into the Principles Which Govern the Amount of Compensation Recovered in Suits at Law* (1847; 2d ed., 1852; 3d ed., 1858), a scholarly as well as practical work. Based on Sedgwick's compilation of English and American statutory and case law and, to some extent, Roman, French, and other civil law jurisprudence on the topic,

the treatise stated and then explained the principles of each division of the law of damages. It was praised for its accuracy and for providing a coherent system for the awarding of damages, then a new area of the law. Particularly important was Sedgwick's treatment of strict liability, the concept that holds that a person who participates in certain types of activities is to be held responsible for any harm that results to others, despite the person's use of utmost care and caution. Sedgwick's general principle, stated in the third edition of his treatise, was that, with some exceptions, the motives of the breaching party are irrelevant to determining damages. The principle was introduced primarily to explain why only compensatory damages—payment for losses actually incurred—and not punitive damages—an award designed to penalize the defendant—are allowed in contract cases. Ordinarily, punitive damages are recoverable only when the breach of contract is shown to be willful, wanton, or malicious. Punitive damages are available, however, if the plaintiff can sue on the basis that an injury or wrong committed against his person or property—a tort—was the result of a bad faith breach. In cases where a loss was aggravated by circumstances of violence, oppression, malice, fraud, or wanton and wicked conduct, a plaintiff can be awarded damages over and above what would barely compensate him for his actual loss(es). Such awards are intended to provide solace to the plaintiff for mental anguish or other aggravations of the original wrong, to punish the defendant, or to make an example out of him. Sedgwick justified his position regarding the consideration of motive in determining damages primarily on the ground that it was necessary to maintain the distinction between contract and tort causes of action. He expressed reservations about the concept of strict liability but based his viewpoint on the law as it existed at that time. It was only in the eighth edition of the treatise that his son Arthur G. Sedgwick, who continued the work, believed that the law had changed significantly enough to justify substantial changes in the text.

Whereas Sedgwick strongly supported the concept of punitive damages, Harvard law professor Simon Greenleaf opposed it, asserting that punitive damages had no doctrinal basis in the American legal tradition and that they constituted a de facto form of compensation. Sedgwick criticized Greenleaf's position for ignoring the well-recognized social functions performed by punitive damages, which, he argued, serve as both punishment and warning in cases of "oppression, brutality or insult in the infliction of a wrong" and thus set an effective example for the community. The Greenleaf-Sedgwick debate continued for several decades, but by the turn of the century, the concept of punitive damages was well established in the United States.

Sedgwick's influential treatise on statutory interpretation, *A Treatise on the Rules Which Govern the Interpretation and Application of Statutory and Constitutional Law*, was published in 1857; a second edition, with additional notes by John Norton Pomeroy, was published in 1874. In it, Sedgwick discussed the danger of ambiguity in law, an unavoidable problem resulting from the uncertainties inherent in language: "The imperfection of language is a serious evil when it occurs in those legislative commands on which the repose, discipline, and well being of society depend." This second treatise provided a theory of interpretation that dealt with the entire Constitution to that time. At least partly with the intention of limiting judicial discretion, Sedgwick proposed a set of general rules to be applied when interpreting the constitutional limits of legislative authority.

Sometime after the Crystal Palace Exhibition, Sedgwick retired to Stockbridge, where his health began to improve. In 1858, having earlier declined the posts of minister to the Netherlands and assistant secretary of state, Sedgwick accepted the position of U.S. district attorney of the southern district of New York. Beginning the next year, his illness made him unable to take an active role in the duties of that department, which fell to his assistants, but he served in that capacity until his death, of neuralgia, at Stockbridge.

• Sedgwick's correspondence as president of the Crystal Palace Association is in the New-York Historical Society. His other papers are held with the Sedgwick family papers at the Massachusetts Historical Society and in various collections at the New-York Historical Society. Transcripts of Sedgwick's letters to his son Arthur and Arthur's unpublished biographical memoirs of his father are at the New York Public Library. Sedgwick contributed largely to *Harper's Monthly* and *Harper's Weekly* and, under the pseudonym Veto, to the *New York Post*. He also published a biography of his great-grandfather, *A Memoir of the Life of William Livingston* (1833). His other writings include: *What Is Monopoly?* (1835); *A Statement of Facts in Relation to the Delays and Arrears of Business in the Court of Chancery of the State of New York* (1838); *Review of the Memoirs of the Life of Sir Samuel Romilly* (1841); *Constitutional Reform* (1843), a collection of articles previously published in the *Albany Democratic Reformer*; *Thoughts on the Proposed Annexation of Texas to the United States* (1844), a series of articles in opposition to the measure previously published in the *New York Post*; and *The American Citizen* (1847), an address given at Union College. Sedgwick also edited *A Collection of the Political Writings of William Leggett* (1840). Leggett, a prominent political writer who died in 1839, had addressed some of the leading issues of his day, including slavery and controversy surrounding the Bank of the United States. Henry D. Sedgwick, *The Sedgwicks of Berkshire*, vol. 3 of Berkshire Historical and Social Sciences Collections (1900), and Benjamin W. Dwight, *The History of the Descendants of John Dwight of Dedham Massachusetts*, vol. 2 (1874), pp. 744–45, contain important biographical information. Obituaries are in *Harpers Weekly*, 31 Dec. 1859; *Solicitors' Journal and Reporter* (London), 14 Jan. 1860; the *New York Daily Tribune*, 10 Dec. 1859; and the *New York Evening Post*, 9 Dec. 1859.

CHRISTOPHER ANGLIM

SEDGWICK, William Thompson (29 Dec. 1855–21 Jan. 1921), biologist and educator, was born in West Hartford, Connecticut, the son of William Sedgwick and Anne Thompson. His father died when Sedgwick was eight, but despite attendant obstacles he completed his schooling. He graduated from Yale's Sheffield Scientific School in 1877 and immediately enrolled in the Yale School of Medicine. Two years later he accepted a fellowship to study physiology at Johns Hopkins University under Henry Newell Martin, intending to return to medicine the following year. When the academic spirit and challenge of laboratory science whetted his interest in biology he changed his plans, remaining at Hopkins to complete the Ph.D. in 1881 and spending two additional years there as associate in biology. He married Mary Katrine Rice of New Haven; they had no children.

Sedgwick accepted a position as assistant professor of biology at the Massachusetts Institute of Technology (MIT) in 1883. President Francis A. Walker invited him to "open out" his "specialty," assuring him that in two years he would head a large department "with an opportunity for almost indefinite expansion" (Sedgwick papers, Yale). Promoted to associate professor in 1884 and to professor in 1891, he remained a stalwart member of the MIT faculty until his death.

Sedgwick's academic career followed an unusually smooth trajectory and reflected his commitment to broaden the intellectual parameters of scientific education at MIT and to align biological science with public service. The biology laboratory he established was an innovation in an engineering college, justified as preparatory to medical education before most medical schools instituted such requirements. In addition to biology, an array of courses in comparative physiology, anthropology, and the history of natural science encouraged a spirit of inquiry. Under Sedgwick's guidance, sanitary science (public health) was soon the mainstay of a new curriculum; as postbaccalaureate scientific education became crucial for technical specialization, Sedgwick's appointment as consulting biologist to the Massachusetts State Board of Health in 1888 opened unique research opportunities at the Lawrence Experiment Station and other sites. Sedgwick's students went on to become spokesmen for standards of safe drinking water at the turn of the century, and experts whose understanding of the bacteriology and epidemiology of waterborne disease helped resolve costly interurban conflicts involving water sources. In 1913 he joined two colleagues from Harvard to establish the Harvard-Technology School of Public Health, the first academic program designed specifically to train public health professionals. He served as chair of its administrative board until 1921.

Throughout his academic career Sedgwick served local, state, and federal public health agencies, reinforcing links between science and public policy. His investigative research established the epidemiologic techniques for tracing the origins of typhoid outbreaks, despite ambiguous bacteriologic and clinical evidence. When Congress considered reorganizing the U.S. Public Health Service in 1910, Sedgwick proposed that a better-informed staff would emphasize laboratory and engineering sciences rather than medicine. At the same time he cautioned President Taft against heeding the expansive administrative proposals of "enthusiasts" and "recent converts to public health" rather than the experienced voice of the surgeon general. Sedgwick was also sensitive to the potential for misplaced faith in sanitary measures; although he vigorously advocated pasteurization, he distinguished between safety and quality, urging that food inspectors not condemn products of lower quality that could be sold at lower prices.

Late in his career Sedgwick recalled that while in medical school he had been dismayed to learn that everything important was already known or else too difficult to study (Jordan, p. 14). Once established in his own research, he vigorously opposed this perspective, training bacteriologists and sanitary engineers for university classrooms, laboratories, and health departments all over the United States. Sedgwick and his personally selected faculty introduced Thomas Huxley's books on education and biology to give a broad foundation to the study of sanitary science, and they instructed students in the practical implications of organic evolution. Sedgwick transformed his basic lecture course into a pioneering text, *Principles of Sanitary Science and the Public Health* (1902), which emphasized "the significance of the actions, reactions and interactions which necessarily go on between organisms and their environments" (pp. 67–68). A leader in situating biology at the center of twentieth-century public health, Sedgwick was a founding member of the Society of American Bacteriologists and the Laboratory Section of the American Public Health Association; he was a member of the Massachusetts Public Health Council, the Advisory Board of the U.S. Public Health Service, and the International Health Board of the Rockefeller Foundation. He was nonetheless modest in advancing the claims of his own field, cautioning, "The application of many results of experimental science to the welfare of man, extensive and valuable though they are, must still wait until their relations to everyday life become clearer" (*Principles*, p. ix).

Sedgwick was convinced that studying the history of scientific progress offered moral as well as material benefits. He published *A Short History of Science* (1917), a survey of Western civilization from antiquity to 1900 that was derived from his popular undergraduate course, as well as several other books and numerous articles of general as well as technical interest. He introduced bacteriology to lay audiences in lectures at Boston's Lowell Institute in 1893. Four years later he became permanent curator of this privately endowed public forum. He warmly supported civil service reform and women's higher education, although he and his wife opposed women's suffrage.

Age and coronary disease prevented military service in World War I, and he was dismayed at how quickly Americans lost interest in reconstruction after the Armistice. An ardent internationalist, he addressed an international congress on public health in Brussels in 1920, followed by a European tour and lectures at the universities of Cambridge and Leeds. Shortly thereafter he died from a heart attack as he walked to his Boston home during a snowstorm.

Sedgwick influenced the application of biological standards and statistical criteria to the protection of water supplies and general public health. He emphasized the authority of technical knowledge when it was sharply focused, and he personally inspired and promoted the careers of many scientists, physicians, and engineers who applied research in the biological sciences to public health. He forged valuable connections between academic life and public service that soon became routine.

• A collection of Sedgwick's letters (1878–1920) and miscellaneous papers is in the Yale University Library Manuscripts and Archives. In addition to the books cited above, Sedgwick coauthored two widely praised textbooks, *General Biology* (1886), with E. B. Wilson, and *The Human Mechanism* (1906), with Theodore Hough. E. O. Jordan, E. C. Whipple, and C. E. A. Winslow (former students) wrote a biographical memoir, *A Pioneer of Public Health, William Thompson Sedgwick* (1924), which includes a list of his publications and a partial record of his students. See also G. C. Whipple, "The Public Health Work of Professor Sedgwick," *Science*, n.s., 53 (25 Feb. 1921): 171–78. For the historical context of his career, see Barbara Gutmann Rosenkrantz, *Public Health and the State, Changing Views in Massachusetts, 1842–1936* (1972), chap. 4. Also useful is Carolyn G. Shapiro-Shapin, "'A Really Excellent Scientific Contribution': Scientific Creativity. Scientific Professionalism and the Chicago Drainage Case, 1900–1906," *Bulletin of the History of Medicine* 71 (1997): 385–411. An obituary is in the *New York Times*, 27 Jan. 1921.

BARBARA GUTMANN ROSENKRANTZ

SEDRIC, Gene (17 June 1907–3 Apr. 1963), jazz tenor saxophonist and clarinetist, was born Eugene P. (or Hall) Sedric in St. Louis, Missouri, the son of Paul Sedric, a ragtime pianist; nothing is known of his mother. Having played clarinet since at least age ten, in early 1922 he joined Charlie Creath's band at the Alamac Hotel in St. Louis and later worked on the riverboats and at other locations with the bands of Fate Marable, Dewey Jackson, and Ed Allen. A job playing in the traveling burlesque show *Black and White Revue* took him in late 1923 to New York City, where he freelanced until joining Sam Wooding's Orchestra at the Club Alabam. In May 1925 he sailed to Europe with Wooding as a member of the *Chocolate Kiddies* revue, which opened on 25 May at the Admiralspalast in Berlin. Besides Sedric, the eleven-piece band included other jazzmen such as trumpeter Tommy Ladnier, trombonist Herb Flemming, and multi-reedman Garvin Bushell. In addition to the band the show boasted more than thirty singers and dancers from the worlds of vaudeville, musical comedy, and cabaret, including future stars Adelaide Hall and Edith Wilson.

After leaving Berlin the show appeared in Hamburg, Stockholm, Copenhagen, Zurich, Barcelona, Paris, Nice, and in Moscow and Leningrad for more than two months between March and May 1926. So popular was the band that in virtually every country it visited the troupe was asked to stage command performances before royalty and heads of state. After leaving Russia the show concluded its tour in Danzig, but Wooding's band remained intact and moved on to play concerts and residencies in Turkey, Egypt, Rumania, Hungary, and other neighboring countries. In the spring of 1927 the orchestra sailed from France to Argentina for a brief South American tour before returning to New York that summer, the most widely traveled jazz-oriented orchestra in the world. Among the offers the band received in New York was one from the new Cotton Club, but because the men preferred to return to Europe, where they were treated like celebrities, Wooding turned down the December opening, which then went to the fledgling Duke Ellington Orchestra.

Sedric stayed with Wooding during the intervening period and returned to Europe in June 1928 with a band that now included Doc Cheatham and Ladnier on trumpets, trombonist Al Wynn, clarinetist Jerry Blake, and pianist Freddie Johnson. For three years the Wooding men toured Germany, France, Scandinavia, Italy, Spain, Rumania, and Turkey before finally disbanding in Belgium in the fall of 1931. After he returned to the United States, Sedric continued to work with Wooding from the summer of 1932 on. He also played for a short while with both Luis Russell and Fletcher Henderson before joining Fats Waller in 1934 as a regular member of his touring and recording band. Although he remained in that capacity until 1942, during November 1937 and the winter of 1938–1939, when Waller went on solo tours, Sedric also worked with Mezz Mezzrow's Disciples of Swing and the Don Redman Orchestra.

In late 1942 Waller decided to concentrate exclusively on solo appearances, which contributed to Sedric in March 1943 forming his own small group, which played at clubs in New York, Chicago, New Jersey, Boston, and Detroit. In late 1944, after recovering from an illness, he joined the Phil Moore Four for a short time and then, in late 1945, toured with the Hazel Scott show. Sedric left Scott in the summer of 1946 and formed another band that played relatively long engagements in New York. Starting in 1950 Sedric played clarinet frequently at the Friday night all-star jazz concerts at Stuyvesant Casino and Central Plaza, and in the spring of 1951 he joined Bobby Hackett's sextet for a residency at Lou Terrasi's. After a stint in Jimmy McPartland's band, Sedric returned to France in February 1953 to tour with Mezzrow. In August 1953 he again appeared at Central Plaza, this time with film actor–trombonist Conrad Janis, in whose band he remained on and off until late 1961, when he became too ill to continue playing. He died in New York's Goldwater Memorial Home.

Primarily because of his extended absences from New York during the mid- and late 1920s and the scarcity of new American jazz records overseas, Sedric's style on clarinet and saxophone remained rooted in the syncopations of his most formative years. Thus, although smoothly played in the conventional dance band manner, his saxophone solos on the Wooding records from 1925 through 1929, as recorded in Berlin, Barcelona, and Paris, scarcely compare with the contemporaneous work of Coleman Hawkins or Prince Robinson in the United States. Wooding wanted his orchestra to combine the best elements of Paul Whiteman and Fletcher Henderson; that is, to have the versatility to play symphonic overtures, classically arranged "American" themes, and novelty popular songs, yet also to be able to incorporate the rhythmic vitality and improvising skills of the best Afro-American hot dance music. To be sure, some of Wooding's arrangements come close to the mark of the best early big band jazz, but the majority is of the sort that most bands played to satisfy the tastes of polite society. From 1934 on Sedric participated in scores of recording sessions, most with Waller, but also several with Alex Hill, Redman, James P. Johnson, Pat Flowers, Cliff Jackson, McPartland, Janis, Louis Metcalf, and others. In 1953, as a member of Mezzrow's band in Paris, he recorded in concert with Buck Clayton and Big Chief Moore. He last appeared on record in 1961 on sessions by Dick Wellstood and Elmer Snowden.

There is no doubt that Sedric enjoyed a far better lifestyle playing in Europe during the twenties than did many of his colleagues back home. But from a strictly musical point of view, he paid a price for it. Because of Wooding's commercial obligations very little time was devoted to hot jazz, either in the form of swinging arrangements or creative solo improvisation. Similarly, in his eight years with Waller, Sedric merely served as a backdrop for the ebullient singer and pianist. Although he soloed on almost all of Waller's many recordings during the 1934–1942 period, his efforts rarely rose above the ordinary. By the same token, when he started concentrating on clarinet during the Dixieland revival of the fifties, he was at a clear disadvantage in comparison with other clarinetists who had been playing pure jazz for decades. Pee Wee Russell, Edmond Hall, Albert Nicholas, and Omer Simeon were unquestionably the preferred artists in this milieu, and Sedric had to resort to vaudevillian mugging and purposefully contrived tricks to attract the public's attention. In sum, Sedric was a reliable journeyman rather than a significant jazz stylist, one whose abilities as a showman often obscured to the public his limited gifts for creative expression.

• Much can be learned about Sedric's activities during the 1920s from the chapter on Sam Wooding in Chip Deffaa, *Voices of the Jazz Age* (1992), and from relevant sections in Albert McCarthy, *Big Band Jazz* (1974). Understandably, Sedric figures prominently in Laurie Wright, *Fats in Fact* (1992), but this is a biodiscography that tells more about the recordings he appears on than about the man himself. Also of interest is Ed Kirkeby, *Ain't Misbehavin': The Story of Fats Waller* (1966). Because Sedric was outside the course of American jazz development for most of the 1920s, his name rarely appears in general histories, while Waller was such a major figure that his sidemen, even one so long-serving as Sedric, seldom receive more than passing mention. Complete discographical listings are in Brian Rust, *Jazz Records, 1897–1942* (1982), and Walter Bruyninckx, *Traditional Jazz Dis-*

cography, 1897–1988 (6 vols., 1989) and *Swing Discography, 1920–1988* (12 vols., 1989). An abbreviated career chronology is in John Chilton, *Who's Who of Jazz* (1985).

JACK SOHMER

SEEGER, Alan (22 June 1888–4 July 1916), poet and soldier, was born in New York City, the son of Charles Louis Seeger, an importer-exporter, and Elsie Simmons Adams. Seeger's childhood was spent on Staten Island. When the Seeger and Guernsey Company failed in 1900, Charles Seeger took his family to Mexico City where he had originally started in business. The beauty of Mexico City and the surrounding areas were later to have a great effect on Alan Seeger's poetry. "An Ode to Antares" and his longest poem, "The Deserted Garden," are full of memories of the Mexican countryside.

It was in Mexico that Seeger started to write, albeit for a private publication, the Seeger family magazine *The Prophet*. He wrote a column, "News about the House," as well as stories and poetry. His brother noted that eventually Alan wrote most of the magazine himself.

In Mexico, Alan, his brother Charles, and his sister Elizabeth, were privately tutored by Edward Harwood until 1902 when Alan and Charles returned to the United States to attend the Hackley School in Tarrytown, New York. At Hackley, Seeger announced that his purpose in life was to find "truth and beauty." This search was always to set him apart from his classmates and later from his fellow soldiers. He edited the school newspaper, *The Hackley*.

After graduating in 1906, Seeger studied at Harvard. Never a part of the social scene, he found his niche in his last two years with "Harvard's rebels," a group of brilliant young men in revolt against the status quo. John Reed, who was later to write *Ten Days That Shook the World*, was a part of this group. Seeger did a great deal of writing, especially poetry, and served as editor and a contributor of verse for the *Harvard Monthly*.

Graduating in 1910, Seeger headed to New York City to become a poet. His one job on a little magazine lasted less than a week. As his biographer notes, "This was Alan's first and last stab at steady employment" (Werstein, p. 22). Odd jobs, such as tutoring, writing assignments, checks from his father, and handouts from his friends were the means by which Seeger made his living. In 1912 Seeger went to Paris. He loved Paris and began writing poetry in earnest. His work appeared only in small literary magazines. By the beginning of July 1914 he was satisfied enough with his poetry and called the collection "Juvenilia," but he had no luck finding a publisher in Paris or London. On his way back to Paris via Belgium he stopped in Bruges. There, Seeger found a printer who, although he agreed to publish the poems, was unable to do so. With the German army at the gates of the city, the printer took the manuscript to the U.S. Embassy in Antwerp. Eventually, it was returned to Seeger in Paris.

Back in Paris, Seeger found that many of his friends had joined the Foreign Legion of France; Seeger promptly followed suit. Seeger was fascinated with war and imagined the time "when courted Death shall claim my limbs" in "the tide of war's tumultuous waves." After preliminary training at Rouen, he was sent to Toulouse and finally into action "with the lightest of light hearts."

Seeger liked being a soldier. He wrote to his mother, "This experience will teach me the sweetness and worth of the common things of life. The world will be more beautiful to me in consequence." At the front, although occupied with fighting and the less glamorous side of war such as ditch digging and carrying wood, Seeger continued to write letters to family, diary entries, and poetry. When some poems of his were published by *Atlantic Monthly*, he was overjoyed. Seeger also became a war correspondent, for both the *New York Sun* and the *New Republic*.

At the end of January 1916, worn out by eighteen months at the front, Seeger was hospitalized with bronchitis. During his convalescence he wrote "I Have a Rendezvous With Death," the poem that made him instantly famous when it was published in the *New Republic*. To many, its sense of fatality and acceptance represented the tragedy and waste of war.

The American colony in Paris asked Seeger to write a poem commemorating American volunteers killed fighting for France. He was to read his "Ode in Memory of the American Volunteers Fallen for France" in a Memorial Day celebration on 30 May. Unfortunately, Seeger was unable to get leave to come to Paris. Ironically, the French bureaucracy had confused Memorial Day and Independence Day. Seeger's pass was for 4 July. But on 4 July he was dead. Seeger was killed near the village of Belloy-en-Santerre, having taken part in the Somme offensive. The dead were buried in a mass grave that was later obliterated by a German barrage. Seeger who had developed a deep love for France was awarded its highest military honor, the Croix de Guerre, in 1916 and later the Medaille Militaire, in 1924.

Poems by Alan Seeger was published in late 1916 and was very popular, going into numerous reprints. The *Letters and Diary of Alan Seeger* (1917) was also well received. On 4 July 1923 a monument dedicated to the American volunteers who were killed fighting for France was unveiled in the Place des Etats Unis, Paris. The statue of the soldier had the features of Alan Seeger, and verses from his "Ode" were inscribed on the pedestal.

As a poet, Seeger had promise that was not to be fulfilled. He wrote in a highly romantic mode. Poems about the war, like "The Aisne," although depicting some of the reality of war, saw warfare as enobling and glorious, as "more than dull Peace," as a way to teach "the dignity of being men." Such sentiments were in stark contrast to those espoused by the English poet Wilfred Owen, who also died in World War I.

In a letter to his mother (18 June 1915), Seeger reflected on the possibility that he might die in battle; he wrote: "There would be nothing to regret, for I could not have done otherwise than what I did, and I think I could not have done better. Death is nothing terrible after all." It is a fitting epitaph.

• Seeger's papers are in the Houghton Library, Harvard University, the Library of Congress, and the New York Public Library. Irving Werstein, *Sound No Trumpet: The Life and Death of Alan Seeger* (1967), is a basic source. William Archer's introduction to *Poems by Alan Seeger* (1916) includes biographical information. Michael Rubin, *Men without Marks: Writings from the Journals of Modern Men* (1980), focuses on Seeger's diary. See also James A. Hart's article in *American Poets, 1880–1945*, ed. Peter Quartermain (1986). Personal anecdotes about Seeger are in Walter A. Roberts, "The Alan Seeger I Knew," *Bookman*, Aug. 1918, pp. 585–90, and "Front Matter," *New Public Library Bulletin* 78 (Summer 1975): 393–95. A highly romanticized critique of Seeger's poetry is in T. Sturge Moore, *Some Soldier Poets* (1920). For a tribute to Seeger, see "The Point of View," *Scribner's Magazine*, Jan. 1917, pp. 123–26.

MARCIA B. DINNEEN

SEEGER, Charles (14 Dec. 1886–7 Feb. 1979), musician and polymath, was born Charles Louis Seeger, Jr., in Mexico City, Mexico, the son of Charles Louis Seeger, a businessman, and Elsie Simmons Adams. The first child of well-to-do parents, Seeger was descended from several generations of New England Yankees. His father was a successful businessman, and the family moved between Mexico City and New York City several times during his precollege years. His schooling was by tutor in Mexico, later at the Hackley School in Tarrytown, New York, run by Unitarians (the family faith), and then Harvard College, where he earned a B.A. in music in 1908.

Soon after graduation Seeger left to spend several years in Europe, where he met many of the rising stars in the composition world and did a considerable amount of composing himself. He also became an assistant conductor of the Cologne Opera.

Seeger returned to New York in 1911 to try to make a career as a composer and performer-accompanist. That year he met and married his first wife, the violinist Constance Edson, a protégé of the Damrosch family. The following year the Seegers were off to California at the invitation of Benjamin Ide Wheeler, then president of the University of California. Seeger became the then-youngest full professor at the University of California, located at Berkeley, and the Seegers spent nearly seven years there.

Seeger faced many challenges and accomplished much during his tenure. He began a Department of Music, designed and offered the first full curriculum of music and the first musicology course to be given in an American university, began the development of the music library, discovered the impressive Native American cultures through the fabulous collection of wax cylinders of their music in the university's museum, promoted performances by the department, earned a reputation as a fine teacher (Glen Haydon was the first student to graduate in musicology in the

United States; Henry Cowell became Seeger's first student of composition), gained his first thorough exposure to the intellectual life, and experienced the awakening of his social consciousness.

In late 1918 Seeger left on his sabbatical but, because of health problems and political differences with the university administration, did not return to Berkeley. Instead, the years from 1919 to 1930 were spent mostly in New York, except for a brief period when he and Constance—and their sons, Charles, John, and Peter—decided to tour the country and, in a sense, proselytize European art music by bringing "good music" to the people. When that scheme faltered they returned to New York, where, thanks to Constance's connections to the Damrosches, Seeger taught at both the Institute for Musical Arts—later Juilliard—and the New School for Social Research. But on that trip Seeger had become cognizant of musics outside the concert-hall sphere, and he began to question trying to compose and perform music in the written tradition for those who created and performed in the oral tradition. For this and other philosophic reasons to which he alluded in several articles, he ceased composing and increased his teaching, promoting musicology and the then relatively new field of comparative musicology, later known as ethnomusicology.

Seeger and Constance divorced in 1932, and he married Ruth Porter Crawford, then a rising star in the composition world. He continued his teaching and exploration of new ideas in music and became a founding member of several scholarly societies, among them the American Musicological Society. During the first half of the 1930s Seeger also became affiliated with the Composers' Collective and wrote music criticism for the *Daily Worker*, for political reasons using the pseudonym Carl Sand. Seeger never alluded much to his political views or activities, probably because throughout his life he was ambivalent about his heritage as a privileged "Brahmin," raised with certain attitudes about his class and position, juxtaposed with his strong social conscience, which impelled him to at least write on behalf of the disadvantaged. Like many of his fellow members in the Composers' Collective, such as Aaron Copland, Seeger was not a member of the Communist party, but like the composers, artists, and intellectuals drawn to the collective, Seeger was looking for solutions to the political and economic problems that were exploding throughout the world.

In 1934 and 1935 his role of writing music reviews for the *Daily Worker* drew together several prongs of his professional interest: his teaching, research, and writing on issues of music scholarship, his social concerns for the plight of the proletariat, and his increasing preoccupation with the nation's values and its uncritical and "lowbrow" tastes. Seeger then still considered art music to be "good" music and folk music to be lowbrow; only later in his life did he come to respect the cultural wealth inherent in a variety of other musics as well as that "of the people." In his reviews Seeger tackled the question of the relative importance of music and language for promoting ideology and social change. He also challenged the established music critics on modern music, definitely standing in favor of the innovative works of Berg, Schönberg, and Shostakovich, which still had not won favor among mainstream critics.

By 1935 he and other members had begun to question the collective's and their own political and musical assumptions and to doubt whether they would ever achieve their goal of meshing music with social concern. Although he cultivated the worker ideology, Seeger never truly relinquished his membership in the establishment. He claimed always to have been interested in the bourgeois-proletarian opposition, but he pitied those who made an ideology out of it.

At the end of that year he left New York and began nearly two decades of happy life and important work in Washington, D.C. From 1935 to 1941 Seeger was first technical adviser in the Resettlement Administration, then shifted to the Works Progress Administration to be second-in-command of the Federal Music Project. He also was intimately involved with the Library of Congress, particularly the Archive of American Folk Song. In 1941 he became head of the Music Division of the Pan American Union, a post in which he remained until 1953.

In his Washington years, particularly, and in his various official capacities he became acquainted with folklore and diverse folk musics and promoted them along with American musics. He also was able to encourage the dissemination of Latin American music and foster its appeal throughout the Western Hemisphere. And it was in Washington that he became highly involved in music education in the United States and in the international sphere. This led to his leadership as a founder or cofounder of several international music education organizations, such as the International Society for Music Education, the International Folk Music Council, and the various music councils of the United Nations Educational, Scientific, and Cultural Organization (UNESCO).

In 1953, shortly after he retired, his beloved Ruth died, leaving him with their four children—Michael, Peggy, Barbara, and Penny. Soon thereafter he moved with the two youngest to Massachusetts to be close to his oldest daughter Peggy, who was then attending Radcliffe. In 1955 he married a childhood sweetheart, the widowed Margaret Adams, and moved to her home in Santa Barbara, California.

During the early 1950s Seeger widened his horizons of interests and accomplishments. He became a founding member of the Society for Ethnomusicology and strongly promoted the tenets of that new field of study, encouraging music scholars not only to study musics of other cultures but also to look at the study of any music in terms of its cultural context. Not content with theory and writing, Seeger also became intensely interested in mechanical and technological aids to understanding music. He was already well into his work on phonophotography—a process of graphing music—and his analysis through electronic aids to capture the techniques of a music process by carriers of a tradition led to development of the melograph that bears his name. For the rest of the 1950s Seeger pushed the development of ever more sophisticated versions of the melograph, a machine that renders a graphic image of musical sounds.

As a result of his work in this area and his new interest in ethnomusicology, he met Mantle Hood, who was creating the soon-to-be-famous Institute for Ethnomusicology at the University of California at Los Angeles. Seeger was concerned with music as a whole, focusing nondiscriminantly on all musics as equally worthy of study because each music is valued by its own culture. In the 1950s he had become greatly taken with the developing field of ethnomusicology, which he viewed as the best disciplinary approach to the study of any and all kinds of musics. Hood invited Seeger to UCLA in a quasi-official capacity and in 1960, when Seeger divorced his third wife, appointed him to be a research musicologist in Los Angeles. There, until university policy forced his retirement, Seeger conceived, wrote, and refined some of his more enduring scholarly tracts. He continued this program of writing and teaching, traveling throughout the country and the world promoting his ideas, until he died in Bridgewater, Connecticut.

In his years as an active composer Seeger wrote a considerable number of compositions, few of which survived the 1923 Berkeley fire. Those that do survive and commentaries from his contemporaries indicate that he was on the cutting edge of composition in the early twentieth century. Once he abandoned composition he began a different kind of composing—that of the written word—and in 1930–1931 wrote a typescript on theory and composition. Published by the University of California Press as section one of *Studies in Musicology II*. Seeger's *Tradition and Experiment in (New) Music* in two parts—"Treatise on Musical Composition" and "Manual of Dissonant Counterpoint"— was a pioneering work. For over seven decades he authored dozens of articles ranging from brief comments on an idea to densely argued, long essays on philosophical, linguistic, and systematic aspects of music. Some of his major pieces and seminal works are published in *Studies in Musicology, 1935–1975* (1977) and its sequel, *Studies in Musicology II, 1929–1979* (1994). The two taken together offer a major "selected edition" of his output.

For music scholars, historians of music theory, theorists, and composers his work is of historic value, a broad canvas of ideas to the music profession. But Seeger himself had a strong idea about which elements of his work he considered the most important and valuable and merited wider circulation. He considered his most important contributions to be his theoretical and philosophical writings. Theoretical musicology was the heart of his work, its ideas those with which he wrestled throughout his life. Certain characteristics of Seeger's thought as well as his dogged pursuit of key concepts are present throughout all of his writings. His main concerns are language, logic, speech, sound, fact, and value in a few extraordinary themes: speech and the linguocentric predicament; the dichotomy between historical musicology (diachronic) and systematic musicology (synchronic); the space-time/music-space-time and the general-space-time continuums; the attempt to understand music in its own terms and in the cultural context within which it operates; fact and value, the fact of valuing, and the valuing of fact. His preoccupation with Kant, Wittgenstein, and Hegelian ideas, particularly dichotomies, also dominates his works. Questions such as "how things were, how things are, and how things came to be what they are and are not" are integral to propositions that Seeger propounded.

Briefly enunciated, key points in these focal concepts are as follows. As regards speech and music, Seeger believed that many disciplines, musicology in particular, use the power of the art of speech but suffer the limitations of the semantics of the art of speech. He argued that language and music both communicate a content but that the particular nature and extent of the relationship between language and music have been ignored. And he suggested that the linguistic study of music—musicology—must be made to bend its efforts to the freeing rather than the further imprisoning of music by language. Within the context of his discussions about language and music, Seeger also focused on fact and value. He saw a constant struggle between these antipodes, and, with respect to music and language he analyzed the struggle thusly: that there is an art of music and an art of language, that they enter into relations with one another, and in some respects are homologous is a fact; that they are peers and are as much alike as they are different is a value.

While recognizing differences between them, Seeger focused on the complementarity and interdependence of historical and systematic orientations in musicology, saying that while students of musicology lean toward one or the other methodology, a balance should be made between the two. It was in his efforts to distinguish between historical and systematic approaches to the study of music that he advanced his ideas on general space-time and musical space-time. According to Seeger, the distinction between historical and systematic orientation in musicology could be best made on the basis of two separate but related concepts of space-time, general and musical. The historical or diachronic approach saw music as occurring in time and space, that is, in general space-time, while the systematic or synchronic approach viewed music—music as time itself and space itself—as occurring within a smaller time and space, or music space-time—tempo, duration, beats, and such.

As for Seeger's position on viewing music in terms of itself as well as within the cultural context in which it is developed, it is probably this development in his thinking that led to his espousal of and interest in the relatively new field of ethnomusicology. It first appeared on the music scholarship horizon as comparative musicology, a method to further enlighten music study through comparisons of different musics. Then, with gathering interest in musics other than European

art music and due to the involvement of anthropologists in the study of musics in various societies, the rubric shifted to "ethnomusicology." Seeger, however, eschewed this term, saying that it had two meanings, neither of which he endorsed: the first implied that ethnomusicology was limited to the study of musics other than one's own, while the second implied that the study of music was limited to its cultural functions. Rather, he suggested that ethnomusicology should be seen as a discipline that studies music both in a culture and in view of itself. With the term "ethnomusicology" then properly understood, the prefix "ethno-" could be removed and the discipline could become simply musicology, or the study of any music both within its culture and in terms of itself.

Other preoccupations, with America and the Americas from the perspectives of the arts and politics, music in the international sphere, music in culture and society, and a deep and abiding concern for music education, were also important. He endorsed an applied musicology that would integrate music knowledge and music practice and advocated that government either facilitate this and/or regulate it. He saw the arts as useful in the development of political relations among nations and spoke to the relationship between arts and politics in such articles as "Music and Government: Field for Applied Musicology" and "The Arts in International Relations."

It is possible to trace a coherent line of development from Seeger's first writings on composition (1920s–early 1930s) through the essays from 1939 to the 1960s to the theoretical and abstract tracts of his last years. But he also cared deeply about justice, ethics, morality, and fair play in both his life and his career. These concerns are much in evidence in his social writings and particularly those that deal with folk, popular, and American musics. Indeed, some of his most valuable writings were in American music. Although he considered his work in this area very important, he really did not want to be known as an American music specialist and, especially, a folk music specialist. Nonetheless, his contributions are permanent in those areas, for aside from his writings, three of his own children—Peter, Michael, and Peggy—have achieved world renown in folk and American music.

Charles Seeger was one of the most important and probably the most original thinker about music in the twentieth century. By his early involvement as a performer, conductor, and composer, and later as a scholar, theorist, administrator, international official, and, most importantly, as a teacher and philosopher, he looms over the larger sphere of American music during this century. There is no single statement by Seeger himself that could encapsulate the man as well as the tribute Henry Cowell wrote in "Charles Seeger," in *American Composers on American Music: A Symposium*: "Charles Seeger is the greatest musical explorer in intellectual fields which America has produced, the greatest experimental musicologist . . . he has solved more problems of modern music theory, and suggested more fruitful pathways for musical composition . . . than any other three men. . . . One could go on indefinitely and not exhaust the number of subjects in which he has been a pioneer" (1962, pp. 119–24).

• The Library of Congress houses the major collection of all of Seeger's papers, along with those of some of his family members and of his second wife, Ruth. Known as the Seeger Collection, it includes music scores, much original documentation, and copies of most of his published works. It also holds two of the four versions of "Tradition and Experiment in (the New) Music." Other smaller collections are at the Music Library of the University of California, Berkeley, and the Wesleyan University Ethnomusicology Archives. Seeger's major published books are *Studies in Musicology, 1935–1975* (1977) and *Studies in Musicology II, 1929–1979* (1994). The former includes a complete bibliography of Seeger's published works. Ann Pescatello, *Charles Seeger: A Life in American Music* (1992), contains not only a full bibliography of his work but also information on the contents of all of the items in the library and archival collections mentioned above. His son Michael holds a small selection of very personal papers, accessible by permission only. An obituary is in the *New York Times*, 8 Feb. 1979.

ANN M. PESCATELLO

SEEGER, Ruth Crawford. *See* Crawford-Seeger, Ruth Porter.

SEELYE, Julius Hawley (14 Sept. 1824–12 May 1895), clergyman, educator, and U.S. congressman, was born in Bethel, Connecticut, the son of Seth Seelye, a merchant and farmer, and Abigail Taylor. Nearsighted as a child, he was mistakenly considered unintelligent by his parents, who originally planned a career in his father's store for the boy. Seelye, however, doggedly pursued a course of self-education, and in January 1846, on the advice of a friend, he entered the freshman class at Amherst College. He graduated in 1849 and immediately began study at the Auburn Theological Seminary, completing the course in 1852. Seelye had been offered a tutorial position at Amherst in 1851 but instead went to Europe, where he studied philosophy at the University of Halle. Returning to the United States in 1853, he was ordained to the ministry on 10 August of that year in Schenectady, New York, where he held the pastorate of the First Reformed Dutch Church for the following five years. During this period he continued the study of Kantian philosophy under the direction of his uncle Dr. Laurens P. Hickok, who was at the time the acting president of Union College. Seelye married Elizabeth Tillman James of Albany, New York, in 1854; they had four children.

In 1858 Seelye returned to Amherst as professor of mental and moral philosophy. Hardworking and industrious, he soon became a respected member of the faculty. He accompanied college president Edward Hitchcock on a trip around the world in 1872. The chief destination of their voyage was India, where, with the assistance of the American Board of Commissioners for Foreign Missions, he delivered a series of lectures (with the goal of proselytizing among the Hin-

dus) that was later published as *The Way, the Truth, and the Life* (1873).

Seelye also found time for public service. In June 1874 he was named by the governor of Massachusetts to a three-man commission charged with exploring possible revisions to the tax laws of the commonwealth. This service, combined with dissention in the local Republican party, caused friends to urge Seelye to run for the U.S. House of Representative in 1874 as an independent candidate. Refusing to spend money or even campaign, he was elected to represent the Tenth District of Massachusetts in the Forty-fourth Congress, where he served on the Committee on Indian Affairs and the Committee on Coinage, Weights, and Measures. His most notable activity in Congress was his opposition to the actions of the Electoral Commission regarding the 1876 presidential election. Although Seelye had voted for Rutherford B. Hayes, he believed that Samuel J. Tilden had, in fact, been the rightful winner of the contest.

After the death of Amherst president William Stearns on 8 June 1876, Seelye became a candidate for that position. Forsaking a seemingly bright future in partisan politics, he was formally installed as president on 27 June 1877. In addition to presiding, Seelye served as pastor of the college church and also taught classes in philosophy. His administration was marked by an increase in both the endowment and the faculty size, and the library expanded in both size and professional management. During Seelye's administration an Amherst student, Melville Dewey, developed the classification system that was to remain a standard of the library for years to come.

Seelye's administration was also noted for its development of the "Amherst Plan," a system of student self-government that featured a college senate presided over by the college president and consisting of ten students from each of the four classes. The system greatly influenced the development of student governmental systems throughout the country. Seelye also introduced changes in the student code of conduct, which, while still strict, placed more emphasis on individual responsibility and downplayed the college's role as the ultimate arbiter of student behavior.

While progressive in his educational policies, Seelye remained orthodox, even reactionary, in his religious beliefs. As a product of Amherst himself, Seelye accepted the college's position (dating from its founding) as a Congregationalist bulwark against the Unitarian "heresy" of Harvard as well as a hedge against the potential failure of fellow Congregationalist institution Williams College. Even as the college advanced intellectually, Seelye clung to the notion that the development of student piety took precedence over academic achievement. His faculty, however, contained an ever-increasing number of scholars who had received their training in German graduate programs (programs that—at the time—far exceeded anything available in the United States); the faculty still consisted largely of Amherst graduates with the same fervent evangelical background as Seelye himself, but the influence of overseas training began to make itself felt in subtle ways. Rote classroom recitation was gradually replaced by the give-and-take of the seminar, and the classical subjects that had held center stage in the educational process were joined by instruction in the physical and social sciences. These changes, combined with an increased emphasis on pure scholarship, resulted in a gradual shift within the student body; Amherst became less of a moral finishing school and more a modern college.

Seelye served other educational institutions besides Amherst; his efforts were particularly notable on the Board of Visitors of the Andover (Mass.) Theological Seminary, when in 1887 he became involved in a heresy case. Five professors stood accused after controversial efforts to apply modern scholarship standards to existing theology were advanced in the *Andover Review*, a faculty-produced periodical. One of the men, Egbert Coffin Smyth, lost his teaching position as a result of the controversy. Seelye voted against the majority of the board, urging "Admonition" in lieu of more severe punishment. (The case, after appeals that went as far as the Massachusetts Supreme Court, ended in the dismissal of the charges.)

In addition to various sermons and periodical articles, Seelye published *Christian Missions* (1875), *Duty* (1891), and *Citizenship* (1894). He also translated Albert Schwegler's *History of Philosophy* (1856) and edited and revised Hickok's *Empirical Psychology* (1882) and *System of Moral Science* (1880). Seelye resigned as college president in 1890 and lived quietly in Amherst, where he died.

Though regarded as successful, the presidency of Julius Seelye was tinged with irony. As the first Amherst alumnus to hold the post, Seelye cherished the orthodox, evangelical faith in which the college had been steeped at its founding. Determined to preserve this heritage, he undertook academic reforms with a view toward better preparing his students in the upholding of that original faith. Many of his reforms, however, ultimately worked to create an increasingly secular college.

• The papers of Julius Seelye are housed at the Amherst College Archives, Amherst, Mass. Thomas Le Duc, *Piety and Intellect at Amherst College, 1865–1912* (1969), contains valuable information on his career. The best source remains Claude M. Fuess, *Amherst: The Story of a New England College* (1935). An obituary is in the *New York Times*, 13 May 1895.

EDWARD L. LACH, JR.

SEELYE, Laurenus Clark (20 Sept. 1837–12 Oct. 1924), founding president of Smith College, was born in Bethel, Connecticut, the son of Seth Seelye and Abigail Taylor, merchant farmers and advocates of education. Seelye was prepared, by members of his family, ministers, and educators, for entrance to Union College, from which he graduated in 1857. He studied for the ministry at Andover Theological Seminary, but his studies there were interrupted within a year by ill

health. In October 1859 he left for what became three years of travel and recuperation in Europe and the Middle East. There he developed a knowledge of the art and architecture of Italy, France, Spain, the Holy Land, and Egypt. In 1861–1862 he completed his studies in theology at Heidelberg and Berlin.

On his return to the United States, Seelye was ordained to the Congregational ministry and in January 1863 was appointed to the pastorate of the North Congregational Church of Springfield, Massachusetts. In November 1863 he married Henrietta Chapin, daughter of Lyman Chapin of Albany, New York, a graduate of the Albany Seminary. They had five children.

A return of the threats to his health, which were a feature of his life, persuaded Seelye to resign his pastorate after just over two years to accept an appointment as professor of rhetoric and literature at Amherst College. He enjoyed a highly successful eight years at Amherst, where his brother Julius served as professor of philosophy and later as president.

In 1871 a bequest of approximately $400,000 by Sophia Smith of Hatfield, Massachusetts, to found a college for women was entrusted to a board of trustees closely associated with Amherst College. Seelye became involved and interested in the planning for this new experiment, and early in the discussions he was approached to accept appointment as its president. Understandably reluctant to cast his lot with a venture so controversial and only marginally endowed, he at first refused, only to be persuaded and finally to accept on 17 June 1873 "with a deep sense of its responsibilities." Seelye spent the following summer months in Europe studying higher education, particularly for women, and particularly at Girton College for women, which had opened in 1873 at Cambridge University in England.

In 1872 the trustees of Smith issued a prospectus of the proposed college for women. The requirements for admission that they established firmly rejected the preparatory concessions then current in the few institutions open to women in higher education. Smith would be one of the few women's colleges that did not maintain a preparatory department. This challenge to applicants considerably reduced the number of students accepted for the first class. Smith opened in September 1875 with an enrollment of fourteen first-year students.

There ensued years in which Seelye joined a cohort of women's college advocates who wrote and spoke patiently and tactfully to debate, persuade, and defend and to prove to a biased public that higher education for women posed no threat to their health and morality or to the sanctity of the home. He succeeded and Smith grew rapidly with each new class. In two years it was necessary to build a second dormitory, followed by others in 1878 and 1879. The young president also proved to be a thrifty administrator who won confidence and elicited additional funds. By the turn of the century, Smith was the largest private college for women in the United States with an international student body and instruction at the graduate level.

A pioneer educator with an encompassing vision, Seelye introduced in 1877, against determined opposition even from his own faculty, college education in music and art. After a decade he had assembled a collection of original works of art, still distinguished for their quality and for early recognition of American painters. He appointed a faculty in the arts and in 1882 provided buildings for the adjunct departments of art and music, anticipating the foundation of college museums and instruction in those disciplines.

Seelye's taste in architecture and the arts extended to his determination to ensure quality in the construction of a growing campus. In spite of economic constrictions, he employed the distinguished landscape architect Frederick Law Olmsted to design the campus grounds and provide planting designed to offer specimens in horticulture.

In 1910, after thirty-seven years as president, Seelye resigned from Smith. He left a national institution that was respected, capably endowed, and revered by a host of alumnae. Seelye died in Northampton.

• Seelye's papers are in the Smith College Archives. For examples of Seelye's own work, see his *The Early History of Smith College* (1923) and *Prayers of a College Year* (1925). See also Harriet Seelye Rhees, *Laurenus Clark Seelye* (1929); Vida Scudder, "Seelye of Smith," *New Republic*, 14 Jan. 1925, pp. 193–94; "President Seelye," *Smith College Alumnae Quarterly* 16 (Nov. 1924): 1–7; and a series of articles about Seelye in the *Smith Alumnae Quarterly* 16 (May 1925), including Harriet Seelye Rhees, "A Biographical Sketch," pp. 267–75; Mary Augusta Jordan, "Some Overtures of Greatness," pp. 277–80; and Jennette Lee, "The Unfinished Portrait," pp. 281–85. Obituaries are in the *New York Tribune*, the *Boston Herald*, and the *Springfield* (Mass.) *Republican*, all 13 Oct. 1924.

ELEANOR TERRY LINCOLN

SEGAR, Elzie Crisler (8 Dec. 1894–13 Oct. 1938), cartoonist and creator of the comic strip character Popeye, was born in Chester, Illinois, the son of Amzi Andrews Segar, a house painter and paper hanger, and Erma Irene Crisler. Segar's initial contact with the world of entertainment came at the age of twelve when he worked at the Chester Opera House, where he drew posters and advertisements and learned to operate a projector for film showings (MPO, for "motion picture operator," was reportedly tattooed on his forearm). His interest in drawing led him to complete the W. L. Evans correspondence course in cartooning, through which many young artists of the day learned the rudiments of the profession. With no further training, Segar moved to Chicago in 1916 and was hired by the Chicago *Herald*, according to some accounts through the intercession of Richard Felton Outcault, creator of the Yellow Kid and Buster Brown for the Sunday comic sections.

Segar's first assignment was to take over the recently acquired feature *Charlie Chaplin's Comic Capers*, which he drew from March 1916 to April 1917. Despite his early exposure to silent film comedy, Segar was unable to transfer successfully Chaplin's special brand of visual humor to the comic strip format, so the strip was canceled, although a series of reprint anthologies appeared in 1917. Then for a year Segar drew his own title, *Barry the Boob*, about an inept soldier in the European war. In 1918 Segar created his first popular feature in *Looping the Loop* for William Randolph Hearst's *Chicago American*. This was a vertical column of small cartoons about daily events and attractions in the downtown Chicago Loop area.

Hearst asked Segar to create a new feature for the evening *New York Journal*, which began under the title *Thimble Theatre* on 19 December 1919. As the title suggests, the daily strip was partly intended to compete with Ed Whelan's popular comic strip satire of the film world, *Midget Movies* and later *Minute Movies*. It featured a variety of characters but focused mainly on the nondescript Ham Gravy, his ungainly girlfriend Olive Oyl, her argumentative and ambitious brother Castor Oyl, and their parents, Cole and Nanna Oyl. The gag-a-day format and satire of the melodramatic stage conventions of the day soon yielded to story continuity, dramatic conflict, and adventure, as Segar began to move the comic strip in the direction of compelling adult mystery and suspense, while still retaining the appearance of comic exaggeration and caricature. Pure humor was reserved for a second title for train commuters called *The Five-Fifteen*, which began on 20 December 1920 in the morning *New York American* and depicted the comic predicaments of John Sappo and his wife Myrtle. The steadily increasing popularity of *Thimble Theatre* through national circulation led to the beginning of a Sunday page in color on 18 April 1925 in the *New York Journal*, to which *Sappo* (formerly *The Five-Fifteen*) was added as a tandem feature at the top of the page on 5 March 1926.

Many grotesque characters and strange events would occupy the stage of *Thimble Theatre* before true inspiration struck with the introduction on 17 January 1929 of a crusty sailor named Popeye. At first simply a hired hand to accompany the Oyls on a fortune hunt, his aloof independence, uncontrollable temper, and desire to speak his own mind (albeit in an odd, ungrammatical dialect) made him the center of attention, and, despite his bizarre physical appearance, he promptly won the enduring affection of Olive Oyl. During a sequence of extreme violence, Popeye would demonstrate his special powers of survival by enduring with impunity a dozen bullet holes in his body. He was, then, one of the first superheroes in the comics, anticipating Superman by nine years. On 6 November 1929, after an altercation, Popeye stated in its first form his singular credo of independence, self-knowledge, and integrity that eventually became: "I yam what I yam an' tha's all I yam." It was not until 14 September 1932 that spinach would be mentioned incidentally as a source of strength for Popeye, and only later would the vegetable occupy a place of importance in the strip.

Segar went on to surround Popeye with an intriguing set of characters rivaling those of Charles Dickens in their bold outline and exaggerated vitality: J. Wellington Wimpy, Alice the Goon, the Sea Hag,

Swee'pea, Poopdeck Pappy, and the magical creature known as the Jeep. The popularity of Popeye was phenomenal. The character was widely merchandized in books, games, toys, puzzles, and a variety of other products. In 1933 Max Fleischer of Paramount Studios began releasing a widely screened series of short animated films usually featuring Popeye, his nemesis Bluto (later Brutus), and the object of their competition, Olive Oyl.

Segar married Myrtle Annie Johnson in 1917; they had two children. Because of his interest in fishing, Segar took his family to Florida for awhile but then moved to Los Angeles. Finally, they settled in Santa Monica. Among Segar's other hobbies were hunting, skeet shooting, basement carpentry, oil painting, and playing several musical instruments. In order to avoid interruptions in meeting his deadlines, he would write and draw his comic strip during the night and sleep during the day. He was slight in build, five feet four inches in height, and wore glasses. His son does not remember him as an affectionate person, and he had a volatile temper, but he had a large circle of friends who called him by the nicknames of "El" or "Smoke." At the height of his success, Segar died prematurely at home in Santa Monica of Hodgkin's disease.

Thimble Theatre was continued under other artists and writers, including Tom Sims, Doc Winner, Bela Zaboly, Ralph Stein, Bud Sagendorf, and Bobby London, but Popeye became in their hands and those of the film animators a milder, more civilized, and less brutal character, intended to be more endearing to the child reader. During the last decade of his life, Segar created a body of work that stretched the boundaries of comic strip art. His narratives were moral fables of life and society, reflecting on the complexities of human conflict in modes both tragic and comic. He gave to the English language several new words, including *goon* and *jeep*, credited to him in most dictionaries. He created in Popeye a character so original in conception and so powerful in depiction that he has become a part of American folklore, an appealing symbol of the aggressive pursuit of truth and justice.

• There is no biography of Segar, but the basic facts can be gleaned from the following sources: the entries on Segar by Bill Blackbeard, in *The World Encyclopedia of Comics*, ed. Maurice Horn (1976); and by Robert C. Harvey, in *The Encyclopedia of American Comics*, ed. Ron Goulart (1990); Bill Blackbeard, "The First (Arf, Arf) Superhero of Them All," in *All in Color for a Dime*, ed. Dick Lupoff and Don Thompson (1970); M. Thomas Inge, *Comics as Culture* (1990); Bud Sagendorf, *Popeye: The First Fifty Years* (1979); and Coulton Waugh, *The Comics* (1947). Anthologies of Segar's work with useful introductions and commentary include *Thimble Theatre, Starring: Popeye the Sailor* (1971) and *Thimble Theatre Introducing Popeye* (1977), with introductions by Bill Blackbeard; Rick Marschall, ed., *The Complete Segar Popeye* (11 vols., 1984–1990); Bill Blackbeard and Martin Williams, eds., *The Smithsonian Collection of Newspaper Comics* (1977); and Alan Gowans, *Prophetic Allegory: Popeye and the American Dream* (1977). Thomas Elzie Segar and Marie Segar Clausen have provided additional personal information.

M. THOMAS INGE

SEGHERS, Charles Jean (26 Dec. 1839–28 Nov. 1886), Catholic archbishop and Alaskan missionary, was born in Ghent, Belgium, the son of Charles Francis Seghers, a florist, and Paulina (née Seghers), a cook. His parents later became moderately wealthy shopkeepers. At the age of twenty he became the sole survivor of his parents and siblings, most of whom died from tuberculosis. Upon graduating from a local Jesuit college in 1858, Seghers entered the city's diocesan seminary. Despite weak health he enrolled in 1861 in the American College of Louvain, founded to train clergy for missionary careers in the United States. His intelligence, unassuming piety, and pleasant disposition led teachers and classmates to view him as an ideal seminarian. Ordained a priest in 1863, Seghers emigrated to the Pacific Northwest in hopes of ministering to Native Americans; instead his fluency in English and poor health kept him in Victoria where he served as parish priest and assistant to Modeste Demers, bishop of Vancouver Island. During the bishop's absences from the diocese Seghers acted as his replacement. Demers, expecting that the consumptive young priest would not live long, invited Seghers to travel with him to Rome as his secretary for the First Vatican Council. Upon returning to Victoria, Seghers assumed increasingly more responsibilities when Demers's own health began to fail. In 1873, two years after Demers's death, 33-year-old Seghers became his successor.

A strong advocate of parochial schooling, Bishop Seghers opposed public education, believing its eschewal of religious instruction weakened society's moral foundation. The principle that guided his educational policies was "No morality without religion." However, attempts to find more religious teachers for his understaffed and poor diocese were largely unsuccessful. In 1875 he oversaw the completion of St. Joseph's Hospital in Victoria, the first Catholic hospital in the city. Dedicated to missionary work, the bishop made several visits to the Nootka and other tribes on the west coast of Vancouver Island, including the Hesquiats for whom he established a permanent mission in 1875. To natives on the eastern side of the island he sent newly arrived missionaries from Belgium.

Beginning in 1873 Seghers undertook frequent trips to Alaska, then part of the diocese of Vancouver, to promote Catholic missionary work and to scout sites for missions. During his second trip in 1877–1878 he spent over a year traveling more than 2,500 miles. Using Nulato as his base of operations, he instructed native peoples in the vast interior of the Yukon River basin, intending to follow up on his expedition by founding a permanent mission in the Yukon. However, upon returning to the United States in 1878, he learned that he had been appointed assistant, with right of succession, to Archbishop François Norbert Blanchet of the archdiocese of Oregon. Before departing for Portland the following year, Seghers made a trip to Alaska during which he founded a mission at the trading post of Fort Wrangell, to which he assigned John Althoff, the first resident Catholic missionary in Alaska.

A year after his transfer to Oregon, Seghers inherited full responsibility for the archdiocese when Blanchet retired. Much of his time was spent visiting the churches, Indian missions, and schools under his jurisdiction in a vast area embracing the present-day states of Oregon, Idaho, and Montana. During his administration he struggled to reduce the debt of the archdiocese, fought to maintain Catholic teachers on Indian reservations, persuaded Benedictine nuns and monks to take up work in his archdiocese, and promoted parochial education. Largely through his insistence a separate administrator was appointed for the church in Montana in 1883 by the creation of the Helena diocese. During his years in Oregon, Archbishop Seghers maintained his interest in Alaska. Concerned about the languishing state of church affairs there, in 1883 he volunteered to resume responsibility for that region. While in Rome on church business he persuaded Pope Leo XIII and Vatican officials to reappoint him to his former post in the diocese of Vancouver Island, which had been for several years without a bishop. In hopes of attracting missionaries and funds for his renewed Alaskan project, he spent a year lecturing on Alaska in Europe and the United States before returning to Victoria.

After participating with other North American bishops at the Third Plenary Council of Baltimore in 1884, the following year Seghers organized a missionary expedition to Alaska to establish permanent Catholic missions at Juneau and Sitka. In 1886 he traveled to the interior of Alaska to investigate sites for a mission along the Yukon River. He was accompanied by two Jesuit priests, Pascal Tosi and Aloysius Robaut, and a lay assistant named Frank Fuller, whom he had met two years earlier at Sacred Heart Mission in Idaho. Tosi and others, believing Fuller was mentally unstable, urged the bishop to drop him from the trip, but Seghers refused. The party, split by dissension over Fuller and physically exhausted, reached the confluence of the Stewart and Yukon rivers on 7 September 1886. There the bishop received news that a Protestant rival was about to found a school at a site near Nulato that Seghers had selected for his future mission. Fearing that delay would damage the Catholic cause, Seghers, still undeterred by the criticism of Fuller, decided to split the party and to continue on along the Yukon. Tosi declined to join him. Accompanied only by Fuller and native guides, he rushed on toward his destination. Entries discovered later in Seghers's diary reveal that he, too, began to doubt Fuller's sanity, but it was too late. While they were camped about ten miles east of the confluence of the Koyukuk and Yukon rivers, Fuller, for unknown reasons, shot Seghers, killing him instantly. The slain bishop attracted more notice in death than he had in life. His dramatic and tragic murder brought worldwide publicity to the struggling Catholic missionary effort in the Yukon. It also attracted new missionaries to the area, including the Sisters of St. Ann and the Jesuits, who undertook permanent work there in 1888. Although imperious and stubborn, Seghers exerted a formative influence on the evolution of the Catholic church in Alaska and the Pacific Northwest. The missionary Joseph Cataldo, a widely experienced churchman who had frequent dealings with him, considered Seghers one of the few great men he had known in his life.

• Unpublished letters from Seghers and other primary sources are preserved in the American College Archives, Louvain, Belgium; Archives of the Propagation of the Faith, Paris, France; Archives of the Catholic Archdiocese of Portland, Oreg.; and Jesuit Oregon Province Archives of the Society of Jesus, Gonzaga University, Spokane, Wash. Seghers's letters from the missionary field are published in *Lettres de Jersey* and in *Woodstock Letters*. Biographies include Joseph R. Crimont, *Sketch of the Martyrdom of Archbishop Charles John Seghers* (1944); Maurice De Baets, *The Apostle of Alaska: Life of the Most Reverend Charles John Seghers*, trans. Mary Mildred (1943); and Gerald G. Steckler, "Charles John Seghers, Missionary Bishop in the American Northwest, 1839–1886" (Ph.D. diss., Univ. of Washington, 1963) and *Charles John Seghers, Priest and Bishop in the Pacific Northwest, 1839–1886: A Biography* (1986). Regarding Seghers's murder, see "Alaska," *Woodstock Letters* 16 (1887): 270–82. Obituaries appear in many periodicals, including the *Victoria Daily Standard*, 19 July 1887; the *Portland Daily News*, 20 July 1887; and Henry Van Rensselaer, "The Apostle of Alaska," *American Catholic Quarterly Review* 13 (1888): 95–118.

GERALD MCKEVITT

SEGRÈ, Emilio Gino (1 Feb. 1905–22 Apr. 1989), physicist, was born in Tivoli, Italy, the son of Giuseppe Segrè, a manufacturer, and Amelia Treves. Segrè completed his secondary education in 1922 after attending the primary school in Tivoli and then the Liceo Mamiani in Rome. After studying engineering for five years at the University of Rome, he switched to physics, a field that had interested him since childhood. Another reason for his transfer was that Enrico Fermi, whom he greatly admired, was on the faculty at the university. During his studies in physics he became a friend and colleague of Fermi, and in 1928 he obtained his Ph.D., the first awarded under Fermi's tutelage.

Segrè served his year of compulsory military duty in 1929 as a lieutenant in the Italian army. He then returned to the University of Rome as an associate instructor in physics. In 1930 he was promoted to assistant professor and received a Rockefeller grant that allowed him to study under Otto Stern in Hamburg and Pieter Zeeman in Amsterdam. After two years he returned to Rome and worked as an associate of Fermi.

Segrè's research before 1929 had involved studies of atomic spectroscopy, molecular beams, and X ray. Prior to his military service, Segrè made significant contributions to understanding the splitting of spectral lines by magnetic and electric fields, the Zeeman and Stark effects, respectively.

In his subsequent work with Fermi, Segrè's interest turned to neutron physics. These experiments involved bombing various materials with neutrons. In 1935 they discovered the slow neutron, a subatomic particle whose speed has been slowed by collision with lighter nuclei. The significance of this finding was that some target nuclei capture slow neutrons more readily than fast neutrons and by this capture are made more prone to undergo nuclear reactions.

Segrè was appointed chairman of the physics department at the University of Palermo in 1936. In that year he also made his first trip to the United States, to see the cyclotron at the University of California at Berkeley. Segrè wanted to find the unknown element that should occupy position 43 (with a nucleus containing 43 protons) in the periodic table between molybdenum (42) and ruthenium (44). While he was at Berkeley, Ernest O. Lawrence gave Segrè a sample of molybdenum that had been bombarded with deuterons (hydrogen with an extra neutron). Back in Italy, Segrè and Carlo Perrier analyzed the molybdenum sample and succeeded in demonstrating that it contained small quantities of element 43. Segrè named the previously undiscovered element technetium, from the Greek *technetos*, meaning "artificial," because this was the first element to be artificially produced in the laboratory. Technetium's short halflife has made it extremely useful in medicine for locating sites of cancer. This element does not occur naturally on Earth, but it has been detected spectroscopically in stars.

Segrè visited Berkeley again in 1938. With Dale R. Curson and K. R. MacKenzie, he filled another gap in the periodic table by discovering astatine, another artificial element, with atomic number 85. Later, with Glenn Seaborg, Segrè discovered plutonium 239, with atomic number 94.

When the Italian government passed an anti-Semitic civil service law in 1938, Segrè, a Jew, decided to remain in the United States. He became a U.S. citizen in 1944. Employed as a research associate at Berkeley, he continued his research on artificial radioactivity. With Seaborg he developed valuable chemical techniques for separating nuclear isomers.

Segrè's discovery of plutonium in 1941 was of great significance. The new element was fissionable and was used as the energy source in the atomic bomb dropped over Nagasaki in August 1945. After World War II Segrè worked for a while as a group leader at the Los Alamos Laboratory before returning to Berkeley as a full professor.

In the early 1950s Segrè began a collaboration with Owen Chamberlain to produce an antiproton, a negatively charged twin of the positively charged proton. A positively charged twin of the electron had been proposed earlier by P. A. M. Dirac, and in 1932 Carl D. Anderson announced the discovery of this particle in cosmic rays (high-energy radiation from extraterrestrial sources). This research initiated the search for other antiparticles. The search of Segrè and Chamberlain for the antiproton was hampered because there was no cyclotron available that could develop sufficient energy to produce the antiprotons. Within a short time, however—partly because of Segrè and Chamberlain's experiment—the bevatron was developed. This instrument was capable of propelling particles to energies reaching billions of electron volts and sufficient to produce antiprotons. Although theoretical calculations

indicated that the bevatron would develop sufficiently large energies to produce the antiproton, they also showed that the particle would be short-lived and difficult to detect. To overcome these difficulties, Segrè and Chamberlain devised ingenious techniques for identifying elusive particles, such as using magnets and magnet-focusing devices to sort out particles with the masses expected for the antiproton, and electronic counters and timers to clock the particles as they traveled a known distance. To depict the antiproton-proton annihilation, they allowed the event to take place in a photographic emulsion, which recorded the starlike spray tracts of the five mesons produced each time an antiproton collided with and destroyed a proton.

Segrè and Chamberlain announced their conclusive evidence for the antiproton in 1955. Their work further established that antiprotons can be produced only in proton-antiproton pairs, much as positrons are produced in electron-positron pairs. For their discovery, Segrè and Chamberlain received the Nobel Prize in 1959. Segrè continued to work in physics at Berkeley until 1972. In 1974 he was appointed professor of physics at the University of Rome, and in 1975 he became professor emeritus.

In 1936 Segrè had married Elfriede Spiro; they had three children. She died in 1970, and two years later Segrè married Rosa Mines. Later in his career, Segrè popularized physics by writing a biography of Enrico Fermi, as well as other books on physics. He was an enthusiastic fisherman and mountain-climber. He died in Lafayette, California.

• Segrè's writings include *Experimental Nuclear Physics* (1953), *Nuclei and Particles* (1964), *Enrico Fermi, Physicist* (1970), and two volumes on the history of physics, *From X-rays to Quarks* (1980) and *From Falling Bodies to Radio Waves* (1984). He also wrote an autobiography, *Autobiografia di un fisico* (1995). More about Segrè can be found in Tyler Wasson, ed., *Nobel Prize Winners* (1987), Bernard S. Schlessinger et al., eds., *Who's Who of Nobel Prize Winners, 1901–1990*, 2d ed. (1991), L. M. Libby, *The Uranium People* (1979), R. H. Stuewer, ed., *Nuclear Physics in Retrospect* (1984), and H. A. Boorse and L. Motz, *The World of the Atom*, vol. 2 (1996). An obituary is in the *New York Times*, 14 Aug. 1989.

DAVID Y. COOPER

SEGUIN, Arthur (7 Apr. 1809–13 Dec. 1852), and **Anne Seguin** (c. 1809–24 Aug. 1888), opera singers, were born, respectively, Edward Arthur Sheldon Seguin and Anne Childe, both in London, England. The names of Arthur Seguin's parents cannot be ascertained. Anne Seguin was the daughter of James W. Childe, an artist (her mother's name is not known). Anne and Arthur met at the Royal Academy of Music in London, where their professional training began. They married in 1832 and had five children.

Arthur Seguin made his professional debut in 1831 at the Queen's Theatre in London as Polyphemus in Handel's *Acis and Galatea*. During the 1830s he sang at Covent Garden (1833–1834), Drury Lane (1835–1838), the King's Theatre, and the English Opera

House; he also performed with the Concerts of Antient Music and at various festivals. In 1838 Arthur Seguin and his wife Anne traveled to the United States, where he was engaged to perform opera in New York with two other British singers, Jane Shirreff and John Wilson. His American debut was at the National Theatre in New York on 15 October 1838 in William Michael Rooke's *Amilie; or, The Love Test*. Arthur Seguin's deep bass voice was highly praised by contemporary critics; he was described as one of the finest English-opera singers active in the United States during the antebellum period. His intonation was precise, his enunciation clear, and his execution skillful; he was also praised lavishly for superlative acting. A critic in the *Spirit of the Times* described him as "accomplished, well educated, gentlemanly and judicious. . . . We have never seen a better singer-actor on the stage. His voice was a basso of fine quality . . . while his acting was admirable" (18 Dec. 1852).

Anne Seguin made her debut in 1836 at Her Majesty's Theatre in the Haymarket, where she appeared with Maria Malibran and Giulia Grisi in Domenico Cimarosa's *Il matrimonio segreto*. She subsequently sang at Covent Garden, Drury Lane, and the Concerts of Antient Music before moving to the United States in 1838. Her American debut occurred at the National Theatre on 11 February 1839 as Rosina in an English version of Gioacchino Rossini's *The Barber of Seville*. Anne Seguin did not elicit universally laudatory praise from American critics; a reviewer writing in the *Dramatic Mirror* in 1842, for example, described her as "beautiful, very correct, and very cold," with a "thin" voice that had "wiry and harsh" upper notes. Despite occasional complaints, however, she was generally described in a positive manner; contemporary critics declared her a "pleasing and accomplished singer" and as a "correct" and "very beautiful musician." According to music historian Nicholas Tawa, Americans found her "handsome, graceful, and vivacious, as well as an accomplished actress."

It is unknown whether the Seguins intended to remain in the United States permanently when they arrived in 1838, but (excepting several trips to England) they spent the rest of their lives there. In 1840 or 1841 they formed the Seguin Opera Company, a small itinerant troupe (generally comprising four to six singers) that performed opera all over the eastern United States and in Canada until 1852. The troupe was particularly successful in New York, Boston, Charleston, and Philadelphia. Beginning with a lengthy excursion to the southern part of the United States (including stops in Richmond, Charleston, Augusta, Mobile, and New Orleans) in 1841 and continuing with tours each year until 1852, the ensemble performed English opera—or at least opera in English—all over eastern North America. They traveled to what was then the American West, performing in St. Louis and Cincinnati in 1843 and 1851, and they made three visits to Canada, appearing in Montreal in 1840, 1841, and 1847. The company also visited the American South regularly.

The Seguin Opera Company was particularly successful with translations and adaptations of such continental operas as Rossini's *Cinderella*, Donizetti's *The Elixir of Love*, Bellini's *Norma* and *La Sonnambula*, Auber's *Fra Diavolo*, and Weber's *Der Freischütz*. The ensemble's most enduringly successful work was *The Bohemian Girl*, by the Irish composer Michael William Balfe. The Seguin company mounted the U.S. premiere of the opera in New York in November 1844; it remained a staple of their repertory until the troupe disbanded. The Seguin Opera Company is also remembered for the premiere performance of William Henry Fry's *Leonora* on 4 June 1845 in Philadelphia. This work, a three-act opera in English, was the first grand opera composed by an American to be produced; the title role was written for Anne Seguin.

The Seguin Opera Company was an important transitional ensemble in the history of opera performance in the United States during the first half of the nineteenth century. The troupe started out as a small ensemble of vocal stars that traveled from city to city on the theatrical circuit; the singers of the ensemble typically performed the "star" roles in operas mounted by the stock companies of local theaters. As the demand for the more difficult bel canto operatic repertory grew among Americans during the 1840s, the Seguin troupe expanded to include additional singers in order to insure that all the important roles of the operas they performed were sung by trained singers. By the mid-1840s the troupe generally numbered six to eight performers and functioned more as a small opera troupe than as a group of itinerant vocal stars.

The Seguins enjoyed unprecedented success in the United States from 1841 through 1847; during this period, in fact, the Seguin Opera Company dominated the performance of English-language opera in the United States to the extent that the name "Seguin" became all but synonymous with the term "English opera." In 1847, however, the company began to lose popularity. The British opera singer Anna Bishop arrived in New York that year for an extended stay, providing the Seguins with their first real competition in years. Furthermore, by the late 1840s Americans had become more familiar with Italian opera performed in Italian and were developing a taste for foreign-language opera. Several Italian opera troupes were based in New York, and in 1847 the Havana Opera Company of the Tacon Theatre, a large and formidable troupe that included several important European stars in its ranks, visited the United States. This company, which performed in the United States during several subsequent years, almost completely eclipsed the Seguin troupe.

The Seguins continued to perform with diminished success until 1852, when Arthur Seguin, who had been ill, disbanded the troupe. English opera companies that succeeded the Seguins during the 1850s tended to be larger and more complete ensembles; this increase in size was a response to the success of the larger, more self-sufficient Italian opera companies that began to proliferate during this time. The Seguin ensemble, however, had served as a bridge between the small vocal-star troupes of the 1820s and 1830s and the larger, more self-sufficient English opera companies active in the United States during the late 1840s, 1850s, and later. The Seguins were also important for the role they played in the promotion of opera as a musical and theatrical form in the United States during the 1840s. After Arthur Seguin's death in New York City from heart disease, Anne Seguin retired from the stage and devoted herself to teaching. She died in New York City.

• The most detailed modern account of the activities of the Seguin Opera Company is in Katherine K. Preston, *Opera on the Road: Traveling Opera Troupes in the United States, 1825–1860* (1993). Playbills from productions of the company are extant in numerous theater and music collections, including the Graphic Arts Collection of the American Antiquarian Society in Worcester, Mass., the Harvard Theatre Collection, and the playbill collections of the Philadelphia Free Library, the New York Public Library, and the Boston Public Library. Additional information is in Francis C. Wemyss's entertaining and useful account of his life on the stage, *Twenty-Six Years of the Life of an Actor and Manager* (1847); and in George Seilhamer's interview of Anne Seguin several years before her death, which he published as *An Interviewer's Album*, no. 9, *Anne Seguin* (1881). See also the entry on Anne Seguin in *Appleton's Encyclopedia of American Biography* (1888). Frequent mention of the activities of the Seguin company is made in most accounts of the American stage during the period, including George C. D. Odell, *Annals of the New York Stage* (1927–1949; repr. 1970); William Clapp, Jr., *A Record of the Boston Stage* (1853; repr. 1969); and W. Stanley Hoole, *The Ante Bellum Charleston Theatre* (1946). Obituaries for Arthur Seguin are in the *New York Daily Times*, 14 Dec. 1852; *Dwight's Journal of Music*, 18 Dec. 1852; and *The Athenaeum*, 22 Jan. 1853; and an obituary for Anne Seguin is in the *New York Times*, 25 Aug. 1888.

KATHERINE K. PRESTON

SEGUIN, Edouard O. (20 Jan. 1812–28 Oct. 1880), physician and educator, was born in Clamecy, France, the son of T. O. Seguin; his mother's name is not recorded. He began his education at Auxerre and at the Lycée St. Louis in Paris. His degree was not in medicine. It is unclear whether his specialty training was in education, physiology, or some allied field.

In 1837, at the invitation of the director of a children's hospital in Paris, the 25-year-old Seguin, under the mentorship of Jean-Marc-Gaspard Itard, began an endeavor to educate a young boy diagnosed as an idiot. Itard had already established his reputation as an educator of intellectually handicapped children through his work with the "wild boy of Aveyron" and with deaf-mute children at the National Institute for Deaf-Mutes in Paris, of which he was medical director.

Seguin's efforts with his first patient and student, under Itard's tutelage and using his methodology, met with some success. At the same time, through trial and error, Seguin was developing his own methods for working with the boy and constructing a theoretical framework based on his experiences. In 1839 Seguin opened a private school for the education of the men-tally retarded, the first ever founded. In 1841 he was invited to demonstrate his method at a public institution, La Salpêtrière; and a year later, a portion of the Bicêtre, another public hospital in Paris, was set apart for the instruction of idiots. Seguin was appointed its first director. His first published works on the results of his efforts were *Théorie et pratique de l'éducation des idiots. Leçons aux jeunes idiots de l'hospice des incurables* (1842) and *Traitement moral, hygiène, et éducation des idiots, etc.* (1846). Educators from around the world, including George Sumner of New York and Horace Mann of Massachusetts (American pioneers in the education of the mentally defective child) were attracted to Seguin's methods because of the success of his programs. Within a few years schools for the mentally retarded based on Seguin's methods were established in England and on the Continent, as well as in the United States.

Seguin's therapeutic work rested on a functional theoretical base. In *Idiocy and Its Treatment by the Physiological Method*, Seguin wrote, "Some Idiots are more afflicted in their minds, even to the verge of insanity, and others in their motor and sensory functions, even to the point of paralysis or anesthesia, but in either form their treatment must proceed more from training of the senses in order to improve the mind, than from education of the mind with a view of developing the sensory aptitudes." In converting this theory to practice, Seguin insisted on a pleasant and stimulating environment, a one-on-one relationship with a teacher, an emphasis on motor skill training, and a gradual increase in the complexity of tasks. The students engaged in exercise, strong sensory stimulation, and group activity, proceeding from motor and sensory training to speech training and the development of realistic work skills. Seguin recommended the use of reward and punishment during training.

The political unrest created by Louis Napoleon's ascendancy as French emperor induced Seguin to leave France in 1848 and emigrate to the United States. He settled first in Cleveland, Ohio, and later in Portsmouth, Ohio. He spent about ten years in Ohio before moving to New York City. There he enrolled at the University of the City of New York and received his medical degree in 1861 at the age of forty-nine. He was instrumental in establishing the Randall's Island School for Defectives in 1863. He was the principal U.S. delegate to the Vienna Conference on Education of Retarded Children in 1873, and he was active in founding in 1876 the Association of Medical Officers of American Institutions for Idiotic and Feebleminded Persons, serving as its first president. Seguin was honored by the French Academy of Science and received a commendation from Pope Pius IX.

With the help of his son—Seguin's English was not good enough to write well in the language—he published his definitive text on his theories and methods, *Idiocy and Its Treatment by the Physiological Method* (1866). Additionally, after receiving his medical degree, he became interested in the study of animal body heat and medical thermometry. His publications on thermometry in 1871 and 1876 helped to popularize the use of the thermometer in clinical practice.

Seguin was described as a modest, almost shy man, dedicated to his work with defective children and to his interest in the arts. In addition to reading poetry and the classics, he composed verse and was an ardent amateur painter. He married twice. The name of his first wife is not recorded, but they had one child; his second marriage was to Elsie Mead in 1880, shortly before his death. He died probably in Mount Vernon, New York.

In a letter to Charles L. Dana, quoted in the *Annals of Medical History* (1924), Walter E. Fernald wrote, "[Seguin] was a remarkable man. He anticipated modern psychiatry, modern psychology and modern pedagogy in a remarkable way so that his treatise on Idiocy is the best guide for the understanding and training of the types of defect which were recognized in his day. His work profoundly affected general pedagogy. The work of Montessori was entirely based upon Seguin's principles."

• The earliest biographical information regarding Seguin is George E. Savage, "In Memory of Edouard Seguin, M.D., Being Remarks Made by Some of His Friends at the Lay Funeral Service, Held October 31, 1880," *Journal of Mental Science* 27 (1881): 421–25. Charles L. Dana, "The Seguins of New York," *Annals of Medical History* (1924): 477–79, chronicles his life as well as that of his son and contains a portrait of him. A detailed account of Seguin's professional work can be found in Harlan Lane, *The Wild Boy of Aveyron* (1976). For a comprehensive statement of his theories and methods, see H. Holman, *Seguin and His Physiological Method of Education* (1914), and Ivor Kraft, "Edouard Seguin and Nineteenth-century Moral Treatment of Idiots," *Bulletin of the History of Medicine* (1961): 393–418. An obituary is in the *New York Tribune*, 29 Oct. 1880.

STANLEY L. BLOCK

SEGUIN, Edward Constant (1843–19 Feb. 1898), neurologist, was born in Paris, the son of Edouard Seguin, a pioneer in special education. His father brought the family to Ohio in 1850, due to the political crisis in France. Edward attended schools in Cleveland and Portsmouth, Ohio. After graduating from high school, he served a year-long apprenticeship as a wheelwright, as family circumstances precluded a college education. Moving to New York in 1861, he began medical studies with his father as preceptor, attending three courses of lectures at the College of Physicians and Surgeons. These were interrupted by Civil War service from 1862 to 1864 as a dresser for the United States Sanitary Commission and as a medical cadet in the United States Army. Seguin received his medical degree in 1864 and returned to the army as a surgeon for eight months in 1864–1865, contracting lung disease in the process. He served as intern and house physician at New York Hospital from 1865 to 1867. When the lung disease returned, Seguin resigned this post and enlisted for another term of army duty. This was apparently arranged with the special help of the surgeon general, who assigned Seguin to New Mexico posts where he would have the chance to recover his health.

During 1869 and 1870 Seguin pursued the special study of diseases of the nervous system in Paris, one of the leading centers of the world in this specialty, where he worked with Charles-Edouard Brown-Sequard, Victor Cornil, Louis-Antoine Ranvier, and Jean-Martin Charcot. He returned to New York in 1870 to join the practice of William H. Draper and was soon accorded a place among New York's leading physicians, an unusual accomplishment for an outsider. He was named in 1871 to a chair of diseases of the nervous system at the College of Physicians and Surgeons, founding in 1873 both a clinic in that specialty and one of the first departments in nervous diseases in the country. His published lectures on the physiology of the nervous system, and on the therapeutics of nervous diseases, enlightened medical colleagues on both sides of the Atlantic, as well as his students.

In 1876 he ended his association with Draper in order to limit his practice to neurology. He was a founding member of the New York Neurological Society and the American Neurological Association, in both of which he participated actively in scientific and administrative work. He achieved recognition for his work on cerebral localization but was known mainly as a teacher and a clinician. He was credited, for example, with introducing the "American system" of administering large doses of potassium iodide for syphilitic paraplegia.

Seguin's influence was not limited to his chosen specialty. In 1873 he helped Brown-Sequard edit the *Archives of Scientific and Practical Medicine and Surgery*, and in 1879 he founded the *Archives of Medicine*. He participated in the New York Pathological Society, the New York County Medical Society, and the New York Academy of Medicine. With Draper, he had helped to introduce medical thermometry to American practice in the late 1860s. Seguin insisted that neurology was an integral part of internal medicine. His carefully monitored quantitative methods of assessing the efficacy of particular remedies were considered a model of the new scientific approach to clinical medicine.

Seguin married Margaret Amidon, the sister of a medical associate, in 1874. The marriage ended in tragedy on 31 October 1882, when Mrs. Seguin shot and killed all three of their children and then herself. She had a history of depression but not of violence; the coroner's verdict was "a fit of mental aberration." Many found it ironic that her husband, an expert on insanity, had been unable to predict or prevent the disaster. His article on "The Treatment of Mild Cases of Melancholia at Home," originally published in 1876, had even included a case history of a low-spirited young married woman who experienced impulses to kill her children and herself.

Seguin was deeply shaken and was unsure whether he would ever practice medicine again; partly for this reason, Royal W. Amidon, Seguin's brother-in-law, had Seguin's published works reprinted in one volume, *Opera Minora* (1884). Immediately after the disaster, the neurologist left for an indefinite stay in Europe. His "Notes on Spanish Asylums for the Insane," published in the *Journal of Nervous and Mental Diseases* in late 1883, suggest that he turned to work as an escape from his profound despair.

On his return, Seguin lived for a year in Providence, Rhode Island, visiting New York weekly to resume care of a large following of patients. He continued to publish original articles on clinical neurology and cerebral anatomy. He returned to New York to practice but resigned in 1885 from his teaching position.

In the winter of 1894 Seguin's health began to fail; in July 1896 he retired from practice. He died in New York City of cirrhosis of the liver.

• See "Edward Constant Seguin, M.D.," *Journal of Nervous and Mental Diseases* 25 (1898): 233–36; also, Bernard Sachs, "A Review of Dr. Seguin's Contributions to Medicine," *Medical News* 72 (1898): 582–86; and Charles L. Dana, "The Seguins of New York," *Transactions of the American Neurological Association* 50 (1924): 4–10. The more important of Seguin's earlier works are collected in Edward Constant Seguin, *Opera Minora: A Collection of Essays, Articles, Lectures and Addresses from 1866 to 1882* (1884). On the family tragedy, see the *New York Times*, 1–4 Nov. 1882.

BONNIE ELLEN BLUSTEIN

SEGUÍN, Juan Nepomuceno (27 Oct. 1806–27 Aug. 1890), military and political figure, was born in San Antonio, Texas, the son of Erasmo Seguín, a merchant and postmaster, and María Josefa Becerra. Seguín was born four years before the outbreak of the Mexican War of Independence. He witnessed the family's loss of property and position when royal authorities accused his father of collaborating with insurrectionists. Restored to a leadership position by the time of independence, his father represented Texas at the Mexican constitutional convention of 1823–1824, while Seguín helped his mother run the post office and farm. Through his father's efforts on behalf of colonization projects, Seguín became a strong supporter of Anglo-American settlement and, like him, an outspoken proponent of states' rights liberalism.

Seguín followed his father into a career of business and public service. Also, before and after Texas independence, Seguín involved himself in minor land speculations and did some ranching. Despite the unsettled condition of Texas during the 1820s, Seguín's prospects were secure enough by 1826 that he married María Gertrudis Flores de Abrego, a member of one of San Antonio's important ranching families. They had nine children who survived infancy.

As a member of one of the city's prominent families, Seguín was expected to be politically active. His election as one of San Antonio's two aldermen (*regidores*) in 1829 was a tribute to his maturity and talents. Subsequently, he served on the district electoral assembly and was elected to the office of city magistrate (*alcalde*) for 1834. He served only three months, however, spending the rest of the year as interim lieutenant governor (*jefe político*) for the San Antonio district.

As a liberal associated with Mexico's states' rights party (Federalists), Seguín opposed conservatives working to establish a strong centralized government. When fighting erupted between Texas settlers and the Mexican army in 1835, Seguín reported for service. Seguín, commissioned a captain of cavalry, organized a company that helped drive the Mexican army out of San Antonio in December 1835. When Santa Anna advanced on San Antonio in February 1836, Seguín entered the Alamo as a defender but escaped the fate of the others when he was sent out with a request for assistance. Seguín's service continued after Texas declared its independence in March 1836. Seguín organized a new company and served as a rear guard for the retreating Texans. Seguín's unit was the only company of native-borns to participate at the Texan victory at San Jacinto, which won independence from Mexico. Afterward, his company monitored the enemy's retreat from Texas. During his tenure as military commander of San Antonio, from June 1836 to May 1838, Seguín, now a colonel, had the distinction of burying the remains of the Alamo defenders.

Seguín resigned his commission after being elected senator from Bexar County and served in the second, third, and fourth congresses of the Texas Republic (1838–1840). Despite his need for a translator, Seguín was chair of the military affairs committee and held a seat on the committee of claims and accounts. Seguín also served as mayor of San Antonio in 1841–1842, but he fled the city in the spring of the latter year. Having made enemies among squatters on city property whom he tried to evict as well as among rival land speculators, he found himself accused of collaborating with the Mexicans. One rumor had it that he betrayed the Texan Santa Fe Expedition of 1841 by reporting its departure to the Mexican government.

Seguín's life was imperiled when a Mexican force occupied San Antonio in early 1842 and the accusations were reinforced. For his foes, Seguín's counsel that San Antonio be abandoned before the Mexican army arrived was proof of his correspondence with the enemy. His flight to Mexico did not bring peace, however. Mexican authorities gave him a choice of prison or military service. With his family to care for and no other prospects, Seguín assisted in a fall 1842 invasion of Texas by a Mexican division. He continued to serve as commander of a cavalry unit stationed on the Rio Grande frontier and fought for Mexico during the Mexican War.

The Texas question having been settled by the Treaty of Guadalupe Hidalgo, the Mexicans no longer had need of Seguín, whose financial situation was precarious. In the spring of 1848 Seguín brought his family back to Texas, where he lived first with his father and then on his own ranch in what is today Wilson County. Aside from trade, Seguín appears to have occupied himself with ranching during this time. He soon returned to public life, serving as a justice of the peace and an election precinct chairman in Bexar County. In 1855 he was one of the founding members of the Democratic party in Bexar County. Seguín's last public office was Wilson County judge during the last months of 1869. Shortly thereafter Seguín took those of his family still living with him to the home of his son Santiago in Nuevo Laredo, Mexico, where he later died.

• Material relating to Seguín's tenures as a Mexican-period official are in the Bexar Archives at the Barker Texas History Center, University of Texas at Austin. Records on his military and congressional service are found in various Republic of Texas record groups and the A. J. Houston Collection at the Archives Division of the Texas State Library. Transcriptions of his memoirs and more important writings, along with a lengthy biographical essay, are in Jesús F. de la Teja, ed., *A Revolution Remembered: The Memoirs and Selected Correspondence of Juan N. Seguín* (1991). See also Ida Vernon, "Activities of the Seguins in Early Texas History," *West Texas Historical Association Year Book* 25 (1949): 11–38, and Richard Santos, "Juan Nepomuceno Seguín, espía tejano en la comandancia del noreste de México," *Humanitas: Anuario del Centro de Estudios Humanísticos de la Universidad de Nuevo León* 17 (1976): 551–67.

JESÚS F. DE LA TEJA

SEIBERLING, Franklin Augustus (6 Oct. 1859–11 Aug. 1955), industrialist, was born on the family farm near Western Star, Ohio, the son of John Franklin Seiberling, a farmer and mechanic, and Catharine L. Miller. After devising an improvement for mechanical reapers, his father entered business in 1861, manufacturing agricultural machinery as well as licensing other producers. The family moved in 1865 to Akron, Ohio, where the elder Seiberling established the Empire Mower and Reaper Works and later added interests in milling, strawboard manufacture, and a theater—an eclectic mix of investments that foreshadowed young Frank Seiberling's early career.

Frank attended Heidelberg College between 1875 and 1877 but left before graduation. After beginning as a salesman with the family firm, he became secretary and treasurer and invested in real estate, fire insurance, gold and copper mining, and printing, twine, and jewelry businesses. The Seiberling family was involved in building and operating street railways around Akron and Cleveland and briefly owned the Akron India Rubber Company. Frank Seiberling's links to the local business community were strengthened by his marriage in 1887 to Gertrude Penfield, a member of a wealthy family with interests in clay products; the couple had six children. The Seiberlings' reaper and mower business failed in 1898 in the face of depression and competition from larger firms. Frank Seiberling retained a range of business interests, including a turpentine firm, mining investments, a lemon grove, and a glass factory, as well as organizing the Woodruff Automobile Company, a short-lived venture.

In 1898 Frank and Charles Seiberling, one of his brothers, established the Goodyear Tire and Rubber Company with financial support from his wife's brother and local business acquaintances. Frank Seiberling was general manager and had the key role of raising new capital from local banks. The business struggled during the early 1900s because of slack demand and patent restrictions on bicycle and carriage tires, initially the major lines. By developing modified tire designs and succeeding in patent litigation, Goodyear established a modest base. Seiberling took out some patents, largely for tires and later for a tire-building machine, but his skill lay in financing developments rather than making technical breakthroughs himself. In 1905 Seiberling, then age forty-six, wrote, "I am along in years to that time when I must make good within the next five years or not at all." The opportunity to realize his ambition came from the dramatic expansion of the automobile industry, with its associated demand for tires, which transformed Akron's rubber industry into the center of tire manufacturing. Over the next fifteen years Seiberling's willingness to expand share capital and to reinvest profits in new capacity and machinery enabled Goodyear to expand rapidly, overtaking more established tire manufacturers like Goodrich and U.S. Rubber. The firm's share of the tire market increased from 5 percent to 25 percent between 1909 and 1912, and four years later the company was the world's leading tire producer; only the neighboring Firestone Company achieved comparable growth. Goodyear extended its distribution systems nationally, which was a vital element in obtaining original equipment contracts with leading automobile manufacturers, including the constituent parts of General Motors and Ford. Frank Seiberling mapped out Goodyear's initial development as a multinational manufacturer with the establishment of a Canadian factory in 1910, the creation of overseas sales branches, and the purchase of a rubber plantation in Southeast Asia in 1916 in response to high raw material prices. More extensive overseas manufacturing was anticipated but was not brought to fruition until the 1920s.

Driven by concern about high rates of labor turnover, Goodyear developed a program of employee benefits, including pensions, recreation facilities, and housing developments, which placed it in the forefront of such welfare capitalism in American manufacturing. Seiberling's personal wealth increased in line with the rising value of Goodyear stock plus his policy of making lucrative dividend payments. The symbol of this wealth was the 3,000-acre Stan Hywet estate in Akron, where Frank and Gertrude had a Tudor revival style house built between 1912 and 1915; it was by far the grandest of the estates established by the city's rubber industry executives.

In common with other industrialists, Seiberling's postwar plans for Goodyear's expansion involved the accumulation of substantial inventories, which became a serious liability following the deflation of the 1920–1921 recession. The Goodyear Tire and Rubber Company was brought to the brink of bankruptcy, exposing the risks of Seiberling's strategy of expanding share capital and dividends and reinvesting profits in greater capacity rather than maintaining reserves. It also showed the difficulty created by his disdain for bankers as unduly cautious, which resulted in a lack of favorable connections to financial institutions. Temporary financing was obtained through Goldman, Sachs before another New York investment bank, Dillon, Read, assumed the leading role in an $87.5 million refinancing. As late as March 1921 Frank Seiberling hoped to retain control, but he was forced to resign by Dillon, Read's representatives.

Frank and Charles Seiberling remained in the tire business by establishing Seiberling Rubber in 1921, acquiring a small factory near Akron. Several former Goodyear executives were hired. Though Seiberling's finances were precarious because of the depressed state of industry profits and the reduced value of his own Goodyear stock, his prestige and contacts allowed Seiberling Rubber to operate as a notable small producer, surviving as most small tire firms perished during the 1920s and 1930s. He had a significant role on behalf of small- and medium-sized firms in the introduction of the National Recovery Administration code for tire manufacturing during 1933 and 1934. Frank Seiberling maintained a varied portfolio of investments; he founded the Akron Aviation Company in 1912, invested in the Akron, Canton and Youngstown Railroad, and was a director of the National City Bank and the Akron Hotel Company, as well as participating in the Lincoln Highway Association. He was among the founders of the People's Hospital in 1914 and supported local colleges.

Frank Seiberling was dubbed the "Little Napoleon" of the rubber industry in newspapers. Goodyear's factory manager later commented on the two Seiberling brothers, saying, "People admired Frank but they loved Charlie. One was the head, the other the heart." A genial family man, Frank Seiberling's enthusiasm for business focused in the financial possibilities of an always highly varied collection of investments. He handed the presidency of Seiberling Rubber to one of his sons, J. Penfield Seiberling, in 1938, and, though he was chairman until 1950, Frank Seiberling played a less active role in corporate affairs. He lived at Stan Hywet Hall until his death.

• Seiberling's papers are in the Ohio Historical Society, Columbus, Ohio; the same location holds related material, including the draft of an unpublished autobiography, in the J. Penfield Seiberling Collection. On Seiberling's role at Goodyear, see Maurice O'Reilly, *The Goodyear Story* (1983), and Hugh Allen, *The House of Goodyear* (1937). For his later career, see Michael French, "Structure, Personality, and Business Strategy in the U.S. Tire Industry: The Seiberling Rubber Company, 1922–1964," *Business History Review* 67, no. 2 (1993): 246–78. On multinational developments, see French, "The Emergence of a U.S. Multinational Enterprise: The Goodyear Tire and Rubber Company, 1910–39," *Economic History Review*, 2d ser. 40, no. 1 (Feb. 1987): 64–79. On one of his investments, see H. Roger Grant, "Frank A. Seiberling and the Formative Years of the Midland Continental Railroad, 1912–1920," *North Dakota History* 43 (1976): 28–36.

MICHAEL FRENCH

SEIBERLING, Henrietta Buckler (18 Mar. 1888–5 Dec. 1979), member of a Christian fellowship, the Oxford Group, who brought together and inspired the cofounders of Alcoholics Anonymous, was born in Lawrenceburg, Kentucky, the daughter of Judge Julius A. Buckler and Mary Maddox. Henrietta's childhood was spent in Texas, where her father was judge of the common pleas court in El Paso. She attended and received an A.B. degree from Vassar College, majoring in music with a minor in psychology. She met J. Frederick Seiberling, the son of Akron's rubber industry leader, Frank A. Seiberling, while he was serving as a lieutenant in the Ohio National Guard on duty in Texas. They were married in 1917 in Akron, Ohio, at the Seiberling estate, "Stan Hywet Hall." The couple had three children.

Henrietta Seiberling was an avid student of the Bible and a member of the Presbyterian church. In January 1933, distressed over family and financial problems, she was attracted to the Oxford Group meetings, held in Akron on the invitation of Harvey Firestone, Sr. The Oxford Group called itself "A First Century Christian Fellowship" and stressed achieving a "maximum experience of Jesus Christ" through return to the principles and practices of first-century Christianity. The group was affiliated with no particular church, had no specific membership, and proclaimed itself nondenominational. Participation in the group had enabled a number of alcoholics, including Russell Firestone, son of Harvey Firestone, Sr., to be relieved, through conversion experiences, of their obsession for alcohol.

At the widely publicized Akron Oxford Group meetings, group founder Frank N. D. Buchman was in attendance, accompanied by a "team" of Oxford Group activists, who witnessed and also shared their life-change experiences in many of Akron's Protestant pulpits. Seiberling and three friends went to several of these meetings. One of the friends was Anne Ripley Smith (later called the "Mother of AA"), who was married to an Akron surgeon, Robert Holbrook Smith, an alcoholic. Smith later became a cofounder of Alcoholics Anonymous and came to be known as "Dr. Bob."

Seiberling set about reading most of the Oxford Group books, and all those of the 1930s, including *Soul-Surgery, For Sinners Only,* and *What Is the Oxford Group?,* together with spiritual titles by many Protestant leaders of the day. She read most of the books by an American Oxford Group leader, the Reverend Samuel Moor Shoemaker, Jr., rector of the Calvary Episcopal Church in New York, who is credited by some as the major source of the biblical/spiritual principles of Alcoholics Anonymous. Seiberling conducted Oxford Group meetings at the home of two non-alcoholic founders of AA—T. Henry and Clarace Williams—in Akron.

Concerned about her friend Anne Smith and the drinking problem of Anne's husband, Seiberling was instrumental in persuading Robert Smith to join his wife at the Oxford Group meetings. Members studied the Bible, read Christian literature, shared their conversion experiences, confessed their shortcomings, and witnessed to victory over their problems through the transforming power of Jesus Christ. They prayed together, engaged in quiet time—listening for the guidance of God—and endeavored to learn and practice Oxford Group principles. These included belief in and surrender of one's life to God through following the 5 Cs (Confidence, Confession, Conviction, Conversion, and Continuance) that led to a "changed life"; making restitution for harms done; adhering to principles taught by Jesus and known as the Four Absolutes—Absolute Honesty, Purity, Unselfishness, and Love; achieving a vital religious experience, or "God consciousness," as it was called; and then, in turn, helping others to change their lives by "giving their lives to God." These Oxford Group principles—which were said to be the principles of the Bible—later became the foundation for most of the basic ideas that AA borrowed from religion and incorporated in its twelve-step spiritual program for recovery from alcoholism.

In the spring of 1935 a newly sober Oxford Group member, William Griffith Wilson, an alcoholic from New York, came to Akron on a business venture. When his venture failed, he suddenly felt the need to work with and carry the Oxford Group message to another alcoholic in order to stay sober himself. Led by what Oxford Group people believe was the guidance of God, Wilson telephoned Walter Tunks, an Episcopalian priest in Akron, who was Harvey Firestone's pastor and a member of the Oxford Group. Tunks suggested some phone numbers that Wilson used and that led him to call Henrietta Seiberling. Seiberling and the Oxford Group had been praying for Dr. Bob Smith's deliverance from alcoholism, and Seiberling proclaimed Wilson's call "manna from heaven."

Anxious to help Dr. Bob achieve sobriety, Seiberling introduced the two alcoholics to each other on Mother's Day 1935 at her home in the gatehouse at the Seiberling estate. The two men talked for hours. Within three weeks Wilson was living with Dr. Bob and his wife at the Smith home at 855 Ardmore Avenue in Akron, recognized as the birthplace of Alcoholics Anonymous. Dr. Bob went on one last alcoholic spree and then, working with Wilson, determined to give himself completely to the spiritual program. He abandoned drinking on 10 June 1935, the accepted date of the founding of Alcoholics Anonymous.

For the next three months Seiberling, Wilson, Dr. Bob, and Anne Smith studied the Bible and Christian literature, prayed together, discussed spiritual principles, sought out other alcoholics to help, and attended Oxford Group meetings. Alcoholics who attended these meetings called themselves "the alcoholic squad of the Oxford Group." Wilson said that the teachings of Seiberling provided AA's cofounders with much-needed "spiritual infusion," and she continued for many years to remain their friend, counselor, and supporter. When the Ohio contingent of AA broke with the Oxford Group in 1939, Seiberling followed them.

Seiberling stressed the following ideas to the AA fellowship: (1) God helps us if we let God direct our lives. (2) There must be great reliance on guidance (of God) and quiet times. (3) Reliance on outside money could mean the destruction of the AA program. (4) The AA program should be anonymous, not depending on prominent names for endorsement. (5) "If you [AAs] don't talk about what God does, and your faith, and your guidance, then you might as well be the Rotary Club . . . because God is your only source of power." (6) "It is my great hope that they [AAs] will never be afraid to acknowledge God and what He has done for them."

Henrietta Seiberling died in New York City. On her gravestone in Lawrenceburg, Kentucky, is an inscription familiar to members of the Oxford Group and to AA: "Let go and let God."

• For conference-approved literature of Alcoholics Anonymous that provides some details on Henrietta Seiberling's contributions, see *Alcoholics Anonymous Comes of Age* (1957), *Dr. Bob and the Good Oldtimers* (1980), *Pass It On* (1984), and *The Language of the Heart* (1988). See also "Origins of Alcoholics Anonymous," *Employee Assistance Quarterly* 1 (1985): 33–39, a transcript of remarks by Henrietta B. Seiberling prepared by Congressman John F. Seiberling of a telephone conversation with his mother in the spring of 1971. For an extensive treatment of the role of Henrietta Seiberling in Alcoholics Anonymous, see the following books by Dick B., published by Glen Abbey Books: *The Akron Genesis of Alcoholics Anonymous* (1993), *The Oxford Group and Alcoholics Anonymous* (1992), *Anne Smith's Spiritual Workbook* (1993), and *The Books Early AAs Read for Spiritual Growth* (1993). See also Mel B., *New Wine: The Spiritual Roots of the Twelve Step Miracle* (1992), and Ernest Kurtz, *Not-God: A History of Alcoholics Anonymous* (1991).

BILL PITTMAN
RICHARD G. BURNS

SEIDEL, George Lukas Emil (13 Dec. 1864–24 June 1947), first Socialist mayor of Milwaukee, Wisconsin, was born in Ashland, Pennsylvania, the son of Prussian immigrants, Otto Carl Ferdinand Seidel, a carpenter, and Henrietta Christine Frederika Knoll. The eldest of eleven children, Seidel attended school in Milwaukee until the age of thirteen, when he was apprenticed as a woodcarver. A modest, earnest, and unassuming individual, he was soon active in the labor movement and became a representative of the local Wood Carvers Association of the Knights of Labor. From 1886 to 1892 he lived in Berlin, where he perfected his craft and joined the German Socialist Democratic party. On his return to Milwaukee, he worked as an industrial patternmaker. In 1895 he married Lucy Geissel; they had two children.

In the 1890s Seidel joined the Socialist Labor party and the Social Democracy of America, and in 1901 he became a founding member of the Socialist party. His socialist career occurred within the context of the Socialist party. In 1902 he ran on its ticket for the governorship of Wisconsin but was defeated. He subsequently was elected three times to the city council of Milwaukee, and in 1910 he was elected mayor.

A bilingual labor unionist, Seidel was an ideal candidate for office. His election as mayor occurred in the midst of a Socialist sweep of city and county offices based on the respect party members had won earlier in public office, the corrupt record of the opposing parties, and systematic propaganda and organization. Seidel established a reform-minded administration that resembled urban nonsocialist Progressive administrations elsewhere. His mayoralty promoted factory regulation and labor legislation; pioneered arbitration and municipal employment policies; policed corporations; appointed housing and harbor commissions; established health, cultural, recreational, and city beautification programs; and stood for honest and cost-efficient government. His highest priorities were the legitimization of labor as an interest group and the enhancement of educational opportunities for the whole community. The epitome of "sewer socialism" in its pragmatism, the Seidel mayoralty was stymied in its more ideologically ambitious efforts to establish municipal lodging houses, markets, and other services, leading Seidel to focus on the goal of home rule. He was defeated in 1912 by a fusion ticket.

Seidel entered the national scene by running for the vice presidency on a ticket headed by Eugene Debs in 1912. In 1916 he again was elected to Milwaukee's city council. That same year, another Socialist mayoralty, under the city attorney of Seidel's term, Daniel W. Hoan, assumed office (and held it for twenty-four years). In World War I Seidel helped spearhead Milwaukee's opposition to American intervention and was a leader in the local branch of the People's Council, opposing conscription and favoring a negotiated peace. After the Socialist party declined in the post–World War I era, he remained a Socialist party activist and public speaker. Nominated for various local and state offices in the 1920s, he won election to the city council again in 1932.

Although often overshadowed by the acknowledged leader of the local party, Congressman Victor L. Berger, Seidel was a key figure in the most electorally successful social democratic party in American history. During his most politically active years, the party in Milwaukee built its strongest branch on the basis of its close ties to the German-dominated trade unions. He retired from electoral politics in 1936 but remained active within the party until his death in Milwaukee.

• Seidel's papers are in the Emil Seidel Collection at the Milwaukee County Historical Society in Milwaukee. Additional materials pertaining to his career are in other collections in that society and in collections at the State Historical Society of Wisconsin. Seidel published an article on his administration and the local socialist movement, "Milwaukee's Achievements," in *American Labor Year Book*, I (1916). Published works touching on his career include Frederick I. Olsen, "Milwaukee's First Socialist Administration, 1910–1912: A Political Evaluation," *Mid-America* 43 (July 1961): 197–207; Sally M. Miller, "Of Ethnicity and Labor," in *Socialism and the Cities*, ed. Bruce M. Stave (1975); and Miller, "Casting a Wide Net: The Milwaukee Movement to 1920," in *Socialism in the Heartland: The Midwestern Experience, 1900–1925*, ed. Donald T. Critchlow (1986). An obituary is in the *New York Times*, 26 June 1947.

SALLY M. MILLER

SEIDL, Anton (7 May 1850–28 Mar. 1898), conductor, was born in Pest (present-day Budapest), Hungary. The names of his parents are apparently unknown. Seidl studied at the university and conservatory in Leipzig. Through the aid of his mentor, the conductor Hans Richter, from 1872 Seidl served for several years as amanuensis for composer Richard Wagner, assisting in the preparation of final scores and performances of the *Ring of the Nibelungs*, including their first integral performance at the Bayreuth Festival in 1876. Seidl became conductor of the Leipzig Opera in 1879. In 1881–1882 he conducted a European tour of the Wagner operas. On 29 February 1884 he married soprano Auguste Kraus (1853–1939), who had been one of the performers in the tour; they had no children. From 1883 Seidl conducted opera in Bremen.

In 1885 Seidl made his American debut at the Metropolitan Opera, conducting *Lohengrin* on 23 November. He was subsequently appointed to conduct German repertory at the Metropolitan, following the death of Leopold Damrosch. In subsequent years there he led the American premieres of all the major Wagner operas, including *Die Meistersinger von Nürnberg* (4 Jan. 1886), *Tristan und Isolde* (1 Dec. 1886), and the complete *Ring* cycle (4–11 Mar. 1889).

In 1889 a Seidl Society was formed by Laura Langford to provide summer evening concerts conducted by Seidl at a large concert pavilion at Brighton Beach. The Seidl Society sold very inexpensive tickets to women and encouraged them to take the train out to the concerts. Although the venture had a slow start, it eventually became quite successful, especially after improvements in train access after 1894. Seidl, or his assistant Victor Herbert, conducted two concerts each day over a season of up to nine weeks. The Brighton Beach phenomenon was a very democratic affair, bringing working people together with New York City's intellectuals for inexpensive, high-quality music. The concerts were discontinued after 1896 but not before influencing John Philip Sousa, who was at that time in the first stages of his career as the nation's bandleader.

After discontinuation of German opera at the Metropolitan, Seidl succeeded Theodore Thomas as conductor of the New York Philharmonic in 1891, a post he held until his death. In the same year he became a naturalized American citizen. Among his accomplishments with the Philharmonic was conducting the premiere of the *New World Symphony* by Dvořák (15 Dec. 1893). Seidl was editor in chief of a two-volume, lavishly illustrated account of *The Music of the Modern World* (1895–1897), for which he wrote an essay, "On Conducting." He returned to the Metropolitan in 1895–1897, again conducting the German repertoire, especially Wagner. During 1897 Seidl traveled to Europe to conduct special performances at Covent Garden in London and at Bayreuth. He refused further engagements abroad after a group of his American supporters formed a permanent Seidl Orchestra for the 1898–1899 season and guaranteed its expenses. Unfortunately, Seidl died suddenly of food poisoning and this project was never realized. His funeral, held on the stage of the Metropolitan Opera, was attended by thousands of supporters.

Seidl's long and intimate association with Wagner and his operas made him the most effective and successful conductor of those works during his lifetime. Seidl and Theodore Thomas, who during the 1890s conducted the newly formed Chicago Symphony, established the tone of the art music world in the United States from the 1880s to about the turn of the century. No one else had the prestige and influence to decide what was heard and, perhaps just as importantly, how it was heard. Both men believed music to be a harbinger from a higher world and worked to educate their audiences in the proper appreciation and understanding of the music of the "masters." Of the two, Seidl was perhaps more in tune with his times through his popular Wagner concerts and democratic leanings. But memory of the importance of Wagnerism in the United States and Seidl's paramount importance in that movement were victims partly of the fact that Seidl was not a composer and that he lived before the era of sound recording (although he would have been recorded if he had lived a normal lifespan), but also partly because of the paranoid anti-Germanism of the period of the First World War. Seidl's achievements stand as emblematic of his time and its embracing of Wagnerian communalism.

• Major holdings of Seidl's papers are housed in the Anton Seidl Archive at Columbia University's Butler Library and the Seidl Society Archives at the Brooklyn Historical Society. Early appreciations of Seidl by close associates include Henry Krehbiel, *Anton Seidl* (1898), and Henry Finck, *Anton Seidl: A Memorial by His Friends* (1899). Elise K. Kirk, "'Ring'-Master–Conductor Anton Seidl Proved an Ideal Leader for the First American 'Ring,'" *Opera News* 57, no. 14 (27 Mar. 1993): 8–12, and Joseph Horowitz, "Coming to America," *Opera News* 57, no. 14 (27 Mar. 1993): 14–20, 49, are brief summaries of Seidl's accomplishments. The best source, not only for Seidl but for American concert music of this period generally, is Horowitz, *Wagner Nights: An American History* (1994), which closely examines Seidl's career and its importance in establishing the tone of American concert music at the end of the nineteenth century and the early decades of the twentieth. An obituary is in the *New York Tribune*, 29 Mar. 1898.

RON WIECKI

SEIFERT, Elizabeth (19 June 1897–18 June 1983), novelist, was born in Washington, Missouri, the daughter of Richard Chester Seifert, railroad engineer, and Anna Sanford. In 1918 Elizabeth Seifert received an A.B. degree from Washington University, St. Louis, where she majored in English. She wanted to be a doctor and had enrolled in the university's medical school, the only woman in her class. She dropped out of the program after a year and a half, however, be-

cause her family did not encourage her in her ambition, and university officials told her that, as a woman, she could finish her medical training but could not get a degree. She still took some medical courses at the university: anatomy, physiology, and medical dietetics. She also audited a creative writing class there and so impressed her instructor that he predicted she would become a professional writer. She worked at various times in hospitals as a clinical clerk and secretary and in the Social Hygiene Bureau during World War I.

In 1920 Seifert married John J. Gasparotti, a World War I veteran; they had four children. The family moved to Moberly, Missouri, where Gasparotti built and operated an ice plant. Moberly remained Seifert's home for life.

In 1926 John Gasparotti began having medical problems, caused by having lain wounded on a European battlefield for five days. The deadline for injured war veterans to claim benefits had already passed. In 1937 Gasparotti was declared totally disabled, although he lived until 1959. With four teenage children to educate and little money in the bank, Seifert found a job working in various capacities at the Woodland Hospital in Moberly. She had been interested in writing since the age of ten, and in 1937, because of the need for more money, she began more serious writing in her spare time.

When Seifert finished her manuscript of *Young Doctor Galahad* she sent it to her older sister, Shirley Seifert, a noted writer of historical fiction. Shirley was not impressed, but she sent it to her publisher, who thought it was one of the best novels he had ever read. When entered in a contest for first novels, it won a $10,000 Redbook Award.

Following the publication of *Young Doctor Galahad* in 1938, Seifert quit her job at the hospital and began to write full-time, setting herself the goal of producing two novels a year. Published under her maiden name, all her stories dealt with professional and personal problems of doctors. Her other books included: *Hillbilly Doctor* (1941); *Army Doctor* (1942); *Take Three Doctors* (1947); *Hospital Zone* (1948); *Miss Doctor* (1951); *Hometown Doctor* (1959); and *Rival Doctors* (1967). She also published stories in *Redbook*, *Cosmopolitan*, *American Magazine*, *McCalls*, and other magazines.

Not one of her more than eighty books was rejected by a publisher. Most were translated into several languages, all were serialized through King's Syndicate, some appeared in pocketbooks and large print, and several sold more than a million copies. She retained the same publisher and agent throughout the years. Her reading audience waited eagerly for each new novel. Unfortunately, Moberly citizens sometimes saw themselves as the undesirable characters, despite Seifert's insistence that her characters were fictitious. Her books were romantic but did not contain explicit sex. The formula for each book included a doctor, a hospital, a girl, symptoms, complications, and a cure. She followed a rough outline, typed, and then rewrote her books three or four times.

Seifert's work schedule began at the typewriter at 7:00 A.M. She took a break at 10:30 for a short walk and then continued writing until 1:00 P.M. After lunch she read newspapers and medical journals for story ideas, bits of information, and recent discoveries that would interest her readers. She once said that her one gift was to know a good story when she saw it.

Seifert's hobbies included reading and travel, and she traveled widely in the United States and Europe until she fell in the late 1970s, crushing her shoulder. She continued her busy writing schedule, but her shoulder remained weak so she taught herself to type with one hand.

After she became established, Seifert spoke at clubs, schools, and women's organizations. Always generous with her time, she held memberships in a number of organizations, including Authors League of America, Women's Book Association, Missouri Historical Society, State Historical Society of Missouri, Beta Sigma Phi, and the Ozark Folk Lore Society.

Elizabeth Seifert, the author of eighty-six novels, died in Moberly.

• Short biographies of Elizabeth Seifert appear in Mary K. Dains, ed., *Show Me Missouri Women: Selected Biographies* (1989); Ann Evory, ed., *Contemporary Authors*, vol. 2 (1981), and Hal May, ed., *Contemporary Authors*, vol. 110 (1984), listed under Gasparotti; and *Current Biography* (1951). Elizabeth Seifert's scrapbook of newspaper clippings and correspondence is available in the Western Historical Manuscript Collection, University of Missouri-Columbia, Columbia, Mo. An article about Seifert by Frank J. Rossi, "The Nonstop Writer," appeared in *NRTA Journal* 31 (Jan.–Feb. 1980); and obituaries appeared in the *Chicago Tribune*, 19 June 1983; *New York Times*, 21 June 1983; *Washington Post*, 22 June 1983; and *Publishers Weekly*, 8 July 1983.

MARY K. DAINS

SEISS, Joseph Augustus (18 Mar. 1823–20 June 1904), clergyman and author, was born in Graceham, Maryland, the son of John Seiss and Eliza Schuler, farmers. Although his father strongly encouraged him to follow in his footsteps as a farmer, Seiss resisted, drawn instead to academia and theology. His father nicknamed him "Dreamer Joseph" because he would lie on his back in the fields at night for hours, staring at the stars. He attended the local Moravian church school, receiving extra tutelage in Latin, history, and biblical studies. At age sixteen he was confirmed in the Moravian church. In 1839, against his parents' wishes but with the help of Lutheran minister Reuben Weiser, Taylor entered Pennsylvania College in Gettysburg, an institution affiliated with the Lutheran church, in order to get the education required to become a minister. He learned enough Greek to read the New Testament in the original. However, financial shortages soon compelled him to interrupt his studies and support himself by teaching full-time. His monetary worries prompted him to accept the Lutheran Synod's unusual offer to license the nineteen-year-old Seiss to

preach if he would begin work immediately. He agreed and began missionary work in 1842 in Mount Sidney and Harrisonburg, Virginia. He married Elizabeth Barnitz in 1843; they had five children.

Ordained as a Lutheran minister in 1844, Seiss served as the pastor in Martinsburg and Sheperdstown, Virginia, from 1843 to 1847; in Cumberland, Maryland, from 1847 to 1852; and in Baltimore, at the Second English Lutheran Church on Lombard Street, from 1852 to 1858. During this time, he published his first theological works, *Popular Lectures on the Epistle to the Hebrews* (1846), *The Baptist System Examined* (1854; rev. ed., 1858), and *The Last Times* (1856), and he served as the president of the Lutheran Synod of Maryland (1852–1858). Moving to Philadelphia in 1858, Seiss was given a pastorate at St. John's Lutheran Church. Continuing to write prolifically, Seiss published *The Lutheran Church* (1859), *Holy Types* (1860), *Petros; or, The Wonderful Building* (1862), and *Lectures on the Gospels of the Church Year* (1868). He edited two religious newspapers, the *Prophetic Times* (1863–1875) and the *Lutheran* (1867–1879). Stricken by illness, Seiss was granted a leave of absence from St. John's in 1864 and went, with the financial sponsorship of his congregation, on a convalescent voyage to Europe and the Near East. He visited Palestine and Egypt, and on his return to America he gave lectures and wrote pamphlets describing his experiences. In 1865 Seiss was made the president of the board of directors of the Philadelphia Lutheran Theological Seminary, a position he retained until his death.

After some debate, the congregation of St. John's agreed to sponsor the construction of a new church to serve the population in the growing areas of western Philadelphia. Seiss supervised the construction of the monumental Church of the Holy Communion, located at the corner of Broad and Arch streets. He resigned his position at St. John's in September 1874 to become the pastor of the new church, serving there until his death. In 1888 Seiss was elected as the president of the General Council of the Evangelical Lutheran Church in North America, an organization he had helped found. He died in Philadelphia.

In addition to his direct involvement with the church in Philadelphia, Seiss exerted lasting influence on the international Lutheran church through his writings and sermons. His publications number more than 100, the most notable of which is a collection of sermons appropriate for different festivals in the ecclesiastical calendar. The careful construction and attention to language evidenced in his sermons helped set the standard for both quality and style in American Lutheran preaching. He is also noted for his works on the liturgy, hymns, and biblical prophecy, especially in the books of Daniel, Ezekiel, Zechariah, and the Apocalypse.

Seiss's belief in chiliasm, or millenarianism, which asserts that Christ will return to reign on earth for 1,000 years immediately prior to the Day of Judgment, was unusual and caused comment when espoused by a church official of his prominence. Seiss was a premillennialist, believing that before the return of Christ the world would deteriorate. (Postmillennialists believed that the world would steadily improve as the date of Christ's return to earth neared.) In his most pointedly chiliastic work, *The Last Times and the Great Consummation* (1856), Seiss wrote, "Some thought the great Bible, Sunday School, and missionary movements would soon win the nations to faith in Jesus . . . they see signs of promise in the movements of reform. . . . I have no confidence in such hopes. . . . I see more promise in the darkest features of the times than in all these pious dreams" (p. 157). Seiss also urged that the Lutheran church continue the use of confession, a practice that many wished to eliminate.

• The best source for Seiss's life is his memoir, *Notes of My Life* (1982), transcribed by Henry E. Horn and William M. Horn from a manuscript at Lutheran Theological Seminary. See also G. W. Sandt, "Dr. Seiss Has Passed Away," *Lutheran*, 23 June 1904; "Lutheran Leaders as I Knew Them: J. A. Seiss," *Lutheran Church Review* (Jan. 1918); and Jens Christian Roseland, *American Lutheran Biographies* (1890). Information on Seiss's involvement with St. John's and the building of the Church of the Holy Communion is in E. E. Sibole, *Centennial of St. John's Church, Philadelphia, 1806–1906* (1906). Other tributes include G. F. Krotel, "Joseph Augustus Seiss, D.D., LL.D., L.H.D.," *Lutheran*, 30 June 1904; and H. E. Jacobs, "Joseph Augustus Seiss," *Lutheran*, 14, 21, and 28 July 1904. An obituary is in the *Philadelphia Public Ledger*, 21 June 1904.

ELIZABETH ZOE VICARY

SEIXAS, Gershom Mendes (14 Jan. 1745–2 July 1816), Jewish religious leader, was born in New York City, the son of Isaac Mendes Seixas, a merchant, and Rachel Levy. His father was born in Lisbon, Portugal, into a crypto-Jewish community. He fled Portugal, arriving in New York via Barbados in 1730 (or 1738).

Little is known concerning Seixas's education. He likely attended the school operated by Congregation Shearith Israel, the only synagogue in New York City at the time. He gained competence in the synagogue ritual through his regular attendance at services. He also probably received instruction from Joseph Jessurun Pinto, a native of Amsterdam who became the congregation's hazan (reader and religious leader) in 1759.

In 1768 the office of hazan of Shearith Israel was available, and Seixas applied. In spite of his relative youth, he was unanimously elected to the position. Although he was not an ordained rabbi, Seixas was for all practical purposes the religious leader of the Jewish community of New York City. He conducted the synagogue services and was a teacher of the young, a pastor, and the community resource for matters of Jewish law and tradition. He devoted much of his time to study and reading, and through his self-education he grew in knowledge and communal stature. He became a *mohel* (ritual circumciser) and was also competent in *shehitah* (ritual slaughter).

In 1775 Seixas married Elkalah Myers Cohen; they had four children before her untimely death in 1785.

In July 1776 it became clear that New York City would fall to British troops. Seixas, an avid patriot, urged that the synagogue be closed and that the community flee New York rather than live under British rule. On 22 August, five days before General George Washington evacuated New York, Seixas and his family left for Stratford, Connecticut. He took Torah scrolls and other artifacts of the synagogue for safekeeping. In 1780 he and his family moved to Philadelphia, where he assumed the position of hazan at Congregation Mikveh Israel. Among the members of the Philadelphia congregation were many New Yorkers who had moved to Philadelphia for the duration of the war.

On 25 November 1783 the British left New York City, and New Yorkers began to return home. A high percentage of the men of Shearith Israel had served the cause of the American Revolution as soldiers and patriots. In the spring of 1784 Shearith Israel invited Seixas to resume his position as hazan of the congregation. After some discussion and negotiation, Seixas agreed. In 1786 he married Hannah Manuel; they had eleven children. The Seixas family was well known for its hospitality; their house was always open to congregants and visitors. Seixas enjoyed the friendship and goodwill of his community. From time to time he was called on to help raise funds for the synagogue. The board of trustees informed him that "we know you to have more influence with the whole of the Congregation than any other person."

On 26 November 1789 Seixas preached a sermon at Shearith Israel to commemorate the first Thanksgiving Day of the United States. In his address Seixas expressed thanks to the Almighty for his divine providence and for his mercy toward the people of the United States. He noted that the Jewish people had reason to rejoice "as we are made equal partakers of every benefit that results from this good government; for which we cannot sufficiently adore the God of our fathers who hath manifested his care over us in this particular instance; neither can we demonstrate our sense of His benign goodness, for His favourable interposition in behalf of the inhabitants of this land."

Seixas represented Jewish interests in communal matters. As early as 1784 he was elected to serve on the Board of Regents of the University of the State of New York. He was one of the incorporators of Columbia College and served as a trustee of the college from December 1784 through July 1814. He mingled freely with the intellectual, religious, and business leaders of New York. Christian scholars of Hebrew sought his instruction, and he was glad to share whatever knowledge he had with all those who made inquiries of him.

Seixas inspired his congregation to develop charitable organizations and societies. In 1802 he was the moving spirit behind the formation of the Hebra Hased Va-Amet, a society devoted to providing care for the dying, the dead, and mourners. His career at Shearith Israel spanned a period of nearly fifty years. During this time he proved himself to be a devoted servant of the Jewish community and a worthy citizen of his city, state, and country. He was an affable autodidact, the first American-born Jewish religious leader in New York City, where he died.

Seixas's funeral was held at the Shearith Israel Synagogue on Mill Street; the funeral address was delivered by Jacob de la Motta, who said that "Seixas, from an early period in life, was endowed with no commonplace intellect . . . pursuing undeviatingly the most correct deportment; admired by all; esteemed alike in every grade of society. . . . [He prosecuted] uninterruptedly a line of conduct that obtained for him the love, respect, and esteem of all sects."

• The archives of Congregation Shearith Israel in New York City contain records and minutes that often refer to Seixas. Some of the original records were published in the *Publications of the American Jewish Historical Society* 21 (1913). His "A Religious Discourse: Thanksgiving Day Sermon, November 26, 1789" was published by the Jewish Historical Society of New York in 1977 with an introduction by Isadore S. Meyer. The best and most authoritative biographical information about Seixas is in David de Sola Pool, *Portraits Etched in Stone* (1952). Other biographical information is in Pool, *An Old Faith in the New World* (1955). A sketch of the life and thought of Seixas is in Jacob Rader Marcus, "The Handsome Young Priest in the Black Gown: The Personal World of Gershom Seixas," *Hebrew Union College Annual* 40–41 (1969–1970): 409–67. Also see Thomas Kessner, "Gershom Mendes Seixas: His Religious Calling, Outlook, and Competence," *American Jewish Historical Quarterly* 58 (June 1969): 445–71.

MARC D. ANGEL

SÉJOUR, Victor (2 June 1817–21? Sept. 1874), playwright, was born in New Orleans, Louisiana, the son of Juan François Louis Victor Séjour Marcou, a small businessman, and Eloisa Philippe Ferrand. His father was a black native of the West Indies, and his mother, a Creole from New Orleans. Séjour attended an academy in New Orleans for the children of free men of color. As a young man he was an active member of the Artisans, a middle-class Creole society. In 1836 Séjour was sent to Paris to finish his studies. In that same year, his short story "Le Mulâtre" was published in *La Revue des Colonies* (Paris). Another early literary success was a poem, "Le Retour de Napoléon," first published in Paris (Dauvain et Fontaine, 1841), then in New Orleans (H. Lauve et Compagnie, 1845).

Séjour made his playwriting debut at the Théâtre-Français on 23 July 1844 with *Dégarias*. The central character of the play—set in fifteenth-century Spain—is a persecuted Jew who must hide his identity because he married a Christian woman. This was followed by *La Chute de Séjan*, which opened at the same theater on 21 August 1849. During this time, Séjour became involved in Paris literary circles that included Emile Augier, Alexandre Dumas, and Jules Janin. Like certain other Louisiana blacks, he found he could live a life in Paris relatively free of the racial prejudice that would have hounded him in the United States.

Using Shakespeare and Victor Hugo as models, Séjour spent most of his career writing serious plays—some in verse and some in prose—that varied in genre from vast historical dramas to musical melodramas.

After his initial successes at the Théâtre-Français, the bulk of his earlier plays was produced at the Porte-Sainte-Martin: *Richard III* (1852), *Les Noces Vénitiennes* (1855), *Le Fils de la Nuit* (1856), *Le Paletot Brun* (1858), *La Tireuse de Cartes* (1859), and *Les Volontaires de 1814* (1862). Like most of Séjour's plays, these often revolve around relationships that are strained by religious, ethnic, or political differences. Two were produced at the Odéon—*André Gérard* (1857) and *Les Grands Vassaux* (1859). *L'Argent du Diable*, a collaboration with Jaime [Adolphe] fils, opened in 1854 at the Théâtre des Variétés. At the Théâtre Impérial du Cirque, Séjour saw two of his major spectacles mounted: *Les Massacres de la Syrie* (1860) and *La Prise de Pekin* (c. 1860).

Séjour's later plays were produced at the "Boulevard Theatres"—the Ambigu-Comique and the Gaité. The first produced *Le Martyr du Coeur* (1858), a collaboration with Jules Brésil; *Compère Guillery* (1860); *Les Mystères du Temple* (1862); and *Les Fils de Charles-Quint* (1864). At the Gaité, *Les Aventuriers* (1860) and *Le Marquis Caporal* (1864) were produced, as well as two collaborations with Théodore Barrière—*Les Enfants de la Louve* (1865) and *La Madone des Roses* (1868). At the time of Séjour's death, *Le Vampire* (1874) had been accepted for production at one of the two Boulevard theaters. No matter what the subject matter, the theme of tolerance was always important to Séjour.

The question of Séjour's importance during his lifetime has been debated by scholars. At least one contemporary critic, Théophile Gautier, was fond of him; another, L. Félix Savard, felt his work—violent, unrealistic, and overwritten—exerted a "détestable influence" on the theater of his time (*Chronique Littéraire* 2 [1862]). Séjour's dramatization of the Mortara Case (in which a young Jewish girl had been kidnapped and brought up as a Christian)—*La Tireuse de Cartes*—sparked an ongoing controversy as to the political and religious (but not the ethnic) nature of the playwright. Séjour's reply was that he was a Christian who despised intolerance and a man of "sentiment" not of politics.

Several of Séjour's plays were translated and occasionally produced in other countries during the nineteenth century: *Les Noces Vénitiennes* became *The Outlaw of the Adriatic* (London), *André Gérard* was published in Portuguese (Lisbon), and *Le Martyr du Coeur* in Turkish (Constantinople). *La Tireuse de Cartes* was published in Lisbon as *A Mulher Que Deita Cartes* and in Rotterdam as *De Kaartlegster*. *Richard III* was translated into Spanish and produced at the Teatro del Principe in Madrid just months after its Paris opening; two different Spanish versions were published shortly afterward. The play was also produced and published in New Orleans in the original French. Also in New Orleans, *Le Paletot Brun* was produced six months after its run in Paris. In the twentieth century, the play has been translated twice into English: once for publication (1970), and once for a New York production at Circle in the Square (1972).

Jean-François-Constant Mocquard (also known as Moquart)—playwright, Napoleon III's private secretary, and friend to Séjour—arranged for Séjour to write a trio of plays in honor of the monarch. He also wrote *André Gérard* for the great Romantic actor, Fréderick Lemaître. After the play's initial success at the Odéon in 1857, Lemaître revived the title role at the Gaité in 1861.

Séjour died in Paris of tuberculosis; he was working on a *Cromwell* at the time. Almost twenty years later, the critic Francisque Sarcey was still making references to him in reviews of other plays—as the representative of a style of melodramatic playwriting that the critic abhorred. Minor playwright or not, he was still a reference point for the French audience many years after his death.

Séjour's plays are best remembered for their themes of social protest, especially his concern with anti-Semitism. As well as being one of several playwrights of color in nineteenth-century Paris, such as Dumas, Séjour is now considered part of the growing canon of African-American playwrights.

• All of Séjour's plays and contemporary reviews are in Paris at the Bibliothèque Nationale. Most secondary sources of information on Séjour's life and works are contradictory in both fact and opinion, but the most important studies are John Richard Cottin, "Victor Séjour: Sa Vie et Son Théâtre" (Ph.D. diss., Univ. of Montreal, 1957), and Era Brisbane Young, "An Examination of Selected Dramas from the Theater of Victor Séjour Including Works of Social Protest" (Ph.D. diss., New York Univ., 1979). See also T. A. Daley, "Victor Séjour," *Phylon: The Atlanta University Review of Race and Culture* 4 (1943): 5–17; J. John Perret, "Victor Séjour, Black French Playwright from Louisiana," *French Review* 57 (1983): 187–93; Bernard L. Peterson, Jr., *Early Black American Playwrights and Dramatic Writers* (1990); and Edward Laroque Tinker, *Les Écrits de Langue Français en Louisiane au XIXe Siècle* (1932). Jacques de Plunkett, *Fantômes et Souvenirs de la Porte-St. Martin* (1946), contains an account of Séjour's relationship with Napoleon III.

NADINE D. PEDERSON

SELBY, William (1739–8 Dec. 1798), organist, composer, and music teacher, was born in London, England, the son of Joseph Selby, a fishmonger and merchant. His mother's name is not known. His early musical training is unknown, but at the age of only fourteen he competed (unsuccessfully) for the organist's position at St. Edmund's Church. Three years later, in 1756, he secured the position of organist at the Church of All Hallows, Bread Street, in preference to the composer Jonathan Battishill, and in 1758 his first known composition, a secular song, was published in Roberts's *Clio and Euterpe, or British Harmony*, volume 2.

In 1760 Selby was appointed as one of the organists at St. Sepulchre's Church, while retaining his position at All Hallows. In 1762 he was elected a member of the Royal Society of Musicians, and in the same year both he and his younger brother John contributed psalm tunes to William Riley's *Parochial Harmony*. He must have married at around this time, for his eldest son

was born in 1765, although not until after Selby's death did historians discover that his widow's name was Sarah. Still retaining his other two posts, Selby took a third in 1766 as organist of Magdalen Hospital, a "charity school" for young women, and in the same year he was admitted as a Freeman of the Worshipful Company of Musicians. Shortly afterward, Magdalen Hospital issued a collection of psalms and hymns, to which Selby contributed nine tunes. From 1765 to 1770 he was quite active as a composer, publishing at least three secular songs in addition to psalm tunes. He also contributed an organ voluntary to a collection published c. 1770.

Selby's younger brother John had been appointed organist of the Church of St. Mary Woolnoth in London in 1764, but in 1771 he resigned the position and crossed the ocean to Boston, where in the fall of that year he began a tenure as organist of King's Chapel. It is probable that it was John who influenced William to also immigrate to the colonies, for in the fall of 1773 Selby resigned his London positions and sailed to Newport, Rhode Island, to assume the position of organist at Trinity Church. Very shortly afterward he placed a notice in a Newport paper advertising that he was available to "teach the violin, flute, harpsichord, and other instruments in use" as well as dancing. John and William were also active in promoting concerts in Boston and Newport in the prerevolutionary period.

The American War of Independence disrupted the lives of the Selby brothers. In 1776 King's Chapel was closed, and John cast his lot with the Loyalists. Along with the rector and many members of King's Chapel, he was deported to Halifax, Nova Scotia, where he carved out a new career as a bandmaster and also became the organist of St. Paul's Church. William remained in Newport, but in the summer or fall of 1776 he moved to Boston, where he became organist of Trinity Church, the only Anglican church then remaining open. He remained in this position until 1780, during which time three of his children were baptized and his eldest son died. Although his activities between 1780 and 1782 are uncertain, Selby appears to have briefly been the proprietor of a shop that sold wines and groceries during this period, rather than during the Revolution, as some accounts suggest. Then, in 1782 King's Chapel, where his brother had previously served as organist, reopened, and Selby was appointed as organist there, retaining the position to the end of his life.

His appointment at King's Chapel also began a period of considerable activity for Selby, both as a composer and as a promoter of concerts. In 1782 he played an organ concerto in a concert given at King's Chapel "for the Benefit of the Poor of Boston." Subsequent concerts, usually for charitable purposes, included an ambitious program at King's Chapel in 1786, in which selections from Handel oratorios were featured, along with a Handel organ concerto and an overture by J. C. Bach. At one of Selby's concerts in 1789, George Washington was present, one of the selections being a "Patriotic Ode" set by Selby; in 1790 Selby also gave a benefit concert for fellow musician William Billings. His concerts were not confined to King's Chapel, however. In 1788 he gave a concert at Christ Church; in 1790 he gave a concert at St. Peter's Church in Salem for the benefit of the organ repair fund; and in 1792 and 1793 he presented a series of subscription concerts at Deblois's Concert-Hall in Boston.

Selby's compositions during this period covered a wide range. One of the first, which is now lost, was an anthem composed in 1782 for the reopening of the Old South Church in Boston, which, like King's Chapel, had been closed during the years of the Revolution. In the same year he published two anthems for mixed voices, *O Be Joyful* and *O Praise the Lord*. These, along with another anthem from around the same period, *Behold, He Is My Salvation*, became quite popular and continued to be reprinted in collections as late as the mid-nineteenth century. Four hymn tunes appear to date from the last years of Selby's life and were published in collections dating 1795, 1802, and 1804.

Although his brother John had remained loyal to King George, Selby turned his talents toward the patriotic fervor of the postrevolutionary period and in 1786 and 1787 published musical settings of two odes, one in honor of General Washington and the other for the anniversary of independence. In 1789 one of his secular songs appeared in *Town and Country Magazine*, and in 1789 and 1790 four others were published in the *Massachusetts Magazine*.

Selby also made two attempts to establish a musical periodical in Boston. In 1782 he advertised for subscriptions to a monthly collection to be called *The New Minstrel*, but apparently there were no takers, and there is no evidence that any issues were ever published. In 1790 he tried again, this time under the name of *Apollo and the Muse's Musical Compositions*. At least one issue seems to have appeared, and a fragment survives in the Massachusetts Historical Society that contains, among other music, a *Christmas Anthem*, two secular songs, and two keyboard pieces (a *Lesson* and an organ voluntary), all believed to have been composed by Selby.

The last few years of Selby's life appear to have been uneventful, and it is possible that although he was only in his fifties, his health was failing. Although he continued as organist of King's Chapel and it is believed that he still taught music lessons, no concerts under his direction are recorded after 1793, nor are any compositions recorded, unless the four hymn tunes previously mentioned belong to this period. In 1798 he saw the birth of a granddaughter and the death of his eighteen-year-old son, and in December of that year he died at his home on Tremont Street and was buried at King's Chapel, which bore part of the funeral costs.

A product of post-Handelian England, Selby might have lived out his days in relative obscurity as a competent parish church organist and minor composer in London. Instead, he immigrated and during the postrevolutionary era in Boston became a leader in the city's musical life as a teacher, an impresario, a church musician, and a champion of the works of Handel. His compositions are well crafted and typical of the rapidly fading late baroque aesthetic. Although his songs, like those of most of his English contemporaries, have fallen into oblivion, his anthems remained sporadically in print and in use during much of the nineteenth century, and along with his few keyboard compositions, they can still be found in modern editions.

• Much information on Selby's career in London is found in the archives of the London Guildhall. All of his compositions known to have been published in England can be found in the British Library; most of his American publications are found in the Massachusetts Historical Society and the American Antiquarian Society. Information on Selby's American career is in the records of King's Chapel and Trinity Church, Boston, and Trinity Church, Newport. Important source material on his American career is contained in Barbara Lambert, ed., *Music in Colonial Massachusetts 1630–1820*, vol. 2 (1985). For more information about his London career see Donovan Dawe, *Organists of the City of London, 1666–1850* (1983). Selby is also briefly mentioned in many general histories of American music, but the first in-depth study was David McKay, "William Selby, Musical Émigré in Colonial Boston," *Musical Quarterly* 57 (1971): 609–27, which gives much information on concert activities, but unfortunately sometimes confuses William with John and cites some incorrect statistics, such as Selby's death date. A more current account of both John and William Selby is found in Barbara Owen, *The Organs and Music of King's Chapel, 1713–1991* (1993). Two of Selby's organ voluntaries were recorded by Barry Turley on the CD *Historic King's Chapel* (1990).

BARBARA OWEN

SELDEN, Elizabeth S. (1888–at least the early 1960s), dancer and writer, was born in Europe. There is no information about her parents or the exact location of her birth. Very little is known about Selden's life. She reportedly received her dance training in Germany and Switzerland from such notable European dance artists as Mary Wigman, Rudolf von Laban, and the Wiesenthal sisters. Before 1930 she immigrated to the United States and at some point became an American citizen. She was living in Connecticut in 1930 and in California later in the 1930s, and apparently gave dance concerts in both New York and California. In 1932 she spent time in Europe updating her knowledge of the modern dance scene there. Selden attended the University of California at Berkeley, where she earned a bachelor's degree in 1935 and a master's in German in 1936. Her M.A. thesis was on late Romantic era German interest in Chinese culture. She may have begun work on a doctoral degree because from 1942 to 1944 she taught Spanish as a teaching assistant at UC Berkeley. She began writing at least as early as 1926 and published two books on dance, *Elements of the Free Dance* (1930) and *The Dancer's Quest: Essays on the Aesthetic of the Contemporary Dance* (1935). She identified herself as primarily a dancer but one also engaged in "research in the comparative study of modern dance" (*Dancer's Quest*, p. xi). In addition to the two books, Selden wrote some articles on dance for the *New York Evening Post*.

Selden's educational breadth was impressive. Her writings demonstrate a familiarity not only with the modern dance of both Europe and the United States and the literature of dance but also with world literature and current writings in philosophy, aesthetics, and the history of art and theater. In addition to her dance works, she also published *China in German Poetry from 1773 to 1833* (1942) and *The Book of Friendship: An International Anthology* (1947), which included poetry she had translated from German, French, Spanish, Italian, and Portuguese. It is her dance writings, however, for which she is remembered.

As she explains in her preface to *The Dancer's Quest*, Selden's first book, *Elements of the Free Dance*, was an attempt to identify the common theoretical and practical components of the twentieth-century concert dance forms that had been developing in Europe up to 1914 and in the United States until about 1924. She wished "to sum up, . . . the accomplishment of that important first epoch of the Free Dance which forms the basis of the present" (p. xii). The dance forms of that "first epoch" were variously called "barefoot dancing," "free dance," and "natural dance," among other things, and were characterized by an exploration of expressive movement possibilities in contrast to adherence to a codified vocabulary and formal choreographic principles such as prevailed in the ballet. *The Dancer's Quest* addresses the subsequent developments in Europe and the United States and includes essays written from 1926 to the mid-1930s. By the 1930s the new concert dance, or "modern dance" as it was called in the United States, had taken on a more identifiable character, which included an emphasis on contemporary thematic material and attention to form and style. The movement vocabularies developed by various leaders in the field as well as their training methods stressed the use of space, design, dynamics, rhythm, and the body's weight as expressive means. Selden discusses the theory and practice of the new dance in general and how they were realized in the work of particular dancers and choreographers, including Mary Wigman, Doris Humphrey, and Martha Graham.

Contemporary reviews of *The Dancer's Quest* were mixed. John Martin, noted dance critic for the *New York Times*, criticized the book as dated and setting up a formalistic approach that negated the experimental nature of modern dance (*New York Times*, 12 Jan. 1936). The reviewer for *Theatre Arts Monthly*, in contrast, praised the work as a serious study covering all aspects of the new dance in Europe and the United States (Dec. 1935, p. 956). Despite Martin's negative view, *The Dancer's Quest* was a seminal work in the early literature of the modern dance and provided a theoretical and practical text for the educational modern dance that was growing in American colleges and universities.

The place of Selden's death is unknown, but it was perhaps in northern California. In the early 1960s she gave some of her collection of materials to two University of California, Berkeley, employees, a librarian and a dance teacher, so it is known that she lived at least

until then. The dearth of material on Selden is probably due to the fact that although she performed and choreographed, she never became one of the major or even secondary figures in the practice of dance, and after *The Dancer's Quest* she seems to have abandoned her dance involvement for academic studies.

• A clipping file on Selden was in the Dance Collection of the New York Public Library, but apparently it has been permanently lost. A small collection of materials is in Special Collections, University Library, University of California, Irvine. For a discussion of Selden's theories see Judith Alter, *Dance-Based Dance Theory: From Borrowed Models to Dance-Based Experience* (1991).

NANCY LEE CHALFA RUYTER

SELDEN, George (14 May 1929–5 Dec. 1989), children's author, was born George Selden Thompson in Hartford, Connecticut, the son of Hartwell Green Thompson, a physician, and Sigrid Johnson. Introduced to opera by his mother and to a love of reading by his father, Selden developed an early interest in writing, music, and his two other lifelong passions, nature and archaeology. After receiving a B.A. in 1951 from Yale University, where he was a contributor to the college literary magazine, he studied Latin and Greek in Italy, and Perugia, on a Fulbright scholarship.

In a 1974 interview with Lee Bennett Hopkins included in *More Books by More People*, Selden revealed that "I realized early that I wanted to be a writer." He was a voracious reader of children's literature as a child, a practice he continued as an adult. Upon returning from Europe, he embarked on his dream of becoming a published author. Selden was unsuccessful as a playwright, but a friend in the publishing business suggested that he try his hand at children's literature, and a distinguished career was launched.

His first book, *The Dog That Could Swim Under Water*, was published by Viking Press in 1956 and was based on his memories of his own childhood pet. *The Garden Under the Sea* (1957), was inspired by childhood family vacations on the Long Island Sound. Later reprinted as *Oscar Lobster's Fair Exchange* (1966), *The Garden Under the Sea* was a fantasy about a group of sea animals who are upset with humans who have been removing "souvenirs," such as shells, from the shore. The three main characters, a lobster, a crab, and a starfish, retaliate by scavenging for human possessions to teach the children in the story a moral lesson about nature and conservation.

Selden's books were known for their gentle humor, readability, and celebration of friendship and loyalty. The accompanying drawings were by Garth Williams, the famous illustrator of numerous major children's books. Selden's most famous work, the now classic *The Cricket in Times Square* (1961), was cited as a Newbery Honor Book and also received the Lewis Carroll Shelf Award. The book was made into an animated television show by ABC in 1973. A fantasy tale about a musically talented cricket named Chester from

Connecticut, and Tucker Mouse and Harry Cat, the new friends he meets in New York City's subway system, *The Cricket in Times Square* tells the story of how the three save the Bellini family's failing newsstand. Selden's love of music, nature, animals, and New York City are all creatively interwoven into the plot. Like all of Selden's books, the story was inspired by his own experiences. While waiting for a subway train in New York City one day, Selden was surprised to hear one of the familiar sounds of his boyhood—the chirping of a cricket.

Tucker's Countryside (1969), the first sequel to *The Cricket in Times Square*, focused on Selden's interest in nature and conservation. It recounted the country adventures of the three animal friends and was set in the meadow across the street from Selden's boyhood home. It was the most successful of the Chester Cricket sequels (five in all) and received the 1969 Christopher Book Award. *Harry Cat's Pet Puppy* (1974), a story written for younger readers, captured the William Allen White Children's Award. Selden's knowledge of archaeology was evident in the two biographies for children that he wrote: *Henrich Schliemann, Discoverer of Buried Treasure* and *Sir Arthur Evans, Discover of Knossos* in 1964.

The Genie of Sutton Place (1973) was adapted from a 1957 television play Selden co-authored. In this book Selden's fantasy centered on his interest in archaeology and involved Dooley, a 1,000-year-old genie who comes to the rescue of a New York City boy named Tim and his dog Sam. A 1973 review in the *Horn Book* described it as a "Felicitous combination of wit and fantasy, hilarity and wisdom." *The Genie of Sutton Place* was optioned by Disney, but was never made into a film. Altogether, Selden wrote fifteen children's books, two plays, and two biographies. He died before he could realize his additional goals of writing screenplays and completing a novel for adults.

Selden died in New York City. A bachelor all his life, Selden lived alone in a small apartment overcrowded with furniture and his favorite books and records. Although he made his home in New York City's Greenwich Village, his affection for his small town and country American roots was evident in most of his fiction.

• Biographical information on Selden is rather scarce and reveals very little about his personal life. Information can be found in Lee Bennett Hopkins, *More Books by More People* (1974); and a variety of book reviews, including the *New York Times Book Review*, 24 June 1973; and the *Horn Book*, Aug. 1969. An obituary is in the *New York Times*, 6 Dec. 1989.

JEANNE ABRAMS

SELDEN, George Baldwin (14 Sept. 1846–17 Jan. 1922), patent attorney, was born in Clarkson, New York, the son of Henry Rogers Selden, an attorney, judge, and lieutenant governor of New York, and Laura Anne Baldwin. After graduating from St. Albans (Vt.) Classical Preparatory School, Selden attended the University of Rochester from 1861 to 1864, Yale College in 1865–1866, and Yale's Sheffield Scientific School from 1867 to 1869, but he never completed a college degree. After joining the law offices of his father and uncle he studied law for three years and was admitted to the New York bar in 1871. In that same year he married Clara Drake Woodruff of Rochester; they had two sons and two daughters.

Selden, who had long been interested in mechanical things, continued to experiment with engines when not engaged in his patent law practice. In 1875 he built an engine fueled by kerosene and nitrous oxide, but it never ran. His other engineering ventures were more successful. Between 1875 and 1877 he obtained six patents covering a machine for the mechanized forming of barrel hoops. Foreshadowing what was to come, he was able to sell these patents, albeit at a small profit. Turning his attention to self-propelled vehicles, he fastened on a stationary engine invented by George Brayton. This two-stroke design used one upward and one downward movement of a piston to produce a single power stroke. Selden first saw the Brayton engine at the 1876 Philadelphia Centennial Exhibition; ironically, this was the year that a far better internal combustion engine was first put into operation by Nicolaus Otto in Germany. With the help of a local machinist, Selden built a three-cylinder version of the Brayton engine (although only one cylinder was actually operational) but was unable to get it to run for more than five minutes.

In the closing decades of the nineteenth century it was increasingly evident that a vehicle powered by an internal combustion engine would become a practical reality. Had Selden persisted with his efforts to develop the engine and then install it in a carriage of some sort, he might have gained credit as the builder of one of the first internal combustion–powered road vehicles. Instead, Selden was able to convert his vision into a considerable amount of money, not by manufacturing an automobile, but by exploiting a patent on it. Well situated to take advantage of this opportunity, he ingeniously combined his interest in mechanical things with his legal acumen and on 8 May 1879 applied for a patent for an "improved road-engine." His application was supported by a drawing of a Brayton-powered carriage and a nonworking model. At the time of the application a patent would have been of little value as a source of royalties because a working automobile had not yet been built, much less commercially marketed. Selden accordingly postponed the actual issuance of the patent by adding amendments from time to time and employing other delaying tactics. Sixteen years later, on 5 November 1895, he was awarded U.S. patent number 549,160.

Selden clearly intended to use his patent not to protect a manufacturing enterprise of his own but to extract royalties from firms that were actually engaged in the construction of automobiles. Selden anticipated, however, that these firms would contest the patent, and he did not have the financial resources necessary for protracted suits. In 1899 he transferred his license to the Electric Vehicle Company, although he retained a portion of any royalties earned by the patent. The Electric Vehicle Company was in considerable financial distress as a result of the failure of an electric cab venture, and in 1900 it turned to the Selden patent as a means of recouping its financial losses.

Within a few years the holders of Selden's patent had developed a subtle scheme for exploiting it. Realizing that legal actions against members of the growing automobile industry would evince continual hostility and large legal expenses, an executive of the Electric Vehicle Company devised a patent pool that would benefit all who subscribed to it. Selected manufacturers would be licensed to use the Selden patent in return for a royalty payment of 1.25 percent of the retail price of every gasoline-powered car they produced. Those not admitted to the pool would be barred from the manufacture of gasoline-powered automobiles; in this way the Selden patent could be used as a powerful tool for suppressing competition. In March 1903 the pool was organized as the Association of Licensed Automobile Manufacturers.

Selden's agreement with the ALAM gave him one-fifth of the gross royalties, half of which he had agreed to turn over to George H. Day, the organizer of the ALAM. While receiving substantial royalty payments, Selden was little more than a spectator in the drama that followed. Members of the ALAM were for the most part manufacturers of expensive cars. Henry Ford's Ford Motor Company, in contrast, was committed to the building of cheap cars for the masses, but its plans were threatened when the ALAM refused to grant it a license. Ford's company went on making cars (and not paying royalties), and in 1903 it was sued for patent infringement. The suit was upheld in 1909, but in 1911 an appeals court reversed the previous decision, ruling that the Selden patent applied only to automobiles powered by the Brayton engine, which had been extinct for many years.

Perhaps in an effort to demonstrate that he was more than a passive extractor of patent royalties, Selden in 1906 established the Selden Motor Vehicle Company (but only after first having obtained an ALAM license from the defunct Buffalo Gasolene Motor Company). After several years of financial losses, production of Selden automobiles ceased in 1914. Selden had been served much better by his patent. Although he reportedly sold his share of the patent in 1907, his income from it totaled approximately $200,000. After the death of his first wife in 1903, he married Jean Shipley in 1909. They had no children. He died in Rochester.

The Selden patent may have ultimately benefited Henry Ford more than George Selden because Ford's willingness to fight the Selden patent had put him in the role of champion of the "little man" in the battle against trusts and monopolies. For many years afterward, automobile manufacturers avoided further conflicts over patents by forming cross-licensing arrangements that gave everyone the right to use inventions patented by one firm.

• There is no known collection of Selden papers. The Selden patent is covered in histories of the automobile industry, including James J. Flink, *The Automobile Age* (1988), J. R. Doolittle, ed., *The Romance of the Automobile Industry* (1916), and T. F. MacManus and Norman Beasley, *Men, Money, and Motors* (1929). For a more detailed account, including many aspects of Selden's life, see William Greenleaf, *Monopoly on Wheels: Henry Ford and the Selden Automobile Patent* (1961).

RUDI VOLTI

SELDES, Gilbert Vivian (3 Jan. 1893–29 Sept. 1970), critic and writer, was born in Alliance, New Jersey, the son of George Sergei Seldes, a pharmacist, and Anna Saphro, who died when Gilbert was three. His only sibling, George Seldes, became a distinguished journalist known for his coverage of European affairs between the world wars. Their father, a freethinker of Russian Jewish descent, sought to convert his farm into an anarchist utopian colony. When that did not succeed, he entered the drugstore business. He enjoyed friendships with Emma Goldman, William D. "Big Bill" Haywood, and other prominent radicals. At age forty-two Seldes recalled that his father in 1900, allowed him and his brother great "freedom of choice, threw so many decisions upon us, left us too independent. . . . We never had the pleasure of reading forbidden books because no books were forbidden."

After graduating from Philadelphia's prestigious Central High School in 1910, Gilbert attended Harvard where he studied literature, was influenced by the philosopher George Santayana, and participated in literary publications and the dramatic club. He was determined to become a "writer," which initially meant fiction. Although he later published three minor novels (1927–1929), Seldes's skills were better suited to journalism, nonfiction assessments of popular as well as high culture, social history and criticism. He became a versatile author in every aspect of these broad categories: vaudeville, jazz, theatricals, film, radio, television, public affairs, and the economic circumstances of middle-class America—with which he explicitly identified.

After finishing at Harvard in 1914 and forming enduring friendships with the poet E. E. Cummings, the novelist John Dos Passos, and others, he pursued a career as a newspaperman in Philadelphia and Washington, D.C., and as a war correspondent in England during World War I. Following a brief stint as an editorial writer for *Collier's Weekly* (1918–1919), Seldes joined the staff of the *Dial*, regarded by many as the preeminent journal in the United States of literature and the arts. As managing editor, Seldes expanded his network to include T. S. Eliot, Sherwood Anderson, Van Wyck Brooks, D. H. Lawrence, and Marianne Moore.

Although he was the *Dial*'s drama critic from 1920 to 1929, Seldes went to Europe in 1923 to write a book in praise of American popular culture, a bold step at that time for an intellectual associated with an avant-garde, highbrow journal. *The Seven Lively Arts* emerged as a manifesto on behalf of popular culture by demanding that highbrows pay it closer attention and apply to it the same critical standards they reserved for opera, ballet, and drama; it appeared in 1924 to considerable acclaim and remains Seldes's best-known work. The monthly column that he wrote for *Esquire* magazine during the 1930s and 1940s was called "The Lively Arts"; and starting in 1955 he hosted a weekly radio program with the same name.

In 1923 he married Alice Wadhams Hall, an Episcopalian from a socially prominent family. They had two children. Alice Seldes died in 1954, and Gilbert never remarried. They were an extremely sociable couple. Following several trips to Europe during the mid-1920s, they lived primarily in midtown Manhattan. Seldes did not drive a car, he said, because his intense concentration on ideas diverted his attention from traffic.

From 1925 onward Seldes produced an immense number of daily, weekly, and monthly essays for the *New Republic*, the *Saturday Evening Post*, *Scribner's*, *Harper's*, the *Atlantic*, *Esquire*, the *New York Evening Journal* (1931–1937), the *Saturday Review*, and other magazines concerned with the arts and other topical subjects, ranging from public affairs to education. He was not sympathetic to the cause of the expatriates, the so-called lost generation, even though some of its members, such as F. Scott Fitzgerald, were close friends. He disliked the fashionable "debunkers," those who derided American culture. He found much to admire (though also to criticize) in his native land. Predictably, he crossed swords with H. L. Mencken and those who found the United States shallow beyond redemption. Seldes called them "boob haters."

Seldes's major books include *The Stammering Century* (1928), a crisp interpretation of American culture in the nineteenth century; *The Years of the Locust: America, 1929–1932* (1933); *An Hour with the Movies and the Talkies* (1929); *Mainland* (1936), an assessment of American civilization during the depression; *The Movies Come from America* (1937); *Your Money and Your Life: A Manual for the "Middle Classes"* (1938); *Proclaim Liberty!* (1942); *The Great Audience* (1950), a pessimistic look at the prospects for film, radio, and television; and *The Public Arts* (1956), a more sanguine evaluation of the media and the emergence of mass culture. He also wrote an adaptation of Aristophanes' *Lysistrata* that became a huge Broadway hit in 1930. Other theatrical endeavors were less successful, including an ambitious 1939 adaptation of Shakespeare's *Midsummer Night's Dream* called *Swingin' the Dream*, which featured African-American stars such as Louis Armstrong and Jackie "Moms" Mabley in an 1890s New Orleans setting.

Seldes served as the first director of television programs for the Columbia Broadcasting System from 1937 to 1945; he had several unhappy attempts as a writer in Hollywood; and he became the founding dean of the Annenberg School of Communications at the University of Pennsylvania from 1959 to 1963. He wrote numerous radio series, served on talk shows, wrote television scripts, and produced documentaries about many aspects of American history and culture, most notably the radio program "Immigrants All—Americans All" in 1938–1939.

"In my own lifetime," he wrote in 1966, "I have witnessed more changes in the modes of communication than occurred in all recorded history before." Because of his penchant for reconciling potential opposites, he supported what seemed best in high culture, especially modernism, but also in popular culture. He insisted that commercial television could combine "actuality and imagination" through, for example, educational programs, high-quality daytime serials, and serious drama. He dedicated *The Public Arts* to two men he deeply admired: nightclub comedian Jimmy Durante and respected broadcaster Edward R. Murrow. If Seldes had bifocal vision, he managed to look high and low for all that seemed best in the American scene.

Seldes considered himself an "adjustor" with a distaste for extreme positions. His admirers invariably referred to him as a "responsible" critic, though he could be fearless in provoking disagreements with persons whose views seemed snobbish (like the cynical Algonquin Circle) or who disparaged mass and "midcult" taste (like Dwight Macdonald). Seldes was an unabashed patriot, a loving critic who nonetheless disdained uncritical lovers of the United States because they lacked discrimination. He believed in American exceptionalism—the idea of a distinctive civilization—for better and for worse, but mostly better. He died at his home in New York City.

In 1965, when preparing a memoir that he never completed, Seldes summarized his two lifelong passions: "the popular arts and the nature of American society." In his work Seldes combined a commitment to cultural democracy with the assumption that it was possible to "level up." He led the way in calling for socially responsible television criticism, and he urged those who controlled programming to broaden rather than narrow the public's range of interests. Seldes was also distinctive among the cultural critics of his generation because he believed strongly in the need for historical perspective in understanding social patterns and cultural phenomena. Ultimately, Seldes was a well-educated intellectual who loved popular entertainment, explained the genius of those who supplied the best of it, and chastised those who praised high culture just because it was "high" rather than for being first-rate. He believed that the same critical standards should be applied to the arts at all taste levels, hence his important role as a democratic and pluralistic critic of the arts.

• Seldes's papers are scattered in many archival repositories, including the papers of the *Dial* and of Edmund Wilson at Yale's Beinecke Library; the papers of Amy Lowell and E. E. Cummings in Harvard's Houghton Library; the papers of F. Scott Fitzgerald, Allen Tate, John Peale Bishop, and the publisher Charles Scribner's Sons in the Special Collections at Princeton University Library; and the papers of John Dos Passos at the Alderman Library, University of Virginia. The New York Public Library has Seldes materials in assorted manuscript collections at the main branch and substantial clippings of essays and reviews at the Billy Rose Library for the Performing Arts. The Manuscript Division of the Library of Congress includes Seldes materials in the papers of Edward R. Murrow, William Allen White, and Archibald MacLeish and in a collection of CBS radio scripts (and related correspondence) from the 1930s–1940s. His unfinished autobiography, his early journals, correspondence with his brother, other letters, and numerous clippings remain in the possession of his daughter Marian Kanin in New York City. Seldes's autobiographical reports to Harvard College, published in the annual *Class Reports*, are helpful, especially those of 1929 and 1939. A source for Seldes's youth is George Seldes's autobiography, *Witness to a Century* (1987). For biographical details, see "Talk with Gilbert Seldes," *New York Times Book Review*, 8 July 1956. For assessments of *The Seven Lively Arts* and *The Great Audience*, see Edmund Wilson, *The Shores of Light* (1952), and Michael Kammen, *The Lively Arts: Gilbert Seldes and the Transformation of Cultural Criticism in the United States* (1996). An obituary is in the *New York Times*, 30 Sept. 1970.

MICHAEL KAMMEN

SELEE, Frank Gibson (26 Oct. 1859–5 July 1909), baseball manager, was born in Amherst, New Hampshire, the son of Nathan P. Selee, a Methodist-Episcopal clergyman, and Annie Marie Cass. The family moved to Melrose, Massachusetts, where Selee attended grammar school, played amateur baseball, and went to work for the Waltham Watch Company. He and his wife May (maiden name and date of marriage unknown) had no children. In 1884 Selee quit his job to organize a town baseball team in the Massachusetts League, one of a growing number of minor leagues. He played some and raised capital to fund the team, but he found his true calling as a manager.

Over the next five seasons (1885–1889) he moved successfully to more competitive leagues, managing teams in Haverhill, Massachusetts; Oshkosh, Wisconsin; and Omaha, Nebraska. Selee's 1889 pennant-winning Omaha team in the Western Association featured the pitching of Charles "Kid" Nichols, whose superior ability attracted the attention of William Conant, a coowner of the National League's Boston Beaneaters. Boston signed both Selee and Nichols to contracts. Nichols won 27 games in his rookie year, but the Beaneaters, decimated by player defections to the upstart Players League, finished in fifth place. In 1891 Selee augmented the Boston roster with players from several minor leagues plus returnees from the Players League, which expired after one season. Boston rose to first place as pitcher John Clarkson won 33 games, and Nichols added 30 more wins. The Beaneaters won four more pennants during the next seven years, and Selee established himself as the first great manager not himself to have played. Throughout the 1890s only Selee and Ned Hanlon, manager of Baltimore and then Brooklyn, managed teams that won National League titles.

A small man, Selee was a courteous and mild-mannered leader in a rowdy period. "If I make things pleasant for the players, they reciprocate," he once said. "I do not believe that men who are engaged in such exhilarating exercise should be kept in straitjack-

ets all the time, but I expect them to be in condition to play." He chose his players carefully and schooled them to play a superior brand of what was then called "inside baseball." Boston excelled at the hit-and-run play, timely bunting, and keen defense that employed shifts and signals and introduced the 3–6–3 double play (the first baseman to the shortstop covering second base and back to the first baseman). Second baseman Bobby Lowe recalled that Selee did not blame his players "if they took a chance that failed. He believed in place-hitting, sacrifice-hitting, and stealing bases."

In 1892 the Beaneaters became the first National League team to win more than 100 games. The league split the season into halves, with Boston taking the first-half pennant and the Cleveland Spiders the second. In a postseason championship series the Beaneaters, after a first-game tie, swept Cleveland in five games.

Boston won its third consecutive pennant in 1893 and finished first in 1897 and 1898. But it was Selee's third-place club of 1894 that proved to be his most powerful. This team scored a major-league record of 1,220 runs with seven regulars each tallying more than 100 runs. Combined, the Boston players hit 103 home runs, a mark not topped by any other major league team from 1884 until 1920. Boston was not shut out over 133 games. Yet the club finished eight games behind the Baltimore Orioles and five behind the New York Giants. The Beaneaters' 1897 pennant ended a string of three straight championships for Baltimore, generally considered the greatest team of the decade.

After three straight years without a championship, Boston released Selee following the 1901 season. The Chicago Cubs, not having won a pennant since 1886, promptly signed him. The Cubs finished fifth in 1902, third in 1903, and second in 1904 as Selee again proved a shrewd judge of talent. During his first season he shifted Frank Chance, a catcher-outfielder, to first base, moved minor league third baseman Joe Tinker to shortstop, and acquired second baseman Johnny Evers from Troy of the New York State League. The Tinker-to-Evers-to-Chance double play combination quickly became three-fourths of baseball's most famous infield.

With the Cubs on the verge of greatness, Selee resigned midway through the 1905 season. Ill with tuberculosis, he was granted an indefinite leave of absence and retired to Denver. He bought an interest in the Pueblo Indians club of the Western League and a share in a Denver hotel, never returning to the major leagues.

During sixteen major league seasons, Selee's teams won 1,284 games and lost 862, for a .598 winning percentage, fourth-best in baseball history. He won five pennants, and the Cubs' team that he built went on to finish first in 1906, 1907, 1908, and 1910. Selee has not been elected to Baseball's Hall of Fame, but eight Beaneaters who played when he managed, including Nichols, and four Cubs have. He died in Denver.

• No biography of Selee has been published. The statistics of his career are given in *Total Baseball* (1995). For background, see George L. Moreland, *Balldom* (1914), MacLean Kennedy, *The Great Teams of Baseball* (1928), Harold Kaese, *The Boston Braves* (1948), and Lee Allen, *The National League Story* (1961). An obituary is in the *New York Times*, 6 July 1909.

STEVEN P. GIETSCHIER

SELFRIDGE, Thomas Oliver, Jr. (6 Feb. 1836–4 Feb. 1924), naval officer, was born in Charlestown, Massachusetts, the son of Thomas Oliver Selfridge, an officer in the U.S. Navy, and Louisa Cary Soley. A midshipman in the class of 1854 at the U.S. Naval Academy, Thomas, Jr., was the first officer to receive a graduation diploma under the present-day system adopted by that institution in 1850 whereby cadets no longer spent three years at sea after their second year at Annapolis, shortening enrollment from seven years to four.

After early duty in the South Pacific and in the African Squadron, Selfridge joined the USS *Cumberland* in 1860 as a lieutenant. Aboard this steam sloop, he participated in the seizure of the Confederate fortifications at Hatteras Inlet in August 1861 and then in the famous engagement with the CSS *Virginia* (ex-USS *Merrimack*). As officer in charge of the forward battery, he fought his guns until almost every man in his division was killed or wounded by fire from the Confederate ironclad. Selfridge was among the last to leave the sinking Union warship. He then briefly commanded the *Monitor* after that ship's duel with the *Virginia* and later the experimental submarine *Alligator*.

Promoted to the rank of lieutenant commander in July 1862, he joined the Mississippi Squadron in its campaign against Vicksburg. As part of that force, he commanded the *Cairo* from August and took the armored gunboat on the Yazoo River expedition, where the vessel was sunk at Haines Bluff in December by a Confederate "torpedo" (in later terminology, a mine). Transferred to the gunboat *Conestoga*, he led the attack on Palmyra, Tennessee, in April 1863. During the final stages of the Vicksburg siege, Selfridge directed a naval battery ashore. Following the surrender of that city in July 1863, he returned to the *Conestoga* and, leading a gunboat squadron, over the next nine months captured the Confederate steamers *Elmira* and *Louisville* and made incursions up several local waterways. When his vessel was sunk in a collision in March 1864, he moved to the ironclad *Osage* for the famous and ill-fated Red River expedition. To extricate the Union flotilla from the shallow waters of the Alexandria rapids, Selfridge helped build the Red River dam and, once that was breached, led the entire Union force past it.

Having attracted the eye of Rear Admiral David Dixon Porter, Selfridge returned to the Atlantic coast with that officer late in 1864. On the screw steamer *Huron*, Selfridge took part in the unsuccessful December attack on Fort Fisher guarding the entrance to Wilmington, North Carolina, the last important Con-

federate port city. In a second assault the next month, he personally led a landing force of marines and sailors against the fort and then participated in the occupation of the city. His wartime conduct was so exemplary and his personal gallantry so conspicuous that the Navy Department proposed his advancement of thirty places on its list of officers. Congress, however, never acted on this recommendation.

Selfridge married Ellen F. Shepley in August 1865; they had four sons. In the postwar navy, Selfridge taught at the Naval Academy and then performed notable service on expeditions to map parts of Latin America. Promoted to commander in 1869, he oversaw in the next four years three surveys of Panama for a canal and explored deep into Colombia. His reports, published in 1874, ultimately won for him the Legion of Honor from France and honorary membership in the Royal Geographical Society of Belgium. Four years later he took the gunboat *Enterprise* on a surveying voyage to the upper Amazon and Madeira rivers. In 1879 he represented the United States at the congress in Paris on interoceanic canals organized by Ferdinand de Lesseps.

Selfridge's later naval employment was equally varied and fruitful. Promoted to captain in 1881, he took command of the new Naval Torpedo Station at Newport, Rhode Island, and began experimentation with offensive employment of and defenses against the untried underwater weapon. Following sea duty on the Asiatic Station and service on the Board of Inspection and Survey, he commanded the Boston Navy Yard (1890–1893) and then headed the commission that determined the location of the Puget Sound Navy Yard. Promoted in 1894 to commodore and to rear admiral the next year, his last command was of the prestigious European Squadron (1895–1898) with the new armored cruiser *New York* as his first flagship. At the coronation of Czar Nicholas II in 1896, Selfridge was the senior U.S. Navy representative. He retired from active duty in February 1898. His wife died in 1905, and in 1907 he married Gertrude Wildes. Selfridge spent his last years composing his memoirs, which were published in the year of his death. He died in Washington, D.C.

Selfridge's career was in many ways emblematic of the U.S. Navy itself in the last half of the nineteenth century. Distinguishing himself during the Civil War on both land and water and serving both on blockade duty and in the "brown water navy" operating against the heart of the Confederacy, Selfridge took a prominent part in the first combat against an ironclad warship and survived the sinking of three of his own vessels. During his remaining thirty-three years in uniform after the war, he helped develop the weapons and supporting shore establishment pivotal to the American naval renaissance of the 1880s and 1890s. His memoirs remain one of the important sources for the U.S. Navy during this period.

• Selfridge's papers are held by the Library of Congress. Aside from two articles in the U.S. Naval Institute *Proceed-*

ings, his major published work is *Memoirs of Thomas O. Selfridge, Jr., Rear Admiral, USN* (1924). Biographical sketches are contained in William B. Cogar, *Dictionary of Admirals of the U.S. Navy*, vol. 1 (1989), and in Clark G. Reynolds, *Famous American Admirals* (1978). A tribute to Selfridge on the occasion of his retirement is in the *New York Times*, 24 Jan. 1898, p. 2.

MALCOLM MUIR, JR.

SELIG, William Nicholas (14 Mar. 1864–16 July 1948), pioneer movie producer, was born in Chicago, Illinois, the son of Joseph Francis Selig, a shoemaker, and Antonia Lunsky. He attended public schools in Chicago and for a time worked as an upholsterer. Then, dubbing himself "Colonel," he went into show business as a magician and as manager of what most sources call a touring minstrel troupe, though film historian Gene Fernett identifies it as a "fly-by-night medicine show" (p. 209).

In 1895 Selig, who had long been interested in photography, saw a demonstration of an Edison Kinetoscope, a primitive film projector, while on tour in Dallas, Texas. Recognizing its commercial potential, he developed and patented his own motion picture projector, the Selig Polyscope. After studying other motion picture cameras, he developed and patented his own camera, the Selig Standard Camera. In 1896 he went into manufacturing both machines in Chicago and prospered. (The similarity of his machines to those he had studied, however, kept him in litigation for patent infringement from 1900 to 1907.)

Beginning in 1896 Selig also produced short films that were used as novelties in vaudeville theaters; he described them as one-scene shots of action in everyday life. In 1897 he produced *The Tramp and the Dog*, a comedy using a hired vaudeville actor in which a bulldog chased a tramp who had stolen a pie and grabbed him by the seat of the pants when he was about to climb a fence. "The climax came when the fence broke under the weight of the tramp," he said, "which was not at all in the scenario, but that gave it a concluding punch. That picture was more than a sensation, it was a riot" ("Cutting Back," pp. 44–45). He married Mary Pinkham in 1900; the couple had no children.

After nickelodeon theaters became a national craze, Selig began to produce single-reel narrative films. One of them was *Trapped by Bloodhounds; or, The Lynching at Cripple Creek* (1905). This "western" was filmed in Chicago, and the lynch mob reportedly consisted of patrons of a local saloon whose pay was free lunch and a barrel of beer. A number of Selig one-reelers from 1905 through 1907 were the work of G. M. "Broncho Billy" Anderson as actor and director.

Selig lost his patent infringement case in 1907. Nevertheless, Selig Polyscope became a member of a pool of ten patent holders, led by the Edison company, who for a fee licensed other movie makers to use the cameras and other machines under patent. By 1909 this had become the Motion Picture Patents Company, a trust that controlled the burgeoning movie industry by giving or refusing licenses. Again Selig prospered. Expanding his company's movie making, he sent a company to Louisiana in 1908 to shoot films on location; weather conditions caused the director to move the company to California, and they filmed the exterior scenes of a one-reel *Count of Monte Cristo* (1908) on a Los Angeles rooftop. It was the beginning of the film industry's move to the West. In 1909 Selig established a fledgling movie studio in downtown Los Angeles, while keeping up production in Chicago.

Though Selig Polyscope films were far from innovative, several productions are of note for various reasons. One was *Big Game Hunting in Africa* (1909), which exploited public interest in Theodore Roosevelt's African hunting safari that year. When Roosevelt refused to let Selig send a cameraman along on the expedition, Selig hired a vaudeville actor who did imitations of Roosevelt, bought an aged lion from a menagerie owner, used black Americans as "Africans," and simulated the big game hunt, climaxing with the shooting of the lion. Though the name of Roosevelt was not used, the public thought it was seeing a record of his expedition. The film was a great success with everyone but Roosevelt.

In *Ranch Life in the Great Southwest* (1910), a cowhand first appeared who would become one of the great stars of westerns: Tom Mix. Mix stayed with Selig Polyscope until 1916. Replicas of the Niña, Pinta, and Santa Maria left over from the Chicago World's Fair of 1893 were utilized anew in *The Coming of Columbus* (1912). The film was hand-tinted, the first all-color feature movie, and won Selig a medal from Pope Pius X.

Two of Selig's productions have found places in American film history. *The Spoilers* (1914), based on Rex Beach's novel, made a film star of stage actor William Farnum and became legendary for its epic, brutal fist fight between Farnum and actor Tom Santschi. *The Spoilers* was also phenomenally successful with the public. *The Adventures of Kathlyn* (1913–1914) was a true film innovation, the first "cliffhanger" serial of a spunky heroine braving death in every episode. Selig, ever the shrewd promoter, arranged for it to be released in tandem with a print version of the serial that ran in Hearst newspapers nationwide. Its success started a whole film genre.

By 1914 Selig's company was at its crest. Besides an enlarged Los Angeles studio, the Chicago plant was still in operation, and Selig had film units at work in Florida, Arizona, and Colorado. He had also assembled a studio menagerie of animals that were used in many films. In 1916 he built a thirty-two acre Los Angeles studio around the "Selig Zoo" near Lincoln Park that was open to visitors. But Selig Polyscope by then was losing actors and directors to more progressive studios that better kept abreast of the movies' rapid advances both as art and industry. In 1918 his studio ceased production. Only the zoo remained in operation, a Los Angeles tourist attraction until 1940.

Selig was involved personally in a few more productions until 1922, but in essence he retired a wealthy man in 1918. He had foreseen early that movies would have a devouring need for good stories and, as he recalled in a 1920 article, he started buying up "film rights to books and plays when authors and playwrights thought it a joke, albeit a well-paying one, to receive fifty dollars [for those rights]. . . . Since then I have resold the rights to some of these for many times what I paid for them." He also had income from continuing calls for Selig Polyscope films such as *The Spoilers*. "I'll never suffer poverty while 'The Spoilers' lives and it bids fair to live forever," he commented ("Cutting Back," p. 130).

The trajectory of Selig's career shows him to have been a person who was both showman and shrewd business opportunist. Away from the studio, he lived quietly with his wife. Though content to retire from active film work, he showed in his later years an abiding love of the industry he had pioneered. The *New York Times* obituary says that in old age Selig "spent much of his time in poring over the archives of the Motion Picture Academy of Arts and Sciences." A few months before his death in Los Angeles, he received a special Academy Award for contributions to the development of the movie industry.

• Materials on the life and career of Selig are in the Billy Rose Theatre Collection at the New York Public Library for the Performing Arts, Lincoln Center. Selig's reminiscences of his career as producer are in "Cutting Back," *Photoplay*, Feb. 1920, pp. 43–46, 130. A selected list of films he produced is in the *International Dictionary of Films and Filmmakers* vol. 4 (1987). Many of Selig's early films are preserved at the Library of Congress. They are cataloged and described in Kemp R. Niver, *Motion Pictures from the Library of Congress Paper Print Collection, 1894–1912*, ed. Bebe Bergsten (1967). The history of the Selig Polyscope movie studio is summarized in Gene Fernett, *American Film Studios: An Historical Encyclopedia* (1988). Obituaries are in the *New York Times*, 17 July 1948, and *Variety*, 21 July 1948.

WILLIAM STEPHENSON

SELIGMAN, Edwin Robert Anderson (25 Apr. 1861–18 July 1939), economist, educator, and government consultant, was born into a prominent Jewish family in New York City, the son of Babette Steinhardt and Joseph Seligman, a distinguished financier and founder of J & W Seligman & Company. Seligman was educated by a private tutor in preparation for entering Columbia Grammar School and later Columbia College. After his college graduation in 1879, Seligman spent three years in Europe, mostly at the University of Berlin and at the University of Heidelberg, where he was influenced by economist Karl Knies and other members of the German historical school. Seligman there developed a lifelong interest in the fields of public finance and policy analysis and would use this knowledge to support practical social reform in the United States as the historical school had done in Germany.

After his return to New York City in 1882, Seligman entered Columbia College's law school and its new School of Political Science, from which he received his LL.B. and M.A. in 1884 and his Ph.D. cum laude one year later. His illustrious teaching career began at Columbia College (later Columbia University) in 1885, and in 1888 he married Caroline Beer, with whom he had at least two children. Seligman was named to the McVickar Professorship in Political Economy in 1904. Serving in this post with dignity and distinction until his retirement in 1931, he was widely recognized as a leading American economist.

Among Seligman's many achievements as an academic economist were efforts along with Richard T. Ely to establish the American Economic Association in 1885. Subsequently, Seligman served as its first treasurer and in 1902–1903 as its president. Along with Henry Carter Adams of the University of Michigan, Seligman gave shape to the fledgling field of "public finance economics," with its numerous inquiries about the goals and consequences of different patterns of taxation and how such taxes affect economic outcomes. Seligman's classic book *The Shifting and Incidence of Taxation* (1899; 5th ed., 1926), broke new ground by exploring the interrelationships between two contrasting distinctions in tax theory, namely, the distinctions between "direct" and "indirect" taxes, on the one hand, and "shifted" and "nonshifted" taxes, on the other. In 1905 Seligman wrote a bestselling economics text, *Principles of Economics, with Special Reference to American Conditions*, which went through twelve editions and a number of translations, including Russian, French, and German in his lifetime. Later editions of Seligman's book contained a detailed discussion of information sources in economics, noting especially where to find quantitative studies about economic subjects in the United States, Britain, and elsewhere. Also addressing policy questions, the book featured discussions of typically American problems such as the "trust" problem in business, the regulation of the railroads, and debate about bank and monetary reform. While acknowledging abuses of protectionism in subsidizing unproductive businesses, Seligman concluded that, on balance, protectionism had been a wise policy for the United States because it worked to hasten industrial development.

In addition to dealing with questions of public policy toward business, Seligman pioneered the study of the history of economic thought, especially by calling attention to the vast literature on economics and other related questions. He assembled a library of books, pamphlets, and broadsides totaling 20,000 rare volumes in the history of economic thought; it helped give shape to this specialty and is now housed at Columbia University Library. Seligman's stimulating article, "On Some Neglected British Economists," which appeared in the *Economic Journal* (13 [1903]: 335–63, 511–35; repr. in his *Essays in Economics* [1925], pp. 64–121), called attention to several unrecognized contributions to economics and subsequently inspired much original research. Seligman's knowledge of economics and its history informs all of his scientific writings. During his retirement years, he worked as general editor on the massive, fifteen-volume *Encyclopedia of the Social Sciences* until its completion in 1935.

Seligman was a mainstream economist with "historical school" leanings, who generally faulted economists for the error of drawing policy conclusions from simple deductive models. Still, unlike many hostile critics of theoretical economics, Seligman appreciated the theoretical economist's taste for "unyielding abstraction" and called it "absolute theory," suggesting that it played a role in establishing a baseline for more practical discussion (*The Shifting and Incidence of Taxation*, p. 151). In the history of economic thought course that he taught at Columbia, he stated that "all theories are relative and they are bound up with peculiar institutions of the time and place" ("Notes from Edwin R. A. Seligman's Lectures on the History of Economics, 1927–1928" in *Research in the History of Economic Thought and Methodology*, ed. Warren J. Samuels [1992], p. 205). Indeed, Seligman devoted his own career to the reform of several American institutions. In addition to tax reform, Seligman once tried to organize the New York City tailors into producer cooperatives on the model of the early Christian Socialist movement. In his later writings he sadly concluded that "with human nature as it still is found in the ordinary man, co-operation is even less than profit sharing a social panacea or an immediately practicable means of escape from modern industrial evils" (*Principles of Economics*, 12th ed. [1929], p. 446).

Seligman embraced many of the programs now associated with the European reformist movement, such as the enactment of a progressive tax on income in which the *rate* of taxation (not only the absolute amount owed) would go up with the level of income earned. In Seligman's day, the definition of "income" and its measurement was in the process of rapid conceptualization by economists (and accountants), and Seligman believed that it was income and not general property that should be the center of tax-collection efforts. Although his support of "progressivity" in the tax structure was qualified at best, it demonstrated that even respectable scholars could find merit in what opponents viewed as a radical socialist scheme. Seligman's position in *Progressive Taxation in Theory and Practice* (1908), *Studies in Public Finance* (1925; repr., 1969), and *Essays in Taxation* ([1895; repr. 1969], pp. 69–97) helped to pave the way for the adoption of both income tax and progressive rate structures on both the federal and state levels. In 1919 New York State followed Wisconsin's lead and adopted a progressive state income tax system. This development reflected, in part, Seligman's untiring efforts to persuade policy makers to tax "earned income" rather than just real estate and other fixed items of wealth.

In 1896 Seligman was described by an editor of *Nature* as "one of the few economists that have influenced politicians" ("Taxation," *Nature*, 19 Mar. 1896, p. 458). Much sought-after for his opinions by the national press associations, Seligman would be regarded today as a successful "media economist." He did not hesitate to take positions, and his pronouncements on many important, contemporary issues were reported in the leading newspapers of his day. He died in Lake Placid, New York.

• Seligman's papers, extensive correspondence, and related materials are housed in the Rare Book and Manuscript Library at Columbia University in New York City. Seligman, whose work was casual and not rigorous on many points of analysis, was sharply criticized for his lack of mathematical rigor; see F. Y. Edgeworth, "Professor Seligman on the Theory of Monopoly" in *Papers Relating to Political Economy* (3 vols., 1925), pp. 143–71). For a more accepting treatment of Seligman's style, see Walter J. Blum and H. Kalven, Jr., *The Uneasy Case for Progressive Taxation* (1953). Seligman's contributions to practical policy analysis are covered in Joseph Dorfman, *The Economic Mind in American Civilization*, vols. 1–5 (1949, 1959; repr. 1969). Additional material about Seligman and his contributions is in Mark Blaug, "Seligman, Edwin, Robert Anderson," in *Great Economists before Keynes* (1986), pp. 218–19), and F. Rozwadowski, "From Recitation Room to Research Seminar: Political Economy at Columbia University," in *Economists and Higher Learning in the Nineteenth Century*, ed. William J. Barber (1993), pp. 169–202. An obituary is in the *New York Times*, 19 July 1939.

LAURENCE S. MOSS

SELIGMAN, Isaac Newton (10 July 1855–30 Sept. 1917), financier and civic leader, was born in Staten Island, New York, the son of Joseph Seligman, an investment banker, and Babette Steinhardt. He was educated at Columbia Grammar School (as a small boy he was tutored by Horatio Alger), and Columbia University, from which he received the A.B. with honors in 1876. While at Columbia, he was a member of the university rowing crew; after graduation he was active in the alumni association.

In 1876 Isaac Seligman began his business career in the New Orleans branch of J. & W. Seligman & Co., the investment banking firm founded by his father and uncles. General practice in the firm was to appoint family members to head branch offices. He transferred to the New York office in 1878 and became a partner in the firm in 1881. In 1894, after the death of Jesse Seligman, who had succeeded their father, Isaac Newton Seligman became president of the company. Under his leadership the firm retained its connections with the financial operations of the U.S. government established by Joseph Seligman. The firm had frequently served as an adviser to the treasury on new bond issues and refinancing. It was also one of seven major negotiators of U.S. railroad securities. J. & W. Seligman & Co. had been one of the first investment banks to place American securities with Continental investors.

Under the new president Seligman & Co. supervised the financial reorganization of the Pere Marquette and other railroads as well as those of the American Steel and Wire Company and the Cramp Steamship Company as part of its U.S. activities. At the turn of the century operations were expanded beyond its traditional sale and servicing of U.S. securities in Europe; the firm participated in loans to Venezuela and facilitated the financial rehabilitation of that country. Loans to other South American, Central American, and Asian countries were also marketed. Seligman & Co. failed to match the growth of other U.S. investment banks in this period; its Frankfurt office (Seligman & Stettheimer) closed in 1900 and the Paris branch in 1910. In at least one case a branch was closed because no family member was available to operate it. By 1914 Seligman & Co. was no longer one of the top five U.S. investment banks. Nevertheless, the firm did participate in loans to France in 1914.

Isaac Newton Seligman was a trustee of the U.S. Savings Bank and the Munich Reinsurance Company and a director of the Lincoln Trust Company, in addition to his activities with his own firm. He was also a member of the Sound Money League.

Seligman's career as a civic, charitable, and cultural leader was one of deep and wide-ranging commitments. His efforts and accomplishments followed a family tradition: his father had also been active in such pursuits, but the son's efforts far surpassed them. He served as treasurer of so many charitable and civic efforts that his absence from the firm was cause for comment. His civic interests included the Citizens' Union and the City and Suburban Homes Company (an organization promoting model tenements), for both of which he served as treasurer. He was vice president of the People's Institute and the New York Chamber of Commerce; he chaired the chamber's committee on taxation. He was the head of the Civic Forum and one of the founders of the Child Labor Association. Seligman was a trustee of the McKinley Memorial Association, the Legal Aid Society, the National Civic Federation, the Civic Forum, and the Association for the Preservation of the Adirondacks as well as a director of the New York Forest Preserve Association. He promoted civil service reform and fought the "social evil" (prostitution) as a member of the Committee of 14 and the Committee of 7. A lifelong Republican, he served on the party's national committee.

Seligman's charitable and religious activities were equally impressive. He served as vice president of United Hebrew Charities and as a trustee of Temple Emanu-El. He was an officer of St. John's Guild, a charity hospital for children. New York governor Levi P. Morton appointed him a trustee of the Manhattan Hospital for the Insane in 1896, a post to which he was reappointed by Governor Theodore Roosevelt. He assembled one of the world's largest collections of Washington Irving manuscripts, which were donated to the New York Public Library on his death.

Seligman's cultural interests centered on music. He was a trustee of the New York Symphony and the New York Oratorio Society. He was among the founders of the Institute of Musical Art and a member of the New York Philharmonic Society. He demonstrated personal artistic ability in music and drawing.

Seligman had married Guta Loeb in 1883. Her father was a partner in the Kuhn, Loeb investment banking firm. They had four children; two apparently died in infancy. Seligman died in New York City as the result of a fractured skull suffered in a fall from his horse.

Isaac Newton Seligman inherited his business position and a strong sense of public duty. His contributions to his city included efforts to improve conditions of life, labor, and justice for ordinary people both by changes in institutions and through direct charity. He also contributed to the religious life of his city and supported the musical arts. In all such efforts he was a founder or an active operating officer, notably generous with both time and means, rather than a mere celebrity figurehead. His efforts constitute a model for effective participation in public service.

• George S. Hellman, ed., *The Family Record of the Descendants of David Seligman* (1913), places Isaac Newton Seligman's career in the context of his remarkable family. More recent sources are Mira Wilkins, *The History of Foreign Investment in the United States to 1914* (1989), pp. 721, 734, 736; Vincent P. Carosso, *Investment Banking in America: A History* (1970), p. 207; and, especially, Barry E. Supple, "A Business Elite: German-Jewish Financiers in Nineteenth-Century New York," *Business History Review* 31 (Summer 1957): 143–78. An obituary is in the *New York Times*, 1 Oct. 1917.

ROBERT C. PUTH

SELIGMAN, Jesse (11 Aug. 1827–23 Apr. 1894), international banker and philanthropist, was born in Baiersdorf, Bavaria, the son of David Seligman, a farmer and woolen merchant, and Fanny Steinhardt, a storekeeper. Jesse left for the United States in 1841, at the behest of his older brothers, who had already established a successful merchant business in New York City. By 1843 the entire Seligman clan of eight brothers (Joseph, William, James, Jesse, Henry, Abraham, Leopold, and Isaac), three sisters (Babet, Rosalie, and Sarah), and their widower father had immigrated to the United States. Jesse managed one of the brothers' merchandise stores in Clinton, Alabama, from 1843 to 1848 then, after selling the store, rejoined his brothers in New York. In 1850 he left the management of another of the brothers' stores in Watertown, New York, to head for California's gold fields.

Seligman opened a general merchandise store, J. Seligman & Company, in San Francisco. His business was one of the few survivors of a fire that swept the city in 1851. He had leased a brick building for his store, preventing disaster in a town built mostly of wooden structures. He did not take undue advantage of his success, however. With his competition wiped out, Seligman continued to offer the same prices after the fire. He joined Howard Fire Company Number 3, the unit that saved his building, in appreciation for the firemen's efforts. He also became a member of the Original Vigilance Committee, an organization designed to maintain law and order. He joined after a stranger shot at him and narrowly missed, only to realize he had mistaken Seligman for someone else. In 1852 Seligman added to his community service by becoming a member of the San Francisco Committee of Twenty-One, a vigilance organization that supervised elections and supported city and state candidates who maintained clean and honest images. Seligman visited Munich in 1852, where he became engaged to Henrietta Hellmann, whose brothers later became business partners of the Seligmans. They were married in 1854 and had seven children.

The Seligmans' family business endeavors continued to expand. Though he did not return to New York until 1857, Seligman was an important financial contributor toward his brothers' eastern successes. In 1853 he became an active member of New York based W. [William] Seligman & Company, Dry Goods. Jesse and his brothers Joseph and James moved the family into investment banking in 1864, and Jesse was especially capable at attracting business and managing social affairs. Upon Joseph's death in 1880, Jesse became the head of the banking house.

The Seligman firm rose to national prominence during the Civil War. Their early merchandising experiences in the South and their northern financial successes familiarized them with the monetary situations within each region. Their strongest ties, however, lay with the Union, where they had both personal and business connections. In 1848, shortly after opening the store in Watertown, Jesse had met young Lieutenant Ulysses S. Grant. They became close friends, and Seligman later urged President Abraham Lincoln to put General Grant in command of the Union forces.

The Seligman bank was one of the few investment banks able to help the Union during the war. President Lincoln relied on the Seligman firm for national support and international legitimacy. The brothers had survived earlier economic pitfalls, such as the panic of 1857, by liquidating their assets and keeping their money out of circulation. They also kept several of their stores after moving into banking, which enabled them to fill some of the Union's clothing contracts during the war. The Seligmans joined thirty-five other merchants in 1861 in contributing equal sums toward clothing for the Union's Seventh Regiment. In addition, Jesse and Joseph Seligman organized the sale of close to $200 million worth of U.S. bonds in Frankfort (in what is now Germany). This move helped the Union at a time when other European countries like England and France hesitated to become involved.

The Seligman firm maintained its close relationship with the federal government after the war. The bank, J. and W. Seligman & Company, established branches in London, Paris, Amsterdam, Frankfort, San Francisco, and New Orleans. International expansion helped the company survive amidst a bleak domestic economy. The brothers were particularly interested in the possibilities associated with southern railway links to Mexico. As early supporters of western expansion, they invested money in the Atlantic and Pacific Railroad (later renamed the Santa Fe and the St. Louis–San Francisco Railway Company). In 1880 Jesse Seligman became director of the railroad. He was also head of the investment syndicate that placed U.S. shares in the Panama Canal. Railroad speculation again brought the Seligman firm into contact with other merchants. They dealt with Daniel Drew, James Fisk, and Jay Gould over Erie Railroad negotiations. Gould in particular benefited from the alliance: the Seligman firm guaranteed his bail bond when he was imprisoned for attempting to corner the gold market.

Jesse Seligman's interest in people extended beyond his ties to the family. In San Francisco and in New York City he became well known as a philanthropist and community leader. In 1859 Jesse and his brother Joseph founded the Hebrew Benevolent and Orphan Asylum, a special source of pride for Jesse. He also was a director of both the New York Association for Improving the Condition of the Poor and the American Museum of Natural History. Twice he declined the Republican nomination for mayor of New York City. One of his political connections, however, ended bitterly. He resigned as an officer of the Union League Club in 1893 after twenty-five years of membership, the last fourteen of which he served as vice president. His son Theodore Seligman, a Harvard graduate and a lawyer, was rejected for admission into the club when several younger members blackballed him. Jesse blamed the incident on anti-Semitism and never again entered the club.

In 1894, facing declining health, Seligman traveled by private rail to California. The trip included his lone visit to the town of Seligman, Arizona, which was named for him. He died at Coronado Beach, California.

• An organized collection of published as well as unpublished material on Seligman and his family network is in the Bass Collection at the University of Oklahoma (Norman). A helpful source that includes the brothers' nonbanking enterprises is H. Craig Miner, *The St. Louis–San Francisco Transcontinental Railroad: The Thirty-fifth Parallel Project, 1853–1890* (1972). The story of the firm, beginning with Seligman and his brothers and continuing into the twentieth century, is told in Ross L. Muir and Carl J. White, *Over the Long Term: The Story of J. and W. Seligman & Company* (1964). An obituary is in the *New York Times*, 24 April 1894.

KELLY L. LANKFORD
DANIEL A. WREN

SELIGMAN, Joseph (22 Nov. 1819–25 Apr. 1880), merchant, investment banker, and New York civic leader, was born in Baiersdorf, Bavaria, the son of David Seligman and Fanny Steinhardt. Joseph, who excelled in literature and in the classics, graduated from the Erlangen Gymnasium and started to study medicine. Resentful of the economic and sociopolitical restrictions against Jews in the Germanies, he decided against a career in medicine and against one in the wool-weaving business of his father and in 1837 made the long journey on the ship *The Telegraph* from Bremen to New York. He then went to Mauch Chunk, Pennsylvania, to be with his cousin Lewis Seligman and was introduced to Asa Packer, the owner of a canal boat construction company. Seligman acquired business skills while working between 1837 and 1839 for Packer, first as a clerk and then as his secretary.

Seligman, who left Packer in 1839, became a merchant who established himself as the patriarch of a family business. Operating a peddling business in the vicinity of Lancaster, Pennsylvania, Seligman sold clothing and jewelry to farmers. In 1839 he opened a store in Lancaster and that same year brought his brothers William and James from Bavaria to assist him in its operation. In 1841 Seligman, who realized that business was becoming intensively competitive in Lancaster, moved the family business to the South. Seligman and his brothers, including a third, Jesse, who had just arrived, established a dry goods store in Selma, Alabama, and also successfully peddled in the town's hinterland. The increased business activities of the Seligmans enabled Joseph to bring even more brothers to America: Abraham, Isaac, and Leopold in 1842; Henry in 1843. After these other brothers arrived in Alabama, Joseph Seligman opened three additional stores near Selma. In 1848 the autocratic Seligman, thinking that the business environment would be better in the North, quickly sold out his stores both in and near Selma. With James and William, he went that year to New York City and established J. Seligman and Brothers at 46 Pine Street. In October 1848 Seligman married Babette Steinhardt, with whom he had nine children.

Primarily directed by Joseph, J. Seligman and Brothers evolved into a leading clothing and importing operation. From the profits of the business, Joseph established branch stores in Watertown, New York, in St. Louis, and in San Francisco. By 1857 Seligman displayed acumen and shrewdness, centralizing the capital of the firm's operations and paying for European merchandise with gold bars from the San Francisco branch, which had been directed by Henry. Seligman and his firm also became involved in the sectional strife between the North and the South. On 20 April 1861, eight days after the shelling on Fort Sumter, Seligman, who vehemently opposed slavery, was selected as a vice president of a large Union meeting in New York City. During the autumn and winter of 1861, he made frequent trips to Washington and entered into contracts to supply military clothing to Union armies.

Recognizing the potential of profits in the world of finance, in 1862 Seligman formed the international banking firm of J. and W. Seligman and Company; he headed this firm in New York City and empowered his brothers to direct the activities of branches in San Francisco, New Orleans, London, and Paris. Seligman traveled to Germany in the summer of 1862 to concentrate his efforts on the sale of Treasury securities; he set up a Frankfurt branch, known as Seligman and Stettheimer, and authorized his brothers Abraham and Henry to direct the operations.

The Frankfurt branch experienced great success during the Civil War, especially by finding European buyers for Treasury bonds with a coupon of 6 percent. Because there were few buyers of Union debt either in England or in France, the sale of about $200 million worth of government securities by Seligman's agency corresponded in importance to the victory of the Union at Gettysburg (W. E. Dodd, *Robert J. Walker* [1914], and Hugh McCulloch, *Men and Manners of*

Half a Century [1888], pp. 183–84). Seligman engaged during the late 1860s in other financial activities to bolster the strength of his banking firm. He derived profits from the timely buying and selling of foreign currencies and of discounted cotton bills.

Seligman, a friend of Ulysses S. Grant, played an important role in attempting to resolve major financial and economic problems arising in the nation during the 1870s. The Seligman houses in New York, London, and Frankfurt were named in 1871 as fiscal agents for the State and Navy departments. That year Seligman also became involved with the question of refunding Treasury securities; he worked with Treasury Secretary George Boutwell to develop a refunding formula and on 28 February 1871 secured Boutwell's consent for the Frankfurt house to serve as the agent for the conversion of the 5-20s to new bonds with a coupon of 4.5 percent. Seligman knew that the coupon of these bonds was a half percent too low and that this offering would not go well. On 11 August of that year, Boutwell gave consent for Seligman's Frankfurt and London branches to participate in the syndicate of Jay Cooke for the successful conversion of $130 million of 5-20s from a 6 percent to a 5 percent coupon.

With the panic of 1873, Seligman, along with other investment bankers, met with Grant on 21 September in New York and proposed remedies for the ailing economy. Seligman suggested that the Treasury should purchase bonds and deposit currency into major banks so that the economy would gradually recover. After this conference he was asked by the president to head the Treasury Department; he graciously turned down this offer, believing that he should concentrate on promoting the interests of his banking house. The year after the panic, Seligman, who offered to Treasury Secretary Benjamin Bristow an impressive plan for the lowering of government interest payments, negotiated with this department on 28 July 1874 a contract to serve in a syndicate with the Rothschilds to offer $55 million worth of Treasury securities. During the last half of the 1870s Seligman negotiated five contracts with the Treasury Department and worked in syndicates with the Morgan, Belmont, and Rothschild houses to complete the department's refunding program through the sale of Treasury securities with coupons of 5 percent or less (*John Sherman's Recollections of Forty Years*, vol. 1 [1895], p. 570).

Seligman, too, was a participant in numerous activities and organizations in New York City during the last half of the nineteenth century. As a Republican who favored municipal reforms, he served on the Committee of Seventy and helped to bring to an end the "Tweed ring" and its corrupt governance of the city (*New York Times Supplement*, 5 Sept. 1871). Seligman was a member of the New York Board of Education between 1873 and 1875, having been appointed by the reformist Republican mayor William Havemeyer. Mayor William H. Wickham named him as one of the five commissioners of rapid transit for the city; this commission, which elected Seligman as its chairman, reported on the creation of an elevated railroad system for the city and helped to establish the Manhattan Railway Company (J. B. Walker, *Fifty Years of Rapid Transit* [1918], pp. 107ff.). Seligman also was associated with the club life of nineteenth-century New York, belonging to the Harmonie Club and serving as vice president of the Union League Club.

Actively involved in Jewish activities and organizations, Seligman in 1860 organized the German Hebrew Orphan Asylum and served as its president. He belonged to Temple Emanu-El, the locus of German Jewry and Reform Judaism in New York; in 1870 Seligman was a member of the temple's building committee. He also served as president of the American Romanian Society and in 1871 funded Benjamin Peixotto in his efforts to stop attacks against Jews in that Balkan state. A man of diverse cultural interests, Seligman helped Felix Adler to establish the Society for Ethical Culture in 1876 and endorsed the movement's central principles of universal morality, humanism, and social reforms; Seligman was elected as president of the society in 1877 and held the position for more than three years. He provided funds for its free kindergartens and industrial school, supported its activities at settlement houses, and recruited to its ranks his friends from Temple Emanu-El.

Though a prominent leader of the American Jewish community, Seligman on 31 May 1877 became a victim of discrimination. Judge Henry Hilton, then the administrator of A. T. Stewart's estate and a former member of the Tweed gang, denied Seligman and his family entry to Stewart's Grand Union Hotel in Saratoga, New York. Hilton was condemned for his prejudicial act by Bret Harte, by Henry Ward Beecher of Brooklyn's Plymouth Church, and by some Protestant financiers in New York. Three years after the Grand Union Hotel affair, Seligman died suddenly while visiting his daughter and her family in New Orleans.

Seligman was a major contributor to nineteenth-century America. This German immigrant started as a peddler, directed a family retail business, and then headed an international investment firm. Seligman secured needed funds for the Union and proffered financial and economic advice to presidents and government leaders. He was also a philanthropist and occupied numerous leadership positions in New York City. Even the incident at Saratoga, which marked the beginnings of social anti-Semitism in America, accentuated Seligman's significance as one of the most prominent leaders of the American German Jewish elite in both New York City and the nation.

• Some letters of Seligman were in the possession of George S. Hellman. Other Seligman letters and significant primary sources relating to his career are housed in the New-York Historical Society in New York City, the American Jewish Archives in Cincinnati, and the Bass Collection of the University of Oklahoma at Norman. Secondary sources and primary materials available for the study of Seligman's career include George S. Hellman, ed., *The Family Register of the Descendants of David Seligman* (1913), which details his life, and the short profile in *The Jewish Encyclopedia*, vol. 2

(1905). His career is described in Linton Wells, "The House of Seligman" (unpublished manuscript, New-York Historical Society, 3 vols., 1931); Hellman, "Joseph Seligman, American Jew," *Publication of the American Jewish Historical Society* 41 (Sept. 1951): 27–40; and Elliot Ashkenazi, "Jewish Commercial Interests between North and South: The Case of the Lehmans and the Seligmans," *American Jewish Archives* 43 (Summer 1991): 25–39. For perceptive interpretations of Seligman's career as a financier, see Ross L. Muir and Carl J. White, *Over the Long Haul: The Story of J. and W. Seligman and Company* (1964); Vincent P. Carosso, *The Morgans: Private International Bankers, 1854–1913* (1987); Barry E. Supple, "A Business Elite: German-Jewish Financiers in Nineteenth-Century New York," *Business History Review* 31 (Summer 1957): 143–78; and Carosso, "A Financial Elite: New York's German-Jewish Investment Bankers," *American Jewish Historical Quarterly* 66 (Sept. 1976): 67–78. Seligman's role in the New York Jewish community is examined by Stephen Birmingham, *Our Crowd: The Great Jewish Families of New York* (1967). The importance of the Grand Union Hotel affair is evaluated by E. Digby Baltzell, *The Protestant Establishment: Aristocracy and Caste in America* (1964); Jacob R. Marcus, *United States Jewry, 1776–1985*, vol. 3 (1993); and Leonard Dinnerstein, *Antisemitism in America* (1994). For Seligman's involvement in the Society for Ethical Culture, see Benny Kraut, *From Reform Judaism to Ethical Culture: The Religious Evolution of Felix Adler* (1979), and Horace L. Friess, *Felix Adler and Ethical Culture: Memories and Studies* (1981). Obituaries are in the *New York Times*, *New York Herald*, and *New York Tribune*, 27 Apr. 1880.

WILLIAM WEISBERGER

SELIJNS, Henricus (bapt. 23 Mar. 1636–Sept. 1701), clergyman, was born in Amsterdam, Holland, the son of Jan Hendrickszoon Selijns, a merchant, and Janneken de Marees. The family had a tradition of active participation in, and had provided several ministers to, the Dutch Reformed church. Selijns was educated in the Amsterdam Reformed church school. In March 1657 he matriculated at the University of Leiden for the study of theology. He passed his examinations in October of that same year and was authorized by the Amsterdam Classis to begin officiating as a *licentiate* in the Reformed church. At Leiden, he came under the influence of the liberal theology of Johannes Cocceius, and thereafter remained a proponent of Cocceian doctrine.

In 1660 the *Deputati ad Res Indicas* (Deputies for Foreign Parts) of the Amsterdam Classis chose Selijns for the ministry in New Netherland. He was called for the Breuckelen (Brooklyn) congregation and was ordained in February; nearly three months after his arrival in New Amsterdam, he was installed on 3 September 1660. Selijns found that the Breuckelen congregation was unable to pay his promised salary, offering him instead 300 guilders' value of grain. Selijns agreed to also preach each week in Director General Petrus Stuyvesant's Bouwerie chapel to increase his compensation. He occasionally preached on Staten Island as well.

Selijns was a popular preacher, garnering approbation from the New York consistory in 1670. He strenuously maintained the independence of the church from the interference of the magistrates in ecclesiastical matters. Under his guidance the Breuckelen congregation developed rapidly. In 1662 he married Machtelt Specht; they had two daughters, both of whom died young.

In 1664, at the expiration of his contract, he returned to Holland. In September 1666 he became minister to the village of Waverveen. During the Franco-Dutch War of 1672, the French occupied Waverveen and burned a good portion of the village. Selijns fled to Amsterdam. He did not return to Waverveen until July 1673. He was absent again from May to November 1675, when he served as an army chaplain to the regiments of the counts of Waldeck and Erpag.

In 1682 after turning down two earlier requests, he reluctantly accepted a call to fill the vacancy left by the death of New York City minister Willem van Nieuwenhuizen. This time he obtained a contract guaranteeing him a salary of 1,000 guilders in cash, passage to America, and other considerations. He began preaching in New York in August 1682. In addition to Sunday services, he held a weekly catechism class and preached occasionally at Bergen, East Jersey, and at Harlem.

Selijns's second tenure in the New World was not harmonious. Under English rule, the Reformed in New York were treated as dissenters, and prudence was necessary to preserve the church. His attempts to placate the Catholic James II's government alienated his more orthodox communicants, who were outraged by his performance of thanksgiving services for the defeat of the Protestant duke of Monmouth's rebellion and for the birth of a Catholic heir to the English throne. Moreover, James's policy of religious toleration allowed numerous sects to flourish. Anabaptists, Brownists, Labadists, and Quakers, among others, proselytized and won adherents from among Selijns's communicants. He summed up his rocky relations with his flock when he labeled them the "wild pigs and bulls of Basham."

Additional difficulties arose for Selijns when, eight months after the death of his first wife, in 1686, he married Margaretha de Riemer, widow of Cornelis Steenwijck, New York's wealthiest citizen. His aggressive attempt to gain control over Steenwijck's estate at the expense of the other heirs estranged him from many. Difficulties came to a head with the 1689 overthrow of James II's New York government. Selijns took sides against popular leader Jacob Leisler, thus antagonizing most of his congregation. His house was searched, his correspondence was seized, and his services were disrupted. Selijns rejoiced at the downfall of Leisler in March 1691. He preached on the occasion, "I had fainted unless I had believed, to see the goodness of the Lord in the land of the living." It was reported that he provided the ladder for Leisler's execution. Thereafter a large segment of his congregation withheld his salary and opposed his ministry.

Despite these difficulties, Selijns continued to work to maintain the independence of the Reformed church in the presence of increasing pressures on behalf of the Church of England. In 1693 Governor Benjamin Fletcher procured the Ministry Act establishing the Anglican church in New York. Selijns and his consistory applied for, and on 11 May 1696 received, a charter guaranteeing the freedom of the Dutch Reformed church. This was the first church charter issued in the colony. Selijns's adept political maneuvering is best illustrated by the fact that when the Anglicans called William Vesey as the first rector of Trinity Church, he assisted in the installation services.

Selijns maintained an extensive correspondence with Dutch, French, and English Reformed ministers and was a noted poet. He prefaced a long Latin poem to Cotton Mather's *Magnalia Christi Americana* (1702). Mather remarked of him, "He had so nimble a faculty of putting his devout thoughts into verse, that he signalized himself by the greatest frequency, perhaps, which ever man used, of sending poems to all persons, in all places, on all occasions; and upon this, as well as upon greater accounts, he was a David unto the flocks of our Lord in the wilderness" (Corwin, p. 76).

Selijns's persistent efforts preserved the Dutch Reformed church in New York and placed it on an equal footing with the Church of England. Moreover, his liberal attitudes toward other denominations greatly contributed toward New York's enduring tradition of religious toleration. He died in New York City.

• Selijns's papers, including his poetry, are in the New-York Historical Society; his Amsterdam correspondence and Brooklyn church book are in the Gardner A. Sage Library, New Brunswick, N.J.; his New York City period church book and related papers are in the Collegiate Reformed Dutch Church, New York, N.Y.; papers relating to his Waverveen period are in the Hervormde Kerk, Waverveen; and additional papers are held by the Amsterdam Gemeentearchief, the Public Record Office, London, and the New York State Library, Albany, N.Y. For Selijns's Brooklyn period see A. P. G. Jos van der Linde, trans. and ed., *Old First Dutch Reformed Church of Brooklyn, New York, First Book of Records, 1660–1752* (1983). For his Waverveen period see A. Eekhof, "De Noord-Amerikaansche predikant Henricus Selijns in de gemeente Waverveen (1666–1682)," *Nederlandsch Archief voor Kerkgeschiedenis* (1916), pp. 97–157. A selection of his correspondence is in Edward T. Corwin, ed., *Ecclesiastical Records, State of New York*, vols. 1–2 (1901–1916). Poetry is in Henry C. Murphy, *Anthology of New Netherland* (1865; repr. 1969). Biographical sketches include Corwin, *A Manual of the Reformed Church in America, 1628–1902* (1902); and Eekhof, *De Hervormde Kerk in Noord Amerika (1624–1664)* (2 vols., 1913) and "Selijns," *Nieuw Nederlandsch Biografisch Woordenboek* 3 (1914): 1159–66. The most recent assessments are Jos van der Linde's essay, "HENRICUS SELIJNS (1636–1701), Dominee, dichter en historicus in Nieuw-Nederland en de Republiek," in *Geen Schepsel Wordt Vergeten* (1985), ed. J. F. Heijbroek et al., pp. 37–59. A portrait is mentioned in Charles Knowles Bolton, *The Founders: Portraits of Persons Born Abroad Who Came to the Colonies in North America before the Year 1701* (1926), p. 994.

DAVID WILLIAM VOORHEES

SELLARO, Vincenzo (24 Apr. 1868–28 Nov. 1932), physician and founder of the Order Sons of Italy in America, was born in Polizzi Generosa in the province of Palermo, Sicily, the son of Giuseppe Sellaro, a shoemaker, and Serafina Polizzotto. As was customary for the first boy in many southern Italian families, he was named after his paternal grandfather. He received his medical degree in 1895 from the University of Naples and immigrated in 1897 to the United States, where he settled in New York City. Following postgraduate courses at the Cornell Medical School, he obtained his medical license in 1898 to practice in New York State.

After establishing his private practice in 1898 at 203 Grand Street in the "Little Italy" section of Manhattan, he noticed that many Italian immigrants were often placed in life-threatening situations because of difficulties in understanding and in being understood by doctors, nurses, and other medical personnel at local hospitals, where only English was spoken. For this reason in 1899 he headed an ad hoc committee of bilingual doctors born in Italy to attack the problem. With financing raised privately from mutual aid societies in the large Italian-American community of New York City, he founded the Columbus Italian Hospital in 1900. By 1902 the building was complete and he became the chief gynecologist. He in 1903 joined the American Medical Association and conducted research on diabetes and cancer. Subsequently, in 1904 at the urging of his wife, he organized a school for midwives under the auspices of the New York City Health Board. This school was a predecessor and eventually was merged a decade later with others into the famous school at Bellevue Hospital.

In 1903 Sellaro married Maria Lignante, a native of Naples; they had three children. He became a naturalized U.S. citizen in 1904 and sent one-way boat tickets for his two brothers and two sisters in Italy. His widowed father also came to New York City but shortly returned to Italy.

Based on his experience in founding the Columbus Italian Hospital, Sellaro realized that for most immigrants to the United States and Canada mutual aid societies had provided opportunities for them to speak their native tongues and to keep their Old Country customs alive. For Italian immigrants, the mutual aid societies were often more tightly knit by ties to the same town or province. Italian-American mutual aid societies were important outlets for assistance to the immigrants, particularly those from small rural agricultural areas, in adjusting to living in large urban industrial cities. Such assistance usually took the form of providing information about job opportunities, giving English-language classes, conducting social events on weekends, and rendering financial aid to members during illnesses or to families when members died. These societies became so widespread in America by the turn of the century that there were about 2,000 such Italian groups in New York City alone.

During 1904 Sellaro conceived the idea of uniting all Italian Americans into one large fraternal organization. On 7 June 1905 an organizational meeting held at his home was attended by lawyer Antonio Marzullo, pharmacist Ludovico Ferrari, sculptor Giuseppe Carlino, and barbers Pietro Viscardi and Roberto Merlo.

The first formal meeting of the order was held three weeks later. At that meeting Sellaro was elected supreme venerable (national president) of the Supreme Lodge of the Sons of Italy. The name of the group was soon changed to the Order Sons of Italy in America (OSIA). A golden lion was adopted as its emblem, and "Liberty, Equality & Fraternity" was chosen as its motto. Its stated goals were to reunite in one single family all Italians scattered throughout the Americas and Canada; to promote moral, intellectual, and material betterment among them; to be a school of mutual benevolence and humanitarian foresight; to participate with all its forces in protecting each member; to keep alive the culture of Italy; and to spread the conviction that participation in American and Canadian political life is a factor of social betterment. It also aimed to provide for the spread of the Italian language, to help in welfare activities on behalf of Italians, and to champion all those causes that infuse the conviction that Italians are valuable workers. Sellaro then proceeded to write a national constitution and a ritual. He also founded the first local OSIA lodge, the Mario Rapisardi Lodge Number 1, with 75 to 100 members, on 31 August 1905. (Initially, lodges were named after Italian heroes and places; Rapisardi was a poet and a professor of literature.) By the end of 1905, there were eight local lodges in New York City and one in nearby Paterson, New Jersey.

As with any rapidly expanding new organization there were growing pains. In absorbing many mutual aid societies, most rank-and-file members were in favor of the OSIA's uniform system of nonsalaried management, although the majority of paid society officers were opposed to it. Even after a mutual aid society voted to join the OSIA as a new lodge and held elections, the former officers with vested financial interests would continue to fight the national leadership by filing lawsuits and by engaging in other obstructive activities. Because of this internal discord, Sellaro resigned on 9 July 1908 and formed the Independent Order of the Sons of Italy.

After Sellaro's successor was expelled in 1909, however, the new supreme venerable, Achille Sabatino, initiated reunification talks. In February 1910, after agreeing to small salaries for some national officers and to the creation of intermediate state lodges, Sellaro and the six lodges that seceded with him rejoined the OSIA. On 10 January 1911 the first Grand Lodge was formed in New York State to oversee the local lodges within its boundaries. The tradition of unpaid volunteer workers serving as local lodge officers continues today. More rapid growth followed with the absorption of many more previously independent mutual aid societies as new lodges. The first Supreme (national) Convention was convened in Paterson, New Jersey, on 18 and 19 April 1914. In the following year a weekly (later a monthly) newspaper *Bollettino Ufficiale* (Official Bulletin) was commenced. The name was subsequently changed to the *OSIA News*.

When the United States entered World War I in 1917, Sellaro was elected president of the Insurance

Fund of the Grand Lodge of New York, a position he held for the remaining fifteen years of his life. During the war, approximately 28,000 members of the OSIA served in the U.S. military, of whom more than 2,000 were killed or wounded. The order gave monthly financial aid in the form of small welfare checks to families of members who were on active duty. By the time the war ended in 1918, the order had attracted 125,000 members in 960 lodges throughout twenty-four states and two Canadian provinces. The wartime assistance was a primary reason why about 20 percent of these new members joined the OSIA. In 1922 Sellaro was knighted by the Italian government for his aid to the Italian-American community and for establishing the OSIA.

Sellaro later became interested in the Masons, even though they were reputed to be anti-Catholic, and was elected by the Garibaldi Masonic Lodge as a grand master. When questioned about this affiliation, he would later write in the *OSIA News* that he joined "in order to emancipate (them) from every prejudice." In 1928 Governor Alfred E. Smith gave Sellaro the key to New York State in recognition of his medical and social contributions. On 18 September 1932 Sellaro was admitted as a patient to the hospital he had founded. He was suffering from the effects of kidney disease, heart disease, diabetes, and arteriosclerosis. After seventy-two days, he lapsed into a coma and died.

Sellaro's greatest contribution remains the founding of the OSIA, which continues to be the largest and longest-surviving Italian-American organization. Since its establishment, the OSIA has evolved from being primarily a large mutual aid society for Italian immigrants to being a social, patriotic, and charitable fraternity for second- and third-generation Italian Americans. By 1995 OSIA had chartered almost 2,700 lodges throughout the United States and Canada, although only about 800 of them have continued to operate with about 80,000 members.

• The most complete collection of documents about Sellaro and the OSIA is maintained by the Immigration History Research Center at the University of Minnesota at St. Paul. For information about the collection, see *Guide to the Records of the OSIA* compiled by John Andreozzi in 1989. A copy of Sellaro's birth record is at the City Hall of Polizzi Generosa in Italy and a copy of his death certificate is available at the Municipal Archives in New York City. A brief biography of Sellaro and a history of the early years of the OSIA were written in Italian in 1925 by Baldo Aquilano, *L'ordine figli d'Italia in America*. An English version was prepared by Ernest L. Biagi, *The Purple Aster* (1961). The only known obituary of Sellaro appears in Italian in *Il progresso* (Progress), a daily newspaper published in New York City, 29 Nov. 1932.

JOSEPH SCAFETTA, JR.

SELLARS, Roy Wood (9 July 1880–5 Sept. 1973), philosopher and educator, was born in Seaforth, Ontario, Canada, the son of Ford Wylis Sellars, a teacher and physician, and Mary Stalker. Soon after Sellars was born, he and his two young siblings moved with their parents to Ann Arbor, where their father completed his medical education at the University of Michigan. The family eventually located in Pinnebog, a rural community in northern Michigan, where Sellars spent his formative years. He took full advantage of his father's well-stocked library and spent many hours talking to him about medicine, science, and history. After a year at the Ferris Institute in Big Rapids to prepare himself for the university and another year teaching at the local one room schoolhouse, he headed for Ann Arbor.

In 1899 Sellars enrolled in the University of Michigan, where Alfred Henry Lloyd and Robert Mark Wenley kindled his interest in philosophy despite great differences between his philosophical disposition and theirs, and he graduated in 1903. He continued his study of philosophy at Hartford Theological Seminary, the University of Wisconsin, and the University of Chicago. Sellars was invited back to the University of Michigan in 1905 as a replacement instructor, and he stayed on, receiving his doctorate in 1908 and remaining a member of the teaching faculty for forty-five years. He spent the academic year 1909–1910 in France and Germany, where he became acquainted with Henri Bergson and Hans Driesch, in sharp contrast to whom he began to develop his own version of evolutionary naturalism. In 1911 he married a cousin, Helen Maud Stalker, and in the next two years two children were born.

At the University of Michigan Sellars regularly taught courses in the philosophy of science, and his closest associates included several biologists and experimental psychologists. A particularly close associate was the distinguished neural anatomist C. Judson Herrick, with whom he frequently discussed scientific perspectives on the mind-body problem. In this scientific environment Sellars's own philosophical perspective was formed and came to fruition. He published prolifically and received recognition from the philosophical community. In 1918 he was elected vice president of the Eastern Division of the American Philosophical Association, and in 1923 he was elected president of the Western Division of the association. He retired from the University of Michigan in 1950 and moved to Ontario and New York, where he continued a very active life of writing and lecturing. His daughter was killed in an automobile accident in 1954, and his wife died in 1962. He then moved back to Ann Arbor, where he continued an active life of writing, on some occasions taking up issues developed by his son Wilfrid—an eminent philosopher first at Yale and then at the University of Pittsburgh. He was honored by a special symposium at the University of Notre Dame on the occasion of his ninetieth birthday. He died in Ann Arbor.

Sellars was a systematic philosopher, and epistemology was the keystone of his philosophical system. As an alternative to the established idealism and the then fashionable varieties of direct realism, he articulated a theory of the nature, conditions, and reach of human knowledge that he called "critical realism." His first book, *Critical Realism* (1916), and his contribution to the cooperative volume *Essays in Critical Realism* (1920) were devoted to articulating an account of knowledge where in a mind-independent object was directly known through the mediation of subjective meanings. Perception was the basic cognitive unit but in itself was seen as a complex act consisting of the interpretative comprehension of external things causally guided by subjective sensory presentations. Perceptual knowing on this account does not terminate in subjective states of mind but in an enduring public object to which we must adjust. Sellars, then, was not faced with the daunting task of inferring external things from the knowledge of internal states, since what is directly though mediately known is the external thing via internal discriminations and cues. By means of higher levels of knowing built upon this basic perceptual knowledge, the independent world initially disclosed in perception is elaborated in more fine-grained detail by scientific theorizing. Human knowing in its basic instances is a matter of levels of disclosure of the structure of the physical world with which we interact.

By virtue of this realistic theory of knowledge, Sellars felt that he had positioned himself to articulate a naturalistic metaphysics and philosophy of mind. He had shown how we could have cognitive access to an independent reality whose structure and characteristics he could now discuss. On the general ontological level Sellars was a materialist at a time when such a view was not at all fashionable. The entities that ultimately constitute the world are physical systems characterized by intrinsic endurance. The macrocosmic systems we directly encounter are secondary endurants that are ultimately composed of primary endurants, the structure and characteristics of which it is the business of physics to determine.

Sellars made an effort to avoid the pitfalls of older forms of materialism by stressing the dynamism and organization of matter is such a way as to account for emergent novelty. His acceptance of the significance of organization led him beyond reductive materialism to an evolutionary account that involved emergent properties as a function of organization. In his *Evolutionary Naturalism* (1922) he presented a theory of evolutionary levels in nature wherein the higher levels were characterized by genuinely novel properties that emerged from the integrative causality at the lower level. He argued that there are junctures in nature at which critical organization occurs, giving rise to novel properties describable by a different kind of law. The levels he distinguished were matter, life, mind, and society; the differences, though real, were seen ultimately to be a matter of degree.

At the level that Sellars characterized as most complex, beings become capable of storing and using past experience to guide their responses to their environment. Organisms capable of this kind of relatively sophisticated behavior are characterized as "minded," and together they constitute the level of mind. This general picture served as the background for Sellars's efforts to deal with what he regarded as the pivotal problem of philosophy, namely, the mind-body problem. He knew that older materialisms foundered on their inability to do justice to the categories of mind and consciousness, and he accepted the burden of showing that his materialism was not similarly deficient. Armed with his critical realist epistemology and his emergent cosmology, he tackled the mind-body problem. The knowing system is basically the organism, and the mind most specifically is the brain in the context of the central nervous system. Sellars was well aware, however, that this quasi-behavioral account of mind did not of itself do justice to the subjective dimension of human experience, the dimension of consciousness. Moreover, we have an acquaintance with ourselves that is not reducible to knowledge about ourselves even as minded. His behavioral account of mind had to be supplemented by an explanation of the privacy of consciousness as well as the phenomenon of introspection.

In contrast to those who maintained that the fact of consciousness points to something other than the brain-mind, Sellars responded that we are not here concerned with two things but simply with two kinds of knowledge of the same thing. Objective psychology and neurophysiology present us with a knowledge of the brain-mind of the same kind as our knowledge of any other physical system. Consciousness, however, is a function of our bearing a unique relation to one physical system, namely, our own brain, the relation of being literally on the inside of it participating in its function. Our consciousness is the inner qualitative content of that physical system that is our brain, which we also know from the outside. Its evolutionary role would appear to be related to the level of guidance required for our sophisticated responses to environmental pressures. Sellars presented an integrated view of these various aspects of his philosophy in *The Philosophy of Physical Realism* (1932).

Although Sellars's reputation was made primarily by his work in epistemology and metaphysics, from his earliest years he was also concerned with the dimension of value, both ethical and religious. Early in his career he published *The Next Step in Democracy* (1916) and *The Next Step in Religion* (1918), and one of his very last efforts was *Social Patterns and Political Horizons* (1970). Consistent with his overall vision, he argued for a critical naturalism in values, scientific humanism in religion, and what he called social realism in politics. Against the background of a general theory of value, he developed an account wherein moral rules and standards were to be constructed, informed by a detailed knowledge of the human situation and guided by moral sensitivity. These standards, which are then the expression of a balance of knowledge and feeling, evolve over time with the changing human situation. Second, he viewed religion as a pervasive cultural force but one that now should give way in favor of a responsible scientific humanism. He was one of the drafters of the *Humanist Manifesto* (1933) and at around the same time wrote a number of articles for the *New Humanist* explaining and defending humanism as a religion. Although one of his earliest books was in political philosophy, most of his work in this area was done late in life. Here his concern with genuine participative democracy led him in a socialist direction, not a utopian socialism but one tempered with an understanding of political realities.

Sellars was a powerful systematic thinker. In publications that spanned more than sixty-five years, he articulated a coherent vision of humanity's place in the world, a vision informed by contemporary science and motivated by a genuine humanism. The general tenor of his reformed materialism is more fashionable now that it was in his day, but it has always been one of the grand alternatives and in him it had one of its clearest modern expressions.

• In addition to numerous articles and contributions to other works, Sellars authored thirteen books. Those not mentioned in the text include. *The Principles and Problems of Philosophy* (1926); *Religion Coming of Age* (1928); *Lending a Hand to Hylas* (1968); *Reflections on American Philosophy from Within* (1969); *Principles, Perspectives and Problems of Philosophy* (1970); *Principles of Emergent Realism*, ed. William Preston Warren (1970); and *Neglected Alternatives*, ed. Warren (1973). Three notable studies of Sellars's philosophy are Norman Melchert, *Realism, Materialism and the Mind* (1968); C. F. Delaney, *Mind and Nature: A Study of the Naturalistic Philosophies of Cohen, Woodbridge, and Sellars* (1969); and Warren, *Roy Wood Sellars* (1975).

C. F. DELANEY

SELLARS, Wilfrid Stalker (20 May 1912–2 July 1989), philosopher, was born in Ann Arbor, Michigan, the son of Roy Wood Sellars, an eminent Critical Realist philosopher, and Helen Maud Stalker. After spending his early years in Ann Arbor, Sellars studied at the Lycée Louis le Grand in Paris and the University of Munich (1931) before returning to the University of Michigan (A.B., 1933) and then going to the University of Buffalo (A.M., 1934). He went on to Oxford University (Oriel College) as a Rhodes scholar, where he was awarded a B.A. with first class honors in philosophy, politics, and economics (1936; M.A., 1940). This was followed by a year at Harvard. His first academic position was as assistant professor of philosophy at the University of Iowa (1938–1943).

Sellars saw active duty as a U.S. Naval Reserve officer, first as an ensign and later a lieutenant, assigned to Air Combat Intelligence, Atlantic Fleet Anti-Submarine Development. In 1945–1946 he was assigned to the Navy Department. In 1946 he became assistant professor of philosophy at the University of Minnesota. He was promoted to professor in 1951 and chaired the philosophy department from 1952 to 1959. On leave from Minnesota in 1958–1959, he visited at Yale University and moved there as professor of philosophy (1959–1963). In 1963 he moved to the University of Pittsburgh as university professor of philosophy and research professor of the history and philosophy of science, a post he held until his death.

At various times after coming to Pittsburgh, Sellars visited at the Universities of Arizona, Illinois, Indiana, and Massachusetts, and at Princeton and Rockefeller Universities. While at Minnesota he had been special lecturer in philosophy at the University of London in 1956, delivering the lectures that were published as "Empiricism and the Philosophy of Mind," his master work. He gave the John Locke Lectures for 1965–1966 at Oxford, the John Dewey Lectures for 1973–1974 at the University of Chicago, the Paul Carus Lectures for 1977–1978 at the Eastern Division meetings of the American Philosophical Association, and the Ernst Cassirer Lectures at Yale in 1979. He served as president of the APA Eastern Division in 1970–1971.

Sellars's first wife, Mary, a writer of short stories, died in 1970, after a long illness. He married his longtime companion Susanna Felder Downey in 1988, shortly before his death in Pittsburgh.

From the beginning, Sellars was a resolutely systematic philosopher, who saw all philosophical problems as both intimately interrelated and ultimately unintelligible apart from an appreciation of their deep roots in the history of philosophy. Both of these commitments distinguished him from most of his colleagues in the Anglo-American tradition that came to be known as "analytic philosophy"—a tradition in which he was nonetheless firmly situated by his concern for careful logical analysis and the philosophy of science. Richard Rorty, on whom he had a great influence, described his distinctive approach as "the spirit of Hegel, bound in the fetters of Carnap." The permanent significance of Sellars's work lies as much in the synoptic character of his philosophical vision as it does in his many detailed contributions to philosophers' understanding of particular issues. But that same systematicity contributes also to the notorious difficulty of his thought. The fact that one needed to read what he wrote on so many different topics in order to make sense of what he said about any one of them (what he himself referred to as the "flower in the cranied wall" character of his writing) too often led to Sellars being more admired than understood.

Sellars is perhaps best known for his arguments (in "Empiricism and the Philosophy of Mind") against the "Myth of the Given," the Cartesian, foundationalist idea that there can be mental occurrences whose mere uncontexted occurrence can constitute awareness that something is the case. Against this traditional idea, he maintains that "all awareness is a linguistic affair," because no state or act can be counted as a belief or a thought unless it stands in inferential relations to other beliefs and thoughts. "In characterizing an episode or state as that of *knowing*, we are not giving an empirical description of that episode or state; we are placing it in the logical space of reasons, of justifying and being able to justify what one says." Knowledge, even of the contents of one's own mind, is always a matter of the application of concepts. Grasping a concept is in the first instance practically mastering the use of a word—paradigmatically its use in the game of giving and asking for reasons. So we learn to think only as one aspect of learning to talk.

In this same essay, Sellars offers an important and influential diagnosis of the nature of the incorrigibility of reports on how things merely *seem* to us, by contrast to claims about how things really *are*—the phenomenon, he claims, that misled Descartes into his fateful treatment of awareness of the contents of our own minds as immediate. "Seems" talk is not an autonomous stratum of language; its concepts are parasitic on those of robust, fallible "is" talk. The fundamental practice from which the empirical content of our concepts derives is that of making perceptual reports on how things are—for instance, claiming that that ball, there, is red. This involves two dimensions: reliable noninferential dispositions to respond differentially to red things (which we can share with pigeons and photocells), and an inferentially articulated commitment or endorsement (whereby one who is master of the relevant justificatory practices, in making the claim thereby becomes committed to something entailing that the ball is colored, and incompatible with the ball being green). Against the background of such a practice, it is possible to master the use of *"looks* red," as in order when one is otherwise disposed noninferentially to report the presence of something red, but because of collateral beliefs (say, about the nonstandardness of the viewing conditions) is unwilling to undertake the commitment that disposition usually engenders. Thus there is no appearance/reality distinction of the sort evinced by the difference in fallibility between "That is red*"* and "That (merely) seems (looks) red," possible for "That seems red*"* and "That (merely) *seems* to seem red." But the incorrigibility of how things merely seem is not metaphysically deep, as Descartes thought, but trivial: one cannot be wrong about how things merely seem to one because in saying how they seem, one has withheld an endorsement, merely expressing a noninferential disposition without making a substantive claim or report.

From his very earliest writings, Sellars insists that semantical and intentional concepts are *normative* concepts. This is a lesson he learned from Kant, the figure he always cited as having the greatest influence on his thought. The "logical space of reasons" is a normative space. A fruitful, essential, and characteristic strategy of natural science since the seventeenth century has been to extrude explicitly normative concepts from its explanatory armamentarium. This creates the characteristic philosophical problem of modernity: to explain the relations of mutual inclusion between what Sellars calls "the scientific and the manifest images" of people and their world—the one naturalistic, the other normative. In this sense, for Sellars modern philosophy *is* philosophy of science. He contributed greatly to the development and professionalization of this important subfield of philosophy. Among his many technical innovations might be mentioned his critique of the "layer cake" model of scientific theories, in which theoretical terms are conceived as part of an inferential superstructure optionally added to an in-principle autonomous layer of purely observational terms. Closely related is his rendering of the theory/observation distinction as not an ontological one (as instrumentalism and certain sorts of realism alike maintain), but merely a methodological one—theoretical objects just being those that at the moment are accessible only inferentially, and not also noninferentially.

Wilfrid Sellars is regarded by many as the greatest American philosopher since Charles Sanders Peirce, with whom he shares many notable traits, not the least of which are the scope, depth, and difficulty of his thought. Sellars lived the life of the mind. He once said that the two activities in which he felt himself most truly alive were teaching and writing. He was indeed a spell-binding lecturer and a masterful dialectician. He was revered by generations of students who came to know him in those capacities. Sellars described his life's task as coaxing analytic philosophy from its Humean to its Kantian phase, and although he remained confident that this transition would eventually be effected, in his later years he was saddened by the realization that he would not live to see it completed.

• Sellars's papers are part of the Archive for Scientific Philosophy at the University of Pittsburgh. He published six books: *Science, Perception, and Reality* (1963); *Science and Metaphysics* (1967); *Philosophical Perspectives* (1967); *Essays in Philosophy and Its History* (1975); *Pure Pragmatics and Possible Worlds: The Early Essays of Wilfrid Sellars*, ed. J. Sicha (1980); and *Naturalism and Ontology* (1980). Among his most important articles are three reprinted in *Pure Pragmatics and Possible Worlds*: "Concepts as Involving Laws and Inconceivable without Them" (1948), "A Semantical Solution to the Mind/Body Problem" (1953), and "Inference and Meaning" (1953). Several more are reprinted in *Science, Perception, and Reality*: "Some Reflections on Language Games" (1954), "Empiricism and the Philosophy of Mind" (1956), "Philosophy and the Scientific Image of Man" (1962), "Truth and Correspondence" (1962), and "Phenomenalism" (1963). Another important article, "Language as Thought and Communication" (1968), is reprinted in *Essays in Philosophy and Its History*. Two more articles of note are "Imperatives, Intentions, and the Logic of 'Ought,'" *Methodos* 8 (1956): 228–68, and "Counterfactuals, Dispositions, and the Causal Modalities" in *Minnesota Studies in the Philosophy of Science*, ed. H. Feigl et al. (1958), pp. 225–308. For a useful book-length treatment of Sellars's work and a bibliography of his writings, see C. F. Delaney et al., eds., *The Synoptic Vision* (1977).

ROBERT BRANDOM

SELLERS, Isaiah (1802–6 Mar. 1864), Mississippi River steamboat pilot, was born in Iredell County, North Carolina. Nothing is known of his parentage, and according to later comments by his contemporaries, he received only a limited formal education. In his classic *Life on the Mississippi*, Mark Twain wrote that Sellers had been a keelboat pilot before entering steamboating. Sellers's own diary, which was extant at the time of his death, started with his 1825 experience as a steamboat pilot in the trade from Florence, Alabama, the head of navigation on the lower Tennessee River, to New Orleans. By 1828 he had moved to St. Louis, where in his subsequent 36-year career, he established his fame as the premier pilot of the lower Mississippi. Completing 460 round trips from St. Louis to New Orleans, he navigated a total of 1.4 million miles. Sellers's marriage, which produced two children, ended in 1843 when his wife Amanda died. Her maiden name and the date of their marriage are unknown.

Sellers's career spanned the period when St. Louis grew from a small frontier city into a bustling metropolis. By mid-century the city had about 3,000 steamboat arrivals annually and ranked only behind New York City and New Orleans in steam tonnage receipts. As this lively business accelerated after the panic of 1837, the "time is money" principle caused steamboat designers and owners to construct faster boats. Highly regarded by his peers, Sellers was one of the two pilots of the *J. M. White* (the second boat with that name), which in 1844 made the record run of only ninety-four hours and nine minutes from New Orleans to St. Louis. This trip, which was a calculated time trial, was not surpassed until twenty-six years later when, because of improvements in straightening channels, the distance had been shortened.

Because Sellers was widely known as the pilot who had never lost a boat, his steamers were in demand by passengers. Sellers's concern for safety extended beyond the management of his own boats. In 1826, while piloting the *General Carroll*, he initiated the practice of ordering soundings to be taken by tapping the bell. This signaling method was much clearer and more efficient than the traditional shouted commands. Twenty years later the disastrous collision of the *Maria* and *Sultana*, which was believed to have been caused by a misunderstanding of shouted passing commands, inspired him to propose the much more effective method of signaling by tapping the roof bell. This idea was later adopted by the federal government, which oversaw steamboat inspections and issued uniform traffic rules and regulations. Sellers shared his vast knowledge of the lower Mississippi's ever-shifting channels and stages in reports that he began writing around 1850 for the (New Orleans) *Picayune* under the pseudonym of "Mark Twain." According to the second and more famous Mark Twain, Sellers discontinued these plainly worded, practical observations sometime in the late 1850s, soon after one of his reports was lampooned by the then cub pilot Samuel Langhorne Clemens. Clemens, who assumed the nom de plume Mark Twain only after Sellers's death, later regretted having insulted so distinguished a man.

Sellers was not only admired for his part in establishing a speed record and his accident-free career in a business that was fraught with sinkings and collisions, but also for his remarkable memory of river details and steamboating history. Late in life, he achieved the status of the river's grand old man, who had witnessed the development of the trade and of the lower Mississippi River valley longer than any of his peers. Tall, erect, and handsome, with dark hair that he retained to his death, Sellers was a striking figure. By all accounts he was unfailingly gracious and modest. Although he worked in a group with a reputation for coarse and vulgar language, he refrained from profanity. He died from pneumonia in Memphis on what proved to be his final run from St. Louis. When his body was returned for burial in St. Louis on the *Henry von Phul*, the flags on all docked steamboats were flown at half mast. His grave in Bellefontaine Cemetery was marked by a large white marble monument that depicted a tall man in frock coat and cap standing at a steamboat wheel.

• The fate of Sellers's diary is unknown. A biographical sketch is in the archives of the Missouri Historical Society, St. Louis, and the society's library has newspaper clippings from 1935 and 1956 about Sellers. Information on some of the steamboats piloted by Sellers are in Frederick Way, Jr., comp., *Way's Packet Directory 1848–1983* (1983). For Mark Twain's appreciation of Sellers, see *Life on the Mississippi* (1883). Sellers's career is also described in John F. Darby, *Personal Recollections* (1880). The most extensive biographical sketch is in E. W. Gould, *Fifty Years on the Mississippi* (1889). The story of the *J. M. White* is covered in Herbert Quick and Edward Quick, *Mississippi Steamboatin'* (c. 1926). For the history of lower Mississippi steamboating during Sellers's era, see Louis C. Hunter, *Steamboats on the Western Rivers: An Economic and Technological History* (1949); William Hyde and Howard L. Conard, eds., *Encyclopedia of the History of St. Louis* (1899); and J. Thomas Scharf, *History of St. Louis City and County* (1883). Obituaries are in the (St. Louis) *Daily Missouri Democrat* and the *Missouri Republican*, both 10 Mar. 1864.

WILLIAM E. LASS

SELLERS, Peter (8 Sept. 1925–24 July 1980), actor and comedian, was born Peter Richard Henry Sellers in Southsea, Hampshire, England, the son of William Sellers, a pianist, and Agnes Marks, an actress. At age five Sellers made his stage debut in a modestly successful musical comedy revue, *Splash Me*. After attending St. Aloysius College in London, Sellers worked as a drummer in a dance band. From 1943 to 1946 Sellers served in the Royal Air Force and toured with the "Gang Show" in the Middle East before being discharged as a corporal. Prior to his 1951 film debut in *Penny Points to Paradise*, Sellers worked as an entertainment director for a holiday camp (1946–1947) and in British vaudeville beginning in 1948. He continued in vaudeville through the early years of his film career and made his first appearances on BBC (British Broadcasting Corporation) radio in 1952, subsequently appearing as a regular on "Show Time," "Ray's a Laugh," and most memorably with "The Goon Show," which remains a cult favorite for comedy fans. The seven-year run of this series, which also featured Harry Secombe, Spike Milligan, Eric Sykes, and Michael Bentine, was marked by the irreverent humor that would be evident in Sellers's greatest films.

On the screen Sellers appeared in numerous movies before scoring a major success. The best of these were *The Ladykillers* (1955), *The Man Who Never Was* (1955; as Winston Churchill's voice), *The Smallest Show on Earth* (1957), and *The Naked Truth* (1958). In 1959 Sellers appeared in two films that elevated him to screen stardom: *The Mouse That Roared* (in which he expertly played three roles, including an elderly duchess modeled on actress Margaret Rutherford) and the popular *I'm All Right, Jack*. Sellers's fame spread outside England during the early 1960s, and his outrageous virtuoso comic acting—which combined a sophisticated level of improvisatory skill and the ability to inhabit a remarkably wide variety of characters—shone in many films during that era. Most outstanding among these were two Stanley Kubrick films: *Lolita* (1962), in which he played an intellectual impersonating a series of characters, and *Dr. Strangelove; or, How I Learned to Stop Worrying and Love the Bomb* (1964), in which he again played three roles: a mild-mannered president of the United States, a stiff-upper-lipped Royal Air Force commander, and a wheelchair bound ex-Nazi scientist with a speech impediment. As film historian Raymond Durgnat has written, Sellers's three characters in *Dr. Strangelove* "separately and together, hauntingly disassociated logic, purpose, and emotion," helping the film to achieve its unique balance between absurd comedy and nuclear-age anxiety.

Sellers's ability to inhabit so many diverse characters with such ease made his own persona difficult to ascertain. He once told an interviewer, "As far as I'm aware, I have no personality of my own whatsoever to offer the public. I have nothing to project." He was at his best in roles that permitted him ample opportunity to demonstrate his improvisatory genius and physical adeptness, while also permitting him to indulge in a wide array of accents and vocal tics. In fact, as he once said, "I always think of the voice first. Perhaps this comes from my radio days. The voice determines everything else."

The Pink Panther (1963), in which Sellers played the hilariously accident-prone Inspector Clouseau, was the first of his memorable "Pink Panther" films. The Pink Panther sequels, which include *A Shot in the Dark* (1964), *The Return of the Pink Panther* (1974), *The Pink Panther Strikes Again* (1976), and *The Revenge of the Pink Panther* (1978), provided Sellers with a perfect comic character through which he could improvise outrageous bits of comedy. Despite his fine performances in numerous other films, most movie fans associate Sellers primarily with the Pink Panther series.

In 1960 Sellers produced a short film, *The Running, Jumping, and Standing Still Film*, directed by Richard Lester (the film won a Golden Gate Award at the San Francisco International Film Festival as best fiction short subject), and in 1961 he directed and starred in the modestly received *Mister Topaze*. Sellers acted in many films throughout the 1960s; most were unsuccessful. Aside from the Pink Panther entries, the best of his 1960s films were *Waltz of the Toreadors* (1962), based on the old stage play; *The Dock Brief* (1963), with an outstanding script by John Mortimer; *The World of Henry Orient* (1964), which allowed Sellers again to play a multitude of characters; and Woody Allen's *What's New Pussycat?* (1965).

Of Sellers's highly improvisatory, lunatic screen acting, producer Charles Feldman once noted: "The only way to make a film with him is to let him direct, write and produce it as well as star in it." When Sellers worked with strong directors there was frequently

strife, as was the case of *Kiss Me Stupid* (1964), directed by Billy Wilder. The two did battle over the script and Wilder's interpretation of Sellers's character; neither remembered the experience positively. During the 1970s Sellers continued to work in film, with more disappointments than triumphs. However, he generally gave outstanding performances, as in Neil Simon's *Murder by Death* (1976) and the Pink Panther sequels. Sellers's most outstanding role of the 1970s was as Chance in a screen version of Jerzy Kosinski's novel *Being There* (1979). Sellers had in fact hounded Kosinski to let him have the rights to make a film of the novel (sending Kosinski almost daily letters and telegrams signed "Chance"), and, under director Hal Ashby, Sellers gave a beautifully modulated performance as a simple-minded gardener mistaken for a genius by some wealthy and high-powered individuals. His remarkable performance was acknowledged by a well-deserved Academy Award nomination for best actor. Colleagues and friends noted that Chance may be the character most like Sellers in real life since he, too, was an extremely shy, withdrawn man off camera.

Sellers suffered from serious heart trouble in his later years and completed only one more film after *Being There*. *The Fiendish Plot of Dr. Fu Manchu* (1980) was not his best effort, but it offered some serviceable opportunities for him to demonstrate his comic versatility. In 1982 Blake Edwards, director of the Pink Panther films, released *The Trail of the Pink Panther*, in which Sellers is seen as Inspector Clouseau for the last time in a film made up of outtakes from previous Pink Panther movies.

Sellers was married four times. His first marriage was in 1951 to actress Anne Howe; they had two children before divorcing in 1964. That same year Sellers married Swedish actress Britt Ekland; they had one daughter. That marriage ended in divorce in 1969. Sellers was next married to Miranda Quarry from 1970 to 1974, and three years later, following a highly publicized romance with actress Liza Minnelli, he married actress Lynne Frederick. Sellers died in London after suffering a massive heart attack.

• For information on Sellers, see Steve Allen, *Funny People* (1981); Eric Braun, "Authorized Sellers," *Films*, Aug. 1982; *Current Biography*, Dec. 1960; Peter Evans, *Peter Sellers: The Mask behind the Mask* (1968); Ellen Gilchrist, "Growth in Spring," *Sight and Sound*, Sept. 1991, p. 35; Roger Lewis, *The Life and Death of Peter Sellers* (1991); Lewis, *Peter Sellers* (1990); D. McGillivray, "Peter Sellers," *Focus on Film* (Spring 1974); and D. McVay, "The Man Behind," *Films and Filming*, May 1963. Also see M. Millar, "Goonery and Guinness," *Films and Filming*, Jan. 1983; Spike Milligan, *The Book of the Goons* (1974); Gerald Peary, "Peter Sellers," *American Film* 15 (Apr. 1990): 54–56; Michael Sellers, *P.S. I Love You: An Intimate Portrait of Peter Sellers* (1982); and M. Sinoux, "Bye Bye Birdie—num-num," *Positif*, Feb. 1981. Other works on Sellers include Graham Stark, *Remembering Peter Sellers* (1990); Michael Starr, *Peter Sellers: A Film History* (1991); Derek Sylvester, *Peter Sellers* (1981); D. Thomson, "The Rest Is Sellers," *Film Comment*, Sept.–Oct. 1980; Alexander Walker, *Peter Sellers: The Authorized Biography*

(1981); Elisabeth Weis, ed., *The National Society of Film Critics on the Movie Star* (1981). An obituary is in the *New York Times*, 24 July 1980.

JAMES FISHER

SELZNICK, David O. (10 May 1902–22 June 1965), film producer, was born in Pittsburgh, Pennsylvania, the son of Lewis Joseph Selznick, a Russian-born jeweler, and Florence Sachs. The family moved to New York City in 1910, where Selznick's father, who had a passion for self-promotion, opened the "world's largest jewelry store." The enterprise failed in 1912, and the elder Selznick entered the movie business, then in its infancy. During the next decade he made and lost a fortune, while introducing sons Myron and David to the production, distribution, exhibition, and advertising end of motion picture making. When his debt-ridden father suffered a debilitating stroke in 1923, Selznick dropped out of Columbia University, added the middle initial "O" for effect, and plunged full-time into moviemaking.

His first two pictures were short subjects, one with heavyweight boxer Luis Firpo, the second with matinee idol Rudolph Valentino. The films made him enough money to produce his first feature, *Roulette* (1924). Through family friend Harry Rapf, Selznick was hired as a reader for Metro-Goldwyn-Mayer, at $75 a week. His "unending" flow of ideas, communicated in memoranda several pages in length, led to a job as associate producer in charge of a Tim McCoy western. By combining sets and adjusting production schedules, Selznick made two westerns for not much more than the price of one, *Spoilers of the West* (1927) and *Wyoming* (1928). These were followed by *White Shadows of the South Seas* (1928), but when the youthful Selznick, whose assertiveness struck some coworkers as arrogance, quarreled with director Robert Flaherty he was fired.

Through director William A. Wellman, a friend, Selznick became an associate producer at Paramount. There his story ideas and detail work with producers and writers won praise from production chief B. P. Schulberg. Selznick facilitated Paramount's transition to talkies by recutting and adding sound to *The Four Feathers*, the studio's most popular picture of 1929. Selznick's work with Nancy Carroll in *Dance of Life* (1929) and *Honey* (1930) made her the most popular star of 1930. *Street of Chance* (1930) starred William Powell. *Sarah and Son* (1930) and *Manslaughter* (1930) gave impetus to the career of Fredric March, and *The Texan* (1930) was a success for Gary Cooper. Selznick left Paramount in June 1931 to form his own production unit and make films free from the assembly-line constraints of major studios.

Selznick married Irene Gladys Mayer, daughter of MGM chief Louis B. Mayer, in 1930, despite Mayer's prediction that "no good will ever come of the Selznick boys." The couple had two children. Mayer's warning was not heeded by David Sarnoff, who made Selznick vice president in charge of production at RKO with the promise of autonomy. Selznick responded with "a thorough and heated commitment to his work," characterized by eruptive memos and relentless verbal prodding of cast and crew. His name appeared on twenty pictures in fifteen months, including the blockbuster *King Kong* (1933) and *A Bill of Divorcement* (1932), which introduced Katharine Hepburn to screen audiences. Mayer, admitting his mistake, asked Selznick to return to MGM. Selznick refused until his father-in-law promised him artistic freedom.

Selznick's three-year stay at MGM as producer and vice president was an artistic and financial triumph both for the studio and its "boy wonder." The films reflected Selznick's careful cultivation of every aspect of the production process, from the selection and final polishing of scripts, to the choice of director and cast, to the supervision of editing, postproduction, publicity, and exhibition. *Dinner at Eight* (1933), directed by George Cukor, parlayed an all-star cast and a critique on New York society into the year's biggest hit. *Dancing Lady* (1933) introduced Fred Astaire to the screen, while resuscitating the career of Joan Crawford. *Viva Villa!* (1934) provided Wallace Beery with his greatest role. *Manhattan Melodrama* (1934) with Clark Gable, William Powell, and Myrna Loy received the unexpected boost of being the film that John Dillinger went to see before federal agents gunned him down as he left the theater in Chicago. *David Copperfield* (1935) introduced Freddie Bartholomew to American audiences and reflected Selznick's career-long passion to bring famous literary works to the screen. *Anna Karenina* (1935) with Greta Garbo and Fredric March and *A Tale of Two Cities* (1935) with Ronald Colman were completed as Selznick prepared to leave MGM, once again, to begin his career as Hollywood's most famous independent producer.

Selznick International continued the producer's streak of lavishly mounted motion pictures that did big box office. *Little Lord Fauntleroy* (1936), starring Bartholomew, cost $590,000 to make and eventually grossed $1.7 million. *The Garden of Allah* (1936) starred Marlene Dietrich and Charles Boyer and was one of the earliest films photographed in the three-color Technicolor process. *A Star Is Born* (1937) received seven Academy Award nominations. *The Prisoner of Zenda* (1937) was made for $1.3 million and made $2.8 million. *Nothing Sacred* (1937) teamed Carole Lombard and March under Wellman's direction and became a comedy classic. *The Adventures of Tom Sawyer* (1938) has become a piece of Americana despite mixed reviews and disappointing box office at its release. *Intermezzo* (1939) introduced Ingrid Bergman to American audiences and confirmed Selznick's reputation as a sharp-eyed discoverer and cultivator of young talent.

Selznick's career reached its apogee with *Gone with the Wind*, the Margaret M. Mitchell romantic epic of the Civil War, produced in 1939 for almost $4.5 million, with a running time of 3 hours, 42 minutes. The project was to dominate two years of Selznick's time and demand the combined efforts of as many as fifteen screenwriters and three directors. The picture, perhaps the most beloved in American cinema history, made $160 million at the box office in the fifty years following its premiere ($841 million, according to a *Variety* estimate, in 1987 dollars), profits that mostly went to MGM for contributing Clark Gable to the cast. The film received a record ten Academy Awards, including best picture, and Selznick was honored with the Irving G. Thalberg Memorial Award for his outstanding contribution to the industry.

Rebecca (1940), Selznick's first film with noted British director Alfred Hitchcock, also won best picture honors and was followed by Selznick-Hitchcock collaborations on *Spellbound* (1945), *Notorious* (1946), and *The Paradine Case* (1948). Selznick's postwar work, however, failed to meet the standard he had set during his thirties. Part of the reason appears to have been his declining health and personal habits. Selznick's dependence on Benzedrine as a stimulant during his most productive years and heavy losses in gambling left him physically ruined and financially strapped. His divorce in 1948 and marriage to contract player Jennifer Jones in 1949, with whom he had one child, accelerated his creative decline. Selznick devoted himself to Jones's career, producing *Duel in the Sun* (1946), which met with critical disdain but success at the box office, though high production costs made it a money loser, and *Portrait of Jennie* (1948), which received indifferent critical and public response.

Selznick tried his hand at co-productions in the 1950s, the most memorable of which is *The Third Man* (1950). Although its box-office receipts were relatively good, *A Farewell to Arms* (1957), starring Jones, proved a costly failure to Selznick because of his financial arrangements with the distributor, 20th Century-Fox. He was planning a comeback when he died in Hollywood.

Selznick's legacy is a long line of outstanding motion pictures, distinguished by good scripts and authentically detailed production values. Selznick's shrewd taste in talent and material set a standard by which all Hollywood producers have been measured. His passion for quality and originality marked his contribution to the art of motion picture making.

• Primary material on Selznick abounds in the oral history archives of the American Film Institute, the University of California at Los Angeles, and the University of Southern California as well as the production files of RKO Radio Pictures and Metro-Goldwyn-Mayer and the archives of the Academy of Motion Picture Arts and Sciences. Also see Rudy Behlmer, ed., *Memo from David O. Selznick* (1972); Ronald Bowers, *The Selznick Players* (1976); Bob Thomas, *Selznick* (1971); Ronald Haver, *David O. Selznick's Hollywood* (1980); Irene Mayer Selznick, *A Private View* (1983); George Wead, *Gone with the Wind: A Legend Endures* (1983); Leonard J. Leff, *Hitchcock and Selznick* (1983); and David Thomson, *Showman: The Life of David O. Selznick* (1992). An obituary is in the *New York Times*, 23 June 1965, and an appreciation in the *New York Times*, 26 June 1965.

BRUCE J. EVENSEN

SEMMES, Raphael (27 Sept. 1809–30 Aug. 1877), Confederate rear admiral, was born in Charles County, Maryland, the son of Richard Thompson Semmes, a tobacco farmer, and Catherine Middleton, the daughter of Arthur Middleton, a signer of the Declaration of Independence. Raised by two uncles after his parents' death during his childhood, Semmes attended private schools in Georgetown and spent a brief period at Charlotte Hall Military Academy. He was named a midshipman in 1826.

Semmes's first assignment was aboard the sloop *Lexington*, which took him to Trinidad and many exotic ports in the Mediterranean and Caribbean seas. During extended leaves of absence, he read law with his brother Samuel Semmes and was admitted to the Maryland bar in 1834. Apparently dissatisfied with life in Maryland, Semmes in 1834 moved to Cincinnati. In 1837 he married Anne Elizabeth Spencer; they had six children. For the next several years he spent considerable time at sea in the Gulf of Mexico and at Pensacola as a surveyor of the Gulf Coast. He soon purchased a plot of land in Baldwin County, Alabama, and thereafter considered himself a citizen of that state. Though he was indifferent toward slavery, Semmes genuinely sympathized with southerners, whom he thought victimized by incessant economic oppression at the hands of northern businessmen and politicians.

With the outbreak of hostilities against Mexico in 1846, Semmes was assigned duty aboard the frigate *Raritan*, one of the principal ships assisting General Winfield Scott's landing at Veracruz. Semmes assisted with the assault on the city, commanding a mortar battery placed on the beaches. Though strictly a navy man, he accompanied Scott's forces to Mexico City and saw action at the battles of Cerro Gordo, Churubusco, and Chapultepec. With the surrender of Anotonio López de Santa Anna's armies, Semmes returned to Alabama in November 1847 and over the course of the next three years wrote *Service Afloat and Ashore during the Mexican War*, which was published in 1851 and enjoyed considerable success as a popular account of the war. In late 1856 Semmes was made inspector of lighthouse stations in the Gulf of Mexico, and two years later he became secretary of the Lighthouse Board in Washington.

After Alabama seceded in January 1861, Semmes resigned his commission in the U.S. Navy and offered his services to the Confederate government in Montgomery. He learned from Jefferson Davis that the Confederacy's principal naval strategy involved destroying the Union's commercial fleet to deprive the northern people of basic commodities and thereby weaken their will to fight. The difficulty with this program, however, was that the South owned no cruisers. A number of nonmilitary, seagoing ships had been seized by the Confederates, but most of these, including a 500-ton steamer, the *Havana*, were hardly capable of naval engagement. Nevertheless, anxious to confront Union blockading and merchant vessels, Semmes quickly outfitted the *Havana* with various-sized guns and converted it into a respectable fighting vessel. On 18 April, four days after Fort Sumter surrendered, Semmes received command of this ship, which was recommissioned the CSS *Sumter*. When Semmes steamed into the Gulf of Mexico aboard his new command, his commerce raider was the sole ship in the Confederacy's fleet, which faced a formidable Union navy with nearly 1,800 guns.

Because the *Sumter* was equipped with a low-pressure steam engine capable of maintaining upwards of ten knots, it held considerable advantage over slower sailing vessels. During the next six months, Semmes commanded the *Sumter* through numerous engagements against Union blockading ships, and he eventually took eighteen prizes. Pursued across the Atlantic by several Union vessels, the *Sumter*, with badly damaged boilers, became trapped off the coast of Gibraltar. Consequently, Semmes decided to sell his frigate, and he soon thereafter traveled to England in hopes of obtaining a new ship.

Confederate agent to England James D. Bulloch had skillfully arranged the construction of several cruisers in the Laird shipyards in Liverpool, despite thunderous objections from the U.S. government. One of these ships, the CSS *Alabama*, slipped outside of English waters in August 1862 and sailed to Terceira Island, where Semmes and 82 sailors waited to board it.

The *Alabama* was 200 feet long, over 1,000 tons, and outfitted with eight guns of various sizes and two 300-horsepower engines. Designed with a minimal fifteen-foot draft, it was built exclusively to strike at vessels and then to outrun any pursuers. Under favorable sea conditions, Semmes's ship could make fifteen knots, clearly faster then most other oceangoing vessels. During twenty-two months at sea, Semmes sank, burned, or captured sixty-nine vessels, a remarkable achievement that greatly endeared the *Alabama*'s captain to supporters of the Confederacy.

However, by late spring 1864 the *Alabama* was showing signs of considerable wear, and Semmes was forced to sail for France for repairs. Soon after arriving off the coast of Cherbourg in June, he learned that the USS *Kearsarge*, a frigate of over 1,000 tons, equipped with eight eleven-inch guns, and commanded by Captain John A. Winslow, was sailing within striking distance. Often considered his most ill-advised decision, Semmes ordered his crew to pursue and destroy Winslow's vessel despite his ship's less than perfect condition. On 19 June, as the *Alabama* steamed toward the Union vessel at full power, Winslow ordered the *Kearsarge* to turn and face its pursuer. Semmes waited until the *Alabama* was within one mile of Winslow's ship and then ordered a full barrage of both shot and shell into the *Kearsarge*'s port side. Winslow's well-trained gunners directed their fire at the *Alabama*'s hull beneath the water line, producing two gaping holes in Semmes's ship that rendered it all but defenseless against Winslow's repeated barrages. Forty-five minutes later the *Alabama* sank into the Atlantic about five miles off the coast. Thus ended the career of the South's most feared and successful commerce raiding vessel.

Semmes was rescued by a British yacht cruising in the area, and after touring Europe for several months, he returned to the Confederacy and a hero's welcome. He was subsequently commissioned rear admiral and given command over the James River squadron charged with protecting the capital from amphibious assault. When Richmond was evacuated on 2 April, Semmes ordered all of his ships burned. He then joined the fleeing Confederate government but was forced to surrender to Federal forces at Greensboro, North Carolina.

Semmes received a presidential parole in May 1865, and he immediately returned to Mobile. Upon arrival in South Alabama, though, Semmes was rearrested by order of the secretary of the navy and was sent to Washington to be tried on what amounted to charges of international piracy. After being held for three months, Semmes was released without trial and was allowed to return to Alabama. He was soon thereafter elected probate judge of Mobile County, but the turbulence of congressional Reconstruction politics forced him to leave that office soon after the election. In the fall of 1866 he accepted a teaching post at Louisiana State Seminary, but he likewise felt it necessary to resign that post because of political pressures. After a brief stint as editor of the *Memphis Daily Bulletin*, he returned to Mobile and opened a private law practice in that city. He died at Point Clear, across Mobile Bay.

• Semmes spent considerable time after the Civil War defending the Confederacy and his record at sea. His *Memoirs of Service Afloat during the War between the States* (1868), a work of nearly 800 pages detailing his voyages aboard the *Sumter* and the *Alabama*, is invaluable but largely self-serving. Many of Semmes's papers, drafted while he commanded the *Alabama*, were published as *The Cruise of the "Alabama" and the "Sumter," from the Private Journals and Other Papers of Commander R. Semmes, C.S.N., and Other Officers* (1864). A complete biography of Semmes is John M. Taylor, *Confederate Raider: Raphael Semmes of the "Alabama"* (1994). Also useful but lacking in scholarship and occasionally inaccurate is John T. Foster, *Rebel Sea Raider: The Story of Raphael Semmes* (1965). An outdated and often polemical study is Colyer Meriwether, *Raphael Semmes* (1913). Those interested in a detailed study of the *Alabama-Kearsarge* clash should consult William Marvel, *The "Alabama" & the "Kearsarge": The Sailor's Civil War* (1996). An obituary is in the *Mobile Daily Register*, 31 Aug. 1877.

ROBERT SAUNDERS, JR.

SEMPLE, Ellen Churchill (8 Jan. 1863–8 May 1932), geographer, was born in Louisville, Kentucky, the daughter of Alexander Bonner Semple, a businessman, and Emerin Price. Semple was raised in comfortable upper-middle-class circumstances because of her father's profitable business transactions with both northern and southern interests during the Civil War; this allowed her in later years a measure of freedom to pursue activities of her choosing. She lived in a predominantly female household owing to parental separation (though not divorce) and the departure from home of her oldest brother. Her mother presided firmly over the family, expecting from each of her children their best effort at whatever they undertook. Her uncompromising high standards were particularly influential on her scholarly and brilliant youngest daughter, whose professional work was always guided by those high expectations.

The combination of high family expectations and the education Semple received at public and private schools in Louisville enabled her to gain admittance to Vassar College at the age of fifteen in 1878. She profited enormously from her Vassar years. "I can relate my subsequent work to college training, power of organizing data and drawing conclusions, habits of intellectual work, and of expression secured by English department training," she later wrote. These solid foundations manifest themselves in all of her professional writings, which are notable throughout for their unity of style and engaging expression.

Semple graduated in 1882 with honors and a generalist bachelor of arts degree. She occupied much of her time after graduation teaching Latin, Greek, and ancient history at the Semple School in Louisville, which her oldest sister founded and ran, and traveling. During a visit to London in 1887, she met Duren John Henderson Ward, who was returning home to America from the University of Leipzig. Ward spoke highly to Semple of one of his teachers at Leipzig, the geographer Friedrich Ratzel, who had founded an academic discipline he called anthropogeography, or what is now referred to as human geography. Over the next several years Ward sent her some of Ratzel's writings. Ward and she met at intervals and developed a strong intellectual relationship that also led to a growing personal relationship and to discussion of marriage. Concurrent with this developing bond, Semple was completing her thesis, "Slavery: A Study in Sociology," for a master of arts degree from Vassar, which was granted in 1891. She left later that year to initiate the first of two terms of study with Ratzel. Having decided that for her it would not be possible to combine marriage with a career, she never saw nor corresponded with Ward again.

Semple's work at Leipzig with Ratzel and other renowned teachers came at a time when German universities were the centers of world scholarship; the experience gave her the professional focus she had been seeking for almost a decade. Semple did not earn a degree, but with Ratzel's sustained encouragement and criticism she began her geography writing (her first effort was published in 1894) and became the principal exponent of his ideas in America. In 1901 she published in the *Geographical Journal* a detailed, field-based article, "The Anglo-Saxons of the Kentucky Mountains: A Study in Anthropogeography." It described the eastern part of her native state before it was profoundly altered by coal mining and remained one of her most cited writings. The conclusion of her first decade of geography writing was marked by her first book, *American History and Its Geographic Conditions*, which appeared in 1903. The book established her

professional reputation and led to charter membership in the Association of American Geographers the following year. She was one of only two women so honored along with forty-six men. It led also to an appointment in 1906 as an occasional lecturer in geography at the University of Chicago, a position she held until 1924.

Semple's second book and her most controversial, *Influences of Geographic Environment*, appeared in 1911 and introduced her interpretation of Ratzel's principles of anthropogeography to the English-speaking world. Though widely praised at the time of its publication, over the years it has provoked criticism intermittently for its alleged misstatement of Ratzel's ideas and for its perceived avowal of environmental determinism, the view that the natural environment controls the course of human action, a perspective in geography that increasingly gained disfavor from the 1920s onward.

The principles that Semple enunciated in *Influences of Geographic Environment* informed all her work. In interpreting Ratzel's difficult German for her readers, Semple tested his themes with concrete examples she selected on the basis of wide inductive research and personal observations. She sought to isolate the elements of the natural environment, including that of space, for their significance in history and human progress. In doing so, she warned that the complexity of her subject demanded that precipitate or rigid conclusions be avoided. Yet the declarative force of her narrative style often resulted in assertions that negated her scholarly warning and offered fuel to critics of environmental determinism with its perspective of human response to physical factors. Semple, living at a time when prevailing scientific concepts postulated an orderly universe of cause and effect, was part of a mainstream that accepted environmental determinism.

In 1921 Semple received her first full-time academic appointment as professor of anthropogeography at Clark University's new Graduate School of Geography. The school's trustees paid her $500 a year less than the full-time male professors, who were neither as productive nor as renowned as she, on the grounds that she was a woman and without dependents—"a mid-Victorian argument from a group of modern capitalists," she observed. On her deathbed a decade later she retaliated by revoking a promised gift of a thousand dollars to the university. The year of her appointment at Clark was also the year she became president of the Association of American Geographers, the first woman to hold her profession's highest elected office. It would be sixty-three years before another woman held that position.

The last twenty years of Semple's life were focused on her third book, *The Geography of the Mediterranean Region: Its Relation to Ancient History*, published in 1931, less than six months before her death in West Palm Beach, Florida. She thought it her best book, and classical scholars have praised it, but her geography colleagues, with few exceptions, ignored the work, likely doing so because they wished to dissociate themselves from an author identified with the now passé doctrine of environmental determinism. The fact that few geographers then or later had a substantial interest in the book's time period also figured in its neglect.

Ellen Churchill Semple introduced anthropogeography into America, where she was an influential pioneer woman in academic geography in the first third of the twentieth century and exercised her influence in several ways. She was an effective writer, speaker, and teacher who reached educated lay audiences through her three books and through public lectures. She had a range of teaching experience that few could equal, from elementary school classes to graduate seminars in geography, and her audience of graduate students was probably the largest of her generation because she taught at Chicago and Clark, the two universities in her time that produced the largest number of postgraduates in geography. Indeed, she was the only woman in her day who regularly conducted graduate classes in a Ph.D.-granting department of geography. As such she was an influential role model for women who aspired to a research career in a discipline where such examples were almost nonexistent. Her influence as a role model continued after her death and may be her most enduring legacy. Despite this, none of Semple's students, nor anyone else, emerged as inheritor and disseminator of her ideas. Nor did she encourage it, for she believed that "no scholar was ever made by slavish submission to the ideas of another." Environmental determinism, the idea with which she is correctly associated, has never regained the place in academic geography circles that it had early in the twentieth century, although its easily comprehended physical cause–human effect relationship may resonate with uncritical lay readers today as it did in the past when they encounter the evocative prose of someone like Ellen Churchill Semple.

• Letters by Semple are found in the Wallace W. Atwood Papers at Clark University and in a collection bearing her name at the University of Kentucky; the latter also contains some of her research notes and memorabilia. The most comprehensive modern assessment is Allen D. Bushong, "Ellen Churchill Semple, 1863–1932," *Geographers: Biobibliographical Studies* 8 (1984): 87–94. The career of her most controversial book is traced by John K. Wright, "Miss Semple's *Influences of Geographic Environment*: Notes toward a Bibliography," *Geographical Review* 52 (1962): 346–61. Gender inequity is addressed by Mildred Berman, "Sex Discrimination and Geography: The Case of Ellen Churchill Semple," *Professional Geographer* 26 (1974): 8–11. The most informative obituary is Charles C. Colby, "Ellen Churchill Semple," *Annals of the Association of American Geographers* 23 (1933): 229–40.

ALLEN D. BUSHONG

SENEY, George Ingraham (12 May 1826–7 Apr. 1893), banker and railroad promoter, was born in Astoria, New York, the son of Robert Seney, a Methodist minister, and Jane A. Ingraham. The couple sent the young man to Wesleyan University, but he transferred to what is now New York University, from which he graduated in 1847. He immediately entered on a career in banking in New York City, first with the Gallatin Bank, then with the Bank of North America. In 1849 he married Phoebe Moser, with whom he had nine children. In 1853 he became paying teller at the Metropolitan Bank, the institution with which he was identified throughout his later career. He became cashier in 1857 and was chosen president in 1877.

In 1879 Seney embarked on a series of ventures in railroad finance that were to make him a sizable fortune. He formed a loose association of financiers and railroad executives that quickly came to be known as the Seney Syndicate. The principal figures were Columbus R. Cummings of Chicago; Calvin S. Brice, an Ohio lawyer; General Samuel R. Thomas; Charles Foster, who became governor of Ohio in 1880; Dan Parmelee Eells, a leading banker of Cleveland; and William B. Howard of Illinois. The Seney Syndicate entered railroading mainly by gaining control of railroads emerging from receivership in the late 1870s, reorganizing them, and then extending them by merger and additional construction. Typical was formation of the Peoria, Decatur & Evansville Railway on 9 December 1879 out of the bankrupt Decatur, Mattoon & Southern and the Pekin, Lincoln & Decatur, with Cummings as president and Seney as a director. Eells gained control of the Ohio Central Railroad when it was sold under foreclosure in March 1878 and brought it to completion between Toledo, Columbus, and the Hocking Valley coalfield in 1880. The most important of these operations was the syndicate's consolidation of the La Fayette, Bloomington & Muncie and Lake Erie & Louisville railroads into the Lake Erie & Western Railway on 4 August 1879. With some additional construction, the LE&W by 1881 had a continuous railroad from Sandusky, Ohio, to Bloomington, Illinois. The route was good, but the railroad was handicapped by dependence for traffic on a hostile connection—the New York Central's Lake Shore & Michigan Southern at Fremont, Ohio. The syndicate's other important investment was in the East Tennessee, Virginia & Georgia Railroad, a major regional railroad that became one of the principal components of the Southern Railway system. Seney and Brice became directors of the ETV&G in 1881. Seney and his associates had vague plans for connecting their railroads, especially in effecting a connection between the Ohio Central and the ETV&G, but nothing was accomplished to this end.

Rather, the syndicate embarked on a major project, the New York, Chicago & St. Louis Railway, which almost immediately became known as the Nickel Plate Road when an editorial recommended public support for it. The syndicate met on 3 February 1881 at Seney's office in the Metropolitan Bank, quickly subscribing $14,666,667 to the enterprise; thus, it was exceptionally well financed by the standards of the time. The plan was to build a main line from Buffalo through Cleveland to Chicago, essentially duplicating the western portion of the New York Central's main line. One of the motivations was to provide a friendly connection to the Lake Erie & Western. A branch was projected from Fort Wayne to St. Louis but never built. This was the period in which the incentives in the industry produced a large number of so-called "unnecessary railroads," duplicating existing carriers; a separate project, unrelated to the Seney Syndicate, the New York, West Shore & Buffalo, was paralleling the New York Central main line from Buffalo to New York. William H. Vanderbilt of the New York Central was overtly hostile to the Nickel Plate Road, reportedly offering Seney and his associates in 1881 a million dollars to drop their project. Seney declined and the Nickel Plate was brought to fruition quickly. The main line was completed with a bridge over the Cuyahoga River at Cleveland on 25 August 1882.

Apparently to keep the line out of the hands of his principal rival, Jay Gould, Vanderbilt arranged with Brice on 25 October 1882—only two days after the road had been opened for business—to buy a 53 percent interest in the Nickel Plate for $7,205,000. Vanderbilt replaced Cummings as president of the railroad on 5 January 1883 and most of the Seney Syndicate's directors resigned. They had, however, made a huge profit on the transaction, estimated by Brice at 75 percent of their investment. Seney was reported to have made some $9 million from his various railroad activities and about 1883 to have had a net worth between $12 million and $20 million.

Thereafter his fortunes faded quickly. In spite of his reputation as a conservative banker, his Metropolitan Bank failed on 14 May 1884. The financial writer Henry Clews accused him of stock watering, wash sales, or fictitious transactions, and other reckless behavior in his railroad dealings. Seney liquidated most of his railroad holdings, gave up his directorships, and devoted himself to resolving the problems of his bank. He sold part of his extensive art collection and otherwise devoted his personal fortune to a successful effort to reopen the bank without loss to its depositors. His fortune recovered, partly from appreciation of some ETV&G stock that he had retained, but his syndicate had broken up and he was never again an important figure in railroading. On his death in 1893, none of the major railroad journals noted his passing. His obituaries in New York newspapers noted his benefactions to Wesleyan University, Emory University, the Metropolitan Museum of Art, and several other cultural institutions.

• For additional information on Seney, see Henry Clews, *Fifty Years in Wall Street* (1908); John A. Rehor, *The Nickel Plate Story* (1965); Taylor Hampton, *Nickel Plate Road* (1947); and Maury Klein, *The Great Richmond Terminal* (1970), especially pp. 48–49. An obituary is in the *New York Times*, 8 Apr. 1893.

GEORGE W. HILTON

SENN, Nicholas (31 Oct. 1844–2 Jan. 1908), surgeon and author, was born in Buchs, north-central Switzerland, the son of John Senn and Magdelena (maiden name unknown), farmers. The family came to the United States in 1852 and settled in Ashford, Fond du Lac County, Wisconsin. In 1864 Senn graduated from Fond du Lac High School. He then taught school for two years while he studied medicine and botany with a local doctor, Emanuel Munk. He grew up fluent in French and German, languages spoken in his home.

In 1866 Senn entered the Chicago Medical College. His thesis dealt with the therapeutic uses of digitalis; much of it was based on experiments Senn performed on himself. The thesis successfully contradicted the contemporary belief that digitalis was a cardiac sedative. Senn received his M.D. in 1868 and shared the top honors in the internship examination for Cook County Hospital. The next year he married Aurelia S. Muehlhauser of La Crosse; the couple had two sons, both of whom became physicians.

After his eighteen-month internship (1868–1869) Senn moved to Elmore, Wisconsin, near Ashford, and opened a general practice. His skills as a diagnostician soon brought him a growing practice throughout the region. By 1871 his interests were primarily in surgery. He early saw the importance of medical societies in furthering the education of practicing physicians, joined the Wisconsin State Medical Society in 1870, and regularly gave papers at its meetings.

In 1874 Senn moved to Milwaukee and became an attending physician at the Milwaukee Hospital. His private practice brought him $10,000 in his first year and grew rapidly. He was not modest, either about his ability or his being an authority in his field. Early in his career he became interested in the scientific side of medicine; he had a laboratory constructed in his basement, and he spent many evenings there working especially on gastrointestinal surgery in dogs. He traveled to Germany in 1877, studied at the University of Munich, and obtained a second M.D. in 1878.

The College of Physicians and Surgeons in Chicago appointed Senn professor of surgery in 1884, but he did not choose to move to that city until seven years later. Two or three days a week he traveled eighty-eight miles to give his lectures and conduct his clinics. He became a success not only with the students but also with the physicians and surgeons in Chicago. His operative procedures for fractures of the neck of the femur and his work on the surgery of the pancreas were widely studied. Senn early recognized the three main elements in progressive contemporary surgery: clinical microscopy, animal experimentation, and antiseptic surgical technique.

In 1886 the College of Physicians and Surgeons named Senn professor of the principles and practice of surgery. Rush Medical College offered him the newly created chair of surgical pathology in 1887, but he declined. However, in 1889 Senn accepted Rush's invitation to become professor of the principles of surgery and surgical pathology. Two years later his title was changed to professor of the practice of surgery and clinical surgery; late in 1901 Senn became professor of military surgery. He also served as professor of surgery at the Chicago Polyclinic, a postgraduate institution.

In 1888 Senn reported his test for the diagnosis of injuries to the gastrointestinal canal. He accomplished this by forcing hydrogen through the rectum and into the intestines, a test he developed by performing experiments on himself. His book *Experimental Surgery* (1889) collected much of his early work. Senn reported his pioneering experimental investigation of surgical connections in the gastrointestinal system in an influential 1893 paper. He also made important contributions to plastic surgery, especially in suturing and in providing a satisfactory blood supply; these efforts were especially useful in correcting harelip and after extirpation of tubercular glands. In 1903 Senn became one of the first to use X-rays in the treatment of leukemia.

The military formed an important part of Senn's life. A frequently reproduced portrait shows him in his uniform, with a firm, proud expression. Senn was appointed surgeon general of the Wisconsin National Guard in 1882. In 1891 he founded the Association of Military Surgeons of the National Guard of the United States and twice served as its president. In Illinois, Governor Altgeld appointed him brigadier general in 1892. Senn initiated a careful physical examination program for the National Guard, considerably improving the quality of its soldiers. He served in Cuba during the Spanish-American War and did much to improve the removal of the wounded. He also became known for his conservative surgery on gunshot wounds.

Senn served as surgeon in chief at both St. Joseph's and Presbyterian hospitals in Chicago and as surgeon to Passavant Hospital. He donated two rooms for physicians to St. Joseph's and later died in one of them. Drawing on his considerable income, he donated a $100,000 building for clinical and laboratory purposes to Rush, and $25,000 for the Nicholas Senn Professorship of Surgery. He built up a 10,000-volume library of clinical and research books and journals in many languages and gave it to the Newberry Library; the collection was later moved to the John Crerar Library of Chicago.

In 1896 Senn gave the surgical oration before the American Medical Association; he served as its president in 1897. That year he was chosen as one of ten to address the full meeting of the Twelfth International Medical Congress in Moscow. He was president of the American Surgical Association in 1892.

Senn was an inexhaustible traveler and wrote several travel books, the most popular being *Around the World via Liberia* (1902) and *Tahiti, the Island Paradise* (1906). Travel ultimately led to his death. While climbing a mountain in South America, he suffered an attack of myocarditis; he barely made it back to Chicago before he died.

Senn made experimental work an important part of surgery, developed useful procedures in abdominal and plastic surgery, and furthered both undergraduate and postgraduate medical education. He considerably improved techniques of military surgery. His philanthropy benefited generations of physicians and medical students.

• The University of Chicago Library, Special Collections Department, has a large collection of Senn's manuscripts, lectures, and notes on lectures and clinics. Additional books by Senn include *Intestinal Surgery* (1889), *Surgical Bacteriology* (1889), *Principles of Surgery* (1890), *Pathology and Surgical Treatment of Tumors* (1895), *War Correspondence* (1899), and *Medico-Surgical Aspects of the Spanish-American War* (1900). Ella M. Salmonsen, "Nicholas Senn, M.D., Ph.D., LL.D. (1844–1908): Master Surgeon, Pathologist, and Teacher; Biographical Sketch, with a Complete Bibliography of His Writings," *Bulletin of the Society of Medical History of Chicago* 4 (1928–1935): 268–94, is basic. Also helpful are F. M. Sperry, comp., *A Group of Distinguished Physicians and Surgeons of Chicago* (1904), pp. 15–31; Samuel C. Stanton, "Editorial Expression: Vale, Nicholas Senn," *Military Surgeon* 22 (1908): 144–51; A. R. Koontz, "Nicholas Senn, Surgeon and Soldier; A Happy Combination in Military Medicine," *Military Medicine* 125 (1960): 203–6; P. Natvig, "Nicholas Senn of Milwaukee and Chicago: His Contributions to Plastic Surgery," *Plastic and Reconstructive Surgery* 61 (1978): 167–76; and H. M. Brown, "Reminiscences of Dr. Senn," *Milwaukee History* 4 (1981): 87–94.

WILLIAM K. BEATTY

SENNETT, Mack (17 Jan. 1880–5 Nov. 1960), movie industry pioneer, was born Michael (or Mikall) Sinnott in Danville, Quebec province, Canada, the son of John Francis Sinnott and Catherine Foy, farmers. Michael was a large, energetic boy who did poorly at school. In 1897 the Sinnotts moved to East Berlin, Connecticut. Michael took a job as an ironworker, though he hoped to become a singer. When the family resettled in Northampton, Massachusetts, young Sennett—armed with a letter of introduction from local lawyer Calvin Coolidge—sought out stage star Marie Dressler, who was in town with a touring company. She steered Sennett to producer David Belasco in New York City. As a courtesy to Dressler, Belasco auditioned Sennett in 1900, but he saw no future for him in musicals; the most that could be said for Sennett's untrained bass voice was that it was loud. The producer recommended that the oversized, awkward, clownish twenty-year-old try burlesque.

Sennett's stage career began at the Bowery Theater in 1900. He played the rear end of a two-man burlesque horse. After learning the rudiments of performing in burlesque, Sennett got chorus work in musicals and bit parts in plays, including *Piff! Paff!! Pouff!!!* (1904), *Mlle. Modiste* (1905), and *The Boys of Company B* (1907). In 1908 he caught on with the American Mutoscope and Biograph Company, one of the leading companies in the burgeoning movie industry. By then he was using the name Mack Sennett. In his early days at Biograph, Sennett worked frequently with prolific director D. W. Griffith, though usually in small parts. Linda Arvidson (Mrs. D. W. Griffith), an actress at Biograph, thought Sennett had no future in films. She did not like his crude clowning and his pushiness, though she conceded in her memoir *When the Movies Were Young* (1925) that "he got by pretty well when any social flair was unnecessary" and "was very serious about his policeman and his French dude" (p. 78).

Sennett first made his mark in films playing a comic Frenchman in Biograph's short comedy *The Curtain Pole* (1908). Having made a close study of French comedian Max Linder's films, Sennett fashioned elements of French slapstick and American burlesque into his own distinctive acting style. Sennett's passion for comedy set him apart at Biograph, a studio dominated by Griffith, who specialized in melodramas, social commentary, and sentimental love stories. Griffith had little interest in (or talent for) comedy, but he encouraged Sennett to develop comic scenarios and even direct short comedies. Sennett went at the task with his characteristic energy, even while maintaining a busy acting schedule. By 1910 Biograph had entrusted him with all its comedy productions.

In 1912 Sennett became production head of the Keystone Film Company, newly formed by investors Adam Kessel, Jr., and Charles O. Baumann to mass-produce comedies for distribution by their New York Motion Picture Company. Sennett received a one-third interest in Keystone and a weekly salary. He set up operations in California at the facilities of the recently defunct Bison company and recruited a stock company of talented young performers, including Fred Mace, Mabel Normand, and Ford Sterling from his comedy unit at Biograph. Normand became Keystone's principal leading lady (and Sennett's love interest). Sennett allowed her to direct and even put her in charge of a production unit.

Sennett himself wrote (or improvised) scenarios and directed many Keystone comedies, but even those done by others followed the Sennett formula. He borrowed the ethnic stereotypes of burlesque, the knockabout routines of the music hall, and the slapstick of early French comedy films and added the sense of movement, speed, and space made possible by the moving picture camera and location shooting. Keystone comedy also reflected Sennett's exuberant, brash, irreverent personality. At Biograph he had maintained that authority figures were inherently ridiculous, but Griffith was unconvinced; at Keystone Sennett proved his point with the klutzy, madcap Keystone Kops.

In Keystone pictures emotion and motivation were mere plot devices to generate gags and action. And what action there was! Sennett knew that by manipulating camera speed, people and machines could be turned into on-screen projectiles. The pace was frenzied; chaos was the norm on screen and off. To save money and hasten production Sennett decreed that scenes should be shot only once. He normally had two or three production units at work. By sticking to his comedy formula and maintaining a breakneck production schedule Sennett's fun factory turned out as many as a dozen films in a month.

As the industry's leading supplier of comedy, Sennett had to employ many talented people to meet audience demand for laughs and excitement. Keystone (and Sennett's subsequent production companies) spawned director Frank Capra; actresses Marie Dressler, Gloria Swanson, and Carole Lombard; and comic stalwart Ben Turpin, Mack Swain, Al St. John, Edgar Kennedy, Charley Chase, Fatty Arbuckle, Harry Langdon, and many others. Even Charlie Chaplin, whose comic sensibility was so different from Sennett's, learned the rudiments of moviemaking at Keystone and created his "little tramp" persona there.

In 1915 Keystone's principal investors joined other movie moguls to create the Triangle Film Company. Triangle would finance and market the films of Sennett, Griffith, and Thomas Ince, the industry's most successful producers. Sennett continued to operate Keystone as a unit of Triangle. The new arrangement came at a time when audiences wanted longer, more technically proficient features. Sennett's pictures came to rely less on frenetic slapstick and more on plot and acting. He already had demonstrated a knack for this evolving style with *Tillie's Punctured Romance* (1914), a feature-length comedy starring Normand, Chaplin, and, in her first movie role, Dressler. (Although a path-breaking effort for Sennett and Keystone, the director could not resist bringing in his Kops for a chase sequence.)

Triangle broke up in 1917 when first Griffith, then Sennett, wanted out. Keystone ceased to exist, but Sennett hired many of its actors and technical people for his new company, Mack Sennett Comedies. During the 1920s he enjoyed some success with vehicles for Mabel Normand and Harry Langdon, but by 1929 he was reduced to working for Educational Pictures, a poverty-row studio. In the 1930s Sennett declared bankruptcy and became a minor figure in Hollywood, though he did some comedy shorts with W. C. Fields and Buster Keaton and received a special Academy Award in 1937 for his contributions to screen comedy. In 1947 choreographer Jerome Robbins drew on the Keystone tradition for his highly regarded *Mack Sennett Ballet*. Sennett's early work enjoyed a revival on television during the 1950s, and he brought out a memoir, *King of Comedy*, in 1954. He spent his last years in relative poverty at the Motion Picture Country Home, a charity operation. Sennett, who never married, died in Hollywood.

Sennett's reputation among critics and film scholars was not diminished by his meager and undistinguished output during the sound era. James Agee, in his influential *Life* magazine essay "Comedy's Greatest Era" (3 Sept. 1949), credited Sennett with launching the art of silent comedy. Raymond Durgnat's study of Hollywood comedy, *The Crazy Mirror: Hollywood Comedy and the American Image* (1969), concluded that "Sennett's films have the richness to gain, rather than lose, from the sea-changes of time" (p. 75). In his *Dictionary of Filmmakers* (1972), Georges Sadoul proclaimed Sennett "one of the three great pioneers who fashioned the art of the American Cinema" (p. 230). Walter Kerr, author of *The Silent Clowns* (1979), dissented, finding Sennett's comedies unfunny and insensitive, but Gerald Mast, in *The Comic Mind* (1973) and other publications, depicted Sennett as the central figure in a collective enterprise that generated "a unique, memorable, and unduplicatable, type of comedy that has assumed its place, not only in the history of cinema, but in the much longer history of comedy itself" (Mast [1984], p. 495). Cultural historian Robert Sklar stressed the chaotic element in Sennett's comedies, observing that they "gave audiences their first glimpses of a social perspective that was to become one of the most emotionally powerful of Hollywood formulas—the anarchic individual pitted against disordered violent authority" (p. 109).

Except for the occasional academic seminar or scholarly article, Sennett's work attracted little critical interest during the 1980s and 1990s. He came in for predictable disapproval for his use of ethnic stereotypes, his exploitation of bathing beauties, and his glorification of the machine, but otherwise a new generation of historians and critics concentrated on Keystone's production and marketing strategies within the broader context of the entire industry. This "materialist" film history calls into question such "slapstick connoisseurs" as Walter Kerr, who denigrated Sennett's Keystone comedies in comparison to the more "artistic" comedies made during the 1920s by Chaplin and Keaton. Such comparisons are invalid, according to the revisionists, because Sennett was working under a much different set of commercial, industrial, and technical conventions. Thus the new film history leaves intact, perhaps even enhances, Sennett's standing as an industry pioneer.

Mack Sennett retains his essential place in the history of motion pictures and, consequently, twentieth-century American culture. He was a true American primitive whose vision and enterprise, for all their brashness and crudity, vitalized the art of film at a crucial stage of its development.

• Sennett's papers are at the Margaret Herrick Library, Academy of Motion Picture Arts and Sciences, Los Angeles. Sennett's memoir, *King of Comedy* (1954), is full of exaggerations and errors. *Father Goose: The Story of Mack Sennett* (1934), a popular biography by Gene Fowler, is incomplete. Kalton C. Lahue, *Mack Sennett's Keystone: The Man, the Myth, and the Comedies* (1971), and Kalton C. Lahue and Terry Brewer, *Kops and Custards: The Legend of Keystone Films* (1968), are informative, though nostalgic. Charlie Chaplin, *My Life in Pictures* (1974), recalls the great comedian's days at Keystone; a less subjective account of the Sennett-Chaplin relationship is in David Robinson, *Chaplin* (1985). For an amusing account of life at the Sennett studio during the 1920s, see Frank Capra, *The Name above the Title: An Autobiography* (1971). Sennett's artistic and romantic involvement with Mabel Normand is recounted, but not adequately documented, in Betty Harper Fussell, *Mabel* (1992). (The same relationship was the inspiration for the 1974 Broadway musical *Mack and Mabel*, featuring Robert Preston as Sennett.) Also relevant are Gerald Mast's articles on Sennett in *The International Dictionary of Films and Filmmakers*, ed. Christopher Lyons, vol. 2 (1984), pp. 491–95, and *World Film Directors*, ed. John Wakeman, vol. 1 (1987), pp. 986–92. James Agee's classic essay, "Comedy's Greatest Era," is reprinted in *Agee on Film* (1958). Robert Sklar, *Movie-Made America* (1975), scrutinizes Sennett's vision from the perspectives of American social and cultural history. Among the articles in Kristine Brunovska Karnick and Henry Jenkins, eds., *Classical Hollywood Comedy* (1995), Doug Riblet, "The Keystone Film Company and the Historiography of Early Slapstick," offers a "materialist" revision of Sennett's place in film history.

WILLIAM HUGHES

SEQUOYAH (1770?–Aug. 1843?), inventor of the Cherokee syllabary, was born in the Cherokee town of Tuskegee in present-day eastern Tennessee, of uncertain parentage. He married Sally (maiden name unknown) in 1815, and they had four children. According to Emmet Starr's *History of the Cherokee Indians* (1921), Sequoyah also married U-ti-yu at an unknown date; they had three children. Sometimes referred to as George Guess, or Gist, he was a silversmith by trade, but he had been a warrior. During the Creek War (1813–1814), he enlisted in Colonel Gideon Morgan's Cherokee regiment and served three months.

Accounts of the inspiration for committing Cherokee to writing vary, but Sequoyah revealed to Samuel Lorenzo Knapp in 1827 that his interest stemmed from the capture of a white soldier in a late eighteenth-century campaign. His war party discovered a letter in the soldier's possession, and the warriors debated "whether this mysterious power *of the talking leaf* was the gift of the Great Spirit to the white man, or the discovery of the white man himself." According to Knapp's account of the conversation, published in his *Lectures on American Literature* (1827), "Most of his companions were of the former opinion, while [he] as strenuously maintained the latter." He then decided to develop a system for writing the Cherokee language. After many years of work, Sequoyah finally created a symbol for each syllable, and in 1821 he unveiled a syllabary of eighty-six characters (later reduced to eighty-five), which reportedly could be mastered by a Cherokee speaker in several days.

At the time Sequoyah introduced his syllabary, he was living in Arkansas rather than in his native Southeast. Cherokees had acquired land in Arkansas in the early nineteenth century, and following land cessions in 1808–1810 and 1817–1819, several thousand Cherokees had moved west. A signatory to an unpopular land cession in 1816, Sequoyah had moved west in 1818. He returned east, however, soon after his invention and introduced his syllabary to Cherokees still living there. The Sequoyah syllabary became an immediate success, particularly among Cherokees who had no knowledge of English and little exposure to Anglo-American "civilization." The highly acculturated leaders of the Cherokee nation, the political entity in the Southeast of which three-fourths of the Cherokees were citizens, seem to have known little about the grassroots movement toward literacy. As Cherokee Elias Boudinot recalled in an article in *American Annals of Education* (1 Apr. 1832), by the time they learned of the invention, "the Cherokees had *actually* become a reading people." By 1835 approximately half of the households in the Cherokee nation had members literate in Cherokee.

Rejecting a rival system for writing Cherokee developed by a white philologist, John Pickering, the Cherokee nation embraced the Sequoyah syllabary and incorporated it into the Cherokee renascence of the 1820s. In 1824 the national council voted to honor Sequoyah with a silver medal. The nation also decided to purchase a printing press and types in Latin letters and the Sequoyah syllabary, and in 1828 the *Cherokee Phoenix*, a weekly bilingual newspaper with a circulation of about 200 copies, began publication. Missionaries and Christian Cherokees began to translate hymns and the New Testament into Cherokee. In the West, the Arkansas Cherokee signed a treaty in 1828 that provided for their removal to what is today northeastern Oklahoma. The treaty promised Sequoyah $500 as a reward for his achievement and the western Cherokees $1,000 for a press. The federal government fulfilled neither promise to the western Cherokees, and soon it even cut short the Cherokee renascence in the Southeast.

At the insistence of southern states, particularly Georgia, the United States began to pressure the Cherokee nation to move west. Ultimately, an unauthorized minority of Cherokees agreed to a removal treaty, which the U.S. Senate ratified in 1836. By 1839 the dispossessed Cherokees from the East had arrived west of the Mississippi, where they outnumbered their well-established kinsmen, who included Sequoyah. A struggle for power that verged on civil war erupted. Sequoyah broke with his fellow western Cherokees (or "Old Settlers"), who wanted to impose their government on the far more numerous newcomers, and appealed to the Cherokees for a new government that encompassed all. In a letter reprinted in Grant Foreman's *Sequoyah*, he encouraged the Cherokees to "talk matters over like friends and brothers." His influence helped make possible a compromise that most Cherokees accepted.

In his new role as national conciliator, Sequoyah decided in 1842 to find a group of Cherokees who, according to unsubstantiated reports, were living in Mexico. He died without having located any Cherokee expatriates. The exact place of his death is unknown.

Sequoyah's syllabary remains a source of pride for Cherokees and a medium of cultural preservation. Albert L. Wahrhaftig's survey of four Oklahoma Cherokee communities in 1964–1965 revealed that 36 to 65 percent of adults were literate in Cherokee. Some Cherokees used the syllabary for personal correspondence and gained information through publications in the syllabary, but writing proved most useful in a religious context. While the desire to read the Bible in their own language inspired many Cherokees to learn the Sequoyah syllabary, a writing system also enabled Cherokee medicine men to record their formulas and preserve an ancient religious tradition. These medicine men probably employed writing in such a sacred task because they perceived Sequoyah's accomplishment as mystical rather than mechanical. Whatever the reason, this particular use of the syllabary as well as its continuing viability elevates Sequoyah's invention above mere antiquarian interest to major historical significance.

• Sequoyah left no collection of papers, although the Thomas Gilcrease Institute in Tulsa, Okla., has four manuscripts attributed to him. The best biography of Sequoyah, although it contains no citations for lengthy quotations, remains Grant Foreman, *Sequoyah* (1938). Recent studies are Willard Walker and James Sarbaugh, "The Early History of the Cherokee Syllabary," *Ethnohistory* 40 (1993): 70–94, and Theda Perdue, "The Sequoyah Syllabary and Cultural Revitalization," in *Perspectives on the Southeast: Linguistics, Archaeology, and Ethnohistory* (1994). On the use of the Cherokee syllabary, see Willard Walker, "Notes on Native Writing Systems and the Design of Native Literacy Programs," *Anthropological Linguistics* 11 (1969): 148–66, and Albert L. Wahrhaftig, *Social and Economic Characteristics of the Cherokee Population of Eastern Oklahoma* (1970).

THEDA PERDUE

SERGEANT, John (1710–27 July 1749), missionary to the American Indians, was born in Newark, New Jersey, the son of Jonathan Sergeant and Mary (maiden name unknown). Sergeant's father died when he was very young, and he was raised by his stepfather, Colonel John Cooper. Because of an injury from a scythe, on his left hand, he decided to pursue an academic life instead of becoming a gentleman farmer as his father and stepfather had been. He graduated from Yale College first in the class of 1729 and was appointed a tutor there in 1731, becoming "one of the most successful holders of that office in the early history of the College" (Dexter, vol. 1, p. 395). Meanwhile he studied theology, in which he received his second bachelor's degree in 1732.

In 1734 the commissioners for Indian Affairs at Boston of the Society for Propagating the Gospel among the Indians of North America, also known as the New England Company, sent two delegates to confer with the Housatonic Indians for the possible establishment of a mission among them. The Indians consented, and the commissioners, having heard of Sergeant's interest in becoming a missionary to the natives, offered him the position.

In October 1734 Sergeant made a brief trip to meet with the Housatonic Indians, who had been living in two places, Skatekook (in Sheffield, Mass.), and Wnahktukook (in Stockbridge, Mass.), and persuaded them to erect a building to serve as school and church on an intermediate spot. When he returned to New Haven to complete his year as tutor at the college, he brought with him two American-Indian boys, who studied English by day and taught him their dialect by night. In July 1735 Sergeant left New Haven, intending to spend the rest of his life with the Housatonics. He was soon ordained to the Congregational ministry and baptized forty Indians within a few months. His annual salary was £150 when he was ordained and reached £300 by the year of his death. Sergeant mastered the Housatonic dialect and translated parts of the

Old and New Testament, some prayers, and Isaac Watt's shorter catechism.

In 1736 the Massachusetts General Court purchased all the Indian land at Skatekook and granted the two Indian groups a township six miles square in Stockbridge. Sergeant and the schoolmaster, Timothy Woodbridge, each received a one-sixtieth part (384 acres). Four carefully selected English families were allowed to live in the town to help the missionaries. A meeting house and a school were soon built. The Indians' activities, such as maple sugar making and hunting, however, undermined the effectiveness of the school. This problem was somewhat alleviated by Isaac Hollis, a London clergyman, who provided funds for the cost of lodging, diet, clothing, and tuition for twelve Indian boys, allowing them to study without seasonal interruptions. Another British donation of £100, which Sergeant set aside for the education of girls, was never fully utilized because the Indian girls did not want to stay away from home.

At the age of twenty-nine, Sergeant in 1739 married Abigail Williams, nineteen-year-old daughter of Colonel Ephraim Williams of Stockbridge and half sister of Ephraim Williams, Jr., the founder of Williams College. Although he came to be allied with the powerful Williams family and lived in an impressive Georgian mansion, instead of a plain cottage among the Indians, Sergeant continued to maintain the trust and affection of his native congregation. During his fourteen years at Stockbridge, the Indian population increased from less than 50 to 218, 129 of whom he had baptized.

To Sergeant, the American Indians were "a very miserable and degenerate Part" of the human race, who had "their own foolish, barbarous, and wicked Custom," knew "nothing like Government among themselves," and had "an Aversion to every Thing that restrains their Liberty." He became convinced, as other missionaries did, that missionary efforts would be fruitless unless the Indians became reasonably "civilized" and learned English. Nor, he believed, would the American-Indian children placed in unsupervised English families improve their moral or social fortunes. Thus in 1743 Sergeant proposed the establishment of a boarding school, requesting a grant of 200 acres of land, on which a building would be erected to house Indian boys and girls aged ten to twenty, a farm would be maintained, and stock and cattle would be raised. The children were to be kept busy under two masters (one to supervise them in their work and the other in their study) because the job would be "too tedious a Task for one." Although many Englishmen responded generously, support from the Bay Colony was meager. King George's War and subsequent difficulties prevented the completion of the school until the summer of 1749, shortly before Sergeant died of a nervous fever in Stockbridge.

There was an ironic twist to Sergeant's missionary enterprise. His wife, aged twenty-nine when he died, was a strong-minded woman whose father was mainly interested in promoting his personal interest. She tried to entice Ezra Stiles, a Yale tutor and five years younger than she, to take Sergeant's position as Indian missionary, a situation that, she might have hoped, would lead to their marriage, but Stiles declined. The post was given to Jonathan Edwards in 1751. Abigail Sergeant then became mistress of the Indian girls' school due to the efforts of her father and her cousin, who had urged the general court and the commissioners for Indian Affairs of the New England Company to provide funds to educate Indian girls, "according to the Plan of the late Reverend Mr. Sergeant." Sergeant's widow proved unpopular in this new capacity, however. She was accused of using the Indian girls to do her chores instead of educating them. The Indians complained that Joseph Dwight, a 49-year-old politician, general, long-time friend of the Indians, and admirer of Edwards, had greatly changed since his marriage to Abigail Sergeant in 1752 and that he and his wife took over the entire Indian affairs. In 1754 the New England Company commissioners took matters out of the general's hands, forcing the couple eventually to remove to the North Parish of Sheffield (later Great Barrington).

John and Abigail Sergeant had had three children. Their daughter, Electa, the first white child born in Stockbridge, married Colonel Mark Hopkins. Their elder son, Erastus, became the first physician in Stockbridge, and the younger son, John Sergeant, Jr., only two when his father died, studied at Princeton for two years, was ordained to the Congregational ministry, and in 1775 took charge of the Indian congregation in Stockbridge. In 1786 the Housatonic Indians moved to New Stockbridge, New York, where the Indians formed two factions. One group invited John Sergeant, Jr., to become its pastor, while the other retained Sampson Occum as its pastor. After Occum's death, the two groups united under Sergeant, who divided his time between New and Old Stockbridge, where his family lived.

• Sergeant's published writings include one of his sermons, *The Causes and Danger of Delusions in the Affairs of Religion Consider'd and Caution'd against, with Particular Reference to the Temper of the Present Times* (1743); *A Letter from the Revd. Mr. Sergeant of Stockbridge to Dr. Colman of Boston; Containing Mr. Sergeant's Proposal of a More Effectual Method for the Education of Indian Children* (1743); and his commencement address printed in 1882 from the manuscript in possession of Williams College, *A Valedictorian Oration, by John Sergeant, Delivered at Yale College in the Year 1729*. The major secondary works on Sergeant are James Axtell, "The Rise and Fall of the Stockbridge Indian Schools," *The Massachusetts Review* 27 (1986): 367–78; Franklin B. Dexter, *Biographical Sketches of Graduates of Yale College*, vol. 1 (1885), pp. 379, 384–97; Patrick Frazier, *The Mohicans of Stockbridge* (1992); Samuel Hopkins, *Historical Memoir Relating to the Housatunnuk Indians* (1753), reprinted in *Magazine of History*, extra no. 17 (1911); Electa F. Jones, *Stockbridge, Past and Present; or, Records of an Old Mission Station* (1854); and William B. Sprague, *Annals of American Pulpit*, vol. 1 (1857), pp. 388–94.

YASUHIDE KAWASHIMA

SERGEANT, John (5 Dec. 1779–23 Nov. 1852), attorney, diplomat, and congressman, was born in Philadelphia, Pennsylvania, the son of Jonathan Dickinson Sergeant, a member of the Continental Congress and attorney general of Pennsylvania during the American Revolution, and Margaret Spencer. His father fell victim to yellow fever in 1793, only six years after his mother's untimely death. Left on his own, young John graduated from the College of New Jersey (now Princeton University) in 1795, three years before his brother Thomas Sergeant, and then apprenticed briefly in the Philadelphia financial house of Ellison and Perot. Settling on law instead of banking, he studied with Jared Ingersoll in 1797 and joined the bar two years later.

Political opportunity for Sergeant came first with the faction of the Jeffersonian party headed by Pennsylvania governor Thomas McKean, a snobbish former Federalist who once referred to common Pennsylvania voters as "clodpoles." McKean men broke with more radical Jeffersonians by defending the state judiciary—mostly Federalist appointees—against a movement in the legislature to impeach them. In 1800, as reward for early political support, McKean appointed the temperamentally reserved young lawyer as deputy attorney general for Chester County, and two years later President Thomas Jefferson named him commissioner of bankruptcy for Pennsylvania. Elected to the Pennsylvania Assembly twice, in 1805 and 1807, Sergeant did the bidding of influential Philadelphians. Transportation improvements and banking were his primary concerns, and he chaired the committee on roads and inland navigation during the 1807 session. In 1813 he married Margaretta Watmough of Philadelphia; the couple had ten children.

Sergeant's association not only with McKean but also with Philadelphia Federalists like Joseph Hopkinson and Joseph Dennie made him a Jeffersonian who appealed to both sides. To replace the late Jonathan Williams, voters elected Sergeant to the U.S. House of Representatives, where he remained from 6 December 1815 to 3 March 1823 and where he sat on the Judiciary Committee. In 1816 Congress dispatched Sergeant on a financial mission to Great Britain, with instructions to borrow up to $5 million in specie for the newly chartered Second Bank of the United States. The result was a bargain in London with Baring Brothers and Reid, Irving, and Company for more than $3 million in silver for twenty months at five percent interest. In other matters of political economy, he promoted eastern woolen interests who wanted protective tariff laws and an American home market, pushed for a uniform bankruptcy law, and supported national funding for internal improvements. Strongly opposed to slavery, Sergeant resisted the admission of Missouri to the Union in 1820, provoking the wrath of House Speaker Henry Clay, whose politics he otherwise embraced. "What is to be tolerated in the old states, only because it cannot be avoided, is unnecessary, and of course criminal, in Missouri," Sergeant insisted. After preferring his Philadelphia law practice to reelection in 1823, he served for one year as president of the Pennsylvania Board of Canal Commissioners in 1825.

As President John Quincy Adams's choice, with Richard C. Anderson of Kentucky, to represent U.S. interests at the 1826 Panama Congress, Sergeant again prepared to go abroad. Though southern members opposed the appointment because of his antislavery views, the Philadelphian gained Senate approval for the mission by a vote of twenty-eight to eighteen. To avoid the disease-ridden tropics during summer, however, he received permission to delay the journey until the delegates reconvened in Mexico City. Sergeant's diplomatic presence from January to July 1827 was of little consequence, but he took interest in Mexico's fear of American designs on Texas: "At present, the Mexicans are much disposed to hold us accountable for whatever occurs in that quarter, as well as to impute to us a violent desire to possess ourselves of their country."

Profoundly disturbed by the growing Jacksonian movement in Congress—"the most ferocious that has existed under our government"—Sergeant won back his old House seat in 1826, a few months prior to leaving for Mexico. His personal following neither strictly Democratic nor Federalist, his was a narrow victory over the Jacksonian candidate, Henry Horn, requiring two elections to settle after the first came out a tie. Perhaps because of Sergeant's prominence among Adams's forces, he lost to Joseph Hemphill in the 1828 Jacksonian sweep of city, state, and congressional offices. During the next four years his public energies turned chiefly to promoting Henry Clay for the presidency in 1832 and to the rallying of anti-Jackson elements in Pennsylvania. Andrew Jackson as chief executive, he thought, was a dreadful "military experiment," incongruous with republican tradition. In the Supreme Court cases of *Cherokee Nation v. Georgia* (1831) and *Worcester v. Georgia* (1832), Sergeant argued for Native American rights against the Jacksonian policy of removal from their traditional lands. The December 1831 National Republican convention in Baltimore nominated Clay for president, and Sergeant, because of the keystone state's anticipated electoral importance, was their choice for vice president.

The major issue in the campaign of 1832—the Second Bank of the United States—touched Sergeant closely. He understood the economic importance of the institution and had been a loyal personal friend of the bank's president, Nicholas Biddle, for many years. In 1824, with Clay and Daniel Webster, he successfully defended the bank before the Marshall Court in *Osborn v. Bank of the U.S.* He served not only as legal counsel for the bank but sat on its board of directors from 1829 to early 1832. Partly on Sergeant's urging, Biddle decided to seek early charter renewal from Congress in 1832, hoping to pressure Jackson to either sign the bill or commit himself by vetoing it prior to the election. In a way, the president's bank veto in July heightened the meaning of Sergeant's candidacy.

Though Jackson's reelection in 1832 ended his chance for a leading role, Sergeant remained active in state politics and returned to Congress, serving from 4 September 1837 to 15 September 1841. He was president of the Pennsylvania Constitutional Convention in the winter of 1837–1838. As chair of the House Banking Committee, Sergeant and his Senate counterpart, John M. Berrien, were asked by party leaders to design the Fiscal Corporation of the United States as a substitute for the Fiscal Bank bill that President John Tyler vetoed in 1841. Unhappily for the Whig majority, the new bill met the same fate. Resigning from the House soon afterward, Sergeant stayed in private life and practiced law until his death in Philadelphia.

• Most of the papers of John Sergeant are stored in the Historical Society of Pennsylvania. On Sergeant and the Second Bank of the United States, see the Nicholas Biddle Papers, Library of Congress, Washington, D.C., and Bray Hammond, *Banks and Politics in America* (1957). For his association with the National Republicans, see Mary W. M. Hargreaves, *The Presidency of John Quincy Adams* (1985), and *The Papers of Henry Clay*, ed. James F. Hopkins et al. (10 vols., 1959–1991). His career in the Fourteenth through Seventeenth Congresses may be followed in the *Annals of Congress, 1789–1824* (42 vols., 1834–1856); in the Twentieth Congress in the *Register of Debates in Congress, 1825–1837* (29 vols., 1825–1837); and in the Twenty-fifth to Twenty-seventh Congresses in the *Congressional Globe* (46 vols., 1833–1873). Sergeant's obituary is in the *Public Ledger* (Philadelphia), 25 Nov. 1852.

JOHN R. VAN ATTA

SERKIN, Rudolf (28 Mar. 1903–8 May 1991), pianist, was born in Eger (now Cheb), Bohemia, the son of Mordko Serkin, a businessman, and Augusta Scharg, who were partly of Russian-Jewish descent. His father, a failed basso singer who turned to business, encouraged his son's early signs of musical talent by giving him lessons on the piano and violin. Young Rudolf learned music before he could read or write and first played the piano in public at age six. His parents moved to Vienna so that he could have leading musical teachers and grow up in a cultured environment. Serkin studied the piano with Richard Robert and composition with Joseph Marx and Arnold Schoenberg. He made his concert debut with the Vienna Symphony Orchestra at the age of twelve in Mendelssohn's Piano Concerto No. 1 in G Minor.

In Vienna Serkin was much influenced by the presence of Schoenberg, Alban Berg, and Anton Webern, who were then at the forefront of modernism in music. He became friendly with a number of influential creative figures, including the artist Oskar Kokoschka and the poet Rainer Maria Rilke, and educated himself with sustained reading on art, music, philosophy, and literature. After completing his musical studies in 1920, he earned a living by teaching piano to the children of wealthy families and giving concerts and recitals. He remained in Vienna and was introduced to the violinist Adolf Busch. Their meeting was an important turning point; after playing sonatas together for several hours, Busch invited Serkin to serve as his accompanist on recitals and tours and became his benefactor.

For the next fifteen years much of Serkin's career consisted of performances with the Busch family. Concentrating on the classical and romantic repertoire, Serkin appeared in Berlin and throughout Europe with the Busch Quartet and the Busch Chamber Players. His debut at the Salzburg Festival came in 1925. He continued to live with the Busch family in Berlin, Darmstadt, and Basle, and he took out Swiss citizenship when Hitler came to power in Germany. In 1935 Serkin married Busch's eighteen-year-old daughter, Irene, a talented violinist. They were to have six children, including one son, Peter, who later established his own career as a concert pianist.

Word of Serkin's prowess as a pianist spread beyond Europe, and in 1933 he made his debut in the United States with Adolf Busch at the Coolidge Festival in Washington, D.C. His first American appearance as soloist with orchestra followed three years later when he played Wolfgang Amadeus Mozart's Piano Concerto No. 27 in B-flat Major (K. 595) with the New York Philharmonic under Arturo Toscanini's direction. In 1937 Serkin gave his first solo recital in New York. All of these appearances were widely acclaimed by critics, and they established an American career that lasted until his death. Serkin and his wife divided their homes between Switzerland and the United States for several years until World War II. They appreciated the hospitality they received in the United States and decided to live there permanently after Serkin acquired American citizenship in 1939.

From 1936 on, especially after World War II, Serkin made many concert tours throughout the world. The State Department of the United States sponsored his tour of the Orient in 1961, and he later toured Australia and New Zealand in 1975. He appeared with all the world's leading orchestras, giving innumerable solo recitals and chamber music concerts. He was a frequent guest at many festivals, notably at the Pablo Casals Festivals at Prades and Perpignan from 1950 on. In 1949 he helped to found the Marlboro School of Music, a summer school for gifted musicians near the vacation farm he and his family had acquired at Guilford in the Green Mountains of Vermont. A year later he established the annual summer Marlboro Music Festival as a memorial to Adolf Busch, who died in 1952, and following an artistic collaboration of thirty-two years with Serkin. Besides serving as president and artistic director of these twin institutions, Serkin also devoted much time to teaching. He joined the faculty of the Curtis Institute of Music in Philadelphia in 1938, became head of the piano department a year later, and served as director of the institute from 1968 until 1976. His teaching inspired other musicians to strive for high artistic ideals.

Serkin's piano playing was renowned for its command of the most complex fingerwork, its full range of dynamics, its classical sense of style and proportion, and its poetry, probity, and purity of feeling. The pianist who influenced him most from an earlier generation was Artur Schnabel. In his early years Serkin championed avant-garde music by the Second Viennese School and frequently played romantic music by Frederick Chopin, Edvard Grieg, and Franz Liszt. As he grew older, he concentrated on the classical repertoire, displaying particular affinity for piano music by Johann Sebastian Bach, Mozart, Ludwig van Beethoven, Franz Schubert, Robert Schumann, and Johannes Brahms. But he retained an interest in playing pieces outside the established piano repertoire by composers such as Antonín Dvořák, Max Reger, and Ferruccio Busoni. His technical prowess enabled him to present a number of contemporary pieces very effectively. He gave the premiere of Bohuslav Martinů's Piano Sonata (of which he was the dedicatee) in 1957 and the U.S. premiere of Serge Prokofiev's Fourth Piano Concerto (for the left hand) in 1968. He made many recordings, primarily for the Columbia label, and was awarded no less than eleven Grammys.

Serkin's achievements were widely honored. In 1963 he was presented the Presidential Medal of Freedom by Lyndon B. Johnson. He performed at the White House in 1966 and 1970. In 1967 he became the first recipient of the Governor's Award of Excellence in the Arts from the Vermont Council of the Arts. In 1971 he received the Fifth Annual Pennsylvania Award for excellence in the performing arts. In 1972 he became an honorary member of the New York Philharmonic in recognition of one hundred performances with the orchestra. In 1988 he was awarded the National Medal of the Arts. He died at his home at Guilford, Vermont.

• Serkin was a modest, private man who avoided public interviews as much as possible. However, his career and approach to music-making are summarized in "Rudolf Serkin Talks to Alan Blyth," *The Gramophone* 46 (May 1969): 1548, and "Serkin: As Interviewed by Dean Elder," *Clavier* 9, no. 8 (Nov. 1970): 8–15, 38–39. Two other useful interviews are in *The Etude* (Mar. 1941) and *Piano Quarterly* (Winter 1977–1978). See also Joachim Kaiser, *Great Pianists of Our Time*, 1st English ed. (1965); Robert M. Jacobson, *Rudolf Serkin* (1973); David Ewen, *Musicians since 1900: Performers in Concert and Opera* (1978); Claude Frank, "Rudolf Serkin: Servant of Music," *Keynote* (Mar. 1983); John Gillespie and Anna Gillespie, *Notable Twentieth-Century Pianists: A Bio-Critical Sourcebook* (1995); and David Dubal, *The Art of the Piano: An Encyclopedia of Performers, Literature and Recordings* (1989). Serkin's collaboration with Adolf Busch is illuminated by Tully Potter's notes accompanying *The Busch/Serkin Duo: Public Performances, 1934–49* (Music & Arts CD-877, 1995). Tributes to Serkin and a discography are included in the notes for *Rudolf Serkin on Television: The 75th Birthday Concert at Carnegie Hall* (Columbia Masterworks, two 33⅓ rpm discs, M35300-35301, 1977–1978).

KENNETH MORGAN

SERLING, Rod (25 Dec. 1924–28 June 1975), television writer and producer, was born Rodman Edward Serling in Syracuse, New York, the son of Samuel Serling, a grocer and butcher, and Esther Cooper. In 1926 Serling's family joined a growing Jewish community in Binghamton, New York. As editor of *Panorama*,

Binghamton Central High School's newspaper, Serling urged students to support the effort to win World War II. Following graduation, he enlisted in the 511th Parachute Infantry Regiment of the Eleventh Armored Division. While stationed in New Guinea, Serling wrote his first plays, which were used as radio propaganda against the Japanese. He survived battles in the Philippines, on Leyte Island and near Manila, with minor injuries, and he was discharged in May 1945; his experience left him with traumatic memories.

Serling enrolled as a physical education major at Antioch College in Yellow Springs, Ohio, in 1946. After a first-year writing course, he changed his major and began writing short stories on boxing and war experiences in the style of Ernest Hemingway. "The Good Right Hand" was published in *The Antiochan* in March 1948. Taking advantage of Antioch's work-study program, Serling interned as a radio scriptwriter at WNYC in New York City, WINR in Binghamton, and WMRN in Marion, Ohio.

In 1948 Serling married Carolyn Louise Kramer in Yellow Springs. They had two daughters. In November Serling was hired as manager of the Antioch Broadcasting System. Writing dramatic scripts for his first anthology show, he explored sound effects and the use of parable in the vein of Orson Welles and "Mr. Radio," Norman Corwin. After resigning in February 1949 to focus on freelance scripts, Serling won third prize and $500 for "To Live a Dream" and appeared on "The Dr. Christian Show."

Serling received his B.A. in 1950, moved to Cincinnati, Ohio, and worked as a television staff writer for WLW. That same year he sold his first script, "Grady Everett for the People," to the network anthology series "Stars over Hollywood." From July 1951 to February 1953 Serling contributed to another series, "The Storm," for Cincinnati's WKRC-TV. Author Gordon F. Sander wrote that "like most writers . . . attempting to make the transition from radio to television, Serling still wrote for the ear rather than the eye. He had yet to master the quick character development and punchy dialogue that TV required" (Sander, p. 74). Serling's early characters were clichéd, mostly men in "crude military morality plays," such as the soldier in "The Sergeant" (1952), whose cowardly screams during combat result in the deaths of several fellow soldiers.

While Serling's writing matured with "a gripping, well-turned plot, taut dialogue, believable characters . . . a definite point of view" and "aural details," his powerful visual images helped make television a force in the 1950s, superseding radio and theater. Through television Serling could best convey his criticism of war, prejudice, and corporate business. His breakthrough came in 1955 with "Patterns," for which he won his first Emmy Award for best television writing. He received a second Emmy the following year for "Requiem for a Heavyweight." Thereafter Serling wrote and produced television scripts for "Lux Video Theatre," "Kraft Television Theatre," "Studio One," "Hallmark Hall of Fame," "U.S. Steel Hour," and

"Playhouse 90," among others. Serling received a third Emmy Award for "The Comedian" for "Playhouse 90" and in December 1957 moved his family to Los Angeles.

When corporate sponsorship began to influence program content, Serling's image as one of the industry's "angry men" blossomed. He constantly fought with sponsors who argued that his moralistic scripts with their "agonistic characters and downbeat themes" contradicted the upbeat, simplistic message of their commercials. Although Serling made attempts to cross over into film, according to Sander, "television . . . was not only the medium best suited to Serling's talents, it was also the one best suited to his intense, quirky personality" (Sander, p. xix). In addition to his sense of humor and good looks, Serling had become known for his incessant chain smoking, his noisy antics, and his intense desire to appear on screen.

"The Twilight Zone," running from 1959 to 1964, confirmed Serling's mastery of television's half-hour dramatic form. Furthermore, his on-screen introductions to the episodes satisfied his desire for recognition. Through "parable and suggestion," Serling finally found what Sander called "a personal bully pulpit to comment metaphorically on the aspects of human behavior and the human condition that made him angry" (Sander, p. 169). Much of "The Twilight Zone" is rooted in autobiography, based on Serling's Binghamton childhood, war experiences, or life in the upper-middle-class suburban town of Westport, Connecticut, where he lived from 1954 to 1957. As a writer-producer of the program, Serling fought with the network for creative control and passed on this courtesy to those who worked for him. He was rewarded with two Emmy Awards for outstanding writing achievement in drama in 1960 and 1961.

Serling took a year to write and teach at Antioch College, and in 1963 he received his sixth and final Emmy for the adaptation "It's Mental Work," for NBC's "Bob Hope Presents the Chrysler Theatre." Pressured in 1963 and 1964 to adapt "The Twilight Zone" to hour slots and challenged by the audience's waning interest in dramatic content, Serling produced a few standout shows before finally selling his rights to the series. To his dismay, "The Twilight Zone" made a fortune for CBS in syndication. While president of the National Academy of Television Arts and Sciences in 1963 and 1964, Serling fought the industry's commercialism.

Serling wrote and introduced one last series, "Night Gallery," from 1970 to 1973. Although many thought he should never have stopped writing for television, Serling spent his final years as a commercial spokesman and as a teacher both at Sherman Oaks Experimental College in southern California and at Ithaca College in Ithaca, New York. He died in Rochester, New York, during open heart surgery. In 1983 he was honored with *Twilight Zone: The Movie* by four directors, including Steven Spielberg, who at age nineteen was given the opportunity to direct a Serling teleplay.

• The University of Wisconsin at Madison holds eight boxes of Serling archival material at the State Historical Society. A smaller collection is at the Department of Special Collections at the University of California, Los Angeles. Antioch College maintains a definitive collection of Serling clippings. Biographies on Serling include Joel Engel, *Rod Serling: The Dreams and Nightmares of Life in the Twilight Zone* (1989), which is written with the cooperation of Serling's brother Robert, drawing anecdotes about Serling from personal and printed interviews; and Gordon F. Sander, *Serling: The Rise and Twilight of Television's Last Angry Man* (1992), which, though not authorized, is quite thorough and, unlike Engel's book, includes an index, bibliography of secondary sources such as interviews and articles, and reference lists to Serling's teleplays, films, and awards. An obituary is in the *New York Times*, 29 June 1975.

BARBARA L. CICCARELLI

SERRA, Junipero (24 Nov. 1713–28 Aug. 1784), Roman Catholic missionary, was born Miguel José Serra in Petra on the Spanish island of Mallorca, the son of Antonio Serra and Margarita Ferrer, farmers. His parents, poor and without formal education, enrolled him in a Franciscan primary school. At age fifteen Serra traveled to the Mallorcan capital, Palma, to study philosophy and theology at the Convento de San Francisco. In 1731, following a year of training, Serra joined the Order of Friars Minor (Franciscans) and took the religious name Junipero. In this he identified with the original Junipero, a companion of St. Francis whose simplicity and good humor were exemplary.

Serra was ordained as a priest in 1738. In 1742 he received his doctorate in theology and served as professor at Palma's Lullian University until 1749. That year Serra pursued correspondence with the commissary general of the Indies, seeking permission (from Francisco Palóu, his future biographer) to become an apostolic missionary. His request was granted, and in 1750 he traveled to Cadiz, where he met others preparing for Christian mission in the New World. While awaiting the Atlantic crossing he wrote a letter to the parish priest in Petra, including the phrase that became his personal motto: "Always go forward, never turn back."

In the Americas Serra worked among the natives in the Sierra Gorda region north of Mexico City. For eight years he translated Christian doctrine and prayers into the language of the Pames Indians. With them, in the mid-1750s, Serra also helped to build a large stone church in Jalpan (in the state of Queretaro in the Sierra Gorda Mountains), which is still used for worship today. His intensity, hard work, and uninhibited delight in God's creation impressed his companions.

In 1758 Serra was reassigned to the Mexican capital, where he undertook the duties of administrator at the College of San Fernando and the ministries of a traveling missionary priest. During this time, plagued by asthma and a painful leg injury, Serra increasingly identified with the Catholic mystical tradition that sought spiritual purification through suffering.

In early 1767 King Charles III suddenly expelled the Jesuits from Spain and its colonies. The following year Serra was placed in charge of the orphaned Jesuit missions on the Baja (lower) California peninsula. Moreover, with the Russians moving from Alaska down the western coast of North America, the Spanish charged him to establish missions in Alto (upper) California. It was this final venture that became Serra's greatest legacy.

At the age of fifty-five Serra accompanied the overland "Sacred Expedition" under Gaspar de Portolá, which reached San Diego in the summer of 1769 and founded the first mission in American California there on 16 July. The next objective was Monterey, some 400 miles to the north, where the second mission, San Carlos Borromeo, was founded on 3 June 1770. Fortified by its presidio, Monterey served as the capital of California and as Serra's headquarters as he served as the father president of the missions for the next fourteen years. Under his direction, nine California missions were founded, teaching the Indian peoples Christian doctrine, literacy, agricultural techniques, building, pottery making, and other skills. Following the teachings of his order and the ideals of Catholic Spain, Serra administered a mission system that helped to transform tribal hunting and gathering economies with loose social organization into more settled, regimented communities that sought to "prepare souls for heaven." By the time of Serra's death an estimated 5,000 neophytes were living in the missions along with 500 Spanish soldiers and settlers.

While some aspects of eighteenth-century mission culture (for example, the experience of discipline and disease) could be harsh, Serra insisted on personal care and community celebrations as well. Moreover, missions such as San Diego and Monterey were relocated some distance from the presidios to improve living conditions. Serra once observed: "The only quality that I can feel fairly sure I have by the kindness and grace of God is my good intentions."

Serra died at the mission San Carlos Borromeo, by then located on the Carmel River. Because of his accomplishments and exemplary life he was declared venerable by Pope John Paul II in 1985, was beatified in Rome in 1988, and is under consideration for canonization as a saint by the Roman Catholic Church. His sculpted likeness, representing the state of California, stands in Statuary Hall in Washington, D.C.

• Serra's papers and manuscripts are collected at the Mission (Santa Barbara, Calif.), the Bibliotheca Nacional and Archivo General de la Nación (Mexico City), and the Archivo General de Indias (Seville, Spain). The best compilation of Serra's works is Antonine Tibesar, ed., *Writings* (4 vols., 1955–1966). The foundational biography is by Serra's eighteenth-century colleague Francisco Palóu, *Life of Fray Junipero Serra*, trans. and ed. Maynard Geiger (1945). Geiger, *The Life and Times of Fray Junipero Serra* (2 vols., 1959), is a detailed and comprehensive classic. Some updating has been provided by Don DeNevi and Noel Moholy in their *Junipero Serra* (1985). A brief, helpful discussion of California's first mission and its founder is Iris H. W. Engstrand, *Serra's San Diego* (1982). A useful bibliography is Francis J. Weber, "California's Serrana Literature," *Southern California Quarterly* (Dec. 1969): 325–42. See also the beautifully illustrated volume by Martin Morgado, *Junipero Serra: A Pictorial Biography* (1991).

JAMES D. SMITH III

SESSIONS, Roger Huntington (28 Dec. 1896–16 Mar. 1985), modernist composer, influential teacher of composition, and writer on music, was born in Brooklyn, New York, the son of Archibald Lowery Sessions, an attorney, and Ruth Gregson Huntington. When Sessions was four years old, his family moved to Hadley, Massachusetts, where his mother's family had lived for nearly three centuries. There he began to study piano at the age of five with local teachers and after 1908 with his mother, who had been trained at the Hochschule für Musik in Leipzig. Once Sessions determined as a child to become a composer, he never wavered from that ambition. His first composition was an unpublished opera, "Lancelot and Elaine" (1910), based on Tennyson's *Idylls of the King*.

Sessions came from a religious family. His great-grandfather had been an Episcopal clergyman, and his mother's father had served as the bishop of central New York State. Another member of the Huntington family, his uncle James, had founded the Order of the Holy Cross. Sessions was educated at the Kent School in Kent, Connecticut, which was affiliated with the Episcopal church. He credited his education, as well as the influence of his parents, with giving him his sense of high idealism. Sessions graduated from Kent in 1911 and entered Harvard University, where he studied composition with Edward Burlingame Hill. At Harvard, Sessions edited and wrote articles for the *Harvard Review*. During this time, Sessions became familiar with the music of Arnold Schoenberg, who had introduced the twelve-tone idiom into modern composition. Although Sessions did not become a proponent of Schoenberg's style, he remained throughout his career profoundly influenced by the Viennese composer's sense of discipline and commitment to the highest compositional standards.

After graduating from Harvard in 1915 Sessions studied composition at Yale University with Horatio Parker, the teacher of famous composers such as Charles Ives. While at Yale, Sessions won the Steinert prize for his *Symphonic Prelude* (1917). He earned a bachelor of music degree from Yale in 1917. In that year he began teaching music theory at Smith College, where he remained until 1921, when he joined Ernest Bloch, with whom he was studying in New York, at the Cleveland Institute. As a student of Bloch's, Sessions composed incidental music to Leonid Andreyev's *The Black Maskers*, which was first performed as the commencement play at Smith College in June 1923 and was premiered by Leopold Stokowski and the Philadelphia Orchestra as a four-movement orchestral suite in 1933. Of the earlier performance at Smith, the critic Paul Rosenfeld wrote that this "beautiful, moving work" was characterized by "great strength in the movements; powerfully pulsing rhythms, long melodic lines that flow and continue and extend in beauty; no padding, no waste."

From 1926 to 1933 Sessions lived in Italy and Germany, supported by Guggenheim fellowships, a Prix de Rome, and a Carnegie Foundation grant. Unlike many American composers at this time, Sessions did not study with Nadia Boulanger. Having been introduced to her by a letter from Bloch, he came to know the famous French teacher but, according to his account, did not become her student because he was already associated with Bloch. He did show her some of his compositions, including the First Symphony (1926–1927), which received its premiere with the Boston Symphony under Serge Koussevitzky on 22 April 1927. This creative period also saw the completion of his Sonata no. 1 for piano (1930) and "On the Beach at Fontana" (1930), a song based on a poem by James Joyce. In Europe, Boulanger introduced Sessions to Igor Stravinsky, whose music Sessions greatly admired, and to Aaron Copland, with whom he produced the Copland-Sessions concerts of modern music between 1928 and 1931. Most of these performances were held in New York, but the fifth in the series was produced in Paris with the support of Boulanger. From Europe and after his return to the United States, Sessions contributed articles to the journal *Modern Music*.

With the continuing spread of fascism in Europe, Sessions returned to the United States permanently. He taught at a number of different institutions, then became a member of Princeton's music faculty in 1935. In 1936 his sixteen-year marriage to Barbara Foster ended in divorce after a long separation. He married Sarah Franck in November 1936 and had two children. Sessions taught at Princeton until 1944, when he became a professor of music at the University of California at Berkeley. He returned to Princeton in 1953 and codirected the Columbia-Princeton Electronic Music Center starting in 1959. Sessions retired from Princeton in 1965 but remained active as a teacher (Juilliard), lecturer (Harvard, Berkeley), writer, and composer. Indeed, his career extended almost until his death in Princeton, New Jersey.

Sessions's admiration for Stravinsky is apparent in his creative use of polytonality, chords based on fourths, and bright orchestral sounds. Nevertheless, Sessions was not an imitator of Stravinsky, Schoenberg, or any other composer. During the 1920s and 1930s, when many American composers experimented with the rhythms and colors of jazz and the familiar melodies of American folk music, Sessions wrote dense, large orchestral pieces that could not be labeled "American" based on any derivative qualities. His Violin Concerto makes a clear attempt to extend the boundaries of the tonal system. A difficult work to execute, this piece received its premiere on 8 January 1940 with the Illinois Symphony and violinist Robert Gross.

After World War II, having spent years writing, as he put it, "on the brink of serialism," Sessions completed the String Quintet (1958), which utilizes the twelve-tone technique. Other pieces from this period include the Concerto for Piano and Orchestra (1956) and the Mass for Organ and Unison Chorus of the same year. The mass was commissioned to celebrate the fiftieth anniversary of the Kent School. Sessions wrote other commissioned works, including Symphony no. 3 for the Boston Symphony's seventy-fifth anniversary (1957), Symphony no. 4 to celebrate the centennial of the state of Minnesota (1958), and Divertimento for Orchestra (1958) for the centennial of state of Oregon. Symphonies no. 5 (1964) and no. 6 (1966) were also commissioned pieces. Sessions was known for large-scale works that often took years to complete, including his three-act opera, *Montezuma*, which took twenty-eight years to compose and which received its first performance at the Berlin Deutsche Oper under the auspices of the U.S. Department of State on 19 April 1964.

Critics often commented on the challenges that Session's music posed for listeners. His friend and colleague Alfredo Casella commented that his music seemed to have been "born difficult." Sessions maintained that the modern composer did not need to make concessions to current trends. Indeed, to be consistent with his own compositional principles, the modern composer had to write what he or she heard. "All that the contemporary composer demands," he said, "is an open mind and a willing ear—and also a gracious ear." The power and beauty of his music was recognized by the larger public relatively late in his life, although Sessions had long held the respect of his peers and colleagues. Northwestern University and the Fromm Music Foundation of Chicago held a retrospective of the composer's works in January 1961, and New York's Museum of Modern Art held an all-Sessions program in October of that year. On 7 February 1973 the Performers' Committee for Twentieth Century Music held a retrospective concert at Columbia University's McMillan Theatre (now the Miller Theatre) that ranged from *The Black Maskers* to *Canons*, a 1971 piece commemorating the work of Stravinsky.

In addition to an influential career as a composer, Sessions is remembered as a teacher and writer. He made a career of university teaching and included among his students Milton Babbitt, David Del Tredici, Donald Martino, Leon Kirchner, and Hugo Weisgall, among many others. In addition to his numerous articles, Sessions is the author of *Harmonic Practice* (1951); *The Musical Experience of Composer, Performer, Listener* (1950), lectures presented at the Juilliard School in 1949; *Reflections on the Musical Life in the United States* (1956); *Questions about Music* (1971); and *Roger Sessions on Music: Collected Essays*, ed. Edward T. Cone (1979).

Sessions is remembered as an uncompromising and independent musical spirit. A modernist, he maintained an almost classical adherence to musical principle and to the integrity of his art, with no bows in the direction of contemporary fad or fashion. Copland called him a musical "philosopher," and others referred to him as a "composer's composer." Sessions's works transcend a particular decade or nationality. By maintaining an internationalist cultural perspective, Roger Sessions enhanced the cause of American musical composition in the twentieth century.

• The papers and musical scores of Roger Sessions are housed in the Special Collections of the Firestone Library at Princeton University. Sessions's own writings provide the best window into his thinking about critical issues such as modernism, nationalism, and internationalism in music, and the relationship of the composer and his art to audiences and critics. Andrea Olmstead, *Roger Sessions and His Music* (1985), is a definitive biography and analytical work. Olmstead also edited *Conversations with Roger Sessions* (1987). Paul Rosenfeld included a piece about Sessions that incorporated comments on the first performance of *The Black Maskers* in his *Port of New York: Essays on Fourteen American Moderns* (1924; repr. 1961). A year after Sessions's death, the Kent School, his alma mater, devoted an entire issue of the *Kent Quarterly* to Sessions: *An Appreciation: Roger Sessions, 1896–1985* (1986). Sessions's musical style was also the subject of numerous articles in *Modern Music, Tempo, Musical Quarterly*, and the *New Yorker*, among others.

BARBARA L. TISCHLER

SET-ANGYA (1800?–8 June 1871), Kiowa war chief, was born probably in the Black Hills region. His name means "Sitting Bear." He was also referred to as Satank by the white settlers. Little is known of his birth and parentage. He had three wives, Ta-lai-ty, Tsa-yu-mah, and Kau-ye-atty, four sons, and three daughters.

By the late 1700s nomadic bands of Kiowas had arrived on the Southern Plains. In 1837 the government signed at Fort Gibson the first treaty with chiefs of that tribe. In that same year warriors led by Set-angya intercepted about forty Cheyenne Bowstrings raiders in the Texas Panhandle area and killed the entire party. A bloody war existed between the Kiowas, allied with the Comanches, and the Cheyennes and Arapahos over horse raiding. In 1840 Chief Dohason and Set-angya were instrumental in negotiating a lasting intertribal peace with the Cheyennes and Arapahos. Set-angya gave 250 of his horses to individual Cheyennes in a gift exchange that sealed the peace. The possession of such a large herd was a symbol of the successful warrior and high rank. The Kaitsenko warrior society, an exclusive group of ten of the bravest men, was led by Set-angya. In battle this society put their lances down through their sashes, anchoring themselves facing the enemy. They were never to retreat unless rescued by a comrade. Also, Set-angya was the keeper of one of the sacred "Ten Grandmother" medicine bundles, another sign of his stature in the tribe.

On 27 July 1853 Set-angya signed the Treaty of Fort Atkinson, pledging peace with whites and permitting the construction of roads and forts in Kiowa country. Later he was given a President Buchanan Peace Medal. In 1865 Set-angya was pressured into signing the Treaty of Little Arkansas, which moved the Kiowa westward to make room for whites. In October 1867 the government again convened the Southern Plains tribes for the purpose of further divesting them of their lands. Under terms of the Treaty of Medicine Lodge the Kiowa lost all their hunting lands and were forced to accept a reservation in Oklahoma. After signing the treaty, Set-angya captivated the gathering with a brief but moving speech. "The white man once put his trust in our friendship and wanted no shield but our fidelity," he told the commissioners. He once "bade us hunt the game," but now he "tells us to be gone, as an offended master speaks to his dog." Holding up the medal that hung around his neck he said, "Look at this medal I wear. By wearing this, I have been made poor. Before I was rich in horses and lodges. Today I am the poorest of all. When you gave me this silver medal, you made me poor." But he added a conciliatory note: "We thank the Great Spirit that all these wrongs are now to cease. . . . Do for us what is best. Teach us the road to travel. . . . You may never see me more, but remember Satank as the white man's friend."

Reservation life turned out to be an ordeal for Set-angya and his people. When he realized that the goal of the government's reservation policy was the total destruction of Indian culture, he felt betrayed. Angry hunting and raiding parties frequently left the reservation. In spring 1870 Young Set-angya, favored son of the chief, was killed by settlers while raiding in Texas. Set-angya was left inconsolable. He recovered his son's bones and placed them in a special tipi. He spoke of the boy as if he were only sleeping, and placed food and water for him. He took the bones with him wherever he went, leading a horse carrying the bundled remains of his son. From then on he was an embittered man ready to wreak havoc upon the Texans.

In May 1871 Set-angya accompanied Set-tainte (Satanta) on a raid into Texas. At Salt Creek Prairie they ambushed a wagon train, killing seven teamsters. Set-tainte brazenly boasted of this deed at Fort Sill, and he, Set-angya, and Addo-etta (Big Tree) were arrested. General William T. Sherman ordered that they be sent to Jacksboro, Texas, for trial.

Set-angya was handcuffed, hobbled with chains, and tossed on a corn wagon. He complained in a loud chanting voice that he was being treated like a dog. He did not want to leave his son. He was a member of the Kaitsenko, under solemn vow to return from every engagement with honor or not at all. He saw no possibility of an honorable return from this trip. He pointed to a tree up ahead and said he would not pass it alive. He prayed and called out loudly to his dead son to light the pipe, for he was lonesome and would soon join him. Finally, he broke into the Kaitsenko society song, which became his death song. In a suicidal act, Set-angya suddenly tore his hands from the manacles, stabbed a guard, and grabbed his gun. Before he could fire, he was shot down by the accompanying cavalrymen and thrown off the wagon. As the wagons moved on toward Texas, Addo-etta looked back and saw Set-angya lying on the roadside mortally wounded, blood pouring from his mouth, still trying to sing his death song, "Only the earth and the sun endure, but we Kaitsenko must die." His body was buried at Fort Sill.

Set-angya was one of the most renowned warriors and respected diplomats in Kiowa history. His leadership contributed to making the Kiowas one of the most powerful and feared tribes in the West. Of all the Indians at Medicine Lodge, Set-angya was the one who most impressed the commissioners and correspondents. Yet Quaker agent Enoch Hoag called him the worst Indian on the reservation, and non-Indians generally viewed him only as a bloodthirsty savage. Crushed by the forces of American expansion, Set-angya's last years were filled with grief, disillusionment, and bitterness. He stopped wearing the silver medal that had made him poor. He no longer cared to be remembered as the white man's friend. In a sense, the old patriarch's violent death symbolized the end of the ancient Kiowa way of life.

• An essential primary source on the Kiowas is James Mooney, *Calendar History of the Kiowa Indians* (1898). N. Scott Momaday, *The Way to Rainy Mountain* (1969), provides a literary study of Kiowa origins, migrations, and culture. For a general history of the Kiowas, see Mildred P. Mayhall, *The Kiowas* (1962). Set-angya's relations with the army are discussed in Wilbur S. Nye, *Carbine and Lance: The Story of Old Fort Sill* (1942) and *Bad Medicine and Good* (1962). See also Bernard Mishkin, *Rank and Warfare among the Plains Indians* (1940), on the Kiowa martial culture. Set-angya's role at the Medicine Lodge Council is described in Douglas C. Jones, *The Treaty of Medicine Lodge* (1966). On Set-angya's conduct on the reservation as perceived by the Indian agents, see Lawrie Tatum, *Our Red Brothers and the Peace Policy of President Ulysses S. Grant* (1899; repr. 1970).

MARVIN E. KROEKER

SETCHELL, William Albert (15 Apr. 1864–5 Apr. 1943), botanist, was born in Norwich, Connecticut, the son of George Case Setchell (occupation unknown) and Mary Ann Davis. Setchell attended Norwich Free Academy, where he early demonstrated an interest in natural history and, especially, botany. While at the academy he read Harvard botanist Asa Gray's *Lessons in Botany* and spent his leisure time collecting and identifying plant specimens in the Norwich area. Along with friend George R. Case, who was deputy collector of the internal revenue for the Norwich district, he published a descriptive list of all plants in the Norwich region in 1883. Entering Yale University in the same year, Setchell drew the attention of noted fern expert Daniel Cady Eaton when Eaton noticed Setchell's discovery of a specimen of the fern *Asplenium montanum* far to the west of its known range. Because Yale had little to offer in the way of formal botanical training, Eaton personally took over Setchell's education and encouraged him to use Eaton's own private collections and library. Setchell's lifelong interest in algae also began at Yale, as the result of an acquaintance with amateur botanist Isaac Holden.

After graduating from Yale with an A.B. in 1887, Setchell became a Morgan Fellow at Harvard University, where he immersed himself primarily in botanical study with noted Harvard botanists and studied some zoology. He fell under the influence of the professor of cryptogamic botany, William Gilson Farlow, with whom he did graduate research. Farlow recognized his pupil's talents early on and considered Setchell to be one his most promising students. From Farlow, who was familiar with the latest European advances, Setchell learned the latest microscopic techniques and procedures. Shortly after receiving a Ph.D. in botany from Harvard in 1890, Setchell secured appointments first at Harvard, then at Yale, but gave up the later position when he received an offer from the newer University of California, Berkeley, to become professor of botany and chair of the botany department, serving as successor to E. L. Greene. Setchell was associated with the botany department at Berkeley from 1895 until his death. He became professor emeritus in 1934.

Although Setchell occasionally studied fungi and higher plants, the bulk of his work was on algae, their taxonomy, and their distribution, especially along temperature gradients within the field known as geobotany or phytogeography. While he was still on the East Coast he frequented the Marine Biological Laboratory at Woods Hole, Massachusetts, and taught summer courses there in proximity to his collecting sites. After he moved to Berkeley, he became an unquestioned authority on Pacific algae and distinguished himself in the study of the Laminariaceae, the giant kelps of the Pacific Coast. Along with his collaborator, Nathaniel Lyon Gardner, Setchell published, beginning in 1919, a series of monographs that became classics in the taxonomy of Pacific algae, *The Marine Algae of the Pacific Coast*. Among his contributions to phycology was a detailed study of the relationship between ambient water temperature and the distribution of algal forms. While the bulk of his studies on the Laminarias focused on their systematics and distribution, one of his studies explored the use of kelp as a natural fertilizer; his findings were subsequently published as an important Senate document.

Setchell also distinguished himself in the completion of the *Phycotheca Boreali-americana*, a project that involved the compilation of dried specimens (exsiccatae) of algae. The series, completed with the assistance of Isaac Holden and a second amateur botanist, F. S. Collins, ran to approximately 3,000 specimens and was circulated widely to an international audience of taxonomists. Many of the specimens had been collected by Setchell.

Setchell made two world tours. He devoted the first, in 1903–1904, to his taxonomic activity, both collecting and identifying specimens in international herbaria that he came to know; the second tour, in 1926–1927, permitted him to explore his secondary interest in the geographical distribution of plants. He made detailed studies of the role of algae in coral-reef formations and of seaweed distribution and abundance. His observations later enabled him to complete important work on the morphology, taxonomy, and distribution of the genus *Zostera*.

In the capacity of teacher and adviser, Setchell appears to have been especially popular with undergraduates, who sought his advice on personal matters. As chair of the botany department, he served as an effective leader who helped shape the character of the department and of the University of California at an especially critical time in its development. Among his contributions to the running of the department was the establishment of extensive phycological and mycological collections (he retained his early interest in cryptogams as a whole), and as director of the botanic garden he supported the hybridization research on tobacco that was carried on by Robert E. Clausen and Thomas Harper Goodspeed. Another noteworthy contribution that stemmed from his interest in geobotany and ethnobotany was the celebrated pipe collection he donated to the university's Robert H. Lowie Museum of Anthropology.

Setchell earned the respect and appreciation of most of his colleagues, who found him an amiable, entertaining, and witty individual who enjoyed lively discussions. Especially fond of the arts and literature, he was, like many taxonomists of his day, well versed in the classics. He also had an avid interest in the history of botany and taught the first history of science course at Berkeley.

Among Setchell's many honors were the Berkeley Faculty Lectureship in 1931 and fellowships in the California Academy of Sciences, American Academy of Arts and Sciences (Boston), American Philosophical Society, Linnean Society of London, Torrey Botanical Club, Washington Academy of Sciences, and the American Association for the Advancement of Science, for which he served as vice president. He was also a member of the American Anthropological Association, the American Geographical Society, Sigma Xi, Phi Beta Kappa, Alpha Zeta, Phi Sigma (he was national president), Alpha Epsilon Sigma, the Authors' Club (London), and the Bohemian Club (San Francisco).

In 1920 he married Mrs. Clara Ball Pearson Caldwell of Providence, Rhode Island, with whom he shared many of his botanical explorations. The two traveled together for the next twelve years, especially in the Pacific regions and in Alaska. She also assisted him assiduously in his laboratory work. (The marriage was childless.) His other noted long-term assistant, N. L. Gardner, continued to assist with laboratory preparations and in revisions of their joint monographs on the Pacific algae. Shortly after the deaths of these two special assistants, Setchell himself was invalided but continued to write at home and visit his laboratory occasionally. He died in his home in Berkeley, California. He is now generally recognized as a pioneer in phycological research and in the development of California botany.

• Setchell's papers, in the University Herbarium Archives of the University of California, Berkeley, include his letters, bound by year; his correspondence; and many of his manuscripts. The most thorough biographical essay is by his Berkeley colleague Thomas Harper Goodspeed in *Essays in Geobotany in Honor of William Albert Setchell*, ed. T. H. Goodspeed (1936). Other biographical sketches include D. H. Campbell, "William Albert Setchell," National Academy of Sciences, *Biographical Memoirs* 23 (1945): 123–47; Francis Drouet, "William Albert Setchell," *American Midland Naturalist* 30 (1943): 529–32; and Herbert L. Mason, "William Albert Setchell," *Madrono* 7 (1943): 91–93. For a history of botany at Berkeley see Lincoln Constance, *Botany at Berkeley: The First Hundred Years* (1978). Setchell is included in Harry Baker Humphrey, *Makers of North American Botany* (1961). For an overview of Setchell and American botany see Joseph Ewan, ed., *A Short History of Botany in the United States* (1969). An obituary by A. D. Cotton is in *Proceedings of the Linnean Society* 156 (1943–1944): 232–33.

VASSILIKI BETTY SMOCOVITIS

SETON, Anya (1904?–8 Nov. 1990), author of historical fiction, was born in Manhattan, New York, the daughter of Ernest Thompson Seton, a celebrated author, artist, and naturalist, and Grace Gallatin, a writer of travel books about the Orient and Near East. She was christened Ann but was known by the sobriquet of Anya, a variation of a Native American word meaning "cloud gray eyes." The name had been bestowed on Seton by her father's friend, a Sioux Indian chief. Raised on the large family estate in Cos Cob, Connecticut, Seton was primarily educated at home by private governesses but graduated from the Spence School in New York and later took courses at Oxford University in England. Twice married (the first time at age eighteen) and twice divorced, Seton raised one son and two daughters. Her second husband, Hamilton Chase, was a successful investment adviser, and the couple built a home along the coast in Old Greenwich, Connecticut.

Seton attributed her affinity for all things English to her British-born father, who hailed from Tyneside in Northumberland. As a child, Seton spent four years in England and developed an appreciation for her own family history as well as the wider British culture. By the time she was thirteen, she was a seasoned traveler, having crossed the Atlantic Ocean eight times, and she later stated that she had spent at least a quarter of her life in Great Britain. England served as the setting for several of her most successful novels. Seton identified herself as an Episcopalian but attributed her lifelong interest in comparative religion, mysticism, and reincarnation to the influence of her mother's belief in Theosophy. This theme was developed in Seton's last two books, *Green Darkness* (1972) and *Smouldering Fires* (1975).

Medicine was Seton's initial passion, and she briefly studied to become a doctor at a French hospital in Paris but did not complete her studies. She later worked for a time in medically related fields as a nurse's aide and as a secretary in a mental health clinic. However, in 1937, at the height of the Great Depression, she followed in her parents' literary footsteps and turned her hand to writing in order to earn a living while remaining at home to care for her children. She began by writing short pieces for newspapers and sold her first story for five dollars. Her first novel, *My Theodosia*, a fictionalized treatment of the life of Aaron Burr's daughter, who drowned under mysterious circumstances in 1813, was published by Houghton Mifflin in 1941. The book was serialized in the *Ladies' Home*

Journal and was chosen by the Dollar Book Club as a featured selection. Writing proved to be a lucrative career and a personally rewarding decision as Seton acquired an international reputation for highly readable, meticulously researched historical novels. All of her books were chosen as book club selections, and each was translated into several languages. Two of her early works, *Dragonwyck* (1944), a Gothic romance set on the Hudson River, and *Foxfire* (1951), with early Arizona as its location, were made into popular films. The film version of *Dragonwyck* starred Vincent Price and Gene Tierney and served as the vehicle that launched director Joseph Mankiewicz on his long Hollywood film career. *Foxfire* featured Jane Russell and Jeff Chandler and was inspired by Seton's trips to the American West. Seton never wrote about a locale she had not personally visited. She was also the author of two books for children, *Mistletoe and Sword: A Story of Roman Britain* (1955) and *Washington Irving* (1960).

The 1941 publication of *My Theodosia* launched Seton's prolific writing career as a novelist, which spanned nearly forty years. Producing a new book involved a long period of intense research, sometimes more than two years in duration, and then a year of actual writing. She considered research her main hobby and greatest pleasure. Most of her writing was done in her house in Old Greenwich, not far from her childhood home. Seton's commitment to exhaustive research and historical accuracy reflected her belief that "one must never distort history. There is a code of honor involved." Such sentiments were unusual in a popular author whose books sold in the millions. In the author's note introducing *The Winthrop Woman* (1958), Seton revealed that she had spent more than four years researching and writing the story of Puritan leaders Elizabeth and John Winthrop, Jr. This included two trips to England and numerous hours at the Massachusetts Historical Society poring over the original handwritten Winthrop family papers. *The Winthrop Woman* was possibly her most critically acclaimed work and successfully combined her interest in both the British and the American experience.

Seton's books generally focused on talented, strong-willed heroines in a variety of historic periods. Some characters were fictitious, but the aforementioned Theodosia Burr, Elizabeth Winthrop, and Katherine Swynford (*Katherine* [1954]), mistress and, later, wife of John of Gaunt, for example, were real historical figures. Seton preferred to classify herself as a "biographical novelist" rather than a writer of historical fiction because of the depth of her research. In her author's note to *The Winthrop Woman* she emphasized that "my determination to present authentic history has necessitated a scrupulous adherence to the findings of research."

Seton died at her home in Connecticut. Although her obituary in the *New York Times* listed her age as eighty-six, her year of birth is in question. Seton was praised as one of the premier American historical novelists of her era. Critic Edward Fuller, writing in the *Saturday Review* in 1958, observed she had elevated the historical novel to "a true art." During her career Seton penned more than a dozen books, most of which became bestsellers and were translated into a dozen languages. She set a standard for historical accuracy and research that has seldom been duplicated among her peers, while also entertaining and educating a generation of avid fans on both sides of the Atlantic.

• Biographical information on Anya Seton can be found in *Current Biography* (1953) and *Something about the Author*, vol. 66. Seton's books were reviewed in a variety of magazines, including the *Saturday Review*, 15 Feb. 1958, and the *New York Herald Tribune Books*, 2 Mar. 1962). For information on Seton's philosophy and style of research and writing, see "The Treasure Hunt of Research," *The Writer*, Apr. 1962. The author's notes to Seton's books also reveal interesting insights into her family background and literary approach. An obituary is in the *New York Times*, 10 Nov. 1990.

JEANNE ADAMS

SETON, Elizabeth Ann Bayley (28 Aug. 1774–4 Jan. 1821), founder of the American Sisters of Charity and Roman Catholic saint, was born probably in New York City, the daughter of Richard Bayley, a prominent surgeon, and Catherine Charlton. Raised by an unloving stepmother and, except for her education, a negligent father, she evidenced in her loneliness a religious bent but immersed herself in the social and cultural life of New York. She developed several close friends among the leading matrons, with whom she would, after her marriage, organize the Society for the Relief of Poor Widows and Small Children. For their many good works they would be called "the Protestant Sisters of Charity."

In 1794 Elizabeth was married by Bishop Samuel Provoost of the Episcopal diocese of New York to a young merchant, William Magee Seton, with whom she had five children. It was a happy marriage except for the realization, almost from the start, that William was dying of consumption. Financial reverses and the hope for William's recovery sent the couple and the oldest of their three daughters to Italy in 1803; William died at Pisa at the end of the year. Two of his Italian business associates, the brothers Antonio and Filippo Filicchi, took charge of the young widow and familiarized her with the teachings and devotions of the Catholic church. After her return to New York she determined to join the Church of Rome, much to the dismay of her family, friends, and spiritual adviser, the Reverend John Henry Hobart. Under the direction of Antonio Filicchi, who had accompanied her home, of Bishop John Carroll of Baltimore, and of two future bishops, John Cheverus of Boston and Louis William DuBourg, a Baltimore Sulpician, Seton made her submission to the Catholic church at St. Peter's Church, Barclay Street, on 14 March 1805. Her inability to support her children adequately as a teacher, plus outbursts of anti-Catholicism in New York City, one occasioned by the conversion of her sister-in-law, Cecilia Seton, for which Elizabeth Seton was blamed, led her to accept the proposal of Father DuBourg to open a school in Baltimore, where she moved with her children.

In a modest house on Paca Street she began classes in September 1808 with the possible intention of forming a sisterhood under the direction of the Sulpicians, who conducted the adjacent St. Mary's Seminary. In October she wrote to Cecilia Seton, "It is expected I shall be the mother of many daughters." She was joined in the course of the school year by four other women, who under the direction of Father DuBourg adopted a religious habit on 1 June 1809. That same month they moved to Emmitsburg, Maryland, where a sizable property had been purchased for them by a young seminarian, Samuel Cooper, eager to put his fortune to good use. At Emmitsburg the sisters were joined by others, including Cecilia Seton, the first to die in the order. The school for boarders that had begun in Baltimore attracted the daughters of the leading Catholic families of Maryland. A separate school for the poor children of Emmitsburg was commenced on 22 February 1810. Though not the first parochial school, as often claimed, it was the first parish school free to those who could not pay to be taught by religious.

The early years of the foundation were a time of trial for Mother Seton. Father DuBourg resigned as director when she and other sisters complained of his refusal to allow the priest they had chosen as their confessor in Baltimore to visit them. The second director, John Baptist David, also a Sulpician, attempted a number of changes in both the sisterhood and the school without consulting Mother Seton. These included a union with the Daughters of Charity in France founded by St. Vincent de Paul. Seton raised no objection to the union, but it was not effected in her lifetime. A rule modeled on that of the Daughters of Charity, which David had obtained, was adopted for their American counterparts in 1812 under their third director, Father John Dubois, founder of Mount St. Mary's College and Seminary in Emmitsburg. The next year the sisters pronounced their first vows. In these founding years Mother Seton was also afflicted by the death of two sisters-in-law and a daughter, all claimed by the "Seton enemy"—consumption. For the sisters in general they were years of great privation.

Under Dubois the sisterhood and its two schools in Emmitsburg prospered. In 1814 the sisters took charge of an orphanage in Philadelphia and in 1817 another in New York City, a work much to Mother Seton's liking. Although in an act of incorporation by the state of Maryland in 1817 one of the chief goals of the Sisters of Charity of St. Joseph, as the order was now officially known, was the care of the sick, the principal ministry of the Daughters of Charity in France, this goal was never realized in the founder's lifetime. In her last years Mother Seton was troubled by the death of another daughter and the irresponsible behavior of her two sons, but her life was enriched by the friendship of Simon Gabriel Bruté de Rémur, future bishop of Vincennes, Indiana. Historians have sometimes characterized Elizabeth Seton as an indulgent mother,

and from the start she made it clear that her "dear ones" had the "first claim which must ever remain inviolate." Yet she never neglected her spiritual children. Often ignored by historians, because they are poorly documented, were Mother Seton's day-to-day activities as religious superior, organizer, and pedagogue, all roles in which she excelled. She won easily the affection of her religious sisters and her pupils and evidenced a remarkable balance of the practical and mystical. She died, in Emmitsburg, of consumption at age forty-six and was buried at the motherhouse.

By 1963, when Mother Seton was beatified by the Catholic church, some 11,000 Sisters of Charity in the United States, divided into six distinct religious orders that claimed her as their founder, were engaged in education, health care, and social work. Elizabeth Ann Bayley Seton left a large body of writings in the form of journals and correspondence, from which could easily be traced her growth in sanctity. On 14 September 1975 she was canonized the first native-born saint of the United States.

• The scattered writings and correspondence of Mother Seton are found mainly in the archives of the Daughters of Charity, Emmitsburg, Md., the Sisters of Charity, Mount Saint Vincent, N.Y., the archdiocese of Baltimore, the University of Notre Dame, and the Postulator General, Rome, Italy. Of her many biographies and published works the most noteworthy are Charles I. White, *Life of Mrs. Eliza Seton* (1853); Robert Seton, ed., *Memoir, Letters and Journal of Elizabeth Seton* (2 vols., 1869); Annabelle M. Melville, *Elizabeth Bayley Seton, 1774–1821* (1951); Joseph I. Dirvin, *Mrs. Seton: Foundress of the American Sisters of Charity* (1962); and Ellin M. Kelly and Annabelle M. Melville, eds., *Elizabeth Seton: Selected Writings* (1987).

THOMAS W. SPALDING

SETON, Ernest Thompson (14 Aug. 1860–23 Oct. 1946), naturalist, artist, writer, and lecturer, was born Ernest Evan Thompson in South Shields, England, the son of Joseph Logan Thompson, a businessman, and Alice Snowden. Joseph Thompson claimed famous Scottish ancestry, including a title, never legally established, deriving from the fifth earl of Winton, Lord Seton. Ernest legally adopted the surname Seton in 1901.

When the family shipping business failed in 1866, Joseph Thompson emigrated with his family to a Canadian farm but, within four years, sold out to a neighbor, William Blackwell. The Thompsons then moved to Toronto, but Ernest's experience with country life had already convinced him to become a naturalist. While in Toronto Collegiate High School, he became ill and was sent to stay with the Blackwells, where he recovered quickly. His famous boy's book *Two Little Savages* (1903) is a fictional account of his adventures there.

Returning to Toronto in 1876, Seton apprenticed himself to a portraitist, acceding to his father's wish that he become an artist. He attended the Ontario School of Art and in 1879 won a gold medal. That same year he persuaded his father to finance a trip to

London, where he studied mammalian anatomy at the London Zoo and British Museum. Although he won a tuition scholarship in 1880 to the Royal Academy School of Painting and Sculpture, ill health, his periodic bane, soon forced him home in poor spirits.

Seton lived briefly on his brother's farm in Manitoba, then took up a claim of his own nearby. Unready to settle down, he spent most of the next five years trapping, drawing, collecting, and hunting on the Manitoba prairie. During these years Seton became a self-trained field researcher and was appointed naturalist to the government of Manitoba. In 1884 he was invited to join the new American Ornithologists Union by its secretary, C. Hart Merriam, and began contributing articles to its journal, the *Auk*.

Soon Merriam invited Seton to visit him in upstate New York. The American used one of Seton's drawings in his *Mammals of the Adirondacks* (1884) and later commissioned a number of them for government publications. For three years, Seton lived at intervals in New York City, working briefly for a lithographer and studying at the Art Students League. During this time, his first scientific work, *A List of the Mammals of Manitoba* (1886) was published, followed by *The Birds of Manitoba* (1891).

Through a contract to make a thousand nature drawings for the *Century Dictionary* (1889–1891), Seton met prominent American ornithologist Elliott Coues, the dictionary's zoological editor. Coues introduced him to J. A. Allen, William Brewster, Robert Ridgway, and other ornithologists. Because of his eccentricity and egotism, Seton repelled some colleagues of more conventional temperament. He did, however, befriend Frank M. Chapman, of the American Museum of Natural History, who gave Seton work as an illustrator and textual contributor to his *Handbook of Birds of Eastern North America* (1895) and *Bird Life* (1897).

In 1890 Seton went to Paris, where he trained at Julian's Academy. The next year, his oil painting of a sleeping wolf was chosen for display in the Grand Salon. His Paris studies in anatomy led to his later book *Studies in the Art Anatomy of Animals* (1896), which, according to editor John Samson, "could stand today as a textbook for veterinarian medicine [because the] illustrations are marvels of study and work."

On his return to the United States in 1892, Seton achieved his first literary success. Hired as a wolf killer in New Mexico, he learned to eliminate these predators, which, at the same time, he grew to admire. These experiences he turned into the first of his famous animal stories, "The King of the Currumpaw," published in *Scribner's Magazine* (1894). The plot of this tale served as a pattern for numerous others in which some animal successfully copes with a series of perils, only to die courageously in the end. Seton felt this sequence was typical in nature.

After further travel in the West, Seton undertook more art study in Paris. In 1896 he married Grace Gallatin, the daughter of California financier Albert Gallatin. His wife, an author and social leader, aided him in editing and designing his books. The couple had one daughter, Ann, who became the novelist Anya Seton. Almost from the beginning, the Setons' lives diverged, though they remained on cordial terms.

The next decade Seton spent exploring wild areas of North America, including the Yellowstone, Wind River, and Jackson Hole. In 1900 he took a trip to Norway, and in 1907, a 2,000-mile Canadian canoe trip that nearly reached the Arctic Circle. During this time, Seton had camped in most U.S. and Canadian wilderness areas and produced and illustrated some twenty books. *The Arctic Prairies* (1911), a lengthy account of Seton's seven-month north Canadian canoe trip, revealed, in addition to other things, his mixed response to the Indians of his day and their life styles. Early editions antagonized some biologists who resented Seton's failure to acknowledge the contribution of Edward A. Preble, his guide and a U.S. Biological Survey staff member, to the success of the trip.

By 1910, Seton was one of the country's leading nature writers and illustrators; his popularity as a public speaker brought him up to $12,000 annually. *Wild Animals I Have Known* (1898) was easily his most successful literary effort. A bestseller in its time, it has been continuously in print since its original publication. With this book, Seton invented a tradition of animal stories, which later attracted such writers as Jack London and earned him the friendship of President Theodore Roosevelt. His literary friends included Mark Twain, William Dean Howells, and Hamlin Garland, together with John Burroughs, the outstanding nature essayist of the period.

Seton's reputation, however, was not invulnerable. In an article in the *Atlantic* (Mar. 1903), Burroughs made him a major target as one of the "Nature Fakirs," who attributed powers of reason to animals and insisted that such characterizations were factual. Roosevelt and Chapman, realizing the value of Seton's work, advised Burroughs against further attacks. Burroughs; sequel article (July 1904) ranked Seton first among contemporary younger naturalists but warned that his stories required the reader to separate truth from fantasy. Roosevelt was among those who persuaded Seton to back up his stories with the publication of facts.

Seton set to work; *Life Histories of Northern Animals* (1909) dealt with sixty of the more common North American mammals. Critical response was highly favorable. The work received the Camp Fire Gold Medal. The next fifteen years were chiefly devoted to producing the massive *Lives of Game Animals*, a four-volume work published between 1925 and 1929, which won him the coveted John Burroughs (1926) and Daniel Giraud Elliott (1928) medals. By ably blending his field experiences with the writings of zoologists and other observers, Seton had created a work that was eminently readable, yet reflected the latest scientific thinking. His landmark insights into animal psychology and emphasis on life histories gave the work its standing as a classic.

As an artist Seton has never been recognized as being of first rank. Most of his mammal paintings were good, if academic, but he is considered to have been best at producing pen and ink field sketches. His forte was depicting quadrupeds, but his quick sketches of birds were also evocative. Although Seton never mastered the look of flight, he devised the field identification system later developed in Roger Tory Peterson's *Field Guides*. As an illustrator, Seton set the standard for later work done by Louis Agassiz Fuertes and others. His unique combination of writing and illustration made him an exceptionally effective publicist for nature.

In 1910 Seton played an important role in the formation of the Boy Scouts of America, writing the original handbook, *The American Boy Scout: The Official Handbook of Woodcraft for the Boy Scouts of America* (1910), and serving as chief scout until 1915. Seton, however, wanted scouting to emphasize campcraft and Indian ways instead of uniforms, discipline, and slogans; he later broke with other leaders of the movement, notably William Hornaday, to give greater attention to his own organization, the Woodcraft Indians, which he had founded in 1902 and which idealized Indian life and lore.

In 1930 Seton became a U.S. citizen and left the East to settle in New Mexico. Purchasing 2,500 acres near Santa Fe, he built "Seton Castle," a structure of stone and adobe whose thirty rooms contained most of his 8,000 paintings and drawings, 13,000 books, and 3,000 mammal and bird skins. Here he established his College of Indian Wisdom. In 1935, four days after divorcing his first wife, Seton married Julia M. Buttree, a student of Indian lore who was almost thirty years his junior. The couple later adopted a daughter. He died at his home near Santa Fe and was cremated in Albuquerque. His home is maintained as a museum and center for the study of Indian life.

• Most Seton material, principally illustrations and papers, is in the Ernest Thompson Seton Memorial Museum at the Philmont Boy Scout Reservation, Cimarron, N.M. There and at Seton Castle in Santa Fe, N.M., owned by his adopted daughter, Beulah Seton Barbour, are 2,000 of Seton's best paintings, drawings, and etchings. Thirty-eight volumes of his journals, sold at auction by his wife's direction in 1965, are held in the Rare Book Room of the American Museum of Natural History, New York City. Seton's autobiography, *Trail of an Artist-Naturalist: The Autobiography of Ernest Thompson Seton* (1940), was reprinted in 1978. Useful compilations of Seton's writings include *The Best of Ernest Thompson Seton*, ed. W. Kay Robinson (1949); *Ernest Thompson Seton's America*, ed. Farida A. Wiley (1954); *By a Thousand Fires: Nature Notes and Extracts from the Life and Unpublished Journals of Ernest Thompson Seton*, ed. Julia M. Seton (1967); and *The Worlds of Ernest Thompson Seton*, ed. John G. Samson (1976). Of his roughly fifty books, several are anthologies of articles previously published in such periodicals as *Scribner's*, the *Century*, *Ladies' Home Journal*, *Country Life in America*, *St. Nicholas*, *American Magazine*, *Forest and Stream*, *Bird-Lore*, *Boy's Life*, *American Boy*, and *Recreation*; these collected tales include *Wild Animal Play for Children* (1900), *Animal Heroes* (1905), *Natural History of the Ten Commandments* (1907), *Wild Animals at Home* (1913), *Wild Animal Ways* (1916), *Woodland Tales* (1921), and *Cute Coyote and Other Animal Stories* (1930). His outdoor guides included *American Woodcraft for Boys* (1902), *The Birchbark Roll of the Woodcraft Indians* (various editions, 1906–1931), *The Forester's Manual* (1911), *The Book of Woodcraft and Indian Lore* (1912), *The Woodcraft Manual for Girls* (1916), *The Woodcraft Manual for Boys* (1917), and *Sign Talk* (1918). A number of scientific articles appeared in the *Auk* and the *Journal of Mammalogy*, among others. Biographical studies include John Henry Wadland, *Ernest Thompson Seton: Man in Nature and the Progressive Era, 1880–1915* (1976) which provides the most comprehensive listing of Seton's books and articles; Betty Keller, *Black Wolf: The Life of Ernest Thompson Seton* (1984); and H. Allen Anderson, *The Chief: Ernest Thompson Seton and the Changing West* (1986). Ralph H. Lutts, *The Nature Fakers: Wildlife, Science and Sentiment* (1990), places Seton in the context of the Nature Faker controversy of the early twentieth century. An obituary is in the *New York Times*, 24 Oct. 1946.

KEIR B. STERLING

SETON, Grace Gallatin Thompson (28 Jan. 1872–19 Mar. 1959), explorer, writer, and suffragist, was born in Sacramento, California, the daughter of Albert Gallatin, the president of the largest steel and iron business on the West Coast, and Clemenzie Rhodes. Grace Gallatin's parents were divorced in 1881. After the divorce, Clemenzie Gallatin moved to New York City, taking with her only Grace, the youngest of her four children.

Grace Gallatin graduated from the Packer Collegiate Institute in 1892 and subsequently studied bookmaking and printing in Paris, France. While in France, she began a career as a journalist, writing articles for San Francisco newspapers. It was also in France, in 1894, that Gallatin met her future husband, Ernest Thompson Seton, a naturalist, artist, and writer. The couple married in New York in 1896 and set up houses in both New York City and Greenwich, Connecticut.

Seton helped her husband with the design and layout of his books on naturalism and accompanied him on many of his travels. As she worked with him, she discovered her passion for exploring. In his autobiography, *Trail of an Artist-Naturalist*, Ernest Thompson Seton remarks on his wife's abilities in the outdoors: "As a camper she was a great success, never grumbled at hardship, or scolded any one. She was a dead shot with the rifle, often far ahead of the guides, and met all kinds of danger with unflinching nerve." In her first two books, *A Woman Tenderfoot in the Rockies* (1900) and *Nimrod's Wife* (1907), Grace Gallatin Seton humorously tells of her experiences traveling through the Rockies and Sierras with her husband. As a result of their shared commitment to naturalism, in 1910 the Setons helped found the Girl Pioneers, an organization that was soon renamed the Camp Fire Girls.

The Setons had one child, Ann (nicknamed Anya), born in 1904. Though she was a loving and devoted mother, Grace Seton felt constrained by the traditional duties of a housewife. In *Nimrod's Wife* she comments on the effort it took to achieve a short trip on the Ottawa River in 1904 and indicates the reward for that effort: "Much violent uprooting from home duties had been required to accomplish it, but the precious freedom was ours."

When her daughter was too young for Seton to enjoy the freedom of travel, she concentrated on helping women gain the freedom to vote. She fought for woman suffrage throughout the first quarter of the twentieth century, serving as vice president and later president of the Connecticut Women's Suffrage Association (1910–1920). In this capacity Seton engaged in numerous speaking tours. Many of the pamphlets and press releases issued by the Connecticut Votes for Women League reveal her opinion that woman suffrage is essential to democracy. As an activist for women's rights, Seton also attended four Pacific conferences for women between 1928 and 1937.

During World War I Seton raised the money necessary to purchase, equip, and operate six trucks for transportation service between the front lines and Paris, where medical help was available for the soldiers. For two years she directed this women's motor unit of the Le Bien-être du Blessé, a Franco-American society founded in 1914. She was awarded a medal of honor by the French government for this work.

Seton had a sustained interest in women's writing. She was president of the National League of American Pen Women from 1926 to 1928 and from 1930 to 1932. In that position she doubled the number of branches of the organization. As chair of letters of the National Council of Women from 1933 to 1938, she established the *Biblioteca Femina*, a collection documenting more than 2,000 volumes written by women and representing thirty-seven countries and five continents. Invaluable in keeping many women writers from obscurity, this resource was later donated to Northwestern University Library.

By the late 1920s their individual interests had led Seton and her husband to travel separately a great deal. Unlike in the early days of their marriage, they no longer shared in each other's work. In 1935, after their daughter had grown and married, the Setons finally divorced.

Between 1920 and the late 1930s Grace Gallatin Seton traveled in more than twelve countries, exploring places that tourists rarely saw. Above all else, her interest in women influenced where she went and what she studied there. In the course of her travels, Seton spoke with politicians, women, and progressive leaders in each country she visited. She attended the First International Congress of Women in Chile and sought the matriarchal society of the Mois in Indochina. She traveled in Egypt, China, Japan, Indochina, India, and South America and wrote five books reflecting her abiding interest in the lives and rights of women: *A Woman Tenderfoot in Egypt* (1923), *Chinese Lanterns* (1924), "*Yes, Lady Saheb*" (1925), *Log of the "Look-See"* (1932), and *Poison Arrows* (1938). Seton lectured extensively on her work as an explorer and was a charter member of the Society of Woman Geographers.

Two of Seton's books were recognized for their exceptional writing and their comment on the progress of women. *A Woman Tenderfoot in Egypt* was selected by the Century of Progress exposition in Chicago as one of the best books by women in the preceding century. "*Yes, Lady Saheb*" was selected by the League of American Pen Women as the best book of 1926.

Grace Gallatin Seton no longer traveled as extensively in her later years. Yet until her death in 1959 she continued to travel within the United States and remained active in various organizations. She also continued to write, publishing a collection of poems, *Singing Heart*, in 1958. In the course of her long life Seton wrote song lyrics, newspaper articles, letters of protest, studies in mysticism, and seven books. She remained a steadfast advocate of women's rights. She died in Palm Beach, Florida.

• Seton's papers can be found in two separate collections. Materials regarding her suffrage work and family life reside at the Schlesinger Library at Radcliffe College, while her manuscripts, correspondence, and a clipping file are at the Sophia Smith Collection at Smith College. The entry on Seton in Marion Tinling, *Women into the Unknown: A Sourcebook on Women Explorers and Travelers* (1989), is an important source of information on Seton's travels and travel writing. Two other sources that offer insight into the life and work of Seton are *Trail of an Artist-Naturalist: The Autobiography of Ernest Thompson Seton* (1940) and Betty Keller, *Black Wolf: The Life of Ernest Thompson Seton* (1984). Information about her involvement in the early days of the Camp Fire Girls organization can be found in *Wo-He-Lo: The Story of Camp Fire Girls, 1910–1960* (1961). Seton's obituary is in the *New York Times*, 20 Mar. 1959.

MARLOWE A. MILLER

SETTLE, Thomas, Jr. (23 Jan. 1831–1 Dec. 1888), federal judge, state supreme court justice, and politician, was born in Rockingham County, North Carolina, the son of Thomas Settle and Henrietta Graves. His father was a distinguished judge on the state superior court (1833–1854), Speaker of the North Carolina House of Commons, and congressman (1817–1821). The younger Settle graduated from the University of North Carolina in 1850, served as private secretary to Governor David Settle Reid, his brother-in-law and first cousin, and read law under Judge Richmond M. Pearson. Licensed to practice law in 1854, Settle immediately launched his political career by election to the North Carolina General Assembly. Serving three successive terms, he was elected Speaker of the House of Commons for the 1858–1859 session. He accepted appointment to the Board of Trustees of the University of North Carolina in 1856 and served until 1874. Settle married Mary Glen in 1859, and they had nine children who survived infancy, including Thomas Settle III (1865–1919), who served two terms in Congress (1895–1899).

Unlike his father, who was a Whig, the younger Settle joined the Democrats, influenced by his kinsman Governor Reid, who led the fight for free suffrage (the removal of the 50-acre qualification to vote for state senators) in North Carolina during the 1850s. In 1856 Settle accepted his party's nomination as a Buchanan elector. During the sectional crisis of 1860–1861, Settle was a Unionist and vigorously supported the presidential candidacy of Stephen A. Douglas, to whom he was related through marriage. When North Carolina held an election to call a secession convention in February 1861, Settle ran as a Unionist delegate and handily defeated his old mentor Governor Reid. However, he did not serve, because the call was narrowly defeated. Though he had been a strong opponent of secession, Settle volunteered for the Thirteenth Regiment, North Carolina Troops, in May 1861, serving one year as captain of Company I. When his term expired, he declined election as colonel of the Twenty-first Regiment and returned home to serve as solicitor of the Fourth Judicial Circuit, a position he held until 1868.

As the war dragged on, Settle grew increasingly critical of Jefferson Davis, the "destructives" who insisted on continuing the conflict, and Confederate "military despotism." He publicly supported the peace movement in North Carolina in 1863–1864 and called on Governor Zebulon B. Vance to convene a state convention to negotiate a separate peace. At the conclusion of the war Settle played a leading role as a delegate to the constitutional convention of 1865. He chaired the respective committees that drafted ordinances abolishing slavery and repudiating the Confederate war debt. That same year he was elected to the state senate and was chosen Speaker.

In 1860 Settle owned twenty-six slaves. During the war he denounced the secessionists for bringing about the destruction of slavery. At the constitutional convention of 1865, according to a northern journalist, Settle even favored the deportation and colonization of the freedmen. Yet Settle chose to cast his political fortunes with the Republican party. He compared the Republicans of the 1860s with the Democrats of the 1850s, because both parties advocated much-needed reforms. In a remarkable speech to a mass meeting of whites and blacks in Rockingham County in June 1867, Settle proclaimed his support for "Union, Liberty and Equality before the Law." He was a supporter of black suffrage. Arguing for sectional and racial harmony, he welcomed northern investment and industrialization in the South and championed the education of "our laboring classes" as the best means of promoting prosperity. In particular, he warned that the peace and abundance of postwar society would depend "upon the good feeling that ought to exist between the two races." When President Andrew Johnson's Reconstruction policies failed, Settle endorsed the congressional Reconstruction program and recommended the early adoption of the Fourteenth Amendment.

In April 1868 Settle was elected associate justice of the North Carolina Supreme Court, where he wrote clear, concise opinions that went directly to the heart of a case. Though he tended to defer to discursive justices like Pearson and Edwin G. Reade on matters of legal principle and philosophy, Settle supported opinions that evinced a democratic sympathy for the laboring classes. Settle showed concern for those subject to oppressive government, negligent corporations, fence laws designed to protect the open range for livestock, and unfair sharecropping contracts that threatened to create a "new *regime*" under conditions "worse than slavery." During his tenure on the court Settle also actively tried to quell the Ku Klux Klan in his native county, testified before the Select Committee of the Senate to Investigate Alleged Outrages in the Southern States, and according to oral tradition, moved his residence to Greensboro in 1870 after receiving assassination threats. In 1871 President Ulysses S. Grant appointed Settle minister to Peru. Illness and a hearty dislike for the climate and country prompted his precipitate resignation in 1872. Settle returned to the United States, chaired the Republican National Convention in Philadelphia that nominated Grant for reelection, and ran unsuccessfully for Congress. He lost by only 268 votes out of 21,000 cast.

Appointed associate justice of the state supreme court once more in December 1872, Settle served until 1876, when he resigned to run against Vance in the gubernatorial election. In what is considered one of the greatest campaigns in the state's history, Settle and Vance conducted a joint canvass that drew huge crowds. A powerful orator, Settle proved the superior debater, but Vance's personal popularity as North Carolina's wartime governor as well as his homespun humor and appeals to white supremacy secured his election by 13,000 votes out of 233,000 cast.

Regarded by his supporters as the "foremost man of his party in the south," Settle received a judicial appointment from President Grant to the U.S. District Court for the Northern District of Florida in 1877. Though his name was often mentioned for cabinet and other prominent positions during Republican administrations, Settle remained in the Jacksonville judicial post until his death. He died in Greensboro.

Settle and his wife belonged to the Baptist church in Greensboro. Handsome, magnetic, and personable, Settle did not generate the choleric hatreds reserved for other southern "scalawags," such as William W. Holden, his close friend and political ally. Most political opponents respected Settle's intellect, integrity, and fairness. His strong Unionist sentiments undoubtedly eased his transition from Douglas Democrat to postwar Republican. Settle's relatively progressive views on race and the shape of the New South's political and economic order placed him in the forefront of southern reformers, who willingly acknowledged, in Settle's words, "There has been a general breaking up of old ideas, and we are now taking a new start in the world."

• Settle's extensive papers are in the Southern Historical Collection at the University of North Carolina at Chapel Hill. Early biographical treatments of Settle appear in John H. Wheeler, *Reminiscences and Memoirs of North Carolina and Eminent North Carolinians* (1884); and *North Carolina Reports*, vol. 139, pp. 649–707, as the "Address" of William P. Bynum, Jr., on the presentation of Settle's portrait to the North Carolina Supreme Court on 7 Nov. 1905. Most standard histories and monographs about N.C. in the Civil War and Reconstruction period mention Settle and his activities, especially J. G. de Roulhac Hamilton, *Reconstruction in North Carolina* (1914). Examples of Settle's postwar political and judicial philosophy can be seen in the *Journal of the Convention of the State of North-Carolina at Its Session of 1865–66*; Sidney Andrews, *The South since the War* (1866); and *North Carolina Reports*, vols. 63–65 and 68–75. Carl N. Degler, *The Other South: Southern Dissenters in the Nineteenth Century* (1974), and James L. Lancaster, "The Scalawags of North Carolina, 1850–1868" (Ph.D. diss., Princeton Univ., 1974), place Settle's career in a broader, comparative context. Also see Sandra P. Babb, "The Battle of the Giants: The Gubernatorial Election of 1876 in North Carolina" (master's thesis, Univ. of N.C., Chapel Hill, 1970).

JEFFREY J. CROW

SEUSS, Dr. *See* Geisel, Theodor Seuss.

SEVAREID, Eric (26 Nov. 1912–9 July 1992), journalist and author, was born Arnold Eric Sevareid in Velva, North Dakota, the son of Alfred Eric Sevareid, a bank teller, and Clare Pauline Elizabeth Hougen. He enjoyed setting type at the weekly *Velva Journal*, owned by a friend of his father's. When wheat-killing droughts closed many local banks, the Sevareids moved in 1925 to Minot, North Dakota, and a year later to Minneapolis, where Sevareid attended high school. He said that the only thing he learned there was how to manage the school paper. Upon his graduation in 1930 Sevareid and a friend took a 2,200-mile canoe trip from Minneapolis to York Factory on Hudson Bay. (He later wrote a book for juveniles based on this adventure, titled *Canoeing with the Cree* [1935].)

In 1930 Sevareid went to work as a copy boy for the *Minneapolis Journal* and soon became a reporter there. In 1931 he enrolled at the University of Minnesota, majoring in political science and economics. While there he worked on the *Minnesota Daily*, the campus papers, and also for city newspapers. He married Lois Finger shortly before graduating with an A.B. in 1935. He was a reporter for the *Journal* until 1936. He studied at the London School of Economics and at the Alliance Française in Paris in 1937. He worked as a reporter and city editor for the Paris edition of the *New York Herald Tribune* in 1938 and 1939 and as United Press night editor in Paris in 1939, changing his byline to Eric Sevareid.

The renowned Columbia Broadcasting System (CBS) radio commentator Edward R. Murrow hired Sevareid in August 1939 as a European correspondent. Once World War II erupted a month later, Sevareid began to cover events in the so-called phony war. He visited the stagnant "front" between the Maginot Line and the Siegfried Line, and in a radio broadcast he described the soldiers on both sides as "schoolboys of Europe . . . sent against each other." In April 1940 his wife Lois gave birth to twins in Paris. In May the Germans, having perfected their blitzkrieg tactics elsewhere, smashed through the Netherlands, Belgium, and Luxembourg, flanked the Maginot Line, and headed straight for Paris. Sevareid sent his family home via Genoa, Italy, broadcast from Paris, Tours,

and finally Bordeaux, and on 16 June was the first journalist to report the surrender of France. He then escaped via a Belgian freighter to England.

Sevareid joined Murrow, whom he came to revere and even idolize, in broadcasting news of the German air raids on London. Later in 1940 Sevareid moved to CBS's Washington office to report on President Franklin D. Roosevelt and the ongoing U.S. war effort. Sevareid covered Mexican president Manuel Avila Camacho's inauguration in Mexico City in December 1940 and Undersecretary of State Sumner Welles's work at the Pan-American Conference in Rio de Janeiro early in 1942. In 1943 CBS dispatched Sevareid to the China-Burma-India theater. When his C-46 transport developed engine trouble, he and nineteen others parachuted into the Burmese jungle. After a month-long trek to safety in India, Sevareid boarded another C-46 and flew without incident on to Chungking, China. Next he reported on Allied advances in Italy, observed partisan activities in Yugoslavia, accompanied American troops during the invasion of southern France, and went with them north and on across the Rhine River into Germany.

After the war Sevareid published *Not So Wild a Dream* (1946), a distinguished, erudite autobiography. He covered the founding of the United Nations, returned to the Washington bureau of CBS, and in time covered presidential nominating conventions and elections in 1948, 1952, and 1956. He became a roving correspondent in Europe (1959–1961). Beginning in 1961 he appeared on a variety of CBS programs produced in New York City. Sevareid was distressed when in 1962 Walter Cronkite was chosen over him for the "CBS Evening News" anchor position. That same year he divorced Lois Sevareid.

In 1963 Sevareid began to do commentaries on Cronkite's evening news program and also married Belén Marshall, a musician; they had one child. In 1964 Sevareid became a roving correspondent for CBS—a moderator, a narrator, a host of various informal but highly informative "conversations," and a participant in many news programs. He covered the 1964 presidential nominating conventions. Two years later he was touring battlefields in Vietnam and broadcasting commentaries on the evening news and in specials. He was reluctant to oppose the Vietnam War, perhaps in part because of unswerving devotion to fighting men regardless of their mission, but in the course of time did so. In 1970 and 1971 he participated objectively with other leading television correspondents in two one-hour discussions with President Richard M. Nixon. However, he televised gravely worded denunciations of both Nixon and Vice President Spiro Agnew shortly after the Watergate scandal broke in 1973. That same year Sevareid and his second wife divorced.

Upon reaching sixty-five, Sevareid retired from CBS but remained as a consultant and also anchored several specials and series—including the 1978 "Between the Wars, 1918–1941" and the 1982 "Eric Sevareid's Chronicle." In 1979 he married Suzanne St.

Pierre, a CBS television producer; they had no children.

Despite worsening health, Sevareid played engaging bit parts in a 1980 segment of the television series "Taxi" and in three movies—*Night Crossing* (1982), *The Right Stuff* (1983), and *The Jigsaw Man* (1984). Late in his career, he declined to do commercial endorsements that would have paid him more than $1 million for minimal work. He wanted, as he put it, to keep his name "untarnished." Sevareid died in Washington, D.C.

Sevareid combined profound learning with smooth objectivity and controlled warmth in all of his work. Beginning as a campus radical and pacifist, he later defined himself as a cultural conservative and a political liberal. He believed in the sanctity of the individual, supporting the rights of minorities and third-world citizens and deploring the materialistic power struggle engaged in by American and Soviet leaders. Sevareid won Emmy Awards in 1973, 1974, and 1977 for television reporting and was inducted into the Television Academy Hall of Fame in 1987. He also won several other awards, notably the Foster Peabody Award for radio reporting (1949, 1964, and 1968) and the Fourth Estate Award given by the National Press Club (1984).

• The Library of Congress has the Arnold Eric Sevareid Collection of manuscripts of his radio and television commentaries. Some of Edward R. Murrow's papers at the Fletcher School of Law and Diplomacy, at Tufts University, Medford, Mass., concern Sevareid. Among his books, in addition to his 1946 autobiography, may be mentioned *In One Ear: 107 Snapshots of Men and Events, Which Make a Far-Reaching Panorama of the American Situation* (1952), a collection of brief, pro-liberal comments on American and world events; *Small Sounds in the Night: A Collection of Capsule Conversations on the American Scene* (1956), an anthology of his broadcasts during President Dwight D. Eisenhower's years in office; *Candidates 1960: Behind the Headlines in the Presidential Race* (1959), his compilation of essays by others concerning John F. Kennedy, Nixon, and five other candidates; *This Is Eric Sevareid* (1964), ten previously published essays on American politics; and *You Can't Kill the Dream: Reflections*, ed. Malcolm Boyd (1968). See also his updated autobiography, *Not So Wild a Dream* (1976). Sister M. Camille D'Arienzo, R.S.M., "Eric Sevareid Analyzes the News" (Ph.D. diss., Univ. of Michigan, 1973), discusses his commentaries. Raymond A. Schroth, *The American Journey of Eric Sevareid* (1995), is a detailed biography. Sevareid is represented in *Reporting World War II*, vol. 2: *Part Two American Journalism, 1944–1946* (1995). The following include discussions of Sevareid and his fellow correspondents and broadcasters: David Halberstam, *The Powers That Be* (1979); Barbara Matusow, *The Evening Stars: The Making of the Network News Anchors* (1983); A. M. Sperber, *Murrow: His Life and Times* (1986); Bill Leonard, *In the Storm of the Eye: A Lifetime with CBS* (1987); Joseph E. Persico, *Edward R. Murrow: An American Original* (1888); Edward Bliss, Jr., *Now the News: The Story of Broadcast Journalism* (1991); and Stanley Cloud and Lynne Olson, *The Murrow Boys: Pioneers on the Front Lines of Broadcast Journalism* (1996). An obituary is in the *New York Times*, 10 July 1992.

ROBERT L. GALE

SEVERANCE, Caroline Maria Seymour (12 Jan. 1820–10 Nov. 1914), clubwoman, was born in Canandaigua, New York, the daughter of Orson Seymour, a banker, and Caroline Maria Clarke. Late in life Severance recalled her childhood as having been marked by the death of her father when she was four, a traumatic event that, along with her mother's "constant mourning," made her a "super-sensitive child." She sought comfort in the religious revivals of the Second Great Awakening but was haunted nonetheless by fears of personal damnation.

She graduated with honors from Elizabeth Ricord's seminary in Geneva, New York, in 1835 and then found employment as a teacher. In 1840 she married Theodoric Cordenio Severance, a banker and abolitionist. They moved to Cleveland where over the next seven years she had five children, four of whom survived to adulthood. She later said that her marriage to a family of reformers freed her from "bondage to authority, dogmas and conservative ideas." Encouraged by the Severances, she became involved in abolitionism, temperance, and women's rights. She helped establish the Ohio Woman's Rights Association and presided over the first annual meeting in 1853, early illustrating her organizational skills.

In 1855 the Severances moved to Boston where she became a convert of Theodore Parker's Unitarianism, adopting his faith in individualism, skepticism of Christian dogma, and commitment to reform. She worked with William Lloyd Garrison on the abolitionist circuit and served as president of the New England Woman's Rights Convention in 1859. During the Civil War she belonged to the Sanitary Commission, a relief organization for Union soldiers.

In 1868 Severance organized the New England Woman's Club (NEWC) and served as its first president, the achievement for which she is best remembered. Severance believed that woman's advancement depended on self-development through education and on actions to improve society in ways that benefited women as well as men; the NEWC, therefore, served as a study club and a center of reform. Members gave papers and listened to speakers while also engaging in reform efforts, especially those geared toward expanding women's options in the paid labor market and their rights as citizens. The club's early reforms included establishing a horticultural school for women and placing four women on the Boston school board. The NEWC was not the first woman's club, but it served as an influential model for the woman's club movement nationwide.

In 1875 the Severances, both suffering stress and strain from their activities in the East, moved to Los Angeles to improve their health. Theodoric became a gentleman orange grower until his death in 1892, while Caroline transformed female reform within the city. She founded two short-lived Los Angeles woman's clubs, which, despite their brief existence, engaged in many reforms, including the establishment of a kindergarten system in Los Angeles by 1889. In 1891 Severance organized the Friday Morning Club, which became a center of progressive reform in the city and the state. Over the next three decades the club supported woman suffrage, demanded and received more public services for women and children, and helped put women into public office. In the late 1890s Severance became a Christian Socialist and helped build a women's movement that included Socialist women as well as clubwomen.

As Severance aged, however, she took some positions that were uncharacteristic of a former abolitionist and a Socialist. At the 1902 General Federation of Women's Clubs convention in Los Angeles, federation members grappled with the issue of whether or not to admit black women's clubs. The federation voted in favor of a policy of racial exclusion, which Severance, a highly honored and powerful participant at the convention, backed, arguing that to do otherwise would "jeopardize the fine helpful fellowship between the northern and southern clubs." For almost the next ten years Severance, by now an octogenarian, campaigned for suffrage as a clubwoman and a Socialist; after suffrage was won in California in 1911, the state women's movement chose her as the first woman to vote in California, but when Severance cast that first vote, in a decisive Los Angeles city election, she publicly supported the Progressive candidate, not the Socialist. Again exhibiting more pragmatism than idealism, she told her Socialist sisters that their candidate would not win and other clubwomen that a Socialist victory, so soon after women had won the vote in California, would set back the national suffrage movement. She died three years later in Los Angeles.

Severance frequently said, "Nothing is impossible for organized womanhood." Her greatest achievement is that so many women believed her.

• The Severance papers and the records of many of the organizations she established in Los Angeles are at the Huntington Library, San Marino, Calif. Her letters are in several other collections as well. Some are in the Alice Park Papers and the Elizabeth Boynton Harbert Papers at the Huntington; others are found in the Lucy Larcom Papers, the Clemens family collection and the Isabella Beecher Hooker Papers, all at the Library of Congress. Severance letters are also in the Alma Lutz Collection and the Briggs family papers at the Schlesinger Library, Radcliffe College, which also houses the records of the New England Woman's Club. Some Severance correspondence is in the Sarah Brown Ingersoll Cooper Papers at the Cornell University Library and in the John Greenleaf Whittier Collection at the Essex Institute, Salem, Mass. Severance did not write an autobiography, but *The Mother of Clubs: Caroline M. Seymour Severance* (1906), ed. Ella Giles Ruddy, contains more primary material from Severance than any other published source; see also Severance's *Report of the Women's Rights Meeting, at Mercantile Hall, May 27, 1859* (1859). The *California Outlook* dedicated its 12 Dec. 1914 issue to Severance. Karen J. Blair, *The Clubwoman as Feminist* (1980), discusses the significance of the New England Woman's Club; for Severance's accomplishments in California, see Sara Essa Gallaway, "Pioneering the Woman's Club Movement: The Story of Caroline Maria Severance in Los Angeles" (Ph.D. diss., Carnegie-Mellon Univ., 1985). Sherry J. Katz provides detailed information regarding Severance's activities as a Socialist; see "Dual Commitments: Feminism, Socialism, and Women's Political Activism in California, 1890–1920" (Ph.D. diss., Univ. of California, Los Angeles, 1991). An obituary is in the *Los Angeles Times*, 11 Nov. 1914.

GAYLE GULLETT

SEVERANCE, Louis Henry (1 Aug. 1838–25 June 1913), capitalist and philanthropist, was born in Cleveland, Ohio, the son of Solomon Lewis Severance, a dry goods merchant, and Mary Long. His father died shortly before his birth, and his newly widowed mother moved with Louis and his older brother to the home of her father, David Long, Jr., the first physician in the city of Cleveland. The boys grew to maturity there, with Louis completing his education in the Cleveland public schools. At the age of eighteen he took a job with the Commercial National Bank of Cleveland. In August 1862 Severance married Fannie Buckingham Benedict, with whom he would have four children. In 1863, with the American Civil War raging, Severance entered the Union army as a "100-day" volunteer, during which time he participated in the defense of Washington, D.C. Following his discharge he sought his fortune within the embryonic oil industry. Moving to Titusville, Pennsylvania, in 1864, Severance spent the next ten years working in oil production. He also became an elder in the local Presbyterian church; these two associations provided the focus for the rest of his life.

In 1874 Severance's wife died. That same year he returned to Cleveland, where he first became associated with John D. Rockefeller's Standard Oil alliance. Severance served Standard Oil as both cashier and treasurer from 1876 until his retirement eighteen years later, and although he was not a prominent leader of the firm, he was quick to realize its potential as an investment. He first acquired Standard Oil stock in 1876 and remained a stockholder throughout his life. His equity holdings increased in value as the firm prospered; at the time of his death, they were worth an estimated $8 million. Seeking diversity in his investments, Severance also acquired interests within the steel, salt, and oil-related industries; perhaps the most prominent association of his later years was with the sulfur industry. He assisted Herman Frasch, Frank Rockefeller, and F. B. Squire in the formation of the Union Sulfur Company, which after 1891 used a Frasch-patented process of dissolving underground sulfur deposits with superheated water that greatly improved mining efficiency. The firm's activities assisted in transforming the United States into an exporter of sulfur, rather than an importer.

With his personal fortune secure, Severance turned to philanthropy in his later years, as did many of his industrial counterparts, donating both time and money to educational and religious causes. Severance served as a trustee of Oberlin College from 1892 until his death, providing the school with both an endowed chair of chemistry and a new chemistry building. Smith took time from his numerous charitable endeavors to marry Florence Harkness of Cleveland in September 1894. She died ten months later. He also served as a trustee of Western Reserve University (now Case Western Reserve University) and the College of Wooster in Ohio. The latter school, a Presbyterian institution, was the largest beneficiary of Severance's largess; following a disastrous fire in 1901 that resulted in its near-total destruction, he almost single-handedly rebuilt the campus.

A devoted Presbyterian, Severance resisted few calls to assist in its advancement. In addition to his work at Wooster, he gave generously and often to a wide range of church related activities. Overseas missions held a special place in his heart; his donations helped to build churches and hospitals in India, Japan, and Korea. In Korea, the Severance Hospital and Severance Medical College in Seoul were the most outstanding examples of his beneficence.

Severance undertook a world tour in 1907–1908, during which time he inspected numerous missions and their efforts. Following his return he became a member of the Presbyterian Board of Foreign Missions. Severance also served at various times as a member of the denomination's College Board and as assistant moderator of its general assembly. Severance likewise held a deep interest in the activities of both the Young Men's Christian Association and Young Women's Christian Association and supported the efforts of the organizations both in the United States and abroad. His interest in evangelizing the Orient culminated in a stint as president of the board of trustees of Nanking University in China. He died at his son-in-law's home in Cleveland.

While not a leader in the formation of Standard Oil, Severance gave yeoman service to the firm for many years. Through shrewd investing he acquired a personal fortune, and in the generous sharing of his wealth he provided valuable support to a variety of educational institutions as well as to his church both at home and abroad.

• Severance's papers have not survived, and information on his life and career is scarce. While he receives brief mention in Ralph W. Hidy and Muriel E. Hidy, *History of Standard Oil (New Jersey): Pioneering in Big Business, 1882–1911* (1955), the best source remains E. M. Avery, *A History of Cleveland and Its Environs*, vol. 2 (1918). An obituary is in the *Cleveland Plain Dealer*, 26 June 1913.

EDWARD L. LACH, JR.

SEVERSKY, Alexander de. *See* de Seversky, Alexander Procofieff.

SEVIER, Ambrose Hundley (4 Nov. 1801–31 Dec. 1848), lawyer and politician, was born in Greene County, Tennessee, the son of John Sevier, Jr., a lawyer, and Ann Hundley. Sevier's parents moved to Tennessee the year before he was born. He was educated in the county schools and in 1820, following the deaths of both parents, moved to Arkansas to live with his uncle, Henry W. Conway. The latter had recently been appointed receiver for the newly created Public Land

Office. After serving as Conway's assistant for a brief time, Sevier was appointed clerk of the house of representatives on 21 October 1820. For the rest of his life he held public office.

In 1823 Sevier was elected to represent Pulaski County in the territorial assembly, then he was chosen prosecuting attorney for one term before returning to the legislature in 1825 and again in 1827. His principal legislation was a bill to prohibit dueling. Ironically, his uncle, Conway, was killed in a duel in the aftermath of a dispute that developed in the 1827 campaign for territorial delegate to the U.S. Congress. Sevier was elected to fill Conway's vacant seat and six years later also faced the challenge of a duel. He avoided his uncle's fate.

In 1827 Sevier married Juliet (Juliette) Johnson, daughter of Benjamin Johnson, then a judge for the territorial circuit court, and a relative of Richard M. Johnson, who served as vice president of the United States from 1837 to 1841. The Seviers had two children. The union of these two politically influential families, coupled with the added influence of the Conways, gave Sevier a kinship connection that made him a highly successful public official. For example, he persuaded Congress to pass legislation that allowed salaries of the territory's legislators to be paid by the U.S. government. He also convinced federal officials to grant Arkansas ten sections of public land, proceeds from which would go to building a permanent capitol, and was instrumental in getting numerous appropriations to open public roads and improve river navigation. He was chosen as the senior senator to the U.S. Congress when Arkansas was admitted as the twenty-fifth state in 1836. He was reelected in 1842.

As senator Sevier used the longtime political friendships developed while he was a territorial delegate to strengthen his position in the Democratic party. He was a staunch advocate of westward expansion and for land allotments for new settlers in Oregon Territory. He was also an outspoken critic of the British interest in the Northwest and was prepared to go to war with England to secure Oregon. In private he took an active role in healing divisions in the Democratic party and was credited with holding the party together in the face of mounting sectional divisions. In his second term Sevier served as chairman of the Foreign Relations Committee. However, his public image was tainted in Arkansas when he mixed revenue from the sale of state bank bonds with his personal expense account and failed to report it until asked to do so by state officials.

In 1848 Sevier resigned his Senate seat to accept an appointment from President James K. Polk to serve as a member of the team to negotiate an end to the Mexican War. Conflict with Nicholas P. Trist and declining health from a "severe cold" caused him to resign from the commission in less than a year.

Returning to Arkansas, Sevier tried to regain his seat in the Senate but was defeated by Solon Borland, who had previously been chosen to fill the unexpired term. Faced with his only political defeat in over forty years, Sevier retired to his plantation in Jefferson County. He never fully regained his health and died there some six weeks before the treaty ending the Mexican War was ratified.

• No significant body of Sevier's personal papers has been discovered in archival sources. Brief biographical treatment is given in John Hallum, *Biographical and Pictorial History of Arkansas*, vol. 1 (1887); Fay Hempstead, *A Pictorial History of Arkansas: From Earliest Times to the Year 1890* (1890); and Dallas T. Herndon, *Centennial History of Arkansas*, vol. 1 (1922). Period monographs that include extensive information on Sevier include Lonnie J. White, *Politics on the Southwestern Frontier: Arkansas Territory, 1819–1836* (1964); and Margaret Ross, *Arkansas Gazette: The Early Years, 1819–1866* (1969).

C. FRED WILLIAMS

SEVIER, John (23 Sept. 1745–24 Sept. 1815), soldier, governor, and congressman, was born near the present town of New Market, Virginia, the son of Valentine Sevier, a farmer, trader, and merchant, and Joanna Goade. He attended school briefly when the family lived in Fredericksburg and in Staunton and at the age of sixteen was married to fifteen-year-old Sarah Hawkins; the couple had ten children. Very shortly after her death in 1780, he married Catherine Sherrill, with whom he had eight children. For a decade after his first marriage, Sevier moved about in the Shenandoah Valley, operating a tavern and store, and farming, trading, and speculating in land. In 1773, joined by his parents and several brothers, he moved to the southwest and settled on the Holston River. Why Sevier and family members would leave the rich lands of the valley is unknown, except perhaps that the valley lands rapidly were filling and the Holston area offered cheap land certain soon to become more valuable.

In 1776 Sevier took up land on the Watauga River near present-day Elizabethton, Tennessee. Already a commissioner and member of the court of the Watauga Association, he was chosen as a delegate to the provincial congress of North Carolina. Soon commissioned a lieutenant colonel in the state militia, he spent much of the next five years fighting to protect the frontier against invasion from the British and the Cherokees.

In the fall of 1780 he commanded troops at the battle of King's Mountain and there won wide recognition and renown. British forces, not achieving the desired military success in the northern colonies, turned in 1778 to the soft underbelly of the South, where they found little resistance and considerable Loyalist support. After seizing Savannah and Charleston, Major General Charles Cornwallis ran at will over South Carolina and Georgia and then looked to the West, where Sevier and others commanded troublesome bands of patriots. Cornwallis placed a seasoned veteran named Patrick Ferguson in charge of a detail of men with orders to destroy with "fire and sword" those "settlers from the extreme backwoods, rough, half-civilized men," who opposed them with arms. Assembling on the Watauga in late September, Sevier and several thousand men marched to meet Ferguson and in early October found him ensconced on the King's Mountain range about a mile and a half south of the North Carolina line. On 7 October they assaulted the enemy and within an hour had received his surrender. After that significant victory, Sevier and several hundred Wataugans aided Francis Marion in South Carolina in guerrilla action against the British and Loyalists.

Soon after the Revolution, Sevier joined with others in Greene, Sullivan, and Hawkins counties in forming the "State of Franklin" (1784–1788). Franklin leaders probably had been encouraged by members of the Continental Congress, who suggested the formation of new western states, and by Thomas Jefferson, who had proposed as many as eighteen states in the West. But North Carolina and national leaders refused to accept this early attempt at separatism. Sevier, although not originally a part of the movement, accepted the office of governor but was opposed by a strong local faction supporting North Carolina. Franklin collapsed in 1788, and Sevier was arrested and accused of treason but never tried. Before the year had ended, the North Carolina Assembly had pardoned him of any taint of treason, commissioned him a brigadier general, and received him into the senate as a duly elected member from Greene County.

Sevier supported ratification of the U.S. Constitution and then was elected to Congress, where he served one term. He supported the cession of North Carolina's western lands and the creation of the Southwest Territory, and, within the territorial government (1790–1796), he served as a member of the legislative council and supported the movement for statehood.

In March 1796, while Congress debated the admission of the new state, Tennesseans organized a government and chose Sevier governor. The state constitution, drafted in January, provided for a two-year term for the governor, except that the first term would expire in September 1797. Sevier was reelected in 1797 and 1799 and then again for three terms beginning in 1803.

Although Sevier prospered politically under the Federalist presidencies of George Washington and John Adams, he was Jeffersonian in his politics. He warmly supported Jefferson's Louisiana Purchase and championed his efforts toward internal improvements. Always popular, only near the end of his gubernatorial service did he develop some opposition, chiefly from sectionalists in Nashville and the midstate counties.

During his dozen years as chief executive, Sevier confronted the usual problems of establishing a government on the frontier. Indian relations became the basis for major concern, and internal improvements, land claims and disputes, and bitter contests for militia commands took much of his time. When war with France threatened near the end of the century, he prepared to assume a field command. Perhaps best remembered from his years as governor were the state's tremendous population growth—from about 85,000 in 1796 to 250,000 when he concluded his last term in 1809—and his continuing feud with Andrew Jackson.

Jealousies between Jackson and Sevier had emerged even before Sevier became governor, and it is quite possible that Jackson had tried to lead opposition to his candidacy in 1796. Then, when Sevier sought to return to the governorship in 1803 after Archibald Roane had served one term, Jackson joined Roane in denouncing Sevier and in accusing him of land frauds. Finally, in October 1803, when Jackson, then judge of the superior court, held hearings in Knoxville, they chanced to meet near the courthouse. Neither was in a conciliatory mood. Both displayed weapons, and only the intervention of friends averted trouble. Jackson retreated to his hotel where he penned a challenge—an action that set off an exchange of letters and counter-challenges but did not result in a duel. Both of course returned to public life in the state, but friendships were never renewed.

Like many men of the time, Sevier speculated in land and from time to time would own thousands of acres in his own name and in partnership with others. His chief biographer, Carl Driver, has referred to him as a "frontier land gambler." Enemies besides Jackson joined in accusing him of land frauds, but none was able to prove guilt.

Sevier was elected to the state senate from Knox County without opposition a few months after his final term as governor. Two years later he was elected to Congress and served there until his death. He supported other western and southern congressmen in their efforts toward expansion and warmly urged on the War Hawks as they talked of war with England.

In March 1815 President James Madison appointed Sevier to a commission that would survey and establish a border between claims of the Creek Indians and the U.S. territory in Alabama. He began work in early June and continued through the summer and early fall. Death apparently was sudden as he reclined in his tent on the Tallapoosa River near Fort Decatur. He was buried there, but in 1887 his body was removed to the courthouse lawn in Knoxville.

• Some of John Sevier's public papers have been collected in Samuel Cole Williams, ed., "Executive Journal of Governor John Sevier," East Tennessee Historical Society *Publications* 1–7 (1929–1935). For additional biographical information, see Carl Driver, *John Sevier, Pioneer of the Old Southwest* (1932), and Cora Bales Sevier and Nancy S. Madden, *Sevier Family History, with the Collected Letters of General John Sevier, First Governor of Tennessee* (1961). Also useful is Robert H. White, ed., *Messages of the Governors of Tennessee, 1796–1821* (1952).

ROBERT E. CORLEW

SEWALL, Arthur (25 Nov. 1835–5 Sept. 1900), shipbuilder and railroad and bank president, was born in Bath, Maine, the son of William Dunning Sewall, a shipbuilder, and Rachel Trufant. Sewall received a common school education in Bath. He was subsequently sent to Prince Edward Island to learn how to cut ship timber, and soon he was able to perform every job required in a shipyard. In 1854, during a peak period of wooden shipbuilding, he founded the firm of E. & A. Sewall with his older brother Edward and took over his father's firm. When Edward died in 1879, the name was changed to Arthur Sewall & Co. Beginning with the 1,000-ton *Holyhead* in 1855, at his yard at Kennebec, Sewall produced eighty sailing ships during the next fifty years, twenty-five of which he owned and operated at one time. Sewall's enterprise moved against the dominant technological forces of the day, since iron, steel, and steam vessels, beginning with the transatlantic run of the British steamer *Sirius* in 1838, would eventually put sailing ships out of competition. Certainly not a technological follower at the time, Sewall also was not an opportunist politically. Because he refused to transfer his ships to British registry during the Civil War, his *Vigilant* was captured by the Confederate raider *Sumter*.

During the years 1873 to 1877, when demands for ships revived, Sewall produced ten excellent ships. Innovative in design, his five "down-easters" reached the acme of perfection in the California wheat trade. The next decade, however, was a depression period during which he did not produce his usual "ship a year." He rebounded during the 1890s, when he built four 3,000-ton wooden full-rigged ships of the *Roanoke* class—the last of their kind ever built, for they failed to restore the American merchant marine to its former prestige. After learning how to use iron at the Bath Iron Works, and during a visit to England, reluctantly perhaps, he was the first American to build steel sailing ships. The first was the *Dirigo* (1894), which carried 14,000 yards of canvas. Three others followed. Yet his importance as a builder rests on the fact that he built, owned, and operated more wooden ships than any other American during the last half of the nineteenth century. In addition, he was at various times president of the Eastern Railroad and the Central Railroad, a director of the Boston & Maine Railroad, and, from 1871 until his death, president of the Bath National Bank.

Sewall won election only as a Bath councilman and alderman. However, he attended every Democratic National Convention from 1872 to 1900 and from 1892 until his death served on the executive committee of the Democratic National Committee.

The Democratic National Convention of 1896 chose as its presidential candidate William Jennings Bryan, an anti-imperialist, tariff-for-revenue only man, and a free silverite. In contrast, Sewall was an imperialist, tariff protectionist, and gold-standard man until he declared for silver just before the Chicago convention. Vice presidential hopefuls included midwesterners Richard P. Bland (Mo.), Horace Boies (Iowa), John R. McLean (Ohio), and Claude Matthews (Ind.), and only two easterners, John W. Daniel (Va.) and Sewall. Of these, only Bland had a popular following. McLean had money, but Bryan held him to be insincere about free silver and an "immoral" man who sought to buy the vice presidential nomination. Bryan also had to decide whether he wanted a poor man as his running mate for a campaign to be waged against privilege or an angel with a barrel. Sewall's pronouncement in favor of free silver just before the convention won over Bryan. Sewall had shown himself to be one of the relatively few businessmen who believed that inflation of the currency would stimulate depression-bound industry. Serious opposition to Sewall on the floor ended when Bland and McLean threw their votes to him.

The nomination of Sewall, a political unknown, surprised the nation. The choice appeared to be an excellent one, however; age was joined to youth, business to the law. Thus the Democratic party was relieved of the charge of being sectional. The Democratic platform recognized the free silver sentiment of the East, and free silverites used to their advantage a leading New England businessman worth $5 to $6 million. Delegates to the Populist National Convention faced the dilemma of joining Bryan or finding new issues and followers only three months before the elections. Fusionists who evaluated Bryan's platform as being quite similar to theirs of 1892 succeeded in naming him as their presidential candidate. Mid-roaders, however, said that Sewall would foul every plank in their platform and named as the Populist vice presidential candidate Thomas E. Watson of Georgia. Despite vigorous campaigning by Bryan and Sewall, they lost the election. Among the major reasons for their defeat were more Republican money and better campaign management, some coercion of labor to vote Republican, opposition to Bryan, especially by foreign-born gold-standard Democrats, and the prediction that the adoption of free silver would cause inflation injurious to the working classes. Workers took to heart the Republican pledge of revived prosperity by means of increased protective tariffs. And finally, the vice presidential vote was split between Sewall and Watson. In the Maine elections, Republicans rolled up their largest majorities in history.

Sewall had married Emma Duncan Croker in 1859, and they had three children, two of whom survived him. He died at his summer home at Stony Point, near Bath.

• Concise narratives of Sewall's life appear in obituaries published in the *Bath Times* and the Portland, Maine, *Daily Eastern Argus*, 6 Sept. 1900. His shipbuilding activities are traced in Wiliam A. Baker, *A Maritime History of Bath, Maine, and in the Kennebec River Region* (2 vols., 1973), and in William H. Rowe, *The Maritime History of Maine* (1948). He is referred to in Democratic National Committee, *Democratic Campaign Book. Presidential Election, 1896* (1896). His political influence is evaluated most extensively in Paolo E. Coletta, *William Jennings Bryan*, vol. 1: *Political Evangelist, 1860–1908* (1964), and in Stanley L. Jones, *The Presidential Election of 1896* (1964); and it is examined briefly in Leroy Ashby, *William Jennings Bryan: Champion of Democracy* (1987); Robert W. Cherny, *A Righteous Cause: The Life of William Jennings Bryan* (1985); and Paul W. Glad, *The Trumpet Soundeth: William Jennings Bryan and His Democracy, 1896–1912* (1960).

PAOLO E. COLETTA

SEWALL, David (27 Oct. 1735–22 Oct. 1825), lawyer and judge, was born in what is now York, Maine (then part of Mass.), the son of Samuel Sewall and Sarah

Bachelor. He was a cousin of Massachusetts chief justice Stephen Sewall and of Loyalist lawyer and royal vice admiralty judge Jonathan Sewall. Sewall graduated from Harvard College in 1755. He then undertook the study of law in Portsmouth, New Hampshire, with William Parker, a leading lawyer later appointed to the New Hampshire Superior Court. Sewall's Harvard M.A. thesis topic had reflected his interest in astronomy, and in 1757 he joined with the Reverend Samuel Langdon of Portsmouth in initiating the publication of a series of astronomical almanacs. In 1762 he married Judge Parker's daughter, Mary Parker. The couple had no children.

In 1760 Sewall was admitted to the bar of the York County Inferior Court of Common Pleas and began the practice of law in the town of York, where he was the only formally trained lawyer. At the June 1763 term of the superior court he was admitted as a barrister. In 1774 his Harvard classmate and fellow lawyer John Adams reported in a letter to his wife that Sewall "never practices out of this County [York], has no Children, has no Ambition, nor Avarice they say, (however Quaere). His business in this County maintains him very handsomely" (*Adams Family Correspondence*, ed. Lyman H. Butterfield et al., vol. 1 [1963], p. 113).

In the years prior to the Revolution, Sewall was appointed to a variety of county offices, including collector of excise (1763), register of probate (1766), and justice of the peace (1767). According to Adams, writing in his diary in 1770, local Whigs viewed him as "not of the Liberty Side," one of a group of officeholders who "rather than hazard" their commissions "would ruin the Country" by abstaining from support of pro-liberty measures. Sewall's commissioning as a captain in the York County militia in 1772 indicates that he enjoyed the favor of royal governor Thomas Hutchinson.

In York County, which was viewed by Boston's radical Whigs as a hotbed of Toryism, Sewall's moderate politics ultimately were radical enough to bring him to the revolutionary side. He was elected to the York County Congress in 1774, chaired a committee that drafted very conservative instructions for the town of York's representative to the Second Provincial Congress in January 1775, and served on the town committee of correspondence. His participation in these local activities was sufficient to commend him to the revolutionary government of Massachusetts, which appointed him a notary public and reappointed him register of probate and justice of the peace. In 1776 and 1777 the House of Representatives elected him to the council, a body that exercised executive authority because the office of governor had been declared vacant.

Despite Sewall's protests, the council appointed him a justice of the superior court on 11 September 1777. Citing the time demands of judicial office, he declined to be considered for reelection to the council in May 1778. He continued to serve as York County register of probate, however, because no one else was qualified to assume that position. As a York County delegate to the Massachusetts Constitutional Convention of 1779–1780, he served on the drafting committee that framed the Constitution of 1780. He was a member of a commission appointed in November 1780 to revise the laws. When he was appointed to the Supreme Judicial Court, the constitutional successor of the superior court, on 16 February 1781, he resigned as register of probate. The new Constitution prohibited Supreme Judicial Court judges from holding any other office.

A staunch Federalist, Sewall served as a presidential elector in the first federal election in 1789. He was commissioned judge of the U.S. District Court for the District of Maine (a separate district within what was still the state of Mass.) on 26 September 1789. After completing a final circuit of the Supreme Judicial Court, he took the federal oath of office on 1 December 1789 and resigned from the state court. In June 1790 Sewall exercised the full criminal jurisdiction given to the district court for the District of Maine under a special provision of the federal Judiciary Act of 1789. The trial, conviction, and resultant execution of Thomas Bird for mutiny and murder on the high seas were the first capital proceedings in the new federal court system.

Apparently anticipating a less demanding docket, Sewall sought and won election to the Massachusetts House of Representatives in 1790. After extensive debate, that body found him ineligible and declined to seat him. If his docket book for 1800–1803 is typical, his judicial duties were indeed frequently routine, consisting mainly of forfeiture actions for violations of federal customs and excise laws, with an occasional admiralty or other civil case.

In any event, Sewall made good use of the time thus spared as an active participant in the many philanthropic and intellectual enterprises that flourished in the new nation. A founder of the American Academy of Arts and Sciences in 1780, he was elected a member of the Massachusetts Historical Society at its founding in 1791 and was one of its corporators in 1794. He was also a corporator of the Maine Historical Society, founded in 1822 after the separation of Maine from Massachusetts. Some of the fruits of his own antiquarian research were published by these societies. Sewall was a member of the Board of Overseers of Bowdoin College from its establishment in 1794 until 1815, serving as president of the board for many years. He contributed a Latin prize (still awarded) to the college, which gave him the honorary degree of LL.D. in 1812. A Congregationalist, he was trustee of the First Congregational Society of York from 1803 to 1808. Sewall's first wife had died in 1788, and he subsequently married Elizabeth Langdon, daughter of his early colleague, the Reverend Samuel Langdon, in November 1790. His second marriage was also childless.

In 1818 Sewall resigned his judgeship, advising President James Monroe in a letter on 9 January "That not with standing his powers of Body & mind remain [strong], yet he is Admonished by his advanced years

that they are diminishing, and claim a relief from the cares of a publick nature." For the remainder of his life, he continued active in intellectual and social pursuits and his role as the genial host of his York mansion, "Coventry Hall." He died in York.

Sewall is an exemplar of the generation of prerevolutionary lawyers who survived both the military and the political struggles of 1776 to contribute sound conservatism, professional skills, and high intellectual and moral values to the leadership of the new republic. At the same time, he gave his talents to the intellectual and social life of his region and community. As his epitaph in the Old York Burial Ground put it, his "elevated benevolence was happily directed by an enlightened intellect. . . . Piety with patriarchal simplicity of manners conspired to secure him universal esteem. His home was the abode of hospitality and friendship. In him, the defenceless found a Protector, the poor a Benefactor, the community a Peacemaker, Science, Social Order, and Religion an affectionate Patron."

• Sewall's manuscripts are scattered, with a few papers, including his 1790 charge to the Bird grand jury and his docket book for 1800–1803, in the Maine Historical Society. His law practice and state judicial service (1760–1789) are documented in the Massachusetts Superior Court and Supreme Judicial Court records and files, Massachusetts State Archives, and in the records of the York County Inferior Court of Common Pleas, Office of the York County Clerk of Courts, Alfred, Maine. The records of his federal judicial service are in the Federal Records Depository, Waltham, Mass. His published works include *An Astronomical Diary; or, An Almanack for . . . 1758* (1757); "Topographical Description of York," Massachusetts Historical Society, *Collections* 3 (1794; repr. 1810): 6–11; "Extracts from the Records of York County," Maine Historical Society, *Collections*, 1st ser., 1 (1831; 2d ed., 1865): 363–91; "Of Father Flynt's Journey to Portsmouth," Massachusetts Historical Society, *Proceedings* 16 (1878): 5–11; and "Destruction of the Town of York," *New England Historical and Genealogical Register* 29 (1875): 108. The fullest account of Sewall's life is Clifford K. Shipton, *Sibley's Harvard Graduates*, vol. 13 (1965), pp. 638–45. See also Edward P. Burnham, "Memoir of Judge David Sewall, LL.D.," Maine Historical Society, *Collections and Proceedings*, 2d ser., 2 (1891): 300–317, which contains several letters concerning Sewall's judicial appointments. His epitaph, and those of his two wives, are transcribed in "Inscriptions from the Old York Burial Ground," *New England Historical and Genealogical Register* 5 (1851): 69–70. For Coventry Hall, see Richard M. Candee, "The Appearance of Enterprise and Improvement," in *Agreeable Situations*, ed. Laura F. Sprague (1987), pp. 75–79.

L. KINVIN WROTH

SEWALL, Henry (25 May 1855–8 July 1936), physiologist and physician, was born in Winchester, Virginia, the son of Thomas Sewall, a Methodist Episcopal clergyman, and Julia Elizabeth Waters. Sewall's father, who was soon called to a Baltimore pulpit, died of tuberculosis when Henry was fifteen. In 1871 Sewall entered Wesleyan University in Connecticut, where as a clergyman's son he had reduced fees. There he took the newly established "scientific course" and studied under the influential teacher William North Rice, but because previous schooling had left him poorly prepared, he did not earn a B.S. until 1876. Poverty thwarted Henry's desire to attend Harvard Medical School, and he returned to Baltimore. A family friend introduced him to Newell Martin, the Anglo-Irish protégé of Thomas Henry Huxley and Michael Foster, who had just been appointed professor of biology at Johns Hopkins University. Martin together with William K. Brooks made the Hopkins department the leading American center for graduate training in biology. That same year Martin hired Sewall as his assistant, and Sewall earned the first American Ph.D. in physiology in the rich intellectual environment of Martin's department in 1879. Sewall spent 1879–1880 in Europe on a fellowship working under Carl Ludwig in Leipzig, Willy Kühne in Heidelberg, and J. N. Langley in Cambridge. Upon returning to Martin's laboratory, Sewall taught the physiology course in 1880–1881 while continuing physiological research.

The faculty of the University of Michigan's Department of Medicine and Surgery began to reform its program in 1877 by adopting a three-year graded curriculum, and in 1880 it assigned Victor Vaughan, an assistant professor of physiological chemistry, the task of finding a qualified full-time physiologist. Vaughan consulted Henry Pickering Bowditch of Harvard, who nominated Charles Sedgwick Minot and Newell Martin of Johns Hopkins, who nominated Sewall. Sewall moved to Ann Arbor with his mother and two brothers, each of whom had tuberculosis, in 1881. He married Isabel Josephine Vickers of Toronto, Ontario, in 1887; they had no children.

In 1882 Sewall introduced a modern physiology course at Michigan that consisted of lectures and demonstrations. Among his first students were the future surgeon William J. Mayo and the future anatomist Franklin P. Mall. Sewall also began a vigorous research program in which he made two particularly important observations. The first was that in the rabbit an increase in pressure in the heart and aorta is the stimulus for reflex slowing of the heart and vasodilatation. This observation provided early evidence of cybernetic control of the circulation. Second, he demonstrated that repeated subcutaneous injections of sublethal but increasing doses of rattlesnake venom into pigeons induce immunity so that the bird eventually tolerates five or more times the previously fatal dose. In doing these experiments, Sewall hoped to stimulate research into whether resistance against germ-caused diseases can be induced by injection of suitable extracts of the germs. Sewall published his results in the British *Journal of Physiology* in 1887, but there is no evidence that any of the European founders of the science of immunology saw it before 1905. Gerald Webb, Sewall's disciple and biographer, believed that Pierre Roux, Emil von Behring, Robert Koch, and even Paul Ehrlich engaged in a "conspiracy of silence" to deny Sewall credit for making a fundamental contribution to immunology (Webb and Powell [1946]; Clapesattle [1984]).

Sewall resigned from Michigan in 1889 because of his tuberculosis. He and his wife moved to Denver, Colorado, where she contracted typhoid fever. During her long illness Sewall taught at the Denver and Gross Medical School and qualified for an M.D. from that institution that allowed him to practice medicine. After spending a year at the Trudeau Adirondack Cottage Hospital (Saranac, N.Y.) as resident physician as well as patient, Sewall returned to Denver, where he recovered his health. He taught physiology and medicine at the University of Colorado until 1917 while he also practiced medicine, specializing in tuberculosis. He quickly rose to local and then to national prominence. Sewall was secretary to the Colorado State Board of Health and an officer and Trudeau medalist of the National Tuberculosis Association. In 1915 he was a founder of the National Board of Medical Examiners. He was elected to the elite Association of American Physicians in 1900, was its president in 1916, and received its Kober Medal for lifetime achievement in 1931. Sewall died in Denver.

• Sewall's "Day Book of Operations in the Physiological Course, J[ohns]. H[opkins]. U[niversity], Sept. 1880," editions of his *A Topical Synopsis of Lectures on Animal Physiology* (1885, 1888), and his official university correspondence are in the University of Michigan's Bentley Historical Library. Gerald B. Webb and Desmond Powell, *Henry Sewall: Physiologist and Physician* (1946), is weak on Sewall as a physiologist but strong on his Denver years; it contains a complete list of his publications. Helen Clapesattle, *Dr. Webb of Colorado Springs* (1984), has many references to Sewall in Colorado. Horace W. Davenport, *Physiology, 1850–1923: The View from Michigan* (1982), describes the University of Michigan medical background and contains a critical analysis of Sewall's physiological accomplishments as well as an account of Newell Martin and his Johns Hopkins laboratory in Sewall's time.

HORACE W. DAVENPORT

SEWALL, Jonathan (17 Aug. 1728–26 Sept. 1796), lawyer and Loyalist, was born in Boston, Massachusetts, the son of Jonathan Sewall, a merchant, and Mary Payne. Orphaned at the age of three, Sewall was heir to the substantial social and political connections that his family, one of the most important in Massachusetts, offered. However, his father's financial failures had left him penniless. He was raised by family and friends who made sure that he was prepared for college, and his uncle, Chief Justice Stephen Sewall, enrolled him at Harvard. Finishing undergraduate work, he went on to get a master's degree. After graduation Sewall taught at a school in Salem, Massachusetts. With the help of a family friend, he began to study law during his free time. In 1756 he left teaching to serve as a legal apprentice to Chambers Russell, a vice admiralty judge. His experience with Russell not only afforded him exposure to practical legal proceedings but also supplied him with a familiarity with the political world of the province. Through the help of Russell he moved to Charlestown and set up his own practice.

Shortly after, Sewall befriended John Adams, and the relationship that ensued lasted far beyond their early days as young lawyers despite the gulf that separated their political views. Commenting on Sewall's character, Adams wrote, "He possessed a lively wit, a pleasing humor, a brilliant imagination, great subtlety of reasoning, and an insinuating eloquence." In 1764 Sewall married Esther Quincy; they had two children. Over the course of three years, 1767 to 1769, his professional competence solicited his appointment to four important posts: solicitor general, advocate general, attorney general, and judge of admiralty.

Sewall's success shaped his political orientation and confirmed his belief that the current social system was just and rewarding. Throughout the 1760s many of his friends, such as Adams and John Hancock, came to believe otherwise. While Sewall claimed that he sought neutrality through his professional integrity, his opponents argued that the interests of the Crown and the province were no longer mutual. Sewall's continuation in appointive office was seen as proof of his stance in the growing conflict. Sewall contended that his actions expressed his opposition to irresponsible agitation. In his political essays, he wrote that he did not envision any alternative to the British constitutional government. Convinced of the speedy defeat of the patriots, he attempted to dissuade Adams from attending the First Continental Congress in Philadelphia.

Sewall's allegiance to the Crown was met with heavy criticism. After a mob attacked his home in September 1774, he left Cambridge for Boston. Early in 1775 he sailed for England—one of the earliest of the Tory refugees. Although he always believed that he would return to his home province, Sewall would never again set foot in Massachusetts. In exile he was extremely depressed and drained by the lack of activity. He was among the Loyalists who were named in the Act of Banishment of 1778, and in April 1779 the state of Massachusetts seized his property.

By 1783 Sewall began to withdraw into himself. In the summer of 1785 he composed a "Plan of the Union" for the Canadian provinces. To Sewall, the lesson learned from the American Revolution was that a successful colonial government must act to safeguard against rebellion and provide a remedy against republicanism. His vision called for an indigenous Canadian oligarchy backed by the British government. In exchange for support, the oligarchy was committed to the province's allegiance to the Crown. Rather than analyzing the success of the American situation, Sewall was reacting against the political change that had disrupted his life and ended his career at its peak. In 1787 he left for Halifax, where he was judge of the admiralty for Nova Scotia and New Brunswick. Prior to leaving London, he arranged a meeting with Adams, and regardless of their political positions, the two men met as friends. In Canada, Sewall's personal disintegration continued. His final defeat came when the British government abolished his vice admiralty court. He died in St. John, New Brunswick.

Both of Sewall's sons went into law. Jonathan Sewall, Jr., became chief justice of Lower Canada (now Quebec), and Stephen Sewall became solicitor general of Lower Canada. Sewall's political essays appeared frequently in the press. Relative to the writings of other Loyalists, Sewall's contributions, which appeared under the names of "Philanthrop" and "J," constitute some of the more talented written defenses of the prerevolutionary system of government.

• The largest collection of Sewall's papers, in the Public Archives of Canada at Ottawa, includes documents dating from 1731 to 1791. Also in the collection are the Papers of Ward Chipman, Sewall's son by sentiment if not by birth. Other manuscript materials are at the Massachusetts Historical Society in the Sewall-Robie Collection, which includes forty years of correspondence between Sewall and his cousin Thomas Robie, and among the papers of several of his friends, including the Adams papers, the Coffin papers, the William Heath Collection, the Higginson Collection, the Hutchinson-Watson Collection, the Smith-Carter papers, and the Lee Family Papers. The most complete modern assessment is Carol Berkin, *Jonathan Sewall: Odyssey of an American Loyalist* (1974), which contains a comprehensive annotated bibliography. For additional secondary sources see Bernard Bailyn, *The Ordeal of Thomas Hutchinson* (1974); Mary Beth Norton, *The British Americans: The Loyalist Exiles in England, 1774–1789* (1972); William Nelson, *The American Tory* (1968); and Thomas Hutchinson, *History of the Colony and Province of Massachusetts-bay*, ed. Laurence Shaw Mayo (1936).

CAROL BERKIN

SEWALL, Lucy Ellen (26 Apr. 1837–13 Feb. 1890), physician, was born in Boston, Massachusetts, the daughter of Samuel E. Sewall and Louisa Maria Winslow. Her father was a lawyer, politician, and activist on behalf of the abolition of slavery and the promotion of women's rights. Her mother came from a prominent Quaker family in Portland, Maine.

Lucy Sewall lived in Boston, Roxbury, and Melrose, Massachusetts, during her childhood. There is no record of her early schooling, which was limited by poor health, but she was known to have been liberally educated in foreign languages and classical studies and to have possessed a remarkably retentive mind. When she was twelve years old her mother died and Lucy took over management of the household. She also ran a children's school, an appropriate occupation for young ladies of the day.

In 1856 Lucy Sewall became acquainted with Dr. Marie Zakrzewska, who was seeking support from Samuel Sewall on behalf of the Blackwell sisters' New York Infirmary for Women and Children. Lucy admired Zakrzewska's dedication to medicine, and when she realized that a medical career need not detract from femininity, she decided to pursue the same profession. Few people in the nineteenth century approved of female physicians, even though the era valued the "female virtues" of modesty and sensitivity, and many sick women were afraid to consult a male physician, often delaying needed treatment until too late. Lucy Sewall's commitment to medical care for women and children and to the advancement of women in the medical profession animated the rest of her life.

In 1857 her father married the widowed sister of his first wife, Harriet Winslow List, who was also an abolitionist and feminist as well as a poet. Both parents supported Lucy's ambitions. Her father's remarriage freed her to pursue an education in medicine, but there were very few medical schools open to women. In 1859 Zakrzewska, with encouragement from Samuel Sewall, became professor of obstetrics at New England Female Medical College in Boston, and Lucy enrolled as her private pupil as well as a student in the college. Its standards were not high, but Zakrzewska's tutelage made up for its omissions. Despite chronic bronchitis, Sewall diligently pursued her studies, often sleeping only four hours a night. Her graduation thesis dealt with two topics—erysipelas (an acute skin disease), and the necessity for female physicians. She received her M.D. in March 1862. Because there were few opportunities for women to train in American hospitals, she spent the following year in England and France, where her gentle ways and feminine manners, coupled with her medical knowledge and skills, gained the respect of important medical men and access to hospitals and clinics where she could observe disease and therapeutics.

In 1862 Zakrzewska left the Medical College and, with the help of Samuel Sewall and other Boston feminists, founded the New England Hospital for Women and Children. The following year Lucy Sewall returned to Boston to become its resident physician. For the remainder of her life she was intimately connected with the hospital, as resident physician for six years, attending physician from 1869 to 1887, and advisory physician thereafter until her death. Many patients insisted on receiving their care only from her. She served without monetary compensation, subsisting on her private practice and a trust fund inherited from her mother. Under the leadership of Zakrzewska and Sewall, the hospital and outpatient department provided medical and obstetrical care to women of all classes, races, and ethnicities, many of whom came great distances to avail themselves of a medical staff that was almost entirely female. In part because nineteenth-century American medicine was threatened by unorthodox systems that disclaimed traditional theories and practices and embraced women practitioners, the leaders of the New England Hospital insisted on high standards that would demonstrate the ability of orthodox women physicians.

The hospital was also a training site for women physicians, and Sewall was instrumental in attracting other young women to medicine. Sophia Jex-Blake, an Englishwoman who was one of her most intimate friends as well as her protégée, spent several years at the hospital before she decided to be a physician and returned to lead the feminist assault on medicine in Great Britain. Susan Dimock, who followed Sewall as resident physician, and Mary Putnam Jacobi, who interned at the hospital before going to Paris to continue her studies, are two of many who achieved fame as pioneer women physicians.

A photograph of Sewall shows a demure, almost childlike face, shyly looking downward. This image contrasts with her colleagues' praise for her rigorous intellect, strong will, and determination, "a thoroughly scientific physician" (Jex-Blake, Intro.). She was reputed to be a skillful operator who handled obstetrical and gynecological instruments with ease and assurance. She traveled alone by horse and carriage, day or night, to her patients' homes. Her New England conscience required that "life must be duty, not pleasure" (Todd, p. 329), yet she could also be a warm friend and a sincere counselor to young women who sought her advice, and a compassionate healer to women and children in pain. She actively promoted the admission of women to Harvard Medical School (unsuccessfully) and to the Massachusetts Medical Society. When the Medical Society finally admitted women late in her lifetime, she refused to submit to its examination on the grounds that her years of medical experience should obviate the necessity for it.

Sewall also had a busy private practice, with patients of all social classes; the poor were charged no fees. However, she struggled continually with her own poor health, and in the final years of her life she was practically an invalid. She died from heart disease at her home in Boston. Two years later the New England Hospital for Women and Children dedicated the Sewall Maternity Building in honor of Samuel E. Sewall and Dr. Lucy E. Sewall. It was a fitting tribute to a woman whose example of courage and determination and high standards of medical care inspired many other women to become physicians.

• Not many of Sewall's letters are known to exist; the Caroline Dall Collection at the Massachusetts Historical Society has a few, as well as some of Samuel E. Sewall. The Countway Library, Harvard Medical School, also has a few letters, including correspondence regarding the admission of women. The Case Books of the New England Hospital for Women and Children are also held at the Countway Library; the Medical Case Records, 1866–1868, are almost entirely gynecological cases signed by Sewall as resident physician. The Schlesinger Library, Radcliffe College, holds nonmedical records of the New England Hospital as well as papers of some of the women on its board.

Information about Sewall's personal and professional life may be gleaned from biographies of her associates: Agnes C. Vietor, *A Woman's Quest* (1924); Virginia E. Drachman, *Hospital with a Heart* (1984), Sophia Jex-Blake, *Medical Women: A Thesis and a History* (1886), Margaret Todd, *The Life of Sophia Jex-Blake* (1918), and Shirley Roberts, *Sophia Jex-Blake* (1993). Nina Moore Tiffany, *Samuel E. Sewall, a Memoir* (1898), includes references to Lucy Sewall's childhood. Zakrzewska wrote a long obituary in the *Woman's Journal*, 22 Feb. 1890. Other obituaries are in the *Boston Post* and the *Boston Transcript*, both 19 Feb. 1890. Finally, *L'Union Medicale* 19 (1863) has a long letter written by Dr. A. Chereau, with whom Sewall became acquainted in Paris, describing her ability and urging the French medical profession to accept women physicians.

AMALIE M. KASS

SEWALL, May Eliza Wright (27 May 1844–23 July 1920), suffragist and educator, was born in Greenfield, Wisconsin, the daughter of Philander Montague Wright, a schoolteacher and farmer, and Mary Weeks Brackett. Sewall was taught at home by her father and in local public schools. She graduated from Northwestern University in Evanston, Illinois, with the degree mistress of science in 1866 and master of arts in 1871. She went on to pursue a career in teaching in Corinth, Mississippi, Plainwell, Michigan, and Frankfort, Indiana. In 1872 Sewall married Edwin W. Thompson and moved to Indianapolis, Indiana, where both taught high school; they had no children. Following Thompson's death in 1875, she continued to teach, and in 1880 she married Theodore Lovett Sewall, a graduate of Harvard College and founder of a classical school for boys in Indianapolis; they had no children. In 1882 she and her husband founded the Girls' Classical School of Indianapolis, where Sewall continued as principal for twelve years after the death of her husband in 1895.

After moving to Indiana, Sewall participated actively in the Indiana women's club movement, the Indiana woman suffrage movement, and the National Woman Suffrage Association. In 1878 she cofounded the Indiana Equal Suffrage Society, which affiliated with the National Woman Suffrage Association (NWSA) in 1887. From 1882 to 1890 Sewall served as chair of the NWSA's executive committee. She was also a founding member of the Association of Collegiate Alumnae (1882) and the Western Association of Collegiate Alumnae (1883), of which she served as president in 1886 and again in 1888–1889. She became the first president of the Indiana Federation of Women's Clubs in 1889. Along with suffrage and education, Sewall's wide-ranging interests included the founding of the Indianapolis Art Association (1883), dress reform, and social purity as well as the Ramabai Circle, an organization dedicated to raising the position of Indian women by founding schools for widows.

Sewall is most widely known both abroad and within the United States as a founding member of the International Council of Women (ICW) and the American National Council of Women, whose histories she documented in her *Genesis of the International Council of Women and the Story of Its Growth, 1888–1893* (1914) and *Transactions of the Third Quincennial Meeting of the ICW in Berlin, 1904* (1910). The ICW was an international women's network first organized in 1888 in the United States to celebrate the fortieth anniversary of the American woman suffrage movement. Sewall took the lead in promoting the international council, serving as its president from 1899 to 1904. In order to bring new members into the ICW Sewall traveled to Paris in 1889 to speak before the International Congress of Women sponsored by the French government, and she spoke as well in Zurich and Geneva. As part of her efforts to popularize the ICW, Sewall returned to Europe again in 1891–1892 and met with heads of women's organizations in France, Italy, Belgium, and Germany.

In 1893 Sewall served as president of the meeting of the ICW held in conjunction with the World Columbian Exhibition in Chicago, during which women from across the globe gathered as "representatives of all worthy organizations of women, whatever their nationality or their specific object." As a second-generation suffrage leader, the ICW embodied Sewall's hopes that an international arena would provide a forum in which suffragists might work closely with other reform-minded women to whom woman suffrage was only one of many other social goals. In the course of her work as a member of the ICW, Sewall corresponded extensively with women reformers abroad and within the United States on woman suffrage, internationalism, and American women's leadership role in a global context.

After resigning from the presidency of the ICW, Sewall worked actively to promote world peace and international arbitration. From 1904 to 1914 she served as convener of the first ICW standing committee on peace and international arbitration, and in April 1907 she addressed the National Arbitration and Peace Congress in New York. She also helped organize and presided over the International Conference of Women Workers to Promote Permanent Peace convened in San Francisco in July 1915.

In the years following her husbands' deaths Sewall became deeply interested in spiritualism and published *Neither Dead nor Sleeping* (1920). A dedicated worker in the women's movement, she was both a highly successful organizer and public speaker. Her commitment to the international dimension of women's reform efforts included suffrage, temperance, peace, and education. Her belief in the necessity of cross-national cooperation between women remained a central aspect of women's organizing well into the twentieth century. She died in Indianapolis.

• Sewall's papers are at the Marion County Public Library, Indianapolis, Ind. Other works authored and edited by May Wright Sewall include *The World's Congress of Representative Women* (1894), *Higher Education of Women in the Western States of the U.S.A.* (1887), and *Women, World War and Permanent Peace* (1915). Accounts of Sewall's activities can be found in the records of those organizations in which she actively participated, including the National Council of Women, the International Council of Women, the National Woman Suffrage Association, and the General Federation of Women's Clubs. See also International Council of Women, *Women in a Changing World: The Dynamic Story of the International Council of Women since 1888* (1966); Anna Garlin Spencer, *The Council Idea: A Chronicle of Its Prophets and a Tribute to May Wright Sewall* (1929); Elizabeth Cady Stanton et al., *History of Woman Suffrage*, vols. 3–6 (1881–1922); Jane C. Croly, *The History of the Woman's Club Movement in America* (1898); and Louise Barnum Robbins, ed., *The History and Minutes of the National Council of Women of the United States: 1888–1898* (1898). Obituaries are in the *Indianapolis News*, 23 July 1920, and *New York Times*, 24 July 1920.

ALLISON L. SNEIDER

SEWALL, Samuel (28 Mar. 1652–1 Jan. 1730), colonial merchant, judge, and philanthropist, was born at Bishop Stoke, Hampshire, England, the son of Henry

Sewall, a pastor, and Jane Dummer. Sewall's father had immigrated to Newbury, Massachusetts, in 1634, and although he was admitted to freemanship in 1637, he returned to England in 1646 and subsequently took the pulpit of North Baddesley. The family returned to Massachusetts in 1659.

The scion of wealth on both sides of his family, Sewall was educated from an early age, attending grammar school in Romsey, England, and later in Massachusetts with Thomas Parker, the pastor of the Newbury Church. He entered Harvard, graduating in 1671. Undecided between a career in commerce or the ministry, he was appointed a resident fellow (1673) and the library keeper. At his M.A. commencement, Sewall was required to respond affirmatively to the question *An Peccatum Original sit & Peccatatum & Poena*, a study on whether original sin was both sin and punishment. After receiving his degree in 1674, Sewall dallied with various activities, declining a call to a pulpit at Woodbridge, New Jersey. Despite his indecision, he married into a prosperous family, marrying Hannah Hull in 1675. They had fourteen children, five of whom survived to adulthood. Hannah died in 1717, and Sewall married Abigail Melvyn Woodmansy Tilley in 1719. After she died in 1720, he conducted an extensive courtship of the widow of Wait Still Winthrop; however, their plans foundered over her concern for her children. In 1722 he married Mary Shrimpton Gibbs, the widow of Boston merchant Robert Gibbs. He had no children with his last two wives.

Sewall's first marriage brought a large dowry and focused Sewall's calling on commerce. He soon took over many of his father-in-law John Hull's mercantile activities. When the elder Hull died intestate in 1683, Sewall entered into "an Estate that might afford a competent Subsistence." His wife Hannah received two-thirds of the estate while her mother received a one-third life interest. Sewall became one of the wealthiest men in Boston, with rentals from properties in the city, the Narragansett region, Newbury, Woburn, Braintree, and other parts of the colony.

After 1683 Sewall also became a major political force. He was elected to the General Court from Westfield in Hampden County and then to the Court of Assistants in 1684. With the revocation of the charter in 1684, he continued to serve as a justice of the peace and a captain in the militia but was passed over for one of the new council appointments. In 1688 concern for the certainty of his property titles in New England and the need to administer his father's and his own properties in England took him to London. While in London, he helped Increase Mather lobby for the old charter. During Sewall's absence from Massachusetts, Governor Edmund Andros and the Dominion of New England were replaced with an interim council. Upon his return to Boston, Sewall became a member of that council and, with the arrival of the new charter, was retained in the upper house in 1691. He held the post until he declined to stand for election in 1725.

One of the first actions of Sir William Phips, the first governor under the new charter, was to appoint a special court of oyer and terminer to hear the witchcraft accusations that had proliferated in Salem over the winter of 1691. He named Sewall to serve on the court. The court used spectral evidence—the "appearance" of the accused to the afflicted—as definitive in its condemnation of witches. This type of prosecution was innovative and ultimately controversial, leading Sewall subsequently to regret his participation in the trials and to issue a public apology at the Old South Meeting House in 1697.

In addition to his activities as a justice of the peace and a member of the court of oyer and terminer, Sewall had a long career as a judge. In December 1692 he was appointed to the Superior Court of Judicature, Massachusetts's highest court, and was elevated to chief justice in 1718; in 1715 he also became judge of the probate court of Suffolk County. Sewall's appointment to these posts illustrates the criteria used for selecting magistrates well into the eighteenth century. Chosen purportedly for their wisdom rather than their legal knowledge, judges in colonial Massachusetts reflected the patterns of a deferential world order based on social status. Beyond the initial appointment, judges learned to cope with the technical demands of the common law either through experience or education. Increasingly the bench came to be composed of trained lawyers like Benjamin Lynde and Paul Dudley, while untrained jurists like Sewall learned through practice.

Sewall also participated in a large number of philanthropic activities. In 1699 he became the treasurer and commissioner of the (Puritan) Society for the Propagation of the Gospel, not to be confused with the more controversial (Anglican) Society for the Propagation of the Gospel in Foreign Parts founded in 1701. He was responsible for administering lands owned by the society and for supervising the disbursement of funds in support of Native American Christian churches. Sewall made extensive contributions toward the support of Indian Christians throughout his life. As early as 1691 he used an unpaid debt to procure land that was then turned over to support an Indian ministry. He also donated land to support a meetinghouse in Kingston and to fund scholarships for Indian students at Harvard.

Sewall, opposed to slavery, wrote *The Selling of Joseph: A Memorial* (1700) in response to the growth of African slavery in the colony. Part of an ongoing debate over slavery, Sewall's book described cases like that of John Saffin's slave Adam. Saffin rented out a farm stocked with horses, cattle, and Adam. After promising Adam he would be set free after seven years of service, Saffin reneged. The case was first heard before Sewall, who urged Saffin to free Adam; meanwhile Saffin was appointed to the superior court, which was then designated to hear the case. Sewall became even more critical of Saffin when he would not remove himself from hearing the case and when he, as Sewall suspected, tampered with the jury. Saffin responded with a pamphlet attacking the premises of

The Selling of Joseph. Ultimately, Saffin's view of race relations and slavery prevailed. In 1705 the deputies passed a bill punishing blacks with whipping and exile for having sexual relations with whites while also barring interracial marriage. Sewall's only consolation was his belief that his opposition had made the terms less severe by legalizing marriages between blacks.

Sewall was also the author of a number of other titles, but his major literary accomplishment was his manuscript diary. In the diary, Sewall revealed the subtle complexities of his many activities and of the colony's affairs at a crucial moment in its transformation from Puritan colony to English province. Covering the period from 1674 to 1729 (with a gap between 1677 and 1684), the diary also provides an intimate view of his life. Sewall appears not only as a merchant and a politician standing at the center of a network of Massachusetts Bay Colony elites but also as a grieving father, a fearful city dweller, a troubled sinner, and a pious believer. The diary gave order and comfort to Sewall and provides us a window into the world of the Puritan laity and popular religion. Sewall died in Boston.

• Sewall's diary and other manuscript materials may be found at the Massachusetts Historical Society in Boston. His business journal is at the Baker Library of the Harvard Business School. A collection of his letters was published in the *Massachusetts Historical Society Collections*, 6th ser., vols. 1–2 (1886–1888). A superb edition of Sewall's diaries is M. Halsey Thomas, ed., *The Diary of Samuel Sewall, 1674–1729* (1973). Theodore Benson Strandness, *Samuel Sewall: A Puritan Portrait* (1967), and Ola E. Winslow, *Samuel Sewall* (1964), are useful biographies. More specialized studies are Joab L. Blackmon, Jr., "Judge Samuel Sewall's Efforts in Behalf of the First Americans," *Ethnohistory* 16 (1969): 165–66; Charles G. Steffen, "The Sewall Children in Colonial New England," *New England Historical and Genealogical Register* 31 (1977): 163–72); and Lawrence W. Towner, "The Sewall-Saffin Dialogue on Slavery," *William and Mary Quarterly*, 3d ser., 21 (1964): 40–52. David D. Hall, *Worlds of Wonder, Days of Judgment: Popular Religious Belief in Early New England* (1989), is especially useful in its close analysis of the diary.

JONATHAN M. CHU

SEWALL, Stephen (14 Dec. 1702–10 Sept. 1760), judge, was born in Salem, Massachusetts, the son of Stephen Sewall, the clerk of court at the Salem witchcraft trials, and Margaret Mitchel. He was a nephew of Chief Justice Samuel Sewall, who sat at the witchcraft trials, and the uncle of Loyalist lawyer and royal vice admiralty judge Jonathan Sewall. David Sewall, the first federal judge in the District of Maine, was a cousin. Stephen received his A.B. at Harvard in 1721. After teaching school in Marblehead for a brief period, he returned to Harvard and received his M.A. in 1724. Apparently drawn to the academic life, he remained at Harvard, serving in various administrative positions, including librarian, until he was appointed a tutor in 1728. He served in that role for the classes of 1731, 1735, and 1739, establishing a strong reputation as a scholar and a greatly beloved teacher. Throughout his

years in Cambridge, Sewall continued his study of theology and sought to obtain appointment to a Boston pulpit. He was unsuccessful, despite his reputation as an outstanding preacher.

Rejecting an offer from the Marlborough church, Sewall undertook the study of law, apparently on his own. Though never admitted to the bar, he was widely recognized for the breadth of his legal knowledge and in 1739 was appointed by Governor Jonathan Belcher to the Superior Court, the highest court in the province. As a later commentator noted, "His appointment . . . is pretty good evidence, either that the proper qualifications for the office were little regarded by Governor Belcher, or that it was reverted to as an expedient often adopted, to quiet the claims of rival candidates, by selecting some third one of unexceptionable qualities" (Washburn, p. 295). In 1752 Governor William Shirley appointed Sewall chief justice, again causing political controversy. Sewall's general reputation for fair, intelligent, and compassionate adjudication quickly overcame these objections. Though he protested against the idea of dual officeholding, in 1752 he accepted election to the Council (the upper house of the legislature), serving as a councillor until his death. He was widely regarded as distinguished and nonpartisan in the office of councillor.

Events surrounding Sewall's death helped to usher in the progression to revolution. In 1755 he presided when the Superior Court granted the application of the British customs officers in Boston for a writ of assistance (a general warrant) to search for smuggled goods. A new application was presented to the court in October 1760. Sewall had evidently come to doubt, according to John Adams, "the Legality and Constitutionality of the Writ" (*Diary and Autobiography of John Adams*, ed. Lyman Henry Butterfield, vol. 3 [1961], p. 275). Posthumous deference to those doubts and the lack of a chief led the surviving justices to postpone a decision. Meanwhile, Thomas Hutchinson, a Crown supporter, was appointed chief justice despite the efforts of James Otis, Sr., to obtain the office. This contest for Sewall's seat produced fateful consequences. When the application for the writ finally came up for hearing in February 1761, it was brilliantly, though unsuccessfully, opposed on behalf of Boston's merchants by James Otis, Jr. Adams's report of Otis's fiery argument that the writ was an unconstitutional exercise of Parliament's power helped to crystallize colonial sentiment against British rule.

Sewall died in Boston, where he had moved upon his appointment to the bench in 1739. His funeral brought forth a large crowd of distinguished mourners and an array of lengthy and effusive obituaries. In a funeral sermon separately published in pamphlet form, Rev. Jonathan Mayhew, minister of Sewall's church, eulogized him at length and in fulsome terms. One diarist said, "He has left few or none behind him equal to him upon all accounts; being eminent both in Gifts & Graces; above others & yet remarkable for his Modesty & Goodnature to all." Another evaluation, in a New Hampshire obituary, stated:

Sewall the just, the generous, and the wise,
Sewall has left us, and ascends the Skies.
Clement in Justice, and unbrib'd his Hand
Patient to hear and quick to understand.
(*New Hampshire Gazette*, 3 Oct. 1760)

Sewall never married. In Boston, he was active in civic affairs and raised his brother's orphaned children, though he had no personal wealth. His generosity to these charges and others was said to have "bordered upon injustice to himself and his creditors" (Washburn, p. 293). His estate was insolvent, and his nephew and administrator, Jonathan Sewall, unsuccessfully sought a discharge of his debts from the legislature. This failure is said to have helped turn Jonathan Sewall toward his ultimate espousal of the Loyalist cause.

Despite the political factors that may have influenced Sewall's appointments to the bench, he was widely recognized as an outstanding judge by lawyers, other judges, and informed citizens of all parties. Hutchinson, from the Crown perspective, wrote that Sewall gave "universal satisfaction to the people of the province" (*History of the Colony and Province of Massachusetts Bay*, vol. 3 [1767], p. 63n). Adams, recalling Sewall's views on the writs of assistance, described him, in a letter written in 1817, as "an able man, an uncorrupted American, and a sincere friend of Liberty, civil and religious" (*The Works of John Adams*, ed. Charles Francis Adams [1850–1856], vol. 10, p. 247).

• Sewall's judicial service is documented in Massachusetts Early Court Files, 1739–1760, Massachusetts Archives, Boston. Sewall's life is best described in Clifford K. Shipton, *Sibley's Harvard Graduates*, vol. 6 (1942). See also Emory Washburn, *Sketches of the Judicial History of Massachusetts, 1630–1775* (1840). For Sewall and the writs of assistance case, see M. H. Smith, *The Writs of Assistance Case* (1978). Jonathan Mayhew's sermon was published as *Discourse Occasioned by the Death of . . . Stephen Sewall* (1760). Extensive obituaries are in the *Boston News-letter*, 18 Sept. 1776; the *Boston Gazette*, 22 Sept. 1760; and the *New Hampshire Gazette*, 3 Oct. 1760.

L. KINVIN WROTH

SEWARD, Frederick William (8 July 1830–25 Apr. 1915), diplomat, journalist, and author, was born in Auburn, New York, the son of William Henry Seward, a powerful Whig and Republican party leader, and Frances Miller, the daughter of an influential Upstate New York lawyer. Fred, as he was called, graduated from Union College at age nineteen. After serving briefly as secretary for his father (who was then in the U.S. Senate), he joined the bar in 1851 at his father's urging. However, Fred Seward was most interested in journalism. In 1852 he became associate editor of the Albany *Evening Journal*, whose editor, Thurlow Weed, was a leading Whig party political strategist and William Seward's closest political adviser.

In 1854 Seward married Anna Wharton; they had no children. She became a popular and influential Washington hostess after William Seward and Fred Seward accepted Abraham Lincoln's offer to become

secretary of state and assistant secretary of state, respectively, in early 1861. Anna Seward ran the secretary of state's busy Lafayette Square household during his 1861–1869 tenure. Fred Seward not only oversaw the work of U.S. consuls who served abroad but often decided which dispatches from American diplomats deserved his father's attention. William Seward broke tradition by often having his son take his place at cabinet meetings. Fred Seward thus attended Lincoln's last cabinet meeting of 14 April 1865, for which the assistant secretary left behind an important historical record.

When Lincoln was shot that night, another assassin, Lewis Payne, was to kill the secretary of state, who was recovering in bed from an accident. Fred Seward stopped Payne outside his father's bedroom. Payne tried to shoot him, but the pistol misfired. Payne pistol-whipped Fred, fracturing his skull. The assassin then slashed William Seward, who eventually recovered. Fred lay unconscious for days before beginning to improve. By early 1866 both Sewards had returned to the State Department, where William plotted a vast postwar expansionist policy to obtain Caribbean bases and trading outlets in the Pacific Ocean–East Asian regions.

In December 1866 Fred Seward went to Santo Domingo with Vice Admiral David D. Porter to negotiate the sale or lease of the magnificent Samaná Bay. Discovering that the surrounding heights controlled the bay, they demanded this land as well. The Dominican government refused, and the mission failed. Later in 1867 the Dominicans did sign a treaty, but it was rejected by the U.S. Senate, whose Radical Republicans had broken with both the more conservative president, Andrew Johnson, and William Seward. The secretary of state's expansionist plans were largely unrealized except for the purchase of Alaska from Russia in 1867. During these talks, Fred Seward successfully lobbied the unpredictable chair of the Senate Foreign Relations Committee, Charles Sumner, to obtain his necessary support for the treaty.

In 1869 the Sewards retired from office. Fred and Anna bought and restored a house, "Montrose," on a magnificent site overlooking the Hudson River. In 1874 Seward won election to the New York State Assembly. Although in the minority Republican party, he successfully introduced constitutional amendments providing for a superintendent of prisons and also a superintendent of public works. He carried on a strong family interest in internal improvements by helping to create the first of their kind street railroads in New York City. He lost the race to be New York secretary of state in 1876.

On 21 March 1877 Seward returned to Washington, D.C., as assistant secretary of state in Rutherford B. Hayes's administration. He worked with Samoan delegates, who hoped the United States would offset the German and British encroachments on their islands. Despite Seward's fears that the racist, antiexpansionist U.S. Senate would object, in 1878 the senators ratified a treaty that gave the United States special rights to use

Pago Pago harbor in return for offering good offices if Samoa had a dispute with another power. The treaty led to the division of the islands between the United States and Germany in 1899 and the creation of American Samoa. Seward also handled many of the potentially explosive negotiations with Mexico that led to the recognition of Porfirio Díaz's regime in 1880. Seward had retired on 31 October 1879, but Díaz was to be Mexico's dictator for another thirty-one years.

In the 1870s Seward helped Weed write his recollections and also edited a three-volume autobiographical work that his father had partially prepared just before his death in 1872. He was state commissioner at the Yorktown Centennial Celebration (1881) and president of the Union College Alumni Association (1900) and of the Society of Cayugas (1902). Also in 1902 he entered the debate over an Alaskan-Canadian boundary dispute by writing the *New York Tribune* to demand the squashing of the "monstrous demands" from "Canadian schemers," who, he charged, only wanted to kill the growing British-American friendship. For his own reasons, President Theodore Roosevelt (1858–1919) fulfilled Seward's demand. In 1904 Seward presided at the semicentennial of the Republican party in Saratoga and that same year was a member of the International Arbitration Conference in Washington, D.C. He also served as vice president of the Hudson-Fulton Commission (1908–1909) and as chairman of its Plank Scope Committee (1908–1909). In February 1915 Seward strongly supported woman suffrage in a letter to the *New York Times*: "Women are not asking for benefits. What they demand is justice, and justice always benefits."

At his death at Montrose, Seward left an estate valued at $100,000 and a long manuscript, "Reminiscences of a War-Time Statesman and Diplomat, 1830–1915," which he wanted published posthumously. The volume, like its author, was tolerant and usually kind in its evaluation of others' political performances, modest and straightforward, and most interesting for its firsthand observations of the Civil War era.

• The most important biographical source is Frederick W. Seward, *Reminiscences of a War-Time Statesman and Diplomat, 1830–1915* (1916), although it needs to be used carefully, especially in its hagiographic handling of William Seward's career. Glyndon G. Van Deusen, *William Henry Seward* (1967), is helpful on the family background and Frederick's work in the State Department during the 1860s. A long obituary is in the *New York Times*, 26 Apr. 1915.

WALTER LAFEBER

SEWARD, George Frederick (8 Nov. 1840–28 Nov. 1910), diplomat and business executive, was born in Florida, New York, the son of George Washington Seward and Tempe Wicke Leddell. George Frederick attended Seward Institute in his hometown and Union College in Schenectady, New York, but left before graduation to take charge of his family's affairs. In 1861 his uncle, Secretary of State William Henry Seward, appointed him U.S. consul at Shanghai, China. The post was elevated to consul general in 1863, and

he served in that capacity until his appointment in January 1876 as U.S. minister to China. In August 1870 he married Kate Sherman; they had four children.

Seward's fifteen years of consular experience well qualified him for the position of chief U.S. diplomat in China, but controversy accompanied his transfer to Beijing (Peking). European and American merchants and missionaries were pressing China to accept Western technology and culture. In the bustling port of Shanghai, Seward had supported foreign commercial efforts and the introduction of inventions such as the telegraph. He encouraged Western construction of the first steam railway in China, a twelve-mile line from Shanghai to Wusong (Woosung). Although he was apparently not an investor in the project, he advised the American and British developers how to circumvent official Chinese objections to the construction. With Seward's knowledge, for example, the builders purchased the railroad right-of-way for the ostensible purpose of constructing a "horse road." After Seward went to Beijing, Chinese authorities purchased and dismantled the line and charged that he had deceived them about the purpose of the project. The way that the railway was built violated the Burlingame Treaty of 1868, which gave the Chinese control over when and how such innovations would occur. For this transgression and for allegedly realizing unauthorized financial gains from his consular post, Minister Seward became the object of an impeachment move by a Democratic-controlled committee of the House of Representatives in 1879. Three separate investigations had found irregularities in Seward's Shanghai accounts, but his longtime aide removed the financial records from the consulate general. Claiming his rights under the Fifth Amendment, Seward refused to turn over the records or to testify about their content. Republicans blocked his impeachment with a parliamentary maneuver on the House floor, but Seward had become a political liability. President Rutherford B. Hayes recalled him from his post prior to the 1880 elections.

Despite Seward's firm conviction that westernization was in the best interest of China, he believed with equal certainty in a friendly approach to the proud Chinese mandarins. This sensitivity made him an outspoken critic of the anti-Chinese sentiment that erupted in California as Chinese laborers immigrated there in search of jobs. Before his dismissal as minister, he began work on a treaty to limit Chinese immigration by mutual agreement. Upon his return to the United States, he published a book, *Chinese Immigration in Its Social and Economical Aspect* (1881), that argued against unilateral exclusion. He asserted that the Chinese would never willingly agree to allow Western influence in their country if Americans arbitrarily excluded Chinese from the United States. He subsequently wrote other books and numerous articles on U.S. relations with Asia.

His diplomatic career over, Seward turned to several business ventures in the 1880s. He became president of the Fidelity and Casualty Company of New York in 1892, and the firm expanded dramatically under his direction. Also a prominent figure in the New York State Chamber of Commerce, he was in line to become its president when he died in New York City.

• Seward's personal papers are in the New-York Historical Society, New York City. His diplomatic correspondence is in the General Records of the Department of State, National Archives, Washington, D.C. His other publications include *The United States Consulates in China* (1867), *The Treaty with Spain* (1898), *The Russian-Japanese War* (1904), and *Insurance Is Commerce* (1910). See also Paul H. Clyde, "Attitudes and Policies of George F. Seward, American Minister in Peking, 1876–1880," *Pacific Historical Review* 2 (1933): 387–404, and David L. Anderson, *Imperialism and Idealism: American Diplomats in China, 1861–1898* (1985). Obituaries are in the *New York Times*, 29 Nov. 1910, and the *Monthly Bulletin of the Fidelity and Casualty Company of New York*, Jan. 1911.

DAVID L. ANDERSON

SEWARD, Theodore Frelinghuysen (25 Jan. 1835–30 Aug. 1902), music educator and editor, was born in Florida, New York, the son of Israel Seward and Mary Johnson, farmers. He was educated at Seward Institute, which was founded by his great-uncle, Samuel S. Seward, the father of William Henry Seward. After studying music with Lowell Mason and George F. Root, he taught in New London, Connecticut, from 1857 to 1859. In 1860 he married Mary Holden Coggeshall; they had three children. In 1862 Seward made New York City his headquarters for editorial work, compiling tunebooks and editing the *New York Musical Gazette* from its inception in 1866. He continued as editor of the *Gazette* when it was taken over in 1869 by Biglow & Main, a firm specializing in music for evangelical groups.

When the Fisk Jubilee Singers met with success in New York in 1871, demands for copies of their songs led their sponsor, the American Missionary Association, to seek a transcriber. How Seward was selected for this assignment can only be conjectured. He may have been recommended by Biglow & Main, as both a musician and a devout Christian. He apparently had no previous experience with folk music, with blacks, or with the South. His published writings display no recognition of the distinctive qualities of African-American music, for which the notational system made no provision.

Far from appreciating a culture different from his own, Seward described the Jubilee Singers as having "no musical cultivation whatever." His only explanation for the excellence of the spirituals was "true inspiration . . . [from] an ever watchful Father." He was the first to claim that his transcriptions captured the music precisely as it was performed. These transcriptions, which included characteristic European harmonies, were widely accepted as authentic and remained the most influential versions of the spirituals until after 1920.

The first publication, *Jubilee Songs*, containing twenty-four songs, was issued in 1872. In December of that year, Seward resigned as editor of the *Musical Gazette*. The success of *Jubilee Songs* led to a full-length book by Gustavus Pike, *The Jubilee Singers and Their Campaign for Twenty Thousand Dollars* (1873), with a musical supplement of sixty-one songs, a volume that was reissued many times with an increasing number of songs. It was succeeded by J. B. T. Marsh's *The Story of the Jubilee Singers* (1875), also reissued in numerous editions, with increasing numbers of songs, all transcribed by Seward. His association with the Jubilee Singers, as transcriber and conductor, continued to 1878, when Fisk University dissociated itself from the group.

While touring with the group in England in 1875–1877, Seward had become interested in the tonic sol-fa method of teaching musical notation. In 1881 he began to edit the *Tonic Sol-Fa Advocate*, continuing until 1886 when it was superseded by the *Musical Reform*, which he edited until 1888. His later years were devoted to religious writing and the organization of societies like the Brotherhood of Christian Unity. He died in East Orange, New Jersey.

• Letters to and from Seward are in the American Missionary Association Archives, Amistad Research Center, Tulane University, New Orleans. Some letters describing a European tour appeared in the *New York Musical Gazette* in 1869. Articles, reviews, and speeches by him appeared in that journal and in the *American Missionary*. The preface to *Jubilee Songs* states his approach to transcriptions. No biography has been written beyond contemporary sketches in W. S. B. Mathews, *A Hundred Years of Music in America* (1889; repr. 1970), and F. O. Jones, *A Handbook of American Music and Musicians* (1886; repr. 1971). D. J. Epstein's "Theodore F. Seward and the Fisk Jubilee Singers" appears in *A Celebration of American Music: Words and Music in Honor of H. Wiley Hitchcock* (1990). An obituary is in the *New York Times*, 1 Sept. 1902.

DENA J. EPSTEIN

SEWARD, William Henry (16 May 1801–10 Oct. 1872), governor, senator, and secretary of state, was born in Florida, Orange County, New York, the son of Samuel Sweezy Seward, a prosperous farmer and land speculator, and Mary Jennings. Young Seward displayed a quick mind and an independent streak. Defying his overbearing father, he interrupted his studies at Union College to teach for a semester in rural Georgia. Seward graduated from Union in 1820 and soon after completing his legal training (he read law with several private attorneys in Goshen and New York City between 1819 and 1822) moved to Auburn in upstate New York. In 1824 he married Frances Adeline Miller, the daughter of his prominent law partner. The Sewards had five children, four of whom survived to adulthood. His devout wife influenced her more worldly husband, especially on matters regarding slavery, but she never could accept his all-consuming political ambition, which made him increasingly a stranger in his own home.

A supporter of John Quincy Adams, Seward moved from the National Republican party to the Antimasonic party in 1829. Antimasonry, which had its core support in upstate New York, introduced an egalitarian moralism to American politics. It also brought Seward together with Thurlow Weed, establishing a remarkable and durable partnership. Weed, a newspaper publisher and behind-the-scenes political manager par excellence, recognized in Seward a rising star. The two became inseparable lifelong friends. In 1830 Weed masterminded Seward's first bid for elective office, which resulted in a four-year term in the state senate. Like almost all Antimasons, Seward gravitated into the Whig party, a coalition of Andrew Jackson's opponents. Weed enabled his protégé to win the 1834 Whig nomination for governor. Seward ran a vigorous but losing race against the incumbent Democrat, William L. Marcy. Seward carried the Erie Canal region west of Albany, which nurtured reformist and utopian urgings, but he lost the Hudson Valley and New York City. Four years later, amid hard times, Seward defeated Marcy for the governorship. Narrowly reelected in 1840, he served as governor from January 1839 to January 1843.

As governor, Seward promoted internal improvements and education. He bid unsuccessfully to expand the Erie Canal system and enlarge the state's railroad network. He optimistically predicted that increased canal revenues would cover the costs of transportation improvements and generate sufficient new wealth to open more public schools, but legislators, anxious about state indebtedness, rebuffed his scheme. Ethnic and religious rivalries also endangered Seward's educational hopes. Aware that German and Irish Catholics considered the schools in New York City tainted by a Protestant bias, he recommended state aid for schools conducted by teachers who professed the same faith and spoke the same language as their students. His controversial proposal aroused the ire of nativist Protestants, forcing the governor to backtrack. He won passage, instead, for an enlarged system of nonsectarian public schools, conducted in English and administered by elected school boards. Because it allowed New York City schools to gain autonomy from the anti-Catholic Public School Society, Seward's compromise proposal was warmly received by the prominent Catholic spokesman, Bishop John Hughes.

Governor Seward's reform agenda had several features: he wanted prisons to rehabilitate rather than punish; he advocated more humane treatment for the insane; he publicly embraced the antiliquor crusade, though he was hardly temperate himself; and above all, he made himself a leader of the political antislavery movement. Seward convinced the legislature to approve a jury trial in fugitive slave cases, he refused to extradite to the South persons alleged to have aided fugitives, and he urged repeal of New York's racially discriminatory qualifications for voter eligibility. Nationally ambitious and keenly aware that slavery had become the most riveting political issue of the era, he resisted overtures from the Liberty party while attempting to bring his fellow Whigs to a more advanced position. He anticipated that enlightened southerners would presently favor peaceful, voluntary, compensated emancipation.

In 1849 New York Whigs recaptured the state legislature following a fratricidal rupture of Democratic ranks, thereby enabling Weed to engineer Seward's election to the U.S. Senate. The freshman senator quickly established an influential relationship with the new president, Zachary Taylor. Although a slaveholder, Taylor ignored southern demands for concessions when California applied to enter the Union as a free state, and he opposed Henry Clay's compromise efforts. Seward went further. In his first major Senate speech he proclaimed that both the Constitution and a "higher law" required development of the unsettled West by free rather than slave labor. Seward's "higher law" speech was a political bombshell. It pleased antislavery enthusiasts, who were his most loyal supporters in the New York Whig party, but it estranged him from Taylor and marked him to many as a dangerous provocateur. To make matters worse, Taylor died unexpectedly in July 1850. His successor was Millard Fillmore, a procompromise conservative from Buffalo, who stood outside the Seward-Weed wing of the New York Whig party. With Fillmore's support, the Compromise of 1850 was finally enacted.

Between 1850 and 1856 the Whig party was torn asunder by the twin forces of sectional recrimination and nativism. Antislavery Whigs were strong enough to deny Fillmore the 1852 nomination. By so doing, however, they weakened the southern wing of the party, already on the defensive because northern Whigs appeared hostile to the 1850 compromise. The explosive Kansas controversy originated in 1854, when Democrats repealed the Missouri Compromise restriction against slavery in territory north of 36°30′. In opposing the Kansas-Nebraska Act, Seward hurled down the sectional gauntlet, telling its supporters, "We will engage in competition for the virgin soil of Kansas, and God give victory to the side which is stronger in numbers as it is in right." Anti-Nebraska insurgents, who included a complement of free-soil Democrats, began to supplant the northern Whig party, undermining Seward's hope that Kansas might prove a winning Whig issue. A simultaneous eruption of anti-immigrant sentiment also eroded Whig loyalties. Capitalizing on popular alarm over the recent surge of immigration, the Know Nothings, or American party, suddenly emerged as a powerful political force. Confronted by partisan chaos in 1855, Weed secured Seward's reelection to the Senate by putting together a coalition of antislavery Whigs and anti-Nebraska elements in the politically divided legislature.

A new political party, the Republicans, emerged from the antisouthern and anti-immigrant upheavals. Erstwhile Whigs such as Seward and Weed joined the new party in late 1855. By June 1856 Republicans had become the principal non-Democratic party in the North. As the most renowned antislavery politician in the country, Seward could probably have gained the Republican presidential nomination, even though he was anathema to many Know Nothings because he had long championed fair treatment for immigrants. Fearing that no Republican could win in 1856, Weed persuaded the sorely tempted Seward to wait until 1860.

During the next four years Seward maintained a high level of public visibility. He called for a transatlantic telegraph cable, a transcontinental railroad, river and harbor improvements, free homesteads, a protective tariff, and the expansion of American commerce in the Pacific. His comments on North-South issues attracted particular attention. Insisting that free labor and slavery were in "irrepressible conflict," Seward confidently predicted that free labor would prevent slavery from expanding into the territories, that free labor would soon "invade" the slave states, and that the United States was destined to become "entirely a free-labor nation." Not long afterward, when abolitionist John Brown (1800–1859) attacked the federal armory at Harpers Ferry, Virginia, southerners and Democrats claimed that Brown was Seward's pawn, obliging the New Yorker to distinguish sharply between Brown's violent deeds and his own hope for voluntary, peaceful emancipation.

Although Seward was widely considered a radical, some Republicans thought him an unprincipled opportunist, whose only compass was his presidential ambition. They frowned on his fraternizing across sectional and party lines (he was on sociable terms with Jefferson Davis and Varina Howell Davis; he and Stephen A. Douglas worked together during the concluding stages of the Kansas controversy). Seward's critics also feared that Weed's unsavory dealings might undercut Republican promises to sweep clean the scandal-plagued presidency of Democrat James Buchanan. Seward remained, however, the odds-on favorite for the 1860 Republican nomination, and he was received as a soon-to-be head of state during a long European tour in 1859.

Republican strategies needed a candidate in 1860 who could carry key states in the lower North (N.J., Pa., Ind., and Ill.), which the party had lost in 1856. Seward's higher law and irrepressible conflict phrasemaking, together with his views about immigrant rights, raised doubts about his ability to win over conservative ex-Whigs and former Know Nothings. At the Republican National Convention in Chicago in June 1860, Abraham Lincoln's managers exploited Seward's weaknesses, and on the third ballot Lincoln was nominated, ending Seward's long quest. Notwithstanding his disappointment, Seward loyally campaigned for Lincoln. He characterized the election as a referendum on the proslavery policies of the Democratic party and a national opportunity to affirm the advantages of free labor.

Lincoln's election triggered a grave crisis, as secessionists gained the upper hand in seven deep South states. Most Republicans dismissed secession as a bluff, but Seward judged otherwise. Although displaced as party leader by Lincoln and deeply distrusted in the South, Seward recognized the imminent peril and threw himself into the struggle to save the Union.

He reached out to beleaguered Unionists in the upper South, hoping to quarantine secession and to set in motion a restoration of the Union. He left to Weed the unpleasant task of persuading Republicans to offer concessions. Weed proposed that Republicans allow southerners a theoretical but otherwise barren right to take slaves to territory south of 36° 30′, the old Missouri Compromise line. This idea was entirely at variance with the view that Seward had championed for a dozen years and was received coldly by Lincoln and most Republicans. Weed also advised Lincoln to include in his cabinet at least two Unionists from the upper South who had no previous ties to the Republican party. Lincoln agreed that Weed could offer a portfolio to North Carolina congressman John A. Gilmer, but Gilmer proved unwilling to accept the overture.

Having already received from Lincoln an offer to serve as secretary of state, Seward found himself regarded as a spokesman for the incoming administration. As such, he could not support a symbolic concession on the territorial issue that upper South Unionists urgently sought. Had Seward been left to his own devices, he might well have done so. He confidently expected slavery to decline, so long as the Union was preserved and war avoided. He did persuade Lincoln to omit from his inaugural address on 4 March 1861 an apparent threat to use armed force, and he also inspired the new president's eloquent peroration, telling southerners, "We are not enemies, but friends. We must not be enemies."

During the six crucial weeks between the inauguration and mid-April, decisions of unlimited magnitude had to be made. Seven deep South states had formed an independent government, the Confederate States of America, but eight slave states remained in the Union. Seward hoped the Confederacy would self-destruct if peace could be preserved and Unionists maintained control in the upper South. To prevent any armed clash, southern Unionists such as Gilmer and Virginia's George W. Summers urged Seward to remove federal troops from Fort Sumter, a key Union-controlled outpost in the harbor of Charleston, South Carolina. Seward and a majority of the cabinet voted to relinquish the fort, and Seward thought Lincoln would soon do so. Assuming that he would be the real power in the administration, Seward promised Virginia Unionists that Sumter would be abandoned. He relayed similar reassurances to three Confederate commissioners in Washington, who had unsuccessfully sought an official interview. Lincoln worried, however, that a withdrawal from Sumter would split the Republican party and create the impression that he had acquiesced in secession. While Seward insisted that peaceful reunion remained possible, Lincoln feared that his options had narrowed to peaceful separation or war, and he decided tentatively to reprovision Sumter.

On 1 April 1861 Seward presented to Lincoln a document entitled "Some Thoughts for the President's Consideration." The "Thoughts," revealed for the first time by Lincoln's biographers in 1890, have since been the best-known and most notorious document

Seward ever wrote. By attempting to hold Sumter, Seward contended, the administration would look as if it sought narrow partisan advantage, but by yielding Sumter Lincoln could show that he put national interests ahead of party interests. Seward instead proposed that a naval expedition reinforce Fort Pickens, offshore from Pensacola, Florida, thereby demonstrating that the federal government had not acquiesced in Confederate independence. Moreover, Seward urged Lincoln to "rouse a vigorous continental spirit of independence" by threatening war against Spain and France for meddling in the Caribbean and Mexico. Long regarded as a muddleheaded proposal to instigate foreign war just as the United States stood on the verge of civil war, Seward's "Thoughts" were instead a strategy to maintain the peace both at home and abroad. Seward wanted a foreign crisis, not a foreign war; his principal objective remained peaceful reunion. A century of misinterpretation regarding his 1 April memorandum has obscured what Frederic Bancroft justly considered "the hour of Seward's supreme greatness"—his months-long struggle to avert the greatest bloodbath in American history (Bancroft, vol. 2, p. 37).

Lincoln rejected Seward's advice, which was echoed by a secret last-minute emissary from the Virginia Convention, John B. Baldwin. The attempt to resupply Sumter led to the outbreak of hostilities. Following the bombardment and surrender of the fort, Lincoln issued on 15 April a proclamation for 75,000 troops to reestablish federal authority in the deep South. In response Virginia, North Carolina, Tennessee, and Arkansas seceded.

Although selected as secretary of state for reasons that had more to do with domestic than foreign policy, Seward was well prepared for the office. He had traveled extensively overseas and had given substantial thought to the position of the United States in the world. He judged his country uniquely well positioned to promote the spread of liberal institutions. Regarding international commerce as the key to progress, Seward advocated global telegraphic communications and a single standard of world coinage. He also hoped to see a canal constructed through the Isthmus of Panama, and he sought island bases for the United States in the Caribbean and the Pacific. His most famous triumph, the purchase of Alaska from Russia in 1867, reflected both his wish to enlarge American commerce in the Pacific and his hope that Canada might yet choose to join the United States.

With the outbreak of war, the most pressing problem facing Seward was the conduct of relations with Great Britain and, secondarily, France. The two European powers had to be treated with sufficient firmness to dissuade them from aiding the Confederacy. At the same time, however, Seward dared not provoke a direct confrontation. He handled this challenge deftly. Seward sowed suspicions among the diplomatic community that he was potentially reckless, but privately he counseled caution. In late 1861, when Union naval commander Charles Wilkes seized Confederate diplomats James M. Mason and John Slidell from a British ship, the *Trent*, the British suspected that Seward wanted war. Seward wanted no such thing, and he persuaded Lincoln to defuse the *Trent* crisis by releasing Mason and Slidell. To assuage northern public opinion, Seward issued a clever vindication of Wilkes's action. Seward also worked adroitly to prevent the European powers from recognizing the Confederacy or offering to mediate the conflict between North and South. Both Britain and France seriously contemplated mediation in 1862, when the war appeared stalemated and cotton shortages became severe. British support for mediation cooled after Lincoln enlarged Union war aims to include emancipation and as alternate cotton supplies increased. France, hoping for division of the Union, remained interested in mediation. The impetuous Napoleon III installed a puppet, Maximilian, on the Mexican throne in 1864. Seward waited until the end of American hostilities before quietly pressuring Louis Napoleon to abandon his New World ambitions. Seward also acted firmly in 1863 to block private British shipbuilders from outfitting the Confederates with powerful warships: he successfully demanded that the British government prevent the so-called Laird rams from leaving port.

Seward's wartime responsibilities extended beyond foreign policy, although there is little substance to the accusation that he presided over military arrests of antiadministration civilians. He grew to admire Lincoln, and by 1862 Seward was the one cabinet member whom the president consulted freely on a broad range of political and military matters. Their rapport sparked jealousy and resentment, most particularly during the so-called cabinet crisis of December 1862, when Seward's enemies unsuccessfully attempted to have him removed. Already suspect because of his role in the secession crisis, Seward further estranged radicals with his lukewarm attitude regarding emancipation. Long hopeful that slaveholders would voluntarily renounce slavery, he opposed making emancipation an explicit Union war aim. He grudgingly accepted Lincoln's Emancipation Proclamation only because he recognized the need to recruit black soldiers. As late as February 1865, at the Hampton Roads Conference where Lincoln and Seward met with three Confederate commissioners, the secretary of state hinted that emancipation might be delayed or slaveholders compensated in exchange for reunion.

When the war ended, Seward favored a lenient Reconstruction policy. He did support the Thirteenth Amendment, abolishing slavery. Indeed, he and Weed provided essential secret lobbying to secure the amendment's approval by Congress. Seward believed, however, that the welfare of the freedmen would be better secured by the goodwill of former slaveholders and ex-Confederates than by enacting additional legal safeguards. Reflecting the ascendant scientific racism of his age, Seward believed white direction was needed to make black labor productive. He also favored rapid readmission of southern states to the Union. His position placed him increasingly at odds with Republicans in Congress, as did his misgivings about the Fourteenth Amendment, which disqualified many former Confederates from holding office and promised to reduce the representation of southern states that did not allow blacks to vote.

Seward enjoyed a far less comfortable and influential relationship with President Andrew Johnson than he had with Lincoln. Johnson was rigid and ultimately self-destructive. Under circumstances in which Lincoln would have worked to accommodate moderate Republicans, Johnson quite blindly spurned any compromise. Remaining in office until the end of Johnson's disastrous term, Seward was held hostage by circumstances beyond his control. Although unable to acquire Hawaii or island outposts in the Caribbean, Seward demonstrated his political resourcefulness by winning approval for the Alaska purchase from a Congress that soon impeached Johnson.

Although Seward and John Quincy Adams are generally considered the two greatest secretaries of state in American history, Seward's latter years in the office were personally harrowing. He was badly injured in a carriage accident in early April 1865. Soon afterward, on the same night that John Wilkes Booth assassinated Lincoln, the bedridden Seward and his son Frederick Seward, who served his father as assistant secretary of state, were each gravely wounded by a knife-wielding Lewis Powell, another of the conspirators. Two months later Seward's wife died, and their only daughter, Fanny, his favorite child, died a year later. Seward commented ruefully in 1867 or 1868, "I have always felt that Providence dealt hardly with me in not letting me die with Mr. Lincoln. My work was done, and I think I deserved some of the reward of dying there" (F. W. Seward, *Seward at Washington*, vol. 2, p. 538).

After his retirement, Seward traveled compulsively, including a spectacular round-the-world jaunt with his adopted daughter, Olive Risley Seward. He started but failed to complete his autobiography. Increasingly paralyzed, he died at his home in Auburn, New York.

Seward's biographers have repeatedly noted that he exhibited two contrasting political tendencies. "John Quincy Adams Seward" championed righteous causes—education, prison reform, and fair treatment for immigrants. He challenged forthrightly the caste system, which enslaved most black Americans and deemed all unworthy of equal citizenship. Seward shared his patron's confidence that economic development and international commerce would raise the United States to the first rank among nations and assure the triumph of liberal nationalism (Bancroft, vol. 1, pp. 200–201). He had "a vision of the good society that transcended any desire for power or place" (Van Deusen, *Seward*, p. 198). On the other hand, "Thurlow Weed Seward" understood best the art of the possible. This Seward, who cut deals over cigars and wine, was a hard-eyed political realist who knew when to "drop the theoretical for the practical" (Bancroft, vol. 2, p. 526). Each Seward was, of course, a caricature, and both tendencies, at once symbiotic and contradictory, existed in tandem. Boldly confident that the passage of time would bring about both the triumph of free labor and the fulfillment of America's national destiny, Seward preferred tactical flexibility in dealing with southern slaveholders and international rivals. He believed that his ends could be secured by peaceful means.

Seward and Lincoln were the two most important leaders spawned by the intersection of antebellum idealism and partisan politics. Lincoln, of course, will always overshadow Seward. Before 1860, however, Seward eclipsed Lincoln. Seward was governor of New York while Lincoln toiled in the Illinois legislature; Seward was the most prominent antislavery leader in the U.S. Senate when Lincoln's national stature, such as it was, resulted from a strong but losing Senate race. The war that Seward did his utmost to prevent bound together the oddly juxtaposed duo. At once fulfilling the most explosive promise of the liberal reform agenda and at the same time shattering hopes that moral suasion and enlightened amelioration could propel the engines of political change, war taught Lincoln and Seward that all ultimately depended on having stronger, more durable armies. The would-be "peacemaker," memorably celebrated during the secession crisis by the Quaker poet John Greenleaf Whittier, had to protect from foreign interference a Union war effort that employed unlimited violence to destroy the slave system. Perhaps fittingly, Seward remained ambivalent about his legacy.

• The Seward papers are housed at the University of Rochester Library. Glyndon G. Van Deusen, *William Henry Seward* (1967), is the only modern biography based on deep familiarity with the Seward papers. Some aspects of Seward's political career are explained more fully in Frederic Bancroft, *The Life of William H. Seward* (2 vols., 1899–1900). Frederick W. Seward, *Seward at Washington* (2 vols., 1891), is a memoir written by Seward's son that incorporates considerable primary material. See also Frederick W. Seward, *Reminiscences of a War-Time Statesman and Diplomat, 1830–1915* (1916). William H. Seward, *William H. Seward: An Autobiography from 1801 to 1834* (1891), covers only through 1834 and includes additional material on 1834–1846 written by Frederick Seward. Many of Seward's public papers may be found in George E. Baker, *The Works of William H. Seward* (5 vols., 1884). For a readable brief overview of Seward's life, see John M. Taylor, *William H. Seward* (1991). An incisive essay on Seward's thought may be found in Major L. Wilson, *Space, Time, and Freedom: The Quest for Nationality and the Irrepressible Conflict* (1974).

William E. Gienapp, *The Origins of the Republican Party, 1852–1856* (1987), is definitive on Seward's course during the key years of party realignment. Van Deusen's parallel biography, *Thurlow Weed: Wizard of the Lobby* (1947), necessarily has much to say about Seward. On Seward's course during the secession crisis see David M. Potter, *Lincoln and His Party in the Secession Crisis* (1942); Kenneth M. Stamp, *And the War Came: The North and the Secession Crisis, 1860–61* (1950); Richard N. Current, *Lincoln and the First Shot* (1963); and Daniel W. Crofts, *Reluctant Confederates: Upper South Unionists in the Secession Crisis* (1989).

Burton J. Hendrick, *Lincoln's War Cabinet* (1946), and Mark E. Neely, Jr., *The Fate of Liberty: Abraham Lincoln and*

Civil Liberties (1991), offer perspective on Seward's wartime career. On wartime foreign policy issues see Norman B. Ferris, *Desperate Diplomacy: William H. Seward's Foreign Policy, 1861* (1976) and *The Trent Affair* (1977); Brian Jenkins, *Britain and the War for the Union* (2 vols., 1974–1980); Gordon H. Warren, *Fountain of Discontent: The Trent Affair and Freedom of the Seas* (1981); Howard Jones, *Union in Peril: The Crisis over British Intervention in the Civil War* (1992); Lynn M. Case and Warren F. Spencer, *The United States and France: Civil War Diplomacy* (1970); and David P. Crooks, *The North, the South, and the Powers, 1861–1865* (1974). Ernest N. Paolino, *The Foundations of the American Empire: William H. Seward and U.S. Foreign Policy* (1974), emphasizes Seward's efforts to promote American commerce, as does Walter A. McDougall's imaginative epic, *Let the Sea Make a Noise: A History of the North Pacific from Magellan to MacArthur* (1993).

The only study of Reconstruction politics to make extensive use of the Seward papers is LaWanda Cox and John H. Cox, *Politics, Principle, and Prejudice, 1865–1866: Dilemma of Reconstruction America* (1963). Olive Risley Seward, ed., *William H. Seward's Travels around the World* (1873), became a posthumous bestseller. An obituary by Charles Francis Adams is *The Life, Character and Services of William H. Seward* (1873).

DANIEL W. CROFTS

SEWELL, Frank (24 Sept. 1837–17 Dec. 1915), college president and clergyman, was born in Bath, Maine, the son of William Dunning Sewell, a shipbuilder and farmer, and Rachael Allen Trufant. As a young man, he developed artistic skill and sensitivity in music, painting, and literature that characterized his later ministry. He graduated first in his class from nearby Bowdoin College in 1858, after which he toured Europe for three years, studying art and theology in Italy, Germany, and France.

The Sewell family was active in the Church of the New Jerusalem (often called the New Church, or Swedenborgian church), which views itself inaugurating a new era of Christianity. The New Church developed out of the theological writings of Emanuel Swedenborg, the eighteenth-century Swedish nobleman, scientist, philosopher, and religious visionary. In his numerous theological writings, Swedenborg described the inner meaning of the Bible, the spiritual realms of heaven and hell, and the heavenly origins of a universal "new church." Sewell was licensed to the ministry in the Church of the New Jerusalem in 1862 on his return from Europe and ordained a year later. His first parish was Glendale, Ohio, north of Cincinnati, where he served from 1863 to 1870.

While attending a New Church gathering in Philadelphia, Pennsylvania, Sewell met Thedia Redelia Gilchrist, whom he married in October 1869. He took an active interest in the liberal education of their five daughters, including their spiritual development through music, art, play, home festivals, and worship.

From Glendale, Sewell was called in 1870 to be president of Urbana University in Ohio. At the same time he also became pastor of the Urbana New Church. He took on the formidable challenges of building the struggling school into a uniquely New Church college, which he guided with a firm hand for the next sixteen years. He modeled the curriculum after preparatory schools in England, his study at Bowdoin, and European universities; he also introduced the study of Swedenborg's scientific, philosophical, and theological works. In addition, he rebuilt a qualified faculty and increased enrollment of New Church students. Although he was a creative and energetic administrator, the school was constantly short of the funds it needed to operate. Differences with the trustees over funding and his determined pedagogical style led to his resignation in 1886.

Following a brief pastorate in Glasgow, Scotland, and travel with his wife and daughters in Europe, Sewell accepted the pastorate of the Washington, D.C., Swedenborgian society in 1889. Unfortunately, a fire destroyed the church building shortly after his appointment. Sewell, who had also studied church architecture, took an active interest in the design of a new building. While still in Europe he sent the building committee sketches for an Italian Romanesque edifice that in his view integrated New Church doctrine with the functions of the building. The committee, however, preferred an English Gothic design; Sewell's influence, however, may be seen in the plan for the stained glass windows and other refinements. The National Church of the Holy City was dedicated in 1896 and stands at 1611 Sixteenth Street, Northwest, in Washington.

Through his preaching, teaching, and writing Sewell's influence spread throughout Washington. A pastor of intellectual and philosophical vigor, he took an active interest in the artistic and literary affairs of the city. He was a member of the Cosmos Club, the Washington Choral Society, the Sophocles Club (dedicated to reading Greek dramas), the Philosophical Society, and the American Federation of the Arts.

Until his death in Washington, Sewell remained busy in denominational leadership, serving on various boards and committees, including the New Church Board of Publications (1883–1902) and Board of the New Church Theological School (1877). His literary and linguistic skills, as well as his keen interest in music and liturgy, gave him a prominent role in the preparation of the Swedenborgian *Book of Worship* (1913). He had long believed that the New Church should have a formal liturgy, and he based it in part on Anglican services.

Sewell was also the founding president of the Swedenborg Scientific Association (1898), an organization devoted to bringing Swedenborg's philosophical and scientific works to a wider audience. Annually reelected its president, he took an active interest in translating these works from Latin. In addition, he was the first president of the Evidence Society (1895), which sought to demonstrate Swedenborg's influences in literary circles and correct misconceptions about his life and teachings.

Sewell was the author of several books, including *The New Ethics* (1881), *Is a New Church Possible?* (1884), *The New Metaphysics* (1888), and *Swedenborg and Modern Idealism* (1902). This latter work explored philosophical trends from Kant to pragmatism from a Swedenborgian perspective.

• Sewell's papers have not been preserved. Besides works noted above, his publications include the *New Churchman's Prayer Book and Hymnal* (1867), translations of Swedenborg's *Rational Psychology* (1887) and *The Worship and Love of God* (1914), *Swedenborg and the 'Sapienta Angelica'* (1912), and various essays in early issues of the *New Philosophy*, journal of the Swedenborg Scientific Association. His life has been sketched by a daughter, Alice Archer Sewell James, in a series of articles: "Frank Sewell as a Young Man," *New Church Review* 23 (Jan. 1921): 29–51; "Frank Sewell at Bowdoin," *New Church Review* (Apr. 1921): 284–306; and "Frank Sewell's Student Life in Italy," *New Church Review* (Apr. 1923): 188–209. See also "Biographical Glimpses of Frank Sewell" (unpublished ms., n.d.), Henry James, Sr., File, General Convention Archives, Swedenborg School of Religion. Sewell's contributions to the Swedenborgian church are covered in Lewis F. Hite, "Mr. Sewell's Work for the Church," *New Church Review* (Apr. 1916): 280–86; "In Memoriam," *New-Church Messenger*, 19 Jan. 1919, pp. 41–56; and Marguerite Beck Block, *The New Church in the New World* (1932; rev. ed., 1984). His Urbana presidency is surveyed in Francis P. Weisenburger, *A Brief History of Urbana University* (1950?). A complete description of the National New Church and Sewell's work as pastor is in Sue A. Kohler and Jeffrey R. Carson, *Sixteenth Street Architecture*, vol. 1 (1978), pp. 197–226.

DAVID B. ELLER

SEWELL, Joe (9 Oct. 1898–6 Mar. 1990), baseball player, was born Joseph Wheeler Sewell near Titus, Alabama, the son of J. Wesley Sewell, a physician and farmer, and Susan Hannon. As a boy, Sewell worked on the family farm and assisted his father in his medical practice; he aspired to be a doctor. After completing elementary school in Titus, he commuted by horseback to Wetumpka High School and graduated in 1916. An avid baseball player, he practiced year-round with his younger brother, James "Luke" Sewell, and he honed his batting reflexes by constantly swinging a broom handle at various objects. In 1916 Sewell and his brother enrolled as premedical students at the University of Alabama, where both became star athletes. Sewell lettered in three varsity sports, but he concentrated most on baseball and played second base for Alabama during four championship seasons. After brief service in the U.S. Army in 1918, he returned to the university, and the following summer, after playing semipro baseball with Birmingham of the Tennessee Coal and Iron League, he tried out with the professional New Orleans Pelicans of the Southern League.

In 1920, after helping the University of Alabama team win the Southern Conference championship, Sewell began his professional career with New Orleans. The rookie shortstop played in 92 games and batted .289 on a team that won the Southern League title. He was playing with the Pelicans when Ray Chapman, the shortstop for the Cleveland Indians, died after being struck on the head by a pitched ball. Sewell was chosen to replace Chapman, who had been his role model as a player, and he made his major league debut in September.

In twenty-two games with the Indians, Sewell batted .329 and helped Cleveland win the American League pennant by two games. Given special dispensation by the league to play in the World Series, Sewell appeared in every game at shortstop as the Indians defeated the Brooklyn Robins. For his contributions, his Cleveland teammates voted him a winning player's share of the World Series receipts ($3,900).

Following his whirlwind 1920 rise from amateur player to professional major leaguer, Sewell in 1921 completed his B.S. degree requirements and rejoined the Indians. That season he played in every game and batted .318. In December he married Willie Veal; they had three children.

During his eleven seasons with Cleveland, Sewell excelled as a batter and fielder. The 5'6½" Sewell batted left-handed and hit above .300 nine times, batting as high as .336 in 1925. He attributed his bat control to keen eyesight, saying, "All through my career in baseball I could see the ball leave my bat." Indeed, no player since Willie Keeler was harder to strike out than Sewell; in 7,132 official major league at bats he struck out only 114 times. In 1925, one of his best years, he averaged only one strikeout for every 170 plate appearances. Slight in physical stature, he still used a forty-ounce bat—unusually heavy by modern-day standards. As a shortstop, he three times led the league in fielding percentage and four times in either assists or putouts. He was a durable player as well; from 1922 to 1930 he played in 1,155 consecutive games, including 1,103 at shortstop.

By 1929 Sewell had been moved to third base. After batting .289 in 1930, he was sold to the New York Yankees, where he batted .302 the following year and .272 for the 1932 pennant-winning team. Playing in his second World Series, Sewell batted .333 as the Yankees defeated the Chicago Cubs in four games. After the 1933 season the 35-year-old Sewell ended his major league career. During fourteen seasons he compiled a .312 batting average with 2,226 hits; in 1977 he was voted into the Baseball Hall of Fame.

Two of Sewell's brothers also played major league baseball, Tommy, who appeared in one game with the Chicago Cubs, and Luke, who was Sewell's teammate at Cleveland during ten seasons. A reliable catcher, Luke Sewell played in the majors for twenty years and was a major league manager for ten.

After retiring from active play, Sewell coached for the Yankees in 1934 and 1935 and helped groom Red Rolfe as his replacement at third base. During 1936–1951 he operated a hardware store in Tuscaloosa, Alabama. From 1952 until 1962 he scouted for the Cleveland Indians and in 1963 for the New York Mets. From 1964 through 1968 he coached at the University of Alabama and was named Southeastern Conference coach of the year when his 1968 team won the championship. During these years Sewell also owned a hardware store and did public relations work for a dairy company. He died in Mobile, Alabama.

• The National Baseball Library at Cooperstown, N.Y., has a newspaper clipping file on Sewell's career. His 1920 major league debut is covered in Mike Sowell, *The Pitch That Killed* (1989). For his Cleveland career, see Franklin Lewis, *The Cleveland Indians* (1949), and Morris Eckhouse, *Day by Day in Cleveland Indians History* (1983); for his years with the Yankees, see Frank Graham, *The New York Yankees* (1943); for background on the era, see David Q. Voigt, *American Baseball*, vol. 2 (1983). A lengthy biographical sketch based on interviews is Eugene Murdock, "Joe and Luke: The Sewell Story," in *Baseball History: An Annual of Original Baseball Research*, ed. Peter Levine (1989). Articles on Sewell's accomplishments as a player include F. C. Lane, "The Man Who Never Strikes Out!" *Baseball Magazine*, Feb. 1927; John J. Ward, "Joe Sewell—Steady and Dependable," *Baseball Magazine*, Nov. 1932; and L. Robert Davids, "Sewell Was a Real Fox at the Plate," *Baseball Research Journal* 5 (1976). Sewell's record as a player is in John Thorn and Pete Palmer, eds., *Total Baseball*, 3d ed. (1993); his playing record in two World Series is in Richard Cohen et al., eds., *The World Series* (1976). An obituary is in the *New York Times*, 8 Mar. 1990.

DAVID Q. VOIGT

SEXTON, Anne Gray Harvey (9 Nov. 1928–4 Oct. 1974), poet and playwright, was born in Newton, Massachusetts, the daughter of Ralph Harvey, a successful woolen manufacturer, and Mary Gray Staples. Anne was raised in comfortable middle-class circumstances in Weston, Massachusetts, and at the summer compound on Squirrel Island in Maine, but she was never at ease with the life prescribed for her. Her father was an alcoholic, and her mother's literary aspirations had been frustrated by family life. Anne took refuge from her dysfunctional family in her close relationship with "Nana" (Anna Dingley), her maiden great-aunt who lived with the family during Anne's adolescence. Sexton's biographer, Diane Middlebrook, recounts possible sexual abuse by Anne's parents during her childhood; at the very least, Anne felt that her parents were hostile to her and feared that they might abandon her. Her aunt's later breakdown and hospitalization also traumatized her.

Anne disliked school. Her inability to concentrate and occasional disobedience prompted teachers to urge her parents to seek counseling for her—advice her parents did not take. In 1945 they sent her to Rogers Hall, a boarding school in Lowell, Massachusetts, where she began to write poetry and to act. After graduation she briefly attended what she called a "finishing" school. Sexton's beauty and sense of daring attracted many men, and at nineteen she eloped with Alfred "Kayo" Sexton II, even though she was engaged to someone else at the time. Then followed years of living as college student newlyweds, sometimes with their parents. Later, during Kayo's service in Korea, Anne became a fashion model. Her infidelities during her husband's absence led to her entering therapy. In 1953 Anne gave birth to a daughter, and Kayo took a job as a traveling salesman in Anne's father's business.

Depressed after the death of her beloved Nana in 1954 and the birth of her second daughter in 1955,

Sexton went back into therapy. Her depression worsened, however, and during times when her husband was gone, she occasionally abused the children. Several attempts at suicide led to intermittent institutionalization, of which her parents disapproved. During these years, Sexton's therapist encouraged her to write.

In 1957 Sexton joined several Boston writing groups, and she came to know such writers as Maxine Kumin, Robert Lowell, George Starbuck, and Sylvia Plath. Her poetry became central to her life, and she mastered formal techniques that gained her wide attention. In 1960 *To Bedlam and Part Way Back* was published to good reviews. Such poems as "You, Doctor Martin," "The Bells," and "The Double Image" were often anthologized. Like such other so-called confessional poets as W. D. Snodgrass and Robert Lowell, Sexton was able to convince her readers that her poems echoed her life; not only was her poetry technically excellent, but it was meaningful to the midcentury readers who lived daily with similar kinds of fear and angst.

In 1959 Sexton unexpectedly lost both of her parents, and the memory of her difficult relationships with them—so abruptly ended—led to further breakdowns. Poetry seemed the only route to stability, though at times the friendships she made through her art, which led to sexual affairs, also were unsettling. Her marriage was torn by discord and physical abuse as her husband saw his formerly dependent wife become a celebrity.

In 1962 Sexton published *All My Pretty Ones*. So popular was her poetry in England that an edition of *Selected Poems* was published there as a Poetry Book Selection in 1964. In 1967 Sexton received the Pulitzer Prize for poetry for *Live or Die* (1966), capping her accumulation of honors such as the Frost Fellowship to the Bread Loaf Writers' Conference (1959), the Radcliffe Institute Fellowship (1961), the Levinson Prize (1962), the American Academy of Arts and Letters traveling fellowship (1963), the Shelley Memorial Prize (1967), and an invitation to give the Morris Gray reading at Harvard. To follow were a Guggenheim Fellowship, Ford Foundation grants, honorary degrees, professorships at Colgate University and Boston University, and other distinctions.

Sexton's reputation as poet peaked with the publication of *Love Poems* (1969), an off-Broadway production of her play *Mercy Street* (1969), and the publication of prose poems in *Transformations* (1972). Clearly her most feminist work, the pieces in *Transformations* spoke to a different kind of reader. The Sexton voice was now less confessional and more critical of cultural practices, more inclined to look outside the poet's persona for material. In 1963 Sexton had traveled in Europe, and in 1966 she and Kayo had gone on an African safari. In 1970 she had helped him start a business of his own after he broke associations with her father's former company. Contrary to her seemingly confident public manner, however, Sexton was heavily dependent on therapists, medications, close friends—particularly Maxine Kumin and, later, Lois Ames—and lovers. Continual depressive bouts, unexpected trance states, and comparatively frequent suicide attempts kept her family and friends watchful and unnerved. Finally, in 1973, Sexton told Kayo she wanted a divorce, and from that time on a noticeable decline in her health and stability occurred as loneliness, alcoholism, and depression took their toll.

Estranged from many of her former friends, Sexton became difficult for her maturing daughters to deal with. Aware that many of her readers did not like the religious poetry that she had recently begun writing with her more personal themes, Sexton became nervous about her poetry. Readings had always terrified her, but now she employed a rock group to back up her performances. She forced herself to be an entertainer, while her poems grew more and more privately sacral. In 1972 she published *The Book of Folly* and, in 1974, the ominously titled *The Death Notebooks*. Later that year, she completed *The Awful Rowing toward God*, published posthumously in 1975. Divorced and living by herself, Sexton was lonely and seemed to be searching for compassion through love affairs. She continued to be in psychotherapy, from which she evidently gained little solace. In October 1974, after having lunched with Maxine Kumin, Sexton asphyxiated herself with carbon monoxide in her garage in Boston.

Other posthumous collections of her poems include *45 Mercy Street* (1976) and *Words for Dr. Y: Uncollected Poems with Three Stories* (1978), both edited by Linda Gray Sexton. The publication of Sexton's work culminated in *The Complete Poems* in 1981. Sexton also wrote important essays about poetry and made insightful comments in her many interviews. She understood the fictive impulse, the way the writer uses both fact and the imagination in creation; and, like Wallace Stevens, she saw her art as the "supreme fiction," the writer's finest accomplishment. Much of what Sexton wrote was in no way autobiographical, despite the sense of reality it had, and thus criticisms of her writing as "confessional" are misleading. She used her knowledge of the human condition—often painful, but sometimes joyous—to create poems readers could share. Her incisive metaphors, the unexpected rhythms of her verse, and her ability to grasp a range of meaning in precise words have secured Sexton's good reputation. Though comparatively short, her writing career was successful, as was her art.

• Anne Sexton's papers are housed at the Harry Ransom Humanities Research Center, University of Texas, Austin. The authorized biography is Diane Wood Middlebrook, *Anne Sexton: A Biography* (1991), controversial in part because of the information supplied by Sexton's first therapist. The major critical study is Diana Hume George, *Oedipus Anne: The Poetry of Anne Sexton* (1987). Collections of criticism by various critics are Diana Hume George, *Sexton: Selected Criticism* (1988); J. D. McClatchy, *Anne Sexton: The Artist and Her Critics* (1978); Frances Bixler, *Original Essays on the Poetry of Anne Sexton* (1988); Steven E. Colburn, *Anne Sexton: Telling the Tale* (1988); and Linda Wagner-Martin, *Critical Essays on Anne Sexton* (1989).

Cameron Northouse and Thomas P. Walsh published *Sylvia Plath and Anne Sexton: A Reference Guide* (1974), but no complete bibliography exists. Diane Wood Middlebrook and Diane Hume George coedited *Selected Poems of Anne Sexton* (1988), and Linda Gray Sexton and Lois Ames edited *Anne Sexton: A Self-Portrait in Letters* (1977). Steven E. Colburn edited *No Evil Star: Selected Essays, Interviews and Prose* (1985), a collection of Sexton's previously published prose.

LINDA WAGNER-MARTIN

SEYBERT, Henry (23 Dec. 1801–3 Mar. 1883), scientist and philanthropist, was born in Philadelphia, Pennsylvania, the son of Adam Seybert, a scientist, apothecary, and politician, and Maria Sarah Pepper. Seybert studied chemistry, geology, and mineralogy at the École des Mines in Paris from 1819 to 1821; his scientific education was paid for by his father who had, at an earlier period, been one of Philadelphia's most prominent scientists, a member of the Chemical Society of Philadelphia and the American Philosophical Society, and a candidate for the chair of chemistry at the University of Pennsylvania. After returning to Philadelphia, Seybert began a series of chemical analyses of minerals and thus transmitted to the United States this method of classification (as opposed to the classification of minerals by external characteristics or by crystal structure).

Since 1800 mineralogy had become popular among the scientific clerisy of the United States; it had been taught at various times at the leading colleges, and in New York the scientific community supported the American Mineralogical Society and Archibald Bruce's *American Mineralogical Journal*, both of which, however, survived for only a few years. Seybert's first paper on mineralogy, on the presence of fluorine in chondrodite, appeared in the *American Journal of Science and Arts* in 1823 and secured his election to the American Philosophical Society on 16 January 1824. In March 1824, at a meeting of the society, he read an account of the discovery of glucinium in crystals of chrysoberyl; this analysis appeared in the *Transactions of the American Philosophical Society* in 1825. During the same period, Seybert analyzed, among others, tourmalines, fluosilicate of magnesia, manganesian garnet, tabular spar, pyroxene, and colophonite and in 1830 published an analysis of meteoric rock found in Tennessee.

His father's death in 1825 and his consequent inheritance of $300,000 effectively ended Seybert's scientific research. For the remainder of his life he divided his time between Europe and the United States, living for extended periods in Paris, studying science and attending lectures on subjects such as history and chemistry. His principal concern, however, was philanthropy: in Philadelphia, Seybert financed temperance concerns, the manufacture in 1876 of a new bell for Independence Hall, and investigations into the composition of bread sold in the city. He contributed mineral specimens, chemical apparatus, and books to the Academy of Natural Sciences of Philadelphia. His interest in spiritualism and the afterlife resulted in his donation of $60,000 in railroad bonds to the University of Pennsylvania to establish the Adam Seybert Chair of Moral and Intellectual Philosophy on condition that the incumbent investigate "all systems of morals, religion or philosophy which assume to represent the Truth, and particularly of modern Spiritualism." Seybert died in Philadelphia after a long illness. He had never married. His will contained 160 specific bequests; the remainder was left to the city of Philadelphia to establish an institution for the care and education of abandoned children, a bequest that resulted in the establishment in 1914 of the Adam and Maria Sarah Seybert Institution for Poor Boys and Girls.

• More than one hundred letters from Henry Seybert are in the Adam and Henry Seybert Correspondence in the Edgar Fahs Smith Collection at the University of Pennsylvania; these letters, written from Paris from 1825 to 1837 and 1847 to 1856, concern cultural life, commerce, and medicine in Europe and contain comments on political events in Philadelphia. Seybert's most significant contributions to mineralogy are "On the Discovery of Fluoric Acid in the Chondrodite," *American Journal of Science and Arts* 6 (1823): 356–61, "Analyses of the Chrysoberyls from Haddam and Brazil," *Transactions of the American Philosophical Society*, n.s., 2 (1825): 116–23, and "Tennessee Meteorite," *American Journal of Science and Arts* 17 (1830): 326–28. Edgar Fahs Smith, *Chemistry in Old Philadelphia* (1919), includes an informed analysis of Seybert's contribution to mineralogy. John C. Greene, "The Development of Mineralogy in Philadelphia, 1780–1820," *Proceedings of the American Philosophical Society* 113 (1969): 283–95, is indispensable for understanding the local context for Seybert's scientific research. A florid biography is in Moncure Robinson, "Obituary Notice of Henry Seybert," *Proceedings of the American Philosophical Society* 21 (May 1883–Dec. 1884): 241–63; a short but useful obituary is in the *American Journal of Science*, 3d. ser., no. 25 (1883): 320.

SIMON BAATZ

SEYBERT, John (17 July 1791–4 Jan. 1860), first constitutional bishop of the Evangelical Association of North America, was born near Manheim, Pennsylvania, the son of Susan Kreuzer and Henry Seybert, farmers. His father had been conscripted to serve as a Hessian soldier with the forces of British king George III during the revolutionary war. Although his parents enrolled him in a catechism class in the Lutheran church at the age of twelve, he confessed in his journal that this in no way tempered his godless, licentious lifestyle and that they wisely withdrew him from the class rather than permit him to be confirmed as an ungodly youth. While enmeshed in an irreligious culture, Seybert was drawn to a "protracted meeting" of the "Albright people" (*Albrechts Leute*) and there in 1810 fell under the deep penitential conviction that was described by the term *Bußkampf*, or the "penitential struggle," by the German Pietists.

The Albright people, officially known as the Evangelical Association (*die Evangelische Gemeinschaft*), had been organized in 1803 by the followers of Jacob Albright, a Pennsylvania-born lay evangelist who sought to extend the Methodist revival to the German population of the Middle States. He had relied on the doctrine of John Wesley and on Methodist patterns of organization, as these were translated and articulated after 1809 in the nomenclature of the German Pietists. Their preachers, to whom Seybert was drawn, were regarded as "bush meeting" preachers, to distinguish them from the more formal and antirevivalist "church Dutch" (Lutherans and Reformed) and "plain Dutch" (Mennonites and other Anabaptists). Their central message was the "new birth" (*die Wiedergeburt*), an experience of regeneration in Christ that was to inaugurate a life of scriptural holiness, or sanctification, resulting in "entire sanctification," or perfection in love.

Seybert wrote that his "breakthrough" (*Durchbruch*) into the new birth occurred while gazing into the well at his father's farm, where "the Lord converted me deep into eternal life." Reflecting on his spiritual pilgrimage in the language of the prodigal son in Luke 15, Seybert reported that his newly redirected appetites and thirsts for God led him into a disciplined program of theological reading—largely in the Luther Bible, the Evangelical *Discipline* and hymnal, and in German devotional resources, such as Thomas à Kempis and Gerhard Tersteegen, the leading German devotional writers in the fourteenth and eighteenth centuries. He would later personally transport thousands of such books over the Allegheny Mountains into the German settlements of the Midwest.

Seybert was licensed to preach in 1819; he was subsequently ordained as deacon and then elder. After several years as a circuit preacher and presiding elder in Pennsylvania, he was elected bishop by the General Conference of 1839. The office of bishop had remained vacant since the untimely death of Albright in 1808, even though the *Book of Discipline* (*Kirchenordnung*) of 1809 had made constitutional provision for the office. Although Seybert deemed himself unworthy, he was unanimously elected and subsequently reelected bishop every four years, in accordance with the *Discipline*, until his death.

As a frugal, bachelor bishop, Seybert was primarily responsible for extending the operation of the association from eastern Pennsylvania into the Midwest and Canada. According to his unpublished journal, running from 1821 to 1855, he traveled by horse and later by buckboard more than 175,000 miles. In addition, he preached 9,850 times, made about 46,000 pastoral visits, and held about 8,000 prayer and class meetings besides visiting at least 10,000 of the sick and afflicted.

Seybert's mystical piety, which included a sense of guidance from the Holy Spirit through his prayer life and from his interpretations of his dreams, was matched by his untiring evangelistic burden to bear witness to the gospel among the far-flung German settlements of the frontier. He preached in homes and in large camp meetings, and he was instrumental in effecting the great revival at Orwigsburg, Pennsylvania, in 1823. He held the first German worship services in Chicago and organized new annual conferences (that is, preaching districts organized under episcopal supervision) in Illinois, Indiana, Michigan, Wisconsin, Iowa, Minnesota, and Ontario. He made conference sessions times of revival. His compassion was ever keen toward persons with physical and temporal needs, as on one occasion when he entered an auction to bid for a widow's farm so that he might restore her deed to her and prevent a foreclosure. The incident, as Seybert's journal unpretentiously records it, resulted in the conversion of the widow's family.

Seybert became the first president of the newly formed missionary society of his denomination in 1840, and in 1848 he inspired and supervised the founding of its German mission, which later grew to become a free church tradition in Germany and Switzerland.

From the beginning of Seybert's ministry to the time of his death at Bellevue, Ohio, the membership of the Evangelical Association grew from a few hundred to more than 40,000 members, and the number would increase to more than 330,000 in the twentieth century. The bishops who succeeded Seybert, including W. W. Orwig, J. J. Esher, and Rudolf Dubs, would become embroiled in political and theological disputes that laid the basis for the division of the denomination between 1891 and 1922. Three-fifths of the membership continued under the name the Evangelical Association, and two-fifths reorganized in this period under the name the United Evangelical church. Both groups looked on Albright and Seybert as their founders. Seybert's life and ministry were guided by his ardor for the beatific vision and for manifesting a full submission to the sanctifying grace of God in Christ. Although thrust into episcopal leadership, he was never a partisan of ecclesial politics.

His biographer, Samuel Spreng, remarked, "John Seybert lived for the unseen world, and therefore this present world has largely forgotten him." His ministry was a unifying spiritual presence as he traveled throughout his denomination, and it was the most effective embodiment of fruitful missionary ardor in the annals of the Evangelical church. The church for which he labored was renamed the Evangelical church (1921), and that later merged with the Church of the United Brethren in Christ to form the Evangelical United Brethren church (1946). This united body joined with the Methodist church to form the United Methodist church (1968), which resulted in the largest American Protestant denomination of that time.

• The unpublished journal of Seybert, from 1821 to 1855, is available (in German and English) at the United Methodist Commission on Archives and History at Madison, N.J. Seybert's nineteenth-century biographers included Solomon Neitz, *Das Leben und Wirken des seligen Johannes Seybert* (1862), and Samuel Spreng, *The Life and Labors of Bishop John Seybert* (1888). Denominational histories that treat Seybert include Raymond W. Albright, *History of the Evangelical Church* (1942), and Bruce Behney and Paul Eller, *History of the Evangelical United Brethren Church* (1979). A twentieth-century biographical and theological work on the subject is J. Steven O'Malley, *Touched by Godliness: Bishop John Seybert and the Evangelical Heritage* (1986).

J. STEVEN O'MALLEY

SEYMOUR, Charles (1 Jan. 1885–11 Aug. 1963), historian and Yale University president, was born in New Haven, Connecticut, the son of Thomas Day Seymour, a Yale professor of Greek, and Sarah Melissa Hitchcock. Seymour was linked with Yale University from his birth to his death. He graduated from high school at sixteen years of age and first took a bachelor's degree in 1904 at King's College, Cambridge, before matriculating at Yale for a second B.A., which he earned in 1908. Repeating this pattern on the graduate level, he studied at several European universities before earning a Ph.D. in history at Yale in 1911. He immediately joined the Yale History Department, where he quickly distinguished himself as a scholar. His second monograph, *The Diplomatic Background of the War, 1870–1914* (1916), thrust him into the making as well as the writing of contemporary history. In 1911 he married Gladys Marion Watkins; they had three children.

The defining event of Seymour's scholarly career was his participation in the American delegation to the Paris Peace Conference. His diplomatic study earned him an invitation to join "The Inquiry," a confidential group that worked in 1917–1918 to assemble information bearing on the forthcoming peace settlement. Seymour was then chosen as one of the "experts" included on the American Commission to Negotiate Peace. With principal responsibilities for American policy toward the former Habsburg Empire, Seymour was delegate to the territorial commissions for Rumania, Yugoslavia, and Czechoslovakia. He typified Wilsonian ideals for a just peace, which were substantially compromised in the final settlement. Seymour's posthumously published *Letters from the Paris Peace Conference* (1965), remain a valuable source for conveying the atmosphere and personal factors that surrounded these fateful events. Most influential for Seymour, however, was the close relationship he developed with Colonel E. M. House, a confidential adviser of President Woodrow Wilson, until their estrangement after the Peace Conference.

Returning to Yale, Seymour was promoted to a distinguished Sterling professorship in 1922. He and House published *What Really Happened at Paris* (1921), and he wrote *Woodrow Wilson and the War* (1921). Seymour was then enlisted by House to present the latter's contributions to the momentous events of the Wilson presidency. House donated his extensive papers to Yale in 1923 with the understanding that Seymour would be curator—a position that Seymour retained for the rest of his life. Seymour worked very closely with the subject in preparing *The Intimate Papers of Colonel House* (4 vols., 1926–1928), which portrayed the important role filled by House in the Wilson administration but skirted the sensitive issue of the personal break between the two men. That issue was only clarified by Seymour twenty-five years after House's death, in a 1963 article in *American Heritage*.

Seymour continued to write on the entry of the United States into World War I even after he became provost of Yale in 1927, but for the next twenty years university administration became the focus of his career. Seymour's ten years as provost under President James Rowland Angell were in some ways more accomplished than his presidency. These years saw Yale's affluence and eminence at a zenith, and Seymour's dual commitment to scholarship and undergraduate education resonated perfectly with the elite ideals of the institution and its alumni. Yale was essentially rebuilt during these years, despite the onset of the depression. Seymour shepherded the great gift of Edward S. Harkness into the realization of a system of residential colleges. He drew upon his experience at King's College to fashion new patterns of undergraduate life, becoming himself the first master of Berkeley College. As the individual most responsible for faculty appointments, Seymour's provostship saw Yale achieve perhaps its greatest eminence in the humanities and certain social sciences. When president Angell retired in 1937, Seymour, "the quintessential Yale man" (Kelley, p. 393), was the obvious choice to be his successor.

The times were less kind to Seymour as president. He began his administration with initiatives to broaden participation in university administration and to strengthen both the curricular and extracurricular side of undergraduate education. He was soon confronted, however, by the disruptions of the impending war, wartime conversion to military training programs, and then the frenetic conditions of the postwar "GI Bill" years. He provided leadership during the unstable prewar period and competent steady administration throughout the emergency, but his preference for consensual process and his strong attachment to Yale traditions made Seymour ill suited for the new postwar environment. Though instinctively defensive toward pressing changes, he bowed to necessity in the end. Thus, he initially distrusted federal support for university research but belatedly began to redress Yale's deficiencies in the natural sciences so that it too might benefit. Similarly, he slowly came to back the abandonment of discriminatory practices in admissions and hiring. He was also reluctant to face the palpable need for major additional financial resources. Upon retirement in 1950 he ceded these responsibilities to his successor, A. Whitney Griswold. Having played an important role for two decades in shaping modern Yale University, he devoted the remainder of his life to those interests formed by the Paris Peace Conference of 1919.

• Seymour's presidential and personal papers, as well as those of the Seymour family, are found in the Yale University Archives. Besides the writings mentioned in the text, Seymour wrote *Electoral Reform in England and Wales* (1915), *American Diplomacy during the World War* (1934), and *American Neutrality, 1914–1917* (1935). A biographical sketch of Seymour appears in Reuben A. Holden, *Profiles and Portraits of Yale University Presidents* (1968). The fullest treatment of his presidency is in Bruce Mather Kelley, *Yale: A History* (1974); of his provostship, George W. Pierson, *Yale: The University College, 1921–1937* (1955).

ROGER L. GEIGER

SEYMOUR, Horatio (31 May 1810–12 Feb. 1886), presidential candidate and governor of New York, was born in Pompey Hill, near Syracuse, New York, the oldest son of Henry Seymour, a storekeeper, entrepreneur, and political activist, and Mary L. Forman, the daughter of a prominent Madison County landowner. Seymour was educated in several local academies and then studied law in Utica, where the family had moved. Admitted to the bar in 1832, he moved in 1833 to Albany. He immediately became involved in state Democratic politics, drawing particularly close to William L. Marcy, whom he served as military secretary during the latter's terms as governor in the 1830s. In 1835, Seymour married Mary Bleecker, the daughter of a well-established landholding family descended from Dutch settlers in New Netherlands. They had no children.

Seymour's career as a loyal member of the Democratic party prospered in the 1840s. He was elected to the state assembly in 1841 and became mayor of Utica in 1842. Defeated for reelection after a year, Seymour returned to the legislature in 1844, distinguishing himself there by his forceful advocacy for improvements to the Erie Canal. In 1845 Seymour became Speaker of the assembly, but, after a bitterly divisive session in which the Democratic coalition split, he declined renomination and devoted himself to managing his family's properties and investing in land in the West.

Seymour was a member of Marcy's Hunker, a conservative faction of the New York Democracy, who opposed Martin Van Buren's attempts to limit government intervention in economic affairs. The Hunkers were friendlier to banks at the state level than were Van Buren's Barnburners and willing to permit New York's government to engage in more energetic involvement in other areas of economic development as well. In the mid- and late 1840s, the two factions persistently fought each other for control of the party. Their disagreements over the national controversies stimulated by the annexation of Texas and the proposed cession of other Mexican territories further fueled their hostility to one another. The Hunkers supported the Polk administration's slavery extension policies, which culminated in the Barnburners bolting the party in the presidential election of 1848. Seymour played some role in this battle, but, not holding office, he was not among the most prominent figures in the divisive disputes that occurred. With the Hunkers in control of the state party after 1848, he ran for governor in 1850 and lost but was elected two years later as the Democracy slowly reunited. While in office, however, he was caught up in and victimized by powerful movements to restrict liquor sales, immigration, and the extension of slavery. These issues produced a nationwide electoral realignment beginning in 1854. Seymour strongly opposed nativism, and he vetoed the antiliquor Maine Law passed by the legislature, believing it an unacceptable extension of state power personal behavior. He lost his bid for reelection in 1854, a victim of the widespread northern U.S. reaction against the Democrats that resulted in massive electoral losses to the emerging Know Nothings and Republicans.

Seymour returned to his private business pursuits until 1860, settling on a farm in Deerfield, on the Mohawk River near Utica. He continued to be politically involved in state politics and was a delegate to the Democratic National Convention in 1856. He worked behind the scenes in the late 1850s to reinvigorate and reunite the national Democratic party. Now a member of its "Soft" wing, which supported Stephen A. Douglas and popular sovereignty in the territories, Seymour fought for Douglas's election in 1860 and then joined Douglas in seeking compromise without war in 1860–1861. Once the Civil War began, however, Seymour emerged as a leader of the Democratic party's "respectable" group, who cautiously supported the northern war effort in contrast to continued resistance to military coercion by the "Peace" Democrats behind Clement Vallandigham and Fernando Wood. At the same time, fearing the power of the "violent and revolutionary" radical faction of the Republican party as the war progressed, Seymour became an outspoken and persistent critic of what Democrats believed were the extremist tendencies of the Lincoln administration. Fearing the growth of centralized power, emancipation, and war-induced limitations on press freedoms and civil liberties, Seymour was drawn into the controversies surrounding the war after he was elected governor of New York in 1862. In particular, he fought the Lincoln administration's efforts in 1863 both to suppress the "Peace" Democrats by closing their newspapers and harassing their leaders and to extend the coercive power of the national government by instituting a military draft.

Seymour successfully delayed and limited the draft's operation in New York State. When the draft began, however, it met stiff resistance, culminating in the New York City draft riots in early July 1863. He went to the city and, among other things, addressed a restive crowd in a controversial speech, which the Republicans ever after used as a club against him. Seymour saw himself as trying to calm the dangerous forces unleashed by the excesses and failures of the Lincoln administration. The latter saw things differently. Most Republicans did not distinguish between Seymour's brand of partisan criticism and Vallandigham's appeal to end the war, considered Seymour to be "in fact a traitor at heart," and successfully tarred Seymour and others like him with the brush of treasonous activity—why else had Seymour addressed a mob of rioters as "my friends"?

Seymour was briefly considered as a possible Democratic presidential nominee in 1864. He was defeated for re-election for governor that fall but remained active as a leader of Democratic conservatism, becoming one of the party's prime spokesmen in its efforts to regain national power after the war. With other Democrats, he tried to bury the issues of the war and to focus, instead, on the excesses of radical Reconstruction: the drive for guaranteed civil rights and congressional attempts to improve the condition of former slaves. With other Democrats, Seymour drew close to President Andrew Johnson's conservative notions about the restoration of former slave states without extensive reconstruction. Still fearing Republican excess, Seymour was nominated in 1868 as a compromise candidate for president at the deadlocked Democratic National Convention in New York City. The convention was particularly split over national financial policies between its traditional conservative wing who opposed the issuance of paper money and those pushing an inflationary monetary policy. Seymour was acceptable to the latter due to his strong wartime opposition record.

Although a reluctant candidate, Seymour ran an energetic campaign, articulating the brand of conservatism and limited government activity in both economic and social affairs that remained a Democratic hallmark for much of the nineteenth century. The Republicans' counterattack, behind Ulysses S. Grant, was predictable: they once more waved the bloody shirt of war memories, the alleged treason of the Democrats, and Seymour's association with the draft rioters. Although weakened by running mate Francis P. Blair, Jr.'s (1821–1875) strongly stated pro-southernism, Seymour ran a respectable race, only to lose by a relatively close margin in the popular vote. His more than 47 percent national vote was the highest Democratic showing since 1852.

After 1868 Seymour remained involved in politics, mostly as an elder statesman and mentor to the rising generation of Democrats, such as Samuel J. Tilden. He was often mentioned for office and actually nominated for governor by the state convention in 1876, but he declined to run. He died at his sister's home in Utica after a brief illness.

• The main collection of Seymour's correspondence is in the New York State Library, Albany. There is a smaller collection in the New-York Historical Society in New York City. The William L. Marcy Papers in the Library of Congress and the Samuel L. M. Barlow Papers in the Huntington Library contain many letters to and from Seymour. The only full-scale biography is the somewhat outdated Stewart Mitchell, *Horatio Seymour of New York* (1938). New York State politics in Seymour's day have been extensively covered. Among many studies, DeAlva Alexander, *Political History of the State of New York* (4 vols., 1906–1924) retains much usefulness. Concerning the national scene, see Joel H. Silbey, *A Respectable Minority: The Democratic Party in the Civil War Era, 1860–1868* (1977).

JOEL H. SILBEY

SEYMOUR, John (c. 1730s–21 Aug. 1818), cabinetmaker, was born in or near Axminster, Devon, England. Although his parentage is unknown, he was certainly a member of the clan of woodworking Seymours established in the Devon area. Little is known of his years in England, although aspects of construction and decoration of surviving furniture reveal English training. He emigrated from Lyme Regis, Devon, with his family in November 1784. Thomas Hopkins, another

Axminster emigrant and a merchant from whom Seymour would purchase furniture hardware in the American colonies, owned the ship on which they sailed. The Seymours arrived in Falmouth (now Portland), Massachusetts (now Maine), by 4 December 1784. The seacoast of Maine, New Hampshire, and Massachusetts was similar to the Devon area and attracted many emigrants from southwestern England.

Seymour resided in Falmouth until December 1792. He spent approximately 75 percent of his time as a cabinetmaker and the balance on miscellaneous jobs, including general carpentry, outfitting ships, and property repairs. It was during these years that he trained his sons, particularly Thomas, in the woodworking trades. (Details regarding his married life are unknown and have been cited inaccurately in various sources.) Seymour is last recorded working in Falmouth in December 1792. The "Taking Books of Assessors of the Town of Boston [Massachusetts]" list "John Seamore" as residing and working in 1793 as a wheelwright. In the same records, for the year 1794, his residence is given as Ward 5, and his occupation is recorded as "Cabinet Maker." His son Thomas Seymour, a "single cabinetmaker," is listed as his partner.

John Seymour & Son, cabinetmakers, remained in business in Creek Square, Boston, from 1793 to 1803. Early American furniture collector Phillip Flayderman purchased the first labeled Seymour piece, a tambour ladies' secretary desk. This desk was sold to Henry Francis du Pont at the auction of Flayderman's collection at the Anderson Galleries in New York City (2–4 Jan. 1930). Based on this initial example, the Seymours' work was recognized as among the finest examples of neoclassical cabinetwork made in Boston during the Federal period. The desk is now in the collection of the Winterthur Museum, Winterthur, Delaware. The secretary is also initialed "J.S." on a drawer bottom.

Since that time, hundreds of pieces of furniture have been attributed by American furniture collectors and dealers to the Seymour shop, although only about a dozen are actually labeled or signed. Approximately the same number have reliable provenances associating them with the Seymour shop. Firm attribution to the Seymours is especially difficult given the increasing collaboration of specialist craftsmen (carvers, inlay makers, joiners, turners, gilders, and so forth) working in Boston during this time.

Furniture associated with the cabinetmaking partnership of John and Thomas Seymour has several distinctive characteristics that are atypical of Boston furniture of 1790–1805: fine construction techniques more typical of English work; superb veneer and inlay work; the use of ash, chestnut, and oak as secondary woods; the use of concealed locking devices; and the use of tambour shutters. Seymour's English training and his knowledge of English and Continental furniture prototypes and construction methods continued to be evident in his craft. He consistently used English woods in his furniture rather than adopting the less expensive indigenous American woods. He often painted the interiors of case pieces—again an English trait. It should be noted, however, that the evidence of interior robin's-egg blue paint or red paint applied to the undersides of tables and the backs of larger pieces does not automatically ascribe the piece to the Seymour shop.

Contemporary scholarship continues to challenge traditional attributions of furniture to specific cabinetmakers or their shops. Several pieces of furniture attributed by Vernon Stoneman to the Seymours are now believed to have been made by Portsmouth, New Hampshire, cabinetmakers. Other reattributions continue to be published. John Seymour's "bespoke" furniture, created for a specific patron rather than produced for a casual clientele, was instrumental in the introduction of new furniture forms to the colonial market. The tambour desk, based on a Continental design, was virtually unique in Boston and the American colonies. As early as 1785, during his tenure in Falmouth, he billed Thomas Robison for a mahogany commode card table, what today would be described as a serpentine-shaped card table. This description predates the popularization of neoclassical forms through published design or pattern books—such as George Hepplewhite's *Cabinet-Maker and Upholsterer's Guide* (1788) or Thomas Sheraton's *The Cabinet-Maker and Upholsterer's Drawing Book* (1791–1794). John Seymour's understanding of neoclassical designs and the introduction of the style to both Portland and Boston clients is as important as the actual furniture.

Surviving documented furniture and various records indicate that Seymour & Son supplied primarily "bespoke" work for specific clients. From tax records, it is apparent that their financial success was limited, especially when compared with other cabinetmakers working in Boston during this time period. They were listed as "poor cabinetmakers, living in two rooms" at the same time that John Seymour's furniture was sufficiently recognized to be included in Josiah Flagg's auction notice: "all the Household Furniture vis. Beds Carpets Chairs China Mahogany Dining Pembroke and Card Tables of the workmanship of Mr. Seymour" (*Russell's Gazette*, 28 June 1798).

John Seymour continued to work as a cabinetmaker in Creek Square with his son Thomas until 1803. According to the *Boston Directories* he lived on Common Street in Boston, still listed as a cabinetmaker, until approximately 1813. His business relationship with his son is uncertain during these years as he had moved to Portland Street by 1813. In 1816 he was committed to the Alms House, where he died. He was buried in the South Burial Grounds, Boston, on 22 August 1818.

• Receipts documenting Seymour's work survive in the Deering and Robison papers at the Maine Historical Society, Portland. For citations to the Deering and Robison papers, see Laura F. Sprague, "John Seymour in Portland, Maine," *Magazine Antiques* 131, no. 2 (Feb. 1987): 444–49. The "Taking Books of Assessors of the Town of Boston" are in the Rare Book Room, Boston Public Library. The standard reference works, albeit with some errors, are Vernon C. Stoneman's

John and Thomas Seymour: Cabinetmakers in Boston, 1794–1816 (1959) and *A Supplement to John and Thomas Seymour: Cabinetmakers in Boston, 1794–1816* (1965). Seymour and related English Seymour craftsmen are noted in Geoffrey Beard and Christopher Gilbert, *Dictionary of English Furniture Makers, 1660–1840* (1986). An excellent article that outlines some problems in the attribution of Seymour furniture is Richard H. Randall, Jr., "Seymour Furniture Problems," *Bulletin of the Museum of Fine Arts, Boston* 57 (1959): 102–13. See also Anne Rogers Haley, "John and Thomas Seymour in England," *America in Britain* 33, no. 2 (1995): 5–9. Seymour's death notice is in the Alms House Records, Massachusetts Historical Society, Boston.

ANNE ROGERS HALEY

SEYMOUR, Mary Foot (1846–21 Mar. 1893), journalist and businesswoman, was born in Aurora, Illinois, the daughter of Ephraim Sanford Seymour, a lawyer, and Rosette Bestor. Her father, who graduated from Middlebury College and practiced law in Galena, Illinois, published the *Galena Directory and Miner's Annual Register* and wrote *An Emigrant's Guide to the Gold Mines of Upper California, Illustrated with a Map* (1849) and *Sketches of Minnesota, the New England of the West* (1850). He died while traveling to California on business in 1851, at which time the family moved to Wilbraham, Massachusetts.

Seymour was educated at private schools in Wilbraham and in Somerville, New Jersey, finishing in 1864 at New York's Twelfth Street School. Her early career included stints at two fairly traditional women's occupations: writing for children and teaching. Having been a composer of poems and stories since she was eight years old, she produced a number of children's stories for various periodicals, as well as moral essays that appeared pseudonymously under the heading "Table Talk of Grandmother Greyleigh." She taught in schools in New York City and Jersey City during the 1870s, although poor health repeatedly forced her to give up her positions.

During periods when her health kept her from schoolteaching, Seymour moved into the less traditional portion of her career by teaching herself stenography, becoming one of the first women in New York to work in a business office. Finding that she could make a much higher salary as a clerical worker in business than she had teaching school, she decided to help other women enter the new field of stenography (or "type-writing," as it was called at that time). In 1879 she opened the Union School of Stenography at 38 Park Row, New York City. It became the largest such school in the city, and Seymour established three more schools, as well as a firm that employed twenty-five stenographers, the Union Stenographic Company. She also opened an employment agency, the Union Stenographic and Typewriting Association.

To further assist women entering jobs in business offices, a field opened up by the marketing of the first efficient typewriters during the late 1870s, Seymour began a bimonthly magazine in January 1889. The *Business Woman's Journal*, which Frank Luther Mott describes as the leading magazine for businesswomen during the 1890s, included sketches of successful women in business and articles of interest to women in business, as well as departments focusing on women's sports, the home, and women's organizations. Seymour herself apparently provided many of the unsigned contributions, as well as an advice series, "Practical Hints to Stenographers and Type-writers," which was later published separately.

After its first year the *Business Woman's Journal* was put under the control of the Mary F. Seymour Publishing Company, a firm whose officers were women and whose stock was kept in the hands of women. This company, which had $50,000 capital, was controlled by Seymour as president and Isabella Beecher Hooker, May Wright Sewall, Lady Henry Somerset, and Frances E. Willard as vice presidents. The journal was priced at $1 per year and attained a circulation of about 5,000. In an effort to further widen its readership, in October of 1892 the *Business Woman's Journal* was turned into one department of Seymour's new *American Woman's Journal—Business Woman's Journal*. In addition to the department on business, the expanded magazine included sections on investments, women's occupations, woman suffrage, and domestic advice. Seymour edited the journal until her death. The journal would later evolve into *American Woman's Magazine and Business Journal* in 1895, *American Woman's Magazine* in 1896, and *American Magazine* in 1896.

Along with her efforts to assist women seeking business careers, Seymour was involved in woman suffrage work and helped expand women's career options through her example. She was named in 1884 as a commissioner of deeds for New Jersey, an appointment that required an appeal to the legislature to allow a woman to fill the position. She assisted and supervised the staff that prepared the 470-page stenographic report of the first meeting of the International Council of Women in Washington, D.C., in 1888. Seymour delivered a speech, "Occupations of Women to Date," at the First Triennial Council of the National Council of Women in 1891 as a delegate of the Women's Press Club of New York and served as commissioner of the federal Court of Claims for New York City and as vice president at large of the American Society of Authors.

After only a few days' illness, Seymour died of pneumonia at her home in New York City. She is remembered as a pioneer businesswoman and as a founder and editor of women's periodicals.

• Files of Seymour's most important publication, the *Business Woman's Journal*, may be found in the Kansas State Historical Society; microfilm is in the Schlesinger Library at Radcliffe College. Frank Luther Mott mentions *Business Woman's Journal* and its successors in *A History of American Magazines, 1885–1905* (1957). For more on Seymour's life, see Frances E. Willard and Mary A. Livermore, eds., *A Woman of the Century*, vol. 2 (1893). Obituaries are in the *New York Times*, 22 Mar. 1893, and the *New York Daily Tribune*, 22–24 Mar. 1893.

JENNIFER HYNES

SEYMOUR, Thomas (14 Feb. 1771–9 May 1848), cabinetmaker and furniture seller, was born in Axminster, Devon, England, the son of John Seymour, a cabinetmaker. He arrived with his family in Falmouth (now Portland), Maine, by 4 December 1784. He served an informal apprenticeship with his father, where in addition to making furniture, he performed general tasks associated with house carpentry and shipfitting. His cabinetmaking training was considerably less regimented than his father's. In much of the furniture attributed to the Seymours during their Boston years, the construction techniques and attention to detail is less refined in Thomas Seymour's work. In 1793 he is noted in the "Taking books of Assessors of the Town of Boston [Massachusetts]" as a single cabinetmaker residing with his father. John Seymour had moved to Boston from Falmouth in 1792, and his son followed, likely for economic reasons. The furniture partnership of John Seymour & Son, located in Creek Square, Boston, dates from 1793 until approximately 1803.

Thomas Seymour speculated in the Boston real estate market in 1799, purchasing property on Back Street in partnership with Benjamin Proctor, a sailmaker. In 1800 he conveyed his portion of the property to Proctor for a small gain. He was involved in a variety of ventures and partnerships throughout his lifetime. He was more involved in the furniture trade as a production business, rather than as a "bespoke" craft. Furniture warehouses were established in England in the eighteenth century with a variety of furniture from different sources being sold in one shop. Seymour's pioneering ventures in developing a similar market for Boston cabinetmakers was an important commercial development.

Seymour married Mary Baldwin on 2 December 1804. She was the daughter of Enoch Baldwin, a local ship captain and victualer. During their marriage they had at least five children. Two days after his marriage Thomas announced the opening of the Boston Furniture Warehouse:

"The Subscriber Respectfully informs the Public that he has taken and fitted up in a most commodious manner those extensive premises at the bottom of the Mall (lately occupied as the Washington Museum) for the purpose of a Commission Furniture Warehouse where he now offers for sale a handsome assortment of Cabinet Furniture, Chairs, Looking Glasses; and from the daily additions to his Stocks and to the prices of the Furniture he flatters himself that persons purchasing any of the above articles will find it to their advantage to call as above." (*New England Palladium*, 4 Dec. 1804)

He was involved in the Boston Furniture Warehouse until 1811, enlarging it in 1805 and adding additional services, including upholstery and the sale of carriages. The Furniture Warehouse was torn down in 1811.

During and after his tenure at the Warehouse, Seymour had a number of brief partnerships with other cabinetmakers including John Cogswell (1809–1812)

and Isaac Vose (1824). Furniture produced during those partnerships has not been identified due partly to the degree of specialization in the furniture trade and the use of retail shop labels on furniture produced by others. Other occupants at the Boston Furniture Warehouse included Henry Ayling, turning manufacturer; Samuel Gragg, patent chairs; and Charles Tuttle and Levi Ruggles, cabinetmaker furniture manufacturers. The documented furniture produced in 1809 for the wealthy divorcée, Mrs. Elizabeth Derby West, attests to the number of craftsmen involved in one commission. Seymour supplied a demi-lune commode to Mrs. West; however, the carving was done by Thomas Whitman, and the painting on the top was done by John Ritto Penniman. The commode and related objects are in the Oak Hill Rooms, Museum of Fine Arts, Boston.

Seymour became a U.S. citizen in 1812 at the March session of the Superior Court of Judicature in Boston. He announced the opening of a new establishment that May: The Ware Room of the Boston Cabinet Manufactory. "Useful and ornamental cabinet furniture" was sold, "all made by or under the inspection of Thomas Seymour" on Congress Street until the 1820s. Subsequent listings in the *Boston Directories* document his movements along Washington Street, a thoroughfare associated with cabinetmaking shops that connected Boston with Roxbury and the surrounding towns. Thomas worked at various addresses on Washington Street until his move to Lunenberg, Massachusetts, in 1843, where he died.

A large selection of federal furniture has been attributed to Thomas Seymour and to his father John. Some of the attributions have been and will be challenged by new scholarship. Seymour furniture is generally of finer workmanship and proportions than the average Boston products, particularly in the last decade of the eighteenth century. However, the degree of specialization within the Boston furniture trade and the overlapping retail labeling makes definitive attributions at best difficult, especially after 1800. Seymour carried on the English craft traditions of his father, and introduced the development of mass marketing within his trade. His opening of the Boston Furniture Warehouse in 1804 was an early attempt at commercializing a hitherto bespoke and piecework economy. The first decades of the nineteenth century saw the demise of many small family-based shops, which yielded to capitalist methods of labor organization. The establishment of premises where cabinetmakers' wares could be sold to the public was an idea that fit the economic changes occurring in Boston. That Thomas Seymour's two successive ventures into a large retail furniture showroom and a furniture manufactory foundered on economic difficulties caused by Jefferson's embargo of 1808 and the War of 1812 should not negate his pioneering attempts.

• The standard reference work, albeit with some errors, is Vernon C. Stoneman, *John and Thomas Seymour: Cabinetmakers in Boston, 1794–1816* (1959), which includes an illustration of his naturalization papers, and his *A Supplement to John and Thomas Seymour: Cabinetmakers in Boston 1794–1816* (1965). The years in Portland, Maine, are briefly noted in Laura F. Sprague, "John Seymour in Portland, Maine," *Magazine Antiques* 131, no. 2 (Feb. 1987): 444–49. See also Ethel Hall Bjerkoe, *The Cabinetmakers of America* (1957). Elizabeth Page Talbott, "The Furniture Industry in Boston 1810–1835" (M.A. thesis, Univ. of Delaware, 1974), discusses Seymour's involvement within the artisanal community. Richard H. Randall, Jr., illuminates the Oak Hill commission in his article, "Seymour Furniture Problems," *Bulletin of the Museum of Fine Arts, Boston* 57 (1959): 102–13.

ANNE ROGERS HALEY

SEYMOUR, Thomas Day (1 Apr. 1848–31 Dec. 1907), classical philologist, was born in Hudson, Ohio, the son of Nathan Perkins Seymour, a professor of Greek and Latin at Western Reserve University, and Elizabeth Day. At age sixteen Seymour was sent to Hartford to work for his uncle Thomas Seymour, the editor of the *Hartford Courant*. Young Seymour entered the Christian Commission, an evangelical organization, and accompanied the Army of the Potomac into Richmond after General Robert E. Lee's surrender. He later undertook undergraduate studies at Western Reserve, where he was active in social, literary, and musical affairs. He graduated as class valedictorian in 1870. The same year his father resigned, and Seymour was appointed professor of Greek, with a two-year leave to spend in Europe to prepare himself for his duties. He studied at Leipzig, Berlin, and Athens. "Perhaps [Seymour's] caliber can best be measured by the fact that he devoted his two years of study to preparation for his teaching and refused to spend the time seeking the doctor's degree," wrote Oberlin classicist Louis E. Lord. Seymour began teaching at Western Reserve in the fall of 1872. In 1874 he married Sarah Melissa Hitchcock, the daughter of the president of Western Reserve. They had three children.

In 1880 Seymour was called to a professorship of Greek at Yale. In 1884, upon the death of Lewis R. Packard, he was appointed Hillhouse Professor of the Greek Language and Literature. The dean of American classicists, Basil Lanneau Gildersleeve, wrote to Daniel Coit Gilman, president of the Johns Hopkins University, "Nothing would seem to me more clearly to indicate the dearth of first class men than the appointment of Seymour to the chair of Greek in Yale. . . . some of S[eymour]'s papers had proven to me that he was sadly lacking both in accuracy and reach" (8 Aug. 1880). Gildersleeve, a master grammarian, was especially irritated by Seymour's articles on grammar. Gildersleeve wrote Gilman, "Seymour produced a halting and jejune affair about the aorist participle—as poor a piece of grammatical work as I ever desire to see" (16 July 1881). Seymour made a concerted effort to get along with Gildersleeve, and they became good friends. After Seymour's death Gildersleeve praised *Life in the Homeric Age* as "the crowning service rendered to Homeric studies by America's leading Homerist" but refused to allow a "formal review" of the volume (Miller, p. 159).

Seymour devoted much of his professional time to administrative matters. "The tale is told in Cambridge that he never refused service on a committee," wrote his friend John Williams White of Harvard. He was chairman of the managing committee of the American School of Classical Studies in Athens (ASCSA) from 1887 to 1901, succeeding White. His fourteen-year tenure was an important period in the school's development. The ASCSA established its long-lived and important excavations at Corinth. Publication of the Argive Heraeum, and several volumes of *Papers* initiated a long and distinguished history of scholarly publication. Cooperation with the British and German schools was established, and Wilhelm Dörpfeld and Karl Wilhelm regularly lectured at the school. The separate positions of permanent director and professor of Greek were, after difficulties, firmly established. There were fellowships open to merit. (In 1899–1900 there were fifteen students, of whom eight were women.) From 1903 until his death, Seymour was president of the Archaeological Institute of America (AIA), which had founded the school. He was president of the American Philological Association in 1888–1889 and an editor of the English *Classical Review* from 1889 until his death.

Beginning in 1884 Seymour served with White as an editor of Ginn and Company's College Series of Greek Authors, to which he contributed many school texts of various parts of the Homeric poems, based explicitly on work by other scholars, *Introduction to the Language and Verse of Homer* (1885) and *Select Odes of Pindar* (1882). He compiled the family tree of *The Family of the Rev. Jeremiah Day* (1900).

Seymour's masterpiece was *Life in the Homeric Age* (1907), a thorough summary of the internal evidence of the *Iliad* and the *Odyssey* for daily life. The work sticks closely to the text and is often a summary of the plots of the two epics. Despite his long association with ASCSA and AIA, he used relatively little archaeological evidence. The book largely ignored philological issues that interested European classicists, and in turn it was itself ignored by leading European Homeric scholars.

Seymour's family connections helped him to obtain two chairs of Greek. His contributions to his field through administration and editing were fruitful and valued. Lord wrote in 1947, "In the youth of the generation now drawing to its close he was one of the 'Big Four'—Gildersleeve, [William Watson] Goodwin, Seymour, White." The work of the other three is still essential for active scholars. Seymour was an administrator whose published work was without lasting importance. He died in New Haven.

• Seymour produced a regular series of articles in the standard American journals, for example, *Transactions of the American Philological Association* and *American Journal of Philology*. Evaluations of him come from *The Letters of Basil Lanneau Gildersleeve*, ed. Ward W. Briggs, Jr. (1987), esp. pp. 120 and 145 for early criticism and pp. 258–59 for the later personal friendship; Louis E. Lord, *A History of the American School of Classical Studies at Athens 1882–1942* (1947); and

John Williams White, *Thomas Day Seymour, 1848–1907* (1908). For Gildersleeve's comments on Seymour's scholarship, see *Selections from the Brief Mention of Basil Lanneau Gildersleeve*, ed. C. W. E. Miller (1930), pp. 159–60; repr. *American Journal of Philology* 29 (1908): 118–19.

E. CHRISTIAN KOPFF

SEYMOUR, Truman (24 Sept. 1824–30 Oct. 1891), soldier, was born in Burlington, Vermont, the son of Truman Seymour, a Methodist minister, and Ann Armstrong. Truman attended Norwich University from 1840 to 1842, after which he received an appointment to the U.S. Military Academy. He graduated nineteenth in the famous class of 1846, which included Thomas J. "Stonewall" Jackson and George B. McClellan, and was assigned to the First Artillery at Fort Pickens, Florida, as a brevet second lieutenant. During the Mexican-American War, 1847–1848, he served with distinction with the First Artillery at the battles of Cerro Gordo, Conteras, and Churubusco and the assault and capture of Mexico City, earning two brevets for gallant and meritorious conduct. On 3 March 1847 he was promoted to second lieutenant and on 26 August 1847 to first lieutenant, evidence that his performance in Mexico was noted by his superiors. Following the war Seymour returned to routine garrison life, serving at Fort Hamilton, New York, from 1848 to 1849 and at Fort Columbus, New York, from 1849 to 1850. From Fort Columbus he returned to the Military Academy, where he was assistant professor of drawing until 26 November 1853. There he also met and married Louisa Weir, the daughter of Robert W. Weir, the professor of drawing. Seymour was assigned to Fort Moultrie, South Carolina, until 1856, then he participated in the conflict with the Seminoles in Florida in 1856–1858. At the cessation of these hostilities he went on recruiting duty followed by a leave of absence to visit Europe from 1859 to 1860. Upon his return, Seymour was ordered back to Fort Moultrie and was promoted to captain in the First Artillery on 22 November 1860.

At the opening of the Civil War, Seymour commanded one-half of the Charleston, South Carolina, garrison. He took a prominent role in the defense of Fort Sumter, earning a brevet to major. Following the evacuation from Fort Sumter, he returned to Fort Hamilton for three months, then joined the newly formed Fifth U.S. Artillery, He subsequently went on recruiting duty until given command of the camp of instruction at Harrisburg, Pennsylvania, on 24 September 1861. December 1861 found him in the defenses of Washington, D.C., where he remained until 28 April 1862, when he was promoted to brigadier general of volunteers and assigned to command a brigade in the Pennsylvania Reserve Division in George A. McCall's division. Seymour and his command participated in some of the fiercest fighting of the Peninsula campaign during the Seven Days' battles (25 June–1 July), suffering 559 casualties. His brigade fought effectively at Beaver Dam Creek and Gaines' Mill, but at Glendale it was swept from the field. Seymour's horse

was killed under him, and he came away with a bullet hole in his hat. From the Virginia Peninsula, McCall's division was transferred to northern Virginia, and Seymour participated in the Union defeat at Second Manassas (29–30 Aug. 1862). He and his command then accompanied the army into Maryland to confront Robert E. Lee's invasion. Seymour's brigade played an integral role in turning the left of the Confederate position in the engagement at South Mountain (14 Sept. 1862). The reserves division commander, General George G. Meade, who personally disliked Seymour, nevertheless gave him high praise, writing that he was "greatly indebted to General Seymour for the skill with which he handled his brigade on the extreme right flank, securing by his maneuvers the great object of our movements." Three days later, at the battle of Antietam, Seymour again won praise from Meade for the handling of his brigade, and he was awarded brevets to lieutenant colonel and colonel for his gallant service in these two engagements.

Although he fought with courage and skill during the Maryland campaign, Seymour did not enjoy the confidence of his men. One soldier wrote after the war, "The men in the division had no confidence in Gen. T. Seymour, especially after the Peninsula Campaign." Apparently he had few friends in influential positions as well, for despite the praise of Meade and his two brevets, Seymour was passed over for promotion. In poor health, he sought a transfer and in November 1862 was sent to the Department of the South to serve as chief of staff, chief of artillery, commander of the Beaufort and Hilton Head garrison, and commander of the Second Division, Tenth Corps, remaining in each position only a short period of time. In July 1863 he led the ill-fated assault against Fort Wagner and suffered a severe wound. He recovered in time to lead an expedition designed to recover Florida for the Union and suffered a disastrous defeat at the battle of Olustee (20 Feb. 1864).

Seymour returned to the Army of the Potomac in the spring of 1864 and assumed command of a brigade in the Sixth Corps "Milroy's weary boys" because of their unfortunate experiences with General Robert H. Milroy in the Shenandoah Valley in 1862 and 1863. Bad luck continued to plague the brigade in the battle of the Wilderness. Although they fought with courage in savage afternoon combat on 6 May 1864, that evening they were routed by a Confederate flank attack. One diarist wrote that Seymour "seemed to be dazed" during the afternoon fighting, and General Ulysses S. Grant reported Seymour's brigade gave way "almost without resistance, carrying good troops with them." Seymour suffered further humiliation in this action when he was captured by the Confederates. He was exchanged on 9 August 1864 and assigned to command of the Third Division, Sixth Corps, on 28 October 1864. He performed competently throughout the Petersburg campaign. At the battle of Sayler's Creek during Lee's retreat from Petersburg, Seymour handled his command aggressively and skillfully and won the praise of General Philip Sheridan. By the time of

Lee's surrender at Appomattox (9 Apr. 1865), Seymour won brevets to major general in the volunteer and the regular army.

When the war ended, Seymour reverted to his regular army rank of major in the Fifth Artillery. He served without promotion at various forts along the Atlantic Coast and on the Artillery Board until he retired on 1 November 1876. He and his wife moved to Florence, Italy, where Seymour developed into a talented artist. He died in Florence.

Seymour's reputation for bravery is unquestioned as he won seven brevets for gallantry during his military career. He was a man of contrasts. An uninspiring soldier, he nevertheless took good care of his troops. Impetuous but of high intellect and a reserved nature, he was also resilient, which helped him rally from his severest defeats and go forward.

• Seymour's Civil War reports and some correspondence are in U.S. War Department, *The War of the Rebellion: A Compilation of the Official Records of the Union and Confederate Armies* (128 vols., 1880–1901). Seymour's military record is in George W. Cullum, *Biographical Register of the Officers and Graduates of the U.S. Military Academy* (1879). Some details of his Civil War service are Stephen Sears, *To the Gates of Richmond* (1992) and *Landscape Turned Red* (1983), and Gordon Rhea, *The Battle of the Wilderness* (1994). Obituaries are in the *New York Times*, 5 Nov. 1891, and the *National Tribune*, 12 Nov. 1891.

D. SCOTT HARTWIG

SEYMOUR, William (19 Dec. 1855–2 Oct. 1933), actor, stage manager, and director, was born William Gorman Seymour in New York City, the son of James Seymour (originally Cunningham), a popular Irish actor, and Lydia Eliza Griffith, a successful actress; both parents were members of the Broadway Theatre company. In 1857 his parents joined the Varieties Theatre company in New Orleans. There Seymour made appearances as an infant, being carried onstage by his mother in *The Rent Day* before he was two years old. The family moved back to New York in 1860, but when James Seymour developed a drinking problem, young William and his mother removed to New Orleans. Seymour never again saw his father, who died in 1864 of alcoholism.

The young actor played his first speaking role in 1862 in the farce *To Parents and Guardians*, also appearing as the Duke of York to the Richard III of Lawrence Barrett. He remained in New Orleans for some time, playing children's roles in support of most leading actors of the time, including Edwin Booth, Joseph Jefferson III (with whom he toured for a season), Edwin Adams, John E. Owens, Frank Chanfrau, Matilda Heron, Mme Celeste, and Charlotte Cushman. He went to New York in 1869 and served as callboy (used to notify actors of their cues) at Booth's Theatre for two seasons, appearing as the Player Queen in Edwin Booth's *Hamlet* and the boy Hendrick in Jefferson's *Rip Van Winkle* (for 149 consecutive performances). In 1871 he moved to the Globe Theatre in Boston as prompter and stock actor, appearing on 2 April 1872 as François to Edwin Forrest's Richelieu (Forrest's last performance on any stage). After appearing in St. John's, Canada, Seymour returned to New Orleans and by age eighteen became the stage manager of the Varieties Theatre under Lawrence Barrett. He remained with Barrett until autumn 1875, serving as a manager, advance agent, stage director, and principal supporting actor.

Seymour next moved to New York as stage manager of Palmer's Union Square Theatre, where he remained for two seasons, also directing productions of *King Lear* and *Julius Caesar* at Booth's Theatre. For a brief time Seymour was stage manager of the Park Theatre in New York City under A. M. Palmer. In 1877, under the management of John McCullough, he went to San Francisco to manage Baldwin's Theatre. During the winter of 1877–1878 he directed the controversial production of *The Passion Play*, in which James O'Neill played Christ. In 1879 Seymour managed Barrett's company as they toured the West, then he arrived in Boston to assume the management of the Boston Museum, a position he retained almost continuously until 1888. While in Boston he appeared in roles such as Dolly Spanker in *London Assurance*, Sir Benjamin Backbite and Moses in *The School for Scandal*, Sir Lucius O'Trigger in *The Rivals*, Danny Mann in *The Colleen Bawn*, Modus in *The Hunchback*, the First Gravedigger in *Hamlet*, Uncle Rufus in *Held by the Enemy*, Squire Western in *Sophia* (a dramatization of *Tom Jones*), and Cis Farringdon in *The Magistrate*. As an actor Seymour won praise as "a careful and painstaking artist," "a decided hit," and "thoroughly charming." For the 1881–1882 season Seymour managed the Madison Square Theater in New York City. Toward the end of the same season he took part in organizing the Actors' Fund, of which he was the first secretary. Seymour married May Davenport, daughter of tragedian Edward L. Davenport, in 1882. They had five children.

After Seymour left the Boston Museum in August 1888, he comanaged Thomas W. Keene and Julia Marlowe, then contracted with producers Abbey, Schoeffel, and Grau, for whom he directed *Antony and Cleopatra*, starring Kyrle Bellew and Cora Urquhart (Mrs. James Brown) Potter. In October 1889 he became manager of the Tremont Theater in Boston, remaining there until 1896–1897. He then stage managed Sol Smith Russell for the 1897–1898 season. He stage managed at the Columbus Theatre in Harlem for a season, then contracted with Daniel Frohman to direct E. H. Sothern in *The King's Musketeer* (1899). Beginning a long relationship under Charles Frohman's management, Seymour then in 1899 directed Julia Marlowe in *Colinette* and Maude Adams in *Romeo and Juliet*. During two decades Seymour directed over eighty productions for Charles Frohman. In the autumn of 1899 he directed Henry Miller in *The Only Way* and Julia Marlowe in *Barbara Frietche*. In October 1900 he contracted as stage manager for the Metropolitan Opera House in New York City.

Seymour also wrote a few play scripts of no special significance, but he was rather more successful as a "play doctor," that is, one who adapted and rearranged scripts written by others. Seymour scripts receiving professional productions included *Salviati; or, The Silent Man* in 1881, *Favette, the Story of a Waif* in 1885, and *The Long Branch* in 1880.

Seymour retired in 1917 but continued to contribute his time and expertise to various projects, such as a special benefit performance of *Out There* for the American Red Cross war effort. He managed and acted with Helen Hayes on tour and in 1922 directed an all-star cast in *The Rivals* for The Players. As late as 1927 he was engaged to direct *Trelawny of the Wells*, the rehearsals for which were interrupted by the illness and death of his wife, May Davenport Seymour. His final professional direction was of The Players' production of *She Stoops to Conquer* in 1928. After several years of retirement, he died in Plymouth, Massachusetts.

Seymour saw during his career the demise of the repertory company in America, the rise of realism in the drama, and the emergence of the director as the dominant influence on production. It was in his direction that Seymour as an exemplary man of the theater made his greatest contributions to the American theater as, as his biographer Ralph Earl Miller put it, "one of the foremost successful, artistic, commercial American directors of the late nineteenth and early twentieth centuries."

• The Seymour Collection at Princeton University consists mainly of materials dealing with the Boston Museum and the Empire Theater in New York City; for a detailed description and a brief biography of Seymour, see Mary Ann Jensen, "The William Seymour Theatre Collection, Princeton University Library," *Theatre and Performing Arts Collections* (1981). A substantial treatment of William Seymour is Ralph Earl Miller, "William Seymour, American Director, 1855–1933" (Ph.D. diss., Wayne State Univ., 1973), which includes a substantial bibliography. The *New York Dramatic Mirror*, 24 Dec. 1898, published a lengthy interview with Seymour. See also Jay Dee, "William Seymour, a Prominent Stage Manager and a Clever Comedian," *Boston Sunday Review*, 28 Nov. 1886; "William Seymour, Veteran among Stage Managers," *New York Sunday Telegraph*, 24 Apr. 1904; and John Bouvé Clapp and Edwin Francis Edgett, *Players of the Present* (1901). Seymour amassed a considerable collection of theatrical memorabilia, which he donated to the Theatre Collection at Princeton University.

STEPHEN M. ARCHER

SEYMOUR, William Joseph (2 May 1870–28 Sept. 1922), Pentecostal minister, was born in Centerville, Louisiana, the son of Simon Seymour and Phillis Salabarr, former slaves. Few specific details are known about Seymour's early life. There is no extant data on the family's occupation(s) or Seymour's formal education, but denominationally, Seymour's roots were in the Methodist and Baptist traditions.

In 1895 Seymour migrated to Indianapolis, where he attended Simpson Chapel of the predominantly white Methodist Episcopal Church (North). From 1900 to 1903 he lived in Cincinnati, where he joined the Holiness movement, which emphasized Wesleyan entire sanctification or perfectionism as a second work of grace. During that time he joined the Evening Light Saints, a small Holiness group that later merged with the Church of God (Anderson, Ind.) and reluctantly accepted ministerial ordination from the "Saints."

In 1903 Seymour moved to Houston, where in July 1905 Charles Fox Parham, a white Methodist-Holiness minister who in 1901 had founded the Pentecostal movement, conducted evangelistic services. Parham advocated the traditional Holiness teachings of salvation and sanctification but added a third work of grace, which became the hallmark doctrine of the Pentecostal movement, the baptism in the Holy Spirit with the initial physical evidence of glossolalia, or speaking in unlearned tongues. Its purpose was to empower spiritually the believer in acts of Christian service. Seymour readily accepted Parham's novel teaching.

In late 1905 Seymour was invited to preach at a small Holiness assembly in Los Angeles. However, immediately after his arrival in February 1906 Seymour's Pentecostal understanding of Spirit-baptism was rejected by the established Holiness churches, so he began to organize informal religious services in private homes. In early April Seymour and some of his followers experienced their Spirit-baptism accompanied by speaking in unknown tongues. As news of these events spread through the Holiness community, crowds gathered around Seymour's ministry, and a religious revival ensued. By 14 April he had secured a small, former African Methodist Episcopal building on Azusa Street for use by his rapidly growing, multiracial disciples and for it adopted the name Apostolic Faith Mission.

Seymour's revival received widespread publicity. On 18 April 1906 the *Los Angeles Daily Times* described it under the headline "Weird Babel of Tongues; New Sect of Fanatics Breaking Loose; Wild Scene Last Night on Azusa Street." Nonetheless, from this Azusa Street revival the nascent Pentecostal movement gained extraordinary force, eventually becoming one of the most influential religious movements of the twentieth century.

In the fall of 1906 Seymour incorporated his fellowship as the Pacific Apostolic Faith Movement with a board of twelve elders. In September he began publishing the *Apostolic Faith* journal, distributed on an irregular basis from September 1906 through May 1908. The *Apostolic Faith* started with a circulation of 5,000 and soon exceeded 50,000. It became the most influential literary organ in early Pentecostalism and was instrumental in spreading or accelerating the Pentecostal movement in many parts of the world. During the peak of the revival, from late 1906 through 1909, thousands of pilgrims flocked to Seymour's mission. Parham arrived by invitation in October 1906 but was appalled at the noisy worship, the mingling of the races, and the nature of its glossolalic speech. When Seymour refused to change his church's practices, Parham left in disgust, labeling Seymour's work a "counterfeit Pentecost."

In 1908 Seymour married Jennie Evans Moore, a staff volunteer at his church. The couple had no children but may have adopted a daughter. Seymour's marriage led to a serious division within the leadership. Clara Lum, mission secretary, disapproved of Seymour's matrimony in light of the expectation of the imminent return of Jesus. In retaliation, she confiscated the mailing list of the *Apostolic Faith* and moved to Portland, Oregon, to assist an Azusa Street itinerant, Florence Crawford. Seymour refused to sue for the return of the journal's subscribers, and the loss crippled the outreach of his ministry. In 1911 a permanent division developed within the American Pentecostal movement when William Durham challenged Seymour on the Holiness doctrine of entire sanctification. Seymour strongly defended the necessity of a second instantaneous work of sanctifying grace before Spirit-baptism, but Durham's non-Holiness views prevailed in many quarters of Pentecostalism.

Seymour's final years were spent in relative obscurity. By World War I attendance at the Apostolic Faith Mission had declined to approximately twenty people, and its racial composition had homogenized. In 1915 Seymour revised the mission's "Constitution" and "Doctrines and Discipline," expressing his hope that the church "won't have any more trouble and division spirit" and establishing that his successor as head of the organization would always be "a man of color." Seymour died in Los Angeles of a heart attack. His wife succeeded him as pastor of the mission. She died on 2 July 1936.

Assessments of Seymour and his role within American Pentecostalism have varied. Before the 1970s historians tended to downplay his contribution, stressing his dependence on Parham for the doctrinal formulation of evidential tongues in Spirit-baptism. Later interpreters have given him more credit for being the catalyst for the revival that brought widespread public attention to the Pentecostal movement and that catapulted it beyond the American scene.

• Seymour's extant writings are scarce but not difficult to obtain. His mission's "Constitution" and the "Doctrines and Discipline of the Azusa Street Apostolic Faith Mission of Los Angeles, Ca., with Scripture Readings by W. J. Seymour, Its Founder and General Overseer," both written in 1915, can be found at the Assemblies of God Archives in Springfield, Mo., and the David J. du Plessis Archives at Fuller Theological Seminary in Pasadena, Calif. His journal, the *Apostolic Faith*, has been reprinted by Fred T. Corum, *Like as of Fire* (1981). Secondary works on Seymour also are few in number. A substantial Ph.D. dissertation on Seymour, Douglas J. Nelson's "For Such a Time as This: The Story of Bishop William J. Seymour and the Azusa Street Revival" (Univ. of Birmingham, England, 1981), is uncritical and romantic in its interpretation but provides valuable primary information on Seymour's life and his famous revival. Though not exclusively devoted to Seymour, Vinson Synan, *The Holiness-Pentecostal Movement* (1971), and Robert Mapes Anderson, *Vision of the Disinherited: The Making of American Pentecostalism* (1979), constructively place Seymour in the context of the Holiness and the early Pentecostal movements. Cecil M. Robeck, Jr.'s essay, "William J. Seymour and 'the Bible Evidence,'" in *In-*

itial Evidence, ed. Gary B. McGee (1991), examines carefully Seymour's position on evidential glossolalia and the baptism in the Holy Spirit.

MICHAEL THOMAS GIROLIMON

SHABENI (c. 1775–17 July 1859), a northern Illinois Potawatomi village chief of Ottawa tribal origin, was born in Canada. His parentage is uncertain, but Shabeni was later reputed to have been a "nephew" (in Ottawa kinship reckoning, likely meaning he was a younger clan-mate) of Pontiac, the intertribal Ottawa leader famed for his prominence in the anti-British rebellion of 1763. Shabeni (variously spelled Shabbona, Chamble, and other ways), meaning He-Has-Pawed-Through, spent his early years near Detroit, where his family moved from his birthplace, perhaps on Manitoulin Island.

With other Ottawas involved in the late nineteenth-century Western Indian Confederacy, as a youth Shabeni fought against American expansion into the western Great Lakes. About 1800 he settled among the Potawatomi near Shabbona's Grove, DeKalb County, Illinois, where he took his senior wife, Bear Woman or Mkonokwe (commonly misspelled Pokanoka). This marriage enabled him to become a village *wkama* (leader), one of no special prestige or influence among other neighboring Potawatomi *wkamek* of his era. A traditional polygynist, during his lifetime Shabeni had at least three, perhaps four or more wives, serially or simultaneously, who together bore him a dozen or more children. In effect, his village was his own multigenerational, polygynous extended family.

Tecumseh, the Shawnee intertribal leader, recruited Shabeni as one of many allies about 1807. For the next several years, Shabeni traveled with Tecumseh on diplomatic missions to other tribes in the Great Lakes area and perhaps the Southeast, working unsuccessfully to generate concerted intertribal support for a major alliance against American expansion. He then joined Tecumseh's supporters and their British allies in ultimately disastrous military operations during the War of 1812. He fought at Frenchtown, Fort Meigs, and other battles and, like hundreds of other frontier personalities, later claimed he was an eyewitness to Tecumseh's fatal wounding in 1813 at the Moravian Town debacle. After this defeat, by American forces invading the Ontario Peninsula from the west of the retreating intertribal-British forces, Shabeni, like most other British allies, made his separate peace with the Americans and returned to Illinois.

Thereafter, Shabeni's so-far modest career turned around: he became identified as a pacific friend to and collaborator with Illinois settlers and officials. Usually, he operated as a lesser compatriot of the Anglo-Mohawk merchant Captain Billy Caldwell and the Scots-Ottawa trader Alexander Robinson. Noteworthy for actively supporting land-cession treaties desired by the United States, he also helped to maintain peace on a still conflicted settlement frontier, and he worked to control alcohol abuse within his own community. During the 1827 Red Bird affair (or "Winnebago war") in Wisconsin, a minor frontier conflict that escalated into a substantial American military confrontation, he successfully resisted efforts of the Winnebago to get the Potawatomi involved, as he did six years later during the tragic Black Hawk conflict. Similarly, during the Black Hawk War he enlisted in a troop of Potawatomi militia, organized as scouts to defend the Chicago area and to serve in the pursuit of Black Hawk's "British Band." On several occasions during these operations, Shabeni supposedly risked his life to restore peace.

Between 1825 and 1833 Shabeni figured in the negotiation of and signed several land-cession treaties. The last and most important was the 1833 Treaty of Chicago, in which the Potawatomis sold their remaining lands in Michigan, Illinois, and Wisconsin and were obligated to abandon these areas promptly and resettle in western Missouri or Iowa. For his collaboration with American authorities, as one of numerous accommodationists, Shabeni was rewarded with a life annuity of $200 and a substantial 1,280-acre personal reservation near De Kalb, Illinois.

During his later years Shabeni regularly traveled west, spending much time there, first on the temporary Platte Purchase reservation, then the Council Bluffs Potawatomi lands, and finally the Kansas River reservations. Originally, he was employed by Americans to effect the relocation, required by the 1833 treaty, of the Illinois and Wisconsin Potawatomi bands from the Lake Michigan area, first to the Platte Purchase and then to Council Bluffs and, after the 1846 treaty, from western Iowa to the eastern Kansas Potawatomi "national" reservation. In part, these travels were personally necessary, since by treaty Shabeni could only draw his extended family's share of Potawatomi tribal annuities, as well as installments of his own life annuity, where disbursements were made—on tribal reserves in the West. Like many of his generation in the prairie bands of Potawatomi, Shabeni was adapted to horse nomadism, extensive seasonal travel, and big-game hunting; so he used these occasions for pursuing buffalo on the Kansas and Nebraska prairies.

During one prolonged absence, squatters secured the fee title to Shabeni's personal property, which supposedly was held in trust for him by the president. Later, the United States, as his trustee responsible for this improper transaction, made partial recompense. He was payed $1,600—at the official land-office rate of $1.25 per acre—for the loss, but by that time these prime northern Illinois farm lands were more valuable. Seeing that Shabeni and his kin-group were landless, Illinois friends raised funds and purchased a home for the old man and his extended kin-group near Morris, Illinois, where he died. Little is known about any of his descendants.

The late nineteenth-century legend of Shabeni is as interesting as the few known details of his life are. The serially embellished product of Illinois raconteurs, old settlers embroidering reminiscences, and imaginative local historians, this frontier fiction took the form of hagiographic folklore, containing more fanciful elabo-

ration and hyperbole than documented information. Its central theme was the then popular stereotype of the "Vanishing Indian Hero," who first struggled courageously against the onrush of Civilization, then saw the error of his ways and helped in establishing that civilization. It was this fictional Shabeni, set in print, that was presented to readers in the first *Handbook of North American Indians* (1910). In the dominant antistereotype that grew up in the late twentieth century, however, accommodationists like Shabeni were adjudged, in contrast, as "traitors to their race." The powerful themes of both the older and the newer stereotypes must be understood if personages such as Shabeni are not again to be misrepresented. In fact, Shabeni never identified with an "Indian race," and contemporary shibboleths such as multiculturalism and sovereignty were unknown to him. His first and overriding loyalty was to his immediate kin-group. An ordinary man who lived in extraordinary times, he devoted the last decades of his life—when his options were sharply limited—to providing security for his own kin. Shabeni's modest fame stemmed from the events of his last years when—judged by the popular stereotype of late nineteenth-century America—he became known as an especially good "friend to the Whiteman." Following his death he was remembered fondly by Illinoisans, not by the Potawatomi.

• Some papers documenting the life of Shabeni are in the archives of the Chicago Historical Society and the Illinois Historical Society, the Lyman Draper Collections of the State Historical Society of Wisconsin, and files concerning the Illinois Potawatomi in Record Group 75 of the National Archives. No full-scale scholarly biography of Shabeni has been published. The best of several local-history studies is James Dowd, *Built Like a Bear* (1979), which also contains a comprehensive bibliography of secondary and primary sources and printed copies of many pertinent, not easily accessible documents. Nehemiah Matson, *Memories of Shaubena* (1878), illustrates the older, folkloristic treatment. Shabeni appears in a cultural-historical context in James A. Clifton, *The Prairie People: Continuity and Change in Potawatomi Indian Culture, 1665–1965* (1977).

JAMES A. CLIFTON

SHADD, Furman Jeremiah (24 Oct. 1852–24 June 1908), physician and educator, was born in Washington, D.C., the son of Absalom Shadd, a prosperous restaurateur, and Eliza Brockett. About 1855 Absalom Shadd sold his business and, following his brother Abraham's example, relocated his family to Canada in Chatham, Ontario, where he took up farming. Following Absalom's untimely death, the family returned to the United States.

In August 1867 Shadd began a 38-year affiliation as student, educator, and administrator with Howard University and its associated institutions. He first enrolled in the preparatory course at the model school administered by the university. Graduating from the model school, he became one of Howard's first university students. He earned his B.S. in 1875, followed by his M.S. in 1878 and his M.D. in 1881. He was selected valedictorian of both his undergraduate and his medical convocations.

While pursuing his own education, Shadd served from 1874 through 1878 as a tutor of mathematics at Howard University's normal school, then as assistant principal in 1878, and as principal from 1879 until 1881, when he completed his medical studies. In 1882 he married Alice Parke; they had three children.

Charles Burleigh Purvis, surgeon in chief of Freedmen's Hospital, offered Shadd the position of assistant surgeon and resident physician in October 1881. Freedmen's Hospital had been established in 1863 to serve African-American civilians and soldiers during the American Civil War. When the medical department at Howard University was established in 1868, Freedmen's became the teaching facility for the university. Shadd was the third African American to receive a faculty appointment in the university's medical department, an appointment he held until 1895. For a period of time he was also responsible for the dispensary and clinic at the hospital.

Shadd's tenure at Howard University's medical department was a lengthy one, both as an educator and as secretary-treasurer for the medical department, dental college, and pharmaceutical college. From 1885 through 1908 he taught primarily materia medica and therapeutics, but he also lectured in such subjects as clinical gynecology, pharmacology, and medical jurisprudence. In 1891 he was made a full professor. As an African-American physician, Shadd in 1891 joined the ranks of Purvis, Alexander Thomas Augusta, and Alpheus Tucker, who had previously attempted to join the local chapter of the American Medical Association only to have their petitions denied solely on the basis of their race. When the opportunity presented itself, Shadd continued his quest for knowledge. In 1893 he consulted with Rudolph Virchow, a renowned German pathologist who was visiting Washington, D.C., at the time. While traveling through Europe in 1906, Shadd met with another specialist, Robert Koch, a famed bacteriologist of the era.

In the community, Shadd served from 1890 to 1896 on the board of trustees for the District of Columbia public schools, sixth division, where he was noted for his advocacy for industrial training and egalitarian education. He participated in the first sessions of the American Conference of Education held in Washington, D.C., in 1890 and became chairman of what was perceived as a radical organization, the District of Columbia branch of the Afro-American Council, which was dedicated to increasing the educational, moral, and political ranking of African Americans.

Outside of education, Shadd was a trustee with the Fifteenth Street Presbyterian Church, a member of the Bethel Literary and Historical Association, a patron of the Samuel Coleridge Taylor Choral Society, and chairman of the Citizen's Committee of the New Building Campaign of the African-American branch of the Young Mens' Christian Association. Cognizant of the value of money and the need to save, Shadd was the founder and director of the Industrial Building and Savings Company. He died in Washington, D.C.

• The Raleigh Township Centennial Museum, North Buxton, Ontario, has "Record of the Shadd Family in Canada" and a family tree of the Shadd descendants. A limited discussion of Shadd and an example of an advertisement for the medical department that he penned are in Herbert M. Morais, *The History of the Negro in Medicine* (1970). The principal sources of biographical information on Shadd are articles by Henry S. Robinson, "Medical History: Furman Jeremiah Shadd, MD, 1852–1908," *Journal of the National Medical Association* 72, no. 2 (1980); and "Biographical Sketches: The Bruce and Related Families" (1982), in the possession of the Shadd family. Another biographical sketch is Daniel Smith Lamb, "Furmann Jeremiah Shadd, A.M., M.D.," in *Howard University Medical Department, Washington, D.C.: A Historical, Biographical and Statistical Souvenir* (1900; repr. 1971).

M. DALYCE NEWBY

SHAFROTH, John Franklin (9 June 1854–20 Feb. 1922), attorney and statesman, was born in Fayette, Missouri, the son of John Shafroth, a merchant, and Anna Aull. Shafroth graduated from the University of Michigan in 1875 and then studied law in the offices of Samuel C. Major of Fayette. He was admitted to the Missouri bar in 1876. In 1881 he married Virginia Talbott Morrison; they had five children, three of whom survived their parents.

Shafroth moved from Fayette to Denver, Colorado, in 1879, where he practiced law and served as city attorney from 1887 to 1891. Elected in 1894 to the U.S. House of Representatives as a Republican, he helped organize the Silver Republicans in 1896 and the same year backed the pro-silver Democrat William Jennings Bryan for the presidency. Reelected as a Silver Republican in 1896 and 1898, he retained his seat in 1900 as a fusion candidate supported by Bryan Democrats and Silver Republicans. In 1901 he encouraged the permanent amalgamation of the nearly moribund Silver Republicans with the Democrats. Evidence of fraud in the 1902 election, in which he was returned as a Democrat, triggered his resignation from Congress on 15 February 1904. His friends dubbed him "Honest John" because he exited voluntarily, but he failed to be reelected to Congress later that year.

Congressman Shafroth unsuccessfully urged the federal government to inflate the currency by purchasing and coining large amounts of silver, a panacea dear to Colorado's silver producers. He also warned against U.S. imperialism and argued against the annexation of Hawaii. His 1897 proposal to amend the Constitution to eliminate the lame-duck congressional session proved to be more than thirty years ahead of its time. Benefiting from the support of women, who had gained suffrage in Colorado in 1893, he championed women's rights. Granting women the vote, he argued, had not subjected them to debasement: "In Colorado I find no tendency in men to omit the politeness and gallantry to woman which she has always commanded" (*Women's Journal*, 25 Nov. 1905, p. 186).

Elected Colorado's governor in 1908 and reelected in 1910, Shafroth proved himself an effective progressive reformer by securing laws mandating state inspection of factories, prohibiting employment of children under fourteen, providing for primary elections, establishing a state tax commission (which helped insure that assessed property valuations reflected actual values), creating a state highway commission, and protecting the right of workers to join unions. He secured a voter registration law and supported a bill insuring bank deposits, which failed because of alleged constitutional defects. His campaign to regulate railroads was not fully effective, despite a law banning rebates and exorbitant freight rates. To curb the power of special interests, he backed legislation that provided for partial state financing of political campaigns, a measure that suffered constitutional challenge and eventual repeal. By calling a special legislative session in 1910, he pressured lawmakers into approving a state constitutional amendment providing for the initiative and referendum. Voters approved the measure in November. In 1912 he used the initiative to win approval of a constitutional amendment giving voters the power to recall certain elected officials. His crusade for laws limiting women and miners to eight-hour work days and his advocacy of coal mine inspection legislation also eventually bore fruit.

Shafroth's election to the U.S. Senate in 1912 took him back to Washington, D.C., where as a member of the Committee on Banking and Finance he helped craft the Federal Reserve Act (1913). He also supported the Clayton Antitrust Act (1914), the imposition of federal income and inheritance taxes, and the League of Nations. His partisans claimed in 1918 that he had done much for Colorado, including securing a $2 million contract for the Yule Marble Company to supply Colorado marble for the Lincoln Memorial and assisting in locating a large army hospital (later named Fitzsimons Hospital) near Denver. A defender of western development, he argued that the federal government should not perpetually retain vast amounts of land in states such as Colorado. "He has stood," wrote Nevada senator Key Pittman, "as an impassable human barrier to the efforts of certain nature fakers and theorists in the far East in their effort to take away from the people of the West their lands, their mines and their timber for the purpose of constituting them into a grand park for the amusement of the effete East" (*Denver Post*, 24 Oct. 1918).

Despite his accomplishments, Shafroth failed in his 1918 reelection bid, losing to the Republican, multimillionaire businessman Lawrence C. Phipps, in a campaign made difficult by the raging influenza epidemic, which caused officials to ban mass meetings. On leaving the Senate he chaired a federal commission to settle claims against the government arising from the curtailment of mineral production when World War I emergency demand ceased. He died in Denver.

Shafroth's advocacy of woman suffrage and his anti-imperialism put him well in advance of much of the country. His 1913 scheme to redesign the national flag

died quickly, but his efforts to safeguard bank deposits, to limit the power of special interest money in elections, to protect labor, to limit child labor, to eliminate the lame-duck session of Congress, and to inaugurate the president in January all proved prophetic. Even his seemingly ill fated silver campaign came to something because the Federal Reserve System, which he helped create, allowed for expansion of the money supply, one of the silver proponents' chief wishes. Few Colorado leaders have been as politically successful as Shafroth was, have achieved as much, or have shown as much foresight.

• Shafroth papers are located in Denver at the Colorado Historical Society, the Colorado State Archives, and the Denver Public Library's Western History Department. Among Shafroth's more important speeches in the *Congressional Record* are his remarks on silver, 54th Cong., 1st sess., 5 Feb. 1896; his attack on imperialism, 55th Cong., 2d sess., 14 June 1896; his espousal of woman suffrage, 63d Cong., 2d sess., 2 Mar. 1914; his presentation opposing federal leasing of public lands, 63d Cong., 2d sess., 21 Mar. 1914; and his defense of Philippine independence, 64th Cong., 1st sess., 7 Jan. 1916. William C. Ferril, *Sketches of Colorado* (1911), includes material on Shafroth family history. Little has been published on Shafroth. E. K. MacCool, "John Franklin Shafroth, Reform Governor of Colorado, 1909–1913," *Colorado Magazine* 39 (Jan. 1952): 37–51, gives a succinct account of his gubernatorial career. Additional detail is provided by Lloyd K. Musselman, "Governor John F. Shafroth and the Colorado Progressives: Their Fight for Direct Legislation, 1909–1910" (M.A. thesis, Univ. of Denver, 1961), and Gerald D. Welch, "John F. Shafroth, Progressive Governor of Colorado, 1910–1912" (M.A. thesis, Univ. of Denver, 1962). An obituary is in the *Rocky Mountain News*, 21 Feb. 1922.

STEPHEN J. LEONARD

SHAFTER, William Rufus (16 Oct. 1835–12 Nov. 1906), military officer, was born in Galesburg, Michigan, the son of Hugh Morris Shafter, a pioneer farmer, and Eliza Summer. Growing up in western Michigan when the region was emerging from its frontier past, he received enough education to meet the modest requirements in 1856 to become a country school teacher.

When the Civil War started in 1861, Shafter joined the Seventh Michigan Infantry Regiment as a first lieutenant. He participated in the battle of Ball's Bluff (1861) and the Peninsula campaign (1862), distinguishing himself at the battle at Fair Oaks (1862). Although wounded, his action at Fair Oaks on 31 May 1862 earned Shafter (on 12 June 1895) the Congressional Medal of Honor, his commander reporting that he "furnished beautiful exhibitions of gallant conduct and intelligent activity." While on military leave, he married Harriett "Hattie" Amelia Grimes in 1862; they had one child. Taken captive after the battle at Thompson's Station, Shafter remained a prisoner from March to May 1863. He earned promotions to major of the Nineteenth Michigan Infantry on 5 September 1862 and to lieutenant colonel of the Nineteenth Michigan on 5 June 1863. In late 1863 he organized and trained the Seventeenth U.S. (Colored)

Infantry Regiment, one of the army's first African-American regiments. Promoted to colonel on 19 April 1864, he led his regiment at the battle of Nashville (1864). On 13 March 1865 he received promotion to brevet brigadier general of volunteers.

In the army's postwar reorganization, Shafter in 1867 received appointment as lieutenant colonel of the Forty-first Infantry, a black regiment. He joined it in Louisiana, but shortly afterward it was transferred to the lower Rio Grande Valley. In 1868 the regiment moved to Fort Clark on the Texas frontier, and the next year it consolidated with the Thirty-eighth to form the Twenty-fourth Infantry.

Shafter served nearly eighteen years on the frontier, most of them in Texas. He spent much of the time exploring western lands, building forts and roads, erecting telegraph lines, and guarding stagecoaches. Perhaps his most important contribution in Texas was the exploration of the Llano Estacado. For five months in 1875 Shafter and his troops crisscrossed the ranging West Texas tableland over a veritable maze of trails, marking roads, locating water sources, and noting its rich ranching potential. Within a year of his well-publicized report, cattlemen and sheepherders entered the high plains country.

Shafter's troops also fought Native Americans and guarded the Rio Grande border. Tough, aggressive, and considered the most energetic man of his rank in the Department of Texas, Shafter with his troops pursued Apaches, Comanches, Kiowas, and Kickapoos across Texas and the greater Southwest. To protect the Rio Grande border, Shafter on several occasions in 1873, 1876, and 1877 illegally crossed the river with his black troops to attack villages in Mexico, where horses and cattle stolen from Texas ranches were held. After a final crossing in 1878, the border troubles declined.

In 1879 Shafter received promotion to colonel of the First Infantry. The assignment took him briefly to the Dakotas before his new regiment returned to the Southwest. In the 1880s he invested in a successful silver mining venture in Texas and served briefly in New York and Arizona before the army in 1886 assigned him to duty in northern California. In 1890–1891 he took his regiment to South Dakota during the Ghost Dance/Wounded Knee troubles, and during the Pullman strike in 1894 he guarded the mails and maintained the peace in Los Angeles. Promotion to brigadier general came in 1897.

Shafter is best remembered for his role in the Spanish-American War in 1898. Grossly overweight and suffering from gout and varicose veins, he led American land forces to Cuba, where in less than four weeks his command gained its objective and encouraged serious negotiations for peace. However, his aggressive manner with reporters, his inability to cooperate in joint army-navy operations, and deficiencies in supplies caused him to become associated with military blunders in the war.

Problems were plentiful in Cuba. Short of landing craft, the men forced their horses and mules out of the ships and into the sea, hoping that the animals would swim to land. Several of them swam away from shore and drowned. The advance troops had been issued only three days of rations. It rained nearly every day for the first two weeks, and the roads—only narrow jungle trails—turned to quagmires, making conditions difficult to get supplies and reinforcements to the front. Some outmoded weapons used shells that when fired gave off black smoke, thus revealing the gunman's position. There were few assault weapons with which to attack entrenched enemy lines. Some American soldiers had been issued uniforms designed for winter campaigning on the northern plains. When he ordered the attack at San Juan hill, Shafter divided his command, a decision that nearly resulted in disaster.

Nonetheless, Shafter, who had moved an army of 16,000 men 1,200 miles by water from Tampa, Florida, landed at Daiquirí on Cuba's southeastern coast on 22 June. In ten days he drove the Spanish forces back to their last line of defense in front of Santiago de Cuba. The most significant fighting occurred on 1 July, when his army killed or wounded more than 2,000 Spanish troops and captured thirty wagonloads of prisoners. Knowing that an attempt to storm the city without sufficient artillery to blast through the barbed wire and the entrenched enemy positions would be suicidal, Shafter on 4 July opened negotiations with Spanish officers. When the conferences broke down, sporadic fighting occurred on 10 and 11 July. Renewing the peace talks, Shafter convinced the Spaniards on 17 July to surrender not only the city but also the entire eastern district of Cuba and an army of 24,000 men. On 7 August his troops started home, and on 25 August Shafter left the island. Although the impression in the summer of 1898 was that Shafter was "criminally incompetent," President William McKinley remarked that Shafter "embarked his command and set sail, well knowing that there were deficiencies in his equipment. But instead of waiting for what he wanted, he took what he could get, and brought back what he went for."

After the war, Shafter served briefly in New York but in October 1898 returned to his former command of the Department of California. Although he retired from the regular army on 16 October 1899, he retained his volunteer status and his position at the Presidio in San Francisco.

In 1901, upon receiving special promotion to major general, Shafter retired to his small ranch near Bakersfield, California, where he died several years later. A complicated individual, he was coarse and profane but also kind and sentimental. Called "Pecos Bill" by his black troops, Shafter spent much of his long career at military posts on the western frontier, where he displayed courage, zeal, and intelligence and where, although he had trouble getting along with subordinates, was known as an officer who got results. In 1898 he was often pictured as a buffoon, but in Cuba he carried out a swift and highly successful operation that ensured a quick and satisfying end to the Spanish-American War.

• Shafter's papers, including scrapbook materials, are at Stanford University. Additional collections are at Texas Tech University, the University of Michigan, and Western Michigan University. Department of War records such as field correspondence, post and regimental returns, and especially Shafter's large ACP file in the National Archives are valuable. Also useful are various government documents from House and Senate investigating commissions, annual reports of the secretary of war, and the Navy Department's 1898 annual report. The most complete modern assessment is Paul H. Carlson, *"Pecos Bill": A Military Biography of William R. Shafter* (1989), which emphasizes the frontier years. For the Spanish-American War see David F. Trask, *The War with Spain in 1898* (1981), and Graham A. Cosmas, *An Army for Empire: The United States Army in the Spanish-American War* (1971). For the frontier period see Arlen L. Fowler, *The Black Infantry in the West, 1869–1891* (1971); William H. Leckie, *The Buffalo Soldiers: A Narrative of the Negro Cavalry in the West* (1967); and Robert M. Utley, *Frontier Regulars: The United States Army and the Indian, 1866–1891* (1973). For the Texas-Mexico border troubles see Clarence C. Clendenen, *Blood on the Border: The United States Army and the Mexican Irregulars* (1969). An obituary is in the *New York Times*, 13 Nov. 1906.

PAUL H. CARLSON

SHAHAN, Thomas Joseph (10 or 11 Sept. 1857–9 Mar. 1932), Catholic clergyman, educator, and church historian, was born in Manchester, New Hampshire, the son of Maurice Peter Shahan and Mary Anne Carmody, Irish immigrants. He grew up in Millbury, Massachusetts, where his father owned a shoe store. After attending public schools there, he went in 1872 to the Sulpician Collège de Montréal (a minor seminary) for his classical and philosophical studies and there was introduced to neo-Thomism. In 1878 he became a seminarian at the North American College in Rome and a student of theology at the Urban College of the Propaganda Fide, where one of his professors was Francesco Satolli, a promoter of the Thomistic revival; he was also strongly influenced by the expert in Christian archaeology Giovanni Battista de Rossi. He was ordained priest on 3 June 1882 for the Diocese of Hartford (Connecticut) and was awarded the doctorate in theology.

After serving in his diocese as an assistant pastor for one year and as chancellor and secretary to the bishop for five, he was invited to join the faculty of the Catholic University of America in Washington, D.C., which was to open in the autumn of 1889. To prepare himself to teach canon law, he returned to Rome and earned the licentiate's degree *in utroque jure* (in canon and civil law) in 1889. Having been asked to change his field to church history (which he had long preferred), he studied in Berlin and Paris under famous scholars such as Adolf von Harnack and Louis Duchesne. In the autumn of 1891 he began teaching at the Catholic University; his areas were ancient and, later, medieval ecclesiastical history and patrology. In addition, from 1900 on he offered courses for the women at Trinity College. He gave frequent lectures outside Washington and at the same time wrote numerous articles, some of which, along with lectures and addresses, he

collected in books. In 1895, together with other faculty members, he helped to launch the quarterly *Catholic University Bulletin* and became its first editor; during the fourteen years of his editorship he insisted on high standards of scholarship. From late 1904 on, he was one of the five editors of the *Catholic Encyclopedia* (16 vols., 1907–1914), to which he contributed more than 200 articles besides rewriting or translating more than 100 others.

In 1909 he was appointed acting rector of the university by the Holy See and shortly thereafter was elected rector by the board of trustees. He was reelected in 1915 and again in 1922 and retired in 1928, having had the longest tenure of any rector or president in the history of the institution. In 1909 he was also invested with the rank of domestic prelate of His Holiness; in 1914 he was raised to the office of titular bishop of Germanicopolis and was consecrated in Baltimore on 15 November.

During the nineteen years of his rectorship the university grew in several respects. The faculty, whose divisiveness along national and ideological lines he pacified, increased from twenty-nine to 115, and the student body from 225 to 892; the land holdings were expanded from seventy to 270 acres; many buildings were constructed, most notably the Mullen Memorial Library; and the number of books rose from 53,500 to 273,674. More religious orders established houses of study in the vicinity. Although he developed endowed scholarship funds, he never fully solved the financial problems he had inherited from his predecessor. To upgrade and standardize the Catholic school system in the United States, an affiliation program for colleges and high schools was begun in 1912, and the program for seminaries was expanded. New institutions, namely, the Summer School (for training teaching sisters and laywomen, the first of its kind under Catholic auspices in the country, in 1911) and its branches, Catholic Sisters College (on a separate campus, also in 1911), Basselin College, and the Knights of Columbus Evening School, were associated with the university; in 1923 the National Catholic School of Social Service became part of the university. Several learned journals were established by or at the university, including the *Catholic Educational Review* (1911), the *Catholic Historical Review* (1915), of which Shahan was editor in chief until 1928, the *Catholic Charities Review* (1917), the *New Scholasticism* (1927), and *Primitive Man* (1928); the *Ecclesiastical Review* was transferred to a professor of sociology, William J. Kerby, in 1927 and later to the university itself. Thus Shahan strove to realize the initial objective of making the Catholic University the capstone of the American Catholic educational structure and a coordinating agency that would extend its influence throughout the country.

For the same purpose Shahan assumed the presidency of several national Catholic organizations. As long as he was rector he was president of the Catholic Educational Association (since 1927 the National Catholic Educational Association). In 1910 he brought together at the university leaders of Catholic charitable work; thus the National Conference of Catholic Charities was founded, and Shahan was elected its president; he held that office for eighteen years. He was also elected president of the Catholic Anthropological Conference when it was founded in 1926. Finally, he was director of the International Federation of Catholic Alumnae from 1916 to 1928.

Early in his rectorship Shahan conceived the idea of building a university church that would be a center of devotion to the Virgin Mary for American Catholics. In 1913 the National Organization of Catholic Women began to collect funds for it. The foundation stone of the National Shrine of the Immaculate Conception was laid in 1920, but only the crypt was finished during Shahan's lifetime. In the 1920s he was criticized for devoting more time to this project than to academic matters. After he retired as rector of the university, he continued to be director of the shrine.

Shahan's prominence was recognized in signal ways. He was elected president of the Association of American Universities in 1913. In 1923 the Catholic University of Louvain conferred on him an honorary doctorate in theology (a rare distinction). Three years later he was elected one of the first thirty fellows of the Mediaeval Academy of America. After his retirement Pope Pius XI elevated him to the honorable position of assistant at the Pontifical Throne, which entitled him to a prominent place at papal ceremonies. He died in Washington and was entombed in the crypt of the national shrine.

Shahan had a kindly and amiable, gentle and benign personality, but his temperament was also highly emotional and easily excitable. From middle age on, he suffered increasingly from deafness. He was not merely a learned, but a cultured scholar, an avid collector of books, and a holy and zealous churchman. In matters of faith he was conservative, but in social questions he tended to be liberal. He was always loyal to his Irish ancestry and sensitive about the minority status of American Catholics. A man of vision, he was fertile and original in conceiving grand plans and enthusiastic, as well as willing to take risks, in realizing them. Besides extolling the power of the arts to ennoble humanity, he promoted a militant educational philosophy, upholding spiritual values against the materialism, relativism, and pragmatism of secular education. His whole professional career was a sustained effort to activate the educative potential of the church and to transmit to posterity in ways adapted to modern times his profound understanding and appreciation of the Catholic heritage.

• Shahan's papers are deposited at the Catholic University of America. His longer books are *The Beginnings of Christianity* (1903), *The Middle Ages: Sketches and Fragments* (1904), and *The House of God* (1905). Some of his shorter books or booklets are *The Blessed Virgin in the Catacombs* (1892), *John Baptist de Rossi, Founder of the Science of Christian Archaeology* (1895), *Giovanni Baptista de Rossi (1822–1894), Founder of the Science of Christian Archaeology* (1900), *The Civil Law of Rome* (1896), *Catholicism in the Middle Ages* (1902), and *Saint Patrick in History* (1904). Shahan is the subject of an unpublished Ph.D. dissertation written by Blase Robert Dixon, T. O. R., "The Catholic University of America, 1909–1928: The Rectorship of Thomas Joseph Shahan" (Catholic Univ. of America, 1972), and he is treated at length by C. Joseph Nuesse in *The Catholic University of America: A Centennial History* (1990). Obituaries are in the *Catholic Educational Review* 30 (Apr. 1932): 193–217, and the *New York Times*, 10 Mar. 1932.

ROBERT TRISCO

SHAHN, Ben (12 Sept. 1898–14 Mar. 1969), painter and graphic artist, was born Benjamin Shahn in Kovno (Kaunas), Lithuania, the son of Hessel Shahn, a carpenter and woodcarver, and Gittel Lieberman. Kovno was located in the area of czarist Russia known as the Pale of Settlement, where Russian Jews were legally allowed to settle. In 1906 the family was forced to flee the pogroms, government-sponsored massacres of Jews, that swept through the Pale at the turn of the century. They took refuge in the United States and settled in Brooklyn. In 1913 Shahn was taken out of school and began an apprenticeship as a lithographer at Hessenberg's Lithography Shop in Manhattan. During the next four years he not only mastered the skill of lettering but also developed a distinctive, incised line that would become a hallmark of his later work as a painter and graphic artist. During his apprenticeship he also attended night school in order to complete his high school diploma and enrolled briefly, in November 1916, in classes at the Art Students League in New York.

Shahn used his skills as a lithographer to finance his later studies at New York University (1919–1921), the City College of New York (1922), and the National Academy of Design (1922). He also financed two trips to Europe and North Africa, one in 1924–1925 and one in 1927–1929. He was accompanied on these trips by Mathilda ("Tillie") Goldstein, whom he had married in 1922. They had two children.

After Shahn returned from his second trip, he shared a studio with the photographer Walker Evans and became interested in recording instances of political injustice in his work. In 1930 he executed a series of watercolor portraits of the major characters in the Dreyfus Affair, the case of the French Jewish military officer charged with treason, found guilty, and later acquitted after it was revealed that the evidence against him had been fabricated and that he had been the target of anti-Semitism. Two years later, in 1932, Shahn created a series of twenty-three gouaches and two tempera panels on the trial and execution, for robbery and murder, of the two Italian-American anarchists Nicola Sacco and Bartolomeo Vanzetti. The case had gained international attention because of the anti-Italian and anti-anarchist biases of the presiding judge. The following year Shahn painted a third series of images, this time on the trial of the labor leader Tom Mooney, who was, once again, the victim of a corrupt justice system.

Shahn's Sacco and Vanzetti series caught the attention of the Mexican muralist Diego Rivera, who agreed to write the foreword to the catalog for the Mooney show and who hired Shahn to help him on a mural he was creating for Rockefeller Center (the mural was destroyed before it was finished, ostensibly because of the inclusion of the head of Lenin). This experience led to further mural ventures in the 1930s. In 1933 Shahn designed a mural on the theme of Prohibition for the New York City Public Works of Art Project, but the mural was vetoed by the Municipal Art Commission. This same commission prevented the execution of a second mural project for the Public Works of Art Project, which Shahn worked on from 1934 to 1935 with the muralist Louis Block. The two artists created a series of mural designs for the Rikers Island Penitentiary, contrasting prison systems of the present and the past. Although the designs were approved by Mayor Fiorello La Guardia and August McCormick, the commissioner of correction, the Municipal Art Commission ruled they were "unsuitable" for the intended location. In 1932 Shahn and his wife divorced, and three years later he married Bernarda Bryson, with whom he had three children.

Shahn was then hired, in 1935, by the federal Resettlement Administration, subsequently renamed the Farm Security Administration (FSA). He worked with this agency as an artist and photographer until 1938. He had become interested in photography while sharing a studio with Walker Evans and took a number of photographs to help in the preparation of the Rikers Island Penitentiary studies. While in the employ of the FSA he made three photographic trips throughout the South and Midwest, recording the effects of the depression on the country's rural and small-town population. These photographs (which numbered over six thousand) are marked by scenes of rundown houses and poverty-stricken women and children staring blankly at the camera. Shahn entered enthusiastically into this government work, feeling that Franklin D. Roosevelt's reform agenda was the only way to get the country back on its feet. He was accompanied on his photographic trips by his wife Bernarda, who was also an artist.

Before leaving the employ of the FSA, Shahn painted a mural in the community center of Jersey Homesteads, New Jersey (1937–1938), one of the first of the resettlement communities built in the 1930s. In this work Shahn presented the history of the Jewish garment workers for whom the town was built, from their arrival in the United States to their work in the sweatshops of New York City to the organization of the International Ladies Garment Workers Union (ILGWU) to, finally, the building of Jersey Homesteads. Shahn also included Albert Einstein in the center of the immigrants arriving in the United States and, in the top left corner, a Nazi soldier in front of a sign reading "Germans, beware. Don't buy from Jews." Ultimately, the mural was a celebration of organized labor, particularly the ILGWU, and the Roosevelt administration. In 1939 Shahn and his family moved to Jersey Homesteads, where he lived for the rest of his life.

Shahn received three more government mural commissions. In 1939 he and Bernarda Bryson painted thirteen tempera panels in the Bronx post office showing individuals working at various occupations such as harvesting wheat, picking cotton, and building hydroelectric dams. That same year Shahn also painted a mural for the Jamaica, New York, post office on the theme of the four freedoms guaranteed by the first amendment. His final mural commission was for the Social Security Building in Washington, D.C. (1940–1942), which highlighted the gains in social security that had been made during the Roosevelt administration.

Shahn's Social Security mural contains many vignettes from paintings he had executed in the late 1930s. These works differed from his earlier paintings in that they no longer focused on public instances of political injustice; instead, they portrayed private moments in working people's lives. They showed people walking through an open field, sitting on a hillside, playing handball in a vacant city lot. He later wrote that this shift from "social realism" to "personal realism" was prompted by his photographic trips across the United States, where he came into contact with all manner of people who were persisting in the face of great hardship. He wanted to convey the personal qualities of these people's daily lives.

Shahn's work underwent another shift as a result of World War II. From the fall of 1942 to the summer of 1943 Shahn was employed by the Office of War Information (OWI) as a graphic artist, and he saw vast numbers of photographs of the devastation taking place in Europe and the South Pacific. In his OWI posters he attempted to convey the horror of these events, yet in his paintings he searched for a more symbolic imagery to convey the extent and nature of this suffering.

During the war Shahn also worked for the Political Action Committee of the Congress of Industrial Organizations (CIO-PAC), creating posters and other graphic material for Roosevelt during the 1944 presidential campaign. He also worked for the CIO-PAC during the 1946 congressional campaign. Shahn valued his work with labor unions because it brought him into touch with such a vast audience. He severed his ties with the CIO-PAC in 1947, however, when the labor federation began purging members of the Communist party and other leftist organizations from its leadership and rank and file. Shahn was outspoken in his criticisms of the political persecution and censorship that was carried out during the Cold War in the name of protecting the United States against communism. He joined the Progressive party in 1947 and worked for its presidential candidate Henry Wallace in 1948. His most famous image from the Wallace campaign is the large poster of President Harry S. Truman and Republican candidate Thomas Dewey that appeared behind Wallace at the Progressive party convention in July of 1948.

Many of the paintings that Shahn produced in the late 1940s and 1950s grew out of commissions he was given to illustrate articles in magazines like *Harper's* or the *Nation*. Although the drawings were highly descriptive of the events presented in the text, the paintings were more often symbolic or allegorical. For example, the painting *Allegory* (1948) is meant to convey, in Shahn's words, "the emotional tone that surrounds disaster," rather than the particular disaster (a tenement fire in which four children had been killed) that had been the subject of the *Harper's* article for which he had created the drawings. Shahn's style also changed at this time. In his early work the narrative subject was clearly articulated, with recognizable historical characters located in settings that often contained carefully rendered architectural details. Now, his backgrounds were becoming more abstract and the foreground figures more schematized, often appearing as mere outlines against the abstract background. Despite this increasing abstraction, Shahn remained a committed proponent of humanistic content in art and argued that artists needed to remain politically engaged in order to help preserve democracy in the United States. He was an avid supporter of the civil rights and peace movements and produced many posters and prints to raise money for these causes. In 1959 he was called before the House Un-American Activities Committee to justify the inclusion of his work in a government-sponsored art exhibition sent to Moscow that summer.

Shahn also gained an international reputation in the 1950s. He was one of two painters representing the United States (the other was Willem de Kooning) at the 1954 Venice Biennial. By the early 1960s Shahn had also gained a following in Southeast Asia. From 1960 to 1962 Shahn created a series of ten paintings on the story of the Japanese fishing boat *The Lucky Dragon*, which had wandered into the area where the United States was testing a hydrogen bomb on 1 March 1954 and been covered with radioactive fallout.

In the last decade of Shahn's life he also designed a series of mosaic murals and stained-glass windows, primarily on religious themes, and created a number of portraits of major political figures, such as Dag Hammarskjöld (1962) and Martin Luther King, Jr. (1966). He also turned his attention increasingly to the Hebrew alphabet and to the illustration of religious texts, creating two deluxe books, *Ecclesiastes* (1965) and the *Haggadah* (1966). Although he is best known today for his work of the 1930s and 1940s, which dealt with instances of political injustice and the public and private lives of working-class Americans, he is also well known within the Jewish community as an artist who conveyed a strong sense of spirituality in his later work. He died in New York City.

• The majority of Shahn's papers are in the collection of the Archives of American Art, Smithsonian Institution, and are available through interlibrary loan on microfilm. John D. Morse edited a collection of Shahn's writings, *Ben Shahn* (1973). *The Shape of Content* (1957) records talks Shahn presented at Harvard in 1956–1957. See also Selden Rodman, *Portrait of the Artist as an American* (1951); James Thrall Soby, *Ben Shahn: Paintings* (1963); Mirella Bentivoglio, *Ben Shahn* (1963); Martin H. Bush, *Ben Shahn: The Passion of Sacco and Vanzetti* (1968); Bernarda Bryson Shahn, *Ben Shahn* (1972); Kenneth Wade Prescott, *The Complete Graphic Works of Ben Shahn* (1973); Davis Pratt, ed., *The Photographic Eye of Ben Shahn* (1975); Kenneth Wade Prescott, *Prints and Posters of Ben Shahn* (1982); Frances K. Pohl, *Ben Shahn, New Deal Artist in a Cold War Climate, 1947–1954* (1989); and Pohl, *Ben Shahn* (1993). An obituary is in the *London Times*, 17 Mar. 1969.

FRANCES K. POHL

SHAKESPEARE, Edward Oram (19 May 1846–1 June 1900), physician, bacteriologist, and public health advocate, was born in New Castle County, Delaware, the son of William McIntire Shakespeare and Catherine Haman. Shakespeare's eulogists omit reference to his parent's occupations but mention that he was a descendant of English dramatist William Shakespeare's brother and that his family had been established in Delaware for several generations at the time of his birth. Shakespeare attended Reynolds' Classical Academy in Dover, Delaware. While an undergraduate at Dickinson College, Shakespeare served as an apprentice to two physicians in Dover. After earning an A.B. in 1867, he entered medical school at the University of Pennsylvania, from which he graduated in 1869. He then spent less than five years in partnership with Isaac Jurup, "an old established physician of large practice" in Dover (Watson, p. 163) before returning to Philadelphia, where he remained an active member of the medical scene until his death. He had a number of institutional affiliations, but none occupied him full time or defined his career. In 1889 he married Mary Louise Baird, the daughter of an officer of the Baldwin Locomotive Works; they had two children.

Early in his career Shakespeare established himself as an ophthalmologist, building his reputation on his 1876 invention of a new type of ophthalmoscope. In the early 1880s he was among the first Americans to experiment with cocaine as a therapeutic and an anesthetic for the eye. By the early 1880s he also held appointments in eye surgery and refraction at Philadelphia General Hospital and the University of Pennsylvania. In forging an ophthalmology practice, Shakespeare participated in the beginnings of specialization in American medicine. At the same time, his aspirations in science and social reform led him to accept a number of unpaid positions in other fields.

As early as 1872, Shakespeare was performing autopsies at Philadelphia General, and during the late 1870s he did similar work for the county coroner. As the hospital's curator from 1880, pathologist from 1882, and bacteriologist from 1889, he had access to bodies for dissection and the opportunity to help develop the hospital laboratory as a site for diagnostic work. Shakespeare also used his fine microscope, acute vision, and skills in photography and drafting in original pathological investigations. By undertaking experiments with animals, he helped to establish a role for investigative medicine in American hospitals and medical schools. His interest in advancing science within medicine led him in 1876 to join the well-respected Pathological Society of Philadelphia, whose members met every two weeks to present specimens and discuss cases. He served as the society's president in 1884–1885.

Shakespeare distinguished himself on several occasions as a scientific consultant to governmental bodies. In 1885 he visited Plymouth, Pennsylvania, at the request of the mayor of Philadelphia, to determine the cause of a devastating outbreak of typhoid fever. His report confirmed that the excreta of a single victim of typhoid, even after months of being frozen in snow, had contaminated the town's water supply. His findings added greatly to a growing understanding of the importance of a pure water supply: both the degree to which the Plymouth disaster had been publicized nationwide and the meticulousness of his investigations heightened the significance of Shakespeare's report.

Later that year, bearing a commission from President Grover Cleveland, Shakespeare traveled to Italy and Spain to study the cholera epidemic that was then receding from Europe. Although he came to no conclusions about the cause of cholera, his thousand-page report, published in 1890, was regarded as a significant contribution to the epidemiology and natural history of the disease. Because of his reputation as a cholera expert, Shakespeare was asked to serve as port physician of Philadelphia during the 1892 cholera scare. While in that post, he suspended his own private practice and not only took charge of the city's maritime commerce but also investigated cholera in his laboratory at Philadelphia General. Just before leaving office he prepared a report that urged the establishment of a municipal laboratory for the bacteriological analysis of the city's milk supply. His assertions about impure milk as a cause of infant mortality and tuberculosis helped set the tone for future discussions of milk regulation.

Shakespeare's final government appointment, overwork at which may have contributed to his early death in Philadelphia from heart disease, was with U.S. Army physician Walter Reed and bacteriologist and public health physician Victor Vaughan on a commission charged with investigating health conditions in army camps during the Spanish-American War. The 1904 Reed-Vaughan-Shakespeare report (of which an abstract was published in 1900, not long after Shakespeare's death) unprecedentedly discounted the results of clinical examinations when they were contradicted by bacteriological findings. The report established that virtually all cases diagnosed as malaria were actually typhoid fever and were therefore being improperly treated. The commission's call for proper prophylactic measures (especially general hygiene and cleanliness) caused a stir in both the military medical establishment and the public health community.

Shakespeare was particularly fascinated by tuberculosis, the leading cause of death in his day and a disease that was generally assumed to be hereditary until German bacteriologist Robert Koch discovered the tubercle bacillus early in 1882. Shakespeare joined the

international medical pilgrimage to Koch's laboratory in Berlin in 1883 and returned a few weeks later to Philadelphia a dedicated proponent of the germ theory. Back home, Shakespeare's success in defending Koch's claim established his reputation as "the earliest and most distinguished Philadelphia pioneer" of bacteriology (McFarland, p. 153).

In 1886 Shakespeare was one of ten Philadelphians invited to be charter members of the elite Association of American Physicians. At the 1890 AAP meeting, he linked current scientific views of tuberculosis to questions of social policy, contrasting the continued absence of a cure with the potential for preventive work inherent in new knowledge of the cause. Shakespeare was one of a small number of doctors to participate in the tuberculosis movement in its early days, and his concern about the contagiousness of tuberculosis helped determine that movement's orientation.

The last quarter of the nineteenth century was a transitional period in the development of biomedical science in the United States, and the type of voluntary positions that Shakespeare filled would soon disappear as pathology, bacteriology, and epidemiology became institutionalized. Shakespeare's own scientific and institutional efforts contributed to these changes in the structure of medical practice and research, and he was an important participant in the importation of scientific medicine to the United States.

• Manuscript materials relating to Shakespeare's career are at the University of Pennsylvania Archives, the College of Physicians of Philadelphia, and in the Walter Reed Papers at the National Library of Medicine. No comprehensive bibliography of Shakespeare's publications has been published. His epidemiological reports include, with Morris French, "Epidemic of Typhoid Fever at Plymouth, Pennsylvania," *Proceedings of the Philadelphia County Medical Society* 7 (1884–1885): 300–333; *Report on Cholera in Europe and India* (1890); and, with Walter Reed and Victor Vaughan, *Report on the Origin and Spread of Typhoid Fever in U.S. Military Camps during the Spanish War of 1898* (1904). His ideas for tuberculosis control appear in "What Can and Should Be Done to Limit the Prevalence of Tuberculosis in Man?" *Medical News* 57 (1890): 201–13. For an overview of Shakespeare's position on port quarantine, which included immigration limitation, see "Necessity for a National Quarantine," *Forum* 14 (1893): 579–90.

Shakespeare's work in Philadelphia is best described in Edward T. Morman, "Scientific Medicine Comes to Philadelphia: Public Health Transformed, 1854–1899" (Ph.D. diss., Univ. of Pennsylvania, 1986); and the pathology enterprise is discussed in Morman, "Clinical Pathology in America, 1865–1915: Philadelphia as a Test Case," *Bulletin of the History of Medicine* 58 (1984): 198–214. For information on Shakespeare as a bacteriologist, see Joseph McFarland, "The Beginning of Bacteriology in Philadelphia," *Bulletin of the History of Medicine* 5 (1937): 149–98. A useful sketch of his work in the tuberculosis movement is in E. G. Price, *Pennsylvania Pioneers against Tuberculosis* (1952), p. 122. See also Irving A. Watson, *Physicians and Surgeons of America* (1896), pp. 163–64.

EDWARD T. MORMAN

SHAKOW, David (2 Jan. 1901–26 Feb. 1981), psychologist, was born in New York's Lower East Side, the son of Abraham Shakow, a cloth merchant, and Eva Leventhal. Shakow later commented that, in spite or because of its economic deprivation, his place of birth had a resilient vitality that manifested itself in family life and social institutions like the schools. It is evident from an oral history that Shakow felt that a Madison Settlement House on the East Side had a great influence on his early education, more than did his formal public schools. At this house he had the guidance of a Mr. Bradstreat, who introduced him to the writing of Carleton H. Parker, an ardent contemporary socialist. There he found mention of Sigmund Freud, whom he proceeded to read avidly at the age of fourteen and fifteen. From Bradstreat he also learned about philosophers John Dewey and William James, and James became a lifelong part of Shakow's ego-ideal.

The James's connection with Harvard University inspired Shakow to attend that institution, from which he received a B.S. in 1924. In the year of his graduation he served as an assistant in psychopathology at the famous McLean Hospital in Waverly, Massachusetts. The next year he worked under F. L. Wells, an inspiring leader, as a psychology intern at the Boston Psychopathic Hospital (subsequently known as the Massachusetts Mental Health Center). In 1926 he married Sophie Harap; they had four children. In 1927 Shakow was awarded a master's degree in psychology at Harvard.

In 1928 Shakow began work as a psychologist at the Worcester State Hospital in Worcester, Massachusetts, where he pursued a productive multidisciplinary research program devoted to the causes and treatment of schizophrenia. This program was supported by the McCormick and Rockefeller foundations. During the years of the Great Depression the work attracted numerous medical specialists, some as refugees from Nazi-occupied Central Europe, as well as aspiring beginners in the mental health sciences. For the latter Shakow organized and directed a pioneer internship program in clinical psychology in this clinical-scientific environment. From 1937 on Shakow was certified as a diplomate in clinical psychology by the American Board of Examiners in Professional Psychology. Shakow "interrupted" his various research and professional efforts to complete a dissertation on the classic problem of deterioration in schizophrenia and received a Ph.D. in psychology from Harvard in 1942.

Shakow served for eighteen years as chief psychologist and director of psychological research at the Worcester State Hospital with a secondary appointment at the Worcester Child Guidance Clinic. In 1946 he became a professor of psychology at the University of Illinois College of Medicine, and from 1948 to 1954 he was a professor at the University of Chicago. From 1954 to 1966 he was chief of the laboratory of psychology, National Institute of Mental Health, Bethesda, Maryland, and from 1967 to 1981, he was senior research psychologist. From 1974 to 1981 he was scientist emeritus, National Institutes of Health.

Throughout his career of extensive professional and scientific activity, Shakow prominently participated in the work of the American Psychological Association. He played a central role on the Policy and Planning Board, was president of the Division of Clinical Psychology in 1948, chaired the APA's Committee on Training in Clinical Psychology from 1947 to 1949, and was the association's representative to the World Federation of Mental Health from 1970 on.

He actively contributed to his profession through various adjunct appointments. From 1946 to 1955 he was consultant in clinical psychology to the Veterans Administration; from 1948 to 1954, he was consultant in psychology to the Surgeon General's office; from 1950 to 1953, he was a member of the Division of Anthropology and Psychology, National Research Council; from 1953 to 1957, he was a member of the selection committee, NIMH Career Investigator grants; and from 1959 to 1962, he was a member of the advisory committee on psychology for the Fulbright Commission.

Cooperating editorially in the publication of various psychological journals, Shakow served as consulting editor of *Psychologia* (1964–1970), associate editor of *Psychoanalytic Review* (1966–1981), *Journal of General Psychology* (1967–1969), and *Journal of Genetic Psychology* (1969–1981), and editor and advisory board member of *Schizophrenia Bulletin* (1969–1981).

The recipient of numerous honors and awards, Shakow received the first American Psychological Association Annual Distinguished Scientist Award in 1971. In the same year he received the Salmon Medal for distinguished service in psychiatry. In 1975 he was awarded the APA certificate for distinguished scientific contributions, and in 1976 its certificate for distinguished professional contributions.

Until his death while at work in his office at the Clinical Center of the National Institutes of Health in Bethesda, Maryland, Shakow had continued his daily office regimen of writing articles and working on his memoirs.

Shakow is notable for several major influences on psychology during his long professional career. First, he provided an impetus to clinical psychology as a research-oriented endeavor in addition to its more obvious applied dimension. Second, he initiated and guided in that setting an internship training program for scores of young psychologists, which served to shape similar training programs nationally. Third, he was a strong force in fashioning the new psychology as a combined scientific and professional discipline. Fourth, he pursued a persistent and positive multidisciplinary orientation in the study and understanding of the still enigmatic problem of schizophrenia. Finally, he supported and promoted the beleaguered cause of psychoanalysis in psychology by contributing a historically grounded perspective in which the role of research in psychopathology was joined with the educational advantages of psychoanalysis toward self-understanding. As an exemplar of dedicated scientific endeavor, he provides a model for the moral educator of youth.

• Shakow's personal and professional papers are at the Archives of the History of American Psychology, University of Akron. A 1973 taped interview with Shakow is in the Milton Senn Collection on Child Development, National Library of Medicine. In 1976 Shakow produced an oral history regarding his early life and the development of his interest in psychology, which is in the possession of his son Alexander Shakow, Washington, D.C. For full details about Shakow's professional career, see N. Garmezy and P. S. Holzman, "Obituary of David Shakow (1901–1981)," *American Psychologist*, 39 (1984): 698–99. Shakow's own survey of his professional participation in psychology and psychiatry is *Clinical Psychology as Science and Profession* (1969). His three other major publications are *The Nature of Deterioration in Schizophrenic Conditions* (1946); *Adaptation in Schizophrenia: The Theory of Segmental Set* (1979); and *The Influence of Freud on American Psychology*, with David Rapaport (1964). Shakow effectively described the historically significant research program at the Worcester State Hospital in "The Contribution of the Worcester State Hospital and Post–Hall Clark University to Psychoanalysis," in *Psychoanalysis, Psychotherapy and the New England Medical Scene: 1894–1944*, ed. G. E. Gifford, Jr. (1978), pp. 29–62. A vivid portrayal of this milieu is Saul Rosenzweig, "The Way It Was: Remembering David Shakow," *American Psychologist* 40 (1985): 1140f.

SAUL ROSENZWEIG

SHALER, Nathaniel Southgate (20 Feb. 1841–10 Apr. 1906), geologist, geographer, and educationalist, was born in Newport, Kentucky, the son of Nathaniel Burger Shaler, a medical doctor, and Ann Hinde Southgate, the daughter of a prominent legal and land-holding family.

Prior to his enrollment in Harvard's sophomore class of 1859, Shaler—due to ill health—had been educated informally by a Swiss tutor, Johannes Escher, who instructed him in classical languages and initiated him into the rudiments of German idealist philosophy. With such a preparation Shaler turned first to the study of the humanities at Harvard, but he soon abandoned what he considered mere scholasticism to enlist as a student of Louis Agassiz in Harvard's Lawrence Scientific School. He remained one of Agassiz's favorite pupils and would become his assistant after graduating in 1862 with an S.B. summa cum laude. Before taking up that position, however, Shaler married Sophia Penn Page—they would have two daughters—and returned to his native Kentucky, where he obtained a commission as captain of the Fifth Kentucky Battery during the Civil War, although his period of active service on behalf of the Union cause was curtailed because of illness.

Returning to Cambridge, Massachusetts, in 1864 with his wife, Shaler began the task of classifying the Museum of Comparative Zoology's accumulated store of fossils. Agassiz had set him to work on this task, no doubt, because as an undergraduate Shaler had carried out research on the brachiopoda phylum and produced an early paper that greatly pleased his Swiss mentor. Its anti-Darwinian thrust, however, would in

due course be muted as he came more and more to appreciate the evolutionary perspective—though never in a classical Darwinian mode, preferring instead the neo-Lamarckian version that a number of Agassiz's students were cultivating.

During Agassiz's expedition to Brazil in 1865, Shaler was in charge of geology and paleontology. In the interim, and prior to taking up his tenured teaching post, however, Shaler had traveled extensively in Europe working on Alpine glaciers and visiting numerous museums. On his return he participated in fossil excavations at Big Bone Lick in Kentucky, which led to a variety of publications on the historical range of the bison in the American Southeast. He also engaged in summer field excursions that provided the stimulus for the famous Anderson School of Natural History at Penikese—a precursor of the Harvard summer school of which he was subsequently to become director.

In 1872 Shaler returned again to Europe, and during this trip he met such outstanding British naturalists as Darwin, Lyell, Huxley, Tyndall, and Galton. While in England he received his first appointment as director of the Kentucky Geological Survey. Under his administration the first triangulation survey of the state was completed, publications on aspects of the state's environment from geology to forestry appeared, and an inventory of its natural resources was produced for the 1876 Philadelphia Centennial Exposition. At this stage, too, Shaler began developing an interest in sea level change, publishing one of the earliest systematic formulations of the principle of glacial isostasy.

After a third visit to Europe in 1881, Shaler occupied from 1884 to 1900 the position of director of the Atlantic Coast Division of the U.S. Geological Survey under the management of John Wesley Powell. In this capacity he published reports on a wide range of geological phenomena, including a study of the nature and origin of soils (12th Report) described by one observer as "a landmark in the history of soil concepts." Shaler also published many more popular pieces in journals such as the *Atlantic Monthly*, *North American Review*, *Scribner's Magazine*, *Chautauquan*, and the newly established nativist weekly *America*. While many of these pieces dealt with popularizations of physiography, he also addressed numerous social issues on topics ranging from race relations to education. Accordingly, at various times he served as commissioner of agriculture for the State of Massachusetts; as a member of the Massachusetts Highway Commission, the Gypsy Moth Commission, and the Topographic Survey Commission; as vice president of the Immigration Restriction League of Boston; and as vice president of the Massachusetts Society for the Promotion of Good Citizenship. Moreover he established one of the earliest laboratories in the United States for the testing of road materials.

In 1891, the year in which Shaler became dean of the Lawrence Scientific School (a position he held until 1904), his celebrated *Nature and Man in America* made its appearance, a work that would be reissued in new editions until well into the twentieth century. As well as outlining the continent's geological structure, it dealt with such themes as prairie homesteading, folk tillage practices, the "Great American Desert," the use of anthropometric and actuarial data to assess population quality, and aesthetic responses to landscape. The following year he delivered the Winkley Foundation Lectures at Andover Theological School on the relations of science and religion; published as *The Interpretation of Nature* (1893), these lectures revealed Shaler's commitment to a teleological view of humanity's place in nature. His 1905 *Man and the Earth* represents the culmination of his thinking on natural resources, going well beyond George Perkins Marsh's diagnoses by focusing on mineral exhaustion, land reclamation, and the need for alternative sources of energy and by reiterating his earlier warnings about soil erosion and deforestation.

Possessing a warm and engaging personality, Shaler was one of Harvard's most popular teachers; his annual enrollments for his famous Geology 4 course reached 500. He authored several student texts, including *A First Book in Geology* (1884), which was translated into both Polish and German, and *The Story of Our Continent* (1892). In addition, he published a five-volume dramatic romance entitled *Elizabeth of England* and a collection of poems that appeared in 1906, *From Old Fields: Poems of the Civil War*.

During his latter years Shaler's mind turned increasingly to matters of civic concern. To this end he produced a trilogy on social theory that bore the stamp of his close friendship with William James and other pragmatist philosophers at Harvard—*The Individual: A Study of Life and Death* (1900), *The Citizen: A Study of the Individual and the Government* (1904), and *The Neighbor: The Natural History of Human Contacts* (1904). But despite this evident productivity, these years brought perhaps the greatest disappointment of his career. Having worked long and hard on behalf of the Scientific School, Shaler secured in 1903 a bequest from Gordon McKay for the teaching of applied science. During his final trip to Europe in 1904, however, proposals were considered for rationalizing technical education in Massachusetts—plans that would divert the McKay funds to the Massachusetts Institute of Technology. Deeply dispirited, Shaler embarked on another campaign of support for his school; the new scheme was scuttled over a legal technicality, and the days of the Lawrence Scientific School were numbered. Shaler's last contribution to Harvard was his participation in the formulation of a new project to establish a Graduate School of Applied Science. Within a few days of the final approval of the plan, Shaler died in Cambridge.

Shaler occupies a strategic place in the history of American science and education during the Darwinian era. The broad, prolific, and lucid nature of his writings fostered his image as purveyor of science to the nation, especially in providing a "scientific" perspective on issues of burning sociopolitical concern.

• Papers of Shaler are available in the Pusey Library, Harvard University, which also houses the materials of the Lawrence Scientific School, although much of his correspondence is scattered. Besides the books mentioned in the text, Shaler also authored *Thoughts on the Nature of Intellectual Property and Its Importance to the State* (1878), *Kentucky: a Pioneer Commonwealth* (1884), *Directions for the Teaching of Geology* (1888), *Aspects of the Earth: A Popular Account of Some Geological Phenomena* (1889), *American Highways: A Popular Account of Their Conditions and of the Means by Which They May Be Bettered* (1896), and *Outlines of the Earth's History: A Popular Study in Physiography* (1898). Autobiographical materials are in *The Autobiography of Nathaniel Southgate Shaler with a Supplementary Memoir by His Wife* (1909). A scientific biography, which includes a complete bibliography (comprising over three hundred books and articles), is David N. Livingstone, *Nathaniel Southgate Shaler and the Culture of American Science* (1987). Numerous other sketches include the *Harvard Engineering Journal* 5 (1906): 129–38, and the *Boston Transcript*, 18 July 1906. An obituary is in the *Boston Transcript*, 10 Apr. 1906.

DAVID N. LIVINGSTONE

SHANE, Charles Donald (6 Sept. 1895–19 Mar. 1983), astronomer, was born on a ranch near Auburn, California, the son of Charles Nelson Shane and Annette Furthey, both schoolteachers who ultimately became county superintendents of education. C. Donald Shane did his undergraduate and graduate work at the University of California, earning his bachelor's degree at Berkeley in 1915 and his Ph.D. in 1920. During World War I he taught navigation to budding merchant marine officers from 1917 to 1919. Shane did his thesis at Lick Observatory on the spectra of carbon stars, under the supervision of W. W. Campbell, its director.

After receiving his doctorate, Shane became an instructor in mathematics at Berkeley in 1920, then assistant professor of astronomy in 1924, and worked up the ladder in that field to professor in 1935 and to chairman of the astronomy department in 1941. At Berkeley Shane taught all the astrophysics courses in a department otherwise largely devoted to celestial mechanics and orbit calculations. Since in those years the University of California turned out many research astronomers, chiefly observational astrophysicists, his influence was widely felt. He did little research of his own at Berkeley, mostly high-dispersion spectroscopy of the sun. Through this work he became familiar with the techniques of laboratory spectroscopy, which led him to originate the idea of using an echelle spectrograph on an astronomical telescope. Part of the design he suggested to Robert H. Wood, Johns Hopkins University spectroscopist, in 1946 was to use a prism as a cross disperser, to separate the different orders that the echelle (or "echellette," as coarse reflection gratings were then sometimes called) produced. Shane's idea was quickly adopted by Wood and by Massachusetts Institute of Technology spectroscopist George R. Harrison, and echelle spectrographs have come to be widely used for astronomical research. Shane was also heavily involved in faculty activities. Deeply interested in education, he was both personable and hardworking and made a host of friends through the Faculty Club, the center of the professors' network in pre–World War II Berkeley. He served on key university committees and became a confidant of and advisor to President Robert G. Sproul.

During World War II Shane served from 1942 to 1945 in the Manhattan (atomic bomb) Project, first as assistant director for scientific personnel of the Radiation Laboratory at Berkeley (under Ernest O. Lawrence) and subsequently in the same position at Los Alamos (under Robert J. Oppenheimer). In 1944 Sproul appointed Shane, then on leave at Los Alamos, to head a committee to plan a large reflecting telescope to be built after the war had ended at Lick Observatory, the University of California's astronomical research center, located on Mount Hamilton near San Jose. The committee had worked largely by mail, drawing heavily on the experience of several of its members who were Mount Wilson Observatory astronomers and California Institute of Technology physicists involved as leaders in building the Palomar 200-inch telescope. When the war ended, Shane helped Sproul shepherd the budget for the Lick telescope, a 120-inch reflector that when completed would be the second largest in the world, through the California legislature. Then he supervised the astronomers and engineers who designed and built it.

In late 1945 Shane became director of Lick Observatory, inheriting the proper-motion program conceived by earlier director William H. Wright that was based on using distant galaxies to define a natural reference system, fixed in the universe. Wright had seen the 20-inch astrograph, a wide-field astronomical camera especially designed for this program, through to completion before he left Mount Hamilton. Shane took over the program, brought the astrograph into adjustment himself, and with assistant Carl Wirtanen began taking the first-epoch plates. These would be compared with second-epoch plates, obtained a quarter of a century later, to measure the small apparent motions of the stars on the sky. Shane brought Latvian-born astronomer Stanislas Vasilevskis to Lick Observatory to develop the mass-production measurement and reduction techniques that would be necessary to complete the program. Meanwhile he and Wirtanen used the first-epoch plates to count the number of galaxies per unit area over the sky. These counts became important data for analyzing the structure of the universe, as Edwin Hubble had originally advised Shane they would.

In 1917 Shane had married Ethel L. Haskett, who died in January 1919, two weeks after their son Charles was born. In 1920 he married Mary Lea Heger, with whom he also had a son. Mary Lea Shane was an astronomy graduate student when the couple met, and she received her Ph.D. after they were married. Although she never worked professionally in astronomy, she kept her interest in it, and years later, in the 1960s, founded the Archives of Lick Observatory, which now bears her name.

In 1958, when Sproul retired as president, Shane decided to step down as director of Lick Observatory but continued as an astronomer on the faculty until 1963, when he retired. His successor as director, Albert E. Whitford, completed the 120-inch telescope in 1959, and it was named the Shane reflector in 1978. After his retirement, Shane and his wife lived at their home in Scotts Valley, California, near the new Santa Cruz campus of the University of California, of which Lick Observatory had become a part. He died in Santa Cruz.

Shane was an important figure in teaching Berkeley graduate students who became the research leaders of the generation after his own, in building the Lick Observatory telescope, and in beginning the observations of a massive proper-motion program that provided, as a by-product, information on cosmology and the clustering of galaxies in the universe.

• Most of Shane's papers are in the Mary Lea Shane Archives of the Lick Observatory, McHenry Library, University of California, Santa Cruz. They include his correspondence as director and much of his personal scientific correspondence. Some additional papers of his are in the Department of Astronomy Papers in the University Archives, Bancroft Library, University of California, Berkeley. A published memorial biography is Stanislas Vasilevskis and Donald E. Osterbrock, "Charles Donald Shane," National Academy of Sciences, *Biographical Memoirs* 58 (1989): 489–511; it contains a complete bibliography of Shane's published scientific papers. Among the most important of them are "The Program of the Carnegie 20-inch Astrograph," *Publications of the Astronomical Society of the Pacific* 59 (1947): 182–83, and "The Distribution of Galaxies," *Publications of the Lick Observatory* 22, no. 1 (1967): 1–59. See also Osterbrock et al., *Eye on the Sky: Lick Observatory's First Century* (1988), which includes a chapter on Shane's directorship.

DONALD E. OSTERBROCK

SHANNON, Del (30 Dec. 1934–8 Feb. 1990), singer, songwriter, and performer, was born Charles Weedon Westover in Coopersville, Michigan. Shannon began learning the guitar and singing at the age of fourteen, profoundly influenced by the lonesome, heart-rending balladry of Hank Williams. Having grown up in an agrarian Christian town, although his own family neither farmed nor attended church, Shannon felt like an outsider and feverishly practiced playing so that he could make a home for himself. Upon graduating from high school in 1957, he joined the army and became involved in musical productions while stationed in Germany. In 1958 he married Shirley (maiden name unknown); they had three children before they divorced in 1985.

After his tour of duty Shannon worked in a carpet store by day and took on the name of Del Shannon while performing nights at local rock-and-roll clubs. Local disc jockey Ollie McLaughlin of WHRV in Ann Arbor, Michigan, saw Shannon's stage show and recommended him to managers Harry Balk and Irving Micahnik of Embee Productions. Although the Shannon-Embee relationship would dissolve in 1966 in acrimony, lawsuits, and accusations of willful financial mismanagement, Balk and Micahnik did manage to find Shannon a recording deal with Bigtop Records. His first release, "Runaway," was a million-selling hit single, remaining at number one on the *Billboard* chart for four weeks in the spring of 1961. It spawned more than 200 cover versions (including ones by Elvis Presley and Lawrence Welk) and defined Shannon as a rock-and-roll artist.

"Runaway" was written by accident during a rehearsal session at the Hi-Lo Club in Battle Creek, Michigan, with keyboardist Max Crook. It featured the striking minor to major chord changes that became a trademark of the Shannon sound. Throughout the 1960s he utilized this device as a way of musically illustrating sharp emotional shifts in his lyrics. The record benefited from the instantly memorable high-pitched solo performed by Crook on his self-developed Musitron, an early forerunner of the synthesizer. The simultaneously joyful and haunting solo is one of the most recognizable in rock history and provided a perfect counterpoint to Shannon's bittersweet vocal and forlorn lyric. "Runaway," which also served as the theme for the mid-1980s NBC-TV series "Police Story," represented the first of Shannon's string of sixteen "Hot 100" *Billboard* chart entries from 1961 to 1966. During a time in rock history characterized by bland, formulaic, producer-driven hit records from photogenic teen idols, Shannon wrote, performed, and sometimes produced his own material, which gave range to a wider palette of emotions than those previously seen on recordings by rock-and-roll artists. Shannon's tales of romantic betrayal, jealousy, ultimate doom, shadowy pursuers, and failed relationships resonated with audiences worldwide.

Besides releasing hits such as "Hats Off to Larry" and "Little Town Flirt," Shannon also became the first American artist to record a Beatles song. His version of "From Me to You" attained minor hit status in 1963 and charted higher than the Beatles version of the song. Shannon met them when they opened for him on an English tour, and he suggested doing a cover of the song to earn them more exposure stateside. He left Bigtop in 1963 and was forced to create his own Berlee record label (named after his parents) when Balk and Micahnik threatened to sue any established record label that signed Shannon. Berlee released two Shannon singles and folded. Soon thereafter, Shannon had a rapprochement with Balk and Micahnik and signed in 1964 with Amy Records, where he had the uncharacteristically buoyant hit cover of "Handy Man." Five months later he scored his last Top Ten hit on both sides of the Atlantic with what may have been his best recording, "Keep Searchin' (We'll Follow the Sun)."

In 1966 Shannon signed with Liberty Records for a three-year period. Despite working with numerous well-known producers and songwriters, no hit singles resulted. Much of the reason for the failure appeared to be a lack of faith in Shannon's talent. The label issued an album of Shannon performing staid covers of other writers' hit songs titled *This Is My Bag* in 1966, yet an album recorded with Rolling Stones producer Andrew Loog Oldham, featuring a mixture of Shannon originals and songs written by young British rockers, was unjustly shelved for nearly a decade. In the late 1960s Shannon focused on developing new artists, including the group Smith and his friend Brian Hyland, as head of his own production company.

The 1970s proved to be a troublesome decade for Shannon, mostly because of his addictions to alcohol and pills and his battles with manic depression. Collaborations with established admirers of his, such as Jeff Lynne and the Electric Light Orchestra (1973) and Nick Lowe and Dave Edmunds (1974), failed to initiate commercial sparks though, as shown by his ecstatic reception on his 1973 album, *Live in England*, Shannon retained a loyal fan base, especially in Britain. By the late 1970s Shannon joined Alcoholics Anonymous and began turning his life around. In 1982 he released *Drop Down and Get Me*, a comeback album produced by Tom Petty. The album yielded some fine new Shannon compositions, but it was a cover of "Sea of Love" that cracked the *Billboard* Top 40 charts. Despite a big splash of press coverage and a financially successful tour, the album only reached number 123 on the *Billboard* chart.

Two years later Shannon returned to his roots in country music by signing a deal with the country division of Warner Brothers Records, where he had one minor hit single. When Warner insisted that he pursue a more commercial sound, Shannon angrily quit the label, and a completed album has remained unreleased. Following his 1985 divorce, Shannon married Bonnie Gutierrez in 1987; they had no children. Financially secure as a result of wise investments, Shannon could have easily quit the music business, but he still loved to tour. During the late 1980s he was mostly relegated to rock-and-roll revival tours, performing at more than a hundred such dates in the last year of his life alone. Shannon was actively being considered as a replacement for the recently deceased Roy Orbison in the superstar musical group Traveling Wilburys (which featured Bob Dylan, George Harrison, Jeff Lynne, and Tom Petty) when he committed suicide with a rifle in Santa Clarita, California.

In Shannon's music one had a sense of rock music "growing up" and expressing as well as appealing to the concerns of a more adult audience. The brooding, angst-ridden vision in his work proved to be a major influence on the direction that rock music took in the 1970s and 1980s. Dan Bourgoise, Shannon's friend, occasional songwriting partner, and post-1974 manager, told *Rolling Stone* in 1990 that Shannon "in a lot of ways . . . was the character in his songs. All those demons he wrote about—the guy being chased in *Stranger in Town*—were real to him." In a 1982 interview Shannon seemed to agree: "I *was* that person. I've lived most of those songs at one time in my life. . . . I'm very happy today but I can tap into that anytime. It's like pressing a button in my mind. Sad songs just seem to come out of me, from where I don't know. I don't have a clue."

• There are several revealing interviews and critical essays available about Del Shannon. *Rolling Stone's* tribute to Shannon, 22 Mar. 1990, and the CD liner notes for the Shannon albums *The Liberty Years* (1991) and *Greatest Hits* (1990) all provide useful basic biography. The best discographies are M. C. Strong, *The Great Rock Discography* (1994), pp. 646–47, and Terry Hounsome, *Rock Record*, 3d ed. (1987), pp. 510–11. The "Rue Morgue, 1960" chapter of Nik Cohn's book *Pop from the Beginning* (1969) places Shannon in the context of the pop music scene of his time. There are also numerous interviews of Shannon from 1982, when his comeback record was released, which feature him musing about his life and career. Probably the best of these is by Jon Young in the June 1982 issue of *Trouser Press*.

HARVEY COHEN

SHANNON, Fred Albert (12 Feb. 1893–4 Feb. 1963), historian and college professor, was born in Sedalia, Missouri, the son of Louis Tecumseh Shannon and Sarah Margaret Sparks, tenant farmers. Shannon moved with his family across the rural midwest as a child and worked in mills and factories as a teenager. He received a B.A. from Indiana State Teachers College in 1914 and earned his M.A. in history from Indiana University four years later.

Shannon began his professional career as an elementary school teacher in Indiana in 1914. He also married Edna May Jones in 1914; The couple would have five children. From 1915 to 1919 he served as a high school principal while completing his master's degree. Shannon's first college teaching job began in 1919 at Iowa Wesleyan College, where he served as the entire history faculty. In 1924 he completed his Ph.D. in history at the University of Iowa, studying under Arthur Meier Schlesinger. He taught at Iowa State Teachers College that year, and then moved to Kansas State College of Agriculture (later Kansas State University) in 1926. He remained at Kansas State until 1938, when he took a one-year appointment in economic history at Williams College. In 1939 he moved to the University of Illinois's Department of History, and he remained there until his retirement in 1961.

College teaching was both Shannon's great passion and the source of great personal frustration. He devoted many summers to teaching on college campuses across the nation, including Harvard, Stanford, Columbia, Wisconsin, and Ohio State. At Illinois he specialized in American agricultural and economic history; he also taught courses on the Civil War and Reconstruction. As a graduate advisor who supervised numerous dissertations, Shannon was known as a hard taskmaster. Early in his career, however, Shannon was frustrated by his inability to find a position at a major research university, in spite of having earned numerous awards and prizes. In 1937, when he was still at Kansas State, his wife Edna wrote to his mentor Schlesinger, explaining that Shannon found it "humiliating to be still teaching in a school of this kind." Shannon's career difficulties can be partly explained by his staunchly populist politics and his socialist sympathies.

Shannon's scholarship was characterized by the mass of evidence he compiled for all his works. He has been described as a "hyperempiricist," with little patience for historians who generalized without supporting evidence. His rigorous standards for writing history were most clearly articulated in his legendary book reviews and comments at professional meetings. In print and in public, Shannon was known for his highly critical and occasionally impolitic remarks. Walter Prescott Webb—the victim of his most famous attacking review—once remarked that "if anybody ever sets up a Pulitzer Prize for criticism, [Shannon] will have a good claim to several ex post facto awards."

The Organization and Administration of the Union Army, 1861–1865 (1928), an elaboration of his dissertation, was Shannon's first important scholarly work. This massive two-volume study narrates the wartime struggle between local and national authorities in the North. Shannon's narrative focused on the rise of centralized state authority and its unintended consequences. Chapters on "The Concession to the Bourgeoisie" and "The Slacker Problem" analyze both politics and daily life during the Civil War in terms of social class. Shannon won the Pulitzer Prize for History and the Justin Winsor Prize of the American Historical Association, rare honors for a historian's first book.

Shannon turned to economic history in 1934 with the publication of the first edition of his textbook *Economic History of the People of the United States*. Shannon's text was written within the context of the Great Depression, paying great attention to labor relations, the small farmer, and the tariff question. Using a wealth of statistics and charts, Shannon argued for increased regulation of the American economy. His closing chapter announced "The Passing of Rugged Individualism." Shannon saw great danger in the crisis of the 1930s, warning of the possibility of "state capitalism under a fascist regime" in America. The text was revised in 1940 and retitled *America's Economic Growth*. Throughout the 1940s and 1950s Shannon's text was widely used in introductory college courses on economic history.

The most controversial episode in Shannon's long career occurred in 1939. As part of a Social Science Research Council conference on Walter Prescott Webb's *The Great Plains*, Shannon wrote a scathing book-length critique. Shannon found fault with nearly everything about Webb's book, particularly its habit of broadly generalizing with insufficient evidence. The resulting conference was remarkably heated for a gathering of professional historians: Webb would not even respond to Shannon's attack and other participants engaged in intense debates. The proceedings of the conference—including Shannon's long appraisal of *The Great Plains*—were published in 1940.

Shannon played a leading role in the creation of one of the postwar era's first important multivolume histories. He worked with Henry David Harold, Harold U. Faulkner, Louis M. Hacker, and Curtis P. Nettels in planning and editing the nine-volume *Economic History of the United States*. Shannon's contribution, *The*

Farmer's Last Frontier, Agriculture, 1860–1897 (1945), was the first volume to appear. The work was noteworthy for emphasizing the impact of environmental factors on the history of the American West and Shannon's placement of agrarian protest movements at the center of his history. In 1947 Shannon edited *The Civil War Letters of Sergeant Onley Andrews*. In this return to his original field of research Shannon attempted to present the daily life of "the common soldier in the ranks" while also railing against the "evils" produced by the warmaking bureaucracies.

In 1953 Shannon was elected president of the Mississippi Valley Historical Association. His 1954 presidential address, "Culture and Agriculture in America," included an attack on what he perceived to be the increasingly urban focus of the study of American culture. His *American Farmers' Movements* (1957) narrates the sweep of American history from the seventeenth to the nineteenth centuries in terms of rural protest movements, including those of the American Indian. *The Centennial Years* (1967) is a posthumous collection of Shannon's writings on American life in the last quarter of the nineteenth century. Shannon died in Wickenburg, Arizona.

• The Shannon papers at the University of Illinois provide a detailed record of his career. Overviews and reminiscences of Shannon's life are found in the *Mississippi Valley Historical Review* 50 (June 1963): 175, and 50 (Sept. 1963): 355; *Agricultural History* 37 (Apr. 1963): 117–19; and Robert Huhn's Introduction to *The Centennial Years* (1967). Peter Novick's *That Noble Dream* (1990) repeatedly holds Shannon up as an example of broader trends among American historians between the two world wars. An obituary is in the *New York Times*, 7 Feb. 1963.

DAVID QUIGLEY

SHANNON, Wilson (24 Feb. 1802–30 Aug. 1877), lawyer and politician, was born at Mount Olivet in Belmont County, Ohio Territory, the son of George Shannon and Jane Milligan, farmers. After farming until sixteen, Shannon attended Ohio University in Athens from 1818 to 1819 and Transylvania University in Lexington, Kentucky, from 1819 to 1821. In 1822 he left college without graduating and returned to Ohio to study law in St. Clairsville. In 1825 he married Elizabeth Ellis. They had one child. Admitted to the bar in 1826, Shannon started a law practice and soon entered politics. He unsuccessfully sought a judgeship in 1830 and in 1832 lost a congressional election. Elizabeth Shannon had died in 1831, and in 1832 he married Sara (or Sarah) Osbun; they had seven children. In 1833 and 1835 voters elected him county prosecuting attorney, and in 1838 he realized his ambitions by winning the governorship on a Democratic antibank platform. Despite reforming banks and stabilizing the state debt, Shannon lost his reelection bid in 1840 to Thomas Corwin. He bested Corwin in 1842, but his determination to regulate rather than destroy banking alienated hard-money Democrats and

paralyzed his administration. In April 1844 he resigned the governorship after President John Tyler nominated him as minister plenipotentiary to Mexico.

The Mexican government refused to recognize the independence of Texas and insisted that its annexation by the United States would constitute a declaration of war. Undeterred, Secretary of State John C. Calhoun armed Shannon with instructions denying Mexico's claim to Texas and later had Shannon warn the Mexicans against attempting to reconquer Texas. When the Mexican foreign minister charged the U.S. government with conspiratorially abetting Texas's treasonable revolt, Shannon demanded a retraction. After several bitter exchanges, Shannon precipitously suspended diplomatic relations. From November 1844 to May 1845, during which time Texas was annexed by a joint congressional resolution, the United States had no official communication with Mexico. President James K. Polk dismissed Shannon in March 1845 but could not rescind his tactlessness.

Shannon returned to St. Clairsville and practiced law. In 1849, infected with gold fever, he organized and financed an expedition of sixty "Argonauts" to California. Sacramento yielded no riches, and he returned to Ohio in 1851. Persuaded to run for Congress in 1852, he won easily and voted for the Kansas-Nebraska Bill in 1854, basing his decision on adherence to party, commitment to popular sovereignty, and diffidence to slavery's expansion.

Trouble began in Kansas almost immediately. Although territorial governor Andrew Reeder guaranteed fair elections, Missourian "border ruffians" illegally elected a proslavery territorial legislature in March 1855. Reeder begged President Franklin Pierce to uphold popular sovereignty, but the president cashiered him, replacing him with Shannon on 10 August 1855. Although well-meaning, Shannon erred by aligning with proslavery forces upon arrival. On 1 September he declared publicly that the territorial legislature was legal and that he would enforce its decrees. Inaccurately reporting that Shannon had advocated slavery in Kansas, antislavery journalist James Redpath dealt a devastating blow to Shannon's prestige. However, the proslavery tint to Shannon's policies was unmistakable, and he did consider opposition to established territorial law to be revolutionary. In response to free-state settlers' repudiation of the "bogus" legislature and their determination to elect their own government, Shannon on 14 November chaired the proslavery "law and order" convention, which pledged to "crush" the traitors.

The Wakarusa War illuminated the building tensions in Kansas. On 27 November fifteen free-state vigilantes escaped to Lawrence after seizing a prisoner arrested by proslavery county sheriff Samuel Jones. Eight hundred free-state settlers gathered at Lawrence to fortify the city, while Jones recruited a militia of 1,200 Missourians to enforce the law. Having authorized Jones to use the territorial militia but not a Missouri militia, Shannon realized by 1 December that the situation had spun out of control. Unable to secure

Pierce's permission to deploy the army to keep the peace, Shannon rushed to Lawrence to negotiate a settlement. He averted the crisis on 8 December in a signed agreement with free-state leaders Charles Robinson and James Lane. Shannon affirmed that he had not requested the services of the Missourians to enforce territorial law, and Robinson and Lane pledged to aid in the execution of the law under properly constituted authority.

In the aftermath of the Wakarusa War Shannon requested power to unilaterally deploy federal troops when necessary to keep the peace. Pierce demurred, maintaining policies that delimited the governor's jurisdiction. After a proslavery federal court indicted elected free-state leaders for treason, U.S. marshal Israel Donelson in May 1856 summoned a proslavery posse to help him serve warrants in Lawrence. Lane had already left Kansas, but Donelson hoped to locate free-state U.S. senator-designate Reeder. Shannon asked Donelson to use federal troops, but when Donelson refused Shannon lacked official authority to intervene. The infamous "sack of Lawrence" followed on 21 May, when the undisciplined posse lawlessly destroyed a hotel, two presses, and Robinson's dwelling. On 24 May John Brown retaliated by murdering five proslavery settlers at Pottawatomie, thus triggering an eruption of guerrilla warfare. In June Shannon deployed the army to pacify Kansas, and he attempted to head off another outburst by dispersing the free-state legislature on 4 July but succeeded instead in angering free-state settlers. Lane relit the smoldering fire in August when he reentered Kansas with a small force and attacked proslavery settlements. Shannon negotiated a truce on 17 August but resigned in disgust a day later, aware Pierce had already removed him because the president considered him a political liability during an election year. Kansas had broken him. "Govern the Kansas of 1855 and '56," he declared years later, "you might as well have attempted to govern the devil in hell" (Day, p. 304).

Shannon remained in Kansas, where he was a distinguished member of the bar. His tumultuous life ended peacefully in Lawrence. He remains notable for his failure to keep the peace in Kansas, thus stimulating the dynamic growth of the antislavery Republican party in 1856 and the eventual election of Abraham Lincoln.

• Shannon's papers are in the Kansas State Historical Society at Topeka and the Ohio Historical Society at Columbus. His "Executive Minutes," *Kansas Historical Collections* 3 (1886): 283–337; "Correspondence of Governor Wilson Shannon," *Kansas Historical Collections* 4 (1890): 385–403; and "Administration of Governor Shannon," *Kansas Historical Collection* 5 (1896): 234–64, are invaluable collections of primary sources. The fullest account of Shannon's life, including an excellent bibliography, is Donald Eugene Day, "A Life of Wilson Shannon, Governor of Ohio, Diplomat, Territorial Governor of Kansas" (Ph.D. diss., Ohio State Univ., 1978). While Day applauds Shannon for his moderate statesmanship, earlier historians criticize Shannon for permitting lawless violence in Kansas. William E. Connelley portrays Shannon as a proslav-

ery partisan in *Kansas Territorial Governors* (1900), while Alfred Theodore Andreas considers him a noble-hearted dupe of the Missourians in *History of the State of Kansas*, vol. 1 (1883; repr. 1976). For Shannon's political career in Ohio see Francis P. Weisenburger, *The Passing of the Frontier, 1825–1850*, vol. 3 of *The History of the State of Ohio*, ed. Carl Wittke (1941); for his relationship with Pierce see Roy Nichols, *Franklin Pierce: Young Hickory of the Granite Hills*, rev. ed. (1958); and for an extensive treatment of territorial politics in Kansas consult Alice Nichols, *Bleeding Kansas* (1954). Obituaries are in the *Lawrence Tribune*, 31 Aug. 1877, and the *New York Times*, 1 Sept. 1877.

GRAHAM ALEXANDER PECK

SHAPERO, Lillian (17 Jan. 1908–19 Apr. 1988), dancer, was born in New York City, the daughter of Morris Shapero and Jennie (maiden name unknown). Lillian grew up in a Chasidic family in the city's Jewish neighborhood on the Lower East Side. After the age of six, when her mother died, she was raised by her grandparents. During her grandfather's observant life attending a small synagogue, or shtible, he encouraged her to participate in traditional songs and dances, which had a profound effect on her. When she became a trained performance dancer, interested in expressing Jewish themes, she was able to draw on her childhood experiences for choreographic material.

Shapero first studied dance with Estelle Harriton at the Neighborhood Playhouse, then part of the Henry Street Settlement House; these classes were in the style of Isadora Duncan. Further modern dance lessons followed with Bird Larson and Michio Ito, and then Shapero was discovered by the important dance composer and editor of the magazine *Dance Observer*, Louis Horst, who brought her to the attention of Martha Graham. Shapero danced in Graham's first modern dance company from 1929 to 1935. Shapero's power as a performer led Graham to choose her as the first dancer to take over Graham's own solo role in what became the seminal modern dance work, *Primitive Mysteries*. This dance was choreographed in 1931; those performing in it moved Graham and her company "into the center of modern dance development." The powerful Graham style and dance technique influenced Shapero.

The verve and creativity of this period matched Shapero's drive. Her first solo recital was given in 1931 in the Graham studio. Shapero's own choreographic fame was made with Maurice Schwartz's production of *Yoshe Kalb*, which had a long run at the Yiddish Art Theatre in 1933. *Yoshe Kalb* (Joe the Calf) was a play about the fate of a rabbi's son manipulated during the time of the great Chasidic rabbis in Poland in the eighteenth century. Shapero recreated her landmark choreography for a revival of the production in 1972 at the Eden Theatre in New York.

Shapero's dance ideas for the Yiddish theater were used successfully in other productions for Maurice Schwartz's Yiddish Art Theatre as well. She choreographed *The Wise Men of Chelm*, *The Water Carrier*, *The Three Gifts*, and *The Dybbuk* between 1932 and 1952. At the Shubert Theatre she choreographed *The*

Bridal Dance, a two-act play by William Siegel with music by Maurice Rauch. From 1936 to 1939 she had her own dance group; in 1939 she created dances for the Jewish Pavilion at the World's Fair in New York. She also did Chanukah Festival pageants for the Jewish community at Madison Square Garden. Sometimes the Yiddish Art Theatre provided her with production and stage help. Her program shown on 7 June 1947, while held at the Yiddish Art Theatre, had several works beyond the Yiddish theater milieu. In this program her company of nine dancers performed in *Two Songs from the Burning Ghetto* and *Two Songs from America* with sections titled "I Am a Jew" and "Go Down, Moses."

Writing about Jewish dance in an article published in the *Dance Observer* called "Chasidic Dance in the Jewish Theatre," Shapero recognized the deep-rooted dance tradition to which she was contributing. She wrote that in the Yiddish theater she drew on folk idioms of Russia, the Ukraine, and Poland and the high, wide arm and head gestures of Chasidic celebrations. In the 1960s Shapero, by then considered an authority on Jewish dance, was hired by the Jewish Community Center of Cleveland to stage a production of *The Dybbuk*.

In addition to Jewish themes, Shapero used political themes in her modern dances. Her group dance *Dance for Spain—No Pasaran* was seen in the 1930s. Collin Wilsey, in a critical review written for *Dance Observer*, said, "Miss Shapero has reached a difficult stage. She is too experienced to be a promising beginner; yet she has not found her direction. . . . There is enough dance material in [her dances] to give hope; she is not given to the over-simplification which results in the popular social cliches and she is apparently trying to turn away from too dry abstraction."

Shapero toured widely and performed in Paris, London, and Moscow, where she was the guest of the Soviet Theatre Festival in 1937. The two types of dances she favored thematically were recognized in an 18 October 1943 review in the *New York World Telegram* as "revolutionary dances on American themes and dances based on Jewish folklore." The concert being reviewed included "Dances of the Oppressed" and "Anti-War Dance." On 25 April 1937 she performed her dance cycle called *Crisis*, with sections including "Venture," "Aggressors," "Compulsion," "Modernity," and "Convergence," at the Guild Theatre. It was termed "a serious attempt at a broad social comment and contained many possibilities for original and significant development." Her performances in this period at the Labor Stage Theatre included *Workaday Song* and *Young America*. In a *Dance Observer* review of this period, it was noted that Shapero "always has shown a great talent for group choreography, and her own personal charm and warmth added a great deal to the occasion." In 1952 her works were seen at Carnegie Hall, and *Dance Observer* noted that the music to her dances was composed by Maurice Rauch, conductor of the Jewish People's Philharmonic Chorus. Her last choreography was for the 1982 television production "Higher than Heaven," composed by Rauch to a story by the Yiddish writer Itche Goldberg.

Shapero often worked with Rauch, who served as her pianist and music director. He was a noted composer and conductor for Yiddish theater and also was acknowledged for his Jewish choral music work. Shapero and Rauch married on 29 January in the early 1920s and had one son. Shapero died in New York City following a stroke.

• Representative photos and reviews of Shapero's performances are housed at the Dance Collection of the New York Public Library for the Performing Arts, Lincoln Center. Key references in *Dance Observer* are Naum Rosen, "The New Jewish Dance in America" (June–July 1934); review of "Lillian Shapero and Group" at the Mecca Temple on 13 Apr. 1935 (May 1935); review of "Lillian Shapero and Dance Group" at the Civic Repertory Theater on 22 Mar. 1936 (May 1936); review of the Guild Theater performance on 25 Apr. 1937 (June–July 1937); and review of Carnegie Hall performance on 3 May 1952 (Aug.–Sept. 1952). See also the *Moscow Daily News*, 18 Oct. 1943, for a review of the Central Jewish Workers Club performance on 11 Sept. 1937. An obituary is in the *New York Times*, 22 Apr. 1988, and *Dance Magazine*, Sept. 1988.

JUDITH BRIN INGBER

SHAPLEY, Harlow (2 Nov. 1885–20 Oct. 1972), astronomer, was born in Nashville, Missouri, the son of Willis Shapley, a farmer and schoolteacher, and Sarah Stowell. Lacking a formal high school education, Shapley nevertheless enrolled in 1907 at the University of Missouri, where he studied astronomy. In 1911 he obtained a fellowship to Princeton University and became the first graduate student of astronomer Henry Norris Russell. Undertaking an investigation of eclipsing binary stars, Shapley made nearly 10,000 individual observations and derived the orbits for ninety of them in order to establish the sizes and masses of their components (only about ten such orbits had previously been determined). In 1913 he won a position at the Mt. Wilson Observatory in California; his ambitious dissertation on eclipsing binary stars was completed in 1914 and published in 1915. On his way to Pasadena in April 1914, he married a former Missouri classmate, Martha Betz, who eventually collaborated with Shapley on several papers and who independently became an authority on eclipsing binaries. The couple had five children.

With its 60-inch reflector (and a 100-inch reflector under construction), Mt. Wilson was in 1913 the world's largest observatory. On arrival, Shapley began an intense observational program of investigating variable stars in globular clusters. Approximately 100 of these massive, highly stable clusters were known, and Shapley photographed them repeatedly in order to find the variable stars whose light varied systematically. Early in 1917 he wrote to the Dutch astronomer Jacobus Kapteyn that "the work on clusters goes on monotonously . . . but give me time enough and I shall get something out of the problem yet." Within the next twelve months, several lines of reasoning fell into place with surprising swiftness. After devising a method for finding the distance to these clusters, Shapley obtained an astonishing result: the clusters lay about ten times farther away than any astronomical distance that had previously been derived. Furthermore, he noticed that the majority of these clusters were concentrated in a relatively small area of the sky along the southern Milky Way in the constellation of Sagittarius. Shapley conjectured that the clusters delineated the position of a distant, unseen nucleus of the Milky Way, which lay in the direction of Sagittarius.

Shapley's distance method rested on an ingenious calibration of the so-called period-luminosity law of Cepheid variable stars, a relationship that had been discovered in 1912 at Harvard Observatory: the greater the intrinsic brightness of a Cepheid star, the longer the period of its cyclic variation in light intensity. By establishing the absolute brightness of a six-day Cepheid, he could use a "faintness means farness" principle to find the distances of those clusters that contained Cepheid variable stars. To the entire, disk-like Milky Way system Shapley assigned a diameter of 300,000 light years. Many astronomers found these results incredible because the commonly accepted diameter of our stellar system was only about 10,000 light years.

As a result of Shapley's claims for the enormous size of the Milky Way, his observatory director George Ellery Hale invited him to debate with Lick Observatory astronomer Heber D. Curtis before the National Academy of Sciences in April 1920. This Shapley-Curtis debate subsequently achieved almost mythic proportions among astronomers, for it was a confrontation not only with respect to the size of the Milky Way, but also on the status of the spiral nebulae, which Curtis believed lay outside a relatively modest Milky Way. Shapley was reluctant to accept this latter view because the spirals seemed so small in comparison with his measurements of the Milky Way, a discrepancy that was partly accounted for a decade later when the discovery of interstellar absorption showed that Shapley's estimate of the size of the Milky Way was approximately three times too large. He approached the debate in Washington with some trepidation because by this time he was under consideration for the directorship at Harvard Observatory and knew that Harvard representatives would be watching his performance. Unaccustomed to public speaking, he performed badly, with the result that he was invited to Harvard, but not yet as director of its observatory.

At Harvard, Shapley's pre-college background as a teenage newspaper reporter served him well. A steady stream of astronomical news from the observatory quickly established Shapley's reputation. Within a few months he was offered its directorship, which he held until 1952. Throughout his tenure at Harvard, Shapley worked aggressively for the popularization of science through lectures, articles, and books; he arranged one of the earliest series of science radio broadcasts in 1926, organized a series of semi-popular titles for advanced amateurs, the Harvard Books on

Astronomy in the 1940s, and played a key role in the young Science Service, a news service whose press releases informed the public about current science. During the 1930s, Shapley was the most widely cited astronomer in the American press.

Meanwhile, Shapley pursued a vigorous program of research into the larger structures of the cosmos. Shapley's 1918 calibration of the period-luminosity law enabled astronomer Edwin Hubble, in 1924, to establish the great distances of several spiral nebulae. Thereafter Hubble continued to have regular access to the giant telescopes at Mt. Wilson, whereas the telescopic arsenal at Harvard consisted largely of smaller, survey instruments. A considerable rivalry developed between the two coasts, and the designation of the spirals became a shibboleth for distinguishing the two camps: astronomers on the West Coast tended to stick with Hubble's rather clumsy "extragalactic nebulae," while the East and Midwest generally adopted Shapley's "galaxies," the term now universally accepted. With an assistant, Adelaide Ames, Shapley produced a comprehensive catalog of over a thousand galaxies that were brighter than the thirteenth magnitude (1932); in a modern revision, the *Shapley-Ames Catalogue* continues to be a standard reference work. Ames's tragic death by drowning in 1930 dampened Shapley's enthusiasm for astronomical research, although he continued to publish a steady stream of scientific papers, including, in 1938, the discovery of two faint dwarf members of our local family of galaxies (the so-called Scuptor and Fornax systems). At the same time, he organized extensive galaxy counts, which demonstrated the clumpiness of their distribution. Hubble and other Mt. Wilson astronomers resisted accepting this result because it challenged the homogeneity that cosmological models seemed to require. Today such large-scale structure is well-documented, and the large concentration of galaxies in Centaurus is sometimes called the Shapley supercluster.

During the 1930s and 1940s, Shapley chafed under a considerable disadvantage vis-à-vis the rival Mt. Wilson Observatory, which had both larger telescopes and much better weather atop its elevated observing site. He hoped that the Harvard-operated telescopes in the southern hemisphere would enable him to overcome some of these disadvantages, especially because the nearest galaxies to the Milky Way, the Magellanic Clouds, were in the southern skies. In 1925 he persuaded the Rockefeller Foundation to donate funds for a 60-inch reflector, which he placed in Bloemfontaine, South Africa, pairing it with a 61-inch reflector in Massachusetts. Shapley reasoned that a southern 60-inch telescope working on the Magellanic Clouds would be as effective as a 200-inch telescope exploring the more distant Andromeda galaxy and consequently organized a systematic photographic campaign of the Magellanic Clouds. But his equation did not take into account the advantage that creative astronomers had by working in proximity with their instruments (as at Mt. Wilson and Palomar) compared with operating a remote field station.

A major astronomical discovery was waiting to be made in the Magellanic Clouds, but unluckily for Shapley, he was preempted in 1951 by the related work of Walter Baade at Mt. Wilson and very quickly thereafter by A. D. Thackeray and A. J. Weselink in Pretoria, South Africa. Shapley (and everyone else) had failed to realize in 1918 that the Cepheid variable stars actually come in two different types; to discover the second type in the Magellanic Clouds required looking for somewhat fainter stars than Shapley was accustomed to searching for. After the discoveries of the 1950s, Shapley scrambled to take part of the credit for a venture in which he had for so long, but unsuccessfully, engaged.

Increasingly in the late 1930s Shapley turned to international problems, and he assisted many European scientists, refugees from the Nazi tyranny, to find positions in the United States. After World War II he took an active part in the formation of United Nations Educational, Scientific, and Cultural Organization, and well-qualified observers report that Shapley was the one who "kept the S in UNESCO." He yearned to play a greater role in the International Astronomical Union as well, but the coastal rivalries in American astronomy insured that a more neutral party would be selected for its presidency.

Shapley's internationalism made him in 1946 a target for Representative John Rankin, then chairman of the House Un-American Activities Committee, and in 1950 for Senator Joseph McCarthy's anti-Communist campaign. He had joined with former vice president Henry A. Wallace and others to form the Progressive party in 1948 but broke with them after Communist elements took too much control of the platform at the party convention. Although Shapley entertained liberal political views, he was never a Communist. Feeling that serious, international science was under attack from all sides, he took a particularly vehement stand in 1950 against Immanuel Velikovsky's *Worlds in Collision*, a popular and much-touted catastrophist account of planetary history and chronology; largely through Shapley's campaign, Macmillan sold off the title and removed it from their publishing list.

For his earlier astronomical researches Shapley won the Draper Medal of the National Academy of Sciences (1926), the Rumford Medal of the American Academy of Arts and Sciences (1933), the Gold Medal of the Royal Astronomical Society (1934), as well as membership in the National Academy of Sciences and numerous foreign academies. He served from 1939 to 1944 as president of the American Academy of Arts and Sciences, which he helped to revitalize, and he was especially active in America's oldest scientific academy, the American Philosophical Society. Although a religious agnostic, Shapley was an early and regular member of the "Star Island" group for the study of the relation of science and religion, and he edited *Science Ponders Religion* (1960). A lucid and witty speaker, Shapley was widely sought as a popular lecturer. Even his detractors admitted that he was one of the most stimulating conversationalists they had ever

known. In his declining years Shapley went to live with one of his sons in Boulder, Colorado, where he died.

Shapley pioneered methods for astronomical distance determinations that led to his discovery of the large size of our Milky Way galaxy. Later, he mapped the distribution of galaxies and was among the first to appreciate their large-scale clustering properties. As founder of the Harvard graduate school in astronomy and of their influential summer school in astronomy, he strongly molded pre–World War II astronomical education, and in the postwar era he also helped in the formation of the National Science Foundation.

• Shapley's extensive papers are in the Harvard University Archives. His anecdotal, seemingly larger-than-life but actually quite accurate autobiography is *Through Rugged Ways to the Stars* (1969). Bart J. Bok, *Biographical Memoirs, National Academy of Sciences* 48 (1976), includes Shapley's extensive bibliography of approximately 600 items. For views of Shapley's early career, see Michael Hoskin, "The 'Great Debate': What Really Happened" in his *Stellar Astronomy: Historical Studies* (1982), and Owen Gingerich, "How Shapley Came to Harvard, or Snatching the Prize from the Jaws of Debate," *Journal for the History of Astronomy* 19 (1988): 201–7. Concerning his later career, see Gingerich, "Shapley's Impact," in *The Harlow-Shapley Symposium on Globular Cluster Systems in Galaxies*, ed. Jonathan Grindlay and A. G. Davis Philip (1988), and "Through Rugged Ways to the Galaxies," *Journal for the History of Astronomy* 21 (1990): 77–88. For Shapley's work with refugee scientists, see Bessie Z. Jones, "To the Rescue of the Learned: The Asylum Fellowship Plan at Harvard, 1938–1940," *Harvard Library Bulletin* 32 (1984): 205–56.

OWEN GINGERICH

SHARAFF, Irene (1910?–16 Aug. 1993), costume designer, was born in Boston, Massachusetts. Nothing is known of her parents. She graduated from Wadley High School in New York City. Originally planning to be a painter, she studied at the Art Students League (now the Parsons School of Design), the New York School of Fine and Applied Arts, and in Paris. While taking art classes in New York in 1928 she met Aline Bernstein who offered her a position as her assistant for costumes, scenery, and properties at Eva Le Gallienne's Civic Repertory Theatre. Her creativity coupled with her artistic education enabled her to do historical research and to draw blueprints, so she quickly became a valuable assistant despite her lack of theatrical experience. Sharaff assisted Bernstein for three years on many productions, including *The Lady from Alfaqueque*, *The Cherry Orchard*, and *Romeo and Juliet* in an intense apprenticeship in theater design. When the Civic Repertory Theatre closed in 1931 because of the depression, Sharaff traveled to Europe to study at the Grande Chaumière in Paris, where she also was exposed to haute couture and the work of leading European theatrical designers such as Christian Bérnard and Pavel Tchelitchev. Le Gallienne visited her in Paris and invited her to design a production of *Alice in Wonderland* to reopen the Civic. After studying the story and the illustrations by Sir John Tenniel that were to be adapted for the stage, she agreed and returned to New York, where the production became her professional debut. She received accolades for her sets and costumes when the play opened in 1932, launching her distinguished career as a costume (and occasionally scenery) designer for theater, film, and ballet that lasted more than fifty years. She also won the first of her many major prizes for theatrical design, the Donaldson Award. In his review of *Alice in Wonderland*, *New York Times* theater critic Brooks Atkinson commended her creative use of color, which became one of the defining elements of her designs.

After seeing her work, Broadway director Hassard Short asked her to create costumes for two numbers, "Eastern Parade" and "Comic Strip," in the musical review he was beginning to rehearse. With the opening of *As Thousands Cheer* in 1933, she made her debut on Broadway. These whimsical flamboyant costumes led to her next commission, designs for the Ballets Russes de Monte Carlo. Sharaff became the first American to design for that company when she created scenery and costumes for *Union Pacific* in 1934.

When Sharaff began her career, the scenic designer for a production was also responsible for costumes, properties, and sometimes even lights. Following the guidance of her mentor, Bernstein, she followed this model. As specialization in one facet of design became common, however, Sharaff concentrated on costume design, becoming both one of the originators of the field and one of its greatest practitioners. The procedures she developed within the specialization have become standard practice. A perfectionist, she painted meticulous sketches of costumes that were appropriate for a production's characters and had great style but were also based on historical research. She then worked closely with the workshops that made the costumes, being especially concerned with fabric choice and color as well as demanding high standards in the construction of garments and accessories.

Until 1942, when she went to Hollywood to design costumes for the Arthur Freed Unit at Metro-Goldwyn-Mayer, she worked continuously on Broadway, mainly designing musical revues and comedies: *The Boys from Syracuse* (1938); *Lady in the Dark* (1941), starring Gertrude Lawrence; *Idiot's Delight* (1936), starring Lynn Fontanne and Alfred Lunt; and *On Your Toes* (1936), with choreography by George Balanchine for whom she subsequently designed the dance *Jeu de Cartes* (1937).

Sharaff relocated in the early 1940s to Hollywood, where she was in great demand primarily due to her innovative use of color—at the time motion pictures were making the transition from black and white to Technicolor. She was under contract initially at MGM and later worked briefly for Sam Goldwyn at Goldwyn/RKO. She often collaborated with another former New Yorker who was equally adept at musical comedy, Vincent Minnelli. Among her first movies were *Girl Crazy* (1943) and *Meet Me in St. Louis* (1944), both starring Judy Garland. She was successful not only in creating the lavish costumes specific to

musicals but was sensitive to the particular needs of dancers. For *An American in Paris* (1951) she created the costumes as well as the scenery for the entire ballet sequence featuring Gene Kelly. She won her first Academy Award for *An American in Paris*; her striking and original designs evoked and revered the great French painters of the late nineteenth and early twentieth century. Also in 1951 she designed the Broadway production of *The King and I*, for which she won the Antoinette Perry Award and another Donaldson Award. Her costumes created a popular demand for the richly colored Thai silks that she imported for the production.

From the 1950s through the mid-1970s she divided her time and energy among the Broadway stage; ballet companies such as the American Ballet Theatre, the Royal Ballet (London), and the New York City Ballet; and the movie industry. She refused to limit herself to one medium and was equally successful in each. Sharaff had the exceptional ability to design for stage as well as for film and did both the original Broadway productions and the film versions of *The King and I*, *West Side Story*, *Flower Drum Song*, and *Funny Girl*. The movies she designed during this period were mainly musicals and period costume dramas, although her credits also include *A Tree Grows in Brooklyn* (1951), *The Sandpiper* (1965), and *The Other Side of Midnight* (1977). She was nominated for sixteen Academy Awards and received five Oscars, for *An American in Paris* (1951), *The King and I* (1956), *West Side Story* (1961), *Cleopatra* (1963), and *Who's Afraid of Virginia Woolf?* (1966). Her designs for Elizabeth Taylor and Barbara Streisand are especially notable. She emphasized Taylor's glamour in *Cleopatra* and *The Taming of the Shrew* (1967) and brilliantly dressed her as the frumpy, alcoholic professor's wife in *Who's Afraid of Virginia Woolf?* For Streisand she created a wide variety of costumes, including those for the character Fanny Brice in *Funny Girl* (1968), who makes a transition from wearing outrageous theatrical costumes to glamorous gowns, the period garments in *Hello, Dolly!* (1969), and the contemporary clothing for *The Way We Were* (1973).

In the mid-1970s she wrote an account of her life and career as the designer of so many successful movies and stage productions. *Broadway and Hollywood: Costumes Designed by Irene Sharaff* (1976) is a lively discussion of many of her projects and some of the performers she costumed, including Gypsy Rose Lee, Sammy Davis, Jr., Rex Harrison, Yul Brynner (whom she induced to shave his head), Debbie Reynolds, and Mary Astor. The book is illustrated with many of her original designs. She also devoted more time to her first love, painting, which she had only pursued intermittently throughout her career.

During the 1970s and 1980s she designed a few more movies, among them *Mommie Dearest*, and the stage revivals of *West Side Story* and *The King and I*, for which she had created the original designs. She devoted the same careful attention to these revivals as she had to the originals, never taking her former designs for granted but rather reworking the designs and often creating new ones. For her final Broadway credit, *Jerome Robbins' Broadway* in 1989, she designed new costumes for the numbers from *Billion Dollar Baby*, *West Side Story*, and *The King and I* that were part of the production.

The extent of Sharaff's talent is confirmed by her enormous body of work as well as her numerous awards. Her originality, meticulous research, carefully chosen fabrics, and especially her color combinations all contributed to her success. Occasionally producers for stage and film would seek her participation in a project because she had not only an aura of style but one of success. In all, her sixteen nominations and five awards from the Academy of Motion Pictures Arts and Sciences is an amazing proportion of her film credits. On Broadway, she received six Antoinette Perry nominations and won one, again remarkable among her sixty credits, of which more than half were musicals.

She is the only costume designer to be honored with a special tribute at the Department of Film of the Museum of Modern Art. At the Academy Award ceremony following her death in New York City, homage was paid to her through a retrospective of her designs. One final aspect of her legacy is that many of the costume designers who came to prominence in the 1980s and 1990s began their careers as her assistants. Sharaff, simply stated, was the greatest costume designer of musical comedy in the twentieth century.

• Original Sharaff designs are in the collections of the Shubert Archive and the Victoria and Albert Museum. Besides her book, *Broadway and Hollywood*, see the conversation between her and Meredith Brody in the magazine *Interview*, Aug. 1989, pp. 127–29. For additional information on Sharaff see Elizabeth Leese, *Costume Design in the Movies*, rev. ed. (1991); W. Robert Lavine, *In a Glamorous Fashion* (1980); Ann Lee Morgan, ed., *Contemporary Designers* (1984); and Bobbi Owen, *Costume Design on Broadway* (1987). Obituaries are in the *New York Times*, 17 Aug. 1993; *The Times* (London) and the *Los Angeles Times*, both 18 Aug. 1993; the *Independent*, 25 Aug. 1993, *Variety*, 30 Aug. 1993; and *Dance Magazine* and *Theatre Crafts International*, both Nov. 1993.

BOBBI OWEN

SHARKEY, William Lewis (12 July 1798–30 Mar. 1873), Mississippi chief justice and politician, was born near Muscle Shoals in Holston Valley, East Tennessee, the son of Patrick Sharkey, a farmer, and his wife, the daughter of Robert Rhodes, a frontiersman. At the age of six he moved with his family to a Warren County, Mississippi, farm. His parents died during his youth, after which he took over the responsibility of providing for himself and his orphaned brothers. He joined the American forces during the War of 1812 and served under Andrew Jackson at the crucial battle at New Orleans.

After the war, Sharkey received preliminary schooling in Tennessee and began the study of law. Concluding his studies under Judge Edward Turner in Natch-

ez, Mississippi, he set up a legal practice in Warrenton, Mississippi, in 1825. Once he had established himself, he acquired sixty-five slaves and a plantation in Warren County. He married Minerva Wren; they had one adopted child. In his treatment of his slaves, Sharkey was a fairly typical planter. An 1842 contract with his overseer instructs him that "on no account is cruel or unusual punishment to be inflicted," and "strict discipline is to be kept up with the negroes." He never really understood the lives of blacks. At the end of the Civil War he went so far as to proclaim that the former slaves would soon be "extinct" and erroneously asserted that over half of the black population of Mississippi had perished since the war.

Sharkey eventually confronted many of the issues associated with slavery from the state's highest court. In 1832 he was elected to the Mississippi High Court of Errors and Appeals, even though he did not favor popular judicial elections. Selected by his colleagues on the court as its chief justice in 1832 he served in that capacity, until 1851. Not the least of the cases that involved slavery that came before his court concerned Mississippi's policy of prohibiting the importation of slaves into the state for the purpose of sale. The Mississippi high court refused to uphold the claims of slave traders that were based upon unpaid promissory notes for such slaves. Although the U.S. Supreme Court ruled the other way in *Groves v. Slaughter* (1841), Sharkey wrote, in *Brien v. Williamson* (1843), that the state policy would prevail. His unionism did not extend to deference to the justices in Washington.

In *Mahorner v. Hooe* (1848), Sharkey upheld an 1842 state prohibition against emancipations by last will even though the will that affected some slaves in Mississippi was probated in Virginia, where other slaves were also to be freed. The state policy was valid and "paramount" to the normal "rule of comity," even though it was one slave state versus another. Within the criminal jurisprudence of slavery, however, Sharkey proved to be more sensitive than judges in some other southern courts. He ruled in *Isham (a slave) v. State* (1841), for instance, that "in prosecutions for offences, negroes are to be treated as other persons."

The Sharkey court also confronted public policy in the area of the law that concerned banking institutions. During the 1840s the court affirmed the state's policy of hostility toward banks. In *Commercial Bank v. State* (1846), the court upheld a forfeiture proceeding against a bank because it had failed to resume specie payments on its notes. It ruled that this requirement, which had been imposed by an 1840 law, did not violate the charter of the bank and hence did not violate the obligation of the contracts clause of the federal constitution. Sharkey clearly was concerned with the rights of debtors of banks and shared a general hostility to the irresponsible policies of state banks.

Sharkey retired from the court in 1851. Also in 1851 he declined the offer of a cabinet post by President Millard Fillmore. Instead, he became consul to Havana, Cuba, in 1851; he resigned after a brief tenure because the pay was too modest. On the great issue of the 1850s—preservation of the Union—he showed himself to be a conservative Unionist who repudiated the constitutional notions of radical firebrands who followed the ideas of John C. Calhoun. Nonetheless, he was the president of the ardently prosouthern Nashville Convention of 1850 and believed firmly that the South had as much right to take slaves into the territories acquired from Mexico as northerners had to take their property there. There is no doubt that, though a Unionist, he was also thoroughly committed to his state of Mississippi. That did not mean that he uncritically accepted whatever his fellow citizens did no matter the perceived provocation.

Sharkey strongly opposed secession and refused to support the Confederacy even while he remained in Mississippi. That position cost him a short time in jail because he refused to sell goods to Confederate officers. As early as 1863 he took the Oath of Allegiance to the United States and worked diligently for the restoration of Mississippi to the Union. He hated Jefferson Davis and sarcastically noted that because Davis had said the fall of Vicksburg meant the end of the Confederacy, "I take him at his word."

In the summer of 1865 Sharkey was appointed provisional governor by President Andrew Johnson after being sent to Washington, along with former state supreme court justice William Yerger, to discuss the conditions for re-admission. He was deeply committed to Johnsonian Reconstruction and presided over the state constitutional convention of 1865. While he generally supported the laws that became known as the black codes (designed to keep blacks in a state as close to slavery as possible), he did try to dissuade the legislators from too radical a restriction on freedmen's rights; he argued, for instance, that it was foolhardy to restrict their rights to own property. He fought against congressional Reconstruction policies and turned to the U.S. Supreme Court to deflect them. He argued the cases of *Mississippi v. Johnson* (1867), which sought an injunction against the enforcement of the Reconstruction Acts, and *Ex parte McCardle* (1868) to turn aside military trials in the South. A conservative who believed in the Union, property rights, and white supremacy to the end, Sharkey died in Washington, D.C., before the end of a radical Reconstruction he deplored.

• There is no complete collection of the personal papers of Sharkey, but a modest collection of useful material is in F. Garvin Davenport, "Judge Sharkey Papers," *Mississippi Valley Historical Review* 20 (1933): 75–90. No full-scale biography has been published. The best general sketch of his life remains Dunbar Rowland, *Courts, Judges, and Lawyers of Mississippi 1798–1935* (1935). For information on his tenure on the Mississippi high court, see Meredith Lang, *Defender of the Faith: The High Court of Mississippi 1817–1875* (1977). His involvement in presidential Reconstruction in Mississippi is treated in James W. Garner, *Reconstruction in Mississippi* (1901); William Harris, *Presidential Reconstruction in Mississippi* (1967); and L. Marshall Hall, "William L. Sharkey and Reconstruction," *Journal of Mississippi History* 27 (1965):

1–17. His position in the slaveowning hierarchy can be gleaned from Charles S. Sydnor, *Slavery in Mississippi* (1933). His challenge to congressional Reconstruction is best followed in Charles Fairman, *History of the Supreme Court of the United States: Reconstruction and Reunion 1864–88*, pt. 1 (1971).

THOMAS D. MORRIS

SHARP, Katharine Lucinda (21 May 1865–1 June 1914), librarian and library educator, was born in Elgin, Illinois, the daughter of John William Sharp, a salesman and commission merchant, and Phebe Thompson. Sharp's mother died when Katharine was seven years old, and she was raised by maternal relatives in Elgin, where she attended the progressive Elgin Academy, from which she graduated in 1880. In 1881, she matriculated at Northwestern University in Evanston, Illinois, earning a bachelor of philosophy with honors in general, Latin, and special scholarship in 1885 and a master of philosophy in 1889. After receiving her Ph.B. from Northwestern, Sharp returned to the Elgin Academy as an instructor in Latin, French, and German from 1886 to 1888. In October 1888, she accepted her first library position as assistant librarian at the Scoville Institute, later to become the public library, in Oak Park, Illinois, where she stayed for two years until she enrolled at the New York State Library School, Albany, in the fall of 1890. She earned the bachelor and master of library science from the Albany school in 1892 and 1907, respectively.

The Albany school was the first formal educational program established solely to educate for library work; the majority of its early graduates became leaders in the emerging profession as well as pioneer library educators. The school's founder was Melvil Dewey, a charismatic and controversial nineteenth-century statesman of libraries and library economy. Sharp's career was strongly influenced by Dewey's philosophies on formal education for librarians, the systematization and organization of library collections, and the extension of library services, as well as by his key role in placing his colleagues and students in significant library-related posts. Through his influence, Sharp was appointed librarian and head of the department of library economy that opened in September 1893 at the Armour Institute in Chicago—the first school for librarians opened in the Midwest and the fourth in the United States.

The Armour Institute library school achieved early acceptance by the profession and, as their reputation grew, Sharp and the library economy program in Chicago were sought out by two midwestern universities, the University of Wisconsin and the University of Illinois. In 1897 Sharp selected Illinois, and the library training school, its teaching resources, and several of its students and faculty were transferred to the university's campus in Champaign-Urbana. Sharp was appointed professor of library economy, head librarian, and director of the Illinois State Library School, a position she held until she resigned in 1907. The transfer produced an expanded curriculum, significantly improved resources, and the first actual degree, the bachelor of science, associated with a degree-granting university in the United States. Sharp's efforts thus were instrumental in the recognition of the need for formal preparation for a library career. For the next decade, Sharp fought to strengthen admission requirements, employ qualified faculty, initiate an innovative and practitioner-oriented curriculum built on experiential instruction and library internships, and place her graduates in libraries across the country. Sharp was perceived by the profession to be a key figure in the library education movement, and her school was among the first accredited by the profession. When Sharp died, a notice in *Library Journal* (July 1914) pointed out that "not only was Miss Sharp an inspiring teacher imbued with the highest ideals of librarianship, but she strove earnestly and successfully to transmit to her students the vision of a broader scholarship and the better professional training which should characterize the librarian of the future."

Sharp's ten years at Illinois were also noteworthy because of her efforts to develop the university's library. Prior to her arrival in 1897, little had been done to organize the collection or to lay the groundwork essential for a strong academic library. When Sharp left in 1907, the collection was inventoried, organized, and administered by a staff of trained librarians; it had also grown threefold, and a solid core of administrative policies had been formulated.

Sharp was active in numerous local, state, and national educational, library, and social organizations, where she served on committees and held several leadership positions, including the council of the American Library Association. She established a statewide bureau of information that supplied data to Illinois libraries, led in the formation of the Illinois Library Association, and influenced the development of traveling library collections for rural communities. Her ideas were articulated in a series of concise and pragmatic articles that were published in several of the major library journals. Her writings articulated the components of professional library education, advocated the implementation of higher standards in all library situations, and emphasized the unique educational value of libraries and the need for widespread access to well-organized collections of resources. In addition, she compiled a five-part work, *Illinois Libraries*, published from 1906 to 1908, that described the current status of free public libraries in the state.

Katharine Sharp never married but focused her interests on her profession. She traveled widely in the United States and had numerous friends with whom she kept in close contact—many of them had studied or worked with her in Illinois. In 1907 Sharp resigned from the University of Illinois and accepted a post as vice president at Melvil Dewey's Lake Placid Club, a recreational, social, cultural, and educational center located in the Adirondack Mountains of New York. Dewey and his wife were not only professionally significant to her but had become beloved members of an extended family. Her last years at Illinois had been frustrated by poor health, personal tragedy in the deaths of her father and stepbrother, and a changed university administration that did not support the library school to the degree that Sharp believed essential. She died in Saranac Lake, New York, from head injuries caused by an automobile accident.

Her zeal for living, her personal drive to achieve her goals, and her vision of the power of the library to influence material, intellectual, and moral advancement were transmitted to those with whom she worked or taught. For fourteen years, she offered a creative and compelling leadership that helped establish recognition of the profession of librarianship as well as a definition of its educational requirements and structure. During her years at the University of Illinois, she demonstrated, through her administration of the university library, the principles and standards that are requisite to effective organization and service. In sum, she defined the nature of library education for several decades into the twentieth century and brought the University of Illinois library to a point that it could and would evolve into one of a dozen outstanding research collections in the world. F. K. W. Drury, who studied under and worked with her at Illinois, described her legacy in a letter to Dewey: "There was no need to undo any piece of work that she had authorized and the foundation laid by her was firm and stedfast (*sic*). She built for the future" (21 Sept. 1914).

• The Katharine L. Sharp Papers are located in the University Archives, University of Illinois, Champaign-Urbana. Additional resources are found in the Melvil Dewey Papers, Columbia University, New York City. The major biographical study of Sharp is Laurel A. Grotzinger, *The Power and the Dignity: Librarianship and Katharine Sharp* (1966). This volume was originally prepared as a doctoral thesis and makes extensive use of the Sharp papers located at Illinois. Two monograph chapters written by Grotzinger that also note Sharp's contributions to the Illinois State Library School are found in *Reminiscences: Seventy-five Years of a Library School* (1969) and *Ideals and Standards: The History of the University of Illinois Graduate School of Library and Information Science, 1893–1993* (1992). Biographical sketches are found in several sources, including Harriet E. Howe's admiring commentary in *Pioneering Leaders in Librarianship* (1953), Suzanne Hildenbrand's brief professional assessment in *Handbook of American Women's History* (1990), and Rudolf Engelbarts's accurate analysis in *Librarian Authors: A Bibliography* (1991). Sharp's work is also reviewed in a number of Grotzinger articles, notably "Women Who 'Spoke for Themselves,'" *College and Research Libraries* 39 (1978): 175–90. A 1955 unpublished doctoral thesis at the University of Illinois by Wayne Stewart Yenawine, "The Influence of Scholars on Research Library Development at the University of Illinois," has a brief introductory section on Sharp's efforts to develop and administer the university library. A review of her role as a pioneer library educator in relationship to other early library educators can be found in Sarah K. Vann, *Training for Librarianship before 1923* (1961), and Carl M. White, *The Origins of the American Library School* (1961). An obituary is in *Public Libraries* 19 (July 1914): 287–88.

LAUREL A. GROTZINGER

SHARP, Malcolm Pitman (20 Nov. 1897–12 Aug. 1980), lawyer and teacher, was born in Madison, Wisconsin, the son of Frank Chapman Sharp, professor of philosophy at the University of Wisconsin, and Bertha Pitman, who for a time served as a city commissioner in Madison. Malcolm Sharp attended public schools in Madison. During his early years, he was also educated in the classics by his aunt, Anne M. Pitman, who taught Greek and Latin at the University of Wisconsin. Sharp graduated from Amherst College in 1918 and then served in 1918–1919 as a navy pilot and flight instructor. He returned to Madison and attended the University of Wisconsin, earning an M.A. in economics in 1920. Because of his earlier classical education, he was able in his senior year to teach Greek at Amherst, and in 1919–1920 he taught economics at the University of Wisconsin. He received his LL.B. (1923) and LL.D. (1927) in law from Harvard. In 1924 Sharp married Dorothy Reed Furbish, a librarian; the couple had two children.

After receiving his LL.B. in 1923, Sharp practiced law on Wall Street and taught law at the University of Iowa for a year before joining the law faculty at Wisconsin. He was with educator Alexander Meiklejohn (president of Amherst when Sharp was an undergraduate) during the exciting years (1927–1932) of the Experimental College at the University of Wisconsin, where he had a joint appointment in the college and the law school. Sharp became deeply involved in the excitement of breaking new ground in undergraduate education through the design of the Experimental College, based on a thorough grounding in the humanities. Unfortunately, the college was phased out by 1933. Alexander Meiklejohn and his idealistic and valiant young colleagues (including Sharp) simply could not survive the combination of a depression economy, conservative state politics, and the opposition of a powerful group of traditionalists at the university. In the interim, Sharp also served as a consultant to Governor Philip La Follette (a childhood friend and the son of Senator "Fighting Bob" La Follette) of Wisconsin in his 1931 campaign and later in his administration.

In 1933 Sharp accepted a position as professor of law at the University of Chicago, where he remained until 1965. During these years Sharp's political and economic positions became clearly defined. A colleague at Chicago, Harry Kalven, Jr., described Sharp as follows: "He is not only the university professor who teaches in a law school. He is the signer of petitions, the supporter of causes, the liberal who is independent. He is the quiet, stubborn, unselfrighteous champion of lost causes. . . . Yet in economic matters he is staunchly conservative" (*University of Chicago Law Review* 33, no. 2 [Winter 1966]: 194).

Sharp worked on the steel code for the National Recovery Administration during 1933–1935. However, a U.S. Supreme Court decision in 1935 that led to the demise of the National Recovery Administration (NRA) was a blow to Sharp's hopes and those of the other young, forward-looking lawyers and economists to encourage industrial recovery and combat widespread unemployment by adopting more than 500 fair practice codes for various industries. Although the Supreme Court decision made the NRA ineffective, many of its provisions (such as the Wages and Hours Act passed in 1938) were reenacted in later legislation.

Sharp returned to the navy during World War II, serving from 1942 to 1943. He also participated in contract renegotiations in the Army Ordnance Office in Chicago toward the end of the war.

Following the war Sharp was drawn into the controversy surrounding the death sentence of accused atomic spies Ethel and Julius Rosenberg. He had read the newspaper accounts of the case and at first saw no reason to question the verdict of guilty. When asked to represent a committee of eminent scholars at the University of Chicago who questioned the severity of the sentence, Sharp, the only lawyer in the group, read the record of the trial, which convinced him that there was reasonable doubt about the guilt of the Rosenbergs. Sharp traveled to New York to represent the Chicago group, where he was asked to join the Rosenberg defense team as an associate of defense counsel at the appeal stage of the trial (1953). The appeal was denied, and the Rosenbergs were executed, after which Sharp became trustee for their two sons. His book *Was Justice Done?—The Rosenberg-Sobell Case* (1956) and numerous articles on the subject continued examination of the case and its outcome.

Following the Rosenbergs' execution, Sharp continued in his battle to preserve civil liberties. As a charter member of the National Lawyers Guild (1936) and first president of the Chicago chapter, he took on the presidency of the guild again for two terms beginning in 1954 to help in their eventually successful efforts to convince the Justice Department that the guild was not subversive and should therefore not be added to the U.S. attorney general's list of subversive organizations. He also worked tirelessly during the 1950s in the cause of a young and favorite student, George Anastaplo, in his highly publicized confrontation with the Character and Fitness Committee of the Illinois Bar Association over Anastaplo's refusal as a matter of principle to answer questions about possible Communist or Nazi associations. In 1961 the U.S. Supreme Court ruled against Anastaplo 5–4. The only consolation was the ringing dissent of Justice Hugo Black, a dissent that many consider one of the best opinions Black ever wrote.

Along with these cases, Sharp championed the cause of Morton Sobell—a supposed member of the Rosenberg "spy ring"—working for his release from Alcatraz, which took place in 1962. His civil rights interests also extended to race issues; he was tireless in testifying as a friend of the court in law school desegregation cases in the South during the 1940s and 1950s.

Sharp retired from the University of Chicago Law School in 1965, having taken only two years of his three-year extended-tenure arrangement, to accept a teaching position in the law school at the University of New Mexico. In 1970 he retired from UNM. In 1971–

1972 he worked for the Albuquerque law firm of Lyon & Ottinger, which had been formed by former students of Sharp's at UNM. The firm specialized in legal matters involving the poor, and Sharp was admitted to the New Mexico bar by legislative act as a professional courtesy so that he could appear in court on litigation.

In 1972 he was named professor and chair of the political science department at Rosary College in River Forest, Illinois. He said on more than one occasion in personal communications that his final years of teaching were in many ways the most satisfying, given the range of courses he taught—constitutional law to biochemical mysteries, problems in war and peace to a course on the nature of proof in philosophy and the law, the technicalities of business law and economics, and all kinds of public policy questions, past and present. In 1974 Sharp received from the Illinois Division of the American Civil Liberties Union its first annual Harry Kalven Freedom of Expression Award. He taught at Rosary until his death in a Chicago hospital.

An education in the classics, training as an economist and lawyer, a devotion to teaching, and a hopeful view of life's possibilities—together with a love of paradox and a playful wit—helped Sharp to express his true nature and overcome disappointments along the way. In the process he made significant contributions in the fields of commercial and international law, civil liberties, and higher education.

• Sharp authored or coauthored three books: *Social Change and Labor Law*, with Charles Gregory (1939), *Contracts: Cases and Materials*, with Fritz Kessler (1953), and *Was Justice Done?: The Rosenberg-Sobell Case* (1956). He also wrote numerous articles and book reviews for scholarly journals, including "Promissory Liability (Parts 1–2)," *University of Chicago Law Review* 7 (1939–1940): 211; "Aggression: A Study of Values and the Law," *Ethics* 57, no. 4, part 2 (1947): 1–39; "Graduated Unilateral Disarmament," *Bulletin of the Atomic Scientists* 17 (1961): 113–14; and "The Conservative Fellow Traveler," *University of Chicago Law Review* 30 (1963): 704–20. He was a regular contributor to the *Bulletin of the Atomic Scientists* on a variety of subjects. Between 1941 and 1954 Sharp was a participant in more than twenty-five University of Chicago Round Tables on radio, also on a variety of subjects.

JONATHAN SHARP

SHARP, Zerna Addas (12 Aug. 1889–17 June 1981), elementary teacher and principal and reading consultant, was born in Hillisburg, Indiana, the daughter of Charles Sharp, owner of a general store, and Charlotta E. Smith. At age five Sharp learned to read by herself and at sixteen graduated from high school. She took a summer course at Marion Normal College and passed the state teachers' examination shortly thereafter. In 1905 she began teaching first grade in her hometown. The next year she taught in Circleville and Kirklin, both in Indiana. During this time she continued her education at Columbia University; however, she did not obtain a degree. Around 1920 Sharp became an elementary school principal in LaPorte, Indiana; she continued to teach as well.

During her time in LaPorte, Sharp became increasingly aware of the lack of interest her students showed in reading. Attributing this in part to the unimaginative textbooks being used in the classrooms, she put her thoughts in writing, sending frequent letters of complaint to the textbook manufacturer Scott, Foresman & Company. The company was impressed by Sharp's concern and as a result, hired her as a traveling consultant. In that job she visited schools in Illinois, Michigan, Iowa, Wisconsin, and her home state. As she talked with teachers and observed the children, she learned that they struggled with reading and did not enjoy it. According to Sharp, children could not read well because they had to read too many words at a time and deal with unfamiliar subject matter.

Now that Sharp had identified the problem facing young readers, she sought a solution. In her new post as textbook editor for Scott, Foresman (she accepted this job in 1924 and moved to Chicago), Sharp worked with a team of assistants on a fresh approach to teaching children to read. But their brainstorming sessions were not successful. Then on a day off, Sharp went to the beach, where she observed the activities of children and listened to their conversations. She paid attention not only to how they talked and what they talked about, but also to what they enjoyed doing. She noticed that the children talked in short sentences, using simple words, and that their conversations dealt with everyday things like helping their parents and playing. They seemed just to have fun. Inspired by what she observed, Sharp returned to Scott, Foresman with an idea: to be successful, a new series of textbooks would have to be based on activities familiar to children, ones in which they actually took part. This idea later blossomed into the Dick and Jane stories.

Sharp chose the names of Dick, Jane, and other characters in the new books (Spot, the dog; Puff, the cat) because children could sound them out easily. While Sharp never actually wrote the stories, she designed the format for them and oversaw the submission of material, rejecting ideas she did not like. The technique she developed involved the use of one new word per page, with the words all being used together after three pages. Each story would contain a maximum of five different words, and along with the text, there would be four-color pictures. To keep the realism in the stories, clothes and other items were modeled from the contemporary store catalogs of Sears, Roebuck or Montgomery Ward. Schools adopted the stories as they became a preeminent series; 85 percent of schools in the United States used the books at one point. The series was regarded as the most widely accepted since the McGuffey readers. Children showed such interest in the stories that they wrote letters to Scott, Foresman asking about the last name of the characters.

In the early 1970s the Dick and Jane stories came under fire from representatives of the women's movement who felt that males and females were always shown in traditional roles: mothers kept house, boys always took the lead and were in controlling leadership roles, and girls were always the followers or at the periphery. In interviews Sharp displayed great annoyance with this view, arguing that those were the opinions of adults, while children accepted the stories quite well. Perhaps due in part to this criticism, Scott, Foresman decided in 1973 to eliminate the series.

Sharp worked for Scott, Foresman until 1964. During her time with the company, the editorial force grew from eight to sixty-three in the reading department alone. She retired to Seal Beach, California, but in 1977 returned to Indiana to live in Wesley Manor in Frankfort. She was alert and active until a few months before her death, when she lost her eyesight due to a failed cataract operation. Sharp, who never married, died in Frankfort.

Sharp helped change the way American children learned to read, and the Dick and Jane stories, used in American classrooms for nearly fifty years, created indelible images of an idealized middle-class existence for those who learned from them. As long-standing assumptions of cultural homogeneity began to be questioned and abandoned, however, Dick and Jane no longer struck a chord in many American children. Once seemingly timeless figures, Sharp's creations entered history.

• Papers and newspaper articles on Sharp are at the Frankfort Museum, Frankfort, Ind. Sharp's nephew, Robert L. Sharp, also holds some papers. Other records are at Scott, Foresman Publishing, Glenview, Ill. Articles that provide information on her life and work include Dennis F. Hensley, "Good-by Dick, Good-by Jane, Good-by Zerna Sharp," *Indianapolis Star Magazine*, 18 Oct. 1981; Wes Smith, "See Dick and Jane," *Chicago Tribune*, 10 Mar. 1994; and Jim Leman, "Dick and Jane: Millions Grew Up with Them," the *Frankfort Times*, 27 May 1977. Obituaries are in the *Chicago Tribune* and the *New York Times*, both 19 June 1981; the *Washington Post*, 20 June 1981; and *Time*, 29 June 1981.

MARY ELLEN COLLINS

SHARPE, Horatio (1718–9 Nov. 1790), military officer and governor, was born in Hull, Yorkshire, England, the son of William Sharpe and Margaret Beake, whose father was principal secretary of Maryland, 1714–1732. Nothing is known of Horatio's childhood, but he apparently was well educated. His brother John Sharpe served as guardian to the minor Frederick Calvert, sixth lord Baltimore. Sharpe's early career was in the military with the Twentieth Regiment of Foot in Scotland, as captain of marines, and in the West Indies, as lieutenant colonel of foot. In 1753 Frederick, Lord Baltimore, commissioned Sharpe governor of Maryland.

Sharpe arrived in the colony in August 1753, just as hostilities between the British and French were beginning on the western frontier. After the French defeated Virginia troops commanded by Captain George Washington at Fort Necessity in July 1754, the British command dispatched Sharpe to take charge of its forces in the West. Sharpe assumed command of the troops at Fort Cumberland in western Maryland and reconnoitered the area in the winter of 1754–1755.

Sharpe provided logistical support to General Edward Braddock, who arrived in America in February 1755 as commander in chief of the British forces. After Braddock's defeat and death on the Monongahela River in July 1755, Sharpe traveled west again to supervise construction of defenses at Fort Cumberland on Maryland's vulnerable frontier. He also participated in British military councils in New York in 1755 and Philadelphia in 1757.

While Sharpe's military background enabled him to address effectively the military exigencies he faced in his first years as Maryland's governor, his frequent absences from Annapolis meant that he could not exert as much political control over the colony as he would have liked. The British government demanded that Sharpe raise money, men, and matériel to support the war with France. Frederick, Lord Baltimore, hounded Sharpe to increase the income from rents and fees he was due as proprietor. The lower house of the general assembly had long sought to increase its power and independence at the expense of both the proprietor and the Crown. Since it controlled the colony's purse, every wartime emergency afforded the lower house the opportunity, Sharpe wrote, to pursue its "determined resolution to make his majesty's service and his lordship's interest clash" (Barker, p. 239).

Governor Sharpe managed the colony's affairs as best he could, playing one side against the other and capitulating to lower house demands only when dire military circumstances required it. The results of Sharpe's balancing of the demands of Crown, proprietor, and lower house satisfied none of the parties entirely. Maryland contributed to the British cause in the war but not as much as it could have. The proprietor got administrative changes in the colony that increased his revenue but not as much as he wanted. The lower house of the general assembly emerged from the war stronger and more confident but still short of its goal of complete control over the colony and its destiny.

The French and Indian War dominated virtually the entire decade of Sharpe's tenure as Maryland's executive. British victory brought only a brief hiatus in the colony's political turmoil. Parliament's decision to raise additional revenue from the colonies reenergized the lower house of the assembly. Opposition to the Stamp Act of 1765 was so widespread in Maryland that Sharpe could neither protect the colony's stamp distributor, Zachariah Hood, nor prevent the lower house from adopting resolutions against the act and dispatching delegates to the Stamp Act Congress.

Political passions had barely begun to cool following Parliament's repeal of the Stamp Act when they were aroused again over the issue of the proprietary prerogative. Maryland's proprietor had vast powers, including the right to appoint a host of provincial and local officeholders. Popular leaders often accused proprietary appointees of being inept or corrupt, and restricting the proprietor's prerogative over appointments was a primary goal of the lower house of the assembly. Sharpe considered "the art of disposing of places so as to avoid offense" one of his most onerous duties as governor, and the task was made more difficult by the greed and guile of the proprietor. In 1763 Sharpe expressed his frustration over the patronage issue to his brother, writing that if he could establish himself in business in England he would "not for the sake of getting something more make my happiness dependent on the caprice of others as is the ease and happiness of every governor in America."

While the increasingly antagonistic agendas of Parliament, the proprietor, and the public limited Sharpe's political effectiveness, his amiable disposition and engaging personality earned him the respect of friend and foe alike. As a result, Sharpe was able to administer the colony effectively during difficult and dangerous times. Whatever the controversy, Sharpe tried to mediate or to keep the most belligerent opponents apart. When a directive from Parliament or the proprietor seemed certain to heighten tensions, Sharpe usually found a way to avoid implementing it without openly defying his superiors. Some thought his behavior weak and vacillating. In fact, Sharpe simply understood better than many what was possible and what was not.

Sharpe enjoyed the social life of Annapolis and was well liked by the provincial elite. A lifelong bachelor, he hosted lavish parties and was a frequent guest at affairs given by others. He was also an avid horseman who imported and raced purebred horses. In 1764 Sharpe began work on "Whitehall," a country house seven miles outside Annapolis that a modern architectural historian has called "one of the most interesting and important houses of the eighteenth century."

On 20 July 1768 Lord Baltimore dismissed Sharpe as governor. Surprised by the action, Sharpe later learned that the proprietor had relieved him to make the position available for his brother-in-law. By the time his successor Robert Eden arrived in 1769, Sharpe had served as Maryland's governor for sixteen years, longer than any previous chief executive of the colony.

In 1773 Sharpe sailed for England on family business. Before he could return, political unrest in the colonies reached fever pitch, making the return trip inadvisable. Marylanders retained their high regard for Sharpe, however, and specifically exempted him from the 1781 act of the general assembly that confiscated Loyalist estates.

Sharpe died in Hampstead, England. Of Sharpe as Maryland's governor, William Eddis wrote, the "invariable rectitude of [Sharpe's] conduct, the affability of his manners, and his unremitting attention to the happiness and prosperity of Maryland had established a well-merited popularity which during an administration of sixteen years continued in full force and secured him the unabated love and attachment of a grateful people" (Edgar, p. 248).

• The largest collections of Sharpe letters are in the Calvert papers and Sharpe papers at the Maryland Historical Society in Baltimore and in the Ridout papers at the Maryland State Archives in Annapolis. Most of this correspondence has been published in William Hand Browne et al., eds., *Archives of Maryland*, vols. 6, 9, and 14 (72 vols., 1883–1972). Some interesting personal letters are in Aubrey C. Land, ed., "The Familiar Letters of Governor Horatio Sharpe," *Maryland Historical Magazine* 61 (Sept. 1966): 189–209. Lady Edgar, *A Colonial Governor in Maryland: Horatio Sharpe and His Times, 1753–1773* (1912), is still worth reading, despite its age and obvious errors. A brief but accurate biographical sketch of Sharpe is in Edward C. Papenfuse et al., eds., *A Biographical Dictionary of the Maryland Legislature, 1635–1789*, vol. 2 (2 vols., 1979, 1985). The historian who best depicts Sharpe's administration is Charles Albro Barker, *The Background of the Revolution in Maryland* (1940). Two contemporaries who knew Sharpe and who provide differing views of his abilities as an administrator are William Eddis, *Letters from America*, ed. Land (1969), and Jonathan Boucher, *Reminiscences of an American Loyalist, 1738–1789*, ed. Jonathan Bouchier (1925).

GREGORY A. STIVERSON

SHARPE, Robert Redington (4 Dec. 1904–14 May 1934), theatrical designer, was born in Boston, Massachusetts, the son of George Bertram Sharpe, an advertising executive, and Leslie Redington. When he was eight years old, his mother began taking him to the theater in New York, where the family lived. She also encouraged his interest in drawing. As a child, Sharpe made elaborate model theaters that exhibit the qualities of his mature work: vivid color, decorative line, sensuous texture, and a preference for fantasy.

In 1919 the family moved to Cleveland, where Sharpe studied at the Cleveland Art Institute while attending high school. In the summer of 1921 he had his first association with the professional theater, when he apprenticed at the Ohio Stock Company as an actor in small parts and as a scene painter.

In 1922 Sharpe went to New York to study scene design with Norman Bel Geddes, a leading exponent of the "new stagecraft," a radical simplification of all the visual arts of theater. The style was not congenial to Sharpe's talent. He later observed, "My first models and sense of color were better in my early work than when I finished art school. Instinctively I put colors together when I was a kid that later I didn't dare mix."

In 1924 Sharpe moved to Los Angeles, hoping to design for the movies. There he met Gilmor Brown, director of the Pasadena Community Playhouse, a pioneer of the American community theater movement. Brown invited Sharpe to join the Playhouse as its first art director. Over the next two years, Sharpe designed forty-one productions in the most creative and productive period of his life. He experimented with a wide range of theatrical styles and techniques: both selective and detailed realism, expressionism, futurism, the painterly style, symbolism, abstraction, and fantasy.

Sharpe left Pasadena in 1926 for a two-year stay in Paris and Berlin. He studied the work of avant-garde directors and designers and served briefly as art director of the Theater am Kurfürstendamm in Berlin.

Sharpe moved to New York in 1928 and almost immediately obtained a commission from the Theatre Guild to design a revival of George Bernard Shaw's

Major Barbara. The fact that Sharpe was designing on Broadway at age twenty-three was noted in prominent articles in the *New York Times* and the *New York World*.

Despite an encouraging beginning, the momentum of his career was stalled by the depression. In the fall of 1933, however, he was engaged to design the setting and costumes for *Tobacco Road*, Jack Kirkland's dramatization of the Erskine Caldwell novel. Sharpe hit upon the idea of reproducing the look—and even the smell—of the yard and shack of a Georgia share-cropper. He piled tons of dirt on the stage, along with rusty cans, corncobs, and inner tubes. Instead of de-signing the costumes, he asked a member of the cast who had a farm in South Carolina to telephone the caretaker for clothes belonging to the farm workers.

Tobacco Road opened on 4 December 1933 at the Masque Theatre. Although the critics panned the play, they praised Sharpe's setting. Gilbert Gabriel, a critic writing in the *New York American* (5 Dec. 1933) observed: "Every time any of the characters sits down on the ground the air grows soupy with dirt. All the crevices of the old shack drip with dirt. So do all the pants-bottoms and the hair-braids." Stark Young in the *New Republic* (20 Dec. 1933) called Sharpe's set-ting of shanty, skeletal tree, shed, well, and deep-ground dirt "better drama than most decor or most plays."

Tobacco Road came close to folding very soon after it opened. It survived only through the commitment of the producer and through an agreement on the part of the performers to work for a percentage of the (very low) ticket sales. But shortly after Christmas the audi-ences began to grow, and by the middle of January 1934 the play was established as a hit. It eventually ran for eight years, with road tours by three companies.

Sharpe met with a violent and tragic death. He was found early on the morning of 12 May 1934 in the sub-way station at Sixth Avenue and Waverly Place, un-conscious. He had evidently been robbed. Taken to Bellevue Hospital, he died two days later of head inju-ries.

Although not the originator of a distinctive style, Sharpe was an imaginative designer who eagerly ab-sorbed the latest artistic and theatrical currents of the early twentieth century. His association with the Pasa-dena Community Playhouse, the Theatre Guild, and *Tobacco Road* earned him a respected place among his contemporaries at an early age.

• Sharpe's scrapbooks and designs are at the Harvard Thea-tre Collection. Arnold Wengrow, *Robert Redington Sharpe: The Life of a Theatre Designer* (1990), the catalog of an exhibi-tion at the Harvard Theatre Collection, includes a biography and a checklist of designs. See also Wengrow, "Robert Red-ington Sharpe: A Designer Rediscovered," *Theatre Design and Technology* 27 (Winter 1991): 14–23.

ARNOLD WENGROW

SHARPLES, James (1751 or 1752–26 Feb. 1811), por-trait painter, was born in Lancashire, England, of Ro-man Catholic parents whose names are unknown but who were of some means. His brother Henry became a timber merchant in Liverpool, and a half sister, Mrs. Talbot, was subprioress at a Catholic school. At some point Sharples received a bequest from an uncle. His parents sent him to France to study for the priesthood, but he chose instead to become an artist. He may have studied with portrait painter George Romney. In 1774 he exhibited "a portrait and two small oval portraits, possibly miniatures" (Foskett, p. 502) at the first exhi-bition of the Liverpool Society of Artists; these are un-located. Five years later he exhibited two portraits at the Royal Academy, London. Settling in Bath by 1781, he advertised in the *Bristol Journal* on 28 July as a "Portrait Painter in Oil and Crayons" who exhibited at his temporary place of business in Bristol "upwards of one hundred specimens of known characters" (Knox, pp. 3–4). He used this technique later to at-tract patrons in the United States. He again exhibited portraits at the Royal Academy in 1782, 1783, and 1785, including one crayon; none of this early work is located today. By this time he had moved to London and had married twice; the names and dates of these two wives are not known. Two children, George, the son of his first wife, and Felix Thomas, the son of his second wife, both became artists. After his second wife's death, Sharples returned to Liverpool. He mar-ried Ellen Wallace, a Quaker, who was a pupil in an art class that he taught in Bath. They had two chil-dren, James, Jr., and Rolinda, who also became art-ists.

Sharples came to the United States in the 1790s with his wife and three youngest children. They perhaps ar-rived as early as 1794, after spending seven months in captivity in Brest, France, when their ship was cap-tured by a privateer. They apparently settled first in New York. Ellen Sharples noted in 1809 in her diary that they had tried to purchase a house at Red Hook "fifteen years ago" (Knox, p. 35). However, Sharples's earliest documented American portraits were made in Philadelphia. They were paid for by George Washing-ton on 10 May 1796 and represent George Washington Motier Lafayette, the son of the Marquis de Lafayette, and George Washington Parke Custis, the president's adopted grandson. Judge William Cushing, writing to his niece Esther Parsons, from Philadelphia on 19 Jan-uary 1797, commented that "Mr. Sharples from New York has been here some weeks, taking portraits" (Knox, p. 15).

According to the 1834 account of American painter William Dunlap, Sharples carried letters of introduc-tion to "persons distinguished, either military, civil or literary, with a request to paint their portraits for his collection. This being granted, and the portrait fin-ished in about two hours, the likeness generally in-duced an order for a copy, and brought as sitters all who saw it. His price for the profile was $15; and for the full-face (never so good) $20." The portraits were on thick, textured, gray paper measuring about nine by seven inches. The outlines of the bust-length por-traits were apparently drawn with a mechanical instru-ment to ensure physiognomic accuracy. The powdered colors, applied with a fine brush, were predominantly black, gray, and white, with flesh tones for the faces and blue for the backgrounds. Dunlap, whose portrait was made by Sharples, called his works "strikingly like" and described him as "a plain, well-disposed man, and accumulated property by honest industry, and uncommon facility with his materials." Among Sharples's sitters in Philadelphia were John Adams, James and Dolley Madison, Benjamin Rush, Thomas Jefferson, and George and Martha Washington. G. W. P. Custis later described Sharples's portrait of Washington, the last for which the president sat, as "an admirable likeness, the profile taken by an instrument, and critically correct" (Floyd, p. 898). Ellen Sharples made duplicates of his portraits, noting in her diary that in Philadelphia "copies were frequently required; these I undertook and was so far successful as to have as many commissions as I could execute; they were thought equal to the originals, price the same" (Knox, p. 13). She continued to do this for many years, bringing confusion to later attempts to attribute individual works.

By October 1797 Sharples and his family settled in New York City, where directories for 1798–1800 list him as a portrait painter, occasionally misspelling his name "Sharpless." In 1801 the entire family returned to England, concerned about their house and investments and about the possibility of war with France. There Sharples made portraits and exhibited the American pastels. James, Jr., and Felix Sharples came back to the United States in 1806 and began careers as pastel portraitists in upstate New York and Virginia. Sharples, his wife Ellen, and daughter Rolinda returned in 1809, settling again in New York City. Sharples made trips to Niagara Falls and Philadelphia but grew weak after a heart attack. He died in New York and was buried in St. Peter's Roman Catholic Church. Ellen Sharples offered his "Collection of Original Portraits of Distinguished American Characters" for sale (New York *Public Advertiser*, 6 Apr.–10 July 1811), and then returned to England with Rolinda and James, Jr. Felix Sharples, who remained in the United States, kept many of his father's unsold drawings, which now form the collection of Sharples's work at Independence National Historical Park, Philadelphia. Ellen Sharples later bequeathed a second large collection of portraits to the Bristol Fine Arts Academy, England, that are now owned by the City Art Gallery, Bristol.

Sharples's portraits owe their accuracy in part to his mechanical talents. He was described by Dunlap as a "man of science and a mechanician, as well as a painter." Three patents that he took out in England, in 1791, 1802, and 1804, describe design changes in mechanical technology ranging from the mechanical power available to steam engines to the reduction of friction in machinery. Two articles, in Nicholson's *Journal of Natural Philosophy* (vol. 7, 1804) and in the *American Medical and Philosophical Register* (vol. 1, 1810), describe some of his observations. The patents were not significant; Mrs. Sharples wrote that "Mr. S.

had greater talents for inventing than bringing his inventions into use—always more disposed to apply to something new" (Knox, p. 4). However, they indicate the mechanical aptitude that aided him in his American career, when he designed a special carriage to carry his family and drawing materials, and apparently used a tracing device to make the portraits.

Sharples's approximately two hundred American pastel portraits are valued today for their accuracy, delicacy, and liveliness, as well as for the prominence of his sitters. He shared with many contemporaries an interest in recording likenesses of leaders of the American Revolution, recognizing their commercial and historical value.

• Sharples is mentioned in William Dunlap's *History of the Rise and Progress of the Arts of Design in the United States* (2 vols., 1834; repr. 1969), vol. 2, pp. 70–72. The full study of his work is Katharine McCook Knox, *The Sharples; Their Portraits of George Washington and His Contemporaries: A Diary and an Account of the Life and Work of James Sharples and His Family in England and America* (1930; repr. 1972). Aspects of his work are more recently discussed by Andrew Oliver, *Portraits of John and Abigail Adams* (1967), pp. 75–91, 247; Arnold Wilson, "The Sharples Family of Painters," *Antiques* 100 (Nov. 1971): 740–43; William Barrow Floyd, "The Portraits and Paintings at Mount Vernon from 1754 to 1799, Part II," *Antiques* 100 (Dec. 1971): 894–99; Daphne Foskett, *A Dictionary of British Miniature Painters* (2 vols., 1972), vol. 1, pp. 502–503; John C. Milley, "Thoughts on the Attribution of Sharples Pastels," *University Hospital 1975 Antiques Show* (exhibition catalog; Philadelphia, 1975), pp. 59–63; and David Meschutt, "Portraits of Anthony Wayne: Re-identifications and Re-attributions," *American Art Journal* 15, no. 2 (1983): 32–42.

ELLEN G. MILES

SHARPLESS, Isaac (16 Dec. 1848–16 Jan. 1920), college president, was born in Birmingham Township, Chester County, Pennsylvania, the son of Aaron Sharpless and Susanna Forsythe, farmers. A Quaker educator, Sharpless helped shape the new model for elite liberal arts colleges emerging at the turn of the century. Born to a family with several generations of Quaker connections, he was educated in the local Friends school and then at the prestigious Orthodox Quaker Westtown School. He remained at Westtown as a teacher for five years (1867 to 1872) before going to Harvard's Lawrence Scientific School for a year, receiving a B.S. degree in 1873. He returned to teach at Westtown for two more years before being appointed instructor of mathematics and astronomy at Haverford College, where he spent the rest of his career. In 1876 he married Lydia Cope; they had five daughters and a son.

As a faculty member from 1875 to 1884, Sharpless taught a variety of mathematics and science courses and published two textbooks: *The Elements of Plane and Solid Geometry* (1879) and *Astronomy for Schools and General Readers* (1882). He was promoted to dean of the college (1884) and then president (1887) in rapid succession.

His scholarly ambitions for Haverford College quickly outran the vision and pocketbooks of more traditional Orthodox Quakers on the governing Board of Managers. Sharpless's election had been quite contentious, and he quickly alienated some managers. He used an astronomical expedition to Moscow to view an eclipse in the summer of 1887 as an opportunity to recruit his first new faculty member, a Cambridge graduate then teaching in Bath, England. He soon hired several other graduates of leading European and American graduate schools in his first years, raising both the faculty's reputation and deficits. Since many members of the Board of Managers believed the college should be self-sustaining and should remain within traditional Quaker learning, they used Sharpless's 1890 through 1891 study leave in Europe to oust him. Sharpless resigned, but supporters had him reinstated.

With increased financial support from the managers and alumni, Sharpless continued to recruit faculty from English and American graduate schools rather than Quaker academies and to build the college. During his thirty years as president (1887–1917), the endowment rose from $211,000 to $2,578,000, a modest campus of four buildings became a well-equipped modern campus, and the library grew from 17,000 to 72,000 volumes, while the student body was only increased from 94 to 157. The combination of resources, talented faculty, and small student body raised Haverford's academic reputation within and outside the denomination, but it disappointed more traditional Orthodox Quakers.

Although raised in a traditional Quaker home, Sharpless became associated with liberal Quaker ideas. He abandoned the external trappings of Quaker traditional Quakerism, such as distinctive dress, while remaining loyal to many Quaker principles. One was the concept of a "guarded education" in which all students were to live on campus and have continual contact with and oversight by faculty. He also remained steadfastly pacifistic. In 1904 Sharpless abolished football due to its un-Quakerly violence and for nearly a decade succeeded in substituting cricket as the college's principal sport. When the United States entered World War I, Sharpless was one of the few college presidents who refused to have a branch of the Student Army Training Corps on his campus, despite the defection of nearby Quaker Swarthmore College.

Sharpless helped shape a new mission for Quakerism, which was suffering a serious identity crisis in the early twentieth century. Most young Quakers rejected the traditional Quaker lifestyle and found "Quietism," the longstanding rejection of political engagement, anachronistic in an increasingly interdependent world. Although some Quakers wanted to be indistinguishable from other denominations, others searched for a distinctive new role. Sharpless and some of his faculty were leaders in reuniting the Orthodox and Hicksite factions around a new commitment to service, institutionalized in the American Friends Service Committee. As a supporter of the reforms and activism associated with the Social Gospel and progressivism, Sharpless was a leader in shaping a new version of socially and politically committed Quakerism.

Sharpless was also active in county and state politics. He worked at the federal level as a spokesman for Quaker views in international affairs, especially in favor of arbitration as a substitute for war. Despite his training in science, he later developed a scholarly interest in the history and practice of applying Quaker principles to government and published the two-volume *A History of Quaker Government in Pennsylvania* (1898), *A Quaker Experiment in Government* (vol. 1) and *Quakers in the Revolution* (vol. 2); *Quakerism and Politics* (1905); and *Political Leaders of Provincial Pennsylvania* (1919). Sharpless was also a founder and president of the Friends Historical Society. He was appointed to the commission to revise the Pennsylvania constitution shortly before his death at Haverford.

Sharpless's greatest influence was as an educator. He was inspired by his experiences at Oxford in 1890 and 1891 to create one of the first honors programs in an American college. By raising admissions standards while keeping the student body small and rejecting technical and vocational courses, Sharpless led Haverford into a modernized liberal arts curriculum similar to that being adopted by Woodrow Wilson's Princeton and other influential colleges. Sharpless led the transformation of Haverford College into an elite institution with academic and social prestige that extended beyond Quaker circles.

In the latter years of his career Sharpless became a national spokesman for the new style of elite liberal arts college that emerged after the turn of the century. He spoke at many meetings of educators who were shaping the new educational order, published regularly in educational journals, and wrote *The American College* (1915) and *The Story of a Small College* (1918). With long experience in what Quakers called "guarded education," Sharpless was a knowledgeable spokesman for the emerging ideal of residential, four-year liberal arts colleges. The Haverford molded by Sharpless was an early example of the type of college that became such an effective rite of passage to the American elite and upper middle class throughout the twentieth century.

• The Sharpless papers are in the Quaker Collection, at Haverford College. The *Bulletin of the Friends' Historical Society of Philadelphia* 9 (May 1920): 90–99, has a useful obituary and a lengthy bibliography listing 19 books and over 100 articles by Sharpless. There is also a biographical sketch in Hugh Barbour and J. William Frost, *The Quakers* (1988). Rufus Jones, *Haverford College: A History and an Interpretation* (1933), is an excellent history of Haverford College written by one of Sharpless's colleagues. Philip S. Benjamin, *Philadelphia Quakers in the Industrial Age, 1865–1920* (1976), places Sharpless in the context of liberal Quakerism, progressive reform, and the peace movement.

W. BRUCE LESLIE

SHARSWOOD, George (7 July 1810–28 May 1883), lawyer, judge, and professor, was born in Philadelphia, Pennsylvania, the son of George Sharswood, a merchant, and Esther Dunn. Sharswood graduated from the University of Pennsylvania in 1828 and proceeded to study in the chambers of a noted Philadelphia lawyer, J. R. Ingersoll. He was admitted to the bar on 15 December 1831 and began a career during which he became noted not only for his legal knowledge but also for his broad acquaintance with classical literature and belles-lettres. Sharswood actually had three careers. From his admittance to the bar in 1831 until his appointment as an associate judge of the District Court in Philadelphia in 1845, Sharswood carried on the practice of law. Beginning in 1837 he also dabbled in politics and was elected both to the state legislature and to the Philadelphia Select Council. During this period he also made his first forays into legal scholarship. In 1841 he wrote a report to the stockholders of the Bank of the United States, commenting on certain problems with the bank, and in 1843 he became an editor of the *American Law Magazine*. Beginning in 1838, Sharswood also began his career as an annotator of British texts, including Leigh's textbook on Nisi Prius, Stephen's textbook on Nisi Prius, and Russell's textbook on crimes.

In 1849 Sharswood married Mary Chambers; the couple had one son. Four years before their marriage, with his appointment as an associate judge, Sharswood began a distinguished judicial career, which was to last the remainder of his life. In 1848 he was elected to serve as the president of the District Court of the City and County of Philadelphia. He remained on this court until 1867, during which period he was said to have heard over 4,000 cases. Of these, 156 were sent on appeal to the supreme court of the state; 124 of these were affirmed. In 1867 Sharswood was made an associate justice of the Supreme Court of Pennsylvania. By the tradition of that court, the chief justiceship rotated to the most senior associate justice. Thus, in 1879 Sharswood became chief justice of the Supreme Court of Pennsylvania, an office he held until his retirement at the end of 1882. During his time on the district court and the supreme court Sharswood obtained a reputation for being both a fair and a learned judge. He was well liked by the bar. During his long judicial career, Sharswood was involved with a number of extremely important cases, perhaps the most important of which was *Borie v. Trott*, popularly known as the Legal Tender Case. In this case, which determined the constitutionality of the Legal Tender Act of 1862, Sharswood dissented.

Sharswood's third career was as a law teacher. In the eighteenth century, the University of Pennsylvania had been one of the first American universities to teach law. James Wilson, a signer of the Declaration of Independence, gave a series of lectures on law there. But over the decades after Wilson, the school's law program had declined. In 1850 Sharswood was hired by the university as a lecturer in law, an appointment that revitalized the law department. Within a short period a full faculty had been hired, and Sharswood had been elected to the professorship of the Institutes of Law. He served on the Pennsylvania faculty until shortly af-

ter his appointment to the Pennsylvania Supreme Court (1867). This period was his most fruitful as a legal scholar. As an annotator of legal texts, in 1852 he issued the American edition of Byles's textbook on bills. Most importantly, in 1859 he published an American edition with annotations of Blackstone's *Commentaries on the Laws of England*, a text that rapidly became the standard edition in this country. Throughout his period as a law teacher, Sharswood also lectured on a vast number of subjects, and his introductory lectures were published as *Lectures Introductory to the Study of the Law* (1870). His most important publication from this period was his lectures on professional ethics, first published under the title *A Compend of Lectures on the Aims and Duties of the Profession of Law*, which, under the title *An Essay on Professional Ethics*, was reprinted four times during his life and several times posthumously (including in 1906 at the behest of the American Bar Association). Sharswood's work on professional ethics, one of the first American attempts to systematically study this subject, exercised great influence on the development of the first codes of lawyer conduct a half century later.

At the end of 1882 Sharswood retired from his position as chief justice and was feted by the Pennsylvania and Philadelphia bars. His role as author, founding professor of the University of Pennsylvania School of Law, and long-sitting judge assured him a respected place in the history of American jurisprudence. He died in Philadelphia a few months after his retirement.

• The best nineteenth-century studies of Sharswood's life are S. Dickson, "George Sharswood," in *Great American Lawyers*, vol. 6, ed. W. D. Lewis (1909), and G. W. Biddle, *A Sketch of the Professional and Judicial Character of the Late George Sharswood* (1883). There is also an excellent memoir of Sharswood contained in the fifth edition of G. Sharswood's *An Essay on Professional Ethics* (1884). On the history of the Philadelphia bar by a contemporary of Sharswood, see the two-volume study by D. P. Brown, *The Forum; or, Forty Years Full Practice at the Philadelphia Bar* (1856).

MICHAEL H. HOEFLICH

SHATTUCK, George Cheyne (22 July 1813–22 Mar. 1893), physician and medical educator, was born in Boston, Massachusetts, the son of George Cheyne Shattuck, a physician, and Eliza Cheever Davis. Shattuck entered Harvard College in 1827 and received his B.A. in 1831. After a year at the Harvard Law School he entered the Harvard Medical School, where he received his M.D. in 1835. After graduation he took additional medical courses from his father's former pupil Benjamin Lincoln at Burlington, Vermont, and at Bowdoin College.

Shattuck then sailed to Europe, where he spent nearly three years studying medicine, chiefly in the clinics and dissecting rooms of Paris, a course that had become commonplace for the professionally ambitious young physician from an affluent family. In Paris, Shattuck, along with his compatriots Henry Ingersoll Bowditch and Alfred Stillé, became an ardent disciple of the clinician and teacher Pierre C. A. Louis. Louis had established typhoid fever as a distinct disease in 1829, but many physicians still wondered if the typhoid fever Louis had studied in Paris might be the same as British typhus fever. At Louis's suggestion, Shattuck traveled to Britain to study typhus, especially at the London Fever Hospital, where he both observed symptoms at the bedside and performed postmortem examinations.

Returning to Paris in 1838, Shattuck reported on his British observations at a meeting of the Société Médicale d'Observation, a group presided over by Louis. Shattuck seconded the French clinician's assertion that typhoid and typhus fever were separate diseases. Along with observations made in Philadelphia in 1836 by Louis's American disciples William Wood Gerhard and Caspar Wistar Pennock, Shattuck's work, published in the Philadelphia *Medical Examiner* as "On the Continued Fever of Great Britain" (1840), not only helped establish the distinction between typhoid and typhus fever but also exemplified the clinical value of symptom-lesion correlation—that is, the matching of particular signs and symptoms observed at the bedside with specific structural lesions revealed at autopsy— that was a hallmark of the Paris School. With Louis's encouragement, Shattuck also translated his 1829 *Anatomical, Pathological, and Therapeutic Researches on the Yellow Fever of Gibraltar of 1828*, published in Boston in 1839.

In 1839 Shattuck returned to Boston to begin medical practice with his father, and in the following year he married Anne Henrietta Brune; they had three children. Shattuck's experience abroad had transformed him into a committed disciple of the Paris Clinical School and its epistemological ideals, and he hoped to transmit to the medical profession in his own country the Parisians' commitment to conducting medical research through empirical observation of the living and dead body, rather than through the more speculative investigation that remained common in the United States. He also wanted to promote a program of clinical teaching and investigation modeled after what he had witnessed in the great hospitals of Paris. Like other American physicians who returned from study in France, however, Shattuck was frustrated by the lack of medical facilities in his own country comparable to what he had enjoyed in Paris.

For nearly a decade Shattuck was without either a hospital or a medical school appointment that would enable him to express his Parisian commitments. Instead, to provide a forum for teaching, shortly after his return he established a private clinic, which he used for private training of medical students. To promote Louisian ideals of medical research, Shattuck, along with Louis's other Boston pupils Bowditch and Oliver Wendell Holmes, founded the Boston Society for Medical Observation. Like its model, Louis's Société Médicale d'Observation in Paris, this organization eschewed the political concerns that preoccupied most contemporary medical societies in the United States and devoted its meetings solely to reports by members on their medical investigations.

In 1849 Shattuck succeeded Holmes as visiting physician to Massachusetts General Hospital, a post he occupied until 1885. He became a professor of clinical medicine at the Harvard Medical School in 1855 and held that position until 1859, when he became professor of the theory and practice of medicine. He was appointed dean of the faculty in 1864. At the time, Harvard, like most American medical schools, was a proprietary institution owned and controlled by its small faculty and operated for their professional and financial profit. During Shattuck's tenure as dean, however, Harvard was among the first American schools to significantly expand their curriculum and raise their standards.

Shortly after his marriage Shattuck left the Unitarians to become an Episcopalian, and throughout his life he was an ardent supporter of the Protestant Episcopal church. He helped to found and supported the Church of the Advent in Boston. In addition, he became a trustee of the General Theological Seminary. After his father's death, in 1855 Shattuck endowed St. Paul's School in Concord, New Hampshire, and donated his country estate as a site for the new institution, which was to combine moral, physical, and spiritual education for boys. He was also a founder of the Shattuck School of Fairbault, Minnesota, a missionary school for Native Americans.

Shattuck was president of the Massachusetts Medical Society from 1872 to 1874. He held his professorship at Harvard until 1873. Through correspondence and visits to France, he remained in contact with his French mentor until Louis's death in 1872, and, through communications with a wider network of American physicians who had studied in Paris, he continued to reaffirm the commitments he had taken up in France. Shattuck died in Boston.

• Most of Shattuck's papers are deposited at the Francis A. Countway Library of Medicine, Boston, and at the Massachusetts Historical Society. Biographical sources include Caleb Davis Bradlee, "George Cheyne Shattuck, M.D.," *New-England Historical and Genealogical Register* 48 (1894): 277–80; and Alfred Stillé, "Notice of the Life and Character of George Cheyne Shattuck, M.D.," *Transactions of the College of Physicians of Philadelphia*, 3d ser., 15 (1893): lxvi–lxxvi. An obituary is in the *Boston Medical and Surgical Journal* 128 (1893): 354–55.

JOHN HARLEY WARNER

SHATTUCK, Lemuel (15 Oct. 1793–17 Jan. 1859), statistician and public health pioneer, was born in Ashby, Massachusetts, the son of John Shattuck and Betsey Miles, farmers. In 1794 the family moved to rural New Ipswich township, in southern New Hampshire, where Shattuck lived until 1816. As a boy, his studies at the local common school averaged in length only five or six weeks a year, and he attended Appleton Academy but two quarters. However, between farm labors he managed to read widely on his own.

As a young man Shattuck began part-time school teaching in order to supplement the family income. After leaving New Hampshire in 1816, he made his living for some time as a teacher, for two years in Troy and Albany, New York, followed by four years in Detroit, Michigan. While in Detroit he also organized and conducted the first Sunday school in Michigan. In 1823 he returned to New England to join his brother in running a general store in Concord, Massachusetts; the partnership continued ten years. Shattuck married Clarissa Baxter in 1825; they had five children. In 1834 and 1835 he operated a store in Cambridge, Massachusetts; then in 1835 the family moved to Boston, where he had moderate success as a bookseller and publisher until his retirement from business in 1839.

During Shattuck's adulthood, many Massachusetts citizens were passionately grappling with such issues as how to preserve the old Puritan values and how to cope with the problems growing out of immigration, industrialization, and urban growth. Seeking solutions to these issues, along with social reform generally, do-gooders were gathering in well-organized groups to advance such causes as temperance, prison reform, public education, the abolition of slavery, and improved care of the mentally and physically ill, while others worked for public sanitary programs. For all of these movements, the compilation of statistical information became of central importance in demonstrating the need for the reforms and justifying their continuance.

In early manhood Shattuck began to participate in several of these civic and reform movements, and ultimately he gained his reputation largely from them. One of these, the pursuit of local history and genealogy, quickly became a central and far from casual avocation for him. Shattuck's early short articles on these topics were eventually expanded into a substantial work, *A History of the Town of Concord* (1835). While researching this volume, he became active in both the Massachusetts Historical Society and the American Antiquarian Society, and in 1845 he was a founder of the New England Historic Genealogical Society. Shattuck published several practical works for genealogical researchers, chief of which was his *A Complete System of Family Registration* (1841). Later his *Memorials of the Descendants of William Shattuck* (1855) became known as a model for family histories.

Shattuck likewise became an energetic and productive public servant. In Concord, as a member of the town's school committee during the early 1830s, he reorganized school finances, prepared new regulations, and initiated the submission of annual school reports, a procedure that he persuaded the legislature to enact into state law in 1838. Between 1837 and 1841, as a Whig member of the Boston City Council, he resisted costly city undertakings, introducing instead numerous modest measures to improve government. Among these were the preservation and publication of city documents, creation of a municipal library, and preparation of an annual city register. As a member of the Massachusetts General Court for two terms (1838–1839, 1849–1850), Shattuck continued his efforts for local school reforms throughout Massachusetts (similar to his initiatives in Concord), sponsored improve-

ments in the state library, and introduced measures to expand governmental fact-finding. By far his most significant contributions, in fact, at both the state and city levels, were his introduction of workable statistical mechanisms and his proposals for systematic public health inquiries.

As a leader of the first generation of American statisticians, Shattuck corresponded widely with British and European "statists," exchanged statistical publications with them, and introduced their methods into the United States. He was principal founder of the American Statistical Association in 1839 and served as secretary of that organization during its early years. Partly as a result of his inability to obtain adequate vital statistics data for his *History of Concord*, but increasingly through his realization of the importance of such data for assessing public health needs and measures, Shattuck became a vigorous advocate for fuller and more accurate public registration of births, marriages, and deaths. In 1842 he was instrumental in obtaining passage of a new registration law for Massachusetts, and through the 1840s he pressed successfully for further improvement of the law. By 1849, through his efforts, the Massachusetts registration system was easily the best of its kind in the United States, while its annual statistical reports were among the most useful of their kind for sanitarians and public officials. In 1845 Shattuck designed and carried out a census of Boston; his comprehensive *Report* (1846) also became a model for American officials and statisticians. He subsequently played a leading role in the designing of the federal census of 1850.

Shattuck's involvement in public health grew mainly out of his statistical activity. In 1841 he published a valuable retrospective study of Boston's vital and disease statistics, and subsequently he analyzed the mortality data of several of the early Massachusetts registration reports. In 1846 and 1847 Shattuck assisted a committee of the American Medical Association in preparing a standard nomenclature of diseases. And in the late 1840s, in professional and reform circles as well as in the Massachusetts legislature, he led agitation for a sanitary survey of the state. Subsequently, as a member of the legislative commission established for such a survey, Shattuck drew up a remarkably far-seeing blueprint for a permanent state and local public health structure in Massachusetts, including comprehensive proposals for its activities. Prominent were its provisions for environmental sanitation, health education, inspection of food and drugs, and regular vaccination as well as the central roles envisaged for epidemiology and statistical analysis. The legislature published and distributed this work, the *Report of a General Plan for the Promotion of Public and Personal Health . . . of the State* (1850), but it failed to enact these or comparable proposals into law until 1869, a decade after Shattuck's death in Boston. Despite this, however, the report became a major influence in the post–Civil War shaping of America's public sanitary institutions and health pursuits.

A self-educated man, Shattuck did more than almost anyone of his generation to introduce applied statistics into American public health, medicine, and social inquiry. A do-gooder, he showed how health professionals could make cities better places in which to live. A businessman, he was outdone by few if any reformers of his day in the effort to make governments as responsive to human needs as to commercial interests.

• The principal collection of Shattuck's papers is at the Massachusetts Historical Society; there is a smaller collection at the Huntington Library in San Marino, Calif. Short autobiographical accounts appear in Lemuel Shattuck, *Memorials of the Descendants of William Shattuck* (1855), and M. M. Quaife and Florence Emery, eds., "Lemuel Shattuck and the University of Michigania," *Michigan History Magazine* 18 (1934): 225–52. Appreciations by contemporaries are Charles Hudson, "Memoir of Lemuel Shattuck," *Proceedings of the Massachusetts Historical Society* 18 (1880): 155–65, and John Ward Dean, "Lemuel Shattuck," *Memorial Biographies of the New England Historic Genealogical Society* 3 (1883): 290–321. Shattuck's statistical innovations are summarized in Walter F. Willcox, "Lemuel Shattuck, Statist, Founder of the American Statistical Association," *Journal of the American Statistical Association* 35 (1940): 224–35. For his public health contributions, see John B. Blake, "Lemuel Shattuck and the Boston Water Supply," *Bulletin of the History of Medicine* 29 (1955): 554–62; Barbara Gutmann Rosenkrantz, *Public Health and the State: Changing Views in Massachusetts 1842–1936* (1972), particularly pages 14–36; and James H. Cassedy, "The Roots of American Sanitary Reform: Seven Letters from John H. Griscom to Lemuel Shattuck," *Journal of the History of Medicine and Allied Sciences* 30 (1975): 136–47.

JAMES H. CASSEDY

SHATTUCK, Lydia White (10 June 1822–2 Nov. 1889), botanist, was born in East Landaff (later Easton), New Hampshire, the daughter of Timothy Shattuck and Betsey Fletcher, farmers. Shattuck's interest in botany blossomed during her childhood. She spent days exploring the streams, hills, and even nearby Mount Kinsman with her brother William, learning both the common and botanical names of the neighborhood flora. Her formal college education was sporadic, largely because she began teaching in public schools at the age of fifteen. While she taught, she continued her own learning through the next decade, briefly studying at an academy in Haverhill, New Hampshire (1838) and schools in Center Harbor, New Hampshire (1845) and Newbury, Vermont (1847).

Shattuck finally settled as a student at Mount Holyoke Seminary at the age of twenty-six. Mount Holyoke was a leader in developing science education for women. One of Shattuck's mentors was the school's founder, Mary Lyon, who encouraged her love of botany. Shattuck was in the final class taught by Lyon before the latter died in 1849.

After graduating with honors in 1851, Shattuck remained at Mount Holyoke as a teacher until her death. One of the highlights of her teaching career was getting distinguished scientists, such as James D. Dana, to teach brief courses there. Although best known for her skill in botanical collecting and classification, Shattuck also taught astronomy, chemistry, physiology, and physics. The traditional roles for women interested in the natural sciences in the nineteenth century were as collectors and describers of specimens, and Shattuck excelled at both. her fieldwork took her as far as Europe (1869) and Hawaii (1886–1887). On the Hawaiian Islands Shattuck collected specimens and information on tropical flora and named many previously undescribed plants. She also made botanical trips to sites closer to home: an island in Lake Superior (1868) and Montreal and the Saguenay (1878). She traveled to various expositions, such as the 1884 event in New Orleans, to further her scientific education.

Shattuck continued learning in both the field and the classroom. In 1873 she was a student at the first Anderson School of Natural History on Penikese Island, off the coast of Massachusetts, attending classes taught by the renowned naturalist Louis Agassiz; she also studied marine biology. Elizabeth C. Agassiz wrote in Shattuck's *Memorial*, "I remember Miss Shattuck in our first summer at Penikese, as one who gave character to our little community by her earnestness in work, her trained powers of study and observation, and her high standard in all questions, whether moral or intellectual. She won the respect and affection both of teachers and students, and we looked upon her presence there as a help to us all" (p. 46). These summer opportunities in 1873 and 1874 brought a community of scientists together to do advanced field research and created future field opportunities for women in science.

Shattuck was a gifted teacher. One of her students was the zoologist Cornelia Maria Clapp, whom Shattuck interested in natural history; Clapp had been teaching gymnastics and mathematics. Clapp, the first woman to hold a research post at the Woods Hole Biological Laboratory, said in a 1921 interview that Shattuck was an inspiration to younger teachers and "probably the most honored person at Penikese" (Shmurak and Handler, p. 129). But the way was not always easy; for example, although Shattuck helped form the American Chemical Society after attending the 1874 Priestley Centennial, neither she nor any of the other women scientists present were permitted to sit for the official photograph.

Throughout her career Shattuck corresponded with Agassiz and other notable scientists. Her advice and opinions were much sought. Harvard University botanist Asa Gray was another colleague with whom she kept up a lengthy correspondence on scientific ideas. Shattuck promoted the revolutionary Darwinian theory of evolution at Mount Holyoke and joined the company of scientists like Gray who supported Darwin.

Shattuck also influenced the growth of Mount Holyoke Seminary. In addition to her correspondence, she kept abreast of new ideas by being a corresponding member of scientific organizations such as New York City's Torrey Botanical Club. Shattuck was also responsible for gathering specimens, interest, and financial support for a botanical garden and a greenhouse at the school. Students who traveled or worked abroad sent her specimens for the herbarium, enriching the collection begun by Shattuck. Her efforts were not restricted to the academic realm: Shattuck led an initiative to raise money for a hydraulic elevator, which was installed in 1880. She also served as president of the Connecticut Valley Botanical Association.

The last year of Shattuck's life was filled with honors, including election as a corporate member of the Marine Biological Laboratory at Woods Hole. That same year Shattuck officially retired after thirty-eight years of teaching. She was named professor emeritus at Mount Holyoke, and a new chemistry and physics building was named Shattuck Hall in her honor when it opened in 1893. Shattuck never married. She was a member of the Methodist church all her life. She died in South Hadley, Massachusetts.

Shattuck was one of the foremost American botanists of the mid- to late nineteenth century. Charles A. Young of Princeton University, who lectured in physics and astronomy at Mount Holyoke in the early 1880s, described her "attainments as a botanist and student of natural history" as "remarkable for the time, and then there were very few women in the country who could be ranked with her in that respect. She was almost a pioneer in such studies" (*Memorial*, p. 45). Shattuck was known not only as a stimulating teacher but also as a scientist who brought back to her classroom the knowledge gained from trips abroad and correspondence with scientific leaders.

• Mount Holyoke's College Archives and Special Collections, South Hadley, Mass., holds Shattuck's papers, including correspondence dating from 1841, verses on college life, notes on chemistry experiments, journal entries from her 1869 trip to Europe, and photographs. The archives also has the 46-page *Memorial of Lydia W. Shattuck* (1890), with biographical essays and tributes from colleagues, students, and friends, and Arthur C. Cole, *A Hundred Years of Mount Holyoke College: The Evolution of an Educational Ideal* (1940). For Shattuck as a teacher see Carole B. Shmurak and Bonnie S. Handler, "Lydia Shattuck: 'A Streak of the Modern,'" *Teaching Education* 3, no. 2 (Winter–Spring 1991): 127–31, which includes a bibliography on Shattuck. See also Charlotte Haywood, "A Scientific Heritage," *Mount Holyoke Alumnae Quarterly* 43, no. 3 (Fall 1959): 122–25. Margaret Rossiter, *Women Scientists in America: Struggles and Strategies to 1940* (1982), offers context for the work of women scientists in the nineteenth century, with a few references to Shattuck and an outline of the role played by Mount Holyoke Seminary and the Marine Biological Laboratory at Woods Hole.

MARIANNE FEDUNKIW STEVENS

SHAUGHNESSY, Clark Daniel (6 Mar. 1892–15 May 1970), football coach, best known for his invention of the modern T formation, was born in St. Cloud, Minnesota, to Edward Shaughnessy and Lucy Ann Foster. He did not play football until the age of seventeen, when he tried out for the University of Minnesota team. Three years later, the six-foot, 200-pound Shaughnessy, who was large for that era, had become a skillful and versatile player. A good passer as a full-

back, he also played tackle and end. He was named to the All-Big Ten team and to the Walter Camp All-America third team as a tackle in 1912. He received his B.A. degree from Minnesota in 1918.

In 1917 Shaughnessy married Louvania Mae Hamilton; they had three children.

Two years earlier, in 1915, Shaughnessy became football coach at Tulane University. He quickly overhauled a weak football program and turned Tulane into one of the powers of southern football. In eleven seasons (1915–1926, excluding 1921) the Green Wave's record was a solid 57–28–7. However, the university president declined an invitation for the 1925 Rose Bowl because he believed the team too small and light and at risk for injury. In 1927 Shaughnessy became head coach at Loyola of New Orleans, where he persuaded the college president to have the school's name changed to Loyola of the South. Shaughnessy transformed a weak program into a small-college football power, amassing a seven-year record of 38–16–2.

The University of Chicago hired Shaughnessy as coach in 1933. Over the years he had become well known in the press and among fellow coaches as a player's coach, careful to protect injured players, and a hard worker. He often rose at 3 A.M. and held staff meetings over breakfast at 6:30 A.M. At Chicago, Shaughnessy began to use the T formation, an outdated offense in which the quarterback lined up directly behind the center and the other three backs formed a line behind him parallel to the linemen. He opened up the T formation's style of play by adding flankers and putting a halfback in motion before the ball was centered. Nevertheless, Shaughnessy won few games in the powerful Big Ten Conference at Chicago because the university's president, Robert Hutchins, deemphasized football during the 1930s. When Hutchins abolished the sport in 1939, Shaughnessy's seven-year record at Chicago stood at 18–33–4.

Shaughnessy then moved to Stanford University, where his 1940 season proved to be one of the most spectacular in football history. He inherited a team that had won only one game the previous season and quickly installed his revised T formation, which was ideally suited to the talents of his quarterback, Frankie Albert, a wizard at handling the ball and an excellent left-handed passer, and Norm Standlee, a tanklike 220-pound fullback. To the surprise of every college football prognosticator, Stanford went undefeated through its nine-game schedule and completed the storybook season by defeating Nebraska, 21–13, in the Rose Bowl. Shaughnessy was named coach of the year by the American Football Coaches Association, and within a few years most colleges had adopted his version of the T formation.

During World War II Shaughnessy left Stanford for Maryland in 1942, moved to the University of Pittsburgh from 1943 through 1945, and came back to Maryland in 1946. He completed thirty-one years of college coaching with a career record of 148–117–17.

After a season as an assistant coach with the Washington Redskins of the National Football League,

Shaughnessy was named head coach of the Los Angeles Rams in 1948. By the late 1940s he was recognized by both sportswriters and other football coaches as a brilliant football technician, but he became exceedingly more difficult to work with. He had little tolerance for human error and had difficulty communicating his ideas about football to the players because the ideas were so advanced. He led the Rams to an 8–2–2 record and the 1949 western division championship, but he was fired by the Rams after some players complained to owner Dan Reeves, who also found Shaughnessy quarrelsome. Shaughnessy joined his old friend George Halas and the Chicago Bears in 1951. For the next twelve years he held the titles of vice president, technical adviser, and defense coach, until 1962, when he resigned following a heated argument with Halas.

Shaughnessy retired from football that year but continued an active interest in his son's publishing company. He died in Santa Monica, California.

• Shaughnessy wrote *Football in War and Peace* (1943) and coauthored *The Modern T Formation and Man-in-Motion* (1941) with Ralph Jones and George Halas. There is no book-length biography of Shaughnessy, but Edwin Pope's *Football's Greatest Coaches* (1955) has a one-chapter biography. Excellent articles about his career include Bob Oates, "Shag: Expert Grid Strategist," *Sporting News*, 30 May 1970; Ron Fimrite, "A Melding of Men All Suited to a T," *Sports Illustrated*, 5 Sept. 1977; and William Barry Furlong, "How the War in France Changed Football Forever," *Smithsonian*, Feb. 1986. An obituary appears in the *New York Times*, 16 May 1970.

C. ROBERT BARNETT

SHAVERS, Charlie (3 Aug. 1917–8 July 1971), jazz trumpeter, arranger, and composer, was born Charles James Shavers in New York City. His parents' names are unknown, but his father ran a barbershop underneath the Savoy Ballroom in Harlem. Shavers recounted that the family was poor but not destitute. His father, also an amateur musician, played banjo and trumpet, and from his grammar school years onward Shavers played piano, banjo, guitar, and string bass before settling on the trumpet.

Shavers became devoted to music while in high school. In trumpeter Carl "Bama" Warwick, who lived at Shavers's home and went to school with him, he had a companion with whom he could practice. "I always think of him as my real brother," Shavers told writer Sinclair Traill. The two trumpeters played in lesser-known bands and joined Laurie Simmons in New York when Shavers was only fifteen. They then moved on to the Hardy Brothers band in Washington—Shavers had presumably dropped out of high school by this point—and then to Frankie Fairfax in Philadelphia in 1936. Fairfax's trumpet section also included Dizzy Gillespie, whose early style was shaped when he and Shavers worked together imitating Roy Eldridge's recorded solos. The brotherly partnership of Shavers and Warwick continued with work in Tiny Bradshaw's big band, which they joined in

Baltimore in 1936, and in Lucky Millinder's big band from early 1937 onward.

In November 1937 Shavers left both Warwick and big bands to replace trumpeter Frankie Newton in string bassist John Kirby's sextet at the Onyx Club on Fifty-second Street in New York. Working with singer Maxine Sullivan, Kirby's unusually quiet instrumental swing sextet was popular in its day. The group had come into existence on the strength of Sullivan's swing-era adaptation of the Scotch-Irish ballad "Loch Lomond," but in large part it owed its character to Shavers, who achieved his first fame as a discreet player and writer. He composed "Rehearsin' for a Nervous Breakdown" and the hit song "Undecided," preserved at Kirby's first recording session in October 1938. He arranged "Anitra's Dance," recorded in 1939, and wrote politely jazzed-up arrangements of classical themes. Pianist Billy Kyle and Shavers were the sextet's finest soloists. In this capacity Shavers occasionally played open trumpet, as heard on "Royal Garden Blues" (also recorded in 1939), but his normal procedure was to use a trumpet mute to muffle both volume and tone quality.

Kirby's sextet held a long engagement at the Onyx, in the course of which it became the first African-American band to have its own sponsored network radio show, "Flow Gently, Sweet Rhythm." Engagements followed at the Famous Door in New York and the Pump Room of the Hotel Ambassador East in Chicago. From 1942 to 1944, when Shavers finally quit, the band gradually disintegrated: Kirby and Sullivan's marriage broke up; drummer O'Neill Spencer became terminally ill, dying in 1944; and reed players Buster Bailey and Russell Procope were drafted. In later decades Kirby's band faded from importance, its music seeming excessively cute and of little historical consequence, but Shavers late in life named the sextet as the favorite by far of all the bands in which he played.

Independent of Kirby, Shavers contributed to historic sessions, recording "Melancholy" (Jan. 1938), with clarinetist Johnny Dodds; "Them There Eyes" (July 1939), with singer Billie Holiday; and "I'm Coming, Virginia" (Sept. 1941), "Texas Moaner" (Sept. 1941), and "Mood Indigo" (Oct. 1941), with clarinetist and soprano saxophonist Sidney Bechet. In 1943 he worked on the staff of CBS radio as a member of Raymond Scott's orchestra, while doubling with Kirby and, by one account, also making his first guest appearances with trombonist Tommy Dorsey's big band. In 1944, his final year with Kirby, he played in Benny Goodman's big band and recorded the ballad "Stardust" under his own name.

Shavers joined Dorsey in February 1945, and until the leader's death in 1956 they toured regularly, at one point performing for two months in Rio de Janiero, Brazil. In marked contrast to Kirby's sextet, Dorsey's band featured the trumpeter's exhibitionist upper-register playing, heard, for example, on numerous performances of "Well, Git It!" Apart from Dorsey, Shavers participated in Kirby's unsuccessful attempt to revive the sextet in 1946, and the following year he recorded another celebrated version of "Stardust" at a concert in Pasadena with vibraphonist Lionel Hampton's Just Jazz All Stars. In 1950 he co-led a sextet with drummer Louie Bellson and vibraphonist Terry Gibbs. As a member of Jazz at the Philharmonic, Shavers also recorded solos on "What Is This Thing Called Love?" and "Funky Blues" at a concert in July 1952. He toured with this aggregation, visiting Europe and, in 1953, Japan. He was a member of Benny Goodman's small group in Chicago in 1954. Shavers's other notable recordings from these years include pianist and comedian Steve Allen's album *Jazz for Tonight* (1955) and, under the name of the All Stars, the album *Session at Riverside* (1956).

From 1956 into the 1960s Shavers led bands and worked with tenor saxophonist Coleman Hawkins, clarinetist Buster Bailey, and other swing-era jazz celebrities at the Metropole nightclub in New York. In 1959 he recorded tenor saxophonist Hal Singer's album *Blue Stompin'*. At some point during this period he also performed at the Embers nightclub in New York. By 1964 Shavers had returned to Dorsey's big band, now a memorial group under the direction of tenor saxophonist Sam Donahue. After performances in England in 1964, international tours continued from 1965 into 1966 under the leadership of singer Frank Sinatra, Jr. Shavers returned to Europe as a soloist in 1969 and 1970. He gave his last performance as a guest with the J. P. J. Quartet, which comprised tenor saxophonist Budd Johnson, pianist Dill Jones, bassist Bill Pemberton, and drummer Oliver Jackson, at the Half-Note in New York in May 1971. Shavers died in New York City of throat cancer. He was survived by his widow, Blanche. Her maiden name and details of the marriage are unknown.

In both his writing for Kirby and his decades of recordings as a trumpeter, Shavers often lacked taste, his music suffering from ideas that might be considered pretentious, technical, bombastic, schmaltzy, corny, or squealing. Two tracks from a Jazz at the Philharmonic concert in Tokyo in November 1953, the swing tune "Cottontail," in which he engages in a showy solo contest with trumpeter Roy Eldridge, and the ballad "Embraceable You," are typical representatives of these failings. Nevertheless, at his intermittent and unpredictable best—in, for example, his composition "Undecided," on lovely versions of "Stardust," in a bluesy, emotional, sprightly solo on "The Man I Love" from the aforementioned Just Jazz group (but without Hampton), and in a lyrical solo and ensemble lead that blossoms from delicacy into forthrightness at the end of Allen's "Limehouse Blues"—Shavers must be reckoned among the leading swing musicians.

• Surveys and interviews are by Tony Hassell, "Charlie Shavers," *Jazz Monthly* 10 (Mar. 1964): 6; Steve Voce, "What'd I Say? Jug and Trumpet," *Jazz Journal* 16 (Mar. 1964): 12; Sinclair Traill, "Charlie Shavers," *Jazz Journal* 23 (May 1970): 8–9; Les Tomkins, "Playing Soft for the Fun of It," *Crescendo International* 8 (June 1970): 12; and Raymond Horricks, "The Man They Called Firecracker: Charlie Shavers," *Crescendo International* 21 (Feb. 1983): 23–24. See also Arnold Shaw, *The Street That Never Slept* (1971; repr. as *52nd Street: The Street of Jazz* [1977]). The most accurate chronological outline is in John Chilton, *Who's Who of Jazz: Storyville to Swing Street*, 4th ed. (1985). For musical descriptions, see Owen Bryce, "Charlie Shavers: An Appreciation," *Jazz Journal International* 32 (Nov. 1979): 16–17; Chilton, *Sidney Bechet: The Wizard of Jazz* (1987); Gunther Schuller, *The Swing Era: The Development of Jazz, 1930–1945* (1989); and Albert McCarthy, *Big Band Jazz* (1974). For information concerning Shavers's influence on Dizzy Gillespie, see Dizzy Gillespie with Al Fraser, *To Be, or Not . . . to Bop: Memoirs* (1979). Obituaries are in the *New York Times*, 9 July 1971, and *Jazz Journal* 24 (Aug. 1971): 4–5.

BARRY KERNFELD

SHAW, Albert (23 July 1857–25 June 1947), editor and publisher, was born in Paddy's Run, Ohio, the son of Griffin Shaw, a physician and small-town merchant, and Susan Fisher. Despite the death of his father when Shaw was only six, his mother had adequate funds for him to complete school in Ohio and then attend Iowa College (subsequently renamed Grinnell) in Grinnell, Iowa, where the Shaws had relatives. Shaw graduated in 1879 and acquired a half-interest in the *Grinnell Herald*, a biweekly publication through which he hoped to learn the newspaper trade.

To further his knowledge of history, government, and economics—subjects he believed essential for an aspiring editor—Shaw took a leave from the *Herald* in 1882 to enroll at the Johns Hopkins University, where he pursued work for a doctorate in history and political economy. There Shaw was surrounded by able scholars such as fellow students Woodrow Wilson and J. Franklin Jameson and young faculty members Herbert Baxter Adams and Richard T. Ely. Shaw flourished in this atmosphere and, after severing his connections with the *Herald*, took on part-time work as an editorial writer with the *Minneapolis Tribune*, a Republican morning daily. In 1884 Shaw completed his dissertation on an Icarian socialist settlement near Corning, Iowa, and moved to Minneapolis to become the *Tribune*'s chief editorial writer. He interrupted his work in 1888–1889 to tour and study the governments of the great cities of Europe. He hoped to derive lessons that might be applied to improve government in the United States. His efforts led to the publication of a series of articles in the *Century Illustrated Monthly Magazine* and in 1895 of two highly regarded books, *Municipal Government in Continental Europe* and *Municipal Government in Great Britain*.

His work so enhanced Shaw's scholarly credentials that he could have left the *Tribune* for any of several academic positions, including a professorship at Cornell, but he found more appealing the chance to begin an American edition of a new magazine, the *Review of Reviews*, founded in London in 1890 by journalist and reformer William T. Stead. For a time the British edition, a monthly of eighty-four small-quarto pages, was reprinted in the United States, but the results had disappointed Stead, who decided to publish a separate American edition and offered Shaw the editorship.

The American edition of the *Review* first appeared in April 1891 and, like Stead's prototype, featured an editorial section called "The Progress of the World," a selection of editorial cartoons that had first appeared in other publications, as well as a character sketch of some prominent individual. The magazine's title derived from two sections, each approximately twenty pages long. "Leading Articles in the Reviews" was a monthly summary of noteworthy articles published in other journals, and "The Reviews Reviewed" was a survey of various English and American magazines. It also included examples of Western European and Russian publications as well as articles from specialized journals. Each issue also contained a major book review, a short list of other new books, and an index to current periodical literature.

From the outset Shaw enjoyed much autonomy and changed the magazine to make it more appealing to the American middle class. To improve the magazine's appearance Shaw contracted with a printing firm that employed higher-grade paper and utilized printing technology that was superior to both what the English edition and the reprinted edition had used. Shaw also added more illustrations and political cartoons and gave more space to original articles. Shaw appreciated the chance to abandon the hectic pace of a daily paper, thinking that he could write more reflectively for a magazine. It was therefore natural that Shaw expanded "The Progress of the World," writing every paragraph of this wide-ranging assessment of domestic and international affairs himself. For a time Shaw thought he might still be able to accept an academic position as well as edit the *Review*, but the burdens of running a business made him realize he could not possibly combine the two careers.

During its first years the *Review of Reviews* was on shaky ground financially, partly because of the inevitable difficulties in starting a new publication and partly because of Stead's other ventures, which led him to borrow money and to mortgage the *Review of Reviews*, the American edition included. Shaw, however, succeeded in raising sufficient funds to keep the magazine afloat. At the end of 1892 he persuaded Stead to sell him controlling interest and to incorporate the American *Review* as a separate entity. Shaw insisted on a board of his own choosing.

With the magazine's finances stabilized, Shaw was able to take off much of 1893 to travel and recuperate from digestive and nervous ailments. During the course of his travels he met Elizabeth Bacon, whom he married later that year. The couple had two children, both sons who made their careers at the *Review of Reviews*.

The *Review of Reviews* occupied a unique position in American journalism, although *World's Work*, founded by Walter Hines Page in 1900, and Isaac K. Funk's weekly *Literary Digest* (its format inspired by Stead's original *Review of Reviews*) each had a few similar features. The *Review* used neither fiction nor muckraking but did incorporate feature articles by highly qualified contributors on economic, political,

social, and scientific topics. Each issue contained 128 pages of text; in some months there were even more pages of advertising. At its height, from about 1893 to 1910, the *Review* was widely read, its monthly circulation reaching more than 205,000. It was said that six people read each copy of the *Review*. Shaw was proud to know that many students, teachers, clerics, and businessmen read the magazine. In managing the *Review*, Shaw had the assistance of several able men, notably Charles Lanier, who handled business affairs, and Robert Finley, William Menkel, and George Pettengill, all of whom held subordinate editorial positions.

Shaw's status as both scholar and editor made him a public figure, and civic groups and universities sought him as a speaker. In addition to lecturing, Shaw was a director of the Southern Education Board and the Rockefeller General Education Board and also participated in civic affairs in New York City. On several occasions his name appeared in connection with various university presidencies or with appointive public office, but he had no intention of leaving the *Review of Reviews*.

Shaw's primary forum was "The Progress of the World," which ran about twenty pages and became the centerpiece of the magazine. A progressive Republican, Shaw stood for efficient, nonpartisan government on the local level, government regulation of big business, conservation, and the future of the United States as a world power. In the early years of the new century he supported the policies of his friend Theodore Roosevelt and later became an admirer of Herbert Hoover. In his last years as an editor Shaw was a caustic opponent of the New Deal, which he believed threatened to sap the vitality of communities and to undermine the initiative and resourcefulness of Americans.

Throughout his publishing career Shaw maintained control over all aspects of the *Review*'s editing and management. As business manager and (after Stead's death in 1912) a major stockholder, Lanier could make recommendations but could not make substantive changes without Shaw's approval. In 1908 the *Review*'s circulation declined slightly and suffered a more substantial drop four years later. The slump should have warned Shaw that troubles were facing his magazine, but the heated presidential campaign of 1916 followed soon by American entry into the First World War helped revive the circulation of the *Review of Reviews* and allowed Shaw to remain complacent about the magazine's future. Shaw's partisan commitment to Theodore Roosevelt at a time when the ex–Rough Rider was causing dissent in the Republican party might have been a factor in the *Review*'s prewar drop in sales, but after the war the magazine declined again. In the early 1920s Albert Shaw, Jr., reinvigorated the publication and was able to stem the tide for a while. The younger Shaw played a major role in the magazine's business affairs and eventually replaced Lanier, who sold out to the Shaws in 1928.

By that time, however, the nature of American journalism had changed. A monthly review of news events was no longer adequate, thanks in good measure to the emergence of news magazines such as Henry Luce's *Time*. From its founding in the 1920s *Time*, a weekly, possessed the enormous advantage of immediacy, and it had a zest that the dignified *Review* lacked. The establishment of the *Reader's Digest* as an outlet for reprints also hurt. Circulation of the *Review* fell to its lowest level in two decades, and with advertisers abandoning his weary monthly, Shaw belatedly began to acquiesce to changes. Many were simply cosmetic, but the *Review* also shrank in size as it lost advertising and as traditional departments had to be shortened or eliminated for economy's sake. In its last efforts to survive, the *Review of Reviews* in 1932 assumed the mailing list of the declining *World's Work*, which had been its chief rival, and in 1937 acquired the *Literary Digest*, which had been undergoing its own difficulties. Shaw hoped that publishing his magazine as a weekly would help and used the title *The Digest* beginning that same year. The arrangement lasted only a few months before Shaw's declining health led him to sell the fading periodical to some younger staff members for a nominal sum. Luce ultimately bought the rights to the *Literary Digest* title from them.

Shaw's wife had died in 1931, and two years later he married Virginia McCall, his secretary. Profits from the lucrative years of the *Review of Reviews* and wise investments had made Shaw a millionaire, and he lived comfortably in retirement. He undertook various projects but published only *International Bearings of American Policy* (1943), in which he argued for a return to the Wilsonian principles of arms control and establishment of an association of nations in which the United States would play a key role. Shaw died in New York City.

As editor and publisher of the *Review of Reviews*, Albert Shaw was a major figure in American periodical journalism for nearly half a century. Shaw modified Stead's concept of the *Review* to suit the expanding white-collar class as its influence grew in the late nineteenth and early twentieth centuries. In addition to being treated to a variety of informative articles, readers of the *Review* were able to scan the contents and ascertain the point of view of other magazines while at the same time reading Shaw's lucid interpretations of the major events of the preceding month in his column, "The Progress of the World." The *Review of Reviews* had its greatest success when a significant proportion of educated Americans shared his optimism and when a monthly analysis of public affairs was sufficient.

• The papers of Albert Shaw are at the New York Library. Lloyd J. Graybar, *Albert Shaw of the Review of Reviews: An Intellectual Biography* (1974), provides a thorough list of Shaw's many publications. Unsurpassed at establishing the *Review's* place in periodical publishing is Frank Luther Mott, *A History of American Magazines*, vol. 4, *1885–1905* (1957). John Tebbel and Mary Ellen Zuckerman, *The Magazine in America, 1741–1990* (1991), should also be consulted. Otis L. Graham, Jr., *Encore for Reform: The Old Progressives and the New Deal* (1967), furnishes perspective on the political thought of Shaw and other progressives. See also Robert P. Sutton, *Les Icariens: The Utopian Dream in Europe and America* (1994). An obituary is in the *New York Times*, 26 June 1947.

LLOYD J. GRAYBAR

SHAW, Anna Howard (14 Feb. 1847–2 July 1919), minister and woman suffragist, was born at Newcastle upon Tyne, England, the daughter of Thomas Shaw, a wallpaper maker, and Nicolas Stott. The family moved to Massachusetts in 1851. In 1859 Thomas Shaw settled his wife and younger children in an unfinished cabin on Michigan's frontier while he returned east. Anna's bitter recollections of the responsibilities that fell to her in the next decade make up the most powerful section of the memoirs she published as *Story of a Pioneer* (1915).

Vowing to avoid dependency, Anna prepared herself for the ministry. With the energy that marked her entire adult life, she entered high school in Big Rapids, Michigan, at age twenty-three, went on to Albion College and Boston University Theological School, where she earned a diploma in 1878, and was licensed the same year by the Methodist Episcopal church. From her pastorate at East Dennis, Massachusetts, she sought ordination but was denied on account of her sex. The Methodist Protestant church ordained her in 1880. While ministering at East Dennis, she earned an M.D. from Boston University Medical School in 1886.

By the time Shaw acquired her credentials, she had lost interest in the professions they opened to her but discovered her gift for oratory. Lecturing for temperance and woman suffrage became her trade. Lucy Stone welcomed her to the movement in Massachusetts, Frances Willard tapped her for the Woman's Christian Temperance Union, but ultimately Susan B. Anthony won her undying loyalty. Shaw cemented their intimacy when she chose Anthony's niece, Lucy E. Anthony, as her companion for life, and "Aunt Susan" sponsored Shaw's ascendancy in the National American Woman Suffrage Association (NAWSA), as national lecturer in 1890 and vice president at large in 1892. Despite her feelings for Shaw, Anthony chose Carrie Chapman Catt, a more astute and experienced politician, to succeed her as president of the NAWSA in 1900. Shaw, however, replaced Catt in 1904. Eleanor Flexner first drew attention in 1959 to Shaw's ineptitude as a leader, observing that her "devotion was complete and her gifts were many, but administrative ability was not among them" (Flexner, p. 256). Shaw rewarded personal loyalty at the expense of experience and presided over bitter upheavals in the leadership each year after 1909. She failed to grasp the need for a national strategy, whether it be to coordinate campaigns initiated by local leaders to amend state constitutions or to launch a new campaign for the federal amendment. Her most enduring administrative failure was the emergence of the Congressional Union as a serious and hostile rival to the NAWSA after 1913. Shaw would not accommodate Alice Paul's efforts to design a federal strategy, forcing Paul out of the association, where she became a magnet for people fed up with Shaw.

Story of a Pioneer documented Shaw's intransigence at the end of her presidency. Written by Elizabeth Garver Jordan from interviews with Shaw, the book pictures Shaw as Susan B. Anthony's true heir, a portrait that sanctified Shaw's leadership of the NAWSA and challenged Alice Paul's references to Anthony as the model for her militance and federal strategy. Hostile to militance (it was "un-American") and defiant of all critics, Shaw declared her intention to stay in office until voted out. A month after the book appeared in the fall of 1915, she chose not to force a vote when Catt, pressed by dissidents, agreed to return as president.

Even opponents conceded the greatness of Shaw's talent on the podium, and she continued to speak for the cause after her resignation. "Her voice was rich and musical," according to her friend Ida H. Harper, and it projected through any hall in the country. To the leader's obligation to encourage believers and define the enemy, she brought the zeal of the Methodist minister. Her sermons and lectures reiterated arguments and definitions used by her mentors since the Civil War, but she crafted a distinctive platform persona that won popular approval despite its sarcasm and irreverence.

A sense of her directness can be gleaned from stenographic reports of lectures. Countering advice that women model themselves after the biblical Rachel, Shaw offered her own exegesis.

[Rachel] had a high sense of the subserviency of woman to man that, while the lazy shepherds lay about gazing at each other, and at the skies, and perhaps at her, she left them gazing while she went to the well and drew the water to water the flocks. That may be the Bishop's idea of God's woman, but it is hardly my idea of the proper division of labor between the sexes. I should prefer to let the Bishop draw the water while I gazed. ("God's Women," 1891)

To meet antisuffragists' objection that voting would oblige women to serve on juries, she declaimed, "I have seen some juries that ought to be sat on and I have seen some women that would be glad to sit on anything. When a woman stands up all day behind a counter, . . . and when she stands for seventy-five cents she would like to sit for two dollars a day" ("The Fundamental Principle," 1915).

When the United States entered World War I, Shaw interrupted her tours for suffrage to lead the Woman's Committee of the Council of National Defense. Although the committee's charge seemed simple enough—coordinate women's relief work and channel the council's directives to women—Shaw found herself contesting archaic ideals of women as well as rival relief agencies. In a faint reflection of her administration at the NAWSA, she could not unravel the conflicts but did serve well as a lecturer who infused patriotic appeals with the message that on the home front no distinction between men's and women's work should survive. Congress awarded her the Distinguished Service Medal in May 1919.

Shaw gave her final service to Woodrow Wilson's peace treaty, joining William Howard Taft and Abbott Lawrence Lowell on a national tour for the League to Enforce Peace in the late spring of 1919. At Springfield, Illinois, she collapsed with severe pneumonia and died weeks later at her home in Moylan, Pennsylvania.

• Shaw's chief collection of papers lies within the Dillon collection at the Schlesinger Library, Radcliffe College. Containing papers of both Shaw and Lucy E. Anthony, the series includes Shaw's speeches, diaries and appointment books, newspaper clippings, and personal correspondence, most notably letters written home to Anthony from meetings and tours. Though Anthony censored and selectively destroyed letters from Shaw, an intimate record of Shaw's work remains. To reconstruct Shaw's presidency of the NAWSA, historians have relied on collections in which her political correspondence was retained, especially the Laura Clay Papers (University of Kentucky), the Catherine Waugh McCulloch Papers (Schlesinger Library), and the National American Woman Suffrage Association Papers (Library of Congress). Elizabeth Garver Jordan's papers (New York Public Library) also include correspondence with Shaw pertinent to understanding *Story of a Pioneer*. The National Archives holds the Council of National Defense Papers with records of its Woman's Committee.

Later volumes of the *History of Woman Suffrage* prepared by I. H. Harper provide valuable reference to Shaw's leadership but obscure deep schisms in the suffrage movement, while burnishing Shaw's reputation. Eleanor Flexner's narrative and analysis of Shaw, *Century of Struggle* (1959), set the tone for most studies done after 1959. Paul Fuller, *Laura Clay and the Woman's Rights Movement* (1975), incidentally documents Shaw's machinations as president of the NAWSA. Wil A. Linkugel has edited Shaw's speeches in "The Speeches of Anna Howard Shaw" (Ph.D. diss., Univ. of Wisconsin, 1960), a two-volume compilation, and, with coauthor Martha Solomon, selected speeches in *Anna Howard Shaw: Suffrage Orator and Social Reformer* (1991). Unfortunately this volume is also the only modern biography of Shaw, and it is uninformed by history of the suffrage movement. Shaw's wartime service receives attention in Barbara J. Steinson, *American Women's Activism in World War I* (1982).

ANN D. GORDON

SHAW, Arnold (28 June 1909–26 Sept. 1989), music business executive, composer, and writer, was born Arnold Shukotoff in New York City; his parents were of Russian Jewish extraction. He received his B.A. at the City College of New York in 1929 and his M.A. two years later at Columbia University, both in English literature. In college he played the piano in his combo, the Harmony Collegians, and did some composing, which he continued throughout his life. He taught in the English department of the City College of New York throughout the 1930s, where he was active in the Anti-Fascist Association of the Staffs of the City College, in the Instructional Staff Association, and in the College Teachers Union. During this time, he married Hanna Wiltchik. His leftist political activities led to his being fired, along with about forty others, following an investigation of the Rapp-Coudert Committee of the New York State legislature. Soon he and his wife were divorced, and he changed his surname to Shaw. He was to be married two more times: first to Frances Schillinger; then to Ghita Milgrom, with whom he had a child and who survived him. He had another child from a previous marriage.

In 1944–1945 Shaw began his career in the music publishing industry as advertising and publicity manager for the Robbins Music Corporation. During 1945 he also edited the magazine *Swank*. He moved that year to the Leeds Music Corporation, where he was advertising and publicity director until 1949. During this time, he coedited the fourth edition of *The Schillinger System of Musical Composition* (1946); his own *Mathematical Basis of the Musical Arts* followed in 1948. Shaw became vice president and general professional manager of the Duchess Music Corporation in 1950, the same year that he published his *Lingo of Tin Pan Alley*. He became an executive at Hill and Range Songs in 1953, when his novel about Tin Pan Alley, *The Money Song*, appeared, and two years later he began his association with the Edward B. Marks Music Corporation, where he remained until 1966.

During the 1950s Shaw became known for publishing and promoting songs and for producing records for RCA Victor, Capitol, and King Records. He recognized Elvis Presley's talent early in the singer's career and helped promote him on northern radio stations, particularly in Cleveland. A champion of rock 'n' roll well before it became a mainstream form of music, he published the songs "Sh-boom," considered the first crossover hit from rhythm and blues to pop, and "Lollipop"; he also was co-composer of "Dungaree Doll." Among the songwriters whose work he published were Paul Simon, Rod McKuen, and the team of Hal David and Burt Bacharach.

Shaw moved to Las Vegas in 1966 and in the years thereafter was a prolific writer of books. His book *Sinatra: Twentieth-Century Romantic* appeared in 1968; it was followed in close succession by *The Rock Revolution: What's Happening in Today's Music* (1969), *The World of Soul: Black America's Contribution to Pop Music* (1970), *The Street That Never Slept: New York's Fabled 52nd Street* (1970), and *The Rockin' 50s: The Decade That Transformed the Pop Music Scene* (1974). At the same time, he was composing more extended music, including *Mobiles: Graphic Impressions for the Piano* (1966), *Stabiles: 12 Images for Piano* (1968), *Plabiles: 12 Songs without Words for Piano* (1971), *A Whirl of Waltzes for Piano* (1974), and *The Mad Moppet: 7 Nursery Rip-Offs for Piano* (1974). The year that he wrote his *Bubble-Gum Waltzes*, 1977, he began teaching at the University of Nevada, Las Vegas; from 1981 to 1988 he held the post of adjunct professor of music there. He started the Research Center for Popular Music on the UNLV campus in 1985 and was the center's director until his death. Shaw's prolific writing of books continued into the 1980s. In addition to another

volume about the singer Frank Sinatra, he published works on rhythm and blues, rock 'n' roll, black popular music, and popular music of the 1920s.

In most of his writings, Shaw drew heavily on his own experiences in the music industry, giving his insights an insider's slant. He prided himself on having accepted and promoted the latest teenage musical fads: "Although I grew up with the pop of the older generation, the '50s were my era. As a publisher, record producer-and-promoter, I early learned to like and work with the new sounds—as a list of hits I picked amply reveals" (*The Rockin' 50s*, p. xvi). Although he was heavily involved in promoting black music—a cause influenced by his early political involvements—he was nevertheless criticized for slighting the contributions of African Americans to the nation's culture. In a review of Shaw's *Black Popular Music in America* (1986), the performer Johnny Otis complained, "How refreshing it would be to one day read a chronicle of black music that went beyond the eternal search for the great white hope. . . . If the over-inclusion of white emulators in a book ostensibly about black music is irritating, the omission of important black artists is unforgivable." Somewhat anticipating that kind of complaint, Shaw explained in the book's introduction, "In recognizing that white musicians, singers, and songwriters have profited greatly—I have used the word *rip-off* in some of my writing—and that blacks have suffered economically and in other ways, we have tended to disregard the *musical* contribution made by whites. Whether we approve or like what white musicians have done in adapting, polishing, refining, and commercializing a black style, it is those changes that have created an audience for the 'original'" (p. viii).

While marred by some slights and inaccuracies, Shaw's books have added considerably to an understanding of the scope and development of popular music in the twentieth century, which he helped to craft and promote. During his career he received three Deems Taylor Awards from the American Society of Composers, Authors and Publishers. Shaw died in Las Vegas.

• Shaw's papers are housed in the Arnold Shaw Research Center for Popular Music at the University of Nevada, Las Vegas. Books by Shaw not identified above include *Belafonte* (1960), *Honkers and Shouters: The Golden Years of Rhythm and Blues* (1978), *Dictionary of American Pop/Rock: From Blue Suede Shoes to Blondie* (1982), *The Jazz Age: Popular Music in the 1920s* (1987), and the posthumous *Let's Dance: Popular Music of the 1930s* (1998). Biographical information is scant, apart from the details appearing in Shaw's own books and those provided in reference work entries; his early political troubles are discussed in "Arnold Shaw (June 28, 1909–Sept. 26, 1989)," *Jewish Currents*, Jan. 1990, pp. 18–19. Obituaries appear in the *Los Angeles Times*, 6 Oct. 1989, and the *New York Times*, 7 Oct. 1989.

RONALD D. COHEN

SHAW, Henry (24 July 1800–25 Aug. 1889), frontier merchant and philanthropist, was born in Sheffield, England, the son of Joseph Shaw, a manufacturer, and

Sarah Hoole. After elementary education near his home town of Sheffield, Shaw attended Mill Hill, a Dissenters' school near London. He developed an interest in the ancient classics as well as English and French literature. At this school, which had formerly been the home of botanist Peter Collinson, he also became interested in trees and flowers on the school grounds.

After six years Shaw returned to his home town, presumably to help his father in business. In the meantime, though, the once highly successful manufacturer had jeopardized his family's economic future by borrowing money from a brother-in-law to finance an American acquaintance in selling Sheffield ware in the New World. It turned out to be an unwise investment, as the American partner neglected his side of the arrangement. As a result, Joseph Shaw decided to sail for Canada in 1818, taking Henry with him and leaving his brother-in-law in distress. Shortly after arriving in the New World, Henry went to New Orleans, where he recovered his father's Sheffield ware. In the spring of 1819, Henry moved upriver to the small town of St. Louis, soon to become the Gateway to the West. There he began selling the cutlery he had retrieved. Four groups in the area needed these goods: the residents of the town, soldiers at the frontier posts, farmers on the rich agricultural acres nearby, and pioneers moving west.

Shaw had an amazing capacity for keeping records of all business details. Further, he did not pay for shipments of English ware in coin. Instead he sent back to England in exchange tobacco, cotton, furs, and other American products. An uncle, James Hoole, acted as his agent in London. Shaw soon prospered and brought his mother and two sisters, Sarah and Caroline, to the United States. They settled with his father in the vicinity of Rochester, New York, because Mrs. Shaw refused to move to Missouri, a slave state.

Shaw's successful business arrangements came to an end in 1840 when high tariffs restricted imports and the canals opened the midcontinent to American goods. By that time, however, Shaw was a relatively rich man. He loaned money with property as security and began to pick up lands southwest of the city at sheriff's sales and foreclosures. On his own initiative Shaw sent money to his aunt and uncle to help ease the financial burden that his father's bad investment had placed on them.

In July 1840 Shaw visited his family in upstate New York and then toured Europe and the Near East, where he developed a great interest in music—attending concerts and operas and going to churches to hear the choirs. After two years he returned to St. Louis and on 4 July 1843 became an American citizen. His sister Caroline came to St. Louis to handle his business affairs while he went on a three-year tour of Europe. Sometime after his return he assisted Caroline and her young husband, Julius Morisse, in getting a start in the hardware business.

In 1849 he commissioned architect George I. Barnett to build a house in town and an Italianate villa on his property several miles beyond the city limits. Two years later he made his will. In it he provided generously for his relatives in England and his two household servants and left the bulk of his property to his two sisters. Shaw mentioned no plans to establish a botanical garden. Yet that same year, while visiting "Chatsworth," the estate of the duke of Devonshire, he decided to do just that, to establish a botanical garden in St. Louis to bear the name Missouri Botanical Garden. He sought advice from Sir William Jackson Hooker, director of the Royal Gardens at Kew near London; from Asa Gray, Harvard botanist; and from George Englemann, St. Louis gynecologist and amateur botanist. On a trip to Europe in 1858, Englemann purchased for Shaw books on botany and the entire herbarium of Johann Jakob Bernhardi in Leipzig. These purchases formed the basis of the excellent library and herbarium, which in turn paved the way for the garden to become a research center in later years. Shaw commissioned architect Barnett to prepare plans for a library, museum, and herbarium. Shaw supervised the planting of countless trees of many American and European varieties. On 14 March 1859 the Missouri state legislature authorized the opening of the Missouri Botanical Garden, which remained a private institution open to the general public. Later that same year, C. M. Hovey, editor of the *Magazine of Horticulture*, brought national attention to Shaw's gift (vol. 25, p. 425).

In the meantime, an attractive young woman by the name of Effie Carstang had sued Shaw for breach of promise and won a judgment of $100,000. Shaw's lawyers appealed, and the higher court reversed the decision. Shaw never married.

During the Civil War Shaw served on the mayor's commission that called for the establishment of a city park. When the residents voted down the recommendation, Shaw decided to give an oblong tract of 276 acres adjacent to the garden to the people of St. Louis. He planned a Victorian strolling park with broad carriage ways, shady walks, benches, ten gazebos, statues, and a "ruins" to suggest antiquity. The city government agreed to an annual budget to support the project. Shaw's gardeners planted 20,000 trees on the once-open prairie. Tower Grove Park, as it was called, was the first large park in St. Louis.

Shaw sought no public office and took no part in political parties or the chamber of commerce. He early supported a railroad to the West, purchased a library of western books for the Missouri Historical Society, and gave property and seed money for St. Luke's Episcopal Hospital. He also advocated the preservation of forests. He spent most of his time overseeing the park and garden and keeping tabs on his rental properties in the city and on his many acres to the west.

Shaw read widely in French and English literature and in colonial American history, especially of the Mississippi Valley. He wrote extensively on historical topics, birds, and trees but published only two small books, *The Rose* (1879), a history of the flower, and *The Vine and Civilization* (1884), in which he advanced the theory that the production and consumption of wine make a country great.

In 1885 Shaw decided to set up the School of Botany at Washington University in St. Louis. At Asa Gray's recommendation, he recruited William Trelease of the University of Wisconsin to head the school. Trelease proved to be an excellent choice, and after Shaw's death in 1889, he was named director of the Missouri Botanical Garden. Under his leadership, this splendid display garden gained recognition as a center of botanical study and research.

Shaw died in St. Louis. In his will, he left the bulk of his estate, estimated at $2.5 million, to the trustees of the garden as a permanent endowment. The Missouri Botanical Garden soon ranked high among the world's gardens. A century later, the director of the Royal Gardens at Kew, E. Arthur Bell, rated it one of the few great botanical gardens in the world (*Missouri Botanical Garden Bulletin* 70 [Sept.-Oct. 1982]: 6).

• The entire collection of Shaw's business papers, copies of his two books, and some of his personal letters and scrapbooks are in the Archives of the Missouri Botanical Garden. William Barnaby Faherty, S.J., *Henry Shaw: His Life and Legacies* (1987), is the most complete modern assessment. The same author's *A Gift to Glory: One Hundred Years of the Missouri Botanical Garden, 1859–1959* (1989), devotes eleven pages to the life of Shaw and 234 pages to his legacies. The entire summer 1984 issue of *Gateway Heritage* is devoted to the Missouri Botanical Garden. NiNi Harris described the garden, the park, and the surrounding neighborhood in *Grand Heritage* (1984). Various issues of the *Missouri Botanical Garden Bulletin* carried articles on the garden and its founder, beginning with Thomas Dimmock's reminiscences (1889), pp. 7–25. David MacAdam described the park in *Tower Grove Park* (1883), and Harris discussed its most recent history in *Henry Shaw's Living Legacy* (1986).

WILLIAM B. FAHERTY

SHAW, Henry Wheeler. *See* Billings, Josh.

SHAW, Howard Van Doren (7 May 1869–6 May 1926), architect, was born in Chicago, Illinois, the son of Theodore A. Shaw, a prosperous dry goods dealer, and Sarah Van Doren, an artist. Shaw's privileged upbringing included attendance at the Harvard School, a preparatory school in Chicago, where he earned early acceptance to the class of 1890 at Yale University. Shaw's formal architectural training, which began when he entered the Massachusetts Institute of Technology in 1891, was balanced by an extensive, eighteen-month trip abroad to Germany, France, Italy, Spain, and England, where he sketched measured drawings of significant architecture. In the winter of 1893 he returned to Chicago and started working in the office of Jenney and Mundie, the firm notably recognized for William Le Baron Jenney's invention of the steel frame, which enabled construction of the skyscraper, and as the training ground for Chicago School architects such as Louis Sullivan. In April of that same

year, Shaw married writer Frances Lillian Wells, daughter of Chicago businessman M. D. Wells. The Shaws would have three daughters.

After establishing his own firm in 1894, Shaw continued to collaborate with Jenney on small residential projects in Riverside, Illinois, a planned community Jenney had designed with Frederick Law Olmstead. In 1896 Shaw received his first large-scale industrial commission, for Reuben Donnelley's Lakeside Press in Chicago. Until then, Shaw had established himself in Hyde Park by designing individual residences near the campus of the University of Chicago. His largest commission, R. R. Donnelley and Sons Company headquarters building in Chicago, which later expanded in four phases to its new location at the lake front, was viewed by architects attending the American Institute of Architects (AIA) National Convention in 1933 as an innovative industrial design noted for its beauty and grace. Some of his other major works include the renovation of Second Presbyterian Church in Chicago (1900), the 1914 designs of the Fourth Presbyterian Church in Chicago with the Boston firm of Cram, Goodhue and Ferguson, the Quadrangle Club at the University of Chicago (from 1922), and the Goodman Memorial Theatre in Chicago (from 1926). Market Square in Lake Forest, Illinois (1912–1916), was the first American shopping center to be organized around a green space adjacent to a commuter rail line and to feature a parking area for automobiles.

Through membership in the Chicago Arts Club, which exhibited at the Art Institute of Chicago, Shaw found time to collaborate with other architects and to join a lunch club known as The Eighteen. The group, which met to share ideas about modern architecture, are now referred to as the Prairie School, a term that, while historically excluding Shaw's work, shares Arts and Crafts–inspired principles. Shaw later moved his office to Dearborn Street in downtown Chicago and eventually to the Monroe building on Michigan Avenue. He employed a number of architects, including David Adler and Ralph Milman, both of whom went on to establish their own successful practices. In addition, Shaw collaborated with engineer George Eich of the firm Eich and Treat and with landscape architect Jens Jensen. He was influenced by many great artists and architects, among them Frederick Law Olmstead, James Renwick, Louis Sullivan, and Frank Lloyd Wright.

Shaw's work tended to be historically based, and most of the forty-plus country estates he designed in the Midwest between 1897 and 1910 were derivations of the English Gothic or Tudor styles he studied during his numerous trips to England. Shaw loved the patina of weathered materials and utilized a combination of brick, limestone, copper, and slate in his work. Shaw's individual style was eclectic; deriving its impetus from the individual client, it sought to create humanistic solutions. Reuben H. and Thomas E. Donnelley, Clayton Marks, and Edward Larned Ryerson, to name a few, were among the established Chicagoans who commissioned Shaw to design country houses that were convenient to the golf courses and riding stables of suburban Chicago, where many of Shaw's clients spent the summer months. In his 37-year career—basically coinciding with the period between the 1893 and 1933 Chicago World's Fairs—Shaw designed more than 100 country houses. Few architects of his day, or since, could boast such a prolific output. Most of his country houses have plans that reach into the landscape and include formal gardens. Commenting on the historic nature of one of Shaw's houses, Frank Lloyd Wright said he could not imagine "someone entering it otherwise than in costume."

Shaw was also involved in the Arts and Crafts movement, both through his architecture and through performances and poetry readings of the literary club called the Little Roomers. He assisted in casting, acting, and directing original plays, some written by his wife, that were performed by the group in his outdoor theater at "Ragdale," the Shaws' summer home in Lake Forest. Shaw's granddaughter Alice Ryerson Hayes later established the property as the Ragdale Foundation for artists and writers to work.

During World War I Shaw's firm produced designs for more than 400 houses for steel workers employed in munition factories. Marktown steel workers' housing near Gary, Indiana, designed in 1915 for steel manufacturer Clayton Mark, though only partially built, was recognized for its consideration of the individual as part of a planned community as well as for its urban scale. Shaw planned various housing types, both multiple and individual, along a grid of streets that connected open parks and culminated in a public market square. At the time of his death, Shaw was involved in several important commissions, including the World War I Memorial planned for Brest, France, and Flanders Field government work. These commissions and others were carried out by members of his office who as Howard Shaw Associates continued work on the firm's projects well into the 1930s.

Among his honors and accomplishments, Shaw was a governing member and trustee of the Art Institute of Chicago, a trustee of Illinois College, a fellow of the American Institute of Architects at age thirty-eight, a member of the National AIA Headquarters Building Committee, a governing member of the United Charities from 1913, and a member of the state and executive art commissions. In 1926 Shaw was awarded the AIA Gold Medal, one of the most prestigious awards in architecture both in the United States and abroad, in "recognition of distinguished service to the profession of architecture and the Institute." Shaw had been scheduled to deliver a speech at the AIA National Convention in Washington, D.C., but had to cancel because of illness. According to his wife's memoirs he did learn of the executive board's decision to award him the AIA Gold Medal and was pleased by it. He died shortly thereafter in Baltimore, Maryland, of pernicious anemia, the cure for which was discovered just a few years after his death. He was buried in Graceland Cemetery in Chicago.

As an architect, Shaw is best described as an eclectic whose historically based English traditions naturally led him into the midst of the Arts and Crafts movement. In a memorial article written for *Architectural Record*, Thomas E. Tallmadge described the great impact of a man who was at heart a very modest person: "If I wanted to find him at a convention of the Institute . . . I always looked for him in the back row. Nevertheless, the world beat a track to his retreat."

• Shaw's surviving sketchbooks and drawings are housed primarily at the Art Institute of Chicago. Contemporary assessments of his work include two by Herbert Croly: "Some Recent Work of Mr. Howard Shaw," *Architectural Record* 22 (Oct. 1907): 421–53, and, with C. Matlack Price, "The Recent Work of Howard Shaw," *Architectural Record* 33 (Apr. 1913): 285–341. For more on his professional impact see Leonard K. Eaton, *Two Chicago Architects and Their Clients: Frank Lloyd Wright and Howard Van Doren Shaw* (1969). Thomas Tallmadge's memorial was published in *Architectural Record* 60 (July 1926): 71–73. An obituary is in the *New York Times*, 8 May 1926.

VIRGINIA A. GREENE

SHAW, Irwin (27 Feb. 1913–16 May 1984), writer, was born in the South Bronx, New York, the son of William Shamoroff and Rose Tompkins. Shaw's father was a Russian-Jewish immigrant, and his mother was an American-born daughter of a Lithuanian-Jewish family. The Jewish immigrant experience was central to the future writer's childhood and furnished material for later stories. When Shaw was seven, the family moved to Brooklyn where for the next seven years he enjoyed a stable and secure childhood. In 1923 William Shamoroff changed his name to William Shaw and began, in partnership with his two brothers, a real estate brokerage firm that initially prospered. The process of assimilation into mainstream American society seemed well on its way to a successful social and financial resolution for the Shaw family. But in 1928 the real estate firm began to lose money, and in 1932 it had to close. William Shaw was never again able to support his family. This domestic tragedy at the onset of the Great Depression left its scars on a young Irwin Shamoroff, who independently kept the original family name until his high school graduation at age sixteen. Throughout his life, even after phenomenal financial success as a writer, he was haunted by fears of imminent and total economic disaster.

Money problems aside, Shaw entered tuition-free Brooklyn College in 1929 with his family's new last name; he graduated in 1934 with a B.A. While in college he was prominent on the varsity football team; athletics would remain important to him throughout his life. After graduation, he held a number of temporary jobs to support his family. The most important was writing adventure serials for radio. Turning out episodes of "Dick Tracy" and "The Gumps" hardly constituted the creation of genuine literature, but it enabled Shaw to support his parents and his brother and to become, in the most literal sense, a professional writer. In addition, when he could find the time he was writing ambitious short fiction and a one-act play. In 1936 Shaw enjoyed his initial breakthrough as a serious writer. His play, an experimental antiwar drama entitled *Bury the Dead*, was produced in New York to critical acclaim, and its 23-year-old author was called a major new voice in the American theater. This sudden success would prove to have its ironic side, however. Despite several attempts, Shaw would never again enjoy an unqualified triumph as a playwright. *Bury the Dead*'s success did result in offers to write for movies, and Shaw produced his first screenplay, *The Big Game*, a forgettable thriller with a football motif, for RKO, in 1936. Of much more importance were the screenplays for *Act of Love*, a 1953 film directed by Anatole Litvak depicting a tragic love affair in occupied Paris, and the 1963 film *In the French Style*, adapted by Shaw from two of his short stories. Shaw also adapted Eugene O'Neill's *Desire under the Elms* for the screen in 1958. Shaw would work in films often during his life; they provided money for his serious work and for his stylish living, but he was embarrassed by a great deal of his work in Hollywood, frustrated by the writer's lack of control, and regretful of the time he gave over to that work.

In 1939 Shaw published his first collection of short fiction, *Sailor off the Bremen and Other Stories*, and witnessed the production in New York by the Group Theatre of his most ambitious play, *The Gentle People*. Several stories from the book, including the title story and the frequently reprinted "Girls in Their Summer Dresses," had previously appeared in the *New Yorker*. In the late 1930s and the 1940s Shaw established himself as a leading practitioner of *New Yorker* short fiction, modernist stories distinguished by consciously controlled narrative technique and a detached sophisticated authorial consciousness. "Sailor off the Bremen" and "The Girls in Their Summer Dresses" illustrate two dominant elements in Shaw's fiction—social protest with a strong undercurrent of violence and studies of adultery and troubled marriages. "Sailor off the Bremen" is a deliberately shocking warning against the rise of international fascism and its threat to world peace and stability, while "The Girls in Their Summer Dresses" is a tense and controlled portrayal of a married couple quarreling over the man's threatened infidelities.

The Gentle People, especially as performed by the leftist Group Theatre, cemented Shaw's early reputation as a protest writer. Subtitled "A Brooklyn Fable," it depicts two modest and aging Brooklyn fishermen's successful defiance of a gangster who is clearly intended as a personification of international fascism. In the late thirties Shaw felt an obligation to warn his fellow Americans of the dangers represented by Hitler and Mussolini. His writing during this period occasionally advocates armed resistance to the fascist threat. This militant posture prompted some critics to accuse Shaw of betraying the pacifist spirit of *Bury the Dead*. In fact, Shaw was never a philosophical pacifist, and his understanding of Hitler's terrifying intent toward Jews made it impossible for him to ignore events in Europe, for he knew they related directly to all Jews.

Despite a remarkable cast including Sam Jaffe, Franchot Tone, Karl Malden, Sylvia Sidney, Elia Kazan, and Lee J. Cobb, *The Gentle People* was only a modest commercial success. Subsequently, without entirely abandoning the theater, Shaw increasingly turned from drama to fiction. On 13 October 1939 he married Marian Edwards, but virtually from the start of married life, he engaged in frequent, often public, affairs with other women. Not surprisingly, the marriage, while complex, was often stormy.

During World War II Shaw served as a noncombatant in a documentary filmmaking unit under the command of Hollywood director George Stevens. Although not in combat, Shaw was present during or shortly after some of the war's most dramatic events—the campaign in North Africa, the Normandy invasion, and the Allied liberation of Paris. His experiences inspired a new and memorable stage of his career. In 1945 his play *The Assassin*, which dramatizes the assassination in Algiers of a pro-German French admiral by the French Resistance, opened in New York after a successful London production. Wounded by lukewarm reviews, the play closed after a ten-day run. For the 1946 publication of *The Assassin* by Random House, the embittered playwright wrote a preface condemning the New York theater as being dominated by artistic compromise and creative cowardice. At this point Shaw had seen seven of his plays produced in New York with steadily diminishing success. His disappointment was intensified by the largely unappreciated artistic integrity of *The Assassin*, which remains an undervalued work. Although he would publish one more ambitious play (*Children from Their Games* in 1962), the critical and commercial failure of *The Assassin* accelerated his retreat from the theater.

His war fiction, in contrast, was consistently well received. "Walking Wounded," an atmospheric study of the loneliness and desperation of a young British soldier trapped in a tedious, noncombatant post in Egypt, won the 1944 O. Henry Memorial Award First Prize. The next year "Gunners' Passage," an elegiac account of the painful fragility of friendship in wartime, was awarded the O. Henry Second Prize. "Act of Faith," published in the *New Yorker* in 1946, treats the theme of friendship in war against a backdrop of anti-Semitism in the U.S. Army and on the home front. One of Shaw's most frequently anthologized pieces, it served as the title story for his 1946 collection, *Act of Faith and Other Stories*.

In 1948, at thirty-five, Shaw published his first novel, *The Young Lions*, an ambitious and panoramic fictional treatment of World War II. The novel interweaves the lives of three protagonists (an innocent Jewish-American enlisted man, a cynical intellectual from Broadway and Hollywood, and a fanatical Austrian Nazi) into a realistic allegory of the war and its immediate aftermath. A considerable critical and commercial success, *The Young Lions* inaugurated a new stage of Shaw's career. Eleven more novels appeared before his death, and he increasingly became known as a novelist.

His second novel, *The Troubled Air*, published in 1951, a denunciation of McCarthyism in postwar America, dramatizes the destruction of individual careers that resulted from blacklisting in the entertainment industry. Never associated in any way with the Communist party, Shaw was briefly blacklisted largely because of the pacifist overtones of *Bury the Dead* and his financial support for the Loyalists during the Spanish Civil War. Two of his best short stories, "Goldilocks at Graveside" and "The Green Nude," also satirize McCarthyism. While not achieving the overwhelming success of *The Young Lions*, *The Troubled Air* was still well received. However, five years after its publication, Shaw's critical reputation as a major American writer began to deteriorate.

Shortly after the birth of their only child in 1951, the Shaws, who for some time had lived and vacationed in Europe, began a 25-year voluntary exile, with a grand residence in Paris, a chalet in Klosters, Switzerland, and various summer homes in the south of France. While living in Paris, Shaw would increasingly be charged with abandoning his American roots as a writer and indulging in a life-style devoted to materialistic excess. The attacks on Shaw's Parisian life-style became reminiscent of the criticism directed against F. Scott Fitzgerald during the 1920s; also like Fitzgerald, Shaw suffered from alcoholism, though he worked every morning of his life and never lost the capacity to order his hours at the typewriter.

In 1956 his third novel, *Lucy Crown*, was widely condemned as representing a betrayal of its author's artistic principles, and none of his other expatriate works would receive high critical regard, even though the novels *Two Weeks in Another Town* (1960) and *Evening in Byzantium* (1973) and the story collection *God Was Here But He Left Early* (1973) are much underrated serious works. Shaw's personal life was troubled as well; in 1970 the Shaws' marriage was interrupted by divorce.

Despite the critical attacks on it, the fiction that Shaw produced during his expatriate years fared well with the reading public; 1970 saw the publication of his most commercially successful book, *Rich Man, Poor Man*, a sweeping fictional treatment of two generations of an immigrant family. The even more successful 1976 television miniseries adaptation of the novel assured Shaw the widest public recognition of his literary career, and in 1977 he published a sequel, *Beggarman, Thief*. After his earlier recognition as a radical playwright, a master of the social protest short story, and a major war novelist, there was no little irony in his final reputation as a bestselling popular novelist.

In 1976 he left Paris to divide his time between Long Island and Klosters. Two years later, he published the most important book in his long, prolific career, *Short Stories: Five Decades*, an omnibus collection of sixty-three of his stories. The volume clearly demonstrates his major contributions to the development of the American short story. Shaw's short fiction stands as the cornerstone of his artistic achievement. His personal triumph at the appearance of *Short Stories: Five Decades* was marred by a series of illnesses, however and in 1981 he discovered that he was suffering from cancer of the prostate. He credited Marian with saving his life during several medical crises, and the two reconciled and remarried in 1982. They remained together until Shaw's death in Davos, Switzerland.

Despite the critical reaction against his work during the last thirty years of his life, Shaw remains an important American writer. Besides his paramount achievement in short fiction, he produced one of the major American World War II novels, *The Young Lions*, and two political plays that make intriguing use of experimental techniques, *Bury the Dead* and *The Gentle People*. In addition, the novels *Two Weeks in Another Town*, *Evening in Byzantium*, and *Bread upon the Waters* (1981) are masterfully crafted modernist fiction, while *The Assassin* is a powerful exercise in traditionally realistic political drama. If the range and scope of Shaw's literary achievement have rarely been appreciated, almost all of his work is distinguished by flawless literary craftsmanship.

• The manuscript of *The Young Lions* is housed at the Pierpont Morgan Library in New York City. Boston University and Brooklyn College have collections of Shaw papers, including letters. Michael Shnayerson's *Irwin Shaw: A Biography* (1989) is the only comprehensive biography of the writer. Other Shaw novels are *Voices of a Summer Day* (1965), *Nightwork* (1975), *The Top of the Hill* (1979), and *Acceptable Losses* (1982); his short fiction appears in *Welcome to the City and Other Stories* (1942), *Mixed Company: Collected Short Stories* (1950), *Tip on a Dead Jockey and Other Stories* (1957), and *Love on a Dark Street and Other Stories* (1965). The only book-length critical studies of Shaw's work are by James R. Giles, *Irwin Shaw* (1983) and *Irwin Shaw: A Study of the Short Fiction* (1991). See also Chester E. Eisinger, *Fiction of the Forties* (1963); Peter G. Jones, *War and the Novelist: Appraising the American War Novel* (1976); and Ross Wetzsteon, "Irwin Shaw: The Conflict between Big Bucks and Good Books," *Saturday Review*, Aug. 1981.

JAMES R. GILES

SHAW, John (1773–17 Sept. 1823), naval officer, was born in Mountmellick, Queen's County, Ireland, the son of John Shaw and Elizabeth Barton. His father was an English cavalry officer who, owing to the poverty of subsistence farming, persuaded his sons to emigrate to America in December 1790. Shaw settled in Philadelphia, where he found work as a deckhand and made several voyages to the East Indies and China. Shaw joined the navy as a lieutenant on 3 August 1798 and fought with distinction during the Quasi-War with France. For several months he served as first officer on the converted merchantman *Montezuma* and performed convoy duty. In December 1799 he received command of the schooner *Enterprise* and commenced a celebrated eight-month cruise that scoured the Caribbean for French privateers. He captured no less than eight enemy vessels, including the *Flambeau*, which possessed a larger crew and armament. This July 1800 action was one of the most hotly contested of the war and resulted in forty French casualties to an American loss of ten. Shaw also liberated eleven American prize vessels before illness necessitated returning to America.

Shaw resumed active duty in 1802 as commanding officer of the *George Washington* and cruised the Mediterranean for several months. He was furloughed the following year and captained a merchant vessel bound for Canton. Shaw advanced to master commandant on 2 May 1804 and volunteered to lead a squadron of gunboats against the Tripolitan pirates; instead he was transferred to the frigate *John Adams* as senior officer. Upon quitting the Mediterranean in 1806, he arrived at New Orleans to direct construction of a gunboat squadron. Shaw became a captain on 27 August 1807 and subsequently testified at the trials of Aaron Burr and Captain James Barron. Between 1808 and 1810 he also functioned as commandant of the Norfolk, Virginia, navy yard, but Shaw was reassigned to New Orleans during the War of 1812. In April 1813 his flotilla ferried the troops of General James Wilkinson during the occupation of Mobile. The following year he relieved Stephen Decatur as commander of a squadron blockaded at New London, Connecticut. Shaw remained on station there until the war's end.

In 1815 Shaw transferred to the frigate *Constitution* as part of Commodore William Bainbridge's squadron in the war with Algiers. When a treaty was concluded in September, he assumed command of a naval squadron consisting of his ship, the frigate *United States*, and the sloops *Erie* and *Ontario*. Shaw cruised the Mediterranean for two years before ending his seagoing career in December 1817. He was appointed to take charge of the Charlestown navy yard, Boston, where he clashed with Commodore Isaac Hull. Shaw had communicated to the Navy Department allegations of Hull's fiscal irregularities. When Hull found out, he had Shaw arrested on 14 February 1822. The ensuing court-martial found Shaw guilty of "unofficer-like conduct" and imposed a six-month suspended sentence. He subsequently commanded the naval station at Charleston, South Carolina. Shaw died in Philadelphia. He had been married twice; to Elizabeth Palmer of Philadelphia, a Quaker, at an unknown date, and to Mary Breed of Charlestown, Massachusetts, in 1820. His first marriage produced two daughters.

Shaw was a capable seaman and distinguished himself in the early wars of the republic. He and other officers of his generation laid the groundwork for success in the War of 1812 and the growth of naval professionalism. His Quasi-War cruise aboard the *Enterprise* was justly celebrated, and he received a personal commendation from President John Adams. Shaw also accepted the unpopular gunboat service without complaint, and his New Orleans command was the only gunboat station to acquire distinction. Shaw fully embodied the latent talent and growing professionalism of American naval tradition.

• Shaw's official correspondence is in Record Group 45, Captain's Letters, National Archives, Washington, D.C. Personal letters are in the Manuscript Division, Library of Congress; the Historical Society of Pennsylvania; and the Clements Library, University of Michigan. See also Dudley W. Knox, ed. *Naval Documents Related to the Quasi-War with France* (6 vols., 1939–1944). For personal information consult James F. Cooper, *Lives of Distinguished American Naval Officers* (2 vols., 1846), and John Shaw, *Trial of Captain John Shaw* (1822). Much of Shaw's naval activity is covered in Spencer C. Tucker, *The Jeffersonian Gunboat Navy* (1993), and Michael A. Palmer, *Stoddert's War* (1987).

JOHN C. FREDRIKSEN

SHAW, John (4 May 1778–10 Jan. 1809), poet and physician, was born in Annapolis, Maryland. The names of his parents are unknown. A linguistically precocious boy, Shaw read classical literature at an age when most children were still mastering English. At age eleven he became one of the original students at St. John's College of Annapolis, and he published poetry of his own when he was twelve. Shaw received a bachelor's degree from St. John's in 1796, then began two years of medical apprenticeship under John Thomas Shaaff of Annapolis.

In the fall of 1798 Shaw went to Philadelphia to begin medical studies at the University of Pennsylvania. After only a couple of months, however, acting on whim (which he later agonized about in his letters and diaries), Shaw signed on as ship's surgeon with an American flotilla bound for Algiers. The flotilla consisted of a naval vessel, which was carrying American consuls to Tunis and Tripoli, and three ships being delivered to the ruler of Algeria. Once in North Africa, Shaw acquired a working knowledge of Italian and French as well as a bit of Arabic and stayed on as secretary to the American consulate in Tunis. A futile and eventually aborted effort to reach England in 1800 forced him to make extensive stays at various points around the western Mediterranean, and his writings described items of interest from North African forts to opera performances in Messina.

Having had his foreign fling, Shaw decided he disliked both the prospects of becoming a naval officer (most of whom he considered "ignorant profligates") and the frustrations of diplomacy and returned to Annapolis. But by 1801 he was off again, this time to Scotland to study medicine at Edinburgh. Edinburgh was then the medical school of choice for Americans, because they admired the practical approach of the Scots. After a couple of seasons at Edinburgh, which he considered a rather inhospitable place, Shaw agreed in 1803 to serve the earl of Selkirk as physician to the latter's Canadian settlement schemes. First in the maritime provinces and then on the prairies above Detroit, Shaw labored hard but rather ineffectually against the fevers and infections rampant in Selkirk's settlements. Shaw was fortunate to survive typhoid fever himself and returned again to Annapolis in 1805.

Shaw married Jane Selby of Annapolis in 1807 and moved to Baltimore in search of a larger medical practice. The number of their children, if any, is unknown. Victory in a hotly contested municipal election won him appointment as a Baltimore dispensary physician, and he served as treasurer for the Medical and Chirurgical Faculty of Maryland, the state medical society. With James Cocke and John B. Davidge, Shaw founded the College of Medicine of Maryland (later the University of Maryland) in Baltimore in 1807 and became its first professor of medical chemistry. Shaw had accomplished all of this without ever actually completing a medical degree, evidence of the characteristically flexible definition of medical professionals in the early American republic. Shaw was styled doctor in later years only because a member of the Maryland legislature thought anyone establishing a medical college should be called "doctor of medicine" and inserted the title after Shaw's name in the medical school charter.

In the fall of 1808 Shaw came down with a serious respiratory condition and determined to seek a warmer climate for the winter. He sailed to Charleston, South Carolina, where he boarded a ship bound for the Bahamas. He died on that ship before he could reach the Caribbean. Hearing of his death, some of Shaw's admiring friends, including Francis Scott Key, compiled as many of Shaw's poems as they could find and published them posthumously in 1810. The collection, which was more than one hundred pages, included odes, elegies, sonnets, English translations of classical poetry, songs, and descriptive pieces, the most interesting of which drew on his travels. Though stiff and sentimental by modern standards, Shaw's poems were likened by critics at the time to those of the better-known Francis Hopkinson and Philip Freneau. Through the rest of the nineteenth century, various Shaw poems were regularly included in anthologies of American poetry, and more people ultimately knew his name as a minor poet than as the founder of a medical school.

• There is no known repository of Shaw's papers. The principal source of information about his life is *Poems by the Late Doctor John Shaw, to Which Is Prefixed a Biographical Sketch of the Author by J. E. Hall* (1810). Hall's biographical preface is a hundred pages long and contains generous excerpts from Shaw's own letters and diaries. On the founding of the College of Medicine of Maryland, see Eugene F. Cordell, *University of Maryland, 1807–1907* (1907).

JAMES C. MOHR

SHAW, Lemuel (9 Jan. 1781–30 Mar. 1861), chief justice of the Massachusetts Supreme Judicial Court, was born on Cape Cod, Massachusetts, the son of Oakes Shaw, a Congregational minister, and Susanna Hayward. After receiving tutoring from his father, Shaw entered Harvard at fifteen and graduated Phi Beta Kappa at nineteen. He briefly taught school and worked for the Federalist *Boston Gazette*. He read law under David Everett (Aug. 1801 until Sept. 1804) and in September and November 1804 was admitted, respectively, to the New Hampshire and Massachusetts bars.

From 1804 until 1830 Shaw practiced law in Boston while also serving as a justice of the peace (1810), member of the Massachusetts house (1811–1815, 1820–1821, and 1829), state senator (1821–1822), delegate to the state constitutional convention of 1820, and president of the Suffolk County bar (1829–1830). In 1822 Shaw served as a commissioner to revise the state's statutes. In 1822 he also wrote Boston's first city charter, which remained in effect until 1913. Shaw became chief justice of Massachusetts on 30 August 1830 and served until he resigned on 21 August 1860.

In 1802 Shaw became engaged to Nancy Melville, but she died before they were married. In 1818 he married Elizabeth Knapp of Boston, who died in 1822, leaving Shaw with a son and a daughter. In 1827 Shaw married Hope Savage of Barnstable, with whom he had two more sons. Shaw's daughter from his first marriage eventually married author Herman Melville, the nephew of Shaw's deceased fiancée. Some scholars believe that Shaw's sometimes harsh decisions on slavery influenced Melville's writings, especially *Benito Cereno* and *Billy Budd*.

By the mid-1820s Shaw was earning $15,000 to $20,000 a year (a very large sum at that time), advising the emerging financial, commercial, manufacturing, and transportation interests in Massachusetts. He also served as a bank director and personally invested in banks, insurance companies, and other commercial enterprises. In 1830 he reluctantly accepted the chief justiceship of the Massachusetts Supreme Judicial Court, at a salary of $3,500 a year. Daniel Webster later claimed that his greatest service to Massachusetts was persuading Shaw to accept this post. With the exception of serving on the Harvard Board of Overseers from 1831 to 1854, Shaw ceased all political activity until he left the bench in 1860.

Politically conservative, Shaw was successively a Federalist, Whig, and Constitutional Unionist. On the eve of secession, when compromise was no longer plausible, Shaw clung to the old formulas of sidestepping the problem of slavery to preserve the Union at any cost.

A strong chief justice, Shaw dominated his court. His squat, massive body with its large head and lined face seemed to be a physical manifestation of the power of his office and the force of his logic. He wrote more than 2,100 opinions but only three dissents. In his fifty constitutional opinions Shaw spoke for a unanimous court forty-seven times. His colleagues and the bar revered him. A fellow judge described a debate over the election of judges as a discussion of "whether Chief-Justice Shaw is a divine institution or a human contrivance" (Levy, p. 27). The attorney Rufus Choate, who was often rebuffed by Shaw, nevertheless advised a fellow attorney not to respond to the chief justice in anger or haste because "with him, and under him, life, liberty, and property are safe" (Chase, p. 289).

Shaw decided important cases on railroad law, the law of industrial accidents, labor law, and such noneconomic issues as separation of church and state, the insanity defense in criminal cases, school segregation, slavery, and the fugitive slave laws.

Shaw's use of common law adjudications to facilitate the transformation of the country from an agrarian economy to an industrial one typified the role of antebellum jurists in aiding manufacturing and commercial interests—what historian J. Willard Hurst called the release of creative energies. Although personally and politically conservative, Shaw's opinions were not doctrinally or jurisprudentially conservative. He often eschewed doctrine, precedent, and procedural technicalities in favor of logic, reason, common sense, and a utilitarian approach to economic and social development. Nor did he see his role as protecting vested property interests from the legislature. In his expansive interpretation of the concepts of "public use," the police power, and the power of eminent domain, Shaw supported legislative and private initiatives to foster new industries at the expense of older technologies and more traditional users of water and land resources.

Shaw's most important antebellum precedents—cited favorably throughout the nation—affected industrialization, torts, and race relations. Shaw's influence was not limited to his own era. Well into the twentieth century courts cited his opinions and applied the concepts he articulated.

Shaw usually deferred to legislative initiatives on economic regulation. In these cases Shaw helped transform the nature of property rights in the United States by allowing the public to destroy vested rights. Shaw supported legislative efforts to redefine the "public" to include privately owned corporations that often did not directly benefit all, or even a majority, of the people whose property they took. Rather than protecting vested property rights, Shaw's decisions encouraged the state government to actively alter property relationships. Courts throughout the nation followed Shaw's precedents, supporting similar legislation. Shaw consistently held that through its "police" and "eminent domain" powers the legislature had authority to regulate private property in any way that might be beneficial to the state.

In *Commonwealth v. Alger* (1851), which many other states followed, Shaw upheld the state's police powers to regulate private property rights. Alger, who was prosecuted for extending his wharf beyond a limit set by the legislature, claimed that a 1641 grant and statute allowed him to build the wharf. His attorney, future Supreme Court Justice Benjamin R. Curtis, argued that the statute under which Alger was prosecuted violated his contractual rights as well as his property rights. Furthermore, Curtis argued, and the state conceded, that Alger's wharf did not interfere with navigation. Therefore Curtis asserted that the statute was an unconstitutional violation of Alger's rights.

Shaw answered these assertions with "a majestic statement on the paramountcy of public over property rights" (Levy, p. 249). He declared that "every holder of property, however absolute and unqualified may be his title, holds it under the implied liability that his use of it may be so regulated" by law "necessary to the common good and general welfare." In *Alger* Shaw declared that the government could regulate property, just as it could other social rights. He found that the rights of property, like all other social rights, "are subject to such reasonable limitations in their enjoyment . . . as the legislature, under the governing and controlling and expedient." Shaw found that the prosecution of Alger for illegally extending his wharf was not a taking, for which compensation would be required, but rather a mere limitation on the use of property.

In addition to cases like *Alger*, upholding the power of the state to limit the use of private property, Shaw's decisions allowed privately owned industries to harm the property rights of other individuals. His application of "mill-dam acts" to iron mills and textile factories illustrates this. Preindustrial mill-dam acts had allowed grist mills, lumber mills, and similar enterprises to dam up small streams and flood nearby farms on the theory that such mills were both a necessity and a scarce public resource. Courts and legislatures believed that the value of such mills to farmers outstripped any loss they may have suffered because without the grist mill a farmer could not bring his crop to market.

By the 1830s newer technologies such as textile factories and iron mills received legislative permission to flood larger streams and rivers, often permanently destroying the value of nearby farms. Opponents argued that such laws were "not a matter of public convenience and necessity, but of private speculation" (Levy, p. 257). It was clear that the farmer whose land was flooded did not benefit from a textile mill the way he might have from a grist mill. Shaw, however, consistently held for the newer technologies, allowing new factories to flood larger streams and rivers, often permanently destroying the value of nearby farms.

Opponents of these acts argued such laws only benefited stockholders and not the general public. But Shaw did not look at the immediate beneficiaries, or victims, of a new factory. Rather, he looked to the greater gains for the entire society. Shaw's opinions were "premised on the desirability of maximizing economic development" even if preexisting users of land and water resources might be harmed in the process (Horwitz, p. 41). Typical of Shaw's approach was his assertion in *Hazen v. Essex Co.* (1853) that "the establishment of a great mill-power for manufacturing purposes" served the "public interest, especially since manufacturing has come to be one of the great public industrial pursuits of the commonwealth." Here he upheld the legislature's "exercise of the right of eminent domain" on behalf of a private corporation. Thus Shaw favored newer technologies and industries and allowed older participants in the marketplace to be quite literally washed away.

Shaw's jurisprudence was vital to the development of railroads. He held that railroads, as public utilities, were immune from private nuisance suits. Similarly, Shaw altered the common law rules of liability for common carriers to make railroads immune for non-negligent losses for goods in a railroad's warehouse. Here Shaw clearly favored railroads at the expense of shippers.

Shaw protected railroads by refusing to alter the traditional notion that no one could recover damages in a wrongful death action. Thus, when railroads injured passengers and pedestrians they might be held liable, but if they killed them the railroads would not be liable. Shaw did, however, alter traditional American tort law in ways that benefited America's emerging industries. In *Farwell v. Boston and Worcester Railroad* (1842) Shaw held that a railroad engineer injured by the negligence of a railroad switchman could not sue the railroad but could only sue the switchman, his "fellow servant." The switchman was simply another worker on the railroad and had no money.

In this case Farwell could recover no money to compensate for his injury. In a thoroughly unrealistic assessment of working conditions in America's emerging industries, Shaw argued that Farwell should have observed the work of his fellow servant to make sure it was done properly. However, to do that Farwell would have had to stop his train at every switch, which would have destroyed the efficiency of the railroad. This decision, which was widely accepted, shifted the costs of industrial accidents from corporations to individual workers. To this day *Farwell* is good law in many jurisdictions, although its harsh result—that workers injured on the job could not be compensated—has been partially overcome by workers' compensation laws and insurance programs.

Farwell rested on a very narrow concept of "fault." In Shaw's view the railroad was not at fault when a worker was injured. This notion of fault reemerged in *Kendell v. Brown* (1850). There Shaw developed the modern principles of fault and contributory negligence in tort cases. He required that people be prudent and careful in their activities; those who were not could not expect to recover damages. While *Kendell v. Brown* involved private parties, the principle of fault and contributory negligence was beneficial to emerging industries.

Shaw was not always prorailroad or antilabor. He upheld statutes and local ordinances requiring railroads to operate in a safe manner. In 1857 he upheld the largest monetary damages awarded up to that time against a railroad. He consistently upheld the right of the state to regulate railroads in a variety of ways. Shaw also wrote the opinion in *Commonwealth v. Hunt* (1842), which has been called, with some exaggeration, the magna carta of labor law. Before this decision labor unions had almost always been considered criminal conspiracies. As he did in so many other areas of the law, here Shaw ignored precedent and came to a remarkably fresh result. He noted that the workers had organized to persuade all in their place of employment to join the union. Shaw concluded that their purpose, to gain members for their union, was "not unlawful." Nor was their ultimate goal of higher wages and better working conditions.

Shaw further held that their tactic of refusing to work with nonunion laborers also was not illegal. If individual workers had a right to quit, then they had a right to do so collectively as well. Because the union had not used force or violence, it had broken no laws. *Commonwealth v. Hunt* was the first Anglo-American decision to reject the traditional notion that labor unions and strikers were unlawful conspiracies. However, the use of injunctions later in the century undermined much of the value of this precedent.

Shaw's conservatism became apparent in cases on such social issues as church-state relations, blasphemy, race relations, and slavery. Shaw upheld the nation's last blasphemy conviction in *Commonwealth v. Kneeland* (1838). Kneeland was a radical Jacksonian while Shaw was a conservative Whig who had helped lead the opposition to Jackson in 1828. These political considerations did not dictate the outcome of this case, but they dovetailed perfectly with the result. Similarly, Shaw's active participation in the Unitarian church and his strong belief in public morality coincided with his support for the Unitarian plaintiffs and the continuation of an established church in Massachusetts in *Stebbins v. Jennings* (1830).

Shaw's social conservatism was also apparent in his jurisprudence on the most important social issues of the age: slavery and race. Like most northerners, Shaw found slavery distasteful and abhorrent. In his precourt career he publicly denounced the African slave trade. During the Missouri Crisis he argued that slavery contradicted American ideals, but he also admitted that it was a "necessary" evil "too deeply interwoven in the texture of society to be wholly or speedily eradicated." Although Shaw thought slavery was wrong, he thought abolitionist agitation endangered the Union. His jurisprudence reflects this ambivalence.

In *Commonwealth v. Aves* (1836) Shaw held that a slave girl, Med, brought into Massachusetts became immediately free. Citing the British precedent of *Somerset v. Stewart* (1772), the Declaration of Independence, and the Massachusetts Constitution of 1780, Shaw found that "slavery was abolished in Massachusetts, upon the ground that it is contrary to natural right and the plain principles of justice." Finding no positive law allowing Med's enslavement, Shaw freed her. Shaw reaffirmed his holding in *Aves* in subsequent cases. In the next twenty-four years all but three or four northern states adopted the principles of *Aves*, which had became the key American precedent in the development of a law of freedom in the North.

Shaw had limited his holding in *Aves* to cases involving slaves in transit and explicitly asserted that the right of a master to hold a fugitive slave was protected by the U.S. Constitution. After 1836 Shaw rarely offered fugitive slaves protection or due process. In 1842 he refused to enforce a writ of habeas corpus that would have released the fugitive slave George Latimer from the custody of the local sheriff. Shaw felt obligated to uphold the federal law and the U.S. Constitution. In this case he did not actually order Latimer returned to slavery, he simply refused to interfere with the rendition process.

In 1851 Shaw refused twice to intervene on behalf of alleged fugitive slaves. In February he rejected an application for a writ of habeas corpus for the fugitive slave Shadrach, who was later rescued. Later that year Shaw heard full arguments in favor of a similar writ for the fugitive slave Thomas Sims. Here he wrote an elaborate opinion of over twenty pages along with an eight-and-a-half-page "note" supporting the constitutionality of the federal fugitive slave law of 1850, even though no federal court had ruled on its validity. In refusing to grant the writ to Sims, Shaw was able to avoid actually sending a fugitive back to slavery; again he merely refused to interfere in the process.

The last major fugitive slave case in Boston was the rendition of Anthony Burns in 1854. At the time of the case the federal government rented facilities in the courthouse of the supreme judicial court. While Burns was in custody federal officials ringed the courthouse with soldiers and federal deputies and placed heavy chains around the building. Shaw did not protest this visual example of the power of slavery in America. The courthouse remained in chains and the chief justice was required to stoop under them to enter his own chambers. While taking no part in the Burns rendition, Shaw publicly acquiesced in the national government's show of military force.

In *Roberts v. Boston* (1849) Shaw upheld the practice of the city of Boston in segregating its public schools. The antislavery attorney Charles Sumner argued that segregated schools were inherently unequal because they forced black children to travel extra distances to school, created segregated neighborhoods near black schools, created a hereditary distinction based on race, and denied black children equality before the law. Sumner observed that "this compulsory segregation from the mass of citizens is of itself an *inequality* which we condemn" (*The Works of Charles Sumner*, vol. 2 [1875–1883], p. 364). Shaw rejected these arguments. He asserted that racial prejudice was neither caused nor abetted by segregated schools.

In *Roberts* Shaw found that black children had "access to a school, set apart for colored children, as well conducted in all respects, and as well fitted, in point of capacity and qualification of the instructors, to advance the education of children . . . as other primary schools." He believed there was nothing either illegal or unconstitutional about this system of education. Thus, Shaw developed the concept of "separate but equal" nearly two decades before the adoption of the Fourteenth Amendment. His decision in *Roberts* remained good law in much of the United States for more than a century. It did not, however, remain good law in Massachusetts for very long. In 1855 the Massachusetts legislature prohibited segregated schools in the state.

In *McCrea v. Marsh* (1858) Shaw's court upheld the right of a theater owner to refuse to seat blacks. Shaw did not write the opinion in this case, but he agreed with it. The court ruled that the ticket was a "license

legally revocable" at the discretion of the theater. The court also held that McCrea was entitled to recover for the value of the ticket. For the second time in less than a decade Shaw's court upheld segregation in Boston.

Shaw's decisions on slavery and race were conservative and cautious. He freed slaves brought to Massachusetts because his state did not recognize or allow the institution. But he would not risk any conflict with the national government or the South over the status of fugitive slaves. Nor did he demand "equality before the law" for the black citizens of Massachusetts. Shaw's vision of blind justice was clearly not color blind.

In August 1860 the 79-year-old Shaw resigned from the bench. He died seven months later in Boston and was buried at Mount Auburn cemetery. He was the most distinguished state judge of his age and probably of the entire century. A key figure in the development of American law, few judges have delivered as many opinions, and no antebellum state jurist has been cited as often. Some of Shaw's jurisprudence has lasted until the late twentieth century. His impact on property law, eminent domain, labor law, torts, and race relations was profound. Shaw developed new and flexible rules that generally helped emerging industries at the expense of existing economic enterprises and workers and gave great latitude to the legislature to develop policies that aided some property holders and harmed others. Shaw resisted social change at the very time his decisions on economic questions led to changes in communications, labor relations, religious practices, and the nature of the federal union.

• The best sources for understanding Shaw are the official reports of the Massachusetts Supreme Judicial Court for the thirty years he was on the bench. Some of his personal papers are at the Massachusetts Historical Society and the Boston Social Law Library. A full bibliography of Shaw's public addresses and other writings is in Leonard W. Levy, *The Law of the Commonwealth and Chief Justice Shaw* (1957), which is also the best biography of Shaw. Also useful is Frederick H. Chase, *Lemuel Shaw, Chief Justice of the Supreme Judicial Court of Massachusetts, 1830–1860* (1918). G. Edward White offers a good sketch of Shaw in *American Judicial Tradition: Profiles of Leading American Judges* (1988). J. Willard Hurst, *Law and the Conditions in the Nineteenth Century United States* (1956), Lawrence M. Friedman, *A History of American Law* 2d ed. (1985), and Morton J. Horwitz, *The Transformation of American Law* (1977), place Shaw's economic decisions in a larger context. Paul Finkelman, *An Imperfect Union: Slavery, Federalism, and Comity* (1981), and Robert M. Cover, *Justice Accused: Antislavery and the Judicial Process* (1975), discuss Shaw's jurisprudence on slavery and race and its impact on American law.

PAUL FINKELMAN

SHAW, Mary (25 Jan. 1854–18 May 1929), actress and suffragist, was born in Boston, Massachusetts, the daughter of Levi W. Shaw, a carpenter and builder, and Margaret Keating. After graduating from Boston's Girl's High and Normal School in 1871, Shaw taught school from 1873 to 1878. When her voice weakened from constant classroom use, she decided to study elocution. These lessons piqued her interest in the theater, and eventually she left teaching. After becoming involved with various amateur theater groups, Shaw joined the Boston Museum stock company (1879), where she first appeared as a chorus member in the spectacle *A Robisonade*. Through the assistance of actress Fanny Davenport, with whom she had worked at the Boston Museum, Shaw was cast as Lady Sneerwell in Augustin Daly's 1881 New York production of Richard Sheridan's *The School for Scandal*.

In 1883 Shaw received her first important opportunity when she was hired by Madame Helena Modjeska's company. She acted with Modjeska's repertory troupe for four seasons, playing numerous roles, including Celia in *As You Like It*, Hero in *Much Ado about Nothing*, and Mariana in *Measure for Measure*. In 1890 she toured with Julia Marlowe as Cynisca in *Pygmalion and Galatea*, Helen in *The Hunchback*, Celia in *As You Like It*, and in various other plays. Her first starring role, Herthe, in the touring production of *A Drop of Poison* in 1890, proved to be only modestly successful. Although Shaw was often praised for her technique and ability, she usually found herself relegated to supporting parts and touring companies. During the remainder of the century, she appeared as Marian in *Tess of the d'Urbervilles* with Minnie Madern Fiske, Gretchen in *Rip Van Winkle* with Joseph Jefferson, and Roxy in *Pudd'nhead Wilson* with Frank Mayo.

In 1899 Shaw created the character of Amrah in the popular dramatization of Lew Wallace's novel *Ben Hur*. That same year she played Helene Alving in a limited engagement of Henrik Ibsen's controversial *Ghosts*, a role that would define her career. Shaw used this role and others like it to create debate about women's rights. Four years later she played Helene Alving on Broadway, and in 1904 she toured the country in *Ghosts*, giving America its first extended exposure to the drama. While on tour Shaw often spoke publicly of women's rights and woman suffrage. Her determination and commitment was captured in a 1903 *Washington Post* interview when she noted: "God did not ask man whether woman should have power. He gave it to her, and this dramatist [Ibsen] realized that this power she should use in one way or another, if not legitimately then to make mischief." She acted in *Ghosts* intermittently for the next twenty-five years.

For much of her career Shaw persisted in portraying controversial women and received acclaim for her interpretations of Ibsen's Hedda Gabler and George Bernard Shaw's Mrs. Warren, the brothel keeper in *Mrs. Warren's Profession*. Her first attempt at performing Mrs. Warren on Broadway was steeped in controversy. Prior to the production, America's eminent guardian of public morals, Anthony Comstock, sent a letter to the *New York Times* demanding that the play be canceled. Mayor George McClellan then ordered the police commissioner to close the production down if it did premiere. The commissioner did just that and arrested all involved after the 30 October 1905 opening night performance. The producer, Arnold Daly, then

abandoned the project, but Mary Shaw persisted and obtained the rights to the play, touring in it from 1907 through 1908.

Shaw appeared in and also wrote various plays specifically concerned with woman suffrage. In 1909 she played Vida Lovering, the lead in Elizabeth Robins's *Votes for Women*, and in 1912 a playlet she wrote for the suffrage movement, *An Impressionistic Sketch of the Anti-Suffragists*, was performed by the Twenty-fifth District Players in the Hotel Astor at the Equal Suffrage meeting. This same group also performed her second short play, *The Parrot Cage*, which dealt with a group of parrots who argue against woman suffrage and are eventually converted by a suffragist parrot. In 1913 Shaw and other women sought to create the Women's National Theatre but failed to raise adequate financial support.

Other feminist plays in which Shaw appeared included *Divorce* (1909), *Polygamy* (1914), and *The Melody of Youth* (1916). She reprised the role of Helene Alving in 1917 and 1922, and she continued to appear in various plays through 1925.

Shaw married twice. Little is known about her first husband, with whom she had one son, the actor Arthur Shaw. Her second marriage in 1885 to French actor-director M. de Brissac was short-lived and also ended in divorce. Shaw performed her last stage role in 1928, the year before her death, in the Civic Repertory Company's production of *The Cradle Song*. She died at her residence at the Hotel Wellington in New York City.

A fine actress, Shaw gave credibility to and made popular some of the most controversial stage characters of her time. With her commitment to women's rights, she encouraged debate and action through her work on and off stage, leaving a legacy as one of the first successful American actresses to interpret the independent and free-thinking "New Woman" created by Ibsen and George Bernard Shaw.

• Shaw wrote "My 'Immoral' Play: The Story of the First American Production of 'Mrs. Warren's Profession,'" *McClure's*, Apr. 1912. For information regarding Shaw's work for women's rights, see Albert Auster, *Actresses and Suffragists: Women in the American Theatre, 1890–1920* (1984), and Robert A. Schanke, "Mary Shaw: A Fighting Champion" in *Women in American Theatre: Careers, Images, Movements*, ed. Helen Krich Chinoy and Linda Walsh Jenkins (1981). For reviews see the *Dramatic Mirror*, 10 June 1899, and *Literary Digest*, 9 June 1917. See also "Mary Shaw: A Woman of Thought and Action," *Theatre Magazine*, Aug. 1902. An obituary is in the *New York Times*, 19 May 1929.

PAUL MROCZKA

SHAW, Nathaniel, Jr. (5 Dec. 1735–15 Apr. 1782), merchant and naval official, was born in New London, Connecticut, the son of Nathaniel Shaw, a ship captain and merchant, and Temperance Harris. He probably received his elementary education at the local town school. There is no record of Shaw's secondary level training, but it can be assumed that he acquired his knowledge of maritime and business matters on an apprenticeship basis or from working at the trade. In 1758 Shaw married Lucretia Rogers; they had no children. During the 1760s Shaw assumed direction of his father's extensive mercantile enterprises, which included commerce with England and other continental colonies but centered primarily on West Indian trade. Under his shrewd management, business flourished to such an extent that he was able to provide New London with an imported fire engine and the seaport's first lighthouse. During this period Shaw became increasingly involved in colonial opposition to Britain's restrictive trade legislation and royal customs collection. In 1769 he was accused of abetting the sinking of the customs ship *Liberty* at Newport, Rhode Island, although Shaw denied these charges. His anti-Crown activism continued, however, and by the eve of the American Revolution he was seeking stocks of gunpowder from New York and the West Indies.

After the outbreak of hostilities, Connecticut's council of safety commissioned Shaw as their agent for gathering naval supplies, dispatching fast ships to the West Indies and elsewhere for gunpowder, and caring for sick seamen in New London. He performed these duties with assistance from his brother, Thomas Shaw, who served as his deputy. He also complied with additional requests from the council, such as procuring the arms, ammunition, and other supplies for fitting-out privateers; acquiring the manpower and equipment for fortifying New London; and disbursing the requisite monies involved in these projects.

The Continental Congress appointed him a naval agent in April 1776, and in this capacity he expanded his activities to include supervising the sale of captured prizes, recruiting sailors, securing pilots for American and French ships navigating on Long Island Sound, furnishing transports and provisions for Continental army troops, and overseeing Connecticut's treatment of prisoners of war as well as prisoner exchanges. On 21 October 1778 the Connecticut General Assembly named Shaw as its marine agent, thus giving him sole command over all privateers and the vessels in Connecticut's state navy. He used his exclusive maritime powers not only for the patriot cause but also to increase his personal wealth and expand his commercial connections. In addition to these naval assignments, Shaw served during the war years as a county justice of the peace and a deputy for New London to the general assembly.

Benedict Arnold's sudden and destructive raid on New London in September 1781 resulted in severe financial losses for Shaw. Three months after the raid came a personal loss when his wife died from a "putrid fever" she caught while nursing sick prisoners. Shaw himself died suddenly shortly thereafter as the result of a self-inflicted, accidental wound he received when a musket misfired during a hunting trip near New London.

• The most abundant and most useful sources relating to the career of Nathaniel Shaw, Jr., are in the Connecticut Historical Society, the Connecticut State Library, the New London Historical Society, and, to a lesser extent, the Yale University Library. Other repositories that hold some manuscript materials concerning Shaw's activities include the Massachusetts Historical Society, the Rhode Island Historical Society, the Rhode Island State Library, the Library of Congress, and the National Archives. The most worthwhile items from printed records dealing with Shaw appear in Charles J. Hoadly, ed., *Public Records of the Colony of Connecticut*, vols. 12–15 (1881–1890), and Hoadly and Leonard W. Labaree, eds., *Public Records of the State of Connecticut*, vols. 1–4 (1893–1942). An earlier, though valuable, primary and secondary source work pertaining to Shaw's lifetime is Frances M. Caulkins, *A History of New London, Connecticut . . .* (1852). This New Londoner's naval achievements during the American Revolution are best followed in William B. Clark and William J. Morgan, eds., *Naval Documents of the American Revolution*, vols. 1–9 (1964–1986); Charles H. Lincoln, comp., *Naval Records of the American Revolution, 1775–1788* (1906); Louis F. Middlebrook, *History of Maritime Connecticut during the American Revolution*, vols. 1–2 (1925); Charles O. Paullin, ed., *Out-letters of the Continental [Congress] Marine Committee . . .* (1914); and Ernest E. Rogers, "Connecticut's Naval Office at New London during the War of the American Revolution," New London County Historical Society, *Collections* 2 (1933).

SHELDON S. COHEN

SHAW, Oliver (13 Mar. 1779–31 Dec. 1848), first prominent U.S. songwriter, was born in Middleborough, Massachusetts, the son of John Shaw and Hannah Heath. Beginning in 1796 he attended the Bristol Academy of Taunton, Massachusetts, and from 1800 to 1805 he received musical instruction, largely at the hands of European immigrants, especially John L. Berkenhead in Newport, Rhode Island, and the better-known Gottlieb Graupner in Boston.

In his maturity, Shaw was blind. An accident with a penknife in early childhood deprived him of sight in his right eye, and a fever condition combined with eyestrain led to the loss of sight in his left eye by the age of twenty-one. This physical condition, remarkably, did not greatly restrain his various musical activities.

Shaw's professional life began about 1805 with a move to Dedham, Massachusetts. There he associated with Herman Mann, a publisher and the author of the words of Shaw's first song, "Address to a Tuft of Violets: A New Song," which was included in the anthology Shaw compiled, *A Favourite Selection of Music Adapted to the Piano Forte* (1806). In 1807 Shaw moved to Providence, Rhode Island, which became his permanent home. In 1812 he married Sarah Jencks; they had five children. A son, Oliver J. Shaw, Jr., achieved some prominence as a musician, and two daughters, Sarah Shaw and Abbie Shaw, took part in musical activities.

Shaw participated fully in the musical life of the Providence community as a composer, publisher, teacher, church organist, and tenor soloist; as an organizer and leader of musical societies; and generally as a musical entrepreneur. He published more than seventy songs and thirty or more instrumental works. From 1809 to 1832 he was the organist of the First Congregational Church of Providence. Also during those years he brought together and presided over an amateur choral group, named the Psallonian Society, which was incorporated in 1816 and dissolved in 1833. This society paralleled on a smaller scale the Handel and Haydn Society of Boston, founded in 1815, with which Shaw was also associated from time to time. On 5 July 1826 Shaw performed one of his best-known songs, "Mary's Tears," as a tenor soloist at a Handel and Haydn Society program for President James Monroe at the First Church in Chauncy Place in Boston. The Mozart Musical Society of Pawtucket, Rhode Island, also listed Shaw as a member. Such societies normally aimed to improve choral singing through the rehearsal and performance of oratorios, programs consisting mainly of various movements of European masterworks by composers such as George Frideric Handel, Franz Joseph Haydn, Wolfgang Amadeus Mozart, Ludwig van Beethoven, and Ludwig Felix Mendelssohn.

Shaw was a music teacher for his own children, and during his Dedham years he gave lessons to Lowell Mason, who became one of the dominant figures in American musical life during the nineteenth century. A number of Shaw's publications were dedicated to his students, including "The Blue Bird. Composed & Dedicated to His Friend & Pupil Miss Mary B. Bush by O. Shaw" (1823–1827).

Other well-known vocal pieces include "There's Nothing True but Heav'n" (1817), "The Polar Star" (1817–1823), and "As Down in the Sunless Retreats" (1817–1821), all settings of religious poetry. Shaw also composed hymn tunes such as "Taunton," "Bristol," and "Weybosset," conventionally named after nearby places, for example, Weybosset Street in Providence. In 1807 he published *For the Gentlemen*, a tutorial anthology for winds. The work begins with a segment of one of the war-horses of the late eighteenth and early nineteenth centuries, "Turkish March in the Battle of Prague" by František Kočžwara, and continues with various marches, minuets, waltzes, and other compositions, the majority by Shaw. It is one of the earliest books of its kind by a native American composer. Shaw also wrote a number of dedicatory marches for governors and military figures. On the occasion of the marquis de Lafayette's triumphal return to the United States in 1824, Shaw wrote "Welcome the Nation's Guest: A Military Divertimento for the Piano Forte. Composed & Respectfully Dedicated to Genl. LaFayette on His Visit to Providence" (1824?).

The annual output of Shaw's song publications reached a peak of about twenty individual pieces in 1835 and declined somewhat from then until the end of his life. In 1846 he issued his final work, a vocal duet, "Home of My Soul. Sacred Duett." Shaw died in Providence.

• The most extensive work on Shaw is Bruce N. Degen, "Oliver Shaw: His Music and Contribution to American Society" (D.M.A. diss., Univ. of Rochester, 1971). Earlier biographies that remain valuable are Frederic Denison et al., eds., *Memorial of Oliver Shaw* (1884), and Thomas Williams, *A Discourse on the Life and Death of Oliver Shaw* (1851). Shaw's involvement with the Psallonian Society is described in detail in Joyce Mangler Carlson, "Early Music in Rhode Island: Part V. Oliver Shaw and the Psallonian Society," *Rhode Island History* 23, no. 2 (1964): 35–50. Also not to be overlooked is the article by Herbert C. Thrasher, "Oliver Shaw," *Books at Brown* 8, no. 4 (1945–1946): 1–4.

JOHN DRUESEDOW

SHAW, Robert Gould (10 Oct. 1837–18 July 1863), soldier, was born in Boston, Massachusetts, the son of Francis George Shaw, a merchant and social reformer, and Sarah Blake Sturgis, an abolitionist. Shaw was born into one of the wealthiest families in the country, linked by marriage to Boston merchant dynasties such as the Cabots and Russells. The Shaw home sat next to George Ripley's utopian community Brook Farm in West Roxbury, Massachusetts, and was a gathering spot for abolitionists and reformers.

Despite a stern upbringing, Shaw's early life was one of privilege, fun, and security. He had many cousins to play with and attended Miss Mary Peabody's school. His extended family encompassed eighty-five first cousins and twenty-three aunts and uncles, most of whom lived in the Boston area. In 1847 his family moved to Staten Island, New York. The move upset young Shaw, and the nine-year-old clung to his mother. Adding to his melancholy, he was placed in Herr Marschalk's private school on Staten Island, which he hated. Upon the advice of his uncle, Joseph Coolidge Shaw, a devout Jesuit, the Shaws then sent Robert to a Catholic boarding school, St. John's College at Fordham. The Shaw letters reveal a young child feeling rejected by his parents. His behavior deteriorated, and he ran away from St. John's twice. Each time, at the urging of his mother, he was returned by his father.

In January 1851 Shaw's father took the whole family on a tour of Europe. Placed in Monsieur Roulet's private school in Neuchâtel, Switzerland, Shaw began to challenge his mother's stern abolitionism and her expectations for him. He wrote to her that he did not "see how one man could do much against slavery. . . . I don't want to become a reformer, an apostle, or anything of that kind." Horrifying his mother, Shaw stated that he planned to join the army, for, as he explained, "what else can I do? . . . I don't want to be a merchant, or Doctor, or minister, or anything like that" (Shaw, *Letters* 1864, pp. 40, 15–16). At age sixteen, Shaw left Neuchâtel for Hanover, Germany, to continue his studies. In Hanover he drank heavily, gambled, and found himself in constant debt.

In 1856 Shaw returned to the United States to begin college. He preferred to attend Columbia or New York University so he could be close to his family. They insisted, however, that he enter Harvard. Crestfallen, he spent two lackluster years there. Ranking in the bottom third of his class and with severe disciplinary problems, he left Harvard for good in 1858. Returning home, Shaw took a job at his uncle's Manhattan mercantile firm, H. P. Sturgis and Company. For two years he worked in the counting room. Shaw showed no enthusiasm for his work and admitted to a friend that he felt enslaved by his job. At age twenty-two, Shaw viewed his life as a failure.

The outbreak of the Civil War in 1861 provided the young aristocrat with a new lease on life. Serving first as a private in the Seventh Regiment New York National Guards and then as a second lieutenant in the Second Massachusetts Infantry, he distinguished himself as a soldier. Shaw was wounded twice and miraculously survived the bloody encounters at Antietam and Cedar Mountain. He loved the military and seemed to have finally found his calling. In August 1862 he received a captain's commission in the Second. Also that year Shaw secretly became engaged to a wealthy New Yorker, Annie Kneeland Haggerty. Against his mother's wishes, Shaw married her in 1863; they had no children.

After the Emancipation Proclamation of 1863, Massachusetts governor John Andrew hurried to organize the North's first "colored" volunteer regiment, the Fifty-fourth. With abolitionist parents and a sound military record, Shaw was Andrew's first choice to lead the new regiment. Without hesitation, Shaw refused the commission. Never considering himself an abolitionist, he did not want the responsibility of leading the much-publicized first black regiment raised northeast of the Mississippi. Deeply ashamed, his mother wrote to Andrew that her son's decision caused her the "bitterist [sic] disappointment."

After a barrage of telegrams and enormous pressure from his mother, Shaw changed his mind reluctantly and accepted the colonelcy of the Fifty-fourth. In February 1863 Shaw supervised the training of African-American volunteers. "Shaw's method," explained second in command, N. P. Hallowell, "was the method of coercion. . . . The unruly members . . . were stood on barrels, bucked, gagged and, if need be, shot" (Hallowell, p. 33). In May the untested regiment was sent to Hilton Head, South Carolina. The Fifty-fourth's first engagement proved an embarrassment to Shaw and his men. Despite Shaw's objections, the regiment took part in the burning of the undefended port town of Darien, Georgia.

On 16 July the Fifty-fourth had the opportunity to recoup its self-esteem when Confederate forces waged a surprise attack on James Island, South Carolina. A group of 250 members of the Fifty-fourth held off repeated assaults, giving the Federal troops time to organize a defensive retreat. Two days later, on Morris Island, Shaw proudly volunteered his regiment to lead the assault on the impregnable Fort Wagner, the first step in an offensive on the Confederate stronghold of Charleston, South Carolina. When the Fifty-fourth charged the fort, 272 were killed, wounded, or captured. One of those who fell was Shaw. Although the assault failed, the bravery of the Fifty-fourth proved the ability of African-American troops in battle. In death, the young Shaw was ennobled as a martyr to freedom and as a symbol of enlightened sacrifice. He and the Fifty-fourth were later memorialized by Augustus Saint-Gaudens's mythic monument placed on the Boston Common.

• Shaw's letters and papers are in the Houghton Library, Harvard University; the Massachusetts Historical Society; and the Rare Books and Manuscripts Division of the New York Public Library. Many of these have been edited and published in Robert Gould Shaw, *Letters: RGS* (1864), which provides letters from Shaw's early life, and *Letters: RGS* (1876), which holds his wartime correspondence. Russell Duncan, *Blue-Eyed Child of Fortune: The Civil War Letters of Colonel Robert Gould Shaw* (1992), provides an excellent biographical sketch of Shaw's early years as well as an annotated compilation of his letters during the Civil War. Shaw's only modern biographer is Peter Burchard, *One Gallant Rush: Robert Gould Shaw and His Brave Black Regiment* (1965). Thomas Wentworth Higginson, "Robert Gould Shaw," in *Harvard Memorial Biographies*, vol. 2 (1866), offers a useful contemporary account of Shaw's life. George M. Fredrickson, *The Inner Civil War: Northern Intellectuals and the Crisis of the Union* (1965), devotes a chapter to Shaw that brilliantly traces the changing meanings Shaw's death symbolized for northern intellectuals. For information on the Fifty-fourth Regiment, see Luis F. Emilio, *A Brave Black Regiment: History of the Fifty-fourth Regiment of Massachusetts Volunteer Infantry, 1863–1865* (1891). Joseph T. Glatthaar, *Forged in Battle: The Civil War Alliance of Black Soldiers and White Officers* (1990), provides an in-depth analysis of the relationship between African Americans and whites within the Union army. Norwood Penrose Hallowell, *Selected Letters and Papers of N. P. Hallowell* (1896; repr. 1963), provides a contemporary's account of Shaw and the Fifty-fourth.

MATTHEW H. CROCKER

SHAW, Samuel (2 Oct. 1754–30 May 1794), revolutionary war officer and consul, was born in Boston, Massachusetts, the son of Francis Shaw, a prominent merchant, and Sarah Burt. After study at the Latin School in Boston, Shaw worked in a countinghouse. He entered military service as a second lieutenant in the militia during the siege of Boston; on 10 December 1775 he received a commission as second lieutenant in the Continental Artillery. In May 1776 he became adjutant of his regiment; he was promoted to first lieutenant of the Third Continental Artillery on 1 January 1777 and to captain on 12 April 1780. Shaw commanded at Fort Washington from August to October 1776, being relieved shortly before the post fell to the British. Shaw served throughout the war, mostly in the capacity of a staff officer—adjutant, brigade major, and, from 1779 to 1783, as aide-de-camp to General Henry Knox, chief of the Continental Artillery. Shaw was present at the battles of Trenton, Princeton, Brandywine, Germantown, Monmouth, and Yorktown.

Shaw's personal letters during the war are revealing of military actions and especially specific episodes, such as the mutiny of the Pennsylvania Line in 1781 and the Newburgh conspiracy of 1783. He helped Knox to form the Society of the Cincinnati and reputedly wrote the constitution of that organization. Despite a busy life in war, further public service, and commerce, Shaw acquired a knowledge of Latin and became well read in ancient Roman history and poetry. An obituary states that in 1790 he received an honorary M.A. degree from "the University of Cambridge" (probably Harvard) in absentia and "without his knowledge, at the solicitation of several gentlemen of eminence in literature." On 25 August 1792 he was elected a Fellow of the American Academy of Arts and Sciences.

Signing on as a supercargo, Shaw sailed on the *Empress of China* from New York City on 22 February 1784 for Canton, China. He served without pay but shared in the profits. The vessel, carrying mainly ginseng, was the first to open up an American-Chinese trade; Great Britain, France, Holland, and Denmark were already involved in the Chinese trade. The *Empress of China* sailed by way of the Cape of Good Hope, reaching Canton, the world's largest tea market, on 30 August 1784. Though at first they took the Americans for Englishmen, the Chinese, according to Shaw, "styled us the *New People*." The ship, laden with tea, silk, and other commodities, arrived at New York City on 11 May 1785. In November 1784 Shaw, his comrades, and the Europeans had almost fought a naval battle with the Chinese, a situation dubbed the "Canton War"; the cause of friction had been the accidental killing of a Chinese man by a British seaman firing a cannon salute. The crisis was defused when the British surrendered the gunner to the Chinese, who presumably put the offender to death. In his report to John Jay, the American secretary for foreign affairs, Shaw announced that the American flag had been "treated with respect in that distant region."

Shaw next held a clerkship in the War Office and accompanied Secretary of War Knox on a tour of magazines in the southern states. Appointed consul at Canton in January 1786, he resigned his post at the War Office and sailed from New York City for Canton on the *Hope* on 4 February 1786. He returned to New York City on 17 July 1789. As consul, Shaw advised Americans trading with the Chinese on protocol and regulations, and he worked with Chinese leaders and European representatives to promote a mutuality of interests. By 1789 fifteen American vessels were engaged in the China trade. Shaw achieved literary distinction for his careful journals of his first two voyages to China. These accounts were published after his death. For the third voyage Shaw went on his own ship, the *Massachusetts*, at 820 tons America's largest merchant vessel. It left Boston in March 1790. Shaw sold the ship to the Portuguese in Macao, located on an estuary of the Canton River. Here Shaw resided most of the time while in China; foreign trading vessels were not allowed to go beyond the deep harbor at Whampoa, twelve miles east of Canton. Shaw returned to the United States in January 1792.

Shaw married Hannah Phillips, daughter of William Phillips (1751–1827), in 1792. The couple did not have children. He was appointed a major in the Massachusetts militia on 30 August 1792. President George Washington renewed Shaw's appointment as consul to Canton; wedded for only a few months, Shaw again set out for the Orient. Because of typhoons he was delayed for several months in Bombay, eventually reaching Canton on 2 November 1793.

While in Bombay, Shaw had contracted a liver disease. Finding no cure in China, he left for the United States aboard the *Washington* on 17 March 1794. Eight months and ten days after he had become sick, he died on ship near the Cape of Good Hope and was buried at sea. Shaw was universally admired, though, as Amassa Delano, who sailed with him aboard the *Massachusetts*, said, Shaw "placed so high a value upon the sentiments of honour that some of his friends thought it was carried to excess."

• Shaw's journals of his first two voyages and a trip to Bengal, personal letters, reports to John Jay, and his biography are published in Josiah Quincy, *The Journals of Major Samuel Shaw . . . with a Life of the Author* (1847; repr. 1968). The third voyage is described in Amassa Delano, *Narrative of Voyages and Travels in the Northern and Southern Hemispheres* (1817). The Papers of the Continental Congress (National Archives) contains letters from Shaw, and the Henry Knox Papers (Massachusetts Historical Society, microfilm) has letters from Shaw to Knox and Knox correspondence in Shaw's handwriting from when Shaw was an aide to Knox during the war. Also see "Captain Samuel Shaw's Revolutionary War Letters to Captain Winthrop Sargent," *Pennsylvania Magazine of History and Biography* 70 (1946): 281–324. Francis Wharton, ed., *The Diplomatic Correspondence of the United States . . . 1783 to . . . 1789* (7 vols., 1833–1834), has consular letters. Brief biographies are found in Freeman Hunt, *Lives of American Merchants*, vol. 2 (1858), pp. 201–22, and James M. Bugbee, *Memorials of the Massachusetts Society of the Cincinnati* (1890), pp. 432–36. A good view of Shaw's role in China is Foster Rhea Dulles, *The Old China Trade* (1930). An obituary is in the Boston *Columbian Centinel*, 20 Aug. 1794.

HARRY M. WARD

SHAW, Wilbur (31 Oct. 1902–30 Oct. 1954), race car driver and race track official, was born Warren Wilbur Shaw in Shelbyville, Indiana, the son of James Shaw, a police officer and sales representative, and Mary King. Wilbur dropped out of high school and apprenticed as a plumber with his stepfather in Indianapolis, where he had grown up. In 1926 he married Beatrice Patrick, who died while giving birth. Young Shaw's passion for sports and speed led him to build and drive race cars. After some success on the small-time dirt tracks of the Midwest, Shaw returned to Indianapolis for the 1927 running of the 500-mile race.

Shaw's initial run at the Indianapolis 500 came in an infamous car that was entered as the "Jynx Special." One of the celebrated Miller racers from California, it had been built for Jimmy Murphy, a popular driver who had won the 1922 Indianapolis 500 but who had died after crashing the car in 1924. Three years later Shaw persuaded an Indianapolis entrepreneur to purchase the rebuilt Miller, now known as the "Murphy Death Car," and to rename it the "Jynx Special" after a new product, Jynx Liquid, which was supposed magically to seal punctured tires. Surprisingly, Shaw, with relief help from Louis Meyer, drove the car to a fourth-place finish in 1927.

A favorite among veteran drivers, especially Peter De Paolo and Tommy Milton, Shaw embraced the simple strategy of putting his race car in front and keeping it there. By adopting this approach to racing, particularly on the popular board tracks of the 1920s, "you just counted on spending a certain amount of time in the hospital," Shaw later recalled. This hell-bent style proved more effective for setting land-speed records and for competing at the smaller dirt tracks than at Indianapolis's Brickyard. Shaw set several speed records on the sands at Daytona Beach, Florida, and he won the first six races of the American Automobile Association's (AAA) 1929 season. But while Meyer, Shaw's relief driver in 1927, won the Indianapolis 500 in 1928, 1933, and 1936 (making him the race's first three-time winner), Shaw had to settle for two second-place finishes, to Meyer in 1933 and to Kelly Petillo in 1935. Finally, in 1937 he drove his own "Shaw-Gilmore" special to a narrow victory over the second-place finisher Ralph Hepburn, averaging just over 113 miles per hour in the process. By this time Shaw had developed a relatively cerebral approach to racing and had gained the reputation of a skilled technical innovator. He was the first racer, for example, to use a custom-fitted steering wheel in order to improve a car's handling and a driver's own comfort. In 1929 Shaw married Catherine Stearns; the couple had one son.

After coming in second in 1938 (his third second-place finish at Indianapolis), in his own "Shaw Special," Shaw made a unique deal to drive a Maserati in the next 500-mile race: he promised his sponsor that he would drive for free if he did not win the race. Shaw not only won the 1939 contest in the "Boyle Valve Special," but he repeated in 1940, making Shaw the first back-to-back winner at Indianapolis, a feat that had eluded his idol Tommy Milton. In 1941 Shaw enjoyed a comfortable lead in the Boyle Valve Special when it went over the wall on the 151st lap. Shaw, who had pioneered the use of crash helmets by drivers in 1932, survived but never raced competitively again.

After working in aviation sales for the Firestone Tire and Rubber Company during World War II, Shaw decided to return to auto racing as an official. He convinced the millionaire Indianapolis industrialist Anton "Tony" Hulman, Jr., to purchase the famed Brickyard, which had fallen into disrepair during the war as no 500-mile races had been run. The Indianapolis 500 of 1946, with Shaw serving as the speedway's president and general manager, proved a great success.

While eschewing any return to competition, Shaw never lost his fascination with machinery and with speed. He worked as a consultant to motor companies, volunteered as a test driver, drove speedboats and motorcycles, and flew his own airplane. He even dreamed of setting a new land-speed record in the "Novi Special," the "death car" in which his old rival Ralph Hepburn had died in 1947. Shaw never made his run in the Novi, as he himself perished in a plane crash while returning to Indianapolis after having test-driven several new Chrysler cars in Detroit, Michigan.

By the time of his death Shaw had become nearly as famous as a race official as he had been as a driver. He helped establish a far-flung radio operation in order to broadcast the Indianapolis 500 on Memorial Day. Recognizing the importance of tradition, Shaw also made a point of inviting back famous drivers from the past—including Ray Harroun, the first Indianapolis 500 winner in 1911; Ralph De Palma, whose record of leading the Indianapolis race for 610 laps during ten races in the 1910s and early 1920s even topped Shaw's own total of 508, achieved in thirteen races between 1927 and 1941; and De Paolo, winner of the 1925 Indianapolis race and one of auto racing's most articulate boosters. In 1949 Shaw even persuaded Milton, a former two-time winner at Indianapolis and by then a wealthy manufacturer, to serve as the chief steward of the 500-mile race. Fueled by Hulman's money and Shaw's expertise, the Indianapolis 500 became more than an auto race and established a claim to be the most important one-day event in the world of sports.

• Shaw's ghostwritten autobiography, published after his death, is *Gentlemen, Start Your Engines* (1955). See also Lyle Kenyon Engel, *The Indianapolis "500": The World's Most Exciting Auto Race*, rev.ed. (1972); Brock Yates, *The Indianapolis 500* (1956); Jack C. Fox, *The Indianapolis 500* (1967); Fox, *Illustrated History of the Five Hundred* (1985); and Al Bloemker, *500 Miles to Go: The Story of the Indianapolis Speedway* (1966). An obituary is in the *New York Times*, 31 Oct. 1954.

NORMAN L. ROSENBERG

SHAW, William Smith (12 Aug. 1778–25 Apr. 1826), bibliophile, lawyer, and presidential secretary, was born in Haverhill, Massachusetts, the son of the Reverend John Shaw, a minister, and Elizabeth Smith. Accident-prone in youth, Shaw also suffered his entire life from chronic febrile and rheumatic complaints. He was, however, bookish at an early age, having acquired a classical taste from his father, who supplemented his income by preparing young men for college.

Shaw's mother, who was Abigail Adams's sister, was a source of direction and discipline throughout her son's life. Among her dictums were: "I have long been of the opinion that *midnight oil* never enriched the mind or the purse" and "there is no condition [marriage] in life which may be so productive of genuine happiness." After graduating from Harvard in 1798, Shaw was taken on as John Adams's summer secretary at Quincy and given the task of arranging Adams's book room, "sorting and separating papers with strict order and method so that no trouble occurs in searching." He met this challenge, and the president took him to Philadelphia as his private secretary when he returned to the seat of government in November. Shaw's initial youthful bumptiousness and immature hand settled. "Your punctuality and attention deserve commendation," wrote Abigail Adams, with whom he corresponded frequently, "and claim a pardon for any inaccuracies of Stile, or manner, which escape your pen." The president found him "very good, attentive and obliging." Shaw, who was well read in the classics and whose personal correspondence ran to both political and literary interests, found that Philadelphia "was pure enjoyment in abundance of books and a few choice friends." However, the District of Columbia, when the administration settled there, was much less attractive as, he complained, "I lose my way in the woods, or stumble over piles of bricks, or fall into some new cellar." Moreover, he found the inhabitants so immersed in real estate speculation that he derived "little improvement or happiness from their society." He lived three years with the Adams family, where he was both enjoyed and useful. "As to William, we have rubd of so many of his peculiarities that he has scarcely one left to laugh at, he is a good creature," Abigail Adams reported. Shaw himself recorded: "Notwithstanding my arms are so stiff, that I can scarcely move them, occasioned by cutting venison for twenty eight very hungry men." Upon the death of General George Washington, Shaw was selected to deliver to his widow the resolution of Congress honoring the former president. During his years in Washington he started what was to become a distinguished collection of American pamphlets.

At the conclusion of Adams's term in 1801, Shaw returned to Massachusetts politically well connected, and in April he began to read law in the Boston office of William Sullivan. He was admitted as an attorney at the court of common pleas two years later and was appointed as clerk of the federal district court for Massachusetts in the spring of 1806, a position in which he served for twelve years.

In 1805, as an outlet for his literary interest, Shaw began an association with Boston's Anthology Society, which met weekly to socialize and also published the *Monthly Anthology and Boston Review*. He contributed occasional writings and functioned as the society's treasurer. The following year the society began collecting periodicals, with Shaw making a substantial gift, and a year later it voted a reading room into existence. On 13 February 1807 the library's trustees incorporated as the Boston Athenaeum—modeled on the Liverpool Athenaeum and Lyceum—for the stated purpose of providing "a reading room, a library, a museum, and a laboratory" for its members. Shaw became its librarian and secretary in his spare time. His efforts on behalf of the Athenaeum were prodigious and thorough. Of him it was noted (and recorded by him): "That dog Shaw goes everywhere. He knows everybody. Everybody knows him. If he sees a book, pamphlet, or manuscript—Oh Sir! The Athenaeum must have this. Well, *have it he will and have it he must* and have it he does, for he seldom goes out of a house without having something under his arm." To him Josiah Quincy wrote, "I am always willing that you should get up on your hobby, and ride down half the letter on pamphlets and Anthologies." In turn Shaw instructed Henry Higginson, "for it is a great object with me to procure every book, in every language, that was ever written respecting our own country." No need was too minor—he drafted instructions for the janitor—no source overlooked. "These institutions [foreign libraries] must receive . . . duplicates," he insisted, "which they do not care to preserve, and would

be willing to send us. . . . no vessel should sail for Boston without some papers for us."

Known locally as "Athenaeum" Shaw, he served unstintingly as librarian until 1822 and as secretary until 1823, "occupying himself almost exclusively in collecting rare books, pamphlets, coins, and interesting relics of antiquity." He entered private practice, but his health was failing, a condition captured in his 1824 portrait by Gilbert Stuart which hangs in the Athenaeum. He died unmarried in Boston. So tangled was his personal estate with the affairs of the Athenaeum that his executor and brother-in-law, Joseph Barlow Felt, could only resolve the problem by awarding everything to the Athenaeum.

Shaw essentially gave his life to broadening and increasing public access to knowledge through many specific acts of giving—library materials, money, and support for individual scholars such as Hannah Adams, an early compiler of historical data. His one enduring monument, the Boston Athenaeum, is a tribute to his involvement as a founder of a major American library and as a charter member of the movement to create American libraries.

• Shaw's papers are at the Boston Athenaeum. The sum of Shaw's life is embodied in Joseph Barlow Felt, *Memorials of William Smith Shaw* (1852), which follows his life through his correspondence. In it, the full force of his absorption in collecting library materials and his commitment to the Boston Athenaeum emerges. Shaw's diary, mentioned in this work, has not surfaced. In the *Athenaeum Century* (1972), by the staff of the Boston Athenaeum, the structure and progression of affairs of this institution is chronicled. Some light is shed on his connection with the Adams family in Page Smith, *John Adams*, vol. 2 (1962), but a full analysis of his role in the presidential years has yet to be made.

JOHN D. KNOWLTON

SHAW, Woody (24 Dec. 1944–9 May 1989), jazz trumpeter, was born Woody Herman Shaw, Jr., in Laurinburg, North Carolina, the son of Woody Shaw, Sr., and Rosalie Pegues, factory workers. The family had settled in Newark, New Jersey, when his mother returned to the South to have him. She brought the two-month-old Shaw back to Newark, where he was raised. Named after both his father and the bandleader Woody Herman, Shaw was steeped in music and later recalled childhood nights of listening to his father's gospel group, the Diamond Jubilee Singers, rehearsing in their home.

After taking up single-valve bugle in the Junior Elks and Junior Masons Drum and Bugle Corps, Shaw switched to trumpet in June 1956 and studied with Jerry Zierling (or Ziering—published accounts are conflicting) at Cleveland Junior High School. By this time he was already suffering from a hereditary disease that caused night blindness (retinitis pigmentosa), a considerable handicap for someone whose profession would bring him regularly into the murky world of nightclubs. At about age fourteen he was caught for vandalism—evidently his poor vision impeded his escape—but in lieu of traditional punishment a sympathetic security guard brought him into the Newark YMCA (Young Men's Christian Association) big band under the rigorously disciplined leadership of Lavozier Lamar, whose young musicians included saxophonist Wayne Shorter.

Shaw had been an outstanding student who skipped directly from seventh to ninth grade, but to his parents' dismay he lost interest in school. Devoted instead to music and women, he dropped out of Newark's Arts High School before finishing. In 1963, after many local professional jobs and jam sessions, he joined percussionist Willie Bobo's band, which included pianist Chick Corea and tenor saxophonist Joe Farrell. While with Bobo, Shaw also performed alongside vibraphonist Bobby Hutcherson as a member of wind player Eric Dolphy's band for rehearsals in New York, performances in Pittsburgh, and the recording of Dolphy's album *Iron Man*. The next year Dolphy invited Shaw to Paris, but shortly before Shaw's departure Dolphy died. Shaw decided to make the trip nonetheless, and he found steady work with saxophonist Nathan Davis and such veteran expatriate American musicians as Bud Powell, Kenny Clarke, Johnny Griffin, and Art Taylor. He performed in Paris, Berlin, and London with a group that included organist Larry Young.

Shaw returned to the United States in May 1965 and the following month joined Horace Silver's quintet, with which he recorded the albums *The Cape Verdean Blues* (1965) and *The Jody Grind* (1966). Silver's formidable tenor saxophonist Joe Henderson was replaced by Shaw's friend Tyrone Washington in 1966, and, according to Shaw, he and Washington preferred melodic improvisations that sometimes utilized phrases of free jazz playing. These solos carried the band in a stylistic direction that the leader disliked, and consequently Silver disbanded the group.

Shaw also recorded two sessions with Young (*In the Beginning* and *Unity*; as a leader and as a sideman late in 1965), and he made albums with Corea (*Tones for Jones Bones*, 1966), alto saxophonist Jackie McLean (including *Demon's Dance*, 1967), and McCoy Tyner (*Expansions*, 1968), this last as a member from about 1968 to 1970 of a group that the members jokingly called the starvation band, because during this golden age of rock the great pianist Tyner could scarcely find work in jazz. In 1968 Shaw also began to work occasionally with drummer Max Roach, appearing with him at a festival in Iran. But by 1969, when he recorded with pianist Andrew Hill, Shaw had become a heroin addict, and Roach let him go. Shaw then worked temporarily as a studio musician and in pit orchestras for Broadway musicals.

In 1970 Shaw formed a quintet with Joe Henderson and recorded the album *Blackstone Legacy* as a leader. He toured with drummer Art Blakey's Jazz Messengers (1971–1972) before settling in San Francisco. Shaw played on Blakey's albums *Anthenagin* and *Buhaina*, recorded in Berkeley in March 1973, while working with the drummer at the Keystone Korner in San Francisco. He briefly led a group with Hutcherson that performed at the Montreux Jazz Festival in Switzerland in July. Details of his first marriage are unknown, but in a 1978 interview he mentioned in passing that the marriage disintegrated during these years.

In December 1974 a new contract brought Shaw to New York to record the first of several albums for the Muse label, *The Moontrane*, with trombonist Steve Turré, pianist Onaje Allan Gumbs, and drummer Victor Lewis. By this point Shaw's drug problems were under control, and he had begun teaching at jazz clinics, an activity that he continued into the mid-1980s. As a jazz educator he was concerned with upholding the hard bop tradition in the face of popular jazz-rock and jazz-soul styles that he felt to be musically shallow, and he was concerned with trying to bring young African-American musicians into jazz.

Shaw returned to San Francisco from February to July 1975 and then moved to New York City to join the Louis Hayes–Junior Cook Quintet, which after tenor saxophonist Cook's departure became the Woody Shaw–Louis Hayes Quintet. Cook was soon replaced by Rene McLean and then by expatriate tenor saxophonist Dexter Gordon, who adopted the band for his acclaimed homecoming performances after his return from Paris late in 1976, an event that marked the beginning of the revival of the bop style in the United States.

Shaw, however, began to feel hemmed in by this style, and from mid-1977 onward he worked as the sole leader of small groups still oriented toward bop but that also incorporated the comparatively static accompanimental patterns of modal jazz and some of the harmonic and expressive freedom of free jazz. In 1977 he also made his farthest venture into free jazz on several tracks of his album *The Iron Men*, recorded by ad-hoc small groups featuring saxophonists Anthony Braxton and Arthur Blythe, pianist Richard Muhal Abrams, and bassist Cecil McBee. Also in 1977 Shaw's manager Maxine Gregg secured a Columbia recording contract, a consequence of his well-publicized work with Gordon and of the support and encouragement of Miles Davis. Shaw and Gregg married, probably that same year; they had one child. Among Shaw's regular sidemen during this period were saxophonist Carter Jefferson, Gumbs, bassist Stafford James, and Lewis, all heard on his albums *Rosewood* (1977), featuring Shaw's big band, and *Stepping Stones* (1978), presenting the quintet live at the Village Vanguard in New York's Greenwich Village. From 1980 to 1983 his quintet included Turré, pianists Larry Willis or Mulgrew Miller, James, and drummer Tony Reedus. Their albums include *United* (1981) and *Master of the Art* (1982), the latter recorded live at the Jazz Forum in New York with vibraphonist Hutcherson added to the quintet after a six-week European tour.

Unfortunately Shaw's personal life plunged from great promise to tragedy as he became overwhelmed by artistic dissatisfaction, the pressures of leadership, and the effort to achieve financial stability via his recordings for Columbia. As his dependency on drugs increased, he began to have trouble keeping his sidemen. Instead he toured and recorded with groups of constantly changing personnel. And yet the effect on his music was not at all obvious. Not only *Setting Standards*, from 1983, but even albums as late as *Solid* (1986) and *Imagination* (1987) find Shaw playing consistently well and offering no clues of his ongoing personal crises. His sight was deteriorating, and he was suffering from AIDS, contracted from injecting narcotics with a contaminated syringe. Finally, he began to lose his teeth, and by 1989 he could no longer play. On 27 February 1989 he fell down the stairs of a Brooklyn subway station, rolled in front of a train, and lost his left arm. He spent his last months in Bellevue Hospital in New York City. Published reports attribute his death variously to kidney disease, pneumonia, and a heart attack, any or all of which presumably were consequences of AIDS.

Like many brass players of his era, Shaw doubled on flugelhorn (particularly during the mid- to late 1970s on record), but his trumpet sound was so inherently deep and rich that he scarcely needed the flugelhorn to achieve the fuller sound that other trumpeters were seeking from this instrument. Indeed at those sessions on which his choice of instrument is not differentiated track-by-track in the album liner notes, it is not always a simple matter to decide which he is playing. Presumably on Gordon's album *Homecoming* (1976) his flugelhorn is on the ballad "'Round Midnight," where Shaw's tone seems even broader than usual. From 1977 to 1978 Shaw sometimes recorded on cornet rather than trumpet, but with the same characteristic timbral breadth and warmth; it may be heard on "The Jitterbug Waltz" from *The Iron Men* and on *Stepping Stones*.

Shaw's beautiful sound was matched by his brilliant technical control of the instrument. He could improvise rapid, precise, subtle melodies in the tradition of Clifford Brown's trumpeting, while also slotting in dissonant phrases or an impassioned brassy shout. Early in his career Shaw was often mistaken on recordings for another of Brown's disciples, Freddie Hubbard, who had taken an identical stylistic path. Later their paths diverged. Although Shaw never stooped to Hubbard's penchant for crassly commercial jazz, badly done—for which the always outspoken Shaw criticized Hubbard repeatedly in published interviews—he never achieved the brilliant originality and conceptual perfection of Hubbard's finest work.

• Informative surveys and interviews include Arnold Jay Shaw, "Woody Shaw," *Down Beat*, 24 Apr. 1975, pp. 34–35; Eugene Chadbourne, "Woody Shaw," *Coda* 144 (Jan.–Feb. 1976): 10–12; Steve Lake, "The Intimidator," *Melody Maker*, 2 Oct. 1976, p. 48; Les Tomkins, "Keeping Jazz Alive . . . Our Way: Louis Hayes and Woody Shaw," *Crescendo International* 15 (Oct. 1976): 20–22; Woody Shaw, "My Approach to the Trumpet and to Jazz," *Crescendo International* 15 (Mar. 1977): 14–15; and Chuck Berg, "Woody Shaw," *Down Beat*, 10 Aug. 1978, pp. 22–24, 49–50, 52. See also Amiri Baraka, liner notes to the album *Woody III* (issued in 1979); repr. in Amiri Baraka and Amina Baraka, *The Music: Reflections on Blues and Jazz* (1987), pp. 193–206; "Woody Shaw," *Jazz Forum* 57 (international ed. 1979): 19; Bob Rusch, "Woody Shaw: Interview," *Cadence* 7 (Jan. 1981): 12–15; and Linda R. Reitman, "Woody Shaw: Linked to a Legacy," *Down Beat*, Jan. 1983, pp. 18–21. A catalog of Shaw's recordings is in *Swing Journal* 36 (1982): 242–47; a fuller and annotated catalog of his recordings exists in electronic form on the World Wide Web, Todd Poynor, "Woody Shaw Discography" (1994). An obituary is in the *New York Times*, 12 May 1989.

BARRY KERNFELD

SHAWN, Ted (21 Oct. 1891–9 Jan. 1972), dancer, was born Edwin Meyers Shawn in Kansas City, Missouri, the son of Elmer Ellsworth Shawn, a newspaperman, and Mary Lee Booth, who was related to the Booth family of actors. As a youth, Shawn wanted to be both an actor and a preacher. He entered the University of Denver and studied for the Methodist ministry until, in his junior year, he contracted diphtheria. Experimental medication left his lower limbs temporarily paralyzed. To speed their recovery, he enrolled in a local ballet class. This conspicuous and courageous act shaped the eighteen-year-old Shawn's future. Then in 1911 he saw for the first time Ruth St. Denis, in her ballet *Egypta*, and he determined to study with her. Toward that end, he moved to Los Angeles to continue dance lessons while earning his living as a typist and an exhibition ballroom dancer. By early 1914 he managed to reach New York City, where he auditioned for St. Denis and was immediately engaged by her as a partner. The famous older artist and her neophyte companion soon discovered that they shared similar personal philosophies as well as unconventional ideals of dance. St. Denis and Shawn were married in August 1914 during their first tour together.

In 1916, they cofounded Denishawn, the school and company that inspired significant first-generation American modern dance figures such as Jack Cole, Martha Graham, Louis Horst, Doris Humphrey, Pauline Lawrence (Limón), John Martin, Barton Mumaw, Gertrude Shurr, Walter Terry, and Charles Weidman, as well as many other teachers, performers, writers, composers, and choreographers who notably influenced various fields of the new dance art in the United States.

St. Denis contributed her experience with Oriental cultures to the institution of Denishawn, while Shawn incorporated François Delsarte's theories of bodily movement into his teaching. Both he and St. Denis experimented with Music Visualization choreography, which St. Denis defined as "the scientific translation into bodily action of the rhythmic, melodic and harmonious structure of musical composition, without intending to 'interpret' it."

Shawn considered dance to be all-inclusive, basing many of his works on his study of Americana; these included his 1921 Aztec dance-drama *Xochitl*, which featured the young Martha Graham and was described by Robert Coe in his book *Dance in America* (1985) as "the century's first dance created on an American theme"; his 1924 Hopi Indian ballet *The Feather of the Dawn*; and his 1937 full-evening program *O, Libertad!* In *Credo* (private printing, c. 1970), his last published work, he expressed his deepest convictions:

I believe that dance is the oldest, noblest, and most cogent of the arts.... I believe that dance communicates man's deepest, highest, and most truly spiritual thoughts and emotions far better than words, written or spoken.... The dancer who has great depth of feeling but refuses to submit to the demands of good theatre, fails to communicate. The choreographer who achieves good theatre ... but communicates only what is thin or empty still has not achieved the true art of the dance. Only when great content and great power of communication are combined do we have the great art of the dance.

From such ideals evolved the brilliantly choreographed and staged Denishawn programs that taught American audiences to accept new dance. In just the three seasons between 1922 and 1925, St. Denis, Shawn, and their Denishawn Dancers gave 556 concerts in 193 U.S. and Canadian cities. Then, for an exceptional fifteen months in 1925–1926, they toured every major country of the Far East, the first Western modern dance company to do so. For the next five years, they resumed their annual tours of the United States. Shawn continued to supervise the many Denishawn schools that, in addition to those in Los Angeles and New York, he had set up in Boston, Dallas, Berkeley, Rochester, Wichita, Minneapolis, and elsewhere. He led summer classes at Carnegie Hall, where he also rehearsed the company for the coming season. A prolific writer of articles and books on the dance, he was a popular lecturer at clubs and colleges as well.

Although they never divorced, Shawn's personal and professional partnership with St. Denis broke up in 1931. It was then that he began his struggle for the right of men to be respected as serious dancers by introducing simple dance forms into the athletic courses of several all-male colleges. From among the most promising students, Shawn formed a small professional ensemble called the Men Dancers. In 1933 he set out with them by car and truck on the first of the seven tours that he led through the United States and into Canada, Cuba, and England. By the time World War II forced his group to disband, they had given more than 700 concerts for increasingly enthusiastic audiences. Shawn's crusade prepared the American public for the advent of the many distinguished dance companies headed by men—Merce Cunningham, Paul Taylor, Erick Hawkins, Alwin Nikolais, and Mark Morris, to name but a few.

In 1933 Shawn established in Becket, Massachusetts, a school, performance center, and annual dance festival named Jacob's Pillow, which was destined to become world-renowned. He helped design the first theater in the United States constructed and used only for dance (built in 1942), and there he functioned as impresario, headmaster, and director for the rest of his life.

The character of the man who was able to realize these achievements is most accurately summarized by critic John Martin in his book *America Dancing* (1936): "He was keen of wit, caustic of tongue, avid of interest, terrifically temperamental, of inexhaustible energy, tenacious, aggressive, indomitable ... obviously of the stuff to break down barriers and become the first male dancer in America to achieve a position of influence and importance." One way Shawn exerted that influence was by booking black dancers on concert programs at Jacob's Pillow in an era when they faced enormous difficulty in becoming acknowledged artists. He was the first manager regularly to present Arthur Mitchell, Carmen de Lavallade, Alvin Ailey, Pearl Primus, Geoffrey Holder, and many other African-American companies and soloists.

But he dared not at the same time openly advocate the rights of homosexuals, in which he also believed, because to have done so during that closeted period would have seriously jeopardized the recognition of male dancers for which he was struggling. Shawn and those closest to him had, therefore, to remain discreet about his relationship with Barton Mumaw, the young Denishawn pupil who became featured soloist with the Men Dancers. Their companionship sustained Shawn through fourteen of his most creative independent dance years, and then survived as an indispensable friendship for the rest of his days.

Shawn built a winter house and studio in Eustis, Florida, on property adjoining the home of Mumaw's parents, with whom he was friends. He spent the months of October to May there with the associate director of Jacob's Pillow, John Christian, preparing the next season's schedule of concerts and classes. Interrupted only by their trips abroad in search of new talent, Shawn also wrote articles and worked on his autobiography *One Thousand and One Night Stands* (1960). He produced detailed annual letters that recorded his professional activities between 1945 and 1971, mailing them out to hundreds of supporters of Jacob's Pillow. In Florida he also became an expert gardener as well as a sculptor in wood whose works were displayed in several galleries.

The king of Denmark made Shawn a knight of Dannebrog for his sponsorship at Jacob's Pillow of the Royal Danish Ballet's first American appearance. Shawn was given the Capezio and the Dance Magazine awards, and his name was inscribed on the Benefactors' Column in the main foyer of the New York Public Library, in recognition of his generous donations of memorabilia to its Dance Collection.

But toward the end of his long and fruitful life, Shawn failed to receive any of the government or corporate funds that were then beginning to be granted to dancers. Upon his death in Orlando, Florida, the *New York Times*'s front-page obituary quoted his statement, "I have been burdened all the time with the simple fight for survival" (10 Jan. 1972). Yet this was the man of whom the critic Clive Barnes could write, "There is not a modern dancer in the world today who cannot trace his pedagogical heritage to Shawn."

Shawn is called the Father of American Dance for his pioneer work as a choreographer and as a performer. As did Isadora Duncan and Ruth St. Denis, he explored free forms of movement through theatrical expression in the 250 solos, ensembles, and ballets he created between 1914 and his retirement as a dancer in 1964. His ashes are buried at Jacob's Pillow, where his legacy persists.

• The Ted Shawn Papers, along with photographs, choreographic notes, films, and other memorabilia, are in the Dance Collection of the New York Public Library for the Performing Arts. Additional collections are in the Ruth St. Denis Archives at the University of California in Los Angeles and at Jacob's Pillow, Becket, Mass. Among Shawn's published books, *The American Ballet* (1926) expresses his philosophy of, and hopes for, dance; *Gods Who Dance* (1929) details the ethnic dance cultures he experienced in the Far East, Spain, and North Africa; and *Every Little Movement* (1963) explains the theories of François Delsarte as Shawn applied them to dance.

Katherine S. Dreier, *Shawn: The Dancer* (1933), provides a beautiful study in prose and photographs of Shawn in Denishawn. Suzanne Shelton, *Divine Dancer: A Biography of Ruth St. Denis* (1981), covers the period of his life with St. Denis; and Jane Sherman and Barton Mumaw, *Barton Mumaw, Dancer: From Denishawn to Jacob's Pillow and Beyond* (1986), records aspects of his later years until his death. Sherman, *Denishawn: The Enduring Influence* (1983), emphasizes Shawn's religious choreography and contains a bibliography; Sherman, *Soaring* (1976), reports on the Denishawn tour of Asia; and Sherman, *The Drama of Denishawn Dance* (1979), contains complete descriptions of twenty-eight dances that Shawn choreographed from 1915 to 1926.

JANE SHERMAN

SHAWN, William (31 Aug. 1907–8 Dec. 1992), editor, was born in Chicago, Illinois, the son of Benjamin W. Chon and Anna Bransky. His father ran the Jack Knife Shop, a successful cutlery store, and the family was well-to-do. Interested in becoming a writer, Shawn changed his name from Chon early in his career because he thought the new name sounded more writerly and was less likely to be mistaken for an Asian name. Shawn's formal education ended with two years at the University of Michigan (1925–1927), after which he dropped out and began his career in journalism. In 1928 Shawn married Cecille Lyon, a feature writer (later editor) for the *Chicago Daily News*. They had three children, including Wallace Shawn, the playwright and actor.

In 1928 Shawn worked for a news service, the Las Vegas (New Mexico) Optic; he then moved back to Chicago and in 1929 became midwest editor of a photo service, International Illustrated News. When the Chicago office closed, Shawn and his wife went to Europe. They stayed there the better part of a year, and Shawn played piano in Paris nightclubs. Upon their return, Shawn freelanced for Chicago papers and published short fiction in the Sunday supplements under various pseudonyms.

Shawn was an avid reader of the *New Yorker* from its early years, and in 1932 he became a freelance reporter for the magazine's "Talk of the Town" section. Shawn's first job at the magazine was to generate information for stories in this section and give the notes to E. B. White, James Thurber, or whoever was handling them at the time; he was hired for the "Talk" staff in 1933. Shawn's greatest talent was generating ideas, not reporting or writing: the only signed piece he published in the magazine in fifty-five years was a short story, "The Catastrophe," in 1936.

In 1935 the *New Yorker*'s editor, Harold Ross, gave Shawn a position compiling ideas for several nonfiction sections of the magazine; Shawn then became associate editor of the *New Yorker* until 1939, managing editor from 1939 to 1952, and editor for the next thirty-five years. For all his anonymity as a writer, Shawn was one of the greatest presences in twentieth-century American letters because of his influence as an editor on the content of one of the most influential magazines of the century. Shawn was known for his respect for writers and their craft, and his own insatiable curiosity. Notable among his accomplishments are his encouraging the single-issue publication of John Hersey's "Hiroshima," which was the only article published in the 31 August 1946 issue of the magazine. Shawn encouraged Ross to take this risk, and the resulting issue was snatched off the newsstands.

As editor, Shawn sent Hannah Arendt to Israel for the trial of Adolf Eichmann ("Eichmann in Jerusalem") and Truman Capote to Kansas to cover a murder ("In Cold Blood"). The magazine also offered readers Rachel Carson's defense of the environment and James Baldwin's confrontation of racial injustice, as well as other compelling political writing. Shawn allowed his writers to work freely to pursue their own ideas; some pieces ran to a length of fifty or sixty thousand words, while others were published long after their purchase. He disliked gory details in writing, although some were published in the magazine of necessity; what went unpublished were the particular words that Shawn asked his writers to avoid, such as "gadget," "workaholic," "tycoon," and "balding."

Shawn's dismissal from the *New Yorker* was international front-page news. He was fired by the magazine's new owner (as of 1985), S. I. Newhouse of Advance Publications, on 12 January 1987, approximately one year after he had referred to Shawn in a speech as "what the *New Yorker* itself is all about." The suddenness with which Shawn was replaced by an editor outside the magazine was regarded as scandalous. The new editor, Robert Gottlieb of the book publishing house Alfred A. Knopf, was greeted with a letter signed by 154 contributors to the *New Yorker* asking him to refuse the post. On 12 February 1987, the day before he left the magazine, Shawn wrote a letter to the staff that began, "My feelings at this perplexed moment are too strong for farewells" and included such statements as "Love has been the controlling emotion, and love is the essential word." After leaving the *New Yorker*, Shawn became an editor at Farrar, Straus & Giroux, where he remained until his death.

Shawn's courteous manner was as famous as his editing. He was notably reluctant to precede anyone through a door and was known as "Mr. Shawn" to virtually all who knew him. One exception to his formal demeanor seems to have occurred during musical evenings at his house, where he relaxed playing jazz piano. An idiosyncratic man, he ate almost the same lunch in the same place every day: orange juice, coffee with hot milk, Special K, and occasionally some toasted pound cake, in the Rose Room of the Algonquin Hotel. A man given to phobias, he disliked automatic elevators, air-conditioning, riding in airplanes, and driving over bridges.

Shawn died in his apartment in New York City. In an obituary that he wrote for a fellow editor, Shawn reflected that the editor's art is an anonymous one, and the success of an editor is reflected in the success of others. Shawn's own urge to remain anonymous cannot mask his triumph as an editor: his presence lingers in the dedications of at least forty books, including J. D. Salinger's *Franny and Zooey*, in which Salinger calls Shawn a "lover of the long shot, protector of the unprolific." With his great affection for fact, Shawn changed American journalism, a shift first evident with the *New Yorker*'s coverage of World War II and its focus on the ordinary soldier's experience. Shawn's magazine was more politically involved and intellectually stimulating than the magazine that Ross edited. The high level of accuracy and rigor of thought found in contemporary American journalism and literature can be traced in part to Shawn's editorial vigor, morals, and influence.

• Shawn's papers are in the New York Public Library's Rare Books and Manuscripts Division, which houses the *New Yorker*'s vast archival material. A thorough description of Shawn's editorial style is in Thomas Kunkel, *Genius in Disguise: Harold Ross of the New Yorker* (1995). Also see E. J. Kahn, *About the New Yorker & Me: A Sentimental Journey* (1979), and Brendan Gill, *Here at the New Yorker* (1975); the latter includes the text of some obituaries that Shawn wrote for others. For a discussion of Shawn's youth and excerpts from his early writings, as well as an analysis of his relations with the business end of the magazine, see Gigi Mahon, *The Last Days of the New Yorker* (1988). A particularly controversial article about Shawn that engaged writers such as J. D. Salinger, E. B. White, and Ved Mehta in Shawn's defense, is Tom Wolfe, "Tiny Mummies! The True Story of the Ruler of 43rd Street's Land of the Walking Dead!" in the supplement to the *New York Herald Tribune*, 11 Apr. 1965. There are two exceptional memorials to Shawn: one is an unsigned editorial, "Comment," in the *New Yorker*, 21 Dec. 1992, pp. 4–6, and the other is "Remembering Mr. Shawn," the *New Yorker*, 28 Dec. 1992–4 Jan. 1993, pp. 134–45, composed of thoughts about the editor written by *New Yorker* writers, editors, and artists, including Jamaica Kincaid (married to Shawn's son Allen), Calvin Trillin, and John Updike. An obituary is in the *New York Times*, 9 Dec. 1992.

ELLEN FERGUSON

SHAWNEE PROPHET. *See* Tenskwatawa.

SHAWNEE WARRIOR. *See* Cheeseekau.

SHAYS, Daniel (1747?–29 Sept. 1825), revolutionary officer and leader of the eponymous "Rebellion" of 1786–1787 in western Massachusetts, was born in Hopkinton, Massachusetts, the son of Patrick Shays (or Shay or Sheas) and Margaret Dempsey. While working as a hired laborer in Brookfield he married Abigail Gilbert in July 1772. He then moved to Shutesbury where he purchased a farm shortly before the war. In 1780 he moved to Pelham, Hampshire County, where he was a middling farmer until driven from Massachusetts in the wake of the rebellion in 1787.

Shays rose through the ranks during his extended service in the Continental army from 1775 to 1780. First serving during the Lexington alarm of April 1775, Shays fought at Bunker Hill, where he was promoted to sergeant in recognition of gallant conduct. He was soon commissioned lieutenant in James M. Varnum's Rhode Island regiment and then captain in Rufus Putnam's Massachusetts regiment in January 1777; he received a commission in the Continental army at this rank in 1779. Shays distinguished himself in the American victory at Saratoga in April 1777 and in the capture of British fortifications at Stony Point, New York in July 1779. The young Marquis de Lafayette presented Shays with a ceremonial sword in recognition of his efforts at Saratoga. He later sold the Lafayette sword, perhaps because of his straitened circumstances.

In October 1780 Shays resigned his commission and returned to his farm in Pelham. He was quickly recognized as a leader in this poor upland community, serving on the Committee of Safety (1781–1782), as town warden, and as a delegate to county conventions. After the Revolution rural communities were particularly hard hit by deflation, credit contractions, and hard currency shortages, particularly when the state government sought to service its wartime debt. According to a 1784 tax valuation, Shays was slightly more prosperous than the average resident of Pelham, but he was twice taken to court in debt actions by innkeeper William Conkey. Depressed conditions throughout the western counties set the stage for popular mobilization against the courts beginning in August 1786. An angry crowd at Northampton prevented the court of common pleas from sitting on 29 August, the first in an escalating series of confrontations that led Governor James Bowdoin (1726–1790) to outlaw the movement's leaders and resulted in the death of two "Regulators" by gunfire at the Springfield arsenal on 25 January.

Shays did not take part in the march on Northampton but was drawn into the movement that would soon bear his name. Captain Shays, who had a reputation for moderation as well as military skill, kept the insurgent forces under strict control at Springfield (26 Sept.), where he was met by a roughly equal number of Hampshire militiamen under General William Shepard. After the superior court agreed to suspend its operations, both sides disbanded without incident. This fragile peace deteriorated, however, after Bowdoin and the General Court refused to meet the Regulators' demands for debt and tax relief and prepared to move vigorously to put down the resistance. Because of the persistence of economic grievances and the apparent jeopardy of Shays and their other leaders, the Regulators failed to take advantage of an amnesty act. After Shephard routed the Shaysites at Springfield, a large force under General Benjamin Lincoln (1733–1810) pursued Shays and the remnant of his supporters from Pelham, to Hadley, Hatfield, and finally Petersham where 150 insurgents were captured on 2 February. Numerous other regulators dispersed to their homes or found refuge in Vermont and New York.

Shay's Rebellion was depicted by nationalist reformers who promoted a more powerful national government as symptomatic of incipient anarchy. Just as in Massachusetts, where Shays's supposedly dictatorial ambitions were vastly exaggerated by progovernment polemicists, Shays was described by the Federalists as a would-be tyrant and despot. But Shays was a reluctant leader of a loosely organized campaign for limited goals that was suppressed with relative ease, although Shaysite exiles conducted a series of violent actions from neighboring states after the Petersham rout.

Shays himself avoided arrest by hiding in Vermont until he and his coadjutors were pardoned in June 1788. Thereafter he migrated westward to a series of new homes in New York State. During this period his first wife died and he married Rhoda Havens, the widow of a Sparta innkeeper. With the proceeds of his military pension (granted in 1818), he built his final home in Scottsburgh, New York, where he lived in modestly prosperous circumstances until his death.

• Shays left no personal papers. Numerous historians have described the rebellion, beginning with George Richards Minot's *History of the Insurrections, in Massachusetts, in the Year MDCCLXXXVI, and the Rebellion Consequent Thereon* (1788; repr. 1971). Shays's career is traced in Marion L. Starkey, *A Little Rebellion* (1955). For studies emphasizing the sociocultural and institutional settings of the rebellion see David Szatmary, *Shays' Rebellion* (1980); Martin Kaufman, ed., *Shays' Rebellion: Selected Essays* (1987); and John L. Brooke, "To the Quiet of the People: Revolutionary Settlements and Civil Unrest in Western Massachusetts, 1774–1789," *William and Mary Quarterly* 46 (July 1989): 425–62. The most recent scholarship on Shays may be found in Robert A. Gross, ed., *In Debt to Shays: The Bicentennial of an Agrarian Rebellion* (1993).

PETER S. ONUF

SHEA, John Dawson Gilmary (22 July 1824–22 Feb. 1892), historian of American Catholicism, was born in New York City, the son of James Shea, an educator, and Mary Ann Flannigan. Called by many the "father of American Catholic history," Shea was educated first at the Sisters of Charity school, then at the Columbia Grammar School, graduating in 1837. After working in business, Shea studied law and was admitted to the New York bar in 1846. That same year he became a member of the New-York Historical Society, having written several articles about Catholic martyrs in the United States.

Joining the Society of Jesus in 1848, Shea adopted the middle name Gilmary, which means servant of Mary. In preparation for ordination, Shea studied at St. John's College, Fordham University, in New York City from 1848 to 1850 and at St. Mary's College in Montreal, Canada, from 1850 to 1852. While at St. Mary's, Shea was influenced by Canadian Jesuit historian Felix Martin. Under the guidance of Martin and through a friendship with Edmund Bailey O'Callaghan, Shea continued to develop his interest in history with an emphasis on the importance of documents and sources. This heavy reliance on primary sources drove Shea's work for his entire life.

As a result of poor health, Shea left the Jesuit novitiate in 1852. In 1854 he married Sophie Savage, with whom he had two daughters, who later helped him in his work. Without the benefit of a family fortune and without an academic job, Shea pursued his historical studies while working full time at several publishing houses and then as the editor in chief for the Frank Leslie magazines *Popular Monthly*, *Chimney Corner*, and *Sunday Magazine*. Even though he could not dedicate all of his time to historical writings, Shea nonetheless was an extremely productive scholar, publishing more than 250 books and articles during his lifetime. Many of Shea's writings were designed as beginning texts and simplistic narratives for popular audiences, but Shea's scholarly work also attracted attention. Beginning in 1852 with the publication of *Discovery and Exploration of the Mississippi Valley* and continuing with *History of the Catholic Missions among the Indian Tribes of the United States, 1529–1854* (1855), Shea attracted attention as an important historian outside of Catholic circles. He was offered membership in many regional historical societies, including societies in Wisconsin, Iowa, Massachusetts, and Maryland. Shea was also the first American member of the Royal Academy of Madrid, elected in 1883 based on his biography of a Spanish cardinal. Shea's scholarly work included several essays in Justin Winsor's *Narrative and Critical History of America* (8 vols., 1884–1889), as well as editing the *Library of American Linguistics* from 1860 to 1874. He also translated (1856) and expanded and revised (1879) Henri de Courcy's *The Catholic Church in the United States*.

Shea's accomplishments did not go unrecognized by fellow Catholics. Although he was never given an academic post, in 1883 Shea was the first recipient of Laetare Medal from the University of Notre Dame, an honor bestowed on prominent American Catholics for their contributions to American society. In 1884 Shea was the primary organizer of the U.S. Catholic Historical Society, which he served as its secretary and later president. In 1890 Shea was honored with a special medal from Georgetown University at its centennial.

Shea told the story of the Catholic church in America from the perspective of the bishops and hierarchy, a style reflected in his crowning achievement, *History of* the Catholic Church in the United States (4 vols., 1886–1892). According to Shea, the true church resided in the hierarchy that found its center in Rome. In accordance with these ideas, Shea's history centered on the activities of the bishops and was based on sources gathered from them. Primary sources were the mainstay of Shea's writing. However, the objective and "scientific" approach he helped to pioneer was implemented within distinct theological assumptions, including a strong belief that the Catholic church was the only way toward salvation and that Protestantism was therefore inherently degenerative.

Shea, however, wrote for both Catholic and non-Catholic audiences. Writing for Catholics, Shea sought to increase Catholic pride and to counter the defeatism brought on by Protestant prejudice. He emphasized the significant role that Catholics played in the discovery, exploration, and founding of America, supporting Catholic claims to have always been true Americans and essential contributors to American success. For non-Catholics, Shea wrote to affirm the American loyalties of Catholic citizens and counter the claims of nativism. Shea also detailed the history of this anti-Catholic prejudice, contrasting it with his view of Catholicism's role in building the foundations of American religious liberty. Beginning with George Calvert, Lord Baltimore, Shea traced the origins of religious liberty in America.

Through his scientific use of sources for historical research and emphasis on patriotism and religious liberty in American Catholicism, Shea made a lasting impact on Catholic identity in America. His magnum opus, *History of the Catholic Church in the United States*, finished just before his death, sealed his position as the "father of American Catholic history." Shea died in Elizabeth, New Jersey.

• The most thorough biography on Shea is Peter Guilday, *John Gilmary Shea: Father of American Catholic History, 1824–1892* (1926), which contains a complete bibliography of Shea's published writings. Also helpful is J. Douglas Thomas, "A Century of American Catholic History," *U.S. Catholic Historian* 6 (1987): 25–49. To put Shea in the context of his contemporaries see Henry Warner Bowden, *Church History in the Age of Science: Historiographical Patterns in the United States, 1876–1918* (1971).

RANDY HEINIG

SHEAN, Al (12 May 1868–12 Aug. 1949), comic actor, was born Albert Schonberg in Dornurm, Germany, the son of Louis Schonberg, a magician and comic ventriloquist, and Fanny (maiden name unknown), a harpist. The Schonberg family immigrated to the United States in 1876. Educated in New York City public schools, he ushered and pressed pants before organizing in 1884 a vaudeville act called the Manhattan Comedy Four, at which time he changed his name to "Shean." In 1891 he married Johanna Davidson; they had one child.

Called by Douglas Gilbert "one of the most popular four-acts of the period," Shean's group was noted for "advanced songs and smart, robust comedy." They helped popularize songs such as "After the Ball" and specialized in a "husky, sensible knockabout realization of life." In 1900 Shean formed a partnership with a straight man, Charles Warren; they played a ragtag skit, "Quo Vadis Upside Down," for ten years.

Shean's success has been called part of a master plan devised by his sister Minnie, who served as his publicist, booking agent, and manager; she was also the mother of the five Marx Brothers. Groucho and Gummo Marx made their earliest appearances in versions of "Quo Vadis Upside Down," and Shean wrote robust sketches such as "Fun in Hi Skool" (1912) and "Home Again" (1914) for all the young Marxes. He advised Harpo to play in pantomime, an idea Harpo at first rejected. In 1910 Shean met the veteran straight man Edward F. Gallagher in Chicago, and the two formed a partnership, at first in *The Big Banner* on the Keith-Albee Eastern Vaudeville Wheel.

Gallagher and Shean made their Broadway book musical debut in *The Rose Maid* (1912). After the team's first breakup in 1914 Shean varied his career with further appearances in musical comedy; these included *Princess Pat* (1915) and *Flo Flo* (1917). In these and subsequent shows, Shean usually played comic Germanic characters named Schike, Schmalz, Moskowitz, Moser, Zwimmer, or Lessing. But by 1920 Shean had been out of work for a year and a half. Reunited that year through Minnie Marx's best efforts, Gallagher and Shean became the stage sensation of their era. They created "Mr. Gallagher and Mr. Shean in Egypt," a song-sketch that soon joined the *Ziegfeld Follies of 1922* for a 67-week run. It elevated their salaries to $2,500 weekly and created an environment within which Shean would relax for the rest of his life. Shean, who had no previous musical credits, claimed to have written the simple but catchy music for "Oh! Mr. Gallagher and Mr. Shean." After an unsuccessful lawsuit brought against the partners by Brian Foy (who claimed he had written the entire thing), Shean held a half interest in the most successful song in the land.

In "Mr. Gallagher and Mr. Shean in Egypt," Shean was the short one with a funny walk, wearing a frock coat, a fez perched on his head, his hands always folded behind him. Gallagher, nominally "straight man" to Shean's capering, mugging, and funny pronunciations, was tall, boatered, and dapper. It was Shean who opened, "Oh! Mister Gallagher . . . Oh! Mister Gallagher!" and Gallagher who replied, "Hello, what's on your mind this morning, Mister Shean?"

Gallagher moderately thoughtful and Shean flapping-armed agitated, they commented on events of the day in nonsense doggerel, parodying the ignorant certainties that pass for everyday conversation and surprising audiences by letting Gallagher have the apparent punch—"Cost of living went so high / That it's cheaper now to die." Yet the real payoff, no matter how bizarre the previous nine or ten lines, was the confident refrain "Positively, Mr. Gallagher?" "Absolutely, Mr. Shean." And on they went to even more surreal verses. Gallagher and Shean's act was immediately burlesqued and parodied. Shean later said that thousands of additional verses were sent to the partners, "including 56 by one professor of language," but they all lacked the necessary "punch line."

"Positively, Mr. Gallagher / Absolutely, Mr. Shean" remained a well-known catchphrase for decades, and Shean's peculiar, swingy pronunciation of Gallagher's name—more like "Gellikhah!"—was equally well known. The song itself, with further new lyrics, was recorded by Bing Crosby and Johnny Mercer in 1939. After *The Greenwich Village Follies* (1923–1924) the Gallagher-Shean partnership broke up for good. In 1926 Shean appeared in the Ziegfeld–Rodgers and Hart musical *Betsy*. In 1928 Shean sued Gallagher, in part claiming that Gallagher had withheld Shean's share of one year's royalties. By 1929, the year of Gallagher's death, Shean was back in vaudeville, using their song in a new act called "Business is Business."

In 1930 Shean appeared on Broadway in *The Prince of Pilsen* and *Light Wines and Beer*. In the same year, with "Chills and Fever," he began to appear in films, at first as an old-time entertainer but eventually perfecting a kindly, avuncular persona. Shean played in many films, including *San Francisco* (1936), *Fifty-second Street* (1937), and *The Great Waltz* (1938). As himself, he was in *Ziegfeld Girl* (1941) with Charles Winninger as Gallagher; in 1944 Shean again played himself, and Jack Kenney was Gallagher, in *Atlantic City*. During these years Shean presented the familiar act on the radio with various "Gallaghers" so effectively that many listeners believed Gallagher was still alive. Onstage, Shean occasionally performed the sketch solo, switching from the fez to the boater and back again.

Shean's best notices in noncomic roles came in the 1932 Jerome Kern musical *Music In the Air*, for which Brooks Atkinson credited him with knowing "how to touch the heart gently," and *Father Malachy's Miracle* (1937). Shean claimed that Roman Catholic priests had told him his "Father" was a better one than theirs. Other stage credits included *The Music Master* (1938), *Popsy* (1941), *Meet a Body* (1944), and *Windy City* (1946). Shean died in his suite at the Ansonia Hotel in New York City.

• An envelope of clippings regarding Gallagher and Shean is listed in the Robinson Locke Collection at the New York Public Library for the Performing Arts, Lincoln Center. He is partially re-created in works such as Joe Adamson, *Groucho, Harpo, Chico, and Sometimes Zeppo* (1973), and Harpo Marx with Rowland Barber, *Harpo Speaks!* (1961). Shean's career before Gallagher is discussed in Douglas Gilbert, *American Vaudeville* (1940). Litigations involving Gallagher and Shean are reported in contemporary issues of the *New York Times*.

JAMES ROSS MOORE

SHEARER, Norma (11 Aug. 1902–12 June 1983), film actress, was born Edith Norma Shearer in Montreal, Quebec, Canada, the daughter of Andrew Shearer, a business owner, and Edith Fisher. When Shearer was in her teens the comfortable life that she and her two siblings had enjoyed crumbled along with the fortunes of their father's lumber and contracting business. Though her mother had hoped that Shearer might become a concert pianist, the family's lack of money made an acting career more practical.

In 1920 Shearer's piano was sold, and the proceeds were used to send Shearer, her sister Athole, and their mother to New York. While waiting for an audience with showman Florenz Ziegfeld, Shearer worked as a background extra in such films as *The Flapper* and *Way Down East* and played a supporting role in the B movie *The Stealers*. When she finally met Ziegfeld, he told her she wasn't attractive enough to be a star. The verdict was seconded by director D. W. Griffith, who said her eyes wouldn't photograph well. Shearer soon found work as an advertising model and was featured on a large Columbus Circle billboard as Springfield Tires' Miss Lotta Miles. During 1922 and 1923 she appeared in six low-budget films. Her performance in one, *Channing of the Northwest* (1922), led to a contract with Metro Goldwyn Mayer (MGM), arranged by that studio's "boy wonder" vice president, Irving Thalberg.

By 1927 Shearer had become a popular star of mostly forgettable films, with occasional good roles in *He Who Gets Slapped* (1924), *Lady of the Night* (1925), and *The Student Prince* (1927). In late 1927 Shearer married Thalberg, prompting Joan Crawford, her ambitious studio rival, to make the famous complaint, "What chance do I have now? Norma sleeps with the boss!" In fact, marriage to Thalberg did not immediately guarantee Shearer good parts, but it upgraded her social standing. Thalberg, whose film judgment was so unerring that he was nicknamed the Oracle, produced such landmark films as *The Crowd* and *Grand Hotel* and made stars out of Greta Garbo and Jean Harlow. He later would be the inspiration for Monroe Starr in F. Scott Fitzgerald's unfinished novel, *The Last Tycoon*. With Thalberg, Shearer became a regular guest of Mary Pickford and Douglas Fairbanks, Sr., at Pickfair and of William Randolph Hearst and Marion Davies at Hearst Castle. The couple were photographed together for *Vanity Fair*, and invitations to gatherings at their Santa Monica beach house were prized. Fitzgerald incorporated the events of one of their tea parties into his short story, "Crazy Sunday."

Shearer's people skills were instrumental in elevating her career. She developed a knack for spotting undiscovered talent and for employing innovative artists and techniques, a practice that built careers and improved her own films in the bargain. She was responsible for the Hollywood career of her brother Douglas, who eventually won twelve Academy Awards for achievement in sound. In 1928 an inexperienced Douglas Shearer became MGM's "one-man sound department," and in 1929 the studio released its first all-talking drama, *The Trial of Mary Dugan*, starring Norma Shearer. Playing a showgirl accused of murdering her rich lover, Shearer struck a *Los Angeles Times* reviewer as "a definitely compelling actress of greater individuality than she has ever revealed in silent pictures." She followed this film with *The Last of Mrs. Cheyney* (1929), in which she played a jewel thief tripped up by love, and *Their Own Desire* (1930), which earned her an Oscar nomination. In *The Divorcée* (1930), for which she took home an Academy Award, Shearer excelled in playing the elegant, sexually adventurous heroine, though even her husband had resisted giving her the role.

Only after she had produced glamour shots taken by portrait photographer George Hurrell (then an unknown) did Thalberg see her possibilities as a femme fatale. She portrayed more worldly women in *Strangers May Kiss* and *A Free Soul*, which teamed her with newcomer Clark Gable and brought her another Oscar nomination. Shearer's popularity soared, as she balanced her spicy onscreen image with her offscreen role as wife and mother (Irving, Jr., was born in 1930, and daughter Katharine, in 1934). Thalberg sought to broaden and then refine his wife's screen image. She was tagged "Queen of the Lot," and from 1931 on she performed almost exclusively in films drawn from Broadway plays, playing roles originated by Gertrude Lawrence, Katharine Cornell, and Lynn Fontanne. *Private Lives* (1931), based on the Noël Coward comedy, was mildly successful; Eugene O'Neill's *Strange Interlude* (1932), costarring Clark Gable, lost money. Shearer rebounded with the hit *Smilin' Through* (1932), a sentimental period piece in which she played a double role.

In 1932 Thalberg, a workaholic whose health had always been poor, suffered his second heart attack. While he was recuperating in Europe, MGM was reorganized, and Thalberg's position as head of production was eliminated. He returned to the studio as the leader of an independent production unit. The unit's first film, *Riptide* (1934), starring Shearer, was a disappointing if stylish melodrama. *The Barretts of Wimpole Street* (1934), was better, and Shearer's portrayal of poet Elizabeth Barrett Browning brought her another Oscar nomination. Based on the performance, Thalberg judged her ready for classics and mounted an elaborate *Romeo and Juliet* for her. Starring 34-year-old Shearer and a 44-year-old Leslie Howard as Shakespeare's teenaged lovers, the film received respectful but not enthusiastic reviews and ultimately lost money.

Two weeks after the film premiered in Los Angeles, Thalberg died of pneumonia, and soon after, Louis B. Mayer and MGM corporate secretary J. Robert Rubin claimed his substantial profit participation as their own. Shearer fought the takeover and captured public sympathy, which forced the two men to back down. The Thalberg estate was granted 6 percent of continuing profits from MGM films produced between April 1924 and December 1938. Television rights later made this deal especially profitable. Not long after, Shearer signed her own contract with MGM. Her first film under the new contract was *Marie Antoinette*, which Thalberg had developed for her. Her performance as the doomed French queen is widely thought to be one of her best, and it provided Shearer with her final Oscar nomination. In *Idiot's Delight* (1939), based on Robert Sherwood's Pulitzer Prize–winning play, Shearer played an ex-vaudevillian masquerading as a Russian countess. In 1939 she headed an all-star cast, which included longtime rival Joan Crawford, in George Cukor's *The Women*. After *The Women*, Shearer's career began to slide. She turned down the leads in *Gone with the Wind*, *Pride and Prejudice*, and *Mrs. Miniver*, choosing instead a supporting role in *Escape* and light comedic parts in *We Were Dancing* and *Her Cardboard Lover*. In 1942 she married ski instructor Martin Arrouge.

Though she never made another film, Shearer retained power within Hollywood by way of her MGM stock and reputation. She discovered actress Janet Leigh, whose father clerked at a ski lodge Shearer frequented, and actor-producer Robert Evans, whom she selected to play Thalberg in *Man of a Thousand Faces*. In later years Shearer's sight failed, and she moved to the Motion Picture Country Hospital in Woodland Hills, California, where she died.

Shearer's work, largely forgotten or discounted by critics for many years, has enjoyed something of a revival in film festivals and on specialty cable movie channels. "At her best," wrote critic Mick La Salle in 1994, "in films such as *Strangers May Kiss*, *The Divorcée*, *The Barretts of Wimpole Street* and a good half dozen others—Shearer conveys a depth of emotion no film actress of her time surpassed."

• Main sources include Gavin Lambert, *Norma Shearer: A Life* (1990), and to a lesser extent, Lawrence Quirk, *Norma: The Story of Norma Shearer* (1988). Other sources include Roland Flamini, *Thalberg: The Last Tycoon and the World of MGM* (1994), and Bob Thomas, *Thalberg: Life and Legend* (1969). Mick La Salle's appreciation of Shearer is in the *San Francisco Chronicle*, 5 Sept. 1994. An obituary is in the *New York Times*, 14 June 1983.

DIANA MOORE

SHECUT, John Linnaeus Edward Whitridge (4 Dec. 1770–1 June 1836), botanist, medical practitioner, and author, was born in Beaufort, South Carolina, the son of Abraham Shecut and Marie Barbary. His Huguenot forebears had left France and settled in Switzerland, but his parents had come to America about 1768 and settled in Beaufort. They moved to Charleston before Shecut was ten years old. At sixteen he studied medicine under David Ramsay, a pupil of Benjamin Rush. No record of Shecut's having attended medical classes at the University of Pennsylvania has been found, but he may have been a private pupil, as references to a Philadelphia residence between 1786 and 1790 recur. He then returned to Charleston and began his practice. By his first marriage, to Sarah Cannon of Edisto Island in 1792, he had four children. By his second marriage, to Susanna Ballard of Georgetown, South Carolina, in 1805, he had five children. His predilection for unusual names is reflected in those given to his two sons, Abraham Homespun and Linnaeus Americanus.

Volume 1 of Shecut's planned two-volume *Flora Carolinaeensis* was published in 1806. He reported that it took twenty months to produce and cost him more than $1,800 to publish. The subtitle, "Being a collection or compilation of the various plants hitherto discovered," belies the presumptuous nature of its 579 pages and the vague botanical or geographic limits he set. Benjamin Smith Barton is alleged to have threatened Shecut with prosecution for plagiarizing from his *Elements of Botany* (1803). Thomas Jefferson cordially thanked Shecut for his gift of the book, pleased perhaps for two reasons, because Shecut's Linnaean classification supported Jefferson's own view on method of classification and because it was written in layman's language.

In 1808 Shecut undertook a business venture, founding the South Carolina Homespun Company, perhaps the earliest cotton mill in the state. The company was sold at a loss four years later. Meanwhile he collected subscriptions for the second volume of his projected *Flora*. Acceptance of his work was justifiably guarded. The physician-botanist William Baldwin, who met Shecut in Charleston in December 1811, reported to Reverend Henry Muhlenberg, a botanist in Lancaster, Pennsylvania, that Shecut had "at least some zeal for Botany." In reply, evidently to a remark of the prominent Charleston botanist, Stephen Elliott, Muhlenberg on 14 February 1812 dismissed Shecut as "no botanist."

The founding of the Antiquarian Society of Charleston, later the Literary and Philosophical Society, by Shecut and associates in 1813, with its incorporation the following year, was the forerunner of the Charleston Museum, an early center for natural history in the United States. The museum survived the Civil War and has continued to flourish.

Shecut hoped to publish "Elements of Medicine" but was "repelled," he said, by the University of Pennsylvania. John Torrey and David Hosack, botanists in New York City, also failed to support this venture, although Shecut wrote Torrey on 8 October 1816 from Charleston that he had more than 230 subscribers for the book in Charleston alone. On 24 December 1817 he wrote physician-naturalist Samuel Latham Mitchill in New York seeking unsuccessfully an honorary M.D. degree. Meanwhile he was using electricity in his practice to stimulate circulation in atrophied or paralyzed limbs. Although his use of an electric machine was announced in his *Medical and Philosophical Essays* (1819), historians have disregarded Shecut's efforts to revive the use of electricity in treatment. (Benjamin Franklin had experimented in 1757 with the use of electricity to stimulate muscular activity with patients suffering from paralysis.) Believing that yellow fever was related to the reduction of "electric fluid" in the air, Shecut rejected both bleeding and mercury for treating that illness.

By 1826 he remarked to Mitchill that he was suffering "neglect and poverty." He wrote two Indian romances, neither published in his lifetime, *Ish-noo-ju-lutche; or, The Eagle of the Mohawks* (2 vols., 1841), which recalls in a nostalgic vein the eighteenth-century naturalist Cadwallader Colden, a correspondent of Linnaeus; and its sequel, *The Scout; or, The Fast of St. Nicholas* (1844). His interests not satisfied by science, medicine, or literature, Shecut also dabbled in theology. He is presumed to have died in Charleston. "This colorful and energetic practitioner" was a "rather erratic character," in the view of medical historian Joseph I. Waring. Whether deserved or not, Shecut's reputation as a botanist did not long survive him. When William Darlington wrote his sixteen-page "Progress of Botany in North America" (1849), he did not mention Shecut.

• Scattered correspondence by Shecut is in the Thomas Jefferson letters (166, Manuscript Division) in the Library of Congress; the Henry Muhlenberg correspondence in the Historical Society of Pennsylvania; the John Torrey correspondence at the New York Botanical Garden; and the Simon Gratz Collection (Scientists) at the Historical Society of Pennsylvania. The principal source on Shecut is Joseph I. Waring, *History of Medicine in South Carolina, 1670–1825* (1964). For Shecut's role in the Charleston Botanic Society and Garden, founded in 1805, see his *Medical and Philosophical Essays* (1819), pp. 44–47, and U. P. Hedrick, *History of Horticulture in America* (1950), pp. 424–25. Evidently Shecut's aborted *Flora* aimed to inform physicians and visitors to the garden, but without "a practical botanist," according to William Baldwin, its future was in doubt (William Darlington, *Reliquiae Baldwinianae* [1843; facsimile, 1969], pp. 54–55). Various botanical details are provided in Frans A. Stafleu and Richard S. Cowan, *Taxonomic Literature*, vol. 5 (1985), p. 557. The larger place of Shecut and Charleston in the "Growth of Learned and Scientific Societies in the Southeastern United States to 1860" is noticed by Joseph Ewan in Alexandra Oleson and Sanborn C. Brown, eds., *Pursuit of Knowledge in the Early American Republic* (1976), pp. 208–18, especially p. 212. *Shecutia* was proposed by Julius Arthur Nieuwland (*American Midland Naturalist* 4 [1916]: 379) as a renaming of the fungus genus *Libertiella* Speg. & Roem.

Shecut, who identified himself as "Practitioner of Physic," also published *An Essay on the Prevailing, or Yellow Fever, of 1817; Together with Preliminary Observations, and an Enquiry into the Causes Which Produced It* (1826), *Elements of Natural Philosophy* (1826), and *A New Theory of the Earth (1826)*. A complete bibliography of his diverse writings has yet to be published, but Sabin's *Dictionary* is useful.

JOSEPH EWAN

SHEDD, John Graves (20 July 1850–22 Oct. 1926), retail merchant, was born near Alstead, New Hampshire, the son of William Shedd and Abigail Wallace, farmers. The youngest of eight children, Shedd completed high school in 1867 and went to work in a fruit store in Bellows Falls, Vermont. Three years later he moved to Rutland, Vermont, where he also worked as a store clerk. In 1872, the year after the Chicago Fire, he traveled to Chicago and landed a job as a stock boy for Field, Leiter, & Company, then a small retail outlet, after a brief but impressive interview with the store's founder, Marshall Field. Shedd advanced quickly and became a sales associate in less than a year in the men's linen department, where he made an important discovery that caught Field's eye. Shedd noticed that odd sizes of gloves, collars, and stockings seemed to accumulate rapidly on counters while more common sizes sold very quickly, so he suggested a scientific way of buying. Inventory purchases should be planned on how much of a particular size sold over a period of time, he suggested, rather than on a buyer's whim. Field soon adopted this policy for his whole store, and Shedd earned a promotion and a raise. Shedd loved to collect proverbs and maxims. His favorite was "The man who is continuously at work is the man who is happy and continuously successful." He followed this advice diligently and by 1893 had become a full partner in Chicago's largest and most elegant department store, which had been renamed Marshall Field and Company in 1878. While working his way up the ladder, in 1878 he had married Mary Roenna Porter of Walpole, New Hampshire, and they had two children.

An austere, hardworking executive, whom Field called "the greatest merchant in the United States," Shedd introduced several important innovations in merchandising, including the "factory system" under which Field's bought goods made exclusively for it at various factories throughout the world. The retail company owned cotton mills in North Carolina, lace factories in Illinois, a towel factory in Virginia, and rug and carpet factories in China and the Philippines. Everything sold at Field's had to meet rigid standards that Shedd established. He argued that independent companies and brands never willingly met these precise specifications; he believed that unless Field's produced its own quality goods wholesalers and manufacturers would fill the store with shoddy merchandise that would damage the store's image. Inferior products would not only ruin Field's reputation but would also set a bad example for other stores, Shedd explained, warning his buyers during one meeting that "a little poison will soon permeate the whole system." The best way to keep customers coming back was to ensure that they always got what they wanted and that everything Field's sold was the best available even if it cost more. Shedd wanted upper-income shoppers, and he realized that they would be willing and able to pay higher prices for their merchandise as long as they received good service and could easily return items with no questions asked.

After Field died in 1906, Shedd became company president and oversaw the opening of a large new store on State Street in 1907, "the world's largest store," as it was dubbed. "Believe in yourself," he told his assistants, "then you are never timorous." Shedd maintained an active interest in local politics and was a Republican. He also contributed his time and money to the Young Men's Christian Association. A Temperance man and a prohibitionist, he donated money to the Anti–Saloon League and would not allow a drop of liquor to be sold by Field's. He hated unions and forbade his employees to organize or even to join one. He assured that Field's never employed children under sixteen, an unusual move for a Chicago businessman in an age when child labor was then just beginning to be viewed as a problem. In place of a union he established a welfare department for his employees, where people with marriage or economic problems could seek aid, and he encouraged his sales staff to join the company chorus, which gave seasonal concerts. Shedd stepped down as president in 1923 and took the less active role of chairman of the board, which he retained until his death. In his last years he collected art and donated several paintings to Chicago's Art Institute. Shedd is most well known, however, for establishing a $3 million trust fund to build the public aquarium on Chicago's lakefront that bears his name. He died in Chicago.

Shedd contributed several significant ideas to modern merchandising and made his store into a virtual museum of modern culture. His commitment to selling only the highest-quality goods and to providing extraordinary service to customers made Marshall Field's the most successful retail store in Chicago. His notion of private-label merchandise manufactured to exacting standards was soon emulated by other retailers throughout the United States.

• No collection of Shedd's papers exists. The best account of Shedd's career is in Herman Kogan and Lloyd Wendt, "*Give the Lady What She Wants*": *The Story of Marshall Field & Company* (1952). A more formal history of Field's and its merchandising innovations that gives Shedd much credit for making Field's into a great store is Robert W. Twyman, *History of Marshall Field & Company, 1852–1906* (1954). An obituary is in the *Chicago Tribune*, 23 Oct. 1926.

LESLIE V. TISCHAUSER

SHEDD, William Greenough Thayer (21 June 1820–17 Nov. 1894), theologian, was born in Acton, Massachusetts, the son of Marshall Shedd, a Congregational pastor, and Eliza Thayer, daughter of a wealthy Boston merchant. After graduating from the University of Vermont in 1839, he taught for a year in New York City and resolved to enter the ministry. He studied at Andover Theological Seminary, and following graduation in 1843 he served for two years as pastor of the Congregational church in Brandon, Vermont. He had been influenced in college by philosopher James Marsh, absorbing his teacher's concern to balance emotion and reason in religion as well as his interests in Romanticism, the Cambridge Platonists, and Samuel Taylor Coleridge. He was called back to the university as professor of English literature in 1845. He was married at that time to Ann Myers of Whitehall, New York; four children were born of the union.

Shedd's extensive literary knowledge, broadened in his seven years at the University of Vermont, was displayed in many of his later books, essays, and sermons, notably in his seven-volume edition of the works of Coleridge (1853). Andover seminary called him back to teach sacred rhetoric, 1852–1854; then he became professor of church history at the Presbyterian seminary at Auburn, New York, where he served for eight years. He returned briefly to pastoral duties at Brick Presbyterian Church in New York City in 1862 and the next year was named professor of Bible at nearby Union Theological Seminary, becoming the first Baldwin Professor of Sacred Literature two years later. He followed strictly the historico-philological method of his Andover teacher Moses Stuart, in which the precise meaning of the text was sought in its original setting, making use of new materials from philology and textual criticism.

In 1874 he was transferred to the Roosevelt Professorship of Systematic Theology, and it was in this role that he is especially remembered. He was honored for his sincerity, firm convictions, and adherence to truth as he saw it. As a systematician he was steeped in the patristic, medieval, and reformation periods and was especially influenced by Augustine and Calvin. His crowning work was *Dogmatic Theology* (3 vols., 1888–1894). As a Presbyterian he became a defender of the Old School position that the whole Bible was inspired and inerrant, which put him in tension with Union's New School background and its acceptance of what came to be called the higher criticism, a method of study that deals with matters of authorship, dates of writing, and original meanings of the biblical books, using approaches developed by archaeology, literary criticism, and the history of religion, among others. Though Union Seminary backed Charles A. Briggs, the leading biblical scholar of the New School, during the trials that led to his suspension from the Presbyterian ministry in 1893, Shedd did not; the two colleagues criticized each other's views publicly. Shedd was given emeritus status in 1890 but taught for three more years while his successor was being sought, until illness made it impossible for him to continue. He died in New York City.

Shedd's writings were direct, logical, and lucid; for him theology was a science, understood in Baconian terms, developed from the philosophy of Francis Bacon into the science-oriented empirical and inductive methods of Enlightenment thought as interpreted by Scottish commonsense realism. His other well known works include *History of Christian Doctrine* (1863), *Literary Essays* (1878), and *Orthodoxy and Heterodoxy* (1893). His later teaching showed an increasing conservatism. Originally from the Old School branch of his communion before the reunion of 1869–1870, Shedd increasingly sided with that tradition as developed at Princeton Seminary under the teachings of Charles Hodge and Benjamin B. Warfield, and he rejected the higher criticism of the Bible. Some of his works, in print more than a century after their publication, have been used particularly by fundamentalists and conservative evangelicals. A versatile, lucid, prolific scholar, teacher, and writer, Shedd moved away from some of his earlier literary and philosophical interests as he staunchly defended orthodox Calvinism in his later work.

• Shedd's other works include an edition of Augustine's *Confessions* (1877), *Discourses and Essays* (1856), *Lectures upon the Philosophy of History* (1856), *Sermons to the Natural Man* (1871), *Commentary on Paul's Epistle to the Romans* (1879), *Sermons to the Spiritual Man* (1884), and *Doctrine of Endless Punishment* (1885). A biographical sketch is in George L. Prentiss, *The Union Theological Seminary in the City of New York: . . . Another Decade of Its History* (1899). See also Cushing Strout, "Faith and History: The Mind of William G. T. Shedd," *Journal of the History of Ideas* 15 (1954): 153–62, and Robert T. Handy, *A History of Union Theological Seminary in New York* (1987). For the context of Shedd's opposition to Briggs, see Lefferts A. Loetscher, *The Broadening Church: A Study of Theological Issues in the Presbyterian Church since 1869* (1954). An obituary is in the *New York Tribune*, 18 Nov. 1894.

ROBERT T. HANDY

SHEED, Francis Joseph (20 Mar. 1897–20 Nov. 1981), Catholic street preacher and book publisher, was born in Sydney, Australia, the son of John Sheed, a draftsman, and Mary Maloney. Sheed's family background prepared him for a lifetime of religious controversy. His father's family were Scottish Presbyterians with a bitter animus against Roman Catholicism, while his father was a Marxist as well as a violently abusive alcoholic. His Irish mother, however, remained a devout Catholic all of her life and insisted that her son be baptized in the Roman church. For some inexplicable reason, his father insisted that the son attend Methodist Sunday school. This gave Frank a lifelong love for Wesleyan hymns and a very Protestant attraction to the person of Jesus. At the same time, it seems to have confirmed his Catholicism by driving it underground and giving it a whiff of martyrdom.

His father also insisted that Frank not begin school until age eight. Thereafter, he advanced swiftly through public elementary and high school and won a scholarship to Sydney University, where he earned a degree in literature in 1918. He completed two years of a four-year law course at Sydney University, then decided to travel to England and Ireland in 1920.

While in London he encountered the Catholic Evidence Guild, a group of street preachers founded in 1919, and was attracted to their work and to one of their leaders, Maisie (Mary Josephine) Ward. Throwing himself into soapbox oratory, he worked for four years as a volunteer for the Catholic Evidence Guild, supporting himself by working for another society that published Catholic pamphlets and tracts.

Street preaching became Frank Sheed's school of theology. He liked the instant feedback from a crowd, which simply walked away if he failed to interest them. He taught orthodox Catholicism and did not shy away from difficult or abstract ideas. Indeed, he found that street crowds were fascinated by the doctrine of the Holy Trinity. He also learned practical rules of ecumenism from this work: "that we must not attack other religions, but must find out what they meant to those who held them. . . . One must never talk for victory. . . . If you talk for victory, sooner or later you will cheat" (*The Church and I*, pp. 55 and 64).

In 1924 Frank Sheed was twenty-seven years old, in love with Maisie Ward, but without any money or a career, so he returned to Australia, by way of a lecture tour in the United States, and finished the rest of his law studies in one year. He earned a law degree from Sydney University in 1926, but he never practiced. Instead, he returned to England, married Maisie Ward on 27 April 1926, and, with financial help from her family, began a religious publishing house named Sheed & Ward.

Maisie Ward came from an upper-class English family that had converted to Roman Catholicism during the Oxford Movement. This was a "high church" movement within Anglicanism that produced much brilliant scholarship and led many of its adherents to convert to Rome. Her father was editor of the *Dublin Review* and wrote biographies of prominent Catholics; her mother wrote novels with a Catholic slant. Maisie's brother Leo once remarked, "Religion was simply what Wards did." Maisie's work as a writer and lecturer complemented that of her husband for the next fifty years. Frank's interests were more purely theological: hers tended more toward social action. Both, however, were powerful speakers and effective writers. Their son, the novelist Wilfrid Sheed, later described their work as "a Siamese twin of a vocation that neither could have pursued solo" (*Frank and Maisie,* p. 60).

Their publishing firm became the center of what was called the Catholic intellectual revival of the 1920s and 1930s. Catholicism in England had been an underground, defensive church since the time of the Reformation; but in the twentieth century, brilliant converts to Catholicism, such as G. K. Chesterton and Ronald Knox, gave it new intellectual respectability. Sheed remarked that converts could make a greater impact as Catholic intellectuals because they "have studied the faith as grown-ups."

Frank Sheed and Maisie Ward made two lecture tours to the United States, in 1931 and 1932, then opened a New York branch of their publishing house in 1933. They found American audiences more polite but more self-conscious than the English hecklers in Hyde Park, and street preaching never caught on in the United States. Instead, they crisscrossed the nation delivering paid lectures at Catholic colleges and universities. This became their congregation and the major market for the books they wrote and published. They moved to the United States with their two children during World War II, though Frank crossed the Atlantic fifteen times during the war in order to keep both the London and New York branches going. They lived in or around New York City for the rest of their lives but were constantly in motion on the lecture circuit and could never be said to have settled down anywhere.

The decade or so after World War II was the period of Frank Sheed's greatest influence in the United States. He wrote a commonsense primer of theology titled *Theology and Sanity* (1946), which sold very well and was widely used as a textbook in Catholic colleges and even some seminaries. His lectures were in great demand, and the publishing firm remained solvent.

In 1956, while lecturing, he suffered a mild stroke and fell from the platform. Although he recovered, he slowed his pace somewhat and relinquished day-to-day control of the publishing business. He welcomed most of the changes brought about by the Second Vatican Council (1962–1965), yet he resented the fact that the church so easily abandoned many teachings he had spent a lifetime defending. The aftermath of the council quickly eroded the parochial Catholic market that had sustained both his lecturing and his publishing, so he sold the American business of Sheed & Ward to the Andrews & McMeel publishing firm in 1973. His wife died in 1975, and he died in Jersey City six years later.

Before the Second Vatican Council, the American Catholic church was doctrinally orthodox, morally prudish, and anti-intellectual but politically liberal on economic issues. Frank Sheed fit all of these descriptions, except the anti-intellectual label. As a speaker, a writer, and a publisher, his life's work was to break through the stifling anti-intellectualism of English-speaking Catholicism. His son summed this up best, "If one had to boil the Sheed/Ward American mission down to one sentence, it would be that Frank and Maisie finally gave Catholics permission to think without benefit of clergy" (*Frank and Maisie,* p. 101).

• Frank Sheed and Maisie Ward's family papers, covering the period from 1832 to 1982, are at the University of Notre Dame archives. Business documents from the New York office of the Sheed & Ward publishing firm are housed at the same location. Sheed wrote an intellectual biography, *The Church and I* (1974), which tells more about his theological views than his life. In addition, he wrote at least a dozen books, most notably, *Communism and Man* (1938), *Society and Sanity* (1953), and *Is It the Same Church?* (1968). Maisie Ward wrote two autobiographical volumes, *Unfinished Business* (1964) and *To and Fro on the Earth* (1973). Probably the most revealing book about Sheed's life is the memoir by his son, Wilfrid Sheed, *Frank and Maisie: A Memoir with Parents* (1985). Obituaries are in the *New York Times,* 21 Nov. 1981, and *Commonweal,* 4 Dec. 1981.

EDWARD R. KANTOWICZ

SHEELER, Charles (16 July 1883–7 May 1965), painter and photographer, was born Charles Rettew Sheeler, Jr., in Philadelphia, Pennsylvania, the son of Charles Rettew Sheeler, an employee of the Clyde Line of Norfolk, a steamship company, and Mary Cunningham. His family was solidly middle class. After attending local high schools Sheeler (with his parents' encouragement) attempted to enroll at the Pennsylvania Academy of the Fine Arts but was dissuaded by its director. He instead began his artistic training at the School of Industrial Art, affiliated with the Pennsylvania (now Philadelphia) Museum of Art. Three years later, in 1903, he again sought training at the Pennsylvania Academy. There he met Morton Schamberg, with whom he worked closely for the next fifteen years. Both students came under the influence of William Merritt Chase, the dynamic impressionist painter who taught the life and paintings classes. In both 1904 and 1905 Sheeler went to Europe while enrolled in Chase's classes. In 1908 he went abroad again with his parents and Schamberg, visiting Naples, Rome, Venice, Milan, Florence, and Paris. That same year Sheeler and Schamberg began sharing a studio on Chestnut Street in Philadelphia; he had his first solo paintings exhibition at the McClees gallery, also in Philadelphia; and he exhibited a few paintings with the prestigious New York dealer William Macbeth.

Although Sheeler's training with Chase prepared him for a career as a plein-air painter, using bright colors and a bravura style, he soon found his own voice. The paintings he produced after his third trip to Europe reflect the influence of the European avant-garde, especially Paul Cézanne. Sheeler's work from this period is marked by a concern for architectonic design and restrained paint handling. His subjects are primarily still lifes and architectural studies, themes that were a mainstay for the rest of his career.

In 1910 Sheeler and Schamberg rented a small, eighteenth-century stone farmhouse in Doylestown, Bucks County, Pennsylvania. The house and the vernacular architecture of the surrounding countryside became an important subject for Sheeler during this period. At about the same time he began doing serious work in photography. Sheeler had been given a camera as a teenager, and he found photography to be an avenue for financial security as well as an extremely satisfying means of artistic expression. Sheeler soon embarked on a successful career as a commercial photographer, photographing local houses for area architects. In the late teens he made a series of photographs of Bucks County barns and another series, elegant and austere, of the interior of the Doylestown house. These photographs were shown at Marius de Zayas's Modern Gallery in New York in 1917, and two of them won prizes at the prestigious John Wanamaker Exhibition of Photographs held in New York in March 1918, for which photographer Alfred Stieglitz served as principal juror.

Sheeler's careers as a photographer and a painter developed in tandem: his paintings frequently address themes similar to those found in his photographs, and in a number of cases the composition of a photograph contributed to the design of a painting or drawing. He submitted six paintings to the landmark International Exhibition of Modern Art in New York (the Armory Show) of 1913, including *Red Tulips* (1912; Regis Collection, Minneapolis), *Landscape* (1913; private collection, Boston), *Dahlias and Asters* (1912; Corcoran Gallery of Art, Washington, D.C.), and *Chrysanthemums* (1912; Whitney Museum of American Art, New York City). Although none of them sold his participation won him the notice of such important supporters of the avant-garde as painter Arthur B. Davies and collector John Quinn. Sheeler was one of only seventeen artists included in the 1916 Forum exhibition, which featured "the very best examples of the more modern American art." In a number of his works from this exhibition Sheeler approached an orthodox cubist style,

using many of the pictorial devices developed by Georges Braque and Pablo Picasso. Although Sheeler worked in this cubist manner for only a few years, the fundamental premises of the style—objectivity, truth telling, and freedom from the restraint of a single viewpoint—became a lifelong quest.

Late in 1919 Sheeler moved to New York City. The change was precipitated by the deaths in 1918 of Schamberg and his friend the adventurous painter H. Lyman Sayen and by the fact that, as Sheeler noted, "Life in Philadelphia seemed much like being shipwrecked on a deserted island. Whatever was happening that was stimulating and conducive to work was taking place in New York." Once in New York Sheeler became part of the avant-garde circle that met regularly in the apartment of noted collectors and patrons of the avant-garde Walter and Louise Arensberg. Sheeler's photographs of the apartment from about 1918 record their radical collection of contemporary art, which was hung above colonial American furniture—a simultaneous dedication to the avant-garde and the antique that Sheeler shared. His photographs also reveal the high regard in which the Arensbergs held Sheeler's art, for his drawings of Bucks County barns were juxtaposed with works by Picasso and experimental artist Marcel Duchamp. Sheeler also maintained connections with other outposts of progressive art in New York—his friends included artists Duchamp, Francis Picabia, and Man Ray, the dealers Stephan Bourgeois, de Zayas, and Charles Daniel (who first showed his paintings in 1919), and, through Daniel, the daring collector Ferdinand Howald of Columbus, Ohio, who became one of Sheeler's most important patrons.

Sheeler continued to exhibit his photographs as well as his paintings during this period. In 1920 he had a solo exhibition of thirty-nine photographs at de Zayas's gallery. Through Stieglitz Sheeler met the photographer Paul Strand, and in 1920 the two collaborated on a 6½ minute film, *Manhatta*, a celebration of lower Manhattan's dramatic vistas and towering skyscrapers. Eschewing featured characters and narrative content (the text was drawn from Walt Whitman's poems "Crossing Brooklyn Ferry" [1856] and "Manahatta" [1860]), Sheeler and Strand filmed many scenes from high angles, with rapid camera movement and shots following one another quickly to express the excitement and vitality of the urban experience. The new New York became Sheeler's subject matter in all media, and scenes from *Manhatta*, as well as from the still photographs he made at the same time, are reflected in many of his best-known oils of the period, such as *Church Street El* (1920; Cleveland Museum of Art) and *Skyscrapers* (1922; Phillips Collection, Washington, D.C.). In these paintings Sheeler abandoned the cream, blue, and lavender palette with which he had been working since the early teens in favor of ochers, rusts, and browns. His shapes became thoroughly geometric, his perspectives vertiginous. Instead of suggesting forms bathed by natural light he showed buildings as if lit from within; they seem to glow and pulse forward, expressing the energy and novelty of urban life.

In 1921 Sheeler married Katharine Baird Shaffer, a vivacious woman two years his senior. In the early years of their marriage (which was childless) they changed addresses several times and he showed with at least six different galleries. Their rootlessness continued until 1923, when Juliana Force, director of the Whitney Studio Club (later the Whitney Museum of American Art), gave Sheeler a two-year tenancy in the apartment above the Whitney on West Eighth Street in Greenwich Village.

Sheeler's involvement with the Whitney began around April 1921, when his photograph of a Gothic Madonna appeared as the frontispiece of *The Arts*, a magazine affiliated with the organization. By 1923 Sheeler had become the Whitney's photographer, one of its exhibitions managers, and a frequent contributor to its paintings and drawings shows. In March 1924 he had a solo exhibition at the Whitney; the show included a few of his abstract New York pictures but consisted primarily of still lifes and landscape vignettes that demonstrated his new commitment to realism. These works were admired for their meticulousness. Sheeler himself remarked that he aspired to reveal "the absolute beauty [of] . . . objects suspended in a vacuum"; works such as *Still Life and Shadows* (1924; Columbus Museum of Art) are characterized by a visual purity and classical grace.

Sheeler continued to show and work at the Whitney until 1926, when "fed up with the city," he and Katharine moved to South Salem, New York. He nonetheless maintained a studio in Manhattan, which he used primarily for commercial photography. In 1926, sponsored by well-known photographer Edward Steichen, he secured a job with Condé Nast publications. He soon was contributing as many as twenty photographs a year (mostly fashion photographs and celebrity portraits) to *Vogue* and *Vanity Fair*. He also did freelance work for several advertising agencies, which led to the most important commission of his career: in 1927 he was hired by N. W. Ayer & Son to document the new Ford Motor Company plant in River Rouge, Michigan.

Sheeler spent six weeks in Michigan in the fall of 1927 and ultimately submitted thirty-two prints in fulfillment of the commission, although he undoubtedly made many more photographs while he was there. These images did not present a comprehensive portrait of the plant's activities—the River Rouge plant produced the new Model A Fords and boasted a specially designed assembly line—or a narrative of the manufacture of an automobile. Nor did the photographs promote Ford's products: no cars, and no readily recognizable parts, appear in the photographs. Instead, Sheeler focused on the machines, their awesome bulk and heroic power; he also celebrated the plant's architecture, emphasizing the rhythm of the girders, cranes, and conveyers soaring overhead. Sheeler clearly responded to the formal geometry of the architecture and machinery of the River Rouge plant. His im-

ages also suggest that he saw the plant as emblematic of American industry as a whole, as a visionary place that was awe inspiring not because of what was produced there but because of the grandeur of its conception.

The Rouge photographs were immediately successful, both as advertising images and as works of art. They were reproduced on the covers of *Ford News* and were featured in the pioneer dealer Julien Levy's inaugural show, American Photography, held in November 1931 in New York City. As was often the case with Sheeler's photography, the Rouge photographs stimulated work in other media—an experience that he described in terms of revelation: "I was out there on a mission of photography. Period. And when I got there, I took a chance on opening the other eye and so then I thought maybe some pictures could be pulled out." Over the next several years—beginning with the modest watercolor *River Rouge Industrial Plant* (1928; Carnegie Museum of Art, Pittsburgh), a study for a major oil, *American Landscape* (1930; Museum of Modern Art, New York), and culminating with *Classic Landscape* (1931; Collection of Mr. and Mrs. Barney A. Ebsworth Foundation)—Sheeler produced a number of relatively large-scale, majestic oils that present the same idealized view of industry he had introduced in the photographs. *Classic Landscape* in particular transforms a cement plant into a modern Parthenon set in a pristine industrial landscape. Through these works Sheeler came to be identified with the Machine Age.

Classic Landscape was first exhibited in November 1931 at the Downtown Gallery, then the most adventurous showcase for contemporary American art in New York. Its director, Edith Halpert, had included a few of Sheeler's works in a group show the previous year. She subsequently offered to become his exclusive dealer and gave him a solo show in 1931 (his first since 1924), the one in which *Classic Landscape* appeared. Also in that exhibition were a series of interiors, including representations of his Manhattan studio and of his South Salem home, the latter of which contained his collection of American antiques, largely Shaker furniture. These works are often witty and ironic: *Home Sweet Home* (1931; Detroit Institute of Arts) shows an eighteenth-century rush-seated armchair pulled up to an oil burner rather than to a cozy hearth; *View of New York* (1931; Museum of Fine Arts, Boston) shows not the bustling streets and soaring skyscrapers that mark his earlier images of Manhattan but rather a blue sky filled with soft pinky-white clouds. These works have an autobiographical quality as well. The South Salem interiors address the conjunction between the traditional and the modern that pervaded Sheeler's art and life, while *View of New York* shows Sheeler's photo studio as he prepared to leave it (camera covered, lamps turned off) not at the end of a work day but for good. Halpert, concerned that Sheeler's photography was detrimental to his productivity as a painter and to the reception of his paintings, counseled him to curtail his photographic work, despite the financial security and visibility it offered him. Accordingly, after his 1931 show at Downtown, Sheeler resigned from Condé Nast, declined other commercial assignments, virtually ceased exhibiting his photographic work, and thereafter dedicated himself almost entirely to painting.

In 1932 the Sheelers moved to Ridgefield, Connecticut. The following summer Katharine Sheeler died, and for the rest of the decade Sheeler's despondency took the form of a kind of artistic retrenchment. Although the greatest of the domestic portraits, *American Interior* (1934; Yale University Art Gallery), depicts the Ridgefield house, for the most part Sheeler's pictures were drawn from his repository of photographic images from the 1910s and 1920s. The connection is especially evident in a group of conté crayon drawings produced between 1930 and 1937. With their rich, velvety textures, their intricate designs, and their smooth, nongestural surfaces, they are in Sheeler's view, the works that "most closely approach photographs" and that "were made to see how much exactitude I could attain." He used cropping, strong back lighting, and other photographic devices in many of these hauntingly empty drawings to create nocturnal effects and eloquent silhouettes.

At the same time, thanks to Halpert's promotion of his paintings and drawings, Sheeler's visibility and market improved. Halpert arranged that his work be featured in such important museum exhibitions as Painting and Sculpture by Living Americans at the Museum of Modern Art (1930) and the Whitney Museum's 1935 Abstract Paintings in America. She was also successful in placing Sheeler's works in prestigious museums—the Fogg Art Museum at Harvard bought *Upper Deck* (1929) in 1933; the Museum of Fine Arts, Boston, acquired *View of New York* two years later; and the Worcester Art Museum purchased *City Interior* (1936) the year after it was painted. Most important, Halpert introduced Sheeler's work to a new group of patrons, principal among them Abby Aldrich Rockefeller (Mrs. John D. Rockefeller, Jr.). Rockefeller bought eight Sheelers—including several major drawings and *American Landscape*—from the Downtown Gallery between 1929 and 1933. She subsequently gave them to the Museum of Modern Art, making that institution one of the richest repositories of Sheeler's work in the country.

By the end of the decade Sheeler was receiving national exposure. He was featured in a four-page article, "Charles Sheeler Finds Beauty in the Commonplace," that appeared in *Life* magazine on 8 Aug. 1938; he was one of the first American painters to be so honored. Constance Rourke's sympathetic biography, *Charles Sheeler, Artist in the American Tradition*, based on Sheeler's own notes, also appeared in 1938. In 1939 Sheeler was commissioned to make a series of six paintings on the theme of power for *Fortune*, which enabled him to visit such spectacles of modern engineering as Boulder Dam and the Tennessee Valley Authority. The six paintings were reproduced in *Fortune* in December 1940 and were given a special exhibition

at the Downtown Gallery, where several sold promptly. *Rolling Power* (1939), for example, was acquired by the Smith College Museum of Art in Northampton, Massachusetts.

In October 1939 the Museum of Modern Art gave Sheeler a retrospective exhibition. Organized by associate curator Dorothy Miller and with a catalog essay by one of Sheeler's close friends, poet William Carlos Williams, the exhibition included 105 paintings and drawings made between 1910 and 1939 and seventy-three photographs. The latter group included some of the Rouge pictures, thirteen of the photographs Sheeler made of Chartres Cathedral during his last trip to Europe in 1929, and a few of the works resulting from his only major commission of the decade, the documentation of Colonial Williamsburg in Virginia, recently restored under the sponsorship of John D. Rockefeller, Jr. Response to the show was mixed: although some critics praised Sheeler's "universal clarity of vision, sensitivity to structure, and meticulous technique," others were troubled by the smooth, detailed realism of Sheeler's most recent paintings and (as Halpert had feared) criticized their closeness to his photographs. Nonetheless, the exhibition greatly enhanced Sheeler's reputation, and at the age of fifty-six he was recognized as a leading figure in American art in two mediums.

In the late 1930s and 1940s Sheeler increased his activity as a photographer, while continuing to paint. In 1942 he worked with the photographer Edward Weston in Connecticut. Also in 1942 Sheeler moved to Irvington-on-Hudson, New York, with his second wife, Musya Sokolova, whom he had married in 1939. To sustain himself during the war years he served as senior research fellow in photography at the Metropolitan Museum of Art. After the war Sheeler worked as artist in residence at Phillips Academy in Andover, Massachusetts (1946), and at the Currier Gallery of Art in Manchester, New Hampshire (1948). During his residencies at Andover and Manchester, his longstanding interest in vernacular architecture inspired a series of photographs and paintings of abandoned mill buildings. The first of these works were relatively descriptive, but as Sheeler generated variations on his themes, they became increasingly abstract. Continuing his practice of using photographs as "shorthand notes," Sheeler began experimenting with a new method of devising compositions. Superimposing two negatives, he would print a composite photograph that evoked the actual site while creating an original, abstract design. At first he used multiple views of the same place, but in later works, such as *New England Irrelevancies* (1953), he conflated two distinct settings to arrive at an image uniting the remembered and the observed, or in his words, "the memory and the present."

Sheeler's career in the late 1940s and 1950s was filled with commissions that yielded both photographs and paintings. He worked for Kodak, U.S. Steel, and General Motors, and he used the photographs made on these jobs to suggest designs for paintings that are both evocations of industry and abstract compositions.

During this period he renewed his friendships with the great artists of his generation: he visited the photographers Ansel Adams (in San Francisco) and Edward Weston (in Carmel). In 1955 Sheeler summered in Cape Split, Maine, home of the watercolorist John Marin, a friend from his early days at the Downtown Gallery.

Also during this period Sheeler was honored with a number of retrospective exhibitions: at the Art Galleries of the University of California, Los Angeles (1954), at the Allentown (Penn.) Art Museum (1961), and at the University of Iowa Art Galleries (1963). The Downtown Gallery continued to feature his work, in a retrospective show in 1956 and in a show of new paintings in 1958. In his seventies Sheeler enjoyed the role of elder statesman, accepting awards and serving on juries, although he had previously declined such opportunities. In 1957 he received the Philadelphia Museum School of Art's Alumni Award for Distinguished Achievement. In 1962 the American Academy of Arts and Letters presented him with their Award of Merit Medal for painting; the next year he was elected to the National Institute of Arts and Letters. In 1959 Sheeler suffered a stroke that left him unable to paint or use a camera. He died in Dobbs Ferry, New York.

• Many of Sheeler's papers, including autobiographical notes and transcripts of interviews with the artist, are in the Archives of American Art, Smithsonian Institution. Important appreciations of Sheeler appear in the 1939 exhibition catalog prepared by the Museum of Modern Art, New York, and in Frederick S. Wight's exhibition catalog for the Art Galleries, University of California, Los Angeles, *Charles Sheeler: A Retrospective Exhibition* (1954). Lillian Dochterman, "The Stylistic Development of the Work of Charles Sheeler" (Ph.D. diss., State Univ. of Iowa, 1963), contains a catalogue raisonné of his paintings. The first scholarly discussion of Sheeler as a photographer is Charles Millard's essay "Charles Sheeler: American Photographer," which constitutes *Contemporary Photographer* 6 (1967); an abridged version appears in the exhibition catalog *Charles Sheeler* (National Collection of Fine Arts, Smithsonian Institution, 1968), which also contains essays by Bartlett Hayes and Martin Friedman. Friedman wrote the monograph *Charles Sheeler*, which was published in 1975. There are a number of studies of particular aspects of Sheeler's work, among them Patrick L. Stewart, Jr., "Charles Sheeler, William Carlos Williams, and Precisionism," *Arts Magazine*, Nov. 1983, pp. 100–114; Susan Fillin-Yeh, *Charles Sheeler: American Interiors* (Yale University Art Gallery, 1987); and Karen Lucic, *Charles Sheeler and the Cult of the Machine* (1991). In 1987 the Museum of Fine Arts, Boston, organized a retrospective exhibition of Sheeler's work. The catalogs of that exhibition, by Carol Troyen and Erica Hirshler (*Charles Sheeler: Paintings and Drawings*) and by Theodore Stebbins and Norman Keyes (*Charles Sheeler: The Photographs*), are the most complete modern assessment of his work. An obituary is in the *New York Times*, 8 May 1965.

CAROL TROYEN

SHEEN, Fulton John (8 May 1895–9 Dec. 1979), Roman Catholic bishop and electronic evangelist, was born in El Paso, Illinois, the son of Newton Morris Sheen and Delia Fulton, farmers. Although he was baptized Peter, he adopted his mother's maiden name as a youth and used it throughout his career as one of the most famous American Catholic priests of the twentieth century.

Sheen attended high school at Spalding Institute in Peoria, graduating in 1913. Following a vocation sensed at an early age, he continued his education at St. Viator's College and Seminary in Bourbonnais, Illinois (B.A., 1917; M.A., 1919), where he excelled as a member of the debating team, and at St. Paul's Seminary in St. Paul, Minnesota. He was ordained to the priesthood for the Diocese of Peoria on 20 September 1919. Recognized for his intellectual talents, he went on to the Catholic University of America (J.C.B., S.T.L., 1920) for more theological study and was sent by Bishop Edmund Dunne to the University of Louvain, where he earned his Ph.D. in 1923. After further studies at the Sorbonne and the Collegio Angelico in Rome (S.T.D., 1924), he taught dogmatic theology for a brief period at St. Edmund's College in Ware, England.

Sheen's doctoral dissertation was published as the book *God and Intelligence in Modern Philosophy* in 1925. The first of his more than sixty books, it won the Cardinal Mercier Prize for International Philosophy and acclaim for its author as one of the leading Catholic philosophers of the period. Sheen also was awarded the prestigious Agrégé en Philosophie degree at Louvain, the first American to be so honored.

After returning to the United States, Sheen served for a year as a curate at St. Patrick's Church in Peoria. He was then appointed to the faculty at the Catholic University of America in 1926, and he began his multifaceted career as a Scholastic philosopher and Catholic apologist, teaching both philosophy and theology until 1950. He vowed to bridge the gap separating the church from the modern world, and to do so he set out to answer the errors of modern thought in light of the philosophy of Thomas Aquinas. Moving beyond the walls of the traditional classroom, he won a national reputation as a dynamic orator, preaching regularly at St. Patrick's Cathedral in New York City and lecturing on world affairs as well as religion.

In 1930 Sheen became a pioneer of the electronic gospel as the featured speaker on the NBC radio network's "Catholic Hour Broadcasts." Sponsored by the National Council of Catholic Men, the program was designed to overcome misunderstanding and prejudice by making the doctrines and teachings of the church better known to the American people. From 1930 to 1952 he gave a regular Lenten series of talks on such topics as "The Eternal Galilean" (1934), "Peace: The Fruit of Justice" (1940), and "The Crisis of Christendom" (1943). Sheen's popularity as a radio evangelist soared; his audience was estimated at four million listeners. Feeling "called by God to reach the masses," his focus was on Christian witness rather than proselytizing, and the broadcasts served not only the cause of religion, but of democracy and education.

Sheen's growth as a public figure coincided with his rise in the ranks of the church. In 1934 he was appointed papal chamberlain, and the following year he was elevated to domestic prelate: right reverend monsignor. In 1951 he was consecrated titular bishop of Caeseriana and auxilary bishop of New York.

Sheen's fame in addition to his personal magnetism led many potential converts to the Catholic faith to seek him out for instruction. His convert successes ranged from his humble housekeeper to many celebrities. Headlines were made when Sheen welcomed prominent figures into the church, including Henry Ford II, the journalist Heywood Broun, and Congresswoman Clare Booth Luce. Perhaps Sheen's most noteworthy convert was former Communist party member Louis Budenz, who had been editor of the *Daily Worker*; Budenz was dramatically introduced as a Catholic by Sheen in 1945 at St. Patrick's.

Because Sheen enjoyed such ready access to the media, he was able to serve as an American Catholic spokesman during the times of crisis surrounding World War II. He employed a double-edged sword in his basic message, speaking both as an advocate of social justice and as an avid crusader against communism. Viewing the world situation from a religious perspective, he pronounced that the war was a "judgment of God"; speaking as an American, his sermons were a blend of patriotism and piety. He taught that social reconstruction was a by-product of spiritual regeneration and that the church's program of reform and Catholic Action, occupying the middle ground between liberal capitalism and communism, offered the best hope for the future.

As the prophet and philosopher of American Catholic anticommunism, Sheen was passionate in his opposition to Marxist ideology. In *Communism and the Conscience of the West* (1948) he stated that "the philosophy of communism, and to some extent the Revolution of Communism, are on the conscience of the Western world." He taught that the Western world must repent and put its own house in order by returning to Christianity. Nevertheless, as a patriot, he also described communism as the "epitome of both irreligion and un-Americanism," reminding his fellow citizens of the "service" Catholics were performing for the nation and paving the way for the church's greater participation in American life.

The Catholic church made its way into the American mainstream during the culmination of the national postwar religious revival. The decade of the fifties marked the apex of Sheen's influence and popularity. In 1950 he was appointed national director of the Society for the Propagation of the Faith. For the next sixteen years he led the evangelization efforts of the organization, and he raised millions of dollars for Catholic world missions. He also wrote two newspaper columns, "Bishop Sheen Writes" and "God Love You," that were syndicated in the secular and Catholic press. As an author, Sheen wrote several books in the religious-inspirational genre, including *Peace of Soul* and *Life of Christ*, that were bestsellers. For many non-Catholic Americans, Sheen was the first association they could make with the church, and he projected a warm, friendly image. His projection of that image through the new medium of television best explains the fifties' phenomenon of Bishop Sheen, Catholic star.

From 1951 until 1957 Sheen's television show, "Life Is Worth Living," was an unparalleled success, watched by thirty million viewers on the DuMont and ABC networks. He inspired and instructed many people of an entire generation, offering them a skillfully presented mixture of common sense, logic, and Christian ethics. For his efforts, he won an Emmy award in 1952, and his status as a celebrity was assured when he made the cover of *Time* magazine (14 Apr. 1952). He was described as a "microphone Missionary," "perhaps the most famous preacher in the United States," certainly "America's best known Roman Catholic priest," and the "newest star of television."

The sixties became a decade of transition for both Sheen and the Roman Catholic church. At the Second Vatican Council he participated as a member of the Commission on the Missions. In 1966 he was appointed by Pope Paul VI as bishop of Rochester, New York, where he embarked on a path of controversial innovation, determined to implement the reforms of Vatican II in his "demonstration diocese." He is remembered for attempting to focus the nation's attention on the plight of the poor in the inner city and for his ecumenical overtones to the community. After a stormy tenure, he resigned from his post in 1969 and was named titular archbishop of Newport, Wales. Insisting that he was "regenerating" rather than retiring, he devoted his last years to continued writing and lecturing, reflecting on his career as a priest. He died in New York City.

Sheen's life was dedicated to "working out a Christian response to the challenge of the times." By adopting the persona of an intellectual popularizer early in his career, he was able to succeed as professor, radio and television preacher, missionary, bishop. In no small measure his work broke down walls of prejudice and enhanced the image and prestige of the Catholic church in the United States. Sheen was memorialized by John Tracy Ellis as "the greatest evangelizer in the history of the American Catholic Church," one of the "greatest preachers of the twentieth century," and the "most eloquent exponent and effective champion of the Catholic faith in the United States."

• The Archbishop Fulton Sheen Archives, located at St. Bernard's Institute in Rochester, N.Y., contain copies of Sheen's published works, his personal library and papers, photographs and memorabilia, and a large set of audio and visual recordings of his television shows. His other more popular and representative books include *Religion without God* (1928), *Old Errors and New Labels* (1931), *The Mystical Body of Christ* (1935), *The Cross and the Crisis* (1938), and *Preface to Religion* (1946). *Treasure in Clay: The Autobiography of Fulton J. Sheen* (1980) was published posthumously. For assessments of Sheen's life and work, see Daniel P. Noonan, *The Passion of Fulton Sheen* (1972), a flawed critique written by a former associate; John Tracy Ellis, *Catholic Bishops: A Memoir* (1983); and Kathleen Riley Fields, "Bishop Fulton J.

Sheen: An American Catholic Response to the Twentieth Century" (Ph.D. diss., Univ. of Notre Dame, 1988). Also see *The Quotable Fulton Sheen* (1989), ed. George J. Marlin et al.

KATHLEEN RILEY

SHEHAN, Lawrence Joseph (18 Mar. 1898–26 Aug. 1984), Roman Catholic cardinal and archbishop of Baltimore, was born in Baltimore, Maryland, the son of Thomas Patrick Shehan, a traveling salesman, and Anastasia Dames Schofield. A product of the parochial schools, he attended St. Mary's Seminary, Baltimore, and the North American College in Rome before his ordination to the priesthood on 23 December 1922 in Rome. In June 1923 he received a doctorate in sacred theology from the Urban College of the Propaganda Fide. Assistant and then pastor at St. Patrick's Parish, Washington, D.C., he also served as director of Catholic Charities for the District of Columbia. On 17 November 1945 he was appointed auxiliary bishop for the archdiocese of Baltimore-Washington and on 12 December was raised to the episcopacy by the apostolic delegate, Archbishop Amleto Cicognani, at St. Patrick's. On 25 August 1953 Shehan was named first bishop of the diocese of Bridgeport, Connecticut, which in eight years he endowed with an impressive array of churches, schools, and other institutions. On 12 July 1961 he was named coadjutor to the ailing archbishop Francis P. Keough of Baltimore, whom he succeeded on 8 December 1961.

Shehan surpassed all former archbishops of Baltimore as a fundraiser and builder. In a special campaign in 1965, he collected nearly $12 million, most of which was expended for larger homes for the aged and for delinquent girls, a school of special education for black children, and four new Catholic high schools. It was in his pastoral role, however, that Shehan was outstanding. The four major goals of his administration were interfaith harmony, liturgical reform, empowerment of the laity, and racial justice.

To coordinate interfaith affairs, in 1962 he created the first Catholic ecumenical commission in the nation. The unobtrusive but crucial role he played at Vatican Council II (1962–1965) derived largely from his ecumenical concerns. A member of the Secretariat for the Promotion of Christian Unity, he was chosen by the American bishops as spokesman to defend the American principle of separation of church and state. He took an active part in drafting the Declaration on Religious Liberty and the conciliar statement on the Jews. At the fourth session he was named one of the twelve council presidents and on 7 December 1965 headed the delegation sent by the pope to meet with Patriarch Athenagoras in Istanbul to lift the centuries-old mutual excommunication of the Roman Catholic and Orthodox churches.

In the course of the council, Shehan was elevated to the College of Cardinals; appointed to two curial bodies at the Vatican, the Consistorial Congregation and the Congregation of the Holy Office; and was the only American named to the Commission for the Revision of Canon Law. At the same time, the American bishops elected him a member of the administrative board of the National Catholic Welfare Conference, chairman of its press department, and chairman of its newly created Committee for Ecumenical Affairs. In December 1965 the National Conference of Christians and Jews bestowed upon him its highest honor, the National Brotherhood Award.

In pursuance of his second goal, liturgical reform, the cardinal conducted personal visitations of his archdiocese to familiarize Catholics with the teachings of the Vatican Council on this and on other matters. Even before the council, he had begun to involve the laity in the governance of the church, his third goal. Afterward he promoted the formation of parish councils, created an archdiocesan pastoral council, and appointed laypeople to a number of boards and administrative positions that had formerly been held by the clergy.

In the area of racial justice, his fourth goal, Shehan integrated all Catholic institutions in his first months as archbishop of Baltimore and composed a forceful pastoral letter explaining the need to uproot local prejudices. In July 1963 he created an urban commission to address the problems of the inner city and was both jeered and applauded when he testified before the city council in favor of open housing. In 1966 he issued the first pastoral of an American Catholic bishop on the moral implications of the military action in Vietnam.

If the first six and a half years of Cardinal Shehan's administration were a time of optimism, the last six were a time of contention. In 1968 the Baltimore riot following the murder of Dr. Martin Luther King, Jr., the antiwar protest of the Catonsville Nine, and the appearance of *Humanae Vitae*, the papal encyclical upholding the ban on artificial birth control, all had unnerving effects on the oldest American Catholic see. Though as a member of the papal commission on birth control Shehan had been on the side of change, he demanded the adherence of dissenting clergy to the encyclical as the official teaching of the church. He allowed them, however, to explain their divergent views in the classroom and pulpit. Increasingly thereafter he felt compelled to defend the pope not only in the matter of birth control, but also in his opposition to married priests and the ordination of women. The cardinal's decision to visit two of his antiwar priests who were jailed on charges of conspiracy against the government further polarized the Catholics of the archdiocese. In his final six years of office the cardinal was also beset by a financial crisis caused by the many institutions he erected and by programs emanating from Vatican Council II. His inherent conservatism in doctrinal matters reasserted itself in these later years, but he remained committed to his four major goals, particularly racial justice.

In 1973 Shehan offered his resignation at the mandated age of seventy-five but was allowed to stay on another year. In retirement he was increasingly a father figure. "He was a priest's priest, a gentleman's gentleman, and the essence of kindness and gentleness," said Cardinal John Krol of Philadelphia, echoing the prevailing opinion upon Shehan's death in Baltimore. In an era of unprecedented change within the Catholic church, Shehan brought a quiet and effective leadership to turbulent times.

• Cardinal Shehan's papers are in the archives of the archdiocese of Baltimore. In 1982 he published his autobiography, *A Blessing of Years: The Memoirs of Lawrence Cardinal Shehan.* Its contents, however, should be supplemented by recourse to the *Catholic Review*, the archdiocesan weekly, where his pastoral letters are found. He wrote several essays for the *Homiletic and Pastoral Review*; especially significant is "Humanae Vitae: 1968–1973," 74 (Nov. and Dec. 1973): 14ff. and 20ff. See also Thomas W. Spalding, *The Premier See: A History of the Archdiocese of Baltimore, 1789–1989* (1989). An obituary is in the *Baltimore Sun*, 27 Aug. 1984.

THOMAS W. SPALDING

SHEIL, Bernard James (18 Feb. 1886–13 Sept. 1969), Roman Catholic prelate, was born in Chicago, Illinois, the son of James Sheil, a coal merchant, and Rosella Barclay. He was educated in the parochial schools of Chicago and, beginning in 1904, at St. Viator's College in Bourbonnais, Illinois. A promising athlete, he turned down offers from several professional baseball teams and entered St. Viator's seminary. Sheil was ordained to the priesthood in 1910. He subsequently served as a curate in Chicago parishes and performed chaplaincy services at the Great Lakes Naval Training Station during 1918–1919, being decorated for the latter work. In the 1920s Sheil became chaplain for the Cook County jail and through his work with juvenile offenders committed himself to preventing young people from embracing a life of crime.

Sheil's star rose steadily under Archbishop George Mundelein. He was appointed vice chancellor of the archdiocese in 1923 and chancellor the next year. Mundelein assigned the young priest to organize the Eucharistic Congress held in Chicago in 1926 and ultimately tapped him for the position of auxiliary bishop. Mundelein consecrated Sheil in May 1928. Sheil was later appointed pastor of St. Andrew's parish on the near north side of Chicago and lived in its rectory, but he left the day-to-day operation of the parish to a staff of clerical assistants.

Unaccustomed by temperament to sitting in the shadows and skilled in self-promotion, Sheil set to work developing the youth apostolate that he had committed himself to during his jail chaplaincy. By 1930 he had consolidated a variety of existing youth programs and created some of his own to form one of the most popular youth organizations in American Catholic history, the Catholic Youth Organization (CYO). Under CYO auspices, Sheil ran educational programs, camps, and summer schools that served thousands of youngsters. The main thrust of the organization was its extensive athletic program, open to Chicago youth of all creeds and colors. Especially popular were the local boxing competitions, which led up to a major boxing tourney attended by thousands. Although criticized for encouraging a morally dubious sport, Sheil stoutly defended his programs as a way to rehabilitate

tough urban youth who otherwise would have turned to gangs and a life of crime. The success of the CYO made Sheil a popular figure in Chicago and nationally. Many dioceses replicated CYO organizations, but since they remained locally led, Sheil never headed a national CYO body.

With the success and visibility that his CYO endeavors gave him, Sheil began to expand his political interests. Building on Cardinal Mundelein's close relationship with President Franklin Roosevelt and assisted by his personal lawyer (later federal judge) William Campbell, Sheil began to cultivate his own contacts in the Roosevelt administration, especially Thomas G. "Tommy the Cork" Corcoran. Sheil endeared himself to Roosevelt and his advisers by orating against the administration's clerical nemesis, Father Charles Coughlin. Sheil's prominence increased in 1937, when he appeared on the dais of a huge public rally called to support the efforts of the Congress of Industrial Organizations (CIO) to organize Chicago meat packers. His presence and his warm endorsement of John L. Lewis gave him a lifelong reputation as a supporter of organized labor. Subsequently, Sheil would attempt unsuccessfully to act as an intermediary between Lewis and Roosevelt.

After the death of his patron Mundelein in 1939, Sheil briefly cherished the hope that he would be selected to succeed him. Officials of the Roosevelt administration even made efforts to secure the post for Sheil. Instead, he was passed over for Milwaukee archbishop Samuel A. Stritch. Not wishing to be subordinate to Stritch and desperately wanting to have his own diocese, Sheil pinned his hopes for ecclesiastical advancement on a carefully calculated program of self-promotion focused on the CYO. Toward the end of the 1930s he had begun to restructure the organization, moving it away from a heavy emphasis on athletics and attempting to give it more of an intellectual and academic direction. A number of bright young Catholic intellectuals whom he recruited as a brain trust composed speeches that Sheil, through the 1940s, delivered to a variety of groups, including labor unions and congressional committees. During World War II he was especially eloquent on the subject of American democracy, arguing forcefully that its benefits must be more liberally extended to all citizens. He was one of the first American bishops to speak out against racism, and he denounced anti-Semitism with equal ferocity. The CYO developed an educational arm called the Sheil School of Social Studies, which amplified many of the bishop's speeches as well as offering a host of adult education programs in everything from Catholic theology to languages and art. The Sheil School lasted nearly a decade—until 1954—and thousands of Chicagoans frequented the institution, making it in the words of one observer "a kind of Catholic Times Square." Despite these efforts and a constant stream of rumors that he was to be appointed bishop of Washington, D.C., or St. Louis, Sheil never left Chicago.

Sheil's many travels and his increasingly far-flung social welfare enterprises created serious financial difficulties for the CYO. Sheil periodically reshuffled the organization's administrators, abruptly firing long-serving staffers and replacing them with outsiders. Keeping up his public speaking engagements, Sheil often jousted with conservatives on a variety of issues. In April 1954 he leveled a blast against the tactics of Roman Catholic U.S. senator Joseph McCarthy in a speech at a labor convention. The following September, Sheil dramatically resigned from the leadership of the CYO and announced that he would return to full-time parish life.

The timing of Sheil's departure, so soon after the McCarthy attack, led many to believe that Sheil was being punished for attacking the senator. In fact, the CYO's deteriorating financial position compelled him to resign. After a brief flurry of press interest, Sheil resumed his pastorate of St. Andrew's parish and slowly faded from the scene. The CYO's indebtedness was absorbed by the archdiocese of Chicago, and its various programs were either phased out or subsumed under other diocesan agencies. Sheil periodically reemerged from his self-imposed seclusion, securing for himself an honorary archbishop's title in 1959 and a place on a committee at the Second Vatican Council. However, he never attended a session and was largely a forgotten man. In 1966 Archbishop John Cody forcibly retired him from his pastorate, and he moved to Tucson, Arizona, where he later died.

• Sheil left behind few personal papers. What remain are in the Archives of the Archdiocese of Chicago and at the Chicago Historical Society. See also Edward Kantowicz, *Corporation Sole: Cardinal Mundelein and Chicago Catholicism* (1983); Steven M. Avella, *This Confident Church: Chicago Catholicism 1940–1965* (1992); Roger L. Treat, *Bishop Sheil and the CYO* (1951); and Mary Elizabeth Carroll, "Bishop Sheil: Prophet without Honor," *Harper's*, Nov. 1955, pp. 45–51. An obituary is in the *New York Times*, 14 Sept. 1969.

STEVEN M. AVELLA

SHELBY, Evan (Oct. 1719–4 Dec. 1794), frontiersman and soldier, was born in Tregaron, Cardiganshire, Wales, the son of Evan Shelby and Catherine (maiden name uncertain, possibly Davies). In 1735 the family immigrated to Pennsylvania, and in 1739 they moved to a 1,000-acre land grant near Hagerstown, Maryland. In 1744 Shelby married Letitia Cox; they had seven children. Letitia died in 1777, and he married Isabella Elliott in 1787; they had three children.

After his father died in 1750, Evan continued to acquire land. He also served as lieutenant in the militia. In 1758, as captain of a company of rangers accompanying General John Forbes (1710–1759) on an expedition against Fort Dusquesne, Shelby blazed a trail from the Potomac River to Fort Cumberland that eventually became part of the Old National Road. After this mission, he and two partners formed Evan Shelby and Company, which sold general merchandise and traded with the Indians. Although they met with initial success, with contacts as far as Green Bay, the business was disrupted by Pontiac's Rebellion. To satisfy creditors, Shelby borrowed heavily and sold

land. After his two partners fled, he became involved in numerous civil suits. During this time he also served as justice of the peace, received land grants, and in 1765 was granted £200 by the Maryland General Assembly for his military service.

In 1768 Shelby purchased 700 acres in Rowan County, North Carolina. After the October 1770 Treaty of Lochaber opened to settlement former land of the Cherokees, Shelby moved his family to southwest Virginia. He purchased land on Beaver Creek near present-day Bristol, Tennessee, naming it "Sapling Grove." His trading post and fort, established in 1772, became a major gathering point and way station on the Wilderness Road and an important defensive position in the Holston Valley.

In March 1774 Indian hostilities forced the Holston settlers into forts, including Shelby's. Shelby was appointed captain of the Fincastle County militia. In August Shelby's 59-man company, with his son Isaac as lieutenant, marched to New River and down the Kanawha to join 1,000 men under Colonel Andrew Lewis on an expedition to defend the settlers against the Indians. On 10 October they were attacked by 1,000 Indians led by Cornstalk. During the battle of Point Pleasant, Shelby exercised effective command and led the militia to victory after all the higher ranking officers were killed or wounded.

In early 1776, Shelby was elected to the Fincastle Committee of Safety. In August, as a major, he accompanied Colonel William Christian's expedition against the Cherokees. After returning in November, Shelby commanded a garrison of 600 men at Fort Patrick Henry. In December 1776 Shelby was appointed militia colonel and justice of the peace for newly created Washington County. Representing Virginia, he helped negotiate the Treaty of Long Island of the Holston on 20 July 1777.

In January 1779 Governor Patrick Henry asked Shelby to lead an expedition against the Chickamaugas in the Chattanooga Country. In April, with a small force of Virginia and North Carolina militia, Shelby surprised and routed the main town of the Chickamaugas. He was rewarded with an appointment as brigadier general of the Virginia militia.

After a 1779 survey revealed that Sapling Grove was in North Carolina, in March 1781 General Nathanael Greene appointed Shelby one of the North Carolina commissioners to negotiate a new Indian treaty at Long Island. That same year Sullivan County elected Shelby to the North Carolina Senate. In 1786 he was appointed brigadier general of the militia for the Washington District of North Carolina.

Shelby played a pivotal role in the controversy over the state of Franklin, which had been organized in 1784 on land formerly part of North Carolina. In March 1787 Shelby and Franklin's governor John Sevier worked out a compromise to prevent hostilities, but the Franklinites undermined Shelby's efforts. In May he and other officials advised Governor Richard Caswell that force might be necessary to restore order. Retaining the respect of both sides in the dispute,

Shelby was nominated to succeed Sevier as governor but declined. In October he resigned his militia commission and retired to Sapling Grove. He died at Sapling Grove and was buried there, but later his body was reinterred at the East Hill Cemetery in Bristol, Virginia.

Evan Shelby was an important figure in frontier settlement and the American Revolution. His son Isaac was one of the heroes of the battle of Kings Mountain during the Revolution and went on to serve as the first governor of Kentucky.

• The most complete account of the life of Evan Shelby is a 41-page typescript sketch written in 1959 by Cass Knight Shelby, a great-great grandson of the subject. A copy of the biography, based on family documents as well as historical records, along with a few brief sketches of other family members, comprises the Shelby Family Collection, Archives of Appalachia, East Tennessee State University. Much of the official correspondence of and about Shelby can be found in Walter Clark, ed., *The State Records of North Carolina*, vols. 18–24 (1896–1905), and William P. Palmer, ed., *Calendar of Virginia State Papers and Other Manuscripts*, vols. 1–6 (1875–1886). For accounts of Shelby's life and career, see Oliver Taylor, *Historic Sullivan: A History of Sullivan County, Tennessee, with Brief Biographies of the Makers of History* (1909), and Samuel Cole Williams, "Shelby's Fort," *Publications of the East Tennessee Historical Society* 7 (1935): 28–37. For historical background, see Elizabeth Meek Fels, "The Battle of Point Pleasant: Its Relation to the American Revolution and to Tennessee," *Tennessee Historical Quarterly* 33 (1974): 367–78; J. T. McAllister, "The Battle of Point Pleasant," *Virginia Magazine of History and Biography* 10 (1903): 75–82; Robert S. Loving, *Double Destiny: The Story of Bristol, Tennessee-Virginia* (1955); Lewis Preston Summers, *History of Southwest Virginia, 1746–1786, Washington County, 1770–1870* (1903); and Williams, *History of the Lost State of Franklin* (1933).

DALE J. SCHMITT

SHELBY, Isaac (11 Dec. 1750–18 July 1826), first governor of Kentucky and revolutionary war hero, was born near Hagerstown, Frederick County, Maryland, the son of Evan Shelby and Letitia Cox, farmers. The Shelby family originally came from Wales to Pennsylvania and then to Maryland. In 1773 the family moved to the Holston area of western Virginia, where they established a fort and small trading post.

In 1774 Shelby served as a lieutenant in Lord Dunmore's War against the Indians. He fought bravely in the battle of Point Pleasant in October 1774 and became a frontier hero. In July 1775 Shelby surveyed land in Kentucky for the Transylvania Company. The following year he returned to Kentucky to improve his own land claim of 1,400 acres. However, in 1777 Virginia governor Patrick Henry appointed Shelby as a commissary agent for the Continental army to secure much-needed supplies for American outposts along the frontier. Faith in Shelby's leadership abilities was demonstrated in 1779, when he was chosen as a representative to the Virginia legislature for Washington County. In July 1780 Shelby joined with General Charles McDowell to attack British and Loyalist forces in western North Carolina. Minor American victories,

however, were soon overshadowed by the defeat of General Horatio Gates's Continental forces at the battle of Camden in August 1780. Shelby and his men retreated to their homes across the Appalachian Mountains. The British commander in western North Carolina, Major Patrick Ferguson, sent a warning to the frontier settlements to make no further attacks against British forces. Shelby and other frontier leaders, incensed by Ferguson's warning, became determined to initiate further attacks on the British.

Shelby, John Sevier, and other frontier leaders planned a campaign against the British and Loyalists in late 1780. Shelby enlisted 240 men for the campaign. By the time the Americans met Ferguson and his force at Kings Mountain, South Carolina, on 7 October 1780, their number exceeded 1,000 men. In an intense battle, Major Ferguson was killed and his forces were defeated. A few months later Shelby assisted in another American victory at the battle of Cowpens. At Shelby's insistence, the American forces planned to drive the British and Loyalists from the area of Fort Ninety-six and Augusta in South Carolina. Shelby believed that the Cherokee Indians were being armed and incited to attack the frontier settlements from these positions. Generals Daniel Morgan and Horatio Gates agreed with Shelby to march against the British. However, Lord Charles Cornwallis learned of the American advance on Fort Ninety-six and sent Banastre Tarleton with a force of 1,000 men to defeat the Americans. The British encountered the Americans at Cowpens, South Carolina, on 17 January 1781. What followed was a brilliant victory by the Americans. British casualties were estimated to be about 600, while American forces lost 72. The British advance into North Carolina was delayed. The Continental Congress and the North Carolina Legislature voted resolutions of thanks for his services at the battle of Kings Mountain. Shelby continued his service to the American cause by raising 500 troops who joined the command of Colonel Hezikiah Maham of the Carolina Dragoons and captured the British stronghold of Fair Lawn, South Carolina, in 1781. During this campaign, the popular Shelby was elected as a representative to the legislature of North Carolina. Shelby lived in North Carolina during the latter part of the revolutionary war and was considered a resident. He was reelected to the legislature in 1782.

In 1783 Shelby moved to Kentucky and on 19 April of that year he married Susannah Hart, the daughter of Nathaniel and Sarah Simpson Hart. The couple would have eleven children.

Because of his military exploits, Shelby became one of the most influential men in Kentucky. In 1783 he was appointed a trustee of the newly established Transylvania Seminary (later Transylvania University). Shelby also served as a justice of the peace and a commissioner of the Lincoln County court. In 1784 Shelby was elected chairman of the first Kentucky statehood convention. Due to his enormous popularity, Shelby was elected the first governor of the Commonwealth of Kentucky in June 1792. Throughout his first term as governor, Shelby's primary concerns were the problems of establishing Kentucky's new government and providing for the safety of his frontier state against Indian raids by creating an effective militia. He also pressured the federal government to help defend the frontier. In 1792 President George Washington appointed General Anthony Wayne commander of the Northwest Territory with the goal of removing the Indians from the territory. Wayne decisively defeated the Indians in the battle of Fallen Timbers on 20 August 1794, thus ending the immediate fear of an Indian invasion of Kentucky.

The Shelby administration also found itself involved in international affairs when in 1793 Edmond Genet, the French minister to the United States, sent four agents to Kentucky to secure a base for attacks against Spanish possessions in the West. Shelby did not believe that the French would be successful in their plans and did not actively support them. Although he was sympathetic to the French cause, he was relieved when Genet was discredited and recalled as minister, an act that resulted in the collapse of French intrigues. Shelby did not want Kentucky to become involved in a European power struggle.

Another concern of the Shelby administration was the navigation of the Mississippi River. Kentucky's commercial welfare depended on the commonwealth's right to send agricultural goods down the Mississippi to the New Orleans markets. The Spanish government, hoping to stem the growing influence of the United States on Spanish territories, had closed the Mississippi to American trade. Shelby pressured the federal government to relieve an intolerable situation for Kentucky commerce. The needs of the West were met when, on 27 October 1795 a treaty was signed with Spain that opened the Mississippi River to American trade.

With a sense of accomplishment, Shelby completed his first term as governor in June 1796. Under Shelby's guidance, Kentucky secured an organized government. Internal improvements such as the Wilderness Road were achieved during his four years in office. After leaving office, Shelby retired to his plantation at "Traveler's Rest" in Lincoln County to pursue his agricultural interests. As owner of some 6,000 acres, Shelby used the labor of both tenants and slaves to cultivate his properties. The Shelby estate raised cattle, hogs, horses, and mules along with grain crops. Shelby displayed a keen interest in the scientific breeding of livestock. As early as 1787 he helped organize the Kentucky Society for Promoting Useful Knowledge, which encouraged agricultural and livestock improvements.

Concern over the impending war with Great Britain interrupted Shelby's contented agrarian lifestyle. In 1812 the 62-year-old Shelby consented to run for a second term as governor of Kentucky. Despite the opposition's attacks about his advanced age, Shelby easily defeated his opponent, Gabriel Slaughter. The War of 1812 would dominate Shelby's second administration. He formulated a more stringent militia law, which made males between the ages of eighteen and forty-five (except ministers) eligible for military service. Shelby also encouraged the women of Kentucky to produce clothing and other items for the war effort.

Kentucky troops suffered a disastrous defeat in 1813 at the battle of the River Raisin. Outraged, Shelby raised more than 3,000 militiamen and joined forces with General William Henry Harrison against the British and Indians under the command of General Isaac Proctor and the famous Shawnee chief, Tecumseh, at the battle of the Thames on 5 October 1813. The brief but intense battle was a victory for the Americans. Tecumseh was killed, and what was left of the British army retreated. A grateful Congress bestowed a gold medal on Shelby for his services to the nation.

The remainder of Shelby's term as governor resulted in little legislation of any importance. When he left office in 1816, he was determined to remain a private citizen. In 1817 Shelby refused an appointment as U.S. secretary of war, citing his advanced age. However, Shelby did help Andrew Jackson negotiate a treaty with the Chickasaw Indians in 1818 to purchase their lands west of the Tennessee River. Also in 1818 Shelby was elected president of the Kentucky Agricultural Society, and in 1819 he became a trustee of Centre College in Danville, Kentucky. Shelby died at his home in Lincoln County.

In many respects Isaac Shelby was Kentucky's George Washington. To his fellow citizens he became a symbol of leadership and stability on the American frontier. Although he was not a brilliant statesman, Shelby's contemporaries greatly admired his devotion to duty. Shelby's place in history is secured as well by his military exploits during the revolutionary war and the War of 1812.

• Many of Isaac Shelby's papers are in the collections of the Kentucky Historical Society in Frankfort and at the Filson Club in Louisville. A large collection of Shelby papers is in the Margaret I. King Library at the University of Kentucky. The most complete biography of Shelby is Sylvia Wrobel and George Grider, *Isaac Shelby: Kentucky's First Governor and Hero of Three Wars* (1974). An excellent overview of Shelby's role at the battle of Kings Mountain is Lyman C. Draper, *Kings Mountain and Its Heroes* (1881). Patricia Watlington, *The Partisan Spirit* (1972), gives an in-depth study of the early political situation in Kentucky. Among the several articles pertaining to the life and career of Shelby are Charles R. Staples, "Kentucky's First Inauguration Day," *Register of the Kentucky Historical Society* 31 (1933): 146–51, which describes the beginning of Shelby's first administration, and Archibald Henderson, "Isaac Shelby and the Genet Mission," *Mississippi Valley Historical Review* 6 (1920): 451–69, which explores the controversial Genet mission to the United States and Shelby's role in the French intrigue.

RON D. BRYANT

SHELBY, Joseph Orville (12 Dec. 1830–13 Feb. 1897), planter and soldier, was born at Lexington, Kentucky, the son of Orville Shelby and his second wife, Anna Boswell. "Jo" Shelby studied at Transylvania University (1845–1848), followed by one year in Philadelphia. At age nineteen he moved to Lafayette County,

Missouri, taking up planting and the manufacture of rope. He acquired a fortune but was increasingly distracted by the slavery controversy in "bleeding Kansas." The slaveholding Shelby led proslavery volunteers in several raids but resumed his economic pursuits when antislavery forces triumphed in Kansas. In 1858 he married a distant cousin, Elizabeth Shelby; they had seven children.

After the Civil War erupted, Shelby, like many others in badly divided Missouri, could have joined either side, but his southern heritage and proslavery views bonded him to the Confederacy. He organized a company of cavalry and led his men into action at Boonville (where they captured the steamship *Sunshine* on the Missouri River) and Wilson's Creek in 1861. Soon thereafter, Shelby followed Major General (former Missouri governor) Sterling Price into Arkansas.

Although lacking formal military training, Shelby demonstrated leadership and a natural talent for martial endeavors. He led his company in the defense of Corinth, Mississippi, in 1862, earning enough favorable notice to be promoted to colonel and authorized to raise troops in Missouri. Returning to Lafayette County, Shelby soon had enough recruits to form a cavalry regiment.

Attached to John S. Marmaduke's division, Shelby proved a resourceful soldier. Leading what soon came to be called his "Iron Brigade," he distinguished himself on virtually every significant battlefield of the Trans-Mississippi theater, especially in Missouri and Arkansas. At Pea Ridge, Newtonia, Cane Hill, Prairie Grove, Cape Girardeau, Helena, and dozens of other engagements, Shelby cut a colorful figure, riding a large horse and sporting a black plume in his hat. His lack of military schooling proved no hindrance as he instinctively mastered cavalry warfare. He grasped the importance of a swift, mobile offensive, which made him particularly effective as a raider, but unlike others of that ilk Shelby was a complete soldier. He devised a "rolling" form of rearguard action that forced pursuing foes to deploy completely and repeatedly against successive temporary lines of resistance that fell back over each other in a "leapfrog" fashion.

Shelby demonstrated his capacity for independent command during his famous raid into Missouri in 1863, one of the most successful such actions of the war. In late September he led 1,000 men across the western half of Missouri as far north as the Missouri River. Although opposed by Federal forces outnumbering him more than five to one, by the time he reentered Arkansas in late October, Shelby had covered over 1,000 miles at an average pace of 36 miles per day; killed, wounded, or captured over 1,000 Federal troops; added hundreds of recruits to his command; completely reequipped his men; brought out thousands of horses and mules; and inflicted nearly $2 million in damage on railroads and Federal property.

Promoted to brigadier general in December 1863, Shelby spent much of 1864 fighting Union forces invading Arkansas, yet he remained anxious to lead another raid into Missouri. In September 1864 he got his chance, not independently but as a division commander under Price. Price led 12,000 Confederate horsemen (many of them unarmed) into Missouri, hoping to capture supplies and recruit 30,000 men. Price quickly abandoned his plan to capture St. Louis, instead moving westward across Missouri with Federal forces closing from several directions. Near Kansas City, superior Union forces caught Price, and in the battle of Westport on 23 October, the Confederates escaped complete destruction due chiefly to Shelby's daring tactics and fierce rearguard actions. In his official report, Price wrote of Shelby, "I consider him the best cavalry officer I ever saw" (*O.R.*, vol. 41, part 1, p. 639). Federal major general Alfred Pleasonton, who fought the renowned "Jeb" Stuart in Virginia and engaged Shelby at Westport, agreed, "Shelby was the best cavalry general of the South" (Foote, vol. 2, p. 776).

At the Confederacy's collapse in April-May 1865, many of Shelby's men wanted to continue the fight, but he persuaded them to go to Mexico. Leading 1,000 men, Shelby was offered by the mayor of Austin, Texas, the $300,000 in specie in the Confederate subtreasury there, but Shelby refused, noting, "I went into the war with clean hands, and by God's blessing I will go out of the war with clean hands" (*New York Times*, 14 Feb. 1897). In Mexico City, Shelby offered to raise an American army of 40,000 men, but Emperor Maximilian declined. After two years in Mexico as a freight contractor, Shelby returned to his Missouri farm in 1867.

Appointed U.S. marshal for western Missouri by President Grover Cleveland in 1893, Shelby sparked controversies. His vigorous suppression of labor unrest during the railroad strike of 1894 led Governor William J. Stone to protest what he considered violations of state sovereignty, but Shelby responded, "The question of State rights was decided by the war, and settled for all time when Lee surrendered at Appomattox" (*St. Louis Globe-Democrat*, 14 Feb. 1897). Shelby also shocked Missourians by appointing an African American as one of his deputies, then a bold move in a former slave state. To his critics, Shelby replied, "The young man is competent. . . . I appointed him for efficiency, and . . . I trust that this is the last I shall have to say in defense of my official action. I am right in what I have done and by the right I propose to stand" (*New York Times*, 14 Feb. 1897). These tempests notwithstanding, Shelby remained popular with his fellow citizens, and a number of localities vied to be his burial place when he died near Adrian, Missouri.

Like many men of his generation, Shelby was thrust into a military life for which he had not prepared. Unlike most of his contemporaries, however, Shelby demonstrated military genius, and he is widely regarded as one of the most talented of the numerous "amateur generals" on either side during the Civil War.

• For primary source references on Shelby's military career, there is no substitute for *The War of the Rebellion: A Compilation of the Official Records of the Union and Confederate Armies*

(128 vols., 1880–1901), commonly referred to as the *O.R.* Shelby appears in many of the volumes, but those of most utility are vol. 22, parts 1–2 (Cane Hill, Prairie Grove, Helena, Cape Girardeau, and other operations with Marmaduke and Shelby's own 1863 raid into Mo.); vol. 34, parts 1–4 (1864 operations in Ark.); vol. 39, part 2, and vol. 41, part 1 (Price's 1864 Mo. raid); and vol. 46, part 3, and vol. 48, parts 1–2 (1865 operations). The only full biography of Shelby is David O'Flaherty, *General Jo Shelby: Undefeated Rebel* (1954). Another helpful source is Clement A. Evans, ed., *Confederate Military History*, vol. 9: *Missouri* (1899), which also has much useful information on Shelby's life before and after the war, and vol. 10: *Arkansas* (1899). See also Wiley Britton, "Résumé of Military Operations in Missouri and Arkansas, 1864–1865," in *Battles and Leaders of the Civil War*, vol. 4, ed. Clarence C. Buel and Robert U. Johnson (1888). Because the Trans-Mississippi theater of operations in the Civil War has received relatively less coverage than the others, secondary sources are concomitantly less plentiful. In terms of the large, multivolume histories, the best for information on Shelby and his campaigns is Shelby Foote, *The Civil War*, vol. 2: *Fredericksburg to Meridian* (1963) and vol. 3: *Red River to Appomattox* (1974). Articles of interest for readers seeking more detail include D. Alexander Brown, "The Battle of Westport," *Civil War Times Illustrated*, July 1966, pp. 4–11, 40–43; William C. Davis, "The Battle of Prairie Grove," *Civil War Times Illustrated*, July 1968, pp. 12–19; and Samual [*sic*] T. Gill, "Liberator Unmercifully Hounded," *America's Civil War*, Sept. 1988, pp. 34–41. Obituaries are in the *New York Times* and the *St. Louis Globe-Democrat*, 14 Feb. 1897.

BROECK N. ODER

SHELDON, Charles Monroe (26 Feb. 1857–24 Feb. 1946), Congregational minister and social reformer, was born in Wellsville, New York, the son of Reverend Stewart Sheldon, a Congregational pastor, and Sarah Ward. Stewart Sheldon moved his family from successive church appointments in New York, Missouri, Rhode Island, and Michigan before settling on a farm near Yankton, South Dakota, in 1867. In his later years, Charles Sheldon rejoiced in recollections of the family values, hard work, and self-reliance that characterized his youth on the farm. He went east to study at Phillips Academy in Andover, Massachusetts, where he graduated in 1879; at Brown University, where he received a B.A. in 1883; and Andover Theological Seminary, where he earned a B.D. in 1886. Ordained in the Congregational ministry in 1886, Sheldon served a church in Waterbury, Vermont, until 1888, when he accepted a call to Central Congregational Church in Topeka, Kansas. On 20 May 1891 he married Mary Abby Merriam of Topeka; they became the parents of one child.

By 1890, Topeka had begun to shed its frontier character to participate in the promise and distress of industrial America. As an important railroad shipping center, it attracted a large number of working-class African Americans and immigrants whose lives were largely alien to those of Sheldon's white, middle-class congregation. Responding to his alienation from "the great world of labor," in 1891 Sheldon announced that he would spend some time living among the city's African Americans, industrial and railroad laborers, and

the unemployed. His plan to spend a week in Topeka's black ghetto, "Tennesseetown," stretched to three weeks, during which he studied the effects of race prejudice, poverty, and vice. Thereafter, Sheldon and the youth of his church's Christian Endeavor Society organized a Christian social settlement, where they assisted and worshiped with the black residents of Tennesseetown.

Sheldon drew upon his experiences with Topeka's working-class residents in writing several series of stories that he read to his Sunday evening congregation and published serially in the *Advance*, Chicago's Congregational periodical. *Richard Bruce* (1892) and *The Crucifixion of Philip Strong* (1894) appeared as books, but Sheldon's fiction won little notice until 1897, when he published *In His Steps*. A simple story with little literary merit, *In His Steps* is set in a midwestern railroad town that is transformed when Reverend Henry Maxwell challenges his middle-class congregation to direct their lives by answers to the question "What would Jesus do?" The subsequent plot touches on issues of class conflict, corporate ethics, labor relations, political corruption, and the slums, but the heart of the novel turns on the efforts of its earnest, middle-class characters to relate to the lives of working-class people.

Like his earlier novels, *In His Steps* was serialized in the *Advance* and published in a paperback format, but unlike them it was a sales success. When a flaw in its copyright allowed for competing editions of the book, sales reached into the millions. Sheldon's claim that *In His Steps* sold thirty million copies within forty years seems unlikely, but even a more reasonable estimate of six million copies sold would place it among the best-selling books of all time. Only one publisher, however, paid its author more than token royalties. Made into a movie in 1936, *In His Steps* has continued to appear on the lists of several publishers. Its remarkable initial success has been explained by its appearance at a time when middle-class Americans were disturbed by the social issues it addressed. The book's continued popularity, however, suggests that it appeals to an audience motivated by more than periodic social crises.

In 1900 Sheldon launched a widely publicized experiment by editing the *Topeka Daily Capital* for a week, during which time the newspaper emphasized the moral side of the news and excluded material that Sheldon thought objectionable. Sheldon's editorial policy shunned sensational reports of crime and scandal; it excluded accounts of prize fights and even most stock market reports as exploiting human inclinations to violence and gambling. He refused advertisements for alcohol and tobacco but also for land and stock investments, women's undergarments, patent medicines, and other products that Sheldon thought were of dubious value. National publicity raised the newspaper's circulation from 12,000 to 350,000 during the experiment, but it ended because of the newspaper's contractual obligations to a more traditional editorial control. As a writer, Sheldon published more than fifty books, hundreds of articles in religious and secular periodicals, and poems, hymns, and plays, but he never repeated the popular success of *In His Steps*. He produced *Jesus Is Here!* (1913) as a sequel to *In His Steps* and *In His Steps Today* (1921) as a nonfiction report on the church's progress since 1896.

Sheldon was a tireless pastor, lecturer, and reformer, who affirmed the Social Gospel's claim that the Kingdom of God was to be established here on earth. He defended the civil rights of African Americans, Jews, women, and other minorities. As a religious reformer, he advocated prohibition, Protestant ecumenism, and world peace. In 1900 and in 1917–1918 he toured the British Isles in behalf of prohibition, and in 1914–1915, at the end of a three-year leave of absence from his pulpit, he joined a "Flying Squadron" of prohibitionists who spoke in 247 American cities in 245 days. In 1919, following a severe illness, Sheldon resigned as pastor of Topeka's Central Congregational Church.

During the latter part of his career, Sheldon worked for the *Christian Herald*, a nondenominational Protestant monthly periodical. He was editor in chief from 1920 to 1925 and a contributing editor from 1926 to 1946. Although Sheldon was a theological liberal, he remained aloof from the fundamentalist-modernist controversy of the 1920s. After the repeal of Prohibition in 1933, he remained interested in pacifism and Protestant ecumenism, continuing to be active into old age. Sheldon died in Topeka two days before his eighty-ninth birthday. His life, ministry, and published work were an unsophisticated monument to the hope of evangelical Protestant social Christianity.

• Large collections of Charles M. Sheldon's manuscript and print documents are at Central Congregational Church and the Kansas State Historical Society in Topeka and at the University of Kansas in Lawrence. Sheldon's autobiography, *Charles M. Sheldon: His Life Story* (1925), is superficial. The standard biography is Timothy M. Miller, *Following in His Steps: A Biography of Charles M. Sheldon* (1987), but Paul Boyer's article, "*In His Steps*: A Re-appraisal," *American Quarterly* 23 (Spring 1971): 60–78, is a fine short introduction. Clinton N. Howard, "In Memoriam: Dr. Charles M. Sheldon, Kansas," *Progress* 46 (Mar. 1946): 3, is a useful obituary.

RALPH E. LUKER

SHELDON, Edward Austin (4 Oct. 1823–26 Aug. 1897), educator, was born near Perry Center, Wyoming County, New York, the son of Eleazer Sheldon and Laura Austin, farmers. He received his early education at the local district school, an institution that, like most of its counterparts, was poorly equipped and run by teachers with uneven credentials. Sheldon's initial exposure to education was unimpressive, and he noted in his *Autobiography*, "I didn't care a fig about learning to spell. I utterly despised learning of all kinds" (Sheldon, p. 29). However, he later found his studies at the newly founded Perry Center Academy more to his liking. Under the influence of the academy's master, Charles Huntington, Sheldon was to prepare for college. He entered Hamilton College in Clin-

ton, New York, in 1844 and found his classwork both challenging and worthwhile. However, an attack of pleurisy derailed his formal education in 1847, and Sheldon was forced to leave Hamilton.

In an effort to regain his health, Sheldon spent the summer of 1847 working in the nursery business of Charles and Andrew Jackson Downing in Newburgh, New York. In the fall of that same year, he accepted an offer from J. W. P. Allen of Oswego, New York, to enter into a nursery partnership in that city. Although still troubled by his health, Sheldon borrowed $500 from his father and entered the horticultural business with high hopes. The partnership soon failed, however, and Sheldon took ownership of a block of Oswego property lots in exchange for his share of the business. He noted that he "was once more free, and without any plans for life . . . [and] began to look around eagerly for some occupation" (Sheldon, p. 69). After an abortive search for employment in New York City, he returned to Oswego and entered into his life's work—education.

At loose ends, Sheldon decided "to investigate the condition of the poorer classes in the city of Oswego" (Sheldon, p. 74). Shocked by the lack of educational opportunities for poor children, he was moved to action. With the help of a few friends, he enlisted the support of locally prominent citizens and formed the Orphan and Free School Association of Oswego on 28 November 1848. Initial community response was positive; subscription lists were soon passed through the city in an effort to raise funds for clothing for the children as well as books. Sheldon realized that he had entered into his new enterprise "unpremeditatedly and unintentionally" but "felt that something ought to be done here; and I knew it would not be done until some one should offer himself a sacrifice to the work and lead it on" (Sheldon, p. 76). With his health now fully restored, Sheldon had anticipated entering the Auburn Theological Seminary; however, events forced a permanent change in his plans. Although he protested to the organizing committee of the Orphan and Free School that "I cannot teach the school; I never had any such idea. I never taught school in my life and do not know how to teach," he was engaged as the first teacher at a salary of $300 a year (Sheldon, p. 77). Sheldon opened his so-called "ragged school" in Oswego in the fall of 1848.

Beginning with some 120 students, most of whom had never been in a classroom, Sheldon proceeded more on enthusiasm than theory, later claiming, "One thing is surely true: if any principles of pedagogy were applied in this school, they were either intuitive or accidental. I had never read any theories of school teaching, and certainly had none of my own at the onset; at least, all my work was haphazard. About all I knew was that these children were poor, neglected, and ignorant, and needed sympathy and help; and these I certainly could give them" (Sheldon, p. 79). In addition to his weekday instructions, Sheldon also engaged in home visits on Saturdays. He married Frances Ann Bradford Stiles of Syracuse in 1849; the couple eventually had five children, one of whom, Mary Downing Sheldon Barnes, also became a leading educator.

Sheldon's efforts with the school led to his advocacy of free schools for all children within the city of Oswego. Here Sheldon ran into opposition; while some objected to the expense, others objected to the plan as a "Protestant plot" to undercut local Catholic schools. At the same time, local enthusiasm and financial support for the school began to wane, and Sheldon, faced with additional responsibilities following his marriage, left his post in 1849 and took over a local private school. His "Oswego Seminary," originally a girl's school, became coeducational and enjoyed a period of success before it, too, suffered a decline in support. With the free school movement still in limbo, Sheldon left Oswego in 1851 and assumed the post of superintendent of schools in Syracuse. In addition to improving his income, Sheldon also recorded several major accomplishments in Syracuse, including the establishment of evening classes, an improved school library system, and an improvement in the gradation and classification of the schools within the system. Additionally, he managed to secure improvements in the physical plants of the local schools and managed to establish harmonious relations between his teachers, the school board, and parents.

The free school movement in Oswego continued following Sheldon's departure. Efforts to implement the new system were rewarded in 1853 with the passage of a bill in the New York state legislature authorizing its creation. With the organization of the first board of education on 11 May 1853, Sheldon was offered the position of secretary (in effect, the superintendent) of the newly created system. Although Sheldon had formed many warm relationships in Syracuse, he found the possibilities in Oswego too great to ignore, noting that he "would have the advantage of organizing a system from the start, in accordance with my own views. This would be better than to try to patch up and reorganize one already established. I would have the pleasure of carrying out and perfecting plans I had already laid out" (Sheldon, p. 94).

Upon his return to Oswego, Sheldon immediately set out to obtain better quality teachers, to reorganize courses of study, and to systematically grade and classify schools. He also rearranged the city into twelve primary school districts. Enjoying the full support of his board, Sheldon's plans soon prospered and gained him recognition; he was elected president of the state teachers' association in 1860 and in the same year also agreed to serve as an editor of the *New York Teacher*.

Sheldon's success was almost too complete; he soon found that he was training teachers only to lose them to other school systems. Accordingly, with his encouragement the Oswego Primary Teachers' Training School opened in May 1861. An instructor from the London, England, Home and Colonial Training Institution, Margaret E. M. Jones, was secured on a one-year contract, and the school, based on the principles first outlined by Johann Heinrich Pestalozzi, soon prospered. The first city "Teachers' Training" school

in the country, it differed from the first normal schools, originally established in Massachusetts, by offering both practice teaching and a model school.

Sheldon assumed the duties of principal of the training school in its second year of operation (1862), continuing in the position until his death. In 1863 the state began to provide not only recognition but financial support for the school; in 1866 it was renamed the Oswego State Normal and Training School. The following school year (1866–1867) provided the most tangible evidence of Sheldon's success, as six additional normal and training schools were organized in New York State along the lines of his Oswego school. Imbued with the then-radical principles of Pestalozzi (which included gradual instruction of the child as a child—as opposed to an adult in miniature—and making allowances for differences between children), the Oswego school became (through its graduates) a major center of influence in American educational thought and theory.

Relinquishing his duties as school superintendent in 1869, Sheldon devoted the remainder of his life to the running of Oswego State Normal (now the State University of New York at Oswego). Amid his many other labors he found time to author several educational texts, including *A Manual of Elementary Instruction* (1862), *Lessons on Objects* (1863), *First Reading Book and Phonic Cards* (1863), and *Teachers' Manual of Instruction in Reading* (1875). His wife died in 1896, and Sheldon himself died at his home in Oswego the next year.

Having entered his chosen field almost by accident, Sheldon provided numerous innovations to the field of education in the areas of administration and teacher training. While not an original thinker, his effective advocacy of the principles of Pestalozzi, as well as his now universally used program of practice teaching, places him solidly within the ranks of such educational pioneers as Horace Mann and Samuel Gridley Howe.

• The papers of Sheldon are held at the State University of New York archives, Oswego, New York. The *Autobiography of Edward Austin Sheldon* (1911) was edited by his daughter Mary Sheldon Barnes and is an invaluable source of information on his life and career. Also useful are Dorothy Rogers, *Oswego: Fountainhead of Teacher Education* (1961), and N. H. Dearborn, *The Oswego Movement in American Education* (1925). Obituaries are in the *New York Tribune* and the *New York Times*, both 27 Aug. 1897.

EDWARD L. LACH, JR.

SHELDON, Edward Brewster (4 Feb. 1886–1 Apr. 1946), playwright, was born in Chicago, Illinois, the son of Theodore Sheldon and Mary Strong. To his family and friends he was always "Ned"; his middle name he bestowed upon himself on entering Harvard in 1904. The family lived comfortably, cushioned by the substantial wealth that Theodore Sheldon derived from Chicago real estate. Henry Strong, Sheldon's maternal grandfather, who was a former president of the Atchison, Topeka & Santa Fe Railroad, possessed an even greater fortune.

In early boyhood Sheldon revealed the enthusiasm for the theater that was to become the central interest of his life. Encouraged by his mother, he put on plays at home and attended touring productions as they reached Chicago. At fourteen he was sent to the Hill School, in Pennsylvania, to prepare for Harvard. After his graduation in 1903, Sheldon's parents sent him to the Milton Academy, in Massachusetts, for an additional year of preparation. He was not happy in the school, however, and withdrew before the year was over. Back in Chicago he was tutored privately for the Harvard entrance examinations.

At Harvard Sheldon was both an academic and a social success. He made friends easily and dazzled young women with his dark good looks and conversational grace. He attended the theater in Boston as often as his allowance permitted and graduated in 1907 with high honors after only three years. The most important event of his undergraduate career was his admission, in freshman year, to Professor George Pierce Baker's renowned English 47, ostensibly a course in dramatic literature, but in fact a course in dramaturgy for would-be playwrights. Baker liked the play that Sheldon wrote for the course and recommended that he send it to an agent. Sheldon did so, but the agent, Alice Kauser, did not pull the play of the pile on her desk and read it until the summer of his graduation. Finding it promising but not stageworthy, she asked Sheldon to write another play and submit it to her. At Harvard, where he was enrolled for a year of graduate study, Sheldon tried again, managing both to turn out a new play and earn a master of arts degree in English. The play was *Salvation Nell*, a melodrama of a young woman with a grim past who joins the Salvation Army and becomes so effective as a street preacher that she can redeem even her drink-sodden former lover. Kauser placed it with the actress Minnie Maddern Fiske, who opened in it to generally favorable reviews in the fall of 1908.

Although Sheldon had taken his M.A. with the thought of teaching, he was now a confirmed man of the theater and chose to live in New York, the center of his profession. Eight plays followed *Salvation Nell* in rapid order; among them were five successes: *The Nigger* (1909, performed in repertory with plays by other writers, not for a regular run), a melodramatic portrait of a southern white-supremacist politician who discovers that he himself is of mixed ancestry; *The Boss* (1911), a depiction of the desensitizing effects of power and wealth; *The High Road* (1912), starring Fiske, the portrait of a woman married to a presidential candidate and for that reason forced to reveal the sins of her past; *Romance* (1913), the tearfully sentimental tale of a young minister's love for a worldly opera singer; and *The Song of Songs* (1914), the dramatization of a novel by Hermann Sudermann. All are closely plotted, well-made plays.

Romance, ultimately Sheldon's most popular play of all, starred Doris Keane, a young actress whom Sheldon met while still at Harvard; over a period of thirteen years she acted the role of the opera star in New York, on the road, and in England and Scotland, and in 1920 appeared in a film version. A second film version was produced in 1930, starring Greta Garbo. Sheldon and Keane had become engaged when he wrote the play. Some time before it opened, however, Sheldon broke the engagement. Long after the event, Keane told a friend that he had said, "I would make a very poor sort of husband for you, Doris."

In 1915, only twenty-nine and at the peak of his youthful fame, Sheldon received his first intimation of the crippling arthritis that would drastically alter his way of life. It began with a stiffness in his knees and gradually worsened until, by 1919, he could scarcely walk. Various treatments were prescribed and tried, but none proved helpful. In 1920 he became permanently bedridden and soon could not even turn his head. Fortunately, his royalties and the family's wealth protected him from what might have been long years of bleak confinement to a hospital room. He could afford a comfortable apartment, servants, and the best orthopedic care. His charm and enthusiasm never left him; friends were delighted to receive his invitations to lunch or dinner, and he never lacked for visitors stopping by for a chat at his bedside.

The theater remained Sheldon's dominant passion until the end. Despite his illness, he continued to write until 1930. In 1917 he adapted *The Lady of the Camellias*, by Alexandre Dumas fils, for Ethel Barrymore. In 1919 he adapted Sem Benelli's *The Jest* for Lionel Barrymore and John Barrymore. Eight more works followed these, three of which could be counted successes: the melodramatic *Lulu Belle* (1926), written with Charles MacArthur; *The Age of Innocence*, an adaptation of the novel by Edith Wharton, written with Margaret Ayer Barnes and starring Katharine Cornell; and *Dishonored Lady* (1930), the pulse-raising depiction of a crime of passion, also written with Barnes and starring Cornell. Possibly of greater importance to the theater, however, was the counsel that Sheldon gave to the many playwrights and actors who sought him out, among them Thornton Wilder, Robert E. Sherwood, Helen Hayes, Ruth Gordon, Cornell, and the Barrymores. John Barrymore, to whom his emotional attachment would seem to have been the strongest of Sheldon's life, wrote in 1926, "No one since I have been a serious actor has been more helpful to me than Edward Sheldon; in fact, I am not sure that he didn't make me a serious actor."

In 1930 Sheldon's vision began to fade, and he soon lost it altogether. Even this extreme deprivation did not take away his zest for living. Visitors continued to share their experiences with him. Authors read to him from works in progress; notable musicians performed privately for him. He died at his home in New York.

• Sheldon's papers are in the Special Collections of the Houghton Library at Harvard. Reviews of his plays are gathered in the Robinson Locke Collection of the New York Public Library of the Performing Arts. Biographies of Sheldon include Eric Wollencott Barnes, *The Man Who Lived Twice* (1956), and Loren K. Ruff, *Edward Sheldon* (1982). He is mentioned in the memoirs of many of his friends; see especially John Barrymore, *Confessions of an Actor* (1926); Lionel Barrymore, *We Barrymores* (1951); Barrett H. Clark, *Intimate Portraits* (1951); and Van Wyck Brooks, *Scenes and Portraits: Memories of Childhood and Youth* (1954). Margot Peters provides an analysis of Sheldon's friendship with John Barrymore in *The House of Barrymore* (1990). An obituary appeared in the *New York Times*, 2 Apr. 1946.

MALCOLM GOLDSTEIN

SHELDON, William Herbert (17 Nov. 1898–16 Sept. 1977), psychologist and physician, was born in Warwick, Rhode Island, the son of William Herbert Sheldon, a jeweler, and Mary Abby Greene. Little is known about Sheldon's parents, but the psychologist was very close to his father, an amateur naturalist, hunting guide, and professional breeder as well as a judge of sporting dogs and poultry. William Herbert Sheldon, Sr., who is said to have been a close friend of psychologist and philosopher William James, chose the Harvard professor as his son's godfather. Sheldon reiterated the important influence of these two men throughout his controversial career.

On the eve of World War I Sheldon began his undergraduate studies at Brown University. He received his A.B. in 1918 and then pursued his master's degree in psychology at the University of Colorado (awarded in 1923). In 1925 Sheldon married Louise Steiger; they divorced in 1928. Sheldon took his Ph.D. in psychology and his M.D. from the University of Chicago in 1926 and 1934 respectively. During Sheldon's doctoral work under Chicago psychophysicist L. L. Thurstone, he began to develop the "somatotype" system for rating human physique, the anthropometric technique for which he became famous. The somatotype is a measurement of the degree to which three components—endomorphy (soft roundness) mesomorphy (squareness, firm muscularity), and ectomorphy (linearity, fragility)—are represented in one's physique. Each factor is quantified on a seven-point scale, with the ultimate well-balanced physique receiving a 4–4–4. Sheldon believed one's somatotype was genetically determined and thus immutable over his or her lifetime, even though an individual's "shape" might change with fluctuations in his or her weight. One's somatotype was thus a measure of his or her "constitution," or hereditary biological endowment.

Sheldon was an instructor in psychology at the University of Chicago between 1924 and 1927 and was an assistant professor at the University of Wisconsin from 1927 to 1930. After completing a pediatrics internship in 1934, Sheldon received a two-year traveling fellowship from the National Council on Religion and Higher Education to study child psychology in Europe. Returning to the United States in 1936, Sheldon joined the faculty at the Chicago Theological Seminary and that same year wrote his first book, *Psychology and the Promethean Will*. Sheldon interpreted religion in rather secular terms as a means of realizing the divine possibilities of human nature; he likewise regarded psychology, particularly the psychology of individual

differences and of personality development, as an essential ingredient in furthering religion. Armed with an appreciation of one's potential, obtained through psychological analysis, an individual might be better able to achieve his or her own divine possibilities.

In 1938, under the auspices of physical anthropologist Earnest Hooton, Sheldon left Chicago for Cambridge, Massachusetts, to assume a combined research associate and lecturer position in Harvard's anthropology and psychology departments. While at Harvard, Sheldon refined his somatotyping technique, working with psychophysicist S. S. Stevens, whose interest in the quantitative side of the somatotyping led him to build Sheldon a somatotype calculating machine. Sheldon wrote two books during his four years at Harvard: *The Varieties of Human Physique: An Introduction to Constitutional Psychology* (1940) and *The Varieties of Temperament: A Psychology of Constitutional Differences* (1942). *Human Physique* set forth Sheldon's schema for classifying humankind by body type; *Human Temperament* correlated body type with behavior, connecting endomorphy, mesomorphy, and ectomorphy with three generalized character traits—relaxed sociophilia, aggressive vigor, and nervous intelligence. Sheldon's somatotyping scheme was hailed as a milestone in the objectification of body typing technique and adopted widely by physicians, criminologists, nutritionists, and physical educators. Social scientists approached Sheldon's correlation of temperament and body type with skepticism, but it was well received by the popular press as championed by Aldous Huxley, Earnest Hooton, and others. In 1943 Sheldon married Milancie Hill; they had two children.

In 1946, after two years in Texas somatotyping prospective pilots for the U.S. Army Air Corps, Sheldon succeeded George Draper, pioneer in American constitutional medicine, at the Constitution Clinic at Columbia's College of Physicians and Surgeons. There Sheldon wrote *Varieties of Delinquent Youth: An Introduction to Constitutional Psychiatry* (1949), extending his correlational analysis to the realm of psychopathology. Sheldon always had written in a lively, tongue-in-cheek style. In *Delinquent Youth*, however, the psychologist turned social critic and eugenicist, lamenting the rampant reproduction of the world's unfit and urging radical social and political measures that would favor the biologically superior, particularly those of Anglo-Saxon heritage. Words such as these, however strongly felt, were particularly distasteful to the post–World War II social science profession and elicited a strong negative reaction. Sheldon's work also was criticized as being tainted by rater bias; that is, Sheldon rated both physique and temperament, and the strong correlations he found between physique and temperament types might have reflected the power of his own preconceptions rather than actual relationships. In 1954 controversy erupted again with the publication of *Atlas of Men* (1954), a virtual "how-to" manual for somatotyping, complete with thousands of nude photographs that included some of the most prominent men of science, letters, and politics of the day (without their permission). Columbia closed the constitution laboratory in 1959. Fortunately for Sheldon, he had the backing of Dallas businessman and cofounder of Texas Instruments Eugene McDermott, who had supported his work since 1949. With McDermott's financial assistance, Sheldon established the Biological Humanics Foundation in Cambridge, Massachusetts, and continued his somatotyping research on a freelance basis. Sheldon died of a heart ailment at his office in Cambridge, attempting to complete an atlas for somatotyping women. Sheldon's penchant for classification extended to numismatics. He was a renowned collector and taxonomist of early American cents.

However eccentric Sheldon's work might seem by today's standards, his interests were not unique. Between 1916 and 1956, American, British, and European medicine and social science experienced a renaissance of interest in human constitution. Thousands of studies explored the relationship between body type and athletic performance, behavior, criminality, susceptibility to disease, and occupational aptitude. With his somatotype, Sheldon offered constitutional researchers a new gauge of physical type, both enlivening the field and capturing the public's imagination. Ultimately, however, the heterodox political and social views that framed Sheldon's work may have discredited the research of constitutionalists as much as his innovative technique advanced the field's development.

• Sheldon's research papers and a portion of his photographic archives are on file at the National Anthropological Archives of the Smithsonian Institution. Other texts Sheldon wrote are *Early American Cents, 1793–1814* (1949), *Prometheus Revisited* (1974), and *Penny Whimsey* (1976). The most revealing of his biographical sketches are found in Barbara Honeyman Heath and J. E. Lindsay Carter, *Somatotyping— Development and Applications* (1990); Richard Osborne, "William H. Sheldon," in *International Encyclopedia of the Social Sciences*, ed. David Sills (1968); and Gardner Lindzey, "Sheldon's Constitutional Psychology," in Lindzey and Calvin S. Hall, *Theories of Personality*, 3d ed. (1978). For a popular treatment of Sheldon's work, see Robert Coughlin, "What Manner of Morph Are You?" *Life*, 9 July 1951. Sheldon's involvement in the college "posture picture" phenomenon is discussed in Ron Rosenbaum, "Exposed: A Bizarre Ritual: The Posture Photo Scandal," *New York Times*, 15 Jan. 1995. In 1982 several of Sheldon's colleagues—Emil Hartl, Edward Monnelly, and Roland Elderkin—completed *Physique and Delinquent Behavior: A Thirty-year Follow-up of William H. Sheldon's "Varieties of Delinquent Youth,"* a volume that discusses Sheldon's earlier work. For more on constitutional medicine and social science historically considered, see Sarah W. Tracy, "George Draper and American Constitutional Medicine, 1916–1946: Reinventing the Sick Man," *Bulletin of the History of Medicine* 66 (1992): 53–89, and Tracy, "An Evolving Science of Man: The Transformation and Demise of American Constitutional Medicine, 1920–1950," in *Greater Than the Parts: Holism in Biomedicine, 1920–1950*, ed. George Weisz and Christopher Lawrence (1998), pp. 161–88. Sheldon's obituary is in the *New York Times*, 18 Sept. 1977.

SARAH W. TRACY

SHELFORD, Victor Ernest (22 Sept. 1877–27 Dec. 1968), ecologist, was born on a farm in Chemung County, New York, the eldest son of Alexander Hamilton Shelford and Sarah Ellen Rumsey, farmers. After ten years of schooling, he taught in Chemung County in 1894, then spent two years attending Cortland Normal and Training School to earn a teaching certificate. He taught in Chemung County again from 1897 to 1899, then entered West Virginia University, where he was strongly influenced by his uncle, William E. Rumsey, assistant state entomologist. Two years later the university's president, Jerome H. Raymond, accepted a professorship at the University of Chicago and obtained a scholarship there for Shelford.

The University of Chicago had two experimental zoologists who had ecological interests. Charles M. Child, an embryologist, taught field zoology and became both undergraduate mentor and graduate school adviser to Shelford. Charles B. Davenport, an experimental evolutionist and geneticist, persuaded Shelford to study the variations and life history of tiger beetles. One of America's first plant ecologists, Henry C. Cowles, also at Chicago, helped to broaden Shelford's interests. Cowles had studied plant succession on the dunes along the south shore of Lake Michigan, and Shelford decided that for his dissertation he would build on both his own and Cowles's earlier studies and investigate the distribution of tiger beetles among those successional environments at the lake.

Shelford received his doctorate on 11 June 1907, and the next day he married Mary Mabel Brown, with whom he had two children. The University of Chicago retained Shelford as an instructor until 1914. He then went highly recommended to the University of Illinois, where he spent the rest of his career until his retirement in 1946.

During his instructorship at Chicago he broadened his research to other groups of animals, especially fish, while preparing his *Animal Communities in Temperate America as Illustrated in the Chicago Region* (1913). This was probably the first attempt by an ecologist to synthesize for a region the accumulating knowledge in animal ecology, plant ecology, and limnology. It contained experimental as well as observational data, including his law of toleration, which states that a species is most abundant where its environmental needs are most amply met and that its range is restricted by adverse amounts of any environmental requirement. At the University of Illinois he expanded his already broad research interests to include applied ecology, especially the impact of water pollution on fish and the use of ecology in controlling insect pests.

Shelford and other ecologists of his generation organized the Ecological Society of America (ESA) in 1916 and elected him its first president, an appropriate choice because he was virtually the only ecologist who had a serious research interest in all four subdivisions, plant, animal, and marine ecology, and limnology. He led ESA committees that studied conservation and preservation issues and became involved in political advocacy. In 1946, when ESA decided that it was inappropriate for a scientific society to be engaged in political advocacy, Shelford responded by helping to form the Ecologists' Union and served on its first board of governors. In 1950 it broadened its membership beyond professional ecologists and changed its name to Nature Conservancy, which has grown steadily ever since in membership and in importance.

An early ESA committee on the preservation of natural conditions that Shelford chaired compiled a *Naturalist's Guide to the Americas* (1926), under his editorship. It became a steppingstone toward his last and largest book, *The Ecology of North America* (1963). Both works are ecological geographies, studies of the distribution and abundance of species and the factors that influence those distributions. Shelford's investigations in ecological geography extended from Hudson Bay to Panama and included the forty-eight contiguous states. He took along students on field trips to diverse parts of the continent.

Shelford's *Animal Communities in Temperate America* was among the first works that could be used as a textbook in ecology courses. Shelford took teaching as seriously as he did research (even if his lectures lacked polish), and he published two editions of a laboratory manual for animal ecology (1929, 1939); in the second edition he was assisted by Orlando Park and Warder Clyde Allee. Shelford attempted to overcome the strong tendency of ecologists to work in only one subspecialty by coauthoring a textbook, *Bio-Ecology* (1939), with plant ecologist Frederic E. Clements. Shelford was graduate adviser and dissertation supervisor for twenty-five doctoral students and fifty-one master's degree students. Mabel Shelford died in 1940 of malaria on their return journey from a summer of research in Panama. Shelford died in Urbana, Illinois.

Shelford became the most prominent animal ecologist of his generation. His influence was widespread because of his many publications of research and synthesis, his teaching and dissertation supervision, and his participation in ESA and conservation affairs.

• About ninety publications that Shelford authored or coauthored are listed in the bibliography of Robert A. Croker, *Pioneer Ecologist: The Life and Work of Victor Ernest Shelford, 1877–1968* (1991). One of Shelford's doctoral students, S. Charles Kendeigh, wrote an appreciation, "Victor Ernest Shelford, Eminent Ecologist," *Ecological Society of America Bulletin* 49 (1968): 97–100. For placement of Shelford's achievements and career within the broader context of American ecology, see Robert L. Burgess, "The Ecological Society of America: Historical Data and Some Preliminary Analyses," and Robert P. McIntosh, "Ecology since 1900," both in *History of American Ecology*, ed. Frank N. Egerton (1977); Warder Clyde Allee et al., *Principles of Animal Ecology* (1949), chap. 3; and Gerald E. Gunning, "Illinois," in *Limnology in North America*, ed. David G. Frey (1963). An obituary by John D. Buffington is in *Annals of the Entomological Society of America* 63 (1970): 347.

FRANK N. EGERTON

SHELIKHOV, Grigorii Ivanovich (1748–20 July 1795), fur trader and founder of the first permanent Russian settlement in Alaska, was born in the small southern Russian trading center of Rylsk, Kursk gubernia, the son of Ivan Shelikhov, a merchant. His mother's name is unknown. In 1772 his father sent him to Siberia to promote family interests and to escape a plague. There in 1774 he became a partner of P. S. Lebedev-Lastochkin, a merchant of Irkutsk engaging in fur-trading ventures in the Kurile and Aleutian islands. Traveling northward down the Lena River to Yakutsk, and from there by the tortuous overland route to the port and maritime fur trade center of Okhotsk, Shelikhov became involved in companies sending out trading vessels and soon concentrated on the Aleutian Island trade. In 1775 he married Natalia Alekseevna Kozhevina; they had six children. In 1778, short of money, Shelikhov became a *prikazchik* (agent) for the merchant Ivan Larionovich Golikov.

Deploring the wasteful competition among many companies in the Aleutian Islands, which resulted in virtual extermination of the valuable sea otter, Shelikhov and Golikov proposed during a trip to St. Petersburg in 1780 that they be given a monopoly on trade throughout the islands and on the coast of the American mainland, and they asked for government aid. Empress Catherine II, a free trader, refused their requests. Shelikhov and Golikov and his nephew, Captain M. S. Golikov, then formed the American Northeastern, Northern and Kurile Company, with the intention of establishing a permanent settlement as a base for further hunting and exploration. They chose the island of Kykhtak (Kodiak) as the most suitable location, although the native Koniags had driven off previous Russian groups. Backed by wealthy friends, Shelikhov and his associates built three galliots, lightweight merchant ships, near Okhotsk: the *Tri Sviatitelia* (Three Prelates, commonly mistranslated as Three Saints), the *Sv. Semeon* (St. Simeon), and the *Sv. Mikhail* (St. Michael).

The flotilla sailed on 16 August 1783 with 192 officers and men, Shelikhov, and his family. The *Sv. Mikhail* was separated from the others early in the voyage but reappeared two years later. The other two vessels continued to Bering Island, where the expedition spent the winter. In June 1784 the two vessels set out again and on 3 August reached Kodiak, where they anchored in a bay, now known as Three Saints Bay, which Shelikhov named after his vessel. The native Koniags resisted but were defeated by the well-armed Russians. In the main action Shelikhov and his men routed "a great number" who had taken refuge on a rocky spur on Sakhlidak Island; some of the resistance leaders were put to death, a number of the children were kept as hostages, and the remainder was released. The rest of the islanders soon capitulated. Shelikhov later reported their number as 50,000, but the total more likely was about 5,000. He established a school where twenty-five boys were taught to read and write Russian and to garden.

The winter of 1784–1785 was hard, with several deaths from scurvy. In the spring Shelikhov sent out parties to subjugate natives on other islands and on the mainland and to collect furs. The 1785–1786 winter passed more easily. In the spring of 1786 Shelikhov prepared to return to Okhotsk with the *Tri Sviatitelia*. The vessel bore a twelve-man crew, Shelikhov and his family, and forty natives—adults and children—who were said to have come "at their own wish" or as prisoners. Some were to be sent to the court of Catherine II, and the rest were to be taught "useful things" in Siberia. Their fate is unknown; most probably died of smallpox, the usual fate then of Alaska natives taken to Siberia.

In August the *Tri Sviatitelia* anchored at the mouth of the Bolshaia River, Kamchatka. While Shelikhov was ashore buying provisions, a strong wind tore the vessel from its anchors, carrying it far out to sea and on its way to Okhotsk. Shelikhov had to make the long journey overland to Okhotsk by dog team, arriving on 27 January 1787; his vessel had arrived safely months before. After settling matters regarding the cargo and giving orders for the return voyage, he and his wife made the two-month journey to Irkutsk, the capital of Siberia, arriving on 6 April.

In Irkutsk, Shelikhov submitted reports, plans for trade and exploration, and requests for loans and reinforcements. Shelikhov, his wife, and Ivan Golikov then left for St. Petersburg, where in February 1788 he and Golikov submitted a petition to the empress stressing their love of country and zeal for the welfare of the empress's new subjects and their need for at least 200,000 rubles and troops. However, Russia was then at war with Turkey and Sweden, and the petitioners had to return to Irkutsk with only an award of gold medals and silver sabers and a citation lauding them for their achievements.

In 1790 Shelikhov enlisted Aleksandr Andreevich Baranov, a merchant from Kargopol and a veteran of Siberian trade, to head the company's enterprises in North America. His selection was perhaps Shelikhov's greatest achievement; the pragmatic Baranov would run the colonies for the next twenty-eight years. At the same time Shelikhov hired Second Lieutenant James Shields, an Englishman in Russian service with earlier training as a shipwright, to go to North America to build ships. Shields built the three-mast *Phoenix* at Resurrection Bay (now Seward), the first large vessel built on the Pacific Coast.

In 1793 Empress Catherine granted Shelikhov's requests for clergy and colonists, and in 1794 a spiritual mission of ten clergymen and fifty-two craftsmen and peasants and their families arrived in Kodiak. The mission made wholesale conversions of Alaska natives to Christianity, laying the basis for later Russian Orthodox church activities in the region. The colonists were used to start a settlement at Yakutat, which by 1806 was overrun by the Tlingit and destroyed.

Shelikhov's interest in trade in the Kurile Islands and Japan continued, and in 1794 he sent an expedition to the Kuriles to establish a colony on Urup Island. In May 1795 he planned a joint expedition with the army captain Adam Laksman for scientific observation, trade, and establishment of relations with the Japanese.

Shelikhov's sudden death in Irkutsk, at age forty-eight, halted execution of most of his plans. After the death of Empress Catherine the next year, other merchants tried to wrest control of the company from Shelikhov's wife. Disgusted by reports of abuses against the natives of the Aleutian Islands, Emperor Paul I was about to abolish the company's privileges. However, through Natalia Shelikhov's determination and the efforts of her highly placed son-in-law, N. P. Rezanov, the emperor was persuaded to decree on 8 June 1799 the formation of the Russian-American Company, vested with the long-sought monopoly on trade. Built on the foundation laid by Shelikhov, it would rule Russian America until 1867.

A self-serving patriot and visionary, Shelikhov was ambitious, at times ruthless, and stern both with native peoples and his own men. His fame is derived partly from his *Stranstvovanie . . .* (Journey), published in St. Petersburg in 1791. A slightly revised version of his 1787 report to the governor general of Siberia, it contains many exaggerations of his achievements. To later editions the publisher added other materials, which some scholars have erroneously attributed to Shelikhov. Shelikhov's name is borne by the strait between Kodiak Island and the Alaska Peninsula, a bay on Kruse Island, a gulf between Kamchatka and the Siberian mainland, several small towns in Russia, and streets in Alaska towns.

• Shelikhov's *Stranstvovanie . . .* has been translated into English by Marina Ramsay under the title *A Voyage to America, 1783–1786*, ed. Richard A. Pierce (1981). Two works in Russian about the explorer are Leonid Aleksandrovich Sitnikov, *Grigorii Shelikhov* (1990), and A. I. Andreev, ed., *Russkie otkrytiia v Tikhom Okeane i Severnoi Ameriki v XVIII veke* (Russian discoveries in the Pacific Ocean and North America in the eighteenth century) (1948).

RICHARD A. PIERCE

SHELLABARGER, Samuel (10 Dec. 1817–6 Aug. 1896), lawyer and politician, was born in Clark County, Ohio, the son of Samuel Shellabarger and Bethany McCurdy, farmers. The family was strictly Presbyterian, and Samuel was sent to college to prepare for the ministry. He graduated from Miami University in Oxford, Ohio, in 1841 and alienated his father by pursuing a career in law instead of the church. In 1848 he married Elizabeth Brandriff; they had five children, one of whom died in infancy.

Shellabarger served on the executive committee of the Whig party for Clark County from 1848 until the party's collapse in 1854. He was a Whig member of the Ohio House of Representatives from 1851 to 1853.

Shellabarger came to national attention in the first Civil War Congress, 1861–1863, representing Ohio's Eighth Congressional District. In this Congress he defended President Abraham Lincoln's right to suspend the writ of habeas corpus under the war powers of the president. He anticipated the conflict between the Congress and the president in the conduct of the war. Disagreeing with Congressman Thaddeus Stevens from Pennsylvania, Shellabarger introduced resolutions acknowledging the different responsibilities of the two branches of government and calling for support of President Lincoln. He argued that the U.S. Constitution incorporated international law, and therefore during wartime or insurrection the government possessed all the war powers delineated as belonging to a belligerent power and could exercise them. He also argued that, apart from a constitutional amendment, the Congress could not abolish slavery. Only slaves actually captured in war could be freed under the war powers of the president. Shellabarger worked closely with Salmon P. Chase, secretary of the Treasury, to put war finances on a sound footing. He advocated the first income tax in U.S. history, supported the issuance of paper currency, and endorsed the creation of a national banking system.

With President Andrew Johnson's succession to the presidency after Lincoln's assassination, Shellabarger became a leading spokesman for the Radical Republicans in the Reconstruction debate. Some historians have called Shellabarger a "Thaddeus Stevens Radical," and others have called him "a more practical radical." At key points in the debates he suggested compromises that brought moderates and Radicals close enough together to pass legislation, such as the Civil Rights Act of 1866, the Military Reconstruction Bill, and the Fifteenth Amendment. Congressman James G. Blaine and President Rutherford B. Hayes credited Shellabarger with the rationale that brought most Republican factions to an acceptance of congressional rather than presidential control of Reconstruction. Blaine said that his theory of Reconstruction, which argued that secession was void but that the states' governments had collapsed in rebellion, opening the way for the federal government to intervene and "reconstruct" republican forms of government embracing the outcomes of the war, was a far stronger case than that presented by Stevens.

From 1869 to 1870 Shellabarger served briefly as minister to Portugal. During his term of service there, a treaty was signed authorizing an undersea cable from the United States to Portugal. Though he was personally opposed to American imperialism, he advised President Ulysses S. Grant of the availability for purchase of various Portuguese colonial possessions.

Shellabarger completed his last of four terms in Congress in 1873. He had served in the Thirty-seventh (1861–1863), Thirty-ninth (1865–1867), Fortieth (1867–1869), and Forty-second (1871–1873) Congresses. During the Forty-second Congress, he wrote and managed through the House the Ku Klux Klan Bill outlawing that organization in the South. He also championed a more active federal role in promoting business through the creation of the National Board of Commissioners of Commerce, which would later become the Department of Commerce, and promoted the revival of the U.S. merchant fleet by federal subsidy. He also served on one of the committees investigating the Crédit Mobilier scandals involving particular congressmen and the Union Pacific Railroad. Following Shellabarger's congressional service, Presi-

dent Grant named him to the Civil Service Commission. He was a strong advocate of civil service reform but resigned in 1875 when Congress failed to appropriate funds to continue the commission.

In the disputed election of 1876, Hayes selected Shellabarger as his personal attorney. While party leaders and attorneys worked out the understandings that led to the resolution of the dispute—what historians have called the Compromise of 1877—Shellabarger kept Hayes at arm's length from all such discussions. After visiting in South Carolina and holding extensive consultations with Grant and with party leaders in Louisiana and Florida, Shellabarger insisted that the federal government enforce the laws enfranchising African Americans. If "tainted" election results were excluded, Shellabarger assured Hayes, then he was legally entitled to be president. Shellabarger then served on the team of attorneys who successfully argued the Republican position to the special Electoral Commission created by Congress to resolve the dispute. After Hayes was declared the winner, Republicans overcame a Democratic filibuster aimed at preventing a final electoral count by agreeing to certain demands of southern leaders to withdraw federal troops from the South. Cries of a dishonest bargain were raised by northern Democrats. Shellabarger responded that Hayes had not been party to any bargains or deals that politicians in Washington may have made.

When his service in Congress and on the Civil Service Commission ended, Shellabarger had remained in Washington as an attorney. The publicity generated by his role in the Hayes-Tilden election dispute gave his career an immediate boost. In an early case he represented 1,000 taxpayers in Washington, D.C., who protested the high cost of city improvements and charged District of Columbia boss Alexander R. Shepherd with fraud. A member of the congressional investigating committee was Jeremiah M. Wilson, who designed a new governmental system for the District of Columbia. Upon completion of his term, Wilson became Shellabarger's law partner in Washington, a partnership that lasted until Shellabarger's death.

The firm of Shellabarger and Wilson devoted itself chiefly to arguing cases before the U.S. Supreme Court, the Supreme Court of the District of Columbia, federal commissions, and congressional investigating committees. The firm served as Washington attorneys for the Union Pacific Railroad Company, the Central Pacific Railroad, the Sutro Tunnel Company, and other large corporations. It also represented the Mormon church and the Choctaw Indian tribe. Shellabarger and Wilson served from 1881 to 1883 as defense attorneys in the Star Route mail fraud cases, involving contracts for carrying the mails, and they were defense attorneys in 1895 for Elverton R. Chapman and John W. McCartney, who refused to answer questions during the Senate investigation of bribery of senators by the Sugar Trust. The firm's involvement in important cases for twenty-one years earned it a reputation as one of the capital's most influential.

Although Shellabarger had been an early advocate of the income tax in 1861 as a means to finance the war, his last case, in 1896, was one of the many brought before the federal courts to set aside the income tax as unconstitutional. During the administrations of Presidents Hayes, James A. Garfield, and Benjamin Harrison, Shellabarger and his family frequently visited the White House, and he served Hayes and Harrison as an informal adviser. He and his wife attended President Hayes's silver wedding anniversary party. His daughter Mary became a childhood friend of the president's daughter Fanny, and she was invited to attend classes with Fanny's governess at the White House.

Shellabarger remained active in the Republican party. He was a delegate to the 1884 Republican convention that nominated Blaine for president, and he campaigned for Blaine. When Blaine served as secretary of state in Harrison's administration, Shellabarger took Blaine's son Walker Blaine into the firm of Shellabarger and Wilson so he could be near his father and serve informally as his assistant.

When his own son died in 1889, Shellabarger assumed responsibility for raising his grandson and namesake, Samuel Shellabarger. The grandson attributed his later successful career as a biographer and novelist to those years in his grandparents' household. Shellabarger died in Washington, D.C.

• Shellabarger's papers are for the most part in the private collections of his descendants and with his biographer. A few are in the Clark County (Ohio) Historical Society, which published a brief monograph, William A. Kinnison, *Samuel Shellabarger (1817–1896): Lawyer, Jurist, Legislator* (1966). A collection of letters from Shellabarger to Hayes is at the Rutherford B. Hayes Memorial Library in Fremont, Ohio, and other correspondence is in the James M. Comly Papers, Ohio Historical Society Library, Columbus. Shellabarger's grandson wrote a fictionalized account of the attorney's life, Samuel Shellabarger, *Tolbecken* (1956). Obituaries are in the *Washington Star* and the *Washington Post*, both 7 Aug. 1896.

WILLIAM A. KINNISON

SHELLABARGER, Samuel (18 May 1888–21 Mar. 1954), novelist and biographer, was born in Washington, D.C., the son of Robert Rodgers Shellabarger, a lawyer, and Sarah Rivera Wood. After the death of both parents when he was a baby, he was raised by his grandfather Samuel Shellabarger, a lawyer and one-time congressman and minister to Portugal. The younger Samuel Shellabarger was educated at private schools in Washington and in Pottstown, Pennsylvania, and from 1905 to 1909 was an honor student at Princeton University, where he majored in English and won all of the school's literary prizes. In 1910 he studied in Germany at the University of Munich and the next year at Harvard Law School before entering the graduate school at Princeton to continue his studies in English. He was an instructor in the English department there from 1914 to 1917, when he received a Ph.D. In the summer of 1914 he visited Sweden,

where he met Vifvan Georgia Lovegrove Borg, whom he married the next year. The couple had four children, one of whom died in infancy.

Shellabarger served as a first lieutenant in the Ordnance Department of the army in 1917. The next year he was transferred to military intelligence, promoted to captain, and made assistant military attaché at the U.S. legation in Stockholm. He held that post until 1919, when he returned to Princeton as assistant professor of English. Interested in writing since his youth, he resigned from Princeton in 1923 to allow himself more time for it. He and his family settled in Lausanne, Switzerland, and traveled extensively through Italy and France until 1927, when they returned to Princeton. Shellabarger resumed his post at the university there, and in 1928 he published his first book, *The Chevalier Bayard*, a well-documented biography of the sixteenth-century French military hero and model of chivalry. Though praised by the *Saturday Review of Literature* as "an excellent example of graceful and valuable scholarship" (22 Dec. 1928, p. 539) and by *Outlook* as "vivid with bright pictures of the pageantry of Renaissance courts" (17 Oct. 1928, p. 994), it was not commercially successful, and, determined to make himself professionally independent, he tried his hand at a contemporary mystery thriller, *Door of Death*, published the same year. A combination of crime detection and Gothic terror, it was well received, and he followed it with a romantic adventure novel, *The Black Gale*, in 1929. That year the Shellabargers again traveled to Europe, where they lived in France and England for the next two years. In 1930 Shellabarger published *Voodoo*, a murder mystery set in Harlem, Cuba, and Haiti. All three works of popular fiction appeared under the pseudonym John Esteven to keep Shellabarger's careers as a scholar and creative writer separate.

In 1931 Shellabarger returned to Princeton, where he gave his full time to writing. In 1935 he published a second biography, *Lord Chesterfield*, placing the eighteenth-century British diplomat and wit's famous *Letters to His Son* in a cultural and historical perspective. Although the book, published under his own name, was well received, its sales were insufficient to support his family, and Shellabarger continued to turn out popular fiction as John Esteven. He contributed short stories to such national magazines as *McCall's* and *Cosmopolitan* and published several more mysteries. *By Night at Dinsmore* (1935), *While Murder Waits* (1937), and *Graveyard Watch* (1938) were all moderately successful, their sinister atmosphere earning critical notices that described them as "actually scary" and "agreeably creepy." In 1938 he also published *Grief before Night*, a romance, and the next year *Miss Rolling Stone*, an adventure story, both under the pseudonym Peter Loring. In 1939 his last mystery, *Assurance Doubly Sure*, appeared as by John Esteven.

Although his fiction provided a sufficient income, Shellabarger had not lost his devotion to education, and from 1938 to 1946 he served with distinction as headmaster of the Columbus, Ohio, School for Girls.

During those years, which he considered "among the most creative and valuable of [his] life," he abandoned his pseudonyms and produced his most popular and commercially successful novel, *Captain from Castile* (1945), a swashbuckling historical romance whose hero escapes the Inquisition to join Cortés's expedition to Mexico. It was coolly received by critics (George Mayberry in the *New Republic* [15 Jan. 1945, p. 89] called it "neither better nor worse than most of its swollen genre"), but it topped the *New York Times* bestseller list for months, became a selection of the Literary Guild, received translations into eighteen languages, and was made into a lavish motion picture. Almost equally popular were his next three historical novels: *Prince of Foxes* (1947), a tale of romance and intrigue set in fifteenth-century Italy; *The King's Cavalier* (1950), the last of his Renaissance novels, dealing with the Bourbon conspiracy in France; and *Lord Vanity* (1953), a picaresque novel set in eighteenth-century England. Although sometimes criticized for wooden characterization, all were praised for their historical accuracy and their dramatic, action-filled narrative, and all were great popular successes. Two further historical novels—*The Token* (1955), a romantic fable of medieval France, and *Tolbecken* (1956), a family saga set in the United States from 1898 to 1920—were published posthumously.

Shellabarger's popular fiction, though sensational in nature, never descended to gratuitous violence or explicit sex. A meticulous scholar, he reportedly had a fluent command of French, German, Swedish, Dutch, Italian, and Spanish, as well as classic Latin and Greek, and drew on the extensive research he did for his biographies to give accuracy to the language and settings of his six period romances. He was methodical in his work habits, devoting seven hours a day to his writing, and conservative in his personal life, maintaining a professorial dignity in striking contrast to the flamboyant characters he created. He was also a conservative in his political views and actively supported the Republican party, for which he served as chairman of the Princeton Citizens for Eisenhower–Nixon in the 1952 presidential campaign. Although his historical novels received little serious attention from critics, they were respectfully treated by historians and were among the bestselling examples of their type, both in the United States and abroad, in the 1940s and 1950s. Shellabarger died at his home in Princeton.

• Shellabarger's personal papers and manuscripts are in the Princeton University Library, and a brief account of his life and work is in Harry R. Warfel, *American Novelists of Today* (1950). Reviews of most of his work appeared in the popular press from 1928 until 1956, and a profile, "Imperturbable Man," is in the *New York Times Book Review*, 11 July 1947, p. 8 An obituary is in the *New York Times*, 22 Mar. 1954.

DENNIS WEPMAN

SHELLY, Mary Josephine (1902–5 Aug. 1976), administrator for the arts and for service women's organizations, was born in Grand Rapids, Michigan, the daughter of Irish-American parents whose names are unknown. She was raised by her older sister, whose husband, a prominent attorney, impressed upon Shelly the value of intellectual discipline. In 1922 she began teaching in the public schools of Grand Rapids and Battle Creek, Michigan, and she attended the Kellogg School of Physical Education; Martha Hill, the dance teacher there, became one of Shelly's lifelong friends.

From Battle Creek, Shelly went on to the University of Oregon, where she taught physical education from 1924 to 1928 while earning her B.A. She received her M.A. in 1929 from Teachers College, Columbia University. She remained in New York to teach physical education at Teachers College and at the pioneering New College of Columbia University, where she taught until 1935.

Shelly's great interest in dance and theater blossomed when she began studying with Martha Graham in New York. Her experiences with Graham led her to search for ways of integrating dance into the physical education curriculum, a pursuit she continued when she began teaching at the University of Chicago in 1935. While retaining her position as associate professor of physical education, Shelly became assistant to the dean of students and also directed the Ida Noyes Gymnasium, a building housing physical education and dance facilities.

In 1934 Hill, who was teaching dance both at New York University and at Bennington College in Vermont, was asked by Bennington president Robert Devore Leigh to organize a summer school of dance. In doing so, Hill approached the four leading modern dance artists of the day: Graham, Doris Humphrey, Charles Weidman, and Hanya Holm. They were to be responsible for teaching and for choreographing world premieres that incorporated their own dancers, who were in residence, and some of the students. Hill, the artistic director of the program, asked Shelly to serve as administrative director. The two women were an exceptionally productive combination, making the school a mecca for modern dance students and teachers. Hill wove the dreams, and Shelly revealed an ability to make practicable the pursuit of excellence. No mere keeper of accounts, she was a lively, enterprising young woman whose artistic vision equaled Hill's; she seemed to know instinctively how to facilitate effective theater in a time of economic depression. By 1940 Bennington had changed the name of the summer school from School of the Dance to School of the Arts. Shelly was appointed cofounder and administrative director. In 1938 she joined the Bennington winter staff as educational assistant to President Leigh.

With the advent of World War II, Shelly took the first of several leaves of absence from Bennington. In 1942 she became a lieutenant in charge of physical education and drill in the Women's Naval Reserve. She was also among the first lieutenants commissioned in the Women Accepted for Volunteer Emergency Service (WAVES). Within a month she had become assistant to the director of training for the Women's Reserve. In this capacity she directed the expansion of WAVES schools from one to thirty-two. Three years later, with the rank of commander, Shelly transferred to the inactive reserve and oversaw the demobilization of the WAVES from their wartime strength of 85,000. Her accomplishments earned her a citation from James V. Forrestal, secretary of the U.S. Navy.

Shelly returned to Bennington in 1946 and became director of admissions. Five years later she took another leave, this time to become a colonel in the air force. It was her task to direct the women in the air force and to increase the recruitment of women during the Korean War. She returned to Bennington in 1954 as director of student personnel. She left a year later to become director of the Girl Scouts of America, a position she held until her retirement in 1966.

Shelly was a stylish woman who possessed a ready wit and keen intelligence. She was also a colorful conversationalist and a generous fount of human insight. Although she was a diffident public speaker, she was much in demand as a speech writer, especially during her years in the service. Shelly never married; she died in New York City.

• For information on Shelly, see Sali Ann Kriegsman, *Modern Dance in America: The Bennington Years* (1981). An obituary is in the *New York Times*, 6 Aug. 1976.

DORIS HERING

SHELTON, Ev (12 May 1898–16 Apr. 1974), basketball coach, was born Everett F. Shelton in Cunningham, Kansas. The names and occupations of his parents are unknown. Shelton won twelve letters in baseball, football, and basketball at Cunningham High School. After graduating in 1916, he enlisted in the U.S. Marine Corps and served until 1919. For the next four years he attended Phillips University in Enid, Oklahoma, where he again earned twelve letters in the three sports. In his senior year he made the all-conference team as a quarterback, and he captained the basketball team.

After graduating with a bachelor's degree in chemistry in 1923, Shelton spent one year coaching at Clarmore, Oklahoma, High School before returning to Phillips University in 1924 as head coach of the basketball and football teams. In three years his basketball teams won 48 games while losing 29. For the next two seasons (1927–1928) Shelton worked as a sporting goods salesman while he coached Sterling Milk, an American Athletic Union (AAU) basketball team out of Oklahoma City. One of Shelton's players on this team was Henry Iba, who became one of college basketball's leading coaches. From 1929 to 1936 Shelton coached at Christian Brothers High School in St. Joseph, Missouri; he also kept his hand in AAU basketball by coaching Cripes Bakery in St. Joseph (1929–1930) and the St. Joseph Boosters Club (1932–1933).

In the summer of 1936 William Haraway, regional manager of the Denver Safeway Stores, after unsuccessfully attempting to recruit Iba, hired Shelton to coach his AAU team. In recommending him, Iba said that he had learned much of his own system from Shelton while playing under him. For several years Haraway had been recruiting basketball players to work for the grocery store chain and play for his team in an effort to bring Denver an AAU championship. The most celebrated players were Jack McCracken and Ace Gruenig. Shelton helped to make Haraway's dream come true by directing Denver to its first national title in 1937. The following year Shelton guided Safeway to the championship game, but the team lost in the last minute of play to the Kansas City Healy Motors, 40–38. Following that game, Safeway dropped its basketball sponsorship, and Shelton found himself without a coaching position. In 1938–1939 he coached the Colorado Springs Antlers, a team that reached the quarterfinals of the AAU tournament. On 29 March 1939, however, Shelton's career took a new direction when the University of Wyoming appointed him head basketball coach.

In Shelton's second year the Cowboys won the first of eight conference titles. This team included Curt Gowdy, who would become a successful sports announcer, and Bill Strannigan, who would succeed Shelton at Wyoming in 1959. In 1942–1943 Shelton and Wyoming would enjoy their most memorable season. The Cowboys had a perfect 10–0 record in conference play, two wins over AAU powerhouse Phillips 66, and a 23-game winning streak at one point in the season. They tuned up for the NCAA tournament by taking third place in the 1943 national AAU tournament. After winning two tough NCAA regional games against Oklahoma and Texas in Kansas City, the Cowboys traveled to Madison Square Garden where they outscored Georgetown 15–3 in the last four minutes to win the NCAA championship game, 46–34. Two nights later, Wyoming faced St. John's University, the National Invitational Tournament champion, in a charity game for the Red Cross. Billed as the game to determine the real national champion, Wyoming turned back the Redmen 52–47 in an exciting overtime period. Wyoming's leading scorers that season were Milo Komenich, Kenny Sailors, and James Weir. The most celebrated player of the three, Sailors, was generally credited with inventing the jump shot and was named 1943's college player of the year.

Because of World War II, Wyoming canceled its 1943–1944 season, and Shelton coached the Dow Chemical AAU team from Midland, Michigan. He then returned to Wyoming where he coached through 1958–1959. Although he won six more conference titles, his last four seasons resulted in an uncharacteristic 30 wins and 74 losses. Amid mounting criticism, he resigned after a disappointing 4–22 mark. His resignation, however, coincided with the announcement that he had accepted a position as head basketball coach at Sacramento State College. Shelton indicated that he would miss competing at the higher levels of collegiate competition, but he admitted some disaffection with "the fierce struggle of recruiting the best players, which as a younger man I relished completely." He said he looked forward to ending his coaching career at a school where they played "for fun only."

Shelton coached at Sacramento State for ten years and compiled a record of 188 wins and 188 losses. In the NCAA College Division championship game, his 1962 team lost 58–57 to Mount St. Mary's in double overtime. After the 1967–1968 season Shelton turned seventy, retirement age. He became the first commissioner of the Far Western Conference in 1968, a position he held until he died while vacationing in Capistrano Beach, California.

Shelton's teams amassed a record of 850 wins and 437 losses over his career as a high school, AAU, and college basketball coach. His 328–201 record at Wyoming has not been surpassed by any of the school's later coaches. Shelton was recognized by other coaches and his players as an outstanding defensive strategist, a master at dissecting opponents' offenses. He possessed strong self-discipline, and his teams reflected this quality. In 1979 he was honored posthumously by induction into the National Basketball Hall of Fame.

• The best source of information on Shelton is the University of Wyoming's 1992–1993 media guide. The *Denver Post* and the *Rocky Mountain News* also have material, and the Sport Information Center at the University of Wyoming and the archives at Sacramento State have clipping files on him.

ADOLPH H. GRUNDMAN

SHEPARD, Charles Upham (29 June 1804–1 May 1886), mineralogist, educator, chemist, and natural historian, was born in Little Compton, Rhode Island, the son of Mase Shepard, a Congregational minister, and Deborah Haskins. Shepard began collecting rocks and minerals while attending grammar school in Providence, Rhode Island. He entered Brown University in 1820, but his father died during his first year, and his mother then moved with her family to Amherst, Massachusetts, where Shepard entered the sophomore class at the newly founded Amherst College.

As a student at Amherst, Shepard explored the area's minerals and plants. He accumulated specimens and in time made exchanges with the Austrian Consul General, adding European examples to his growing mineralogical cabinet. Of his Amherst professors, he was most impressed by botanist and geologist Amos Eaton, and he was able to provide the illustrative examples for Eaton's lectures from his own specimens. He set up a laboratory downstairs in his mother's home and began to give instruction there. During his senior year he sent a notice to Professor Benjamin Silliman at Yale, describing his mineral observations in the hope that they might be included in the *American Journal of Science and Arts*, and from that time he was a steady contributor to the *Journal*.

After graduating with an A.B. from Amherst in 1824, Shepard spent a year in Cambridge studying natural history with the botanist and mineralogist Thomas Nuttall. Shepard taught botany and mineralogy privately in Boston and meanwhile traveled to mineral localities; he traded specimens not only with Nut-

tall and other collectors but, on finding outstanding tourmalines in Maine, with the British Museum (Tyler, p. 623). He decided to devote himself to the natural sciences and not a profession, although this was against the advice "not to depend on so uncertain means of support" (Hitchcock, p. 101).

Shepard was in New Haven pursuing further studies in natural science when Benjamin Silliman, who encouraged his interest in the chemistry laboratory and the mineralogical cabinet and noted his background in natural history, gave him the opportunity to become his assistant in the laboratory at Yale. Shepard was assistant in chemistry from 1826 until 1831, when he was named lecturer on botany in Yale College.

In 1831 Shepard undertook the direction for a year of the Franklin Institution, established by James Brewster in New Haven to provide popular lectures and instruction in the sciences. That year Shepard married Harriet Taylor, of New Braintree, Massachusetts, in whom the Sillimans had taken a parental interest; this brought a close and lasting relationship between the two families. The Shepards had three children.

When the secretary of the treasury in 1832 requested Benjamin Silliman to investigate and prepare a report on the culture of sugar cane and methods of sugar refining and manufacture throughout the United States, Silliman enlisted the assistance of Shepard and Oliver Payson Hubbard. Shepard was charged with visiting the southern states, with especial attention to Georgia and Louisiana, for the inquiry, and he traveled through the South during the winter; his results became part of the report submitted to the government. Appointed lecturer in natural history at Yale College from 1833 to 1847, Shepard gave lectures in conchology, which he correlated with fossil shell examples and geological connections. His *Treatise on Mineralogy* (1832–1835) dealt with "Mineralogy as an Independent Science" (*American Journal of Science*, 1832 review) and went through three editions up to 1852–1857. He contributed papers on mineralogy, geology, and meteorites to the *American Journal of Science* for more than sixty years.

Shepard was appointed professor of chemistry in 1835 at the Medical College of South Carolina in Charleston, where he taught for part of each year until 1861 and from 1865 to 1869, when his son, Charles Upham Shepard, Jr., followed him in the professorship.

In 1835 Shepard joined Dr. James Gates Percival, a geologist, in conducting the first geological survey of Connecticut; they traveled together throughout the state, with Shepard concentrating his inquiries on the mineralogy in each area, giving particular attention to the economic potential for development. Shepard published *A Report on the Geological Survey of Connecticut* in 1837 and compiled a corresponding collection of almost 800 specimens for exhibit at the State House, to "communicate a correct general impression of our minerals and rock formations." Percival completed his report on Connecticut's geology five years later.

In 1845, when Edward Hitchcock was appointed president of Amherst College, Shepard accepted an appointment as professor of chemistry and natural history at Amherst and gave up his lectureship at Yale in 1847. Scientific colleagues, both had formerly assisted Benjamin Silliman in his chemistry laboratory at Yale and had been early contributors to Silliman's *Journal*. From 1852 Shepard was professor of natural history at Amherst and from 1877, emeritus professor. He divided his teaching between the Charleston medical school and Amherst, although for most of his years his home was New Haven.

Shepard brought his cabinets to Amherst in 1847, a fireproof building having been provided for them as agreed, with arrangements for their purchase by the college at a later date. About the collections, President Hitchcock observed that "simple minerals and meteorites have been the first objects of his labors, while geology and zoology have come in, as it were, incidentally; and yet the incidental results are often superb" (Hitchcock, p. 102). Shepard had collected meteorites and meteorite observations and information since 1828, and by 1859 Shepard's *Notice of Collections in Natural History, Preserved in the Shepard Cabinets at Amherst College, (Massachusetts.)* remarked that they included meteoric specimens from 124 localities; the mineralogical collection held more than 10,000 specimens. That year the report of a visit to Shepard's mineralogical collections at Amherst during the meeting of the American Association for the Advancement of Science noted: "In the richness and splendor of its selections, the mineral species are nowhere in America and seldom anywhere so well represented" (*American Journal of Science*, p. 293).

Shepard continued his mineralogical journeys and explorations, and by 1863 it was said that he had visited, and often returned to, virtually every significant mineral location, however wild the terrain, in travels to Georgia and Arkansas and west to the Rocky Mountains. The duplicate minerals he collected proved invaluable in trade for specimens obtained during trips abroad. Shepard made twelve European trips in all to augment his collections and bought important fossils for the college. The collections had been bought by the college upon Shepard's retirement and moved to another building when they were destroyed by a fire in the spring of 1882 that spared only a vault with meteorites and some specimens.

Shepard and his son hoped to replace the loss, as they were both unceasing collectors; the elder Shepard had built fireproof storage for his collections in New Haven. After his death in Charleston, his son gave the largest part of his collection to Amherst in his father's name and deposited minerals and meteorites at the National Museum in Washington. The Amherst collection of meteorites has since been bought by the Center for Meteorite Studies at Arizona State University in Tempe, Arizona.

• Biographical material, notebooks, and letters are in the Charles Upham Shepard Papers, and letters and material on his cabinets are in the Pratt Museum Papers in the Amherst College Archives; further sources are the Silliman Family Papers in Manuscripts and Archives, Yale University Library, and the Charles Upham Shepard Papers in the Smithsonian Institution Archives. Nelson Horatio Darton, *Catalogue and Index of Contributions to North American Geology 1732–1891* (1896), lists Shepard's papers. Shepard's meteorites are listed under "The C. U. Shepard (1884–1886) Meteorite Collection Acquired from Amherst College in 1980," in Charles F. Lewis et al., *Catalogue of Meteorites in the Collections of Arizona State University*, pp. 271–74. Edward Hitchcock gave a history of Shepard and his cabinet in *Reminiscences of Amherst College, Historical, Scientific, Biographical, and Autobiographical, also of Other and Wider Life Experiences* (1863), pp. 101–3. W. S. Tyler quotes Shepard in *History of Amherst College during Its First Half Century, 1821–1871* (1873), pp. 80–88, 622–25. Benjamin K. Emerson, "The Geological and Mineralogical Collections of Amherst College," *Amherst Graduates' Quarterly* 5 (1915–1916): 17–25, 97–102, describes the various Shepard cabinets at Amherst College, with recollections of Shepard and the fate of his collections. Biographical articles include Gloria Robinson, "Charles Upham Shepard," in *Benjamin Silliman and His Circle*, ed. Leonard G. Wilson (1979), pp. 85–103, and Arthur Roe, "The C. U. Shepard Mineral Collection and the Two Drs. Shepard," *Mineralogical Record* 5 (1975): 253–57. Obituaries are in the *Charleston News and Courier*, 2 May 1886, and *American Journal of Science*, 3d ser., 31 (1886): 482–83.

GLORIA ROBINSON

SHEPARD, Odell (22 July 1884–19 July 1967), writer and college professor, was born in Rock Falls, Illinois, the son of William Orville Shepard, a Methodist bishop, and Emily Odell. Shepard worked as a journalist in Chicago, after studying literature, journalism, and music at Northwestern University. He married Mary Farwell Record in 1908; they had one child. Shepard taught English at the University of Southern California from 1909 to 1914. He returned to school for doctoral studies in English and in 1916 was awarded a Ph.D. from Harvard University. In 1917 Shepard made his home in Connecticut, where he was Goodwin Professor of English at Trinity College for some twenty-five years, becoming one of the college's most distinguished faculty members, known for his idealism, good conversation, and an abiding love of the Connecticut landscape.

Shepard sparked controversy in the Hartford academic and business communities because of what some considered to be his excessive devotion to New Deal politics. The controversy culminated in his resignation from Trinity College in 1946 after he charged that the "autocratic" new president of the college, George Funston, had unfairly refused him a leave of absence. Though Shepard's friends rallied around him, Trinity's executive committee, composed of conservative Hartford businessmen who had long disapproved of Shepard's notions about banks, utilities, and big business, decided in favor of the president.

In 1941 Shepard cofounded the Thoreau Society of America; he served as lieutenant governor of Connecticut from 1940 to 1943 on a three-year leave from teaching; and he was adopted into the Mohegan tribe under the name "Chief Many Sons" in 1941. He died in New London, Connecticut.

His trademark was variety, as he ranged from criticism and teaching to editing and the writing of nonfiction, fiction, and poetry. During Shepard's career, he edited collections of American fiction, poetry, and essays that reflected his interest in nineteenth-century American literature. He edited, among other works, Henry David Thoreau's *Week on the Concord and Merrimack Rivers* (1921), *Poems of Longfellow* (1934), and Bronson Alcott's *Journals* (1938). His works of nonfiction include a history, *The Lore of the Unicorn* (1929); a fishing book, *Thy Rod and Thy Creel* (1930); and a history of his home state, *Connecticut Past and Present* (1939). Shepard liked best *The Lore of the Unicorn*, a history of the unicorn as literary motif and a chronicle of the imaginary beast's decline in symbolic power because, in Shepard's words, "there [is] no longer any sufficient capacity for a faith unsustained by the senses"; humanity has made "fact decisive where it should have least weight." The book's plates were destroyed in London, which Shepard attributed to wartime "enemy action."

His creative writing includes books of verse, collections of personal essays, and two historical romances coauthored with his son Willard, *Holdfast Gaines* (1946) and *Jenkins' Ear* (1951). The latter was a Book-of-the-Month selection, while the *New York Times* called *Holdfast Gaines* "an unusually ambitious and unhackneyed novel."

His essays often turn to the Connecticut landscape. *The Harvest of a Quiet Eye* (1927) contains prose and poetry that offer a sometimes nostalgic commentary on his home, what he called his "little country" and a "manageable and man-sized territory." One critic said of Shepard's writing, "While footslogging his way over most of the highways & byways of the Nutmeg State, Odell Shepard has peddled such friendly wares as good talk, homely poetry, corny songs and New Deal politics" (*Time*, 13 May 1946). Shepard said that, while he would have liked to write about "the history of solitude," he never published one word on the subject. Nonetheless, one can detect the solitary's approach to the landscape in several of his poems and essays, as in the following from "Sunshine and Shadow," "The road I walked that afternoon ran all the way through pure and uncontaminated Connecticut."

Shepard is best known for his Pulitzer Prize–winning biography, *Pedlar's Progress: The Life of Bronson Alcott* (1937), about the influential Transcendentalist and father of Louisa May Alcott. *Time* said of Shepard and his work, "Alcott was a failure at almost everything he tried: Shepard has been a success" (13 May 1946). The biography won wide acclaim as a model for that genre, exploring not only an individual's life but also its cultural context; Shepard's research brought to prominence a man of American letters who might otherwise have been ignored, and it detailed the cultural background of the era now known as the American Renaissance. By way of introduction to the biography, Shepard forestalled criticism for writing about an "atypical" and "unrepresentative" American, asking, "And how have you grown so sure about what is 'typical' and 'representative'? Is it not possible that you are generalizing too soon? Perhaps the examples are not all in. At any rate, add this one." Shepard's strength was his attention to the unattended, as he celebrated Americans who found themselves solitary either by choice or coincidence in a world of competing values and traditions.

• Shepard's work is available at most major libraries. There is no indepth study of Shepard's life to date, though critical reviews of his work may prove helpful; see "Alcott and His New England," *New York Times Book Review*, 9 May 1937, pp. 1, 27, and Ernest Sutherland Bates, "*Pedlar's Progress*," *American Historical Review* 43, no. 1 (Oct. 1937): 160–62. For an account of the Trinity College controversy, see *Time*, 13 May 1946, pp. 80–81. An obituary is in the *New York Times*, 20 July 1967.

KELLY CANNON

SHEPARD, Thomas (5 Nov. 1605–25 Aug. 1649), New England Puritan minister, was born in Towcester, Northamptonshire, England, the son of William Shepard, a grocer, and his wife (name unknown), a grocer's daughter. Shepard's mother died when he was about four years old; his father, when the boy was about ten. He was brought up by his oldest brother, John. The family inclined toward the emergent Puritan movement, into which Shepard was initiated by Towcester schoolmaster and preacher William Cluer and Emmanuel College fellow Daniel Cockerell. He entered Emmanuel as a pensioner on 10 February 1620, earned the bachelor of arts degree in 1624, and was ordained to the priesthood soon after receiving the master of arts degree in 1627. At Cambridge, under the inspiration of such Puritan leaders as Laurence Chaderton, John Preston, and Thomas Goodwin, he experienced a protracted and stressful religious conversion that fixed the pattern of his mature piety.

Shepard became a minister just as Bishop William Laud was mobilizing the Anglican church against Puritan reforms and reformers. Late in 1630, after serving some three years as lecturer (preacher) in Earles-Colne, Essex, he was suspended by Laud for Nonconformity; the shock confirmed his commitment to the Puritan cause. Shepard found refuge as chaplain to Sir Richard Darley in Buttercrambe, Yorkshire, where, in 1632, he married Darley's cousin and servant, Margaret Touteville. The marriage lasted until her death in 1636 and produced one surviving child. After a brief pastorate in Heddon, near Newcastle in Northumberland, Shepard preached for a time at large while keeping ahead of episcopal surveillance, then went into hiding. In 1635 he sailed with his wife and son in the ship *Defense* to New England. The party landed in Boston on 3 October.

Soon after arriving the Shepards and some of their fellow passengers bought homes from members of the Cambridge (then called Newtown) congregation who were moving to Connecticut. In Cambridge on 1 February 1636 the newcomers formed a church and chose

Shepard as their pastor in a ceremony recorded as a model by John Winthrop (1588–1649) in his journal. He served as pastor of the Cambridge church until his death.

Knowledge of Thomas Shepard's life comes primarily from the short autobiography that he left to his son Thomas, who followed him into the ministry. This document recounts and interprets the experience of a Puritan minister in England and New England. Most of the narrative describes his life in England and gives details of Shepard's personal and pastoral life. The pages for New England chiefly concern public affairs—the Antinomian controversy, the Pequot War, and the founding of Harvard College—but biographical details are obtainable from other sources, including his private journal. The autobiography records Shepard's second marriage, in 1637, to Joanna Hooker, daughter of Thomas Hooker, who preceded Shepard as minister in Cambridge; the birth of four children, two of whom survived; and Joanna's death in childbirth in 1646, where the text breaks off with a moving expression of Shepard's love and grief. In 1647 Shepard married Margaret Boradel, with whom he had one child.

Shepard's pastorate stands among the models for the pioneer generation in New England. He carefully nurtured and guided his flock's religious lives. His powerful preaching and pastoral vigilance kept his congregation free of strife during the Antinomian agitation of the mid-1630s. In 1636 the colony's magistrates acknowledged his reputation as spiritual and moral counselor by siting Harvard College in Cambridge, where the students came under Shepard's pastoral charge. No outbreaks of heterodoxy are recorded in his church, and the only serious breach of discipline involved Nathaniel Eaton, whose abuse of office as the college's first master escaped Shepard's watchfulness for a time and caused him retrospective anguish.

Although younger than such eminent colleagues as Hooker, John Cotton, and Richard Mather, Shepard made noteworthy contributions to the distinctive ecclesiastical forms and practices of the so-called New England or Congregational way. Committed to the principle of exclusivity—that true churches should comprise none but true saints—he helped develop and police the requirement of an acceptable confession of religious experience and faith for admission to membership. In 1636 his objections to deficiencies of certain confessions in Dorchester delayed the founding of a church there. In addition Shepard or a lay leader recorded as many as sixty-seven confessions made by applicants to his own church between 1638 and 1649. These narratives provide unparalleled documentation of the religious travels and travails of ordinary women and men in Puritan Massachusetts.

Despite chronic ill health Shepard took an active part in New England's public affairs. Gravely alarmed by the movement of dissent fomented by Anne Hutchinson and seemingly countenanced by Cotton, he helped organize and manage the synod in Cambridge in 1637 that condemned the insurgents' supposed theological errors, and he testified against Hutchinson at her trial before the General Court in 1637 that resulted in her banishment. In support of the college in 1644, when the region's economy was severely depressed, he persuaded the commissioners of the united New England colonies to adopt a plan for funding the maintenance of indigent students by voluntary contributions. With John Allin he published *A Defence of the Answer . . .* , (1648), justifying the worship and discipline of New England's Congregational churches against sharp criticism from British Presbyterians. He had a hand in the synod of 1648 that codified the Congregational system in *The Cambridge Platform of Church Discipline*. He assisted the Indian mission of his friend John Eliot, whose work began in Cambridge in 1646.

Shepard ranks third behind Cotton and Eliot among first-generation New England ministers in number of titles printed and second to none in total pages. His principal works are sermon series—*The Sincere Convert* (1641), *The Sound Believer* (1645), and *The Parable of the Ten Virgins Opened and Applied* (1660), the last of these his successful effort to immunize his congregation against Antinomianism. In addition to *Theses Sabbaticae* (1649), a treatise on the doctrine of the Sabbath, he produced several tracts of a theological or moral nature, two pieces promoting the conversion of Indians, and a catechism. *The Sincere Convert*, his most popular work, remained in print in one American and numerous English and Scottish printings for half a century; twenty-one editions are reported to 1812. Most of his writings received a modernized edition in 1853 (repr. 1967).

Recognized in his time as an exemplary pastor and preacher, Shepard represented a strain of Puritan piety and personality that was highly charged with emotions of anxiety and aspiration. In his journal (of which the portion for 1640 to 1644 survives) as well as in his autobiography, he describes his inner life as a constant, urgent quest for assurance of the love of God. In his outer life he strove to exhibit convincing evidence of divine acceptance while agonizing privately over his shortcomings. "The greatest part of a Christian's grace," he noted in a characteristic passage, "lies in mourning for the want [i.e., lack] of it." No minister grappled more earnestly with the Puritan problem of imperfect or ambiguous assurance than Shepard; none analyzed the psychology of hypocrisy more acutely. As Shepard's theological writings have informed our understanding of Puritan religious thought, so the records of his and his people's spiritual distresses and comforts have profoundly influenced current interpretations of Puritan psychology. He died in Cambridge.

• The manuscript of Shepard's journal is at the New York Public Library. The manuscript of his autobiography is owned by the First Church in Cambridge, Congregational. His manuscript records of confessions of applicants for membership in the Cambridge church are at the New England Historic Genealogical Society (Boston) and the American Antiquarian Society (Worcester, Mass.). John A. Albro, "Life of Thomas Shepard," in *The Works of Thomas Shepard*, ed. Albro, vol. 1 (1853; repr. 1967), pp. vii–cxcii, remains the amplest biography. For a study of Shepard's character, thought, and rhetoric, with a list of his writings, see Thomas Werge, *Thomas Shepard* (1987). Werge, "Writings about Thomas Shepard, 1702–1974," in *Early Puritan Writers: A Reference Guide*, ed. Edward J. Gallagher and Werge (1976), provides an annotated bibliography. Context for Shepard's pastoral work is supplied by David D. Hall, *The Faithful Shepherd: A History of the New England Ministry in the Seventeenth Century* (1972), and Charles Hambrick-Stowe, *The Practice of Piety: Puritan Devotional Disciplines in Seventeenth-Century New England* (1982). Professions of religious experience and belief by applicants to Shepard's church are recorded in George Selement and Bruce C. Woolley, eds., *Thomas Shepard's Confessions*, Publications of the Colonial Society of Massachusetts: Collections, vol. 58 (1981), and Mary Rhinelander McCarl, "Thomas Shepard's Record of Relations of Religious Experience, 1648–1649," *William and Mary Quarterly*, 3d ser., 48 (1991): 432–66. These records are discussed in Charles L. Cohen, *God's Caress: The Psychology of Puritan Religious Experience* (1986), and Patricia Caldwell, *The Puritan Religious Experience* (1986), and Patricia Caldwell, *The Puritan Conversion Narrative: The Beginnings of American Expression* (1983). See also Andrew Delbanco, *The Puritan Ordeal Expression* (1989), and Amanda Porterfield, *Female Piety in Puritan New England: The Emergence of Religious Humanism* (1992). For Shepard's autobiography and journal, with an interpretive introduction, see Michael McGiffert, ed., *God's Plot: The Paradoxes of Puritan Piety* (1972), and *God's Plot: Puritan Spirituality in Thomas Shepard's Cambridge* (1994). The latter volume contains professions of the Cambridge laity with a new introduction.

MICHAEL MCGIFFERT

SHEPARD, William (1 Dec. 1737–16 Nov. 1817), soldier and congressman, was born in Westfield, Massachusetts, the son of John Shepard, a tanner, and Elizabeth Noble. Reared in an atmosphere of Congregational rectitude (his father was a deacon of the church) and educated in the public schools of Westfield, he grew to adulthood as a sober, honest citizen whom his neighbors respected. He had his first experience of soldiering at the age of seventeen, when he enlisted as a private in the Massachusetts militia during the French and Indian War. Gaining valuable experience in the profession of arms during that long conflict, he served for seven years and achieved the rank of captain under Sir Jeffrey Amherst's command. Among other campaigns, he participated in operations against Forts William Henry and Crown Point. He married Sarah Dewey in 1760, and when the war ended he settled with her on a farm near his native village.

There Shepard lived peacefully for the next few years, serving as a selectman, until growing tensions between America and Great Britain caused him to take a more active public role. In 1775 he was chosen by his fellow citizens to be a member of the local committee of correspondence, and when all-out war flared between the patriots and British, he returned to military duty as a lieutenant colonel in Timothy Danielson's regiment. While serving at the siege of Boston in January 1776 he was appointed lieutenant colonel of the Third Continental Infantry. Nine months later he was promoted to colonel, with his seniority in that rank

backdated to May. He was at New York in July 1776, when General William Howe commenced operations against the American army under General George Washington, and was driven northward from the city along with his fellow soldiers in the general rout of patriot forces. He fought valiantly under Colonel John Glover in the battle of Pell's Point on 18 October, when the patriots unsuccessfully attempted to stop the British from moving toward Eastchester, New York. In 1777 he campaigned against John Burgoyne in upstate New York and spent the following winter at Valley Forge. Transferring to the Fourth Massachusetts Infantry in 1778, he returned to his native state on recruiting service. He continued in the Continental army for the remainder of the war, and when he mustered out on 1 January 1783, after having fought in twenty-two military engagements, he had achieved a reputation as a courageous and efficient officer.

With peace restored and the American republic established, Shepard returned to his Massachusetts farm and his wife and nine children. However, public service beckoned again in 1785, and in that year he was elected to the first of two terms in the state legislature. In 1786 he was commissioned major general in the Hampshire County militia, in which role he became embroiled in the popular uprising called Shays's Rebellion. (Led by Daniel Shays, hundreds of indebted farmers rose up in protest against high taxes and debt foreclosures.) As it happened, Shepard's duty as a militia general was to defend the federal arsenal and protect the dignity of the courts in Springfield. On 26 September 1786 he mustered several hundred militiamen to assure the opening of the Supreme Judicial Court but was chagrined when insurgents collected in overpowering numbers and forced the court to adjourn. Thereupon, he concentrated his few available troops around the Springfield arsenal to make sure that the valuable facility did not fall into the hands of the rebels. Two months later Shepard watched helplessly as Shays's men closed the Springfield Courts of Common Pleas and General Sessions. In early 1787 he was greatly relieved to learn that the Massachusetts government had ordered an army of 3,200 men under Benjamin Lincoln to join him as quickly as possible at Springfield. But on 25 January before Lincoln arrived, he was attacked at the arsenal, and although Shays's men were easily repelled, Shepard was anxious for the safety of both the arsenal and the town of Springfield. Therefore, he sent express riders thundering toward Lincoln's army, which was encamped at Worcester. The next day, much to Shepard's relief, Lincoln reinforced him with a regiment of infantry and a small squad of cavalry. On the twenty-seventh, Lincoln and the rest of his command arrived, thus relieving Shepard of any more responsibility during Shays's Rebellion.

In 1789 Shepard was chosen by the people of Massachusetts as one of the first presidential electors under the new federal Constitution, and four years later he acted in the same role. In the meantime, in 1792, he became a member of the governor's council, an office that he filled for five years. In 1796 he stood for election to the federal House of Representatives. Succeeding to that position, he filled it for three terms, finally retiring on 3 March 1803. He spent the remaining years of his life in modest seclusion at Westfield, where he died, serving like his father before him as a deacon of the Congregational church and playing the role of famous citizen. Sadly, he was compelled to live in somewhat straitened circumstances, never having been compensated for personal expenditures during Shays's Rebellion and having suffered damage to his property by the rioters. The commonwealth owed him that, for his intelligent and courageous defense of the Springfield arsenal was the major achievement of his career and of great importance in suppressing the revolt.

• The Library of Congress holds a few Shepard papers, but they are not very useful. Biographical details of Shepard's life are in Isaac Knapp, *A Sermon, Delivered at Westfield, November 18th, 1817; at the Funeral of Maj. Gen. William Shepard, Aged Eighty* (1818), and Francis B. Heitman, *Historical Register of Officers of the Continental Army during the War of the Revolution* (1893). James M. Bugbee, ed., *Memorials of the Massachusetts Society of the Cincinnati* (1890), is also useful. William Abbatt, *The Battle of Pell's Point (or Pelham), October 18, 1776* (1901), covers one important episode in Shepard's military career. His role in Shays's Rebellion is described in Charles Martyn, *The Life of Artemas Ward* (1921). See also Robert A. Feer, *Shay's Rebellion* (1988). For his life in Westfield, see John H. Lockwood, *Westfield and Its Historic Influences, 1669–1919* (2 vols., 1922), and Frank Grant, *History of the Celebration of the Two Hundred and Fiftieth Anniversary of the Incorporation of the Town of Westfield* (1919).

PAUL DAVID NELSON

SHEPPARD, Eugenia (1900?–11 Nov. 1984), journalist and author, was born in Columbus, Ohio, the daughter of James Taylor Sheppard and Jane Benbow. Her parents' occupations are unknown. After attending the Columbus School for Girls, she went to Bryn Mawr, where she majored in French and English and from which she graduated in 1921.

Sheppard began her journalistic career as a reporter for the society department of her hometown newspaper, the *Columbus Dispatch*. In 1938 she moved to New York as a fashion writer for *Women's Wear Daily*. Her personal drive and ambition in fulfilling this job produced the chance she needed to advance in the field of women's journalism. In describing her first big break Sheppard later stated: "I was so crazy to get along that I used to coax to get on an assignment." This desire produced an assignment to cover a fashion show in Brooklyn during bad weather. Sheppard was the only reporter at the press table. While there, she met the fashion announcer for the show, Katherine Vincent, who was also fashion editor for the *New York Herald Tribune*. Six months later, Vincent offered Sheppard a job to cover home furnishings for the *Herald Tribune*. Sheppard concluded that "the moral of that tale is that if you go over to Brooklyn on a very bad night you'll get a good job."

For seven years Sheppard worked as a writer in the women's features department of the *Herald Tribune*. She slowly increased her coverage from home furnishings to beauty, fashion, and makeup. Her beauty column, published on Wednesdays, appeared under the pseudonym of Sara Sutton. After the retirement of Vincent in 1947, Sheppard became the *Herald Tribune*'s fashion editor. When she originally took over the position, she was forced to delegate to others her favorite subject among the various women's features: home furnishings. At that time she was not strongly enthusiastic about fashion reporting. That attitude slowly changed, and it was through her fashion reporting that Sheppard became a power in the world of journalism.

When Sheppard became fashion editor, the *Herald Tribune* allotted a page for women's material only as long as it could be completely filled. The paper's editor felt free to use any leftover space for other stories. Sheppard worked diligently to fill the entire page in hopes of making the women's page a permanent part of the newspaper. An experience that occurred before Sheppard became fashion editor provided the primary impetus for her efforts. In 1945 a carefully planned story on beauty parlors filled only part of the available space. The rest of the space was filled with a story titled "Blast in Beauty Parlor Kills Five Women." Sheppard, working to avoid such questionable editing decisions, succeeded in making the women's page a daily feature of the *Herald Tribune* in 1949.

A regularly published women's page was only the first of Eugenia Sheppard's successes in the world of fashion reporting. In 1951 she convinced her editor to send her to Europe to cover the Paris fashion shows directly, a move that became common practice in later years. Sheppard began causing stirs in the fashion community because of her willingness to criticize the new fashions and their designers. For a time, some designers tried to bar her from their fashion-collection previews. Sheppard, however, continued to do more than just describe the newest fashions. In 1956 she introduced her column "Inside Fashion." Originally used for leftover information and personal opinions, the column quickly became required reading for anyone, man or woman, who wanted to be informed about the fashion world.

"Inside Fashion" made Eugenia Sheppard famous and, according to the *New York Times*, "one of the most influential fashion observers of the 1950's and early 1960's." At the height of her career, designers waited for Sheppard's arrival before starting their show even when she was late. She maintained her influence despite her bad eyesight and her refusal to wear glasses. Whoever sat next to her at a fashion show often described to her what was being shown. Beginning as a biweekly column, "Inside Fashion" grew into a daily production that was syndicated in 150 newspapers across the United States.

Sheppard became women's editor for the *World Journal Tribune* in 1966, following the merger of several newspapers. After the demise of the paper, her column appeared for a while in *Women's Wear Daily*. In

1968 she became society editor of the *New York Post*, where she continued writing her column into the 1970s. By this time, however, her influence had waned, and her column eventually ceased publication. In her later years, Sheppard wrote a column, "Around the Town," for Publishers Hall, a New York features syndicate. She also coauthored two novels, both set in the world of the fashion and beauty industry, with Earl Blackwell, *Crystal Clear* (1978) and *Skyrocket* (1980). Sheppard died in New York.

Sheppard was a very private person and refused to discuss her personal life during interviews. As a result, very little specific information is available concerning her life outside of the newsroom. She was married three times. She married Samuel Black shortly after graduating from Bryn Mawr. The marriage ended in divorce. Her second marriage, to Preston Wolfe, also ended in divorce. Her third husband, Walter Millis, was an editorial writer and military historian for the *Herald Tribune*. He died in 1968. Sheppard had only one child, Sheppard Black, a son by her first husband.

Although Sheppard's impact was felt in many ways during her more than forty years as a fashion and society reporter and editor, it was her column that made her a truly influential journalist. Described as having power "because she took it," Sheppard used "Inside Fashion" to carve out a niche for herself in the newspaper world. Geraldine Stutz, president of Henri Bendel, described Sheppard's impact in this way: "'Inside Fashion' was an enormous revelation. Up until then, fashion reportage was description of clothes. Eugenia was fascinated by fashion and began to talk about the people who made the clothes and the people who wore the clothes. She personalized fashion. It was the beginning of modern fashion reporting." After Eugenia Sheppard, the women's page would never be the same again, for she transformed fashion news from a dry description of clothes to a spirited discussion of the lives of the people involved in the international fashion industry.

• No book-length biography of Eugenia Sheppard exists. For how she came to work for the *Herald Tribune*, see "Covered Story on 'Bad Night'; Landed H-T Job," *Editor & Publisher*, 28 Feb. 1948. Barbaralee Diamonstein, *Open Secrets: Ninety-four Women in Touch with Our Time* (1970), contains an interesting interview with Sheppard. Two articles, Allene Talmer, "Four Unique Columnists," *Vogue*, 1 Nov. 1958, and "Men Read Her," *Newsweek*, 18 June 1962, provide descriptions of Sheppard at work. An obituary is in the *New York Times*, 12 Nov. 1984.

CAROL SUE HUMPHREY

SHEPPARD, Melvin Winfield (5 Sept. 1883–4 Jan. 1942), Olympic gold medalist and track coach, was born in Almonesson, New Jersey, the son of Harry Sheppard and Alice (maiden name unknown), farmers. He attended the Brown Preparatory School in Philadelphia, where the sturdily built 5'8", 165-pound young man played football, won cross-country races, and set an interscholastic two-mile record of 9:57.4. After graduating in 1902, Sheppard moved to New York City and went to work at the John Wanamaker Department Store as both a salesman and recreation director. The company sent him in 1904 to St. Louis, where he won the exhibition half-mile (880 yards), part of the Olympic Games festival. He was invited that year to join the prestigious Irish-American Athletic Club, and his athletic career began in earnest.

In 1908 Sheppard married a young woman from his home town, Estelle Simon. They had two children. That year he was selected as a member of the U.S. Olympic team, and at the games in London, England, the aggressive-running Sheppard won the 800 meters in 1:52.8, a new Olympic and world record. He won the "metric mile" (1500 meters) in a new Olympic record of 4:03.4, and on the last day of competition, he won a third gold medal in the 1600-meter medley relay (200, 200, 400, 800). Sheppard's "anchor leg" was run in 1:55.4. He returned home, the star of the games, and for the remainder of his career was called "Peerless" Mel Sheppard.

In between Olympic games, he ran and won hundreds of races, winning championships in both the United States and Canada, posting the world's fastest times at 500, 700, and 800 yards; at two-thirds of a mile; and on world record–breaking mile and two-mile relay teams. Sheppard's "splendid turn of speed" got him on the 1912 Olympic team and an opportunity to face the markedly improved group of international middle-distance runners gathered in Stockholm, Sweden. Sheppard ran well at 400 meters but failed to win a medal. In the 1500-meter final he ran faster than his winning time in 1908 but finished in sixth place. In the 4 × 400-meter relay, Sheppard ran first; his team won first place and four gold medals, plus set a world record time of 3:16.6. The very busy "Shep" was at his best in the 800-meter final, called "the greatest Olympic footrace up to that time." Sheppard swept through the initial 400 in 52.5 seconds, followed closely by the brilliant American 19-year-old, Ted Meredith. In a whirlwind rush down the home stretch, the courageous 29-year-old Sheppard was unable to hold the lead into the finish line. Meredith's 1:51.9 was a new Olympic and world record, as was Sheppard's 1:52.0, some 18 inches back. Sheppard's silver medal and four gold medals in two Olympic Games competitions was unprecedented.

Sheppard's career ended in 1915 when he tripped on a loose board in Madison Square Garden. Two years later he was in the U.S. Army, serving during World War I as physical fitness director at several army camps. He also served with the American Sixty-ninth Infantry during the Mexican border "unrest." For twenty years after the war he continued working for the John Wanamaker store and coaching at the New York City Millrose Athletic Association. He died of a heart attack in Queens, New York.

• There is a delightful sketch of Sheppard in Richard Schaap, *An Illustrated History of the Olympics* (1963). See Sheppard statistics in Cordner Nelson and Roberto Quercetani, *Runners and Races* (1973), and Ray Krise and Bill Squires, *Fast*

Tracks: The History of Distance Running (1982). More can be found in David L. Porter, ed., *Biographical Dictionary of American Sports: Outdoor Sports* (1988); Frederick Webster, *Olympic Cavalcade* (1948) and *Great Moments in Athletics* (1947); David Wallechinsky, *The Complete Book of the Olympics* (1992); Reid M. Hanley, *Who's Who in Track and Field* (1978); and *The Fourth Olympiad London 1908 Official Report* (1909). Obituaries are in the *New York Times*, 4 Jan. 1942, and the *New York Herald Tribune* and the *Washington Post*, both 5 Jan. 1942.

JOHN A. LUCAS

SHEPPARD, Morris (28 May 1875–9 Apr. 1941), lawyer, U.S. congressman, and U.S. senator, was born John Morris Sheppard near Wheatville, Morris County, Texas, the son of John Levi Sheppard, a lawyer, and Margaret Alice Eddins, a member of a politically active Louisiana family. Sheppard's father held a succession of political and judicial offices, including district judge (1888–1896) and U.S. congressman (1899–1902). His political loyalties placed him among the progressive Democrats. On the state level he supported the programs of Governor James Stephen Hogg, and on the national level he campaigned for William Jennings Bryan.

In 1891 Morris Sheppard entered the University of Texas, where he participated in debate and public speaking and wrote for the student newspaper. He received a B.A. in 1895 and an LL.B. in 1897, having worked his way through school as a night watchman. After graduating he entered Yale University and received the master of laws degree in 1898. In 1896 he joined the Woodmen of the World, held several offices in that fraternal insurance organization, and gave speeches around the country for the group.

After graduating from Yale, Sheppard returned to Pittsburg in Camp County, Texas, and joined his father's law practice. In 1899 he moved his practice to Texarkana. When his father died in October 1902, Sheppard ran for and won the open seat in Congress. Identifying himself as a progressive Democrat, Sheppard was disenchanted with the conservative Republican power structure he encountered in Congress. He supported moral, social, and economic reforms, but his committee assignment, Public Buildings and Grounds, provided little opportunity for promoting these interests. Instead he developed a reputation as a gifted orator and a partisan critic of the Republican party. Sheppard fought high tariff rates from his earliest days in Congress and attacked the privilege of free railroad passes for members, but he did not overlook the more immediate needs of his constituents. He advocated a series of water projects that would further the industrial development of northeast Texas. After several of his reform initiatives, including an income tax measure, were defeated by Republican Speaker of the House Joseph G. Cannon, Sheppard grew vitriolic, arguing that the GOP had "drifted into a complete paralysis, a hopeless inertia." By 1909 the emerging split within the GOP provided Sheppard, other reform Democrats, and insurgent Republicans with greater legislative opportunities in Congress. In that year Sheppard married Lucile Sanderson. The couple had three daughters.

After the midterm elections in 1910, the Democrats regained control of Congress, and Sheppard assumed the chair of the Public Buildings and Grounds Committee. He researched the safety of government buildings. Aware of the need to safeguard valuable government documents from fire and other hazards, he passed legislation authorizing the construction of the National Archives.

In 1913 the Texas legislature elected Sheppard to the U.S. Senate. He was more progressive than Woodrow Wilson and hoped the new president would adopt a more liberal stance on issues such as woman suffrage and child labor. Sheppard supported the income tax, the creation of the Federal Reserve System, and the establishment of the Federal Trade Commission. He joined with other progressive southern Democrats in pushing the administration to adopt the Federal Farm Loan Act in 1916. Known as the father of national Prohibition, Sheppard crusaded for temperance reform. He argued that alcohol was "a source of danger to posterity because the alcoholic taint foredooms the unborn millions to degeneracy and disease. I shall oppose this scourge from hell until my arm can strike no longer and my tongue can speak no more." On 10 December 1913 he introduced a constitutional amendment providing for nationwide Prohibition. The measure passed in 1917 and was ratified as the Eighteenth Amendment in 1919. The Texas senator had earlier advised the White House on foreign policy problems stemming from the Mexican Revolution and split with a number of other progressives in backing Wilson's preparedness program. A member of the Military Affairs Committee since 1914, Sheppard lobbied for Wilson's defense program in 1916. "We cannot blind ourselves to the fact that force is the final arbiter among nations," he told his colleagues. He supported the expansion of military aviation and training within the armed forces and the construction of additional military posts along the Texas-Mexico border. After World War I he backed Wilson's peacemaking efforts and the League of Nations.

Sheppard's progressivism generated heated outcries from the more conservative wing of the Democratic party in Texas, and in the postwar years the senator fought off criticisms from Joseph Weldon Bailey and James E. Ferguson, both political titans in Texas. Yet these attacks did not deter Sheppard, because he remained popular with the state's more progressive Democrats and its many "drys." The senator pushed for what he called "humanizing legislation" during the 1920s. Among these measures were infant welfare, maternity benefits, and agricultural relief. The Sheppard-Towner Act, passed in 1921, resulted from a Department of Labor study that attributed deaths of women and children during and after childbirth to a lack of adequate knowledge about hygiene and health care. Sheppard firmly believed that "if there is anything which the state should guarantee it is the safety of each new borne [*sic*] baby." The new law provided money for a federal investigation by the U.S. Children's Bureau and appropriated funds to the states for medical services for mothers and infants.

In 1921 Sheppard joined with other senators and representatives in organizing the "Farm Bloc," which advocated tariff protection for agriculture. He deviated from his previous opposition to the tariff in the name of preserving the farmers' position within the larger national economy. Two years later Sheppard joined with Robert La Follette, George Norris, Hiram Johnson, William E. Borah, Arthur Capper, Smith W. Brookhart, and Lynn D. Frazier in the creation of the "Progressive Bloc," which pushed Congress to provide farmers with equal access to the credit sources used by businesspeople and backed various electoral reforms. Sheppard himself advocated a system of crop insurance and lobbied for government aid to small businesses and the decentralization of industry.

The 1930s and the presidency of Franklin D. Roosevelt provided Sheppard with increased political visibility. Much of his time in the early years of the decade was spent fighting for the retention of national Prohibition. Despite Roosevelt's support for its eventual repeal, Sheppard supported the new president's economic and social program. Sheppard introduced and passed legislation providing for the federal credit union system so that low-income Americans could gain access to banking facilities with nominal interest rates. Unlike some other Democrats, in 1937 he stayed with the administration when the president introduced a plan to increase the size of the Supreme Court after several key New Deal measures had been overturned. Yet in 1938, when he chaired the special Senate Investigating Committee on Campaign Expenditures, he criticized the political activities of the Works Progress Administration in that year's elections. As a result of his findings, Congress passed the Hatch Act in 1939, a measure that limited political activity by government employees.

As hostilities developed in Europe, Sheppard's duties as chair of the Military Affairs Committee increased. He usually managed the administration's programs on the Senate floor. He sought a stronger peacetime army during the mid-1930s and supported changes in the Neutrality Act and the Embargo Act and provisions for the sale of military equipment on a cash-and-carry basis. He backed Roosevelt's plan for compulsory military training, and in 1940 he guided the Burke-Wadsworth Selective Service Bill through to passage, resulting in the first peacetime draft in the United States. He helped secure authorization of legislation providing greater military responsibilities for the National Guard. These legislative battles in the summer of 1940 taxed Sheppard's strength, yet in February 1941 he spoke on behalf of Roosevelt's lend-lease proposal, which passed the following month. This was Sheppard's last fight. He died in Washington, D.C.

• Sheppard's papers are at the Center for American History (CAH), University of Texas, Austin. Information about Sheppard is also in the Albert Sidney Burleson Papers, the Oscar B. Colquitt Papers, the Will C. Hogg Papers, and the Sam Rayburn Papers, all in the CAH. The center also has a copy of a typescript by his daughter, Lucile Sheppard Keyes, "Morris Sheppard" (1950), and a useful biographical file. Additional Sheppard materials are in the Albert Sidney Burleson Papers, the Thomas Watt Gregory Papers, the Harold Ickes Papers, the Robert Lansing Papers, the Theodore Roosevelt Papers, the William Howard Taft Papers, the Joseph Tumulty Papers, and the Woodrow Wilson Papers, all in the Library of Congress. Ample materials on Sheppard's career are in the Herbert Hoover Presidential Library, West Branch, Iowa; the Franklin D. Roosevelt Presidential Library, Hyde Park, N.Y.; and the Lyndon B. Johnson Presidential Library, Austin, Tex. Sheppard wrote several pieces himself, including *Fraternal and Other Addresses*, 2d ed. (1914); *What Shakespeare Says about It*, comp. and titled by Morris Sheppard (c. 1935); and "The Mexican Situation," *American Review of Reviews* 49 (Apr. 1914): 431–32. Sheppard is the subject of Richard Bailey, "Morris Sheppard of Texas: Southern Progressive and Prohibitionist" (Ph.D. diss., Texas Christian Univ., 1980); Escal F. Duke, "The Political Career of Morris Sheppard, 1875–1941" (Ph.D. diss., Univ. of Texas, Austin, 1958); and Karen Jeanette Salas, "Senator Morris Sheppard and the Eighteenth Amendment" (M.A. thesis, Univ. of Texas, Austin, 1970). See also Bailey, "Morris Sheppard—A Prohibitionist in the Liberal Tradition," *Studies in History* 6 (1976): 75–81; Lewis L. Gould, *Progressives and Prohibitionists: Texas Democrats in the Wilson Era* (1973); Dewey Grantham, Jr., "Texas Congressional Leaders and the New Freedom, 1913–1917," *Southwestern Historical Quarterly* 53 (July 1949): 35–48; and J. Stanley Lemons, "The Sheppard-Towner Act: Progressivism in the 1920s," *Journal of American History* 55 (Mar. 1969): 776–86. An obituary is in the *New York Times*, 9 Apr. 1941.

NANCY BECK YOUNG

SHEPPARD, Samuel Edward (29 July 1882–29 Sept. 1948), chemist, was born in Hither Green, Kent, England, the son of Samuel Sheppard, a market gardener, and Emily Mary Taplin. "A naturally insatiable but quite general curiosity turned me into science," he wrote later ("Autobiographical Sketch," p. 1). Sheppard attended Deal College in Kent, a preparatory school, and then entered St. Dunstan's College in Kent, a technical school. There he began his lifelong association with Charles Edward Kenneth Mees, a fellow student who was keenly interested in the chemistry of photography. Sheppard and Mees entered University College in London in 1900, where they studied under chemist William Ramsay, and both received the B.Sc. in chemistry in 1903. Sheppard set up a chemical laboratory at home and published several papers jointly with Mees; in 1906 he received the D.Sc. in chemistry from University College. His doctoral research and that of Mees were published together in 1907 as *Investigations on the Theory of the Photographic Process*, which became widely used in the profession.

Sheppard received an 1851 Exhibition Scholarship in 1907, and went to Marburg University in Germany for more than a year of research with Karl Schaum, professor of photochemistry, and physicist Franz Richarz. There Sheppard used a spectrophotometer to analyze the color-sensitizing action of newly developed dyes for use in photography; he was able to distinguish between the true solutions and colloidal solutions among them. This was the first use of the spectrophotometer to analyze the spectra, or bands of colors, in dyes. Sheppard also spent some time at Jena, Germany, studying advanced microscopy. For another year and a half of the scholarship period he worked at the Sorbonne in Paris with Victor Henri to continue studies of the colloid properties of photosensitizing dyes and "at the same time gained much experience in general colloid chemistry" ("Autobiographical Sketch," p. 2).

Back in England in 1910, Sheppard began work for Wratten and Wainwright in Surrey, a company that manufactured photographic equipment; Mees was also working there. Sheppard left the firm in 1911 to study agricultural chemistry at the School of Agriculture, Cambridge University. There he carried out research on the chemistry of gluten in wheat flour; he also completed the manuscript of *Photochemistry* (1914). In 1912 he married Eveline Lucy Ground; they had one son.

In 1912 Mees became head of the newly established research laboratory of Eastman Kodak Company in Rochester, New York, and at his invitation, the next year Sheppard joined that laboratory as a colloid and physical chemist. In 1920 he became head of the combined departments of physical, inorganic, and analytical chemistry. In 1921 he was put in charge of developing the company's X-ray intensifying screens; he later organized the department established to manufacture the screens. In 1924 he became assistant director of research, a position he held until 1948, retiring only a few months before his death. He did not become a U.S. citizen.

During World War I, when Kodak was asked by the Submarine Defence Corporation, a British group, to advise on the use of coal dust as a fuel, Sheppard determined that a colloidal mixture could be made from resin soaps and the fine coal mixed into fuel oil. This was successful and provided an economic use for coal dust, which had previously been discarded.

At Kodak Sheppard's projects were concerned chiefly with the chemical and physical properties of gelatins, in which light-sensitive materials are contained, and of cellulose esters, which are fundamental compounds used in photography. His work on gelatins included determination of their structure, setting and melting points, and drying and swelling, as well as measurements of their viscosity, strength, and elasticity. About 1921 he concluded that the sensitivity, or speed, of film was proportional to the size of the grains of silver in the emulsion and that larger grain size in the emulsion increased the film speed. He followed up on this by analyzing the mechanism of precipitation of silver halide and its growth into grains. This led to the development of methods to measure the distribution and size of grains in the emulsion. Sheppard's research on this topic, coauthored with A. P. H. Trivelli, was

published as *Silver Bromide Grain of Photographic Emulsions* (1921), the first in a Kodak monograph series on the theory of photography. Sheppard also wrote *Gelatin in Photography* (1923), the third monograph in the series.

By 1925 Sheppard had observed that the reaction of gelatin with silver bromide was affected by sulfur compounds, which were present in the better gelatin samples. He determined that the sulfur was derived chiefly from wild mustard plants eaten by cattle from which the gelatin was manufactured. These analyses made it possible for manufacturers to create uniform emulsions on photographic paper and to develop films of greater speed. Much of Sheppard's later work was concerned with sensitizing dyes; these are adsorbed onto grains of silver halide in an emulsion and increase its sensitivity to certain colors. He analyzed the absorption spectra of dyes in various solvents to determine the manner in which they were able to absorb light.

A project not related to photography was Sheppard's development in 1921 of the first successful technique for electroplating rubber and rubber compounds, which became the basis for a new industry.

Sheppard's work was fundamental to the theory of the photographic processes. Through his chemical analyses of complex compounds, he placed the field of photography on a much more scientific footing. He received more than sixty patents. In addition to several books, he wrote almost 200 scientific papers and a few chapters in technical books. For his accomplishments, he was awarded the Progress Medal of the Royal Photographic Society of England (1928), the Adelsköld Medal of the Swedish Photographic Society (1929), and the Nichols Medal of the American Chemical Society (1930). He died in Rochester, New York.

• Some biographical records of Sheppard are in the archives of Eastman Kodak Company, including a three-page "Autobiographical Sketch," with a bibliography to 1929. See also a memorial, by C. E. K. Mees, "Samuel Edward Sheppard," *Journal of the Chemical Society, London*, pt. 1 (1949): 261–63.

ELIZABETH NOBLE SHOR

SHERA, Jesse Hauk (8 Dec. 1903–8 Mar. 1982), librarian, educator, and author, was born in Oxford, Ohio, the son of Charles Hypes Shera, a dairyman, and Jesse Hauk. Shera grew up in Oxford, attending William McGuffey High School. He was a member of the debating team, as well as a drummer, a cheerleader, and the 1921 senior class president. Although he was interested in a career in chemistry, his poor eyesight prevented him from pursuing this interest. Remaining in Oxford, he graduated with honors from Miami University in 1925 with an A.B. in English. Shera earned tuition by selling typewriters from door to door and working at a local soda fountain. From Miami he went to Yale University, where he graduated in 1927 with a master's degree in English literature.

Employment for English professors in those pre-depression years was difficult to find, so Shera returned to Oxford and took a position in Miami University's library. There he met his future wife Helen May Bickam, whom he married in 1928; they had two children. Set to enter Columbia University's library school in the fall of 1928, Shera instead accepted a research associate and bibliographer position at Miami University's Scripts Foundation for Research in Population Problems, a position he held until 1940. At Scripts he performed population studies using Hollerith machines to calculate and tabulate data. This early exposure to computers and their statistical capabilities began a lifelong interest in the electronic organization of information.

Taking leave from Scripts for two years, Shera finally entered library school at the University of Chicago as a doctoral candidate in 1938. During the war years he was appointed as chief of the Library of Congress's 1940 census project. From 1941 to 1944 Shera served as department chief of the Central Information Division in the Office of Strategic Services, gathering and organizing military intelligence. Using IBM punch cards, he created computerized subject access to mail that the United States received from foreign countries. Shera later applied this experience to library automation. Returning to the University of Chicago, he completed his doctorate in 1944 and subsequently held a series of management positions in technical and public services at the university. From 1947 to 1952 he also taught in the library school.

Three significant events in 1952 proved to be momentous to Shera's career. First, he was selected as dean of the Western Reserve Library School by that university's progressive president, John Schoff Millis. Shera expanded the faculty fivefold and added a doctoral program by 1956. Increasingly he became interested in automation and computerization and its practical application to libraries. Also in 1952 Shera met James W. Perry, a chemist from the Massachusetts Institute of Technology working on the application of automation and mechanization to scholarship. Shera brought Perry and his colleague Alan Kent to Western Reserve's library school faculty. With Perry and Kent, Shera established in 1955 the Center for Documentation and Communications Research (CDCR) to advise business, industry, government, higher education, and librarianship on creating methods of organization for recorded or stored information.

Finally, in 1952 Shera reorganized the American Documentation Institute (ADI) and the following year brought the editorial offices of the organization's journal *American Documentation* to Western Reserve. Founded in the 1930s for the purpose of preserving information, primarily in microformat, the ADI was transformed by Shera and others to investigate the application of electronics to information preservation.

While the majority of the profession was not yet interested in automation, Shera organized numerous conferences on employing information systems in libraries, including the 1957 conference Systems for Information Retrieval. However, 1961 brought a schism in the CDCR that resulted in Perry's departure. Perry had devised his own system of information organization and focused the center's activities solely on his system and its scientific applications. This split marked the beginning of the polarization of the library community between those who ascribed to a scientific, analytical methodology and those who believed in a predominantly humanistic approach to librarianship and bibliographic control. Eventually the CDCR was absorbed by the university's library school.

Beginning in the late 1940s and continuing well into the 1960s, Shera wrote prolifically and held various editorships of journals and presses, including the *Library Quarterly* (1947–1955), *American Documentation* (1953–1959), the *Journal of Cataloging and Classification* (1947–1957), and the Western Reserve University Press (1954–1957). He also wrote a regular column in the *Wilson Library Bulletin* titled "Without Reserve" in the early 1960s. His awards and public service record was also quite lengthy. He was a recipient of the Melvil Dewey Award from the American Library Association (1968) and the Kaula, a gold medal from India (1976). He held many national and state offices in professional library and educational associations, and he was a delegate for the National Science Foundation to an international conference on classification in 1957. In 1965 Shera was named to Lyndon Johnson's Presidents Committee for Employment of the Handicapped, an issue of interest because of his lifelong struggle with strabismus and his partial blindness. With the merger of Western Reserve University and Case Institute of Technology in 1967, Shera's beloved library school fell in priority in the new Case Western Reserve University. In June 1970 he retired as dean, but he continued to teach and be active in the profession until his death in Cleveland Heights, Ohio.

Shera's mark on librarianship and on the education of librarians is unmistakable. Although the ADI eventually became the American Society for Information Scientists, Shera was never convinced that librarianship could become wholly a science. He warned against the dehumanizing effects of technology, fearing that librarians would become mired in the mechanics of information technology and ignore the philosophy of information. He believed that librarians needed a well-rounded undergraduate education as well as a specialty within library science. Shera's tireless devotion to the professionalization of librarianship led to new educational methodology in library schools across the country. In his last years Shera foretold the information explosion of the 1980s that would result from mechanical technology's inability to deal with the twentieth century's symbolism in human terms.

• Shera's papers are held at Case Western Reserve University. Several bibliographies attempt to collect all of his writings: H. Curtis Wright, *Jesse Shera: Librarianship and Information Science* (1988); Laurie P. Ruderman, "Jesse Shera: A Bio-Bibliography" (master's thesis, Kent State Univ., 1968); and the *Encyclopedia of Library and Information Science.* All of these sources contain biographical information. At the time of Shera's death many tributes and assessments of his career were written. An obituary is in *American Libraries* 13 (Apr. 1982): 220ff.

JENNY L. PRESNELL

SHERBURNE, Henry (16 Feb. 1675–29 Dec. 1757), mariner-merchant and politician, was born either at Little Harbor (now Newcastle, N.H.) or in Hampton (at that time part of Massachusetts), the son of Captain Samuel Sherburne and Love Hutchins. Sherburne's father, who owned extensive property in Portsmouth and Little Harbor, had moved to Hampton in 1675, where he became an innkeeper, selectman, and captain of the Hampton militia. He was a strong advocate of Hampton remaining under Massachusetts's jurisdiction after 1679, when New Hampshire, with Hampton, became a separate royal colony. Young Henry, baptized in Newbury, Massachusetts, grew up in Hampton's frontier atmosphere of violent Indian wars, chaotic provincial politics, and the Masonian proprietary threats to the security of his father's property. Captain John Mason's 1635 land claims to the colony of New Hampshire were assumed by Robert Mason during the 1670s and Samuel Allen in the 1690s, each of whom sought their enforcement and the collection of annual quitrents from the New Hampshire settlers.

In 1691, after his father's death in a battle with Indians during King William's War, Sherburne went to sea, probably under the tutelage of his uncle John Sherburne of Little Harbor, a mariner involved in the coastal trade in lumber and fish. By the late 1690s Sherburne was a mariner of enough prominence to join in marriage with Dorothy Wentworth, the youngest daughter of the Portsmouth merchant-innkeeper Samuel Wentworth, and the sister of John Wentworth, who would later become lieutenant governor. The couple had seven children. By 1699 Sherburne, now living in Portsmouth, was first mate to John Wentworth, who commanded ships carrying masts to England. Soon after, Sherburne commanded his own vessels carrying lumber and fish to the West Indies and, occasionally, to Spain or Portugal. From the 1720s (when the shipping returns begin to indicate vessel ownership) until the late 1740s Sherburne and his sons were second only to the mast contractors for the royal navy in total volume of overseas trade from Piscataqua. By 1710 Sherburne had become a Portsmouth retail merchant as well as a mariner, and he was consistently among the top ten Portsmouth taxpayers from 1713 through the mid-1740s. He and his family lived in a two-story brick mansion at the head of Sherburne pier "in almost Royal style." In 1710, concerned about receiving proper social recognition, he traced his genealogy to a knight, Sir Richard Sherburne of Stonyhurst, and assumed his arms and pedigree.

Sherburne entered politics with his election to the New Hampshire Assembly as a Portsmouth representative in 1720. The assembly immediately elected him clerk of the assembly and placed him on committees that corresponded with the provincial agent in England and sought to create legislation issuing new paper currency. His staunch advocacy of paper money probably contributed to his failure to win reelection in 1722, although his attendance was irregular enough that he lost his position as clerk in 1721. He served as a Portsmouth selectman in 1723, 1725, 1726, and 1728, and then Lieutenant Governor Wentworth appointed him to the New Hampshire Council, where he served from 1728 to 1757.

Unlike most of the Portsmouth merchants on the council, Sherburne had family and property connections in Hampton, Dover, and Newcastle and was related to the Waldron family, as well as the Wentworths, through his cousin Mary Sherburne's marriage to Thomas Westbrook, father-in-law of Richard Waldron III. When Jonathan Belcher became governor of Massachusetts and New Hampshire in 1730 and Lieutenant Governor Wentworth died, Sherburne joined the Belcher-Waldron alliance in ousting Wentworth relatives from all provincial offices, extending the provincial courts to the major towns outside Portsmouth, and seeking to strengthen New Hampshire's ties with Massachusetts. The outcome of these changes was a political war between the new alliance and the Wentworth faction. As a reward for Sherburne's support, Belcher had promised him the vacant post of lieutenant governor, but he was unable to deliver on that promise. Consequently, Belcher provided Sherburne with a colonel's commission, appointed him provincial treasurer and chief justice of the superior court of judicature in 1732, and made his mansion a center of political and social activity by using it as his residence during visits to New Hampshire.

As the political warfare increased during the 1730s, Sherburne's Wentworth relatives agitated and manipulated him. His two younger sons supported the Wentworth side, and all three sons joined the new Portsmouth Anglican church against his wishes, as he was a member of the north parish Congregational church. Belcher lamented to Waldron that he had to be very guarded in his correspondence with the "honest, tho brittle" Sherburne ("old H") and that, while Sherburne was "an honest friend," at times he was an "old Fool," "unsteady," and "a compound of Ignorance, jealousy, and brittleness" (Belcher to Waldron, 2 May 1737, Belcher papers, Massachusetts Historical Society). Belcher sought to keep him "steady" by appointing his cousin Joseph Sherburne to the council and even nominating Sherburne's oldest son, Samuel, as well. Sherburne's only major political disagreement with Belcher involved the issuance of paper currency: Sherburne pushed its expanded use, through land banks if necessary, while Belcher opposed any further expansion. As the prospects for a Wentworth clan victory and the creation of separate governors for New Hampshire and Massachusetts became imminent, Sherburne's vote in 1740 made a majority for the council's petition to the Crown defending Belcher's administration and requesting that New Hampshire be annexed to Massachusetts. The petition, however, was unsuccessful. The Wentworth faction obtained victory, and by 1742 the new and separate New Hampshire governor, Benning Wentworth, had stripped Sherburne of all political offices except his council membership. For Sherburne, ambition and principles had brought his political downfall.

From 1742 until his death Sherburne, shattered, embittered, and in ill health, crippled by gout, remained on the fringes of politics, attending the council irregularly through 1754, when his wife died, and supporting those who opposed Wentworth's administration. He was delighted to see his son Henry's conversion during the Great Awakening and his election to the assembly, where he led the opposition to the Wentworths from the mid-1740s on. In 1745 the assembly appointed both Sherburne and his son Henry to an executive committee in charge of outfitting and supplying New Hampshire's contribution to the Louisbourg expedition. This was Sherburne's final official responsibility. He died in Portsmouth.

In retrospect, Sherburne's economic success exemplified the transition from mariner to merchant, a major avenue to wealth in northern New England. Moreover, although his life spanned all the major changes that occurred in the Piscataqua region except the American Revolution, Sherburne remained true to the general values of his earliest years, promoting pro-Massachusetts political and religious approaches. His doing so indicated both the lasting impact of Massachusetts in New Hampshire and the existence of a variety of outlooks within Portsmouth's merchant aristocracy.

• Manuscripts relating to Sherburne are in the shipping returns for the port of Piscataqua, British Public Record Office, CO 5, nos. 967, 968; the State Papers, New Hampshire Archives; the Belcher papers and the Waldron papers, New Hampshire Historical Society; the Belcher papers, Massachusetts Historical Society; and the Portsmouth Town Records, New Hampshire State Library. Published sources are scattered in Nathaniel Bouton et al., eds., *New Hampshire Provincial and State Papers*, vols. 3–6, 9, 17–19, 36 (40 vols., 1867–1943); W. M. Sainsbury et al., eds., *Calendar of State Papers, Colonial Series, America and West Indies, 1574–1738* (44 vols., 1850–1969); "Belcher Papers," Massachusetts Historical Society, *Collections*, ser. 6, vols. 6–7. Short sketches are in Sybil Noyes et al., *Genealogical Dictionary of Maine and New Hampshire* (1928–1939); *New England Historical and Genealogical Register* (1904); John Wentworth, *Wentworth Genealogy* (1878); and Charles Brewster, *Rambles about Portsmouth*, 2d ser. (1869). Works placing Sherburne in historical context are Charles E. Clark, *The Eastern Frontier: The Settlement of Northern New England, 1610–1763* (1970); Jere Daniell, *Colonial New Hampshire: A History* (1981) and *Experiment in Republicanism: New Hampshire Politics and the American Revolution, 1741–1794* (1970); and David E. Van Deventer, *The Emergence of Provincial New Hampshire, 1623–1741* (1976). Still useful is Jeremy Belknap, *The History of New Hampshire*, ed. John Farmer (1831).

DAVID E. VAN DEVENTER

SHERIDAN, Martin Joseph (28 Mar. 1881–27 Mar. 1918), track and field athlete, was born in Bohola, County Mayo, Ireland, the son of Martin Sheridan and Jane Dierken. With his older brother Richard he immigrated to the United States in 1897; he would not visit Ireland again until after the 1908 Olympics in London. Richard Sheridan quickly established himself in the United States as a discus thrower. Martin Sheridan also took up the event and quickly became the best in the world at it. Both brothers competed mostly for New York's Irish-American Athletic Club.

Many of the top weight throwers in the world in the early 1900s were Irish immigrants, often termed the "Irish whales," since most of them were quite large and often overweight. Sheridan stood 6'3", but he weighed 195 pounds in his prime and was actually quite trim. This enabled him to excel also as a jumper and an all-around athlete.

During the era in which Sheridan competed, there was no official governing body that recognized world records. Various sources credit him with between seven and sixteen world records. He set his first world mark on 14 September 1901, when he threw the discus 120'7¾" (36.77 meters) at a small meet in Paterson, New Jersey, while his last world record was the 142'10¼" (43.53 meters) recorded at Celtic Park, New York, on 10 October 1909. Sheridan's longest recorded throw, however, was the 143'4" (43.69 meters) with which he won the First Regiment Irish Volunteer's Athletic Association Annual Meet on 10 September 1905; but it was not recognized as a record, for reasons that are not clear.

Sheridan's Olympic fame rests primarily on his winning three Olympic gold medals in the discus. His first came in 1904 in St. Louis, Missouri, where he tied for the lead and then won a throw-off for the championship. In 1906 he won the gold medal in the Intercalated Olympic Games at Athens, Greece, by throwing a world record 136'0" (41.46 meters). Sheridan's final discus gold medal came in London in 1908 when he led an American sweep, with Merritt Giffin and Bill Horr earning the other medals.

Sheridan was far more than just a discus thrower. Overall, he won four medals, three of them gold, at the 1904 and 1908 Olympics. At the 1906 Olympics, termed unofficial by some purists, Sheridan won five medals, two of them gold. In 1908, in addition to the discus gold, he earned the gold medal in the Greek-style discus throw, which was contested only at the 1906 and 1908 Olympics, and the bronze medal in the standing long jump.

At the 1906 Intercalated Olympics, Sheridan had his greatest performance. He entered 14 events, but competed only in seven of them. In those seven, he won gold medals in the discus throw and shot put, and silver medals in the stone throw, the standing high jump, and the standing long jump. He was fourth in the Greek-style discus throw and did not finish the pentathlon. Sheridan later called his failure to finish the pentathlon his greatest athletic disappointment; he was heavily favored, but a knee injury forced him to withdraw after he finished second in the first event, the standing broad jump.

At the 1908 Olympics, Sheridan also gained fame for a comment he made after Ralph Rose, a shot putter and the U.S. flag bearer, did not dip the U.S. flag to the king of England during the opening ceremonies. Although Rose carried the flag during the opening ceremonies, it is often mistakenly believed that Sheridan was the flag bearer. This legend seems to have arisen because several days later, when asked about Rose's actions, Sheridan proclaimed, "This flag dips to no earthly king!"

Sheridan was a superb jumper and weight thrower, but he displayed his other talents in the all-around championship, the early American forerunner of the decathlon. Sheridan entered and won three all-around events in his athletic career: the AAU national championships of 1905, 1907, and 1909. In so doing he broke the world record each time, finally setting a mark of 7,385 points, which Jim Thorpe broke by only a few points in 1912. Sheridan also won AAU discus championships in 1904, 1906, 1907, and 1911, the last one occurring just before his retirement as an athlete.

Off the field, Sheridan worked as a policeman (1902–1918), as did many of the Irish-American athletes. His fame led him to be a personal bodyguard for the governor of New York on occasions when the governor visited New York City. Sheridan never married and died without issue from pneumonia in New York City only seven years after he retired from athletics. In the *New York Herald Tribune* (28 Mar. 1918), his obituary proclaimed him to be the greatest all-around athlete ever known in the United States—greater even than Thorpe, who was quoted as saying, "Sheridan was the greatest athlete in the world. He could do things I never could."

• Information on Sheridan's athletic accomplishments is in Richard Hymans and Ekkehard zur Megede, *Progression of World Best Performances and Official IAAF World Records* (1991); Bill Mallon, "The Pre-IAAF Discus Throw Record Progression," in *International Athletics Annual 1986*, ed. Peter Matthews (1986); Mallon and Ian Buchanan, *Quest for Gold: The Encyclopaedia of American Olympians* (1984); Peter Matthews, Buchanan, and Mallon, *The Guinness International Who's Who of Sport* (1993); D. H. Potts and Scott Davis, *The United States National Record Progression from 1877* (1983); and David Wallechinsky, *The Complete Book of the Olympics*, 3d ed. (1991).

BILL MALLON

SHERIDAN, Philip Henry (6 Mar. 1831–5 Aug. 1888), U.S. Army general, was born while his family was en route from Ireland to Somerset, Ohio, the son of John Sheridan, a laborer, and Mary Meenagh. In 1830 John Sheridan had sold his leasehold on a small farm in County Cavan in north-central Ireland and bought passage to the United States. The following year, after finding no opportunities at Albany, New York, he was given work on the National Road—then being extended toward St. Louis, Missouri—and settled in the village of Somerset, Ohio. Whether Philip was born at sea, in Albany, or in Somerset has never been clearly established.

At the age of ten, Philip Sheridan began attending the one-room school in Somerset. His was a typical nineteenth-century frontier education; brief (four years in duration), rudimentary, and punctuated by frequent whippings. Being slight of stature and a member of the much-maligned Irish ethnic group, Sheridan suffered more than his share of hazing and gained a reputation for a short temper and ready fists.

In 1845, his schooling complete, Sheridan went to work as a bookkeeper for Fink and Dittoe's dry-goods store in Somerset. Despite his scanty education, he became, he recalled in his *Personal Memoirs* (1888), "quite a local authority in history, being frequently chosen as arbiter in discussions and disputes that arose in the store."

Intrigued by stories of the Mexican War of 1846–1848, Sheridan resolved to become a soldier. When he learned in 1848 that a young man who had been nominated to the U.S. Military Academy at West Point had failed the entrance examination, he wrote to his congressman asking for the appointment, "reminding him that we had often met in Fink & Dittoe's store, and that therefore he must know something of my qualifications." This rather slim claim to preferment was successful.

Sheridan compensated for his lack of academic training and skills with dogged persistence and maintained a place in the middle of his class rankings. During a dress parade in September 1851, the beginning of Sheridan's final year at West Point, cadet sergeant William R. Terrill gave him an order in what Sheridan considered to be an "improper tone." Sheridan threatened Terrill with a bayonet, and after Terrill reported the incident, Sheridan attacked the much larger Virginian with his fists.

Sheridan was suspended from West Point for one year. When he finally graduated, in June 1853, he ranked thirty-fourth in a class of forty-nine, a standing not high enough to give him any choice of arm or assignment. He was made a brevet second lieutenant in the First Infantry Regiment. Sent with his regiment to Fort Duncan, Texas, in 1854, the next year he was transferred to the Fourth Infantry Regiment at Fort Reading, California. For the next five years Sheridan's principal work was policing an American Indian reservation in western Oregon.

Not until March 1861, on the eve of the Civil War, did Sheridan win promotion to first lieutenant. Soon thereafter Fort Sumter fell, and still Sheridan remained in his remote western fort (although he was promoted again, in May, to captain). "I earnestly wished to be at the seat of war," he wrote, "and feared it might end before I could get East."

Finally, on 1 September 1861 the 30-year-old captain was ordered to join a new infantry regiment in Missouri. Major General Henry W. Halleck, commanding the Union's Western Department, assigned Sheridan to head a board of auditors, and the former bookkeeper displayed such talent as a military accountant that he was named chief commissary and quartermaster for the little Army of the Southwest

Missouri District. While the Federal Army of the Mississippi fought off Confederate attacks at Inka and Corinth, Sheridan's fervent desire to command troops in the field went unfulfilled.

On 6 April 1862 the "forlorn and disheartened" Captain Sheridan was in Chicago buying horses when Ulysses S. Grant's Federals won the largest battle of the war thus far at Shiloh in southern Tennessee. Sheridan, deeply frustrated, went to the area to seek a line command.

On 25 May the governor of Michigan offered Sheridan the colonelcy of the volunteer Second Michigan Cavalry. Regular officers were not supposed to command volunteer organizations, but Sheridan somehow won General Halleck's approval, took command of the regiment, and immediately led it on a four-day raid into Mississippi. On 11 June Sheridan's brigade commander was promoted, and Sheridan succeeded him.

On the morning of 1 July nearly 5,000 Confederate cavalrymen launched a surprise attack on Sheridan's 800 troopers in their camp at Booneville, Mississippi. Instead of retreating, Sheridan executed a complex counterattack and routed the Confederates. A telegram sent shortly afterward to General Halleck, signed by five brigadier generals, read, "The undersigned respectfully beg that you will obtain the promotion of Sheridan. He is worth his weight in gold."

Now a brigadier general, Sheridan commanded the Eleventh Division of the Federal Army of the Ohio at Perryville, Kentucky, on 8 October 1862. His division led the army into battle and seized the vital high ground in the center of the Federal line. While the Federal left was driven back, Sheridan's division fended off several attacks and then counterattacked, driving into the town of Perryville. The advance was not supported, and the battle ended a draw, although the Confederates relinquished the field the next day. Sheridan enjoyed his first taste of fame as some newspapers dubbed him the "Paladin of Perryville."

On 31 December 1862, when the Confederates attacked along Stones River, southeast of Nashville near the town of Murfreesboro, they routed two Federal divisions then came up against Sheridan, who counterattacked. Overwhelmingly outnumbered, he was forced to fall back, but he did so stubbornly, keeping his men well in hand. After another day of fighting, the Confederates left the field and yielded the victory.

On 19 September 1863 the armies engaged again along the Chickamauga River. The battle was confused, with each side feeding units into the fighting piecemeal. Early the next day, a misunderstood command opened a gap in the Federal line next to Sheridan's division, into which two Confederate divisions attacked. Sheridan was overwhelmed as the Federal army was driven from the field and returned to Chattanooga. Union forces were pinned down as Confederate troops occupied the high ground ringing the town. Alarmed authorities in Washington named a new department commander, Grant, who on 25 November launched an attack.

Sheridan's division was in the center of the advance against the Confederate line on Missionary Ridge. His men overran their objective—a line of enemy entrenchments at the bottom of the ridge—and, instead of stopping there as ordered, began to scramble up the steep, 400-foot face of the ridge toward the main enemy line. While Grant watched in admiring disbelief, Sheridan joined his division as they clambered up the slope, cracked the Confederate center, took 1,762 prisoners, captured 17 guns—Sheridan straddling one of them and howling in triumph—then chased the retreating army off into the twilight.

When Grant was named general in chief of the Union armies on 12 March 1864, he appointed Sheridan chief of cavalry for the Army of the Potomac. On his way east to his new assignment, Sheridan was presented to President Lincoln, who later described the bantam officer as "a brown, chunky little chap" with "not enough neck to hang him." To Grant, Lincoln opined that Sheridan was "rather a little fellow to handle your cavalry." Grant's reply was serene: "You will find him big enough."

Sheridan found the cavalry units in Virginia widely scattered, their camps filthy, the horses broken down, and the men poorly armed. While he straightened out the routines, reestablished discipline, and cleaned up the camps, he became convinced that the Cavalry Corps was being misused carrying messages, escorting infantry officers, patrolling enemy territory, and guarding a perimeter sixty miles in circumference.

As Grant's brutal overland campaign toward Richmond began in the spring of 1864, Sheridan argued repeatedly with the commander of the Army of the Potomac, Major General George G. Meade, over the proper use of cavalry. After one especially heated exchange on 8 May, Sheridan, flirting with insubordination, demanded permission to mass the cavalry, go out into enemy territory, and whip the enemy cavalry under the legendary Jeb Stuart. When Meade complained to Grant, the general in chief responded mildly, "Did he say that? Well, he generally knows what he is talking about. Let him start right out and do it."

Sheridan headed toward Richmond with 10,000 men and thirty-two guns in a column thirteen miles long that took four hours to pass a given point on its route. Instead of the usual tactics for such a raid—racing through enemy territory, doing some damage, and getting back to safety—Sheridan walked his horses toward Richmond, knowing that Stuart would have to find and engage him. The steadiness of the pace, wrote one cavalryman, "calmed the nerves, strengthened self-reliance, and inspired confidence."

On 11 May 1864 Stuart managed to get in front of Sheridan with 4,500 exhausted troopers a mere six miles from Richmond, near a crossroads inn called Yellow Tavern. The southerners dismounted and withstood attack after attack until a Federal private got off a lucky shot and killed Stuart. Sheridan's men bulled their way to the first line of Richmond defenses and could have gone into the city, but Sheridan, seeing "no permanent advantage," declined the temptation to make headlines.

With his victory, Sheridan had made a dramatic point about the proper use of the mounted arm, had shattered the myth of the innate superiority of southern horsemen, and had confirmed General Grant's high opinion of him. Grant used Sheridan to draw off Robert E. Lee's cavalry while the Army of the Potomac crossed the James River east of Richmond in June. In July, when a Confederate force under Jubal Early regained supremacy of the Shenandoah Valley, invaded the North, and threatened the defenses of Washington, Grant sent Sheridan west to retake the valley.

Sheridan took command of the reorganized Army of the Shenandoah on 7 August then spent five weeks maneuvering and skirmishing. He measured his opponent, probing with his cavalry and prodding with infantry reconnaissances. Sheridan attacked Early's widely separated forces at Winchester at dawn on 19 September 1864.

The attack was flawed by an early morning traffic jam and a slightly skewed advance. By midday the Federals had been stopped, and Sheridan spent the afternoon fuming and building a new plan of attack from the wreckage of his old one. At 4:00 P.M. he unleashed a massive flanking maneuver that, combined with one of the largest cavalry charges of the war, smashed the Confederate formations and sent them, as Sheridan's prompt telegram to Washington phrased it, "a whirling through Winchester."

Sheridan followed up the rout with another at Fisher's Hill three days later, chased Early's army into the Blue Ridge Mountains, and took possession of the Shenandoah Valley. To deny its abundance to future Confederate military operations, he burned the mills and barns and confiscated the livestock from Staunton north to Cedar Creek, near Middletown, where he camped while he argued with Washington authorities over his next assignment.

Sheridan was in Winchester, twelve miles north of Middletown, when at dawn on 19 October 1864, Early launched a surprise attack that routed the Federal army. Arriving at his lines at midday, Sheridan galvanized his men with a dramatic ride along their lines and in late afternoon counterattacked, driving Early's army from the field again. The dramatic victory, celebrated in a poem titled "Sheridan's Ride" by Thomas Buchanan Read, helped lift the North's deep war weariness and contributed to the reelection of Lincoln. It was Sheridan's finest hour.

After a final humiliation of Early's remaining Confederates in the spring of 1865, Sheridan led his cavalry east to rejoin Grant in the siege of Richmond and Petersburg. On 29 March, while the Federal infantry moved to sever Lee's last railroad connections to the south and west, Sheridan took the cavalry wide to the west and on 1 April destroyed a Confederate blocking force at Five Forks. The next morning Grant smashed through the Petersburg entrenchments, but Lee got most of his army away on a desperate run to the west.

Sheridan ran faster. At Sailor's Creek on 6 April he caught and helped capture 6,000 men and five generals. The remainder of Lee's army was desperate for food, and Sheridan found out where its cache was located—the village of Appomattox, twenty-six miles farther west. Sheridan got there before Lee did.

On the morning of 8 April the Confederates attempted a breakout, but Sheridan held them long enough; Federal infantry arrived, the white flag went up, and Lee began negotiating the surrender of his army. A Federal staff officer heard Sheridan raging, "Damn them, I wish they had held out for an hour longer and I would have whipped hell out of them." Grant recalled that Sheridan "wanted to end the business by going in and forcing an absolute surrender by capture." Sheridan stood fuming with disappointment in the parlor of the McLean house while men of larger spirit ended the war that had made him famous.

While thousands of men went home to savor the peace or to Washington to enjoy a victory parade, Sheridan was sent urgently to New Orleans. There he took command of the Military Division of the Gulf and maneuvered his troops along the Rio Grande in front of a small French army placed in Mexico to see what advantage might be gained over a war-ravaged United States. After two years of being intimidated by Sheridan, the French withdrew. Appointed military governor of Louisiana and Texas, Sheridan used a heavy hand to deal with the political and racial upheaval racking both states. He issued edicts and had them enforced at gunpoint; he removed from office the elected governors of both states; and he ignored orders from President Andrew Johnson to moderate his approach. After three months he was removed from office. He is remembered in the state for his comment, "If I owned both Hell and Texas, I'd rent out Texas and live in Hell."

In September 1867 Sheridan was given a job to which he was much better suited by experience and temperament, the suppression of the western American Indians. For the next sixteen years, except for a two-year tour as an observer with the German army in the Franco-Prussian War, Sheridan presided over the relentless hounding of the Plains Indian tribes, first leading a campaign against the Oklahoma Cheyenne that ended in the winter of 1868 with a massacre by a force under George Custer of a Cheyenne village on the Washita River. He also directed the 1876 campaign against the Southern Plains Indians that is remembered for the massacre of Custer and his Seventh Cavalry by the Sioux and their allies at Little Big Horn. On hearing a Comanche chief identify himself as a "good Indian," Sheridan responded with an instant aphorism for his fellow Indian fighters: "The only good Indians I ever saw were dead."

In the spring of 1875 a Chicago newspaper ran the headline: "Great Cavalry Leader Vanquished by a Blonde." In June the 44-year-old Sheridan married his quartermaster's animated 22-year-old daughter, Irene Rucker. Thereafter he moderated his behavior, was steadfast in his admiration of her, and fathered four children.

Sheridan was named general in chief of the U.S. Army in 1883. It was an army with virtually nothing to do. Sheridan seemed to take deep pleasure from his family but otherwise was mostly bored for five years. In the spring of 1888 he was ravaged by a series of heart attacks. He was only fifty-seven, but he knew the wound was mortal. He had himself set out on the porch of his new summer cottage at Nonquitt, Massachusetts, and there on a summer Sunday afternoon, while watching the waves roll in, he died.

Sheridan was an outstanding warrior who knew how to lead men in battle and how to make them want to follow him. Grant, who expressed envy of Sheridan's hold on the private soldier, called him "the embodiment of heroism, dash and impulse." Although hardly scholarly or reflective, Sheridan intuitively grasped the tactical implications of changing conditions on the battlefield, as for example, when he demonstrated the use of massed cavalry.

Sheridan enunciated his own best epitaph when he told a West Point class, "Whatever I took up, even if it were the simplest of duties, I tried to do it better than it had ever been done before. In the second place I always looked out for the common soldier. Trust your reputation to the private and he will never let your military fame suffer."

• Sheridan's papers are in the Library of Congress. His *Personal Memoirs* (1888) are unusually well written and objective for the genre. For a comprehensive and evenhanded appraisal of Sheridan's life as well as his role in the Civil War, see Paul Andrew Hutton, *Phil Sheridan and His Army* (1985), supplemented by Stephen Z. Starr, *The Union Cavalry in the Civil War* (1981). The best close-up, first-person observations of Sheridan at work are provided by George Forsyth, his wartime aide, in the memoir *Thrilling Days in Army Life* (1900). See also Richard O'Connor, *Sheridan the Inevitable* (1953), and Roy Morris, Jr., *Sheridan: The Life and Wars of General Phil Sheridan* (1992). An obituary is in the *Washington Post*, 6 Aug. 1888.

THOMAS A. LEWIS

SHERIF, Muzafer (29 July 1906–16 Oct. 1988), social psychologist, was born Muzaffer Serif Basoglu in Oedemis near Izmir (Smyrna), Turkey, the son of Sherif Basoglu (occupation unknown) and Emine (maiden name unknown). He grew up in Turkey, where he received a B.A. from the International College at Izmir and an M.A. in 1929 from Istanbul University. Later that year he came to the United States on a fellowship and enrolled in graduate work at Harvard. In 1932 he obtained an M.A. in psychology, with an experiment on "prestige suggestion" as his thesis. After a brief visit to Berlin, where he attended lectures by Gestalt psychologist Wolfgang Koehler, he returned to Turkey as an instructor at Gazi Institute in Ankara. There he started to work on his group experiments on social influence.

In 1934 Sherif returned to Harvard to work under psychologist Gordon Allport. Leaving soon after to work with Gardner Murphy at Columbia University, he received a psychology Ph.D. in 1935 for his group experiment with the autokinetic phenomenon (a stationary point of light that appears to move in an otherwise dark room). The experiment was designed to study a laboratory version of the real-world formation and internalization of social norms. Introducing Sherif's concept of "frame of reference" (the surround or context that strongly affects the perception of even simple visual stimuli), the experiment became one of the classics of social psychology. After spelling out the implications of his work in *The Psychology of Social Norms* (1936), Sherif returned again to Turkey via Paris. Serving on the faculty of Gazi Institute and of Ankara University from 1937 on, he was promoted to professor in 1944. His active opposition to Nazi influence and race doctrines in Turkey brought him political difficulties, which apparently included his arrest and imprisonment in 1944. He obtained his release through the intervention of the U.S. State Department upon the urging of his American psychologist friends, among them Hadley Cantril, Leonard Doob, and Gardner Murphy.

In 1945 a State Department fellowship brought Sherif back once more to the United States. He worked for two years at Princeton University, where he met Carolyn Wood, his future wife and co-worker. Married in 1945, they eventually had three children. In collaboration with Hadley Cantril of the Princeton psychology department, Sherif wrote *The Psychology of Ego-involvement* (1947) before moving to Yale University for a two-year Rockefeller Research Fellowship. His work with Carl Hovland at the Yale psychology department resulted in the joint publication of *Social Judgment: Assimilation and Contrast Effects in Communication and Attitude Change* (1961), which showed the importance of the individual's own anchor points in the judgment of social stimuli.

In 1949 Sherif joined the University of Oklahoma as professor of psychology and in 1952 became the director of its Institute of Group Relations. There he began an extremely productive period of laboratory and field studies on social judgment, intergroup relations, adolescents, and inner-city youth. His best-known study, the "Robbers Cave" series of experiments in *Intergroup Conflict and Cooperation* (1961), demonstrated the emergence of prejudice and negative stereotypes in situations of conflict between arbitrarily created groups. The creation of "superordinate," that is, shared goals requiring cooperation between the two groups was shown to be the best method to resolve intergroup hostility. It became a paradigm for the liberal integrationist approach to the social psychology of race relations of the civil rights era. Although his wife, Carolyn, had always worked together with him as full partner, her name did not appear as coauthor of the early publications. When, as a faculty wife, she remained ineligible for a tenured position at Oklahoma even after receiving a Ph.D. in psychology from the University of Texas in 1961, the couple decided to move to Pennsylvania State University in 1966. There Carolyn held a tenured appointment in the psychology department until her death in 1982, and Muzafer became professor of sociology. He retired from that position in 1972.

Together with his wife, Sherif was a prolific researcher and writer, publishing more than twenty scientific books and three times as many chapters or articles in other publications. His influence on the early shape of social psychology was considerable, especially through his ingenious and paradigmatic studies of social norm formation, intergroup conflict and stereotype development, and conflict resolution. Creating his own procedures, such as a novel way to measure attitudes, and his own method of combining field research and experimental techniques, he refused to be boxed in by traditional disciplinary boundaries. His theoretical approach, which emphasized the individual's perceptions, provided an alternative to the behavioristic stimulus-response paradigm that dominated American psychology before the "cognitive revolution." This unorthodox orientation caused Sherif to feel, not without justification, that he and his work were never completely accepted into the mainstream of U.S. academic psychology. His lively temperament, which displayed manic-depressive tendencies, and perhaps his cultural background also may have contributed to his somewhat marginal position. Nevertheless, the American Psychological Association honored him with its Distinguished Scientific Contribution Award in 1968, and the American Sociological Association recognized him with its first Cooley-Mead Award. He also received both a Guggenheim Fellowship and the Kurt Lewin Memorial Award from the Society for the Psychological Study of Social Issues in 1967. He died in Fairbanks, Alaska.

• Some correspondence from Sherif dating from the 1930s can be found in the Gordon Allport Papers at Harvard University. A list of Sherif's publications up to 1969 is given in the *American Psychologist* 25 (1968): 865–67. Works of his not cited in the text above include *Groups in Harmony and Tension* (1953) and *Reference Groups: Exploration into Conformity and Deviation of Adolescents* (1964), both written with Carolyn M. Sherif, and *In Common Predicament: Social Psychology of Intergroup Conflict and Cooperation* (1966). Obituaries are in the *American Psychologist* 44 (1989): 1325–26, and the *New York Times*, 27 Oct. 1988.

FRANZ SAMELSON

SHERMAN, Forrest Percival (30 Oct. 1896–22 July 1951), admiral and Chief of Naval Operations, was born in Merrimack, New Hampshire, the son of Grace Allen and Frank James Sherman, a textbook salesman. Sherman entered the Massachusetts Institute of Technology in 1913, but the following year was admitted as a midshipman to the U.S. Naval Academy in Annapolis, Maryland. At the academy, Sherman excelled academically, displaying even then the studiousness, leadership, and driving sense of professional accomplishment that would distinguish him throughout his naval career. Graduating second in his class in 1917, Sherman reported for duty aboard the USS *Nashville*, then serving in Mediterranean waters. After

subsequent assignments aboard destroyers and battleships, his first command came in 1921 with the *Barry*, an understrength destroyer. Two years later he married Dolores Brownson; the couple had one child.

Sherman had become a naval aviator in 1922, and through the 1920s and 1930s his assignments would chiefly involve this increasingly vital component of the navy's mission. He served successively as executive officer of a fighter squadron in the Battle Fleet, director of combat training at the air station in Pensacola, on board the carriers *Lexington* and *Saratoga*, on the staff of the Battle Fleet's commander of aircraft, and as instructor of flight tactics at Annapolis. By 1932 Sherman was commander of Fighting Squadron One aboard the *Saratoga*. From 1933 to 1936 he directed the Aviation Ordnance Section at the Board of Ordnance. After service aboard the carrier *Ranger*, Sherman in 1937 became aviation officer on the staff of Admiral C. C. Bloch, who commanded the Battle Fleet.

Carrier officers and aviators like Sherman were destined to play an outsized role in U.S. naval operations during the Second World War. As war clouds gathered in Europe and the Pacific, Sherman was assigned in 1940 to the War Plans Division, Office of the Chief of Naval Operations. He drafted plans for hemispheric defense that focused on protecting approaches to the Panama Canal. He also served on the U.S.–Canadian Permanent Joint Board of Defense and as a naval aviation adviser at the Atlantic Charter Conference in August 1941. Promoted to captain, Sherman returned to sea in May 1942, commanding the aircraft carrier *Wasp*. Part of the covering force during the U.S. Marine landings on Guadalcanal, the *Wasp* was torpedoed and sent to the bottom by a Japanese submarine that September. Not held responsible for the loss of the ship, Sherman, who had suffered internal injuries during the sinking, was instead cited for "extraordinary heroism" and awarded the Navy Cross. He was next assigned to Pearl Harbor, to serve as chief of staff for Vice Admiral John H. Towers, commander of the Pacific Fleet's air forces. In that capacity he was involved in planning air operations, deploying aircraft, and arranging for logistical support and training.

Sherman's talent for staff work impressed Admiral Chester Nimitz, the commander in chief of the Pacific Area of Operations. Determined to appoint a naval aviator as his planning officer, Nimitz, in November 1943, had Sherman transferred to his staff and shortly thereafter advanced him to the rank of rear admiral. Eventually deputy chief of staff (plans), the cerebral Sherman became a key figure in shaping the amphibious drive against the Japanese. Rated by one historian as "Nimitz's right arm if not a major part of his brain" (Reynolds, *Fast Carriers*, p. 386), Sherman helped determine which Pacific islands would be attacked and which bypassed, worked to put the ideas of both Nimitz and his own staff into operation, and sometimes spoke for his commander before their superiors in Washington. In recognition of his part in the navy's Pacific successes, Sherman stood alongside Nimitz and William Halsey during the Japanese surrender ceremonies aboard the *Missouri* in September 1945.

Returning to the United States at the end of 1945, Sherman was promoted to vice admiral and named Deputy Chief of Naval Operations. As did many of his contemporaries, he soon became caught up in the struggle over the creation of an independent air force, a move he vigorously opposed, and in the associated debate over the consolidation of the armed forces. Most navymen welcomed the prospect of a unified military no more than that of a separate air force, but Sherman became persuaded that unification was inevitable and acted as a force for compromise. After protracted negotiations, Sherman, together with the army's representative, Major General Lauris Norstad, drafted the plan that provided for a single Department of Defense headed by a civilian secretary who oversaw what would remain distinct branches of service: the navy, the army, and the newly minted U.S. Air Force.

As the Cold War developed, Sherman became involved, too, in planning responses to potential Soviet operations in Europe. He outlined in great detail the threat posed by Soviet forces in the Mediterranean, pointing out to President Harry Truman that Russia could launch an all-out attack against Turkey and Greece, thereby menacing Western Europe's exposed southern flank and endangering vital oil supply routes from the Middle East. His advice became influential in the formulation of the Truman Doctrine, which proposed to help "free peoples" resist "subjugation by armed minorities or by outside pressures"—in this instance by rushing aid to Greece and Turkey in early 1947. The Truman administration also readily accepted Sherman's suggestion that a permanent U.S. naval presence be established in the Mediterranean and in December 1947 made him commander of U.S. Naval Forces, Mediterranean (reorganized later as the Sixth Task Fleet)—his first assignment at sea since the sinking of the *Wasp*.

In the aftermath of public protests by navy leaders against the apparent dwindling of their branch's clout within the unified Defense Department, Sherman in November 1949 succeeded Louis Denfeld as Chief of Naval Operations—the navy's representative on the Joint Chiefs of Staff. Promoted to admiral, Sherman was the youngest man to that time to become CNO, his appointment probably being intended to mollify naval aviators who had had to acquiesce in the creation of the air force. Among the many controversial issues he faced, none was as vexing as the status of the marine corps. Sensitive to any relinquishment of the navy's authority over the marines, Sherman refused to allow the corps' commandant to have equal status on the Joint Chiefs. Initially, Sherman also faced the prospect of reductions in aircraft, personnel, facilities, and ship construction. But in the wake of the Soviets' explosion of an atomic bomb, and especially with the outbreak of the Korean War, the budget cuts were reversed. Sherman went to Korea in August 1950, helping to plan the Inchon landings. On a diplomatic and military mis-

sion to Europe the following year, Sherman died of a heart attack in Naples, Italy.

• The U.S. Naval Historical Division in Washington, D.C., holds Sherman's official papers dating from 1947 to 1951. Biographical information is in the U.S. Navy Biographic Information Bureau publication *Admiral Forrest Percival Sherman, U.S. Navy, Deceased* (1951, 1958). There are also essays on Sherman in Robert Love et al., *Chiefs of Naval Operations* (1960); Clark Reynolds, *Famous American Admirals* (1978); James I. Matray, *Historical Dictionary of the Korean War* (1991); and *Current Biography 1948*. See also Reynolds, *The Fast Carriers: The Forging of an Air Navy* (1968); Demetrios Caraley, *The Politics of Military Unification: A Study of Conflict and the Policy Process* (1966); and Edward S. Miller, *War Plan Orange: The U.S. Strategy to Defeat Japan* (1991). An obituary is in the *New York Times*, 23 July 1951.

LEO J. DAUGHERTY III

SHERMAN, Frederick Carl (27 May 1888–27 July 1957), naval officer, was born in Port Huron, Michigan, the son of Frederick Ward Sherman, a newspaper publisher, and Charlotte Esther Wolfe. He graduated from the U.S. Naval Academy in 1910, and during the next three years he served on the armored cruiser *Montana*, the battleship *Ohio*, and the armored cruiser *Maryland*. He was commissioned an ensign in 1912. In 1914 Sherman was transferred to submarine duty, and after serving on the tender *Cheyenne* and submarine *H-3*, he commanded submarine *H-2* in 1916–1917. In 1915 Sherman married Fanny Jessop; they had one son. With the rank of lieutenant commander, Sherman commanded submarine *O-7* in 1918–1919, and in early 1919 he served briefly as navigator of the battleship *Minnesota*.

Between 1919 and 1940 Sherman rotated between shore and sea duty while rising to the rank of captain. He served in the Bureau of Engineering (1919–1921), commanded Submarine Division Nine (1921–1924), was a student at the Naval War College (1924–1925), served in the Division of Fleet Training in the Office of the Chief of Naval Operations (1925–1926 and 1931–1932), was gunnery officer on the battleship *West Virginia* (1926–1929), served in the Bureau of Navigation (1929, 1931), was navigator of the cruiser *Detroit* (1932–1933), commanded Destroyer Division Eight and then Destroyer Division One (1933–1935), and for a brief period in 1934–1935 was aide to the commandant of the Eleventh Naval District in San Diego, California. In 1935–1936 Sherman changed the direction of his career by earning his wings as a naval aviator after completing flight training at Pensacola, Florida. Over the next years he was executive officer of the aircraft carrier *Saratoga* (1936–1937), executive officer of the Naval Air Station at San Diego (1937–1938), commander of Patrol Wing Three in the Canal Zone (1938–1939), and a student at the Naval War College (1939–1940). By June 1940, when he was given command of the carrier *Lexington*, Sherman had become a fervent advocate of naval aviation. A stern taskmaster, he insisted on rigorous training of his pilots, and during the months before American entry into World War II in December 1941 he worked with his squadron commanders to develop new tactics for carrier-based planes.

At the time of the Japanese attack on Pearl Harbor, which crippled the battleship division of the U.S. Pacific Fleet and rendered Hawaii vulnerable to invasion, the *Lexington* was at sea near Midway Island, and for several days afterward Sherman, in an atmosphere of agonizing uncertainty over the enemy's plans and location, searched unsuccessfully for the Japanese task force. In February 1942 Sherman's planes attacked the Japanese base at Rabaul on New Britain Island, and in March they struck at Lae and Salamaua in New Guinea. Two months later Sherman participated in the battle of Coral Sea, the first naval battle fought totally by aircraft. Planes from the *Lexington* sank the Japanese light carrier *Shoho*, but Sherman eventually had to scuttle the *Lexington* after Japanese bombs and torpedoes crippled the ship.

During these early battles Sherman earned a reputation as a ready fighter and a skilled tactician and ship handler, and even though he had lost the *Lexington* he was quickly promoted to rear admiral. After spending the summer of 1942 in Washington, D.C., as assistant chief of staff to Admiral Ernest J. King, commander of the U.S. Fleet and chief of naval operations, Sherman was given command of Carrier Division Two in October 1942. Over the next months he supported operations in the Solomon Islands while testing new carrier formations, especially concentrating them into multicarrier task forces to provide maximum air defense. Like other air admirals, Sherman believed that naval air forces were the key to victory in the Pacific war and urged that surface ships be integrated with them, not the reverse as had been the practice. At one point, in a preview of sorts of the famous "Revolt of the Admirals" in 1949, in which naval airmen argued vigorously for the central role of naval aviation in the nation's defense strategy, he even suggested that aviators should have the dominant voice in determining all naval policy and that only aviators should be in command of task forces that included carriers. In another instance he proposed that all the carriers should be placed under a commander, carriers Pacific, and that he be given the job with the rank of vice admiral. Despite his outstanding combat record, Sherman's opportunity for higher command was hampered by his zealous advocacy of naval aviation, self-promotion, showy style, and acerbic personality.

Nevertheless, Sherman was recognized as one of the ablest and most experienced carrier men in the navy, and between July 1943 and March 1944, as commander of Carrier Division One, he again demonstrated his aggressiveness and tactical skills in raids against the Japanese bases at Rabaul and Kavieng on New Ireland Island and in support of the landings at Bougainville Island and the Gilbert Islands. At Rabaul planes from the carriers *Saratoga* and *Princeton* severely damaged seven Japanese heavy cruisers in a raid on 11 November 1943, neutralizing Japanese naval power in the northern Solomons. In a raid against Kavieng on 25 December 1943 Sherman launched his planes before dawn and was able to catch the Japanese off guard at daylight. When the Japanese counterattacked that night, Sherman avoided any damage to his own ships through radical evasive maneuvers.

After two years of nearly continuous duty as a combat commander, Sherman was given a rest with the command of the West Coast Air Fleet. He returned to command of Carrier Division One in August 1944, and during the next ten months he participated in the landings in the Philippine Islands; the battle of Leyte Gulf, in which his planes helped sink the superbattleship *Musashi* and several other major Japanese ships; and the Iwo Jima and Okinawa operations. In July 1945 Sherman was promoted to vice admiral and given command of the First Fast Carrier Force, Pacific, and from January 1946 to September 1946 he commanded the Fifth Fleet in the western Pacific.

Sherman retired in March 1947 with the rank of admiral. He wrote about naval affairs for the *Chicago Tribune* until 1948, and in 1950 he published *Combat Command*, a brief history of the carrier war in the Pacific from his perspective.

Sherman, known to his friends as "Ted," was one of the best naval aviators in the Pacific war. He stood out especially for his long combat record, advancement of multicarrier task force formations, and dynamic leadership. He died in San Diego.

• A summary of Sherman's career is in Clark G. Reynolds, *Famous American Admirals* (1978). For Sherman's service during World War II see Samuel Eliot Morison, *History of United States Naval Operations in World War II*, vols. 4 (1949), 5 (1949), 6 (1950), 12 (1958), and 14 (1960); Clark G. Reynolds, *The Fast Carriers* (1968) and *Admiral John H. Towers: The Struggle for Naval Air Supremacy* (1991); and John B. Lundstrom, *The First Team: Pacific Naval Air Combat from Pearl Harbor to Midway* (1984). An obituary is in the *New York Times*, 28 July 1957.

JOHN KENNEDY OHL

SHERMAN, Henry Clapp (16 Oct. 1875–7 Oct. 1955), chemist and nutritionist, was born near Ash Grove, Virginia, the son of Franklin Sherman and Caroline Clapp Alvord, farmers. After receiving an education in a rural, ungraded school, Sherman entered Maryland Agricultural College (now the University of Maryland) and earned a bachelor of science degree in 1893. He was an assistant to the state chemist of Maryland until 1895, when he began graduate study in chemistry at Columbia University, becoming in 1897 the youngest person to receive a Columbia Ph.D. From 1897 to 1899 he was an assistant in analytical chemistry at Columbia and also assisted Wilbur Atwater in his investigation of the energy of metabolism at Wesleyan University.

Sherman rose through the faculty ranks at Columbia, becoming professor of organic analysis in 1907, professor of food chemistry in 1911, and Mitchell Professor of Chemistry in 1924. He also headed the Department of Chemistry from 1919 to 1939. He retired in 1946. His only separation from Columbia came during wartime, when he served first as a member of the 1917 American Red Cross mission to Russia to study the food situation there and then in 1943 as chief of a new Bureau of Nutrition of the U.S. Department of Agriculture, with the charge of solving the food problems arising from a wartime economy. In 1903 he married Cora Aldrich Bowen; they had four children. His daughter, Caroline Lanford, was an authority on nutrition and coauthor of two of her father's twelve books.

Much of modern nutritional science developed during Sherman's lifetime, and he made valuable contributions to the knowledge of proteins, vitamins, and minerals as essential nutrients. Trained as an analytical chemist, he devoted much of his research to the quantitative measurement of nutrients in foods and the establishment of their nutritional requirements. As a lecturer at Columbia in 1899 he was given the opportunity to offer courses for the first time on quantitative organic analysis and food chemistry. His first book, *Methods of Organic Analysis* (1905), was the fruit of that experience, with the application of organic analysis to foods comprising the greater part of the book.

From 1910 to 1934 Sherman investigated the chemistry of enzymes and proteins, especially the starch-splitting amylases. In sixteen papers in collaboration with Mary Caldwell, his Ph.D. (1921) student and later a professor of chemistry at Columbia, he developed methods to obtain highly purified enzymes and to precisely measure their activities. In 1931 Sherman and Caldwell crystallized pancreatic amylase and presented compelling evidence of its protein nature, a view then under attack by proponents of enzymes as nonprotein, low molecular weight catalysts. Sherman also established the nutritional value of several proteins and in 1925 proved cystine to be an essential amino acid.

Sherman's studies of minerals focused on calcium and phosphorus. Between 1907 and 1922 he determined the average human requirements for these minerals. Between 1934 and 1944 he published sixteen papers on calcium utilization, an investigation that stemmed from his wondering why vegetable calcium was less readily utilized than milk calcium. In 1935 he revealed that the oxalic acid in some vegetables combined with the calcium present, rendering the mineral useless nutritionally. Thus, spinach, which had both high calcium and high oxalic acid content, was a poor source of calcium in the diet, with about 95 percent of it unavailable. He made national headlines with his *Science of Nutrition* (1943), which claimed that spinach was a relatively poor choice as a calcium source among green-leaf vegetables.

Sherman began his research career before vitamins had been discovered, and in the 1920s none of these proposed nutrients had been isolated or shown to be specific chemical entities. Between 1921 and 1933 he developed quantitative bioassay methods for vitamins A, B_1, B_2, and C and used these to get a quantitative measure of the vitamins needed to overcome the deficiency diseases of scurvy, beriberi, and pellagra. He

was largely responsible for placing the bioassay of vitamins on a quantitative basis, which became the foundation for the identification of vitamins as pure compounds and for the establishment of their nutritional value in foods. In 1921 he discovered how to induce and control rickets, providing thereby a foundation for much of the subsequent study of vitamin D.

Among Sherman's final investigations were his life span studies with Columbia colleague H. Louise Campbell. He and Campbell fed rats adequate diets that differed from each other only in having a higher proportion of one specific nutrient. They examined the effect of the diets on growth rate, size, vigor, reproduction, and longevity, showing that one diet was superior to another if it had, for example, more milk powder. These studies were important for determining the optimal intake of nutrients. Sherman used his findings in the 1940s to argue that the quality of human life can be changed through better nutrition and that a diet rich in protective foods, such as fruits, vegetables, and milk, can ward off disease, delay the onset of old age, and increase life span.

Much in demand by government and private organizations for his expertise on food values, Sherman was chair of the Committee on Nutritional Problems of the American Public Health Association from 1919 to 1933 and wrote many reports on food and nutrition for APHA as well as for Department of Agriculture publications. He was a research associate with the Carnegie Institution from 1912 to 1929 and from 1933 to 1939, and his annual reports on enzymes appeared in the Carnegie Institution Yearbook from 1912 to 1945. He was president of the American Institute of Nutrition from 1931 to 1933 and 1939 to 1940. In the 1940s he was chair of the Committee on Dietary Allowances of the Food and Nutrition Board of the National Research Council. The committee published tables on the amounts of protein, vitamins, and minerals needed for persons of various ages to be used by the government in planning the food requirements for the nation. *Chemistry of Food and Nutrition* (1911) was the most influential of his twelve books. Used internationally by health and educational institutions, it underwent eight printings, with a final edition in 1952.

Sherman died in Rensselaer, New York. He was little known to the public, being a retiring and self-effacing person. His influence as a nutritionist came primarily from his writings and his creation of a premier school of nutrition within the chemistry department at Columbia University.

• Sherman's colleagues honored him with *The Selected Works of Henry Clapp Sherman* (1948), which contains reprints of his most important papers, a bibliography of his publications, and biographical notes. Charles Glen King wrote Sherman's biography for the National Academy of Sciences, *Biographical Memoirs* 46 (1975): 397–433. Edward C. Kendall, his graduate student and a Nobel Prize winner, assessed his mentor's career in "Henry Clapp Sherman," *Journal of Chemical Education* 32 (1955): 510–13. Paul L. Day gives a more detailed account of his research in "Henry Clapp Sherman," *Journal of Nutrition* 61 (1957): 1–11. An obituary is in the *New York Times*, 8 Oct. 1955.

ALBERT B. COSTA

SHERMAN, John (10 May 1823–22 Oct. 1900), senator, secretary of the treasury, and secretary of state, was born in Lancaster, Ohio, the son of Charles Sherman, a judge on the Ohio Supreme Court, and Mary Hoyt. Sherman was only six years old in 1829 when his father died, leaving a widow with eleven children. The family's financial situation forced Sherman's mother to send many of the children to relatives, and in 1831 Sherman moved to Mount Vernon, Ohio, to live with his father's cousin. He returned to Lancaster four years later. His decision to quit school at the age of fourteen may have been motivated by a determination to help provide for the family. Sherman spent the next two years outdoors, apprenticing to engineers working on river improvements in Ohio. In 1840 he moved to Mansfield, Ohio, to study law. When Sherman turned twenty-one in 1844, he was admitted to the bar and established a practice. He married Margaret Stewart four years later. They adopted one child.

Sherman entered political life as a Whig in the late 1840s. Within a few years, however, outrage over the Kansas-Nebraska Act, which made it possible to establish slavery in those territories, led to formation of a coalition in Ohio among Whigs, some Democrats, and members of the antislavery Free Soil party. Nominated by this coalition to run for a seat in the House of Representatives in 1854, Sherman rode the tide of sentiment against the Kansas-Nebraska Act to win by some 300 votes. He became a "founding father" of the Republican party in Ohio.

Never an abolitionist, Sherman quickly emerged as an articulate spokesman for the moderate Republicans, those who would not interfere with slavery where it existed but who absolutely opposed the extension of slavery into the western territories. After being reelected twice, Sherman emerged as a candidate for Speaker in 1859 in a bitterly divided House of Representatives but withdrew from the contest and became chair of the Ways and Means Committee. He thus took the first step toward establishing himself as the leading Republican figure in the conduct of the nation's financial and monetary affairs over the next thirty-five years.

Sherman won a fourth term in the House in 1860, and he had reason to believe that every Republican would support him for Speaker. Instead, when President Abraham Lincoln chose Senator Salmon P. Chase of Ohio to become secretary of the treasury in 1861, the Ohio legislature selected Sherman to replace Chase for a full six-year term in the Senate just as the nation plunged into the Civil War. While his older brother, General William Tecumseh Sherman, helped lead the North to victory, Sherman played a critical role as well as a member of the Senate Finance Committee. To pay for the war, in 1862–1863 he vigorously supported the temporary use of hundreds of millions of dollars in paper money without gold backing, or "greenbacks"; the first income tax in the history of the nation; and the creation of the National Banking System.

The Ohio legislature voted in 1866 to return Sherman to the Senate for a second term. As a moderate in his approach toward the defeated South, he hoped that President Andrew Johnson and the leaders of Congress would cooperate on a policy that would bring the South back into the nation as quickly as possible. Sherman came to believe, however, that the president's determination to control Reconstruction threatened to divide the Republican party. When Johnson vetoed the Civil Rights Act of 1866, the first attempt to extend the protection of the federal government to the freedmen, or former slaves, Sherman concluded that the president had abandoned the party.

Driven into the camp of the Radical Republicans as much by the president's actions as by the mistreatment of the freedmen and the abuses of the Ku Klux Klan in the South, Sherman took the lead in the Senate in writing the Reconstruction Act of 1867, providing for military occupation of ten states. Each state could return to the nation only when it ratified the proposed Fourteenth Amendment to the Constitution, the "civil rights" amendment. After the House of Representatives voted overwhelmingly for impeachment of President Johnson, the Senate conducted the trial in 1868, and Sherman joined those who found the president guilty. The Senate came within one vote of removing Johnson from office.

In 1867 Sherman became chair of the Finance Committee, a position he would hold for a decade. He quickly emerged as the central figure in the post–Civil War controversy over monetary policy. He opposed contraction of the amount of greenbacks in circulation, advocating instead that the nation resume specie payments—that is, make greenbacks redeemable in gold coin—by adopting financial policies that would bring the greenbacks to a value at par with gold coins. At the same time, however, he supported the effort to eliminate the silver dollar from the nation's coinage. Sherman insisted that any attempt to circulate a silver dollar at face value would undermine confidence in the nation's currency.

Elected to a third term in 1872, Sherman began to stand out from the crowd among national leaders, particularly when Congress, at his urging, discontinued coinage of silver dollars in 1873. That same year the economy collapsed in a "panic," and Sherman eventually became a target for those who tied the hard times to what they came to call the "crime of 1873," the decision to demonetize silver. Sherman did not hesitate to defend his position on this controversial issue or any other, but he apparently failed to understand that political courage did not necessarily help one's presidential ambitions. Following Sherman's lead, Congress voted in 1875 to keep $300 million in greenbacks in circulation and to resume specie payments as of 1 January 1879.

Sherman continued to build his reputation during the presidential election of 1876. It appeared that Republican governor Rutherford B. Hayes of Ohio had lost the election to Democrat Samuel J. Tilden until Republican leaders realized that a bloc of contested electoral votes could produce victory for Hayes. After a commission awarded all of the contested votes to Hayes, producing a Republican victory by one electoral vote, Sherman participated in the February 1877 "Wormley" conference in Washington, D.C., at which leaders of both parties worked out a deal to persuade the Democrats to accept the outcome of the election.

President Hayes asked Sherman to become secretary of the treasury. Ironically, Sherman now had the responsibility for implementing specie payments at the beginning of 1879. He made significant changes in the process of floating bond issues and accumulated enough gold to guarantee specie payments. At the same time, however, he had to deal with the growing sentiment in favor of reviving the coinage of silver dollars. After the House of Representatives voted in favor of the unlimited coinage of silver dollars in 1877, Sherman worked closely with leaders of the Senate to secure passage of a compromise, the Bland-Allison Act of 1878, which provided for the coinage of only $2 million to $4 million worth of silver dollars each month. As it turned out, Sherman's career peaked in 1879, when the resumption of specie payments went into effect without the slightest disruption of the nation's finances.

Hayes did not seek a second term as president in 1880. A historic deadlock at the Republican National Convention pitted those who supported the nomination of Ulysses S. Grant for an unprecedented third term as president against those who sought the nomination for James G. Blaine, then representing Maine in the Senate. Sherman, who received ninety-three votes on the first ballot, behind only Grant and Blaine, believed all along that the deadlock would force the delegates to compromise and award him the nomination. However, Sherman did not tally more than 120 votes on any ballot, and the delegates settled on another Ohioan, representative James A. Garfield, who had come to the convention as a supporter of Sherman.

Ironically, the Ohio legislature had chosen Garfield for a full term in the Senate that was to begin in 1881. When Garfield won the presidential election, Sherman returned to the Senate. Along with other Republicans, Sherman could not hope for the same influence and power in the 1880s, particularly after Democrat Grover Cleveland won the presidential election of 1884. Sherman did not accept the idea that it was Blaine's turn for the presidential nomination in 1884, and he was an undeclared candidate for the nomination, once again hoping for a deadlock. Sherman placed fifth on the first ballot and never became a factor at the convention, leaving Blaine to become the first Republican to lose a presidential election since 1856.

The Ohio legislature gave Sherman a fifth term in 1886, and he began to believe that the delegates at the national convention might come to the conclusion that Sherman's turn had arrived in 1888. Yet Blaine remained the favorite of many Republicans, even among the Ohio delegation. Much of Sherman's support came from beneficiaries of Treasury Department patronage. These officeholders, many of them African Americans, represented states in the South that Republicans could not hope to carry in the late nineteenth century.

With fourteen candidates nominated, Sherman led with 229 votes on the first ballot, a total more than double that of any other candidate but barely one-quarter of the votes cast. Sherman needed 416 votes, a number never within his grasp. Thereafter Benjamin Harrison of Indiana, a former Civil War general and former senator, gained momentum and won the support, among others, of the New York delegation, by far the largest in the convention. Sherman could not win, but he refused to withdraw, demonstrating, in the words of one scholar, that "staying in the presidential race when others would have been hopelessly discouraged was an old Sherman habit" (Marcus, p. 111). Harrison took the lead from Sherman on the seventh ballot, then won the nomination.

The question remains: why did Sherman's presidential ambitions fail so miserably? The answers all relate to Sherman's personality. He has been described as the "Ohio Icicle" (Marcus, p. 37; Morgan, p. 40), his quest for the presidency doomed because he "carried the political cross of dullness" (Mayer, p. 199). More specifically, he faced two insurmountable obstacles. Ohio Republicans, with more than their share of potential presidential candidates, never truly united behind him at any national convention. Additionally, he was a colorless man, and it was his misfortune that every four years he had to contend for the nomination against his opposite, Blaine, the "Plumed Knight," who captured the imagination of the American public.

Sherman experienced a sort of last hurrah after the Republicans regained the White House in 1888. He helped write what became known as the Sherman Silver Purchase Act of 1890, even though he accepted it only as an alternative to the unlimited coinage of silver dollars. The law provided that the federal government would purchase virtually all of the silver produced in the United States each month but would have the option of coining the silver or holding it in reserve. Sherman understood this as guaranteeing that no increase would be made in the coinage of silver dollars.

Finally, on 4 December 1889, Sherman, as chair of the Finance Committee, introduced in the Senate the bill that became, after amendments and major revisions, the Sherman Anti-Trust Act of June 1890. This law was the first attempt to control the power of big business in the history of the nation, and it remained in effect more than a century later. The tremendous growth of the nation's economy in the last third of the nineteenth century had led to the development of ever larger corporations and, in the 1880s, to the combination of such corporations into "trusts" that monopolized various segments of the economy. A tide of public opinion that demanded federal regulation of the trusts produced bipartisan support in Congress for such legislation. Although the Judiciary Committee wrote the final version of the law that passed the Senate by a vote of 52–1, it remained the Sherman Anti-Trust Act, perhaps to retain the support of the influential senior senator from Ohio, to honor Sherman, and to attach the prestige of Sherman's name to the historic law.

In his bid for a sixth term in 1892, Sherman faced serious opposition for the first time from the much younger Joseph Foraker, who had served two terms as governor of Ohio. Foraker, then forty-five years old, was one of the many Ohioans with presidential ambitions and had been in conflict with Sherman throughout the 1880s. When Foraker had first run unsuccessfully for governor in 1883, some had talked of nominating Sherman instead of Foraker, who was only thirty-seven years old at the time. Foraker became governor in 1885.

Though Sherman had supported Foraker's successful bid for a second term in 1887, he began to see Foraker as a potential rival for the presidential nomination in 1888. At the state convention in 1887, Sherman insisted that Ohio Republicans endorse him for the nomination. Governor Foraker initially opposed that action, understanding that such an endorsement would eliminate him as a potential candidate and believing that it would hurt his chances for a second term by alienating those who supported Blaine for another nomination. In 1889 Foraker lost his bid for a third term as governor, and he became determined to move up to the Senate in place of Sherman, who was then sixty-eight years old.

Sherman won the contest in the Ohio legislature and began the last phase of a distinguished career doomed to an unfortunate ending. Once again Sherman believed that a Republican convention might turn to him. President Harrison won the nomination, however, and the presidential election of 1892 brought Cleveland back to the White House. When the nation's economy suffered a complete collapse in 1893, Sherman, who never believed in the law named for him, did not hesitate to support Cleveland's demand for repeal of the Sherman Silver Purchase Act.

As of mid-June 1894 Sherman set a record for longevity in the Senate. Soon, however, contemporaries would have reason to recall the stories about Sherman never being able to remember names. During the presidential campaign of 1896, the 73-year-old Sherman occasionally experienced complete loss of memory, perhaps a first indication of the onset of senility. Nevertheless, President William McKinley of Ohio shamelessly used Sherman, asking him to serve as secretary of state so a Senate seat would become available for McKinley's political mentor, the wealthy industrialist Mark Hanna.

During a year as secretary of state, Sherman repeatedly demonstrated that he suffered from an almost total loss of hearing and could not concentrate for prolonged periods. Gradually his responsibilities were delegated to others. By 1898 he sometimes would not recognize old acquaintances. He resigned at the end of April 1898, shortly after the United States went to war with Spain. Differences over expansionism, some degree of awareness that others had taken over his responsibilities, and suggestions from colleagues that the time had come to leave public office all may have contributed to his decision. Sherman then identified with other prominent individuals who opposed creation of an American empire in the aftermath of the Spanish-American War, but he did little more than lend the use of his name to the anti-imperialist movement. He died in Washington.

• Sherman's papers, a vast collection in 619 volumes, are in the Manuscripts Division, Library of Congress. Sherman published his memoirs as *John Sherman's Recollections of Forty Years in the House, Senate and Cabinet: An Autobiography* (2 vols., 1895). Two old biographies are Theodore Burton, *John Sherman* (1906), and Winfield S. Kerr, *John Sherman: His Life and Public Services* (2 vols., 1907). The most informative sources on the details of his lengthy career are George H. Mayer, *The Republican Party, 1854–1964* (1964); Robert D. Marcus, *Grand Old Party: Political Structure in the Gilded Age, 1880–1896* (1971); and H. Wayne Morgan, *From Hayes to McKinley: National Party Politics, 1877–1896* (1969). See also David J. Rothman, *Politics and Power: The United States Senate, 1869–1901* (1966), on his career in the Senate; Kenneth E. Davison, *The Presidency of Rutherford B. Hayes* (1972), and Ari Hoogenboom, *The Presidency of Rutherford B. Hayes* (1988), on his term as secretary of the treasury; and Robert L. Beisner, *Twelve against Empire: The Anti-Imperialists, 1898–1900* (1968), for his connection to the anti-imperialists.

ALLAN BURTON SPETTER

SHERMAN, Mary Belle King (11 Dec. 1862–15 Jan. 1935), woman's club leader and conservationist, was born in Albion, New York, the daughter of Rufus King, a publisher, and Sarah Electa Whitney. She spent her early years in Rochester, New York, and moved with her family to Chicago when she was twelve years old. There she attended the Park Institute, an academy for girls. In 1887 she married John Dickinson Sherman, a journalist who was associate editor of the *Inter Ocean* and director of the Western Newspaper Union. They had one child.

Sherman became active in the Chicago Woman's Club at the turn of the century, serving as its recording secretary, press committee chairperson, and legislative committee's authority on parliamentary law. In fact, she became so knowledgeable on parliamentary law that she taught the subject at John Marshall Law School of Chicago and published *Parliamentary Law and Rules of Procedure* (1901). She also became active on the national club scene, serving as recording secretary of the General Federation of Women's Clubs (GFWC) and its second vice president from 1908 to 1910. She accompanied federation president Eva Perry Moore on a 1907 tour of women's clubs in the Panama Canal Zone, where she was stricken with an undiagnosed illness that "almost cost her life and left a permanent legacy of physical suffering." Recuperating at Tahosa, a retreat in Estes Park, Colorado, that she had acquired in 1909, she developed an appreciation of nature and became a public supporter of conservation issues.

Sherman would win the title "National Park Lady" from federated clubwomen by creating and chairing the Conservation Department of the GFWC (1914–1920). In that capacity she lobbied for national parks, a national park service, and the protection of forests. Sherman promoted conservation and the celebration of National Garden Week in speeches to countless women's organizations, school groups, and civic clubs. She also represented clubwomen as a member of the National Parks Association and vice president of the American Forestry Association. During World War I, Sherman was appointed special assistant director of the U.S. School Garden Army of the Bureau of Education (1918), which urged voluntary organizations to encourage students to plant school gardens. She was the only woman on the National War Garden Commission.

After chairing the GFWC's Department of Applied Education from 1920 to 1924, Sherman was elected president of the two-million-member federation in 1924. During her four-year term she presided over a series of controversies that made her administration the most notorious in the history of the organization. She had moved to headquarters in Washington, D.C., after her husband's death in 1926 and faced difficulties in three arenas. First, she designed policies to strengthen centralization of power at the top and to apply efficient methods of management, systems that many clubwomen regarded as unwelcome. She also invited criticism of the work of the Department of the American Home, which she created. Its ambitious Home Equipment Survey identified the dearth of labor-saving devices in a half million urban homes, and the study was later expanded to include rural households with funding from the National Electric Light Association and its state affiliates. Critics charged that the study's call for more labor-saving electrical appliances was proof that utility companies had commercialized and compromised the survey. Nonetheless, the final five-part *Home Equipment Primer* emphasized the labor of women within the household and helped persuade the Bureau of the Census to create a new category, "homemaker," where "not employed" had been used before. Finally, Sherman suffered attacks by patriotic women's organizations, via *Woman Patriot* magazine, which claimed that Bolsheviks had corrupted the organization to support such radical causes as the League of Nations, international peace, child labor laws, federal support for maternal and infant care, and a U.S. Cabinet post for education. In fact, the GFWC had supported these progressive programs long before Sherman's administration. The outraged federation membership weathered the storm gracefully, standing by their leader for two terms in the highest office. Sherman's administration came under attack despite the fact that its emphasis on home economics repre-

sented the most conservative impulses in the organization.

Sherman was appointed by President Calvin Coolidge to the George Washington Bicentennial Committee (1925) and served on the Advisory Council of the National Broadcasting Corporation from 1926 until her death. She published dozens of articles in popular magazines about the findings of the Home Equipment Survey. She died in Denver, having devoted her career to organizing women in voluntary organizations to cooperate for social reform.

• The General Federation of Women's Clubs in Washington, D.C., has a President Sherman file containing biographical materials. Sherman wrote *Parliamentary Law at a Glance* (1901). Her *Parliamentary Law and Rules of Procedure* went through several editions from 1901 to 1916. See also Mildred Marshall Scouller, *Women Who Man Our Clubs* (1934), and Frances D. McMullen, "The National Park Lady," *Woman Citizen*, 17 May 1924. Obituaries are in the *New York Times* and the *Washington Post*, both on 16 Jan. 1935.

KAREN J. BLAIR

SHERMAN, Roger (19 Apr. 1721–23 July 1793), merchant and revolutionary leader, was born in Newton, Massachusetts, the son of William Sherman and Mehetabel Wellington, farmers. He moved with his family two years later to the part of Dorchester that became Stoughton and is now the town of Canton, Massachusetts. He grew up on his father's farm and attended district schools, an apt student with a particular interest in arithmetic. William Sherman was somewhat downwardly mobile and had reduced his farm from 270 acres to 73 acres by the time of his death in 1741.

Roger's older brother, William Sherman, had taken up a small parcel of family-owned land in New Milford, Connecticut, in 1740. At his father's death, Roger bought a farm in that part of New Fairfield that became the town of Sherman. He moved there around 1742, taking his mother and younger siblings with him.

In Connecticut Sherman began his ascent to leadership. At some point he had learned the craft of cordwainer. His family no doubt worked the farm in New Fairfield, and perhaps, as tradition has it, he continued cobbling as a way to sit still so he could study surveying. At any rate, within a few years Sherman was appointed New Haven County surveyor, a position of great activity in that rapidly populating frontier area along an only recently resolved New York–Connecticut boundary. When Litchfield was created in 1752, Sherman became one of two official surveyors for that county. Surveying fees provided Sherman with a considerable income, and by 1745 he had given up cobbling. The surveying business had opened up opportunity for land speculation, and ultimately Sherman, while still in his late thirties, became the largest landowner in Litchfield County.

In 1748 Sherman moved to the central village of New Milford to enter into a partnership in a general store with his brother William. The Sherman store was a tightly run business with books cleared uncommonly often, and apparently it thrived. At the age of twenty-seven Sherman bought one of the finest houses in the village, journeyed back to his home town in Massachusetts, and married Elizabeth Hartwell. They had seven children, three of whom died in infancy. Sherman gave up his surveyorship around 1758. He continued to operate the store with his brother and kept up activities designed to bring attention to himself and to promote his ambitions. From 1750 to 1760 he published a series of annual almanacs of the sort then common that included astronomical data, quotations from poems by Englishmen of letters, and homilies and aphorisms, some of which he may have written himself.

Sherman enjoyed upward political mobility that paralleled his economic success. In 1748 he began his career in public office, which was broken only by his death. He moved rapidly through lesser local offices to become one of five selectmen, who administered town affairs, in 1753 and two years later one of New Milford's two deputies to the Connecticut General Assembly, the pinnacle of local elected office. He continued in those positions until he left New Milford in 1761, adding, in 1755, the prestigious position of justice of the peace for New Milford and Litchfield County.

Meanwhile, Sherman had been reading law, and in 1754 he was admitted to the bar. His law business soon became his primary occupation, though he still dealt in land, operated his store, published almanacs, and held increasingly responsible public offices.

William Sherman died in 1756, and Roger took on Anthony Carpenter as a partner to run the store, but Carpenter, too, soon died. When Sherman's wife died in 1760, he sold out and relocated to the town of New Haven, which was one of Connecticut's busiest ports and, with Hartford, the cocapital of the colony. It was a place of unbounded commercial and political opportunity for a merchant-lawyer of unlimited energy and ambition. He married Rebecca Prescott in 1763. She was only twenty, half his age, but of a social standing well above that of his first wife. They had eight children. Sherman was elected to represent New Haven in the general assembly three years after he moved there, extraordinary for a man so new to town. In 1765 he was appointed a justice for New Haven County.

The mid-1760s was, of course, a time of great political ferment in all the mainland British colonies. Imperial politics could make and break careers, and Sherman apparently determined to see that his was made. His principal strengths were his unrefined and plain-speaking representativeness, his incisive manner of thought, and his rationality. To these he added a reputation for absolute integrity. His pastor, who knew him well, said, "His abilities were remarkable, not brilliant, but solid, penetrating, and capable of deep and long investigation. In such investigation he was greatly assisted by his patient and unremitting application and perseverance." He was six feet tall, wore his brown hair short, and had steel blue-grey eyes. He claimed to have controlled his passions by the time he was twenty, and none of his contemporaries ever had reason to question the claim.

Sherman's political practice was to listen a lot, hedge his positions, sniff the wind sharply, and join the leading wave as he saw it building. He always managed to stay just a bit ahead of the dominant thrust of public opinion, but it is unlikely that he ever championed a cause he did not think was right for his constituents and right under God.

During the Stamp Act controversy of 1765, Sherman was among Connecticut's moderate radicals, and it was he who wrote the assembly's instructions to the delegates sent to the Stamp Act Congress in New York. His position was antistamp, of course, but he also protested the taxation without representation and trials without juries that the act implied. The instructions, which no doubt reflect a consensus rather than Sherman's own position, were moderate and well short of the desires of the most radical members of the assembly but closer to their views than to those of the conservatives led by Governor Thomas Fitch.

Indeed, the actions of Fitch and other conservative members of the council and house led to their defeat at the next colonywide elections. One of the replacements on the twelve-man council—the upper house—was Sherman. From 1766 on, the Connecticut government, with its popularly elected executive and legislature, was securely in the hands of anti-Parliamentary forces. Thus in 1774, when a call came to send delegates to a Continental Congress, the "patriots" had things their own way. Sherman was sent with two others to represent them.

Sherman's participation in the First Continental Congress marks the beginning of nearly two decades of activity on the national political scene. In the Congress he was, in John Adams's (1735–1826) words, "one of the soundest and strongest pillars of the Revolution." "I have no expectation that [the British] administration will be reconciled unless the Colonies submit to their arbitrary system," said Sherman in 1775, adding portentously, "or convince them that it is not in their power to carry it into execution." If the British persist in their military activities, he said just after Lexington and Concord, "I hope every Colony will take Government fully into their own hands."

Sherman early saw that there was no logical way to connect a self-governing people to an imperialist system. The Townshend taxes were "as unconstitutional as the Stamp Act," he had written in 1767, and each colony had "distinct and complete powers of legislation . . . [and are not] in any proper sense subordinate to the Legislature of Great Britain." By 1776 his views were well known, and it made sense to put him on Congress's five-man committee to write a Declaration of Independence. No evidence exists that Sherman made any verbal contribution to the text of that document but that it reflects his views is beyond doubt. Connecticut, where he was a—if not *the*—major figure in shaping intercolonial policy, had voted its own very similar declaration the previous month.

Sherman was consistently reelected to the upper house in Connecticut, a position that carried with it a seat on the state's supreme court. He was also returned as a delegate to the Continental Congress, where he sat on the committee that wrote the Articles of Confederation. The Articles restricted the terms of delegates, but Sherman served as often and as long as permissible and was in attendance about half the time between 1774 and 1789. He actually served in the various national Congresses during that period more days than any other man.

By 1787, when he went as a delegate to the Constitutional Convention, no one had more national legislative experience than Sherman. He appeared so wise and so skillful that he developed the reputation of being nearly always successful in carrying out his objectives. "He is an able politician, and extreamly [sic] artful in accomplishing any particular object," wrote an observer at that convention, "—it is remarked that he seldom fails." He had, said one who knew him well, "acute discernment and sound judgement, but especially . . . knowledge of human nature. He had a happy talent of judging what was feasible and what was not feasible, or what men would bear, and what they would not bear in government. And he had a real talent of prudence, or of timing and adapting his measures to the attainment of his end." Sherman's rule in politics, he once told a young friend, was "minorities talk; majorities vote."

It was natural, then, at the Constitutional Convention of 1787 that Sherman—the dominant figure of the state's three-man delegation—should play the role of compromiser. Over and over again he proposed solutions on the floor or engaged in back room negotiations to bring about arrangements satisfactory to his state and acceptable to a majority of the other delegations. One high-flown and wealthy Hartford merchant, who was afraid that Sherman only wanted to "patch up" the old system, warned other delegates that "he is cunning as the Devil, and if you attack him, you ought to know him well; he is not easily managed, but if he suspects you are trying to take him in, you may as well catch an Eel by the tail."

Sherman's basic objectives at Philadelphia were two: strengthen the central government so it could pay its debts, negotiate effectively with foreign governments, and maintain domestic tranquility; and protect state autonomy. "Each state," he said, "had its particular habits, usages and manners, which constituted its happiness." The Constitution should not "give to others a power over this happiness, any more than an individual would do, when it could avoid it."

Thus he brought about the alliance of New Englanders and deep southerners that forced the constitutional prohibition on export duties on the middle states. He was instrumental in giving each state one vote in the presidential election when the electoral college fails to produce a majority. His greatest triumph was, beyond any doubt, his engineering of the famous Connecticut Compromise. As the most effective states' rights delegate at the convention, Sherman was determined to block the Madisonian effort to institute proportionality in both houses of Congress. His political machinations are shadowy, but again he succeeded. The state equality in the Senate is largely his doing.

Sherman participated in all the debates concerning all the great documents of the nation's founding, and he actually signed more of them than any other person: the Declaration and Resolves of 1774, the Declaration of Independence, the Articles of Confederation, and the U.S. Constitution.

After working for ratification of the Constitution in Connecticut, Sherman was elected to the House in the First Congress and to the Senate in the second. He joined forces with the economic nationalists but continued to work hard at protecting states' rights. For these efforts and those at the Philadelphia convention, the great states' rights philosopher John C. Calhoun later listed Sherman as one of three men to whom we are indebted for "a federal government instead of a national government."

As part of this determination to protect the states from federal intrusion and also because he hated quick change, Sherman resisted the development of a national bill of rights. Sherman himself wrote that frequent elections were "a much greater security than a declaration of rights or restraining clauses on paper." He failed, of course, in his effort to prevent the enumeration of rights in the Constitution, but he succeeded—virtually singlehandedly—in having them added at the end instead of inserted piecemeal at appropriate places throughout the document as James Madison (1751–1836) wanted.

Sherman was an honest politician, not a man easy to like, perhaps, but one easy to respect. "That is Mr. Sherman of Connecticut," Thomas Jefferson told a young friend at the end of Sherman's career, "a man who never said a foolish thing in his life." At his funeral in New Haven, where he died, the president of Yale College told the dead man's neighbors, Sherman had "that Dignity which arises from doing everything perfectly right. He was an extraordinary man—a venerable uncorrupted patriot."

• No corpus of Sherman papers exists. Yale University has the largest collection: one box in Beinecke Library containing a few letters, a couple of account books, and miscellaneous papers; and about 200 items in a single box in the Historical Manuscripts Room at Sterling Memorial Library, the largest group consisting of letters taken from the Baldwin Family Collection covering only the last five years of Sherman's life. Forty-one papers and a notebook are at the Library of Congress. Several letters and papers are located at the American Antiquarian Society in Worcester, Mass. Groups of letters can be found at the Massachusetts Historical Society, the New Haven Colony History Society (where the collection includes an account book), the Historical Society of Pennsylvania, and the Connecticut Historical Society. Dartmouth, Harvard, and Brown Universities also have about a half-dozen letters each. The Litchfield Historical Society has a few writs and orders of Sherman's as a justice of the peace, and the New-York Historical Society has three letters of little significance.

No collection of Sherman's almanacs has been preserved, but Victor Hugo Paltsits published "The Almanacs of Roger Sherman" in the *Proceedings* of the American Antiquarian Society 18 (1907): 213–58. Sherman himself published three pamphlets, *A Caveat against Injustice by Philoeunomes* (1752), an argument against paper money; and two religious tracts, *A Short Sermon . . .* (1789) and *A Vindication of Presbyterian Ordination . . .* (1768).

The only scholarly full-length biography is Christopher Collier, *Roger Sherman's Connecticut: Yankee Politics and the American Revolution* (1971), which includes the most complete bibliography of sources. Two older book-length biographies are Lewis Henry Boutell, *Life of Roger Sherman* (1896), which is especially strong on Sherman's legal activities; and Roger Sherman Boardman's more popular *Roger Sherman, Signer and Statesman* (1938). Two shorter works are Collier, *Roger Sherman: Puritan Politician* (1976), and John G. Rommel, *Connecticut's Yankee Patriot: Roger Sherman* (1980). Sources for the study of Connecticut during Sherman's era are discussed in Christopher Collier and Bonnie Collier, *The Literature of Connecticut History* (1982).

CHRISTOPHER COLLIER

SHERMAN, Stuart Pratt (1 Oct. 1881–21 Aug. 1926), critic and professor of English, was born in Anita, Iowa, the son of John Sherman, a druggist and farmer, and Ada Pratt. Sherman's family moved to Los Angeles in 1887 and after his father's death in 1892 joined maternal relatives in Dorset, Vermont. He graduated from Williams College in 1903 and received a Ph.D. in English at Harvard in 1906. He married Ruth Mears that same year; they had one son. After a year at Northwestern University (1906–1907), he moved to the University of Illinois, where he taught for seventeen years, serving as acting chair of the English department in 1910 and as chair from 1914 until 1924. He then left the university to serve as literary editor of the *New York Herald Tribune*.

Sherman was strongly influenced by the new humanism of his Harvard professor, Irving Babbitt; Babbitt also introduced him to the work of another conservative critic, Paul Elmer More. Sherman shared Babbitt's conviction that literature needed aesthetic and moral standards derived from Christian and classical traditions—traditions producing balance and self-restraint. He also shared Babbitt's conviction that contemporary American writers influenced by European naturalism and symbolism were slipping into vulgarity and moral chaos.

Sherman first received attention as a writer with a signed letter in the *Nation*, "Graduate Schools and Literature" (14 May 1908), which attacked the rigidity and deadliness of graduate schools in English, with their excessive emphasis on medievalism and esoteric languages. This letter launched Sherman as a regular contributor to the *Nation* and the *New York Evening Post* and as an occasional contributor to other periodicals. As a rule, Sherman avoided traditional scholarship.

Although he called for freshness in pedagogy, Sherman's early criticism was savagely xenophobic. In *On Contemporary Literature* (1917) he suggests that John Millington Synge's exuberance is a disguise for symbolist morbidity and speaks of Synge "looking into the noisome grave" (p. 210). Of Theodore Dreiser's first five novels Sherman writes:

I do not find any moral value in them, nor any memorable beauty—of their truth I shall speak later; but I am greatly impressed by them as serious representatives of a new note in American literature, coming from that "ethnic" element of our mixed population which, we are assured by competent authorities, is to redeem us from Puritanism and insure our artistic salvation. (p. 87)

According to Sherman, Dreiser's naturalism was "based upon a theory of animal behavior," and applying it to modern man was an "artistic blunder" (p. 101). In the *Nation* (29 Nov. 1917), he attacked H. L. Mencken for preferring European culture (especially German culture) to American and for flaunting his German heritage. Speaking for the Allied cause to the National Council of Teachers of English on 1 December 1917, he denounced Mencken as a promulgator of Nietzschean philosophy.

Throughout the early 1920s Sherman was a conservative force of growing importance, frequently publishing articles, reviews, and collections of his work and interacting with other prominent critics. However, he began to drift away from conservatism. In *The Genius of America* (1923) he argues that modern literature is at odds with the fundamental culture of the United States and that American literature should "make Puritanism beautiful" (p. 32). To Sherman, Puritanism meant, as it is usually understood to mean, hard work, moral restraint, and deferred gratification, but he also found it to be "one of the vital, progressive, and enriching human traditions" (p. 53). Its consistent impetus "is the passion for improvement. . . . the immortal urgent spirit that breaks from the old forms, follows the new vision, seriously seeks the discipline of the higher life" (p. 56). Thus Sherman, by juxtaposing ideas seemingly at odds with each other, was becoming receptive to the innovations of modern literature. As literary editor of the *New York Herald Tribune* he wrote primarily favorable essays on D. H. Lawrence, Sherwood Anderson, and others. Sherman's most drastic reversal was his eulogistic review of Dreiser's *An American Tragedy* in 1926, although he carefully explained that Dreiser had matured into a true realist (*New York Herald Tribune*, book review section, 3 Jan. 1926).

While vacationing at Dunewood, a Michigan resort he shared with friends, Sherman died of a heart attack following a canoeing upset. Despite his prominence in his own day, he has subsequently been given little attention either as a practicing critic or as a literary theorist. When he is mentioned at all, it is usually by those sympathetic to Dreiser and H. L. Mencken, who believed Sherman had tried to turn the anti-German hysteria of the World War I period against them. Writing in 1929, Jacob Zeitlin and Homer Woodbridge offered in their biography of him measured praise that avoided the issue of posthumous opinion: "It may be too early to attempt an estimate of Sherman's definite place in American criticism, but there can be little question of his importance among contemporary critics and of the value of his work in a consideration of the literary currents of our time" (p. vii). By contrast, Mencken was blunt in dismissing Sherman. He refused Sherman's hand, saying, "I'd rather pass into heaven without the pleasure of his acquaintance. He is a dirty fighter" (Nolte, p. 158). Posterity has proven to be kinder to Mencken than to his adversary.

• Sherman's papers are at the New York Public Library, at the University of Chicago, and at Harvard and Princeton Universities. Jacob Zeitlin and Homer Woodbridge, *Life and Letters of Stuart P. Sherman* (1929, 1971), is very thorough and has a good bibliography. Sherman's own critical works include *Matthew Arnold: How to Know Him* (1917), *Essays and Poems of Emerson* (1921), *Americans* (1922), *Critical Woodcuts* (1926), *The Main Stream* (1927), and *Shaping Men and Women: Essays on Literature and Life*, ed. Zeitlin (1929). He is coeditor of the four-volume *Cambridge History of American Literature* (1917–1921). His doctoral dissertation is the source for his one-volume edition of two John Ford plays, *'Tis Pity She's a Whore and the Broken Heart* (1915). Several books on Mencken and Dreiser contain accounts of their feuds with Sherman. An excellent discussion is in William H. Nolte, *H. L. Mencken: Literary Critic* (1966, 1967). An obituary is in the *New York Times*, 23 Aug. 1926.

MARYJEAN GROSS
DALTON GROSS

SHERMAN, William Tecumseh (8 Feb. 1820–14 Feb. 1891), soldier, was born in Lancaster, Ohio, the son of Charles R. Sherman, a state judge, and Mary Hoyt. His father died when Sherman was nine years old, leaving the family penniless. Sherman grew up in the family of Thomas Ewing (1789–1871), a noted politician, and Maria Boyle. At sixteen he received an appointment to the U.S. Military Academy at West Point through his foster father's influence, graduating sixth out of a class of forty-one.

Though he chafed under the restrictive military academy environment, he came to see the army as his family, a substitute for the familial relationship he felt he had lost with the death of his father. He respected Ewing enormously and tried to gain his approval but always saw himself as only a poor orphan ward.

After graduation, Sherman served a variety of military assignments, mostly in the South. He participated in the difficult Seminole War in Florida from 1840 to 1842. At Fort Morgan in Mobile, Alabama (1842), and Fort Moultrie in Charleston, South Carolina (1842–1846), Sherman became intimately acquainted with southern people and geography, two areas of knowledge that were to influence his later military career.

When the Mexican War broke out in 1846, Sherman was on recruiting duty in Pittsburgh, but he soon received orders for California. A 198-day sail around the Horn of South America brought him to Monterey, where he served until 1850. He experienced no combat, his main excitement being the famous gold rush.

Sherman was happy in 1850 to leave California for Washington, carrying military messages to President Zachary Taylor and to Winfield Scott, the army's commanding general. His lack of combat experience still worried him, and his marriage that year to Ellen Ewing (with whom he had eight children) added to his burdens. Ellen, a staunch Catholic tied very closely to her family, insisted that he accept her religion (he expressed no denominational preference) and that he leave the army and find civilian occupation, but only in Lancaster, Ohio, where her parents still lived.

However, Sherman remained in the army until 1853, serving in St. Louis and New Orleans in the commissary service. Ellen spent as much time as she could in Lancaster, giving birth to two children there during these years. Sherman remained unhappy at their frequent separations and because of his concern that the army did not provide the financial security he believed his family needed if it were to avoid the disaster he had experienced as a child when his father had died. When a St. Louis banker friend and former military colleague in California, Henry S. Turner, offered him the management of a branch bank in San Francisco, Sherman accepted it hesitatingly. Ellen remained opposed to any move that took her far away from Lancaster and her family.

Sherman's four-year stint (1853–1857) as a California banker was filled with financial problems, highlighted by a run on all San Francisco banks in 1855. He weathered the panic well, however, gaining the admiration of the city's businessmen. In May 1856 he found himself in the middle of a vigilante crisis. Though he headed the local militia and had the support of the state's governor, Sherman found himself helpless in the face of the determined extralegal movement. He had to stand by while vigilantes took over the city; he resigned his militia commission to try to protect his bank.

Sherman's personal life was similarly unsettling. In return for Ellen's departure for California, Thomas and Maria Ewing insisted that the older of the two Sherman children, the two-year-old Maria (Minnie), remain with them in Lancaster. Ellen thus found herself torn between California and Ohio, and she spent one seven-month period in Lancaster visiting father and daughter. Throughout the four California years, Sherman suffered sometimes incapacitating asthma attacks. Depression plagued him, the result of worry about his health, business, and family. In late 1856, because of their concern over Sherman's increasingly pessimistic reports about his health and California's financial climate, the St. Louis bankers decided to close their San Francisco branch.

Sherman accepted management of a new branch in New York City, but the panic of 1857 sank the St. Louis bank and forced the closing of the New York branch, too. Depression overwhelmed him, as he faced his greatest fear: inability, like his father, to support his family. He dreaded becoming Ewing's poor ward again. Ellen's happiness that events were driving him inexorably to Lancaster only made his depression worse.

Sherman thrashed around trying to discover some way out of his financial and personal abyss. He felt forced to accept Ewing's offer to manage the family's coal and saltworks in nearby Chauncey, Ohio. At the last minute, he gained a reprieve. His brothers-in-law, Thomas Ewing, Jr. (1829–1896), and Hugh Boyle Ewing, offered him a part in their legal and real estate business in Leavenworth, Kansas.

Business never materialized the way the three men had hoped, and young Tom Ewing, much to Sherman's disgust, spent more time in antislavery politics than in real estate. In 1859, despaired of success in Kansas, Sherman tried to get back into the army. There were no openings, however, and he was not interested in managing a London bank in which the Ewings had an interest. At the last minute, thanks to some former army friends, he gained the position of superintendent of the newly established Louisiana Military Seminary (forerunner of Louisiana State University).

Sherman's life in Louisiana from the fall of 1859 to February 1861 was one of the happiest periods in his life. Students, parents, and the state's politicians were impressed with his accomplishments at the school and with his proslavery attitude. Ellen remained in Lancaster with their five children. She and her father kept telling Sherman that he should come home or, at least, accept the banking position in London. Sherman, growing in confidence everyday as he experienced a success he had seldom before felt in his life, insisted that he would stay in Louisiana.

Unfortunately, secession forced Sherman to a major turning point. After a hard struggle, he decided to leave Louisiana. He took a job as president of a street railway company in St. Louis, words of praise from Louisiana people still ringing in his ears. He witnessed the chaos created by Federal volunteer Home Guards in their clumsy attempt to rid the city of equally incompetent pro-Confederate state militia. He determined to stand aside until the Union war effort became more organized and orderly.

In May, owing to the influence of his brother and the Ewings, Sherman was offered and accepted the colonelcy of a regular army unit. Winfield Scott appointed him an inspector general, and on 30 June 1861 Sherman was made commander of the Third Brigade of the First Division in Irvin McDowell's army preparing to invade Virginia. Sherman quickly whipped his volunteer unit into shape and led them admirably at the battle of Bull Run (Manassas). The Union debacle devastated him, however; all his fears about volunteer incompetence and Union disorganization were played out before his eyes. Press criticism reawakened his long-held animosity against reporters. He wondered if, once again, his hopes for success were to be dashed.

In August 1861 Abraham Lincoln named him Robert Anderson's second in command of the Department of the Cumberland (Ky. and Tenn.), promising, as Sherman requested, that he would never be called upon to lead. The situation there proved even more chaotic than in Washington, and when Anderson, the hero of Fort Sumter, broke under the pressure, Sherman was forced to take over, Lincoln's promise notwithstanding. Sherman found the task overwhelming, exaggerating a bad situation until it appeared hopeless. He freely spoke of imminent Confederate victory and danger to bordering northern states. He demanded to be relieved of command, and the Lincoln administration sent Don Carlos Buell to replace him.

Sherman moved to Missouri under Henry W. Halleck's command; he so vociferously continued expressing his pessimism about the war that Halleck sent him home to Lancaster for a rest. Newspaper reporters, angry at having been excluded from his camps, took advantage of the situation to label him insane. He developed such severe depression that he contemplated suicide. Sherman was given troop training duty at Benton Barracks, Missouri, but he did not rebound fully until he became associated with Ulysses S. Grant and saw that the Union cause was indeed not doomed. In April 1862 he distinguished himself at Shiloh. He received a hand wound as Confederates overran his position, but he maintained his composure and conspicuously rallied Union troops around him in the face of the hard-charging enemy, demonstrating to himself and to others that he was an excellent battlefield leader. Simultaneously he drew inspiration from Grant's reversal of the Union debacle on the first day into the victory of the second. Participation in Halleck's capture of Corinth in June 1862 increased this newfound optimism. He even talked Grant out of quitting in despair over his seeming demotion after Shiloh.

When Memphis fell into Union hands in June 1862, Sherman became its military governor. There he battled guerrillas more than Confederate regulars and came to recognize that this war was between two societies more than it was between two armies. He punished civilians when they harbored partisans or tried to sabotage Union forces or installations. He similarly inspired Union sentiment in Memphis, leaving the post for active field activity in the fall of 1862 pleased with his popularity and content that he had finally achieved the success that had so long eluded him.

This feeling of accomplishment quickly melted away when, in December 1862, Sherman failed to defeat Confederate troops at Chickasaw Bayou near Vicksburg. His troops valiantly battled the watery terrain and charged the entrenched enemy on the Walnut Hills but suffered a discouraging repulse with terrible casualties. Newspaper charges that he had made an insane attack reopened old wounds, and in reaction Sherman court-martialed Thomas Knox of the *New York Herald*, the only such proceeding against a reporter in American history.

The early months of 1863 continued to be frustrating. Sherman lost his command to political general John McClernand, who took credit for the successful capture of Arkansas Post in January 1863. Grant made repeated attempts to take Vicksburg and failed each time, Sherman sharing in the frustration. Sherman strongly advised Grant to return to Memphis and begin anew, but Grant saw the political suicide in such a retreat. Instead Grant ordered the brilliant but dangerous flanking of the city and the positioning of the Union troops between Joseph E. Johnston's force in Jackson and John Pemberton's (1814–1881) troops in Vicksburg. Sherman made an elaborate feint at Snyder's Bluff above Vicksburg to try to shield Grant's activities below the city. Having achieved his purpose, he raced his army to rejoin Grant's force. He participated in chasing Johnston out of Jackson and destroyed its military capability. His troops were active participants in Grant's May attack on Vicksburg, and then he organized the force Grant sent to the Big Black River east of Vicksburg to thwart any efforts by Johnston to break the Union siege of the city. When Grant forced Vicksburg into a 4 July surrender, Sherman shared the excitement. Once more he experienced success, but this time the death of his beloved son, Willie, during a family visit to the area in the fall of 1863 caused a wound that never healed.

In the fall of 1863, when Grant became overall head in the West, Sherman became commander of the Department of the Army of the Tennessee. He participated in the successful battle of Chattanooga and then returned to Mississippi to put into practice the concept of war he had been contemplating since Memphis. During the Meridian campaign in February 1864, Sherman cut a swath of destruction from Jackson to Meridian, Mississippi, utilizing property damage and warfare against the southern psyche to achieve the victory he believed the mayhem of battle could not accomplish as quickly or as effectively. When Grant was made general in chief of all Union armies in March 1864, Sherman became commander of the Military Division of the Mississippi, head of all military operations in the West.

Grant and Sherman now planned coordinated military activities throughout all the theaters of the war. On 5 May 1864, as Grant began his movement against Robert E. Lee in Virginia, Sherman departed from Chattanooga and moved against Johnston and his Army of Tennessee in Georgia. For the next four months, in a series of flanking movements that required not only tactical, but logistical skill, Sherman pushed Johnston back toward Atlanta. He almost crushed the Confederates at Snake Creek Gap near Resaca in the opening days of the campaign, but the failure of General James B. McPherson to follow up his advantage prevented this success. Sherman failed at several other flanking movements, pushing Johnston back but unable to land a killing blow. Exasperated, he unwisely made a frontal attack at Kennesaw Mountain, only to be severely repulsed with large losses. He went back to his flanking activities and forced Johnston into the Atlanta defenses. At this time Confederate president Jefferson Davis replaced Johnston with John Bell Hood. The aggressive Hood went on the offensive, but Sherman successfully repulsed each of his attacks and took command of the

city in September 1864, just in time to help salvage the presidential reelection of Lincoln.

Despite initial opposition from Lincoln and Grant, Sherman implemented his philosophy of psychological warfare and property destruction. He saw pillage as a preferable substitute for the continued carnage of battle. He did not want to kill southerners, people he still considered his friends; he wanted to convince them to stop the war. Beginning in early November 1864, he marched through Georgia to the sea at Savannah, and in early 1865 he marched through the Carolinas. He had his soldiers live off the land, taking what they needed and destroying anything associated with slavery and the Confederate war effort. Private homes were not normally destroyed, but Sherman's men (as well as Confederate cavalry, deserters from both sides, and fugitive slaves) frequently looted these dwellings. Sherman preached the doctrine of hard war and soft peace. Once the Confederates stopped their war effort, he promised, he would support their return into the Union with no further punishment. This psychological warfare worked. Casualties to military men and civilians were small on the marches; property destruction was widespread. Confederate desertions increased, and the people's will to continue fighting deteriorated.

When General Johnston approached him in April 1865 about ending the fighting, Sherman jumped at the offer. In fulfillment of his hard war, soft peace doctrine, he agreed to terms that were so generous to the defeated Confederates that Washington politicians and the nation's newspapers, reeling from Lincoln's assassination, accused him of treason. Sherman was forced to renegotiate the treaty. He was so angered to see himself defamed once more that, during the Grand Review of Union Armies in Washington in May 1865, he snubbed his chief critic, Secretary of War Edwin Stanton, on the reviewing stand.

Sherman came out of the war with the success he had always craved. He enjoyed his popularity but wanted only to go back to the army and society as he remembered them before secession. However, the war had changed the United States, and the Reconstruction following the war was a difficult time. Sherman supported the old-line leaders in the South. Though he knew slavery was dead, he thought that the freed people should be kept in a subordinate status. When Andrew Johnson tried to use him in his battle with Congress, Sherman refused to become involved, insisting that the only answer to the imbroglio was a return to the prewar years.

When Grant became president in 1869, Sherman succeeded him as commanding general, a post he was to keep until his retirement. He found the job frustrating. Grant did not support him in his battle with the secretary of war over command jurisdiction, causing a rupture in their friendship that was never totally healed. He was regularly upset as Congress continually cut army strength and military salaries. Politicians ignored his military counsel, even when it came to waging the difficult American Indian wars. As a result, Sherman left Washington whenever he could, spending a year on tour in Europe and the Middle East (1871–1872) and another eighteen months (1874–1876) in St. Louis. He particularly enjoyed visiting the West, and in 1879 he received a friendly welcome when he revisited scenes of his wartime exploits in the South. In 1875 he published his memoirs and weathered the criticism he received from Union friends and Confederate foes for his interpretation of wartime events. His major imprint on the postwar army was improving military education, including the establishment of a school for officers at Fort Leavenworth, Kansas.

When he officially retired in 1884, Sherman continued attending veterans' gatherings, and he was president of the Society of the Army of the Tennessee from the late 1860s until his death. He was one of the most popular after-dinner speakers in the nation, still "Uncle Billy" to his aging soldiers and the esteemed approachable Civil War hero to the nation's civilians. He saw himself as defender of the history of the Union cause, writing articles and giving speeches insisting on the moral superiority of the Unionists and defending his own and his army's role in the war. In the process, he engaged in numerous feuds, notably in the late 1880s with Jefferson Davis. In 1880 Sherman coined the phrase that was shortened to "war is hell," and when in 1884 he refused, yet again, to run for the presidency, he said, "I will not accept if nominated and will not serve if elected."

Sherman was crushed when his oldest son, Tommy, became a Jesuit priest. Ellen's health grew increasingly worse, and she became a near recluse, dying in 1888 in the New York City house he had bought for her that same year. Sherman maintained an active social life. He loved the theater and was a favorite among New York's actors and actresses. He regularly rode the elevated trains with ordinary citizens and enjoyed taking his visiting grandchildren to the circus, wild west show, or Central Park. He gained a reputation for kissing young women, and he sought feminine companionship every chance he had. The sculptor Vinnie Ream was a particular favorite.

When Sherman died in New York City, the outpouring of national mourning expressed the public's admiration for him. It was only in later years that the growth of the southern Lost Cause interpretation of the Civil War created his reputation as a villain who practiced senseless barbaric destruction. In truth, Sherman was a pioneer of purposeful psychological and total war, one of the major figures in American military history.

• Sherman's papers are located in libraries and manuscript depositories all over the nation. The most important papers are found in the Library of Congress, the Archives of the University of Notre Dame, and the Ohio Historical Society. See also *Memoirs of General William T. Sherman* (2 vols., 1875 and 1886; new ed., 1990). Joseph H. Ewing, ed., *Sherman at War* (1992), is a collection of Civil War letters. A modern biography is John F. Marszalek, *Sherman: A Soldier's Passion for Order* (1993); it contains a complete listing of Sherman's

papers. Dated but still worthwhile are Lloyd Lewis, *Sherman, Fighting Prophet* (1932); Basil H. Liddell-Hart, *Sherman, Soldier, Realist, American* (1929; repr. 1958); and James M. Merrill, *William Tecumseh Sherman* (1971). On total war, see Charles Royster, *The Destructive War: William Tecumseh Sherman, Stonewall Jackson and the Americans* (1991). An insightful study of Sherman's soldiers is Joseph T. Glatthaar, *The March to the Sea and Beyond: Sherman's Troops in the Savannah and Carolinas Campaigns* (1985). A study of Sherman's hostile relationship with newspaper reporters is Marszalek, *Sherman's Other War: The General and the Civil War Press* (1981). A critical assessment of Sherman's Atlanta campaign is Albert Castel, *Decision in the West: The Atlanta Campaign of 1864* (1992). John B. Walters, *Merchant of Terror: General Sherman and Total War* (1973), is severely hostile to Sherman's psychological warfare, while Charles Edmond Vetter, *Sherman, Merchant of Terror, Advocate of Peace* (1992), views his subject more objectively. A front-page obituary is in the *New York Times*, 15 Feb. 1891. *Literary Digest*, 21 Feb. 1891, pp. 20–21, provides synopses of a host of obituaries in the nation's press.

JOHN F. MARSZALEK

SHERRILL, Henry Knox (8 Nov. 1890–11 May 1980), Episcopal clergyman, was born in Brooklyn, New York, the son of Henry William Sherrill and Maria Knox Mills, farmers. In 1907 he entered Yale College, after a preparatory year at the Hotchkiss School. For the next four years he attended St. Paul's Episcopal Church in New Haven, Connecticut, where James DeWolf Perry, later the eighteenth presiding bishop of the Episcopal church, was the rector; Sherrill taught Sunday church school under Perry's direction. At the end of his junior year Sherrill decided to study for the ministry. The religious atmosphere of his home prepared him for this decision, and the preaching of John R. Mott and Henry Coffin "gave a relevance of the Gospel to contemporary society" that he could not forget. Sherrill wrote, "There grew upon me gradually the conviction that the world needed Christ" (*Among Friends*, p. 26). He graduated from Yale in 1911 and in the fall entered the Episcopal Theological School in Cambridge, Massachusetts, from which he received his B.D. in 1914. He was ordained deacon on 7 June 1914 and priest on 9 May 1915.

Sherrill began his ministry as assistant minister at Trinity Church, Boston, and remained there until 1917, when he became chaplain of the Massachusetts General Hospital, later known as Base Hospital Six. Later in 1917 he and others from the hospital were sent to Europe, where they took over a hospital in Talence, France, about three miles from Bordeaux. Most of Sherrill's ministry as a chaplain consisted of visiting through the wards, with special attention to critical cases. Here he saw men of all faiths and no faith and was impressed by their need for prayer. This experience convinced him of the truth of the statement, "Man is incurably religious" (*Among Friends*, p. 73). In 1919 he was discharged from the army.

When he returned to Boston, Sherrill had three calls: the Episcopal Theological School wanted him to be an instructor; St. Paul's Cathedral, Boston, wanted him to become their first canon; and the wardens and vestry of the Church of Our Saviour, Brookline, wanted him as rector. He accepted the job of rector and stayed at the Church of Our Saviour until 1923. While there he met Barbara Harris, and they were married in 1921. They had four children.

In 1923 Sherrill became the twelfth rector of Trinity Church, Boston, remaining there until 1930. While at Trinity Church he also taught pastoral care and homiletics at the Episcopal Theological School, and pastoral care at the Boston University School of Theology. He was a member of the board of preachers of Harvard University, a trustee of the Massachusetts General Hospital, and president of the Greater Boston Council of Churches. The last position introduced him to the possibilities of the ecumenical movement.

On 8 May 1930 Sherrill was elected the ninth bishop of the Diocese of Massachusetts. He was consecrated at Trinity Church, Boston, on 14 October 1930, and served in that position until 1 June 1947, when he resigned on being chosen presiding bishop. During these seventeen years the diocese grew, and Sherrill became widely known for his ability as an ecclesiastical leader, especially with regard to his ecumenical activities and his managing one of the largest dioceses in the Episcopal church. From 1940 until 1947 he also served as chairman of the Commission on Army and Navy Chaplains.

At the General Convention of 1946 Sherrill was elected the twentieth presiding bishop of the Episcopal church. Until 1943 the presiding bishop had also continued to be the bishop of his diocese, but a canon passed in 1943 required the presiding bishop to resign his previous jurisdiction. Sherrill was the first presiding bishop chosen after this canon was passed, and so he resigned as bishop of Massachusetts on 1 June 1947. He served as presiding bishop from 1 January 1947 until 14 November 1958.

During Sherrill's tenure as presiding bishop the Episcopal church moved forward on a number of issues. Under his strong and constructive leadership the church's organization was strengthened with regard to missionary work. Sherrill led in the organization of the Episcopal Church Foundation, with a large revolving loan fund to lend dioceses money for the construction of church buildings. He participated in the establishment of the Seabury Press, which opened officially on 1 January 1952 as the publishing firm of the Episcopal church. Sherrill also encouraged the Builders for Christ campaign, a stewardship program. He established the Presiding Bishop's Fund for World Relief, the Episcopal church's primary relief agency. Sherrill also supported the work of Christian Social Relations, and he was a leader in the forthright stand by religious leaders against the anti-Communist hysteria of the McCarthy era.

One of Sherrill's major areas of leadership was in the ecumenical movement. The World Council of the Churches of Christ, formed at an assembly in Amsterdam in 1948, brought together 135 denominations. Sherrill was one of six presidents, who formed a presidium, from 1954 until 1961. The National Council of

the Churches of Christ in the U.S.A. was organized at a 1950 meeting in Cleveland, Ohio; Sherrill was elected its first president and served from 1950 until 1952.

Sherrill was also a leader in the civil rights movement. The 1955 General Convention of the Episcopal Church had been scheduled to meet in Houston, Texas. In the spring of 1954, however, several dioceses and church leaders raised concerns about Houston's having segregated housing facilities for conventions. Sherrill studied the situation and decided to move the convention to Honolulu. This helped to move the Episcopal church into the center of the civil rights movement, where it remained for years. During his lengthy retirement, Sherrill traveled and lectured. He died in Boxford, Massachusetts.

Sherrill was presiding bishop of the Episcopal church during a difficult time in American history. Courage and daring were major characteristics of his leadership.

• Sherrill's papers are in the Archives of the Diocese of Massachusetts in Boston and in the Archives of the Episcopal Church in Austin, Texas. His insightful autobiography is *Among Friends* (1962). Sherrill also published *William Lawrence: Later Years of a Happy Life* (1943), a study of the seventh bishop of Massachusetts, and *The Church's Ministry in Our Time* (1949), a collection of his Lyman Beecher Lectures on Preaching at Yale Divinity School. An obituary is in the *New York Times*, 13 May 1980.

DONALD S. ARMENTROUT

SHERWIN, Belle (25 Mar. 1868–9 July 1955), suffragist and civic leader, was born in Cleveland, Ohio, the daughter of Henry Alden Sherwin, an industrialist, and Mary Frances Smith. Her father, the founder of the paint-manufacturing Sherwin-Williams Company, was an influential citizen in Cleveland, and because of his example in particular she developed a strong work ethic. From 1886 to 1890 she attended Wellesley College, where she earned a B.S. in history. Some of her professors, particularly Katharine Coman, professor of history and economics, are credited with encouraging her interest in social issues. Sherwin later served as a Wellesley trustee (1918–1943; emerita, 1944–1952) and as chair of the Building and Grounds Committee (1922–1940). The college recognized her contributions by awarding her an honorary degree (1950).

Before pursuing graduate study in history at Oxford University between 1894 and 1895, Sherwin taught for a brief time at her high school alma mater, St. Margaret's School in Waterbury, Connecticut. In 1898–1899 she made another attempt at teaching, at Miss Hersey's School for Girls in Boston, but in 1899 she returned to Cleveland, where she initially organized English classes for Italian immigrants at a local social service agency called Alta House. Sherwin reportedly left teaching because her energy level was too high and her range of interests too varied "for the quiet backwater of teaching in girls' schools" (Prescott, p. 9).

In 1900 Sherwin organized the Cleveland Consumers' League, the first consumer-oriented organization established in the United States, and for much of that decade she managed the league's investigations into alleged improprieties. From 1899 to 1924 she was a director in the newly established Public Health Nursing Association. Sherwin served on the board of the Visiting Nurses' Association in 1902. From 1900 to 1914 she was director of the Cleveland Welfare Federation and as such is credited with integrating a visiting nurse program into the city's public health system. In addition to her civic work, Sherwin joined the College Equal Suffrage League in 1910 and began to put her managerial skills to work for the cause of woman suffrage. In 1916, responding to the formation that same year of the National Association Opposed to Woman Suffrage, she formed the Women's City Club, intended to be a forum for reasonable debate, as women in the city had become heatedly divided on the suffrage issue.

Sherwin's suffrage activities were interrupted during U.S. involvement in World War I. From 1917 to 1918, as chairman of the Woman's Committee of the Ohio branch of the U.S. Council of National Defense, she oversaw sixty Cleveland women's groups that were involved in such wartime efforts as food conservation and production, industrial recruitment, and social welfare. In 1919, her war service completed, Sherwin became president of the Cleveland Suffrage Association. The following year she helped to found the National League of Women Voters which was formed out of what had been the National American Woman Suffrage Association, and in 1921 she was elected vice president of the league as well as chairman of the committee charged with training women for civic affairs. In 1924, succeeding Maud Wood Park, Sherwin was elected the league's second president, a post she would hold until 1934. Her experiences as vice president had taught her that women would have to be educated in the political process before they would become motivated to use their newly won right to vote. At the league headquarters in Washington, D.C., she began her term by unifying the administration of the organization toward the goal of political education. That the League of Women Voters has earned a reputation for being a nonpartisan organization known for publishing accurate and objective educational materials is directly the result of Sherwin's leadership. During the period in which she served as president, the league supported U.S. entry into the League of Nations and the adoption of a child labor amendment to the U.S. Constitution; it also called on Congress to establish a federal department of education.

An advocate for equal economic and educational opportunities for women, Sherwin was an early and persistent supporter of the right of women to serve on juries, and she encouraged women to take a more active part in politics. In 1933 she was the only nongovernmental person present at the signing of the Tennessee Valley Authority. In 1934 President Franklin D. Roosevelt appointed her to the National Consumers' Advisory Board of the National Recovery Administration and to the Federal Advisory Committee of the U.S. Employment Service.

Sherwin was called "Boo" by her niece and nephews, one of whom described her as "a determined intellectual, an emancipated champion of worthy causes, a fighter for women's rights, a woman of tireless energy, great intellectual capacity and absolutely no sense of humor." A commanding presence, she was inclined to take charge of any situation and through her work made many lasting friendships. In her later years she had the bearing of a "vigorous and intellectual Queen Victoria" (Prescott, pp. 9–10). Upon completion of her government service, Sherwin returned to Cleveland and divided her time between the family estate in nearby Kirtland and the townhouse in Cleveland that she designed. She died in Cleveland.

• The records of the League of Women Voters of the United States, deposited in the Manuscript Division of the Library of Congress, contain papers relating to Sherwin's presidency of that organization. The Schlesinger Library of Radcliffe College, Cambridge, Mass., has a collection of Sherwin's personal papers, including a photo album and scrapbooks relating to her family and career. That library's Woman's Rights Collection also contains papers relevant to her work for suffrage. Biographical information is available from Jean Glasscock, *Wellesley College, 1875–1975: A Century of Women* (1975), and in the autobiography of Sherwin's nephew, Orville Prescott, *The Five-Dollar Gold Piece: The Development of a Point of View* (1956). Sherwin's involvement with the League of Women Voters is discussed in J. Stanley Lemons, *The Woman Citizen: Social Feminism in the 1920s* (1973). See also Marian J. Morton, *Women in Cleveland: An Illustrated History* (1995), and David D. Van Tassel and John J. Grabowski, eds., *The Encyclopedia of Cleveland History* (1987). An obituary is in the *New York Times*, 10 July 1955.

KAREN VENTURELLA

SHERWOOD, Isaac Ruth (13 Aug. 1835–15 Oct. 1925), editor, soldier, and politician, was born in Stanford, Dutchess County, New York, the son of Aaron Sherwood and Maria Yeomans. Orphaned at age nine, he lived thereafter with his uncle Daniel Sherwood, who served in the New York State legislature. After attending local schools Isaac was able to study at the Hudson River Institute in Claverack, New York, from 1852 to 1854 and at Antioch College from 1854 to 1856. He briefly read law with Judge Hoogeboom in Hudson, New York, and he then attended Ohio Law College in Poland, Ohio, graduating in 1857.

While in college, Sherwood wrote many newspaper articles, and although he continued to pursue a legal education, his interest in journalism grew. Finally, in 1857 he abandoned law and purchased a weekly newspaper, the *Williams County Gazette*, in Bryan, Ohio. One of his early, memorable experiences as an editor came after publishing a favorable review of Walt Whitman's *Leaves of Grass* (1855), when the author sent him a letter of thanks and an autographed portrait. Sherwood was notable as an outspoken abolitionist, putting his paper in full mourning when John Brown was hung following his raid on Harpers Ferry, Virginia, in 1859. That year he married Katharine Margaret Brownlee; they had three children.

Sherwood's second profession, which was intertwined with his journalism, was politics. Soon after moving to Bryan, he served as town mayor, and in October 1860 he was elected probate judge of Williams County. However, after the outbreak of the Civil War and Abraham Lincoln's call for volunteers on 15 April 1861, Sherwood left his paper in his wife's hands and enlisted as a private. He was mustered out in August 1861. In September 1862 Sherwood resigned his judgeship, closed his paper, and reenlisted as a first lieutenant. During the war he saw considerable action and was steadily promoted, finally being brevetted brigadier general on 16 February 1865.

When the war ended Sherwood resigned his commission and moved to Toledo, where he had two important contacts: James Steedman, a journalist who had been his commander and friend during the war, and Alexander Brownlee, a former mayor (1857–1861) and a relative by marriage. Sherwood resumed his journalism career, becoming editor of the *Toledo Daily Commercial* as well as writing political editorials for the *Cleveland Leader*. Shortly after his arrival, Sherwood again sought public office, winning election as secretary of state for Ohio in 1868 and in 1870. His most notable action in this office was establishing the Bureau of Statistics in 1869. He was next elected to Congress, serving from 1873 to 1875.

At this point of rising expectations and prominence, Sherwood's political career was abruptly interrupted by a policy difference that changed his party allegiances. Because he opposed a strict hard money policy in favor of a more flexible currency system, he was denied renomination by the Republican party in his district. As a consequence he left the GOP for the National Greenback party, but in 1879 he responded to appeals from the Ohio Democratic party platform and its gubernatorial candidate, and thereafter he associated with that party.

Upon leaving Congress Sherwood purchased the *Toledo Journal*, which he edited until 1884, when he moved to Canton to edit the *Stark County Democrat* (later the *Canton News-Democrat*) until his return to Toledo in 1898. Except for election as a probate judge in 1878 and in 1881 (first as a Greenbacker and then as a Democrat), Sherwood did not seek office again until 1906, when he was seventy-one years old. Elected to Congress in that year, he was part of the Democratic resurgence in Ohio and other states from Illinois to New York that brought the party to majority status in the House in 1910.

Sherwood's activities in the House were very much shaped by his memories of the Civil War and his sense of the horrible consequences of war. Serving on the Committee on Invalid Pensions, of which he was chair from 1910 to 1918, he was an aggressive advocate of higher pensions for veterans. He sponsored over fifty pension bills, most notably a "Dollar-a-Day Pension Law" for Civil War veterans, which passed in 1912 and set a sliding scale of benefits. This committee experience also kept fresh in his mind the results of war, and as World War I was fought in Europe, Sherwood opposed American involvement. He was a vocal opponent of expenditures for military preparedness in 1916, and he was one of fifty congressmen—and only sixteen Democrats—who opposed the war declaration in 1917.

Despite the political jeopardy his antiwar vote created and the rising Republican tide in 1918, Sherwood survived that election, while five of his Ohio Democratic colleagues did not. However, he could not withstand the Republican landslide of 1920 and criticism of his opposition to the Volstead Act, and he suffered his first loss. He ran again in 1922 and won 51.3 percent of the vote, but in the following election he suffered his final defeat. He died in Toledo from complications stemming from a fire in his Toledo apartment.

Sherwood combined his military experience and his writing ability in two publications, *The Army Grayback, a Reminiscence* (1889), a humorous poem, and *Memories of the War* (1923). He shared an interest in writing with his wife, who published memorial poems relating to the Civil War and was an active journalist, working with Isaac on the *Toledo Journal*, writing features for the *National Tribune*, and serving as vice president of the Toledo Press Club.

Besides his activities regarding pensions and war, Sherwood achieved little national visibility. While he was not a major political leader, his combination of journalism and politics illuminates a pattern common to the era, and his departure from the Republican party over the money question reveals an important undercurrent in party politics of the Gilded Age. Finally, his attitude toward World War I reflects not only the view of other Democrats but also a distaste for war felt by many of the remaining Civil War veterans of both parties.

• Two useful articles are Virginia E. McCormick, "The Talented Sherwoods: Poets and Politicians," *Northwest Ohio Quarterly* 52 (1980): 244–53; and Francis P. Weisenburger, "General Isaac R. Sherwood," *Historical Society of Northwestern Ohio Quarterly Bulletin* 14 (1942): 42–54. Additional information is available in various biographical volumes, including Henry Howe, comp., *Historical Collections of Ohio* (1904); Harvey Scribner, *Memoirs of Lucas County and the City of Toledo* (1910); and N. O. Winter, *A History of Northwest Ohio* (1917). Sherwood's electoral fortunes are most easily seen in the *Guide to U.S. Elections* (1975), which lists his county and district votes for Congress, and in *Annual Report of the Secretary of State* (1868 and 1870), listing his votes for secretary of state. The most detailed study of his later political career is Walter A. Shreffler, "Toledo's Grand Old Warrior: The Congressional Career of General Isaac Ruth Sherwood, Civil War Hero and World War I Pacifist, 1906–24" (M.A. thesis, Univ. of Toledo, 1973). An obituary is in the *Toledo Blade*, 16 Oct. 1925.

PHILIP R. VANDERMEER

SHERWOOD, Lorenzo (1810–12 May 1869), attorney and politician, was born in Hoosick, Rensselaer County, New York, the son of Lemuel Sherwood, a merchant, and Sharon (maiden name unknown). Lorenzo Sherwood attended Bennington Academy in nearby Bennington, Vermont, and was for a short time its principal. He studied law, opened a practice, and at the same time edited a newspaper at Hamilton, Madison County, New York. His law partner was James Warren Nye, a Free Soil Democrat who joined the Republican party in the 1850s, was named governor of Nevada territory in 1861, and was elected U.S. senator from that state in 1865. In 1834 Lorenzo married Elsie Starr. That marriage ended soon after, and at some time in the 1830s he married Caroline Eldridge; they had one son.

In 1843 Sherwood was elected to the New York legislature, where he established a reputation as an expert on fiscal matters and government finance of internal improvements. He supported Michael Hoffman, an assemblyman from Herkimer County, who called for state financed and operated railroads rather than loaning government funds to private corporations. Sherwood also was a member of the State Constitutional Association, which lobbied for the New York constitutional convention of 1846.

Sherwood moved in 1849 to Galveston, Texas, where he established a law practice representing foreign shipping concerns in the local courts. He also became a major spokesman for the development of banking and railroads in Texas. As in New York, he supported the idea of state construction and operation of railroads. Backing what became known locally as the "State Plan" or "Sherwood Plan," he spoke at public meetings across the state and appeared at railroad conventions in 1853 and 1855. In 1853 he backed state senator John Dancy for the Democratic nomination for governor because of Dancy's support for his railroad ideas. In 1855 Sherwood ran successfully for the state legislature, promising to push a state program of railroad construction.

Sherwood had powerful allies, including Governor Elisha M. Pease, who had been converted to the plan, but his activities also put him into direct conflict with other powerful Democratic politicians and merchants. William P. Ballinger, Guy M. Bryan, Francis R. Lubbock, and Ashbel Smith were among these men. They supported private corporate development of railroads, backed by state credit, and saw Sherwood's proposals as a threat to their interests. As Sherwood secured more and more backers for his plan, his opponents destroyed him politically by accusing him of being an abolitionist. Sherwood was not an abolitionist, although he thought slavery was inefficient and immoral, but his opponents did not even allow him to defend himself. When he offered to explain himself in a public speech, they threatened dire consequences should he attempt it, and Sherwood was forced to resign from the legislature, effectively ending his chances to carry through the railroad plan.

Following this experience Sherwood withdrew from politics and devoted his attention to the support of several private railroads proposed out of Galveston. At the outbreak of the Civil War he was in the North buying railroad steel, and he remained with his family in New York City. During the war Sherwood associated with prominent abolitionists and Republican congressmen. He actively worked to secure help for Texas Unionist refugees and personally assisted William Alexander, another lawyer from Galveston.

Sherwood emerged from the war with radical views about Reconstruction. He advocated strong action against former secessionists and a military occupation of the South. He publicly opposed the policies of President Andrew Johnson, and he played a role in the organization of the Southern Loyalists convention that met at Philadelphia on 3–7 September 1866. At the convention he joined with other radicals proposing that suffrage be extended to blacks in the southern states as the only way that a loyal government could be secured.

In addition to his role in Reconstruction, Sherwood was active in New York Republican politics. He was also president of the National Cheap Freight Railroad League. He continued to practice law, and in 1866 he wrote the brief and delivered oral arguments before the U.S. Supreme Court in *The Steamer Peterhoff v. The United States*, which fixed principles for government blockade and contraband policies during wartime. He successfully argued on behalf of the owners of the English vessel—which had been seized by the U.S. Navy off St. Thomas and contained cargo destined for Matamoros for movement into the Confederate states—that the United States had no power to restrict trade between neutrals, even though the cargo consisted of contraband material intended for the South.

He died in Brooklyn at the home of a relative following a short illness.

• Sherwood left no personal papers. A collection of his published works, primarily newspaper and magazine clippings, that details some of his early career is in the Rosenberg Library, Galveston, Tex. The fullest description of his career can be found in Earl W. Fornell, *The Galveston Era: The Texas Crescent on the Eve of Secession* (1991). His obituary is in the *New York Times*, 13 May 1869.

CARL H. MONEYHON

SHERWOOD, Mary (31 March 1856–24 May 1935), physician, was born in Ballston Spa, New York, the daughter of Thomas Burr Sherwood, a lawyer and farmer, and Mary Frances Beattie. Sherwood was one of six children in an academic family: her sister Margaret Pollack Sherwood was a professor of English at Wellesley College, and her brother Sidney Sherwood was an associate professor of economics at the Johns Hopkins University until his premature death. After graduating Phi Beta Kappa from Vassar College in 1883, Sherwood taught chemistry at Vassar from 1883 to 1885 and astronomy and mathematics at the Packer Collegiate Institute in Brooklyn, New York, in 1885–1886. Faced with few choices for medical training in the United States, from 1886 to 1890 Sherwood studied medicine at and received her M.D. from the University of Zurich. There she met fellow physician Lilian Welsh, who became her professional partner and lifelong companion. The two women studied under some of the most brilliant scientists of the day and took one of the first courses in bacteriology ever given in the world.

In 1890 Sherwood joined part of her family in Baltimore, where her brother Sidney was working on his doctorate at the Johns Hopkins University. She established a medical practice in Baltimore and spent 1890–1891 as a graduate student in pathology at the Johns Hopkins University Medical School. There she worked in the laboratory of pathologist William Henry Welch and on the wards of physician William Osler and gynecologist Howard Kelly. In 1891 Sherwood was offered the prestigious position of a residency under Osler on the condition that another woman accept a residency at the same time. The second woman who was offered this position married before the position was to start, and because the hospital refused to accept a married woman as a resident, both women were denied this opportunity. Although disappointed, Sherwood was soon offered an assistantship to Kelly in his private work from 1891 to 1893. In the summer of 1892 Kelly gave Sherwood a place on his staff in gynecology at Johns Hopkins. According to a Vassar alumnae magazine, Sherwood received a substitute appointment in 1893 as a resident gynecologist at Johns Hopkins, "but by a recent resolution of the Medical Board no woman physician can hold a bona fide medical position" (*Vassar Miscellany* 23, no. 6 [1894]: 242).

In spite of the difficulty of becoming accepted into the local medical community, Sherwood persevered. In 1892, fourteen months after her arrival in Baltimore, Welsh joined her, and the two women established an office together. Sherwood lectured in pathology at the Woman's Medical College of Pennsylvania from 1893 to 1897 and in hygiene at Bryn Mawr College from 1894 to 1898. She simultaneously began working in the public health positions for which she is most remembered.

In 1894 Sherwood became director of health at the Bryn Mawr School for Girls in Baltimore, where she served until her death. From 1892 to 1910 she and Welsh worked as physicians to the Evening Dispensary for Working Women and Girls of Baltimore and as members of its board of managers. In their work at the dispensary, the two physicians, as Welsh explained, used "all our opportunities to instruct women in the hygiene of maternity and infancy, and to lead women to demand more enlightened care for themselves in childbirth and for their children" (Welsh, p. 58). After several decades of service to women and children, in 1919 Sherwood organized and developed the Baltimore City Health Department's Bureau of Child Welfare, which addressed the health and welfare of mothers and children, specifically focusing on prenatal care, care of mother and baby during the birthing process, and care of young children. Serving as its first director from 1919 to 1924, she became the first woman to head a municipal bureau in Baltimore.

While holding these professional positions, Sherwood also served on a number of municipal and state committees related to her work in medicine and public health. She was a member of the executive committee of the Babies' Milk Fund Association of Baltimore from its organization in 1904, member of the Board of Trustees of the Thomas Wilson Sanitarium, member of Baltimore's Public Bath Commission, member of the Board of Supervisors of City Charities (1896–1900), chair of the Midwifery Committee of the Medical and Chirurgical Faculty of Maryland (the state medical society; 1908–1916), and vice president and first female officer of the Medical and Chirurgical Faculty (1898–1899). In addition to her work on health care, Sherwood was also a suffragist, an active member of the League of Women Voters, and a trustee of Goucher College from 1923 until her death.

Sherwood died at her home in Baltimore. An editorial in the *Baltimore Sun* (26 May 1935) memorialized her as a "pioneer," "unconventional for her day in her ambitions," and "part of a determined movement which opened the halls of the universities and medical schools to women ambitious for professional achievement and which stirred a civic consciousness in women of charitable intentions."

• A few of Sherwood's letters from 1924 can be found in the Florence Rena Sabin Papers at the American Philosophical Society in Philadelphia. The best sources for Sherwood are Lilian Welsh, *Reminiscences of Thirty Years in Baltimore* (1925), and Florence R. Sabin, "Doctor Mary Sherwood," *Goucher Alumnae Quarterly* 13 (July 1935): 9–13. For information on Sherwood's position in the Medical and Chirurgical Faculty of Maryland, see Joseph E. Jensen, "Taking Stock: Med-Chi and Its Women Members," *Maryland State Medical Journal* 32 (Oct. 1983): 787–90. Other useful information is found in the Bryn Mawr School archives and the Vassar College alumnae records. An obituary is in the *Baltimore Sun*, 25 May 1935.

LAURA E. ETTINGER

SHERWOOD, Mary Elizabeth Wilson (27 Oct. 1826–12 Sept. 1903), socialite and writer, was born in Keene, New Hampshire, the daughter of James Wilson and Mary Richardson. Her father was a general in the U.S. Army and served as a congressional representative from New Hampshire. Known in the family as "Lizzie," she began to write for publication when young. Some contemporary sources say an essay on *Jane Eyre* in the *New York Tribune* appeared when she was just fifteen years old, another source reports she sold her first work at seventeen. In her memoir *An Epistle to Posterity* (1898) she says she was first published in Livermore's *Social Gazette* while still in school in Keene. Later she was sent to a boarding school in Boston to complete her education.

After the death of her mother, she became her father's hostess in Washington, D.C. (1847–1850), where she met many of the prominent literary and public figures of her day. Her delight in her experiences in Washington never left her. Comparing Washington's social life with her earlier life in Keene and a sojourn in the frontier cities of Chicago and Dubuque with her father in the early 1840s, she was convinced of the superiority of comfort and the civilized life. For the rest of her life she aggressively pursued high society, striving to keep a place for herself in the drawing rooms of the rich and famous in both the United States and Europe.

She married lawyer John Sherwood in 1851, and after a honeymoon trip in the West Indies they moved to New York City, where over the course of her life she resided in several hotels. They had four sons, two of whom died before her. After her marriage Sherwood gave readings in her home, some as benefits for the restoration of Mount Vernon, and she was also a volunteer worker for the Sanitary Commission during the Civil War. At the same time she wrote hundreds of poems, short stories, essays, and "letters" from her various travels, all written during the intervals of an intense social life.

Sherwood's poems, usually published either anonymously or under the initials M.E.W.S., are little distinguishable from the average newspaper verse of the mid-nineteenth century. These lines from a sonnet on the death of William Prescott, whom she had known as a young girl (first printed in a newspaper and then in George Ticknor's biography of Prescott), are typical: "Two worlds shall weep for thee, the Old, the New, / . . . / While angels on imperishable scroll / Record the wondrous beauty of thy soul."

In contrast to the florid style of her poetry, her gossipy insider reports in *Royal Girls and Royal Courts* (1887) and on her travels were written in a clear, often humorous style. Her writing was lively and descriptive. But she was an inveterate name dropper, ever ready to sprinkle a page with references to men and women who were famous, infamous, or rich, even if only peripherally connected to the subject at hand.

Sherwood's delight in "society," her yearly travels to Europe, and what her grandchildren remembered as an extravagant taste in clothing, jewelry, and household items, soon placed the family in serious financial difficulties. An additional stress came when John Sherwood developed mental and physical disabilities that greatly curtailed his ability to help Mary sustain the life to which she had grown accustomed. While maintaining a genteel fiction that she wrote merely because "hers was not a nature to be idle" (Harvier, p. 13), she wrote increasingly more, usually reworking her experiences into pieces for the periodicals. She tried a novel in 1878, *The Sarcasm of Destiny; or, Nina's Experience*, another in 1882, *A Transplanted Rose*, and a final attempt at the long form with *Sweet-Brier* in 1889. None of these was very successful. However, her opinions on society and manners were well received (in her obituary the *New York World* characterized her as a "female Ward McAllister"), and her *Manners and Social Usages* (1884) went through multiple editions. Sherwood recognized that Americans felt most comfortable in a freer, less-constricted social atmosphere, but she also knew that those who were new members of the middle and upper classes were unsure of themselves and interested in acquiring skill in the activities that represented and maintained class distinctions. She was trusted by her readers as a guide who knew the intricacies of European etiquette and had adapted what was best in that practice to American culture.

After her husband died, Sherwood continued to write. Her own health was precarious during her later years, but even while invalided by arthritis she managed to continue producing criticism and memoirs. Her obituary in the *New York Times* (15 Sept. 1903) noted that she had been writing for the *Times's Saturday Review of Books* for the last ten years. She died in New York City, still interested in a social world that had changed greatly but which she still admired. She ended *An Epistle to Posterity* with some sorrow that ostentatious displays of wealth were no longer admired ("Whose business is it how rich people spend their money? . . . formerly we accepted the situation . . . and enjoyed the ball") but also with admiration for what she saw coming ("The young women, what can they not learn, what can they not achieve, with Columbia University annex thrown open to them? In this great outlook for women's broader intellectual development I see the great sunburst of the future").

• Sherwood's *Here & There & Everywhere* (1898) and her other prose works are probably the best sources of information on this complex woman, since they reflect both her positive and negative qualities. Contemporary references to Sherwood, such as the entry in Frances E. Willard and Mary A. Livermore, *A Woman of the Century* (1893), and Frances W. Halsey, *Women Authors of Our Day in Their Homes* (1903), are uniformly positive. Particularly admiring is Evelyn Baker Harvier's biographical sketch, which was printed as an introduction to the collection of Sherwood's poetry that Harvier edited in 1892. John Mason Brown's treatment of Sherwood in his biography of her grandson Robert E. Sherwood, *The Worlds of Robert Sherwood* (1962), is much less sympathetic.

JoAnn E. Castagna

SHERWOOD, Robert Emmet (4 Apr. 1896–14 Nov. 1955), writer, editor, and critic, was born in New Rochelle, New York, the son of Arthur Murray Sherwood, a stockbroker and member of the New York Stock Exchange, and Rosina Emmet, an artist and illustrator. He was named for an ancestor, Robert Emmet, the Irish patriot. When Sherwood was one year old, the family moved to New York City. After 1906, summers were spent at Skene Wood, in Westport, New York, on Lake Champlain, "the most beautiful place in the world." Sherwood's writing career began at age seven, when he edited a hand-printed magazine called *The Children's Life*. However, the magazine had limited circulation, with Sherwood the main contributor and his sisters the sole subscribers. A year later he rewrote the ending of Charles Dickens's *A Tale of Two Cities* and an ending to Dickens's unfinished *The Mystery of Edwin Drood*. By age eleven he had written his first play, *Tom Ruggles' Surprise*.

In 1905 Sherwood was sent to the Fay School in Southborough, Massachusetts, but health problems necessitated his leaving after two years. From 1909 to 1914 Sherwood attended Milton Academy in Massachusetts, where he published stories and poems in the school's monthly magazine, *Orange and Blue*. Although his poor scholastic record yielded no diploma, ironically, the student body elected him class valedictorian. After a summer of intense tutoring, he entered Harvard in the fall of 1914. He was editor of the freshman *Redbook* but failed freshman English. His grades were poor, but he wrote for both the *Harvard Lampoon* and the Hasty Pudding Club. As a junior he edited the *Lampoon* (Sherwood's father was a founder of the magazine). One of his best issues was a parody of the magazine *Vanity Fair*.

Sherwood's first play for Hasty Pudding was *A White Elephant*, staged during the spring of 1916, but because of academic problems, his name was not on the program. In 1917 he wrote *Barnum Was Right* with Samuel P. Sears; the production was canceled because of war. In June 1917 Sherwood left Harvard to serve in the First World War. He was rejected by both the U.S. Army and the navy because of his unusual height of six feet, seven inches. Undaunted, Sherwood took the train to Montreal and on 3 July 1917 enlisted in the Canadian Expeditionary Force. He was assigned to the Forty-second Battalion of the Fifth Royal Highlanders, the Canadian Black Watch. On active duty in France, he was gassed at Vimy ridge in July 1918. He insisted on walking back to his unit after treatment and suffered permanent heart damage. In August he went "over the top" at Amiens and was gassed again and hit in both legs with shrapnel. He spent the rest of the war in military hospitals. After his discharge in January 1919, he returned home to New York City.

In May 1919 Frank Crowninshield, editor of *Vanity Fair*, remembering the *Lampoon* parody, offered Sherwood a job. His first article was "The Bloodlust on Broadway," a review of violent death in contemporary drama. Two lifelong friendships with Robert Benchley and Dorothy Parker sprang from his brief tenure at the magazine. With them, Sherwood became part of the Round Table at the Algonquin Hotel, a select gathering of Broadway writers, critics, and playwrights. When Parker was fired from *Vanity Fair*, Sherwood left in protest. He was hired by Harvard's Hasty Pudding Club to rewrite and produce *Barnum Was Right*.

In 1920 Sherwood began work for *Life* magazine and was joined almost immediately by Benchley and Parker. At *Life* Sherwood became a film reviewer, and by January 1921 he had his own column, "The Silent Drama." He also reviewed films for the New York *Herald*, *McCall's*, and *Photoplay*. Sherwood was a pioneer movie critic, and his "generally thoughtful" comments were highly regarded. In 1924 Sherwood assumed editorship of *Life*, where he remained until a difference of opinion forced his resignation in 1928. After a brief stint as literary editor at *Scribner's*, Sherwood quit the job market to concentrate on his burgeoning career as a playwright.

While working for *Life*, Sherwood continued to frequent the Algonquin Round Table. One of the members was Mary Brandon, an actress remotely related to Booth Tarkington. She and Sherwood married in 1922; they had one daughter. The marriage ended in divorce in 1934. In 1935 Sherwood married Madeline Hurlock Connelly, former wife of playwright Marc Connelly. They had no children.

Stimulated by his successful *Barnum Was Right*, Sherwood wrote his first professional play, *The Dawn Man*, in 1922. It was not well received. Undeterred, Sherwood continued to write. His first success was the 1927 comedy *The Road to Rome*. His next play, *The Love Nest* (1927), closed after twenty-three performances. His subsequent plays—*The Queen's Husband* (1926), *Waterloo Bridge* (1930), *Reunion in Vienna* (1931), and *The Petrified Forest* (1935)—were all hits.

Sherwood's first Pulitzer Prize was awarded for *Idiot's Delight* (1936), starring Alfred Lunt and Lynn Fontanne. *Abe Lincoln in Illinois* (1938), Sherwood's most famous play, secured him a second Pulitzer Prize. This play was also the first production of the Playwrights Company formed in March 1937, with Sherwood, Maxwell Anderson, S. N. Behrman, Sidney Howard, and Elmer Rice as partners. Sherwood was the company's first president.

There Shall Be No Night (1940), about the Russian invasion of Finland, earned him a third Pulitzer and brought the horror of the war in Europe to Broadway. Concerned with the inroads of fascism in Europe, the pacifist Sherwood donated most of his royalties from the play to aid Finland and Britain. Sherwood became a member of the Committee to Defend America by Aiding the Allies in 1940. After Pearl Harbor he became a speech writer for President Franklin D. Roosevelt. In 1942 he was appointed director of the Overseas Branch of the Office of War Information in London. Having worked closely with Roosevelt and Works Projects Administration head Harry S. Hopkins, Sherwood, after their deaths, wrote *Roosevelt and Hopkins, an Intimate History* (1948). Sorting through forty filing cases of paper that Hopkins had accumulated, Sherwood spent thirty months writing this "perceptive, detailed study." The book resulted in a fourth Pulitzer Prize, this one in history.

Sherwood was also in demand as a screenwriter. From 1926 to 1953 he worked on twenty-three films. In 1924 he rewrote the subtitles for *The Hunchback of Notre Dame*, and in 1931 he wrote "snappy dialog" for Howard Hughes on *The Age of Love*. Other films included *The Scarlet Pimpernel* (1935), written with Arthur Wimperis; *The Ghost Goes West* (1936); *The Adventures of Marco Polo* (1938); *Rebecca* (1940), written with Joan Harrison; and *The Bishop's Wife* (1947), with Leonardo Bercovici. Sherwood wrote the screenplay to his own plays *Idiot's Delight* (1939) and *Abe Lincoln in Illinois* (1940). His screenplay *The Best Years of Our Lives* (1946) won an Academy Award for best picture. He continued to write until his death in New York City.

Although known principally as a playwright, Sherwood was a talented screenwriter and historian. In an increasingly violent world, Sherwood, an ardent pacifist since the First World War, was sympathetic to the individual. Yet his burning desire for peace warred with his knowledge that, in order to accomplish this peace, fighting was sometimes necessary to ensure freedom. In the words of Dr. Valkonen in *There Shall Be No Night*, "There is no coming to consciousness without pain."

• Promptbooks and typescripts of published and unpublished plays, scrapbook clippings, and photographs are in the Billy Rose Theatre Collection at the New York Public Library for the Performing Arts, Lincoln Center. The Houghton Library at Harvard and the Wisconsin Center for Film and Theatre Research at the University of Wisconsin, Madison, also have materials. Books published on Sherwood include John Mason Brown, *The Worlds of Robert E. Sherwood: Mirror to His Times, 1896–1939* (1965) and *The Ordeal of a Playwright: Robert E. Sherwood and the Challenge of War* (1970). See also Walter J. Meserve, *Robert E. Sherwood: Reluctant Moralist* (1970), and S. N. Behrman, "Old Monotonous," in his *The Suspended Drawing Room* (1965). Maxwell Anderson, "Robert E. Sherwood," *Theatre Arts*, Feb. 1956, pp. 26–27, and Anderson's "Eulogy," delivered at Sherwood's funeral and published in the *New York Times*, 17 Nov. 1955, are testaments to Anderson's relationship with Sherwood. An obituary is in the *New York Times*, 15 Nov. 1955.

MARCIA B. DINNEEN

SHERWOOD, Thomas Adiel (2 June 1834–11 Nov. 1918), lawyer and judge on the Supreme Court of Missouri (1872–1902), was born in Eatonton, Putnam County, Georgia, the son of Adiel Sherwood, a clergyman and educator, and Emma C. Heriot. In 1832 his father, a Baptist minister in Georgia, founded a school in Eatonton that later became Mercer University. In 1841 Adiel Sherwood left his professorship at Mercer to become president of Shurtleff College in Upper Alton, Illinois. In 1848 he moved to the presidency of Masonic College in Lexington, Missouri, and a year later to a ministry in Cape Girardeau, Missouri. The father's professional path shaped the son's education. Along this way Sherwood, like his father, became a dedicated Baptist.

Thomas Sherwood began his undergraduate education at Mercer and finished at Shurtleff College. After moving to Missouri in 1852, he taught school from time to time. He studied law and graduated from the Cincinnati Law School. By the time Sherwood graduated in 1857, the school had become one of the more prominent in the field of legal education.

Sherwood was admitted to the bar at Charleston in Mississippi County, Missouri, in 1857. He moved to southwestern Missouri and practiced in Neosho and Mount Vernon, where he married Mary Ellen Young in 1861. They had eight children. In 1863 Sherwood and his brother-in-law Henry C. Young became law partners at Springfield. He "rode circuit," but his legal tastes ran to office and appellate practice rather than trial work. Although Sherwood was affiliated with the cause of the Union during the Civil War and was known as a "Union man," he did not serve in the Union army.

Sherwood was elected to the Supreme Court of Missouri in 1872 in an era of Democratic party domination

of the state that lasted until the turn of the century. His stance as a Democrat of conservative leanings fit the times, and important party figures were instrumental in his nomination. Sherwood was reelected in 1882 and again in 1892 to ten-year terms, and served as chief justice by seniority from 1876 to 1883 and by election from 1891 to 1892.

In judicial outlook and temperament he leaned toward strict construction of constitutions, careful maintenance of separation of powers, and distrust of concentrations of federal power at the expense of state governments or private individuals. These sentiments were not unusual for a state appellate judge in post–Civil War America. Sherwood developed a reputation for frequent and effective dissents, and he was seldom ambiguous in his disagreement with his colleagues. Sherwood dissented in *Fields v. Maloney* (1883), which concerned judicial jurisdiction over land disputes. His dissent, which branded his colleagues "radically wrong," later became law and allowed for the sensible and practical amendment of pleadings. Such was the case with many of Sherwood's dissents in areas ranging from forgiveness of technical error to allow a widow's dower rights, as in *Lincoln v. Thompson* (1882), to a criminal defendant's plea of alibi without fully establishing its existence, as in *State v. Jennings* (1883). These dissents contributed to his reputation as a protector of individual rights. And as one newspaper noted concerning his nationally significant opinion in *Marx & Haas Jeans Clothing Co. v. Watson* (1902), in which the First Amendment precluded an injunction against a labor boycott, there is not "an atom of aristocratic or plutocratic tendency in his composition."

Sherwood's public persona included a reputation for "caustic severity," tendencies to the austere, and "an iron will that nothing save reason can swerve." In private and among intimates he was known to sing a good song and tell a good tale.

In 1902 he sought and expected nomination to run for a fourth term. After an intense nightlong session of the Democratic State Judicial Convention, however, he was not among the three nominees selected from a field of twelve. Sherwood's own "strong following . . . was unable to break the strong combination against him." This was the apparent consequence of the accumulated enmities of three decades on the bench and concerns about his age. Nothing ever came of the occasional mention of his name "for higher judicial honors."

After leaving the bench, Sherwood wrote *Commentaries on the Criminal Law of Missouri* (1907), a thousand-page treatise, both descriptive and argumentative, "with words of disapprobation where disapprobation seemed to be demanded." In 1915 he wrote a short and less formal monograph, *An Inquiry into the Constitutional Validity of Divers Acts of the Present Occupant of the Presidential Chair*. Its thesis was that a president is restricted to the powers literally conferred on him by the Constitution, and that President Woodrow Wilson had exceeded those because of "overvaulting and unscrupulous ambition." Thus, he argued that Wilson had no authority to send a representative to California to lobby the legislature not to enact an "anti-alien land law." Similarly, he felt that Wilson departed from constitutional principles requiring separation of powers when he recommended amendment of existing federal statutes or opposed pending bills. To Sherwood such actions took the president into the constitutional domain of Congress. Sherwood thought impeachment the appropriate remedy for Wilson's misconduct but considered it unlikely because, he believed, Wilson controlled Congress.

Also after leaving the court Sherwood practiced law in St. Louis with his son in 1903–1904 and then in Springfield with the firm of Sherwood, Young and Lyon. Several years before his death he and his wife moved to Long Beach, California, where another son was an attorney. Thomas Sherwood died in Long Beach and was buried there.

Thomas Adiel Sherwood was perhaps the dominant figure in the Missouri judiciary in the late nineteenth century. With his emphasis on constitutional literalness and a fierce determination to preserve individual rights, Sherwood contributed to the creation of a jurisprudential model that became a theme and a characteristic of much in the Missouri judiciary in the twentieth century.

• For further information on Thomas Adiel Sherwood see J. O. Boyd, "Thirty Years a Justice," *American Law Review* 48 (1914): 481–97; Howard L. Conard, *Encyclopedia of the History of Missouri*, vol. 5 (1901); A. J. D. Stewart, *The History of the Bench and Bar of Missouri* (1898); Return I. Holcombe, ed., *History of Greene County, Missouri* (1883); and Louis C. Krauthoff, "The Supreme Court of Missouri," *The Green Bag* 3 (1891): 185–87. Obituaries are in the *Springfield Daily Leader*, 25 Nov. 1918, and the *Jefferson City Democratic Tribune*, 26 Nov. 1918. A "Memorial of Hon. Thos. A. Sherwood" is in *Proceedings of the Missouri Bar Association* 5 (1919): 217.

ALFRED S. NEELY

SHERWOOD, Thomas Kilgore (25 July 1903–14 Jan. 1976), chemical engineer and educator, was born in Columbus, Ohio, the son of Milton Worthington and Sadie D. Tackaberry. His family soon moved to Montreal, Quebec, Canada, where he spent his youth.

After completing his bachelor of science degree at McGill University in 1923, Sherwood began graduate studies at the Massachusetts Institute of Technology (MIT), a leading center for chemical engineering education, where he worked with W. H. Adams and Warren K. Lewis. An outstanding student, he served as assistant or research assistant from 1924 (when he received his S.M.) to 1928. In the meantime, he began pursuing doctoral research on drying solids under Lewis. Sherwood married Betty Macdonald in 1927 while still attending MIT. They had three children before her death in 1950. Sherwood remarried, to Virginia Howell Smith, in 1953; they had no children.

In 1928 Sherwood was appointed assistant professor of chemical engineering at Worcester Polytechnic Institute. While teaching at Worcester, he completed his dissertation, receiving his Sc.D. from MIT in 1929. In 1930 he returned to MIT as an assistant professor. He remained there for the next thirty-nine years. He was promoted to associate professor in 1933 and to professor in 1941. For twelve years (1934–1946) he was the principal administrator of the graduate program in chemical engineering. He also served six years (1946–1952) as MIT's dean of engineering, guiding its engineering programs through the difficult post–World War II transition. He concluded his career at MIT as its first Lammot duPont Professor of chemical engineering (1965–1969).

Sherwood made numerous contributions to chemical engineering pedagogy, publishing seminal textbooks in a number of areas. His key work was *Absorption and Extraction* (1937), which was revised with coauthors as late as 1975 (under the title *Mass Transfer*). As the first substantive text dealing with mass transfer and a standard reference work for decades to come, it significantly influenced the field. In 1939 Sherwood published *Applied Mathematics in Chemical Engineering* with C. E. Reed. It, too, went through several revisions, the last in 1957. In 1958 he coauthored *Properties of Gases and Liquids*; subsequent editions appeared in 1966 and 1977. He also coauthored *The Role of Diffusion in Catalysis* and *A Course in Process Design* in 1963.

Sherwood's pedagogical contributions went beyond authoring the textbooks used by his and others' students. He was very well liked by the graduate students who worked under him. They appreciated his warmth, charm, thoughtfulness, and sense of humor. When dealing with students, Sherwood generally focused on the positive, but when he had to criticize, he did it in a jovial and caring manner that made the criticism easy to swallow.

Sherwood's research work at MIT focused on "mass transfer," the movement of chemical substances from one phase (gas, liquid, solid) to another. He carried out pioneering work on controlled mass transfer in packed absorption towers and on both the absorption and diffusion of substances in gas streams. He also followed up his dissertation work on drying with additional research on heat transfer phenomena. By the end of the 1930s Sherwood was perhaps the leading American authority on mass transfer under molecular and turbulent flow conditions and mass transfer theory. He was an important consultant in the development of the first commercial, heat-operated, absorption refrigeration equipment for air conditioning.

In 1940, as World War II approached, Sherwood worked with the National Defense Research Committee of the Office of Scientific Research and Development (OSRD) to identify and recruit chemical engineers for defense-related projects. From 1940 until 1946 he served as technical aide, section chief, and division member of the National Defense Research Committee. He worked on or helped supervise the development of low-temperature hydraulic fluids, antifouling paints, large smoke-screen generators, concentrated hydrogen peroxide, photoflash bombs, and aviation oxygen masks. In 1942 he also served as a consultant to the Baruch Committee on synthetic rubber development, and in 1944 he served as a member of the Whitman Committee, which was concerned with jet propulsion. In 1944 OSRD sent Sherwood to Europe to gather scientific intelligence, and in 1948 the government awarded Sherwood the U.S. Medal of Merit for his services.

After World War II, Sherwood continued his research in mass transfer and heat transfer phenomena. In 1950, for example, Sherwood published a seminal paper on turbulent transport phenomena, quantifying hitherto unquantified relationships relating to the viscous sublayers and initiating modern research in turbulent transport phenomena.

Because Sherwood recognized the limits of mathematical analysis in practical chemical engineering and because separation processes involving mass transfer were central to the chemical industry, Sherwood was extensively used as an industrial consultant. He worked for many years with companies such as Pfizer and Union Oil. As a consultant, he contributed to the development of chemical processes involving sulfur dioxide removal from stack gases, penicillin manufacturing, freeze-drying of blood, and manufacturing of vinyl acetate and oxo alcohols. He also served as technical adviser of the Office of Saline Water of the U.S. Department of the Interior (1952–1961) and on the National Research Council's Committee on Air Quality Management (1967–1973).

Sherwood was a prolific author; he published around 120 technical papers in addition to the books noted above. In several areas he developed procedures and data still used by engineers in the design of chemical process equipment.

In Sherwood's later years he received numerous honors. In 1958 he was elected to the National Academy of Sciences, and he was a founding member of the National Academy of Engineers (1964). He received an honorary life membership in the Canadian Institute of Chemistry. The American Institute of Chemical Engineers presented him its William H. Walker Award (1941), Founder's Award (1963), and Warren K. Lewis Award (1972), and the American Chemical Society presented him its E. V. Murphee Award (1973). But perhaps his most important honor came from his colleagues, who named the dimensionless number used in mass transfer correlations the "Sherwood number" in his honor.

Sherwood retired from MIT in 1969 but immediately accepted an appointment as a visiting professor at the University of California at Berkeley. He continued in that position until his death in Berkeley.

• Sherwood's papers are located in the Archives and Special Collections of MIT, although the collection is rather small. The best published source for biographical information is the opening pages of *Industrial and Engineering Chemistry Fundamentals* 16, no. 1 (1977), published at his death. It includes short remembrances by several former associates. The Na-

tional Academy of Engineering, *Memorial Tributes* 1 (1979): 246–50, and *Modern Scientists and Engineers*, vol. 3 (1960), also have short biographical sketches.

TERRY S. REYNOLDS

SHERWOOD, William Hall (31 Jan. 1854–7 Jan. 1911), piano virtuoso and music educator, was born in Lyons, New York, the son of Lyman H. Sherwood, an Episcopal minister, and Mary Balis. Sherwood's early musical instruction came from his father, who in 1854 had established the Lyons Musical Academy, and from Edward Heimberger in Rochester and Jan Pychowski in Geneseo. His progress was rapid, and in 1866 he became a teacher in his father's academy. While still in his mid-teens, Sherwood attended William Mason's Normal Institute in Binghamton.

Encouraged by Mason, Sherwood went to Germany, where, between 1871 and 1876, he studied theory and composition with Ernst Richter, Karl Doppler, and Carl Weitzmann; organ with Scotson Clark; and piano with Theodor Kullak, Ludwig Deppe, and Franz Liszt. During these years he performed with notable success throughout Germany. He was particularly praised in Berlin for his playing of the Chopin Fantasy in F Minor on a program in March 1872 shared with fellow budding virtuosos Moritz Moskowski, Jean-Louis Nicodé, and Xaver Scharwenka. The following season Sherwood's performance of Beethoven's *Emperor* Concerto, conducted by Royal Cappellmeister Richard Wüerst, was enthusiastically received, and additional performances had to be scheduled. Sherwood met Edvard Grieg in Leipzig and received coaching from the composer on Grieg's Piano Concerto in A Minor, which Sherwood performed with the Hamburg Philharmonic and later introduced to American audiences.

Sherwood returned to the United States in 1876 and began teaching at the New England Conservatory of Music in Boston. In the early summer of 1876 he made his American debut as a soloist with the Theodore Thomas Orchestra at the Philadelphia Centennial Exhibition, performing the Schubert-Liszt "Wanderer" Fantasy in C Major. The ovation of the large audience—8,000 people according to some reports—paved the way for ten more appearances with that orchestra during the following year. In the late 1870s Sherwood played many joint recitals with his first wife, Mary Fay, an American pianist whom he had married in Germany in 1874; they had three children. (Liszt was godfather to their first daughter.) Throughout his life Sherwood maintained an arduous schedule of recitals and appearances with major orchestras. He is reported to have had more than 100 playing engagements during 1908 and 1909.

In the late 1880s Sherwood moved from Boston to New York. Following his divorce he married one of his Boston students, Estelle Abrams of Monongahela, Pennsylvania, in 1887; they had two children. In New York Sherwood had "every expectation of permanence," but he was soon offered a position at the Chicago Conservatory of Music. In a letter dated 12 October 1888 to Frederick Grant Gleason, the composer and critic who later became director of the theory department of the conservatory, Sherwood stated his desire for "superior studio facilities," "control of the Piano Department," the use of some of his pupils as assistants, and $10,000 a year.

Sherwood moved to Chicago and joined the faculty of the Chicago Conservatory in September 1889. In addition to his usual touring, he appeared in many faculty concerts, often providing comments about the compositions played. He thus pioneered the idea of the lecture-recital. Sherwood regularly programmed music by American composers such as Edward MacDowell, John Knowles Paine, Gleason, Edgar Stillman Kelley, and William Mason.

Sherwood himself wrote well-crafted piano pieces, which were published under fifteen opus numbers, and made piano arrangements of music by other composers, including an organ fugue by Rheinberger, a gavotte from Gleason's opera *Otho Visconti*, and the "Royal Gaelic March" from Kelley's *Music to Macbeth*. Sherwood prepared many instructional editions of works from the standard piano repertory. He often employed symbols of his own invention to indicate refinements of accentuation, phrasing, pedaling, and dynamic shading, and he sometimes included extended introductory remarks. He also published short articles and pamphlets concerning piano technique and music education.

In the summer of 1889, a few weeks before he began work at the Chicago Conservatory, Sherwood became head of the piano department at the Chautauqua Assembly in western New York. He returned to Chautauqua each summer for twenty-two years, and there he offered interpretation classes and lectures with illustrations as well as individual piano lessons. He gave solo recitals, joint recitals with the resident violin virtuosos—Bernhard Listemann from 1893 to 1898, and Sol Marcosson in later years—and played musical examples for lectures given by other faculty members. Sherwood's extensive repertory, prodigious memory, gracefulness as a commentator, and his uncompromising artistic idealism made him admirably suited to the cultural and educational atmosphere at Chautauqua.

The New York Symphony Orchestra, under Walter Damrosch, gave a concert at Chautauqua in July 1909. The orchestra returned the next summer, and Sherwood was the featured soloist in a performance of the first movement of the MacDowell Piano Concerto no. 1 in A Minor. The orchestra's concerts stimulated an interest in symphonic music at Chautauqua, which led to the establishment of summer residencies by visiting orchestras and eventually, in 1929, to the founding of the Chautauqua Symphony Orchestra.

Sherwood's tenure at the Chicago Conservatory terminated when he established his own school in 1897. In the August 23–24 issue of the *Chautauqua Assembly Herald*, an advertisement appeared for the Sherwood Piano School in Steinway Hall, Chicago. The advertisement stated, in part: "Among the most necessary accessories of piano playing are harmony, counterpoint and general musical analysis. These studies will be taught with particular reference to their relation to piano playing and interpretation." The name of the school was soon changed to the Sherwood Music School and later to the Sherwood Conservatory of Music. Over the years not only the name but also the character of the school changed. At one time, the institution included extension centers with affiliated teachers who, using specially edited music and texts, made instruction resembling that offered at the main school in Chicago available in geographically scattered locations. In the early 1990s the school phased out its collegiate programs and has since operated as a community-focused music school. In every stage of its evolution, the Sherwood Conservatory has reflected the educational ideas and standards of its founder. Sherwood died in Chicago following a stroke.

• Several brief biographical sketches were published during Sherwood's lifetime. One article, "Mr. and Mrs. Wm. H. Sherwood," appeared in *Brainard's Musical World*, vol. 17 (1880), pp. 66–67. A "Biographical Sketch of W. H. Sherwood," *The Etude* 2 (1884): 207–8, includes an extensive repertoire list and selected press notices. W. S. B. Mathews, "Sherwood: An American Master of Piano" *Music* 11 (Feb. 1897): 339–47, is both a personal memoir and an appreciative evaluation by a friend and fellow pianist. A later perspective on Sherwood's career is found in Edith Bane, "How an American Pioneer Blazed a Trail in His Native Land" *Musical America*, 27 June 1925, pp. 7, 19. Information concerning Sherwood's student years in Germany is scattered in the collection of Amy Fay's letters, published as *Music Study in Germany* (1881). Many of Sherwood's performances during his years of residence in Boston are reported in various issues of *Dwight's Journal of Music* (1876–1880), and many of his programs at the Chicago Conservatory are contained in the personal scrapbooks of Frederick Grant Gleason, now at the Newberry Library, Chicago. Sherwood's activities at Chautauqua are recounted in L. Jeanette Wells, *A History of the Music Festival at Chautauqua Institution 1874 to 1957* (1958), and in the files of the *Chautauqua Assembly Herald* (later the *Chautauquan Daily*) and the *Chautauquan Weekly* in the Smith Memorial Library at Chautauqua. Informative notices and tributes following his death include those in the *Chicago Tribune*, 8 and 15 Jan. 1911, the *Rochester Democrat Chronicle*, 8 Jan. 1911, the *Chautauquan Weekly*, 12 and 19 Jan. 1911, and *The Musician*, Apr.–May 1911.

HERBERT S. LIVINGSTON

SHEVLIN, Thomas Leonard (1 Mar. 1883–29 Dec. 1915), college athlete and football coach, was born in Muskegon, Minnesota, the son of Thomas Henry Shevlin, a wealthy lumberman, and Alice Hall. A capable student at the Hill School in Pottstown, Pennsylvania (1897–1902), Shevlin starred in football, baseball, and hockey (he was captain of the 1902 team). In 1902 he threw the twelve-pound hammer a world record 187'9". To keep himself in physical condition, he employed a personal trainer. During four years at Yale College (B.A., 1906), Shevlin played varsity football (he was captain his senior year) and was on the track team. At the summer 1904 dual track meet in which Harvard-Yale competed against Oxford-Cambridge, Shevlin placed first with a twelve-pound hammer throw of 152′8″. However, he left the varsity baseball team after his freshman year, because his play fell short of his expectations.

Strength and speed made the 5′9″, 190-pound Shevlin one of Yale's most outstanding football players. After being shifted from right tackle to right end on the "Irish Line," Shevlin claimed, "In the four years I played football no one ever made a run around my end!" He twice ran back opponents' kickoffs for touchdowns. From 1902 through 1905 Yale teams won 42 games, including 35 shutouts, four of them over Harvard. Yale defeated Princeton three times, losing only in 1903. Their only other loss during his playing days came in 1904 to the U.S. Military Academy, with which Yale also had its only tie in 1902. Under the flamboyant Shevlin as captain, Yale was undefeated in 1905, scoring 222 points to 4 against ten teams and shutting out nine of them. Yale became the Big Three champion and was co-national champion with the University of Chicago. To Yale's 20–0 defeat of Army, Shevlin contributed a two-point safety. The Yale players took off their pads to gain speed in their 53–0 victory over Columbia. In Yale's shutout of Harvard, Shevlin tackled an opponent who, although it was not called by the umpire, had made a fair catch. Indeed, the general roughness, even brutality, of play in 1905 led to the establishment of the Intercollegiate Athletic Association of the United States (which in 1910 became the National Collegiate Athletic Association) and the legalization of a limited forward pass.

Three times Shevlin was one of twelve players chosen by Walter Camp for his first-team All-America football squad (1902, 1904, 1905); in 1903 Shevlin was on Camp's second team. He also was selected as an end on four All-Time All-Player teams: by Camp (1910), by Fielding Yost and by John W. Heisman on their separate lists in *Leslie's Weekly* (1920), and by Walter W. Liggett in *Sportlife* (1925). Shevlin was among the ends on Allison Danzig's all-time specialists list. In 1954 he was elected to the National Football Foundation Hall of Fame and the Helms Athletic Foundation College Football Hall of Fame.

Yale president Arthur Twining Hadley complimented Shevlin on "wisely" spending his generous allowance and on financially helping other students. But Shevlin also liked to race his Mercedes against trains, and he was occasionally fined for speeding. While he did not drink, he began smoking high-priced cigars during his senior year. Perhaps because of his boastfulness he was not tapped by any of Yale's senior societies.

After a year learning the lumber business in the Northwest, Shevlin became his father's assistant in the firm. In 1909 he was named company secretary and then vice president. He married Elizabeth Brannin Sherley of Louisville, Kentucky, in 1909; they had two children. On his father's death in 1912, he and his two sisters formed the Shevlin Company, of which he was president, to control the $1.5 million family estate.

For several seasons assisting University of Minnesota football coach Henry L. Williams, a Yale alumnus, Shevlin also helped the Yale team before major games. Called to Yale as an emergency football coach in 1910 to replace Ted Coy, Shevlin recognized that its graduate coaching system was antiquated and that it must hire a full-time professional coach, as Harvard alumni had in 1908. Wearing a big fur coat, boutonniere, and derby and carrying a diamond-studded cane, he galvanized Yale with his enthusiasm and taught the players the "Minnesota shift," an offensive maneuver designed to catch the defensive team somewhat off-guard. Yale, despite defeats by Army and Brown and a scoreless tie with Vanderbilt, overcame Princeton and held Harvard to a scoreless tie, thereby becoming Big Three champion. Helping out from 1911 through 1913, Shevlin was again called back in 1915 to coach a weak, fumble-prone Yale team to a 13–7 win over Princeton. But in losing for the fourth year in a row to Harvard, Yale suffered its worst defeat (41–0) and its first losing season (4–5). Afterward, Shevlin commented, "You just can't make two lemonades out of one lemon."

A cold that Shevlin contracted developed into pneumonia after he returned home from a rest in California. Although he was examined by four physicians and a specialist, he died in Minneapolis. "No one among the Yale graduates," wrote Robert N. Corwin, chairman of the Yale Athletic Committee, in *Thomas Leonard Shevlin in Memoriam, 1883–1915* (1916), "was so generous of his time and effort" in helping "a discouraged football team." Describing him as "one of the most magnetic characters that ever came to Yale," Camp paid tribute to Shevlin as "the ideal All-American end for there was no department of play in which he did not stand without a peer."

• For Shevlin's overall football career, see Tim Cohane, *The Yale Football Story* (1951), and Marcia G. Synnott, "Thomas Leonard Shevlin," *Biographical Dictionary of American Sports: Football*, ed. David L. Porter (1987), pp. 540–41. For football statistics and big plays of major games, see L. H. Baker, *Football: Facts and Figures* (1945); Thomas Bergin, *The Game: The Harvard-Yale Football Rivalry, 1875–1983* (1984); Allison Danzig, *The History of American Football: Its Great Teams, Players, and Coaches* (1956); and John McCallum, *Ivy League Football since 1872* (1977). Brief biographies of Shevlin are in Ralph Hickok, *Who Was Who in American Sports* (1971); McCallum and Charles H. Pearson, *College Football U.S.A., 1869–1973* (1973); and Ronald L. Mendell and Timothy B. Phares, *Who's Who in Football* (1974). Albert Beecher Crawford, ed., *Football Y Men—Men of Yale Series*, vol. 1, *1872–1919* (1962), is a useful reference. For supplementary personal details, see "Thomas Leonard Shevlin," biographical sketches in *History of the Class of 1906, Yale College*, vol. 1; senior year album (1906); and the memorial on his death. See also "Shevlin of Yale, a Model of the Modern College Athlete," *Boston Herald*, 16 Oct. 1904. His illness and death were reported in the *New York Times*, 29 and 30 Dec. 1915, and in the *New York Evening Post*, 29 Dec. 1915.

MARCIA G. SYNNOTT

SHIBE, Benjamin Franklin (28 Jan. 1838–14 Jan. 1922), baseball executive, was born in Philadelphia, Pennsylvania, to parents whose names are unknown. He grew up without formal education in Kensington, a working-class section also known as Fishtown. Working for a horse-drawn streetcar company, he developed a knack for mechanics and an ability for fashioning leather goods like plaited whips, watch fobs, and blackjacks. He also took an interest in sports despite a leg injury that caused him to wear a brace and eschew participation.

Enthusiasm for baseball boomed after the Civil War. Shibe began making baseballs with his nephew and then formed a partnership with his brother, John D. Shibe & Co., to do the same. The firm prospered after Shibe invented an automatic winding device that made possible the manufacture of balls of uniform quality. The Shibes turned out several brands, with names such as Skyrocket and Bounding Rock. Cheaper varieties were intended for boys at play, and the most expensive balls for the top teams of the day. Shibe married and had four children, but his wife's name is unknown.

In 1882 Shibe withdrew from the partnership to form a new business with Alfred J. Reach, one of baseball's first and most prominent professional players. He had capitalized on his fame by opening a retail cigar and sporting goods store, Reach & Johnson, but soon came to realize that Shibe's products were superior to his own. The new firm, Reach & Shibe, was a success and in 1889 changed its name to the A. J. Reach Co. In time the Reach Company struck a deal with A. G. Spalding & Bros., the country's other large sporting goods firm. Reach abandoned retail trade to Spalding and concentrated on manufacturing. Al Reach supplied the sales skills, and Shibe provided the manufacturing knowledge. He devised so many mechanical innovations in the production of baseballs that the company acquired a virtual monopoly. Shibe invented the two-piece baseball cover, which remained in use throughout the twentieth century, and in 1909 he introduced the cork-center baseball, a durable product that retained its bounce and shape.

As his partnership and friendship with Reach grew, Shibe developed an interest in owning baseball teams. From 1877 through 1880, when there was no major league team in Philadelphia, he organized and supported the semiprofessional Shibe Club. He also bought stock in a minor league team and in the Philadelphia Athletics who played in the major league American Association. Following the association's demise after the 1891 season, Shibe consistently voiced his support for two major leagues despite the fact that his partner Reach was co-owner of the National League's Philadelphia Phillies.

When Ban Johnson reorganized the American League as a second major league in 1901, he sent Connie Mack from Milwaukee to establish a franchise in Philadelphia. Mack signed several established National League players and recruited Shibe as half-owner and president. With Mack running the team on the field and making all personnel decisions, and with Shibe and his sons managing the business side, the Athletics became the new league's most successful franchise. From 1901 through 1914 the A's won six pennants and three World Series titles and finished second three times. The profits the Athletics made during these years permitted Shibe to finance the construction of Shibe Park, baseball's first steel-and-concrete ballpark and a marked advance over the wooden parks then extant. Opened in 1909, it was immediately hailed as an architectural showplace and a monument to the sportsmanship of its creator.

In his later years Shibe was known affectionately as "Uncle Ben," a tribute to his plain, unassuming manner. He remained as president of the Athletics even after being injured in an automobile accident in August 1920. He died in Philadelphia.

• Clipping files on Shibe are at the National Baseball Library, Cooperstown, N.Y., and at the archives of the *Sporting News*, St. Louis, Mo. For background, see Bruce Kuklick, *To Every Thing a Season: Shibe Park and Urban Philadelphia, 1909–1976* (1991); and Peter C. Bjarkman, *Encyclopedia of Major League Baseball Team Histories: American League* (1991). Obituaries are in the *Sporting News*, 19 Jan. 1922; the *New York Times*, 15 Jan. 1922; and the *1922 Reach Official American League Guide* (1922).

STEVEN P. GIETSCHIER

SHICKELLAMY (fl. 1728–1748), Iroquois sachem, was probably the son of a French trader and a Cayuga mother. Reportedly captured and adopted by the Oneida at about two years of age, he was regarded as a strong and visionary leader. His name, which one finds spelled in a variety of ways, means "he causes it to be light" or "he enlightens us." He was sometimes referred to as "Our Enlightener."

Shickellamy undoubtedly attained prominence early on but entered history in 1728, when he protested the unregulated sale of rum to Indians before the Pennsylvania Provincial Council at Philadelphia and arranged the attendance of an important Delaware leader named Sasoonan at the request of Pennsylvania governor Patrick Gordon. He already served as representative from the League of the Iroquois to such tribes as the Conestoga, Mohican, Delaware, Nanticoke, Shawnee, and Ganawese, who lived as their tributaries in Pennsylvania's Susquehanna Valley. The British called Shickellamy "vice regent" or "half-king"—revealing their inclination for titles—but there is little indication that the league bestowed any title beyond that of sachem, nor could any Indian have exercised the authority such a title suggested.

After 1728 Shickellamy became a vital link in colonial Indian policy, acting as intermediary between the Iroquois, the Susquehanna tribes, and the British. He brought Iroquois representatives to Philadelphia in August 1732 and helped negotiate a treaty that radically altered the relationship between Iroquois and Pennsylvania authorities. Because the British feared French presence in Canada and the Ohio Valley, particularly their penchant for forging trade and military alliances with Indians, Governor Gordon made the Iroquois a primary partner in Pennsylvania and charged them with policing the region, monitoring tribes, and discouraging trade with the French. In return, the Iroquois attempted to control other tribes, complete with British backing. This arrangement made Shickellamy both intermediary and the man primarily responsible for peaceful Indian-white relations in western Pennsylvania. He even agreed to force the Shawnee back to Pennsylvania from Ohio, where they had gone to escape Iroquois interference and British settlers.

Shickellamy and Conrad Weiser, his friend and renowned interpreter, negotiated another treaty in 1736 that deeded Iroquois land to Pennsylvania and the landmark Lancaster Treaty of 1744, which forced Virginia and Maryland to recognize Iroquois claims in these colonies and, thus, pay for the land. They obtained travel rights for the Iroquois in Virginia and Maryland, compensation for land, and support for Iroquois authority. Despite his vow, however, Shickellamy was unable to bring the Shawnee back to the Susquehanna Valley or to halt the rum trade he so rigorously opposed.

As regional policeman, Shickellamy arrested alleged criminals and turned them over to white authorities for punishment, sometimes creating animosity among Indians. One of these, a Delaware named Musemeelin, was accused in 1744 of tomahawking two white traders to death. Captured by Shickellamy and then released by his own sons, Musemeelin was eventually recaptured and tried in Philadelphia but not convicted. Shickellamy interceded in intertribal disputes and kept track of French movements in Canada during King George's War.

He resided until 1738 on the intersection of the Catawba and Wyoming trails at a place called Shickellamy's Town, about one-half mile below present-day Milton, Pennsylvania. In 1738 he moved to Shamokin, near today's Sunbury. After the Lancaster Treaty, Weiser and several German settlers built him a 49½′ × 17½′ shingled house to replace his traditional dwelling. Also following the 1744 treaty, Shickellamy negotiated a peace between Iroquois and Catawba in Virginia and Carolina, made several trips to Onondaga in New York—the chief council fire of the league—and met with British authorities in Philadelphia. During one trip he reportedly slipped on ice and tumbled down a precipice; his life was saved only because the string on his backpack hooked onto a tree stump and broke the fall. On another journey he and his companions nearly died when they stumbled into a nest of angry rattlesnakes.

In summer 1747 Shickellamy's health failed. Considered an old man by this time, he contracted a fever, as did his wife, who apparently died of it, a daughter, three sons, and three grandchildren. Shickellamy recovered, although not completely. He went to Philadelphia in April 1748, became ill again, and returned home. In November he visited Moravian missionaries in newly established Bethlehem, Pennsylvania, but grew gravely ill and barely made it back to Shamokin.

Shickellamy had been converted by Moravians shortly before his death—although reportedly he had been baptized as a child by Jesuits—which probably explains his untimely trip. According to Weiser, Shickellamy's relapse was aggravated by starvation, since the winter was hard and game in the Susquehanna Valley was almost depleted. Shickellamy died in Shamokin; his funeral was conducted by Moravian bishop David Zeisberger. He was buried in Sunbury below a rock formation sometimes called "Shickellamy's Profile."

Shickellamy has been called a visionary, an Iroquois leader able to see the benefit of peaceful Indian-British relations. He has also been accused of sacrificing Indians to the white onslaught. The truth no doubt lies in between. He probably saw little chance in stopping white encroachment and hoped to negotiate the best deal he could for his people. He was considered kind, an enemy of alcohol, and a man whose opinion mattered greatly to Iroquois and British alike. Both made it a point to frequently recognize Shickellamy's authority with words and gifts, and for twenty years, Iroquois leaders repeatedly affirmed him as their spokesman among whites and other tribes. In 1915 the Augusta Chapter of the Daughters of the American Revolution and the Pennsylvania Historical Commission erected a boulder monument to Shickellamy near his grave.

• *Minutes of the Provincial Council of Pennsylvania*, vols. 3–5, and the *Pennsylvania Archives* contain information on Shickellamy and colonial authorities. Other primary documents include *The Moravian Journals Relating to Central New York, 1745–1766* (1916) and John Bartram et al., *A Journey from Pennsylvania to Onondaga in 1743* (repr. 1973). C. Hale Sipe, *The Indian Chiefs of Pennsylvania* (1927; repr. 1971), has several chapters on Shickellamy but provides no bibliography or footnotes. Paul A. W. Wallace, *Conrad Weiser, 1696–1760, Friend of Colonist and Mohawk* (1945), leads serious researchers to paper collections and manuscripts, mostly located in Pennsylvania and New York. Wallace, *Indians in Pennsylvania* (1961), gives a short biographical sketch. Richard Aquila, *The Iroquois Restoration* (1983), takes a more critical look at British policy that jeopardized Iroquois and tribes such as the Shawnee and Delaware. C. A. Weslager, *The Delaware Indians, a History* (1972), also states that by promoting Iroquois hegemony, the British strengthened their hold over the area, something they intended but that the Iroquois did not envision. Neither the whites nor the League of the Iroquois anticipated or recognized the seething anger of Delaware and Shawnee, he claims. Joseph J. Kelley, *Pennsylvania, the Colonial Years, 1681–1776* (1980), has a good bibliographic essay, but endnotes fail to specify sources adequately. Anthony F. C. Wallace, *The Death and Rebirth of the Seneca* (1970), reports that Shickellamy's family accused several Delaware of using witchcraft to hasten his death. Also of interest is Nancy L. Hagedorn, "A Friend to Go Between Them: The Interpreter as Culture Broker during Anglo-Iroquois Councils, 1740–79," *Ethnohistory* 35 (Winter 1988): 60–80.

KATHLEEN EGAN CHAMBERLAIN

SHIELDS, George Oliver (26 Aug. 1846–11 Nov. 1925), author, editor, and conservationist, was born in Batavia, Ohio, the son of John F. Shields and Eliza J.

Dawson. He attended public school in Delaware County, Iowa, for only three months, which was the extent of his formal education. In late 1863 or early 1864 he enlisted in the Union army. He took part in Sherman's "march to the sea" and was wounded in action at Resaca, Georgia, in May 1864. Shields was discharged from the army in July 1865, following what appears to have been a lengthy convalescence. After his discharge he traveled west, serving for a short time as an immigration agent in New Mexico. By some accounts, Shields was probably married, although few details are actually known.

Shields was an avid hunter, and his first published articles described his experiences hunting and fishing in various western locales. These articles, often written under the pseudonym "Coquina," were published in a number of popular magazines including *Harper, Outing,* and *American Magazine.* In 1883 Shields published his first book, *Rustlings in the Rockies,* a collection of first-person narratives primarily dealing with his hunting and fishing experiences. His second book, *Cruisings in the Cascades* (1889), followed a similar pattern. Shields also wrote or edited several instructional books on outdoor life, including *The Big Game of North America* (1890), *Camping and Camp Outfits* (1890), *The American Book of the Dog* (1891), and *American Game Fishes* (1892).

During his years traveling in the West, Shields also became interested in Native American history and culture, about which he frequently lectured in later years. *The Battle of the Big Hole* (1889) is a detailed account of the Montana conflict between the Nez Percé and troops commanded by General Gibbon that led to the defeat of the Nez Percé and their renowned leader, Chief Joseph. *The Blanket Indian of the Northwest* (1921) is a somewhat nostalgic portrayal of the West and Shields's "personal reminiscences of Indians I have known, hunted with, feasted with, and starved with." Shields's portrayals of Native Americans are generally sympathetic, although he does reflect some of the cultural biases of his time. Shields expressed a simple yet eloquent appreciation for many aspects of a culture and a way of life that he had personally witnessed, writing, "Of course we all approve the action of the Federal Government and of the missionaries in educating and attempting to civilize the red people; but at the same time we deplore the great loss we have sustained in consequence" (*The Blanket Indian of the Northwest,* p. 9).

The latter part of Shields's career was spent primarily as editor of two popular magazines: *Recreation,* from 1894 to 1905, and *Shields' Magazine,* from 1905 to 1912, the latter of which was sponsored by the New York Zoological Society. It was during this period that Shields made his reputation as a staunch, if sometimes strident, advocate for wildlife conservation. Like his contemporary Theodore Roosevelt, Shields believed that outdoor life was crucial to the health and well-being of the individual, and he sought to instill this belief in the American public through his magazines and through the formation of organizations such as the

Camp Fire Club, which he presided over from 1897 to 1902. In 1898 Shields also founded the League of American Sportsmen, serving as that organization's president from 1898 to 1919. Using that position, his editorship of *Recreation,* and later his editorship at *Shields' Magazine* ("the official organ of the League of American Sportsmen"), Shields fought vigorously to enact and enforce stricter game laws on the federal and state levels. In *Our Vanishing Wildlife* (1913), William Hornaday noted that Shields's harsh attacks on "game-hogs" had earned him numerous political enemies, but he lauded Shields's efforts to protect songbirds and game species, declaring that during his "war with the game-hogs . . . Mr. Shields's name became a genuine terror to excessive killers of game; and it is reasonably certain that his war saved a great number of game birds from the slaughter that otherwise would have overtaken them" (Hornaday, p. 58). Despite the importance of his work to the crucial task of garnering public support for wildlife and songbird protection, Shields's contribution during the critical early years of the conservation movement in the United States has generally been overlooked. Shields lived in the Bronx during the last few years of his life, with his health and financial circumstances both in decline. He died at St. Luke's Hospital in New York City.

• Relatively little biographical material on Shields, other than that contained in his own essays, has been published. *American Authors 1600–1900* (1938) contains a brief biographical profile of Shields. Various articles about Shields that are not mentioned in the text appear in *Shields' Magazine* (Mar. 1905), *Back-Log* (May 1930), and *Outdoor Life* (Nov. 1931). For a discussion of Shields's contribution to wildlife protection, see William T. Hornaday, *Our Vanishing Wildlife* (1913), and Peter Matthiessen, *Wildlife in America* (1959).

DANIEL G. PAYNE

SHIELDS, James (6 May 1806–1 June 1879), soldier and politician, was born in Altmore, County Tyrone, Ireland, the son of Charles Sheals, a shopkeeper, and Katherine MacDonald. A general in two wars and the only man to be elected a U.S. senator from three states, Shields was a Jacksonian Democrat whose political career eventually foundered because of the sectional crises.

Information regarding Shields's early life, including his date of birth and the spelling of his father's surname and his mother's maiden name, is fragmentary. It is clear, however, that he was raised in a Catholic middle-class family in the northern part of Ireland, where he received a formal education. Poor economic conditions in Ireland convinced James to emigrate in 1827. Sailing from Ulster, he probably followed the route of many Irishmen, landing in Montreal and then traveling by land to New York. Shields finally settled in Kaskaskia, Illinois, in 1828.

Shields's command of Latin, French, and Spanish helped him in his first job in Kaskaskia as a schoolmaster. While teaching, he studied law and joined the practice of U.S. Senator Elias Kent Kane, a leader in the Democratic party. In 1832 he was admitted to the bar. In 1836 he was elected to the Illinois legislature. He was not yet a naturalized citizen, but Illinois allowed immigrants to vote and hold office after only six months of residence. Like other Democrats in Illinois, Shields favored internal improvements and took a moderate antibank stand.

Shields did not run for reelection in 1838, but he remained politically active, accepting a post on the Board of Public Works and an appointment as state auditor in 1841. Shields had supported the acceptance of bank notes at face value in payment of taxes, but the bankruptcy of the state banks forced him to issue a proclamation declaring that the state would accept notes only at their market value. In the storm of protests that followed, Shields challenged Abraham Lincoln to a duel, accusing Lincoln of writing three letters to Illinois's leading Whig newspaper in which Shields was called a "dunce" and a "liar and a fool." Lincoln chose broadswords as the weapons, and the men met on "Bloody Island" in Missouri in October 1842. When Lincoln revealed that he had not written the letters, Shields withdrew the challenge. The following year, after unsuccessfully attempting to win the Democratic party nomination for Congress from the Belleville district, Shields was named to the Illinois Supreme Court by Governor Thomas Ford. In 1845, President James K. Polk appointed Shields as federal commissioner of public lands.

When the Mexican War began, Shields resigned his position and returned to Illinois to raise a regiment. Commissioned a brigadier general, Shields fought in a number of engagements, including Tampico, Cerro Gordo, where he was severely wounded, Contreras, Churubusco, and Chapultepec, where he was again wounded.

In 1847 Shields left Mexico a hero. Capitalizing upon his military fame, Shields decided to run for the U.S. Senate. He crisscrossed Illinois giving speeches and soliciting support, and he won Stephen Douglas's endorsement by promising to support the "Little Giant's" presidential ambitions. President Polk tried to save the Senate seat for the incumbent, Sidney Breese, by offering Shields an appointment as governor of the Oregon Territory, but Shields declined. On 12 January 1849, the General Assembly elected Shields to the U.S. Senate. The Senate, however, denied Shields his seat since he did not satisfy the constitutional requirement that a senator be a citizen for nine years. Breese declared that he had naturalized Shields on 21 October 1840, so Shields was nine months short of being eligible. Shields was livid, at first fabricating stories about his citizenship and then threatening Breese. The governor called a special session of the legislature to meet in October to elect a senator, and after twenty-one ballots Shields was once again elected.

Shields's career as a U.S. senator was generally undistinguished. He initiated no major legislation and made no inspired speeches. Shields supported Douglas on the major issues of the day: the Compromise of 1850, land grants to railroads, the Gadsden Purchase,

homestead legislation, and the Kansas-Nebraska Act. His support of the Kansas-Nebraska Act doomed his political ambitions in Illinois. Anti-Nebraska forces won control of the legislature, which in 1855 deadlocked between Shields and Lincoln in trying to choose a new senator before selecting instead Lyman Trumbull. Shields was bitterly disappointed, particularly since Trumbull had been a hated rival since Shields's congressional campaign in 1843.

Martial in manner, arrogant, and sensitive to any perceived affront to his dignity, Shields left Illinois almost immediately, moving to Minnesota in April 1855. He began speculating heavily in a land boom and became financially involved in railroad promotion. In October 1857, Minnesota voters ratified a state constitution and elected Shields's business partner, Henry Hastings Sibley, as governor. The new state legislature elected Shields a U.S. senator. Drawing the short term ending in March 1859, Shields took his seat in the Senate once Minnesota was admitted to the Union in May 1858. He sided with Douglas in opposing the proslavery Lecompton constitution, but in 1859 the Republican party swept the state elections and defeated Shields's reelection bid to the Senate. With dim political prospects and near financial ruin in the wake of the panic of 1857, Shields left for California in April 1860. When Shields arrived in San Francisco, he opened a law office and immediately engaged in politics, campaigning for Stephen Douglas. At the age of fifty-five, Shields married a 25-year-old Irish immigrant, Mary Ann Carr, with whom he had five children, two of whom died in their youth.

Following the outbreak of the Civil War, Shields was appointed a brigadier general. He took the field in March 1862, joining Nathaniel P. Banks's command in the Shenandoah Valley, where on 23 March he repulsed Stonewall Jackson at Winchester. Two months later Jackson easily defeated Shields's exhausted and poorly supplied division at Fort Republic. Following reassignment of the remnants of Shields's division, Lincoln recommended his promotion to major general, but the Senate denied confirmation. Without a command or hope of promotion, Shields accepted an assignment in the Department of the Pacific. He resigned his commission on 28 March 1863 while on his way back to San Francisco.

Shields resumed his law practice and again became involved with railroads, accepting an appointment as a California state railroad commissioner. In May 1866, Shields moved his family to Carrollton, Missouri. A part-time lawyer, farmer, lecturer, and politician, Shields ran for Congress in 1868, campaigning on the need for reconciliation with the South. His apparent victory was overturned by the U.S. House of Representatives on the basis of voter fraud. The panic of 1873 devastated what was left of Shields's resources, so to supplement his military pension he traveled extensively on the lecture circuit. Never abandoning politics, however, he was elected to the Missouri legislature in 1874 and 1875 and was appointed to the Missouri Railroad Commission in 1876. In January

1879 the legislature elected Shields to the U.S. Senate to complete an unexpired term. Declining to seek re-election, he served until March 1879. While on a lecture tour in Ottumwa, Iowa, Shields died of an apparent heart attack.

Shields was closely involved in the crucial American events of the mid-nineteenth century: the Bank War, the Mexican War, the sectional crisis, and the Civil War. His private and public fortunes closely paralleled those of the Democratic party. While not a particularly gifted politician or statesman, he rose quickly to prominence in the fluid society of antebellum America. But the events of the Civil War and Reconstruction created a new generation of heroes and politicians and relegated Shields to local politics. The state of Illinois placed a statue of Shields in Statuary Hall in the U.S. Capitol.

• Shields's papers are in the Illinois State Historical Society library (Springfield), and a collection of his letters is at the Chicago Historical Society. Other letters of Shields may be found in the Stephen A. Douglas Papers at the University of Chicago and the Henry Hastings Sibley Papers at the Minnesota Historical Society (St. Paul). An important primary source is Gustave Koerner, *Memoirs of Gustave Koerner*, ed. Thomas J. McCormack (2 vols., 1909). The most complete biography is Judith Moran Curran, "The Career of James Shields, an Immigrant Irishman in Nineteenth Century America" (Ed.D. diss., Columbia Univ. Teachers College, 1980). Curran provides the most reliable and convincing evidence regarding Shields's date of birth and the spelling of his father's surname and his mother's maiden name. Other sources include William H. Condon, *Life of Major-General James Shields, Hero of Three Wars and Senator from Three States*, (1900); John G. Coyle, "James Shields, Soldier, Justice, Senator," *United States Catholic Historical Society, Historical Records and Studies* 19 (1915): 41–52; Archbishop John Ireland, "Address at the Unveiling of the Statue of General Shields in the Capitol of Minnesota, October 20, 1914," *Minnesota Historical Society Collections* 15 (1915): 731–40; Francis O'Shaughnessy, "General James Shields of Illinois," *Illinois State Historical Society Transactions* 21 (1915): 113–23; and James Purcell, "James Shields, Soldier and Statesman," *Minnesota Historical Society Collections* 15 (1915): 73–86.

STEPHEN L. HANSEN

SHIELDS, Larry (13 Sept. 1893–21 Nov. 1953), jazz clarinetist and composer, was born Lawrence James Shields in New Orleans, Louisiana, the son of James Michael Shields, a house painter, and Emma Puneky. Shields came from a family of musicians: his brother Harry played the cornet and clarinet, his brother Eddie played the piano, and his brother Patrick (who died young) played several instruments, including the trombone, guitar, and bass. An older half-brother, James Ruth, played the mandolin and guitar.

Shields's formal education was perfunctory. After observing the chaotic nature of elementary education in practice at the time, his father withdrew him and his brothers from grammar school and enrolled them in a music school, where at age fourteen Shields began the formal study of the clarinet. As a beneficiary of a long tradition of New Orleans–trained reed players that included the brothers Achille and George Baquet, John-

ny Dodds, Jimmie Noone, and Omer Simeon, he quickly gained a reputation as a competent player among the emerging group of white musicians in the city. Music historian William Shafer calls Shields a true representative of the New Orleans clarinet tradition who directly benefited from his association with black musicians—especially Achille Baquet, whom Shafer describes as a "black clarinet teacher/player who crossed the 'color line' and worked with many musicians of Shields' circle" (p. 1). Shields's playing, Shafer observes, "is in the tradition of the best black musicians . . . and on recordings like 'Tiger Rag,' 'Ostrich Walk' or 'Clarinet Marmalade,' the busyness and bravado of the clarinet idiom shines clearly" (Shafer, p. 1).

While living in New Orleans, Shields played with a number of quasi-jazz bands, including one led by cornetist Nick LaRocca. But in 1915 he answered a call from bandleader Tom Brown, a New Orleans–born musician living in Chicago, who recruited Shields for another Chicago band, led by Bert Kelly. Shields, who had never learned to read music, soon grew frustrated in this new setting; he left Kelly, first to join a group led by Brown himself and later, in October 1916, to accept an offer to replace clarinetist Alcide "Yellow" Nunez in LaRocca's newly formed Original Dixieland Jazz Band (ODJB). Shields prospered in the band and soon became its most accomplished player and musical improviser.

In January 1917 the ODJB began a particularly successful engagement at Reisenweber's Cafe in New York City. The band then made what was to be history's first phonograph recordings of jazz for Victor Records the following month. The success of "Livery Stable Blues" and "Original Dixieland Jazz Band One-Step" (released on 17 Mar. 1917) propelled the group toward national acclaim and a string of engagements, including one at the Amsterdam Theater, where they appeared in the Ziegfeld *Midnight Follies*. Shields married Clara Bell Ferguson in Chicago in 1919; then had no children.

The ODJB's New York successes led to a European tour (the first ever for a jazz band) in 1919 and 1920. Upon returning from Europe, Shields continued with the ODJB until 1921, after which he worked briefly with bandleader Paul Whiteman in New York City before moving to the West Coast. He spent the rest of the 1920s in California, leading bands at various venues in Los Angeles and touring with a number of music reviews, at least one of which featured songstress and comedienne Sophie Tucker.

But Shields's days as a performing jazz musician appeared to be on the wane: on more than one occasion he returned to New Orleans seeking work during the early 1930s. Then in 1936 LaRocca revived the ODJB first in its original five-piece combo configuration and then, with the addition of nine new members, as a fourteen-piece band. Shields became the featured soloist in the fourteen-man combination and began being touted as the rival of Benny Goodman. The new ODJB did live performances, radio broadcasts, a

"March of Time" newsreel, and some recording sessions, during which it rerecorded some of the earlier hits. The revival (the last one to be organized by LaRocca) lasted until February 1938. Shields remained in New York City for the next couple of years, performing with some of the original ODJB members before returning to California, where he would live the remainder of his life.

By virtue of his excellent musicianship, as well as his fortuitous position of being the first clarinetist to record jazz, Shields became the model for many younger jazz clarinetists, including a young Goodman, who recounted, "I was playing jazz on my clarinet when I was eight years old, listening to the records of the Original Dixieland Jazz Band, which made a terrific impression on me" (Brunn, p. 205).

In his role within the ODJB, Shields was known for his strong melodic lead and may have been one of the early practitioners of the so-called "noodling" style—a practice adopted by Goodman and virtually every other clarinetist of the swing era. Defined as the "embroidering [of] a counterpoint with overly decorative, busy or distracting figures, as in Jimmy Dorsey's sardonic set-piece 'Oodles of Noodles'" (Shafer, p. 2), noodling created a competitive contrapuntal line to the cornet's melodic lead. In addition, many of Shields's imaginative "breaks" and definitive solos on New Orleans classics were performed intact by jazz clarinetists of subsequent generations, thus setting the stage for the rise of the clarinet as a virtuoso solo instrument in the hands of later performers such as Jimmy Dorsey, Artie Shaw, Benny Goodman, and Woody Herman. Shields died in Los Angeles.

• The principal source of information on Shields and the Original Dixieland Jazz Band is H. O. Brunn, *The Story of the Original Dixieland Jazz Band* (1960), which also contains the complete discography of recordings made by the group, along with tables that identify the fluctuating personnel and the band's original compositions and their composers. William J. Shafer, "Clarinet Kings," *Mississippi Rag* 10, no. 11 (Sept. 1983): 1–5, gives a detailed assessment of the musical contributions of Shields and his contemporaries with particular emphasis on the early development of the clarinet as a solo instrument in jazz. A firsthand account of hearing the Original Dixieland Jazz Band is Ed Blizard, "The Original Dixieland Jazz Band, the *Saturday Evening Post* and Bix," *Tailgate Ramblings* 21, no. 7 (July 1991): 5–6. Shields's predecessors and the dynasty of New Orleans clarinetists who followed Lorenzo Tio, Jr., is discussed in Lloyd Levin, "Lou'siana Swing," *Jazz Journal International* 39, no. 8 (Aug. 1986): 13. Other sources of information on Shields include Max Jones, "The Days When Jazz Was Young," *Melody Maker*, 28 Nov. 1953, p. 14, and Al Rose and Edmond Souchon, *New Orleans Jazz: A Family Album* (1967). An obituary is in the *New York Times*, 23 Nov. 1953.

CHARLES BLANCQ

SHIELDS, Thomas Edward (9 May 1862–5 Feb. 1921), Catholic priest and educator, was born in Mendota, Minnesota, the son of John Shields, an immigrant Irish farmer, and Bridget Burke. The year that Thomas was born, a Minnesota Sioux uprising forced the

Shields to take refuge at Fort Snelling. In his early youth, Thomas was known as an "omadhaun," a Gaelic term for fool or simpleton, because he was thought to be uneducable. Through the efforts of a parish priest, however, he learned to love reading and study.

In 1882 Shields's parents sent him to three years of higher education at the College of St. Francis in Milwaukee, Wisconsin. In 1885 he attended the Seminary of St. Thomas Aquinas in St. Paul, Minnesota, where he studied for the priesthood. He was ordained in 1891, and after a year as a curate at Archbishop John Ireland's (1838–1918) cathedral, he was sent to St. Mary's Seminary in Baltimore, where in 1892 he obtained a master's degree in theology, and to Johns Hopkins University, where he studied biology and experimental psychology, obtaining a doctorate in 1895.

From 1895 to 1902, Shields taught psychology and biology at the Seminary of St. Paul, where Archbishop Ireland intended for him to introduce clerical students to a competent dialogue between theology and the modern sciences. Because of his reputation for scholarship, in 1902 he was hired by the Catholic University of America in Washington, D.C., as an instructor in psychology. Shortly after joining that faculty, however, Shields focused his interest on the application of biology and psychology to the field of education. In 1905 he established a correspondence course, supplemented by diocesan summer institutes, for the numerous teaching sisters in the rapidly expanding Catholic school system across the nation. He also founded the university's Department of Education in 1909. To provide further for the professionalization of Catholic teachers, he conducted the first summer institute for teaching sisters and built the Sisters College at the university in 1911.

Shields was a strong advocate of higher education for women and women religious, believing that the teaching sisters in particular needed professional training and graduate degrees to meet the demands of state certification and the rising standards of education within the nation. His support for higher education for women was considered innovative in the early twentieth century when many at the Catholic University of America, as elsewhere in Catholic higher education, resisted the trend.

Shields was a Catholic representative of the Progressive Era in American education. Along with John A. Ryan in social thought, Edward Pace in philosophy, and William Kerby in sociology, he was one of the progressive faculty members at the Catholic University who sought to develop creatively a rapprochement between Catholic theology and modern science and philosophy. Shields became a national Catholic leader in developing a Christian view of education. He was clearly influenced by his own education in biology and experimental psychology and by the child-centered approaches to education of the Progressive Era. In 1907 and 1908, Shields entered into a major national debate with Father Peter Christopher Yorke at the Catholic Education Association's national meetings on religious education. Yorke emphasized content, and

Shields argued that more emphasis ought to be placed upon the method of teaching and the teacher's awareness of the student's learning readiness and psychological capacity. Shields opposed the method of memorization that was common in the catechisms. He wanted to correlate the content with the psychological growth of the student. In 1908, such an approach was considered revolutionary.

Shields's primary study, *The Philosophy of Education* (1917), incorporated the thought of many of the educational reformers of his day. Shields wanted educators to supplant the passivity of the old educational system with activities within the normal experiences of childhood. Like John Dewey and other innovators, Shields believed that children learned best by doing, by becoming active in the pursuit of knowledge, not only through books and teaching lessons but also through music, signs, symbols, and liturgical activity. Education should correspond to the actual stage of the child's psychological development. Shields also believed, like Dewey, that students needed some means of linking together the various subjects presented to them. Unlike Dewey, however, he believed that religion could provide that integrating and directive link. Shields believed in developing the child according to the laws of his or her own nature, but he asserted that nature itself needed the guidance of revelation and religion to direct the child's total development.

To propagate his revolutionary new methods of teaching, Shields edited with Pace six elementary textbooks and readers in the *Catholic Education Series* (1908–1915), set up his own Catholic Education Press, founded the *Catholic Educational Review* (1911), conducted lectures at convents and diocesan educational conventions across the country, and wrote numerous articles and books on education.

Shields was an American-Irish activist whose Progressive Era energy and optimism made him attractive to the students who attended his classes at the university. His innovations in teaching methods and his attempts to chart new directions in the teaching of religion, however, also produced enemies and critics within American Catholicism. Although the old methods of education prevailed throughout the first half of the twentieth century, Shields's new methods gradually helped to transform the education of women religious who attended summer schools and the Sisters College at the Catholic University of America, and through those women religious the new methods were put into practice in the American Catholic school system.

After 1916 Shields suffered with valvular heart trouble; he died in his Washington, D.C., home.

• Shields's letters and unpublished papers are located primarily in the Archives of the Catholic University of America, Washington, D.C. Among his more important published works are *Twenty-Five Lessons in the Psychology of Education* (1905–1907), *The Education of Our Girls* (1907), *The Teaching of Religion* (1907), *The Making and the Unmaking of a Dullard* (1909), and *Teachers Manual of Primary Methods* (1912). The only biography is *Thomas Edward Shields, biologist, psychologist, educator* (1947) by Justine Bayard Cutting Ward, one of his students and admirers.

PATRICK W. CAREY

SHILTS, Randy Martin (8 Aug. 1951–17 Feb. 1994), journalist, was born in Davenport, Iowa, the son of Bud Shilts, a salesman of prefabricated housing, and Norma (maiden name unknown). Neither of his parents graduated from high school. They raised four sons in a politically conservative Methodist family. Young Randy Shilts grew up in Aurora, Illinois, a suburb of Chicago, where he organized a local chapter of Young Americans for Freedom and graduated from a public high school. Shilts entered the University of Oregon in 1969. Two years later he openly acknowledged his homosexuality and became a leader in the Gay People's Alliance in Eugene. In his senior year Shilts ran unsuccessfully for student body president on the slogan "Come Out for Shilts." After completing requirements for graduation with honors in English literature, Shilts decided that he "didn't know how to write." Changing his major to journalism, he learned that he could write well, won several journalism awards, and served as managing editor of the campus newspaper. In 1975 Shilts graduated at the top of his class with a B.S. in journalism.

Unable to find work in mainstream journalism because of his open homosexuality, Shilts became the Northwest correspondent for the *Advocate*, a national lesbian and gay periodical then based in San Mateo, California. Six months later he moved there and worked as an *Advocate* staff journalist for three years. In February 1977, as large numbers of gay and lesbian people moved into the Bay area, San Francisco radio station KQED hired Shilts to cover gay community news. As he expanded his coverage to include city politics and urban affairs, Shilts got to know San Francisco's new gay city commissioner, Harvey Milk, and learned that they both came from backgrounds in the libertarian strand of conservative Republican politics. When former city commissioner Dan White assassinated Mayor George Moscone and Commissioner Milk on 27 November 1978, it was Randy Shilts's story. In 1979, after riots following the murders, Oakland's independent television station KTVU hired Shilts to cover city hall and the gay community for its evening news.

Shilts used the money that he earned in television to launch a career in freelance journalism, publishing articles in *Christopher Street*, the *Columbia Journalism Review*, the *Village Voice*, and the *Washington Post*. His *Christopher Street* article on the death of Harvey Milk led to a contract for a book, which took him three years to write. "I couldn't deal with it emotionally," he recalled. "I'd never known anybody before who'd gotten killed" (Current Biography Yearbook [1993], p. 526). Writing under the influence of authors John Irving, James Michener, and Mike Royko, Shilts produced his first book, *The Mayor of Castro Street: The Life and Times of Harvey Milk* (1982). The biography of the nation's leading gay officeholder became a major work of investigative journalism in big city politics and a vehicle for telling the story of the gay liberation movement.

When he joined the staff of the *San Francisco Chronicle* in 1981, Shilts was the first openly gay reporter on a major American newspaper. Yet, because of his television exposure, he was more widely known than most print journalists. By 1983 Shilts had persuaded the *Chronicle*'s editors to let him work full time covering the new plague, acquired immunodeficiency syndrome (AIDS), which had begun to decimate San Francisco's gay community. By exposing the role of bathhouses as centers for anonymous sex, he risked the hostility of many gay men. Shilts's reports reinforced homophobia, they charged, and he was called a "gay Uncle Tom." Clarifying his position, he called for eliminating in bathhouses certain sexual practices that were high risks for spreading the disease. Having patronized the baths himself, Shilts was tested for the AIDS-causing HIV virus in 1986. He delayed learning the results of the test until he finished his second book manuscript, *And the Band Played On: Politics, People, and the AIDS Epidemic* (1987), however, lest the information influence his reporting. Shilts's history of the AIDS plague severely criticized the Ronald Reagan administration, the news media, the scientific establishment, and some segments of the gay community for their slow, contorted response to the crisis. His book was widely praised and was a finalist for a National Book Award in nonfiction. He was named the outstanding author of 1988 by the American Society of Journalists and Authors.

On 16 March 1987 Shilts learned that he had tested positive for the HIV virus. Sustained by AZT, the drug that inhibited HIV, and with a fine journalist's sense of news agenda and a near $1 million advance, Shilts turned from the AIDS crisis to a study of homophobia in the armed forces. He obtained 15,000 pages of documents through the Freedom of Information Act and conducted more than 1,100 interviews with veterans. As AZT began to lose its inhibiting effect, Shilts's health deteriorated. He developed pneumocystic carinii pneumonia, an AIDS-related infection, in August 1992, and his HIV-positive status became full-blown AIDS. When Democratic presidential candidate Bill Clinton announced that if elected he would end the ban on gays and lesbians in the military, Shilts's publisher was anxious to put *Conduct Unbecoming: Lesbians and Gays in the U.S. Military* (1993) into the national debate. On 24 December 1992 Shilts's left lung collapsed, and he worked from a hospital bed with an editor to finish the book.

When Shilts publicly acknowledged his HIV-status in February 1993, he summarized the thesis of *Conduct Unbecoming* for *Newsweek* (1 Feb. 1993): "From the first days of the Defense Department's antigay regulations in the early 1940s, the government was willing to waive the for-heterosexuals-only requirement for military service if barring gays interfered with manpower exigencies." Shilts found a pattern of relative toleration in wartime but of coercive homophobia in peacetime. *Conduct Unbecoming* won generally positive reviews. Some gay activists criticized Shilts for refusing to reveal the homosexuality of prominent figures, including two four-star generals. Former secretary of the navy John Lehman spoke for much of the military establishment in dismissing Shilts as exemplifying the "schizophrenia of the radical gay movement" in his "loathing of the military" and "genuine ignorance of its ways." Yet another critic said that *Conduct Unbecoming* bore the same relation to gay liberation that Betty Friedan's *The Feminine Mystique* and Rachael Carson's *The Silent Spring* bore to the modern feminist and environmental movements. On 31 May 1993 Randy Shilts and his companion, Barry Barbieri, a film student, held a ceremony honoring their commitment to each other. Shilts died of complications related to AIDS at his home in Guerneville, California.

• Randy Shilts published no autobiographical work, but his papers are in the Gay and Lesbian Archives at the San Francisco Public Library. The best secondary sources include *Contemporary Authors*, vol. 127, pp. 400–405; *Current Biography Yearbook* (1993), pp. 525–29; Sharon Malinowski and Christa Brelin, eds., *The Gay and Lesbian Literary Companion* (1995), pp. 459–73, 574–75; and Claude J. Summers, ed., *The Gay and Lesbian Literary Heritage: A Reader's Companion to the Writers and Their Works, from Antiquity to the Present* (1995), pp. 659–60. For an obituary, see the *New York Times*, 18 Feb. 1994.

RALPH E. LUKER

SHINDLER, Mary Dana (15 Feb. 1810–8 Feb. 1883), songwriter and advocate of reform, was born Mary Stanley Bunce Palmer in Beaufort, South Carolina, the daughter of Benjamin Morgan Palmer and Mary Stanley Bunce. In 1814 her father, a Princeton graduate, became co-pastor of Charleston's Independent (Congregational) Church. Mary attended a prestigious school for girls in Charleston and received a lady's education at seminaries conducted by clergymen in Connecticut and New Jersey. Some of her juvenile poems were published in a periodical that was edited locally. Through family connections she met many of antebellum America's leading clergymen, foreign and domestic missionaries, and women involved in church work and charities.

After marrying Charles Eleutheros Dana, a native of Vermont, in 1835, she moved to New York City. A son was born in 1837. The Danas migrated westward in 1838, settling in a Mississippi River town (now Muscatine) in Iowa Territory. After her husband and son died during an epidemic of "congestive fever" in the summer of 1839, she returned to South Carolina, where she began writing poems about love and loss and publishing them in periodicals. Thereafter her life and writings were closely connected.

Conventional in form and content, her sentimental and elegiac poems affirmed the consolations of religion. In *The Parted Family, and Other Poems* (1842) she requested "indulgence" for unpolished lyrics written in sorrow and published for the benefit of other mourners. In accordance with contemporary practice, reviewers commended her faith and sentiments and suggested that she publish more selectively.

She continued to write copiously during her widowhood. Writing served her as an emotional outlet and a means of serving others. It was also a respectable source of income, a motive that she acknowledged privately. Noting a dearth of suitable music for domestic use on Sundays, she set original religious lyrics to familiar tunes that she arranged for piano and guitar. Her first songbooks, the *Southern Harp* (1841) and *Northern Harp* (1842), yielded a comfortable income for several years. Another songbook, *The Temperance Lyre* (1842), states a purpose characteristic of much of her writing: to serve a worthy cause by "invok[ing] the potent aid of poetry and song."

In the mid-1840s she regularly published religious lyrics and prose regional sketches in the *Southern Literary Messenger*, *Augusta Mirror*, *Graham's Magazine*, and the *New York Observer* (a Presbyterian paper). As a regular contributor to New York's *Union Magazine*, she published a series of sketches of life in the South and West. Her moral tales *Charles Morton, or, the Young Patriot: A Tale of the American Revolution* (1843) and *Forecastle Tom: Or, the Landsman Turned Sailor* (1846) were noticed favorably in southern periodicals. *The Young Sailor: A Narrative Founded on Fact* (1843), a volume included in Harper's School District Library, was reprinted three times. "Pass under the Rod," a poem that interprets affliction as evidence of divine love, was widely popular. Another lyric, "O Sing to Me of Heaven," was published in many hymnbooks and songbooks.

Following a year of intense reading and reflection, she converted to Unitarianism in early 1845. Wounded by harsh criticism of her change of allegiance, she published *Letters Addressed to Relatives and Friends, Chiefly in Reply to Arguments in Support of the Doctrine of the Trinity* (1845). While explaining her own rejection of Calvinism and reasoned commitment to liberal religion, she appealed for greater public charity and toleration.

Her parents, on whom she had relied since losing her own family, died unexpectedly in 1847. The next year she married Robert Doyne Shindler, an Episcopal clergyman from western Virginia, and soon afterward renounced Unitarianism. In 1852 she bore a son and published her last literary sketch in *Godey's Lady's Book*. Handicapped by a throat condition, Robert Shindler found preaching difficult. As he struggled to support his family by teaching, the couple lived briefly in Maryland and Kentucky, returning periodically to South Carolina in search of meaningful work. While he was principal of the Female Institute in Ripley, Tennessee, Mary taught music there. She published a *Song Book* (1858) for schools and families and *The Western Harp* (1860), another collection of "Sunday Music." During the Civil War the Shindlers lived in western Tennessee, a predominantly pro-Confederate region. Although Mary longed to return to Charles-

ton, they spent their last years together in San Augustine and Nacogdoches, Texas, where Robert taught and held pastorates.

Widowed again in 1874, Shindler returned to journalism and songwriting. The new cause that integrated her talents and enthusiasms was spiritualism. Bereaved more often than she could bear as an orthodox religionist, she found in spiritualism assurance that her loved ones had merely "gone before" to a different phase of existence. After attending seances in New England and New York, she wrote *A Southerner among the Spirits: A Record of Investigations into the Spiritual Phenomena* (1877). Based on a journal she kept during her research and interlarded with quotations from spiritualist publications, this 169-page book recounts the process by which she came to "KNOW" that open-minded persons can communicate with the dead.

Shindler lived briefly in Memphis with a female medium with whom in 1878 she coedited the *Voice of Truth*, a weekly paper committed to the advancement of spiritualism and, its masthead proclaims, "all other reforms." Purposely nonhierarchical, the spiritualist movement welcomed women as mediums and lecturers. Although Shindler was not a public speaker, spiritualism—which she regarded as "a science, and not merely a religion" (*Southerner*, p. 17)—provided an alternative to an authoritarian belief system that failed to satisfy her intellectual and emotional needs.

She continued to think of herself as a Christian and to quote the Bible. In prose she retained the style characteristic of evangelicalism. She wrote a letter to the leading spiritualist paper to deny a rumor that she had abandoned the movement: "God forbid" that she should "repudiat[e] a truth which is dearer to me than life itself, for which I have suffered severely in my social relations, and which has made a lonely widow one of the happiest of God's creatures." Certain of "the truth of spirit return and communication," she declared that she had "'kept the faith'" and anticipated receiving "'crowns of glory'" (*Banner of Light*, 18 Dec. 1880, p. 3). Most of her religious poems written before her affiliation with spiritualism cannot be differentiated from those written afterward.

Her last book, *The U.S. Labor Greenback Song Book* (1879), was a collection of original campaign songs set to popular tunes to promote the Labor Greenback party, a precursor of the populist movement. She died in Nacogdoches, Texas.

It was not uncommon for nineteenth-century Americans to change denominations or creeds. Many women found in religion and reform their justification for authorial careers suitable for ladies. Shindler is also representative of many contemporaries who abandoned sectarianism while maintaining the ethic of serving God by serving humanity. But her evolution from strict Calvinist to spiritualist, reformer, and populist must be considered extraordinary for a woman of her background whose father and cousin (also named Benjamin Morgan Palmer) were eminent Southern Presbyterian divines. Other American women writers questioned orthodox religion in their fiction; few of

Shindler's generation openly engaged in theological controversy.

• Duplicate copies of the Shindler-Palmer Family Papers are at the South Caroliniana Library, University of South Carolina, and in the Steen Library, Stephen F. Austin State University, Nacogdoches, Tex. The best nineteenth-century biographies are in John S. Hart, *Female Prose Writers of America* (1852); Ida Raymond [pseudonym of Mary Tardy], *The Living Female Writers of the South* (1872); and Sam H. Dixon, *The Poets and Poetry of Texas* (1885). Shindler's parlor music is discussed in Judith Tick, *American Women Composers before 1870* (1983).

For information on the Palmer family, see Thomas C. Johnson's biography of Shindler's cousin, *Life and Letters of Benjamin Morgan Palmer* (1906). For religious history relevant to her life and writings, especially her adoption of Unitarianism, consult George Howe, *History of the Presbyterian Church in South Carolina* (1883), and George N. Edwards, *A History of the Independent or Congregational Church of Charleston, South Carolina* (1947). Also useful is Ann Braude, *Radical Spirits: Spiritualism and Women's Rights in Nineteenth-Century America* (1989).

MARY DE JONG

SHINGAS (fl. 1740–1763), king, speaker, and war captain of the Ohio Delawares, also called Shingas the Terrible. His name means "wet, marshy ground" or "swamp person" in the Delaware language. A member of the Turkey group of Delawares, Shingas was the brother of Sassoonan and Tamaqua (or Tamaque, better known as Beaver), both of whom were Delaware chiefs. A prominent tribal member, Shingas originally had lived in the Susquehanna River valley but moved westward to the Ohio River valley in western Pennsylvania. His settlement, known as Shingas's Town, was located in the vicinity of present-day McKees Rocks, just north of Pittsburgh, Pennsylvania, on the Ohio River, and his followers became known as the Delawares on the Ohio.

As the younger brother of Sassoonan, Shingas was eligible to become chief of the Delawares when his brother died in 1747. However, Sassoonan favored Pisquetomen, his nephew, to succeed him, and it was not until 1752 that the Delawares on the Ohio selected Shingas as their chief and crowned him king with the approval of colonial officials in Virginia and Pennsylvania. Speaking for the Delawares, Tanacharison declared, "We let you know that it is our Right to give you a King, and we think it proper to give you Shingas for your King, whom you must look upon as your Chief & with whom all publick Business must be transacted between you & your Brethren the English" (Weslager, pp. 209–10). The ceremony took place at Logstown; however, Shingas was not present, so Tanacharison put a laced hat on the head of Tamaque, who was acting as Shingas's proxy. Not all Delawares supported Shingas, but because his crowning had been supported by colonial officials and the Iroquois, the Ohio Delawares had little choice in accepting him. Delawares in New Jersey and those living along the Susquehanna River, however, followed their own chiefs.

In the fall of 1753 George Washington was dispatched by Virginia officials to order the French out of the Ohio country. During the journey, Washington visited Shingas at his new home about two miles south of present-day Pittsburgh. Washington and Shingas attended a council at Logstown, where the Indians dispatched messengers to the French ordering them to abandon the territory. In addition, Shingas and Tanacharison pledged their full support to the Virginia effort to drive the French out of the Ohio country.

Shingas's support of the English waned following Washington's abandonment of Fort Necessity in the spring of 1754 in the face of a superior French force. With Washington fled the English traders upon whom the Delawares had become dependent for guns, powder, lead, knives, cooking pots, blankets, and other manufactured products. By the fall of 1754 Shingas, Tamaque, and Pisquetomen were beginning to doubt their alliance with the British. The final break came in June 1755 when British Major General Edward Braddock summoned Shingas and five other Indian chiefs to his camp and asked them for help in his planned assault on the French at Fort Duquesne. When Shingas asked what would happen to the land once the French were driven out, Braddock answered that the English would "Inhabit & Inherit" and that "no Savage Should Inherit the Land" (Weslager, p. 225). Dismayed at the answer, Shingas and the other chiefs asked the question the following morning. The answer was the same. This time the Indians told Braddock that if they could not live on the land they would not fight for it.

As Shingas explained, "the Greater Part [of Delaware] remained neuter till they saw How Things wou'd go Between Braddock and the French" (Weslager, p. 224), and when Braddock was defeated by a combination French and Indian force on 9 July 1755, they allied themselves with the French during the French and Indian War. Open warfare started on 16 October 1755 when a party of Shingas's warriors attacked a white settlement on Penn's Creek south of present-day Selinsgrove, Pennsylvania. Bitter fighting raged throughout the Pennsylvania frontier. So great were the depredations committed by Shingas's followers that Pennsylvania offered a reward of 700 pieces of eight for his scalp, and Virginia offered to pay 100 pistols for his death.

Shingas's raids were based out of another village he had established at Kittanning on the Allegheny River. On 8 September 1756, however, a group of Pennsylvania militia led by Colonel John Armstrong (1717–1795) attacked and destroyed Kittanning. Afterward Shingas and his followers moved to Saukunk, or Shingas's Old Town, near present-day Beaver, Pennsylvania. By 1757 Shingas was attempting to realign the Delaware with the English, and he sent two of his sons to negotiate peace. The following year, 1758, he joined fourteen other Delaware leaders to sign a letter stating, "We long for that Peace and Friendship we had Formerly." Living in fear of being captured and executed, Shingas abdicated in favor of his brother Tamaque, and peace returned when colonial officials promised to keep white settlers off the Delaware homeland and to provide them with trade goods.

Following the war Shingas migrated westward from Pennsylvania to Ohio and established a new tribal town near present-day Bolivar, Ohio. Called the Tuscarawas, Beaver's Town, or Shingas's Town, the settlement contained about forty huts. Shortly afterward he again moved and established another settlement, called Hockhocking or Beaver's New Town, near Standing Stone, present-day Lancaster, Ohio.

With the outbreak of Pontiac's Rebellion in 1763, Shingas again led his followers against the British and attacked colonial settlements in the Juniata, Tuscarora, and Cumberland valleys and, along with Tamaque, unsuccessfully attempted to persuade Captain Simeon Ecuyer to evacuate Fort Pitt. Although Pontiac's Rebellion was characterized by torture on both sides, Shingas refused to harm his prisoners and in one instance adopted two young white boys who had been captured as his own sons. The defeat of the rebellion ended Shingas's influence over the Delawares. When the tribe sued for peace in 1765, he had been replaced in his leadership position and did not take part in the negotiations.

• C. A. Weslager, *The Delaware Indians: A History* (1972), contains much information describing Shingas's role in Delaware and colonial politics. Anthony F. C. Wallace, *King of the Delawares: Teedyuscung, 1700–1763* (1949), provides information on Shingas's life during the conflict in western Pennsylvania. The official records of the Delaware War can be found in *Pennsylvania Colonial Records* (16 vols., 1852–1853). An account of Shingas's role in the westward migration of the Delawares is in Weslager, *The Delaware Indian Westward Migration: With the Texts of Two Manuscripts (1821–22) Responding to General Lewis Cass's Inquiries about Lenape Culture and Language* (1978). See also Michael N. McConnell, *A Country Between: The Upper Ohio Valley and Its Peoples, 1724–1774* (1992).

PAUL F. LAMBERT

SHINN, Asa (3 May 1781–11 Feb. 1853), Methodist clergyman and an architect of the Methodist Protestant church, was born in New Jersey, the son of Quaker parents Jonathan Shinn and Mary Clark. Little is known about his parents and early life except that he was reared in Harrison County in western Virginia.

Shinn's circumstances did not offer opportunities for formal education. It is said that he had some primary education under the tutelage of a disabled sailor who earned a living by teaching mountain children the rudiments of reading and writing. In 1798, when he was about seventeen, Shinn was aroused to Christian faith through the efforts of a Methodist circuit preacher, the Reverend Robert Manly; within three years Shinn himself had become an itinerant Methodist preacher. Encouraged by a ministerial colleague, he mastered English grammar by studying a book he had purchased. As his contemporary, the Reverend Andrew Lipscomb, president of the University of Georgia, described him, Shinn was "a self-made man. . . .

the fresh, earnest, independent man came right out in all his discourses" (quoted in Sprague, p. 367).

Shinn began his itinerant ministry in 1800 by preaching in a circuit that included Pittsburgh. For the next seven years his assignments followed westward expansion. In 1801 he was admitted as a member (on trial) of the Baltimore Conference of the Methodist Episcopal church (MEC). After several assignments in southwestern Pennsylvania, West Virginia, and Ohio, Shinn spent two years traveling circuits in southern Kentucky. Beginning in 1807 the balance of his career with the MEC was divided between the region of the Monongahela watershed in southwestern Pennsylvania and northern (now West) Virginia and the city of Baltimore. Also in 1807, while working near Fairmont, (West) Virginia, Shinn met Phebe Barns; they were married later that same year. The couple had four children, only two of whom survived to adulthood, before Phebe Shinn's death in 1819. In 1825 Shinn married Mary Bennington Wrenshall Gibson, the widow of Woolman Gibson; they had one child.

Shinn earned a reputation as an extraordinary preacher. The Reverend George Brown, who heard him preach in 1813 at a camp meeting near Baltimore, later recalled that Shinn "was strong in argument, apt and clear in illustration, and fervent and impressive in manner" (quoted in Sprague, p. 365). The leadership of the MEC recognized Shinn's talents and assigned him to increasingly more populous circuits as well as to leadership positions in the church, for example, presiding elder of the Monongahela District (1818–1819) and the Pittsburgh District (1825–1826).

Beginning in 1824 Shinn began to identify himself with the cause of reform within the MEC. Viewing the authoritarian polity of the MEC as strangely out of step with the era of Jacksonian democracy, Shinn, along with Nicholas Snethen, Alexander McCaine, and others, advocated reforms that would make the church less hierarchical and more amenable to lay participation. In 1824 the reformers established a monthly periodical, *The Mutual Rights of Ministers and Members of the Methodist Episcopal Church*, through which Shinn, Snethen, and McCaine pressed for reforms that included limitations on episcopal authority, the election rather than appointment of presiding elders, and lay representation at legislative conferences. In 1827 the Baltimore Annual Conference censured, and subsequently expelled, ministers Dennis Dorsey and William Poole for their reforming activities. The churchwide General Conference of 1828 became a battleground between traditionalists and reformers; the reformers brought a legislative platform that was rejected, and despite Shinn's oratorical support, the appeal for reinstatement made by Dorsey and Poole failed by the slim majority of twenty votes.

After the General Conference of 1828 the "Associated Methodist Churches," as the reforming congregations called themselves, gathered into annual conferences in anticipation of forming a new church. On 2 November 1830 these churches sent delegates to a general conference, held in Baltimore, and through their efforts the Methodist Protestant church (MPC) was born. The new church was to be Methodist in its theological posture but nonepiscopal in its polity. The reformers' attempt to bring a greater degree of democracy to the MPC was reflected in a polity that granted greater congregational autonomy, eschewed the leadership of bishops, and allowed laymen to join clergy in voting at legislative conferences.

Shinn played a major role in the founding conference of the MPC and continued to exercise leadership in the church until mental illness forced him from active service in 1843. He was elected president of several annual conferences, including the Ohio Conference (1829–1830) and the Pittsburgh Conference (1833). He served influential MPC pastorates in Cincinnati (1830, 1837), Pittsburgh (1831–1832, 1837–1840, 1842–1843), and Allegheny City (1841). In 1834 he was appointed joint editor, with Nicholas Snethen, of the denominational periodical, the *Methodist Protestant*. In 1842 he was elected president of the General Conference of the MPC. Shinn also authored two significant theological books. The first, *An Essay on the Plan of Salvation* (1812), was one of the first systematic theologies produced by an American Methodist. It examined the biblical and rational evidences that undergird the doctrine of redemption. His second book, *On the Benevolence and Rectitude of the Supreme Being* (1840), took a similar approach to investigating the nature of God. His reforming vision anticipated many subsequent developments, such as lay participation in the governance of the church, in the Methodist tradition. An ardent abolitionist, Shinn labored unsuccessfully to convince the MPC to take an official stand against slavery.

Although Shinn overcame a lack of formal education to become an effective minister, church leader, religious journalist, and author of several significant books, his ministry was frequently interrupted by failing health and mental illness. He was placed in supernumerary (nonactive) status in 1816–1817, 1820–1821, 1828, and from 1844 until the end of his life. Bouts with mental illness persisted, and Shinn's last decade of life was spent in an asylum in Brattlebourgh, Vermont, where he died.

• Shinn authored two pamphlets not mentioned above, *An Appeal to the Good Sense of the Citizens of the United States* (1826) and *A Finishing Stroke to the High Claims of Ecclesiastical Sovereignty* (1827). R. F. Shinn, *A Tribute to Our Fathers* (1853), and J. H. Shinn, *The History of the Shinn Family in Europe and America* (1903), are significant biographical sources from the memoirs of family members. Articles in Matthew Simpson, *Cyclopedia of Methodism* (1878), T. H. Colhouer, *Sketches of the Founders* (1880), and by Guy Smeltzer in *Encyclopedia of World Methodism* (1974) outline the significance of Shinn's career in the larger context of Methodist history. Important contemporary information and personal reminiscences are contained in the lengthy article in W. B. Sprague, *Annals of the American Pulpit*, vol. 7 (1859). An obituary is in the Pittsburgh *Daily Commercial Journal*, 18 Feb. 1853.

JOHN R. TYSON

SHINN, Earl (8 Nov. 1838–3 Nov. 1886), art critic, was born in Philadelphia, Pennsylvania, the son of Earl Shinn, secretary of the Bricklayers' Society, and Sarah Comfort. He entered the Westtown School, a progressive Quaker academy, in 1853 and for the rest of his life was a Friend, affiliated with the Philadelphia Monthly Meeting for the Southern District. His faith and middle-class background help explain the pragmatic standards and zeal for educating readers that distinguished him from other leading critics, uniformly patrician, whose tastes and vocabulary more often alienated than persuaded unsophisticated readers.

By 1859, although working as a real-estate title examiner, Shinn felt called to a life devoted to "Art, Poesy, [and the] Imagination." His activities of the early 1860s are unknown. If he served in the Union army, he, like so many other Quakers forced to serve against their wills, never mentioned this then or later. By January 1865 he lived in New York City and was associated with Frank Leslie's Publications, a magazine publisher. With the death that year of his rigidly orthodox parents, who abhorred the visual arts, he felt free to pursue his dream of becoming a painter, and using his modest inheritance, he sailed for Europe in April 1866 to study art in Paris, France. Upon his arrival he discovered that foreign students were being excluded from the École des Beaux-Arts, France's official academy. He persuaded the American legation to protest this exclusion, and soon he and several other young Americans, including his good friend Thomas Eakins, won admission to the École.

Like Eakins and most other Americans, Shinn chose to study in the atelier of Jean-Leon Gérôme. He described his art classes and the social scene in Paris in letters that appeared in the *Philadelphia Evening Bulletin* in 1866–1867 under the byline "Rash Steps" by L'Enfant Perdu. He began contributing similar articles to the *Nation*. Vague but persistent eye problems, however, ended Shinn's painting career. Returning to Philadelphia he joined the *Bulletin*'s staff.

Moving to New York in 1872, Shinn worked for the *Nation* until 1881 as its principal art critic. He adopted the pseudonym Edward Strahan for all of his writing to shield "his father's revered name." (Earl Shinn, Sr., had published regularly on Quaker matters, and his son avoided embarassing him posthumously by linking the name Earl Shinn and the visual arts.) He contributed regularly to numerous journals and newspapers, especially *Lippincott's*, the *Art Amateur*, and the *New York Evening Post*. His periodical writings will never be fully documented, because to earn a living he wrote anonymous "paid praise" that masqueraded in newspapers as columns, in such quantity that, in Shinn's own words, "it outweighs in amount, and in the effect it makes, voluntary contributions."

Shinn's importance lies less in such ephemeral writings, however, than in the lavish volumes he aimed at affluent collectors and art lovers. In a long association with Philadelphia publisher Gebbie & Barrie, he celebrated the art of the 1876 Centennial Exhibition, familiarized Americans with leading French painters, especially Gérôme, and documented the contents of America's most important art collections in his monumental *Art Treasures of America* (1879–1883).

Shinn first began to survey private collections in *Lippincott's* in 1871. Additional articles on collections appeared there and in the *Art Amateur*, beginning with its inaugural issue in 1879. His fascination with the wealthy and his desire to improve their tastes led him to visit collections around the country. His decade-long research resulted in the *Art Treasures of America*, three folio volumes issued by Gebbie & Barrie to 1,000 subscribers between 1879 and 1883. He discussed in depth 23 collections, supplied briefer surveys of 100 others, and listed the contents of 90 collections. He illustrated this set with 142 full-page photogravures of collectors' favorite and most prestigious works, and several hundred smaller illustrations in a variety of media. Like all critics, Shinn sought to educate readers' tastes, but unlike his patrician peers he did not reject, and he never ridiculed, collectors' existing tastes. Instead, even as he praised collectors' favorite works, he steered readers to styles and subjects he considered nobler.

Shinn was the last prominent proponent of the traditional belief that excellence was objective and criticism a science. He assured readers that good taste was not innate or inbred but only acquired through experience and education. He thus stood opposed to the elitist concept of inborn genius and sensibility then beginning to dominate art criticism. He told readers to educate their eye by looking at all kinds of paintings. He insisted that excellence took many forms and was present in competing styles. Shinn helped popularize the still-controversial Barbizon school by comparing and equating Jean-François Millet with revered academicians like Gérôme. He was the only major critic of his era who recommended equally the best academic painters, such as Gérôme and Ernest Meissonier, and so-called progressive artists, such as Millet and Camille Corot.

Shinn's final major project, *Mr. W. H. Vanderbilt's House and Collection* (1883–1884, repr. 1972), published for 500 subscribers paying $400 a set, may have been the most lavish celebration of a private home ever published. Its double-elephant-folio format, hand-colored illustrations, and exhaustive descriptions of the architecture, decorations, and furnishings of this long-vanished New York City mansion, make it the ultimate apotheosis of wealth and display during the Gilded Age. He spent 1882 in Paris supervising its production.

Although friendly with many artists—he was an original member of the Tile Club, a recreational group for leading young artists whose activities he publicized—Shinn was of a retiring disposition and "few persons, even in New York art circles, knew him personally" (*Art Amateur* 16 [Dec. 1886]: 3). He died in New York following years of ill health.

Shinn is the most obscure important critic of his era because he was never close to the patrician writers and "progressive" artists who soon wrote the memoirs and histories of art that remain our starting points for exploring American art during this period. Despite his obscurity today, he was the writer most responsible for educating—and documenting—the tastes of nouveau-riche collectors following the Civil War.

• Shinn's papers survive primarily in the Richard Cadbury Tapper Papers in the Friends Historical Library, Swarthmore College. A diary Shinn kept is in the Historical Society of Pennsylvania. His major publications as Edward Strahan remain critical primary sources for scholars. In addition to *Art Treasures of America* and *Mr. W. H. Vanderbilt's House and Collection*, scholars rely heavily upon his *The Masterpieces of the Centennial International Exhibition* (1876–1878); and *The Book of the Tile Club* (1886), completed after Shinn's death by F. Hopkinson Smith. Like so many writers of his day, he also published poetry; see his *The New Hyperion* (1875). The one monograph about him is a rare, fifteen-page pamphlet: William Walton, *Earl Shinn* (1887), repr. in Josiah H. Shinn, *The History of the Shinn Family in Europe and America* (1903). Shinn has primarily interested modern scholars in the context of his close friendship with Thomas Eakins. See Lloyd Goodrich, *Thomas Eakins* (1982), and Gordon Hendricks, *The Life and Work of Thomas Eakins* (1974). He also turns up in studies of American art students in France. See H. Barbara Weinberg, *The Lure of Paris: Nineteenth-Century American Painters and their French Teachers* (1991), and David Sellin, *Americans in Brittany and Normandy* (1982). Brief obituaries appeared in the *Art Amateur* 16 (Dec. 1886): 3; *Nation* 63 (11 Nov. 1886): 394; and several Quaker journals.

SAUL E. ZALESCH

SHINN, Everett (7 Nov. 1876–1 May 1953), painter and illustrator, was born in Woodstown, New Jersey, the son of Isaiah Conklin Shinn, a bank teller, and Josephine Ransley. Both parents were Quakers. Shinn attended Bacon Academy and then the Spring Garden Institute in Philadelphia, Pennsylvania, where he studied mechanics. At the institute he designed one of the first rotary engines. After graduating he got a job designing lighting fixtures, but he soon was caught sketching street scenes while on the job and fired. In 1893 he matriculated at the Pennsylvania Academy of the Fine Arts, where he studied under Thomas P. Anschutz.

Through the Pennsylvania Academy and his part-time position as a staff artist at the *Philadelphia Press*, Shinn became friends with fellow artists William Glackens, George Luks, and John Sloan. They often painted together at the studio of Robert Henri and became known collectively as the "Philadelphia Four," noted for their depictions of urban realism. In 1897 the Pennsylvania Academy held an exhibition of Shinn's work, featuring both his urban scenes and his theatrically themed sketches, both done primarily in pastels. He married Florence Scoval, an author and illustrator, in June 1898; they had no children. After moving to New York City, Shinn supported himself by working as an illustrator for several newspapers—the *World*, the *Herald*, the *Journal*—and for *Harper's Magazine*. In 1900 he went on a brief trip to London, where he painted one of his better known works, the *London Hippodrome*.

In 1908 the Macbeth Galleries in New York held a major exhibition of the work of Shinn and seven other artists: Henri, Sloan, Glackens, Luks, Arthur B. Davies, Ernest Lawson, and Maurice Prendergast. Collectively known as "The Eight," short for the "Eight Men of Rebellion," they were united in opposition to the conservative policies of the National Academy of Design. Their critics later dubbed the group the "Ashcan school," a name reflecting their predilection for painting stark city scenes. In the preface to a catalog for a 1943 retrospective of the group at the Brooklyn Museum, Shinn stressed the group's repudiation of the "monotony of pretty falsification," which they saw as prevalent in late nineteenth-century painting.

The city of Trenton, New Jersey, commissioned Shinn to paint a mural for its city hall. Unveiled in 1911, the work won praise for its realism and artistic sincerity. After a divorce from his first wife, Shinn married Corinne Baldwin in 1913; they had two children. In 1917 he began experimenting in the film genre, working as art director for three releases: *Polly of the Circus* (1917), *The Bright Shawl* (1923), and *Janice Meredith* (1924). After a second divorce, he married Gertrude Chase in 1924. Many exhibitions of Shinn's work were held in New York City in the 1930s; these included shows at the Fifty-Sixth Street Gallery in 1930, the Metropolitan Galleries in 1931, and the Morton Galleries in 1935. His third marriage also ended in divorce; he wed Paula Downing, thirty-six years his junior, in 1933. In 1951 he was elected to the American Academy of Arts and Letters. Shinn died in New York City.

An American impressionist, Shinn was part of a new wave of interest in urban realism within American painting. The theater influenced his style, which grew increasingly dramatic and, in later years, mannered. Other frequent subjects included circus scenes and ballet dancers. His preferred medium was pastels. In addition to painting, Shinn created sets for plays and illustrated numerous books, including Charles Dickens's *A Christmas Carol*, Oscar Wilde's *The Happy Prince*, and *The Sermon on the Mount*.

• The permanent collections of the Metropolitan Museum of Art, the Whitney Museum of American Art, and the Art Institute of Chicago include works by Shinn. A self-portrait (1901) is owned by the National Portrait Gallery, Washington, D.C. Collections of biographic materials are held in the Archives of American Art in the National Collection of Fine Arts in Washington, D.C., and in the Delaware Art Museum in Wilmington, Del. Edith DeShazo, *Everett Shinn, 1876–1953: A Figure in His Time* (1974), offers a complete bibliography of Shinn's work. For further information on Shinn and his circle of painters, see Valerie Ann Leeds, *The Ashcan School and Their Circle, from Florida Collections* (1996); Rebecca Zurier, *Metropolitan Lives: The Ashcan Artists and Their New York* (1995); Bennard Perlman, *Painters of the Ashcan School: The Immortal Eight* (1988; reissue of *The Immortal Eight*, 1962); John Sloan, *The Gist of Art* (1939); Ira Glackens, *William Glackens and the Ashcan Group* (rev. ed., 1984); and J. J. Kwait, "The Genius of Everett Shinn, the Ashcan Painter," *Journal of the Modern Language Association of America* (Mar. 1952). An obituary in the *New York Times*, 3 May 1953, incorrectly gives Shinn's year of birth as 1873.

ELIZABETH ZOE VICARY

SHINN, Milicent Washburn (15 Apr. 1858–13 Aug. 1940), writer, editor, and psychologist, was born in Niles, California, the daughter of James Shinn and Lucy Ellen Clark, who operated a farm and tree nursery. Following high school graduation in 1874 she enrolled at the University of California and, after taking a leave of absence to acquire necessary funds by public school teaching, received her A.B. in 1880.

Shinn's early career, devoted to literature and publishing, began while she was in college on the editorial staff of the *San Francisco Commercial Herald* (1879–1881). She then contributed both poetry and prose to the magazine *Californian* and assumed the post of editor in 1883 after acquiring copyright to revive for its use the title *Overland Monthly*, a name that had earned much national respect before the demise of the publication several years earlier. A contemporary who succeeded her as editor, Charles S. Greene, attested that the publication "had in Miss Shinn editorial ability of the highest sort" (*Overland Monthly*, Sept. 1902). Operating with quite limited financial resources, Shinn carried a heavy responsibility for business affairs and production as well as for the magazine's literary content, much of which she wrote. Both as writer and editor, she thereby played an influential role in promoting the development of literature in the West. Shinn's motivation was to use the magazine as a means of elevating the intellectual life of her region, in her words "the possible germ of much civilization" (1882 letter to Daniel Coit Gilman, cited in Scarborough and Furumoto, p. 56).

A family event occasioned Shinn's shift in career from literature to psychology and formed the basis of work that won her international recognition in the field of child psychology. In 1890 she was living with her extended family on the homestead in Niles when a daughter was born to her brother Charles and his wife, Julia. Fascinated by the baby, Shinn took meticulous notes on her growth, paying special attention to the development of her senses and motor activities, and thereby produced a large mass of data chronicling the emergence of the child's physical and mental abilities. She was invited to present her observations of the infant's first two years at an international conference on education held in conjunction with the 1893 World's Columbian Exposition in Chicago. Shinn's work was enthusiastically received and regarded as complementing William Preyer's observational study of his son, first published in Germany in 1882 and translated as *The Mind of the Child* (1888–1889). She was urged to continue her observations and undertake graduate study at the University of California. She resigned as editor of the *Overland Monthly* in 1894, returned to the Berkeley campus, and pursued a rich course of study that resulted in her becoming the first woman and eleventh person to receive the doctorate from California when she graduated in 1898.

Shinn's doctoral dissertation consisted of observations based on her niece's development (which she continued to record through the child's seventh year) and the conclusions she drew for pedagogical applications. Her work was published in three installments by the university under the title *Notes on the Development of a Child*, and in 1900 it was published as *The Biography of a Baby*, a popular version that was widely used by parents and students. Shinn's pioneering study became a classic in the field of child psychology and a model of systematic observational research. She and Preyer are typically credited with setting the standard for this type of child study, and her book continues to be cited in infant and child development literature.

The Biography of a Baby traced the child's first year, recording and interpreting behaviors as they emerged and changed month by month. A quotation from the sixth month provides an example of both observation and explanation and demonstrates how Shinn made her scientific work accessible to a general audience:

Our baby, for instance, first used her intelligence to steer her toe into her mouth, and the way she did it, compared with the way she slowly settled on the proper movements for getting her rattle into her mouth, shows clearly the practical difference between unintelligent and intelligent action, even if both are at bottom made of the same psychological stuff. . . . Of all a baby's doings this toe business is the one that people find it most impossible to regard with scientific seriousness. But its indirect usefulness is considerable. The cooperation of different parts of the body that it teaches is remarkable; and it must have great influence in extending the sense of self to the legs and feet, where it has hitherto seemed but weakly developed. (pp. 164–66)

Despite the thoroughness of her training and the significance of her professional contributions, Shinn's career in psychology was short-lived. She never held employment as a psychologist and apparently never sought a professional position following her doctoral training. Her decision to pursue graduate studies was based not on a desire to become a psychologist but rather on the belief that her observational project had merit and that its publication would benefit both the University of California and the work of educators. The close family ties that provided the opportunity for her data gathering, however, also prevented her from continuing the scholarly pursuits she so enjoyed. Following the receipt of her doctorate at age forty, she found it necessary to turn her energies to retiring a heavy mortgage on her parents' ranch. Her ailing mother, for whom Shinn felt a special responsibility as the only daughter, also needed much attention. Though she maintained contact with friends and colleagues through correspondence, she had to keep "constant vigilance" over her mother in the family home where she also provided tutoring for a younger brother's children. By her mid-fifties she had developed a disabling heart condition that increasingly cur-

tailed her activities until her death in either Niles or Alameda County, California.

Energetic until her health failed, Shinn was active in a number of national and regional societies. She promoted the Association of Collegiate Alumnae (now the American Association of University Women) by organizing a branch in California and heading a national committee on child development from 1895 to 1909. She supported woman suffrage, the League of Nations, the eugenics movement, a local anti-saloon organization, and the Save-the-Redwoods League.

Shinn's obligations as a daughter, sister, and aunt anchored her in the homestead where she lived all her life. Nevertheless, during the 1880s and 1890s she engaged in an interval of professional and scholarly involvement that produced a highly significant intellectual legacy.

• Shinn's papers are in the California Historical Society, Sacramento, and the Mary Lea Shane Archives of the Lick Observatory, Santa Cruz. A detailed account of her personal life is in Elizabeth Scarborough and Laurel Furumoto, *Untold Lives: The First Generation of American Women Psychologists* (1987). An obituary is in the *New York Times*, 15 Aug. 1940.

ELIZABETH SCARBOROUGH

SHIPLEY, Ruth Bielaski (20 Apr. 1885–3 Nov. 1966), government administrator, was born in Montgomery County, Maryland, the daughter of Alexander Bielaski, a Methodist minister, and Roselle Woodward Israel. She grew up in comfortable circumstances on her grandfather's Maryland farm and at the family's Washington, D.C. residence. She received a high school education in Washington.

In 1903 Shipley took her first job as a clerk in the U.S. Patent Office. She remained there until 1909, when she married Frederick van Dorn Shipley and resigned to live with him in the Panama Canal Zone. They had one child. In 1914 Frederick Shipley's illness required them to return to Washington. With the help of Ruth Shipley's brother, A. Bruce Bielaski, who was chief of the Justice Department's Bureau of Investigation, Ruth obtained a temporary clerk's job in the Department of State, where she remained for forty-one years. Her husband died in 1919.

At the State Department Shipley became special assistant to Assistant Secretary Alva A. Adee and then assistant to Margaret M. Hanna, chief of the Office of Coordination and Review, who was then the highest paid woman in the department. In 1928 Shipley's apprenticeship ended with her appointment as the first permanent chief of the Passport Division, a job previously rotated among foreign service officers for limited periods. At the time when male supervisors and female clerks were the rule in the federal workplace, she supervised seventy employees and her salary, then about $4,000 a year, was among the highest paid to a woman in the government.

In 1930 Shipley was a U.S. delegate to the Conference on the Codification of International Law at The Hague, Netherlands, but otherwise she shunned the spotlight. She disliked publicity, the Washington social scene, and even having her picture taken. In the 1930s and 1940s the work of her office grew dramatically, and with it grew her superiors' respect for her integrity and efficiency.

The Neutrality Acts of the 1930s and World War II required Shipley's office to restrict travel in war zones. In the early Cold War her personal control over the issuance of passports and her fervent anticommunism put her at the center of a growing debate about a citizen's right to travel abroad. In 1856 Congress gave the secretary of state the exclusive right to issue passports, and in the war emergencies of 1918 and 1941 Congress empowered the executive branch to stop citizens from going abroad without passports. In 1950 the McCarran Internal Security Act authorized denying a passport to any member or former member of an organization that was listed as Communist or subversive by the attorney general. Under these authorities Shipley denied passports to well-known American leftists, including Paul Robeson, Arthur Miller, Rockwell Kent, Leo Szilard, Linus Pauling, W. E. .B. Du Bois, Clark Foreman, Elizabeth Gurley Flynn, and Herbert Aptheker, on the ground that their travel was "prejudicial to the interests of the United States." She rarely explained her decisions, from which until 1953 there was no formal and until 1955 no independent appeal. When she did give reasons, they were overtly political, as when she told physicist Martin Kamen that he had not been candid when he testified before the House Un-American Activities Committee.

The controversy made Shipley the subject of public debate in 1952, when Senator Pat McCarran (D.-Nev.) and Secretary of State Dean Acheson defended her office against Oregon Republican senator Wayne Morse's charges that the passport denials were "tyrannical and capricious." Shipley's objectivity was suspect not only because of her own conservative views but also because of the activities of her brother Frank B. Bielaski. He was a private detective with a checkered reputation who, while working for the Office of Strategic Services in 1945, had broken into and illegally seized evidence at the offices of the pro-Communist magazine *Amerasia*. In 1950 he made unsupported claims about what he had found there to the Senate Foreign Relations Subcommittee. Shipley was at most a minor player in McCarthyism and certainly not as much of an ideologue as her successor Frances Knight. Nonetheless she became the object of liberal scorn. Thus the woman admired in *Fortune* (Nov. 1945) as "a good-looking woman . . . whose "alert gray eyes appraise you long and thoughtfully" became to blacklisted screenwriter Lillian Hellman, who was seeking permission to work in Europe, "a severe looking lady with a manner made more severe by its attempt not to be" (*Scoundrel Time* [1976], p. 79). Yet, as Hellman admitted, Shipley granted her a passport.

It took years to adjudicate the travel rights of citizens. In the 1950s a federal appeals court established the courts' right to review the State Department's procedures in denying passports. In *Aptheker v. Secretary of State* (1964) the Supreme Court ruled that the State Department must afford both procedural and substantive due process to applicants before denying them a passport.

When Shipley retired in 1955 at age seventy, the State Department honored her with its Distinguished Service Award. She had served presidents from Calvin Coolidge to Dwight D. Eisenhower and secretaries of state from Frank Kellogg to John Foster Dulles. The passport controversy should not obscure her long service nor the fact that she was a much-admired civil servant whose example helped open doors for women in government. She died in Washington, D.C.

• Shipley was a private person who left no collection of personal papers or writings in a public depository. The most comprehensive source for her personal life and career is the *Washington Star* clippings file about her in the Washingtonian Room of the Martin Luther King, Jr., Public Library, Washington, D.C. During her career she was profiled in popular magazines, including H. W. Erskine, "You Don't Go if She Says No," *Collier's* 132 (1953): 62–65; and André Visson, "Watchdog of the State Department," *Independent Woman* 30 (1951): 225–26, which was condensed as "Ruth Shipley, the State Department's Watchdog," *Reader's Digest* 59 (1951): 73–76. The Cold War passport controversy is explored in Leonard B. Boudin, "The Constitutional Right to Travel," *Columbia Law Review* 56 (1956): 47–75; "Passport Refusals for Political Reasons: Constitutional Issues and Judicial Review," *Yale Law Journal* 61 (1952): 171–203; and, with greater perspective, Alan Rogers, "Passports and Politics: The Courts and the Cold War," *Historian* 47 (1985): 497–511. Civil liberties aspects of the passport controversy are discussed at length in Stanley I. Kutler, *The American Inquisition: Justice and Injustice in the Cold War* (1982), although it mostly covers Shipley's successor. Obituaries are in the *New York Times* and the *Washington Post*, both 5 Nov. 1966.

CHARLES HOWARD MCCORMICK

SHIPMAN, Ellen Biddle (1869–29 Mar. 1950), landscape architect, was born probably in Philadelphia, Pennsylvania, the daughter of James Biddle, a career officer in the U.S. Army, and Ellen McGowan. Her family's domicile was determined by her father's military orders. A book titled *Reminiscences of a Soldier's Wife*, written by her mother and privately printed in Philadelphia by Lippincott in 1907, gives the reader a sense of Ellen's solitary and unusual childhood. She attended the Harvard Annex (later Radcliffe College) for a year, leaving in 1893 against her parents' wishes to marry the poet and playwright Louis Evan Shipman.

Seminal to Ellen Shipman's future and the development of her career as a landscape designer was the couple's decision in 1895 to summer in the artists' colony at Cornish, New Hampshire, formed a decade earlier around the sculptor Augustus St. Gaudens. For two summers in the mid-1890s the newlyweds shared a house with Herbert D. Croly, editor of *Architectural Record*, and his wife Louise, who was Shipman's college housemate. The Shipmans then became "chickadees," or year-round residents, buying their own house, "Brook Place," in nearby Plainfield, New Hampshire, where their three children were raised.

Cornish was the embodiment of the American Renaissance, with its emphasis on artistic interactions and collaborations. Frequent visits by talented residents enhanced and magnified aesthetic considerations, making them a part of daily life. Everyone was affected by the beauty of the gardens, the near landscape, the vistas, all culminating in the towering, ever-present Mount Ascutney. Frances Grimes's "Reminiscences," an undated manuscript at Dartmouth College Library, gives the flavor and some details of these halcyon days.

While bringing up her children at Brook Place, Shipman planted gardens. She also drew plans for "dream houses and dream gardens." At the end of her career, after a lifetime of successful gardenmaking, she wrote in her "Garden Note Book," "As I look back, I realize it was at that moment that a garden became for me the most essential part of a home." She was recalling her visit to Annie Lazarus's "High Court," with its garden designed (1890–1891) by Charles Adams Platt. Platt, an etcher, landscape painter, and nascent architect, had just published his influential book *Italian Gardens* (1894). A Cornish resident, he noticed, appreciated, and encouraged Shipman. One Christmas around the turn of the century he gave her a complete set of drafting tools, with a note saying, "If you can do as well as I saw, you better keep on."

In the *Ladies' Home Journal* (Sept. 1911), Shipman published an article titled "Window Gardens for Little Money." In 1913 she identified herself on her letterhead as a "landscape gardener." Platt's encouragement became collaboration. He invited her to create planting plans for his garden designs. In an exhibition of Cornish artists at Dartmouth College in March 1916, her work was shown alongside Platt's. An early example of this collaboration (1917) is the Mr. and Mrs. Russell Alger estate, the "Moorings," Grosse Pointe Farms, Michigan. The Algers continued as Shipman's clients until 1937.

Platt's encouragement, tutelage, and eventual collaboration launched Shipman's professional career. Her increasingly unhappy marriage ended in divorce (probably around 1920). Also in 1920, while retaining Brook Place, Shipman moved to New York City and set up her own office as a landscape architect next door to her house at 21 Beekman Place. Her collaboration with Platt continued, but she immediately developed her own clientele. Her innate talents, hard work, and faithfulness to her design principles resulted in a busy practice. Shipman insisted the first essentials were a paper, pencil, and eraser. Primarily a garden must have a well-defined plan: "It must have design. It must have privacy and it must have greenery." Her extraordinary way with plant material became legendary, as was her insistence on proper, if sometimes backbreaking, soil preparation. She understood the qualities of plants, and the abundance of her borders was an outstanding characteristic.

Shipman's attention to the requirements of both the site and the client was paramount. At the outset of each new commission, Shipman intently studied the general location and actual site of the projected garden. In her Garden Note Book she wrote, "I took two or three days driving about the country to note the native growth and natural combinations." In a letter of 28 June 1945 to Mrs. L. Wilmont, she wrote, "I feel strongly that each garden that I do is like a portrait of the person and should express their likes and dislikes and be nearly as they would have made themselves had they the training to do so."

Shipman's work was predominantly residential and mostly on the East Coast. Eventually, she executed commissions in twenty-five states as far afield as Texas, Colorado, and California. One example of her work now open to the public is Longue Vue Gardens in New Orleans. Shipman worked with Edith and Edgar Stern for three decades refining these brilliantly designed garden rooms on their eight-acre place.

Shipman's public commissions were the Bronx Botanical Garden (1928, 1931), Bronx, New York; the Sarah P. Duke Gardens (1937), Duke University, Durham, North Carolina; Lake Shore Boulevard (1931–1932), Grosse Pointe, Michigan; the Museum of Fine Arts (1934–1935), Colorado Springs; the Aetna Life Insurance Company (1931), Hartford, Connecticut; and the United States Military Academy (1936), West Point, New York. She also worked on the reshaping of the St. Gaudens gardens as they were prepared for the transition from a private to a public site.

Aware of her lack of formal training in a field becoming increasingly professionalized, Shipman, while overseeing a burgeoning practice, enrolled (class year unknown) in the Lowthorpe School of Landscape Architecture and Horticulture for Women, Groton, Massachusetts. Eventually she became an instructor and member of the board. Shipman hired only women and became an outspoken protagonist for women working in the field. In a 13 March 1938 *New York Times* interview, Shipman affirmed, "Before women took hold of the profession, landscape architects were doing what I call cemetery work. Until women took up landscaping, gardening in this country was at its lowest ebb. The renaissance of the art was due largely to the fact that women, instead of working over their boards, used plants as if they were painting pictures as an artist would."

In June 1933 *House & Garden* proclaimed a Gardening Hall of Fame. It included Louise Payson, Agnes Selkirk Clark, Rose Greely, Annette Hoyt Flanders, and Romney Spring. Ellen Shipman was cited as "the Dean of American women landscape architects, in a manner of speaking; for adding immeasurably to garden industry in many states; and for having been so long a sane, understanding leader in her profession."

A creator of splendid residential gardens during a period of unparalleled national affluence, Shipman was forced to alter her practice after the onset of the depression. Always interested in the dynamic interaction of the transitions between interior and near and far exterior spaces, she successfully adapted to the economic climate and began in 1931 to offer her clients interior design services.

With the advent of World War II, Shipman volunteered for work in the U.S. Army Camouflage Unit. She was turned down because of her age; she was seventy-two. She began her own war effort. She devised an eight-week program and taught girls drafting skills. She traveled, at her own expense, giving lectures on how to make a victory garden.

Although she did not receive official recognition during her lifetime, Shipman's work was widely published in periodicals. Late in her life, with a possible eye toward publication, Shipman began a Garden Note Book. It remains an unpaginated manuscript. In it, she recounts her experience and techniques and elucidates her design philosophy. Shipman did not invent a garden style. Rather, she constantly worked to refine her medium, one characterized by tight, formally organized spatial relationships, the use of architectural elements (walls, different levels, benches), and abundant plant material. She felicitously utilized native plants and plant groupings. She juxtaposed the formal with the informal with consummate skill. She said, "I stress simplicity of design with privacy to be secured, as a garden is intended to be a place of beauty where one can go to rest and meditate." Shipman died in her house in Bermuda.

• Ellen Shipman's archives are at the Carl A. Kroch Library, Cornell University, Ithaca, N.Y. Shipman gave her correspondence to the World War II paper drive. Smaller holdings of Shipman materials can be found within other collections at the Dartmouth College Library; the Rhode Island School of Design Library, Providence; the St. Gaudens National Historic Site, Cornish, N.H.; the Office of Horticulture, Smithsonian Institution, Washington, D.C.; and the University of Oregon, Eugene, Special Collections (Lord & Schryver Archives Collection no. 98). Several unpublished papers give information about Shipman. They are Ann F. Bloom, "Ellen Biddle Shipman," Radcliffe seminar paper, 1986, Carl A. Kroch Library, Cornell University; Jane A. Knight, "An Examination of the History of the Lowthorpe School of Landscape for Women, Groton, Massachusetts, 1901–1945" (master's thesis, Cornell Univ., 1986); and Deborah Kay Meador, "The Making of a Landscape Architect: Ellen Biddle Shipman and Her Years at the Cornish Art Colony (master's thesis, Cornell Univ., 1989). Two works by Dan Krall, an authority on Shipman, are useful: A Half Century of Garden Designs: The Drawings of Landscape Architect Ellen Shipman (exhibition brochure, Cornell Univ., Apr. 1986) and Early Women Designers and Their Work in Public Places, paper presented at the "Landscapes and Gardens: Women Who Made a Difference" Symposium, East Lansing, Mich., 9–10 June 1987. An excellent and generously illustrated general source is the chapter on Shipman in William H. Tishler, ed., American Landscape Architecture: Designers and Places (1989). Shipman is discussed in Catherine R. Brown and Celia Newton Maddox, "Women and the Land: A Suitable Profession," Landscape Architecture, May 1982, pp. 65–69. An obituary is in the New York Times, 29 Mar. 1950.

CATHA GRACE RAMBUSCH

SHIPPEN, Edward (1639–Aug. 1712), merchant, religious martyr, and political leader, was born in Yorkshire, England, the son of William Shippen, a prominent landholder, and Mary Nunnes (or Nuns). Although his older brother earned degrees at Oxford and became an Anglican clergyman, Edward in 1668 emigrated to Boston, Massachusetts, a wilderness town of about 3,500. In 1671 he married Elizabeth Lybrand; they had eight children during their seventeen years together. Not long after he joined an artillery company, Shippen converted to his wife's faith and became a member of the Society of Friends.

His decision to join the Quakers identified Shippen as an outsider in New England and strongly circumscribed the role he might play in Massachusetts. Positive consequences of this conversion included business connections that Shippen made with Quakers in Rhode Island, New York, and Pennsylvania and the stature he later gained in the Quaker colony during the last eighteen years of his life. The immediate effect of his conversion was humiliation. Quakers had been persecuted ever since their arrival in Boston in 1656. Before 1661 four had been hanged and others whipped or mutilated. Overt hostility abated during the decade following 1664 but revived in 1675. On two occasions in August 1677 Shippen was arrested and publicly whipped for attending Quaker meetings. Years later, when attitudes in Boston changed, Shippen erected as a monument two posts at either end of the pit into which the corpses of "martyrs for the truth" had been tossed.

Like many New England merchants, Shippen utilized family connections. He traded with England and Jamaica, and later with Boston. He also relied on Quaker connections. Shippen's economic base expanded considerably following an inheritance from his father, who died in 1681. He owned several wharves near Faneuil Hall and several houses in Boston. Within thirteen years he invested more than £1,000 in real estate. New men, with roots in Restoration England, coalesced into a powerful group that took advantage of opportunities created as the founding generation of Puritans disintegrated during the 1680s, but Shippen remained an outsider. New and old groups agreed that the zealots, or Quakers, with their "superadded presumptions and incorrigible contempt for authoritie" had no place in Massachusetts.

In 1686 Shippen bought a house in Philadelphia, the capital of William Penn's recently established Quaker colony. The death of Shippen's wife and two of his children, his commercial dealings with Quakers in New York and Pennsylvania, and his marriage in 1689 to Rebekah Richardson, a widow whose sister had moved to Philadelphia, helped persuade Shippen to relocate there in 1690. The move, coupled with Shippen's family and religious connections, his reputation, personality, and great wealth, gained him immediate gratification in a world of power and politics that Puritan Boston had stifled.

The social structures of Philadelphia and Pennsylvania were very fluid and rather undifferentiated. Unlike most immigrants, Shippen entered at the top of society. His fortune, reputedly £10,000 sterling, made him one of the wealthiest men in the Delaware Valley; it is unlikely that anyone's economic resources equaled his. In 1693 only four estates had been valued for tax purposes at more than £1,000, and no one who died in seventeenth-century Pennsylvania left an estate valued at more than £2,800. Shippen owned at least 500 acres, plus an estate in England and property in Boston. A man of Shippen's economic stature, who had also suffered physically as a strong witness to "the Truth," exhibited the qualities that William Penn sought in leaders of the province. Shippen impressed others as a natural leader, for immediately upon his arrival settlers elected him Speaker of the assembly. From then until his death Shippen took full advantage of his power and abilities. He figured prominently in local and provincial affairs and expanded his economic base, rose in political stature, and firmly established his family's position. In the process, he contributed to the rise of Philadelphia, of Pennsylvania, and of the nascent elite.

Shippen continued to trade with merchants in England, the West Indies, Boston, New York, and elsewhere. He also invested in land, owning 250 acres adjoining the southern city boundary as well as property within the Philadelphia city limits. His mansion, with attractive views of the city and of the Delaware River, became the showplace of the province. In 1699 Penn used it as the governor's mansion when he visited his province. Shippen's lifestyle stretched to the limit the wealthy Quakers' affinity for "the best sort, but plain." He rode to town in what many claimed was the largest coach in the province, and the fact that he owned a coach set him apart from most in this pioneer society where coaches and carriages probably numbered fewer than a half dozen. Shippen also had his portrait painted, for which he wore a deep brown coat of fine material, white scarf, ruffled cuffs, and powdered, curled white wig. In 1706 Shippen arranged the marriage of his 22-year-old daughter with Thomas Story, a middle-aged English Quaker who styled himself a gentleman. This alliance with wealth and power—Story held several offices including membership in the provincial council—suggests Shippen's ambitions.

In 1694, 1700, and 1705 Shippen was elected to the provincial assembly, and in July 1695 he became Speaker of the assembly. While the provincial council was an elective body, he was chosen a member in 1696 and "returned every year at the fresh elections." As early as 1697 he apparently served as its president. Although the Charter of Privileges of 1701 made no provision for an upper house in Pennsylvania, Penn created a governor's council and appointed Shippen to it. Shippen served as the council's first president, and in this capacity he acted as chief executive of Pennsylvania from 1703 to 1704, before a new governor was appointed. Because of his close association with William Penn, Shippen often facilitated cooperation between the council and the assembly. Although he sometimes took an independent stand, people looked on him as a strong supporter of Penn. He later served as an executor, trustee, and overseer of Penn's will. Shippen was chief justice of Pennsylvania in 1699 and in 1701 served as a provincial judge. From 1701 to 1712 he served as commissioner of property.

The first mayor of Philadelphia, serving from 1701 until 1703, Shippen remained in the Philadelphia city corporation after it was reformed as the governing board of the city in 1704. He continued as an alderman until his death, and from 1705 to 1712 he was city treasurer. Shippen played a relatively minor role in the Philadelphia Monthly Meeting; his most important assignment was as a member of the building committee that erected the 1696 meeting house.

The Quaker Meeting carefully scrutinized the activities of all of its members, even the most wealthy and politically powerful. In 1705 Shippen's second wife died. The following year, with almost irreverent haste, he married Esther Wilcox James, the widow of Philip James, a wine cooper. Although her brother Joseph was a merchant and mayor of Philadelphia, and Esther owned valuable property, one critic described it as "one of ye darkest weddings . . . ever." James Logan, not yet a prominent Pennsylvanian but rather an unsuccessful suitor for Shippen's daughter, wrote that "ye old Lecher" had outraged the Society of Friends because they discovered his intended bride's "apron to rise too fast." The birth of John in early 1707 confirmed the charge that the bride was pregnant. For the next year the couple suffered humiliation; the Quakers suspended meetings at Shippen's house and caused the couple to condemn their behavior in writing. The final humiliation occurred when Shippen stood before the meeting while his kinsman read Shippen's testimony. The testimony was sent to Friends in several mainland colonies, the West Indies, and London who might use it "for the service of Truth . . . only as the Wisdom of God" suggests. Shippen remained a Quaker until his death. Although he resumed his minor role in the meeting, his bequest of £50 to the meeting for the support of the Friends school and the poor suggests that the richest man in the colony remained angry about the censure. The city government had tried to lessen the blow to his pride by electing Shippen mayor in 1707, a vote facilitated by the fact that one-third of the members of the body that elected him were his relatives. He declined the honor.

Shippen remained forceful and energetic throughout his life. When he died in Philadelphia, he left a foundation upon which later generations built one of the great colonial families. Shippen's stature as one of the wealthiest men in the colonies, a powerful political office holder, and a martyr for religious freedom provided a strong economic and emotional legacy for later generations. The Shippen family drew strength from this "reference ancestor," his impressive "symbolic estate," and his financial fortune.

• Useful material is in the Shippen, Penn, and Logan manuscripts, Historical Society of Pennsylvania; and in the manuscript records of the Society of Friends, Philadelphia. Although the Shippen family papers are extensive, most focus on later generations. References to Shippen appear in a dozen manuscript collections at the Historical Society of Pennsylvania, which has photographs and engraved reproductions of Shippen portraits. Randolph Shipley Klein, *Portrait of an Early American Family: The Shippens of Pennsylvania across Five Generations*, chap. 2 (1975), provides the fullest biographical sketch. Other works dealing with Shippen include John W. Jordan, ed., *Colonial and Revolutionary Families of Pennsylvania* (3 vols., 1911); Charles P. Keith, *Provincial Councillors of Pennsylvania* (1883); Craig W. Horle et al., *Lawmaking and Legislators in Pennsylvania: A Biographical Dictionary*, vol. 1 (1991); Edward Armstrong, ed., "Correspondence between Wm. Penn and James Logan," *Memoirs of the Historical Society of Pennsylvania* 9–10 (1870–1872); H. H. Martin, *Martin's Bench and Bar of Philadelphia* (1883); T. W. Balch, *The English Ancestors of the Shippen Family and Edward Shippen of Philadelphia* (1904); Thomas Balch, *Letters and Papers Relating Chiefly to Pennsylvania* (5 vols., 1855); Edwin B. Bronner, *William Penn's "Holy Experiment"* (1962); Carl Bridenbaugh, *Cities in the Wilderness* (1962); Gary Nash, *Quakers and Politics* (1968); Frederick B. Tolles, *Meeting House and Counting House* (1963); and Tolles, *James Logan and the Culture of Provincial America* (1957). A portrait of Shippen hangs in the mayor's reception room in Philadelphia's City Hall.

RANDOLPH SHIPLEY KLEIN

SHIPPEN, Edward IV (16 Feb. 1729–15 Apr. 1806), member of the governor's council and chief justice of Pennsylvania, was born in Philadelphia, Pennsylvania, the son of Edward Shippen III, a merchant and office holder, and Sarah Plumley. He had much to live up to because the Shippens had cut large figures in economic and political circles. Shippen was apprenticed to Tench Francis, Pennsylvania's attorney general. At age nineteen he continued his legal training at Middle Temple. After completing his studies in London, he traveled in France before returning to Philadelphia in 1750. In 1753 Shippen married Margaret Francis, his preceptor's daughter; they had nine children, and the marriage lasted until her death more than four decades later. Kinship ties with Chief Justice William Allen, Deputy Governor James Hamilton, and others provided Shippen with political offices. In 1755 he became a judge of the admiralty, and in 1758 he entered the Philadelphia Common Council. Soon Shippen rode in a four-wheeled carriage and lived in the "great house" in Philadelphia, which he rented from his father, close to many kinsmen. Although his father and the chief justice were Presbyterians, Shippen became an Anglican.

During the 1760s and 1770s the power, structure, and functioning of the Shippen family gave a certain character to society. In 1764 Benjamin Franklin, Joseph Galloway, and the Quaker party tried in vain to overthrow the proprietary form of government and make Pennsylvania a royal colony. As the imperial crisis intensified, the Shippens were caught in an ambiguous position. They opposed efforts to increase British control by converting Pennsylvania into a royal colony and broader efforts to tighten the empire. On the other hand, they did not sympathize with aspects of the protest movement directed against the old-style politics. When the Stamp Act crisis began, Shippen remarked that his namesake was born just in time "to breath[e] about three weeks the Air of Freedom; for [soon] . . . we may call ourselves the Slaves of England." With misgivings, Shippen and his brother Joseph Shippen III, secretary of the province, defied the parliamentary measure. Shippen also supported Chief Justice Allen, who called a mass protest meeting at the state house.

Following the Boston Tea Party in December 1773, Shippen feared a civil war. He began to hedge. Although he identified with Americans as "neither natural or unatural [*sic*] Rebels," he also "as if by accident" let people know that ill health and old age would prevent him from being a delegate to the provincial convention. "A most extraordinary *Pamphlet* entitled, Common Sense," frightened Shippen, for it "openly avows an absolute Independency of Great Britain" (Shippen papers, vol. 7, p. 149). Shippen hoped in vain as Lord North's conciliation plan failed; his fears rose as Timothy Matlack and "a number of other violent wrongheaded people of the inferior Class" tried to replace the assembly with a radical provincial convention. Both Shippen and his brother moved their families out of Philadelphia; Shippen's family went to his farm in Amwell, New Jersey.

Indeed, the Pennsylvania Constitution of 1776 served as a ringing denunciation of many activities and practices of the Shippens and other colonial families. The authors of this revolutionary document adopted more than a dozen statements that stand as indictments of the Shippens and their friends. Multiple office holding was singled out; hence Shippen lost his appointments as judge of the admiralty court, prothonotary of the Supreme Court of Pennsylvania, and member of the governor's council. Extensive power given to "the people," term limits, and rotation in office were concepts diametrically opposed to the system Shippen favored. In 1776 Philadelphians abolished the Common Council of Philadelphia, of which Shippen and his kinsmen had comprised a majority.

The Shippens were not Tories, for they harbored no desire to increase the royal prerogative. Like many other officials of the colonial government, Shippen signed a parole but declined to swear allegiance to the revolutionary constitution. The parole document essentially imposed house arrest. It enabled proprietary government officers to avoid prison by promising not to flee the area or interfere with the new government. With concern for his family and his professional stature uppermost in his mind, he moved dextrously through the tortuous course of revolution. In 1776, when Shippen feared General William Howe's advance through New Jersey, he moved his family back to Philadelphia. Much to Shippen's chagrin, his only son, Edward V, jeopardized the family's neutrality when he was taken prisoner by the Continental army at Trenton. Shippen wrote, "Though I highly disapproved of what he had done, yet I could not condemn him so much as I should have done if he had not been inticed to it" by his cousins the Allens (Shippen-Balch papers, vol. 2, p. 35). The son had no British commission; hence a family friend got him an immediate discharge, and the family's neutrality remained intact.

During 1777 Shippen lived in constant fear of arrest by the radicals and felt increasing burdens of trying to support his family, which included four daughters with expensive tastes. When the British army marched on Philadelphia, Shippen signed a parole and thus avoided exile to Virginia. He remained in town during the British occupation in order to protect his property from plunder and to assess the chances of a British victory. His daughters proved popular with young British officers. Major John André courted Peggy Shippen, and a young lord was obliged to apologize for brazenly kissing Salley Shippen in public. Beyond that, Shippen avoided identification with the occupying force. Although the Continental army suffered at Valley Forge, the British failed to convince Shippen they could win. The Shippen family was not among the 3,000 civilians who accompanied the British army when it retreated from Philadelphia to New York.

That exodus played a decisive role in committing Shippen and his family to the rebel cause. Before the end of the year he gladly announced that his daughter Betsy had married her cousin Major Edward Burd, prothonotary of the Supreme Court, and "my youngest daughter [Peggy] is much solicited by a certain General on the same subject." The "certain General" was Benedict Arnold, one of the more successful American officers, then in charge of the military administration of the nation's capital.

Betsy Shippen's lavish wedding, which included no less than twenty-five bridesmaids, served notice that Shippen and his family had not been cast aside by the Revolution. Even after he sold his 370-acre farm and gristmill in New Jersey to help finance the weddings and dowries, Shippen felt financial strains. During the next few years he contemplated moving to Lancaster to reduce expenses and frequently complained about high taxes. Nevertheless, Shippen provided a handsome dowry to nineteen-year-old Peggy, including "Mount Pleasant," one of the finest country seats in North America. Ironically, this effort to identify with the American cause connected the family with a treacherous villain. Within days of General Arnold's flight from West Point, Peggy Shippen Arnold returned to her father in Philadelphia. Revolutionary authorities dismissed accusations of her involvement in the plot or other intrigues, but they ordered her into exile.

The revolutionary years caused a startling decline in Shippen's wealth and power. Although the Shippens lost no property other than offices, the elaborate extended family network, covering three generations and lateral kinsmen, suffered extensive damage. Death had removed important figures, including Shippen's father. The value of Shippen's connection with the Allens and the Penns declined tremendously when the Penns lost the government and millions of acres in Pennsylvania.

During the 1780s Shippen and his brother Joseph tried with little success to squeeze profits from their real estate holdings in Philadelphia, Shippensburg, and less-developed areas of Pennsylvania in what became Northampton, Bedford, Cumberland, Allegheny, and Westmoreland counties. Shippen overestimated the value of his undeveloped lands and rarely found a buyer. He and his brother often failed to pay taxes on their lands until they feared a sheriff's sale. Fortunately, by 1789 it became evident that "Shippensburg appears now in a much more thriving State than it has ever been and will probably improve & increase . . . [because of] the Trade of the back Country" (Shippen papers, box 1).

Despite setbacks and frustrations, Shippen yearned for the power and influence that he previously enjoyed. He derived some income from the law and real estate. He also reduced expenses by relying on products from his farm and moved out of the dilapidated house on Fourth Street into a more modest dwelling. Still, Shippen's financial straits were evident as he tried to collect 25-year-old debts and borrowed money from his son-in-law. His eldest son and two daughters could not marry until their late twenties.

Shippen returned to public life in 1784 as a justice of the peace and president of the Court of Common Pleas for Philadelphia County. The following year he was elected a magistrate in Philadelphia. "Th[ough] I dislike the business & know it will be burthensome," he admitted, he accepted it in hopes that it would lead to "something more to my mind" (Shippen papers, vol. 8, p. 127). At this time Shippen also became judge of the orphans court, a position he held until 1789. These offices provided more burdens than rewards. In 1786 he resigned as justice of the peace and president of the Court of Quarter Sessions of the Peace in order to focus on the more important office of president of the Court of Common Pleas for Philadelphia County. He retained the latter position until 1790.

Upon the creation of the federal judiciary system in 1789, Shippen's friends, including the attorney general, recommended him as district judge of Pennsylvania. His supporters believed that "far superior knowledge and Capacity for the station" based on his knowledge of common, maritime, and civil law made him preferable to the leading candidate. The position was not offered. Not long after this the government of Pennsylvania relied in part on Shippen's advice in setting up an entirely new arrangement of the courts in the commonwealth. In 1791 he was appointed to the Pennsylvania Supreme Court. There he joined his former students and kinsmen Jasper Yeates and Edward Burd. Shippen continued in that body for fifteen years, becoming chief justice of Pennsylvania in 1799.

Shippen's opinions rested on solid legal principles and were not distorted by his affiliation with the Federalists. In 1804, however, the opposition party in the state assembly impeached him and two associates. The charges arose from the Passmore case in which Thomas Passmore, a prickly and vindictive merchant, charged that a court ruling against him was "pregnant with so many alarming consequences to the rights of the people" that he petitioned for impeachment. Without the benefit of a trial by jury, or even being present in the courtroom, he was sentenced to a short jail term and modest fine. His offense fell within the English concept of "constructive complaints" and was part of the legal customs of Pennsylvania. The prosecutor relied on rhetoric rather than evidence, for the charges were flimsy, and the trial rested on politics, not principles. The Pennsylvania Senate acquitted the chief justice and his associates in January 1805. Shippen retired later in 1805 and died at home in Philadelphia. He had played a major role in establishing law as a skilled profession in the nation's largest city and one of the largest states.

• The Shippen Family Papers at the Historical Society of Pennsylvania, the American Philosophical Society, and the Library of Congress are extensive, and references to Shippen also appear in many other manuscript collections at those institutions. Randolph Shipley Klein, *Portrait of an Early American Family: The Shippens of Pennsylvania across Five Generations* (1975), provides much information about Shippen. Other works dealing with Shippen include John W. Jordan, ed., *Colonial and Revolutionary Families of Pennsylvania* (3 vols., 1911); Charles P. Keith, *Provincial Councillors of Pennsylvania* (1883); H. H. Martin, *Martin's Bench and Bar of Philadelphia* (1883); T. W. Balch, *The English Ancestors of the Shippen Family and Edward Shippen of Philadelphia* (1904); Thomas Balch, *Letters and Papers Relating Chiefly to Pennsylvania* (5 vols., 1855); Carl Bridenbaugh's *Cities in Revolt* (1964) and, with Jessica Bridenbaugh, *Rebels and Gentlemen* (1962); Edward Potts Cheyney and Ellis Paxson Oberholtzer, *University of Pennsylvania: Its History, Influence, Equipment, and Characteristics, with Biographical Sketches and Portraits of Founders, Benefactors, Officers, and Alumni* (2 vols., 1901–1902); James H. Hutson, *Pennsylvania Politics 1746–1770* (1972); Gary Nash, *Quakers and Politics* (1968); Lily Lee Nixon, *James Burd: Frontier Defender, 1726–1793* (1941); Theodore Thayer, *Pennsylvania Politics and the Growth of Democracy, 1740–1776* (1953); Frederick B. Tolles, *Meeting House and Counting House* (1963); and Whitfield J. Bell, Jr., *Patriot-Improvers: Biographical Sketches of Members of the American Philosophical Society*, vol. 3 (1998). Details on Shippen's impeachment are in William Hamilton, *Report of the Trial and Acquittal of Edward Shippen* (1805). A portrait of Shippen by Gilbert Stuart is in the collection of the Corcoran Gallery of Art.

RANDOLPH SHIPLEY KLEIN

SHIPPEN, William, Jr. (21 Oct. 1736–11 July 1808), physician and teacher of anatomy and midwifery, was born in Philadelphia, Pennsylvania, the son of William Shippen II and Susannah Harrison. William, Jr., was often referred to as "Dr. William Shippen, Jr.," which distinguished him from his father, an important medical man in Philadelphia. Young Shippen received a sound classical education intertwined with firm religious guidance at the Reverend Dr. Samuel Finley's academy in West Nottingham, Chester County, Pennsylvania, and at the College of New Jersey in Princeton. At commencement exercises in 1754, eighteen-year-old Shippen's valedictory address impressed Ezra Stiles as an "ingenious oration," and George

Whitefield compared Shippen's eloquence to that of Roman orators. Shippen next served a medical apprenticeship under his father in Philadelphia. The older Shippen had built on his success as an apothecary and had recently been appointed a physician to the Pennsylvania Hospital, the only informally trained practitioner thus honored. With financial aid from his uncle Edward Shippen III, young Shippen continued his training abroad.

In England Shippen obtained practical experience at St. Thomas's Hospital, Guy's, St. George's, and St. Bartholomew's, which emphasized obstetrics and midwifery under Colin Mackenzie and anatomy under William and John Hunter. Upon the advice of John Fothergill, a mentor to many Pennsylvanians interested in science, Shippen continued his education at the University of Edinburgh. He studied with the Monros, William Cullen, and others and in 1761 received an M.D. Shippen's dissertation, "De Placentae cum Utero nexu," was dedicated to "the best of fathers" and five other physicians of the Pennsylvania Hospital. Shippen returned to London, saw the coronation of George III, and then traveled in France. During these years abroad, dedication to his profession and the control of emotion characteristic of surgeons replaced this Presbyterian's family values rooted in the religious enthusiasm of the Great Awakening. Back in London before returning to Philadelphia, Shippen in 1762 married 26-year-old Alice Lee of Virginia. The couple moved into Shippen's father's spacious house and eventually had two children.

The father and son became partners. William, Jr., cherished the hope of bringing to fruition "a School for Physick . . . that may draw students from various parts of America & the West Indies & at least furnish them with a better Idea of the Rudiments of their Profession" (Morton and Woodbury, p. 357). With his father's assistance, on 16 November 1762 he inaugurated a series of lectures on anatomy, surgery, and the practice of midwifery "for the advantage of young gentlemen . . . whose circumstances and connections will not admit of their going abroad for improvement" (*Pennsylvania Gazette*, 11 Nov. 1762). Shippen used anatomical drawings and casts sent by Fothergill as a gift to the hospital. The pictures were by the famous Dutch painter Jan Van Rymsdyk, who had done most of the illustrations for William Hunter's great work on the gravid uterus. The drawings became an important part of the collections of the Pennsylvania Hospital, where Shippen also lectured. By 1765 he offered a complete course in midwifery to men and women. Rocks shattered windows in his lab and nearby public lamps, and mobs burst into his dissecting rooms, for some believed rumors that Shippen robbed graves, while others found male midwifery offensive. This medical pioneer defied controversy; in fact, he seemed to thrive on it, and in this instance he became increasingly successful.

In 1765 Shippen's friend and fellow Philadelphian John Morgan returned from medical training abroad. Three years earlier Morgan and Shippen had discussed with Fothergill plans for establishing a medical school in the colonies. Although Morgan went beyond those talks, he acted alone to implement his "Discourse upon the Institution of Medical Schools in America." On 3 May Morgan was appointed by the trustees of the College of Philadelphia as professor of the theory and practice of medicine. Morgan, not Shippen, became the founder of the first medical school in British North America and held the first medical professorship. Morgan took "full credit for the Medical School" and made no mention of Shippen's preparatory work or role. He thus reaped all the public acclaim for what was publicly described as "Morgan's Plan" and also the perpetual enmity of the Shippens, which had grave consequences for the development of medicine in the colonies and early republic. Morgan exacerbated the situation in 1766 when he founded a medical society and again ignored the Shippens. Shippen did not agree that medical practitioners trained through traditional apprenticeship methods should be excluded from the emerging profession. The public and private feud over who originated the medical school and other professional and personal matters divided the medical community and poisoned the atmosphere until Morgan's death in 1789.

Although Shippen signed the Non-Importation Agreement during the Stamp Act crisis, he lacked his father's ardent commitment to the American cause. Private ambitions to advance professionally, socially, and economically explain his wartime conduct. In July 1776 Shippen became chief surgeon of the Flying Camp in New Jersey. In October he gained appointment as head of all hospitals west of the Hudson River. He challenged Morgan's authority. Abruptly in January 1777 Congress relieved Morgan of his post as director general of hospitals. In March it adopted Shippen's plan for reorganizing the army medical department and on 11 April appointed Shippen in his stead. Blinded by vindictive rage, Morgan forgot the many causes that brought about his dismissal. He fixated on the "Machiavelian . . . conduct" of Shippen and his fellow conspirators, including Shippen's brothers-in-law, the Lees of Virginia. Morgan presented his case in *Vindication of His Public Character* (1777).

Benjamin Rush, a physician and the first professor of chemistry at the College of Philadelphia, entered the controversy against Shippen when he publicly expressed concern that "our hospital affairs grow worse and worse. . . . The fault is both with the establishment and in the Director-General. He is both *ignorant* and *negligent* in his duty" (letter to John Adams, 21 Oct. 1777). Fearing a congressional whitewash, Rush refused to divulge evidence except to a court-martial board. In January 1780 Shippen was arrested, and five specific charges were presented. Essentially his accusers claimed that Shippen speculated with supplies such as wine and sugar when the sick and wounded needed them, and they also asserted that his incompetence caused needless suffering and death. Shippen escaped conviction by one vote, following a highly irregular trial, during which the board's composition changed and the accused privately entertained the board members with fine food and mocking imitations of his chief detractor. Although the court-martial board concluded that "Dr. Shippen did speculate in and sell hospital stores . . . which conduct they consider highly improper and justly reprehensible," it refused to convict him (*Pennsylvania Packet*, 25 Nov. 1780). Shippen's friends in Congress blocked efforts to censure or discharge him, but Congress refused to confirm or sanction the acquittal. Shippen remained director general another five months. Morgan attacked him in a handbill, and the two doctors hurled acrimonious epithets at one another in newspapers during the remainder of the year. Shippen's defense of his conduct confirmed the opinion that he was insensitive to human suffering; as director general he never visited the sick, dressed wounds, or comforted soldiers but admitted that he speculated in hospital stores.

Despite the scandal, Shippen's stature rose. When the revolutionary government of Pennsylvania revoked the charter of the College of Philadelphia in 1779 and created the University of the State of Pennsylvania, Shippen accepted a position in the new institution. During the 1790s Shippen was physician to President George Washington. When the University of Pennsylvania emerged in 1791, he was appointed professor of anatomy, surgery, and midwifery. In the same year he rejoined the staff of the Pennsylvania Hospital and served it until 1802. This charter member of the College of Physicians of Philadelphia became its president from 1805 to 1808.

Shippen's attempt to ally the family with the powerful Livingstons of New York proved a disaster. His immature daughter, Nancy, and her peculiar husband, Henry Beekman Livingston, separated soon after the birth of their daughter. Nancy lived with her father and, like her own mother, became clinically depressed and led a very unhappy life. Shippen's only son, Thomas Lee Shippen, studied law with his kinsman Edward Burd and at Middle Temple and thoroughly enjoyed spending his father's money abroad. He married a seventeen-year-old widow from Virginia and died of tuberculosis at age thirty-three while under his father's care. Shippen informally adopted his grandchildren, which enabled the twice-widowed woman to remarry. Shippen's wife of thirty-nine years and his father both died in 1801. Although Shippen continued to lecture on anatomy at the college, his health soon failed. He died from an attack of anthrax at his home in Germantown, Pennsylvania.

Shippen contributed significantly to the establishment of medicine in America as a profession based on university training. He also pioneered courses in midwifery, despite opposition from "the unskilled old women" whose methods, he believed, caused needless suffering and sometimes death. He provided scientific knowledge about women's diseases and appropriate treatments, along with "necessary cautions against the dangerous and cruel use of instruments." Although some have claimed that his medical lectures on anatomy, midwifery, and surgery at the state house in 1762 were the origin of America's first medical school, scholars rightly give the credit to the more ambitious undertaking by his rival in 1765. Shippen's rivalry with other physicians and his record as a revolutionary administrator caused great complications and controversy in the nation's medical and political capital and sometimes damaged the profession that he held so dear.

• Extensive Shippen family papers exist at the American Philosophical Society, the Historical Society of Pennsylvania, and the Library of Congress. The Benjamin Rush Papers at the Library Company of Philadelphia (and the selection edited by Lyman Butterfield) are very helpful. The fullest sketch of Shippen is Betsy Copping Corner, *William Shippen, Jr.: Pioneer in American Medical Education* (1951). Important coverage appears in Randolph S. Klein, *Portrait of an Early American Family: The Shippens of Pennsylvania across Five Generations* (1975); Whitfield J. Bell, Jr., *John Morgan, Continental Doctor* (1965); Bell, "The Court Martial of Dr. William Shippen, Jr., 1780," *Journal of the History of Medicine and Allied Sciences* 19, no. 3 (1964); and Bell, *Patriot-Improvers: Biographical Sketches of Members of the American Philosophical Society*, vol. 3 (1998). Other sources include Caspar Wistar, *Eulogium on Doctor Wm. Shippen, Delivered . . . 1809* (1818), reprinted in *Philadelphia Journal of the Medical and Physical Sciences* 5 (1822); Charles Caldwell, *Extract from the Eulogium on Wm. Shippen* (1818); and Ethel Armes, ed., *Nancy Shippen, Her Journal Book* (1935). Other accounts appear in Edward Potts Cheyney and Ellis Paxson Oberholtzer, *University of Pennsylvania: Its History, Influence, Equipment, and Characteristics, with Biographical Sketches and Portraits of Founders, Benefactors, Officers, and Alumni* (2 vols., 1901–1902); George W. Norris, *The Early History of Medicine in Philadelphia* (1886); John F. Watson, *Annals of Philadelphia* (1844); Thomas G. Morton and Frank Woodbury, *The History of the Pennsylvania Hospital* (1895); W. S. W. Ruschenberger, *An Account of . . . the College of Physicians of Philadelphia* (1887); Joseph Carson, *A History of the Medical Department of the University of Pennsylvania* (1869); and Roberdeau Buchanan, *Genealogy of the Descendants of Dr. William Shippen* (1877). A portrait of Shippen, attributed to James R. Lambdin, after an original by Gilbert Stuart, is at the Historical Society of Pennsylvania.

RANDOLPH SHIPLEY KLEIN

SHIRAS, George (26 Jan. 1832–2 Aug. 1924), associate justice of the U.S. Supreme Court, was born in Allegheny County, Pennsylvania, the son of George Shiras, Sr., a wealthy brewery owner, and Eliza Herron. Shiras graduated from Yale College in 1853, was admitted to the Pennsylvania bar in 1855, and shortly afterward married Lillie Kennedy of Pittsburgh. They had two sons. In 1862 Hopewell Hepburn, Shiras's law partner and former preceptor, died; thereafter, he worked alone. As the Pittsburgh economy grew, so did Shiras's practice. His clients included the Baltimore & Ohio Railroad Company and the region's major industrial enterprises; by 1880 his annual income was said to be $75,000, an enormous sum at that time. Although a wealthy man with genteel tastes and conventional social attitudes, Shiras was something of a nonconformist. He wore long sidewhiskers long after they went out of fashion and never used the telephone. Shiras had no interest in either the ostentatious world of Gilded Age high society or the spoils-oriented world of Pennsylvania politics, and he shunned even collegial bar association gatherings throughout his life.

Shiras had no experience in public life before his nomination to the Supreme Court by President Benjamin Harrison (1833–1901) on 19 July 1892. The death of Justice Joseph P. Bradley, who came from New Jersey and represented the Third Circuit, comprising New Jersey, Pennsylvania, and Delaware, had resulted in a vacancy on the Court. Judicial tradition and political logic indicated a Pennsylvania Republican as Bradley's replacement, but President Harrison was at odds with James D. Cameron and Matthew Quay, bosses of the Pennsylvania Republican machine. For six months after Justice Bradley's death, President Harrison looked for a political unknown whose nomination would be greeted enthusiastically by the Pennsylvania bar yet would not antagonize Republican politicians loyal to Cameron and Quay. Shiras was his man.

The 1890s was a transitional period in American history, and the questions that crowded the Court's docket indicated the increasing scope and intensity of government interventions in economy and society. Three major classes of constitutional issues came up during Shiras's tenure; not surprisingly, he charted an independent course. One class of cases involved petitioners who sought enlarged judicial protection under the Fourteenth Amendment for "liberty of contract" in the face of state laws regulating labor relations or the price of essential services. They got no encouragement from Shiras. In *Brass v. North Dakota* (1894), a grain elevator case, he upheld a price-fixing law even though the affected firms did not have a "virtual monopoly" at particular locations. He also spoke for the Court in *Knoxville v. Harbison* (1901), sustaining a Tennessee statute that barred payment of wages in company-store scrip. Justices David Brewer and Rufus Peckham, the Fuller Court's leading apostles of laissez-faire, dissented in each instance.

Yet Shiras was consistently aligned with Brewer and Peckham in the second class of cases, including *United States v. E. C. Knight Co.* (1895) and *Champion v. Ames* (1903), involving federal authority under the commerce clause in policy domains traditionally reserved to the states. For Shiras, congressional regulation of manufacturing corporations and public morals were illegitimate innovations in the organization of constitutional power.

Shiras wrote his most powerful opinions in the third class of cases, involving petitioners whose liberty or property was jeopardized by intensified federal activity in areas of acknowledged federal competence. In *Wong Wing v. United States* (1896) Shiras spoke for a unanimous Court that finally curbed Congress's draconian anti-Chinese program at the point where immigration officials were authorized to sentence illegal aliens to as much as one year of hard labor prior to deportation. The sentence of hard labor was an "infamous" one, Shiras explained, which could be invoked only after the Fifth and Sixth Amendment requirements of due process and trial by jury had been met. He also dissented in *Brown v. Walker* (1896), contending that a federal immunity statute for persons required to testify before the Interstate Commerce Commission was an inadequate substitute for the Fifth Amendment right against selfincrimination.

At the time of his appointment, Shiras vowed to retire at seventy to avoid burdening his brethren because of age. He underscored his habitual divergence from conventional norms by carrying through his resolve. His retirement in 1903 attracted little notice, and his death in Pittsburgh, more than twenty years later, even less. Shiras's jurisprudence was simply too idiosyncratic to generate a significant following at the bar, in the law schools, or among the general public.

• The standard biography of George Shiras is Winfield Shiras, *Justice George Shiras, Jr. of Pittsburgh* (1953). See also Arnold Paul, "George Shiras, Jr.," in *The Justices of the United States Supreme Court, 1789–1969: Their Lives and Major Opinions*, ed. Leon Friedman and Fred L. Israel (1969).

CHARLES W. MCCURDY

SHIRAS, Oliver Perry (22 Oct. 1833–7 Jan. 1916), federal district court judge, was born in Pittsburgh, Pennsylvania, the son of George Shiras and Elizabeth Herron, farmers. He was raised close by the Ohio River in a strong Presbyterian family, and his brother George Shiras would become an associate justice of the U.S. Supreme Court. Shiras attended public schools as a child and completed his undergraduate work at Ohio University, receiving his A.M. in 1856. He then spent a year doing postgraduate work in the Department of Philosophy and Art at Yale University and completed his law degree at the same time. He immediately entered practice, persuaded by his old friends the Herron brothers to settle in Dubuque, Iowa. In 1857 he wed Elizabeth Mitchell; they had four children, one of whom died in infancy.

In August 1862, Shiras joined the Union army, commissioned as a first lieutenant and quartermaster of the Twenty-seventh Iowa Volunteer Infantry. He served as a judge advocate for the campaigning Army of the Western Frontier. He resigned in December 1863 and returned to Dubuque, where he was elected city councilman, serving for a year. He then returned to his law practice with the firm of Shiras, Vanduzee & Henderson and gained a reputation as an excellent trial lawyer. The firm was the most successful in the area during the 1870s.

Shiras's practice was interrupted again when his firm was dissolved by political preferment. For a short time he practiced alone, but in 1882 President Benjamin Harrison nominated him to the federal bench, despite his lack of judicial and public service experience. Two factors seemed to be critical to his nomination. First, his roots were in the same geographical area as his predecessor on the court, and second, he was not part of the anti-Harrison faction of the Pennsylvania Republican party. In 1882 he was appointed judge of the U.S. District Court for the Northern District of Iowa, where he remained until retiring in 1903. His first wife died in 1885, and in 1888 he married Hetty E. Spaulding Cornwall.

On the federal bench, Shiras's reputation was stellar though complex. He was credited with possessing "wisdom, integrity, and precise reasoning." A man of scholarly bent, his strong professional interest was in equity, and he wrote a small but well-respected book titled *Equity Practice in the United States Circuit Courts*, published in 1889.

It has been said that Shiras made the Sixteenth Amendment necessary. In 1890 he participated in a decision to strike down the proposal of an income tax in *Pollock v. Farmer's Loan and Trust Co.* In addition, he opposed the laissez-faire vision of the court during 1892–1903 and was reluctant to strike down state laws through the due process clause of the Fourteenth Amendment. However, his was not a political vision but a legal mind born from the soil of many years of practice. Hence, he took a very fact-specific approach to cases and was attentive to precedent. He was much more open to employing the due process clause as a protector of civil liberties.

Shiras's most important contribution to jurisprudence was his concept of a national common law detailed in his opinion in *Murray v. Chicago & Northwestern* (1894). The conflict arose over the railroad's attempt to avoid regulation of interstate traffic during 1875–1887, just prior to when Congress assumed control in 1887. A businessman brought a complaint against the railroad for its rates, and the case was removed to federal court and Judge Shiras. The railroad based its defense on the ground that regulation of interstate commerce was in the exclusive control of Congress and, when the plaintiff's shipments occurred, no regulation existed pertaining to the several states.

Shiras resolved the issue before him by application of a theory of national common law. The opinion is noteworthy for its detail and method of reasoning. Indeed, although a district court opinion, it was approvingly cited by the U.S. Supreme Court on several occasions. Shiras employed numerous precedents to demonstrate that the Constitution did not abrogate the common law but assumed it was applicable both in the states and at the national level, depending on the matter. Since Congress was silent and interstate travel was a federal matter, the court must base its decisions upon common law principles. Beyond arguments from precedent, Shiras engaged in both interpretive and structural analyses of the Constitution in far greater detail than had previous federal courts, including the well-known case of *Swift v. Tyson* (1842). Shiras declared that the Constitution explicitly gave the federal courts the power to enforce principles of the law of nations, the law of maritime, and equity. Given that the common law was part of this preexisting system, he reasoned that the document also gave the federal courts power to apply the national common law when appropriate. Jurisprudentially, he made the point that, if the Constitution were not based upon something, it would be a meaningless piece of paper born out of the void. "When searching for that something," said Shiras, "one found principles of common law." Though his nonpositivist stance was not unusual for the day, the breadth of the opinion was.

The second most important dispute to come before Shiras was an equity suit stemming from years of controversy over the Des Moines River improvement land grant. The government presented a bill to confirm the title of certain settlers to land they supposedly received from the United States. Shiras felt bound by the law to dismiss the settlers' claim but urged Congress on grounds of equity to compensate the settlers. The U.S. Supreme Court approved the decision, and Congress eventually took Shiras's advice.

Shiras retired from the bench at the age of seventy in 1903 and devoted his attention to civic affairs. He was a trustee and president of the Dubuque Public Library, a trustee for Dubuque Finley Hospital, chairman of the public park board, and a member of the Dubuque County Bar Association. He took his philanthropy seriously and was dubbed "Father of the Dubuque County Park System."

• The Federal Judicial Center in Washington, D.C., has compiled a biographical file on Shiras for use by the public. Other than that, little written information is available. Some is in E. H. Stiles, *Recollections and Sketches of Notable Lawyers and Public Men of Early Iowa* (1916). Mention of Shiras is made in the *Dubuque Times-Journal*, 7 and 16 Jan. 1916. He is also noted in the *Proceedings of the Iowa State Bar Association* in 1916.

TRISHA OLSON

SHIRER, William Lawrence (23 Feb. 1904–28 Dec. 1993), journalist and historian, was born in Chicago, Illinois, the son of Seward Smith Shirer, an assistant U.S. attorney, and Josephine Tanner. When Shirer's father died of appendicitis in 1913, finances forced a move to his mother's family home in Cedar Rapids, Iowa. Shirer worked as sports editor of the *Cedar Rapids Republican* while attending Coe College from 1921 to 1925. He graduated with a degree in history.

While on a summer visit to Europe following graduation, Shirer was hired as a reporter for the European edition of the *Chicago Tribune*. From 1925 to 1927 he also took courses in European history at College de France in Paris. The young journalist's efforts were rewarded in 1927 when he was made a foreign correspondent for the Chicago edition of the *Tribune*. During these Paris days Shirer met such American expatriate writers as Ezra Pound, Ernest Hemingway, and F. Scott Fitzgerald; James Thurber was his friend and co-worker at the Paris *Tribune*. He interviewed dancer Isadora Duncan and author Gertrude Stein and covered Charles Lindbergh's landing at Le Bourget.

Shirer became chief of the *Tribune*'s Central European Bureau in Vienna in 1929. In this capacity he covered the rise of Hitler and the Nazi party in Europe. He also spent time in 1930 and 1931 on special assignment in India with Mahatma Gandhi. In 1931 Shirer married Theresa Stiberitz, an Austrian. They had two daughters; they were divorced in 1970.

After Shirer lost vision in one eye in a skiing accident he spent a year in Spain writing a novel based on his Indian experiences. In 1934 Shirer returned to journalism. He became a reporter for the Paris *Herald*, an American paper, taking the only job he could get. Later that year, when he was offered a position in Berlin writing for the Universal Service—a news agency that provided copy to the Hearst papers and other subscribing journals—he gladly accepted. Shirer's characterization of the 1936 Olympic Games in Berlin as propaganda to hide Nazi anti-Semitism drew denunciation from the German press and threats of expulsion from the government.

Edward R. Murrow hired Shirer in 1937 to prepare radio broadcasts from Vienna for the Columbia Broadcasting System. Between 1938 and 1940 Shirer struggled against Nazi censorship, threats of arrest, and the dangers of war to report the Änschluss, or German annexation of Austria; the Munich conference where Adolf Hitler negotiated with Britain and France for his takeover of the Sudetenland from Czechoslovakia; and the fall of Poland, Denmark, Norway, and France, as well as the Battle of Britain. As a pioneer radio journalist, Shirer withstood the dangers and helped develop the techniques and potential of broadcast reporting of foreign wars. He also helped open American eyes to the evils of Nazism.

By 1940 Nazi hostility to the United States resulted in increased censorship of Shirer's broadcasts. He believed he could no longer report the truth and feared he might be falsely accused of spying. His family had already fled to America, and in late 1940 Shirer flew out of Germany to join them. He published *Berlin Diary: The Journal of a Foreign Correspondent, 1934–1941* in 1941. This work was based on his notes, supplemented by his broadcast scripts, dispatches, and memory. Its subject is Hitler's rise to European dominance, and it warns of "the Nazi blight and the hatred and the fraud and the political gangsterism and the murder and the massacre and the incredible intolerance and all the suffering and the starving and cold and the thud of a bomb blowing the people in a house to pieces, the thud of all bombs blasting man's hope and decency." Eventually translated into French, Spanish, Swedish, and Portuguese, *Berlin Diary* was a Book-of-the-Month Club offering that sold nearly 300,000 copies in a year. Going through nineteen printings, the Knopf American edition matched those sales for the same period.

Shirer moved with his family into a Manhattan home and spent the rest of World War II in the United States doing broadcasts for CBS and writing a syndicated column for the *New York Herald Tribune*. He won the 1946 Peabody Award for news commentary. In 1947 Shirer was dropped from his CBS program by a sponsor. Hoping to continue the broadcast with another advertiser, he turned to his boss Edward R. Murrow for support. Murrow withheld it, and Shirer left CBS, believing he had been fired. His departure stirred controversy in the media about sponsor control of news and commentary.

Shirer moved from New York to live in Torrington, Connecticut. He signed on with the Mutual Broadcasting System and completed a book, *End of a Berlin Diary* (1947). This sequel to the *Berlin Diary* tells of the close and immediate aftermath of World War II in Germany. Shirer won the Wendell Willkie One World Award in 1948. He was dropped as a columnist by the *Herald Tribune* the same year. His broadcast was discontinued by Mutual in 1949. Shirer believed advertisers considered him too liberal to work as a journalist. In 1950 a group called American Business Consultants published *Red Channels*, which suggested that Shirer was sympathetic to the Communist party. In this period of McCarthyism and blacklisting, Shirer thought such innuendo had made him unemployable as a journalist. He decided to write books for a living.

Shirer completed a novel, *The Traitor*, in 1950. It treats a character based on American correspondent Bob Best of United Press who made treasonous broadcasts for the Nazis during World War II. This novel and Shirer's two others, *Stranger Come Home* (1954) and *The Consul's Wife* (1956), drew mixed reviews from literary critics and were less popular with readers than his efforts at nonfiction had been. Besides these fictional works, Shirer wrote two other books in the 1950s: *Midcentury Journey: The Western World through Its Years of Conflict* (1952) and *The Challenge of Scandinavia: Norway, Sweden, Denmark, and Finland in Our Time* (1955). Although neither of these books ranks among Shirer's major accomplishments, *Midcentury Journey*, a Literary Guild selection, anticipated his later analyses of the fall of France to Hitler and the rise of Nazi power in Germany.

Though his publisher and his agent discouraged him, Shirer spent the last half of the decade researching a history of the Third Reich. By 1960 he completed the manuscript, and Simon & Schuster accepted it for publication. *The Rise and Fall of the Third Reich* (1960) was a history book 1,245 pages long, bristling with notes, and expensive at ten dollars. Nonetheless, it sold over a million copies its first year in print. It was abridged and serialized in *Reader's Digest* in 1962 for a readership of twelve million and won the National Book Award and the Carey-Thomas Award, a prize for creative publishing. The book then sold another two million copies as the bulkiest, most expensive paperback book printed up to that time. Translated into Chinese, French, German, Greek, Hebrew, Italian, Persian, Portuguese, and Spanish, *The Rise and Fall of the Third Reich* was a landmark nonfiction bestseller.

Although received less warmly by historians than by journalistic critics, the history was generally praised for its compelling narrative and its coherent synthesis. Shirer blamed the Germans for the rise of Hitler and Nazism rather than explaining it in the context of emergent European totalitarianism, a theory offered by some unfriendly reviewers. Except in West Germany, the critical and popular reception of the book was favorable. As Gaveriel Rosenfeld notes in his 1994 analysis of the reception of the history, "few works have achieved as enduring a reputation or attained as unique a commercial success" (p. 95).

Two related books by Shirer about World War II followed: *The Rise and Fall of Adolf Hitler* (1961) and *The Sinking of the Bismarck* (1962). The former is a biography for young readers, and the latter is based on material Shirer gathered while writing his history of the Third Reich. He next began researching and writing his detailed account of France's defeat by the Germans in World War II, *The Collapse of the Third Republic* (1969). The appearance of this history of French decline between the world wars was a major publishing event, and the work was a Book-of-the-Month Club selection. Still, it was not the popular or critical success that *The Rise and Fall of the Third Reich* had been.

Living in Lenox, Massachusetts, since his 1970 divorce, in 1976 Shirer published the first part of his three-volume autobiography, *20th-Century Journey—A Memoir of a Life and the Times: The Start, 1904–1930*. As the title suggests, this book treated the author's life in its historical context. Some reviewers complained that it told too little about the writer as it surveyed the times. For instance, Shirer discusses striking labor unions, lawyer Clarence Darrow, author Theodore Dreiser, and gangster Al Capone while describing his own childhood in Chicago. The second volume, subtitled *The Nightmare Years, 1930–1940*, appeared in 1984. When the third volume, *A Native's Return, 1945–1988*, was published in 1990, emphasis shifted to the writer's life, with Shirer even telling about extramarital affairs that led to his divorce. The controversy over his departure from CBS, which was described in this book, was renewed in some reviews. He concluded the autobiography: "Whatever happens now, and whenever, I am glad to have lived through the turbulent, tumultuous twentieth century, with all its tremendous changes, despite all its upheavals and violence."

Shirer intended to include his impressions of Gandhi in the second volume of *20th-Century Journey* but was discouraged by his publisher, who felt that book should focus on European conflicts. So the author's admiring recollections of the Indian leader appeared in 1979 as *Gandhi: A Memoir*.

In 1982 Shirer began to study Russian and visited the Soviet Union. He returned there in 1986 to gather information that was used in his posthumously published *Love and Hatred: The Troubled Marriage of Leo and Sonya Tolstoy* (1994). Shirer's companion on this trip was a Russian, Irina Alexandrovna Lugovskaya, who had become an American citizen; he married her in 1989. Shirer died in Boston, Massachusetts.

William L. Shirer enjoyed a long and sometimes controversial career as a journalist and author. His work reveals him to be an idealistic, compassionate, articulate, honest, and opinionated man. He witnessed and reported some of the most important events of the twentieth century. As one of the first foreign correspondents to use radio, he was a trailblazer in broadcast journalism. His conflicts with sponsors and media management defined persistent concerns about the interference of advertisers and political interest groups in news programming. He was a tireless researcher and writer, with a gift for synthesis. His broadcasts and his writings sometimes lacked objectivity and revealed his politics, stirring controversy. Shirer is best remembered for his *Berlin Diary*, for the pioneering broadcast work it describes, and for *The Rise and Fall of the Third Reich*.

• Manuscripts of a few short works as well as letters by, about, and to Shirer can be found in the Martha Dodd Papers at the Library of Congress and in the archives of Story Press and of the P.E.N. American Center at Princeton University. The only book on Shirer is Uwe Siemon-Netto, *The Fabricated Luther: The Rise and Fall of the Shirer Myth* (1995). However, Siemon-Netto mentions Shirer but briefly as the popularizer of a theory—originated by Thomas Mann and others—that Luther's influence on German thought and character explains Hitler's ascendancy. Gavriel D. Rosenfeld, "The Reception of William L. Shirer's *The Rise and Fall of the Third Reich* in the United States and West Germany, 1960–1962," *Journal of Contemporary History* 29 (1994): 95–128, contains useful information about his most important book. Edward Bliss, *Now the News: The Story of Broadcast Journalism* (1991), discusses Shirer's career and summarizes both his and Murrow's accounts of their differences. Three Murrow biographies discuss Shirer: Alexander Kendrick, *Prime Time: The Life of Edward R. Murrow* (1969); Joseph Persico, *Murrow: An American Original* (1988); and A. M. Sperber, *Murrow: His Life and Times* (1986). Bill Moyers, *A Witness to History with William Shirer*, PBS Video (1990), is an interview with Shirer treating his impressions of Nazi leaders, the German people, and Ghandi. An obituary is in the *New York Times*, 29 Dec. 1993.

ANDREW T. CROSLAND

SHIRLEY, William (2 Dec. 1694–28 Mar. 1771), colonial governor of Massachusetts, was born in London, England, the son of William Shirley, a London textile merchant and landowner, and Elizabeth Godman. The Shirleys, who had connections among the leading English politicians, decided that William should have a university education and law career. He attended the Merchant Taylors' School in London, Pembroke College in Cambridge, and the Inner Temple.

About 1719 Shirley married Frances Barker, the heir of a London merchant; they had nine children. Shirley first was a clerk in the London government, and on being admitted to the bar in 1720, he began to practice law. Speculation in the ill-fated South Seas project and other enterprises, depression, and general dissatisfaction with his opportunities led Shirley to seek a position in the colonial government. In 1731 he emigrated to Boston, Massachusetts. Help and encouragement eventually came from the duke of Newcastle, an acquaintance of the family, who handled some patronage for the Robert Walpole ministry. In 1733 Shirley was named judge of the vice admiralty court in New England and later advocate general (prosecutor) of that court. A law practice supplement-

ed his income and involved him in Massachusetts politics. Shirley associated with a group, timber merchants and landowners in particular, who desired the removal of Governor Jonathan Belcher. Opposition organized in Boston and London (where Shirley's wife was his representative) took advantage of a banking and credit crisis caused in part by Belcher's rash actions. While Shirley managed to avoid outward involvement, he positioned himself nonetheless to be Belcher's successor.

In London, dissenting politicians were also forcing a change in Walpole's foreign policies. War had broken out in the Caribbean, and colonial cooperation was essential. Shifts in cabinet leadership gave Newcastle an opportunity to replace Belcher with Shirley in 1741. Shirley was expected to support the war against Spain in America and to dampen the bitter political situation in Boston. He thus entered office in crisis. His first duty was to suppress the rival banks as ordered by the British government and to secure the cooperation of the shareholders. By providing paper credit in anticipation of taxes, with tight controls for the redemption of the paper currency as taxes were collected, Shirley managed the liquidation of the banks and restoration of public credit. While economic conditions improved, Shirley attempted to control widespread smuggling, appeasing the merchants by favoring one of the group, Christopher Kilby, as colonial agent and by seeking war contracts and commissions. As opposition mounted, Shirley persuaded Newcastle to permit some relaxation in enforcing trade laws.

During these years, Shirley won a group of supporters through war trade, contracts, and commissions. He managed to be on the popular side of trade issues and grew in power as governor. His popularity certainly increased in 1745 when he backed a successful Massachusetts-led attack on the French fortress of Louisbourg at Cape Breton following the entry of France into the European-colonial war in 1744. Shirley and many New Englanders saw the possibility of both increased trade and an enlarged empire that might extend to the Mississippi River and also include Canada. The Louisbourg expedition brought Massachusetts help from neighboring colonies and monetary and military aid from the British government. Shirley and his associates won popularity and economic reward. A legislative effort to bring about a new hard currency, which Shirley had pledged in return for British aid, involved a bittersweet union of the old bankers of the 1740s, who joined Shirley's friends to make the new currency possible.

The war ended with the Treaty of Aix-la-Chapelle in 1748, which included establishment of a boundary commission in Paris to settle issues affecting the empires. Shirley was named to that commission and sailed for Paris in 1749. In Paris, he met and married a woman by the name of Julie (maiden name unknown); Shirley's first wife had died in 1747); they had no children. Meanwhile, he and three others sought ways to divide the American West and to establish title to disputed Caribbean islands. For the expansionist Shirley, who wanted the British empire extended at least into the Ohio Valley, the strain of working under orders from the London government was severe. The ministry generally wanted a broad international zone separating the empires. Shirley's experiences in Paris were frustrating. Realizing that France was developing a basis for an enlarged empire with many frontier forts in areas close to British colonial settlements, he welcomed the opportunity to return to Massachusetts in 1753.

About the time of his arrival, a Virginia expedition commanded by the young George Washington had already clashed with the French and their Indian allies and had been forced to surrender at Fort Necessity in western Pennsylvania. Britain reacted to the threat to frontier peace by calling a conference of the colonial governments to plan defensive measures and to mobilize friendly Indians. Shirley favored some plan of union of the colonies and leaned strongly to a military solution for meeting the crisis. The conference brought forth the Albany Plan of Union, which provided for a loosely organized association of the colonies, but only in Massachusetts was there a legislative review of the plan. The British government finally decided on a limited operation to end encroachment along the frontier. General Edward Braddock was put in charge of a small military force, but the colonies were also expected to raise two regiments and auxiliaries. Shirley was chosen colonel of one regiment.

Evaluating British efforts, Shirley decided that a partial military mobilization was necessary. Conferences with neighboring governors resulted in the raising of troops in Nova Scotia, New York, and New England. A plan of attack was developed, and when Braddock arrived in America in 1755, he was presented with a substantial increase in his forces. He then selected Shirley as second in command and put him in charge of a force to attack Fort Niagara by way of Oswego. He agreed as well to attack Crown Point in New York and French forts on the Bay of Fundy. Much depended, however, on Braddock to move against Fort Duquesne and to coordinate the movement. Unfortunately, with Braddock's surprise by the French near Fort Duquesne and his death from his wounds, Braddock's forces disintegrated. Though Shirley succeeded Braddock as commander of British forces in North America, he had neither the military know-how nor the authority over subordinates to succeed. Only in Nova Scotia did the expedition achieve its objectives.

By 1756, plagued by international rivalries, questions of his authority, lack of funds, and British indecisiveness regarding its plans for America, Shirley faced an impossible political and military situation. He nonetheless raised additional military forces and on his own authority pledged funding from the British government for the costs of recruiting and supply. He planned to follow loosely what had been ordered by Braddock, but anticipating that the ministry would choose a new commander, he moved slowly—too slowly, as it turned out. The French took advantage of the delay, attacked Fort Oswego, and captured it, which proved a major disaster.

By the early summer, a new British commander, Lord Loudoun, and a considerable army arrived in New York. Loudoun accused Shirley of ineptitude because of his inaction in the spring, the loss of Oswego, and other military irregularities. Shirley was ordered to London and was eventually removed from his post as governor. An extended investigation into his actions continued into 1758, but little was ever found to reveal anything other than irregularities. He languished in England for nearly three years, while the war effort continued, until William Pitt and Newcastle arose as leaders of a new coalition that brought the war to a successful conclusion with the Treaty of Paris in 1763.

Meanwhile, Shirley had petitioned Newcastle in 1757 for help with his future, and finally, late in 1758, Shirley gained the honorary rank of lieutenant general and the governorship of the Bahama Islands. His arrival in Nassau on 31 December 1759 marked the beginning of seven years of service in a thinly populated colony, where the simplicity of life provided little formal business for government. But he turned his attention to the administration, bringing friends from Massachusetts to serve in some key positions, and worked to improve education, control smuggling, and make the court system more efficient. He was lonely, with only a grandson, William Hutchinson, as his secretary. (The fate of his second wife is unknown.) In 1767 Shirley's son Thomas succeeded him as governor. Shirley retired to his country place in Roxbury, Massachusetts, where he died.

• The extensive Shirley correspondence is widely scattered. Charles Henry Lincoln drew together the official British letters in *Correspondence of William Shirley* (2 vols., 1912). The Massachusetts Historical Society, the Huntington Library, and the Library of Congress house many of the remaining letters. George Arthur Wood published a single volume of a projected two-volume study, *William Shirley, Governor of Massachusetts* (1920). Shirley's most recent biography is John A. Schutz, *William Shirley* (1961).

JOHN A. SCHUTZ

SHIRREFF, Jane (1811–23 Dec. 1883), soprano, was born in Scotland, but the exact location is not known; her parents' names also are unknown. Very little can be ascertained about her early years. She studied for five years with T. Essex, who trained her for concert singing; she also became proficient on the piano under his tutelage. Shirreff made her professional debut at the Oratorios in England on 5 March 1828. Shortly thereafter she began to study with Thomas Welsh, a celebrated London voice teacher and composer, who prepared her for the stage. Shirreff's operatic debut occurred at Covent Garden on 1 December 1831, when she sang Mandane in Thomas Arne's *Artaxerxes*. In 1832 she performed with the Concerts of Antient Music in London and also appeared at the Philharmonic Concerts and at the Gloucester Festival. Two years later, Shirreff sang at the Westminster Abbey Festival. From 1832 until 1838 she sang regularly on the stage, at both the Covent Garden (1831–1835; 1837–1838) and Drury Lane (1835–1837) theaters. Her roles included Isabella in the Covent Garden premiere of Giacomo Meyerbeer's *Robert le diable*, as adapted by Michael Rophino Lacy (1832); Oscar in the London premiere of Daniel-François-Esprit Auber's *Gustavus III* (1833); and Zerlina in Mozart's *Don Giovanni* (1834). She also appeared in Ferdinand Hérold's *Le Pré aux clercs* (1834) and Auber's *Lestocq* (1835), both as adapted by Thomas Cooke. During this period she performed with an impressive number of other Covent Garden singers who, at one time or another, appeared in the United States, including Miss Inverarity (who appeared at New York's Park Theatre in 1839 as Mrs. Martyn), Thomas Reynoldson, John Braham, Henry Phillips, Theodore Victor Giubilei, John Wilson, A. Edward Seguin, and William Harrison.

In 1838 Shirreff accompanied Wilson and Seguin to New York, where they were engaged for a season of opera at the National Theatre. Her American debut, on 15 October 1838, was in the title role of William Michael Rooke's opera *Amilie, or the Love Test*, a character that she had created at the work's premiere performance on 9 December 1837 at Covent Garden. The New York production of *Amilie* proved to be the operatic and theatrical hit of the dramatic season. Shirreff, Wilson, and Seguin, along with a chorus composed of various singing actors and actresses from the National Theatre, performed in several East-coast cities during the fall and winter of 1838–1839. Shirreff subsequently spent twenty highly successful months in North America, touring with Wilson (who assumed the role of her protector) and, for a time, with Edward and Anne Seguin. They appeared in English operas and in English adaptations of European operas in New York, Boston, Providence, Washington, Baltimore, Philadelphia, and Charleston during 1838, 1839, and 1840. Shirreff and Wilson also undertook two extensive concert tours, the first in the summer of 1839 and the second in the fall and winter of 1839–1840. They performed in concerts that included operatic arias as well as traditional ballads and popular songs; they sang in both small towns and large cities in an area bounded by Detroit to the west, Montreal to the north, and Savannah to the south. Shirreff and Wilson remained in the United States until May 1840. During these twenty months they functioned as a very important part of an operatic craze, centered in New York, that gripped the country in the late 1830s and early 1840s. On her return to England, she married J. Walcott, who was secretary of the Army and Navy Club; the number of children they had is unknown. Once back in England, Shirreff retired permanently from the stage. She died in Kensington, London.

Shirreff was an attractive and skillful actress. She had perfect intonation and a full, powerful voice. Her upper notes were described by contemporary critics as "clear and bell-like." According to theater historian Joseph Ireland, she was the "most admired English prima donna between the days of Mrs. Wood and those of Louisa Pyne" (vol. 2, p. 276). Francis Wemyss, another contemporary, wrote that Shirreff's success in the United States gave her "fame and reputation throughout the United States superior to any she enjoyed in London." Indeed, Shirreff was fabulously successful during her twenty-month sojourn in the United States, both artistically and financially. As one of the most popular and successful British singers to visit the United States during the first half of the nineteenth century, Shirreff played a crucial role in the development of American musical culture of the antebellum period. She and the other singers with whom she worked introduced hundreds of thousands of Americans to operatic music, in both staged and concert formats. Furthermore, Shirreff's enthusiastic reception by Americans and her artistic and pecuniary success here certainly encouraged other British musicians to try their luck in the United States, which undoubtedly resulted in an increased number of professional musical performers and performances here during the 1840s and 1850s.

• Shirreff's personal papers, along with a journal kept by Mary Blundell, a friend who accompanied Shirreff on her travels, can be found in the Jane Shirreff Collection, Billy Rose Theatre Collection, New York Public Library. For contemporary biographical accounts, see Francis C. Wemyss, *Twenty-Six Years of the Life of an Actor and Manager* (1847); and William H. Husk's article on Shirreff in *Grove's Dictionary of Music and Musicians* (1890). On her operatic career in the United States, see Joseph N. Ireland, *Records of the New York Stage from 1750 to 1860* (2 vols., 1866–1867; repr. 1968); George C. Odell, *Annals of the New York Stage*, vol. 4 (1927–1931; repr. 1970); Katherine K. Preston, *Opera on the Road: Traveling Opera Troupes in the United States, 1825–1860* (1993); and Preston, "The 1838–40 American Concert Tours of Jane Shirreff and John Wilson, British Vocal Stars," in *Essays in American Music*, ed. James Heintze (1994).

KATHERINE K. PRESTON

SHOCKLEY, William Bradford (13 Feb. 1910–12 Aug. 1989), physicist, was born in London, England, the son of William Hillman Shockley, an American mining engineer, and May Bradford, a mineral surveyor. When he was three years old, his family returned to the United States and settled in Palo Alto, California, where he received his early education. His interest in science was stimulated by a neighbor who was a physics professor at Stanford University. After graduating from Hollywood High School in 1927, Shockley spent one year at the University of California, Los Angeles, and then transferred to the California Institute of Technology, where he received his B.S. in physics in 1932. He obtained a teaching fellowship to support his graduate work and received his Ph.D. from the Massachusetts Institute of Technology in 1936; the subject of his thesis was "Calculation of Wave Functions for Electrons in Sodium Chloride Crystals."

Shockley went to work at the Bell Telephone Laboratories in Murray Hill, New Jersey. His first assignment was to design an electron multiplier vacuum tube amplifier. Later he turned his attention to solid state physics and attempted to design a solid state amplifier to replace vacuum tubes; however, he was unable to develop a solid state amplifier because the necessary components were not then available. Shockley's knowledge of electronics, however, was applied to Bell's program of replacing the mechanical switching system of its exchanges with an electronic one.

During World War II Shockley worked at Bell Labs on military projects for the navy. In 1945 he became director of Bell's solid state physics program, with John Bardeen and Walter H. Brattain as collaborators. This group resumed an investigation of semiconductors begun before the war.

Early radios had employed a semiconductor crystal of galena attached to a "cat's whisker" (coil of wire) to rectify antenna signals picked up from radio waves. Soon vacuum tube amplifiers replaced the crystals; however, vacuum tubes were short-lived and fragile, and they required power to heat the cathode. Shockley's group aimed at replacing the vacuum tube amplifier with a rectifying semiconductor. Originally Shockley wanted to apply the principle of the vacuum tube to control current by applying an electric field across a semiconductor. He reasoned that, by applying an electric field on the semiconductor, he could produce amplification of the input current, but this experiment failed. Bardeen suggested that the applied field was probably prevented from penetrating the interior of the semiconductor by electrons trapped at the surface layers. This suggestion prompted the semiconductor research group to study the surface effects of applied currents.

Previous work had shown that conduction in semiconductors results from two kinds of charges—electrons and "holes." The electrons available for conduction are those that are in excess of the number required to maintain the semiconductor's crystal structure. Holes represent missing electrons and therefore behave as positive charges equaling the negative charges of electrons. When an electron moves forward, it leaves a new hole behind, so it appears the hole is moving backward. Shockley's calculations emphasized the importance of hole flow. This information resulted in the introduction of materials into pure crystals that did not exactly fit into the structure; this increased the number of excess electrons or holes, depending on the materials introduced. Materials that increased electrons were designated n-type, and those that increased holes were p-type.

Bardeen and Brattain made the first semiconductor amplifier transistor in 1947. It consisted of a block of n-type germanium with two closely spaced point contacts on one face of the crystal and a broad metal electrode on the opposite face. To one contact (the emitter) a small positive voltage was applied in relation to the broad electrode (the base), and a large negative voltage was applied to the second contact (the collector). Shockley found that when a signal voltage was applied to the emitter in series with the base voltage, it was greatly amplified in the collector circuit. This amplification resulted from the introduction of holes in the germanium by the emitter contact. These newly generated holes flowed to the collector, thus increasing the current in the collector circuit.

Shockley improved the original transistor by placing a rectifying junction between the p-type and n-type regions. This device, called a junction transistor, consisted of a thin p-region sandwiched between two n-regions. All the regions had separate contacts. This transistor functioned more efficiently and soon replaced the point contact version. This improvement, together with better methods of growing, processing, and purifying silicone crystals, resulted in the realization of Shockley's original idea: a field effect transistor. The junction transistor revolutionized electronics when the transistor principle was applied to silicon chips, and integrated circuits containing thousands of minute transistors were developed. The integrated circuits made possible the introduction of the modern computer, the hand-held calculator, new kinds of communications equipment, control instruments, and many other medical and electronic devices. Shockley, Bardeen, and Brattain were awarded the 1956 Nobel Prize for physics for developing the transistor.

Shockley remained at Bell Labs until 1955. He then formed the Shockley Semiconductor Laboratory, later Shockley Transistor Corporation, a subsidiary of Beckman Instruments, Inc. The firm closed in 1968 after two ownership changes.

Shockley was a guest lecturer at Princeton University in 1946. After leaving industry, he was appointed the first Alexander M. Poniatoff Professor of Engineering and Applied Sciences at Stanford University in 1962; he held this chair until 1976.

While at Stanford Shockley became interested in finding out what factors might improve thought processes and thereby facilitate the development of scientific thought. His thinking on how society might be improved, influenced by the eugenics movement of the early twentieth century, led him to propose controversial theories concerning human genetics. He became convinced that the average intelligence of the U.S. population was being lowered because people with the lowest intelligence produced the most children. Shockley's writing on this subject gradually took on racist overtones, and in 1976 he told an audience at the National Academy of Sciences that the main cause of "the Negro problem" was racially genetic. For this he was severely criticized.

Shockley had married Jean Alberta Bailey in 1933; they had three children. The marriage ended in divorce in 1955. His second marriage was to Emily I. Lanning, a psychiatric nurse. In his youth Shockley was an avid mountain climber; in later life he enjoyed sailing, swimming, and skin-diving. He died in Palo Alto.

• Most of Shockley's papers are in the archives of Stanford University; others are in the archives of the Hoover Institute, Palo Alto. An oral history on Shockley is at Columbia University. His papers on genetics are collected in *Shockley on*

Eugenics and Race: Application of Science to the Solution of Human Problems, ed. Roger Pearson (1992). For more information on Shockley see *Current Biography,* Dec. 1953; Shirley Thomas, *Men of Space,* vol. 4 (1963); National Geographic Society, *Those Inventive Americans* (1971); Rae Goodell, *The Visible Scientists* (1977); John Daintith et al., eds., *Biographical Encyclopedia of Scientists,* vol. 2 (2 vols., 1981); Tyler Wasson, ed., *Nobel Prize Winners* (1981); *Science 84* (Nov. 1984); and Bernard S. Schlessinger et al., eds., *Who's Who of Nobel Prize Winners, 1901–1990,* 2d ed. (1991). An obituary is in the *New York Times,* 14 Aug. 1989.

DAVID Y. COOPER

SHOLES, Christopher Latham (14 Feb. 1819–17 Feb. 1890), printer, journalist, and inventor, was born on a farm near Mooresburg, Pennsylvania, the son of Orrin Sholes, a cabinetmaker; his mother's name is not known. His parents moved soon after to Danville, Pennsylvania, where he attended school until age fourteen. He worked as an apprentice printer for the editor of the *(Danville, Pa.) Intelligencer* for four years, then moved to Green Bay, Wisconsin, to live with a brother and to work on the house journal of the territorial legislature. At age twenty Sholes went to Madison and took charge of the *Wisconsin Inquirer,* owned by his brother Charles. A year later he moved to Southport (later Kenosha), Wisconsin, and established the *Telegraph* with his friend Michael Frank. In 1851 he met and married Mary Jane McKinney; they had six sons and four daughters.

Sholes was appointed postmaster in 1851. This work, combined with his journalistic career and passion to defend the underdog, led him into politics. Raised as a Democrat, he later joined the Free Soil movement. He served two terms as state senator (1848–1849 and 1852–1853) and one term in the state assembly (1856–1857). An advocate of abolition, he later helped to found the Republican party in Wisconsin.

In 1860 Sholes moved to Milwaukee, where he assumed the post of editor of the *Sentinel.* He soon gave up that position to become customs collector of the port of Milwaukee at the request of President Abraham Lincoln. Sholes's varied activities reflected his enthusiasm for new subjects and issues. By the end of the Civil War he had a dual career as a journalist and politician but had earned no honors. However, he had already exhibited signs of his inventiveness in the course of his publishing activities.

Early in his editorial work Sholes devised a system to print the names of subscribers in the margin of the front page, a process intended to save time in distribution. He did not pursue any of his inventions or innovations; it was typical of him to move from one interest to another. Once he became customs collector, however, he had more leisure time and a steady income. He and Samuel W. Soulé, a machinist, devised a series of mechanical printing devices which they patented. Working in a mechanic's shop, they perfected and patented a machine designed to number the pages of blank books. They shared their shop with a third inventor, Carlos Glidden, who reportedly suggested to Sholes that his numbering machine provide the basis for a lettering machine similar to that devised by John Pratt in London.

The invention of personal typing machines had been attempted time and again since the early eighteenth century, but none of the prototypes constructed were practical enough for mass production and use. Working from a *Scientific American* article describing the Pratt "pterotype," Sholes in 1867 set about devising a practical model. That summer he had a working model, limited to printing a single letter. By September he was able to type his name and the date, all in capitals. The patent for this machine, which was made of wood and had eleven piano keys, was granted in June 1868; two later improvements were also patented in Sholes's name. The machine Sholes patented was similar to earlier models by other, unsuccessful inventors in that it used a circular disposition of letters that responded to impact on the keyboard. As soon as the letter was printed, the carriage, which was above the character reel, moved one space to the left. The lasting innovation in Sholes's invention, however, was the keyboard layout. After many experiments he found that a keyboard with letters in alphabetical order caused the levers to tend to collide, jamming the device. Sholes rearranged the letters so that the upper row of keys began with the letters QWERTY. This arrangement, although challenged by other manufacturers, was soon adopted by typing schools and remains the standard layout for American English keyboards, even though others have been suggested as more efficient. A shift-key allowing the use of both upper-case and lower-case letters was added to the machine in 1878.

Although Sholes displayed inventive genius, he was unsuccessful at raising the capital necessary to launch mass production of his machine. In the meantime he benefited from the encouragement and criticisms of acquaintances, particularly James Clephane, a stenographer in Washington, D.C. His reports and those of other testers, as well as the encouragement of James Densmore, a lawyer and investor, led Sholes to improve his machines, producing as many as fifty by 1873. He failed, however, to market them successfully, and most were given away for publicity or to hold off creditors. As a result, Sholes's partners eventually relinquished their rights to his invention, and in 1873 Sholes sold the production rights to the Remington company in New York. The first Remington machines were marketed the following year. Sholes carried on work on the typewriter, communicating each improvement to the Remington factory. His last patent was granted in 1878. He spent the remainder of his life fighting tuberculosis, which eventually caused his death in Milwaukee.

Although Sholes was not the first to invent a typing machine, he was the first to devise a practical model, which he called the "type-writer." He was aware of the value of his invention and later described it as a means for women to "more easily earn a living" and to achieve entrepreneurial independence. Despite his talents as a journalist and inventor, his idealism and passion often prevented him from persevering in a methodical way; this explains his lack of success when his inventions reached the marketing stage. He deserves credit, however, for being the first to devise a practical individual printing machine.

• A collection of Sholes's papers are at the Smithsonian Institution's National Museum of American History. See also Richard Nelson Current, *The Typewriter and the Men Who Made It* (1954); Arthur Toye Foulke, *Mr. Typewriter* (1961); Wilfred A. Beeching, *Century of the Typewriter* (1974); and Frank J. Romano, *Machine Writing and Typesetting* (1986).

GUILLAUME DE SYON

SHOOK, Karel (29 Aug. 1920–25 July 1985), ballet teacher and company director, was born in Renton, Washington, the son of Walter Shook and Ida Marie Tack. His father, an American from a Pennsylvania Dutch family, joined the British army in World War I, when he met and married Shook's Belgian mother. He returned to the United States to work as an engineer, but the depression reduced the family's circumstances to small-scale farming. Karel decided while still a child to be an actor, and at the age of thirteen he auditioned at the Cornish School of Allied Arts in Seattle. Nellie Cornish predicted an American renaissance in dance and urged the boy to study dance as well as acting. He was invited to join the Ballet Russe de Monte Carlo and made his debut in 1939 at the Metropolitan Opera House in New York City in Léonide Massine's ballet *St. Francis*. Shook soon understood he needed stronger technique, so he left to study with master teacher Edward Caton, then Anatole Oboukoff, Felia Doubrovska, and Pierre Vladimiroff. In later years he always expressed admiration for good teachers and mentioned them by name.

When Shook rejoined Ballet Russe de Monte Carlo in 1941 he knew his path led toward teaching and directing but regarded performing as a necessary preparation. The next seven years were constant touring and nightly performances. In 1948 he took off a year "to study and starve" and immersed himself in music, languages, and writing. When it came time to work again he toured in the Broadway shows *Song of Norway* and *The Chocolate Soldier*. Then he joined George Balanchine's New York City Ballet for one season. He returned in 1950 to Ballet Russe de Monte Carlo as a dancer and assistant ballet master.

In 1952, Syvilla Fort, a former Cornish classmate who was directing the Katherine Dunham School, invited Shook to join the faculty, and he immediately took the job. The Dunham school was the center of dance training for black artists in New York, and Shook's classes attracted a galaxy of promising dancers, including Pearl Reynolds, Alvin Ailey, Donald McKayle, and Louis Johnson. Mary Hinkson, a dancer in the Martha Graham Company, told him about one of her students at New York City's High School of Performing Arts who wanted to be a ballet dancer. Ballet companies at that time offered jobs only to white dancers, and the school was urging this black student toward modern dance because of his color. Shook gave the young man, Arthur Mitchell, a scholarship and said, "Don't worry about what people tell you. Just do it and see what happens."

Shook opened his own Studio of Dance Arts when the Dunham school closed in 1954 but found the business aspects of maintaining a studio tedious, and after two years he joined the faculty of the June Taylor School. The choreographer Alvin Ailey writes in his autobiography, *Revelations* (1995), "Karel Shook attracted black dancers because nobody else wanted us to study with them. He welcomed us. We all owed him money, but he insisted that we still come to class. . . . Arthur Mitchell, at the time, lived with Shook on Thirty-fourth Street and First Avenue. He was not yet in the New York City Ballet. I used to go to their place, and they would feed me. . . . Shook used to cook and also supervised Arthur's rehearsals. . . . He was a real mentor. . . . I spent a lot of time with Arthur and Karel Shook" (pp. 76–77).

In 1959, when Shook was offered the position of ballet master with the Netherlands Ballet, he was ready to try life in Europe. The Netherlands Ballet was at a weak point when Shook joined the staff. Amid upheavals of artistic administration, in a highly politicized atmosphere in which many experienced dancers had departed to form another company, Shook became a steadying influence. The responsibilities of a ballet master include the day-to-day work of rehearsing the ballets and teaching the daily technique class. He worked to give the dancers consistent technical style and strength.

In a review of the company's season at Monte Carlo, Irene Lidova in *Dance and Dancers* (Mar. 1960, p. 21) acknowledges Shook's contribution of a ballet *Jazz Nocturne* and the presence of several promising American dancers. The Dutch government united the Netherlands Ballet and the Amsterdam Ballet in 1960, and the new entity became the Netherlands' National Ballet. The group was extremely large, nearly 100 dancers, with a big repertory of sixty ballets and a constant touring schedule. "Everyone asked me how I did it," Shook told interviewer Tobi Tobias (1973, p. 68). "I just went in and did what needed to be done, enormously long hours." Shook's language skills in French, Dutch, Russian, and English helped the process. By 1964 critic Oleg Kerensky remarked on the dancers' high technical level. During these years Shook also choreographed more than twenty works for stage and television but decided his gift was in teaching.

Arthur Mitchell, during the years that Shook lived in Europe, had become a respected star dancer of the New York City Ballet, the company's only black dancer. In the late 1960s he was also beginning to direct, having established a ballet company in Brazil. The Martin Luther King assassination in 1968 was a turning point for Mitchell, and he decided to apply his experience and skills in America so that other black dancers could have serious careers in ballet. Mitchell asked Shook to join him in this new venture. Dance Theatre of Harlem's school and the performing company developed simultaneously. Classes began in June 1968 with thirty students; by summer's end there were 400. Lecture-demonstrations and performances were started so students could see the result of their studies.

While Mitchell concentrated on choreography and fundraising, Shook concentrated on the technical training of the dancers; artistic and administrative decisions were discussed jointly. Growing beyond workshop performances, the company performed in 1970 at Jacob's Pillow in Massachusetts, an important summer showcase. In 1971 Dance Theatre of Harlem presented its New York debut at the Guggenheim Museum, followed by a brief spring season at the ANTA Theater in New York City. Annual New York seasons continued, augmented by tours to Chicago, Los Angeles, Boston, and Washington, D.C. Dance Theatre of Harlem danced its first London season in August 1974, with outstanding success.

Mitchell, in a *Dance and Dancers* interview (1974, p. 17), addresses the inevitable question about a white man in the midst of a black company: "Many [white] people make a mistake when dealing with [black students]," Mitchell responds, "even though their heart is in the right place, they don't know how to talk to people. This is something Mr. Shook understands, he has taken the time to understand black people. There never has been the feeling that he was a white person working with blacks; he was a person who *believed* that you could do something."

Shook staged *Le Corsaire Pas de Deux* and *Don Quixote Pas de Deux* but otherwise concentrated on teaching and supervising rehearsals. In 1977 he published his text *Elements of Classical Ballet Technique*, in which he outlined the training profile he developed at Dance Theatre of Harlem. Former students speak of his calm nature, his clear explanations, and the sense that he knew exactly what he wanted from the class. Mitchell said, "Shook knows how to guide people into doing things the correct way."

Dance Theatre of Harlem grew steadily, although several times it weathered financial crises caused by rapid expansion, adding performance weeks, and increasingly prestigious engagements. By the mid-1980s, at the time of Shook's death at his Englewood, New Jersey, home, it had become a major American ballet company.

• Most of Shook's papers are in inaccessible private storage, but those of the last two years of his life are housed in the library of Dance Theatre of Harlem. His manual, *Elements of Classical Ballet Technique* (1977), is the authoritative source for his approach to training. An extensive interview with Tobi Tobias, "Talking with Karel Shook," was published in *Dance Magazine*, Jan. 1973, pp. 65A–71. Transcripts of brief interviews by John Gruen with Karel Shook, 19 May 1971 and 14 Oct. 1975, and with Arthur Mitchell, 27 May 1971, are in the Dance Collection of the New York Public Library. A book about ballet teachers, *Behind Barres* (1980), by Joseph Gale, contains a chapter on Shook. "Dance Comes to Harlem" and "Harlem Comes to London" are in *Dance and Dancers*, Oct. 1974. Additional material is from conversations with Iris Cloud, Rose Anne Thom, and Arthur Mitchell. Obituaries are in the *New York Times*, 27 July 1984, and *Dance Magazine*, Oct. 1985 both of which give a wrong date of birth.

MONICA MOSELEY

SHOPE, Richard Edwin (25 Dec. 1901–2 Oct. 1966), animal pathologist and virologist, was born in Des Moines, Iowa, the son of Charles Cornelius Shope, a physician, and Mary Hast. Shope attended medical school in Iowa City, receiving the M.D. in 1924. For a brief time he was instructor in pharmacology at the State University of Iowa. In 1925 he married Helen Madden Ellis; they had four children.

In 1925 Shope was asked by Paul A. Lewis to come to the Princeton branch of the Rockefeller Institute for Medical Research to work on tuberculosis. He remained with the Rockefeller Institute for most of his career. While studying hog cholera in the late 1920s, Shope observed an outbreak of swine influenza, and together with Lewis he isolated *Haemophilus influenzae suis* (related to Pfeiffer's bacillus). In 1931 Shope also isolated a so-called filterable virus that causes the "filtrate disease" of swine influenza. Only the simultaneous presence of *H. influenzae suis* and the virus was found to produce full-blown disease. Shope's work on filterable virus inspired a British team of investigators (Wilson Smith, P. Laidlaw, and Christopher H. Andrewes) to search for a human influenza virus, a task in which they succeeded in 1933 by using ferrets as the experimental animal. This resulted in lifelong cooperation and friendship between Shope and Andrewes.

The synergistic effect of swine influenza virus and *H. influenzae suis* and the erratic appearance of influenza epidemics led Shope to assume one or more intermediate hosts in the natural history of swine influenza. In the 1940s he proposed a controversial model of "complex infection," in which swine influenza virus was supposed to be present in the ova of lungworms, which were passed in the pig's feces, to be taken up by earthworms, which were subsequently eaten by pigs. He assumed the virus to be present in lungworms in an inapparent, or "masked," state. This scheme was not widely accepted, and Shope's biographer Andrewes concluded that if the infectious cycle does exist, it is of no great epidemiological importance.

Soon after the discovery of swine influenza virus Shope discovered two other agents of infectious animal disease, the virus of infectious fibroma and that of rabbit papilloma. Shope's infectious fibroma was isolated from a cottontail rabbit and was a tumor only in a very broad sense. Shope and Andrewes found that the virus isolated from the fibroma could change into a virus with much greater virulence for rabbit cells. They suggested the term "mutation" for this process, making their report one of the earliest on the explicit experimental observation of the mutation of viruses. Furthermore, extensive studies of Shope's fibroma in the laboratories of Shope, Andrewes, Peyton Rous (Rockefeller Institute, New York City), and others led to the conclusion that the distinction between infection and neoplasia (abnormal cell growth) was not a strict one, the dichotomy being bridged by conditions such as Shope's fibroma.

The third virus discovered by Shope was that of a rabbit papilloma. These papillomas, or warts, could be transmitted in series by a filtrate containing the virus in cottontail rabbits but not in domestic rabbits. Further studies by Shope and by Rous showed the papilloma virus to be present in domestic rabbits in a "masked" state. This process was later shown to be more or less analogous to the "proviral," or "latent," state of bacteriophage (the so-called prophage). The confused state of contemporary thinking on latent viruses and the importance of Shope's work is apparent from his contribution "'Masking,' Transformation, and Interepidemic Survival of Animal Viruses" (*Viruses 1950*, ed. Max Delbrück [1950], pp. 79–92).

It was furthermore shown, by Rous, that domestic rabbit papillomas could become malignant, a finding that stimulated research into the viral etiology of cancer. Together with the observation that papilloma virus was not demonstrably present in papillomas in domestic rabbits, this led Shope to pose the rhetorical question "Are Animal Tumor Viruses Always Virus-Like?" (*Journal of General Physiology* 45 [1962]: 143–54), which constitutes a landmark in tumor virus research.

In the early years of World War II Shope worked on a Canadian-American project for the development of an effective vaccine against rinderpest, a virus infection of cattle, sheep, goats, pigs, and other animals, by means of culture and attenuation of the virus in embryonated eggs. In the late 1940s the Princeton branch of the Rockefeller Institute was closed; Shope resigned and became assistant director of the Merck Institute for Therapeutic Research in Rahway, New Jersey. In 1952 he moved to the Rockefeller Institute's main laboratories in New York City. Among the many awards he received were the U.S. Army Legion of Merit and the Albert Lasker Award. He died in New York City.

Several of the viruses discovered by Shope were crucial for developments in cancer research in the 1950s and 1960s in that they became animal models for carcinogenesis studies, resulting in a new concept of (animal) virus. It was Shope's generosity in letting others participate in the study of these viruses that contributed to cancer research's entering a new phase; he helped to build a network of scientists studying cancer viruses in the United States and England.

• A biography of Shope is Christopher H. Andrewes, "Richard Edwin Shope—December 25, 1901–October 2, 1966," National Academy of Sciences, *Biographical Memoirs* 50 (1979): 353–75, which includes a bibliography of Shope's published papers. The landmarks among them include "Swine Influenza. III: Filtration Experiments and Etiology," *Journal of Experimental Medicine* 54 (1931): 373–85; "A Transmissible Tumor-Like Condition in Rabbits: A Filterable Virus Causing a Tumor-Like Condition in Rabbits and Its Relationship to *Virus Myxomatosum*," *Journal of Experimental Medicine* 56 (1932): 793–822; "Infectious Papillomatosis of Rabbits," *Journal of Experimental Medicine* 58 (1933): 607–24; with Andrewes, "A Change in Rabbit Fibroma Virus Suggesting Mutation. III: Interpretation of Findings," *Journal of Experimental Medicine* 63 (1936): 179–84; and "Complex Infections," *Archives of Pathology* 27 (1939): 913–32.

TON VAN HELVOORT

SHOR, Toots (6 May 1903–23 Jan. 1977), restaurateur and bon vivant, was born Bernard Shor in Philadelphia, Pennsylvania, the son of Abraham Schorr, a shirtmaker and cigar and candy store owner, and Fanny Kaufman. Shor's father (who had his surname changed from "Schorr" by a hurried immigration officer), though of Jewish background, settled his family in a Christian working-class community of South Philadelphia. Under the pressure of the anti-Semitism of the time, the young Shor quickly learned to fight and to live by his wits. There, he also developed a strong sense of friendship and loyalty qualities that became inviolable watchwords throughout his life. His nickname came from his boyish long, blond curls.

From grammar school onward Shor was obsessed with sports and soon became more adept at baseball, pool sharking, and gambling than at schoolwork. As he grew to over six feet and 180 pounds, his first ambition was to become a boxer. This youthful goal, however, was vehemently discouraged by his parents. Reluctantly, he attended the Drexel Institute and Wharton School of Business but earned no advanced degrees. Before Shor reached twenty-one, his mother was killed in an accident, and his father committed suicide. Despite these early tragedies, Shor remained fun loving and hopeful about his uncertain future.

After a brief, unsuccessful career as a salesman and a stint as a pool hustler, Shor drifted to New York City in 1930. After living on the edge of poverty for months, Shor caught on as a greeter and bouncer at the 5 O'Clock Club in Manhattan, an establishment run by Owney Madden and George "Big Frenchy" La Mange, prominent gangsters of the Prohibition era. Shor's bold personality, his willingness to fight, and his hard-drinking style fit perfectly with this high-living crowd. Already, at twenty-six, Shor basked in the presence of major celebrities such as Florenz Ziegfeld, James Cagney, Georgie Jessel, and Charles "Lucky" Luciano. Over the next four years, Shor amassed more than $300,000 in salary and gambling winnings. In 1934 he married Marian "Baby" Volk, a Ziegfeld girl. They had four children. By the end of the 1930s Shor was again in financial trouble due to major gambling losses; however, by then he knew almost every prominent restaurant owner in New York. Through his loyalty, sense of class, and general moxie, he developed a host of friends who could be counted on to follow him wherever he worked. He drank with famous athletes, sportswriters, radio, film and Broadway stars, and sports franchise owners. Shor's credo during this exciting period was, "I don't wanna be a millionaire. I just want to live like one."

Shor eventually gathered enough financial backing to open his own restaurant and saloon at 51 West Fifty-first Street. On 30 April 1940 Shor was on his way toward earning the title of the "world's greatest saloon keeper." During the nineteen years that Shor operated his first and most famous restaurant, his personal legend grew in direct proportion to the popularity of his establishment. The years between 1940 and 1959 were rich and memorable in the lore of the big (now 230 pounds) and boisterous proprietor of Toots Shor's. He perfected the persona of the heart of gold under an insulting exterior. If Shor publicly insulted someone, that person (always male) was welcome. His avowed goal was "to make every day Mardi Gras and every night New Year's Eve." Though by conventional standards he was a respectable businessman (his "store" grossed about $2 million per year), he was known to personally eject occasional unruly customers. As colorful as he was, however, Shor was never profane. His boldest expletive was "Jiminy crickets!" and the worst name a Shor foe could be called was "a piece of raisin cake." So strenuous was Shor's hard living that gossip columnist Earl Wilson once wrote, "Overheard at Toots Shor's—Toots Shor."

The cast of characters that frequented Toots Shor's during the 1940s, 1950s and 1960s was remarkable. Four U.S. presidents dined there, and Shor himself dined at the White House twice: once with Harry Truman, and most notably in 1944 with Franklin D. Roosevelt in the company of the young Frank Sinatra who substituted for Shor's ailing wife. The glittering list of his friends bridged sociological gaps from Cardinal Spellman and the nuns at Marymount to gangsters Frank Costello and Abner "Longy" Zwillman; from Babe Ruth, Casey Stengel, and Groucho Marx to William Randolph Hearst, Jr., Edward R. Murrow, playwright Robert Sherwood, and Sir Alexander Fleming, the discoverer of penicillin. After prizefights, Shor would spend hours discussing the bout over brandies and soda (his favorite drink) with Ernest Hemingway. Yankee slugger Joe DiMaggio, the ultimate ballplayer in Shor's eyes, regularly played on the charity softball team sponsored by the restaurant.

Among Shor's innermost circle (members of his "liquid church," as Joe Flaherty put it in *Esquire*, Oct. 1974) were comedians Jackie Gleason, Joe E. Lewis, and Bob Hope; movie stars Sinatra, Bing Crosby, Don Ameche, Pat O'Brien, and Orson Welles; sportswriters Jimmy Cannon, Red Smith, Bob Considine, and Red Barber; sports heroes Jack Dempsey, Billy Conn, Rocky Graziano, Eddie Arcaro, Ben Hogan, Leo Durocher, Yogi Berra, Mickey Mantle, Whitey Ford, DiMaggio, and Babe Ruth, whom Shor worshipped. In fact, when Ruth was dying of cancer, Shor sent great portions of lobster bisque to the Babe's hospital room each night for "proper nourishment." Other regular members of Shor's "palship" were former New York City mayor Jimmy Walker; Horace Stoneham, owner of Shor's beloved New York Giants; lawyer Edward Bennett Williams; the Kentucky Derby's Bill Corum; writers Hemingway, Sherwood, and Quentin Reynolds; and columnists Considine, Wilson, Bugs Baer, and Mark Hellinger, Shor's early mentor.

In those prime years, Shor raised huge sums of money for various charities, was always the first to loan his "flat pocket" friends needed cash, and came up with some of the most colorful quotes on record. (He often said that "whiskey helps you when you're feelin' good *and* when you're feelin' bad.") During World War II, when customers complained about the midnight curfew imposed on New York bars, Shor exclaimed, "Any bum can't get drunk by twelve o'clock ain't trying."

Over he years Shor had many offers to purchase his restaurant, and finally in July 1959 he sold it for $1.5 million. Just before the closing, 250 of his closest friends arranged a nostalgic farewell dinner that Red Smith described as "hideously sentimental." On the day Toots Shor's closed, one New York paper noted, "Thousands of bums will be homeless."

Shor opened a second restaurant at 33 West Fifty-second Street in December 1961. Among the first-night patrons was Earl Warren, chief justice of the Supreme Court. Although the opening was promising, Shor's glory days had passed. The new restaurant was not successful, due to miscalculation of the inflated costs of food and drink and the migration of the best New York habitués to Hollywood. By 1975 Shor had lost two places in a row for nonpayment of taxes. His last job was as consultant to New York's Offtrack Betting Corporation.

Although Shor did not exhibit personal ambition beyond the managing of a popular, successful restaurant and meeting place, during his unique career he was influential far beyond his station in life. He supported countless charities and other good causes; he socialized with cardinals, notorious gangsters, the greatest of American sports heroes, movie stars, writers, and politicians; and late in life he boasted that he drank with seven U.S. presidents. His restaurant at 51 West Fifty-first Street became one of the most famous eating spots in American history and brought joy to countless patrons. Its success was primarily due to the sheer force of Shor's personality. He was a fiercely loyal friend, an astute businessman, a father confessor, and generous to a fault, doing much more good than harm during his eventful life. Shor may well be thought of, as his friend Quentin Reynolds anointed him, the American Falstaff. He died in New York City.

• Shor left no body of writing or papers. The best biography is Bob Considine's highly anecdotal *Toots* (1969), but it does not include the last eight years of Shor's life. Another book-length study is John Bainbridge, *The Wonderful World of Toots Shor* (1951), first excerpted in the *New Yorker* 26 (Nov. 1950): 50–52. Mention of Shor is substantial in George Frazier, *The One with the Mustache Is Costello* (1947). Uncritical articles include Quentin Reynolds, "Falstaff of the Fifties," *Colliers* 118 (Oct. 1946): 70ff; "My Life with Toots," by his wife Marian, with Tom Meany, *Colliers* 128 (Sept. 1951): 23ff; John Lardner, "The Life of T—ts Sh-r," *Newsweek* 28 (Nov. 1946): 91; Charles Champlin, "A Laugh and a Tear for Toots," *Life*, July 1959, pp. 84ff; and Gay Talese's articles in the *New York Times*, 8 Oct. 1960 and 28 Dec. 1961. The most balanced later article is Joe Flaherty, "Toots Shor among the Ruins," *Esquire*, Oct. 1974. David Halberstam focuses on Shor's influence on baseball celebrities in *Summer of '49* (1989). See also Leslie Bennetts, "Toots Shor" in *Biography News* 2 (May–June 1975): 651–52. Obituaries are in the *New York Times*, 24 Jan. 1977, and in *Variety*, 26 Jan. 1977.

BRUCE L. JANOFF

SHORE, Dinah (1 Mar. 1917–24 Feb. 1994), singer and television show host, was born Frances Rose Shore in Winchester, Tennessee, the daughter of Solomon A. Shore, a dry goods merchant, and Anna Stein. Shore made her singing debut at the age of fourteen in a Nashville nightclub and her first radio performance on Nashville's radio station WSM while a sophomore at Vanderbilt University. After graduating in 1938 with a degree in sociology, she moved to New York City.

Shore first worked as an unpaid singer on radio station WNEW, where she met musical director Ticker Freeman, who would become her longtime accompanist and musical adviser. Shortly after arriving in New York, she dropped her childhood nickname of "Fanny Rose" in favor of "Dinah," reportedly because of the growing popularity of her rendition of the song "Dinah." She legally adopted the name Dinah in 1944.

In January 1939 Shore sang with the Leo Reisman orchestra, where she was noticed by band leader Xavier Cugat. He asked her to join him in a series of records for RCA Victor, which began with "The Breeze and I." Between 1940 and 1955 she recorded seventy-five hit records, including "Yes, My Darling Daughter," "Blues in the Night," and "I'll Walk Alone." Her sultry, "torchy jazz" vocal style was popular with both the public and the critics, who compared her early work to Mildred Bailey and Ethel Waters. She later adopted a more rapid and upbeat delivery, similar to Doris Day and Jo Stafford, but never limited herself to a single style. Commenting on her recording career, in 1965 she stated, "That may be the only reason I've survived. I certainly haven't had many big sellers. I've always tried to stay current."

Shore later sang with Ben Bernie's orchestra on the Columbia Broadcasting System radio network, joined the "Chamber Music Society of Lower Basin Street" on the National Broadcasting Company (NBC) radio network, and had a three-year run on Eddie Cantor's radio show from 1940 through 1942. The *Motion Picture Daily Fame*'s annual poll in radio listed her as the top female vocalist in 1941 and in every year thereafter until 1961.

A film offer from Warner Brothers Studios led to Shore's appearances in *Thank Your Lucky Stars* (1943) and *Till the Clouds Roll By* (1946), as well as several other movies for different studios, including *Up in Arms* (1944). Advisers in the movie industry persuaded her to change her appearance, and she dyed her dark hair honey blonde and had plastic surgery on her nose. She did not become a favorite with movie audiences, however, and her final film was *Aaron Slick from Punkin Crick* (1952). She later explained that she

"bombed" as a movie star because she was "just not photogenic."

During World War II Shore's work in the Hollywood studios was punctuated by a large number of appearances for U.S. troops at hospitals and servicemen's canteens and by tours of army camps in Europe and Japan with the United Service Organization (USO). While in Hollywood Shore met actor George Montgomery, whom she married in 1943. The couple had two children, one of whom was adopted; they divorced in 1962.

Shore's lack of movie success did not detract from her popularity on radio or on the new medium of television. She made several appearances on special programs hosted by Bob Hope during 1950 and 1951, and she started her own fifteen-minute variety show, "The Dinah Shore Chevy Show," which ran on NBC from 1951 to 1956. The show was enlarged to an hour weekly program and renamed "The Dinah Shore Show" in 1956, with the Chevrolet division of the General Motors Corporation remaining her sponsor until 1962. She and the automobile company became fused in the public mind with the musical jingle, "See the U.S.A. in Your Chevrolet"; eventually she found the association too much of a gimmick and sought other sponsors and other roles in other shows. In 1961 she starred in a television version of Noël Coward's *Brief Encounter*.

Following her divorce from Montgomery, Shore temporarily retired from television and limited her performances to nightclubs and charity benefits. In May 1963 she married professional tennis player Maurice Fabian Smith; the couple was divorced in 1964. She returned to television to host "The Dinah Shore Special" on NBC on 20 January 1963 and hosted several other occasional "specials" for NBC during 1963–1969.

Shore switched formats and started one of the first television talk shows, "Dinah's Place," which ran on NBC from 1970 to 1974. She also continued to perform in occasional television specials, make guest appearances in television series such as "Mary Hartman, Mary Hartman," "Alice," "Hotel," and "Murder, She Wrote," and appeared in the television movie *Death Car on the Freeway* (1979). She also hosted several other talk shows that were broadcast over the Nashville Network; her final television show was "A Conversation with Dinah," which ran from 1989 to 1991. During the early 1970s she became the subject of publicity because of her long-term romantic involvement with Burt Reynolds, an actor nineteen years her junior, whom she met when he appeared on her talk show.

An avid golfer, Shore was instrumental in advancing the status of women's professional golf. She was a founder and financial sponsor of the Colgate–Dinah Shore–Women's Circle Ladies' Professional Golf Association Tournament, which began in 1970 at Palm Springs, California, and subsequently became known as the Dinah Shore Classic. She was also the author of three cookbooks, *Someone's in the Kitchen with Dinah* (1971), *The Dinah Shore Cookbook* (1983), and *The Di-*

nah Shore American Kitchen (1990). She died at her home in Beverly Hills, California.

• Bruce Cassiday, *Dinah!* (1979), is a biography based on interviews with Shore. She wrote the foreword for, and is discussed in, George T. Simon, *The Best of the Music Makers* (1979). She was profiled in Judy Klemsrud, "Dinah Reveling in Her 60's," *New York Times*, 26 Apr. 1981, and in "Ten Years for Dinah," *TV Guide*, 1 Oct. 1960, reprinted in Jay S. Harris, *TV Guide: The First 25 Years* (1978). See also David Ewen, *All the Years of American Popular Music* (1977), and Burt Reynolds, *My Life* (1994). Obituaries are in the *New York Times*, 25 Feb. 1994, *Variety*, 28 Feb. 1994, and *Billboard*, 12 Mar. 1994.

STEPHEN G. MARSHALL

SHOREY, Paul (3 Aug. 1857–24 Apr. 1934), classical scholar, was born in Davenport, Iowa, the son of David Lewis Shorey and Maria Antoinette Merriam. His father was a prosperous lawyer, later a judge, then trustee of the University of Chicago. The family early moved to Chicago, where Shorey passed most of his life. He graduated from Harvard College in 1878 and next worked in his father's law office, gaining admittance to the Illinois bar in 1880. Law did not appeal to him, and he spent the next three years studying in Europe, at Leipzig, Bonn, the American School in Athens, and lastly in Munich, where he wrote his dissertation in Latin on Plato's theory of forms under the Hellenist Wilhelm Christ.

Shorey joined the faculty of the newly founded Bryn Mawr College in 1885. He taught Latin, philosophy, and Greek; met the Hopkins classicist Basil Lanneau Gildersleeve; and began work on his Horatian commentary. In 1892 William Rainey Harper appointed him first professor of Greek at the new University of Chicago. He married a Latin student, Emma L. Gilbert, in 1895. He remained at Chicago until his retirement in 1927. His *Horace Odes and Epodes* (1898) became a standard and often reprinted textbook. He next published a controversial essay, *The Unity of Plato's Thought* (1903), which revived the view of the German theologian Friedrich Schleiermacher that Plato early conceived his main ideas and later simply polished them. The book argued against contemporary opinion that postulated a development in Plato's thought away from Socrates beginning with *Apology* and continuing to his last work, *Laws*. Apart from several polemical contributions to metrical studies and a famous paper on the ethics and psychology of Thucydides (1893), Shorey's scholarly publications were confined to Greek philosophy, especially Plato. *What Plato Said* (1933) is his enormously intelligent "résumé of the entire body of the Platonic writings" (p. v) with frequent peppery criticism of what others believed Plato to have said. His two-volume edition of Plato's *Republic* in the Loeb Classical Library (1930, 1935) has long been the pride of the series. It contains an authoritative text but also an expert's translation that is both eloquent and accurate.

Shorey took an active, even militant, part in the cultural politics of his time. He was a regular contributor to the *Atlantic* and the *Nation*. He was a conservative and a patriot, if not a chauvinist. He admired German scholarly professionalism against Oxbridge dilettantism, but he insisted that American scholars must emancipate themselves from their German masters and strike out on their own. He welcomed American entry into World War I and in 1919 delivered a violent harangue, embarrassing today, against the great German achievement in classical scholarship. He was a founder and managing editor (1908–1934) of the Chicago journal *Classical Philology*, to which he devoted much of his time. He was Theodore Roosevelt Exchange Professor at the University of Berlin in 1913. He received eleven honorary degrees. He was often difficult, ready to see a slight where none was intended, and more at ease with students than with colleagues. He directed some seventy outstanding dissertations, built up the Classics Library at Chicago, and with his contemporaries, Gildersleeve and W. A. Oldfather, was one of the founders of scientific classical research in the United States. That contributed immeasurably to the serious study of the humanities in America. He is the only American whose elucidations of Plato are ranked with those of the great Europeans, upon which indeed he occasionally improved. A modern historian of Platonic exegesis warns, "What Shorey looks for and finds in Plato is not so much theoretical thought as moral edification, as understood by a serious-minded American academic, with a transcendentalist heritage and a utilitarian outlook, who tends to regard philosophical speculation as a loss of time if not worse" (Tigerstedt, 55). Shorey's weakness was in his generalizations. His strength remained the precise philological exegesis of Greek philosophical texts. He was a significant figure in the creation of Bryn Mawr College, where a professorship preserves his name, and in the formative years of the University of Chicago. His doctoral students influenced three generations of American classical scholars. His greatest student and his successor at Chicago was Benedict Einarson. He died in Chicago.

• Published sources for Shorey's life are John Francis Latimer, "Paul Shorey: A Bibliography of his Classical Publications," *Classical Philology* 81 (1986): 1–29; E. Christian Kopff, "Paul Shorey," in *Classical Scholarship: A Biographical Encyclopedia*, ed. Ward W. Briggs and William M. Calder III (1990), pp. 447–53 (the authoritative life, with an extensive bio-bibliography); Paul Shorey, "Evolution: A Conservative's Apology," *Atlantic Monthly*, Oct. 1928, pp. 475–88; E. N. Tigerstedt, *Interpreting Plato* (1977), pp. 52–56. Shorey papers are at the Newberry Library, Chicago, and the University of Chicago Library, where there is an unpublished catalogue by Margaret A. Fusco (1984). The informative papers of Shorey's biographer, John Latimer, are at the University of Illinois at Urbana-Champaign. Much material not available elsewhere is there.

Aside from the ones mentioned in the text, Shorey's principal publications are *De Platonis Idearum Doctrina atque Mentis Humanae Notionibus Commentatio* (Munich, 1884), reprinted with facing English translation (by R. S. W. Hawtree) as *A Dissertation on Plato's Theory of Forms and on the Concepts of the Human Mind* in *Ancient Philosophy* 2 (Spring

1982); "On the Implicit Ethics and Psychology of Thucydides," *Transactions of the American Philological Association* 24 (1893): 66–88 (= *Papers* 1:192–214); "Fifty Years of Classical Study in America," *Transactions of the American Philological Association* 50 (1919): 33–61; *Selected Papers* (2 vols., 1980).

WILLIAM M. CALDER III

SHORT, Charles (28 May 1821–24 Dec. 1886), classical scholar and professor, was born in Haverhill, Massachusetts, the son of Charles Short and Rebecca George (information on the occupation of Short's parents has not been found). He pursued classical studies at Harvard College, which he entered after two years of teaching. He graduated in 1846 and did postgraduate work under Evangelinus Apostolides Sophocles. Short taught at his former school, Phillips Academy, Andover, and then was headmaster of Roxbury Latin School from 1847 to 1853, before founding his own school in Philadelphia. In 1849 he married Anne Jean Lyman; they had four children.

In 1863 Short left Philadelphia to become president of Kenyon College (in Gambier, Ohio), which prospered during his stay; but in 1867, as a result of an academic controversy, he resigned—the exact nature of the dispute is not clear from published sources. In 1868 Short was elected professor of Latin at Columbia College, New York, where he continued for the rest of his career. At Columbia he had both detractors (such as the administrators Nicholas Murray Butler and John W. Burgess, who regarded Short as a pedant) and admirers (such as the literary figures Brander Matthews and Harry Thurston Peck, who praised Short's immense learning and love of literature). His distinctive teaching manner may be sampled in a privately printed volume titled *Short Commentaries on the Latin Language and Literature* (1905), a collection of eccentric anecdotes taken down by Peck during Short's classes.

As early as 1866, Short had been engaged by Harper and Brothers to plan and undertake a thorough revision of their *Latin-English Lexicon*, edited by Ethan Allen Andrews (1851). His intention was to revise the etymologies, introduce words of ecclesiastical Latin, and otherwise expand and improve the work. But progress was less than rapid, and in 1874 the publisher secured the efficient services of Charlton T. Lewis as a collaborator. Initially Short completed the revision of the text for letters *A* through *C*, but the manuscript of the text for *B* and *C* was lost, and those portions of the final work were written by Lewis. Short's plan for revision and his learned exertions under the letter *A* constitute his most enduring contribution to classical scholarship, since the dictionary, published as *Harpers' Latin Dictionary* (1879) and known as "Lewis and Short," became the most useful work of its scope in the English-speaking world, although the *Oxford Latin Dictionary* (1968–1982) superseded it in certain respects.

Other important works of classical scholarship by Short were a lengthy and elaborate study titled "The Order of Words in Attic Greek Prose" prefixed to Charles Yonge's *English-Greek Lexicon*, as edited by Henry Drisler (1870); and a series of minutely detailed articles published under the general title "The New Revision of King James' Revision of the New Testament" in the *American Journal of Philology*, vols. 2–7 (1881–1886). He died in New York.

• A detailed biographical and bibliographical account is given in the memoir by Charles Lancaster Short, *Charles Short* (1891). Numerous other biographical references are given in the fully documented article by F. J. Sypher, "A History of *Harpers' Latin Dictionary*," *Harvard Library Bulletin* 29, no. 4 (1972): 349–66. An obituary notice appears in the *New York Tribune*, 25 Dec. 1886.

F. J. SYPHER

SHORT, Charles Wilkins (6 Oct. 1794–7 Mar. 1863), physician, botanist, and medical educator, was born at "Greenfield," Woodford County, Kentucky, the son of Peyton Short, a Kentucky state senator and gentleman farmer, and Maria Symmes. When he was age six, his mother died, and he was sent to Lexington, Kentucky, to live with paternal relatives, at which time he may have begun his schooling at Joshua Fry's school in Danville, Kentucky. Short's father married Jane Henry Churchill, a widow, in November 1802, and Charles and his brother and sister returned home. Short received a bachelor's degree from Transylvania University in 1810 and then began an apprenticeship in medicine under his uncle, Dr. Frederick Ridgely of Lexington. In November 1813 he enrolled at the University of Pennsylvania Medical Department.

Having had Caspar Wistar as his mentor during the first of two required sessions of medical lectures, the following April Short became a private pupil of physician Nathaniel Chapman and enrolled in the private surgery course of Thomas T. Hewson at the Philadelphia Alms House and in Dr. Benjamin Smith Barton's botany course. The latter was Short's first formal course in botany, which became a lifelong interest.

In April 1815 Short submitted a thesis on *Juniperis Sabina* and received an M.D. from the University of Pennsylvania. He returned to Kentucky to look for a place near his family to begin practice. He again returned to the East, living in towns in Pennsylvania and New Jersey, and in November 1815 married Mary Henry Churchill, his stepsister. The following spring, they traveled by wagon to Lexington, Kentucky. Here Short met the British botanist Thomas Nuttall, and together they made several botanical excursions around Lexington and Cincinnati, Ohio.

During this time in Lexington, Short decided to practice in Hopkinsville, Christian County, Kentucky, a region called the "Barrens." Rural practice did not appeal to Short, but the opportunity to botanize in new and unfamiliar flora interested him and made practice tolerable. In 1815, at the request of William P. C. Barton, M.D., nephew and successor to his former professor of botany, Short began a correspondence and exchange of botanical specimens that eventually evolved into his distributing 28,918 specimens to fellow botanists in the United States, England, and Europe. By 1819, he had acquired a national reputation as an expert on western botany and was elected to membership in the Academy of Natural Sciences of Philadelphia.

After having refused several opportunities to assume the chair of materia medica and medical botany at Transylvania University's medical department, Short finally (Aug. 1825) decided to abandon his rural practice and accept the appointment, beginning the most productive period of his life (1825–1838). He served as dean of the faculty from 1827 to 1837 and in 1828, with his colleague John Esten Cooke, M.D., founded the *Transylvania Journal of Medicine and the Associate Sciences*. This journal was to be a forum for publications of the faculty and graduates through which they and their school might become widely known. In it, Short published twenty-five of his twenty-nine scientific publications while he was a professor at Transylvania. All but eight of his contributions to the literature were on botanical subjects. While a professor at the Louisville Medical Institute (1838–1846) and the medical department of the University of Louisville (1846–1849), he published the remaining four papers, three of which appeared in the *Western Journal of Medicine and Surgery*.

The medical faculty constructed a new Medical Hall at Transylvania in 1827, and prospects for the medical department seemed bright. Although an economic decline was beginning locally in response to Lexington's isolation—not being on a major waterway—the city continued to be the cultural center of the state. The tranquility sought in Lexington was disrupted when dissention within the medical faculty arose concerning a proposed removal of the school to Louisville. Teaching became less attractive to Short as his botanical studies assumed greater personal importance. Correspondents sought his expertise in identifying unknown plants and requested opportunities to exchange specimens. Short's name and fame spread in England and Europe following the reprinting of his "Sketch of the Progress of Botany in Western America" in Sir William J. Hooker's *Journal of Botany* in November 1840. In recognition of his contributions to scientific botany, Short was elected a member of the American Philosophical Society in Philadelphia (1835).

Offered the chair of materia medica and medical botany when a new medical school, the Medical Institute of the City of Louisville (commonly known as the Louisville Medical Institute, or LMI), was established in 1837, Short at first declined, but the following year he accepted, attracted by the excellent and congenial medical faculty in Louisville. He served from 1838 to 1841 as dean of the faculty. Although disinterested in teaching, he continued his quest to improve the financial prospects of the faculty by attempting to attract more students with better teaching facilities. The faculty in 1840 authorized the construction, at their own expense, of an amphitheater connected to the Louisville Marine (City) Hospital for presenting medical cases, surgical operations, and autopsies to medical students. Short, as dean, recruited Samuel David Gross, M.D., an able teacher, dissector, and anatomist, as professor of surgery at LMI in 1840.

In April 1840 Short was confronted with town and gown difficulties that had been escalating since the medical institute had opened and the medical faculty had had exclusive care of the patients in the Louisville Marine (City) Hospital. The problem was resolved by an ordinance, which allowed two private physicians from the community to join four from the faculty to attend patients at this hospital.

Having received a valuable legacy following the death of his uncle, William Short, Short purchased the 230-acre "Hayfield" farm, five miles south of Louisville. Here, during his summers, Short cultivated many plants collected by him and by his correspondents from various parts of the world, continued his correspondence, and added to his herbarium. Plagued by illness, he resigned in 1849 from the faculty. He gave his herbarium to the Academy of Natural Sciences of Philadelphia, where it was used by scholars for many generations.

Short's contributions to botany were recognized by his peers by their naming several plants and grasses in his honor—*Shortia galacifolia*, *Myosurus Shortii* (now called M. minimus), *Aster Shortii*, *Vesicaria Shortii*, *Solidago Shortii*, *Gonalobus Shortii*, and *Carex Shortiana*.

Because of the proximity of Confederate forces in the surrounding area, the Shorts moved from their farm into Louisville in late fall 1862. Short became gravely ill in early spring 1863 and died of typhoid pneumonia at his home in Louisville.

As a teacher, administrator, and medical editor, Short contributed to the dissemination of medical knowledge. His pioneering studies of western flora, exchange of well-prepared specimens, and prolific correspondence with botanists throughout the world assisted in the development of botanical sciences and established his international reputation.

• Major collections of Short's letters and publications are in the Filson Club, Louisville, Ky.; the American Philosophical Society Library, Philadelphia, Pa.; and the Southern Historical Collection, University of North Carolina, Chapel Hill. Several well-documented biographies are, by Samuel D. Gross, in *Proceedings of the American Philosophical Society* 19 (1865): 171–86; Deborah S. Skaggs, "Charles Wilkins Short: Kentucky Botanist and Physician, 1794–1863" (M.A. thesis, Univ. of Louisville, 1982); and P. Albert Davies, "Charles Wilkins Short, 1794–1863, Botanist and Physician," *Filson Club History Quarterly* 19 (1945): 131–55 and 208–49, which contains Short's bibliography (pp. 236–49). An obituary is in the *Louisville Daily Journal*, 9 Mar. 1863.

EUGENE H. CONNER

SHORT, Hassard (15 Oct. 1877–9 Oct. 1956), theatrical director, was born Hubert Hassard Short in Edlington, Lincolnshire, England, the son of Edward Hassard Short and Geraldine Blagrave, both of inherited means. At age fifteen Short left the Charterhouse School in Surrey, searching for a life in the theater. By

1895 he had made his London acting debut and had appeared with Lily Langtry. He caught Anglophile producer Charles Frohman's eye and by 1901 was appearing for Frohman on Broadway. There, supporting headliners such as John Drew and John Barrymore, Short eventually became stereotyped as a "heavy" or a silly Englishman.

As early as 1912 Short, who was said to be both fussy and understated, was directing musical shows such as *Dance Dream*, a revue, for one of his clubs, the Lambs. In the crucial early years of Actors Equity (1919–1922) Short, an active supporter of the strike that established Equity's status as bargaining agent for legitimate performers, took charge of the five-week Equity shows, the Metropolitan Opera House Equity program that celebrated the strike's end, and the three subsequent Equity Met shows. Although his *Honeydew* (1920) was hailed as "brilliant work" in *Theatre Magazine*, Short came into his own only when Irving Berlin hired him to direct at his new Music Box Theatre; in 1930 *Theatre Magazine* called Short the "Master of the Revue."

Although the Music Box was small by Broadway standards, there, said Berlin's biographer Lawrence Bergreen in *As Thousands Cheer*, Short developed a talent "for filling a stage from one end of the proscenium to the other." For the first *Music Box Revue* (1921) Short invented a traveling stage platform and the "Hassard Short [backstage] elevator," which hoisted sixteen chorus girls into their positions on a giant black iridescent fan.

The newly arrived stars of *Charlot's London Revue of 1924* were awed—according to one of them, Gertrude Lawrence—by what they believed to be normal Broadway procedure: a theater filled with the scent of orange blossoms. In fact, Short nightly activated tiny valves beneath each seat that released the fragrance as Grace Moore and John Steel strolled among onstage trees while singing Berlin's "An Orange Grove in California." Seventeen of Short's fifty Broadway shows were directed for producers who liked large effects: Sam Harris, Max Gordon, and Mike Todd. Though Short sometimes produced his own shows, such as *Hassard Short's Ritz Revue* (1924), generally his talents were for hire. Occasionally Short was hired to "save" a show after the original director had been fired; such directors included Jerome Kern and Vincente Minnelli.

Of Short's innovations, the most important was his use of light and color. He discovered a way to paint gauze, and he claimed that another "discovery"—approximating pure black and white lighting—stemmed from a mistake in changing gels (the colored slides used to create lighting effects) that he had witnessed in Europe. Short came to believe that lighting was the most important aspect of a revue. The opening night audience at *Three's a Crowd* (1930) grumbled when the footlights were turned out, but they were assuaged when they realized that Short had hung spotlights under the balcony, producing exciting new effects. The audience was also quickly won over by the opening scene: as a husband was about to discover his wife's lover under a bed, the stagehands removed the bed and an actor announced that it wouldn't be *that* kind of show. Clifton Webb and Tamara Geva danced "Body and Soul" silhouetted on a green-lit stage, while small spotlights isolated their hands, feet, and torsos. In *The Band Wagon* (1931) Short created a device whereby the audience saw a mirror image of itself as the curtain went up. He also integrated designer Albert Johnson's twin revolving stages into musical numbers and sketches, including a waltz sequence in which a beggar falls asleep on the steps of the Vienna Opera, his dream unfurling as the stage revolves to the theater's interior; "Two Hoops," in which Adele Astaire and Fred Astaire wreak havoc rolling hoops against the flow of humans on a crazily revolving stage; and "I Love Louisa," which features the entire cast on a Bavarian merry-go-round.

Teaming again with Berlin, Short directed *As Thousands Cheer* (1933) and its London adaptation, *Stop Press* (1935), using a newspaper headline format to introduce topical songs and sketches. He underlined the mockery of public figures, and as Bergreen reported in his biography, the American audience felt "on equal terms or superior" to them, which was "good news in 1933." *Stop Press* differed markedly from *As Thousands Cheer*, in part because Short cannibalized numbers from other productions as far back as the Music Box revues. In addition, he eliminated the political mockery in *As Thousands Cheer*: "We can't have that sort of thing for London. . . . In America politicians don't mind because . . . they are used to defending and explaining themselves." Short added that in the United States people who were lampooned onstage regularly came backstage to congratulate him. Among visual splendors in *Stop Press* were "Easter Parade," lit in the sepia tones of the newspaper's rotogravure, and "A Sequin Serenade," in which, according to the *Times* drama critic, James Agate, "the dancers moved in and out of pools of light, trailing rivers of illumination."

Short's *The Great Waltz* (1934) had a tryout as *Waltzes from Vienna* in London, where he was presented to King George V and Queen Mary. In this inaugural performance at the 3,822-seat Radio Center Theatre, Short managed twenty-three actors, seventy-seven singers, thirty-three ballet dancers, fifty-three musicians, ninety backstage workers, and a wardrobe of more than five hundred costumes.

Short continued to direct distinguished musicals, including the Weill-Gershwin *Lady in the Dark* (1941), with its stylized circus scenes, and the Oscar Hammerstein II adaptation *Carmen Jones* (1943); his overall design for the latter, entirely in primary colors, won particular acclaim. During the mid-1940s the type of theater with which Short was associated began to be eclipsed by the newer sort of musical play, such as *Oklahoma!* (1943); choreographers increasingly supplanted directors, and book shows increased in popularity. Short's *Make Mine Manhattan* (1948) for producer Max Leibman was called the last of the traditional Broadway revues, and his last show opened in 1952. Short, a lifelong bachelor, died while vacationing in Nice, France.

London director Robert Nesbitt noted Short's "style, taste and subtlety," and theater historian Gerald Bordman praised him for his "impeccable . . . gift for theatrical movement." Between 1920 and 1950 Short innovated lighting and mechanical effects that became standard in the theater. Short's achievement is glimpsed in the words of the musical theater historian Ethan Mordden: "From Julian Mitchell to John Murray Anderson to Hassard Short to Rouben Mamoulian, there have been directors of such stature that at times they are larger than the shows they stage."

• Clippings, theater programs, and other material relating to Short's career are in the New York Public Library for the Performing Arts (Lincoln Center) and the Theatre Museum, London. A biography of Short has yet to be published. The flavor of his shows can be inferred from books such as Ethan Mordden, *Broadway Babies* (1983); Lawrence Bergreen, *As Thousands Cheer* (1990); Stanley Green, *Broadway Musicals Show by Show* (1985); and Gerald Bordman, *Chronicle of the American Musical Theatre* (1992).

JAMES ROSS MOORE

SHORT, Joseph Hudson, Jr. (11 Feb. 1904–18 Sept. 1952), journalist and presidential press secretary, was born in Vicksburg, Mississippi, the son of Joseph Hudson Short, clerk of the U.S. Court for the Southern District of Mississippi, and Irene Elizabeth Jones. Friends remember the "tall Short boy" as quiet and meditative, like his father, and interested in a career in the military. Both of his grandfathers had been Civil War veterans, one a civilian clerk on the staff of General Ulysses S. Grant, the other a soldier under General Robert E. Lee. Short attended Marion (Alabama) Institute and received his B.A. from Virginia Military Institute in 1925; he ranked eighty-third in a class of 101 students. The standing reflected Short's preoccupation editing *The Cadet*, a campus newspaper, and his decision, under the tutelage of Professor William M. Hundley, a former reporter on the *Baltimore Sun*, to become a journalist.

After graduation Short earned twenty dollars a week as a copyreader and reporter for the *Jackson* (Miss.) *Daily News*, returning to that newspaper in 1927 after a year at the *Vicksburg Post and Herald*. His work in 1929 at the *New Orleans Times–Picayune* covering a bitter streetcar strike led to a job in the Richmond, Virginia bureau of the Associated Press. Two years later he was transferred to AP's Washington bureau, where he covered the eviction of the so-called Bonus Army in 1932 and then traveled with the Democratic presidential candidate Franklin Roosevelt. In 1937 Short married Elizabeth (Beth) Roberta Campbell, a colleague at AP. In 1936, after seven years as a newspaper reporter, she had become the only woman on AP's general staff of eighty-eight. He covered President Roosevelt and the White House, while she was assigned Eleanor Roosevelt.

In 1939, Short was named chief of AP reporters covering the House of Representatives, and a year later Beth resigned to have the first of the couple's three children. Short resigned from AP in 1941 to become a Washington correspondent for the *Chicago Sun*. Two years later he joined the Washington bureau for the *Baltimore Sun*. When he was assigned to Harry Truman's vice presidential campaign train in 1944, "Truman didn't know my name," Short recalled. The trip's major gaffe occurred in Providence, Rhode Island, when Truman agreed with Short's observation that there was little difference between isolationist Republicans and Democrats. The statement triggered national headlines and reflected Truman's tendency to "shoot from the lip."

While covering the Democratic vice presidential candidate, Short initially doubted Truman's capacity to be president. His estimation of Truman, however, "went up daily." As the Washington-based reporter for the *Sun*, Short accompanied Truman, who became president following Roosevelt's death in April 1945, during domestic and foreign trips. He logged more than 125,000 miles with the president and became a frequent poker partner aboard the presidential yacht, once losing $400 to Truman. A mutual admiration grew between the two. Short was impressed with Truman's "courage" and decisiveness. Truman considered Short a "crackerjack" reporter of rare qualities who had won the respect of fellow journalists. Indeed, in 1948 Short was elected president of the National Press Club.

When presidential press secretary Charles G. Ross died in December 1950, veteran reporters Merriman Smith and Raymond P. Brandt were among those who urged Truman to pick Short as Ross's replacement. Short accepted the appointment, despite his concern that he "might not prove as useful to the president as Ross," who had known Truman since childhood. His first act as press secretary was symbolic. He cut the red velvet cord that kept reporters out of the press secretary's office. Two weeks later, he named two assistants, Irving Perlmeter and Roger Tubby, to facilitate press contacts.

Short was the first White House reporter to move directly to the position of presidential press secretary. His tenure, however, was not an altogether happy one. Newspaper reporters who had admired Short's "attention to detail" and "fierce loyalty" as a reporter now thought him "too protective" of Truman. Many charged that his new rules preventing direct contact between the press and members of the executive branch "built a wall between the Truman administration and the press." Some felt "betrayed" by a former colleague who, they felt, had grown insensitive to the demand of deadlines.

Short's defensiveness grew from his struggle to reverse a slide in Truman's popularity, which had been hastened by the stalemate in the war in Korea and then by the firing of General Douglas MacArthur in April 1951. His determination "to take the administration's message to the American people" made him "a top-level voice on general policy" within Truman's "inner circle," according to White House aide Richard E. Neustadt. Friends worried that Short was too "emotionally involved" in his work and feared for his health. A viral infection led to his hospitalization on 9 September 1952. His death from a heart attack in Alexandria, Virginia, shocked Truman, who felt he had lost "a loyal friend, a member of my own family."

• Short's papers are at the Harry S. Truman Library in Independence, Mo., along with an unprocessed collection at the National Archives in Washington, D.C. The Truman Library also has an oral history given by Short's widow, Beth Campbell Short, in 1971, and interviews with members of the press corps who covered the Truman White House. The best of these are by Edward T. Folliard, Jack L. Bell, and Robert G. Nixon, longtime acquaintances of Short. The best of the secondary sources is Francis H. Heller, ed., *The Truman White House: The Administration of the Presidency, 1945–1953* (1980), particularly the reminiscence of special assistant to the White House Richard E. Neustadt. For background on Short's relationships with other members of the Truman administration, see Donald R. McCoy, *The Presidency of Harry S. Truman* (1984); Cabell Phillips, *The Truman Presidency* (1966); and Robert H. Ferrell, *Harry S. Truman and the Modern American Presidency* (1983). For Short's role in the development of presidential press relations, see M. L. Stein, *When Presidents Meet the Press* (1969); Douglass Cater, *The Fourth Branch of Government* (1959); James E. Pollard, *The Presidents and the Press: Truman to Johnson* (1964); and Elmer E. Cornwell, Jr., *Presidential Leadership of Public Opinion* (1965). Important newspaper accounts of Short's career are found in the *New York Times*, 9 Dec. 1950, 19 Sept. 1952, and 20 Sept. 1952; the *Baltimore Sun*, 4 Mar. 1949, 9 Dec. 1950, 19 Sept. 1952, and 20 Sept. 1952; the *Jackson* (Miss.) *Clarion-Ledger*, 20 Sept. 1952; and the *Vicksburg Evening Post*, 20 May 1984.

BRUCE J. EVENSEN

SHORT, Luke (19 Nov. 1908–18 Aug. 1975), western novelist, was born Frederick Dilley Glidden in Kewanee, Illinois, the son of Wallace Dilley Glidden, a boiler-company secretary, and Fannie Mae Hurff, who after her husband's death in 1921 taught high school English and later became dean of women at Knox College in nearby Galesburg. Frederick Glidden's brother, Jonathan H. Glidden (1907–1957), became the western novelist Peter Dawson. Frederick Glidden graduated from Kewanee High School, attended the University of Illinois at Urbana, transferred to the University of Missouri at Columbia, and graduated in 1930 with a bachelor's degree in journalism. He became a fur trapper in northern Alberta, Canada (1931–1933), worked as an archaeologist's assistant in and near Santa Fe, New Mexico (1933–1934), and married Florence Elder in Grand Junction, Colorado, in 1934. He began writing fiction for pulp magazines in Pojoaque (outside Santa Fe), engaged New Yorker Marguerite E. Harper as his literary agent (1934), sold his first short story (1935), and adopted the pen name Luke Short, evidently before realizing that there had been a real-life Dodge City gambler and gunfighter with the same name.

Short's first novel, *The Feud at Single Shot*, soon followed (1936). His wife wrote and marketed a few "ranch romances" herself at this time. During the rest of the 1930s Short averaged about $800 a month through the sale of a dozen more novels, first seeing print in pulp magazines, including *Argosy, Blue Book, Star Western*, and *Western Story*. Only one novel up to this point is vintage Luke Short. It is *Hard Money* (1939), located in a booming mine town and featuring a tender-tough hero who helps a rich old miner defeat assorted villains. From the outset, Short wrote formulary westerns; that is, they center on the actions of a gunslinging loner who achieves justice by violence and cunning in a setting of authentic scenery and action but little or no historically valid ambience, and a heroine who is defined by her relationship to males.

The 1940s were happy for Short. Between 1940 and 1942 he and his wife had their three children. He spent some time writing in Hollywood (1941–1943). Kept from military service during World War II because of poor eyesight, he put in a year at the Office of Strategic Services in Washington, D.C. When the war ended, his career blossomed. He began his lucrative association with Bantam Books in 1946, returned to Hollywood that same year to help convert his excellent novel *Ramrod* (1943) into a successful movie, and in 1948, thanks to his Hollywood agent, the legendary H. N. Swanson, saw four more of his novels made into motion pictures: *Albuquerque*, based on *Dead Freight for Piute* (1940); *Blood on the Moon*, based on *Gunman's Chance* (1941); *Coroner Creek*, based on the 1946 novel of the same name; and *Station West*, based on the 1947 novel of that name.

In 1947 Short and his wife bought and moved into a Victorian house in Aspen, Colorado. By that time Short had deserted the pulps, which had published most of his hundred-odd stories and serialized several of his novels in prebook form; he arranged instead for the *Saturday Evening Post* to serialize nine new novels. However, in 1942, after *Post* editors rejected Short's fine cavalry novel *And the Wind Blows Free* because its youthful narrator catches his adult idol in an extramarital love affair, Short's agent sold its serial rights to the pulp magazine *Short Stories* (10, 25 Feb. 1943) and hardbound book rights to Macmillan (1945). Although other firms were publishing Short in hardbound by this time, it was Bantam, the paperback leader, that paid him the largest sums. Soon he was being translated into French, German, Spanish, and other languages and was even paid the ultimate compliment of being shamelessly plagiarized both by a Dutch publisher and also by an American in England.

The 1950s were unsettled for Short, whom success seemed to bore. In 1950 his film agent sold the movie rights to *High Vermilion* (1948) and *Ride the Man Down* (1942), the latter cleverly featuring rival ranchers and a schoolmarm too timid for the West. In 1952 he wrote the lyrics and an Aspen friend provided the tunes for *I've Had It*, a musical comedy that pleased audiences in Aspen and Denver. Broadway hopes for it came to nought. Also during those years, Short flew north of Alberta to observe uranium mining (1953), visited a Utah uranium mine owned by a friend (1954), and produced *Rimrock* (1955), the strongest of his relatively few novels set in contemporary times; it pits a uranium-seeking hero and a venomous villainess. Short's efforts to found a thorium company proved fruitless, as did a brief writing stint in 1955 with television stars Desi Arnaz and Lucille Ball. When he completed *Summer of the Smoke* and could not place it in any periodical, Bantam ballyhooed it as "first time published anywhere!" (1958). It has shopworn ingredients and seventeen killings.

In 1960 Short's son James Dilley Glidden drowned at the age of nineteen in the Princeton University swimming pool. Short buried himself in work after this personal sorrow, and title after title followed. The quality fell off, though sales did not. *The Some-Day Country* (1964), which concerns illegal immigrants and would-be homesteaders, is his weakest effort. While vacationing with his wife in the Virgin Islands (1963), he attempted in *Pearley* a *Cannery Row*–like story of an aging alcoholic's fight against a heartless pipe-laying company; the novel was never published. In 1964 Short signed a lush contract with Bantam, which from that time advertised him as "today's best-selling western writer" and "the master storyteller of the West" and guaranteed him a minimum of $15,000 per original paperback. He began an ambitious series of novels set in or near a fictitious Colorado town he christened Primrose and populated with politicians, mine owners, saloon and hotel keepers, a corrupt newsman, indifferent lawmen, women of varied morals, and other characters. He drew up street plans and floor plans for several town buildings, and in a letter to his literary agent (4 May 1965) he compared his Primrose to William Faulkner's Yoknapatawpha County. Had Short lived longer, his eight *Primrose* novels—*First Campaign* (1965), *The Primrose Try* (1967), *Debt of Honor* (1967), *The Guns of Hanging Lake* (1968), *Donovan's Gun* (1968), *The Deserters* (1969), *Three for the Money* (1970), and *Man from the Desert* (1971)—might have been only the beginning of a saga anticipating Louis L'Amour's later series of novels featuring the Sackett family.

The most meritorious non-Primrose novel by Short during his Primrose phase is *Paper Sheriff* (1966), the horrors of which prefigure his sadly bitter 1970s work. In it, a decent rancher is elected parttime sheriff, only to discover that his slatternly wife is a criminal protected by her vicious clan. In 1969 Short developed severe eye trouble and, five years later, terminal throat cancer. To the end, however, he remained productive. He died in Aspen Valley Hospital. Although his final novels are unremittingly grim, he remains one of the most readable of all western novelists. His well-paced plots, his easy and sometimes salty dialogue, and his hardbitten heroes meeting challenges on cattle ranges and Native-American reservations, in the desert, in mines and at army forts, and along railroad tracks heading west have become part of the myth of the American West.

• A wealth of unpublished material by and about Short is deposited in the library of the University of Oregon at Eugene. Four essays by three fellow western novelists who admired their friend are Steve Frazee, "Meet Fred Glidden," *Roundup*, Oct. 1955, pp. 3–4; T. V. Olsen, "Luke Short, Writer's Writer," *Roundup*, Mar. 1973, pp. 10–11 and "Lauds Luke Short as Tops in Field," *Roundup*, Oct. 1975, p. 10; and Brian Garfield, "The Fiddlefoot from Kewanee," *Roundup*, Nov. 1975, pp. 6–7, 11. Phillip D. Thomas, "The Paperback West of Luke Short," *Journal of Popular Culture* 7 (Winter 1973): 701–8, is a reliable early study. Robert L. Gale, *Luke Short* (1981), emphasizes the literary quality of Short's work. Richard W. Etulain, "Luke Short (Frederick D. Glidden) (1908–1975)," in *Fifty Western Writers: A Bio-Bibliographical Sourcebook*, ed. Fred Erisman and Richard W. Etulain (1982), covers Short's biography, his themes, and criticism of his output. J. Golden Taylor et al., eds., *A Literary History of the American West* (1987), has brief commentaries on Short, always in praise. Gale, "Luke Short," in *Bibliography of American Fiction: 1919–1988*, ed. Matthew J. Bruccoli and Judith S. Baughman, vol. 2 (1991), includes primary and secondary items. A useful obituary is in the *New York Times*, 19 Aug. 1975.

ROBERT L. GALE

SHORT, Robert Earl (20 July 1917–20 Nov. 1982), businessman, political activist, and sports franchise owner, was born in Minneapolis, Minnesota, the son of Robert Lester and Frances Niccum. His father, a brewery driver, fireman, union official, and Democratic alderman in the city's fourth ward, had his son distributing political literature at age nine. By the time Short graduated from North High School in 1936, he was interested in a career in law and politics. He received his bachelor's degree from the College of St. Thomas in 1940, studied law at several universities, and served in the U.S. Navy before earning a law degree from Georgetown University in 1947. He then served as assistant to the U.S. district attorney, both in Washington, D.C. (1947–1948) and in Minneapolis (1949–1950).

In 1947 Short married former model Marion McCann, with whom he had seven children. Finding it difficult to support his family on a government salary, he left law for business in 1950, borrowing money to invest in the Mueller Transportation Company, a small trucking firm in St. Paul operating between the Twin Cities and Chicago. He acquired McKeon Transportation Company in 1956 and in 1961 bought Merchants Motor Freight, Inc., for $10 million, merging it with his other company to form Admiral-Merchants Motor Freight, Inc. Acquisition of the Dixie Highway Express Company, based in Birmingham, Alabama, in 1967 greatly expanded his business.

While trucking formed the base of Short's fortune, he moved into other industries in the 1960s. In late 1964 he purchased the Leamington Hotel in Minneapolis and added to his holdings the Francis Drake Hotel (1969) and the Dyckman Hotel (1975) in Minneapolis and, in 1971, the St. Paul, Lowry, and Karl hotels in St. Paul. By 1978 he also owned ten parking facilities in the Twin Cities area, additional business and apartment buildings, and Minneapolis radio station WWTC, purchased in 1977. Between 1968 and 1972 Short was in the aviation business, operating Gopher

Aviation, Inc., an aircraft sales and service company. In 1978 he estimated his wealth at between $4 million and $10 million.

Short's success in business was not replicated in his political endeavors. He lost the 1946 Democratic-Farmer-Labor party primary for the U.S. congressional seat from Minnesota's third district, and in 1956 he chaired the Minnesota delegation to the Democratic National Convention after he challenged the party's state leaders by supporting Tennessee senator Estes Kefauver, who defeated Adlai Stevenson in the state's presidential primary. In 1966 he ran unsuccessfully for lieutenant governor of Minnesota on the Democratic-Farmer-Labor party ticket. As a result of his friendship with Hubert H. Humphrey, Short became active in national politics, serving as the coordinator of Humphrey's vice presidential campaign in 1964. In August 1968 Humphrey appointed him treasurer of the Democratic National Committee, where he faced the task of raising money to finance Humphrey's presidential campaign and then resolving the party's nearly $7-million debt; Short resigned the post in March 1969. He had long coveted a place in the U.S. Senate, and in 1978 he ran for the seat left vacant by Humphrey's death. He narrowly won the party primary but was defeated soundly by David Durenberger in the general election.

Outside Minnesota, Short was best known for his ownership of two sports franchises. His involvement with professional sports began in 1957 when he and more than a hundred local businessmen paid $150,000 for the struggling Lakers' franchise in the National Basketball Association in order to keep the team in Minneapolis. Short soon acquired nearly all of the stock in the team, which continued to have financial problems. In 1960 he moved the Lakers to Los Angeles, where, led by Elgin Baylor and Jerry West, they enjoyed greater success on the court and at the box office, enabling Short to sell the team to Jack Kent Cooke in 1965 for $5 million. This was among the highest prices paid for an NBA franchise up to that time.

In December 1968 Short bought another struggling franchise, the Washington Senators major league baseball team, for $9.4 million. His controversial personnel moves, including the signing of former stars Curt Flood and Denny McLain and his enticing of the great hitter Ted Williams to manage, failed to improve the team's performance or its finances and often angered its fans. Near the end of the 1971 season, the unpopular owner announced that he would move the team to Arlington, Texas, for the next season. In 1974 Short sold the Texas Rangers franchise for $9 million to a group of local investors. Short's approach to the business of sports apparently concerned even other owners. In 1976 he and a local investor tried to buy the San Francisco Giants, but other team owners insisted that majority ownership rest with the local investor, not with Short, and the deal collapsed.

Short tirelessly combined careers in business, sports, and politics, but his blunt manner and obvious ambition made him a controversial figure in all three fields. Energetic, impatient, and demanding in his business dealings, he readily professed his desire for power and recognition. Critics argued that he often put personal ambition above loyalty to party, his team's fans, and sound business practices; to Short and his defenders, however, he was an honest, straightforward businessman who knew what he wanted and had the ability to get things done.

A Roman Catholic, he was a devoted family man and a philanthropist whose charitable gifts often went to Catholic institutions. He served on the board of trustees of the College of St. Thomas and of St. Mary's Hospital in Minneapolis, and he was on the advisory board of the University of Notre Dame Law School. He died in Minneapolis.

• The Minnesota Historical Society has a short bibliography of articles and biographical sketches about Short and a file of clippings about him but no manuscript material. Short's ownership of the Lakers is discussed in Scott Ostler and Steve Springer, *Winnin' Times: The Magical Journey of the Los Angeles Lakers* (1986). His ownership of the Washington Senators/ Texas Rangers is discussed in Shelby Whitfield, *Kiss It Goodbye* (1973); Al Hirshberg, *Frank Howard: The Gentle Giant* (1973); and Peter C. Bjarkman, "Washington Senators–Texas Rangers: There Are No Dragons in Baseball, Only Shortstops," in *Encyclopedia of Baseball Team Histories: American League*, ed. Peter C. Bjarkman (1991). His political career, especially his work for Hubert Humphrey, is mentioned in Carl Solberg, *Hubert Humphrey: A Biography* (1984); Albert Eisele, *Almost to the Presidency: A Biography of Two American Politicians* (1972); and Theodore White, *The Making of the President—1968* (1969). The best overview of Short's business career is Wayne Christensen, "Bob Short: Why He Keeps on Truckin'," *Corporate Report*, May 1978, pp. 39–41, 84–89. Obituaries are in the *Minneapolis Tribune* and the *St. Paul Pioneer Press*, 21 Nov. 1982, and the *New York Times*, 22 Nov. 1982.

KENNETH W. ROSE

SHORT, Walter Campbell (30 Mar. 1880–3 Sept. 1949), soldier, was born in Fillmore, Illinois, the son of Hiram Spait Short, a physician, and Sarah Minerva Stokes. He graduated Phi Beta Kappa from the University of Illinois with a B.A. in 1901, spent a brief time as an instructor in mathematics at the Western Military Academy, and then accepted a commission as a second lieutenant in the U.S. Army in 1902.

Short's life over the next forty years mirrored the history of the pre–World War II army. He served in the Philippines (1907–1908) and with General John Pershing during the campaign against the Mexican bandit and revolutionary Pancho Villa (1916). During World War I he participated in the Aisne-Marne, St. Mihiel, and Meuse-Argonne offensives, and at war's end he also served with the occupation forces in Germany. Short's administrative virtues were soon rewarded with the Distinguished Service Medal for "conspicuous service in the inspecting and reporting upon frontline conditions" and for his skill in machine-gun instruction. In 1914 he married Isabel Dean; they had one child.

Training, reporting, inspecting, and the routine of military bureaucracy forced the substance of Short's postwar résumé. His textbook, *Employment of Machine Guns* (1922), confirmed him as an authority on the use and deployment of automatic weapons. He attended the School of the Line (1921) and the Army War college (1923).

These achievements were reflected in his steady advancement in rank to major general by 1940. On 8 February 1941 General George Carlett marshall appointed Short commandant of the U.S. base at Pearl Harbor, Hawaii. Within a year, however, his military career had ended in ruin. In the aftermath of the Japanese attack on Pearl Harbor, Short resigned from the army.

A bill of particulars in a case against Short includes first his failure to understand the true nature of his mission. He apparently believed that the defense of the Hawaiian base and the island itself was primarily the navy's responsibility. The Japanese would never attack Pearl Harbor, he reasoned, as long as the ships were there. It proved a fatal misjudgment. The Japanese sought the destruction of the American fleet and its air defenses and not the military installations under Short's command. His mission was properly the defense of the fleet and the base. The army was there to defend the fleet, not vice versa.

In addition, Short failed to develop an effective command relationship with Admiral Husband E. Kimmel, commander of the Pacific Fleet. Of course this was not entirely Short's responsibility. Short and Kimmel were amiable colleagues, and apparently each believed that friendly relations were sufficient to ensure success. They met often to discuss issues and mutual concerns and played a round of golf now and then, but they never created a truly coherent system of cooperation. Nothing illustrates this better than the failure of Short and Kimmel to construct a long-range reconnaissance system that might have alerted Hawaii to an approaching danger.

Short also failed to understand modern air power. He was in temperament and training a regimental infantry officer. When asked later about his inadequate air defenses, Short revealed that he had no clear idea how an air attack might even be repelled. He had certainly considered the possibilities of an air attack, but he did not consider air defenses as an essential element. He concentrated on how a Japanese amphibious landing would be repulsed. Once the attack began, Short set up his command post at Aliamanu Crater on Oahu in a bunker some fifteen feet below the ground. There with energy, determination, and no little courage, he planned to repel the invasion that never came.

Short is not without defenders. They argue that hardly anyone, including the high command in Washington, D.C., expected the Japanese to attack Pearl Harbor. They also highlight the fact that Short had, in response to a "war warning" from Washington, notified his superiors that he was emphasizing land defense and anti-sabotage measures and had purposely avoided a full alert to avoid unsettling the civilian population of the islands. No one in Washington objected to these plans, and Short took this as concurrence with his preparations.

A small minority also held that Short fell prey to a scheme to entice the Japanese into war. According to this theory, President Franklin D. Roosevelt was determined to enter the European war on the side of Britain. Because opinion in America was divided and an anti-interventionist lobby had stymied his diplomatic and military objectives, the president sought to lure the Japanese into a war and thereby involve the United States in a global conflict. An unprovoked attack by the Japanese would galvanize American public opinion into full support for the president's foreign policy. Thus, Short was simply a pawn in one of the most reprehensible conspiracies in history. Few credible historians, however, accept this "backdoor to war" thesis.

But it is also necessary to put the Pearl Harbor defeat and Walter Short's culpability into proper perspective. Any explanation for the defeat has as much, perhaps more, to do with the mix of meticulous planning, excellent equipment, remarkable courage, and extraordinary luck on the part of the Japanese navy as with American errors, omissions, or conspiracies. Whatever the truth, many agree that Short received an unfair proportion of the blame for a failure for which America's civil and military leadership was collectively to blame. His death has been attributed, in part, to the stress and humiliation of his defeat at Pearl Harbor.

Short died in Dallas, Texas.

• In the absence of a biography, Short's role is best understood through the studies of Pearl Harbor produced by Gordon W. Prange, with the assistance of Donald M. Goldstein and Katherine V. Dillon, *At Dawn We Slept: The Untold Story of Pearl Harbor* (1981), *Pearl Harbor: The Verdict of History* (1986), and *December 7, 1941: The Day the Japanese Attacked Pearl Harbor* (1988). Short's testimony is found in the *Hearings before the Joint Committee on the Investigation of the Pearl Harbor Attack*, 79th Cong., 1946, 39 parts.

FRANK J. WETTA

SHORT, William (30 Sept. 1759–5 Dec. 1849), diplomat, was born in Surry County, Virginia, the son of William Short IV, a planter, and Elizabeth Skipwith, the daughter of Sir William Skipwith, a baronet. He attended the College of William and Mary (graduating in 1779), where he was a founder of Phi Beta Kappa and a classmate of James Monroe. He and John Marshall studied law under George Wythe. He had family ties with Martha Jefferson, but Thomas Jefferson, as adviser on Short's studies and career, called him an "adoptive son." Thanks to Jefferson's influence, Short was elected to the Virginia Executive Council of State (then a check on the governor) and became a U.S. diplomat.

In 1784 Jefferson as minister to France made Short his secretary. Short helped conclude the U.S.-Prussian commercial treaty of 1786. In 1789 he made an extensive grand tour of southern France and Italy. After Jefferson's return to America in 1789, Short as chargé d'affaires oversaw U.S. interests in France. As his country's sole fiscal agent, he also borrowed about $12 million from bankers at Amsterdam and Antwerp in order to pay for new governmental expenses, to refinance revolutionary loans, and to repay debts to France, to Spain, and to foreign officers who had helped win American independence. Disappointed at not succeeding Jefferson as minister to France, Short settled in 1792 for an appointment as U.S. minister to the Netherlands. There he was unable to do much to help Lafayette, who, after leaving his army command in northern France claimed neutral status as an American when he was captured by the Austrians.

By September of 1792 Short was alarmed by French radicalism after his friends Lafayette and La Rochefoucauld had lost influence. When the latter was assassinated, Short's duties delayed his consoling in person "Rosalie," the widowed duchesse de La Rochefoucauld, whose lover he was. He was able to safeguard much of her fortune by placing it in his name, but she declined to marry him because there was no one else to care for her mother-in-law, the dowager duchesse.

In January 1792 Short joined William Carmichael in Spain where, as joint treaty commissioner, he sought a trade treaty, recognition of neutral rights, and recognition of U.S. navigation rights on the Mississippi with a designated place to deposit goods. Spain's war with France and alliance with Great Britain, however, postponed conclusion of such a treaty. In 1795 Carmichael died as he was about to sail for America. Short settled with the Spanish many of the terms of the subsequent Treaty of San Lorenzo, especially reciprocal trade between the United States and European Spain and the Spanish grant to Americans of the right to deposit goods free of tariffs near the mouth of the Mississippi. Ignorant of Short's progress, the Washington administration sent Thomas Pinckney to supersede him. Magnanimously, Short remained at Madrid to help the new envoy until the conclusion of the treaty in mid-1795. Thereafter, he returned to France, where he lived with Rosalie.

In 1802 he finally heeded Jefferson's advice to refresh himself in his Americanism. At Monticello he incurred James Madison's lasting enmity when he derided as naive Madison's belief that the French directors were virtuous republicans. Although Jefferson, as Short's attorney, had bought for him a farm near Monticello, Short decided to reside at Philadelphia, where he could better supervise his investments. In 1803 he visited in Kentucky, Virginia, and the District of Columbia. He dined regularly at the White House but neither won the friendship of U.S. senators nor formed a good opinion of them. In 1808 Jefferson gave Short a recess appointment as minister to Russia with the goal of encouraging Tsar Alexander I to form a league of armed neutrals that might compel France and Great Britain to recognize neutral rights on the high seas. Short went no farther than Paris, where the Russian foreign minister, Count Nicholas de Romanzoff, awaited Britain's response to Russia's peace proposals. Desiring this mission to be secret as long as possible, Jefferson did not submit Short's nomination to the Senate until the eve of his leaving office nor did he lobby for it. Declaring that no minister to Russia was needed, the Senate declined to confirm Short. After Madison took office he nominated John Quincy Adams for the same assignment and, after much lobbying, got him confirmed. Short did not blame Jefferson, but his bitterness against Madison strained Short's friendship with Jefferson. Short might have remained in France but for Rosalie's marriage to her cousin Comte Boniface de Castellane.

In 1810 Short returned to Philadelphia, where for the next thirty-nine years he managed his investments and was a philanthropist. Already a millionaire, he shifted his investments from government bonds, first to land in upstate New York, then to canals, and finally to railroads. A benefactor of the American Philosophical and American Colonization societies, he was a long-term vice president of the latter. After 1836 he helped his nieces and nephews save his brother Peyton Short's encumbered properties in Kentucky. After several years of declining health, he died at Philadelphia.

Except for his friend Monroe, Short was the most successful of Jefferson's protégés. In their elevated correspondence of more than fifty years concerning the French Revolution, religion, and slavery, Short drew back from too sharp or persistent disagreement with his mentor, but he believed that the president was too optimistic of the French Revolution, too trusting of the French revolutionaries, and too laggardly in opposing slavery. He helped recruit faculty for the University of Virginia, but in 1824 he timed his inspection of it—and his last visit to Monticello—so as to avoid James Madison.

• The Short and the Jefferson papers in the Library of Congress are the principal sources for Short's official and personal life. The Coolidge Collection of Jefferson papers at the Massachusetts Historical Society and the Short–La Rochefoucauld letters at the American Philosophical Society are important supplements. Julian P. Boyd et al., eds., *The Papers of Thomas Jefferson* (25 vols., 1948–), and Andrew A. Lipscomb and Albert E. Bergh, eds., *The Writings of Thomas Jefferson* (20 vols., 1903–1904), contain most of the Jefferson-Short correspondence. Harold C. Syrett et al., eds., *The Papers of Alexander Hamilton* (27 vols., 1961–1987), contains most of Short's correspondence concerning the U.S. debt. George Green Shackelford, *Jefferson's Adoptive Son: The Life of William Short* (1993), is the only full-length biography.

GEORGE GREEN SHACKELFORD

SHORT BULL (c. 1847–1935?), member of the Burned Thighs (Sicangu) Lakota tribe, often referred to by its French appellation, Brulé, emerged as one of the most influential proselytizers of the Ghost Dance (1890), an important Plains Indian millenarian movement. Short Bull (Tatanka Ptecela) was born probably in Nebraska's Niobrara River country around 1847, and although little pre-1890 information exists about him, his life undoubtedly followed the usual patterns of Plains Indian culture. He participated in the Plains

Indian wars of the 1860s and 1870s, fought at the battle of the Little Bighorn (1876), and experienced the vicissitudes of the reservation period. Short Bull attracted U.S. government attention in 1879, when troops apprehended him leading Brulés in an attempted escape from South Dakota's Rosebud Reservation. Responding to the agent's threatened ban of the Sun Dance, an early summer ritual of universal renewal, Short Bull intended to join nonreservation Lakotas in self-imposed Canadian exile. By the late 1880s he was a leader of the "non-progressive," or antiassimilationist, faction in tribal religious and political life.

For most Lakotas, reservation life meant cultural disintegration, a desperate condition that led to a search for equally desperate solutions. In 1889 Short Bull heard about the millenarian teachings of Wovoka, a Paiute living at Pyramid Lake, Nevada. That fall, Lakota elders meeting at Pine Ridge, South Dakota, requested that Short Bull, his brother-in-law Kicking Bear, and eight other tribesmen learn about Wovoka's doctrine firsthand. An intertribal delegation representing the Lakotas, Arapahos, and Cheyennes traveled by horse, foot, and trains to meet Wovoka. The delegation achieved its goal and returned to Pine Ridge in the spring of 1890. After arriving home, Short Bull depicted Wovoka in messianic terms and his message in an apocalyptic light, reporting that Lakotas could make the whites disappear, bring back the buffalo herds, and achieve reunion with dead relations by dancing and singing. This religion came to be called the Ghost Dance.

Short Bull, one of the Ghost Dance's leading apostles, assured believers that sacred designs painted on their shirts and dresses rendered them invulnerable to bullets. Fearing a general uprising, the government rushed troops to Lakota reservations in North and South Dakota. In December 1890 the Ghost Dance climaxed with the slaughter of Lakotas by troops at Wounded Knee, South Dakota. Short Bull, who led a few hundred followers to safety in the Badlands, surrendered to General Nelson A. Miles at Pine Ridge on 15 January 1891. The government imprisoned him and eighteen other Lakotas at Fort Sheridan, Illinois, before transferring them to the custody of William F. "Buffalo Bill" Cody, who employed them as performers in his Wild West show. Short Bull appeared with Buffalo Bill in Europe in 1891 and 1892 and the next year at the World's Columbian Exposition in Chicago. In 1894 Thomas A. Edison filmed the two men conversing in Plains Indian sign language at the inventor's New Jersey laboratory. For the remainder of his life, Short Bull stayed closer to Pine Ridge, where in the fall of 1913 he and General Miles appeared in Buffalo Bill's filmed reenactment of the Ghost Dance and Wounded Knee.

Although the Ghost Dance failed, Short Bull's status among Lakota traditionalists apparently remained undiminished. In 1894 James R. Walker, agency physician at Pine Ridge, asked Lakota elders for help in preserving knowledge of vanishing ways. They responded, nine years later, that interviews could take place but only if Short Bull received a vision sanctioning the sessions. Short Bull approved, and the resulting flow of information formed the basis for significant ethnographic works by Walker.

Around 1906 folklorist Natalie Curtis spent time with Short Bull at Pine Ridge, where he was revered "as a great medicine-man, a prophet, and a worker of miracles." She obtained five songs from him and a notebook, since dispersed, containing autobiographical drawings recounting pre-1877 horse-raiding expeditions and battles against enemy tribes. Additional Short Bull drawings are located in Hamburg (Museum für Volkerkunde) and Leipzig (Museum für Volkerkunde). In 1912 Walker commissioned two paintings by Short Bull of Sun Dance scenes on large sheets of canvas for New York's American Museum of Natural History. Short Bull also maintained a winter count, a series of mnemonic drawings on paper through which he recorded the most memorable event of each winter, or Lakota year as measured from the first snowfall of one year to that of the next. This chronicle, now at the Sioux Indian Museum in Rapid City, South Dakota, apparently covers the 1840–1920 period.

Hardly anything is known about Short Bull's private life, though he was married at least once and evidently fathered several children. The actual year of his demise remains in doubt partly because his name was not an uncommon one among Lakotas of his generation. He may have been photographed as late as 1933, and it appears likely that he died at Pine Ridge, South Dakota.

Short Bull's life exemplifies the persistence of Lakota religion in the face of officially sanctioned efforts to replace it with Christianity. Faced with the dire conditions of reservation life, Short Bull sought to preserve his culture through the Ghost Dance's redemptive, albeit apocalyptic, goals. Although the violence at Wounded Knee undercut the Ghost Dance, Short Bull remained a significant factor in Lakota spiritual life for another four decades. His cooperation with pioneering ethnographers and creation of descriptive drawings and paintings aided in the preservation of much information about prereservation Lakota culture.

• Short Bull has not commanded the attention of a book-length biography, and given the fragmentary nature of information about his life it is difficult to see how such a project could be realized. Two articles offer comprehensive coverage of his life: Ron McCoy, "Short Bull: Lakota Visionary, Historian, and Artist," *American Indian Art Magazine* 17, no. 3 (Summer 1992): 55–65, and Wilhelm Wildhage, "Material on Short Bull," *European Review of Native American Studies* 4, no. 1 (1990): 35–42. For his role in the Ghost Dance, see James Mooney, "The Ghost-Dance Religion and Wounded Knee," in *Fourteenth Annual Report of the Bureau of Ethnology to the Secretary of the Smithsonian Institution, 1892–93*, pt. 2 (1896). One of Short Bull's drawings and five of his songs are in Natalie Curtis, *The Indians' Book* (1907). For the products of James R. Walker's labors, in which Short Bull played such a pivotal role, see Raymond J. DeMallie and Elaine A. Jahner, "James R. Walker: His Life and Work," in Walker's *Lakota Belief and Ritual* (1980), pp. 3–61.

RON McCOY

SHOTWELL, James Thomson (6 Aug. 1874–15 July 1965), historian and internationalist, was born and raised in Strathroy, Ontario, the son of John Blansfield Shotwell, a teacher and farmer, and Anne Thomson. In 1894 Shotwell entered the University of Toronto, from which four years later he graduated with a degree in history and a determination to do graduate work. Upon discovering that no Canadian university offered a Ph.D. degree in history, he entered Columbia University in 1898 to work with James Harvey Robinson in medieval history. In 1902 he married Margaret Harvey. They had two children.

Shotwell excelled in graduate school and quickly established himself as one of the leading advocates of the New History, a concept that rejected traditional political and diplomatic history as too narrow. It called for an interdisciplinary approach to the study of the past and emphasized socioeconomic factors in explaining how political institutions developed. In 1903 he received his Ph.D. and two years later accepted a position as adjunct professor of history at Columbia. In 1908 he was promoted to full professor and remained associated with Columbia until his retirement in 1942 as Bryce Professor Emeritus of the History of International Relations.

Although trained as a medievalist, Shotwell early in his career became interested in the impact of science and technology on Western civilization. In his lectures and writings, he focused on three major themes: the persistence of superstition and magic in human thought, the influence of science and technology, and the growth of critical thought in Western civilization. Accepting a progressive view of history, he believed that rational thought and scientific inquiry helped free humankind from the superstition and taboos that dominated earlier generations. These themes pervade both his famous essay "History," which appeared in the eleventh edition of the *Encyclopaedia Britannica* (1910–1911), and *The Religious Revolution of To-Day* (1913).

World War I presented a major challenge to Shotwell's core belief that organized intelligence and scientific inquiry could solve even the most difficult social problems in a democratic context. It caused him to broaden his perspective to include an examination of international conflict and the possibilities of its elimination. If scientific inquiry could enhance democracy in the industrialized world, could it not also reform the international system and promote peace?

In 1917, following America's entry into the conflict, Shotwell took up residence in Washington, D.C., in order to help organize the National Board for Historical Service, an agency created by the nation's leading historians to explain the war and its implications to the American people. Soon afterward, he joined Walter Lippmann and Edward M. House in the Inquiry, a committee charged by President Woodrow Wilson with studying the major political, economic, legal, and historical questions likely to arise at a future peace conference. Two years later, along with other Inquiry members, he accompanied Wilson to the Paris Peace Conference. Although he played a minor role as an adviser, he did assist in establishing the International Labor Organization.

Following the war, Shotwell became one of America's leading exponents of liberal internationalism, arguing that only collective security and free trade could prevent future armed conflicts. Combining advocacy and activism with scholarship and teaching, he undertook a variety of activities that promoted peace and kept alive the Wilsonian vision. In 1919 he initiated the *Economic and Social History of the World War* for the Carnegie Endowment for International Peace. The project, which consisted of 152 volumes and took seventeen years to complete, sought to determine the true impact of modern warfare. As general editor, Shotwell believed that the massive study proved that war was no longer a viable instrument of national policy.

In 1924 Shotwell took a position with the Carnegie Endowment and lobbied for American entry into the League of Nations, the World Court, and the International Labor Organization. In addition, he worked tirelessly to unify the diverse factions of the American peace movement into a coherent political force. He advocated arms reduction and planted the seed that ultimately led to the Kellogg-Briand Peace Pact. Hoping to find a way to align America more closely with the League of Nations, he proposed to the French foreign minister, Aristide Briand, that the United States and France negotiate an agreement renouncing war between the two nations. Briand liked the concept and proposed it as his own. Unfortunately, from Shotwell's perspective, the negotiations that followed led to a broad multilateral treaty renouncing war, eventually signed by some sixty-four nations, that had little real meaning and took the United States no closer to the European security system.

Throughout the 1930s Shotwell continued to agitate for internationalist causes and for a more activist world role for the United States. He wrote extensively on international issues, arguing that the United States should either join the League of Nations or, failing that, unilaterally align its power with the league system. He served as the American representative to the League of Nations Committee on Intellectual Cooperation and from 1935 to 1939 served as president of the League of Nations Association.

The start of World War II in 1939 reaffirmed Shotwell's belief that the only way to establish a peaceful and democratic international system was through world organization and collective security. In order to promote these ideas, he and Clark Eichelberger, executive director of the League of Nations Association, established the Commission to Study the Organization of Peace, which sought to provide a practical blueprint for a new world order. During the war he also served on the Advisory Committee on Post-War Foreign Policy established by the State Department, and in 1945 he became chairman of a consultants group to the American delegation to the United Nations Conference in San Francisco. At the conference he worked diligently to promote human rights and to strengthen those sections of the UN Charter dealing with the social and economic activities of the organization.

In 1948 he assumed the presidency of the Carnegie Endowment for International Peace and retired two years later to devote himself to research and writing. During the next decade, he published two major books, an autobiography, a book of poetry, and numerous articles. Although his later work received few scholarly accolades and attracted little public attention, it did reaffirm his belief that the creation of an international system based on free trade, collective security, and world organization was the surest path to peace. He died at home in New York City.

Shotwell's contribution to twentieth-century America was not as a policymaker, although he aspired to be one, but as the most important and articulate advocate of internationalism and the Wilsonian tradition in the United States. His extensive list of publications on world affairs, which included more than a dozen books and four hundred articles, brought him to the attention of both political leaders and the general public as a committed champion of peace and internationalist principles. Although his dream of a new world order based on collective security was doomed to failure in an age of rising nationalism, he understood the importance of finding alternatives to war and creating institutions through which international problems might be resolved.

• Shotwell's papers are deposited in the Butler Library at Columbia University, as are the archives of the Carnegie Endowment for International Peace, which contain much Shotwell material. For additional material, see *The Autobiography of James T. Shotwell* (1961) and his "Reminiscences" (1964) in the Oral History Research Office at Columbia University.

Shotwell was the author of 18 books and over 400 articles. In addition, he edited some 200 volumes, including the massive *Economic and Social History of the World War* (1921–1940). Among his most important works are *An Introduction to the History of History* (1922); *War as an Instrument of National Policy and Its Renunciation in the Pact of Paris* (1929); *On the Rim of the Abyss* (1936); *At the Paris Peace Conference* (1937); *What Germany Forgot* (1940); *The Great Decision* (1944); *Lessons on Security and Disarmament from the History of the League of Nations*, with Marina Salvin (1944); *The United States in History* (1956); *The Long Way to Freedom* (1960); and *The Faith of an Historian and Other Essays* (1964).

The most extensive biography of Shotwell is Harold Josephson, *James T. Shotwell and the Rise of Internationalism in America* (1975), which analyzes his career and provides a useful bibliography of his writings. Also of value are Charles De Benedetti, "James T. Shotwell and the Science of International Politics," *Political Science Quarterly* 89 (June 1974): 379–95; and De Benedetti, "Peace Was His Profession: James T. Shotwell and American Internationalism," in *Makers of American Diplomacy*, vol. 2, ed. Frank J. Merli and Theodore A. Wilson (1974). His obituary appears in the *New York Times*, 17 July 1965.

HAROLD JOSEPHSON

SHOUMATOFF, Elizabeth (18 Dec. 1888–30 Nov. 1930), portraitist, was born in Kharkov, Ukraine (then part of Imperial Russia), the daughter of Nicholas Avinoff, a general in the Russian army, and Alexandra

Lukianovitch. She grew up in St. Petersburg and at the Avinoff family's country estate, "Shideyevo," near Poltava, Ukraine. She early displayed an aptitude for drawing and had her first art lessons from her British governess, Frances Whishaw, from whom she also learned English. By the time she was ten, Elizabeth had painted several creditable watercolors. "But I felt I could not be a real artist unless I painted in oils" (E. Shoumatoff, p. 5), and at the age of fourteen she began working in oils. She continued to do watercolors, however, and much of her work was in this medium.

In 1913 she married Leo Schumacher, a Baltic German who Russianized his family name to Shoumatoff in 1916; they had three children. In October 1917 Leo Shoumatoff took the family to the United States on official business for the provisional government of Alexander Kerensky. On their arrival they learned that the Kerensky government had fallen and been replaced by the Bolshevik regime of Vladimir Lenin. Fiercely anti-Communist, the Shoumatoffs elected to remain in the United States. Elizabeth's brother, Andrey Avinoff, who had already moved to the United States, lived with them for a short while; he eventually became director of the Carnegie Museum of Natural History in Pittsburgh.

The Shoumatoffs had not been able to bring much money with them from Russia, but they had enough to buy an old dairy farm near Pine Brush, New York. At first their standard of living was barely above subsistence level. Elizabeth had brought with her a few of the watercolors she had painted in Russia. George Inness, Jr., the son of the well-known artist and himself a painter, saw and admired them. He commissioned her to paint a miniature of himself and paid her $250, the first money she had ever made from her art. News of her skill in portraiture spread, and she soon was receiving commissions from prominent men of business such as Harvey Firestone and Edsel Ford. She also painted a charming watercolor of the Nobel Prize–winning poet Rabindranath Tagore.

The Shoumatoffs moved from Pine Brush to the village of Napanocch, twenty miles deeper into the Catskills, in 1920. There Elizabeth Shoumatoff continued to paint, although she still regarded her activity as more of an avocation than a vocation. Her husband went into business with the helicopter pioneer Igor Sikorsky and was successful enough for her to consider retirement from portrait painting. Leo's untimely death in 1928, however, caused her to abandon that idea. She brought a house in Locust Valley, Long Island, and began to paint in earnest. "I never considered myself a professional artist," she later wrote. "I had no real artistic training and always shunned publicity. But I had a God-given talent to capture the likeness of a person" (E. Shoumatoff, p. 13).

Shoumatoff achieved great success as a society portraitist, painting in her preferred medium of watercolor the likenesses of America's socially prominent families. Her brush captured Mellons, du Ponts, Fricks, and some self-made millionaires like Robert Woodruff (of Coca-Cola). In 1937 she did a portrait of Mrs. Winthrop Rutherfurd (Lucy Mercer), and this encounter led eventually to Shoumatoff's best-known work.

Lucy Mercer Rutherfurd had been romantically involved with Franklin D. Roosevelt during the First World War and remained devoted to him. In the spring of 1943 she commissioned Mrs. Shoumatoff to do a portrait of President Roosevelt. The sittings took place in the White House, and the result was a small (twelve by ten inches) watercolor showing the president wearing his U.S. Navy cape over a gray suit and blue tie. Roosevelt's friends and colleagues liked the portrait, although Shoumatoff later came to feel that it was too flattering. Mrs. Rutherfurd, however, was quite pleased with it. Two years later, in April 1945, she arranged for Mrs. Shoumatoff to travel to FDR's vacation home in Warm Springs, Georgia (the "Little White House") to do another portrait of him. Shoumatoff was shocked by Roosevelt's careworn appearance and ashen complexion. But she commenced the portrait on the morning of 12 April, painting the head and sketching in the body. She was just putting the finishing touches to the face when Roosevelt suffered a cerebral hemorrhage; he died later in the afternoon.

That FDR was posing for his portrait when he died soon became widely known, and Shoumatoff, who abhorred publicity, was besieged by the press. She handled celebrity gracefully but never enjoyed fame. Her portrait of FDR was widely reproduced, and it brought her further commissions, including a number from crowned and elected heads of state. One of the more interesting of these was a portrait of Liberian president William Tubman, which she executed in 1956. Never having painted a black man before, she studied historical portraits of blacks by Sir Joshua Reynolds and other artists before flying to Liberia to paint Tubman. She enjoyed the experience and wrote at length about it in her autobiography.

In 1968 Shoumatoff painted another American president, Lyndon B. Johnson. A great admirer of FDR, he chose Roosevelt's best-known portraitist to do his own official likeness for the White House collection. Johnson's features are accurately rendered with an uncharacteristically thoughtful expression; he liked the portrait very much. It was subsequently reproduced on a U.S. postage stamp. Shoumatoff painted Mrs. Johnson's official portrait as well. Both were rendered in oils, a medium with which she now felt more comfortable, although most of her work continued to be in watercolor. In 1966 she painted an oil portrait of Roosevelt based on her 1943 watercolor; it also hangs in the White House.

Mrs. Shoumatoff remained active until just three weeks before her death. She died in Glen Cove, New York, and was buried in the Locust Valley cemetery. With the exception of her portraits of Roosevelt and the Johnsons, her work remains little known, because the bulk of it is still in the possession of the families for whom it was painted. "Having a watercolor by Madame Shoumatoff in your living room was . . . a mark of standing," writes her grandson Alex. "It went with dressing at Brooks Brothers and being in the Social Register . . . she painted the good families, the captains of industry, the heads of state" (A. Shoumatoff, p. 29). Shoumatoff was famous for capturing accurate likenesses. That she could also capture a person's character can be seen in her best-known work, the unfinished portrait of FDR, described by the *Philadelphia Inquirer* as "the picture of a man thinned by illness, pitifully aged by world care, spiritualized by high purpose." "Left as it was, hardly begun," writes Alex Shoumatoff, "the portrait has a great sadness, as if the man were almost fading away before you."

• Elizabeth Shoumatoff's papers remain in the possession of her family. The best accounts of her life are her own autobiography, *FDR's Unfinished Portrait: A Memoir by Elizabeth Shoumatoff,* published posthumously in 1990, and Alex Shoumatoff, *Russian Blood: A Family Chronicle* (1982), an account of the Shoumatoff and related families by the artist's grandson. An obituary is in the *New York Times,* 1 Dec. 1980. The unfinished portrait of FDR belongs to the Little White House Historic Site, Warm Springs, Ga.

DAVID MESCHUTT

SHOUP, David Monroe (30 Dec. 1904–13 Jan. 1983), U.S. Marine Corps officer and commandant, was born in Battle Ground, Indiana, the son of John Lemar Shoup and Mary Layton, farmers. While studying mathematics at DePauw University in Greencastle, Indiana, Shoup enrolled in the Reserve Officers' Training Corps (ROTC) program in order to receive the small stipend that was provided. After graduating in 1926 Shoup sought and received a commission as a second lieutenant in the marines. Although he entered the military mostly out of economic need, Shoup became a highly successful career officer. In 1931 he married Zola De Haven; they had two children.

First sent to Philadelphia for training, Shoup then served in Tientsin, China (1927–1928), followed by a tour aboard the USS *Maryland* (1929–1931). During the 1930s Shoup returned to China for assignments in Shanghai and Peking before he was appointed an instructor at the marine base in Quantico, Virginia. In 1940 Shoup was sent to Iceland. After U.S. entry into World War II Shoup was ordered to the Pacific theater. Once there, he participated in the Guadalcanal and the Solomon Islands campaigns. His major wartime contribution came in November 1943, when he commanded all the marine forces marshalled to take the Tarawa atoll as the first step in the U.S. Navy's strategy to "island-hop" toward Japan by moving through the central Pacific. In this first fully amphibious assault of the war, U.S. forces attempted to overtake fortified positions with an invasion force supported solely by naval artillery and carrier-based aircraft. Shoup's personal heroism and leadership were critical to the U.S. victory. The invasion was hampered at the start because the marines had to wade ashore through intense Japanese fire. Coming ashore early in the assault, Shoup immediately began to regroup his battered troops, despite his being wounded by a mortar shell. Refusing to rest until victory was assured, Shoup personally directed all the American land forces for the first two days of battle. Although the United States was victorious, the assault on Tarawa claimed more than three thousand casualties (including close to one thousand dead) and was the bloodiest American battle to that date in the war. For his valor Shoup was awarded the Congressional Medal of Honor, which recognized, according to his citation, that he was "largely responsible for the final decisive defeat of the enemy" at Tarawa. Shoup later served in the Saipan and Tinian campaigns in the Mariana Islands.

In late 1944 Shoup was assigned to marine headquarters in Washington, D.C.; then in 1947 he returned to Asia for service with the Pacific Fleet until 1950, when Shoup became commandant of the Basic School at Quantico. During the 1950s he emerged as a critical troubleshooter within the marines. In 1953 Shoup became the first fiscal director for the marines. He was charged with rationalizing the budgetary system to accommodate the marines' post–Korean War expansion in size and mission as the corps began to maintain fully prepared expeditionary forces in the Western Hemisphere, the Mediterranean, and Asia. Shoup was appointed as the first inspector general of recruit training in 1956. The post was created in response to public outrage at the drowning of six marine recruits at the Parris Island, South Carolina, boot camp. Shoup worked to defend the basic concepts and methods of marine basic training while imposing new reforms to prevent future tragedies.

In 1959 President Dwight Eisenhower, impressed by Shoup's advocacy of interservice cooperation, bypassed nine higher-ranking marines to nominate Shoup as the next commandant. Conflict among the different branches of the U.S. military had been a constant problem throughout the twentieth century, and the role of the marines in this struggle had grown as the marines gained greater autonomy from the navy after the Korean War. During the 1950s the position of the marine commandant was elevated to a status equivalent to the chief of naval operations and was granted a position on the Joint Chiefs of Staff (JCS) for the first time.

As commandant from 1960 to 1963, Shoup successfully molded internal policy for the marines. Within the corps he improved combat readiness, and he reorganized the whole supply system bureaucracy. These reforms helped the marines meet their constantly expanding mission to be the initial landing force of any overseas military intervention. Shoup also resisted outside pressure from Congress to interfere with marine training. In 1962 several conservative senators tried to impose greater anticommunist indoctrination in marine training, but Shoup adamantly refused, successfully arguing that marines should be taught how to fight, not how to hate.

Beyond the corps, Shoup had little success shaping national security policy. Although President John F. Kennedy eventually viewed Shoup as his favorite member of the JCS, Shoup's concept of military professionalism and his personality limited his influence outside of the marines. As commandant, Shoup believed that his primary role was to implement the orders of the president rather than to shape policy. He frequently argued that his objective was to "ensure that our Corps is always ready, willing, and able to carry out efficiently any mission that we may be assigned" (quoted in Heinl, p. 599). Within the corps Shoup acquired a reputation as an exacting commander who frequently disciplined subordinates, but within the larger circles of the U.S. government he was perceived as shy and reticent. Theodore Sorensen, a longtime Kennedy aide, later described Shoup as having all the "charisma of a Treasury clerk" (*Kennedy Legacy*, p. 88).

Shoup also lacked a strong bureaucratic base from which to influence policy. Among the joint chiefs, Shoup's seat as commandant was the newest post, and technically he was only allowed to comment on JCS matters that directly affected the marines. The more established JCS members in the army, navy, and air force dominated most meetings and were more vocal when the JCS met with the president. Kennedy, moreover, relied more heavily on his civilian appointees, such as Secretary of Defense Robert McNamara, than on his career military advisers.

Although Shoup opposed military interventions in Cuba and Vietnam, he was unable to effectively voice his opposition on these issues. During the Cuban missile crisis of 1962 Shoup was the only member of the JCS to stress the difficulties involved with an American invasion to remove the nuclear missiles, recalling the heavy losses the United States had suffered in taking Tarawa and predicting the same or higher level of casualties in any invasion of Cuba. But Shoup's cautions proved less influential than the advice of McNamara and Attorney General Robert Kennedy in prompting Kennedy to reject the JCS recommendation to invade. With regard to Vietnam, Shoup privately opposed the increasing American commitment to preserve an independent, anticommunist South Vietnam. He reasoned that South Vietnam was not important enough to the United States either strategically or economically to justify a major American military presence there. Shoup also interpreted the warfare in South Vietnam as primarily an internal civil conflict in which the United States should allow the Vietnamese to determine their own political future. His only action, however, was to restrict the number of marine advisers sent to train the South Vietnamese military.

After his retirement in 1963, Shoup became a vocal critic of President Lyndon Johnson's decision in 1965 to send large numbers of combat troops to Vietnam. In articles, public speeches, and an appearance before the Senate Foreign Relations Committee in 1968, Shoup challenged the president's view of the conflict in Vietnam and his rationale for committing U.S. forces. In 1969 Shoup wrote an article for the *Atlantic Monthly* in which he expanded his criticism to include not only the American war in Vietnam but also the larger role of the military in shaping government policy and American values. He lamented that the United States had "become a militaristic and aggressive nation" (*Atlantic Monthly*, Apr. 1969, p. 51).

Shoup's career paralleled the rapid expansion of the U.S. military during World War II and the Cold War. He helped to prepare the marines to fulfill their role in the increasing number of U.S. interventions abroad, yet as commandant he developed reservations about the most significant of these operations. He died in Alexandria, Virginia.

• Shoup's papers are in the Hoover Institution on War, Revolution and Peace in Stanford, Calif. The John F. Kennedy Presidential Library in Boston, Mass., contains an oral history by Shoup. A section of his private papers has been published as Howard Jablon, ed., *The Marines in China, 1927–1928, the China Expedition Which Turned Out to Be the China Exhibition: A Contemporaneous Journal* (1987), which includes a biographical essay on Shoup. Shoup's testimony before the Senate Foreign Relations Committee has been published as *The Present Situation in Vietnam* (1968). See also Shoup, "The New American Militarism," *Atlantic Monthly*, Apr. 1969, pp. 51–56. On Shoup's activities during World War II, the most important sources are Robert Lee Sherrod, *Tarawa: The Story of a Battle* (1944); and Richard Wheeler, *A Special Valor: The U.S. Marines and the Pacific War* (1983). For Shoup's actions within the U.S. Marine Corps during the 1950s and early 1960s, see Robert Debs Heinl, Jr., *Soldiers of the Sea: The United States Marine Corps, 1775–1962* (1962). No single work covers Shoup's activities within the larger context of policymaking during the Kennedy years. Two works by Theodore C. Sorensen, *Kennedy* (1965) and *The Kennedy Legacy* (1969), provide some insight into the perceptions of Shoup held by other policymakers. An obituary is in the *New York Times*, 16 Jan. 1983.

BARNEY J. RICKMAN III

SHOUP, Francis Asbury (22 Mar. 1834–4 Sept. 1896), Confederate soldier, clergyman, and educator, was born in Laurel, Indiana, the son of George Grove Shoup, a merchant and politician, and Jane Conwell. He attended Asbury College (now DePauw University), before deciding on a military career. Given his family's local prominence, he easily secured an appointment to West Point, from which he was graduated in 1855. As an artillery subaltern, he did garrison duty in Florida and South Carolina and served in the Seminole War of 1856–1858. During these formative tours of duty, Shoup forged close friendships with many southern-born soldiers and civilians, whose aristocratic pretensions he shared; apparently he came to consider himself a southerner at heart if not by birthright. When he resigned from the army in 1860, he returned to his native state but the following year settled in St. Augustine, Florida, where he practiced law.

When civil war engulfed the nation in mid-1861, Shoup offered his services to his adopted state. The governor of Florida promptly dispatched him to Fernandina, a potential objective of Union land and naval forces. In that island village Shoup erected a battery and other defenses that helped quell the invasion fears of local residents. When the provisional Confederate army was organized, Shoup joined it as his old-army rank, but in October 1861 he was promoted to major

and was sent to Cave City, Kentucky, to command a twelve-gun battalion under Major General William J. Hardee.

Early in 1862 Hardee's command was transferred to the Mississippi-Tennessee theater. On the first day at Shiloh, 6 April, Shoup, commanding Hardee's artillery, emplaced the batteries that eventually forced the surrender of the Union salient known as the Hornets' Nest. For this deed the major won the praise of his superiors and, ultimately, command of all the cannon in the Army of Mississippi.

Considering Shoup a talented and versatile officer, the Confederate War Department appointed him a brigadier general and in September sent him to the Trans-Mississippi Department, where he was assigned a brigade of infantry under Major General Thomas C. Hindman. Shoup quickly rose to divisional command; in the December battle at Prairie Grove, Arkansas, he led eight infantry regiments and three batteries in helping repulse a heavy Federal assault. Again he received official commendation, this time for his "noble" leadership in a critical situation.

Four months after Prairie Grove, Shoup returned to artillery service in Major General Simon B. Buckner's (1823–1914) command, then fortifying Mobile, Alabama. A few weeks later, however, Shoup traveled to Mississippi, where he was assigned an infantry brigade under Lieutenant General John C. Pemberton. Shoup's small command—six Louisiana infantry regiments plus five cannon—guarded Vicksburg's riverfront during Ulysses S. Grant's investment of that city. On 19 May and again three days later, Shoup's brigade won wide notice by repulsing enemy assaults. When, despite all efforts, Vicksburg fell on 4 July, Shoup and a dozen other generals accompanied their troops into captivity.

After being paroled and exchanged, Shoup returned to Mobile, where in late September 1863 he was assigned to Major General Dabney H. Maury's District of the Gulf. Until he fell ill in December, he commanded a demi-brigade of troops of all arms. By early 1864, for unknown reasons, Shoup was in bad odor with General Maury; thus he sought a transfer to Joseph E. Johnston's Army of Tennessee, where a vacancy existed in infantry brigade command. Instead, in February Shoup was sent to central Mississippi to command several batteries under Lieutenant General Leonidas Polk (1806–1864), then opposing William T. Sherman's Meridian campaign.

In early May, when Polk's command was absorbed into the Army of Tennessee, Shoup became Johnston's artillery chief; a compromise candidate for the position, his selection calmed passions aroused by factional infighting. In his new position Shoup served ably if not brilliantly throughout the Georgia campaign. Observers as diverse as General Braxton Bragg, military adviser to Confederate president Jefferson Davis, and Brigadier General William N. Pendleton, Robert E. Lee's artillery chief, lauded Shoup's talents as both an artillerist and a military engineer. Moreover, Shoup is usually given credit for the

Army of Tennessee losing not a single cannon during its many retreats from Dalton to Atlanta. Even so, the paucity of tactical authority granted general officers of artillery reduced Shoup's role to that of a staff officer. Arguably, his greatest contribution to Confederate operations in Georgia was the formidable defenses erected under his supervision along the Chattahoochee River—defenses that General Johnston abandoned four days after occupying them in early July.

When John Bell Hood replaced Johnston in command of the army on 17 July, Hood named Shoup his chief of staff. The brigadier remained in this position until mid-September, when Hood relieved him at his own request. Shoup stepped down only two weeks after the evacuation of Atlanta, during which a large quantity of quartermaster's and ordnance stores fell into Union hands—a circumstance for which he received a certain amount of criticism, although a court of inquiry absolved him of blame. Shoup's career through the remainder of the war is veiled in obscurity. Early in 1865 the Confederate War Department ordered him to take command of Hardee's artillery in North Carolina then assigned him, instead, to Johnston, who was trying to organize an army large enough to stop Sherman's march from Savannah. Before Shoup could join Johnston, however, the latter informed the war office that he did not wish to be reunited with his old artillery chief. As a result, Shoup was without a command as the war ended.

Shoup's postwar career was less obscure and more rewarding. Soon after hostilities ceased, he was elected professor of applied mathematics at the University of Mississippi. A wartime convert to the Episcopalian faith, he took holy orders in 1868 and, concurrent with his academic duties, served as rector of St. Peters's Church, Oxford, Mississippi. In 1869 he moved to Sewanee, Tennessee, where he served as faculty member and chaplain of the University of the South. In Sewanee he authored textbooks on algebra and metaphysics and in 1870 married Esther Habersham Elliott, daughter of an Episcopal bishop. They had three children. Six years later he left the teaching profession to serve as rector of a parish in Upstate New York, followed by ministries in Nashville and New Orleans. He returned to the University of the South in 1883 as professor of engineering and physics and later regained his position in the mathematics department. He died at Columbia, Tennessee.

Shoup's Civil War record obscures as much as it reveals, as if critical information has been suppressed. A soldier of marked intellectual ability, he was also a gifted and versatile tactician. Not only did his artillery and infantry service win commendation, he also wrote well-regarded treatises on the tactics of both arms. His stint as chief of staff of the Army of Tennessee, while brief, appears to have been unexceptionable, and his involvement in the loss of supplies at Atlanta should not have harmed his career. Reports he compiled on such diverse subjects as the raising of black Confederate units and the production of munitions in the Trans-Mississippi gained him the high regard of many officials, including President Davis.

Despite the variety and magnitude of his contributions, General Shoup (whom President Davis called that "much-abused officer") traveled from one army and theater to another, was tendered smaller and smaller commands, and was given less and less time to organize them. In late 1863 General Maury permanently reassigned Shoup's brigade to another officer the minute Shoup took sick leave. In early 1865 Johnston, under whom Shoup had served faithfully on the road to Atlanta, took the unusual step of protesting Shoup's assignment to his undermanned command, which could have used all the senior-officer expertise it could get. Possibly some fatal flaw, some streak of incompetence or ill luck that escaped revelation in print cost Shoup command after command and left him in limbo as the war wound down. Perhaps his northern birth or his endorsement of black troups led military and civilian superiors to question his loyalty and commitment to the Confederate cause, as appears to have been the case with other Yankees in gray, such as Pemberton, Major General Franklin Gardner, and Brigadier General Roswell S. Ripley.

• The shadows that cloud Shoup's career are not dispelled by collections of personal papers accessible to the public. A small selection of his correspondence on postwar academic interests, however, forms part of the Albert G. A. Balz Papers, University of Virginia. *The War of the Rebellion: A Compilation of the Official Records of the Union and Confederate Armies* (128 vols., 1880–1901) contains Shoup's Vicksburg campaign report (ser. 1, vol. 24, pt. 2) and the headquarters journal of events he kept as chief of staff of the Army of Tennessee (ser. 1, vol. 38, pt. 3, and vol. 39, pt. 1). In addition to his published works on *Infantry Tactics* (1862) and *Artillery Division Drill* (1864), Shoup's contributions to Confederate military fortunes can be traced in two articles he published: "How We Went to Shiloh," *Confederate Veteran* 2 (1894): 137–40, and "Dalton Campaign—Works at Chattahoochee River," *Confederate Veteran* 3 (1895): 262–65. A biographical sketch is in Clement A. Evans, ed., *Confederate Military History*, vol. 11 (1899). Modern works that chronicle Shoup's service as artillery commander under Johnston and chief of staff to Hood include Thomas L. Connelly, *Autumn of Glory: The Army of Tennessee, 1862–1865* (1971); Richard M. McMurry, *John Bell Hood and the War for Southern Independence* (1982); Larry J. Daniel, *Cannoneers in Gray: The Field Artillery of the Army of Tennessee, 1861–1865* (1984); James Lee McDonough and James Pickett Jones, *War So Terrible: Sherman and Atlanta* (1987); Craig L. Symonds, *Joseph E. Johnston: A Civil War Biography* (1992); and Albert Castel, *Decision in the West: The Atlanta Campaign of 1864* (1992). A representative obituary is in the *Nashville American*, 5 Sept. 1896.

EDWARD G. LONGACRE

SHOUP, George Laird (15 June 1836–21 Dec. 1904), governor and U.S. senator, was born in Kittanning, Pennsylvania, the son of Henry Shoup and Anne Jane McCain, farmers. Shoup attended public school in Pennsylvania until 1852, when the family moved to Galesburg, Illinois. After farming with his family for awhile, to participate in the gold rush Shoup moved in

1859 to Colorado, likely near Denver, and became a merchant. When the Civil War began, he enlisted as a scout in the West and was eventually promoted to colonel in the Third Colorado Cavalry. He served as a delegate to the state's constitutional convention of 1864, but two years later he packed up his belongings and headed north to Montana. He opened a store in Virginia City, Montana, then relocated to the recently settled town of Salmon, Idaho, the next year. In 1868 he married Lena Darnutser, with whom he had six children.

Shoup achieved rapid success as a merchant and soon translated that success into a political career. He served as one of the first commissioners of Lemhi County and became the county superintendent of schools in 1872. In 1874 he was elected to the lower house of the territorial legislature and moved to the upper chamber in 1878. He served intermittently on the Republican National Committee from 1880 to 1900. It was his active role in pushing for statehood that endeared him to Idaho's voters. After President Benjamin Harrison appointed him territorial governor in 1889, Shoup followed in the footsteps of his predecessor by calling for a constitutional convention. Once the convention adopted a constitution and Idaho's voters approved it, Shoup went to Washington to lobby for statehood. When criticized for leaving the territory for an extended period, he threatened to resign in order to stay in Washington, but that was unnecessary. Congress approved statehood for Idaho on 3 July 1890.

Shoup was honored with the Republican nomination to be the new state's first governor. His real ambition, however, was to be elected to the U.S. Senate. Fearing that an active gubernatorial campaign would hurt his chances of becoming a senator, he allowed others to do most of his campaigning while he positioned himself for a battle over the senatorial nomination. He was elected governor, but his elevation to the Senate would be complicated by sectional rivalry. Representatives from the northern section of the state were adamant that one of their number receive one of the Senate seats. The two leading candidates, Shoup and Fred T. Dubois, were both from southern towns. The legislature reached a compromise when Congress permitted the state to elect three senators, one term for the current Congress, which would expire in two months, one term to expire in four years, and one for the full six years. The Republican caucus in the state legislature chose Dubois for the full term, and finally Shoup and William J. McConnell, the candidate of the northern counties, agreed to draw straws for the two short terms. Shoup drew the longer one. William Claggett, the leader of the northern counties, refused to accept this compromise and led an attempt the next year to overthrow the elections. Congress, however, was tired of the squabbling and quietly accepted Shoup's credentials. Shoup was reelected to a full term in 1894 but was defeated in 1900, when his lack of full support for free silver proved a liability with both Republican and Democratic legislators.

Shoup's term as governor lasted two and a half months, too short to accomplish anything of substance. He was widely criticized in the press for failing to mention the issue of silver coinage in his first message to the state legislature. He made amends by issuing a supplement recommending free coinage, but the silver issue remained vexacious and would continue to trouble him in the Senate. He adamantly opposed the repeal of the Sherman Silver Purchase Act in 1893, participating in the filibuster that delayed that action, and he addressed the convention of the Idaho Bimetallic League, urging acceptance of a compromise based on coinage of silver at a rate lower than sixteen to one. His support of free silver, however, was unsteady, and his support of William McKinley in 1896 hurt him in 1900. When Senator Dubois led the Idaho delegation out of the Republican convention of 1896, Shoup took his place on the convention floor, exciting wild admiration from the delegates but permanently damaging his popularity in Idaho. After 1896 Shoup fell in line with the party regulars in the Senate and supported the gold standard. He retired from public life after his defeat in 1900. He died in Boise.

By leading the fight for statehood, Shoup became the most popular politician in the state, resulting in nearly simultaneous selection as governor and senator. This popularity, however, could not withstand the tribulations of free silver. Shoup faced the dilemma of many western Republicans. Because his state produced silver, his constituents were greatly in favor of free coinage. To support such a position, however, meant defying the national party and allying with Democrats. Shoup's bold stand at the 1896 convention marked a turning point, both for his position on the issue of silver coinage and for his political future. He dared the wrath of Idaho's voters to remain loyal to his party, and the choice cost him his office.

• Shoup's papers are located at the Idaho Historical Society and the University of Idaho. William B. Mathews, *Sketch of the Life and Services of the Hon. George L. Shoup* (1900), and David L. Crowder, "Pioneer Sketch: George Laird Shoup," *Idaho Yesterdays* 33 (1990): 18–22, are both informative. Regarding the senatorial elections of 1890, see Margaret Lauterbach, "A Plentitude of Senators," *Idaho Yesterdays* 21 (1977): 2–8. A particularly useful source of information about Shoup and about Idaho politics generally is Leo W. Graff, Jr., *The Senatorial Career of Fred T. Dubois of Idaho, 1890–1907* (1988).

WILLIAM T. HULL

SHOUSE, Jouett (10 Dec. 1879–2 June 1968), politician, was born in Midway, Kentucky, the son of John Samuel Shouse, a notable Disciples of Christ minister, and Anna Armstrong. After graduating from high school in Mexico, Missouri, where his family had moved in 1892, Shouse enrolled in the classic curriculum of the University of Missouri in 1895. He worked at the *Mexico Ledger* and *Columbia Herald* until he quit school after his junior year.

In 1898 Shouse returned to Kentucky, where he was a reporter and managing editor at the *Lexington Her-*

ald, of which he became part owner. He founded and edited the *Kentucky Farmer and Breeder*, primarily devoted to thoroughbred horses, and organized the Home Telephone Company to protest inferior Bell Telephone services.

Shouse married Marion Edwards in 1911; they had two children before divorcing in 1932. Soon after his marriage, Shouse went on what he thought would be a short visit to aid his banker father-in-law in Kinsley, Kansas. Instead, he stayed in Kinsley to farm, ranch, and engage in business and banking. His first Kansas political venture was to help successfully commit the state's 1912 Democratic presidential delegation to candidate James "Champ" Clark, a family friend and Speaker of the U.S. House of Representatives. Urged to seek office himself, Shouse ran on the 1912 Democratic ticket for the state senate in the heavily Republican Thirty-eighth District. His close rapport with voters, a strenuous grass-roots campaign, and a solid party organization resulted in his victory. As chairman of the Senate Ways and Means Committee, Shouse wielded broad influence and thereby gained statewide notice.

In 1914 Shouse won the U.S. Seventh Congressional District seat in a narrow upset victory. Serving on the House Banking and Currency Committee, he was a framer of the 1916 Federal Farm Loan Act and key amendments to the Federal Reserve Act. He loyally supported the World War I policies of President Woodrow Wilson and earned the esteem of many important House members. In the Republican sweep of the 1918 congressional elections, Shouse was soundly defeated in his third-term bid.

In 1919 Secretary of the Treasury Carter Glass appointed Shouse assistant secretary and placed him in charge of customs, internal revenue, and the War Risk Bureau, which handled insurance and various allotments for military personnel. By actions such as cutting the bureau staff by two-thirds, Shouse transformed the agency and earned Wilson's praise for "intelligent and effective" service before he resigned in late 1920.

Although not abandoning politics, Shouse prospered in business during the 1920s. Along with Dudley Doolittle, a former Kansas Democratic congressman, he maintained tax counseling offices in Kansas City, Missouri, and Washington, D.C. He was also the vice president of the Orient Railroad, and he started a practice after studying law. Keeping active in party affairs and gaining respect for political astuteness, Shouse was chairman of the Kansas delegations at the 1920, 1924, and 1928 Democratic presidential conventions. As a shrewd adviser to presidential candidate Alfred E. Smith, Shouse duly impressed John J. Raskob, the chairman of the Democratic National Committee.

Ten years of Democratic losses convinced Raskob that a full-time functioning political apparatus was necessary to revitalize the party. In 1929 Shouse agreed to Raskob's entreaty that he head the permanent Washington, D.C., headquarters. The position of chairman of the Executive Committee of the Democratic National Committee was created specifically for Shouse, whose responsibility was to devise and coordinate party strategy. An able administrator who possessed rare political instincts and was willing to take risks, he inflicted incalculable harm on the Republican party. The Democratic gains in the 1930 congressional elections were attributed in large part to Shouse. He boldly set the party against Prohibition in 1931, which paid huge political dividends. His Democratic operatives shrewdly and relentlessly dumped the total responsibility for the Great Depression on President Herbert Hoover. A Democratic victory was thereby nearly ensured in the 1932 presidential election.

A pivotal figure in the Democratic resurgence, Shouse was expected to play a significant role in the 1932 national party convention and ensuing campaign. Shouse was maneuvered from any position of authority, however, by Franklin D. Roosevelt because of his close ties to Smith, who was by now a political adversary of the party's presidential candidate. Participating minimally in the 1932 campaign, Shouse's vote for Roosevelt was his last for a Democratic presidential nominee. In 1932 he married heiress Catherine Filene Dodd. There is no record of their having children together.

Alienated from the party that he had helped to achieve political victory, Shouse's split with President Roosevelt sharpened when Shouse served as the only president of the American Liberty League during its six-year history more from conviction than for pay. Ostensibly founded in 1934 as a nonpartisan organization to combat radicalism, the league was fiercely anti–New Deal. It portrayed Roosevelt's policies as patent quackery and part of a sinister conspiracy to subvert the Constitution, destroy democracy, and implant a dictatorship by expanding federal authority. Prestigious members like Smith and rich benefactors like Pierre du Pont enabled the league to grab headlines for several years.

After the league was dissolved, Shouse concentrated on his Washington, D.C., law practice and manifold business interests and publicly endorsed Republican presidential nominees. His interest abided in thoroughbred horses, including breeding and racing his own, and racing-related issues, and he also showed champion boxer dogs. The Wolf Trap Cultural Center is located on land donated by Shouse. He died in Washington, D.C., on the day it was named as the center's site.

A leading national political figure for a generation, Shouse's biggest imprint was as an architect in the revival of the Democratic party and its long-term political hegemony. Paradoxically, he is better remembered as a testy critic of the very political change he fostered.

• Shouse's papers, which deal largely with his post-1914 career, are located at the Margaret I. King Library at the University of Kentucky. Leslie Wallace, "The Kansas Optimist," *Outlook and Independent* 160 (1932): 109–10, 115, 128, is a useful biographical summary and character sketch. A brief complimentary evaluation of Shouse as chairman of the party Executive Committee is in "Shouse Rules," *Collier's* 87 (1931): 69; and detail on his breach with Roosevelt is available in Charles Michelson, *The Ghost Talks* (1944). On Shouse and the Liberty League, see George Wolfskill, *The Revolt of the Conservatives* (1962); and George Creel, "The True Friend," *Collier's* 96 (1935): 15, 46. Robert F. Burk, *The Corporate State and the Broker State: The Du Ponts and American National Politics, 1925–1940* (1990), is first-rate on conservative politics. Shouse's obituary is in the *New York Times*, 3 June 1968.

PATRICK G. O'BRIEN

SHRADY, Henry Merwin (24 Oct. 1871–12 Apr. 1922), sculptor, was born in New York City, the son of George Frederick Shrady, a surgeon and medical writer who had been physician to President Ulysses S. Grant, and Mary Lewis. Shrady served in the New York National Guard from 1889 to 1896, studying languages and literature at Columbia University from 1890 to 1894 and entering Columbia Law School after graduation. However, for reasons that are not clear, he soon left his studies to take a position in 1895 as assistant sales manager at the Continental Match Company, where he remained until 1900. He married Harrie Eldridge Moore in 1896; they had four children.

An aura of mystery surrounds Shrady's early artistic career. Some sources state that he began drawing as a diversion while recovering from typhoid fever, while others say that the failure of the match company turned his interests to art. Lorado Taft suggests that his artistic talents developed naturally in the leisure time afforded by his office job. By 1898 Shrady was modeling and exhibiting small bronze animal and equestrian figurines, working out of a spare room at home. He came to the attention of New York jeweler Theodore B. Starr, who became his dealer and partner. Starr probably introduced Shrady to Karl Bitter, an Austrian sculptor who was also director of sculpture for the 1901 Pan-American Exposition in Buffalo, New York. Bitter liked Shrady's bronze and invited him to enlarge a moose and a buffalo for the exposition grounds. When Shrady expressed some concern about the large scale of the project, Bitter offered him the use of his own studio and instruction in the necessary technique.

From 1901 on Shrady had no trouble gaining commissions and honors. The success of his animal sculptures brought an invitation to compete for the commission of an equestrian statue of George Washington for the Brooklyn end of the Williamsburg bridge. His model was chosen over those of more experienced sculptors such as Charles Henry Niehaus, and he was awarded a prize of $50,000. He also was elected to the National Sculpture Society in 1902.

In 1901 the Society of the Army of the Tennessee finally succeeded after six years of pressure in persuading Congress to fund a Washington, D.C., monument to their former commander, Ulysses S. Grant. Shrady and architect Edward Pearce Casey entered the design competition for the monument in 1902, and their model was eventually selected from a pool of twenty-seven designs by a jury including Generals John McAllister Schofield and Wesley Merritt, architects Daniel Hudson Burnham and Charles Follen McKim, and sculptors Augustus Saint-Gaudens and Daniel Chester French. Shrady's selection sparked a bitter protest by his more experienced competitors, particularly Niehaus (who said that Shrady's design would run over the allotted budget of $250,000) and John Massey Rhind. Others suggested that his connections to wealth and power (his brother-in-law was the son of railroad magnate Jay Gould) had influenced the panel's decision. A runoff competition was held from which Shrady emerged the winner in February 1903.

The Grant memorial was Shrady's life's work and his masterpiece. It was an ambitious design, consisting of a 252-foot marble base, two bronze groups depicting cavalry and artillery charging into battle, and an equestrian statue of Grant in the center, rising serene and calm forty-four feet above the ground. The cavalry group alone, when completed by the Roman Bronze Works in 1916, was said to be the largest group yet cast in the United States, standing eleven feet high and weighing 31,400 pounds. The statue of Grant when finished was the second largest equestrian statue in the world. Many writers of the time remarked not only on the scale of the monument, but also on Shrady's mastery of the details of military equipment, which he had placed himself in a position to observe by rejoining the national guard in 1902.

Shrady accepted other commissions while working on the Grant memorial. In 1903 he won a commission from the Holland Society in New York for a statue of William the Silent, who led the Netherlands in a revolt against Spanish rule and was the Netherlands' first hereditary Stadholder. In 1909 he was honored by induction as an associate in the National Academy of Design and by memberships in the National Institute of Arts and Letters and the Architectural League of New York. He sculpted an equestrian statue of General Alpheus Starkey Williams for Belle Isle Park in Detroit, Michigan, and a figure of Jay Cooke for Duluth, Minnesota, both completed in 1921. He also designed a bust of Ulysses S. Grant for the New York University Hall of Fame (now the Hall of Fame for Great Americans at Bronx Community College). He started work on an equestrian statue of Robert E. Lee for Charlottesville, Virginia, which he did not finish, although his model is at the Jefferson Madison Regional Library in Charlottesville. The statue itself was completed by Leo Lentelli. If Shrady's sculpting career was interrupted at all, it was by World War I, when he served in the reserve corps and as an artillery instructor at Columbia University.

Shrady never got to see the dedication of the Grant memorial on which he labored for so many years. He fell ill and died in New York City two weeks before the monument was unveiled on what would have been Grant's one-hundredth birthday, 27 April 1922.

Shrady is one of a group of artists who benefited from a flurry of urban renewal projects being undertaken in American cities in the late nineteenth century. The Grant memorial was part of one such project to implement Pierre L'Enfant's original plan for the Mall area of Washington. Shrady's style was outside any particular school of art, but its qualities of romance, heroism, and gravity were prized by art critics and patrons of the time. The fact that Shrady was self-taught also must have enhanced his reputation with contemporary art patrons, who as entrepreneurs believed in the power of the individual to shape his own destiny. These factors, combined with Shrady's natural talent, brought him the kind of overnight success rare for artists of any age.

• Shrady's papers are at the Archives of American Art in Washington, D.C. Important contemporary sources are Adeline Adams, *The Spirit of American Sculpture* (1923), Lorado Taft, *The History of American Sculpture* (1924), and Michigan State Library, *Biographical Sketches of American Artists* (1924). For the Grant memorial, see Helen Wright, "The Grant Memorial in Washington," *Art and Archaeology* 13 (Apr. 1922): 185–87; *The Grant Memorial in Washington* (1924), and Dennis R. Montagna, "Henry Merwin Shrady's Ulysses S. Grant Memorial in Washington D.C." (master's thesis, Univ. of Delaware, 1987). For the Jay Cooke memorial, see Timothy J. Garvey, "The Jay Cooke Monument as Civic Revisionism: Promotional Imagination in Bronze and Stone," *Old Northwest* 9 (Spring 1983): 37–57. An obituary is in the *New York Times*, 13 Apr. 1922.

MELISSA L. BECHER

SHREVE, Henry Miller (21 Oct. 1785–6 Mar. 1851), steamboat captain, army engineer, and steamship designer, was born in Burlington County, New Jersey, the son of Israel Shreve and Mary Cokely, farmers. During the American Revolution British forces had destroyed the Shreve home, so Shreve's father took his family to the frontier in Fayette County, Pennsylvania, when Henry was about three years old.

With the death of his father in 1799, Shreve began serving as a laborer for captains on a variety of barges and keelboats floating down the nearby Monongahela to Pittsburgh and the Ohio River. By 1807 he had acquired experience and funds enough to build his own barge, load it with goods, and take it down the Ohio and up the Mississippi to St. Louis. The French fur traders were delighted to receive his hardware and trinkets, which he swapped for furs. He loaded his barge with the pelts and returned to Pittsburgh, where middlemen threatened to absorb all his profits. Tolerating the threat only briefly, Shreve purchased a wagon and personally delivered the pelts to Philadelphia. Shreve's profits were substantial, in part because his was the first load of furs ever to reach Philadelphia from St. Louis. He was not yet twenty-two. The voyage opened his eyes to other ventures, and soon he was prospering further in the lead trade down the Mississippi from the Galena, Illinois, mines to New Orleans.

On 28 February 1811 he married Mary Blair at Brownsville, Pennsylvania. The couple had three children; apparently only one reached adulthood.

In 1812 Shreve put into service his own 95-ton barge, which he had built and which he used in the Pittsburgh–New Orleans trade for four years. But the western movement was creating a demand for powerful steam engines to cope with the swift river currents. Several inventors designed a variety of steamships, the most practical of which was Robert Fulton's *Clermont*, put into operation in 1807 on the Hudson.

Fearing Fulton's plans to move into the Mississippi trade, Shreve sought a better ship and designed and helped fund a different style of ship, an 80-foot sternwheeler, called *Enterprise*, which Shreve captained to New Orleans. In 1814–1815 he supported General Andrew Jackson's forces in the defense of New Orleans by bringing supplies and munitions from upriver. Shreve also engaged in prisoner exchanges, the evacuation of women and children from the besieged city, and transporting troops back to their posts after the war.

Shreve's postwar plans for an enlarged freight and passenger service were threatened by Fulton and his partner, Edward Livingston of New Orleans. These men had obtained trade monopolies for the Hudson and the Mississippi from the state of New York and the territory of Louisiana, respectively. Ignoring Livingston's injunctions, Shreve continued to trade, and *Enterprise* became the first steamer to travel from New Orleans back to the Monongahela. (In 1824 the U.S. Supreme Court ruled against Livingston, declaring unconstitutional such state assertions of power over interstate commerce, thereby throwing all the western waters open to competition.)

Shreve returned home and built the *Washington*, a new departure in steamers. Launched at Wheeling, Virginia, in 1816, this ship blew its boiler on its first voyage, killing fourteen men, the first among scores of steamship accidents of the nineteenth century. Nevertheless, Shreve made corrections, and the ship succeeded. Its new design became the standard. About 150 feet long, *Washington* was the first steamer with two decks. The high-pressure steam engine was located on the main deck with the freight rather than in the hold. For comfort the passengers were carried on the second deck. Equally important was its flat hull, which provided greater speed and the possibility of steaming into the shallow waters of the upper reaches of many rivers. *Washington* was something of a floating hotel, with fine furniture and carpeting and an elegant dining room.

Shreve's design made river travel luxurious and fun, but it was also dangerous. Captains overfired boilers to surpass other ships' speed records, a risky practice but one that, in theory, was subject to congressional oversight. Seemingly beyond control, however, were the driftwood and uprooted trees, washed from the banks by floods, then trapped in sand or other trees. At times these snags grew large enough to cause major rivers to divert their channels. Choked in this fashion, the Mississippi and all its tributaries posed great risk to the most experienced of pilots. The steamboat era could not long tolerate the loss of lives, time, and goods that resulted. The War Department asked several engineers to attempt to clear the rivers; they all failed. Henry Shreve claimed to have a new method of removing the logs and was allowed to assume the task. Almost by default Shreve became superintendent of western river improvement in 1826.

Three years passed before the government appropriated sufficient funds to build *Heliopolis*, the first "snag boat." Designed by Shreve, the boat looked like a giant claw—twin hulls, eleven or twelve feet apart, connected mid-ship by a huge, but sharp, beam that served as a battering ram. Shreve's tactic was to drive his boat against each partly submerged tree, ramming it again and again until it broke loose from the river's grip. A steam-propelled windlass hauled each tree on deck; powerful steam saws cut the logs into small pieces and dumped them into the river to float harmlessly downstream. *Heliopolis* took a terrible pounding, attacking trees six feet in diameter and even boulders, but it did the job. Meanwhile, workers stood in the rushing waters, chopping and sawing at the smaller trees. Within months Shreve and his seven crews totally cleared the Ohio and Mississippi rivers. In 1830 not a single ship was lost to a snag in the entire length of those two rivers. Then Shreve turned to the Red River.

The Red posed the most stupendous task of clearance that the nation had ever known. The "Great Raft," as pioneers called it, was a raft, or logjam, that stretched at least 150 miles north from present-day Alexandria, Louisiana, totally blocking steamer passage. The raft was not solid, but rather a series of rafts, frequently broken by large lakes. Some jams were so thick with trees and brush that men crossed them on horseback, and even pirogues could not snake through. This accumulation of centuries crippled commerce and hampered the army's ability to support its posts in the upper Red River country.

In 1833 Shreve, with 160 men and the new snag boat *Archimedes*, assaulted the Red. In his first year, operating from his headquarters in what is now the city of Shreveport, Louisiana, he cleared about seventy miles, allowing the river to run free to the Mississippi. The lower Red never closed off again, turning the region into a delta country with scores of rich plantations below Shreveport, but new rafts continued to grow in the upper reaches of the Red. Shreve's work became more and more intermittent upstream as government interest and funds turned toward railroads and sectional grievances. When Shreve retired to his farm in 1841, he was still fighting to clear the entire river. His wife died in about 1846, and Shreve married Lydia Rodgers of Boston about a year later; they had two children. He died in St. Louis.

• Family history and a good chronology of Shreve's life can be found in Florence Dorsey, *Master of the Mississippi* (1941), written largely from family correspondence in widely scattered, unnamed repositories. The terrors and frustrations of navigating western waters are evident in military annals before 1800; vivid descriptions of such surveys can be found in Thomas Freeman, *An Account of the Red River* (1806), and Timothy Flint, *Recollections of the Last Ten Years* (1826). A clarifying study of the Red River Raft and attempts to remove it is Norman Caldwell, "The Red River Raft," *Chronicles of Oklahoma* 19, no. 3 (1941): 253–68. Material on Shreve and his snag boats is in Louis C. Hunter, *Steamboats on the Western Rivers* (1949). Samuel Lockett, *Louisiana as It Is* (1969), and Carl Tyson, "The Red River in Southwestern History," (Ph.D. diss., Oklahoma State Univ., 1975), narrate the continuing struggle to navigate the Red.

THOMAS L. KARNES

SHREVE, Richmond Harold (25 June 1877–10 Sept. 1946), architect, was born in Cornwallis, Nova Scotia, Canada, the son of Richmond Shreve, an Anglican priest, and Mary Catherine Parker Hocken. In 1885 he moved with his family to Albany, New York, where he attended public and private schools. After graduating from high school, he worked for three years as an office boy and junior draftsman for the New York State architect in Albany. He then entered the College of Architecture at Cornell University in 1898 and graduated in 1902.

Shreve spent the ensuing four years on the architecture faculty at Cornell and as a graduate-level student of structural engineering and design. In 1905–1906 he supervised the construction of two buildings still standing on the Cornell campus, Goldwin Smith and Rockefeller halls, both designed by the prestigious firm of Carrère & Hastings. His management skills impressed John Mervin Carrère, who invited Shreve to join his New York City offices following completion of the buildings in 1906. In that year Shreve became a U.S. citizen and married Ruth Bentley, a classmate from Cornell; they had three children.

Shreve's association with the "old-school silk-hat" firm of Carrère & Hastings lasted for eighteen years. From this experience he acquired a firm adherence to the rationalism of the Beaux-Arts, and, throughout his career, "order, forethought, [and] system" characterized his work.

In 1920, when Thomas Hastings retired, Shreve and William Frederick Lamb advanced to junior partners within the firm, which was reorganized as Carrere & Hastings, Shreve & Lamb. Four years later, he and Lamb formed an independent partnership, Shreve & Lamb. Shreve managed the business aspects of the firm and the production schedules for projects under construction; Lamb and Arthur Loomis Harmon, who joined the collaboration in 1929 when it was reconstituted as Shreve, Lamb & Harmon, concentrated on design.

In 1926 Shreve was one of the founders of the Building Congress, an organization created to promote cooperation among the building trades in New York City. As president of the organization for three years, he brought widespread attention to his firm and boosted its ability to compete for large commissions from major corporations.

The work of Shreve and his associates on the General Motors Building (New York, 1928) maneuvered them into the forefront of architectural firms identified with the design of stately office towers. While working on the General Motors project, Shreve and his associates also came to the attention of John J. Raskob, a business investor and vice president of General Motors. In 1929, Raskob joined with Alfred E. Smith to plan construction of what was to be the world's tallest building, the Empire State Building, but he had already approached Shreve & Lamb in 1928 with the proposition of designing the extraordinary project. Shreve participated in all phases of the planning and construction for the 102-story building (1931). He synchronized the complex technical, logistical, and production requirements of the prodigious undertaking so that construction proceeded "with the precision of army mobilization."

In 1932, in recognition of his work on the Empire State Building, Shreve was elected to a fellowship in the American Institute of Architects, and he received a gold medal from the New York Chapter of the institute. Recognition of his administrative talents and ability to manage large projects also led to numerous offers to serve on professional and governmental boards, including the Real Estate Board of New York.

In 1933 Shreve was appointed director of the Slum Clearance Committee of New York. For the duration of his career, the challenge of rebuilding American cities and providing housing for the "slum-bound ten million" absorbed much of his time and interest. As early as 1934, he advocated massive and long-term financial commitments from the federal government to subsidize the construction of new housing. He subsequently acted as chief architect for the design and construction team responsible for the first government-assisted projects of the New York Housing Authority: the widely acclaimed Williamsburg Houses (Brooklyn, 1937), a 1,622-unit complex designed in part with William Lescaze; and Vladeck Houses (Manhattan, 1940). He also acted as chief architect for Parkchester (Bronx, 1938–1942), a colossal, privately funded apartment complex designed for 40,000 residents, and three similar housing developments in Manhattan: Stuyvesant Town, Riverton, and Peter Cooper Village, all completed in 1947. In managing the construction of these housing projects, he often reassembled teams of builders (Starrett Brothers & Eken) and architects (Irwin Clavan) who had worked with him on the Empire State Building.

From 1937 to 1939 Shreve served on the Board of Design for the New York World's Fair and coordinated the activities of the distinguished roster of architects who participated in that event. His firm designed one exhibition building for the Johns-Manville Corporation. Labeled the Glass Center in architectural journals, it was a striking Bauhaus-influenced composition with a tower executed in blue glass. Noted for its conservatism and equivocation about European modernism, Shreve's firm, during his lifetime, was responsible for only one other significant work in a modern idiom, an academic building for Hunter College on Park Avenue in New York (1940, with Harrison & Fouilhoux).

In 1941 Shreve was elected as president of the American Institute of Architects. During his two terms as president, he encouraged architects to plan for postwar reconstruction of cities. He also urged architects and engineers to work in partnerships on the planning and design of military facilities. His firm, active in several of these cooperative ventures, designed military bases in Newfoundland and Greenland and on Long Island.

When he died in Hastings-on-Hudson, New York, Shreve was a nationally prominent figure in American architecture. Beyond his notable contributions to the development of the vertical corporate skyscraper in Manhattan during the 1920s and 1930s, he was instrumental in the planning, design, and construction of some of the largest public and private housing projects that emerged out of the slum clearance and social welfare initiatives of the Great Depression.

• A collection of items on Shreve (including the unpublished memoirs of Harold C. Bernhard, his colleague at Shreve, Lamb & Harmon) is in the Carl A. Kroch Library at Cornell University. Additional sources include an interview in an article by Henry H. Saylor, "The Firm of Shreve, Lamb & Harmon," *Architectural Record* 90 (Aug. 1941): 73, 77–78, and Alan Keller, "They Build New York," *New York World Telegram*, 18 Feb. 1938. For his role in the construction of the Empire State Building, see John Tauranac, *The Empire State Building: The Making of a Landmark* (1995). Obituaries are in the *Journal of the American Institute of Architects* 7 (Jan. 1947): 18–23; *Empire State Architect* 7 (Sept.–Oct. 1947): 34–36; and the *New York Times*, 11 Sept. 1946.

JEFFREY CRONIN

SHRYOCK, Richard Harrison (29 Mar. 1893–30 Jan. 1972), historian, was born in Philadelphia, Pennsylvania, the son of George Augustus Shryock, a manufacturer of binding boards, and Mary Harrison Chipman. Graduating from Central High School, Philadelphia, in 1911 with a degree of bachelor of science, Shryock would have studied medicine, but, as this was financially impossible, he prepared for a career in teaching. He graduated from the Philadelphia School of Pedagogy in 1913, then taught in the city's public schools and in 1917 received the degree of bachelor of science in education from the University of Pennsylvania.

Assigned to the Sanitary Corps and the Army Medical Library in World War I, Shryock had the opportunity to read medicine. On his discharge he entered the graduate school of the University of Pennsylvania, hoping to study the history of public health in the United States. The subject was judged by his advisers to be "interesting, but not history," and he received his doctorate in 1924 for a study of Georgia and the Union in 1850 (1926). He taught at Ohio State University (1921–1924) and the University of Pennsylvania (1924–1925), and in 1925 joined the history department of Duke University. Returning to the University of Pennsylvania in 1938, he played a large part with Roy F. Nichols and Robert E. Spiller in inaugurating the Department of American Civilization, then a pioneering interdisciplinary graduate program. He married Rheva Suzetta Ott, a fellow graduate of the University of Pennsylvania who had been trained as a bacteriologist, in 1921; they had two children.

One of the sources for Shryock's dissertation had been the letters of Dr. Richard D. Arnold, mayor of Savannah and first secretary of the American Medical Association. Study of these for publication (1929) reinforced Shryock's interest in medical history, and in 1936 his researches culminated in *The Development of Modern Medicine: An Interpretation of the Social and Scientific Factors Involved*, a work of broad scope that he described as "an attempt to portray certain major aspects of medical development against the background of intellectual and social history in general." Hitherto most medical history had been written by physicians and surgeons, who focused on the great figures, discoveries, and publications in their disciplines but paid scant attention to outside influences or consequences; while general historians, if they mentioned health and disease at all, only alluded to a few catastrophes, like the Black Death and the Philadelphia yellow fever epidemic of 1793. Shryock insisted that "medical history involves social and economic as well as biologic content and presents one of the central themes in human experience" (*Medicine in America*, preface). Medical historian Guenter B. Risse likened Shryock's fresh and fruitful approach to "a Copernican revolution" because it shifted medical historical writing from a physician-centered historiography to "a society-centered cosmos," in which the physician was just one "amid a galaxy of factors shaping human health and disease" (*Journal of the History of Medicine* 29 (1974): 5). Shryock's approach was so novel in 1936 that neither historical nor medical journals knew what to make of it. Not for five years, after a German translation of *The Development of Modern Medicine* had appeared, did the *American Historical Review* notice it.

This seminal work, which was published also in England, France, and Japan, was followed in the next thirty years by books and articles that extended or refined its author's view of medical science and practice as an integral part of the history of any society. Thanks in part to Shryock's work and influence and in part to the inherent appeal of the subject, medical history by 1970 was firmly established as an academic discipline. Although physicians and surgeons continued to write on traditional topics, most of the research and publication was by professionally trained historians, who had a national association, two national journals, and a number of university graduate programs and departments. Almost all their work illustrated and extended Shryock's studies of the "interplay of scientific and social factors" in the history of medicine.

While continuing his work in medical history, Shryock also presented significant insights into several aspects of more general American history. Without ever proclaiming himself a "revisionist," he displayed a skeptical, sensible attitude toward some widely accepted historical interpretations. His paper on "American Indifference to Basic Science in the Nineteenth Century" (*Medicine in America*, pp. 71–89) provided an integrating principle for much research and writing in the ensuing thirty years; and three perceptive papers on the colonial Pennsylvania Germans and their patterns of agriculture challenged conclusions too easily drawn from the influential "frontier hypothesis" of Frederick Jackson Turner. In these and other publications Shryock made effective use of comparisons to question generally accepted interpretations. "We should guard against the assumption that all major outcomes must have been for the best," he warned (*Medicine in America*, p. 108). Never dogmatic, always questioning easy generalizations of economists, psychiatrists, statisticians, environmentalists, and other system-makers, he called for particulars, relying on no single explanation, whether Marx, Freud, or "the hand of God." Shryock founded no "school," and, though he had many students (who were devoted to him), he had no disciples, for he believed that "schools" and discipleship require a suspension of critical judgment.

In 1949 Shryock became director of the Institute of the History of Medicine of the Johns Hopkins University. In addition to conducting his research and publication in medical history, he enlarged the scope of the institute's interests to include science generally, bringing visiting scholars and postgraduate fellows to Baltimore to study subjects other than medicine. Retiring from Johns Hopkins in 1958, he returned once more to Philadelphia. As librarian of the American Philosophical Society there, he extended the scope of the library's interest beyond its emphasis on Benjamin Franklin and the eighteenth century to include nineteenth-century science, the history of evolution and genetics, twentieth-century physics, even American Indian linguistics, and he encouraged publication of the papers of Joseph Henry and Charles Darwin. As professor of history at the University of Pennsylvania once more, he helped organize the university's Department of the History of Science. He retired from the librarianship after a heart attack in 1965 but continued to write and publish as before.

Shryock was president of the History of Science Society in 1941–1942 and of the American Association for the History of Medicine in 1946–1947 and received the principal award of each. He was an honorary fellow of the College of Physicians of Philadelphia and for several years delivered a course of lectures under its auspices to the students of Philadelphia's five medical schools. He was acting director of the American Council of Learned Societies in 1946–1947. Always interested in the education profession, he wrote a history of the faculty of the University of Pennsylvania (1959) that was virtually a history of college and university teaching in the United States, and he was president of the American Association of University Professors in 1950 and of the International Association in 1964.

Shryock died suddenly while on vacation in Fort Lauderdale, Florida.

• Many of Shryock's papers are in the American Philosophical Society. Those relating to his work in the history department of the University of Pennsylvania are in that institution's archives. *Medicine in America: Historical Essays* (1966) contains a selection of Shryock's most characteristic and perceptive essays. A bibliography of his writings to 1967 was published in *Journal of the History of Medicine* 23 (1968): 8–15; a complete bibliography is in American Philosophical Society. Biographical and critical assessments are, in *Journal of the History of Medicine* 29 (1974), Merle Curti, "The Historical Scholarship of Richard H. Shryock," 7–14, and Whitfield J. Bell, Jr., "Richard H. Shryock: Life and Work of a Historian," 15–31; Nathan Reingold, "Richard H. Shryock, 1895 [sic]–1972," *Isis* 64 (1973): 96–100; Lloyd G. Stevenson, "A Salute to Richard Shryock," *Journal of the History of Medicine* 23 (1968): 1–7; and Esmond R. Long, "Richard Harrison Shryock (1893–1972)," American Philosophical Society, *Year Book* (1973), pp. 150–56. Shorter accounts are by Owsei Temkin in *Journal of the History of Medicine* 27 (1972): 131–32, and, all by Bell, in *Bulletin of the History of Medicine* 46 (1972): 499–503; *American Historical Review* 77 (1972): 1203–5; and College of Physicians of Philadelphia, *Transactions and Studies*, 4th ser., 40 (1973): 202–4.

WHITFIELD J. BELL, JR.

SHUBERT, Lee (15 Mar. 1873?–25 Dec. 1953), theater producer and owner, was born Levi Shubert in Neustadt, Prussia, the son of David Shubert, a peddler, and Catherine "Carrie" Eldridge(?). Lee emigrated with his family to Syracuse, New York, sometime between 1880 and 1882. With poverty a constant threat, he and his younger brother Sam entered the workforce while still small boys, selling newspapers on the streets of downtown Syracuse.

The Shubert brothers discovered the world of the theater while selling papers to audiences on their way to and from Syracuse's several playhouses and by attending as many cheap matinees as they could manage to get themselves into. Sometime around 1888 the ingratiating Sam was offered the position of program boy at the Grand Opera House. Lee, meanwhile, entered the cigar-making business in 1889, where he remained until 1893, when he became a haberdasher. About 1895 he teamed up with Jesse L. Oberdorfer to form a men's furnishings business, which he maintained even as he turned his attention to a career in the theater. In 1897, while operating a men's furnishings store with his brother Jacob (known as "J. J."), Lee took over as treasurer of the Wieting Theatre for Sam, who had vacated that position in order to manage the touring company of Charles Hoyt's *A Texas Steer*. He also wrote a short musical spoof entitled *A Trip to the Bowery* (it was never produced) and became manager of the Bastable Theatre, which Sam had leased.

In 1898 Lee became a partner with Samuel Mirbach in the Shubert and Mirbach haberdashery, and with the income derived from the store as well as the financial backing of several Syracuse businessmen, Lee, Sam, and J. J. Shubert quickly added to their theatrical holdings. By the end of 1899 they had built the Baker Theatre in Rochester and had acquired additional theaters in Utica, Troy, Albany, and Syracuse. They also formed several resident stock companies.

In 1900 the Shubert brothers obtained the U.S. touring rights to the great British musical success *The Belle of New York*. Also at this time Sam and Lee began to shift their focus to New York City, where they established an office, while J. J. assumed primary supervision of the upstate holdings. They obtained a lease on the Herald Square Theatre in May of that year, and it was here that they produced their first original production in New York, *The Brixton Burglary*. The play opened on 20 May 1901 and ran for forty-eight performances, a not atypical run for a play of that time. Shortly they acquired the Casino, Princess, and Madison Square theaters in New York, built with composer Reginald DeKoven their first theater in New York's Times Square, the Lyric, and acquired leases on playhouses in Boston, Buffalo, Cleveland, Chicago, and St. Louis.

The Klaw and Erlanger Theatrical Syndicate, which had a stranglehold on the booking of theaters across the United States at the turn of the century, soon began to look askance at the upstarts from Syracuse who were, it seemed to them, assembling a small competing empire. At first the Shuberts tried to cooperate with the Syndicate, but by 1903 conflict had arisen over the latter's restrictive business tactics. As the Shuberts became increasingly aggressive, acquiring more and more theater buildings and theatrical properties, their opposition to Klaw and Erlanger grew more vocal. They very publicly advocated a policy whereby managers and producers would gain more personal control over bookings without having to agree to share large percentages of their profits with the Syndicate. Many independent managers and performers rallied around the Shubert cause.

In the early stages of the Shubert-Syndicate war, tragedy struck the Shubert brothers. In 1905, on his way to take part in a legal action against the Syndicate related to the Duquesne Theatre in Pittsburgh, Sam Shubert was killed in a train crash. His family was devastated, and Lee, who was in London overseeing the building of the Waldorf Theatre, the Shuberts' first venue in that city, was prostrate with grief. Many in the industry, including Klaw and Erlanger, believed that this would be the end of the Shuberts' theatrical ventures, because Sam had always been the driving force behind the brothers' activities. But instead, Sam's death galvanized Lee and J. J., making them more determined than ever to carry out their late brother's dreams of an industry free of Syndicate control.

Lee, assisted now by J. J., added rapidly to the Shubert Theatrical Company's holdings. They acquired leases to existing venues and commenced new theater construction. By 1911 the brothers controlled seventeen theaters in New York City alone, and at the height of their empire in the late 1920s they either owned, leased, or booked productions into over one thousand theaters in North America. In 1913, after much battling, the Syndicate, now a shadow of its former self, joined forces with the Shuberts, although Lee always maintained that the old war wounds never fully healed. The Syndicate officially dissolved in 1919, and in the ensuing years many in the industry accused the Shuberts of being as abusive of their power as the Syndicate had ever been.

While J. J.'s main interests were with the musical productions, it was Lee who often strove for more serious and artistic fare. In 1909 he joined a group of prestigious and wealthy businessmen in building the New Theatre on Central Park West. Meant to be an "art theater" on an elaborate scale, it was to be the home for an American repertory company on the model of the Moscow Art Theatre and the Comédie Française. The venture, however, was unsuccessful.

As producers the Shuberts became known as presenters of mainstream revues, operettas, light comedies, and popular dramas. Their *Passing Show* and *Artists and Models* revues of the 1910s and 1920s were created to rival Florenz Ziegfeld's *Follies*. Later revues of the 1930s such as *At Home Abroad, Life Begins at 8:40*, and the various editions of the *Ziegfeld Follies*, to which Lee bought the title and production rights after Ziegfeld's death in 1932, were critically praised. Operettas like *Maytime* (1917), *Blossom Time* (1921), and *The Student Prince* (1924) were immensely popular with audiences, and the Shuberts sent out touring companies of these shows year after year. While few of the comedies and dramas that they produced have stood the test of time, many were nonetheless successful in their day. Plays like Clyde Fitch's *The City* (1909), Maurice Maeterlinck's *The Blue Bird* (1910), Luigi Pirandello's *As You Desire Me* (1931), and J. B. Priestley's *Laburnum Grove* (1935) received considerable public attention. Twice the Shuberts attempted to enter the profitable vaudeville field—once in the form of the U.S. Amusement Company, established in 1906 in partnership with their archrivals Klaw and Erlanger, and once in the form of Shubert Vaudeville, established on their own in 1922. Both of these attempts were disastrous.

Lee had a special knack for spotting and appreciating talent. Among the stars whom he discovered or nurtured were Jack Benny, James Cagney, Lucille La Sueur (later known as Joan Crawford), Eddie Foy, Willie Howard, Eugene Howard, Al Jolson, Archibald Leach (later known as Cary Grant), Jeannette MacDonald, Marilyn Miller, Carmen Miranda, Alla Nazimova, John "Ole" Olsen and Harold "Chic" Johnson, Laurette Taylor, and Mae West. Lee also realized early the money-making potential of motion pictures. Beginning in 1913 with the formation of the Shubert Feature Film Booking Company and continuing up through the early 1920s, when his involvement with the World Film Corporation ceased, Lee was an active player in film production and booking. He also helped to capitalize Marcus Loew's motion picture theater company, Loew's Incorporated, was a significant stockholder and organizer of the Goldwyn Picture Company, and had a financial involvement later in Metro-Goldwyn-Mayer.

Among many other business ventures, Lee and J. J. acquired large parcels of valuable properties in New York and other major cities. These investments guaranteed the security of their theaters against outside real estate speculators and also provided them with equity and a large rental income.

Like many other businessmen, the Shuberts were severely hurt by the Great Depression. They had to sell some theaters, give up the leases on others, and scale back their producing activities. In 1931 the Shubert Theatrical Corporation went into receivership. But Lee, as astute and determined to succeed as he had ever been, formed a new company called Select Theatres and bought the assets of the old company at a bankruptcy auction in 1933. From this point on the Shuberts produced fewer and fewer shows. Although they had significant hits in the late thirties—Olsen and Johnson's *Hellzapoppin'* (1938) was an extremely popular and influential example—the Shuberts were content to remain behind the scenes as investors in other people's shows, as theater and property owners, and as participants in other business enterprises. The post-depression Shuberts operated an extremely profitable company.

Lee, always secretive about his private life, was known throughout the theatrical community as a workaholic for whom fifteen-hour workdays spent in his office above the Shubert Theatre were not unusual. He was believed to have been a longtime bachelor, but in 1948 Marcella Swanson, a former musical comedy actress, surprised the world by publicly filing for divorce from Lee on the grounds that keeping their marriage secret for twelve years constituted an act of cruelty. They were divorced but remarried the following year. They had no children.

Lee loved the theater passionately, and despite his constant battling with the press and with creative personnel, he cared deeply about the industry's future. Some called him a "wooden Indian" for his stiff, impenetrable demeanor and ruddy complexion, while others described him as cold, ruthless, and stingy. Still others, however, knew him as a generous but awkwardly shy man. The many causes to which he donated time and money, as well as the charitable foundation that he and J. J. established in 1945, stand as testaments to that generosity.

In 1950 the U.S. government filed an antitrust suit against the Shuberts. Lee, who died in New York City three years later, never saw the end result of that litigation, which required the divestiture of several theatrical properties in New York and other cities. J. J. continued his involvement in the business until his death in 1963, at which point others assumed control.

Lee Shubert played a key role in defining and establishing the Broadway theater industry. Were it not for the contributions of Lee and his brothers, the structure of the business and even its physical appearance (the result of the numerous theaters they constructed that have been landmarked) would be radically different entities.

• Lee Shubert's papers (as well as those of his brothers Sam and J. J.) are in the Shubert Archive, New York City, which also contains an extensive collection of playbills, photographs, set and costume designs, business contracts, and architectural plans. In addition, the archive publishes a bi-annual newsletter, the *Passing Show* (1977–), that contains numerous articles relating to Shubert history. There are two books on the Shuberts: Brooks McNamara, *The Shuberts of Broadway* (1990), and a not very reliable or well-documented source, Jerry Stagg, *The Brothers Shubert* (1968). A three-part article by A. J. Liebling, "The Boys from Syracuse," *New Yorker*, 18 Nov. 1939, pp. 26–30; 25 Nov. 1939, pp. 23–27; and 2 Dec. 1939, pp. 33–37, provides a fairly extensive portrait of the Shuberts up through the 1930s. For Lee's early career see especially Julian Johnson, "The Little Brown Buddha of the Play," *American Magazine*, July 1913, pp. 73–77; Lee Shubert, "The Truth about Commercialism in the Theatre," *Theatre Magazine*, Apr. 1924, p. 9; and Keene Summer, "Sometimes You Fight Better If You're Driven to the Wall," *American Magazine*, Oct. 1921, p. 20. An important summary of the Shuberts' involvement in the film industry is provided by Kevin Lewis, "A World across from Broadway," parts 1 and 2, *Film History* 1, no. 1 (1987): 39–52; and no. 2 (1987): 163–86. Other informative sources include Ruth Gordon, "Remembering Mr. Lee," *New York University Magazine*, Spring 1986, pp. 28–29; Norman Nadel, "When the Shuberts Fit," *Horizons*, Oct. 1981, pp. 54–59; Ed Sullivan, "Mister Lee," *Daily News*, 12 Dec. 1953; and Peter Wynne, "The Shuberts Centerstage," *New York University Magazine*, Spring 1986, pp. 20–27. Obituaries are in the *New York Times* and the *New York Herald Tribune*, both 26 Dec. 1953.

MARK E. SWARTZ

SHUBRICK, John Templer (12 Sept. 1788–July 1815), naval officer, was born on Bull's Island, South Carolina, the son of Thomas Shubrick, a revolutionary war officer, and Mary Branford. Shubrick attended grammar school in Charleston, South Carolina, and a private seminary in Dedham, Massachusetts, before studying law in the office of William Drayton in Charleston for two years. Young Shubrick's temperament was not suited to the sedentary life of an attorney, however, and, after numerous entreaties, his father obtained for him in August 1806 a midshipman's warrant in the navy. The allure of the navy was strong then, as the successful exploits of American seamen engaging the Barbary pirates was exciting reading for the youth of the period. Shubrick joined the service in the wake of congressional legislation expanding the navy after a five-year period of retrenchment.

Shubrick's first assignment in the peacetime navy aboard USS frigate *Chesapeake* was a lesson in preparedness and national honor for Shubrick. The British ship *Leopard* confronted this American warship off Cape Henry, Virginia, on 22 June 1807 for allegedly harboring British deserters. The *Leopard*'s broadsides forced the *Chesapeake* to strike her colors after firing only one gun in her own defense. *Chesapeake*'s guns were not primed for action, and confusion on board the ship precluded an immediate response. As a result Commodore James Barron surrendered, a humiliating act that emboldened the eighteen-year-old Shubrick never to be caught unprepared again. Shubrick remained on the *Chesapeake* for another year while the

renowned Stephen Decatur, Jr., was in command. Decatur restored order and pride to the humiliated ship, and Shubrick actively sought to serve with the naval hero throughout his career.

Assigned to the brig *Argus* from 1808 to 1810, Shubrick served under Master Commandants P. C. Wederstrandt and Samuel Evans and Lieutenant Jacob Jones. During this period the navy routinely cruised the coast of the United States, enforcing the Embargo Act of 1807. Shubrick participated in this often mundane activity, but he also acquired nautical skills such as tracking the land along the coast and taking soundings near capes and ports. In the aftermath of the *Chesapeake/Leopard* affair, Congress reconsidered its reliance on gunboats for defense and refitted several larger vessels, including the frigate *United States*, which Decatur assumed command of in 1809. The Navy Department granted Shubrick's request for a transfer to the *United States*, but he remained on that vessel only a few months in 1810 before Decatur reassigned him to the brig *Viper*, promoting him to acting lieutenant. Shubrick served on the *Viper* and on the brig *Siren* at the New Orleans station, protecting trade and enforcing the embargo, until he was ordered to Washington in December 1811. War fever was strong in the capital early in 1812 and the Navy Department was busy refitting and recruiting in anticipation of hostilities with Great Britain.

Shubrick received his lieutenant's commission, to date from 28 May 1812, just days before Congress declared war on 18 June. As the fifth lieutenant on the frigate *Constitution*, commanded by Isaac Hull, Shubrick participated in a tiring but successful three-day struggle in July to evade an English squadron of five vessels. After a short port call, the *Constitution* departed Boston in early August for a cruise in the Gulf of St. Lawrence. Off the coast of Newfoundland on 19 August, the *Constitution* captured and destroyed the British frigate *Guerrière*, and Shubrick commanded the quarterdeck guns during the engagement. The *Constitution* returned to Boston in late August, its command having devolved to William Bainbridge by seniority. Two of Hull's lieutenants left the ship with him, thus permitting Shubrick to advance to third lieutenant under Bainbridge.

On 26 October the *Constitution* left for the coast of Brazil for commerce raiding. Shubrick acquitted himself well during the three hour and fifteen minute engagement with HM frigate *Java* on 29 December in which the latter was so badly damaged she had to be destroyed. Shubrick was transferred to the sloop of war *Hornet* and participated as acting first lieutenant in that ship's capture of the British brig *Peacock*, off Demerara, Guiana, on 24 February 1813. In his after-action report, the *Hornet*'s captain, James Lawrence, recommended Shubrick to Secretary of the Navy William Jones for his "coolness and good conduct."

After returning to New York and awaiting the *Hornet*'s refitting, Shubrick, always seeking adventure, volunteered in April 1814 to serve on the *Argus* to search for an enemy vessel that was disrupting the coasting trade in Long Island Sound. Shubrick returned to the *Hornet* after this brief, unsuccessful sojourn on the *Argus*. Meanwhile, Decatur had formed a squadron consisting of the *United States*, the frigate *Macedonian*, and the *Hornet* to cruise off Charleston, South Carolina. Despite the tightening British blockade, the squadron attempted to escape from New York in May but was chased into the Thames River in June.

The blockade idled Shubrick's naval career during the summer of 1813, giving him the opportunity to marry Elizabeth Matilda Ludlow of New York. They had one son. But marriage and shore duty lacked the adventure that Shubrick desired, and so he transferred to the *United States* knowing that its captain, Decatur, would eventually get another ship and another chance to cruise against the British. When the Navy Department shifted Decatur to the *President* in 1814, he brought many of his officers, including Shubrick, along with him. But the British offensive in the summer of 1814 precluded any cruise, and Decatur and his crew were diverted to shore defenses around New York. On 14 January 1815 the *President*, with Shubrick as second lieutenant, attempted to breach the British blockade, but a squadron of four enemy vessels captured her off New York the following day. The crew of the *President* spent a short time in captivity in Bermuda before being released when peace was declared.

Shubrick returned to New York in March 1815 but left in May with a Mediterranean expedition assigned to redress the dey of Algiers's harassment of American commerce. Decatur had specifically requested Shubrick to be first lieutenant on his flagship, the frigate *Guerrière*. The squadron quickly subdued the dey's forces, and the commodore dictated a treaty by 30 June, just forty days after leaving America. Decatur entrusted Shubrick with taking the treaty back home in the sloop of war *Epervier*. Sailing from Algiers early in July, the *Epervier* passed through the Straits of Gibraltar on 14 July and disappeared while at sea.

Although his naval career spanned a short nine years, Shubrick participated in many of the most significant engagements of America's fledgling navy. During this time he saw action in six battles, but he never suffered injury in any of them. He actively sought situations that would place him "in harm's way," but his untimely death was probably due to a gale in the Atlantic.

• Official naval correspondence is at the National Archives, RG 45, Naval Records Collection of the Office of Naval Records and Library, 1775–1910. Shubrick's letters to the secretary of the navy are in M148, "Letters from Officers of Rank Below That of Commander"; letters from the secretary of the navy to Shubrick are in M149, "Letters to Officers"; his service record can be found in RG 24, M330, "Abstract of Service Records of Naval Officers." Other useful information is in correspondence of his commanding officers with the secretary of the navy, RG 45, M125, "Captains' Letters." Biographical essays on Shubrick date from the nineteenth century and include James F. Cooper, *Lives of Distinguished American Naval Officers*, vol. 1 (1846), pp. 147–70; *The Analectic Magazine, and Naval Chronicle* 8 (Sept. 1816): 247–51; and *The Portfolio* 19 (May 1825): 360–63.

CHRISTINE F. HUGHES

SHUBRICK, William Branford (31 Oct. 1790–27 May 1874), naval officer, was born at Belvedere Plantation, Bull Island, South Carolina, the son of Thomas Shubrick and Mary Branford, planters. His father had been a colonel in the Continental army during the American Revolution, serving with Generals Nathanael Greene and Benjamin Lincoln in the South. William Branford Shubrick attended Harvard College in 1805, then entered the navy as a midshipman in 1806, enlisting with his older brother, John Templar Shubrick.

Shubrick served aboard the *Wasp*, first in the Mediterranean and then in U.S. waters enforcing the embargo, until 1810. Aboard the *Wasp* he met and befriended James Fenimore Cooper. During the War of 1812, Shubrick served aboard the *Hornet* (1812), on the *Constellation* (1812–1813), and on the *Constitution* (1813–1815). On 20 January 1812, commanding a small gunboat, he led an attack against the British ship *Juno* and then commanded a gun ashore. The *Constellation* remained blockaded within Hampton Roads, and he transferred to the *Constitution* ("Old Ironsides"). He saw action off Portugal against the *Cyane* and the *Levant*, leading the party that took possession of the *Levant* on 20 February 1815. Aboard that vessel, he was struck by a portion of falling mast, which dented a helmet he was wearing. He bore a mark of the blow later in life and was awarded the Eagle of Cincinnati medal by the state of South Carolina for the action.

In 1815 Shubrick married Harriet Cordelia Wethered; they had one child. In 1820 he was commissioned commander, took charge of the *Lexington*, and cruised the waters off Labrador in protection of American fishing rights there. He later sailed to the Caribbean to retrieve the remains of Commodore Oliver Hazard Perry, hero of the battles on Lake Champlain. In 1831 Shubrick was commissioned captain, and in the mid-1830s he took up ordnance duties. In 1838 he was given command of the West Indian Squadron, and in 1840 he was put in charge of the Norfolk Navy Yard. With the organization of the bureau system, he was made chief of the Bureau of Provisions and Clothing, 1844–1846.

During the war with Mexico, Shubrick was ordered to the Pacific Coast, where he took charge of U.S. forces at Monterey, California. He then led the blockade of Mazatlán on the West Coast of Mexico. He later took Guaymas, at the head of the Gulf of California, and the town of San Jose, in Lower California. On 11 November 1846 Shubrick led the force that captured the city of Mazatlán. After occupying other towns in the vicinity and setting up shore administration, he had too few troops to attempt to take Acapulco as well. On the conclusion of peace in July 1848, he sailed back to the East Coast aboard the *Independence*.

From 1849 through 1853 Shubrick held a variety of shore assignments, including president of the board to revise regulations for the Naval Academy (1849), president of the Board of Naval Examiners (1850), commander of the Philadelphia Navy Yard (1850), inspector of ordnance and ammunition (1851–1852), and member of the Lighthouse Board (1853–1855). In 1852–1853 Shubrick served as chief of the Bureau of Construction and Repair.

In 1853 Shubrick sailed aboard the *Princeton* for Nova Scotia, where he negotiated outstanding issues regarding fishing with a British naval officer and reached a temporary agreement until a treaty could be arranged. His next five years were spent on shore duty, including service on the Lighthouse Board.

In 1858, after the U.S. survey ship *Water Witch* was fired on by the armed forces of the dictator of Paraguay, Shubrick led an expedition of nineteen ships to South America. He was in charge of "showing the flag," and U.S. forces were well received in Paraguay and Argentina. Heading the expedition aboard the *Sabine*, he reached Asuncion, Paraguay, on 25 January 1859 and secured an apology and a cash indemnification for the attack on the *Water Witch*. In Argentina the president of the confederation presented Shubrick with a sword, which by act of Congress, he was allowed to keep.

At the outbreak of the Civil War, Shubrick remained in Washington and offered his services to the Union, despite efforts to recruit him to the Confederate cause. In 1861 he was placed on the retired list, then promoted to rear admiral in 1862. He continued to serve as chairman of the Lighthouse Board until 1871. He died in Washington, D.C.

Shubrick is remembered as a veteran of the War of 1812 and as a leading officer of the period of the war with Mexico. He earned his greatest renown for the capture of cities and towns on the coast of Mexico. His negotiations with the British over fishing rights and during his visit to South America served as early examples of the naval officer as diplomat. A native of South Carolina, he was praised by his admirers for declining to join the Confederacy and offering his services to the United States.

• Shubrick wrote "Paraguay Expedition and Brazil Squadron," which is available in microform at the Naval Historical Center, Washington, D.C. A report by Shubrick regarding the fisheries negotiation of 1853 is in the National Archives in RG 45. He was also the author of "Despatches of Commodore Shubrick, Containing an Account of His Proceedings on the West Coast of Mexico," which was reprinted in *Message from the President of the United States to the Two Houses of Congress, December 5, 1848* (1848), pp. 1065–1161. Sources include William Cogar, *Dictionary of Admirals of the U.S. Navy* (1989), and Susan Fenimore Cooper, "Rear Admiral William Branford Shubrick, A Sketch," *Harper's New Monthly Magazine*, Aug. 1876, pp. 400–407. An obituary is in the *Washington Evening Star*, 27 May 1874.

RODNEY P. CARLISLE

SHUFELDT, Robert Wilson (21 Feb. 1822–7 Nov. 1895), naval officer and diplomat, was born in Red Hook, New York, the son of George Adam Shufeldt, a lawyer, and Mary Howey Wilson. He attended Middlebury College in Vermont from 1837 to 1839 but before graduating, joined the navy. After cruises in the Home Squadron (1839–1840) and the Brazil Squadron (1840–1843), he graduated as a midshipman from the Naval School, Philadelphia, in June 1845. Service followed with the Coast Survey (1845–1846, 1849) and the West African Squadron (1846–1848). In 1848 he married Sarah Hutchins Abercrombie; the couple had three sons who survived infancy (three children did not). After placement during 1850–1851 as acting lieutenant aboard Edward Knight Collins's steamship *Atlantic* plying between New York and Liverpool, Shufeldt resigned from the navy in 1854 to become a merchant steamship captain between New York, Havana, and Mobile, and eventually, from 1856 until 1860, for the Louisiana-Tehuantepec Company. Shufeldt mingled with New Orleans and New York business visionaries hoping to control a transit road across the Mexican Isthmus of Tehuantepec.

At the outbreak of the Civil War, Secretary of State William H. Seward appointed Shufeldt consul general at Havana. Shufeldt advised Captain Charles Wilkes to seize John Slidell of Louisiana (whom he had known in New Orleans) and his fellow Confederate commissioner James M. Mason of Virginia from the Royal Mail packet *Trent*, but he escaped the later censure of Wilkes. Shufeldt also reported on Confederate shipping and, from November 1861 to February 1862, provided detailed reports on the British, Spanish, and French tripartite expedition to Mexico. Seward sent Shufeldt to Mexico City to report on Mexican resistance, but Shufeldt exceeded his instructions in suggesting to Foreign Minister Manuel Doblado a treaty to colonize "contrabands" (freed American slaves) at Tehuantepec and offering to provide Secret Service funds. Seward recalled him, and Shufeldt resigned in April 1863 to rejoin the navy. He commanded the USS *Proteus* (1863–1865) and the USS *Miantonomoh* (1869–1870) in Theodorus Bailey's East Gulf Squadron.

After the Civil War Shufeldt became flag captain of the USS *Hartford* in Admiral Henry Haywood Bell's Asiatic Squadron. He commanded the USS *Wachusett* in the Yangtze River, observed American vessels in the opium and coolie trades, and promoted surveys of the Yangtze, Korea, and Japan. While investigating a massacre of the crew of the schooner *General Sherman* on the west coast of Korea in 1867, he called for annexation of Korea's Nan Hoo Islands.

In the post–Civil War era, three areas of the world occupied Shufeldt's attention, Tehuantepec, Korea, and Africa. From 1870 to 1871 he led a navy survey for an interoceanic canal across Tehuantepec, advocating an American-controlled canal with 140 locks in 144 miles to cost between $69 million and $109 million. Such a canal would stimulate an American presence in the Pacific. In April 1870 he declared, "The Pacific Ocean is to be hereafter the field of our commercial triumphs. . . . [It] is & *must* be essentially *American*. Through it & by us—China and Japan must acquire a new civilization & adopt a new creed—for it is in this sense that 'Westward still, the Star of Empire takes its way'." The Tehuantepec route was rejected by President Ulysses S. Grant's Interoceanic Canal Commission in 1876 in favor of Nicaragua.

From 1875 to 1878, as chief of the Bureau of Equipment and Recruiting, Shufeldt directed modifications in the navy's harsh punishment code, advocated better pay and working conditions for sailors, diminished desertion rates, and encouraged recruitment of American boys for an American navy. In 1878 he published a pamphlet specifying the need to revive U.S. commerce, especially exports, and preaching that the navy and merchant marine were "joint apostles" and "pioneers of commerce."

Convinced that the United States had to find new markets for agricultural and industrial surpluses, Shufeldt persuaded Secretary of the Navy Richard W. Thompson to authorize a world cruise for him aboard the steam corvette *Ticonderoga*, "with a view to the encouragement and extension of American Commerce." In an extraordinary two-year circumnavigation (1878–1880) of 35,000 miles, the *Ticonderoga* anchored at forty-three ports in European colonial possessions on both African coasts, Zanzibar, Muscat, Aden, the Persian Gulf, India, Southeast Asia, Japan, Korea, China, and Hawaii. Shufeldt reported extensively on the commercial opportunities of all countries visited and called for a greatly expanded consulate service for Africa. Existing treaties with Liberia, Muscat, and Zanzibar were renewed and new treaties negotiated in Madagascar, with the chiefs of the Malagasy and Sakalava tribes, and with the sultan of Johanna (Comoro Islands).

Shufeldt's most important task was opening Korea to U.S. influence and trade. He had to first counter an assumption by the Korean court that war existed with the United States following the ill-fated Low-Rodgers expedition in 1871, when American forces killed 800 Korean troops in the Han River forts. In spring 1880 the Japanese minister for foreign affairs, Inoue Kaoru, gave Shufeldt letters of introduction to Korean authorities and charts of the Korean coasts, but the Korean minister of ceremony, under pressure from *Ajon* (nobles) and *yangban* (gentry), brusquely declared that Koreans would never consent to a treaty with the country that had made war. Thwarted, Shufeldt sought the help of Li Hung-chang, the powerful viceroy of Chihli, the northern provinces of China, before taking the *Ticonderoga* to the Sandwich Islands (Hawaii) and San Francisco in November 1880.

Shufeldt returned to China when Li suggested a position as grand admiral in the Chinese navy. Secretary of State James G. Blaine and Secretary of the Navy William H. Hunt both authorized Shufeldt to negotiate a Korean treaty. He was caught between competing Chinese and Japanese attempts to control Korea and the power struggle in the Korean court that deadlocked decision making. Only the king's intervention in favor of negotiations enabled a Korean envoy and a seventy-man trading mission to proceed to Tientsin to meet Shufeldt. Blaine provided new instructions authorizing him to negotiate.

Li and the Chinese Tsungli Yamen wanted an article inserted into the United States–Korean treaty indicating that "Chosen" (Korea) was a dependency of China. An appeal by Shufeldt to Blaine's successor, Frederick T. Frelinghuysen, to indicate his sentiments on the dependency clause was ignored as Frelinghuysen reviewed his predecessor's policies. This first treaty opening Korea, negotiated entirely in Tientsin and signed in Korea on 22 May 1882, omitted the dependency clause. It permitted American citizens to trade and erect residences and warehouses in the open ports; set a tariff of 10 percent on necessities, 30 percent on luxuries, and 5 percent on export duties; established rights for victims of shipwrecks; provided for diplomatic and consular representatives; prohibited the opium trade; and granted the United States extraterritorial jurisdiction and most favored nation privileges. It also plunged the United States into the arena of Far Eastern rivalry over Korea, involving Russia, Japan, and China, in the last two decades of the nineteenth century.

Shufeldt's impatience over delays in 1881 led him to write a letter to Senator Aaron A. Sargent of California damning China and its armed forces as decadent and the empress as "an ignorant, capricious and immoral woman." He argued that force was the only solution. Realizing its importance in the politics of Chinese exclusion in California, Sargent published the letter in the *San Francisco Bulletin*, 20 March 1882. The resultant criticism almost terminated Shufeldt's career in the navy and undermined his health. His treaty met opposition in the Senate for being negotiated by an "executive agent," appointed without the advice and consent of the Senate, before being ratified in the Senate on 9 January 1883, ratified in Korea on 19 May 1883, and proclaimed on 4 June 1883.

Secretary of the Navy William E. Chandler appointed Shufeldt president of the Second Naval Advisory Board to superintend the designs and contracts for the navy's first all-steel vessels, *Atlanta*, *Boston*, *Chicago*, and *Dolphin*. When Shufeldt retired in 1884, somewhat embittered, he lived in Nagasaki, Japan, from 1885 to 1889, from whence he preached a gospel of commercial expansion in Africa and Asia and the annexation of the Sandwich Islands once a canal was constructed. After the Republicans recaptured the presidency, he returned to the United States in 1889 and was offered but declined the position of minister to China. He lived in Alexandria, Virginia, cared for by his niece Molly, whom he adopted, until his death in Washington, D.C. Shufeldt's surveys, his cruise in the *Ticonderoga*, his opening of Korea, and his work for the new steel navy were achievements that opened new avenues for the United States overseas in the 1880s and the 1890s.

• Shufeldt's papers are in the Library of Congress Manuscript Division along with a two-volume manuscript, "The Cruise of the *Ticonderoga*," edited by his son Mason Shufeldt. Shufeldt published *The Relation of the Navy to the Commerce of the United States* (1878). His canal report on Tehuantepec, "Report of Captain R. W. Shufeldt, USN, to Hon. George M. Robeson, Aug. 11, 1871," is in Senate, 42d Cong., 2d sess., 1872, S. Exec. Doc. 6. The most detailed biography is Frederick C. Drake, *The Empire of the Seas: A Biography of Rear Admiral Robert Wilson Shufeldt, USN* (1984), which includes a bibliographic essay. A good account of Shufeldt's naval significance is in Kenneth J. Hagan, *American Gunboat Diplomacy and the Old Navy, 1877–1889* (1973). Significant readings are Drake, "Robert Wilson Shufeldt: The Naval Officer as Commercial Expansionist and Diplomat," in *Captains of the Old Steam Navy: Makers of the American Naval Tradition, 1840–1880*, ed. James C. Bradford (1986); Hagan, "Showing the Flag in the Indian Ocean," in *America Spreads Her Sails*, ed. Clayton R. Barrow, Jr. (1973); and David Long's comparative study of nineteenth-century naval diplomats, *Gold Braid and Foreign Relations: Diplomatic Activities of U.S. Naval Officers 1798–1883* (1988). Older accounts include Henry G. Appenzeller, "The Opening of Korea: Admiral Shufeldt's Account of It," *Korean Repository* 1 (1892): 57–62; Charles O. Paullin, "The Opening of Korea by Commodore Shufeldt," *Political Science Quarterly* 25 (1910): 470–99; and A. S. Hickey, "Rear Admiral Robert Wilson Shufeldt, United States Navy, Gentleman and Diplomat," *United States Naval Institute Proceedings* 69 (1943): 73–80. Newspaper reports of the cruise of the *Ticonderoga* are in the *New York Herald* and the *New York Daily Graphic*, 1879–1880. Obituaries are in the *New York Daily Tribune*, 8 Nov. 1895; *United States Army and Navy Journal* 33 (9 Nov. 1895): 169, and (16 Nov. 1895): 175; the *Washington Post*, 8 Nov. 1895; and the *Chicago Tribune*, 8 Nov. 1895.

FREDERICK C. DRAKE

SHULER, Nettie Rogers (8 Nov. 1865?–2 Dec. 1939), suffragist and clubwoman, was born Antoinette Rogers in Buffalo, New York, the daughter of Alexander Rogers, a clerk for the American Express Company, and Julie Antoinette Houghtaling. Her father had emigrated from County Perth, Scotland. Her mother's family had been in America since the Revolution. Nettie Rogers graduated from Buffalo Central High School. In 1887 she married Frank J. Shuler, a bookkeeper. They had one child, a daughter named Marjorie.

In her day Shuler was one of only two women to have served as president of both the New York State (1912–1914) and the New York City (1929–1931) Federation of Women's Clubs. In 1908, as president of the Western New York Foundation of Women's Clubs, she addressed the annual convention of the National American Woman Suffrage Association (NAWSA), meeting in Buffalo. In 1909 the 32,000-member Western Federation, the first chapter in the national federation to admit suffrage clubs as affiliates, passed a resolution in support of woman suffrage. That same year the New York legislature held hearings on the issue of woman suffrage, and Shuler was a member of the delegation that advocated on behalf of a suffrage amendment to the state constitution. After Shuler moved to New York City from Buffalo in 1917, she continued as

honorary president of the Western Federation until her death.

Although Shuler was an uncommonly active clubwoman, after her husband's death in 1916, she concentrated her efforts toward promoting the cause of woman suffrage, a movement embraced by her daughter as well. Shuler established a reputation as an organizer by leading the western New York campaign for the state suffrage party, a two-year campaign that led in 1915 to a referendum. The referendum was lost, but in 1917 Shuler was chosen by NAWSA president Carrie Chapman Catt to replace Hannah Jane Patterson of Pennsylvania as the association's corresponding secretary. Throughout the four years that she worked in the national office in New York City, Shuler continued to participate in the New York state campaigns, building up support that was fundamental to congressional passage of the suffrage amendment. As chair of Campaigns and Surveys for the national association, she helped to train field organizers, supplying them with information on the history of suffrage and the legislative process as well as teaching them how to organize, raise money, and publicize their activities. In January 1917 she was an instructor at the second suffrage school, sponsored by the NAWSA in Portland, Maine.

Often assisted by her daughter, Shuler addressed countless public meetings and testified before committees of state legislatures, working tirelessly in Maine, Massachusetts, Maryland, Michigan, New Hampshire, Oklahoma, Rhode Island, South Dakota, and West Virginia. Along with Catt, she spent many evenings addressing mass meetings and many days holding conferences with field workers. After the Nineteenth Amendment was passed in August 1920, Shuler and Catt continued to work together. Their coauthored book, *Woman Suffrage and Politics*, published in 1923, is a short narrative history of the suffrage campaign beginning with the Seneca Falls Convention in 1848.

In addition to her club work, Shuler was a member of the Buffalo Chapter of the Daughters of the American Revolution, president of the Erie County Political Equality Society, an honorary member of the Buffalo Society for Mineral Painters, an honorary member of the Teachers Educational League of Buffalo, and a member of the Woman's Investigating Club. Marjorie Shuler was a staff writer for the *Christian Science Monitor*. Nettie Rogers Shuler, a Baptist for much of her life (and at one time a member of the woman's society of Delaware Avenue Baptist Church in Buffalo), later became a Christian Scientist, even serving for a time as second reader of the Seventh Church of Christ, Scientist, in New York City. A member of the Republican party, she actively supported enforcement of Prohibition and opposed passage of an equal rights amendment to the U.S. Constitution as first drafted by Alice Paul in 1923. Shuler died in New York City.

• For additional information on Shuler's involvement in the suffrage movement see Ida Husted Harper, *History of Woman*

Suffrage, 1900–1920, vols. 5 and 6 (1922; repr. 1969). Also see Angela Howard Zophy, ed., *Handbook of American Women's History* (1990), pp. 434–35. An obituary is in the *New York Times*, 3 Dec. 1939.

KAREN VENTURELLA

SHULL, George Harrison (15 Apr. 1874–29 Sept. 1954), botanist and geneticist, was born on a farm near North Hampton, Ohio, the son of Harrison Shull and Catherine Ryman, farmers. A devout member of the Old German Baptist Church, Shull's father was also an unpaid lay minister; his mother, an avid reader, eventually became an accomplished horticulturist after her children were raised. Shull's formal education was sparse. It is estimated that he only spent 46.5 months in formal school before he entered college and never spent a full year in school at a time. Despite these trying circumstances, George and his seven siblings were educated with the help of their mother, who encouraged study. Stimulated by a rural background that provided him proximity to both wild and agricultural plants, Shull's interest in plants was apparent by the age of sixteen.

Shull's thirst for knowledge appears to have been so great that it carried him over many educational hurdles. At the age of seventeen he published his first paper in the *American Garden*. He taught at county schools in rural Ohio until he was twenty-three, when he entered Antioch College. At college he supported himself by arising at four A.M. to light the furnaces, serving as head janitor, college plumber, and performing other odd jobs to support himself. In what little spare time he had, he continued to explore the countryside, collecting and identifying plants. He received a B.S. in 1901 and obtained a position to survey Tennessee forests with the U.S. Bureau of Forestry just before his graduation. In 1902 he was appointed to the National Herbarium in Washington and transferred to the Bureau of Plant Industry of the Department of Agriculture to study the flora of Chesapeake Bay.

At the same time that he was seeking employment, Shull began graduate work at the University of Chicago. Entering officially in 1901, he met Charles B. Davenport, who was then engaged in biometrical studies. The meeting was especially fortunate because Davenport permitted his new student to use a statistical study of variation on *Aster prenanthoides*, the plant on which Shull had already worked for his undergraduate thesis project. In 1904 Shull obtained a Ph.D. from the University of Chicago for this work. Two months later Shull was appointed to the Station for Experimental Evolution, newly founded by the Carnegie Institution of Washington at Cold Spring Harbor. Among his projects, he was sent by the Carnegie Institution to examine the celebrated claims of the breeder and plant "wizard" Luther Burbank. From 1906 to 1911 Shull spent half of his year at Santa Rosa, California, examining Burbank's work. He concluded that many of Burbank's claims were unreliable as a result of unsystematic and unscientific procedures. Finally, in 1915, Shull was offered the position of professor of botany

and genetics at Princeton University, a position he accepted and held until 1942, when he became professor emeritus. He married Ella Amanda Hollar in 1906. They had one daughter. After the death of his wife in 1907, he married Mary Julia Nicholl in 1909; they had six children.

While Shull started his career with an interest in botany, a subject he continued to teach every spring semester at Princeton, he distinguished himself as a pioneer in plant genetics and breeding. The first to describe the phenomenon called hybrid vigor, or "heterosis" in plants, Shull's work became a landmark in the history of genetics and plant breeding. Using the economically important and tractable experimental organism of maize, Shull demonstrated how Wilhelm Johannsen's concept of pure lines operated in that species. Following this, he demonstrated how progressive self-fertilization resulted in inferior inbred lines but also demonstrated how hybrid crosses between these inbred lines could result in improved and more vigorous hybrid forms. This phenomenon, which he termed "heterosis" in a lecture he delivered in Göttingen in 1914, became a key concept not only in theoretical genetics but also in applied plant breeding. Though Shull suggested a practical method for commercial production of hybrid corn in 1909, his suggestions were not put into effect until 1922 in the United States. With the increasing implementation of practical methods of producing hybrid corn, agricultural production in the United States was improved drastically, especially during the war years. Later, hybrid corn was introduced on a global scale, greatly increasing world food production.

Shull was responsible not only for demonstrating heterosis in maize but also for introducing other terms important to genetics, including the use of "gene" for "factor," "duplicate genes," and "sibs," as well as the present spelling of gene, allele, and clone, with a terminal "e." In addition to researching maize genetics, Shull worked on other plants until his retirement, including *Oenothera* (evening primrose) and *Capsella* (shepherd's purse), and showed an interest in plants like *Isoetes*. An avid conservationist, Shull was active in helping to make a wildlife sanctuary of Island Beach, New Jersey, the last undeveloped dune land in the region.

Shortly after his arrival at Princeton, Shull founded and then edited one of the foremost journals of the new field, *Genetics*. It was largely at his initiative that Princeton University Press agreed to undertake publication of this journal; and it was through his efforts to raise subsequent publication funds that publication of the journal was possible. He served as managing editor for the first ten years of the journal, 1916–1925, and served as associate editor until his death.

Shull's many honors included presidencies of the American Society of Naturalists (1917) and the Torrey Botanical Club (1947). He was also a member of the American Philosophical Society, the Ecological Society of America, the Eugenics Society of America, and the American Association for the Advancement of Science. He received the Marcellus Hartley Medal of the National Academy of Sciences in 1948 for his pioneering work in hybrid corn, the De Kalb Agricultural Association Medal in 1940, the John Scott Award of the City of Philadelphia in 1946, and the Agricultural Annual Citation for Distinguished Service to Agriculture in 1945. He was included as one of the fifty most important men in science and engineering by *Popular Mechanics'* Fiftieth Anniversary Hall of Fame in 1952.

Shull was devoted to his family, with whom he spent much leisure time. He died in Princeton, New Jersey. Shull's earlier interests in botany have largely been forgotten; he is primarily known for his pioneering work in understanding the phenomenon of hybrid vigor, in being one of the breeders of hybrid corn, and his editorship and founding of the journal *Genetics*.

• Shull's papers are located in the genetics collections of the American Philosophical Society Library in Philadelphia, Pa. The most complete biographical essay is by Herbert Parkes Riley, in *Bulletin of the Torrey Botanical Club* 82 (1955): 243–48. See also Paul C. Mangelsdorf, "George Harrison Shull," *Genetics* 40 (1955): 1–4, and Herbert Parkes Riley, "George Harrison Shull, 1874–1954," *Journal of Heredity* 46 (1955): 65–66. The interaction between Shull and Burbank is discussed by Bentley Glass, "The Strange Encounter of Luther Burbank and George Harrison Shull," *Proceedings of the American Philosophical Society* 124 (1980): 133–53. For an early history of hybrid corn and Shull's contributions to its development see A. Richard Crabb, *The Hybrid Corn Makers: Prophets of Plenty* (1948); see also H. K. Hayes, *A Professor's Story of Hybrid Corn* (1963). For a more recent account of the business history of hybrid corn see Deborah Fitzgerald, *The Business of Breeding: Hybrid Corn in Illinois, 1890–1940* (1990). Obituaries are in the *New York Herald Tribune*, 30 Sept. 1954; *Time*, 11 Oct. 1954; and *Nature*, 8 Jan. 1955.

VASSILIKI BETTY SMOCOVITIS

SHUMLIN, Herman (6 Dec. 1898–14 June 1979), producer and director, was born in Atwood, Colorado, the son of George Shumlin, a one-time farmer, factory worker, and merchant, and Rebecca Slavin. The family moved around a great deal during the early part of his life. A farming venture in Colorado failed, and the family moved to West Pullman, Illinois, when Shumlin was two years old. Financial hardships often kept the family on the move looking for work. When it was time for Shumlin to attend high school the family was in New Jersey, where he attended the Barringer School for one year before he was forced to quit and work in a factory. Shumlin was fired from the factory and labeled a "socialist" when he complained about the workers' safety. His father fostered these ideas by subscribing to a liberal newspaper for his son and prompted him to become politically active. After his father died in 1915, Shumlin supported his mother until she remarried.

Shumlin's mother loved the arts and had exposed him to the theater at an early age. When he was ten his interest in theater grew after seeing Sir Johnston Forbes-Robertson play Hamlet. Shumlin would combine the interests of his father and mother into politically active theater. He landed a job in the advertising department of Metro Pictures until 1924, when his friend Jed Harris became managing editor of the *New York Clipper* and hired Shumlin as a theater reviewer. As a reviewer he was permitted to sneak into rehearsals and spent hours learning how directors worked. He would later say he learned as much about directing during this period than in any other. The next year Shumlin reviewed films for *Billboard* magazine and then moved on to do publicity for Schwab and Mandel, an important production house, before again joining Harris, now at his own production house. Shumlin worked as a press agent alongside other up-and-comers S. N. Behrman, Arthur Kober, and Lillian Hellman.

Despite his friendship with Harris, Shumlin found the atmosphere at Harris's office stifling and left in 1927 to form his own company in partnership with Paul Streger. Their first venture was to produce *Celebrity*, which opened at the Lyceum Theatre on 26 December 1927. When it failed Streger left and Shumlin produced three other losing ventures before the depression hit Broadway hard in 1929. Shumlin did not give up on producing and in 1930 scored his first big hit with *The Last Mile* at the Sam H. Harris Theatre. His success continued when he produced Vicki Baum's *Grand Hotel* at the National Theatre. The play, which opened on 13 November 1930, was also Shumlin's directing debut and ran for 257 performances. From this time on in his career, he often performed the dual role of producer and director, and the plays he chose usually had a theme of political or social significance. Also in 1930 Shumlin married Rose Keane; they had no children.

In 1934 Shumlin reached his maturity as a director with Hellman's *Children's Hour*. The production, which opened at the Maxine Elliott Theatre on 20 November, ran into censorship problems because of its lesbian themes when it transferred to Boston. Shumlin launched a campaign that resulted in a revision of Massachusetts state laws. The play also marked the start of an important collaboration between Shumlin and the playwright. Over the next ten years he would produce and direct four other plays written by her, *Days to Come* (1936), *The Little Foxes* (1939), *Watch on the Rhine* (1941), and *The Searching Wind* (1944). He also directed the film version of *Watch on the Rhine* in 1943, with some critics calling it the best film of the year.

The collaboration with Hellman was beneficial for both parties even though not all the productions proved successful. In her introduction to a volume of her first four plays, Hellman said of Shumlin, "He has done more than interpret these plays; he has wrung from them more than was in them, and hidden things which should not be seen. . . . He is one of the few directors who believes in the play . . . who has the sharp clarity, the sensitivity, the understanding, which should be the director's gift to the play." The collaboration worked because Shumlin and Hellman shared a moralistic worldview—their commitment both to the theater and to political causes enhanced their production work.

During the production of *The Little Foxes*, the professional collaboration developed into a more intimate relationship, even though Shumlin was still married (the couple divorced in 1941) and Hellman was involved with the writer Dashiell Hammett. As the personal relationship soured, so did the professional one, and after the production of *The Searching Wind* failed, the love affair ended with Hellman and a number of critics blaming Shumlin's direction.

Despite his break with Hellman, Shumlin continued to produce and direct, mostly successfully, for the next twenty years. One critic suggested that one of Shumlin's weaknesses as a director became apparent after his successful years with Hellman: he would rush into rehearsals for plays for which he had no conviction simply to keep busy and in an effort to repeat his earlier successes. Shumlin was successful again in 1955 when he teamed with another influential director, Margo Jones, for the New York premiere production of *Inherit the Wind*. The production opened on 21 April at the National Theatre to critical success. The *New York Times* critic Brooks Atkinson said Shumlin "meticulously balanced the whole production."

Another great success for Shumlin was his last directing effort, *The Deputy*, which opened on 26 February 1964 and ran 316 performances. *The Deputy* was controversial, condemning the pope for failing to save Jews during World War II, and had been turned down by producers Billy Rose and Elia Kazan before Shumlin acquired the rights. A risky production that attracted hate mail and picketing, staging *The Deputy*, according to one critic, "was an act of bravery" and brought Shumlin a Tony Award as producer and a nomination as director.

Shumlin was authoritarian and perfectionist as a director. Eugene Earl, an actor whom Shumlin directed in *The Searching Wind*, said he was almost "always somber and in dead earnest," rarely relaxing his guard while demanding the same concentration from his casts. Julie Harris recalled that Shumlin concerned himself with what she considered minor details, which often made the actors feel trapped by such concentration on the mechanics rather than the emotions of the character. Claudia Morgan, who starred in Shumlin's production of *Wine of Choice*, said, "He ran a tight ship: there was no nonsense." In crowd scenes, Shumlin would give each actor lines and names rather than have them mumble, and he looked closely at every detail of an actor's performance. Nevertheless, Shumlin's success as a director, despite such a dictatorial approach, was based on his kind and gentle nature. The actors saw him as basically a kind man who did not raise his voice or have temper tantrums as many directors did unless he truly felt the actors were not giving their best effort. Actors claimed they tolerated his strict directing style because they liked the man.

Some actors benefited from Shumlin's distinct style. Tallulah Bankhead, who portrayed Regina in *The Little Foxes*, recalled in her autobiography that Shumlin could be extremely sensitive with his actors, but he would not tolerate their questioning of his instructions. Despite their frequent disagreements during rehearsals, Shumlin taught Bankhead a great deal about acting—he knew how to get the best performances he could from his actors. A part of Shumlin's contribution to theater was personal—his personal interest and encouragement of actors such as Bankhead, Paul Muni, and Ethel Barrymore enriched their performances.

As a director Shumlin's strengths lay in his ability to focus on the script and the importance he placed on casting. With the exception of two plays, Shumlin directed only new scripts and worked closely with the authors to communicate the heart of the meaning of their works clearly to audiences. Shumlin believed the director should be invisible—the play speaks for itself and the director's goal should be to serve the play. Consistent with his meticulous manner of directing, Shumlin would not produce a show unless he had the cast he had envisioned. He sought actors in summer stock and off-Broadway and discovered Ann Revere, Ann Blythe, and Richard Waring, among others.

Shumlin's major limitation as a director was his inability to visualize a set based on the designs or models and to communicate to his designers what he wanted. Shumlin worked with well-known designers such as Jo Mielziner and Howard Bay, but tension often resulted when Shumlin first saw a set that he believed did not resemble his interpretation of the design.

Whatever his limitations, Shumlin was a successful producer and director. A key figure on Broadway for four decades, he directed thirty-eight plays and produced twenty-eight, serving as both producer and director of twenty-one of these productions. Shumlin's chief contribution as a director/producer is in his encouragement and respect of the playwright and his willingness to bring new plays to the stage. Hellman was only one of the playwrights he encouraged and collaborated with on their early efforts. Others included Rolf Hochhuth, Aimee Stuart, and James Bridie. Shumlin's belief that the theater is where convictions and ideas should be challenged and explored led him to produce and direct plays that not only were artistically sound but also often socially or politically motivating. Shumlin died in New York City.

• The most thorough sources of Shumlin's life and career are Gary Blake, "Herman Shumlin: The Development of a Director" (Ph.D. diss., City Univ. of New York, 1973), and Samuel L. Leiter, *The Great Stage Directors* (1994). Other useful sources are Ted Goldsmith, "The Man behind *Grand Hotel*," *Theatre Magazine*, Mar. 1931, pp. 13ff; Murray Schumach, "Monkey Trial Staged," *New York Times*, 17 Apr. 1955; and Enid Bagnold, "The Flop," *Atlantic Monthly*, Oct. 1952, p. 62. A complete listing of his stage and film work can be found in the *Biographical Encyclopedia and Who's Who in the American Theatre* (1984). Sources that deal specifically with Shumlin's relationship with Hellman (both professional and personal) include Richard Maney, "From Hellman to Shumlin to Broadway," *New York Times*, 9 Apr. 1944; Richard Moody, *Lillian Hellman* (1972); Carl Rollyson, *Lillian Hellman: Her Legend and Her Legacy* (1988); and Hellman's memoirs, collectively titled *Three* (1979). An obituary is in the *New York Times*, 15 June 1979.

MELISSA VICKERY-BAREFORD

SHURCLIFF, Arthur Asahel (19 Sept. 1870–12 Nov. 1957), landscape architect, was born in Boston, Massachusetts, the son of Asahel Milton Shurtleff, an inventor and manufacturer of surgical instruments, and Sarah Ann Keegan. Shurcliff changed his last name in 1930, in order, he said, to have it conform to the ancient spelling of the family name. He and his four siblings spent their early years in a loving environment, with parents who fostered an appreciation of painting, poetry, music, and all forms of creative endeavor. His father taught the boys carpentry, an avocation Shurcliff pursued throughout his life. Winters the family dwelt in Boston; summers were spent in various country retreats where Shurcliff developed a deep appreciation for the natural world.

Shurcliff, who described himself as a "natural born mechanic," studied mechanical engineering at the Massachusetts Institute of Technology, in preparation for entering the family business. He states in his memoirs, however, that his interest in the natural world—in camping, mountain climbing, bicycling, landscape painting—along with the works of Emerson and Thoreau, drew him "toward scenery, toward planning and construction for scenes of daily life." After graduating from MIT in 1894, Shurcliff headed for the Brookline, Massachusetts, offices of the most prominent practicing landscape architect in the United States, Frederick Law Olmsted (1822–1903). There the gifted Charles Eliot guided Shurcliff to further studies at Harvard University where, with Eliot's aid, he pieced together a program ranging from fine arts to surveying, emerging with a second B.S. in 1896. At that time he sailed abroad to study parks, gardens, and planning, a pattern he repeated periodically throughout his life.

Shurcliff spent the next eight years in the Olmsted firm. In 1899 he aided Frederick Law Olmsted, Jr. (1870–1957), in establishing a four-year landscape program at Harvard, the first in the nation. He was a member of the faculty there until 1906. In 1904 he set up his own practice in Boston, and the following year he married Margaret Homer Nichols. Both Shurcliffs, influenced by the Arts and Crafts Movement, pursued wood carving and furniture building together throughout their lives, also teaching the craft to their six children.

Initially Shurcliff emphasized his experience as a town planner; as early as 1907 he was making major highway studies for the Boston Metropolitan Improvement Commission and the Massachusetts State Highway Commission. This resulted in numerous commissions for town planning in surrounding communities. During World War I Shurcliff designed model war housing in Bridgeport, Connecticut. He also laid out industrial towns and mill villages. For example, as early as 1910, and again in 1918–1919, he provided plans for highway construction in Hopedale, Massachusetts,

and sited over one hundred single- and two-family structures there. In 1918 he designed street patterns and decided on the location of schools, playgrounds, mills, and approaches in the new town of Bemiston, Alabama. For many years, beginning in 1905, he served as consultant to the Boston Parks Department and the Metropolitan District Commission. And over the years he received multiple commissions for public works in the Boston area, including the Charles River Basin and Storrow Drive, as well as reservoirs, the zoological gardens, and recreational spaces from small parks to large reservations.

In addition to creating hundreds of private gardens, Shurcliff contributed to the design of many college campuses including Johns Hopkins, Wellesley, Amherst, and Brown, and of several secondary schools such as Groton, Deerfield, and St. Paul's.

The single largest commission of his career, and certainly one of the most important, began in 1928 when he was asked to produce the initial planning report for the restoration of Williamsburg, Virginia, undertaken by John D. Rockefeller, Jr. Shurcliff served as chief landscape architect for Colonial Williamsburg until 1941. In this capacity he was able to integrate his avocational interests in American history, handicrafts, and old garden design, with the professional skills of design and planning acquired in over thirty years of practice. In 1938 he participated in the initial planning and siting of Old Sturbridge Village in Massachusetts.

He was a member of the American Society of Landscape Architects, serving as president from 1928 to 1932. He was a member of the American City Planning Institute and of the Massachusetts Art Commission. He died in Boston.

Shurcliff lived and worked during a transitional moment in American life, when the country was moving from its nineteenth-century agrarian culture to the fast-paced industrial and urban demands of the twentieth century. Imbued with a profound love of the natural world, and trained in the Olmsted tradition, he was prominent among the next generation of landscape architects who extended that tradition into the community and into the rapidly changing landscape. His long and prolific professional career is characterized by his ability to infuse his sensitivity to the beauty of the natural world into all of his professional work, combining it with a practical and sophisticated knowledge of engineering and a felicitous capacity to integrate the two into a harmonious whole.

• Shurcliff's papers are located at the Massachusetts Historical Society, the Loeb Library of the Harvard Graduate School of Design, and the Archives and Records Office of the Colonial Williamsburg Foundation. His memoirs, written in the winter of 1943–1944 and the summers of 1946 and 1947, were collected in *Autobiography of Arthur Asahel Shurcliff 1870–1957*, which was printed in 1981 by his daughter Sarah Shurcliff Ingelfinger and his grandson Arthur Asahel Shurcliff II. His own publications include four books of reflections and numerous magazine articles.

ELIZABETH HOPE CUSHING

SHUSTER, George Nauman (27 Aug. 1894–25 Jan. 1977), educator and Catholic layman, was born in Lancaster, Wisconsin, the son of Anton Schuster, stone mason, and Elizabeth Nauman. (Shuster later changed the spelling of his surname.) He graduated from the University of Notre Dame in 1915. He served with U.S. Army Intelligence in France during World War I (1917–1919), taught English at Notre Dame for five years, and in 1924 married a former student, Doris Parks Cunningham.

Moving to New York soon after, Shuster taught English at St. Joseph's College for Women in Brooklyn (1924–1935) and joined the staff of the Catholic weekly, *The Commonweal*, at the time of its third issue, in November 1924. He remained with the journal for twelve years, contributing articles and reviews, often under pseudonyms, and serving first as assistant editor and then, starting in 1928, as managing editor. He made three trips to Europe in the 1930s and published widely on German culture and the rise of Adolf Hitler. He resigned from the journal in 1937 in disagreement with *The Commonweal*'s support of General Francisco Franco in the Spanish Civil War.

In 1939 Shuster was appointed acting president of Hunter College, one of the largest colleges for women in the world. After a year he was named president. Also that year he received a Ph.D. in English literature from Columbia University. During the two decades of his presidency, Hunter College's liberal arts curriculum was strengthened, professional courses or what he termed "vocational inlays" were added, a concert series and opera workshop were begun, President Franklin D. Roosevelt's nearby townhouse was purchased as a social and religious center for the college, a School of Social Work was established, and the college was opened to men as well as women.

During his years at Hunter, Shuster was also drawn into public service. He served on the General Advisory Committee of the State Department's Division of Cultural Relations after 1941, was a member of two Enemy Alien Boards in 1942, and chaired a war department commission sent to Europe in 1945 to interview prominent German prisoners of war. In 1950 and 1951 he served as land commissioner (governor) of Bavaria for the American occupation and represented the United States on the executive board of UNESCO from 1958 to 1962.

Shuster returned to Notre Dame in 1961 as assistant to the president, Rev. Theodore M. Hesburgh, CSC, and director of a newly established institute, the Center for the Study of Man in Contemporary Society. Until his retirement in 1969, he sponsored significant studies of Catholic elementary and secondary education, the relationship of science to religion, population problems and trends, poverty and delinquency, and social and economic conditions in Latin America.

Shuster and his wife, who were married fifty-two years, had one son; several foster children also lived with them from time to time. He was the author of approximately twenty books and 300 articles, chiefly in literature, history, and public affairs. Kindly, soft-spoken, and deeply religious, he was often a gentle dissenter from the more conservative stands of the Catholic Church. He died in South Bend, Indiana.

• The major collection of Shuster's papers is preserved in the Archives of the University of Notre Dame, although important materials are also available in the Hunter College Archives and in the pertinent government collections in the National Archives. Valuable autobiographical studies are his "Spiritual Autobiography," in *American Spiritual Autobiographies*, ed. Louis Finkelstein (1948); "An Autobiography," in *Leaders in American Education: The Seventieth Yearbook of the National Society for the Study of Education*, ed. Robert J. Havighurst (1971); and especially, *The Ground I Walked On* (2d ed., 1969). Other significant publications of Shuster include *The Catholic Spirit in Modern English Literature* (1922), *The Catholic Spirit in America* (1927), *The Germans: An Inquiry and an Estimate* (1932), *Strong Man Rules: An Interpretation of Germany Today* (1934), *Like A Mighty Army: Hitler versus Established Religion* (1935), *The English Ode from Milton to Keats* (1940), and *Catholic Education in a Changing World* (1967). Biographical information can also be found in Thomas Blantz, "George N. Shuster and American Catholic Intellectual Life," in *Studies in Catholic History*, ed. Nelson H. Minnich et al. (1985); William M. Halsey, *The Survival of American Innocence: Catholicism in an Era of Disillusionment, 1920–1940* (1980); and Vincent P. Lannie, "George N. Shuster: A Reflective Evaluation," also in Havighurst, ed., *Leaders in American Education*.

THOMAS E. BLANTZ

SHUTE, Denny (25 Oct. 1904–13 May 1974), golfer, was born Hermon Densmore Shute in Cleveland, Ohio, the son of Hermon Bryce Shute and Alice Densmore. Shute began playing golf at age three with miniature clubs made for him by his father, who had been a clubmaker in England before emigrating to the United States and becoming head professional at the Huntington, West Virginia, Country Club. Shute competed with members when he was only five. As a teenager, when he could find no opponents, he played against himself, using two balls and playing right-handed and left-handed.

Shute first played in a national championship, the U.S. Amateur, in 1923, advancing to the third round before losing. After winning state amateur championships in West Virginia in 1925 and Ohio in 1927, he turned professional in 1928. He soon tasted victory and disappointing defeats. He won two Ohio open championships in 1929 and 1930, but he lost in the U.S. Open in 1929 because he did not equal par on the last three holes. After claiming his first national title in 1930 at the Los Angeles Open, he then lost in the final match of the 1931 P.G.A. championship. By this time Shute had developed a permanent reputation as good with a short game, cautious and cool in temperament, and a golfer and man colorless and plain. In April 1930 he married Hettie Marie Elizabeth Potts; they had one child.

At the 1933 British Open at St. Andrews, Shute played golf that better embodied his skill and spirit than at any other time in his career. Sportswriters paid him little attention, however, filing their copy largely on Craig Wood, a powerful driver, and other frontrunners. Shute posted four consecutive 73s to tie Wood at the end of regulation play. In the thirty-six hole play-off, although usually forty to sixty yards behind Wood off the tee, Shute led early and won by five strokes, demonstrating "mastery of his irons and the consistency of his rusty old putter"; his very conservative game, one writer noted, was a "most utterly safe and blameless golf." It was a satisfying victory for him as the first American to win the British Open in thirteen years.

Shute did not play regularly on the tour through the 1930s because his duties as the head professional at the Llaanerch Country Club near Philadelphia consumed much of his time and energy. He remained, nonetheless, an excellent player, capturing the PGA title in 1936 and 1937, which made him the last golfer to win it in consecutive years up to the mid-1990s. He nearly won the 1939 U.S. Open, tying Bryon Nelson and Craig Wood in regulation play before losing in the playoff. He played on the Ryder Cup squad for four years in the 1930s, and he defeated U.S. Open champions Jimmy Thompson and Ralph Guldahl in 1933 and 1937 challenge matches, but he lost to Henry Cotton, the British Open Champion, in a 1937 match touted as a contest to decide the world's unofficial championship.

After finishing second in the U.S. Open in 1941, Shute seldom played on the tour. For twenty-seven years beginning in 1945 he served as the head professional at the Portage Country Club near Akron, Ohio, and earned a reputation as an excellent instructor. Altogether, he won sixteen professional events, including two PGA tournaments and a British Open, as well as local and state competitions. He was elected to the PGA Hall of Fame in 1957. Although not a dramatic figure, he was one of a company of good golfers who increasingly popularized the professional tour in the 1930s.

In many respects Shute complemented his golfing era of players in long-sleeved white shirts, bow ties, and often presenting a tone of grace and formality. He remained a model of reserve and quiet concentration in play. Slender at 5'11" and about 140 pounds, he did not hit long off the tee, but he was deft around the green. He played an extremely conservative game, saying once that "I learned never to take a chance." But he was a fierce competitor, one opponent calling him "a mean, brutal fellow" on the links. A former caddy recalled that Shute was not a pleasant golfer to carry clubs for: "He would fix a frozen smile in his face for the gallery and all the while would be giving me the devil down the fairway for misguiding him." He was always a determined player. On one occasion, resolved to break his father's recent record of thirty-one for nine holes, he played six rounds in one day and finally shot a thirty. Late in his forties, after Ben Hogan had shot a good round in the National Golf Day competition, he went out at Portage, "just for the challenge," and fired a sixty-one.

Shute, an avid stamp collector, used every tour event to search for good copies of modestly priced nineteenth-century U.S. stamps. As in his golf, he displayed tenacity and caution. He was especially shrewd in assessing stamps by their cancellations and perforations. He amassed a collection valued at more than $200,000 on his death. One sportswriter has seen in his approach to his hobby a conservatism typical of his golf, suggesting that had he been more adventuresome in avocation and vocation, he might have accomplished more. Shute died in Akron, Ohio.

• Professional golf in Shute's era is described in Benjamin G. Rader, *American Sports: From the Age of Folk Games to the Age of Spectators* (1983). Contemporary accounts of his personality and play appeared in "British Open Golf Captured by Shute" and "Shute Began to Swing Golf Clubs at 13," *New York Times*, 9 July 1933; Bernard Darwin, "Shute Is Hailed as Real Champion," *New York Times*, 9 July 1933; editorial, *Akron Beacon Journal*, 15 May 1974; Pat Jordan, "Shopwalk," *Sports Illustrated*, 5 May 1975, p. 4; and Jack Patterson, "Denny Shute's Achievements Will Live On," *Akron Beacon Journal*, 14 May 1974. Obituaries are in the *Akron Beacon Journal* and the *New York Times*, both 14 May 1974.

CARL M. BECKER

SHUTE, Samuel (12 Jan. 1662–15 Apr. 1742), British army officer and colonial governor of Massachusetts and New Hampshire, was born in England, the son of Benjamin Shute and Patience Caryl, daughter of the Reverend Joseph Caryl, the noted Nonconformist minister and a brother of Lord Barrington. Shute was educated by the Puritan Charles Morton, admitted to the Middle Temple on 23 November 1683, and on 12 December 1683 was accepted in Christ's College, Cambridge, but did not receive a degree. Shute continued his education at Leyden and then served as a captain in the War of the Austrian Succession (1689–1697).

A captain in Marlborough's army during the War of the Spanish Succession (1702–1713), Shute was wounded at the 1704 battle of Blenheim. In 1712 he was promoted to lieutenant colonel of the Third Dragoon Guards. In April 1716 the Whig ministry named Shute as governor of Massachusetts and New Hampshire; the post was a reward for Shute's military service. The Whigs had been in control of government and patronage since the 1714 accession of George I to the British throne. Shute arrived in Boston on 4 October 1716 and was warmly welcomed by the Puritan minister Cotton Mather. Shute, who was a Nonconformist by birth, by then was a member of the Church of England. To placate the Massachusetts Puritans, Shute attended services in both Puritan and Anglican churches. Despite his efforts to appease local leaders, Shute immediately became embroiled in a struggle for power with the assembly. Massachusetts, virtually a self-governing commonwealth until the loss of its charter in 1684, resented the limited autonomy granted to it with the new 1691 charter. Since that date the assembly had been engaged in an ongoing attempt to limit the authority of the royal governor while enhancing its own.

The first issue to divide the governor and assembly was related to the lack of specie in the colony. The assembly, during the War of the Spanish Succession (known in the colonies as Queen Anne's War), issued paper bills of credit, including £40,000 to finance a military expedition against Canada. The colony had little or no gold or silver, the medium of exchange in the greater market economy of which it was a part. The war, which ended in 1713, was followed by a severe economic depression and rampant inflation, devastating to those on fixed incomes.

Solutions to the crisis were offered by various factions, with political allegiances frequently determining an individual's conviction. One group, headed by Boston physician and assemblyman Elisha Cooke, Jr., favored the establishment of a private bank to issue paper bills of credit. An opposing faction rejected the idea of a bank and wanted the assembly to authorize another emission of bills, with the money to be loaned to people with collateral. The interest from the loans was to be applied to the support of government. A third and smaller group favored a return to the exclusive use of gold and silver.

Shute quickly allied with the group that favored a new emission of paper money, thereby alienating the supporters of the bank and their influential leader Cooke. The majority of the representatives agreed with Shute and voted to authorize a loan of £100,000. Despite the influx of cash, trade did not improve, and the economy worsened as the paper money rapidly depreciated. Shute was paid with local currency, and the assembly refused to raise his salary to compensate for depreciation. The assembly ignored his call to enact measures to halt the inflation. Many representatives were themselves in debt and content with the prospect of repaying loans with depreciated currency. The frugal assembly, which had the Crown-assigned task of raising money for all government expenses, also rejected Shute's demand that it guarantee him a permanent salary, as stated in the Crown's instructions. Instead the assembly demanded the right to audit the governor's warrants on the treasury.

Shute recognized that Cooke was the leader of the opposition. His resentment of Cooke escalated when the latter in 1718 attacked the honesty of the Crown's surveyor general, John Bridger, whose responsibilities included preventing Maine residents from cutting white pine trees, reserved by law for the exclusive use of the Royal Navy. Cooke charged that Bridger had taken bribes and permitted cutting to occur. Bridger filed a complaint with Shute, who defended his actions, while Cooke enlisted the backing of the assembly.

The split between Shute and Cooke widened when Shute heard that Cooke had called him a "blockhead." In retaliation, Shute removed Cooke from his post as clerk of the supreme court and in 1718 refused to let Cooke serve when the legislature elected him councillor. In 1720 the assembly voted Cooke its Speaker, a choice promptly rejected by Shute. Both Cooke and the assembly were furious at what they considered an invasion of the latter's rights. Shute pointed out that he had precedent for his action, because former gover-

nor Joseph Dudley had also rejected the house's choice of Speaker, none other than Cooke's own father, Elisha Cooke, Sr. On the refusal of the house to make a new selection, Shute dissolved the assembly and called new elections. When the assembly met on 13 July, its first official act was to protest the dissolution of the preceding assembly and to defend the assembly's right to select its Speaker.

Shute next asked the assembly to provide money for presents to placate the Penobscot Indians, who were threatening Massachusetts's borders. The assembly refused at first to vote any money at all for presents, and when asked to reconsider voted only the paltry sum of £10. When Indian war broke out later that year, the assembly, to conserve expenditures, voted to reduce Shute's half-year salary from £600 to £500 paid in depreciated currency. When the assembly adjourned for six days, Shute protested its action vigorously, claiming that the power to adjourn the assembly was his alone. The assembly insisted that it had the same right of self-adjournment as did the British House of Commons.

Shute's task in New Hampshire was considerably easier than in Massachusetts. Although Shute was named governor, the day-to-day governance of the province was in the hands of a lieutenant governor. Contention between opposing factions broke out over which faction would control the lieutenant governor. One faction was led by William Vaughan and Richard Waldron, who were opposed by John Wentworth and his followers. When Shute arrived in New Hampshire he found supporters of Vaughan and Waldron in control of the powerful council. Shute quickly surmised that Vaughan and Waldron had divided the colony and determined to reduce their influence by allying with Wentworth. He called assembly elections but dissolved that body when he found it was packed with opposition supporters. To counter the influence of the Vaughan and Waldron faction, he named Wentworth as lieutenant governor, a choice that was confirmed in 1717 by the king. A new assembly was called, this time with a Shute-Wentworth majority. Shute completed his triumph by suspending Vaughan from his council seat. Wentworth secured his power, and that of Shute, by naming supporters to key civil and military posts in the government.

Such a victory eluded Shute in Massachusetts, where issues were more complex and passions ran deeper. Shute unexpectedly returned to England early in 1723 after a gunshot narrowly missed him as he sat in his home. The shot, possibly an assassination attempt, led Shute to board a ship in the harbor. He was, in any event, disgusted with Massachusetts politics and determined to get backing from the ministry by filing formal complaints against the Massachusetts assembly with authorities in England. The assembly, fearful of Shute's influence, promptly dispatched Cooke to England to answer Shute's charges. Cooke's mission was fruitless as the attorney general, the solicitor general, the Board of Trade, the Privy Council, and the king all backed the royal governor. The Crown forced the Massachusetts assembly to accept an amendment to its 1691 charter in the form of an explanatory charter. This document, which further limited the powers of the Massachusetts assembly, gave the governor the right to veto the house's choice of Speaker and limited the time the assembly could adjourn itself to two days. The Massachusetts assembly feared that if it refused to accept the explanatory charter, the 1691 charter would be recalled, leading to further curtailment of its rights and privileges. In 1726 the changes were accepted by the assembly with a vote of 48 to 32.

After the decision, Shute delayed his return to Massachusetts. In 1727, with the death of George I, his commission was invalidated. George II transferred Governor William Burnet from New York to Shute's Massachusetts post. A relieved Shute remained in England, trying to collect the arrears of his salary from the Massachusetts assembly, which just as consistently refused to pay. He was awarded a Crown pension of £400 a year and remained a private citizen until his death in England. It is not known whether he married or had children.

Shute's short but frustrating career as governor of Massachusetts and New Hampshire highlights the inherent problems in colonial administration. Governors were given extensive theoretical power in their posts, more power in the colony than the monarch enjoyed in England, but lacked the means to enforce that power. They were at the mercy of the assembly, which controlled the purse strings. A governor like Shute, who refused to compromise, was at a distinct disadvantage, particularly when faced with a determined and forceful opposition leader such as Elisha Cooke. Any governor who could not raise essential money for defense from the legislature jeopardized the safety of the colony and lessened respect for the English Crown and its government.

• For Samuel Shute's correspondence and reference to him, see Noel Sainsbury et al., eds., *Calendar of State Papers, Colonial Series, America and West Indies* (1860–); *Journal of the Commissioners of Trade and Plantations* (1920–1928); William H. Whitmore, *The Massachusetts Civil List for the Colonial and Provincial Periods, 1630–1774* (1870; repr. 1969); and *Journals of the House of Representatives of Massachusetts* (1919–). See also Elisha Cooke, Jr.'s pamphlet, *A Just and Seasonable Vindication* (1720), and Cotton Mather's response, *News from Robinson Cruso's Island* (1720).

For early histories of Massachusetts that deal in part with Shute see Thomas Hutchinson, *History of the Colony and Province of Massachusetts Bay*, vol. 2, ed. Lawrence Shaw Mayo (3 vols., 1936; repr. 1970), and John Gorham Palfrey, *History of New England* (5 vols., 1859–1890). For modern works that deal with Shute's governorship, see Richard L. Bushman, *King and People in Provincial Massachusetts* (1985), and Kenneth Silverman, *The Life and Times of Cotton Mather* (1984). For Shute's career in New Hampshire, see Jere R. Daniell, *Colonial New Hampshire* (1981).

MARY LOU LUSTIG

SHUTZE, Philip Trammell, II (18 Aug. 1890–17 Oct. 1982), architect, was born in Columbus, Georgia, the son of Philip Trammell Shutze I, a banker, and Sarah Lee Erwin. His family moved to Atlanta and later West Point, Georgia, after Shutze's father was shot and killed by a deranged bank employee in 1900. In 1908, following graduation as class valedictorian from public high school in West Point, Shutze obtained a scholarship to attend the architectural program at the Georgia Institute of Technology. Concurrent with his years at Georgia Tech, Shutze was employed as a draftsman in the Atlanta firm of Hal Hentz and Neel Reid, who encouraged him to pursue further academic study. He enrolled in the School of Architecture at Columbia University in the fall of 1912, earning a second Bachelor of Architecture degree in 1913. Shutze then worked with the Hentz & Reid office until 1915, when he won the architectural design award in the American Academy's Rome Prize competition, which carried a stipend of $3,000 and three years study in Italy.

In contrast with Paris's École des Beaux-Arts formal program of architectural history, theory, and instruction, the Rome scholarships were designed "for the man approaching thirty years of age, fully developed in technique with some years of practical experience in his profession. . . . Coming after years of projects and the steady grind of preparatory work, this three-year period offers the artist a breathing spell to 'find' himself, and at the same time the opportunity to acquire culture and taste in the most inspiring environment the world possesses" (Charles Henry Cheney, "The American Academy in Rome," *Architectural Record* 31 [Mar. 1912]: 254). The architecture of the Italian Renaissance, particularly of the romantic country villas with their weathered facades, delicate coloration, and lushly landscaped terraces, proved an enduring influence on Shutze's later residential work.

Serving with the Italian Red Cross during the last years of World War I, Shutze returned to Atlanta in 1920. He again found work in the office of Hentz & Reid, now known as Hentz, Reid & Adler, increasingly supplanting an ailing Neel Reid as the firm's chief designer. During this phase of his career, Shutze was involved in the design of Atlanta's Howard Theatre (1919; demolished 1960, facade partially preserved as part of a private residence in Moultrie, Georgia), the Villa Apartments (c. 1920, extant), the Italian-style Andrew Calhoun Residence (1922, extant), the Garrison Apartments (1923, extant), and Rich's Department Store Building (1924, extant). Between 1923 and 1925 Shutze attempted to establish a practice in New York City, working briefly with architects F. Burrall Hoffman, Mott B. Schmidt, and Frank Markoe, but returned once again to Atlanta and the Hentz, Reid & Adler firm as an ultimately fatal brain tumor curtailed Neel Reid's ability to work. Between 1925 and 1926 Shutze worked on designs for the Massee Apartments in Macon, Georgia (extant), the Atlanta Athletic Club (demolished 1973), and the Joseph Rhodes residence in Atlanta's Buckhead district (extant). Following Neel Reid's death in 1926 Shutze was elevated to the position of chief designer in the reorganized firm of Hentz, Adler & Shutze.

During the next three decades, Philip Trammell Shutze designed more than 750 buildings of all varieties for Hentz, Adler & Shutze and its successor firms, Shutze, Armistead & Adler (1944), Shutze & Armistead (1945–1950), and Philip Trammell Shutze (1950–1982). Among the best known of Shutze's commercial works are Atlanta's Davison/Paxton (now Macy's) Department Store (1927, extant), an Italian Renaissance–inspired remodeling of the Citizens & Southern (now Nation's) Bank Headquarters (1929, extant), a number of suburban branch banks for the same C & S Bank, retail stores for Sears, Roebuck & Company, local exchange buildings for the Southern Bell Telephone Company in both Georgia and South Carolina, and numerous commissions for the U.S. government. Prominent institutional works include the interior remodeling of the East Lake Country Club (1927, extant), the Piedmont Driving Club (c. 1927, extant), and the Spring Hill Mortuary (1928), all in Atlanta; the Library at Wesleyan College in Macon, Georgia (1928); the Journalism Building at the University of Georgia in Athens (1934); the Harris Nurses' Home (1928), Glenn Memorial Church (1930), Whitehead Memorial Annex to the University Hospital (1945), Business Administration Building (1946), Kappa Alpha and Chi Phi Fraternity houses (dates unknown), and University Gates (date unknown), all at Atlanta's Emory University; the Temple of the Hebrew Benevolent Congregation (1931), North Fulton (County) High School (1932), and the Standard Club in Atlanta (1929); the Academy of Medicine, Atlanta (1940); additions to the Henry W. Grady High School, Atlanta (1949); and, in collaboration with the firms of A. Ten Eyck Brown, Crook & Ivey, and F. P. Smith, the Clark Howell Homes Public Housing Project (1941), also in Atlanta.

It is nevertheless Shutze's distinctive residential work, with its evocative Renaissance-inspired villas surrounded by meticulously designed, lush garden settings, that gave rise to his enduring reputation as a brilliant architectural designer. Best known among these works is undoubtedly the "Swan House," built in 1926–1928 for Edward and Emily Inman and now the property and headquarters of the Atlanta Historical Society. An amalgam of English and Italian Renaissance elements set upon a richly landscaped and terraced hillside, Swan House is perhaps the most complete realization of Philip Shutze's eclectic ethos. Another noted Atlanta residential commission, the English Regency–inspired James Goodrun House of 1929 now serves as the Southern Center for International Studies. Prominent examples of Shutze's residential work are to be found throughout Atlanta's affluent Buckhead section, as well as in Macon, Savannah, and Sea Island, Georgia, and Greenville, South Carolina.

A traditionalist by both taste and training, Philip Shutze opposed the modern movement that ultimately came to dominate postdepression American architecture. Though elected a fellow of the American Institute of Architects in 1951, his output and reputation suffered the derision of champions of modernism and neglect by the most influential of the national architectural periodicals. A reappraisal of his contribution to American architecture was first stimulated by an exhibit of his work at the Atlanta Historical Society in 1976, followed in 1977 by the publication of an essay by Henry Hope Reed in *Classical America*, which judged Shutze to be the nation's "greatest living classical architect." In 1978 Shutze received the Georgia Governor's Award for the Arts and the following year an honorary Doctor of Humane Letters from Emory University. In 1980–1981 the student chapter at Georgia Tech established the Philip Trammell Shutze Distinguished Alumni Award whose namesake became its first recipient in 1982.

A lifelong bachelor, Philip Trammell Shutze died in Atlanta. Dedicated to the philosophy and traditions of Italian Renaissance design, his elegant residential structures have at long last emerged from the obscurity imposed upon them by the dogma of the modernist movement to testify to their creator's brilliant abilities as a master of eclecticism.

• Architectural drawings and documents by Shutze and his partners are in the collections of the Atlanta Historical Society and the University of Georgia. Elizabeth Meredith Dowling, *American Classicist: The Architecture of Philip Trammell Shutze* (1989), is the most exhaustive study of Shutze's architectural accomplishments. Also of note is Henry Hope Reed, "America's Greatest Living Classical Architect: Philip Trammell Shutze of Atlanta, Georgia," *Classical American* 4 (1977): 5–46, and James Grady, *Architecture of Neel Reid in Georgia* (1973).

WILLIAM ALAN MORRISON

SIBERT, William Luther (12 Oct. 1860–16 Oct. 1935), military engineer, was born in Gadsden, Alabama, the son of William J. Sibert and Marietta Ward, farmers. He studied at the University of Alabama from 1878 to 1880 when he was appointed to the U.S. Military Academy, from which he graduated seventh in the class of 1884. Commissioned as a second lieutenant in the Corps of Engineers, he studied for an additional three years at the Engineer School of Application at Willett's Point, New York. In 1887 he married Mary Margaret Cummings, with whom he had seven sons (two of whom died as infants) and one daughter. Promoted to first lieutenant in the same year, he was assigned to harbor work at Cincinnati, Ohio, and repair of locks and dams on rivers in Kentucky. From 1892 to 1894 he worked with Colonel Orlando Metcalfe Poe on the famous Poe Lock of the Soo Canal. In 1894 he assumed independent command of the Little Rock, Arkansas, river and harbor district and was promoted to captain in 1896. Though he sought command of a volunteer unit in the Spanish-American War, he was assigned in 1898 to teach civil engineering at the Engineer School of Application.

Sent to the Philippines in 1899 to reconstruct the Manila & Dagupan Railway, he was soon made chief engineer and general manager of the line and appointed chief engineer of the Eighth Army Corps. The following year he was sent to Louisville, Kentucky, and later to Pittsburgh, Pennsylvania, with responsibility for improvements to the Allegheny, Monongahela, and Ohio rivers. In this post he maintained and repaired fourteen canal locks, built fifteen more, and constructed a nine-foot channel in the Ohio River from Pittsburgh to Cairo, Illinois. He was promoted to major in 1904. His skill, his energy, and his forcefulness in dealing with the objections of civilian transportation interests led President Theodore Roosevelt (1858–1919) to appoint him to the Isthmian Canal Commission in 1907. Although he found him "cantankerous and hard to hold" in meetings, Colonel George W. Goethals soon entrusted Sibert with the Atlantic Division of the Panama Canal project, including construction of the Gatun locks and dam, the breakwater in Colon Harbor, and seven miles of canal from Gatun to the sea. Sibert continued to clash with Goethals and to air his views to political allies, so Goethals considered firing him. The commission reported to the secretary of war that Sibert was disloyal to the project. His competence and the support of the chief of engineers saved him, and he was promoted to the rank of lieutenant colonel in 1909. A large and physically vigorous man, Sibert kept hounds on this assignment and hunted deer in the jungle. He also kept a boa constrictor to which he fed live possums.

Returning from Panama in 1914, he went immediately to China to chair a board of engineers studying flood control in the Huai River Valley for the American Red Cross and the Chinese government. The outbreak of the First World War ended the project. His wife died in 1915, the same year that Congress commended the Isthmian Commission and Sibert was promoted to brigadier general in the line of the army. He was given command of the Coast Artillery of the Pacific Seaboard. Promoted to major general in 1917 just after the United States entered World War I, he was given command of the First Division and married Juliette Roberts of Pittsburgh shortly before taking the division to France. The second senior officer in France after the American Expeditionary Force commander in chief, John J. Pershing, Sibert was handicapped by his unfamiliarity with line responsibilities and his lack of tactical command experience. Excessively dependent on his staff and interested in entrenchment rather than preparation for warfare in the open, he let his division decline in efficiency. After being rebuked by Pershing in front of fellow officers for an inadequate critique of tactical maneuvers, he was relieved of duty and sent home before the year's end to command the Southeastern Department headquartered at Charleston, South Carolina. In the spring of 1918 he was directed to create the Chemical Warfare Service out of several smaller organizations, a task he successfully completed by the war's end. His wife died later that year in the influenza epidemic. Shortly before the chemical service he commanded was made a permanent part of the army in 1920, Sibert retired to his farm in Bowling Green, Kentucky, where he bred Jersey cattle and hounds.

In 1922 he married Evelyn Clyne Bairnsfather. From 1923 to 1929 he chaired the Alabama State Docks Commission and was chief engineer and manager responsible for building an ocean terminal at Mobile. In 1928 President Calvin Coolidge named him chair of the Boulder Dam Commission examining the feasibility and economic consequences of the project that became the Hoover Dam. He died in Bowling Green.

• With J. F. Stevens, chief engineer of the Panama Canal, Sibert wrote *The Construction of the Panama Canal* (1915), a report of technical rather than autobiographical interest. The only full-length biography of Sibert is Edward B. Clark, *William L. Sibert: The Army Engineer, Major General, Retired* (1930). Useful obituaries are in the *New York Times*, 17 Oct. 1935, and the *Army and Navy Journal*, 19 Oct. 1935.

JOSEPH M. MCCARTHY

SIBLEY, Henry Hastings (20 Feb. 1811–18 Feb. 1891), soldier, congressman, and governor, was born in Detroit, Michigan Territory, the son of Solomon Sibley, a territorial delegate to Congress and justice of the Michigan Supreme Court, and Sarah Sproat. Educated at a local academy, he also received two years of tutoring in the classics. In his late teens Sibley studied law, but in 1828 he began to clerk for an army sutler and the following year for the American Fur Company. In 1834, by which time he had become the company's chief factor on the upper Mississippi, Sibley entered into a partnership with two veteran fur traders. Together, they operated trading stations at Mackinac, Michigan Territory, and Fort Snelling, Minnesota Territory.

From his earliest years in the fur trade Sibley spent much time among the Native Americans of his region. He became especially well acquainted with several tribes of the Sioux nation. About 1838 he took a Sioux wife, Red Blanket Woman, with whom he had a daughter. He lived with his Indian family in the first stone residence in the Minnesota Territory, which he built near Mendota in 1835. At some point Sibley separated from his wife and daughter, although it is reported that he continued financial support to the child. In 1843 he married Sarah Jane Steele; they had six sons and three daughters.

In the 1840s Sibley continued his trading, explored uncharted regions of the Minnesota and Wisconsin territories, and in his spare time wrote articles about frontier life for sporting magazines. In 1848 he entered Democratic party politics and was elected a delegate to Congress from Wisconsin. Taking his seat in the House of Representatives, he devoted much of his time to organizing Minnesota for statehood. From 1849 to 1853 he represented that territory in the House of Representatives. Refusing a third term, he returned to the Northwest, helped frame Minnesota's constitution, and after the territory's admission to the Union in 1858 was elected its first governor. He promoted internal improvements, cautiously fostered railroad expansion, protected public school lands, and helped to create a powerful militia.

During the second year of the Civil War Sibley was entrusted with a field command. In August 1862 several of the lower Sioux tribes, quiescent since signing treaties with the federal government in the early 1850s, rose up against the white citizens of southwestern Minnesota. Within days of the outbreak, Governor Alexander Ramsey appointed Sibley a colonel of militia and provided him with 1,600 state troops to subdue the hostiles. On 23 September, after raising the siege of Birch Coulee and marching to Wood Lake near Fort Ridgely, Sibley's troops evaded an ambush planned by Little Crow and in the fight that ensued made casualties of sixty-five Indians and forced hundreds of others to retreat. Three days later Sibley reestablished contact with the fugitives, took numerous prisoners, and freed 241 of their captives. At the general's urging, Abraham Lincoln approved death sentences for those judged most culpable for the massacre; thirty-eight were hanged en masse at Mankato, Minnesota, on 26 December. For his role in the subjugation of the marauders, Sibley was appointed a brigadier general of volunteers on 20 March 1863.

In the summer of 1863 Sibley led an expedition into the Dakota Territory, where he established garrisons and trading posts, opened trails of settlement toward Idaho, and again defeated the Sioux in a series of skirmishes. The following summer Sibley, from his headquarters at St. Paul, guarded settlements along the southern and western borders of his state. Thanks to his vigilance, anticipated raids by Sioux and Chippewa warriors failed to materialize within his District of Minnesota.

In April 1866 Sibley was mustered out of federal service as a brevet major general of volunteers. To maintain the peace he had helped to establish in the Northwest, he served for two years on a board of Indian commissioners established by President Andrew Johnson. In 1871 he returned to political office as a member of the Minnesota legislature. Residing in St. Paul, he became president of a gas company, an insurance firm, and a bank. He also served on the board of regents of the state university and helped found the Minnesota Historical Society, serving as its first president and contributing frequently to its artifact collections and publications. He died in St. Paul.

Despite his impressive list of political, commercial, and scholarly accomplishments, Sibley's place in history rests on his military campaigns against the Sioux. Apparently he received command of his first expedition because of his "understanding of the Indian character and ways" and the credibility he enjoyed among the Native Americans of his state. He urged the government to adopt a lenient policy toward the tribes of the Northwest and to fulfill the terms of the various treaties it had signed with the Sioux and Chippewas in the 1840s and 1850s. Sibley's view of treaty making, however, displayed his ambivalence about Native Americans: While he believed they should be permitted to live in peace, he wished them to remain far from

the paths of white society. When campaigning against the Sioux in 1862 and 1863, he revealed his acceptance of the racial stereotypes of his era and region. Appalled by the brutality of the "monsters in human form," he vowed to "chastise the miserable savages."

Though generally successful in the field, Sibley was neither a brilliant strategist nor an accomplished tactician. He lacked imagination and the ability to plan ahead, and he too often overestimated the numerical strength of his opponents, which he used as a pretext to obtain more troops and supplies for his district. He was also lax at reconnaissance and, unless prodded by his superiors, tended to move at a glacial pace. In battle he relied on superior firepower, especially light artillery, to carry the day. In the final analysis, therefore, Sibley was neither an influential politician nor an accomplished soldier. He made his most enduring contributions as a supporter of regional history, especially as a founder of and benefactor to his state's historical society.

• Sibley's voluminous unpublished correspondence is housed at the Minnesota Historical Society. Jane Spector Davis, comp., *Guide to . . . the Henry Hastings Sibley Papers* (1968), facilitates research and provides an insightful biography. Also at the Minnesota Historical Society are the papers of many of his military, political, and business associates, which include substantial numbers of Sibley letters, especially the Henry B. Whipple, William Pitt Murray, and Charles Powell collections. Further, the society has the papers of a score of participants in Sibley's 1862–1863 campaigns. Records of the American Fur Company covering Sibley's years with the corporation are at the Minnesota Historical Society and the Newberry Library in Chicago. Sibley's military operations are detailed in his letters and telegrams to his superiors, collected in *The War of the Rebellion: A Compilation of the Official Records of the Union and Confederate Armies* (128 vols., 1880–1901). Studies of Sibley's campaigns include Chester M. Oehler, *The Great Sioux Uprising* (1959); Kenneth Carley, *The Sioux Uprising of 1862* (1961); and Wallace J. Schutz and Walter N. Trenerry, *Abandoned by Lincoln: A Military Biography of General John Pope* (1990).

EDWARD G. LONGACRE

SIBLEY, Henry Hopkins (25 May 1816–23 Aug. 1886), Confederate general, was born at Natchitoches, Louisiana, the son of Samuel Hopkins Sibley, a parish public official, and Margaret I. McDonald. He was the grandson of the influential Louisiana planter, American Indian agent, and prominent Whig State senator John Sibley (1757–1837). When Sibley was seven his father died, and the boy was taken by his mother to live with an uncle in St. Charles, Missouri. He received an early education at the Grammar School of Miami University at Oxford, Ohio. After returning to Louisiana to live with his grandfather, who became the boy's legal guardian, he was able to obtain an appointment to the U.S. Military Academy, largely through the efforts of his influential grandfather. Although set back one year, he graduated from West Point in 1838.

Commissioned a second lieutenant in the Second Dragoons, Sibley saw action in the Second Seminole War. While on leave, he married Charlotte Kendall in

1840; they had two children. In the Mexican War, Sibley was brevetted a major for bravery at Medellin outside Veracruz and fought at Cerro Gordo, Contreras, Churubusco, and Molino del Rey. In Mexico he became temporarily snow blind while attempting an ascent of the snow-capped volcano Popocatépetl.

From 1850 to 1854 Sibley was stationed on the Texas frontier at Fort Graham, Fort Crogan, Phantom Hill on the Clear Fork of the Brazos, and Fort Belknap. While at Fort Belknap, in the early spring of 1855, he conceived the idea of the Sibley tent, which was modeled after a tepee he had observed during a visit to a Comanche village. He was sent to Kansas to help quell violence over the slavery question, and in the winter of 1857 he marched with Colonel Philip St. George Cooke to join the punitive Mormon expedition at Fort Bridger. In Utah Sibley was court-martialed as a result of a personal feud with Cooke, his regimental commander; the court-martial had no apparent effect on his career.

Sent to New Mexico Territory, Sibley was in the unsuccessful 1860 Navajo campaign and was stationed at Fernando de Taos and later at Fort Union. Resigning from the army in May 1861, he went to Richmond, Virginia, where he convinced Jefferson Davis of a grandiose plan to seize not only New Mexico but also Colorado and California for the Confederacy, in the hope that a transcontinental Confederacy would gain European diplomatic recognition. Commissioned a brigadier general, Sibley went to San Antonio, Texas, where he helped organize three regiments of Texans into the Sibley Brigade. Marching his army across the Trans-Pecos to Fort Bliss at El Paso, Sibley launched an invasion of New Mexico and defeated the Federals under Colonel Edward R. S. Canby near Fort Craig in the bloody battle of Val Verde on 21 February 1862. Moving up the Rio Grande, the "Army of New Mexico" seized Albuquerque, Santa Fe, and moved on Fort Union, a major Federal supply base. High in the Sangre de Cristo Mountains at Glorieta Pass, Sibley's Texans beat a Federal force comprising hastily recruited Union volunteers known as Colorado "Pikes Peakers" on 28 March 1862 but lost their entire supply train to a raiding party of Federals in Apache Canyon. Forced to evacuate the territory, Sibley began a disastrous retreat through the mountains west of the Rio Grande. He reached San Antonio in the summer of 1862, having lost one-third of his men in the New Mexico campaign.

Summoned to Richmond, Sibley was forced to answer charges filed against him as a result of his inebriation and poor leadership during the New Mexico campaign. After he assumed leadership of his brigade in southwestern Louisiana again in 1863, his lack of leadership and heavy drinking became especially evident during the battle of Bisland, and he was ordered court-martialed by General Richard Taylor (1826–1879). Although acquitted, he spent the remainder of the war without a command.

After the war Sibley traveled through New Orleans and Richmond on his way to join his wife in New York, where he was recruited into the Egyptian army as a general in 1869. In Egypt he was placed in charge of the construction of coastal fortifications, but because of his growing alcoholism and incompetence, he was dismissed by the khedive in 1873. Sibley spent the last years of his life in poverty in Fredericksburg, Virginia, where he lived with his daughter. He wrote magazine articles, taught French, worked on several military inventions, and continued legal efforts to obtain royalties on the Sibley tent. He died in Fredericksburg.

• Martin H. Hall, *Sibley's New Mexico Campaign* (1960), remains the definitive study of that chapter of Sibley's life. For a biography of Sibley see Jerry D. Thompson, *Henry Hopkins Sibley: Confederate General of the West* (1987).

JERRY THOMPSON

SIBLEY, Hiram (6 Feb. 1807–12 July 1888), business leader, was born in North Adams, Massachusetts, the son of Benjamin Sibley and Zilpha Davis, farmers. Sibley attended village schools in North Adams, where he worked as a sawyer and shoemaker while also honing his skills as a practical mechanic. At age sixteen he left home for the Genesee Valley of New York, where he worked briefly as a wool carder. In 1830 he set up a successful machine shop in Lima, New York, and the following year he and a partner purchased a machine shop in nearby Mendon from Giles Tinker, a fellow North Adams native. Sibley remembered Tinker's daughter, Elizabeth, from his youth, and married her in 1833. The couple had five children. Between 1831 and 1837 Sibley supervised a team of eighty artisans who manufactured wool carding machinery and agricultural implements. In 1838 Sibley moved to Rochester, New York, where he expanded the range of his activities still further by engaging in banking and real estate. Between 1843 and 1847, he also served as sheriff of Monroe County.

Sibley's involvement with electric telegraphy grew logically from his residence in Rochester. In this period Rochester was a thriving wheat-processing center in which up-to-date commodity price information was a critical business asset. Like several of his Rochester neighbors, including Henry O'Rielly and James D. Reid, Sibley recognized that the telegraph could greatly increase the speed and reliability of this information, thus ensuring the fortunes of those entrepreneurs who could exploit it in a systematic way.

Sibley's first major foray into the telegraph industry came in 1849, a mere five years after Samuel F. B. Morse had demonstrated its commercial feasibility. At the suggestion of a friend, Sibley secured control of certain telegraph patents held by inventor Royal House. Two years later Sibley established the New York & Mississippi Valley Printing Telegraph Company, using House's patents to avoid a legal challenge from Morse. Sibley quickly recognized that Morse's technology was superior to House's and consequently bought a stake in Morse's patents as well. Sibley's goal was not merely to establish one more telegraph line but, rather, to combine the various lines west of Buffalo into a consolidated system. Sibley reasoned that if he could gain control of the principal lines in the West, he could generate enough revenue to cover his costs. Although his vision was greeted with considerable skepticism by his Rochester backers, Sibley's confidence ultimately prevailed, and in 1854 he secured $100,000 in investment capital, a considerable sum for the day.

After a few lean years Sibley's idea proved sound. By obtaining key patents, securing favorable contracts with railroads, and outmaneuvering his principal rivals, Sibley established a formidable enterprise. In 1856 his firm became the nucleus of Western Union, with Sibley as its first president. Although Sibley's former competitor, Ezra Cornell, got the honor of naming the new firm, this was strictly a consolation prize, since it was Sibley, rather than Cornell, who had made the key strategic decisions that resulted in the consolidation.

Sibley quickly oversaw the further consolidation of the industry by drafting a legally binding agreement known as the "six-party contract" or the "Treaty of the Six Nations" in 1857. This agreement laid the groundwork for the formal establishment of the North American Telegraph Association (NATA) one year later. NATA regulated interfirm competition until 1866 when Western Union bought out its leading competitors to become the first national monopoly in the United States.

Sibley's interests in telegraphy extended beyond the consolidation of existing lines. In 1857 he supported the construction of a transcontinental telegraph, and in 1860 he helped secure passage of federal legislation that subsidized the construction of a telegraph line from Omaha, Nebraska, to the West Coast. Sibley bid on the contract, secured it, and oversaw the construction of the line, which was completed in October 1861, thus rendering the Pony Express, the transcontinental horse express that a rival group of entrepreneurs had established the previous year, virtually obsolete.

Having linked the Atlantic and the Pacific by telegraph, Sibley soon turned his attention to Europe. Like many of his contemporaries, he doubted the technical feasibility of Cyrus W. Field's Atlantic telegraph, proposing instead an alternative way of reaching Europe by way of Alaska, Siberia, and the Bering Strait. To smooth the way, in 1864 Sibley traveled to St. Petersburg to meet Czar Alexander II, eventually securing Russian approval for the venture. Unfortunately, he had already begun to string wires across Siberia when news of Field's success rendered the project superfluous, saddling Western Union with a considerable loss. Sibley's project was not a total failure, however, since it enabled him to learn, during a casual conversation in St. Petersburg with a Russian diplomat, that the Russian government would be willing to sell Alaska to the United States for a surprisingly reasonable price. Sibley passed this information on to Secretary of State William Seward who, already thinking along similar lines, ultimately negotiated the Alaska purchase in 1867.

Sibley's active involvement in the telegraph industry ceased with his retirement as Western Union president in 1865. During the final two decades of his life, Sibley invested widely in railroads, timber stands, salt mines, and various other industrial enterprises. His most notable business venture during this period began in 1875, when he purchased Briggs & Brothers, one of the many agricultural supply firms located in Rochester.

Sibley renamed the firm Hiram Sibley & Company and quickly turned it into one of the most innovative firms of its kind in the United States by marketing seeds to 40,000 retail outlets throughout the country. Sibley's land holdings during this period were also significant and included experimental farms in Canada, England, France, Germany, the Netherlands, and Italy; a 3,500-acre reclaimed swamp in upstate New York; and the Burr Oaks Farm in central Illinois, an enormous 17,000-acre tract upon which Sibley grew hybrid corn and peas.

Plain spoken and blunt, Sibley was an excellent conversationalist who was widely praised for his energy, determination, and business acumen. While Sibley himself had little formal schooling, he placed great faith in education as a tool for self-advancement. He contributed generously to Cornell University, where he established the Sibley College of Mechanical Arts, or what is now the Sibley College of Mechanical Engineering. "One thing is damn sure," Sibley declared, in explaining his bequest, "you can't take away from a fellow what he puts into his head and into his hands" (Bishop, p. 97). Sibley also donated large sums to various public institutions in Rochester, including the University of Rochester, to which he gave a library.

Sibley died in Rochester. Though his interests were varied, his most notable contribution remains his pivotal role in the consolidation of the telegraph industry. More than any other single individual, Sibley transformed Western Union from a struggling regional firm into a cornerstone of the national communications infrastructure.

• There is a large collection of Sibley's papers at the University of Rochester. Additional correspondence can be found in the Ezra Cornell papers at Cornell University. The fullest account of Sibley's life is Harper Sibley, Jr., "The Biography of Hiram Sibley" (B.A. thesis, Princeton Univ., 1949). Among its contributions is Harper Sibley's persuasive debunking of the frequently repeated story that Sibley played a major role in securing congressional support for Morse's telegraph. See also Hiram W. Sibley, "Memories of Hiram Sibley," *Rochester Historical Society Publication Fund Series* 2 (1923): 127–34. On Sibley's role in the telegraph industry, the best source is Robert Luther Thompson, *Wiring a Continent* (1947). For additional details, see Robert Sobel and David B. Sicilia, *The Entrepreneurs: An American Adventure* (1986), and James D. Reid, *The Telegraph in America* (1879). On Sibley's role in the purchase of Alaska, see Ronald J. Jensen, *The Alaska Pur-*

chase and Russian-American Relations (1975). On his role as a philanthropist, see Morris Bishop, *History of Cornell* (1962). An obituary is in the *New York Times*, 13 July 1888.

RICHARD R. JOHN

SIBLEY, John (19 May 1757–8 Apr. 1837), physician and Indian agent, was born in Sutton, Massachusetts, the son of Timothy Sibley and Anne Waite, possibly farmers. After medical study under Dr. John Wilson, he served as surgeon's mate with the American forces during the Revolution. At war's end he entered practice at Great Barrington (Mass.) and in 1780 married Elizabeth Hopkins, with whom he had two children. Ever restless, in 1784 he moved his family to Fayetteville, North Carolina, where he briefly published the Fayetteville *Gazette*. Following the death of his first wife in 1790, he married Mary White Winslow, a widow who bore him two more children, but the union seems to have been an unhappy one, and in July 1802 he resettled in Louisiana, Mary remaining in North Carolina until her death in 1811.

A journey up the Red River in March 1803 so committed Sibley to the region that he established himself permanently at Natchitoches, the oldest and most western settlement in the still Spanish-controlled colony, where he became surgeon to the American troops stationed at Fort Claiborne after the Louisiana Purchase. William C. C. Claiborne, governor of the Territory of Orleans, early on became Sibley's champion, extolling his knowledge of the western country and its Indian population in letters to Washington and naming him to his own advisory council. In 1805 Sibley sent a copy of his journal of the Red River exploration to General Henry Dearborn, secretary of war, and soon thereafter directed to President Thomas Jefferson his "Historical Sketches of the Several Indian Tribes in Louisiana South of the Arkansas River, and between the Mississippi and the River Grande," together with a series of reports on surveys he had made as far west as Santa Fe. These proved so valuable to the president in his intensive search for information on the newly acquired Louisiana that he appointed Sibley in October 1805 to the post of Indian agent for Orleans Territory and the region south of the Arkansas River. At the president's request, Sibley also prepared compilations of the vocabularies of the Indian tribes of the territory, but the extent of his surveys is uncertain. His questioning of old settlers in the Natchitoches area led to discovery of a manuscript copy of Bernard de la Harpe's early eighteenth-century *Journal Historique de L'Etablissement des Francais à la Louisiane*, which both Jefferson and James Monroe would rely on extensively in their arguments defending American positions in the southwestern boundary disputes with Spain.

From the beginning of his residency at Natchitoches, Sibley worked assiduously to block Spanish influence along the American border, enticing Indian tribes of the area to friendship with the United States and arguing for annulment of the agreement creating the Neutral Ground between Texas and the territory of the United States. He worked closely with William

Shaler, appointed by Secretary of State James Monroe to report on revolutionary movements in Mexico, gave open support to Jose Bernardo Gutierrez and Augustus William Magee in their attempts to liberate Texas from Spanish control, and provided Washington with the most detailed account of their activities in Mexico from 1812 to 1813. These efforts and his success in diverting Indian trade from Mexican markets to the United States factory at Natchitoches led Nemisio Salcedo, commandant of New Spain's Interior Provinces, to denounce him as "a revolutionist, the friend of change, and a most bitter enemy of public peace" (Garrett, vol. 45 [1941]: 289).

Some of Sibley's activities, such as his sponsorship of an 1808 trading expedition into what was clearly Spanish territory, began to raise questions in Claiborne's mind as to his reliability, doubts that grew with charges in the New Orleans newspapers that Sibley had abandoned his family in North Carolina and was planning a bigamous marriage in Natchitoches. Jefferson refused to move on these unproven allegations and Sibley retained his position, but for reasons still not clear his tenure as Indian agent was ended in January 1815.

Following his removal, Sibley remained active in Louisiana affairs, serving as Natchitoches justice of the peace, parish judge, captain of militia, and member of the state senate. Joining Colonel James Long's 1819 raid into Texas, he participated in the taking of Nacogdoches and acted briefly as a member of the supreme council of the captured post before returning to his plantation at Grand Ecore in Natchitoches to expand his flourishing business interests there. A highly successful planter, he shipped the first Red River cotton to New Orleans in 1810, engaged in the production of salt from Drake's Salt Lick near Natchitoches, and developed an extensive cattle ranching enterprise.

In 1813 Sibley married Eudalie Malique of Louisiana, mother of his last four children. He died at his plantation in Natchitoches.

• Letters from Sibley may be found in the Thomas Jefferson Papers at the Library of Congress, in the records of the adjutant general at the National Archives, and in collections held by the Missouri Historical Society, the American Antiquarian Society, and Lindenwood College, St. Charles, Mo., which also has segments of a journal kept by him during his life in Louisiana, a portion of which has been published in G. P. Whittington, "Dr. John Sibley of Natchitoches, 1757–1837," *Louisiana Historical Quarterly* 10 (1927): 467–73. Most valuable for the period after 1820 are letters to his daughter Ann Eliza and her husband, U.S. Senator Josiah Stoddard Johnston of Louisiana, in the latter's papers in the Historical Society of Pennsylvania. His report to Dearborn in 1805 and his historical sketches of the Indian tribes may be found in *American State Papers, Indian Affairs* 1, no. 113, and in *Annals of Congress*, 9th Cong., 2d sess., 1075–1104. His anti-Spanish activities are detailed in a series by Julia Kathryn Garrett, "Doctor John Sibley and the Louisiana-Texas Frontier, 1803–1814" *Southwestern Historical Quarterly* 45–49 (1941–1946), which contains all letters from Sibley as Indian agent to the secretary of war. Sibley figures prominently as well in Clarence E. Carter, comp. and ed., *Territorial Papers of the United States*, vol. 9, *The Territory of Orleans, 1803–1812* (1940), in Dunbar Rowland, ed., *Official Letter Books of W. C. C. Claiborne, 1801–1816* (1917), and in Charles Wilson Hackett, ed., *Pichardo's Treatise on the Limits of Louisiana and Texas* (1934).

JOSEPH G. TREGLE, JR.

SIBLEY, John Langdon (29 Dec. 1804–9 Dec. 1885), librarian and historian, was born in Union, Maine, the son of Jonathan Sibley, a physician, and Persis Morse. His father's medical practice was more "extensive than gainful." Sibley was educated at home, except for two years (1819–1821) at Phillips Exeter Academy, where he was provided free tuition and living expenses. He graduated from Harvard College in the class of 1825, having supported himself in college through a series of jobs, including work in the library. Following graduation he was appointed assistant librarian to librarian Charles Folsom, for whom the position was part-time. Upon Folsom's resignation in 1826, the position was made full-time, at twice the salary, which left no funding for an assistant. Sibley enrolled in Harvard Divinity School.

Ordained at Stow, Massachusetts, in 1829, Sibley is said to have been highly successful in the pastoral side of his duties, but he missed Cambridge and its library; and he resigned in 1833. He took a room in Harvard's Divinity Hall, which he was to occupy until his marriage to Charlotte Augusta Langdon Cook in 1866, and he devoted himself largely to a number of editorial enterprises. His chief project was the *American Magazine of Useful and Entertaining Knowledge*, which began publication in 1834 and failed in 1837.

During the 1830s Sibley also performed unofficially various services for Harvard's library. He became assistant librarian in 1841, the year when the library's move into a new building, Gore Hall, necessitated another staff member. Named librarian in 1856, he continued in that position until 1877.

Throughout those thirty-six years, during which little money was available for books, Sibley labored indefatigably to build the collections by donations, particularly of source materials: pamphlets, old newspapers, and government documents. When he became assistant librarian, gifts amounted to about 160 volumes a year; by his first year as librarian the collection numbered 3,906 volumes and 2,498 pamphlets. He published annual reports that contained lists of donors, distributed a circular to alumni at commencement, graciously welcomed visitors to the library, carried on an extensive correspondence, installed exhibition cases in 1860, was always ready to travel to view a potential gift, and was quick to follow up on rumors of material being discarded.

Sibley also sought funds from alumni, and in 1859, for the first time, the library became able to purchase new publications systematically. His success can be measured statistically: volumes, exclusive of pamphlets, numbered about 41,000 in 1841 and 164,000 in 1877, while the income from endowments had increased from $250 to $170,000. The growth of the collections meant that Gore Hall became filled, and this forced on Sibley numerous makeshift arrangements for housing the collections. The inadequate amount of space and its inappropriateness for books (frost or green mold formed on the walls, depending on the season) led Sibley to urge college authorities—in vain—to act on the need for a new building.

Sibley did, however, have many administrative achievements, among them a great expansion of the library's hours. This was not, though, accomplished without repeated and strong assertions of the need for additional staff members. A major accomplishment of the Sibley years, a classed card catalog, begun in 1861, seems to have been the first publicly available card catalog in the United States. Though it was, in its execution and perhaps conception, the work of Assistant Librarian Ezra Abbot, Sibley was supportive.

Sibley's career began at a time when the library added very few books and was open only short hours. His successors made the library into a "workshop" and built collections that transformed it into one of the world's largest international libraries. Sibley was a transitional figure. He was able to build a research collection only in American history, but his tireless propagandizing on behalf of the library helped bring in the book funds that made possible later expansion of the library's scope.

Sibley's success in obtaining donations came in part from knowledge derived in editing, beginning in 1842, twelve Triennial Catalogues, works whose accuracy and completeness required a large correspondence with alumni. From 1850 to 1870 Sibley also edited Harvard's Annual Catalogue. In 1873 Sibley published the first volume of his *Biographical Sketches of Graduates of Harvard University*, generally known as "Sibley's Harvard Graduates," which continues to be compiled under the auspices of the Massachusetts Historical Society, in part with funds bequeathed by Sibley. Although nearly blind by retirement in 1877, Sibley continued his biographical work, the third volume of which, closing with the class of 1689, was published in 1885.

Sibley's very simple life enabled him to accumulate surplus funds, which he expended in personal charity to poor students and in the creation of an endowment for poor students at Phillips Exeter Academy, into which he also paid his father's bequest to him. Throughout most of the last decade of Sibley's life, a friend managed his money so successfully that additional bequests to institutions were possible. In addition to belonging to the Massachusetts Historical Society, Sibley was a member of the New England Historic, Genealogical Society and of the American Academy of Arts and Sciences. He died in Cambridge, Massachusetts.

• Sibley's library correspondence, personal diary, and other correspondence are in the Harvard University Archives, along with his Librarian's Diary. An outgrowth of Sibley's work with the Annual and Triennial catalogs was his *Notices of the Triennial and Annual Catalogues of Harvard University, with a Reprint of the Catalogues of 1674, 1682, and 1700* (1865), in which he also described his own work. Sibley also published *A History of the Town of Union* [Maine], in 1851. The most important contemporary account of Sibley's life is Andrew P. Peabody, "Memoir of John Langdon Sibley, A.M.," *Proceedings of the Massachusetts Historical Society*, 2d ser., 2 (1886), also published separately in 1886, and the same author's sketch in his *Harvard Reminiscences* (1888). Crucial for Sibley's work as librarian is Clifford K. Shipton, "John Langdon Sibley, Librarian," *Harvard Library Bulletin* 9 (1955): 236–61.

KENNETH E. CARPENTER

SICARD, Montgomery (30 Sept. 1836–14 Sept. 1900), naval officer, was born in New York City, the son of Steven Sicard, a merchant, and Lydia Hunt. His mother was the sister of U.S. Supreme Court justice Ward Hunt. Steven Sicard died in 1840, and the family moved to Lydia Sicard's home town of Utica, New York. Montgomery entered the U.S. Naval Academy in 1851 and graduated with the class of 1855.

Sicard performed sea duty in the Mediterranean and off China and was promoted to lieutenant on 31 May 1860. When the Civil War broke out he initially saw action against Confederate forts near New Orleans, Louisiana, as the executive officer of the USS *Oneida*. He then participated in the Vicksburg action and in July 1862 was promoted to lieutenant commander, the rank he retained throughout the war. In 1863 he married Elizabeth Floyd, a direct descendant of William Floyd, a signer of the Declaration of Independence. The couple had three children. Sicard next served with the *Susquehanna* off Mobile, Alabama, then transferred to the *Ticonderoga*, where he remained from early 1863 until late 1864. In the fighting at Fort Fisher, he was in command of the gunboat *Seneca*, and in the 15 January 1865 Union landing on Fort Fisher he commanded the left wing of the Second Naval Division.

Sicard's postwar career was marred by a tragic accident. After a tour of duty at the Naval Academy, he was assigned to command the *Saginaw* and was promoted to commander on 2 March 1870. During a Pacific cruise on 29 October 1870, the ship wrecked on Ocean Island. Sicard tried to get assistance by dispatching five of his crew in the *Saginaw*'s small gig to Hawaii, some 1,200 miles from Ocean Island. Only one of the five reached Hawaii. Sicard and the other survivors were rescued after spending two months on Ocean Island.

Sicard made a name for himself in the field of naval ordnance. Assigned to the New York Navy Yard after the shipwreck incident, he began working on designs for a steel, breech-loading gun. He continued his work in Washington, D.C., during 1872–1877. His efforts resulted in the U.S. Navy's first steel breech-loader, and in 1876 he published a pamphlet, *Description of Naval 3-Inch Breech-loading Howitzers*. In conjunction with a coauthor, he revised *Ordnance Instructions for the United States Navy* in 1880. Promoted to captain in 1881, he subsequently headed the Ordnance Bureau for ten years. During this duty he helped create the Washington Gun Factory and oversaw great progress in U.S. naval armament. Sicard headed the Steel Inspection Board during 1890–1891, then he returned to sea as the skipper of the monitor *Miantonomah* from 1891 until 1893.

Sicard commanded the Portsmouth, New Hampshire, Navy Yard in the first part of 1894, and in July of that year he was promoted to commodore. With this promotion, he was dispatched to the Brooklyn Navy Yard as commanding officer. Promoted to rear admiral in April 1897, he was placed in command of the North Atlantic Squadron, reflecting the high regard his superiors had for his judgment and leadership.

Sicard missed the Spanish-American War, although his guns performed well during the conflict. When the USS *Maine* exploded in Havana harbor, he was poised with his squadron at Key West, Florida. He fully expected to play a significant role in the war since his squadron would be the American mainstay against the Spanish fleet. But Sicard was stricken with malaria and, on the advice of a medical board, relinquished his position to his next in command, Captain William T. Sampson. Partially recovered, Sicard later served as president of the Naval War Board of Strategy while the war was in progress. Bitterly disappointed at his inability to see action and retain his command, he retired on 30 September 1898, when he passed the age limit. He died in Westernville, New York.

Sicard's greatest contribution was not as a battle commander but as a farsighted naval ordnance technician. The introduction of steel, breech-loading weapons was highly controversial. Traditionalists resisted the change, but Sicard's steady performance and patient explanations encouraged the guns' ultimate acceptance. He proved the merits of his new designs, and the U.S. Navy was not long in reaping the benefits of his competent work.

• Sicard's career is traced in L. R. Hamersly, *The Records of Living Officers of the U.S. Navy and Marine Corps*, 6th ed. (1898). An account of the wreck of the *Saginaw* is G. H. Read, *The Last Cruise of the "Saginaw"* (1912). The incident at Key West is recounted in W. A. M. Goode, *With Sampson through the War* (1899). Obituaries are in the *Washington Post* and the *New York Times*, both 15 Sept. 1900.

ROD PASCHALL

SICKELS, Frederick Ellsworth (20 Sept. 1819–8 Mar. 1895), inventor, was born in Gloucester County, near Camden, New Jersey, the son of John Sickels, a physician, and Hester Ann Ellsworth. He grew up in New York City where his father practiced medicine. Although his formal education was limited to grade school, he maintained an interest in mechanics and physics and read about the subjects whenever possible. At sixteen he worked briefly as a rod man for the Harlem railroad. The following year he became an apprentice machinist of James Allaire of the Allaire Works, manufacturers of steam engines, in New York City.

Sickels's reputation as an inventor is based largely on two important patents. His first and most significant invention (Pat. No. 2,631) was an improved valve gear for steam engines, which he created in 1842 while working for Allaire. With an increasing dependence throughout the nineteenth century on the steam engine to power ships as well as American industry, any method of improving its efficiency was much sought after. The volume of steam used, and therefore of fuel consumed, were critical concerns in the operation of any engine. Economy depended, in large part, on the effective operation of the valve gear. Sickels's method of lifting, tripping, closing, and damping his drop-cut-off valve was a breakthrough in steam engine design, since it admitted no more steam than was necessary, and the full advantage of the expansive force of the steam was realized. Commercial production of stationary engines using this valve gear began in about 1845 with the sale of the land rights to his patent, and Sickels profited greatly. But, much of his fortune was spent between 1850 and 1865 on an unsuccessful and costly patent infringement suit against inventor George Corliss, who also devised a drop-cutoff valve gear. Although he won in the lower courts, Sickels finally lost on Corliss's appeal to the U.S. Supreme Court. There it was determined that each inventor had an exclusive right to his particular form of valve mechanism.

His second most widely known invention was a marine steam-powered steering gear. Until the introduction of the steering gear in 1853 at the Crystal Palace in New York, two or more men were needed to operate the helm of a large ship. The Sickels gear enabled one person to guide the largest and most powerful vessel. By coupling two small steam engines and their controlling valve directly to the ship's wheel and mechanism, the engines would actually move the rudder and hold it steady until the wheel was moved again. Despite the significance of this invention, Sickels's efforts to promote the idea in the United States met with little success. Although there were several installations, he was unable to convince either maritime interests or the government of its value. The steering gear was simply perceived as being impractical. Hoping foreign enthusiasm for his invention would spur demand at home, he displayed an example of the steering gear at the London Exhibition of 1862. He fared no better there, and after four years abroad he returned home. Rejection resulted not only from the same unfounded reasoning, but also from prejudice against Americans, which had been heightened by the Civil War. While Sickels faced financial ruin and was forced to abandon the device in the early 1870s, inventors in England and Europe had picked up on the idea and were successful in marketing the concept. But by the 1890s, when the steering gear was finally in widespread use, Sickels's patent was no longer in effect.

A poor businessman, Sickels profited little from his inventions, in spite of holding some thirty patents. Although he invented such things as a machine brake (1848) and dumping scow (1882), the focus of his work was on improving the steam engine valve gear and steam steering apparatus. His interests turned toward civil engineering after the Civil War. In 1870 he devised a means for sinking pneumatic piles, and in 1892, in what was to be his last patent, he invented a method for anchoring bridge piers. In the early 1870s he joined his brother, civil engineer Theophilus E. Sickels, in work on the Union Pacific Railroad. Their most notable accomplishment was the Omaha and Council Bluffs Missouri River tubular iron-pier bridge, which opened in March 1872. In 1883, while still with the Union Pacific, he was put in charge of the construction of a plant for processing sulfate soda into caustic soda. Problems discovered in the completed plant hurt his reputation. Not only were the furnaces too small, but also the piping burst as it was buried above the frost line, equipment was defective, and several essential structures were lacking. By 1889 he was appointed chief engineer of the New York-based National Water Works Company office at Kansas City, Missouri. He held that position until his death in Kansas City.

He was survived by his wife, Rancine Shreeves Sickels and five children.

• Sickels wrote little, and the personal papers generated during the critical years of his career were lost in the great Chicago fire of 1871. Information about his patents and inventions can be found in the records of the U.S. Patent Office. Genealogical information on the Sickels family is included in original correspondence in the Frederick E. Sickels biographical file in the Division of Engineering & Industry, National Museum of American History, Smithsonian Institution. Maury Klein, *Union Pacific: Birth of a Railroad 1862–1893* (2 vols., 1987), gives brief mention of Sickels's work for the railroad and his experience with the soda works. His life and especially his role in the engineering community are discussed in detail in the "Memoirs of Deceased Members" that appeared in the *Proceedings of the American Society of Civil Engineers* 22 (1896): 130–34, and the *Transactions of the American Society of Civil Engineers* 36 (1896): 577–82. Both entries are by the noted nineteenth-century mechanical engineer Robert H. Thurston. The most informative article concerning his steam-powered steering gear appeared as part of a lengthy obituary in the *American Machinist*, 4 Apr. 1895, pp. 261–64. Other obituaries are in the *Kansas City Journal*, 9 Mar. 1895, the *Kansas City Star*, 8 Mar. 1895, the *New York Tribune*, 9 Mar. 1895, and *Scientific American*, 30 Mar. 1895.

WILLIAM E. WORTHINGTON, JR.

SICKLES, Daniel Edgar (20 Oct. 1819–3 May 1914), politician, soldier, and diplomat, was born in New York City, the son of George Garrett Sickles, a lawyer, and Susan Marsh. Young Sickles briefly attended New York University prior to entering law practice in 1840; he was admitted to the bar in 1843 and soon became affiliated with Tammany Hall, the Democratic political machine that controlled New York City.

In 1847 Sickles won election to the New York State Assembly. Six years later, in January 1853 he was appointed corporation counsel of New York City, but he resigned after eight months to become secretary of the American legation in London. While serving under

Ambassador James Buchanan, Sickles had a hand in drawing up the notorious Ostend Manifesto, the document that claimed America's right to seize Cuba, thereby embarrassing the Franklin Pierce administration. While attending a U.S. Independence Day dinner in Richmond on the Thames in 1854, in a spate of nationalistic fervor, Sickles refused to rise from his seat when a toast was offered to Queen Victoria; this affront to British dignity caused an outcry on both sides of the Atlantic.

Sickles returned to New York later in 1854 and resumed his law practice. After winning a seat in the New York Senate (1855–1857), the rising Democrat won election to the U.S. House of Representatives (1857–1861). It was during his stay in Washington, D.C., that Sickles first attracted widespread national fame. Although he had married sixteen-year-old Teresa Bagioli in 1852 and fathered a child, Sickles was widely known for his infidelity and womanizing. Teresa started an extramarital affair of her own with Philip Barton Key, the U.S. attorney for the District of Columbia and son of "Star-Spangled Banner" author Francis Scott Key. Once Sickles was informed of his wife's affair, he took matters into his own hands. On 27 February 1859, as Key loitered near Sickles's house on Lafayette Square, Sickles confronted Key and shot him dead. The murder trial resulted in his acquittal on the ground of temporary insanity, the first instance in U.S. history that this plea was used. Although most friends sympathized with Sickles, he enraged society by publicly forgiving his wife and taking her back. This act derailed Sickles's political career and led to his widespread shunning.

The Civil War revived Sickles's aspirations. Although lacking military experience, he raised a five-regiment brigade of New York troops (the "Excelsior Brigade") and was appointed brigadier general of volunteers on 3 September 1861. However, the Senate revoked Sickles's commission on 17 March 1862. President Lincoln and Secretary of War Edwin Stanton worked to reverse the Senate's decision, and Sickles was finally confirmed on 13 May 1862.

By this time Sickles's unit was part of Joseph Hooker's division, Third Army Corps, Army of the Potomac. Sickles acquitted himself well at Fair Oaks on 1 June 1862, then at Oak Grove on 25 June as the Seven Days' Battles opened. He was promoted to major general of volunteers on 29 November 1862 and commanded a division during the battle of Fredericksburg (13 Dec. 1862), where his troops were held in reserve.

Following Hooker's promotion to army command, Sickles was given the Third Corps and led his troops well at Chancellorsville (2–3 May 1863), where they located Stonewall Jackson's flanking march, moved in pursuit, then were cut off temporarily when Jackson attacked the Union right flank.

At Gettysburg on 2 July 1863, Sickles did not like the position assigned to his troops and against orders moved his corps forward to the Peach Orchard line. Before General George G. Meade could move Sickles's men back to Cemetery Ridge, Confederates assaulted the new position and Meade was forced to send reinforcements into the battle piecemeal. As his corps was withdrawing under enemy pressure, a cannonball smashed Sickles's right leg. It was amputated that night.

In the spring of 1864 Sickles busied himself with damaging General Meade's reputation by using the Joint Congressional Committee on the Conduct of the War. Meade believed Sickles had blundered at Gettysburg and indicated in his official report that Sickles had misinterpreted his orders; Sickles thought that Meade was incompetent and did not hesitate to cover his own conduct by blasting his superior before the committee. Sickles maintained that Meade never issued him orders, that his original position was weak, that his troops had saved the day by forcing a southern attack, and that Meade had wanted to retreat from Gettysburg but was prevented from doing so by Sickles's advance. Although Meade emerged from the hearings still in command, Sickles and his allies had effectively sullied Meade's reputation.

Later in 1864 Lincoln sent Sickles on a tour of the occupied South to assess the progress of Reconstruction, then dispatched him on a diplomatic mission to Colombia, South America. In September 1865 Sickles was placed in command of the reconstruction of South Carolina, then in June 1866 elevated to command of the Second Military District, which embraced the Carolinas. President Andrew Johnson relieved Sickles of command in August 1867 because Sickles defied a court order that had released men accused of slaying some Union soldiers.

Sickles then became a Republican and worked for Ulysses S. Grant's presidential bid. He was rewarded by being named minister to Spain, a position he held from 1869 to 1874. While in Madrid, Sickles worked behind the scenes to free Cuba from Spanish control. When the *Virginius*, a ship used to land munitions to aid Cuban insurrectionists, was captured by Spain in 1873 and its mostly American crew shot, the outraged Sickles, although instructed by the U.S. government not to raise any public outcry, seemed bent on helping to start a war with Spain. The Madrid government bypassed Sickles and negotiated a settlement directly with Secretary of State Hamilton Fish. Mortified at such treatment, Sickles resigned. His wife Teresa had died in 1867, and Sickles married Caroline Martinez Guerrera de Creagh in 1871. Sickles converted to Roman Catholicism and fathered two more children. He acquired the nickname "Yankee King of Spain" in part from his romantic involvement in Paris with Spain's deposed Queen Isabella II.

Meanwhile, Sickles was instrumental in forcing Jay Gould to quit the Erie Railroad after the financier had ransacked the railroad of a fortune. Sickles came back to New York and the March 1872 confrontation with Gould garnered national headlines for Sickles, who had spent years preparing for this battle.

After leaving Spain, Sickles remained in Europe until 1879, when he returned to the United States to live. His family remained in Europe, and his second wife only attempted reconciliation in 1914. In addition to his law practice, Sickles was sheriff of New York County (1890), U.S. congressman (1893–1895), and chairman of the New York Civil Service Commission (1897).

Gettysburg remained Sickles's lifelong concern. He was chairman of the New York Monuments Commission from 1886 to 1912, when he was removed amidst embezzlement charges. In addition to defending his battle record, in 1895 Sickles proposed legislation that transferred the growing Gettysburg park from a private memorial association to federal control. In 1897 he belatedly received a Congressional Medal of Honor for gallantry at Gettysburg.

Sickles's contemporaries either adored or despised him; there never seemed to be halfway ground where he was concerned. As his biographer noted, Sickles "was always in some sort of crisis, be it financial, legislative, sexual, or homicidal, and these situations invariably galvanized him into action, not always wise." Sickles died in New York City and was buried in Arlington National Cemetery.

• Major collections of Sickles papers are located in the New-York Historical Society and the New York Public Library. The Library of Congress has three boxes of Sickles's diplomatic papers, and Duke University has a letterpress book (1889–1912). Sickles himself never wrote much, although he authored articles in the *Journal of the Military Service Institute of the United States* (June and Sept. 1885 issues) and the *North American Review* (Mar. 1891). Post–Civil War newspapers contain many accounts of his speeches and comments on his controversies with General Meade and others.

The biography by Edgcumb Pinchon, *Dan Sickles: Hero of Gettysburg and "Yankee King of Spain"* (1945), is unfootnoted and overly laudatory. W. A. Swanberg, *Sickles the Incredible* (1956), still remains the best source for the general's life. For a brief review, see Edward G. Longacre, "Damnable Dan Sickles," *Civil War Times Illustrated* 23 (May 1984): 16–25. Nat Brandt, *The Congressman Who Got Away with Murder* (1991), details Sickles's murder of Key and the resulting trial. For a documented study of Sickles's role at Gettysburg and the controversy surrounding it, see Richard A. Sauers, *A Caspian Sea of Ink: The Meade-Sickles Controversy* (1989). An obituary is in the *New York Times*, 4 May 1914.

RICHARD A. SAUERS

SIDIS, Boris (12 Oct. 1867–24 Oct. 1923), psychologist, physician, and pioneer in the field of psychopathology, was born in Kiev, Russia, the son of Moses Sidis, a well-to-do merchant and intellectual, and Mary Marmor, both Ukranian Jews. Under his father's tutelage, Boris showed early intellectual promise, developing an interest in poetry, languages, and history. During the czarist pogroms against the Jews in the 1880s, he was arrested for teaching peasants how to read and write. He spent two years in solitary confinement and withstood beating and torture before his father was able to secure his freedom. He immediately escaped from Russia and went, nearly penniless, to New York in 1887. While tutoring Russian immigrants, he met Sarah Mandelbaum. In 1891 Sidis went on to Boston, where Mandelbaum soon joined him. She enrolled at

the Boston University Medical School, and he continued to work and study. At her urging, he qualified to enter Harvard as a special student in 1892, and he received an A.B. in 1894. Also in 1894 he married Mandelbaum; they had two children.

Sidis attracted the friendly attention of the Harvard philosopher-psychologist William James, who encouraged him to enter psychology. Under James's guidance, Sidis earned an M.A. in 1895 and a Ph.D. in 1897. His dissertation, *The Psychology of Suggestion*, a treatise on the hypnotic suggestibility of crowds, was signed by George Herbert Palmer, Josiah Royce, and E. B. Dellabarre, in addition to James. Published by Appleton in 1898 with a preface by James, the work subsequently launched the so-called Boston school of psychotherapy and also had a major impact on the continued evolution of experimental social psychology in France.

After leaving Harvard, through a contact that James had with a former student, Theodore Roosevelt, then governor of New York, Sidis became an associate in psychopathology at the recently established Pathological Institute of the New York State Hospitals under Ira van Gieson. While there, Sidis influenced such budding psychotherapists as William Alanson White. In 1901 Sidis became director of the psychopathic hospital and laboratory at the New York Infirmary for Women and Children.

During this time, Sidis embarked on a systematic experimental analysis of the subconscious, particularly focusing on the diagnosis of multiple personality. From this research, he produced an in-depth study of a single case, Rev. Thomas C. Hanna, who, after a severe accident, had become a dual personality. Hanna's life was one identity before the accident and a completely different one after. Through Sidis's intervention, however, the personalities were successfully merged, and the case of Hanna, described in Sidis's work with S. P. Goodhart, *Multiple Personality* (1904), became a milestone in the scientific literature on dissociation, the reigning theory of the subconscious, which posited mental states as either integrated or dissociated from one another. Sidis's various works on psychotherapy and the subconscious soon became internationally known as standard texts in the field.

Sidis returned to Harvard in 1904 and began work on an M.D., studying primarily under neurologist James Jackson Putnam. He also came under the influence of the physiologist Walter Bradford Cannon. Sidis's perspective on psychotherapy thus became more biological and psychiatric. He lived in Brookline with his wife and young son, William James Sidis, who later became known as a prodigy, and he maintained a private practice in psychotherapy while he went to medical school.

Beginning in 1904, Sidis rendered translations of Ivan Petrovich Pavlov and Sigmund Freud for the staff at the Massachusetts General Hospital (with the assistance of the young Dr. Harry Linenthal). Sidis's most important studies at this time, however, were on hallucinations, sleep, and the galvanometric measurement of psychophysical responses. He crowned this period with articles in the *Journal of Abnormal Psychology* in which he described a method subsequently used widely by psychopathologists to tap into forgotten subconscious memories. Using light hypnosis, the method involved suspending consciousness between waking and sleeping in the so-called hypnogogic state, where abstract thoughts could be translated into prolific mental images.

Sidis received an M.D. from Harvard in 1908 and a year later opened the Sidis Psychotherapeutic Institute in Portsmouth, New Hampshire. The facility encompassed a palatial estate, complete with rolling fields, well-trimmed lawns, large spouting fountains, and numerous elegant buildings. Previously called "Maple Wood Farms," the house and grounds had been given to him by a grateful patient, Mrs. Frank Jones, to establish a private hospital that employed the latest psychotherapeutic techniques from Europe and America for wealthy neurasthenic patients.

From this vantage point, for the following decade and a half, Sidis continued to work and publish on scientific psychotherapy, a field that already was rapidly changing toward the radically different model of Freudian psychoanalysis and away from the classic nineteenth-century model of dissociation, to which he had so mightily contributed. Nevertheless, Sidis continued to publish treatises on psychotherapy, among them *The Foundations of Normal and Abnormal Psychology* (1914), *Symptomatology, Psychognosis, and Diagnosis of Psychopathic Diseases* (1914), and *The Causation and Treatment of Psychopathic Diseases* (1916).

Meanwhile, Sidis also branched out into psychology and education with his *Philistine and Genius* (1911) and into psychology and literature with *The Psychology of Laughter* (1913). He was also passionately interested in languages, political economics, and philosophy.

Personally, according to his friend and colleague Linenthal, "he possessed a genial and kindly nature, but was apt to express his opposition to what he considered fraudulent or dishonest with abruptness and vigor." Sidis died suddenly of a cerebral hemorrhage in Portsmouth.

• The most complete bibliography of Sidis's books and articles is on file in the Rare Books Department, Countway Library of Medicine, at Harvard Medical School. A less complete version is in the *Twenty-fifth Anniversary Report of the Harvard Class of 1894* (1919). Still the best statement on Sidis's personality is the entry by Harry Linenthal in *The Dictionary of American Biography*. Additional biographical details of Sidis's life can be gleaned (with some caution) from Amy Wallace, *The Prodigy* (1986), a biography of the son, William James Sidis. The psychotherapeutic scene in which Sidis operated has been circumscribed in George E. Gifford, Jr., *Psychoanalysis, Psychotherapy, and the New England Medical Scene, 1894–1944* (1978); Nathan G. Hale, Jr., *Freud and the Americans: The Beginnings of Psychoanalysis in the United States, 1876–1917* (1971); and E. I. Taylor, *William James on Exceptional Mental States* (1982). Obituaries are in the *Portsmouth (N.H.) Herald*, the *Boston Transcript*, and the *New York Times*, 25 Oct. 1923.

EUGENE TAYLOR

SIEGEL, Bugsy (1906–20 June 1947), gangster, was born Benjamin Siegel in Brooklyn, New York, the son of parents whose lives remain obscure. As a youth Siegel joined one of the many gangs that were so common on New York's Lower East Side in the early years of the twentieth century. His volatile personality, which combined intelligence with charm, generosity, irrational rages, and violent behavior, earned him his nickname of "Bugsy" early in life.

As with so many other major underworld figures, Siegel owed his eventual prominence to a combination of his own ability, key relationships, and good luck. While still a teenage hoodlum, he formed a lasting friendship with Meyer Lansky that became the basis for much of Siegel's personal success and notoriety.

Prohibition provided the first major opportunity for Siegel and Lansky to create significant careers in crime. With the financial backing of Arnold Rothstein, New York's premier underworld figure at the time, they established a car and truck rental company on Cannon Street on the Lower East Side. Eschewing the more dangerous aspects of bootlegging, the two partners offered transportation facilities to bootleggers seeking ways to deliver their products to thirsty customers around the city. By controlling such a crucial aspect of the bootlegging business, Siegel and Lansky became major figures in the distribution of alcohol in the New York region. By 1929 their organization was regarded as one of the Big Seven, an informal title for the seven most important illegal liquor operations in the northeastern United States. In 1929 he married Esther Krakower. They had two daughters.

Like many other bootleggers, Siegel continued his association with liquor when Prohibition ended, but in strictly legal ways. He invested with Lansky, Joe Adonis, and Frank Costello in Capitol Wines and Spirits, one of the larger liquor distributors in New York. Siegel also participated in another favorite post-Prohibition activity among former bootleggers by investing in gambling. In the early 1930s he operated crap games and a bookmaking business. At a time when several other major underworld figures such as Lansky and Costello were experimenting with gambling ventures in Florida, Arkansas, Kentucky, and Louisiana, Siegel decided to explore the investment possibilities in southern California. George Raft, one of his lifelong friends from the Lower East Side, provided an entrée into high society in Hollywood, which Siegel first visited in 1933. In 1935 or 1936 Siegel moved permanently to Hollywood, where he initially made his living by investing in floating crap games in private homes, in bookmaking at the Santa Anita track, and in gambling ships off the California coast. These business activities introduced Siegel to many members of southern California's gambling fraternity, men who had developed successful careers independent of their more famous East Coast peers.

Siegel is perhaps most remembered in popular crime lore as the inventor of the Flamingo, supposedly the casino that transformed Las Vegas into America's gambling playground. His claim to fame in this instance is not well supported by the known facts.

Siegel's initial acquaintance with Las Vegas developed from his bookmaking interests. In 1939 or 1940 the Al Capone syndicate in Chicago founded Trans-America, a wire service for bookies, and Siegel agreed to develop the West Coast market for the new company. He visited Las Vegas in 1941 as Trans-America's representative and established several partnerships with local bookies.

Since Siegel also invested in a casino called the Colonial Inn in Hallandale, Florida, with his old friend Meyer Lansky in the early 1940s, he may have developed a simultaneous interest in owning a Las Vegas casino. His desire to expand this aspect of his business activities to Las Vegas first emerged in 1943, when he attempted unsuccessfully to buy El Rancho Vegas, which had been built by California gambling entrepreneurs in 1941, and which was the first major luxury hotel-casino in Las Vegas. Two years later he formed a syndicate consisting of California and East Coast associates (including Lansky) to buy El Cortez, a casino in downtown Las Vegas.

The opportunity to build the Flamingo occurred only because its original developer, Billy Wilkerson, needed money to complete his dream. Wilkerson was a major figure in Hollywood, owning a newspaper and several famous restaurants. He was also an important figure in the gambling fraternity, and it was Wilkerson who conceived of the Flamingo as a new kind of casino featuring major Hollywood stars as one of its prime attractions. When his grandiose plans outran his financing, Wilkerson sought help from additional investors.

Siegel used Wilkerson's plight as his own opportunity. He persuaded his partners in El Cortez to sell out and invest their handsome profits in the Flamingo. Once in control (the Siegel syndicate owned 66 percent of the Flamingo), Siegel proceeded to embellish Wilkerson's original concept in an extravagant fashion that cost his partners much more money than they had intended to spend.

The Flamingo opened for business on 26 December 1946 and promptly suffered huge losses. Business was so bad that the casino had to close at the end of January 1947. Siegel promptly sought further funding from his partners, but they reputedly had run short of patience with his extravagance. The Flamingo reopened successfully in March, but Siegel's managerial deficiencies continued to threaten the economic well-being of his partners. When an unknown assassin murdered Siegel in Beverly Hills, California, his partners immediately assumed control of the Flamingo's management and turned it into a premier Las Vegas attraction.

Unlike his friend Meyer Lansky, Siegel lacked the temperament and skills to be a major innovator in the world of illegal enterprise. His reputation as a charming killer (who boasted that he had murdered twelve men) and, more importantly, as a close associate of Lansky, enabled Siegel to enjoy a relatively successful criminal career. But his stewardship of the Flamingo revealed his fundamental inability to manage a major project in a manner that could satisfy the strict accountability standards of his peers.

• Siegel's notoriety has attracted the attention of two biographers: David Hanna, *Bugsy Siegel: The Man Who Invented Murder, Inc.* (1974), and Dean Jennings, *We Only Kill Each Other: The Life and Bad Times of Bugsy Siegel* (1967). Both need to be read with care. Robert Lacey, *Little Man: Meyer Lansky and the Gangster Life* (1991), contains much useful information about Siegel and is essential for anyone seeking to place Siegel in the context of his times. An obituary is in the *New York Times*, 22 June 1947.

DAVID R. JOHNSON

SIGEL, Franz (18 Nov. 1824–21 Aug. 1902), soldier, educator, and politician, was born in Sinsheim, Grand Duchy of Baden, the son of Franz Moritz Sigel, a chief magistrate, and Maria Anna Lichtenauer. Sigel graduated from the military academy at Karlsruhe in 1843 and entered the service of the Grand Duke of Baden as a lieutenant. He played a conspicuous role in the revolutionary ferment that swept Baden five years later. During the 1848 revolt for unification of the German states along liberal constitutional lines, he held a command in the revolutionary army in Baden. Defeated by the Prussian army, he fled to Switzerland. In 1849, after a revolutionary government came to power, Sigel returned to Baden and became secretary of war. Prussian troops entered Baden soon after to restore the deposed government. Sigel took the field as adjutant to the commander of the army, which was defeated at the battle of Waghäusel. With the revolution over, Sigel took command of the beaten army and conducted a difficult retreat to Switzerland. He would be fondly remembered by his fellow exiles as a magnificent failure in a memorable cause.

After spending some time in Switzerland, Sigel moved to England in 1851 and to New York City in 1852. He taught at a private school for German Americans and became active in the New York state militia. In 1854 he married Elise Dulon, daughter of the revolutionary writer and educator Dr. Rudolph Dulon; they had five children. Moving to St. Louis in 1857, Sigel became an instructor in the German-American Institute and director of all the city's schools. Throughout his pre–Civil War years in the United States, Sigel maintained ties with the German immigrant communities of the North's major cities. Unlike other Forty-Eighters, he avoided a visible role in national politics.

Throughout the Civil War, Sigel enthusiastically supported the Union cause. He helped to rally German-American support in St. Louis and became colonel of the Third Missouri Infantry on 4 May 1861. On 10 May he participated in the capture of the pro-Confederate Missouri State Militia at Camp Jackson. Sigel led his first independent command in the battle of Carthage, Missouri, on 5 July. Although forced to retreat, he achieved national fame. On 10 August 1861 he commanded a wing of the federal army at the battle of Wilson's Creek, contributing to the Union defeat with his inept handling of his troops. Yet Sigel was widely praised in the German-American and Republican press, which had also celebrated his promotion to brigadier general on 7 August 1861, to date from 17 May.

At Sigel's favorable press coverage grew, his career and influence blossomed. When he was passed over for an independent field command in Missouri in December 1861, Sigel offered his resignation in protest. Public support from immigrants and many native-born Americans helped to convince his superiors to retain his services. Sigel commanded two divisions at the battle of Pea Ridge, Arkansas, 6–8 March 1862. He contributed modestly to the Union victory there, but friendly newspapers proclaimed him the true genius behind his army commander, Brigadier General Samuel Ryan Curtis, and he was promoted to major general on 21 March 1862.

Sigel was transferred to a more politically visible command in Virginia and was lionized by adoring fans during his train journey from Missouri. His modest performance as a corps commander in Major General John Pope's (1822–1892) Army of Virginia, which suffered an overwhelming defeat at Second Manassas (Bull Run) in late August 1862, was largely overlooked by the press.

Sigel's reputation deteriorated when he testified before an army court of inquiry into the conduct of Major General Irvin McDowell, one of Pope's corps commanders. Sigel had started rumors that McDowell had tried to sabotage Pope's battle plans, but he could not prove them. Sigel commanded a Grand Division in the Army of the Potomac, but his men did not participate in the battle of Fredericksburg on 13 December 1862. In February 1863, when he was demoted to command of his old Eleventh Corps, he again offered his resignation as a protest. This time, no one came to his support.

Sigel was shunted into insignificant posts. He took charge of a district in Pennsylvania, where he organized militia troops during the Confederate invasion that ended at Gettysburg. Sigel began to lobby vigorously for command of the Department of West Virginia, banking on the Republican need to curry favor among the German Radicals in preparation for the upcoming presidential election. He received the appointment on 29 February 1864. This, his first department command, resulted in the most thorough and humiliating defeat of his career at the battle of New Market, 15 May 1864.

Sigel finally ended his Civil War career in July 1864, when, confronted by Confederate general Jubal Early in the Shenandoah Valley, he retreated to Harpers Ferry without offering resistance. He was promptly relieved of his command and formally resigned from the army on 4 May 1865. Despite his many failures, Sigel retained the respect of many German Americans after the war. After editing a German-language newspaper, the *Baltimore Wecker*, for two years, he made New York City his home. He was active in Republican politics and served as pension agent, collector of internal revenue, and city registrar. Sigel continued to edit periodicals that served his immigrant constituency, including the *Neu Yorker Deutsches Volksblatt* and the *New York Monthly*. Sigel died in New York City.

Throughout the early part of his public life, Sigel's motives were sincere. Inspired by the liberal themes of the French Revolution of 1848, he genuinely supported the Baden revolution and the war against the Confederacy. However, by 1862 he began to manipulate the press and the public that had showered him with undeserved praise. By 1865 most of his supporters and all of his superior officers abandoned him because they came to realize his accomplishments did not match the promise of his publicity. Nevertheless, he was the most famous German-American general in the Union army and the most visible symbol of immigrant support for the Union cause.

• Sigel's papers are held by two archival repositories, the New-York Historical Society and the Western Reserve Historical Society. The National Archives has two categories of manuscript material that contain Sigel documents. The General's Papers comprise documents that detail his Civil War career, and Sigel's telegrams, dispatches, and reports are in the records of the military divisions, departments, and armies to which he was assigned. Many of Sigel's dispatches and reports were printed in *The War of the Rebellion: A Compilation of the Official Records of the Union and Confederate Armies* (128 vols., 1880–1901). Sigel wrote his reminiscences of the Baden revolution in *Denkwürdigkeiten aus den Jahren 1848 und 1849* (1902). The only book-length biography is Stephen D. Engle, *Yankee Dutchman: The Life of Franz Sigel* (1993). Works that deal with selected aspects of his Civil War career include Earl J. Hess, "Sigel's Resignation: A Study in German-Americanism and the Civil War," *Civil War History* 26 (1980): 5–17; William L. Shea and Earl J. Hess, *Pea Ridge: Civil War Campaign in the West* (1992); and William C. Davis, *The Battle of New Market* (1975). An obituary is in the *New York Times*, 22 and 23 Aug. 1902.

EARL J. HESS

SIGERIST, Henry Ernest (7 Apr. 1891–17 Mar. 1957), medical historian, was born in Paris, France, the son of Ernst Heinrich Sigerist, a Swiss shoe executive, and Emma Wiskemann. In 1901 he moved with his family to Zurich, Switzerland. His secondary education instilled in him a fascination for ancient languages, and after its completion in 1910 he studied Arabic, Hebrew, and Sanskrit for a year at the universities of Zurich and London. Unwilling to specialize in one language to the exclusion of the others, he decided instead to study languages as an avocation and to make medicine his career. Over the next six years he served intermittently in the Swiss Army Medical Corps while studying medicine at the universities of Munich and Zurich. During this period he decided to become a medical historian and combine his love of ancient languages with his medical knowledge. In 1916 he married Emmy Minna Escher, with whom he had two children. The next year he received his M.D. from Zurich and was commissioned a lieutenant in the medical corps. Two years later, he was promoted to first lieutenant and permitted to engage in postgraduate studies in Germany at the University of Leipzig's Institute of the History of Medicine (LIHM), the premier institution of its kind in the world.

In 1921 Sigerist became Privatdozent (assistant professor) of medical history at Zurich; he was promoted to titular (full) professor three years later. In 1925 he returned as professor and director to LIHM, where he wrote his two most memorable works. *Einführung in die Medizin* (1931), translated into English as *Man and Medicine* (1933), addressed the educated general public and examined the evolution of the philosophy of medicine as well as of medical knowledge and technique. *Grosse Aerzte* (1932), translated as *Great Doctors* (1933) and considered by many to be his finest endeavor, presented a nontechnical history of medicine by focusing on the lives and achievements of sixty of the world's foremost physicians.

In 1931 Sigerist was invited to present a series of lectures throughout the United States under the auspices of Johns Hopkins University. As a result of the tour's success, his belief that the United States would soon eclipse Germany as the center of medical innovation, and Adolf Hitler's impending rise to power in Germany, in 1932 he accepted an appointment as Hopkins's William H. Welch Professor and director of its institute of the history of medicine. He also edited *Publications of the Institute of the History of Medicine, the Johns Hopkins University* from 1934 to 1947, and from 1942 to 1945 he served as acting librarian of Hopkins's William H. Welch Medical Library. In these capacities he implemented the first graduate-level program in medical history in the United States and transformed Hopkins's institute into LIHM's equal, if not better. He also played an instrumental role in establishing medical history as a vibrant discipline in the United States by founding the *Bulletin of the History of Medicine* in 1933 and serving as its editor until 1947 and by reorganizing the American Association for the History of Medicine (AAHM) during his presidency in 1937.

While Sigerist's published work at Zurich and Leipzig was concerned primarily with philology and philosophy, his Hopkins endeavors mostly involved sociology. *Amerika und die Medizin* (1933), translated as *American Medicine* (1934), and *Socialized Medicine in the Soviet Union* (1937) were based largely on observations he made while touring those countries and reflected his growing interest in the social aspects of disease and the degree to which the medical profession is responsible to the public. Moved by the suffering he saw in the United States during the Great Depression and informed by a naive acceptance of Soviet medical statistics, Sigerist became an outspoken proponent of socialized medicine; in 1939 he taught the first course in practical socialized medicine offered in the United States. He believed that medicine should offer humanity far more than an opportunity for a select few to make a comfortable living and argued forcefully that the dispensation of proper medical care was a service that every state owed its citizens. *Medicine and Human Welfare* (1941) and *Civilization and Disease* (1943) continued to mine the sociological vein by discussing the historical relationship between disease and the entire material and intellectual fabric of human society.

In 1947, four years after he became an American citizen, Sigerist retired to Pura, Switzerland, although he maintained his standing in the academic community by becoming a research associate of Yale University. He devoted his remaining years to lecturing throughout the world and to writing an eight-volume history of world medicine. Health problems forced him to curtail the latter project after completing one volume on primitive and archaic medicine, which addresses its development as a sociological event involving the combination of magic, religion, and empiricism, and a significant portion of another on the medical practices and beliefs of the early Greeks, Hindus, and Persians.

Sigerist was president of the History of Science Society (1939–1940) and vice president of the International Society of the History of Medicine (1938–1941) and of the American Association for the Advancement of Science's section L (1943). He edited the *American Review of Soviet Medicine* from 1943 to 1948. He was chief consultant to the U.S. Board of Economic Warfare (1943–1944), commissioner of the Saskatchewan Health Services Survey Commission (1944), adviser to the Government of India Health Survey and Development Committee (1944), and member of a World Health Organization panel of experts on social medicine and occupational health (1951). In 1933 he was awarded the Karl Sudhoff Medal of the German Society for the History of Medicine, the Natural Sciences and Technology, and in 1950 the AAHM awarded him the William Henry Welch Medal. He died in Pura.

Sigerist was the foremost medical historian of his day. He contributed to the advance of medicine by helping to incorporate an awareness of the evolution of medical theory and practice into the basic medical curriculum in the United States and by making medical history more accessible to the educated general public.

• Sigerist's papers are in the Historical Library of Yale Medical School. An autobiography is *Henry E. Sigerist: Autobiographical Writings*, trans. Nora Sigerist Beeson (1966). Information on his life and writings is in Genevieve Miller, ed., *A Bibliography of the Writings of Henry E. Sigerist* (1966). Much biographical information is in "Henry E. Sigerist Valedictory Number," *Bulletin of the History of Medicine* 22 (Jan.–Feb. 1948): 1–93, and "Henry E. Sigerist Issue," *Journal of the History of Medicine and Allied Sciences* 13 (Apr. 1958): 125–250. On obituary is in the *New York Times*, 18 Mar. 1957.

CHARLES W. CAREY, JR.

SIGOURNEY, Lydia (1 Sept. 1791–10 June 1865), woman of letters and philanthropist, was born Lydia Howard Huntley in Norwich, Connecticut, the daughter of Ezekial Huntley, a gardener and handyman, and Zerviah Wentworth. Her childhood was passed on the estate of Jerusha Talcott Lathrop, widow of a prosperous Norwich pharmacist, who treated her as a protégée and encouraged her love of reading and writing, especially after her parents took her out of school to help her ailing mother. After Lathrop's death in 1806, Lathrop's nephew Daniel Wadsworth of Hartford assumed responsibility for Lydia's well-being.

In 1811, after a few months of advanced schooling in Hartford, Lydia Huntley and a friend, Nancy Maria Hyde, opened a girls' school in Norwich. This enterprise came to a halt when Hyde became ill. After Hyde's untimely death in 1816, Huntley published a memorial volume, *Life and Writings of Nancy Maria Hyde*, as a "solace" to her own feelings and a "source of profit to the bereaved mother" (Sigourney, p. 326). In 1814 she moved to Hartford to conduct a school for upper-class young ladies in Wadsworth's home. The favored subjects were geography and history, approached through a strongly Bible-centered Protestant perspective that would dominate her work throughout her career. Wadsworth also arranged publication of her first book in 1815, *Moral Pieces in Prose and Verse*, subscribed to by many leading families from Hartford, Norwich, and the surrounding towns and counties.

In 1819 she married Charles Sigourney, a widower with three children, at the time a prosperous hardware merchant. They had two children, a son who died in 1850 at age nineteen and a daughter who survived her mother and oversaw posthumous publication of Sigourney's autobiography, *Letters of Life*, in 1866. The marriage was unhappy, in part because Charles disapproved of Sigourney's literary efforts, which, nevertheless, she pursued. *Traits of the Aborigines*, a six-canto scholarly historical epic about the destruction of Native American tribes, appeared anonymously in 1822. In 1824 she published *Sketch of Connecticut, Forty Years Since*, a fanciful depiction of Norwich in the 1790s centered on the figure of a benevolent widow very much like Lathrop. Written much later, the quasi-autobiographical *Lucy Howard's Journal* (1857) looked back to the early years of the nineteenth century.

By the mid-1820s Charles Sigourney was suffering serious financial losses, and from then on Lydia Sigourney's literary work provided the family's income. She wrote prolifically and enjoyed enormous success; at her death she was the best known woman poet in the United States, according to her own tally having authored or compiled some fifty-six books as well as having contributed hundreds more uncollected poems and sketches to numerous periodicals. Except for a trip to England and France in 1840 that resulted in a travel book of mixed prose and verse—*Pleasant Memories of Pleasant Lands* (1842)—Sigourney resided in Hartford throughout her adult life, lending her name to a range of public causes including temperance, peace, missionary societies, women's education, Native American rights, and institutionalized care for the disadvantaged. She supported African-American schools and churches in Hartford and was an early benefactor of Thomas Gallaudet's Hartford institution for the deaf. A strong advocate of a separate sphere of activity for women, taking into account their physical weakness relative to men, Sigourney included a range of public activities within that sphere. She argued that since women often needed to earn their own livings or support their families, they had the rights to education and access to respectable and decently paying work. She viewed literary production as entirely appropriate for women. While insisting that the home was women's particular responsibility, she defined domestic women as teachers, disciplinarians, and patriots as well as nurturers.

Most of Sigourney's writing falls into three categories: prose sketches—chiefly pious, legendary, or historical; didactic works—including exemplary biographies, histories, and advice manuals; and poetry. Among her didactic books the most popular was *Letters to Young Ladies* (1833), which had almost thirty editions in England and the United States during Sigourney's lifetime. Her first book, *Poems*, came out in 1827. In 1834 she published *Select Poems*, a collection of her most popular poetry, which she reissued in updated editions for the rest of her life. Among several other collections of poetry are *Zinzendorff, and Other Poems* (1835), *Pocahontas, and Other Poems* (1841), and *Western Home, and Other Poems* (1854). Sigourney wrote long and short poems in a variety of verse forms and on a range of topics. She was regularly asked by friends, acquaintances, and even strangers to write original poetry for various uses. As she commented in *Letters of Life*,

Churches requested hymns, to be sung at consecrations, ordinations, and installations; charitable societies, for anniversaries; academies and schools, for exhibitions. "Odes were desired for the festivities of New Year and the Fourth of July, for silver and golden weddings, for the voyager wherewith to express his leave-taking, and the lover to propitiate his mistress. Epistles from strangers often solicited elegies and epitaphs." (Sigourney, p. 368)

Sigourney complied with most of these requests, partly from good nature and partly from a sense of the commercial value of goodwill. The poetry for which she became especially known were her consolation and obituary verses; as Sarah Hale wrote in *Woman's Record* (1852), "Her Muse has been a comfort to the mourner."

Sigourney was a good businesswoman who made literature into a successful career. Never interested in being a great or major poet, she wrote as a professional for her own time and place. During her lifetime she was criticized for imitating the English poet Felicia Hemans; after her death she was alternately belittled or neglected. She presents an image of the woman poet considerably at odds with stereotypes of nineteenth-century women as passive and submissive. Her success indicates that her activist image did not deter the public from appreciating her work, while also testifying to the important place given to poetry among the general public.

• Collections of Sigourney's papers exist in the Connecticut Historical Society at Hartford and the Yale University Library. Sigourney's autobiography, *Letters of Life* (1866), is an important source. The only full-length biography, Gordon S. Haight, *Mrs. Sigourney: The Sweet Singer of Hartford* (1930), is not sympathetic. Work attempting to recover Sigourney in context includes Emily Stipes Watts, *The Poetry of American Women from 1632 to 1945* (1977); Sandra Zagarell, "Expanding 'America': Lydia Sigourney's Sketch of Connecticut, Catharine Sedgwick's Hope Leslie," *Tulsa Studies in Women's Literature* 6 (1987): 225–45; Annie Finch, "The Sentimental Poetess in the World: Metaphor and Subjectivity in Lydia Sigourney's Nature Poetry," *Legacy: A Journal of Nineteenth-Century American Women Writers* 5 (1988): 3–18; Zagarell, "'America' as Community in Three Antebellum Village Sketches," in *The (Other) American Traditions: Nineteenth-Century Women Writers*, ed. Joyce Warren (1992); Nina Baym, "Reinventing Lydia Sigourney," in *Feminism and American Literary History: Essays* (1992); and Patricia Okker, "Sarah Josepha Hale, Lydia Sigourney, and the Poetic Tradition in Two Nineteenth-Century Magazines," *American Periodicals* 3 (1993): 32–43.

NINA BAYM

SIGSBEE, Charles Dwight (16 Jan. 1845–19 July 1923), naval officer, was born in Albany, New York, the son of Nicholas Sigsbee and Agnes Orr. Although his family history did not include any naval service, Sigsbee sought admittance to the U.S. Naval Academy. With the help of Erastus Corning, the Democratic congressman and industrialist, Sigsbee entered the academy in 1859. Because he was extremely young when he started at Annapolis, he was "turned back"—that is, held back as an acting midshipman—for a year in 1860. He graduated in 1863 in the midst of the Civil War and was appointed acting ensign on the steamship *Monongahela* of Admiral David Farragut's West Gulf Squadron. The following year Sigsbee was assigned to another squadron ship, the *Brooklyn*, under the command of Captain James Alden, and performed brilliantly in the battle of Mobile Bay on 5 August 1864. He was later transferred to duty with the North Atlantic Blockading Squadron and participated in Admiral David Porter's attacks on Fort Fisher on 24–25 December 1864 and 13–15 January 1865. He was then assigned to the Asiatic Squadron aboard the *Wyoming*, where he remained until 1867.

Despite the lack of opportunity in the post–Civil War navy, Sigsbee's career advanced rapidly, with promotions to master in 1866, lieutenant in February 1867, and lieutenant commander in March 1868. From 1869 to 1871 he was an instructor at the Naval Academy, where he began a class in nautical drawing. He was a proficient cartoonist, and a number of his drawings were published in the *New York Daily Graphic*, which offered him employment. He refused, preferring to remain in the navy. In 1870 he married Eliza Rogers Lockwood, the daughter of army general Henry Hall Lockwood. They had four children.

While most of Sigsbee's naval peers were concerned with the business of fighting at sea, his interest was in the field of marine science. In particular he focused on charting the ocean floor and surveying coastal ledges. After commanding the *Worcester* (1871–1873), from 1873 to October 1878 he used these skills on assignments in the Hydrographic Office and Coast Survey of the navy. He commanded the survey ship *Blake* and made extensive explorations of the Gulf of Mexico. Working with the internationally known marine biologist Alexander Agassiz, Sigsbee discovered the deepest spot in the gulf, which was named the Sigsbee Deep in his honor, and a rare species of ocean-bottom fauna, which was designated *Sigsbeia murrhina*. He explored along the coast of Cuba, where he discovered new types of sea lilies. This exploration would have a deeper meaning twenty years later, when he was commander of the *Maine*. He also invented a number of deep-sea sounding devices, like the parallel ruler for mechanical drawing, which earned him the decoration of the Red Eagle from Prussia and a gold medal at the 1876 International Fisheries Exhibition in London.

Also in 1876 another of Sigsbee's inventions, the deep-sea sounding machine, was exhibited by the Navy Department at the Philadelphia Centennial Exposition. Sigsbee published his research observations in 1880 in the highly acclaimed *Deep-Sea Sounding and Dredging*. His work in marine science earned him a promotion to commander in May 1882, and he returned to the Naval Academy until 1885. He commanded the *Kearsarge* in the European Squadron for two years before returning to the Naval Academy, then he was placed in command of the training ship *Portsmouth*. He was promoted to chief of the Hydrographic Office, serving in this capacity from 1893 to 1897. In March 1897 he was promoted to captain and one month later was given command of the battleship *Maine*.

When relations between the United States and Spain suffered over the question of Cuban independence, President William McKinley in January 1898 ordered the *Maine* with 328 men and 36 officers to Havana as a show of support for the Cuban insurgents and to protect threatened American lives and property. On 15 February 1898, while the *Maine* was anchored in Havana Harbor, an explosion in the forward deck of the ship ignited its magazines, and it rapidly sank. Although Sigsbee escaped the ordeal unharmed, 260 of his officers and men were killed or wounded. When news of the disaster was released, certain members of the press and several war-hungry politicians presumed the Spanish government to be guilty and sought revenge. To Sigsbee's credit, the calm tone of the cables he sent from Havana was primarily responsible for preventing a premature reprisal against the Spanish.

Ultimately, relations worsened between the two countries after the sinking of the *Maine*, and the United States declared war on Spain on 25 April 1898 (retroactive to 21 April). The cry "Remember the *Maine*" resounded throughout the United States. On 20 April 1898 the U.S. Navy appointed Sigsbee commander of the auxiliary cruiser *St. Paul*, and on 25 May 1898 that ship captured a British collier carrying a vital supply of coal intended for Rear Admiral Pascual Cervera and his fleet at Santiago. Under Sigsbee's command, the

St. Paul also defeated the destroyer *Terror* and the cruiser *Isabel II* on 22 June 1898.

After the Spanish-American War Sigsbee published his own theories on why his ship exploded in *The "Maine:" An Account of Her Destruction in Havana Harbor* (1899). The navy honorably advanced him three numbers in rank "for extraordinary heroism displayed during the war with Spain." His postwar service included chief intelligence officer of the navy from 1900 to 1903, commandant of the navy yard at League Island for one year, then commander of the Caribbean Squadron for two years. On 18 June 1905 he sailed for Europe, where he was entertained by various heads of state. On his return trip to the United States aboard the flagship *Brooklyn*, Sigsbee carried the remains of John Paul Jones from Cherbourg, France, to reinterment at the Naval Academy. His final assignment was command of the Second Squadron, North Atlantic Fleet in 1906.

On 16 January 1907 Sigsbee retired from naval service as an admiral and settled in New York City. He died at his home in New York City and was buried with full military honors at Arlington National Cemetery. Although Sigsbee's heroism during the Spanish-American War won him great acclaim, he is best remembered for his inventions and contributions to the field of marine science.

• Sigsbee's papers are in the New York State Library, Albany, N.Y. His military service is documented in his personnel record, which is on file at the Military Personnel Records Center in St. Louis, Mo.; *Army and Navy Register*, 28 July 1923; L. R. Hamersly, *The Records of Living Officers of the U.S. Navy and Marine Corps* (1898); *The Official Records of the Union and Confederate Navies in the War of the Rebellion* (30 vols., 1894–1922); and *Report of the Secretary of the Navy* (1898–1907). An obituary is in the *New York Times*, 20 July 1923.

MITCHELL YOCKELSON

SIHLER, Wilhelm (12 Nov. 1801–27 Oct. 1885), evangelical Lutheran theologian, pastor, and founder of Concordia Seminary and Concordia Teachers College (Fort Wayne, Ind.), was born near Breslau, Silesia, Germany, the son of Christian Georg Sihler, a Prussian army officer; his mother's maiden name was Wiesner. He studied at the University of Berlin, 1826–1829, where he was influenced by the theology of Friedrich Schleiermacher, a student of Immanuel Kant and the founder of modern Protestant theology. After teaching a year as a private tutor in Breslau, 1820–1830, he taught at a private college in Dresden.

At first he was a rationalist in religion, with an admixture of Schleiermacher's notions of faith as a feeling of absolute dependence, presumably on God. But he came under the influence of Johann Gottfried Scheibel, a professor at Breslau University, and Andreas Gottlob Rudelbach, a conservative confessional Lutheran educated in Copenhagen and a pastor and the superintendent in Glochau, in Saxony. Sihler visited three Bohemian Brethren settlements and was

deeply impressed by their hard work, consecration, personal faith, and missionary drive.

For five years (1838–1843) Sihler served as a domestic tutor in the Baltics, and then for another two years he taught in the household of retired Russian officer Major von Tunzelmann, a good Lutheran whom he had met in Dresden, on the island of Sarema in the Baltic Sea near the coast of Estonia. He later moved to Riga, the capital of Latvia, where he served as a tutor in the house of a merchant named Lösewitz in 1840 and where he had opportunity to study the Lutheran Confessions (symbolical books), including a detailed study of the Formula of Concord. During this period his faith in Christ as an existential and immediate experience was gradually merged with his concern for the correct exposition of the Christian faith. In this far-off corner of Europe, where Johann G. Hamann, the magus of the North, instilled his mystical spirit into Johann Herder, Sihler experienced an ever growing intensity of religious fervor. There he developed a strong desire to enter the ministry and serve the evangelical Lutheran Church.

In 1843, while visiting an evangelical pastor in Riga, he was given a copy of Friedrich Wyneken's *Notbrief*, a call for help for Lutheran ministers, since the number of German immigrants in the United States was swelling to one third of the country's population. With the encouragement of the mission-minded theologian Wilhelm Löhe, who directed many young Lutheran missionaries to America, Sihler emigrated to America. He was ordained as a minister in the Evangelical Lutheran Joint Synod of Ohio and other states in June 1844. In the spring of 1845 he served as a preacher in Pomeroy, Ohio, and in July 1845, was called to Fort Wayne, Indiana, to St. Paul's church, which remains a thriving congregation. He left the Ohio Synod and was, along with Dr. C. F. W. Walther and Friedrich Wyneken, a leader in the organization of the Lutheran Church of Missouri, Ohio, and other states (known later as the Missouri Synod). He served as the president of the Central District of the Synod, 1854–1860. He helped to establish the Theological Seminary in Fort Wayne and served as a professor and the president, 1846–1861. It was known as the "Practical Seminary" designed to produce ministers for the frontier churches in the West. He was also the president of the teachers training school after it was moved from Milwaukee to Fort Wayne. The school had been founded for the education of parochial schoolteachers and was later moved to Addison, Illinois.

Sihler published a number of books all practical in nature from a pastoral perspective. *A Conversation between Two Lutherans on Methodism, The Life of William Sihler, Sermons for Sunday and Festival Gospel Days of the Church Year, Time and Occasional Sermons, Sermons on the Sunday and Festival Epistles of the Church Year.*

Confessional Lutheranism as Sihler represented it meant loyalty to and faith in the three ecumenical creeds of the Christian Church and acceptance of the specifically Lutheran confessions stated under duress in the first century of the sixteenth-century Reformation: the Augsburg Confession (Melanchthon and Luther), 1530; the Apology of the Augsburg Confession (Melanchthon); the Smalcald Articles (Luther); the Small and Large Catechisms (Luther); the Formula of Concord, 1577; and Book of Concord, 1580 (Jakob Andreae *et alii*). Sihler died in Fort Wayne.

• The basic sources of information to consult are W. Sihler, *Lebenslauf von Wilhelm Sihler* (2 vols., 1879–1880); Lewis W. Spitz, *Life in Two Worlds: A Biography of William Sihler* (1968); E. G. Sihler, "Memories of Dr. William Sihler (1801–1885)," *Concordia Historical Institute Quarterly*, 5 (1932–1933): 50–57; Robert E. Smith, "Laborers in the Harvest Field: The Practical Seminary, Concordia Theological Seminary, 1846," *Seminary Publication* (Fall 1995): 16–18; and J. H. Jox, "Zum Ehrengedächtniss des am 27 October 1885 selig heimgegangenen Dr. W. Sihler, treuverdienten Pastor zu St. Paul in Fort Wayne, Ind." *Der Lutheraner* 42 (1886): 17–18, 26–28, 34–35, 42–43, 50–51, 59–60, 67, 69, 83–84, 91–92.

LEWIS W. SPITZ

SIKORSKY, Igor Ivanovich (25 May 1889–26 Oct. 1972), helicopter and aircraft designer, was born in Kiev, Russia (now Ukraine), the son of Ivan Alexis Sikorsky and Zinaida Stepanovna, both physicians. Sikorsky's father played a prominent role in the development of psychiatry in prerevolutionary Russia. Sikorsky received a great deal of affection and attention from both his parents and his siblings. Encouragement by his family to appreciate and explore the arts and sciences at an early age helped to nurture an inquisitiveness that would become an important part of his persona. In 1903 Sikorsky enrolled in the Imperial Russian Naval Academy at St. Petersburg. After reading about the first Wright brothers flights in the United States, he resigned from the naval academy in 1906 to pursue engineering studies in Paris. In 1907 he returned home and enrolled in the Polytechnic Institute of Kiev. While in attendance he built and experimented with a variety of mechanical devices.

In the summer of 1908, while on vacation with his father in Germany, Sikorsky read the newspaper reports of the Wrights' airplane flights in Europe as well as the dirigible flights of Count von Zeppelin. Inspired by these accounts, he decided to pursue a career in aviation. He began experimenting while in Germany, drawing sketches of helicopter designs and building a model rotor to test lift potential.

In December 1908 Sikorsky left for Paris to learn more about aviation firsthand and to buy a motor for his helicopter. Meeting with some of the early builders and fliers in France proved inspirational as well as educational. In 1909–1910 he constructed two twin-rotor helicopter designs, both of which proved to be unsuccessful.

Undaunted, Sikorsky then turned to the design of his S series airplanes. These proved more successful, and in 1911 he was awarded his F.A.I. (Fédération Aéronautique International) pilot's license by the Imperial Aero Club of Russia.

Sikorsky's seventh airplane, the S-6A, took first place in the national military competition of 1912, establishing Sikorsky as one of Russia's premier aircraft designers. He was hired by the Russo-Baltic Railroad Car Works that same year as their chief designer and engineer. Between 1912 and 1917 Sikorsky designed more than fourteen aircraft in the S series, including the world's first four-engine enclosed cabin airplane, the Grand, in 1912. This aircraft marked the first of three milestones in a career spanning six decades. A variant of the Grand, the Il'ya Muromets, proved to be a remarkable aircraft and became the backbone of the world's first long-range strategic bomber and reconnaissance squadron, with more than seventy built for the Imperial Russian Air Force.

The advent of the 1917 Russian Revolution profoundly altered the course of Sikorsky's life. Fleeing the Bolsheviks, he arrived in France in early 1918 and worked briefly to design a bomber for the French military. With the end of hostilities in Europe, he immigrated to the United States. Before he left Russia, he divorced his first wife, Olga Fyodorovna Simkovitch, with whom he had one child.

After a difficult period of transition Sikorsky formed the Sikorsky Aero Engineering Corporation in 1923 with financial support from members of the Russian émigré community. In 1924 he married Elisabeth Semion; they had four children. In the spring of 1924 he built and flew his first American design, the S-29A, a large multiengine enclosed-cabin aircraft. He then collaborated with René Fonck, a rival of Charles Lindbergh, in the design of the ill-fated S-35, which was modified in order to fly across the Atlantic with a crew of four. Crashing and burning on takeoff, the plane was destroyed with the loss of one crew member in 1926.

Sikorsky ultimately overcame this reversal and established himself as a major American designer with the S-38 amphibian. Sikorsky's amphibian played an important role in the opening of the South American and Caribbean air routes by Pan Am. With the massive increase of commercial air transport during the early 1930s, large orders were placed for Sikorsky's flying boat designs. He developed a number of new and innovative designs, many of them international record holders. By the late 1930s land-based aircraft began to dominate the commercial airways, and orders for Sikorsky's flying boats decreased dramatically.

The decline of interest in flying boats set the stage for a new and innovative period for Sikorsky, who now turned his attention to an old idea, the building of a helicopter. A pioneer in vertical flight, Sikorsky built the first practical single-rotor helicopter in 1939, the VS-300. Within four years, Sikorsky and his team had resolved the massive engineering hurdles that were required to build a practical working helicopter. By 1943 the Sikorsky R-4, which was designed for the U.S. Army, was in full production. As Sikorsky had predicted, the helicopter became an invaluable tool in missions of rescue and supply. Sikorsky's active years as a designer ended with his retirement in 1957.

Having lived through war and revolution, Sikorsky was profoundly troubled by the course of the twentieth century. As early as 1942 he turned to religious and philosophical writings as a vehicle to express his ideas. Sikorsky drew inspiration from his Russian Orthodox faith and a humanitarian outlook. He died at home in Easton, Connecticut.

Sikorsky's aeronautical contributions over the years are significant; they span from the infancy of modern aviation to its maturity. All multiengine aircraft are the direct descendants of his original aircraft design. Commercial air travel became a reality in part because of his successful flying boat designs. The development of the helicopter represents the culmination of a lifelong quest, a concept that resulted from the practical application of divergent technological ideas and Igor's faith of his place and purpose in the world.

• Sikorsky's papers are in the Sikorsky Aircraft corporate archive in Stratford, Conn.; the Library of Congress in Washington, D.C.; and the Connecticut Aeronautical Historical Association housed at the New England Air Museum in Windsor Locks, Conn. These collections include manuscripts, log books, scrapbooks, correspondence, and artifacts. Material pertaining to his work in Russia can be found in the Russian Aviation Collection Archive at the National Air and Space Museum, Smithsonian Institution, Washington, D.C. Sikorsky recounted his career in *The Story of the Winged-S: An Autobiography* (1938; rev. ed., 1958). His philosophical and religious treatises include *The Message of the Lord's Prayer* (1942) and *The Invisible Encounter* (1947). A complete bibliography of aviation articles and reprints of lectures pertaining to aeronautics by Sikorsky appears in Dorothy Cochrane et al., eds., *The Aviation Careers of Igor Sikorsky* (1989). General works include Robert M. Bartlett, *Sky Pioneer: The Story of Igor I. Sikorsky* (1947); Frank J. Delear, *Igor Sikorsky: His Three Careers in Aviation* (1969), Konstantin Nikolayevich Finne, *Igor Sikorsky, the Russian Years*, ed. Carl J. Bobrow and Von Hardesty (1987).

CARL J. BOBROW

SILL, Anna Peck (9 Aug. 1816–18 June 1889), evangelical educator and seminary founder, was born in Burlington, Otsego County, New York, the daughter of Abel Sill and Hepsibah Peck, farmers. Both of her parents were descendants of early Puritans, and she grew up in a very devout, Calvinist family that valued both strong religious conviction and education for girls as well as boys. As was typical of many such households, prayer was an intimate part of each day, and the Bible and the Book of Common Prayer were among Peck's early books. At age four she began to walk a mile each way to the rural schoolhouse where she learned spelling, grammar, and geography. Her mother, well educated in her own right, trained her in household duties and was a strong influence on her, especially after 1824, when Sill's father died; she was only seven.

The many religious revivals of the 1830s had a great effect on Sill, and in 1831 she dedicated her life to God. Choosing education as her field of service, at age twenty she became a teacher in the district school in Barre, New York. Her early household training

helped her to survive, as she was able to augment her meager income ($2 a week) by spinning and weaving. She continued her own education in the district schools during her vacation at Albion, the site of Miss Phipps' Union Seminary, which she entered in November 1837 and where she remained until 1843, becoming a teacher there in 1838. Her next two assignments were also in New York State. In 1843 she founded and for three years headed her own female seminary in Warsaw. The seminary was prosperous, but Sill closed it in March 1846, perhaps because she did not have adequate resources available to manage its growth. In August of that year she became preceptress of the girls' branch of the Cary Collegiate Institute in Oakfield, which maintained high standards of scholarship.

Sill experienced a minor spiritual crisis during these years as she tried to decide where her next service to God should take place. Her interest in evangelism guided her toward joining a foreign mission, but her dedication to education convinced her instead to remain in the United States and to migrate even further along the frontier, where the need was greater. Sill's work as an educator was known among Presbyterians and Congregationalists in the West, and that reputation led the citizens of the northern Illinois town of Rockford to ask her to come there. On 11 July 1849, in a modest boardinghouse supplied by the town, she founded a private school for the education of girls. Townspeople raised funds to construct the school's first building, but it quickly became insufficient, and Sill traveled back to the East, where she raised additional funds to construct a second building. On 15 July 1852 Sill's school became Rockford Female Seminary under the control of the Society for the Promotion of Collegiate and Theological Education. Sill was named its first principal, a position she retained until her retirement in 1884. She then remained on campus as principal emerita until her death there five years later.

With the support of a board of trustees that served both Rockford and Beloit College in Wisconsin, Sill conjoined her ideas of religion and education toward the goal of training the young women to be Christian missionaries and mothers for the evangelization of the West. A central object of the course of education was conversion, a crucial aspect of Sill's core beliefs. The three-year program, patterned after that at the esteemed Mount Holyoke Seminary, featured courses in math, the natural sciences, and literature as well as mental and moral philosophy and biblical languages. Bible study and work in the classics were stressed. The low fees were to Sill's liking, as she was concerned about the education of all classes of girls.

Sill worked hard to improve facilities and the teaching faculty, and she often seemed to be more successful at fundraising than at teaching. The number of students increased rapidly, but so did concerns about her strict rules and regimen. Sill was able to compromise on some of her more stringent rules concerning women's public roles and coeducation, but her missionary zeal never wavered, and she never stopped encouraging girls to follow in her footsteps; nor did she change her ideas about proper female behavior.

The founding of new secular colleges for women in the East forced Sill to reevaluate Rockford's future as an educational institution, and in the 1870s she started to push for a change in the status of the seminary to that of a college. However, while she sought collegiate status for the school, she never abandoned her deeply religious standards or her conviction that such beliefs should remain the central focus of the curriculum. Sill finally achieved her goal in 1882, when the seminary began awarding degrees. It officially became Rockford College in 1892. Sill's thirty-five years as principal of the Rockford Female Seminary had allowed her to influence several generations of young women, many of whom undoubtedly found their calling through her evangelical inspiration.

• Some of Sill's correspondence is in the Rockford College Archives. Her addresses are reprinted in the following issues of the *Rockford Seminary Magazine*: Dec. 1884, pp. 60–61; Mar. 1879, p. 77; June 1883, p. 186; Oct. 1885, p. 277; and July 1886, p. 216. For more information on Sill's tenure at Rockford, see the following college publications: *Profiles of the Principals of Rockford Seminary and Presidents of Rockford College, 1847–1947* (1947) and *Memorials of Anna P. Sill, First Principal of Rockford Female Seminary, 1849–1889* (1889). Also see Thomas Woody, *A History of Women's Education in the United States*, vol. 1 (1929); Lucy Forsyth Townsend, *The Best Helpers of One Another: Anna Peck Sill and the Struggle for Women's Education* (1988); and Charles A. Church, *History of Rockford and Winnebago County Illinois: From the First Settlement in 1834 to the Civil War* (1900).

RITA S. SASLAW

SILL, Edward Rowland (29 Apr. 1841–27 Feb. 1887), educator and writer, was born in Windsor, Connecticut, the son of Theodore Sill, a physician, and Elizabeth Rowland. Childhood illness and the deaths of his only sibling in 1847, mother in 1852, and father in 1853 contributed to Sill's sense of the power of fate and a lack of clear purpose or accomplishment in his life. The orphaned Sill attended Phillips Exeter Academy in New Hampshire and then the preparatory school at Western Reserve College in Ohio; he lived with uncles in Pennsylvania and Cuyahoga Falls, Ohio. There he fell in love with his cousin Elizabeth "Bess" Newberry Sill. In 1857 he entered Yale College, where he made important lifelong friends, adopted often heterodox views, and distinguished himself as a poet and as a writer and editor for the *Yale Literary Magazine*. He graduated with a B.A. in 1861.

Scorning commerce, uninterested in politics or the Civil War, and seeking health, Sill spent ten years in search of a meaningful vocation that would combine social usefulness with intellectual stimulation without depleting his meager energy. Following graduation, he and his closest Yale friend, Sextus Shearer, who shared Sill's rebellion against materialism and conservatism, sailed for California. Sill's clipper ship voyage is recorded in *Around the Horn. A Journal: December 10, 1861 to March 25, 1862*, which was not published until 1944. For four years, Sill unsuccessfully sought a teaching position; he also considered law, medicine, and reporting. Relatives and friends helped him find positions in a post office and a bank. He was also writing poetry. *Man the Spirit*, a long philosophical poem strongly influenced by Darwinian science, was read in June 1865 before the Associated Alumni of the Pacific Coast, a regional society of East Coast–educated men based in Oakland.

By that time Sill and Shearer had decided to return to New England. Before sailing, Sill began selecting poems and translating from the German. This work resulted in *The Hermitage and Other Poems* (1867) and *Mozart: An Historical Romance* (1868), from the German of H. Rau. These were his only volumes published during his lifetime, from the fledgling firm of Yale classmate Henry Holt.

Arriving in New York in November 1866, Sill soon arranged to publish his poems, and to enter divinity school in Cambridge, Massachusetts. In 1867, overcoming worries about consanguineous marriage, he married his cousin Elizabeth in Cuyahoga Falls; they had no children. Sill proceeded to Harvard, chosen for its liberal religious views. Within four months he was disillusioned about Unitarian ministers who, he wrote, "have made religion mockery & forgotten that truth is always safe." In Brooklyn, New York, he worked briefly as an editor for the *Evening Mail*, took other unfulfilling positions, and came to detest city life. In 1868 the Sills returned to Ohio, where he began teaching in a country school. Soon he became principal of the high school and superintendent of schools in Cuyahoga Falls. Throughout this period his poems were published regularly.

Compared to the vitality of California, the East seemed conservative and the Midwest intellectually impoverished. Helped by California friends, in 1871 Sill became assistant principal of the new high school at Oakland, where he taught Latin, Greek, history, rhetoric, physical geography, art, music, and the natural sciences. From 1874 to 1882 he was professor of English literature at the University of California in nearby Berkeley. The teacher's task, he believed, was "to nourish intelligence in a world maddened by material desires." In his years at the university, Sill worked to improve the inadequate library, revised the English curriculum, attracted new students, nurtured talented young writers, and hired philosopher Josiah Royce as his assistant. Although teaching left little time for his own literary interests, in these years Sill published more than forty poems, including his most popular, "The Fool's Prayer" and "Opportunity." In essays like "The Best Uses of Wealth," "Shall We Have Free Schools?" "What Is a University?" and "The Doctrines of Ralph Waldo Emerson," he engaged important social and cultural issues. The ideal university, he believed, would be free of both church and state control. But California businessmen sought a more practical vocational curriculum, and Sill felt his liberal views were ignored. In 1882, at the age of forty-one, soon after his only trip to Europe, Sill resigned his professorship. When his father-in-law insisted they return to Ohio, "duty" won out. As his farewell to California, Sill privately published *Venus of Milo and Other Poems*, gathering published and unpublished verse written after *The Hermitage*—including the 1882 Smith College commencement poem "Field Notes" and the lovely "California Winter."

In Ohio, still a cultural backwater, Sill worked to establish the first circulating library in Cuyahoga Falls, read, and wrote. Increasingly he published anonymously or pseudonymously because his family disapproved of his literary career and because he shrank from public disclosure. Liberated by his pseudonyms, Sill doubled his productive work in the last two years of his life, publishing poems (as "Anthony Morehead") in the *Century Magazine*, the *Overland Monthly*, and (as "Andrew Hedbrook") in the *Atlantic Monthly*. He produced signed articles supporting female education and unsigned table-talk on various topics—music, language, dreams, memories, science, nature—in the "Contributor's Club" section of the *Atlantic Monthly*.

In ill health in 1886–1887, Sill planned a trip to Colorado that he was not to take. A few days after surgery in Cleveland, he suffered a minor stroke and died.

Sill is regarded as a minor author. Posthumous publication brought him new fame as an inspired ethical poet, essayist, and letter writer, struck down by an untimely death. Newton Arvin considered Sill, Emily Dickinson, and Sidney Lanier the only "worthwhile" poets of the post–Civil War period. Alfred Ferguson saw him as representative of the shifting currents of a turbulent age, caught between faded optimism and scientific questioning, and admitted that his language frequently lapsed into a "sentimental counterfeit." Alfred Kreymborg, defending the label "minor" for a writer of "perfectly sustained lyrics," called him the "purest artist in Nineteenth Century Poetry."

• Sill's papers are in the Bancroft Library, University of California; Yale University Library; Johns Hopkins University Library; Houghton Library of Harvard University; and other repositories. *The Prose of Edward Rowland Sill* (1900) collects published and unpublished familiar and critical essays, mostly from Sill's last years; its long introduction consists primarily of familiar letters from and to Sill. *The Poetical Works of Edward Rowland Sill*, ed. William Belmont Parker (1906) collects about 200 of Sill's published poems.

William Belmont Parker, *Edward Rowland Sill: His Life and Work* (1915), the first biography, draws heavily on Sill's correspondence. Barbara Simison Damon published "Letters to Yale Friends from Edward Rowland Sill" in the *Yale University Gazette* 41 (Apr. 1967): 146–65 and 42 (July 1967): 21–33. A modern biography is Alfred Riggs Ferguson, *Edward Rowland Sill: The Twilight Poet* (1955). It ends with a chronological list of all located Sill publications. Tributes include Elizabeth Stuart Phelps, "Edward Rowland Sill," *Century Magazine* 36 (Sept. 1888): 704–8; and E. L. Baker, "Edward Rowland Sill, Poet-Teacher," *Overland Monthly* 83 (Apr. 1925): 154–55, 175–76. Assessments of his poetry can be found in William F. Dix, "The Poems of Edward Rowland Sill," *Outlook* 72 (Nov. 1902): 554–56; W. H. Carruth, "Great Poets or Great Poems?" *Poet Lore* 17 (June 1906):

78–85; Newton Arvin, "The Failure of E. R. Sill," *Bookman* 62 (Feb. 1931): 581–89; and Alfred Kreymborg, *A History of American Poetry* (1934).

NANCY CRAIG SIMMONS

SILLIMAN, Benjamin (8 Aug. 1779–24 Nov. 1864), scientist and educator, was born in North Stratford (now Trumbull), Connecticut, the son of Gold Selleck Silliman, a lawyer and brigadier general in the Continental army, and Mary Fish Noyes. Silliman entered Yale College when he was thirteen, graduating in 1796. After spending two years at home and teaching at a private school, he began the study of law and was admitted to the bar in 1802. During this time he was also a tutor at Yale (1799–1802), where his interest in the natural world began. Yale's president, Timothy Dwight, was convinced that chemistry and natural philosophy should be part of the curriculum and induced Silliman to abandon the practice of law and to teach chemistry and natural philosophy. Since Silliman knew little about science, he studied chemistry at the University of Pennsylvania, where he made a lasting friendship with Robert Hare, the inventor of the oxyhydrogen blowpipe. He also met Joseph Priestly and Benjamin Rush. John Maclean of the College of New Jersey (now Princeton) informed him of the most important works in chemistry to be read and instructed him in the art of teaching chemistry.

After giving the very first courses in chemistry at Yale, in 1804 and 1805, Silliman visited Britain to complete his studies and to buy books and equipment. Handsome, personable, and intelligent, Silliman traveled in the loftiest circles, meeting John Dalton, Humphrey Davy, W. H. Wollaston, Joseph Banks, William Wilberforce, and Benjamin West. He also examined mines and canals and saw the slave ships docked in Liverpool, which confirmed his abolitionist sentiments. His grounding in geology originated in his association with John Murray and Thomas Hope, both of Edinburgh, who were investigating the origin of the earth's surface and the formation of rocks and minerals. Murray was an advocate of James Hutton's theory, which attributed geological change to the internal heat of the earth. Heat, according to this view, caused the elevation of continents, the winds that eroded exposed rock, and the currents that carried detritus to deep seas where it accumulated and, by the agency of heat, formed new rock. Hope, by contrast, was an enthusiastic supporter of the ideas of Abraham Gottlob Werner, who identified water as the principal agent of geological change and believed that rocks crystallized out of ocean waters or were formed by the pressure of water acting on sediments. Silliman generally favored Werner's "neptunism," although he wrote a judicious critique of both theories. After returning to America, where he introduced the formal teaching of geology, Silliman used Werner's practical system of geology, which favored the characterization of minerals by color, hardness, texture, taste, and smell rather than by chemical composition, crystalline structure, and other properties that required instrumentation for measurement. Silliman's experience abroad was recounted in his popular *A Journal of Travels in England, Holland, and Scotland in 1805–06* (1810).

He returned to Yale in 1806, lecturing in chemistry, mineralogy, and geology (which he continued to do for the next half century). Through his lectures, based on the latest European thinking, students were introduced to new concepts of heat and chemical equivalency (combining weights and the law of definite proportions). His teaching was enhanced by the superb Gibbs collection of minerals, which through Silliman's efforts was loaned to the college and eventually purchased in 1823. He completed a geological survey of the New Haven area and also carried out research, reported in about sixty papers, which while of interest, were not highly original; he was more the verifier, expander, and publicizer of others' work.

In 1807 Silliman did the first analysis of meteoric material that fell in America, near Weston, Connecticut, work that was discussed in Europe. Using Hare's blowpipe, which achieved temperatures never before attained, he was able to reduce materials that had been previously considered by European Scientists to be elements, and he observed the melting of lime, magnesia, beryl, corundum, rock crystal, and other substances (1811). Using Hare's Galvanic deflagrator, he studied both the fusion and the volatilization of carbon with its transfer from the positive to the negative pole. These he communicated as letters in the *American Journal of Science (and Arts)*, giving full credit to Hare and complaining that some Europeans "reinvented" Hare's apparatus and repeated his and Hare's experiments, without giving due credit to them.

Beginning in 1808 some of Silliman's lectures were opened to the public in New Haven; these were so warmly received, he was prompted to increase his public lecturing. Particularly adept at translating scientific concepts into language everyone could understand, he strove to inform and interest the public in the application of science to mining, agriculture, and industry. In 1809 he married Harriet Trumbull; they had nine children. Harriet died in 1850. The following year he married Sarah Webb.

Deeply religious from his student days on, Silliman took it upon himself in his lectures to defend science against charges that it was atheistic, insisting that science and religion were compatible and that there was no conflict between the biblical version of genesis and geological theory. He discussed these matters in the appendix to the third American edition of Robert Bakewell's *Introduction to Geology*, published in 1839.

At Yale, Silliman advocated the founding of the Medical School (1813), where he taught chemistry. In 1818 he founded the *American Journal of Science (and Arts)* (commonly called Silliman's Journal), based on European models, which he edited and assiduously promoted by soliciting articles and financial support. In a decade it was self-supporting and was widely regarded as America's premier scientific journal, publishing papers of both theoretical and practical interest from the United States and Europe. He was sole editor until 1838, when his son Benjamin, Jr., assumed some editing responsibility; in 1847 his son-in-law James Dwight Dana joined the editorial board. Silliman also edited and adapted English texts on chemistry and geology and wrote a widely used *Elements of Chemistry in the Order of the Lectures Given in Yale College* (1831), which went through several editions. Accounts of his travels, in which he combined business with pleasure, were recorded in *A Short Tour between Hartford and Quebec* (1820) and *Narrative of a Visit to Europe* (1853). In 1839–1840 he gave the inaugural lectures at the Lowell Institute in Lowell, Massachusetts, speaking on geology. In 1853 he became professor emeritus at Yale. Ten years later he was one of the founding members of the National Academy of Sciences (1863). He died in New Haven.

Silliman became a national figure in American science through his lecturing and teaching, his popular books, and the scientific journal he created. He trained many of the future leaders in science. But he was not an original thinker or discoverer. An industrious administrator, with a practical bent, he was largely responsible for the conversion of Yale College to Yale University, with strong medical and scientific departments.

• Silliman's numerous letters are in the New-York Historical Society, the Historical Society of Pennsylvania, the Library Company of Philadelphia, and the American Philosophical Society; his diaries and other extensive writings are in the Yale University Library. There are several biographies of Silliman. See George P. Fisher, *Life of Benjamin Silliman, M.D., LL.D.* (1866), John F. Fulton and Elizabeth H. Thomson, *Benjamin Silliman, 1779–1864, Pathfinder in American Science* (1947), Chandos Michael Brown, *Benjamin Silliman: A Life in the Young Republic* (1989), and Alexis Caswell, "Memoir of Benjamin Silliman, Sr., 1779–1864," National Academy of Sciences, *Biographical Memoirs* 1 (1877): 99–112. See also George P. Merrill, *The First 100 Years of American Geology* (1924), E. S. Dana et al., *A Century of Science in America, with Special Reference to the American Journal of Science, 1818–1918* (1918).

LEONARD WARREN

SILLIMAN, Benjamin, Jr. (4 Dec. 1816–14 Jan. 1885), chemist, was born in New Haven, Connecticut, the son of Benjamin Silliman, a noted Yale scientist, and Harriet Trumbull. Interested in science from an early age, the younger Silliman attended lectures on chemistry, mineralogy, and natural history as he followed the traditional liberal arts curriculum offered by Yale College. He graduated in 1837 and served as an assistant in several science departments while pursuing an independent course of study that led to an M.A. in 1840. Silliman also assisted his father in editing the *American Journal of Science*, beginning an association with the journal that lasted throughout his career. In 1840 Silliman married Susan Huldah Forbes of New Haven. This marriage produced seven children, five of whom reached maturity.

While lecturing and serving as laboratory assistant in the chemistry, mineralogy, and geology departments, Silliman began to attract a small group of students who were interested in applied chemistry. Although this study group enjoyed access to campus facilities, its position within the college remained nebulous. In 1846, with the support of his father and other science faculty, Silliman proposed a more formal organization of a curriculum in practical and applied science that would emphasize laboratory instruction as well as lectures. This proposal led to his appointment as professor of applied chemistry, in which position he taught chemistry, mineralogy, and metallurgy. Yale established the School of Applied Chemistry the following year; the fledgling facility retained an informal connection with Yale College but received only minimal financial support. It became the Sheffield Scientific School in 1861.

Silliman's growing family responsibilities and his relatively low Yale salary convinced him to accept a position with the medical department of the University of Louisville in 1849. His duties as professor of medical chemistry and toxicology at the Kentucky school included a series of lectures given from November through March, after which he would be free to return to New Haven. Silliman's salary was based on the fees paid by students, as was common practice in medical schools of the period, but the medical department's enrollment was never sufficient to provide him with the remuneration he expected. Silliman left Louisville in 1854, following his father's retirement from Yale. He was appointed to the faculty in both the medical and academic departments at his alma mater, holding the position of professor of general and applied chemistry.

In addition to his activities as a lecturer and laboratory instructor, Silliman remained active as a textbook author. His *First Principles of Chemistry* appeared in 1847 and underwent major revisions in 1848 and 1852. By the 1870s this clearly written text had sold approximately 50,000 copies. *First Principles of Physics* was also widely used in both its original 1859 edition and the revision that followed two years later. In 1866 Silliman coauthored a brief volume with fellow chemistry text author George F. Barber. Their *Principles of Modern Chemistry* discussed the new chemistry based on the atomic system codified at the Karlsruhe Conference of 1860 and represented the first American textbook to incorporate these ideas.

As was the case with many scientists of the mid-nineteenth century, Silliman's academic career provided opportunities for consulting activity. During the 1840s he shared his expertise with local businesses and government in the New Haven area, but by the middle of the next decade Silliman's consulting activity had become a major aspect of his professional life. In 1855, for example, he traveled to western Pennsylvania to analyze the "rock oil" that oozed from the ground in Venango County. Using the relatively new technique of fractional distillation, Silliman isolated several useful or potentially useful products, including kerosene, paraffin, various lubricants, and gasoline. His report alerted interested investors to the potential of petrole-

um and led to the drilling of Edwin Drake's successful oil well on this property in 1857. Silliman's consulting activity continued to grow over the next few years, providing him with income that far exceeded his Yale salary.

Silliman's growing reputation as a consultant led to his association with various eastern financiers who had interests in the American West. In March 1864 he embarked on an extensive consulting trip to California, Nevada, and Arizona to investigate various mineral deposits. His favorable reports concerning petroleum deposits in southern California led to a frenzy of speculative activity by eastern and local investors. Silliman was similarly impressed with gold and silver properties in California, western Nevada, and northwestern Arizona, preparing reports that were frequently published as pamphlets by the mining companies involved. Following his return to New Haven in January 1865, however, many of these speculative ventures collapsed, leading to criticism of the Yale chemist's work. Questions concerning Silliman's professional objectivity were raised by various scientists, including Yale colleagues and members of the California Geological Survey. During the early 1870s, while continuing his consulting activity in the West and elsewhere, Silliman found himself the target of a growing campaign to challenge his credibility. Accusations that he had written excessively positive evaluations of properties to justify the high fees paid by his employers were offered as explanation for the failure of these ventures. Silliman's critics attempted to remove him from the Yale faculty and from the National Academy of Sciences, despite his status as a charter member of the latter. Although these campaigns were unsuccessful, Silliman's reputation suffered. Increasingly isolated from the Yale academic community, Silliman's only formal connection with the college was his faculty position in the medical department.

The last decade of Silliman's life focused principally on consulting activity and editorial duties for the *American Journal of Science*. His service as a consultant involved significant travel, including extended visits to Pennsylvania and the American Southwest during the early 1880s. Although financially profitable, this activity did little to redeem his damaged reputation. The establishment of the petroleum industry in southern California and the economic viability of several of the mining properties Silliman had praised earlier came too late to convince critics of his professional integrity. He died in New Haven.

• The primary manuscript source for Silliman is the Silliman Family Papers in the Yale University Library. Other Yale collections that relate to Silliman's career are the William Henry Brewer Papers and the Whitney Family Papers. Silliman's publications include more than 100 articles and reports, most of which were published in *American Journal of Science*. His analysis of Pennsylvania oil was published as *Report on the Rock Oil, or Petroleum, from Venango Co., Pennsylvania* (1855). A survey of Silliman's career, which includes a list of his major publications, is Arthur W. Wright, "Benjamin Silliman, 1816–1885," National Academy of Sciences,

Biographical Memoirs 7 (1911): 117–41. Selected aspects of Silliman's life and career may be found in Leonard G. Wilson, ed., *Benjamin Silliman and His Circle: Studies on the Influence of Benjamin Silliman on Science in America* (1979), a study of the elder Silliman. Details of Silliman's western explorations and their impact are discussed in Gerald T. White, *Scientists in Conflict: The Beginnings of the Oil Industry in California* (1968). An obituary is in the *New York Times*, 15 Jan. 1885.

GEORGE E. WEBB

SILLIMAN, Gold Selleck (7 May 1732–21 July 1790), Continental and militia officer in the revolutionary war, was born in Fairfield, Connecticut, the son of Ebenezer Silliman and Abigail (Gold) Selleck. His father was prominent in Fairfield County politics and was elected in 1739 to the colony's Council of Assistants, the elite group of twelve men who advised the governor and served as the upper house of the legislature.

Gold Selleck Silliman matriculated at Yale in 1749 and graduated with the class of 1752. He was appointed county surveyor immediately on his return to Fairfield. After declining the offer of a tutorship at Yale, he studied law and embarked on a successful legal career. In 1766 his father was one of several Assistants voted out of office by the colony's freemen for administering an oath to Governor Thomas Fitch, required by the Stamp Act, to enforce the hated tax. Nonetheless, Gold Selleck Silliman was appointed king's attorney for Fairfield County in 1769 and justice of the peace in 1772, commissions that were renewed annually for many years by the General Assembly. Simultaneously he rose through the ranks of the militia, being appointed captain of a troop of horse in 1769, major of the fourth militia regiment in May 1774, lieutenant colonel the following October, and colonel in May 1775.

He married Martha Davenport in 1754. She died in 1774, leaving only one surviving child. Ten months later he married Mary (Fish) Noyes, with whom he had two sons. The youngest, Benjamin Silliman (1779–1864) became Yale's first professor of chemistry and an influential figure in the development of American science during the early nineteenth century.

Gold Selleck Silliman's war service began in March 1776 when he was ordered to New York with a detachment of militia on temporary duty. On his return he accepted command of the first additional "New Levy" regiment that Congress had asked Connecticut to raise in response to the unexpectedly large British force deployed in North America during the campaign of 1776. The unit joined George Washington's forces in New York in early July as part of the Continental army. It was rotated to the rear on the day of the battle of Long Island, but was one of the last evacuated to Manhattan when the army retreated several days later. Silliman was the senior Continental officer in command of the regiments stationed at the southern tip of Manhattan on 15 September when the British attacked the island. Though initially reluctant to withdraw

without orders, he eventually extricated most of the men under his command from envelopment by the enemy. Subsequently he served with distinction at the battle of White Plains (28 Oct. 1776).

After retiring from the Continental army at the end of 1776, Silliman accepted the commission of brigadier general in command of the state's newly formed fourth militia brigade, a position that placed him in charge of defending Connecticut's exposed southwestern frontier. Fairfield County contained the largest concentration of disaffected persons in the state, which complicated his task. In addition to coping with repeated raids by small parties of Loyalists, which were abetted by many local residents, he also had to organize the coastal militia's response to larger enemy operations. The greatest challenge he faced was an invasion by a British force of 1,800 on 24–26 April 1777 that destroyed the Continental depot at Danbury. But he was also called on to lead a large detachment of militia to reinforce the Continental army at the Highlands during the final phase of the campaign that ended in John Burgoyne's surrender at Saratoga. Silliman had little aptitude as a military tactician and the occasions on which he exercised independent command damaged his reputation among the residents he was assigned to defend. Yet he displayed great courage under fire and inspired confidence among the men he commanded in the field.

On the night of 1 May 1779 he was kidnapped from his home by a band of Loyalists and remained a captive on Long Island for almost a year until he was exchanged for the Loyalist judge Thomas Jones, who had been kidnapped for this purpose. He resumed command of the fourth brigade on his return from Long Island, but the year of captivity had broken his health and impoverished his family. Although he represented Fairfield in the state legislature in October 1780 and October 1781, he resigned his military commission at the end of 1781. He resumed acting as state's attorney during 1782, but he was unable to recover his prewar legal business or to restore the family's fortunes after the conclusion of the war. When he died at Fairfield his estate was thought to be insolvent, though his wife, through prudent management, was eventually able to settle all just claims against it.

Silliman was a traditionalist by temperament who felt disoriented in the unchartered waters of revolutionary change. Many others shared this disability with him, and his career highlights some of the pitfalls encountered by revolutionary leaders called upon to fill roles for which neither past training nor inclination equipped them.

• The Silliman Family Papers are deposited in the Yale University Manuscript Collection. The early material in the file includes the extensive correspondence between Gold Selleck and his second wife, Mary Fish Noyes, and her father, Joseph Fish. Additional Silliman letters, largely of an official nature, can be found in the Jonathan Trumbull Papers and the Connecticut Archives Revolutionary War Series, both in the Connecticut State Library, Hartford. The Fairfield Historical Society holds a few items bearing on Silliman's first marriage, and the New Canaan Historical Society's collection of Noyes papers contains somewhat more material bearing on his second marriage. The only secondary source that tells his story is Katherine Hewitt Cummin's hagiographic *Connecticut Militia General, Gold Selleck Silliman* (1979). A biography of his second wife by Joy Day Buel and Richard Buel, Jr., *The Way of Duty* (1984), examines Gold Selleck's life in detail from the beginning of the revolutionary war until his death. Chandos Brown's *Benjamin Silliman: A Life in the Young Republic* (1989) covers some of the same ground.

RICHARD BUEL, JR.

SILLS, Milton (12 Jan. 1882–15 Sept. 1930), actor, was born in Chicago, Illinois, the son of William H. Sills, a dealer in mica, and Josephine Troost. His mother belonged to a wealthy banking family. He completed his education at the University of Chicago, with an A.B. in philosophy (1903), but he had already been active in college dramatics. After two years of graduate work, as scholar and fellow in philosophy at the University of Chicago, he entered the professional theater in *Dora Thorne* (1906) as a member of a touring company. Until 1909 he acted with stock and repertory companies, including Charles Coburn's Shakespearean company (1908).

Sills's first appearance on Broadway was in *This Woman and This Man* (1909), in which he played a leading role. Other male leads followed in New York and on the road. Sills could say he had never appeared as anything but a leading man on the Broadway stage. During a tour of *The Servant in the House* (1909) he met actress Gladys Wynne, and the two were married in 1910. His years on the stage continued until 1916 and gave him opportunities to play opposite numerous female stars of the day. His last appearance was in *Any House* (1916).

From 1914 on Sills became increasingly involved in motion pictures. After his first appearance on the screen in *The Pit* (1915), which he had filmed in 1914 while appearing at the same time in a stage play, he made four more films in 1915 and two in 1916. He further appeared in a fifteen-part serial, *Patria* (1916–1917). His tall good looks and virile manner made him an ideal leading man for female film stars of the day such as Clara Kimball Young, Gloria Swanson, and Colleen Moore. Assured of a steady and rising income as an actor for the screen and seeking a more settled life with his wife and young daughter, Sills moved to Hollywood in 1916.

In the next few years, Sills made an increasing impression on the public in numerous films. He made as many as eight movies a year, all of them romantic melodramas. Whatever the setting, from frozen wastes to desert sands, the films followed standard plot devices of the time. Yet the skill and distinctiveness of his acting for film was sometimes noted. The *New York Times* reviewer of *Behold My Wife* spoke of Sills's being "more vigorous, more free and easy" in the picture, "but without loss of the restraint that always marks his acting and helps to make it telling" (11 Oct. 1920). Another review, of *Flowing Gold*, voiced regret

at the hokum of the movie: "[Sills] ought to be cast in more plausible stories, as his ability is worth something better than he is offered in 'Flowing Gold'" (*New York Times*, 10 Mar. 1924).

One of Sills's outstanding successes was *The Sea Hawk* (1924), in which he played the swashbuckling role of an English lord who is betrayed by the treachery of a brother and sold to be a galley slave but is able to fight his way to escape and to justice. With its great success, Sills became one of the highest-paid stars of silent films. But his roles in succeeding films for First National, where his contract had two years to run, did not allow him any wider scope. The reviewer of *The Silent Lover* typified him as "the portrayer of hard-fisted fighters who never go down to defeat. . . . In all his pictures, Mr. Sills gets his man, invariably after a hard and mighty battle. This current photoplay is no exception" (*New York Times*, 15 Nov. 1926).

The sameness of his parts in so many routine melodramas apparently made Sills restless to break out. In 1924 he was reported to be anxious to direct. In January 1926 he gave a speech in which he deplored the hack work of screenwriters and called for higher script standards. That year he wrote his own screenplay for *Men of Steel*. In addition, relentless typecasting caused viewers at times to consider his performances routine or indifferent. For instance, in *I Want My Man*, he was described as "too stiff and stagey in most of the scenes to be effective" (*New York Times*, 6 Apr. 1925). The best that could be said of another film was that "Mr. Sills . . . gives the average cinema goer his money's worth" (*New York Times*, 5 Dec. 1927).

Sills was known by associates as a very different person offscreen from the one he played in his dozens of films. At home, he reverted to being the well-educated man from a wealthy family that he was in fact. His personal library included books of philosophy in several languages, and with Ernest S. Holmes, he worked on a book that would be called *Values: A Philosophy of Human Needs* (published posthumously in 1932). A lover of flowers, he spent many hours creating an English garden for his Santa Monica estate. During this period he contributed to the founding of the Academy of Motion Picture Arts and Sciences.

In 1925, at age forty-three Sills entered a time of emotional upheaval. He became attracted to actress Doris Kenyon, his costar in two films that year. He was divorced from his wife of fifteen years in 1925 and married Kenyon in 1926. In spite of advancing years, he maintained a constant round of filmmaking and physical exercise. A son was born in 1927. In 1928 he made the stressful shift to talking pictures successfully, using his stage-trained voice for the first time in *The Barker* (1928). In 1929 he suffered a severe nervous collapse and had to enter a sanitarium in the East for an extended rest. Back in Hollywood in 1930, he starred in a romantic drama, *Man Trouble*. A tale of derring-do, *The Sea Wolf* (1930), proved to be one of his outstanding films, and also his last. In the midst of a tennis game at his home in Santa Monica, he suffered chest pains, insisted on completing the game, and died of a heart attack on the court. He was forty-eight years old. The *New York Times* reported that his autopsy showed death "was due to angina pectoris, probably of five years standing" (18 Sept. 1930).

Though one of the great movie stars of his day, Milton Sills has fallen into obscurity since his death. Many of his films are no longer available for public viewing; some are "lost" and others are in private collections only. Part of his decline may be attributed to the severe upheaval that the film studios were undergoing in 1930 with the triumph of talking pictures. Other actors with good speaking voices were quickly developed as stars to play the kinds of roles Sills had played. Also, he made many forgettable films and few that were outstanding. Reviews of his films often dismissed his work as "capable." Even in his greatest success, *The Sea Hawk*, he was described by the *New York Times* reviewer only as "exceptionally capable" (3 June 1924). He remained until his death a tall, handsome, well-built, virile "matinee idol" of screen romances for women to sigh over and men to identify with. The *New York Herald Tribune*'s obituary summarized his achievement: "In a sense Milton Sills was much too handsome for his own benefit. A splendid physique and a kind of masculinity that appealed to both the men and women of his audiences more than likely kept him from [a] career as a dramatic actor [and from] fulfilling the promise he showed on the stage before he turned to the motion pictures."

• Materials on the life and career of Milton Sills are in the Billy Rose Theatre Collection at the New York Public Library for the Performing Arts, Lincoln Center. An extensive biographical sketch is in George Katchmer, *Eighty Silent Film Stars* (1991); it includes a filmography. Another informative biographical sketch is in Kalton Lahue, *Gentlemen to the Rescue* (1972), which includes photographs from Sills's films. Other portraits and production stills are in Daniel C. Blum, *A Pictorial History of the American Theatre* (1960) and *A Pictorial History of the Silent Screen* (1953). A front-page article on Sills's death is in the *New York Times*, 16 Sept. 1930, and an obituary is in the *New York Herald Tribune*, 16 Sept. 1930.

WILLIAM STEPHENSON

SILVER, Abba Hillel (28 Jan. 1893–28 Nov. 1963), rabbi and Zionist leader, was born Abraham Silver in the Lithuanian village of Neustadt-Schirwindt, the son of Rabbi Moses Silver, a proprietor of a soap business, and Dina Seaman. The family immigrated to the United States in stages, settling on New York City's Lower East Side in 1902, when Silver was nine years old. He attended public school in the mornings and Jewish religious seminaries in the afternoons yet still made time for his growing interest in the fledgling Zionist movement. He and his brother Maxwell founded the Dr. Herzl Zion Club, one of the first Zionist youth groups in America, in 1904. On Friday evenings, Silver attended the mesmerizing lectures of Zvi Hirsch Masliansky, the most influential Zionist preacher of that era. "I can still taste the sweet honey of his words," Silver remarked many years later. Inspired by Masliansky, Silver soon developed a reputation of his own

as an orator, equally eloquent in Yiddish, Hebrew, and English. He addressed the national Federation of American Zionists convention when he was just fourteen.

During his high school years, Silver excelled in secular studies and increasingly moved away from his Orthodox religious upbringing. Upon graduation, in 1911, he enrolled at the University of Cincinnati and the Hebrew Union College, the rabbinical seminary of Reform Judaism. He was not fazed by the Reform movement's anti-Zionism; indeed, it may have whetted his appetite. He organized Zionist activity on campus, edited student publications, won prizes in public speaking contests, and graduated in 1915 as valedictorian of his class.

At his first pulpit, in Wheeling, West Virginia, Silver soon earned a local and regional reputation as an orator. He also earned the enmity of more than a few Wheeling residents by his involvement in controversial causes, especially his sponsorship of a lecture in 1917 by Senator Robert M. LaFollette, who opposed U.S. entry into World War I. That summer, Silver was lured away from Wheeling to Cleveland, Ohio, to become the spiritual leader of the Temple (Tifereth Israel), one of the country's most prominent Reform congregations. In Cleveland he continued to attract public attention, usually as an outspoken defender of labor unions, and frequently sparred with groups such as the Daughters of the American Revolution, which denounced him as a dangerous radical.

Still, it was the cause of Zionism that was closest to Silver's heart, reinvigorated by a visit to British-administered Palestine in the summer of 1919. Soon he was speaking throughout the United States on behalf of the Zionist movement, attracting large audiences and rave reviews. "Many who heard him last night pronounced him as one of the greatest orators the Jews possess," a newspaper in Texas declared after one of Silver's addresses. In 1923 he married Virginia Horkheimer; they had two sons. While two assistant rabbis handled the bulk of the Temple's routine rabbinical duties, Silver rose to prominence on the national Jewish scene. As leader of Cleveland's Zionists—who comprised one of the largest districts of the Zionist Organization of America (ZOA)—he spearheaded protests against British restrictions on Jewish immigration to Palestine and organized boycotts of products from Nazi Germany.

The escalating Nazi persecution of Jews, the apathetic response of the Roosevelt administration to news of Hitler's atrocities, and England's refusal to open Palestine to refugees from Hitler, stimulated a mood of growing militancy in the American Jewish community during the late 1930s and early 1940s. Silver both symbolized American Jewish militancy and helped encourage its spread. In August 1943, he was appointed co-chair of the American Zionist Emergency Council (AZEC), a coalition of the leading U.S. Zionist groups, alongside Rabbi Stephen Wise. Until then Wise had been widely regarded as the most powerful leader of the American Jewish community. Silver's elevation to the co-chairmanship of AZEC launched a bitter political and personal rivalry between the two men that would endure for years.

While Wise, a loyal Democrat, was reluctant to criticize the Roosevelt administration's hands-off attitude toward Palestine and European Jewry, Silver did not hesitate to speak his mind. Silver's followers characterized the contrast between the two as "Aggressive Zionism" versus "the Politics of the Green Light [from the White House]." Within weeks of assuming the AZEC co-chairmanship, Silver spoiled Wise's plan to downplay the Palestine issue at that year's American Jewish Conference. Wise had hoped to mollify Washington and London, as well as Jewish critics of Zionism, by skirting the Jewish statehood issue, but Silver electrified the delegates with an unannounced address in which he vigorously demanded Jewish national independence. The "thunderous applause" that greeted his speech said as much about Silver's new prominence as it did about the American Jewish mood.

Under Silver's leadership, American Zionism assumed a vocal new role in Washington, D.C. Mobilized by AZEC, grassroots Zionists deluged Capitol Hill with calls and letters in early 1943 and late 1944, urging the passage of a congressional resolution declaring U.S. support for creation of a Jewish national home in Palestine. The opposition of the War and State Departments stalled the resolution in committee but did not deter Silver from campaigning in the summer of 1944 for the inclusion of pro-Zionist planks in the election platforms of the Republican and Democratic parties that summer. Silver's ability to maneuver the two parties into competition for Jewish electoral support was a testimony to his political sophistication even if, much to Wise's chagrin, the Republican platform went beyond what AZEC requested by denouncing FDR for not challenging England's pro-Arab tilt in Palestine.

While successfully usurping Wise's leadership role in the Jewish community, Silver took care to guard his own right flank. He quietly hired several militant Revisionist Zionists to help shape AZEC policy and guide its public information campaigns. He also engineered a public reconciliation between the Revisionists' U.S. wing and the mainstream Zionist movement.

During the postwar period, Silver and AZEC stepped up their pressure on the Truman administration with a fresh barrage of protest rallies, newspaper advertisements, and educational campaigns. Silver's effort in early 1946 to link postwar U.S. loans to British policy in Palestine collapsed when Wise broke ranks to lobby against linkage. More successful were Silver's behind-the-scenes efforts to mobilize non-Jewish Americans on behalf of the Zionist cause. AZEC sponsored the American Christian Palestine Committee, which activated grassroots Christian Zionists nationwide, and the Christian Council on Palestine, which spoke for nearly 3,000 pro-Zionist Christian clergymen.

Although the Truman administration wavered in its support for the 1947 United Nations plan to partition Palestine into Jewish and Arab states, a torrent of protest activity spearheaded by Silver and AZEC helped convince the president to recognize the new State of Israel just minutes after its creation. Silver's protests against the U.S. arms embargo on the Middle East, however, were consistently rebuffed by the administration.

In the aftermath of Israel's birth, Silver pressed for a clear separation between the new state and the Zionist movement, insisting that Israel should not control the World Zionist Organization or other Diaspora agencies. The leaders of the ruling Israeli Labor party had always viewed Silver with some suspicion because he preferred the free market advocates of the General Zionist party to the socialists of Labor. His effort to break Israeli hegemony over the Diaspora enraged Prime Minister David Ben-Gurion. The Labor leadership threw its support behind a faction of disgruntled ZOA members who resented Silver's prominence, and together they forced Silver and his followers from power in 1949.

Silver resumed full-time rabbinical duties at the Temple, with only an occasional and brief foray into the political arena when he could utilize his Republican contacts to lobby on Israel's behalf. He turned his attention to religious scholarship, reading voraciously and authoring several well-received books on Judaism. He died suddenly at a family Thanksgiving celebration in Cleveland.

Silver's reign marked a political coming of age for American Jewry. His lobbying victories infused the Jewish community with confidence and a sense that their agenda was a legitimate part of American political culture—no mean feat for a community comprised largely of immigrants and children of immigrants. The Silver years left their mark on the American political scene as well. After the inclusion of Palestine in the 1944 party platforms, Zionist concerns assumed a permanent place in American electoral politics. Additionally, the swift U.S. recognition of Israel in 1948, a decision made, in large measure, with an eye toward American Jewish opinion, was a first major step in cementing the America-Israel friendship that has endured ever since.

• Silver's papers, including his manuscript sermons, are in the Archives of the Temple, Cleveland, Ohio. The most significant documents pertaining to his career as a leader of the American Zionist Emergency Council and the Zionist Organization of America are in the Central Zionist Archives, Jerusalem. Silver himself authored *A History of Messianic Speculation in Israel: From the First Through the Seventeenth Centuries* (1927), a booklet titled *The Democratic Impulse in Jewish History* (1928), *Where Judaism Differed* (1956), and *Moses and the Original Torah* (1961). Four volumes of Silver's sermons and essays have been published: *Religion in a Changing World* (1931); *The World Crisis and Jewish Survival* (1941); *Vision and Victory: A Collection of Addresses by Dr. Abba Hillel Silver, 1942–1948* (1949); and Herbert Weiner, ed., *Therefore Choose Life: Selected Sermons, Addresses and Writings of Abba*

Hillel Silver (1967). A perceptive biography of Silver is Marc Lee Raphael, *Abba Hillel Silver: A Profile in American Judaism* (1989). The most useful scholarly assessments of Silver's Zionist activity are in Doreen Bierbrier, "The American Zionist Emergency Council: An Analysis of a Pressure Group," *American Jewish Historical Quarterly* 60 (Sept. 1970): 82–105; Zvi Ganin, "Activism Versus Moderation: The Conflict Between Abba Hillel Silver and Stephen Wise during the 1940s," *Studies in Zionism* 5, no. 1 (Spring 1984): 71–95; and Melvin I. Urofsky, "Rifts in the Movement: Zionist Fissures," in *Essays in American Zionism, 1917–1948*, ed. Urofsky (1978), pp. 195–211. An academic conference on Silver's career was held at Brandeis University in 1996; a number of the papers delivered at the conference were subsequently published in the *Journal of Israeli History* 17, no. 1 (Spring 1996).

RAFAEL MEDOFF

SILVERHEELS, Jay (26 May 1919–5 Mar. 1980), actor, best known for his role as Tonto in 221 television episodes of "The Lone Ranger," was born Harold J. Smith on Six Nations Reserve, Ontario, Canada, the son of A. G. E. Smith, a captain in the Canadian army; his mother's name cannot be ascertained. Silverheels was brought up in the traditions of his Mohawk family. Before he went to Hollywood in 1933, Silverheels was a lacrosse player, and it was as a member of a touring lacrosse team that he first visited California. Before moving to the screen, he was both an amateur and a professional boxer. Beginning in the early 1940s he became an actor in movies and on television, playing opposite Tyrone Power, Elizabeth Taylor, and Errol Flynn. Silverheels played the Apache chief Geronimo in three films: *Broken Arrow* (1950), *The Battle at Apache Pass* (1952), and *Walk the Proud Land* (1956). In *Brave Warrior* (1952), he portrayed Tecumseh, and in the screen version of James Fenimore Cooper's *Pathfinder* (1952) Silverheels played the noble American Indian Chingachgook.

Although he had roles in over forty films from 1947 to 1973, Silverheels gained fame as Tonto, the sidekick to the Lone Ranger, a character first played by John Hart and later by Clayton Moore in the television series "The Lone Ranger." Silverheels starred in every television episode from 1949 to 1957 and in two movies, *The Lone Ranger* (1956) and *The Lone Ranger and the Lost City of Gold* (1958), which were spinoffs from the television series.

Conscious of the mounting criticisms during the civil rights era of the 1960s of his portrayal of the loyal Indian accompanying the masked white hero, Silverheels was a major force in the movement to form the Indian Actors' Guild in Los Angeles in 1966 to promote the employment of American Indian people in Native American roles, to promote training Indians in horsemanship, and to promote the teaching of acting skills to Indians. In 1963 he helped to form the Indian Actors' Workshop at the Los Angeles Indian Center along with Buffy Sainte-Marie, Iron Eyes Cody, and Rodd Redwing. In recognition of Silverheels's support of Indian actors, the American Indian Registry for the Performing Arts in Los Angeles dedicated its 1984 *American Indian Talent Directory* to his memory. In spite of often negative responses to the role he played as Tonto, Silverheels symbolized for many Indian actors the potential for employment in the visual media, an area that had long been dominated by white actors playing "Indian."

In 1974, near the end of his acting career, he began a new career as a harness racing driver and raced competitively at such places as Vernon Downs Racing Track and Churchill Downs. In 1979 Silverheels became the first American Indian to have a star in Hollywood's Walk of Fame along Hollywood Boulevard. He married Mari DiRoma in 1946, and they had four children. Silverheels died at the Motion Picture and Television Country House in Woodland Hills, California, from complications of pneumonia. A sports center in his honor was erected on his home reservation on ten acres of land donated by his mother.

• Information on Jay Silverheels is sparse and is limited to short pieces in Marion E. Gridley's *Indians of Today* (1971); David Ragan's *Who's Who in Hollywood, 1900–1976* (1976); Ephraim Katz's *The Film Encyclopedia* (1979); and Roland Turner's *The Annual Obituary, 1980* (1981). Brief obituaries appear in *Newsweek*, 17 Mar. 1980, p. 86; *Time* 17 Mar. 1980, p. 65; and the *New York Times*, 6 Mar. 1980.

GRETCHEN M. BATAILLE

SILVERS, Phil (11 May 1911–1 Nov. 1985), comedian, was born Philip Silver in Brooklyn, New York, the son of Russian immigrants Saul Silver, a former tinsmith who worked as a sheet metal worker on New York skyscrapers, and Sarah (maiden name unknown). Philip attended Hebrew School and public schools sporadically. He began his theatrical career singing for gangsters and pugilists in Willie Beecher's neighborhood gymnasium, was a "reel-break-down" singer at a local movie house, and briefly joined a song-and-dance team called Bud and Buddy Jr. In 1923 the family moved to Bensonhurst, where he frequented the Brighton Beach Theater. At age twelve he joined Gus Edwards's *Newsboy Revue* in Philadelphia. At thirteen he was home for his bar mitzvah and briefly attended New Utrecht High School. He then joined the vaudeville team of Morris and Campbell, touring for six years. By 1932 he was marking time on the Borscht Circuit in the Catskills, where he developed longtime friendships with Jack Albertson and Rags Ragland. He toured with Minsky's burlesque troupe from 1934 to 1939 and adopted his trademark black horn-rim glasses, a penchant for gambling, and his fast-paced style. Describing it, Pete Martin later said of him, "Thoughts poured from him as if bottled under pressure" (p. 231).

Warner Bros. hired Silvers to make two-reel movies, and then he broke into legitimate theater on Broadway as Punko Parks in *Yokel Boy* (1939), a musical with Buddy Ebsen. Seeing this, Louis B. Mayer signed him for MGM. His screen test as an English vicar in *Pride and Prejudice* "killed a year" for him in Hollywood because he was unsuited for the part and this test was sent to studios requesting information on him. However, he made many Hollywood friends, including Judy Garland, Gene Kelly, Frank Sinatra, and Bing Crosby, and performed in benefits and nightclubs. Classified by the draft board as 4F because of his poor eyesight, Silvers worked for the USO during World War II. His big movie break came as the wise-cracking ice cream man in *Tom, Dick, and Harry* (1941). Darryl Zanuck of 20th Century–Fox saw it and signed him. "Gladda see ya!" became his stock line. During the next nine years he appeared in over twenty movies and was loaned to other studios. Most of the films he was in were made to cheer the troops overseas; among them were *Footlight Serenade* (1942), *My Gal Sal* (1942), and *Cover Girl* (1944), with Rita Hayworth and Gene Kelly. He characterized himself as "Blinky," the guy who never won the girl but always told the heroine in the last reel that the hero really loved her. In 1945 he met and married Jo-Carroll Dennison, Miss America of 1942. They had no children.

Silvers went to New York in 1946 to do a radio variety show. It did not last; however, in 1947 his musical comedy career took off. He played Harrison Floy, "a Bilko in spats," in *High Button Shoes*, with Nanette Fabray. The show ran 727 performances, longest running of the 1947–1948 season. "The Phil Silvers Variety Show" on NBC-TV, which ran concurrently with *High Button Shoes*, lasted only thirteen weeks. In 1950 he made the movie *Summer Stock* with Judy Garland and toured the country in a nightclub act. He was divorced that year. In *Top Banana* (1951) he played Jerry Biffle, a character patterned after ex-vaudevillian Milton Berle, and won a Tony Award for best actor in a musical in 1952. The show ran for 350 performances before touring.

Silvers continued to perform in movies and as a comic master of ceremonies for functions such as the Radio and TV Correspondents' dinner in 1954. But he is best known for his role in a TV series written by Nat Hiken. Tim Brooks wrote, "This burlesque comic created one of the most memorable characters in the annals of TV—the brash, beaming, fast-talking con man Sgt. Ernie Bilko" (p. 779). The original title of the show, "You'll Never Get Rich," was soon changed to "The Phil Silvers Show." It surpassed Milton Berle's popular program in the ratings, ran from 1955 to 1959, and won the Sylvania Award for best comedy show on TV. It also won five Emmys and numerous other awards, proving even more popular in reruns. In 1955 Silvers met Evelyn Patrick, former Miss Florida. They were married in 1956. The marriage produced five children. When the Bilko show ended in 1959, Silvers continued to do TV specials. One of these featured him with Jack Benny as "The Slowest Gun in the West." In 1960 he was in New York playing the role of Hubie Cram in Garson Kanin's musical *Do Re Mi*. In 1963, back in Hollywood, he starred in "The New Phil Silvers Show" on TV playing a Bilko-like character, but the show lasted less than a year. He continued to perform in movies and TV, appearing in *It's a Mad Mad Mad Mad World* (1963) with other zany comedi-

ans. His energetic lifestyle combined work, play, and family life. Daughter Nancey, interviewed by Bob Greene, said, "It's no secret that my dad gambled—a lot. All of the TV sets and radios in the house were always turned on, because he always had to know the sports results. There was probably never a day when he didn't have a bet down." He subsequently suffered health problems. In spite of depression and poor eyesight, he played the role of Marcus Lycus in a film version of *A Funny Thing Happened on the Way to the Forum* (1966), with Zero Mostel. After a period of medical treatment, he and Evelyn were divorced in 1966.

Silvers's movie and TV career continued. He did six episodes with Buddy Ebsen in "The Beverly Hillbillies," continued nightclub performances, and made a Disney movie, *The Boatniks* (1970). He appeared in his only nonmusical play, *How the Other Half Loves* (1971), and made guest appearances on sitcoms such as "Gilligan's Island," "The Lucy Show," and "The Love Boat." In 1971 he opened in a revival of the musical *A Funny Thing Happened on the Way to the Forum* as Pseudolus. He won a Tony Award for best actor in a musical in 1972 but suffered a severe stroke, and the show closed. He recovered and continued doing television shows. In 1973 he published his autobiography with Robert Saffron, *This Laugh Is on Me*. It appeared a year later in Great Britain as *The Man Who Was Bilko*. He was a member of the Friars Club and performed in various benefits and skits for them. One song is attributed to him, "Nancy (with the Laughing Face)," which he co-wrote with Jimmy Van Heusen for Sinatra's daughter in 1945. He died at home in Los Angeles.

• Silvers's autobiography is an important source. A revealing interview with Silvers is in Pete Martin, *Pete Martin Calls On . . .* (1962). After Silvers's death Tim Brooks highlighted his career in *The Complete Directory to Prime Time TV Stars, 1946–Present* (1987). A comprehensive overview of his early career is in *Current Biography Yearbook* (1957). Bob Greene's interview with Silvers's daughter Nancey in 1991 is in the *Chicago Tribune*, 14 Aug. 1991. Obituaries are in the *Los Angeles Times*, the *New York Times*, and the *Washington Post*, all 2 Nov. 1985. For a list of his TV appearances, refer to *The Complete Actors' Television Credits, 1948–1988* (1989).

ELIZABETH B. NIBLEY

SIMEON, Omer Victor (21 July 1902–17 Sept. 1959), jazz clarinetist and saxophonist, was born in New Orleans, Louisiana, the son of Omer Simeon, a cigar maker. His mother's name is unknown. His family moved to Chicago in 1914. Four years later he began taking lessons from clarinetist Lorenzo Tio, Jr. After working with his brother Al Simeon's Hot Six, he joined Charlie Elgar's Creole Orchestra as an alto saxophonist and clarinetist in 1923, later taking up soprano saxophone as well. The band played mainly in Milwaukee at the Riverview Ballroom and the Wisconsin Roof Garden, but it also worked in Chicago. There Simeon met Jelly Roll Morton, and after returning to Milwaukee with Elgar he commuted to Chicago to play on the first sessions by Morton's Red Hot Peppers (1926). The first and greatest record of this session, "Black Bottom Stomp," exemplifies Simeon's prominent, busy, cleanly articulated, bluesy playing, bright in the clarinet's high range and full-bodied in its lower register. On one title, "Someday Sweetheart," Simeon's part was a compositional gimmick; he reluctantly agreed to play a slow melody on a rented bass clarinet, thereby making an early and inconsequential claim for the instrument's place in jazz. Otherwise, these are all classic performances by the clarinetist.

In April 1927, when King Oliver's Dixie Syncopators played one night at the Wisconsin Roof, Simeon left Elgar to join Oliver. They toured colleges, performed in St. Louis, and then finished the month with two weeks at the Savoy Ballroom in New York, during which time they recorded. On these titles Simeon's tone is even more brilliant than with Morton, his clarinet sounding almost like a violin ("Showboat Shuffle") and his soprano saxophone almost like a clarinet ("Willie the Weeper"), possibly because of the tinniness of the recording fidelity rather than any fundamental change of approach. As a soprano saxophonist, his slow, slippery blues playing is featured on "Black Snake Blues."

Leaving New York, Oliver's group played assorted one-night stands before becoming stranded in Baltimore in May 1927 without further work. Simeon rejoined Elgar at the Eagle Ballroom in Milwaukee and at Dreamland in Chicago. In the summer of 1928 he returned to New York to join Luis Russell at the Nest Club for about three months. He also replaced Russell Procope in Morton's band for a recording session, performed with Morton's band for one week at Rose Danceland, and recorded again with Oliver.

In the fall of 1928 Simeon joined Erskine Tate in the pit band at the Metropolitan Theater in Chicago in order to be with his family. He remained with Tate until 1930, while working on occasion with Elgar at Chicago's Savoy. During this period he recorded regularly with Jabbo Smith's small groups (1929). These sessions afford an extended opportunity to hear Simeon playing clarinet, alto sax, and tenor sax in a freewheeling style, paired with Smith's own audacious approach, as on the deceptively named "Take Your Time" (they do not), and in pretty, deliberate melodies serving as a foil for Smith's playing, as on "Sweet and Low Blues." After playing in Dave Peyton's orchestra at Chicago's Regal Theater, Simeon became the lead alto saxophonist in Earl Hines's orchestra at the Grand Terrace in March 1931. Except for a two-week stint with Fletcher Henderson in 1936 as a replacement for Buster Bailey, and a long stay in the big band of Horace Henderson after a dispute over money between Hines and his sidemen (Aug. 1937–Sept. 1938), Simeon remained with Hines until 1940. He was, Hines said, "a very quiet sort of fellow, and very serious about his work. He always stayed by himself and didn't hang out with the wilder guys." On Hines's recordings he seems to have fashioned an improvisatory style in which rhythm and volume operated in

spurts and bursts of sound. "Rock and Rye" (1934) is characteristic, and it additionally provides a typical example of him leading the saxophone section through a florid line in rhythmic unison.

Simeon joined a big band led by Hines's former trumpeter Walter Fuller, again at the Grand Terrace (1940). After playing with Coleman Hawkins (1941), he returned to Fuller from late that year until the summer of 1942, playing mainly at the Happy Hour in Minneapolis. He was in Jimmie Lunceford's big band from 1942 until 1950, with Eddie Wilcox taking over its leadership after Lunceford's death in 1947. "Back Door Stuff" (1944) offers a beautifully fluid, bluesy solo on clarinet.

While touring with Lunceford, Simeon became involved in the New Orleans jazz revival, most notably by recording with Kid Ory in Hollywood in 1944, including "Do What Ory Say," and 1945. In 1951 he joined Wilbur De Paris's band, which toured Africa in the spring of 1957 but mainly held residencies in New York City, where Simeon died of cancer.

Simeon's place in jazz would be assured, had he done nothing other than play clarinet for Morton on one of the most significant bodies of recordings in the music's history. As it stands, this was only the beginning—albeit an illustrious one—of a career as a versatile performer in early jazz and swing styles.

• An interview with Simeon of 10 Dec. 1948 is summarized in "The Walter C. Allen Interviews," *Storyville*, no. 147 (1991): 87. An interview from 18 Aug. 1955 is in the archives of Tulane University. Simeon recalls Morton in Alan Lomax, *Mister Jelly Roll: The Fortunes of Jelly Roll Morton, New Orleans Creole and "Inventor of Jazz"* (1950), pp. 191–92; and in Simeon, "Mostly about Morton," *Selections from the Gutter: Jazz Portraits from "The Jazz Record,"* ed. Art Hodes and Chadwick Hansen (1977), pp. 92–93. Brief biographies include Herman Rosenberg and Eugene Williams, "Omer Simeon," *Jazz Information* 2, no. 1 (1940); and Hugues Panassié, "Omer Simeon," *Bulletin du Hot Club de France*, no. 92 (1959): 3–6. See also Laurie Wright, *Mr. Jelly Lord* (1980) and *Walter C. Allen and Brian Rust's "King" Oliver* (1987), and Stanley Dance, *The World of Earl Hines* (1977). For lists of recordings and musical analysis, see John R. T. Davies, "The Curious Case of the Forgotten Years," *Storyville*, no. 1 (1965): 8–9; Gunther Schuller, *Early Jazz: Its Roots and Musical Development* (1968), pp. 211–13; H. Openeer, Jr., "Omer Simeon," *Doctor Jazz*, no. 42 (1970): 6–8, no. 43 (1970): 4–7, and no. 45 (1970–1971): 25; and William J. Schafer, "Clarinet Kings," *Mississippi Rag* 10 (Sept. 1983): 1–5.

BARRY KERNFELD

SIMKINS, Francis Butler (14 Dec. 1897–9 Feb. 1966), historian, was born in Edgefield, South Carolina, the son of Samuel McGowan Simkins, a lawyer and circuit judge, and Sarah Raven Lewis. Simkins wrote that his family history scrapbook was read as often as "our Shakespeare and our Bible." Surrounded by memories of the past, Simkins turned his hand to history.

Having attended public and private school in Edgefield, Simkins received his B.A. from the University of South Carolina in 1918. After spending 1918–1919 in the military, he enrolled at Columbia University, where he earned an M.A. in 1920 and a Ph.D. in 1926. While he was at Columbia, Simkins became fascinated with Latin American history. At the invitation of fellow student Gilberto Freyre, Simkins spent the summer of 1924 in Brazil, where he viewed another variant of race relations. One of his first published articles pertained to Latin America. Before and after receiving his doctorate, Simkins held a series of temporary appointments at Randolph-Macon Woman's College in Lynchburg, Virginia, the University of North Carolina at Chapel Hill, and Emory University before accepting a position in 1928 at Longwood College in Farmville, Virginia, where he remained until his retirement in 1966. His career at Longwood was interrupted only by visiting professorships at Louisiana State University (1948–1951), Princeton University (1953–1954), and the University of Texas (1957). Simkins married Edna Chandler on 16 August 1930. After this marriage ended, on 7 June 1942 he married Margaret Robinson Lawrence; they had one son, Francis Butler Simkins, Jr.

Simkins effectively caught his students' attention by pointing out the humor in a person or an event. His penchant for the occasional extravagant statement endeared him to students and faculty, as when he remarked that Thomas Jefferson "was not too simple to live in a Roman mansion instead of a log cabin and to drink madeira instead of cider." He was an excellent undergraduate teacher, at ease and unaffected with his students. His undergraduates at Louisiana State University rated him a superior teacher. Devoted to his students, Simkins challenged them to think for themselves. Fond of inviting students to lunch for discussion, he neither dominated the conversation nor attempted to influence the thinking of his guests.

Simkins was an active researcher, publishing eight books, numerous scholarly articles, and an abundance of miscellaneous work, including book reviews, edited works, and encyclopedia articles. Though his research interests were broad, two themes characterized his work. First, Simkins believed that the South ought to be treated on its own terms. Tired of northerners who interpreted the South through the lens of presentism, Simkins attempted not to moralize but to understand the South. Second, he believed that the South possessed cultural characteristics that were different from the rest of the nation. Simkins paid a price for his adherence to these themes. Often viewed as too conservative, Simkins frequently had to alter his work to get it published. Toward the end of his career, he advised students "not to stay with the South." He never acquired a permanent appointment at a major institution. Stories conflict on why he left Louisiana State University; it was not his choice.

Simkins's contributions to southern history were enormous. In one of the first scholarly articles to buck the "Birth of a Nation" mythology that glorified the Ku Klux Klan and presented African Americans in a negative light, Simkins in a 1927 article in the *Journal of Negro History* detailed the violence, corruption, atrocities, and pretensions of chivalry of the extralegal terrorist organization. In 1932 he won the Dunning prize for his *South Carolina during Reconstruction*, written with Robert Moody. In it, he argued that the Reconstruction era was not the miserable, frenzied period characterized by other historians. Although African Americans were given the right to vote, white supremacy dominated the majority of southern institutions. Reconstruction was not a period of social revolution. Despite an increase in poverty, Simkins argued that social relations between blacks and whites were, for the most part, undisturbed. According to early revisionist Simkins, the image of Reconstruction, as depicted by historians such as William Archibold Dunning, had been more pernicious than the period itself. Simkins argued that the myth of "Black Reconstruction" created by the South and perpetuated by historians had helped to excuse the disfranchisement of African Americans and the institutionalization of Jim Crow in the 1890s. In 1938 Simkins read the provocative paper "New Viewpoints of Southern Reconstruction" to an overflowing crowd at the Southern Historical Association annual meeting. Introducing the research of modern anthropologists contradicting the prevailing assumption of innate Arican-American inferiority, Simkins's provocative paper developed the thesis, shocking for its day, that the behavior of former slaves during Reconstruction must be explained on grounds other than race. Moreover, he prophesied that these anthropological findings suggest "the rejection of the gloomy generalization that the race, because of its inherent nature, is destined to play forever its present inferior role." He called for objectivity in the study of all aspects of Reconstruction.

In 1936, along with James Patton, Simkins published *The Women of the Confederacy*, one of the first serious scholarly studies of women in southern history. Using the unpublished diaries of a number of southern women, the work illustrated the critical role that women played in the Confederate war effort.

Simkins's monumental biography *Pitchfork Ben Tillman* was completed in 1944. Through it, Simkins traced the life of the famous South Carolinian from upcountry beginnings through his career as a U.S. senator. The definitive work on Tillman, the book was praised for its thoroughness and objectivity. Simkins placed Tillman squarely in an agrarian reform tradition, attempting to explain the extreme racism of Tillman without judgment, despite his disagreement with it.

In 1947 Simkins finished *The South: Old and New: A History, 1820–1947*, which became a major textbook for southern history, revised in 1953 as *A History of the South*. Simkins intended to show how the South had evolved into a region cognizant of its own identity. He also expressed pessimism about whether the white South would allow blacks to be incorporated into the mainstream of southern society. The book reflects Simkins's own ambivalence on race, and it has come to be considered very old-fashioned on racial matters. In

1956 he founded the Institute of Southern Culture at Longwood College.

Finally, in 1963 Simkins published a collection of essays, *The Everlasting South*. Each essay stressed the distinctiveness of the South from the rest of the nation in its geography, climate, and views on race and religion.

The scholarly community generally believes that Simkins made an important contribution to southern history. A check of references to Simkins in the 1965 and 1987 historiographical collections *Writing Southern History* and *Interpreting Southern History* reveals the extent and continuing significance of his work. The unorthodox Simkins was something of a gadfly; he delighted in challenging the intellectual pretensions of other scholars yet remained on good terms with them. Although his research methods were unusual and his notetaking somewhat disorganized, he is still respected for his attention to detail and, as critics continually pointed out, his knowledge of sources. Overall, his work was judged as balanced and fair.

Simkins was loyal to the prevailing traditions of the South. Although he looked with disapproval on the shameful treatment of African Americans, he also criticized federal intervention in civil rights. The South, he believed, must arrive at its own solution on race. In a certain sense, Simkins was caught between two hostile positions. As one of the first revisionists in the history of Reconstruction, he was attacked by conservatives for his lack of orthodoxy on the race issue. In 1948 fellow southerner Frank Lawrence Owsley, in a review of Simkins's *South: Old and New*, condemned Simkins for crusading for African Americans. "Not once does the author really grapple with the race problem of the South with all its complexities and ramifications. At times, he seems to feel that race adjustment is something that Federal legislation—imposed on the South by non-southerners—can accomplish; that folkways can be repealed by act of Congress" (*Sewanee Review* 56 [1948]: 716–20).

At the same time, Simkins did not move fast enough for liberal critics. In a 1964 review of Simkins's *Everlasting South*, fellow southerner Dewey Grantham criticized Simkins for minimizing "the importance of such developments as recent political shifts and the new generation of Negro Southerners in reflecting and promoting change in the contemporary South" (*Journal of American History* 51 [June 1964]: 113). Significantly, in the 1960s Simkins's close friend and coauthor of *South Carolina during Reconstruction*, Robert Woody, broke with Simkins over the civil rights movement.

Simkins is one of the most intriguing intellectual forces of his generation. As a scholar, he questioned conventional thinking and helped lay the foundation for the civil rights movement. Yet he could not keep pace with the very changes that he had helped engineer. When the momentous events of the 1950s and 1960s challenged the traditional order in the American South, Simkins discovered much in the old South to be conserved, and he became a spokesman for tradition. Thus, contradicting his 1937 call for racial equity, in his presidential address at the Southern Historical Association in 1954 he proclaimed: "The historian of the South should accept the race and class distinctions of his region unless he wishes to deplore the region's existence. He should display a tolerant understanding of why in the South the Goddess of Justice has not always been blind, why there have been lynchings and Jim Crow laws." His devotion to the older enduring South inhibited his ability to accept the new. A complex man, not easily understood, he would not want to be pigeonholed ideologically.

• Simkins's papers are at the Southern Historical Collection at the University of North Carolina at Chapel Hill. He wrote several books during his career. Representative are *The Tillman Movement in South Carolina* (1926; repr. 1963), *The South: Old and New: A History, 1820–1947* (1947), and *Reconstruction in the South* (1952). Important articles are "The Election of 1876 in South Carolina," *South Atlantic Quarterly* 21 (July 1922): 225–40 and (Oct. 1922): 335–51; "The Ku Klux Klan in South Carolina, 1868–1871," *Journal of Negro History* 12 (Oct. 1927): 606–47; "Reflections on the Study of History," *Virginia Journal of Education* 21 (Mar. 1928): 313–15; "Ben Tillman's View of the Negro," *Journal of Southern History* 2 (May 1937): 161–74; and "Tolerating the South's Past," *Journal of Southern History* 21 (Feb. 1955): 3–16. Simkins's family published a memorial pamphlet, Augustus Greydon, et al., *Francis Butler Simkins, 1897–1966* (n.d.). Other treatments of his life and significance are E. Stanley Godbold, Jr., "Francis Butler Simkins," in *The Encyclopedia of Southern History*, ed. David C. Roller and Robert W. Twyman (1979), and Grady McWhiney, "Historians as Southerners," *Continuity* 9 (Fall 1984): 1–32. There are two worthwhile obituaries by colleagues: by Charles P. Rolland and Bennett H. Wall in the *Journal of Southern History* 32 (Aug. 1966): 435; and by Robert Hilliard Woody in the *Journal of American History* 53 (Sept. 1966): 439.

ORVILLE VERNON BURTON

SIMMONS, Al (22 May 1902–26 May 1956), baseball player, was born Alois Szymanski in Milwaukee, Wisconsin, the son of Polish immigrants John Szymanski, a brush factory foreman, and Agniszka Czarniecki. At some point in his childhood, possibly at the time of his confirmation, his name was changed to Aloysius Harry Szymanski. His father's death made him the family's breadwinner at age nine. During the next nine years he worked as a newspaper peddler, messenger, shoe factory laborer, truck driver, and glove manufacturer's employee. He found time, though, to develop his baseball skills on neighborhood sandlots. In 1921 he played for semiprofessional teams in Juneau and Stevens Point, Wisconsin. That autumn, Stevens Point Normal School recruited him for football, but an injury suffered in his first game prompted him to quit both football and the college.

Adopting the name Simmons, which he saw on a hardware company billboard, he unsuccessfully petitioned Connie Mack, the Philadelphia Athletics owner-manager, for a tryout. Soon he was signed for the Milwaukee Brewers (American Association) by Eddie Stumpf, a scout who had seen him play at Juneau. Batting .365 for Aberdeen, South Dakota, of the Dakota

League in 1922 and .360 for Shreveport, Louisiana, of the Texas League in 1923, Simmons was recalled to Milwaukee near each season's end. Nevertheless, the Brewers' owner, Otto Borchert, shared with others the belief that Simmons would not be able to hit major league curveballs because he stepped toward third base while swinging, a lifetime habit for which he was dubbed "Bucketfoot Al."

But in 1924 Mack purchased Simmons's contract from Milwaukee on the recommendation of Shreveport manager Ira Thomas, a former Philadelphia Athletics catcher who recognized the young player's natural talent. Simmons starred with Philadelphia from 1924 through 1932. In the 1929, 1930, and 1931 World Series for the American League champion Athletics, he batted .333 with six home runs and 17 runs batted in. His home run in the seventh inning of the fourth game of the 1929 Series started a dramatic 10-run rally against the Chicago Cubs, which overcame an eight-run deficit and led to a Philadelphia championship in five games.

Financial difficulties forced Mack to sell his star, who at the time had a three-year $100,000 salary, and two other players to the Chicago White Sox (American League) for $150,000 after the 1932 season. During three seasons with Chicago, Simmons batted .331, .344, and .267. Traded to Detroit in 1936, Simmons hit .327, but with his skills obviously eroding, he finished his 16 years as a regular player with Washington (American League) in 1937 and 1938, and Boston and Cincinnati (National League) in 1939. He returned to the American League as a part-time player for the Athletics in 1940, 1941, and 1944 and for the Boston Red Sox in 1943. He also coached for Philadelphia from 1940 through 1949, except in 1943, and for the Cleveland Indians in 1950 before retiring because of ill health.

The black-haired "Duke of Milwaukee" compiled a career batting average of .334 with 2,927 hits—539 doubles, 149 triples, and 307 home runs—and 1,827 runs batted in. After being named the American League's Most Valuable Player in 1929, he won the league's batting crown in 1930 with a .381 average and in 1931 with a .390 average. From 1927 through 1934, he was an all-star outfield selection six times. His record from 1924 through 1934 illustrates his greatness: during each of those years, he was an exceptional fielder and clutch hitter, batting above .300 and driving in 100 or more runs. In that span he hit .354 and averaged 125 RBIs per season, led the majors in total hits and ranked second only to Babe Ruth in runs scored, runs batted in, extra base hits, and salary earned.

A muscular right-handed player at 6' and 200 pounds, Simmons was cocky and hard-nosed. He frequently expressed his hatred for pitchers and refused to fraternize with opponents on the field. His acute baseball instincts led his contemporaries to say that he never threw to a wrong base or erred in making a quick decision as a player or coach. Awaiting a pitch, he would stand deep in the batter's box with his feet together; as he swung, he moved his body into the pitch with a long stride toward third base. Using a narrow 38-inch bat, he drove balls to all fields with equal power. His greatness as a hitter tends to overshadow his stature as a fielder blessed with sure hands and a quick throwing release. After four seasons as a center fielder for the Athletics, he was shifted by Mack to left field to reduce the strain on his body and prolong his career. Left field was in fact his natural position. He particularly excelled at cutting off hits over third base and holding potential doubles to singles.

Simmons's marriage to Doris Lynn Reader in 1934 produced one son and ended in divorce in 1941, leaving him a lonely man who drank to excess and became overweight. He was elected to the Baseball Hall of Fame in 1953. After suffering a coronary attack, he died in Milwaukee.

• Ed "Dutch" Doyle, *Al Simmons, the Best* (1979), a biography, covers Simmons's career through 1932. Simmons is a subject in numerous collective biographies, including Tom Meany, *Baseball's Greatest Hitters* (1950), and Bob Broeg, *Super Stars of Baseball* (1971). His personal reminiscences are related in J. G. Taylor Spink, "Down Memory Lane with Al Simmons," *Sporting News*, 5 Nov. 1942. His career statistics appear in *The Baseball Encyclopedia* 9th ed. (1993), John Thorne and Pete Palmer, eds., *Total Baseball* 3d ed. (1993), from which the statistics used in this article were taken; and Craig Carter, ed., *Daguerreotypes*, (8th ed., 1990). The most significant articles about Simmons in *Baseball Magazine* are F. C. Lane, "Simmons a Candidate for Babe Ruth's Crown," Feb. 1934, and John Ward, "That Fading Star—Al Simmons," Mar. 1937. Obituaries appear in the *New York Times*, 27 May 1956, and *Sporting News*, 6 June 1956.

FRANK VAN RENSSELAER PHELPS

SIMMONS, Calvin Eugene (27 Apr. 1950–21 Aug. 1982), conductor, was born in San Francisco, California, the son of Henry Calvin Simmons, a dock hand and church official, and Mattie Pearl (maiden name unknown), a registered nurse and church musician. His mother's work as a choral conductor and pianist attracted the boy to music. By the time he was eight, he had begun to perform in public and the next year joined the San Francisco Boys Chorus, directed by Madi Bacon, which was called on for occasional performances with the San Francisco Opera. Bacon offered Simmons his first conducting lessons. While at a summer camp, Simmons began the study of theory with William Duncan Allen, trying his hand at composition during his mid-teens. At age sixteen he was appointed pianist for the San Francisco Boys Chorus and won the attention of Kurt Herbert Adler, who granted him access to the opera rehearsals. In commemoration of the death of Reverend Martin Luther King, he conducted Mozart's *Requiem* while yet in high school.

Simmons began his college days as a student at the University of Cincinnati (1968–1970). There he was befriended by the vocal coach Sylvia Olden Lee and the conductor Max Rudolf (whose textbook he had studied while still in junior high school). When his conducting teacher left Cincinnati the next year for a post at Philadelphia's Curtis Institute of Music, Simmons followed. In addition to the continuation of his work in conducting, he was accepted in the piano studio of Rudolf Serkin. During this time he served as pianist to Maria Callas, who, like many, initially thought him a servant because he was black.

Following graduation in 1972 Simmons made his formal debut as conductor in San Francisco's production of *Hänsel und Gretel* (with which he also made his Metropolitan Opera debut in 1978). As assistant director of the Western Opera Theater, he gave performances on tours from Arizona (where operas were presented to a Navaho audience) to Alaska (where they performed for Eskimo children in a village of fewer than 100 residents). This was consonant with his dedication to the presentation of music to new audiences, including many concerts for children and even opera productions on the street corners of San Francisco. In 1974 he was engaged by England's Glyndebourne Opera Company with the London Philharmonic Orchestra, principally for performances of Mozart's *Così fan tutte* and *Le nozze di Figaro*, both at the Glyndebourne estate and on tours. He moved to the Los Angeles Philharmonic Orchestra as assistant to Zubin Mehta in 1975 with a grant from the Exxon Corporation and made his first recording with that ensemble.

In 1978 he was appointed music director of the Oakland Symphony, the first African American after Henry Lewis (with the New Jersey Symphony Orchestra in 1968) to have full artistic authority over an American orchestra. In this post he was both aggressive and imaginative in selling the orchestra to a large public, raising the orchestra's standards as well as its budget. Frequently engaged as a guest conductor for most major orchestras, he was selected to lead the debut of *Juana la loca*, an opera by Gian Carlo Menotti, with Beverly Sills in her final opera performance, and of that Shostakovich opera which, as *Lady Macbeth of Mtsensk*, had infuriated the Soviet government. His St. Louis performance of *Così* in 1982 created a sensation, and numerous bookings reached into the future. Among the soloists for this production were two newcomers to the opera scene, Jerry Hadley and Thomas Hampson. "A more provocative and consistent *Così* you are not likely to come across in a lifetime of opera-going," stated a review in the *New York Times*. That summer, while relaxing at Lake Placid, his canoe overturned in the icy waters, and Simmons was drowned.

His funeral was held in San Francisco's Grace Cathedral. Musical tributes were offered by a string quartet from the Oakland Symphony and by mezzo-soprano Marilyn Horne. The orchestra's hall was subsequently named in his honor when its schedule was resumed; it then became known as the Oakland East Bay Symphony.

Simmons was unmarried and childless. He was well known for his irrepressible and spontaneous humor, which often was manifest at unexpected moments. Although he took music very seriously, he enjoyed playing pranks in public and was quick to improvise, particularly when this could ease tensions. His antics did not diminish the respect he earned from such figures as Elizabeth Schwarzkopf, Birgit Nilsson, and the appreciative critics who attended his American and European performances.

• An important source on Simmons is Rinna Evelyn Wolfe, *The Calvin Simmons Story; or, "Don't Call Me Maestro"* (1994). See also Jane Eshleman Conant, "Musician of the Month: Calvin Simmons," *Musical America* 29, no. 3 (Mar. 1979): 6–7; A. Ulrich, "Calvin Simmons, Oakland's Paramount Talent," *Focus* 29, no. 3 (1982): 30; and Eileen Southern's entry on Simmons in *Biographical Dictionary of Afro-American and African Musicians* (1982). An obituary is in the *New York Times*, 24 Aug. 1982.

DOMINIQUE-RENÉ DE LERMA

SIMMONS, Edward Emerson (27 Oct. 1852–17 Nov. 1931), painter, was born in Concord, Massachusetts, the son of George Frederick Simmons, a Unitarian minister, and Mary Emerson Ripley. His father and grandfathers were stern Unitarian ministers who preached against slavery before it was fashionable. At an early age the sheltered, timid, yet inquisitive Simmons was grief-stricken when his father suddenly died, leaving the family in poverty. Simmons was raised in Concord's Old Manse by his mother, grandmother (an amateur botanist), and his Bible-toting grandfather, whose relatives had come from England on the Mayflower.

From childhood into early adulthood Simmons lived with and liked to listen to stories told by his famous cousin Ralph Waldo Emerson, whom he idealized as a man "who rendered the commonplace sacred" (*From Seven to Seventy*, p. 22). Surrounded by creative writers and men of the cloth, Simmons was inspired to learn all he could about natural history, literature, and art, but because his family had little money, experiences outside of Concord were limited. Throughout his staunch, New England upbringing his favorite activities were drawing and reading.

Simmons entered Harvard in 1870. He found the academic environment exhilarating, even though classmates joked about his lack of experience and nicknamed him "Wambat." As the Hasty Pudding Club ushered him into manhood, Simmons helped to found the *Harvard Crimson*, then called the *Magenta*, and was secretary of the art club. After obtaining his A.B. in 1874, Simmons went to New York City with the intention of becoming an architect, but architect Russell Sturgis convinced him to become a painter.

Desperate to seek adventure and to leave New England and his austere relatives, in 1874 the ever-cautious Simmons packed a loaded gun and went to look for work in Cincinnati. One day, after failing at attempts to become a salesman and a tutor of young boys, he boldly knocked on a door that read "Artist." He had done so out of curiosity, and as luck would have it, the famous painter Frank Duveneck answered the knock, greeted Simmons, and allowed him to enter the first artist's studio he had ever seen. From that day forward Simmons was determined to save enough money to train in Europe and become a professional painter.

With an introductory letter from Emerson, Simmons went to San Francisco in 1875 and secured a part-time job as drama critic for the *Chronicle* and a teaching position for $75 a month at the Strawberry Valley School. Simmons enjoyed socializing with painters William Keith and Thomas Hill as well as living and working in San Francisco, but in 1877, after a close friend was shot and killed on a city street, he decided he had experienced enough excitement and soon returned to Boston.

At Boston's Institute of Technology Simmons met painter William Rimmer, who encouraged him to study at Boston's Museum School with Frank Crowninshield. Simmons did so and after a few months with Crowninshield, drew well enough to sail for France. He arrived at the Hotel de Londres, located along the rue de Douai in the Montmartre section of Paris, in 1878. For thirty francs a month he rented an unheated, sixth-floor room with two iron cots and a trap door for a window. He studied with C. R. Boulanger, who instilled in Simmons the importance of being able to draw the human form with anatomical perfection, and J. J. Lefebvre at the Académie Julian in Paris. By 1881 he had become a friend of James Abbott McNeill Whistler and won one hundred francs at the académie for finishing the best drawing; in 1882 his *La Blanchisseuse* won an honorable mention at the Paris Salon.

In 1881 Simmons moved to a wheat loft in Breton on the coast of Concarneau, where for the next five years he painted genre scenes of peasants working and playing in the streets and fields and on hillsides. Joining him to paint in Concarneau and Pont Aven were Willard Metcalf, Theodore Robinson, Edmund C. Tarbell, Bastein-Lepage, and other famous painters. In December 1883 Simmons married writer Vesta Schallenberger; their son was born the following year. From 1887 to 1891 the family lived in St. Ives in Cornwall, England, where Theodore Robinson accompanied Simmons as he painted the cliffs, coasts, and local fishermen. Summers were spent sketching in Denis, Montreuil, and Grez, France; in Stuttgart, Germany; and in the Forest of Fontainebleau outside of Paris. He divorced his first wife and in 1903 married Alice Ralston Morton, who gave birth to their son in 1904.

In 1891, having received a commission to design and construct a stained glass window for Harvard, Simmons returned to New York City to complete the project. For the 1893 World's Columbian Exposition in Chicago Simmons, along with Robert Reid and Elihu Vedder, was chosen by Frank Millet to decorate the domes of the Manufacturer's Building. From then on Simmons resolved to devote his energies to mural painting and the painted decoration of buildings. The act of "painting pictures to be hung on the wall by strings . . . in the wrong light" was no longer satisfactory. "But given a certain space to beautify . . . where one was reasonably sure his work would remain permanently—that was worth doing" (quoted in Hoeber).

Simmons had a nationalistic spirit, and his realistic murals were attempts to dissociate American art from European tendencies and to present views of American life. In New York, famous architect Stanford White became Simmons's closest patron and friend. Through him Simmons joined the city's Player's Club and Vaudeville Club, painting the latter's library ceiling in 1893; joined Boston's St. Botolph Club; and received an award winning commission to paint the Criminal Court House in New York City. Their camaraderie also stimulated Simmons's imagination and helped to develop in him an exacting sense of design. His murals appeared on the Astoria Hotel in New York; the Boston State House; the Library of Congress; state capitol buildings in St. Paul, Minnesota, and Pierre, South Dakota; the Massachusetts State House; and the halls of the Panama-Pacific International Exposition held in San Francisco in 1915. In 1898 he joined The Ten—a group of American impressionists who wanted to exhibit independently, outside the National Academy, without rigid jury scrutiny—and became the group's most prolific, award-winning muralist.

Having for some time associated with some of the most innovative, inspired artists and architects of his day, by 1890 the once-shy Simmons had become one of the most extroverted, high-strung, impulsive men in American art. Throughout his life, however, Simmons remained an inquisitive artist who, until the day of his death in Baltimore, Maryland, sought to paint, in a realistic and impressionist manner, exquisite aspects of nature.

• For a personal account of his life and times see Edward Simmons, *From Seven to Seventy: Memories of a Painter and a Yankee* (1922); for an artist's view of Simmons see Arthur Hoeber, "Edward Emerson Simmons," *Brush and Pencil*, Mar. 1900, pp. 210–15; for a complete history and lists of awards, studios, murals, and memberships see Patricia Jobe Pierce, *The Ten* (1976); for his mural decorations see Pauline King, *American Mural Painting* (1902); for his Concarneau years see Henri Belbeoch, *Les Peintres de Concarneau* (1994). An obituary is in *American Art Annual*, vol. 38 (1931), p. 417.

PATRICIA JOBE PIERCE

SIMMONS, Franklin (11 Jan. 1839–6 Dec. 1913), sculptor, was born in Lisbon (later Webster), Maine, the son of Loring Simmons and Dorothy Batchelder. At the age of fifteen, while employed in the counting room of a cotton mill in Lewiston, he took drawing lessons and began modeling in clay. Encouraged by the favorable reception of his early efforts, Simmons went to Boston in 1856 and briefly studied the rudiments of sculpture with John Adams Jackson. Then he established studios in Lewiston, Bowdoin, and later Portland, Maine, where he specialized in executing portrait busts of local citizens. In 1864 he married Emily J. Libbey of Auburn, Maine.

In 1865 Simmons went to Washington, D.C., after being commissioned by a foundry owner from Providence, Rhode Island, to produce a series of medallion portraits representing Abraham Lincoln, his cabinet, and some military heroes who had played prominent roles in winning the Civil War. Called the National Bronze Picture Gallery, this unusual series of at least thirty-one medallions was exhibited in a number of American cities. (The Union League of Philadelphia is in possession of the most complete set.) At the recommendation of Ulysses S. Grant, Simmons was commissioned by the state of Rhode Island in 1867 to make a full-length statue of Roger Williams for Statuary Hall in the U.S. Capitol. That year he took his wife to Italy, visited Florence, and commenced work on the statue in Rome. Although Simmons visited the United States several times, he became an expatriate and remained in Italy until his death. In Italy he turned his attention away from American subjects and sculpted a series of ideal statues in the neoclassical style, representing biblical and classical figures such as *Mother of Moses (Jochebed)* (1872) and *Penelope* (c. 1880).

During the last two decades of the century Simmons reverted to a more animated naturalistic style and created imposing public monuments honoring heroes of the Civil War, most notable among them the *Naval Monument* (1877, Washington, D.C.), the complex *Soldiers and Sailors Monument* (1891, Portland, Maine), and the equestrian *General John A. Logan* (1897–1901, Washington, D.C.). The latter has a bronze base decorated with two large reliefs. His unusually lifelike seated figure of Henry Wadsworth Longfellow (1888, Portland) is noteworthy for its monumental simplicity. Numerous wealthy Americans visited Simmons's studio in the Villa San Nicolo Tolentino to have their bust portraits modeled; although these commissions are generally unremarkable, they made the sculptor wealthy. In 1892, twenty years after the death of his first wife, Simmons married Ella, baroness von Jeinsen; the couple had no children. Several years later the Grand Army of the Republic commissioned him to make a life-size marble statue of Grant. After the first version (Portland Museum of Art) was rejected for not representing the subject in a martial attitude, he made a second that was unveiled in 1900 and later placed in the Capitol.

During the last fifteen years of his life Simmons worked on portrait statues, ideal pieces, and a large-scale neoclassical *Hercules and Alcestis* that never went beyond the plaster model stage. Simmons died in Rome, where he was buried in the Protestant Cemetery. He willed many of his sculptures to the Portland Museum of Art.

Wayne Craven noted that Simmons devoted his career to "the attempt to perpetuate a pure classical ideal in the second half of the nineteenth century." His earliest works are characterized by their bland naturalism and expressionless quality. The neoclassical ideal pieces from the early Roman period possess a noble delicacy, with their polished, smooth surfaces and attention to detail. Simmons's greatest accomplishments were his large Civil War memorials, in which he combined heroic grandiosity with an animated, spontaneous naturalism that was rivaled only in the best work of his contemporary Augustus Saint-Gaudens.

• Henry Burrage, "Franklin Simmons, Sculptor," *Maine Historical Memorials* (1922), pp. 109–47, and Stephen Camett, "Franklin Simmons: A Maine-Born Sculptor," *Pine Tree Magazine* 8 (1907): 92–96, provide basic biographical information. Lorado Taft, *The History of American Sculpture* (1903), p. 248; Wayne Craven, *Sculpture in America* (1984), pp. 295–300; and Jan Seidler Ramirez, *American Figurative Sculpture in the Museum of Fine Arts, Boston* (1986), pp. 186–87, provide surveys of his career. See also E. F., "Artisti stranieri residenti in Italia," *L'Arte Italia* 5 (Apr. 1873): 60; "A Veteran Sculptor," *Outlook*, 27 May 1911; and Lilian Whiting, *International Studio* (May 1905), supp. An obituary is in *La Tribuna* (Rome), 10 Dec. 1913.

ROBERT WILSON TORCHIA

SIMMONS, Furnifold McLendel (20 Jan. 1854–30 Apr. 1940), politician and lawyer, was born in Jones County in eastern North Carolina, the son of Furnifold Green Simmons, a plantation and slave owner, and Mary McLendel Jerman. After experiencing the turmoil of the Civil War and Reconstruction, he attended Wake Forest College (now Wake Forest University) from 1868 to 1870 and graduated from Trinity College (now Duke University) in 1873. He read law and practiced in New Bern and Raleigh until 1901. In 1875 he married Eliza Humphrey, who died in 1883. They had three children. He married Belle Gibbs in 1886; two children were born of this marriage.

Although twice defeated for the state legislature, Simmons was chosen in 1884 to chair the Democratic Executive Committee of his district, the famous "Second," a notoriously gerrymandered one designed to have a black voting majority. In 1886 the Republicans, probably as a result of Democratic maneuverings, nominated two blacks for Congress, thus dividing the Republican vote, and Simmons was elected congressman. Two years later he lost his seat to a black. In 1892 he was chosen chair of the Democratic State Executive Committee. The Democrats carried the state that year, and Simmons was rewarded by being appointed collector of internal revenue for the Fourth District in North Carolina. Although he was a white supremacist, he was personally sympathetic to individual black Carolinians. Likewise, as one who came from a farming family, he sympathized with the complaints of farmers but was cautious about endorsing anything that he considered politically radical. Both his white-supremacy views and his views on farm issues were subordinate to his loyalty to the Democratic party.

Populist-Republican fusionists won most state offices in the next two elections, and in 1898 the Democrats again asked Simmons, the architect of their last state victory, to chair their executive committee. He accepted and held that office until 1907. In 1898 he reestablished his precinct-by-precinct organization of 1892 and launched a campaign marked by intimidation of blacks, ballot-box corruption, and the preaching of white supremacy. The Democrats gained control of the legislature, and in Wilmington, the state's largest city, a band of several hundred armed white men, enraged by the views of a black newspaper editor and by fusion successes in local elections, burned the newspaper building and after driving out the city government installed their own.

Although during the campaign Simmons had denied planning the disfranchisement of any voters, immediately after the election he began to organize the party to elect a governor in 1900 and to disfranchise black voters, most of whom were Republicans. Again Simmons's organization was effective. Charles Brantley Aycock, the Democratic candidate, was elected governor, and a constitutional amendment was approved providing for a literacy test, a poll tax, and a "grandfather" clause designed to protect illiterate white voters whose forebears had been on the voting rolls from disfranchisement. Simmons had shaped these campaigns to appeal to the racism of white voters, but, while believing in white supremacy, he was more politically concerned with cutting the ground from under the state's Republicans by disfranchising a large bloc of their party. At the same time he courted the business class by claiming that the Democrats were its protection against Populist-Republican fusion.

Democratic voters rewarded Simmons by nominating him in 1900 in the first senatorial primary held in the state, and the Democratic legislature elected him senator, an office he was to hold for three decades. In the Senate he was especially noted for his service on the commerce and finance committees. On the Commerce Committee he supported federal financing of highways and such internal improvements as the Intracoastal Waterway. He made his principal contributions as chair of the Finance Committee during the Wilson administrations, where he had the responsibility of guiding through Congress the Underwood-Simmons Tariff and unprecedented war revenue measures. With the return of the Republican Congress in 1919, he became the ranking Democrat on the Finance Committee and tried in vain to find a compromise that might secure senatorial approval of the Versailles Treaty. In the 1920s he opposed the Fordney-McCumber and Smoot-Hawley Tariffs, supported adjusted compensation for veterans and immigrations restriction, and dueled with the Republicans over the Mellon tax proposals.

Over the years, a myth inspired by Simmons's political enemies developed that a "Simmons Machine" controlled North Carolina politics. True, Simmons had built up an effective organization of his political friends, many of whom continued to turn to him for advice, and his office in Washington did many favors for constituents. However, he rarely if ever interfered in county politics, and he claimed little responsibility for state legislation, except for the passage of laws in 1903 and 1905 that prohibited the sale of liquor anywhere in the state except in large towns. He did take a great interest in the campaigns for governor, and he and his personal secretaries, especially A. D. Watts and Frank Hampton, used all the influence they could muster to support gubernatorial candidates, but Simmons was probably enthusiastic about the outcome in only four of the eight elections while he was senator.

Simmons's personal popularity is suggested by the fact that he had significant opposition in only three of his six senatorial primaries. His last primary was in 1930, two years after he, a consummate Democratic partisan, opposed Alfred E. Smith, his party's nominee for the presidency of the United States. He opposed Smith not because Smith was a Roman Catholic, or because Smith was opposed to prohibition, or because Smith was from Tammany Hall, but because these and other factors represented a brand of the Democracy that threatened the historic domination of the party by southern Democrats. Simmons thus helped to organize the anti-Smith Democrats, who provided sufficient votes (with the always substantial Republican vote in N.C.) to defeat Smith in the state. This "bolt" encouraged those Democrats who were not friends of Simmons to support Josiah W. Bailey in the senatorial primary of 1930. By that time, Simmons's organization was falling apart; his closest friends were old, or dead, and in the primary, the 76-year-old man was overwhelmed.

Simmons retired to his farms near New Bern. He had been a hard-working, conscientious senator, conservative but usually willing to compromise, an authority on taxes and tariffs, persuasive rather than oratorical, who continued to boast about his role in the white supremacy campaigns. He suffered from financial stringency and ill health throughout the twenties and thirties. Ten years after his loss to Bailey, he died in the home of one of his daughters near New Bern.

• The Simmons papers and the Josiah W. Bailey Papers are in the Perkins Library at Duke University. There is no biography of Simmons, but J. Fred Rippy edited a short memoir and some key addresses in F. M. Simmons, *Statesman of the New South, Memoirs and Addresses* (1936). For his congressional career, see the *Congressional Record*. See five articles by Richard L. Watson, Jr.: "A Political Leader Bolts: F. M. Simmons in the Presidential Election of 1928," *North Carolina Historical Review* 37 (Oct. 1960): 516–43; "A Southern Democratic Primary: Simmons vs. Bailey in 1930," *North Carolina Historical Review* 42 (Winter 1965): 22–46; "Furnifold M. Simmons, Jehovah of the Tar Heels," *North Carolina Historical Review* 44 (Spring 1967): 166–87; "Principle, Party, and Constituency: The North Carolina Congressional Delegation, 1917–1919," *North Carolina Historical Review* 51 (July 1979): 298–323; and "Furnifold Simmons and the Politics of White Supremacy," in *Race, Class and Politics in Southern History: Essays in Honor of Robert F. Durden*, ed. Jeffrey Crow et al. (1989). See also Eric Anderson, *Race and Politics in North Carolina, 1872–1901* (1981); Helen Edmonds, *The Negro and Fusion Politics in North Carolina* (1951); Paul D. Escott, *Many Excellent People, Power and Privilege in North Carolina, 1850–1900* (1985); and Robert H. Wooley, "Race and Politics: The Evolution of the White Supremacy Campaign of 1898 in North Carolina" (Ph.D. diss., Univ. of N.C., Chapel Hill, 1977). A lengthy obituary is in the Raleigh *News and Observer*, 1 May 1940.

RICHARD L. WATSON, JR.

SIMMONS, George Henry (2 Jan. 1852–1 Sept. 1937), physician, editor, and administrator, was born in Moreton-in-Marsh, Gloucestershire, England, the son of George Simmons and Sarah Louise Clifford, farmers. While son George was still a child his parents died, and he was brought up by his maternal grandfather. Seeking greater opportunities, George left England in 1870 and sailed to the United States, settling in the Midwest.

After attending Tabor College in Iowa from 1871 to 1872, Simmons spent the next four years at the University of Nebraska at Lincoln. In college Simmons became known as a leader in various reform movements. One of these, an effort to remove the city government from the hands of machine politicians, led the Chamber of Commerce to pass a resolution underlining the citizens' debt to Simmons for much of Lincoln's "political cleanliness and financial soundness." Simmons later worked as editor of the *Nebraska Farmer*, assistant city editor of the *Nebraska State Journal*, and field correspondent of the *Omaha Republican* and the *Kansas City Journal*.

Simmons finally decided on medicine as his career and obtained his first M.D., from the Hahnemann Medical College of Chicago, in 1882. Taking 1883–1884 for postgraduate education in Europe, especially at the Rotunda Hospital in Dublin, where he studied obstetrics and gynecology, Simmons then returned to Lincoln, Nebraska, where he practiced medicine for the next fifteen years.

He founded and edited the *Western Medical Review* in Omaha from 1896 to 1899. He served as secretary of the Nebraska State Medical Society from 1895 to 1899 and of the Western Surgical and Gynecological Society from 1896 to 1899. Late in 1898 the American Medical Association (AMA) selected Simmons from several candidates as its editor. The board of trustees also approved his appointment as secretary of the association, but without additional compensation. One of his first editorial actions established a much-needed annual index for the AMA's *Journal*.

Chicago was not unfamiliar to Simmons because of his studies at Hahnemann. Also, during the early 1890s, he had enrolled at Rush Medical College, attended lectures on various trips to that city, and obtained his second M.D. in 1892. Simmons, a developing medical politician, undoubtedly recognized the value of a degree from a regular medical college.

The AMA, founded in 1847, had spent most of its first half-century in discussion of subjects such as medical ethics rather than in accomplishment. Membership was limited to specially elected individuals from medical societies and other organizations. Simmons envisioned a much more active role for the association and soon initiated a small committee to reorganize the AMA. Simmons had himself named secretary of the committee; J. N. McCormack of Kentucky became chairman.

The committee visited practically all of the county and state medical societies in the country, urging their members to affiliate with the AMA. This affiliation would make the association much more representative and would also give it considerable power as the national spokesman for the medical profession. The association adopted the committee's new constitution and proposals at the annual meeting in St. Paul, Minnesota, in 1901. Membership now became tripartite: all members of the AMA had to be members of their state medical societies, and these had to be members of the appropriate county societies. The state and national organizations elected members to the AMA House of Delegates, which was designed to accomplish the association's policies and programs. The AMA now began gradually to build up its power to direct medical and lay opinion on public hygiene, medical education, and other matters affecting the profession.

With this reorganization Simmons became general manager of the association, increased his power as editor, and obtained administrative charge over the headquarters and its staff. Councils and boards were established on medical education (1904), pharmacy and chemistry (1905), and public instruction (1907). Quacks and quackery were a special target, and Simmons pushed the attack by eliminating patent medicines and unscientific therapy from the advertising pages of the *Journal*.

The AMA also revised its code of ethics at the turn of the century. Simmons, who held both homeopathic and regular degrees, pushed for these major changes, which made feasible consultation between regular physicians and homeopaths and other sectarian physicians. In addition, the AMA's structural reorganization brought in state and county medical societies, several of which (New York leading the way) had opened their membership to homeopaths and others.

Simmons also improved medical education by establishing a special annual issue of the *Journal* to report the results of state licensing examinations for alumni of the various medical schools. He pushed for the four-year curriculum as a standard and for full-time faculty, especially in the basic sciences. He also inaugurated other special issues on internships, residencies, and hospitals. Simmons started specialty journals in internal medicine (1908), pediatrics (1911), neurology and psychiatry (1919), dermatology and syphilis (1920), and surgery (1920). Realizing the growing value and complexity of the medical literature, Simmons founded the *Quarterly Cumulative Index Medicus* (1916) to make it easier for physicians to find needed material for clinical and research work. He also inaugurated the biennial *American Medical Directory* (1906), a national listing of physicians with related information.

The Army Medical Reserve Corps commissioned Simmons a first lieutenant in 1908. Promoted to major in 1917, he served as a member of the General Medical Board's busy committee on promotions. For this work, much of it in Washington, he was awarded the Distinguished Service Medal in 1921.

In 1924 Simmons left the AMA as editor and general manager emeritus and moved to Hollywood, Florida. He had earlier married a woman physician, who unfortunately became a morphine addict. After their divorce, he married Kate Vedder Monell; the couple had no children. When his second wife died, a niece,

Annie Nicholls, came from England to Florida to take care of Simmons for the rest of his life. He often traveled back to Chicago, and it was there that he was operated on for diverticulitis, dying in that city from complications of the operation.

George Henry Simmons could be called the creator of the American Medical Association as the dominant national spokesman for organized medicine and as the improver and watchdog over medical education and medical literature.

• Simmons destroyed his private papers when he retired. Morris Fishbein, *A History of the American Medical Association 1847 to 1947* (1947), includes much on Simmons, especially in the biographical section entitled "Dr. George Henry Simmons—Editor." The pamphlet *Testimonial Banquet with Presentation of Portrait to Dr. George Henry Simmons on the 25th Anniversary as Editor of JAMA* (1924) contains essays by well-known colleagues. Biographical sources include Morris Fishbein's obituaries in the *Journal of the American Medical Association* 109 (4 Sept. 1937): 807–08, and the *Proceedings of the Institute of Medicine of Chicago* 11 (1937): 397–401. An obituary is in the *New York Times*, 2 Sept. 1937.

WILLIAM K. BEATTY

SIMMONS, Henry Martyn (20 Aug. 1841–26 May 1905), Unitarian clergyman, was born in Paris Hill, Oneida County, New York, the son of Phillip T. Simmons and Miranda Head (occupations unknown). After graduating at the head of his class from Hamilton College in 1864, he moved to Kenosha, Wisconsin, to become principal of the local high school. A year later he entered Auburn (N.Y.) Theological Seminary to prepare for the Presbyterian ministry. After graduation (probably in 1868) he began serving a church in Salina, New York. In 1868 he married Florence A. Head, with whom he had three children.

Simmons found that he could not in good conscience subscribe to the Westminster Confession and so was denied ordination as a Presbyterian. In 1868 he began ministering to two small-town churches (Ilion and Herkimer, near Troy, N.Y.) under Unitarian auspices. In 1871 he returned to Kenosha as a Unitarian minister; he remained there for eight years, serving concurrently as superintendent of schools. In 1878 Unitarians in Madison, Wisconsin, reopened their church and called Simmons to serve it. After three years at Madison, in 1881, he moved to Minneapolis. He remained minister of the First Unitarian Society in that city until his death there.

Simmons was one of the group of ministers in the Western Unitarian Conference who founded *Unity*, the conference's semi-official organ, in 1878. (The first few issues appeared under the name the *Pamphlet Mission*.) He edited the paper for one year in 1879 and served on the editorial board for as long as he lived. During the 1880s and early 1890s the editorial board of *Unity* was made up of six men, Jenkin Lloyd Jones, William Gannett, Frederick Hosmer, John Learned, James V. Blake, and Simmons. These "Unity men," as they were called, were the leaders of the Western Conference during its most exciting years. They led it into

greater independence from Boston Unitarian influence and greater institutional effectiveness, establishing regionally centered structures for missions and education. During this period the conference stood on the advancing edge of liberal religious thought and practice, embracing critical biblical scholarship, scientific knowledge, and sociological insights. Eventually, however, the radicalism of the Unity men outpaced the more traditional religious views of Unitarians in some parts of the conference. A protracted schism, known as "The Issue in the West," began in 1886, and it generated much bitterness. Simmons was the first to break ranks with the Unity men and welcome a compromise, affirming a theistic Christianity. When the issue was finally resolved by compromises in 1892 and 1894, the influence of the Unity men was broken; leadership passed to younger men and women.

Even in an age when the scholarly cleric was not a rarity, Simmons's erudition was seen as remarkable. He was as fluent in classical and modern European languages as he was in English, and he was a master of literary classics and contemporary biblical criticism. More significant, though, was his scientific knowledge, especially in botany, geology, and astronomy. During his holidays these were his chief pursuits. A major theme of his sermons was the religious value of evolutionary thought and scientific knowledge, and his two published books were expositions on scientific subjects. *The Unending Genesis*, a guide to the religious significance of evolutionary science compiled for the Western Unitarian Sunday School Society, was published in 1882. After his final illness was diagnosed, Simmons spent his last days preparing *New Tables of Stone and Other Essays*, a collection of his sermons on the sciences, published in 1904.

In his sermons Simmons was also an outspoken critic of social trends of which he disapproved. For example, he preached against protectionism and labor unions and in favor of free silver and the single tax. The Spanish-American War ignited his total opposition to war. At the time of his death, he was serving as vice president of the Anti-Imperialist League.

Simmons began to lose his hearing in his forties, and by his fifties he was entirely deaf. Although he continued to preach effectively, he withdrew from most other ministerial activity. Nevertheless, those who knew him well noted his consistent sunny temperament and sense of humor.

Henry Simmons was one of a group of men (and women) who helped to create a vital Unitarian presence in the Midwest in the last half of the nineteenth century. His special contribution, however, was to spell out the religious values of science.

• Some letters of Simmons are in the two Jenkin Lloyd Jones archives, the Joseph Regenstein Library and the Meadville-Lombard Library, both on the University of Chicago campus. The best biographical source is the *Unity* tribute issue, 12 Oct. 1905. The article in Samuel A. Eliot, *Heralds of a*

Liberal Faith, vol. 4, *The Pilots* (1953), is useful but inaccurate in some details. An obituary is in the *Minneapolis Journal*, 27 May 1905.

THOMAS E. GRAHAM

SIMMONS, Roscoe Conkling Murray (20 June 1878–27 Apr. 1951), orator, politician, and writer, was born in Greenview, Mississippi, the son of Emory Simmons, a principal of a black school in Hollandale, Mississippi, and Willie Murray. He grew up in Aberdeen, Mississippi, and worked for a time as Ohio senator Mark Hanna's office boy. In 1895 he entered Tuskegee Institute in Alabama, studying under Booker T. Washington, who had married Simmons's aunt, Margaret Murray. After graduating in 1899, he took a job as a reporter for the *Pensacola Daily News* and a year later moved to the Washington, D.C., *Record*, where he began his political involvement. Simmons worked for a time as a teacher in Holly Springs, Mississippi, and once tried selling cigars, but his ambitions lay in journalism and politics. When his uncle offered him a teaching position at Tuskegee Institute, Simmons declined, replying, "I have been called to teach, but the rostrum and the public hall will be my classroom" (*Chicago Defender*, 5 May 1951).

Simmons continued to work in journalism as a reporter for the Mound Bayou, Mississippi, *Demonstrator* from 1902 to 1904 and, from 1904 to 1913, as editor and contributor to three New York publications, the *Age*, the *Colored American Magazine*, and the *National Review*. Simmons campaigned in New York for William Howard Taft's 1908 run for the Republican presidential nomination and in exchange received party funding for his *National Review*. In his political and journalistic activities during this period, Simmons received funding and direction from his uncle Booker and often acted as a promoter of Tuskegee. In 1912 Simmons established a national reputation as an orator while campaigning for Theodore Roosevelt among blacks in New York City and in the South. After hearing him speak, William Jennings Bryan reportedly predicted Simmons would become one of the world's greatest orators. Simmons developed a long-lasting alliance with *Chicago Tribune* publisher Joseph Medill McCormick, who later became a senator from Illinois. In 1913, at the urging of Washington, Simmons left the *Age* to start his own newspaper, the *Sun*, in Memphis, Tennessee. The paper, which extolled the Tuskegee philosophy of self-help, folded after one year.

Shortly after the *Sun*'s demise, Simmons began working for Robert Abbott's *Chicago Defender* as a columnist and promoter. The relationship proved mutually beneficial. Simmons became one of the highest paid employees in black journalism, and the *Defender*'s circulation increased dramatically, becoming the first black-owned, mass circulation newspaper. Simmons toured the South, recruiting distribution agents and speaking to crowds that sometimes numbered in the thousands. He plugged the *Defender* while speaking on the events of the day. "We go forth," he told a Memphis audience during World War I, "to make the world safe for democracy. After that job is well done we will make the United States safe for the Negro" (*Chicago Defender*, 7 July 1917). Even whites, according to the *Defender*, 1 June 1918, thought Simmons's wartime speeches were "surcharged with loyalty and patriotism, delivered by a master of all the arts and graces of the genuine orator."

Simmons continued with the *Defender* until 1925, when he was implicated with three others in a scheme to expropriate funds. Abbott did not bring formal charges and a few years later rehired Simmons, who was released again in the mid-1930s, when the depression forced staff reductions. Simmons then parlayed his friendship with the McCormick family into a job as feature writer and columnist for the daily *Chicago Tribune*. His column, "The Untold Story," highlighted cooperation between blacks and whites.

Simmons made his greatest mark as a political orator on behalf of conservative Republican candidates. He visited Presidents Theodore Roosevelt, Warren Harding, and Herbert Hoover in the White House and became a fixture at Republican National Conventions, where he delivered speeches from the podium. He acted as chairman of the party's colored speakers' bureau in 1920, 1924, and 1928; seconded the nomination of Hoover in 1932; and was a delegate to the Republican National Convention several times. While promoting Republican presidential nominee Alf Landon in 1936, he declared, "My countrymen, on one side are *Landon* and *Liberty*; on the other side are *Roosevelt* and *Ruin*" (Boulware, p. 132).

Trezzvant W. Anderson, writing for the *Pittsburgh Courier*, 5 May 1951, called Simmons a "silver-tongued orator who wove a spell of beauty and delight." A professor of speech called his speaking style "impressive . . . without being pretentious" (Boulware, p. 132). Yet Simmons's oratorical talents were not enough to win him a political office. In 1930 he lost his bid to take the Republican nomination for U.S. congressman from Chicago's incumbent, Representative Oscar S. DePriest, the only black member of Congress. Two years later Simmons lost a race for the state senate.

Simmons's racial philosophy of "undefeated *patience*" (Boulware, p. 131) tied him to the earlier period when Washington was influential and left him out of touch with an increasingly militant and Democratic black majority. As most black voters joined Franklin D. Roosevelt's New Deal coalition, Simmons remained loyal to the Republicans until his death and became irrelevant to the black struggle for equality. During his prime, however, he had been a major spokesman for African Americans to leading Republicans, a key figure in the development of African-American journalism, and a spellbinding orator.

Simmons married twice. With his first wife, whose name is not known, he had one child. With his second wife, Althea, a schoolteacher, he had two children. He died in Chicago.

• Some of Simmons's letters are in the Theodore Roosevelt Papers in the Library of Congress and *The Booker T. Washington Papers*, ed. Louis R. Harlan and Raymond W. Smock (1972–1989). On Simmons's place in black history, see "The Twilight of Two Eras," *Ebony*, Aug. 1951, p. 102. On his Memphis newspaper and a speech on the South Lawn, see David M. Tucker, *Lieutenant Lee of Beale Street* (1971). On his career with the *Chicago Defender*, see Roi Ottley, *The Lonely Warrior: The Life and Times of Robert S. Abbott* (1955). On his oratorical abilities, see Marcus H. Boulware, "Roscoe Conkling Simmons: The Golden Voiced Politico," *Negro History Bulletin* 29 (Mar. 1966): 131–32. Obituaries are in the *New York Times*, 29 Apr. 1951; and the *Baltimore Afro-American*, *Chicago Defender*, and *Pittsburgh Courier*, all 5 May 1951.

WILLIAM JORDAN

SIMMONS, William James (26 June 1849–30 Oct. 1890), Baptist leader, educator, and race advocate, was born in Charleston, South Carolina, the son of enslaved parents, Edward Simmons and Esther (maiden name unknown). During his youth, Simmons's mother escaped slavery with him and two of his siblings, relocating in Philadelphia, Pennsylvania. Simmons's uncle, Alexander Tardieu (or Tardiff), a shoemaker, became a father for the children and a protector and provider for the fugitive slave family. He moved them among the cities of Philadelphia, Roxbury, Massachusetts, and Chester, Pennsylvania, constantly eluding persistent "slave catchers," before permanently taking residence in Bordentown, New Jersey. While Simmons never received formal elementary or secondary school education, his uncle made a point of teaching the children to read and write. As a youth Simmons served as an assistant to a white dentist in Bordentown. At the age of fifteen he joined the Union army, participating in a number of major battles in Virginia and finding himself at Appomattox in 1865. After the war, Simmons once again worked briefly as a dental assistant. He converted and affiliated with the white Baptist church in Bordentown in 1867, announced his call to the ministry, and ventured to college with the financial support of church friends.

Simmons attended Madison (later Colgate) University in 1868. Leaving Rochester University in New York after a brief stay because of eye trouble, Simmons enrolled in Howard University in Washington, D. C., in 1871 and earned B.A. and M.A. degrees, respectively, in 1873 and 1881.

To secure additional requisite funds for living expenses while pursuing his education, Simmons taught school in Washington, D. C., serving for a time as principal of Hillsdale Public School. In August 1874 he married Josephine A. Silence of Washington, a union that produced seven children.

For five years the family lived in Florida, where Simmons, after attempting a living from investments in lands and orange farming, returned to teaching, becoming principal of Howard Academy. He also pastored a church and became deputy county clerk and county commissioner. After returning to Washington for several years of teaching, the young Baptist relocat-

ed once again in 1879, this time to Lexington, Kentucky, to pastor the First African Baptist Church. In 1880 the fledgling Normal and Theological Institution chose Simmons as its president, and under his leadership it attained university status in 1884. The name of the institution was changed to State University of Louisville, Kentucky, and in 1918 was changed once again to Simmons University. The school offered the only college education for blacks in the state after the Kentucky legislature outlawed integrated education at Berea College in 1905 and was the only African-American institution of higher learning offering undergraduate, law, and medical degrees. Prizing vocational training as well as classical education, Simmons established the Eckstein Norton Institute in Cane Spring, Kentucky, in 1890.

Simmons played major roles in a number of black Baptist conventions, including the Baptist Foreign Mission Convention, established in 1880 to pursue African missions. His role in the formation and presidency of the American National Baptist Convention (ANBC) in 1886 laid the foundation for the emergence in 1895 of the enduring National Baptist Convention, which resulted from a merger of the ANBC and two other groups. Appointed missionary to the South by the predominantly white, northern-based American Baptist Home Mission Society in 1887, Simmons organized churches and advocated black Baptist unity.

Simmons participated in a number of black state conventions, assemblies of race leaders dealing with critical issues facing African Americans, and remained vigorously opposed to and outspoken about Jim Crow segregation and all forms of racial discrimination, especially as exercised by state and local governments. While essentially a Republican, he called for blacks to place their interests above any particular political party. In the 1880s he predicted that the state governments, not the federal government, were increasingly the places to work for racial progress.

While many Baptist leaders strongly opposed the organization of women's conventions, Simmons heartily encouraged and supported such groups, opening the organizing session of Kentucky women that led eventually to the establishment of the Baptist Women's Educational Convention of Kentucky. In 1882 the Baptist leader founded the *American Baptist* newspaper, in which he as editor called for racial and denominational unity. In addition, Simmons established a publication, *Our Women and Children*, calling for racial progress, particularly for women and youth. Significantly, Simmons opened the pages of the magazine to an ecumenical array of women writers who published articles dealing with domestic life. Simmons achieved lasting fame for his *Men of Mark*, published in 1887, showcasing the triumphs of black males, most of whom had surmounted the horrors of childhood enslavement with the clear intention of banishing the increasingly academically respectable notion of black innate inferiority and of promoting a thirst for education among black youth. Interestingly, Simmons planned a sequel outlining the achievements of prominent women, but his premature death interrupted those plans. He died in Cane Spring.

With his contributions regarding denominational unity and missions, racial unity and progress, gender equity, journalism, and politics, Simmons, despite his relatively short life span, emerged as one of the major American leaders of the nineteenth century.

• The impact of Simmons in both the wider world of American history and his denominational context is described in Henry M. Turner's introduction to William J. Simmons's *Men of Mark* (1887; repr. 1968) and in Albert W. Pegues, *Our Baptist Ministers and Schools* (1892). James M. Washington, *Frustrated Fellowship: The Black Baptist Quest for Social Power* (1986), and Leroy Fitts, *A History of Black Baptists* (1985), capture his place in the development of the denomination. Sandy D. Martin, *Black Baptists and African Missions* (1989), illustrates Simmons's involvement in the development of African missions, particularly regarding the Baptist Foreign Mission Convention (1880–1894). Evelyn Brooks Higginbotham, *Righteous Discontent: The Women's Movement in the Black Baptist Church, 1880–1920* (1993), is a very good source for contextualizing the significance of Simmons's support of gender equity. For more recent biographical collections that update Simmons's and Pegues's accounts, see the *Encyclopedia of African-American Culture and History* (1996) and the *Dictionary of American Negro Biography* (1982). Finally, Edward M. Brawley, *The Negro Baptist Pulpit: A Collection of Sermons and Papers by Colored Baptist Ministers* (1890; repr. 1971), contains a sermon, "The Lord's Supper," written by Simmons especially for that publication that demonstrates the African-American leader's sophisticated treatment of theological and doctrinal issues, along with his concerns about ecclesial and racial unity and progress. Obituaries are in the *Louisville Courier-Journal*, 31 Oct. and 3 Nov. 1890; and the *New York Age*, 8 Nov. 1890.

SANDY DWAYNE MARTIN

SIMMONS, William Joseph (6 May 1880–18 May 1945), founder and imperial wizard of the modern Ku Klux Klan, was born in Harpersville, Alabama, the son of Calvin Henry Simmons, a physician, and Lavonia David. A talent for oratory led Simmons into the ministry at an early age. "When I was fourteen years old I was a regular leader of the mid-week evening prayer meetings in our Methodist Church," Simmons told an interviewer for *Collier's* in 1920. At age eighteen Simmons fought in the Spanish-American War. After his return, he attended the Southern University for a time and was licensed to preach for the Methodist church (probably in 1899). When he turned twenty-one he was given a circuit of small churches in Florida and Alabama to pastor. Finding it hard to support himself on his small salary, Simmons frequently held revival meetings to raise extra money. At an unknown date he married Bessie, whose full name is not known. They had at least one son.

In 1912 Simmons and the Methodist church parted ways. Simmons claimed the break came because of the church's failure to give him the promised pastorship of a big city church. Church officials reported that Simmons was denied a pastorship because of "inefficiency." Regardless of the reason, Simmons turned to building fraternal organizations. While he later claimed to belong to more than a dozen fraternal organizations, his greatest success was as a promoter for the Woodmen of the World. He moved to Atlanta, became the district manager for the order, and made a comfortable income in the process.

In 1915 Simmons fulfilled what he claimed had been his goal of many years, the establishment of a new order of the Ku Klux Klan. The idea of forming the Klan grew out of childhood memories of descriptions of the original Klan. As an adult these portrayals still fascinated him, and he decided to act while recuperating from an automobile accident. During his recovery, Simmons planned the robes, masks, rituals, and terminology. He recruited the charter members from various fraternal lodges. He also placed advertisements in Atlanta newspapers in close proximity to advertisements for the upcoming opening of D. W. Griffith's *Birth of a Nation* to capitalize on the film's sympathetic portrayal of the Klan. The group first met in October, and on Thanksgiving Day 1915 the first initiation took place on top of Stone Mountain, Georgia, under the light of a fiery cross. By 1916 Simmons had legally established the Klan by obtaining a corporate charter from the state of Georgia.

The new Klan saw slow but steady growth until 1920–1921, when a great surge in publicity helped its membership skyrocket. In 1920 Simmons hired the Southern Publicity Association, run by Edward Y. Clarke and Elizabeth Tyler, to increase Klan membership. Taking advantage of free publicity and postwar societal jitters, Clarke and Tyler were able to dramatically increase the membership from a few thousand to well into the millions. The exact number is unknown, since few membership rolls have survived, but the conservative estimate is two million members. Each new enrollee paid an initiation fee of ten dollars, most of which went to the Southern Publicity Association. While it was originally thought that most members were rural, poor, and uneducated, new studies have contradicted this view. Studies of Klaverns in Indiana, California, Utah, and other places have shown that Klan membership included many sophisticated urbanites as well as people of different class and educational levels. A series of articles in the *New York World* exposing Klan practices and violence led to a congressional investigation in October 1921.

As the Klan grew in size, Simmons gradually lost control over the organization. By the spring of 1922 he was convinced to take a six-month "vacation" and named Clarke as the interim imperial wizard. Clarke soon ran into problems of his own. Dogged by rumors of infidelity and indicted for mail fraud, Clarke resigned from the top position in October 1922. Hiram Wesley Evans, an assistant to Clarke and former leader of the Dallas, Texas, Klavern, stepped into the leadership void. In November 1922, at the national convention in Atlanta, Evans, along with several other state Klan leaders, orchestrated a coup against Simmons and convinced the delegates to elect Evans as the new imperial wizard. Simmons was given the largely symbolic title of emperor. Evans consolidated his power by canceling the Klan's contract with the Southern Publicity Association and banning Clarke from membership in the Klan.

Simmons did not fade away quite as easily as the new leaders hoped. In the spring of 1923 he tried to merge the women's Klan auxiliary, where he had significant support, into the main Klan organization, but Evans managed to block this move. Next Simmons tried to regain control by summoning an emergency session of the executive committee while Evans was out of town. Evans declared Simmons's tactics illegal and threw the matter into the courts. The protracted legal battle stretched into 1924. Eventually an out-of-court settlement was reached, wherein Simmons agreed to "sell" his interest and copyrights back to the Klan for a reported $90,000.

This ended Simmons's involvement in the Klan he had founded, but it did not end his involvement in fraternal organizations. Soon after he severed his ties with the Klan, he began a new order called the Knights of the Flaming Sword. Clearly intended to be a rival to the Klan, the new order managed to draw some former Klansmen into its circle but never caught on in large numbers. The Klan itself was also fading by 1924. Growing prosperity and immigration quotas skewed against southeastern Europeans blunted the anti-Catholic, anti-Jewish, anti-radical fearmongering that had fed the growth of the Klan in the immediate postwar years.

As the Knights of the Flaming Sword faded into obscurity, so did Simmons. He apparently lived out the last years of his life in a state of quasi-retirement, writing and giving occasional lectures. He died in Atlanta, Georgia.

• Simmons left no known papers, and his life must be followed by tracing the Ku Klux Klan. Simmons's book, *The Klan Unmasked* (1923), is a good source for his ideas. Because they are based on extensive interviews, the most helpful articles are by William G. Shepherd, including "How I Put Over the Klan," *Collier's* 82 (14 July 1928): 5–7, 32, 34–35; "Ku Klux Koin," *Collier's* 82 (21 July 1928): 8–9, 38–39; and "The Fiery Double Cross," *Collier's* 82 (28 July 1928): 8. Also of interest are Charles O. Jackson, "William J. Simmons: A Career in Ku Kluxism," *Georgia Historical Quarterly* 50 (Dec. 1966): 351–65; and Robert L. Duffus, "Salesmen of Hate: The Ku Klux Klan," *World's Work* 46 (May 1923): 31–38. The standard works on the Klan include David M. Chalmers, *Hooded Americanism* (1965), and Kenneth T. Jackson, *The Ku Klux Klan in the City, 1915–1930* (1967). For a good summary of recent revisionist views see Shawn Lay, ed., *The Invisible Empire in the West: Toward a New Historical Appraisal of the Ku Klux Klan of the 1920s* (1992). Obituaries are in the *Atlanta Constitution* and the *Atlanta Journal*, 21 May 1945.

MARK N. MORRIS